April 18–23, 2015
Seoul, Republic of Korea

Association for
Computing Machinery

Advancing Computing as a Science & Profession

SIGCHI

I0888102

CHI 2015
CROSSINGS

CHI 2015

Proceedings of the

33rd Annual CHI Conference on Human Factors in Computing Systems

Sponsored by:

ACM SIGCHI

Supported by:

Samsung, Golfzon, Google, Microsoft, NAVER, SK Planet, AutoDesk, Daumkakao, Disney Research, FuturePlay, Hyundai Motor Group, Language Grid, LG, NSF, Adobe Systems, H9Works, Yonsei University, KIPFA, and Samsung Art & Design Institute

Association for
Computing Machinery

Advancing Computing as a Science & Profession

The Association for Computing Machinery
2 Penn Plaza, Suite 701
New York, New York 10121-0701

Notice to Past Authors of ACM-Published Articles
ACM intends to create a complete electronic archive of all articles and/or other material previously published by ACM. If you have written a work that has been previously published by ACM in any journal or conference proceedings prior to 1978, or any SIG Newsletter at any time, and you do NOT want this work to appear in the ACM Digital Library, please inform permissions@acm.org, stating the title of the work, the author(s), and where and when published.

ISBN: 978-1-4503-3145-6 (Digital)

ISBN: 978-1-4503-3772-4 (Print)

Additional copies may be ordered prepaid from:

ACM Order Department
PO Box 30777
New York, NY 10087-0777, USA

Phone: 1-800-342-6626 (USA and Canada)
+1-212-626-0500 (Global)
Fax: +1-212-944-1318
E-mail: acmhelp@acm.org
Hours of Operation: 8:30 am – 4:30 pm ET

Printed in the USA

From the General and Technical Program Chairs

Welcome to CHI 2015, the premier international forum for human-computer interaction (HCI). In its early days, HCI focused on optimizing interactions between a user and a computer. Today, computers pervade our world, impacting our lives in varied and subtle ways. By never focusing solely on technology itself but always on innovations and their effects throughout human lives, HCI has increasingly come to mean *human-centered innovation*.

The theme for the conference this year is *CROSSINGS* which represents our excitement about crossing into Asia and also reflects CHI's core principle of crossing disciplines, crossing people and technology, crossing research and business, crossing physical and digital, ... crossing you and me.

This year's conference brings CHI to Asia for the first time in its 33-year history, continuing the SIGCHI commitment to making CHI a truly international community. The city of Seoul represents one of many innovation centers in Asia and provides a fantastic opportunity to showcase groundbreaking content from across the region. In addition to an exciting technical program, we are holding four special symposia devoted to breakthrough insights and innovations from the Chinese, Japanese and ASEAN research communities.

The exciting keynote program features speakers who will bring fresh perspectives to CHI including Dean ***Lou Yongqi*** of Tongji University, China, a prominent global thinker on social and sustainable design; Executive VP ***Donghoon Chang***, MFA, head of Samsung Electronic's design strategy; Senior Research Fellow ***David Min***, PhD, head of the Software Center at LG Electronics; and ***PSY***, the media record breaker and innovator discussing creative methods and the impact of social media on to cross cultural boundaries.

CHI is honored this year to be the forum chosen by the recipient of one of ACM's top awards, the Athena Lecturer Award, ***Susan T. Dumais*** who developed novel algorithms and interfaces for interactive retrieval that have made it easier for people to find, use and make sense of information. She will present insights from her experiences at a special keynote session at the conference.

CHI 2015 includes two days of focused workshops and four days of technical content, including CHI's prestigious technical program, with 16 parallel sessions of rigorously reviewed research Papers, engaging Panels, Case Studies and Special Interest Groups (SIGs), an extensive Course program and invited talks from SIGCHI's award winners: Leysia Palen, Jean Scholtz, Michel Beaudouin-Lafon, Jim Hollan, Susan Dray and the new inductees to the CHI Academy.

We also host student research, design, and game competitions, and last-minute SIGs for discussing current topics. The popular alt.chi forum entered its tenth year of provocation to the HCI community. Interactivity's hands-on demonstrations showcase the best of interactive technology and innovation. The program also highlights more than 200 Work-In-Progress posters. Evening events include the CHI 2015 conference reception, Sponsors and University events, local performances and the Job Fair. Across all tracks, CHI received over 2800 submissions and accepted nearly 1000 that will appear in the ACM Digital Library.

We are deeply indebted to an enormous number of volunteers, without whom CHI 2015 would not be possible, including over 3800 reviewers, over 200 senior members of the program committee, nearly 100 members of the CHI 2015 conference organization committee and, of course, the more than 180 student volunteers. We are also deeply grateful to the ongoing support of the Korean HCI society who demonstrated incredible hospitality by moving their own conference's time and location to make room for

CHI in Seoul and who provided tremendous resources from their membership to support CHI logistically and in attracting novel content from around Asia.

We hope you will see fresh insights, strengthen connections and find new collaborators in Asia. *Above all, we hope you enjoy this unique experience of CHI 2015!*

General Conference Chairs

Bo Begole
Huawei, USA

Jinwoo Kim
Yonsei University, Korea

Technical Program Chairs

Kori Inkpen
Microsoft Research, USA

Woontack Woo
KAIST, Korea

From ACM SIGCHI's President and Vice President for Conferences

SIGCHI is proud to sponsor the premier annual conference in the field of human-computer interaction. We are extremely grateful to the CHI 2015 Conference Chairs Jinwoo Kim and Bo Begole, to Technical Program Chairs Woontack Woo and Kori Inkpen, and to their wonderful crew, who succeeded to build an impressive program and experience.

CHI 2015 is in Seoul, Korea, the first CHI ever in Asia. CHI started in Gaithersburg, MD, USA, in March 1982. That first conference in Gaithersburg drew over 900 attendees, and since then CHI, with the official name: "ACM Conference on Human Factors in Computing Systems" moved to annual, originally moving between the USA and Canada. Starting with 1993 CHI traveled between locations in Europe and North America. This year is another big step forward, made possible thanks to the Korean HCI Society that helped understand and navigate the local context, that moved its annual conference 3 months earlier to December 2014, and at the same time supported CHI's Technical Program meeting.

CHI has continued to grow and broaden its range of topics and contributing disciplines: the founding psychologists and software engineers began to meet new visions from ethnography, sociology, communication sciences and arts, among others. Relevant industries, as well as research institutes and academia, showed an increasing — and often long-lasting — interest and involvement (through volunteers and through sponsorship for conference expenses). This year's Conference Committee truly succeeded in crossing borders of all kind, providing new and unique opportunities for all participants to meet something entirely different.

CHI is an ideal forum for people to meet formally as well as informally, to exchange knowledge and views, to share experiences, and to learn. The CHI conference brings together professionals from research and practice; people from industry, academia, and from government; long-term veterans of HCI, young professionals and students; all in an environment designed to encourage interaction. We invite you to actively participate in that interaction: introduce yourself to people, interact with presenters and speakers, renew old friendships and make new ones

CHI is organized on behalf of ACM's Special Interest Group on Computer-Human Interaction (SIGCHI), an international community of professionals who share an interest in the many diverse facets of HCI. SIGCHI is committed both to advancing the field of HCI, to facilitate exchange of information within the SIGCHI community, and to support students to enter the domain.

The CHI conference is arguably the single most visible activity of SIGCHI, but we also sponsor and support a wide range of specialized conferences and workshops in areas ranging from interactive systems design to user interface technology to computer-supported cooperative work to "intelligent" user interfaces. Visit the SIGCHI website at **http://www.sigchi.org** to find our conference schedule, listing upcoming as well as past conferences.

SIGCHI and ACM produce some of the most respected publications in the field. All members receive interactions, a highly-acclaimed magazine covering the broad field of HCI and user interface design. ACM Transactions on Computer-Human Interactions (ToCHI), now in its 21st year, is our flagship journal – a quarterly publication with the top-quality archival research aimed at researchers and those translating research into practice.

SIGCHI is truly an international organization, with around 40 local chapters and 3 student chapters in 25 countries on 6 continents. We encourage all SIGCHI members to join their local chapter — or if there isn't one in your area, we would love to help you create one. And don't forget virtual communities! SIGCHI hosts dozens of electronic mailing lists on topics ranging from HCI and the Web, to HCI educations, to public policy and beyond. Those lists range from dozens of subscribers to thousands, and are an excellent way to keep up with the field and with friends and colleagues.

Finally, on behalf of ACM SGICHI, we again want to thank the conference committee and all of the hundreds of volunteers who make this conference possible. Their work makes this a rewarding experience for all of us.

Gerrit C. van der Veer
SIGCHI President

John "Scooter" Morris
SIGCHI Vice-President for Conferences

About SIGCHI

CHI 2015 is sponsored by ACM's Special Interest Group on Computer-Human Interaction (ACM SIGCHI). ACM, the Association for Computing Machinery, is an educational and scientific society uniting the world's computing educators, researchers, and professionals to inspire dialogue, share resources, and address the field's challenges. ACM strengthens the profession's collective voice through strong leadership, promotion of the highest standards, and recognition of technical excellence. ACM supports the professional growth of its members by providing opportunities for life-long learning, career development, and professional networking. ACM offers its more than 100,000 worldwide members cutting edge technical information through world class journals and magazines, dynamic special interest groups, and globally recognized conferences.

Visit www.acm.org for more information about the ACM.

SIGCHI is the premier international society for professionals, academics, and students who are interested in human-computer interaction (HCI). We provide a forum for the discussion of all aspects of HCI through our conferences, including our flagship CHI conference, publications, web sites, email discussion groups, and other services. We advance education in HCI through courses, workshops, and outreach, and we promote informal access to a wide range of individuals and organizations involved in HCI. Members can be involved in HCI-related activities with others in their region through local SIGCHI chapters. Come to the SIGCHI Town Hall meeting on Wednesday, April 22, at 12:50 to 14:30 in Room 308 or visit www.sigchi.org to learn more about SIGCHI.

Membership Information

Please contact ACM's Member Services Dept.
Online: www.acm.org
Tel: +1-800-342-6626 (USA/Canada)
+1-212-626-0500 (International)
Fax: +1-212-944-1318
Email: acmhelp@acm.org

Write:

Association for Computing Machinery, Inc.
General Post Office
P.O. Box 30777
New York, NY 10087-0777, USA

CHI 2015 Papers and Notes Chairs' Welcome

The CHI Papers and Notes programme is continuing to grow and this year! We are pleased that CHI continues to be the leading conference for research in human-computer interaction.

This year we considered more than 2120 submissions, ~600 of which were notes. This represents a continuation of ~4% annual growth in submissions. We accepted 486 submissions (~23%): 379 papers and 107 notes.

The CHI review process demands a tremendous amount of work from all areas of the human-computer interaction community. As co-chairs of the process, we are amazed at the ability of the community to organize itself to accomplish this task. We would like to thank the 2809 individual reviewers for their careful consideration of these papers. Every submission received at least three external reviews.

We also deeply appreciate the huge amount of time donated to this process by the 225-member program committee, who paid their own way to attend the face-to-face program committee meeting, an event larger than most ACM conferences.

We are proud of the work of the CHI 2015 program committee and hope that you enjoy these papers and notes, which represent the best research in human-computer interaction.

CHI 2015 Paper and Notes Chairs

Andy Cockburn
University of Canterbury

Janna McGrenere
University of British Columbia

Table of Contents

Visualizing Data

Session Chair: Christophe Hurter, *IRIT, France*

Interaction in 3D Space

Session Chair: Kening Zhu, *City University of Hong Kong, China*

Understanding & Evaluating Performance

Session Chair: Richard Davis, *Singapore Management University, Singapore*

Music & Art

Session Chair: Jonathan Hook, *University of York, UK*

Supporting Change in Developing Countries

Session Chair: Anirudha Joshi, *Indian Institute of Technology, Bombay, India*

Privacy, Security & Interruptions

Session Chair: Emilee Rader, *Michigan State University, USA*

Making & Sharing Assistive Technologies

Session Chair: Suranga Nanayakkara, *Singapore University of Technology and Design, Singapore*

Matching & Facilitating Social Interactions

Session Chair: Jofish Kaye, *Yahoo!, USA*

Family Communication

Session Chair: Siân Lindley, *Microsoft Research, UK*

Crowdsourcing Fans & Friends

Session Chair: Shaun Lawson, *University of Lincoln, UK*

Managing Personal Privacy

Session Chair: Sameer Patil, *Yahoo Labs, USA*

Health Sensors & Monitoring

Session Chair: Regan Mandryk, *University of Saskatchewan, Canada*

Kids Haptic, Wearable, Tangible Learning

Session Chair: Shuli Gilutz, *Interdisciplinary Center (IDC) Herzliya, Israel*

Motivation & Participation

Session Chair: Meredith Morris, *Microsoft Research, USA*

Sustainability & Recycling

Session Chair: Adrian Clear, *Lancaster University, UK*

The Value of the Village in Caregiving

Session Chair: Lena Mamykina, *Columbia University, USA*

I Like What I See - Interface Aesthetics

Session Chair: Simon Bowen, *Newcastle University, UK*

Supporting Creativity through UX Design

Session Chair: Luciano Gamberini, *University of Padova, Italy*

Smartwatch Interaction

Session Chair: Daniel Ashbrook, *Rochester Institute of Technology, USA*

Healthcare Bias, Engagement & Adaptation

Storytelling in InfoVis

Grip, Move & Tilt: Novel Interaction

Interactive Video & Collaborative Annotations

Session Chair: Amy Ogan, *Carnegie Mellon University, USA*

HCI for the Elderly

Session Chair: Maria Wolters, *University of Edinburgh, UK*

The Impact of Crowd Work on Workers

Session Chair: Jaime Teevan, *Microsoft Research, USA*

Social Media and Mobile Camera Privacy

Session Chair: Pam Briggs, *Northumbria University, UK*

Understanding & Extending Touch Interfaces

Session Chair: Theophanis Tsandilas, *INRIA, France*

Sharing & Collaboration @ Work

Session Chair: Steven Drucker, *Microsoft Research, USA*

Families and Their Use of Technology

Session Chair: Jennifer Marlow, *Carnegie Mellon University, USA*

Understanding Crowdwork in Many Domains

Session Chair: Uichin Lee, *Korea Advanced Institute of Science and Technology, South Korea*

Eco-Green: Encouraging Energy Conservation

Session Chair: Germaine Irwin, *University of Maryland Baltimore County, USA*

Sports Tracking & Training

Session Chair: Hao-Hua Chu, *National Taiwan University, Taiwan*

Feeling & Communicating Emotions

Session Chair: Rongrong Wang, *Samsung Research America, USA*

Critical Design

Session Chair: Giulio Jacucci, *University of Helsinki, Finland*

HMDs in Augmented & Virtual Reality

Session Chair: Shahram Izadi, *Microsoft Research, UK*

Tangible Interaction with Phones

Session Chair: Shengdong Zhao, *National University of Singapore, Singapore*

UI Impact on Performance & Decisions

Session Chair: Tom Gross, *University of Bamberg, Germany*

Telepresence Video, Robots, and Walls

Experience Design for Games

Digital & Materials Fabrication

Tactile Notifications for Phones & Wearables

HCI for Civic Engagement

Security Feedback & Warnings

Wellness & Wearables

Task Interruption & Resumption

Using Random Body Parts for Input

Session Chair: Patrick Baudisch, *Hasso Plattner Institute, Germany*

Brain & Physiological Data use for HCI

Session Chair: Jacob Robert, *Tufts University, USA*

Software Engineering Tools

Session Chair: Feng Tian, *Chinese Academy of Sciences, China*

HCI at Home

Session Chair: David Geerts, *Social Spaces, Belgium*

Digital Collections, Practice & Legacy

Session Chair: Will Odom, *Simon Fraser University, Canada*

Multilingual Communication

Session Chair: Hao-Chuan Wang, *National Tsing Hua University, Taiwan*

Empowering Users

Session Chair: Maarten Thissen, *The Hague University of Applied Sciences, The Netherlands*

Accessibility for Vision Impaired Users

Session Chair: Xiaojuan Ma, *Huawei Technologies, Hong Kong*

Interactive & Multi-Surface Maps

Session Chair: Brent Hecht, *University of Minnesota, USA*

Robot Personalities

Session Chair: Malte Jung, *Cornell University, USA*

Mid-Air Gestures and Interaction

Session Chair: Yang Li, *Google Research, USA*

MOOCS & e-Learning

Session Chair: Juho Kim, *Massachusetts Institute of Technology, USA*

Understanding Gamers

Bridging Communities

Gender & Technology

Coping & Wellbeing Through HCI

Session Chair: Jina Huh, *Michigan State University, USA*

Interacting with Floors & Situated Displays

Session Chair: Diego Martinez Plasencia, *University of Bristol, UK*

Multi-Device Interaction

Session Chair: Michael Nebeling, *ETH Zurich, Switzerland*

Speech & Auditory Interfaces

Session Chair: Cosmin Munteanu, *University of Toronto Mississauga, Canada*

Email & Social Media at Work

Session Chair: Pernille Bjorn, *IT University of Copenhagen, Denmark*

Understanding & Protecting Kids Tech Use

Session Chair: Svetlana Yarosh, *University of Minnesota, USA*

Social Media & Citizen Science

Session Chair: Elena Glassman, *Massachusetts Institute of Technology, USA*

CHI 2015 Organization

General Conference Chairs
Jinwoo Kim, *Yonsei University, Korea*
Bo Begole, *Huawei, USA*

Technical Program

Technical Program Chairs
Woontack Woo, *KAIST, Korea*
Kori Inkpen, *Microsoft Research, USA*

Papers
Andy Cockburn, *University of Canterbury, New Zealand*
Joanna McGrenere, *University of British Columbia, Canada*
Jun Rekimoto, *University of Toyko, Japan*

Case Studies
Danielle Cooley, *DGCooley Consulting, USA*
Joonhwan Lee, *Seoul National University, Korea*

Courses
Regina Bernhaupt, *ICS-IRIT, France*
Matt Jones, *Swansea University, UK*

Interactivity
Julie Rico Williamson, *University of Glasgow, UK*
Juhyun Eune, *Seoul National University, Korea*

Video Showcase
Jinwook Seo, *Seoul National University, Korea*
Rodrigo de Oliveira, *Google, USA*

SIGs
Enrico Rukzio, *Ulm University, Germany*
Simone Barbosa, *PUC-Rio, Brazil*

Doctoral Consortium
Si-Jung "Jun" Kim, *University of Central Florida, USA*
Jaime Teevan, *Microsoft Research, USA*
Sue Fussell, *Cornell University, USA*

Workshops
Juergen Steimle, *Max Planck Institute for Informatics, Germany*
Bongshin Lee, *Microsoft Research, USA*

Works in Progress
Shamsi Iqbal, *Microsoft Research, USA*
Shaun Lawson, *University of Lincoln, UK*
Shendong Zhao, *National University of Singapore, Singapore*

Student Research Competition
Seungyon "Claire" Lee, *Google, USA*
Geehyuk Lee, *KAIST, Korea*

Student Design Competition
Youn-Kyung Lim, *KAIST, Korea*
Anirudha Joshi, *ITT Bombay, India*

Student Game Competition
Floyd Muller, *RMIT University, Australia*
Alessandro Canossa, *Northeastern University, USA*
Soojin Jun, *Yonsei University, Korea*

alt.chi
Silvia Lindtner, *University of California, Irvine, USA*
Morgan Ames, *Intel, USA*
Henry Duh, *University of Tasmania, Australia*

TOCHI Papers
Jeffrey Nichols, *IBM Research, USA*

Best of CHI Awards
Mark Billinghurst, *University of Canterbury, New Zealand*

Panels
Khai Truong, *University of North Carolina, Charlotte, USA*
Elaine M. Huang, *University of Zurich, Switzerland*

Conference Theme Chair
Kyle Hyunsuk Kim, *Hongik University, Korea*

Industry Liaison
Garett Dworman, *TecEd, USA*

Operations

Chair's Assistant
Yoojin Lee, *Yonsei University, Korea*

Chair's Assistant
Nik Martelaro, *Stanford University, USA*

Student Volunteer
Jon Haber, *University of Calgary, Canada*
Siroberto Scerbo, *Virginia Tech, USA*
Jieun Wee, *Seoul National University, Korea*

Technology Liaisons
Sara Drenner, *University of Minnesota-Twin Cities, USA*
Scooter Morris, *University of California, San Francisco, USA*

Webmaster
Juho Kim, *MIT, USA*
TJ Monserrat, *National University of Singapore, Singapore*

Social Media
Max Wilson, *Nottingham University, UK*
Kwangsu Cho, *Sungkyunkwan University, Korea*

Data Managerment
Max Van Kleek, *University of Southampton, UK*
BoYu Gao, *Konkuk University, Korea*

Proceedings
Deana Brown, *Georgia Tech, USA*
Jaejeung Kim, *KAIST, Korea*

Infrastructure Accessibility Chair
Jongbae Kim, *Yonsei University, Korea*

Digital Accessibility Chair
Jeff Bigham, *University of Rochester, USA*

Scheduling
Christophe Hurter, *ENAC, France*
Juho Kim, *MIT, USA*

Mobile Apps
Stephen Oney, *Carnegie Mellon University, USA*
Eiji Hayashi, *Carnegie Mellon University, USA*
Jason Wiese, *Carnegie Mellon University, USA*
Célia Martinie, *Université Paul Sabatier, France*

Video Previews
Fanny Chevalier, *INRIA, France*
Stéphane Huo, *Université Paris-Sud, France*

Posters
Hyun Joo Song, *Seoul National University, Korea*

Translations
Sue Fussell, *Cornell University, USA*
Naomi Yamashita, *NTT, Japan*

Local Hospitality
Junho Choi, *Yonsei University, Korea*

Sponsors, Exhibits & Recruitment
Carol Klyver, *Foundations of Excellence, USA*

Registration
Yvonne Lopez, *Executive Events, Inc. USA*
Brooke Daley, *Executive Events, Inc. USA*

PCS Liaisons
Max van Kleek, *University of Southampton, UK*
Carol Klyver, *Foundations of Excellence, USA*
Scooter Morris, *University of California, San Francisco, USA*

bioLogic: Natto Cells as Nanoactuators for Shape Changing Interfaces

Lining Yao[1], Jifei Ou[1], Chin-Yi Cheng[2], Helene Steiner[3], Wen Wang[4], Guanyun Wang[5], Hiroshi Ishii[1]

[1]MIT Media Lab
Cambridge, USA
{liningy, jifei, ishii}
@media.mit.edu

[2]Design Computation
MIT, USA
chinyich@mit.edu

[3]Royal College of Art
London, UK
helene.steiner@network.rca.ac.uk

[4]Chemical Engineering
MIT, USA
wwen@mit.edu

[5]Zhejiang University
Hangzhou, China
guanyun@zju.edu.cn

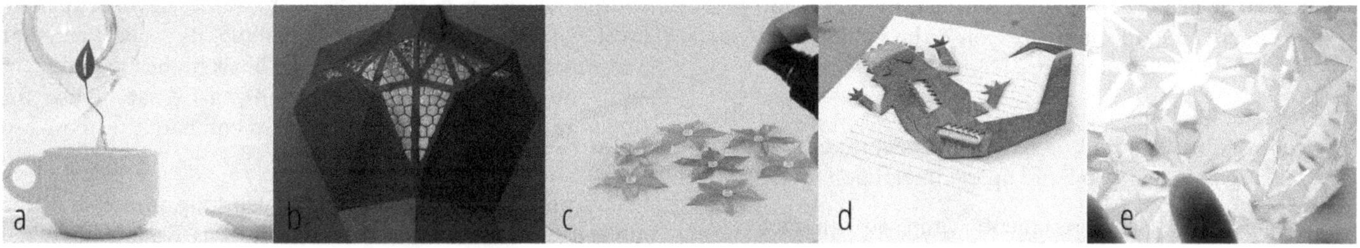

Figure 1: Example applications. (a) Living teabags; (b) "Second Skin" as responsive clothing; (c) Animated origami toys; (d) Artificial plants that change both form and color; (e) Transformable lampshade.

ABSTRACT

Nature has engineered its own actuators, as well as the efficient material composition, geometry and structure to utilize its actuators and achieve functional transformation. Based on the natural phenomenon of cells' hygromorphic transformation, we introduce the living *Bacillus Subtilis* natto cell as a humidity sensitive nanoactuator. In this paper, we unfold the process of exploring and comparing cell types that are proper for HCI use, the development of the composite biofilm, the development of the responsive structures, the control setup for actuating biofilms, and a simulation and fabrication platform. Finally, we provide a variety of application designs, with and without computer control to demonstrate the potential of our bio actuators. Through this paper, we intend to enable the use of natto cells and our platform technologies for HCI researchers, designers and bio-hackers. More generally, we try to encourage the research and use of biological responsive materials and interdisciplinary research in HCI.

CHI 2015, April 18 - 23 2015, Seoul, Republic of Korea

http://dx.doi.org/10.1145/2702123.2702611

Author Keywords

Biology; Biological Material; Shape Changing Interfaces; Smart Material; Programmable Material; Bio-printing; Hygromorph.

ACM Classification Keywords

H.5.2. User Interfaces: Haptic I/O; Prototype

INTRODUCTION

Looking into nature, from the wilting of flowers to the opening of fallen pinecones, biological sensors as well as actuators are omnipresent. Utilizing such mechanisms from nature through the integration of living organisms into design and engineering has gained increasing interest amongst scientists and engineers [3][16]. On the other hand, in the field of Human-Computer Interaction (HCI), material-based interface design and shape-change interfaces are emerging topics[24]. Ishii describes "Radical Atom" and suggests the dynamic manifestation of digital information in the physical world [9]. To add one more type of smart material for such research, we introduce a biological cell actuator, *Bacilus Subtilis* natto that responds to moisture changes to design interactive objects.

Using living cells as an actuator has several distinctive advantages: electronic free, safe and edible, the lack of wires or tubes, quiet transformation, potential biological synthesis, self-reproduction and flexibility of deposition as a liquid form. However, there are still challenges when we seek to use living cell actuators in the HCI context. For example: how to gain access and use the material in a common prototyping environment while reducing biosafety level concerns? How to synthesize material on a macro scale with nano scale actuators? How to integrate digital fabrication for more precise manufacturing in order to embed a certain level of programmability to achieve desired transformation? How to integrate the human factor and digital controllability into a hydromorphic actuator that responds to the change of relative humidity? Through this work, we hope to address those challenges.

In this paper, our main contribution, particularly compared with the closely related technique - *Bacillus Subtilis* endospore [1] based bio actuator, includes:

- Introducing natto cells as nanoactuators for designing transformable thin sheet materials that respond to humidity change. Based on our test, the natto cell has stronger force and faster response time compared with *Bacillus Subtilis* endospore [1].
- Integrating the nanoactuator with a digitally controllable humidity changing system, as well as sensing composite to build up the interaction loop.
- Developing the experiment setup to characterize performance of the nanoactuator.
- Implementing application prototypes that either use biofilm as a self-contained sensing and actuation mechanism, or use biofilm within a computer modulated interaction loop to demonstrate the wide design space with the cell actuator.
- Developing digital simulation and fabrication tools to facilitate HCI design study.
- Providing transformation structure examples that cell actuators can achieve.

INTRODUCING NATTO CELLS AS ACTUATORS

Cells' hygromorphic phenomenon has been well studied, especially in some plants such as pinecones and wheat awns[1]. In collaboration with biologists, we observed a similar hygromorphic behavior from the *Bacillus Subtilis* natto cell. By varying the relative humidity (RH) around the cells, the size of the cells can change by 50%. With the natto cell, we introduce the idea of developing cell-hybrid biofilms that can transform with the change in relative humidity.

Originally, we began our exploration with the *Bacillus Subtilis* endospore, which was reported as one option for biological actuators [3]. Through the process, we fortuitously found that the vegetative natto cells perform even better (Figure 2d). Our comparison test shows that the cell-hybrid film has an average bending curvature that is 5 times greater than that of the spore-hybrid films, with a 2.5 times more rapid response. For example, under the condition of 40% relative humidity and 3.6 μm cell thickness, the natto cell based film can reach an average bending curvature of 470 degrees (Table 2), while the endospore based film can reach an average of 80 degrees.

While the endospore solution requires mixing with Polylisine in order to be attached to latex surfaces, the hygromorphic bonds between natto cells and latex substrate behave as natural glue that can resist up to a 2 minute flush of water. Culturing cells also takes a much shorter time and poses fewer technical requirements than culturing spores. Since natto cells have been used to ferment food in Japan since 1906 [25], they are safe for use and do not require a lab environment with specified biosafety levels.

Beyond natto cells, we have also tested a variety of other cells, e.g., E. coli and yeasts. Natto cells were eventually chosen based on a few criteria: biosafety level, expertise level to handle, synthesis complexity and actuator performance. For example, E.coli has a higher requirement on its bio-safety level; and, although yeast is safe to use, the actuating performance is inadequate compared to the natto cell.

Our hypothesis on the natto cells' working principle at the molecular level is as follows: it was found that the functional layer of the endospore system is the "cortex" composed of peptidoglycan (protein and sugar) [3]. In our living cell system, there is no cortex but proteins. We hypothesized that cell expansion behavior is due to water absorption by intracellular proteins. We further strengthened our hypothesis by testing out that pure proteins have hygromorphic behaviors as well, but with a much longer response time, possibly due to the lack of cellular scaffolds. In the future, more scientific study will be conducted to establish the underlying mechanisms.

DEVELOPMENT OF BIOFILMS

A *composite biofilm* contains two layers: the cell layer and the substrate layer. The biofilm can vary the bending curvature triggered by the RH change (Figure 2b,c). We obtain the composite biofilm by applying cell-water solution onto the substrate layer and vaporizing the water content (Figure 2a). The ideal substrate material includes 0.2mm thick latex, 0.3mil Kapton and 0.3mil PET.

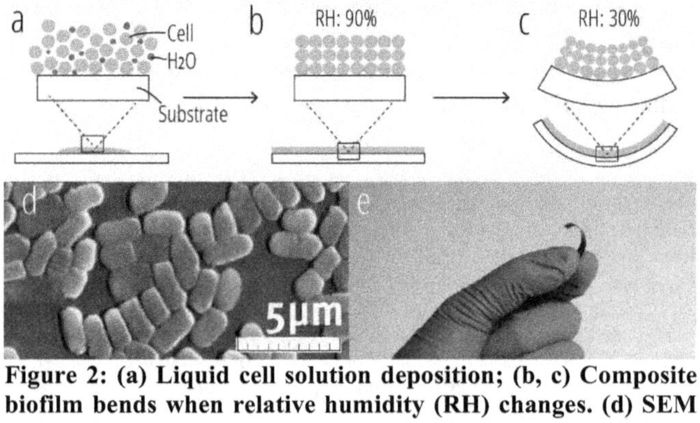

Figure 2: (a) Liquid cell solution deposition; (b, c) Composite biofilm bends when relative humidity (RH) changes. (d) SEM image of the nanoactuators, natto cells; (e) Composite biofilm.

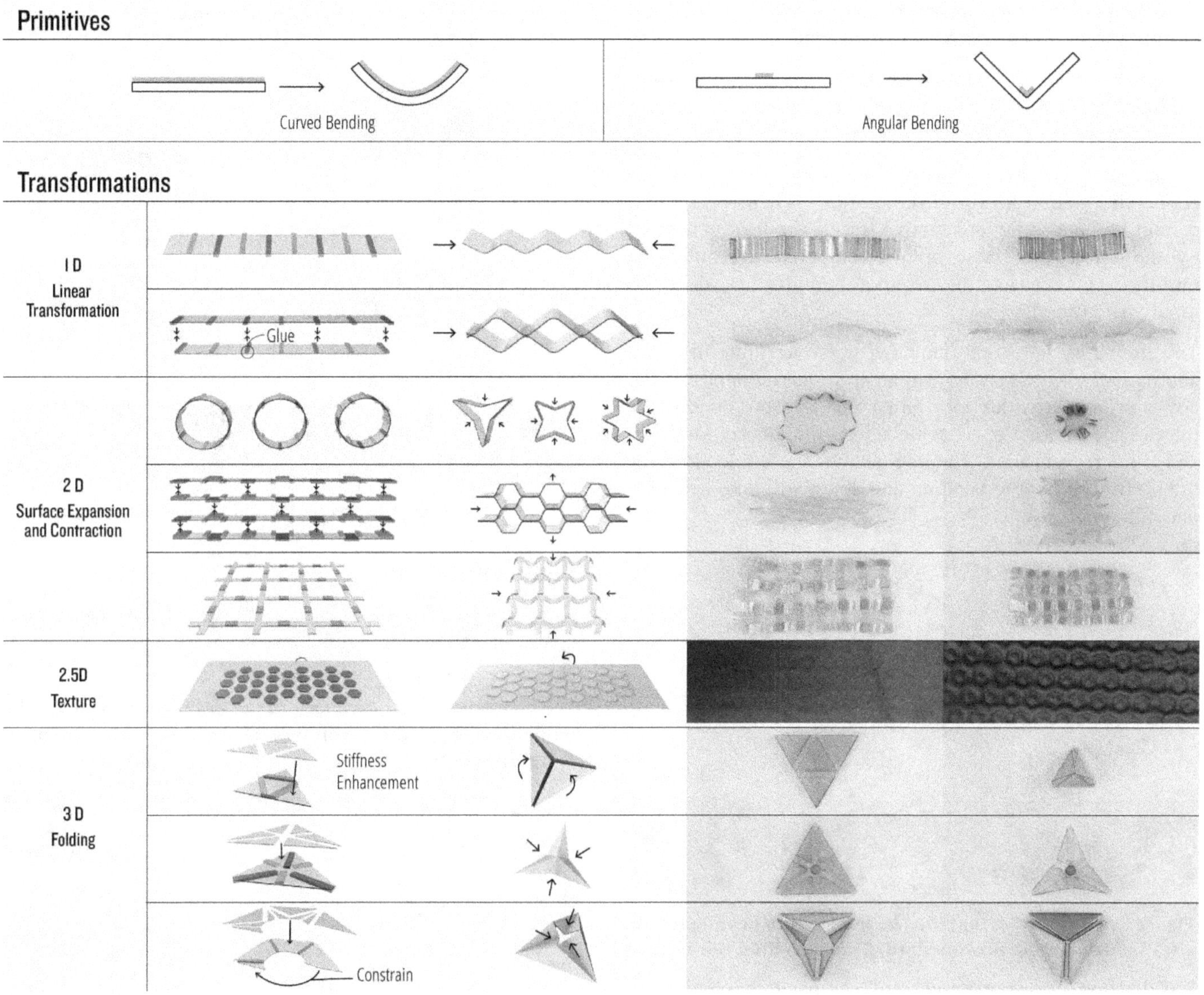

Table 1: Design of Responsive Structures. Two basic bending primitives can be translated into 1D linear transformation, 2D surface expansion and contraction, 2.5D texture change and 3D folding.

DEVELOPMENT OF RESPONSIVE STRUCTURES

With biofilm as the basic building blocks, we design responsive structures and transformations, which can be referenced when we try to achieve a certain shape change in the design of HCI systems. The detailed simulation and fabrication process will be described in the later chapter of the paper.

Transformation design is based on two bending primitives: (Table 1): Curved bending is for more organic transformation; angular bending is for more geometric transformation. To achieve a curving transformation, cells were applied across the entire strip; for an angular transformation, cells were applied in lines. In the latter case, a stiffer material can be attached to substrate regions without cell actuators, to stabilize the structure and enhance the effect of a sharp fold.

Through combining the bending primitives across different dimensions, we can create a variety of responsive transformations including lD linear transformation, 2D surface expansion and contraction, 2.5D texture change and 3D folding (Table 1).

CONTROL OF THE BIOFILMS

To design interactive systems using our biofilm, we seek ways to modulate the regional relative humidity around our biofilm samples in a relatively fast manner.

To quickly raise the relative humidity, we set up a water bubbler that can convert dry, compressed air into wet air that reaches above 90% relative humidity (Figure 3).

To quickly lower the relative humidity, we composite conductive traces on top of the biofilm. When we apply a certain voltage to the conductive traces, the heat generated by the traces will raise up the temperature around the biofilm. This causes the relative humidity to decrease rapidly (Figure 3).

To alternate the high and low relative humidity, we alternatively switch on the wet air from the bubbler and the power which provides a certain voltage to the conductive traces. The alternation is achieved by three relay switches and a microcontroller. Figure 3 shows one circle time for the biofilm sample to bend up and down will take less than one minute.

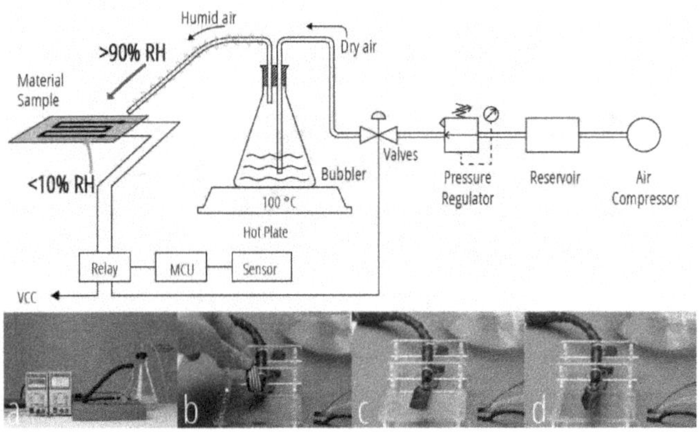

Figure 3: (a) control setup; (b) The sample with heating traces (c) Control button pressured; (d) Control button released;

We develop our own process of compositing conductive traces to the existing biofilm. To maintain the flexibility of the biofilm for transformation purpose, a flexible conductive ink (125-19, Creative Material, Inc.) customized for silicone substrates is applied to the biofilm through a screen printing process. To enable faster iterations of prototyping, rather than customize a photo-emulsion screen, we laser cut double-sided tacky paper to create masks. The mask is then placed on the back of a screen (××8, Blick) (Figure 3a). Squeegees are used to apply the conductive ink to the latex substrate (Figure 4). We have successfully printed conductive traces between 0.35mm and 2mm using this method.

The same conductive traces can potentially be used as sensing elements as well. For example, the resistance of the conductive traces is changing as the biofilm bends at varying curvatures. With precise calibration, the bending angle can be read directly. A single conductive trace can serve either as a capacitive sensor or heating element through the use of two relay switches. "Responsive Plants" in the application section is an example of this technique (Figure 11).

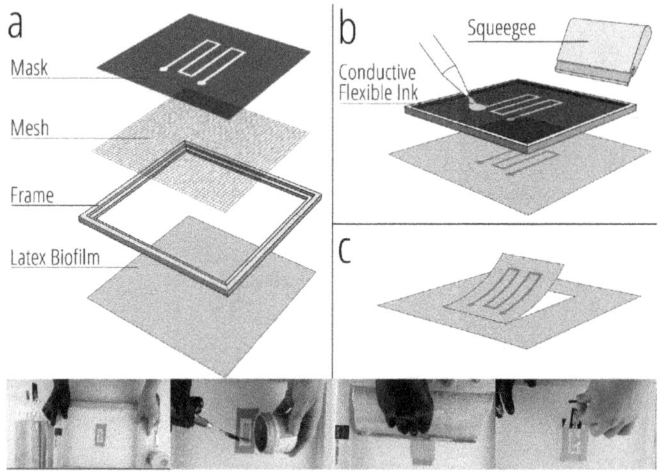

Figure 4: Process of screen printing flexible circuit onto the biofilm

DESIGN PROCESS

Our design process contains three steps: mechanical characterization, simulation, and fabrication.

Mechanical Characterization

We characterize the mechanical performance of the biofilm with the consideration of two factors: bending curvature and response time.

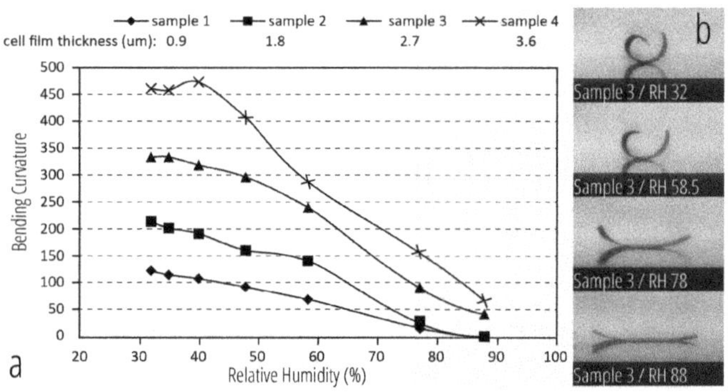

Table 2: (a) Bending curvature versus RH curve; (b) Contrast of bending curvature of Sample 1 at different RH.

Table 2 measures the curvature changes on four biofilm samples, which are prepared on the same 0.2mm latex substrate with varied film thickness of cells. Firstly, the bending curvature becomes smaller as the relative humidity is decreased. Second, under the same relative humidity, the thicker the cell layers are, the bigger the bending curvature is. The sample with the most cell layers has the maximum bending angle at the lowest relative humidity.

Table 3 describes the response time of the biofilm to reach its maximum curvature under two alternated RH conditions. It shows that it takes 9.04s for sample 1 to reach its maximum curvature and it takes longer (14.98s) when layer thickness is increased for sample 2.

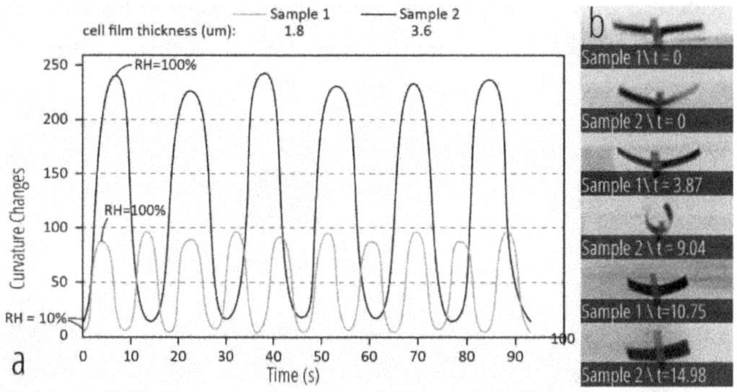

Table 3: RH alternates between 10% and 100%, the curvature changes versus time.

Simulation

In order to better design and predict the transformation behavior and produce digital files for fabrication (geometry for cell printing and substrate film), we developed a digital material design and simulation platform within Rhinoceros 5 and Grasshopper. It includes two main functions: design and simulation. At the design stage, users can define the geometry of the substrate and regions for actuator application sequentially; and, at the simulation stage, the process of transformation can be animated with the change of RH (Figure 5). Experimental data from Table 2 is integrated into the software for physical simulation. And, as examples of cases used, all of the transformation structures from Table 1 were designed and simulated with this platform.

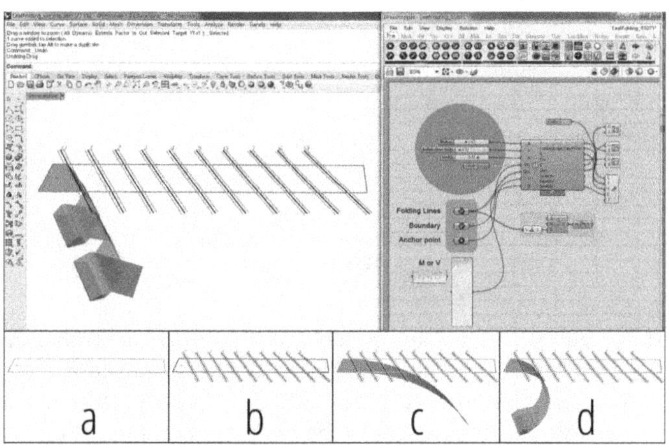

Figure 5: Design and simulation platform. (a) Defining substrate; (b) Defining actuators; (c) Simulating in high RH; (d) Simulating in low RH.

In terms of molding methods at the back end of our software, the central part of our simulation is to simplify the model into curves, divide them into consecutive units, and then calibrate the inner stress and moment equilibriums through evolutionary computing[5] (Figure 6a).

To reduce the calculation time, we create a database that contains a group of pre-calculated curves that are under various boundary conditions (Figure 6b). To simulate a model, we firstly simplify the model into a combination of basic curves, depending on whether they have the cell actuators on top of the substrate material or not. Then, we look into the database and obtain the shape of each basic curve through the interpolation of the existing data. Those curves are then connected to achieve a rough shape of our model. To refine the rough simulation, we apply the same evolutionary computing method to the entire model within a reduced range of possible solutions.

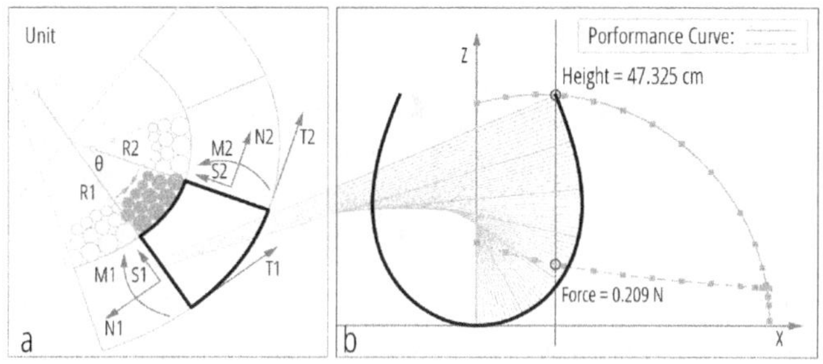

Figure 6: (a) The analysis of force and moment in a single unit with the cell stress and geometric constraint; (b) The shape of basic curve generated by interpolating data from the database.

Fabrication with Bioprinters

Beyond manual pipetting, which is a common liquid application technique in wet labs, we have explored other digital fabrication techniques for more precise deposition of liquid cell solution. Inkjet printing and atomizing are presented as two platforms, one for precise placement of the cell solution for smaller scale and the other for large-scale application (Figure 7).

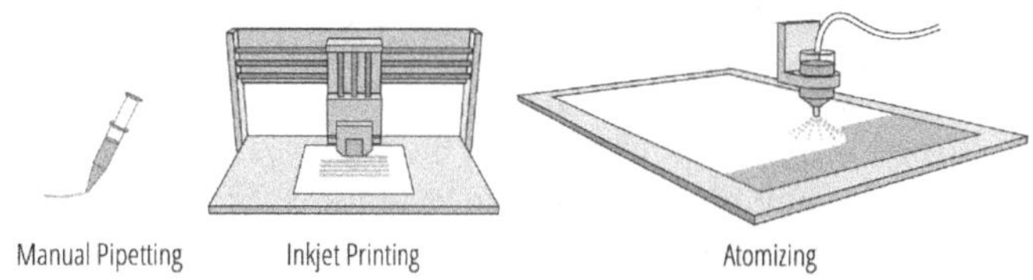

Figure 7: Three fabrication tool options

In both cases, since Table 2 describes that the maximum bending curvature is tightly related to the layer thickness of the cells, we need to control cell layer thickness through a combination of the flow rate and the machine feedrate. To reach a certain curvature under certain RH conditions, we can refer to Table 2 and interpolate a suggested cell layer thickness t. And to reach t, it takes time T:

$$t \times S = v \times T \quad (1)$$

Where S is a certain surface area, v is the machine flowrate.

To allow the deposition to cover the whole surface area S:

$$f \times T \times w = S/z \quad (2)$$

Where f is the machine feedrate, w is the width of the droplet coverage, and z is the stepover of the CNC machine.

Machine feedrate v can be calculated based on (1) and (2):

f = v/ (t × z × w) (3)

Inkjet Printer

In order to achieve a higher accuracy of deposition, we assembled an inkjet-based print head (HP C6602A) with a 3-axis computer numeric control system (Zentoolworks). We designed a custom printhead to hold the inkjet cartridge carrier in place, and stabilize two pneumatic tubes to accelerate the drying process of the cell solution by constantly blowing gentle air onto the substrate while printing. Figure 8 shows the printing process. Ultrasonic cleaning is necessary before the filling of empty cartridge.

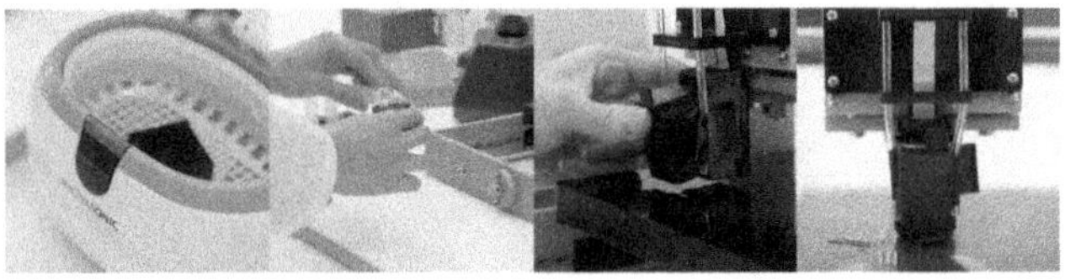

Figure 8: Inkjet printing process on a desktop CNC machine.

On the software side, we customize the G-code generated by standard CNC toolpath software (Makercam in our case), to disable the control of spindle and Z-axis, and add the control of printhead to make sure that the ink spray will be paused when the printhead has to be lifted up and move to a new location.

Atomizer

We modified a medical atomizer (Model 286-RD, DeVilbiss) that can create a fine mist and connect it to a regulated air supply. The device is mounted to a stationary CNC router (PRSalpha, Shopbot), and the production process can be easily translated and used in an industrial context (Figure 9). Atomizing is good for creating homogeneous coating on a large scale, but is less feasible for depositing arbitrary patterns. The way we create patterned deposition is through masking: laser cut mask with photo-mount spray is attached to the substrate surface before the atomizing process.

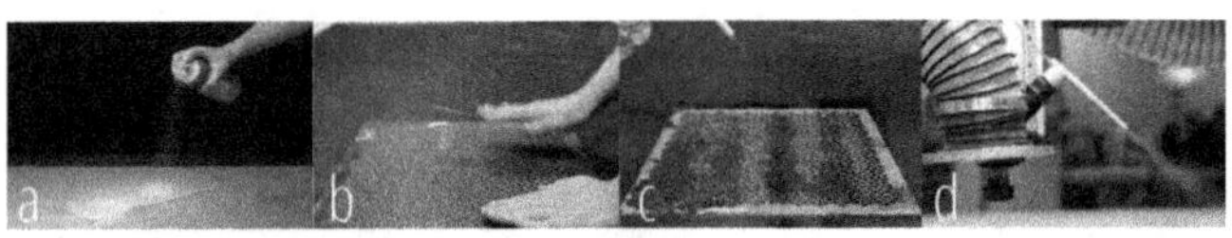

Figure 9: Masking and Atomizing process on a stationary CNC machine.

APPLICATIONS

We consider two methods for applying the use of our composite biofilms for the design of responsive interfaces: biofilm as self-contained sensing and actuation system (Figure 10a), and biofilm within a computer modulated interaction loop (Figure 10b). In the self-contained biofilm method, human behavior plays a role in causing the change of RH in the biofilm, so it can be utilized as both an organic sensing and actuation mechanism without additional sensors. In the computer modulated biofilm method, human interaction can be sensed by additional sensing mechanisms to control the RH level for actuation.

We provide five example applications, two using self-contained biofilm methods in "Living Teabags" and "Second Skin;" three using computer modulated biofilms in "Artificial Plants," "Responsive Lamp" and "Animated Toys."

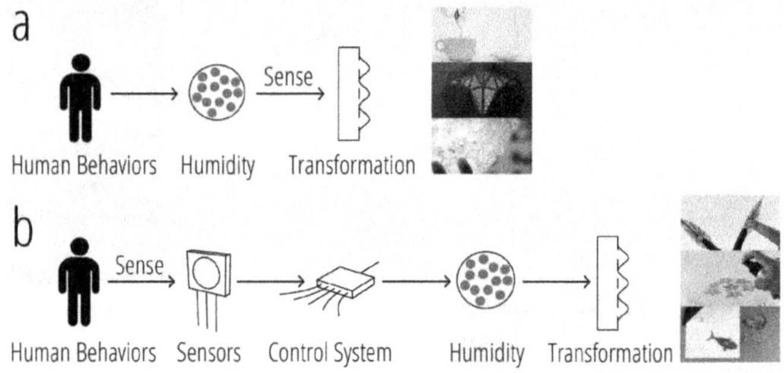

Figure 10: Interaction Loops. (a) Self-contained system with biofilm functions as both sensor and actuator; (b) Computer modulated biofilm incorporates other sensing mechanisms in the interaction loop.

Living Teabag

The leaf on top of the tea bag is curled up in the beginning. After pouring hot water into the teacup, the curled leaf will slowly unwrap to indicate the tea bag is fully soaked in water. Once the tea is ready and the tea bag is pulled out of the cup, the leaf will curl up again to indicate the end of its life (Figure 11). The unwrapping can be triggered by either the steam coming from the hot water, or the capillary force that comes all the way up from the tea bag. Since we can control the length and timing of the capillary movement, the leaf's unwrapping can more precisely indicate the timing of when tea is ready.

Figure 11:Living teabags

Second Skin

If we choose thin Kapton substrate (0.3mil) to synthesize the biofilm, it gets so thin that it reacts to raised human body temperature (Figure 12b,c). We prototype a responsive suit that reacts to the body temperature. It opens up when the skin raises its temperature during running and sweating (Figure12a,d,e). The responsive "Second Skin" creates an ecosystem between the human body and the covering.

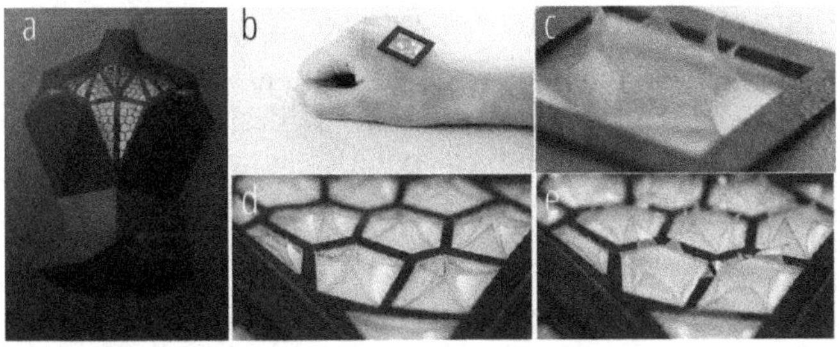

Figure 12: (a, b, c) Biofilm with 0.3mil Kapton substrate reacts to raised skin temperature. (d, e,f) Design of the "Second Skin" as a piece of responsive cloth

Responsive Plants

We print the cell actuators following the vein structure of certain leaves, which creates biomimetic transformation that resembles real, natural organisms (Figure 16). Considering many natural leaves transform due to the gain and loss of water inside the veins, cell actuators swell and shrink to create a similar effect.

With a closed control loop, artificial plants that respond to various stimuli are designed as educational toys. In order to mimic the natural flower changing shape and color at the same time, we mix thermochromic paint into liquid latex and produce our own color-changing film substrate. A flower bouquet is designed to transform in both shape and color (Figure 13a,b,c). When we spray water on them, they change from being curled and umber to expanding and red. The control logic is: the heating circuit below the plate is always on until an equipped humidity sensor detects a water spray.

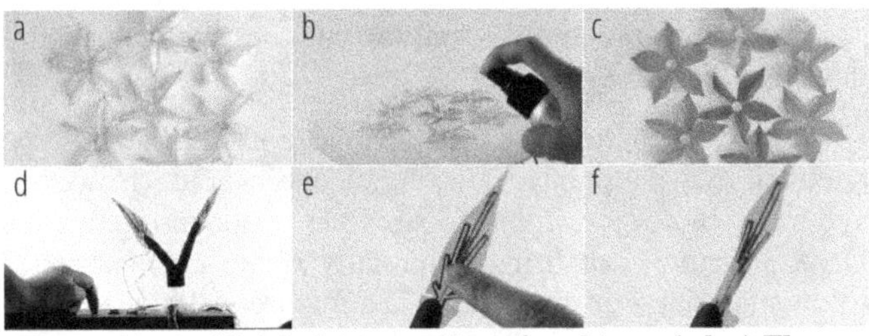

Figure 13: Artificial plants as educational toys. (a,b,c) Flower bouquet that changes both color and form. (d,e,f) Biomimetic leaves that respond to human touch.

Figure 13d,e,f depicts another way to interact with the artificial plants. This leaf mimics the movement of Mimosa, which closes when people touch it. Capacitive sensing uses the same circuitry for heating. Two relay switches control the embedded conductive traces to be connected to either a capacitive sensing board or a direct voltage source for heating.

Animated Toys

Previously, research has used other smart materials to make responsive origami and related objects[13][22][27]. We built a flexible heating board on paper with heating traces made of copper tapes. By folding and unfolding the corner of the card, the heating platform is switched on and off. The paper animals designed with hinges made of biofilm can be animated in real time (Figure 14).

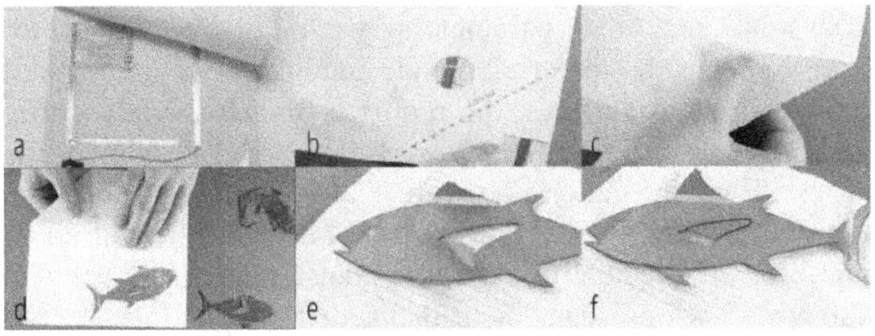

Figure 14: Animated origami toys.

Responsive Lamp

Using one of the 3D folding primitives mentioned earlier, we are able to design a responsive lamp that closes up its lampshade when it is off, and opens up to leak light and create lighting patterns when it is on (Figure 15). Through this example, we intend to demonstrate the fabrication techniques we suggested are easily extendable to more complex systems with more transforming units. All of the actuators on this lamp are fabricated within 12 hours with two experienced fabricators.

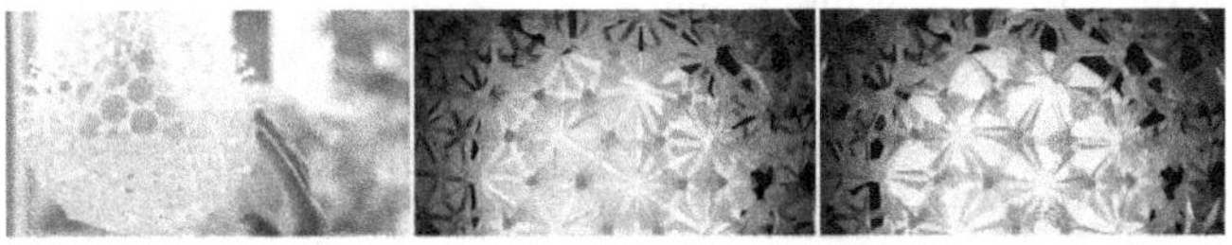

Figure 15: Transformable lampshade.

RELATED WORK

Bio-hybrid Cell-based Actuators

As the development of microsystems, such as microrobots, micropumps and micromotors, bio-hybrid cell-based actuators are emerging[2]. Common stimuli types for those actuators include temperature, pH, ionic strength, light and humidity. A tissue engineered robotic jellyfish was created with rat cells [20]. Elastin-like polypeptides (ELPs) are one such class of biopolymers that respond to temperature change [18]. Based on the swelling effect of paper, smart material composited from cellulose has been developed [23].

Based on Carlsen and Sitti's review paper on bio-hybrid cell-based actuators[2], we conclude that so far all the reported systems in this field are submerged in fluid, and none of them utilize relative humidity change as actuation stimuli. In this sense, we introduce a concept to fill in the blank of the non-fluidic humidity responsive cell actuators. The fact that our actuator is simple to fabricate also makes it stand out from other bio-actuators.

Shape Transformation in Soft Material

Kempaiah and Nie have published a review paper summarizing recent progress of shape transformation using soft materials [10]. While mentioned materials in the paper are mainly inorganic or nonliving, we emphasize the natto cell is a living, food-safe organism. The bio-film we produced can be safely integrated into food, wearable and living environments.

For some technical parameters, we compare with other state-of-art soft materials, and conclude the natto cell performance as follows: the required time for synthesizing is moderate, the required expertise level is low, the accessibility for material resources is high, the scalability is high, and the response time is fast. The main limitation of our biofilm is the limited force transferred from cells to substrate, which can be enhanced through introducing covalent binding in the future.

Unconventional Actuators for Shape Change in HCI

Beyond common electric motors, many more types of actuations have been adapted to design shape changing interfaces: Pneumatic actuation [11][26], shape memory alloy [4][8], piezo actuators [19], jamming material [7][21], ferromagnetic fluids [12], etc. Different techniques have their unique benefits: fast prototyping (electric motors), big force and compliant to malleable surfaces (pneumatic actuators), silent and flexible (shape memory alloy), phase transition (ferromagnetic fluids). In this paper, we try to demonstrate both the advantages and challenges of our bio-actuator for HCI.

Hygromorphic Materials

Many natural and artificial materials respond to humidity change by swelling or shrinking, from the fiber in wood to fallen pine cones. Hygromorphic natural materials have been introduced in both scientific and design fields. Scientists have focused on studying and explaining the mechanism behind the hygromorphism of different organisms [6]. A bio-inspired polymer composite actuator was invented to harvest energy through continuously flipping sides [16]. Additionally humidity-reactive wood has been utilized by designers to build architecture scale, transformable installations [17]. Faz pavilion exemplified that humidity reactive natural wood can achieve simple yet ecologically embedded architecture in reaction to its surrounding environment.

Living Organisms in HCI

Study of utilizing living organisms, especially the field of synthetic biology, has gained increasing attention from HCI and the design community. DIYbio has initiated events and hackerspaces around the topic of synthetic biology and has been inspirational to the interdisciplinary research combining biology with HCI and design [15]. Machines, toolsets and communities have emerged in the field of manipulating DNA and life.

Biological sensors have been explored in interface design as well. The importance of including living organisms such as plants and animals into the current sensing mechanisms was addressed [14].

DISCUSSION AND FUTURE WORK

Collaboration Between HCI and Biology

Materiality/matter based interface design and shape changing interfaces are emerging topics in HCI that are gaining more and more attention. By introducing natto cell-hybrid films, we try to broaden the material library that designers in HCI can use. At the initial stage of exploration, collaborating with experienced biologists was critical. Their intuition and expertise led to the accidental finding and the following quantitative characterization of the natto cell actuator. As the project moved to the step of biofilm development, chemical and mechanical engineering knowledge started to play a more important role. For the structure and application design, HCI researchers with design backgrounds played an essential role.

As the collaboration progressed, HCI designers were empowered with an interesting material that has both unique functions and provocative bio-potentials. On the other hand, our biologist collaborators also commented that this was the first time they perceived and studied cells for their actuation capability, rather than their growth, physiology or DNA synthesis. The scientists mentioned they were surprised to see how designers scale up their research results from glass tubes and pipette tips to objects on the table, ceiling and even human body.

Biological Challenges and Opportunities

The uniqueness of self-evolving, self-duplication and self-assembly of living organism can potentially give rise to critical design concepts. For example, we can design shape-change interfaces that grow. With synthesized life, the "behavior" of the transformation can be evolved as life develops.

Until now, the natto cells that have been used are wild-type bacteria and they have not been engineered. However, synthetic biology, which focuses on engineering of the DNA structure, can bring potentially richer characteristics to the material. For example, it is a mature technique to add genes for bioluminescence into the cells. So, potentially, we could engineer our nanoactuators and make them glow in a dark environment.

Engineering Challenges and Opportunities

It has been proven that the cell has a very high energy density, considering a single layer cell (1μm in thickness) can lift up 0.2mm thick latex film. However, simply adding more cell layers will not help to lift up thicker materials, since each layer of cells needs to tightly connect to each other and to the substrate. Also, adding cell layer thickness will increase the time for humidity diffusion and lower the response time. More multidisciplinary engineering research has to be included in the research on bonding method, material processing, mechanical structure design, and stable control of relative humidity for suitable applications.

Design Challenges and Opportunities

Natural-natural hybrid material is an exciting direction. Combining natural organisms with different characteristics dates back to grafting fruits. As one example, by compositing the spore actuators to natural willow leaves, we could make the leaves transform in a desired way when it is about to rain. Thus, the willow tree becomes a transformable and natural installation and also an environmental sensor.

Since the *Bacillus subtilis* natto is food safe, one potential space is actuated food. Food is inevitable for daily life. Rather than just focusing on the taste and presentation, adding interactivities into the experience of eating can be interesting. For example, shape changing food that indicates when the temperature is right for eating.

CONCLUSION

In this paper we have introduced the development of a new biofilm based on living natto actuators for humidity responsive transformable interfaces. As designing shape-change interfaces draw more and more attention in HCI, materiality becomes one of the important aspects we need to be concerned with in design. Through this research, we hope to look beyond hard and inorganic material and reflect: how can we grow living materials and incorporate them into our man-made interaction systems? How do they enable a bigger design space in the myriad of life - things we eat, drink and wear? We believe the unique properties of the cell actuator - being electronic-free, humidity responsive, safe and edible – can enable the design for improving everyday life.

REFERENCES

[1] Burgert, I. and Fratzl, P. 2009. Actuation systems in plants as prototypes for bioinspired devices. *Phil. Trans. R. Soc. A*. 367, (Apr. 2009), 1541–1557.

[2] Carlsen, R.W. and Sitti, M. 2014. Bio-hybrid cell-based actuators for microsystems. *Small (Weinheim an der Bergstrasse, Germany)*. 10, 19 (Oct. 2014), 3831–51.

[3] Chen, X., Mahadevan, L., Driks, A. and Sahin, O. 2014. Bacillus spores as building blocks for stimuli-responsive materials and nanogenerators. *Nature Nanotechnology*. 9, January (2014), 137–141.

[4] Coelho, M., Ishii, H. and Maes, P. 2008. Surflex. *Proceeding of the twenty-sixth annual CHI conference extended abstracts on Human factors in computing systems - CHI '08* (New York, New York, USA, Apr. 2008), 3429.

[5] Eiben, A.. and Smith, J.E. 2003. *Introduction to Evolutionary Computing*. Springer,Natural Computing Series.

[6] Erb, R.M., Sander, J.S., Grisch, R. and Studart, A.R. 2013. Self-shaping composites with programmable bioinspired microstructures. *Nature communications*. 4, (Jan. 2013), 1712.

[7] Follmer, S., Leithinger, D., Olwal, A., Cheng, N. and Ishii, H. 2012. Jamming user interfaces: programmable particle stiffness and sensing for malleable and shape-changing devices. *Proc. of UIST 2012* (2012), 519–528.

[8] Gomes, A. and Nesbitt, A. 2013. MorePhone : A Study of Actuated Shape Deformations for Flexible Thin-Film Smartphone Notifications. (2013), 583–592.

[9] Ishii, H., Lakatos, D., Bonanni, L. and Labrune, J. 2012. Radical Atoms : Beyond Tangible Bits , Toward Transformable Materials. *Interactions*. 19, 1 (2012), 38–51.

[10] Kempaiah, R. and Nie, Z. 2014. From nature to synthetic systems: shape transformation in soft materials. *Journal of Materials Chemistry B*. 2, 17 (2014), 2357.

[11] Kim, S., Kim, H., Lee, B., Nam, T.-J. and Lee, W. 2008. Inflatable mouse. *Proceeding of the twenty-sixth annual CHI conference on Human factors in computing systems - CHI '08* (New York, New York, USA, Apr. 2008), 211.

[12] Koh, J.T.K.V., Karunanayaka, K., Sepulveda, J., Tharakan, M.J., Krishnan, M. and Cheok, A.D. 2011. Liquid interface. *Computers in Entertainment*. 9, 2 (Jul. 2011), 1–8.

[13] Koizumi, N., Yasu, K., Liu, A., Sugimoto, M. and Inami, M. 2010. Animated Paper: A Toolkit for Building Moving Toys. *Computers in Entertainment*. 8, 2 (Dec. 2010).

[14] Kuznetsov, S., Odom, W., Pierce, J. and Paulos, E. 2011. Nurturing natural sensors. *Proc. of UbiComp '2011* (ACM Press, 2011), 227–236.

[15] Kuznetsov, S., Taylor, A.S., Regan, T., Villar, N. and Paulos, E. 2012. At the Seams : DIYbio and Opportunities for HCI. *Proc. of DIS 2012* (2012), 258–267.

[16] Ma, M., Guo, L., Anderson, D.G. and Langer, R. 2013. Bio-inspired polymer composite actuator and generator driven by water gradients. *Science (New York, N.Y.)*. 339, 6116 (Jan. 2013), 186–9.

[17] Menges, A. and Reichert, S. 2012. Material Capacity: Embedded Responsiveness. *Archit Design*. 82, (2012), 52–59.

[18] Meyer, D.E. and Chilkoti, A. 2004. Quantification of the Effects of Chain Length and Concentration on the Thermal Behavior of Elastin-like Polypeptides. *Biomacromolecules*. 5, 4 (2004), 846–851.

[19] Miyaki, T., Ding, Y., Banitalebi, B. and Beigl, M. 2011. Things that Hover : Interaction with Tiny Battery-less Robots on Desktop. *Proc. of CHI EA 2011* (2011), 531–540.

[20] Nawroth, J.C., Lee, H., Feinberg, A.W., Ripplinger, C.M., McCain, M.L., Grosberg, A., Dabiri, J.O. and Parker, K.K. 2012. A tissue-engineered jellyfish with biomimetic propulsion. *Nature biotechnology*. 30, 8 (Aug. 2012), 792–797.

[21] Ou, J., Yao, L., Tauber, D., Steimle, J., Niiyama, R. and Ishii, H. 2014. jamSheets : Thin Interfaces with Tunable Stiffness Enabled by Layer Jamming. *Proc. of TEI 2014* (2014), 65–72.

[22] Probst, K., Seifried, T. and Haller, M. 2011. Move-it: interactive sticky notes actuated by shape memory alloys. *Proc. of CHI EA 2011* (2011), 1393–1398.

[23] Qiu, X. and Hu, S. 2013. "Smart" Materials Based on Cellulose: A Review of the Preparations, Properties, and Applications. *Materials*. 6, 3 (Feb. 2013), 738–781.

[24] Rasmussen, M., Pedersen, E., Petersen, M.G. and Hornbæk, K. 2012. Shape-changing interfaces: a review of the design space and open research questions. *Proc. of CHI 2012* (2012), 735–744.

[25] Shurtleff, W. and Aoyagi, A. 2012. *History of Natto and Its Relatives*. Soyinfo Center.

[26] Yao, L., Niiyama, R., Ou, J., Follmer, S., Silva, C. Della and Ishii, H. 2013. PneUI : Pneumatically Actuated Soft Composite Materials for Shape Changing Interfaces. *Proc. of UIST 2013* (2013), 13–22.

[27] Yasu, K. and Inami, M. 2012. POPAPY : Instant Paper Craft. *Proc. of ACE 2012* (2012), 406–420.

Control of Non-Solid Diffusers by Electrostatic Charging

Deepak Ranjan Sahoo, Diego Martinez Plasencia, Sriram Subramanian
Department of Computer Science, University of Bristol, UK
{deepak.sahoo, diego.martinez-plasencia, sriram.subramanian}@bristol.ac.uk

ABSTRACT
The form factors of displays using fog or water surface are limited by our ability to control the non-solid substances used as the diffuser. We propose a charging technique for polar aerosols (e.g., mist or fog) that allows control of the shape and trajectory of such non-solid diffusers using electric fields. We report experiments that allowed us to design a charging mechanism that produces charged fog aerosols with homogeneous electrical mobility. We illustrate our idea by demonstrating how electric fields can be used to control the shape of a fog display and the trajectory of a bubble display.

Author Keywords
Non-solid diffusers; Shape changing; Aerosol; Polar molecules; Diffusion charging; Electrostatic field; Control.

ACM Classification Keywords
H.5.2. [Information interfaces and presentation] : Prototyping

INTRODUCTION
There is a growing tendency towards using touchless interaction. Commercially available devices, such as Kinect or Leap, allow us to interact with rich and expressive input in mid-air. But even if input can be sensed anywhere, the display requires a solid substrate such as LCD or projection surface. This can constrain users' movements, i.e., hands cannot pass through the display, or force the display to stay at a distance, making input and output non-collocated.

Some display technologies have been proposed that use non-solid diffusers (e.g., water or mist) as the display surface. These approaches offer interesting interaction opportunities and allow interaction to happen anywhere around the user, while not adding architectural barriers due to display walls or projection surfaces. Rakkolainen et al. [8] proposed a fog display that presents imagery floating in mid-air that users can reach and even walk through. AquaTop [7] uses top projection on a bath tub, allowing interactions underneath and above the surface. The multi-layered water display [1] and MisTable [6] use water and mist respectively to create a 3D volume within which users can interact. SensaBubble [9] and FRAGWRAP [5] use fog

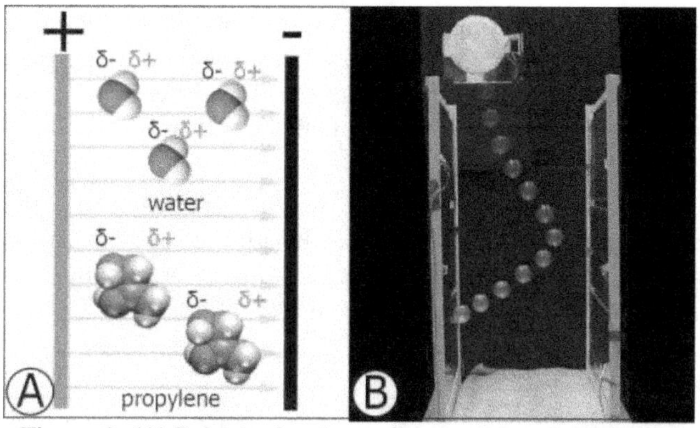

Figure 1: (A) Polar molecules such as water and propylene glycol are mobile in electric fields, and are proposed to make non-solid displays. (B) A time-lapse photo of a charged fog filled bubble display that was steered by electric fields is shown to demonstrate the proposed technique.

filled bubbles as display surfaces that could potentially float anywhere in the room.

While the potential of these display technologies seems remarkable, their design and form factors are limited by our ability to control the shape of the non-solid diffusers used. Using laminar air-flow to constrain fog allows for flat vertical surfaces, e.g., fog screen. Using accurate synchronization allows the multi-layered water display to create several non-occluding projection surfaces. Bubble displays use bubbles as a way to carry fog and shape the display. These examples illustrate how the technique to control and shape the non-solid diffuser is one of the main elements guiding the design of such display technologies.

Here we propose a novel technique to control the shape and position of non-solid diffusers using electric fields and polar molecules, which have asymmetric charge distribution in their molecular structure that makes them react to electric fields (see Figure 1.A), as well as help maintain charge compared to non-polar molecules. We leverage these features and present an aerosol, made from a mixture of glycol and water, i.e., typically used as a non-solid diffuser, with accurate control of the charge, size and speed of each nanometer-scale aerosol particle. This is used to control the trajectory and shape of the non-solid diffusers as illustrated in Figure 1.B.

Here we contribute a method to create electrically charged aerosol particles. We illustrate the utility of the proposed method using two novel example applications: a shape changing fog display, and a trajectory controlled bubble display.

CHI 2015, April 18–23, 2015, Seoul, Republic of Korea.

http://dx.doi.org/10.1145/2702123.2702363

CHARGING AEROSOLS FOR NON-SOLID DIFFUSERS

Charging aerosols has been addressed in certain engineering domains, mostly with the intention to remove charge (e.g., dust removal in the industry), rather than to induce it. Applications such as electrostatic spray painting involve charging of particles; but the particles are not filtered by size and their speed is not controlled.

In order to provide accurate control of non-solid diffusers, aerosol particles need to have homogeneous electrical mobility. That is, particles must be homogeneous in terms of charge, size and speed, so that they all react similarly when travelling through an electric field.

This section describes our choice of the aerosol and the charging method, while the evaluation of the electrical mobility and interference of the charging mechanism on the aerosol are described in the following section.

Polar molecules, surface tension and charging

Polar molecules are inherently reactive to electric fields (see Figure 1.A). However, their dipole moments, e.g., 3.6 Debyes for glycol and 1.85 Debyes for water, are too weak to allow us to use them as non-solid diffusers in a usable range, i.e., in tens of centimeter range, using electric field.

The dipole moment of polar molecules makes them align and bond to other polar molecules with hydrogen bonds, which is stronger than that among non-polar molecules. This feature grants polar droplets a higher surface tension, which allows them to hold larger amounts of charge before they break down into smaller droplets. This also makes it more difficult for them to lose charge due to diffusion.

Charging aerosol particles

Diffusion charging is the most common technique for charging aerosol particles [2]. In this method, particles pass through an ionized gas, colliding with the ions and causing their charge to be diffused into them. This can be achieved using photoelectric, radioactive or corona discharge methods [3], with the later one offering higher extrinsic charging efficiency (up to ≈ 86%) and stable operation.

Many designs of corona based chargers are reported in the literature [3]. Our initial "needle-to-plate" designs could not provide enough throughputs. Our current charger has a "wire-to-cylinder" design; see Figure 2. A copper wire of 0.8 mm diameter is located along the axis, and is connected to the positive terminal of a Glassman MJ1500 10kV DC variable voltage supply. The copper cylinder has 20 mm inner diameter, 1 mm thickness and 18 cm length, and is connected to the ground terminal. A highly non-uniform electric field is created around the wire, which ionizes the nearby molecules in the air, producing positive ions and free electrons by corona discharge. The positive ions while slowly repelled towards the ground electrode diffuse into the aerosol particles and charge them via random collisions. The free electrons are rapidly attracted towards the positive wire because of their low mass and are quickly dissipated before diffusing into and neutralizing the charged aerosol.

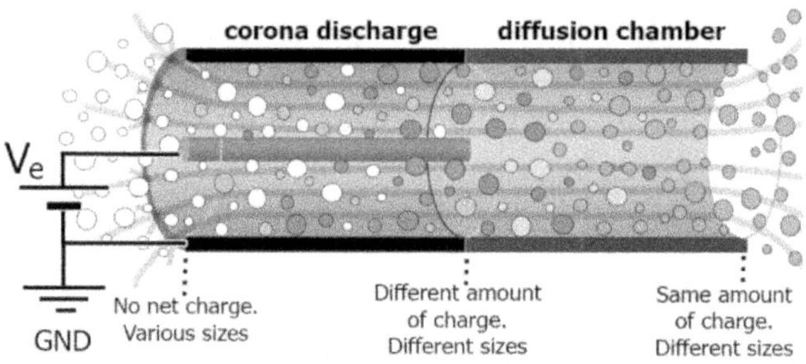

Figure 2: A cross-section of the charging and diffusion chambers is shown. First, the fog passes through a corona-discharge chamber, which contains a positive wire (shown in red) surrounded by a ground cylinder (shown in black). The fog then flows into a diffusion chamber to homogenize the charge in the fog particles (best viewed in color).

The aerosol particles may have different levels of charge when leaving the corona charger. However, charge diffuses among the charged air and aerosol particles while traveling through the pipe and reach a (statistically) homogeneous charge distribution.

The speed (v) of each charged aerosol particle in air in uniform electric field (E) is given by, $v = \mu E$, where the constant μ is their *electrical mobility*. Figure 3 illustrates this effect. If particles with two different electrical mobility are present, then two trajectories are observed; see Figure 3.A. If particles have similar electrical mobility, then a single trajectory is observed; see Figure 3.B. Thus, homogeneous electrical mobility is required to effectively control the non-solid diffuser.

HOMOGENEOUS ELECTRICAL MOBILITY

Electrical mobility is defined by $\mu \propto q/m$, where q and m are the charge and mass of the particle, respectively. Our charging mechanism provides enough ions and time for diffusion to produce particles with homogeneous volumetric charge (q) density. However, homogeneous electrical mobility also requires homogeneous particle sizes (m), even after charging. To ascertain this, we performed the following two experiments using an electrical mobility analyzer, i.e., a Differential Mobility Analyzer (DMA) plus a Condensation Particle Counter (CPC) from GRIMM Aerosol Technik, to measure the particle size distribution.

In the first experiment, the particle size distribution of the aerosol produced by two entry level commercial fog machines: a Chauvet Hurricane 700 and a LEX F500 were analyzed. The fog followed the same path that it would in any real application, so that any possible condensation effects produced within the pipes were also considered. The fog machine was connected to a reservoir with fans, as described in [6], to assure a continuous flow of fog. The charging mechanism was placed between the reservoir and the DMA. The fog was not charged in this experiment. The Chauvet Hurricane 700 showed two dominant particle size distributions around 60 nm and 4000 nm (see Figure 3.C), resulting in two trajectories as shown in Figure 3.A. The LEX F500 showed a single particle size distribution around

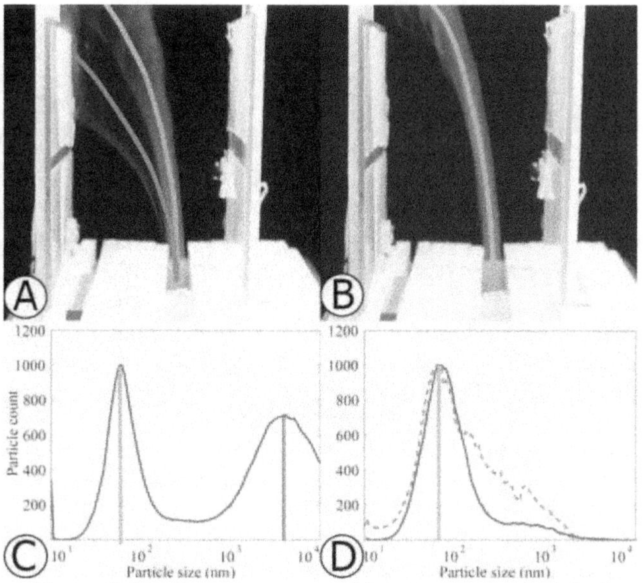

Figure 3: Nonhomogeneous and homogeneous electrical mobility distributions of fog particles are shown to follow different trajectories in A and a uniform trajectory in B, respectively. Nonhomogeneous and homogeneous particle size distributions measured using a Differential Mobility Analyzer are shown in C and D using fog from a Chauvet hurricane (C) and a LEX F500 (D), respectively.

70 nm (blue graph in Figure 3.D), resulting in a single trajectory as shown in Figure 3.A.

In the second experiment, we tested if charging affected the particle size. We used the LEX F500 and applied 5.5 kV to our corona-discharge charger; above this limit fog became thin as the particles exploded due to electrostatic repulsion, which countered surface tension. The size distribution after charging, shown as red graph in Figure 3.D, was similar to the size distribution before charging. The peak was slightly smaller (≈ 68 nm) due to electrostatic repulsion. Due to collisions during charging some particles aggregated.

These two experiments suggest that we can use a simple corona discharge based charger with a LEX F500 fog machine to create novel interactive applications.

CONTROL PARAMETERS

The trajectory of charged bubbles and fog particles in an electric field can be modeled as a first order ODE, resulting in the well-known exponential solution for projectile motion. The maximum displacement (D) and switching time (T) of trajectory are given by $D/T^2=Vq/md$, assuming that the effect of drag is minimal at low velocity. Thus, our technique can produce trajectories with high curvature and sharp shapes by adjusting voltage (V), charge (q) and bubble/particle mass (m). The separation between the electrodes is denoted by d. Moreover, the trajectory of the bubbles and shape of the fog display can be accurately controlled by dynamically adjusting V in closed loop. Good closed loop performance is achievable due to the fast response time of the power supplies (e.g., 0 to 10kV change in 50ms in our device) and the high mobility of the bubbles and fog particles, and is recommended for a useful display.

EXAMPLE APPLICATIONS

The application of the charging mechanism enables an additional level of control for the design of interactive experiences involving aerosols as non-solid diffuser. This section describes two example applications of our approach, one using charged fog flowing freely in midair, and another one using soap bubbles concealing the charged fog.

Shape changing fog screen displays

In our fog-display prototype, the fog charger is connected to the inlet of a fog screen unit, designed as described in [4]. The fog screen is placed between two arrays of transparent electrodes (see Figure 4.A). Modulation of the voltage signals applied to the electrodes (see Figure 4.B) allows to control the shape of the fog screen, and to adapt its shape to the projected graphics. Our current implementation used two transparent electrodes on either side of the charged fog screen to control its curvature. The electrodes are placed 8cm apart. The protective laminar flow was designed and tuned to create a display of 12x12 cm^2 (i.e., bigger displays are possible using a bigger honeycomb). A 4 mm thick fog screen offered adequate visual effects. The initial velocity of fog is 100cm/s (i.e., measured using an anemometer), so particles take 120ms to reach the top of the display. 4kV DC voltage is applied, particles deflect 5 cm horizontally (i.e., 16.9cm radius of curvature in Figure 4.C). Higher curvatures can be produced by increasing voltage. A 2D array of electrodes would allow more complex shapes and higher shape resolution to create interesting depth effects.

The electrodes can be placed further apart to allow users to directly touch and interact with the shape-changing fog screen. Also, a single electrode fog display (i.e., to allow direct touch) can be built, as the charged fog particles are also repelled from a single charged electrode. Making a large shape changing fog screen would require bigger electrodes and larger amount of charged fog. Our charging mechanism is scalable using higher voltage and current power supplies, and using multiple units in parallel, which would meet this requirement. The shape-changing fog-display can adapt its shape to a projected object to give a strong depth perception cue, similar to Mistable [6]. It could also be used to create evocative and compelling experiences in amusement parks. For example, a talking head projected on the fog can challenge a user in her path and the face can change shape to give different emotions.

Trajectory controlled bubble displays

Control of the position and trajectory of the bubbles is one of the design parameters described in [4], and it still remains as a challenge. As described in [9], fans can only provide coarse control, and use of air pressure waves has not been demonstrated. FRAGWRAP [5] uses electric induction (i.e., a technique to impart temporary charge separation) on the soap solution, but no specific details, i.e., voltages and charging mechanism, are provided.

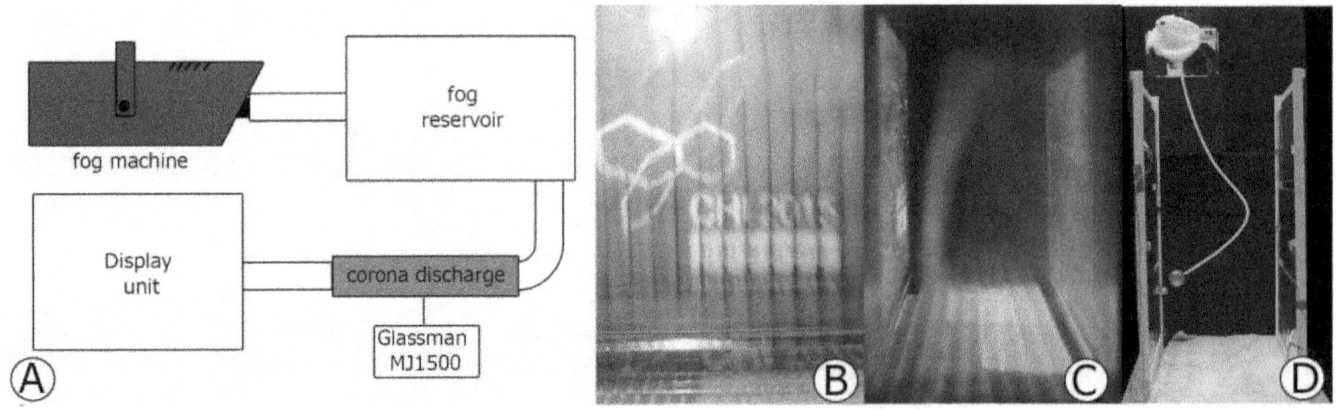

Figure 4: (A) Schematic of the prototypes used in the example applications. (B) Front view of a charged fog screen contained between two transparent electrodes. (C) Side view of the shape-changed fog screen; peak curvature 16.9 cm created using 4kV DC. (D) Side view of a bubble-display; trajectory controlled using three switched electric fields; peak curvature 12.8 cm created using 10kV DC.

In our bubble-display prototype, the charger is connected to the inlet of a bubble maker [9]. Positively charged bubbles are released between three pairs of electrodes of 45 cm x 24 cm size, 50 cm separation (*d*) and connected to a 10 kV variable DC voltage supply. A typical bubble has 8 cm diameter and zero initial vertical velocity. It moves by 40cm horizontally within 500 ms and 1 m of vertical travel. The peak radius of curvature in Figure 4.D is 12.8 cm. The bubble trajectory could be controlled using the voltage signal, and more complex trajectory could be generated using more electrode pairs. Time multiplexing of voltage applied to the electrodes can allow individual control of several bubbles, as long as they are not in the same section. Other form factors, e.g., depth can also be considered.

As part of user-experience in amusement attractions or in malls, the bubbles can be directed towards specific user-groups. In an amusement attraction, when users enter dark tunnels or mazes, the bubble could be an agent of goodwill or evil. For example, a little fairy concealed inside a bubble could suggest users to follow her if they look lost in a forbidden tunnel. The walls of the maze or tunnel can serve as electrodes to steer the bubbles.

Our techniques pose no health and safety risk to the users. Charged fog filled bubbles hold little charge, and inductively charged bubbles are neutral overall. The electrodes can be placed out of reach and danger to the users. The human body has 100pF capacitance and 1.5kΩ series resistance; the users will build up very low charge standing between the electrodes with voltages up to 100kV. Wind is known to affect bubble and fog displays; our technique could be used to counteract it.

CONCLUSION

We reported a technique to charge aerosols that allow them to be used as controllable non-solid diffusers for displays. We explain our choice for aerosol made of polar molecules, e.g., availability and charging efficiency. Our experiments show how corona discharge and appropriate choice of a fog machine can be used to produce fog aerosols with an almost homogeneous electrical mobility of their particles. We have illustrated the applicability of our technique in two prototype applications: a shape changing mechanism for fog displays, and a trajectory control mechanism for bubble displays, both requiring no mechanically moving parts.

ACKNOWLEDGMENTS

We thank Professor Jonathan P. Reid and Dr Allen Haddrell for their valuable suggestions and help with electrical mobility analysis. This work is supported by the European Commission 7th framework programme through European Research Council (Starting Grant agreement no. 278576) and FET Open Scheme (grant agreement no. 309191).

REFERENCES

1. Barnum, P.C., Narasimhan, S.G., and Kanade, T. A multi-layered display with water drops. In *Proc. SIGGRAPH'10. 2010. ACM.*
2. Hinds,W.C., *Aerosol technology* (1999) J. Wiley & Sons.
3. Intra, P. and Tippayawong, N., An overview of unipolar charger developments for nanoparticle charging. *Aerosol and Air Quality Research* (2011) 11, 187-209.
4. Kataoka, A. and Kasahara, Y., Method and apparatus for a fog screen and image-forming method using the same (1993) US patent 5,270,752.
5. Kyono, Y., Yonezawa, T., Nozaki, H., Nakazawa, J., and Tokuda, H. FRAGWRAP: fragrance-encapsulated and projected soap bubble for scent mapping. In *Proc. UbiComp'13,* ACM (2013).
6. Martinez, D., Joyce, E., and Subramanian, S. MisTable: reach-through personal screens for tabletops. In *Proc. CHI'14,* ACM (2014).
7. Matoba, Y., Takahashi, Y., Tokui, T., Phuong, S., and Koike, H. AquaTop display. *Proc. VRIC,* ACM (2013).
8. Rakkolainen, I., Hollerer, T., Diverdi, S., and Olwal, A., Mid-air display experiments to create novel user interfaces. *Multimedia Tools Appl.,* 44 (2009) 389-405.
9. Seah, S.A., Martinez, D., Bennett, P.D., Karnik, A., Otrocol, V.S., Knibbe, J., Cockburn, A., and Subramanian, S. SensaBubble: a chrono-sensory mid-air display of sight and smell. *Proc. CHI'14,* ACM (2014).

Investigation of Material Properties for Thermal Imaging-Based Interaction

Yomna Abdelrahman, Alireza Sahami Shirazi, Niels Henze, Albrecht Schmidt
VIS, University of Stuttgart
Stuttgart, Germany
{firstname.lastname}@vis.uni-stuttgart.de

ABSTRACT

Recent work demonstrated the exciting opportunities that thermal imaging offers for the development of interactive systems. It was shown that a thermal camera can sense when a user touches a surface, performs gestures in the camera's direct field of view and, in addition, performs gestures outside the camera's direct field of view through thermal reflection. In this paper, we investigate the material properties that should be considered for detecting interaction using thermal imaging considering both in- and outdoor settings. We conducted a study to analyze the recognition performance for different gestures and different surfaces. Using the results, we derive guidelines on material properties of surfaces for detecting on-surface as well as mid-air interaction using a thermal camera. We discuss the constrains that should be taken into account using thermal imaging as the sensing technology. Finally, we present a material space based on our findings. The space depicts surfaces and the required properties that enable the different interaction techniques.

Author Keywords

thermal imaging; roughness; conductivity; interaction

ACM Classification Keywords

H.5.2 Information interfaces and presentation: User Interfaces

INTRODUCTION

There is an ongoing trend to extend the interaction with computers to a broad range of situations. Different situations require different interaction techniques. As a result new means to sense the user need to be developed. An example is the Kinect that was initially designed to increase the immersion when playing games by enabling interaction without a physical controller. The Kinect can sense a user and derive a 3D model of the scene by exploiting near-infrared light patterns projected on the scene.

One of the main reasons that makes the Kinect suitable for usage in daily life is the use of a non-visible light spectrum. The user cannot see the projected pattern and therefore it does not intervene with the experience. Recent work proposed to go even further in the light spectrum from near-infrared light to the far-infrared band [7, 12]. Thermal cameras are used to sense heat traces that are left behind when a user moves a finger across a surface [7] or to sense mid-air interaction besides and behind a thermal camera's field-of-view (FOV) through thermal reflection [12]. As a novel sensing technology for human-computer interaction, thermal imaging offers exciting opportunities for the development of interactive systems. Prior work only provided details about detection accuracy for interaction on surfaces but not for mid-air interaction. Further, prior work did not assess the properties of materials which can be used for creating interactive surface using thermal imaging. For a sensing system to be competitive compared to current RGB and near-infrared depth cameras the individual advantages and limitations have to be identified.

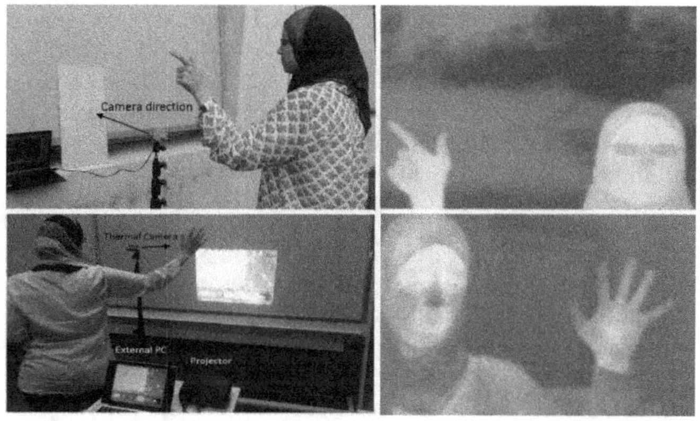

Figure 1. (top) the outdoor setup with the thermal view of tile as the reflective surface (bottom) the indoor setup with the thermal view of glass as the reflective surface.

In this paper, we present a study that assesses the recognition accuracy of mid-air gestures sensed through thermal reflection using different surfaces in indoor and outdoor setups to complement the work presented by Sahami Shirazi et al. [12]. Further, we provide holistic insights on the surfaces' properties that should be considered when it comes to sense interactions on the surface and/or mid-air using a thermal camera. Based on the identified properties, we provide a material space describing surfaces that enable interaction on the surface and/or mid-air interaction through thermal reflectivity. The guidelines enable to select materials for creating interactive surfaces using thermal imaging.

RELATED WORK

A large body of work combined projectors and sensing cameras to build interactive projected surfaces. Initially, RGB cameras were used to detect hands and fingers [6, 8]. Such systems typically use skin color detectors or template match-

CHI 2015, April 18–23, 2015, Seoul, Republic of Korea.

http://dx.doi.org/10.1145/2702123.2702290

ing to segment the hand and then calculate contour and convexity defects to identify fingers. A major challenge of such systems is the sensitivity for different light conditions.

Research prototypes have used infrared imaging [3] and depth cameras to enable multi-touch and mid-air gestures when interacting with projection screens and tabletop setups. In such systems, the space behind the screen is typically illuminated with an infrared source. Using an infrared-pass filter, all lights except the infrared light is blocked for the infrared camera. Using a depth camera, the depth information can be used to detect touch and hand gestures on projected screens [9, 14]. Such systems generally utilize either a 2D view above the surface [9] or a selective 2D projection of 3D sensed data [14] for processing users' input on or above the surface using common 2D computer vision techniques.

Using existing computer vision techniques, thermal imaging can be used to detecting interaction on surfaces as well as mid-air gestures. Two thermal properties have been leveraged for monitoring interactions. First, heat traces that are left on a surface due to the temperature difference and the heat transfer between hands and surfaces. Such traces have been used to detect interactions and pressures on surfaces [5, 4, 7]. The second property is thermal reflectivity which is the result of radiations' reflection when striking a surface. Sahami Shirazi et al. [12] propose to use specular reflectivity for extending the mid-air interaction space behind the camera's direct field-of-view and detecting mid-air gestures. However, they did not report the recognition accuracy of mid-air gestures in the extended space. In contrast, this paper investigates the recognition accuracy of mid-air interaction using thermal reflectivity. Further, we provide a holistic overview on surface properties which should be considered for creating an interactive setup using thermal imaging as the sensing technology.

RECOGNITION ACCURACY OF MID-AIR GESTURES

We conducted a study in both indoor and outdoor settings to assess the detection accuracy of mid-air gestures performed in the reflected space sensed using thermal reflectivity. We replicated the system reported in [12]. We recruited 30 participants (11 female, with an average age of 26 years, SD=3.8) using our university's mailing lists. All participants were students in different majors. Three participants were left handed. None had experience with thermal cameras. The participants were divided in two groups of 15, one group used the indoor setup, and the other used the outdoor setup.

Apparatus

The indoor and the outdoor setup were identical, including a projector and an Optris PI160 contactless thermal camera with 23° x 17° field of view(Figure 1). The projector was connected to a PC and displayed the tasks on a surface. The camera was mounted on a tripod and faced toward the surface from a distance of 50 cm to cover and capture the thermal reflection of the surfaces with a dimension of 30x60 cm. Since the setup was stationary no dynamic calibration was required. No special light source or illumination conditions were requisite as the thermal camera operates independent of illumination. We considered four common surfaces, also used in [12], for the experiment: glass, tile, MDF, and aluminum.

To detect mid-air gestures we implemented the algorithms described in [7, 12]. We used OpenCV for the hand and finger tips extraction. The frame extraction from the thermal imaging is done through the dynamic link library (DLL) the Optris camera provides. The image analysis covered the steps reported in [12] including pre-processing, noise and background removal, and thresholding. The feature extraction, i.e., the hand and finger information, was computed from the hand contour, convex hull, and convexity defects. The mid-air gesture detection was based on a view-based approach where the fingers positions and their relative distance were used to match the predefine gesture.

Tasks & Procedure

To assess the detection accuracy we considered three different gestures: (1) mid-air pointing interaction using one finger, (2) continuous interaction using one finger, and (3) mid-air hand postures using two fingers. We considered different tasks for each gesture. For the mid-air pointing 5 points were randomly projected on the surface. Participants were asked to point at the points in-air. We considered the dragging task for the continuous interaction. A pair of points were projected and users were asked to drag an object from the start point to the end point. Users repeated this task three times. For the mid-air posture, users were asked to perform a pinch and a pan gestures. For this task, users had to use two fingers.

After welcoming participants, we described the purpose of the study. We showed them where they had to stand and where to perform the gestures. Each participant performed the tasks for four different surfaces resulting in 12 tasks (3 tasks x 4 surfaces). The order of the tasks and surfaces were randomized per participant. The light condition of the indoor setup was constant during the whole study. The outdoor setup was in a shadow for the projection to be visible and the temperature was constant (24°C). The study took approximately 30 minutes per participant. We recorded the study on video and stored the thermal video for later analysis as ground truth. The time between the camcorder and the thermal camera was synchronized. To calculate the accuracy, an experimenter watched the videos and counted the number of times a gesture was correctly recognized by the software.

Results & Discussion

Table 1 includes the recognition accuracy of all tasks in indoor and outdoor setups. We found very similar results for both setups. Using the glass surface resulted in the highest accuracy followed by tile, MDF, and aluminum. Considering the roughness of the surfaces reported in [12] the Pearson coefficient revealed a strong inverse correlation between the accuracy and the roughness (r= -.98). Surfaces with lower roughness result in more mirror-like reflectivity, respectively, sharper images and higher recognition accuracy. Whereas, surfaces with higher roughness have hazy reflectivity, hence, lower accuracy.

In this study, we investigated the recognition performance of the gestures performed by single and multiple fingers. However, our system could support any arbitrary gestures by feeding the tracked fingers positions to either $1 or $N gesture recognizers which recognize arbitrary gestures formed of single or multiple strokes [1, 15].

Surface	Setup	R_a	Task: Pointing		Task: Continuous		Task: Posture		$b_{surface}$	$T_{surface}$	T_c
Glass	Indoor	.004	97%	SD=.17	95%	SD=.22	93%	SD=.26	1288	17	21
	Outdoor		96%	SD=.20	95%	SD=.21	93%	SD=.26		22.7	24.9
Tile	Indoor	.04	86%	SD=.35	88%	SD=.33	89%	SD=.31	3852	18	21
	Outdoor		87%	SD=.34	88%	SD=.33	89%	SD=.31		20.5	22.9
MDF	Indoor	.11	85%	SD=.35	86%	SD=.33	88%	SD=.36	365	19	22
	Outdoor		83%	SD=.37	86%	SD=.35	87%	SD=.36		27.05	27.9
Aluminum	Indoor	.33	56%	SD=.50	67%	SD=.48	46%	SD=.51	22265	14	14.07
	Outdor		58%	SD=.50	64%	SD=.48	47%	SD=.51		24	24.03

Table 1. It depicts two information: (1) the recognition accuracy of mid-air interactions for indoor and outdoor setups based on the experiment conducted (2) temperature at the contact point (T_c) calculated using Equation 1 with T_{skin} = 30°C and b$_{skin}$= 1000 $JS^{-1/2}m^{-2}K^{-1}$. The difference between T_c and $T_{surface}$ should be $>$ 0.08°C to be detected by the Optris PI160 thermal camera.

THERMAL IMAGING & INTERACTIVE SURFACES

Thermal imaging as sensing technology has shown promising potentials for interactive surfaces beyond traditional imaging systems. The robustness of different lighting conditions and the thermal properties allows further flexibility. The results of our study and a review of prior work reveal that surfaces with specific properties should be used to create interactive surfaces using thermal imaging. Based on both findings, we derive properties of surfaces that should be considered to support these interactions. We divide the interaction with a surface into two spaces: (1) interaction on the surface through touch, (2) mid-air gesture interaction in the extended FOV using thermal reflectivity as discussed in [12].

On surface interaction using heat traces

Tracking interaction on a surface using a thermal camera relies on heat traces left behind by the contact of the finger with the surface. The thermodynamic laws state that heat goes from a warm object to a cold object. Hence, the heat transfer between the finger and surface occurs as far as their temperature differs. The amount and direction of heat transferred principally relies on the surfaces material property knowing as the thermal contact conductance [2]. The thermal contact conductance refers to the conductivity of heat between two objects in contact. The amount of heat transferred (conducted) between the hand and the surface in contact could be either reflected or absorbed by the surface.

To determine on-surface interaction, we are interested in the heat trace and the temperature change at the point of contact. Ray suggests a simple model that calculates the temperature at the contact point [11]. Hence, T_c ($°C$) the temperature at the contact point between human's skin and the surface is as follows:

$$T_c = \frac{b_{skin}T_{skin} + b_{surface}T_{surface}}{b_{skin} + b_{surface}} \quad (1)$$

$$b = \sqrt{K.P.C} \quad (2)$$

The T_c depends on the temperature of the two contact points (T_{skin} and $T_{surface}$) as well as their thermal penetration coefficient (b). The b depicts the amount of heat penetrated and absorbed by a surface. It is expressed in terms of thermal conductivity (K), thermal density (P), and specific heat capacity (C) [10] (Equation 2). The b of human skin for short contact is 1000 $JS^{-1/2}m^{-2}K^{-1}$ [10]. On the other hand, the detection of temperature changes at the contact point depends on the camera's sensitivity. The changes must be higher than the camera's temperature sensitivity to be visible by the camera.

To detect heat traces, it is necessary to consider its decay time. Based on the Netwon's law of cooling, the rate of heat loss of a body ($Rate_{cooling}$) is proportional to the temperature difference between the body and its surrounding. The higher the difference is, the lower is the cooling rate, thus, the trace lasts longer. If the cooling rate ($Rate_{cooling}$) is smaller than the time one frame lasts ($1/FrameRate_{camera}$), the camera can not sample the trace before it decays. It should be mentioned that the cooling rate depends on other additional factors such as the surface area of the heat being transferred and the heat transfer coefficient between surfaces.

We calculated T_c for the surfaces used in the study by measuring the T_{skin}, the $T_{surface}$, and obtaining the $b_{surface}$ from [10] (Table 1). The sensitivity of the camera used is 0.08°C and it's frame rate is 120Hz. Based on our camera property, the change in temperature at the contact point should be bigger than 0.08°C and should last at least 8.3 milliseconds. The result unveiled that the difference between T_c and $T_{surface}$ is more than the threshold for all surfaces except for aluminum. Thus, the temperature changes on aluminum surfaces is invisible to our camera. In [12], it is empirically tested and reported that no trace can be detected on aluminum using this thermal camera. A camera with higher sensitivity and/or a higher frame rate may reveal other results.

Mid-air gestures through thermal reflectivity

For mid-air interaction specular thermal reflectivity is required which depends on the roughness of a surface. It is reported that the roughness (R_a) of the surface should not exceed 1/8 of the human body radiation, i.e., 1.18 micrometer, to recognize interaction behind the camera's direct FOV [12]. The results of our study reveals that the lower the roughness the sharper the rendered image from the reflection, respectively, higher is the recognition performance. Otherwise, the interaction in extended space is too blurry and cannot be used.

Material Space for Interactive Surfaces

Our investigation reveals that knowing certain information about a surface enables us to determine whether it can support on surface interaction and/or mid-air interaction using thermal reflectivity. Based on our study and prior work we derived a material space for an Optris PI160 thermal camera (Figure 2). As previously described, for on surface interaction the temperature at the contact point (T_c) and its decay

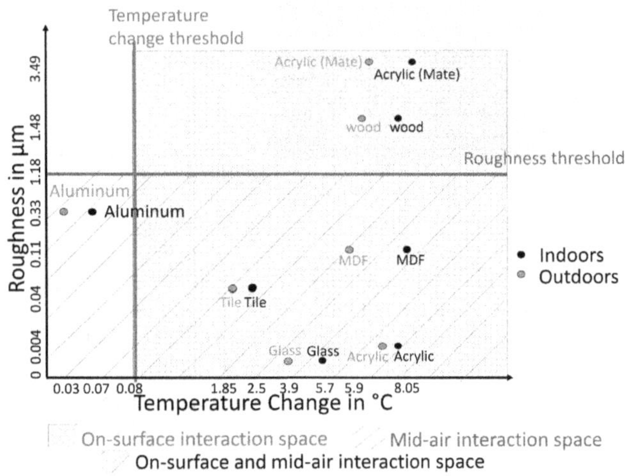

Figure 2. Material space for the Optris PI160 thermal camera: it depicts which materials support on-surface and/or mid-air interaction.

rate should be taken into account (T_c decay_rate 8ms). For For mid-air interaction using thermal reflectivity the surface's roughness should be smaller than 1.18 micrometer.

Based on our setup and our thermal camera, surfaces such as glass, MDF, and tile can be used for both types of interaction. Whereas, aluminum can be used only for mid-air interaction and wood only for on surface interaction.

Constrains

Thermal imaging has shown promising potentials for interactive systems. However, there are still limitations and constrains concerning deploying thermal cameras as sensing technologies. Sensitivity of the camera and its frame rate are one of the main constraints. Furthermore, it effects the sharpness of reflected images rendered. The resolution of the camera should be also considered. We report the material space (Figure 2) for a specific thermal camera (Optris PI160). Using the approach described above, it can be easily derived for cameras with improved properties.

CONCLUSION

In this paper we assessed the recognition accuracy of mid-air interactions sensed through thermal reflectivity using surfaces with different reflection characteristics in indoor and outdoor setups. We further derived the material space and the constraints of interaction enabled through thermal imaging. The guideline allows identifying whether a surface supports on-surface interactions and/or mid-air gestures using a thermal camera as the sensing technology. Knowing the thermal penetration coefficient of a surface, it is possible to determine if heat traces last long enough at the contact point on the surface to be detected by the thermal camera. Further, it is possible to find out if the mid-air interaction space can be extended beyond the camera's direct FOV through thermal reflectivity by knowing the roughness of the surface.

Our work as well as previous work that uses thermal imaging for interactive systems uses standard computer vision techniques originally developed for the visual spectrum. This approach already provides reasonable performance. However, significant improvements can be expected when using algorithms specifically designed to exploit the characteristics of thermal imaging. To sense users through thermal reflection techniques that were initially designed to remove reflections from recorded thermal images [13] could be applied. By separating the scene sensed through reflection and the directly observed, both scenes could be analyzed independently. A further improvement could be achieved by using more advanced thermal cameras. While such cameras were only available for the military, they currently become also available for normal use.

ACKNOWLEDGMENTS

This work is funded by the German Research Foundation within the SimTech Cluster of Excellence (EXC 310/1).

REFERENCES

1. Anthony, L & Wobbrock, J. A lightweight multistroke recognizer for user interface prototypes. In *Proc. GI* (2010).
2. Cooper, M., Mikic, B., and Yovanovich, M. Thermal contact conductance. *International Journal of heat and mass transfer 12*, 3 (1969).
3. Hilliges, O., Izadi, S., Wilson, A. D., Hodges, S., and et al. Interactions in the air: adding further depth to interactive tabletops. In *Proc. UIST* (2009).
4. Iwai, D., and Sato, K. Heat sensation in image creation with thermal vision. In *Proc. ACET* (2005).
5. Iwai, D., and Sato, K. Limpid desk: see-through access to disorderly desktop in projection-based mixed reality. In *Proc. VRST* (2006).
6. Kane, S. K., Avrahami, D., Wobbrock, J. O., Harrison, B., and et al. Bonfire: a nomadic system for hybrid laptop-tabletop interaction. In *Proc. UIST* (2009).
7. Larson, E., Cohn, G., Gupta, S., Ren, X., Harrison, B., Fox, D., and Patel, S. Heatwave: thermal imaging for surface user interaction. In *Proc. CHI* (2011).
8. Manresa, C., Varona, J., Mas, R., and Perales, F. Hand tracking and gesture recognition for human-computer interaction. *ELCVIA 5*, 3 (2005).
9. Murugappan, S., Vinayak, and et al. Extended multitouch: recovering touch posture and differentiating users using a depth camera. In *Proc. UIST* (2012).
10. Parsons, K. Contact between human skin & hot surfaces equivalent contact temperature. In *Proc. ICEE* (1992).
11. Ray, R. The theory and practice of safe handling temperatures. *Applied ergonomics 15*, 1 (1984).
12. Sahami Shirazi, A., Abdelrahman, Y., Henze, N., and et al. Exploiting thermal reflection for interactive systems. In *Proc. CHI* (2014).
13. Vollmer, M., Henke, S., Karstädt, D., and et al. Identification and suppression of thermal reflections in infrared thermal imaging. In *Proc. Inframation* (2004).
14. Wilson, A. D., and Benko, H. Combining multiple depth cameras and projectors for interactions on, above and between surfaces. In *Proc. UIST* (2010).
15. Wobbrock, J. O., Wilson, A. D., and Li, Y. Gestures without libraries, toolkits or training: a recognizer for user interface prototypes. In *Proc. UIST* (2007).

ShapeClip: Towards Rapid Prototyping with Shape-Changing Displays for Designers

John Hardy, Christian Weichel, Faisal Taher, John Vidler, Jason Alexander
School of Computing and Communications
Lancaster University, UK
{j.hardy, c.weichel, f.taher, j.vidler, j.alexander}@lancaster.ac.uk

ABSTRACT

This paper presents ShapeClip: a modular tool capable of transforming any computer screen into a z-actuating shape-changing display. This enables designers to produce dynamic physical forms by 'clipping' actuators onto screens. ShapeClip displays are portable, scalable, fault-tolerant, and support runtime re-arrangement. Users are not required to have knowledge of electronics or programming, and can develop motion designs with presentation software, image editors, or web-technologies. To evaluate ShapeClip we carried out a full-day workshop with expert designers. Participants were asked to generate shape-changing designs and then construct them using ShapeClip. ShapeClip enabled participants to rapidly and successfully transform their ideas into functional systems.

Author Keywords

Shape-changing Displays; Actuated Displays; Shape Displays; Reconfigurable; ShapeClip; Tool;

ACM Classification Keywords

H.5.3. User Interfaces: Graphical User Interfaces, Input devices and strategies, Interaction Styles.

INTRODUCTION

Actuated shape-changing displays transform our interactions with technology by exploiting perceived affordances inherent in physical form [9, 22]. However, despite being a powerful technology with transformative potential [9, 18, 31, 32] such systems are still too difficult to construct and deploy, even for those with the essential, highly specialist, technical skills. These barriers prevent those with different expertise (e.g. designers) from engaging with shape-change and thus iteratively evaluating and improving it as a community. We argue that creating and deploying applications and motion designs for shape-change should take hours, not weeks.

CHI 2015, April 18 - 23 2015, Seoul, Republic of Korea
Copyright 2015 ACM 978-1-4503-3145-6/15/04...$15.00
http://dx.doi.org/10.1145/2702123.2702599

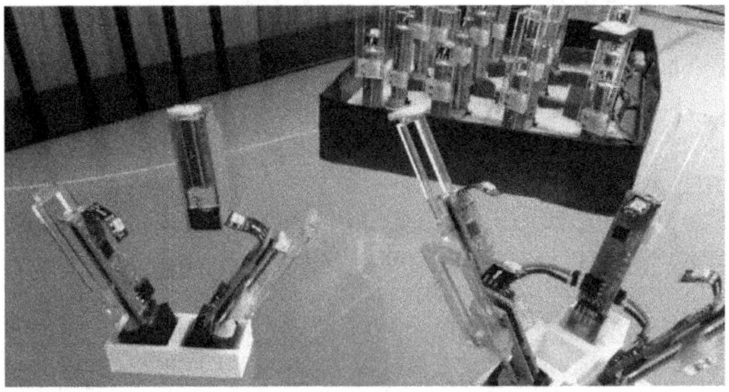

Figure 1: ShapeClip in 4 different configurations deployed on a Microsoft SUR40.

To overcome these barriers, we present *ShapeClip*: a modular tool capable of transforming any computer screen into a z-actuating shape-changing display (Figure 1). By significantly lowering the cost, complexity, time, and skills required to develop shape-changing displays we are able to engage a wider community of non-technical designers. ShapeClip displays are composed of multiple shape-pixels or '*clips*' that actuate when placed on standard displays (Figure 1). Clips can be re-arranged into different topologies, added and removed at runtime, and support varying degrees of scale and density. Battery powered clips enable portability, and a graphical control system removes the need for control circuitry whilst encouraging designers to quickly evaluate shape-change in different configurations.

To evaluate ShapeClip and learn from its strengths and limitations, we organised a full-day workshop and invited seven experienced designers to participate. During the workshop participants proposed and constructed six shape-changing prototypes, with the option to collaborate and use a range of materials (e.g. fabrics, cardboard, plastic, etc.). We focused our analysis on determining if participants were able to immediately 'pick up and construct' their ideas and leverage existing design skills and familiar tools. All participants successfully constructed one or more functional prototypes and reported spending more time on design than shape changing implementation. Post-session feedback also provided insight into strengths, limitations, and important features for expanding the range of shape-changing toolkits.

The paper is structured to draw out the foremost contributions:

1. **Concept and Implementation:** The open-source concept, design, and implementation of hardware, software, and firmware applied to a range of actuators and performance tested on a range of displays.
2. **Capability Demonstration**: A description of the key capabilities and validation that they operate together in a cohesive manner through five demonstration applications.
3. **Workshop Findings**: Evaluation of the suitability for adoption by designers leveraging their ability to use existing skills to implement their ideas, and lessons learned that can inform future toolkit requirements.

RELATED WORK

Prototyping tools in HCI and computer science are strong drivers of experimentation and innovation [11, 12, 14]. The design of ShapeClip is guided by the study of tools that support user innovation [17] in concert with the unique requirements of the shape-change research community. Effective tools allow end-users to quickly and inexpensively explore new designs, reduce the cost/risk of failure, and allow use in a flexible and reconfigurable manner that can be easily deployed.

The Range of Shape-Changing Displays

Shape-changing displays are visual output surfaces that support dynamic physical reconfiguration. Coelho et al. [7] review the design space of self-actuating shape-change, categorising devices by their materially or surface properties and Rasmussen et al. [31] by their topological form, transformation, and interaction. Displays' geometry can be described using 'shape-resolution' [32].

The community has explored a range of self-actuated shape-changing device forms. InFORM [9], Lumen [30], Feelex [19], and Relief [25] provide various scales and densities of z-actuation with either top-projected visuals or coloured bars. Portable and mobile form factors have also garnered significant attention. Tilt Displays [1] added tilt to z-actuated OLED displays to a tablet-sized device, Hemmert explored tapering [15] and weight-shifting [16] phones, Morphees [32] explored a range of advanced material implementations, MorePhone [10] added SMA's to a thin-film e-ink display for corner-bending notifications, and Dimitriadis et al. [8] evaluated volume expansion, protrusion and corner-bending for in-pocket mobile notifications. Surflex [6] used SMAs embedded in foam, and BubbleWrap [2] enclosed actuators in fabric, to explore the design of programmable surfaces. Pneumatics [13] and microfluids [5] can produce on-demand buttons on touch-screens. Sublimate [24] addresses the challenge of combining high-resolution visuals and high-resolution physical output through augmented reality. Within this range, ShapeClip focuses on providing the most prominent form, z-actuation, whilst supporting dynamic scales, densities, topologies, and runtime reconfiguration.

Towards Prototyping Support for Shape-Change

The community has amassed a range of implementations that explore the design space of shape-change. However, significant challenges remain in their construction, restricting accessibility to non-technical audiences. A primary challenge is reducing the complexity of mechanical components and control systems. These factors currently limit physical resolution[1] and changes in scale and configuration require significant re-assembly.

One approach to overcome this complexity is to use existing display technologies to communicate in parallel with multiple components placed on a screen: Sugimoto et al. [34], Hairlytop [26, 28], and HamsaTouch [21] have shown how this is possible. Of these, the closest to ShapeClip is HairlyTop [26, 28] which uses changes in display brightness to simultaneously control multiple 'smart hairs' made from SMA wire. ShapeClip extends this approach with a digital circuit and adopts LDRs rather than photodiodes for increased information bandwidth. HamsaTouch [21] shows how display images can be directly converted into tactical feedback to achieve a tactile visual substation system. WebClip [23] shows how two-way serial communication can be achieved on touch screens.

Although requiring a screen suggests that designers may only work with a fixed flat surface, display devices are available in a variety of sizes and shapes that make the concept applicable to a range of scales (i.e. large LCD screens through to small wearable devices). In the near future OLED technology promises bendable displays [10] and projector-based control could support multiple devices over wider areas on non-planar surfaces [27, 33]. ShapeClip steers designers away from monolithic system architectures that limit on-the-fly re-configurability and transference to other application scenarios. Follmer et al. summarise the current state of design: "*Most current shape-changing interfaces that address on-demand affordances provide a specific transformation, which limits their use for general purpose UIs and 3D interaction*" [9].

CONCEPT

The goal of ShapeClip is to remove complexity from the process of building shape-changing displays and re-focus effort on design of applications rather than engineering.

This is achieved through the removal of hardware barriers: (1) engineering complexity, (2) fixed actuator arrangements, (3) control circuitry, (4) low failure tolerance, (5) large build-footprints and, (6) scalability challenges. Interactive motion designs can be produced with no programming knowledge, embedded firmware, cross-platform support, or software tools.

---

[1] MIT's inFORM [10] provides the highest resolution to date with 30×30 actuated pixels.

Figure 2 illustrates the components needed to construct a ShapeClip display. *Clips* are placed on a *control surface* (i.e. LCD Screen). Light Dependent Resistors (LDRs) in each Clip sense changes in screen brightness to adjust actuation height and output color. Touch events can be 'forwarded' to capacitive surfaces using thin wires run down the length of the Clip to copper tape on the base.

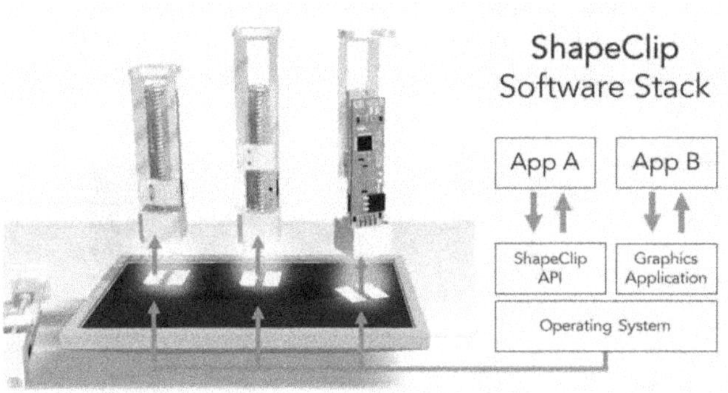

Figure 2: ShapeClip display hardware and software components (not to scale).

This approach enables individual Clips to be added, removed, repositioned, and re-oriented at runtime. A small, light, design allows several Clips to fit onto small screens (e.g. phones and tablets) and many to pack onto larger displays (e.g. televisions and touch surfaces). Clips can be *augmented* with different covers/casings to change their appearance or interactive qualities (i.e. hard or spongy to the touch). It is also possible to place Clips into *assemblies* that add new functionality through the combination of clips (e.g. tilting).

The light based control approach allows program code to be replaced entirely with graphics animations—making it accessible to non-programmers and children. Those with programming experience can control the Clips with a provided JavaScript API. Advanced users may edit the Clip firmware directly. The modularity of ShapeClip removes the need for fixed hardware configurations, and a graphical control system replaces complex bespoke circuitry with a system that can quickly adapt to configuration change. These features ease the prototyping phase as they enable quick iteration over different application ideas.

IMPLEMENTATION

To validate the ShapeClip concept we fabricated 100 Clips. All of the resulting outputs (hardware, firmware, web-graphic API, and applications) are made available[2] under the MIT license.

Clip Hardware

Standard Clips are constructed from a bespoke circuit board containing an ATmega328p (compatible with the Arduino tool chain), two LDRs, a stepper motor (as used in DVD drives), a corresponding 3D printed base, and a WS2812B LED for RGB color output. For interactivity, Clips are able to forward touch events to capacitive screens using copper tape and thin wire, or stream data from an optional force sensor attached at the top. Heads and bases tailored to suit different applications can be attached to the motor or screwed onto the actuator. It is also possible to change the actuator to support other kinds of shape-change (i.e. rotary, pneumatic). This is achieved using auxiliary output pins that support standard control slide potentiometers and servos (Figure 3). A separate pin in the power connector supports different motor voltages.

Each standard Clip weighs ≈30g, and is 20×20×80mm when closed, and costs ≈USD$15. The selected stepper motor has 60mm of travel. Under stress, individual Clips draw between 60–540mA at 5V, enabling small groups to be powered via USB. To power larger numbers, our designs specify appropriate power supply requirements. An independent on-board power circuit separates motor voltage from logic in order to increase the travel speed above the standard 80mm/s. Clips are 'clipped' together with pin connectors that double up as a power transmission method. To enable portability, an accompanying LiPo battery pack can continuously actuate a Clip for ≈30mins.

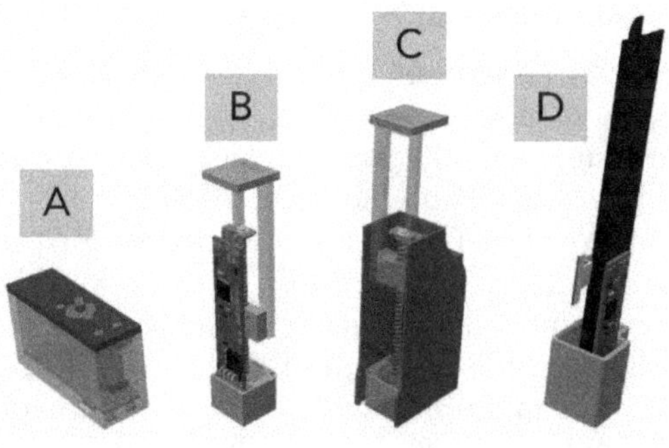

Figure 3: Different Clip actuator configurations. (A) SG90 Servo, (B) Standard Clip, (C) Standard Clip + Battery Pack, and (D) MD100AM2BF motorized slide potentiometer.

Clip Firmware

The Clip firmware samples pixel brightness and converts it into control signals for the actuators and RGB LED. If needed, users can select different modes that optimize for different requirements (i.e. trade speed for precision):

Height Mode (default): Both LDRs are used to sample height, RGB output is disabled. This mode is useful for orientation independent applications and can be driven purely by graphics. Samples are analogue (every 10ms). This mode continues to operate if an LDR is damaged.

Sync Pulse Mode: One LDR samples height, whilst the other looks for a regular sync pulse (Figure 4, top). This is used as a timing signal so that RGB values can be sampled at appropriate offsets (typically 200ms apart). This method can reliably update the RGB LED just over once per second without compromising stability.

[2] https://github.com/LUHCI/ShapeClip

Serial Mode: Both LDRs are used to transmit arbitrary digital data to the Clip using a tri-state auto-adjusting differential transmission method (Figure 4, bottom). One parity bit and two stop bits provide error checking and can achieve a stable transmission rate of ≈9.8 bits/s. A simple protocol layer interprets height and color changes, but is significantly slower than the other analogue modes. It is useful for advanced users who require reliability when extending the Clip firmware or hardware. The use of differential light levels means it can run concurrently with the other modes without interrupting their operation.

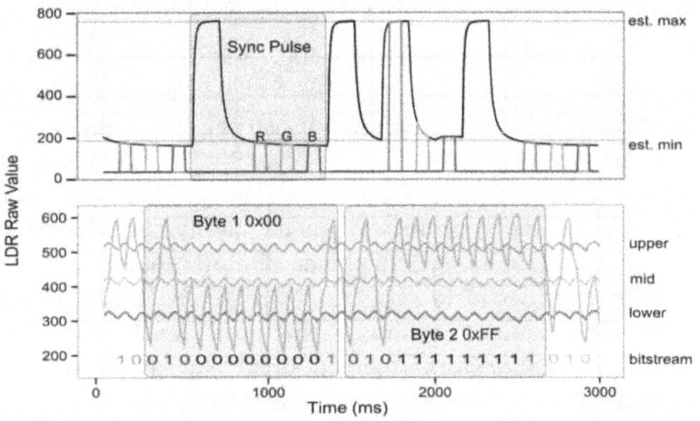

Figure 4: Sync Pulse LDR behavior showing RGB samples (top). Serial-over-screen LDR behavior showing two bytes: 0x00 and 0xFF (bottom).

End User Development

In support of non-programmers, motion designs can be created using well known graphics packages such as Adobe Illustrator, Photoshop, Microsoft PowerPoint, and MSPaint. As ShapeClip is not restricted to any particular software package, users are free to work with the tools they are familiar with. Interactivity can be direct (i.e. next slide when a clip is touched) or simulated via wizard-of-oz using a multi-monitor system. For programmers seeking greater control, a web-graphic based API (HTML5, CSS, and JavaScript) wraps common and advanced functionality. This API has the ability to encode serial messages into the on-screen graphics using the methods described above. It also contains a WebSocket-to-Serial bridge (for Clip profiling and debugging from within the browser), and a Clip arrangement tracker compatible with the Microsoft Surface SUR40 that detects topologies at interactive rates.

This approach to end user development make it easy to test motion designs immediately without re-compilation, enables Clip operation across multiple devices and platforms, and easily integrates rich graphics, multimedia, and traditional UI components into ShapeClip applications.

System Performance

The primary technical challenge was achieving screen-based communication that worked reliably across a wide variety of consumer displays and devices. Our approach is influenced by the limitations of commodity screens (low screen fill/refresh rates, varying brightness and contrast levels) and the sensing characteristics of the LDRs (≈66ms response time to recognize a 0%–100% brightness transition). Many displays are gamma-corrected to optimize for human perception; creating artifacts in the transmission process (Figure 5). To correct for this without affecting the visual appearance of surrounding graphics, a profiler application compares expected LDR values against actual LDR samples for specific displays; reducing the error to a negligible value.

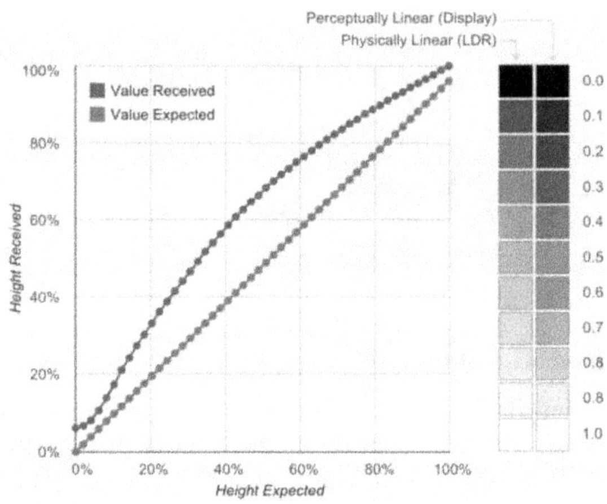

Figure 5: Expected vs received LDR analogue values (left). Illustrated mismatch between 'perceptually linear' display luma and 'physically linear' LDR samples (right).

ShapeClips successfully operate without profiling on a wide range of consumer displays. We specifically tested them on: an iPad mini (Gen 1), Microsoft SUR40, Microsoft Surface Tablet, Nexus 5, Samsung Galaxy SII, and a various Dell monitors (LED, LCD, and IPS).

To enable bi-directional communication between Clip and screen, we implemented an in-circuit representation of the human-body-model [20] and the method described by Kubitza et al. [23]. Although these worked individually, we were unable to reliably communicate with multiple Clips. As an alternative, we support interactivity through capacitive forwarding, resistive pressure, and serial-streamed force sensing on selected Clips.

CAPABILITY DEMONSTRATION

ShapeClip provides nine capabilities that facilitate different rapid prototyping scenarios. In order to validate these operate cohesively, we implemented five scenarios to cover a range of requirements (Table 1).

Portability: By combining battery-powered Clips with a mobile device it is possible to produce portable shape-changing displays. Figure 6H shows a portable augmented magazine, with ShapeClips assembled on an iPad.

Interaction: Beyond capacitive forwarding, Clips can be made to react to gesture (i.e. depth camera data), force, or signals from an external data source.

Variable Scale: No limits are imposed on the size of the control-display surface, including the number of Clips that can be placed on it.

Variable Topology and Density: ShapeClip displays do not require a fixed arrangement; allowing users to place and reconfigure Clips at-will. Density is limited by the physical Clip size and available screen space. Topology is limited by line-of-sight to the control surface.

Variable Orientation: Clips can be re-oriented locally (i.e. turned to face a user) or globally (i.e. moved as the display moves). When operating in sync-pulse mode local orientation interrupts operation. It is possible to operate a ShapeClip display on its side or upside-down.

Hot-swappable: Like all mechanical systems, Clips are subject to mechanical failure. Should a Clip fail, it can be easily replaced on-the-fly, without stopping the software or hardware (if not part of a shared power rail).

Augmented: Clips may have additional materials added to change appearance (i.e. covers, casings) or interactive capabilities (e.g. force sensor). Augmentations can apply to individual Clips or to groups (i.e. a top-mounted deforming membrane).

Assemblies: Clips can be arranged into assemblies which achieve specific objectives (e.g. tilting, stacking, pushing, levering). Specific 3D printed bases are also available that hold Clips at different angles to achieve expanding volume style deformation.

Scenario \ Capability	Portable	Interaction	Variable Scale	Variable Density	Variable Topology	Variable Orientation	Hot Swappable	Assembly Based	Augmented
PortableClips	✓	✓				✓	✓		
LensClips			✓	✓	✓	✓	✓		✓
PaintClips					✓	✓	✓	✓	✓
TangibleClips		✓	✓			✓		✓	✓
ForceClips		✓					✓	✓	✓

Table 1: Map of capabilities to application scenarios.

Scenarios

LensClips create a shape-shifting magic-lens [3] that visualizes population density over a map. It demonstrates variable densities and topologies by running the same application code on a SUR40 and a tablet PC. On smaller displays (Figure 6A) a user places Clips in interesting locations to 'physicalise' population. On larger displays (Figure 6B) the user moves a lens (clips in a grid assembly that can be moved as one) to reveal trends.

PaintClips allow users to define motion behaviors by drawing them on an interactive surface. This example shows a teddy bear (Figure 6C) whose arms wave as a child moves her across the display. A 'fill' tool is used for rapid state changes and a gradient tool is used for subtle changes or slower movements.

ForceClips demonstrate Clips used in an (8×6=48) array to create a large shape-display that reacted to force (Figure 6D, Figure 6E). A spandex sheet was spread across the clips. A FingerTPS[3] pressure sensing glove made the table react to different interaction pressures across a continuous surface.

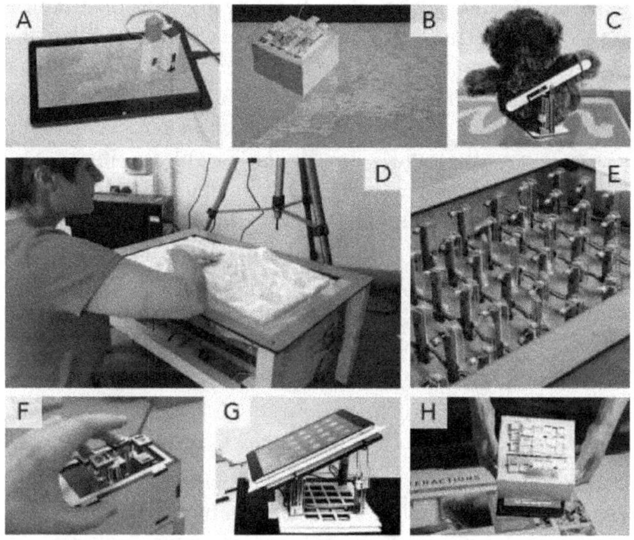

Figure 6: Montage of scenarios that demonstrate capabilities of ShapeClip. Photographs are described inline.

TangibleClips demonstrate augmenting physical objects with Clips. Clips are used to prototype a shape-changing TV remote control embedded within a sofa; controls appearing when required (Figure 6F). A smartphone provided a compact control surface. Additionally, four Clips are used to create a Tilt Display [1] inspired assembly that re-orients an iPad in response to gestures detected by a Microsoft Kinect (Figure 6G).

PortableClips is a magazine based data-visualization that renders on-screen bar-charts as physical data on a tablet (Figure 6H). Clips are attached to the device on-the-fly as appropriate content becomes available. They are secured by a laser-cut template. Users can perform touch interactions on the chart to inspect specific values.

EVALUATION WORKSHOP

To evaluate ShapeClip's suitability for adoption within the designer community, we wanted to determine whether designers with diverse skillsets were able to seamlessly 'pick up and construct' their own shape-changing ideas; leveraging existing skills and familiar tools.

Workshop Format

We organized a full-day workshop and invited seven experienced designers to lead the construction of multiple

[3] http://www.pressureprofile.com/finger-tps

shape-changing display prototypes. The day was divided into four stages: (S1) introduction to ShapeClip and shape change generally, (S2) ideation and concept design, (S3) rapid prototyping, and (S4) reflections and feedback.

During the ideation stage (S2), participants were asked to brainstorm ideas for shape-changing technology, and record their ideas on post-it notes on a large wall. For half of the session, we used fast paced (30sec) themed idea generation via a verbal stimulus. During the construction stage (S3), participants constructed their ideas from the previous session. They were welcome to form new ideas or implement multiple prototypes. A range of materials were provided to assist construction, such as fabrics, plastic, wood, Lego®, cardboard, tablets, interactive surfaces, projectors, and 3D-printed baseplates with various shapes and angles for the Clips The final session (S4) involved a reflections period during which participants were asked to identify the strengths and weaknesses of ShapeClip, the problems they encountered, ideas for enhancements and future explorations, and to describe how closely their prototype matched their intended outcome.

Participants were free to use any tools they wished, collaborate, and form groups. This approach aimed to create an ecologically valid environment that reflected processes found in a typical design studio setting [4], rather than isolating participants in a controlled environment. Questionnaires were provided at the start and end of the workshop. The entire workshop was recorded with audio and video to document processes and physical outcomes.

Participant Demographics

The workshop consisted of seven participants within the age ranges of 18–44 (µ30 years). All participants were formally trained in one or more design domains, predominantly: (P1) graphic design and advertising, (P2) sound and multimedia, (P3) UX design and digital fabrication, (P4) materials, (P5), cartographic design, (P6) graphics and multimedia, (P7) audio-visual engineering. Six participants had previously seen demonstrations of shape-changing technology, but had no previous direct interaction experience. All but one (P5) indicated more experience with graphics and media visualisation than programming.

Brainstorming

The brainstorming stage resulted in a diverse range of shape-changing applications. Of the 86 ideas generated, 88% were technically feasible for ShapeClip in its current state. The domains included, but were not limited to: augmented living (12), public transport (11), graphic design (11), gaming (9), wearables (8), concerts (8), sports (6), aviation (6), and advertising (6). While many ideas were technically feasible, others were beyond the practical scope of ShapeClip or already existed (e.g. adaptable landing gear and wings on an airplane).

Prototype Construction

Several functional shape-changing prototypes were developed during the workshop (Figure 7), including: two physical sound equalizers, a dynamic terrain elevation map, a shape-shifting advertisement, a portable exposure analyser, and a shy robot concept. The motivation behind each prototype tended to mirror the experience background of the participants who created them.

Sound Equalizer

Participants P3 and P7 collaborated to construct a graphical equalizer using a row of eight Clips (Figure 7D). They used the Processing library to detect input sound through a microphone and converted the frequency values into colour brightness levels (i.e. higher frequencies would drive a ShapeClip up and vice versa). The Clips were mounted on top of an LCD display (connected to a laptop) that displayed eight circular pads that were positioned beneath the Clips. P3 and P7 spent approximately 2 hours to complete the prototype.

P2 also developed a sound equaliser but adopted an approach that did not involve programming (Figure 7B) and used battery packs so that he could test it around the room. This involved downloading a frequency analyser application that visualized the frequency as a white wave on a dark background. He placed 10 Clips in two rows on an LCD display connected to his laptop. The movement of the wave controlled the heights of the Clips; the first row detected high gain and the second row detected low gain. This was achieved in approximately 30 minutes.

Dynamic Physical Elevation Map

Participants P5 and P6 constructed a display that rendered graphical terrain and physical elevation using a mixture of projection and Clips placed on an SUR40 (Figure 7C). A greyscale height map was produced using QGIS[4] and then overlaid onto an interactive map created using Leaflet.js[5]. A grid of 4×4 Clips (300×230mm) was placed on top of this and covered with a sheet of white spandex material to create a continuous surface between the actuators. The corresponding graphical terrain (i.e. roads, lakes, etc) was projected on top of the material. Using the computer arrow keys, the projected terrain would shift in alignment with the map, and the Clips automatically adjusted to show corresponding elevation. Constructing this prototype took approximately 2 hours.

Shape-shifting Advertisement

P1 constructed a poster that displays an actuating question mark (Figure 7G). Her aim was to draw attention from passers-by through movement and enable users engage with the content by feeling parts of the poster. P1 used

---

[4] QGIS: Open source Geographic Information System http://www.qgis.org/

[5] JavaScript library for producing interactive maps. http://leafletjs.com/

graphics from a previous project and arranged Clips into a question mark shape on an LCD screen. Lego® was used to build up the sides of the monitor to the closed height of the clips, and a poster sheet was attached over the top that would be raised in different areas as the clips actuated. The movement of the Clips was controlled through Adobe Photoshop (Figure 7F) and a brightness control slider on the connected laptop. The moving poster took approximately 1.5 hours to complete.

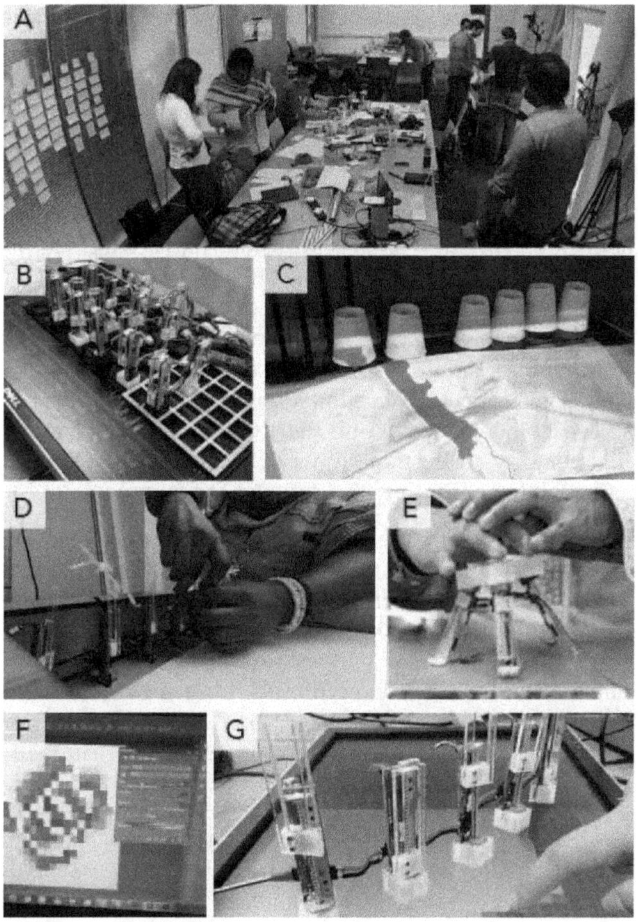

Figure 7: The workshop setting (A), a shape-changing sound equalizer (B), a terrain map that shows elevation data (C), figures being attached to another sound equalizer during construction (D), a shy robot concept (E), and graphical software used to create a digital poster (F) and the poster in development (G).

Shy Robot

P4 explored a playful interaction concept by attaching four Clips to a 3D printed baseplate and turning it upside down such that the Clips behaved as limbs (Figure 7E). As a user's hand was hovered over the device, the Clips contracted due to the reduction in light intensity. They then quickly expanded again once the user removed their hand. This created an effect of "shyness". This concept was realized within minutes, as it was simply a case of attaching the Clips to pre-fabricated baseplates and powering them on. It was an unexpected use of the technology (using the LDRs as presence sensors) and stimulated discussion about use of other types of sensor.

Portable Exposure Analyser

Within minutes of the prototyping session starting, P2 produced a portable Clip attachment for a DSLR camera that indicated the exposure setting to the user whilst allowing them to continue looking through the eyepiece. This approach exploited the light sensing capability of the LDRs. Realizing this concept involved simply using tape to attach a Clip to the eye-piece of a digital camera.

Analysis

The overall reception of ShapeClip was positive (Figure 8). All participants agreed that the technology was easy to understand and work with. Deeper analysis of post-hoc feedback confirmed many of ShapeClip's expected strengths (i.e. simplicity, non-technical control, modularity, variable topology) and exposed areas for immediate improvement that we had not initially considered as significant (i.e. expanded range of end-adaptors and input sensors).

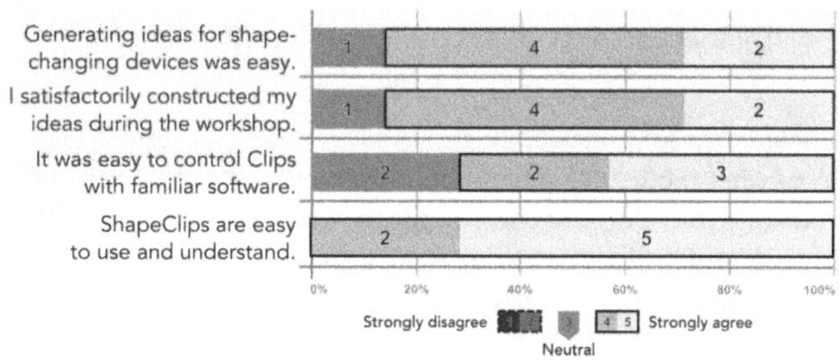

Figure 8: Responses to post-session feedback questions.

Controlling Actuation

All but one participant (P4) agreed or strongly agreed that they were able to satisfactorily construct their ideas within the prototyping session. A wide array of tools were used to control the Clips, including web browsers, Adobe Photoshop, Processing, sound visualisation, and simply blocking natural light. No participants indicated that they could not satisfactory control the Clips. Their comments included:

"It was a really good idea to use colour as an input variable as I didn't even need to use code to control the system" – P1.

"Implementing the idea was simple enough. I need a grid to put the ShapeClips in and a screen to connect my laptop" – P2.

"Easy to control because you are not locked in a set of tools. You can use anything from Scratch to PPT [Microsoft PowerPoint]" – P7.

Extension with Materials and Assemblies

Participants typically used familiar software and hardware tools in order to configure the ShapeClips. For instance, P5 used GIS software and P1 used graphic design packages. Hardware used included attaching materials like fabrics, cardboard, plastic, and Lego® to the Clips. P6 attached a sheet of fabric to the top of 16 Clips using cardboard and two-sided adhesive pads. In the post-hoc feedback four participants indicated better attachments would have assisted their process; suggesting Velcro® and Lego® connectors. Six participants stated that most of their time was spent on the design process of their prototype (i.e. creating the applications, attaching materials), rather than the control of shape-changing hardware components:

"We probably spent half the time on data and software, and half trying to attach some spandex to the shape clip matrix" – P5.

"Very little [time spent on ShapeClip] - mostly the time was used to create the [equalizer] visualization" – P3.

Participants particularly liked that ShapeClip did not require technical expertise and it was clear that no significant technical learning curve impacted the process. The main confusion stemmed from the power cable orientation being initially unclear. However, P1, P2 and P4 all independently worked out they could chain the Clip power connectors to create arrangements.

Modularity and Flexibility

We observed the participants freely repositioning and moving the Clips, experimenting with different densities and layouts. The modular nature of the Clips led them to be shared between different groups in the session. For instance P3 and P7 started with two rows of eight Clips for their equalizer, but later changed it one row of eight. P5 and P6 encountered a faulty Clip whilst setting up their terrain mapping prototype. The faulty ShapeClip was easily replaced by the two participants:

"The modular system works well. One module broke but was easy to replace" – P6.

The post-workshop reflections also evidenced the value of modularity and flexibility through the number and range of prototypes developed in a short space of time featuring different configurations and control mechanisms. This strengthens the argument for modular and flexible approaches to actuation in shape-change prototyping toolkits.

Size and Resolution

The constructed prototypes ranged from using individual clips through to grids (4×4=16) and rows (8×2=16). P5 expressed an interest in using more of the Clips at a later date to continue development of their terrain map. Beyond construction cost (which was not a factor in this study) the main complexity for increasing resolution was powering more ShapeClips. Without prompting, participants sought out more Clips to expand their displays size or resolution. Doing so did not require modifying their underlying design architecture. To support a larger Clip layout, P2 reduced the resolution settings of his computer to that the visualization covered a larger physical space. This suggests that it might be prudent to provide desktop application software that can selectively scale regions of a display, perhaps by applying a contrast filter.

Limitations and Suggested Improvements

During the workshop one ShapeClip failed due to a mistake with wiring. Although additional durability testing and refinement of the power connectors is required, we are confident that Clips are structurally robust and suitable for rapid prototyping. Towards the end of the workshop participants remarked on the heat generated by the motors after extensive use. We aim to address this issue in the future with more durable motors.

Participants felt that the ShapeClips generated too much noise and would benefit from being smaller, with faster actuation. This was in contrast to our initial expectations of demand for larger travel lengths. Better support for attaching materials was suggested via the inclusion of interchangeable caps and the use of Velcro®. Furthermore, motion-sensing, touch detection, and adding sound and direct replication of visual outputs (i.e. on-screen colour displayed on the RGB LED) were among functionality suggestions. This is because the sync-pulse approach to controlling the LDR was too complex.

A difficultly with the current Clip design is that the vibration of the stepper motor can cause a Clip to travel across the screen when not in a fixed assembly. When Clips are tightly packed there is a risk of actuators snagging on their neighbors as a result of this movement. Future iterations will experiment with a lower center of gravity and different base materials (e.g. rubber). It may also be possible to exploit this property to create self-propelled tangibles.

DISCUSSION

Concept Validation

We evaluated ShapeClip and validated our design through implementation, application scenarios demonstrating its capabilities, and exposing the Clips to a full-day workshop with expert designers. The designers were able to use them to construct functional prototypes based on their own ideas and backgrounds. In terms of effectiveness as a prototyping tool we observe similarities to other foundational technologies that allow for a trial-and-error approach to design—reducing the costs of failure and enabling runtime adjustment to designs.

The workshop demonstrated that no programming knowledge is required to rapidly produce functional prototypes, motion designs, and thought-provoking effects. We believe this approach has the potential to enable people of all ages and skillsets to engage with shape-change. Combining shape-change with rapid-fabrication tools (i.e. 3D printing and laser-cutting) means that designs can be quickly iterated and easily transferred into presentation-ready systems.

Engaging with ShapeClip

ShapeClip is open source and designed for easy replication and extension. Its construction uses low-cost commercially available components and 3D printed structures. We found it possible to assemble 100 Clips in our lab in less than two weeks.

While developing our own ShapeClip based displays, the power of the graphical control scheme became apparent. Even as technical users, we would find ourselves using motion graphics to achieve our goals. The inherently spatially-connected design makes applications trivially simple to deploy, with both small and large numbers of Clips. The use of graphical tools as a programming and control environment was intuitive and allowed non-technical designers to implement their ideas without obstruction. We hope that this level of user-accessibility and the number of transformations / configurations / assemblies enabled by the modular nature of ShapeClip can be combined with other tools (e.g. Bosu [29]) to help to overcome the challenge of limited applicability of single-transformation in shape-change described by Follmer et al. [9].

Risks

ShapeClip is based on linear-actuation, as this is currently the most common type of shape-change present in the literature. However, there is a risk that this decision could restrict or influence decisions designers make when developing shape-change. The brainstorming session validated that ShapeClip did not restrict ideation. The flexibility of ShapeClip also means that other types of actuation (such as rotary motors) can be substituted. The open-source nature of ShapeClip readily invites other researchers and developers to build on the concept as new and different types of shape-change emerge.

We also note that the nature of our workshop may encourage use of ShapeClip in a playful manner. More advanced motion designs may require simulation and timing that are yet to be explored.

Future Development

Display-based Control: The use of LDRs for analog communication is sufficient for many applications, but is inherently subject to limited bandwidth and accuracy—in particular the update rate of the RGB LED was too slow and would likely see increased usage if it were as easy to control as the height. It may be possible to detect full 24-bit colour using LDRs with filters applied to block certain light colours.

Scalability: The graphical control system can drive as many Clips as can be packed onto a display. However, large floor or wall sized displays introduce new scale-based challenges. We intend to examine the potential for in-place firmware upgrades using serial-over-screen to flash thousands of Clips in parallel.

Motion Design Toolkits: Although ShapeClip is primarily a hardware-oriented toolkit, it simplifies the end user development of motion design by expanding the range of tools/methods available. There is a clear opportunity to extend this research with more effective methods for creating, simulating, and debugging physical motion designs. We hope that future toolkits can be adopted and extended for this purpose.

Integration with Construction Kits: To support rapid-prototyping, the workshop demonstrated the need for ShapeClip to support attachments that connect to various types of construction kits (e.g. Lego, K'nex, etc.). We intend to develop a range of 3D-printable base- and top-plate connectors that are compatible with these popular construction kits.

CONCLUSION

ShapeClip provides researchers and designers with the ability to prototype programmable physical forms by simply 'clipping' actuators to screens. We demonstrated the robust, flexible nature of ShapeClip through a series of application scenarios that demonstrate novel capabilities, and a workshop that evaluated its effectiveness when used by a range of real designers to implement their own ideas.

This work has helped to solidify the requirements for the design of shape-changing toolkits for designers. Such toolkits must easily integrate quickly and easily with existing tools and skillsets, be 'readily available' (i.e. immediately usable without detailed training), and even if complex APIs are provided, it's probable they will be subverted to better suit expertise.

ShapeClip is open-source and actively supported to encourage the wider community to engage with and improve upon its design; allowing anybody to turn a screen into a shape-changing display. It is our intention that the concept, open-implementation, and the results from our workshop will help encourage others to join an active and innovative shape-changing community.

ACKNOWLEDGEMENTS

This work forms part of GHOST, a project funded by the European Commission's 7th Framework Programme, FET-Open scheme (Grant #309191). Many thanks go to Matthias Schittenhelm for his assistance with assembly.

REFERENCES

1. Alexander, J., Lucero, A., and Subramanian, S. *Tilt Displays: Designing Display Surfaces with Multi-axis Tilting and Actuation*. in *MobileHCI '12*: ACM.
2. Bau, O., Petrevski, U., and Mackay, W. *BubbleWrap: A Textile-based Electromagnetic Haptic Display*. in *CHI '09*: ACM.

3. Bier, E.A., Stone, M.C., Pier, K., Buxton, W., and DeRose, T.D., *Toolglass and Magic Lenses: The See-through Interface*, in *SIGGRAPH '93:* ACM: p. 73-80.
4. Bull, C.N., Whittle, J., and Cruickshank, L., *Studios in Software Engineering Education: Towards an Evaluable Model*, in *ICSE '13*. IEEE Press. p. 1063-1072.
5. Ciesla, C.M. and Yairi, M.B., *User Interface System and Method*. 2012.
6. Coelho, M., Ishii, H., and Maes, P. *Surflex: A Programmable Surface for the Design of Tangible Interfaces*. in *CHI '08 EA*: ACM.
7. Coelho, M. and Zigelbaum, J., *Shape-changing Interfaces*. Personal and Ubiquitous Computing, 2011. **15**(2): p. 161-173.
8. Dimitriadis, P. and Alexander, J. *Evaluating the Effectiveness of Physical Shape-Change for in-pocket Mobile Device Notifications*. in *CHI '14*: ACM.
9. Follmer, S., Leithinger, D., Olwal, A., Hogge, A., and Ishii, H. *inFORM: Dynamic Physical Affordances and Constraints through Shape and Object Actuation*. in *UIST '13*: ACM.
10. Gomes, A., Nesbitt, A., and Vertegaal, R. *MorePhone: A Study of Actuated Shape Deformations for Flexible Thin-film Smartphone Notifications*. in *CHI '13*: ACM.
11. Greenberg, S., *Toolkits and Interface Creativity*. Multimedia Tools and Applications, 2007. **32**(2): p. 139-159.
12. Greenberg, S. and Fitchett, C., *Phidgets: Easy Development of Physical Interfaces through Physical Widgets*, in *UIST '01*, ACM. p. 209-218.
13. Harrison, C. and Hudson, S.E. *Providing Dynamically Changeable Physical Buttons on A Visual Display*. in *CHI '09*: ACM.
14. Hartmann, B., Klemmer, S.R., and Bernstein, M., *d. tools: Integrated Prototyping for Physical Interaction Design*. IEEE Pervasive Computing, 2005.
15. Hemmert, F., Hamann, S., Löwe, M., Zeipelt, J., and Joost, G. *Shape-Changing Mobiles: Tapering in Two-dimensional Deformational Displays in Mobile Phones*. in *CHI EA '10*: ACM.
16. Hemmert, F., Hamann, S., Löwe, M., Zeipelt, J., and Joost, G. *Weight-Shifting Mobiles: Two-Dimensional Gravitational Displays in Mobile Phones*. in *CHI EA '10*: ACM.
17. Hippel, E.v., *User Toolkits for Innovation*. Product Innovation Management, 2001. **18**(4): p. 247-257.
18. Ishii, H., Lakatos, D., Bonanni, L., and Labrune, J.-B., *Radical Atoms: Beyond Tangible Bits, Toward Transformable Materials*. Interactions, 2012. **19**(1): p. 38-51.
19. Iwata, H., Yano, H., Nakaizumi, F., and Kawamura, R. *Project FEELEX: Adding Haptic Surface to Graphics*. in *SIGGRAPH '01*: ACM.
20. JEDEC/ESDA, *Electrostatic Discharge Sensitivity Test - Human Body Model (HBM) - Component Level*. 2012.
21. Kajimoto, H., Suzuki, M., and Kanno, Y., *HamsaTouch: Tactile Vision Substitution with Smartphone and Electro-tactile Display*, in *CHI EA '14*, ACM p. 1273-1278.
22. Klemmer, S.R., Hartmann, B., and Takayama, L., *How Bodies Matter: Five Themes for Interaction Design*, in *DIS '06*, ACM. p. 140-149.
23. Kubitza, T., Pohl, N., Dingler, T., and Schmidt, A., *WebClip: A Connector for Ubiquitous Physical Input and Output for Touch Screen Devices*, in *UBICOMP '13*, ACM. p. 387-390.
24. Leithinger, D., Follmer, S., Olwal, A., Luescher, S., Hogge, A., Lee, J., and Ishii, H. *Sublimate: State-Changing Virtual and Physical Rendering to Augment Interaction with Shape Displays*. in *CHI '13*: ACM.
25. Leithinger, D., Lakatos, D., DeVincenzi, A., Blackshaw, M., and Ishii, H. *Direct and Gestural Interaction with Relief: A 2.5D Shape Display*. in *UIST '11*: ACM.
26. Nojima, T., Ooide, Y., and Kawaguchi, H. *Hairlytop Interface: An Interactive Surface Display Comprised of Hair-like Soft Actuators*. in *WHC '13*.
27. Oguchi, R., Kakehi, Y., Takahashi, K., and Naemura, T. *Photonastic Surface: Pin Matrix Type Display Controlled with Light*. in *ACE '08*: ACM.
28. Ooide, Y., Kawaguchi, H., and Nojima, T., *An Assembly of Soft Actuators for an Organic User Interface*, in *UIST Adj. Proc. '13*. ACM p. 87-88.
29. Parkes, A. and Ishii, H., *Bosu: A Physical Programmable Design Tool for Transformability with Soft Mechanics*, in *DIS '10*. ACM. p. 189-198.
30. Poupyrev, I., Nashida, T., and Okabe, M. *Actuation and Tangible User Interfaces: The Vaucanson Duck, Robots, and Shape Displays*. in *TEI '07*: ACM.
31. Rasmussen, M.K., Pedersen, E.W., Petersen, M.G., and Hornbæk, K. *Shape-Changing Interfaces: A Review of the Design Space and Open Research Questions*. in *CHI '12*: ACM.
32. Roudaut, A., Karnik, A., Löchtefeld, M., and Subramanian, S. *Morphees: Toward High "Shape Resolution" in Self-Actuated Flexible Mobile Devices*. in *CHI '13*: ACM.
33. Schmidt, D., Molyneaux, D., and Cao, X. *PICOntrol: Using a Handheld Projector for Direct Control of Physical Devices through Visible Light*. in *UIST '12*: ACM.
34. Sugimoto, M., Kodama, K., Nakamura, A., Kojima, M., and Inami, M. *A Display-Based Tracking System: Display-Based Computing for Measurement Systems*. in *ICAT '07*.

FluxPaper: Reinventing Paper with Dynamic Actuation Powered by Magnetic Flux

Masa Ogata[1,2,3]
[1]Keio University [2]JSPS Research Fellow
Yokohama, Japan
ogata@ayu.ics.keio.ac.jp

Masaaki Fukumoto[3]
[3]Microsoft Research
Beijing, China
fukumoto@microsoft.com

Figure 1. FluxPaper and its applications: (a) Basic structure of FluxPaper, (b) Automated To-do list by whiteboard and electromagnet header behind the board, (c) Creating picture puzzle using 25 pieces of self-aligned paper, (d) Tetrahedron model using self-aligned paper.

ABSTRACT
FluxPaper is a new paper-based medium that enables physical movement and dynamic interaction between a high-power magnetized paper and a programmable magnetic field. FluxPaper has a very thin patterned magnetic layer (0.1 mm) pasted behind the paper. A thin but strong neodymium-based magnet realizes fast, powerful, and precise physical actions while retaining the original characteristics of the paper that is widely used in our daily lives. Owing to an effective magnetic pattern and a computer-controlled magnetic field, FluxPaper can add new interaction modality to ordinary paper. We describe the functions of magnetized paper; challenges through realization; and the interaction scenarios in several applications, such as self-alignment, self-construction, floating on the board, and quickly picking out a target card from a stack.

Author Keywords
Active paper; paper interaction; magnetic flux; shape-changing;

CHI 2015, April 18 - 23, 2015, Seoul, Republic of Korea
Copyright 2015 ACM 978-1-4503-3145-6/15/04···$15.00
http://dx.doi.org/10.1145/2702123.2702516

ACM Classification Keywords
H.5.m. Information interfaces and presentation (e.g., HCI): Miscellaneous.

INTRODUCTION
Paper is a common material used for several functions such as printed media for knowledge productive work, material for packaging, and folding into aesthetic designs (i.e. origami). In HCI research, as paper has become a common and affordable medium of user interaction and design, paper can be applied to computer manipulation. There are some existing concepts of enhancing regular paper such as moving or shape-changing functions [3]. In many cases, shape memory alloy (SMA) or other kinds of temperature-controlled materials are attached on the paper for deformation [12, 18, 19]. The system can control and change paper shape by adding heat with electricity or laser to the material. External energy is required for actuation, and complex wiring is often needed on the paper for controlling individual moving joints.

In this work, we reinvent paper with dynamic actuation powdered by magnetic flux. We create a magnetically controllable paper named FluxPaper and establish the technology to manipulate the paper's physical actuation by both of self-actuation (actuation without applying external energy), and computerized electromagnetic control. Our approach provides self-actuation capability to ordinary paper without applying external energy and removes complex wirings on the paper for controlling actuation.

In this paper, we will describe:

- Envisioning the future of paper interaction with magnetic manipulation by showing several possible applications
- Providing methods and techniques for producing thin and powerful magnetized paper
- Describing effective design for both pasting and magnetizing patterns and control systems, to build the application of magnetically actuated paper.

FLUXPAPER

FluxPaper is a magnetically controllable paper, and has a very thin patterned magnetic layer pasted or printed behind the paper (Figure 1 (a)). Although the magnetic layer is very thin (0.1 mm), a neodymium-based powerful magnet provides enough attractive or repulsive force for physically moving the pasted paper material. The cost of the magnetic layer actually used for proposed application is about U.S. $0.15 per a sheet of sticky note size.

FluxPaper can be handled in the same way as ordinary paper. According to the thickness of general paper, such as Post-it® sticky notes (0.1mm thickness) and general printer paper (72 g/m^2, 0.092mm thickness), we targeted to make the magnetic layer as thin as a paper substrate, thus current FluxPaper consists of 0.1 mm paper and 0.1 mm magnetic layer. Magnetic layer is usually placed on the bottom side of FluxPaper, so the face side can be used for printing. To make 0.1mm thickness of magnetic layer, we molded magnet powder made of very small magnet particles with epoxy resin. By using neodymium-based magnet powder, we succeed in generating a flexible but powerful magnetic paper.

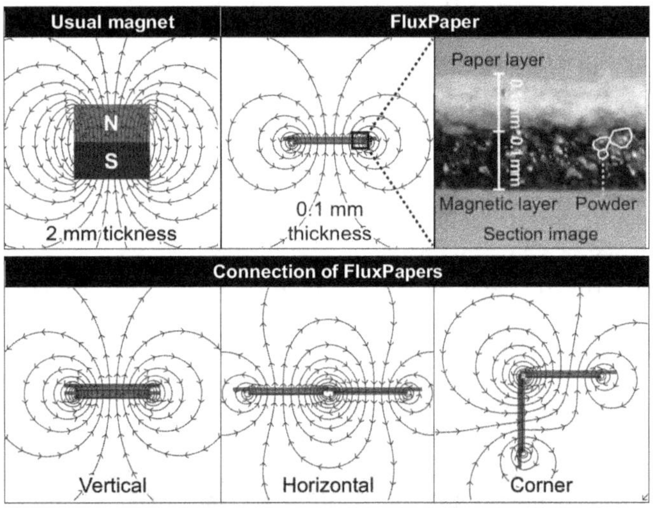

Figure 2. Illustration of FluxPaper and magnetic pole.

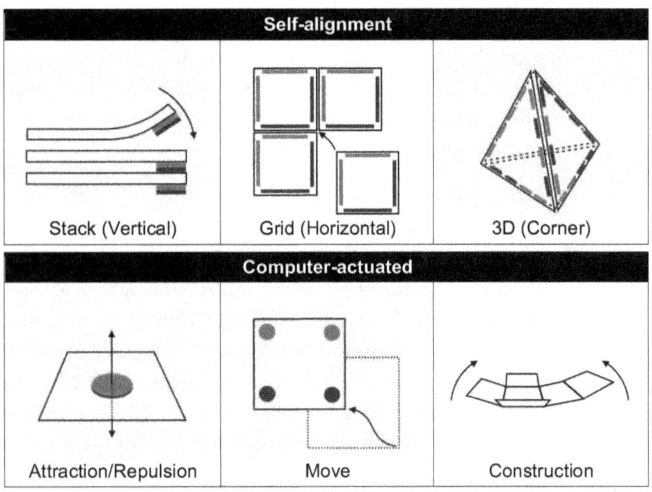

Figure 3. Possible design with FluxPaper.

Figure 2 shows the composite details of FluxPaper and compares these with an ordinary magnet, where lines of magnetic flux are simulated in a condition that relative permeability of the paper is the same as free space. According to the magnetizing direction, magnetic flux penetrates the paper surface (= surface normal direction), thus they can be used for stacking FluxPapers vertically. The magnetic flux around edge can be used for connecting FluxPapers horizontally and also making three-dimensional (3D) structure.

FluxPaper can add two kinds of actions to ordinary paper; self-alignment: the paper can attract other pieces of paper without external force; and computer-actuated: the paper is actuated by an external magnetic field. Figure 3 shows typical design and actuation patterns of FluxPaper. In self-alignment, it can be actuated without applying any external energy, and used for self-alignment functions for vertical stacking, horizontal connection with a grid, and making 3D shapes. In computer-autuated, an external electromagnetic field, such as computer-controlled electromagnets, can actuate FluxPaper, enabling many complex functions without attaching a bunch of wires on the paper material.

PAPER PRODUCTION

Figure 4 shows current "laboratory-level" production process of FluxPaper. It does not require huge plants and much electrical power. The process is as follows:

1. Mix the two mediums of epoxy in a bowl. Place the magnet powder in and mix again evenly.
2. Place the magnet paste on the paper and mold it by leveling off. Wait until it finishes hardening.
3. Cut and reshape the magnetic layer.
4. Magnetize it with a magnetizer by using two permanent magnets.

Magnetic Powder

The magnetic layer of the FluxPaper consists of bonded neodymium magnet powder and epoxy resin. We used the neodymium bond magnet powder (Molycorp Magnequench's MQFP 14-12-20000 [16]) that has a strong magnetic flux of 780–840 mT [mili Tesla] and is usually used for plastic magnets. The size of the particle is around 5 μm, which is small enough to make the composite thin magnetic layer pasted on the paper.

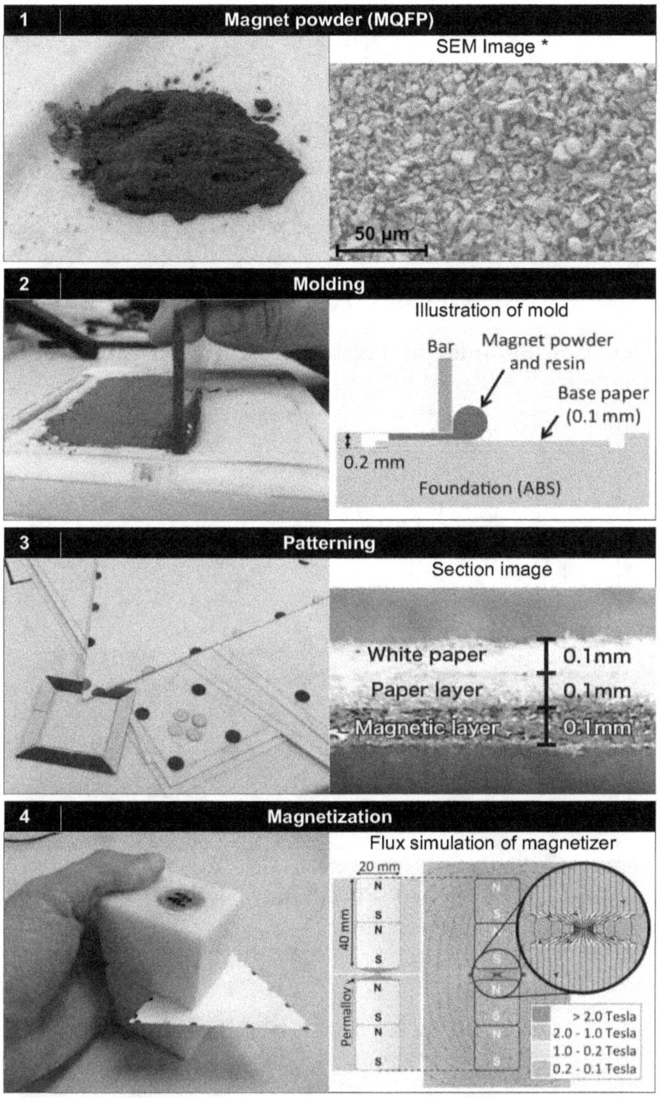

Figure 4. Laboratory-level production process. (*SEM image is cited from Magnequench's document [16].)

Solidification

Epoxy resin is one of the best solid preparations to make a strong conjugation between the paper and magnetic layers. We selected two-liquid epoxy adhesives (Loctite® E-20HP Hysol) for solidifying the magnet layer. Preliminary experiment reveals that the best mixing ratio of magnet powder to epoxy resin is around 5:1 in gram units. The density of the epoxy resin is 1.10 g/cm^3; the apparent density of magnet powder is 1.69 g/cm^3, with a theoretical density of 7.4 g/cm^3; and the actual volume ratio of magnet to epoxy resin is 3.25:1, thus the content of magnet powder in the composite is about 76.5% by volume.

Molding and Patterning

Shaping and molding the magnet layer is particularly challenging. Because of its thickness of 0.1 mm, we had to design a special apparatus for molding. Since there are no tools that can process a rolling mill in a normal laboratory, we leveled off the magnet epoxy paste on the paper before hardening the epoxy. We made an ABS plate with a level of 0.2 mm (= 0.1mm paper + 0.1mm magnetic layer) by a milling machine. For molding, we put the paper on the lower level and level it off by placing a straight stick on the upper level. After the leveling, the polypropylene sheet should be placed on the leveled magnetic layer to flatten the surface. After the magnetic layer hardens, the FluxPaper is cut and pasted on the other paper substrate (White paper in Figure 4 (3, right)). Therefore, current FluxPaper's thickness is not 0.2 mm but 0.3 mm, however, magnetic power is still enough for proposed applications.

Magnetization

Generally, magnetization of neodymium magnets requires a high magnetic flux density by emitting the pulse current about 10,000 A. However, it is difficult to use or build such a danger high-voltage apparatus in a normal laboratory. Our approach was to use a non-electronic device to generate a large magnetic field at the thin gap between two magnets. We placed two pieces of magnetic yoke made by PB permalloy between the two magnets. PB permalloy is a type of Ni-Fe alloy and has high permeability that allows magnetic flux to more easily pass through. Figure 4 (4, right) shows the design of the non-electronic handy magnetizer. In this apparatus, we use two cylinder shaped neodymium magnets (N35, 11900 gauss, 20 mm in diameter and 20 mm in height). The ABS container holds the magnets and permalloy. The surface flux density of the bare magnet is 500 mT. Permalloy-based yoke creates a high magnetic flux density of up to about 3.5 T at the narrow gap between two blocks. As the required magnetic flux density for magnetizing the neodymium magnetic powder is between 1.2 T and 2.0 T, the magnetic flux density of the magnetizer is strong enough for magnetizing the magnetic layer of FluxPaper.

Comparison with Existing Magnet Sheets

There are some magnet sheets for holding small items, and magnet papers for printing labels or pictures. These products are basically made from plastic or rubber sheet that contains the magnetic powder. However, these magnet sheets do not have enough magnetic power for targeted applications. They use low coercivity magnetic powder or density of magnetic powder is reduced for cost reduction. Magnetization patterns are also different. Ordinary magnet papers adopt periodic striped or checkered patterns for increasing the attractive force on the metal plate. On the other hand, by magnetizing with surface normal direction, FluxPaper has large magnetic flux leakage that is used not only for sticking on the metal plate, but also stacking vertically and connecting horizontally with other piece of FluxPaper. Therefore the suitable magnetization pattern may vary from each application. In addition, FluxPaper should be strong against the external magnetic field. For example, when a small neodymium magnet (5mm diameter, 10mm height) is placed on the sheet, FluxPaper can keep the same magnetic flux as when it is magnetized, but the ordinary products lose their magnetic flux and re-magnetized.

Safety and Measures

Small particles of magnet powder (less than 100 µm) are dangerous and fatal to lung health, and its chemical composition contains heavy metal. A dust mask must be worn during treatment and hands should be washed to remove powder from the skin. However, after curing epoxy resin, the magnetic layer is durable, sealed, and as safe as usual magnet products and rubber magnets. Thus the structure of FluxPaper can bear in long-term use. Even if the magnetic layer is cracked, the broken piece is still covered with epoxy resin, which is a safe and popular material for printed circuit boards (PCB) and making waterproof paper.

CHARACTERISTIC ANALYSIS

We analyzed very thin magnetic layers with magnetic field simulation software (ViziMag 3.18) and conducted two types of experiments on the magnetic flux density to compare and verify with normal magnets. These experiments were in preparation to prove the effectiveness of FluxPaper applications. Experiment #1 measured the repulsion force of two types of samples against the magnetic field. And experiment #2 compared the repulsion force among different ratios of magnetic layer areas on the paper.

Magnetic Flux Distribution Analysis

We compared two types of magnetic layers, shown in Figure 5. Each layer has 0.1 mm thick and is magnetized. One has a magnetic layer space of 0.5 mm every 2 mm, the other one is a non-slit type. The total area of the magnetic layer is 1 cm^2 each, thus there is no difference of amounts of magnetic powder between two samples.

The results and analysis are shown in Figure 6, which indicates a section view of samples. The magnetic flux is illustrated as the lines that represent magnetic flux lines, and color is the density of the magnetic flux; red, yellow, and green colors represent strong densities. The paper with the slit has more surface flux density than the paper with no slit, which means that the slit design emits a leakage flux outside. We also check the results with a gauss meter to probe the surface of the samples.

Slit Design and Repulsion (Experiment #1)

We wanted to know whether the gross attraction and repulsion force is different between slit and non-slit designs. This is important for designing the pattern of magnetic layers on the paper to strengthen the attraction and repulsion force affected from the external electromagnetic field.

Figure 7 shows our design of an experimental apparatus and arrangement. For this experiment, we reused the same slit/non-slit samples (Figure 5). We were using electronic weighing instruments—with an accuracy of 0.1 g, up to 200 g—foundations for place, a transparent plastic plate, a

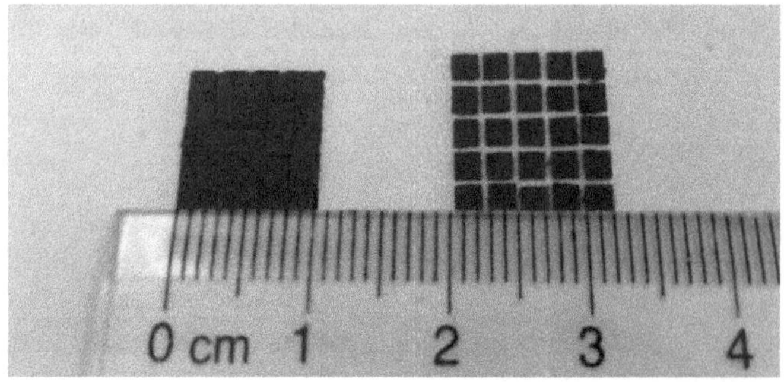

Figure 5. Samples of FluxPaper with non-slit and slit design.

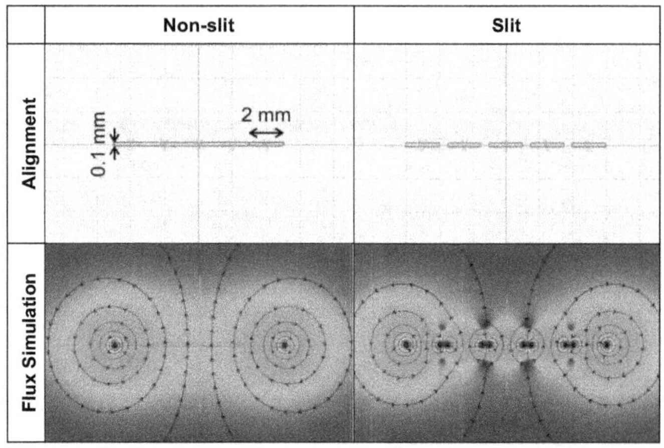

Figure 6. Analysis of magnetic flux for two designs of samples. Slit-designed FluxPaper (right) has a strong magnetic field between slits.

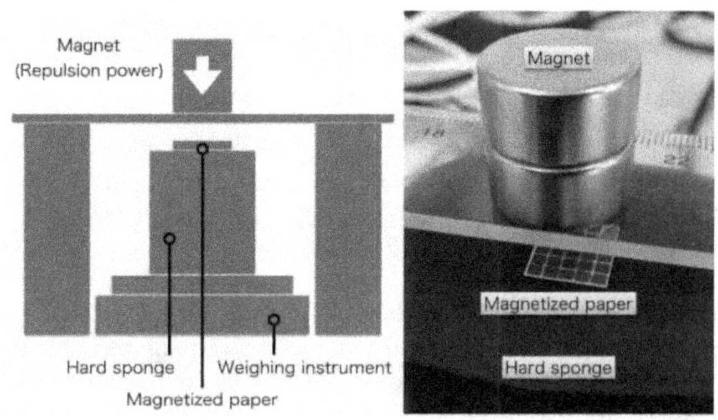

Figure 7. Measurement apparatus for repulsion and actual configuration with the magnet and the sample.

hard sponge, and a magnet—a 20 mm in diameter and 20 mm in height, N35 neodymium magnet. We placed the samples on the hard sponge to avoid the attraction force to the weighing instrument caused by a magnet. Using this apparatus, the distance between the sample and magnet was fixed at 11 mm, enabling the precise measurement of repulsion force. We placed the magnet just above the sample. With this method, we found no difference in repulsion force between the two samples. The average from ten operations was 6.7 g for slit designs, and also 6.7 g for

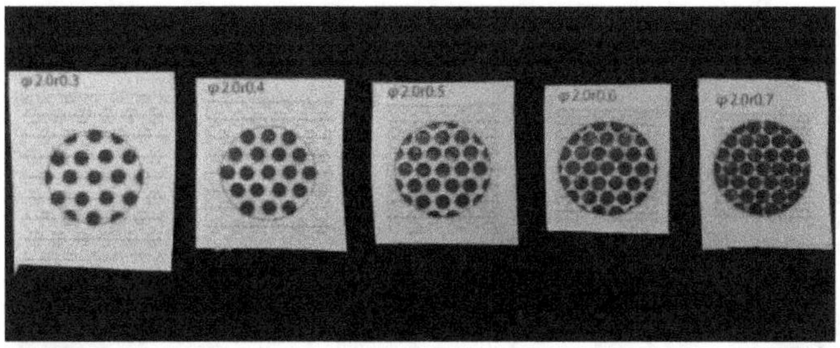

Figure 8. Different area ratio (30%, 40%, 50%, 60%, 70%) of magnetic layer on samples.

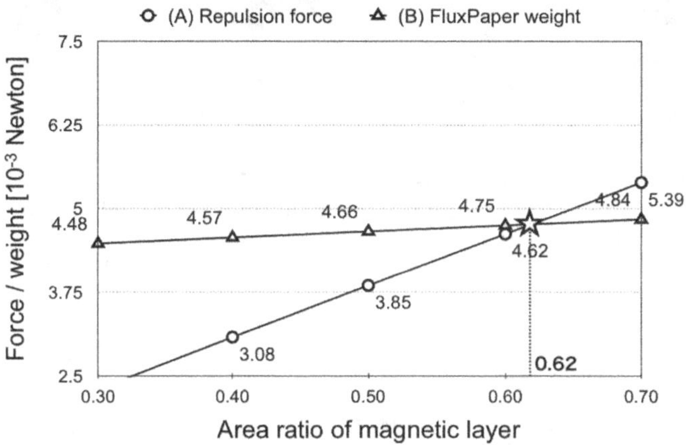

Figure 9. Results of repulsion force against the opposite magnetic field. An equilibrium point of efficient area ratio can be solved from the cross point.

non-slit designs, which means that the slits on the magnet layer do not affect the gross repulsion force of the magnetic layer against the external magnetic field.

Magnetic Area Ratio and Repulsion (Experiment #2)

We prepared five sheets for area ratios at 30%, 40%, 50%, 60%, and 70% of the magnetic layer, as Figure 8 shows. All sheets are magnetized in the same magnetic field (2 Tesla). The experiment was carried out with the same apparatus as shown in Figure 7. In this experiment, the distance between the sample and the magnet was 12 mm.

Figure 9 is a plot of (A) the relationship between gross repulsion force and the area ratio of the magnetic layer and (B) paper weight calculated from the weights of paper (76 mm square Post-it®), magnetic layer (4 points of 13.65 mm diameter, the same as samples). This result described the whole amount of the magnetic layer contributed to the gross attraction (and the repulsion) force to the external magnetic field. In the magnetic field density of 1/20 from experiment #2, the cross point showed that 0.62 was balanced.

These experiments indicated that total repulsion force is just affected by the total amount of magnetic powder and not by the slit design. However, the simulation also indicated that properly designed slit could generate high magnetic field between slits. It can be effectively used for vertically stacking applications.

FLUXPAPER WITH SELF-ALIGNMENT

In this section, we describe three approaches to utilize FluxPaper's magnetic flux attraction force without applying external energy; vertical stacking, horizontal draw-up along the grid, and making a complex structure in three dimensions (Figure 10). Since FluxPaper retains the attraction force between papers loosely, , we can design several re-coupling and movable joint functions. In addition, because of the high flux density on FluxPaper, the magnetic layer can be inserted between the two papers and both surfaces could be used for printing.

Self-stacking, easy to arrange (Figure 10 (a))

The two surfaces of FluxPaper that are magnetized as S and N poles attract each other, which means FluxPapers which have the same magnet layer pattern and the magnetized pole can be stacked in the same row. Even if the paper is thrown and roughly placed on the other paper, the paper moves and stacks automatically. This feature realizes neat desktop even when bunch of documents are piled up.

Horizontal connection with grid (Figure 10 (b))

FluxPaper provides the self-connection function by using leakage magnetic flux on the side of the piece. Pieces of FluxPaper can be connected to the edge of next piece when one piece is coming close to the next piece. In Figure 1 (c), using 25 separated pieces of the square FluxPaper, we built up one photograph. Finally, we could lift a complete puzzle by two hands with one metal bar behind the upper side.

Complex 3D structure (Figure 10 (c, d))

Because of the magnetic flux emitted from the magnetic layer, each FluxPaper has a magnetic flux around the surface or edge. These flux leakages can attract or repel each other, also in the 3D structure. We show an example of using FluxPaper to build a rectangular tetrahedron. In

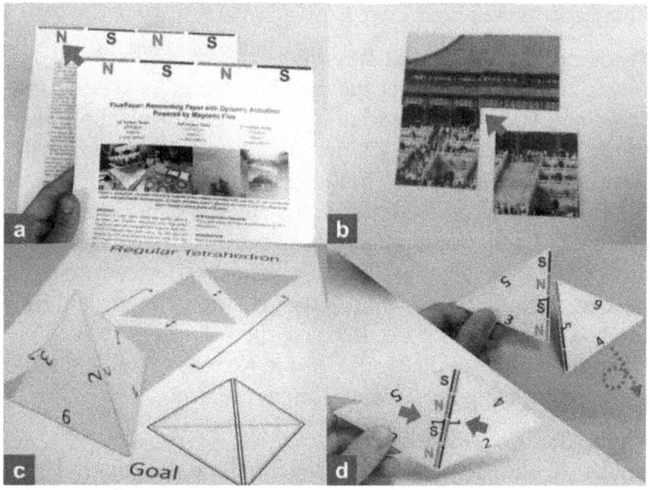

Figure 10. Examples of Self-alignment: (a) Vertical stacking, (b) horizontal connection with grid, (c) Self-connected tetrahedron model, (d) Only a correct combination with the same number of edges, can be connected. S and N indicate internal magnetic pattern.

this example, four pieces were connected to each side of the pieces, and each side had a number that represented the right connection to the other side. Because the magnetic flux has two poles, the paper can attract and repel according to the combination of magnetization patterns. When the combination or direction is wrong, FluxPaper will not be connected and the two sides will repel each other as shown in Figure 10 (d). Users can understand the correct combination or direction from the magnetic repulsion feedback of the FluxPaper.

AUTOMATED WHITEBOARD

A whiteboard is one of good candidate for utilizing FluxPaper's ability. We created an automated whiteboard that has movable electromagnet header with a special XY table behind the board (Figure 11). We also designed the FluxPaper-based sticky memo pad that has specially designed magnetic and adhesive areas.

Hardware Structure

A whiteboard consists of aluminum frames, two motors and belts, one electromagnet header, and one Arduino-based micro controller with a stepping motor and DC motor controllers. The board size was 600 mm x 500 mm (W x H), the XY table moved 400 mm x 320 mm, and the electromagnet header size was 80 mm x 80 mm. The electromagnet header was moved by the XY table with two motors. The header contained 4x4 (total 16) electromagnets. The electromagnet was 20 mm in diameter and had an 8 mm center area of iron core surrounded by a coil. The microcontroller and motor driver IC controlled 16 electromagnets. Each electromagnet consumed 0.25 A when 12 V was applied, then 4 A for all. The average surface flux density was 50 mT when 12.0 V was applied to the coil of the electromagnet. Because of the thickness of the whiteboard (3mm), actual flux density effects to the FluxPaper were about 20 mT.

Tracking, Pointing, and Moving

A whiteboard can detect the paper position as well as the color and text written on the paper by capturing the image of the board on camera. Camera tracking can determine the position of each paper. Through processing with OpenCV, the fluorescent color was extracted and the paper shape was detected. Each paper attached to the board had adhesive area pasted on the backside. By using the electromagnet header, it could be moved to other positions or trashed into the box beside the board. Because the minimum step of the stepping motor was 0.01 mm on the XY table, the XY table could manipulate the head and paper precisely.

Paper Design with Adhesive

Figure 12 shows the magnetic layer behind the paper. There are two kinds of areas, one is the combination area of magnetic layer and adhesive, and the other is the simple magnetic layer. When moving on the whiteboard, non-adhesive magnetic areas are attracted and the adhesive area is repelled by the electromagnet header. When the paper is moved to the destination, adhesive areas are attracted and keep sticking after magnetic power is dissolved. Moreover, when all magnetic areas are repelled, the paper will fall down.

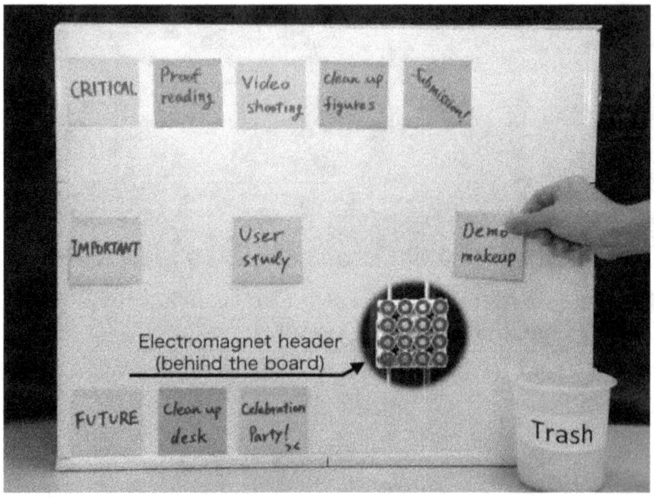

Figure 11. Automated and magnetic white board: Movable electromagnet header behind the board.

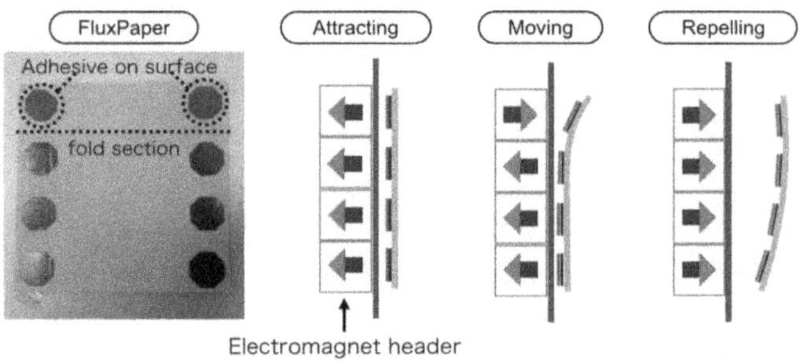

Figure 12. FluxPaper design and actuation patterns. When repelling the top section of the paper, the paper attached on the board with adhesive is taken off.

Paper Expressions

On the whiteboard, designing paper expression realizes a new modality of interaction via magnetically actuated paper media by attracting and repelling with the magnetic field. We designed four patterns of paper expression shown in Figure 13. For example, to provide notification and user attention, changing the magnetic field notifies the users. In addition, by waving or curl-up expression, the system can obtain the user's attention, and by vibration, the system can react to a user's behavior when the user is going to touch or remove the paper. When the user is going to obtain the wrong piece of paper from the whiteboard, the whiteboard attracts the paper so that it cannot be removed from the board.

Practical Tasks

An automated whiteboard and FluxPaper provide many opportunities to design real-world interactions via paper. We show two particularly practical applications.

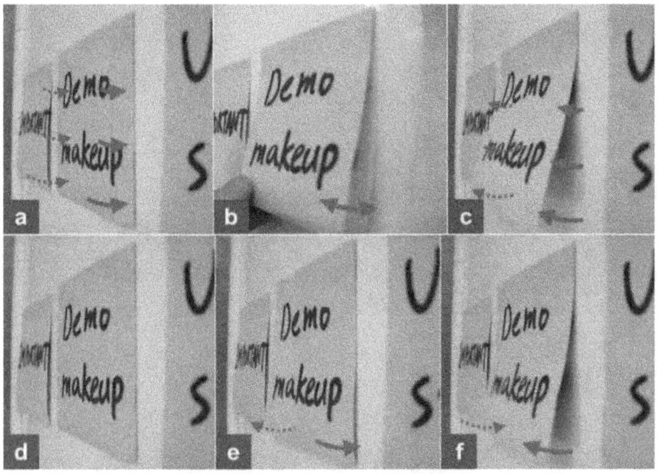

Figure 13. Paper Expressions: (a) attraction to avoid user to remove the paper, (b) vibration to notify the task is not finished or failure, (c) curl-up to get user's attention, (d, e, f) waving makes noise to notify.

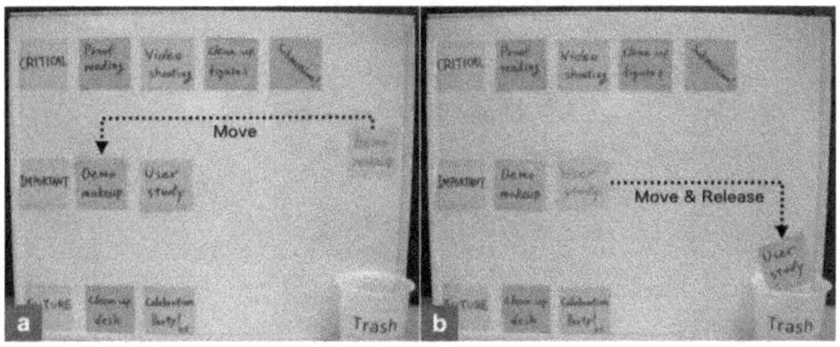

Figure 14. (a) Re-arrangement of paper, and (b) wasting cards.

To-do management (Figure 14)

To-do management is one of the important tasks that a user would require to be managed by computers. FluxPaper and the whiteboard realize the collaboration between human and computer via a medium of paper. When users write something on the whiteboard, they must check and remove it on their own. In FluxPaper application, the system detects and recognizes the text on the paper. For example, the system can be implemented to judge the to-do task with the schedule attribute. Therefore, when the scheduled task reaches its time, the whiteboard starts to notify the paper to the user with several interactive expressions.

Re-arranging and wasting

As people use a piece of paper for brainstorming and collaboration, FluxPaper also can help group interaction with paper items. According to image recognition, FluxPaper pasted on the whiteboard can be arranged by color, order, content, and other attributes related to the items. The system schedules and calculates the trajectory to move the papers to an ideal position while avoiding collision with other papers. When the item is finished or the system judged to trash, the item can be moved to trash automatically.

ONE-TOUCH PICKUP FROM STACKED CARDS

Usually, the card cannot be selected without any preparation, just by scanning the tag information one by one, such as with barcodes or magnetic tape, and it is impossible to select and pick up if it is stacked. FluxPaper enables the direct selection of certain cards from the stack without scanning of each cards.

Hardware and Control

Figure 15 shows a sample configuration of two electromagnet headers designed for selecting 8 FluxPaper-based cards. Top and bottom headers that have 16 electromagnets control magnetic flux to select the paper to be lifted up or allowed to fall down. Electromagnets control the output that matches the paper's magnetic layer that users want to obtain and they are connected to the microcontroller that enables control of the magnetic pole of 32 electromagnets placed on header equipment. There is a handle to grab the header and cables shown in Figure 16 (c). The system must know the pattern of the magnetic layer before operation; however, there is no need to know about the order of papers.

Paper Design

There are eight designs of magnetic layers for 16 points of magnet operation, with 2 points selected for each paper. (Figure 17) The magnet layer of each paper does not overlap the others. Testing with eight pieces of paper, each paper has enough power to lift the other paper up between the attracting header and attracted paper when the electromagnet is operated. Due to the limited number of electromagnet actuators, current patterning design is not rotational invariance, then the orientation of the cards must be aligned before stacking.

SELF-CONSTRUCTION

FluxPaper can be constructed in a magnetic field environment. The magnetic layer repels or attracts the magnetic flux emitted from the electromagnet, and a computer can fold or hold the paper. We are showing one

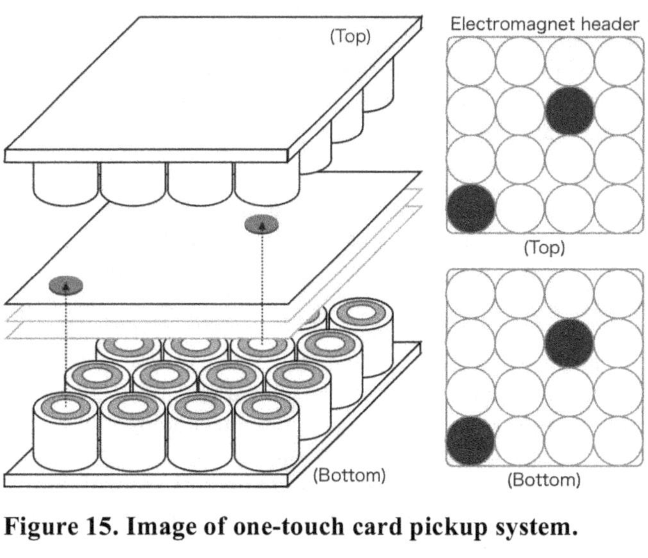

Figure 15. Image of one-touch card pickup system.

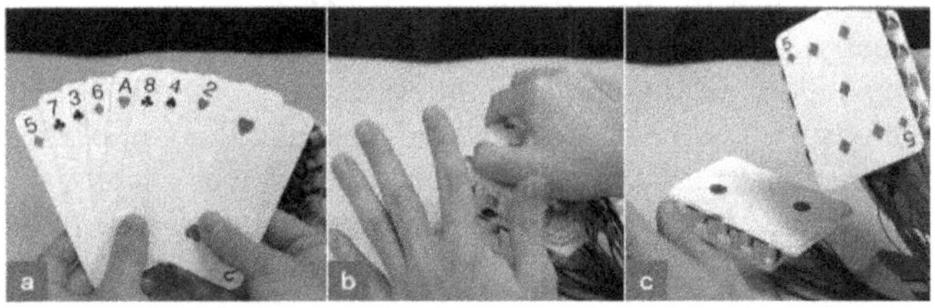

Figure 16. One-touch pickup application: (a) 8 magnetized cards, (b) Stacking cards and electromagnet operated to select 'the five' card, (c) Selecting 'the five of diamonds' from the stack.

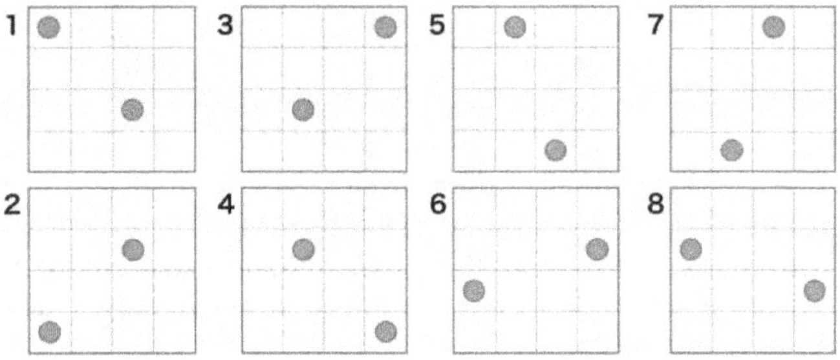

Figure 17. Sample card design of magnetized patterns.

example of a folding design for FluxPaper. Figure 18 shows the folding process to make a regular hexahedron from beginning to end. The paper placed on the electromagnet header has designed pattern on the surface that has two types of magnetic layer shape. The circle-shaped magnetic layer receives attraction force from the electromagnet and a line-shaped layer keeps the connection between sides after movement. Two of the sides support the building of the cube structure.

DISCUSSION AND FUTURE WORKS

Through three entire computer-actuated applications that handle FluxPaper, a magnetic field and its two directional powers actuate and make papers active, organic, and interactive. The shape and size of the electromagnets for generating the magnetic field limit flux density and fineness. The paper should match the apparatus used in this study. However, the functional design and magnetic flux density printed on the FluxPaper was precise and strong enough to realize the activity, shape-changing, and self-constructible paper with magnetic power.

Our future goal is to realize the automated printing system to print both the color ink and the magnetic material on paper to generate FluxPaper (Figure 19). The printer would include the usual inkjet header, special header of magnetic ink or thermoplastic magnetic filament, and computer-controlled magnetizer to magnetize the magnetic layer with a specific pattern. Moreover, by combining Ag ink-based circuit printing [9] and 3D printing technology, we will create many complex objects that include magnetic and electric components. With the help of computational design, users can automatically generate the paper format for building and constructing with a magnetic guide. We

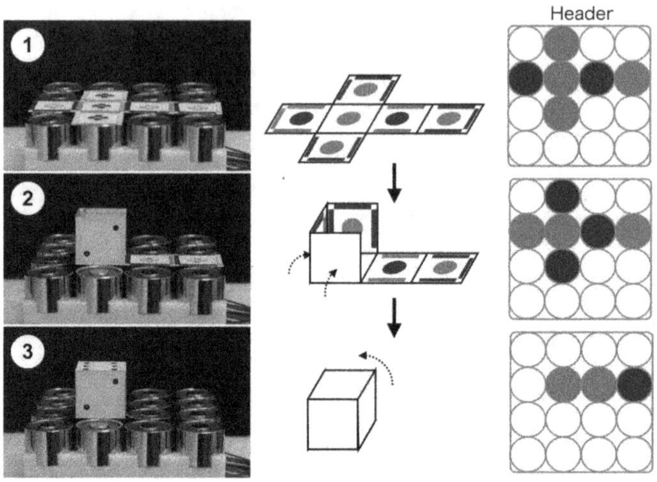

Figure 18. Electromagnet control with order of paper folding and magnetic pattern design.

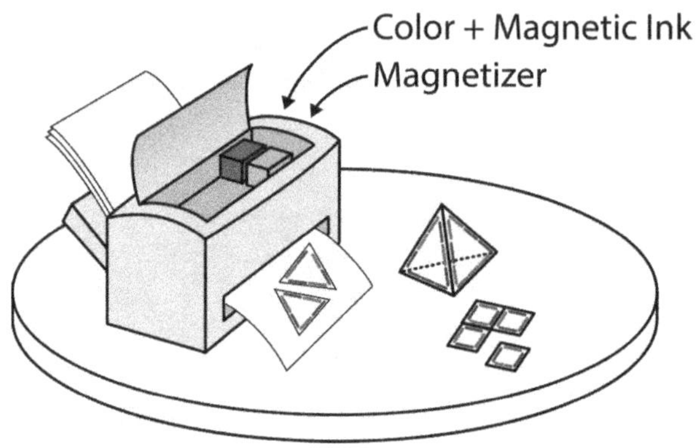

Figure 19. Future image of FluxPaper printing with magnetic ink tank and magnetizer head to print a magnetized magnetic layer on the usual paper.

believe that this ecosystem can cover the entire design of FluxPaper material and will be of great help for personal creation. In the future, according to applications regarding the ability to perform on speed and portability of FluxPaper, soft plastic may be proposed by collaborating with other actuators and materials including SMA enabling several functions for paper motion and the ability to realize geometric motions.

LIMITATIONS

The current method to produce FluxPaper is not automated. However, for the vision of printable FluxPaper, we are considering a way to use thermoplastic resin. Generally, a magnet has a limit temperature to lose magnetic strength, but this issue can be solved by magnetizing after printing the magnetic layer with thermoplastic resin. UV-curable resin based magnetic ink is another possible approach.

The thickness of magnetic layer limits the magnetic force accordingly. Large-scale paper relatively reduces the magnetic force from the magnetic layer. We think a size of around a Post-it® note (76 mm x 76 mm) is appropriate to demonstrate the applications. In addition, FluxPaper in our current applications has double paper layers (0.1 mm each) and one magnetic layer (0.1 mm each) to simplify the production process (see Figure 4). Therefore, an attractive force of stacked FluxPaper becomes weak due to the increment of paper thickness. This limitation will also be resolved by using above-mentioned automated printing system. To establish an effective printing and magnetizing patterns for various applications is also important.

In applications, we succeeded in implementing the self-folding FluxPaper with controlling electromagnets. However, there are several limitations. The size and strength of the magnetic field limit the size of the electromagnets. By using smaller and stronger electromagnets, we can control self-construction precisely. That also can be said for card magic application. The expression of pattern is not much, limited to under eight papers in one task because of the numbers of the header. We can easily manipulate many more papers by increasing the number of electromagnets or using "dithered" magnetization patterns.

RELATED WORKS

FluxPaper has four types of field of HCI research: novel interaction and actuation through magnetism, shape-changing and programmable materials, paper interaction and active paper, and printing and designing paper as a functional material.

There are several approaches to using magnetic power to HCI applications. ZeroN [14] is presented as a tangible user interface that is powered by magnetic levitation. Triangles [6] are also a tangible interface, but the magnet is used for connecting each block of hardware to help a user construct the complex structure by hand. Actuated workbench [17] is a tabletop interface that creates magnetic attraction through electromagnets. Madgets [25] also achieved tabletop interaction actuated by magnetic force. Two sets of research show examples of leveraging magnetic power to make the material active in the spatial interface. Programmable Blobs [24] is a shape-changing material reacting to changes in the magnetic field.

Using other methods, there are still several ways to design shape-changing materials. For example, PneUI [26] is soft composite interface actuated by air pressure. These two materials are designed for special applications. However, there are other bodies of research on actuating paper. POPAPY [27] uses heat-shrinkable tubes on the paper, shrinking when the paper is placed in a microwave. Bridging book [4] is a sensing idea using a compass sensor to count the page numbers of a book. The magnet is installed in each page. However, the thickness of the book becomes large due to the neodymium magnet. Our approach changes the paper from general everyday material to active and programmable material without losing the appearance and function of the paper. The input method to use the metaphor of paper is also achieved by [5, 7, 13].

Other types of paper interaction have been proposed. Saul et al. describe several types of paper designs for actuation and interactive systems by instructing with LED lights for folding [7], and with the SMA to actuate the paper [12, 18, 19, 21, 28]. Though ideas of using SMA tend to use wired designs for the paper, Koizumi et al. [12] consider a wireless method for moving the paper with SMA heating by laser irradiation. In addition, there is the idea of using power transmission via electromagnetic induction on the paper material [28, 29]. Paper material research by Figueiredo et al. [3] changes the shape of paper by heat caused by electricity and makes it possible to build an executable robot structure. As with SMAs on paper, these ideas require heat to change the state of the material to actuate or shape change. FluxPaper does not require heat of electricity on the paper because the magnetic layer reacts to external magnetic fields.

As with FluxPaper, printing or implementing functions on paper is a common way to realize new interactive technology. Paper Generators [9] are designed for acquiring electricity from paper rubbing; Anabiosis [23] and Electric origami [8] have the function to change the color of paper. Pulp-based computing [2] shows the vision of paper-printed sensors and actuators. Klemmer et al. [11] achieved a tangible interface for designers by providing paper-based affordance. Making or implementing the circuit is proposed in much research [2, 15, 20, 22], and the idea of printing with Ag ink [10] makes paper a precise circuit of computer assisted design. Our idea shares the same concept of printing functions and calculates efficient designs for paper media.

CONCLUSION

We have made contributions in producing, designing, and manipulating strong magnetized paper with efficient patterns, and achieved a new modality of paper interaction powered by a magnetic flux generated from the movable or handheld electromagnet apparatus controlled by a computer. By showing Self-alignment and Computer-actuated instances, we have demonstrated the invention of active paper and its fast, powerful, and precise manipulation.

REFERENCES

1. 3M Post-it notes, http://www.post-it.com/
2. Coelho, M., Hall, L., Berzowska, J., and Maes, P. Pulp-based computing: A framework for building computers out of paper. *In Proc. CHI EA '09*. ACM, 3527-3528.
3. Felton, S., Tolley, M., Demaine, E., Rus, D., and Wood, R. A method for building self-folding machines. *Wood Science* 8 August 2014: 345 (6197), 644-646.
4. Figueiredo, A. C., Pinto, A. L., Branco, P., Zagalo, N., and Coquet, E. Bridging book: a not-so-electronic children's picturebook. *In Proc. IDC '13*. ACM, 569-572.
5. Girouard, A., Tarun, A., and Vertegaal, R. DisplayStacks: interaction techniques for stacks of

flexible thin-film displays. *In Proc. CHI '12*. ACM, 2431-2440.

6. Gorbet, M. G., Orth, M., and Ishii, H. Triangles: tangible interface for manipulation and exploration of digital information topography. *In Proc. CHI '98*, ACM Press/Addison-Wesley Publishing Co., 49-56.
7. Huang, Y., and Eisenberg, M. Easigami: Virtual creation by physical folding. *In Proc TEI '12*. ACM, 41-48.
8. Kaihou, T., and Wakita, A. Electronic origami with the color-changing function. *In Proc SMI '13*. ACM, 7-12.
9. Karagozler, M. E., Poupyrev, I., Fedder, G. K., and Suzuki, Y. Paper generators: Harvesting energy from touching, rubbing and sliding. *In Proc UIST '13*. ACM, 23-30.
10. Kawahara, Y., Hodges, H., Cook, B. S., Zhang, C., and Abowd, G. D. Instant inkjet circuits: Lab-based inkjet printing to support rapid prototyping of UbiComp devices. *In Proc. UbiComp '13*. ACM, 363-372.
11. Klemmer, S. R., Newman, M. W., Farrell, R., Bilezikjian, M., and Landay, J. A. The designers' outpost: A tangible interface for collaborative web site. *In Proc UIST '01*. ACM, 1-10.
12. Koizumi, N., Yasu, K., Liu, A., Sugimoto, M., and Inami, M. Animated paper: A toolkit for building moving toys. *Comput. Entertain.* 8, 2, Article 7 (December 2010), 16 pages.
13. Lahey, B., Girouard, A., Burleson, W., and Vertegaal, R. PaperPhone: Understanding the use of bend gestures in mobile devices with flexible electronic paper displays. *In Proc. CHI '11*. ACM, 1303-1312.
14. Lee, J., Post, R., and Ishii, H. ZeroN: Mid-air tangible interaction enabled by computer controlled magnetic levitation. *In Proc. UIST '11*. ACM, 327-336.
15. Mellis, D. A., Jacoby, S., Buechley, L., Perner-Wilson, H., and Qi, J. Microcontrollers as material: Crafting circuits with paper, conductive ink, electronic components, and an "untoolkit". *In Proc. TEI '13*. ACM, 83-90.
16. Molycorp Magnequench MQFP Datasheet, http://www.mqitechnology.com/downloads/brochures_PDF/MQFP-Overview.pdf
17. Pangaro, G., Maynes-Aminzade, D., and Ishii, H. The actuated workbench: computer-controlled actuation in tabletop tangible interfaces. *In Proc. UIST '02*. ACM, 181-190.
18. Probst, K., Haller, M., Yasu, K., Sugimoto, M., and Inami, M. Move-it sticky notes providing active physical feedback through motion. *In Proc. TEI '14*. ACM, 29-36.
19. Qi, J., and Buechley, L. Animating paper using shape memory alloys. *In Proc. CHI '12*. ACM, 749-752.
20. Qi, J., and Buechley, L. Sketching in circuits: designing and building electronics on paper. *In Proc. CHI '14*. ACM, 1713-1722.
21. Saul, G., Xu, C., and Gross, M. D. Interactive paper devices: end-user design & fabrication. *In Proc TEI '10*. ACM, 205-212.
22. Shorter, M., Rogers, J., and McGhee, J. Enhancing everyday paper interactions with paper circuits. *In Proc. DIS '14*. ACM, 39-42.
23. Tsuji, K., and Wakita, A. Anabiosis: An interactive pictorial art based on polychrome paper computing. *In Proc ACE '11*. ACM, Article 80, 2 pages.
24. Wakita, A., Nakano, A., and Kobayashi, N. Programmable blobs: A rheologic interface for organic shape design. *In Proc. TEI '11*. ACM, 273-276.
25. Weiss, M., Schwarz, F., Jakubowski, S., and Borchers, J. Madgets: Actuating widgets on interactive tabletops. *In Proc UIST '10*. ACM, 293-302.
26. Yao, L., Niiyama, R., Ou, J., Follmer, S., Silva, C. D., and Ishii, H. PneUI: Pneumatically actuated soft composite materials for shape changing interfaces. *In Proc. UIST '13*. ACM, 13-22.
27. Yasu, K., and Inami, M. POPAPY: Instant paper craft made up in a microwave oven. *In Proc. ACE'12*, Springer-Verlag, 406-420.
28. Zhu, K., Nii, H., Fernando, O., and Cheok, A. D. Selective inductive powering system for paper computing. *In Proc. ACE '11*. ACM, Article 59, 7 pages.
29. Zhu, K., and Zhao, S. AutoGami: A low-cost rapid prototyping toolkit for automated movable paper craft. *In Proc. CHI '13*. ACM, 661-670.

TabLETS Get Physical: Non-Visual Text Entry on Tablet Devices

João Guerreiro[1,3], André Rodrigues[2,4], Kyle Montague[5], Tiago Guerreiro[2,4], Hugo Nicolau[6], Daniel Gonçalves[1,3]
[1]INESC-ID, [2]LaSIGE, [3]Instituto Superior Técnico / [4]Faculdade de Ciências, Universidade de Lisboa
[5]University of Dundee, [6]Rochester Institute of Technology
joao.p.guerreiro@ist.utl.pt, andrefprodrigues91@gmail.com, kmontague@dundee.ac.uk, tjvg@di.fc.ul.pt, hmnics@rit.edu, daniel.goncalves@inesc-id.pt

ABSTRACT
Tablet devices can display full-size *QWERTY* keyboards similar to the physical ones. Yet, the lack of tactile feedback and the inability to rest the fingers on the home keys result in a highly demanding and slow exploration task for blind users. We present *SpatialTouch*, an input system that leverages previous experience with physical *QWERTY* keyboards, by supporting two-handed interaction through multitouch exploration and spatial, simultaneous audio feedback. We conducted a user study, with 30 novice touchscreen participants entering text under one of two conditions: (1) *SpatialTouch* or (2) mainstream accessibility method *Explore by Touch*. We show that *SpatialTouch* enables blind users to leverage previous experience as they do a better use of home keys and perform more efficient exploration paths. Results suggest that although *SpatialTouch* did not result in faster input rates overall, it was indeed able to leverage previous *QWERTY* experience in contrast to *Explore by Touch*.

Author Keywords
Blind; Text-Entry; Touchscreen; Tablet; Non-Visual Interaction; Bi-Manual Interaction; Spatial Audio.

ACM Classification Keywords
H.5.2. User Interfaces: User-centered design, Input devices and strategies, Interaction styles.

INTRODUCTION
Touchscreens have become pervasive, mostly due to the success of small, portable smartphones. In recent years, we have also seen a shift into tablet devices. Unlike smartphones, these devices are able to accommodate full-size *QWERTY* keyboards, similar to that of a personal computer. However, virtual keyboards lack the tactile feedback, not just in the physical perception of key presses, but also in the ability to feel the home keys (*F* and *J*) [2]. Visually impaired people usually rely on resting their fingers on the home keys to orientate their position within the keyboard and locate desired keys. Still, current accessibility solutions (*VoiceOver*[1] and *Talkback*[2]), do not support screen exploration techniques that would allow blind users to interact this way. These solutions resort to an *Explore by Touch* paradigm where users browse the screen content by moving a single point around the interface that reads aloud the element in focus. This approach tends to be very slow particularly for novice users [7].

Previous research to support non-visual text-entry includes alternative keyboard layouts [1, 6, 7, 9], which enable faster input but require additional learning (e.g. learn *Braille*), as they have not yet offered support for non-visual multitouch exploration of *QWERTY* keyboards (the *de facto* method).

In this paper, we investigate QWERTY text-entry performance in tablets by novice blind users. In detail, we have the following research goals: 1) Assess novice users' text-entry performance with *QWERTY* keyboards in tablets; 2) Compare the performance between single- and multi-touch text-entry approaches; 3) Understand the strategies and advantages of each method. We developed *SpatialTouch*, an input system for blind users that leverages previous experience on physical *QWERTY* keyboards, by supporting multitouch exploration. Our system combines spatial and simultaneous audio feedback with multitouch selection techniques to mimic traditional two-hand keyboard interaction. *SpatialTouch* enables blind users to rest their idle hand on a key (e.g. *F* or *J*), while simultaneously exploring the keyboard with their active hand and receiving auditory feedback about the character location. Our character selection technique allows disambiguating between the different touch inputs, mitigating unintentional insertions from the idle hand. We contribute an analysis and discussion on the performance and emerging behaviors of *QWERTY* tablet text-entry using both *Explore by Touch* and *SpatialTouch*.

CHI 2015, April 18 - 23 2015, Seoul, Republic of Korea
Copyright 2015 ACM 978-1-4503-3145-6/15/04 $15.00
http://dx.doi.org/10.1145/2702123.2702373

[1] apple.com/accessibility/osx/voiceover/
[2] developer.android.com/design/patterns/accessibility.html

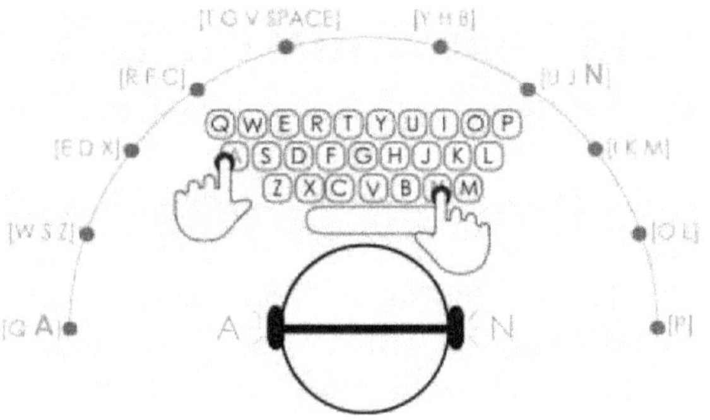

Figure 1. The keyboard and the characters spatial position in the 3D audio space. Example of simultaneous interaction.

TEXT ENTRY ON TABLETS

Mainstream touchscreen technologies support non-visual access through the use of built-in screen readers such as *VoiceOver* and *Talkback*. Still, they restrict the exploration to a single point and therefore don't leverage the multitouch support of such devices. Guerreiro and Gonçalves [4] demonstrated that screen reader users are capable of receiving and interpreting simultaneous speech sources, suggesting that current screen readers could be imposing limitations on the possible interaction methods used for non-visual access of touchscreens. In the particular case of tablets, their dimensions are similar to the ones of a physical *QWERTY* keyboard, where users are able to use two hands. We propose an investigation of non-visual text entry strategies on tablet devices using screen readers that support both single- and multi-touch exploration.

Supporting Multitouch Interaction with *SpatialTouch*

SpatialTouch extended the existing interaction method of *Explore by Touch*, allowing users to interact simultaneously with two fingers and receive independent feedback for each finger. We relied on studies that support the use of concurrent speech and point out configurations that enhance speech segregation and perception [3, 4].

Multitouch Feedback. Previous research has shown that hearing more than two simultaneous sound sources significantly decreases speech perception [3, 4]. Thus, in order to prevent auditory overload, *SpatialTouch* supports two simultaneous input points and voices. To further enhance speech intelligibility, we use different voice genders for each touch input [3]. The first finger to touch the screen is assigned the male voice, whilst the second is allocated the female voice. These assignments are only updated when both fingers are removed from the screen. *SpatialTouch* maps the characters auditory feedback relative to their location in the keyboard. Spatial locations vary on the frontal horizontal plane as illustrated in Figure 1 to help segregate both speech sources [3].

Multitouch Selection. We conducted a pilot study with five users in order to choose the target selection method (release finger vs double tap) and define the parameters that arose from having two possible insertion points. Based on the number of errors and user preferences, we selected the *Talkback* default method where a character is inserted by releasing the finger on the key. The character selection depended on which finger was lifted from the screen. The remaining parameters were reached empirically through the analysis of interaction logs, where we tried different values and chose the ones that provided better results overall. The parameters are: after receiving audio feedback for a character, users have 2 seconds to insert it by lifting their finger, allowing rested fingers to be lifted and repositioned without unintended inserts; to prevent users from inserting erroneous characters from a quick tap on a key, we introduced a 200ms delay between insertions; and we discard a second character when both fingers are lifted at approximately the same time (less than 1 second). When a character is inserted, the system provides a short beep.

USER STUDY

The purpose of the user study was to investigate novice blind users' *QWERTY* text-entry performance and strategies in tablets. We evaluated and compared two interaction methods: *Explore by Touch* and *SpatialTouch*.

Apparatus

We used a Samsung Galaxy Tab2 with a multitouch 10.1 capacitive touchscreen. It was fixed on a table in landscape orientation, connected to a laptop computer via Wi-Fi. The laptop controlled the evaluation stimuli and provided the auditory feedback (via Ozone Onda ST headphones). The spatial audio was provided by *Text-to-Speeches* [4], integrated with *System Wide Assistive Technology* (SWAT) [8] to control and log all interactions.

Procedure

The user study was conducted within an institution for visually impaired people and was divided into two sessions: 1) gathering experience and demographics, 2) and text-entry evaluation. Each session was conducted on separate days to avoid over exerting participants.

Gathering Experience and Demographics. We asked participants to rate their experience and proficiency with touchscreens and *QWERTY* text-entry (on touchscreens and physical keyboard). Moreover, users performed a text-entry test in a computer physical *QWERTY* keyboard (silicon marks on letter *F* and *J*), where they wrote three individual sentences. The session took approximately 15 minutes.

Text-Entry Evaluation. Each participant performed only one interface condition. Once assigned the condition, the participants were given a 10-minute practice with the system, where the researcher explained how the condition behaved. Participants were encouraged to perform simple text-entry tasks such as typing their name, which allowed them to become familiar with the method.

Participants completed five trials. Sentences were randomly selected from written language corpus, each one having five words with an average size of 4.48 characters and a minimum correlation with the language of 0.97. For each trial, the researcher would read aloud the stimulus sentence and then participants repeated it to ensure they understood what was said. Participants would then type the sentence using the current interface condition. Error correction was disabled to ensure that all errors and typing behaviors were captured. Once the participant finished all five trials they were asked to complete an oral questionnaire to obtain subjective opinions regarding the interface condition.

Design and Analysis

To avoid learning and carryover effects, we used a between-subjects design with 30 novice users. It had one independent variable: interface condition (*Explore by Touch* vs *SpatialTouch*). Participants completed 5 randomly selected sentences, making a total of 150 trials. We applied Shapiro-Wilk normality test to observed values in all dependent variables. Parametric tests were applied for normally-distributed variables; non-parametric tests otherwise. There were no significant differences between groups regarding age ($t_{(28)}$=-34, p=.73), self-reported *QWERTY* experience (U= 104.0, z = -.362, p=.76) and *QWERTY* WPM in a physical keyboard ($t_{(22)}$=-.584, p=.56).

We analyzed users' performance in terms of speed (words per minute, WPM) and accuracy (MSD Error Rate). We also analyzed the following path-related metrics:

Starting Offset. It accounted for how close to an inserted character did the user landed his finger on. It was measured both in terms of spatial (in pixels) and key distance. The latter accounted for the number of keys that separated the two if following an optimal path (distance equals one if both keys edges intersect). For instance, *A* had a distance of one from *Q*, *W* and *S*, while a distance of three to *F*. When landing outside the keyboard, we considered the first reached key and added a penalty of one.

Deviation from Optimal Path. For each inserted character, it measured the difference between the actual path (number of keys visited) and the starting offset. For example, from *A* to *S* the optimal path is 1 traveled key; a user that follows that path has a deviation of 0. In contrast, a user that travels *A-Q-A-S* goes through two unnecessary keys.

Participants

30 visually impaired participants, 24 male, were recruited for this study. Their age ranged from 22 to 65 (M=46, SD=11.3) years old. Participants had no previous experience with tablets and only 5 reported having some experience with *QWERTY* in smartphones. However, all users had previous experience with physical keyboards.

RESULTS

No differences in performance. An independent samples t-test ($t_{(28)}$=-1.64, p=.11) revealed that *SpatialTouch* users (M=3.00, SD=1.17) did not write significantly faster than the *Explore by Touch* ones (M= 2.38, SD=0.82). Likewise, a Mann Whitney U test revealed no difference in terms of MSD error rate (U=74.0, z=-1.58, p=.12) between *SpatialTouch* (M=11.52, SD=3.91) and *Explore by Touch* (M=9.95, SD=6.54). Although no significant differences were found in the number of omission and substitution errors, *SpatialTouch* (M=4.72, SD=2.78) users made more erroneous insertions (U=65.0, z=-1.95, p=.05, r=.36) than the *Explore by Touch* users (M=2.83, SD=2.01).

SpatialTouch users landed nearer the targets and followed better paths. Comparisons of both spatial (U=63.0, z=-2.037, p<.05, r=.37) and key starting offsets (U=65.0, z=-1.95, p=.05, r=.36) have shown that *SpatialTouch* users (spatial: M=120.95, SD=7.69; key: M=0.90, SD=0.30) landed closer to the intended characters than *Explore by Touch* users (spatial: M=163.31, SD=17.97; key: M=1.38, SD=0.76). Moreover, an analysis of the *Deviation from Optimal Path* has also shown an advantage ($t_{(28)}$=2.04, p=.05, r=.35) for *SpatialTouch* users (M=.63, SD=.35 vs M=.93, SD=.44 of *Explore by Touch*). It means that *SpatialTouch* users, depending on where they landed their fingers, traveled through less unnecessary keys before reaching the intended target and thus followed better paths.

SpatialTouch performance correlated with physical QWERTY keyboard experience. No correlations were found between physical *QWERTY* WPM scores and *Explore by Touch* metrics. However, *SpatialTouch* users were able to leverage their previous *QWERTY* experience, as shown by strong correlations between their physical keyboard *WPM* scores and their *WPM* (r = .696, p<.01) and *Deviation from Optimal Path* (rho = -.647, p<.05).

SpatialTouch users divided the screen as in physical keyboards. All *SpatialTouch* users divided the screen in half and used the respective hand therein, with two distinct strategies: explore with one hand while keeping the other on the screen as a reference point; or slightly lifting the other finger (but still using it as a reference point). Yet, as aforementioned these strategies did not present a significant influence on performance.

Most actions were performed above the touchscreen. Most users tried to take advantage of their mental spatial model of the keyboard, as they usually aimed at landing their fingers on the next character to insert. In fact, their fingers landing locations are distributed across the keyboard (Figure 2). However, *SpatialTouch* users landed more often on characters that are common in the language and/or near the physical *QWERTY* home keys (and less in between). *Explore by Touch* users landed more in the keyboard borders and other less common characters suggesting they aimed at a different target or landed outside the keyboard.

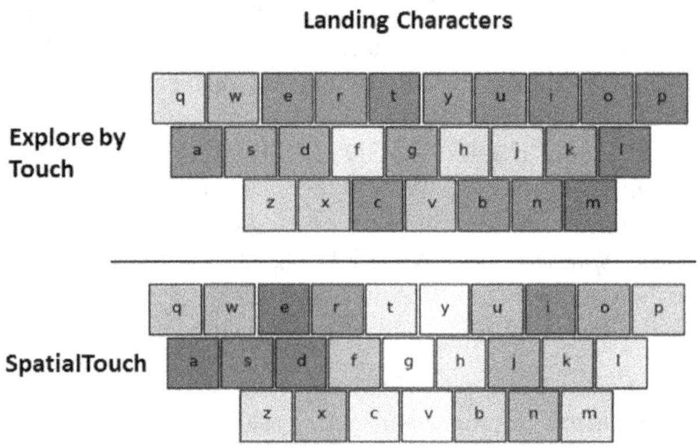

Figure 2. The heatmap of the relative frequency users landed on each character. Lighter means less frequent.

DISCUSSION

New methods needed to speed-up virtual QWERTY input. Participants typed an average of 23.4 WPM (SD=13.0) in a physical *QWERTY* keyboard. Previous research in smartphones contrast with these values, as Oliveira et al [7] reported an average of 2.1 WPM (SD=0.7) in a single session, whilst Azenkot et al [1] reported an average of 3.99 WPM (SD=1.65) after seven sessions, but very similar in the first session. Herein, we provide a baseline for *Explore by Touch* in tablets, which presented similar results (M=2.38, SD=0.82). Moreover, supporting two-handed exploration did not accelerate this task. Despite *QWERTY* being the de-facto standard text-entry method of tablet devices, this study revealed it is still too slow. However, alternative keyboards may require effortful learning. There is a need for new solutions that can still leverage previous knowledge of keyboards and enable higher input efficiency.

SpatialTouch leverages previous QWERTY experience. Two-hand interaction is a common behavior when typing on *QWERTY* keyboards. Users take advantage of the ability to rest their idle hand and quickly locate nearby target keys. This is especially important for non-visual input. *SpatialTouch* enabled users to mimic this behavior and make more efficient onscreen explorations to select target keys, as they landed near the intended targets and followed better paths. Our results suggest that participants were leveraging previous *QWERTY* experience. Future work should seek to exploit natural typing behaviors of blind users by supporting two-hand interaction.

Multitouch input needs better character selection methods. The ability to rest the fingers on a touchscreen was previously explored for sighted users [5], but non-visual input is more demanding. One user searched for the home keys (*F* and *J*) and positioned the other fingers as he usually does to interact with a physical keyboard. This suggests that multitouch may support more accurate reference points, even beyond two-finger interaction provided that the auditory channel is not overloaded. Most users had an accurate mental model of the keyboard layout and were able to leverage two-hand interaction by making more efficient interactions, but with more insertion errors. Having more than one input point adds a selection uncertainty that needs to be effectively addressed. Future research should explore new selection techniques and recognizers for multitouch input. Regarding the audio feedback, participants reported their preference to have each hand associated to a particular voice, instead of being dependent of the touches order.

CONCLUSION

We presented *SpatialTouch*, a non-visual text-entry input system that supports multitouch keyboard exploration. Results show that *QWERTY* is a slow input method in tablet devices and that supporting simultaneous screen exploration was not enough to improve performance. However, *SpatialTouch* showed that, given the ability to interact two-handed, users will leverage their previous *QWERTY* experience by resorting to reference points and taking better paths. This suggests a greater understanding of the keyboard layout. Moreover, faster physical *QWERTY* typists were also faster in *SpatialTouch*, but not in *Explore by Touch*. Future work will explore multitouch selection methods to provide blind users more control over input.

ACKNOWLEDGMENTS

Supported by *FCT* (PEst-OE/EEI/LA0021/2013, PEst-OE/EEI/UI0408/2014; SFRH/BD/103935/2014) and RCUK (EP/G066019/1 - SIDE).

REFERENCES

1. Azenkot, S. et al. Input finger detection for nonvisual touch screen text entry in Perkinput. In Proceedings of Graphics Interface (2012)
2. Barrett, J. Performance effects of reduced proprioceptive feedback on touch typists and casual users in a typing task. Behaviour & Information Tech. 13 (6) (1994).
3. Brungart, D. S., Simpson, B. D. Improving multitalker speech communication with advanced audio displays. Air Force Res. Lab Wright Patterson AFN OH (2005).
4. Guerreiro, J., Gonçalves, D. Text-to-Speeches: Evaluating the Perception of Concurrent Speech by Blind People. *In Proceedings of ASSETS* (2014).
5. Kim, S et al. TapBoard: making a touch screen keyboard more touchable. *In Proceedings of CHI* (2013).
6. Nicolau, H. et al. B#: chord-based correction for multitouch braille input. In *Proceedings of* CHI (2014).
7. Oliveira, J. et al. Blind people and mobile touch-based text-entry: acknowledging the need for different flavors. In Proceedings of ASSETS (2011).
8. Rodrigues, A., Guerreiro, T. SWAT: Mobile System-Wide Assistive technologies. Proc. of BCS HCI (2014).
9. Southern, C. et al. An evaluation of BrailleTouch: mobile touchscreen text entry for the visually impaired. *In Proceedings of Mobile HCI* (2012).

VocalSketch: Vocally Imitating Audio Concepts

Mark Cartwright
Northwestern University, EECS Department
mcartwright@u.northwestern.edu

Bryan Pardo
Northwestern University, EECS Department
pardo@northwestern.edu

ABSTRACT
A natural way of communicating an audio concept is to imitate it with one's voice. This creates an approximation of the imagined sound (e.g. a particular owl's hoot), much like how a visual sketch approximates a visual concept (e.g a drawing of the owl). If a machine could understand vocal imitations, users could communicate with software in this natural way, enabling new interactions (e.g. programming a music synthesizer by imitating the desired sound with one's voice). In this work, we collect thousands of crowd-sourced vocal imitations of a large set of diverse sounds, along with data on the crowd's ability to correctly label these vocal imitations. The resulting data set will help the research community understand which audio concepts can be effectively communicated with this approach. We have released the data set so the community can study the related issues and build systems that leverage vocal imitation as an interaction modality.

Author Keywords
user interaction; vocal imitation; audio software; data set

ACM Classification Keywords
H.5.2 User Interfaces: Input devices and strategies, Interaction styles; H.5.5 Sound and Music Computing: Methodologies and techniques

INTRODUCTION
In audio production applications, users currently communicate audio concepts to the software using low-level technical parameters (e.g. setting parameters on a music synthesizer). For audio search applications (e.g. finding the right door "slam" from a library of 100,000 sound effects), users typically rely on keyword descriptions stored with the audio.

It can be very difficult for a user to communicate via low-level technical parameters if they are unfamiliar with these parameters. When people communicate audio concepts to other people (rather than software), they typically do so using methods such as descriptive language and vocal imitation [10]. While descriptive language can be an effective way of communicating audio concepts [14, 10], audio concepts without broadly agreed upon labels, e.g. most sounds produced by music synthesizers, are difficult to describe with language [10].

CHI 2015, April 18–23, 2015, Seoul, Republic of Korea.

ACM 978-1-4503-3145-6/15/04 ...$15.00.
http://dx.doi.org/10.1145/2702123.2702387

When words fail, we vocally imitate the desired sound. In doing so, one approximates the target audio concept by mapping its pitch, timbre, and temporal properties to properties of the voice. Vocal imitation has been shown to be useful for "vocal sketching" in collaborative design [4]. In recent years, the community has begun building interfaces that use vocal imitation for a variety of tasks. These include searching audio databases for particular songs [6], drum loops [7], or sound effects [1], controlling a music synthesizer [2, 13, 8] and editing audio [12].

Given the recent interest in this area, it is important for interface designers to understand what kinds of sounds may be successfully reproduced by vocal imitation so that appropriate interfaces can be built.

Lemaitre et al have investigated vocal imitation from several angles [9, 10]. In [9], participants freely categorized vocal imitations of 12 identifiable kitchen sound recordings into 4 categories. More recently, Lemaitre et al investigated both vocal imitation and descriptive language as a means of communicating audio concepts [10]. This study used a set of 36 sounds (9 from each of the following categories: 1. *identifiable complex events*, 2. *elementary mechanical*, 3. *artificial sound effects*, 4. *unidentifiable mechanical sounds*). They found vocal imitations no more effective than descriptive language when the sound source is identifiable by name (categories 1 and 2). Vocal imitations were much more effective than descriptive language when the sound sources were not identifiable by name (categories 3 and 4). While their work is excellent, the number of sounds and participants is small, limiting the generalizability of their results.

Eitz et al performed a collection of crowd-sourced visual sketches of 250 everyday objects [3]. The authors of that study created two tasks on Amazon's Mechanical Turk: a sketching task and a recognition task, and they also released their data set to the public for others to use. Inspired by Eitz's work, we collected labels and "vocal sketches" from a large number of participants over Amazon Mechanical Turk. We built on Lemaitre's work, using a much larger set of sounds and larger population to obtain more generalizable results.

METHODOLOGY
In this work, we focus on vocal imitation to communicate audio concepts defined primarily by their timbre. We assembled a diverse set of 240 audio concepts with a wide range of timbres. Most audio concepts were defined by both a sound label (e.g. a 1-4 word description, e.g. "barking dog") and a short (up to 10 seconds) sound recording of a specific instance of the audio concept. 40 of the audio concepts did not have sound labels (discussed later). We then collected thousands

of vocal imitations from workers on Amazon's Mechanical Turk. A second set of workers described the vocal imitations and matched them to their referent audio concept. All workers were first required to pass a simple listening test.

This data set will help address the following questions: What types of audio concepts can be effectively communicated between people via vocal imitation? What are the acoustic characteristics of audio concepts that can be effectively communicated between people? The answers to these questions will clarify what applications this method of communication can be used for. The human-provided labels of the vocal imitations form a performance baseline for automated systems that search for relevant audio based on vocal imitations.

Audio Concept Set
Our audio concept set contains four subsets: *everyday*, *acoustic instruments*, *commercial synthesizers*, and *single synthesizer*. These subsets were chosen with two goals in mind: 1) diversity and 2) applicability to potential applications for vocal imitation (e.g. sound design).

The ***everyday*** subset is a set of 120 audio concepts assembled by Marcell et al [11] for confrontation naming applications in cognitive psychology (i.e. applications in which participants are asked to identify sounds). This set contains a wide variety of acoustic events such as sounds produced by animals, people, musical instruments, tools, signals, and liquids. The set includes a recording and label (e.g. "brushing teeth", "jackhammer") for each of the audio concepts.

The ***acoustic instruments*** audio concept subset consists of 40 primarily orchestral instruments [5]. Each sound recording in this subset is of a single note played on musical pitch C (where applicable) at on octave chosen to be appropriate for the range of each particular instrument. The sound labels for the audio concepts are instrument names and any short notes on the playing technique (e.g. "plucked violin").

The ***commercial synthesizers*** subset consists of 40 recordings of a variety of synthesizers in Apple Inc's Logic Pro music production suite with various popular synthesis methods. This let us explore people's ability to recognize and reproduce sounds that they could not necessarily name and and had not had many years of exposure to (unlike "brushing teeth"). Each recording was created from a "factory preset" (well-crafted settings chosen and named by Apple Inc) and consists of a single note played on musical pitch C (the octave varied according to the intended pitch range of the preset). The labels for this subset are the names of the factory presets, (e.g. "resonant clouds", "abyss of despair").

The ***single synthesizer*** subset consists of 40 recordings of a single 15-parameter subtractive synthesizer (with some limited FM and AM capabilities). Each recording consists of a note played on musical pitch C (the octave varied depending on the parameter settings). This subset was included because we know the parameter settings used, and we have the source code for this synth. This data could be used to learn mappings between vocal imitation features, referent audio features, and synthesis parameters, which is of use to researchers of new music synthesis tools and interfaces. Since these recordings were not derived from presets and are difficult to describe with language, no labels exist for these sound recordings.

Vocal Imitations of Audio Concepts
We designed two tasks for Mechanical Turk in which participants recorded a vocal imitation in response to a stimulus.

The first task addressed the use case where a user seeks a general audio concept (e.g. any church bells). Participants were given a *sound label* (e.g. the text "church bells") from our audio concept set and asked to "imagine a short (less than 10 seconds) sound produced by the following description." Next they were asked to "indicate the degree of confidence you have in your ability to imagine the sound" on a discrete scale. They were then given a simple recording interface and asked to "imitate the imagined sound with your voice as closely as possible." They were told to avoid using conventional onomatopoeia (e.g. "meow"), but that whistles, coughs, clicks, and other mouth noises were okay. Before continuing to the next step they were required to listen again to their recording and to indicate how satisfied they were with the recording. Participants were allowed to rerecord their vocal imitations unlimited times before proceeding. Discarded imitations were saved as "drafts" on our server.

The second task addressed the use case where a user seeks to reproduce the exact sound of a specific instance of an audio concept (e.g. the sound of specific church bells). This task was similar to the first task, but instead of imitating the imagined sound of a description, participants were asked to listen to a reference *sound recording* (e.g. a recording of church bells) and to imitate it with their voice as closely as possible. They were then required to listen to both the reference recording and their own recorded imitation and indicate their satisfaction with the imitation. They were allowed to rerecord their vocal imitations unlimited times until satisfied. They were then asked to "describe the identity of the source of the reference audio" (using less than 5 words) and to indicate their confidence in their description on a discrete scale.

Data Overview
Including all draft imitations, there were 10750 vocal imitations recorded by 248 unique participants. All of the submitted imitations (i.e. non-"drafts") were listened to by one of the authors, and any recordings lacking a vocal imitation or of poor recording quality were removed. The remaining recordings form the subset discussed in the remainder of the paper. This subset contains 4429 vocal imitations (2418 from the *sound recording* stimulus task, 2011 from the *sound label* stimulus task) recorded by 185 unique participants. Of the 175 participants that completed the survey, 100 identified as male / 75 as female, and their mean reported age was 31.8 (SD=8.5). The median number of imitations per participant was 4 (min=1, max=204). There were at least 10 (max of 11) vocal imitations collected for each of the 240 sound recordings and 200 sound labels.

Human Recognition of Vocal Imitations
To establish a human baseline level for the effectiveness of vocal imitations for communication, we had Mechanical Turk workers perform several identification tasks.

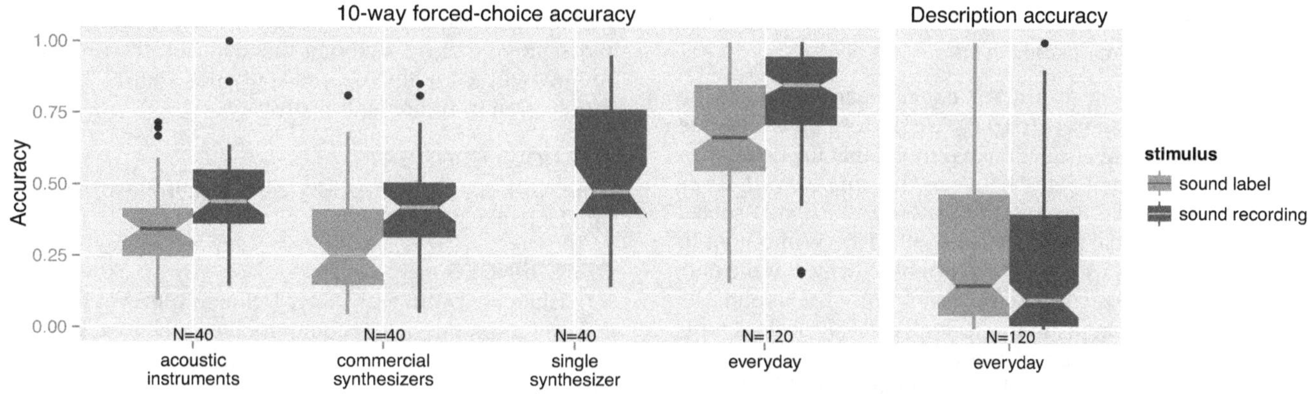

Figure 1. Human recognition accuracy of vocal imitations. The boxes extend from the lower to upper quartiles of the data. The horizontal lines in each box are the medians, and the notches around the median are 95% confidence intervals.

For both the 2418 vocal imitations produced in response to reference sound recordings (a recording of a jackhammer) and the 2011 vocal imitations produced in response to descriptive labels (the word "jackhammer"), participants were presented a randomly selected vocal imitation. They could play this imitation unlimited times. They were asked to describe what it was an imitation of, using five words or less. They were then asked to indicate their degree of confidence in this free-response description on an 5-level scale.

Then, if the vocal imitation had been produced in response to a sound recording, the participant was presented 10 recordings drawn from the same audio concept subset (e.g. if it was an *everyday* sound they were presented 10 distinct everyday sounds): the referent recording and 9 random distractors. After hearing each recording in its entirety at least once, they were presented a 10-way forced choice to identify the recording the imitation was based on. Lastly, they had to indicate their confidence in their choice on a 5-level scale. Participants could play all of the recordings unlimited times.

Similarly, if the vocal imitation had been produced in response to a sound label, the participant was presented a 10-way forced choice between labels from the same audio concept subset. The task was to choose the label that the vocal imitation had been produced in response to. Participants could play the imitation recording unlimited times.

Data Overview

There were at least two (maximum of three) identification task instances assigned for each vocal imitation we collected. There were a total of 9174 identifications by 329 unique participants. The median number of identifications per participant was 10 (min=1, max=424).

RESULTS

In this section, we provide a brief analysis of the human baseline performance on the identification of vocal imitations.

The authors of the *everyday* subset [11] published guidelines for scoring short descriptions of their sound recordings for binary recognition (e.g. description must contain "both the object ('door') and the closing action" for "door closing"). Using these guidelines, we scored our participants' descriptions of the everyday sounds for recognition. We found that our participants' mean recognition accuracy across the 120 *everyday* sounds was 0.80 (SD=0.25). This was similar to that of the previous study: mean=0.78 (SD=0.25). Comparing these to the previous study's results on the same 120 sounds, we obtained a Pearson correlation of r=0.84 (p=0.0), and a paired t-test of t(119)=1.67 (p=0.097). Therefore, our participants via Mechanical Turk performed comparably to lab-consented participants, giving validity to the effort our participants put into the task.

Figure 1 shows the recognition accuracy for the vocal imitations, grouped by audio concept subset and stimulus type. "10-way forced-choice accuracy" refers to the recognition accuracy of the participants' 10-way forced-choice response in the identification task. For the *sound recording* stimulus vocal imitations, the mean recognition accuracy, broken down by audio concept subset was *acoustic instruments*: 0.45 (SD=0.18), *commercial synthesizers*: 0.42 (SD=0.18), *single synthesizer*: 0.54 (SD=0.22), *everyday*: 0.80 (SD=0.17), and mean accuracy for the *sound label* stimulus vocal imitations was *acoustic instruments*: 0.35 (SD=0.16), *commercial synthesizers*: 0.29 (SD=0.19), *everyday*: 0.68 (SD=0.20). Note that chance performance on all these tasks is 0.1.

Comparing each subset by stimulus type, the mean accuracy of the *sound recording* stimulus is greater than the *sound label* stimulus for all subsets (excluding *single synthesizer* since it lacks sound labels) according to one-sided paired t-tests, $p < 0.01$ in all cases. This difference is likely due participants' varied interpretations of what a text-based label means.

Due to space constraints, we focus the rest of our analysis on the vocal imitations from the "sound recording" stimulus tasks. The *everyday* sounds were communicated the most effectively with vocal imitations. This may be due to the familiarity but also reproducibility of the *everyday* subset. Within that subset, imitations with the highest accuracy from the sound recording stimuli were typically sounds easily producible by the voice (human and animal sounds - e.g. "yawning", "wolf") or those with salient time-varied characteristics (e.g. "police siren"). Those with the lowest recognition accuracy were likely harder to accurately imitate with a single voice. For instance "glass breaking" (accuracy=0.20) has many overlapping small sonic events.

After a Welch's f-test to test for equal means between the four audio concept subsets (p=0.0), we performed a pairwise t-test with Bonferroni correction and found that the difference of 0.12 in recognition rates between the *single synthesizer* (0.54) subset and the *commercial synthesizers* (0.42) subset bordered on statistical significance (p=0.058). Without an in depth acoustic analysis it is hard to establish why, but the data set is available to allow this follow-on work. One hypothesis is that the audio concepts in the *single synthesizer* class typically have simpler but strong modulation characteristics (i.e. salient temporal properties) which may have aided in the imitation and therefore recognition of these sounds.

In Figure 1, "Description accuracy" refers to the recognition accuracy of the participants' free-response descriptions *of the vocal imitations* in the identification task. We again used the same scoring guidelines described in [11], and therefore we only scored the *everyday* subset, which was the same set used in their work. The mean recognition accuracy was 0.23 (SD=0.27) for the *sound recording* stimulus vocal imitations, and mean=0.27 (SD=0.27) for the *sound label* stimulus vocal imitations. Some audio concepts had a 0% recognition (e.g. "blinds"), while some had a 100% recognition (e.g. "sheep"). While the free-response recognition accuracy is much lower than the forced-choice recognition accuracy, this is to be expected since the participants must describe the imitation without any additional clues. However, when failing to identify the referent audio concept, participants often described similar (e.g. "motorcycle" instead of "lawnmower") or possibly more general (e.g. "horn" instead of "boat horn") concepts. This implies that more information may be needed help to disambiguate or refine certain concepts. In an audio application, this could be achieved by asking the user for additional information.

DISCUSSION

As this work is primarily about providing a data set for the community to use, the analysis in this work is intended to be illustrative rather than comprehensive. From our analysis, it seems *everyday* audio concepts were communicated the most effectively, though in a real application additional information may need to be provided by a user to disambiguate concepts. In the remaining instrumental subsets, audio concepts from the *single synthesizer* subset were communicated the most effectively, but further acoustic analysis is required to determine what enables some audio concepts to be communicated more effectively than others with vocal imitation. The data set in this paper can be obtained at `http://dx.doi.org/10.5281/zenodo.13862`.

CONCLUSION

In this work we presented a novel data set containing crowd-sourced vocal imitations of audio concepts and identifications of those imitations by other humans. This data set will help the research community understand which audio concepts can be effectively communicated with vocal imitation and what the characteristics of these audio concepts are. It is the authors' hope that by studying this data set, the research community will learn how we can apply this natural form of communication to future audio software.

ACKNOWLEDGMENTS

This work was supported by NSF Grant Nos. IIS-1116384 and DGE-0824162.

REFERENCES

1. Blancas, D. S., and Janer, J. Sound retrieval from voice imitation queries in collaborative databases. In *Proc. of Audio Engineering Society 53rd Int'l Conf.* (2014).
2. Cartwright, M., and Pardo, B. Synthassist: Querying an audio synthesizer by vocal imitation. In *Conference on New Interfaces for Musical Expression* (2014).
3. Eitz, M., Hays, J., and Alexa, M. How do humans sketch objects? *ACM Trans. Graph. 31*, 4 (2012), 44.
4. Ekman, I., and Rinott, M. Using vocal sketching for designing sonic interactions. In *Proc. of the 8th ACM Conf. on Designing Interactive Systems* (2010).
5. Fritts, L. University of iowa musical instrument samples, 2012. `http://theremin.music.uiowa.edu/MIS.html`.
6. Ghias, A., Logan, J., Chamberlin, D., and Smith, B. C. Query by humming: musical information retrieval in an audio database. In *Proc. of the Third ACM Int'l Conference on Multimedia* (1995).
7. Gillet, O., and Richard, G. Drum loops retrieval from spoken queries. *Journal of Intelligent Information Systems 24*, 2-3 (2005), 159–177.
8. Janer Mestres, J. *Singing-driven interfaces for sound synthesizers*. PhD thesis, Universitat Pompeu Fabra, 2008.
9. Lemaitre, G., Dessein, A., Susini, P., and Aura, K. Vocal imitations and the identification of sound events. *Ecological Psychology 23*, 4 (2011), 267–307.
10. Lemaitre, G., and Rocchesso, D. On the effectiveness of vocal imitations and verbal descriptions of sounds. *The Journal of the Acoustical Society of America 135*, 2 (2014), 862–873.
11. Marcell, M. M., Borella, D., Greene, M., Kerr, E., and Rogers, S. Confrontation naming of environmental sounds. *Journal of Clinical and Experimental Neuropsychology 22*, 6 (2000), 830–864.
12. Smaragdis, P., and Mysore, G. J. Separation by "humming": User-guided sound extraction from monophonic mixtures. In *Proc. of IEEE Workshop on Applications of Signal Processing to Audio and Acoustics* (2009).
13. Stowell, D. *Making music through real-time voice timbre analysis: machine learning and timbral control*. PhD thesis, Queen Mary University of London, 2010.
14. Sundaram, S., and Narayanan, S. Vector-based representation and clustering of audio using onomatopoeia words. In *Proc. of AAAI* (2006).

An Evaluation of Multidimensional Controllers for Sound Design Tasks

Robert Tubb and Simon Dixon
Centre for Digital Music
Queen Mary University of London
r.h.tubb@qmul.ac.uk

ABSTRACT
This paper presents an investigation into musicians' ability to control sound synthesiser parameters using various interfaces. The principal aim was to compare separate, 1D parameter controls (touchscreen sliders) to multidimensional controllers (an XY touchpad for 2D, the Leap Motion for 3D). Subjects had to match a target sound as quickly and accurately as possible. Results show that after about two hours of practice, the XY pad is 9% faster than two sliders for no accuracy loss, and the Leap is 17% faster than 3 sliders with 9% accuracy loss. The multidimensional controllers improved most with practice. A new perspective on Fitts' index of difficulty is presented: "Index of Search Space Reduction" (ISSR). ISSR and retrospective accuracy thresholds on the search trajectory are used to obtain straight line plots and throughput values. These plots reveal that the Leap's speed improvement was mainly due to reaction time, but the XY pad traversed the space faster.

Author Keywords
Audio; Parameter Exploration; Synthesiser; Fitts' law; 3D interfaces; Leap Motion

ACM Classification Keywords
H.5.5. Sound and Music Computing: Miscellaneous
; H.5.2. User Interfaces: Evaluation/methodology

INTRODUCTION
Human-computer interaction is generally carried out in a serial fashion. Predominant interaction models tend to assume a single action at a time. However, some domains require more parallelism in the communication channel between the human and machine. One such field is music. To watch the performance of a concert pianist is to witness a virtuoso display of "space-multiplexed" [8] user input. The throughput of this interaction has been estimated at 300 bit/s, contrasting with about 50 bit/s for a good typist, and 5 bit/s for mouse pointing [4]. The increase in speed that comes with virtuosity is obvious, but usually comes at a cost in training time: some tens of thousands of hours in the pianist's case [6]. So a key question is how much practice is required to reach a throughput greater than that of a standard serial interface? This experiment investigates this issue by looking at interaction with a synthesiser, based on a simplified version of a sound design task. Controllers with 1, 2 and 3 DOF (degrees of freedom) are compared for speed, accuracy and throughput.

http://dx.doi.org/10.1145/2702123.2702499

Sound Design and the Digital Musical Instrument (DMI)
The task of sound design in music, film, or computer games is a challenging one. Synthesisers and effects processors often have tens or hundreds of parameters, leading to a huge combinatorial search space. Artists search these large spaces to hand-craft instruments with complex timbres and textures. Often, only a small subset of the parameter space produces pleasing output. Parameters may interact in non-linear and unpredictable ways, and the perceived value of certain sound will change with context. This poses a challenge to interface designers: how to make the search as productive as possible?

The majority of computer music production is carried out using a Digital Audio Workstation (DAW). Despite the increasing sophistication of the sound generators, most DAW interfaces are built around metaphors that hark back to mid-20th century studio technology, namely potentiometer knobs, faders and switches. When operated with a mouse, these GUI items necessitate one at a time adjustments. DAWs are extremely powerful and flexible, but acknowledged to be less musically "expressive" than traditional instruments [17], hence the interest in using high DOF [26] controllers for Digital Musical Instruments (DMIs). This is one focus of the "New Instruments for Musical Expression" research field [20, 2]. Expressiveness is a difficult term to define, but generally implies real-time control of the dynamics and timbre of notes. The more complexity and nuance that can be imparted to a musical event, the greater the expressive range. This implies a link between expressiveness and information transfer rate. Information "throughput" has been discussed in relation to synthesiser interfaces [19], but has not yet been measured experimentally.

Synthesis parameters often correspond to, or at least affect, "perceptual dimensions". Perceptual dimensions have been shown to lie along a continuum between "integral" and "separable" [9]. Integral dimensions tend to be perceived and processed holistically [14] and not analysed in isolation, for in-

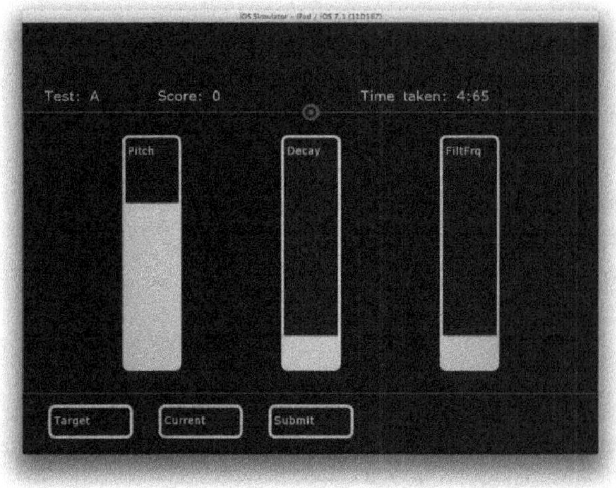

Figure 1. Screen shot of 3 slider interface during the search task. The "Target" button plays the target sound, the "Current" button plays the sound that is being adjusted using the sliders. When the user has matched the two sounds, "Submit" is pressed.

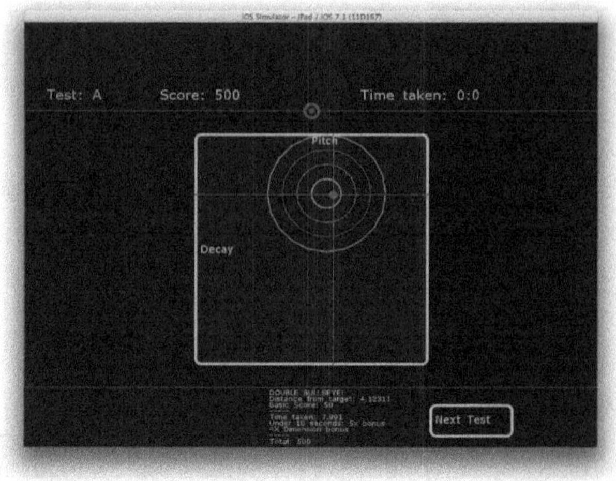

Figure 2. XY pad trial. A successfully located sound has been submitted.

stance hue and brightness. Separable dimensions are those dimensions that are perceived and most easily manipulated separately, for instance size and colour. Timbre dimensions are highly integral. This structure of perceptual space has been shown to be important for HCI by Jacob et al. [13]. This experiment revealed that the integral dimensions were best controlled by multidimensional controllers, and separate one-dimensional controllers suited separable dimensions. They also proposed a general principle that the structure of the interface must match the perceptual structure of the task domain. This has ramifications for timbre navigation and DMI design, as it implies that multidimensional controllers will be more suitable. This was tested in [22], but inaccuracies of early 3-D controllers made results inconclusive. Another influential result is [12], showing that *complex* many-to-many mappings produced better results in a sound matching task than one-to-one mappings. These complex mappings also showed more improvement with practice. A good qualitative analysis of a 4D bimanual timbre controller is found in [1].

In [23] recommendations are made for improving DMI research by borrowing tools from HCI. Fitts' law is mentioned as having potential, but has not yet been fully investigated, perhaps due to lack of a easily applicable methodology. Whilst there are many analogies between visual target pointing and sound target matching tasks, there are a number of differences and extra challenges with an auditory search. These differences must be considered when finding an analogue of Fitts' law for sound target acquisition:

1. *Delayed Assessment.* Differences in position can be assessed virtually instantaneously. Sounds, however, take time to listen to. Some control adjustments may have delayed effects, particularly time envelope controls. Differences between two sounds cannot be easily assessed with them playing simultaneously (with the exception of pitch: identifying intervals is a core part of musical training).

2. *Anisotropy.* Timbre space does not look the same in all directions. Pitch, timbre and temporal features are all very different perceptual qualities. In contrast, 3D space can be considered isotropic, although evidence for some anisotropy in pointing tasks has been found [18].

3. *Low sightedness*: Differences in sounds are harder to judge, and take far more effort to process that differences in position. Parameter spaces could be said to vary between being "sighted", where the distance and direction to the target is predictable, and "blind" where it is impossible to know which direction to move in, or how far away one is from the target. This may depend on the user's expertise.

4. Timbre space possesses a dimensionality far higher than that of ordinary space.

Research into this problem may also be applicable to many other areas where large numbers of unpredictable parameters need to be adjusted to obtain creatively satisfying results: graphic design, animation, architecture and so on.

EXPERIMENTAL METHOD

The study was a within-subjects repeated measure design. 8 subjects carried out 8 blocks of 94 sound matches. Whilst it is generally better to use more subjects for less trials, a pilot study revealed that performance was still improving after numerous runs, so a more longitudinal study was required. "Expert" participants were selected, with at least 5 years experience of music, sound synthesis or working with audio. They were paid 30 GBP for participating. To avoid fatigue, participants completed four blocks on one day, and four the following day. Table 1 shows the sequence of trials for a single block. All users conducted the trials in this order, which was designed to ramp up in difficulty, whilst balancing the multidimensional and separate slider conditions. The sequence could have been better balanced or randomised, but at the expense of a coherently gamified user experience. It was assumed that after 8 blocks the order effects would have balanced out, but this could be a limitation of the study.

REP	DIM	UI	PRC	VIS	MEM	PIT	DEC	FLT
1	1	Slidr	Y	-	-	1	-	-
1	2	XY	Y	-	Y	1	2	-
1	3	Leap	Y	Y	-	1	2	3
2	1	Slidr	-	-	-	1	-	-
2	1	Slidr	-	-	-	-	-	1
2	1	Slidr	-	-	-	-	1	-
4	2	Slidr	-	-	-	1	2	-
4	2	XY	-	-	-	1	2	-
4	2	XY	-	-	-	-	1	2
4	2	Slidr	-	-	-	-	1	2
8	3	Leap	-	-	-	1	2	3
8	3	Slidr	-	-	-	1	2	3
1	1	Slidr	-	Y	-	1	-	-
1	1	Slidr	-	Y	-	-	-	1
1	1	Slidr	-	Y	-	-	1	-
2	2	XY	-	Y	-	1	2	-
2	2	Slidr	-	Y	-	1	2	-
4	3	Slidr	-	Y	-	1	2	3
4	3	Leap	-	Y	-	1	2	3
2	1	Slidr	-	-	Y	1	-	-
2	1	Slidr	-	-	Y	-	-	1
2	1	Slidr	-	-	Y	-	1	-
4	2	XY	-	-	Y	1	2	-
4	2	Slidr	-	-	Y	1	2	-
4	2	Slidr	-	-	Y	-	1	2
4	2	XY	-	-	Y	-	1	2
8	3	Slidr	-	-	Y	1	2	3
8	3	Leap	-	-	Y	1	2	3

Table 1. The trial sequence for one block. All blocks for all users ran in this order. REP column gives the number of repetitions of this trial. PRC indicates a practice run, not scored and not included in results. Controlled conditions were: DIM: number of parameters, UI: interface type, VIS: Visible target, MEM: only one listen to target sound. PIT: indicates which control (if any) operated pitch, DEC: decay time, FLT: filter cut-off. For Multi-D controls 1, 2 and 3 correspond to X,Y and Z dimensions respectively.

The sound generator was a basic digital subtractive synthesizer, constructed in Pure-Data [21]. The sound could be described as a short "pluck" with varying pitch, duration and brightness, as often heard from classic synths such as the Minimoog. The application ran on a multi-touch tablet, the hand's coordinates being sent from the Leap via a MIDI connection. The following parameters were sent to the synth as 7-bit MIDI CC[1] values:

1. Pitch: a one octave range, midi note 40 (E3) to 52 (E4).
2. Decay time: this affected both the decay of the amplitude, and also the rate of decay of high frequencies. Maximum note length was 500ms.
3. Filter cut-off: the cut-off frequency for the resonant low-pass filter.

The Leap Motion is a device that can track the position and shape of hands and fingers. It appears to be the most spatially and temporally accurate consumer device for this purpose [24]. Skeletal hand tracking can generate at least 20 DOF, however the number of parameters was limited to 3: the XYZ position of the hand. More parameters would likely have increased the difficulty of the search beyond many participant's capabilities.

[1]Musical Instrument Digital Interface, Continuous Control

For each trial, after an initial 3 second countdown the user was presented with two sounds: the "target" and the "adjustable" sound. Both sounds parameters were randomised, but with a minimum Euclidean distance between the two[2]. The task was to alter their adjustable sound so that it matched the target sound. For example, the simplest trial featured a single slider controlling pitch: the user had to move this slider up or down until the pitches matched, and then press the submit button. Participants were told that speed and accuracy were equally important, and this was reflected in the scoring system. Controls were adjusted with the right hand, and the results heard by retriggering the sounds with the left[3]. In the standard test, either sound could be triggered whenever the user wished. In the target sound memorisation test (Table 1, MEM condition) the target button would disappear after a single listen. The intention behind this test was to more closely approximate a realistic sound design task, where the user may have a sound "in their head" that they wish to create, but was assumed to be a more difficult condition due to memory fade.

When the user was happy that their settings matched the target, they would press the "submit" button (centre bottom Fig. 1) and were given a score and a visual indication of where the target really was (Fig. 2). A small prize was offered for the best score for one block. Participants stated that "gamification" of the task increased their motivation and engagement.

A number of tests were control tests with a visual target (Table 1, VIS condition). The user simply had to line the controls up with this visual indicator, the sound being irrelevant. This was to test for interface effectiveness independent of the more complex perceptual aspects of sound matching. In the Leap motion case a 3D scene was displayed on the touch-screen, with moveable "jack" crosshairs to be aligned.

For the 3D trials, parameters 1-3 were always assigned to the x (left/right), y (forward/backward) and z (up/down) axes respectively. The 2D tests alternated between pairs of parameters 1 & 2 and 2 & 3. The 1D tests alternated between all 3 parameters. There were an equal number of trials for 2D vs. 3D tasks, sliders vs. multidimensional control types, and normal vs. target memorisation conditions.

The 1D controls were 10cm vertical sliders on the tablet screen. The 2D XY pad's height and width was also 10cm. Users did not have to pick up the position indicator from its current position before moving it. Unfortunately this meant losing data in the VIS scenario, as users could just tap the target and hardly any of the trajectory would be recorded. The iPad was directly in front of the user, and the Leap was positioned 20cm to the right of the top right corner of the iPad. The size of the Leap's active volume was 30cm cubed, 15cm above the device/table. All interaction movements and events were logged at a sample rate of 50Hz.

[2]For the Leap, the initial settings would correspond to wherever the users hand was when the test started. This start position was taken into account when calculating $ISSR$ from distance ratios.

[3]In the pilot test the sounds played automatically in alternation (reducing variability in this part of the task), but people found it too hard to determine which sound was which.

INTERPRETING THE DATA: FITTS' LAW

Fitts' law applies to rapid aimed movements in a single dimension towards a visible target. This law has been extended for more than one dimension [16, 18, 10], but it has not been investigated in non-visuospatial parameter spaces. It is a linear relation between movement time, MT, and an "index of difficulty", ID:

$$MT = a + b \times ID. \quad (1)$$

The ID is a measure of task difficulty in bits. It is calculated from the target width W, and the distance moved to reach the target D. Fitt's original formula for ID [7] can be derived (or at least motivated) by considering the movement as a series of smaller movements with iterative corrections [3, p. 53]. However, there are alternative formulae, and even power laws fit the data well in many cases. The debate continues [5, 25], but the currently accepted standard is derived by considering the nervous system as a noisy communication channel [15]:

$$ID = \log_2 \left(\frac{D}{W} + 1 \right) \quad (2)$$

Fitts' law can be used to predict the time taken for various common interaction tasks, such as moving a cursor to a GUI button. It can also be used to compare the effectiveness of input devices, via the "throughput": the rate at which a user can input information to the system, $TP = ID/MT$.

Throughput seems like it should be a useful measure of progress in this target acquisition task. The question is if the prerequisites for Fitts law apply for this experiment. The search is certainly not "rapid", and may not be "aimed", due to low sightedness. The size of a sonic target is impossible to specify to the user, therefore they cannot implement different accuracy levels to provide a range of values for a regression line. One can calculate W from the standard deviation of the results to obtain the "effective width" $W_e = 4.133\sigma$. However, the high variance in accuracy generates extremely low ID values (for the 3D search in this study $\sigma \approx 10, D/W_e \approx 64/40, ID \approx 2bits$), and this single error distribution would not provide a range of difficulties. On the other hand, we carried out a large number of trials, and have a record of all the search paths, many resulting in high accuracies. Therefore, it would be helpful to have a method of extracting useful information from these accurate trials without artificially selecting unrepresentative data.

Rather than taking the index of difficulty as a independent variable set by the experimenter, we need an equivalent quantity that can quantify, *post-hoc*, the amount of success achieved at a certain task in a certain time. How can we measure the information input without recourse to an end point noise distribution, and how can we extend it to an n-dimensional control space? Can we meaningfully compare information input across different control dimensionalities? We approach these problems by deriving an information measure from "search volume reduction", presented in the next section.

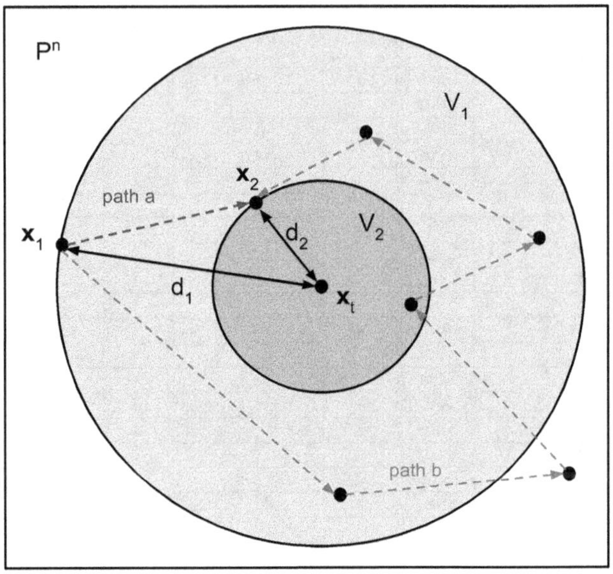

Figure 3. Search space reduction. The target is x_t, x_1 and x_2 are the start and end points of the movement along path a. V_1 and V_2 are the volumes associated with distances to target d_1 and d_2. The logarithm of the ratio between these two volumes gives a measure of information gain. Summing over all the steps of b gives the same amount of information gain as a (Eq. 5).

Index of Search Space Reduction (ISSR)

Both Fitts' and Hick's law [11] are motivated by an assumption of constant information flow through the nervous system. For a human interacting with a computer, this information then flows into the interface, and ultimately to the data artifact that is to be manipulated. The main motivation for developing ISSR is that, for content creation tasks, the ideal point at which to measure information flow is "where the rubber hits the road": precisely how it alters the data toward some desired state. Rather than looking at the capacity of the motor channel, we look at the reduction in the entropy of the point(s) in parameter space.

For an n-dimensional parameter space P^n, a start point $\mathbf{x}_1$, an end point $\mathbf{x}_2$ and a target point $\mathbf{x}_t$ we first calculate the distances to the target before and after a movement,

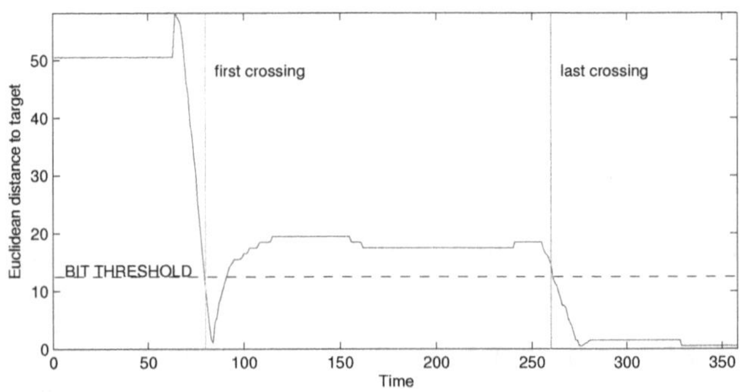

Figure 4. Time-to-threshold is calculated from the last crossing of a distance threshold. In this 1D case search space is effectively quartered, ISSR = 2 bits, MT = 260 samples (5.2 seconds).

$$d_1 = \|\mathbf{x}_t - \mathbf{x}_1\|, d_2 = \|\mathbf{x}_t - \mathbf{x}_2\|.$$

We define the search space reduction factor R as the ratio of the n-volumes corresponding to radii of the distances (see Fig. 3). Volume is calculated as $V = Cd^n$. The exact shape and size of the volume does not in fact matter, as the multiplier C cancels:

$$R = \frac{V_1}{V_2} = \frac{{d_1}^n}{{d_2}^n}.$$

For a path through a space towards a target, the remaining search space will be whatever volume the remaining search path is restricted to.

In general, any search task can be said to be a reduction of a set of possibilities. For an task involving a fixed number of options, the entropy reduction (or information conveyed) by a choosing of a subset of these possibilities will be the logarithm of the number of possible states before the choice was made divided by the number of possible states afterwards. If the remaining search volume is reduced by a factor of two, then we have successfully completed one bit of the search. This gives the "index of search space reduction" (renamed from index of difficulty to avoid confusion),

$$ISSR = log_2\left(R\right) = \log_2\left(\frac{{d_1}^n}{{d_2}^n}\right) = n\log_2\left(\frac{d_1}{d_2}\right). \quad (3)$$

Whilst a negative "difficulty" seems meaningless, it seems reasonable to say that moving away from the target results in lost information, and $ISSR < 0$ when $d_1 < d_2$. If no progress is made and $d_1 = d_2$, then $ISSR = 0$. For MT, dependence on dimensionality is simple: a constant multiplier of the gradient b,

$$MT = a + bn\log_2\left(\frac{d_1}{d_2}\right). \quad (4)$$

In fact this alternative derivation, for the one dimensional case, gives us Fitts' original equation [7]: substituting $n = 1$, $D = d_1$ and taking the target width as twice the final distance to the target centre, $W = 2d_2$ we get

$$MT = a + b\log_2\left(\frac{2D}{W}\right).$$

Interestingly, in 3D it is also yields a very similar equation to the change in entropy of a isothermally compressed gas, $\Delta S = -Nk\log\left(V_2/V_1\right)$, N and k being constants. So we might consider our interaction data set, a coalescing cloud of search paths, as analogous to the paths of a gas particles in a shrinking box.

A further reassuring property of the ISSR is that it conserves information, i.e. the total information gain of a search path can be considered as the sum of the information of all its subpaths, irrespective of how it is divided. The sum of information for M steps is

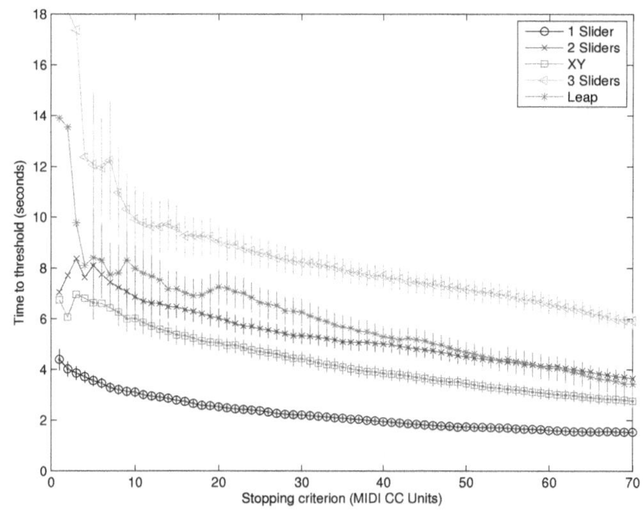

Figure 5. Average time taken to reach a given Euclidean distance threshold for each interface condition, day 2. Whilst different dimensionalities may not be directly comparable here, they are shown on the same plot for brevity. Whiskers display 95% confidence ratios at points where difference between interfaces is significant.

$$\begin{aligned} ISSR &= \sum_{m=1}^{M-1} n\log_2\left(\frac{d_m}{d_{m+1}}\right) \\ &= n\sum_{m=1}^{M-1}\Big(\log_2\left(d_m\right) - \log_2\left(d_{m+1}\right)\Big). \end{aligned}$$

All the terms cancel except the first d_m and the last d_{m+1} term, giving

$$ISSR = n\log_2\left(\frac{d_1}{d_M}\right). \quad (5)$$

This is identical to Eq. 3 for the start and end points of the whole path. It is difficult to see how the ID in Eq. 2 can conserve information in this way.

What difference will this formula give when navigating the search space using one parameter at a time rather than with a multidimensional controller? In the separate case, the total navigation time will be just the sum of navigation times for each 1D control, from Eq. 4:

$$MT_{tot} = na_{sep} + nb_{sep}\log_2\left(\frac{d_1}{d_2}\right). \quad (6)$$

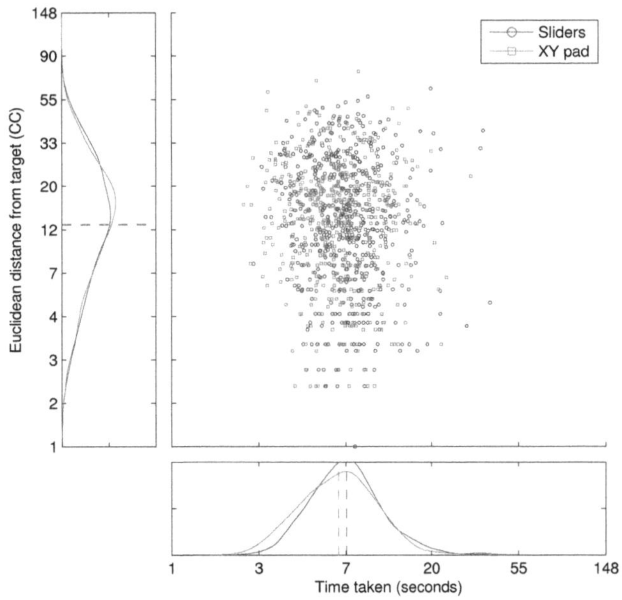

Figure 6. Distributions of log speed and accuracy results for the two parameter case, on the second day of the test. The XY-pad is as accurate as the sliders, but has more fast results under 5 seconds, resulting in a small but significant difference.

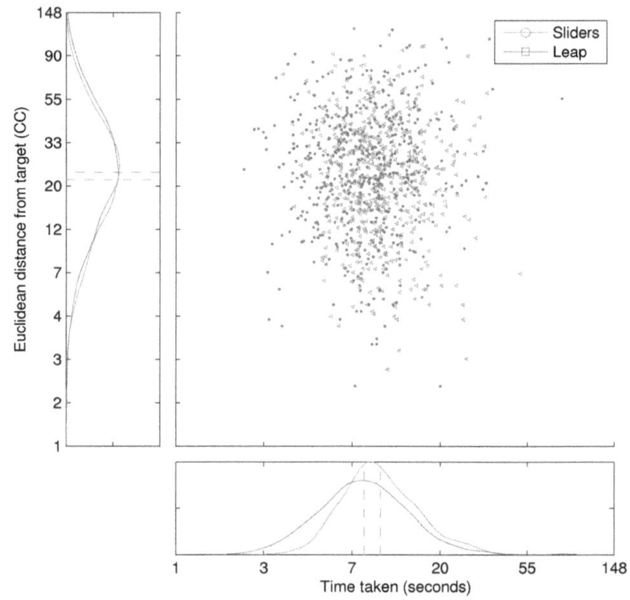

Figure 7. Speed and accuracy results for the three parameter case (day 2). Accuracy is slightly less with the leap but it yields more results under 7 seconds.

In the multidimensional case, however,

$$MT_{tot} = a_{int} + nb_{int} \log_2 \left(\frac{d_1}{d_2} \right). \tag{7}$$

If we assume the difficulty of progress through the space is the same $b_{sep} = b_{int}$, then the only difference between the two formulae will be an offset due to acquisition time. If $a_{int} < na_{sep}$, then integral controllers will be faster. In other words, any slow down seen in the separate case should be entirely explained by a constant offset time, for instance, how long it takes people to swap between sliders.

Alternatively, in light of the result in [13], it seems possible that diagonal movements require quite different cognitive processes, and $b_{int} \neq b_{sep}$.

Time-To-Threshold Plots

We would like a throughput measure that also makes use of all the search path trajectory data, rather than just its end point. As an example of this approach, Jacob et. al. [13] performed a retroactive analysis of the search trajectory that measured the time taken to reach various accuracy thresholds (or stopping criteria). This produces a series of simulated experiments with different target sizes. Figure 4 shows a plot of Euclidean distance to target for an example trial, and shows the last crossing of an accuracy threshold. We can set as many of these levels as we wish, and average many trials to get a mean time-to-threshold. One can then produce plots of time against accuracy (e.g. Fig. 5). For our purposes, these plots have a number of issues:

1. The lines often curve up steeply at smaller thresholds. Straight lines would be preferable, in order to obtain Fitts' law constants a and b.
2. The starting point is not taken into account: if the user starts close to the target, then achieving an absolute distance threshold will be easier.
3. In more dimensions the search space is larger, therefore achieving a given threshold will be harder.

We can avoid these issues by expressing the stopping criterion in terms of the $ISSR$. If sub-sections of the search path also obey Eq. 4 then plotting average MT against ISSR should give straight lines, and reflect the relative difficulties in different dimensionalities.

There is a statistical dilemma with this multiple threshold technique, however. One can include all the trials, but poor performances never reach high bit levels, and will not be represented towards the right of the plot. This will tend to make the lines curve downwards, and become unreliable at high $ISSR$. On the other hand, if the tests where the threshold was never reached are omitted entirely, the good performances are over-represented and significance decreases due to the smaller sample size. The policy here is to use the best half of all the trials for a given condition, i.e. set a threshold at the median $ISSR$ achieved. Any trial that did not reach the median no. of bits are discarded. Whilst this means the final TP values may underestimate the task difficulty as a whole, they should at least provide a *relative* comparison between experimental conditions. Higher $ISSR$s for the successful tests are not featured on the plot, therefore sample size is the same for every point along the line. This should not unfairly favour any particular control device, though it will favour the results from users more comfortable with the task. If the $ISSR$

	Pitch	Decay	Cut-off
1S	5.28	9.21	9.75
2S	4.49	13.94	12.99
XY	6.13	13.76	13.34
3S	6.67	14.79	14.24
LM	7.93	16.07	15.21

Table 2. Inaccuracies (standard deviation from the target in CC units) of individual parameters for all trials. Pitch is always most accurate.

version of Fitts' law holds, then this technique should give straight lines across a range of bit values.

RESULTS

Speed and Accuracy

Scatter plots of speed (time to submit) and accuracy (Euclidean distance to target at submission) for all 2D and 3D trials are shown in figures 6 and 7. Both axes display approximately log-normal distributions. No correlation between speed and accuracy is seen.

Overall, the decrease in completion time compared to equivaluent numbers of sliders is around 8 percent for the XY and 13 percent for the leap. However, people significantly improved across the two days (see later). If we look at results for the last 4 blocks (day 2), post practice the XY was 9% faster (paired T-test between interfaces $t(527) = 5.22, p < 0.01$). The leap was 17% faster than 3 sliders ($t(527) = 9.61, p < 0.01$), for an accuracy reduction of 9% ($t(527) = -2.36, p < 0.05$). Individual analyses for each user reveal similar patterns. Here we assume that different dimensionalities are not comparable, but if 2-way ANOVA is run for both dimensionality and interface type, speed-up is still significant ($F(1,1) = 192.4, p < .01$) and there is a significant interaction ($F(1) = 5.58, p < 0.05$).

Accuracy errors for all trials are given in Table 2, in the form of the standard deviation of the difference between the target value and the value of the parameter at submission. Not surprisingly, the accuracy for each parameter decreases the more sliders need to be set (the one exception being the good result for pitch in the 2D case). Timbre errors were around twice the size of pitch, despite a pitch range of only 1 octave, illustrating the "anisotropy" mentioned earlier.

We may already conclude that the higher DOF controllers are marginally more effective, but it would be preferable to have a single measure of throughput, and trajectory progress plots giving more insight into the cause of the differences.

Throughput

Figure 5 shows the average time taken to reach a given Euclidean distance threshold for all 2 and 3 dimensional trials. The Leap and XY pad are faster than the corresponding number of sliders for thresholds $> 5CC$. Figure 8 shows $ISSR$ plots for day 1 and day 2. Most lines now appear straighter, supporting the idea that a Fitts style law applies. Table 3 shows that if a regression is fit to the raw data, the wide distributions generate low R^2 values, but confidence bounds for the slope and intercept are reasonable.

On day 1 the leap was faster up to 3bits, but the gradient b_{LM} is obviously steeper than for 3 sliders. Day two, the gradients

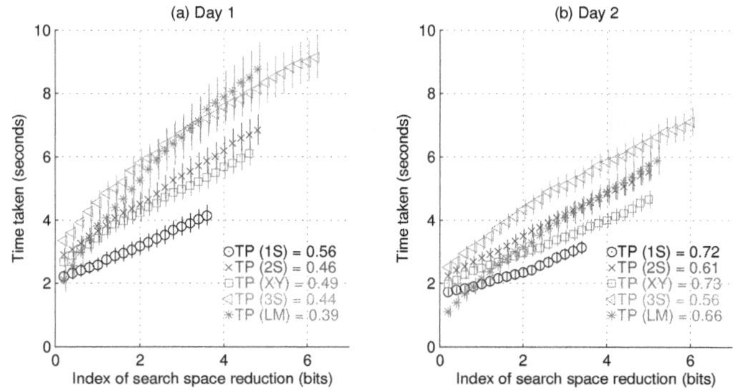

Figure 8. ISSR vs. MT, day 1 and day 2. Colors and markers consistent with Fig. 5. The gradient for the Leap improves with practice to match the sliders, but is about 1 second faster at all bit levels. To obtain cleaner plots, only trials that scored above the median $ISSR$ for that condition are included. TP values are calculated from the average of $MT/ISSR$ for every point along the line.

	1S	2S	XY	3S	LM
Intercept	1.6±0.2	1.8±0.1	2.0 ± 0.1	2.2±0.1	1.2±0.15
Slope (b)	.51±.04	.79±.03	.70±.02	.85±.02	.87±.02
TP (1/b)	1.96	1.26	1.42	1.17	1.14
R^2(all)	0.123	0.204	0.156	0.175	0.156
R^2(mean)	0.984	0.999	0.997	0.990	0.994

Table 3. Results of regression line fitting for each interface on day 2. Throughput here is taken as the reciprocal of the slope.

b_{LM} and b_{3S} appear the same, but the intercept a is lower for the Leap. This pattern is not seen in the 2D case, here a_{XY} and a_{2S} appear equal but b_{XY} is shallower than b_{2S}. The XY pad is faster even on day 1. Throughput values on the plots are calculated by averaging $ISSR/MT$ for all data points.

The intercepts can be largely explained by calculating reaction times, these are shown in Table 5. Firstly, RT is the average time from the presentation of the test until the sound is triggered. Second, listening time, LT, is taken as the time taken from the first sound trigger until the first control adjustment. RTs are the same for all interfaces (around 1s). LT is more variable. With the Leap, people start moving within 0.25s, even before they have time to listen to the sound they are adjusting. This could be just random hand waver triggering the movement threshold (set at 10CC/s), but the advantage carries through to higher accuracies, so it would appear to be real progress. The quick start also seems to explain the lower intercept on the Leap's plots. The question then becomes: what was it about the Leap that enabled people to start making progress sooner? One hypothesis is that people can *categorise* a sound quickly, and associate it with an approximate region in 3D space. On hearing the target, they can move in roughly the right direction without even listening to their current position or considering individual parameters. This

	1S	2S	XY	3S	LM
Time	-22⋆	-21†	-28†	-21†	-37†
Median Acc.	-6	4	9⋆	-3	8
Throughput	27	32⋆	48†	28⋆	70†

Table 4. Percentage difference for time taken, accuracy, and throughput between day 1 and day 2 (See Fig. 8). Two sample t-test, $\star P < 0.05$, $\dagger P < 0.01$.

	1S	2S	XY	3S	LM
RT	0.99	0.99	0.98	0.96	1.03
LT	0.85	1.26	1.05	1.39	0.24

Table 5. Reaction times (RT) and initial listening times (LT) for different interfaces. People seem to start moving much faster with the leap, explaining the lower intercepts.

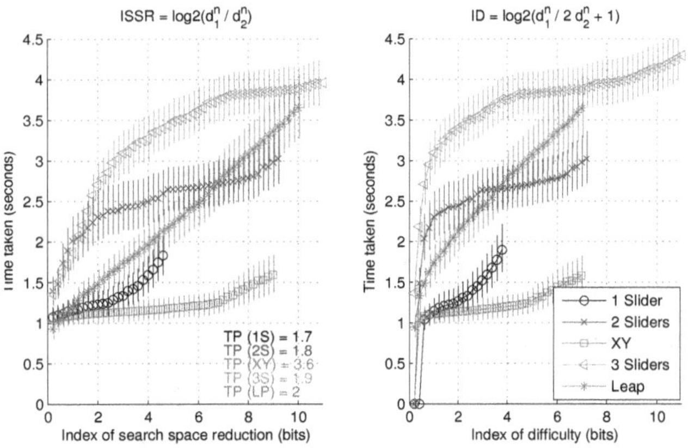

Figure 9. ISSR plot for the visible target condition (left) the kinks in the plots for the sliders are caused by having to swap controls. If we imagine the curves extrapolated onwards to higher accuracies, it seems that the 3 sliders will overtake the Leap. The right hand plot uses MacKenzie's ID, introducing sharp drops at low IDs.

would indicate a completely distinct learning process from that occurring with separate controls, certainly worth investigating further. Alternatively, one could argue that differences in reaction times reveal a flawed methodology, in which case some way of eliminating this effect should be found.

Table 4 summarises the effects of practice. The sliders show around a 21% speed improvement from day 1 to day 2, the XY improves by 28%, the Leap improves 37%. Participants keep their accuracy threshold relatively steady.

Comparisons with Visual Target Acquisition

Figure 9 shows the results for acquisition of the visual targets. Around twice the speed and twice the bit accuracy was achieved compared to the sound task. The only interface that gives a straight line is the Leap. The mostly flat lines for the 1 slider and XY plots are because users could simply tap the target, so the movement data was not recorded until their finger was on the screen for the final adjustments. The kinks in the 2 and 3 sliders' plots are probably caused by swapping time (as predicted in 6). Initial reaction times are similar to the sound task. The second plot shows the lines when a $+1$ is incorporated in the ID calculation (i.e. Eq. 2). This results in a sharp curve when $ID < 1$bit. If a regression line is fitted to the data, this reduces R^2 from 0.32 to 0.24 in the Leap's case. So the $ISSR$ formula does seem more appropriate for handling this time-to-threshold data.

People quite often needed to revisit a slider once the others were closer to the correct values. In theory, setting 3 parameters necessitates 2 slider swaps, in fact the mean number of swaps was 3.3, indicating that adjustments became more difficult if the other parameters were not set. The mean time for a swap was 0.9s. In the 2D case, number of swaps $= 1.7$ and

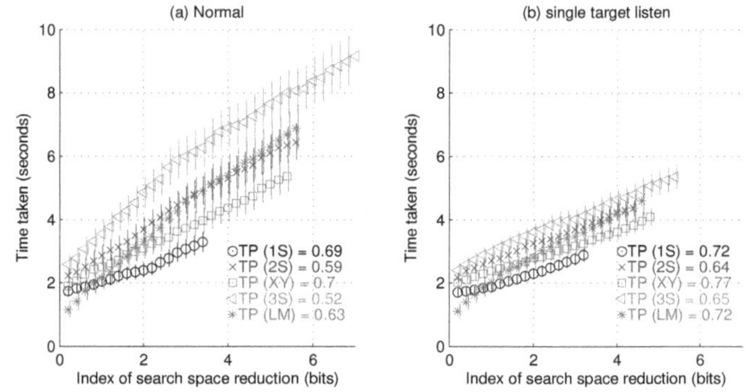

Figure 10. ISSR vs. MT, for MEM and nonMEM case, day 2 only. Not surprisingly, final accuracy has decreased, but the speed up for a given accuracy is quite surprising.

	1S	2S	XY	3S	LM
Mean Accuracy	-6⋆	-15†	-10†	-21†	-18†
Time to mean acc.	−14⋆	−26†	−17†	−33†	−29†
Throughput	8	17	8	26⋆	22

Table 6. Percentage change from normal to MEM condition (See Figure 10). $\star P < 0.05$, $\dagger P < 0.01$

swap time $= 0.86$s. When a visible target was present the swap times were faster: 0.65s. So an extra 0.2s was required to re-orient to another perceptual dimension in the sound task, probably to re-compare the sounds. This complicates the theory behind Eq. 6 somewhat.

Integration: Diagonal Movement

Another quantity of interest is whether people really did operate more than one dimension at a time, i.e. move diagonally in the integral controller case. Diagonal travel is also referred to as "coordination" [26] and "controller integration" [22]. The former is calculated from the correlation of different dimensions, but here, as in [13], integration was calculated from as being the ratio between the amount of time that more than one dimension was moving to the time only one dimension was moving. The speed threshold distinguishing a moving/stationary dimension was set at 10CC/s. Integration values were heavily dependent on the threshold value, but results comparing experimental conditions were not. A scatter plot of diagonality vs. completion speed (Fig. 11) shows that the amount of diagonal travel did slightly correlate with speed, however most navigation was being carried out in a city-block fashion, with integration ratios < 1.

Target Memorisation Test

Fig. 10 shows the differences in the MEM case. Accuracy worsens; participants said that auditioning the sound they were controlling degraded the memory of the target. However it is interesting that the actual time to a given bit threshold is much faster. Table 6 shows percentage differences. So for rough matches it is much faster to not keep re-listening to the target. Nevertheless, participants failed to implement this strategy when they were given the choice, indicating that they underrate their own ability to either memorise a target or predict the effect of parameter adjustments.

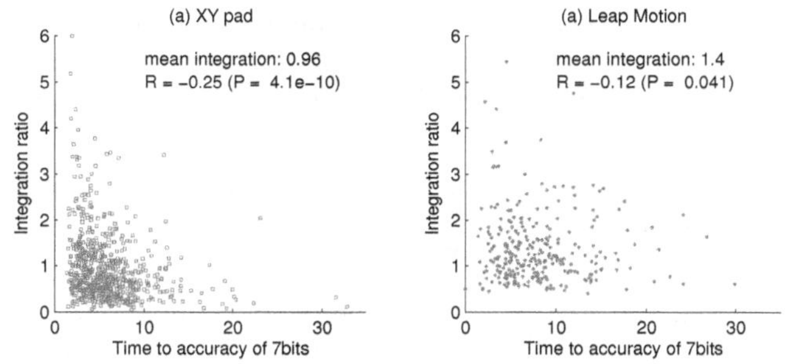

Figure 11. A small but significant correlation between amount of diagonal movement and speed.

Another interesting result was that search trajectories were more diagonal in the single target listen case. For the XY pad, the integration ratio was 1.2 (MEM), vs. 0.8 (non-MEM) $t(1022) = 6.95, p < 0.01$. For the Leap it was 2.2 (MEM) vs. 1.3 (non-MEM) $t(1022) = 7.4, p < 0.01$. It seems that if people are forced not to repeatedly compare the two sounds, they treat the dimensions in a more integral fashion. Could this be because a back and forth comparison encourages a slower, analytical mode of thinking, whereas a sound stored in a short term auditory buffer is treated in a more holistic fashion?

DISCUSSION

It seems the multidimensional controllers are more effective, though not by a huge margin. However, they were showing greater improvements with practice, so may be expected to become faster still. The reasons for the speed improvement appeared different for the different devices, however. The XY pad showed a greater throughput due to a shallower gradient: it was faster traversing the space. The speed gains with the Leap, on the other hand, seemed to be a result of faster reaction time: for some reason people felt they could start the search quicker, without waiting to compare the sounds first. We speculate that this is the result of associative learning of regions of the space. For achieving high accuracies, the sliders were still preferable to the Leap, which was 9% less accurate. Therefore, in terms of sound production work-flow, high DOF controllers would be better for early stage exploratory creativity and live performance, but individual controls better for late stage creativity and fine tuning.

There is a small correlation between diagonal movement and speed, but not yet enough to be the cause of significant speed up for multidimensional control. Far more practice seems to be needed to be able to be completely comfortable taking the shortest path through the parameter space. One user guessed that about 100 hours would be required before they had learned the perceptual space well enough to move directly to the target in 3D. Indeed, one of the most striking findings is how hard the perceptual component of this task is. Even with three simple audio parameters, experienced users, and elimination of the worst half of the results, throughput is only around 0.5bit/s, around a quarter of that for the pointing tasks.

The proposed ISSR characterisation of Fitts' law proved useful for the following reasons:

1. It provided a theoretical baseline of how difficulty should scale with dimensionality, for both integral and separable cases.
2. It measures information throughput at the point of interest: the effectiveness of the search.
3. Where varying accuracy levels cannot be specified in advance, it enables us to extract a range of difficulty values from the trajectory data.
4. For the multidimensional controllers, it generated straight lines near the intercept of movement time plots, and these intercepts agreed well with reaction time measurements.
5. It has a simple and generalisable definition, and could be easily applied to a wide variety of search task situations.
6. Information is always conserved, no matter how convoluted the search path.

What ISSR is not intended to address is accurate *prediction* of movement difficulty. Fitts' law can be used in a predictive sense, in which case subtleties of the human motor system are important, but can also be used in a comparitive/evaluative sense, where we wish to test alternative interfaces for their effectiveness. It is the second scenario that ISSR is deemed appropriate for. Further work is needed to ascertain exactly why the noisy channel approach gives a different formula.

This experiment was probably not precise enough to expose subtle cognitive effects such as integrality or separability of timbre parameters. The bulk of the disparity between interfaces seemed to be attributable to basic manipulation issues, i.e. those revealed in the visual target task. Ideally, individual experiments would be carried out to investigate each of the aspects of this experiment in isolation. More should be done to reduce the variability in participants' performance, perhaps by teaching a consistent technique. An upcoming study will attempt to treat time as the independent variable: users will match a repeating sequence of targets (this time with 6 DOF) along to metronome clicks of varying speeds. Musicians are good at predicting when regular beats will occur, so hopefully reaction times can be eliminated. Also eliminated will be the need for the user to trigger sounds themselves. This task should also be a more appropriate model of live performance. It would also be useful to compare hardware faders and knobs: these are generally preferred by musicians to touch screen controls, and they may exhibit faster acquisition times. However there is a practical difficulty specifying the target in the visual target case, and giving progress feedback to the user. Touch screens are more flexible for such graphical feedback.

There is still a long way to go to get ecologically valid results for a digital musical instrument capable of musically varied sounds. Four hours of interaction time is a fair duration for most interface evaluations, however it is tiny compared to the amount of time serious musicians spend practising. If a practise programme could be designed for a higher dimensional synthesiser interface, analysis based on Fitts' law could provide valuable insights for the instrument designer, the musician, and the HCI community at large.

REFERENCES

1. Adams, A. T., Gonzalez, B., and Latulipe, C. SonicExplorer: Fluid exploration of audio parameters. In *Proceedings of the SIGCHI Conference on Human Factors in Computing Systems*, CHI '14, ACM (2014), 237–246.
2. Caramiaux, B., Tahiroğlu, K., Fiebrink, R., and Tanaka, A., Eds. *Proceedings of the International Conference on New Interfaces for Musical Expression*, Goldsmiths, University of London, UK (2014).
3. Card, S. K., Newell, A., and Moran, T. P. *The psychology of human-computer interaction*. L. Erlbaum Associates Inc., 1983.
4. Despain, A., and Westervelt, R. High performance human-computer interfaces. Tech. Rep. JSR-96-130, Advanced Research Projects Agency (ARPA), September 1997.
5. Drewes, H. Only one Fitts' law formula please! In *CHI '10 Extended Abstracts on Human Factors in Computing Systems*, CHI EA '10, ACM (2010), 2813–2822.
6. Ericsson, K. A. The influence of experience and deliberate practice on the development of superior expert performance. *The Cambridge handbook of expertise and expert performance* (2006), 683–703.
7. Fitts, P. M. The information capacity of the human motor system in controlling the amplitude of movement. *Journal of experimental psychology 47*, 6 (1954), 381.
8. Fitzmaurice, G. W., and Buxton, W. An empirical evaluation of graspable user interfaces: towards specialized, space-multiplexed input. In *Proceedings of the ACM SIGCHI Conference on Human factors in computing systems*, ACM (1997), 43–50.
9. Garner, W. R. The stimulus in information processing. *American Psychologist 25*, 4 (1970), 350.
10. Grossman, T., and Balakrishnan, R. Pointing at trivariate targets in 3d environments. In *Proceedings of the SIGCHI conference on Human factors in computing systems*, ACM (2004), 447–454.
11. Hick, W. E. On the rate of gain of information. *Quarterly Journal of Experimental Psychology 4*, 1 (1952), 11–26.
12. Hunt, A., and Wanderley, M. M. Mapping performer parameters to synthesis engines. *Org. Sound 7* (August 2002), 97–108.
13. Jacob, R. J., Sibert, L. E., McFarlane, D. C., and Mullen Jr, M. P. Integrality and separability of input devices. *ACM Transactions on Computer-Human Interaction (TOCHI) 1*, 1 (1994), 3–26.
14. Kemler Nelson, D. G. Processing integral dimensions: The whole view. *Journal of Experimental Psychology: Human Perception and Performance 19* (October 1993), 1105–1113.
15. MacKenzie, I. S. Fitts' law as a research and design tool in human-computer interaction. *Human-computer interaction 7*, 1 (1992), 91–139.
16. MacKenzie, I. S., and Buxton, W. Extending Fitts' law to two-dimensional tasks. In *Proceedings of the SIGCHI conference on Human factors in computing systems*, ACM (1992), 219–226.
17. Magnusson, T., and Mendieta, E. H. The acoustic, the digital and the body: A survey on musical instruments. In *Proceedings of the International Conference on New Interfaces for Musical Expression* (2007), 94–99.
18. Murata, A., and Iwase, H. Extending Fitts' law to a three-dimensional pointing task. *Human Movement Science 20*, 6 (2001), 791–805.
19. Pennycook, B. W. Computer-music interfaces: a survey. *ACM Computing Surveys (CSUR) 17*, 2 (1985), 267–289.
20. Poupyrev, I., Lyons, M. J., and Fels, S. New interfaces for musical expression. In *CHI'01 Extended Abstracts on Human Factors in Computing Systems*, ACM (2001), 491–492.
21. Puckette, M. Pure Data: another integrated computer music environment. *Proceedings of the Second Intercollege Computer Music Concerts* (1996), 37–41.
22. Vertegaal, R., and Eaglestone, B. Comparison of input devices in an ISEE direct timbre manipulation task. *Interacting with Computers 8*, 1 (1996), 13–30.
23. Wanderley, M. M., and Orio, N. Evaluation of input devices for musical expression: Borrowing tools from HCI. *Computer Music Journal 26*, 3 (2002), 62–76.
24. Weichert, F., Bachmann, D., Rudak, B., and Fisseler, D. Analysis of the accuracy and robustness of the leap motion controller. *Sensors 13*, 5 (2013), 6380–6393.
25. Zhai, S. Characterizing computer input with fitts law parameters, the information and non-information aspects of pointing. *International Journal of Human-Computer Studies 61*, 6 (2004), 791–809.
26. Zhai, S., and Milgram, P. Quantifying coordination in multiple DOF movement and its application to evaluating 6 DOF input devices. In *Proceedings of the SIGCHI conference on Human factors in computing systems*, ACM (1998), 320–327.

AnnoTone: Record-time Audio Watermarking for Context-aware Video Editing

Ryohei Suzuki **Daisuke Sakamoto** **Takeo Igarashi**
Department of Computer Science, The University of Tokyo
rsuzuki@is.s.u-tokyo.ac.jp, {d.sakamoto, takeo}@acm.org

ABSTRACT
We present a video annotation system called "AnnoTone", which can embed various contextual information describing a scene, such as geographical location. Then the system allows the user to edit the video using this contextual information, enabling one to, for example, overlay with map or graphical annotations. AnnoTone converts annotation data into high-frequency audio signals (which are inaudible to the human ear), and then transmits them from a smartphone speaker placed near a video camera. This scheme makes it possible to add annotations using standard video cameras with no requirements for specific equipment other than a smartphone. We designed the audio watermarking protocol using dual-tone multi-frequency signaling, and developed a general-purpose annotation framework including an annotation generator and extractor. We conducted a series of performance tests to understand the reliability and the quality of the watermarking method. We then created several examples of video-editing applications using annotations to demonstrate the usefulness of Annotone, including an After Effects plug-in.

Author Keywords
Video annotation; audio watermarking; video editing interface; context awareness; metadata

ACM Classification Keywords
H.5.2. Information Interfaces and Presentation (e.g., HCI): User Interfaces

INTRODUCTION
In recent years, shooting video footage has become an everyday activity for a large number of people, and the purpose and style of shooting has diversified significantly. For example, various kinds of lecture videos on topics from university-level mathematics to household machine repairs and cooking have been created and shared. Many events, shows, and live concerts are recorded and stored in online archives to provide people all over the world with entertainment. The appearance of compact, low-cost, and high-performance video cameras and smartphones has led to the further widespread use of video recording. Small-sized action cameras such as GoPro are frequently used for recording first-person view of the players of extreme sports such as skydiving and motocross to provide exciting movie contents. These recorded videos may be edited and uploaded to video-hosting services such as YouTube and Vimeo. The recording and sharing of video is an entertainment experience that is available to a great number of end users.

This new form of entertainment has led to the desire to rapidly create attractive movie content from recorded videos, and the demands of non-professional video-editing applications have grown considerably. One problem here is that it is often time-consuming to edit the recorded video, particularly when the editing is dependent on contextual information that is only available during recording. For example, if the user wishes to overlay a map showing the geographical location of the current video frame, they must separately take notes and manually combine this with the video. Even if the needed contextual information can be obtained by watching the video, it is tedious to repeatedly review the video to complete the editing. Our goal in this study was to facilitate such an editing process by allowing the user to embed contextual information directly into the video while it is being recorded, and to use the embedded information to support editing the video after recording.

In this paper, we describe a system called "AnnoTone", which allows the user to embed annotations into video footage during real-time recording as audio watermarks, and to later extract them from the annotated videos during editing. The user simply places a smartphone on top of a video camera, and the watermarking signal is transmitted from the loudspeaker of the smartphone and recorded as inaudible background audio, as shown in Figure 1. The annotation data can be either manually specified by controlling the smartphone, or automatically generated based on sensor data, which may be a global positioning system (GPS) receiver or an external sensor. Our technique can also be used while recording a video with a smartphone. By running a background application that transmits the watermark signals from the loudspeaker on a smartphone, the user may use any camera application on the phone to record a video with embedded annotations.

We evaluated the performance of the watermarking scheme, including limitations regarding the data rate, the distance that the watermark signal can travel in air, the response to audio format conversions, and the influence of the signal on the sound quality of the audio track in the finished video. The results showed that AnnoTone can embed data into a video at a

CHI 2015, April 17–23, 2015, Seoul, Republic of Korea.
Copyright © 2015 ACM 978-1-4503-3145-6/15/04 $15.00.
http://dx.doi.org/10.1145/2702123.2702358

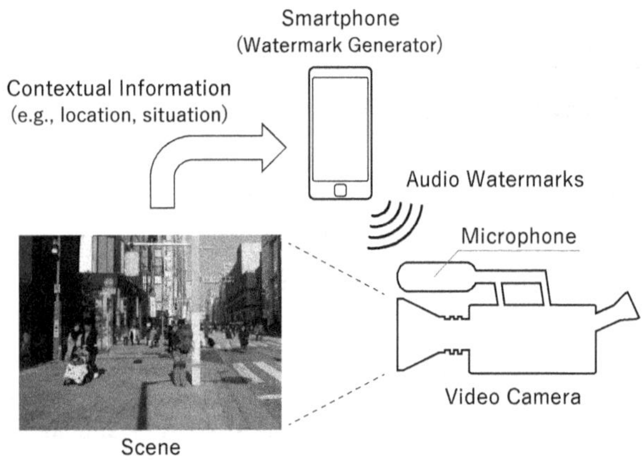

Figure 1. An image showing how annotations are recorded.

bit rate of 400 bps, with adequate reliability in various recording situations, and that the embedded annotations are robust to conversion between several major audio formats. The embedded watermarks do not lead to noticeable loss of listening impression, and they can be removed completely by applying a low-pass filter to the audio signal in the finished recording.

We also investigated several examples of video-editing applications using annotations to demonstrate the possible usages scenarios of AnnoTone. The first application enables automatic segmentation of a recorded video by splitting it into shorter movie clips, which are classified as either success or failure at the positions annotated by the user. The second application utilizes annotations that describe the states of a chess game at each moment to automatically overlay a video with generated graphics to help the watcher understand the game. The third application uses a series of annotations indicating the geo-locations of a moving camcorder to show the path of the camera on a map. These applications demonstrate the potential of annotations in movie editing to reduce the editing workload, and to help create richer content. We also designed a way to integrate the watermark extractor with off-the-shelf video editing programs, and confirmed that AnnoTone can facilitate existing movie-creation workflow by, for example, adding effects automatically based on annotations.

The major contributions of this work can be summarized as follows:

- The creation of a novel video-editing workflow with real-time annotation using audio watermarking.
- Implementation of a prototype system using Dual-Tone Multi-Frequency (DTMF) method.
- Performance evaluation exploring the capabilities and limitations of the method.
- Three example applications that facilitate the AnnoTone and a script to export annotation to video editing software.

RELATED WORK

Digital Audio Watermarking

Digital audio watermarking techniques have been studied mainly for protecting music and movies from piracy by including copyright information in the content. Audio watermarking was first developed in the late 1990s. In 1996, Bender et al. described the basic techniques, including low-bit coding, phase coding, spread spectrum, and echo hiding [5]. Following their pioneering work, many researchers have reported enhanced audio watermarking techniques. An advanced spread spectrum technique, with improved robustness and detection capabilities, which employs a large range of frequencies was reported by Cox et al. [8, 7].

Most watermarking schemes embed audio watermarks into existing audio or video content by analyzing and manipulating the audio signals, so it is not usually possible to add watermarks during real-time recording. Recently, technologies termed *real-time watermarking*, which embed watermarks into audio signals as they are recorded, have been developed. Tachibana described a real-time watermarking scheme named Sonic Watermarking, for live musical performances [23], the aim of which was to prevent surreptitious recording of concerts. In this scheme, the musical performance and watermark signals are played separately from two speakers, and mixed in the air; therefore, audio watermarking is realized without manipulation of the recorded audio signals of the performance. Our method uses a similar technique to mix audio watermarks and environmental sounds in the air to annotate video data without requiring any modifications of the recording instruments.

Audio watermarking techniques have also been used to transmit information to devices to enhance the user experience in entertainment and advertising applications. Matsuoka reported a watermarking framework termed "acoustic orthogonal frequency division multiplexing" (acoustic OFDM) [17] to convey text data, such as a uniform resource locator (URL) to consumer devices during audio broadcasting. Listeners of an annotated audio program can retrieve related information such as song titles using a dedicated smartphone application that can receive watermark signals. Museum installations and live concerts have demand for such communication because they can enhance the interactivity of exhibitions and performances without installing additional devices except for an ordinary loudspeaker and smartphones. Gebbensleben et al. developed an audio guide system for museums and exhibitions that automatically detects objects which the user is seeing using audio watermarking signals, and plays an appropriate audio content [9]. Hirabayashi developed a system called Cryptone [14], which enables interaction between performers and the audience at venues of musical performances using high-frequency acoustic DTMF signaling, in a similar manner to our method; however, this system can only represent a limited number of identifiers and cannot transmit arbitrary information. In contrast, our method, AnnoTone, focuses on a rich array of information, including geo-location data and contextual information. In addition, whereas existing methods use audio watermarking to facilitate interactions between devices, we use it to facilitate video editing.

Video Annotation

As the advances in camera devices have led the proliferation of digital photographs and videos, audio/video annotation techniques to facilitate collecting, browsing and editing recorded contents have been proposed. WillCam [24] is a digital camera system that captures and records contextual information including the location, temperature, ambient noise, and facial expressions of the photographer, and uses these data to provide the user with a means to indicate what is relevant to them in the picture. It simply overlays the pictures with visual icons representing associated contextual information, and simultaneously stores sensor data in extended image format (EXIF). ContextCam [19] is a context-aware video camera for creating archives of home movies, which annotates it with the time, location, people present, and additional contextual information associated with the video, using a collection of sensors and machine-learning techniques to infer higher-level information. With ContextCam, annotations are embedded in the recorded video sequence using least significant bit (LSB) encoding on video frames. These systems enable the recording of contextual information during the shooting of a picture or a video footage, as with our method; however, because they both require specialized hardware, the range of applications of these techniques is limited. However much work also have been done for automated or semi-automated photograph/video annotation [15, 20, 26], there is still little work in intensively utilizing these annotations for editing videos. AnnoTone focuses on providing a novel video-editing workflow with recorded annotations for supporting content creation.

Some commercial products that can record contextual information with video data are already commercially available. Sony's HDR-AS30V/B Action Cam [1] is a compact digital video camera equipped with a GPS receiver to record ones location during the shooting of video footage. The videos recorded by it can be played with overlaid information, including the speed at each moment, together with a map showing the path taken when using a special player. Our method makes it possible to add such functionalities to ordinary video cameras and smartphones, without requiring any special hardware.

Managing Contents with Metadata

Numerous user interfaces have been developed to utilize time-synchronized metadata or annotation to browse, analyze and arrange various kinds of contents including videos. DIVA developed by Mackay and Beaudouin-Lafon [16] is an explaratory data analysis tool for videos with various kinds of annotations, designed for analyzing the work practice of air traffic controllers, and discovering an opportunity for improving their user interface. DIVA provides a sophisticated mechanism to handle multiple streams of annotations, such as boolean operation between streams, and a display interface in which the user can look over the correlations between annotations from above, to facilitate the video analysis task.

SILVER [6] is a digital video editor that simplifies the process of video editing by incorporating semantic annotations about videos into the editing interface. It provides a hierarchical timeline view that enables the user to handle videos by multiple levels of semantics, from frame level to shot level to clip level. It also provides a transcript view in which the user can specify a chunk of video based on the selection of transcript. Using these interfaces fully utilizing annotations, the user can easily edit a video concentrating on the semantics of video, without being bothered by too much low-level operations. As these systems suggested, handling large data such as a video could be significantly simplified by using appropriate annotations and user interfaces. Annotations recorded with videos by AnnoTone could be used from such systems to facilitate managing contents.

ANNOTONE

Workflow

Figure 2 shows the workflow of AnnoTone. We designed the annotation method to convert annotation data into sounds and to transmit them from the loudspeaker of a smartphone. We take advantage of the fact that ordinary video cameras have 44.1 kHz audio sampling frequency and can record sound with frequency up to about 22 kHz, though high-frequency sound above 18 kHz is virtually inaudible for human if it is not too loud [4, 22]. Annotations are represented as audio watermarks, are embedded in the high-frequency range of the audio track of a video recording, and can be extracted after the video is imported into a personal computer (PC) for use to support video editing. Because annotations are embedded as sounds that can be recorded using an ordinary microphone, our technique does not require any special equipment other than a video camera and a smartphone. Audio watermarking also has advantages in terms of the portability and synchronicity between the annotation and a timestamp of a video, because annotations are embedded directly into the time series of the content. Unlike annotation methods that employ external metadata, all of the information is contained in the video file, and synchronization between a moment of a video and a watermark is not lost during video editing. Because AnnoTone uses a specially designed watermarking scheme that employs high-frequency audio (in the range 17.6 - 20.0 kHz), the watermarks are not only inaudible, but also can be easily removed from the video recording by applying a digital filter.

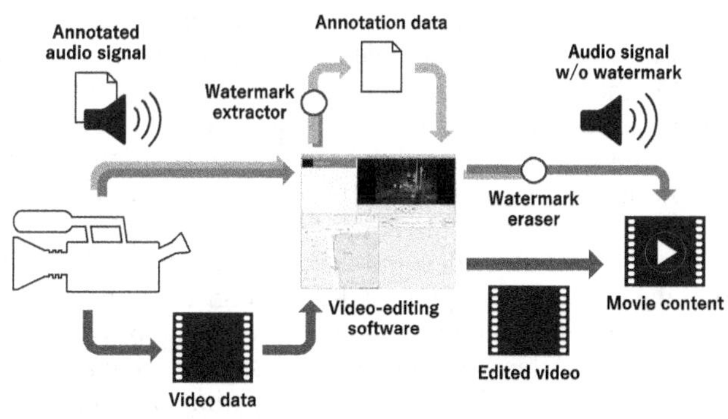

Figure 2. The AnnoTone workflow.

Usage Scenario

The basic usage scenario of AnnoTone is as follows. Users first attach a smartphone to a video camera and then start an application that includes the watermark generator, as shown in Figure 3. Next, they record a scene using the video camera, controlling the smartphone application to embed the annotations they need. After recording the video, the video file is transferred to a PC, and loaded into an annotation-aware video editing application using the watermark extractor. And, then users can create movie content from the imported video, exploiting the functionality provided by the application. Following editing, the watermark is removed using a filter, so that the high-frequency components are not included in the resulting movie. In addition to the a dedicated video editing application, we provide an extensional script to extract and erase the audio watermark, and export to a commonly used video editing application.

The other scenario is that public event. Instead of attaching a smartphone to a video camera, we can share the loud speaker for embedding the audio watermark into not only the video camera, but the other camera phones and smartphones. This is an optional scenario and is not main target usage scenario of the AnnoTone. However, this will be included in the performance evaluation for investigating future implication of the AnnoTone.

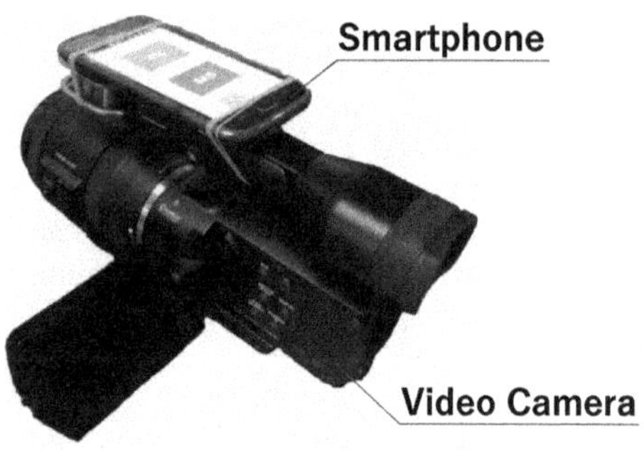

Figure 3. A typical hardware setup to use AnnoTone.

IMPLEMENTATION

The AnnoTone system consists of a watermark generator, extractor, and eraser. The watermark generator is provided as a software library for smartphones. It receives digital data from either the user interface of the application or the sensors on the smartphone, converts them into audio watermark signals, and then transmits the signals from the loudspeaker on the phone. The user should prepare a smartphone application depending on their purpose for the video annotation. The watermark extractor is implemented as a Java program that analyzes video files and extracts the embedded annotation data for use to support video editing. It can be used as a component of a video editing application that provides dedicated user interface and functionalities for specific annotation types, and also can be integrated to existing video editing applications. The watermark eraser is a low-pass filter that removes the high-frequency audio signals (i.e., at frequencies $\geq$ 17 kHz) to eliminate the audio watermarks from the audio track of the finished video.

Watermarking Scheme

The watermarking scheme used with AnnoTone can be considered a derivative of dual-tone multi frequency (DTMF) signaling [21], which is widely used in telecommunications applications. The basics of the DTMF audio watermarking technique can be found in previous works [11, 14, 18]; however, we describe them here briefly for completeness. AnnoTone converts annotation data into modulated sounds that are almost inaudible, at frequencies in the range 17.6 - 20 kHz [4, 22]. A unit signal in DTMF is a composition of two single tones of different frequencies, and the combination of the two frequencies represents the value of the signal. AnnoTone uses seven equally spaced frequencies, and we use 16 combinations of pairs of these frequencies (${}_7C_2 = 21$) to represent four bits per signal. Larger datasets can be sent by rapidly switching the tones. The length of each unit signal was set to 10 ms, giving a gross aggregate bit rate of 400 bps. Figure 4 shows a signal spectrogram of a watermark packet.

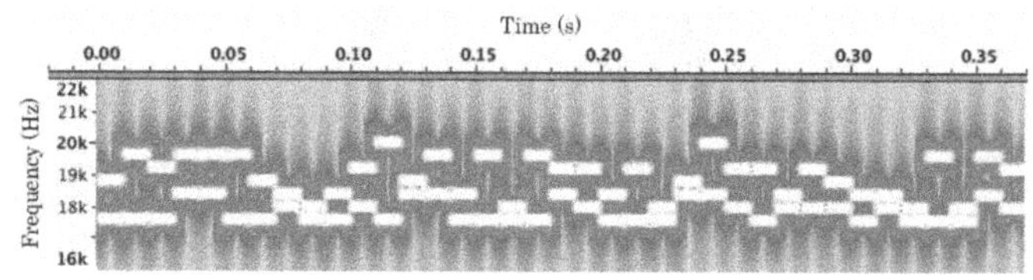

Figure 4. A signal spectrogram of a watermark packet with a 16-byte payload.

Packet Structure

Annotation data are serialized into an array and converted into a structured watermark packet. Figure 5 shows a schematic diagram of the packet structure. Each watermark packet consists of several successive unit signals. The unit signal at the head of a packet is termed the start frame. It is fixed to represent "2", and functions only as an indication of the start position of the packet. The second unit signal is termed the length frame, and specifies the length of the payload region following it to be 2^n bytes, where n is the value of this unit signal. This enables the payload size to vary depending on the annotation. From the third unit signal, the payload region containing the body of the annotation data starts, and continues for the length specified in the length frame. Each byte is encoded using two unit signals: the first represents the lower four bits and the second represents the higher four bits. The unit signal following the end of the payload region represents the annotation type ID, and is a number from 0 to 15, which is used to distinguish the different kinds of annotations, which may be embedded in the same media file. The annotation ID can be determined arbitrarily by the annotation application. Each packet ends with two unit signals representing the cyclic redundancy check (CRC)-8 checksum of the packet for error detection in decoding.

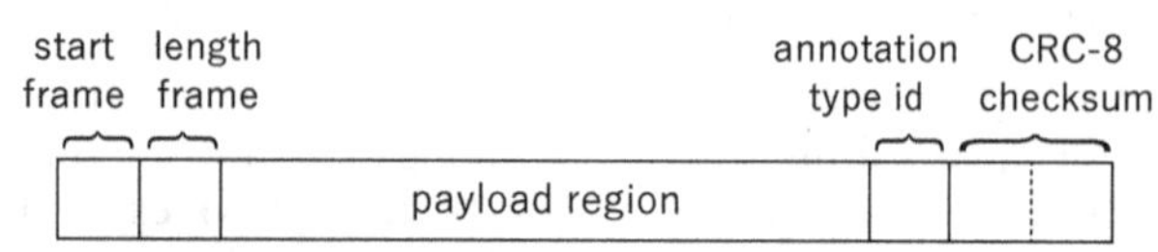

Figure 5. The packet structure used with AnnoTone.

Watermark Generation and Extraction

DTMF watermarks are generated using the following process. First, an annotation of any kind of data are serialized to an array of bytes. Second, a data stream of packets is generated from the array by adding header and footer data, including the CRC-8 checksum. Third, the DTMF pulse-code modulation (PCM) signal is generated as follows:

$$s(t,m) = w(t) \cdot a(m, d(\lfloor \frac{t}{0.01} \rfloor)) \cdot \sin(2\pi t \cdot f(m)) \quad (1)$$

where $s(t,m)$ is the sample value of the m-th sub-carrier at timestamp t (in seconds) counted from the beginning of the watermark packet, $f(m)$ is the frequency (in Hz) of the m-th sub-carrier, $d(n)$ is the n-th 4-bit unit of data in the packet, and $a(m,x)$ is the DTMF encoding function, defined as the (m,x)-th element in the following table.

	0	1	2	3	4	5	6	7	8	9	A	B	C	D	E	F
7	0	0	0	0	0	1	0	0	0	0	1	0	0	0	1	0
6	0	0	0	0	1	0	0	0	0	1	0	0	0	1	0	0
5	0	0	0	1	0	0	0	0	1	0	0	0	1	0	0	1
4	0	0	1	0	0	0	0	1	0	0	0	1	0	0	0	1
3	0	1	0	0	0	0	1	0	0	0	0	1	1	1	1	0
2	1	0	0	0	0	0	1	1	1	1	1	0	0	0	0	0
1	1	1	1	1	1	1	0	0	0	0	0	0	0	0	0	0

Table 1. The DTMF encoding function.

$w(t)$ is an envelope filtering function to reduce low-frequency noise at borders between two unit signals:

$$w(t) = (0.5 - 0.5\cos(2\pi \frac{t \bmod 0.01}{0.01}))^{0.8} \quad (2)$$

The watermark packet $x(t)$ is generated by mixing all of the sub-carrier signals as follows,

$$x(t) = \sum_{m=1}^{7} s(t,m) \quad (3)$$

Because DTMF modulation can be considered a variety of frequency-shift keying (FSK), the watermarks that are embedded in media files using AnnoTone can be easily extracted using common demodulation methods for FSK. Watermarks can be removed by simply applying a low-pass filter, because they are contained in a frequency range that is at the upper limit of the frequency response of the human auditory system, and so is not significant for the listening quality. In the performance evaluation described below, we used a 199-tap finite impulse response (FIR) low-pass filter with a cut-off frequency of 17 kHz to remove the watermarks.

PERFORMANCE EVALUATION

To demonstrate the feasibility of the proposed technique, we conducted a series of performance evaluations of our audio watermarking system. These consisted of three objective evaluations to investigate the robustness of the scheme in practical situations, as well as a field test to show that our method can be used without negatively impacting the sound quality of the final product. In these experiments, we used a typical hardware setup consisting of commercially available consumer products, i.e., a Sony NEX-VG30H digital camcorder and a Samsung Galaxy S smartphone. With the exception of the evaluation of the acceptable distance between camera and smartphone, the smartphone was directly attached to the microphone unit of the camera using a rubber band, so that the distance between the loudspeaker of the smartphone and the microphone was approximately 1 cm, as shown in Figure 3. We found that some other video cameras produce video files with 44.1 kHz or 48 kHz audio track, but actually record sounds in much lower sampling rates (e.g. 32 kHz). AnnoTone cannot be used with such video cameras.

Video data were recorded in MPEG-2 format using standard image quality, and sound was recorded using a sampling rate of 44.1 kHz and 16-bit stereo PCM format. The annotation transmitter application was installed on the smartphone. The volume of the smartphone loudspeaker was manually adjusted to the maximum value that did not result in audible distortion. Videos may be recorded in diverse situations, and the acoustic environment may vary considerably depending on the situation in which a video footage is shot. Taking this into consideration, we did recording experiments in four different environmental settings: a silent room, a public space, a rock music concert, and while playing electronic music.

Limitations of Data Rate

To achieve a high data rate, the amount of data sent per unit time must be large; however, shorter lengths of data packets decrease the correct detection rate (CDR), and so there is an optimum data rate that retains a large CDR, together with a large overall data rate. To determine this optimum and show that our watermarking scheme can transmit practicable amounts of data with good reliability, we recorded video footage with embed watermarks with a range of unit signal lengths, and measured the CDR. We varied the unit signal length in the range 6 - 11 ms at 1 ms intervals. A unit signal length of 6 ms corresponds to a data rate of 667 bps, and a unit single length of 11 ms corresponds to 364 bps. For each recording, 100 watermarks with 16-bytes payload were embedded at 3 s intervals, and the correctly detected watermarks were counted using our watermark extractor after recording.

Figure 6 shows the measured CDRs for each of the environmental conditions. This result shows that sufficient reliability was achieved with all of the recording environments when the unit signal length was set to 10 ms (98 % for the electronic music environment, and 100 % for the others). The CDR dropped rapidly as unit signal length decreased below 10 ms in all acoustic environments. From the result, we conclude that 10 ms is the optimum length of the unit signal, and 50 bytes of data can be sent per second. For comparison, the speed of speaking that the range of people can hear comfortably is 150 - 160 words per minute [25], which corresponds to approximately 12 - 13 bytes per second (assuming an average word length of five characters); therefore, 400 bps is sufficient to embed subtitles of a conversation, for example.

Separation of the Camera and Smartphone

In some situations, it may not be convenient to attach the smartphone directly to the video camera, and is desirable that

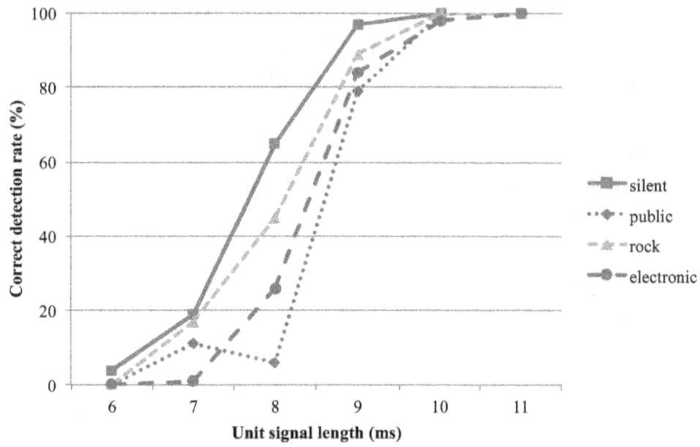

Figure 6. The CDR as a function of the unit signal length.

watermarks are transmitted from a distant device like loud speaker, for example. To investigate the possibility of such usage, we measured the CDR as a function of the distance between the camera and the smartphone.

Figure 7 shows the CDR as a function of the separation between the smartphone and the video camera. A CDR of greater than 80% was obtained when the distance was less than 25 cm. This suggests that watermarking can be achieved without directly attaching a smartphone to the video camera, and annotation is available in various usage scenarios, including, for example, when the camera operator transmits the watermarks from a smartphone in one hand while holding the camcorder in the other hand. However, this distance may be too short for many situations, and so increasing the sensitivity of the watermark detection system is desirable. Improvements in the response of the loudspeaker of the smartphone and the microphone of the video camera at high frequencie range may be expected to enable an increase in this distance.

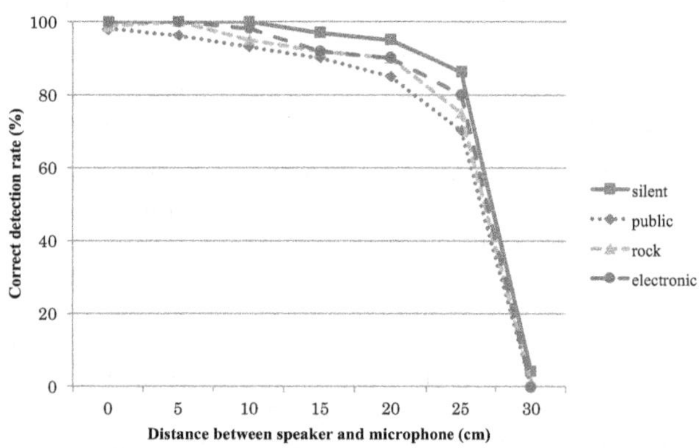

Figure 7. The CDR as a function of the distance between the loudspeaker of the smartphone and the microphone of the camera.

In order to investigate the practicability of diverse use cases, we also conducted a similar experiment using a desktop speaker (28 W Creative GIGAWORKS T20 II) instead of a smartphone, and examined how much distance watermark signals can travel through air if the output volume is much larger than a smartphone. Because of the spatial restriction, we only used a silent room (10 m × 10 m, 3 m height, concrete wall and floor) as the acoustic environment for this experiment. Figure 8 shows that a CDR greater than 80% was obtained when the distance was less than or equal to 5 m. It suggests that we can record watermark signals into a video camera transmitted from a loudspeaker placed remotely. We give some possible applications with such usage in the discussion section.

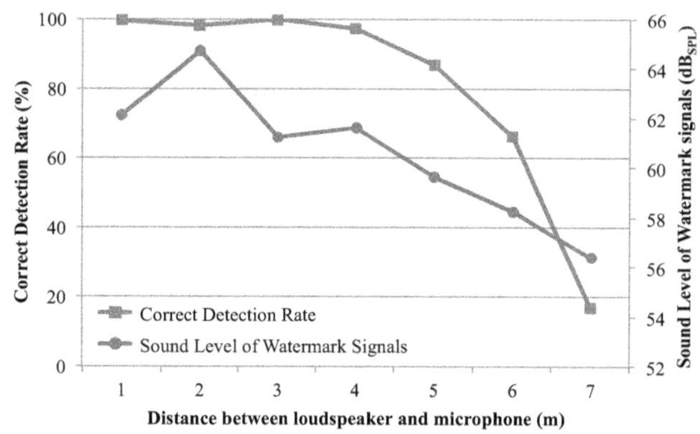

Figure 8. The CDR and the measured sound level of watermark signals at the camera position as functions of the distance between a desktop speaker and the microphone of the camera.

Audio Format Conversion

To assure that the embedded annotations remain throughout the movie-authoring process, it is important to retain the watermarks even when format conversions are conducted. We evaluated the durability of watermarks in regard to format conversions by measuring the proportion of detectable watermarks in videos after applying a variety of audio format conversions. An uncompressed audio file with 10 detectable watermarks was converted into a compressed format, and watermark detection was investigated on the converted file. MP3, Ogg Vorbis, AC-3 (also known as *Dolby Digital*) and AAC formats were used as compression algorithms. For each format, compression was applied with four bit rate settings in the range 128 - 320 kbps to examine the quality requirements necessary to preserve the watermarks with each format. We measured the CDRs of different audio files and calculated the mean CDR for each format and quality setting.

The results are shown in Figure 9; watermarks were preserved almost completely following a format conversion with the Ogg Vorbis and AC-3 formats with a bit rate of $\geq$ 192 kbps. They were also preserved after conversion into AAC format with a bit rate of 320 kbps. This suggests that our method can be used in practical movie-authoring processes because satisfying these format requirements is not difficult. However, the MP3 format did not preserve the watermarks, even at the highest bit rate setting; this is attributed to the characteristics of the compression algorithm, which tends to discard high-frequency components.

Effect of the Watermarks on Audio Quality

We evaluated the audibility of the watermarks via a subjective experiment. Five participants, aged 21, 22, 22, 58, and

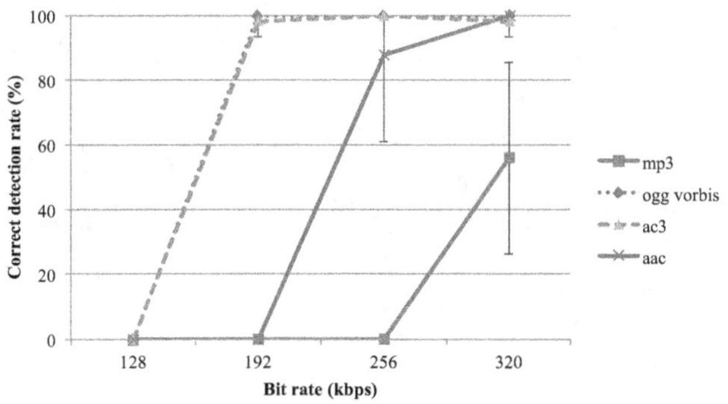

Figure 9. The average CDR following format conversion for a range of compressions.

58 years, were asked to listen to recorded sounds with the embedded watermarks using headphones, and to push a button if they noticed any unexpected or unnatural sounds. The output volume was maintained constant at a volume that was comfortable for the participant to listen to music. The proportion of noticed watermarks was counted for each participant and sound. We investigated whether the watermarks were audible with the four sound settings described above (i.e., silent, public, electronic music, and rock music) to investigate whether the detectability of the watermarks was dependent on the environment of the recording. To verify that the low-pass filter can effectively remove the watermarks from the audio file, we prepared two recordings for each sound setting: one with the filter applied and the other without the filter. In total, eight recordings were used in the experiment. Each recording was 1 min long, and contained 10 watermarks with 16-byte payloads, at randomly selected positions.

The results are shown in Figure 10. The mean rate at which watermarks were detectable by the participants was 30 % prior to applying the low-pass filter in each situation. After applying the filters, the rates at which participants correctly detected the watermarks were negligible, indicating that the watermarks were effectively removed using the filter. Furthermore, the difference in the rate at which participants noticed the watermarks depended on their age, with elder participants being less able to notice watermarks than younger ones. The absolute threshold of hearing is reported to be a sound pressure level (SPL) of 130 dB at 18 kHz in people aged 50 - 59 years, compared to an SPL of 80 dB in people aged 10 - 19 years [22]. Our results are consistent with this age dependence of the frequency response of the human ear.

APPLICATIONS

In this section, we describe three example applications using AnnoTone. Each application is provided as a set of watermark-generating programs running on the camera-mounted smartphone, and a watermark-extracting program running on the PC. Here, we will describe the input to the watermark-generating program and the output of the watermark-extracting program. After that, we show the interoperability of AnnoTone with an off-the-shelf video-editing software, Adobe After Effects.

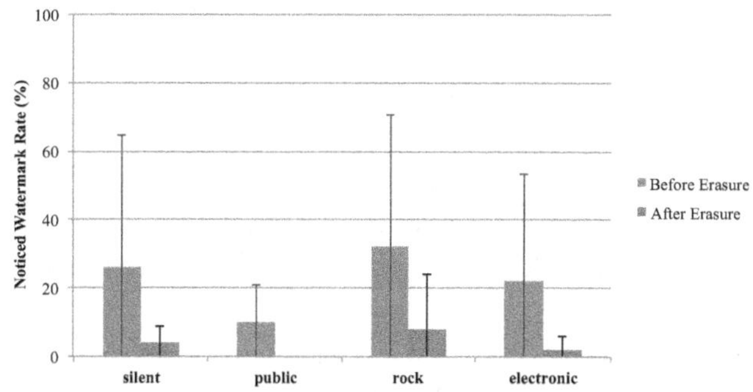

Figure 10. Mean rates of identification of watermarks by listeners for each of the recording conditions.

Record-time Editing

During post-production, a movie creator may carry out a large number of operations, such as deleting scenes, which can be tedious and time-consuming because the user must repeatedly examine the video content. Using AnnoTone, we can embed information required for the editing process into a video during recording, as well as perform automatic editing after the video has been recorded, using that information. We have created a simple video-editing application, which automatically cuts sections containing mistakes from a video, as shown in the right image in Figure 11.

Suppose the user shoots a video lecture, consisting of multiple independent segments. If the lecturer makes a mistake during recording, the segment should be deleted and a new segment needs to be recorded. To facilitate this process, our system allows the camera operator to indicate success or failure of the segment by pressing a button on the smartphone just after recording that segment (Figure 11 left). This success/failure information is recorded as an annotation. After recording, the video-editing application automatically detects the annotations and divides the video into a series of segments according to the annotated timestamps. Then the system automatically removes all of the segments that are marked as failures.

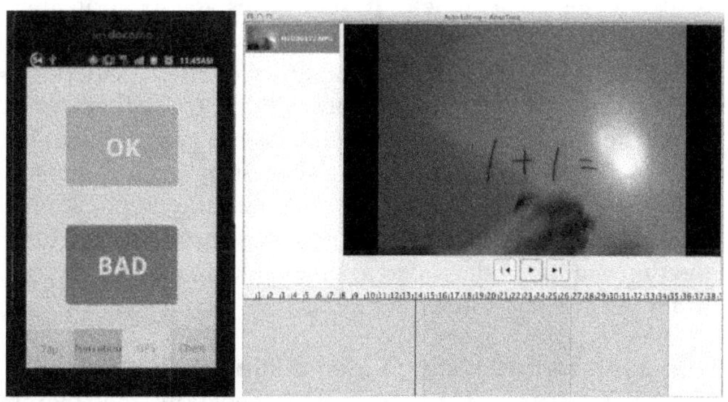

Figure 11. Left: The user interface of the annotation application. Right: The automatic video-cutting application; the good sections are shown in green, the bad sections in red.

Automatic Captions

Much movie content has overlaid captions or images that describe situations and provide supplementary information.

For example, recordings of ballgames typically have a caption containing the score, some television programs related to travel have overlaid maps, and movies of concerts may have captions containing the words of the songs. Creating such captions and overlaying them at the appropriate time is a time-consuming part of the movie-authoring process. In some cases, creating and overlaying captions can be automated by embedding contextual information in videos using AnnoTone.

We developed a system for chess movies, which automatically overlays a video with an animation of a chessboard in sychronization with the game progress using embedded chess notes. The camera operator operates the smartphone application to embed the chess notes in the video. The application provides a simple videogame-style user interface, as shown in the left image in Figure 12. Each chess note is recorded as a line of standard Forsyth-Edwards notation (FEN); therefore, the notes embedded in a video represent all of the information describing the game. The system analyzes the video annotated with the chess notes to determine the state of the chessboard at each timestamp, and generates a series of images to be overlaid as shown in the right image in Figure 12.

Figure 12. Left: The user interface for annotating chess notes. Right: A movie overlaid with a chessboard created by the system.

Geo-location-based Video

Sometimes a video is recorded while the camera operator walks or rides in a vehicle. In such cases, the location at each moment is often significant to the content of the movie. We created a system that can automatically overlay a video showing a corresponding map together with the trail of the camera. The watermarking application embeds the geographical location of the video camera using data from a GPS sensor at intervals of a few seconds. The video-editing application extracts the embedded series of geo-locations associated with the timestamps of the video to obtain a map using the Google Maps API [3], as shown in Figure 13.

Integration with Existing Video-editing Software

So far, we showed three example applications that facilitate the audio watermarking technique. These applications are designed as dedicated video-editing software to provide special functionalities. However, AnnoTone is not limited to this usage, and can be used with off-the-shelf video-editing software to facilitate content creation workflow in general. Some video-editing programs provide end-user scripting mechanisms that allow the user to control effects and objects in the

Figure 13. A video overlaid with a map showing the trail of the camera.

movie by writing a simple program. AnnoTone's annotation data can be used from these mechanisms by implementing an extension or a plugin for the video-editing software that executes watermark extractor and imports extracted data into it. We developed an extension script for Adobe After Effects (AE), a widely used video editing program, to integrate AnnoTone's functionality into it. We employ the end-user scripting mechanism (*expressions*) of AE. The process is simple; just running the extension script once to extract the audio watermark. As a result, a new text layer is generated, and each embedded watermark packet is converted into a key frame of the layer at the corresponding timestamp in the source video. Each key frame contains annotation data represented in the JavaScript Object Notation (JSON) format, which can be accessed from the end-user scripts. User can control many aspects of the behavior of objects and effects in the video using the imported annotation data. For example, users can control the pulse rate of a computer animation of a heart that is overlaid on a sport video, in synchronization with the sequence of output values of a vital sensor that is embedded in the video as annotations (Figure 14).

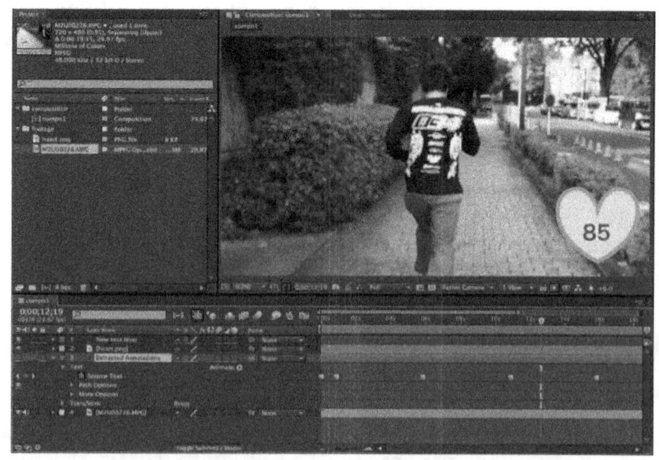

Figure 14. Editing a video of jogger with annotations of his heart rate at each moment in Adobe After Effects. The extension script automatically generates a text layer including keyframes representing the heart rate at each moment as a JSON object. The animation and the number at the lower-right of the movie is associated with the data by end-user scripts.

DISCUSSION

Possible Extensions and Applications

As an extension of AnnoTone, it is possible to change the source of the watermark sound to broaden the use of the technique. As a result of the performance evaluation, we confirmed that audio watermarking from distant place by using 28 watt desktop speaker was successfully embedded information into a video camera. This result suggests that the distance between speakers and a video camera can be longer with a public space-size loud speaker. For instance, using a loud speaker placed in a public space to transmit watermarks containing location-specific data that could allow videos recorded in that space to be used by anyone. Such an installation could offer various kinds of entertainment associated with video recoding, for example, videos recorded at rides and attractions of an amusement park by visitors could be automatically placed on a map after being uploaded to a video-hosting service, and visitors who recorded videos at a specific location could receive promotional material from the park. Publicly transmitted watermarks could also be used to synchronize videos recorded at a sports match or a live performance, and to generate multi-viewpoint video content. According to studies in the past, some kinds of animals such as dogs and cats are sensitive to high-frequency tone [12, 13], therefore publicly transmitted audio watermark signals possibly affect them. Thus, installation of public speakers for transmitting watermark signals should be avoided in places where pets are expected to be brought, such as parks.

Using machine learning or pattern-recognition techniques with the watermark-transmitting program for smartphones could provide more useful applications. For example, annotating an emoticon describing the mood of the camera operator could aid with locating content in a large home video archive [24]. Another possible application of AnnoTone is similar to the Accessible photo album program [10], i.e., supporting people with visual impairments in sharing their memories by recording videos with associated non-visual information that aids in recalling the experiences, such as temperature, textual information describing the scene, and the subjects or camera operators body position.

Meta-data vs. Audio Annotation

An external file called "meta-data" is a common way to add annotation data to videos. For example, Adobe Extensible Metadata Platform (XMP) format [2] is designed to store annotation data with timestamps in the video capturing device, and has the same benefit as AnnoTone from the viewpoint of time-synchronization with the content. Using these formats could be a smarter way when shooting a video with a camera phone. However, in order to generate such meta-data during recording a video, a user should use a specialized camera or a smartphone application that can handle a specific format, thus it is difficult to use them with standard video cameras. AnnoTone can be used with any video camera that does not have a capability of handling digital data except for video, because it only requires a camera to record the high-frequency modulated signals in the audio track of a video. This is advantageous when one wants to record a high-quality video using a dedicated video camera device. Additionally, having time-synchronized information within a single, standard video file is advantageous because one only needs to copy or send a single file, and that one can edit it using standard video editing software. Managing separate files might be trivial for professionals, but it can cause significant confusion and frustration for general users.

The bandwidth of AnnoTone is 400 bps, which is much smaller than other meta-data formats. However, 400 bps = 50 ascii characters/sec, is sufficient enough for storing textual information like subtitles. A combination of location and orientation data, which consists of five or six floating-point values ($\leq$ 4 Bytes $\times$ 6 = 24 Bytes), could be recorded in less than 0.5 sec. This is sufficient for our target application scenarios. If a user wants to record more data than supported by the current bandwidth capabilities, they can record the data separately and use embedded annotations as anchors to them.

Limitations and Future Work

In most cases, the embedded watermarks are imperceptible to human ears; however, the high-frequency sounds are perceptible to some sensitive listeners. Although watermarks can be removed by applying a low-pass filter, these treatments may result in some degradation of sound quality. To overcome this limitation, we could employ more elaborate methods to completely erase the watermarks with less loss of quality using existing noise-reduction techniques. There is also scope for improving the precision and sensitivity of the watermark transmission and receiving. The current watermarking scheme of AnnoTone uses high-frequency DTMF; however, higher data rates and improved reliability may be obtained by introducing a more sophisticated modulation technique, such as spread spectrum audio watermarking.

Finally, our implementation is a proof-of-concept prototype so that AnnoTone requires the user to develop an one-off smartphone application to generate watermarks. Instead, we can provide a pair of applications that generates and extracts watermarks for individual usage scenario. This will be useful and work for the end-users. For the higher level of users, we can provide customizable general-purpose watermarking application that provides basic annotating functions such as sensor logging and detecting touch positions.

CONCLUSION

We presented a video annotating system called AnnoTone, which can annotate a video during recording with little requirements for specific hardware using an audio watermarking technique. AnnoTone is designed to present new video-editing workflow with a handheld device (e.g., smartphone) and a video camera. We demonstrated the use of our annotation system through video-editing applications that utilize contextual information embedded in videos to provide automated video-editing functionality, and demonstrated the feasibility of our watermarking scheme through a series of performance evaluations. We have discussed the limitations of the current implementation of this technique, and identified a number of directions for further development. We believe that our system has considerable potential for creating a new style of video recording and editing, by the inclusion of annotations and non-audio/visual data.

REFERENCES

1. Action cam with gps - hdr-a30v/b review - sony us. `http://store.sony.com/compact-pov-action-cam-zid27-HDRAS30V/B/cat-27-catid-All-Action-Cam`. (Accessed: 2014-09-22).
2. Adobe extensible metadata platform (xmp). `http://www.adobe.com/products/xmp.html`. (Accessed: 2014-09-22).
3. Google maps api. `https://developers.google.com/maps/`. (Accessed: 2014-09-22).
4. Ashihara, K., Kurakata, K., Mizunami, T., and Matsushita, K. Hearing threshold for pure tones above 20 khz. *Acoustical science and technology 27*, 1 (2006), 12–19.
5. Bender, W., Gruhl, D., Morimoto, N., and Lu, A. Techniques for data hiding. *IBM systems journal 35*, 3.4 (1996), 313–336.
6. Casares, J., Long, A. C., Myers, B. A., Bhatnagar, R., Stevens, S. M., Dabbish, L., Yocum, D., and Corbett, A. Simplifying video editing using metadata. In *Proceedings of the 4th conference on Designing interactive systems: processes, practices, methods, and techniques*, ACM (2002), 157–166.
7. Cox, I., Miller, M., Bloom, J., and Miller, M. *Digital watermarking*. Morgan Kaufmann, 2001.
8. Cox, I. J., Kilian, J., Leighton, F. T., and Shamoon, T. Secure spread spectrum watermarking for multimedia. *IEEE Transactions on Image Processing 6*, 12 (1997), 1673–1687.
9. Gebbensleben, S., Dittmann, J., and Vielhauer, C. Multimodal audio guide for museums and exhibitions. In *Electronic Imaging 2006*, International Society for Optics and Photonics (2006), 60740S–60740S.
10. Harada, S., Sato, D., Adams, D. W., Kurniawan, S., Takagi, H., and Asakawa, C. Accessible photo album: Enhancing the photo sharing experience for people with visual impairment. In *Proceedings of the SIGCHI Conference on Human Factors in Computing Systems*, CHI '13, ACM (2013), 2127–2136.
11. Healy, R., and Timoney, J. Digital audio watermarking with semi-blind detection for in-car music content identification. In *Proceedings of the AES 36th International Conference: Automotive AudioSound in Motion* (2009).
12. Heffner, H. E. Hearing in large and small dogs: Absolute thresholds and size of the tympanic membrane. *Behavioral Neuroscience 97*, 2 (1983), 310.
13. Heffner, H. E., and Heffner, R. S. High-frequency hearing. *Handbook of the senses: Audition* (2008), 55–60.
14. Hirabayashi, M., and Shimizu, M. Cryptone: Interaction between performers and audiences with inaudible dtmf sounds. In *SIGGRAPH Asia 2012 Emerging Technologies*, SA '12, ACM (2012), 5:1–5:4.
15. Lavrenko, V., Feng, S., and Manmatha, R. Statistical models for automatic video annotation and retrieval. In *Acoustics, Speech, and Signal Processing, 2004. Proceedings.(ICASSP'04). IEEE International Conference on*, vol. 3, IEEE (2004), iii–1044.
16. Mackay, W. E., and Beaudouin-Lafon, M. Diva: exploratory data analysis with multimedia streams. In *Proceedings of the SIGCHI conference on Human factors in computing systems*, ACM Press/Addison-Wesley Publishing Co. (1998), 416–423.
17. Matsuoka, H., Nakashima, Y., Yoshimura, T., and Kawahara, T. Acoustic ofdm: Embedding high bit-rate data in audio. In *Advances in Multimedia Modeling*. Springer, 2008, 498–507.
18. Nakayama, A., Machino, T., Kitagishi, I., Iwaki, S., and Okudaira, M. Rich communication with audio-controlled network robot. proposal of "audio-motionmedia". In *Proceedings of the 11th IEEE International Workshop on Robot and Human Interactive Communication*, IEEE (2002), 548–553.
19. Patel, S. N., and Abowd, G. D. The contextcam: Automated point of capture video annotation. In *Proceedings of the 6th International Conference on Ubiquitous Computing*, Springer (2004), 301–318.
20. Sarvas, R., Herrarte, E., Wilhelm, A., and Davis, M. Metadata creation system for mobile images. In *Proceedings of the 2nd international conference on Mobile systems, applications, and services*, ACM (2004), 36–48.
21. Schenker, L. Pushbutton calling with a two-group voice-frequency code. *Bell System Technical Journal 39*, 1 (1960), 235–255.
22. Stelmachowicz, P. G., Beauchaine, K. A., Kalberer, A., and Jesteadt, W. Normative thresholds in the 8 to 20khz range as a function of age. *The Journal of the Acoustical Society of America 86*, 4 (1989), 1384–1391.
23. Tachibana, R. Audio watermarking for live performance. In *Electronic Imaging 2003*, International Society for Optics and Photonics (2003), 32–43.
24. Watanabe, K., Tsukada, K., and Yasumura, M. Willcam: A digital camera visualizing users. interest. In *CHI '07 Extended Abstracts on Human Factors in Computing Systems*, CHI EA '07, ACM (2007), 2747–2752.
25. Williams, J. R. Guidelines for the use of multimedia in instruction. In *Proceedings of the Human Factors and Ergonomics Society Annual Meeting*, vol. 42, SAGE Publications (1998), 1447–1451.
26. Yi, J., Peng, Y., and Xiao, J. Exploiting semantic and visual context for effective video annotation. *Multimedia, IEEE Transactions on 15*, 6 (2013), 1400–1414.

Exploring Gesture Sonification to Support Reflective Craft Practice

Thomas Smith[1], Simon J. Bowen[1], Bettina Nissen[1], Jonathan Hook[2], Arno Verhoeven[3], John Bowers[1], Peter Wright[1], Patrick Olivier[1]
[1]Culture Lab, School of Computing Science, Newcastle University, UK
{thomas.smith, simon.bowen, b.s.nissen, john.bowers, p.c.wright, patrick.olivier}@ncl.ac.uk
[2]Department of Theatre, Film and Television, University of York, York, UK
jonathan.hook@york.ac.uk
[3]Edinburgh College of Art, University of Edinburgh, Edinburgh, UK
a.verhoeven@ed.ac.uk

ABSTRACT
Much of the knowing employed in skilled craft practice is difficult to communicate solely through written or verbal description. Consequently, the reflection and development of a craft practice in this manner may miss important nuances of practitioners' skills and experiences. We created digital technologies to sonify (using audio to perceptualize data) a group of craft practitioners' gestures to explore how we can aid their reflection in and on their craft, and consequently develop it. Over a number of workshops, the design of these sonifications were iterated based on how the practitioners responded to them. We found that direct sonification of gesture (sounds generated directly from motion sensor data) helped practitioners understand and reflect upon their own and each other's practice, encouraged discussion and enabled modification of craft technique.

Author Keywords
Craft Skills; Sonification; Reflective Practice

ACM Classification Keywords
H.5.m. Information interfaces and presentation (e.g., HCI)

INTRODUCTION
Craft skill is developed through reflection in and on practice [19] often through practice alongside a more experienced practitioner [24]. In this study we explore how digital systems can support such reflection. By craft skill we refer to the elusive knowing through which practitioners perform and develop their craft. Parts of this knowing can be articulated by the craft practitioner through speech and demonstration [23]. However, other parts are less easily communicated (e.g. how much pressure to apply when working a material) and are frequently learned by *doing*. Such nuance may be reflected in the movements employed in skilled practice, so in this study we chose to investigate how the translation of gesture into sound can support practitioners' reflection upon and consequent development of their craft.

CHI 2015, April 18–23, 2015, Seoul, Republic of Korea.

ACM 978-1-4503-3145-6/15/04…$15.00.
http://dx.doi.org/10.1145/2702123.2702497

We followed a research through design [5][25] approach in which we investigated how transforming practitioners' gestures into sound could facilitate understanding of their craft practice through iteratively designing a digital sonification system. By working with a group of craft practitioners, we designed different forms of sonifications to help practitioners reflect, discuss and in some cases modify their craft techniques over the course of three workshops. Background research, observations made during the workshops and collective critical reflection after each workshop informed our sonification design for subsequent workshops. Our response to the insights that arose from the workshops was to design and develop a system that can replay captured data, along with captured video of the practitioners' gestures while designing sonifications live, allowing us to rapidly prototype the sonifications which we then presented to the practitioners in the following workshop.

We describe our design process for creating a data capture and sonification system and how we explored these sonifications' use throughout the workshops. We present findings on how sonification allowed craft practitioners to reflect on their practice, and discuss the implications for designing digital systems to support reflection upon and development of craft practice. In doing so, we highlight to the HCI community the sonic representation of craft skills as an opportunity for further research.

BACKGROUND

Craft Skills
The practical understanding of craft practice has primarily been investigated from two approaches: firstly through the critical analysis of tools and artefacts that result from the technical process of craft practice; and secondly through reflective descriptions of the process of making by the

practitioners themselves and observers. Although these approaches bring us closer to understanding craft practice, they have recently been found to be incomplete.

Barad [2] discusses the challenges with regard to this material semiotic approach to "things", suggesting that accounts developed by deconstructing artefacts to understand the processes that generate them will be unable to construct a cohesive account of the process. For Barad, any change to the context of an artefact alters the meaning that any future actors and agents might construct, suggesting that any extended interpretations derived from artefacts become contextually sensitive as well. With regard to descriptive accounts by practitioners, Perry & Krippendorff [14] suggest that a use of protocol analysis in design activity may be challenging due to the inability for researchers to come to a consensus when categorizing these descriptions. Wood [23][24] discusses the challenges faced by practitioners in communicating their craft knowledge, for example observing how a bowl turner describes his practice in one way (only using one tool) but her video recording demonstrates that his actions are counter to his description (he changes tools during the process) [23, p.35].

Polanyi [15] introduced tacit knowing (which has subsequently been used to characterize craft skill, e.g. [23][24]), describing it as "we can know more than we can tell" [15, p.4], i.e. some aspects of craft practice become internalized and cannot be articulated by the practitioner. Ingold [10] offers an alternative view by focusing on the 'telling' rather than the 'knowing' and observing that we can tell what we know *"through practice and experience"* [10, p.109], avoiding the problem of specification and articulation Polanyi requires from practitioners. Therefore, through exploring the performance of a craft rather than the verbal articulation of a craft, we may support the understanding of craft skills in additional ways.

The concept of performativity introduced by Butler [3] describes gestures, speech and other performative actions as constructors of identity. From this view gestures are an expression of a craft. Although gesture cannot capture a craft in its entirety (e.g. given the tactile feedback that a craft involves), exploring the craft practitioners' performative gestures during making, rather than analyzing what is made and descriptions of making, could provide some insight into those practices. If performative actions are, to some extent, an expression of a craft, then the use of a body-worn sensor for recording gestures is a possible means for helping practitioners develop their craft. This poses the question: how do we represent this gestural data in a way that is useful to practitioners?

Representing Data

The ability to represent gestural data so that it is meaningful and useful to the target audience is non-trivial. Each set of data is contextual and requires careful thought to be able to be represented effectively. The aesthetic form and function are both important to the effectiveness of a data representation.

Data Visualization

The most common form of representation is visualization. Data visualization has not only become a substantial research area for statisticians and designers but it has also entered the cultural consciousness, and being used by popular magazines and websites. Data visualization refers to the ability to use space, color and other visual properties to help disseminate information from an otherwise complex dataset. Gestural data is seldom visualized due to the fact that it is inherently three-dimensional but a number of art projects have made use of visualization to let users explore the data [7]. For our project, the use of data visualization is not ideal as we do not want to divide the craft practitioners' attention between their craft and a screen when relying on hand-eye coordination [21].

Data Sonification

Using a sense that is less central to a making process would be less disruptive: therefore we are exploring data sonification. Sonification refers to representing data through auditory means. Rather than using visual properties such as space and color to convey the data in a meaningful way, we use amplitude, frequency and temporality. Sonification is defined by Hermann [9] as *"[T]he data-dependent generation of sound, if the transformation is systematic, objective and reproducible, so that it can be used as scientific method."*

Sonification has been explored in many areas where data visualization would not be appropriate – such as when a user's actions would be hindered if their visual attention is divided between the task at hand and a screen, the data is more meaningful when represented temporally or the user is visually impaired. For example, within the ICAD [11] community, there has been much research into using sonifications to aid sports athletes in training [6][17][18]. These projects translate the movement data of the athletes in different ways. Either the sound is generated by passing the data through a design system which is known as *sonification* [9] or directly generated from the movement data which is known as *audification* [8]. Sports activities are comparable to craft practice as both involve repeated movements in a temporal frame. Therefore, the concepts used for sports sonification are viable to explore in craft practices.

The aesthetic design of the sonifications will be significant to how they are perceived. Jensenius' concept of artificial action-sound relationships [12] describes how we design artificial sounds that react to actions (gestures) and discusses the need for practical action-sound design to "enhance the interaction between humans and technological devices".

RESEARCH THROUGH DESIGN

Due to the exploratory nature of this study, we had many decisions to make in terms of how to approach the problem space. We are exploring how sonifications can facilitate craft practitioners' understanding of their own and other's practice by exposing its performative aspects. As sonifications have not been used for craft practice previously, care was needed in approaching the problem. We did not want to restrict the enquiry by pre-defining too many elements of the sonification system, nor did we wish to leave the design of this system completely open and risk lack of progress. We therefore adopted a research through design approach [5][25], drawing on the design strengths of the researchers to design sonifications (and the system to generate them) in direct response to how craft practitioners used them, whilst also establishing an understanding of the effect of such sonifications on craft practice.

We decided to design a sonification system to be used in a series of workshops with a group of craft practitioners. Based on how the practitioners experienced the system, we would form design insights, iterate the design of the system and present the new system back to the participants for further exploration.

Our approach was further informed by the interdisciplinary skills within our research team. The team included an interaction designer, a design researcher with a focus on craft practice and a computer scientist. These different disciplines allowed us to be confident in following a fast-paced, iterative method.

Researchers took field notes, audio and video recordings of the workshops alongside audio and video data recorded by the sonification system, and collectively discussed activities and observations immediately after them. This critical reflection during the project both informed the design work and research enquiry. We include an account of the activities and thinking of our design, so that this research through design is available for others to critique [25]. The findings that we present were made during these post-workshop discussions and our critical reflection of the study as a whole.

Design Choices

The project imposed a practical constraint that we needed to prototype a working sonification system that could be iteratively used by practitioners and re-developed within the project timescale. Design choices were then made at the start of the study to ensure that this was possible.

To frame our initial enquiry we chose a relevant craft domain that was also readily accessible to the research team. This had implications for our choice of technology to capture the craft's performative actions, the group of participants with which we would work, and the system we would create, not only to process and play the sonifications back to the practitioner in real time but also to allow for analysis between workshops and to iterate its design.

Choice of Craft

Craft practice covers a wide range of different activities and processes; some crafts require large and complex machinery while others only require the practitioner's hands. We developed a taxonomy of different crafts according to the tools used and the prevalence of repeated gestures to inform our selection of craft domain (Table 1). We chose to focus on tool-based textile crafts due to the way these crafts are performed. Firstly, the use of the tool is very important and direct in practicing these crafts, allowing us to focus our attention on the gestural use of the tool. Secondly, artefacts are produced by performing a set of repeated gestures, allowing us to focus our sonification designs around these gestures.

Type of tool	Description	Example crafts
Hand	Using hands to affect material	Basket weaving, pottery, origami
Hand Tools	Tool as extension of hand to affect material	Crochet, wood turning, weaving
Machine Tools	Holding material and using machine to affect it	Sewing with machine, furniture making, metalworking
Digital Tools	Affecting material on digital device	Animation, 3D modelling

Table 1. Taxonomy of craft with respect to the tools used.

We decided to focus on two particular textile crafts: crochet and hooky matting. Crochet is a textile craft that has similarities to knitting although only one needle is used with a hook at its tip. The skill of crocheting is in working the hook in one hand while holding the wool in the other hand. In contrast, the craft of hooky matting is a traditional (local) rug making techniques using strips of old fabric. This craft requires the user to control a tool with one hand and the material with the other. We chose to also include the use of hooky matting because of its similarities to crochet, the idea being that this would allow us to explore how participants used the sonifications in a similar, yet foreign, craft.

Another reason for choosing to focus on crochet was that one of the researchers is also a crocheter and therefore had an understanding of the vocabulary and concepts used by the craft practitioners. This researcher also gave us access to a local community of practitioners to work with.

Choice of Technology

In response to the gestures performed in the selected craft practices, the technology we used to capture craft gestures must not hinder the practitioner in performing their craft and must be robust enough to handle the different ways in which different practitioners perform their craft.

We experimented with different technologies that could potentially be used for capturing craft gestures. We first used the vision-based technology LeapMotion [13]. The LeapMotion is a device that can track the positions of hands, fingers and tools in 3D space. Using vision-based sensors, it scans for finger-like objects and, when they are found, maps them to a model of a hand. This allows it to make assumptions as to where occluded fingers and tools are in 3D space. However, through our testing, we found that the crochet material (wool) would confuse the device and tool occlusion was a big problem when we performed crochet gestures.

Due to the many different ways in which practitioners may use the material and the tool, we decided that a vision-based technology was not robust enough for our purposes. Next, we considered a wireless inertial measurement unit called WAX [1] – a small (35.8 x 24.5 x 9.1 mm) and light (7.3g) sensor which includes a 3-axis accelerometer, 3-axis gyroscope, 3-axis magnetometer and a Bluetooth radio. The WAX collects data from these sensors and streams them over Bluetooth to any receiver using a binary or CSV format.

Figure 1. Crochet hook with a WAX device attached.

The WAX device has many benefits for our application. The non-reliance on a vision system means that there is no chance of occlusion of the tool, fingers or the material being used. Also, compared to other devices, the fact that the technology is wireless means that it is not tethered to a machine used to create the sonifications and so does not interrupt the practitioner's movements or force them to move in a different way in which they are used to. The small size and weight of the WAX also means that it will not interfere with the normal use of the crochet hook tool.

Choice of Participants

A range of different experiences and proficiency with crochet and craft practice in general was required for our participant group. A group of experts or complete beginners would give us some insight into how sonifications affect the experience of crocheting, but a group with a range of abilities allows us to explore how their differing proficiencies may give rise to different reactions.

We decided to work with an established crochet group who meet regularly in an informal setting to crochet and socialize. They are therefore comfortable discussing and practicing their craft in the presence of others and do so voluntarily as a social occasion and an opportunity for learning. The group was recruited by one of the authors as she has participated in some of the crochet sessions previously. The group has 8 members (5 or more typically attending each meeting), all of whom are female and are aged between 30 and 60 years. Working with this group meant we could be flexible in our workshop format, asking questions to individuals or the whole group as necessary.

Design of the System for Research

We required a system design that would aid us in iteratively designing and testing our sonifications based on our findings between workshops. Therefore we designed the system so it would not only capture the WAX device's data stream and generate sonifications but also save video and audio of each usage. This allows us to alter the design of sonifications in real-time, using real-world data synced with video of the crafter's gestures.

When the data stream is captured, the system also begins recording video of the practitioner's hands via the webcam, the audio produced by the sonification, and the WAX data. At the end of the session, this audio is merged with the video to create a new video file. This allowed us to analyze the sonification generation with respect to the movements the user was performing. It also allowed us to run the data back through the system using different sonifications. This allowed us to design, test and iterate different sonifications using the same real-world data. The system uses a C# application to communicate with the WAX device and to record the video, audio and data files. The data from the WAX device is then processed and the resulting data is streamed to PureData [16], which generates the audio and allows for real-time editing of the sonifications.

Proposed Workshop Structure

Running craft sonification workshops with multiple participants raised several practical concerns. In structuring the workshops, we decided that participants would use the sonification system consecutively but within the same room. This open and flexible format would allow participants to hear each other's sonifications and discuss their practice as a group, rather than on an individual basis. Due to the iterative nature of the design of our system, we did not know in advance what we would be deploying at each workshop so instead planned that each workshop would engage participants in different ways. This was so we could explore how the technology could facilitate participants from different perspectives of craft practice.

As there would be no findings with which to design sonifications for workshop 1, we designed this workshop as a way for the participants to experience using the sonifications and WAX-augmented crochet hook in an open and flexible manner. Participants would attend their crochet group as normal but they would take it in turns to use our WAX-augmented hook with a set of designed sonifications. Workshop 2 was designed as a personalization workshop, where the participants and researchers would use their reflections from Workshop 1 to help modify sonifications together within the workshop using a simplified software interface created in PureData. Workshop 3 would follow the overall format of workshop 1, but participants would instead be learning hooky matting, allowing us to explore how learning a different but similar craft affected the participants' use of the sonification system.

Workshops 1 and 2 were designed to run for three hours including time for the participants to arrive and depart. Workshop 3 was to take place off-site at a heritage museum offering hooky matting courses and so was designed to run for a longer time of six hours, including time to arrive and depart.

DESIGNING AND DEPLOYING SONIFICATIONS

Our prototyping activity was split into two overlapping activities: designing sonifications based on our observations of and reflections upon their deployment; and subsequent workshops where we explored the use of these sonifications with practitioners. Study findings are presented alongside workshop descriptions to enable the reader to follow how our design work and research inquiry developed according to participants' use and discussion of sonifications.

Initial Design Work

In approaching Workshop 1, we based our designs on our background research, initial experimentation with the technology and early tests of the system with the crocheting researcher (discussed earlier). Our initial design proposal was that, by quantifying the gestural properties involved in crocheting, we could produce a form of 'rating system' that would be used to drive a number of designed sonifications.

Quantifying Gesture

To quantify the gestural properties of crocheting, we first needed to decide which properties were important for efficient crocheting. Based on reflections upon a research team member's personal experiences of crochet we came to the conclusion that a skilled crocheter would perform stitches *smoothly*, and at a constant *rate*. Both of these properties are required for efficient crocheting because we can imagine somebody who can smoothly perform one stitch but then must stop between each stitch or between stitches sporadically. We began to translate the movement data given to us by the WAX device into quantifiable properties using digital signal processing techniques on a sliding window. We decided upon three different techniques to give the input movement a rating.

Firstly, we took the input signals from the accelerometer and gyroscope (50Hz sampling rate) in two data window sizes, a short 20 sample window and a long 100 sample window. We then applied smoothing functions to them. By comparing the smoothed versions of the data to the original, we are able to see how smooth the input movements were. Secondly, we performed Fast-Fourier Transform (FFT) [4] on the smoothed input data (the small sample windows meant this did not introduce any discernible latency) to transform the signal from time domain to frequency domain and observe the distribution of low frequencies and high frequencies in the data. If there were a large percentage of high frequencies, then we could deduce that the movement is somewhat sporadic. Thirdly, we calculated the second order derivative of the smoothed input data. This is used to show us where there is a sudden change in movement. By calculating these properties of the input data, we could infer the smoothness of a crocheter's movements. To calibrate the rating system, we altered the rating system's parameters until our colleague's crocheting received an average to good score. Although we did not know how experienced our colleague was, we decided that if she received a score around the center of the rating, we would have a wide enough range for the participants to explore.

Designing Sonifications

We designed three sonifications using very different approaches to support our open-ended and flexible enquiry. This was so that we would be able to collect a range of opinions on the different designs and aesthetics of sonifications. The first design was a simple sonification that would 'beep' if the user's rating dropped below a threshold. We will refer to this sonification as *coaching*. The second sonification was based on natural aesthetics and would play different sounds based on the user's rating in a range. The user would hear the sound of wind that became more aggressive if the rating was low, or calm if the rating was high. If the user was performing particularly well, they would hear birdsong over the calm wind but if they were performing particularly poorly, they would hear thunder and rain. We will refer to this sonification as *wind*. Thirdly, we designed a sonification based around musicality and longer-term use. This sonification would play the sounds of instruments in a repeating melody. If the user's rating stayed above a certain threshold for a period of time, another instrument would join the piece. There were three thresholds in total that the user would have to stay above to hear all of the instruments. We will refer to this sonification as *buildup*.

We chose to attach one WAX sensor to the end of a crochet hook to capture the participants' gestures. We considered using more sensors, such as one for each hand, as crocheting is a bimanual craft. However, through initial testing with our crocheting colleague, we were able to obtain discernible data from the single sensor setup and translate this into distinguishable sonifications and could see a varied range of ratings within our rating system when different smoothness, speed and stitches were performed.

Workshop 1

Workshop 1 was run with five participants from the local crochet group. The participants had a range of skill levels and experience of crocheting. Pseudonyms are given for individual participants. The workshop was structured in three sections. The participants were first told how each sonification 'worked', after which the participants took it in turns to use the WAX augmented crochet hook to experience each of the three designed sonifications, and finally a focus group-style discussion was held.

Throughout the workshop, one researcher asked questions about crochet and craft practice in general to initiate discussions between the participants. The topics discussed were: learning, teaching, materiality, experience and comparison to other crafts. The questions asked fell into two categories. The first set were deliberately general, to act as impetus for discussion rather constrain discussion to a single topic. The second set asked the participants about their thoughts on the sonification system.

During the course of running workshop 1, we found that the rating system did not work entirely as we expected. When Doris (the most-experienced participant) was very quick at stitching, and in her own words "jerky" and "aggressive". The speed at which she was stitching meant that the system translated her movements into an average-to-low score in the data window we analyzed. The rating system worked much better for the other participants because they were naturally slower in their stitching and therefore, the rating system calculated as much.

However, this problem with the quantitative system was interpreted in an interesting way by the participants. The participants had been told how the *wind* sonification worked, but after Doris played mostly wind rather than birdsong, each subsequent participant tried to match Doris' sound. Therefore, when they generated birdsong they thought they were not doing well because to them Doris must have the best rating. Familiar social interactions in the already established group meant participants tried to emulate the member they perceived to be most experienced.

Aesthetically, the majority of participants preferred *buildup* due to its musical quality. As the participants are friends who meet to crochet weekly, the sessions included casual conversation on familiar topics. Only when *buildup* was being used, everybody was quiet to listen to it. One participant described it as meditative and that it felt like it needed to be given respect. *Wind* was not as popular as *buildup* and one participant said that this was because of the natural sounds. The fact it sounded like nature made it feel like she was in the garden and "*wanted to go back inside*".

When asked the participants about their opinions on the designs of the sonifications, four of the five participants preferred *buildup* to the *coaching* sonification. Hannah expressed "*I felt like I was guiding it* [buildup], *whereas coaching was guiding me*". This remark was met with agreement by most of the other participants, showing us that using the sonification as a reference and allowing the participant to progress at their own pace is preferable to a sonification which requires the participant to follow it. This was further expressed as participants suggested that *coaching* and *wind* could distract them from crocheting.

Post Workshop 1 Design

Observing that participants were trying to match the most-experienced practitioner's sound and the participants' opinions on the aesthetics of the sonifications led us to explore sonification design from a different perspective: designing abstract and ambiguous sonifications from which the participants could derive their own meaning. We used smoothing functions to smooth the accelerometer and gyroscope data coming from the WAX device but then these smoothed signals were what was used to drive the sonifications directly. Due to the way the system is designed, we were able to take the data recordings from Workshop 1 and run this data and the videos recorded through the system again with these new sonifications. By working in this iterative manner, we were able to design a set of simple, *direct* sonifications in which you could hear different properties of the movement. These sonifications are described as the subset of audification. Their advantage lies in allowing the listener to hear repeated phrases in a data set or signal; therefore we believed this would be useful for hearing the repetitive movements of crochet stitching.

These descriptive sonifications were based on the simple concepts of amplitude modulation and frequency modulation. Each data stream could be used to drive amplitude or frequency modulation (or a combination of both) and each resulting signal could be combined with each other. There were eight data streams available: accelerometer x, y and z and average and gyroscope x, y and z and average.

As workshop 2 was intended to be a workshop to explore and personalize sonifications, we developed a new system to support the ability to alter and combine the different descriptive sonifications. The participants had no experience with PureData and therefore, the interface was designed to be as simple to use as PureData allows. The process of capturing and smoothing different data streams (accelerometer and gyroscope) was hidden from the interface. A simple interface was built which only exposed the volume sliders for each data stream for each descriptive sonification, allowing a user to simply use the slider to merge different data streams with the different forms of descriptive sonification.

Workshop 2

Workshop 2 was run with four participants from the crochet group, three of which had attended workshop 1. The workshop was structured around three sections. We began by discussing the new sonifications with the participants and how they worked. Each participant then used the new sonifications and we finished with a focus group-style discussion. One of the researchers asked questions throughout the session to prompt discussion of their experiences of using the new sonifications and comparisons with the sonifications in workshop 1.

Figure 2. Participant using WAX augmented crochet tool.

Doris and Rachel described how they could hear the difference in the stitches being made when the other participants were using the sonification system. Doris said that she could "see the stitch" in her mind's eye. When it was Margaret's turn to use the system, the other participants could not hear the stitches as well as they could when using it themselves. This began a discussion into the differences in Margaret's crocheting technique as the participants tried to understand why it sounded different. The participants discussed how Margaret must have been manipulating the material with her non-hook hand more than the others did. After this discussion, Margaret expressed "*I didn't know we did things so differently*" even though they had been crocheting together for a long time in these crochet sessions.

After this long discussion about differences in technique, Margaret and Shelley continued to compare techniques. Through demonstrating what she heard in the sonification, Margaret taught Shelley her technique. When asked about this during the focus group-style discussion, Shelley said that she has now realized that she is very "uneconomic" in the way that she crochets and that Margaret's technique is much better. Shelley said she was going to attempt to alter her technique to match that of Margaret's. Here we can see that from a direct result of experiencing the sonifications in a group, a discussion led to participants reflecting on their techniques and one participant teaching the other a technique that she had never tried before.

Aesthetically, Rachel described the amplitude modulation sonification as relaxing, while the frequency modulation sonification was energetic. Shelley discussed how it felt like "*a mental reward*" when you could hear you'd done a stitch smoothly, Rachel echoed this by saying that it was nice to be able to make the sound of a stitch and then repeat making it.

One of the main discussion points during the workshop was about learning techniques. One participant described how she used tutorial videos posted on websites such as YouTube while the others learnt through older family members and used diagrammatic crochet books. We then discussed whether hearing a sonification alongside video could be useful for learning which the participants were positive about.

After discussing if they could hear the stitches when another participant was using the system, Doris and Rachel realized they could not only recognize the stitches but them were following the stitches and rhythm of the sonifications when they weren't creating them. This led them to stop crocheting because they were altering their own crochet projects by accident. This prompted a discussion on whether it would be possible to learn a pattern through sound rather than traditional methods (from a crochet pattern book or with an instructor in person).

Post Workshop 2 Design

Given the positive results of the direct sonifications for generating discussion and aiding reflection and technique modification in workshop 2, we decided to use them again for workshop 3. We also designed two exercises based on discussions of potential applications for the sonifications. Firstly, to create our 'stitch-a-long' exercise, our colleague performed a simple crochet pattern with a variety of stitches using the system to generate a crochet 'sound pattern'. We created a number of these 'sound patterns' of differing complexity to play to the participants in workshop 3. Secondly, to create our sonification video, we video recorded our colleague practicing crochet in the style of a YouTube tutorial. She performed a simple pattern using the WAX augmented hook which we filmed from an over-the-shoulder perspective and then overlaid the sonification audio onto the video.

Workshop 3

Workshop 3 was run with four participants from the crochet group, three of whom had attended workshops 1 and 2. The workshop was structured around three sections. We began by discussing workshop 2 and attempting the exercises we developed. The participants were then taught how to hooky by an instructor from a local living history museum, and we finished with a discussion about the workshop activities. During instruction each participant used a WAX augmented hooky tool so we could explore whether the sonification was useful for learning this new craft. During the course of the workshop, a researcher prompted discussions of their experiences of learning hooky matting, as well as the differences and similarities with crocheting.

During the stitch-a-long exercise, the participants listened to the different 'sound patterns' and attempted to discern the different stitches. The more experienced crocheters (Doris and Rachel) were able to hear the differences in the stitches, whereas the less experienced crocheters (Shelley and Margaret) could only hear the rhythm.

When using the YouTube mock-up, each participant attempted to stitch along while watching/listening to it. Ann expressed how she found the sound useful to get into a rhythm and would only glance at the video to see where she was and then continue to use the sound to crochet along to. So she described the sound as another support mechanism.

We then moved on to using the direct sonifications for hooky matting. When practicing their hooky matting, the participants expressed that the sonification helped. Most of the participants expressed that they were using it to try to keep to a rhythm. However, Shelley described how she was not using it to stay in rhythm but was using it to hear when she was doing it incorrectly, this is because her sudden movements would cause a loud peak in the sound. Here we see how different participants made use of the ambiguous sound, some using it as positive reinforcement whereas another using it for discerning errors.

During Doris' turn with the sonifications, she expressed that she thought they were helpful to her. We muted the sound from the speakers to test this at which point Doris stopped hooky matting but could not say why at first. She expressed that she felt like there was something missing and that she was following the sound, when the sound was muted she could no longer follow it.

Again, the participants talked about the aesthetics of the sonifications and created their own personal meaning from them. Ann described the sonifications as sounding like an orchestra tuning up and then falling into a rhythm. When you are in a rhythm it is soothing and meditative, when you are not in a rhythm it is exciting to hear the "tuning up" and anticipating the rhythm. She continued by describing the in-rhythm experience as being "in the zone".

The meditative effects of the sound were also discussed throughout the workshop. While using the YouTube mock-up, Doris expressed how she "*felt hypnotized*" and Ann said she felt like she was "*going into a trance*". When using the sonifications for hooky matting, Margaret expressed that the sound was meditative because it was connected directly to your movements, it was not connected consciously.

Summary of Findings

We found that the sonifications affected participants' practice in several ways: participants attempted to *echo the expert* of the group, manipulating their practice to match her sound; when listening to each other's generated sounds, they were able to *perceive differences* between stitches, rhythms and techniques; participants used sonifications as a *resource for the development of practice*, e.g. when Margaret taught Shelley her technique; participants *engaged through sonifications*, describing their aesthetic and meditative effects throughout the workshops; and perceiving stitches in each other's sound led to an *entanglement with practice* as participants altered their own projects unknowingly.

DISCUSSION

In our workshops we observed that sonifications *can* facilitate craft practitioners in discussing, reflecting upon and continuing to learn from their own and each other's practices. Our system for sonifying textile-based craft gestures has demonstrated how sonifications can enable practitioners to explore their own and each other's practice in new ways. Our observations in workshops and collective critical reflections between them suggested several ways in which this happened. Our central finding was that direct sonifications supported reflection and technique modification for the participants whereas preconfigured sonifications did not. We now discuss the ways in which direct sonifications supported the participants' practice.

Enabling Interpretive Flexibility

Through designing different sonifications over the three workshops and observing how participants used them, our findings show that sonifications should be directly linked to the gestural data rather than have meaning imposed upon them by data transformation. The ambiguous sonifications that result are open to interpretation and so allow the participants to derive their own meaning based on what they perceive and interpret in the sounds.

In workshop 1, we designed the sonifications to react in particular ways based on a rating system. We observed that they were not useful to the participants. By designing preconfigured sonifications, we were making assumptions on what the participants would find useful rather than allowing them to make their own meaning. Only *wind* was useful to us from this first set of sonifications, and only in so much as to show us that participants were deriving their own meaning from the sound based on who they want wanted to emulate rather than adhering to the rules which governed the sound produced. This shows us that our prior conceptions of meaning, as expressed in the computational rules were of no use to the participants beyond attempting to emulate the most-experienced crocheter.

The direct sonifications allowed the participants to reflect on their own and each other's practices because they allowed the participants to make their own meanings. In this respect, the sonifications are an example of the reflective design strategy "provide for interpretive flexibility" [20] where users maintain control of and responsibility for the meaning-making process.

Perceiving Differences

The direct sonifications also enabled the participants to perceive differences in their techniques. We found that using the direct sonifications created a situation where one participant's generated sound was not as clear as the other participants', a discussion arose around why this may be. Only through further use of these sonifications did the participants realize that her technique was different from the others and then they were able to discuss these differences. To enable such opportunities for reflection, designers should tailor direct sonifications to better afford personal interpretation and deploy these sonifications to groups rather than individuals to allow the participants' differing interpretations to prompt discussion.

Supporting Reflection Upon and Development of Collective Practice

The ambiguity of the direct sonifications enabled participants to make use of them as they pleased. Given practitioners of varying experience and skill levels, what they hear in the sonifications is different and therefore they interpret what is useful for the development of their practice. Direct sonification of gestures enabled participants to perceive nuances in each other's practices more readily. This supported the group's learning by *doing* through heightening their sensitivities to patterns of gestures associated with differing levels of ability.

We also saw an unexpected consequence of multiple sonifications in group practice. When one participant was using the direct sonifications, a second participant began following the rhythm of the first. Only after some time, did the participant realize that she was doing this and that this was detrimental to her own crochet project. When this happened, this subconscious entrainment was seen as strange and detrimental but this phenomenon could possibly be further explored and used to facilitate the learning of a rhythmic, repetitive craft using direct sonifications in future work.

Reflections on the Design Process

Over the course of three workshops, we explored how to design sonifications with a group of craft practitioners. The design of the system played a vital role in allowing us to explore these sonifications. The ability to record video of the participants and pair these with the recorded gestural data allowed us to explore different sonification designs without needing the participants present.

The system also allowed us to easily manipulate the sonification designs during workshops, which let us respond to points that the participants were making. For example, during workshop 2 one participant expressed that the sound was droning. We were able to manipulate the sonification and receive more feedback from the participant on this change. Furthermore, the direct sonifications that our participants found useful may not be useful to a group of woodworkers for example. Given the variety of different craft practices and the gestures performed to practice them, developing direct sonifications iteratively *with* craft practitioners (e.g. through workshops) is important in order to develop sonifications that are meaningful within their particular practice. A flexible system for producing such sonifications is essential to this process.

Sonifications as Boundary Objects

Participants each heard different things in the sonifications. For some it was rhythm and for others it was the separate stitches, but the whole group was able to discuss common aspects of their practice with respect to the sonifications. In this manner the direct sonifications can be understood as a form of boundary object [22], being flexible enough that it can be interpreted differently by different communities but robust enough to maintain a common identity across them.

The sonifications also acted as a boundary object between the participants and the researchers. Researchers who do not crochet were able to understand concepts the participants were discussing because the discussions were facilitated by the participants' use of sonifications as a reference point, either describing the sound or verbalizing it to help convey an aspect of the craft.

CONCLUSION

In this paper, we have provided a descriptive account of our design-led approach to iteratively designing sonifications for craft practitioners in response to observations and experiences in running a series of workshops. Through working with a group of craft practitioners of varying skill levels, we were able to iteratively design a set of sonifications and example applications that were useful to their practice. By exploring craft through its performative actions (rather than practitioners' descriptions of their making or a semiotic approach to deconstructing artefacts and tools) we have shown how real-time sonification of gestures can facilitate occasions for reflection and discussion of craft skills.

A limitation of our study is that it only investigates the design of sonifications for a particular group of craft practitioners. Further studies with other crafts and groups of practitioners would develop further understanding on how digital systems can aid practitioners in discussing and reflecting on their craft.

We observed how sonifying practitioners' gestural movements can support reflection in and on practice [19] and help them to modify and develop their techniques. This opens up a possibility for remote and en mass learning: could you access the masters' skill by "hearing" it, at a distance? Further, we have demonstrated how sonification can aid practitioners in developing their craft skills but have not explored how this may then aid the preservation of craft skills (e.g. appending sonifications to current learning tools such as YouTube tutorial videos) or how gesture sonification might be used by complete beginners (working alone or with an experienced practitioner).

During workshops 2 and 3, some of the participants expressed interest in continuing to use the sonification system after our study, e.g. Doris wondered if we could make the technology into an app so that she could use it at home. This highlights an opportunity for longitudinal study, and we have continued to work with participants albeit using different technology – exploring tangible data translation activities utilizing a participatory digital fabrication approach in order to engage craft practitioners in further reflection on their practice.

These limitations notwithstanding, our study opens a space for the sensitive design of digital systems to support reflection in and on craft practice that the HCI community can explore further.

ACKNOWLEDGMENTS

We thank the crochet group who participated in the study. This work was funded by a UK AHRC KE Hub for the Creative Economy (ref: AH/J005150/1 Creative Exchange).

REFERENCES

1. Axivity Limited. http://axivity.com.
2. Barad, K. (2003). Posthumanist Performativity: Toward an Understanding of How Matter Comes to Matter. Signs: Journal of Women in Culture and Society, 28(3), pp.801–831.
3. Butler, J. (1993). Gender Trouble: Feminism and the subversion of identity. Routledge: London.
4. Cooley, J. & Tukey, J. (1965). "An algorithm for the machine calculation of complex Fourier series". Math. Comput. 19: 297–301.
5. Gaver, W. (2012) What should we expect from research through design? In *Proc. CHI 2012*, ACM Press (2012).
6. Godbout, A., & Boyd, J. E. (2010). Corrective sonic feedback for speed skating: a case study. In *Proc. ICAD 2010* (pp. 23-30).
7. Gowtow, B. Kinect hand tracking visualization. [Online]. http://blog.foundry376.com/2011/02/kinect-hand-tracking-visualization/.
8. Hermann, T. & Ritter, H., (2004) Sound and meaning in auditory data display. Proceedings of the IEEE 92(4), pp. 730-741.
9. Hermann, T., & Hunt, A. (2011). *The sonification handbook*. Berlin: Logos Verlag.
10. Ingold, T. (2013). Making: anthropology, archeology, art and architecture. Routledge: Milton Park.
11. International Community for Auditory Display. [Online] http://www.icad.org/.
12. Jensenius, A. R. (2007). Action-Sound, developing methods and tools to study music-related body movement. PhD thesis, University of Oslo, 2007.
13. LeapMotion. [Online]. http://www.leapmotion.com.
14. Perry, G., & Krippendorff, K. (2013). On the reliability of identifying design moves in protocol analysis. Design Studies, 34(5), pp. 612-635.
15. Polanyi, M (1966), *The Tacit Dimension*, University of Chicago Press: Chicago.
16. PureData. [Online]. http://puredata.info.
17. Roberts, J, Jones, R, Mansfield, N, & Rothberg, S. (2005) Evaluation of impact sound on the 'feel' of a golf shot, Journal of Sound and Vibration, vol. 287, no. 4-5, pp. 651-666.
18. Schaffert, N., Mattes, K., & Effenberg, A. O. (2009). A sound design for the purposes of movement optimisation in elite sport (using the example of rowing). In *Proc ICAD 2009*.
19. Schön, D. A. (1983). The reflective practitioner: How professionals think in action. New York: Basic Books.
20. Sengers, P., Boehner, K., David, S. & Kaye, J. (2005) Reflective design. In *Proc. CC 2005*, ACM Press (2005), pp. 49-58.
21. Sodnik, J., Dicke, C., Tomazič, S. & Billinghurst, M. (2008) A user study of auditory versus visual interfaces for use while driving. International Journal of Human-Computer Studies 66(5): 318-332.
22. Star, S. & Griesemer, J. (1989). "Institutional Ecology, 'Translations' and Boundary Objects: Amateurs and Professionals in Berkeley's Museum of Vertebrate Zoology, 1907-39". Social Studies of Science 19 (3): 387–420.
23. Wood. N. (2006). Transmitting craft knowledge: designing interactive media to support tacit skills learning. PhD thesis, Sheffield Hallam University, November 2006.
24. Wood N & Horne G (2008). The new journeyman; the role of an expert learner in eliciting and transmitting skilled knowledge. Proceedings of the Design Research Society Conference, Sheffield, July 2008.
25. Zimmerman J., Stolterman, E., & Forlizzi, J. (2010) An analysis and critique of Research through Design: towards a formalization of a research approach. In *Proc. Dis 2010*, Aarhus, Denmark.

Remote Paper Prototype Testing

Kevin Chen
Northwestern University
Evanston, IL
kevinchen@u.northwestern.edu

Haoqi Zhang
Northwestern University
Evanston, IL
hq@northwestern.edu

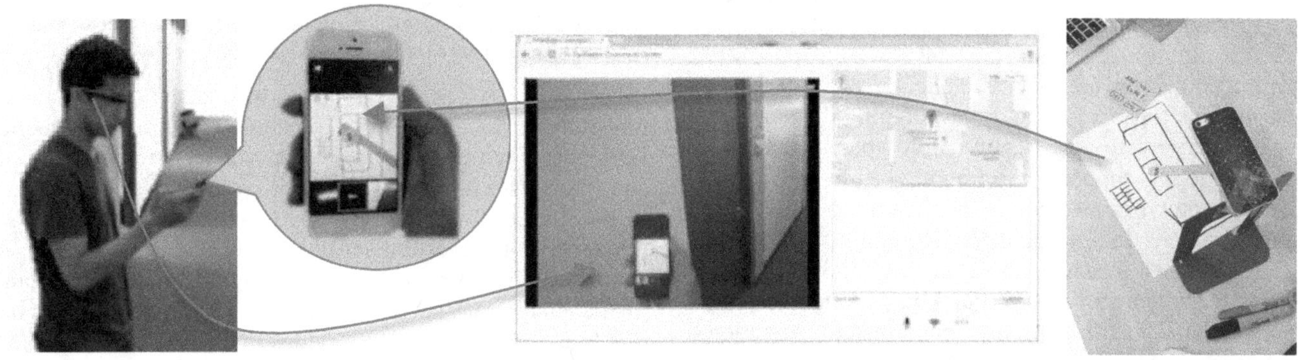

Figure 1. A tester interacts with a paper prototype of a mobile application out of the lab (Left). The designer observes the tester's interactions, first-person perspective, and location data (Center) and remotely wizards the paper prototype (Right).

ABSTRACT

To test paper prototypes of mobile applications, we have been experimenting with *remote paper prototype testing* as an approach and tool for enabling a designer to wizard a paper prototype from afar while a user tests the prototype out of the lab. This paper presents a system for remote paper prototype testing that consists of (1) a video camera placed over a paper prototype, which streams a live audio-visual feed via Google Hangouts to a tester, and (2) Google Glass on the tester, which streams a live audio-visual-data feed to the facilitator and wizard. Results from a pilot study found that remote paper prototype testing helped designers gain valuable insights through use in realistic scenarios.

Author Keywords

Paper prototyping; Lo-fi prototyping; Mobile apps; Design.

ACM Classification Keywords

H.5.m. Information interfaces and presentation (e.g., HCI): Miscellaneous.

INTRODUCTION

Lo-fi prototyping, or paper prototyping, is a powerful tool for designers to test designs with users early in the design process [11]. Paper prototypes are fast and cheap to make, focus on core interactions instead of look and feel, and enable designers to test multiple designs and iterate quickly. Despite these benefits, HCI researchers and design practitioners have argued that paper prototyping is poorly suited for evaluating mobile applications [5]. In particular, they express the need and difficulty in evaluating mobile application designs in environments that surface realistic experiences [1,8,9]. Testing in the lab lacks situational context; for evaluating the *mobile use* of an application, scenarios often feel contrived and the users' experiences fail to reveal major issues in the design [7,8]. Testing out of the lab faces practical challenges. In order to observe the user in context, a facilitator and wizard may need to follow a user around, which may be undesirable. But even if they do, it may be hard to see a user's interactions with a paper prototype and wizard effectively in a mobile setting.

We are experimenting with *remote paper prototype testing* as an approach for lo-fi prototype testing that enables user testing a paper prototype out of the lab while a designer wizards from afar (Figure 1). To explore its use, we developed a tool by building on existing technologies that consists of (1) a smartphone camera pointed at the paper prototype, which streams a video feed through Google Hangouts to the tester's mobile device, (2) Google Glass on the user, which streams a first-person perspective audio-visual-data feed to designer, and (3) a *command center interface*, from which the designers observe and facilitate the session from the lab, and wizard interactions in response to tester actions and changing context.

This paper makes three contributions: (1) an approach for remote paper prototype testing; (2) a tool that implements the approach, built with Google Hangout and Google Glass; and (3) the results of a pilot study, in which three designer-facilitator-wizards prototyped and facilitated the testing of

CHI '15, April 18—23, 2015, Seoul, South Korea.

ACM 978-1-4503-3145-6/15/04···$15.00
http://dx.doi.org/10.1145/2702123.2702423

two location-based mobile applications that were evaluated by five testers. Results indicate that the tool allowed designers to remotely facilitate testing, presented testers with realistic scenarios, and helped reveal critical incidents.

RELATED WORK

To facilitate testing mobile app prototypes under realistic scenarios, previous work focused on tools for creating interactive, higher-fidelity prototypes. For example, Raento et al. [10] introduced ContextPhone, which supports prototyping context-aware mobile applications. Sá et al. [6] introduced tools for mixed-fidelity prototyping that support adding interactivity to low-fidelity prototypes. Numerous commercial tools support wireframing and generating interactive prototypes of mobile applications; Balsamiq, Invision, Framer, Indigo, and Mockingbird are some examples. But while these tools enable higher-fidelity prototypes to be generated more quickly, paper prototypes are easier to make still and may focus testers' attention more on core interactions than on look-and-feel [11].

To address the shortcomings of in-lab testing, *remote usability testing* allows an application developer to view and record a tester's interactions and reactions to an interactive, mobile application prototype. MailChimp, for example, created an early prototype for remote usability testing in which a user holds up their mobile device up to their laptop's webcam while video chatting on Skype. While remote usability testing allows designers to gather feedback on computer prototypes, with remote paper prototype testing we face the added challenge of having to wizard a paper prototype from afar to realize both the benefits of paper prototyping and out-of-the lab testing.

As testers in a remote paper prototyping session interact with a video of the interface and not the paper itself, aspects of the experience are akin to *paper-in-screen* prototyping [4]. For mobile apps, a paper-in-screen prototype digitizes a paper prototype and adds navigational elements by linking drawn interface elements to different views within a mobile interface. One benefit of paper-in-screen prototypes shared by remote paper prototype testing is that users can interact with the interface on their own mobile device, adding to the authenticity of the experience. But while a paper-in-screen consists of a set of pre-determined interactions, remote paper prototype testing supports dynamic updates to an interface with a human wizard.

REMOTE PAPER PROTOTYPE TESTING

We developed a remote paper prototype testing tool to enable designers to observe, facilitate, and wizard a paper prototype testing session in the lab while a tester interacts with the prototype out of the lab. Our prototype tool is built with a combination of existing technologies.

We place a paper prototype on a desk under a smartphone that is attached to a bookstand (Figure 1, Right). The

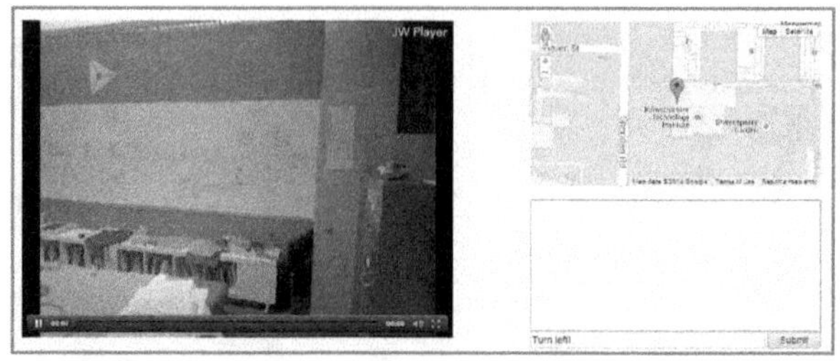

Figure 2. The facilitator's command center interface displays a video stream, location data, and a chat box.

smartphone serves as a makeshift document camera, transmitting a video of the prototype through Google Hangouts (Figure 1, Left). A tester connects to the hangout and interacts with the feed as if it were an actual interface (Figure 1, Left). The tester wears Google Glass running our remote prototype testing software, which streams a video of the tester's first-person perspective, audio, and location data to the facilitator's command center (Figure 2). Based on this live feed, the wizard provides instructions and updates the paper prototype in response to the tester's actions. For example, the wizard might update the interface based on the tester's movement by manipulating a stick that points at the tester's location (Figure 1, Right). At any time, the facilitator can speak to the tester directly or via a message box. Messages are displayed on Glass and also voiced with text-to-speech.

Design Goals

Test mobile apps in realistic environments: Our remote paper prototype testing setup allows a tester to experience an app in the places and situations where they are likely to use it. For example, this setup helps support the testing of location-based mobile applications for social networking (e.g., Foursquare) for which the locational aspects of the interaction may be difficult to replicate in the lab.

Remotely facilitate a testing session and wizard a prototype from the lab: One advantage of facilitating and wizarding from the lab over following a tester out of the lab is that it is easier to manipulate a paper prototype in lab than on-the-move or at remote locations, where holding and updating a prototype can be physically difficult or awkward. The lab also provides easy access to prototype components (e.g., Post-Its, notecards) and resources (e.g., desktop computers).

Provide location-based and situational context: Remote testing can make it difficult for designers to understand user interactions in the context of their surroundings. By streaming the user's first-person viewpoint, our remote paper prototype testing tool shows designers sequences of interactions live and in-situ. For example, being able to see how a user shifts their attention between the app and their environment can provide insights about how interface elements are helping users navigate or complete tasks.

Preserve the affordances of paper prototyping: Despite their seeming simplicity, paper prototypes can be highly expressive and capture the essence of complex interactions.

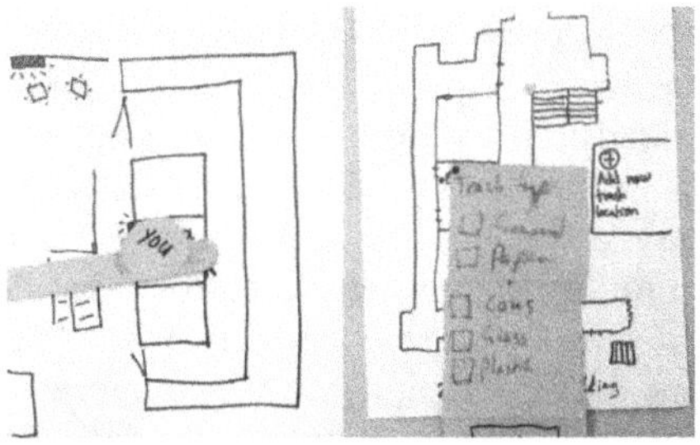

Figure 3. Left: Sugar Rush. Right: Recycle Hunt

Our tool seeks to maintain paper's flexibility while simultaneously enabling remote testing. In contrast to paper-in-screen prototyping [4], we are not limited to a set of predetermined interactions: a wizard can flexibly update the mobile interface based on situations and events.

Implementation

The remote paper prototype testing tool's native Glass component is written in Java and built using Google's Glass Development Kit Preview (API 19). Glass streams its camera video using the libstreaming library to a Wowza media server that handles viewing clients. Native Android functions implement broadcasting location information and viewing text updates from the facilitator and playing them aloud. Parse stores and transmits text updates and location data. The command center is built in HTML, CSS, Javascript, JWPlayer, and Google Maps' Javascript API.

PILOT STUDY

We conducted a pilot study over two days to explore opportunities for using remote paper prototype testing. We recruited a purposive sample of designers and testers. Three designers created and iterated on paper prototypes of two location-based, mobile applications. Five testers evaluated these two prototypes. During testing sessions, designers acted as facilitators, wizards, and observers.

Designers were given 20 minutes to create the prototype. During subsequent testing sessions, they instructed testers on tasks and scenarios, observed their interactions, and wizarded the system. Testers participate through 30-minute sessions. They were instructed to talk aloud while using the application out of the lab. After evaluating both prototypes, testers provided feedback to designers. We interviewed everyone about their testing experience at the end.

Results

Designers prototyped two applications: Sugar Rush and Recycle Hunt. Sugar Rush is a treasure hunt style app for candy (Figure 3, Left). Testers are shown a hand-drawn map with candy cane boxes marking the approximate locations of candy and a "You" pin indicating their current location. The designer moves a popsicle stick to match the tester's location. Recycle Hunt crowdsources the locations of recycle and trash bins (Figure 3, Right). Through a map view, testers can find locations to dispose of trash and add the locations of unmarked trashcans or recycling bins.

Results from the testing sessions demonstrate some of the potential benefits of remote testing and show that the remote paper prototype testing tool supported our four stated design goals:

Test mobile apps in realistic environments

Testers found themselves engaged in the presented tasks as they walked around the building looking for candy or trash bins. Testing revealed a number of critical incidents; for example, a few Sugar Rush testers could not find candy even when they were very close. One designer noted that this was "something we couldn't have found out [in a lab]."

Remotely facilitate a testing session and wizard a prototype from the lab

Designers noted that the first-person perspective streamed from Glass "[allowed them] to be reactive". Despite interacting remotely, designers observed testers interacting with the prototype application like they were trying to actually use their personal phones to complete the task. A tester commented that "seeing the paper and being able to press it seemed real," especially because they were "actually using it in the actual environment."

Provide location-based and situational context

Designers repeatedly expressed the usefulness of being able to see the users' actions in context. A Sugar Rush designer said: "With Glass you get to see what's going on when they switch their focus from the app to the real world...If you're testing in lab, you go like 'Great, you found the candy.' But ...you didn't know what to do when you got to the location." Seeing user actions in context also helped designers identify interactions that confused users. In Sugar Rush, an early prototype provided no feedback when users reached the location of the candy. The designer found that users "tried to click on [the candy icons]" and wondered what to do next. Based on this observation, the designer updated the prototype so that the wizard would shake the user location popsicle stick as feedback for when a user approached candy. This prompted users to look up from their phones and helped them find the candy.

Preserve the affordances of paper prototyping

Designers felt that the ability to prototype on paper and immediately test it in realistic scenarios helped them gather "more insights faster." Designers focused on expressing the core idea behind the application, knowing that there may be flaws but that remote testing would help to "immediately realize all of the ways [they] would fail." For Recycle Hunt, the designer "realized that [users] didn't have any incentive to use the app at the point in which [their] knowledge was useful. If [they] knew where the recycling thing was [they] wouldn't use the app, which shoots down the entire premise." He noted that the flaw he had discovered through testing would be "sort of devastating if you spent a long time on it," but that finding the flaw through remote paper prototype testing "was a very useful place to get to."

DISCUSSION

The Case for Remote Paper Prototype Testing

To facilitate testing prototypes of mobile applications in realistic scenarios, previous work focused on helping designers create higher-fidelity prototypes and provided features for logging and analyzing usage data [6,10]. In contrast, our tool allows designers to create paper prototypes, test them outside the lab, and, unlike paper-in-screen prototyping [4], flexibly update the interface in response to events and situations while testing.

With our remote testing method, designers can use paper prototypes of mobile apps to identify critical incidents and usability problems through actual mobile use cases. Paper prototypes in the pilot took only 20 minutes to create; a computer prototype with comparable functionality may have taken a full day to create. That said, paper prototyping requires continued human involvement during testing, and may not support longitudinal studies. Future work will more carefully investigate the respective benefits and shortcomings of remote paper prototype testing and higher fidelity prototyping in varied use cases.

Technology for Remote Paper Prototype Testing

Remote paper prototyping testing can integrate a variety of technologies to create a more powerful overall experience. In the pilot, we used Glass for its first-person perspective, which allowed designers to remotely observe what users were looking at, their location, and their situational context. More generally, our core approach centers on (1) streaming a live audiovisual feed of the paper prototype to a remote tester, and (2) streaming information from the tester back to the wizard.

Future work will explore the tradeoffs in complexity, cost, and functionality through alternative implementations of our approach. For example, we could create a testing app that (1) use the front facing camera to capture the user's facial expressions, and (2) display street view as testers move about an environment. These technologies offer a substitute for Glass to capture context and user reactions.

In our pilot, wizards expressed that managing multiple technologies while reacting to user actions and changing situations was difficult. To reduce this burden, we will also explore setups that reduce the need of the wizard to shift their attention and the effort required to complete wizarding actions. For example, we will overlay an event stream of user actions on top of the video of the paper prototype in the command center. We will also experiment with augmented reality displays of prototyping materials.

Testing Lo-fi Prototypes in the Wild

Our future work will study the limits while expanding the use of remote testing for lo-fi prototypes to testing in actual locations, times, and situations. For location, pilot testing took place inside an engineering building in which testers and bystanders were tech-savvy and felt little to no aversion to Glass or talk-alouds. We plan to test mobile prototypes in public venues such as parks, coffee shops, and department stores to study if wearing Glass affects testers or bystanders, examining if they feel self-conscious and exploring any social implications of using this technology. For times, pilot testing sessions lasted only half an hour and at scheduled times. Future work will seek to allow testing throughout a user's existing routine, explore methods for (a) notifying wizards of pending interactions, and (b) recruiting a real-time crowd to act as wizards on demand [2,3]. For situations, our pilot focused on mobile apps in which location plays a crucial role in the experience, but the remote testing approach may be useful for a wide range of mobile use cases and contexts. Our future work will explore the advantages and limitations of remote paper prototype testing across a large range of scenarios, such as ones that require inter-personal interactions, that are time sensitive, or that make use of other technologies, such as cameras.

REFERENCES

1. Been-Lirn Duh, H., Tan, G. C. B. and Chen, V. H. 2006. Usability evaluation for mobile device: a comparison of laboratory and field tests. In *MobileHCI '06*
2. Bernstein, M., Brandt, J., Miller, R.C. and Karger, D.R. Crowds in two seconds: Enabling real-time crowd-powered interfaces. In *UIST '11.*
3. Bigham, J., Jayant, C., Ji, H., Little, G., Miller, A., Miller, R., Miller, R. and Yeh, T. VizWiz: nearly real-time answers to visual questions. In *UIST '10.*
4. Bolchini, D., Pulido, D., & Faiola, A. (2009). Paper in screen prototyping: an agile technique to anticipate the mobile experience. *Interactions*, *16*(4), 29-33.
5. de Sá, M. and Carriço, L. 2008. Lessons from early stages design of mobile applications. In *MobileHCI '08.*
6. de Sá, M. and Carriço, L. 2009. A mobile tool for in-situ prototyping. In *MobileHCI* '09.
7. Kjeldskov, J. and Stage, J. New techniques for usability evaluation of mobile systems, International Journal of Human-Computer Studies, Volume 60, Issues 5–6, May 2004.
8. Lumsden, J., MacLean, R. A Comparison of Pseudo-Paper and Paper Prototyping Methods for Mobile Evaluations. MONET '2008, 2008.
9. Nielsen, C.M., Overgaard, M., Pedersen, M.B., Stage, J. and Stenild, S. 2006. It's worth the hassle!: the added value of evaluating the usability of mobile systems in the field. In *NordiCHI '06.*
10. Raento, M.; Oulasvirta, A.; Petit, R.; Toivonen, H. ContextPhone: a prototyping platform for context-aware mobile applications. *Pervasive Computing, IEEE* , vol.4, no.2, pp.51-59, Jan.-March 2005.
11. Rettig, M. 1994. Prototyping for tiny fingers. *Commun. ACM* 37, 4 (April 1994), 21-27.

Controlling In-the-Wild Evaluation Studies of Public Displays

Sandy Claes[1], Niels Wouters[1], Karin Slegers[2], Andrew Vande Moere[1]
[1] Research[x]Design, Department of Architecture, KU Leuven
[2] CUO | Social Spaces, KU Leuven / iMinds
{sandy.claes, niels.wouters, karin.slegers, andrew.vandemoere}@kuleuven.be

ABSTRACT
In this paper, we investigate the potential of controlled in-the-wild studies as an evaluation methodology that merges the benefits of lab-based and in-the-wild studies. Our exploratory investigation builds upon a comparative, between subject experiment benchmarking different interaction features of a custom public installation that visualized a series of urban datasets. In order to evaluate the usefulness of the in-the-wild versus the controlled in-the-wild methodologies, we compared the resulting findings in terms of participant engagement, insight generation, and social interaction. We propose that a controlled in-the-wild study offers a viable alternative when evaluating more complex interaction methods in public space, hereby potentially reducing the practical efforts of in-the-wild studies to involve participants.

Author Keywords
Methods; in-the-wild study; controlled study; evaluation; data visualization; urban visualization; public display.

ACM Classification Keywords
H.5.m. Information interfaces and presentation (e.g., HCI).

INTRODUCTION
As interactive public displays increasingly permeate our urban environment, the need arises to evaluate their effectiveness in purposively engaging passers-by. Typically, longitudinal effects are studied in deployment based research, while early prototypes are studied in lab studies, which aim to minimize the impact of external influences (e.g. [2]), or in-the-wild studies [8], which preserve the ecologic validity of real-life contexts [1]. However, both lab as in-the-wild methodologies are faced with particular shortcomings [4], as lab studies fail to simulate the complex, unpredictable dynamics of the 'real world', and in-the-wild studies tend to be cumbersome in terms of participant commitment (e.g. limited time commitment), preparation (e.g. permits) and privacy regulations (e.g. video logging in public space).

We believe the opportunity exists to merge the qualities of lab-based and in-the-wild studies into a single evaluation methodology, i.e. "controlled in-the-wild studies". Although such methodology would retain ecological authenticity while also enjoying dedicated participant commitment and relatively few unpredictable organizational issues, little is known of its applicability or the validity of its results [3, 7]. Therefore, we have compared the findings from an in-the-wild (ITW) and controlled in-the-wild (CITW) study in order to analyze the qualities and challenges inherent to each methodology. We used the findings of a comparative, between subject evaluation study of an interactive urban installation that compared the impact of three distinct conditions. Observations from each methodology are structured according to user engagement, the depth level of insight discovery, and any apparent social interaction [5]. We believe this knowledge is relevant for research that is highly dependent on real-life contexts, while yielding results in more efficient and flexible ways.

CHI 2015, April 18 – 23, 2015, Seoul, Republic of Korea.

ACM978-1-4503-3145-6/15/04...$15.00.
http://dx.doi.org/10.1145/2702123.2702353

CASE STUDY
We designed an urban installation to inform passers-by of locally situated information. The urban installation had the shape of a telescope (see Figure 2), in order to metaphorically invite people to reflect on their environment by looking through a 'lens' of data. The data consisted of dimensions like local birthrate, total number of inhabitants, average income levels, total energy usage and total amount of waste produced by local households. As we preferred to encourage passers-by to simultaneously observe 3 distinct data dimensions, we felt unsure what interaction technique to deploy in a public setting. Accordingly, we developed 3 distinct conditions that differed in how people could select the 3 data dimensions, as well as the media on which the dimensions were shown, i.e. 1) *touch*, i.e. in which data dimensions were both selected and shown as graphs on a standard touch display; 2) *physical*, in which the data dimensions were shown as graphs on physical discs, which had to be selected by hand; and 3) *mixed*, in which the dimensions were selected by handling physical discs, yet the graphs were shown on a display. Our comparative experiment was thus designed to investigate if the *way* the telescope facilitated interaction influenced the passive and

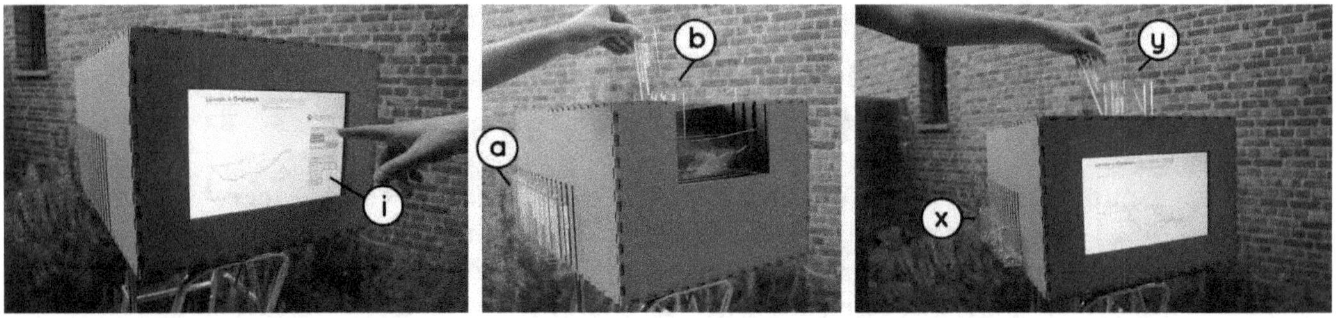

Figure 1. Touch condition (left), physical condition (middle) and mixed condition (right). Note the touch display buttons (i), the series of discs on the left side (a, x) denoting a data dimension each, of which 3 could be slotted at the top (b, y).

active engagement [5] of passers-by, the depth of the discovered insights [6], and the social interaction alongside.

***Touch* Condition.** People were able to select up to 3 different data dimensions by pressing common touch-enabled buttons that were displayed on a (30x40cm) digital screen (Figure 1, left).

***Physical* Condition** contained no display. Instead, a series of transparent thermoplastic (TP) discs were provided on the left, outer side of the telescope, forcing people to solely interact in a tangible way (Fig.1, a). People could insert up to 3 TP discs in the 3 slots on top of the telescope (Fig.1, b). Each disc was specifically laser-cut to state a dimension, and physically resemble the matching line graph.

***Mixed* Condition** featured the same display as in the *touch* condition (Fig. 1, z), yet people could select up to 3 data dimensions in an identical way to the *physical* condition. The according data graphs were shown on the display.

Methods	*ITW*	*CITW*
Observations	Y	Y
Video logging	Y	Y
Semi-structured interviews	Y	Y
Spontaneous user participation	Y	N
User recruitment	N	Y
Between subject design	Y	Y

Table 1. Overview of evaluation methods used in the in-the-wild and in the controlled in-the-wild methodologies.

METHODOLOGY

Next to several other evaluation methods (see Table 1), both ITW and CITW involved semi-structured interviews in order to reveal: 1) why users engaged with the telescope; 2) how they interacted; and 3) what new insights they discovered. In addition, video fragments of each condition were analyzed by categorizing every passer-by according to the Passive, Active Engagement and Discovery (PACD) model [5]: passive engagement comprises of glimpses and glances towards the display, while active engagement occurs when passers-by read or interacted with the display. We also measured the time spent during each engagement phase, and analyzed the *depth* of each reported insight by counting the number of data dimensions that had to be put together to be able to reach the insight.

In-the-wild Study (ITW)

During the in-the-wild study (ITW) the telescope was deployed in 2 divergent locations: a pedestrian shopping street (Fig.2, right) and a square in a residential area, near a major bus stop. Passers-by were thus able to freely walk up to the installation and actively engage with it (or not). Each person who actively engaged with the installation was approached by a (previously concealed) researcher to participate in a semi-structured interview.

Figure 2. Passage (CITW, left). Shopping street (ITW, right).

Controlled in-the-wild Study (CITW)

We set up the controlled version of the in-the-wild study (CITW) at the university campus nearby the city. Local university personnel (e.g. PhD students, administrative and technical staff) were invited via email to participate in an "open study on interactive installations". Individual appointments were made with interested persons who live, or lived, in the city (and thus knew the context of the data). They were asked to keep 30 minutes available of their time. The telescope was placed outside, at one of 2 different locations that resembled the characteristics of the in-the-wild environment. At the start of each experiment, the researcher introduced herself, but not the project. She then left the participant alone with the telescope mentioning an everyday excuse (i.e. toilet break). From that moment, participants were thus free to engage with the telescope or not, which was logged via a nearby video camera. The researcher returned after she noticed that the 'free' user engagement finished, and a semi-structured interview was taken, together with a Likert scale survey.

RESULTS

Passive engagement.

ITW. Our observations indicate that the *physical* condition motivated 34.8% of passers-by (54 out of 155) towards passive engagement (see Table 2).

CITW. During interviews, participants reported the "see-through aspect" of the display in the *physical* condition had attracted them to approach and look through the telescope.

	Touch	*Physical*	*Mixed*
Controlled in-the-wild study (CITW)			
Duration	4h	4h	4h
Passers-by	6	4	8
Participants (N)	8	8	8
Avg. interaction time	2'55" (σ=1'40")	4'42" (σ=2'01")	4'15" (σ=1'20")
Avg. age	42 (σ=11)	38 (σ=11)	32 (σ=13)
Gender	4M, 4F	3M, 5F	4M, 4F
Insights (amount)	30	38	26
Insights-per-participant	3,75 (SD=2,43)	4,75 (SD=4,06)	3,25 (SD=1,48)
In-the-wild study (ITW)			
Duration	4h	4h	4h
Passers-by	134	155	130
Passively engaged	31	54	41
Actively engaged	8	27	19
Interviews (N)	4	14	7
Avg. interaction time	49" (σ=27)	1'40" (σ=45)	2'05" (σ=55)
Avg. age	37,5 (σ=5)	32 (σ=9)	30 (σ=17)
Gender	2M, 2F	6M, 8F	6M, 1F
Insights (amount)	5	19	8
Insights-per-participant	1,67 (SD=1)	2,39 (SD=1,1)	2 (SD=1,41)

Table 2. Demographic participant characteristics of (C)ITW.

Active engagement.

ITW. Out of 130 passers-by, 11 immediately grabbed a TP disc in the *physical* condition (avg. delay: 1" (σ=1), and analyzed its contents. Subsequently, they often searched for additional instructions on what to do next.

CITW. Participants in the *physical* condition revealed they were not hesitant to grab a disc because the installation "*looks playful*" and "*easy to work with*" (n=6). Participants in both other conditions revealed to be more cautious (n=11), mainly because of the perceived technical complexity (e.g. "*I might do something wrong*").

Insight depth.

ITW. In *touch*, participants compared multiple data dimensions, yet never reported any insight that contrasted 2 distinct dimensions. However, both *physical* and *mixed* seemed to motivate participants to explore the relationship between up to 2 dimensions, leading to deeper insights (e.g. "*more green leads to more criminality*", *mixed*).

CITW provided similar results. However, in *physical* and *mixed*, participants also reported comparisons between 3 datasets, the maximum number of possible combinations. During the interviews, almost all participants of *touch* (n=7) indicated they randomly explored the available dimensions, without hypothesizing a relationship between them. In contrast, in condition *physical* (n=7) and *mixed* (n=6), participants said they looked first at all possible dimensions available and then made a choice based on their personal interest to discover a specific relationship.

Social interaction.

ITW. We only noticed honeypot effects (n=4) between strangers during *physical*, such as discussions about the purpose of the telescope. The insights produced by social interactions between multiple passers-by were deeper.

CITW. In the *touch* and *physical* conditions, we noticed honeypot-effects when accidental passers-by asked participants about what they were doing (n=3). However, no insights were discussed with strangers, nor were they invited to join in. It was more evident in the CITW video log analysis that the discs were used without the display in condition *mixed*, and that participants stood at various locations around the telescope (in contrast to the display conditions, which were always manipulated at the front).

DISCUSSION

By evaluating our comparative between-subject experiment results, we observed that many results of ITW and CITW overlap although they were derived by different evaluation methodologies. However, while ITW was more ideal to identify quantitative indications of actual user engagement, CITW yielded more valuable insights on *why* these trends were happening, which allowed us to evaluate the effectiveness of the interaction method.

Participant Involvement

Passers-by in public environments often decline to participate, due to personal time constraints or other social circumstances. They tend to answer only the first few questions willfully, then evade any prolongation of the interview by giving too concise answers, or answers that are socially desirable (e.g. *"The installation was very nice, thank you!")*. Some participants respond in irrelevant ways, incorporating non-relevant topics (e.g. *"I think the city council [...] should not spend time on this kind of stuff!")*. Although ITW generally provided more participants in the same amount of time (4h), eliminating time and social constraints in CITW allowed us to explore the capabilities of the public installation more thoroughly and completely, as participants' answers were more considerate and better expressed. While the number of insights per participant was higher for CITW, ITW demonstrated the same insight distribution over the 3 conditions. ITW also showed that more passers-by interacted with *physical* than the other 2 conditions in identical environments. In CITW, we gained similar knowledge about popularity via interviews, yet also learned that this pattern was the result of the spatially distributed, low-tech and visually playful appearance of *physical.* As CITW supports full control over participant numbers and demographics, it allowed us to benchmark the 3 experimental conditions to each other. However, we remark that as the CITW participants worked in technical or administrative university positions, analytical feedback could have been exaggerated.

CITW leads to more and better qualitative results, which tended to compensate for the lack of quantitative measures.

Ecological validity

As with all in-situ studies [8], CITW balanced the need to control realism and external factors by providing participants with a prescriptive task within a representative environment. Due to its (semi-) public setting, CITW still allowed for unpredictable situations to occur that could influence results, such as curious passers-by, unexpected phone calls, weather elements, or traffic conditions. However, CITW requires a particular research design that facilitates spontaneous participant behavior (e.g. researchers leaving the vicinity unsuspiciously). Ideally, CITW could simulate group-based social interaction by inviting multiple participants. Because of its full control over both participant demographics and social relationships, we propose that this research methodology lends itself well for further research on multi-user and social interactions.

The public setting and absence of researchers allows still semi-realistic situations to occur in CITW, yet it requires a well-considered research design that artificially simulates spontaneous context of use.

Practical Matters

ITW often necessitates obtaining many permissions, such as to occupy public space, survey or film passers-by, respect privacy concerns, or acquire the approval of private persons to use their property. As CITW avoided frequent visual obstructions of unengaged passers-by, its 'cleaner' video logs allowed for a more thorough and efficient analysis of participant behavior. Moreover, as most practical matters and permits can be incorporated from the research design stage, CITW lends itself well for deploying additional or more sophisticated behavioral logging methods. For instance, CITW could include 'fake' participants that might behave in particular ways, or one could deliberately shift between ITW and CITW methodologies to assure ecologically correct participant demographics.

Overall, CITW allows for a more efficient yet controlled research context. Moreover, because of the overlapping results once participants are actively engaged, future ITW studies could consider skipping semi-structured interviews or detailed video analysis when circumstances are complex.

CONCLUSION

We benchmarked an in-the-wild versus a controlled in-the-wild methodology in the context of a-comparative between subject evaluation study. We analyzed their respective ecological validity, participant involvement and practical aspects. We discovered similar results although they were derived by different evaluation methodologies. Therefore, we propose that CITW offers a viable alternative when investigating the effectiveness of more complex interaction techniques in public settings. CITW allows researchers to work more efficiently in terms of participant involvement and the deployment of research methods, while the data is still gathered in relatively ecological valid, spontaneous context. However, we note that CITW should be considered complementary to ITW, as CITW is not yet ideal to capture ecological valid user engagements or quantitative results. In conclusion, as the field of public display progresses and its research questions are becoming more sophisticated, more research is required to investigate the true potential of CITW. For instance, it is still unknown how more complex user behaviors could be staged and analyzed while respecting ecological validity, whether ITW participants could be successfully invited to a CITW in order to increase participant demographics variety, or whether the (C)ITW results are actually representative of longer term usage.

REFERENCES

1. Alt, F., Schneegaß, S., Schmidt, A., Müller, J. and Memarovic, N. How to Evaluate Public Displays. In *Proc. PerDIS'12,* ACM New York, NY, USA, (2012).
2. Beyer, G., Alt, F., Müller, J., Schmidt, A., Isakovic, K., Klose, S., Schiewe, M. and Haulsen, I. Audience Behavior around Large Interactive Cylindrical Screens. In *Proc.CHI'11*, ACM (2011), 1021-1030.
3. Hornecker, E. and Nicol, E. What Do Lab-Based User Studies Tell Us About in-the-Wild Behavior?: Insights from a Study of Museum Interactives. In *Proc. DIS'12* ACM (2012), 358-367.
4. Kjeldskov, J., Skov, M. B., Als, B. S. and Høegh, R. T. Is It Worth the Hassle? Exploring the Added Value of Evaluating the Usability of Context-Aware Mobile Systems in the Field. In *MobileHCI'04*, Springer, 2004, 61-73.
5. Memarovic, N., Langheinrich, M., Alt, F., Elhart, I., Hosio, S. and Rubegni, E. Using Public Displays to Stimulate Passive Engagement, Active Engagement, and Discovery in Public Spaces. In *Proc MAB'12.* ACM (2012), 55-64.
6. North, C. Toward Measuring Visualization Insight. *IEEE CG&A 26*, 3 (2006), 6-9.
7. Oulasvirta, A. Field Experiments in Hci: Promises and Challenges. In *Future Interaction Design Ii*, Springer, 2009, 87-116.
8. Rogers, Y., Connelly, K., Tedesco, L., Hazlewood, W., Kurtz, A., Hall, R. E., Hursey, J. and Toscos, T. *Why It's Worth the Hassle:* The Value of in-Situ Studies When Designing Ubicomp, Springer, 2007.

Evaluation Probes

Anna Luusua[1], Johanna Ylipulli[2], Marko Jurmu[2], Henrika Pihlajaniemi[1], Piia Markkanen[1], Timo Ojala[2]
[1]Oulu School of Architecture, University of Oulu, Finland
[2]Faculty of Information Technology and Electrical Engineering, University of Oulu, Finland
firstname.lastname@oulu.fi

ABSTRACT
We introduce *evaluation probes* for conducting emic, experiential evaluation of urban technologies "in the wild" without direct researcher presence. We commence with a thorough discussion and analysis of the original cultural probes, used by Gaver, Dunne and Pacenti to gain design inspiration, and their subsequent variations. We develop the concept of evaluation probes through careful re-conceptualization and application of the cultural probes in three successive studies conducted in the wild. We recount and reflect on our use of evaluation probes and discuss their merits and limitations in experiential emic evaluation.

Author Keywords
Methodology; evaluation; in the wild; probes; experience.

ACM Classification Keywords
J.5 Arts and humanities; J.4 Social and behavioral sciences.

INTRODUCTION
The experiential evaluation of interactive installations "in the wild" [41] remains a challenge for the urban computing [28] research and design community. As computing becomes ever more pervasive in urban environments, researchers and designers of urban computing applications have become aware of the need to evaluate their works in the wild, i.e. outside of traditional research laboratories [7]. This work has already begun and much research has been conducted to evaluate interactive urban computing systems [27, 32]. However, those approaching the task of evaluative research from an *experiential* point of view [27] have stated that there is a lack of methods in the field. This is no task for strictly itemized check-lists; rather, there is a need to be able to flexibly gauge people's holistic experiences of what it is like to come face to face with interactivity in public urban places. We agree with Rogers [41] that a "central part of designing in the wild is evaluating prototypes in situ. This involves observing and recording what people do and how this changes over suitable periods of time". Researchers' *etic* perspectives on people's behaviour are important; but we also argue in favour of studying people's *emic* experiences with interactive technologies. Etic refers to researcher's own interpretations and categorizations of people's behaviour, whereas emic refers to insider knowledge: how people explain and categorize their own experiences. [3]

CHI 2015, April 18 - 23 2015, Seoul, Republic of Korea

http://dx.doi.org/10.1145/2702123.2702466

The task of developing these methods is not easy, as urban computing as a research field could be seen as involving several existing disciplines, and has strictly post-positivist roots [1, 21, 22]. Yet research questions may come in any form, and they require appropriate research methods in order to be answered. Issues relating to human experience, we argue, seem to be an area where this problematic is particularly visible. There is a crisis of experiential evaluation [2] that it is leading, we argue, to a much larger challenge in the urban computing community. The piecemeal addition and borrowing of individual methods and theories has proven difficult, if not impossible, as there is no common basis or understanding from where to proceed as a community. This, among other things, has led some researchers [e.g. 30, 31] to lament the lack of completely original methods and theories in HCI related fields. However, there is no need to reinvent the wheel many times over. In-the-wild urban computing studies are an inherently multidisciplinary field that must borrow from older research and design disciplines. This is not at all detrimental, and neither is urban computing alone in this regard. In the field of architecture and urban design (which always operates in real-word contexts), a similar variance of research questions and intentions prevails, and researchers in the field must necessarily operate within different research paradigms [20]. This is not seen as a problem, however, but researchers must always carefully state their position in order to avoid confusion and misinterpretation of their research methods and results; and, be keenly aware that all methods always come with epistemological roots and associated practices, accumulated through collective experience. Once care is taken to understand and respect the origins of theories, methodologies and paradigms, we can begin to build upon them, thinking about them in new ways, and finding uses for them outside of their original contexts.

In this spirit, we address the challenge of emic experiential in-the-wild evaluation of urban interactive technologies by introducing *evaluation probes* as a novel adaptation of the probes methodology [17, 18].

PROBES AS METHODOLOGY
Cultural probes were originally introduced by Gaver *et al.* [17] as a set of carefully designed objects that were

personally given to study participants. Importantly, cultural probes were based on the philosophical thinking of *artist-designers*; they could be described both as design research [e.g. 14], and as design through research. This very broad research methodology can be seen as falling under the general paradigm of emancipatory research, as opposed to (post)positivism and naturalism [20]. The profound aim was to inspire design by initiating a creative conversation between elderly people and designers; the probes were interventions meant to provoke new ways of thinking and to stimulate the imagination of both parties by distancing them from routine thinking. Instead of analysing the elderly participants' lives to supply tools to fulfill their needs, the researchers were more interested in opening up new design spaces through creating novel pleasures for them. Further, Gaver *et al.* openly stated that their probes were not intended to be analyzed at all. This is understandable in the research by design paradigm, wherein the act of designing is considered a tool for knowledge production. Overall, their approach was characterized by somewhat rebellious, subversive, critical and reflexive attitude.

Need for epistemological consistency

Cultural probes have been subsequently employed in various ways, raising enthusiasm for their applicability, but also concerns over misuse [4]. The term 'cultural probe' has been used to refer to many different approaches which bear some kind of similarity to the original probes, e.g. 'design probes' [33, 34], 'technology probes' [26] and 'urban probes' [37]. As the originators of the cultural probes approach did not state their epistemological and ontological groundings in much detail, there has been some confusion over their appropriate use. For example, Graham *et al.* [19] stated that probes have been used within different communities of practice, with different notions of vocabulary, practices and rigour; they pointed out that these communities have very different ideas concerning the interpretation of probe data. This also explained their own confusion over the designerly sensibility of cultural probes; they claimed that the discussion around probes cloaked 'design' in mystery, did not acknowledge accountability, and presented a view of design work that was not truly interdisciplinary. In a similar vein, Hemmings *et al.* [23] criticized the original approach, observing that Gaver *et al.*'s "inspiration" was largely a misnomer for acquiring ethnographic understandings, i.e. information about participants. We find these criticisms problematic, since they fail to understand and empathize with the essence of designerly thinking [9] and design research [14], which is based on reflective practice [42]. However, we do acknowledge that design knowledge and practices can appear opaque to readers who are not personally familiar with conducting design processes, as much of design knowledge is tacit [40] and involves lateral thinking [5]. For those interested, the aspect of design thinking and design inspiration in the context of probes has been more thoroughly explicated by Mattelmäki [33].

A fundamental premise in many papers [e.g. 19, 43] is that, as researchers, we must explain *how probes work*. This demand, when taken as a requirement for a more careful description of how knowledge is actually gleaned from acquired research materials, is understandable from a researcher's point of view and it must be taken seriously. However, we argue that rather than passively take the probes simply as they are, as an immutable recipe, we must also actively decide how we want them to work and boldly and reflectively experiment with them. Still, we agree with Boehner *et al.* [4] that methods that draw on cultural probes but change some of their essential aspects "cannot rest on the common acceptance of cultural probes for their validity." As such, "adaptations of the original cultural probes should be grounded in an awareness of which essential aspects of those probes are being adopted and which are not, and should justify those decisions." We agree that using methods without paying any attention to the larger methodology can be considered dangerous. This is comparable to the situation that is very often present in mixed methods research [10]: "Research involves a wide range of methodological tools, and we have to use many of these tools in a concrete research project. In other words, there is often a need to mix methods. However, we argue that this mix cannot be done without taking the ontological and epistemological dimensions into account. We call this perspective a 'critical methodological pluralism'." We deem it important, then, that when taking an approach and using it for other purposes, we must explicitly reflect on: 1) what aspects of the original methodology we are using and what we are leaving out, 2) what does this imply, and 3) what kind of epistemological commitments the methodology has, and does it match with our epistemological premises. In other words, we consider it crucial for the study to explicitly reflect on its *epistemological consistency.*

Essential features and epistemological commitments

To answer these questions, we must first elaborate on what exactly were the central features of probes. Others have also strived to tease out their essence. For example, Boehner *et al.* [4] identified four ways in which probes have been viewed by the HCI community: probes as packets, probes as data collection, probes as participatory, and probes as a sensibility. Graham *et al.* [21] identified five functions of probes common to most studies: to capture artifacts, yield (auto)biographical accounts, make the invisible (i.e. thoughts, attitudes, ideas, practices) visible, frame the participant as expert, and engage them in dialogue and conversation with designers and researchers. We agree that these features are important for the success of probes.

However, we argue that at the very core of the popularity of the methodology is (1) *the powerful metaphor of the "probe"* that effectively conveys the basic idea of how this type of research is carried out: a probe is an *artefact* that is sent into inaccessible places and situations in the real world to advance a researcher's understanding of that place, usually by collecting data. What is significant about the adoption of this metaphor is that it is used for qualitative explorations. A cultural probe bears some similarities to the *diary* method in social sciences [15] through which temporally organized written reflection is collected. While both can be described as participant self-documentation methods, probes are a more expansive and accommodating methodology, owing in large part to the difference in the two metaphors, i.e. diary vs. probe. Probes can contain multiple non-chronological tasks and they allow for various types of materials and modalities to be used, i.e. the use of various media, such as cut-and-paste pictures, photos, postcards and drawings. Further, we consider (2) *the aesthetically pleasing and playful presentation* of the original cultural probes as a central feature that made them work. Gaver *at al.* specifically mentioned that they wanted to make the probe package look like a gift, given to the participants as a gesture of appreciation in order to entice them to truly engage with it. This could take many forms, depending on the task at hand. (3) *Critical participant reflection* was also an inherent and important part of the original cultural probes, to help participants "think outside the box", for example through the use of exciting and unusual exercises or materials. Supporting open-minded or even critical thinking is intended to yield better, more ethical and socially sustainable design ideas. This cannot be done without (4) *developing an adequate rapport with the participants*; as such, it can be considered a crucial part of the methodology. This relationship should ideally be one of (5) *mutual learning/knowledge-production*; i.e. the researcher directs the participants' attention to something in their everyday life, and helps them reflect upon it through the probe materials. The materials in themselves function as an enabler and a reminder on the researchers' behalf. Overall, probes require (6) *open reflection and a critical attitude* in both their design and their analysis (or non-analytic use, as in the case of Gaver *et al.*). It is, then, a typical qualitative method in the sense that the researchers' skill and ethics play a key part in making sense of the results [20]. In our view, then, a probe is an artefact or a collection of artefacts that is intended to both help research participants generate experiential data through reflective assignments, and to collect this data as various kinds of empirical research materials from participants.

It would seem that most of the aspects attributed to probes in this article and in review papers fall under three major umbrella terms: either they describe the ***physical probe*** artefact, the ***participation*** that is inherent to them, or they refer to the ***aims*** of the probe (originally, of course, to gain design inspiration). These are guided by an overall critical and reflexive attitude that is typical to the epistemology of the emancipatory research paradigm [20]. Even though this is not the only way to try to grasp what is essential about probes, we find it nevertheless a very useful one, and for the purposes of our research, we use this framework (Fig. 1) to describe probes.

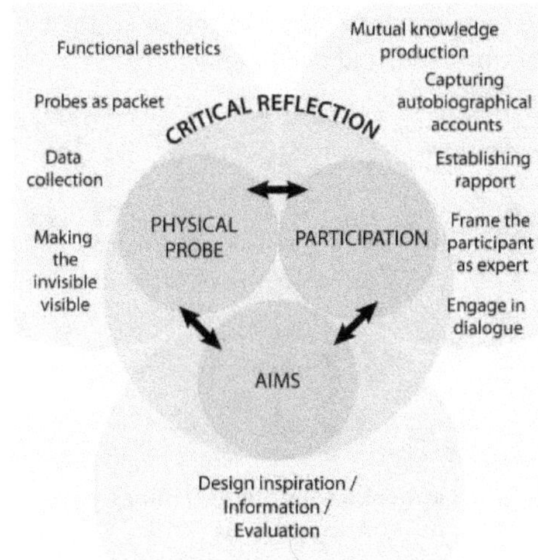

Figure 1. Conceptualizing the central elements of probes. © Anna Luusua 2015

EVOLUTION OF EVALUATION PROBES

Next we describe, in a chronological manner, how the new concept of evaluation probes evolved through our own work. An important first step in their development was the ICT diary probe, whose primary objective was to understand young people's attitudes, perspectives and experiences about information and communication technology and its use. In other words, the overall aim of the probe was to gain information. We conceptualized the ICT diary probe as a hybrid, an evolutionary step between a cultural probe, a diary and an interview [15]. Realizing the vast potential of the approach for real-world evaluation, we developed it further into the concept of evaluation probes in two successive studies. These were "pure" evaluation probes in that enticing materials were linked with designed artefacts. The first was an evaluation of a network of outdoor public displays (Display probe). The second was an evaluation of a more short-term installation of adaptive lighting (Adaptive lighting probe). These experimental studies provide an interesting mix of research contexts and purposes within which probes were used. Their analyses have yielded valuable results detailed in [29, 44, 45, 46]. This paper focuses on the novel method that produced these results.

(1) ICT diary probe

The ICT diary probe study was carried out in Oulu, Finland; a Nordic city of approximately 141 000 inhabitants, in 2011-2012. In this study, we had a broad scope and mainly ethnographic aims; therefore we describe this probe as an information probe. The overall ***aim*** of the study was to map young adults' everyday life with ICT in general, unveiling technology related attitudes, perceptions, experiences, skills and dreams. The motivation to employ a probe instead of more conventional ethnographic methods was the all-encompassing nature of ICT: it is used almost everywhere and in any situation, also in the home, which is a sensitive study site. A traditional ethnographic approach combining participatory observation and interviews was deemed too intrusive and challenging.

Figure 2. Scrapbooks from the ICT diary probe study. © Anna Luusua 2015

Before the probe was designed, the responsible researcher conducted four group discussions with 20 young adults to gain preliminary understanding of the current ICT practices of the target age group. These discussions, carried out in an open and informal manner in local cafes, gave invaluable insights and affected the design of the probe. In addition, before recruiting the rest of the participants, the probe was tested with five persons and polished according to their comments. The final ***physical probe*** was a small, colorful scrapbook, accompanied with three-pages set of printed images and a return envelope (Fig. 2). It included ten different tasks, which required self-expression through cut-and-paste pictures, sketches and informal writing, tracing how and how much young adults use different ICTs; how they use them in different places, both at home and in public; what kind of attitudes they have towards the use and towards particular devices; and what kind technology-related hopes and fears they have. In addition, the diary included a task where participants were asked to go out and try one of the large interactive displays, located in different public places in the city, and write about their experiences. Importantly, this one simple and open-ended task became an inspiration for the later developed evaluation probes.

Concerning ***participation***, participants were asked to keep the scrapbook at least for two weeks and return it to the researcher by mail. Then they were called to participate in group interviews that were conducted in a conversational spirit and structured around the tasks in the scrapbooks. The participants could reflect on the themes and compare their views which also made the differences within the age group very visible for the researcher. The interviews lasted for 1.5-2.5 hours and they were recorded and transcribed. In total, 48 participants filled in the scrapbook and participated in the interviews. The return rate was excellent as the probe was initially given to 56 participants; this was probably due to the fact that the researcher sent polite reminders by email every week and was ready to give extra time for the participants. Further, a majority of the participants reported that they had found completing the diary probe enjoyable. However, some also stated that it was not a conventional diary, reflecting its hybrid nature. The ones completing the diary and interview were rewarded with two film tickets and a chance to participate in a lottery where they could win a gift card to a restaurant.

The returned scrapbooks were filled with essays, shorter notes, drawings, cartoons, sketches of floorplans and picture collages, and hundreds of pages of transcribed interviews. The "thickness" and broadness of the data have allowed us to look at young adults' ICT reality from many different perspectives [29, 44, 45, 46]. This richness can be contrasted with the fact that collecting the material took a long time. However, it probably would not have been any faster to conduct several smaller studies.

(2) Display probe

The Display probe was the first proper *evaluation probe* study, designed to evaluate participants' experiences of a design artefact; in this case a network of public displays in an authentic urban setting. The research site was again Oulu, Finland, where a rich pervasive computing infrastructure has been deployed. This includes a network of 17 situated displays, which have been in operation since 2009. The displays are installed at pivotal indoor and outdoor locations, including the pedestrian area at the heart of the city. As such, these public displays are a familiar sight to the inhabitants of the city. Our study focused on the outdoor displays dispersed around the city center, i.e. at the pedestrian area and the nearby marketplace. At the time of their installation, the displays were a novel technology, and to this day, this network of public interactive displays remains the largest of its kind deployed for research purposes in a city center [36]. As such, it poses a wealth of unanswered research questions.

The ***aim*** of the study was to explore local people's perceptions of the public displays, and how they experience the displays as a part of the streetscape in their everyday living environment from the point of view of aesthetics. The probe, then, can be described as an evaluation probe, as it was intended to specifically evaluate the experience of a particular design artefact. Further, the evaluated artifact, in this case a public display, is an integral part of the evaluation probe package; a necessary feature which sets it apart from cultural probes. This, in turn, affected other aspects of the probe; e.g. the design of the physical probe materials and the manner of participation. The probe was not meant to directly inspire design ideas, but rather to delve deeply into the experiences of our participants. As such, these probes were intended for in-depth qualitative analysis from their inception.

Participants needed to be able to carry the ***physical probe*** materials with them outdoors in winter and autumn conditions, even though they were not required to write on the spot. This is why we decided to gather all the material in a single notebook (Fig. 3). This, we have discovered, was a necessary practicality in the design of the evaluation probe, to enable participants to carry them comfortably. The content of the notebooks was carefully designed to accommodate thoughts, opinions and ideas in an open-ended manner on several themes, e.g. the location of the chosen display, the display itself, and the general environment around it. Participants were instructed to express themselves freely through sketches, writings and photography. We specifically mentioned that the more creative types of writing, such as poetry, drawings and anything else they might deem useful, like cut-and-paste pictures, were allowed. One assignment specifically asked for visual input in the form of a photograph or a drawing. These proved useful, since a few participants clearly favoured visuals to text, and their sketches always conveyed thoughts that were different from their writings. Interestingly, the sketches and the one poem returned all conveyed *emotion*; specifically that the displays sometimes looked *lonely* out there on the streets. The probe methodology, then, not only seems to support different kinds of communication styles, but the different modes of communication seem to yield different kinds of knowledge. This makes the probes methodology more suitable to us than, e.g., the diary method, as we found the more expansive probe metaphor to be more conducive to participant creativity.

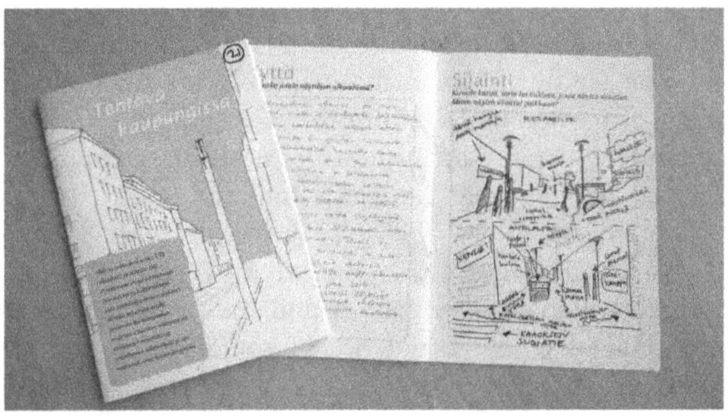

Figure 3. The Display probe notebook. © Anna Luusua 2015

In terms of ***participation***, in accordance with our research agenda, we focused on young adults aged 20-29. The probe was conducted twice: the first probe in the winter (Feb-Mar 2013) had 20 participants and the second probe in the fall (Sep-Oct 2013) had 21 participants. The two probes conducted in different times of the year were motivated by our desire to evaluate seasonal effects on the participants' experiences. We handed out the notebooks individually, instructing and discussing the assignment with each participant. The participants seemed to be highly interested in our study and presented many questions about ourselves and our work. This, we argue, helped us to bridge the distance between our participants and ourselves, and to create a more positive attitude towards the assignment. However, we were pleased to also discover that the participants' answers contained both critical and positive remarks concerning their experience. This might be due to the fact that the two researchers conducting the participant recruitment had not been personally involved in the design of the displays. Thus, they were able to tell the participants that they were merely investigating the deployment and the whole idea of public displays, and that they valued all their opinions. All participants returned the probe notebook, although one had misunderstood the assignment and used an indoor display. The participants were rewarded with movie tickets.

The data gained from the two probes was highly interesting. While it painted a varied picture of experiences and attitudes, several patterns began to emerge already in preliminary analysis. Some of them focused on usability issues, demonstrating that the evaluation probe can certainly help with more open-ended usability evaluation. Many experiences dealt with aesthetic preferences and personal feelings that the participants attached to the displays. They also provided us knowledge about how they viewed this kind of a novel intrusion into their living environment in general. Further, the participants' experiences were found to be strikingly different during the two seasons that posed varied sensory settings [44].

As this was an entirely new application of the probes methodology, needs for further development of the concept did arise. The probes could easily be complemented with group discussions or co-design workshops at the end. After all, the lay expertise developed by our participants would be highly useful in the design of future technologies. Secondly, the probe could be complemented with additional methods, e.g. some preliminary homework or participant video recording; or researchers might conduct traditional semi-structured theme interviews prior to the assignment. This depends largely on research context; what kind of knowledge is sought, and what it will be used for, as illustrated in the Adaptive lighting probe.

(3) Adaptive lighting probe

The ***aim*** of this study was to evaluate people's experiences of an adaptive lighting installation in an indoor commercial space. Specifically, the goal was once again to produce rich data on people's experiences for in-depth analyses. The real-world setting presented many challenges from a research point of view. The objective of the new lighting design was to attract customers to the installation area and to invite them to spend more time browsing the products, thus affecting their shopping behavior. The installation was designed and set up in a relatively small and restricted area in the women's clothing section of a department store. The overall illumination of the area was reduced from its surrounding areas. The merchandise and focal points, such as mannequin dolls and background panels, were accentuated by illuminating them with spotlights of static white light (Scenario 1), adaptive white light (Scenario 2), and adaptive coloured and white light (Scenario 3). Overall, the adaptive lighting was meant to serve customers by enabling them to see the products better and enhance their experience. The lighting installation functioned in Oct-Jan, running continuously in a three-day rotation of Scenario 1, Scenario 2 and Scenario 3. The probe study was conducted during the course of approximately one month in Oct-Nov.

All ***participants*** were females ranging from 35 to 55 years in age since the selected store site contained only women's clothing. The evaluation probe consisted of three visits to the lighting installation site, and a package containing three notebooks and a calendar; however, the probe was also amended with a preliminary semi-structured theme interview lasting approximately 30 minutes. It explored themes relating to commercial spaces, their own shopping behavior, lighting in general, lighting in commercial spaces and the idea of adaptive lighting. The interviews gave us valuable insight into our participants' background and their thoughts about their own shopping behaviour. Several participants noticed the prevalence of lighting related questions. We did not deem it necessary to hide this from our participants; on the contrary, the interviewer told them that they were not test subjects, but partners in the study. The participants were rewarded with cosmetic products of approximately 20 euros in value.

Figure 4. Notebooks in the Adaptive lighting probe package. © Anna Luusua 2015

The ***physical probe*** materials contained three notebooks and a calendar to plan and mark three visits. The notebook format was useful to distinguish the visits from each other, and they were convenient for our participants to carry. A box of items, in the style of cultural probes, would have been a nuisance to carry around. Once again, participants were encouraged to express themselves in any way they preferred; by writing, sketching, or even adding pictures from other sources, e.g. magazines. Each of the notebooks (Fig. 4) was sealed with a sticker, and participants were instructed to break the seals only after having finished the previous notebook. All in all, each participant filled out three notebooks; one for each visit they were required to make in the department store. On each occasion, a different lighting scenario was in operation. The different lighting scenarios, then, were scheduled to rotate on three consecutive days. The participants were given a colour-coded calendar, where each day corresponded with a notebook. The notebooks' colour scheme matched with that of the calendar.

The orchestration of this fairly complex experimental setting proved to be slightly difficult for us and the participants. Some participants actually visited the store on a wrong day. Further, two holidays occurred within the visitation period, which made the schedule even more complex to understand. Therefore, the practicalities of organizing an evaluation consisting of three visits which necessarily must be done in a certain order are probably too much for participants who are operating independently. In future studies, a comparative evaluation of several scenarios using the evaluation probe method could benefit from a setting which would allow the participants to launch each scenario themselves on site by e.g. a mobile device request.

Despite these difficulties, the probe provided us with hundreds of pages and recorded minutes of experiences and perceptions in the form of sketches, writings, pictures and audio/video. The preliminary interview alone provided us with a rich data set that can be analysed from various points of view: either as background information for helping us in analysing the notebooks, or, for example, as stand-alone material for researching and analysing the participants' attitudes concerning commercial spaces and their lighting. Similarly, with the notebooks, we obtained in-depth accounts of the participants' experiences with the three different lighting scenarios in a real department store context [38].

Analysis of evaluation probe data

In all our studies, we used qualitative analysis methods, emphasizing iterative readings of data to understand phenomena. After an initial free-form reading, we structured the materials and our remarks about them into emergent themes [e.g. 6]. These were also organized into matrices to facilitate comparative readings between participants. This thematization and the original data have been analyzed with the aid of theoretical concepts, which have acted as lenses through which we have scrutinized the data. These theoretical lenses include, e.g. *emplacement* [39] and *urban rhythms* [16] in our studies [44, 45]. As previously stated, Gaver *et al.*'s use of cultural probe data was non-analytic. However, we consider the in-depth analysis of the rich evaluation probe data to be central to its utilization and distilling new knowledge.

DISCUSSION

In this paper, we have argued for the re-conceptualization of cultural probes towards evaluative research. Through our methodological discussion of probes, we concluded that the original cultural probes contained finely tuned facets that require thoughtful consideration in their application. We argued for epistemological consistency in the design, execution and analysis of probes, especially in multidisciplinary research settings. We accepted functional aesthetics, critical reflection, establishing a rapport and mutual knowledge production, as well as framing the participant as an expert as central features of the methodology.

Our approach combined these with (1) evaluative aims and (2) in-depth theory-based analysis. Thus, the probe consisted of both the evaluated design artefact as well as the package given to participants. By no means can this new approach be regarded as a cultural probe anymore, and therefore we decided to call it evaluation probes ("EP"). Next we discuss the key benefits and limitations of the evaluation probes discovered in our empirical studies.

Truly "in the wild" with no direct researcher presence

Firstly, using EP we gained *experiences that were as close to real life as possible* in an emic study, since the users were able to choose the location and the time for using the artefacts in peace, without direct researcher presence, taking their time to hang around, observe the locale and play with the artefact. This, we argue, produces more realistic experiences for participants, which is important in in-the-wild studies with the objective to gain real-world knowledge about design artefacts.

Support for different communication styles

Secondly, EP *supports different kinds of participants' communication and learning styles* [12]. This is especially important for in-the-wild studies in which participants experience the research setting with all their senses. In our studies, EP created room for many different kinds of ways to express one's thoughts: some participants clearly preferred writing; some were more visual and expressed themselves with drawings and clippings; and some made only short notes in the notebook but verbalized their perspectives at length in an interview. However, the probe materials gave everybody a similar opportunity to reflect on their experiences or practices over a longer period of time.

Combining a probe with an interview was found useful, especially regarding the studies' aim to produce in-depth qualitative knowledge. For example, in the ICT diary probe study, the scrapbooks acted as a preliminary assignment that led to more profound and mature interviews. Further improvements would include the wider inclusion of different sorts of sensory experiences and learning and communication styles through the use of various media. Participants might be given video cameras or audio devices for these purposes. These methods have already been utilised in sensory ethnography [39].

Critical reflection teases out fresh, unexpected views

Thirdly, EP encouraged the participants to critically reflect upon the artefacts and also their everyday routines. The participants gained a kind of lay expertise on the subject that also challenged the traditional roles of experts and lay persons. For example, while returning the Display probe materials, many participants noted that they now saw the displays differently because they had had a chance to both use them and to reflect upon what the displays meant to them personally. Previously, most participants had not given them as much as a thought in their everyday lives, although they all knew about them. As a result, the participants' view of the world had changed somewhat as a direct result of the probe study. In the ICT Diary probe, some even reported that they had started to observe other people's technology use. Everyday life practices tend to become invisible but the notebook made them visible for the participants. Similarly, the participants of the Adaptive lighting probe noted that they had begun to think of lighting differently over the course of the study.

The thickness and richness of the material itself greatly supports the goal of in-the-wild studies by providing fresh real-world perspectives for designers and researchers. The participants are recruited, and remain, as trusted partners throughout the study. As one possible improvement, the lay expertise created along the study could be later explored further in co-design workshops. As such, EP spans between the information probe and the cultural probe; through understanding participant experiences of the design artefact we can move towards further design ideas rooted in empirical knowledge. We would be especially interested in seeing a process where both cultural probes and evaluation probes would be used at the different stages of a particular design process.

Many types of knowledge from a single EP study

Fourth, *a single EP study can produce many types of knowledge.* EP typically produces information concerning usability on a practical level, but also knowledge relating to e.g. emotional experiences. The latter is encouraged by the multimodal communication styles supported by EP. As such, EP is an efficient method for conducting open-ended, informal and rich evaluation "in the wild". However, *probes are also able to produce much more in-depth knowledge that is valuable in and of itself, and, theorized further, can help build and develop empirically-based design theory* on a more fundamental level, as was the case in our own EP studies. The concept can be compared to ethnography – e.g. in our first case these two were merged – as both are qualitative approaches that enable us to map and understand people's experiences and everyday life.

The outcomes of studies where ethnography and design meet have often been successful [e.g. 8]; nevertheless, Dourish and Bell [13] highlighted how ethnography can produce two kinds of results, both relevant to design: (1) design recommendations, often derived from empirical aspects of ethnographic work, and (2) "profound design guidance" born from the analytical aspects of ethnographical work. The first type of results can provide relatively direct guidelines how to proceed with some limited design challenge; the latter is "where the substantive intellectual achievement can be found", and it tends to open up new design space rather than closing it down towards 'the best solution'. In other words, *we call for profound analysis and the use of theoretical lenses also when analyzing probe materials*, as discussed above; although this was not the initial purpose of Gaver *et al.*, it can result in significant insights when applying probes in different ways.

Efficient and flexible evaluation

Fifth, in our studies we have found that *EP enables researchers and designers to conduct evaluative research efficiently*. If the assignment is carefully designed, the participants are able to proceed fairly independently. EP, then, offers a viable alternative to "rapid ethnography" or "quick-and-dirty ethnography" [35]. Participants are able to spend several days, or even weeks, with the assignment, processing the experience presented to them and exploring their own thoughts. Further, EP is *time flexible*, as demonstrated in the Display probe. While the displays have been deployed in the city for five years, it was especially beneficial that the EP study could be extended for longer or shorter periods of time, and iterated several times over with a reasonable effort. Also, *EP yielded compatible and complementary data to other data sets that we have obtained with other means*. For example, the public displays have generated a wealth of quantitative usage data; the emic, experiential data yielded by the Display probe was able to explain particular phenomena in the quantitative data [44]. Further, our studies show that *EP is able to accommodate different kinds of research settings*. This is especially important in evaluative research, since research settings are as varied as they are numerous.

Meta-participation: participant experiences of probes

The majority of our participants liked the overall experience and tasks, and they found the colorful and playful design of the probes appealing and motivating. However, some of them thought that the openness of the questions was difficult or confusing, and they wished they had been given more specific questions. This attitude was also present in all our probe participants' commentary on the concept. Some participants felt that they had already answered a question on a previous page. This was perfectly acceptable, as the questions were meant as a *reflective* framework for the participants. We conducted our readings very freely to foster their personal communication styles. Furthermore, the tasks and questions in the probes were purposefully meant to be as open as possible to allow for participants' own perceptions.

Limitations and caveats

Although EP produces knowledge through participants' critical reflection, this also presents a limitation to researchers, as these are not unreflective, humdrum everyday experiences. In other words, there can be no reflection without detachment, which can also be seen as a limitation. The experiences recorded through EP are the experiences of actively thinking participants. Obviously, external observation can be used to observe unknowing passers-by, but their thoughts cannot be documented at all. EP takes us to the limits of what we can learn about experiences, but no further.

Furthermore, the critical reflection of the participants and possible subsequent interchange of roles can also complicate the analysis of the EP data. For example, in the Adaptive lighting probe one participant wrote that she was not at all interested in the clothes, as she was really observing the area and taking notes. Some participants commented on other customers' behavior at the study site, clearly adopting the role of an observer. Their perspective is thus moved away from a normal shopping experience, which needs to be acknowledged while analysing the data and interpreting the results, as reflection automatically distances the participants from their daily routines.

In general, the thickness and richness of the EP data can make it relatively hard to analyse. Only the researchers' imagination limits the different communication modalities than can be included in EP. However, the researchers should carefully anticipate the kinds of data that will be produced and ask themselves whether they will be able to make sense of it. Of course, this kind of freedom of expression also requires that participants are ready to use their creativity and invest time in the study. Rapport-building and enticing materials, then, are absolutely necessary ingredients, making the successful implementation of an EP a delicate balancing act between traditional researcher skills and designer skills.

The use of EP is demanding, as it requires a wide array of skills from researchers, from drafting relevant research questions to designing and producing the probe materials and the research setting, all the way to building rapport with participants and conducting possible interviews and co-design workshops. Thus, it is most useful for heterogeneous but closely knit research and design teams where each individual understands the way in which EP produces knowledge. A foundational understanding of qualitative research and analysis can be considered necessary for conducting an EP study. Similarly, an understanding of the design artifact and the basics of design research is useful.

An EP must be tailored for the participant group that we wish to engage; the participants' age, gender, and cultural background play an important part in this. Fortunately, the inherent flexibility of EP and the underlying probes approach enables this. The subsequent analysis of the EP data must be conducted accordingly with the tailoring and the participant group in mind.

The researchers' non-presence also means that no additional questions can be asked while the participant is completing the assignment. Thus, the setting must be carefully considered both in the design and analysis of EP. Overly complex settings are not likely to succeed. Any involved technologies should function at least reasonably reliably to provide the intended experience. If the designed artefact is at its early development stages, or its functionality cannot be guaranteed to a reasonable extent, using EP is probably not the best option. A more suitable qualitative method in these cases might be participant observation coupled with an interview.

However, the lack of researcher presence does not remove the researchers' accountability and subjectivity from the research process. EP is still designed by the researchers and the results are interpreted by them, which calls for highly reflexive attitude [11, 42]. Further, when using EP as a part of a design process, the designer's influence within the process must be acknowledged.

CONCLUSIONS

We presented evaluation probes for conducting emic, experiential evaluation in the wild without researcher presence. We were motivated by the probes methodology being so useful that we deemed it not only acceptable but imperative to develop it for uses outside its original intended domain. However, its use requires open reflection and a highly ethical and critical attitude. Thus, while we are aware of the excited and somewhat haphazard manner in which new types of probes have been developed in design fields, we decided to carefully try and extend it into a new, useful direction. We laid a theoretical foundation for re-conceptualizing and adapting the probe methodology into evaluative in-the-wild practice, basing our approach on a careful analysis of the original cultural probes. Their central features include the functional aesthetics and playful nature of the *physical probe artefacts*; *participation* through building a good rapport with the participants, leading to mutual knowledge production; and the overall *critical and reflexive sensibility* that penetrates the whole methodology. However, we then parted ways with the *aim* of gaining design inspiration of the cultural probes. Throughout the three consecutive studies, we adapted the cultural probe into an evaluation probe that consists of the evaluated design artefact and participant materials, for conducting emic, experiential evaluation of the artefact in-the-wild.

Based on the empirical findings of our studies, we argue that the evaluation probes are highly useful for evaluating urban computing applications from an experiential point of view in the wild. The continued improvement of experiential evaluation methods in urban computing studies is of crucial importance to the well-being and quality of life of urban inhabitants, the number of which is rapidly increasing globally. To introduce computing into the everyday living environment of people is a task that aims to engage the senses, emotions and needs of urban inhabitants on a daily basis. It is the responsibility of the designers and researchers to grasp the consequences of their decisions to the best of their ability. For this purpose, we need methodologies and methods that address these issues.

Finally, evaluation probes are a qualitative research approach which can also be seen as a part of the critical research paradigm, with its accompanying epistemological and ontological groundings. However, through understanding it thoroughly and respecting its qualities, we can also compliment probe materials with other data sets, including quantitative ones. As such, we emphasize the foundational meaning of epistemological consistency and understanding to the larger urban computing research and design community.

ACKNOWLEDGEMENTS

We thank our participants, the Academy of Finland, TEKES, and the Nokia Foundation for their support.

REFERENCES

1. Bardzell, J. and Bardzell, S. A great and troubling beauty: cognitive speculation and ubiquitous computing. *Personal and Ubiquitous Computing* 18, 4 (2014), 779-794.
2. Bargas-Avila, J. A. and Hornbæk, K. Old wine in new bottles or novel challenges: a critical analysis of empirical studies of user experience. In *Proc. CHI 2011*, ACM Press (2011), 2689-2698.
3. Bodley, J. H. *Cultural anthropology: Tribes, states, and the global system*. Altamira Press, Lanham, 2011.
4. Boehner, K., Vertesi, J., Sengers, P. and Dourish, P. How HCI interprets the probes. In *Proc. CHI 2007*, ACM Press (2007), 1077-1086.
5. de Bono, E. *Lateral Thinking*. Penguin Books, London, 1990.
6. Bryman, A. *Social research methods*. Oxford University Press, 2012.
7. Chamberlain, A., Crabtree, A., Rodden, T., Jones, M. and Rogers, Y. Research in the wild: understanding 'in the wild' approaches to design and development. In *Proc. DIS 2012*, ACM Press (2012), 795-796.
8. Clarke, A. J. *Design Anthropology: Object Culture in the 21st Century*. Springer, 2011.
9. Cross, N. Designerly ways of knowing. *Design Studies* 3, 4 (1982), 221-227.
10. Danermark, B., ed. *Explaining society: Critical realism in the social sciences*. Routledge, London, 2002.
11. Davies, C. *Reflexive Ethnography: A Guide to Researching Selves and Others*. Routledge, London, 1999.
12. Denig, S. Multiple intelligences and learning styles: Two complementary dimensions. *The Teachers College Record* 106, 1 (2004), 96-111.
13. Dourish, P. and Bell, G. *Divining a digital future: Mess and mythology in ubiquitous computing*. MIT Press, Cambridge, 2011.
14. Downton, P. *Design Research*. RMIT University Press, Melbourne, 2003.
15. Elliott, H. The use of diaries in sociological research on health experience. *Sociological Research Online* 2, 2 (1997). http://www.socresonline.org.uk/2/2/7.html
16. Galloway, A. Intimations of everyday life: Ubiquitous computing and the city. *Cultural Studies* 18, 2-3 (2004), 384-408.
17. Gaver, B., Dunne, T. and Pacenti, E. Design: Cultural probes. *Interactions* 6, 1 (1999), 21-29.
18. Gaver, W., Boucher, A., Pennington, S. and Walker, B. 2004. Cultural probes and the value of uncertainty. *Interactions* 11, 5 (2004), 53-56.

19. Graham, C., Cheverst, K. and Rouncefield, M. Whose probe is it anyway? Workshop on Appropriate Methods for Design in Complex and Sensitive Settings at OzCHI 2005.

20. Groat, L. and Wang, D. *Architectural Research Methods*. Wiley, New York, 2002.

21. Harrison, S., Sengers, P. and Tatar, D. Making epistemological trouble: Third-paradigm HCI as successor science. *Interacting with Computers* 23, 5 (2011), 385-392.

22. Harrison, S., Tatar, D. and Sengers, P. The three paradigms of HCI. alt. chi 2007.

23. Hemmings, T., Crabtree, A., Rodden, T., Clarke, K. and Rouchefield, M. Probing the probes. In *Proc. PDC 2002,* ACM Press (2002), 42-50.

24. Hogan, R. Engendered autobiographies: The diary as a feminine form. *Prose Studies: History, Theory, Criticism* 14, 2 (1991), 95–107.

25. Hosio, S., Kostakos, V., Kukka, H., Jurmu, M., Riekki, J. and Ojala, T. From school food to skate parks in a few clicks: Using public displays to bootstrap civic engagement of the young. In *Proc. Pervasive* 2012, Springer (2012), 425-442.

26. Hutchinson, H., Mackay, W., Westerlund, B., Bederson, B., Druin, A., Plaisant, C., Beaudouin-Lafon, M., Conversy, C., Evans, H., Hansen, H., Roussel, N. and Eiderbäck, B. Technology probes: Inspiring design for and with families. In *Proc. CHI 2003*, ACM Press (2003), 17-24.

27. Keskinen, T., Hakulinen, J., Heimonen, T., Turunen, M., Sharma, S., Miettinen, T. and Luhtala, M. Evaluating the experiential user experience of public display applications in the wild. In *Proc. MUM 2013*, ACM Press (2013), Article 7.

28. Kindberg, T., Chalmers, M. and Paulos, E. Guest editors' introduction: Urban computing. *IEEE Pervasive Computing* 6, 3 (2007), 18-20.

29. Kukka, H., Luusua, A., Ylipulli, J., Suopajärvi, T., Kostakos, V. and Ojala, T. From cyberpunk to calm urban computing: Exploring the role of technology in the future cityscape. *Technological Forecasting and Social Change* 84 (2014), 29-42.

30. Kuutti, K. HCI and design - uncomfortable bedfellows? In Binder, T. Löwgren, J. and Malmborg, L. *(Re)searching the Digital Bauhaus*. Springer, London, 2009.

31. Liu, Y., Goncalves, J., Ferreira, D., Xiao, B., Hosio, S. and Kostakos, V. CHI 1994-2013: Mapping two decades of intellectual progress through co-word analysis. In *Proc. CHI 2014*, ACM Press (2014), 3553-3562.

32. Marshall, P., Morris, R., Rogers, Y., Kreitmayer, S. and Davies, M. Rethinking 'multi-user': an in-the-wild study of how groups approach a walk-up-and-use tabletop interface. In *Proc. CHI 2011*, ACM Press, 3033-3042.

33. Mattelmäki, T. *Design probes*. Aalto University, Helsinki, 2006.

34. Mattelmäki, T. and Battarbee, K. Empathy probes. In *Proc. PDC 2002*, ACM Press (2002), 266-271.

35. Millen, D. R. Rapid ethnography: time deepening strategies for HCI field research. In *Proc. DIS 2000,* ACM Press (2000), 280-286.

36. Ojala, T., Kostakos, V., Kukka, H., Heikkinen, T., Linden, T., Jurmu, M., Kruger, F. and Zanni, D. Multipurpose interactive public displays in the wild: Three years later. *Computer* 45, 5 (2012), 42-49.

37. Paulos, E. and Jenkins, T. 2005. Urban probes: encountering our emerging urban atmospheres. In *Proc. CHI 2005*, ACM Press (2005), 341-350.

38. Pihlajaniemi, H., Luusua, A., Markkanen, P., Herneoja, A. and Pentikäinen, V. Experiencing Adaptive Retail Lighting in a Real-World Pilot. In *Proc. Experiencing Light 2014,* Eindhoven University of Technology (2014), 90-93.

39. Pink, S. *Doing Sensory Ethnography*. Sage, London, 2009.

40. Polanyi, M. *The Tacit Dimension.* University of Chicago Press, 1966.

41. Rogers, Y. Interaction design gone wild: striving for wild theory. *Interactions* 18, 4 (2011), 58-62.

42. Schön, D. *The reflective practitioner: How professionals think in action.* Basic books, 1983.

43. Wallace, J., McCarthy, J., Wright, P. and Olivier, P. Making design probes work. In *Proc. CHI 2013*, ACM Press (2013), 3441-3450.

44. Ylipulli J., Luusua A., Kukka H. and Ojala, T. Winter is coming: Introducing climate sensitive urban computing. In *Proc. DIS 2014*, ACM Press (2014), 647–656.

45. Ylipulli, J., Suopajärvi, T., Ojala, T., Kostakos, V. and Kukka, H. Municipal WiFi and interactive displays: Appropriation of new technologies in public urban spaces. *Technological Forecasting and Social Change* 89 (2014), 145-160.

46. Ylipulli, J. and Suopajärvi, T. Contesting ubicomp visions through ICT practices: Power negotiations in the meshwork of a technologised city. *International Communication Gazette* 75, 5-6 (2013), 538-554.

Real-World Affinity Diagramming Practices: Bridging the Paper–Digital Gap

Gunnar Harboe **Elaine M. Huang**
University of Zurich
Binzmühlestrasse 14, IFI, 8050 Zürich, Switzerland
{harboe,huang}@ifi.uzh.ch

ABSTRACT
Despite the availability of computer-based alternatives both for desktop and touch screen systems, a number of cooperative work processes still commonly rely on simple paper sticky notes. In this paper, we present the first in-depth investigation of the real-world practices of people who use paper-based affinity diagrams and similar clustering processes in their work, in order to identify challenges and requirements for technology support. Findings from retrospective and artifact-based interviews with 13 participants suggest ways in which the rich interactions and material affordances offered by paper are key to the process. Instead of seeking to replicate interactions with paper on a screen, simpler transfer of information between the physical and digital worlds has the potential to address many of the most pressing problems experienced in practice. We describe different types of technology integration and augmentation, with preliminary recommendations for different situations.

Author Keywords
Affinity diagrams; cooperative data analysis; paper clustering; sticky notes; augmented paper; interview study

ACM Classification Keywords
H.5.m. Information interfaces and presentation (e.g., HCI): Miscellaneous.

INTRODUCTION
A common class of in-person cooperative work in many professions involves arranging pieces of paper (sticky notes, photos, drawings, etc.) on a surface such as a wall or a table. As a particular case of this kind of work we consider *affinity diagramming*, a method that is frequently used for several different purposes in the fields of Human–Computer Interaction (HCI), design, anthropology and management [2,4,22].

Affinity diagramming is a method that has been addressed by a significant number of computer systems designed to support it and remedy perceived problems. However, despite these attempts, going back many years, the method still appears to be predominantly performed on paper. [12]

Design efforts may have been hampered by a lack of data on how people actually perform affinity diagramming currently – their experiences and practices. Empirical study has mainly been limited to user tests staged according to protocols pre-defined by the researchers. Different textbook descriptions differ, and may anyway not be representative of actual practices. We therefore believe that there is a need in the research community for a grounded understanding of real-world practices and the challenges users face.

To fully achieve that will require detailed in-situ observations. As a first step, however, we describe an interview study with 13 participants that looks at how paper-based affinity diagramming and similar methods are practiced "in the wild." Building on our account of this and how it differs from previous literature, we present findings about the pragmatic reasons for and the implications of working on paper. We then describe important variations in the process as well as commonalities with other methods, and discuss the transitions of material into and out of the diagrams and between different forms of representation. Based on these findings, we identify key design factors, and suggest alternative ways digital technology can support the different variations of the method. Our conclusions argue for bridging the gap between paper and digital representations of data, and for devising flexible support suitable to different scenarios. The overall contribution of this work is two-fold:

- We present findings from the first in-depth study of real-world affinity diagramming and similar methods, commonly used in HCI, which differ from previous descriptions on a number of points.
- We interpret these findings to highlight two key factors for design, diagram lifetime and transitions between digital and physical, in order to inform the design of computer support for affinity diagramming, and perhaps for paper-based cooperative work more generally.

BACKGROUND AND RELATED WORK
Affinity diagramming (also known as the KJ method [2,4]) is a technique variously recommended for data analysis, idea-generation/planning, and consensus-based decision-making. The process generally takes the form of arranging paper notes on a surface. In affinity diagramming, items

CHI 2015, April 18 - 23, 2015, Seoul, Republic of Korea

ACM 978-1-4503-3145-6/15/04...$15.00
http://dx.doi.org/10.1145/2702123.2702561

(e.g. ideas, interview quotes, observations) are written down on separate notes, which are placed one by one on a surface such as a table or a wall. As the notes are placed, and in moving them around later, they are clustered based on their *affinity*: their similarity or relevance to a shared topic. This leads to the creation of groups, which are labeled and recursively clustered. The process repeats until the highest level has only a few groups and the initially unstructured items have been organized bottom-up. [2,4,22]

Affinity diagramming, then, is one particular formalization of spatial clustering and organization. As such, it has significant similarities with methods such as card sorting[1], storyboarding, laying out designs visually [16], mind-mapping, etc. Indeed, as we shall see, these methods often blend into each other in actual practice.

Textbook Descriptions

There has been relatively little empirical research into how affinity diagramming is performed "in the wild", so the best descriptions of the method come from the instructional literature, mainly found in textbooks and online references [2,4,10,25]. (The oft-cited original publications by Kawakita [13,14] have proved so difficult to track down that we suspect they may only be in private circulation.) While these sources agree in most general aspects, they differ in important detail: e.g. Brassard [4] speaks of diagrams of slightly more than a hundred notes done in 30–45 minutes by 3–4 people, while Holtzblatt, Wendell and Wood [10] describe diagrams of 500–1000 notes that take 2–20 people 1–3 days, and Beyer and Holtzblatt mention a diagram size of around 1500 notes; in some versions the notes contain ideas, opinions or thoughts of the participants [4,25], and the clustering is done in strict silence, in others the notes are insights or interpretations of observational or interview data [2,10], and discussion is encouraged; different versions also include a moderator [10] or facilitator [25], and specific steps after clustering, such as "walking the wall" and generating design ideas [2,10], and voting on high-priority issues [25].

The literature does call out a number of characteristic features of affinity diagramming: First, it is a collaborative process, always practiced as a group. It is usually characterized as an interpretive, reflective method that is used to achieve new insights and ideas, not to provide definite, objective answers. Most texts emphasize the importance of working intuitively rather than "rationally," and to avoid established patterns of thinking. The mental processes are sometimes called "abductive" reasoning and occasionally linked to grounded theory [22,24], but not all sources agree with this term or demand the deep reflection and imaginative insight it implies.

The variability and lack of consensus among the sources demonstrates the need for empirical investigation. Rather than adopting one particular definition and set of requirements, we take a broad, non-prescriptive view of the method, in order to study affinity diagramming as it is actually practiced.

Empirical Studies

The most in-depth studies to date have been observations of short affinity diagramming sessions to inform the design of digital prototypes.

Judge et al. [12] staged and observed four affinity diagramming sessions, conducted according to a protocol adapted from Beyer & Holtzblatt, but using only 50–279 notes generated by brainstorming (in three sessions). Of 16 participants, only four had any prior experience with affinity diagramming. Judge et al. provide a rich description of participants' detailed interaction with the notes as well as their social interaction around them, focusing on the three themes of shared awareness, cognitive offloading, and understanding, organizing and searching for notes.

Similarly, Geyer et al. [6] arranged for three groups to generate design ideas using affinity diagramming, while observing their physical interactions in detail. All 15 of their participants were novices with the method, and all the diagrams involved less than 100 notes. The reported results mainly address participants' shifts of attention between their individual notes, the shared work area and other participants through different stages of the work (e.g. divergent and convergent phases).

While these studies represent valuable work and interesting findings, they are limited in that they primarily studied novices in the lab, using researcher-defined, non-standard variations of (relatively small) affinity diagrams for design brainstorming or decision-making. Only to a limited extent do they address the question of how affinity diagramming is performed in real-world contexts and for other purposes.

Given the modest amount of prior research and these limitations, we determined at the outset that a complementary approach looking at affinity diagramming more generally would be valuable. We have briefly reported [9] on a preliminary study that involved interviews with 7 participants with affinity diagramming experience. Those interviews were quite short (around 30 minutes or less), and the reported findings focus on problems around locating notes.

Systems and Prototypes

Previous attempts to design for affinity diagramming fall into one of two groups. On the one hand there are numerous desktop-based systems such as GUNGEN [21] , DiscuSys [29] PathMaker,[2] StickySorter,[3] CDTools[4] (now discontinued), AFFINITY,[5] and the Affinity Visualization Tool.[6]

[1] http://www.usabilityfirst.com/glossary/affinity-diagram

[2] http://www.skymark.com/pathmaker/tour/brain.asp

[3] http://allmyapps.com/apps/stickysorter-organize-notes

[4] http://incontextdesign.com/process/cdtools/

[5] http://www.discover6sigma.org/d6slab/affinity/

Despite the easy availability of many of these tools, none of our study participants had ever used any of them.

Secondly, there have been a number of efforts to create applications to support affinity diagramming on large, shared screens. The Designer's Environment [27] uses individual tablets to create notes and an interactive tabletop surface to group them. Similarly, Judge et al. [11] use PDAs for individual notes and a wall-sized multi-display environment to cluster them, while Affinity+ [5] lets users create notes on tablets, smart phones and PCs, and group them on a wall-sized touch screen. Finally, the AffinityTable [6] combines a vertical display, an interactive tabletop, and digital pens to capture and create digital copies of physical notes, which are then grouped digitally.

There are also systems to support other, similar methods. The Designers' Outpost [16] was an early and influential example combining an interactive whiteboard with physical paper notes to support design brainstorming. In Collaborage [20], a camera captures notes tagged with visual markers on a board, creating digital representations of the arrangements or performing commands automatically. Both these systems could be used for affinity diagramming. Our design implications build on all this previous work.

Collaboration around (Augmented) Paper

There has been a great deal of study of other collaborative practices around paper artifacts, e.g. [17,18,28], and digital systems that seek to augment them or create paper-like digital experiences [3,7,19]. Of particular inspiration is Sellen & Harper [23], who point out that by studying domains where computers have not supplanted paper, "we can begin to think about what new kinds of devices and systems might be constructed that would make new kinds of activities possible or better support the kinds of work that people are trying to accomplish." Our study falls into this tradition: the use of paper takes central place, and our design implications look at ways not to *replace* paper, but to incorporate it alongside digital support into one system.

STUDY DESCRIPTION

In view of the scarcity of empirical data, we wished to learn more about how affinity diagramming and similar processes are performed in practice, and about the experiences, attitudes and insights of the people using them. Our research questions focused on practical work processes, problems experienced, and the reasons for engaging in affinity diagramming. To address them, we conducted a semi-structured interview study with thirteen participants, asking about real-life diagrams they had worked on. We had hoped to supplement the interviews with direct observations, but had difficulty recruiting experienced affinity diagrammers for naturalistic observation.

Our participants were recruited through a mailing list and from personal networks; we also asked each interview participant to refer to us anyone else who might be interested. Interviews were conducted in person (4), over video conferencing (5) or phone/audio conferencing (4). Interviews lasted between one and two hours, with 90 minutes as the default, and participants were offered a $40 (or equivalent) incentive, though several declined.

In addition to our semi-structured interview protocol, we asked participants whenever possible to share material from their work with us, and used that as a basis for conversation. Eight participants showed photos of their process or the resulting physical artifacts, or the artifacts themselves. Two participants shared reports or other documents.

We transcribed the interviews and examined the photos and other material. We analyzed this data qualitatively, using open coding, an affinity-like clustering process, and several tables and diagrams to look for patterns and trends. Our findings represent a selection of the themes that emerged.

Participant Characteristics

The thirteen interview participants (six male, seven female) were all based in the US and Europe. Four held PhDs, one was in a PhD program, while the rest held the equivalent of Masters degrees or were currently in a Masters program. Their backgrounds were in social sciences, design, psychology, HCI, computer science and engineering.

Six participants were working in industry (including corporate research labs), four in academic institutions, and four were current Masters students (one of whom also worked in industry). Two pairs of participants (P1–P2 and P4–P5) came from the same teams and had worked on some of the same projects. Ten participants had worked on affinity diagrams, while three (P4, P5, P11) only had experience with *other cluster diagrams* (see below). Of the former group, seven had significant experience (numerous diagrams over several years), while three were relative novices (only 2–3 diagrams or a few months of experience).

Limitations

Many interesting aspects of affinity diagramming can only be investigated through first-hand observation. Due to the retrospective nature of the study, we could not directly monitor the detailed physical and social interactions during diagramming, much less the associated mental processes, and participants were only able to report these activities in quite general terms. On the other hand, retrospective interviews allow us to more easily study long-lasting processes, and to include more of the larger context and outcomes of the work. It also lets us collect the participants' own perspectives. Our findings focus on aspects where we feel their retrospective accounts are reasonably reliable.

While we provide some descriptive statistics to give a general sense of the data collected, we caution against reading too much into the specific figures. Numbers mentioned are based on participant estimates (supported by photos and other artifacts where available), which may not always be precise. Additionally, we do not have all data for

[6] http://www.benjaminkoh.com/AffinityTool.html

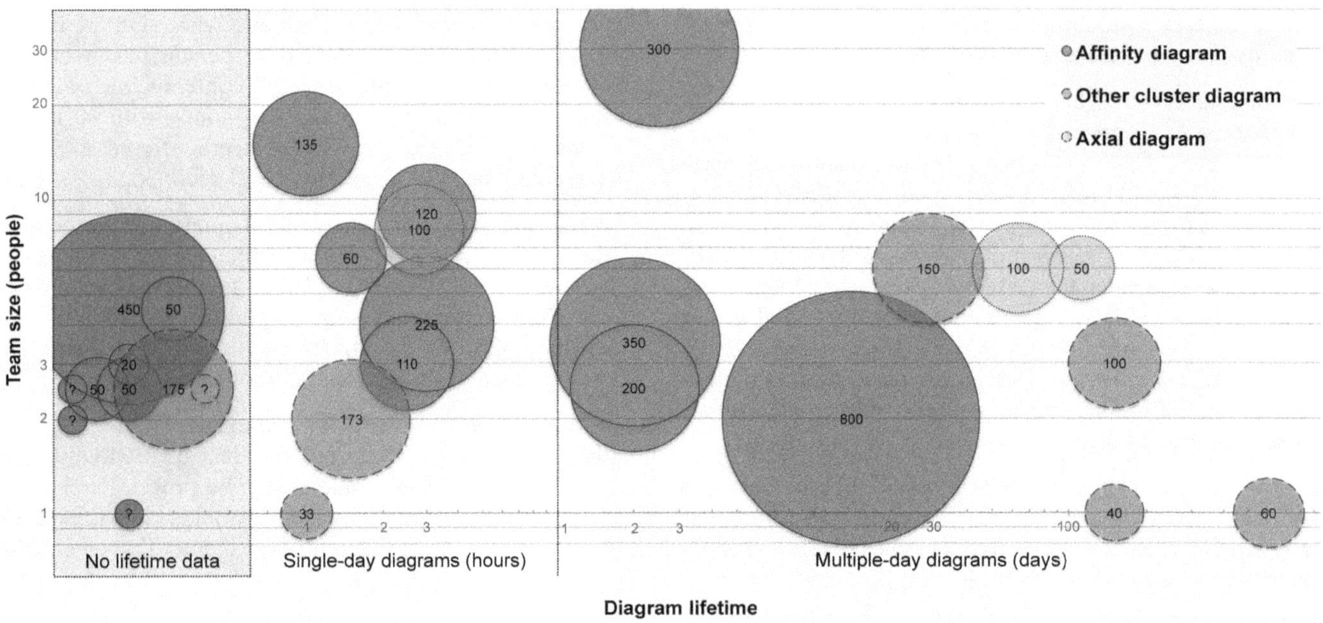

Figure 1: Diagram lifetime, average team size, and diagram size (as bubble area), plotted on a log-log scale. Lifetime information is missing for 10 diagrams, and diagram size for 4 of those. The size of otherwise unspecified "small teams" has been set to 2.5.

every diagram, so specific figures are necessarily based on a subset of cases, and numbers therefore do not always add up. Finally, the results may not be representative of all others using these and similar processes in general.

FINDINGS

We first present a general overview of the participants' practices and the diagrams they created, discussing commonalities and variations, and then delve into three important and interrelated themes: the importance of the physical affordances to the affinity diagramming process; problems caused by the physicality; and the transitions between physical and digital forms of information.

Diagram Characteristics

Altogether, participants discussed 28 examples of using paper note clustering processes (1-4 per person); about 15 of these were described in detail. We classified seventeen of the diagrams as what we call *traditional affinity diagrams*, and eight as *other cluster diagrams*: substantially similar methods with some notable variations (e.g. methods that involved clustering codes from a coding scheme, or where the clusters were not used to form labeled groups). To provide context and discover potential commonalities, we also included in the analysis data on three that we labeled *axial diagrams* (cf. [26]): methods that had similarities to affinity diagramming, but with the significant difference that they used pre-defined dimensions to organize the notes (in two of them, participants organized notes along a timeline, and in the third along multiple predefined axes). These methods were used for project post-mortem review, project planning and design development.

Fit with Literature and Similarities across Variations

Much of what the participants said about their practices can be related back to one or another of the affinity diagramming templates described in the literature. However, few (if any) instances were carried out exactly according to any one textbook description. The processes reported varied significantly, with affinity diagramming shading into other, similar methods such as storyboarding, card sorting and timelining without any sharp dividing line. For example, P11 used a method where sticky notes were initially placed on images rather than on a blank surface, hoping thereby to find connections between the notes and specific things depicted. P10 clustered photos without dividing them into explicitly labeled groups. P13 described using paper notes in a similar way in project post-mortems, but placing them in rough chronological order depending on what stage of the project the point related to. While these examples depart from the principle that notes are placed purely on the basis of "affinity", this rule was not always followed strictly in traditional affinity diagrams either, with special arrangements sometimes used to express particular relationships between notes. Such departures from canonical practices are also known from other HCI methods [30].

Of the traditional affinity diagrams, perhaps the most striking divergence from "textbook" procedure was that most of the reported diagrams (11 out of the 15 that reported this detail) had only one level of hierarchy; groups were created and labeled, but the groups themselves were not organized further. The other four diagrams had two levels; there were no reports of diagrams with more, even though e.g. Beyer and Holtzblatt call for three or more levels of hierarchy [2]. (This is only partially explained by smaller diagram sizes, since not even the largest diagrams in the study used more levels of hierarchy.)

Apart from this, we noted two different kinds of variation. There are *practical variations* in e.g. diagram size, time used and team size, and there are *variations in the purpose of the process,* and hence how it is performed.

Practical Variations

The diagrams reported by participants (cf. Figure 1) varied in size between 20 and 700–900 notes. Ten diagrams had fewer than 100 notes, eight had between 100 and 200, and six diagrams had more than 200 notes. Most of the reported diagrams, then, are relatively small, more in line with the sizes indicated by Brassard [4] than the ones recommended by Beyer and Holtzblatt [2], but the overall range is much greater than any one single reference describes or what has previously been studied. We are aware that even larger diagrams, up to 2000 notes, are sometimes used [1], but these did not appear in the study data.

Although all the literature references characterize affinity diagramming as a team process, our participants reported four diagrams (one traditional affinity diagram and three other cluster diagrams) that were done entirely by one person working alone, and several others where one person worked alone for part of the process. However, other participants said they did not use the technique alone. P7: "I've never done affinity diagramming by myself. I think it's a technique that is mostly useful when done in pairs, at least." P6 expects to use it again in future group projects, but "[when by] myself, I prefer to order information on my computer." Of the other affinity and cluster diagrams, 15 were done by teams of 2–7 people, three by 8–15 people, and one by about 30 people. (As it was common for the number of people involved to vary throughout the process, more precise numbers were difficult to pin down.)

As estimated by the participants, eight diagrams were created in one day, in sessions lasting 1–5 hours, and three were created over 2–3 days. Six were built intermittently over long periods of time, and one over a couple of weeks with an estimated 3–5 days of full-time work. The method of data collection does not provide a solid basis for drawing any statistical conclusions about how these factors are connected, but one apparent trend (see Figure 1) is that large groups tend to get affinity and cluster diagrams done more quickly. We interpret this as more a matter of logistics than of efficiency, since the diagrams with the largest number of participants all took place at off-sites and similar time-limited events, while smaller groups (or lone researchers) could keep working on a diagram for weeks or months. Existing affinity diagramming instructions do not address such long-lasting diagramming processes.

Purpose Variations

Participants used paper-clustering methods for a wide variety of tasks, primarily as a means of exploration. P4: "We use post-its [...] when we want to first expand a lot, and then start narrowing. We don't use them when we know what we really need but we just need to refine it." P12 found paper notes especially useful "when I'm just thinking about it, when I'm just formulating the ideas, trying to figure out what groups make sense." Within this role, traditional affinity and similar cluster diagrams mainly served three separate, though overlapping purposes, which we classify as to *elicit diverse input*, to *organize material*, and to *analyze data.*

To Elicit Diverse Input

In the first case, diagrams were used with a group of people as a way to draw out their individual ideas, opinions or perspectives. Instances included design brainstorming, organizational reflection and project planning. (The same general approach was also used for project post-mortems.) In this variation, notes were generally generated on the fly by participants (often working individually without communication), and a group discussion would generally follow the clustering. There were five instances of this type, including all the diagrams created by large groups (≥8 people), but it was also practiced in smaller teams.

To Organize Material

In about four examples, the main purpose of the process appeared to be simply to put into order already existing material. These cases involved collections of unstructured or badly structured items that were well understood individually, but needed to be organized. A typical example was taking a set of product requirements from various sources and producing a consolidated and structured view of them. Although participants did mention sometimes agonizing over aspects of the grouping, it seems to have been relatively quick and straightforward, demanding only moderate mental effort. As a result, the categories produced were often expected (in some cases partially pre-defined, in another departure from textbook practice).

To Analyze Data

Finally, the most common reported use (with about 16 instances) of affinity and cluster diagrams in this study was as a method of data analysis, to derive insights and ideas from existing material. Typical examples of this variation included analyzing interview data to find themes, and then using these themes to identify design requirements and inspire design ideas. Unlike the examples in the previous category, in these cases the significance of the individual items was not always known in advance, and the categories required more reflection to formulate. This variation of the process, therefore, was slower and more mentally effortful. P6: "Ordering is really cognitively intensive, to try and figure out the groups that we want to see." The instances of lengthy diagramming processes were all of this type.

This tripartite division reflects to some extent the variations found in literature, with the use to elicit diverse input following Brassard or Spool relatively closely [4,25], and also the form predominantly used in previous studies [6,12]. The use for organizing material does not have a clear template, but is probably influenced by card-sorting. When used to analyze data, the method often drew on elements from Beyer and Holtzblatt [2], but as described above, the divergences and degree of variation were considerable, and many participants were explicitly influenced by other analysis techniques, such as grounded theory.

Why Physicality of Paper Is Important

Previous studies on paper-based processes [18,23] have identified a number of crucial benefits of paper, and our participants, several of whom were familiar with that research, made similar observations for affinity diagramming (which they all carried out with paper notes).

Participants expressed a strong awareness of the tangibility of the paper notes, and the physical manipulation of them. Many valued this aspect highly, and even saw it as one of the biggest advantages of the process. P2, about the benefits of working on paper: "You can take it in your hand, you can give it to others, you can put it somewhere... cache it. Maybe the tangibility, that the paper feels good in your hand." Participants also pointed to the size of the working area and the spatial awareness as important benefits. P1: "you have a large canvas, no limitations of a screen where you can only focus on one thing at a time, you can get an overview in one gaze and focus in." P6: "physically ordering in the spatial world facts and things creates opportunities for unexpected conclusions and understandings."

Participants made active and creative use of the physical properties of the diagrams. Most reported improvising ways to adapt the affinity diagrams to particular purposes, and to capture particular information. For example, P1 and P2 attached loose notes with interview excerpts to A4 paper sheets, and wrote little summaries next to them to capture the "gist" or their interpretation. Participants commonly created new notations on a case-by-case basis in order to represent something that was important for that particular diagram, e.g. highlighting points of concern to draw attention to them (P5), adding little flower doodles to distinguish different kinds of notes (P9, Figure 2a), or color-coding data from different participants (P1–P2, Figure 2b).

The ability to flexibly vary the method, to break the "rules" in special cases, was considered important. P13: "My experience is that all these methods should be used with common sense. If it gets very rigid, you get sick of them. [...] I'm very pragmatic about it; I take short cuts. Almost every step of the process can be varied." A number of participants explicitly associated flexibility with working on paper. P6: "There's a degree of nimbleness that comes with [paper] affinity diagrams, even when working on one's own, that is challenging to do any other way."

Paper, then, straightforwardly supports a flexible process with improvised adaptations. This trait would appear to be important for enabling the range of variations and the pragmatic requirements of affinity diagramming, motivating why participants continue to prefer working on paper.

How Physicality of Paper Causes Problems

While participants found the physical nature of the process important, they also reported drawbacks connected with this aspect. One in particular stood out as a major problem for almost all participants: Sticky notes often fall down off the wall, and paper notes on a table can be accidentally disarranged. P5: "I find it very annoying that post-its don't stick to cork quite as well as we would like them to." Participants mitigated the problem in various ways: by using tape or other means to fasten the individual notes more securely, by storing them in folders, and by taking photos of the diagram as backups, should any part be lost or destroyed. Still, these solutions were only partially effective, and notes falling down remained one of the biggest frustrations (cf. [12]).

Participants often had difficulties finding a suitable space for the affinity diagram. Sometimes rooms to work in were not available, or could only be booked for short periods of time. Several participants (P1–P2, P7, P11) were forced to move a diagram-in-progress in the middle of the affinity process. In other cases, the wall or desk space was simply too small for the number of notes. P4: "Last semester we didn't have such a large whiteboard, just a small one. We would take pictures and keep building on that, and I would take care of organizing the data in Excel spreadsheets." Lack of space could lead to clutter and confusion. P9: "We tried to group them, but because they were so many so the groups are not visible any more."

Participants adopted various ways to deal with limited space. Some reduced the number of notes by omitting less important ones. Others merged duplicate or similar notes together to make more space for others. Several worked on only one part at a time (e.g. per session), meanwhile folding, stacking or otherwise packing away the other sections. However, this meant giving up the benefits of overview and direct access to all the items. P2: "It would have been more optimal if the notes could have been spread out so I could see them all at once, but we had to pile them up and stick them under the label because we didn't have enough space." This could cause problems in the analysis. P2: "When you can't keep an overview, you can forget some groups and end up with duplicates or similar groups."

While we might expect space constraints to be a problem mainly for larger diagrams, the issue in fact occurred across the range of diagram sizes. In determining whether and how space will become an issue, other factors such as diagram lifetime and level of accommodation also come into play.

Transitions between Digital and Physical Forms

The instances of affinity diagramming and similar methods we examine are performed on paper, but in all cases they represent only one step of a longer process, and often the steps preceding and following the physical clustering are computer-based. As a result, the transitions between physical and digital forms of representation are a major issue, not explicitly covered in previous affinity diagramming studies, and we will describe it in some detail.

Figure 2: (a) Wall-based affinity diagram with improvised annotations (P9). (b) Table-based affinity diagram with color-coded text, partially collapsed for storage (P1–P2).

Into the Diagram (to Physical Form)

Before the affinity diagramming starts, the content may exist in several different forms. Many participants reported spending significant time turning it into notes suitable for affinity diagramming. In fact, this process could sometimes take as much time as the clustering itself (P3, P9), although it varied considerably.

When the method was used to *elicit diverse input*, the notes were generated on the fly by the team members (although in several instances they referred to existing documents or other material, generally in digital form). In other cases, they may be created from interview transcripts, observational notes, photos, or other documents. These materials are sometimes digital, sometimes analog (handwritten notes), and sometimes a mix. In 12 of the 28 diagrams reported the material was in digital form before clustering.

The transformation of this material into paper notes took some very different forms. One team (P1–P2) printed the notes directly from the digital documents. However, most went through a process where they reviewed the material (digital or analog), usually as a group. The review might mean reading the notes or transcripts aloud (P4–P5, P6, P7, P9), or even reenacting them (P3). In these cases, the choice of handwritten or printed notes seems to have been a pragmatic one; specifically, when the note-making took place during the same session as the clustering, printing out the notes was not considered feasible.

This step served as an opportunity to process the raw data, filtering out irrelevant/redundant information, rearticulating the observations into the team's own terms (sometimes literally translating from one language to another), and making implicit points, interpretations and insights explicit. P7: "For example, maybe the post-it required additional sub-levels or additional specifications, or it pointed to a related question not mentioned elsewhere, so we made extra post-its for that." Its role corresponds closely to the contextual design "interpretation session" [2,10]. While time-consuming, participants appeared to find the work worthwhile, and did not complain about the effort.

Out from the Diagram (to Digital Form)

On the other hand, the job of transforming the finished diagram was a common point of dissatisfaction. Most participants wanted to preserve the diagram in some form, in order to share it with others, go back to it later, or as a record of the work. However, the actual diagram is a hard-to-move installation that takes up significant amounts of space, and is often taken down (destroyed, or more often folded up for archiving) shortly after completion. It doesn't integrate well with other documents, and most participants did not see it as a suitable way to communicate the results to other people who hadn't taken part in the process (in some cases, e.g. P12, P13, they believed that "sticky notes" would not be taken seriously). P2: "We can't deliver the collection of loose paper notes as a report." Participants therefore wanted the outcome in a digital format. P5: "We shouldn't deliver documentation as scanned pictures, so we go in and transcribe." In fact, practically every diagram reported was converted into some digital form.

Different approaches were taken to perform this transfer. Seven participants took photos of the diagram and archived these for reference. Ten transcribed the content and structure of the diagram, and all but one mentioned writing it up as a report, using the diagram as an outline. However, the work of digitizing the affinity diagram information was often found to be very time-consuming and tedious. P9 called it a problem in every project she had worked on, and described transcribing a paper note affinity diagram into Excel: "I was sitting at the computer and one member of my group told me the groups and labels and... yes, it was [slow]." P3 also felt the result was not satisfactory: "If you have huge affinity diagrams it's just a mess [to transcribe into Excel or Word], and it's hard to find everything."

The work can be especially frustrating if the data on the notes started out in the computer. P2: "This isn't a good way. At first they are in a computer. And then you print them and they're in the physical world. And then when you cluster them... they're in a physical world and then you have to turn them into computer again. So it's really slow." P12: "Yeah, I don't think that's always the smartest way of doing things. I'm sure it's not a timesaver. Definitely not."

In addition to being time-consuming, the task of digitizing the diagram is error-prone. Several participants described going back to the physical notes (or photos of the diagram) because they didn't trust the digital version. P3: "We weren't sure whether what we captured is under the right header or requirement." P2: "Now we should check that the attribution of the quotes are correct, because in reading the report I have a feeling some have been misattributed."

In contrast with these findings, textbook instructions describe using the completed paper diagram itself to communicate the results, or for carrying out the next stage of the process, with only Holtzblatt et al. [10] mentioning the possibility of archiving the diagram digitally (using a now discontinued software application). Previous research [6,16] has pointed out the need to digitize the diagram content (design ideas, in their case), and identified it as a problematic aspect, without discussing how it is actually achieved. An important and problematic part of the process remains unaddressed.

DISCUSSION

From our findings we draw a number of insights that motivate our design implications. Our main arguments are that *our model of affinity diagramming should be updated and refined* to better reflect accurate practice, that in designing systems for affinity diagramming, *there is good reason to explore support for paper-based diagrams*, and that the two most important dimensions to consider are: (1) *diagram lifetime and the division of the work into different sessions*, and (2) *how information is transitioned and transformed between digital and physical representations*.

Although the focus of this study was affinity diagramming, the practices reported bleed into similar methods. These commonalities suggest that design implications derived from the study may apply not just to affinity diagrams, but also to collaborative paper diagrams more generally.

Going Beyond "Affinity Diagramming"

We see that while taken as a whole, the literature encompasses many of the actual affinity diagramming characteristics, individual definitions and instructions do not fully or accurately capture how affinity diagramming is performed in practice: few or no reported diagrams conform completely to a specific reference. Furthermore, some findings differ from previous descriptions: there are diagrams that take longer and use less hierarchy than prescribed, and people occasionally work on affinity diagrams by themselves (if only for part of the process). Woolrych et al. [30] argue that such variations are a universal and necessary fact of doing HCI work, and that we should reconceive rigid methods as flexible combinations of "resources." The details of specific practices and the organization by diagram purpose we present above offer the beginnings of such a conception of affinity diagramming.

Working on Paper

The findings provide ample evidence to account for the continued use of paper for affinity diagramming, with particular emphasis on the tangibility, the support for collaboration, the flexibility and the perceived low overhead of paper. While none of the participants in this study had access to wall-sized touch screens in their work, and we therefore could not directly compare touch-screen applications for affinity diagramming, it would seem difficult to replicate the material affordances of paper that enable such rich flexibility on a regular touch screen, and the problems securing ideal, long-term work-spaces show the importance of lightweight solutions that can be quickly set up anywhere. For this reason, we find it likely that paper, or a paper-like digital tangible, will remain the tool of choice for at least some of these diagrams in the future as well, and we focus on addressing the paper-based process.

Practical Issues and Variations

For at the same time, working on paper has drawbacks. The issues identified in this study tend to differ from many that previous systems have attempted to address; the findings offer weak support at best for a need for help to find notes, for remote sharing of or collaboration on the diagram, or for integrating multimedia content. Rather, the bigger challenges that emerge from the interviews are the mechanical aspects of dealing with a physical diagram.

Because they are practical in nature, these problems are liable to be affected by practical circumstances and variations in the process. Of the different dimensions of variation among the diagrams reported in the study, one stands out as particularly important: the working lifetime of the diagram, from the first placing of notes to its completion or abandonment. The diagram lifetime directly affects many of the most critical practical issues mentioned above: the longer a diagram is up, the greater the risk of notes falling off, the more difficult it may be to secure space for it, and the more likely that it will need to be collapsed between sessions.

We therefore propose *diagram lifetime* as a key factor for the design of technologies supporting affinity diagramming and similar methods, with different durations and divisions into separate sessions lending themselves to different technology solutions. (Geyer et al. [6] similarly divide a single diagramming session into phases, and find more need for support in the later, "convergent" phases.) We particularly note that current problems are more acute for longer-lived diagrams (those for analyzing data), which suggests a greater need for technology support.

Transition Issues and Variations

The second major challenge found in the interviews is the transitions between physical and digital forms of the information, particularly the step of converting the analog diagram into digital form at the end of the diagramming process. Here, the variation in practices point to subtle differences in user needs and design potential.

The transition at the beginning of the process is important for how digital technology can be integrated. As we have seen, two things appear to affect how a transition from digital to physical form (if relevant) happens: The lifetime of the diagram, or more precisely whether there are separate sessions for note-creation and clustering; and the degree and form of processing of the material. If it is mere mechanical formatting, a digital process is often used, but when the material must be *transformed* through a creative, collaborative process of rearticulation, working manually on paper is often (as when clustering) more convenient.

When it comes to the transition at the end of the clustering process, we also find that the different reported ways of converting to digital involve different forms and degrees of transformation of the content. Photos of notes on the wall apply little processing, preserving the spatial arrangement of the physical diagram, but they lock the data in a non-editable, non-computer-readable form. A transcription transforms the diagram into a linear document without otherwise greatly changing the content, while rewriting it as a report requires significant further processing.

These options involve tradeoffs, and when the degree of transformation was low, participants felt the work to be tiresome. We propose *degree and form of transformation* at the transitions as another key factor in designing for affinity diagrams and similar methods.

DESIGN IMPLICATIONS

In light of these insights, we propose a design focus on augmenting paper diagrams by bridging the gap between the physical and digital worlds; more specifically, on making it easier to make digital representations of the physical artifacts as well as physical representations of the digital models, and to integrate the two representations. The idea, then, is to find ways to capture paper notes and physical diagrams digitally, and display digital information alongside or as part of the physical diagram. In this manner, digital technology can help address the problems identified in our findings, such as deterioration of the paper diagram (e.g. serving as a backup or helping restore it), size constraints (e.g. by displaying collapsed parts digitally, or supporting the processes of taking down and putting back up the diagram between sessions), and of course the transitions between digital and physical form.

Earlier efforts have explored elements of this basic concept, and our study offers support for many of their design ideas. The Designers' Outpost [16], Collaborage [20], AffinityTable [6] and Harboe et al. [8] all link paper notes with a digital representation and provide possible technical enablements. Note content (text or drawings) can be captured with digital pens [6], by creating the notes digitally and printing them out [8], or using a camera to photograph the notes [16,20]. To capture the spatial arrangement, we can rely on a camera for optical detection (perhaps aided by tagging the notes with fiducial markers) [8,20], or a smart surface may detect notes being placed on it [6,16]. Alternatively, the logical structure may be captured directly by scanning ID barcodes on the notes [1]. To display digital information with or on the physical diagram, a screen may be used as the back surface [6,16], it can be projected onto the wall or viewed through a magic-lens screen [8], or displayed separately on a computer screen [20].

However, while the components of a technical implementation are there, the diagramming variations targeted by previous work encompass just a small part of the practices described in this study, and perhaps as a consequence, the forms of paper-digital integration proposed only cover a limited range of possibilities: all systems to date rely on real-time digitization and tracking of notes. By considering the design factors we have identified, we can make tentative suggestions for other design approaches to explore.

In a paper-digital system, information can exist digitally (i.e. "on-screen"), physically (i.e. in non-augmented analog objects such as plain paper notes), or in a dual state where the representations are synchronized (e.g. a digital tangible or augmented physical object). Transitions between these forms can happen at different stages of the process, depending on the lifetime (1st design factor), and with various forms of transformation (2nd design factor). Based on our findings, we assume that items should exist on paper for the clustering, and that the final output should be available digitally. This leaves us with the questions of when and how the transition between these forms should happen.

When: If the diagram lifetime is short, and the work happens in a single session, many of the identified problems are less acute, and notes are handwritten. In this case it may suffice to simply offer support for the most pressing issue: digitizing the diagram at the end of the process. Similarly, for diagramming instances with longer duration and multiple sessions, many of the most important benefits may potentially be achieved simply by capturing the physical diagrams in digital format at the end of each session, or whenever users desire a "checkpoint."

How: Alternative options for transforming the diagram into digital form offer different types and degrees of transformation, which may be suitable for different purposes. A promising approach could be to build on existing practices, and provide tools to help photograph an affinity diagram (e.g. by automatically stitching multiple photos together, or a diagram viewer to easily switch between affinity overview and note close-up view), to help transcribe an affinity diagram (e.g. quickly capturing the structure by scanning barcodes or fiducial markers, or using handwriting recognition to capture the content), and to help write up an affinity diagram as a report (e.g. by linking parts of the report directly to the relevant sections of the diagram, and allowing users to quickly see which parts of the diagram remain to be written up). Automating the less transformative aspects of the transition in these ways could speed up the process and remove much of the drudgery. However, since the goal of the process is not simply to create the physical artifacts, but (particularly in the *analyze data* case) mentally process the content, designers must be mindful of how efficiency improvements could affect the mental work.

This is not to say that a solution that provides a digital representation of the diagram (alongside the paper notes) throughout the clustering process could not work equally well, since it offers the same end result, and potentially more support during the process. In light of our findings, we would expect the greatest benefits of such a system to be realized in cases where the diagrams are long-lasting, stretching over several sessions, where the notes derive from material in digital form, and possibly when the diagram size is larger than the diagrams in our study. Designers of such systems may wish to focus on these diagramming variations, which have not been explicitly targeted in existing prototypes.

However, digital tool support always involves tradeoffs [6], and in cases where real-time integration is not necessary it might well be beneficial to forgo it. As Klemmer et al. point out, capturing and digitizing the process is not a goal in itself: "it is through the *use* of the captured material that value is produced." [15] Designers should focus on supporting the appropriate digital transformations at the appropriate points in the process.

CONCLUSION AND FUTURE WORK

Practices like affinity diagramming, where multiple people interact within large collections of physical artifacts, using their spatial arrangement and material properties to create rich emergent codes and forms of meaning within a flexible, semi-rigorous framework, represent a challenging target for designing interactive computer systems. We have argued that instead of seeking to replace the paper-based processes for this and similar methods, it might be better to try to build technologies to support and augment it. From an understanding of the characteristics and variations of affinity diagramming as actually practiced, we have identified and proposed alternative approaches for different affinity diagramming situations. And because these characteristics and variations appear to significantly overlap with other types of paper-note diagrams, the same approaches may also be applicable to a wider set of practices. Further studies, particularly in-situ observations, would be valuable to deepen our understanding of affinity diagramming and identify additional issues.

In other work we have begun to explore the directions for design identified in this paper through various prototype systems, building on previous work that was not fully informed by these findings [8]. Our current focus is how to transform information from the diagramming process from analog to digital form, and how to visualize and interact with the digital version of the information.

Our argument that the design of effective interactive systems for techniques like affinity diagramming should, at least for some situations, cede parts of the experience to analog practices, and in effect *do less*, may seem like a retreat from hard problems. However, in fact it leads to new challenges, as it requires the technology to interact more with the physical world in all its variety and ambiguity.

REFERENCES

1. Bentley, F. and Barrett, E. *Building mobile experiences.* The MIT Press, Cambridge, Mass., 2012.
2. Beyer, H. and Holtzblatt, K. *Contextual design: defining customer-centered systems.* Morgan Kaufmann, 1998.
3. Brandl, P. et al. Bridging the Gap Between Real Printouts and Digital Whiteboard. *Proc. AVI* 2008.
4. Brassard, M. *The Memory Jogger Plus + Featuring the 7 Management and Planning Tools.* Goal/QPC, 1996.
5. Burtner, R., et al. Affinity+: Semi-Structured Brainstorming on Large Displays. *CHI Adj. Proj.* 2013.
6. Geyer, F. et al. Designing reality-based interfaces for creative group work. *Proc. C&C* 2011.
7. Haber, J., Nacenta, M.A., and Carpendale, S. Paper vs. Tablets: The Effect of Document Media in Co-located Collaborative Work. *Proc. AVI* 2014.
8. Harboe, G. et al. Two Thousand Points of Interaction. *Proc. DUI* 2012.
9. Harboe, G. et al. Computer Support for Collaborative Data Analysis. *Proc. CSCW* 2012.
10. Holtzblatt, K., Wendell, J.B., and Wood, S. *Rapid contextual design.* Morgan Kaufmann, 2005.
11. Judge, T.K. and McCrickard, D.S. *Collaborating on Affinity Diagrams Using Large Displays.* TR-08-19, Virginia Tech 2008.
12. Judge, T.K. et al. *Studying Group Decision Making in Affinity Diagramming.* TR-08-16, Virginia Tech 2008.
13. Kawakita, J. *The KJ method–a scientific approach to problem solving.* Kawakita Res. Inst., Tokyo, 1975.
14. Kawakita, J. *The original KJ method.* Kawakita Res. Inst., Tokyo, 1991.
15. Klemmer, S.R et al. Integrating physical and digital interactions on walls for fluid design collaboration. *Human–Computer Interaction 23*, 2 (2008).
16. Klemmer, S.R. et al. The designers' outpost: a tangible interface for collaborative web site. *Proc. UIST* 2001.
17. Luff, P., Heath, C., and Greatbatch, D. Tasks-in-interaction: Paper and Screen Based Documentation in Collaborative Activity. *Proc. CSCW* 1992.
18. MacKay, W.E. Is Paper Safer? The Role of Paper Flight Strips in Air Traffic Control. *ACM ToCHI 6*, 4 (1999).
19. McGee, D.R. et al. Comparing paper and tangible, multimodal tools. *Proc. CHI* 2002.
20. Moran, T.P. et al. Design and technology for Collaborage. *Proc. UIST* 1999.
21. Munemori, J. and Nagasawa, Y. GUNGEN: groupware for a new idea generation support system. *Information and Software Technology 38*, 3 (1996), 213–220.
22. Scupin, R. The KJ method: A technique for analyzing data derived from Japanese ethnology. *Human organization 56*, 2 (1997), 233–237.
23. Sellen, A. and Harper, R.H.R. *The Myth of the Paperless Office.* The MIT Press, 2003.
24. Simonsen, J. and Friberg, K. Collective Analysis of Qualitative Data. In Simonsen et al. (ed.), *Situated Design Methods*, (2014).
25. Spool, J.M. *The KJ-Technique.* http://www.uie.com/articles/kj_technique/.
26. Strauss, A.L. and Corbin, J.M. *Basics of qualitative research: Techniques and procedures for developing grounded theory.* Sage Publications, Inc, 1998.
27. Tse, E. et al. Exploring true multi-user multimodal interaction over a digital table. *Proc. DIS* 2008.
28. Vyas, D. et al. Collaborative practices that support creativity in design. *Proc. ECSCW* 2009.
29. Widjaja, W. et al. Discusys: Multiple User Real-time Digital Sticky-note Affinity-diagram Brainstorming System. *Procedia Computer Science 22*, (2013).
30. Woolrych, A. et al. Ingredients and Meals Rather Than Recipes. *Int. Journal of HCI 27*, 10 (2011).

Situational Ethics: Re-thinking Approaches to Formal Ethics Requirements for Human-Computer Interaction

Cosmin Munteanu [1,6]
cosmin.munteanu@utoronto.ca

Heather Molyneaux [2,7]
heather.molyneaux@nrc.gc.ca

Wendy Moncur [3]
wmoncur@dundee.ac.uk

Mario Romero [4]
marior@kth.se

Susan O'Donnell [2,7]
susan.odonnell@nrc.gc.ca

John Vines [5]
john.vines@ncl.ac.uk

[1] Institute of Communication, Culture, Information and Technology, University of Toronto Mississauga, Mississauga, ON, Canada
[2] National Research Council Canada, Human-Computer Interaction Team, Fredericton, NB, Canada
[3] Duncan of Jordanstone College of Art & Design, University of Dundee, Dundee, United Kingdom
[4] Department of High-Performance Computing and Visualization, Kungliga Tekniska högskolan, Stockholm, Sweden
[5] Culture Lab, School of Computing Science, Newcastle University, Newcastle Upon Tyne, United Kingdom
[6] Technologies for Ageing Gracefully, Department of Computer Science, University of Toronto, Toronto, ON, Canada
[7] Faculty of Arts, University of New Brunswick, Fredericton, NB, Canada

ABSTRACT

Most Human-Computer Interaction (HCI) researchers are accustomed to the process of formal ethics review for their evaluation or field trial protocol. Although this process varies by country, the underlying principles are universal. While this process is often a formality, for field research or lab-based studies with vulnerable users, formal ethics requirements can be challenging to navigate – a common occurrence in the social sciences; yet, in many cases, foreign to HCI researchers. Nevertheless, with the increase in new areas of research such as mobile technologies for marginalized populations or assistive technologies, this is a current reality. In this paper we present our experiences and challenges in conducting several studies that evaluate interactive systems in difficult settings, from the perspective of the ethics process. Based on these, we draft recommendations for mitigating the effect of such challenges to the ethical conduct of research. We then issue a call for interaction researchers, together with policy makers, to refine existing ethics guidelines and protocols in order to more accurately capture the particularities of such field-based evaluations, qualitative studies, challenging lab-based evaluations, and ethnographic observations.

ACM CLASSIFICATION KEYWORDS

H.5.2 [User interfaces]: Evaluation/methodology; K.4.1 [Public Policy Issues]: Ethics.

CHI 2015, April 18 - 23 2015, Seoul, Republic of Korea

ACM 978-1-4503-3145-6/15/04$15.00
http://dx.doi.org/10.1145/2702123.2702481

AUTHOR KEYWORDS

Ethics; Research protocol; Field studies; Situational ethics; Vulnerable populations.

INTRODUCTION

Recently we are seeing a wider and changing range of studies, from traditional usability evaluations to ethnographic research and to user-centered or participatory design. Our user populations have also changed; they now often include vulnerable groups – participants who may benefit the most from our research but potentially suffer from researcher engagement. HCI as a discipline has always been dedicated to studying and designing for such user groups which often entails work outside the traditional confines of laboratories. While ethics has long been an essential part of designing research in HCI [21], these practice-based methods can more *dynamically* affect all aspects of ethically conducting the research: privacy, confidentiality, consent, harm and risks, trust and authority.

In most cases, preparing for a study or evaluation involves a formal process of receiving approval from an administrative body responsible for ensuring all research follows sound ethical principles. In Canada, these bodies (Research Ethics Boards – REBs) are present in all universities as well as the National Research Council, and are guided by the formal Tri-Council Policy Statement on Ethical Conduct for Research Involving Humans [31]. In the United Kingdom, research involving human subjects is carried out under the governance of various bodies (professional organizations, universities, the National Health Service - NHS) and their policy statements (Ethical Guidelines for Good Research Practice by the Association of Social Anthropologists of the UK and the Commonwealth). In countries such as the US the ethics guidelines are less centralized (e.g. specific to each university); nonetheless, the principles and implementation are shared across countries and disciplines and the subject of increased scholarly attention (as illustrated by workshops such as [8]).

For most research, the application of such guidelines is straightforward. However in some cases researchers find themselves facing various serious ethical dilemmas when the realities of their field research do not match or even contradict the formal requirements of the ethical approval process [14]. This can be partly due to the bureaucratization of the ethics approval process in its attempt to formalize universally accepted principles (privacy, confidentiality, avoiding risks or harms [13]). However, we are currently witnessing an increase in studies conducted outside traditional contexts (e.g. mobile interfaces providing health or educational support for at-risk user groups [20] or studies using non-traditional sources such as online internet research, requiring a push for interdisciplinary global internet research ethics [3], [6]). Such work is bound to run into ethical challenges similar to those faced by disciplines where fieldwork has long been the norm, resulting in dilemmas (or "moral panics" [14]) not anticipated during the planning and formal approval process, such as changing from covert to overt researcher due to personal ethical qualms [18], resulting in fact in significantly less data being collected, or having ethical and moral concerns related to how difficult it is for a medical anthropologist to "disengage and disentangle … from fieldwork" [16].

In this paper we present some of the ethical challenges encountered in our own research. These examples, while covering a wide range of evaluation methodologies and settings, illustrate a common thesis: that contemporary HCI research often does not fit "traditional" or *static* ethical templates. To a certain extent, the HCI community is adapting to the ethical challenges prompted by the changing nature of the evaluations and field studies: [4], arguing for the consideration of new practices and reconsideration of old research norms to face ethical challenges posed by evaluations with large user groups; [2], bringing attention to ethical issues such as consent related to online social research (or [7], to authorship); [5], calling for further research into how to account for new ethical challenges when designing interactive technology and its evaluations; [19], making the case for greater flexibility of ethics and interpretation of data collected when conducting research that require membership in a community at risk of privacy exposures; or [9], proposing a more ethically-minded approach to technology design. However, in many other cases of both field and laboratory research, the realities of conducting the study can unexpectedly differ from what the researchers have planned for. It is thus time to introspectively look at the ethical implications raised by the ever-changing demands of HCI research that cannot always be anticipated as exemplified by the case studies presented in this paper.

Formal processes and policies have been essential in ensuring that research with human participants is carried out in an ethical manner. In this paper, we focus on the implications of the discrepancies between the formal ethics guidelines and the reality of conducting HCI studies with marginalized populations or in challenging environments. Our rationale is to draw the attention of interaction researchers and policy makers to the *situational* ethics which can be unpredictable and at times called for when conducting fieldwork, especially in novel areas. The rest of this paper is structured around four cases studies. For each of these we present the ethical challenges we encountered during the conduct of the study. Drawing from our experiences illustrated by these case studies, we conclude with a set of recommendations for addressing the ethical challenges posed by the newer real-life contexts and diversity of research method we are now encountering.

EXAMPLE: FIELD STUDY OF A MOBILE LANGUAGE SUPPORT APP FOR LOW-LITERACY ADULT LEARNERS

Context

In Canada, close to 50% of adults are considered to have literacy levels below the minimum functional requirements for today's society [1], and programs designed to provide learning support and resources to low-literacy adults have difficulty reaching and retaining those that would benefit. We[1] developed a mobile language assistant (ALEX) for use both in the classroom and in daily life, in order to help low-literacy adults become increasingly literate and independent. We evaluated ALEX through a six-month exploratory study with 11 adults enrolled in a literacy program. Each participant received one tablet running our app, to be used both in and outside the classroom. We collected data through frequent classroom observations and through participants' own verbal accounts of usage elsewhere. Our study [25] revealed that the app was helpful for activities essential to the literacy program and increased students' independence with respect to the use of literacy skills and their confidence and motivation to learn.

We encountered numerous challenges both in preparing and conducting our research. Most of the methodological issues are described in [26]. Here we elaborate on ethical principles and guidelines that were particularly challenging during our field study. After several iterations during which we have received very useful suggestions[2] from the REB, the approved study protocol covered a longitudinal study to be conducted in-situ with low-literacy adults, and with instruments (e.g. questionnaires, consent forms) adapted to the particularities of our user group. However, as shown here, it was impossible to anticipate and formally capture the challenges encountered during the study proceedings.

Informed consent

The literacy program is geared toward adults who completed only a few years of formal schooling, typically up to middle school. They are able to carry out some non-

[1]This work was conducted while the first author was affiliated with the National Research Council Canada.

[2]Such as allowing participants to take the consent forms home for two weeks and review them with a trusted person.

complex reading and writing tasks, such as some newspaper reading and writing a very simple letter.

Each potential participant received one mobile device running our literacy application, and was instructed on the use of the device and of the application through a one hour long one-on-one session with the researcher. Researchers also explained the details and objectives of the study, informed them of the information described on the consent forms, and encouraged them to review the forms with the teacher (who often acted as a proxy between researchers and participants), a family member, or friend. After a review period of up to two weeks, participants decided if they wanted to continue with the study.

We found that the adult learners struggled to understand the forms, and most signed without reading them. Only one participant read the consent form. One participant jokingly drew the comparison with signing the contract for a new cell phone plan. Despite our efforts to phrase the consent form in accessible, plain language, our final version was still worded in a relatively formal way, to satisfy the requirements of the ethics review process. We found ourselves explaining this form to participants, only to be cut short by them signing it to get the formalities over.

A similar departure from established ethical requirements occurred with the device review process. Normally participants have a few minutes to familiarize themselves with the application before signing the consent form. Our approved protocol allocated a week for this phase, during which we visited the classes daily for technical support. While we were not supposed to be collecting study data at that time, most participants started to offer their feedback, suggestions for improvement, and examples of usage, although they were not officially enrolled in the study. We faced a procedural ethical dilemma of whether we should collect such valuable data, before the consent forms were signed.

Privacy and confidentiality

It is a routine ethical expectation that participant privacy and confidentiality are guaranteed, particularly for research involving vulnerable user groups. Our approved protocol was to collect data through confidential interviews. In practice however, the study details and participants' use of the application were openly discussed in the classroom among participants, and also with non-participant students. While we conducted interviews as privately as possible and no audio was recorded, the daily observations were often a mix of tech support, participants' feedback, and personal stories on using the app, all shared in the classroom.

While ethics guidelines exist for consent forms for studies that are conducted with group interactions in which participants are explicitly informed that their group interactions are not entirely private, our protocol was not designed for this situation. We chose not to revisit the already-signed forms after noticing these group interactions, since signing the consent form was already a tedious task for participants, and since many non-participants were also included in these group interactions. Despite the departure from the privacy protocol outlined in our original REB application we decided to continue collecting data in this manner since privacy risks were minimal – the adult learners were already sharing many personal details in the classroom.

Reflections on research

Voluntary participation

The Policy Statements [31] for human-subject experiments require voluntary enrollment. Not all learners in the classroom enrolled in the study: some simply did not want the burden of having to take care of a device that was not theirs, while others were in the literacy program only for short periods of time. Yet almost all of these non-participants used our application, as most participants willingly lent them their devices while in the classroom. While no one was pressured to enroll in our study, the non-participants who used the borrowed devices became, in a way, involuntary subjects. Their interactions with classmates were described to researchers by the study participants, and on occasion, directly to researchers by these non-participants. This raises the ethical (and moral) question of whether data collected from non-participants should be included in researchers' analysis.

Exposure to risks and harms

Informing participants of any risks to which they are exposed is an essential ethics component of any study. Typically in HCI research, such risks are not greater than those from using everyday technology; such statements still must be disclosed to participants before they enroll in the study. However, such a disclosure is significantly limited when the system to be evaluated is being used by non-participants, a very common occurrence in our field study.

Data collection

Our formal ethics application to the REB allowed for small changes such as the phrasing of a question[3]. However, during the field study we still found ourselves in situations where we needed to improvise, e.g. during data collection. The participants' literacy levels made it difficult to conduct rigorous, structured data collection. Verbally-administered questionnaires, even rephrased with the help of teachers, at appropriate literacy levels, did not elicit meaningful answers. Instead, we conducted semi-structured interviews, adapting the questions for individual participants, or having to set them in the context of a personal story.

Another example of such departure from protocol was the "unplanned" data collection that occurred outside the classroom. Being located in a small city, we encountered

[3]Any significant changes in research instruments were to be submitted to the REB for review.

participants in various public spaces or stores. Participants took advantage of such encounters to ask various technical questions but also to relate their app use experiences. Again as researchers we faced the dilemma of whether to ignore this data. In fact, we suggest it would be impossible and perhaps even unethical to ignore such valuable data.

Participant-researcher rapport
One of the most significant ethical (and moral) challenges was the familiarity between researchers and participants that developed naturally during six months of daily visits. A positive consequence was the participants' unreserved feedback, but also their expectation of researchers becoming intimately involved in the class activities and beyond (e.g. answer questions, share personal details, attend the holiday party, ask for a ride after class, even extending the loan of a device to a participant whose school-aged child started using our app for homework.). While all efforts were made to ensure unbiased data collection [25], it was difficult to maintain a social distance – an increasing occurrence in HCI research as ethnographies become more common (e.g. [32]).

Discussion
A longitudinal, ethnographic evaluation where researchers are immersed in the observed environment for extended periods of time can represent a significant challenge from an ethical perspective for researchers unfamiliar with these methods (as well as for ethics review committees that review only science and engineering research). Informed consent, privacy, confidentiality, or harm are principles that must be evaluated in the particular context of the study, as they can be widely different than the usual template of usability evaluations familiar to HCI researchers.

EXAMPLE: FIELDWORK WITH PARENTS OF SICK NEWBORN INFANTS

Context
This project[4] involved fieldwork with parents of sick newborn infants who were cared for in a Neonatal Unit (NNU) in a large Primary Care hospital in the UK. We [23] designed, developed and evaluated a prototype software tool that mediated the communication of health updates and support needs across the social network on behalf of the parents [22]. A user-centred, Grounded Theory approach was taken [12].

We used focus groups to establish what information parents were willing to share with network members. Full details of the study are available in [22]. Before carrying out fieldwork with parents in the sensitive context of the NNU, we conducted a pilot focus group at a parenting conference with seven mothers, whose children who had been cared for in the NNU but had subsequently been discharged. Participants were asked what information they would want to be sent on their behalf to their friends and relatives about their baby while (s)he was in NNU. The researcher-facilitated focus group lasted one hour.

Following on from the pilot focus group, we intended to run focus groups with parents of babies currently in NNU. Here, we planned to ask participants what information they would want to be sent to their friends and relatives about their baby while (s)he was in NNU. Recruitment criteria to participate were strict: for example, parents would be excluded if it was the first week after admission, if the baby was the subject of a care order (parents legally denied access), or if the parent had a learning disability or mental or terminal illness, was unable to consent for themselves for any reason, or was a Prisoner/ Young Offender.

Formal ethical approval
For the pilot focus group, our university's Ethics Committee carried out the review. For the studies with parents who currently had babies in NNU, ethical approval was obtained from the NHS Local Research Ethics Committee (LREC), and reviewed by university administrators for indemnification. LREC requirements are extensive, with approval required for any research with: *"... patients and users of the NHS. This includes all potential research participants recruited by virtue of the patient or user's past or present treatment by, or use of, the NHS. It includes NHS patients treated under contracts with private sector institutions. Individuals identified as potential research participants because of their status as relatives or carers of patients and users of the NHS, as defined above."* [28]

One of the LREC's main concerns was that we would avoid placing parents under yet more stress: these parents were already under considerable stress because they had a very sick baby. Clearly, ethical approval is essential in carrying out research with sick people (and with parents of sick babies and their supporters). It is not acceptable for participants to be asked questions that might make them even more depressed or worried about their condition, however useful these questions are from the perspective of satisfying research questions. This is an important constraint on working with patients and their carers. In contrast, the sort of knowledge acquisition activities which are carried out with medical staff do not usually have an emotional impact on them – although of course it is not ethically acceptable to make medical staff depressed or stressed either [23].

Advance planning was needed, as the hospital-based research had to be signed off by the LREC. The ethical approval process called for a highly detailed submission, which included a description of the research, the staff involved and their backgrounds, contact points for complaints, participant information and consent forms. The process was time-consuming: it can take up to 60 days to

[4]This research was supported by the UK Engineering and Physical Sciences Research Council, under grant EP/D049520/1 and a doctoral training award.

establish whether initial ethical approval for research will be granted, and a review of substantial amendments to research plans can take up to 35 days. The approval process included attendance at an LREC meeting, where the researcher answered questions about the research from the large committee (approximately 14 people), made up of health professionals and lay members. Advance planning was somewhat at odds with our Grounded Theory approach, which calls for the development of research plans that can flex depending on findings from each incremental study.

Reflections on research

Recruitment and participation

Recruitment for the pilot focus group was successful. The women who attended showed little interest in the 'small print' of the information sheet and consent form. They were enthusiastic about taking part and wanted to get started rather than spend time on paperwork. An eighth participant did not fit the inclusion criteria – she was a childless midwife who had worked in NNU, and was interested to hear women's experiences. Participants were asked if it was acceptable for her to stay, and agreed. The researcher thus asked that she observe but did not contribute actively.

In contrast to the pilot focus group run at the parenting conference, NNU parents were uniformly unwilling to join a group discussion in the hospital. However some were willing to be interviewed by the researcher, either individually or with their partner (n=6: 4 female, 2 male). While it was necessary to adjust the research design to cater for the (much) smaller group size, we used the same discussion stimuli as the focus group, and remained faithful to the ethical approval granted.

Even when parents satisfied ethical criteria and agreed to participate in the hospital study, their attendance was not guaranteed. Attrition prior to participation could occur through lack of availability (e.g. - a mother might be feeding her baby, speaking to medical staff, have friends and family visiting, the baby being discharged early), reorientation of the baby's care from active to compassionate (palliative) care, or parents simply having a bad day and no longer wanting to participate. Amongst those parents who agreed to be interviewed, some interruptions occurred when nursing staff called parents away to attend to their babies or speak to doctors, but the parents returned to complete the interviews.

Involvement

The pilot focus group was highly emotionally charged. Despite the participants' experiences of NNU being up to 11 years ago, all participants ended up crying as they shared vivid memories of their experiences. The focus group was planned to last for 60 minutes, but ran for 90 minutes, until the room was booked for use by another activity. Participants volunteered that the focus group had given them an "invaluable" opportunity to discuss not only the types of information that they gave out when their baby was in hospital, but also their shared experiences of having a very sick baby in NNU, and their frustrations. All of the participants wept freely during the focus group, as they shared their experiences.

The midwife who had joined the group served a valuable role in comforting women who were distressed. As she had experience both in NNU and in caring for new mothers, she was well-placed to take this role. Her tactful intervention also allowed the researcher to keep discussion going in the focus group, and to draw attention away from distressed participants.

Discussion

For the pilot focus group, ethical approval was granted on the basis that participants would provide fully informed consent, fit the inclusion criteria, and participate in a discussion lasting an hour, facilitated by a researcher. What actually happened deviated from this substantially. For the researcher, guiding the focus group to satisfy the research questions in such emotionally charged circumstances was a challenge both professionally and personally (previously highlighted in [24]). Despite this deviation, rich discussion and insight into the experiences of parents were generated. This was valued by the participants, who made clear that they appreciated the opportunity to talk through their experiences of NNU together, as well as by the researcher.

In contrast, participants whose babies were currently being cared for in NNU were not enthusiastic about talking through their experiences in a group. Their intense and traumatic experience of having a very sick baby was immediate, not softened by time, and they were living through a period of uncertainty and worry. Whilst we adhered carefully to the questions we intended to explore in a focus group, and to the ethical approval granted, it was necessary to adjust our methodology by reorienting it to individuals or pairs. This called for a situational interpretation of the granted ethical approval. To have re-applied for ethical approval with such unexpected but minor changes would have led to significant delays and a need to recruit afresh.

The depth of insights delivered by working with parents who had authentic experience of NNU outweighed the disadvantages of (justifiably) strict ethics procedures. Their experiences were quite different to those of parents of well babies, and could be difficult for others to understand [23]. This illustrates the need for a flexible approach when planning the ethical aspects of such research – for example, by providing the option for focus groups *and* interviews in the research design and ethical approval process.

EXAMPLE: A LAB-BASED EVALUATION OF AN INFANTRY TRAINING SIMULATOR

Context

Interaction with serious games systems, such as mixed-reality training simulators, is a cost-effective alternative to field-based courses for military or law enforcement training. A realistic rendering of scenarios and conditions allows trainees to transition from course-based (classroom) instruction to applying their knowledge, skills, and judgment to solving real-life situations.

In partnership with the Canadian Forces, we[5] have developed a flexible mixed-reality infantry training simulator (presented in detail in [11]). Built as a research platform, it supports multimodal interaction between trainees and an immersive serious gaming environment projected onto multiple walls, allowing the re-creation of real-world environments and interactions with life-size characters. The game was developed according to requirements drafted in collaboration with subject-matter experts (e.g. infantry instructors). The customizable simulator supports tangible interactions such as simulated stun grenades and laser rifles for engaging in realistic combat with the game avatars. The system allows trainees to interact and engage in dialogue with virtual characters under different scenarios, by way of automatic speech recognition. The scenarios can be modified on the fly by instructors through a control interface that runs on a tablet.

Study protocol

Building such a complex system required significant user involvement. Beside collecting requirements and receiving feedback from subject-matter experts, extensive user testing was needed to iteratively develop and refine the system. This occurred through several technology demonstrations to our partners, but also through two 3-day testing sessions with a team of five soldiers, carried one year apart. While these two sessions were crucial in the development of the simulator, they have raised several ethical challenges during both the planning and execution phases.

Formal Ethical Approval

The guidelines of the Canadian Tri-Council Policy [31] on conducting ethical research suggests that a formal ethics approval is not needed if participants perform tasks that are part of their routine workplace activities. Soldiers often participate in the evaluation of various simulators as part of their on-the-base training, and engaging in activities that simulate battlefield conditions is also a regular activity. However, carrying out such tasks in our lab for the purpose of fine-tuning an interactive system may not fall as clearly under the definition of "routine work duties". We have described this situation to our Research Ethics Board, who thoroughly analyzed the circumstances and took a proactive role in helping us properly frame the ethical dimensions of our experiment. In the end, the REB judgment was that a formal ethics application was not required for this study. Nevertheless, an uninformed impromptu visitor to our lab could have easily labeled the setup and activities as a rather typical HCI human-subject evaluation.

[5]This work was conducted while the first author was affiliated with the National Research Council Canada.

Reflections on research

Voluntary Participation

Free will is fundamental to conducting ethical research, and experimenters must ensure that participants are voluntarily enrolling. In our simulator's evaluations, the two teams that took part in the trials were not explicitly given such choice. Instead, their superiors (our military collaborators) tasked them with taking part in the trials. One can argue that free will is not typically associated with military duties. Moreover, all of the participants enjoyed themselves during the study, and even took over our lab to take advantage of the opportunity to train using a new simulator, and in a sense welcomed having a break from their usual routine on the base[6]. Nevertheless, we were faced with having study participants being present in our lab[7] not by their own will – an example of the difficult distinction between ethics and morality when conducting human-subjects research.

Researcher-Participant Rapport

Often the relationship between researchers and participants is not symmetrical. In fact, various elements of the formal ethics guidelines (informed consent, no harm, voluntary participation, confidentiality, no-consequence withdrawal) are intended to prevent situations where researchers are in a position of authority over the participants. Yet in our study, we found that this relationship was often challenged with respect to authority (and trust), and left us wondering who is "in control". Soldiers became comfortable with the simulator, the researchers, and the lab – by the end of the second day the soldiers "took over" the lab and the experiment [27]. This entailed using the simulator to draft new training routines, which signified an unconditional technology acceptance, but also left us with very little control over how the evaluation was carried out. Some of the developers and researchers from our team also ended up half-willingly as "living props" in these new training routines, which included various degrees of physical strain. On the other hand, researchers were still in an asymmetrical position of trust, as the identity of soldiers was not anonymous and actions could have been reported to their superiors. Overall the general atmosphere was friendly and resembling the typical military camaraderie, having lunch together, or researchers being challenged to a friendly (virtual) shooting competition. However, the unfolding of the evaluations, mainly the contrast between soldiers taking control of aspects of the evaluation and the researchers'

[6]In a way, one can draw a parallel to the unwitting participation of end users in product improvements or marketing analyses.

[7]The lab is part of a civilian-funded institute, not affiliated with the Department of Defence.

technical collaboration with their superiors, raises the question of who was in a position of authority and trust.

Discussion

The lab-based user evaluation described here seemingly occupied a "gray area" of formal ethics. While approval was deemed unnecessary, the study proceedings raised several questions about what constitutes voluntary participation, and how the relationship between researchers and participants should be managed. Users were never exposed to any harm or privacy violation[8], yet the study could, at best, be described as "unconventional". This raises the questions of how well formal ethics procedures account for such unconventional cases, and also highlights the importance of having, such as in our case, a proactive and well-informed REB that became a partner in deciding how best to approach this study from an ethical perspective.

EXAMPLE: LABORATORY STUDY OF MOBILE TOUCHSCREEN TYPING WITH BLIND PARTICIPANTS

Context

Mobile texting is a ubiquitous form of communication. Yet, mobile text entry is often difficult due to size constraints. Phones have too many buttons, physical or virtual, that are too small. This problem is particularly limiting for the visually impaired, especially on touchscreens. For this, we designed BrailleTouch [29], a software keyboard for touchscreen mobile phones based on braille typing, supporting accessible text entry for the visually impaired on commodity smartphones. We evaluated our app during a laboratory study with 11 visually impaired participants ([30]), through 90-minute text-entry sessions repeated on different days, comparing our app to various text entry alternatives. We collected non-identifiable demographic data, surveys, interviews, typing speed and accuracy, and we recorded participants' voice and video of their hands interacting with the device.

Informed consent procedure

Together with our Institute Review Board (IRB), we designed an informed consent procedure to closely take into account our participants' visual impairment. We carefully crafted a script informing participants of the research questions of the study and their rights. During the design of the study, we had different options of allowing the participants to read the script. They could read it on a braille printout or listen to it with a screen reader. We decided to read the script to them and make it as natural as possible. As a result, we were able to ascertain that the participants had heard and understood the consent form. Furthermore, we recorded the delivery of the script and the acceptance from the participant saying "I consent". While the reading of the consent required more time than it would have taken the participants to read it in braille or with a screen reader, we considered it a courtesy and a crucial step in building trust, especially given that the participant would spend several hours over several days in our study. Participants appreciated our approach.

Given the close ties among members of the visually impaired community, the news of our app spread quickly among potential participants who simply wanted to try the app. In fact, a number of individuals requested that we distribute our app through the app store as soon as possible. To many of them, participation in the study was an opportunity to get early hands on experience with the technology. In fact, we discovered that many visually impaired and blind individuals are actually very early technology adopters. While they wanted to use the technology, they did not necessarily want to go through the long hours of typing the study entailed. For those who signed up for the study, they seemed eager to get on with using the technology and the consent form was simply a formality to get over quickly. They mostly paid attention to the consent form to know more about the details of the study than to ensure we were protecting their privacy. They were not concerned about the consent form. Most significant, they did not express uneasiness about the proposed recording of their interaction. No one asked, for example, for a trusted sighted individual to be present while we recorded to verify that we followed the protocol of not recording participants' faces. This is in stark contrast[9] with the typical ethical approach for conducting research with at-risk users, which in this case proved to unnecessarily exceptionalize our blind participants (a concern often encountered in anthropological research [17]).

Privacy and confidentiality

We recorded video of the participants consenting, in lieu of signatures on paper. We recorded sound and video of their hands interacting with the devices. We informed the participants that we would not use any identifiable data in our publications. We informed participants that the IRB might review our records to audit our adherence to the protocol, including not recording their faces during the typing tests. None of the participants expressed concern over the recordings, even though they could not verify its contents. They simply did not pay any attention to it.

Reflections on research

Recruitment and exposure to harm

Recruiting participants was challenging. Our study demanded around seven hours of participation over five days. We included only legally blind adults proficient in

---

[8]One can argue that even the anonymized reporting, through publications such as the one here, of participants' activities, amounts to exposing them to breaches of confidentiality with respect to their superiors in the workplace.

[9]In fact, this is also in contrast with the situation encountered in the evaluation of the infantry training simulator, where ethical approval was deemed unnecessary, yet several concerns about participants' vulnerabilities emerged later in the evaluation, as described in the previous section.

braille typing. However, braille literacy is the greatest predictor of employment among blind adults, thus making it difficult to recruit among employed adults (despite a financial incentive being offered). Additionally, while we provided courtesy transportation from the participants' location to our laboratory and back to reduce participants' anxiety, this created significant logistical challenges and exposure to risks and harms not anticipated initially.

In retrospect, we learned several valuable lessons about preparing a protocol for this population that could have been included in the ethics review process. For example, we could have conducted the study at participants' locations. The loss of experimental control over environmental variables such as noise and potential interruptions, may have overcome part of the difficulties of recruitment. Furthermore, realizing that our target population consisted of working adults, we could have limited the time participants stayed in the study by, for example, designing a mixed within- and between-subject protocol. Again, we could have traded off individual independent variable evaluation for greater participation, which is what most of the individuals in our target population wanted.

Ownership and involvement

Our users wanted to participate, get their hands on the prototype, tell their friends, and have an opportunity to provide constructive feedback to make a potential product better. They made our goals their own. We could have provided greater and more diverse opportunities for the community to be a part of the study, balancing study control with participant inclusion. In fact, after the release of the results from this study, a major news outlet ran a story on our app and we received over 700 unsolicited emails worldwide for releasing the app on the App store [10]. Currently, we are working towards our most profound goal, to have lasting positive impact in the community of our study, the community of our volunteers, through the release of our app in the App store. Greater participation could have significantly cut the time to release by providing us with greater opportunity to interact with the community.

Discussion

Conducting technology evaluations with people with disabilities can be challenging from an ethical perspective. Clearly, a significant impairment such as blindness needs to be factored in the research protocol to ensure protection of participants' safety, privacy, and dignity. While we took such steps in our study design, we were also confronted with unexpected challenges during the study (e.g. travel) that were difficult to address after the study has started. Several of the ethical principles that we went to great lengths to implement (informed consent, privacy while recording) were of less concern for the participants themselves. This may be due to the study being perceived as less of an experiment and more of a trivial "app testing", but also due to our participants' desire to contribute to what they perceived as important for their community. While this in no way diminishes the importance of a rigorous ethics review, it highlights the need to consider participants as equal research partners instead of human subjects.

SUMMARY

The four cases discussed highlight how disconnections can occur between the protocols approved by research ethics boards and the realities of conducting HCI research in non-traditional environments. In one case where the researchers were able to work through research challenges with the research ethics board, a satisfactory solution was developed. This example highlights the need for researchers to see research ethics boards as partners in the research process. Also, some of the research contexts discussed might be new to HCI researchers accustomed to controlled evaluations of technology, but familiar to many social sciences researchers, suggesting that collaborating with researchers from other disciplines would be fruitful. At the same time there could be challenges involved in presenting protocols that use social science approaches for review by an ethics board comprised solely of members with expertise in computer science and engineering. Taking a long-term view, it is clear that HCI research in non-traditional contexts requiring ethics approval is expanding. Given this situation, it makes sense for HCI researchers to become involved in higher-level activities of developing research ethics policies that are inclusive of these new contexts.

RECOMMENDATIONS

The examples presented in this paper cover a relatively wide range of HCI research. However, an underlying theme can be seen emerging: contemporary HCI research, especially that involving vulnerable or at-risk participants, has its own unique ethical challenges that do not fit the ethical templates which we are accustomed to. Our four case studies provide examples of unanticipated situations, how they relate to the formalities and rigorousness of the ethical process, and how under-prepared researchers can find themselves dealing with such unexpected ethical challenges once their studies are underway.

As a community we need to take an active role in managing such challenges. We presented our case studies as (simple yet telling) examples that may start a longer-term discussion on how we approach HCI research from an ethical perspective. We hope our contribution will lead to the future development of a "situational ethics" framework that will assist HCI researchers as they navigate the challenges of fieldwork. As a first step, and based on the lessons learned from our shared experiences, we propose several recommendations[10] for HCI researchers to address

[10] We believe that any solutions to these ethical challenges will require thorough scrutiny, evaluation, and refinement from the HCI community. As such, we can only suggest recommendations based on our own experiences – we wanted to avoid passing the exact "ethical edicts" (overly rigid and often not applicable to all

the ethical issues posed by the dynamic nature of studies in novel areas:

- Look for "ethical triggers" in their research protocol – elements that indicate potential challenges during the field study: participants that could belong to vulnerable populations, sensitive settings, in-the-wild deployments of technology, and possibility of blurred lines between being a research participant or an end-user. Most researchers, as was the case in our own examples, are trained to detect such triggers. However, a deeper level of scrutiny is often required – as shown, for example, by the evaluation of the infantry training simulator, where the blurring of participant / research line was not anticipated.
- Incorporate into research design the ability to assess ethical risks and adjust protocols responsibly in the field in response to participant needs, particularly in emotionally charged settings or when evaluating technologies as readily available apps "in the wild" (including handling indirect participation or unexpected requests from participants). While researchers often see ethics as a compliance issue [15], a "situational ethics" approach to planning and conducting fieldwork may allow researchers to better adapt to particular unexpected conditions that arise after the design of the research and ethics protocol. To be successful, such an approach may require an improved rapport between researchers and their institutional Ethics Boards, as detailed in our next recommendation.
- Maintain a continuous dialogue with the Ethics Board when navigating the protocol design challenges and during the study. Board members may have encountered similar situations in other disciplines, and can provide guidance on the ethical issues that may arise. The dialogue may be difficult at times but many of the challenges can be addressed head-on by researchers increasing their sharing of experiences and best practices, and by volunteering for such boards. Our own experience is that being pro-active leads to better understandings of the research challenges, as illustrated in this paper and also as witnessed recently by three of the co-authors after having taken on more responsibilities with their respective ethics boards.
- For researchers, assembling multidisciplinary research teams, even when the study goals are relatively set within one area. This is particularly relevant when the participants are vulnerable or at-risk – common cases in social sciences.
- For institutions that have review boards consisting of committees dedicated to separate disciplines, ensuring that members of such committees have a multidisciplinary background – as many research studies are crossing the boundaries of what constitutes a well-defined research area.
- Become involved in the process of revising ethical guidelines. By participating in stakeholder consultations that continually update ethical policies, HCI researchers have an opportunity to take ownership of decisions that affect their research and raise the awareness of the dynamically-changing contexts of HCI research.

forms of research) that we provided evidence against.

CONCLUSION

The formal requirements of the ethics approval process are often at odds with the realities of conducting qualitative field research. With the recent increase in qualitative research being carried out in HCI, particularly on mobile technologies with marginalized or at-risk populations, ethical challenges that are well known in many disciplines will also become an issue in HCI research. As illustrated by recent publications, such challenges are already acknowledged as an essential factor in designing research protocols by the HCI community; however, our own work highlights the discrepancies, from an ethical perspective, between the planning stages of field research in HCI and the realities of fieldwork.

In this paper we presented our own such challenges in conducting various HCI-related field studies. We showed that some of the established ethical guidelines used to develop the study protocols did not provide proper guidance in dealing with specific situations encountered during our study, and left it up to researchers to make decisions based on personal moral principles rather than on meaningful guidelines. Based on our shared experiences, we proposed recommendations for a *situational* approach to such ethical issues in both the planning and execution stages of the research. We hope that, by illustrating these examples, the HCI community will become more aware of the dynamic nature of the ethical challenges of field research, lab-based evaluations, or qualitative research, especially with at-risk or vulnerable users, and will join the inter-disciplinary efforts of creating ethical guidelines and formal review processes that are flexible and reflective of the diversity of research methods and real-life cases that we encounter.

REFERENCES

[1] ABC Canada. Who Wants to Learn? ABC Canada Literacy Foundation Report. 2001

[2] Bos, N. et al.. Research ethics in the Facebook era: privacy, anonymity, and oversight. ACM *CHI 2009.*

[3] Buchanan, E.A. and Ess, C. Internet Research Ethics and the Institutional Review Board: Current Practices and Issues. *SIGCAS Computers and Society* (39:3), 2008

[4] Chalmers, M. Ethics, logs and videotape: ethics in large scale user trials and user generated content. *CHI 2011.*

[5] Detweiler, C. et al. Values in Design - Building Bridges between RE, HCI and Ethics. *INTERACT 2011*

[6] Ess, C. and Jones, S. Ethical Decision-Making and Internet Research: Recommendations from the AoIR Ethics Working Committee. In *Buchanan, E.A. (Ed.), Readings in Virtual Research*. 2004.

[7] Ess, C. Internet Research Ethics. In *Joinson, A. (Ed.), Oxford Handbook of Internet Psychology*. 2007

[8] Ethics Rupture: An Invitational Summit about Alternatives to Research-Ethics Review. St. Thomas University & University of New Brunswick, 2012.

[9] Friedman, B. et al. Value Sensitive Design and Information Systems. *Human-Computer Interaction and Management Information Systems*, 2006.

[10] https://itunes.apple.com/app/brailletouch/id579725651 accessed on 2015/01/07.

[11] Fournier H. et al. A Multidisciplinary Approach to Enhancing Infantry Training through Immersive Technologies. *I/ITSEC 2011*.

[12] Glaser, B.G. and Strauss, A.L. *The Discovery of Grounded Theory*. Weidenfeld and Nicolson, 1968.

[13] Guta, A. et al. Resisting the seduction of "ethics creep": Using Foucault to surface complexity and contradiction in research ethics review. *Journal Social Science & Medicine,* 2012.

[14] van den Hoonaard, W. Is Research-Ethics Review a Moral Panic? *Canadian Review of Sociology (38),* 2001.

[15] Kahn, J.P. and Mastroianni A.C. Moving From Compliance to Conscience: Why We Can and Should Improve on the Ethics of Clinical Research. In *Arch Intern Med.* 161(7) 2001.

[16] Killshaw, S. Ethics in studying contested illness. In *McClancy, J. (Ed). Ethics in the Field.* 2013

[17] Kim, S.N. Whose voice is it anyway? Rethinking the oral history method in accounting research on race, ethnicity and gender. In *Critical Perspectives on Accounting*, 19(8), 2008

[18] Li, J. Ethical Challenges in Participant Observation: A Reflection on Ethnographic Fieldwork. *The Qualitative Report (*13:1), 2008.

[19] Lingel, J. Ethics and dilemmas of online ethnography. *CHI 2012*.

[20] Marsden, G. and Jones, M. Inspiring Mobile Interaction Design. ACM *CHI 2011 Course.*

[21] Mackay, W. Ethics, lies and videotape. ACM *CHI 1995*.

[22] Moncur, W., Masthoff, J., Reiter, E., Freer, Y., and Nguyen, H. Providing Adaptive Health Updates across the Personal Social Network. Human–Computer Interaction 29, 3 (2014), 256–309

[23] Moncur, W., Mahamood, S., Reiter, E., and Freer, Y. Involving healthcare consumers in knowledge acquisition for virtual healthcare. AAAI Fall Symposium Series, AAAI Press (2009), 43–51.

[24] Moncur, W. The Emotional Wellbeing of Researchers: Considerations for Practice. In *Proceedings of the ACM SIGCHI Conference on Human Factors in Computing Systems (CHI)*, 2013.

[25] Munteanu, C., Molyneaux, H., Maitland, J., McDonald, D., Leung, R., Fournier, H., and Lumsden, J. Hidden in plain sight: Low literacy adults in a developed country overcoming social and educational challenges through mobile learning support tools. In the *Journal of Personal and Ubiquitous Computing*, Springer-Verlag, November 2013

[26] Munteanu, C., Molyneaux, H., Maitland, J., McDonald, D., Leung, R., Lumsden, J., and Fournier, H. A Tale of Two Studies: Challenges in Field Research with Low-literacy Adult Learners in a Developed Country. In *Proceedings of the ACM SIGCHI Conference on Human Factors in Computing Systems (CHI).* 2012.

[27] Munteanu C., Fournier, H., Lapointe, J.F., Emond, B., and Kondratova, I. We'll Take it from Here: Letting the Users Take Charge of the Evaluation and Why that Turned Out Well. In *Proceedings of the ACM SIGCHI Conference on Human Factors in Computing Systems (CHI).* 2013.

[28] National Research Ethics Service. *NRES guidance on information sheets and consent forms*. 2007.

[29] Romero, M., Frey, B., Southern, C., and Abowd, G.D. BrailleTouch: designing a mobile eyes-free soft keyboard. In Proceedings of the *ACM International Conference on Human Computer Interaction with Mobile Devices and Services (MobileHCI)* 2011.

[30] Southern, C., Clawson, J., Frey, B., Abowd, G.D., and Romero, M. An evaluation of BrailleTouch: mobile touchscreen text entry for the visually impaired. In Proceedings of the *ACM International Conference on Human Computer Interaction with Mobile Devices and Services (MobileHCI)* 2012.

[31] Tri-Council Policy Statement: Ethical Conduct of Research Involving Humans, 2nd edition, 2010.

[32] Williams, A. et al. Anchored mobilities: mobile technology and transnational migration. *ACM DIS* 2008

The Royal Corgi: Exploring Social Gaze Interaction for Immersive Gameplay

Mélodie Vidal[1], Rémi Bismuth[2], Andreas Bulling[3], Hans Gellersen[1]
[1]Lancaster University, Lancaster, UK. {m.vidal}{h.gellersen}@lancaster.ac.uk
[2]ISART Digital, Paris, France. remi.bismuth@gmail.com
[3]Max Planck Institute for Informatics, Saarbrücken, Germany. andreas.bulling@acm.org

ABSTRACT
The eyes are a rich channel for non-verbal communication in our daily interactions. We propose social gaze interaction as a game mechanic to enhance user interactions with virtual characters. We develop a game from the ground-up in which characters are designed to be reactive to the player's gaze in social ways, such as getting annoyed when the player seems distracted or changing their dialogue depending on the player's apparent focus of attention. Results from a qualitative user study provide insights about how social gaze interaction is intuitive for users, elicits deep feelings of immersion, and highlight the players' self-consciousness of their own eye movements through their strong reactions to the characters.

Author Keywords
Eye tracking; Virtual agents; Immersion; Games

ACM Classification Keywords
H.5.m. Information Interfaces and Presentation (e.g. HCI): Miscellaneous

INTRODUCTION
Social gaze is a powerful medium of nonverbal communication in our daily conversations. We propose to apply it to HCI through what we call *social gaze interaction* as a way to augment user experiences. Social gaze interaction makes the computer react to the user's gaze in typical human-like reactions, with the aim to render interactions more immersive, natural, and make the user aware of the power of their own gaze. We explore this capability through a first-person social game we built for this purpose, where game characters are aware of the player's gaze and react differently depending on how the user socially looks at them.

Decades of psychology research have provided us with a deep understanding of the variety of ways human communication is influenced by the eyes. A look can indicate the desire to start an interaction, but gaze aversion can, in return, demonstrate the will to avoid said interaction, for example to resolve right of passage at intersections [16]. Eye contact during a conversation can indicate attention [1]; but too long a look turns into a stare, which can be interpreted as trying to establish dominance and can result in reactions that range from aggression to submission [8]. Looking at an object during conversation can also confirm mutual understanding of what is being discussed - a process called joint attention [8]. Depending on the culture, maintained eye contact can also show a lack of respect [1]. According to Kleinke, gaze "influences evaluations of liking and attraction, attentiveness, competence, social skills and mental heath, credibility, and dominance" [16].

Figure 1: The player is in conversation with the French ambassador. When the player looks to the side for too long, she interrupts herself and turns to follow the player's gaze.

We propose to adapt this channel for nonverbal communication for HCI and particularly as a game mechanic for interaction with virtual characters. By bringing implicit social interactions such as gaze into the virtual world, we add a layer of nonverbal communication with the computer with which we aim to enhance user interaction. Figure 1 shows a game character a player is talking to; as the conversation goes on, the player is distracted and looks around while she talks. The character realises this, interrupts herself and turns to identify what caught the player's attention. With social gaze interaction, characters become aware and sensitive in a social way to the player's gaze. We believe this holds great potential in terms of immersion, as it enables players to embody their character and interact with virtual characters on a deeper level, closer to what they might do with humans.

In order to study the various possibilities to integrate social gaze in a game, we developed a first-person game from the ground-up. We identified a variety of social gaze effects; for each of them, we designed a character that exhibits this behaviour. The game, entitled The Royal Corgi, requires players to interact with game characters to gain their trust in a quest to become the next Royal Corgi Instructor. During the game, players need to make dialogue choices to attain their goal -

CHI 2015, April 18–23, 2015, Seoul, Republic of Korea.

ACM 978-1-4503-3145-6/15/04 ...$15.00.
http://dx.doi.org/10.1145/2702123.2702163

however, as they gradually discover, their eyes also influence the dialogue depending on the characters' personalities.

This new mode of interaction leads us to study both how possible it is for users to apply gaze mechanisms usually found in human-human conversations to game characters, but also what effects interacting with gaze-aware characters have on a player. As such, we identify three main research themes. First, can players make sense of gaze mechanisms which are generally implicit in face-to-face conversations? It is usually desirable to render a game interface as natural and intuitive as possible. With game controllers such as the WiiMote and the Microsoft Kinect, players can now reproduce real-life movements for gameplay; we wish to investigate whether interacting with the eyes in games can be made natural as well. Second, does using natural gaze patterns to interact with virtual characters have an effect on the player's sense of immersion and presence? In a quest to make gameplay as immersive as possible, researchers have studied what increases enjoyment in games [27] and gaze as an input modality has previously been found to increase immersion in games [15, 24]. Gaze-aware game characters thus may have the potential to impact player's immersion. Finally, we are interested in whether this process has an effect on the player's internal state, including awareness of their own eye movements. Gaze-aware agents have been reported to create positive feelings of rapport [2]. In addition, Grynszpan et al. reports that although we use gaze socially, we are generally not aware of doing so [10]. Gaze mechanisms in gameplay could have an impact on the way people think about their eyes beyond the game and the way it makes them feel.

This paper presents the following contributions. (1) We propose social gaze interaction as a concept for human-computer interaction and explore its consequences on user interaction. (2) We do so through a new game, The Royal Corgi, which we designed with social gaze as a gameplay mechanism from the start and is the first of its kind. (3) Finally, our study provides insights on how social gaze interaction holds great potential for immersive and natural experiences and has an impact on the self-awareness of the users.

RELATED WORK

As an important means of nonverbal communication, gaze has naturally been a topic of focus for interaction with virtual agents and robots. We also explore the ways the eyes have been used to interact with interfaces and more particularly with games.

Interaction with virtual agents and robots

In a human-robot interaction (HRI) context, social gaze can be considered in two directions. First, it can be reproduced by the robot or agent to elicit an emotional response from the human. A vast body of work has shown that providing robots and agents with human-like eye behaviour improves communication and positive feelings of connection with the artificial personality (for an extensive review on the topic, see [23]). In video games, the character's eyes are occasionally leveraged for communication: in The Wind Waker, Link looks to the side to signal to the player when an interesting object is nearby, while L.A. Noire takes full advantage of the nonverbal behaviour of the eyes by challenging the player to determine whether a character is lying depending on his extremely realistic eye movements. However, the player's gaze is not taken into account.

Second, social gaze can be inferred from the human to inform the virtual personality. For example, Eichner et al. presented a showroom where agents adapt their presentation depending on the user's gaze attention [6]. In museum settings, robotic tour guides have been designed to wait to start giving explanations until a visitor presents visual interest in a scene [4], and have been made to detect when a visitor avoids meeting the robot's gaze during a quiz session [17]. Bee et al. have also studied the effects of establishing eye contact with a virtual agent and found that it created positive feelings of rapport [2]. Finally, Ishii et al. studied users' attention while conversing with an agent; when users seemed distraught, the agent would prompt the user with questions. They found that doing so increased perceived agent intelligence and conversation awareness [12].

These works are examples of the potential that social gaze interaction holds and explore single aspects of it. Here we formally introduce social gaze interaction and explore its feasibility and consequences on a players' perceived immersion.

Eye-tracking for interaction and games

By being responsive to the user's gaze, social gaze interaction is in itself an eye-based interaction technique. While there has been extensive research on eye-based interfaces, the majority have been focused on target selection [18] and positioning [28], text entry (see an overview in [20]) or steering [25] panning and zooming [26]. Only few works on using eye tracking to correct the eyes position for videoconferencing [29, 31] and the body of work on virtual agents mentioned above present applications that makes use of the naturally social behaviour of the eyes for interaction.

The lack of eye-based interaction techniques that harvest the natural behaviour of the eyes is particularly acute in games that use the eyes as input. The idea of using the eyes for interaction with games has been explored in a variety of ways, especially to investigate the difference between using the eyes versus the controller a game was originally designed for. Examples include Half Life and Sacrifice [15], a Paddle game [5], Quake2, Neverwinter Nights and Lunar Command [24], World of Warcraft [14] or Mario [21]. Results alternate between reporting increased performance over mouse [5], increasing perceived immersion and fun [15, 24], but also report that the way the eye tracks moving objects results in latency when using the eyes as ways to aim fire in FPS [15, 24]. Finally, Wetzel et al. recently demonstrated how a player's gaze behaviour can be used in real-time to adapt the parameters of a game and provide sufficient challenge while reducing frustration [30].

Isokoski et al. provide an impressive survey of the different ways the eyes have been used for gaming, and highlight that very few have been built from the ground-up specifically to integrate the eyes as inputs [13]. Hillaire et al. adapted

Concept (effect)	Player's action	Effect on character	Example potential for gameplay
Desire for interaction	Looks at character	Looks back at player, awareness of being looked	Possibility to trigger interaction with reluctant character
Avoidance of interaction	When not in a conversation, avoids meeting the eyes of the character	Inability to start interaction, potential frustration	Possibility to avoid a character
Apparent distraction	While in a conversation, looks around repeatedly	Annoyance, potential perceived lack of respect	Penalising the player for inattention
Cultural disrespect	Sustained eye contact	Annoyance, potential perceived lack of respect	Introducing cultural understanding in gameplay
Dominance test	Stares at the character's eyes	Submission to aggression, or aggression back and pride	Confidence training
Gaze following trigger	Insistently or repeatedly looks at something else than the character	Movement of the eyes to follow the player's gaze direction	Distracting the character
Signs of intent	While in an interaction, looks away at specific object or location	Hypothesis and prediction on intent	Bluffing the character
Joint attention	While in an interaction, looks away at specific object or location	Knowledge of the player's object of attention	Influencing game story depending on interest in objects

Table 1: Summary of the social gaze concepts used in the game.

the game's blur and focus to mimic the eyes' reproduction of depth of field, which reportedly increased the sense of realism experienced by the players [11]. Nacke et al. also showed how the eyes could be used as a metaphor from cultural references, such the Medusa's gaze, which freezes a person on eye contact [22]. In the study, players reported the eyes as their favourite biofeedback interaction method. The study also stressed the importance of establishing an intuitive mapping between direct biofeedback (such as gaze) and its effects.

In this work, we create a game from the ground-up in which characters react socially to the player's gaze. Building such a game enables us to study the feasibility of implementing intuitive eye interactions that users may not have to learn to use because they can compare it to social situations with humans.

SOCIAL GAZE INTERACTIONS

Psychology informs us about the wide range of reactions to gaze depending on the perception of the gazing person's competitiveness and status [16], for example. Based on these findings, we identified prominent social gaze interaction concepts that we wished to implement. These are summarised in Table 1 where the concepts are named and which provides details on what the player does, what effect this can have on the game character, and an example of the concept's potential for gameplay in general.

Desire for interaction. Humans have an accurate ability to determine whether they are being looked at [8]. Looking at someone can indicate the desire to enter an interaction, which starts when both parties establish eye contact. This can be seen as ways for the user to influence the game: players may force a character to attend to them if they insistently look at them, forcing the character's awareness of the player's presence.

Avoidance of interaction. In contrast, gaze aversion - avoiding to meet someone's eyes - prevents that person from starting an interaction [16]. This is for example the case at traffic crossings. Here again, players can take advantage of this concept to control the game: if characters are actively seeking eye contact to start a conversation, players can choose to ignore them and divert their gaze.

Apparent distraction. While in a conversation, frequent eye movements directed at something else than the person talking can be interpreted as lack of interest and attention in the interaction. This can potentially trigger annoyance and anger from the person talking [1]. This concept can be used in games as ways to penalise the player for lack of inattention.

Cultural disrespect. Certain cultures may inversely interpret eye contact as a lack of respect [1, 8]. Prolonged eye contact may annoy a person who expects specific displays of respect. This difference can be used for interaction as means to introduce cultural understanding in gameplay.

Dominance test. By extension, staring can be interpreted as aggression. Depending on the character's perception of the staring player and their own personality, he or she may exhibit a submissive behaviour, or excessive pride if the player looks away first. This can potentially be turned into a way to encourage players to exhibit confidence through their eye behaviour.

Gaze following trigger. Gaze following seems to be a behaviour that is "hard-wired" in the brain [7]. When a person looks insistently at a specific location, other people tend to physically follow their gaze to identify what caught their attention. This concept has the potential to allow for playful interactions with a character, for example to voluntarily distract them.

Signs of intent. While engaged in an interaction, people may also infer knowledge from monitoring the other person's gaze and predict what they are interested in or about to do [3]. Purposefully showing signs of intent can be a way for the player to bluff the game characters so that they wrongly predict the player's next action.

Joint attention. When two persons have a conversation and one of them keeps looking at a third object, this can trigger joint attention, where the other person will also look at the object to potentially clarify the topic being discussed. This can be used to influence the game's storyline depending on what the player seems more interested in.

This list of concepts is not exhaustive: social gaze is a broad topic and effects can vary culturally. We have chosen this subset in order to explore a large range of reactions and gameplay possibilities for the players. As Table 1 shows, some concepts share the same action from the player or effect on the character. The ambiguity surrounding the interpretation of social gaze and its effects can be taken as a playful mechanism [9]:

due to context and the high variability of player personalities, the integration of social gaze interactions into gameplay can lead to potentially desirable ambiguous interpretations of the game mechanics and of the virtual personalities. Social gaze is an input mechanism that game designers can play with, and it can be embraced in a wide variety of ways, from the socially accepted to the perhaps playfully anti-social.

THE ROYAL CORGI GAME

We built a game with the intent of implementing these concepts. In order to seamlessly integrate social gaze interaction as part of the gameplay, we made several early design choices. We decided on a first person-style game, where the player sees the viewpoint of their character. Furthermore, we designed it to be a social game, where players have to talk to a lot of characters and interact with them in order to progress in the game. To study whether they could make sense of each gaze concept, we decided to assign each of them to a different character and present players with a wide range of personalities and behaviours.

Because the game is focused on using the eyes as natural controllers, the interface had to be designed so that players could use their eyes as they would in real-life conversations. For this purpose, we recorded voices for the characters instead of displaying dialogues on the screen, which would have required players to read and thus not use their eyes for face-to-face interaction. We also designed the dialogues so that each character would finish their lines by a question to which players could only answer by 'yes' or 'no', again to avoid players having to read potential answers. For example, a character would ask "Do you like dogs?" and wait for the player's answer.

For increased realism, we chose to design the game so that players had to walk up close to a character in order to start a conversation with them. This means that during a conversation, characters were facing the player in a way that resembles a face-to-face conversation. Finally, the player's head-up display (part of the screen informing players of time left, status, etc) was designed so that the player's status was matched by a colour code evolving progressively between red (bad) to green (good). This is so that players could be aware of their status changing using peripheral vision only and not diverting their eyes from the main scene.

Game synopsis

Our game, named The Royal Corgi, takes place in medieval England. The king has just acquired a new Corgi (a breed of dog) which he is fond of, and is looking for an instructor dedicated to his beloved dog. The player impersonates a greedy young lord whose goal it is to gain influence at the court and views the new position as the perfect way to get closer to the king. He needs to gain the trust of the king's counsellors, which will advise the king on who to appoint as instructor. The game can thus be viewed as a networking game.

Characters (see Figure 3) have different levels of influence, which they will grant to the player if they answer correctly to their questions but also if they exhibit certain social gaze behaviours that they are sensitive to. While a player is not

Figure 2: Screenshot of the start of the game. The HUD is visible in the bottom left corner: the yellow colour indicates the influence of the player is average. The player is looking at the Budget Advisor, which is thus turned towards her.

interacting with a character and just walking around the room, characters also turn towards the player if the player is looking at him/her (*Desire for interaction*), then turn back to his/her initial position when they player looks elsewhere.

The game takes place only four minutes before the meeting in which the king will decide who will be the Corgi instructor. The player will only be appointed as Corgi instructor if their influence level is higher than a certain threshold. The player is thus pressed by time to talk to (and please) as many influential people as possible during this time. Players do not know in advance the characters personalities and levels of influence and can only discover it by talking to them.

Characters

The *Military Advisor* is a stern character, whose only concern is to make sure the player is devoted to training the Corgi to be a defensive dog for the king (Figure 3a). He is very influential, but will be offended and dismiss the player if they look away for too long or too many times while they are in a conversation (*Apparent distraction*).

The *Horse Instructor* is also serious, and very proud (Figure 3b). She is influential because she is the instructor of the royal horse, which she considers to be of higher importance than the royal Corgi. The player needs to be humble in front of her, and lower their eyes often while talking to her, otherwise she will take it as a lack of respect (*Cultural disrespect*).

The *Archivist* is a character with ambition but low self-esteem (Figure 3c). The player can make him advocate in their favour to the king if they dominate him and stare him down when he tries to challenge them in a staring contest. If players are not dominant with this character, he will turn against them by gaining confidence and will try to get the position for himself (*Dominance test*).

The *Budget Advisor* is also quite influential (Figure 3d). He just came back from a honeymoon with his new wife, which is next to him. The Budget Advisor is accommodating about the player's answers on how they plan to manage the finances of the royal Corgi if they were to be appointed. However, he is a jealous man and he will monitor whether the player

(a) The Military Advisor gets offended if the player looks around too often.

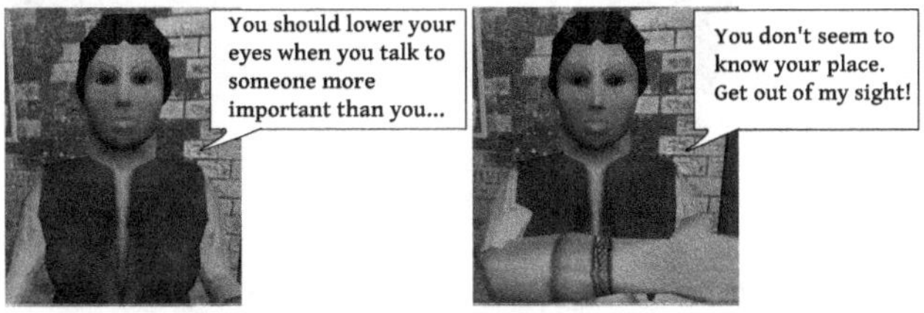

(b) The Horse Instructor first warns the player about the display of respect she expects, then gets annoyed when the user does not comply.

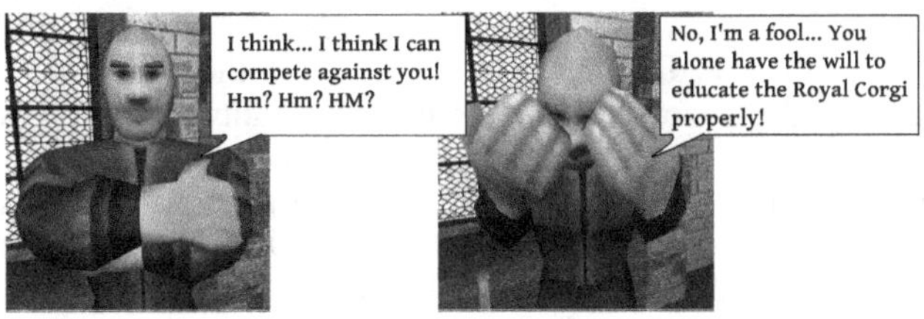

(c) The Archivist challenges the player in a staring contest, then exhibits submissive behaviour if the player did not look away.

(d) The Budget advisor get annoyed if the player spent too long looking at his wife during the conversation.

(e) The Painter exhibits friendly behaviour if the player spent more time looking at the "artistic" painting.

Figure 3: Examples of the effects of the player's gaze on different characters.

glances at his wife while they are talking. He will get angry if this is the case. His dialogue mentions his wife, in order to trigger a glance by the player (*Signs of intent*).

The *Painter* is a jaded character (Figure 3e). He is paid by the king to paint countless paintings of the Corgi (visible in the room) but wishes to paint more challenging and inspiring art. He is placed in between two paintings, one of a Corgi and one of classical art. If the player glances more at the Corgi painting while they talk, he will dismiss them, but if they look more at the other one he will acknowledge them as someone who shares his taste and will give them a small amount of influence (*Joint attention*).

The *French Ambassador* is a character designed to waste the player's time (Figure 1). Instead of waiting for the player to engage a conversation with her, she will come to them as soon as they look at her more than a few seconds. She will then start a lengthy conversation about dogs and cheese, which will never change the player's influence level and can not be interrupted. The only way to escape her is to look away while she talks. She will then turn around, asking whether there is something important happening behind her (*Gaze following trigger*). Only at that moment, the player can interrupt the conversation and walk away. Once they have learnt about her personality, players can also avoid her by not looking at her (*Avoidance of interaction.*).

In order to encourage players to talk to many different characters and to create an even wider variety of personalities, we also placed characters that are not influenced by the player's eyes. We were interested in discovering whether players would start imagining effects that their eyes had on the game, once they learnt that certain characters reacted to them. The *Archbishop* is half-mad and concerned that the Corgi is possessed; he wants the player to swear they will try to exorcise it. The *Fool* does not make sense when he talks but will bring a positive amount of influence if the player takes the time to talk to him. Finally, five competitors are also placed around the room and only dismiss the player when they talk to them.

Implementation

Once the time is up, the game displays the player's score and offers to play again. During a game, players can only talk once to a character; the game is designed to be short in order to give players the opportunity play again and speak several times to the same character to figure out how to win their trust. This short gameplay also provides us with the opportunity to prompt users at several stages of their discovery of the game and its social gaze concepts, and ensure they talk to every character at least once.

Players can move in the environment using the mouse to move their head and the WASD keys to walk; start a conversation with a character by getting close to them and pressing the spacebar; interrupt a conversation by pressing the spacebar again (except the French Ambassador); answer 'yes' or 'no' by using the Q and E keys; and finally, they can hear their character's inner voice by looking at a character and pressing the V key, which will give them insights on who they are and hints on their personalities. For example: "This is the royal

Horse Instructor. She's very proud - better make her think I respect her". The player's gaze is not visible during the game.

The Royal Corgi was developed using Unity3D, custom voices and dialogues, and commercially available 3D models and graphics. The graphics were not detailed enough to allow us to make the character's eyes or face move, but still allow for body animations. While it would have been desirable, the fact that characters can not move their eyes does not impact our goal, which is to implement social gaze interaction from the user's point of view.

The implementation of the gaze concepts is straightforward and very modular. By defining regions of interest (ROIs), characters are made aware whether the player's gaze is located on their faces, on their bodies, or somewhere else. The size of the ROIs varied depending on the object but were generally in the order of 350*350px when viewed while in a conversation. At a viewing distance of about 60cm, this ensures eye tracking accuracy was sufficient for robust selection of ROIs. The amount of time the gaze is located on one ROI was also monitored, and the concepts are implemented depending on the length of the gaze or the frequency it switches to another ROI. Characters can thus be made sensitive to eye contact (and its absence) and the supposed attention or intention of the player. Finally, the eye tracking data was smoothed in real time using a median filter.

USER STUDY

We conducted a qualitative user study with twelve participants (6M, 6F, age M = 26.8 , SD = 5.4). Their background ranged from computer science and design to psychology and occupational therapy. All participants reported playing video games at least monthly, except P1 and P10 who reported having never played; When prompted to rate how used to First-Person shooters they were on a scale of 1 (not at all) to 5 (very used to them), the average was 3.86 (SD = 1.38).

Participants were first introduced to the game and its controls. They were placed around 60cm from the screen and underwent a short 9-point calibration procedure for the eye-tracker, a Tobii TX300 collecting data at 60Hz on a 23" screen with a 1920*1080 resolution. They were also encouraged to explore the game and talk to all the characters, and to voice their thoughts while playing the game. The screen was placed so that players would face characters at eye-level to increase conversation realism (see setup in Figure 4).

Participants were only told how to use the different keys to interact with the game, and that their eyes would also have an effect on the game. They did not know in advance how their eyes would affect the characters. When the game started, players found themselves at the corner of a room and could see several characters in front of them (see Figure 2). They also saw the time ticking down and their influence status on the HUD. They were then free to walk around and choose who they wanted to interact with: each time they played, they interacted with different characters. On average, users interacted with 4.2 (SD = 1.3) characters per game. Excluding competitors and the French Ambassador, interactions lasted for 52 seconds on average (SD = 20.7). The Ambassador's dialogue looped and players could only interrupt interaction by figuring out how to distract her, which is why on average interaction with her lasted for 85.5 seconds (SD = 51.7).

Figure 4: A participant playing the game on the Tobii TX300.

After each four-minutes game, the researcher asked them whether they had noticed any effects from their eyes on the game, and if so, to describe them. Participants played on average 5.3 games (SD = 0.8). The number of games played per participant varies, because we asked them to stop playing only when they had interacted with all the characters at least once and some participants were quicker than others. Participants were then invited to discuss their gameplay experience in a semi-structured interview, always with the same researcher. During the interview, the researcher asked questions such as "When did the game react to your eyes?" "How did it make you feel that the characters responded to your eyes?" and "Did you adapt your behaviour?". Finally, they were asked to complete a questionnaire for demographics. The entire study (which lasted for about an hour) was filmed, then transcribed for analysis.

The analysis of the interview transcripts provided us with a great amount of valuable insights and findings, which we regroup here by theme.

Ease of interaction and naturalness

No participant reported strain on their eyes, despite playing for 20 minutes on average. All participants reported that they had to adapt their behaviour to use the game, and that they had to make conscious efforts to perform the way they were expected for each character, but described it as having to be more focused (*"It was a bit alien 'cause it was a higher level of concentration than if you would just play"* (P6)). In general, they expressed that maintaining control of their eyes was difficult: *"It was difficult, 'cause you're not normally constrained, you can normally look wherever you want"* (P8).

However, this difficulty is contrasted by the fact that all the participants expressed that the interactions were *"real"* (P1, P6, P9) - specifically, that the way they could interact with their eyes was natural but also that the way the characters reacted to their eyes was natural. *"It was the easiest kind of roleplaying. [...] It was very simple to show respect, show disinterest... [...] That's quite easy to do with your eyes"* (P8). Most concepts felt *"obvious"* (P4), especially the ones implemented in the Budget Advisor, the Military Advisor and the Painter, which were often discovered first. *"It's like you're talking to people in real life. That's how people would react in real life"* (P6). *"It made complete sense, that's how I was able to work out the patterns."* (P8).

Participants that were used to video games discovered most gaze concepts after playing three times. On the contrary, the two participants that reported having no prior experience with video games did not discover the concepts after four games until being explicitly prompted about it. We hypothesise that this may be because experienced players may be more used to different types of controllers and thus to the idea that a new part of their body could be having an effect on the game, whereas the two novice players may have been overly focused on using the keyboard and mouse and did not remember that their eyes also had an effect. The Archivist's staring contest was discovered only once, by chance.

Immersion

Social gaze interactions seem to have drawn people into the game. When prompted about how the game made them feel, all participants reported strong feelings of immersion, in that they chose to qualify the game as more *"immersive"* (P1, P5), *"personal"* (P1, P6, P9), *"engaging"* (P7), *"involved"* (P9, P12) than what they are used to and feelings of being *"in the room/game"* (P3, P8, P10). P10 elaborates: *"I really felt like I was having a conversation with these people"*. Several participants never realised that characters turned when they were being looked at. However, it was appreciated when it was noticed: *"It feels like they know your presence there"* (P5) *"It felt like they knew I was there"* (P1).

Some participants also reported wanting to physically nod and mimic characters (P4, P7, P8). Further, several participants reported feeling like they *"acted"* (P5, P11) like their character and described experiences of embodiment: *"I felt like I really was the character. [...] I started to think as myself as yeah, I'm the Corgi instructor. [...] I heard my thoughts, and then I embodied the thoughts."* (P8). P4 said that he occasionally had to remember his *"physiological role"*.

Strong feelings towards the game and the characters

Various participants expressed strong feelings triggered by the fact that they felt the game "knew" what their eyes were doing. We believe this is caused by the strong feelings of immersion reported above. One participant in particular, whose background is psychology, described the experience as being "on show": *"It makes you think like the character is at the will of others [...] It's almost like there's judgement coming from the game. You're on show yourself, you're the one performing for them. [...] It feels like a dangerous environment in some ways"* (P3).

A participant further detailed that he was uncomfortable with having to embody such a greedy character. *"I forgot my character of the greedy young lord [...] It made me more uncomfortable because I didn't like that character, but it made me feel like I had to be that person, I couldn't just press the buttons and press through it, I had to make myself do that, and it was weird, but I liked it. Because I didn't experience it before [...] It is weird... how powerful that is"* (P4).

In addition, we found that participants reacted strongly to particularly polarising characters. The Horse Instructor demanded that players lower their gaze, to which participants generally complied in order to earn more influence. But certain participants decided that they would not, because they felt like they were as good as her - even at the loss of influence. *"She thinks she's better than me, but of course not, I won't do that"* (P11) *"I thought 'I'm as important as you'! I'm not going to lower my eyes for you"* (P12). P1, which complied when prompted to look down, particularly elaborated on her experience with the Horse Instructor: *"It sort of reminded me, all of a sudden I'm in primary school or something. Quite a deep feeling actually [...] It reminded me what it was to feel small, properly small, and a bit inferior."*

The Ambassador was designed to be annoying by wasting the player's time. However, we found that she sometimes triggered unexpected behaviours. Participants either expressed strong feelings of dislike towards her, trying to escape her as soon as possible, or on the contrary thought of her as a *"friend"* (P10). One participant added *"I felt like she was my favourite [...] I feel like I can go and talk to her. You don't get the aggression if you get it wrong"* (P5). It seems that, in an environment where they felt on show and judged for their physiological actions, participants were seeking a figure of reassurance - especially in a challenging game where they had to prove themselves worthy and convince people, such as a networking event. Thus, despite the Ambassador not having an effect on the player's performance, some still enjoyed talking to her. When prompted about trying to interrupt her, they also mentioned trying to do it in a soft way, seeking *"the polite thing to do"* (P3) *"without offending her"* (P10).

We hypothesise these counter-productive behaviours for the game stem from participants getting the impression of being "in" the game and physically identifying with their character. They report to have felt judged, and as a result exhibited various behaviours apparent to coping mechanisms: they fought back and defended themselves or they sought a friendly supporter.

Personal differences

As expected, participants had different expectations about what respect meant in terms of eye behaviour. Some participants found it obvious that the Horse Instructor would require lowering the eyes (*"It's natural, like when you have to look down to respect someone"* (P11)) while others thought it would never happen in real life (*"It was weird looking down, I wouldn't actually expect anyone to say that to me"* (P7)). In a similar fashion, while some participants were at ease with maintaining eye contact with the Military Advisor or the Budget Advisor (*"I knew intuitively that to show respect I had to maintain eye contact"* (P8)), others thought it odd to be always looking at his eyes (*"That's the way people interact, you don't always look at their eyes"* (P3)).

Similarly, some participants found it obvious to look away to distract the French Ambassador (*"If i had someone who enjoyed talking quite a lot that's what I would do. I would try to make a distraction"* (P6)) while others felt it was unnatural (*"I would never normally try to escape someone by looking around at the ceiling while they spoke to me"* (P7)).

Participants also voiced different ideas about how much they think people are aware of their eye movements - and showed different levels of awareness themselves. Some (P3,P5,P8) mentioned that they think people aren't generally aware of it (*"It's something you don't think about when interacting with someone"* (P5)), while others (P6,P7,P10) mentioned being very conscious of it: *"I was consciously making sure my eyes were where they were meant to be, which I always do in real life situations"* (P6).

As a result, participants also had different strategic approaches to how much eye contact is acceptable during face-to-face conversation, which showed in the strategies they chose to adopt. Those who are aware of their eye movements were at ease maintaining eye contact with the Military Advisor and the Budget Advisor, for example, while others found it difficult to keep their attention focused on one character and kept looking away. *"You're just supposed to keep eye contact - It's too awkward, I don't know, I get distracted"* (P2).

Enjoyment

Despite these strong differences in opinion, all participants reported the game as enjoyable, fun and frequently laughed out loud when discovering patterns, such as being caught looking at the Corgi painting or the Budget Advisor's wife. They reported appreciating the wide variety of interactions possible with their eyes - from looking at something to looking away on purpose. *"[about the Ambassador] it's a bit different and it's more playful than just having characters where you have to look in a certain direction to influence them. I really liked it"* (P5).

Participants seemed to enjoy the new modality, which is often the case in eye tracking studies, and the embodiment effect. For example, they mentioned that *"It's more rewarding 'cause I'm not just using my fingers and clicking things"* (P5) and *"It made the game more fun, because it gave an extra dimension to the game"*(P12). The extra dimension highlights the potential of eye tracking to augment existing modalities without replacing them, and provide players with an additional layer of control.

Potential for other games

Participants often expressed how they could envision the eyes being used in the same way for other games, specifically role-playing games such as Assassin's creed, Oblivion, or Fable. Several participants mentioned L.A. Noire as a comparison. *"I could definitely see the eyes taking that button pressing bit out of it and I just think it would be so much fun to play around with it"* (P8). One participant also mentioned how it could be used for pointing at things to be picked up (P12), which has been explored by Smith et al. [24]. Another mentioned that the eyes could also be used to make the screen focus on a particular area (P9), which Hillaire et al. studied [11].

Interestingly, three participants (P2, P3, P4) mentioned that they could envision this kind of technology being used for social therapy training, such as game tailored for persons with autistic symptoms. They thought that, if being played regularly, this kind of game could influence the way people behave socially - and potentially improve their social interactions by learning how people can react to different attitudes without risking real-life repercussions. *"This would actually be a really interesting game for people who don't communicate very well, the concept of that game could be used in order to almost socially train people, train people how to interact in a social setting."* (P3). In a similar way, P1 also mentioned that such technology could be used for social skills such as job interview training, in order to *"convey [personality] traits and be in the best possible light"*.

Game implementation insights

Several participants (P1, P2, P4) reported that the way the Painter was presented helped understanding what was needed of them. It seemed to have been subtle but clear enough for their expectations from games: *"The Painter was pretty obvious, [...] just by the way the camera positioned itself. It's good to get some visual guidance"* (P2) Participants were on the lookout to discover what actions would be triggered by their eyes, *"I really like the fact that the controls weren't so explicit"* (P4). They could not see their gaze on the display, and this occasionally led them to imagine that the game was more reactive than it actually is. For example, one participant thought that all the Corgi paintings scattered around the room could register their gaze, when actually only the painting next to the Painter mattered for interaction. Another one thought that the Archbishop followed his gaze up and down whenever he was next to him, which was simply a coincidence due to the animation.

In general, participants did not notice the Archivist's staring contest - only one person discovered it by chance. When explained later the Archivist's concept, participants suggested using more body language - coming closer, raising eyebrows, to hint players on that fact that something specific is happening. While this was not possible with our 3D models, where the face is static, it is a great insight as to how slightly more obvious body language could allow even more powerful and playful social gaze concepts in future games: *"[the graphics are] intentionally not real, so the cues have to be more pronounced in order to make sense"* (P4).

The limitations from our graphics also came into light with other suggestions from participants, such as making the Ambassador turn only in the direction where the player was looking (P2) (the animation made her turn left and right regardless of the gaze direction), making characters turn only their head instead of their whole body when being looked at (P9), or making more expressive faces.

Despite the care we took in the game design, we omitted to isolate the part of the screen that presented the score as a special region of interest (ROI) to be ignored when the gaze falls onto it. This led to characters such as the Military Advisor misinterpreting the player as inattentive, and players feeling unfairly scowled for their behaviour. In hindsight, we should have isolated this part of the screen to be ignored. This shows that for social gaze interaction, game designers need to keep in mind the different levels of attention their players will experience in the game and the different layers of information available to them - and what this means in terms of gaze behaviour. Players appreciated when the ROIs were carefully divided - such as the distinction between head and body for the Horse Instructor: *"I really liked [...] the details, the Horse Instructor knew about your eye level"* (P5).

Although the interactions were reported as natural, several participants felt that their eyes were restraining them in their interactions: Instead of adding something for the player, they would penalise them if they did the wrong thing. This highlights that social gaze interaction can be made to control the player and penalise them, which might be desirable in certain games, but which is something one should be aware and conscious of when applying social gaze interaction in games.

Finally, one participant mentioned that although the game was using the eyes in an active way, it was not tiring, hinting that it may be because the parts where the eyes are "observed" are divided into units of time - the dialogues. While the player is not talking to anyone, they are free to look around the room in a natural way, which he said allowed the eyes to rest. This is again a useful insight into designing more games that use the eyes in natural ways: *"It was a little bit tiring but it was only for short interactions, because the characters offer a way to chunk up the interactions and you can let your eyes loosen everywhere else"* (P4).

DISCUSSION

These game implementation insights are to be balanced with the hardware we used. In our study, we chose an eye tracker designed for lab studies, whose accuracy and compensation of head movements ensured the data we gathered from players was largely accurate for the size of ROIs we used. Even though our techniques operate with wide ROIs, in future work we plan to test how small the ROIs can afford to be and how precise interactions can be with eye trackers targeted for the general public, such as the Tobii EyeX which is specifically desgined to integrate gaze in games. It would be also interesting to experiment with multi-user eye tracking, or devices that have a larger range of tracking capability, in order to integrate social gaze interactions beyond desktop-bound games - games that are played in the living room, for example.

An obvious limitation to our study is that our characters were not able to move their own eyes. In order to fully study the potential and repercussions of social gaze interaction, it is necessary to evaluate the impact on interaction when both the virtual character and the player can exhibit social gaze behaviour. Nonetheless, this exploratory work provided us with numerous findings and insights on the potential of social gaze interaction as a game mechanic.

One promising field of application are games that train specific behaviour in players, as has been suggested by several participants. Eye-contingent games and virtual agents are already used in clinical situations, for example for autism [19, 10]. We can envision social gaze interaction being a successful candidate to further develop social therapy or cultural training and learn the consequences of one's gaze behaviour in different situations.

In more conventional games, social gaze interaction could be integrated seamlessly along the storyline to allow players to embody their characters. In a spy game, players could consciously have to not look at a particular piece of evidence. We can also imagine a Poker game, where virtual players would be aware of the player's eyes: Poker is a game where the eyes are crucial and can reveal a lot to a seasoned player. It could thus be used to train oneself to bluff or hide giveaway clues.

An important aspect to consider for design with social gaze interaction is the strong feeling of embodiment reported, and what this implies for the players. Having their eyes monitored by other characters made some participants feel on show and judged. By adding social gaze interactions in a game, we also brought in the consequences of the weight of a peer's gaze. In addition, some participants expressed negative feelings about the character they had to impersonate. While they may have felt this way even without gaze interaction, we believe that the fact that they physically embodied the game's greedy character emphasised this feeling. We suggest game designers should be particularly attentive to the role they offer their players and what they want to make them feel.

Finally, the game audience is also an important consideration: social gaze expectations vary depending on culture and personality. A specific angle of approach in terms of audience is that of female players. While we noticed strategies and trends between genders, our participants sample size was not large enough to report specific findings. However, several female participants expressed that they had to remember that their character was a man, which they expressed to be difficult since the interaction style was so embodied. We would like to further our players' gaming experience by creating another version of the Royal Corgi where the main character is female.

CONCLUSION

We introduced social gaze interaction as a game mechanic, and implemented a range of social gaze concepts into a game we built specifically for this purpose. Our study showed that the social gaze concepts were found natural and participants did not have to be taught how to interact. Participants reported experiences of immersion and presence and described strong feelings of embodiment. Finally, they mentioned modifying their physiological behaviour in order to adapt to the game as they discovered different concepts and played with them purposefully. This highlights the potential of social gaze interaction for games as a way to enhance user experiences with virtual characters, and gathers insights for future games wishing to integrate social gaze interaction.

REFERENCES

1. Argyle, M., and Cook, M. *Gaze and mutual gaze.* Cambridge University Press Cambridge, Eng. ; New York, 1976.
2. Bee, N., Wagner, J., André, E., Vogt, T., Charles, F., Pizzi, D., and Cavazza, M. Discovering eye gaze

behavior during human-agent conversation in an interactive storytelling application. In *International Conference on Multimodal Interfaces and the Workshop on Machine Learning for Multimodal Interaction* (2010), 9:1–9:8.

3. Castiello, U. Understanding other people's actions: Intention and attention. *Journal of Experimental Psychology: Human Perception and Performance 29* (2003), 416–430.
4. Das, D., Rashed, M. G., Kobayashi, Y., and Kuno, Y. Recognizing gaze pattern for human robot interaction. In *Proc. of HRI* (2014), 142–143.
5. Dorr, M., Böhme, M., Martinetz, T., and Barth, E. Gaze beats mouse: A case study. In *The 3rd Conference on Communication by Gaze Interaction (COGAIN 2007)* (2007), 16–19.
6. Eichner, T., Prendinger, H., André, E., and Ishizuka, M. Attentive presentation agents. In *Proc. of the 7th International Conference on Intelligent Virtual Agents* (2007), 283–295.
7. Emery, N. J. The eyes have it: the neuroethology, function and evolution of social gaze. *Neuroscience and Biobehavioural Reviews 24* (2000), 581–604.
8. Frischen, A., Bayliss, A. P., and Tipper, S. P. Gaze cueing of attention: visual attention, social cognition, and individual differences. *Psychological bulletin 133* (2007).
9. Gaver, W. W., Beaver, J., and Benford, S. Ambiguity as a resource for design. In *Proc. of CHI* (2003), 233–240.
10. Grynszpan, O., Simonin, J., Martin, J.-C., and Nadel, J. Investigating social gaze as an action-perception online performance. *Frontiers in Human Neuroscience 6*, 94 (2012).
11. Hillaire, S., Lécuyer, A., Cozot, R., and Casiez, G. Using an eye-tracking system to improve camera motions and depth-of-field blur effects in virtual environments. In *VR* (2008), 47–50.
12. Ishii, R., Nakano, Y. I., and Nishida, T. Gaze awareness in conversational agents: Estimating a user's conversational engagement from eye gaze. *ACM Trans. Interact. Intell. Syst. 3*, 2 (Aug. 2013), 11:1–11:25.
13. Isokoski, P., Joos, M., Spakov, O., and Martin, B. Gaze controlled games. *Universal Access in the Information Society 8*, 4 (Oct. 2009), 323–337.
14. Istance, H., Hyrskykari, A., Vickers, S., and Chaves, T. For your eyes only: Controlling 3d online games by eye-gaze. In *Proc. of INTERACT* (2009), 314–327.
15. Jönsson, E. If looks could kill - An Evaluation of Eye Tracking in Computer Games. Master's thesis, KTH Royal Institute of Technology, Sweden, 2005.
16. Kleinke, C. L. Gaze and eye contact: a research review. *Psychological bulletin* (1986).
17. Kobayashi, Y., Shibata, T., Hoshi, Y., Kuno, Y., Okada, M., and Yamazaki, K. Choosing answerers by observing gaze responses for museum guide robots. In *Proc. of HRI* (2010), 109–110.
18. Kumar, M., Paepcke, A., and Winograd, T. Eyepoint: Practical pointing and selection using gaze and keyboard. In *Proc. of CHI* (2007), 421–430.
19. Lahiri, U., Warren, Z., and Sarkar, N. Design of a gaze-sensitive virtual social interactive system for children with autism. *Neural Systems and Rehabilitation Engineering, IEEE Transactions on 19*, 4 (Aug 2011), 443–452.
20. Mollenbach, E., Hansen, J., and Lillholm, M. Eye movements in gaze interaction. *Journal of Eye Movement Research 6(2)* (2013), 1–15.
21. Muñoz, J., Yannakakis, G. N., Mulvey, F., Hansen, D. W., Gutierrez, G., and Sanchis, A. Towards Gaze-Controlled Platform Games. In *Proc. of IEEE Conference on Computational Intelligence and Games* (2011).
22. Nacke, L. E., Kalyn, M., Lough, C., and Mandryk, R. L. Biofeedback game design: Using direct and indirect physiological control to enhance game interaction. In *Proc. of CHI* (2011), 103–112.
23. Ruhland, K., Andrist, S., Badler, J. B., Peters, C. E., Badler, N. I., Gleicher, M., Mutlu, B., and McDonnell, R. Look me in the Eyes: A Survey of Eye and Gaze Animation for Virtual Agents and Artificial Systems. In *EG 2014 - STARs*, Eurographics Association (2014), 69–91.
24. Smith, J. D., and Graham, T. C. N. Use of eye movements for video game control. In *Proc. of ACE* (2006).
25. Stellmach, S., and Dachselt, R. Designing gaze-based user interfaces for steering in virtual environments. In *Proc. of ETRA* (2012), 131–138.
26. Stellmach, S., and Dachselt, R. Investigating gaze-supported multimodal pan and zoom. In *Proc. of ETRA* (2012), 357–360.
27. Sweetser, P., and Wyeth, P. Gameflow: A model for evaluating player enjoyment in games. *Computers in Entertainment 3*, 3 (July 2005), 3–3.
28. Turner, J., Bulling, A., Alexander, J., and Gellersen, H. Cross-device gaze-supported point-to-point content transfer. In *Proc. of ETRA* (2014), 19–26.
29. Vertegaal, R., Weevers, I., Sohn, C., and Cheung, C. Gaze-2: Conveying eye contact in group video conferencing using eye-controlled camera direction. In *Proc. of CHI* (2003), 521–528.
30. Wetzel, S., Spiel, K., and Bertel, S. Dynamically adapting an ai game engine based on players' eye movements and strategies. In *Proc. of the 2014 ACM SIGCHI Symposium on Engineering Interactive Computing Systems* (2014), 3–12.
31. Yang, R., and Zhang, Z. Eye gaze correction with stereovision for video-teleconferencing. In *Proc. of ECCV* (2002), 479–494.

Exploring 3D User Interface Technologies For Improving The Gaming Experience

Arun Kulshreshth
Department of EECS
University of Central Florida
4000 Central Florida Blvd
Orlando, FL 32816, USA
arunkul@knights.ucf.edu

Joseph J. LaViola Jr.
Department of EECS
University of Central Florida
4000 Central Florida Blvd
Orlando FL 32816, USA
jjl@eecs.ucf.edu

ABSTRACT
We present the results of a comprehensive video game study which explores how the gaming experience is effected when several 3D user interface technologies are used simultaneously. We custom designed an air-combat game integrating several 3DUI technologies (stereoscopic 3D, head tracking, and finger-count gestures) and studied the combined effect of these technologies on the gaming experience. Our game design was based on existing design principles for optimizing the usage of these technologies in isolation. Additionally, to enhance depth perception and minimize visual discomfort, the game dynamically optimizes stereoscopic 3D parameters (convergence and separation) based on the user's look direction. We conducted a within subjects experiment where we examined performance data and self-reported data on users perception of the game. Our results indicate that participants performed significantly better when all the 3DUI technologies (stereoscopic 3D, head-tracking and finger-count gestures) were available simultaneously with head tracking as a dominant factor. We explore the individual contribution of each of these technologies to the overall gaming experience and discuss the reasons behind our findings.

Author Keywords
Air-combat game; Finger-Count; Stereoscopic 3D; Head tracking; User Study; Video Games; Game Design; Game-play metrics; Player Behavior; User Experience.

ACM Classification Keywords
H.5.m Information Interfaces and Presentation (e.g. HCI): Miscellaneous.; K.8.0 Personal Computing: Games

General Terms
Design, Experimentation, Measurement, Performance, Human Factors.

INTRODUCTION
3D user interface technologies [4] (e.g., stereoscopic 3D, head tracking, gesture based control, etc.) have the potential to improve game performance and the gaming experience. Such interfaces allow users to use natural motion and gestures to control the game thereby making the whole gaming experience more immersive and engaging. In the past, researchers [9, 10, 11, 18, 19] have studied the benefits of these technologies (e.g. stereoscopic 3D, head tracking, gesture based control, etc.) for video games. But, most of the past work have been focused on these technologies in isolation and it is still unknown how the gaming experience will be affected if several 3DUI technologies are used simultaneously. By designing a game which integrates several 3DUI technologies, we hope to understand the interplay between the technologies and its effect on the gaming experience.

CHI 2015, April 18 - 23, 2015, Seoul, Republic of Korea
Copyright © 2015 ACM 978-1-4503-3145-6/15/04...$15.00
http://dx.doi.org/10.1145/2702123.2702138

Figure 1. A user playing the air-combat game we designed. The game effectively uses stereoscopic 3D, head tracking and finger-count gestures.

Stereoscopic 3D and head tracking are two core technologies for 3DUI applications. Stereoscopic 3D [11, 18, 19] and head tracking [10, 21, 22], in isolation, have been shown to provide a better gaming experience along with performance benefits for some games. Based on these findings, we chose to use stereoscopic 3D and head tracking for our game design. We chose to design an air-combat game since it had tasks (e.g. judge the distance of an enemy, find enemy, etc.) which could benefit from the availability of stereoscopic 3D and head tracking usage. Furthermore, to enhance depth perception and minimize visual discomfort, our game dynamically adjusts the stereoscopic 3D parameters (convergence and separation), based on the user's look direction.

Additionally, we wanted to include a 3DUI input mechanism in our game to create a more inclusive 3D user interface experience and chose a gesture-based interface. Initially, we experimented with several motion sensing devices (e.g. Leap Motion, Microsoft Kinect, etc.) but these devices failed for our purposes for two reasons. First, the gestures recognition accuracy of these devices was not good enough for precisely controlling the aircraft in our game. Second, users needed to continuously control the airplane causing fatigue during our pilot testing sessions (lasting for about 100 minutes). These factors hindered the overall gameplay experience. However, finger-count gestures [9] are well studied in the past and have higher recognition accuracy as well as being easy to use and fast to perform. These gestures could potentially be used as shortcuts in video games. The finger count gestures were well suited for longer use since the user is not using them continuously while playing the game. Therefore, we used these gestures as an alternate to using buttons for switching weapons. We refer to them as finger-count shortcuts.

In this paper, we designed an air combat game (see Figure 1) and conducted a within subjects experiment to evaluate the effectiveness of simultaneous use of these technologies (stereoscopic 3D, head tracking and finger-count shortcuts). We examined the performance data (enemies killed & survival time), head tracking usage data, and self-reported data on user's perception of the game.

RELATED WORK

Stereoscopic 3D has been found useful for games depending upon the game task involved. Stereoscopic 3D has also been found to be helpful in playing simple games where a user is manipulating a single object at a time [6]. Rajae et al. [16] showed that presence of stereoscopic 3D did not help people perform better in a shooter game but people experienced a stronger feeling of presence in stereoscopic 3D mode. Other researchers [13, 18, 19] have also confirmed increased engagement and preference for stereoscopic 3D games.

Creating graphical user interfaces (GUI) for stereoscopic 3D games is a difficult choice between visual comfort and effect. Schild et al. [17] explored GUI design space for a stereoscopic 3D game in order to design comfortable game GUIs (e.g., menus and icons). Their results showed that in-game menus look best when displayed at the bottom of screen with a semi-transparent background. For referencing objects, they found that it is best to show the referencing information at the same depth as the object itself. Deepress3D is a flight game [18] which was custom designed keeping stereoscopic 3D viewing in mind. Their game design featured a stereoscopic specific GUI based on [17] , no real depth illusions in graphics, and optimal parallax budget for stereoscopic viewing. Their results show that the users experienced an enhanced sense of presence in the stereoscopic 3D viewing environment.

Stereoscopic 3D benefits can only be expected if the stereoscopic vision is not accompanied by distortions (e.g., contradicting depth cues, ghosting/cross-talk, exaggerated disparity) [27]. While stereoscopic 3D has shown some positive benefits depending on the task, it also has shown to cause negative symptoms as well, such as eyestrain, headache, dizziness, and nausea [8]. Ware [25] proposed dynamic adjustment of stereoscopic parameters to minimize visual discomfort and optimize stereo depth. Our game design also dynamically adjusts stereoscopic 3D parameters (convergence and separation), based on user's look direction, for a comfortable viewing experience and still enhance stereo depth perception whenever possible.

Wang et al. [24] used face tracking for head gesture recognition. Their evaluation, based on simple game prototypes they developed, showed that the test participants experienced a greater sense of presence and satisfaction with their head tracking technique. However, no performance benefits were found compared to a button based head control. Yim et al. [26] developed a head tracking solution using Wiimotes and their preliminary results show that users perceived head tracking as a more enjoyable and intuitive gaming experience. Sko et al. [21] explored head tracking for first person shooter games. Their study showed that head tracking could be useful for games which are designed with head tracking usage in mind. Kulshreshth et al. [10] explored head tracking for a variety of games and found it to be useful for a few games depending upon the game type and the gaming experience of the participants. However, they used commercial games for their experiment and some of their games may not have been designed with head tracking usage in mind, possibly explaining why they did not find performance benefits in all the games they tested.

For optimal head tracking usage in a game some design guidelines have been proposed [10, 22] which includes proper training for head tracking usage, avoiding awkward head movements, non-isomorphic head rotations with different scaling along different directions, natural movements for tasks and proper calibration of head tracking device. For our air-combat game, we made use of all these design principles to optimize head tracking usage.

Barfield et al. [3] studied the effects of stereoscopic 3D and head tracking on a wire-tracing task. Their results indicated that the task time was the same irrespective of display conditions (monoscopic vs stereoscopic 3D) when head tracking was present. People performed best with stereoscopic 3D when head tracking was absent. McMahan et al. [14] explored the interplay between display fidelity and interaction fidelity. Their results showed that the performance was best with low-display low-interaction fidelity and high-display and high-interaction fidelity. Another experiment involving a spatial judgment task [15] showed that the participants performed better with head-tracking and best performance was achieved when both stereoscopic 3D and head tracking was present. The worst score was achieved with a combination of monoscopic display and no head tracking. However, none of these researchers used complex video games for their experiments.

Finger-Count menus were first proposed for multi-touch surfaces [1] and were later adapted for distant displays [2], using the Kinect as the gestural input device. But, the Kinect based implementation was slow for practical use. Another implementation [9] improved the selection time of this technique by using a faster finger recognition algorithm resulting in an average selection time of under a second. Their study showed that Finger-Count shortcuts have a high accuracy and are layout independent. Finger-Count gestures could also be used as shortcuts in video games. Our game these finger-count shortcuts for switching between weapons.

Figure 2. Air-combat game screenshot

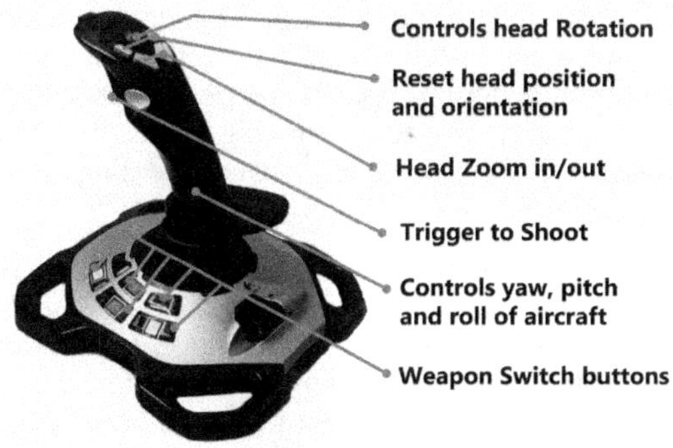

Figure 3. Joystick Controls for the air-combat game

None of the work mentioned above evaluated the affects of using several 3DUI technologies together in complex gaming environments like in modern video games. To the best of our knowledge, our work is the first to systematically explore the combined affect of several 3DUI technologies in a custom designed game with several design optimizations specific to each technique.

DESIGN FACTORS

As mentioned in the introduction, we chose to design an air-combat game since it had tasks which could benefit from availability of stereoscopic 3D, head tracking usage, and finger-count gestures. Furthermore, an air-combat game scene has a lot of depth and using stereoscopic 3D would make the game more immersive. The design of this game includes several optimizations, based on past work, specific to stereoscopic 3D [11, 17, 18, 20] and head tracking [10, 21, 22].

Air-Combat Game

The player has to control an aircraft , using the Logitech extreme 3D Pro joystick, in first person view and shoot enemies (see Figure 2 for a screenshot of the game). The game has five different kind of enemies, each marked with a different color, and five different kind of weapons. The color of the crosshair indicates the color of the currently selected weapon. Each enemy can be killed only with a weapon of the same color and thus requires a user to frequently switch weapons while playing the game. A radar is also available which shows 2D positions of the enemies around the aircraft. To be consistent with the color scheme, the radar uses the same color as the enemy to display its position. The game also featured 3D sound effects for aircraft, weapons and explosions (when enemies are shot dead). An enemy could also be locked (except for yellow and green enemies) by holding the crosshair over it for a short period of time (about two seconds).

The head of the player can be controlled either by using head tracking (a TrackIR 5 device was used) or a combination of the hat switch and buttons on the joystick (see Figure 3). To switch weapons one can use finger-count shortcuts or buttons on the joystick (one button is assigned for each weapon). To avoid any confusion each button is clearly marked with a color on the joystick. In case of finger-count shortcuts, a chart was displayed at the top of the screen indicating the correspondence between finger-count gestures and weapon colors. The game was implemented using the Unity3D game engine and the Air Strike Starter Kit from the Unity Asset Store. For implementing finger-count shortcuts, we used the Intel's perceptual computing SDK.

Stereoscopic 3D features

Dynamic Stereo. Currently, most stereoscopic 3D games fix convergence and separation values for optimal depth budget throughout the game. But, this approach reduces stereo depth when a large object (e.g. gun in FPS games, cockpit in air-combat, etc.) is present in front of the game camera. The reason being the fact that stereo parameters have to be optimized to keep that large object always in focus. However, when the player's head is rotated, that nearby object is not in the players view and stereo depth could be increased. In case of our air-combat game, we optimized stereo parameters under two conditions. First, when the user is looking sideways (left/right) and second, when the user is zoomed into the scene. In both these cases, the user is not looking at the cockpit in front. When the player's head is rotated sideways (left/right), the separation is increased with linear scaling proportional to the heads rotation and the convergence is not changed. When a user zooms in the scene the field of view (FOV) of the camera is reduced proportional to the head's displacement. Thus, in case of zooming, the separation is increased with linear scaling proportional to the camera's FOV. At the same time, the convergence is linearly decreased with the camera's FOV to keep both the crosshair and background in focus. These dynamic parameters ensured a comfortable stereoscopic 3D experience and provided better depth perception for this air-combat game.

Stereoscopic 3D Specific GUI Elements. Based on [17], we optimized our game GUI for stereoscopic 3D usage. All the 2D GUI elements (timer, game stats, etc.) were rendered at screen depth to allow them to be in focus throughout the game. The radar was displayed at the bottom of the screen and was also rendered at screen depth. The chart displaying the correspondence between finger-count gestures and weapon colors was a 3D object rendered at the same depth as the aircraft to be visible all the time without being occluded by other 3D objects in the scene.

Optimal Depth Cues. The game minimized the impact of monocular depth cues. All the enemy ships were colored instead of textured. No dynamic light sources were used and shadows (a known depth cue) were disabled.

Disable Post-processing Image Effects. Some post-processing image effects (e.g. halo effect for lights) do not work well with stereoscopic 3D rendering since these effects are rendered only for one eye making it uncomfortable to look at. Hence, we did not use any post-processing image effects for our game.

Minimized 3D Glasses Flicker. Excessive motion in front of the display may sometime cause the 3D glasses to flicker due to loss of sync signal [11]. In our case head tracking was used only for head rotations & zooming and all other motions were restricted. In case of head rotation, the head position does not change and the head rotation is also limited (about 40 degrees each side). When a user zooms in, the head moves towards the Nvidia IR emitter. Thus, in both these cases the head motion is minimal and does not interfere with 3D sync signal loss. Furthermore, we noticed that Nvidia 3D vision 2 glasses were flickering when used together with the Creative Senzeye3D depth camera (used for detecting finger-count gestures). We suspect that there was some interference between IR blaster inside the camera and the 3D sync signal from Nvidia IR emitter causing the glasses to loose sync signal. However, older Nvidia 3D vision glasses worked fine without any flickering issues. Hence, we used older Nvidia 3D vision glasses instead of newer 3D vision 2 glasses for our experiments.

Head Tracking Features

Natural Head Movements. People are used to rotating their head for looking around. We mapped head tracking to use these natural movements for looking through the sides of the plane and zooming in. Thus, it is very easy to understand the head tracking usage for our air-combat game.

Adaptable Setup. Since every user is different (in terms of height/size and comfortable sitting position), the starting head position in the game was customized for each user. We asked users to sit in their relaxed pose and that was chosen as the starting head position/orientation. The user's motion is then detected relative to that starting pose. Thus, we ensured that each user is comfortable while playing the game.

Training for Head Usage. A prior experiment on head tracking usage in video games [10] found that experienced gamers make better use of head tracking than casual gamers. Casual gamers pay more attention to learning how to play the game and do not use these extra features to their advantage. To avoid this problem, we trained all our participants, irrespective of their gaming experience, to be able to play the game and use head tracking at the same time.

Avoid Awkward Head Movements. We restricted the player's head position/orientation to avoid most awkward head poses. The player's head could only be rotated sideways (left/right) and up/down. The head position was fixed along axes parallel to the display to allow only one directional movement toward display while zooming. These restrictions ensure that the users don't get disoriented while playing thereby reducing head-tracking based motion sickness (nausea).

Non-Isomorphic Head Rotations. When users are looking at the display, they can not rotate their head beyond a certain range depending upon the display size and the player's distance from display. In the past, non-isomorphic rotations seem to have helped in rotation tasks [12] when head tracking is present. We used non-isomorphic rotation scaling for left and right rotations to allow users to see more area on both sides of the plane without rotating his head too much. We thought this would help them quickly scan a large area of the game environment for finding potential enemies.

Why Five Enemies and Five Weapons?

As part of our experiment, we wanted to evaluate the performance of finger-count shortcuts, as a fast way to switch weapons, compared to buttons. Since the user were using one hand to control the plane, only one hand was available for finger-count gestures. This limits the number of finger-count gestures to five. This motivated us to keep five different kind of enemies. Moreover, we wanted people to use these gestures frequently throughout the game play session. Thus, we designed five different kind of weapons and added a restriction that each enemy can be killed only by a specific weapon.

USER EVALUATIONS

We conducted an experiment with our air-combat game to evaluate the combined effect of stereoscopic 3D, head tracking, and finger-count shortcuts on the gaming experience. Additionally, we also looked at the effects of individual technologies to be able to understand their contribution to the overall gaming experience. Based on previous findings in related work and our analysis of the game, we have the following hypotheses:

Hypothesis 1 (H1) : The combined usage of stereoscopic 3D, head tracking and finger-count shortcuts improves user's gaming performance compared to the control condition with monoscopic display, no head tracking and buttons for weapon switching.

Hypothesis 2 (H2) : Stereoscopic 3D improves user's gaming performance compared to the monoscopic display condition.

Hypothesis 3 (H3) : Head-tracking improves user's gaming performance compared to button based head control.

Hypothesis 4 (H4) : User's performance with finger-count shortcuts will be same as with buttons.

Hypothesis 5 (H5) : Participants prefer to use Finger-count shortcuts compared to buttons.

Subjects and Apparatus

We recruited 32 participants (29 males and 3 females ranging in age from 18 to 30 with a mean age 20.84) from the university population, of which four were left handed. Out of all participants, only 4 had prior experience with head tracked games, 8 had played stereoscopic 3D games, and 30 people had played motion controlled games. The experiment duration ranged from 100 to 120 minutes and all participants were paid \$10 for their time.

The experiment setup, shown in Figure 4, consisted of a 27" BenQ XL2720Z 3D monitor, Nvidia 3D Vision kit, a TrackIR 5 with Pro Clip (mounted on a headphone), a Creative Senz3D depth camera, a Logitech Extreme 3D Pro joystick, and a PC (Core i7 4770K CPU, GTX 780 graphics card,

Figure 4. The Experimental Setup.

8 GB RAM). We used the Unity3D game engine and Intel Perceptual Computing Software Development Kit (PCSDK) for implementing the game. The TrackIR 5 camera, the creative camera, and the Nvidia IR emitter were mounted on the top of monitor. Participants were seated about 2 feet away from the display. Since the 3D Vision glasses could impact the subjective feel and comfort level of the participants under different condition, participants were asked to wear them throughout the experiment. In non-stereoscopic condition, the open shutters of the glasses provide an image slightly darker than without glasses but minimally brighter than the stereoscopic 3D version. To make sure that all our participants are able to see stereoscopic 3D, we used Nvidia medical test image to test stereo abilities of participants. All our participants passed the test. All participants preferred using their right hand (despite some of them being left handed people) for joystick control and left hand for weapon switching (buttons or finger-count gestures).

Experiment Design and Procedure

We chose a within-subjects design for our experiments in order to be able to measure and compare user perceptions of the game on a variety of quantitative and qualitative metrics. This within-subjects experiment had 3 independent variables: display mode (Stereoscopic 3D and monoscopic 2D), head control mode (head-tracked and button based head control) and weapon switch mode (finger-count shortcuts and buttons). In total we had $2 \times 2 \times 2 = 8$ conditions and for each condition the user conducted two trials which makes a total of 16 game plays per participant as part of this experiment. Each game trial ends if the player dies (if hit with another plane or ground, shot by another plane) or if the time limit of 5 minutes is reached . Our dependent variables were mean survival time and mean number of enemies killed, where the mean is taken over the two trials for that condition.

The experiment began with the participant seated in front of the monitor and the moderator seated to the side. Participants were given a consent form that explained the experiment procedure. They were then given a modified version of Terlecki and Newcombe's video game experience survey [23] as a pre-questionnaire which collected general information about the participant (age, sex, dexterity) and their prior gaming experience. At the beginning, each participant was trained for about 20-25 minutes on how to play the game under different experimental conditions. Participants then played the game under

	Game Questions
Q1	To what extent did the game hold your attention?
Q2	How much effort did you put into playing the game?
Q3	How mentally demanding was this game?
Q4	Did you feel hurried or rushed when playing this game?
Q5	To what extent you felt frustrated while playing?
Q6	To what extent did you find the game challenging?
Q7	To what extent did you enjoy the graphics and the imagery?
Q8	To what extent you felt that you were part of the game rather than just observing?
Q9	To what extent you felt that you were physically present in the game environment presented?
Q10	How much would you say you enjoyed playing the game?
Q11	Would you like to play the game again?
Q12	Which aspects of the game made your overall game experience better? Stereoscopic 3D, Head-tracking, Finger-count shortcuts?

Table 1. Post-Questionnaire. Participants responded to question 1-11 on a 7 point Likert scale. Question 12 was a multiple choice question.

each condition. Each condition presented to the user in random order based on a Latin square design [5]. We recorded survival time, number of enemies killed and head tracking usage data for each gaming condition presented during experiment. After the experiment, the participant filled out a post-questionnaire with questions about their experiences with the game (see Table 1) including questions about stereoscopic 3D (see Table 2), head tracking (see Table 2), and finger-count shortcuts (see Table 3).

RESULTS

To analyze the performance data, we used repeated-measures 3-factor ANOVA per dependent variable. We did a post-hoc analysis using pairwise sample t-tests. We used Holm's sequential Bonferroni adjustment to correct for type I errors [7] and the Shapiro-Wilk test to make sure the data was parametric. To analyze the Likert scale data, we used Friedman's test and then a post-hoc analysis was done using Wilcoxon signed rank test. For all of our statistical measures, we used $\alpha = 0.05$.

Quantitative Results

Repeated measures 3-factor ANOVA results are shown in Table 4. In terms of enemies killed, significant interactions were found based on the combined usage of all the three technologies (DM×HCM×WSM). People killed significantly more ($t_{31} = -2.546, p < 0.02$) enemies when stereoscopic 3D, head tracking and finger-count shortcuts ($\bar{x} = 18.21, \sigma = 5.70$) were present compared to a condition with monoscopic display, no head tracking and buttons for weapon switch ($\bar{x} = 15.32, \sigma = 4.88$). There was no significant difference in survival time between the above two conditions.

We found significant differences in the number of enemies killed ($F_{1,31} = 14.264, p < 0.005$) and the survival time ($F_{1,31} = 14.215, p < 0.005$) based on the head control mode (NHT vs HT). Participants killed significantly more enemies ($t_{31} = -3.777, p < 0.005$) and survived significantly longer ($t_{35} = -3.770, p < 0.005$) when head tracking was present.

Source	Enemies Killed	Survival Time
DM	$F_{1.31} = 0.876, p = 0.357$	$F_{1.31} = 0.021, p = 0.886$
HCM	$F_{1.31} = 14.264, p < 0.005$	$F_{1.31} = 14.215, p < 0.005$
WSM	$F_{1.31} = 5.320, p < 0.05$	$F_{1.31} = 3.255, p = 0.081$
DM×HCM	$F_{1.31} = 0.103, p = 0.751$	$F_{1.31} = 0.932, p = 0.342$
DM×WSM	$F_{1.31} = 2.601, p = 0.117$	$F_{1.31} = 1.791, p = 0.191$
HCM×WSM	$F_{1.31} = 3.705, p = 0.063$	$F_{1.31} = 0.995, p = 0.326$
DM×HCM×WSM	$F_{1.31} = 6.221, p < 0.05$	$F_{1.31} = 0.009, p = 0.924$

Table 4. Repeated measures 3-factor ANOVA results. DM: Display Mode, HCM: Head Control Mode, WSM: Weapon Switch Mode

	Stereoscopic 3D/Head Tracking Questions
Q1	To what extent did 3D/HT improved the overall experience of the game?
Q2	To what extent 3D/HT was helpful in the game?
Q3	I would choose to play with 3D/HT over normal viewing.
Q4	I felt that 3D/HT enhanced the sense of engagement I felt.
Q5	3D/HT is a necessity for my future game experiences.
Q6	To what extent you felt that the head tracking helped you find enemies in the environment faster?
Q7	Do you feel that 3D/HT helped you to perform better?
Q8	How did 3D/HT help you perform better?
Q9	Do you feel that 3D/HT hurt your performance?
Q10	How did 3D/HT hurt your performance?
Q11	Did you feel any Symptoms from viewing the games in stereoscopic 3D (eye strain, headaches, dizziness, Nausea)?

Table 2. Stereoscopic 3D/Head Tracking Questionnaire. Participants responded to question 1-6 on a 7 point Likert scale. Questions 7-10 were multiple choice and open ended questions to gauge the users perception of the effects of stereoscopic 3D. In question 11, each symptom had a 7 point Likert scale to indicate the extent of each symptom ranging from not at all to very much so.

Mean number of enemies killed and mean survival time under different gaming conditions is shown in Figure 5 and Figure 6 respectively. There was no significant difference in the number of enemies killed or the survival time based on the display mode (2D vs 3D). Compared to monoscopic mode, people killed slightly more enemies when stereoscopic 3D was present. We found significant differences in terms of enemies killed based on the weapon switch mode (buttons vs finger-count shortcuts) but no significance was found in the post-hoc analysis.

Furthermore, the gaming experience of the participants did not play a significant role in the performance of the participants across different gaming conditions. The statistics were same even when we divided the participants in two groups, casual and experienced, and compared performance data for all gaming conditions separately for two groups.

To compare our results with prior research [3, 15], we also looked at the number of enemies killed and the survival times based on only the display mode and the head tracking mode (see Figure 7). We found that people killed most enemies when both head tracking and stereoscopic 3D was present but survival time was slightly more for head tracked (HT) and monoscopic condition. Overall, head tracking played a significant role in performance and stereoscopic 3D had only minor performance impact.

	Finger-Count Questions
Q1	To what extent did the finger-count gestures improved the overall experience of the game?
Q2	To what extent did you feel that the finger-count gestures were helpful while game play?
Q3	To what extent do you think that using a finger-count for weapon switch was better than using buttons?
Q4	The finger-count gestures hurt your performance in the tasks that were presented?
Q5	Do you feel that the finger-count gestures should be used for future games?
Q6	Are there any other game tasks (not specific to this game) where finger-count shortcuts could be used?

Table 3. Finger-Count Questionnaire. Participants responded to question 1-3 on a 7 point Likert scale. Questions 4 and 5 were yes/no questions. Question 6 was an open ended question.

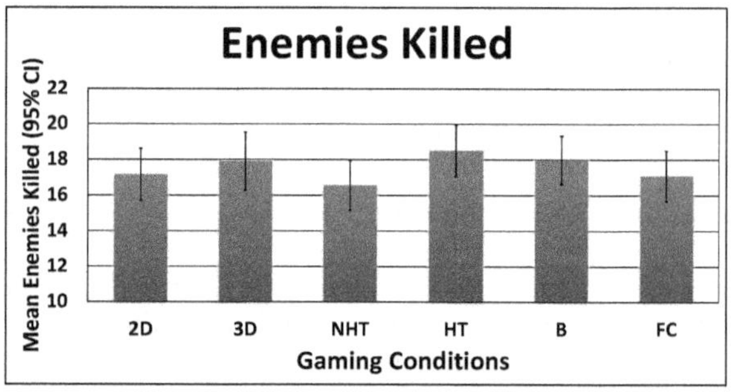

Figure 5. Mean number of enemies killed under different gaming conditions where 2D : Non-stereoscopic 3D, 3D: Stereoscopic 3D, NHT: Non-head-tracked, HT: Head-tracked, B: Button based weapon switch, and FC: Finger-Count based weapon switch.

When head control data (see Figure 8) was analyzed, we found that significantly more people, compared to button based head control, used head controls when head tracking was present ($t_{31} = 6.917, p < 0.005$). We also found that people use zoom (iron sight) more often compared to looking sideways (left/right).

Mean ratings for game post-questionnaire questions 1 to 11 (see Table 1) are summarized in Figure 9. We can see that:

- The game held attention of all the participants and everyone tried their best.
- The game had moderate mental demand and difficulty level.
- Participants did not feel frustrated while playing and indicated that they would like to play the same game again.

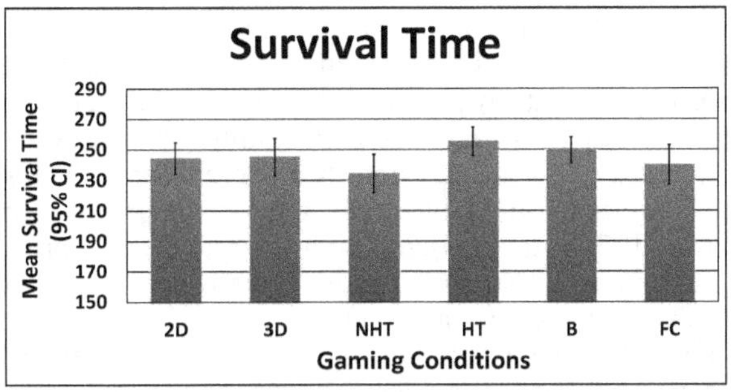

Figure 6. Mean survival time under different gaming conditions where 2D : Non-stereoscopic 3D, 3D: Stereoscopic 3D, NHT: Non-head-tracked, HT: Head-tracked, B: Button based weapon switch, and FC: Finger-Count based weapon switch. Higher survival time is better.

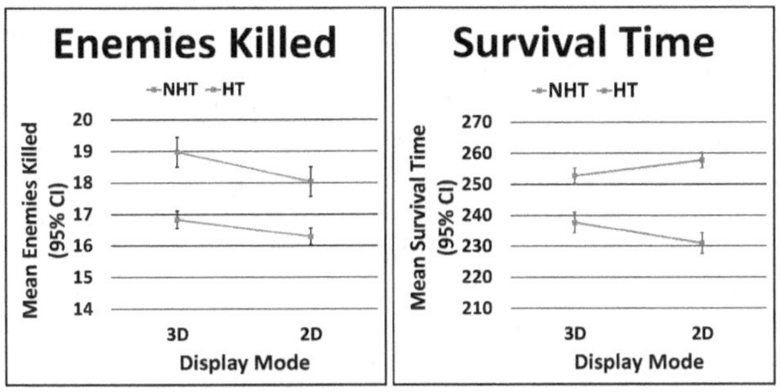

Figure 7. Mean enemies killed and mean survival time irrespective of weapon switch mode where 2D : Monoscopic, 3D: Stereoscopic 3D, NHT: Non-head-tracked mode, and HT: Head-tracked mode.

- Graphics quality of the game was rated as high and people enjoyed the game.

Out of 32 participants, 27 liked head tracking, 22 liked stereoscopic 3D and only 11 liked using finger-count shortcuts (see Figure 10). Majority of participants thought that stereoscopic 3D and head tracking was helpful in the game. Four people thought that stereoscopic 3D hurt their performance and five people thought that head tracking hurt their performance. People were divided about their views on finger-count shortcuts. Out of 32, 17 thought that finger-count shortcuts helped them perform better and 15 thought that it hurt their performance. Nineteen people thought that finger-count gestures should be used for future games.

Users perception of the three technologies revealed some interesting findings. Mean ratings for stereoscopic 3D, head tracking, and finger-count post-questionnaire questions (Q1-Q5 for 3D & HT, Q1-Q3 for FC) are summarized in Figure 11. Overall experience was significantly ($\chi^2 = 11.327, p < 0.005$) different across three technologies. Head tracking provided significantly better ($Z = -2.693, p < 0.01$) overall experience compared to finger-count shortcuts. Helpfulness of technologies was significantly different ($\chi^2 = 7.856, p < 0.05$) across technologies. Head tracking was significantly more ($Z = -2.339, p < 0.02$) helpful than finger-count shortcuts. Preference ratings of the technologies were also significantly different ($\chi^2 = 6.018, p < 0.05$). Head tracking ($Z = -2.249, p < 0.03$) and stereoscopic 3D ($Z = -2.125, p < 0.04$) had significantly higher preference rating than finger-count shortcuts. There was no significance found between head tracking and stereoscopic 3D for necessity ratings. People did not think that stereoscopic 3D or head tracking is a necessity for future games. Except for minor eye strain, none of the participants noticed any symptoms (headache, dizziness, or nausea) from viewing games in stereoscopic 3D.

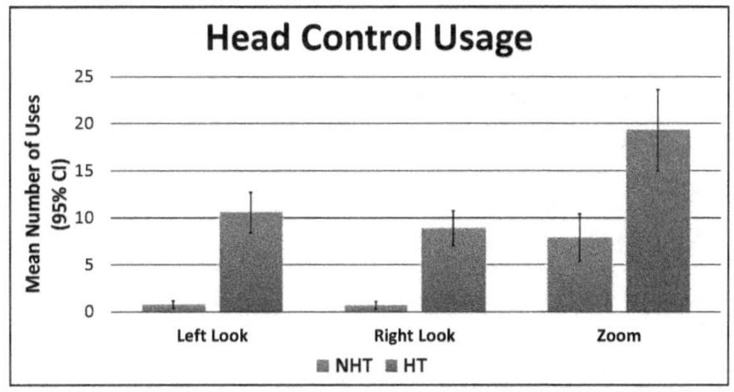

Figure 8. Players head control usage based on head control mode (buttons vs head tracking)

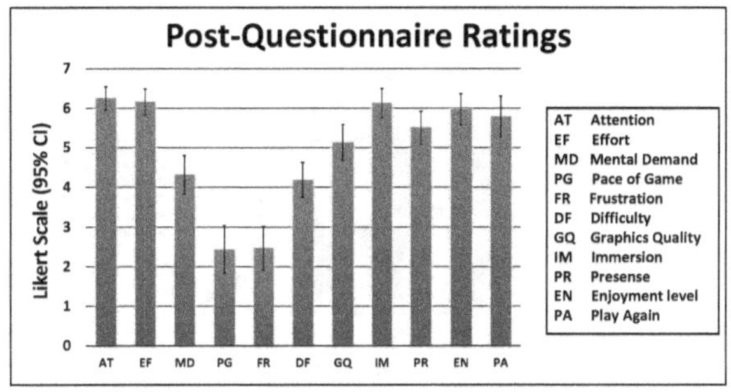

Figure 9. Mean ratings for the game post-questionnaire.

Out of all participants, 17 people thought that the depth perception was better with the presence of stereoscopic 3D, 17 people thought that it was more enjoyable to play with stereoscopic 3D, only 9 people thought that stereoscopic 3D helped them to judge the relative position of the enemies in the game, and 15 people thought that stereoscopic 3D made the game look more realistic. For the head tracking questionnaire, 17 people thought that head tracking added more realism to the game, 26 people thought that it was helping them to find enemies in the game environment, 26 people thought that it was much easier to look around with head tracking, and 25 people thought that zoom feature was helping them shoot distant enemies.

Qualitative Results

When asked about their experience playing the game, participants gave a variety of responses. One participant mentioned that he was very impressed with 3D effects in the game and it distracted him while playing. He occasionally felt like just enjoying the view rather than playing the game. Two of our participants were very sensitive to stereoscopic 3D and mentioned that it was very uncomfortable for them to play the game in 3D. One participant mentioned that it was uncomfortable to wear 3D glasses throughout the experiment. Two participants did not like zooming using head tracking because they felt uncomfortable being close to display screen while playing. Few participants mentioned that it was much easier

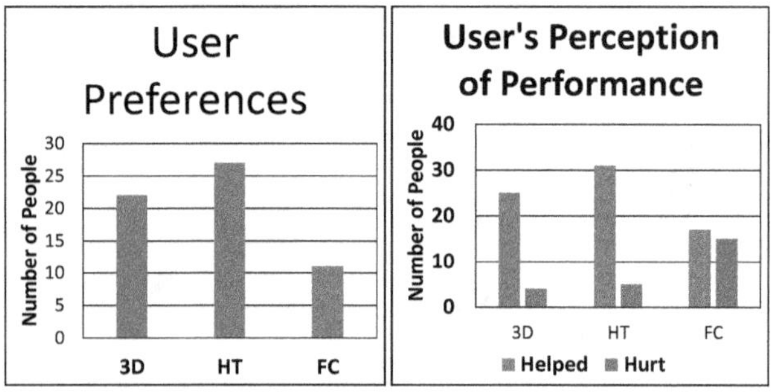

Figure 10. User preferences and user's perception of stereoscopic 3d, head tracking and finger-count shortcuts.

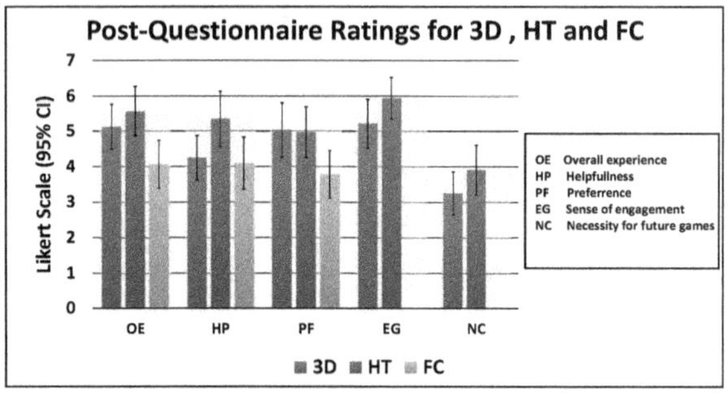

Figure 11. Mean ratings for the stereoscopic 3D, head tracking and finger-count post-questionnaire. Please note that EG and NC ratings were not collected for finger-count shortcuts.

to use finger-count shortcuts than buttons because they don't have to look down to find the button corresponding to a enemy color.

We got some interesting ideas when they were asked for other possible game tasks where finger-count gestures could be useful. One participant suggested to use finger-count gestures to quickly select and send pre-assigned text messages to other gamers in a multiplayer gaming environment. Currently, this task requires using a mouse which may not be the fastest choice. Another participant mentioned that finger-count gestures could be useful to solve some mini-puzzles, requiring selection from a set of items (e.g. Tower of Hanoi puzzle in Mass Effect where the task is to move blocks between towers), in games. A few other comments include using finger-count gestures to switch between different characters in a multi-character game (e.g. Trine), to switch between items in the minecraft game, to teleport a game character to different numbered locations in the game, and to assign a task (from a set of numbered tasks) to a game character.

DISCUSSION

We found significant performance benefits, in terms of number of enemies killed, due to combined usage of stereoscopic 3D , head tracking and finger-count shortcuts. Survival time was similar compared to the condition with monoscopic display, no head tracking, and button based weapon switch. Essentially, it means that people killed more enemies in the same time as in the condition with none of these technologies present. Therefore, the combined usage of the three technologies improved the performance of the users and we were able to accept out first hypothesis H1.

We did not find any significant performance differences based on display mode. These results are not surprising because prior experiments which studied effects of stereoscopic 3D [13, 19, 18] also found similar results. Kulshreshth et al. [11] found performance benefits of stereoscopic 3D for some video games (a pool table game and a game involving manipulation of 3D blocks) depending upon the user's prior gaming experience. But, those games were very different from our air-combat games and had tasks requiring precise motion in three dimensional space. For our game, the aircraft was moving in 3D space and enemies could be locked which does not require that much precision to shoot. Hence, we were not able to accept our second hypothesis H2.

Our experiment indicates that participants performed significantly better, in terms of enemies killed and survival time, when head tracking was present. Availability of head tracking helped participants find enemies faster in the environment without rotating the whole aircraft. When they were using button based head controls, it was not as easy to control the head as in case of head tracking which used natural head movements for controlling the player's head. Occasionally, while turning, participants used head tracking to make sure the turn is safe and would not end up in a collision with mountains or the enemies in the vicinity. Based on these results, we accepted our third hypothesis H3.

Most participants were positive about the game and felt an enhanced sense of engagement while playing when stereoscopic 3D and/or head tracking was present. They mentioned that depth perception, due to presence of stereoscopic 3D, made the game very realistic and more enjoyable. They felt as if they were actually flying that plane. Furthermore, they mentioned that it was very natural to use head tracking for searching enemies and it made the game very realistic. It was also mentioned that the gaming experience was best when both head tracking and stereoscopic 3D was present.

User's performance with finger-count shortcuts was as fast as with buttons and we were able to accept our fourth hypothesis H4. We expected these results based on the fact that the recognition time for our finger-count gestures (under a second) was approximately same as that of a button press. Moreover, it has already been shown that finger-count gestures are easy to learn and fast to perform [9]. Consequently, all participants were able to learn these gestures quickly and use them for weapon switching task in the game.

Interestingly, people were divided about their views on finger-count shortcuts. About half of participants preferred using finger-count shortcuts while another half did not. One possible reason could be familiarity with the button based interfaces (game controllers, keyboard/mouse, etc.) for video games. Most people play games using button based game controllers. Some of them like motion controlled games and some don't. Another possibility could be higher cognitive demand associated with finger-count shortcuts. In case of finger-count shortcuts, they need to control both hands independently and in different spatial areas requiring more cognitive attention than pressing buttons on a joystick. Consequently, we were unable to accept our fifth hypothesis H5.

Gaming experience of participants did not play a significant role in performance across different gaming conditions. In prior experiments with stereoscopic 3D [11] and head tracking [10], it was found that gaming performance across different gaming conditions could be affected by gaming experience of the participants. Casual users focus more on playing the game rather than using added features (head tracking or stereoscopic 3D) to their advantage. Meanwhile, expert users try to use these additional features to improve their game play performance. Our air-combat game was an easy game to play and all participant were allowed to practice the game, for about 20-25 minutes, before the experiment began. This gave them ample time to get themselves familiar with the game and not worry about learning the game during the actual experiment. This could have been the reason we did not noticed any significant interactions based on the participants prior gaming experience.

Compared to prior research [3, 15] , which studied interaction between head tracking and stereoscopic 3D, our results (see Figure 7) were slightly different. In our case, we found that head tracking significantly improved performance but stereoscopic 3D did not. Barfield et al. [3] found that display mode did not affect performance when head tracking was present and performance was better with stereoscopic 3D when head tracking was absent. Regan et al. [15] found that performance was best when stereoscopic 3D and head tracking was used together, but provided little benefit when used individually. One possible explanation of this difference could be the difference in the tasks presented to the participants as part of the experiment. Barfield et al. [3] used a wire tracing task, in which the objective was to move a virtual stylus (controlled by a real stylus) along the path of a virtual wire as quickly as possible without touching the wire. In case of [15], participants inspected cave structures with layers connected by vertical tubes and the task was to count the number of tubes connecting the horizontal layers. In both experiments, these were simple isolated tasks which were very different from playing a video game requiring a user to pay attention to many things while game play.

We found that people used head controls more often when head tracking was present. In case of button based head control, a combination of joystick hat switch and buttons (see Figure 3) was used to control the head of the player. On the other hand, when head tracking was present, natural head head movements were used to perform the same task. Cognitively, using buttons was much more difficult than using head tracking. Hence, while game play people refrained from using head controls frequently when head tracking was absent.

There are a few factors that could have affected our results. Our implementation of stereoscopic 3D, using dynamic stereo parameters, was different from all the past implementations. This could have a minor effect on our results but we still believe that the results will be similar or worse (due to less depth perception) with fixed stereo parameters. The size of display screen used could also have some influence on how much users can turn while using head tracking. The ideal choice would be very wide and curved display, with 180 degree field of view, but such stereoscopic 3D displays are not easily available. Most participants in our user study were males and this gender imbalance could have a minor effect on our results.

CONCLUSION AND FUTURE WORK

We presented an in-depth study which investigates how the combined use of several 3D user interface technologies affects the gaming experience. We designed an air-combat game keeping stereoscopic 3D, head tracking, and finger-count shortcuts usage in mind based on existing design ideas from the literature. A within subjects experiment was conducted where we examined game performance data, head tracking usage data, and data on user perception of the game. Our results show that people perform significantly better with the combined use of these technologies. Additionally, we found that head tracking was a major contributor to these performance benefits. The finger-count shortcuts also did not add much to the performance. However, about half of our participant preferred to use finger-count shortcuts compared to buttons for switching between weapons.

In our experiment we used head tracking data to dynamically optimize stereo parameters. But, head tracking provides only an approximate look direction and requires an user to rotate his/her head. In the future, we would like to use eye tracking to find where the user is looking and then optimize stereo parameters based on that information. Playing the game for different durations (e.g., 20 minutes, 40 minutes, or 60 minutes every other day for two weeks) might affect the game experience and would be interesting to look at in the future. We studied only a single game genre as part of our experiment. In the future, it would be interesting to explore these technologies for other game genres as well.

ACKNOWLEDGMENTS

This work is supported in part by NSF CAREER award IIS-0845921 and NSF awards IIS-0856045 and CCF-1012056. We would also like to thank the other members of ISUE lab for their support and the anonymous reviewers for their useful comments and feedback.

REFERENCES

1. Bailly, G., Lecolinet, E., and Guiard, Y. Finger-count & radial-stroke shortcuts: 2 techniques for augmenting linear menus on multi-touch surfaces. In *Proceedings of the SIGCHI Conference on Human Factors in Computing Systems*, CHI'10, ACM (New York, NY, USA, 2010), 591–594.
2. Bailly, G., Walter, R., Müller, J., Ning, T., and Lecolinet, E. Comparing free hand menu techniques for distant displays using linear, marking and finger-count menus. In *Human-Computer Interaction INTERACT 2011*, vol. 6947 of *LNCS*. Springer Berlin Heidelberg, 2011, 248–262.
3. Barfield, W., Hendrix, C., and Bystrom, K.-E. Effects of stereopsis and head tracking on performance using desktop virtual environment displays. *Presence: Teleoper. Virtual Environ. 8*, 2 (Apr 1999), 237–240.
4. Bowman, D. A., Kruijff, E., LaViola Jr, J. J., and Poupyrev, I. *3D User Interfaces: Theory and Practice*. Addison-Wesley, 2004.

5. Fisher, R. A. *The design of experiments*. Oxford, England: Oliver & Boyd, 1935.

6. Fujimoto, M., and Ishibashi, Y. The effect of stereoscopic viewing of a virtual space on a networked game using haptic media. In *Proceedings of the ACM SIGCHI international Conference on Advances in Computer Entertainment*, ACM (New York, NY, 2005), 317–320.

7. Holm, S. A simple sequentially rejective multiple test procedure. *Scandinavian Journal of Statistics 6*, 2 (1979), 65–70.

8. Howarth, P. A. Potential hazards of viewing 3D stereoscopic television, cinema and computer games: a review. *Ophthalmic & Physiological Optics : The Journal of the British College of Ophthalmic Opticians (Optometrists) 31*, 2 (2011), 111–122.

9. Kulshreshth, A., and LaViola, Jr., J. J. Exploring the usefulness of finger-based 3d gesture menu selection. In *Proceedings of the SIGCHI Conference on Human Factors in Computing Systems*, CHI '14, ACM (New York, NY, USA, 2014), 1093–1102.

10. Kulshreshth, A., and LaViola Jr., J. J. Evaluating performance benefits of head tracking in modern video games. In *Proceedings of the 1st symposium on Spatial user interaction*, SUI '13, ACM (New York, NY, USA, 2013), 55–60.

11. Kulshreshth, A., Schild, J., and LaViola Jr., J. J. Evaluating user performance in 3D stereo and motion enabled video games. In *Proceedings of the International Conference on the Foundations of Digital Games*, ACM (New York, NY, 2012), 33–40.

12. LaViola, J. J., Forsberg, A. S., Huffman, J., and Bragdon, A. The influence of head tracking and stereo on user performance with non-isomorphic 3d rotation. In *Proceedings of the 14th Eurographics Conference on Virtual Environments*, EGVE'08, Eurographics Association (Aire-la-Ville, Switzerland, Switzerland, 2008), 111–118.

13. Litwiller, T., and LaViola Jr., J. J. Evaluating the benefits of 3D stereo in modern video games. In *Proceedings of the SIGCHI Conference on Human Factors in Computing Systems*, CHI'11, ACM (New York, NY, USA, 2011), 2345–2354.

14. McMahan, R. P., Bowman, D. A., Zielinski, D. J., and Brady, R. B. Evaluating display fidelity and interaction fidelity in a virtual reality game. *IEEE Transactions on Visualization and Computer Graphics 18*, 4 (Apr. 2012), 626–633.

15. Ragan, E. D., Kopper, R., Schuchardt, P., and Bowman, D. A. Studying the effects of stereo, head tracking, and field of regard on a small-scale spatial judgment task. *IEEE Transactions on Visualization and Computer Graphics 19*, 5 (2013), 886–896.

16. Rajae-Joordens, R. J. Measuring experiences in gaming and tv applications. In *Probing Experience*, vol. 8 of *Philips Re*. Springer Netherlands, 2008, 77–90.

17. Schild, J., Bölicke, L., LaViola Jr., J. J., and Masuch, M. Creating and analyzing stereoscopic 3D graphical user interfaces in digital games. In *Proceedings of the SIGCHI Conference on Human Factors in Computing Systems*, CHI '13, ACM (New York, NY, USA, 2013), 169–178.

18. Schild, J., LaViola, Jr., J. J., and Masuch, M. Altering gameplay behavior using stereoscopic 3d vision-based video game design. In *Proceedings of the SIGCHI Conference on Human Factors in Computing Systems*, CHI '14, ACM (New York, NY, USA, 2014), 207–216.

19. Schild, J., LaViola Jr., J. J., and Masuch, M. Understanding user experience in stereoscopic 3D games. In *Proceedings of the SIGCHI Conference on Human Factors in Computing Systems*, CHI '12, ACM (New York, NY, USA, 2012), 89–98.

20. Schild, J., and Masuch, M. Fundamentals of stereoscopic 3D game design. In *ICEC, International Federation For Information Processing* (2011), 155–160.

21. Sko, T., and Gardner, H. Head tracking in first-person games: Interaction using a web-camera. In *Human-Computer Interaction - INTERACT 2009*, vol. 5726 of *Lecture Notes in Computer Science*. Springer Berlin / Heidelberg, 2009, 342–355.

22. Sko, T., Gardner, H., and Martin, M. Studying a head tracking technique for first-person-shooter games in a home setting. In *Human-Computer Interaction INTERACT 2013*, vol. 8120 of *Lecture Notes in Computer Science*. Springer Berlin Heidelberg, 2013, 246–263.

23. Terlecki, M., and Newcombe, N. How important is the digital divide? the relation of computer and videogame usage gender differences in mental rotation ability. *Sex Roles 53* (2005), 433–441.

24. Wang, S., Xiong, X., Xu, Y., Wang, C., Zhang, W., Dai, X., and Zhang, D. Face-tracking as an augmented input in video games: enhancing presence, role-playing and control. In *Proceedings of the SIGCHI Conference on Human Factors in Computing Systems*, CHI '06, ACM (New York, NY, USA, 2006), 1097–1106.

25. Ware, C. Dynamic stereo displays. In *Proceedings of the SIGCHI Conference on Human Factors in Computing Systems*, CHI '95, ACM Press/Addison-Wesley Publishing Co. (New York, NY, USA, 1995), 310–316.

26. Yim, J., Qiu, E., and Graham, T. C. N. Experience in the design and development of a game based on head-tracking input. In *Proceedings of the 2008 Conference on Future Play: Research, Play, Share*, Future Play '08, ACM (New York, NY, USA, 2008), 236–239.

27. You, J., Jiang, G., Xing, L., and Perkis, A. Quality of visual experience for 3D presentation - stereoscopic image. In *High-Quality Visual Experience*, M. Mrak, M. Grgic, and M. Kunt, Eds., Signals and Communication Technology. Springer Berlin Heidelberg, 2010, 51–77.

Quantifying and Mitigating the Negative Effects of Local Latencies on Aiming in 3D Shooter Games

Zenja Ivkovic, Ian Stavness, Carl Gutwin, and Steve Sutcliffe
Department of Computer Science, University of Saskatchewan
110 Science Place, Saskatoon, Canada, S7N 5C9
[zenja.ivkovic, ian.stavness, carl.gutwin, steve.sutcliffe]@usask.ca

ABSTRACT
Real-time games such as first-person shooters (FPS) are sensitive to even small amounts of lag. The effects of network latency have been studied, but less is known about *local latency*, the lag caused by input devices and displays. While local latency is important to gamers, we do not know how it affects aiming performance and whether we can reduce its negative effects. To explore these issues, we tested local latency in a variety of real-world gaming scenarios and carried out a controlled study focusing on targeting and tracking activities in an FPS game with varying degrees of local latency. In addition, we tested the ability of a lag compensation technique (based on aim assistance) to mitigate the negative effects. Our study found local latencies in the real-world range from 23 to 243 ms which cause significant and substantial degradation in performance (even for latencies as low as 41 ms). The study also showed that our compensation technique worked extremely well, reducing the problems caused by lag in the case of targeting, and removing the problem altogether in the case of tracking. Our work shows that local latency is a real and substantial problem – but games can mitigate the problem with appropriate compensation methods.

Author Keywords
Local latency; Lag; Aiming; Targeting; FPS games.

INTRODUCTION
Real-time competitive games require quick and timely responses to other players' actions and game events [24]. Any delays in the responsiveness of a game are disruptive because they create mismatches in timing between a player's actions and visual feedback of those actions, opponents' actions, and other game events. Latency on the game output forces players to react based on old information, and input latency adds to the time taken for actions to be registered. In both situations, player performance suffers, either because of a missed opportunity, incorrect response to an opponent's action, or reduced player control. As a further drawback, local latency may be imperceptible to the player, but still cause reduced performance and enjoyment [1].

CHI 2015, April 18 - 23, 2015, Seoul, Republic of Korea

ACM 978-1-4503-3145-6/15/04...$15.00
http://dx.doi.org/10.1145/2702123.2702432

Latency (or *lag*) arising from network communication has been studied in a number of contexts, and delays above 100 ms have been shown to be disruptive to racing games [19] and first-person shooter (FPS) games [2]. However, much less work has examined *local latencies* arising from input devices, displays, and software processing. Whereas the magnitude of network lag is generally decreasing, local latency is often increasing due to the use of wireless input devices and high-latency displays such as living room televisions. Our measurements suggest that local latency in these situations is often above 100 ms.

Previous studies have examined local latency in 2D pointing tasks (e.g., [16, 21]), but it should not be assumed that these results directly translate to FPS-style aiming tasks. FPS games are more complex both due to gameplay elements and the mechanism of aiming, which involves panning the view of the 3D world while the reticule remains centered in the screen (as opposed to translating a cursor over a 2D background). This mode of aiming requires users to process substantially more visual information, which tends to slow down feedback responses [7]. Looser et al. [15] reported that target acquisition in 3D FPS environments is 25% slower than in 2D scenarios. This decrease in performance suggests the effects of latency in 2D and FPS environments may also differ.

While some game genres, such as fighting games, force serious players to become aware of local latency, players of other genres are relatively less informed. Many players of FPS games know that local latency affects performance but the lack of quantification leads to misunderstanding and an underestimation of its impact. Without quantification, it is difficult to judge how severely lag affects different game tasks, to develop effective compensation techniques, to motivate consumers to consider latency when making game system purchases, and to motivate hardware and software developers to minimize local latency in their products.

To provide quantitative information about local latency we carried out three steps: we found the magnitude of local latency in typical real-world systems; we quantified the effects of latency on core FPS aiming tasks (acquisition and tracking); and we evaluated the effectiveness of aim compensation techniques for mitigating the effects of lag.

Our studies provide the following three findings:

- A sample of real-world systems (from PCs with LCD monitors, to gaming consoles with televisions) range in local latency from 23 to 243 ms.
- Local latency had a significant negative effect on both acquisition and tracking at latencies as low as 41 ms.
- Compensation techniques eliminated the negative effects of local latency in target tracking, and significantly reduced the effects in target acquisition.

We provide the first empirical evidence that local latency is a real and substantial problem for FPS games – even at very low levels, and levels lower than were measured in many real-world systems. In addition, we demonstrate compensation techniques that can reduce or even remove the effects of local latency. Our work shows that designers and publishers of FPS games (and other high-speed interactive systems) can benefit from compensating for local latency.

RELATED WORK

Latency and Local Latency

Latency is the measure of time delay between the sending and receiving of a message [8]. Latency is pervasive in digital systems and can vary greatly depending on the device (e.g., some LCD televisions have high latency due to built-in image processing). The negative effects of latency have been reported for a number of computer applications, such collaborative groupware [24], video scrubbing [18], digital sketching [3] and video games [20, 2].

Game system latency arises from a number of sources broadly classified as either network lag or local latency. Network latency occurs in multi-player video games due to delays in the network connection between players [22]. Network latency in video games has been well studied [19, 3]; however, effects of delay in a distributed system are different than the phenomena of local latency.

Local latency occurs in both multi- and single-player video games, because it is caused by delays in components of the game system that process user input and update the video display, rather than the network. Local latency causes delayed visual feedback of a player's own actions.

Local latency has recently become a subject of interest with new types of gaming systems that use high-latency devices, such as gesture input or televisions. Many games also rely on touch devices, such as tablets, mobile phones, or Nintendo's Wii U, that suffer from significant local latency. In a Fitts' law study with direct touch, Jota et al. found that latencies as low as 10ms reduced drag-and-point performance [11].

Aiming with Latency in 2D

Aiming movement can be decomposed into two phases: a *ballistic phase,* an open-loop action meant to arrive at the vicinity of the object; and a *controlled phase*, a closed-loop action relying on visual and kinetic feedback to carefully acquire the target [5]. In FPS games, two common aiming movements are target acquisition and target tracking.

Target acquisition uses both ballistic and controlled phases of movement. MacKenzie and Ware [16] measured acquisition time in four lag conditions using the Fitts' law paradigm. They found that lag had a significant negative effect on acquisition (up to 64% reduction in performance at 225 ms).

Target tracking involves keeping a pointing device over a moving target. Pavlovych et al. [21] examined the effect of lag on target tracking in 2D and found significant interaction between lag and longitudinal tracking errors. However, the 2D target motion in that study used Lissajous curves, which are smooth curves that do not match the horizontal ground-plane movements seen in FPS games. The curved target motion using Lissajous curves may aid the participant's ability to predict the target motion in high latency conditions and may not apply to FPS games.

Aiming in 3D

Target acquisition in full 3D VR environments with tri-variate targets has been shown to be negatively affected by latency [26]. Another 3D VR study suggested that, in the presence of latency, index of difficulty (ID) should include separate factors for target distance and target width [23].

Most 3D environments, such as FPS games, are 2D projections of a 3D scene, and therefore can be modeled as a bivariate pointing task [1,15], though pan-based pointing in 3D also requires angular measures in Fitts' law [12]. Although FPS pan-based targeting has been shown to obey Fitts' Law [15], no studies have been done to examine the effects of latency on targeting in 3D FPS environments.

FPS environments have unique properties that may make latency particularly disruptive. First, shooter games involve fast-paced game events, meaning that quick reflexes and precise aiming are paramount to performance. Second, the first-person perspective means that a player's movements cause the entire view of the 3D scene to shift behind a fixed cursor in the center of the screen. This causes much stronger visual changes (e.g., optical flow and motion parallax) as compared to 2D environments where a small cursor is moved across a fixed background.

Sources of Local Latency

A variety of sources can combine to result in high local system latency. For input devices, input that occurs between samples is not registered until the next time the input device is polled. For instance, USB mice by default are polled at a rate of 125 Hz (8ms intervals) in Windows XP and on, although gaming mice may set rates of up to 1000 Hz.

The display is a main contributor to local latency. Although specialized gaming monitors have low lag, most monitors average about 30-60 ms of latency. Televisions, which are popular in the game console community, often have significantly greater latency than monitors due to internal processing such as motion smoothing. The pixel response time in displays – that is, the time for a pixel to fully transition from one color to another, also contributes to the latency (5-10 ms). Additionally, displays almost always operate at 60

Hz refresh rates, which means that full screen updates cannot be shown any quicker than the refresh rate allows.

The game itself can cause significant amounts of latency. Input and output is processed in discrete intervals called frames, with frame rates typically ranging from 60 Hz in ideal cases (i.e., 16.7 ms periods), to 30 Hz or less, which is very commonly encountered on game consoles and slower computers. Any input received after the start of a frame period must wait until the next period, resulting in additional latency. Furthermore, games may perform input or output buffering, which causes more latency to be added and can contribute as much as 67ms or more.

Two additional software factors that affect latency at the output level are vertical sync (v-sync) and render-ahead. V-sync is used to synchronize game updates to display refreshes, which eliminates screen tearing, but it also caps the game frame rate to the display refresh rate. Without v-sync, a new frame can be rendered and sent to output while the monitor is the middle of a scan-out, which means that partial feedback can happen even quicker than the display refresh rate would suggest. Additionally, vertical sync locks the frame rate to factors of the refresh rate (e.g., a game capable of 55 fps on a 60Hz display would run at 30 fps). Triple buffering eliminates these discrete steps, but is only supported by OpenGL and not Direct3D (which is currently dominant). Instead, Direct3D uses render-ahead, which keeps a buffer of several frames to smooth output and eliminate tearing. The default buffer is three frames, which adds substantial latency [28].

Lag Compensation

Many multi-player games incorporate methods to reduce or compensate for *network* latency. Everquest 2 renders movement locally to reduce transmission rate and allow local queueing of events [6]. Quake IV uses prediction algorithms to compensate for lost data [27], a technique that is common for other FPS games. Another technique to improve aiming performance in lagged settings shows players their delay (a technique called Echoing [4]).

Aiming assistance is common in 3D games, but it is typically intended to reduce game difficulty or overcome controller difficulties, rather than to reduce the negative effects of local latency. The most common aim assists in games are 'gravity' techniques or 'sticky targets', where the cursor is attracted to the target when the player is in close proximity [25]. Others have suggested that eye-tracking technology could be used for aim assistance in games [9].

STUDY 1: LATENCY IN REAL-WORLD SYSTEMS

Although gamers share evidence when discussing game system latency [13], and significant marketing is employed to promote "low latency" input devices and displays, little empirical evidence exists for the local latency associated with different gaming setups. Minimizing latency in VR headset displays has been a recent focus of attention for new products, such as the Oculus Rift (www.oculusvr.com) that include specialized devices to measure latency from "motion-to-photon" while the device is in use. However, efforts to apply such measurement methodologies to typical FPS gaming systems have been uncommon.

We built our own latency measurement apparatus in order to sample a range of typical gaming setups and measure the amount of latency faced by gamers in real-world situations. We also used it with our experimental setup to measure the amount of latency in each latency condition of our user study. Our system measures the latency between an input mouse movement and resulting visible screen motion.

Latency Measurement Apparatus

The measurement apparatus used a high speed video camera (Canon ELPH 300HS digital camera, recording video at 240 frames per second) mounted on a tripod to capture the motion of the input device, e.g. the movement of a mouse on a flat wooden board elevated to the height of the display. This allowed both the mouse and the display to be captured in the camera frame at once.

To obtain a measurement, we ran the game system with a highly visible textured scene to allow for easy observation of movement on the screen. With the camera recording, we struck the input device sharply with a hammer to elicit a change in view direction. We measured the amount of latency by reviewing the recorded footage on a frame-by-frame basis, counting the number of frames elapsed between the mouse initially starting to move and the display changing. An LED light mounted on the device showed exactly when the movement started.

The reported latency period ended when any updates were first seen on the screen. Note that this could mean that only a small portion of the screen has updated at that point. For our experimental setup the display updated at 120 Hz, therefore it would take up to an additional 4 ms for half the screen to update and 8 ms for the screen to fully update.

Our camera makes discrete measurements with a precision of 4.2 ms and the display latency can have some jitter. For these reasons we report the average latency from 4 measurements for each of the real-world systems.

Local Latency of Typical FPS Gaming Systems

We used our latency measurement apparatus to determine the latency of a number of real-world systems. We selected systems from a variety of different types including gaming and office PCs and gaming consoles, and we used different types of input and output devices. Measurements were performed on a number of different games, using the same system settings that would be used during normal gameplay without modification. We found a wide range of latencies from 23ms on a PC with an ultra-fast gaming monitor, up to a surprising 243ms for the best-selling game GTA5, even on a relatively low-latency TV. Although our measurements are not intended to be exhaustive, they are a representative sample of real-world latency. Table 1 shows mean and standard deviation latency results in milliseconds.

System	Game	Input	Display	Lag (s.d.)
Win 7 (G)	Day Z	M, W	Asus VH242H (T)	117 (7)
OS X 10.9 (S)	Zombie count	M, WL	Toshiba PA3769 (VGA) (T)	158 (12)
Win 8.1 (G)	CS: GO	GM, W	Dell UP2414Q (I)	65 (4)
ArchLinux (G)	Path of Exile	GM, W	Overlord X270OC 100Hz (I)	32 (3)
Win 8 (G)	Quake 3	GM, WL	BenQ XL2420T 120Hz (T)	37 (2)
Win 8 (G)	Quake 3	GM, W	BenQ XL2420T 120Hz (T)	23 (2)
Win 8 (G)	Quake 3	GM, W	LG L226WTX (T)	64 (4)
Win 7 (S)	Cut the rope	M, W	Dell S2340Tt (I)	117 (6)
Wii U (C)	Windwaker HD	C, WL	Sony KDL55HX850 (V)	155 (16)
Wii U (C)	CoD Black Ops 2	C, WL	Sony KDL55HX850 (V)	130 (8)
PS4 (C)	Killzone SF	C, WL	Sony KDL55HX850 (V)	148 (8)
PS4 (C)	Watch Dogs	C, WL	Sony KDL55HX850 (V)	175 (16)
Xbox 360 (C)	Battlefield 3	C, WL	Sams. UN60EH6003F (V)	155 (23)
Xbox 360 (C)	GTA 5	C, WL	Sams. UN60EH6003F (V)	243 (60)
Wii U (C)	Bioshock Infinite	C, WL	Sams. UN60EH6003F (V)	192 (9)
Wii U (C)	Windwaker HD	C, WL	Sams. UN60EH6003F (V)	138 (17)

Systems: G = gaming computer (recent hardware, discrete GPU); S = standard computer; C = gaming console. **Input**: M = standard mouse; GM = gaming mouse; C = standard gamepad; W = wired, WL = wireless. **Displays**: T = twisted-nematic; I = in-plane switching or equivalent; V = LCD televisions (IPS with game mode on).

Table 1: Results of field latency sample.

STUDY 2&3: EFFECTS OF LOCAL LATENCY AND LAG COMPENSATION ON FPS TARGETING AND TRACKING

We designed controlled studies of two different FPS game tasks: target acquisition and target tracking. Our goals in these studies were to assess the effect of local latency on task performance, and to determine whether compensation techniques can limit the negative effects of lag.

Experimental Tasks

Our experimental system implemented 3D target tracking and target acquisition. These tasks are representative of primary activities in many 3D game environments: in FPS games, target acquisition is carried out when first encountering an enemy, and then a combination of acquisition and tracking is used until the enemy is eliminated.

Target Acquisition

In each trial, a roughly-spherical stationary target appears in the player's view. Players are instructed to aim at the target and click the left mouse button. If the target is hit, the player's view resets to the base position, and after a 500 ms delay, another target appears in a different position. The view is fixed during the 500 ms delay, ensuring each trial starts from the same position. If the target is missed, the trial continues until the target is hit, although the trial is repeated until completed without misses.

Each lag condition consists of 36 possible target positions within a virtual cone extending from the center of the base view position (Figure 1). The position order is randomized, but the same order occurs within every condition.

The 36 target positions were generated by different combinations of cone variables: angle (0°, 45°, 135°, 180°, 225°, 315° from horizontal), radius (74, 148, and 224 units), and depth from camera (224 units and 448 units, which effectively controls the size of the target). These variables are aggregated into six *Indices of Difficulty* (*ID*). Distance and radius are roughly equivalent to the width and distance variables in Fitts' Law [1]. Since rotation is used to aim, the units used are angular distances [15].

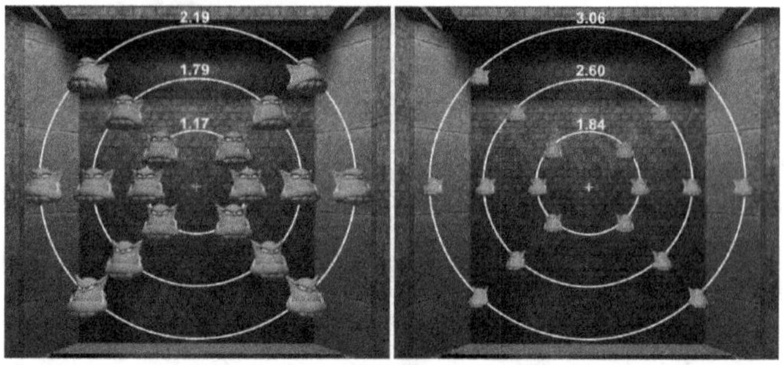

Figure 1: Target acquisition task showing all possible target locations and sizes. The six IDs (numeric labels) were chosen to be typical of targets in FPS games.

Target Tracking

In each tracking trial, a target appears at the same initial position in front of the player. To begin a trial, the player clicks on the target. The target moves horizontally (Figure 2) for 5 seconds and then the trial ends and the target resets. The player's goal is to keep aim on the target for as long as possible. The target turns green when the crosshair is over it. Although horizontal movement is a special case for mouse movement [14], it is the most commonly used tracking axis in FPS games since players often make side-to-side evasive movements along a ground plane.

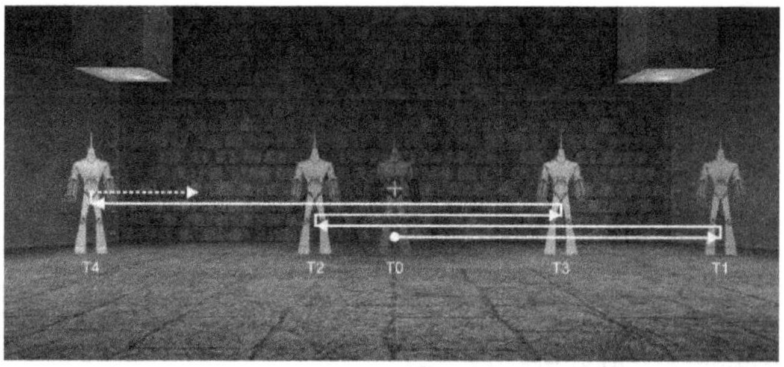

Figure 2: Target tracking task showing target movement from initial position (T0) through four direction changes (T1-4).

The only factor within a lag condition is target speed. Each sequence of trials begins with 4 slower trials at 240 units per second (u/s), followed by 4 trials at 320 u/s. The target's bounding box is 30 units wide and deep, with a height of 56 units. Direction changes take 140 ms to complete and occur at random intervals (taken uniformly from a period of 0.3 to 0.75 seconds, which is similar to player behavior in similar settings) with an average count of 10 reversals per trial. Target size and speed were chosen based on observations of existing games: the higher speed is based on player movement speeds in Quake III Arena, and the lower speed is based on more realistic slower-paced FPS games.

Questionnaire

Participants filled out a questionnaire with a seven-point Likert scale between each change of lag. Questions were "I performed well this round," "lag affected my performance," "this round was frustrating," and "the controls were laggy."

Artificial Local Latency

In order to control the amount of lag in our experiment setup, a system with low baseline lag was used with a technique to artificially increase the amount of latency in a controlled manner. Rather than varying each possible source of local latency, all latency was added at the output stage in order to reduce complexity. This approach is reasonable because input is rarely the primary source of local latency.

Five levels of system latency were used in the study, creating 11 ms, 41 ms, 74 ms, 114 ms, and 164 ms of lag. This covers a reasonable range of latency that matches well with levels found on PC systems in study one while retaining sufficient granularity to evaluate low levels of latency. The lowest achievable level (11 ms) serves as a baseline.

The lowest two latency conditions, 11 ms and 41 ms, were achieved using the natural latency of our system with v-sync disabled (11 ms) and enabled (41 ms). The higher three levels of latency were achieved with artificial latency, added to the graphical output by rendering frames sequentially into a ring buffer of textures. The choice of which frame to use from this buffer determines the amount of latency. To achieve baseline latency, frames are displayed immediately; to achieve two frames of latency, the texture in the buffer from two frames in the past is displayed.

Compensating for Local Latency

We developed compensation techniques based on existing aim assistance methods to mitigate the effects of local latency. The compensation involved aiming assistance that was proportional to the average expected latency. We devised our assistance so that it mitigates local latency rather than serving as a general form of performance boosting. In order to create targeted compensation schemes, we identified two primary ways that local latency affects the two tasks.

Target overshoot during target acquisition. During target acquisition, players tend to keep moving the crosshair toward the target until they observe that they have reached the target. If lag is present, people can overshoot the target because the visual state is behind the true game state. *'Sticky targets'* was chosen to compensate for lag in targeting because it directly combats the target overshoot effect by increasing the width of the target in motor space. Sticky targets reduces the mouse gain (also called *C:D* ratio [17]) while the aim is on the target, and is designed to decrease overshoot due to latency.

Direction changes during target tracking. Each time a target changes direction, players have to change their aiming movement. Perceiving direction changes under local latency can take substantially longer; and once players do react and attempt to change their aim, the target has moved even farther in the other direction. Another aspect to tracking is predicting future target positions and when it may change direction, if a pattern is apparent. Latency interferes with this process by delaying feedback regarding incorrect predictions. *Aim dragging*, an assist found in the Call of Duty games was chosen to compensate for lag in tracking because it provides assistance during direction changes, reducing the amount of time spent off target. *Aim dragging* causes the aim to be partially dragged in the direction of target movement. As in Call of Duty, aim dragging is active even if aiming near the target but not quite on it. The decreased-gain aspect of *sticky targets* is also applied, which mostly compensates for the fact that the tracking assistance could otherwise move the aim too quickly once added to the player's own input, and also provides overshoot protection.

Based on our previous experience with latency, we determined a general desired shape for the assistance strength curves. We then performed an initial pilot study with separate participants in order to tune the constant scalar and exponent terms applied to the lag variable. The formulas used for compensation are as follows:

$$\text{Sticky targets:} \qquad s = \frac{1}{1+10l^{1.2}}$$

where s is the change in mouse gain (with 1 being no change in gain) and l is the amount of lag in seconds. The effect is a roughly linear decrease in sensitivity up to about 100 ms, after which the effect decreases gradually to prevent the gain from being too low at high amounts of lag.

$$\text{Aim dragging:} \qquad d = 1 - \frac{1}{1+2.75l^{1.3}}$$

where l is the amount of lag in seconds and d is the strength of the drag, with 0 corresponding to no assistance and 1 being perfect assistance (auto-tracking). Again, the effect is approximately linear at first, with a gradual decreased slope at high latency. Table 2 shows the resulting assistance values at the latencies used in our experiment.

Factor	41 ms	74 ms	114 ms	164 ms
s	0.82	0.69	0.57	0.47
d	0.10	0.17	0.24	0.31

Table 2: Assistance strength at the experimental lag levels.

Experimental Conditions Used in the Study

Three factors were the same for acquisition and tracking tasks: *Lag*, *Block*, and *Compensation*. The tracking task also had a *Speed* factor for target speed, and the acquisition task had an *ID* factor for index of difficulty.

Lag. Five levels of latency were used in the study, corresponding to 11 ms, 41 ms, 74 ms, 114 ms, and 164 ms of lag. These numbers represent the average latency at that level, and although some frame to frame variation was present, it was minimal. The variation never exceeded one frame, and was on average much less than one frame.

Block. A sequence is a group of trials where all trials have the same level of lag (36 trials for acquisition, 8 for tracking). A block groups five sequences of sequentially increasing or decreasing lag. There were three blocks within each task for each compensated and non-compensated session. The first block increased lag from minimum to maximum. The second block then went from max to min, and the last block once again went from min to max. Blocks were used as a compromise to achieve a degree of counterbalancing, so that lag levels were spread throughout the experiment. This approach minimizes changes in lag at each adjustment, with the goal being to quantify the effect of lag once people have had time to get used to it, rather than observing rate of adaptation.

Compensation. This factor controlled whether lag compensation aiming assists were in use. The assistance strength was directly tied to the amount of lag in the current condition. At the minimum lag level, no assists were given.

Speed. Used only in the tracking task, this factor represented the speed of the target (240 units/s and 320 units/s).

ID. For target acquisition, six IDs were tested, consisting of combinations of target distance and cone radius.

Participants and Apparatus

Eighteen participants were recruited from a local university (15 male, 3 female). All participants had at least some experience with FPS games using a mouse. The same participants performed both studies over two sessions on consecutive days, with one session making use of lag compensation and the other being the baseline, non-compensated condition. The order of conditions was counterbalanced.

Half the participants started with the acquisition task, with the other half starting with tracking. Each task started with two half-duration blocks of training period (not included in the aforementioned 3 blocks).

Both studies were performed on a PC (Intel Core i7 3.2GHz CPU with NVidia GeForce 460GTX video) running GNU/Linux. In order to achieve the lowest minimum latency, we used a gaming mouse with a 1000Hz sampling rate (Razer DeathAdder 3.5G) and an ultra-fast gaming display with a 120Hz refresh rate (BenQ XL2420T).

The experiment was implemented as a C++ program utilizing the open-source Ogre3D (www.ogre3d.com) graphics engine using OpenGL as the rendering back-end. The software ran at a consistent 120 fps while v-sync was enabled.

Latency Measurement

We used the same apparatus as in Study 1 to measure lag in each experimental condition. To assess the latency jitter and ensure that our measurements were accurate, we made 18 measurements at each of the lowest latency levels and report the mean and standard deviation. We also verified that the higher latency conditions with artificial lag have the expected amount of additional latency. The mean baseline latency (no v-sync) was 11.4 ms (s.d. 2.28), and the first latency condition (v-sync on) was 40.8 ms (s.d. 3.13).

Design and Hypotheses

The acquisition study used a 2×3×5×6 within-participants RM-ANOVA with factors *Compensation* (off, on), *Block* (1-3), *Lag* (11 , 41, 74, 114, 164 ms), and *ID* (1.15, 1.76, 1.81, 2.15, 2.54, 3.02). Dependent measures were task completion time and number of errors.

The tracking study used a 2×3×5×2 within-participants RM-ANOVA with factors *Compensation* (off, on), *Block* (1-3), *Lag* (11, 41, 74, 114, 164 ms), and *Target Speed* (240, 320 u/s). The dependent measure was time on target.

Our hypotheses for the studies were:

H1. Tracking time on target would decrease with lag.
H2. Acquisition time would increase with lag.
H3. Acquisition errors would increase with lag.
H4. Lag compensation would reduce the effect of lag on tracking time on target.
H5. Lag compensation would reduce the effect of lag on acquisition time.
H6. Lag compensation would reduce the effect of lag on acquisition errors.

RESULTS

Outliers were removed from the data for both studies by removing the worst 1% of trials within each lag level for each participant (268 total trials removed, equivalent to one-tailed 3σ s.d.). We chose the one-tailed approach because it was impossible for a trial to be too fast in our system, but trials could be too slow if participants moved their hand from the mouse, rested, or asked questions during a trial.

Acquisition Study

Trial completion time included trials with misses. We chose to incorporate error rate into the time metric because this approach reflects the effect of misses in real FPS games.

Effect of Lag on trial completion time

ANOVA showed a significant main effect of *Lag* ($F_{4,60}$=246, $p < 0.0001$), as well as an interaction effect between *Lag* and *Compensation* ($F_{4,60}$=18.7, $p < 0.001$). In the non-compensated case, planned pairwise t-tests (Holm corrected) showed a significant difference between all levels of lag ($p < 0.0001$), with the exception of the 11 ms and 41 ms pair ($p = 0.25$). We therefore accept **H2**.

Figure 3 shows the effect of lag on trial completion time, both with and without compensation (black lines). The effect of 41 ms of lag was negligible compared to baseline, although it becomes substantial and approximately linear at higher levels. Trial completion time increased by 1.5%, 11.0%, 28.5%, and 52.1% compared to baseline at 41 ms, 74 ms, 114 ms, and 164 ms, respectively.

Effect of Compensation

The interaction between lag and compensation also suggests that compensation may have been effective at reducing the effect of lag. However, with compensation enabled, planned pairwise t-tests showed that the same pairs of lag had a significant effect on performance as in the non-compensated case (74 ms and higher). This means that our compensation technique was not able to eliminate the effect of lag. However, Figure 3 shows that compensation did decrease the effect, and follow-up paired t-tests (Holm corrected) confirm a significant improvement at 74, 114, and 164 ms ($p < 0.05$), both when comparing the compensated curve to baseline, and when comparing within the compensated curve at the 11 ms level. We therefore accept **H5**.

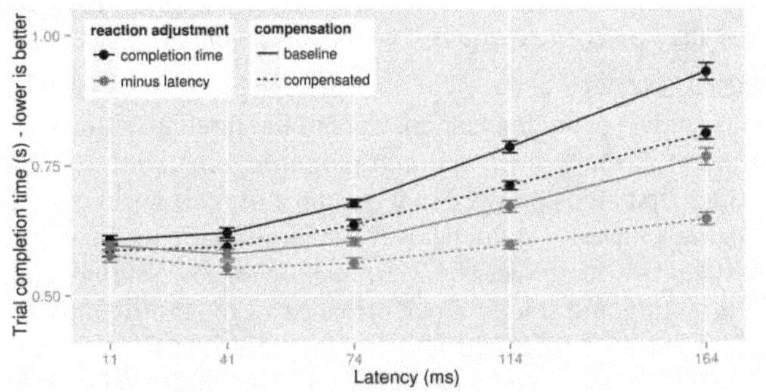

Figure 3: Effect of latency on targeting performance.

Figure 3 also contains dark red lines depicting trial completion time when the amount of latency is subtracted from completion time. With lag, the participant will see the target appear later than when it actually gets created within the game state, and therefore reaction time will be delayed by the amount of latency present. All subsequent figures will display non-adjusted performance (black lines).

Effect of ID

ANOVA showed a significant interaction between *Lag* and *ID* ($F_{20,300}$=8.87, $p < 0.0001$), as well as a three-way interaction between *Lag*, *ID*, and *Compensation* ($F_{20,300}$=2.15, $p < 0.001$). This suggests that lag has a different effect on acquisition performance depending on acquisition difficulty. Figure 4 shows that there actually was a performance decrease between 11 ms and 41 ms of lag at the lower three difficulties, confirmed by a followup paired t-test ($p < 0.001$), although not at higher difficulties ($p > 0.5$). It can also be seen that compensation worked for all *ID* levels.

Figure 5 shows the same *Lag*, *ID*, and *Compensation* factors, but with *ID* on the x-axis. Since the curves are approximately linear, it is appears that the acquisition task in the FPS environment follows Fitts' Law when angular distances are used. Note however the sharp increase in completion time between the very close second and third *ID* at higher latencies. These points are associated with a change in both radius and distance, reinforcing previous results [23].

Effect of Block

ANOVA showed a significant main effect of *Block* ($F_{2,30}$=6.76, $p < 0.05$), indicating that a practice effect was present. Trial completion time decreased by 1.5% in block 2 and 3.6% in block 3 compared to block 1.

Error rate

We also examined the effect of lag on acquisition error rate. ANOVA showed a significant interaction between *Lag* and *Compensation* ($F_{4,60}$=6.32, $p < 0.001$). Without compensation, paired t-tests show that error rate is lower at 41 ms than at 11 ms ($p < 0.01$), and that there is no significant difference between 11 ms and the other levels, so we must reject **H3**. With compensation enabled, paired t-tests show a significant decrease in error rate at 114 ms and 164 ms compared to 11 ms of lag, and no significant difference at 41 ms and 74 ms. We therefore accept **H6**. The decrease in error rate compared to the baseline suggests that our compensation technique could benefit from further tuning.

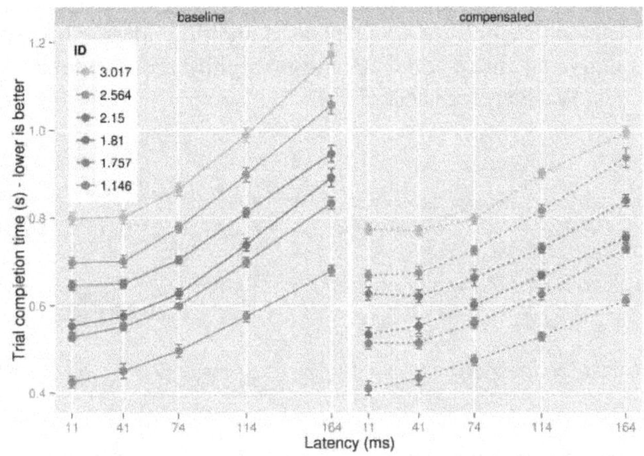

Figure 4: Effect of latency on targeting performance by *ID*.

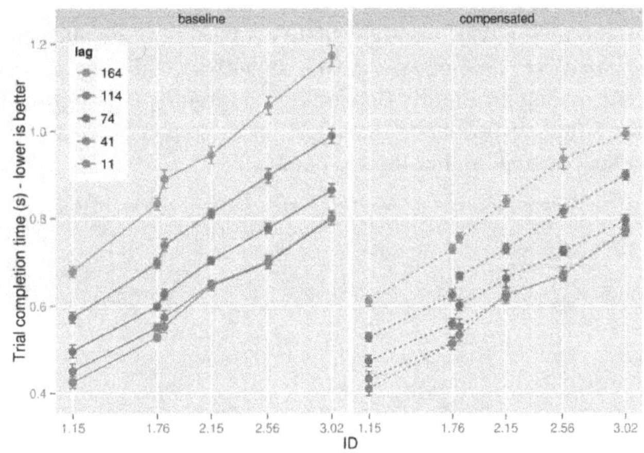

Figure 5: Effect of difficulty on targeting performance by latency and compensation.

Tracking Study

Performance in the tracking study was determined by the mean amount of time successfully spent tracking the target per trial, with maximum possible time being 5 seconds.

Effects of Lag on tracking time

ANOVA showed a significant effect of *Lag* ($F_{4,56}$=39.7, $p < 0.0001$), as well as a significant interaction between *Lag* and *Compensation* ($F_{4,56}$=46.2, $p < 0.0001$). With no compensation, planned pairwise t-tests (Holm corrected) showed a significant decrease in tracking time between each level of lag ($p < 0.01$). We therefore accept **H1**.

As shown in Figure 6, the performance decrease is approximately linear with increasing lag: 94.2%, 87.8%, 77.7%, and 67.3% of baseline latency performance at 41 ms, 74 ms, 114 ms, and 164 ms of latency.

Effect of Compensation

ANOVA showed a significant main effect of *Compensation* ($F_{1,14}$=22.6, p<0.001) and an interaction between *Lag* and *Compensation* ($F_{4,56}$=46.2, p<0.0001), meaning that compensation was effective at reducing the effect of lag. With compensation enabled, pairwise t-tests showed no significant difference in tracking time between any levels of lag ($p > 0.2$). T-tests also showed a significant difference between the baseline and compensated tracking times at all levels above 11 ms ($p < 0.01$), with no significant difference at 11 ms. We therefore accept **H4**.

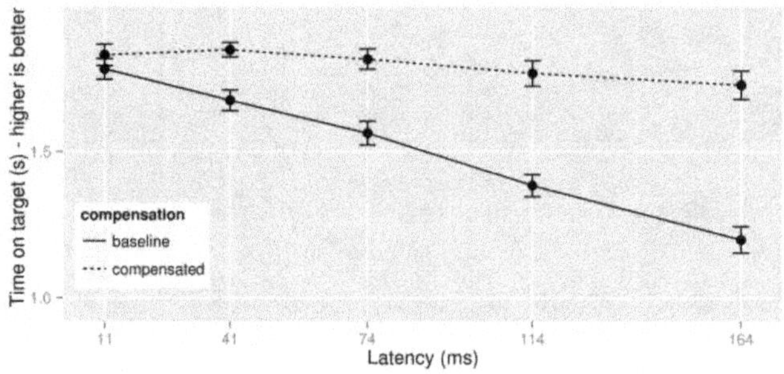

Figure 6: Effect of latency on tracking performance.

Effect of Speed

An interaction was found by ANOVA between *Lag* and *Target Speed* ($F_{1,14}$=4.40, $p < 0.01$), suggesting that lag affects performance differently depending on target speed. Figure 7 shows that performance impact of lag is greater at lower target speeds than higher target speeds.

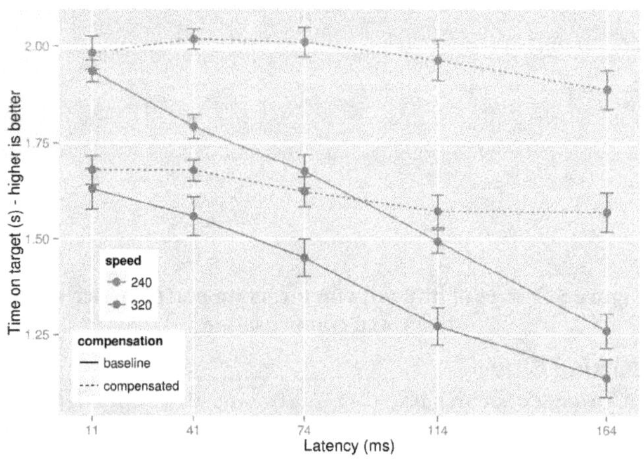

Figure 7: Effect of latency on tracking performance, by speed.

A significant three-way interaction between *Lag*, *Speed*, and *Compensation* was also shown by ANOVA ($F_{4,56}$=3.38, $p < 0.05$). The effectiveness of our compensation technique varies depending on the amount of lag and target speed, with it giving a slight boost compared to baseline performance at lower target speeds at 74 ms and 114 ms.

Effect of Block

ANOVA showed a significant main effect of *Block* ($F_{2,28}$=8.98, $p < 0.001$), suggesting that there was a learning effect present. Tracking time increased by 4.1% in block 2 and 6.5% in block 3, as compared to block 1.

Questionnaire Results

Surveys showed that participants could identify the presence of lag and its effect on performance at 114 ms of lag and higher (MWW test, p<0.05), and could not distinguish between lower levels. With compensation enabled, they felt that they performed equally well at all levels of lag.

DISCUSSION

Our studies provide clear answers to the three questions:

- *What is the prevalence and magnitude of local latency*? Our first study showed that a sample of real-world gaming setups have local latencies from 23 to 243 ms.
- *What are the effects of local latency on 3D aiming*? Both targeting and tracking performance were significantly degraded with local latency. Completion time for target acquisition increased significantly for lag above 41 ms (for higher difficulty targets) and above 11 ms (for lower difficulty targets). Time on target during tracking decreased significantly for lag beyond 11 ms.
- *Does compensation reduce the effects of local latency*? Compensation was very effective. The negative effects of latencies were reduced by up to 40% for target acquisition and eliminated altogether for target tracking.

Explanation and Interpretation of Results

The reasons why local latency causes performance to decrease are likely the same as those discussed for other types of latency – the surprising finding in our study, however, is that even latencies as low as 41 ms can cause significant performance problems for aiming. Few studies have suggested that human reaction time can be affected by latencies this small – although one recent study of ultra-low-latency touch screen hardware also found that latency above 10 ms had a negative effect on touch performance [11].

The difference in sensitivity between targeting and tracking may arise from the added requirements of the tracking task – during tracking, changes in the direction of target movement were observed to cause significant disruption, and direction changes occurred numerous times during each trial. Direction changes cause a double penalty in tracking – not only does it take longer to react to a direction change with lag, but the target has moved farther in the opposite direction.

As with the effects of latency, the reasons for the success of our compensation mechanisms also align with previous work. That is, the techniques worked well because they provided a kind of bridge across the delay-caused gap between the initiation of an action and the display of that action. For targeting, compensation enlarged the effective width of targets by the amount needed to make up for the overshooting that occurred due to latency; for tracking, aim dragging kept the crosshair on the target for the amount of time in which the target's direction change was invisible due to delay.

The difference in compensation effectiveness between targeting and tracking (compensation did not work as well in targeting) arises from the fact that we only compensated for overshooting errors, rather than lateral errors. We initially thought that latency would primarily cause overshooting, but we observed that lateral aiming errors were also common, and the presence of lag hampered the player's ability to adjust their aim through controlled feedback. Future work will examine techniques that take these transverse errors into account (e.g., bullet magnetism [25]).

Again, the surprising finding in our study of compensation techniques was the degree of effectiveness of the technique, even at the highest levels of local latency that are likely to be experienced in the real world. This means that the problem of local latency is one that could potentially be solved if compensation techniques can be successfully deployed.

Generalizing the results to real FPS games

Although our study was (necessarily) a controlled experiment rather than a real-world test in a real FPS game, there are several reasons why our results about the effects of latency will hold in realistic scenarios:

- We tested amounts of latency that are common in gaming systems, and covered a wide range of systems with different input and display devices in various games.
- We tested realistic task elements (targeting and tracking) that are ubiquitous in 3D shooter games. Although there are many differences between our study system and an actual FPS game (e.g., moving while shooting, other visual information), the core mechanics of moving the mouse to acquire or track a target do not change.
- The ways that targeting and tracking work in most FPS games is similar to out experimental tasks. FPS players typically aim for fixed targets in a single aim-and-shoot action, and moving targets typically move along a horizontal plane (e.g., the ground or a ledge) with most evasive action occurring as horizontal direction changes.
- We used an experimental setup that closely mimics a real gaming PC (fast mouse, graphics card, and display), and recruited participants with FPS gaming experience.

There are some differences that should be studied further in a real FPS environment. For example, in the study system the player could not move the character. While player movement is often used as part of tracking in FPS games, this restriction allowed us to focus specifically on mouse input for tracking tasks (although many FPS games encourage the player to stay stationary while firing in the form of reduced accuracy when firing while moving). However, we believe that differences between our testing environment and a real FPS environment will most likely increase the effects of lag. Player movement adds additional complexity when aiming and provides further opportunity for lag to interfere with the feedback processes. Likewise, the combination of movement and pressure to fire accurately encourages players to use the closed-loop feedback phase of aiming which is highly affected by lag due to the need for multiple adjustments with feedback delay between each one. Similarly, mechanics such as gun recoil and bullet spread used by some FPS games introduce an additional feedback loop into the aiming process where lag may have an even greater detrimental effect. Unlike real games, our experiment involved repeated simple aiming motions where participants could easily focus on the open-loop ballistic phase of motion.

Given enough time, players can get used to the latency of a particular system and notice it less. Players often claim that this adaptation reduces the effect of lag, and although that may be true to a small extent, we believe the adaptation effect is limited. Lag reduces the amount of time available to respond to game events. Planned acquisition motions such as open-loop ballistic motion with correctly predicted target locations may become latency-adapted to some extent, but errors are common and would negate adaptation. Likewise, tracking predictable targets may suffer less from lag, but any unexpected path deviations or errors in tracking would suffer from the closed-loop feedback-delay penalty imposed by latency. Our experiment gave players a chance to adapt to lag by making smaller, sequential changes in small steps rather than randomizing latency levels. Since there was no interaction effect between *Block* and *Compensation* in either task, it appears that players were sufficiently adapted.

Our study setup also supports generalization of the effects of compensation to real FPS games. Our compensation technique was designed to be general enough to apply to many common aiming scenarios. Two issues were not studied in our experiment: first, the effects of large required movements to acquire a target (e.g., real gameplay might require the player to perform a rapid 180 degree turn to aim at an enemy); second, the potential effects of distractor targets. Distractors that can appear near the intended target can make aiming assistance techniques less effective [25], even though the technique is designed to only affect a small angle around the targeting cursor. In real FPS scenarios, distractors may be less of an issue because players typically shoot at the nearest target. In addition, modifications to the compensation algorithm – such as determining the size of the effect based on cursor speed – may help to avoid errors.

There are some important challenges in deploying a compensation scheme in a real-world FPS. One main issue is the need to know the amount of local latency in order to set the amount of compensation. If the estimated latency is incorrect, compensation will either work ineffectively or provide an unfair advantage to the player. To accurately determine local latency, measurement tools should be used. These tools are already in use for latency-sensitive devices such as the Rock Band game controller and the Oculus Rift headset. However, to ensure fairness it would be better if latency estimates could be made directly from the hardware components that make up a game system. We envision that the required information could be archived in a database of component latency specifications, ideally created by manufacturers and from crowd-sourced gaming communities. The game could then require that players establish their latency before allowing compensation to be enabled.

Questions for further study

Are target size and target distance independent factors for ID in the presence of latency? So and Chung [23] suggest that target size and distance should not be considered a single effect of ID for tasks involving latency. We included two target conditions with similar IDs, but with different combinations of distance and size. With lag present, the closer and smaller targets had consistently worse performance than the targets with greater distance and size (but similar ID). The performance discrepancy with these similar IDs also increased with lag (Figure 5). This would suggest that smaller targets cause greater problems for local latency. However, this preliminary finding will need to be verified by a more targeted study as future work.

Comparison to latency in 2D tasks. Although existing studies of latency in 2D pointing tasks (e.g., [16]) use different methodologies, conditions, and latency levels than our experiment, it seems that latency may have effects of similar magnitude in 2D pointing as in 3D. However, studies on 2D target tracking under latency show a different scenario. In one study [20], tracking errors were only significantly greater than baseline at 170 ms of latency, as opposed to our results which show degradation from 41 ms.

CONCLUSIONS

This study provides the first empirical evidence quantifying the negative effects of local system latency on aiming in 3D game environments. Our results show that local latency as low as 41 ms caused significant and substantial degradation in aiming performance and that performance degradation increased as latency increased. Our results also show that significant amounts of latency prevail in real-world systems and that aim assistance can mitigate local latency. We show that problems caused by lag can be compensated for, reducing the problems for acquisition and removing them altogether for tracking. Our work shows that local latency is a real and substantial problem – but that games can mitigate the problem with appropriate compensation methods.

REFERENCES

1. Accot, J., and Zhai, S. Refining Fitts' law models for bivariate pointing. *CHI 2003*, 193-200.
2. Beigbeder, T., et al. The effects of loss and latency on user performance in Unreal Tournament. *NetGames 2004*, 144-51.
3. Braga Sangiorgi, U., et al. Assessing lag perception in electronic sketching. *NordiCHI 2012*, 153-161.
4. Chen, L., et al., An HCI method to improve human performance reduced by local-lag mechanism, *Interacting with Computers 19*, 2 (2007), 215-224.
5. Elliott, D., Helsen, W., and Chua, R. A century later: Woodworth's (1899) two-component model of goal-directed aiming. *Psych. Bulletin 127*, 3, 2001, 342.
6. Fritsch, T., Ritter, H., and Schiller, J. The effect of latency and network limitations on MMORPGs: a field study of Everquest2. *SIGCOMM 2005*, 1-9.
7. Ghez, C., & Krakauer, J. The organization of movement. *Principles of neural science 4,* 2000, 653-73.
8. Gutwin, C. The effects of network delay on group work in shared workspaces, *Proc. ECSCW 2001*, 299-318.
9. Isokoski, P., et al. Gaze controlled games. *Universal Access in the Information Society 8*, 4, 2009, 323-337.
10. Jörg, S., Normoyle, A., and Safonova, A. How responsiveness affects players' perception in digital games. In *Proc. Applied Perception 2012*, 33-38.
11. Jota, R., Ng, A., Dietz, P., and Wigdor, D. How fast is fast enough?: a study of the effects of latency in direct-touch pointing tasks. *CHI 2013*, 2291-2300.
12. Kopper, R., et al. A human motor behavior model for distal pointing tasks. *IJHCS 68*, 10, 2010, 603-615.
13. Leadbetter, R. *Console Gaming: the Lag Factor.* (2009) eurogamer.net/articles/digitalfoundry-lag-factor-article
14. Lee, B., Bang, H. A kinematic analysis of directional effects on mouse control. *Ergon. 56*, 11, 2013, 1754-65.
15. Looser, J., Cockburn, A. and Savage, J. On the validity of using First-Person Shooters for Fitts' law studies. *People and Computers 2005*, 33-36.
16. MacKenzie I., Ware C. Lag as a determinant of human performance in interactive systems. *CHI 1993*, 488-493.
17. Mandryk, R.L., and Gutwin, C. Perceptibility and utility of sticky targets. In *Proc. GI 2008*, 65-72.
18. Matejka, J., Grossman, T., and Fitzmaurice, G. Swift: reducing the effects of latency in online video scrubbing. *CHI 2012*, 637-646.
19. Pantel, L. and Wolf, L. On the impact of delay realtime multiplayer games. *Proc. NOSSDAV 2002*, 23-29.
20. Pavlovych, A., and Stuerzlinger, W. Target following performance in the presence of latency, jitter, and signal dropouts. *Proc. GI 2011*, 33-40.
21. Pavlovych, A., and Gutwin, C. Assessing target acquisition and tracking performance for complex moving targets in the presence of latency. *GI 2012*, 109-116.
22. Savery, C., Graham, T.C., and Gutwin, C. The human factors of consistency maintenance in multiplayer computer games. *CSCW 2010*, 187-196.
23. So, R., Chung, G. Sensory motor responses in virtual environments. *IEEE EMBS 2005*, 5006-8.
24. Stuckel, D., and Gutwin, C. The effects of local lag on tightly-coupled interaction in distributed groupware *CSCW 2008*, 447-456.
25. Vicencio-Moreira, R., et al. The effectiveness (or lack thereof) of aim-assist techniques in first person shooter games. *CHI 2014*, 937-46.
26. Ware, C., Balakrishnan, R. Reaching for objects in VR displays: lag and frame rate. *ToCHI 1*, 4, 1994, 331-356.
27. Wattimena, A.F., et al. Predicting the perceived quality of a first person shooter: the Quake IV G-model. *SIGCOMM*, 2006, 42.
28. Wilson, D. *Triple Buffering: why we love it.* Feb 2009. http://www.anandtech.com/show/2794/4.

First Person vs. Third Person Perspective in Digital Games: Do Player Preferences Affect Immersion?

Alena Denisova
Department of Computer Science
University of York
York, YO10 5GH, UK
ad595@york.ac.uk

Paul Cairns
Department of Computer Science
University of York
York, YO10 5GH, UK
paul.cairns@york.ac.uk

ABSTRACT
Contemporary digital game developers offer a variety of games for the diverse tastes of their customers. Although the gaming experience often depends on one's preferences, the same may not apply to the level of their immersion. It has been argued whether the player perspective can influence the level of player's involvement with the game. The aim of this study was to research whether interacting with a game in first person perspective is more immersive than playing in the third person point of view (POV). The set up to test the theory involved participants playing a role-playing game in either mode, naming their preferred perspective, and subjectively evaluating their immersive experience. The results showed that people were more immersed in the game play when viewing the game world through the eyes of the character, regardless of their preferred perspectives.

Author Keywords
Digital games; Immersion; Player experience; Player perspective; Camera point of view.

ACM Classification Keywords
H.5.m. Information Interfaces and Presentation (e.g. HCI): Miscellaneous

INTRODUCTION
Nowadays digital games companies offer a wide range of genres, complexities, and formats of games for the diverse tastes of their players. Due to the existing variety, competitive game designers and developers are concerned with what makes a good game, and the research in the area of player experience (PX) plays a major role in these decisions.

One of the terms used to describe PX is immersion – a state of complete involvement with a digital game [2]. It has consistently proved itself to be an important element of the experience players seek from digital games. Immersion has often been used interchangeably with the term presence [14] – a physical sensation of complete submersion in a digital medium [11]. However, this comparison may not be entirely accurate, as suggested by Cairns et al. [3] – unlike presence, immersion is an all-inclusive experience, which is not fully dependent on only physical dimensions of technology.

Certain components could make a game less or more attractive to its player: graphics, sounds, music, novelty, storyline, challenge, advancements, and others [6]. One of the important components that make a game interactive is the POV by which the player interacts with the game environment. Traditional digital games typically have only one POV through which the player can observe their character and the game environment. However, an increasing number of games allow for a user to switch between perspectives, e.g. between the first person and third person POV. Such choice provides many benefits over the conventional single perspective, however it is argued whether one of these POVs is better at immersing participants in the digital world than the other [13].

This paper sets out to investigate whether playing in first person perspective is more immersive than the third person POV, and whether players' personal preferences in terms of the camera POVs they typically choose have an effect on this.

BACKGROUND
Player perspective is one of the important design choices made when creating a digital game. Traditional camera options include audience, isometric, bird's eye, trailing camera, third person and first person POVs [10]. These views support distinctive experiences of immersion for video game play and different perception of the game space. Many contemporary games are designed such that the player, depending on a situation or personal preferences, can choose a perspective.

It could be suggested that the same game can create different experiences depending on the viewpoint through which the player sees the game world. First person POV allows the player to perceive the game through the eyes of the character, observing the world around them up close, giving a clear view of the scenery in front of them. This perspective is believed to provide the most immersive feel for the player [4, 16].

Alternatively, a third person POV allows the player to observe the main character in action, without giving the player the sense that they actually are the character. Although such camera positioning gives a wider field of view of the surrounding area, it makes it hard for the avatar to accurately gauge its focus of interest [4]. A character's visual focus point is particularly important in games where the player needs to know exactly where to aim, and be able to finely adjust the aim.

CHI 2015, April 18–23, 2015, Seoul, Republic of Korea.

ACM 978-1-4503-3145-6/15/04 ...$15.00.
http://dx.doi.org/10.1145/2702123.2702256

Many contemporary digital games are offering an option to choose between first and third person POV to compensate for the drawbacks of each of the viewpoints. Often, third person perspective is used for exploration and interaction, and first person POV is useful when projective accuracy is required [16]. However, this preference has been the subject of discussion on social networks, and gaming forums and magazines for years [9, 17] – the first and third person perspectives are often argued about, whether either of them makes a player feel more immersed in a game than the other one. In previous work these perspectives were compared with regards to the sense of presence in a digital environment [15], establishing that the greater sense of ownership provided by the first person POV leads to higher presence. While there has been no evidence behind the claims that first person POV leads to higher immersion, it is often assumed that it does, both in the academic literature [4, 12], and anecdotally [9].

This question was addressed by Rouse [13], who argues that third person perspective distances the player from the game world and the character they are playing. Hence, the sense of immersion appears to be significantly reduced. According to Gard [7], one of the greatest appeals of digital games is that they allow the player to feel in control, and to see the consequences of one's own actions instead of the actions chosen by the protagonist. Immersing the player in the game world as much as possible is crucial to this 'ownership' of choices made in the game world [13].

Due to the lack of evidence behind the claims of Rouse [13] and Taylor [16], the aim of this paper is to address this question by measuring and comparing immersion in two groups of participants playing the same role-playing game either in first or third person perspectives while also factoring in their pre-existing preferences for a particular perspective.

STUDY DESIGN

The experimental manipulation was the perspective in which players played the chosen game – in first person or third person POV. The players' preference for a particular perspective was a pseudo-independent variable. The dependent variable was immersion which was measured using the IEQ [8], a 31 item questionnaire with five-point Likert scale items. As well as providing an overall measure of immersion, it can be analysed into five factors of cognitive involvement, emotional involvement, real world dissociation, challenge, and control.

Based on a pilot study giving an estimate of moderate effect size ($d = 0.65$), a sample of 40 participants was recruited (7 women and 33 men) with varying levels of gaming experience. The age range of the participants was between 18 and 41 years, with a mean age of 23.5 ($\sigma = 4.97$). Most participants played several times a week and also played for more than an hour when they did play.

Most participants (26 out of 40) had previous experience of playing video games on a PlayStation 3 (PS3), and were familiar with the controllers. Furthermore, over a half of the volunteers (23 out of 40) claimed that they had played the chosen game on a PC, but none of the total number of 40 volunteers had any experience of playing this game on this particular console.

The game

For ecological validity, the study took place in a living room like environment, similar to a place typically used to play video games. The game used in the experiment was Skyrim [1], a role-playing game (RPG) with a possibility to switch between first and third person POV. The option for changing between the perspectives was disabled manually. It was played on the PS3, a platform that none of the participants had used to play this game. Difficulty level was adjusted to be suitable to the experience of the player.

Following the main storyline of the game, the objective set for the participants was to complete (at least partially) 'The Golden Claw Quest' – one of the very first missions in the game. The quest was easy enough for a novice player to complete, but it was also one of the missions not many experienced players could remember due to its early appearance in the game. The quest also required players to engage in the typical RPG activities including travelling throughout the dungeon, thus giving a good opportunity for immersion and for the perspective to be relevant. The weapons used in the game were also fixed to be a sword and a shield, which are both powerful and equally usable in both first and third person perspectives.

Procedure

Before the start of the experiment, each participant was allocated randomly to one of the two experimental conditions, with 20 people in each. In the beginning each participant had a small tutorial, during which they had an opportunity to familiarise themselves with the controllers. Each tutorial session was set in the same POV as the one participants played in during the main part of the experiment. All participants had the same set of instructions of how to navigate the game with the PS3 controller if they had never used it before.

The players were then left to complete the quest in the game. Regardless of how far from completion participants were, they were interrupted after 15 minutes of playing the game. Once the participant was interrupted, he or she was asked to fill out the IEQ, and then the demographics questionnaire. After that, each participant was asked about their preferred perspectives, and then fully debriefed.

Results

Overall, the hypothesis was supported by the results – participants who played the game in first person POV had higher levels of total immersion ($\overline{X}_1 = 117.25$, $\sigma = 13.28$) than those who watched their character from behind ($\overline{X}_3 = 107.10$, $\sigma = 11.69$). The difference in the results was significant ($t(38) = 2.57, p = 0.014$), with a large effect size – Cohen's $d = 0.79$.

Though preferences were not explicitly controlled, each group of participants had an almost equal split of people who preferred one of these two perspectives over the other. Out of 20 participants playing in first person perspective there were

	Played in First Person				Played in Third Person			
	Prefers First Person		Prefers Third Person		Prefers First Person		Prefers Third Person	
	Mean	Std. Dev.	Mean	Std. Dev.	Mean	Std. Dev.	Mean	Std. Dev.
Total Immersion	117.25	9.63	116.82	16.14	98.00	14.00	112.00	6.63
Cognitive Involvement	37.56	2.40	38.09	5.56	31.86	6.18	34.69	4.13
Emotional Involvement	20.78	3.99	20.36	5.78	17.43	5.44	21.00	3.03
Real World Dissociation	25.78	2.86	25.36	3.35	21.71	3.04	24.46	2.22
Challenge	14.44	1.01	14.91	1.22	10.71	2.56	14.00	1.15
Control	19.22	2.82	18.09	3.53	16.29	2.43	17.85	2.23

Table 1. Total immersion and its components when playing in 1st and 3rd person POV, depending on the preferences of the player.

9 who preferred this POV, and 7 who preferred first person perspective in the third person condition.

A two-way ANOVA showed that the difference between immersion scores in first and third person perspectives was significant ($F(1, 36) = 10.22, p = 0.003, \eta^2_{\text{partial}} = 0.221$). However, the effect of players' preferences was marginally significant ($F(1, 36) = 2.87, p = 0.099, \eta^2_{\text{partial}} = 0.074$), while the interaction between these two factors was approaching significance ($F(1, 36) = 3.78, p = 0.060$), with a small effect size, $\eta^2_{\text{partial}} = 0.095$ (Figure 1).

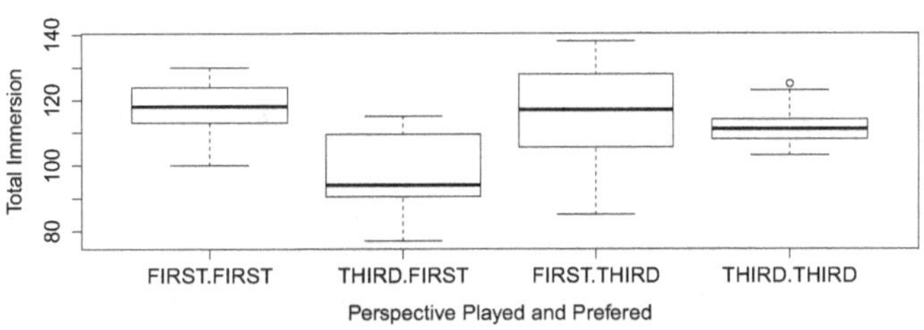

Figure 1. Total immersion depending on the preferred perspectives (right label) and the played perspectives (left label).

In terms of immersion components, significantly different results were found for the real world dissociation, challenge and cognitive involvement of participants. Significance was found in the main effect for real world dissociation ($F(1, 36) = 7.19, p = 0.011, \eta^2_{\text{partial}} = 0.166$), but not in the effect of players' preferences in camera POV ($F(1, 36) = 1, 59, p = 0.216, \eta^2_{\text{partial}} = 0.042$) nor in the interaction of these factors ($F(1, 36) = 2.91, p = 0.096, \eta^2_{\text{partial}} = 0.075$).

The difference between the cognitive involvement scores of those who played in first or third person POV was also highly significant ($F(1, 36) = 8.96, p = 0.005, \eta^2_{\text{partial}} = 0.199$). While in terms of the POV preferences, there was no significant difference found between the two groups of players ($F(1, 36) = 1.23, p = 0.275, \eta^2_{\text{partial}} = 0.033$), nor the interaction of these two factors ($F(1, 36) = 0.57, p = 0.454, \eta^2_{\text{partial}} = 0.016$).

The challenge scores were on par with the results for the total immersion: the main effect was highly significant ($F(1, 36) = 23.38, p<0.001, \eta^2_{\text{partial}} = 0.394$), as was the effect of the preferred perspectives in games ($F(1, 36) = 15.28, p<0.001, \eta^2_{\text{partial}} = 0.298$). The interaction of these two factors on challenge was also highly significant ($F(1, 36) = 8.65, p = 0.006, \eta^2_{\text{partial}} = 0.194$).

Though there was no significance in the main effect, the effect of preferred perspectives, and interaction effect for the emotional involvement and control components of immersion.

In case previous experience of the game was important, immersion was tested against differing levels of experience, but there was no significant difference. Similarly, the level of immersion of those familiar with PS3 controllers and those not did not differ significantly.

Discussion

Following the theoretical discussion in the background section, the results of this study confirmed that first person POV is more immersive than its third person counterpart when playing an RPG game offering this choice. This difference was also seen when preferences were taken into account, though there were indications of more modest effects due to perspective itself, and in interaction with the experimental manipulation. However, previous experience of either the game or the platform did not influence immersion, which suggests that the experiment is reliably reflecting the immersion felt more generally.

Further analysis of these results using the components of the IEQ showed that the main effect of the experimental manipulation was due to effect on real world dissociation, challenge and cognitive involvement. But differences in preference were only seen in the challenge component and no differences at all were seen in the emotional involvement and control aspects. This suggests that players were experiencing similar levels of control in all conditions of the game regardless of their preferences. This is a useful finding, as it is possible that the difference in perspectives from preferred would result in a reduced sense of control.

The main influence of the experimental manipulation was through real world dissociation and cognitive involvement. Following from the theoretical assumptions made by Rouse [13] and Taylor [16], it is not surprising that players' dissociation from the real world was much stronger in first person POV than in third person perspective. In an RPG game, such as Skyrim, in first person POV players feel as if they are a part of the story and the game environment; projecting their thoughts and actions onto their character and taking ownership of them – hence, reducing the distance between the game world and themselves. On the other hand, playing in third person POV distances the player from perceiving themselves as having direct action in the game world, as they watch their character perform actions and make decisions from the viewpoint of somebody who controls the avatar.

It is interesting that this same influence is seen in cognitive involvement. It suggests that the greater sense of being in the game represented by the world is accompanied by a greater cognitive engagement with the world. This might be because the first person POV somewhat restricts the players' ability to see their situation within the game, and hence leads to the greater sense of challenge and requires to be more cognitively engaged to overcome the restriction.

Additionally, challenge was also influenced by preference. This suggests that the preference has led to a certain style or expectation in play, making it easier for players who prefer the first person perspective when they are required to play in the third person POV. It may be that players who prefer the first person perspective do so, because of the greater challenge it presents, and whether or not it is the preferred POV, all players get more immersed because of how it situates them in the virtual world of the game. Indeed, it is widely believed that first person perspective is often chosen by more experienced gamers [17], particularly in shooting games [4], as it requires more skill and better reflexes. While third person POV allows for the easier navigation, and as a result is more suited for people who are less advanced in playing digital games.

It may be this particular aspect that explains why people who are more experienced in playing in first person perspective felt moderately challenged and cognitively involved with the game, while those players who preferred the other viewpoint had higher scores in both immersion components. This also explains why the lowest immersion scores were obtained by players who interacted with the game in third person POV, but normally prefer first person perspective.

Overall then, it seems that regardless of your preference, first person is more immersive, and indeed that if you prefer first person it is 'hard to go back.' This might be because the increased challenge is needed to bring about the greater immersive experience. Interestingly though this contrasts with one of the reasons for offering an option to switch between the camera viewpoints, which is to satisfy the preferences of any gamer, and so increase their involvement in the game. It may be that players perhaps make some progression from a third person perspective, which is less challenging, and therefore more engaging for those learning the game, to a first person perspective, as mastery is achieved because of the greater accuracy that can be attained in that perspective. Perhaps then, rather than offering players the opportunity to have one mode or the other, games could progress from one mode to the other in order to achieve the higher levels of immersion. However, if this results in too high a challenge, it could actually reduce immersion [5], so might be an adaptive element suited to how well players seem to cope with the different modes.

CONCLUSION AND FURTHER WORK

Immersion is one of the various gaming experiences that players believe to be very important when playing a game. This work shows that, as far as immersion is concerned, POV does influence immersion regardless of preferences. Of course gaming experience is much more multi-faceted, and it may be that with first person perspective there might be increased immersion, but at the cost of a reduction in other aspects, say social presence. This is something that requires more detailed investigation. Alongside this, it should be noted that the game chosen here is a particular style of game, and in others, such as racing or shooting games, alternative factors may dominate in the production of immersion and other gaming experiences. Further studies of this sort will reveal how generally important POV is for building up the gaming experience.

REFERENCES

1. Bethesda Game Studios. The Elder Scrolls V: Skyrim. www.elderscrolls.com/skyrim, (2011).
2. Brown, E., and Cairns, P. A grounded investigation of game immersion. In *CHI'04*, ACM (2004), 1297–1300.
3. Cairns, P., Cox, A., and Nordin, A. I. Immersion in digital games: a review of gaming experience research. *Handbook of digital games, MC Angelides and H. Agius, Eds. Wiley-Blackwell* (2014), 339–361.
4. Call, J., Voorhees, G. A., and Whitlock, K. *Guns, Grenades, and Grunts: First-person Shooter Games*, vol. 2. Bloomsbury Publishing USA, 2012.
5. Cox, A., Cairns, P., Shah, P., and Carroll, M. Not doing but thinking: the role of challenge in the gaming experience. In *CHI'12*, ACM (2012), 79–88.
6. Ermi, L., and Mäyrä, F. Power and control of games: children as the actors of game cultures. In *DIGRA Conf.* (2003).
7. Gard, T. Building character. *Gama Network: Gamasutra.com* (2000).
8. Jennett, C., Cox, A. L., Cairns, P., Dhoparee, S., Epps, A., Tijs, T., and Walton, A. Measuring and defining the experience of immersion in games. *International journal of human-computer studies 66*, 9 (2008), 641–661.
9. Kotaku Magazine. First or third person - what's your perspective? `goo.gl/LYlL2W`, Apr 2011.
10. Laramée, F. D. *Game design perspectives*. Cengage Learning, 2002.
11. Lombard, M., and Ditton, T. At the heart of it all: The concept of presence. *Journal of Computer-Mediated Communication 3*, 2 (1997).
12. McMahan, A. Immersion, engagement and presence. *The video game theory reader* (2003), 67–86.
13. Rouse III, R. What's your perspective? *ACM SIGGRAPH Computer Graphics 33*, 3 (1999), 9–12.
14. Ryan, R. M., Rigby, C. S., and Przybylski, A. The motivational pull of video games: A self-determination theory approach. *Motivation and emotion 30*, 4 (2006), 344–360.
15. Slater, M., Spanlang, B., Sanchez-Vives, M. V., and Blanke, O. First person experience of body transfer in virtual reality. *PloS one 5*, 5 (2010).
16. Taylor, L. N. *Video games: Perspective, point-of-view, and immersion*. PhD thesis, University of Florida, 2002.
17. Unity3d Forum. First person vs third person perspective. `goo.gl/m1c4c9`, Aug 2010.

VIZMO Game Browser: Accessing Video Games by Visual Style and Mood

Jin Ha Lee[1], Sungsoo (Ray) Hong[2], Hyerim Cho[1], Yea-Seul Kim[2]
iSchool [1], Human-Centered Design and Engineering [2], DUB Group
University of Washington, Seattle WA 98195, USA
{jinhalee, rayhong, chohr113, yeaseul1}@uw.edu

ABSTRACT
Despite the growing interests in video games as consumer products as well as objects of research, current methods for accessing video games are limited. We present *Vizmo* as a new way of browsing video games based on their visual style and mood. In order to test the usability and usefulness of Vizmo, we asked 19 video game experts to evaluate their interaction with the tool. The results show that experts perceived Vizmo as a novel and aesthetically pleasing game discovery tool which would be most useful for game research on historical and aesthetic aspects. We discuss five key points for improving the design of Vizmo as well as our future plan for the next iteration of this prototype game browser.

Author Keywords
Video games; Visualization; Visual style; Mood; Metadata

ACM Classification Keywords
H.5.0. Information Interfaces and Presentation: General

INTRODUCTION
Video games play an increasingly widespread role in our social, cultural, and economic activities. It is important to provide a useful way to search and browse video games for a growing user base. However, previous research shows that despite increasing interest in and significance of video games, current descriptive practices and access methods are not sufficiently robust [2, 7]. Most of the currently available game-related websites only provide platform and genre as main access points other than basic descriptive information of video games such as game title, publisher, and developer. As a result, it is difficult, if not impossible, to search or browse games based on attributes describing the actual content of the game (e.g., plot, mood, theme, visual style).

Our work aims to fill this gap by exploring a novel method for improving users' access to video games. In particular, we test the usability of a prototype video game browser that allows users to access games based on two types of metadata: mood and visual style. While we envision that Vizmo can potentially be useful for both game experts and general game players, in this paper we specifically study game experts as our first step. We seek to answer the following research questions focusing on the usability and usefulness of our browser:

RQ1. How do game experts rate the usability of our video game browser? How can we improve the user experience?

RQ2. Would browsing games by using mood and visual style metadata be useful? If so, what kinds of professional and personal tasks could benefit from such access methods?

RELATED WORK

Game Research in HCI
A substantial body of research related to various aspects of video games can be found in previous HCI literature including the design of games, usability of game interfaces, gamification, and so on. However, little research has been conducted on designing information retrieval systems for games, or understanding gamers' information behavior as they search, browse, collect, and organize games.

Outside of the video game domain, we found a few studies on designing and developing a browsing tool for other media types such as movies [8], images [14], or music [1]. The latter two studies as well as [5,9], in particular, implement and evaluate a browsing interface utilizing faceted metadata (i.e., data attributes organized into orthogonal set of categories (facets/dimensions) [3]) as an alternative to other dominant search/browse methods based on keywords or similarity [14]. Our design is also based on this approach as mood and visual style are represented as two different facets in Vizmo. Previous usability studies found that facet navigation can be an effective and convenient search method for users [5,14]. Users assessed the idea of using facets very positively [1], and despite the slower response time of their interface, they still preferred it stating the search experience was interesting and enjoyable [14]. Karlson et al. [5] found that facet navigation is especially effective when users are seeking information objects with certain characteristics. These studies highlight the usefulness of facets for accessing media objects.

It is also noteworthy that systems described in studies like [8] or [13] use mood metadata for browsing movies or generating music playlists. We envision that our work can

CHI 2015, April 18–23, 2015, Seoul, Republic of Korea.

ACM 978-1-4503-3145-6/15/04...$15.00.
http://dx.doi.org/10.1145/2702123.2702264.

complement such research by perhaps allowing the use of mood metadata for browsing multiple types of media including movies, music, and video games.

Previous Research Efforts

This work is part of a larger research project by the Game Metadata Research (GAMER) Group at University of Washington Information School and Seattle Interactive Media Museum, aiming to create a standardized metadata schema and a set of controlled vocabularies (i.e., standard lists of terms with definitions and specification of related terms for describing particular metadata elements) for describing video games [7]. In a series of user studies conducted as part of this research effort, both mood and visual style have been identified as potentially useful elements for accessing games. In an online survey involving 1,257 participants, 66.7% responded that mood/affect information would be useful for the games they are currently playing or for seeking new games to play, and 53.4% for visual style [7]. Of the 237 respondents who reported having game-related professions, 70.9% and 55.3% responded positively for mood/affect and visual style, respectively. Interview data from 56 game users [7] also supports the importance of such metadata:

> *P42: Super Mario Bros. where they're like pixelated, my younger kids are going to look at that and go "Oh the graphics, gross" but the patrons my age that grew up with this are going to say "Oh my gosh, flashback to childhood, I want this!" So people have a very strong response to the visual look of the game."*

> *P28: I think [mood] is often times why people choose [certain games], well why did you choose the one where you could only kill zombies with household appliances? I picked it because it was funny...you know, this is a comical way to prevent the apocalypse versus a very serious way to prevent the apocalypse, which I think might be a good way to organize."*

Based on the user data, we decided to include visual style and mood in our video game metadata schema. In order to consistently describe these attributes, it is necessary to establish a controlled vocabulary for each element. We established the initial list of terms by collecting candidate mood terms from a number of media object websites that use mood taxonomy, including Movie Genome Project, gamerDNA.com, allmusic.com, etc. The candidate visual style terms were sourced from previous scholarly literature including [4,6,11] in addition to designer forums and video game art appreciation websites. From the initial lists, duplicate and irrelevant terms were removed. Afterwards, each term was defined, and the hierarchical, equivalent, and associative relationships among terms were identified.

The terms were evaluated based on multiple aspects, primarily their understandability (e.g., do people understand what we mean by "cel-shaded"?) and usability (e.g., can people use these terms to describe the games they played?). Based on the users' feedback, the controlled vocabularies were revised for easier and more consistent application. The two main changes were to 1) simplify the initial list by reducing the number of terms, and 2) removing technical visual style terms (i.e., terms referring to the techniques for rendering certain images such as rasterized or ray traced). More information on this phase can be found in [2].

DESIGN OF VIZMO

Vizmo is a web-based visualization interface built on Javascript and D3 (http://d3js.org/). The interface consists of four main components: selectors, navigable timeline, title list browser, and detailed information box area.

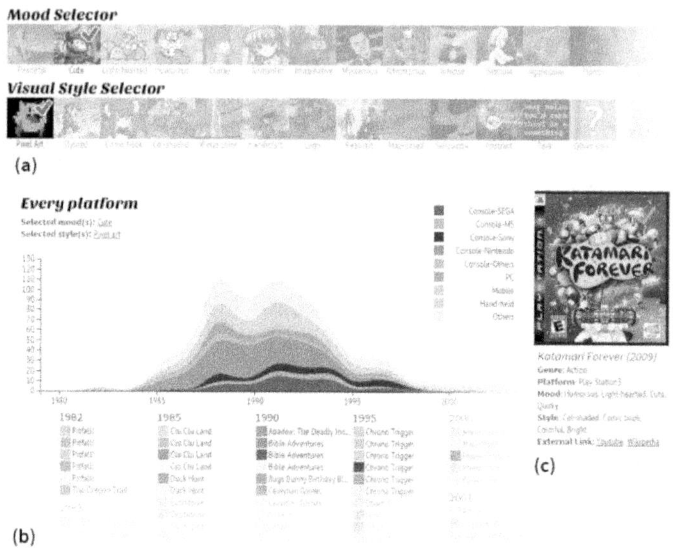

Figure 1. Vizmo visual interface. (a) Mood and Visual style selector; (b) Navigable stack area graph and title browser; (c) Title detail (accessible at: http://vizmo.mooo.com)

The selectors for mood and visual style are prominently positioned at the top of the page. In prior research, we discovered that users had difficulty understanding visual styles of game solely based on terms and definitions; rather, showing examples of games that fit into each category was much more effective [7]. Therefore we created icons based on prototypical examples of games for each visual style, and embedded them in the selector as visual cues. In order to make the interface consistent, we also added icons representing different moods of video games.

The order of the mood terms was determined based on previous research on mood in Psychology, specifically the Tellegen-Watson's circular mood model [12]. Our mood terms were ordered to approximately match the clockwise order of the mood clusters in their model. The selector for visual style has three groups (i.e., style, brightness, and colorfulness) divided by whitespaces. The users can select and unselect the multiple moods and visual styles at the same time and the results showing the relevant games will dynamically change, accordingly.

The navigable timeline is dynamically generated to show the quantity and distribution of the games by platform and published year of the game titles that match the categories of mood and visual style selected by the user. Concurrently, all the selected game titles are listed below. The first layer of the chart is representing nine broad categories of game platforms (e.g., console-MS, console-Sony, console-Nintendo, PC, Mobile). Once the user clicks a specific area in the chart, the result will be divided into sub-categories showing more detailed platform information (e.g., console-Nintendo will be divided into Wii U, Wii, etc.). The colors representing the platforms are taken from the logo of the company (e.g., red for Nintendo) or color of the physical consoles (e.g., gray/black for Sony PlayStation). In the second layer, we applied sequential hue for color coding so that the brightness corresponds to the order of the launching date of the platforms; the newer platforms with darker hues.

In the title list browser, we present the game titles as entry points for users to get to the detailed view. When the users hover over the list of game titles, the pop-up image will show a representative image of the game. Once the user selects a specific game, detailed information will appear in the info box at the right bottom corner. The design of the timeline and info box reflects Shneiderman's principle of interface design that the visualization should give the overview first and provide detail-on-demand [10].

The game data shown in Vizmo is derived from 604 sample video game metadata records [7]. Vizmo is currently in a prototype stage and therefore there are a limited number of records being used to generate the results. For games that have multiple versions (e.g., ports, remakes), the published year is set to represent the year when the original version of the game was published.

USABILITY TESTING

We conducted a usability study involving 19 participants. We specifically recruited users who have game-related professions to explore how useful Vizmo may be for professional game-related information retrieval tasks in addition to personal tasks. Participants were recruited initially through the authors' professional and social networks, and additional participants were found by snowball sampling. While the subjects came from various backgrounds and professions, every one of them had at least one year of work experience in the game industry and had in-depth knowledge of the domain. The participants were asked to freely explore the browser and fill out an online post-task questionnaire. We asked questions regarding their opinions on the usability of the browser, design of the selectors, presentation of results, and usefulness of the tool. They were also encouraged to provide suggestions for improvement.

FINDINGS AND DISCUSSION

Demographics

The age of participants ranged from 20 to 60 with an average of 36, and 68% of participants were male. Eight participants had more than ten years of game-related work experience. Some examples of the respondents' occupations include game designer, developer, analyst, reviewer, researcher, and librarian.

Usability of Vizmo

Overall, 13 respondents expressed that Vizmo was easy to use and the design was intuitive. One user specifically mentioned that he/she appreciated the minimal design:

> *P14: It's all quite easy to use and simple, no need to over complicate something that has a fairly narrow purpose. Honestly I thought the timeline presentation of when the games were released and for which platform was the coolest feature.*

They also noted that the interface is visually attractive (P16) and the selectors provided them with some new insights into how to browse games (P8: "I like these a great deal. They are a fresh way to think about game genres.").

The most common comment was regarding the matching algorithm for selecting games which is set to be additive (search criteria are combined with an OR operator). Seven out of 19 respondents thought they would like to be able to have an 'AND' relationship so that they can narrow down the results, or at least to have options to choose 'OR', 'AND' or 'NOT' for the search.

The intention of using representative icons in the selectors was to provide users with visual cues. However, some users felt that this could potentially be misleading.

> *P9: It makes sense for the VISUAL selector as the combination of the category words and the sample aesthetic from an example game give a good sense of what to expect in results, but using game graphics on MOOD has some side effects: for the gamer who is familiar with the games the example image may be mislead[ing] given their experience of mood in that game, and those unfamiliar are really going on an interpretation of the category word anyway...*

> *P18: The images are somewhat representative, but perhaps not as good as a tooltip with a definition.*

Two respondents (P10, P17) specifically mentioned that they wanted to be able to click the platform legend rather than having to click on the areas in the timeline to pull up the results. One participant suggested the results to be presented in a different way by showing "some top picks from that combination, or something simpler than having to scroll down to find suggestions. (P1)"

Usefulness of Vizmo

We asked how/whether Vizmo would be useful to users personally or professionally. Fifteen participants found Vizmo useful, mainly for video game research as it provides a historical view with the timeline and allows a more aesthetic approach for finding games.

> *P4: It will be useful for analyzing what kinds of game genres were popular over time. I can see visual directors or artists using this to search for games with a similar tone.*

> *P6: Primarily I would find it useful for garnering game ideas, potentially useful in research, or finding a game related to a particular idea or feeling. Being able to find an action game*

whose thematic elements are similar seems really interesting.

P17: As a reviewer, I see myself using this to track trends...I could make statements in my reviews like, "2009 was a rough year for comedic games. The quirky indie explosion of the teens had yet to happen..."

A couple of participants mentioned how Vizmo may appeal more to users who are less knowledgeable about games, and also hinted how it may be improved with personalization features:

P3: The less a player knows about available games, the more they would benefit. If you have a lot of information already, this is less useful, though it might help with jogging one's memory.

P13: The tool asks no questions about the user's preferences or gaming history, and not enough information about the games in the end to help shape a decision of what to play or how the listed games are related or similar.

Although the mood/visual style selectors provide new ways to browse games, the respondents thought providing more options to filter out the games would be useful. Some respondents specifically expressed that this would also help address the subjective nature of metadata.

P9: As-is this is more useful for a media aesthetics approach to games, but if you added some kind of ergodic experience selector...[it] would be quite useful for my teaching goals. Something that lets you search for the kinds of challenge or "non-trivial effort" that the game emphasizes.

P19: They are useful but subjective. It would be useful for searchers to have a place to click for the rating as a third option and single vs. multi-player as a fourth option.

There were several comments about the usefulness of Vizmo in relation to other existing websites (e.g., P3: "Perhaps personally [I would use it] on a service like Steam.") suggesting the importance of seeking collaboration to potentially use information such as play history/personal preference for better browsing experience.

CONCLUSION

Game experts perceived Vizmo to be an aesthetically pleasing game browser, which offers a novel approach to accessing games. Feedback indicates that Vizmo can be useful for game research on historical and aesthetic aspects. The key points from our usability test are:

1. Provide multiple options for selecting categories
2. Provide definitions in addition to icons
3. Make the platform legend selectable in the timeline
4. Provide more filtering options such as genre or rating
5. Seek integration with existing services

In our future work, we plan to conduct a follow-up study with the improved version of Vizmo involving general game players to further evaluate its usefulness and usability. We also plan to expand our selectors to include other novel access methods for discovering games such as tropes, plot, theme, setting, and appeal factors/motivations for playing games in order to increase the usefulness of Vizmo.

ACKNOWLEDGMENTS

We thank Stephanie Rossi, Carl Gellert, and the GA crew at University of Washington iSchool for collecting the data. This research is supported by the UW Office of Research.

REFERENCES

1. Dachselt, R. and Frisch, M. Mambo: a facet-based zoomable music browser. In *Proc. MUM '07,* ACM (2007), 110-117.
2. Donovan, A., Cho, H., Magnifico, C., and Lee, J. H. Pretty as a pixel: issues and challenges in developing a controlled vocabulary for video game visual styles. In *Proc. JCDL '13*, ACM (2013), 412-414.
3. Hearst, M. A. Clustering versus faceted categories for information exploration. *Commun. ACM 49,* 4, (2006), 59-61.
4. Järvinen, A. Gran stylissimo: The audiovisual elements and styles in computer and video games. In *Proc. CDGC,* Tampere University Press (2002), 113-128.
5. Karlson, A. K., Robertson, G. G., Robbins, D. C., Czerwinski, M. P., and Smith, G. R. FaThumb: a facet-based interface for mobile search. In *Proc. CHI,* ACM (2006), 711-720.
6. Kyprianidis, J., Collomosse, J., Wang, T., and Isenberg, T. State of the art: A taxonomy of artistic stylization techniques for images and video. In *IEEE Trans. Vis. Comput. Graphics*, IEEE (2012), 1-20.
7. Lee, J. H., Clarke, R. I., and Perti, A. Empirical evaluation of metadata for video games and interactive media. *JASIST,* in press.
8. Martins, P., Langlois, T. and Chambel, T. MovieClouds: content-based overviews and exploratory browsing of movies. In *Proc. MindTrek '11,* ACM (2011), 133-140.
9. Medynskiy, Y., Dontcheva, M., and Drucker, S. M. Exploring websites through contextual facets. In *Proc. CHI 2009,* ACM (2009), 2013-2022.
10. Shneiderman, B. The eyes have it: a task by data type taxonomy for information visualizations. In *IEEE Sym. on Visual Languages*, IEEE (1996), 336-343.
11. Tavinor, G. *The art of video games.* Wiley-Blackwell, Malden, MA, 2009.
12. Tellegen, A., Watson, D., and Clark, L. A. On the dimensional and hierarchical structure of affect. *Psychological Science, 10*, 4, (1999), 297-303.
13. Van Gulik, R. and Vignoli, F. Visual playlist generation on the artist map. In *Proc. ISMIR '05*, (2005), 520-523.
14. Yee, K-P., Swearingen, K., Li, K., and Hearst, M. Faceted metadata for image search and browsing. In *Proc. CHI 2003,* ACM (2003), 401-408.

"I always assumed that I wasn't really that close to [her]": Reasoning about Invisible Algorithms in News Feeds

Motahhare Eslami, Aimee Rickman†, Kristen Vaccaro, Amirhossein Aleyasen, Andy Vuong Karrie Karahalios, Kevin Hamilton, Christian Sandvig‡
University of Illinois at Urbana-Champaign, †California State University, Fresno, ‡University of Michigan
{eslamim2, kvaccaro, aleyase2, avuong3, kkarahal, kham}@illinois.edu
†arickman@csufresno.edu, ‡csandvig@umich.edu

ABSTRACT
Our daily digital life is full of algorithmically selected content such as social media feeds, recommendations and personalized search results. These algorithms have great power to shape users' experiences, yet users are often unaware of their presence. Whether it is useful to give users insight into these algorithms' existence or functionality and how such insight might affect their experience are open questions. To address them, we conducted a user study with 40 Facebook users to examine their perceptions of the Facebook News Feed curation algorithm. Surprisingly, more than half of the participants (62.5%) were not aware of the News Feed curation algorithm's existence at all. Initial reactions for these previously unaware participants were surprise and anger. We developed a system, *FeedVis*, to reveal the difference between the algorithmically curated and an unadulterated News Feed to users, and used it to study how users perceive this difference. Participants were most upset when close friends and family were not shown in their feeds. We also found participants often attributed missing stories to their friends' decisions to exclude them rather than to Facebook News Feed algorithm. By the end of the study, however, participants were mostly satisfied with the content on their feeds. Following up with participants two to six months after the study, we found that for most, satisfaction levels remained similar before and after becoming aware of the algorithm's presence, however, algorithmic awareness led to more active engagement with Facebook and bolstered overall feelings of control on the site.

Author Keywords
Algorithms; Algorithm Awareness; News Feeds; Hidden Processes

ACM Classification Keywords
H.5.m. Information Interfaces and Presentation (e.g. HCI): Miscellaneous

INTRODUCTION
Today, algorithms curate everyday online content by prioritizing, classifying, associating, and filtering information. In doing so, they exert power to shape the users' experience and even their perception of the world [9]. News feeds, which provide users with frequently updated news, are one application where algorithms play an influential role. An example of a prominent news feed today is Facebook News Feed, which in September of 2014, was viewed by on average 864 million daily active users [12]. This list of updating stories that appears front and center on Facebook home pages displays an algorithmically curated or filtered list of stories selected from a pool of all stories created by one's network of friends.

The increasing prevalence of opaque and invisible algorithms coupled with their power raises questions about how knowledgeable users are and should be about the existence and operation of these algorithms. Whether their understanding is correct or not, users' perceived knowledge about an algorithm can affect their behavior. For instance, believing that posts with commercial keywords were ranked higher by the Facebook News Feed algorithm, some teenagers added product names to their posts in an attempt to manipulate the algorithm and increase their posts' visibility [41]. Other users tended to block new mothers in their feed based on a false assumption that such women posted too many baby pictures, when in fact the prevalence of such images was determined by their popularity among users [27].

However, with no way to know if their knowledge of these invisible algorithms is correct, users cannot be sure of the results of their actions. Algorithmic interfaces in Internet applications rarely include a clear enough feedback mechanism for users to understand the effects of their own actions on the system. Without such feedback, it can be difficult to assess the influence of either algorithm knowledge or ignorance.

To begin to address these issues, we explored users' awareness and perception of the Facebook News Feed curation algorithm (hereafter "*the algorithm*"). This algorithm determines which stories (e.g., status updates, pictures, videos, likes and comments) appear in a Facebook user's News Feed based on social network links and activity on Facebook [28, 29]. We interviewed 40 Facebook users and discovered that more than half (62.5%) were not aware that News Feed hid stories. They believed every single story from their friends and followed pages appeared in their News Feed. To understand why so few participants knew of the algorithm's existence, we conducted interviews to investigate Facebook use.

To assist us in these interviews, we developed *FeedVis*, a Facebook application, to reveal the algorithm to study participants. FeedVis extracted participants' News Feed stories as well as their friends' stories to disclose what we call "*the al-*

CHI 2015, April 18 - 23 2015, Seoul, Republic of Korea

ACM 978-1-4503-3145-6/15/04...$15.00
http://dx.doi.org/10.1145/2702123.2702556

gorithm outputs": the difference between users' News Feeds when they have been curated by the algorithm and when they have not. Using FeedVis, we showed participants alternate views of their familiar News Feed and provided them with an opportunity to modify the algorithm outputs to curate their desired News Feed. We discovered that strong initial negative reactions to the mere presence of an algorithmic filter often subsided once users understood who and what was being hidden. We followed up with participants two to six months later and found that their usage patterns had often changed due to the insight they gained about the algorithm via our study.

RELATED WORK

Many areas of research have examined invisible processes and how people perceive and react to them. Cognitive science and human factors researchers study the mental models people create when they interact with machines and technology [30]. Designers develop new ideas by enacting probes that reveal interactions with hidden and uncertain aspects of people's lives [14]. Related efforts exist in architecture and urban planning, where architects create new spaces based on the study of how people perceive and navigate landscapes [24]. Finally, time and motion studies observe people conducting a task and extract any hidden patterns to find the most productive way to complete it [16]. Studies dealing with hidden or invisible components of daily life have also addressed some aspects of social media. The invisibility of audiences in online environments has prompted research into the imagined audience [23], including quantifying how perceived audiences compare to actual audiences and measuring otherwise invisible patterns of attention on social media [4].

Algorithms

Research attention has recently turned to algorithms as invisible and influential aspects of daily digital life. Many researchers have considered curation algorithms and argued that their effects are important while their operation is opaque [2, 19, 36]. For example, search algorithms structure the online information available to a society, and may function as a gatekeeper [18, 20]. And scientific journal rankings have been found to produce unwarranted perceptions about the importance of some articles over others [6].

Researchers have paid particular attention to algorithms when outputs are unexpected or when the risk exists that the algorithm might promote antisocial political, economic, geographic, racial, or other discrimination. Invisible algorithms in health care, credit scoring and stock trading have aroused interest in recent years [32, 39]. Researchers have looked at dynamic pricing and the possibility of reinforcing biases against rural and poorer areas, which tend to have less competition, thereby "diminish[ing] the Internet's role as an equalizer" [42]. Algorithms that select personalized advertisements have been found to unevenly distribute arrest record ads by race [40]. Controversy over Twitter Trends and accusations of algorithmic censorship of the tag #occupywallstreet throughout the Occupy Wall Street protests led to questions of whether a sorting algorithm can be wrong or unethical under some conditions [17, 35]. Some researchers have even studied unexpected results in the filtering of autocompletion text, finding some algorithms explicitly attempt to make moral judgements, such as removing terms deemed to be related to child pornography [8].

As a result of these concerns, some have argued that increased algorithmic transparency would be beneficial. Designs and recommendations have been developed to reveal the power of algorithms to predict people's interests and to affect their online life [13, 26]. Designers at Ubisoft, a video game company, recently offered personalized inferences that can be made from Facebook profiles as a promotional device for a surveillance-themed game [10].

The prevalence of algorithmically generated feeds in social media such as Facebook News Feed has triggered discussions about the appropriateness of the curation algorithms employed. Some commentators are primarily concerned about friends that "vanish" from the platform [33], and others see an opportunity for profit linked to the position of posts [5]. While other work has attempted to reverse-engineer these algorithmic processes [19] or develop new summaries of algorithmic results [10, 13, 26], to our knowledge no researchers have developed systems to reveal to users the contrast between algorithmically manipulated and unfiltered results.

Case Study: Facebook News Feed

Launched in 2006 [37], the Facebook News Feed curation algorithm has attracted significant attention in recent years, particularly after a recent, controversial study of emotional contagion [22]. Facebook currently uses close to 100,000 factors to algorithmically choose the best stories from the large pool of potential stories for News Feed [25]. Although Facebook has stated it would change how it communicates updates to News Feed due to the large number of user requests [1], there is still little understanding among users or anyone outside of Facebook of how the News Feed curation algorithm works. To shed light on invisible algorithms curating social media feeds and how they impact users, we ask the following research questions:

RQ1. How aware are users of the News Feed curation algorithm and what factors are associated with this awareness?

RQ2. How do users evaluate the curation of their News Feed when shown the algorithm outputs? Given the opportunity to alter the outputs, how do users' preferred outputs compare to the algorithm's?

RQ3. How does the knowledge users gain through an algorithm visualization tool transfer to their behavior?

STUDY DESIGN

To address the proposed research questions, we conducted a mixed-methods study consisting of three phases. First, participants visited our lab and completed a questionnaire and interview to measure algorithm awareness. At this time, we also collected participants' network size, News Feed stories and friends' stories to populate an interface for the next phase. In the second phase, participants used an application (FeedVis) to visualize the algorithm outputs, and we used a long form open-ended interview to discuss them. Third, we e-mailed participants two-to-six months later to ask closed- and open-ended questions to evaluate the consequences of any insight gained by observing the algorithm outputs. All in-person interviews were audio recorded and transcribed for analysis.

Pre-Assessment: Testing Algorithm Awareness

At the beginning of the study, participants answered a demographic questionnaire including measures of their social media use. With one exception, all participants used Facebook at least once a day. To assess their familiarity with the algorithm, we asked a combination of open- and closed-ended behavioral, knowledge, and attitude questions whose answers likely depend upon awareness of the algorithm. First, we asked if and how they used Facebook settings to adjust the content on their News Feed (including sorting the stories of News Feed by recency or top stories, hiding a story, following or unfollowing friends and making Facebook lists). Next, we asked them to imagine they had a "friend," Sarah, and she shared a public story visible on her wall to all her friends. We asked them whether this story would appear in their own News Feed. In addition, we asked whether they missed any stories that they would have preferred to see in their News Feed. If they answered affirmatively, we probed further to understand their reasoning for why they may have missed a story; for instance, whether they thought missing a story would be a result of their own actions such as scrolling past it or a result of a filtering process. During this pre-assessment, we asked participants to use their Facebook accounts to log into our Facebook application, FeedVis. FeedVis extracted and collected the participant's network size, News Feed and their friends' stories. This collected information was used to generate a series of alternate views for the feed.

Main Interview: Algorithm Outputs Disclosure

After understanding the participants' existing News Feed knowledge, we presented them with a series of FeedVis feed views. Paging through these views revealed some algorithm outputs to the participants. If they were not already aware of the algorithm's existence, these views provided the first revelation of News Feed's algorithmic curation. These views were used as prompts in the interview so that participants could react to and discuss stories that actually appeared on their News Feed. As extracting all stories from an entire friend network is process-intensive, we limited the time period of the stories collected to one week or less depending on the number of the user's friends. We briefly describe the four FeedVis views.

The FeedVis Content View: Revealing Content Filtering

The Facebook algorithm shows a user a selection of stories chosen from the universe of all stories contributed by the people and pages that the user follows. In the first view, we aimed to show the user this universe of potential content, highlighting content that the algorithm excluded from display. This view helped the user compare what they saw and what they might have seen in the absence of a filter, or with a different one. The Content View consisted of two columns (Figure 1). The right column, "*Shown Stories*," included only the stories displayed on the user's News Feed. These stories were shown with a blue background. The left column, called "*All Stories*," showed every story posted from all the user's friends. In this column, stories which did appear in the user's News Feed were again shown on a blue background, while stories which did not appear in their News Feed were shown on a white background. The content for the "Shown Stories" view was generated by querying user_id/home/user via the Facebook Graph API. It is important to note that "Shown Stories," while displayed on the user's News Feed, might not have been seen if the user did not scroll far enough. The content for the "All Stories" view is the union of friend_id/feed/ queries for each friend; we extracted all stories that the user would see if she went to a friend's page while logged in. We then used post_ids to determine whether those posts had appeared in the user's News Feed. To verify our operationalization of "Shown Stories," we asked participants if they remembered seeing randomly selected stories in this column. With a few exceptions, they did remember them.

Figure 1. The Content View. Shown stories (in blue) occur across both columns, while the hidden stories (white) appear only in the left column as 'holes' in News Feed. Stories appear in reverse chronological order.

The FeedVis Friend View: Revealing Social Patterns

By filtering content, the Facebook algorithm also creates user perceptions about how other people use Facebook. We built a visualization, the Friend View, to help the user understand which users usually appear and which are hidden. This view divided the user's friends into three categories based on the proportion of each friend's stories that had appeared in the user's News Feed during the previous week: "rarely shown," "sometimes shown," and "mostly shown" friends (Figure 2).

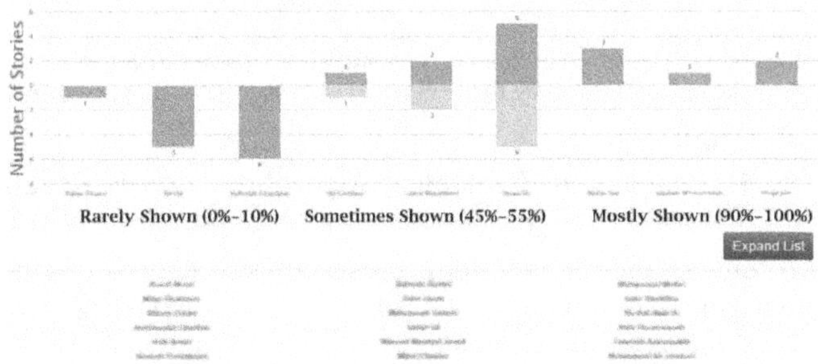

Figure 2. The Friend View. "Rarely shown" includes friends whose stories were mostly hidden (0%-10%) from the user. "Sometimes shown" includes friends who had roughly half of their posts (45%-55%) shown to the user. "Mostly shown" includes those friends whose stories were almost never filtered out (90%-100%) for the user. The number of the shown stories is displayed above the x-axis and the number of hidden stories is below the x-axis. The expand button augments the three category lists below the chart.

The FeedVis Friend & Content Rearrangement Views: Envisioning a Different Algorithm

After exploring the algorithm outputs, we wanted to gauge participants' desire to change them. We created two new

Figure 3. The Friend Rearrangement View. User can move friends between the categories by changing the color of a friend to the destination category's color.

views that invited participants to "tweak" their algorithm. The first view allowed adjustment based on story authorship, the second based on story content. First, the Friend Rearrangement View (Figure 3) presented a list of friends according to the same three categories described above, and invited re-assignment of friends to different categories. Second, the Content Rearrangement View (Figure 4) randomly selected ten shown stories and ten hidden stories, then invited users to indicate whether they would have preferred a "shown" story to be "hidden" or vice versa. The lab portion of this study, including the pre-assessment, lasted one to three hours per participant.

Figure 4. The Content Rearrangement View. User can move a story from its original category to the other by clicking the button beside each story.

Post-Assessment: Evaluating Algorithm Outputs Revelation

To understand the long-term consequences of revealing hidden aspects of a curation algorithm, we contacted participants via e-mail two to six months after conducting the study. We asked two questions and invited any additional comments participants wished to share. The questions were: (1) Has participation in our study resulted in more, less or no change in your satisfaction with Facebook News Feed? (2) Have you changed anything about how you use Facebook in light of what you learned in our study? (e.g., "I 'like' more posts now" or "I view posts using the 'Most Recent' setting instead of the 'Top Stories' setting.").

Participants

We used modified quota sampling to obtain a non-probability sample that is roughly representative of the US population on four dimensions. The national proportions for gender, age, race/ethnicity and socioeconomic status were used as quota targets for recruitment and selection in the Champaign, Illinois and surrounding area. Quotas required an elaborate recruitment strategy including posters in varied public places, e-mails to local online communities and civic organizations, and posts on Facebook. We recruited 40 participants consisting of five students, two faculty members and 14 staff from the University of Illinois and 19 people with other occupations such as homemakers, delivery persons, servers, artisans, performers and writers. Participants received $10/hour for the pre-assessment and main interview; participation in the post-assessment entered them in a lottery for a $50 gift card. The original sample was 60% women and ranged between 18 and 64 years old. 68% of the participants were Caucasian, 15% were Asian and the African-American, Hispanic and Native American participants were nearly equally distributed. Approximately half of the participants' annual income was less than $50,000 and the rest were between $50,000 and $150,000. Our participants are typical of Facebook users in terms of age, gender, race and income [3, 38].

Data Analysis

To organize and conceptualize the main themes discussed by the participants, two researchers used line-by-line open coding to label the pre-assessment, main interview, and post-assessment data under primary categories and subcategories. We used Nvivo [31] to map the interviewees' statements to these categories. Through a collaborative, iterative process, we revised these categories to agreement, then used axial coding to extract the relationships between themes. To further explore our data, we used statistical analysis to support our qualitative findings. For clarity, details of this analysis will be presented later in the paper.

RESULTS

Awareness of the Algorithm (RQ1)

Surprisingly, the majority of the participants (62.5%) were not aware of the algorithm's existence. When asked whether the public story of their "friend," Sarah, would definitely be shown in their News Feed, they answered affirmatively: *"I bet it would be on my News Feed. I probably would catch [it] at some point during the day"* (P30). In their opinion, missing a public story was due to their own actions, rather than to those of Facebook. Importantly, these participants felt that they missed friends' stories because they were scrolling too quickly or visiting Facebook too infrequently. They believed if they *"wanna go back to [a missed story], it's accessible"* (P39) in their News Feed. We refer to this majority as the "Unaware" participants.

The rest of the participants (37.5%) knew that their News Feed was filtered. When answering the question about Sarah's story, they stated that a friend's story might not appear in their News Feed due to a filtering process: *"I don't think everything is supposed to be there. I mean I don't think the News Feed shows everything that everyone puts on Facebook. It's just certain things"* (P22). As a result of their knowledge, these participants stated that they might miss a story because of the Facebook algorithm in addition to their own actions. We refer to them as the "Aware" participants.

Paths to Awareness

We investigated Aware participants' responses further to understand how they became aware when so many others did not. Three learned of the algorithm's existence from external sources such as other people and news articles. However, most Aware participants stated they gained knowledge about the algorithm via one or two of the following common paths: inductively comparing feeds or deductively considering network size.

Inductively Comparing Feeds: Most Aware participants (n=12) compared the quantity of stories from different friends in their News Feed and felt they were seeing some friends' stories much more than others. This observed difference suggested to them the possibility of the existence of a News Feed filtering process: *"I have like 900 and some friends and I feel like I only see 30 of them in my News Feed. So I know that there's something going on, I just don't know what it is exactly"* (P26). Most had observed that interacting with a friend (e.g., visiting their page, liking and commenting on their stories) often resulted in more stories from that friend in their News Feed. A few compared their News Feed to their friends' pages and found that stories were missing.

Deductively Considering Network Size: Seven Aware participants believed a filtering process must logically be part of the News Feed curation, since *"there's too much material in general on Facebook"* (P22). They argued that as the number of friends that people have on Facebook increases, there should be *"some way that filters out those [stories] that you may not be as interested in"* (P31). These participants thought the algorithm was a basic, even obvious, element necessary to curate News Feeds and to avoid overwhelming readers.

Although there were many avenues towards algorithm awareness, more than half of the participants were unaware of the algorithm's existence. This raises questions about their unawareness: While all the participants were exposed to the algorithm outputs, why were the majority not aware of the algorithm's existence? Were there any differences in Facebook usage associated with being aware or unaware of the News Feed manipulation? The following section answers these questions.

Connecting Exposure and Engagement to Awareness

To address the above questions, we investigated the participants' Facebook usage. Some participants engaged with the algorithm outputs *passively* by, for instance, scrolling News Feed and reading the stories as they appeared. Some engaged with the algorithm outputs *actively*, for example, adjusting their News Feed content using the settings Facebook provided. To understand whether this difference in engagement with the algorithm outputs was associated with algorithm awareness and to identify features related to these engagement patterns, we combined our interview material with data we extracted from each participant's Facebook account. We identified three passive and four active engagement features. Each feature was either mentioned by participants or found in their Facebook data.

Passive Engagement: We identified several features that are likely to be related to awareness of the algorithm, but that may not imply any intentional activity by the user or could involve circumstances that are out of their control. These include: *Membership duration*, the number of years a user has been a member of Facebook. *Shown content percentage*, the ratio of the number of stories in a user's News Feed to the number of all the potential stories that could have appeared in an unfiltered News Feed. A smaller shown content percentage means overall the user would expect to read fewer stories from any friend. *Friendship network size*, the number of Facebook friends. Network size can be grown in a relatively passive way — for example, by responding to friend requests initiated by others — and it may reflect social behavior outside of Facebook (such as actual friendships) rather than decisions related to the platform. Network size is related to algorithm awareness because the prioritization in News Feed results in a greater proportion of filtered potential stories by the algorithm when the network is large[1].

Active Engagement: We then identified several features that are related to awareness of the algorithm and are more likely to also indicate platform- or algorithm-related intentional behavior. They are: *Usage frequency*, the number of times per day a participant uses Facebook. Frequent users may be more prone to active engagement with the algorithm outputs. They possibly explore more spaces on Facebook (such as options and settings screens) and may compare different aspects of the site. *Activity level*, a categorization of users as "listeners" (mostly reading the feed without posting a story), "light posters" (posting stories occasionally), or "heavy posters" (posting stories frequently), based on the participants' descriptions of their Facebook usage during the study. A light or heavy poster is more actively engaged with algorithm outcomes than a listener because they receive feedback and attention (likes and comments) to their stories which affect algorithm behavior. This makes a potential filtering process more salient. *News Feed content adjustment*, whether a participant uses settings to control what they see in their News Feed. Sorting stories based on importance, following a friend, hiding a story and making lists are some examples of these settings. Using any of these makes a user more actively engaged with the algorithm outputs because they are intentionally trying to change them. *Facebook page/group management*, whether a user is involved in managing a Facebook page or group. This suggests familiarity with Facebook analytics (information that shows a page manager how many people see a page's story, revealing the possible existence of a filtering process).

We used open coding to find and compare engagement patterns between Aware and Unaware participants using these features, and used statistical methods to support our qualitative analysis. For numerical features, we conducted Welch's test to avoid unequal sample size and variance effects between the Aware and Unaware groups. For categorical features, we used Chi-square tests. We performed Fisher's exact test to confirm Chi-square results due to our small sample size.

We found a significant difference between the Aware and Unaware groups for all of the active engagement features by both

[1]We found friendship network size and shown content percentage have a significant negative correlation; $r = -0.44$, $p = 0.005$

thematic and statistical analysis (Table 1). In terms of usage frequency, we found that all participants who used Facebook more than 20 times per day were aware of the curation algorithm. There was a significant difference in usage frequency between the Aware (M=27.18, SD=33.8) and Unaware participants (M=6.92, SD=5.79). Frequent users were on Facebook *"all day"* (P21), they were *"constantly logged in"* (P33) and looked at Facebook *"too many [times] to count"* (P22). We hypothesize that spending more time on Facebook allowed these participants to explore more stories, features and views (such as others' profile pages) than infrequent users. This exploration led to inductive feed comparisons and consequently new knowledge about News Feed and the algorithm.

Table 1. ***Active Engagement Features***

Active Engagement	t-value§ Chi-square†	p-value	Effect size
Usage Frequency	-2.2§	0.03	0.83
Activity Level	8.57†	0.03	0.46
News Feed Content Adjustment	14.14†	0.00	0.59
Facebook Page/Group Management	4.23†	0.04	0.32

Participants unaware of the algorithm's existence included both posters and non-posters ("listeners"), but in contrast all 15 Aware participants were light or heavy posters. In Aware participants' discussions of their Facebook usage, we found the number of likes and comments on their own stories suggested the possibility of the existence of a filtering process. They found that their popular stories were shown in their friends' News Feeds more often: *"I feel some of the stuff got to reach to [a] certain threshold of comments or number of likes before Facebook thinks that I might be interested in [it] enough; and I experienced in my own post[s] [....] I think it probably has to do with the way Facebook presents [stories]"* (P23).

All six participants who did not apply any settings to adjust their News Feed content were unaware of the algorithmic curation of their News Feed. Conversely, all the Aware participants tried to adjust their News Feed content by using at least one of the options provided by Facebook. Among the participants who did not apply any changes to their News Feed, some believed they *"cannot control the News Feed [since] it's kind of receiving what Facebook gives [us], it's kind of limited"* (P1). The rest believed they could apply settings to adjust their News Feed if they were *"willing to invest the kind of time to find out how"* (P3), but did not invest this time.

There were seven participants involved in Facebook page/group management and all were aware of News Feed curation. These participants mentioned that Facebook provided some analytics for page/group managers such as 'post reach' (the number of people in whose News Feed a page/group story appeared) and 'people engaged' (the number of people who have clicked, liked, commented on or shared a story). They stated that observing this analytic information suggested a filtering process that causes some of their page/group stories to reach more people than the others: *"[My friends] all don't get to see everything, and I've always been suspicious of [Facebook], on how they choose who gets to see it, who doesn't"* (P28). Consistent with theories about the construction of mental models [7, 21], we believe these participants extended their knowledge from a known domain (Facebook page/group) into an unknown domain (personal profile) and used the analogy between these two domains to infer the algorithm's existence in their personal profiles.

In contrast to the active engagement features, we did not find any noticeable difference between the Aware and Unaware groups in terms of the passive engagement features. This suggests that being a periodic Facebook user over many years, having a larger friendship network, or having a smaller fraction of stories from your friends actually shown in your News Feed is not associated with an awareness of the algorithm. These results suggest that simple exposure to the algorithm output is not enough to gain information about the algorithm's existence. To learn about an algorithm without any outside information, active engagement is required.

Reactions to & Expectations of Algorithm Outputs (RQ2)

Once we knew participants' prior awareness of the algorithm's existence, we walked them through the FeedVis tool. We started with the Content and Friend Views, to discover their reactions to an unfiltered alternative. Then we directed them to the Friend and Content Rearrangement Views, allowing them to create their desired Friend and Content Views.

Initial Reactions

Many of the Unaware participants (n=15) were initially very surprised by how long the "All Stories" column was in comparison to the "Shown Stories" column in the Content View (Figure 1): *"So do they actually hide these things from me? Heeeeeeey! I never knew that Facebook really hid something!"* (P1). One participant described it as a completely new idea that she had never considered before, despite using Facebook daily: *"It's kind of intense, it's kind of waking up in 'the Matrix' in a way. I mean you have what you think as your reality of like what they choose to show you. [...] So you think about how much, kind of, control they have..."* (P19).

Observing the algorithm outputs in FeedVis surprised some Unaware participants (n=11) by revealing misperceptions about their friends whose stories were not shown in the participants' News Feed at all. For example, seven of them assumed that those friends simply did not post on Facebook. It was through FeedVis that they discovered these friends did indeed post. A few participants falsely believed that those friends had left Facebook: *"I know she had some family issues so I just thought she deactivated her account"* (P35). Importantly, some participants disclosed that they had previously made inferences about their personal relationships based on the algorithm output in Facebook's default News Feed view. For instance, participants mistakenly believed that their friends intentionally chose not to show them stories because they were not interpersonally close enough. They were surprised to learn via FeedVis that that those hidden stories were likely removed by Facebook: *"I have never seen her post anything! And I always assumed that I wasn't really that close to that person, so that's fine. What the hell?!"* (P3).

A few participants (n=5) were curious and began asking questions about the algorithm. For example, P37 asked: *"Do they choose what they think is the best for me to see? Based on what?"* This curiosity led them to wonder whether *"there is some algorithm or something or some rules to choose these [hidden] things that would not appear [in News Feed]"* (P1). In contrast to Unaware participants, most of the Aware participants did not express surprise or curiosity, because of their previous awareness of the algorithm's existence. They did, however, express dissatisfaction, as we describe below.

Expectations

Along with surprise and curiosity, many participants, Aware or Unaware, (n=19) expressed dissatisfaction and even anger when missing stories were revealed to them on FeedVis because Facebook violated their expectations: *"Well, I'm super frustrated [pointing to a friend's story], because I would actually like to see their posts"* (P3). Participants explained that seeing an otherwise hidden story would affect their behavior toward the friend who posted it: *"I think she needs support for that; if I saw it, then I would say something [to support her]"* (P8). In the Friend View, as with the Content View, many participants (n=19) expected their network to be categorized differently than was reflected on Facebook. This expectation was particularly likely for posts by family members; many participants stated that family members should appear in the "mostly shown" category in the Friend View: *"I cannot really understand how they categorize these people. Actually this is my brother [in 'sometimes shown'] and actually, he needs to be here [in 'mostly shown']"* (P1).

Some participants (n=9) believed it was not Facebook's place to decide what to show in their News Feed: *"It was sort of like someone was deciding what I wanted to see and it kind of made me mad"* (P32). These participants preferred to see every story and use *"manual filtering"* (P23) themselves. However, a few argued that Facebook, as a free service, had the authority to manipulate the feed without concern for the users' desires: *"I feel like I'm a mouse, a little experiment on us. To me, that's the price I pay to be part of this free thing. It's like we're a part of their experiment and I'm okay with it"* (P21).

To better understand how participants' expected outputs compared to the actual algorithm outputs, we asked participants to move friends to their desired categories via the Friend Rearrangement View (Figure 3). On average, participants moved 43% of their friends to another category. This high rate of change demonstrates that the algorithm is not effectively capturing the strong feelings participants had about which friends should appear in their News Feed. In the Content Rearrangement View (Figure 4), participants moved on average 17% of their News Feed content between the "shown" and "hidden" categories (SD = 9%), a noticeably lower percentage.

Despite the frustration in some initial reactions, more than half of the participants (n=21) came to appreciate the algorithm over the course of the study. Even as they first scrolled down the Content View, many mentioned that they began to understand why Facebook hid some stories[2]. For example, many hidden stories were about friends' interactions with each other (e.g., likes, comments, happy birthday messages) that were not relevant to them: *"A lot of what is filtered out are things that don't really pertain to me. I'm so grateful because, otherwise, it would just clutter up what I really want to see"* (P13). Although many participants were initially shocked, concerned or dissatisfied with the existence of a filtering algorithm, they concluded there were few stories they actually wanted to move: *"Honestly I have nothing to change which I'm surprised! Because I came in like 'Ah, they're screwing it all!'"* (P23). This suggests that while filtering is both needed and appreciated, a lack of awareness of the existence of the process leads to dissatisfaction.

[2]As participants explored the algorithm outputs via the Content and Friend Views, we asked them to speak aloud, describing any patterns that might emerge. They described and revised fascinating folk theories explaining the algorithm. These theories are out of the scope of this paper and will be discussed in later work.

From Algorithm Awareness to Future Behavior (RQ3)

During our initial discussions with Aware participants, we found their perceptions of the algorithm already affected their Facebook usage. They stated that awareness of the algorithm led them to actively manipulate their News Feed, using theories they developed about how the algorithm might work. For example, those who believed interacting with their friends would affect the number of stories seen from those friends adjusted their interactions: *"I know that if you don't interact with people you won't see their posts; sometimes I purposely don't interact with people just so that hahaha, [I'm] manipulating the system"* (P20). Others thought the number of stories displayed was limited by the algorithm. They believed if they unfollowed someone, *"there's always a new person that [would] start showing up more"* (P26). In addition to manipulating their own, a few Aware participants (n=4) tried to manipulate News Feeds of others. Participants who believed that stories with more comments and likes would reach more people might comment on their own stories to get into more people's News Feeds. For example, one participant suggested *"if you post a picture, without a comment, it's less likely to show up on your friends' News Feed"* (P21).

Following Up with Participants

To understand whether exposure to the algorithm outputs during the study would prompt similar behaviors in the previously Unaware participants (or reinforce these behaviors among the Aware participants), we contacted our participants two to six months after the study. We asked them whether their Facebook usage or satisfaction with the News Feed had changed as a result of participating in our study. Of the 40 original participants, 30 responded[3].

Usage

Most of the follow-up participants (83%) reported changes in their behavior due to participation in our study. We noted that despite coming into the study with varying levels of awareness, Aware and Unaware participants reported similar changes. The Aware participants specifically noted that FeedVis provided new information to them not available in the existing Facebook interface.

Manipulating the Manipulation: 21 of the 30 who completed the follow-up (both Unaware and Aware) asserted that they started to manipulate what they saw on Facebook, mainly by using News Feed settings or changing their interaction with

[3]We attribute this attrition rate in part to the different incentives for participation in each part of the study. Initial lab visits were paid by the hour, while completing the e-mail follow-up entered participants into a lottery.

friends. Of those who started to use News Feed settings for the first time after the study (n=13), most began using "Most Recent" and "Top Stories" options provided by Facebook to sort stories. Most said that they *"make more of an effort to make sure [their] viewing of posts is more on the 'Most Recent', as opposed to the 'Top Stories' option"* (P35) because they preferred a time-sorted, unfiltered feed to Facebook's "Top Stories." A few stated that they *"tend to switch up between the 'Most Recent' setting and the 'Top Stories' setting"* (P14) to see both the trending and the chronological feed.

Ten participants changed their interaction with their friends in order to affect the stories appearing from those friends in their own News Feed. Some started to be *"more selective about clicking 'like' because it will have consequences on what [they] see/don't see in the future"* (P4). On the other hand, a few participants "liked" more stories than they used to. This was particularly true if they *"may not want to comment on their status but want to make sure that their posts continue to show up in News Feed"* (P31). A few participants changed their interaction with some friends by visiting their personal pages *"so they pop up on News Feed again"* (P11). In addition, a few who realized that they might not see some stories due to the filtering process, said they were *"more likely to visit home pages for certain friends to see if they've posted anything"* (P38). Finally, unfriending people in order to receive updates only from those they were most interested in was a more drastic change some mentioned.

A few participants tried to make their own stories appear on more of their friends' News Feeds. For example, starting to like their own posts *"to give them more visibility"* (P28). Others modified their settings to limit who saw their stories.

Exploration: Four participants began to *"play around with Facebook a little more"* (P25). They stated that after the study, they *"went back and started experimenting a little with the News Feed and discussing with some friends on ways to streamline"* (P10) what they were receiving in News Feed. Some also shared *"what [was] learned from the study with others"* (P18) as they felt more knowledgeable about how Facebook worked. One participant even made their friends aware that the algorithm hid their stories from her News Feed: *"I told some friends that I was not seeing their posts"* (P36).

Decreasing Usage Frequency: Three participants used Facebook less than they had in the past. One reason was the frequent changes to the News Feed settings, including the location of the "Most Recent" story sorting setting, leaving them frustrated with the need to search for and understand settings. In an extreme case, one participant stopped using Facebook as she believed it was not straightforward with its users about News Feed curation: *"After the study, I stopped using Facebook because I felt the way the Feed items were curated had, in some ways, broken the expectations between myself and Facebook [...] By neither showing me everything nor making their actions explicit, I felt like I was being lied to"* (P3).

Overall, participation led to more informed Facebook use, even for those who were previously aware of the algorithm's existence: *"It definitely made me more aware of how I was using it"* (P20). Even from the nine participants who reported no change in their usage, six noted they *"do feel more knowledgeable of the way [Facebook] 'studies' viewing preferences and accordingly adapts News Feed"* (P22) after the study.

Satisfaction

In the follow up, we also asked the participants whether participation in our study affected their satisfaction with News Feed. The majority of the participants (n=24) who answered reported the same or higher satisfaction level with News Feed after the study. However, a few participants (n=6) declared that their satisfaction decreased when they understood that *"some updates were deliberately not shown"* (P9). They explained that worrying they might miss stories they wanted to see made them trust News Feed less: *"I'm disappointed because I keep thinking that I might be missing some of the updates from my friends. [..] I don't really trust the News Feed about giving me updates on everything I want to know"* (P17). They also felt *"less empowered to have an optimal experience [since] the rules can change at any time [...] which makes no promises in terms of permanence"* (P21).

Participants who had the same or higher satisfaction level with News Feed generally discussed how they felt more knowledgeable about the algorithm as a result of participating. For instance, one Unaware participant stated that becoming aware of the algorithm's existence resulted in less dissatisfaction when stories did not receive enough attention from others: *"Because I know now that not everything I post everyone else will see, I feel less snubbed when I make posts that get minimal or no response. It feels less personal"* (P38). Another noted how understanding that Facebook hid some stories they might not be interested in made them *"more interested in checking Facebook because it does not seem as cluttered with random information"* (P10). Overall, gaining insight into the algorithm via FeedVis resulted in people feeling more knowledgeable about Facebook's algorithm and their satisfaction level with Facebook generally remained high.

LIMITATIONS

While our results are suggestive, we hope future research will employ a quantitative experimental design featuring a control group to better establish causal relationships between algorithmic awareness, its antecedents and consequences. Our study employed a non-probability sample and did not vary geographic diversity to match the US population, a dimension that may be important. And although the study was longitudinal, all behavioral assessment was based on self-reports.

As this study focused only on one instance of a curation algorithm, we do not know how far to generalize our conclusions. We suspect different dynamics exist in other contexts and even for other curation algorithms within Facebook (such as the algorithm that selects advertising).

Some FeedVis design decisions were influenced by the query limits in the Facebook API. At the time of our study, the Facebook API permitted 600 queries per minute. Therefore, it took longer to collect data for participants with larger friend networks. The size of a participant's network determined the time duration of the presented data for their FeedVis views.

While validating "Shown Stories" and "All Stories" feeds, we noticed that in a few cases, an expected story was not returned by the Facebook API. This finding has been reported by various developers and Facebook [11]. So this would not affect user perceptions, we used post_ids to ensure that "Shown Stories" were a subset of "All Stories" in the FeedVis views.

DISCUSSION

Users clearly benefit from awareness of an algorithmic curation process and likely from knowledge about how it works. Although algorithm awareness on Facebook was prompted by what we termed "active engagement," most users were not so engaged, and thus were not aware. We suspect that users are not aware of most curation, even when the presence of a filter appears obvious to those with a background in computing.

On Facebook, ignorance of the algorithm had serious consequences. Our participants used News Feed to make inferences about their relationships, wrongly attributing the composition of their feeds to the habits or intent of their friends and family. Users incorrectly concluded that friends had dropped them due to political disagreements or their unappealing behavior. In the extreme case, it may be that whenever a software developer in Menlo Park adjusts a parameter, someone somewhere wrongly starts to believe themselves to be unloved.

This conclusion draws our attention to more than just the danger of misunderstanding a filter. Users felt betrayed when discovering an algorithm that they were unaware of. Yet over time, knowledge about the algorithm increased satisfaction with the product. What are the best ways of alerting users to the presence of these processes? How much information about them is adequate to satisfy both the needs of effective interaction design and of principled, ethical use?

On the first question, as our study suggests that prolonged or passive use of Facebook did not correlate to knowledge of the algorithm at work, some form of direct intervention is required. An alert to the presence of an algorithmic process could take place external to the platform, as did ours, providing a sort of temporary x-ray or ombudsman's perspective into the composition of a normally seamless experience. This approach is consistent with that of interaction designers looking to create trust in critical systems such as voting machines; there, initial training and later auditing ensures trustworthy use [34]. Such an approach would also lend itself to continued "seamless" interaction with algorithmic media, avoiding the regular introductions of "seams" through explanations of algorithms that make interactions less fluid. However, while reverse engineering and explaining algorithms is promising, algorithms often use so many features that educating users about them is unlikely to be meaningful. And training through system help pages or blogs often falls short, both because users are unaware those resources exist and the resources provide too little information to be truly educational.

A different approach to alerting users to the presence and function of these algorithms could be integrated into routine use. Persistent, predictable feedback that enables users to understand a process has long been a staple of interaction design, and perhaps the introduction of new, more predictable capabilities for "tweaking" one's feed, or one's appearance in other feeds, achieves awareness of algorithms without sacrificing fluidity and dependability. Providing a visual narrative for algorithmic processes has the potential to educate users without revealing technical specifications or intellectual property. We argue that providing this kind of feedback requires trusting the user, but we believe all are capable of better understanding how their digital environments work.

In either case, work remains to be done on just how much information is enough to satisfy the needs of trustworthy interaction, civic good, and, pragmatically, the protection of proprietary interest. Our study provides some starting points for this work. It shows that users respond differently to revelations about different features of the algorithm (e.g., friend-based vs. story-based filtering). Tools like *FeedVis* could be extended to other domains or to demonstrate the performance of more than two algorithms. They could also be extended to allow users to create their own curation; related "personally developed" algorithms have been explored in the past [15], and we argue that they will play an increasingly important role in the increasingly personalized online world.

What other insights might we draw from our findings to inform the design of technology? Designers often struggle to determine what parts of a system's operation should be made visible to users. This study shows that the decision to promote a "secret sauce" or to highlight an otherwise hidden process is far more than marketing. Some designers prefer systems that operate as if by magic, delivering results without muddying the user experience with details of a complicated process. In contrast, we suggest that enabling active engagement with the process shows users that an algorithm exists and gives them an important sense that they are not controlled by an algorithm but are a part of one, and can have some influence on its results. Indeed, the algorithm can offer users agency, control, and a deeper relationship with the platform itself.

In conclusion, given the recent rise of concerns over the ethical and social consequences of opaque algorithms in search, news and other applications, it is high time for interaction designers to bring their own approaches to the conversation. Arguments for algorithm transparency by ethicists or journalists may strike more pragmatic developers as unrealistic, and product satisfaction or popularity as a primary standard for evaluating success will strike others as inadequate for ensuring sound civic roles for these powerful platforms. Future work in this area will require contributions from many angles.

Like many complex infrastructures, our algorithmic platforms reflect the influence of economic interests, empirical and design research, and competing foundational assumptions about collective living. If the best systems have achieved success through careful integration of such disparate approaches into the design process, certainly our algorithms deserve the same.

ACKNOWLEDGMENTS

This work was funded in part by the Office for the Vice Chancellor of Research Interdisciplinary Innovation Initiative at the University of Illinois. We would like to thank Roshanak Zilouchian Moghaddam, John Lee, Mary Pietrowicz and Amin Sadeghi for their feedback on this work.

REFERENCES

1. Backstrom, L. News Feed FYI: A Window Into News Feed. `http://on.fb.me/1kz3Yak`.
2. Barocas, S., Hood, S., and Ziewitz, M. Governing algorithms: A provocation piece. In *Governing Algorithms: A Conference on Computation, Automation, and Control.* (2013).
3. Bennett, S. Social Media 2013: User Demographics For Facebook, Twitter, Pinterest And Instagram . `http://bit.ly/1j6g12u`.
4. Bernstein, M. S., Bakshy, E., Burke, M., and Karrer, B. Quantifying the invisible audience in social networks. In *Proc. CHI 2013*, ACM Press (2013), 21–30.
5. Bilton, N. Facebook News Feed Draws More Criticism. *The New York Times*.
6. Brembs, B., Button, K., and Munaf, M. Deep impact: Unintended consequences of journal rank. *Frontiers in Human Neuroscience 7*, 291 (2013).
7. Collins, A., and Centner, D. How people construct mental models1. *Cultural models in language and thought* (1987), 243.
8. Diakopoulos, N. Sex, violence, and autocomplete algorithms, August 2013. `http://slate.me/1hMomGN`.
9. Diakopoulos, N. Algorithmic Accountability Reporting: On the Investigation of Black Boxes. *Tow Center for Digital Journalism* (2014).
10. DigitalShadow. `http://digitalshadow.com/`.
11. Facebook Developers. `https://developers.facebook.com/bugs/576745515760299/`.
12. Facebook newsroom, Company Info. `http://newsroom.fb.com/company-info/`.
13. Floodwatch. `https://floodwatch.o-c-r.org/`.
14. Gaver, W. W., Boucher, A., Pennington, S., and Walker, B. Cultural probes and the value of uncertainty. *Interactions 11*, 5 (2004), 53–56.
15. Gilbert, E. Computing Tie Strength. *UIUC PhD dissertation* (2010).
16. Gilbreth, F. B., and Kent, R. T. *Motion study, a method for increasing the efficiency of the workman.* New York, D. Van Nostrand Company, 1911.
17. Gillespie, T. Can an Algorithm Be Wrong? `http://limn.it/can-an-algorithm-be-wrong/`.
18. Granka, L. A. The Politics of Search: A Decade Retrospective. *The Information Society 26*, 5 (2010), 364–374.
19. Hamilton, K., Karahalios, K., Sandvig, C., and Eslami, M. A path to understanding the effects of algorithm awareness. In *Proc. CHI EA 2014*, ACM Press (2014), 631–642.
20. Introna, L., and Nissenbaum, H. Shaping the Web: Why the Politics of Search Engines Matters. *The Information Society 16*, 3 (2000), 1–17.
21. Kempton, W. Two Theories of Home Heat Control. *Cognitive Science 10*, 1 (1986), 75–90.
22. Kramer, A., Guillory, J. E., and Hancock, J. T. Experimental evidence of massive-scale emotional contagion through social networks. *Proceedings of the National Academy of Sciences 111*, 24 (2013).
23. Litt, E. Knock, knock. Who's there? The imagined audience. *Journal of Broadcasting and Electronic Media 56*, 3 (2012), 330–345.
24. Lynch, K. *The Image of the City*. MIT Press: Cambridge, 1960.
25. McGee, M. EdgeRank Is Dead: Facebook's News Feed Algorithm Now Has Close To 100K Weight Factors. `http://goo.gl/X4yOja`.
26. ProPublica Message Machine. `http://projects.propublica.org/emails/`.
27. Morris, M. R. Social networking site use by mothers of young children. In *Proc. CSCW 2014*, ACM Press (2014), 1272–1282.
28. Facebook Inc. How does News Feed decide which stories to show? `https://www.facebook.com/help/166738576721085`.
29. Facebook Inc. What is News Feed? `https://www.facebook.com/help/210346402339221`.
30. Norman, D. *The Psychology of Everyday Things*. Basic Books: New York, 1988.
31. Nvivo Tool. `http://www.qsrinternational.com`.
32. Pasquale, F. Restoring Transparency to Automated Authority. *Journal on Telecommunications and High Technology Law 9*, 235 (2011).
33. Pegoraro, R. Facebook News Feed filtering can make friends vanish. *The Washington Post*.
34. Pieters, W. Explanation and trust: what to tell the user in security and ai? *Ethics and information technology 13*, 1 (2011), 53–64.
35. Sandvig, C., Hamilton, K., Karahalios, K., and Langbort, C. Re-centering algorithms. In *Governing Algorithms: A Conference on Computation, Automation, and Control.* (2013).
36. Sandvig, C., Hamilton, K., Karahalios, K., and Langbort, C. Auditing algorithms: Research methods for detecting discrimination on internet platforms. In *Data and Discrimination: Converting Critical Concerns into Productive Inquiry* (2014).
37. Sanghvi, R. Facebook Gets a Facelift. `http://on.fb.me/1gd7z1I`.
38. Smith, C. 7 Statistics About Facebook Users That Reveal Why It's Such A Powerful Marketing Platform. `http://read.bi/194eLre`.
39. Steiner, C. Automate This: How Algorithms Came to Rule Our World. *Portfolio: New York* (2012).
40. Discrimination in online ad delivery. *Communications of the Association of Computing Machinery* (January 2013).
41. danah boyd: The kids are all right. `http://www.pbs.org/wgbh/pages/frontline/media/generation-like/danah-boyd-the-kids-are-all-right/`.
42. Valentino-Devries, J., Singer-Vine, J., and Soltani, A. Websites vary prices, deals based on users' information. *Wall Street Journal* (December 2012).

News Feed: What's in it for Me?

Paul Lapides, Apoorve Chokshi, Sheelagh Carpendale, Saul Greenberg
Department of Computer Science, University of Calgary, Alberta, Canada
{plapides, apoorve.chokshi, sheelagh, saul}@ucalgary.ca

ABSTRACT

Over a billion people use social networking sites like Facebook to maintain awareness of their friends. Facebook's News Feed is the primary mechanism by which people are shown updates about their friends' daily activities on the site in the form of an algorithmically curated list of stories. This paper examines how people browse the News Feed, their perceptions and satisfaction while using it, and the interactions they make with their personal social network. We conducted a qualitative study involving think-aloud semi-structured interviews as the participants casually browsed their own feeds. We observed a wide variation in the use of the News Feed ranging from careful consideration of social conventions, judgment of people, and annoyance and frustration towards certain friends. Our findings suggest that people do not deliberately curate their own News Feed either due to lack of awareness or perceived social repercussions.

Author Keywords

Facebook; social networks; News Feed

ACM Classification Keywords

H.1.2. User-machine systems: Software psychology

INTRODUCTION

Today, over a billion people use social networking sites (SNSs) such as Facebook to upload photos, write personal messages, and share digital content [7]. The prevalence and ubiquity of SNSs has begun to complement established mechanisms of communication (in person conversation, telephone, text message) by providing people with a semi-public profile page to which they can post or re-share content that they find interesting or represents their personality or identity [1, 22] – such as textual status updates, photos, videos, news articles, and links to websites. Facebook's News Feed, first introduced in 2006, quickly became a key mechanism to present the posts and activities of friends, as well as entice people to share content of their own [4]. In this paper we present a qualitative study that investigates how people browse their News Feed and the extent to which they feel they can influence its content.

The News Feed highlights or promotes certain stories that are algorithmically identified to be popular or particularly relevant to the reader. This contrasts with other content stream approaches, as used by Twitter, that list tweets chronologically with minimal filtering. One of the primary reasons that a filtered News Feed exists is to show the reader a manageable volume of their friends' stories and to promote certain posts deemed particularly relevant to the reader. Without any filtering, the reader would be overwhelmed with uninteresting stories and unable to find the stories they truly care about.

It is reasonable to assume that Facebook uses a variety of metrics to determine if a story is important to the reader and makes assumptions about what a given person wants to see, which may not be an accurate reflection of their actual tastes [15]. Facebook has been tweaking the News Feed since its creation and has large volumes of logs and tests to guide their design decisions. However, because this is propriety information, others who wish to develop similar approaches to the News Feed cannot rely on Facebook to disclose their trade secrets.

We conducted semi-structured contextual interviews with eleven people while they browsed their Facebook News Feed to gain an in depth and tacit understanding of this interface. In our study we take a fresh look on people's News Feed activities by exploring the interplay between their interactions with the News Feed and their emotions. Limiting our number of interviews allowed us to explore our questions in depth and detail. It also supported a flexible open ended approach allowing us to learn about new factors as they arose. Our questions focused on people's perceptions and emotional responses to News Feed stories. As with the nature of qualitative studies, we received extensive information about our participant's practices with the News Feed and discovered that participants lacked awareness of their own potential to influence the content of their News Feed and that social factors such as judgment stood in the way of this curation possibility.

UNDERLYING SOCIOLOGICAL FRAMEWORKS

The following conceptualizations of social behavior are relevant to our exploration of Facebook's News Feed: Goffman's work that theorizes how people present themselves to each other [12], Coleman's explanations of

CHI 2015, April 18 - 23, 2015, Seoul, Republic of Korea

ACM 978-1-4503-3145-6/15/04 $15.00
http://dx.doi.org/10.1145/2702123.2702554

the workings of social capital [6], and Granovetter's work on social weak ties [13].

Goffman uses a theatre metaphor to explain social interactions: individuals make a *performance* to the *audience* and it is expected that these performances match the individual's *role*. A person may play different performances for different audiences based on their changing role. For example, a person's role with their relatives is different from their role at work, and so their performances are also different. Usually, individuals make performances effortlessly and without any awareness that they are performing; however, in some cases the performance is carefully calculated to give the audience a specific impression of the individual. In addition to performances, an individual's *personal front* – clothing, age, gender, body, posture, speech – are used to establish and communicate their role to the audience. For example, a surgeon's clothing communicates their role to the audience. The audience expects that an individual's performance and personal front be congruent with each other and their role.

Coleman extends the notion of *social capital* from the economic concepts of physical capital (materials and tools) and human capital (skills and knowledge). Social capital is then the relations between people that can be called upon to accomplish tasks, to upkeep societal norms, and to enable information flow throughout the social network. For instance, trustworthiness inside of a social group allows individuals to expect the return of favors they have done for their friends and creates reciprocity obligations for those that receive favors.

Finally, Granovetter explains that a social network broadly consists of closely-knit groups (locally dense) connected together with weak ties (globally sparse). It is through weak ties that new information is shared between closely-knit groups [2] and allows individuals to grow their social capital by creating connections to groups of people they would not normally know.

RELATED WORK

The primary uses of Facebook since its launch in 2004 have been to maintain pre-existing social connections and to learn more about new acquaintances [8, 17, 19, 20, 31]. Many people use Facebook to "lurk" – to read content without liking, commenting, or sharing – as a way to keep up with their friends' activities as well to organize offline activities such as parties, dates, and other spontaneous meetings [3, 25]. In particular, Facebook allows people to communicate more easily with acquaintances and weak or new friends [3]. While these studies primarily target university students, Facebook has also been studied in the workplace setting. A new set of complex social rules emerged when people began to mix personal and professional networks such as: sharing content more carefully; concealing parts of their profile after realizing that senior co-workers could see them; and feeling pressure to accept friend requests from clients [27]. With nearly half of Facebook friends being strangers or acquaintances, people expressed concern about their content being seen by these specific "social insiders" on their friend list rather than "outsiders" or people who they are not friends with on Facebook [10, 16]. Sharing content with selective groups may be a possibility to mitigate this concern [18].

After a period of initial opposition, the News Feed was quickly adopted because it made it easier have "ambient awareness" of social groups and their daily occurrences [30]. Visiting a friend's profile directly was the only way of reading their posts prior to News Feed. Information and ideas are dispersed more widely and more quickly when seen on the News Feed [2, 28]. Facebook users express curiosity when they see their friends' activity on the News Feed and begin to look at their profile to see what they are up to [14]. Seeing friends share content encourages new users to participate by sharing content of their own [4].

The design and consequent social effect of the News Feed has been discussed in the popular media as well. What happens if the News Feed algorithm is given too many signals or purely inauthentic signals – in the form of likes? After two days of liking everything on his News Feed, one author describes his feed being entirely devoid of people – instead a stream of extreme political articles, click-bait [5], and celebrity sensationalism [15]. Others ask if the News Feed shows readers positive "feel-good" content rather than current events or serious topics. In the summer of 2014, two viral trends were circulating in the United States: the first was the "ALS ice bucket challenge", a viral campaign that challenged people to dump water on their heads [29]; the second was the reaction of a fatal police shooting in Ferguson, MI. Many users pointed out that, while their Twitter feeds were primarily filled with tweets about Ferguson, their News Feeds were nearly devoid of this content – favoring the "ice bucket" videos instead [9, 23, 24]. Should SNS designers have a responsibility to show their users a balanced content feed when up to 28% of internet users get their news from SNSs [26]?

STUDYING NEWS FEED ACTIVITIES

Our study goal was to discover people's personal practices and activities when using the News Feed, especially their emotional responses to the stories they are shown. To explore these questions we conducted a qualitative study with semi-structured contextual interviews. We were able to observe Facebook users when interacting with their News Feed and to ask directed questions about their browsing activities as the participants revealed more details. We chose to use a qualitative approach to glean a deeper understanding through gathering a few extensive interviews and conducting in depth analysis. This approach has allowed us to examine complex questions, providing a description that is a rich slice of reality.

Participants and Recruitment

Eleven people from the ages of 19 to 37 (4 male and 7 female) participated in our study. Recruitment was done via notices posted to one researcher's personal Facebook profile, billboard notices posted around the university, and word-of-mouth recruitment. To get a reasonable spread across the ages of the usual Facebook users, we selected approximately two to three participants for each of the following age groups: 18-21, 22-25, 26-29, 30-33, 34+. Our participants came from many disciplines and professional backgrounds: a geologist, programmer, neuroscientist, rock climbing instructor, and undergraduate and graduate students. Participants were remunerated with $20.

Experimental Setup

The study was conducted in a quiet, private room with a chair and a desk and an optional desktop computer. A video camera was placed behind the participant and facing the display of the computer they were using. An audio recorder was placed on the table in front of them to record clear audio of the interview. The researcher sat next to the participant's table. If the participant chose to bring their own device, they placed it on the table in front of them and the video camera was adjusted to bring the device in frame.

Procedure

On confirming the appointment time, participants were asked to refrain from reading their News Feed for four hours prior to the start of the interview so that fresh stories would have time to accumulate. The study had four separate components completed as follows.

Pre-study Questionnaire

Before commencing the News Feed browsing portions of the study, each participant completed a questionnaire that asked personal demographic information and several Facebook-usage questions. Once completed, the rest of the study was explained and any questions were answered. A short demonstration of think-aloud protocol was conducted to familiarize the participant with this technique [21].

Initial News Feed Browsing

The participant was instructed to log into their Facebook account on their chosen computer. They were given several minutes to address any important or routine tasks such as reading notifications or answering private messages and were also instructed to close the chat feature. These steps eliminated any distractions during the browsing sessions.

The participant was then asked to browse their News Feed as they would normally use it on their own, including liking, commenting, and sharing posts, visiting their friends' profiles, looking at photos and videos, and opening links as they wished. Participants were given up to 12 minutes for this portion of the study, or until they began seeing posts that they had already read previously.

This portion of the study was not video or audio recorded, as required by ethics, to address potential privacy and dignity concerns. As the participants were instructed to not read their News Feed for several hours prior to the study, they would not be aware of what posts would appear on feed. Any egregious posts that did appear could be hidden using Facebook's hide feature or the participant could choose to withdraw from the study entirely. Neither of these actions was undertaken by any of the participants.

One researcher was present during this portion and recorded field notes describing any actions the participant made during the initial browsing session to serve as entry points for open ended questions or discussions.

Think-aloud News Feed Browsing

The participant was then instructed to return to the top of their News Feed and to begin browsing while verbalizing what they were doing, thinking, and feeling [21]. This portion and the post-study interview, were video and audio recorded. The researchers prompted the participant with probing questions if they began to quickly skip posts without explanation or if they had non-verbal reactions to a post such as unusual facial expressions, a lengthy contemplative pause, or laughing. Participants were often asked to explain how they knew the friend who was posting, why they were interested or not in the post, and any specific context if the situation called for it.

Post-study Interview

The study concluded with a semi-structured interview intended to further explore any topics that were discovered during the think-aloud portion. The researchers also asked questions that addressed the following topics: perceptions of friends based on their posts; annoyances or negative feelings while browsing; self-censorship; perceived judgments placed on the participant by their friends; emotions regarding unfollowing or unfriending people; perceived online social conventions; and general opinions about Facebook. The participant was encouraged to discuss any additional topics or opinions they held about Facebook, the News Feed, and social networks in general.

Analysis

The think-aloud and interview transcripts were open-coded in two passes as in the constant comparative method [11]. First, three representative transcripts were selected from participants who had explained their emotional decisions, interpersonal relationships, interests, and browsing behavior in great depth. Thus, themes and codes discovered from these interviews would form a good basis for open-coding the other transcripts. One researcher analyzed all three interviews while another researcher analyzed two of the interviews. This independent analysis showed 92% similarity between the two researcher's coding and categorization, demonstrating rigor. Code categories were formulated and the remaining interviews were coded by both researchers independently.

FINDINGS

We have identified six thematic categories that encompass the majority of the browsing actions or emotional affects observed. Loosely summarized, they are: friendship and interest considerations, annoyances and judgment, liking and commenting actions, and News Feed curation.

Friendship Classification

As expected, the type and strength of a friendship makes a large impact in the interest and overall emotional response of the participants. This was mentioned by all the participants when looking at the stories on their News Feed. Participants glanced at the name or profile picture of the story poster to identify who posted it, and used the following sub-categories as metrics to determine if they were interested to read more about the story. *"I always read the names first." (P2)*

Friendship strength and closeness

The type of friendship greatly determined if participants were interested in reading stories from people. Participants classified friendships on a discrete scale typically consisting of three designations: close friend, friend, and acquaintance. Participants referred to people as close friends when they knew them for a considerable period of time, trusted them, socialized frequently, and shared similar values. *"[We were] close friends in high school. We see each other around quite a bit now still." (P7)*

In contrast, "acquaintance" was a loose term and had different meanings between the participants. For instance, one participant described acquaintances as old co-workers or classmates whom they no longer socialize with, another described them as people they simply do not feel a strong personal connection to, and a third explained that an acquaintance could be a complete stranger or someone who they have met face-to-face only once. *"I've had Facebook for 7 years and I have a lot of different ranges of acquaintances. What I mean by this is that I worked with them at a grocery store for a few years when I was in high school. And I have not talked to them since then." (P2)*

The designation, "friend", referred to people who were in neither of the other two groups. These were people such as current co-workers or classmates, people the participant socialized with but did not know well, or even former close friends with whom the participant lost touch. *"I used to go to HS with him and his friends, we lost touch." (P10)*

Frequency of interaction

Participants were more interested in posts from people who they interacted with on a regular basis, either in real life or on Facebook. These "frequent friends" often posted about shared experiences that were relevant to the participant, for example photos of a hiking trip, which invited further socialization either on Facebook or in person. *"...who I'm more apt to spend time looking at or reading posts or commenting on. And I think those are the people who have more regularity in my immediate life right now." (P5)*

Friendship context and history

Participants explained that the context of a friendship was sometimes an important factor when considering posts from friends. This was mostly used to pay attention to former colleagues and classmates, for example, when their friend changed jobs or had career success. *"This person was my ex-colleague but is currently in a position of chief technical officer of a company, so sometimes I read his posts as well." (P3)* Four participants had professional contacts in their friend-list and used Facebook to maintain awareness of the personal lives of their professional network.

Location

Geographic distance between two people played a large role in participants' choice to read stories. As Facebook is used primarily used to keep up with friends' lives, participants were interested in posts from friends living far away. This allowed them to maintain awareness of several people's lives without the need to be in constant contact with them. Participants explained that these stories sometimes spurred them to re-establish contact with friends they haven't talked to in a while. *"He's an Australian friend of mine with a family so I just had a quick look at his kids." (P5)*

Friends' reputations

Many participants had intricate knowledge of the typical stories certain friends shared. Participants explained that they knew that specific friends shared funny or interesting stories most of the time and were eager to pause to read these posts. *"He posts good stuff that I'm interested in." (P5)* Participants readily forgave the situations when reputable friends made posts that were out of character for that particular individual. *"She often posts things that are usually pretty funny, clever, but not this time." (P8)*

Conversely, participants quickly identified people who posted stories that they found boring, did not like, or even were annoyed with. In these cases, participants usually had to be asked specifically about these posts as they often scrolled passed them quickly without explanation. One instance of a negative reputation is when participants were aware what the subject matter of their friends' posts was, and usually it was something of little interest to them. *"I know she posts what she normally posts. I'm just familiar with her posts and a lot about fashion that I'm not interested in." (P5)* Other times, participants expressed that a particular friend simply posted too often, usually with short status updates about their day to day activities such as getting coffee, waiting in lines, or sitting in traffic. *"I think he posts a lot of stuff, so you kind of become numb to it after a while. Maybe if he posted a Facebook status update once a week even, I'd be more interested in reading it but he's posts stuff all the time and I've read enough of them to know I'm not interested." (P2)*

Story Affinity

Personal interest plays a major role for participants. This category encompasses several motivations ranging from curiosity about a friend they want to learn more about, whether the story is written well or has professional photos, or if the story relates to the reader in some way.

Curiosity about friends

Participants want to see stories about the people they care deeply about. Participants were curious to read stories made by their close friends or people who they frequently interacted with and cared less about posts from acquaintances. *"I might have paused to look at this for a sec. It's my uncle and cousins." (P10)* In some cases however, stories from acquaintances were found to be interesting as the participant explained that they had lost touch with that person and were interested to see what they were up to. *"It is our undergrad institutions alumni, they got together recently three or four days ago, I saw many pictures and I like all of them." (P6)* Status updates and photos allowed participants to see what their friends were doing, where they were, who they were with, how they were feeling, and their opinions about topics dear to them.

Personal interest in the content

People are interested to read stories that are about things they are interested in themselves. Participants explained how they scan stories quickly to identify if it relates to them in any way. By glancing at the preview text or picture, they have a cursory idea if the story is worth further investigation or not. *"That's probably my general mode, I'm scanning for key photos that grab my interest or key content." (P5)* Participants cared very little and skipped past stories if they had no interest in its content or any other reason to read it. *"Immediately within the first few words I know it's not something that really relates to me." (P2)*

Participants usually paused to read a story if they believed they could get something out of it. Personal motivations for reading a post can range from curiosity about an unfamiliar topic; prevalence of the story in current events: *"It's about yesterday's game. The Uruguay and Italy, one player bites another." (P3)*; high familiarity about the subject matter of the story: *"I normally read this because it has to do with philosophy." (P10)*; and perceived entertainment value: *"I like animals. The video had a cat and a horse." (P9)*

Personal interest in the stories is also heavily linked to the friendship type and strength. The close friends of the participants – with shared interests and values – posted content that was eagerly read for its subject matter rather than to get an update about that person. Essentially, the participant was interested in similar things that their close friends were interested in. *"I'm friends with them because I have something in common with them. And usually the stuff that they post I would like and be interested in." (P2)*

Stories related to the participant

Participants were interested in stories that direct connected to them. The simplest case of this is when the participant appeared in a photo or was tagged in a photo or status update. The participants stopped to read these stories completely, usually clicking on status updates, photo, and albums to see them in more detail. *"I clicked on the first picture because I'm in the first picture. [laughs]" (P2)*

The story could be about something that the participant and friend had previously discussed, either in person or online. For example, a friend posted travel photos depicting places and experiences that had been specifically shared with the participant a few days ago. *"She had talked specifically about certain experiences that she had in India so I might spend more time on this album looking for the photos that she had talked about." (P2)* Prior to the study, one participant's friend had reached out to her social circle – via Facebook – to ask a technical question for a project she was working on. The participant offered his advice to the friend and explained that he was interested in a video that the friend posted showing her working project. *"This is why this one caught my eye, because it triggered that [previous] conversation." (P11)* In another situation a participant began reading posts from a music festival that he had attended in his home town. *"This is a festival in Nova Scotia that I've gone to once or twice." (P10)*

Story aesthetic and perceived quality

Nearly every story on the News Feed has a short description and preview image that sometimes piques readers' interest because of its perceived quality. In the case when a story was not about a friend and did not seem to have personal relevance, several participants were still drawn to the post because of the preview image or text. One participant explained that they clicked on a story because the preview image appeared to be a professional quality photograph of a person (who they did not know). Another participant followed a link because they found a colorful infographic to be particularly aesthetic. *"I opened this one up, that just looks like an attractive picture." (P10)* Finally, a participant paused to read a long a textual post because the first sentence was written with poetic language. *"I would actually probably read through more of this because it's fairly well written." (P2)*

Annoyances

Some stories on the News Feed were met with negative emotions like annoyance, frustration, and exasperation. Though occurring infrequently, all of the participants expressed some degree of negativity towards specific stories they saw. While these feelings were mostly mild annoyances or quips, a handful of situations arose where participants described feeling offended or frustrated.

Feeling overwhelmed

Most participants expressed frustration at the volume of uninteresting stories being posted by specific people. Described earlier in the friendship section, we found that these people had previously established reputations in the minds of the participants. *"They post a lot of things on Instagram and a lot of things on Facebook and it's always status updates about their life and I just don't have the vested interest." (P2)* The participants described the majority of these people as acquaintances or people they do not know well or spend time with. During some interviews, we observed participants scrolling over dozens of posts at a time – often status updates.

It was not only status updates and posts from acquaintances that were found to be overwhelming. Participants sometimes ignored even close friends when they over-shared any type of story, particularly Instagram photos.

"She posts a lot. I just find that it can be pretty aggressive, it always has a lot of hashtags and a lot of stuff from Instagram too." (P11) Another participant explained that her friend is constantly posting updates from her travels and that she doesn't want to see constantly. *"She's always going away on trips. I don't really need to see all the updates." (P8)* Some participants held the opinion that their friends "lived their life on Facebook", explaining that their entire lives seemed to be documented on their profile. *"I know she's is a pretty high user for Facebook, she posts a lot. 'I'm having a coffee today', so I kind of cruise through her stuff, just because it's shit like this. It's just not interesting. I guess when we first became friends I read all of them and got a general gist of 'she's a Facebook liver', her life is on Facebook." (P5)*

Participants expressed similar annoyances towards subscribed pages that posted content often. These pages usually shared links to articles that the participants were interested to read – they had willingly subscribed to the pages, after all. However, participants explained that some pages shared several links and pictures each day and that they felt overwhelmed by the amount of posts coming at them and began to ignore content coming from those pages. *"Sometimes it has something interesting and I'll take a look, but lately I've been ignoring it because I get bombarded with stuff from them." (P8)*

Rude and offensive stories

While we did not observe this situation occurring during our study, participants explained previous events where occasional stories evoked strong negative emotional responses. One participant explained that they found the post offensive and they went as far as to report it to Facebook for removal. *"The post that showed up was offensive and I even reported it as well." (P11)* The post in question was about an animal rights petition that used graphic imagery to incite people to join the petition. Another participant found a particular story rude but would not go into further detail. *"They posted something that said something bad, it wasn't very nice so I just blocked it." (P9)*

Unsolicited invitations

Lastly, all our participants unilaterally ignored Facebook application invitations and ads. Participants explained that most app invites came from friends who were playing games on Facebook who had invited them to join. *"I find updates from people who play games, like Facebook games, I find that really annoying." (P2)* Likely there are many people who play Facebook games and click on these invitations but not so among our participants. Ads were also ignored, though were less berated by our participants. One person suggested that targeted ads may be welcome, especially if vouched by their friend who had become a "fan" of a brand. *"Suggested posts, I don't look at because first of all there's no personal connection. For the sponsored posts, maybe if there was a really close friend of mine who had liked something might be more intriguing to me." (P1)*

Liking and Commenting

Liking and commenting are the primary mechanisms for people to communicate with their friends about their posted content. We observed several behaviors regarding these mechanisms that make suggestions about broader social conventions between people on Facebook. It is important to remember that likes are one of the main signals that the News Feed uses when predicting what content to show.

'Like' awareness, reciprocation, and obligation

Similar to being aware of friends' posting habits, nine out of eleven participants were aware of what friends consistently liked or commented on their own posted stories. *"I could probably tell you on a small list of who likes things more often than other people." (P5)* In seven of the participants, this awareness contributed to the social behavior of liking posts made by these friends in return. Participants described feelings of obligation to "return the favor" and like posts that they did not necessarily find interesting. *"Maybe there is a friend who always keeps liking my posts and my pictures and stuff, so when they post a picture or post which is probably not very interesting to me, but out of that obligation that they like my posts, I go ahead and like them."* (P1) Others explained that they would only reciprocate if they felt genuine interest toward their friend's post. *"I liked the picture also she generally likes my stuff too, so I feel in some ways you kind of have to reciprocate. If I have friends that always like my stuff, I commonly will like their stuff too, as long as I'm fairly interested in it." (P2)* Participants describe feeling pressure to like posts when they are tagged in them or when posts are shared directly to their profile. *"When posts are directly on my page then I kind of feel pressure. Maybe posts that I was tagged on, I usually like them." (P4)*

In cases when social pressure was not a factor, participants explained that they wanted to show their support by liking posts of friends who were sharing stories about major life events such as birthdays, marriages, career or life advancement – perhaps as a social lubricant. *"I like it because they are my friend and they are getting married and this is very important to her or him, so I liked it. This is not pressure, someone not blaming me, but maintaining good vibes.[laughs]" (P6)* Other times, participants explained how liking or commenting on stories from new Facebook friends is a way of establishing a new friendship. *"It's like a new car smell in a relationship, you put your best foot forward, so times you do it [reciprocate]. It's not like you're not being true to yourself but you just go out of your way to extend a bit of effort to make a comment [or like] with somebody new." (P5)*

Casual, choosy, and genuine 'likes'

We discovered three patterns among our participants for how they distributed likes to the stories they saw on the News Feed. The first was a casual approach, observed in only one participant who liked up to half of the stories presented to her during the first browsing session. Photos, videos, status updates, and links were all given likes without hesitation. It appeared to the researcher that if the participant paused at all to read a post that she would like it. She explained that seeing these stories made her happy and she wanted to express that by liking them.

Conversely, most participants liked stories sparingly during the study and explained that they prefer to "save" their likes for specific stories or people. *"I try to save them [the likes]." (P8)* Some participants explained that they would only like one or two stories from each friend, specifically the posts that they themselves considered important, and refrain from liking the less meaningful posts. *"They got engaged recently and I did like those photos that came out of that but this I'm not going to like." (P2)* This participant also said that she preferred to like stories that did not have many likes to show her support, avoiding liking the stories that many people had already liked. *"If they already have a lot of likes, I don't as much feel the need to like it." (P2)*

Commenting

Commenting on stories was not observed as frequently as the action of liking. In the cases when participants did write comments, they did so for stories they had some affinity or interest to, either because of who posted it, who or what the post was about, or that it was something that they personally related to. Participants commented on stories centered about their friends without much hesitation, using the comment feature to have in situ conversations in the specific context of the post. *"I felt like I had to comment because it seems like, probably an exaggeration, but a lot of his pictures he has a black eye." (P10)* Commenting was also done to ask specific questions about the post or to provide friends with support. Comments were usually short and something the participants were comfortable sharing in public. Participants used Facebook's private chat feature when they wanted to have more in depth conversations or discuss private matters. *"In this particular case I might not comment [...] I'll go back later tonight, I'm going to write a nice note to her or something like that." (P8)*

The action of writing a comment was seen by some participants as a stronger indicator of interest than the action of liking. Commenting required more investment of time and energy, and so they felt that story should really be worthy of their comment. *"I don't often comment on unless I feel like it's good, well written, impactful, socially responsible, moral, funny." (P5)*

Participants were careful about writing comments about articles that they did not fully understand because they did not want to appear unknowledgeable or to express an opinion they did not fully stand behind. In these cases they deferred to not writing anything. *"I don't want to say something completely foolish that doesn't make sense in terms of the article or whatever." (P9)*

Some participants expressed frustration that their friends only liked posts and wished that more people would engage them with comments. Participants occasionally started commented on stories specifically to start a discussion. *"I find that a lot of times on Facebook, you put something up and someone likes it but then they won't comment on it, they won't say anything and sometimes I want to start a discussion." (P8)*

Reading comment threads

Reading a comment thread was an action taken by all participants. Reading the comments or opinions of their friends increases the reader's social capital. Comments give people insights into their friend's personal relationships or their other activities that they might not make explicit posts about. *"I clicked on the comments because I wanted to see if anybody I knew closely was looking for a job." (P2)* The action of opening a comment thread was done much more often if the participant knew that their close friends had made comments while caring little if they did not know who was commenting. *"I see immediately that they're not anybody that I know so I don't read them in detail." (P2)* Others were more interested in the conversations than who was involved. *"I'm more interested in what people are saying than who's saying it." (P5)* Participants were hesitant to comment because there were many non-friends who had already commented on a story, and they preferred to read anonymously rather than engage with strangers. *"All these people that I don't know are commenting on it. I wouldn't comment." (P2)*

Passing Judgment

Passing discreet judgments about other people is a common activity and occurs on Facebook as well. Participants explained that they judged their friends based on the posts they shared and were aware that they themselves were likely being judged by people on Facebook.

Judgment on friends

When asked, eight of the participants explained that they placed judgments onto their friends, particularly acquaintances who they did not know very well. Participants formed opinions about their friends primarily based on the stories they shared or comments that they wrote on other posts. *"I think it's about the post, what the comment is. It's a reflection of that person. There's one particular person who doesn't really think before they speak, puts a lot of silly things out there." (P5)* The posts also served to reinforce the participant's pre-existing opinions formed from previous social interactions outside of Facebook. *"I had the thoughts about her having that baby prior to her posting pictures of it. So I wouldn't say that the posts are what form a negative opinion. I don't really like her anyway so then I find it annoying but it's kind of adding together." (P11)* The posts made by acquaintances combined with new opinion forming allowed participants to gauge whether they wanted to know more about a particular person. *"I have a lot of acquaintances on Facebook that I don't know at ton about. I will definitely gauge whether that it's somebody that I would want to have more contact with based on what they post." (P2)* Participants judged their friends on the extent of how personal their posts were, explaining that they themselves would not share as much detail as their friends. *"I really don't like Facebook sometimes when people start posting a lot of personal, something that they should keep to themselves rather than letting the entire world know. I myself don't do that." (P1)*

One participant humorously explained that passing judgment on his friends can be an enjoyable activity. *"You know what's fun? Judging people." (P5)*

Awareness of judgment from friends

Participants were aware that their friends likely judge their actions in the same ways that they judge others, and this affected their posting behavior. In most cases, participants expressed their desire to not overwhelm their friends with too many of their own stories, preferring to post infrequently about things that are interesting or especially important to them. *"I don't want to flood their News Feed with stuff, I want it to be interesting." (P2)* When asked if outside judgment has changed his posting behavior, one participant explained that he tried to make his posts clear and engaging. *"Maybe it would manifest in terms of wording, how I would phrase it. I tried to a bit more thoughtful and engaging." (P5)*

Outside judgment also affected the participants' commenting and liking behavior. One participant did not want her comments to be misconstrued and took great care to write clearly and edit her comments before posting. *"I'll want it to be something that I have made very clear. I don't like to be misconstrued so I would probably go over it a couple of times." (P11)* A different participant explained that she never likes negative stories because she knows that this action is sent to her friends' News Feeds and does not want to be associated with negativity. *"I do not post any negative kind of things, never ever. I do not even like these posts, because when I like a post that is also notified to my friends' Facebook feed, and I don't want those people to know those posts." (P3)*

Unfriending, Unfollowing, and Hiding Posts

Most participants explained that they do not take any actions to hide or limit posts from their friends. Only two participants explained that they actively unfriended people, which was motivated by the desire to keep their friend-list small and manageable. Often the unfriend action was trigged by a post from that person. *"I'm triggered by it if I see something in my News Feed, 'Oh that person's still on my Facebook? I should unfriend them.'" (P8)*

Although many participants expressed annoyance or frustration at some of their friends' posts, the action to unfollow or unsubscribe from a friend was rarely taken primarily because it was an all-or-nothing action. Participants did not want to miss out on future posts from their friend that they might find interesting. *"Yeah, but there's sometimes something that comes up that I'm interested in." (P10)*

On occasion, participants were not even aware of the unfollow or hide features of the News Feed. *"I didn't know it was a thing." (P2)* In other situations they incorrectly believed their friend was notified when they hid posts from them, and because of this avoided taking the hide action. *"I'm guessing that once you do that, it will let them know. 'So and so blocked your post'" (P9)*

DISCUSSION

In this paper, we closely examine the News Feed browsing behavior of eleven participants in order to shed light on this important and ubiquitous feature of Facebook. Our study was exploratory in nature, examining people's emotional responses, annoyances, and irritations to their own News Feed. Through this qualitative lens we re-affirmed many findings from other studies [3, 8, 17, 19, 20, 25], noted the complex social interplay between friends, the variety of social conventions, and the feelings of pressure and judgment present on Facebook. These findings point towards the broader topic of personal curation.

Social Browsing

Our participants paid more attention to close friends than to acquaintances and were interested to see activity from friends whom they had frequent interactions with. Most participants had pre-existing knowledge of their friends' posting habits; some friends were known for posting "high quality" content such as interesting articles or funny pictures while others made posts that were considered boring or uninteresting. The participants could quickly determine what stories they were interested to read by scanning the preview text or picture for clues about their personal interests. Posts from people living in different cities were also interesting to the reader, even if they were from acquaintances – but only as long as they had some sort of positive emotion about the individual. It could be that people pay attention to acquaintances on the News Feed as a way of maintaining their social capital and using these weak ties to stay connected to distant groups of people, for instance old high school friends from their hometown.

Social Pressure Surrounding Likes

The action of liking stories presented a range of complex decisions for participants. Some participants liked stories casually while the majority made careful considerations about their likes. We observed several cases of *like reciprocation* – liking the posts of someone who likes your posts – a behavior done to "repay" friends for their likes. Other participants described feeling obligated to like their friends' posts as a way to show their support. This behavior could be a mechanism for people to maintain their social capital, similar to returning favors in day-to-day life. By occasionally liking their friends' posts, people are able to meekly maintain their friendships in the absence of other communication. Some participants abstained from liking certain posts out of fear of judgment from their friends, others did not like any posts whatsoever, and others only liked stories from specific people. None of the participants reported that they understood the action of liking is a method of sending signals to the News Feed.

Prevalence of Judgment

Facebook is a SNS consisting primarily of offline friendships where people are not anonymous. There are often many complex social conventions for people to consider before taking actions that may have repercussions in their offline friendships. We discovered that writing comments or liking stories often came with feelings of hesitation or fears of external judgment. Participants sometimes avoided commenting despite wanting to for fear of starting a confrontation or from having their comment misunderstood.

In almost all of the interviews, the participants expressed a sense of judgment about their friends' or their posts, often manifested when considering people who are acquaintances or strangers. Feelings of judgment ranged from minor annoyances to near disdain. Many participants expressed annoyance at people who posted too frequently or shared predictable or uninteresting status updates. The strength of this emotion was reflected when participants explained that they were careful about what and how often they shared.

Invoking Goffman's conceptualization, we suggest that an individual's actions and profile on Facebook extends their real-life *performances* and *personal front*, respectively. In this light, it is not surprising that our participants are so vigilant about what image they portray to their friends through actions of sharing, liking, and commenting. In essence, the individual is charged with creating a single performance seen by different *audiences,* which must be congruent with multiple *roles*.

The Issue of Curation

We found that participants took almost no steps to deliberately curate their News Feed. Most of our findings play into this factor:

- **Unaware**: Some participants were simply not aware that they could hide specific stories or unfollow people if they were not interested in seeing their posts.
- **Reluctance**: Participants were reluctant to take seemingly drastic measures to alleviate minor annoyance from seeing predictable posts from previous acquaintances.
- **Effort**: It was often considered more effort to take the unfollow action than to scroll past the offending posts.
- **Fear of missing out**: More importantly, even when participants expressed a willingness to unfollow someone, they chose against doing so out of fear of missing out on some future posts that might be interesting to them.
- **Social impact**: The perceived social capital of becoming subscribed to an acquaintance was worth putting up with their uninteresting – and sometimes vexing – posts.

LIMITATIONS AND FUTURE WORK

With qualitative studies there is always the possibility of re-examining people's interactions with the News Feed from a different perspective. For instance, how do our findings compare to adolescents or to people from different socio-economic status? It is also possible to take a quantitative approach and conduct extensive surveys that may lose some richness in details but are more generalizable.

As to future research, our findings suggest an opportunity for more discovery in the area of curation. How could SNS recommendation systems like the News Feed incorporate features that give people greater control over what they are shown? Is there a way to give the system clear signals without the social pressures present today? While we do not expect our work to influence Facebook, these questions are worthy of exploration as personal recommendation systems become more pervasive in our lives.

CONCLUSION

From our study we gained a rich reality-based description of how people experience reading the News Feed. While this description may not be exhaustive in the broader population of Facebook users, there are some insights the HCI community may gain from our study.

If personalized recommendation engines such as Facebook's News Feed make incorrect predictions, the reader may not be relied on to correct these mistakes. This lack of action may stem from social protocols that the reader strongly adheres to or it may stem from laziness or apathy. Alternatively, the reader may simply not be aware of how to send signals to the News Feed to help better curate their content, or may not understand how taking or withholding certain actions – such as liking – affects what they are shown.

Perhaps it may be prudent to diminish the effect that publically visible actions on Facebook have on the News Feed given the apparent social implications of these actions. It is conceivable that Facebook could track what posts a reader scrolls past quickly or pauses to read. Could the "hide story" feature instead be re-appropriated to a more prominent (and likely private) dislike button?

Throughout August and September 2014, Facebook has launched a video advertising campaign on its own Facebook page about the News Feed. The videos present several short vignettes where a variety of users ranging from adolescents to seniors describe how to curate their News Feed. These videos explain how actions such as liking, unfollowing, and list management change the News Feed. The hide feature is not presented in these videos.

Has the optimization of the News Feed reached a limit? Is it is now up to us, the users, to start better curating our own feed, and will we be given functional tools to do so? Perhaps of more interest is the possibility of future News Feed-like interfaces outside of Facebook. Our study indicates that there are rich avenues to explore in the area of personally curated content streams, where it might be possible to support more subtle types of curation.

ACKNOWLEDGEMENTS

This research was supported in part by AITF, NSERC, GRAND, SurfNet, and SMART Technologies.

REFERENCES

1. Back, M. Facebook Profiles Reflect Actual Personality, Not Self-Idealization. In *Psychology Science.* (2010), 372-374
2. Bakshy, E., Rosenn, I., Marlow, C., and Adamic, L. The Role of Social Networks in Information Diffusion. In *Proc. WWW 2012, ACM Press* (2012), 519-528.
3. Barkhuus, L., and Tashiro, J. Student Socialization in the Age of Facebook. In *Proc. CHI2010,* ACM Press (2010), 133-142.
4. Burke, M., Marlow, C., and Lento, T. Feed Me: Motivating Newcomer Contribution in Social Network Sites. In *Proc. CHI2009*, ACM Press (2009), 945-954.
5. Click-baiting http://newsroom.fb.com/news/2014/08/news-feed-fyi-click-baiting/
6. Coleman, J. Social Capital in the Creation of Human Capital. *American Journal of Sociology*, Vol. 94, (1988), S95-S120.
7. Company Info, Facebook Newsroom http://newsroom.fb.com/company-info/
8. Ellison, B., Steinfield, C. and Lampe, C. The Benefits of Facebook "Friends:" Social Capital and College Students' Use of Online Social Network Sites. Journal of Computer-Mediated Communication, 12: 1143–1168.
9. Facebook Wants Your News Feed to Reflect What's Happening Right Nowhttps://time.com/3399167/facebook-news-feed-change/
10. Forest, A. L., & Wood, J. V. (2011a). [Closeness of Facebook friends]. Unpublished raw data.
11. Glaser, B., Strauss, A. *The Discovery of Grounded Theory: Strategies for Qualitative Research.* Aldine De Gruyter, NY, USA, 1967.
12. Goffman, E. *The presentation of self in everyday life.* Doubleday, Garden City, NY, USA, 1959.
13. Granovetter, M. The Strength of Weak Ties: A Network Theory Revisited. *Sociological Theory* (1983), 201-233.
14. Hart, J., Ridley, C., Taher, F., Sas, C., and Dix, A. Exploring the Facebook Experience: A New Approach to Usability. In *Proc. NordiCHI 2008*, ACM Press (2008), 471-474.
15. I Liked Everything I Saw On Facebook http://www.wired.com/2014/08/i-liked-everything-i-saw-on-facebook-for-two-days-heres-what-it-did-to-me/
16. Johnson, M., Egelman, S., and Bellovin, S.M. Facebook and Privacy it's Complicated. In *Proc. SOUPS 2012,* ACM Press (2012).
17. Joinson, A.N. Looking at, Looking up or Keeping up with People?: Motives and Uses of Facebook. In *Proc. CHI 2008*, ACM Press (2008), 1027-1036.
18. Kairam, S., Brzozowski, M., Huffaker, D., and Chi, E. Talking in Circles: Selective Sharing in Google+. In *Proc. CHI2012,* ACM Press (2012), 1065-1074.
19. Lampe, C., Ellison, N. and Steinfield, C. A Face(book) in the Crowd: Social Searching vs. Social Browsing. In *Proc. CSCW2006*, ACM Press (2006), 167 – 170.
20. Lampe, C., Ellison, N. and Steinfield, C. Changes in Use and Perception of Facebook. In *Proc.CSCW2008*, ACM Press (2008), 721-730.
21. Lewis, C. and Rieman, J. Task-Centered User Interface Design. Chapter 5: Testing the Design With Users. http://hcibib.org/tcuid/chap-5.html#5-5.
22. Mehdizadeh, S., Self-presentation 2.0: Narcissism and Self-Esteem on Facebook. In *Cyberpsychology, Behavior, and Social Networking.* (2010), 357-364.
23. Michael Brown's shooting in Ferguson lost on social media http://www.cbc.ca/news/technology/michael-brown-s-shooting-in-ferguson-lost-on-social-media-1.2740014
24. Net Neutrality, Algorithmic Filtering and Fergusonhttps://medium.com/message/ferguson-is-also-a-net-neutrality-issue-6d2f3db51eb0
25. Pempek, T.A., Yermolayeva, Y.A., and Calvert, S.L. College students' social networking experiences on Facebook. *Journal of Applied Developmental Psychology 30,* Elsevier (2009), 227–238.
26. Purcell, K., Rainie, L., Mitchell, A., Rosenstiel, T., and Olmstead, K. Understanding the Participatory News Consumer. *Research for Pew Internet*, (2010)
27. Skeels, M. and Grudin, J. When Social Networks Cross Boundaries: A Case Study of Workplace Use of Facebook and LinkedIn. In *Proc. GROUP2009.* ACM Press (2009), 95-104.
28. Sun, E., Rosenn, I., Marlow, C., and Lento, T. Gesundheit! Modeling Contagion through Facebook News Feed. In *Proc. ICWSM 2009*, AAAI Press (2009), 146-153.
29. The Ice Bucket Challenge on Facebook http://newsroom.fb.com/news/2014/08/the-ice-bucket-challenge-on-facebook/
30. Thompson, C. Brave New World of Digital Intimacy. New York Times Magazine. (September 5, 2008)
31. Vitak, J., Ellison, N.B., Steinfield, C. The Ties That Bond: Re-Examining the Relationship between Facebook Use and Bonding Social Capital. *HICSS* (2011)

Understanding User Beliefs About Algorithmic Curation in the Facebook News Feed

Emilee Rader and Rebecca Gray
Department of Media and Information
Michigan State University
{emilee,grayreb}@msu.edu

ABSTRACT

People are becoming increasingly reliant on online socio-technical systems that employ *algorithmic curation* to organize, select and present information. We wanted to understand how individuals make sense of the influence of algorithms, and how awareness of algorithmic curation may impact their interaction with these systems. We investigated user understanding of algorithmic curation in Facebook's News Feed, by analyzing open-ended responses to a survey question about whether respondents believe their News Feeds show them every post their Facebook Friends create. Responses included a wide range of beliefs and causal inferences, with different potential consequences for user behavior in the system. Because user behavior is both input for algorithms and constrained by them, these patterns of belief may have tangible consequences for the system as a whole.

Author Keywords

algorithms; feedback loop; intuitive theories; Facebook News Feed.

ACM Classification Keywords

H.5.m. Information Interfaces and Presentation (e.g. HCI): Miscellaneous

INTRODUCTION

People are becoming increasingly reliant on online socio-technical systems that employ *algorithmic curation*: organizing, selecting, and presenting subsets of a corpus of information for consumption. An algorithm is "a finite, discrete series of instructions that receives an input and produces an output" [16], and systems like Facebook and Google (and many, many others) use algorithms as information intermediaries that determine what information should be displayed and what should be hidden [5].

Because algorithms are automated and usually poorly understood by end users, people often assume that they are objective or impartial [5]. However, just because a system is automated does not mean it is free from the potential for bias. Researchers are becoming increasingly concerned that algorithms enforce biases that are hard to detect, but have potentially negative outcomes [6, 14].

The Facebook News Feed is a socio-technical system composed of users, algorithms, and content. Users produce content items (posts) that become part of Facebook's corpus, which is continuously changing. At the same time, personalization algorithms select a subset of items from the corpus, rank or organize them according to a proprietary algorithm, and present them to users for consumption in their News Feeds. If a user were to contribute a post that the News Feed algorithm does not display near the top of others' News Feeds, that post becomes effectively invisible to those users. Bucher [6] calls this the "threat of invisibility, " or the potential for one's contributions to go unseen by an unknown number of people. If users become aware of this possibility, avoidance of this "threat" can then guide their behaviors and choices as they engage with others via the system.

The potential for negative consequences like the threat of invisibility are presumably the result of feedback loops: situations where the output of a process becomes an input to that same process. This happens in social media because information consumers are also producers; both explicitly via choices to post, comment or "Like", and also implicitly via their behavioral traces recorded in system logs. What users learn about the system when they act as consumers can affect the choices they make as producers of content. Feedback loops make all users gatekeepers for each other, by using as input to the algorithm evidence collected from other users about the value (comments, Likes, shares) of the particular item in question [30]. It is extremely difficult to understand the complex, nonlinear interactions that take place in socio-technical system like the Facebook News Feed where the algorithm, the users, and the corpus of content itself are constantly interacting and evolving [27].

Because of the feedback loop characteristics of these systems, user beliefs about content filtering algorithms work are an important component of shaping the overall system behavior. To better understand the interdependence between users and algorithms, we conducted a study investigating users' beliefs about what the Facebook News Feed chooses to display, and why. We describe the kinds of evidence of algorithm behavior that users notice and respond to and the beliefs they form about algorithm selection and ranking criteria, and we present

CHI 2015, April 18–23 2015, Seoul, Republic of Korea

ACM 978-1-4503-3145-6/15/04...$15.00
http://dx.doi.org/10.1145/2702123.2702174

implications of these beliefs for their own behavior and for the system overall.

RELATED WORK

Content Streams and Recommendations

Recommender systems researchers have explored ways to use algorithms to help users connect with the content they are most interested in on social media sites. Several research teams have proposed different ways to use information about network ties, topic preferences, and characteristics of posts in the system to make recommendations. For example, Sharma and Cosley [28] proposed using information about content preferences from the Facebook profiles of users and their Facebook Friends to help generate recommendations for movies, television shows, and books. Items recommended by the algorithm variant that used Facebook Friends' profile information received the highest number of views. In a follow-up study [29], they found that such social recommendations were more persuasive when they came from people who were close friends whose interests are known to the user.

Much of this research has taken place using Twitter, which has been a more open platform to use for experimentation and evaluation of systems designed to help users with information overload in their content streams and feeds. Chen et al. [7] created a Twitter app to recommend "conversations" (a chain of @replies, or broadcasted messages directed to others via username) to users, to help them focus on the interactions that would be most interesting to them. The algorithm used conversation dimensions such as thread length, topic relevance, and tie strength to make its selections. The algorithm that performed best was a combination of topic and tie strength.

Bernstein et al. [4] also created a Twitter client to help users focus on information that would be most interesting to them. Their tool clustered tweets within a user's stream by topic, and allowed users to browse those topics. This was essentially a way to sort information in the user's feed into groups of similar items to help them focus on more relevant information. They tested a prototype with users (and users' own Twitter accounts) in the lab. They found that while users liked how it helped them read more relevant tweets when they were grouped by topic, they felt like it was harder to make sure they had seen everything. The typical chronological interface was simply "less enjoyable but more comprehensive." However, this finding may not hold on Facebook where it may be more important for relationship maintenance not to miss posts.

One consideration when designing a filtered feed is how to take relatedness of recommended content items into account. Because information appears in the feed rather than being sought out by the user, it can be jarring to encounter content that seems like it does not belong with the rest. Lv et al. [23] emphasize that relatedness is important for keeping users' attention as they browse from item to item. However, they point out that relatedness as operationalized by an algorithm is not necessarily the same as relatedness perceived by a human being, and that accounting for a user's reading interests when recommending content can be difficult.

In addition to relatedness, it is also important for the system to keep track of the timeliness of the items and not fill the user's content stream with outdated items or the same item over and over again. However, in a system where content items are turning over very quickly like Twitter or Facebook, a greater degree of personalization means the system has fewer items it can possibly recommend to the user. This makes it difficult for the algorithm to select items that are both new to the user and relevant to the user's interests [21].

Finally, several researchers have attempted to evaluate whether filter bubbles (recommendations of decreasing diversity over time) are likely to exist in content recommendation systems. Nguyen et al. [25] analyzed a MovieLens dataset and found that both the diversity of items recommended by the system and items rated by users did indeed become less diverse over time, but only slightly. They concluded that this was weak evidence for a filter-bubble-like effect. In addition, in two separate modeling and simulation studies, independent research teams found that some recommendation algorithms are susceptible to a narrowing effect under particular conditions; however, neither paper presented empirical data to verify the simulation results [11, 17].

Research projects like these use various data about users and content available in social media systems as input to algorithms that are designed to prioritize content for display, and direct user attention to information they want to see. However, few projects have explored interaction with algorithmic curation systems with large numbers of users over long periods of time. It is difficult to evaluate algorithms in isolation from their context of use—without data from real users to act upon, one cannot get an accurate picture of performance [13, 21]. Therefore, bias that might be introduced by interdependence between user and algorithm behavior is largely unknown.

The Facebook News Feed

Facebook is the largest social network site (SNS) in the world with over 1.28 billion monthly active users [9] and over 71% of American adults using the site [1]. The Facebook News Feed is a "constantly updating list of stories from people and Pages that you follow on Facebook" [10]. Maintaining relationships is the main reason most people use Facebook [22], and seeing updates and other shared content from Friends is how users stay informed about what Friends near and far are "up to" and is a source of a perpetual feeling of connection with them [18].

According to a post to the "Facebook Newsroom" on August 6, 2013, any time a user visits his or her News Feed there are on average "1500 potential stories from friends, people they follow and Pages for them to see," and the News Feed algorithm prioritizes "an average of 300 stories out of these 1500 stories to show each day" [2]. Facebook allows users to sort the News Feed in two ways: *Top Stories* or *Most Recent*. The *Top Stories* function displays Friends' posts, ranked by the News Feed algorithm. Factors used to determine the ranking include "the number of comments, who posted the story, and what type of post it is (ex: photo, video, status update)" [10]. Users can exert some control over what appears in the News

Feed if they sort by *Most Recent*, which re-orders posts by reverse chronological order within the News Feed (newest items first). Users can also *hide* people, Pages, or groups, *follow* or *unfollow* Friends, and create *Friend Lists* that when selected only display posts from members of the list.

Feedback Loops in the News Feed

The News Feed algorithm has similar goals to other recommender systems: to connect people with information they are likely to want to consume, by making some items easier to access than other items [26]. However, Facebook's News Feed is different from other recommender systems in one important way. A feedback loop exists in the News Feed that has the potential to affect not only the information used for selection and ranking of items, but characteristics of the corpus of posts as well.

In a typical recommender system, item ratings can be susceptible to popularity bias caused by a feedback loop [31]. Items that are very popular may be recommended more often than unpopular items, which means popular items are viewed more and receive more ratings. In other words, the output of the ranking algorithm (popular items are recommended and therefore viewed more) affects the inputs to that same algorithm (items that are viewed more receive more ratings). But the corpus of movies or products is relatively stable over time, and only changes when the company revises its catalog of offerings. In the News Feed, both the item "ratings"—comments, Shares and Likes—and the posts users create can be affected by a feedback loop. This happens because users are both consumers and producers of content on Facebook, and what users learn about the system when they consume posts affects what they choose to post as producers.

The News Feed algorithm *curates* (selects, organizes and presents) a personalized stream of content, instead of offering users a set of alternatives to choose from. This approach changes the interaction between the user and the system from actively specifying preferences and selecting items, to passive consumption of items the system has chosen. For example, if a post from a user's Friend is not highly ranked by the News Feed algorithm, it may not appear in her News Feed. Or, it may appear so far down in the list that the user is unlikely to scroll far enough to see it. If she does not visit the Friend's Timeline, she may never know the post existed.

The posts that users see at the top of their News Feeds are the ones prioritized by the algorithm. Through repeated exposure, users may notice patterns in the characteristics of the posts and Friends they see, and begin to learn about what kinds of posts tend to receive more attention than other posts. If a user were to notice that Facebook posts that contain the word "congratulations" tend to be highly visible, she might learn that the Facebook News Feed prioritizes major life events over other kinds of posts, and subsequently believe that if she doesn't post about celebratory occasions her posts won't be viewed by others [32]. Even if an algorithm's behavior is an invisible part of the system's infrastructure, users can still form beliefs about how the system works based on their interactions with it, and these beliefs guide their behavior [12].

Research Goals

People are naturally very skilled at attending to evidence in the world and forming intuitive theories for why things happen the way they do. These theories help people structure their interactions with the world around them. However, they often contain incorrect or contradictory information, and are constantly updated as people have new experiences and learn new things [12].

Our goal in this study was to elicit users' intuitive theories about the composition of their Facebook News Feeds, so that we can begin to understand the complex interdependencies between users and algorithms that affect system behavior [27]. Users' beliefs about how the system works are an important component of a feedback loop that can cause systems to behave in unexpected or undesirable ways [8, 24]. The output of the News Feed algorithm (the posts that are displayed to users) affects the inputs to that same algorithm (interactions with those posts, and the characteristics new posts that are subsequently created). Understanding users' beliefs is an important first step towards identifying effects of the feedback loop and potentially designing algorithms that are better at taking these effects into account.

METHOD AND PARTICIPANTS

This paper focuses on two questions from a larger survey that was conducted in April 2014, investigating users' beliefs and experiences related to algorithmic curation in the Facebook News Feed. We asked respondents a closed-ended question, "Do you feel like your Facebook News Feed always shows you every post created by your Facebook friends?" to which the possible responses were Yes, Maybe, or No. We designed the closed-ended question to cause respondents to think and anticipated that it might trigger some to wonder about something they had not thought about before. We therefore included "Maybe" as a closed-ended option (in addition to "Yes" and "No") to provide a way for respondents to express uncertainty.

Immediately following the closed-ended question, we asked an open-ended question intended to collect the reasoning behind the closed-ended responses: "Please explain your answer to the previous question." The response field had a minimum length requirement of 150 characters (about three sentences). The median response length was 50 words (Min=26, Max=174). The survey also included questions about basic demographics, frequency of Facebook activity, and number of Facebook Friends. The questions that are the focus of this paper were asked early in the survey, and respondents had not yet been alerted via the survey to the role of the News Feed algorithm on Facebook.

We recruited respondents using Amazon's Mechanical Turk (MTurk) for a paid incentive of $5 for completing the entire survey. MTurk workers were exclusively from the USA and were required to have a 90% or higher approval rating after completing at least 500 HITs. Eligible respondents were at least 18 years old, had more than 20 friends on Facebook, and reported visiting Facebook at least once per week. We recruited Mechanical Turk workers for this study because we wanted to gather beliefs and opinions from members of a population that is typically comfortable using the web and social media, and thus more likely than the general population to be aware of algorithmic curation. In other words, we were hoping to collect data from respondents who had thought about these issues before. Amazon Mechanical Turk workers may be more more knowledgeable about algorithms and internet technologies in general than other Facebook users, and as such they might attend to and remember different things about their News Feeds than a random sample of Facebook users.

A total of 505 respondents completed the survey. We removed cases from the analysis when a respondent answered any of the three attention check questions incorrectly, and when responses to open-ended questions were indecipherable or virtually identical to other respondents' answers. The final number of cases for this analysis is 464.

The median time to complete all survey questions was 19 minutes, with an average of 29 minutes. The sample was 59% male, with a median age range of 26 to 34. Most respondents were white (372) and reported either attending (170) or having graduated from college (161). A large majority reported visiting Facebook several times per day (361) and posting to Facebook less than once per week (170). One hundred fourteen reported having 21-100 Facebook Friends, 208 reported 101-300 Friends, and 142 reported 301-500 Friends (Median=193, Max=2161).

ANALYSIS

People form "intuitive causal explanatory theories" [12] that help them interact with the world and accomplish their goals. These intuitive theories are generated out of each person's unique experiences, and as such are contextual and usually inaccurate in some way [19]. People are most likely to seek explanations for new evidence they encounter when they are faced with inconsistency or a problem to be solved, and as they encounter more evidence they continuously update their beliefs about what is going on [12].

One of the ways people attempt to form intuitive theories about unfamiliar situations is by making predictions and providing explanations that may or may not match the evidence at hand [12]. Our open-ended survey question asked respondents to speculate about why they believed the News Feed does or does not show every post created by their Facebook Friends. This is a very natural activity for people to engage in, and as users of Facebook they are likely already doing this.

We analyzed the open-ended responses using an iterative, inductive coding approach to identify components of respondents' intuitive theories about why they see the posts that they do in their Facebook News Feeds. In the first pass through the data, we coded for emergent similarities across responses, focusing on respondents' beliefs about who or what is in *control* of which posts appear in their News Feeds, and on the *evidence* they provided to support those beliefs.

In our second coding pass we added, removed and combined codes until we had formed a set of *control* codes and a set of *evidence* codes that represented the breadth of the responses. In a third pass through the data we wrote definitions and summaries for each code, and in the process we found that we needed to break up some codes and combine others. We did this to ensure that our codes had descriptions that were internally consistent, and were different enough to easily distinguish them from the other codes. At this stage we also grouped codes into higher-level themes, keeping the *control* and *evidence* codes separate.

The codes and higher-level themes were *not* mutually exclusive. Most responses ended up falling under one of the higher-level *control* themes, and one or two *evidence* themes. For example, the following answer from respondent R9 was coded as *Control: News Feed*, referring to the statement that the entity the respondent believes is in control of prioritizing posts is "it". (Many responses used a pronoun to refer to the News Feed itself, which was mentioned in the question text.) This response was also coded as *Evidence: People I am Close To*, because the respondent stated that he or she mostly sees posts in the News Feed from close friends:

> I usually see posts by the same people every day. This leads me to believe it might prioritize posts by closer friends. For example, with over 200 friends, I can't remember the last time I saw news updates from more than half of them. (R9)

Finally, in the last stage of the analysis we focused on drawing connections across the *control* and *evidence* themes based on code overlap within each response, to identify six intuitive theories (i.e., patterns of causal beliefs) contained in multiple responses.

Having 464 responses from different people allows us to analyze the relative prevalence of certain patterns of responses within the sampling frame we used for this study. Because of our sampling frame and the fact that our study is not a quantitative content analysis, we cannot compare absolute counts across themes to draw generalizable conclusions. However, the relative proportions can be interpreted as a rough indicator of how common one theme is compared with another.

LIMITATIONS

This study was conducted without the involvement Facebook or any of its employees. Therefore, we have no visibility into the details of the News Feed algorithm in use at the time we collected these data, so we cannot comment on the accuracy of respondents' intuitive theories about how the News Feed algorithm works. We have no way of knowing which posts each respondent's News Feed actually did or did not display, and so we have focused our findings on respondents' beliefs and the potential implications of those beliefs for the behavior of the system as a whole. Variation in respondents' perceptions about what causes their News Feeds to look the way they do may actually stem from different users experiencing different versions of Facebook or the News Feed algorithm. For example, we do not know what other research studies (e.g. [20, 3]) or A/B tests these respondents may have experienced prior to or simultaneously with our study that may have affected the composition of their News Feeds. Finally, our data are written statements from respondents and as such contain respondents' self-reported memories of past behavior and subjective interpretation of their experiences. Certain kinds of experiences might be more memorable than others, which could bias our findings.

FINDINGS

A large majority of the responses to the closed-ended question, "Do you feel like your Facebook News Feed always shows you every post created by your Facebook friends?" indicated that most Facebook users in our sample believed they do not see every post their Friends create. Seventy-three percent (N=341) answered *No*, and only 8% (N=38) answered *Yes*. The remaining respondents answered *Maybe* (18%, N=85). The median number of Friends within each closed ended response group was: No=209 (n=341), Maybe=129 (n=85), Yes=122 (n=38). Pew data show that the US median is 200 (Fall 2013, http://pewrsr.ch/1dm5NmJ). Note that differences in medians across response categories are not necessarily statistically or practically meaningful, due to size differences between the categories.

Our findings below focus on patterns of beliefs—intuitive theories—expressed by respondents. The beliefs we identified are not mutually exclusive, and sometimes respondents made contradictory statements within the same response. This is normal; intuitive theories are often not well-formed or well tested, and constantly evolve as people learn new things. We briefly summarize the findings in Table 1, along with the number of responses that exhibit characteristics of each intuitive theory.

Passive Consumption

One hundred three responses contained statements that described a passive approach to experiencing the News Feed. These statements expressed few strong opinions about whether the News Feed shows every possible post. They did not mention steps respondents may have taken to ensure they are seeing the posts they want to see, nor the belief that the system is in control. It was common for *Passive Consumption* responses to speculate about the kinds of symptoms that might indicate that the user is or is not seeing all the possible posts. For example, this respondent ran through possible clues that he or she might have missed a post before concluding that he or she had not experienced any of them:

> Every post I hear people talk about I have read on my Facebook feed. I have never visited someone's profile and saw a post that was never in my feed. I have never had someone tell me about a post that was not in my feed. (R161)

Another respondent mentioned how the volume of information in the News Feed might signal that posts are missing from it, and then concluded that because there are so many posts he or she must be seeing all of them:

> Even though I have a relatively low amount of Facebook friends compared to most, I still see a lot of new posts to wade through no matter how often I check out the feed, so I don't see why it wouldn't be showing them all. (R317)

Evidence about News Feed volume (or lack of it) was used by other respondents to reach the opposite conclusion. Responses like this one present a belief that the News Feed would feel more full, somehow, if every post were displayed:

> I don't think it shows every post created by my friends. If it did, my whole page would be filled with their posts which isn't possible because I have 80+ friends and that would flood my page making it impossible to read every post in a timely manner. (R232)

Assumptions like the above about what the News Feed would look like if it did or did not show all possible posts appear in many of the patterns of causal beliefs that respondents described. However, the group of *Passive Consumption* responses is unique in that the proportion of respondents who answered No (54%) is almost equal to the proportion that answered Maybe or Yes (46%). This indicates that these respondents may not have thought about this issue before and were drawing on their past experience to form plausible explanations on the fly.

Manual Control

Unlike the responses described in the previous section, statements that fall under the *Manual Control* pattern of beliefs described ways in which respondents believed themselves to be in control of what the News Feed displays. Some responses focused on explicit control of the contents of the News Feed by producers who manage their audiences using the privacy controls. Others focused on the ability of the consumer to engage the mechanisms Facebook provides to see more or fewer posts from particular individuals. In other words, these respondents believed that whether posts appear in the News Feed or not is at least sometimes up to them, not an intervention by the system.

Producer Privacy

Statements about privacy controls placed some of the responsibility over whether a post can be seen in the News Feeds of Facebook Friends in the hands of the person who created the post. This signals that some respondents were aware that the system supports a form of access control over posts. Respondents were aware that they might not see everything their Friends post because they themselves could block people from seeing their posts using Facebook settings. By definition, users cannot know if their Friends are doing this because if the producer of the post is successful the consumer will never see the post:

> I know that Facebook allows you to filter who can view your post, and I'm sure that some of the people on my feed filter theirs so that only family, non-coworkers, etc can see it. I do that myself, and have talked to friends that do the same thing. (R305)

> Well, I'm not sure. Some people might have chosen to elect not to show their posts to me in their privacy/post settings. I can't ever be sure if they have or haven't. (R154)

These responses illustrate that respondents are certain that access control is possible but also recognize that there is really

Beliefs	*Responses*	*Summary*
Passive Consumption	103	Respondents consume the contents of the News Feed without thinking too much about why they see the posts they do. Explanations range from never having experienced anything that would cause them to think some posts might not appear, to the belief (without evidence) that because there are so many posts the News Feed can't possibly show them all. *54% No, 46% Maybe/Yes*
Producer Privacy	45	Responses convey awareness that the News Feed might not show every post from Friends because users can use Facebook's audience selector to prevent specific others from seeing their posts. Respondents do not have direct evidence that they are excluded by others but believe this is possible because they do it themselves. *60% No, 40% Maybe/Yes*
Consumer Preferences	130	Respondents believe that without intervention the News Feed will not show them what they want to see. They cope with this by using the mechanisms provided by the Facebook interface for telling the system how they want it to behave, such as specifying (*Top Stories* or *Most Recent*, hiding or following people, etc. *74% No, 26% Maybe/Yes*
Missed Posts	208	Respondents explicitly implicate the News Feed as the agent that causes them to miss posts from Friends. They become aware that they have missed posts when someone they know mentions a post to them that they did not see, or when they visit Friends' Timelines to seek out posts they feel they may have missed. *81% No, 19% Maybe/Yes*
Violating Expectations	216	Respondents describe patterns or regularities in the News Feed that constitute symptoms that the News Feed may not be showing them every post. These symptoms are salient because they violate expectations about how they believe the News Feed should behave. For example, many respondents mentioned posts out of chronological order or older posts that repeatedly appear at the top of the feed as examples. *76% No, 24% Maybe/Yes*
Speculating about the Algorithm	223	Respondents indicate they believe an entity, characterized as Facebook or as an algorithm, prioritizes posts for display in the News Feed. Also, which posts they see depends on what the system knows about their preferences and characteristics, post popularity, and past interaction with other users. *80% No, 20% Maybe/Yes*

Table 1. Patterns of causal beliefs, identified through iterative inductive coding of open-ended explanations for responses to the question, "Do you feel like your Facebook News Feed always shows you every post created by your Facebook friends?" A single response may be represented in multiple rows.

no way to know, short of directly asking someone, whether one is being prevented from seeing particular posts. However, out of the 45 responses in this cluster, none expressed negative sentiments about this.

Consumer Preferences

One hundred thirty respondents expressed a belief that without manual intervention, the News Feed will not show them exactly what they want to see. This intervention was described in two ways: either directing the system *not* to display some or all of the posts from particular people, or directing the system to display *everything* from others by following, sorting, or creating Friend lists. These are the mechanisms that the system provides for users to explicitly state preferences about what they want to see. Respondents had many different names for what they called the activity: hiding (R427), blocking (R127), filtering (R390), unfollowing (R36), unsubscribing (R222), removing (R414), and ignoring (R198). Some described how they used these mechanisms for their intended purpose:

> I have several friends on my list that I don't follow, which means that their posts don't show up on my news feed every time they say something on their account. I do this because I don't like what they post. (R396)

However, others had adopted these controls as workarounds. This respondent created what is essentially a secondary Friend list as an attempt to negate the influence of the News Feed algorithm:

> I have a group called "Everyone" that has ALL of my Facebook friends on it. It doesn't pick and choose and I get to see everyone's posts. When I see something I don't like or someone I might unfriend, instead, I just delete them from the group. (R246)

These are examples of people taking personal responsibility for making sure they see the things they want to see, and they don't see posts that are annoying or upsetting. Unlike the *Passive Consumption* beliefs, these responses indicate an intuitive theory involving less trust that the Facebook News Feed will make good choices on their behalf.

Symptoms of Curation

The most common pattern in respondents' answers was to provide an example of a post they did not see in their News Feeds as evidence that the News Feed does not show every post. Like the *Passive Consumption* beliefs, these statements include symptoms respondents noticed that caused them to speculate about what the News Feed is doing behind the scenes. However, unlike the *Manual Control* beliefs, these statements attribute control over this to the system rather than to other users.

Missing Posts

One form this evidence took was the description of an occasion where someone the respondent knows in real life asked if he or she had seen a particular post. Forty-three responses were like this. In the majority of these responses, the respondent did not remember seeing the post but reported being able to find it on a Friend's Timeline once they tried to do so:

> Sometimes when I see a friend in real life, they will ask if if I saw something that they posted, and at least half of

> the time I haven't seen it. If I go directly to their profile, then I'm able to read it, but so often things don't appear on my newsfeed, which I find annoying! (R193)

One hundred seven responses described a feeling that the respondent had not seen a post from someone lately, and so they decided to find out what that person had been up to:

> Sometimes I feel like I haven't heard anything about a friend for awhile. I wonder if maybe they've quit Facebook, or maybe even unfriended me. Then I go to their profile and look, and they've been posting stuff the whole time. So that means that my News Feed just hasn't been showing what they've posted. (R20)

This is a good example of a respondent recalling a past experience and incorporating it into a causal belief about how the News Feed works. It also indicates that some users have expectations for how often they should see posts from particular people or at least a background awareness of who they regularly encounter on Facebook versus who they do not. Prioritizing some posts over others is the intended behavior of the News Feed algorithm; however, respondents' background awareness of who they had heard from recently and who they had not made this behavior feel unexpected or unwelcome to them in some cases. In fact, seventy responses mentioned the feeling that there were posts missing from the News Feed that respondents really did want to see, like this one:

> I miss posts from people I want to be seeing posts from all the time. Instead I see a bunch of crap that I DON'T care about: ads, comments on events I wasn't invited to, etc etc. There are some friends I see posts from so rarely that I often forget about them. (R173)

Violating Expectations

Two hundred sixteen responses included descriptions of patterns in the News Feed that could only have been noticed through repeated interactions that provided evidence over time. These patterns were incorporated into intuitive theories about the visibility of posts in the News Feed. The patterns also highlight a mismatch between expectations about how the News Feed should work, and the reality of how it does work as experienced by these respondents.

Posts out of order. Respondents seemed to have expectations about the proper order for posts to appear in. This led them to make statements about the News Feed being "out of order" or wanting to see posts in "linear" or "real" order. Signs that the News Feed was selecting some posts to prioritize over others included examples of posts that would "bump" or "bounce" to the top, "pushing" more recent posts down:

> No, the timeline bounces up things from the past back up to the top. Things that may have been more recently get pushed down, if they get pushed down far enough, I may not scroll down far enough to see a friend's post. (R180)

Turnover Rate. Respondents also seemed to have expectations about the expected rate of change or turnover of posts in the News Feed. A violation of this expectation was provided in some responses as evidence that some posts might be left out. Especially in instances of too-low turnover (i.e., repeating too many old posts), respondents wrote about feeling that seeing the same content over and over meant there were posts that were not being displayed:

> I know it does not show me every post. It changes simply by refreshing the page to older posts I have already seen. (R123)

People Represented. The final pattern respondents noticed was seeing the same people represented over and over again in the News Feed. This was a sign for respondents that posts from some Friends were being repeatedly prioritized over others:

> Many people I am friends with do not show up in my newsfeed even though I know that they post to Facebook. I generally only see posts from the same group of people even though I have quite a few friends. (R211)

This "same group of people" pattern was described by some respondents as only seeing posts from close friends; in other respondents' statements it was only posts from friends they are not close to, or even seemingly random friends. No respondents reported being aware that this pattern could have arisen simply because of the power-law pattern in participation: only a few of a given user's friends are likely to be very active, and the posts of these few may in reality just dominate the News Feed. However, it is interesting that respondent perceive this pattern as anomalous in some way.

Speculating about the Algorithm

The responses in this final group illustrate that some respondents were aware of a relationship between their behavior in the system and the content that the News Feed displays for them. These 223 responses contained statements about an entity—usually either "Facebook" or in 42 responses an "algorithm"—making inferences about their preferences. This is a fairly sophisticated understanding of the system, and reflects respondents' attempts to put together pieces of evidence from their own experience into a coherent story about what the News Feed is doing.

Respondents made statements illustrating that they recognize the system is attempting to show them posts that are "relevant" to them in some way, although they weren't always sure how this works:

> I generally feel like Facebook shows me the posts that it 'thinks' I'd be most interested in. I feel like if I want to see all of them, I have to do so manually. (R77)

Many responses focused on the fact that the system knows how often users interact with particular Friends and posts. These responses illustrate that some users understand the system makes guesses about whose posts a user might want to see based on their past behavior. Some respondents even took this a step farther, suggesting that if one were to alter his or her browsing behavior, they might end up changing the composition of posts in the News Feed:

> I know that it shows me the most commented on posts. It also shows the friends' pages that I visit the most. If

> you start 'liking' more posts it may show more posts that I want to see. (R58)

Another group of responses recognized the popularity bias effect on the News Feed, often seen in other recommender systems (popular posts get more attention, which make them more popular). Respondents had noticed that posts with more comments and likes are prioritized over other posts:

> I think that it hides some of them if they are not deemed to be popular. So what likely happens is that a popular person gets many views to their page. So people like a post. This post then gets put in the news feed for more people to like. Posts that have no likes don't always make it to the feed. (R155)

Responses like this indicate that respondents know something is making decisions on their behalf, and that this means some posts will not be as easily accessible through the system as other posts.

Summary of Findings

Our findings describe patterns of respondents' intuitive theories about how the Facebook News Feed works. We focused on intuitive theories because they are learned over repeated interactions with Facebook, and they guide behavior. Respondent beliefs ranged widely, from believing the News Feed shows all possible posts from their Friends, to automated filtering by an algorithm. Some respondents believed that the system could make inferences about their preferences based on which posts they read and whose Timelines they visited. Others noticed evidence of the News Feed algorithm that they interpreted as clues that the system was presenting posts "out of order", including seeing too many or too few posts from particular Friends, or old posts displayed on too many visits. Respondents disliked missing posts from their Friends, and believed that when they did it was evidence of system intervention.

IMPLICATIONS

Algorithm designers should be aware that even if the influence of an algorithm is not made explicitly visible to users, they nevertheless can and do adapt their behavior to correspond with how they believe the system works, in order to accomplish their goals for using the system. This means that there are implications of users' beliefs for their individual interactions with the system, and because of the feedback loop, for the behavior of the system overall. Our findings allow us to draw some conclusions below about how the interdependence of user and algorithm behavior might have system-wide consequences.

Mismatch between User and Algorithm Goals

The News Feed algorithm has (at least) two design goals[1]. One goal is to "show everyone the right content at the right time so they don't miss the stories that are important to them." The second is that the News Feed should display posts more prominently that will generate more interaction or "engagement" [26]. These two goals separate consumption (don't miss important stories) from production (increased engagement).

Some respondents believed that the News Feed is like a river or a force of nature (a flood or flow metaphor was even present in some answers), rather than a road or some other kind of infrastructure that can be altered by human intervention. It was not important to these users to be too involved with manually shaping the composition of their News Feeds. This perspective of the News Feed as something that arises naturally out of Friends' behavior rather than being constructed by the system might cause users not to attempt manual intervention. It is not clear how well the algorithm would perform for people who prefer to passively experience the News Feed, in comparison with others whose intuitive theories lend themselves to a more manual approach. If people were to accept what the system presents and not adjust their behavior to achieve a particular outcome, the impact of a feedback loop might be lessened. However, one respondent actually noticed that the less he or she interacts with others via on Facebook, the less content from friends he or she sees in the News Feed, which could be a symptom of the feedback loop:

> But over the years it seems like I see their posts less often. Its very annoying actually and lately I have been considering quitting Facebook... Only about 50% of my newsfeed is posts from friends. It seems like unless you actually communicate with them often you hardly, if ever see their posts. (R150)

For users whose personal goals for using the system do not match the system's goals, our findings suggest that unexpected outcomes like this may be possible.

Another area in which users' and the system's goals may not be aligned is when producers' privacy settings restrict the visibility of posts. Greater restrictions on who can see a producer's post would decrease the number of users who might be able to see and interact with it. When more private posts are ranked against public posts in preparation for display in the News Feed, they could appear below public posts that were visible to more people and therefore received more interaction. Privacy settings may indirectly prevent users who were in reality granted access from actually seeing the post in their News Feeds. A potential outcome like this would be extremely difficult for users to detect, as well as difficult for designers to explicitly test for. However, generating use cases where user and algorithm goals are in conflict as part of the design process is a good step towards systematic identification of edge cases that result from the interaction between user and algorithm behavior.

It may be that excluding users who do not fit the design goals of the algorithm is a side effect that is more of a feature than a bug; after all, Facebook (the company) has the ability and the right to identify and reward whatever it believes to be appropriate participation. Hallinan and Striphas [14] call this the "court of algorithmic appeal" in which ideas are judged

[1]We assume this based on our understanding of the News Feed FYI blog posts to the Facebook News Room, at http://newsroom.fb.com/news/category/news-feed-fyi/

by system components and not human beings. However, if the operational definition of "appropriate participation" is not an intended consequence, then the algorithm may be creating categories of valid and invalid forms of contribution in ways that are contrary to the overall goals of the system. Identifying undesirable feedback loop effects that occur when the user's goals do not match the system's goals should be an important part of an algorithm designer's role.

Reverse-engineering the Algorithm

Many respondents had sophisticated ideas about what kinds of interactions with content on Facebook brought about specific, repeatable consequences, and wrote about altering their behavior to work within the constraints of the algorithm or to use the mechanisms provided by the system to achieve their goals. What our respondents described is different from systematic attempts by researchers and journalists to perform experiments intended to discover details about the parameters and weighting used by the News Feed algorithm to rank posts for display. Determining the specifics of the algorithm by comparing users' experiences is nearly impossible, because each user has a different network of Friends who serve as the sources of content [15]. However, each user is familiar with who his or her Friends are and may naturally make attributions about how interactions with the system are related to changes in what they see at a later time. Users can't help but informally reverse-engineer the algorithm, and repeated use of the News Feed provides them with ample opportunity to form intuitive theories about how the system works.

The commonalities across respondents in the intuitive theories about how the algorithm works are important for understanding potential effects of feedback loops. For example, consider the large number of our respondents who said they had experienced missed posts. Missed posts are part of the correct operation of the News Feed algorithm, as it prioritizes a subset of posts for display. However, the focus on engagement means that people who create posts that achieve visibility in the News Feed receive more attention, leading to a form of the popularity bias. Our findings suggest that users are aware that this happens, and our respondents mentioned many symptoms of it (for example, low turnover from posts that get stuck at the top of the News Feed because of a highly active comment thread). As consumers, they can use Facebook's mechanisms for hiding posts and Friends to try and control these effects on their News Feeds; they might also cope in other ways, such as forming a routine to visit friends' Timelines directly to stay in touch:

> I have had friends ask me about certain events or occasions in their lives and I had no clue what they were talking about because I'd never seen it in my news feed. I now make a point to visit certain people's timelines to see what they have posted. (R28)

As producers, users can try to create posts that other users find more engaging so their posts get more attention and avoid the "threat of invisibility" [6]. Knowledge about how the algorithm works enables kind of individual experimentation, attempting to train the system through investigating what patterns of input will produce the desired output. Missed posts seem like one symptom of algorithm behavior that is unpleasant enough to trigger users to try and figure out the algorithm. Our findings describe many other forms of expectation violations that might also serve as triggers. Therefore, we suggest that algorithm designers should consider the intuitive theories users learn about how the system works, and what might trigger them to reverse-engineer it, when trying to identify the consequences of feedback loops.

Finally, as Hamilton et al. point out, there is much debate about whether and to what extent automated system processes should be made visible to the humans who interact with them [15]. Although it may be a sign of good design when users do not detect algorithms at work, the consequences of this invisibility may exacerbate the impact of different user and algorithm goals. Our findings show that users don't necessarily need to understand that an algorithm is shaping their experience to adapt their behavior to it. But, it may be possible for designers to leave clues for users to help them inadvertently form intuitive theories that may be more friendly to the intended operation of the algorithm—in effect, using the propensity of users to reverse-engineer the system as a mechanism for controlling some of the second-order effects created by the feedback loop. Future work should investigate the relationship between varying degrees of algorithmic literacy and system-level outcomes.

CONCLUSION

Our goal for this study was to better understand interactions between users and algorithms. While algorithms are designed to achieve particular goals, the consequences of design choices can be hard to predict. We focused on algorithmic curation in the Facebook News Feed as an example of a system in which feedback loops have the potential to affect behavior at both the individual and system level. We identified several patterns of beliefs about the News Feed that have implications for the design of algorithms for organizing, selecting, and presenting information in a complex socio-technical system. Ultimately, users vary widely in the degree to which they perceive and understand the behavior of content filtering algorithms in this online social network context, and these differences affect how they interact with and experience the systems they are using. We used intuitive theories about causal relationships as a lens for identifying implications of feedback loops that algorithm designers may not routinely consider. Algorithmic curation has the potential for generating negative outcomes that could be identified and avoided, if system dynamics like feedback loops are better understood.

ACKNOWLEDGMENTS

We thank Paul Rose for assisting with early stages of the data analysis, and the MSU BITLab research group for feedback on the survey questions. This material is based upon work supported by the National Science Foundation under Grant No. IIS-1217212.

REFERENCES

1. Social Networking Fact Sheet, 2014. http://www.pewinternet.org/fact-sheets/social-networking-fact-sheet/.

2. Backstrom, L. A Window Into News Feed, Aug. 2013. https://www.facebook.com/business/news/News-Feed-FYI-A-Window-Into-News-Feed.
3. Bakshy, E., Rosenn, I., Marlow, C., and Adamic, L. The Role of Social Networks in Information Diffusion. In *WWW 2012* (2012), 519–528.
4. Bernstein, M. S., Suh, B., Hong, L., Chen, J., Kairam, S., and Chi, E. H. Eddi: interactive topic-based browsing of social status streams. In *UIST '10*, ACM (2010), 303–312.
5. Bozdag, E. Bias in algorithmic filtering and personalization. *Ethics and Information Technology 15*, 3 (2013), 209–227.
6. Bucher, T. Want to be on the top? Algorithmic power and the threat of invisibility on Facebook. *New Media & Society 14*, 7 (Oct. 2012), 1164–1180.
7. Chen, J., Nairn, R., and Chi, E. H. Speak Little and Well: Recommending Conversations in Online Social Streams. In *CHI '11* (2011), 217–226.
8. Clegg, C. W. Sociotechnical principles for system design. *Applied Ergonomics* (2000).
9. Facebook. Company Info: Facebook Newsroom. http://newsroom.fb.com/company-info/, 2014.
10. Facebook. How News Feed Works. https://www.facebook.com/help/327131014036297/, 2014.
11. Fleder, D., and Hosanagar, K. Blockbuster Culture's Next Rise or Fall: The Impact of Recommender Systems on Sales Diversity. *Management science 55*, 5 (2009), 697–712.
12. Gelman, S. A., and Legare, C. H. Concepts and folk theories. *Annual Review of Anthropology* (2011).
13. Gillespie, T. The Relevance of Algorithms. In *Media Technologies Essays on Communication, Materiality, and Society*, P. Boczkowski and K. Foot, Eds. MIT Press, 2014.
14. Hallinan, B., and Striphas, T. Recommended for you: The Netflix Prize and the production of algorithmic culture. *New Media & Society* (2014).
15. Hamilton, K., Karahalios, K., Sandvig, C., and Eslami, M. A path to understanding the effects of algorithm awareness. In *CHI EA '14* (2014), 631–642.
16. Hogan, B. From Invisible Algorithms to Interactive Affordances: Data After the Ideology of Machine Learning. In *Roles, Trust, and Reputation in Social Media Knowledge Markets*. Springer International Publishing, Cham, 2015, 103–117.
17. Jannach, D., Lerche, L., Gedikli, F., and Bonnin, G. What recommenders recommend–an analysis of accuracy, popularity, and sales diversity effects. *User Modeling, Adaptation and Personalization* (2013), 25–37.
18. Joinson, A. N. 'Looking at', 'Looking up' or 'Keeping up with' People? In *CHI '08* (Florence, Italy, Apr. 2008), 1027–1036.
19. Jones, N. A., Ross, H., Lynam, T., Perez, P., and Leitch, A. Mental Models: An Interdisciplinary Synthesis of Theory and Methods. *Ecology And Society 16*, 1 (2011).
20. Kramer, A. D. I., Guillory, J. E., and Hancock, J. T. Experimental evidence of massive-scale emotional contagion through social networks. *PNAS 111*, 24 (2014), 8788–8790.
21. Lavie, T., Sela, M., Oppenheim, I., Inbar, O., and Meyer, J. User attitudes towards news content personalization. *International Journal of Human-Computer Studies 68*, 8 (2010), 483–495.
22. Lenhart, A. Adults and social network sites. Tech. rep., Pew Research Center, 2009.
23. Lv, Y., Moon, T., Kolari, P., Zheng, Z., Wang, X., and Chang, Y. Learning to Model Relatedness for News Recommendation. In *WWW 2011* (2011), 57–66.
24. Meadows, D. H. *Thinking in Systems: A Primer*. Chelsea Green Publishing, 2008.
25. Nguyen, T. T., Hui, P.-M., Harper, F. M., Terveen, L., and Konstan, J. A. Exploring the filter bubble: the effect of using recommender systems on content diversity. In *WWW '14* (2014), 677–686.
26. Owens, E., and Vickrey, D. News Feed FYI: Showing More Timely Stories from Friends and Pages. http://newsroom.fb.com/news/2014/09/news-feed-fyi-showing-more-timely-stories-from-friends-and-pages/, September 2014.
27. Rouse, W. B., and Serban, N. Understanding change in complex socio-technical systems. *Information Knowledge Systems Management 10*, 1-4 (Jan. 2011).
28. Sharma, A., and Cosley, D. Network-Centric Recommendation: Personalization with and in Social Networks. In *IEEE SocialCom 2011* (2011), 282–289.
29. Sharma, A., Gemici, M., and Cosley, D. Friends, Strangers, and the Value of Ego Networks for Recommendation. In *ICWSM '13* (2013), 721–724.
30. Singer, J. B. User-generated visibility: Secondary gatekeeping in a shared media space. *New Media & Society 16*, 1 (Jan. 2014), 55–73.
31. Steck, H. Item popularity and recommendation accuracy. In *RecSys '11* (2011), 125–132.
32. Sukumaran, A., Vezich, S., McHugh, M., and Nass, C. Normative influences on thoughtful online participation. In *CHI '11*, ACM (2011), 3401–3410.

Cross-language Wikipedia Editing of Okinawa, Japan

Scott A. Hale
Oxford Internet Institute, University of Oxford
1 St Giles, Oxford, UK OX1 3JS
scott.hale@oii.ox.ac.uk

ABSTRACT
This article analyzes users who edit Wikipedia articles about Okinawa, Japan, in English and Japanese. It finds these users are among the most active and dedicated users in their primary languages, where they make many large, high-quality edits. However, when these users edit in their non-primary languages, they tend to make edits of a different type that are overall smaller in size and more often restricted to the narrow set of articles that exist in both languages. Design changes to motivate wider contributions from users in their non-primary languages and to encourage multilingual users to transfer more information across language divides are presented.

ACM Classification Keywords
H.5.4 Information Interfaces and Presentation (e.g. HCI): Hypertext/Hypermedia; H.5.3 Information Interfaces and Presentation (e.g. HCI): Group and Organization Interfaces

General Terms
Human Factors, Design

Author Keywords
Social Media; Information Discovery; Social Network Analysis; Information Diffusion; Cross-language; Wikipedia; Multilingual

INTRODUCTION
Allowing users to contribute content in multiple languages on user-generated content platforms results in a large difference in the content available in different languages. Within Wikipedia, for example, over 74% of concepts have an article in only one language edition, and more than 95% of concepts appear in six or fewer languages [18]. This finding is not unique to Wikipedia: on Twitter there is also surprisingly little overlap between the top domain names and hashtags used in tweets of different languages [19]. User-generated content platforms face a trade-off on allowing the use of multiple languages. On the one hand, increased language diversity increases the potential number of contributors as monolingual individuals from multiple languages can join. On the other hand, increased language diversity may also increase the risk of fragmenting content and users across languages, particularly if multilingual users who would have used the site in a large, international language move exclusively to smaller language editions. On question and answer platform Stack Overflow, the risk of fragmentation—that is, the risk that multiple language editions of the site would result in fewer users to any one particular language edition and therefore less high-quality answers—has been cited as one of the reasons for the platform to remain monolingual.[1]

Key to the trade-off between the potential increase in other-language users and the risk of fragmentation across languages are the roles technology and users play in facilitating the flow of information between languages. Previous research has suggested multilingual users who read and contribute content in multiple languages may share novel information between languages and broaden the scope of information available to monolingual users online [10, 15, 16, 18]. Research to date, however, has either examined differences in content between languages [6, 8, 18] or examined user behavior [10, 15, 16], but not both. Thus, while 15% of the active editors on Wikipedia contribute to multiple language editions [16], it remains unclear what content multilingual users contribute, how much content they contribute, and how valuable the content they contribute is. These questions are important in understanding the current roles multilingual users play in transferring information between languages as well as gaining insight for designing multilingual platforms in ways that maximize cross-language information transfer. This paper starts to address this gap by examining the content contributed by multilingual users in their primary and non-primary languages on one of the largest multilingual user-generated content platforms online, Wikipedia. The findings lead to a more in-depth understanding of the role multilingual users play on multilingual user-generated content platforms and suggest platform design strategies.

BACKGROUND AND RELATED WORK
Each language edition of Wikipedia exhibits a self-focus: that is, each edition has, in general, more information about the regions where the language of the edition is spoken and less information about the regions where the language is not spoken [18]. Even when corresponding articles for a common concept exist across multiple language editions, there is a surprising diversity in the topics covered in each language edition's article on that concept [5]. For example, the Spanish-

[1] `http://blog.stackoverflow.com/2009/07/non-english-question-policy/`

CHI 2015, April 18–23, 2015, Seoul, Republic of Korea.

ACM 978-1-4503-3145-6/15/04...$15.00
http://dx.doi.org/10.1145/2702123.2702346

language article on psychology contains a section on important contributions from Latin America that is not found in other language editions [18].

The global nature of the Internet allows for the possibility that expatriates, language-learners, and other-culture/language enthusiasts (who Zuckerman [31] has termed xenophiles) can spread information between languages on user-generated content platforms. In a one-month study of edits to the top 46 language editions of Wikipedia, Hale [16] found that approximately 15% of active Wikipedia users edited multiple language editions of the encyclopedia. These multilingual users were distributed across all language editions, but smaller-sized editions with fewer users had a higher percentage of multilingual users compared to larger-sized editions. The percentage of multilingual users primarily editing each language edition was found to negatively correlate with the self-focus of the 15 editions studied by Hecht and Gergle [18]: that is, editions with more multilingual users exhibited less self-focus [16].

Multilingual users are well situated to act as bridges or gatekeepers and transfer content between languages; however, past work points to a more nuanced picture of the extent to which multilingual users actually fulfill this role. Studies of multilingual users on Twitter show they are in structural positions to act as bridges across language groups [10, 15] and that approximately 11% of active Twitter users write in multiple languages [15]. However, a study of multilingual users on Twitter in Switzerland, Qatar, and Quebec using LDA topic modeling found that multilingual users often focused on different topics in different languages [20]. This suggests these multilingual users may not be bridging across languages as much as their structural positions suggest. A similar situation may be present in Wikipedia, where 43% of the multilingual users studied by Hale [16] edited articles about different concepts in their primary and non-primary languages.

The first research question of this paper, therefore, simply asks *what articles do multilinguals edit in their non-primary languages?* (RQ1). This paper compares the articles multilingual users edit in their non-primary languages with the articles edited by other users to understand the scope within which multilingual users may transfer information between languages. The results show that multilingual users edit a narrower set of articles in their non-primary languages and suggest design interventions such as cross-language content recommendation systems could broaden the scope of articles users edit in their non-primary languages.

Beyond what articles users edit in a non-primary language, this paper also asks *what types of edits do multilingual users make in their non-primary languages?* (RQ2) in order to understand the nature and the extent of the information that multilingual users transfer between languages. A first dimension by which to compare contributions is size. Using the meta data available from Wikipedia, Hale [16] analyzed the difference in the size of articles before and after each edit in bytes, but that measure is not the most reliable as an edit that adds a large block of text but also removes a different block of text could result in a size difference very close to zero bytes. Using the content of edits, this study calculates a more nuanced measure of edit size using the number of words added, the number of words removed, and the amount of reorganization performed. A second dimension by which to compare contributions is the types of content changes users make in their non-primary languages. The study of 2010 Haitian earthquake blogs found that the sharing of images and videos was a large motivation for crossing language boundaries among bloggers [14], which suggests adding, removing, or otherwise modifying images might be more prevalent in users' non-primary languages.

The final research question posed in this paper asks *how valuable are the contributions by multilingual users in their non-primary languages?* (RQ3). Given the diversity in information between languages on Wikipedia [18] as well as online more generally, edits by multilingual users have the potential to introduce truly novel and valuable information and sources from one language into articles in another language. Connections across languages may serve as "bridges" and have been compared to the concept of "weak ties" in social network analysis [10, 13], where ample scholarship has shown weak ties to be of critical importance to the spread of information, with benefits ascribed to both the individual and the system/network as a whole [7].

The study of multilingual users on Wikipedia also found a positive correlation between multilingualism and the number of edits users' made in their primary languages: users more active in their primary languages were more likely to edit in multiple languages [16]. This suggests that multilingual users overlap to some extent with the group of very active elite or power users on Wikipedia, on which, like on many other platforms, much of the work is done by a small percentage of very active users [29, 21]. Monolingual studies have found that these users are responsible for a disproportionately large percentage of the content in the encyclopedia [21] and are overwhelmingly responsible for the content that is viewed most frequently [29]. It remains unclear, however, how much content these users contribute and how long it persists when they are editing in their non-primary languages.

In order to investigate both users and content effectively, this paper focuses on content and multilingual user contributions in English and Japanese in a relatively contained geographic area: Okinawa, Japan. Okinawa is an archipelago of small, sub-tropical islands home to a large number of native Japanese speakers and a large number of native English speakers.[2] Geographically closer to Taipei than Tokyo, the islands were once part of a prosperous independent kingdom built on trade in the region. After formal incorporation into Japan at the end of the 1800's, the islands were separated from Japan at the end of World War II and administered by the United States until 1972. Since that time, the US has maintained a strong presence, with half of all US personnel (military, contractors, dependents) in Japan under the US Status of Forces Agreement located in Okinawa. This accounts for

[2]The author has lived in Okinawa and can speak Japanese and English.

just under 50,000 individuals [24] with military facilities occupying just over 18% of the land area of the largest and most populated island [26].

Previous qualitative studies of Wikipedia have found differences in the editing behavior of users editing different language editions of Wikipedia—such as correlations with Hofstede's cultural dimensions [28]. These studies have not examined the roles played by users who edit in multiple languages as is done in this article, but these previous studies do underscore the importance of studying users in multiple languages before making generalizations. Nonetheless, English and Japanese are good initial languages to study given that they are among the most-used languages online, not only on Wikipedia [16], but also on Twitter [15]. Furthermore, speakers in each language play vastly different roles in interlanguage connections [15, 16]. In the one-month study of edits to Wikipedia, Japanese was a major outlier with only 6% of the primary editors of the Japanese edition editing a second edition [16]. In contrast, English was very central in the cross-language movements of users: when non-English users edited a second edition, that edition was most frequently English [16].

DATA

Finding the subset of all articles related to a particular geographic region on Wikipedia involves a trade-off between direct relevance and completeness (or, using the terminology of information retrieval, between precision and recall). Using the Wikimedia Labs[3] infrastructure, three article samples were extracted in October 2013. The *geotag sample* included all articles with geographic information (geotags) physically placing the articles in Okinawa.[4] The *category sample* included all articles in any category that contained the word "Okinawa" for the English edition or "沖縄" (Okinawa) for the Japanese edition. Finally, the *article link sample* included all articles containing a link to an article starting with "Okinawa" for the English edition or to an article starting with "沖縄" (Okinawa) for the Japanese edition. All edits to each article in each sample were then downloaded from the date the article was created until October 2013 using the Wikipedia API.[5]

The article samples were filtered to only include articles in the main, article namespace (i.e. not talk pages, user pages, etc.). The article link sample was also filtered to only include articles that mentioned Okinawa in the main body text of the article (i.e. not transcluded via a template to appear in a sidebar or footer). This was done so that the articles in the sample had a more substantial connection to Okinawa than just being part of a large group of articles linked together by a common portal or category such as "Regions and administrative divisions of Japan" or "USAAF Eighth Air Force in World War II."

[3]`https://www.mediawiki.org/wiki/Wikimedia_Labs`

[4]The bounding box used included articles between 25.75 and 26.9 E and 126 and 129 N.

[5]`https://www.mediawiki.org/wiki/API:Main_page`

Corresponding articles in the English and Japanese language editions were found using the October 2013 database dump from WikiData.[6] Launched in 2012, WikiData centralizes all interlanguage links (and, increasingly, statistics and other structured data) in one location and avoids some previous issues with out-of-date or conflicting interlanguage links when the links were separately maintained in each language edition of Wikipedia. For each non-anonymous user, the Central Authorization database was queried with the username to determine if the username was a global account connected to multiple language editions. If it was, the database for each language edition the user edited was queried to get the total number of edits per language that the user made since creating the account. The language of each user's most edited edition is referred to as the user's primary language throughout this paper while the languages of any other editions edited by the user are referred to as the user's non-primary languages. Users belonging to the (ro)'bot' group or having the 'bot' template on their userpages as well as users that had been suspended for malicious editing were removed in order to focus on the behavior of good-faith, human editors.[7]

Measures of edit size and value

Users contribute value to Wikipedia in many ways. For example, Kriplean et al. [22] found 42 different types of contributions to Wikipedia through an analysis of barnstars (personalized tokens of appreciation given to fellow users). The types of contributions they identified included programming tools/bots, designing templates, performing administrative functions, teaching, and leadership. Welser et al. [30] similarly identified multiple user roles by analyzing the distribution of users' edits across the different namespaces on Wikipedia (articles, article talk pages, user pages, etc.).

In order to have one quantitative measure of the value of edits to articles, this paper uses edit persistence, following past work analyzing Wikipedia in one language [1, 2, 3, 29]. In particular, this paper uses the algorithms developed by Adler et al. [1, 2, 3] for their WikiTrust content-driven reputation system for Wikipedia to compute the extent to which each edit survives through the next six revisions to the article (edit persistence). WikiTrust accounts for some of the complexities of Wikipedia including differences created by rewording and rearranging text, and it also correctly attributes text that is deleted and then restored to the first author who contributed it (rather than to the author who restored it) [2]. Edit persistence is calculated on a word-by-word basis for the next six revisions to each article so that users get partial credit for an edit even when part of their edit is subsequently changed or removed.

WikiTrust also computes a more detailed measure of edit sizes than is reported directly from Wikipedia. The edit sizes reported by Wikipedia simply measure the difference in page

[6]`http://www.wikidata.org/`

[7]The status of user accounts was checked one year after data collection in December 2014 to allow sufficient time for malicious editors to be reported and blocked. The data as well as the code used for data collection and analysis are available at `http://www.scotthale.net/pubs/?chi2015`.

Sample	en-only	ja-only	Both
Geotag	52	185	152
Category	156	2,819	707
Article link	3,411	9,984	5,567

Table 1. The number of unique concepts in each sample. The majority of concepts have an article either only in the English edition or only in the Japanese edition (en-only or ja-only), while a smaller number of concepts have articles in both the English and Japanese editions (Both).

size (in bytes) before and after an edit. In contrast, the sizes computed by WikiTrust and used in this paper are determined by the number of words added, deleted, changed, or moved. New words and deleted words contribute one point each, replacement words contribute 0.5 points each, and moving a word a fraction x of the normalized page length ($0 < x < 1$) contributes x of a point [2].

WikiTrust was developed and tested on languages with spaces between words; however, Japanese is written without spaces between words. Therefore, the Japanese text was first preprocessed to add spaces between words with mecab, an open-source library for text segmentation, part-of-speech tagging, and morphological analysis of Japanese text.[8] The WikiTrust algorithm was then run twice: once over the articles in the English article link sample and once over the articles in the Japanese article link sample. The reputation scores were computed only on the basis of users' edits in the data samples, and not in the full multi-terabyte dumps of all of Wikipedia articles.

RESULTS

This section begins by describing the three article samples in order to understand the article landscape within which Wikipedia users were editing. It then addresses each of the three main research questions in turn:

1. *What articles do multilinguals edit in their non-primary languages?* (RQ1)
2. *What types of edits do multilingual users make in their non-primary languages?* (RQ2)
3. *How valuable are the contributions by multilingual users in their non-primary languages?* (RQ3)

All three article samples (geotag, category, and article link) show differences in the concepts related to Okinawa covered in the Japanese and English editions of Wikipedia. Consistent with previous research [18], there are more concepts with an article in only one language (either Japanese or English) than concepts with articles in both languages (Table 1). The three samples have substantial overlap—all but a small handful of articles in the geotag sample are present in the category sample, and the article link sample contains all the articles in both the geotag sample and the category sample.

In order to investigate the differences between the editions further, the inter-article links that connect articles together within each language were used to construct two networks for each sample. One network for the Japanese edition with each Japanese article in the sample as a node, and one network for the English edition with each English article as a node. Edges in both networks were the inter-article links between articles in the same language edition. Nodes were then ranked using the PageRank method [27]. This algorithm, also used by Google, ranks nodes by the number of links to them weighted by the PageRanks of the nodes from which the links originate.

Within the geotag sample, the top-ranked English-only articles were mainly about US military facilities, equipment, and historic battles, while the top-ranked geotagged Japanese articles included a variety of parks, tourist areas, ports/terminals, and a shrine, reflecting that Okinawa is a Japanese tourist hot spot.

The top-ranked articles within the category and article link samples were very similar to each other. The top-ranked articles appearing only in English in the category and article link samples included many articles related to karate, which started in Okinawa. The top-ranked articles appearing only in Japanese in these samples included historic articles (articles on the reversion of Okinawa from the US to Japan in 1972) as well as articles about Okinawa-based media and transit companies.

Given the substantial overlaps between the samples, the remainder of this paper uses only the article link sample to investigate the roles of multilingual users in the spread of content between the Japanese and English language editions. The article link sample has the benefits that an article link sample can be formed for any seed set of articles and that article links have been better studied on Wikipedia [23] than categories. In particular, Bao et al. [5] examined the frequency with which different language editions were missing article links (that is the frequency with which a concept was mentioned without a link to the article about the concept) and found that the English and Japanese editions were missing possible article links at similar frequencies.

Article selection

This subsection examines what articles users edited, with a particular emphasis on what articles multilingual users edited in their non-primary languages in order to answer the first research question. Most editors were anonymous, had local accounts, or had global accounts that primarily edited the language edition in question (Table 2). The prevalence of edits by anonymous users is consistent with previous research analyzing Wikipedia and not a peculiarity of this sample [4]. It is difficult to calculate per-user statistics for anonymous users since IP addresses change over time and multiple users may edit from the same IP address, but relevant statistics for anonymous users are presented where possible given the size of this group.

A small number of registered users primarily edited either the Japanese or English edition, but also edited the opposite edition: 558 primary editors of the English edition edited articles in the article link sample from the Japanese edition, and 466 primary editors of the Japanese edition also edited articles in the article link sample from the English edition.

[8] `https://code.google.com/p/mecab/` (in Japanese)

	Total users Count	%	Total articles edited Count	%	Articles edited per user Median	Mean	SD	Edit size per user (log) Median	Mean	SD
English edition										
Anonymous	192,839	73.4%	216,840	46.15%						
Local account	15,008	5.7%	58,689	12.49%	1	3.91	21.79	1.79	1.97	1.93
Pri. English	50,038	19.0%	179,951	38.30%	1	3.60	20.74	1.94	2.08	1.97
Pri. Japanese	466	0.2%	1,488	0.32%	1	3.19	7.32	1.16	1.38	1.67
Pri. Other	4,341	1.7%	12,911	2.75%	1	2.97	16.44	0.47	1.13	1.71
Totals	262,692	100.0%	469,879	100.0%	1	3.62	20.67	1.84	2.00	1.96
Japanese edition										
Anonymous	372,852	88.4%	717,608	62.74%						
Local account	9,945	2.4%	109,765	9.60%	2	11.04	47.84	3.09	2.95	1.81
Pri. English	558	0.1%	5,531	0.48%	1	9.91	58.47	0.96	1.55	1.95
Pri. Japanese	37,191	8.8%	301,980	26.40%	1	8.12	43.97	3.00	2.91	1.83
Pri. Other	1,174	0.3%	8,954	0.78%	1	7.63	57.44	0.18	1.07	1.76
Totals	421,720	100.0%	1,143,838	100.0%	1	8.72	45.35	2.97	2.87	1.85

Table 2. User counts, articles edited, and edit sizes. The primary (pri.) language of a user with a global account is the language of the most-edited edition of Wikipedia.

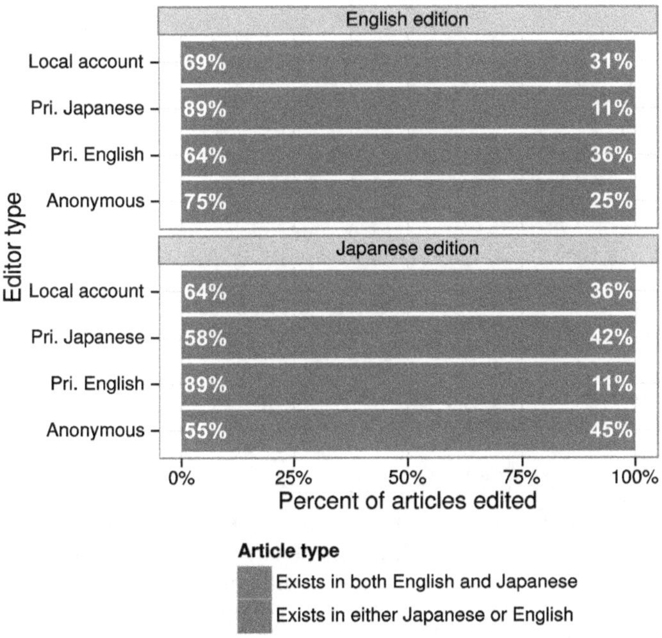

Figure 1. English users editing the Japanese edition are far less likely than other users to edit articles that only appear in Japanese. Similarly, Japanese users editing the English edition are far less likely than other users to edit articles that only appear in English.

The articles users choose to edit reflect how different groups of users distribute their time and energy across articles. Although the previous section showed that most concepts had articles in only one language, the majority of edits by all users were to concepts with articles in both languages (Figure 1). Even so, the edits by multilingual users writing in a non-primary language were significantly more concentrated on concepts with corresponding articles in both languages compared to the edits of other users writing in each language.[9]

[9]The difference in means between any two groups within either edition is significant with $p < 0.001$.

The finding that multilingual users mostly edit articles with corresponding articles in their primary languages is confirmed by a linear regression (Table 3), which also shows the articles users edited in their non-primary languages tended to have more overall edits/editors, more images, and have higher PageRank scores computed as described earlier. The articles Japanese users edited in English also tended to have more links to external sources, but the number of links to external sources was not significantly associated with the number of English users editing an article in Japanese.

These results give a more nuanced understanding of the article selection behavior of multilingual users. Data on the articles that users viewed is not available, and thus it is not possible to say whether multilingual users read (but did not edit) articles in their primary languages before editing the corresponding articles in their non-primary languages. The editing data, however, clearly shows that while multilingual users in this dataset edit similar proportions as other user groups of one- and two-language concepts in their primary languages, they disproportionately edit a smaller amount of one-language concepts in their non-primary languages.

Types of contributions

This subsection addresses the second research question on the size and type of edits multilingual users make. Setting aside anonymous users and local accounts to compare users who have global accounts to one another, a finding in both editions is that those users who edited articles in both Japanese and English in the dataset were very active on their primary language editions. Considering users with global accounts who primarily edited the English edition, about one percent of these users also edited the Japanese edition. However, this group of users was responsible for six percent of all edits to the English edition made by English users. Similarly, Japanese users who also edited the English edition were also about one percent of all Japanese users with global accounts, but they made 13% of all edits by Japanese users in the Japanese edition.

	# of Japanese users editing English		# of English users editing Japanese	
	Estimate	(Standard error)	Estimate	(Standard error)
Exists in both languages	0.641***	(0.024)	3.285***	(0.034)
Total number of editors	0.001***	(0.0001)	0.003***	(0.0001)
PageRank	0.014***	(0.0005)	0.245***	(0.006)
Number of images	0.003***	(0.001)	0.054***	(0.002)
Number of external links	0.001***	(0.0003)	−0.0003	(0.0004)
Constant	0.008	(0.015)	0.029	(0.019)
Observations	5,441		14,825	
Adjusted R^2	0.348		0.572	
Residual Std. Error	0.849 (df = 5435)		1.828 (df = 14819)	
			*p<0.1; **p<0.05; ***p<0.01	

Table 3. Linear regression results fitting the number of primary Japanese users editing each English article and the number of primary English users editing each Japanese article.

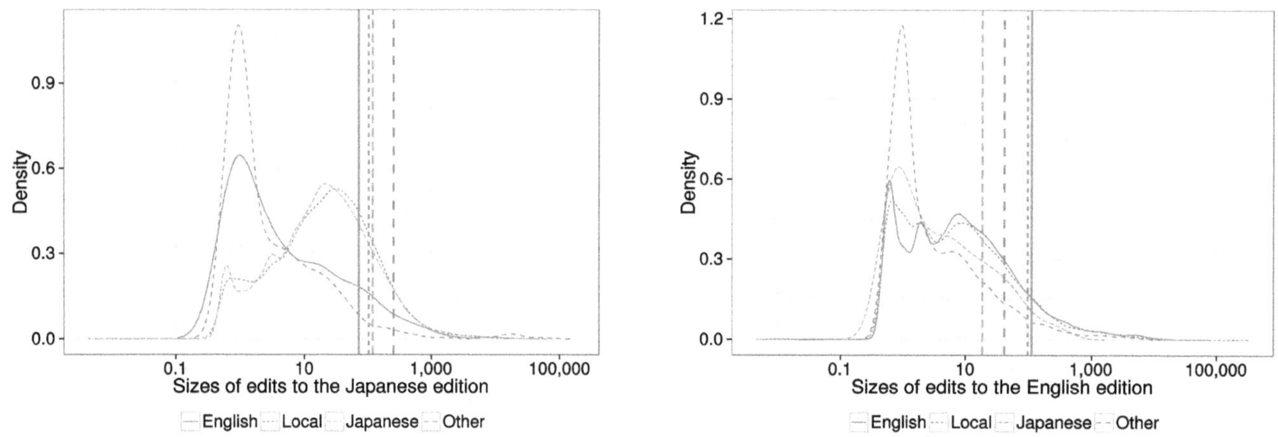

Figure 2. Density plots for non-anonymous users editing articles in the Japanese (left) and English (right) editions grouped by their primary language editions. Vertical lines indicate distribution means.

While multilingual users were very active in their primary languages, a smaller percentage of each user's total edits were to each user's non-primary languages. Overall, 14% of all edits by multilingual users were to their non-primary languages, which is higher than the prior work that found only 2.6% of edits across all language editions for one month were from users writing in their non-primary languages [16]. This could be due to the focus on a geographic region with large numbers of English and Japanese speakers and/or the longer time frame of the analysis.

Edit sizes

Users who edited both the Japanese and English editions have two sets of scores for their edit sizes and edit persistence. One set for the English edition and one set for the Japanese edition. First looking at the scores for users' primary language editions, a consistent finding in both Japanese and English is that those users who edited both editions made significantly larger edits than the users who only edited one edition.[10] Japanese users who also edited the English edition made larger sized edits in Japanese compared to Japanese users who did not edit the English edition (median 3.9 vs. 3.0, mean 3.8 vs. 2.9, sd both 1.8, $p < 0.001$). Likewise, English users who also edited the Japanese edition made larger sized edits in English compared to English users who did not edit the Japanese edition (median 2.4 vs. 1.9, mean 2.5 vs. 2.1, sd 1.9 and 2.0, $p < 0.001$).

While multilingual users made larger sized edits in their primary languages, the analysis of their edits in their non-primary languages reveals a very different picture (Figure 2 and Table 2). The sizes of edits to the Japanese edition by English users were significantly smaller than the sizes of edits to the Japanese edition by Japanese users ($p < 0.001$). Similarly, the sizes of edits to the English edition by Japanese users were significantly smaller than the sizes of edits to the English edition by English users ($p < 0.001$).

Content changes in primary and non-primary languages

In order to better understand the gap between the edit sizes of users in their primary and non-primary languages, a small subset of edits was explored qualitatively. A random set of 70 users who had edited both editions was chosen: 35 users who primarily edited the English edition and 35 users who primarily edited the Japanese edition. Up to five edits from

[10]Given the heavy-tailed distribution of average edit sizes, the results are reported after being transformed with the logarithm.

Edit category	Pri. lang.		Non-pri. lang.		p-val†
Addition	97	31%	47	26%	0.25
Maintenance	103	33%	44	24%	0.04
Deletion/Reversion	37	12%	11	6%	0.03
Image-related	27	9%	32	18%	0.01
Interlanguage links	8	3%	32	18%	0.00
Change	65	21%	34	19%	0.62
Total edits‡	315		181		

Table 4. Exploratory, qualitative coding of edits in users' primary languages (pri. lang.) and non-primary languages (non-pri. lang.). †p-values are for two-tailed t-tests on difference of percentage means. ‡Some edits are assigned to multiple categories and, therefore, the column sums are greater than the total number of edits reported.

each edition were randomly chosen for a total of up to 10 edits from each user. Despite the measures to remove (ro)bots described in the data section, qualitative analysis revealed that one randomly chosen user was a bot: this user was replaced with another randomly chosen user. Not all users had five edits in each edition; so, 496 edits were reviewed in total. This set included edits by English users to the English edition (145 edits) and the Japanese edition (96) as well as edits by Japanese users to the English edition (85) and the Japanese edition (170). The findings suggest that users made different types of contributions in their primary and non-primary languages, which may account for the differences in the computed size of their edits.

Edits made to articles (but not to talk pages, etc.) were examined in order to understand the contributions users made to articles in their primary and non-primary languages. After consulting previous literature [22, 28], initial codes were created through an emergent coding of a subset of the data. These were refined into six (non-exclusive) categories, and the full sample was systematically coded using these categories. Each edit was classified as making an addition (adding new text or references to an existing article or creating a new article), as maintenance (adding, removing, or adjusting templates, categories, links in a "See Also" section, or whitespace changes that did not alter text), as deletion/reversion (reverting an edit or deleting text from an article), as image-related (adding, altering, or removing an image), as altering interlanguage links, and/or as change (edits that changed existing text such as correcting spelling errors or updating facts that had changed like the latest winner of an annual sports tournament).

There was a significant difference between the types of edits users made in their primary languages compared to the types they made in their non-primary languages ($\chi^2 = 48, p < 0.001$, Table 4). Users made significantly more deletions/reversions and maintenance edits in their primary languages compared to in their non-primary languages. On the other hand, users made significantly more image-related edits and added/removed significantly more interlanguage links in their non-primary languages compared to in their primary languages. The findings related to interlanguage links are no longer applicable to Wikipedia as these links are now maintained separately within WikiData. Nonetheless, it is noteworthy that the task of locating a related article and linking it across languages was motivating enough for some users to edit a foreign language edition.

The proportion of addition edits and change edits did not differ significantly between users' primary and non-primary languages. Overall, 15% of the edits made by Japanese users to the English edition concerned fixing incorrect romanizations of Japanese words and/or adding Japanese characters for terms. These types of language-specific edits that are easy for native speakers but harder for non-native speakers illustrate both the value of cross-language collaboration and also why these users may have been making edits of different types in their primary and non-primary languages.

Value of edits

As stated in the Data section, there are many ways in which users contribute value to Wikipedia, but a common, quantitative measure on which to compare the many different types of contributions is how much of each edit is retained through subsequent revisions to the article. Using the WikiTrust algorithms, the next six revisions after each edit were examined to compute how much of the edit was retained (persisted) through these revisions. Each edit was given a normalized score from -1 (edit completely removed) to 1 (edit completely retained). Comparing the mean edit persistent scores showed that the text from edits made by non-primary editors survived at a similar rate to the text from edits made by users who primarily edited each edition.[11]

DISCUSSION

The large differences in content observed between different editions of Wikipedia globally [18] also applied to articles related to Okinawa despite the presence of Japanese and English speakers living on the island. Similarly, the small percentage of users editing multiple editions of Wikipedia [16] applied to this dataset as well. In many ways, Okinawa is a hard case: Japanese and English use very different writing systems, and Japanese users have consistently been observed to engage less with other-language content not only on Wikipedia [16], but also on Twitter [15].

Nonetheless, this work has shed greater light on the selection of articles multilingual users in these two languages edit, the types of contributions they make, and the value of these edits. If further research confirms the patterns found in this paper apply more broadly, then one key challenge for designers of multilingual platforms seeking to facilitate cross-language information exchange is increasing multilingual users' awareness of and contributions to related other-language content. The multilingual users in this study were far less likely to edit articles in their non-primary languages that did not have corresponding articles in their primary languages despite these

[11]The average score for Japanese users editing the English edition (median 0.44, mean 0.38, sd 0.58) was higher but not significantly different from the average score for English users editing the English edition (median 0.47, mean 0.35, sd 0.64, $p = 0.46$). Similarly, the average score for English users editing the Japanese edition (median 0.45, mean 0.44, sd 0.53) was marginally higher but not significantly different from the average score for Japanese users editing the Japanese edition (median 0.37, mean 0.43, sd 0.50, $p = 0.72$).

articles being more numerous. The large difference in content between languages applies not only to the sample used for this study, but also overall on Wikipedia [18], on Twitter [19], and likely to most other user-generated content platforms. The challenge of making users aware of content available in their non-primary languages but not in their primarily languages is thus a challenge likely to be faced by designers of all multilingual user-generated content platforms.

Further research will be needed to understand the precise implications of design on user content selection, but it seems likely that the prominence of interlanguage links connecting related articles across languages on Wikipedia and the lack of other-language discovery tools are partially responsible for the narrow scope of multilingual users' edits in their non-primary languages. Currently, for example, there is no facility to search multiple language editions of Wikipedia simultaneously. So, if a user generally searches only in his primary language, that user may not discover the content that exists in another language if the content has no corresponding article in his primary language even if the user reads the other language. Very often the full text of articles in the Japanese edition includes an English translation of the article's concept, and likewise Japanese terms are often included in Japanese-themed articles in the English edition. If the search interface automatically checked a user's non-primary language editions when no matches were found in the user's primary language edition, that user might discover articles in his non-primary languages that have no article in his primary language.

Another possible design change would be to suggest articles related to a specific theme that exist in users' non-primary languages, but not in their primary languages. Such an approach could employ similar methods to those used here: gathering all articles linking to a given article and computing the PageRank scores or other methods like Latent Dirichlet Allocation (LDA) [17]. In practice, this might look very similar to the valuable SuggestBot [9] tool, which can recommend articles for users to edit based on the articles the users have previously edited in one language. Currently, separate versions of SuggestBot run independently in multiple languages, and a potentially useful (although certainly non-trivial) step would be to extend SuggestBot to offer suggestions across user-selected (or inferred) languages for users who desire such suggestions. That is, based on the articles a user has previously edited in one language, the user could ask for articles in another language that either need work or that have no equivalent in the user's primary language.

A small, but dedicated group of users, who made large-sized edits in their primary languages, also edited articles in a second language. The edits in the users' non-primary languages were smaller in size, but were equally valued by the site's users persisting through subsequent revisions at a similar rate to the edits made by users editing only one language edition. An exploratory analysis of the edits users made in their primary and non-primary languages indicated that the differences in edit sizes were partially due to users making different types of edits in their primary and non-primary languages—multilingual users more frequently edited images and interlanguage links in their non-primary languages. In contrast, they made more maintenance and deletion/reversion edits in their primary languages.

Even if the edits in users' non-primary languages are smaller and of a different type, they still have value. The qualitative exploration of edits revealed many examples of users updating out-of-date information and correcting errors in their non-primary languages. Japanese users also frequently added or corrected relevant Japanese-language text in the English edition. There were also edits of addition and, occasionally, translation into users' non-primary languages.

The Language Engineering team of the Wikimedia Foundation[12] has been actively developing an (open-source) content translation tool to help users translate content between different language editions of Wikipedia.[13] While the integration of machine translation and bilingual dictionaries, the automatic conversion of article links, and the streamlined user-interface of the translation tool will no doubt assist would-be translators, this research indicates that helping users find articles they want to translate will be a major hurdle. Multilingual users in this study clearly made their largest-sized contributions in their primary languages, suggesting that platforms might be more successful in encouraging translation from users' non-primary languages to their primary languages rather than from users' primary languages to their non-primary languages. This would require surfacing content in users' non-primary languages that does not exist in the users' primary languages even while the users are viewing content in their primary languages.

Beyond translation, there are a range of contributions users can make on multilingual user-generated content platforms that require a varying level of cross-language proficiency. Offline data on multilingualism is imperfect and incomplete, but best estimates suggest around half of all humans speak two or more languages [12]. Thus, it might be possible to encourage far more users to contribute content in multiple languages on user-generated content platforms. Survey work suggests that Internet users consume content in multiple languages more frequently than they contribute content in multiple languages (not only on Wikipedia,[14] but also more generally online [11]). The prevalence of image-related edits in this study and the apparent motivation images provide for cross-language linking in the blogosphere [14] suggest multimedia content is a low-barrier entry point for increasing multilingual contributions from users. Designers of multilingual user-generated content platforms wishing to increase multilingual activity could specifically consider and optimize cross-language multimedia content related tasks and other low-barrier entry points for multilingual contributions as one

[12] `https://wikimediafoundation.org/wiki/Language_Engineering_team`

[13] `https://www.mediawiki.org/wiki/Content_translation`

[14] `https://meta.wikimedia.org/w/index.php?title=Editor_Survey_2011/Location_%26_Language&oldid=8409990`

possible way to increase the number of users contributing in multiple languages on their sites.

Adler et al. [1, 2, 3] advocate combining together the measures of edit size and edit persistence to form a reputation score for each user, which their WikiTrust work uses to predict the quality or trustworthiness of users' contributions to Wikipedia. If such a system evaluated the contributions of multilingual users separately for each language, most multilingual users would have low reputation scores in their non-primary languages due to the smaller sizes and smaller number of their edits while they would have large reputation scores in their primary languages. The analysis in this paper, therefore, shows the importance of evaluating multilingual users holistically across their multiple languages to accurately measure their contributions to user-generated content sites.

Successfully combating the risk of fragmenting users and content too thinly across multiple languages on user-generated platforms requires a more advanced understanding of localization and internationalization than traditional principals such as translating interfaces to "speak the user's language(s)" [25]. Multilingual users need to be specifically considered in site design. This involves not only making existing cross-language connections visible, but also designing for the discovery of related foreign-language content not available in users' primary languages. The most active and dedicated users will reach across language boundaries online to contribute to other-language content, but the users in this study made their largest-sized contributions in their primary languages. Thus, successful multilingual user-generated content platforms need to nurture both active, dedicated monolingual communities and also encourage multilingual users to discover other-language content and serve as bridges between monolingual communities. Further research should analyze the extent to which multilingual search, cross-language content recommendation, and optimized low-barrier entry points for multilingual contribution can help multilingual users better understand the differences in content between languages, encourage these users to transfer more information between different languages, and thereby enable wider access for all users to the most interesting and important material that is not yet in their primary languages.

ACKNOWLEDGMENTS

I would like to thank Eric T. Meyer, Taha Yasseri, and Alolita Sharma as well as the anonymous reviewers who provided helpful comments on previous versions of this article.

REFERENCES

1. Adler, B. T., Chatterjee, K., de Alfaro, L., Faella, M., Pye, I., and Raman, V. Assigning trust to Wikipedia content. In *Proceedings of the 4th International Symposium on Wikis*, WikiSym '08, ACM (New York, NY, USA, 2008), 26:1–26:12.
2. Adler, B. T., and de Alfaro, L. A content-driven reputation system for the Wikipedia. In *Proceedings of the 16th International Conference on World Wide Web*, WWW '07, ACM (New York, NY, USA, 2007), 261–270.
3. Adler, B. T., de Alfaro, L., Pye, I., and Raman, V. Measuring author contributions to the Wikipedia. In *Proceedings of the 4th International Symposium on Wikis*, WikiSym '08, ACM (New York, NY, USA, 2008), 15:1–15:10.
4. Anthony, D., Smith, S. W., and Williamson, T. Reputation and reliability in collective goods: The case of the online encyclopedia Wikipedia. *Rationality and Society 21*, 3 (2009), 283–306.
5. Bao, P., Hecht, B., Carton, S., Quaderi, M., Horn, M., and Gergle, D. Omnipedia: Bridging the Wikipedia language gap. In *Proceedings of the SIGCHI Conference on Human Factors in Computing Systems*, CHI '12, ACM (New York, NY, USA, 2012), 1075–1084.
6. Bilic, P., and Bulian, L. Lost in translation: Contexts, computing, disputing on Wikipedia. In *iConference 2014 Proceedings*, M. Kindling and E. Greifender, Eds. iSchools, 2014, 32–44.
7. Burt, R. S. Structural holes and good ideas. *The American Journal of Sociology 110*, 2 (2004), 349–399.
8. Callahan, E. S., and Herring, S. C. Cultural bias in Wikipedia content on famous persons. *Journal of the American Society for Information Science and Technology 62*, 10 (2011), 1899–1915.
9. Cosley, D., Frankowski, D., Terveen, L., and Riedl, J. Suggestbot: Using intelligent task routing to help people find work in wikipedia. In *Proceedings of the 12th International Conference on Intelligent User Interfaces*, IUI '07, ACM (New York, NY, USA, 2007), 32–41.
10. Eleta, I., and Golbeck, J. Bridging languages in social networks: How multilingual users of Twitter connect language communities. *Proceedings of the American Society for Information Science and Technology 49*, 1 (2012), 1–4.
11. Eurobarometer. User language preferences online: Analytical report. Tech. rep., 2011. Survey conducted by The Gallup Organization, Hungary upon the request of Directorate-General Information Society and Media, European Commission.
12. Grosjean, F. *Bilingual: Life and Reality*. Harvard University Press, 2010.
13. Hale, S. A. Impact of platform design on cross-language information exchange. In *Proceedings of the 2012 ACM Annual Conference on Human Factors in Computing Systems Extended Abstracts*, CHI EA '12, ACM (New York, NY, USA, 2012), 1363–1368.
14. Hale, S. A. Net increase? Cross-lingual linking in the blogosphere. *Journal of Computer-Mediated Communication 17*, 2 (2012), 135–151.

15. Hale, S. A. Global connectivity and multilinguals in the Twitter network. In *Proceedings of the SIGCHI Conference on Human Factors in Computing Systems*, CHI '14, ACM (New York, NY, USA, 2014), 833–842.
16. Hale, S. A. Multilinguals and Wikipedia editing. In *Proceedings of the 6th Annual ACM Web Science Conference*, WebSci'14, ACM (New York, NY, USA, 2014).
17. Haruechaiyasak, C., and Damrongrat, C. Article recommendation based on a topic model for Wikipedia selection for schools. In *Digital Libraries: Universal and Ubiquitous Access to Information*, G. Buchanan, M. Masoodian, and S. Cunningham, Eds., vol. 5362 of *Lecture Notes in Computer Science*. Springer Berlin Heidelberg, 2008, 339–342.
18. Hecht, B., and Gergle, D. The Tower of Babel meets Web 2.0: User-generated content and its applications in a multilingual context. In *Proceedings of the 28th International Conference on Human Factors in Computing Systems*, CHI '10, ACM (New York, NY, USA, 2010), 291–300.
19. Hong, L., Convertino, G., and Chi, E. Language matters in Twitter: A large scale study. In *International AAAI Conference on Weblogs and Social Media* (2011), 518–521.
20. Kim, S., Weber, I., Wei, L., and Oh, A. Sociolinguistic analysis of Twitter in multilingual societies. In *Proceedings of the 25th ACM Conference on Hypertext and Social Media*, HT '14, ACM (New York, NY, USA, 2014), 243–248.
21. Kittur, A., Chi, E., Pendleton, B. A., Suh, B., and Mytkowicz, T. Power of the few vs. wisdom of the crowd: Wikipedia and the rise of the bourgeoisie. Presented at alt.CHI, ACM SIGCHI Conference, San Jose, CA, USA, 2007.
22. Kriplean, T., Beschastnikh, I., and McDonald, D. W. Articulations of wikiwork: Uncovering valued work in Wikipedia through barnstars. In *Proceedings of the 2008 ACM Conference on Computer Supported Cooperative Work*, CSCW '08, ACM (New York, NY, USA, 2008), 47–56.
23. Milne, D., and Witten, I. H. An effective, low-cost measure of semantic relatedness obtained from Wikipedia links. In *In Proceedings of the AAAI 2008 Workshop on Wikipedia and Artificial Intelligence*, WIKIAI 2008, AAAI (Chicago, IL, USA, 2008).
24. Ministry of Foreign Affairs of Japan. 米軍人等の施設・区域内外居住者の人数について(全国)(平成20年3月31日時点) (Information on the number of people living on and off US military related facilities [Nationwide][March 31, 2008]). `http://www.mofa.go.jp/mofaj/press/release/h20/6/1181033_910.html`, 2008.
25. Nielsen, J. *Usability Engineering*. Academic Press, 1993.
26. Okinawa Prefecture. 沖縄の米軍基地及び自衛隊基地（統計資料集） (US military bases and Japan Self-Defense Force bases in Okinawa [Compiled statistics]). `http://www.pref.okinawa.jp/site/chijiko/kichitai/toukeisiryousyu2503.html`, 2013.
27. Page, L., Brin, S., Motwani, R., and Winograd, T. The pagerank citation ranking: Bringing order to the web. Technical Report 1999-66, Stanford InfoLab, Nov. 1999.
28. Pfeil, U., Zaphiris, P., and Ang, C. S. Cultural differences in collaborative authoring of Wikipedia. *Journal of Computer-Mediated Communication 12*, 1 (2006), 88–113.
29. Priedhorsky, R., Chen, J., Lam, S. T. K., Panciera, K., Terveen, L., and Riedl, J. Creating, destroying, and restoring value in Wikipedia. In *Proceedings of the 2007 International ACM Conference on Supporting Group Work*, GROUP '07, ACM (New York, NY, USA, 2007), 259–268.
30. Welser, H. T., Cosley, D., Kossinets, G., Lin, A., Dokshin, F., Gay, G., and Smith, M. Finding social roles in Wikipedia. In *Proceedings of the 2011 iConference*, iConference '11, ACM (New York, NY, USA, 2011), 122–129.
31. Zuckerman, E. *Rewire: Digital Cosmopolitans in the Age of Connection*. W. W. Norton & Company, London, 2013.

Societal Controversies in Wikipedia Articles

Erik Borra†,1 Esther Weltevrede† Paolo Ciuccarelli‡
Andreas Kaltenbrunner§ David Laniado§ Giovanni Magni‡
Michele Mauri‡ Richard Rogers† Tommaso Venturini¶
†UvA Amsterdam, NL ‡Politecnico di Milano, Italy §Barcelona Media, Spain ¶Sciences Politiques, France

ABSTRACT

Collaborative content creation inevitably reaches situations where different points of view lead to conflict. We focus on Wikipedia, the free encyclopedia anyone may edit, where disputes about content in controversial articles often reflect larger societal debates. While Wikipedia has a public edit history and discussion section for every article, the substance of these sections is difficult to phantom for Wikipedia users interested in the development of an article and in locating which topics were most controversial. In this paper we present Contropedia, a tool that augments Wikipedia articles and gives insight into the development of controversial topics. Contropedia uses an efficient language agnostic measure based on the edit history that focuses on wiki links to easily identify which topics within a Wikipedia article have been most controversial and when.

Author Keywords
Wikipedia; Controversy Mapping; Social Science; Data Visualization

ACM Classification Keywords
H.5.3 [Group and Organization Interfaces]: Computer-supported cooperative work; D.2.2 [Design Tools and Techniques]: User interfaces

INTRODUCTION

Since its first article in 2001 the English Wikipedia has expanded to more than 4.5 million articles. In addition to covering a growing number of socially relevant topics, Wikipedia is increasingly becoming a rich historical source logging the development of societal controversies over time in its publically available history pages. Reference works, like Wikipedia, "often inherit the conflicts of the external world they seek to document and are being seized upon as exemplars of, and proxies in, those debates" [12].[2]

While the built-in edit history and the talk pages of a Wikipedia article provide a detailed record of present and past changes to the content of articles and the unfolding of discussions, the public usually ignores these pages, as they are too complex to be understood by casual readers and editors of Wikipedia articles. For social researchers—one of the target groups of Contropedia—too, it often remains unclear what has provoked most edit activity and discussion, when and why. In this paper we show how the edit history of an article may be repurposed to map out the specific matters of concern in controversies, as well as the extent to which something is controversial within an article.

The aim of Contropedia is to extract and re-present the information in these pages so that it becomes clear which topics within a page have sparked controversy and why. First, we formulate an easy way to find which topics within an article are disputed most; and second, we provide two visual ways in which the dispute can be analyzed: via an overlay which indicates which topics within a page are most controversial (and why), as well as by a dashboard which ranks the topics by controversialness and shows how the controversy around various topics develops over time.

ALGORITHM

Pre-processing

We retrieve the full edit history for a controversial article, including the wiki text of each revision and the meta data conveying at what time it was edited, who the editor was, as well as the editor's comment (edit summary). Whenever a user makes multiple consecutive edits, we only retain the last version made by the user and discard all intermediate edits. As we are looking for substantive disagreements, we discard vandalism edits and their reverts by identifying whether the comment of a revert contains the word 'vandal', whether the user name making the revert belongs to one of the known anti-vandalism bots, when an IP-edit is reverted within 60 seconds, or when the automatic edit summary (WP:AES)[3] indicates that the content of a page was blanked or replaced by unrelated text such as curse words.

Associating Wiki Links to Edits

We make use of Wikipedia's MediaWiki markup to identify the most relevant elements in an article. In this paper we focus on wiki links, as they identify the key concepts and

CHI 2015, April 18–23, 2015, Seoul, Republic of Korea.

ACM 978-1-4503-3145-6/15/04…$15.00.
http://dx.doi.org/10.1145/2702123.2702436

[1] Corresponding author, borra@uva.nl

[2] 'Wikipedia's list of controversial articles' furthermore mentions that disputed articles, where opinions on a given issue differ, often reflect "the debates of society as a whole". See http://bit.ly/1Fg2pO2

[3] See http://bit.ly/1ujpTIq

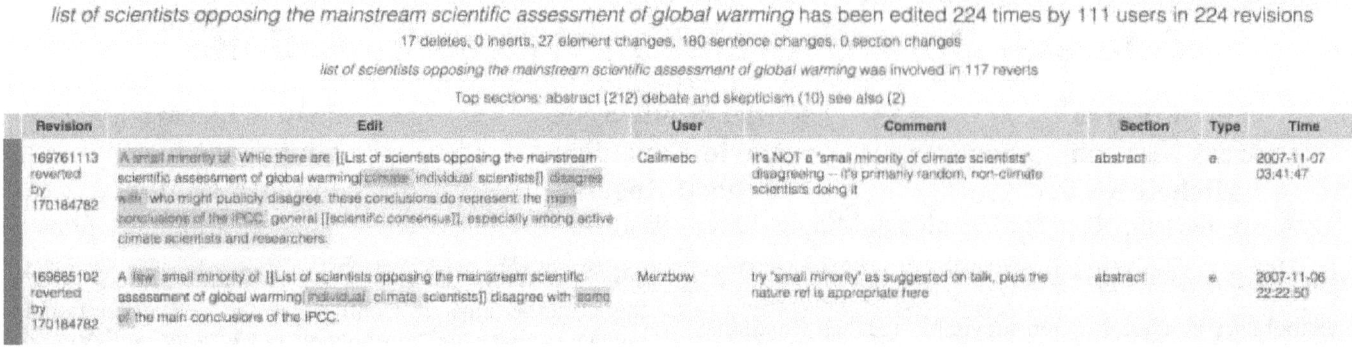

Figure 1: Partial substantive edit history. The red color under the 'Edit' section indicates a deletion and green an insertion of text, with respect to the previous revision. The first (upper) edit involves two links (indicated by double brackets), the second only one.

entities of an article [1, 3, 6]; they are the lenses through which we can look at the substance and activity of controversies within a Wikipedia article. Our approach seeks to associate edits to wiki links by taking the sentences in which these links reside as our basic unit of analysis.

Let $\{R_1, \ldots, R_{r-1}, R_r, R_{r+1}, \ldots\}$ be the set of revisions of a Wikipedia article. As we are specifically interested in disputes related to a wiki link, we consider the edit activity on a sentence level by comparing every revision R_{r-1} with its successor R_r. We split each revision into sections and then pairwise compare corresponding sections of R_{r-1} with those of R_r. If the text of the sections differs, we use a diff algorithm to identify the edited sentences, the exact changes made to them, and the wiki links they contain.

To further assure that edits to sentences containing wiki links convey disagreement, we discard edits where only insertions are made. We also discard full section inserts or deletes (as these are mostly due to renaming of sections). We thus only consider edits that are substantive: the revision is not marked as vandalism; and that show disagreement: the changes should (also) contain a deletion.

Controversy Score

We are interested in finding out how controversial a wiki link W_k is and compare the substantive, disagreeing, edit activity of sentences in which W_k appears. Intuitively, the more wiki links appear in an edited sentence, the less focus there is on one particular wiki link. For every sentence S_j with a substantive disagreeing edit, the weight attributed to a wiki link is thus divided by the total number of wiki links $w(S_j)$ that appear in that sentence.

A controversy score $c(W_k)$ is assigned to every wiki link W_k that appears in a sentence S_j with a substantive, disagreeing edit, of a revision R_i (up to a given revision R_r) as follows:

$$c(W_k) = \sum_{i=1}^{r} \sum_{S_j \in R_i} \frac{1}{w(S_j)} \quad (1)$$

In other words: the number of sentences with substantive, disagreeing, edits that include W_k are summed over all revisions up to R_r. In those revisions where the wiki link W_k appears in an edited sentence with other wiki links, the summand is divided by the number $w(S_j)$ of links involved. A wiki link thus accumulates controversialness through counting and weighting the substantive, disagreeing, edits to the sentences in which it resides.

As an example, consider Figure 1 where two substantive disagreeing edits are shown. The first sentence contains two wiki links[4] ('List of scientists opposing the mainstream scientific assessment of global warming', and 'scientific consensus'), and the second only one ('List of scientists opposing the mainstream scientific assessment of global warming'). If we just take these two edits into account, the first link would get a controversy score of 1.5 (0.5 in the first edit and 1 in the second) and the second link would get a controversy score of 0.5.

To find out which wiki links are most controversial, i.e. around which wiki links most dispute took place, we simply rank the wiki links of the article by their overall controversy score.

INTERFACE

To convey which topics attracted most dispute, two main views have been designed.

Indicating Disputed Content

In the *layer view* the original Wikipedia article layout is reworked and annotated to show which wiki links are controversial and in which part of the article they can be found (Figure 2). A visual contrast has been created among controversial and non-controversial elements. Controversial elements are represented through five color shades, from the most controversial (red) to the least one (pale blue). In the layer view, the assignment of those colors follows a logarithmic scale and the images are converted to grayscale

[4] In MediaWiki links are written as [[anchor | anchor text]], i.e. [[link to article | optional name of link in text]].

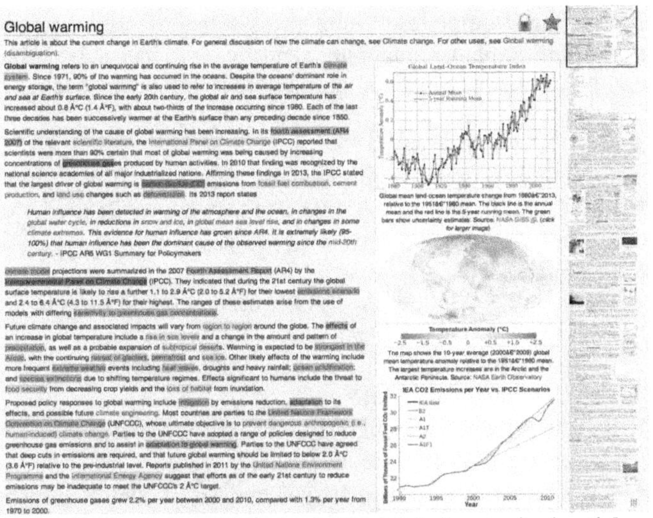

Figure 2: Controversial topics in the 'global warming' article.

to put focus on the controversial elements. On the right-hand side a minified version of the full page is shown so that users can quickly identify which parts of the page contain most controversial wiki links.

When clicking on the highlighted controversial wiki links within an article, a list of edits involving, or with debate about, that wiki link unfolds (see Figure 1). This edit table adopts a classic diff visualization that shows the changed and deleted parts with color-coding. It also shows several other relevant variables like the id of the revision in which the edit was made, the name of the editor, the edit summary, the section in which the edit was made, and the timestamp of the edit.

Since the displayed edits only show the sentences in which the wiki link resides, in contrast with the display of all edits in a revision – as offered by the original Wikipedia interface, this function allows the user to zoom in on a particular wiki link to analyze its controversial history. The edit table thus allows the user to further scrutinize the construction of controversial topics in an article and to gain an understanding of what precisely has been disputed about that wiki link as well as which positions were taken.

Ranking Disputed Topics

The second view, which we call the *controversy dashboard* (see Figure 3), is designed to provide a more analytical view on the data. The dashboard consists of a table listing all the controversial elements, ranked from the most controversial to the least one. Note that the list can also include elements that were removed from the article (e.g. in the article on 'Abortion' the highly controversial wiki link 'death' was removed in 2011). Such elements are struck through (see Figure 3).

Similar to the layer view, the bar on the left represents how controversial a wiki link is through its associated color. A timeline shows the amount of all edits through time, allowing the user to identify historical periods where

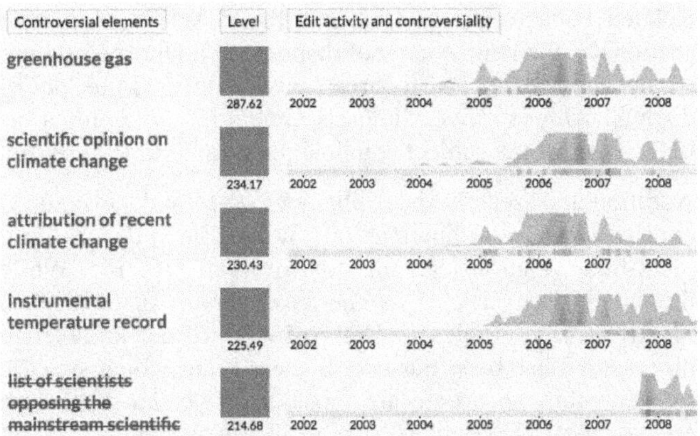

Figure 3: Detail of dashboard view of the most controversial wiki links in the 'global warming' article on 1 August 2014.

several edits affected the same element. When the timeline is clicked, the edit table shows the edits associated to that wiki link (see Figure 1). Underneath the timeline one may find a colored bar indicating at what point in time most controversial edits were made. The higher the share of substantive disagreeing edits made to the wiki link in a particular month, the redder the color for that month. This allows one to quickly locate when the link was disputed most. The same colors are used as in the layer view and the overall ranking of the wiki links; grey is added to indicate the absence of controversial edits.

Both views are accessible via a menu where one can choose an article and the time frame of the analysis. One can thus explore what was more controversial in a given article in, say, 2007. Or what has become controversial since then. It allows one to further study the trajectory of which wiki links were controversial at which time, i.e. at what point a topic was still 'hot' or whether its controversialness has 'cooled down' over time.

When an article is created and news is still uncertain, there may be disputes about what is happening and articles may contain many controversial topics early in their life cycle. That does not mean that those disputes cannot get resolved or that others cannot emerge, as the article on the 'Fukushima Daiichi nuclear disaster' exemplifies. Whereas at its start the main disputes revolved around the accuracy of radioactive measurements and the comparison with the Chernobyl disaster, two years later the disputes concern health effects. By aggregating edit discussions around wiki links our approach thus allows both timely and core controversies to surface.

RELATED WORK

Conflicts in Wikipedia have previously been studied by observing article edit histories [5], by considering reverts [4, 13], by analyzing talk pages [7, 9], or a combination of the aforementioned [14]. Most of these studies were primarily focused on the social dynamics between editors and only few quantitative approaches have taken into account what the controversy is about, as we do.

Related controversy research has found Wikipedia article sections as the main source of dispute [11]. Our method has a finer granularity and focuses on wiki links as the loci of dispute. Others have similarly regarded wiki links as indications of the subject composition of an article [1, 3, 6].

Additional research has characterized and visualized conflict and coordination on Wikipedia [10, 8] and identified which articles are controversial [16, 17]. While the latter uses articles as the basic units of content to identify which articles are controversial, to our knowledge no research has been pursued in identifying which specific topics within an article are most controversial. Although Viégas et al. [15] and Adler et al. [2] show which content remains stable within an article, we are interested in the opposite: which content has been contested the most?

CONCLUSION AND DISCUSSION

Recognizing the potential of Wikipedia's edit histories for providing insight into societal controversies, and recognizing that each link within an article can be seen as a focal point for debate, has allowed us to use Wikipedia articles as interesting sites to map controversies. Wiki links identify the main topics in an article and in this paper we have shown how they may be assigned controversy scores by associating wiki links to substantive, disagreeing, edits and then weighting and counting them. We also introduced a tool with two views that are intended to get a quick overview of what is, or was, controversial in an article, why, where, when and to what extent.

The design, and accompanying open-source demo[5], furthermore allow the users of our tool, Contropedia, to zoom into the specific changes around wiki links in the unfolding debate. During case studies, various social researchers found it an invaluable tool to visualize the dynamics of techno-scientific and other societal debates as they unfold on Wikipedia, displaying the framing and phrasing of issues, and helping to clarify conflicts about the content of an article[6]. We think this software may prove useful for Wikipedians as well, as it allows them to gain insight into the substance and build-up of controversies, and allows them to make informed decisions when managing edit wars and disagreements about the articles' content.

We are further developing the tool presented here as part of an elaborate toolkit to study social life on Wikipedia. We are currently associating discussion threads with wiki links to provide further detail about conflict surrounding wiki links. We are also experimenting with calculating the controversy scores using only the parts of sentences involved in substantial edits (instead of using entire sentences). Furthermore, we intend to use other focal points for measuring dispute such as external links, references, figures, and templates. Using these types of elements our algorithm remains language agnostic and has substantial computational savings compared to text-based approaches.

[5] http://www.contropedia.net

[6] See http://contropedia.net/#case-studies

ACKNOWLEDGEMENTS

This research was supported by EU FP7 EINS grant #288021 and in part by EU FP7 EMAPS grant #288964.

REFERENCES

1. S. Adafre & M. de Rijke. Discovering missing links in Wikipedia. In *Proc. LinkDD*, 2005.
2. B. Adler et al. Assigning trust to Wikipedia content. In *Proc. WikiSym*, 2008.
3. Bao, P. et al. Omnipedia: Bridging the Wikipedia Language Gap. In *Proc. CHI,* 2012.
4. U. Brandes & J. Lerner. Visual analysis of controversy in user-generated encyclopedias. *Information Visualization*, 7(1):34–48. 2008.
5. M. Ekstrand & J. Riedl. rv you're dumb: identifying discarded work in wiki article history. In *Proc. WikiSym*, 2009.
6. B. Hecht & D. Gergle. Measuring self-focus bias in community-maintained knowledge repositories. In *Proc. C&T*, 2009.
7. A. Kaltenbrunner & D. Laniado. There is No Deadline-Time Evolution of Wikipedia Discussions. In *Proc. WikiSym*, 2012.
8. A. Kittur, B. Suh, B. Pendleton & E. Chi. He says, she says: conflict and coordination in Wikipedia. In *Proc. SIGCHI*, 2007.
9. D. Laniado et al. When the Wikipedians talk: network and tree structure of Wikipedia discussion pages. In *Proc. ICWSM*, 2011.
10. C. Li, A. Datta & A. Sun. Mining latent relations in peer-production environments: a case study with Wikipedia article similarity and controversy. *Social Network Analysis and Mining*, 2(3):265–278, 2012.
11. H. Rad & D. Barbosa. Identifying controversial articles in Wikipedia: A comparative study. In *Proc. Wikisym*, 2012.
12. J. Reagle. The Argument Engine, In *Critical point of view: A Wikipedia Reader*. G. Lovink and N. Tkacz (eds). INC Amsterdam, 2011.
13. B. Suh et al. Us vs. them: Understanding social dynamics in Wikipedia with revert graph visualizations. In *Proc. VAST*, 2007.
14. R. Sumi et al. Edit wars in Wikipedia. In *Proc. PASSAT*, 2011.
15. F. Viégas, M. Wattenberg & K. Dave. Studying cooperation and conflict between authors with history flow visualizations. In *Proc. SIGCHI*, 2004.
16. B. Vuong et al. On ranking controversies in Wikipedia: models and evaluation. In *Proc. WSDM*, 2008.
17. T. Yasseri et al. Dynamics of conflicts in Wikipedia. *PloS one*, 7(6):e38869, 2012.

Barriers to the Localness of Volunteered Geographic Information

Shilad W. Sen
Macalester College
St. Paul, MN, USA
ssen@macalester.edu

Heather Ford
Oxford University
Oxford, UK
heather.ford@oii.ox.ac.uk

David R. Musicant
Carleton College
Northfield, MN, USA
dmusican@carleton.edu

Mark Graham
Oxford University
Oxford, UK
mark.graham@oii.ox.ac.uk

Oliver S. B. Keyes
Wikimedia Foundation
San Francisco, CA, USA
okeyes@wikimedia.org

Brent Hecht
University of Minnesota
Minneapolis, MN, USA
bhecht@cs.umn.edu

ABSTRACT
Localness is an oft-cited benefit of volunteered geographic information (VGI). This study examines whether localness is a constant, universally shared benefit of VGI, or one that varies depending on the context in which it is produced. Focusing on articles about geographic entities (e.g. cities, points of interest) in 79 language editions of Wikipedia, we examine the localness of both the editors working on articles and the sources of the information they cite. We find extensive geographic inequalities in localness, with the degree of localness varying with the socioeconomic status of the local population and the health of the local media. We also point out the key role of language, showing that information in languages not native to a place tends to be produced and sourced by non-locals. We discuss the implications of this work for our understanding of the nature of VGI and highlight a generalizable technical contribution: an algorithm that determines the home country of the original publisher of online content.

INTRODUCTION
Over the past decade, *volunteered geographic information* (VGI) has transformed our relationship with the physical world. VGI datasets such as geotagged tweets, Wikipedia articles about places, and eBird observations have opened up novel avenues of research and enabled whole new classes of applications. Much of the promise of VGI has been thought to lie in its ability to engage local content producers. For instance, well-known geographer Michael Goodchild states that VGI "is putting mapping where it should be, which is the hands of local people who know an area well" [18].

The literature on VGI thus far has largely provided support for the optimism surrounding VGI and localness. In particular, research has established an association between the home locations of VGI contributors and the locations about which they create information. For instance, research has shown that Wikipedia editors tend to edit articles about places close to them [14, 16], a large proportion of Flickr photos are taken nearby photographers' homes [6], and Twitter users tend to tweet about locations near them (e.g. [4]). Many researchers see the shift in authorship from paid experts to volunteers — often described as public-participation geographic information science (PPGIS) [25] — as a way to increase local geographic information production, especially among disadvantaged populations.

This localness of VGI has implications well beyond the large group of researchers who use and study VGI. To the extent that locals see their community differently, (non-)local-ness can lead to systemic differences in how people experience and learn about places online. A search for a place name on any large search engine will prominently feature Wikipedia content, user-contributed photos, TripAdvisor reviews, and social media posts. VGI also shapes our physical experiences of places. As some have argued [11, 19], VGI does not just represent the world, but also becomes part of the world. It forms layers of code and information that augment everyday activities: it shapes where we go, what we do, and how we perceive and understand the world that we live in.

This paper is the first to study whether the localness of VGI is a *universal* property. Although research has shown that VGI has a strong overall local component at the repository level, little is known about the *geographic variation in this localness.* Is VGI about certain parts of the world more local than other parts? If so, are there patterns in where VGI is more and less local? Like much of the work on VGI localness (e.g. [14, 16]), we focus on Wikipedia, but we examine 79 different language editions of the encyclopedia. These language editions range from large encyclopedias written in global languages (e.g. English, French) to smaller encyclopedias written in regional languages from around the world (e.g. Latvian, Korean, and Georgian).

We consider localness to be a special case of what we call *geoprovenance*, or the geographic origin of information. Unlike previous research in this area, we consider

CHI 2015, April 18–23, 2015, Seoul, Republic of Korea.

ACM 978-1-4503-3145-6/15/04 ...$15.00.
http://dx.doi.org/10.1145/2702123.2702170

two types of geoprovenance, each of which provides a unique lens on the localness of VGI. *Editor geoprovenance* considers the relationship between the locations of Wikipedia editors and the geographic articles they edit (e.g. "What countries do edits to articles about Iran comes from?"). *Source geoprovenance*, on the other hand, focuses on the *citations* added to Wikipedia articles. It considers the relationship between the location of cited *sources* and the geographic articles the sources describe (e.g. "What countries publish the sources cited in articles about Iran?"). Each source is produced by individuals, organisations and groups based in particular geographic regions and selected by Wikipedia editors to support informational claims in articles. Sources can therefore serve as an important signal about where (geographically) Wikipedia information comes from. To investigate source geoprovenance, we developed a novel algorithm that determines the country of the original publisher of online content with 91% accuracy.

Our analyses reveal extensive inequalities in the localness of Wikipedia VGI around the world. Through visualizations and statistical models we show that these inequalities tend to increase the local perspective in Wikipedia pages about areas with higher socioeconomic status (SES). We also find a powerful role of language in localness, a factor not been carefully considered thus far. More specifically, our findings suggest that if you read about a place in a language that is not commonly spoken in that place, you are unlikely to be reading locally-produced VGI or even VGI that references local sources.

We provide four major contributions: (1) The first global analysis of the variation in the localness of VGI. (2) We find that language can serve as an almost complete barrier to local VGI editors. (3) We find that the degree of a country's source localness primarily reflects the strength of its scholarly media networks. (4) An algorithm that identifies the home country of the original publisher of content posted on the web with 91% accuracy.

Our findings point to the existence of disconnected "VGI bubbles" that conform to language and socio-economic barriers, and suggest that VGI systems need new tools to reveal and overcome these barriers. In addition, our findings provide an empirical foundation to probe the "local = good" assumption present in the vast majority of the VGI literature. To disseminate our results and support future research, we have built a public website that visualizes the geoprovenance of information in 79 language editions of Wikipedia and released the datasets and source code for algorithms described in this paper.[1]

RELATED WORK

In addition to the work mentioned earlier that studies VGI localness at the repository level, this paper draws from research in two additional areas: research on Wikipedia citations and content biases in VGI. We address each of these in turn below.

[1]http://www.shilad.com/localness

Authors such as Luyt and Tan [21] have looked to Wikipedia's sources as a way of understanding from whose point of view and according to which principles and values it is written. They found that Wikipedia history articles are supported by few citations comprised predominantly of US government and online media news sites. Ford et al. [7] examined 500 random citations from the English Wikipedia and found that 80% of publishers of cited source material are located in a country whose primary language is English. This study extends this work beyond the English Wikipedia, considering more citations and leveraging two geoprovenance lenses.

This research builds on work related to geographic content biases in VGI. Research has established that VGI datasets tend to have substantial biases in terms of information quantity, with some areas of the world being covered much better than others. In early research on the subject, Hecht and Gergle [15] found that most language editions of Wikipedia exhibit substantial *self-focus bias*, with more content about places where the language is spoken. Graham et al. [8] found exceptions to this general rule, with some editors creating content far away from their local areas. Neis et al. [24] made a related observation in OpenStreetMap, finding that content coverage decreased with distance from city centers in Germany. Geographic content biases have also been found in Twitter (e.g. [23, 17]), Flickr (e.g. [20, 17]), Foursquare (e.g. [17]), and geographic content on the Web more generally (e.g. [10]).

More recently, researchers have sought a more detailed understanding of the factors that are associated with increased and decreased VGI coverage. For instance, Graham et al. [9] have identified broadband Internet connectivity as "necessary, but not a sufficient" condition for high VGI coverage in Wikipedia. Li et al. [20] found that places where "well-educated people in the occupations of management, business, science, and arts" live are associated with more tweets and geotagged Flickr photos. Other researchers have identified that there is more VGI per capita in urban areas than rural areas [17], and that the accuracy of different types of VGI contributions varies with a country's socioeconomic status [12].

This paper is distinguished from work on geographic content biases in that it does not look at variation in the *quantity* of VGI content around the world, but rather is the first to look at variation in the *localness* and the *geoprovenance* more generally of that content.

EDITOR PROVENANCE DATASET

We study geoprovenance on Wikipedia through two geographic lenses: the editors who create article content and the source publishers who inform article content. This section describes the editor geography dataset.

We extracted all edits to geotagged articles[2] across all Wikipedia language editions between June 6th and

[2]Editors geotag an article by inserting special text specifying an article's latitude and longitude.

lang	geotagged articles	geolocated edits	URLs
EN	937,315	2,357,561	8,228,596
DE	328,625	656,206	2,757,402
FR	299,544	685,920	2,271,618
		36 more langs	76 more langs
total	4,408,100	5,355,530	31,810,797

Table 1: Basic statistics describing the editor and source datasets. Due to anonymization, the editor dataset covers fewer languages.

September 4th 2014. Our data included both anonymous and registered users, but excluded actions by bots. Editors' IP addresses were geolocated to countries using the MaxMind GeoIP database, a technique that has been shown to be 96% to 98% accurate at the country level [27]. Edits that could not be resolved to a valid nation were excluded.

Because a Wikipedia editor's IP address is considered private information, we did not access the raw geolocated edits. Instead, we analyzed an anonymized version of the dataset that aggregated the number of edits for each combination of Wikipedia language edition, article country, and editor country. For example, it indicated that in the Arabic Wikipedia, editors in South Africa contributed 20 edits to all articles about locations in Algeria. To avoid the possibility that even the aggregated dataset would not be anonymous, two anonymity filters were imposed. First, any combination of language edition and article country that did not contain at least 20 distinct articles was removed. Second, any language edition with fewer than 500 distinct articles after filtering was removed. This privacy filtering may introduce some bias in that it cuts out less active language editions and articles. Although our analyses control for language edition as a specific variable, our findings should be interpreted with this limitation in mind.

The final anonymized dataset contained 5M edits from 39 language editions (Table 1). English Wikipedia had the most geolocated edits (937K) followed by German Wikipedia (328K) and French Wikipedia (299k).

SOURCE PROVENANCE DATASET

In addition to editor location, we study geoprovenance as defined by the country of source publishers cited in Wikipedia. Since each language edition uses its own citation syntax (English has dozens of different templates), we took a language-neutral approach that extracts all URLs embedded within articles. Although this choice allows us to compare all language editions, it excludes the roughly 25% of citations without a URL[7].

Table 1 shows background statistics for the languages with the most URL citations. In total, we extracted 31,810,797 URLs from the 79 language editions of Wikipedia with geotagged articles. Because the same URL can appear in multiple articles, these 31M urls represented 9,404,072 distinct URLs. Of the 9,404,072 distinct URLs, 19.9% failed to return web content in some way (e.g. host not found, HTTP 404, etc). This paper analyzes the 7,528,431 successfully crawled URLs.

We created a novel geo-location algorithm that inferred the country of source publisher for each URL. Algorithms exist to geo-locate a specific IP address [27], and identify the geographic topics of a webpage [2]. In addition some previous algorithms used IP and country code top-level domains (CC TLDs) to identify source publisher country [22]. However, ours is the first geolocation algorithm that uses multiple signals to triangulate a web-page's source publisher, enabling it to achieve 91% precision and approach the agreement levels of human coders. The sections that follow define what we mean by "source publisher", describe the human-coded gold standard we collected, list the data sources used by the algorithm, and evaluate the algorithm's effectiveness.

Data coding procedure

To ensure that we created an accurate source provenance dataset we performed human coding to associate 198 randomly chosen URLs with their source publisher country. One member of the team first performed open coding of 90 randomly sampled citations from English Wikipedia to draft a codebook for the location of the publisher of each URL. For publications hosted on third party sites (such as the Wayback machine or a book hosted on Google Books), we looked up the location of the original publisher; for machine translated works we used the original publisher; for human-translated works, we used the translator because of their ability to shape the final source; for Google map citations, we used the copyright information provided at the resolution of the URL in order to look up copyright holder locations in addition to Google. An additional member of the team then used the codebook (which contained no specific examples) to code all 90 examples. Agreeement on these examples was 95%.[3] Both team members then coded 50 URLs chosen across all 79 language editions to ensure the coding applied robustly to non-English Wikipedias, achieving an agreement of 93%. Finally, the team indepedently coded an additional 75 non-English citations, resulting in 90 citations from English Wikipedia, and 125 citations from other languages. 17 of these URLs were no longer available (e.g. dead links) and removed from the dataset, leaving 198 URLs for evaluation purposes.

URL geolocation features

We used four signals to discern a URL's publisher.

Whois records: We obtained the WHOIS record that provides registration information associated with each URL in order to extract the country within them. WHOIS records are maintained by regional internet registries, and are publicly accessible. To gather these records we extracted the top-level "private" domain (TLPDs) for each URL. In total, we identified 1,015,733 distinct TLPDs and retrieved WHOIS records for all TLPDs. We constructed a hand-coded parser that identified administrative contacts in whois records using key

[3] We use simple agreement because, given the 200+ possible codings (i.e. countries), a statistic such as kappa would be extremely high and difficult to interpret.

	overall-share	webpage-language	milgov	whois-structured	whois-freetext	cc-tld	wikidata	baseline	logistic-regression
coverage	100%	96%	8%	40%	16%	49%	19%	100%	100%
accuracy	30%	61%	100%	81%	77%	98%	93%	78%	91%

Table 2: Accuracy and coverage of our web page geolocation algorithm, its component features, and a baseline algorithm.

terms (e.g. the text "admin" and "country").We refer to this data feature as **whois-structured**. When records could not be parsed using the "structured" approach, feature **whois-freetext** extracted country references from anywhere in the free-text WOHIS record.[4]

Web page languages: We detected the language of each of the 7.5M URLs using Python's langid module,[5] which detects 97 different languages with high precision. Each language was mapped to countries weighted by the number of primary and second- language speakers of the language. Our estimates for language speakers is described in the later statistical analysis of localness.

CC TLDs: For all applicable URLs, we extract the country associated with the URL's CC TLD (e.g. Russia for ".ru"). We ignore "generic" TLDs (e.g. ".com" and ".net") and CC TLDs used for their mnemonic characteristics (e.g. ".tv").[6]

Wikidata country: Wikimedia's Wikidata project is a human maintained repository of structured information about entities [29]. We identified all entities in Wikidata that contained an "official URL" and spatial coordinates (about 22K entities covering 95K URLs).

URL geolocation algorithm

We created a machine-learning classifier to infer the location of every URL resource. Country inference is a multiclass machine learning problem (one class per country). However, because training data is unavailable for many countries, we trained a country-agnostic binary classifier. The classifier was invoked for a specific url and country, and returned a single probability indicating whether a URL was published by that country. Given a URL, by repeatedly calling the classifier for all countries, we can infer a probability distribution over countries and, if desired, identify the most likely source country.

The classifier included the five previously described variables: whois-structured, whois-freetext, webpage-language, cc-tld, and wikidata. We also included two other features: overall-share, the fraction of all URLs associated with each country, and milgov, a feature that infers the United States for ".mil" and ".gov" TLDs. Each of these features is specific to a country and url. For example, webpage-language(whitehouse.gov, us) = 0.25,[7] milgov(whitehouse.gov, us) = 1, and milgov(whitehouse.org, ru) = 0. We used a logistic regression classifier to integrate individual features because of its simplicity and transparency.

[4]Names and codes from `http://download.geonames.org`

[5]`https://github.com/saffsd/langid.py`

[6]`https://support.google.com/webmasters/answer/1347922`

[7] The US represents roughly 25% of all people who have at least second-language proficiency in English.

Using the human-coded dataset of 198 URLs described above, we evaluated the accuracy of our geolocation algorithm, each individual geolocation feature, and a baseline algorithm that used the CC TLD if available and predicted US for everything else.

Table 2 shows the accuracy and coverage results. While a language was inferred for almost all webpages (96%), the accuracy of language in predicting publisher country was relatively low (61%) due to the ambiguity of mapping a language to a country (e.g. Spanish is spoken in many countries). Several features (cc-tld, milgov and wikidata) didn't apply to the majority of cases (49%, 8% and 19% coverage respectively), but had near perfect accuracy when they did. The wikidata feature proved particularly useful for locating large multi-national companies and organizations (e.g. UNESCO.org and Nestle.com) who had detailed Wikidata entries.

The machine learning classifier synthesizing these features achieved an accuracy of 91% with cross-validation, approaching levels of human agreement. The classifier also cut error rates by more than half over the baseline (91% vs 78%). More interestingly, for "difficult" urls without a clear cc tld, the classifier achieved an accuracy of 77% versus 51% for the baseline.

Given a particular URL in our human-coded dataset, we evaluated the geolocation classifier accuracy by comparing the top predicted country against the human-coded country. However, this "winner-takes-all" approach would introduce significant bias into our data. For example, for the 6% of web pages whose only applicable feature was the inferred language English, a winner-takes-all approach would always assign the US as the source country, ignoring the United Kingdom, Australia, India, etc. Instead, our data uses a proportional approach, choosing from the probability distribution estimated by the classifier (which we calibrated to be reasonably accurate). This procedure emphasizes distributional accuracy, which is critical to this work, over the accuracy of any single URL.

LOCALNESS

This section analyzes the localness of information in Wikipedia, asking *How much information about a place originates from that place, and what factors explain variations in localness?*

We analyze each country's localness at the language edition level using two lenses: editors and sources. For example, in the Arabic Wikipedia, what percentage of edits to articles about France come from editors in France? And what proportion of sources in those articles are local to France? What about in the French Wikipedia? We investigate these questions through a combination of exploratory visualizations and statistical analyses. We

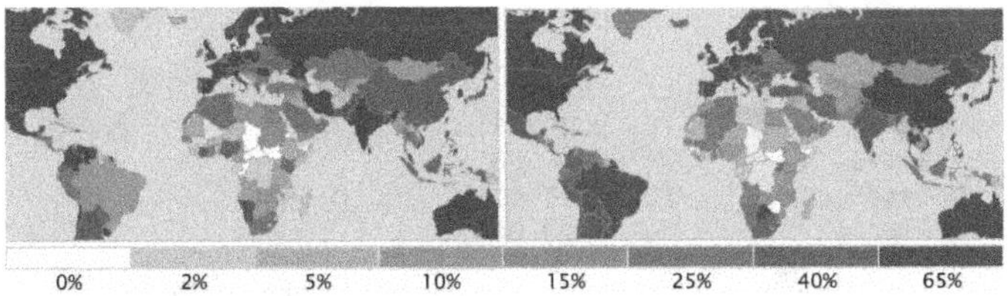

Figure 1: The overall localness of sources (left) and editors (right) across all language editions. Articles tend to have slightly more localness in the sources they cite than the editors that create them. The middle east and Africa show particularly low localness.

encourage readers to use the online visualization tool we created to explore the relationships we discuss.

Exploratory analysis of localness

Figure 1 shows each country's localness, aggregated across all language editions.[8] In this map we see our first evidence of inequalities in the localness of sources and editors. The countries with the highest percentage of local sources tend to be countries with large economies and "nation-states" responsible for a large share of worldwide speakers for their primary language: Sweden (93.0%), the U.S. (90.6%), The Czech Republic (87.9%) and France (86.3%).The countries with the highest percentage of local edits overlap substantially, but the list seems to favor countries that represent the majority of speakers of their primary language: Netherlands (89.2%), Germany (86.8%), and Latvia (86.1%).

Africa and the Middle East stand out as having particularly low localness. For example, many central African countries have less than 0.2% localness in both sources and editors (Chad, South Sudan, Central African Republic, the DRC). Figure 1 points to SES characteristics affecting VGI localness. Many countries in sub-Saharan Africa have per-capita GDPs below $1000 U.S. per year, among the lowest in the world. We return to these ideas in the statistical analysis that follows.

The apparent role of language in these results suggests that we should look more closely at individual language editions of Wikipedia. Figure 2 does so by comparing the localness of the Middle-East and North African (MENA) countries along two axes. The left column shows results for the Arabic Wikipedia while the right column represents the French Wikipedia. The top row shows editor localness, while the bottom row conveys source localness. For example, Algeria's dark color in the top-left map indicates that in the Arabic Wikipedia, a large percentage of edits to articles about Algeria come from editors in Algeria (75%). Comparing the result to the other three maps, we can see that Algeria's editor localness in the Arabic Wikipedia is substantially higher (75%) than its editor localness in the French Wikipedia (39%, upper right) and also higher than its source localness in both language editions (44% and 40% for the Arabic and French Wikipedias in the bottom two maps).

[8]All map visualizations use an identical color scheme. Thematic cartography teaches that, while there are some accepted best practices, choosing an appropriate color scheme for a given map can involve both art and science [28]. We attempted to communicate the percentage associated with each country by using cubed values mapped to a gradient from white to blue. Values above 0.65 receive maximum saturation. This transformation balances between highlighting large and small effects.

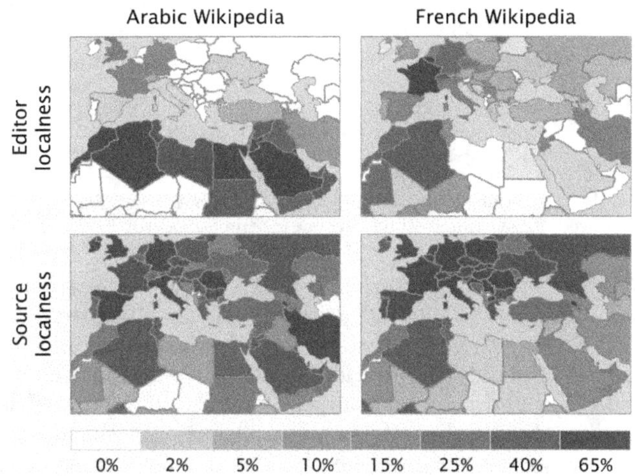

Figure 2: Across all articles about a country, the localness of editors (top) and sources (bottom) for the Arabic Wikipedia (left) and the French Wikipedia (right). For example, Algeria's dark color in the top-left shows that in Arabic Wikipedia, a large percentage of edits to its articles come from editors in Algeria (75%).

The comparison between the French and Arabic Wikipedias reveals how Wikipedia is embedded into a broader system of knowledge. The language that an editor is writing in — and the place that that language originates from — matters immensely to what information can be produced on Wikipedia. If there are few Arabic speakers in Greece, few people in Greece will create content about the country in the Arabic Wikipedia (e.g. none in our dataset). We can see the Arabic Wikipedia's *language barrier* preventing local edits through much of Europe and central Africa. Similarly, local edits in the French Wikipedia are constrained to Europe and former French colonies such as Algeria and Morocco.

While language also shapes source localness, the effects are substantially dampened. Editors proficient in one language seem to be able to draw on a broader array of digital and digitized knowledge in other languages. For example, editors of French Wikipedia can still draw on local sources when authoring articles on Saudi Arabia (12.3%), even though less than 1% of editors are local to Saudi Arabia. This effect persists broadly across our data. Across all 847 project-specific country localness values that have at least 100 edits and sources, 82% have higher source than editor localness.

Overall, we see support for both socio-economic status (SES) and socio-linguistic effects on localness. SES appears to play the primary role in overall localness (Figure 1). However, when considering individual language editions, language also plays an important role, and appears to serve as a near-total barrier to local editors.

Statistical analysis of localness

The visualizations above suggest that language and SES factors both play roles in the localness of content. We performed a statistical analysis to systematically iden-

Localness of sources	coeff	odds-ratio	z-value
intercept	-0.13	0.87	-0.6
log(journals)	0.34	1.41	23.4 ***
log(population)	-0.24	0.78	-13.5 ***
lang-share	1.24	3.45	3.6 ***

Localness of edits:	coeff	odds-ratio	z-value
intercept	-4.10	0.01	-6.6 ***
is-native	1.76	5.83	7.8 ***
log(internet)	0.12	1.12	2.9 **
lang-share	3.04	20.80	4.3 ***

Table 3: Models of source and edit localness for articles in a particular country. Socio-economic variables play a stronger role in sources, followed by language. The reverse is true for editor localness. This paper uses * for $p < 0.05$, ** for $p < 0.01$, and *** for $p < 0.001$

tify country characteristics that explain differences in localness. We included a variety of variables that may correlate with a country's ability to support people editing Wikipedia (population, GDP, broadband penetration [1]), and produce sources that can be cited in Wikipedia (the number of journal articles[9] and the number of newspapers [1] published by a country). Across all explanatory variables, we used raw counts over per-capita numbers because this better reflects the total quantity of volunteer work and citeable information available in a country. Our models also include log-transformed variables for attributes with long-tailed distributions (e.g. population, GDP, num-journals). This (and all future) analysis uses stepwise forward variable selection to isolate the most explanatory model variables.

Based on the language patterns we saw above, the statistical models also included two language variables. First, `is-native` is a boolean indicator that is 1 if a country is a native speaker of the Wikipedia language edition (e.g. Saudi Arabia for the Arabic Wikipedia). Second, `lang-share` represents a country's share of the global population of speakers for the Wikipedia language. For example Saudi Arabia contains 8% of the world's Arabic speaking population, so `lang-share(ar-wiki, Saudi Arabia) = 0.08`. We estimated both variables using data from the Geonames Gazetteer.[10]

Our analysis uses logistic regression to model the fraction of sources or edits that are local. Every data point in the regression is the localness of edits for a particular country, within a particular language edition of Wikipedia. For example, our dataset includes a single record for all 1882 edits to articles about Algeria in the Arabic Wikipedia. The dependent variable in this case would be 0.75 (the localness of edits is 75%). This record's value for GDP would be Algeria's GDP, the `is-native` indicator would be 1, and `lang-share` would be 0.11 (roughly 11% of Arabic speakers live in Algeria).

Table 3 shows the results of the logistic regression model. Both three-variable equations explain significant portions of the overall deviance in localness (27% for source localness, 47% for editor localness). Although both models select similar variables, the importance they place on each of them differs. The statistical model of source localness selects the number of journal articles as the most important factor. Interestingly, though `log(journals)` and `log(population)` are strongly correlated ($\rho = 0.72$), the "non-population part" of the number of journal articles signal seems to matter. A country's share of the Wikipedia project's language also plays an important role, with all three variables being strongly significant ($p < 0.001$). The effect sizes of these variables are substantial. For example, for every doubling in the number of journals, the odds of a country's sources being cited increase by 41%.

The statistical model for editor localness reverses the importance of the two types of variables. A country whose population natively speaks a language corresponding to a Wikipedia language edition (e.g. Saudi Arabia for the Arabic Wikipedia) has 483% higher odds of a particular edit being local. Interestingly, the most predictive SES variable is broadband penetration, which captures an editor's ability to access the Wikipedia site itself. For every doubling in the number of broadband users for a country, its odds of having a local editor increase by 12%.

To summarize, we identify substantial barriers to localness in VGI that explain differences of several orders of magnitude. Source localness is shaped most strongly by the quantity of scholarly publications that a country produces, with language barriers playing a smaller role. However, these language barriers are a huge factor in editor localness with SES characteristics (in particular Internet access) a secondary effect.

Overall, our findings reflect previous findings that SES correlates with the quantity of VGI about places. However, we do find two key differences. First, we illustrate language's key role as a barrier to editors. Although this finding is intuitive, the scale of the effects we see are dramatic, explaining differences in editor localness of several orders of magnitude. Second, localness about a place and the quantity of information about a place need not be correlated. For example, the U.S. is one of the most heavily represented countries in Arabic Wikipedia [8] despite having less than 1% editor localness.

[9] `http://www.scimagojr.com/countryrank.php`

[10] This work focuses on second-language proficiency language speakers who could plausibly make a substantive contributions to a language edition. For example, although only 0.02% of India's population are native English speakers, the over 200 million Indians with second-language proficiency in English represent the fourth most prolific group of editors to English Wikipedia (behind the U.S, U.K., and Canada). Because no dataset of worldwide second-language proficiency exists, we estimated it using the Geonames dataset (`http://www.geonames.org/`), which orders languages by number of speakers. We created an asymptotic function that estimated second-language speakers by combining a country's Geonames' language rank with the country's population. Though this seemed to perform well in practice, more accurate estimates of world-wide second language proficiency may improve the accuracy of our models, and represent a valuable area of future work.

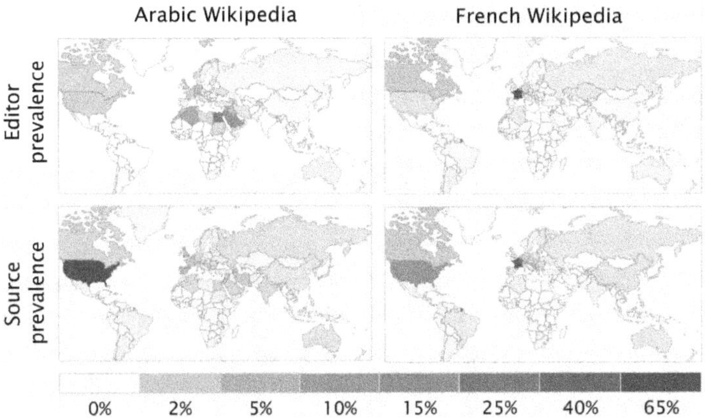

Figure 3: The overall percentage of sources and editors that come from each country. The images visualize differences along two dimensions: editors (top) vs sources (bottom) and Arabic Wikipedia (left) vs French Wikipedia (right). For example, the left images show that while editors from MENA countries constitute the majority of editors to Arabic Wikipedia (top), U.S. sources are most heavily cited (bottom).

Our results indicate that when we experience the world through VGI — either online or in augmented environments – our experience is shaped by many of the historical barriers and inequalities that existed before VGI.

GEOPROVENANCE

Localness tells us how much content is produced and sourced from a particular country, but it does not tell us where non-local content originates. We next move beyond localness to geoprovenance more generally. Specifically, we ask: *What is the worldwide network of sources and editors for articles about a particular country? What factors explain differences between countries and language editions?*

Our analysis of geoprovenance is divided into two parts. First, we study the overall prevalence of source and editor countries within each language edition (e.g. What proportion of edits in the Arabic Wikipedia come from people in Tunisia?). In doing so, we isolate language edition-wide effects due to language, population, demographics, etc. Next, controlling for these top-level language edition effects, we drill down to focus on the results for articles about a specific country, and the worldwide distribution of editors and sources for that country. (e.g. For articles about Iraq in the Arabic Wikipedia, what is the worldwide distribution of sources and editors?)

Top-level effects between language edition and country

We begin by studying the effect of language edition on the overall prevalence of sources and editors from each country (e.g. What proportion of all edits in the Arabic Wikipedia come from people in Tunisia?). Figure 3 shows four example distributions corresponding to the same two axes in the previous section. As an example, the left images show that while editors from MENA countries constitute the majority of editors across all articles in the Arabic Wikipedia (top), U.S. sources are most heavily cited (bottom).

Several clear patterns emerge that resonate with earlier findings about localness. The top row shows that editors in a language edition come almost exclusively from countries that speak the language. Editors of the Arabic Wikipedia come primarily from Egypt (23%), Saudi Arabia (13%), Jordan (8%), Algeria (7%) and Kuwait (5%). Editors of the French Wikipedia come from French speaking countries: France (88%), Belgium (3%), Vietnam (2%), Canada (2%), and Switzerland (1%). Editors from the U.S., for example, who account for 20% of all edits in our dataset, account for less than 1% of edits to both the Arabic and French Wikipedias.

While language appears to serve as an almost total barrier to editor contributions, socio-economic status (SES) factors appear to explain substantial variation within that barrier. For example, the Arabic Wikipedia dramatically under-represents native speaking low-GDP countries such as Sudan and Yemen, which constitute 10% and 7% of worldwide Arabic speakers but only 1% of Arabic Wikipedia edits. The same pattern appears in the French Wikipedia for the Democratic Republic of Congo. The DRC, where 40% of the population speaks French, account for 13% of French speakers worldwide but represent essentially no edits to the French language edition. We do not see the reverse trend occurring. Relatively wealthy, native-speaking countries (e.g. Egypt and Saudi Arabia in the Arabic Wikipedia and Belgium in the French Wikipedia) do not significantly exceed their "fair share" of edits.

As with localness, language does not constitute an absolute barrier for source use. Instead, traditionally dominant places in the geography of media persist, with the U.S. accounting for 61% of Arabic Wikipedia sources, followed by Spain (4%), and the U.K. (3%). While French Wikipedia is dominated by countries with large French speaking populations such as France (54% of sources), Belgium (7%), and Canada (2%), the U.S. also plays a notable role, accounting for 11% of all sources.

The role of the U.S. as the dominant publisher of Arabic Wikipedia sources seems surprising at first glance. This finding reflects the large share of total Arabic Wikipedia citations that occur in articles about the United States (39%) compared to Arabic countries like Egypt (2.5%) and Saudi Arabia (1.6%). This finding also resonates with Graham and Hogan [8], who find that a significant number of editors from MENA countries choose to write about places in North America rather than the MENA region. However, we will see in the next section that this finding also reflects the U.S.'s role as the primary publisher of sources about many Arabic-speaking countries — even in the Arabic Wikipedia.

To unpack these affects, we statistically analyzed the prevalence of source and editor countries for each Wikipedia project (Table 4). The forward stepwise variable selection procedure identified `lang-share` and `log(journals)` as the most explanatory pair of variables for both source publisher country and editor coun-

Source publisher country prevalence:	coeff	odds-ratio	z-value
intercept	-1.79e+1	6.08e-7	-14.1 ***
log(journals)	1.08e+0	2.19e+0	10.6 ***
lang-share	4.27e+0	5.61e+1	10.0 ***

Editor country prevalence:	coeff	odds-ratio	z-value
intercept	-10.50	2.75e-5	-5.3 ***
lang-share	7.46	1.75e+3	10.4 ***
log(journals)	0.45	1.57e+0	3.1 **

Table 4: Model of top-level effects between a language-edition and source or editor country. As with localness, our model for sources identifies SES attributes as primary factors and language as a secondary (but important) effect. The reverse is true for editors.

Country of Article (Country of Publisher in rows)

Country of Publisher	French Wikipedia					Arabic Wikipedia				
	Overall	Egypt	Iran	Iraq	Tunisia	Overall	Egypt	Iran	Iraq	Tunisia
Algeria	0%	0%	0%	0%	0%	1%	0%	0%	0%	0%
Egypt	0%	4%	0%	0%	0%	1%	34%	0%	1%	1%
Iran	0%	0%	10%	0%	0%	2%	0%	73%	1%	0%
Iraq	0%	0%	0%	1%	0%	0%	0%	0%	9%	0%
Saudi Arabia	0%	0%	0%	0%	0%	1%	2%	0%	1%	1%
Tunisia	0%	0%	0%	0%	33%	0%	0%	0%	0%	40%
France	55%	40%	19%	37%	45%	3%	2%	1%	2%	17%
Belgium	7%	1%	1%	1%	1%	0%	0%	0%	0%	1%
Canada	2%	1%	3%	2%	2%	1%	2%	2%	2%	1%
UK	2%	5%	3%	7%	1%	4%	5%	2%	10%	4%
US	12%	37%	46%	37%	9%	62%	37%	13%	44%	16%
Other	22%	12%	18%	16%	8%	24%	17%	9%	29%	20%

;

Country of Article (Country of Editor in rows)

Country of Editor	French Wikipedia					Arabic Wikipedia				
	Overall	Egypt	Iran	Iraq	Tunisia	Overall	Egypt	Iran	Iraq	Tunisia
Algeria	0%	0%	0%	0%	0%	7%	0%	0%	1%	1%
Egypt	0%	0%	0%	0%	0%	24%	65%	36%	4%	8%
Iran	0%	0%	17%	0%	0%	0%	0%	9%	1%	0%
Iraq	0%	0%	0%	0%	0%	4%	3%	24%	35%	1%
Saudi Arabia	0%	0%	0%	0%	0%	13%	5%	8%	7%	3%
Tunisia	0%	0%	0%	0%	12%	1%	1%	1%	1%	51%
France	88%	96%	70%	88%	56%	2%	0%	1%	1%	18%
Belgium	3%	2%	3%	1%	1%	0%	0%	0%	0%	0%
Canada	2%	0%	1%	3%	0%	1%	2%	1%	2%	2%
UK	0%	1%	1%	1%	0%	3%	3%	4%	13%	0%
US	0%	0%	1%	0%	0%	2%	1%	1%	4%	2%
Other	7%	1%	8%	6%	31%	44%	21%	14%	31%	14%

Figure 4: Distribution of source country (left) and editor country (right) for four countries (Egypt, Iran, Iraq, and Tunisia) for both French and Arabic Wikipedias. The table includes 12 key source publisher countries. "Overall" lists the percentage of all sources in the language edition that are published in that country (i.e. the top-level effect modeled at the beginning of this section).

try prevalence. This simple model explains the majority of total deviance in the data (61% and 80% for source and editor country respectively).

Once again, SES indicators play the primary role in the location of source publishers, while language plays the critical role in the location of editors. However, the effects appear more pronounced. For example, for every 10% increase in a country's share of the worldwide speakers of the Wikipedia edition's language, its odds of producing a source increase by 461% and the odds of a particular editor coming from it are 175 times higher.

The model's selection of journal articles as the key predictor of source publisher suggests that the volume of content produced by traditional media industries plays a critical role in a country's prominence as a publisher of sources in Wikipedia. Since journal article numbers correlate with many other SES indicators we probed this finding by replacing `log(journals)`, with other variables (e.g. GDP, Internet, etc.). When we did so, we saw residual deviation increase by 12% to 33%, suggesting that a country's scholarly media environment does indeed capture its likelihood of being a Wikipedia source publisher better than conventional SES indicators.

To summarize, we find that a country's prevalence among both sources and editors at the Wikipedia language edition level can be explained by the size of the country's media network and the fraction they represent of the world's fluent speakers of that language.

Focusing on articles in particular countries

We now shift our focus from broad project-level effects to articles about a specific country, and the worldwide network of sources and editors those articles draw upon.

To provide some intuition for this effect, Figure 4 shows the worldwide distribution of editors and sources for all geotagged articles in four specific MENA countries (Egypt, Iraq, Iran, and Tunisia) in both the Arabic and French Wikipedias. The table columns ("Overall", "Egypt", ...) indicate article country. The rows ("Algeria", "Egypt", ... , "U.S.", "Other") are associated with publisher countries, and the numbers in the cells indicate the percentage of citations in French Wikipedia associated with that country. The "Overall" column shows each country's share of all citations in French or Arabic Wikipedia (analyzed in the previous section).

The left table shows that language plays a large role in the geoprovenance of sources. Sources in France constitute a large share of citations for three of the four countries in French Wikipedia, with 40%, 37%, and 45% of citations for Egypt, Iraq, and Tunisia respectively. Iran serves as a noticeable outlier, having only 19% French citations. In the Arabic Wikipedia, where native speakers are not concentrated in any single country, we see a sharp rise in local sources across all MENA countries (34% to 73%) with Iraq serving as an outlier with only 9% localness. Iraq's low source localness may reflect its lack of web infrastructure; the CIA Factbook ranks it at #218 in number of Internet hosts, with 26 hosts.

Interestingly, although the U.S. does not publish many sources overall in French Wikipedia (12%), it constitutes a large share of citations for articles about many countries in the Middle East. We see similar effects for U.S. sources in Arabic Wikipedia. These findings provide insight into the U.S.'s prevalence in the Arabic Wikipedia broadly, extending results that we saw earlier (Table 3). Across language editions, U.S. sources constitute a large share of citations in articles about MENA countries.

The right table shows similar patterns for editor geoprovenance, with exaggerated language effects. France represents 70% or more of edits to every country except for Tunisia, while the Arabic Wikipedia is dominated by editors from MENA countries. In contrast to our results

Source geoprovenance:

	coeff	odds-ratio	z-value
intercept	-4.16	0.01	-155 ***
top-level(wplang, B)	6.07	432.90	91 ***
is-same(A,B)	3.42	30.84	95 ***
log(migrants A->B)	0.09	1.10	29 ***

Editor geoprovenance:

	coeff	odds-ratio	z-value
intercept	-4.18	0.01	-44.0 ***
top-level(wplang, B)	6.33	563.57	53.0 ***
is-same(A,B)	2.50	12.12	14.3 ***
log(migrants A->B)	0.03	1.03	2.4 *
lang-overlap	-0.58	0.56	-2.3 *

Table 5: Given an article about country A, factors influencing the likelihood of a source or editor coming from a country B. top-level(wplang, B) is the overall prevalence of sources / editors from country B in the language edition (analyzed in the previous section).

for publishers, editors from the U.S. do not play a significant role in either language edition, representing 0% and 2% of editors. Analyzing the outliers in Figure 4 also provides insight into factors that affect geo-provenance. Iran exhibits notable source localness in French Wikipedia (10%), and exceptionally strong source localness in Arabic Wikipedia (73%) despite not being a native language country for either encyclopedia. These effects may be attributed to Iran's educational system, which ranks #7 in total books produced in the world, and a literacy rate of 97% among young adults. However, it does not appear to be solely Iranian editors who are contributing these local sources; Iranians only have an editor localness of 9% in Arabic Wikipedia. Tunisia, whose inhabitants speak both French and Arabic shows high localness in both language editions and source and editor lenses.

Table 5 shows the results of a statistical analysis that seeks to identify underlying factors that explain the worldwide geoprovenance network. More specifically given an article about country A, the model identifies factors influencing the likelihood of a source or editor coming from a country B. Because we seek to study the specific relationship between two countries, we control for the effects of source and editor localness at the Wikipedia language edition and article country level by including a dummy variable for it: `top-level(wplang,B)`. We also include `is-same(A,B)`, a dummy variable for localness that is 1 when A = B.

The statistical models for both publisher and editor identify a strong effect of localness. Migration also seems to be associated with source publishers. For every doubling in the number of people who emigrate from country A to country B, the odds of the country B being a publisher for articles about country B increase by 10%. This can statistically explain relationships such as Tunisia and French Wikipedia in Table 4. However, determining the underlying cause requires more research. Is it migrants who are actually responsible for these edits, or is this a signal of cultural overlap along many dimensions (spatial, religious, lingual, ethnic) that leads to increased knowledge and interest in another country?

To summarize, high-level effects of language edition on geoprovenance show that large differences exist in where different language editions get their content from. Our findings at the project-level mirror our findings for localness. Countries that fluently write in the language of the Wikipedia project contribute more sources and dramatically more edits. SES factors (in particular, the number of journal articles) contribute to both lenses of geoprovenance, but serve as the driving factor for sources. When honing in on the pairwise relationship between an article country and source or editor country, we find language overlap, localness (a boolean indicator), and migration to be indicators of the likelihood of one country to produce sources and editors for another country.

CONCLUSION AND DISCUSSION

This paper presents the first large-scale study of the forces shaping the localness of VGI. We find inequalities in the localness of content of several orders of magnitude, and statistically identify socio-economic and linguistic explanatory factors. The countries most-often cited in VGI are those that are strong publishers of traditional scholarship. For VGI editors, language serves as an almost total barrier, but within that barrier, SES factors (such as Internet penetration) explain large differences in localness. More broadly, our findings suggest that if a place faces serious SES obstacles, or you read about a place in a language that is not spoken in that place, you are unlikely to be reading locally-produced VGI or even VGI that references local sources.

Our findings have important implications for VGI. First, the primary role that SES factors play in localness suggests that VGI may not be the equalizing panacea that it has been portrayed as being. Instead, VGI appears to follow many of the same structural barriers to equality as traditional expert-curated systems, although research must determine whether the strength of these barriers in VGI is different. Barriers to localness may form the contours of "VGI bubbles" (similar to what Eli Pariser called "filter bubbles" [26]). However, our findings indicate these VGI bubbles exhibit unusual topologies. For example, U.S. source publishers seem to straddle nearly all language editions and countries. Future research should more deeply chart the shape of these barriers.

One way to reduce these barriers is by supporting, identifying and encouraging contributions that cross linguistic and cultural lines. For example, the Wikidata project aims to make factual units of information available in all language editions. Hale's work on cross-lingual blog linking [13] suggests that multimedia can also help in this respect, and the Wikimedia Commons project provides a good technical platform for this strategy. VGI barriers could also be reduced by making readers and editors aware of them. For example, a visualization such as Omnipedia [3] could alert readers to differing perspectives in other language representations of a particular artifact.

Several limitations of this study suggest areas for future work. While we analyze a single snapshot of geoprovenance, future research should explore the longitudinal dynamics of this it. In particularly, the effects of translation on localness deserves further study, given English Wikipedia's dominant role as a source of translated Wikipedia articles [30]. We also consider content and people from the same country as "local." We believe this is reasonable given the scale of our analysis and the accuracy of source country prediction, but we would like to study variations in localness at other scales. Following the vast majority of the VGI literature, our work also equates "local" with "good". However, it would not be good if 100% of the sources in, for example, North Korea were local. There is much to be gained from an understanding of the benefits of diversity in creating strong knowledge platforms and conversations. As Elwood stated, "legitimizing VGI based on its locality or the nearness of observer to observed further elevates already-powerful cultural conventions... as valid ways to perceive what is true about the world [5]." Future research could propose frameworks that help us reason about optimal levels of locality.

Finally, we believe the URL geoprovenance algorithm introduced in this paper represents an important new tool for researchers. In addition to supporting analyses of the geographic diversity of viewpoints, it could be used to identify differences in how media from different countries discuss particular issues or it could track geographic flows in online media networks. To support research on improved geoprovenance algorithms, we are releasing our gold standard dataset and a reference implementation of our algorithm.[11]

ACKNOWLEDGEMENTS

We would like to thank Dario Taraborelli and the Wikimedia Foundation for helping to craft the anonymized editor geoprovenance dataset. We would also like to thank Matthew Zook for his advice about geocoding publishers. This research was generously supported by the National Science Foundation (IIS-0964697, IIS-1421655, and IIS-0808692), the John Fell Fund (Oxford Univ.), and an Amazon Web Services Research Grant.

REFERENCES

1. *World Development Indicators 2012.* World Bank, 2012.
2. Amitay, E., Har'El, N., Sivan, R., and Soffer, A. Web-a-where: geotagging web content. In *SIGIR* (2004).
3. Bao, P., Hecht, B., Carton, S., Quaderi, M., Horn, M., and Gergle, D. Omnipedia: bridging the wikipedia language gap. In *CHI* (2012).
4. Cheng, Z., Caverlee, J., and Lee, K. You are where you tweet: A content-based approach to geo-locating Twitter users. In *CIKM* (2010).
5. Elwood, S., Goodchild, M. F., and Sui, D. Z. Researching volunteered geographic information: Spatial data, geographic research, and new social practice. *Annals of the AAG 102*, 3 (2012), 571–590.
6. Fischer, E. Locals and tourists (Flickr), June 2010.
7. Ford, H., Sen, S., Musicant, D. R., and Miller, N. Getting to the source: where does Wikipedia get its information from? In *WikiSym* (2013).
8. Graham, M., and Hogan, B. Uneven openness: Barriers to mena representation on wikipedia. *SSRN* (2014).
9. Graham, M., Hogan, B., Straumann, R. K., and Medhat, A. Uneven geographies of user-generated information: Patterns of increasing informational poverty. *Annals of the AAG* (2014), 1–19.
10. Graham, M., and Zook, M. Augmented realities and uneven geographies: exploring the geolinguistic contours of the web. *Env. and Planning A 45*, 1 (2013), 77 – 99.
11. Graham, M., Zook, M., and Boulton, A. Augmented reality in urban places: contested content and the duplicity of code. *Trans. Inst. of British Geog. 38*, 3 (2013), 464–479.
12. Haklay, M. How good is volunteered geographical information? a comparative study of OpenStreetMap and ordnance survey datasets. *Environment and Planning B: Planning and Design 37*, 4 (2010), 682 – 703.
13. Hale, S. A. Net increase? Cross-lingual linking in the blogosphere. *JCMC 17*, 2 (2012), 135–151.
14. Hardy, D., Frew, J., and Goodchild, M. F. Volunteered geographic information production as a spatial process. *IJGIS 26*, 7 (2012), 1191–1212.
15. Hecht, B., and Gergle, D. Measuring self-focus bias in community-maintained knowledge repositories. In *C&T* (2009), 11–19.
16. Hecht, B., and Gergle, D. The tower of Babel meets web 2.0: user-generated content and its applications in a multilingual context. In *CHI* (2010), 291–300.
17. Hecht, B., and Stephens, M. A tale of cities: Urban biases in volunteered geographic information. In *ICWSM* (2014).
18. Helft, M. Online maps: Everyman offers new directions. *The New York Times* (Nov. 2009).
19. Kitchin, R., and Dodge, M. *Code/space: Software and everyday life.* MIT Press, 2011.
20. Li, L., Goodchild, M. F., and Xu, B. Spatial, temporal, and socioeconomic patterns in the use of twitter and flickr. *CAGIS 40*, 2 (2013), 61–77.
21. Luyt, B., and Tan, D. Improving Wikipedia's credibility: References and citations in a sample of history articles. *JASIST 61*, 4 (2010), 715–722.
22. McCurley, K. S. Geospatial mapping and navigation of the web. In *WWW* (2001).
23. Mislove, A., Lehmann, S., Ahn, Y.-Y., Onnela, J.-P., and Rosenquist, J. N. Understanding the demographics of twitter users. In *ICWSM* (2011).
24. Neis, P., Zielstra, D., and Zipf, A. The street network evolution of crowdsourced maps: OpenStreetMap in Germany 2007–2011. *Future Internet 4*, 1 (2011), 1–21.
25. Obermeyer, N. J. The evolution of public participation GIS. *CAGIS 25*, 2 (1998), 65–66.
26. Pariser, E. *The filter bubble: What the Internet is hiding from you.* Penguin UK, 2011.
27. Poese, I., Uhlig, S., Kaafar, M. A., Donnet, B., and Gueye, B. IP geolocation databases: Unreliable? *ACM SIGCOMM Comp. Comm. Review 41*, 2 (2011), 53–56.
28. Slocum, T. A., McMaster, R. B., Kessler, F. C., and Howard, H. H. *Thematic Cartography and Geovisualization.* Prentice Hall, N.J., USA, 2009.
29. Vrandečić, D. Wikidata: A new platform for collaborative data collection. WWW '12 Comp. (2012).
30. Warncke-Wang, M., Uduwage, A., Dong, Z., and Riedl, J. In search of the ur-wikipedia: universality, similarity, and translation in the wikipedia inter-language link network. In *WikiSym* (2012).

[11] `http://www.shilad.com/localness`

The Heart Work of Wikipedia: Gendered, Emotional Labor in the World's Largest Online Encyclopedia

Amanda Menking
Information School
University of Washington
amenking@uw.edu

Ingrid Erickson
School of Communication & Information
Rutgers University
ingrid.erickson@rutgers.edu

ABSTRACT
This note explores the issue of women's participation in Wikipedia through the lens of emotional labor. Using a grounded theory approach, we detail the kinds of tasks women Wikipedians choose to do and explore why they choose the work they do. We also explore the emotional costs of their labor and their strategies for coping. Our analysis of 20 interviews leads us to posit that the gendered and emotional labor required of many women to participate in Wikipedia's production renders it, problematically, a space of conflicting public and private spheres, motivated by antithetical open and closed values. In addition to other contributions, we believe this insight sheds light on some of the complex dynamics behind Wikipedia's observed gender gap.

Author Keywords
Wikipedia; Women; Gender Gap; Emotional Labor

ACM Classification Keywords
K.4.3. Organizational Impacts: Computer-supported collaborative work

INTRODUCTION
Wikipedia, perhaps the most successful large-scale, online collaboration in the world, is a storied space of democratic values and meritocracy in action—as many within the CHI and CSCW communities have extensively detailed [e.g., 13,18,19,22,23,24]. Yet underneath its idealized veneer, Wikipedia in practice proves to have a notable gender gap. Unlike user distribution reports on social media platforms, which trend more toward representative parity or even a greater number of female users [7], surveys of Wikipedia users indicate the overwhelming majority of contributors are male [14]. Both the popular media [e.g., 9,21,27] and scholars [e.g., 1,6,20] have begun to explore Wikipedia's participation disparities, raising questions about editor recruitment and retention, content coverage and bias, and the tension between diversity and territoriality [10]. Recently, Jimmy Wales, co-founder of Wikipedia, admitted that the Wikimedia Foundation (WMF) has "completely failed" [29] to meet its goal of increasing the number of female participants to 25% by 2015.

CHI 2015, April 18 - 23 2015, Seoul, Republic of Korea
Copyright 2015 ACM 978-1-4503-3145-6/15/04...$15.00
http://dx.doi.org/10.1145/2702123.2702514

In February 2011 in response to an article published in *The New York Times* [5], then Executive Director of WMF, Sue Gardner, asked her Deputy Director Erik Möller to create the Gendergap mailing list, a publicly archived listserv "provided by the Wikimedia Foundation as a communication tool to collectively address the realities of the gender gap" [28]. In September 2014, a male Wikipedian posted the following message to the list: "I think there should be a separate site for the gender gap effort [...] where women and men interested in narrowing the gender gap and documenting the existing problems can exchange views in an atmosphere undisturbed by men pretending to be women, men opposed to narrowing the gender gap, men arguing that it's not really proven that the gender gap is a problem." Even within a dedicated listserv, the topic of gender parity proves to be volatile. Lam et al. [20] confirm this social complexity, noting a "culture that may be resistant to female participation" [20:9].

However, Wikipedia's gender gap is typically framed as a "woman problem" [8]. It has been attributed to women's lack of discretionary time [6], sensitivity to conflict and criticism [6], desire to be more social [21], and hesitancy to learn technical skills such as the Wiki mark-up language [11]. In August 2014, Wikimedia Deutschland published a diversity report indicating that, although the picture is complex, "lack of time, technical usability barriers (e.g. navigation, editability), and a variety of sociocultural and communication issues (style of communication, working atmosphere) can [...] definitely be identified as reasons for low female participation in Wikipedia" [4].

Despite the perception of the gender gap as a "woman problem," women *do* actively contribute to different language Wikipedias across the world. Women lead local chapters, sustain sister projects, and work for and chair the WMF. Women who have similar edit counts to men are more likely to become administrators [21] and make more sizeable revisions [1] than men do. This note reports early findings that suggest there is something to be learned about the possible cause(s) and consequences of Wikipedia's gender gap by looking more closely at the experiences of women actively engaged in the community. What are their experiences like? What challenges do they face? How do they persevere? We posit that many women Wikipedians engage in a form of 'emotion work' [15], also known as emotional labor, that allows them to maintain their participation even as the circumstances in which they engage prove challenging, if not caustic.

THEORETICAL FRAMEWORK

This research draws on the growing awareness among HCI scholars of the need for more nuanced considerations of gender and the careful application of feminist theories in sociotechnical research [e.g., 2,3,16,17,26]. Here we attend particularly to issues of agency, empowerment, and fulfillment [2:1301], drawing on Hochschild's construction of 'emotion work' to identify aspects of Wikipedian participation that might otherwise go unremarked.

Emotion Work

Hochschild [15] defines emotion work as "the act of trying to change in a degree or quality an emotion or feeling…[it is] the effort—the act of trying—and not the outcome, which may or may not be successful […] 'emotion work' refers more broadly to the act of evoking or shaping, as well as suppressing, feeling in oneself" [15:561]. This work is *deep acting*, meaning one tries to alter both the display as well as the originating emotion itself to rectify one's own emotion to the perceived appropriate emotion for the situation. This act of emotional alignment is oriented to a situation's 'feeling rules.' By contrast, the management of one's behavioral expression(s) alone (i.e., controlling what others see) is *surface acting*, which draws on Goffman's dramaturgical notion of the presentation of self.

Like Goffman, Hochschild's construction of emotional labor was conceived with the assumption that interactions take place face-to-face or, at minimum, voice-to-voice. Nevertheless, we believe participation in many of today's sociotechnical environments may also involve forms of emotional labor. Despite their digital nature, online spaces such as Wikipedia engage individuals as whole selves, not only intellectually but also emotionally. By way of edit logs, talk pages, and other digital traces, Wikipedians can engage simultaneously in both surface as well deep acting. Using the lens of emotional labor allows us to better tease apart how Wikipedia's gender gap may relate to prevailing feeling rules or participation strategies; at the same time this work contributes to advancing Hochschild's theory of emotion work for understanding mediated social situations.

METHODOLOGY

This work is part of a larger qualitative project that seeks to understand the participation experiences of Wikipedia editors who self-identify as women.[1] Participants were recruited via a variety of methods, including utilizing the Gendergap mailing list. Selection criteria were twofold: (1) self-identified as a woman, (2) had been editing the English language (EN) Wikipedia for two or more years. (Of the 20 participants interviewed, 15 have edited the EN Wikipedia for 7 or more years.) Study participants ranged in age from 19 to late 60s and derived from the following countries: Australia (1); France (1); Germany (2); India (2); Spain (1); and the United States (13). These women represent a range of gender identities, sexual orientations, life stages, and relationship statuses. The total number of EN live edits for all participants ranges from 112 to 122,828 per user[2], and their user permissions include a wide range of system privileges.

Here we use grounded theory [12] to analyze a set of 20 interviews conducted by the first author between January-July 2014. Each interview was conducted as a semi-structured conversation using instant message (2), email (2), or video conferencing applications (16). No interviews were conducted in person, and all interviews were conducted in English, audio recorded, and transcribed. Participants were invited to review their transcripts and elaborate on their comments post-interview.

FINDINGS

Data analysis revealed three themes related to emotional labor in the collective interviews. Together, these themes provide a glimpse into the strategic work women engage in to adjust their actions and/or feelings to sustain their participation in Wikipedia.

Surface Acting Around Choice and Timing of Work

One key way participants engage in surface acting involves exhibiting agency over what kinds of work they do. Many interviewees stop or avoid certain kinds of work because it involves too much "drama." For example, one women noted that she doesn't experience trolling or harassment because she "actively avoid[s] areas or tasks" she thinks are "stressful" (P12). Similarly, P1 explains why she chooses not to participate on talk pages for controversial articles:

Women are marginalized in Wikipedia because [there are] so few of us. I don't participate in those discussions because I just—that is too much emotional work for me. I have plenty of emotional work to do in real life. […] I think a lot of other women make the same judgment because it's really awful. I hate arguing with people on the Internet. […] I avoid any kind of drama on Wikipedia because I don't have the energy to deal with it.

---

[1] Our theoretical lens was applied *post hoc* to our collected data. This study never set out to explore the phenomenon of emotional labor in Wikipedia, which we acknowledge as a subject inclusive of all genders.

[2] Edit counts in Wikipedia EN as of 19 September 2014.

Interviewees also manage their participation by controlling when they choose to be active. Eight women reported they have taken at least one Wikibreak (e.g., a break from reading, editing, and contributing to Wikipedia) and 2 women switched to a different project. P5 notes, "I didn't ever completely quit, but I did make a deliberate effort to change what I was doing so that I would not have to be faced with seeing really, really disturbing things that people were writing." All 10 of these women say their decision to stop or change their work was the direct result of Wikistress (e.g., stress caused by editing, specifically involving conflict, vandals, trolls, edit wars, and/or incivility); six say their Wikistress was caused by gender-based hostility.

Deep Acting and Gendered Feeling Rules

Participants' *deep acting* emotion work was primarily connected to stories of conflict, being targeted by trolls, or receiving unwanted sexual advances. At these moments, there was common recognition among interviewees that they should "stop behaving like a woman," which reveals the existence of a gendered 'feeling rule' in Wikipedia. P2 articulates the dimensions of this rule,

If you're harassed, there's an expectation that you will behave like a saint. You cannot give into any of the provocation [...] If you manage to successfully deal with the harasser [...] you cannot talk about [your] success. Because in talking about success stories dealing with women's harassment on Wikipedia, you empower the harassers. And that's the view that's being consistently said again and again and again . . . The only acceptable model for behavior on Wikipedia is to behave like a man, which is to ignore all the bullshit.

Similarly, P9 says, "[There was] one time that my sex was used against me in a way that did hurt me. I would appreciate it if you didn't [share the details] because I don't like to show weakness. We have a term for that on Wikipedia. We call it beans."

Emotional Labor, Ideological Gain

According to Hochschild, when people engage in emotion work they do so because they value social participation more than their personal feelings of conflict or despair. This equation expressed itself in our interviews as ideological gain. Despite stories of conflict, trolling, and harassment, participants valorized Wikipedia and the effort they put in to be editors. According to P1, "[Wikipedia] is the way I can reach the most people, and it means a lot to me to have a voice." Other participants note feelings of fulfillment generated by being *productively involved:* "I got this feedback from actual people, who really wanted to learn about the things I knew about" (P7); "I feel so much more connected to my local place [...] I've suddenly got a reputation as a local historian" (P8); "I'm really happy there are articles there because I started them [...] I'm also always really happy when I find a source for something that justifies keeping an article" (P15). Deep acting (or adhering to and accepting the 'feeling rules' of the dominant culture) is the mechanism by which our interviewees authentically engage with the values of Wikipedia (e.g., free knowledge for all, written by anyone and presented from a neutral point of view). Notably, this need for alignment appears to be so fine-tuned in our subjects that it no longer seems discordant to them.

DISCUSSION

Wikipedia is a fluid community, intentionally pushing and crossing boundaries in both formal and semi-structured ways. However, our data suggest that many participants' experiences in the community are shaped by others' perceptions of and responses to their gender. This not only affects participants' choice and timing of work in unintended and unstructured ways—and other community members' responses in turn—but also their engagement with other Wikipedians, friends, partners, and children. If participating in this sociotechnical space requires people of any gender to engage in taxing emotional labor, then it is time to change the collective perception of Wikipedia as a neutral, if not democratic, environment.

Some of the participants interviewed for this study may be acting as proverbial canaries in the coal mine, their emotion work signaling a pernicious environment within Wikipedia. If women who adhere to the underlying mission and epistemology of Wikipedia must engage in forms of deep and surface acting to participate as editors, administrators, and WMF employees, then what does it cost other individuals to conform to the Wiki way [25]? Should emotional labor be considered the cost of enabling such a socially complex project? Moreover, are Wikipedians victimizing themselves by institutionalizing biased 'feeling rules'? As one example, perhaps it is time that policies, guidelines, and essays such as "Assume good faith," "Deny recognition" (redirected from "Don't feed the trolls") and "Don't stuff beans up your nose" be critically interrogated for their normalization of raised—rather than lowered—barriers to full participation.

This brief exposure of women's experiences as editors suggests that the Wikipedia community must decide the gender gap is, first, a problem and, second, a problem worth addressing. Bridging the gap will require more than an increase in female participation; it will require Wikipedia to better understand its own culture of knowledge production. In this same spirit, we acknowledge that the participants interviewed for this study do not represent the entirety of women, genders, or perspectives within the Wikipedia movement, and thus this study cannot and does not speak for all women Wikipedians or those who have left the community. There are many disparate and diverse communities of editors who self-identify as women within the greater Wikipedia community, and factors such as personality type, communication style [16], and lived experience affect the ways in which these women perceive their gender and work. Finally, this study in no way suggests that those who identify as male or any other gender don't engage in emotional labor as well; it is only that this possibility cannot be discussed empirically at this point in our research.

Nascent and non-generalizable as these findings are, they nevertheless provide a new perspective for considering the often overlooked and undervalued work that many people, often those who are socially marginalized, do to participate in online spaces designed, built, and organized—usually without due acknowledgement—according to the norms of a dominant culture.

ACKNOWLEDGMENTS

The research received funding from a Wikimedia Individual Engagement Grant. The first author would like to thank Ellen Chisa for introducing her to Hochschild's work.

REFERENCES

1. Antin, J., Yee, R., Cheshire, C., and Oded, N. (2011). Gender differences in Wikipedia editing. In *Proceedings WikiSym 2011*, ACM Press (2011), 11-14.
2. Bardzell, S. (2010). Feminist HCI: taking stock and outlining an agenda for design. In *Proceedings CHI 2010*, ACM Press (2010), 1301-1310.
3. Bardzell, S and Bardzell, J. (2011). Towards a feminist HCI methodology: social science, feminism, and HCI. In *Proceedings CHI 2011*, ACM Press (2011), 675-684.
4. Charting diversity: Working together toward diversity in Wikipedia. (2014). https://upload.wikimedia.org/wikipedia/commons/5/57/ Charting_Diversity.pdf
5. Cohen, N. (2011, January 30). Define gender gap? Look up Wikipedia's contributor list. *The New York Times*.
6. Collier, B., and Bear, J. (2012). Conflict, criticism, or confidence: An empirical examination of the gender gap in Wikipedia contributions. In *Proceedings CSCW 2012*, ACM Press (2012), 383-392.
7. Duggan, M. and Brenner, J. (2013). The demographics of social media users, 2012. Pew Research Center, Washington, D.C.
8. Eckert, S. and Steiner, L. (2013). (Re)triggering backlash: Responses to news about Wikipedia's gender gap. *Journal of Communication Inquiry*, 37: 284.
9. Filipacchi, A. (2013, April 30). Sexism on Wikipedia is not the work of 'a single misguided editor'. *Atlantic*.
10. Flöck, F., Vrandečić, D. and Simperl, E. Towards a diversity-minded Wikipedia. In *Proc. WebSci '11*, ACM Press (2011).
11. Gardner, S. (2011). Nine reasons women don't edit Wikipedia. *Sue Gardner's blog*.
12. Glaser, B. (1992). *Basics of grounded theory analysis*. Mill Valley, CA: Sociology Press.
13. Halfaker, A., Geiger, R.S. and Terveen, L.G. (2014). Snuggle: Designing for efficient socialization and ideological critique. In *Proceedings CHI 2014*, ACM, Press (2014), 311-320.
14. Hill, B.M. and Shaw, A. (2013). The Wikipedia gender gap revisited: Characterizing survey response bias with propensity score estimation. PLoS ONE, 8:6.
15. Hochschild, A. (1979). Emotion Work, Feeling Rules, and Social Structure. *American Journal of Sociology*, 85:3, 551-575.
16. Iosub, D. et al. (2014). Emotions under discussion: Gender, status and communication in online collaboration. PLoS ONE, 9:8.
17. Kannabiran, G (2014). Ecofeminism and sustainable HCI. In *Proceedings DIS Companion 2014*, ACM Press (2014), 185-190.
18. Kittur, A., Bongwon, S., Pendleton, B., and Chi, E. (2007). He says, she says: Conflict and coordination in Wikipedia. In *Proceedings CHI 2007*, ACM Press (2007), 453-462.
19. Kittur, A., and Kraut, R. (2008). Harnessing the wisdom of crowds in Wikipedia: Quality through coordination. In *Proceedings CSCW 2008*, ACM Press (2008), 37-46.
20. Lam, S., Uduwage, A., Dong, Z., Sen, S., Musicant, D., Terveen, L., and Riedl, J. (2011). WP:Clubhouse?: An exploration of Wikipedia's gender imbalance. In *Proceedings WikiSym 2011*, ACM Press (2011), 1-10.
21. Leonard, A. (2013, April 29). Wikipedia's shame. *Salon*.
22. Niederer, S. and van Dijck, J. (2010). Wisdom of the crowd or technicity of content? Wikipedia as a sociotechnical system. *New Media Society*, 12:1368.
23. Nov, O. (2007). What motivates Wikipedians? *Communications of the ACM*, 50:11, 60-64.
24. Panciera, K., Halfaker, A., and Terveen, L. (2009). Wikipedians are born, not made: A study of power editors on Wikipedia. In *Proceedings GROUP 2009*, ACM Press (2009), 51-60.
25. Van der Velden, M. (2013). Decentering design: Wikipedia and indigenous knowledge. *International Journal of Human-Computer Interaction*, 29:4.
26. Weibert, A., Marshall, A., Aal, K., Schubert, K. and Rode, J. (2014). Sewing interest in E-textiles: analyzing making from a gendered perspective. In *Proceedings DIS (2014)*, ACM Press (2014), 15-24.
27. Where are the women in Wikipedia? (2011, February 2). The Opinion Pages: Room for Debate. *The New York Times*.
28. Wikimedia: Gendergap mailing list. (n.d.). https://lists.wikimedia.org/mailman/listinfo/gendergap
29. Wikipedia 'completely failed' to fix gender imbalance [Video file]. (2014, August 8). *BBC News*.

How Activists Are Both Born and Made: An Analysis of Users on Change.org

Shih-Wen Huang, Minhyang (Mia) Suh, Benjamin Mako Hill, Gary Hsieh
University of Washington
DUB Group
{wenhuang, miasuh, makohill, garyhs} @ uw.edu

ABSTRACT
E-petitioning has become one of the most important and popular forms of online activism. Although e-petition success is driven by user behavior, users have received relatively little study by e-petition researchers. Drawing from theoretical and empirical work in analogous social computing systems, we identify two potentially competing theories about the trajectories of users in e-petition platforms: (1) "power" users in social computing systems are born, not made; and (2) users mature into "power" user roles. In a quantitative analysis of data from Change.org, one of the largest online e-petition platforms, we test and find support for both theories. A follow-up qualitative analysis shows that not only do users learn from their experience, systems also "learn" from users to make better recommendations. In this sense, we find that although power users are "born," they are also "made" through both processes of personal growth and improved support from the system.

Author Keywords
online activism, civic engagement, e-petition, power user, contribution, motivation

INTRODUCTION
In November 2013, 15-year-old high school student Sarah Kavanagh found out that brominated vegetable oil (BVO), a controversial flame retardant chemical, is an ingredient in some Gatorade drinks. She decided to go to Change.org – one of the largest e-petition platforms – to start a petition to ask Gatorade to remove the harmful ingredient. In less than two months, the petition received more than 200,000 signatures from people around the world and was widely discussed in the press. As a result, Gatorade executives agreed to remove the ingredient. Although her petition's wild success is not typical, Kavanagh's experience is not unique. In September 2014, there were hundreds of thousands of petitions on Change.org, and many successful stories like Kavanagh's.

CHI 2015, April 18 - 23 2015, Seoul, Republic of Korea
Copyright 2015 ACM 978-1-4503-31456/15/04...$15.00
http://dx.doi.org/10.1145/2702123.2702559

Figure 1. The petition about removing flame retardant chemicals in Gatorade on Change.org. The campaign was a huge success with more than 200,000 signatures.

Despite this potential for impact, the vast majority of petitions on Change.org have few signatures and more than 99% of petitions are never marked as "victorious." To be successful, e-petitions need signatures – our data shows that victorious petitions on Change.org receive, on average, 20 times more signatures than non-victorious petitions. Because these signatures come from users, it becomes critical for designers and petitioners to understand user behavior in these platforms.

Although e-petitioning has received relatively little study by HCI and social computing researchers, e-petition platforms share many features and qualities with other social computing systems. Users have accounts, profiles, and can create and share content. Like many other social computing systems (e.g., Wikipedia [9]), the most active users are responsible for the majority of contributions. Our data shows that the top 5% of Change.org users make more than 50% of all signatures. As a result, understanding these power signers may be a key to building a successful e-petition platform.

An important issue with any discussion of power users is the degree to which users begin as active contributors and the degree to which they learn to grow into these roles. Often, these debates are framed as whether power users are "born or made" [13, 16]. For example, social computing research on Wikipedia [16] has shown that extremely active users are different from ordinary users in the first days of their lifespans and suggested that these users are inherently different. On the other hand, another body of research suggests that participants in communities learn to become contributors, or even leaders, through situated peripheral participation [11] and can systematically be nurtured by carefully designed systems such as the reader-to-leader framework proposed by Preece and Shneiderman [18].

In this study, we used a mixed analysis to examine these two competing theories. First, we present a quantitative analysis of users' participation in Change.org that aims to test the *born* and *made* theories. In a second study, we present a qualitative analysis of 14 in-depth interviews with Change.org signers that further explores our quantitative findings. Our work makes several theoretical, methodological, and substantive contributions to the literature on social computing and the born or made debate. Our results use qualitative data to reveal previously untheorized mechanisms and extend social computing research to e-petition platforms. Additionally, although previous work on whether users are born or made has focused on the first hypothesis (e.g., [17]), our work tests both and finds support for each. In doing so, we offer a novel approach to the born/made debate and a way to reconcile the apparently contradictory findings.

BACKGROUND

E-petitioning

A classic example of grassroots political activity, petitioning is an act of collective action by citizens where groups place a single-issue request before an authority or organization to undertake or impede certain actions or policies [14]. An online analog, e-petitioning has gained popularity because it features low-commitment action based on easy and convenient tools allowing more people to support causes important to them. From the comfort of their homes, people can quickly and easily sign a petition with a click of a button. E-petition platforms like Change.org, Causes.com, and Moveon.org have rapidly grown and increased in number over the last several years.

Political science researchers have shown a particular interest in e-petition platforms. For example, Hale et al. [7], traced the growth of over 8,000 petitions on the UK Government's No. 10 Downing Street website for two years and found that most successful petitions grow quickly. Jungherr and Jürgens also analyzed 1.5 years worth of data from the German parliament e-petition platform, *epetitionen.bundestag.de* [8] and provided descriptive statistics about its petitions and signers.

Although these studies have explored several characteristics of e-petition platforms, they have been primarily descriptive of how people use the system (e.g., [8] reports the distribution of the number of total petitions and distinct topics supported by signers) or have focused on questions of what *petition* qualities, rather than *user qualities,* lead to more signatures and petition success. Following lessons from human-centered designs, designers also need to understand *users* – petition signers – to effectively improve these e-petitioning platforms.

Change.org

To obtain a broader understanding of e-petition platforms, we studied petition signers on Change.org. Change.org was founded in 2007 as a social network for non-profits and for project-based giving. Used by more than 70 million users in 196 countries, Change.org is the largest and most widely used e-petition platform and has been widely adopted by social movement organizations working on a wide variety of issues. Although it does not substitute for other forms of civic engagement, there are many examples of successful Change.org petitions like Kavanagh's that have led to meaningful social change in the real world. Unlike other e-petition platforms (e.g., We the People, UK No. 10 Downing Street), a *victorious* petition on Change.org does not mean the petition's signature count exceeds a certain threshold. On Change.org, a petition's goal for signatures can be changed once it reaches its original goal and petitioners can declare victory at any point.

Are Power Signers Born or Made

Because the goal of a petition is to accumulate signatures, the success of an e-petition platform requires significant user participation. Reviews suggest that a small portion of users make up a major of the contributors in typical online communities [10]. Our data of Change.org shows that the top 4.6% of users (i.e., "power signers") contribute more than half of all signatures (Table 2). Although increased rates of signing might come at the expense of quality, many signatures point to increased political engagement [7,14] and can be a sign of a system that is effective at helping users find petitions that match their ideals. As a result, understanding user behavior to attract and encourage power signers remains one of the most important questions for e-petition researchers. Research into online participation on other social computing systems offers several competing theories of where "power users" come from, and how one might design to support them.

Born

An influential theory of power users suggests that active participants in online communities are born and not made. For example, research has shown that the most active contributors to Wikipedia are different from other contributors on their first day [16]. Similarly, Panciera et al. [17] find support for the "born" hypothesis in a study of power editors in a Geowiki. Additionally, Muller [13] found that the engagement level of users on enterprise social media is related to stable personal traits. Pal et al. [15] found the experts in a Q&A community contribute significantly more than others at the beginning of their lifespans within the community.

Laboratory experiments have attempted to model individual decisions to participate in petitioning by focusing on qualities of individuals that are unlikely to change with time. For example, Margetts et al. found that more extraverted individuals and people with higher locus of control are more likely to be "starters" – those who sign when petitions are first initiated [12]. In addition, Cruickshank et al. [6] found that petition participation is related to individuals' intrinsic psychological characteristics. This body of work suggests that e-petition signers' behavior may be driven by stable individual characteristics. As a result, we would predict that, like other social computing domains, power signers will be "born," and that users' initial engagement with the platform will predict their long-term activity:

H1: Initial levels of engagement with an e-petition platform will strongly predict users' subsequent levels of engagement.

Made

Another perspective is that power users grow and mature over time. Lave & Wenger discuss the idea of legitimate peripheral participation in their work on general communities of practice and suggest that through interaction and engagement with a community, individuals learn to become experts and core members [11]. Building on this idea, Preece and Shneiderman offer the reader-to-leader framework [18] characterizing online users' participation behavior in terms of four categories that participants move through as they develop in their use of a site: reader (e.g., browsing, searching, returning), contributor (e.g., rating, tagging, reviewing, posting, uploading), collaborator (e.g., developing relationships, working together, setting goals), and leader (e.g., promoting participation, mentoring novices, setting and upholding policies).

In a broader sense, the idea that users' behavior is shaped and driven by their experience over time is central to social computing research, which has frequently focused on ways that users develop identity and commitment over time and respond to social influence [10]. Additionally, a rich literature on organizations points to organizational learning and planned behavior as two of many ways that individual action is shaped, and supports the idea that users of social computing systems learn to be power users.

This perspective suggests that users become more actively involved with communities and more committed to platforms over time and, as a result, participate more often:

H2a: Signers will participate more often as their experience with the platform increases.

Research in other social computing domains also provides support for the idea that learning improves the *effectiveness* of contributors. In their study of Q&A, Ahn et al.'s study of Stack Exchange found that receiving feedback (e.g., votes and favorites) predicts a marginal increase in the quality of question askers' subsequent questions [1]. In a controlled experiment to test donation behavior in crowdfunding sites, Wash & Solomon [19] found that participants could learn to coordinate their efforts and not contribute to high-risk or unfundable projects. In the e-petition context, an improvement in *effectiveness* would mean that signers become better at assessing petitions over time. For example, this might mean that users are more likely to sign petitions that are later declared victorious:

H2b: As their experience with the platform increases, signers will be more likely to sign victorious petitions.

A creator's decision to mark a petition as victorious is a potentially noisy measure of petition quality. A second measure of petition quality is the raw number of signatures that the petition will end up receiving:

H2c: As their experience with the platform increases, signers will sign petitions that eventually get more signatures.

Finally, it is worth noting that it is possible the users are "made" in social computing systems in more than one sense. Users may become more engaged and/or more effective over time not only because they have learned but, rather, because the system has grown to be "better" at supporting them. For example, Cosley et al. [4] utilized the edit history of Wikipedia users to recommend Wiki pages that users might be interested in editing. Others have shown that the same technique is useful in increasing users' contribution in an online movie review forum [5]. In addition, An et al. [2] showed that it is possible to use users' tweets to invite potential investors to fund crowdfunding projects that might interest them. This thread of research demonstrates that social computing systems can use user data to encourage contribution and users can be "made" in the sense that they are supported to become more effective by a system.

STUDY 1: QUANTITATIVE ANALYSIS

The first step in our research seeks to test our hypotheses using public "digital trace" data on users of Change.org published on its website and made available through a publicly accessible API.[1]

Data and Empirical Setting

To build a representative sample of Change.org users, we took advantage of the fact that Change.org user ID numbers increase sequentially. By selecting numbers sequentially, we built a 1% sample of users who created their accounts during the 16-month period between January 2010 and April 2011. From an original sample of 23,000 users, we removed 648 with malformed data (*e.g.*, some users put both city and state information in the city field) and 1,072 users who hadn't signed any petitions. We focused on the

[1] https://www.change.org/developers

Data field	Description
User ID	The unique ID of the user.
User Name	The name of the user.
User location	Comprised of city, state (province), and country.
User Activities	A list of IDs of the petitions the user signed and created.
Petition ID	The unique ID of the petition.
Petition category	The topic (e.g., Animals or Environment) of the petition.
Petition duration	The start date and end date of the petition.
Petition status	A status that shows if the petition is still running (open), has finished but is not successful (closed), or if the creator finished the petition and declared victory (victory).
Petition signatures	The information (name and location) of the signers of the petition and the timestamps of the signatures

Table 1. A summary of the user and petition data retrieved through Change.org API.

remaining 21,280 users in our analysis. Next, we collected information on the 140,866 petitions that these users signed. A description of the data collected is shown in Table 1. Because many users sign petitions in batches, we grouped signatures into "sessions" when the elapsed time between signatures is less than one hour.

Like many measures of social media activity, our continuous measures are highly skewed. For example, about one third of users only sign once in their lifespans, and more than half of the users sign less than 3 times. In contrast, the power users (top 4.6%) on average sign 205 times and contribute more than 50% of all signatures (Table 2). Toward that end, we log transform each of the continuous measures before using them in regression analyses.

Study 1a: Using the First Session to Predict the Level of Activeness of the User

Measures

Testing **H1** requires cross-sessional data with users as the unit of analysis and measures of long term and initial engagement. To capture the level of a user's long term engagement, we use the total number of signing sessions (i.e., groups of signatures separated by less than one hour) that a user engages in between the time they join the site and the point of data collection (September 2014). To measure initial levels of engagement, we use the number of petitions that users sign in their first session.[2]

# of Signatures	Users (%)	Accumulated Users (%)	Contributions (%)	Accumulated Contributions (%)
1	33.2%	33.2%	1.7%	1.7%
2-3	17.0%	50.2%	1.9%	3.6%
4-5	10.2%	60.4%	2.2%	5.9%
6-10	11.6%	72.0%	4.3%	10.1%
11-25	11.7%	83.7%	9.5%	19.6%
26-50	6.6%	90.3%	11.4%	30.9%
50-100	5.1%	95.4%	18.3%	49.2%
Over 100	4.6%	100%	50.7%	100%

Table 2. The distribution of users by their signature count. It shows most users contribute only a few signatures on the platform, while, the top 4.6% of the users contribute more than half of the total signatures.

We also constructed a series of control variables to capture other reasons that might influence users' level of engagement with Change.org. Because users attracted by different types of petitions might have different trajectories, we include stable qualities of the initial petitions signed by users in the form of dummy variables indicating whether initial petitions were created by organizations and whether they were declared victorious. We also include continuous measures of the total signatures received by the first petition signed by each user. To control for other observable qualities of users, we also measure the number of signatures and the age of the first petition signed in days at the point when it was signed by the user in question. Because different issues might attract users who are more or less driven to participate in the future, and because users who join Change.org earlier had more time to engage, we also include fixed effects for both the category of the user's first signed petition (e.g., Animal Rights, Criminal Justice, or Education) and for the month in which the user first signed a petition in a second model.

Methods and Analysis

To test our hypotheses that power signers are born, we first follow Panciera et al.'s approach to studying power editors of Wikipedia [16]. We begin with descriptive statistics of the likelihood the signers will become power signers by looking at the different number of petitions signed in their first session. Although defining levels of activity that constitute "power signing" is necessarily arbitrary, our analysis

[2] We used the first session for our analysis to be consistent with Study 1b. Results using signers' first day instead of their first session were similar.

Signatures in 1st session	Count	Proportion of users	Likelihood of > 1 Session	Likelihood of > 5 sessions	Likelihood of > 20 sessions
1	16336	77%	52%	22%	8%
2	1696	8%	62%	31%	13%
3	1099	5%	69%	35%	13%
4	1580	7%	71%	43%	18%
>=5	569	3%	76%	50%	22%

Table 3. Likelihood of signers becoming active based on the number of signatures in their first session. We report results for > 1 session (50th percentile), > 5 sessions (75th percentile), and > 20 sessions (90th percentile).

suggests, as in previous work [16], that our pattern of results are not sensitive to the threshold we choose.

Beyond these descriptive statistics, we also try to formally test **H1** using a series of fitted regression models. Poisson models are frequently used for counts like the total number of sessions a user makes on Change.org. Like many counts, over-dispersion is a concern in our data so we estimate a quasi-Poisson model. In analyses not reported here, we also estimate negative binomial count models and we find the results are similar.

Results

Table 3 reproduces a table used by Panciera et al. [16] to argue that Wikipedia power users are born, not made. Our results match Panciera et al.'s results from Wikipedia and provide descriptive evidence in support of the claim that users are born. For example, the far right column shows that a larger proportion of users who sign at least 5 petitions will go on to have more than 20 sessions (the 90th percentile) than those who only sign only one petition. This pattern is repeated across all columns which capture the number of sessions users go on to have.

Regression results demonstrate strong support for the born hypothesis as well. Table 4 includes two models with and without controls in the form of fixed effects for first petition category and month of first engagement. Because these are Poisson models, we estimate that, in the model without fixed effects, a log unit increase in the number of signatures in a users' first session will be associated with a 1.5 (or $e^{0.42}$) times increase in the total number of sessions.

To further assist with the interpretation, we fit a series of linear probability models using the right side of the full fixed effects model to describe the model-predicted probability of a user falling into one of the categories described in Table 3. Predicted probabilities from these models with all controls held at their sample medians are shown in Figure 2 and describe a similar pattern of results shown in Tables 3 and 4. They show that users who are more engaged in their very first session are much more engaged in the site over the long term. These analyses provide strong support for H1 and the idea that power signers on Change.org are born.

Study 1b: A Longitudinal Analysis of Users' Petition Signing Behaviors

Measures

Because testing **H2** involves looking for changes in user behavior over time, we construct a longitudinal dataset where the unit of analysis is the user-session. To test **H2a** that users will participate more frequently over time, we construct a measure of time since the previous session.[3] To test **H2b** and **H2c** that users become more effective at assessing petitions, we construct a dummy variable to measure whether a session includes a signature to a petition that will eventually be declared victorious and a measure of the mean number of signatures that petitions in a given session will ultimately receive. Because all three **H2** hypotheses involve looking for change as a user gains experience, our primary independent variable is the session number or sequence for the user in question (i.e., 5 for a user's fifth session).

As we hypothesize, systems may drive what appears to be learning by presenting users with more popular materials over time. To address this in **H2b** and **H2c**, we include our measure of the average number of signatures a petition has at the time the user signed it. In the case of **H2c**, this is a very strong control because this measure is highly correlated with the dependent variable (i.e., the average total number of signatures that petitions in the session receive).

Methods and Analysis

Testing **H2** in our longitudinal dataset includes repeated measures of the same user, which leads to concerns of a lack of independence between observations. To address this, we estimate fixed effects models that are equivalent to fitting a dummy variable for every single user in the dataset. This reflects a very strong test because these fixed effects control for any observed or unobserved quality that

[3] We necessarily omit the first session from this analysis.

	w/o Fixed Effect	w Fixed Effect
(Intercept)	1.57***	1.68***
	(0.12)	(0.19)
# of Signatures in 1st Session	0.44***	0.42***
	(0.03)	(0.03)
1st Pet. By Organization	0.31***	0.26***
	(0.04)	(0.04)
1st Pet. Victory	-0.19***	-0.04
	(0.05)	(0.05)
1st Pet. Popularity	0.04	0.02
	(0.02)	(0.02)
1st Pet. Popularity when Signed	0.01	0.02
	(0.02)	(0.02)
1st Pet. Age	0.00	-0.01
	(0.00)	(0.01)
Fixed Effects		
1st Sig. Category	No	Yes
1st Sig. Month	No	Yes
Deviance	476220	461086
Num. obs.	21280	21280

***$p < 0.001$, **$p < 0.01$, *$p < 0.05$, All the continuous measures were logged.

Table 4. Quasi-Poisson regression models that predict the number of total sessions with and without fixed effects for petition category and the month of users' first activity.

has a consistent user-level effect on our outcomes. As a result, our estimates rely entirely on within-person variation over time.

Results

Parameter estimates for our fitted regression models for our three sub-hypotheses for **H2** are shown in Table 5. **H2a** (that users will contribute more frequently as they gain experience) is tested in $\mathbf{M_{Elapsed}}$ and finds strong support. Because both our dependent and independent variables are log transformed in $\mathbf{M_{Elapsed}}$, we estimate that a 1% change in the session sequence number is associated with a 0.12% decrease in the time between the session in question and the previous session. We also find that our control for the number of petitions signed in a session is related to larger spans of time between sessions.

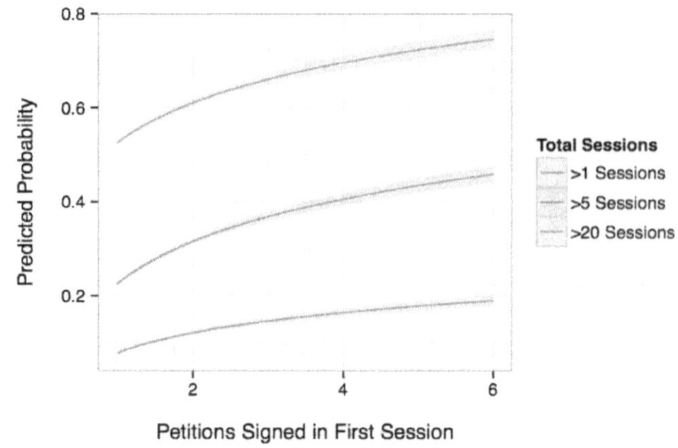

Figure 2. Predicted probability of various level of total sessions based on the number of petition signed in the first session.

In $\mathbf{M_{Victorious}}$, we test **H2b** that users become more effective with experience and sign petitions that are more likely to be declared victorious. Our results are contradictory to our prediction. $\mathbf{M_{Victorious}}$ suggests that controlling for the number of petitions signed and the number of signatures already on a petition when a user signs it, users are *less* likely to sign a victorious petition in a given session as they gain experience on Change.org. Using a linear probability model, we can interpret that a 1% change in session sequence number is associated with a 2% decrease in the likelihood of the session including one petition that will eventually be declared victorious. This finding provides disconfirming evidence for **H2b**.

$\mathbf{M_{Popularity}}$ tests **H2c** that users will sign petitions that will eventually accumulate more signatures. The results provide support for **H2c** in favor of increased user effectiveness. In $\mathbf{M_{Popularity}}$, we estimate that a 1% increase in the session sequence number is associated with a 0.04% increase in the total number of signatures. Although this effect is small, it is worth keeping in mind that this reflects the marginal effect after controlling for the number of signatures at the time that the petition was signed. Controlling for when users sign, and given that they are signing more frequently over time, users sign petitions that end up with more signatures as they gain experience with the site.

Although we find evidence that users are both born and made, the relative importance of these effects is an important question. We can begin to answer this by considering whether stable individual characteristics or changes in behavior over time explain more of the variation in our longitudinal models. Although the models used in Study 1b use within-person fixed effects to offer a strong test of the made hypotheses, this means that we cannot simply add dispositional covariates. Instead, we estimate a series of random effects models otherwise identical to the models in Study 1b that allow us to estimate the intra-class correlation, which reflects the proportion of variance in our dependent

	$M_{Elapsed}$	$M_{Victorious}$	$M_{popularity}$
Session sequence number	-0.12***	-0.02***	0.04***
	(0.00)	(0.00)	(0.00)
# of petitions in session	0.05***	0.07***	-0.07***
	(0.01)	(0.00)	(0.00)
Avg. petition popularity when signed		0.04***	0.74***
		(0.00)	(0.00)
R^2	0.01	0.03	0.72
Adj. R^2	0.01	0.03	0.67
Num. obs.	171282	183091	183091
Num. users	11810	11810	11810

$^{***}p < 0.001$, $^{**}p < 0.01$, $^{*}p < 0.05$, All the continuous measures were logged.

Table 5. Three regression models where the dependent variables are elapsed time from previous session ($M_{Elapsed}$), # of victorious petitions in session ($M_{Victorious}$), and the Avg. petition popularity in session ($M_{popularity}$)

variables that comes from stable individual characteristics. Our results are mixed and suggest that the importance of stable characteristics varies enormously across our three models. We find that 43% of the variance in time between sessions, 3% of the variance in the proportion of editing sessions with at least one victorious petition, and 21% of the variance in average petition popularity is associated with characteristics that are stable across individuals.

Discussion

Our results echo previous research on Wikipedia and show that power signers on Change.org can also be predicted using engagement level in their first session. This supports **H1** that power signers are *born*. We also find the signers sign more frequently and target more popular petitions when they have more experience on the site. Although our test of **H2b** points in an unanticipated direction, it also shows change over time. This provides broad support for **H2** that the power signers are also *made*. Going beyond Panciera et al. [16,17] who tested only whether users were born, our results show that power users can be both born and made, and to varying degrees, along different and important measures of activity. These results have important theoretical implications to social computing researchers used to presenting "born" and "made" as competing hypotheses.

Our results for our test of **H2b** – that users are *less* likely to sign victorious petitions over time – is both surprising and at odds with our finding for **H2c**. That said, the relative infrequency of victorious petitions and the subjective nature of creator-defined "victory" suggests that more complex dynamics may be at play than our quantitative results can uncover.

Even our more intuitive results raise questions that are difficult to answer using only observational data from the Change.org website. For example, although our results show that signers sign more frequently as they gain experience on Change.org, we cannot know whether this is because signers learn to contribute more or because the system learns to better target them.

STUDY2: INTERVIEW OF SIGNERS

In a follow-up qualitative study, we aim to answer two questions raised by our quantitative analyses:

1. Why do people select more popular petitions over time?
2. Does the Change.org system play a role in signers' behavior change?

We conducted semi-structured interviews with a number of individuals who have signed more than one petition on Change.org.

Methods

Interviewees were recruited from Facebook and Craigslist in 10 major cities in the U.S. Potential interviewees completed a short demographic and Change.org usage screening survey. Based on the survey answers, we reached out to 20 people through email, and 14 were willing to be interviewed. All interviews were conducted over the phone or Skype, audio recorded, and transcribed. Interviews lasted about 50 minute on average. As compensation, interviewees could choose between $20 in Amazon gift cards or donating the same amount of money to a charity of their choice. All of the participants joined Change.org over one year ago, four of them signed less than five petitions, five of them signed more than five but less than 50, and five of them signed more than 50 petitions. Eight of the participants were between 20-39 years old, three of them were between 40-59, and three of them were 60 years or older. Ten of the participants were female and four were male. The overrepresentation of women among our interviewees is in line with the distribution of women in the population of Change.org users.[4]

In interviews, we asked users about their first and most recently signed petitions on Change.org, and explored how their motivation and signing behavior has changed over time. Some example lead-in questions were:

- What triggers you to sign petitions on Change.org?

[4] https://chartio.com/blog/2013/12/the-data-behind-online-activism

- How do you search/decide which petition to sign?
- Has your signing behavior on Change.org changed since you first signed? How?

Each of the interviews was coded with inductive codes using Dedoose qualitative data analysis software by two members of our team. Codes were discussed, combined, and interpreted to create themes using a grounded theory approach [3]. Coded responses were analyzed based on categories related to how interviewees responded to the questions.

Results

Signers Become More Selective

In line with our results in **H2c** that users become more effective, interviewees frequently explained that they felt they had become more careful about choosing the petitions they sign as they gained experience with Change.org. First, they explained a growing recognition that some petitions on Change.org are of low quality:

> You can tell that some are just put up there as a joke, or maybe not a serious petition. And, you know, it has to be something I believe very strongly before I even take the time to sign it. (P14)

Also, we found that as signers become more aware of their presence on the site, they choose the petitions more carefully. For example:

> In the beginning, I used to sign in all the time and ... displaying my signature was okay. Now ... I really don't want to put my name on everything. It's a bit overwhelming. I'm careful where I put my name on petitions. (P7)

This provides support for our hypotheses that signers become more selective as they become more experienced on Change.org.

Raising Awareness as Petition Success

The results in our quantitative analyses were surprising in the sense that they suggest that users are selecting more popular petitions but not the ones that are more likely to be declared as victories. Although we did not describe this finding to interviewees, many participants suggested petition success might not only be through a petition accomplishing its stated goal. For example, users found that raising awareness of an issue could be equally, or even more, important:

> I guess the success of a petition, there are two definitions. It would be either bringing more awareness to people on a situation or actually getting a goal accomplished because sometimes, petitions may not be as successful as we want them to but it does bring awareness to people. Sometimes, when I sign it, it may say maybe 10,000 signatures but then when I get an update, it might say 20,000 signatures. Although that isn't a lot, it's still 10,000 people you're reaching out to. (P13)

Another interviewee echoed a similar sentiment:

> If you're getting people thinking about an issue or you're making them feel like it's a passionate issue and you're changing somebody's approach to something ... they're more aware of issues that may be around them. (P2)

In further explanation of our finding in **H2b**, signers emphasized that petition victory is something that is outside of the petitioners' control:

> It doesn't seem like very many petitions are truly successful, maybe they are, but it seems like you'll get all these supporters and still nothing's been changed. But at least you know that you're not the only person that thinks that way. Maybe there's 3,000,000 people who think that GMOs are wrong, but the government's still not listening. (P1)

These explanations suggest that many active signers do not target the petitions based on how likely it is to accomplish its goal (i.e., victory) but rather to find issues that are important and that help them raise awareness. To the extent that this position, common in our interviews of experienced Change.org users, develops in users over time, it may provide an explanation to why our quantitative analysis finds disconfirming evidence for **H2b** but in support of **H2c**.

Signers Are Being Made By the System

Finally, our results in **H2a** suggest that signers sign more frequently over time. As we suggested in our background, it can be difficult to unpack the way that users are made through personal growth and learning or through increased support from a system.

To unpack this issue, we asked all interviewees what prompted them to sign petitions on Change.org. Interestingly, unlike many social computing systems where users actively go to the site to make contributions, our interviewees rarely went to Change.org unprompted. Instead, they returned to the platform when receiving invitations to sign a petition. For many interviewees, this was over email:

> Well, they send me an e-mail. That's the only time I [sign petitions on Change.org]. It's an e-mail about one specific issue and if you want to sign it you click a thing and if you say skip to the next one it skips to another one. Then you read it and if it's something I want to sign, I sign it. (P9)

Other interviewees cited Facebook as the primary prompt for engagement but the pattern of interaction was nearly identical:

> Facebook is actually the quickest way because once you say, "Oh I like it" you get the updates that you want. So that's actually a quicker way, if I don't have patience to just go scroll through the "bajillion" things, I can go through Facebook. (P7)

To the extent that users' engagement is driven by these targeted prompts sent through channels managed by the Change.org platform (i.e., emails from the site and its petitioners and from Facebook channels), this provides evidence that users are not only learning but that their signing behaviors may be shaped by the site.

In further support of this conclusion, signers mentioned that they think Change.org does a good job of modeling their interests and provides useful recommendations to them:

> They must know the topics that I respond to because I will not sign every one. I must read the petition first to make sure it agrees with my principles. (P5)

A common response suggested that, although they did not understand how Change.org worked, users felt it did a good job of recommending petitions to them based on their previous use of the system:

> I don't know how Change.org actually, how the system runs but ... I always get petition for animals. That's the number one thing that I always receive. I guess because it's saved, I guess your likes or your recent signing and petitions, it brings up recommendations of what you're interested in. (P13)

Several interviewees explicitly suggested that many emails for petitions they sign come not from Change.org but from organizations using Change.org as a platform. To the extent that these organizations are also learning, they provide a larger concept of the platform that can effectively target users. For example, one user explained:

> I get a lot of messages from, like, the Freedom from Religion Foundation, for example. I get, you know, e-mails from them, and sometimes they do include links to petitions on Change.org. (P14)

Of course, many other forms of engagement were driven by prompts outside the control of Change.org and petition creators. Many other interviewees suggested that they received petition information from other social media platforms like Twitter and Reddit. That said, these interviews suggested that not only were users learning to be more selective and effective, but that the Change.org system, and the broader ecosystem of petitioners using the system, was also learning to make better recommendations as it collected more data about signers. In this sense, Change.org activists are not only "made" themselves, but also "made" by the system.

DISCUSSION

By examining the born and made hypotheses in a mixed method analysis of Change.org users, our study advances our understanding of user behavior in e-petition systems. Our results also add to the larger theoretical debate about whether users are born or made in social computing systems in general, and suggest that these theories may not be in conflict.

First, in our study on Change.org signers, we found similar results to prior studies that the likelihood of a user becoming a power user can be estimated using initial engagement. Although this provides strong evidence in favor of the claim that power users are born, we found that this is not the full story. A longitudinal analysis of Change.org signers shows that user behavior also changes over time and suggests that both "born" and" made" theories help explain user behavior on Change.org.

This research is an observational study of users. As a result, more research is needed to understand how systems can use both theories to elicit more contributions from users. That said, several implications for design are immediately clear. For example, even though one might be able to identify power users after their initial engagement, a system might still effectively nurture these users.

In strong support of this approach, our in-depth interviews uncovered evidence that the behavior of signers on Change.org changes not only because signers are learning from their own experience in the community, as proposed in research on situated learning and the reader-to-leader framework [10, 18], but also because signers are being "made" into more active and engaged users by the system as the platform itself learns from the history of signers and engages them more effectively. This provides strong support for the idea that social computing systems that utilize intelligent task routing to encourage contributions, like those created for Wikipedia [4] and MovieLens [5], might play an important role for users who were born as active contributors. For instance, a system might actively send out requests to users to better understand their interests by their responses. Then, the system might send requests to users based on their interests to solicit additional contributions.

Limitations

In this study, we analyzed data from 21,280 users who joined Change.org between January 2010 and April 2011 and all the petitions they signed. Although we sampled randomly over this period, this random sample is unlikely to contain extreme outliers that may be of interest to a studies of power users. Because we rely on a random sample, our study is limited to average effects.

Additionally, we cannot be confident in our findings' generalizability to other social computing platforms or even to other e-petition systems. Although it is important to note that general user interaction on e-petition sites are quite similar, and although we have also found that patterns of use on Change.org are similar to what other scholars of e-petition platforms have reported, it is impossible to know how findings gleaned from Change.org can inform our understanding of user behavior on other platforms. This is particularly the case for social computing systems that operate very differently than Change.org. For instance, our "made" effect might be weaker in a platform such as Wikipedia which does not send out emails or systematically recommend that users edit particular pages.

CONCLUSION

In this study, we analyzed petitions and users on one of the most popular e-petition platforms. In particular, we asked whether power signers on Change.org are born or made. Our results found support for both the born and made hypotheses. We found that users who contribute more frequently initially are more likely to be active over their lifespan on the site. We also found that signers' behavior changes over time and that as signers gain experience, they contribute more frequently, sign petitions that are more likely to be popular, and are less likely to sign victorious petitions.

Using data from interviews of Change.org users, we unpack this final finding in ways that lead us to be more confident in our hypothesis that users learn. Additionally, this interview data suggests signers' activity on the site is often prompted by email and social media in ways that suggest that learning is also happening within the system. As signers sign more petitions, the Change.org platform can better model signers' interest to recommend petitions that the signers are more likely to sign. These findings suggest that administrators of e-petition platforms should both find ways to identify power signers early in their lifespans, and devote more resources to encourage users to develop and grow in their activity.

There are many possible directions for future work. One interesting finding from this study is that email and social media seem like important drivers of Change.org signing. Therefore, in the future, we hope to measure activity around petitions outside of e-petition platforms.

ACKNOWLEDGEMENTS
Many thanks to the anonymous reviewers for their valuable comments on how to improve an earlier draft of this work. This paper also benefited from the discussion with Yi-Chen Sung and the UW Prosocial Computing Group.

REFERENCES

1. Ahn, J., Butler, B. S., Weng, C., & Webster, S. Learning to be a better q'er in social Q&A sites: Social norms and information artifacts. In *Proc. the American Society for Information Science and Technology* (2013).
2. An, J., Quercia, D., & Crowcroft, J. Recommending investors for crowdfunding projects. *In Proc. WWW* (2014).
3. Charmaz, K., & Belgrave, L. *Qualitative interviewing and grounded theory analysis.* The SAGE handbook of interview research: The complexity of the craft (2002).
4. Cosley, D., Frankowski, D., Terveen, L., & Riedl, J. Suggest Bot: using intelligent task routing to help people find work in Wikipedia. *In Proc. IUI* (2007).
5. Cosley, D., Frankowski, D., Terveen, L., & Riedl, J. Using intelligent task routing and contribution review to help communities build artifacts of lasting value. *In Proc. CHI* (2006).
6. Cruickshank, P., Edelmann, N., & Smith, C. F. Signing an e-petition as a transition from lurking to participation (2010).
7. Hale, S. A., Margetts, H., & Yasseri, T. Petition growth and success rates on the UK No. 10 Downing Street Website. In *Proc. WebSci* (2013).
8. Jungherr, A. and Jürgens, P. The Political click: Political participation through e-petitions in Germany. *Policy & Internet* (2010).
9. Kittur, A., Chi, E., Pendleton, B. A., Suh, B., & Mytkowicz, T. Power of the few vs. wisdom of the crowd: Wikipedia and the rise of the bourgeoisie. *World Wide Web* (2007).
10. Kraut, R. E., & Resnick, P. Building Successful Online Communities Evidence-Based Social Design (2012).
11. Lave, Jean. & Wenger, E. *Situated learning: Legitimate peripheral participation.* (1991).
12. Margetts, H. Z., John, P., Hale, S. A., & Reissfelder, S. Leadership without Leaders? Starters and Followers in Online Collective Action. *Political Studies* (2013).
13. Muller, M. Lurking as personal trait or situational disposition: lurking and contributing in enterprise social media. In *Proc. CSCW* (2012).
14. Panagiotopoulos, P., & Elliman, T. Online engagement from the grassroots: Reflecting on over a decade of e-petitioning experience in Europe and the UK. In *Empowering Open and Collaborative Governance* (2012).
15. Pal, A., Farzan, R., Konstan, J. A., & Kraut, R. E. Early detection of potential experts in question answering communities. In *User Modeling, Adaption and Personalization,* Springer Berlin Heidelberg (2011).
16. Panciera, K., Aaron, H., and Loren T. Wikipedians are born, not made: a study of power editors on Wikipedia." In *Proc. GROUP* (2009).
17. Panciera, K., Priedhorsky, R., Erickson, T., & Terveen, L.Lurking? cyclopaths?: a quantitative lifecycle analysis of user behavior in a geowiki. In *Proc. CHI* (2010).
18. Preece, J., & Shneiderman, B. The reader-to-leader framework: Motivating technology-mediated social participation. In *AIS Transactions on Human-Computer Interaction* (2009).
19. Wash, R., & Jacob S. Coordinating donors on crowdfunding websites." *In Proc. CSCW* (2014)

Personalized, Wearable Control of a Head-mounted Display for Users with Upper Body Motor Impairments

Meethu Malu
Inclusive Design Lab | HCIL
Department of Computer Science
University of Maryland, College Park, MD
meethu@cs.umd.edu

Leah Findlater
Inclusive Design Lab | HCIL
College of Information Studies
University of Maryland, College Park, MD
leahkf@umd.edu

ABSTRACT
Head-mounted displays provide relatively hands-free interaction that could improve mobile computing access for users with motor impairments. To investigate this largely unexplored area, we present two user studies. The first, smaller study evaluated the accessibility of Google Glass, a head-mounted display, with 6 participants. Findings revealed potential benefits of a head-mounted display yet demonstrated the need for alternative means of controlling Glass—3 of the 6 participants could not use it at all. We then conducted a second study with 12 participants to evaluate a potential alternative input mechanism that could allow for accessible control of a head-mounted display: switch-based wearable touchpads that can be affixed to the body or wheelchair. The study assessed input performance with three sizes of touchpad, investigated personalization patterns when participants were asked to place the touchpads on their body or wheelchair, and elicited subjective responses. All 12 participants were able to use the touchpads to control the display, and patterns of touchpad placement point to the value of personalization in providing support for each user's motor abilities.

Author Keywords
Motor impairments; wearables; mobile accessibility.

INTRODUCTION
For users with upper body motor impairments such as tremor, lack of sensation, or spasm, smartphones and other mobile devices can present accessibility challenges [1,15,26,33]. Basic interactions like multi-touch gestures and text entry can be difficult and sometimes impossible to use [1]. Even pulling the phone out of a pocket or bag when in a mobile context can be an accessibility barrier [26].

In contrast, emerging mainstream head-mounted displays such as Google Glass offer new possibilities for accessible computing. Such devices are always available and offer relatively hands-free interaction, potentially alleviating the manual input challenges of today's smartphones and tablets.

CHI 2015, April 18-23, 2015, Seoul, Republic of Korea.
Copyright 2015 ACM 978-1-4503-3145-6/15/04...$15.00.
http://dx.doi.org/10.1145/2702123.2702188

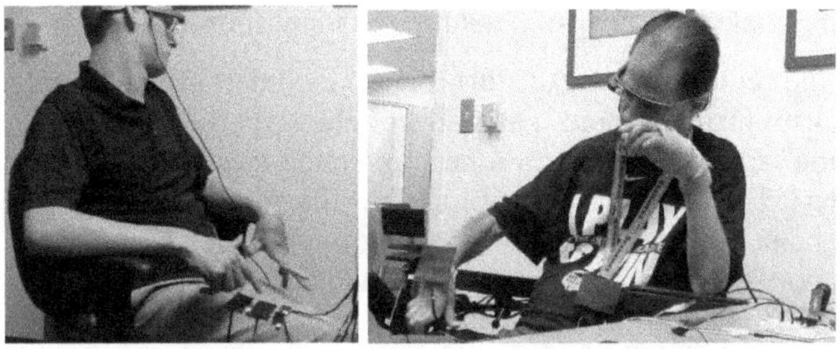

Figure 1. Examples of participants' touchpad placement using a set of four customizable touchpads designed to provide accessible control of a head-mounted display.

Recent work by McNaney *et al.* [25], for example, showed in a field trial with 4 participants with Parkinson's disease that Google Glass provided a sense of independence and security, and that few accessibility issues arose with device interaction. Similarly, Carrington *et al.* [4], conducted participatory design work on input and output opportunities that employ the space around a power wheelchair. Though participants in their study did not use a head-mounted display, several felt that it would be a useful output modality. These studies provide an important first step in demonstrating the potential of head-mounted displays for people with motor impairments. We build on their findings by evaluating the accessibility of Glass with a wider range of users than in [25], and by implementing and evaluating an alternative means of controlling such a display.

This paper investigates the relatively unexplored area of accessible, wearable interaction for users with motor impairments in two ways (Figure 1). First, we conducted a small, exploratory study to assess the accessibility of Google Glass (a head-mounted display) with a diverse set of motor-impaired participants, including those with cerebral palsy, essential and orthostatic tremor, and spinal cord injury. Unlike McNaney *et al.*'s [25] findings for users with Parkinson's disease, our study demonstrates that manual input on the side of the Glass device was difficult or impossible for some participants.

Second, we developed a simple, personalizable interaction approach that employs four switch-based wearable touchpads that can be affixed to the body or wheelchair (Figure 1). The term "wearable" here refers to touchpads attached on body as well as on the wheelchair. These touchpads control what is displayed on Google Glass without having to reach up and touch the side of the device. We conducted a study with 12 participants with motor impairments to assess: (1) baseline input performance with touchpads of three different sizes (2cm, 4cm, and 8cm in width); (2) preferences and rationale for wearable placement of the touchpads; (3) performance when using these customized locations; and (4) overall response to the approach and comparison with Glass's default interaction. Findings show that all participants could independently use the wearable touchpads, choosing to place them in a variety of locations on their body or wheelchair. Rationale for placement and preferences for touchpad size demonstrate the influence of individual motor abilities and further motivate the utility of personalized input for this context.

The contributions of this paper include: (1) a simple, customizable input solution to allow users with motor impairments to control a head-mounted display via switch-based touchpads; (2) empirical results from a performance and subjective comparison among three sizes of touchpads, and, secondarily, between these touchpads and the default Glass controls; (3) characterization of personalization patterns and design considerations to support accessible wearable input for users with motor impairments.

RELATED WORK

We cover accessible mobile and wearable computing, as well as general wearable input and head-worn displays.

Accessible Mobile Computing

Mobile devices can provide a sense of independence for users with motor impairments [15,26], while presenting accessibility challenges [1,15]. For example, findings from Trewin *et al.* [33] and Anthony *et al.* [1] highlight the difficulty of multi-touch gestures. As well, users with motor impairments exhibit more errors with touchscreens than those without motor impairments [6], and users with gross motor impairments exhibit longer dwell times [14].

Approaches for addressing these challenges include making use of the edge of the screen to stabilize gestures [7,35] or using a swiping ("swabbing") interaction rather than tapping, which allows the user to stabilize their finger on the screen [34]. Based on analysis of touchscreen tapping, crossing, and directional gesturing by users with motor impairments, Guerreiro *et al.* [8] also found that targets located at the bottom of the screen and next to the preferred hand were the easiest to select.

These findings highlight both the positive impacts that mobile phones and touchscreen devices can have for users with motor impairments, but also the persistent need for more accessible means of computing in a mobile context.

Accessible Wearable Computing

Wearable device research for users with motor impairments has largely focused on wearable sensors for the diagnosis of medical conditions or in the context of motor rehabilitation; see [38] for a survey. Mazilu *et al.* [24], for example, used an inertial measurement unit to detect freezing of gait in individuals with Parkinson's disease and provided audio feedback to help the wearer continue walking.

More related to our work, however, is accessible wearable *interaction*, that is, techniques to enable users to perform mobile computing tasks. McNaney *et al.*'s [25] study on the applicability of Google Glass for users with Parkinson's disease, and Carrington *et al.*'s [4] participatory design work on wheelchair-based input and output are two examples. In a follow-up to their original study, Carrington *et al.* [5] proposed a pressure-based touchpad input device mounted on the wheelchair's armrest that could be used to control a mobile device. As with the earlier design investigations [4], the focus here was not on controlling information on a head-mounted display; however, the approach could be used in that context. Although not focused on mobile interaction, other projects have investigated wearable input to control wheelchair movement (*e.g.*, using the tongue [12]) or to control desktop computers (*e.g.*, inertial sensors [29])—contexts which differ from a mobile computing scenario and from the head-mounted display scenario that is our focus.

Finally, the idea of using a head-mounted display to provide memory or other cognitive assistance for older adults [19] or users with cognitive impairments [10,36] has been investigated. In semi-structured interviews and shadowing with three older adults using Google Glass, for example, Kunze *et al.* [19] identified short-term memory augmentation, long-term capture and access, timers and reminders, and instructions (*e.g.*, for cooking) as potential application scenarios.

General Wearable Input and Head-mounted Displays

While not focused on accessibility, there is a long history of general wearable input research and research on head-mounted displays. Wearable input devices and techniques have ranged wrist-worn devices (*e.g.*, *GestureWrist* and *GesturePad* [30], *Facet* [21]), to rings (*e.g.*, [2]), to muscle-computer interfaces (*e.g.*, [31]), to on-body or skin-based interaction (*e.g.*, [9,11]). Many of these devices, particularly wrist-worn ones and rings, employ small interaction areas that may be difficult for users with motor impairments. Others could potentially be adapted to support a large input space for users who have difficulty with fine motor movements, such as *OmniTouch* [11], which employs a depth camera and projector to make any surface (including the body) interactive.

Most head-worn display work has occurred in the field of augmented reality (AR), where virtual imagery overlays physical objects in real time [37]. Applications have included such varied areas as military, navigation, industrial design, and medical [17]—even some smartphone apps offer AR functionality (*e.g.*, Yelp). To control the virtual information displayed, tangible user interfaces, gestures (*e.g.*, [20]), gaze tracking [18], speech input (*e.g.*, [27]), and other wearable devices such as Twiddler for text input [22] have all been investigated. In contrast to this previous work, very little attention has been paid to accessibility in AR or more generally in the control of head-mounted display information—the head-mounted display work of McNaney *et al.* [25] and Kunze *et al.* [19] mentioned earlier are two rare examples. Our study begins to address this gap.

ACCESSIBILITY OF GOOGLE GLASS

To collect preliminary data on the potential impacts of a head-mounted display for people with motor impairments, we conducted a small study with one specific, yet popular device: Google Glass. While the findings from this study were limited to Google Glass, they motivated the subsequent and more general study on wearable touchpads.

Method

Six participants (4 female) with upper body motor impairments were recruited. Details are shown in Table 1.

Each session lasted one hour and included a background questionnaire (demographics and current mobile use), tasks with Google Glass, and a semi-structured interview on the experience of using the head-mounted display. Glass provides input through a touchpad on the right arm of the device that senses taps and swipes, and through voice commands. Output is through the head-mounted display that sits in front of the right eye and a bone-conduction headphone. For the Glass tasks, the researcher first demonstrated the touchpad and voice commands. The participant then completed a series of tasks over about 20 minutes, such as viewing activity on the timeline, looking up the weather, and taking pictures. To complete these tasks required at least 8 forward swipes, 3 backward swipes, 11 downward swipes, 12 taps, and 10 voice commands. Because of accidental taps and swipes, these numbers are a lower bound. For participants who could not reach the touchpad, the researcher performed that input.

Following the tasks, participants used 5-point scales to rate the physical comfort and ease of use of the touchpad and the visual display, and ease of use of the voice commands. The session concluded with open-ended questions about the potential impacts of head-mounted displays and brief feedback on design ideas for alternative forms of input beyond the built-in touchpad. Sessions were video recorded and analyzed to observe interaction successes and challenges, and to summarize open-ended responses.

Findings

Table 2 summarizes participant ratings on ease of use and physical comfort. Overall, ratings were neutral to positive.

Input Mechanisms: Touchpad and Voice Commands

The accessibility of the touchpad depended on each participant's motor abilities. For P1, P3, and P5, the

ID	Age	Gender	Diagnosed Med. Condition	Mobile Device
P1	46	Male	Spinal cord injury (C5)	None currently
P2	25	Female	Cerebral palsy	Apple iPhone 5
P3	53	Male	Cerebral palsy	Basic phone
P4	25	Female	Cerebral palsy	HTC smartphone
P5	22	Female	Cerebral palsy	Apple iPhone 5S
P6	53	Female	Essential and orthostatic tremor	Basic phone

Table 1. Study 1 participants. All but P6 used a wheelchair.

ID	Visual Display		Touchpad Gestures		Voice Commands
	Comfort	Ease	Comfort	Ease	Ease
Median	2	2	3	2	1
M	2.2	2.2	3	2.7	1.7
SD	1.2	1.2	2.2	1.9	1.2

Table 2. Ease of use and physical comfort ratings for Glass interactions in Study 1 (1=very easy/comfortable to 5=very difficult/uncomfortable).

touchpad was not accessible at all and the researcher ultimately had to perform their taps and swipes. P1 and P5 could not physically reach the touchpad, although for P5 the touchpad may have been possible to use had it been on the left side of the device; she had limited movement in her right hand. P3, in comparison, could reach the touchpad but could not tap or swipe on it without physically displacing the device. After a few attempts, he asked the researcher to perform the gestures. The other participants, P2, P4, and P6, encountered fewer difficulties, although their error rates when attempting taps or swipes were still 11% (of 61 interactions), 37% (of 93) and 18% (of 65) respectively. For P4, by far the most common problem was that the touchpad did not respond to her input. This issue occurred 16 times, and was perhaps due to the angle at which she was able to approach the touchpad. She also had persistent trouble correctly locating the touchpad, despite intervention.

For voice commands, only P3 encountered difficulty. He had dysarthria (slurred speech) and for him the device only successfully recognized the word 'Google.' P1 and P4 expressed surprise at how well Glass recognized their voices. P2 suggested that Glass should be fully accessible by voice, and wanted voice commands like 'Go Back' or 'Home Screen' to replace swiping or tapping multiple times on the touchpad. These findings are in contrast to McNaney *et al.* [25], whose participants experienced issues with voice input perhaps because they used Glass in a variety of settings and for a wider range of tasks.

Visual Display

All participants were able to read text on the display when prompted. However, P3, P4, and P5 needed the display to be frequently adjusted because it moved when they tapped or swiped. P4 had problems keeping her head upright, which affected her ability to look at the display. During the session, she asked to be strapped to her wheelchair so that she could sit up and see the display better. Participants did not complain about the font size or size of the display.

Potential Impacts of a Head-mounted Display

Comparing Glass to a mobile phone, three participants mentioned the touchpad on Glass as a disadvantage. Advantages, however, included, not having to look down at the display (P2, P4), keeping the hands free (P2, P4, P6) and reducing the risk of dropping and damaging the device (P1). For example, P1 said:

> *"That someone who has limited mobility could wear a technological device without fear of dropping or damaging it that seems a lot more useful than a notepad or a laptop in my aspect, in my living situation." (P1)*

ID	Age	Gender	Reported Medical Condition	Smartphone?	Uses wheelchair?	Dominant Hand	Box-and-Block Test	
							Right	Left
P1	46	Male	Spinal cord injury, C5	Yes	Yes	Left	0	16
P2	25	Female	Cerebral palsy	Yes	Yes	Right	8	2
P3	21	Female	Cerebral palsy	No Phone	Yes	Left	2	12
P4	23	Male	Spastic quadriplegia, neuromuscular scoliosis	Yes	Yes	Right	32	23
P5	25	Male	Cerebral palsy	Yes	Mobility scooter	Right	22	10
P6	23	Female	Cerebral palsy, Spastic quadriplegia	Yes	Yes	Left	0	4
P7	47	Male	Myotonic muscular dystrophy	Yes	No	Right	10	7
P8	31	Male	Spinal cord injury, C6 and C7	Yes	Yes	Right	29	11
P9	53	Female	Essential and orthostatic tremor	Basic Phone*	No	Right	53	48
P10	22	Male	Cerebral palsy	Yes	No	Left	46	46
P11	52	Male	Right side paralysis	Basic Phone*	Yes	Left	7	23
P12	61	Female	Hemorrhagic stroke	Yes	Yes	Right	53	0

Table 3: Study 2 participant demographics, smartphone use, wheelchair use, and Box-and-Block Test results for both hands (higher values represent higher manual dexterity). *P9 and P11 reported iPad use.

P2 expressed the ease of not having to hold her phone:

> *"My hands are free. It didn't require me to pick up anything as opposed to having to pick up this [phone] and you know look down on it and you know I was looking up so I didn't have my head down." (P2)*

Feedback on Alternative Input Ideas

At the end of the session we briefly introduced theoretical alternatives to Glass's touchpad: mid-air gestures, wearable physical buttons, and a portable touchpad. While the responses were generally positive, each participant had different yet specific places where they would like the touchpad to be located, like the armrest, joystick or tray. We explore this finding further in Study 2. Participants also spoke about using body and facial movements and customized voice commands as other alternatives.

Summary and Discussion

For our six participants, Google Glass presented exciting possibilities for mobile information access but also serious accessibility challenges. The always-available nature of Glass allowed easy access to information on the go, without the physical requirement to hold a mobile phone. At the same time, half of the participants could not use the touchpad input. These findings motivated our next study, where we evaluated personalizable wearable touchpads of different sizes to control Glass. Again, our goal is to design and assess alternate input systems for head-mounted displays like Google Glass that can provide mobile information access for users with motor impairments.

STUDY OF PERSONALIZED WEARABLE TOUCHPADS

To investigate the use of configurable, wearable touchpads for accessible control of a head-mounted display, we built a prototype system and conducted a controlled experiment with 12 participants with motor impairments. The study was designed both to assess user performance with different sizes of touchpad as well as to characterize how participants would want to customize touchpad locations.

Method

The study included three tasks: (1) a reciprocal tapping task to measure baseline performance with three sizes of touchpad; (2) another controlled tapping task, but with the touchpads placed at custom locations on the participant's body or wheelchair; and (3) a more realistic task where participants used their preferred touchpad configuration to control a small app on the head-mounted display.

Participants

Twelve participants (5 female) with upper body motor impairments were recruited. See Table 3 for detail. To gain a baseline understanding of manual dexterity and variation across participants, we administered the standardized Box-and-Block Test [23]. This 5-minute test involves moving blocks one at a time across a partition and provides dexterity scores per hand. Typical adult scores range from about 80 for younger adults to about 60 for older adults [23]. Our participants' scores, shown in Table 3, ranged from 0 (no use of the hand) to 53. Three participants (P1, P2, P9) had used Glass in the preliminary study, while the others had no prior experience. All participants were volunteers and were compensated for their time.

Apparatus

We built a custom, reconfigurable system that used four touchpads made of pressure-sensitive conductive sheeting to control a Google Glass device (Figures 1 and 2). The touchpads, each on a piece of flexible foam backing, were connected to an Arduino Uno board that sensed taps using the CapSense library. Touchpads of different sizes could be easily swapped out during the study. A Motorola MotoX phone running Android v4.4.2 acted as a mediator between the Arduino and Glass. The phone was paired with the Arduino via a BlueSMiRF HID Bluetooth modem, and communicated with it via the Amarino app [16]. This app received data about the taps from the Arduino and sent it to a custom Bluetooth chat application on the phone (built in Java), which in turn forwarded the input to Glass. An Android application was written for Glass to display visual task prompts and communicate with the phone. It also logged interactions with the wearable touchpads.

Procedure

Study sessions lasted two hours. The session began with a background questionnaire on demographics and technology experience, followed by the Box-and-Block Test. Participants were briefly introduced to Glass and tried out

Figure 2: P12 performing Task 1 with large touchpads placed 32 cm apart on the table.

Figure 3: P10 performing Task 2 with the medium touchpads. He placed selected locations on the wrist, palm and chest.

swipes and taps on the built-in touchpad. They then completed the three following tasks:

Task 1: Reciprocal Tapping. Participants tapped back and forth between two touchpads placed on a table in front of them (Figure 2). Three touchpad sizes were presented in counterbalanced order: 8 cm (large), 4 cm (medium), and 2 cm (small). The two touchpads (per size) were placed 32 cm apart, as measured from the centers of the touchpads. We chose these widths (*W*) and the distance (*D*) between them to cover a theoretical range of pointing difficulties. The Fitts' law indexes of difficulty (*ID*) were 2.3, 3.1 and 4.0 for the large, medium and small touchpads respectively, where $ID = \log_2(D/W+1)$ [13].

For each touchpad size, participants performed four practice taps (2 on each touchpad) using their dominant hand. The test trials were then presented—16 alternating taps—and participants were asked to tap as quickly and accurately as possible without stopping. The Glass display presented visual prompts to "*tap forward*" (right) or "*tap backward*" (left) for each trial. Success and error sounds played for correct and incorrect taps. The software only advanced to the next trial after the correct touchpad was tapped. After using each size, participants rated ease of use and physical comfort of performing the taps on 5-point scales. Overall feedback was solicited after all three sizes were complete.

Task 2: Location Customization and Tapping. Four touchpads labeled *forward*, *backward*, *select* and *cancel*, based on the four basic manual inputs of Glass were used. Sizes were presented in the same counterbalanced order as in the reciprocal tapping task. For each size, participants were asked to place the four touchpads anywhere on their body or wheelchair that was "accessible and comfortable" for them. The researcher affixed the touchpads to skin, clothing or the wheelchair using Velcro straps, Velcro tape, or adhesive tape (Figure 3).

Participants then tested out the touchpad locations and practiced tapping each one twice (a total of 8 taps), and were given the opportunity to adjust the locations if desired; 6 did so. Then, 32 test trials were presented (8 per touchpad). The order of prompts was randomized, with the constraint that no two consecutive taps could be on the same touchpad. As with the first task, participants were asked to tap quickly and accurately, and success and error sounds played. After each touchpad size, participants rated ease of use and physical comfort on a 5-point scale. They were also asked to provide rationale for their choice of locations. At the very end of the task, we asked about overall size and location preferences.

Task 3: Final Configuration and Realistic Use. Briefly, to provide a reminder of Glass's functionality, we again had participants try the swipes and taps on the default touchpad (~1 minute). Then, to provide a more realistic experience of using wearable touchpads to control a head-mounted display, participants used a simple, custom Glass application. It included pictures, description and weather information on two cities, ordered hierarchically with 3 screens per city. Similar to Task 2, participants created a personalized input system by choosing different locations. In this task, however, they could select any size of touchpad and mix different sizes in case some were deemed to be more useful for particular locations. The four touchpads emulated the functionality of the Glass touchpad: *forward* and *backward* navigated the current level of the hierarchy, *select* provided more detail on an option (*e.g.*, moving down a level in the hierarchy), and *cancel* closed the current page or returned to the previous level. Participants first tapped on each touchpad to make sure they could reach it and were given a chance to change the locations or sizes. Participants were asked to take a few minutes to explore the application, and had to try using each of the four inputs at least three times while doing so.

The session concluded with a final semi-structured interview on the experience of using the wearable touchpads and their potential impacts on accessibility of a head-mounted display. All interviews were audio and video recorded. P7 was not able to see the Glass display due to a visual impairment, so for him all visual prompts were presented on a laptop screen instead.

Design and Counterbalancing

We used a within-subjects design with a single factor of *Touchpad Size.* It had three levels: *small* (2 cm), *medium* (4 cm), and *large* (8 cm). For a given participant, touchpad sizes appeared in the same order for both tasks. Order of presentation was fully counterbalanced, with an equal number of participants randomly assigned to each order.

Data and Analysis

One-way repeated measures ANOVAs with a single factor of *Touchpad Size* were used to analyze the timing data for each of the first two tasks. Post-hoc comparisons were protected against Type I error using Tukey HSD. Our primary performance measure is speed. The system did not advance until the participant had correctly completed the current trial, which means that *speed* includes an implicit error penalty. We do not present a separate error analysis because the system could not detect missed taps, such as hits just outside a touchpad's bounds.

While all participants completed the full study procedure, only 10 participants are included in these performance analyses for Tasks 1 and 2. For both tasks, the log files for P1 were not accurate because of a calibration issue with the touchpads. For Task 1 only, we excluded P6's performance data because we had to reduce the distance between the two touchpads to accommodate her limited range of motion. For Task 2 only, we excluded P4's performance data because he placed the small touchpads very close to each other, which caused interference for the capacitive sensing. In all, we analyze $2 \times 8 \times 3 \times 10 = 480$ trials for Task 1, and $4 \times 8 \times 3 \times 10 = 960$ trials for Task 2 (number of touchpads × repetitions × sizes × participants).

For rating scale data, we used non-parametric Friedman tests. Finally, open-ended responses were analyzed based on themes of interest [3] (*e.g.*, rationale, impacts of motor ability), while allowing for new, emergent themes.

RESULTS

We cover performance and subjective results for Tasks 1 and 2, as well as, based on Tasks 2 and 3, themes in personalization rationale and the experience of using wearable touchpads to control a head-mounted display.

Performance

Task 1: Reciprocal Tapping Task

This task provides a baseline performance assessment for the touchpad sizes in an ideal setup. As expected, *Touchpad Size* significantly impacted tapping speed. As shown in Figure 4, the average tapping time per trial was 2.7s (SD = 1.3) for the small touchpads, 1.8s (SD = 1.0) for medium, and 2.0s (SD = 1.1) for large. A one-way repeated measures ANOVA revealed a main effect of *Touchpad Size* on average trial completion time ($F_{2,18} = 8.57$, $p = .002$, $\eta^2 = 0.49$). Post-hoc comparisons indicated small touchpads were slower than both the medium ($p < 0.01$) and large ($p < 0.05$) sizes. No significant difference was found between medium and large sizes.

For subjective feedback, most participants ($N = 8$) found the large touchpad easiest to use, followed by medium and small ($N = 2$ each). The majority of participants ($N = 7$) also found the large touchpad to be the most physically comfortable, while 4 said medium, and 1 felt all sizes were similar. Participants provided ratings on ease of use and physical comfort, which are summarized in Table 4. While the mean ratings on both measures improve (*i.e.*, become closer to 1) as the target size increases, Friedman tests were not statistically significant for either measure.

Task 2: Location Customization and Tapping Task

As with Task 1, *Touchpad Size* again impacted tapping speed. As shown in Figure 4, average trial times were 3.2s (SD = 1.5) for small, 2.5s (SD = 1.3) for medium, and 2.2s (SD = 0.96) for large touchpads. Across all touchpad sizes, these speeds are only 0.4s more than the baseline tapping speeds collected in Task 1, which shows that the personalized locations offer feasible input performance. A one-way repeated measures ANOVA revealed a significant impact of *Touchpad Size* on tapping speed ($F_{2,18} = 9.55$, $p = .001$, $\eta^2 = 0.51$). Post-hoc comparisons showed that the small touchpads were significantly slower than both the medium ($p < 0.05$) and large ($p < 0.01$) sizes.

Overall, large and medium touchpads appeared to be preferred to small touchpads for this task, with the following distribution of votes for most preferred size: 4 (large), 5 (medium), and 2 (small); one participant could not choose between small and medium. The ease of use and physical comfort ratings, shown in Table 4, support this trend. The mean ratings for the small touchpads were worse than for medium and large touchpads, although a Friedman test did not find a statistically significant impact of *Touchpad Size* on either measure. Encouragingly, the mean ratings for the larger two sizes were about 2 on a 5-point scale, meaning "easy" and "physically comfortable."

Personalization: Touchpad Placement and Rationale

We provide detail on placement and rationale findings from Task 2. Because rationale trends were similar in Task 3, where participants could personalize their input with multiple touchpad sizes at once, we highlight only the choice of sizes selected in that task.

Task 1: Reciprocal Tapping	Small		Medium		Large	
	Comfort	Ease	Comfort	Ease	Comfort	Ease
Median	2	3	2	2	1	2
M	2.4	3.4	2.1	2.5	1.8	2.3
SD	0.9	0.9	0.9	1.2	0.9	1.3
Task 2: Location Customization	**Small**		**Medium**		**Large**	
	Comfort	Ease	Comfort	Ease	Comfort	Ease
Median	2	3	2	2	2	2
M	2.7	2.8	2.0	1.9	2.1	2.0
SD	1.2	1.1	1.0	0.8	1.1	1.1

Table 4. Ease of use and physical comfort ratings for Tasks 1 and 2 (1 = very comfortable/easy and 5 = very uncomfortable/difficult). (N = 12)

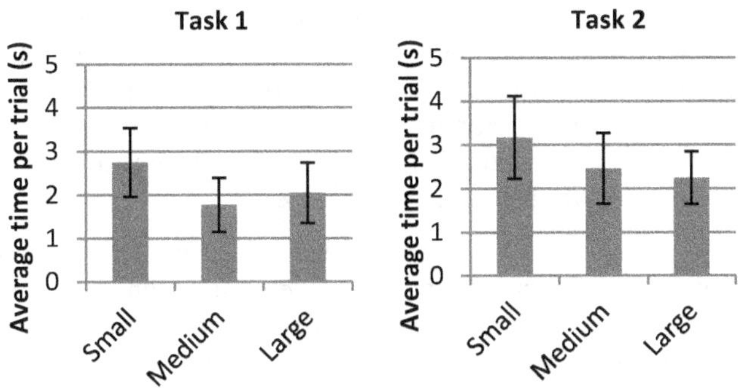

Figure 4: Average time per trial in Task 1 (reciprocal tapping) and Task 2 (location customization). The small touchpads were significantly slower than the other two sizes in both tasks. (N = 10; error bars: 95% confidence intervals).

Placement

In Task 2, participants chose a wide variety of locations for touchpad placement; see Table 5 for detail. Of the 8 wheelchair users, 2 placed all sizes of touchpad on their body only (thigh, wrist, palm, and chest), 3 chose their wheelchair only (tray and joystick), and 3 chose a combination of wheelchair and body locations. P5, on a mobility scooter, placed all touchpads on his body, "*Because I'm not on my scooter all the time, it has to be on my body. It will be easier for me.*" Among all the locations, the most popular choices were the thigh (N = 7) and wrist (N = 5). For wheelchair users, the tray was the most common location, followed by the joystick. While P9 and P12 chose the same locations for all three sizes, P1 and P5 had to adjust their configuration to accommodate the largest size (for P5 this meant using both thighs instead of one).

Rationale

Rationale for touchpad placement was an open-ended question and participants could provide more than one reason for each touchpad size. The reasons were similar across sizes, so we present an aggregate analysis.

As expected, participants' motor abilities impacted their touchpad personalization. Overall, the most common reasons for selecting locations were ease of reach (N = 8) and proximity to the dominant hand/arm (N = 6). For example, P6 had a Box-and-Block score of 4 in her left (dominant) hand and we had adjusted the touchpad locations in the reciprocal tapping task so that she could reach. She accommodated this limited range of motion by placing all touchpads on her tray close to her left hand, saying: "*I didn't have to stretch too far.*" As another example, P7 initially placed all large touchpads on his left arm. After the practice, however, he moved the topmost one to his knee because of the difficulty of lifting his arm high enough to reach it: "*Easier to tap and [on the arm it had been] difficult for my hand to reach as far as I need to.*"

Another anecdote on the impact of personalization comes from P8, who described a problem in how he typically uses his touchscreen phone. He cannot point perpendicularly to

ID	Small	Medium	Large
P1	Joystick, wrist, lanyard on neck	Joystick, wrist, lanyard on neck	Joystick, wrist, thigh, lanyard on neck
P2	Tray	Tray	Tray
P3	Tray, joystick	Tray	Tray, joystick
P4	Fingers	Fingers, wrist	Chest
P5	Thigh	Thigh	Thigh
P6	Tray	Tray	Tray
P7	Wrist	Thigh	Arm, thigh
P8	Thigh	Cushion of wheelchair	Thigh
P9	Thigh	Thigh	Thigh
P10	Chest, neck, palm	Chest, palm, wrist	Thigh, back of hands
P11	Joystick, armrest, wrist, thigh	Joystick, armrest, back of hand	Joystick, wrist, thigh
P12	Thigh, Wrist, Palm	Thigh, wrist, Palm	Thigh, wrist, palm

Table 5. Choice of touchpad locations per participant per size. All but P5, P7, P9, and P10 use a wheelchair.

the screen because the low strength in his hand causes instability when the fingers bend. Instead, he taps the screen with his knuckles. With the personalized layout he placed the touchpad sideways on the wheelchair cushion, which allowed for tapping with the side of the hand; Figure 5. He thought of this option in time for the last touchpad size (medium in his case), saying, *"It was just easy."*

Three participants (P8, P9 and P12) talked about placing the touchpads close to where their hands rest in their natural state. For P9, the desire to rest her hands was due at least partly to her tremor. She said before initial touchpad placement: "*I mean most naturally my hands would rest here [points to thigh] so like I guess on my thighs.*" Other reasons for placement included arranging touchpads based on their meaning (*e.g. forward* in front of *backward*) to remember the order (N = 4), wanting the touchpad to be easily visible (N = 3), reducing interference with the wheelchair (N = 2), and using familiar locations (N = 10).

Finally, three participants commented on the emergent benefit that their touchpad placement allowed for eyes-free use so they could maintain visual attention on the head-mounted display—an important practical consideration for control of such a display.

Interference with Typical Movements

An important potential downside of wearable input is the possibility of interfering with typical body movements or

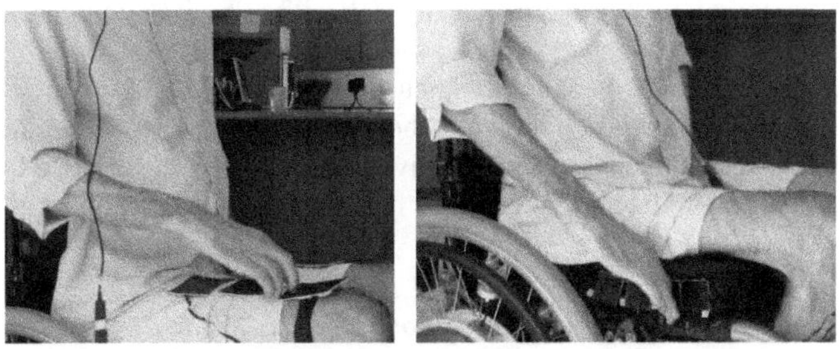

Figure 5. Large and medium personalized touchpad placement for P8, showing a perpendicular approach that requires bending at the knuckles (left) compared to an "easy" approach from the side with vertically placed touchpads (right).

other worn items. The majority of participants ($N = 8$) felt that the large touchpads would interfere with body movements, and few ($N = 4$) also felt they would interfere with items worn on their body. P1, for example, said of the large size, "*…they would alter the way I would normally do things.*" Only at most 3 participants felt the small or medium touchpads would interfere with body movements, worn items, or wheelchair movements. Two participants (P8, P9) had mentioned taking interference into account during touchpad placement. Another issue considered by P12 is that an ideal placement while seated may be different while walking.

Overall Location and Size Comparisons

Preferences regarding the touchpad sizes after Task 2 varied. The surface area of the large touchpads was an advantage for some participants as it did not require precise tapping (P5, P11), but a disadvantage to others, who felt that it led to accidental taps (P6 rested her hand close to the touchpads), was too cumbersome (P9), or took up too much space (P6, P7, P8). The small touchpads, however, provided more options for placement (P6, P9) but required more precise movement (P7, P12). The medium size was a nice compromise for some (P5, P7, P8, P12). When asked to compare locations they had tried across the three sizes, many responses were similar to the earlier rationale responses (*e.g.*, thigh is easy to reach). P1, however, commented that the lanyard placement he had used was difficult because it made for a moving target.

In Task 3, participants mixed different sizes to create a personalized input system with four controls. The variation in choices again supports the need for personalization. Eight out of 12 participants combined different sizes: 4 used medium and large, 3 used small and medium and 1 used all three sizes. Other participants used all small (P1, P9), all medium (P8), or all large (P4) touchpads. Dominant reasons provided for these choices were similar in pattern to those at the end of Task 2, such as ease of reach.

Comparison to Glass's Built-in Touchpad

Participants used Glass's built-in touchpad twice during the study: once as an introduction and briefly as a reminder before Task 3. The wearable touchpads were considered by almost all participants to offer accessible control of a head-mounted display, and compared favorably to Glass's built-in touchpad. While 4 participants (P1, P3, P6, P7) could not reach the touchpad on Glass, all 12 were able to use the wearable touchpads to complete the study tasks. Six of the 8 participants who *could* reach the Glass touchpad still felt that the wearable ones would positively impact their ability to use a head-mounted display, for example, *"More accessible"* (P10), and:

> *"For me, with my arm and hand issues, its much more difficult to keep going here [points to Glass] than it is to rest my hands on my lap and just tap what I need to." (P9)*

When asked how the wearable touchpads would impact their ability to independently use a head-mounted display compared to Glass's touchpad, 9 felt that the wearable option would provide more independent use, and 2 thought the options were similar. That said, one participant (P12) mentioned an important drawback of the wearable approach—that it requires effort to do the customization rather than having an all-in-one device.

As it did with placement rationale, the desire for eyes-free input arose again. Participants were split on how the wearable option would impact their ability to pay attention to their surroundings. On the positive side ($N = 6$) were participants like P9, who felt the wearable touchpads were easy to tap without looking, "*Because I got to choose where they were [...] plus it was all kind of the same movement.*" On the negative side ($N = 2$), P12 appreciated that Glass's default input was designed to not require visual attention.

Social Considerations

Issues such as aesthetic design and social awkwardness are common with wearable devices [28], and, unsurprisingly, a few participants mentioned such concerns. P1 and P9 felt the large touchpads would be awkward to use in a public place. P8, who had placed the touchpads on the cushion of his wheelchair for his personalized setup said:

> *"You're a bit more incognito [than with Glass's touchpad...] I could sit there for a while clicking on [the wearable touchpads] and I bet this [Glass's touchpad] would be weird and stupid and annoying sitting over here tapping on my face for longer than 30 seconds or 8 taps."*

One participant mentioned stigma around assistive technology [32], a concern that could be magnified in the context of wearable devices. P1 said of the large touchpads:

> *"...I don't want to look like R2-D2. I want people to see [name] and not his [wheel] chair so I would not use these big ones [...] they stand out too much."*

Some participants offered new ideas for controlling the head-mounted display, and again social considerations arose. P8 compared head movements to voice input, saying: *"Speaking is not something I want to do in public, only nodding to cancel is something I would want to do."*

DISCUSSION

The two studies presented here extend a small body of recent work [4,25] by both motivating the need for further research on accessible input for head-mounted displays and by providing promising directions for how to provide that input. In Study 1, participants reacted positively to the idea of using a head-mounted display, as embodied by Google Glass. Compared to smartphones, potential advantages included not having to hold the device while interacting with it, not having to look down to see the screen, and not having to worry about dropping the device. While preliminary, these findings suggest that such a device may offer important opportunities to increase mobile computing accessibility for users with upper body motor impairments.

Design Reflections

The findings from Study 2 point to the promise of a wearable switch-based control that can be personalized to a user's motor abilities. All 12 participants were able to use the wearable touchpads to control the display, including those four who could not Glass's built-in touchpad. The relatively small difference between performance in the baseline condition (reciprocal tapping on the table) and the wearable condition supports the feasibility of our approach in terms of providing efficient input. Finally, in contrast to work with wheelchair users only (*e.g.*, [4]), our participants also included non-wheelchair users and one person with a mobility scooter. This diversity provides a degree of generalizability to the population of users with upper body motor impairments, although more work is needed.

The utility of personalizing wearable input to support individual motor abilities was demonstrated in Study 2, and provides evidence to strengthen suggestions made in previous work [4]. Participants selected varied locations (wrist, thigh, arm, tray, armrest) for the wearable touchpads and even mixed sizes when given the opportunity. The most common reason for selecting a location was "ease of reach," with detailed description often revealing the participant's consideration of their motor abilities. A downside of personalization is the effort required (*e.g.*, mentioned by P12) and the potential, particularly for wearable input, that the input device will need to be adjusted each day. An important area of future work is thus to investigate easy-to-adjust wearable mounting mechanisms or permanent placement on the chair itself for wheelchair users. Carrington *et al.*'s [4] chairables work provides guidance in this latter direction.

Wearable touchpads do present some practical issues. The possibility of interfering with everyday activities such as body or wheelchair movements was of particular concern with the large touchpads. Smaller touchpads may mitigate this issue. Capacitive touchpads, as used in Study 2, are also not likely to be the best approach. Although they require little strength to activate, they are also more susceptible to being accidentally triggered than a mechanical button would be. However, the findings from our study should apply to other switch-based input if the goal is to support personalization.

Our focus was to build a solution that could: be socially acceptable, support use in a mobile context, be easy to learn, and be accessible to users with varying levels of physical strength. Our wearable touchpad approach supported these goals, yet is only one potential solution. Alternatives to manual input will also be important to explore. For example, ideas of eye-gaze and head-controlled input were raised by our participants. Expanded speech input offers another possibility for accessible control of a head-mounted display, but it was not usable for one Study 1 participant due to dysarthria, and was mentioned as inappropriate for social reasons in Study 2. The need for accessible manual input remains important.

Limitations

While the wearable touchpad approach should be applicable to head-mounted displays in general, the accessibility findings in Study 1 are specifically limited to Google Glass; different issues may arise with other devices. As well, our evaluations were limited to a lab setting and users with mild to moderate impairments in their hands and arms. To truly understand the impacts of this approach, future work will need to assess performance and user response in a variety of mobile contexts and include users with more severe motor impairments. One Study 2 participant, for example, mentioned the possibility of having multiple sets of touchpads at different locations, like his desk and scooter, for everyday use. Additionally, participants were seated during study tasks and the touchpads were wired, which may have influenced placement (*e.g.*, popularity of the thigh). We note, however, that the wires only rarely interfered with the participant's ability to tap. We plan to create a more robust wireless approach in the future. Finally, we examined switch-based input, which results in the need for multiple controls (in our case four touchpads to control Glass). For users with sufficiently fine motor control, there may be a preference for using a single touchpad that would support swipe gestures instead of having to use four touchpads that only support tapping.

CONCLUSION

We presented two studies investigating accessible control of head-mounted displays for users with upper body motor impairments. The first study, while small, offered potential advantages of a head-mounted display over more widely used mobile computing devices, such as not requiring that it be held during use. At the same time, we identified accessibility challenges with Google Glass. Glass is of course only an early example of mainstream head-mounted displays, and we expect improvements in the coming years. The personalized wearable approach that we proposed and evaluated in Study 2 offers one promising direction.

ACKNOWLEDGMENTS

We thank UCP in Lanham, MD, especially Michael McGee and Melissa Schick, our participants, and Chris Imbriano for early discussions. This work was funded by the National Science Foundation under grant IIS-1350438.

REFERENCES

1. Anthony, L., Kim, Y., and Findlater, L. Analyzing user-generated YouTube videos to understand touchscreen use by people with motor impairments. *Proc. CHI'13,* (2013), 1223–1232.
2. Ashbrook, D., Baudisch, P., and White, S. Nenya: subtle and eyes-free mobile input with a magnetically-tracked finger ring. *Proc. CHI'11,* (2011), 2043–2046.
3. Braun, V. and Clarke, V. Using thematic analysis in psychology. *Qualitative Research in Psychology 3*, 2 (2006), 77–101.
4. Carrington, P., Hurst, A., and Kane, S.K. Wearables and Chairables: Inclusive Design of Mobile Input and Output

Techniques for Power Wheelchair Users. *Proc. CHI'14*, (2014), 3103–3112.

5. Carrington, P., Hurst, A., Kane, S.K. The Gest-Rest: a pressure-sensitive chairable input pad for power wheel-chair armrests. *Proc. ASSETS'14*, (2014), to appear.
6. Duff, S.N., Irwin, C.B., Skye, J.L., Sesto, M.E., and Wiegmann, D.A. The effect of disability and approach on touch screen performance during a number entry task. *Proc. HFES'10*, (2010), 566–570.
7. Froehlich, J., Wobbrock, J.O., and Kane, S.K. Barrier Pointing: Using Physical Edges to Assist Target Acquisition on Mobile Device Touch Screens. *Proc. ASSETS'07*, (2007), 19–26.
8. Guerreiro, T.J.V., Nicolau, H., Jorge, J., and Gonçalves, D. Assessing Mobile Touch Interfaces for Tetraplegics. *Proc. MobileHCI'10*, (2010), 31–34.
9. Gustafson, S., Holz, C., and Baudisch, P. Imaginary phone: learning imaginary interfaces by transferring spatial memory from a familiar device. *Proc. UIST'11*, (2011), 283–292.
10. Ha, K., Chen, Z., Hu, W., Richter, W., Pillai, P., and Satyanarayanan, M. Towards wearable cognitive assistance. *Proc. MobiSys'14*, (2014), 68–81.
11. Harrison, C. and Wilson, A.D. OmniTouch: wearable multitouch interaction everywhere. *Proc. UIST'11*, (2011), 441–450.
12. Huo, X., Park, H., Ghovanloo, M. Dual-mode tongue drive system. *Proc. Wireless Health*, (2012), 1–-8.
13. International Organization for Standardization. *Ergo-nomic requirements for office work with visual display terminals (VDTs)—Requirements for non-keyboard input devices (Ref. No. ISO 9241-9:2000(E))*. 2002.
14. Irwin, C.B. and Sesto, M.E. Performance and touch characteristics of disabled and non-disabled participants during a reciprocal tapping task using touch screen technology. *Applied Ergonomics 43*, 6 (2012), 1038–1043.
15. Kane, S.K., Jayant, C., Wobbrock, J.O., and Ladner, R.E. Freedom to Roam: A Study of Mobile Device Adoption and Accessibility for People with Visual and Motor Disabilities. *Proc. ASSETS'09*, (2009), 115–122.
16. Kaufmann, B. and Buechley, L. Amarino. *Proc. MobileHCI'10*, (2010), 291.
17. Krevelen, D.W.F. Van and Poelman, R. A Survey of Augmented Reality Technologies , Applications and Limitations. *Int'l J. of Virtual Reality 9*, 2 (2010), 1.
18. Kumar, M., Paepcke, A., and Winograd, T. EyePoint. *Proc. CHI'07*, (2007), 421–430.
19. Kunze, K., Henze, N., and Kise, K. Wearable computing for older adults. *UbiComp'14 Adjunct*, (2014), 83–86.
20. Lee, T. and Hollerer, T. Handy AR: Markerless Inspection of Augmented Reality Objects Using Fingertip Tracking. *Proc. ISWC'07*, (2007), 1–8.
21. Lyons, K., Nguyen, D.H., Ashbrook, D., and White, S. Facet: a multi-segment wrist worn system. *Proc. UIST'12*, (2012), 123–129.
22. Lyons, K., Starner, T., Plaisted, D., et al. Twiddler typing: one-handed chording text entry for mobile phones. *Proc. CHI '04*, (2004), 671–678.
23. Mathiowetz, V., Volland, G., Kashman, N., and Weber, K. Adult norms for the Box and Block Test of manual dexterity. *American J. of Occupational Therapy 39*, 6 (1985), 386–391.
24. Mazilu, S., Blanke, U., Hardegger, M., Tröster, G., Gazit, E., Hausdorff, J.M. GaitAssist: a daily-life support and training system for Parkinson's disease patients with freezing of gait. *Proc. CHI'14*, (2014), 2531–2540.
25. McNaney, R., Vines, J., Roggen, D., et al. Exploring the acceptability of Google Glass as an everyday assistive device for people with Parkinson's. *Proc. CHI'14*, (2014), 2551–2554.
26. Naftali, M. and Findlater, L. Accessibility in Context: Understanding the Truly Mobile Experience of Smartphone Users With Motor Impairments. *Proc. ASSETS'14*, (2014), To appear.
27. Olwal, A. and Feiner, S. SenseShapes: Using statistical geometry for object selection in a multimodal aug-mented reality system. *Proc. ISMAR '03* (2003), 300.
28. Profita, H.P., Clawson, J., Gilliland, S., et al. Don't mind me touching my wrist. *Proc. ISWC '13*, (2013), 89.
29. Raya, R., Roa, J.O., Rocon, E., Ceres, R., and Pons, J.L. Wearable inertial mouse for children with physical and cognitive impairments. *Sensors and Actuators A: Physical 162*, 2 (2010), 248–259.
30. Rekimoto, J. GestureWrist and GesturePad: unobtrusive wearable interaction devices. *Proc. ISCW'01*, (2001), 21–27.
31. Saponas, T.S., Tan, D.S., Morris, D., Balakrishnan, R., Turner, J., and Landay, J.A. Enabling always-available input with muscle-computer interfaces. *Proc. UIST'09*, (2009), 167–176.
32. Shinohara, K. and Wobbrock, J.O. In the shadow of misperception. *Proc. CHI'11*, (2011), 705–714.
33. Trewin, S., Swart, C., and Pettick, D. Physical accessibility of touchscreen smartphones. *Proc. ASSETS '13. Article 19*, (2013), 1–8.
34. Wacharamanotham, C., Hurtmanns, J., Mertens, A., Kronenbuerger, M., Schlick, C., and Borchers, J. Evaluating swabbing: a touchscreen input method for elderly users with tremor. *Proc. CHI'11*, (2011), 623–626.
35. Wobbrock, J.O., Myers, B.A., and Kembel, J.A. EdgeWrite: A Stylus-Based Text Entry Method Designed for High Accuracy and Stability of Motion. *Proc. UIST'03*, (2003), 61–70.
36. Yamamoto, G., Kuroda, T., Yoshitake, D., et al. PiTaSu: wearable interface for assisting senior citizens with memory problems. *Int'l Journal on Disability and Human Development 10*, 4 (2011), 295–300.
37. Zhou, F., Duh, H.B.-L., and Billinghurst, M. Trends in augmented reality tracking, interaction and display: A review of ten years of ISMAR. *Proc. ISMAR'08,* (2008), 193–202.
38. Zhou, H. and Hu, H. Human motion tracking for rehabilitation—A survey. *Biomedical Signal Processing and Control 3*, 1 (2008), 1–18.

Designing Conversation Cues on a Head-Worn Display to Support Persons with Aphasia

Kristin Williams[1], Karyn Moffatt[2], Denise McCall[3], Leah Findlater[1]

[1] Inclusive Design Lab | HCIL, College of Information Studies, University of Maryland, College Park, MD

[2] ACT Research Group, School of Information Studies, McGill University, Montreal, QC

[3] Snyder Center for Aphasia Life Enhancement, Baltimore, MD

krismw11@umd.edu, karyn.moffatt@mcgill.ca, dmccall@scalebaltimore.org, leahkf@umd.edu

ABSTRACT

Symbol-based dictionaries of text, images and sound can help individuals with aphasia find the words they need, but are often seen as a last resort because they tend to replace rather than augment the user's natural speech. Through two design investigations, we explore head-worn displays as a means of providing unobtrusive, always-available, and glanceable vocabulary support. The first study used narrative storyboards as a design probe to explore the potential benefits and challenges of a head-worn approach over traditional augmented alternative communication (AAC) tools. The second study then evaluated a proof-of-concept prototype in both a lab setting with the researcher and *in situ* with unfamiliar conversation partners at a local market. Findings suggest that a head-worn approach could better allow wearers to maintain focus on the conversation, reduce reliance on the availability of external tools (*e.g.*, paper and pen) or people, and minimize visibility of the support by others. These studies should motivate further investigation of head-worn conversational support.

Author Keywords

Aphasia; head-worn display; conversational support; wearable computing; accessibility.

ACM Classification Keywords

H.5.m. Information interfaces and presentation (*e.g.*, HCI).

INTRODUCTION

Individuals with aphasia experience a sudden loss of language skills (*e.g.*, due to a stroke) [7]. Because of aphasia's impact on speaking and comprehension, this loss can make even simple day-to-day conversations challenging, leading to a sharp reduction in independence. Computer-based tools to support aphasia typically provide multimodal, symbol-based dictionaries that can be used either as a replacement or prompt for natural speech [7,17].

CHI 2015, April 18 - 23 2015, Seoul, Republic of Korea
Copyright 2015 ACM 978-1-4503-3145-6/15/04...$15.00
http://dx.doi.org/10.1145/2702123.2702484

Figure 1. Participant in Study 2 before entering the market to complete tasks with head-worn vocabulary. Each prompt provides an image, text and audio (*e.g.*, pumpkin is shown, top-right). A wrist-worn touchpad (smartphone) controlled the display for study tasks (bottom-right).

Unfortunately, adoption of these augmentative and alternative communication (AAC) tools remains low [17]. The causes are complex, but evidence points to issues in how external devices disrupt social conversation norms and draw undue attention to the disability [17]. Unlike prosthetics such as eyeglasses or hearing aids, traditional AAC tools, either on dedicated assistive devices (*e.g.*, Dynavox [1]) or more recently as mobile apps (*e.g.*, Lingraphica[2] and Proloquo2Go[3]), are *external* to the user—requiring the user to consciously seek out support and divert attention away from the current conversation (*e.g.*, to retrieve and interact with their device). Multi-tasking while conversing can be challenging for anyone, but for an individual with aphasia, it can significantly impact speech production [25].

In this paper, we investigate the design of vocabulary prompts on a head-worn display for individuals with aphasia (Figure 1). By providing always-available and glanceable support, a head-worn display may enable a fundamentally different communication experience than existing tools—potentially enabling the user to better maintain focus on their communication partner while unobtrusively controlling the conversational support. While research in wearable computing has long employed head-

[1] http://www.dynavoxtech.com/default.aspx
[2] http://www.aphasia.com/
[3] http://www.assistiveware.com/product/proloquo2go

worn displays for contextual information such as just-in-time memory support [24] and cross-language communication [23], supporting communication for individuals with aphasia has not yet been studied.

We conducted two studies to inform the design of head-worn vocabulary support and to assess the potential impacts of such support. Study 1 was an interview study to elicit feedback on the general idea from 8 participants. It included an introduction to and brief use of Google Glass, as well as presentation of two narrative storyboards as a design probe. Guided by findings from that study, we built a proof-of-concept prototype on Google Glass—that we call *GLAAC* (Glass AAC)—and evaluated it with 14 participants with aphasia. In Study 2, participants used GLAAC during conversations in a lab setting with the researcher and *in situ* with unfamiliar conversation partners at a local market.

Combined, our results show head-worn vocabulary prompts to be a feasible approach to conversation support. Findings from Study 2, in particular, suggest that glanceable vocabulary contributed to keeping participants' attention on their conversation partner and helped them stay engaged in the conversation task while seeking out support. While some participants discussed concerns with device input, there was generally a positive response to using head-worn vocabulary in busy contexts where environmental pressures challenge those with aphasia to respond quickly. Our work contributes (1) a proof-of-concept prototype for presenting vocabulary prompts on a head-worn display; (2) a qualitative evaluation of this prototype based on use in lab and field settings; and, (3) identification of potential contexts of use for which head-worn vocabulary prompts may be most beneficial. Secondarily, we reflect on the methods used in our studies and their efficacy for eliciting feedback from individuals with aphasia in the design and prototyping stages of new technology development.

RELATED WORK AND BACKGROUND

We provide a brief background on aphasia, as well as research on computerized AAC and head-worn cognitive and communication support.

Aphasia

Aphasia is an acquired language disorder that occurs from damage to the language areas of the brain [7]. It ranges widely in severity from mild complications in speech production to complete loss of language production and comprehension. Depending on the location and extent of the brain damage, individuals can experience different combinations of deficits in naming, fluency, repetition, auditory comprehension, grammatical processing, reading, and writing [7]. Aphasia affects people of all ages; however, as the most common cause of aphasia is stroke, the prevalence of aphasia increases with age.

Due to impaired language skills, those with aphasia can be perceived as incompetent and can find their opportunities to participate in conversation and decision-making limited [13]; delays while formulating a response can lead to a speaker with aphasia losing their turn [3]. Conversational success often depends on the facilitation skills and cooperation of the conversational partner [3,13]. These barriers to participation are particularly evident in public or community settings where conversation partners may be unfamiliar with aphasia and may not have the same patience and understanding as a more intimate partner.

Computerized AAC for Aphasia

While some research has focused on supporting people with aphasia in activities of daily living (*e.g.*, daily planning [4,20] and cooking [26]), AAC support has been a more dominant theme in the literature. Some high-tech AAC systems focus on storytelling, by enabling access to pre-recorded stories that can be used to introduce topics (*e.g.*, TalksBac [27]). Others provide mechanisms for capturing and accessing photos for use in later conversation [1,2].

Another popular line of work is the use of symbol-based dictionaries of words and phrases—an approach that we use in this paper. These tools typically provide audio and pictures paired with text, and address the problem that individuals with aphasia generally know what they wish to say, but may experience difficulty in expressing the specific words needed. A primary challenge, however, is providing fast access to vocabulary that is typically organized in deep, cumbersome hierarchies. Manual customization is commonly supported, but effortful. Another approach is to reduce navigation time by organizing vocabulary based on semantic associations [21], or dynamically adapting it based on the user's location or conversational partner [14]—some research has begun to explore automated means of generating these contextual predictions [8].

While these approaches provide promising directions for content organization, they ignore how the form factor of the device may impact the user's ability to efficiently integrate support into conversation. For many individuals, the audio and visual stimuli are sufficient for prompting speech. However, because that support is audible and visible to others, the system tends to dominate, replacing rather than augmenting the user [17]. Moreover, use requires that the user turn their attention away from the conversation, which is not only socially awkward, but can impede the use of facial cues as an aid to comprehension [10]. We conjecture that the time to pull out the tool along with the negative implications of turning focus away from the partner compound the effect of navigation time on communication success. We thus explore the use of a head-worn display as an alternative form factor that is also compatible with automated approaches to efficient vocabulary organization.

Head-Worn Cognitive and Communication Support

To our knowledge, no research has investigated head-worn displays to support persons with aphasia, although one project used a head-worn camera to capture content for later use in storytelling [2]. A few studies have looked at head-worn displays to support older adults [16] and persons with

Figure 2. Example frames from the storyboards used as a design probe in Study 1: two frames from the grocery store scenario showing a woman searching for cheddar cheese, and three frames from a man with a migraine visiting the doctor.

cognitive decline [11]; these efforts have identified a number of potential application areas, including short-term memory aids, experience capture, and instructions (*e.g.*, for cooking). In addition, a study of Google Glass with persons with Parkinson's disease found no serious accessibility challenges due to motor impairments [19], a consideration that is also important for persons with aphasia, who often have right-side hemiparesis (weakness or paralysis).[4]

More broadly, the effect of delivering information via a head-worn display during conversation has been studied with unimpaired individuals, but whether these findings extend to the design of AAC remains an open question. One study on the timing and modality of information delivery during conversation found that it should be delivered visually in batches when the wearer is not speaking [22]. Another study showed that delivery during conversation negatively impacted eye contact and attention [18]; however, the information shown was not relevant to the conversation and the display was located just below the wearer's line of sight. It is unclear how these findings will translate when the information plays a direct role in the conversation, as with our approach.

STUDY 1: FORMATIVE INTERVIEWS

We conducted an interview study with 8 participants with aphasia to gauge initial reaction to vocabulary prompts on a head-worn display and to perform a preliminary assessment of the accessibility of Google Glass for users with aphasia.

Method

The study included basic tasks on Glass, and semi-structured interviews with storyboards as a design probe.

Participants

Language ability varies greatly with aphasia, and we predict that our approach will be most useful to persons with good auditory comprehension and mild to moderate verbal production deficits. However, as this first study relied heavily on discussion of the design probe, we targeted recruitment at the higher end of that range. Participants were screened by a licensed speech-language pathologist based on two standardized tests: (1) the Communication Activities of Daily Living (CADL-2), to assess the impact of impairment on daily communication [12], and (2) the Western Aphasia Battery (WAB), which assesses type and degree of aphasia [15]. Criteria for participation included a minimum of the 50th percentile for the CADL-2, and for the WAB, 7/10 for auditory verbal comprehension and 5/10 for information content of spontaneous speech.

Eight participants were recruited at a local community organization for individuals with aphasia.[5] They ranged in age from 45 to 72 (M = 59.8, SD = 8.5); one was female. All participants acquired aphasia from a stroke that resulted in right-side hemiparesis (weakness). As a result, all participants were left-handed post stroke; pre-stroke, S5 was left-handed and S4 was ambidextrous.

Storyboards

Two storyboards depicting everyday conversational tasks were used as a design probe, to elicit feedback on the idea of glanceable, head-worn vocabulary prompts:

- *Grocery store* (Figure 2). A woman visits a grocery store while wearing a head-worn display preloaded with her grocery list. At the store, she cannot locate the cheddar cheese nor can she express the words "cheddar cheese" to ask a clerk where it is. She activates the device, navigates a hierarchy to the entry for cheddar cheese, and taps to play text-to-speech. After practicing saying "cheddar cheese" on her own, she seeks a clerk and successfully asks for help with finding the cheese.
- *Doctor's office* (Figure 2). As a man approaches a clinic, the head-worn device recognizes it and automatically loads personalized medical prompts. Once in the examining room, the man points to his head and the doctor guesses that he has a headache. But, to be more specific, the man accesses two prompts on the head-worn display to help him say that it is a "migraine" and that he wants the medication "Zomig".

The storyboards were initially hand-drawn, revised with image manipulation software, and augmented with comic-book grammar to convey text-to-speech features, GPS triggers, projected displays, and gestural interaction. Finalized panels were printed on paper for a low-fidelity look-and-feel to encourage critical discussion.

Interviewing and Communication Technique

Because communication is inherently difficult with aphasia, past work has proposed guidelines for including individuals with aphasia in the design process. Accordingly, our

[4] Aphasia results from damage to the left side of the brain. As motor-function is contralateral, right-side deficits are common.

[5] A ninth participant withdrew.

method employs aspects such as working one-on-one with participants [9] and phrasing questions in a closed manner when necessary [13]. The lead researcher was also trained in *supported conversation*, a set of methods designed to create opportunities for an individual with aphasia to contribute to the conversation [13]. While we primarily asked open-ended interview questions, we used supporting materials to adapt to each participant's needs: pictures, visual scales with close-ended alternatives to the open-ended questions, paper and pen, and finally, markers, sticky notes, and transparent sheets to annotate the storyboards.

Procedure

We developed protocols in consultation with clinicians, such as an aphasia-friendly consent process; our institutional review board (IRB) approved these protocols. Study sessions were one hour long. Following informed consent, participants were asked demographic questions as well as questions about their current conversation support strategies. The following two parts were then completed:

Part 1: Google Glass Use. The researcher introduced Glass and demonstrated directional swipes (forward, back, and down) and taps on the arm of the device. During this demonstration, participants viewed the effects of the input via screencast on a paired Bluetooth phone. Next, participants put on Glass. After the participant had tried out and confirmed that they understood each gesture, the following set of tasks was presented (~10 minutes): (1) navigate to a photo album, (2) view a recent New York Times article, (3) activate the audio feature to have the headline text read aloud, and (4) return to the home screen. These tasks required at a minimum 3 forward, 3 backward, and 1 downward swipe, and 2 taps. After, participants rated each of the following on 7-point scales (easy to difficult): swiping the touchpad, tapping the touchpad, seeing images/text on the screen, and hearing audio output.

Because 3 of the first 6 participants encountered difficulties in using Glass's touchpad, we adjusted the above protocol for the last 2 participants to include a second input option. These participants completed the task set on the Glass touchpad, and then repeated the task set using the Bluetooth-connected phone as a touchpad to control Glass.

Part 2: Storyboard Scenarios. The storyboards were introduced one at a time (grocery store then doctor's office), and participants were asked to give feedback and discuss the role of Glass in each one. Once both storyboards had been shown, participants were asked open-ended questions about whether and how a head-worn display could provide support during conversation.

Data and Analysis

The entire session was video recorded with the exception of S1, for whom only audio was recorded. Open-ended responses were analyzed for themes of interest [6].

Aspect of Use	Mean	SD	Median	Range
Swiping	4.1	1.0	4.0	2–6
Tapping	3.5	2.1	4.0	1–7
Seeing	3.9	1.6	3.5	2–6
Hearing	4.0	2.3	5.0	1–7

Table 1. Study 1 ratings of Google Glass accessibility, including swiping and tapping on the touchpad, seeing the display, and hearing the audio (1=easy; 7=difficult). (N = 7)

Findings

Participants identified accessibility issues with Glass and offered feedback on the idea of head-worn word prompts.

Accessibility of Glass

While some participants were able to use Glass with relative ease, others encountered substantial challenges. Ease of use ratings were mixed as a result, as shown in Table 1. Based on video analysis, swipes and taps were particularly problematic for 3 participants and the researcher had to step in and control their finger or the device itself to help them complete the tasks. One of the three, S7, was not able to use the touchpad on Glass without the researcher's help, so did not rate its ease of use; he was however able to use the phone as a touchpad and rated its ease of use: swiping, 4; tapping, 1; seeing 2; hearing 1. In total, 6 of the 8 participants expressed a preference for inverting the device's design so that the touchpad and display would be on the left.

In terms of the display, 3 participants gave low ratings for being able to see it, either due to poor eyesight or weakness in the right eye, or a preference for having a display on both sides. Two participants encountered issues with the audio being hard to hear or too fast.

Feedback on Glanceable Vocabulary Prompts

Overall, 7 out of 8 participants spoke positively of the ideas presented in both storyboards. S6 only responded positively to the doctor's office scenario, finding the vocabulary depicted in the grocery store scenario too easy to require support. We summarize the main themes here, particularly focusing on those related to the head-worn form factor.

Enabling stronger conversational roles. Five participants discussed how support during conversation can impact their identity within a group and ability to influence group decisions. Important roles included being a fully informed patient at a doctor's office, providing customer service at work, or asking questions at a board meeting. S1, for example, expressed a desire to return to his previous job as a restaurant owner. To do so, he envisioned using the head-worn display to ask customers for their preferred ingredients while making sandwiches with his hands. As another example, S3 sat on the executive board of a family business, but found his opinion skipped over at meetings when he needed to use paper and pen to communicate. He felt a head-worn display could address this problem.

Privacy & social perception. The privacy of the audio and visual output was seen by two participants as potentially enabling natural speech. S5 liked private access to phonetic cuing because she would still have the opportunity to say the word herself: *"I can't say it...um...but I know what it is...so this device can say it for me, and [then] I'll say it."* S3 wanted access to the audio, text, and visual aspects of the prompts to support his communication without circumventing his place in conversation. When asked why those aspects, he said: *"Because [the prompts are] working now I mean...its...I'm the one asking, not [my wife] or someone else but me."* The ability to retain the ability to speak for oneself while accessing support was important for these participants. None of the participants raised concerns about privacy or negative social perception when asked about the drawbacks of using Glass.

Overcoming contextual pressures. Six of the 8 participants highlighted situational pressures that make timeliness of support important. S3 was keenly aware of having a limited amount of time to find support because otherwise he may lose his turn to ask a question or steer the topic of conversation during group meetings: *"But I can't say it, or write it down, or have me a pen and paper...4 or 5 minutes and then that's it."* S6 provided the example of wanting to use head-worn support when taking the bus so that he could respond to the bus driver's requests: *"talk to bus driver, money, what kind of money, $1 okay."* This hurried context of boarding a bus while retrieving the required fare highlights the potential of glanceable support.

Related, 4 participants described how support mechanisms may be unavailable or misplaced at the time they are needed. A wearable, always-available display could mitigate this issue. S2, for example, uses voice recognition on his phone but sometimes misplaces the phone. In this respect, he viewed Glass positively: *"[taps the side of his glasses] click away and the eyes see it and there is no distractions [like] with 'where's my cell phone?"*

Perceived advantages. Participants additionally noted a number of general advantages relative to their current compensatory strategies. Two mentioned trouble with audio-only conversations, noting the need to both hear and see. S6, for example, explained that he does not use a cell phone because he needs to see facial expressions. This points to problems with assistive tools that require the user to look away from their partner to access the support. A head-worn display would allow the wearer to monitor their partner's facial expressions while accessing support.

Another general advantage, raised by 3 participants, was that while writing was useful, it was also time consuming, inefficient, and dependent upon finding a pen. Particularly relevant to our focus on vocabulary retrieval, 4 participants described elaborate support strategies for when precision is needed. S2 described that when he needs a specific medication he relies on the availability of a particular pharmacist who knows him. S3 described telephoning his wife when stuck, who would then list off possible words until finding the right one. Both of these examples point to the potential of AAC vocabulary support as a solution, though a head-worn display may not be necessary.

Perceived drawbacks. Apart from the widespread concern about the right-sided touchpad on Glass, other concerns that arose regarding head-worn vocabulary support included: one participant who did not like the idea of assistive technology in general (whether a tablet, phone or head-worn display), concern by 2 participants about the learning curve for our proposed solution, and 1 participant who did not want more than five prompts on the device, feeling that it could detract from efficient navigation mid-conversation. Note, however, that this lattermost participant changed his mind after also participating in Study 2.

Summary

Overall, participants responded positively to the idea of head-worn conversational support, seeing potential for it to provide a stronger role in conversation for the wearer and to allow for more efficient communication than existing strategies. While the study did reveal accessibility issues with Google Glass, the use of alternative input options alleviated these concerns.

STUDY 2: PROTOTYPE AND EVALUATION

While the findings from Study 1 suggest promise for head-worn vocabulary support, the experience of using a working prototype could be different. For this second study, we built a proof-of-concept prototype called *GLAAC* and asked 14 participants with aphasia to complete conversational tasks with the prototype in a lab setting and at a public market.

Proof-of-Concept Prototype

For the proof-of-concept prototype, we wrote a custom Android application for Google Glass. The design was informed by common participant feedback in Study 1 (*e.g.*, the need for a different touchpad placement) and user interface guidelines for individuals with aphasia (*e.g.*, [5,10]). Although Study 1 explored the number and types of prompts that should be included in such a tool, these remained open design questions in Study 2.

The prototype consisted of a simple two-level hierarchy of words the user could navigate with swipes and taps (Figure 3). The top-level categories were 'baseball', 'groceries', and 'you', which correspond to the study tasks described below; 'you' was customized to each participant. Each category included five words. Category and word screens consisted of an image, a text label, and an audio prompt (provided by Android's text-to-speech engine). To visually differentiate between category screens and word screens, categories used white icons on a black background, while words included color photos and had the parent category's icon superimposed on the upper-right corner (Figure 3).

Only one screen in the hierarchy was visible at a time. We used standard Glass interactions for navigation: *forward* and *backward swipes* scrolled through items in the current level of the hierarchy, *tap* moved down a level (*i.e.*, from a category to its specific words), *downward swipe* canceled

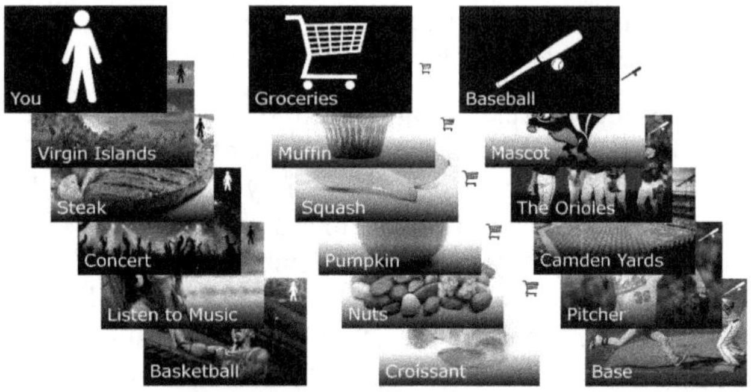

Figure 3. Vocabulary in the proof-of-concept prototype for Study 2. This two-level hierarchy consists of three categories (you, groceries, baseball), and five words in each category. Each screen provides an image, text, and audio. The 'you' category was customized in advance for each participant.

out of a level (*i.e.*, from a specific word back to its category screen). In addition, we implemented a fifth gesture, a *two-finger tap*, to play audio for the current screen.

Because of the difficulties observed in Study 1 with Glass's right-sided touchpad, we used a Bluetooth-paired Samsung Galaxy S4 phone to control the prototype (Figure 1). Pairing the phone in this way mirrors the Glass display on the phone's screen and allows use of the phone's touchpad to control Glass. We covered the phone screen in black tissue paper that still allowed for touch input while visually hiding the display.. The phone was placed in a sport armband, which could then be attached to the user's right wrist to allow for left-handed control of Glass. While this approach is not designed for long-term use, it allowed us to sufficiently circumvent the accessibility issues with Glass's right-sided touchpad to conduct an exploratory evaluation.

Evaluation Method

The proof-of-concept prototype was evaluated with 14 individuals with aphasia to assess usage and response to head-worn vocabulary prompts during conversation.

Participants

We recruited 14 participants (3 female) through our partner organization, including the 8 who had participated in Study 1. As Study 2 relied less on verbal feedback than Study 1, we did not restrict participation to those with high verbal skills. Participants were screened by a licensed speech-language pathologist. Participants ranged in age from 46 to 75 ($M = 61$, $SD = 8.1$). Scores on the CADL-2 ranged from the 31st–99th percentile. Composite scores on the WAB ranged from 51.5–82 ($M = 68.6$), while the sub-component ranges were 5–10 ($M = 7.6$) for information content, and 5.85–9.5 ($M = 8.1$) for auditory verbal comprehension.

Procedure

Study sessions were two hours long and were IRB approved. Participants wore Google Glass and controlled it via the paired Samsung phone, which was attached to their right wrist. The researcher introduced the application and how to control it with the touchscreen gestures by using the 'baseball' category; this category was chosen because it is a popular conversation topic at the partner organization. Participants then completed tasks in two settings: an autobiographical task in the lab with a researcher, and two shopping tasks at a nearby market with unfamiliar store clerks. Finally, a semi-structured interview was conducted.

Autobiographical task. To provide practice using head-worn prompts, the researcher and participant had a brief conversation (~5 minutes) on a familiar topic and in a quiet environment. To support this conversation, the 'you' category was customized in advance based on a short questionnaire on personal interests administered before the session. The researcher then asked 3 open-ended questions, such as "What would you like to do this weekend?" or "What do you enjoy doing in your spare time?" Participants were asked to use the prompts when responding.

Market tasks. During the second hour, participants visited a nearby market with the researcher to use GLAAC for *in situ* conversational tasks with unfamiliar partners (*i.e.*, store clerks). We chose a setting with an unfamiliar partner as it is a challenging—but important [25]—setting for high-tech AAC design. The tasks were: (1) ask for an out-of-season item that would not be easily found (a pumpkin), and (2) ask whether a particular product (a muffin) contained an allergen (nuts). These tasks were chosen because of their everyday nature and because they would be difficult to accomplish through other compensatory strategies like pointing and gesturing. The 'groceries' category contained 5 prompts: 3 ('pumpkin', 'muffin', and 'nuts') to support the tasks, and 2 ('croissant', and 'squash') as distractors.

Before leaving the lab setting for the market, the researcher explained the goal of each market task by using pictures but without verbally naming the items (pumpkin, muffin, nuts). For example, for the second task participants were instructed to clarify whether 'this bakery item contains this common allergen.' Participants were given a chance to ask questions in the lab and again before entering the market.

Semi-structured interview. Finally, upon return to the lab, the researcher asked open- and close-ended questions on the experience of using GLAAC.

Data Collection and Analysis

All interaction with the device was automatically logged. The autobiographical task and semi-structured interview were video recorded, while the market trip was only audio recorded due to IRB concern that video was invasive of bystanders' privacy. Clerks were told about the study in advance, but they were not given detail about the tasks or goals. To supplement the market audio data, the researcher took notes in situ and filled out a more thorough observation sheet immediately following the study session. This sheet included topics like whether the participant said the target vocabulary word or whether the device created noticeable disruption during conversation with the clerk.

Semi-structured interviews were transcribed and coded for themes of interest [6], while allowing for new, inductive codes tied closely to the data to emerge. We developed our themes from 22 codes, such as 'line of vision', 'timing of support', and 'learning curve'. Speaking turn was used as the basic unit of analysis for coding. However, because supported conversation requires the interviewer to act as a resource for the person with aphasia, a "turn" could cover more than one speaker or even the same speaker multiple times [3]. In cases requiring gestures for interpretation, the video data was also referenced. Finally, to validate our approach, a person independent of the research team used the code set to independently characterize participant-initiated topics and to jointly code a transcript with a member of the research team to verify whether consensus held. The two coders disagreed in 65 of 1034 cases, conflicts were resolved through discussion, and when interviewed on issues of bias, completeness, and characterization of participants' responses, the independent coder thought the codes were being applied fairly.

Findings

We begin with an overview of the autobiographical and market task results, focusing on the log data use and Likert scale feedback, before covering the themes that arose in the end-of-session interview portion of the study. Participant numbers for repeat participants are the same as in Study 1.

Overall Task Success

Autobiographical task. Overall, participants responded positively to using GLAAC to answer the researcher's questions about their personal interests (7 positive, 4 mixed, 2 neutral, 1 negative). Negative responses were largely directed at the physical form factor, with 9 participants suggesting modifications (*e.g.*, adding physical buttons, improving gesture detection, and moving to the left the touchpad/display). Four participants criticized the limited vocabulary, wanting it customized to their needs or interests. For example, S2 highlighted how our design does not capture his main need for help linking vocabulary: *"...'how', 'is', 'its', 'have', [...] a lot of times [my conversation partner] can't help me [with those]."* A summary of log data from interactions with the device is shown in Table 2.[6]

Market tasks. Accessing the word prompts appeared to help participants correctly say the target vocabulary while at the market. Based on observational data, 7 participants used the prompts and said the target vocabulary for both the pumpkin and muffin tasks, while 3 more did so for at least one of the tasks (another participant was successful but did not need the prompts at all). The participant who had scored the lowest on the functional language profile of the CADL (S14) was not successful. However, 5 of 7 participants who scored in the middle of the range were successful with at least both tasks—a promising finding particularly given the complexity of using a new device in a busy environment.

Participants rated their use of the prototype at the market highly. The overall average rating of the experience was 7.5 on a 9-point scale, where 9 is positive (*SD* = 1.3, median = 7.5). Participants also felt that they were able to concentrate on conversing with the clerk while using the prototype (*M* = 7.6/9, *SD* = 1.5, median = 8.5), and that the device generally supported rather than disrupted their conversation with the clerk (*M* = 7.1/9, *SD* = 1.4, median = 7.5).

	Lab		Market	
	M	*SD*	*M*	*SD*
Number of prompts used	20.9	12.3	36.7	21.3
Time spent on irrelevant vocabulary (%)	32.3	17.0	69.2	20.0
Number of touch events	26.9	17.5	42.5	26.8
Elapsed time of interaction bursts (s)	1.4	0.2	2.0	0.9
Number of times the most relevant word category was closed	0.7	1.2	3.1	2.2

Table 2. Interactions with GLAAC in the autobiographical (lab) and market tasks. Unsurprisingly, participants encountered more difficulties in the market setting; however, overall subjective response was still positive.

The log data, shown in Table 2, suggests that differences between the lab and market settings impacted use of the device. On average, participants viewed more prompts at the market, spent less time on relevant vocabulary, and interacted with the device both more often and for longer than they did during the autobiographical tasks. This trend is not surprising given the additional distractions in the market setting. Aside from one participant who did not use GLAAC at all during the tasks,[7] all participants viewed the prompt 'muffin' at least once while 11 viewed 'pumpkin' and 9 viewed 'nuts'. On average, each participant activated the 'pumpkin' audio 3.5 times (*SD* = 4.7), but use quickly dropped off for the second task at least partly because the audio was difficult to hear in the noisy environment. Audio use also varied by participant, with 5 participants using it over 6 times, and 4 not using it at all.

Despite these successes, some issues arose. Six participants encountered a problem in at least one of their conversations. S7, S9, S12, and S14 tried using the device during conversation but had to walk away before reattempting. The time it took for them to find the needed word caused either the clerk to excuse themselves and promise to return, or the participant to volunteer to take a moment and return. S6, S7, S9, and S10 got stuck with the device interaction at least once, for example, tapping repeatedly when tapping was not applicable or interacting at length with unrelated vocabulary. Of these 6 participants, 3 had problems saying the target vocabulary in both tasks. The others persevered and successfully completed at least one of the tasks.

Semi-Structured Interview

Our interview results illustrate how GLAAC was perceived as offering support for maintaining conversational focus, reducing reliance on others to support conversation, managing perceptions, and handling stressful conversations.

[6] Log data is unavailable for S1 due to an application malfunction.

[7] This participant was able to complete the tasks without support, as indicated in their feedback and by the researcher's observations.

Important overall feedback was that, though the market was described as a place where it is typically difficult to converse, almost all participants (N = 10) thought that GLAAC had a strong role in such environments. For example, while S3 acknowledged that it was easier to use GLAAC one-on-one in the lab, he stressed it had a bigger role in busy, public places like the market. *"Busy place, and friends or enemies, then [GLAAC has] really [a] much livelier [role]."*

Glanceable display. Nine participants discussed how the glanceable nature of the display allowed them to maintain visual awareness of their conversation partner. S5, for example, said: *"[My focus was] right on the money...he was standing right there and the...I can see him...and I can see the pumpkin"*. One person, S8, discussed being able to pay attention specifically to his partner's nonverbal communication: *"Oh, yeah, I could read her."*

Some scenarios of use for GLAAC envisioned by our participants touched on the ability to immediately access support for time-sensitive exchanges. For example, S8 described how he wanted to be able to be part of a roaring stadium of fans and yell at a soccer player right when they made the wrong play: *"Yeah, 'You're doing the wrong f[*%#]in' thing!'... And they would get it."* S1 similarly expressed the desire to present his personality, by aspiring to be seen as courteous to hostesses. He felt the prototype could support these quick exchanges.

The quick access to support was also seen as helping the wearer reorient himself/herself mid-conversation. S11 described becoming anxious while talking to the clerk, but glancing at the display got him back on track: *"And the glasses, and then...I could do it. And then, other one, muffin, good."* Frequently, participants realized they did not have the word they wanted midway through speaking. S8 said:

> *"Oh yeah. I can see it really, it really come to life. I didn't have it, I can, I...right. And I can't even remember now, the prompts, but...yeah, it came to life."*

This quote describes how GLAAC helped with inserting the needed word into speech mid-conversation. Overall, 11 participants described a halt mid-speech, and 9 described seeing the support vocabulary mid-conversation.

Issues with multitasking. While the display was regarded positively overall, interacting with it was still seen as demanding by some participants. For the autobiographical tasks, 2 participants described feeling time pressure to respond while trying to read the displayed information: *"Five things, six things [on the display] and I thought, so there was no time for me to see them,"* (S8).

The wrist-based navigation was seen as particularly problematic, with 10 participants commenting that it detracted from speaking. For example, S13 felt as if the wrist navigation added a second task in addition to talking:

> *"Well this...[she mimics the swipe gesture on her wrist]. It's very hard to concentrate. Two things. This conversation, two different things of happening." (S13)*

After finishing the market tasks another participant, S6, explained: *"I like talking to people face-to-face... [but] the eye, the arm, and talking, [are] too much [at once]."*

Availability of support. The market task prompted participants to reflect on how their existing support strategies sometimes fail in similar environments. Similar drawbacks arose as in Study 1. S2 again stressed that the wearable display would be useful because it was always easily available and did not require *"fumbling around."* He mentioned the typical experience of needing to ask for help at the grocery store and having to find a paper and pen.

Four participants currently use social support strategies in these kinds of contexts, but desired more independence. S8's wife goes grocery shopping with him and provides vocabulary support, which S8 combines with gestures, but still he does not speak with the clerk in the way he experienced using our prototype. When leaving the market S8 remarked:

> *"I would never thought to do that myself...I wouldn't. [...] No, I would go with my wife. She would help me and I would have to point." (S8)*

Vocabulary prompts could replace strategies that rely on the availability of a partner to fill mid-conversation gaps. S6 uses a similar approach when at the library: he gets the librarian to list off titles until he signals that she has guessed the correct one. He would prefer to use GLAAC to initiate his own request, *"I would. Nobody [would have to] ask me."* He emphasized that their conversation would be more efficient by eliminating the guesswork: *"Oh, I know what you want,"* enabling them to proceed directly to the desired book.

Privacy. While not a common theme, we were interested in comments about discreet use and privacy. S8 stressed the importance of audio for allowing him to feel in control during a conversation: *"if we had so we can hear at the same time... then it would be easier because we can... [take] control of the situation."* S5 also mentioned privacy, in describing wanting to store contact information and vocabulary, but not wanting anyone but her family to have access to this information. Finally, while our study design did not allow us to directly examine third party perceptions of GLAAC use, one anecdote suggests use was relatively inconspicuous: the researcher incorrectly recorded S4 used GLAAC for the word "nuts" during the market task, yet afterward, S4 clarified that he had been able to say "nuts" but "muffin" was hard. The personal display had concealed the exact words used for support.

Summary

Study 2 reinforced our findings from Study 1, with observations and feedback from use in the lab and the market highlighting similar themes, including a better ability to maintain focus on the conversation, reduce reliance on the availability of external tools or people, and minimize visibility of the support by others. Nonetheless, multitasking between accessing the support and engaging in conversation was challenging for our participants and further work is needed to improve input and navigation.

DISCUSSION

Symbol-based dictionaries can help individuals with aphasia find the words they need, but are often seen a last resort because they tend to replace rather than augment the user's natural speech [7]. Our findings, though exploratory, suggest that head-worn support may mitigate this issue. Participants commented on form-factor related aspects such as being able to keep their conversation partner within their line of sight and how the privacy of the audio and visual prompts could support them in speaking for themselves. It may even be possible to provide fully discreet assistance in the future—during the market task, even we had difficulty ascertaining when participants were viewing prompts. Despite this promise, our work is only a first step and raises many challenges and questions for future research.

Reflections on Design

Cognitive demand. Manipulating a wearable device may ultimately be less demanding than using a mobile phone for the same support, not least of all because it does not need to be retrieved from a pocket or bag. Many participants in Study 2, however, found the multitasking demanding and some even needed to step back and re-orient themselves in the middle of an exchange with a clerk. A lack of familiarity with the device most likely contributed to this cognitive demand, since participants had only briefly used it before being placed in a complex, real-world setting. Even with more practice, further refinement of the input mechanism and vocabulary structure will likely be needed.

Toward an accessible head-worn display. The right-sided touchpad of Google Glass was problematic at times due to right-side motor deficits that are common with aphasia. While we circumvented the motor issues by using a Bluetooth-paired phone as a touchpad, it presented its own problems and a more refined solution is needed for long-term practical use. A wristband with physical buttons to support eyes-free input may be effective. We had also expected the visual display location on the right side to be problematic due to right-side visual deficits, but received only a few complaints in Study 1. Still, other display placements should be explored.

Scalability. A notable limitation of our proof-of-concept prototype was that it included only 15 words in three categories. Because our goal is to provide communication support *during an exchange* it is critical that needed vocabulary be available quickly. Any complete system will need to assess how many prompts are appropriate to include for this use scenario, and how these prompts should be created and managed. The most effective solution will likely combine manual customization and automatic context-based adaptation (*e.g.* [14]) to present a short list of words. The user could, for example, enter their grocery list before leaving home; similar desktop-phone hybrids have previously been explored for aphasia [4].

Target users. Aphasia varies substantially in manifestation and severity. We targeted individuals with relatively intact auditory comprehension and mild speech deficits as we see this profile as likeliest to benefit from head-worn vocabulary support. We also targeted interactions with unfamiliar partners as the primary context for use as this is an underserved area. With intimate partners, in contrast, low- and no-tech AAC solutions (such as pointing, gesturing, and drawing) are often sufficient due to the partner's familiarity with the person and with aphasia.

Reflections on Study Method

Although both studies were exploratory, they played different but complementary roles. Study 1 relied heavily on verbal description to collect feedback on early design ideas, which can be challenging for individuals with aphasia [2,9,14]. As such, we recruited participants with high verbal abilities and drew heavily on recommendations for incorporating individuals with aphasia into the design process [14]. Study 2 instead focused on use of a working prototype. This approach greatly broadened the range of feedback we received and allowed us to recruit participants with lower verbal abilities, supplementing their feedback with observation. Success in lab or therapy settings has not always translated to less controlled environments [25]. The fact that so many participants completed the market task successfully despite the prototype's rough edges, receiving little training, an unfamiliar conversation partner (clerk), and a noisy setting (market) is very promising. Due to the complementary successes of both studies, we recommend that this combined method be used more broadly in working with participants with aphasia.

Limitations

Further studies are needed to confirm our findings and to assess detailed impacts on conversation dynamics and long-term use. A main limitation is that we did not employ a control condition in Study 2 due to the early nature of the work. As a result, some positive feedback was not clearly attributable to the head-worn form factor; we have tried when possible to note these cases. A comparison may also have mitigated novelty effects, a common concern in design research. A second limitation is that 8/14 participants in Study 2 also participated in Study 1. This consistency enabled us to iterate on a well-defined set of user needs, but there is the danger that participants felt more invested in the design than they would have otherwise. Finally, data analysis in both studies relied on participant transcripts, which were sometimes difficult to interpret due to communication difficulties. To lessen this concern we referred to video and observational notes to aid analysis, but the sometimes-cryptic nature of the transcripts made it difficult to perform reliability analysis on the coding.

CONCLUSION

We presented two design investigations toward the goal of head-worn conversational support for individuals with aphasia. Study 1 elicited feedback based on a design probe of two narrative storyboards, and the findings further motivated the potential benefits of a head-worn approach over traditional AAC tools. Study 2 evaluated a proof-of-concept prototype in lab and field settings, showing that despite limitations, most participants were able to complete constrained conversation tasks successfully and reacted positively to the experience. While these exploratory studies are only a first step, the findings should motivate further investigation of head-worn conversational support—support that could ultimately improve the wearer's ability to maintain their sense of identity and use their own natural voice for a range of daily interactions.

ACKNOWLEDGMENTS

We thank Theo Lorrain-Hale, Angela Baker, and Yasmeen Shah for providing feedback on this work. Additionally, we thank SCALE and its members for all of their help and support for this research. Icons are from the Noun Project and created by Ed Harrison, Wilson Joseph, Rachel Healey, Gerald Wildmoser, and Farran Brown. This research was funded by a Google Faculty Research Award and a Career Development Grant from AAUW.

REFERENCES

1. Allen, M., McGrenere, J., and Purves, B. The design and field evaluation of PhotoTalk: A digital image communication application for people. *Proc. ASSETS'07*, ACM (2007), 187–194.
2. Al Mahmud, A., Gerits, R., and Martens, J. XTag: designing an experience capturing and sharing tool for persons with aphasia. *Proc. NordiCHI'10*, ACM (2010), 325–334.
3. Ball, M.J., Muller, N., and Nelson, R.L., eds. *Handbook of Qualitative Research in Communication Disorders*. Psychology Press, 2014.
4. Boyd-graber, J., Nikolova, S., Moffatt, K., et al. Participatory Design with Proxies: Developing a Desktop-PDA System to Support People with Aphasia. *Proc. CHI'06*, ACM (2006), 151–160.
5. Brandenburg, C., Worrall, L., Rodriguez, A.D., and Copland, D. Mobile computing technology and aphasia: An integrated review of accessibility and potential uses. *Aphasiology 27*, 4 (2013), 444–461.
6. Braun, V. and Clarke, V. Using thematic analysis in psychology. *Qualitative Research in Psychology 3*, 2 (2006), 77–101.
7. Chapey, R. *Language intervention strategies in aphasia and related neurogenic communication disorders*. Lippincott Williams & Wilkins, Philadelphia, 2001.
8. Demmans Epp, C., Djordjevic, J., Wu, S., Moffatt, K., and Baecker, R.M. Towards providing just-in-time vocabulary support for assistive and augmentative communication. *Proc. IUI'12*, ACM (2012), 333–36.
9. Galliers, J., Wilson, S., Roper, A., et al. Words Are Not Enough: Empowering People With Aphasia In The Design Process. *Proc. PDC'12*, ACM (2012), 51–60.
10. Galliers, O., Galliers, J., Wilson, S., et al. City Research Online Accessibility of 3D Game Environments for People with Aphasia: An Exploratory Study. *Proc. ASSETS'11*, ACM (2011), 24–26.
11. Ha, K., Chen, Z., Hu, W., Richter, W., Pillai, P., and Satyanarayanan, M. Towards wearable cognitive assistance. *Proc. MobiSys'14*, ACM (2014), 68–81.
12. Holland, A., Frattali, C., and Fromm, D. Communication Activities of Daily Living: CADL-2. (1999).
13. Kagan, A. Supported conversation for adults with aphasia: Methods and resources for training conversation partners. *Aphasiology 12*, 9 (1998), 816–830.
14. Kane, S.K., Linam-Church, B., Althoff, K., and McCall, D. What We Talk About: Designing a Context-aware Communication Tool for People with Aphasia. *Proc. ASSETS'12*, ACM (2012), 49–56.
15. Kertesz, A. and Poole, E. The Aphasia Quotient: The Taxonomic Approach to Measurement of Aphasic Disability. *Can. J. Neurol. Sci. 1*, 1 (1974), 7–16.
16. Kunze, K. Wearable Computing for Older Adults – Initial Insights into Head-Mounted Display Usage. *Adj. Proc. UbiComp'14*, ACM (2014), 83–86.
17. Lasker, J. and Bedrosian, J. Promoting acceptance of augmentative and alternative communication by adults with acquired communication disorders. *Augmentative and Alternative Communication 17*, 3 (2001), 141–153.
18. Mcatamney, G., Street, S.V., and Uk, G. An Examination of the Effects of a Wearable Display on Informal Face-To-Face Communication. *Proc. CHI'06*, ACM (2006), 45–54.
19. McNaney, R., Vines, J., Roggen, D., et al. Exploring the acceptability of google glass as an everyday assistive device for people with parkinson's. *Proc. CHI'14*, ACM (2014), 2551–2554.
20. Moffatt, K., Mcgrenere, J., Purves, B., and Klawe, M. The Participatory Design of a Sound and Image Enhanced Daily Planner for People with Aphasia. *Proc. CHI'04*, ACM (2004), 407–414.
21. Nikolova, S., Tremaine, M., and Cook, P. Click on Bake to Get Cookies: Guiding Word-Finding with Semantic Associations. *Proc. ASSETS'10*, ACM (2010), 155–162.
22. Ofek, E., Iqbal, S.T., Strauss, K., and Way, O.M. Reducing Disruption from Subtle Information Delivery during a Conversation: Mode and Bandwidth Investigation. *Proc. CHI'13*, ACM (2013), 3111–3120.
23. Patokallio, J. and Ward, N. A wearable cross-language communication aid. *Proc. ISWC'01*, IEEE Comput. Soc (2001), 176–177.
24. Rhodes, B.J. *Just-In-Time Information Retrieval*. PhD Dissertation, MIT, 2000.
25. Van de Sandt-Koenderman, M. High-tech AAC and aphasia: Widening horizons? *Aphasiology 18*, 3 (2004), 245–263.
26. Tee, K., Moffatt, K., Findlater, L., et al. A Visual Recipe Book for Persons with Language Impairments. *Proc. CHI'05*, ACM (2005), 501–510.
27. Waller, A., Denis, F., Brodie, J., and Cairns, A.Y. Evaluating the use of TalksBac, a predictive communciation device for nonfluent adults with aphasia. *Int. J. Lang. Commun. Disord. 33*, 1 (1998), 45–70.

Head-Mounted Display Visualizations to Support Sound Awareness for the Deaf and Hard of Hearing

Dhruv Jain[1,2], Leah Findlater[3], Jamie Gilkeson[4], Benjamin Holland[4], Ramani Duraiswami[2], Dmitry Zotkin[2], Christian Vogler[5], Jon E. Froehlich[2]

[1]MIT Media Lab, Cambridge, MA
[2]Computer Science, [3]Information Studies, University of Maryland, College Park, MD
[4]Montgomery Blair High School, Silver Spring, MD
[5]Technology Access Program, Gallaudet University, Washington, DC

djain@mit.edu, leahkf@umd.edu, rduraisw@umd.edu, wdz@umd.edu, christian.vogler@gallaudet.edu, jonf@umd.edu

ABSTRACT
Persons with hearing loss use visual signals such as gestures and lip movement to interpret speech. While hearing aids and cochlear implants can improve sound *recognition*, they generally do not help the wearer *localize* sound necessary to leverage these visual cues. In this paper, we design and evaluate visualizations for spatially locating sound on a head-mounted display (HMD). To investigate this design space, we developed eight high-level visual sound feedback dimensions. For each dimension, we created 3-12 example visualizations and evaluated these as a design probe with 24 deaf and hard of hearing participants (Study 1). We then implemented a real-time proof-of-concept HMD prototype and solicited feedback from 4 new participants (Study 2). Study 1 findings reaffirm past work on challenges faced by persons with hearing loss in group conversations, provide support for the general idea of sound awareness visualizations on HMDs, and reveal preferences for specific design options. Although preliminary, Study 2 further contextualizes the design probe and uncovers directions for future work.

Author Keywords
Deaf; hard of hearing; head-mounted display; wearable; sound visualization; conversation support; accessibility.

INTRODUCTION
Persons who are deaf or hard of hearing rely on visual signals such as body language, facial expressions, and lip movement to interpret speech (*speechreading)* [4,5,9]. Knowing where to focus visual attention is a prerequisite for effective speechreading. While hearing aids and surgically implanted devices can improve speech recognition, they generally do not improve sound localization [21,23]. In this paper, we investigate visualizations on a head-mounted display (HMD) to increase sound awareness for the deaf and hard of hearing, particularly for group conversations with oral partners.

Prior work on visual aids for persons with hearing loss has focused largely on non-speech sounds (*e.g.,* an alarm or doorbell) presented on external displays such as desktops or mobile devices [11,17,18,27]. Though promising, these external displays require the user to turn their attention away from conversational partners. Moreover, these designs require algorithms that can accurately identify non-speech sounds, which is still an open area of research (*e.g.*, [34]). More similar to our work, Kaneko *et al.* [14] proposed a wrist-worn device with LEDs to indicate sound in one of eight directions to support group conversation. Their primary emphasis, however, was on sensing rather than visual feedback, and included only a minimal user study (1 participant with hearing loss). Here, we explore a head-mounted approach, which offers potential advantages such as increased glanceability and privacy compared to past solutions (Figure 1).

Figure 1: Our proof-of-concept in use during a group conversation with four people. The wearer (not shown) is seated at the south end of the table. Arrows on the transparent HMD (Google Glass) direct attention toward active speakers. Arrow size indicates loudness. See supplementary video.

To investigate sound awareness visualizations for HMDs, we first developed a taxonomy of eight high-level design dimensions such as *perspective*, *loudness*, and *iconic representations*. For each dimension, we generated 3-12 specific visualizations, which were informed by known sound awareness needs [11,17,18] and our own experiences as persons with hearing loss.[1] We then performed two evaluations: a design probe study (Study 1) with 24 deaf and

[1] Two authors including the first have severe-to-profound hearing loss, which both helps to motivate and inform our work.

CHI 2015, April 18 - 23 2015, Seoul, Republic of Korea

ACM 978-1-4503-3145-6/15/04...$15.00
http://dx.doi.org/10.1145/2702123.2702393

hard of hearing participants and a small, exploratory study (Study 2) of a proof-of-concept HMD prototype with four new participants. Study 1 focused on eliciting feedback and identifying promising visual designs, while Study 2 explored the experience of using real-time, HMD sound localization in group conversations.

Findings from Study 1 extend and reaffirm past work [3,9,28] on challenges in group conversations for people with hearing loss who employ speechreading. Specifically, we further motivate the need for glanceable, unobtrusive, and always-available sound awareness to help localize sound sources, focus attention on active speakers, and assist with speaker transitions. During our design probe, all participants supported the idea of head-mounted sound awareness information. We also identified statistically significant preferences for specific design options—for example, positioning sound indicators on the periphery of the screen and how to represent loudness. While preliminary, Study 2's findings further contextualize the design probe and uncover directions for future work.

In summary, the contributions of this paper include: (i) the introduction of an HMD approach to provide sound awareness for the deaf and hard of hearing, with a delineation of eight relevant design dimensions; (ii) empirical results from a design probe study with 24 lip-reading and signing hard of hearing/deaf participants; (iii) a real-time proof-of-concept system that includes a non-wearable microphone array, and findings from a preliminary evaluation with 4 participants; (iv) design recommendations for HMD sound awareness systems, including visual design and physical form factor aspects. While our long-term goal is to provide sophisticated features such as real-time captioning and speaker identification, our focus here is largely on designing and evaluating ideas for spatially locating sound.

BACKGROUND AND RELATED WORK

We provide background on communication strategies, and cover related work on technology for sound awareness.

Communication Strategies & Sound Awareness

Persons with hearing loss use a variety of strategies to converse with partners who use spoken language, including gestures, two-way note taking, and facial expressions [9]. Researchers have developed classifications for these communication strategies [3,28], which we employ in our analysis. A *maladaptive* behavior detracts or inhibits communication, such as avoiding conversation or feigning comprehension [3]. *Adaptive* behaviors can be verbal or non-verbal, such as asking a speaker to repeat or simplify an utterance, explaining one's hearing loss, or repositioning to improve one's view of the speaker [4,9]. Our head-mounted approach should support non-verbal adaptation by helping to direct visual attention.

Even those who cannot hear any sound often understand at least parts of oral conversation through *speechreading*, where lip-reading combined with visual cues, such as facial expressions and body language, are used to interpret speech [5]. Using a hearing device (*e.g.,* hearing aid or cochlear implant) does not eliminate the need to speechread [*ibid*].

Sound awareness is also important beyond conversations. In interviews with deaf and hard of hearing participants, Mankoff and colleagues asked about awareness needs for *non-speech* sounds [11,18]. Participants emphasized a desire to be more aware of sounds across contexts, including home (*e.g.,* alarms, doorbells/phone), transit (*e.g.,* honking), and work (*e.g.,* activities of coworkers, phones). While valuable, our focus in this paper is *localizing* rather than *identifying* sound. Future work should explore both.

Hearing Aids and Cochlear Implants

Sound localization affects sound awareness and speechreading even for users of hearing devices. Modern devices employ sophisticated digital signal processing that often incorporates noise suppression, dynamic gain control, and directional microphones (*e.g.,* [23,24]). The directional microphones amplify sound in front of the listener while limiting it from the sides and behind [19]; however, they generally do not improve the *localization* of sound without visual stimuli (speaker's face in view) [23]. For bilateral hearing aid users (both ears), each device works independently, which has destructive effects on the binaural cues necessary to locate sound [1]. Even bilateral cochlear implant users encounter difficulties in localizing sound [8,21]. Multisensory hearing devices have also been proposed, such as to direct amplification based on eye gaze [10]; this still requires the user to know where to look.

Visual and Tactile Sound Awareness Approaches

Prior work has explored visual [11,14,17,18,32] and tactile [6,31,33] sound awareness approaches. The visual solutions focus largely on non-speech sounds and non-wearable solutions (*e.g.,* [11,17,18]). Closest to our work is Kaneko *et al.*'s [14] wrist-worn localization display mentioned in the Introduction. In contrast to our head-mounted approach, however, their device is low resolution and requires the wearer to look away from conversation partners.

Translation of speech information (*e.g.,* acoustic properties) to haptic patterns has also been studied [6,31,33]. For example, Yeung *et al.* [31] created a tactile display that transforms pitch information into a 16-channel vibro-pattern on the forearm. While tactile-based studies have generally shown positive outcomes—*e.g.,* in the perceptual enhancement of words and phonemes among lipreaders [6]—tactile devices remain an active area of research. We do not explore haptic feedback in this paper, but consider it complementary to our visual designs.Finally, real-time captioning is an active area of research. Because automatic speech recognition (ASR) is still far from a solved problem, recent work has looked at real-time editing of ASR [30] or forgoing ASR altogether by using crowdsourcing [16]. Sony recently released *Access Glasses* [26], which presents captioned text on glass lenses for moviegoers with hearing loss; however, the captions are prepared *a priori*. Jones *et al.* [13] examined methods to display a sign language interpreter

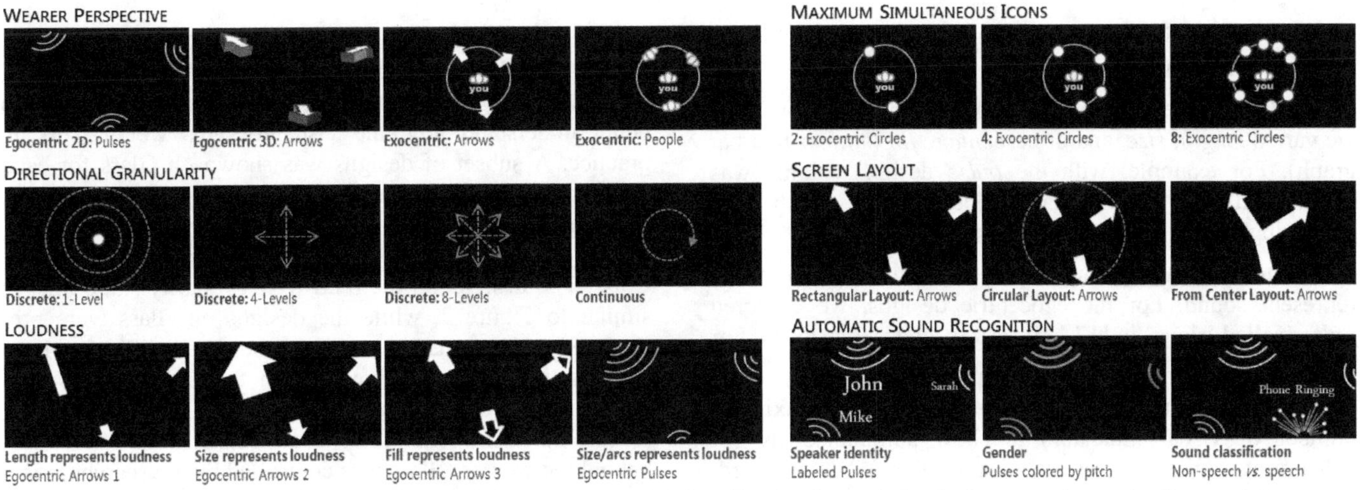

Figure 2: Examples of six of the eight design dimensions: wearer perspective, directional granularity, loudness, maximum simultaneous icons, screen layout, and automatic sound recognition attributes. Different sound indicator icons (*e.g.,* pulse, arrow) are also embedded throughout.

via an HMD. Reactions were mixed—some participants found value in having constant access to the interpreter regardless of head movement. A majority found it difficult to focus on both the interpreter in the HMD and the study tasks (*e.g.,* watching a movie). Though our focus is sound localization, captioning could be incorporated in the future but would also likely demand increased attention from the wearer.

Augmented Reality

Finally, most HMD work has occurred in augmented reality (AR), where virtual imagery overlays physical objects in real time (for reviews, see [15,35]). Though most AR work focuses on augmenting vision, audio has also been explored (*e.g.,* location-based audio cues [22]). Others have investigated how to accurately synthesize spatial audio so that it appears to emerge from AR objects (*e.g.,* [25]). Though AR systems have a potential cognitive cost because they require attentional resources (as with [13]), we could not find design guidelines for displaying peripheral visual cues in HMDs (some work exists for dashboard AR [20]).

DESIGN OF SOUND LOCALIZATION VISUALIZATIONS

We describe our design goals and eight design dimensions.

Design Goals

Informed by the research covered in the Related Work section and our own experiences as persons with hearing loss, we developed the following set of design goals for HMD-based sound visualizations:

- **Localize sound:** The visualizations should provide unobtrusive and accurate indicators of where sound occurs.
- **Glanceable:** The directional information should be easy-to-understand at a glance.
- **Responsive:** The visual cues should render in real-time.
- **Augment, not substitute:** The visualizations should augment and not replace the wearer's own senses and communication strategies. For example, body language, head turns, and eye movements can often indicate who is speaking; the display should supplement these cues.
- **360° sensing:** The visualizations should provide 360° spatial mappings of information. Study 1 investigates precision levels within this range (*e.g.,* 45° steps *vs.* 90°).
- **Adaptable:** Informed by [17,18], visual designs should be customizable to fit each user's needs. Our examination of designs is broad, which helps to isolate specific, promising features that could be customizable in the future.

We also developed a set of secondary goals including: speaker recognition, real-time captions, topic analysis, descriptive conversational statistics (*e.g.,* who speaks the most), and emotion inferences. Though interesting and potentially valuable, most of these secondary aims require sophisticated machine-learning algorithms, which are still active areas of research. Thus, our design work here focuses on sound information that could be gleaned with current technology (*e.g.*, microphone arrays).

Design Dimensions

From the design goals, we generated eight high-level design dimensions (Figure 2). For each dimension, we created at least three different designs by manipulating one or more of the following features: size, shape, perspective, layout, and animation. To simplify our exploration and because Glass has a small color palette [7], we made limited use of color. Similarly, we restricted text use, which may be hard to read at a glance. Below, we describe each design dimension.

1. Wearer Perspective refers to the narrative mode used to render visual information. We evaluated two perspectives: *egocentric*, which presents data from a first-person perspective, and *exocentric*, which presents a disembodied view (*e.g.,* a top-down perspective). For the egocentric designs, we also evaluated 2D *vs.* 3D views. In the 2D view, indicators at the top of the screen correspond to the wearer's front while those at the bottom represent behind.

2. Directional Granularity represents how precisely sound is shown on the display. We explored four levels of fidelity: *continuous*, *8-level discrete, 4-level discrete*, and *1-level discrete*. While continuous shows the exact direction of a sound source, the 8- and 4-level designs visualize data at 45°

and 90° degree discretizations. The 1-level design is binary, showing that sound is occurring but not its location.

3. Loudness represents sound volume. To visualize loudness, we varied *length*, *size*, and/or *percentage fill* (similar to a bar graph). For example, with the *pulse* design, volume was represented by a proportional number of arcs, which were increasingly large for louder sounds.

4. Sound Indicator Icons are the visual shapes used to represent sound. For the egocentric designs, we explored *pulse* (called 'rings' in [17,18]), *arrow*, and *finger* icons. For exocentric, we used *people*, *arrow*, and *circle* icons.

5. Maximum Simultaneous Icons defines the maximum number of visual indicators to show simultaneously for concurrent sounds (*e.g.*, overlapping speakers). We explored: *two*, *four*, and *eight*.

6. Screen Layout refers to where sound indicators are drawn on the display. We explored three layouts: a *rectangular* layout that positions indicators around the screen perimeter, a *circular* layout that positions indicators around a large, centered circle, and *from center*, which draws indicators in the center of the screen.

7. Conveying Sound Source refers to whether indicator icons should point towards the sound source (*i.e.*, directing outward away from the wearer) or follow the path of the sound itself (*i.e.*, directing inward toward the wearer).

8. Automatic Sound Recognition. Beyond localization, we explored more advanced features, including automatically identifying *who* is speaking, highlighting gender, performing sound classification (*e.g.*, visualizing speech and non-speech differently), and real-time captioning.

STUDY 1: DESIGN PROBE AND EVALUATION

To assess our designs and gain a deeper understanding of problems faced in group conversation with oral partners, we conducted a two-part study with 24 deaf and hard of hearing participants.

Method

Participants

Twenty-four volunteers (12 female) were recruited through email and social media. Participants were on average 38.1 years old (*SD*=15.8, range 23–76). Twenty had profound hearing loss, while the remaining four had at least moderate hearing loss. Most reported congenital hearing loss (12) or loss in early childhood (7). Fourteen participants used a hearing device: 7 reported cochlear implants and 8 used digital hearing aids (1 reported using both). Finally, 19 participants (excluding P3, P7, P9, P19, P22) employed lip-reading during conversation at least some of the time. Participants were compensated $50 for time and travel.

Design Probe

The design probe included two visual mediums: an iPad PowerPoint slide deck and a custom Android application for Google Glass. The iPad was used to show a breadth of visualizations for each design dimension, which allowed us to elicit feedback on *overall* ideas rather than specific manifestations of a design. Glass provided a more realistic, medium-fidelity experience and allowed our participants to better understand how the visual designs would work in practice. A subset of designs was shown on Glass for each dimension except for that of maximum simultaneous icons. For example, to compare egocentric 2D *vs.* 3D designs, the iPad included six examples while only two were shown on Glass. The designs on the iPad were primarily static images similar to Figure 2, while the designs on Glass were pre-rendered animations of two common but difficult group conversation scenarios drawn from the first author's own experiences: a small group meeting and a classroom setting (Figure 3). Each scenario has three speakers, one of whom is behind the wearer. Glass was controlled by a researcher via a Bluetooth-paired Android phone.

Procedure

The study procedure took on average 67 minutes (*SD*=13), and included a semi-structured formative interview and a design probe. Participants communicated with the research team verbally (*N*=9) or by typing in two-way chat (*N*=15).

Part One: We began with a questionnaire to collect demographics and background on the participant's hearing loss. The researcher then conducted a semi-structured interview on problems encountered in group conversations, how the participant accommodated those problems, prior experience with computing or mobile devices to support group conversation, and ideas for future technology.

Part Two: At the beginning of the design probe, we introduced the idea of visualizing sound on an HMD, described the meeting table and classroom scenarios in Figure 3 with three animated design examples on the iPad (egocentric pulse, egocentric arrow, and exocentric arrow), and elicited initial feedback. Participants then put on Glass and viewed animated visualizations of the classroom scenario using the exocentric and egocentric arrow designs.

Following this introduction, for each design dimension, we provided a brief textual description, examples on the iPad, and, if applicable, animated visualizations on Glass. We elicited open-ended feedback on the designs and asked for specific preferences along with rationale. To maintain participant engagement and to ensure that they understood the designs, we periodically asked which scenario had been shown on Glass. After completing the first seven design dimensions but before showing examples for automatic sound recognition, we asked participants to describe their ideal designs; participants could do so verbally, textually, and/or with sketches. Finally, the automatic sound recognition examples were shown.

Although not a controlled experiment, to reduce bias we counterbalanced the order in which animated visualizations were shown for each design dimension on Glass. To do so, we created six orderings and assigned an equal number of participants to each ordering. Full counterbalancing was used for sets with 2 or 3 designs, balanced Latin squares for sets of

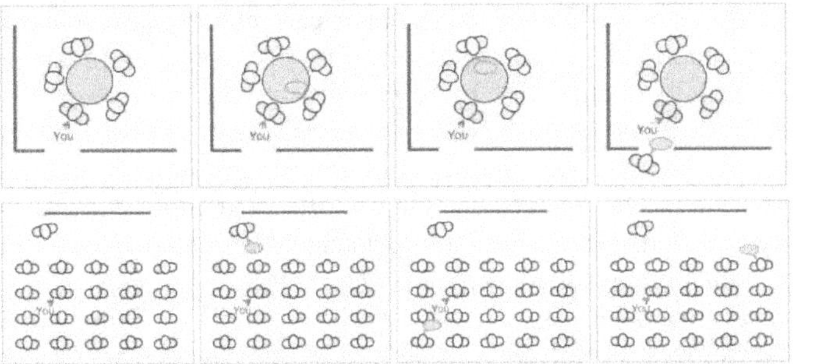

Figure 3: The two scenarios used for animated visualizations in Study 1: meeting table and classroom. Each scenario includes three non-overlapping speakers, one of whom is behind the Glass wearer ('You'). See video.

4 or 6 designs, and no counterbalancing was used for the automatic sound recognition set.

Data and Analysis

Sessions were video and audio recorded. Part One was transcribed for those sessions where participants spoke rather than typed (9 of 24 participants). We then conducted an iterative coding process on these responses [2,12]: (i) one researcher developed an initial codebook for each of 7 sections of the interview; (ii) two independent coders analyzed up to six randomly selected transcripts and met and refined the code set; (iii) the final code set was applied to the remaining transcripts by two independent coders. For this last step, Krippendorff's alpha across all codes was on average 0.68 (*SD*=0.30). Conflicting code assignments were resolved through consensus between the two coders.

For Part Two, we analyzed the distribution of preference votes across options for each design dimension using a chi-square (χ^2) test (except for automatic sound recognition and simultaneous icons, which were open-ended questions). Preference votes were collected verbally and, while we asked participants to make only one selection, they were sometimes unable to decide between multiple options. We note these cases below, for which we divided the participant's vote among their selections; for example, if a participant preferred egocentric and exocentric designs equally, a vote of 0.5 rather than 1.0 was assigned to each. Finally, open-ended justifications for preference were grouped based on emergent themes.

Findings

We first describe participants' experiences and challenges with group communication before discussing findings related to the visual designs. Quotes are pulled from the audio transcripts and two-way chat logs; some are lightly edited to fix typos and grammatical errors.

Part One: Formative Inquiry into Group Communication

Three themes emerged related to group conversation with oral partners: general problems, accommodations, and use of technological solutions.

General Problems. All participants agreed that communicating in a group with hearing persons can be challenging. Over half (15) mentioned problems directly caused by multiple speakers. Commonly, this included issues following speaker transitions, for example:

> *"If one person finishes talking, I do not know who to look at next—that is my problem because hearing people can hear who the next person is, and what they are saying." (P20)*

Other issues included the difficulty of following overlapping speakers and side conversations, and the need to remind people to look at them when speaking.

Accommodations. Participants were asked how they generally accommodate these problems. Fourteen reported using a variety of traditional adaptations, such as hearing aids, captioning services, or interpreters. For example, P3 discussed needing multiple interpreters for group meetings: *"The first interpreter will interpret. If someone interrupts, the second interpreter takes over and so on"* (P3). Nine participants mentioned using verbal accommodations, including asking a speaker to repeat an utterance or explaining about one's hearing loss. For example: *"I usually ask them to talk one at a time, and only when I am making eye contact,"* (P16). Seven participants reported using low- and/or high-fidelity technology such as pen and paper or two-way chat programs: "*I also use paper and pen to communicate if necessary or use computer technology such as Word and instant messaging.*" (P22). Finally, seven participants mentioned maladaptive accommodations [3,28] that would detract from or prevent communication. For example: *"I usually avoid large groups,"* (P16), and "*I almost always interact with Deaf people. When I converse with hearing people it's usually 1:1 with interpreters.*" (P4)

Computer Technology. Participants were asked about current and envisioned technology to support group conversations. For current technology, 16 participants mentioned using a smartphone, tablet, or laptop. For example, *"I use my iPhone notepad to communicate,"* (P10), and *"Colleagues have learned to keep their phone handy or use voice-to-text software,"* (P2). Five participants also cited assistive devices such as CART (Communication Access Realtime Translation), frequency modulation (FM) systems that transmit directly to hearing aids, and UbiDuo, a face-to-face communicator. Participants noted that these did not necessarily work well for group conversation, however. Finally, six participants stated that they had never used technology for group conversation: "*Never, there isn't any that I am aware of that would be helpful or that would enable real-time conversational fluidity,*" (P17).

For envisioned technology, 18 participants mentioned enhancements to common assistive technology devices (*e.g.*, ASR on their mobile phone), 6 suggested technologies to indicate the direction of sound, 5 mentioned help for overlapping speakers, and 3 wanted better *in situ* collaborative typing. Automatic captioning was a dominant theme: *"...it would look as if subtitles are appearing over the person speaking like real-time/real-life transcribing,"* (P17). Still, participants realized that captioning is technologically difficult based on prior ASR experiences.

Part One Summary. Our findings confirm research in communication strategies of deaf and hard of hearing people with oral partners (*e.g.*, [3,9,28]). Our participants used a variety of adaptive and maladaptive strategies for group conversation and expressed key challenges that may be addressed by our approach (*e.g.*, missing speaker transitions, helping follow simultaneous speakers).

Part Two: Design Probe Findings

We provide initial reactions to the idea of head-mounted sound localization feedback, responses to each of the eight design dimensions, suggestions for new features, and an analysis of participant-sketched designs.

Initial Reactions. All 24 participants thought the idea of head-mounted visualizations for sound awareness was useful. A majority of participants (17) expressed that it would be helpful to know who is speaking and/or the direction of the sound source. For example, P7, who reported not being a good lip-reader, said that he would like to know where the speaker is so that the interpreter does not have to convey that information, which can waste time. Others emphasized the benefits to speechreading:

> *"I think it's a great idea, especially for those that can lip read at least above a functional level... It would reduce the amount of time and effort to find the individual speaking if I have information where the sound is coming from, which would lead to less content loss." (P17)*

However, 4 participants also expressed that the direction of sound source combined with lip-reading would be insufficient to understand conversation and more help would be needed (*e.g.* interpreters, captions).

Wearer Perspective. Participants were nearly uniformly split in preference between the exocentric and egocentric wearer perspectives, with 13 and 11 votes, respectively. A chi-squared test on the distribution of votes was not significant ($X^2_{(1,N=24)} = 0.04, p = ns$). By far the most common reason (12/13) for preferring the exocentric perspective was that it showed the location of the wearer in reference to other speakers, which participants felt made it easier to locate direction compared to egocentric. For example, P15 said: *"I can better judge the direction if I have a [top-down] reference to myself. Pointing to front and back are difficult in egocentric."* For participants who preferred egocentric, reasons included that it was more understandable, less cluttered, and easier to interpret.

When asked specifically about preference for 2D *vs.* 3D egocentric designs, participants were again split (12 each). For those who preferred 2D, reasons included simplicity, visual sharpness, and information density (*i.e.*, the same information as 3D but in less space). For those who selected 3D, participants mentioned increased realism and a better sense of direction: *"In 3D, I just follow the arrow while in 2D, I need to remind myself I am in a 3D space,"* (P17).

Direction Granularity. Of the four direction granularities, participants preferred the more precise options ($X^2_{(3,N=24)} = 17.75,\ p < .001$). Fourteen participants selected continuous, the most popular option, because of its precision (*e.g.*, P20 stated: "*The more precise the direction, the better it is.*"). Another perceived advantage, identified by 3 of the 14 participants, was that it could more easily support multiple speakers. The 8-level design was the next most popular (5 votes), with supporters emphasizing the balance between practicality and specificity: *"8 level is easier to locate than 4-level. Continuous is too specific,"* (P1). Only three participants preferred the 4-level and one participant selected the 1-level; these were generally seen as not providing enough information. For example, P20 did not like 1-level because he wanted the display *"to PINPOINT sound exactly where it is coming from."*

Screen Layout. The rectangular and circular layouts were the most popular, with 10 and 9 votes, respectively, and 3 more participants split between the two; only 2 participants chose the from-center layout ($X^2_{(2,N=24)} = 6.81, p = .033$). For participants who liked the rectangular layout, the two most common reasons were that the position on the screen makes it easy to locate sound, and that the aesthetic is uncluttered. However, participants who preferred the circular layout generally found it easier to understand. One participant also mentioned that the circular layout freed up space on the display that could be used for other visual information. P3 captured some of the tradeoffs among the three designs:

> *"I'd prefer circular. Due to spatial orientation -- I know I'm in the middle. I don't like rectangular due to the lack of visual aid to assist in spatial orientation. I don't like from center because those arrows take up too much screen [space]." (P3)*

Sound Indicator Icons. Participants were asked about sound icon preference for both an egocentric design and an exocentric design. With the egocentric design, pulses were the most preferred (14 votes) compared to arrows (6) and fingers (2); two participants were split between pulses and arrows ($X^2_{(2,N=24)} = 10.75,\ p = .005$). The most common reason for preferring pulses was that they represent sound in an intuitive way (9), for example: *"...easy to recognize that that's where the sounds are coming from,"* (P2). For arrows, the most common advantage was that they clearly point to the sound source (3).

With the exocentric design, arrows, people, and circles were equally popular, with 9, 7, and 7 votes, respectively; one participant was split between arrows and people ($X^2_{(2,N=24)} = 0.44,\ p = ns$). The most common reason for preferring arrows, as expressed by 8 participants, was that they explicitly represent the direction of the sound. The people icon was seen as providing a good indication that someone is speaking, as opposed to, for example, a dog barking (of course, such a design would require automatic sound discrimination). Finally, the circles were appreciated for their simplicity. In summary, for the egocentric design, pulses were the most preferred, while for the exocentric design there was no clear preference among icon options.

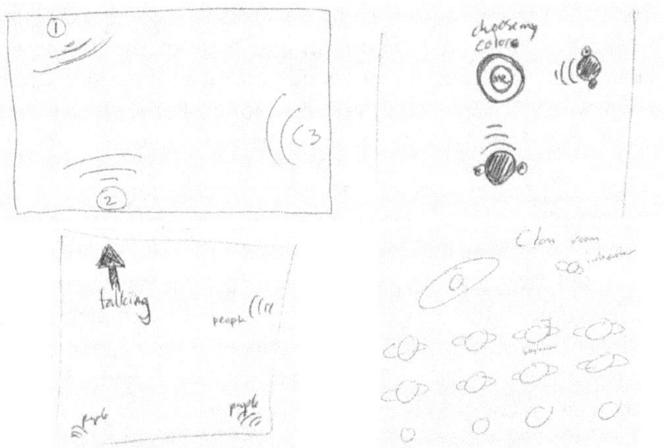

Figure 4: Ideal designs as sketched by our participants. **(a)** P19 extended egocentric pulses with numbers to show recent speaking order. **(b)** P14 drew an exocentric design that visualized all potential speakers; pulses indicate who is talking. **(c)** P14 also created an egocentric design where pulses represent recent speakers and a 3D arrow shows the current speaker. **(d)** P7 drew an exocentric design with room layout and people locations so that he could focus on his interpreter but still know who was speaking.

Conveying Sound Source. There was a strong preference for indicators that point outward to the sound source (17 votes) compared to indicators that point inward (3); four participants had no preference ($X^2_{(1,N=24)} = 7.04$, $p = .008$). The primary reason for choosing the outward indicators was that they target the sound source better, for example: *"Outward tells me where to look. For inward, I'll automatically think as if someone is talking to me,"* (P6). In fact, 4 participants who chose outward mentioned that for inward, it looked like the speaker was talking to them, which may not be the case.

Simultaneous Indicators. Participants were asked how many overlapping speakers they would want to see visualized simultaneously on the display. This was an open-ended question and, as such, no chi-square test was conducted. The most frequent answer was 4 speakers (10 votes), 8.5 participants suggested 5 or more, and 5.5 wanted at *most* three speakers. So, while a maximum of four speakers may be reasonable, the variation in preference suggests that this design dimension should be customizable.

Loudness. We assessed how to visualize loudness by showing six options and soliciting overall feedback: egocentric arrows that varied in fill, size, or length, egocentric pulses that varied in size, and exocentric arrows and circles that varied in size. Among these options, the majority of participants (13.5) preferred egocentric pulses that varied in size to convey loudness. Reasons included that it was intuitive and natural. For example: *"Egocentric pulses, it just seems natural based on my experiences with WiFi signal strength [icons]"* (P17).

A chi-square test on the distribution of votes was significant ($X^2_{(6,N=24)} = 37.98$, $p<.001$). When asked about other ways to represent loudness beyond what we designed, the most common suggestion (4) was to use color, for example: *"red for louder and pink/white very quiet,"* (P10). Animation speed was also suggested by 2 participants: *"the pulses should be way faster if the speaker is loudest,"* (P20).

Automatic Sound Recognition. Finally, we also asked about four advanced features that would require sophisticated sound processing algorithms: speaker identity, discriminating speech *vs.* non-speech sounds, real-time captioning, and gender. Almost all participants wanted the first three: speaker identity (22), non-speech sounds (22), and captions (23). For speaker identity, participants thought that it could make locating a person in a large group more efficient, for example: *"Speaker name is a great idea; it would eliminate the need to look for moving lips"* (P17).

As with the formative findings, real-time captioning was popular. Two new ideas arose about how it could work:

> *"I have to have interpreters anyway; maybe instead of having them follow me around, they could listen to what Glass hears, and caption it remotely." (P3)*

> *"If possible by technology, that would be nice. Just display the nouns, others can be implied. Also, real-time captioning is distracting and all consuming." (P12)*

The majority of participants were not interested in highlighting gender (12); three were unsure. It was deemed unnecessary (*i.e.*, one can see by looking) or socially unacceptable. For the 9 participants who indicated interest in gender, they thought it would reduce visual search time: *"It will help me to identify who is speaking"* (P19).

Other Information. After the last design probe, we asked participants to suggest other information that we did not include in our own designs. Half of the participants wanted more complex cues such as emotion, conversation topics, or information on speakers (*e.g.*, who spoke the most). For example: *"I don't know if Google Glass is able to identify the tone of the person… the emotional tone"* (P6). Two participants wanted additional ways of identifying speakers (*e.g.*, assigning colors to more easily discriminate them). One participant also expressed that too much information could lead to overload, so careful selection is required:

> *"I think it is too much to have names, arrows, circles, and whatever. I think one or the other will suffice." (P4)*

Ideal Design and Rationale. Roughly 70% into the design probe, we asked participants to describe and/or sketch their "ideal design for providing sound awareness feedback" on Glass (Figure 4). We purposely asked this question before showing loudness and automatic sound recognition designs to see if these features would emerge organically. While responses varied, 14 participants described or extended egocentric designs, 7 used exocentric as a base, and 3 participants used one of each. Seven designs included advanced features such as visualizing loudness (4), providing the exact location of people with a floorplan of the room (4), automatically identifying sounds (2), and automatically recognizing when speakers were talking to them (2). When sketching her egocentric 3D design, P20 described her thought process:

> *"The goal of this for me = pinpoint sound in the most exact, realistic way possible. Adding layouts confuses me. I want it to be simple and 'point' to the sound—as if I could 'see' the soundwaves coming towards me." (P20)*

Part Two Summary. Though all participants were supportive of HMD sound visualizations, preferences differed across design dimensions. Participants were split between egocentric and exocentric but preferred precise directional granularity, peripheral screen layouts, and pulse (egocentric) or arrow (exocentric) indicators with up to 4 simultaneous speakers. For advanced features, real-time captions, speaker identity, and discriminating speech from non-speech sounds were nearly uniformly desired.

STUDY 2: PROOF-OF-CONCEPT SYSTEM

To collect preliminary feedback on the experience of using working visualizations, we built a proof-of-concept system using Google Glass and a non-wearable microphone array for sound processing (*VisiSonics RealSpace Audio Sensor* [29]). We implemented two popular yet complementary designs from Study 1—egocentric pulses and exocentric arrows—and evaluated these with four new deaf and hard of hearing participants in lab-based group conversations.

System Description

The RealSpace Audio Sensor is a spherical 64-microphone array for localizing sound in three dimensions. It was connected via USB to a laptop running real-time sound source localization and beamforming software [36]. Every 250ms, the laptop sent a processed audio packet consisting of the intensity, azimuth, and elevation of all co-occurring sounds via WiFi to a custom Android application running on a *Samsung Galaxy Chat* phone. The top four highest intensity sounds were then transmitted to Glass via Bluetooth, which generated the feedback visualizations. While useful for a proof-of-concept assessment, this system had two limitations. First, the audio sensor was 20cm in diameter (*i.e.*, non-wearable), so had to be placed in the middle of the meeting table. As a result, the sensing was slightly offset from the participant and did not adjust to head movement. Second, low frequency voices were occasionally missed. See supplementary video for details.

Evaluation Method

Four new participants were recruited (2 female; 26–42 years old, M=35.0, SD=7.5). Three were profoundly deaf since birth, while R2 had severe hearing loss in both ears since early childhood. R2, R3, and R4 employed lip-reading at least sometimes. Study sessions were one hour long. After a background questionnaire and introduction to HMDs, the participant sat at a meeting table wearing Glass. For each of egocentric pulses and exocentric arrows, the following steps were completed. First, to familiarize the participant with the visualization, a researcher walked once around the room while talking. Second, the participant observed two scripted conversations among research team members: (i) a 2-person conversation with team members seated on opposite sides of the table; (ii) a 4-person conversation with team members around the table, during which one person moved and spoke behind the participant. Third, all four team members and the participant had an open-ended conversation. All three conversations were 2–5 minutes long. Participants were asked open-ended questions about their experiences.

Order of presentation of the two visualizations was fully counterbalanced and participants were randomly assigned to orders. To reduce the impact of a specific conversation, we excerpted two 2-person scripts from the movie *Shawshank Redemption* and two 4-person scripts from *Ghostbusters*, and defined "travel" and "hometown" as open-ended conversation topics. These options were paired with visualization conditions using full counterbalancing.

Preliminary User Feedback

All participants thought the sound visualizations would be useful at least in some contexts. R1 and R3 felt the display helped with following the scripted conversations, for example, *"I think this [display] is very helpful for when somebody is speaking outside my hearing range, like behind me"* (R3). R2 and R4 did not find it useful for the study tasks, but nevertheless appreciated some aspects of it. For example, R2 commented that the "*approach would be helpful because my sound processor is not able to point where the sound was from.*"

Emergent Issues. Two important issues arose that will need to be addressed in future designs. First, the Glass display is slightly above and to the right of the wearer's line of sight, which was problematic for R2 and R4. They found it difficult to attend to the display and lip-read, for example: *"I have to look up [at Google Glass] and look at people's faces. It's pretty hard to do it at once,"* (R4). A second issue was the potential for cognitive overload, mentioned, again, by R2 and R4. R2 found it distracting to simultaneously attend to his hearing aid and Glass, and was confused when multiple icons appeared at the same time. R4 felt that it could be distracting if small sounds frequently popped up (*e.g.*, paper rustling, coughing), although when asked she still wanted those sounds to be shown.

Contexts. Two participants thought that the system would be useful in a public setting when someone is trying to get their attention. For example, R4 felt it would reduce the chance of inadvertently being rude by ignoring someone she could not hear. R3 found it useful for social group settings, when *"everyone's participating in the conversation but I don't know that they are talking."* However, R4 was not convinced that he would use the device with a group of hearing friends:

> *"I might not need it because they would want me to understand better by real conversation rather than expecting to read from Google Glass." (R4)*

Preferred designs. Three participants preferred arrows to pulses because they more clearly showed who was speaking or were bolder and easier to see; the fourth participant (R1) had no preference. This feedback highlights the importance of glanceability: *"Because they [the arrows] were bold, you know, I can see them easier without having to [squint]"* (R3).

The sound indicators changed in size based on loudness, which R4 found useful, but R3 said was information her hearing aid already provides.

DISCUSSION

While participants in both studies had varied reactions to specific design dimensions, *all* were supportive of the general idea of providing sound visualizations on an HMD. Here, we reflect on implications and study limitations.

Design Reflections

Based on the exploration of our eight design dimensions, we provide the following design recommendations:

- **Wearer Perspective.** Both egocentric and exocentric designs were well received, so either could be used.
- **Directional Granularity.** Precision is valued. Use high directional granularity, at least 8-level if not continuous.
- **Screen Layout**. Sound indicators should be positioned on the periphery of the screen rather than in the center.
- **Sound Indicator Icons.** For an egocentric design, pulses are recommended. For an exocentric design, no clear pattern emerged, thus arrows, people, or circles could all be used. Other better options may also exist.
- **Conveying sound source.** Arrow-based sound indicators should point outward toward the sound source. For other indicators (*e.g.*, pulses) preference may differ.
- **Simultaneous indicators.** Visualizing up to 4-5 overlapping speakers should satisfy most users, although some users may want to customize this attribute to suit their needs or the environment.
- **Loudness.** Loudness is a desired attribute. Of the six designs shown, egocentric pulses were the most popular.
- **Automatic Sound Recognition.** Of all design dimensions, advanced features were the most uniformly desired, particularly: speaker identity, differentiating between speech and non-speech sounds, and automatic captioning. Gender was not as popular; however, participants did like having additional information on how voices sounded.

Similar to prior studies [17,18], our findings also support the need for customizability. Though strong preferences existed for certain features (*e.g.,* high directional precision) others were mixed (*e.g.,* egocentric *vs.* exocentric). Moreover, preferences may change depending on context (*e.g.*, conversation with friends *vs.* strangers).

The design probe employed relatively simple visualizations for sound localization. How best to combine these with the more advanced features that were requested by participants is an open question. Some participants recognized the potential for information overload from features such as speaker recognition and captioning—as an example, one suggestion was to show only nouns rather than full captions. Although many of these more advanced features are in themselves open areas of research, once they are feasible to incorporate, the ability to turn them on only as needed will likely be key.

As seen in Study 2, Google Glass is not ideal for HMD sound visualizations. It physically interferes with some cochlear implants and behind-the-ear hearing aids, and the display is not always visible in peripheral vision. An ideal HMD would: accommodate existing hearing devices, include automatic head-tracking that updates visualizations based on head orientation, be lightweight, comfortable, and accurate, and contain a large transparent display superimposed over the eye. Information would need to be presented on the display in a location that does not prevent or distract a person from speechreading. Obviously, a wearable audio sensing solution is also needed, which we did not examine. For accurate sound localization, we predict that at least eight microphones will be needed, which could be positioned on the HMD itself [37]. Our research group is working on a wearable headband version with 16 microphones (extending [37]), which should resolve sound sources with a root-mean-square error of 0.1 radians in the presence of noise.

The visualizations tested were based on a set of design goals informed by past work and our own experiences as persons with hearing loss. The understandability of the localization information, overall positive response from participants, and responsive proof-of-concept system suggest that we were successful in meeting at least some of these goals. However, future work will need to implement and evaluate a completely wearable, interactive system. Properly assessing glanceability and the ability of such a system to augment existing communication strategies, for example, will require observations of conversation dynamics and wearer behavior with realistic use and over a longer time period than our studies allowed.

Limitations

First, most of our study participants had profound hearing loss, but future work should consider a larger, more diverse sample. Second, in the design probe study, we did not show an equal number of all design dimension combinations. Participants had greater exposure to egocentric and outward designs, which may have influenced preferences. Where possible, however, design exposures were counterbalanced (*e.g.,* the order of presenting egocentric *vs.* exocentric designs). Moreover, we solicited preference feedback immediately after first showing a design to mitigate exposure effects. Third, both studies are based on initial reactions in a laboratory rather than long-term use with a working system. Fourth, the audio sensor used in Study 2 had limitations (size, placement, sensing frequency range), which negatively impacted the experience of at least one participant. Future work should apply our findings to a functioning, interactive wearable system that is ultimately deployed and studied longitudinally.

CONCLUSION

As the first work in the area of sound visualizations on HMDs for the deaf and hard of hearing, this paper explored a broad range of novel designs and a preliminary working prototype to examine and uncover promising elements for future work. Study 1, with 24 participants, reaffirmed challenges faced by persons with hearing loss in group conversations and identified design preferences for HMD sound visualizations. Responses highlighted uniform preference for some design dimensions and a need to make others customizable. We then conducted a preliminary evaluation of a proof-of-concept non-wearable prototype with four participants. Participant feedback supported the potential of our approach, and uncovered additional directions for future work. Our findings have implications for HCI and hearing researchers, hardware developers of HMD technology, and persons with hearing loss.

ACKNOWLEDGMENTS

We thank Ji Hyuk Bae, Yumeng Wang, Meethu Malu, and Alina Goldman for their help.

REFERENCES

1. Van den Bogaert, T., Klasen, *et al.* Horizontal localization with bilateral hearing aids: Without is better than with. *J. of the Acoustical Society of America 119*, 1 (2006), 515.
2. Braun, V. and Clarke, V. Using thematic analysis in psychology. *Qual. Research Psych. 3*, 2 (2006), 77–101.
3. Demorest, M. & Erdman, S. Scale Composition and Item Analysis of the Communication Profile for the Hearing Impaired. *J. Sp. Lang & Hear Res 29*, 4 (1986), 515–535.
4. Demorest, M.E. and Erdman, S.A. Development of the Communication Profile for the Hearing Impaired. *Journal of Speech and Hearing Disorders 52*, 2 (1987), 129–143.
5. Gallaudet University. Resources to Develop Speechreading Skills. 2008. http://goo.gl/HALGdz.
6. Galvin, K.L., Ginis, J., Cowan, R.S., *et al.* A Comparison of a New Prototype Tickle Talker™ with the Tactaid 7. *Aus. and NZ Journal of Audiology 23*, 1 (2001), 18–36.
7. Google Inc. Google Developers Glass Style. https://developers.google.com/glass/design/style.
8. Grieco-Calub, T.M. and Litovsky, R.Y. Spatial acuity in 2-to-3-year-old children with normal acoustic hearing, unilateral cochlear implants, and bilateral cochlear implants. *Ear and hearing 33*, 5 (2012), 561–72.
9. Hallam, R.S. and Corney, R. Conversation tactics in persons with normal hearing and hearing-impairment. *International journal of audiology 53*, 3 (2014), 174–81.
10. Hart, J., Onceanu, D., Sohn, C., *et al.* The Attentive Hearing Aid: Eye Selection of Auditory Sources for Hearing Impaired Users. *INTERACT 2009,* 19–35.
11. Ho-Ching, F., Mankoff, J., & Landay, J.A. Can You See What I Hear?: The Design and Evaluation of a Peripheral Sound Display for the Deaf. *CHI 2003*, 161–168.
12. Hruschka, D., Schwartz, D., St. John, D., *et al.* Reliability in Coding Open-Ended Data: Lessons Learned from HIV Behavioral Research. *Fld Methds 16* , 3 (2004), 307–331.
13. Jones, M., Lawler, M.J., Hintz, E., *et al.* Head Mounted Displays and Deaf Children: Facilitating Sign Language in Challenging Learning Environments. *IDC'14*, 317–320.
14. Kaneko, Y., Chung, I., and Suzuki, K. Light-Emitting Device for Supporting Auditory Awareness of Hearing-Impaired People during Group Conversations. i*Systems, Man, and Cybernetics* (2013), 3567–3572.
15. Van Krevelen, D.W.F. and Poelman, R. A Survey of Augmented Reality Technologies, Applications and Limitations. *Intl J. of Virtual Reality 9*, 2 (2010), 1–20.
16. Lasecki, W.S. and Bigham, J.P. Real-time Captioning with the Crowd. *interactions 21*, 3 (2014), 50–55.
17. Matthews, T., Fong, J., Ho-Ching, F., and Mankoff, J. Evaluating non-speech sound visualizations for the deaf. *Behaviour & Information Tech. 25*, 4 (2006), 333–351.
18. Matthews, T., Fong, J., and Mankoff, J. Visualizing non-speech sounds for the deaf. *ASSETS'05*, 52–59.
19. McCreery, R.W., *et al.* An evidence-based systematic review of directional microphones and digital noise reduction hearing aids in school-age children with hearing loss. *American J. of Audiology 21*, 2 (2012), 295–312.
20. Medenica, Z., Kun, A., Paek, T., & Palinko, O. Augmented Reality vs. Street Views: A Driving Simulator Study Comparing Two Emerging Navigation Aids. *MobileHCI'11*, 265–274.
21. Mueller, M.F., Meisenbacher, K., Lai, W., & Dillier, N. Sound localization with bilateral cochlear implants in noise: how much do head movements contribute to localization? *Cochlear Implants Intl 15*, 1 (2014), 36–42.
22. Mynatt, E.D., Back, M., Want, R., Baer, M., and Ellis, J.B. Designing Audio Aura. *CHI'98*, 566–573.
23. Picou, E., Aspell, E., & Ricketts, T. Potential benefits and limitations of three types of directional processing in hearing aids. *Ear and hearing 35*, 3 (2014), 339–52.
24. Picou, E., Ricketts, T., & Hornsby, B. How Hearing Aids, Background Noise, and Visual Cues Influence Objective Listening Effort. *Ear and Hearing 34*, 5 (2013).
25. Sodnik, J., Tomazic, S., Grasset, R., Duenser, A., and Billinghurst, M. Spatial Sound Localization in an Augmented Reality Environment. *OZCHI'06*, 111–118.
26. Sony. Sony Access Glasses. http://goo.gl/0DKFoQ.
27. Tomitsch, M. & Grechenig, T. Design Implications for a Ubiquitous Ambient Sound Display for Deaf. *CVHI '07*
28. Tye-Murray, N., Purdy, S., and Woodworth, G. Reported Use of Communication Strategies by SHHH Members. *J. of Speech Lang & Hearing Res 35*, 3 (1992), 708.
29. Visisonic Inc. VisiSonics RealSpace™ Audio Camera. http://visisonics.com/realspace-audio-camera.
30. Wald, M. Captioning for Deaf and Hard of Hearing People by Editing Automatic Speech Recognition in Real Time. *ICCHP'06*, 683–690.
31. Yeung, E., Boothroyd, A., and Redmond, C. A Wearable Multichannel Tactile Display of Voice Fundamental Frequency. *Ear and Hearing 9*, 6 (1988), 342–350.
32. Yoo, I. & Yook, D. Automatic sound recognition for the hearing impaired. *IEEE Trns CE 54*, 4 ('08), 2029–2036.
33. Yuan, H., Reed, C.M., and Durlach, N.I. Tactual display of consonant voicing as a supplement to lipreading. *J. of the Acoustical Society of America 118*, 2 (2005), 1003.
34. Zhang, Z. and Schuller, B. Semi-supervised learning helps in sound event classification. *ICASSP'12,* 333–336.
35. Zhou, F., Duh, H.B., & Billinghurst, M. Trends in augmented reality tracking, interaction and display: A review of ten years of ISMAR. *ISMAR'08,* 193–202.
36. Zotkin, D.N., *et al.* Chain architecture: An efficient hardware solution for a large microphone array system. *Proceedings of Meetings on Acoustics*, 2013, 3302-3322.
37. Zotkin, D.N., *Duraiswami, R., and Gumerov, N.A.* Plane-Wave Decomposition of Acoustical Scenes Via Spherical and Cylindrical Microphone Arrays. *IEEE Trans Audio, Speech, & Language Processing on 18*, 1 (2010), 2–16.

Using Interactive Machine Learning to Support Interface Development Through Workshops with Disabled People

Simon Katan, Mick Grierson, Rebecca Fiebrink
Department of Computing
Goldsmiths, University of London
s.katan@gold.ac.uk m.grierson@gold.ac.uk r.fiebrink@gold.ac.uk

ABSTRACT
We have applied interactive machine learning (IML) to the creation and customisation of gesturally controlled musical interfaces in six workshops with people with learning and physical disabilities. Our observations and discussions with participants demonstrate the utility of IML as a tool for participatory design of accessible interfaces. This work has also led to a better understanding of challenges in end-user training of learning models, of how people develop personalised interaction strategies with different types of pre-trained interfaces, and of how properties of control spaces and input devices influence people's customisation strategies and engagement with instruments. This work has also uncovered similarities between the musical goals and practices of disabled people and those of expert musicians.

Author Keywords
Interactive machine learning; accessible interfaces; music.

ACM Classification Keywords
H5.2. Information interfaces and presentation: User Interfaces.

INTRODUCTION
Prior work has shown that interactive machine learning (IML) can help people create custom gesturally-controlled systems quickly and without programming, and that these systems can directly encode aspects of embodied practice and "feel right" to use [2,3]. This prior work focused primarily on highly skilled computer musicians creating custom gestural interfaces for experimental music. However, very little work has explored the application of IML to user interface design or customisation in other contexts. A better understanding of how IML can be applied by other end users and developers, and of the challenges that can arise, is needed to inform the development of new IML tools and to guide future research.

We present new work investigating the application of IML

CHI 2015, April 18 - 23, 2015, Seoul, Republic of Korea
Copyright 2015 ACM 978-1-4503-3145-6/15/04...$15.00
http://dx.doi.org/10.1145/2702123.2702474

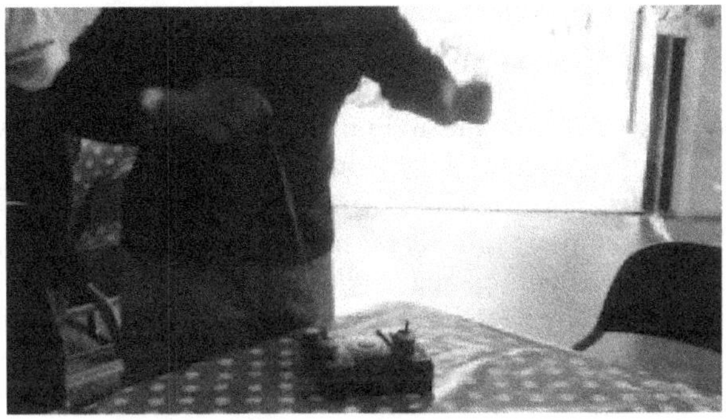

Figure 1: A workshop participant plays a digital instrument built with the Gametrak controller, which senses 3D position of the user's hands using two strings.

to the creation of musical interfaces for people with learning disabilities and physical disabilities. IML is a potentially good match to this domain: disabled people may face insurmountable barriers to playing and becoming proficient on conventional musical instruments, so bespoke computer interfaces can provide a critical creative outlet. However, to our knowledge, IML has not previously been used to create customised interfaces for disabled people, for musical applications or otherwise.

In order to better understand the challenges and benefits of applying IML in this new application space, we partnered with a local community arts centre to conduct a series of workshops in which disabled people interacted with digital musical instruments, built with commercially available and bespoke input devices. IML was used by developers of the instruments and by workshop participants to customise the types of gestures that could be used and the relationships between gesture and sound.

This work presents the first exploration of IML for the development of new interfaces for disabled people. Its primary contributions include insights not only into the challenges and benefits of applying IML to this application space, but also into the ways that properties of the IML process, control space, and input devices impacted on people's customisation of and engagement with gestural interfaces.

RELATED WORK
Machine learning is potentially useful in the creation of software that must understand or respond to human actions. Instead of writing code, a system designer can provide

examples of an action (e.g., a body posture sensed by a Kinect) paired with examples of the appropriate computer response (e.g., sending particular control values to a music synthesiser, or sending a "jump" command to a video game avatar). A supervised learning algorithm can then build a model of the relationship between human actions and computer responses, and this trained model can be incorporated into a real-time software system (e.g., changing sound or controlling a game as the user moves).

Initially proposed in the context of computer vision [1], *interactive machine learning* describes an approach in which a user can iteratively create training examples, examine the resulting trained model, and improve the model by changing the training data and retraining. IML has been investigated by Fiebrink [2,3] in the context of expert musicians building new instruments, by creating training examples from real-time demonstrations of human control movements paired with sounds to be produced by those movements. That work demonstrates that IML can improve interface design by facilitating rapid prototyping, exploration of the design space, and encoding of embodied practices into the interface via the demonstrated examples.

Substantial research has explored approaches for customising interfaces to people with disabilities or impairments, and even early efforts have included data-driven approaches that tailor a device to a user given example measurements of their range of motion [6]. Data-driven methods have also been used to optimise GUIs to individual users [4]. IML has been proposed (but not evaluated) for the end-user customisation of rehabilitation technologies to post-surgery patients [7].

Some high-profile musical projects such as the British Paraorchestra[1] have engaged engineers to create bespoke instruments for disabled musicians. Most often, though, disabled people who cannot play existing instruments are limited to "accessible" music interfaces such as Soundbeam[2] or Skoog[3]. Compared to the instruments that can be built with IML (as used in here), they are still quite limited in terms of customisability and musical breadth.

To our knowledge, this is the first project to apply IML techniques to the creation or customisation of gestural interfaces for people with disabilities. This is also one of the first applications of IML to the creation of gestural control systems with users who are not expert musicians.

METHOD

IML to Meet Varied Requirements of Disabled Users

We partnered with a local creative arts centre, Heart n Soul, who work primarily with adults with various combinations of cognitive, physical and sensory impairments.[4] These adults possess a wide diversity of abilities and preferences. For example, whilst one person might only be able to execute a narrow range of movement, another might find subtle movements difficult, instead preferring large movements. We sought to discover whether IML could be used to adapt gestural interfaces to people with differing ranges and qualities of movements without loss of functionality. We also sought to explore whether it was feasible and useful for such adaptations to be driven by disabled users themselves within a workshop setting.

A Focus on New Digital Musical Instruments

Music is an enjoyable and engaging activity for many people. Further, digital instruments (in which a computer generates sound in response to the actions of a person) can incorporate a huge variety of physical actions and real-time control strategies. By building a set of 12 instruments, each using a different pairing of input sensors and musical output, we were able to observe how users' experiences were affected by diverse physical input devices and control strategies (e.g., recognising one of a known set of gestures versus inviting more free-form control; triggering discrete musical events versus offering continuous control over synthesis parameters or effects).

Workshop Structure

Over two months, we conducted six music-making workshops in collaboration with Heart n Soul. The aims of these workshops were: 1) to create musically engaging experiences for disabled people through the use of digital instruments; 2) to better understand how IML can be used in the development and customisation of such interfaces, and what challenges and benefits may arise; and 3) to inform future research and development work employing IML for interface design.

The workshops included four two-hour sessions with two to four disabled participants, where we introduced people to new instruments developed by our team. The other two workshops were "drop-in" sessions at public events lasting around five hours each, featuring refined versions of our prototypes. These allowed us to observe a wider variety of people (approximately 20 attendees, including disabled people from the arts centre and the wider public).

In each workshop, we placed around a large room two or three of our prototype instruments and a similar number of commercial music interfaces (e.g., Thereminis[5] and iPad sequencer apps, none of which allowed customisation). Participants could move around the room freely, engaging with instruments or listening to others. Members of our team were present to assist and answer questions, but did not provide formal instructions.

Taking into account the diversity of participants' learning and communication difficulties, we sought to understand on

[1] http://www.paraorchestra.com/

[2] http://www.soundbeam.co.uk/

[3] http://www.skoogmusic.com/

[4] The centre do not collect information about people's specific disabilities.

[5] http://www.moogmusic.com/products/etherwave-theremins/theremini

an individual basis how people engaged with each instrument. We observed whether someone spent time actively engaged with an interface, whether they chose to return to the interface on future occasions, the finesse of control demonstrated, and the breadth and quality of musical output. We discussed these observations with participants during the sessions when appropriate and possible. In between workshops, our team discussed our observations and session video logs as we prepared the next set of prototype instruments.

Implementation of Digital Musical Instruments

Each prototype instrument employed one sensing device: Microsoft Kinect for Xbox (using skeleton tracking to identify limb positions), Leap Motion (in-air hand and finger tracking), video with human face tracking, Gametrak (Figure 1), or one of two squeezable tangibles (stuffed with conductive thread).

To link human actions sensed by these devices to control over sound, we used Wekinator [3], an IML toolkit that allows users to provide training examples of input gestures and matching sounds using real-time demonstration. Our prototype instruments employed the same regression and classification algorithms (neural networks, AdaBoost, k-nearest neighbour, decision trees, support vector machines) and the same IML workflow as described in previous work [2,3]. The outputs from Wekinator's trained models linked people's sensed motions to control over music software created by our team. All instruments allowed sound to be controlled based on the position and/or movement of some part(s) of the player's body (e.g., torso (*x*,*y*,*z*) position or direction of hand motion in front of Kinect). Some instruments offered discrete control (e.g., choosing one of four drum loops) and some continuous control (e.g., sweeping a filter, changing synthesis parameters).

We aimed to design instruments that adhered to the principles of "low threshold" and "high ceiling" [5], where users could make a good sound from the beginning but were rewarded sonically for continuing to gain expertise. We designed instruments to be used to navigate spaces of musical patterns, sound textures, or drum beat sequences, rather than select and trigger individual notes. This allowed people to play in a relatively familiar pop/electronica genre, and to expressively explore a wide variety of sounds, without a fear of playing "wrong" notes.[6]

OUTCOMES

Challenges of On-the-Fly End-User Customisation

We initially expected our team to use IML within workshops to modify instruments "on-the-fly," gathering training examples directly from participants and training models for each person. We particularly expected this to be helpful for instruments that used classifiers to recognize distinct gestures, since many participants would have trouble reproducing gestures from a pre-determined vocabulary. However, we observed that people frequently had trouble choosing non-ambiguous gestures that could be accurately discriminated by any classifier, had trouble remembering their custom gesture vocabularies, and had trouble performing gestures in a consistent manner. They also had trouble understanding how the training process was used to build the instrument.

How Control Space Properties Impacted Customisation and User Experience

Nevertheless, we observed that many pre-trained instruments still enabled people to develop effective customisation strategies. These strategies were strongly influenced by the types of control afforded by an instrument, especially whether control was discrete (using gesture recognition to choose among a set of musical events) or continuous (mapping real-time body position or motion properties to a continuous musical parameter space). People engaging with continuous instruments often began by moving in a variety of ways to explore the "sound space" available in an instrument, then gradually settled on a personal gestural vocabulary—a few static positions or types of movement that were relatively easy for them, each resulting in a different sound. People would then play the instrument by switching back and forth among these poses or motions, almost as if the instrument had been trained using a discrete gesture classifier. Unlike the process of training one's own gesture classifier, however, this process allowed people to experiment with a wider variety of gestures, to tailor the set of sounds to their preferences, and to gradually adapt their playing technique without interruptions for model training. People were most successful using this strategy for developing custom control vocabularies when the parts of the continuous musical control space that were accessible using their personal movements offered a large variety in sounds.

Among instruments that recognized discrete gestures, we found that using too many gesture classes (typically, more than 5) produced frustration, as the gesture vocabulary became difficult to remember and classifiers became less accurate. Some of the more engaging discrete instruments used very simple classifiers that left people free to move in ways that were extraneous to the gesture recognition. For example, one popular instrument used centre of mass of a person in front of Kinect to select among four drum samples; many people used their standing position to trivially control the drums while simultaneously dancing expressively to the music.

On the other hand, we observed that instruments with larger discrete control spaces (e.g., selecting among 10–12 percussive samples) could be engaging when they afforded

[6] Additional information about all instruments is documented at http://doc.gold.ac.uk/~mus02mg/soundlab/

use in an exploratory manner, allowing people to discover a variety of sounds and gestures as they moved freely rather than requiring that users memorise and reproduce a specific gesture set. We found that such instruments were easily built by training a regression model and discretising its output, as opposed to providing arbitrarily selected training examples for every discrete "class." Further, the granularity of discretisation could be easily tuned on-the-fly.

IML as a Tool for Developers

Despite challenges of on-the-fly customisation, our team continued to use IML in our development between workshops due to the speed and flexibility with which new prototypes could be created. Further, IML provided a mechanism by which workshop observations could directly influence prototypes, as developers could train new instruments using example movements similar to those observed. However, when input devices did not expose features that could be used in their raw form to train musically interesting instruments from gestures likely to be used by workshop participants, development dramatically slowed. Possible future work might include the exploration of mechanisms for expediting and automating experimentation with feature normalisation, filtering, and common processing heuristics, with the aim of integrating these with existing IML approaches.

Similarities Between User Groups

We did not observe clear differences between the ways that disabled people from the community centre and members of the public engaged with our instruments. In fact, our workshop participants' apparent preference for instruments that invited exploration of rich sound spaces using novel (not pre-determined) performer gestures echoes the preferences of expert composers in prior work [3]. This finding reaffirms our supposition that research into the use of gestural interfaces using IML to meet the needs of disabled users is equally useful for the wider community.

CONCLUSION

Our work demonstrates the utility of employing IML in the design of customised interfaces for disabled people. In exploring this new application area for IML, we draw attention to the following findings that can inform future research related to accessible interfaces and participatory design.

As stated, we observed similarities between the musical goals and practices of people with physical and mental disabilities, and those of expert musicians. This suggests a need for more complex and refined instruments for people with disabilities than those currently commercially available (such as Soundbeam, etc.). This also underscores how existing research on musical expressivity and engagement by musical experts may be relevant to designing instruments for people with disabilities and other user groups.

Our work demonstrates IML's potential value as a design tool, accelerating the design process by allowing the quick translation of participant observations into prototypes. Here, we have highlighted some relevant challenges in using IML in this manner (e.g., participant difficulty in developing memorable gesture vocabularies on the fly) and some ways of addressing those challenges (e.g., using continuous control spaces or larger discrete control spaces that invite exploratory interaction).

Finally, our research shows that the customisation of gestural interfaces can be accomplished not just with custom gesture classifiers tailored to an individual, but by setting up flexible control spaces that allow each user to efficiently explore different motions, simultaneously receiving feedback about how those motions are being interpreted. This allows people to develop new gesture vocabularies that reflect and build on their own abilities, while also accounting for the affordances of the interface, sensors and feature representation. Further, the use of large and flexible control spaces, rather than controls driven by recognition of specific gestures, enables diverse users to experimentally develop bespoke control strategies even while using the same pre-trained interfaces.

ACKNOWLEDGMENTS

This project was funded by the UK NESTA/AHRC/ACE Digital R&D programme.

REFERENCES

1. Fails, J. and D. R. Olsen. 2003. Interactive machine learning. *Proc. IUI*, 39–45.
2. Fiebrink, R., P. R. Cook, and D. Trueman. 2011. Human model evaluation in interactive supervised learning. *Proc. CHI*, 147–56.
3. Fiebrink, R., D. Trueman, C. Britt et al. 2010. Toward understanding human-computer interactions in composing the instrument. *Int'l Comuter Music Conf.*
4. Gajos, K., D.S. Weld and J.O. Wobbrock. 2010. Automatically generating personalized user interfaces with Supple. *Artificial Intelligence* 174(12–13): 910–50.
5. Myers, B.A., S.E. Hudson and R. Pausch. 2000. Past, present, and future of user interface software tools. *ACM Trans. CHI* 7(1): 3–28.
6. Pausch, R., and R. D. Williams. 1990. Tailor: Creating custom user interfaces based on gesture. *Proc. UIST*, 123–34.
7. Xu, Z., R. Fiebrink, and Y. Matsuoka. 2012. Virtual therapist: A Phantom robot-based haptic system for personalised post-surgery finger rehabilitation. *Proc. IEEE Robotics & Biometrics (ROBIO).*

Tongue-in-Cheek: Using Wireless Signals to Enable Non-Intrusive and Flexible Facial Gestures Detection

Mayank Goel[1], Chen Zhao[2], Ruth Vinisha[2], Shwetak N. Patel[1,2]

[1]Computer Science & Engineering | DUB Group
University of Washington
Seattle, WA 98195 USA

[2]Electrical Engineering | DUB Group
University of Washington
Seattle, WA 98195 USA

{mayankg, chzhao, vinisha, shwetak} @uw.edu

ABSTRACT
Serious brain injuries, spinal injuries, and motor neuron diseases often lead to severe paralysis. Individuals with such disabilities can benefit from interaction techniques that enable them to interact with the devices and thereby the world around them. While a number of systems have proposed tongue-based gesture detection systems, most of these systems require intrusive instrumentation of the user's body (*e.g.,* tongue piercing, dental retainers, multiple electrodes on chin). In this paper, we propose a wireless, non-intrusive and non-contact facial gesture detection system using X-band Doppler. The system can accurately differentiate between 8 different facial gestures through non-contact sensing, with an average accuracy of 94.3%.

Author Keywords
Tongue-computer interface; Tongue gestures; Wireless signals; Accessibility.

ACM Classification Keywords
H.5.2. Information interfaces and presentation: User Interfaces – *input devices and strategies.*

INTRODUCTION
Motor neuron diseases such as Amyotrophic Lateral Sclerosis (ALS), as well as serious brain or spine injuries, often cause severe paralysis. Many of these individuals retain strong cognitive abilities, and half of them are between the ages of 16 and 30 years [1]. The debilitating effects of these injuries and diseases impede an otherwise able person from fully participating and engaging with certain aspects of their environment, such as computing technologies. Therefore, there is great value in empowering these individuals by helping them communicate with and control their environments.

Many brain injuries, spinal injuries, and motor neuron diseases that lead to paraplegia, do not however affect the cranial nerves [3]. These nerves control various facial organs such as eyes, jaws, tongue, and cheeks. While the eyes and tongue have been used extensively by researchers for building accessible interaction systems [1,2,3,4,7], many other facial organs also offer advantages for robust and non-intrusive gestural interaction. For example, due to their utility in chewing and vocalization, jaws offer low perceived exertion and, unlike the eye, produce no interference with the user's visual activity. Moreover, most of the tongue-based gesture recognition approaches require varied levels of on-body instrumentation; including magnetic piercings in the tongue [1], dental retainers [3], and an array of eight sEMG sensors attached on the user's face and chin [4,7]. The more invasive technologies, such as the tongue piercing, offer very fine-grained tracking of the user's tongue [1] and can be used for many advanced applications such as controlling wheelchairs or handwriting recognition. However, in cases where the user needs simpler input and does not require fine-grained tracking of tongue, sensing can be significantly less intrusive. Moreover, in many cases, these individuals can still use other parts of their body controlled by the cranial nerves, such as their jaws and cheeks [5]. A system that could non-intrusively track movement of all these body parts can provide additional flexibility for users. The users can then easily switch between the different ways of gesture input depending on their preferences and exertion over time.

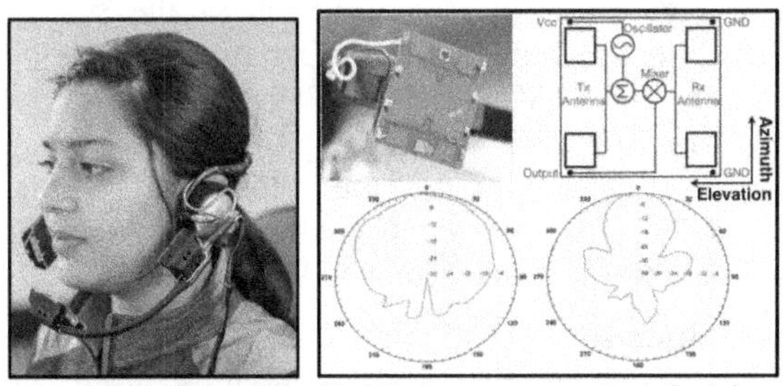

Figure 1. ***(Left)*** Tongue-in-Cheek is a non-contact facial gesture detection system. It is integrated into a pair of off-the-shelf headphones. ***(Right)*** The motion sensor module and Azimuth (bottom-left) and elevation (bottom-right) of the antenna beam pattern.

In this paper, we present *Tongue-in-Cheek* (Figure 1), a system that uses 10 GHz wireless signals to detect different facial gestures in four directions. It detects the movement of cheeks caused by moving different parts of the mouth:

CHI 2015, April 18 - 23 2015, Seoul, Republic of Korea

http://dx.doi.org/10.1145/2702123.2702539

touching of tongue against the inside of the cheeks, puffing the cheeks, and moving the jaws. Tongue-in-Cheek places three small, inexpensive 10 GHz Doppler radar units around a user's face (Figure 1) and measures the Doppler shifts caused by fine movements of the cheeks. Unlike earlier systems, these sensors do not need to be in contact of the user's skin and require no intricate calibration or placement. Tongue-in-Cheek easily integrates with existing headphones and treats motions from the tongue, cheeks, and jaws as the same so that the user can seamlessly switch between these three body parts. This feature also makes the system adaptable to individuals with different variations of paralysis. For example, the system used by an individual with facial paralysis can seamlessly be used by another individual with tongue paralysis.

We evaluated our system design and gesture set with 3 individuals with facial paralysis and 2 of the 3 participants felt Tongue-in-Cheek was perfect suited to their needs. The accuracy of Tongue-in-Cheek was evaluated in a controlled study of 8 participants. The system was tested for eight different gestures performed through three methods: tongue movement, cheek puffing, and jaw movement. Our findings show that Tongue-in-Cheek differentiates between different gestures in four directions: *up, down, left,* and *right,* with an average accuracy of 94.3%. The system requires minimal calibration from the user. It simply checks whether the user has worn the headset properly by asking them to perform one gesture in each of the four directions. On an average, participants took 10.2 seconds to adjust the headset. This adjustment is not significantly different than adjusting one's headphones. Lastly, we also tested the effectiveness of Tongue-in-Cheek for text entry using EdgeWrite [6] and for playing video games.

DESIGN OF TONGUE-IN-CHEEK

The Tongue-in-Cheek prototype consists of three small microwave motion sensor modules. These sensors are attached to a pair of off-the-shelf headphones such that that each sensor covers one of the three sides: *left, right,* and *bottom* (Figure 1, *Left*). The outputs of the sensors are connected to a National Instruments USB-6009 data acquisition unit (DAQ). The unit takes voltage samples at 48 kS/s and digitizes them with 14-bit resolution. The system samples each of the three sensors at 16 kS/s. The output of the DAQ was connected to a computer through USB, where it was processed in MATLAB.

Motion Sensors

The microwave motion sensor modules used in this prototype are X-band bistatic Doppler transceiver modules (Parallax 32213). The module's built-in dielectric resonator oscillator uses a pair of transmitting patch antennas (Figure 1, *Right*) to transmit a 10.5 GHz waveform with a peak power of 5 mW. Another pair of antenna receives the microwave energy reflected by the objects in front of the module. If the object moves, the received frequency is shifted away from the transmit frequency of 10.5 GHz due to the Doppler effect. This frequency-shifted received signal is mixed with the transmitted signal to obtain a low-frequency voltage representing the amount of frequency shift.

Apart from being inexpensive ($4 USD) and easily available, these sensors offer some unique advantages for our purposes. Considering that they operate in the microwave region, the sensing is immune to the effects of temperature (within normal bounds of temperature variation), acoustic noise, light, *etc.* Their low output power also prevents any harm to the human body. These modules are not FCC approved but comply with FCC Part 15 Rules and Regulations. Additionally, our system requires sensors that can be placed in close proximity of the face and can detect subtle facial movements The antennas on these modules are highly directional and have almost uniform beam patterns from -60° to 60°. If the sensors are placed in close proximity of the face, the 60°conical radiation pattern of the antenna in front of the sensors covers the majority of user's cheeks and chins. The system also needs to ensure that the modules do not 'jam" each other as they are running at same frequency. It presents a simple UI to guide the user to adjust the modules such that they are close to the user's cheeks and their face occludes the opposing modules in such a way that the side lobes of the modules do not interfere with one another.

Gestures

Tongue-in-Cheek supports gestures in four directions: *left, right, up,* and *down* and two modes: *tap* and *hold.* In case of *tap* gestures, the user moves the body part with which they want to perform the gesture and then retract to the rest position. For *hold* gestures, the user "holds" the gesture instead of retracting back to the resting position after a tap. All the (both *tap* and *hold*) gestures can be performed either by touching the tongue against the inner side of the cheeks or moving the lower jaw, or puffing the cheeks. In case of puffing of cheeks, the *up* and *down* gestures require the user to puff the upper lip and lower lip portion, respectively. All these gestures result in a, sometimes subtle, motion of cheeks.

We aimed to make our device flexible so that the user could

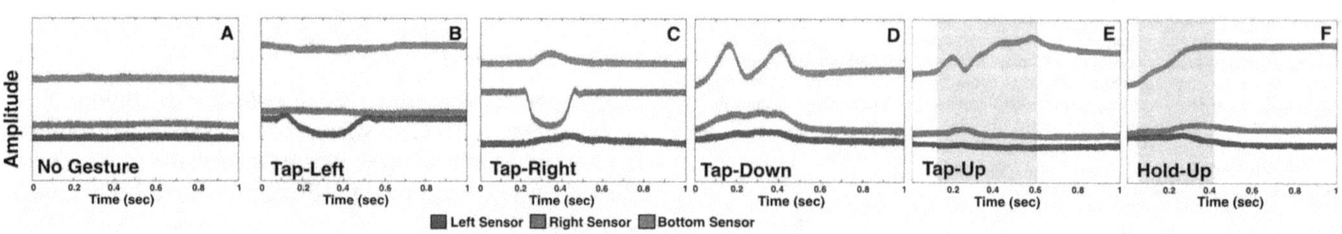

Figure 2. (A-E) Output signal from the each of three microwave Doppler sensors for no-gesture, 4-directional tap gesture. **(F)** *hold-down* gesture. The highlighted part in **E** and **F** shows the difference between a tap and a hold gesture.

switch between different interaction modes. This was motivated by two observations: (1) cranial muscles are not trained for gestures and have a tendency to get tired after prolonged use, and (2) different individuals have different conditions. For example, in our evaluation one participant could not use their tongue for interaction but could easily puff the cheeks. This goal was aided by our choice of sensing approach. The motion sensors used in our prototype sense the direction of the motion. The system is only aware of the direction in which the gesture was performed and not the way the user performed it. This method helps the user to seamlessly switch between the gesture modes without the need to retrain or reconfigure the system. We carefully selected our gesture set to make sure that they are simple and modular. The gestures can be performed in all four directions and the differentiation of *tap* and *hold* means that the gestures can be combined to perform more complicated interactions. The video figure shows one such example for cursor control. The modularity of the gestures helps in overcoming the limitation of discrete gesture detection.

The placement of three sensors around the face enables a simple detection of motion in three directions: left, right, and down. A gesture in one direction changes the signal in the corresponding sensor significantly more than the rest. We do not have a sensor in the *"up"* direction, which adds some complexity. Ideally, the upward motion of the skin would generate a reverse Doppler shift detected by the bottom sensor. However, this simple model does not accommodate the complexity of facial muscle structure; when a user touches their upper lips with their tongue, the entire area around the mouth moves, and all three sensors experience deviations in their low-frequency components. The bottom sensor experiences the most deviation, but not necessarily in the opposite direction as in the case of the *"down"* gesture (Figure 2). In the both the *"up"* and *"down"* gestures, the skin moves out (*i.e.,* away from the user's body) more than it moves up. However, our empirical experiments show that the signal is different for each of the four gestures and can be separately classified using standard machine learning techniques.

Figure 2F shows an example of the observed low frequency signal for a *hold-up* gesture. This signal for bottom sensor is very different from the *tap-up* gesture shown in Figure 2E. In case of *hold*, the magnitude does not oscillate because the muscles do not retract to resting position immediately.

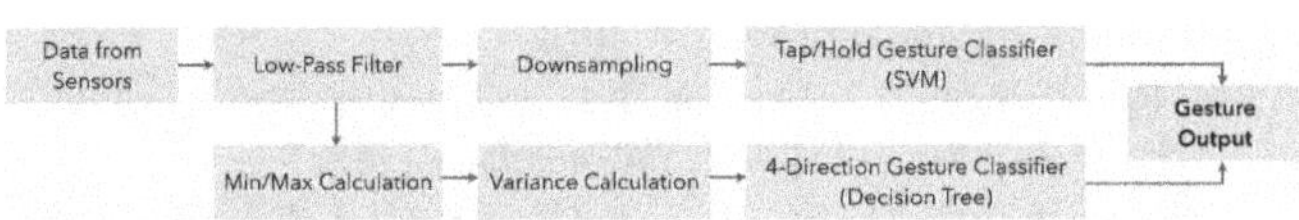

Figure 3. Tongue-in-Cheek's algorithm

Algorithm

The output of the microwave motion sensors is a baseband signal representing the amplitude of the Doppler shift. An analog to digital converter (ADC) first digitizes the output from the motion sensors. Then a third order Butterworth Filter low-pass filters the data up to 15 Hz (Figure 3). After this we use two different processing pipelines to differentiate between *tap* and *hold,* and the four directions. The outputs from both the classifiers are combined in the end to form eight different gestures: *tap-left, tap-right, tap-up, tap-down, hold-left, hold-right, hold-up,* and *hold-down.*

Tap vs. Hold Classification

Figure 2 shows that the signal looks substantially different for the *tap* and *hold* gestures. We use a support vector machine (SVM) classifier here and the features are calculated across 1 sec windows with a 0.8 sec overlap. The overlap of 0.8 sec assumes that the user would not perform two gestures within 0.2 sec. We first use mean filtering to downsample the low-pass filtered signal into 20 samples. These 20 data points from each of the three sensors gives us a total of 60 features for the SVM-based model. This particular processing pipeline does not do any segmentation. It simply calculates features across window. The second processing pipeline that classifies the gesture into one of the four directions performs the segmentation.

Direction Classification

Figure 3 shows that while differentiation between *left, right,* and *down* is very clear, the case of *down vs. up* is not that straightforward. Therefore, we cannot use a rule-based system and use decision trees to classify between the four directions, instead. We also added a class to represent when no gestures is being performed. This helped us in robust segmentation of real-time data. We calculate 3 features for each gesture: minimum, maximum, and variance of each 1 second window. The variance is the most important feature in this classifier because it is clear from Figure 3 that the amount of change in signal is a big differentiating factor. The minimum and maximum features help in overcoming the noise in the data and provide dynamic thresholding to the decision trees. All the features are calculated over 1 second window with a 0.8 seconds overlap.

QUALITATIVE EVALUATION

We evaluated our choice of sensing mechanism and gesture-set by demonstrating Tongue-in-cheek to three individuals with neuromuscular conditions. Two of the participants tried the system for almost 10 minutes each, and commented on the performance and the design. The third participant could not use the system personally and commented on the overall design and utility. P1 could not open his jaw far enough to instrument the inside of the mouth easily. Another side effect of his condition was tongue fasciculation – minor but constant involuntary muscle fluctuations across the tongue. These fluctuations were large enough to make tongue tracking hard, but the cheeks were relatively stable. Therefore, Tongue-in-Cheek was a relatively better approach for him as compared to [1,3]. P2 preferred switching between different modes and said, "the fact that you support several avenues of interaction is great." P3 actually preferred using a magnet attached to her tongue for more fine-grain control, but saw the appeal for people not wanting to place a magnet in their mouth [1]. Tongue-in-Cheek could be useful for a subset of the population due to its flexibility and non-intrusiveness.

TECHNICAL EVALUATION & RESULTS

To evaluate the gesture detection accuracy, the users had to perform repeated sets of gestures and our participants from qualitative evaluation had limited availability; hence we recruited eight participants (3 females) who did not have any neuromuscular condition. They all used the same pair of modified headphones. The initial adjustments were not very different from the kind a user makes when using a pair of headphones, *i.e.,* adjusting the size of the headband and adjusting the angle and reach of the microphone.

For each gesture class, participants had to perform 20 gestures. The order of the gesture classes was random. The participants were told that they could perform the gestures by either using their tongue, moving their lower jaw, or by puffing their cheeks.

The system performs leave-one-out cross validation and the system never uses the data for the same participant in training as well as testing. The models are therefore global and do not need to be adjusted for each user.

The system was able to correctly predict the direction of the gesture with 94.3% accuracy. The confusion was greatest between the *up* and *down* gestures. This was expected since both of these gestures depend heavily on the variation in output of the sensor placed under the user's chin. The accuracy for differentiating between *tap* and *hold* was 97.4%, and the segmentation accuracy for the system was 93.6%.

Tongue-in-Cheek is agnostic to the source of movements, *i.e.,* tongue, cheek, or jaw, and we did not formally evaluate how the system performed for these different movements. The participants were told that they could use the three motions independently.

APPLICATIONS

We applied Tongue-in-Cheek-based input to two different applications. We recruited three of our original eight participants to evaluate the applications (See video figure).

EdgeWrite

Inputting text on computing devices is an important capability. We integrated EdgeWrite [6] into our system to test if Tongue-in-Cheek could be used for text. Each participant was asked to enter three simple English language phrases. All three participants were able to correctly enter the three phrases with an average text entry rate of 9 wpm.

Video Games

In order to test the responsiveness of our gesture detection system, we asked the participants to play two different games: Pac-Man and Contra. All participants were able to play the games and expressed satisfaction with the system's responsiveness.

These are just two example applications for Tongue-in-Cheek. Our evaluation has shown that the system can reliably detect gestures in four directions and can be useful for many other general-purpose applications.

DISCUSSION AND LIMITATIONS

Systems like Tongue-in-Cheek that are designed for users with neuromuscular conditions face an important challenge. In most cases, such systems require the user to change their lifestyle and go through training. Hence the users should be able to use the device properly and actually enjoy using it. Tongue-in-Cheek detects modular, and directional gestures with no contact with the body. However, our interviews highlighted that different individuals have different needs and preferences. For example, Tongue-in-cheek is less intrusive, but it is more visible than [1,3].

Near infrared (NIR) sensors can also be used for proximity and motion sensing. Apart from being susceptible to dust and light, NIR is less immune to physical properties of the reflecting surface, hence might work differently for bearded or clean-shaven user. On the flip side, RF is more prone to ambient motion and headset movement. While this limitation can be largely countered with an Inertial Measurement Unit, we believe that our algorithms will work similarly for both the sensors and the final decision on sensors will depend on the user's preference.

CONCLUSION

Motor neuron diseases such as ALS as well as serious brain or spine injuries often result in severe paralysis. Patients can benefit from systems that allow them to control their environment non-intrusively. We present a facial gesture detection system that robustly detects various facial gestures in four directions. These gestures can be performed using the user's tongue, cheeks, or jaws. This capability allows the user to seamlessly switch between different gesture modalities and potentially feel less exerted.

REFERENCES

1. Huo, X., Wang, J., and Ghovanloo, M. A Magneto-Inductive Sensor Based Wireless Tongue-Computer Interface. *Neural Systems and Rehabilitation Engineering 16*, 5 (2008).
2. Lukaszewicz, K. The Ultrasound Image of the Tongue Surface as Input for Man/Machine Interface. *Proc. INTERACT '03.*
3. Saponas, T.S., Kelly, D., Parviz, B. a., and Tan, D.S. Optically sensing tongue gestures for computer input. *Proc. UIST'09.*
4. Sasaki, M., Arakawa, T., Nakayama, A., Obinata, G., and Yamaguchi, M. Estimation of tongue movement based on suprahyoid muscle activity. *Proc. IEEE Engineering in Medicine and Biology Society. 2013.*
5. Wilson-Pauwels, L., Akesson, E.J., and Stewart, P.A. *Cranial Nerves: Anatomy and Clinical Comments.*1988.
6. Wobbrock, J.O., Myers, B.A., and Kembel, J.A. EdgeWrite: A Stylus-Based Text Entry Method Designed for High Accuracy and Stability of Motion. *Proc. UIST 2003.*
7. Zhang, Q., Gollakota, S., Taskar, B., and Rao, R.P.N. Non-Intrusive Tongue Machine Interface. *Proc. CHI'14.*

MatrixWave: Visual Comparison of Event Sequence Data

Jian Zhao[1] **Zhicheng Liu**[2] **Mira Dontcheva**[2] **Aaron Hertzmann**[2] **Alan Wilson**[2]

[1]University of Toronto [2]Adobe Research

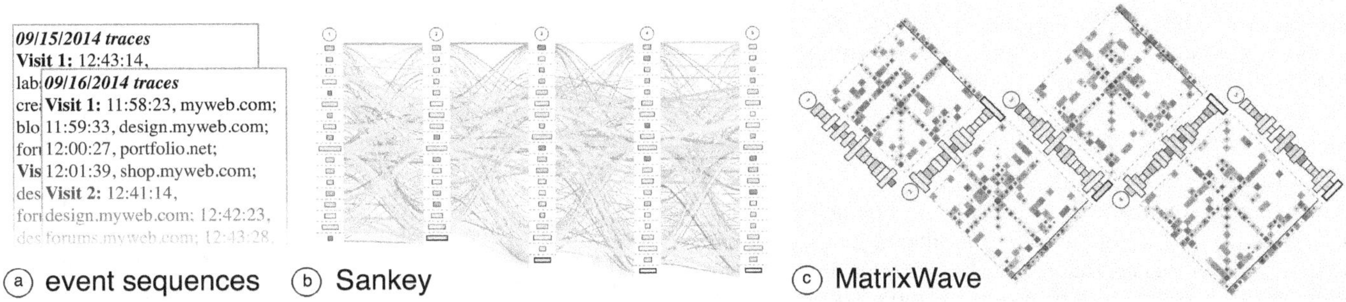

Figure 1. We explore visualization designs for comparison analysis of two web clickstream datasets (a). Node-link diagrams, like the Sankey diagram (b), use a familiar node-link paradigm, but lead to many overlapping edges. In contrast, MatrixWave displays links as with matrices (c) and arranges step-to-step transitions in a zig-zag pattern. Traffic volume is encoded with size, and differences between the two datasets are encoded with color.

ABSTRACT

Event sequence data analysis is common in many domains, including web and software development, transportation, and medical care. Few have investigated visualization techniques for comparative analysis of multiple event sequence datasets. Grounded in the real-world characteristics of web clickstream data, we explore visualization techniques for comparison of two clickstream datasets collected on different days or from users with different demographics. Through iterative design with web analysts, we designed MatrixWave, a matrix-based representation that allows analysts to get an overview of differences in traffic patterns and interactively explore paths through the website. We use color to encode differences and size to offer context over traffic volume. User feedback on MatrixWave is positive. Our study participants made fewer errors with MatrixWave and preferred it over the more familiar Sankey diagram.

Author Keywords

Event sequences; visual comparison; Sankey diagram; matrix representation; information visualization.

ACM Classification Keywords

H.5.2. Information Interfaces and Presentation (e.g. HCI): User Interfaces

INTRODUCTION

Analysts often seek to understand event sequence data, that is, multiple series of timestamped events. Event sequence data arises in many applications. For example, websites log how users navigate their pages, airlines track events during airplane flights, and hospitals record when patients transfer from one part of the hospital to another. A key analysis task is *comparison* between different time periods and different populations. For example, a website analyst asks numerous questions about how users navigate their site. Is traffic increasing or decreasing? Are this week's visitors leaving the site faster than last week's visitors? Are visitors from North America visiting the same parts of the website as visitors from Europe? While several visualization techniques have been designed for event sequence data, such as the Sankey diagram [25] and the LifeFlow [31] and Outflow [30] systems, little attention has been paid to supporting visual comparisons for this type of data.

In this work, we explore visualization designs for *comparative analysis* of two related event sequence datasets. We perform this exploration in the context of web clickstream data, but we believe our findings generalize to other domains. As we began our exploration, we found that visualizing even a single clickstream dataset is not well supported by existing techniques, as clickstream data includes many events and many transitions resulting in complex and unreadable visualizations (Figure 1-b). To handle visualizing real-world clickstream data, we propose the MatrixWave representation. MatrixWave displays a transition matrix [3] for each successive step in the sequence, rotated and concatenated side-by-side in a zig-zag manner (Figure 1-c). This design directly exposes traffic statistics for individual nodes and for step-to-step transitions; moreover, individual navigation paths through the site can be isolated as zig-zag paths through the sequence of matrices. To support comparative analysis of event sequences, we design additional visual encodings using color and size. Using our design, an analyst can get an overall picture of website traffic from the basic visualization, can identify popular nodes and transitions from histogram statistics, and can see how these quantities have changed over time or between user segments. MatrixWave also incorporates flexible interactions, such as filtering, searching, and node reordering, to aid users with the exploration of data.

CHI 2015, April 18–23 2015, Seoul, Republic of Korea.

http://dx.doi.org/10.1145/2702123.2702419

We grounded our design in interviews with expert web analysts and iteratively collected feedback throughout the design process. Additionally, we evaluated how well users perform with MatrixWave and the Sankey diagram from comparison tasks. Although the Sankey diagram is more familiar and MatrixWave requires learning a new technique, the study participants made fewer errors and preferred the MatrixWave representation over the Sankey diagram. Qualitative feedback points to the need for better ways to filter the data and further exploration into layout.

RELATED WORK

Visualizations of clickstream data

Clickstream visualization has received considerable attention. ClickViz [5] and WebQuilt [13] introduced directed graphs for clickstream visualization, but these approaches can only handle dozens of paths. In order to handle larger datasets, some authors have proposed clustering paths [7, 14, 29] and showing summary statistics [17]. These approaches provide a high-level overview of clickstream patterns, but do not allow fine-scale analysis of individual paths. Moreover, the actual set of behaviors may not be represented well by clusters. Commercial systems, such as Google Analytics, use Sankey diagrams to show pages and links with the most traffic, but offer little assistance with comparison.

Visualization of event sequences

Perhaps the most basic approach to event sequence visualization is to display the raw sequences, as done by Lifelines [24, 28], CloudLines [15], and TimeSlice [33]. These methods can provide considerable detail to individual traces, but do not scale to clickstream data, which typically involves thousands of sequences. In order to reduce dataset size, LifeFlow [31] and EventFlow [19] consolidate common subsequences, resulting in a tree-like representation. These representations scale exponentially in the number of event types, and thus are impractical for clickstream data, where each event is typically one of hundreds of webpages.

Several authors have proposed consolidating events into a graph. A state transition diagram [27] is a general graph of state nodes that directly shows all routes between pages. But, this approach does not show step information and does not scale well to highly-connected graphs. In some cases, the scaling issue can be addressed by discovering motifs [18, 23], or conducting interactive queries over event types, event intervals, etc. [10, 20]. The Sankey diagram [25] is a form of graph arranged to show step-by-step transitions; we discuss the Sankey more extensively later in the paper. A number of variants and extensions to the Sankey have also been developed [30].

Two previous methods use sequences of matrices, similar to MatrixWave. MatrixFlow [22] visualizes histories as a sequence of matrices. Though superficially similar to MatrixWave, MatrixFlow does not describe paths through states, as each matrix is a separate, independent visualization, and each matrix is a symmetric correlation matrix rather than a transition matrix. Closest to our own work is GeneaQuilts [4], which visualizes genealogy by alternating individuals with pairs of matrices. This work is specialized to genealogy, in which each child has exactly two parents. The GeneaQuilts graph requires twice as many matrices for the same number of steps as MatrixWave, in order to completely specify ancestry. Although MatrixWave would not be able to precisely show ancestry, it is designed for much denser transition relations where each event may follow many other events, and where there are many more possible events.

Visual data comparison

Gleicher et al. [9] classify visual comparison techniques into three categories: juxtaposition, superposition (e.g., [26]), and explicit encoding (e.g., [11]). Another common approach to reveal differences between data is to use animation (e.g., [2]). Juxtaposed views enable a side-by-side comparison of data, often complemented with interactions highlighting the matches or explicit drawings showing the connections [21, 12, 6, 32]. Superposed views allow an in-place comparison by overlaying multiple objects in one visualization [26, 16]. Explicit encoding techniques compute the differences between related elements and visualize these derived values [11]. Finally, animated views interpolate two visual representations to preserve a viewer's mental map [2]. These prior works on visual comparison primarily focus on trees and graphs, and have not addressed the visualization and comparison of changes between two event sequences. Nevertheless, they provide valuable results to ground our design choices. We employ superposition to combine two related event sequence datasets and use explicit encoding for comparison tasks.

UNDERSTANDING CLICKSTREAM ANALYSIS

We use web clickstream data to ground our investigation in real-world problems. Modern commercial websites track thousands of distinct clickstream sequences each single day. A sequence consists of ordered events, each assigned a step number. Each event is an interaction with the website, including a click on a link, a click on a menu, or filling out a form and pressing return. These sequences are highly variable. Some include only one or two events, while others can include tens or hundreds of unique events.

To better understand the web analysis domain, we interviewed expert analysts who work with clickstream data at large IT companies. We conducted multiple interviews and collected feedback throughout the design process. During the interviews, we presented the prototypes, discussed alternatives for visual encodings and interactions, and collected feedback from the experts to guide our next steps. Although we developed MatrixWave in the context of comparing web clickstream data, the visualization and its interactive features can be generalized to other types of event sequence data.

To ground our design in real work, we distilled the following analysis tasks from our interviews:

Traffic volume: One of the most common analysis tasks is assessing the number of visitors to a site and tracking which pages get the most visitors. Analysts usually compare traffic volume from a given day to volume from the previous day and volume from the same day on the previous week. Volume

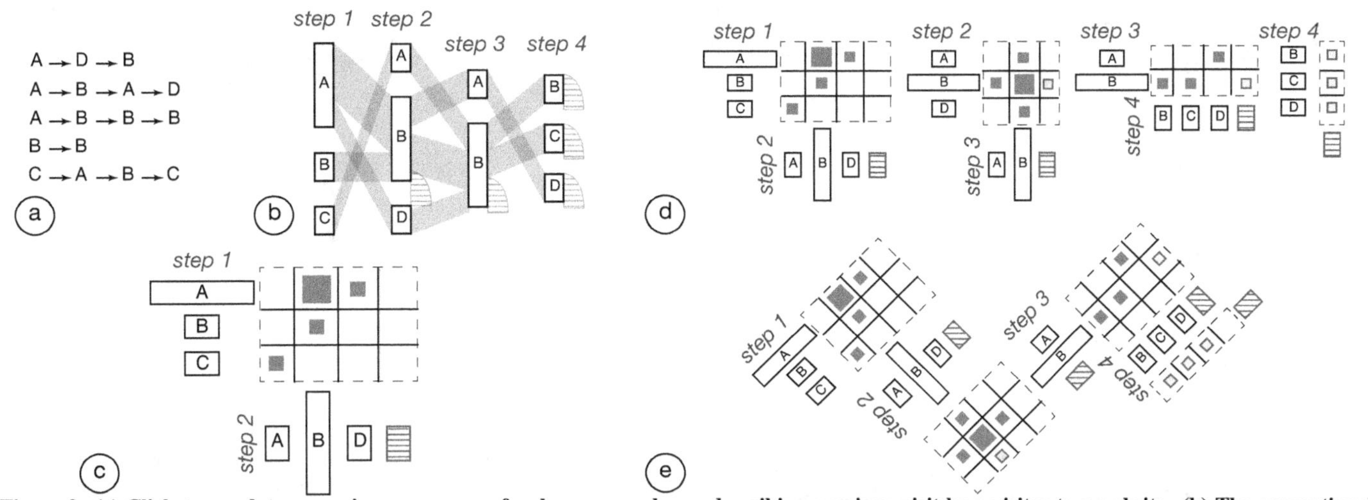

Figure 2. (a) Clickstream data comprises sequences of web pages, each one describing a unique visit by a visitor to a website. (b) The conventional visualization for clickstreams is the Sankey diagram, in which each column of bars represents a step number. But Sankey diagrams can become unreadable due to edge crossings between links. (c) We propose to replace the links with a transition matrix, in which each element in the grid represents the link from one node to the next; here, the size of the gray square indicates the traffic volume in that link. (d) Matrices can be sequenced together. However the notion of a path through the website is lost. (e) To enable path visualization and eliminate duplicating nodes, we chose a zig-zag layout. Drop-off (exit) nodes are filled in with a line pattern.

comparison is also common across steps in the sequence. Volume comparison across steps tells analysts how quickly visitors leave the site.

Entry into the website: Analysts often seek to understand the effect of marketing campaigns: are they bringing more people to the website, and what are these people doing? For this task, analysts break down traffic by entry point (email click, search engine, banner ad, etc.) and study where new visitors go next as compared to other types of visitors. Close inspection of the first one or two steps tells analysts how many people continue deeper into the site.

Exits from the website: Analysts also seek to understand how and when users leave a website. Much of website optimization entails trying to reduce drop-off rates.

Paths through the website: Finally, analysts are often interested in studying specific paths through a website. For example, an analyst might want to see all the paths that take visitors from the home page to the checkout page and how those are different for different types of users. They are interested not only in which pages were visited but also the sequence of those pages. For example, a path that contains many visits to the same webpage can be a sign of a design flaw or bug in the implementation.

There are a number of other important tasks that we do not address in this work, such as optimizing search engine performance or detecting looping behavior where visitors go back and forth between the same set of webpages.

DESIGN OF MATRIXWAVE

We now describe our visualization techniques for studying and comparing event sequence datasets. We discuss the design of the MatrixWave representation, and present techniques for embedding comparisons into the representation.

Visualizing a single dataset

The inputs are sets of event sequences, where each event sequence is a list of *nodes*. For example, we might have four possible nodes A, B, C, and D, and an individual sequence might be $B \rightarrow A \rightarrow C$. This path contains three *steps*. A transition between nodes at a given step is called a *link*. Nodes and links have traffic volumes associated with them. In clickstream visualization, each node represents a webpage view, and a sequence represents a single user's navigation history, e.g., start at page B, go to page A, go to page C, exit. A simple example dataset is shown in Figure 2-a.

Modern visualizations of clickstream data typically employ the Sankey diagram, which offers an aggregate view of paths and offers more details through interaction. A Sankey diagram aggregates clickstream data according to steps (Figure 2-b). At each step, identical pages are aggregated into nodes, and nodes are sized according to their volume. Links connect nodes between steps and are also sized according to volume. For clickstream data, drop-off links show the volume of traffic leaving the site at various steps.

While Sankey diagrams are popular, their major weakness is in handling dense transitions. Even with less than ten nodes and dozens of paths, a Sankey diagram is hard to read due to the multitude of edge crossings.

The approach we propose, MatrixWave, replaces the edge connections between a pair of steps with a transition matrix (Figure 2-c). Each cell in the matrix represents the volume of traffic between the corresponding two nodes. This is inspired by the observation that matrices can effectively display dense graphs [8]. We hypothesize that the advantages of the matrix representation still apply in the context of visualizing clickstream data. Applying the matrix representation to each step in the Sankey representation, we obtain a sequence of matrices placed next to each other in a sequence (Figure 2-d).

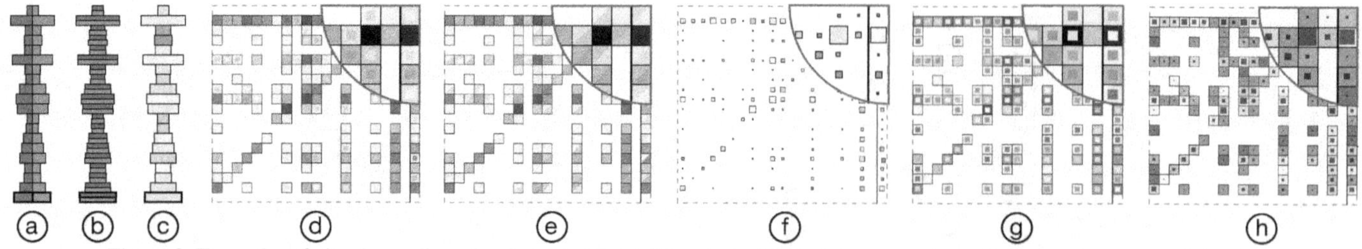

Figure 3. Examples of visual encodings developed in MatrixWave to facilitate data comparison of two event sequence datasets.

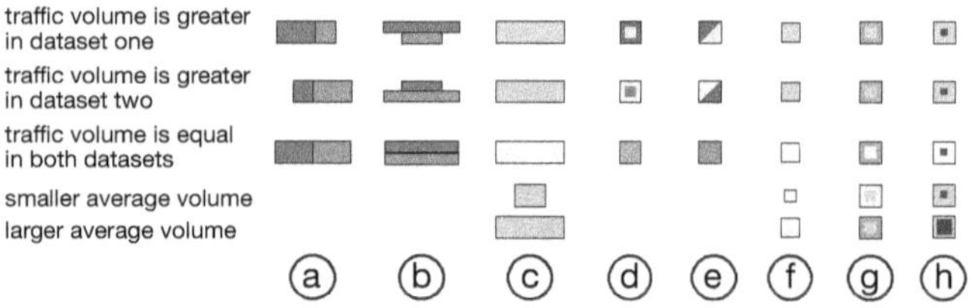

Figure 4. Potential designs for showing differences.

To represent drop-offs, we add an additional drop-off node to each step of the matrices.

One problem with this design is that the notion of a continuous path is lost because the nodes at each step are duplicated. To avoid duplication of nodes, we rotate the matrices 45 degrees and concatenate them. The rotation allows us to use nodes in each step to show both incoming and outgoing links (Figure 2-e). A user can then trace a path in a zig-zag manner.

Visual encodings for comparison

To do comparative analysis of two datasets, we must first place them into correspondence. We assume that most nodes are in common; e.g., the only changes to a website structure might be the addition or removal of a few pages. We match nodes that have the same page name and step number, and links that have the same source and target nodes. If a node or a link only appears in one dataset, the corresponding volume in the other dataset is set to zero. In real-world datasets, a step can include hundreds of distinct page events. We aggregate page events into groups using the website's organizing hierarchy.

We consider four approaches for visual comparison: juxtaposition, superposition, explicit encoding, and animation [9]. In the design of MatrixWave, we apply *superposition* to represent two datasets within one visualization. Showing two separate visualizations side-by-side (juxtaposition) is not effective in comparing complicated structures, because corresponding elements are far apart and difficult to identify [1]. While animations can provide smooth transitions between multiple datasets, they require switching between views repeatedly. Within a visualization, we apply *explicit encoding* to show volume differences in nodes and links. We explain the design of explicit visual encodings below.

Node encoding choices

We apply *explicit encoding* in MatrixWave, where the difference in traffic at each node is computed and directly displayed. It is common practice to map differences to a diverging color scheme, e.g., purple to orange (Figure 3-c), so that it is easy to identify the direction of change. Both relative difference and percentage difference can be mapped to the color-scale. In addition, we use size to show the average volume, as the importance of a difference is often determined by the volume of traffic. Changes on popular pages are more important than changes on pages with less traffic.

A design alternative is to use juxtaposition: for every page group, we have two nodes, each representing the page group in one of datasets. Size is an effective visual variable to encode volume and hue is appropriate for representing dataset membership. We can either align the two nodes along a center line (Figure 3-a) or put them side by side (Figure 3-b) for easier comparison. Figure 4-a to -c show how the potential designs represent differences. Juxtaposition requires analysts to make perceptual judgments about the differences in volume, while explicit encoding is more efficient and provides direct access to this information [9].

Link encoding choices

Differences in link traffic can also be displayed by juxtaposition or explicit encodings. Our final design uses *explicit encodings* with two concentric squares: the inner square size represents the average link volume of the two datasets, and the background hue of the cell encodes the difference in traffic volume (Figure 3-h).

We started by designing two types of glyphs for juxtaposition: one using two fixed-sized concentric squares (Figure 3-d), and the other dividing a cell along the diagonal into two triangles (Figure 3-e). Color intensity of the two regions represents link volume in the two datasets. Previous work has explored other glyphs for encoding differences and found that the square division method outperformed the rest [1].

We also tried to use color to explicitly encode difference and size to represent link volume (Figure 3-f), similar to the node encoding. Due to the limited number of pixels allocated to each cell, this approach results in tiny squares when the link volume is small, making it difficult to read the differences represented as color. We considered swapping the mapping (so that color represents volume and size encodes difference), but size is not effective at indicating the direction of difference, positive vs. negative.

To overcome this problem, we tried representing link volume with two concentric squares with two different colors (Figure 3-g), but found it harder to interpret two different colors representing different types of quantities. In the end, we decided to size a black square inside of each cell according to link volume, and use the hue of the background of each cell to represents the magnitude of difference (Figure 3-h). This design is also consistent with our choice of node encoding.

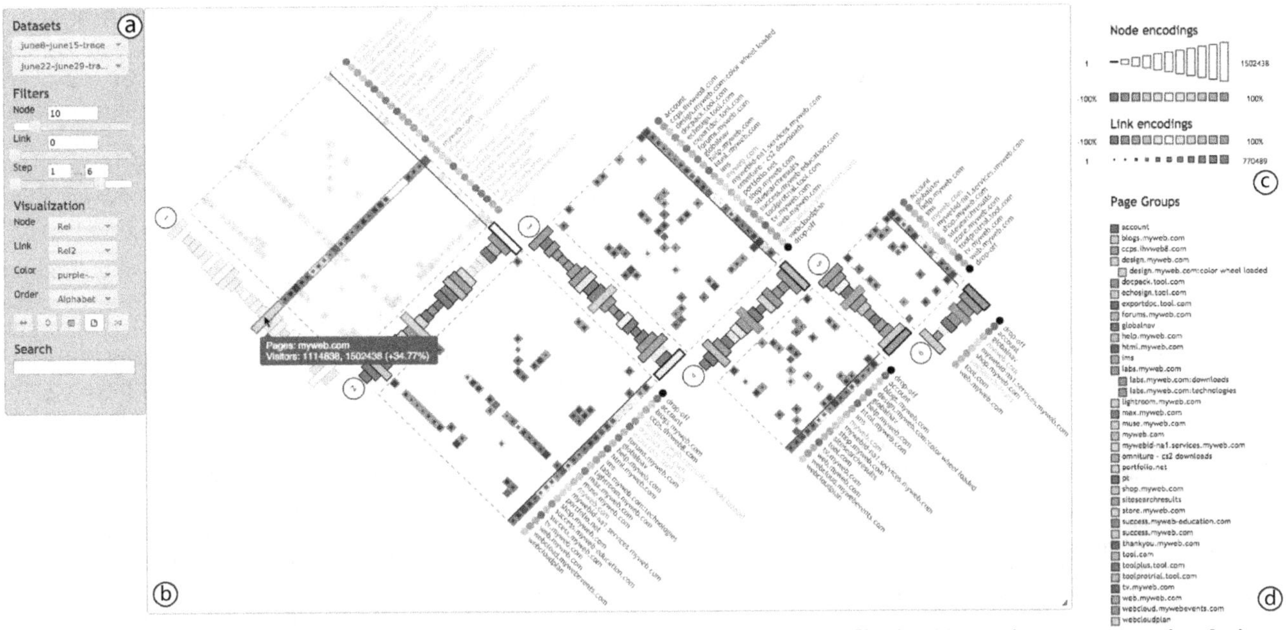

Figure 5. The MatrixWave interface includes a control panel for selecting datasets, sorting, and filtering (a), a main canvas presenting the interactive visualization (b), a legend (c), and a list of page groups (d). Here the user has highlighted a webpage from the first step. The bright orange and purple squares representing links show that there are lots of differences between the two datasets. The user can use the groups in the panel on the right (d) to filter the dataset according to the website structure.

Figure 4-d to -h show those design alternatives for comparing values in two datasets.

In our final implementation, MatrixWave visualizes the event sequence data with the designs shown in Figure 3-c and -h by default, using percentage difference as the measurement. Other alternatives can be accessed in the prototype through the control panel (Figure 5-a). In addition, we display the page group names associated with each group of nodes on the opposite side of each matrix (Figure 5-b).

Interactive Features

MatrixWave incorporates a number of interactions to further facilitate the exploration and comparison of event sequences.

Brushing & linking and selecting: When a user hovers over a node, he sees more information about that page group, including the traffic volume in both datasets and the difference as a percentage. Additionally all the incoming source nodes, outgoing target nodes, and the links across all steps are highlighted (Figure 5-b). Similarly, hovering over a link offers more details about the transition and highlights its source and target nodes. A user can click on a node or a link to select it. When a node or a link is selected, traffic through that node or link is highlighted. To allow users to move around the visualization, MatrixWave supports zooming and panning.

Showing paths: Since analysts are often interested in understanding user paths through a website, we provide a way to overlay path information on top of the matrix representation. When one or more nodes/links are selected, as shown in Figure 6-a, blue lines indicate the underlying event sequences that pass through the selected nodes/links.

The traffic volume of the selected paths is typically only a subset of the overall volume. For example, in Figure 2, if we select the path $A \rightarrow A \rightarrow B$, the third-step volume for B is only a fraction of the overall volume for B at that step. To represent these path-specific volumes, we overlay visuals with the same encodings. In particular, for a node, an inner bar representing the path-specific volume is displayed on top of the overall aggregate volume bar (Figure 6-b); and for a link, the matrix cell is split into two triangles where the right half denotes the path-specific volume and difference (Figure 6-c). This path-specific representation can be turned on or off through the control panel.

Filtering: We developed several filtering mechanisms in MatrixWave. First, users can search for page group names in a search box and select all the matching elements at once (Figure 6-a). This is useful when a user decides to focus on exploring the flow of a specific page group or a subset of page groups in the same name domain. Second, users can filter both nodes and links by volume. Additionally, entire steps can be filtered out to support more advanced exploration, for example, removing unnecessary intermediate steps when only the starting and ending nodes are of interest. Finally, pages can be filtered according to their organization in the website using the tree-structured page listing (Figure 6-d).

Ordering: In order to facilitate comparison, a user can sort page groups alphabetically, by volume, or difference. Sorting can be performed within a specific step or across all steps. Additionally, MatrixWave allows the user to insert proxy nodes for all page groups in the website at each step. This facilitates using spatial positions as anchors into the identity of a page (i.e. the third node in a step will always be the same page or page group). Using proxy nodes can result in very large and sparse matrices, but it makes it easier to get an overview of the entire site and to trace a particular page group across steps. Finally, a user can also fix the ordering

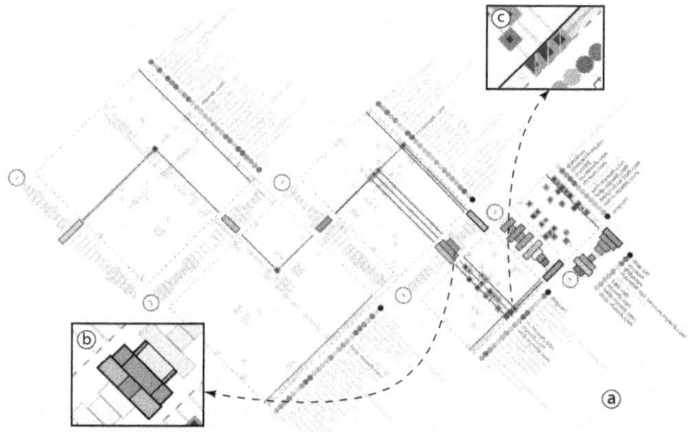

Figure 6. When one or more objects are selected, paths passing through the selected nodes/links are indicated with a blue-line (a). Path-specific differences are overlaid to show how the path volume is different from the aggregate volume (b)(c). In this example, the differences in the path specific volume of the highlighted nodes are the same as the differences in the aggregate nodes (b). The path-specific link information (c), shows that there is an increase in the number of path-specific links from one dataset to the other.

of the nodes in one step and propagate this ordering across steps. This facilitates comparison across steps.

ANALYST EXPERIENCE

We designed MatrixWave iteratively by working with web data analysts. To explain how analysts use MatrixWave let's walk through a typical workflow. For a complete view of the exploration process, please refer to the supplemental video.

John is examining a website following a major redesign. He loads two datasets into MatrixWave for comparison—one from the week before the redesign and one from the week after. At a glance, he sees a lot of differences: there are a lot of pages with bright orange and bright purple colors. He sorts the pages according to changes in traffic.

The homepage immediately pops out. It has many links (Figure 5), but many of them are purple, which means that traffic is down. He hovers over those links and sees that many of those links are no longer visited from the homepage. They are probably no longer on the homepage, John thinks. There is a 35% drop in traffic to the forums pages and a huge jump in traffic to the help pages (390%). He clicks on the link connecting the homepage and the help pages to highlight all traffic that passes through the homepage and the help pages.

From the help pages, he sees people go on to four different types of pages next. There is a huge jump in visits to the video site, where some of the help videos are hosted. He selects the videos site in step 3 to see what happens next (Figure 6). He is surprised to see that everyone leaves after step 4. So, visitors who go to the help site after the homepage, are leaving within a couple of pages. He looks at all the drop off nodes and sees that the drop-off nodes for step 4, 5, and 6 have seen a big increase. Looks like people are leaving the site faster now after the redesign. John needs to investigate further.

ADAPTING SANKEY FOR VISUAL COMPARISON

Since our work is one of the first to investigate comparative analysis of event sequences, there are no existing baselines to compare with our approach. To help us understand the strengths and weaknesses of MatrixWave, we chose to adapt the conventional Sankey diagram. The Sankey diagram is widely used for visualizing large numbers of event sequences in many applications, such as Google Analytics and [30].

We adapted the Sankey for comparison using superposition and explicit encodings (Figure 1-b). Nodes are represented in the same way as in MatrixWave. Unlike the traditional Sankey visualization, we placed the node bars horizontally in each step to allow for easier comparison of page volume. For encoding differences in links, we use smooth-curved ribbons colored according to difference magnitude. The thickness of the ribbon is mapped to the average of the two volumes associated with that link. We used the same divergent color scheme as in the MatrixWave design. Additionally, we replicated all interactions available in the MatrixWave prototype. To highlight paths, we used blue outlines for all the related nodes and links. To encode path-specific volume on top of nodes, we used the same representation as we did in MatrixWave. To encode path-specific volume in links, we extended the overlay paradigm and overlaid smaller ribbons on top of the aggregate ribbons.

EVALUATION

We conducted a laboratory study to investigate the effectiveness of MatrixWave in supporting visual comparison tasks. In the study, we compared MatrixWave with the adapted Sankey visualization we described above. The main goal of the study was to understand the advantages and disadvantages of these two distinct approaches and get feedback from both novice and expert users on their preferences. Since previous work has indicated that a matrix representation is more effective than the node-link diagram for larger and denser data [1, 8], we focused on comparative analysis tasks with two datasets, instead of comparing MatrixWave and the node-link based Sankey for visualizing a single dataset.

Participants and apparatus

We recruited 12 volunteers, 8 males and 4 females, aged 22–53 (mean 42), from a large IT company. Participants were from various technical backgrounds, such as software engineering, product management, data analysis, and graphics design. Six of them had familiarity with website clickstream data, and four considered data analysis part of their job. All participants had normal vision (or corrected-to-normal vision) without color deficiency. The experiments were conducted on a laptop (a MacBook Pro with 2.3 GHz Intel Core i7 CPU and 16 GB memory) connected to a 30-inch Dell desktop monitor. The visualization on the screen was restricted to an area of 1600×1000 pixels. All participants completed the study with a mouse and keyboard.

Data

We created our study datasets from real clickstream data captured on a large organization's website. We visualized the first 6 steps of the 1000 most common event sequences on two different days, where the input data covered 90% of page groups in the entire traces. We used the first 6 steps, in order to allow the visualization to fit on the screen; the first few steps are usually the most important in web clickstream analysis. The final input to the visualization contained 167 nodes and 902 links in total.

Methodology

We performed a within-subject, full factorial design with two experimental conditions and eight tasks. Two different sets of eight task questions were developed to address any memory learning effects. The orders of the techniques and the task sets were counter-balanced using a Latin square. The order of the tasks within each set was fixed.

We created eight study tasks that cover a variety of interactions we saw analysts do with the visualizations during our interviews including: node comparison, link comparison, comparison across steps, and path comparison. Each task included a multiple-choice question and a visualization customized to the question. Customizations included sorting the nodes and highlighting specific nodes and links. As others have shown previously [1], eliminating the task of selecting related visual elements allows us to better isolate the effect visual encodings have on performance. Each task included a "do not know" option to prevent users from randomly guessing. The template we used for task questions is shown in Table 1. We carefully chose the data parameters in task questions to avoid ambiguous answers and to maintain the same level of difficulty across task sets. Each question had only one correct answer.

Node comparison tasks: We found node comparison within a step and across steps to be part of almost every analyst task. For example when looking at overall traffic volume, analysts focus mostly on nodes and look for big changes in color, especially for the popular pages that receive more traffic.

Link comparison tasks: Link comparison invokes comparing the number of outgoing and incoming links and how they are different across datasets. Link comparison is an integral part of understanding entry and exit of the website. To understand where people go when they get to the website, analysts look at the number of links and their connections.

Comparison across steps: Comparison across steps involves comparing nodes across steps and comparing links across steps. This type of comparison is part of understanding whether users are leaving the site faster in one dataset than the other and whether visitors in one dataset are visiting more of the website as compared to visitors from the other dataset.

Path comparison tasks: Path comparison involves selecting two or more nodes and looking at the specific paths between those nodes. In particular, analysts want to know if there are multiple paths and which nodes they include. Path comparison is rarely done today, because analysts do not have the right tools to do it.

Procedure

The study began with a brief tutorial to the participants about the problem domain and the visualizations. Participants then performed four training tasks with each of the techniques (Sankey and MatrixWave) with a separate dataset. During the training session, participants were instructed to think aloud, and the experimenter helped them resolve any questions. Next, the participants went through 8 tasks with each technique for a total of 16 tasks. Each tasks was limited to 2 minutes, after which the system automatically advanced to the next trial. We reminded participants that they could always select the "do not know" option when their confidence was low. We recorded task completion times and users' answers. We also observed how participants performed the tasks and captured the entire session using screen recording software. After the study, participants were asked to specify their preference for a visualization technique, and we conducted a semi-structured interview to collect their feedback. The whole study lasted approximately 1 hour for each participant.

	Type	Question
T1	Node	Pages A and B have been highlighted in steps x, y, and z. Which page has a larger overall volume?
T2	Node	Pages A and B have been highlighted in steps x, y, and z. Which page has a greater overall change?
T3	Link	Pages A and B are highlighted in step x. Which of these two pages has more incoming links with increasing volume?
T4	Link	Pages A and B are highlighted in step x. Among all the outgoing links from these two pages, which has the largest volume?
T5	Step	Is the overall traffic between the highlighted pages in steps x and $x+1$ increasing or decreasing?
T6	Step	Compare the traffic between highlighted pages at step x to $x+1$ and at step y to $y+1$. Which has a larger overall volume?
T7	Path	Observe the paths of traffic going through the highlighted pages. Which page has the largest path-specific volume at step x?
T8	Path	Observe the paths of traffic going through the highlighted pages. Is the overall path-specific volume increasing or decreasing?

Table 1. Experimental tasks.

Hypotheses

We had the following hypotheses about the performance of these two visualization techniques:

H1 For node comparison tasks, we expect Sankey to perform faster, because MatrixWave introduces a rotation making it more difficult to compare nodes; we expect the two techniques to achieve a similar accuracy, because they use the same visual encodings.

H2 For link comparison and step comparison tasks, we expect MatrixWave to perform faster and more accurately, because links are occluded by edge crossings in Sankey.

H3 For path tasks, we expect Sankey to perform faster than MatrixWave, because Sankey is more familiar to users and users do not have to follow a zig-zag to understand the path; for the same reason in H1, we expect the two techniques to achieve a similar accuracy.

Results

Accuracy

On average, MatrixWave achieved an accuracy of 95% (SD=6%) for all tasks, which was much higher than Sankey, which had an accuracy of 79% (SD=17%). Both incorrect answers and "do not know" choices were counted as

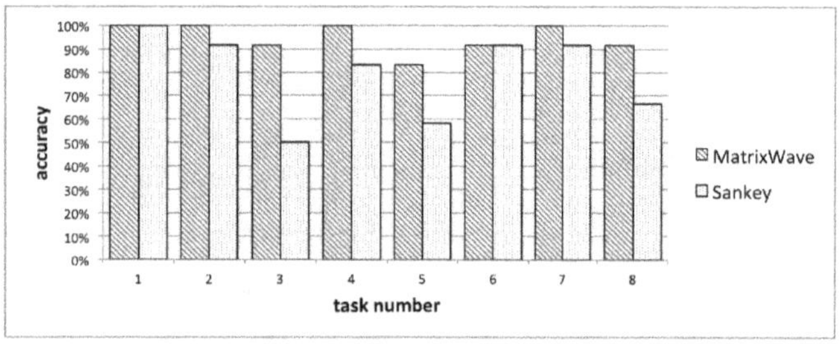

Figure 7. Accuracy of each task

incorrect. There was a significant effect of visualization techniques on task accuracy ($F_{1,14}$=5.918, p<0.01). Figure 7 shows a more detailed picture with accuracy for each task. Despite our expectations that Sankey would outperform MatrixWave for node and path tasks (H1 and H3), both techniques performed equally well for node tasks (T1, T2) and MatrixWave outperformed Sankey in path tasks (T7, T8). The greatest difference in accuracy was for link comparison tasks (T3, T4), where MatrixWave was about 30% more accurate, supporting H2. For the step comparison tasks (T5, T6), we found a different story. While MatrixWave outperformed Sankey for T5, it did about the same for T6. This result might be due to the nature of the task, which does not ask for precise comparison. The participants only had to determine whether one set of links is larger in volume than another set of links. In contrast, T4, which was also about link volume comparison, required users to specify which link was bigger. Thus, tasks that require more precision in link and step comparison are better supported by MatrixWave.

Completion time

We analyzed task completion time for all tasks that were completed correctly. On average, the participants spent 34.0 seconds (SD=16.2) on a task using MatrixWave and 38.2 seconds (SD=19.6) using Sankey. Figure 8 shows the completion time for each task. We found a significant effect ($F_{1,22}$=6.097, p<0.01) of visualization technique for the step comparison tasks (T5 and T6), which asked participants to assess the overall traffic difference between steps. MatrixWave was about 36% faster than Sankey for step comparison tasks, supporting H2. There was no significant effect for other task types. Sankey had an overall higher standard deviation on all tasks, especially in link and step tasks where we expected MatrixWave to be faster, indicating that participants may resort to random guessing more when using Sankey.

Preference and feedback

The preference ratings from all participants were: 2 strongly preferred MatrixWave, 6 preferred MatrixWave, 2 were neutral, and 2 preferred Sankey, indicating that 8 out of 12 participants liked MatrixWave. From the study interviews, we gathered many qualitative comments from participants about the advantages and disadvantages of both techniques.

First impressions: When we presented the two techniques to participants, people felt that the Sankey representation was easy to understand, because the nodes and the links of each step followed a linear left-to-right layout, which is commonly seen in representing data flows. However, participants also felt that it was overwhelming and noisy,

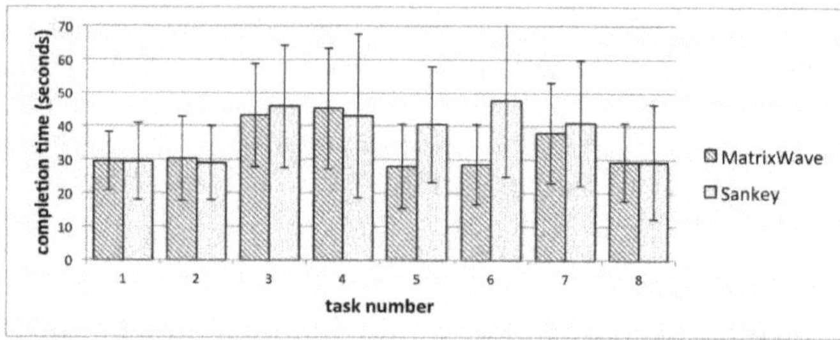

Figure 8. Completion time of each task (errors bars indicate the standard deviation).

because many links with different thicknesses, colors, and curvatures were overlapping with each other. As for MatrixWave, three participants found it difficult to comprehend the zig-zag layout of matrices at first, mentioning "*I need to think about it a bit and try to get used to it*". Some said that they had never seen the matrix representation of graphs and thought that using squares to encode links was less intuitive. However, all participants said that MatrixWave was more concise and clean, making information visible in a compact manner. They also liked the fact that MatrixWave provided a clearer overview of the data, saying that "*the matrices are like a heatmap, clearly telling me what is happening in which part of the website*".

Learning: Although many participants were not familiar with the matrix representation of a graph and the layout of matrices in MatrixWave, they could interpret the visual representations after some explanation. For both visualizations, we also observed that the visual encoding of volume and differences were easy for participants to understand. They did not have any questions about the volume and difference visual encoding following the training tasks. The path-specific visual encoding was more difficult for users, because it required differentiating between aggregate flow and path-specific flow. One user suggested that "*showing only the paths and removing the overall ones could be better*". Four participants had a dramatic change in preferences over the course of the study. During the training sessions, they said to themselves (the think aloud protocol) that Sankey was a lot better than MatrixWave, but after the study, they all agreed that MatrixWave was more useful and preferable.

Ease of use: As expected (H2), participants mentioned that it was extremely difficult to perform link-related tasks with Sankey, because 1) there were too many edge crossings, making the identification of specific links tedious and sometimes impossible, and 2) it was hard to compare the thickness of links with different curvatures. Participants thought the visual design in MatrixWave addressed these problems, commenting that "*it is clearer to see the incoming and outgoing links in the matrix because they are all aligned to the same row [or column]*". Moreover, for path-related tasks, participants generally thought that tracing multiple paths in MatrixWave was much easier with the blue line as a visual cue, even though the Sankey diagram applied similar highlighting. Two participants mentioned that MatrixWave design was evocative of architectural design with the matrices as rooms. One participant, who is an experience designer, said that she felt this design would help her explain the visitor's journey through the website in a way that the Sankey diagram doesn't. Another participant said: *"it [a path] looks like a person enters a room [the matrix] through a door [the node] and find a table [the link square] and exits it through another door"*. Participants also commented that the page labels were difficult to see in the Sankey diagram because they overlapped with the link ribbons, whereas MatrixWave displayed them next to the matrices. But in MatrixWave people needed to rotate their heads to read the labels, which some mentioned was uncomfortable.

Domain-specific usage: From the participants who had experience with analyzing web clickstream data, we collected a number of domain-specific comments. For example, one mentioned that the visual design of encoding volume and differences was effective for real-world cases, because people could related the two aspects to pin-point which pages to examine further, e.g., moderate differences on large-volume pages are more important than large differences on small-volume pages. Another comment was that when pages in each step were properly ordered, the matrix representation in MatrixWave showed a heatmap of traffic across different sections of a website, so that "*hot regions*" would pop up immediately. Moreover, participants pointed out that it was extremely useful to be able to select nodes in examining traffic for anticipated user behaviors. For example, an analyst could select certain entry pages and drop-off points to explore the volumes and differences of the connecting paths. Further, when paths were highlighted, participants thought that the spatial locations of nodes and link cells were strong visual cues indicating where the transitions happened in the website.

DISCUSSION

The results of our laboratory study indicate that MatrixWave is more effective than Sankey for visual comparison tasks. Except for node tasks where we expected the Sankey to outperform MatrixWave, MatrixWave was either more accurate or significantly faster than Sankey.

For link tasks, MatrixWave and Sankey achieved similar completion times, which was a bit surprising, because we expected that edge crossings would lower the performance of Sankey in both time and accuracy. It could be that highlighting/fading out links and nodes helped to resolve the visual clutter common in Sankey. However, even with highlighting, Sankey's accuracy rate is much lower than that of MatrixWave. This effect became more pronounced when participants had to assess a large number of links. For example, in step tasks, MatrixWave significantly outperformed Sankey in both speed and accuracy rate. The results for path tasks were also surprising. Despite the zig-zag paths, MatrixWave achieved a similar completion time and was more accurate than Sankey. Additionally, users preferred the visual representation of paths in MatrixWave in the form of blue lines. Further research is needed to explore different highlighting techniques and how those interact with the visualization for path tasks.

In practice, one should consider many factors beyond just completion time and errors in making design decisions. For example, if the data is sparse and small, a Sankey diagram might be preferable, because it is familiar to users and will not have much visual clutter. Also, if node or step comparison tasks are most important, the Sankey diagram might be sufficient. But, if the dataset is large and dense, MatrixWave is significantly more effective for all levels of comparison tasks once users become familiar with the visual encodings.

One concern with the MatrixWave design is the layout and the rotated matrices. Although the current design offers the best screen real-estate utilization, it also introduces usability issues. For example, users have to compare nodes in a step along a diagonal axis. The experimental results for node comparison tasks seem to indicate that this is not a big factor for performance, however, participants reported discomfort reading the rotated page labels. In future work we plan to explore how we might use interaction to ameliorate some of this discomfort. For example, we can allow users to rotate an individual matrix in place or the whole visualization when necessary. Another solution is to draw the text labels horizontally. However some part of the text may be obscured by the visualization.

In MatrixWave, we did not encode temporal information beyond order. Although in the exploration of web clickstream data, analysts mainly focus on the logical time of events, i.e., steps, temporal information, such as the duration of a event, is often useful in analyzing event sequence data in other application domains. To represent event durations, MatrixWave can easily be extended to include visual encodings similar to the "time edges" in OutFlow [30] next to a node. In addition, to represent event timestamps, a short line can be drawn on top a node with its position mapped to the delay of the event relative to a reference timeframe.

CONCLUSION AND FUTURE WORK

We have presented MatrixWave, a visualization technique for comparing two event sequence datasets. MatrixWave displays step-by-step clickstream data as a series of transition matrices rotated and concatenated in a zig-zag manner. By involving expert web clickstream analysts in the design process, we explored a number of design alternatives to visually represent two datasets using superposition and explicit encoding. Despite a steep learning curve, participants in a lab study preferred MatrixWave over the conventional Sankey and were more accurate in completing comparison tasks.

There are a number of promising future directions. First, we plan to further evaluate MatrixWave and study how domain experts use it in their everyday work. Second, we want to pursue comparison across multiple datasets. For example, it would be great to be able to show how traffic patterns have changed over an entire week rather than just over two days. Finally, we want to combine multiple event sequence visualization techniques including the Sankey, MatrixWave, and Icicle plot [31] into one system and study how they can be used to together to solve tasks and how analysts can smoothly move from one representation to another.

REFERENCES

1. B. Alper, B. Bach, N. Henry Riche, T. Isenberg, and J.-D. Fekete. Weighted graph comparison techniques for brain connectivity analysis. In *Proc. CHI*, 483–492, 2013.
2. B. Bach, E. Pietriga, and J.-D. Fekete. Graphdiaries: Animated transitions and temporal navigation for dynamic networks. *IEEE TVCG*, 20(5):740–754, 2014.
3. J. Bertin. *Semiology of Graphics: Diagrams, Networks, Maps*. University of Wisconsin Press, 1983.
4. A. Bezerianos, P. Dragicevic, J.-D. Fekete, J. Bae, and B. Watson. GeneaQuilts: A System for Exploring Large Genealogies. *IEEE TVCG*, 16(6):1073–1081, 2010.
5. J. Brainerd and B. Becker. Case study: e-commerce clickstream visualization. In *Proc. InfoVis*, 153, 2001.
6. S. Bremm, T. von Landesberger, M. Hess, T. Schreck, P. Weil, and K. Hamacherk. Interactive visual comparison of multiple trees. In *Proc. VAST*, 31–40, 2011.
7. I. Cadez, D. Heckerman, C. Meek, P. Smyth, and S. White. Visualization of navigation patterns on a web site using model-based clustering. In *Proc. KDD*, 280–284, 2000.
8. M. Ghoniem, J.-D. Fekete, and P. Castagliola. On the readability of graphs using node-link and matrix-based representations: A controlled experiment and statistical analysis. *Info. Vis.*, 4(2):114–135, 2005.
9. M. Gleicher, D. Albers, R. Walker, I. Jusufi, C. D. Hansen, and J. C. Roberts. Visual comparison for information visualization. *Info. Vis.*, 10(4):289–309, 2011.
10. D. Gotz and H. Stavropoulos. Decisionflow: Visual analytics for high-dimensional temporal event sequence data. *IEEE TVCG*, 20(12):1783–1792, 2014.
11. J. Guerra-Gomez, M. Pack, C. Plaisant, and B. Shneiderman. Visualizing change over time using dynamic hierarchies: Treeversity2 and the stemview. *IEEE TVCG*, 19(12):2566–2575, 2013.
12. D. Holten and J. J. van Wijk. Visual comparison of hierarchically organized data. *Comp. Graph. Forum*, 27(3):759–766, 2008.
13. J. I. Hong, J. Heer, S. Waterson, and J. Landay. Webquilt: A proxy-based approach to remote web usability testing. *IEEE Trans. Info. Sys*, 19(3):263–285, 2001.
14. S. Kannappady, S. P. Mudur, and N. Shiri. Visualization of web usage patterns. In *Proc. IDEAS*, 220–227, 2006.
15. M. Krstajic, E. Bertini, and D. Keim. Cloudlines: Compact display of event episodes in multiple time-series. *IEEE TVCG*, 17(12):2432–2439, 2011.
16. B. Lee, G. G. Robertson, M. Czerwinski, and C. S. Parr. Candidtree: visualizing structural uncertainty in similar hierarchies. *Info. Vis.*, 6(3):233–246, 2007.
17. J. Lee, M. Podlaseck, E. Schonberg, and R. Hoch. Visualization and analysis of clickstream data of online stores for understanding web merchandising. *Data Mining and Knowledge Discovery*, 5:59–84, 2001.
18. E. Maguire, P. Rocca-Serra, S.-A. Sansone, J. Davies, and M. Chen. Visual compression of workflow visualizations with automated detection of macro motifs. *IEEE TVCG*, 19(12):2576–2585, 2013.
19. M. Monroe, R. Lan, H. Lee, C. Plaisant, and B. Shneiderman. Temporal event sequence simplification. *IEEE TVCG*, 19(12):2227–2236, 2013.
20. M. Monroe, R. Lan, J. Morales del Olmo, B. Shneiderman, C. Plaisant, and J. Millstein. The challenges of specifying intervals and absences in temporal queries: A graphical language approach. In *Proc. CHI*, 2349–2358, 2013.
21. T. Munzner, F. Guimbretière, S. Tasiran, L. Zhang, and Y. Zhou. Treejuxtaposer: scalable tree comparison using focus+context with guaranteed visibility. *ACM Trans. Graphics*, 22(3):453–462, 2003.
22. A. Perer and J. Sun. Matrixflow: Temporal network visual analytics to track symptom evolution during disease progression. In *Proc. AMIA*, 716–725, 2012.
23. A. Perer and F. Wang. Frequence: Interactive mining and visualization of temporal frequent event sequences. In *Proc. AVI*, 153–162, 2014.
24. C. Plaisant, B. Milash, A. Rose, S. Widoff, and B. Shneiderman. Lifelines: visualizing personal histories. In *Proc. CHI*, 221–227, 1996.
25. P. Riehmann, M. Hanfler, and B. Froehlich. Interactive sankey diagrams. In *Proc. InfoVis*, 233–240, 2005.
26. Y. Tu and H.-W. Shen. Visualizing changes of hierarchical data using treemaps. *IEEE TVCG*, 13(6):1286–1293, 2007.
27. F. van Ham, H. Van De Wetering, and J. van Wijk. Interactive visualization of state transition systems. *IEEE TVCG*, 8(4):319–329, 2002.
28. T. D. Wang, C. Plaisant, A. J. Quinn, R. Stanchak, S. Murphy, and B. Shneiderman. Aligning temporal data by sentinel events: Discovering patterns in electronic health records. In *Proc. CHI*, 457–466, 2008.
29. J. Wei, Z. Shen, N. Sundaresan, and K.-L. Ma. Visual cluster exploration of web clickstream data. In *Proc. VAST*, 3–12, 2012.
30. K. Wongsuphasawat and D. Gotz. Exploring flow, factors, and outcomes of temporal event sequences with the outflow visualization. *IEEE TVCG*, 18(12):2659–2668, 2012.
31. K. Wongsuphasawat, J. A. Guerra Gómez, C. Plaisant, T. D. Wang, M. Taieb-Maimon, and B. Shneiderman. Lifeflow: visualizing an overview of event sequences. In *Proc. CHI*, 1747–1756, 2011.
32. J. Zhao, F. Chevalier, C. Collins, and R. Balakrishnan. Facilitating discourse analysis with interactive visualization. *IEEE TVCG*, 18(12):2639–2648, 2012.
33. J. Zhao, S. M. Drucker, D. Fisher, and D. Brinkman. Timeslice: Interactive faceted browsing of timeline data. In *Proc. AVI*, 433–436, 2012.

The Effects of Representation and Juxtaposition on Graphical Perception of Matrix Visualization

Xiaotong Liu
The Ohio State University
liu.1952@osu.edu

Han-Wei Shen
The Ohio State University
shen.94@osu.edu

ABSTRACT

Analyzing multiple networks at once is a common yet difficult task in many domains. Using adjacency matrices for this purpose, however, can be effective because of its superior ability to accommodate dense networks in a small area. We evaluate various representations and juxtaposition designs for visualizing adjacency matrices through a series of controlled experiments. We investigate the effects of using square matrices and triangular matrices on the speed and accuracy of performing graphical-perception tasks. Based on human symmetric perception, we propose two alternative juxtaposition designs to the conventional side-by-side juxtaposition, and study how users perform visual search and comparison tasks regarding different juxtaposition types. Our results show that the matrix representations have similar performance, and the matrix juxtaposition types perform differently. With the design guidelines derived from our studies, we present a compact visualization termed TileMatrix for juxtaposing a large number of matrices, and demonstrate its effectiveness in analyzing multi-faceted, time-varying networks using real-world data.

Author Keywords

Networks; Information Visualization; Adjacency Matrices

ACM Classification Keywords

H.5.2 [Information Interfaces and Presentation]: User Interfaces – Graphical user interfaces

INTRODUCTION

A network is an abstract data type that represents entities as nodes and their relationships as edges. Examples include social networks, computer networks, biological networks, and organizational networks. Network visualization has become an important research topic aiming to gain an effective overview of complex relational data [4, 8, 14, 15, 16]. Introduced by Jacques Bertin [6], adjacency matrices offer an interesting alternative to conventional node-link diagrams, which can suffer from visual cluttering due to node overlapping and edge crossing. An adjacency matrix shows how nodes are connected together through the intersection of the corresponding row and column. When the connections are undirected, the adjacency matrix is symmetric with respect to the main diagonal. Consequently, the same information is shown in both the upper and lower triangular matrices. Adjacency matrices have been shown more readable than node-link diagrams for many graphical-perception tasks, particularly when networks are dense [2, 10, 19]. Since many real-world networks are naturally dynamic and associated with multiple attributes, analyzing multiple networks at once is a common yet difficult task. Therefore, visualizations that aid users to compare and contrast multiple networks are of great importance.

Juxtaposition is an effective visual design that encourages side-by-side visual comparison of multiple facets of a complex data set, without overplotting or occlusion that may occur in *superimposition*, which overlays many objects in a single visualization. Although conventional side-by-side juxtaposition, or small multiples [6, 29], has been applied to adjacency matrices for comparative analysis [4], it predominantly relies on the use of the viewer's memory and attention shifts to make connections between repeated objects [12]. When too much of the comparative burden is added onto the viewer's mental effort, he or she can fail to detect changes even if the information is well represented in the visualization [25]. Designing appropriate juxtaposed visualization for adjacency matrices, which allows visual processing to connect patterns across multiple matrices with less mental effort, is still an open problem. Furthermore, an effective representation of multiple adjacency matrices is an instance of fundamental visualization research: making more effective use of display space to increase the amount of data with which users can effectively work [13, 29]. However, it remains unclear how different matrix representations and juxtaposition designs affect the ability of users to quickly and reliably understand the underlying information.

In this paper, we evaluate the representation and juxtaposition designs for visualizing adjacency matrices through a series of controlled experiments. We investigate the effects of matrix representation on the speed and accuracy of performing graphical-perception tasks. Based on *human symmetric perception*, an automatic visual process that forms an integral part of perceptual organization [30], we propose two alternative juxtaposition designs to the conventional side-by-side juxtaposition, and study how users perform visual search and

CHI 2015, April 18–23, 2015, Seoul, Republic of Korea.

ACM 978-1-4503-3145-6/15/04 ...$15.00.
http://dx.doi.org/10.1145/2702123.2702217

comparison tasks regarding these juxtaposition types. Our results show that triangular matrices are as effective as square matrices, and the juxtaposition types (*side-by-side*, *back-to-back*, and *complementary*) perform differently. With the design guidelines derived from our studies, we present a compact visualization termed *TileMatrix* for juxtaposing a large number of matrices, and demonstrate its effectiveness in analyzing multi-faceted, time-varying networks using real-world data.

RELATED WORK

Previous research related to this work can be classified as follows: matrix visualization, graphical perception, and comparative visualization.

Matrix Visualization

The node-link diagram and adjacency matrix are the most popular for network visualization. Node-link diagrams are generally suitable for sparse networks while adjacency matrices are more effective for dense networks, as shown by Ghoniem et al. [10], Keller et al. [19] and Alper et al. [2]. Many research efforts have recently been made to enhance the usability and readability of matrix-based network visualization. MatrixExplorer [15] couples a node-link diagram and an adjacency matrix representation of the same network by juxtaposed views. MatLink [16] augments matrix representation with links connecting nodes in lines and columns to reconcile the difficulty of path-related tasks in matrix visualization [10]. NodeTrix [14] visualizes community structures (dense sub-networks) as adjacency matrices, which are then reconnected with links that represent the sparse parts of the network. Dinkla et al. [8] exploited the structural characteristics of gene regulatory networks to design compressed adjacency matrices. Behrisch et al. [5] placed matrices of high similarity together in a projection space. However, such automated approach cannot reveal multiple facets of the data, and the order in time is lost after projection, which can make it difficult to identify trends of networks over time. Cubix [4] stacks adjacency matrices over time to form a 3D space-time cube, and supports interactive transitions to projected 2D juxtaposed views. While most previous works employed square matrices for visualizing networks, we explored the effects of triangular matrices and their use in designing compact juxtaposed visualization for showing more readable networks within a limited display space.

Graphical Perception

Graphical perception is defined as the visual decoding of information encoded on graphical displays [7]. Cleveland and McGill [7] established a scientific foundation of graphical methods for data analysis and representation through human graphical perception. Since then, evaluating user performance on graphical perception has been an important research topic in the fields of human computer interaction and information visualization. Lohse [21, 22] developed a cognitive model for perception and understanding of graphs, and performed an empirical study to compare computer-simulated graphical perception based on his model with the actual user performance. Gillan and Lewis [11] also proposed a perceptual model and investigated human interaction with graphs, by asking users to accomplish visual comparison tasks using various visualizations such as line graphs, scatter plots, and stacked bar graphs.

Graphical-perception tasks measure how users interpret the information encoded on graphical displays. The effects of visual variables for various graphical-perception tasks have been explored in the literature. Heer et al. [13] conducted two controlled experiments to measure the effects of chart size and layering on user performance while performing visual discrimination and estimation tasks. Javed et al. [18] evaluated user performance for visual comparison, slope, and discrimination tasks for multiple line graph visualizations. Fuchs et al. [9] investigated user performance of different temporal glyph designs in a small multiple setting. Most recently, Albers et al. [1] measured user performance of several visualization design choices for matching visual encodings to various aggregate comparison tasks. Our work attempts to empirically evaluate the effects of visual representation and juxtaposition on graphical perception of adjacency matrices.

Comparative Visualization

Visual analysis often involves visual comparison of multiple objects. Gleicher et al. [12] described juxtaposition, superimposition, and explicit encoding as three generic design approaches to visual comparison, and suggested that multiple designs can be combined to created hybrid comparative visualization. Meanwhile, Javed and Elmqvist [17] divided the design space of composite visualization into juxtaposition, superimposition, overloading and nesting. Jacques Bertin [6] and Edward Tufte [29] introduced small multiples, the most popular juxtaposition design in both the scientific literature and the mass media. Such side-by-side design has been shown more effective than animation for dynamic networks [3] and trends [24]. Tominski et al. [28] proposed shine-through and folding interactions for visual comparison besides side-by-side comparison. Far more examples are given by Gleicher et al. [12] in a survey of over 110 references on visual comparison for information visualization. Our goal is to obtain a more general understanding about the design of alternatives juxtaposition for adjacency matrix visualization, not just the conventional side-by-side juxtaposition.

STUDY 1: EVALUATING MATRIX REPRESENTATION

As stated in the beginning, a symmetric adjacency matrix can be represented in either a square matrix (Figure 1 (left)) or a triangular matrix (Figure 1 (right)). The goal of the first experiment is to determine the impact of the matrix representation on the user's graphical perception: how does the choice of square or triangular matrices affect user performance?

Tasks

To keep the experiment manageable in time and effort for the participants, we did not include complex tasks related to finding paths and common neighbors since they can be difficult for the given matrix visualization [10]. Rather, such tasks can be accomplished more easily with node-link diagrams [10] or with additional visual cues [16]. Since we were interested in studying the effects of two different representations, tasks that are less relevant to the representation, such as counting

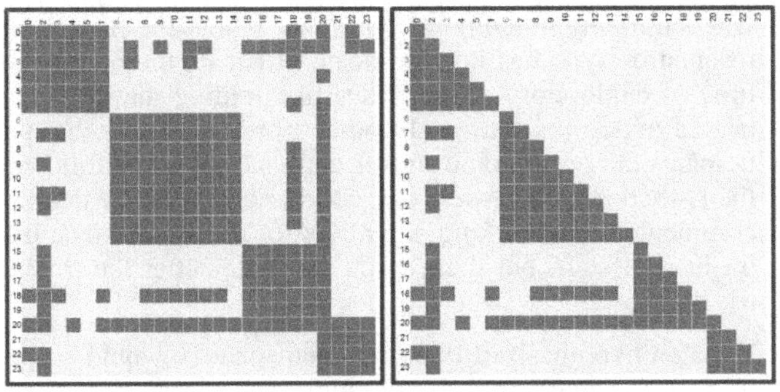

Figure 1. Adjacency matrix representations. Left: a square matrix representation. Right: a triangular matrix representation.

the number of nodes or finding a node given its label [10], were also excluded in our experiment. Finally, three generic tasks were selected in an attempt to capture both overview and detail use cases of matrix visualization:

(T1) *How many communities can you identify in the matrix?*

(T2) *Which node has the maximum number of neighbors?*

(T3) *Are the two specified nodes connected in the matrix?*

T1 is an overview graphical-perception task that represents a common use case of matrix visualization for community detection in networks [14]. T2 is an exploratory visual search task that requires browsing through the visualization to find information. T3 is a confirmatory visual search task that asks the users to make judgments once they locate the specified targets. T1 and T2 are related to the interpretation of blocks (communities) and lines (a node's neighbors), which are categorized as structural features by Mueller et al. [23]; T2 and T3 were also used in previous studies [10, 19].

Hypotheses

(H1) *The square matrix will perform as well as the triangular matrix for overview perception (T1).* For viewing the shapes of communities in a matrix, we believe that squares and triangles should be equally easy for perception.

(H2) *The square matrix will outperform the triangular matrix for exploratory search (T2).* For square matrices, users scan through rows or columns to view the neighbors of one node; for triangular matrices, users need to follow an L-shaped path to view the corresponding neighbors. We expect that following a straight line in rows or columns will have better user performance than following an L-shaped path.

(H3) *The square matrix will outperform the triangular matrix for confirmatory search (T3).* Square matrices encode one connection between two nodes twice in the visualization, while triangular matrices represent the connection exactly once. We predict that the repetition of such information will have a direct effect on user performance.

Experiment Design

The study was conducted as a within-subjects experiment with 2 experimental conditions (matrix representations) and 10 repetitions for each condition. For each repetition, the participant was presented with only one condition. We counterbalanced the selection of condition in the 10 repetitions so that each participant performed the same number of repetitions for both conditions while the choice of condition is random.

In the spirit of classic graphical perception experiments [9, 13, 18], we evaluated the different visual representations alone, disabling selecting, highlighting, zooming, and other interactive operations. Ghoniem et al. [10] have shown that in most cases, matrix visualization was insensitive to size and density variation and no interaction between size and density was found for the matrix representation. Hence, while the size and density of the matrices vary across repetitions for creating diverse experimental datasets, the effects due to size and density were not explicitly studied in our experiment.

We follow the convention of perception studies [13, 18, 20] in using synthetic data to allow control over the characteristics of experimental datasets. We first generated a random number of communities of varying sizes, then added a random number of edges for randomly selected nodes. In order to eliminate any ambiguity with respect to T2, which is to find the most connected node, we added an extra 20% of edges to the most connected node in every matrix. We labeled the nodes numerically according to the order of their creation, and ordered the nodes in such a way that those from the same community are placed together to preserve the community structures in the matrix. In this way, we obtained repetitions of varying number of nodes (from 20 to 50) and edges (density from 0.2 to 0.5), as well as varying number of communities (from 3 to 6). Specifically, the labels of the two specified nodes for T3 are highlighted in a distinct color. Figure 1 shows one example of the datasets we used for this experiment.

20 subjects (14 males, 6 females) were recruited for this experiment. The subjects were graduate students, aged 24 to 32 years. Half of the subjects have backgrounds in computer science, and most are using a computer more than 20 hours per week. All subjects have normal or corrected-to-normal vision. 40% of the subjects said they were familiar with matrix visualization.

We deployed the experiment on the web using HTML5 and JavaScript. Each subject used their own machine and browser, and the visualization images were scaled to fit the corresponding screen space before the test. Due to our within-subjects design, each user performed tasks regarding different representation types on the same screen he or she had. Hence, the influence of screen size has been alleviated when studying the effects of representation types. Prior to the experiment, subjects viewed a tutorial that gave a basic explanation of the two matrix representations, and they performed some training tasks to get familiar with the user interface of the experimental system. We asked the subjects to answer as quickly as possible while trying to make answers accurate. After the subjects finished tasks for all repetitions, they were asked to participate in a semi-structured interview.

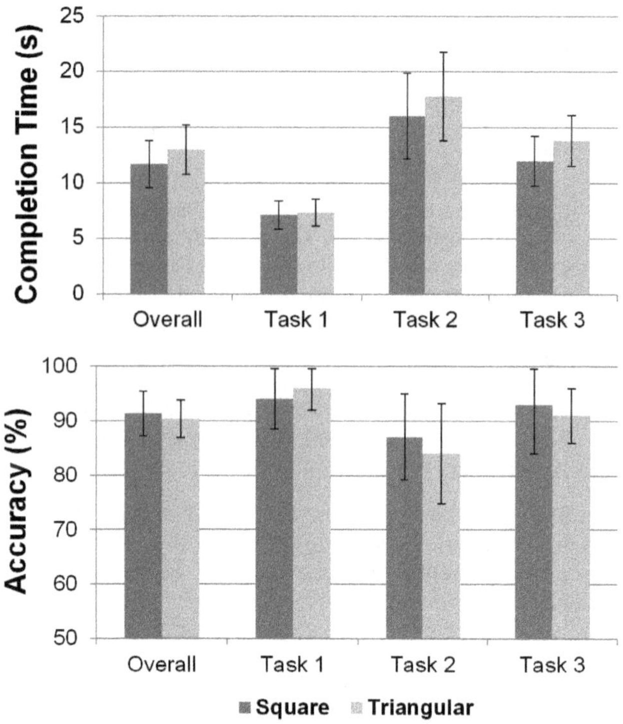

Figure 2. Mean completion time and accuracy for Study 1.

Table 1. RM-ANOVA analysis of results for Study 1.

	Factor	$F_{1,19}$	p
Overall	Time	0.82	0.37
	Accuracy	0.16	0.69
T1	Time	0.08	0.79
	Accuracy	0.40	0.53
T2	Time	0.48	0.49
	Accuracy	0.29	0.60
T3	Time	1.56	0.22
	Accuracy	0.18	0.68

Results and Discussion

We measured the time participants needed to complete each task and the correctness of their reported answers. User performance measures were evaluated using Repeated Measures Analysis of Variance (RM-ANOVA) to test for significant effects. For each participant's performance, we used the average of the repetitions for the following analysis. We report completion time and accuracy in Figure 2 and our RM-ANOVA analysis in Table 1.

Our first hypothesis was that the square matrix would perform as well as the triangular matrix for overview perception. This hypothesis was confirmed. We found that the accuracy and completion time were almost the same across the two representations, which indicates that users were able to interpret communities in both representations.

One surprising outcome of our study is that the matrix representation type has no significant effect on the completion time of exploratory search tasks like finding the most connected node in a matrix. In other words, it seems that participants did not become significantly slower when following the L-shaped path to view one node's neighbors. Participants commented that tracking neighbors for one node was a little bit hard at start, but their speed got faster after the training trials.

We also hypothesized that the square matrix would outperform the triangular matrix for confirmatory search. Contrary to our hypothesis, our quantitative results did not show significant differences between the matrix representations. Rather, these results indicate that the participants performed equally well in the confirmatory search, regardless of the matrix representations.

Overall, results from our first experiment revealed that users were able to interpret triangular matrices correctly, and their task performance with the triangular matrix was comparable to that with the square matrix.

STUDY 2: EVALUATING MATRIX JUXTAPOSITION

The goal of the second experiment is to investigate the effects of juxtaposition types in the presence of multiple adjacency matrices. More specifically, we are interested to see how users perform visual search and comparison tasks under different juxtapositions. Is there a benefit to introducing more types of juxtapositions other than conventional side-by-side juxtaposition?

In our previous experiment we found that square and triangular representations of adjacency matrix had comparable accuracy and completion time, so we removed square matrices from consideration in this experiment and focused on comparing triangular matrices of different juxtaposition types.

Matrix Juxtaposition

We divide the design space of comparative juxtaposition into three general types, based on how the relationships between the related parts of different adjacency matrices are encoded:

Side-by-side juxtaposition (SID), also known as small multiples [29], repeats the same representation multiple times without any modification to the design (Figure 3 (left)), and has been applied to various domains such as system management, quality control, and medical record analysis [29]. This *translational juxtaposition* is the conventional design of comparative juxtaposition.

Back-to-back juxtaposition (BAC), which reverts the order of the rows or columns in one of two matrices to form a symmetric composition (Figure 3 (middle)). This design is motivated by human symmetric perception, which is an automatic visual process that forms an integral part of perceptual organization [30]. Such *symmetric juxtaposition* has been shown effective in identifying similarity and contrasts in computer-aided diagnosis. For example, radiologists are using the differences between the symmetric juxtaposition of left and right breasts in mammograms (photographs of breasts made by X-rays) to help detect certain malignant breast cancers [26].

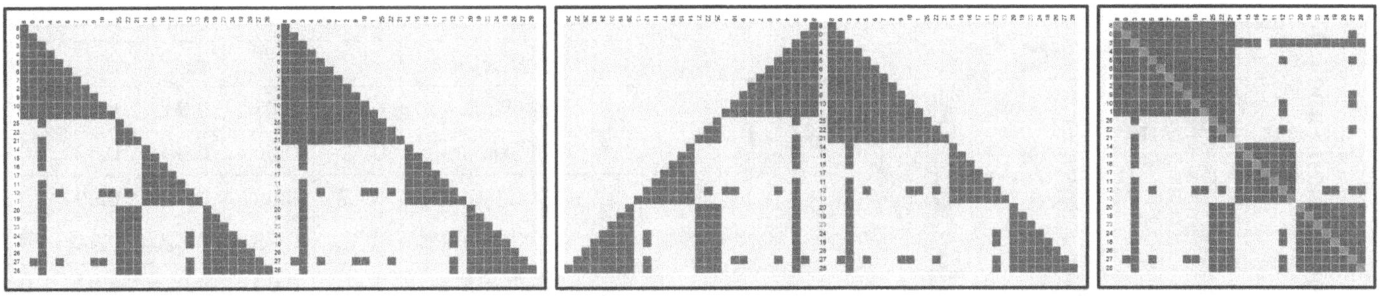

Figure 3. Adjacency matrix juxtapositions. Left: side-by-side juxtaposition (SID). Middle: back-to-back juxtaposition (BAC). Right: complementary juxtaposition (COM).

Complementary juxtaposition (COM), which takes two triangular matrices together to form a compact square matrix. Consequently, the rows and columns in the two matrices are complementary, and the positions of cells in the two matrices are symmetric with respect to the main diagonal (Figure 3 (right)). In other words, two triangular matrices form an asymmetric square matrix. This design is a variant of back-to-back juxtaposition, and only applies to triangular matrices.

We think these three juxtaposition types are *fundamental*: they define the juxtaposed relationship of two matrices (translational juxtaposition for **SID** or symmetric juxtaposition for **BAC** & **COM**), representing the basic cases for comparative visualization. More importantly, they provide the building blocks that can assemble complex juxtaposition of many more matrices. In other words, the three juxtaposition types can be combined to create hybrid juxtaposed visualization.

Tasks

Typical visual comparison tasks often require users to scan and compare related elements simultaneously. Three tasks, modified from the tasks selected in our previous experiment, were included in this experiment:

(T4) *Does the largest community have the same number of nodes in the following matrices?*

(T5) *Does the most connected node have the same number of neighbors in the following matrices?*

(T6) *How many times (0, 1, or 2) are the two specified nodes connected in the following matrices?*

In each task, users were asked to identify multiple targets within two matrices presented in one of the three juxtaposition types, and determine the similarity or difference of the targets. As in our prior experiment, these tasks were selected to represent overview and detail use cases of matrix visualizations, with a balance between task complexity and suitability.

Hypotheses

(H4) *For tasks involving comparison of structures and patterns in matrices (T4, T5), BAC & COM (symmetric juxtaposition) will outperform SID (translational juxtaposition) in task completion time.* The strength of symmetric perception is that it allows easier comparison of shapes across objects. We believe that the mental alignment due to symmetric perception will result in better completion time by connecting patterns and reveal their differences across matrices.

(H5) *When searching and comparing a specific target in matrices (T6), SID, BAC and COM will have comparable performance.* Comparing a specific target requires accurately locating the same item across matrices. We predict that symmetric juxtaposition requires more mental effort to locate a specific target across matrices. However, we think that the easier mental alignment due to symmetric perception compensates this additional effort, resulting in a performance comparable to that obtained using translational juxtaposition.

Experiment Design

The experiment used a 3 (juxtaposition) $\times$ 3 (task) within-subjects design with 9 repetitions. For each repetition, the participant was presented with only one condition. We counter-balanced the repetitions so that each participants performed the same number of conditions for three conditions while the selection of condition in each repetition was random.

We followed the design choices we made in our previous experiment. We first generated matrices that have varying numbers of nodes (from 20 to 50) and edges (density from 0.2 to 0.5), and varying numbers of communities (from 3 to 6). Then for each generated matrix, we randomly assigned several nodes to a different community and added edges for randomly selected nodes to get a new matrix. The two matrices were then grouped using one of the three juxtaposition types. Figure 3 shows one example of the datasets we obtained for this experiment.

We recruited 28 subjects (17 males, 11 females, aged 24 to 39 years), who are graduate students or professionals from the fields of computer science, electric engineering, chemistry, statistics, geographic information science, to name a few. Half of the subjects had previously participated in the first experiment. 36% of the subjects said they had experience with multiple matrix visualization. The experiment follows a similar procedure to the prior experiment. After the subjects finished all tasks, they were asked to rate their satisfaction with **SID**, **BAC** and **COM** in each task on a questionnaire (e.g., *Which view do you think is the best to identify the size difference of the largest community? (A: side-by-side; B: back-to-back; C: complementary; D: no preference)*). Finally, they were asked to participate in a semi-structured interview.

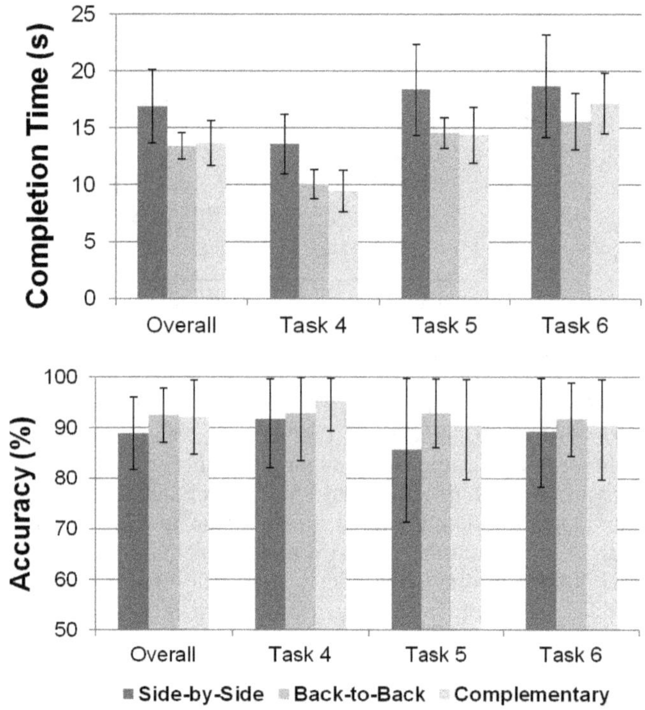

Figure 4. Mean completion time and accuracy for Study 2.

Table 2. RM-ANOVA analysis for Study 2 (s:SID, b:BAC, c:COM).

	Factor	$F_{2,54}$	$p_{s,b,c}$	$p_{s,b}$	$p_{s,c}$	$p_{b,c}$
Overall	Time	4.81	**0.01**	**0.01**	**0.03**	0.77
	Accuracy	0.59	0.56	0.30	0.42	0.91
T4	Time	8.47	**0.001**	**0.003**	**0.001**	0.49
	Accuracy	0.32	0.73	0.82	0.41	0.57
T5	Time	4.30	**0.02**	**0.02**	**0.03**	0.86
	Accuracy	0.73	0.49	0.25	0.49	0.63
T6	Time	1.46	0.24	0.12	0.46	0.26
	Accuracy	0.10	0.91	0.64	0.84	0.81

Table 3. Subjective user preference for tasks in Study 2.

	SID	BAC	COM	None
T4	0%	46%	50%	4%
T5	10%	36%	40%	14%
T6	21%	21%	18%	40%

Results and Discussion

We report completion time and accuracy in Figure 4. Statistical significance was tested for all groups and each pair respectively. Table 2 summarizes all results and highlights the significant ones. The qualitative feedback is shown afterwards in Table 3.

In H4 we hypothesized that **BAC** & **COM** would be faster than **SID** due to their symmetric alignment for detecting changes of structures and patterns in matrices. This hypothesis was confirmed. We found that **SID** took significantly longer time than **BAC** & **COM**. This result validates our design goals: facilitating identification of the repeated patterns and differences of connectivity between juxtaposed matrices. Subject ratings (Table 3) confirmed that most participants preferred either **BAC** or **COM** in accomplishing T4 and T5. Participants commented that **BAC** and **COM** are helpful in connecting the left and right matrices, while **SID** requires more mental effort in certain cases.

Our results confirmed H5: **BAC** & **COM** would not have a negative impact on performance when searching and comparing a specific target in matrices. We found no significant difference between the juxtaposition types in task completion time or accuracy. Participants do not seem to have a strong preference in choosing a particular juxtaposition for T6. Accuracy seems to stabilize at a high rate for each task in any juxtaposition. It indicates that the participants were equally careful in visual comparison, regardless of juxtaposition type.

DESIGN IMPLICATIONS

Based on our experimental results, we offer the following implications for designing adjacency matrix visualizations:

Triangular representation does not hamper graphical perception of adjacency matrices. One unexpected result was that the triangular matrix neither slowed down the task completion time nor hurt the accuracy. The triangular representation cuts the size of the matrix in half without any observed downside, as long as the viewer learns how to interpret the triangular matrix.

Symmetric juxtaposition rather than translational juxtaposition should be preferred for detecting changes of structures and patterns. The mental alignment due to symmetric perception is able to connect patterns and structures across matrices, which facilitates visual comparison with less mental effort.

Complementary juxtaposition is beneficial for optimizing utilization of display space. Since complementary juxtaposition doubles the data density (data marks per display area) compared to other juxtaposition types, we advocate its use when space constraints warrant.

TILEMATRIX: CREATING COMPACT VISUALIZATION BY TILING THE MATRICES

With the design implications, we devise a compact visualization — *TileMatrix*, coupling the side-by-side juxtaposition, back-to-back juxtaposition and complementary juxtaposition to display a large number of adjacency matrices. The TileMatrix representation is inspired by the physical act of laying tiles to cover floors, walls, ceilings and roofs. A *tile* is generally designed in an interlocking pattern so that multiple tiles fit together to have an aesthetic appearance. In TileMatrix, one tile is a triangular matrix. Every two adjacent matrices are placed in either back-to-back juxtaposition or complementary juxtaposition, resulting in a hybrid juxtaposition that also includes side-by-side juxtaposition . In the following sections, we first discuss typical usage scenarios for displaying a large number of matrices, and then describe our TileMatrix system. We demonstrate its effectiveness in a case study using real-world data, and report initial user feedback.

Usage Scenarios

A weighted network associates a weight with every edge in the network, representing the strength of the connection between the entities [2]. In many network applications, the weights of edges can be quite complex and dynamic. On the one hand, the weight of the connection between the entities can change as multiple facets are associated with the connection. For instance, consider a collection of National Basketball Association (NBA) players as the entities, who are connected either strongly or weakly based on the similarity of their performance. Each player is associated with multiple performance facets: points, rebounds, assists, steals, blocks, and many others. Therefore, players can have different weights of connections on different facets. On the other hand, the weight of a connection between the entities can change over time. This is also seen in the NBA players example since their performance often vary in different years.

Visual analysis of such multi-faceted, time-varying weighted networks is challenging as the number of networks grows in both data and temporal domains. Although we can always reduce the number of facets using dimension reduction techniques or aggregate networks over time, we learn little about the heterogeneity nor the dynamics of the network. The reduced dimensions do not always have a semantic interpretation, and the temporal differences are hidden in temporal aggregation. Consequently, we understand neither how to interpret the relationships from multiple perspectives nor how certain temporal trends are formed.

TileMatrix offers one alternative solution to visualizing multi-faceted, time-varying weighted networks without losing information — the matrices of networks are tiled simultaneously in two directions of the display space: matrices in different facets are tiled in columns while matrices over time are tiled in rows. In this way, the viewer can examine and compare networks of multiple facets at a particular time step (horizontally), as well as networks of a particular facets over time (vertically). The repeated patterns and differences in the relationship of entities can be identified, in both data and temporal domains.

Case Study

To demonstrate the effectiveness of TileMatrix, we used our system to explore the NBA statistics dataset [27], which consists of 16 performance facets for NBA players: GP (Games Played), MIN (Minutes Played), PT (Points Scored), AST (Assists), REB (Rebounds), STL (Steals), BLK (Blocked Shots), TO (Turnovers), ORE (Offensive Rebounds), DRE (Defensive Rebounds), FGA (Field Goals Attempted), FGM (Field Goals Made), FTA (Free Throws Attempted), FTM (Free Throws Made), TPA (Three Point Attempted), and TPM (Three Point Made). To view a relatively large number of matrices with TileMatrix, in this study we extracted players that have relatively longer NBA careers (at least 15 years compared to an average career length of 5 years) from 1989 to 2003. This gave us 11 NBA players: Horace Grant, Reggie Miller, Vlade Divac, Avery Johnson, Glen Rice, Karl Malone, Scottie Pippen, Charles Oakley, Kevin Willis, Rod Strickland, and Mark Jackson. The similarity networks for all pairs of players were computed regarding each facet for each year. The corresponding TileMatrix contains $16 * 15 * 11 * 11/2 = 14520$ cells. The color of self-connections is set to grey. Matrices of adjacent facets are assigned similar colors while distant facets are colored differently for overall appearance.

By analyzing the semantic meaning of the performance facets, we roughly categorized them into three groups based on the criteria of the performance measurement: *activity* = {GP, MIN}, *score* = {PT, FGA, FGM, FTA, FTM, TPA, TPM}, *aid* = {AST, STL, BLK, REB, ORE, DRE, TO}. Therefore, we reordered the facets in TileMatrix to place related facets in the same category closer. To highlight the contrasts between highly and weakly connected nodes, we reordered the nodes by the weighted average degree.

Figure 5 shows the resulting TileMatrix visualization after reordering. Facets are labeled on the top of TileMatrix while years are on the left. The names of the players are also labeled accordingly. From the TileMatrix visualization, we had a few key findings on the multi-faceted, time-varying relationships of the NBA players that had relatively longer careers:

Temporal trends regarding a particular facet. To understand the time-varying similarity/dissimilarity of players' performance with respect to one facet, we can simply view matrices form a column of TileMatrix. For example, the left-most column of TileMatrix in Figure 5 shows the time-varying similarity networks based on the number of games the players had played, from which we can observe the following trend: (a) in 1989, 1991, and 1997: one or two players had played quite a different number of games compared to the rest of players, as the their connections to the others were relatively weak (e.g., CO (Charles Oakley) and AJ (Avery Johnson) in 1989, VD (Vlade Divac) in 1991, and SP (Scottie Pippen) in 1997); (b) in 1992, 1993, 1996 and 1999: the number of games played were almost the same among the players, since the matrix cells show very strong connections; (c) during 2000-2003: players started to have distinct degrees of activity, and the differences seemed to reach a peak at the end of this time window (e.g., in 2003, most players were strongly connected to only a few other players while weekly connected to the majority). This could be partly because some players had played for many years, and their performance became diverse compared with their early career.

Repeated patterns across multiple facets at a specific time. As implied from our experiments, the symmetric juxtaposition has significant effects on connecting patterns and structures across matrices. To view the multi-faceted similarity/dissimilarity of players' performance at a specific time, we can focus on one row of matrices in TileMatrix. For instance, the first row of TileMatrix in Figure 5 shows the multi-faceted similarity networks of players in 1989. Approximately repeated visual patterns can be identified between the following groups of facets respectively: FGA & FGM, FTA & FTM,

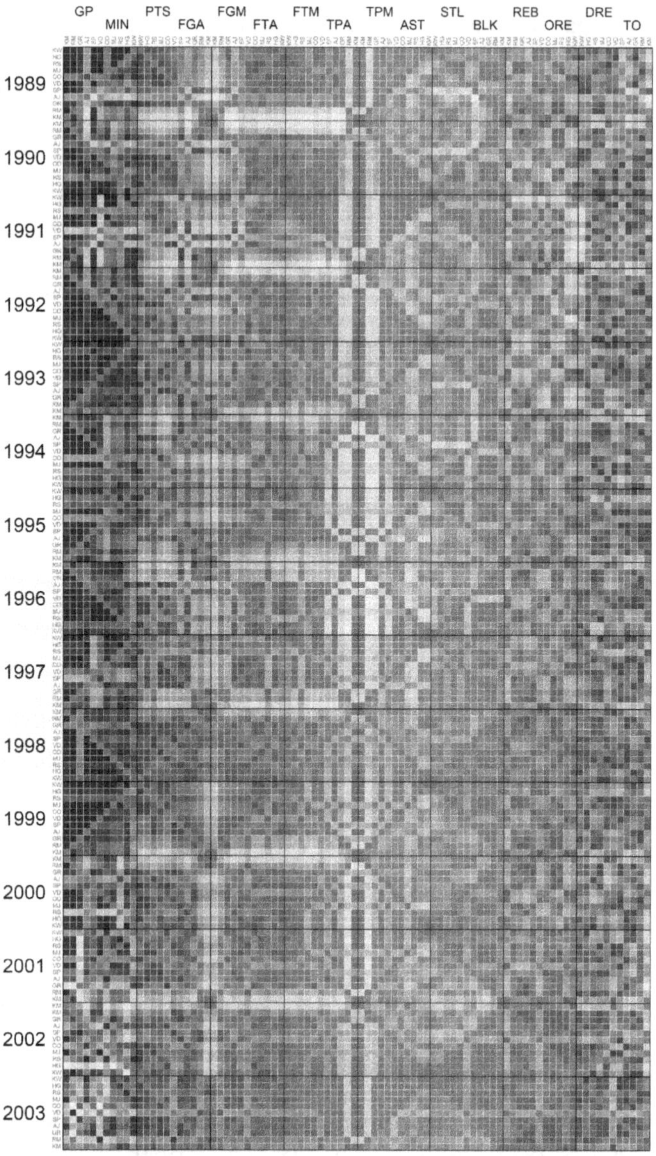

Figure 5. The TileMatrix visualization of 16-faceted similarity networks of National Basketball Association (NBA) players from 1989 to 2003. Matrices of different facets are tiled in columns, while matrices of different years are tiled in rows. The color opacity encodes the strength of the connection.

and TPA & TPM. From a zoom-in view of the facets in Figure 6 (a), we learned that: if one player (e.g., RM (Reggie Miller)) behaved differently from the others in one facet (e.g., TPA), he was very likely to perform differently from the others in another related facet (e.g., TPM); if the performance of a group of players (e.g., KW (Kevin Willis), HG (Horace Grant), RS (Rod Strickland), MJ (Mark Jackson), CO (Charles Oakley), VD (Vlade Divac)) were similar to each other in one facet (e.g., FTM), such similarity relationship could also be found in another related facet (e.g., FTA).

Contrasts between multiple facets at a specific time. Another implication from our experiments is that the symmetric juxtaposition also helps reveal contrasts between adjacent facets. Take the similarity networks on ORE and DRE in

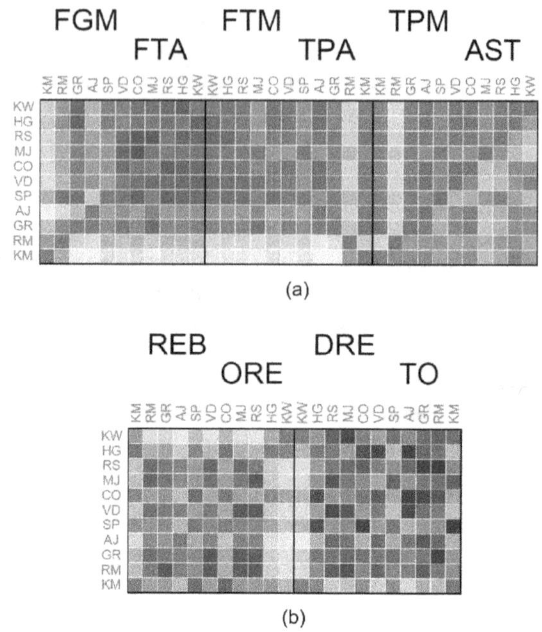

Figure 6. Two zoom-in views of the TileMatrix visualization in Figure 5. (a) Matrices of 6 selected facets (FGM, FTA, FTM, TPA, TPM, AST) in 1989. (b) Matrices of 4 selected facets (REB, ORE, DRE, TO) in 1991.

1991 as an example (shown in Figure 6 (b)). We observed that the degree of dissimilarity to other players are different between offensive rebounds and defensive rebounds for HG (Horace Grant), while it roughly stayed the same for KW (Kevin Willis). A comparison between REB and TO for the connections of KW (Kevin Willis) also highlights the contrasts between these two facets: his performance was more different from others on rebounds than on turnovers.

Temporal trends regarding multiple facets. Because of the two dimensional tiling layout in TileMatrix, we are able to examine the temporal trends of adjacent facets, by viewing matrices in adjacent columns as a whole. For example, the columns of TPA and TPM of TileMatrix in Figure 5 shows a trend for the dissimilarity of players' performance regarding these two facets: (a) starting from 1989, only one player RM (Reggie Miller) performed differently from the others; (b) the difference among players became more and more obvious over the years until it reached top in 1996, when three players performed very differently from the others regarding both three point shots and scores; (c) after that, the degree of dissimilarity among the players dropped; (d) finally in 2003, RM (Reggie Miller) once again became the only one that performed differently compared with the other players, just like how the trend started in 1989. Comparisons between other related facets also revealed interesting temporal trends.

Informal User Feedback

We observed six users (5 males, 1 female) viewing the TileMatrix in Figure 5, and a conventional side-by-side juxtaposed view of square matrices (denoted as SidMatrix) in Figure 7. SidMatrix displays the same number of matrices as TileMatrix with the same color encoding. We explained the designs of TileMatrix and SidMatrix to the users, and how the

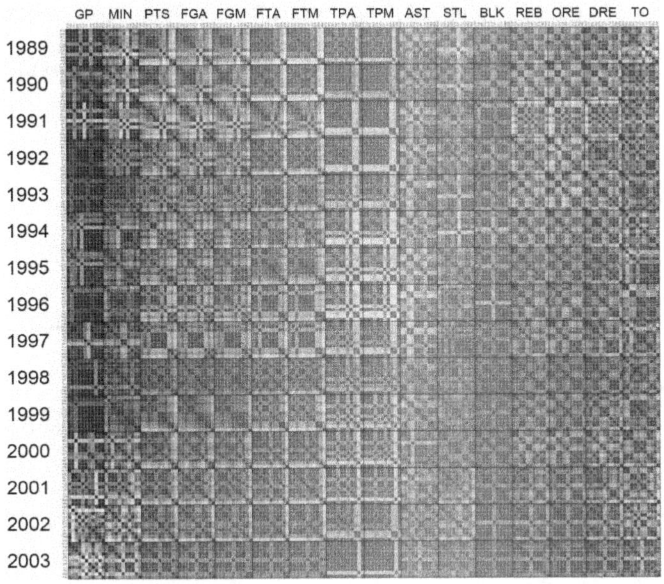

Figure 7. The side-by-side juxtaposed matrix visualization (SidMatrix) for the same data as TileMatrix in Figure 5.

information of the multi-faceted, time-varying similarity networks of NBA players is presented. Our task was very informal, simply asking them to comment on their understanding and visual comfort of the two visualizations, and how easily they could find interesting trends in each visualization. The two visualizations were uniformly scaled to the same width and put side by side for direct comparison.

As initial feedback, all six participants were able to understand TileMatrix as well as SidMatrix. One general feedback is that a cell in SidMatrix is much smaller and less legible than that in TileMatrix. This is expected since the two visualizations display the same number of matrices, square matrices in SidMatrix take double space compared with triangular matrices in TileMatrix, and thus each cell in SidMatirx is displayed in half size of that in TileMatrix. Participants commented that TileMatrix was easier to see details. They were more comfortable in seeing larger cells with more effective information in TileMatrix. Participants also explained that with TileMatrix, it was easier to compare adjacent matrices when they are in back-to-back or complementary juxtaposition, since the symmetric layout helped them to see the subtle differences, which were not as obvious in SidMatrix. However, some participants reported that TileMatrix required more training effort to follow the L-shaped path when viewing the connections of a particular player, while they were used to following straight lines in SidMatrix. This is consistent with the findings in our first controlled experiment.

Our observations partly explained the tradeoffs of introducing hybrid juxtapositions of triangular matrices in visualizing a large number of networks. While such hybrid design makes better use of the display space, and may be useful for identifying repeated patterns and differences across multiple matrices more comfortably and clearly, it requires more training effort than the conventional side-by-side juxtaposed visualization.

DISCUSSION AND FUTURE WORK

As stated in the beginning, the triangular matrix works when the connections in a network are undirected. As for directed networks, it is not possible to increase the data density by juxtaposing triangular matrices. Our experiments considered a small set of generic tasks for matrix visualization. We believe these findings generalize to a wider range of situations, but have not confirmed this empirically. Also we did not include interactive operations in our experiments but only focused on evaluating the effects of different representations and juxtapositions alone. Still, future work is needed to determine the additional effects when visualization is augmented by interaction.

Our TileMatrix design is effective in viewing the similarity and differences in matrices across facets and time, in particular for comparing matrices placed at nearby locations. On the other hand, using TileMatrix requires training to follow L-shaped paths when viewing one node's neighbors, and thus perhaps requiring more effort when tracing one node's neighbors across multiple matrices. Providing additional interactions such as highlighting one's neighbors across matrices when selecting a node could be helpful. Although the effect of colors used in TileMarix was not explicitly studied in our experiments, the design of TileMatrix can be easily extended, and the task performance with additional factors such as colors will be investigated in the future.

The scalability of TileMatrix depends on several factors: the number of attributes (M), the number of time steps (T), and the number of entities per attribute per time step (N). The total number of cells in TileMatrix is $M * T * N * N / 2$. Given a display screen, a tradeoff between N, M and T must be made when using TileMatrix, for example: (1) the network is small so many attributes and/or time steps are shown (as in our case study); (2) the network is medium sized so a medium number of attributes and time steps are shown; and (3) the network is large, thus a few selected attributes and time steps are shown. We note that if the display screen cannot hold all cells, panning and zooming could be provided to view sub-regions on demand. Although we demonstrate the effectiveness of our TileMatrix design with a case study and informal user feedback, the trade-off between design complexity and task performance needs to be better understood in the future.

CONCLUSION

In this paper, we conducted two controlled experiments to assess the performance of adjacency matrices in two representations — square matrices and triangular matrices, and three juxtaposition designs — side-by-side juxtaposition, back-to-back juxtaposition, and complementary juxtaposition. We quantitatively measured speed and accuracy based on generic tasks in each experiment. The results showed that triangular matrices were as effective as square matrices, and the three juxtaposition types performed differently. We showed that back-to-back juxtaposition and complementary juxtaposition are generally a good choice for detecting changes of structures and patterns across matrices due to the mental alignment of symmetric perception. Based on the design guidelines derived from our studies, we propose a compact visualization termed TileMatrix for juxtaposing a large number of matrices, and show its benefits in analyzing multi-faceted, time-varying networks using real-world data.

ACKNOWLEDGMENTS

This work was supported in part by NSF grant IIS-1017635 and IIS-1065025, DOE grant DOESC0005036, and DOE SciDAC grant DE-FC02-06ER25779; program manager Lucy Nowell.

REFERENCES

1. Albers, D., Correll, M., and Gleicher, M. Task-driven evaluation of aggregation in time series visualization. In *CHI* (2014).
2. Alper, B., Bach, B., Henry Riche, N., Isenberg, T., and Fekete, J.-D. Weighted graph comparison techniques for brain connectivity analysis. In *CHI* (2013).
3. Archambault, D., Purchase, H. C., and Pinaud, B. Animation, small multiples, and the effect of mental map preservation in dynamic graphs. *TVCG* (2011).
4. Bach, B., Pietriga, E., and Fekete, J.-D. Visualizing dynamic networks with matrix cubes. In *CHI* (2014).
5. Behrisch, M., Davey, J., Fischer, F., Thonnard, O., Schreck, T., Keim, D., and Kohlhammer, J. Visual analysis of sets of heterogeneous matrices using projection-based distance functions and semantic zoom. *Computer Graphics Forum 33*, 3 (2014), 411–420.
6. Bertin, J. Semiology of graphics: diagrams, networks, maps, 1983.
7. Cleveland, W. S., and McGill, R. Graphical perception: Theory, experimentation, and application to the development of graphical methods. *Journal of the American statistical association* (1984).
8. Dinkla, K., Westenberg, M. A., and van Wijk, J. J. Compressed adjacency matrices: untangling gene regulatory networks. *TVCG 18*, 12 (2012), 2457–2466.
9. Fuchs, J., Fischer, F., Mansmann, F., Bertini, E., and Isenberg, P. Evaluation of alternative glyph designs for time series data in a small multiple setting. In *CHI*, ACM (2013), 3237–3246.
10. Ghoniem, M., Fekete, J.-D., and Castagliola, P. On the readability of graphs using node-link and matrix-based representations: A controlled experiment and statistical analysis. *Information Visualization* (July 2005).
11. Gillan, D. J., and Lewis, R. A componential model of human interaction with graphs: 1. linear regression modeling. *Human Factors: The Journal of the Human Factors and Ergonomics Society 36*, 3 (1994), 419–440.
12. Gleicher, M., Albers, D., Walker, R., Jusufi, I., Hansen, C. D., and Roberts, J. C. Visual comparison for information visualization. *Information Visualization 10*, 4 (2011), 289–309.
13. Heer, J., Kong, N., and Agrawala, M. Sizing the horizon: The effects of chart size and layering on the graphical perception of time series visualizations. In *CHI* (2009).
14. Henry, N., Fekete, J., and McGuffin, M. Nodetrix: a hybrid visualization of social networks. *TVCG 13*, 6 (Nov 2007), 1302–1309.
15. Henry, N., and Fekete, J.-D. Matrixexplorer: a dual-representation system to explore social networks. *TVCG 12*, 5 (2006), 677–684.
16. Henry, N., and Fekete, J.-D. Matlink: Enhanced matrix visualization for analyzing social networks. In *Human-computer Interaction* (2007).
17. Javed, W., and Elmqvist, N. Exploring the design space of composite visualization. In *Pacific Visualization Symposium*, IEEE (2012), 1–8.
18. Javed, W., McDonnel, B., and Elmqvist, N. Graphical perception of multiple time series. *TVCG 16*, 6 (2010).
19. Keller, R., Eckert, C. M., and Clarkson, P. J. Matrices or node-link diagrams: Which visual representation is better for visualising connectivity models? *Information Visualization 5*, 1 (Mar. 2006), 62–76.
20. Lam, H., Munzner, T., and Kincaid, R. Overview use in multiple visual information resolution interfaces. *TVCG 13*, 6 (2007), 1278–1285.
21. Lohse, G. L. A cognitive model for understanding graphical perception. *Human-Computer Interaction 8*, 4 (1993), 353–388.
22. Lohse, J. A cognitive model for the perception and understanding of graphs. In *CHI* (1991).
23. Mueller, C., Martin, B., and Lumsdaine, A. Interpreting large visual similarity matrices. In *International Asia-Pacific Symposium on Visualization* (2007), 149–152.
24. Robertson, G., Fernandez, R., Fisher, D., Lee, B., and Stasko, J. Effectiveness of animation in trend visualization. *TVCG 14*, 6 (2008), 1325–1332.
25. Simons, D. J., and Levin, D. T. Change blindness. *Trends in cognitive sciences 1*, 7 (1997), 261–267.
26. Tang, J., Rangayyan, R., Xu, J., El Naqa, I., and Yang, Y. Computer-aided detection and diagnosis of breast cancer with mammography: Recent advances. *IEEE Transactions on Information Technology in Biomedicine 13*, 2 (March 2009), 236–251.
27. TODAY, U. Online nba statistics. http://www.usatoday.com/sports/nba/statistics/.
28. Tominski, C., Forsell, C., and Johansson, J. Interaction support for visual comparison inspired by natural behavior. *TVCG 18*, 12 (2012), 2719–2728.
29. Tufte, E. *Envisioning Information*. Graphics Press, 1990.
30. Tyler, C. W. *Human symmetry perception and its computational analysis*. Psychology Press, 2003.

g-Miner: Interactive Visual Group Mining on Multivariate Graphs

Nan Cao
IBM Research
nan.cao@gmail.com

Yu-Ru Lin
University of Pittsburgh
yurulin@pitt.edu

Liangyue Li
HangHang Tong
Arizona State University
{liangyue,hanghang.tong}@asu.edu

ABSTRACT
With the rapid growth of rich network data available through various sources such as social media and digital archives, there is a growing interest in more powerful network visual analysis tools and methods. The rich information about the network nodes and links can be represented as multivariate graphs, in which the nodes are accompanied with attributes to represent the properties of individual nodes. An important task often encountered in multivariate network analysis is to uncover link structure with groups, e.g., to understand why a person fits a specific job or certain role in a social group well. The task usually involves complex considerations including specific requirement of node attributes and link structure, and hence a fully automatic solution is typically not satisfactory. In this work, we identify the design challenges for mining groups with complex criteria and present an interactive system, "g-Miner," that enables visual mining of groups on multivariate graph data. We demonstrate the effectiveness of our system through case study and in-depth expert interviews. This work contributes to understanding the design of systems for leveraging users' knowledge progressively with algorithmic capacity for tackling massive heterogeneous information.

Author Keywords
Group Mining; Visual Analysis; Information Visualization

ACM Classification Keywords
H.5.m. Information Interfaces and Presentation (e.g. HCI): Miscellaneous

INTRODUCTION
The visual analysis of networks is an important subject in many domains ranging from social or information networks to power grids or biological networks. With the rapid growth of data available through various sources such as social media and digital archives, the interest in more powerful network visual analysis tools and methods is growing as well. These data often include rich information about the nodes and links and can be represented as *multivariate graphs*, in which the nodes are accompanied with attributes to represent the properties of individual nodes – e.g., the demographic information such as race or gender of the 'people' nodes in social network analysis. Such multivariate graphs provide rich contexts that enable analysts to form hypotheses while exploring the network [30]. An important task often encountered in their analysis is to uncover link structure with groups. For example, in social network analysis, the analysts are interested in understanding why a person fits a specific job or certain role well in a social group, comparing member composition across different groups, or looking for a group with specific link structure or member composition. Finding these groups allows them to determine common or irreplaceable parts of these networks which is for instance of importance for the maintenance in communication networks or discovering specific roles in organization networks.

CHI 2015, April 18–23 2015, Seoul, Republic of Korea.

ACM 978-1-4503-3145-6/15/04...$15.00.
http://dx.doi.org/10.1145/2702123.2702476

Group mining with large-scale, heterogeneous network data is computationally intensive, and hence automatic group identification algorithms have become a popular solution. Recent advances in graph mining techniques, particularly in community detection [13] and team formation [1, 19] algorithms, have been developed to identify subsets from multivariate graph data. However, the automatically generated solutions derived from these techniques are rarely able to satisfy the complex or dynamic criteria that users require for finding desirable groups. More importantly, a fully-automatic approach can never support users' exploratory need, neither does it allow users to evaluate, refine or make sense of different solutions.

This paper presents an interactive system called g-Miner (Fig. 1) that enables visual analysis of groups with large-scale multivariate network data. Our key contributions include:

System. We introduce the problems of *interactive group mining* – concerning mining groups from multivariate network data with the capability to adapt complex or dynamic requirements of the desired group. We identify the system design requirements through a pilot user study. Guided by the design requirements, we integrate a set of graph mining algorithms with novel visualization tools to support iterative group mining with users' feedback in the loop.

Visualization. We proposed two sets of visualization tools for efficiently *locating* and *comparing* groups. (1) Cross-level exploration: The "Hierarchy Explorer" (Fig. 1(4)) allows users to navigate the entire graph dataset following a hierarchical structure. Once a group of interest is located, users can inspect the group via "Group Explorer" (Fig. 1(3)) or find alternatives of the group members via "Candidate Explorer"

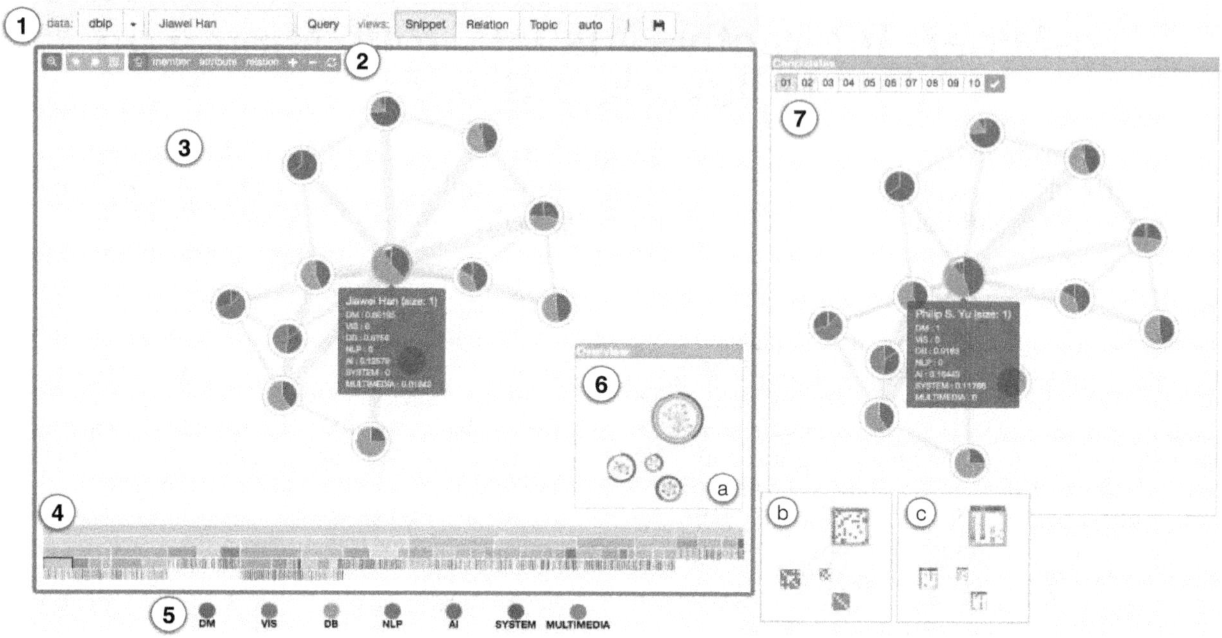

Figure 1. The visualization illustrates an example of using our proposed g-Miner system to find a candidate (e.g., Philip S. Yu) (in 7: Candidate Explorer) to replace the person (Jiawei Han) in the center of the network (in 3: Group Explorer) when that person is unavailable. Users can visually compare the two groups in terms of attribute and relational aspects and observe the candidate has similar expertise and social ties with the rest of the team. The labels from 1 to 7 correspond to the key interaction and visualization components detailed in the paper.

(Fig. 1(7)). (2) Multi-structure group views: Three different glyph-based views are automatically determined based on the topological and attribute structure of the group, including "Graph Snippet" (Fig. 1(a)), "Relation Map" (Fig. 1(b)) and "Feature Map" (Fig. 1(c)). These snippets highlight the relational or content patterns of a group (or group subset), which enables an efficient visual comparison among groups.

Integrated analysis. We introduce an integrated analysis module that is both data- and user-driven. We utilize graph clustering and indexing algorithms to generate an initial hierarchical structure for users to efficiently locate a group of interest from a large dataset. We then integrate a recently developed graph mining algorithm [20] to generate recommendations and help users query and refine a group with flexibly specified criteria.

We demonstrate the effectiveness of our system through case study and in-depth expert interview. The results suggest that our system is particularly useful in exploring rich multivariate graph data, and in tackling non-trivial criteria for forming a group. Our research sheds light on the design of systems for guiding users to explore the possibilities of "organizing things" in a complex setting through leveraging algorithmic solutions.

Throughout the paper, we use the following scenario to illustrate the problem context of interactive group mining and to motivate the system design. **Running example:** In a large-scale company, a manager often needs to build a task force – a team created for a specific project or to solve a particular problem (such teams may vary in size, e.g., ranging from tens to hundreds of members). An effective team requires members with the competencies or complementary skills to carry out the task, and more importantly, who can collaborate well with one another. For example, the manager may want to find members who have successful collaboration among themselves, or find one or more key people that have collaborated well with subsets of the team and can coordinate the communications across subgroups in the team. Hence, the essential criteria for building a team include both attribute (e.g., skill sets) and relational (e.g., collaboration relationship) aspects. Sometimes assembling a team involves more complex considerations such as team members' resource capacity or conflicts of interests. The manager would wish to find a proper set of members by incorporating these complex criteria.

RELATED WORK

We review research related to our work, from the aspects of *visualization* and *analysis*. We focus on (1) visualizing multivariate graphs, (2) visualizing sub-structures and groups, and (3) group mining techniques and applications concerning the use of multivariate networks.

Visualizing and Exploring Multivariate Graphs

Previous work on visualizing multivariate graphs focused primarily on how to represent both the topological structure of the graphs (networked data) and the multivariate attributes of nodes on the graphs. Most of this research leverage existing designs that had been originally proposed for displaying multivariate datasets. For example, to visualize the node or edge distributions in a social network, Bezerianos *et al.*'s GraphDice [2] used an interactive scatterplot matrix, and Shannon *et al.* [25] adopted parallel coordinates [17]. Wong *et al.* [31] used a pixel-based multivariate data visualization to represent node attributes. Xu *et al.*'s GraphSpace [32] is a hybrid visualization that overlays the graph on top of a 3D density map generated using node attributes. In order to tease out the structure of multivariate graphs, visual techniques recently have started employing analytical operations based on node attributes. Lin *et al.* [22] and Cao *et al.* [6] introduced multi-relational graphs that can be used to represent different types of relations involving different node attributes, and Pretorius and Van Wijk [23] developed a technique that allows users to partition or aggregate the graph according to the attributes of nodes or edges.

As for exploring multivariate graphs, various interaction techniques have been proposed. Aggregation of nodes and links based on their attributes are the most common interaction designs, e.g., Pivot Graph [30] and Graph Trail [11]. GraphDice [2] switches between views of different node attributes by rotating a hypercube of attributes via animated transitions. DICON [5] supports splitting and merging functions to enable a flexible attribute summary of any subset of nodes or clusters. General exploring tools like search and filtering have been commonly used for exploring graphs or multivariate graphs [7, 12, 27, 29]. Although these techniques pointed out various possible ways for visualizing and exploring multivariate graphs, they are limited in offering functions to support group mining on multivariate graphs.

Visualizing Sub-structures or Groups in Networks

There has been work focusing on visualizations or exploration of sub-graphs, graph communities or clusters – which can be generally considered as groups. Traditional techniques for visualizing set data can be applied to visualize groups. For example, drawing a "convex hull" [14] of subsets of nodes on top of a graph is a commonly used method. Collions *et al.* [9] introduced BubbleSet that wraps the items belonging to the same set via a non-convex shape to avoid incorrect inclusion of set members. Although these are powerful representations for group membership in a graph, they do not capture richer aspects such as attribute differences of groups and hence cannot be applied directly to compare groups in a multivariate graph. Recent development of iconic representations for clusters makes it possible to compare and interpret clusters in terms of their within-group structures or features [5, 16]. Particularly, Henry *et al.* designed NodeTrix [15] in which graph clusters are shown as adjacency matrices to highlight the relational patterns and can be embedded in a node-link diagram to facilitate tracing links among clusters. Cao *et al.* introduced DICON for exploring feature patterns of groups in multivariate datasets [5]. Our work extends these iconic visualization designs to facilitate efficient characterization, comparison, and manipulation of groups in the process of interactive group mining.

Group Mining Techniques and Applications

A substantial body of graph mining research has focused on detecting groups or communities in graphs [13].Rather than based on pure topological structure, the problem of team assembly concerns extracting groups by considering both connections among and attributes of members [1, 10, 19]. It has been observed that to ensure a team's success, team members should possess the desired skills and have strong team cohesion. In other words, both relational (team members' social ties) and attribute (individuals' skills) structures need to be considered [10]. Such multi-objective requirements have been tackled recently by more sophisticated algorithms [1, 19]. However, the solutions are usually restricted into a ranking list of teams (or team members) based on fixed, predefined criteria, which prevents users' feedback to refine the mining results, or to dynamically incorporate more complex criteria such as the availability of team members.

Our proposed g-Miner goes beyond these solutions by designing an interactive group mining framework that allows users to flexibly and dynamically specify a rich set of criteria to build and refine groups iteratively. We leverage a recently developed algorithm proposed by Li *et al.* [20] which efficiently finds replacements for a given team based on both relational and attribute features. Our extension of this algorithm allows users to incrementally refine any chosen groups, with a new set of interactive visualizations specifically designed to guide users in the interactive group mining process.

SYSTEM REQUIREMENTS AND DESIGN

To better understand the needs for interactive group mining in multivariate graph data, we conducted a pilot study with expert users. Based on their feedback, we identified requirements that guide the design of the proposed system.

Pilot Study and Design Goals

Our pilot study is a multiple-session design process involving two expert users who have worked on team assembly research using social network methodology and machine learning approaches.

Session 1. Initial requirement: We discussed the challenges they encountered during the analysis. The experts pointed out that the most difficult task in their analysis is to *make sense of the results generated by different team assembly algorithms, especially when data involves team members' multivariate attributes and social relationships.* The initial requirement was to design a system that allows users to compare different possibilities of assembling a team with visualization for comparing members' attributes and connections.

Session 2. Prototyping: Based on the initial requirement, we develop the antecedent version of g-Miner.In this prototype system, we visualize a group using a multivariate graph representation where each team member is represented as a circular shaped voronoi diagram (similar to DICON [5]) with each cell representing a kind of expertise of the member, and members are connected by links as in standard node-link diagram representation.

Session 3. User study: We worked with the experts to conduct a preliminary user study. We recruited 20 people to participate in a team selection task using the prototype system. The system generated a set of team assembly results (through different algorithmic configurations such as "relation only," "skill only" and "proposed method") and asked the participants to compare and select the best team results (without knowing which result came from which method). The ages of the participants ranged from 22 to 35, all were college educated, and 2 of them were female. After the completion of the task, we asked users to provide free-form feedback on the system interface. The preliminary study results showed that ,compared with the best alternative choices, our proposed best method achieved 27% and 24% net increase in average recall and precision, respectively. Users' informal feedback suggested our initial design allows users to compare teams by viewing the team members' expertise and connections simultaneously. However, several users commented that functionality is limited and only suitable for making straightforward comparisons between small teams. The feedback led to further discussion with the experts and helped to clarify the limitations and needs for team analysis tasks.

Through the multi-session pilot study, we identify the system requirements and design goals as follows. The first three requirements concern a system's capacity to support group mining tasks in general, followed by three requirements that further specify the goals of group visualization design.

- **R1 Scalability.** Group mining and analysis is most valuable when users have to deal with a huge and heterogeneous dataset. A scalable system that allows users to explore groups from big data, big groups, or small groups within larger groups, is critical.
- **R2 Locating groups of interest.** When dealing with a huge dataset, it is important for users to be able to navigate the entire dataset and quickly identify groups they may be interested in giving a closer inspection.
- **R3 Iterative group refinement.** When an identified group is not satisfactory, users can specify or modify the criteria for making a better group. The system needs to incorporate such users' feedback to efficiently refine the group.
- **R4 Group abstraction.** Groups need to be represented in a way that users can easily spot similarities or differences between groups, as well as to directly manipulate groups.
- **R5 Group characterization.** Groups are formed by members based on their multivariate attributes (e.g., expertise) and connections (e.g., collaboration). The visual representation of a group should highlight different characteristics of a group in terms of these features. This can facilitate efficient group identification and comparison. For example, users can quickly recognize whether a group consists of members with similar or rather complementary expertise, or whether a group has densely connected members.
- **R6 Level of group comparison.** Groups can be compared at different levels, from the attributes of their members, to member composition and connectivity within groups, to connections with other groups. The system should enable making different levels of comparison among groups.

Interactive Group Mining

We design an *interactive group mining* framework as the core of our new g-Miner system to meet the system requirements. As illustrated in Fig. 2, this framework incorporates two components that enable users to easily locate a group of interests from a large dataset (**R1,2**) and to iteratively refine the group according to user-specified complex criteria (**R3**).

Finding initial group. Three different methods are provided for users to locate a group of interest based on different levels of knowledge and expectations about the desirable group:

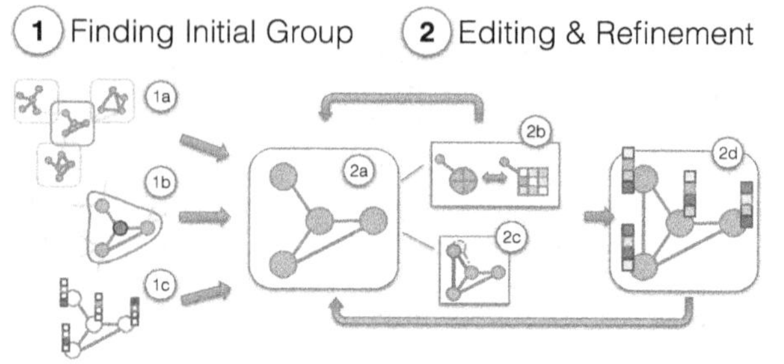

Figure 2. The process of interactive group mining.

Locating a group based on data hierarchy (1a): The system provides a *Hierarchy Explorer* that allows users to navigate the hierarchical structure of entire dataset. This data hierarchy is built based on the connections among individuals. Hence, selecting a densely-connected group from the data hierarchy is particularly efficient when users expect the desirable group to have dense connections among members.
Querying a member's ego-network (1b): If users consider more importantly the desirable group should include a particular member, they can simply query the member by name (Fig. 1(1)). When the system locates the member from the dataset, the ego-network centered on this member will also be shown. Here we show the so-called 1.5-degree egocentric network, i.e., a network consisting of all individuals having direct connections with this member and all connections among them.
Template matching (1c): If users are not concerned with whom should be included in the desirable group, but instead have specific criteria about the members' attributes, connections or overall group structure, users can use a *group editing tool* to flexibly specify complex criteria through building a *template group* and find a group from the dataset that best matches a template group.

Group editing and refinement. Once the initial group is found (2a), users can inspect the group by using the *Group Explorer* (2b). If the initial group found by the previous methods does not completely satisfy users' need, or users may decide to change the group criteria after seeing the actual data, users can refine the group (2c) by further editing the attributes or connections between members. The system then finds a list of candidate refined groups based on the modified criteria and users can compare these candidate groups by using the *Candidate Explorer*. These refinement steps can be continued iteratively until users find a group better meets their expectation (2d).

VISUALIZATION AND INTERACTION DESIGN

This section presents our novel visualization and interaction design, including (1) a multi-level group exploring interface, (2) the multi-structure group viewers, and (3) a group editing tool for users to flexibly specify the criteria of forming a group. We then provide a use case scenario to demonstrate the functionalities of these novel tools.

Multi-level Exploring Interface

As shown in Fig. 1, the user interface comprises three different exploring tools that allow users to explore and compare the group data at different levels:

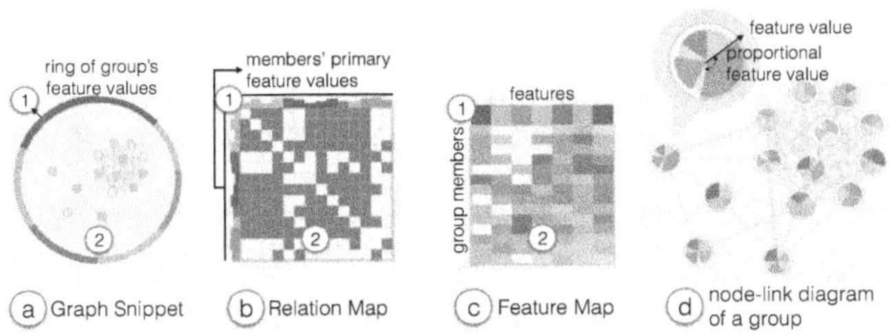

Figure 3. Visualization for characterizing a group: (a) Graph Snippet, (b) Relation Map, (c) Feature Map, and (d) Node-Link Diagram.

Group Explorer (Fig. 1(3)) represents a group of interest that can be selected from a hierarchical graph representation [12, 4, 26]. We use a fast greedy graph clustering algorithm [24] to hierarchically partition the entire network into groups, sub-groups and so on. Such a representation [12] offers an intuitive way to effectively make a big graph navigable (**R1**) and allows users to inspect the sub-structure of the group (**R6**). Alternatively, the focused group can be further presented by the multi-structure visualization tool (**R4,5**) detailed in the next subsection.

Hierarchy Explorer (Fig. 1(4)) visualizes the hierarchical clusters in an icicle tree view [18], providing an overview of the data hierarchy and supporting fast navigation (**R1**). In the tree view, leaves are individuals and the intermediate nodes represent clusters. Clicking any intermediate node makes the corresponding cluster a focused group to be visualized in the Group Explorer. Users can then narrow down the search and focus on replacing the undesirable part of the focused group (**R2,3**). This design follows the "overview first, zoom and filter, then details-on-demand" visualization guideline [28].

Candidate Explorer (Fig. 1(7)) allows users to compare the focused group with the list of candidate groups recommended by the system based on users' specified criteria. Users can switch between these candidates. Candidates are shown via multi-structure visualization as the focused group. The consistent representation of multiple groups enables detailed comparison at different levels of group structure in iterative group refinement (**R3,6**).

We proposed a multi-structure visualization design to represent the focused and candidate groups in both Group Explorer and Candidate Explorer.

Visualization Design

The multi-structure group visualization combines three different types of iconic views: Graph Snippet, Relation Map and Feature Map. The iconic views are designed to capture the characteristic properties of a group by encoding different information aspects, such as the graph topological structure, sub-structure, and attribute distribution, into a compact representation to facilitate group summarization and comparison (**R5**). We use a consistent visual encoding scheme across all three views: color hues encode different attributes (as in Fig. 1(5)), color opacity encodes values of attributes, and icon size encodes number of members of a group. At the same time, the iconic representation allows users to directly manipulate groups (**R4**): dragging to move a group, clicking to zoom-in the next level of the group, and selecting multiple sub-groups to aggregate their characteristic properties. We now describe the details of the three iconic representations.

Graph Snippet (Fig. 3(a), Fig. 1(a)) uses a node-link diagram that intuitively captures a group's topological structure. We generate a thumbnail of a node-link diagram (Fig. 3(a2)) and pack this thumbnail inside a ring with a circularly surrounding bar chart summarizing the attribute values of the group (Fig. 3(a1)). The ring sectors with different colors indicate different attributes. The arc length of each sector is proportional to the corresponding within-group attribute value. The height of each sector indicates the attribute value normalized across all groups in the dataset, which facilitate a comparison within and across different groups. Each node in the diagram is either a sub-group or an individual (i.e., a leaf in the data hierarchy). When the node represents an individual, it is visualized as a pie-chart-like icon (Fig. 3(d)). Similar to the ring encodings, each pie area encodes the corresponding attribute value relative to the member's other attribute values, and the height of each sector indicates the attribute value normalized across all individuals in the dataset.

Relation Map (Fig. 3(b), Fig. 1(b)) extends the design proposed in NodeTrix [15] to capture a group's relational patterns. It shows a matrix reflecting a group's connections among members. In this matrix, each row and column represent a member node in the graph and the opacity of each matrix entry encodes the connection strength between a pair of nodes in the group (Fig. 3(b2)). We visualize each node's primary attribute value via a small rectangle attached on the top and left of the corresponding row and column (Fig. 3(b1)). The rectangle is colored according to the primary attribute and sized by attribute value. To enhance visual patterns, we reorder the rows and columns of the matrix either by their primary attributes or by innate connection of the nodes inside the group (reordering methods can be chosen by users).

Feature Map (Fig. 3(c), Fig. 1(c)) employs a heatmap representation to capture the patterns of attribute values of each node in the group. In the heatmap, the header row shows attributes in different colors (Fig. 3(c1)). The remaining rows indicate nodes' attribute values encoded by color opacity (Fig. 3(c2)). The rows are reordered based on similarity of the feature vectors.

View Aggregation

The above view designs support flexible aggregation mechanism in which users can brush to select a set of (intermediate or leaf) nodes and groups to merge them together, forming a new group. A group can also be split into individual nodes by brushing it again. After aggregation, the views of the groups are updated based on the new set of nodes and links.

View Recommender

Each of the three views described before can be most suitable for capturing the characteristic properties of some groups but not others, depending on the structure of the group data. To help users choose a proper view, we further introduce an algorithm to automatically choose the most informative view for representing a group. Let a group G consist of n nodes with m attributes and their xy-coordinates indicating their locations on the two dimensional space. The information can be formally described into three matrices: $\{\mathbf{A}_{n\times n}, \mathbf{F}_{n\times m}, \mathbf{X}_{n\times 2}\}$, where $\mathbf{A}$ is the adjacency matrix representing the connections, $\mathbf{F}$ is attribute matrix, and $\mathbf{X}$ is the 2D coordinate matrix. To make these matrices comparable, we compute the $n \times n$ similarity matrices $\mathbf{S}_F = \mathbf{F}\mathbf{F}^T$ and $\mathbf{S}_X = \mathbf{X}\mathbf{X}^T$ for estimating similarities of nodes corresponding to their attributes and coordinates respectively.

To determine the most informative view, we compute the informativeness score of an input matrix $\mathbf{M} \in \{\mathbf{A}, \mathbf{S}_F, \mathbf{S}_X\}$ based on information entropy. In brief, this algorithm computes an average entropy score of the rows in a row normalized matrix. The entropy of each row in the matrix suggests to what extent we can differentiate a node's neighbor based on the adjacency matrix or similarity matrices. Thus, a matrix with larger entropy is more "informative" (easy to be differentiated). Visually, this means the corresponding view has a more distinguished structure in terms of relations, attributes, or coordinates. When $\mathbf{A}$ is considered to be the most informative, we choose the Relation Map for a direct representation of $\mathbf{A}$. Similarly, when $\mathbf{S}_F$ is considered to be the most informative one, the Feature Map is selected. Otherwise, Graph Snippet is chosen to represent the group.

Group Editing

A set of group editing tools (Fig. 1(2)) are provided for users to flexibly specify criteria to form or refine a group: (1) *Member editing* allows adding or deleting member nodes in a group. (2) *Attribute editing* allows adjusting attribute values of each member in a group by clicking the sectors in the pie-chart-like icon. (3) *Relation editing* allows adding new edges between group members, removing existing edges from the group, or adjusting the weight of a selected edge via a slider. This function allows users to specify a particular link structure, e.g., to find a coordinate person with strong links with multiple sub-groups. View aggregation is supported in the editing mode.

Case Study with the Publication Dataset

We demonstrate the effectiveness of our visualization and interaction designs using a real-world paper publication dataset which contains multivariate graph information.

Dataset. This demonstration[1] is based on a paper publication dataset that comprises papers mostly in the Computer Science domain[2]. We transformed the data into a multivariate graph, in which nodes are researchers (authors) and edges are co-authorships with the weights representing the number of co-authoring papers. An author's expertise is represented by a seven-dimensional vector where each dimension represents the number of papers the author published in one of the seven research fields, including "data mining (DM)", "visualization (VIS)", "database (DB)", "nature language processing (NLP)", "artificial intelligence (AI)", "system", and "multimedia.". Both edge weights and expertise vectors are normalized for visualization purpose. The graph contains 78,997 nodes and 423,388 edges in total.

[1]The same dataset is used for conducting the interview with experts.
[2]http://arnetminer.org/download

Data Overview. The dataset contains four major research groups that are displayed as four big bubbles labeled by 1, 2, 3, and 4 (Fig. 4(A:a)). Each bubble contains several nodes in different colors, indicating sub-groups with different research interests. They are connected by links representing the collaborations across different groups or sub-groups.

Group Insights. Fig. 4(A:a) illustrates many high level differences of groups in terms of group size, primary research interests, and sub-structure. For example, group 4 is the largest group with three primary research interests including system (green), multimedia (brown), and database (orange). The sub-structure differences among groups can be captured in Fig. 4(A:b). For example, group 4 contains a central node that connects to all other nodes, reflected as a "cross" pattern in the matrix. The subgroups in group 3 are highly connected, shown as a clique in Figure 4(A:a) and as a dense matrix in Fig. 4(A:b). Both groups 1 and 2 contain multiple leading nodes (several crosses in the Relation Map). Fig. 4(A:c) displays group differences in terms of their research interests. For example, the members in group 3 have more diverse research interests as shown in Fig. 4(A:c), suggesting people in this group have comprehensive expertise.

As shown in Fig. 4(A:d), users can continuously zoom into their interested groups (e.g., group 4) guided by research topics (e.g., data mining and database), until reaching a cluster at the bottom of the hierarchy. From Fig. 1(3) users can clearly see that this is a star-shaped network centered on a person who has strong expertise in data mining and database. If the central person is unavailable, the team's coordination may be significantly affected. In this case, our system provides Candidate Explorer that allows users to query and find a most suitable candidate with similar skills and connections as the central person (Fig. 1(7)).

ANALYSIS: GRAPH MINING ALGORITHMS

We implement the group mining algorithm based on a fast Team Member Replacement algorithm ("TMR algorithm" for short) proposed by Li *et al.* [20]. The original TMR algorithm was designed to search the best replacement of a team member from multivariate graph data. The authors proposed the approximation method and demonstrated that this algorithm can efficiently generate high quality results in very large real-world datasets. This feature uniquely meets the scalability requirement (**R1**). This section first summarizes the key ideas in TMR algorithm, and describes how the algorithm is extended to support two core group mining tasks.

Team Member Replacement Algorithm

Considering a team in which a team member p is about to leave and the team needs a replacement, the goal of TMR algorithm is to find a similar person q to replace the current team member p. An ideal replacement q should not only have a similar skill set as p, but also have the proper connections with the rest team members so that the whole team can work together harmoniously.The algorithm was designed to solve the two-fold problem: (1) *skill matching*: the new member should bring a similar skill set as the current team member p; (2) *structural matching*: the new member should have a similar network structure as team member p in connecting

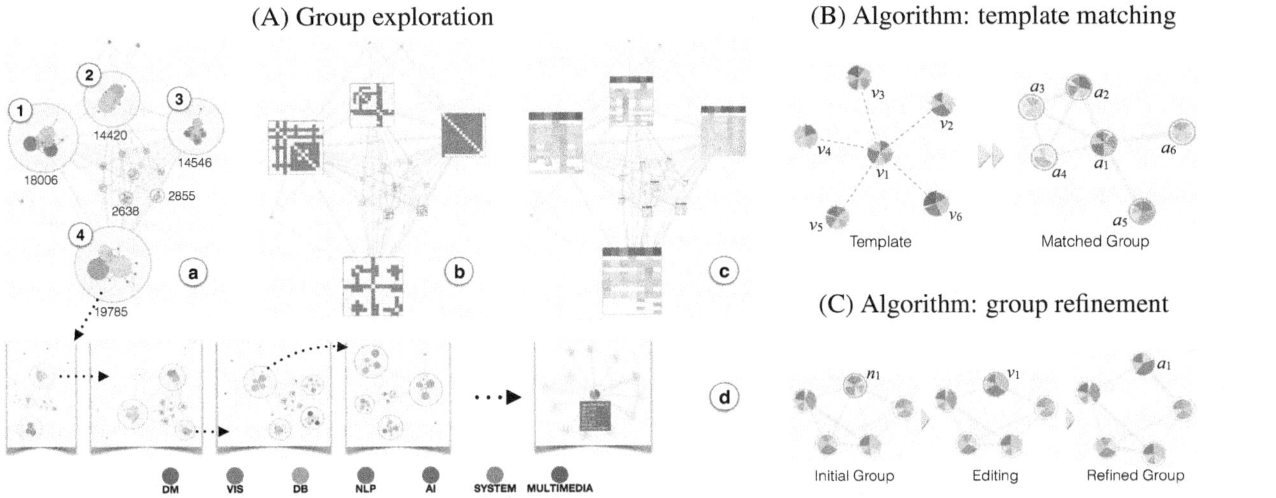

Figure 4. (A) An example of exploring groups in publication data using g-Miner. (B) An illustration of template matching. (C) An illustration of group refinement.

the rest of the team members. The objective can be formally described as:

$$q = \arg\max_{j \notin \mathcal{T}} Ker(G(\mathcal{T}), G(\mathcal{T}_{p \to j}))$$

where $\mathcal{T}$ is the set of nodes representing the members in the given team, $G(\mathcal{T})$ is the induced subgraph by the set $\mathcal{T}$ from a multivariate graph where each node is associated with a vector representing the values of the node attributes (e.g., skill set), and $G(\mathcal{T}_{p \to j})$ is the multivariate subgraph after the team member p is replaced by another individual j in data. The function $Ker(\cdot)$ is the graph kernel between these two labeled graphs. The intuition behind this optimization objective is to make the new team after the replacement as similar to the original one as possible. Here, a graph kernel function is used to compute the similarity between the two input graphs by considering both team member skills and relationships. A random walk graph kernel [3] is used in the algorithm implementation. The above model can be efficiently solved via an approximate algorithm and more details can be found in [20].

We extend the original TMR algorithm to support two core group mining tasks in g-Miner: (a) template-based group builder, and (b) group refinement recommender.

Template-based Group Builder

The template-based group builder allows users to build a group from scratch using a template graph. The template graph can be flexibly generated by using the graph editing tools provided in g-Miner. It is used to specify the desirable expertise features of group members (the attribute or content of nodes) and the desirable relational features within the group (the graph structure defined by the edges). Given the input template graph, the algorithm finds a subgraph that is most similar to the features defined in the template graph. This novel function enables users to explore a wide range of different possible group combinations from the data. It is particularly useful, for example, when a project leader seeks to create task forces for new tasks.

As shown in Fig. 4(B), the input of template-based group builder is a template graph consisting of virtual nodes (i.e., nodes not in the actual network) and edges. The goal is to find a subgraph in the data that best matches the given template. Note that if no such nodes exist in the data with the exact skill and relation configuration specified as in the given template, the output will be a subgraph that most resembles the given template.

To find the best matching subgraph, we iteratively find a match for each vertex at a time. This is to avoid dealing with the combinatorial problem – that is, to compute a similarity score for every possible subgraph in the network with the same size.

Group Refinement Recommender

Group refinement recommender is designed to refine an existing group by replacing some of the group members selected by users. For example, users may seek to find a person outside a team with better or similar connections and skills to replace one or more members who cannot be in the team for certain reasons (e.g., conflicts of interests or resource capacity).

As discussed in our pilot study, evaluating the results derived from an automatic approach for team refinement is challenging. More importantly, users may need to change their evaluation criteria flexibly and iteratively in the context of different applications (**R3**). Our group refinement recommender is designed to address these issues.

We use the TMR algorithm along with the interactive group mining interface to recommend a set of best replacement candidates. When users specifically add a new member with particular skills and connections, the TMR algorithm cannot be directly applied as it is designed to replace a current member with another one in the dataset, rather than "refine" the team with desirable member properties. We provide a solution similar to our template-based group builder: to find a candidate that best matches to a virtual group member with desired attributes and connections. This virtual group member can be generated by editing the member that is going to be replaced in the existing group (Fig. 4(C)). The editing includes adding or removing links of the node and adjusting its attributes to the desired values.

EVALUATION VIA EXPERT INTERVIEW

This section presents our evaluation through an in-depth expert interview process.

We conducted interviews with three domain experts to fully understand the design and functionality of the proposed system. Two experts were first interviewed (interview study I & II), helping diagnose usability issues in interaction components and the overall mining pipeline. The identified usability issues were addressed before we conducted the interview with the third expert (interview study III), who provided feedback on the final design.

Procedure. We started each interview with a tutorial explaining the goals and features of g-Miner followed by a detailed demonstration of the system. The experts were then asked to use the system[3]. After they fully explored the system's functionality, we conducted a semi-structured interview covering questions on aspects of visual design, interactive group mining, overall usefulness, ease of use, and general pros and cons. Further, as the three expert users have different backgrounds and expertise, we asked them to elaborate on their opinions based on their expert domain knowledge. Each interview study lasted approximately 1.5 hours. Interviews were recorded and notes were taken.

Summary of interview study I & II. The first expert is a professor who also had worked with us for developing the prototype system in the pilot study. Familiarity with our system requirements allows him to offer detailed assessment of the new system. The second expert is a senior manager in an IT company. His team developed the first enterprise-wise expert recommendation system, SmallBlue [21].

Both experts were impressed by the system's capability, particularly on offering the interactive group mining capacity that allows mining large graph in real time, and on the amount and levels of information shown in the visualization. Expert #2 especially appreciated the idea of leveraging group mining algorithms to enable iterative group refinement, which he believed "a very powerful function that is missed in the SmallBlue system". Expert #1 noted the advantages of the multi-structure group visualization: "helps provide a more comprehensive picture of the sub-graphs from various aspects". Both experts described the iconic summary "can easily identify the differences [of groups]." Moreover, both experts commented that the Hierarchy Explorer and Group Explorer are the most efficient tools for fast data navigation.

Lessons learned from studies I & II. The two experts also raised several usability issues potentially undermining the interaction support in the group mining framework. After collecting their feedback and identifying the key usability issues, we incorporated solutions to address these issues into a final design as shown in Fig. 1. We summarize the key issues and our solutions as follows.

1. *Parallel views are not always useful.* The system we used in the first two interview studies inherited a similar look as the prototype system , which comprises Group Explorer and Candidate Explorer on two parallel aligned panels. Both experts believed the two views may not be used simultaneously. **Solution**: In our final design (Fig. 1), we reserved most of the visual space for Group Explorer and placed the Candidate Explorer into a floating window (Fig. 1(7)). This window will only show up when needed.The size of this floating window is the same as the size of Group Explorer. Users can drag this window on top of the Group Explorer and make a 1:1 visual comparison between the focused group and the recommended group in the Candidate Explorer.
2. *Missing hierarchical context while zooming-in.* Expert #2 pointed out that when he zoomed into the next level of a group, the context of the upper level is completely missing. **Solution**: We added an inset window inside the Group Explorer to display the upper-level graph of the focused group when applicable (Fig. 1(6)).
3. *Too many interaction functions to learn.* Expert #1 highlighted this learnability issue. **Solution**: We simplified the interactions in the entire group mining pipeline. The new interaction design simply requires standard mouse operations, such as dragging and clicking.

Summary of interview study III. The third expert is a research consultant working for an international IT company with more than 200,000 employees. A major part of her job is building teams in which the members can effectively propose IT solutions for resolving various customer problems. The customers come from diverse domains including Healthcare, Finance, etc., and the final solution usually covers the aspects of hardware, software, and services. She has worked in this position for more than five years and has abundant knowledge and experience in identifying experts from over 2000 employees with various background to form effective teams that can support her work. The dataset we used in the study has similar contexts as the data she is used to dealing with (both have individuals' expertise information and the collaborations among them). She was asked to build research teams using the final version of g-Miner and provide comments.

She immediately appreciated the design of g-Miner. After seeing our demonstration, she confirmed that the system has great novelty compared with any existing tools she knew: "existing tools I used can only recommend experts, but it is far from enough to build a temporary consulting team as the experts are usually unavailable [because of the conflict of the schedule, lack of interests, etc.]" She believed this system will be very useful for her to build teams and find replacement when candidates are unavailable. In the exploration process, she first chose to query a person, a data scientist whom she knew to start with. After briefly exploring the person's ego-network in the Group Explorer, she then removed some of the team members and replaced existing members with some new members iteratively via Group Editing and Refinement Recommender. She commented when using the tools: "it

[3]The system was developed using HTML5, JavaScript, D3.js (front-end) and Python CGI (back-end) and was deployed on an Amazon EC2 server. The expert users test the system by using Chrome browser with a 27-inch iMac.

runs very fast", "it is very nice that I can edit the attributes and connections of the team members to enter my requirements", and "it really finds a candidate for me [to replace another person in the team], and this guy is even better!"

Her response to the question, "which is the most problematic part of the system?", is very valuable. She felt building a team based on the Template Matching is a nice feature; however, the current implementation is not sufficiently effective because "it does not start with the people I'm familiar with" and "the system doesn't allow me to add multiple people that I know well into a template at the same time". She also pointed out three issues about the visualization design: (1) The outer parts of the Graph Snippet and Relation Map (expertise ring and bar chart, respectively) still require some effort of learning to understand. However, she agreed that these designs are extremely informative once the users learn about what is encoded in the visualization. (2) Comparing groups in the same window (e.g. Group Explorer) is sometimes difficult when group sizes are highly uneven. This leads to the readability issue: the iconic views of small groups may not be readable when a very large group exists in the same viewing space. (3) Too little textual information: Additional context information such as statistic of groups and topic keywords describing a person or a group's skills can also be very useful.

DISCUSSION

In the real world, team assembly requires tremendous human judgment and contextual knowledge that goes beyond the power of automatic learning and mining algorithms. Our g-Miner aims to facilitate the process through an interactive group mining system. The set of functionalities offered in g-Miner was mostly well accepted by the domain experts we interviewed. However, the current design still has limitations. We discussed these limitations and ways to improve them.

Bridging query and template-matching. As noted by expert #3, the current implementation of g-Miner does not support matching a template graph that comprises one or multiple default members. The current query function only allows users to find a single individual from the data and fetch his or her existing ego-network. This restricts users' options to either start with a (single) selected member (by querying), or specified structure (by template-matching), but not both. A more powerful query mechanism can be achieved by combining both query and template-matching such that when building a template, users can query and assign members to any nodes on the template.

Overcoming the readability of iconic representation. Our visualization design employs iconic representation to offer an abstract but characteristic view of a group in order to facilitate group manipulation and comparison. The iconic representation has a resolution limit as it captures group (topological or attribute) structure independent of the visualized icon size. This issue can be addressed in different ways: (1) When displaying groups with highly uneven sizes in the same view space, non-linear scaling (e.g., log-scale) should be used to enable more effective visual comparison among groups. Proper legends should be included to ensure the correct interpretation of icon size. (2) Interaction techniques such as fisheye and focus+context [8] can be used to enlarge a small icon with users' focus.

More details are on demand. Although g-Miner provides a large set of functionalities to make group mining more efficient, users usually need more detailed information to support their decision making after finding a group. This can be achieved by providing more context and information details or a statistical summary about the groups or group members (e.g., topic keywords, attribute values, group size, number of edges and more graph-based metrics) via additional views or tool-tips. By providing more detailed information when it is demanded in the context of exploration, the system can be potentially used as resource browser for discovering organizational knowledge.

Design implication for interacting with large multivariate graph data. Although this work focuses on addressing the technical challenge of team assembly, the graph-mining based interactive design solution can be widely applicable. On one hand, the interactive pipeline enables users to start with partial knowledge about a group and progressively form more complicated queries in the context of refining a group. On the other, the algorithms are able to take into account both users' new requirements and the group to be refined to generate a new solution and progressively refine the solution based on users' feedback. This idea of interactive group mining can also be applied to other scenarios that involve exploratory needs in heterogeneous data. For example, user-generated content, such as e-mails and photos, consists of rich information (e.g., topics and users' social networks) and users are often unable to determine how they wish to organize or explore the content beforehand. Our design concept can be potentially used in bridging users' partial knowledge and the capacity of advanced algorithms for tackling large heterogeneous datasets.

CONCLUSIONS AND FUTURE WORK

We have presented g-Miner, the first interactive group mining system that allows users to efficiently explore heterogeneous graph data and from which to progressively select and replace candidate members to form a group based on user-specified criteria. Our solution incorporates the design of interactive group mining pipeline, glyph-based group visualization and manipulation, and an integrated algorithmic component. Our system addresses the technical challenge of team assembly by connecting users with algorithmic solutions. In future work, we plan to explore new applications of the proposed framework. In addition, we plan to improve our current implementation by addressing the limitations discussed in the previous section, such as offering more flexible template-matching and incorporating proper interaction techniques to guide in-depth exploration.

ACKNOWLEDGMENTS

This material is partly supported by the U.S. Defense Advanced Research Projects Agency (DARPA) under the Social Media in Strategic Communication program under Contract Number W911NF-12-C-0028, by the NSF under Grant No. IIS1017415, and by the Army Research Laboratory under Cooperative Agreement Number W911NF-09-2-0053. The views and conclusions contained in this document are those of the author(s) and should not be interpreted as representing the official policies, either expressed or implied, of DARPA or the U.S. Government, and no official endorsement should be inferred. The U.S. Government is authorized to reproduce and distribute reprints for Government purposes notwithstanding any copyright notation here on.

REFERENCES

1. Balog, K., Azzopardi, L., and De Rijke, M. Formal models for expert finding in enterprise corpora. In *ACM SIGIR*, ACM (2006), 4350.
2. Bezerianos, A., Chevalier, F., Dragicevic, P., Elmqvist, N., and Fekete, J.-D. Graphdice: A system for exploring multivariate social networks. In *Computer Graphics Forum*, vol. 29, Wiley Online Library (2010), 863872.
3. Borgwardt, K. M., Schraudolph, N. N., and Vishwanathan, S. Fast computation of graph kernels. In *NIPS* (2006), 1449–1456.
4. Buchsbaum, A. L., and Westbrook, J. R. Maintaining hierarchical graph views. In *SODA*, Society for Industrial and Applied Mathematics (2000), 566–575.
5. Cao, N., Gotz, D., Sun, J., and Qu, H. DICON: Interactive visual analysis of multidimensional clusters. *IEEE TVCG 17*, 12 (Dec. 2011), 2581–2590.
6. Cao, N., Sun, J., Lin, Y.-R., Gotz, D., Liu, S., and Qu, H. FacetAtlas: Multifaceted visualization for rich text corpora. *IEEE TVCG 16*, 6 (2010), 1172–1181.
7. Chau, D. H., Kittur, A., Hong, J. I., and Faloutsos, C. Apolo: making sense of large network data by combining rich user interaction and machine learning. In *ACM SIGCHI*, ACM (2011), 167176.
8. Cockburn, A., Karlson, A., and Bederson, B. B. A review of overview+ detail, zooming, and focus+ context interfaces. *ACM CSUR 41*, 1 (2008), 2.
9. Collins, C., Penn, G., and Carpendale, S. Bubble sets: Revealing set relations with isocontours over existing visualizations. *IEEE TVCG 15*, 6 (2009), 1009–1016.
10. Cummings, J. N., and Kiesler, S. Who collaborates successfully?: prior experience reduces collaboration barriers in distributed interdisciplinary research. In *Proc. of 2008 ACM CSCW*, ACM (2008), 437446.
11. Dunne, C., Henry Riche, N., Lee, B., Metoyer, R., and Robertson, G. GraphTrail: Analyzing large multivariate, heterogeneous networks while supporting exploration history. In *SIGCHI*, ACM (2012), 16631672.
12. Elmqvist, N., and Fekete, J.-D. Hierarchical aggregation for information visualization: Overview, techniques, and design guidelines. *IEEE TVCG 16*, 3 (2010), 439–454.
13. Fortunato, S. Community detection in graphs. *Physics Reports 486*, 3 (2010), 75–174.
14. Graham, R. L. An efficient algorith for determining the convex hull of a finite planar set. *Information processing letters 1*, 4 (1972), 132–133.
15. Henry, N., Fekete, J., and McGuffin, M. J. Nodetrix: a hybrid visualization of social networks. *IEEE TVCG 13*, 6 (2007), 1302–1309.
16. Henry, N., and Fekete, J.-D. Matlink: Enhanced matrix visualization for analyzing social networks. In *INTERACT*. Springer, 2007, 288–302.
17. Inselberg, A., and Dimsdale, B. Parallel coordinates for visualizing multi-dimensional geometry. In *International Conference on Computer graphics*, Springer-Verlag New York, Inc. (1987), 25–44.
18. Kruskal, J. B., and Landwehr, J. M. Icicle plots: Better displays for hierarchical clustering. *The American Statistician 37*, 2 (1983), 162–168.
19. Lappas, T., Liu, K., and Terzi, E. Finding a team of experts in social networks. In *ACM SIGKDD* (2009), 467476.
20. Li, L., Tong, H., Cao, N., Ehrlich, K., Lin, Y.-R., and Buchler, N. Replacing the irreplaceable: Fast algorithms for team member recommendation. *WWW* (2015).
21. Lin, C.-Y., Ehrlich, K., Griffiths-Fisher, V., and Desforges, C. Smallblue: People mining for expertise search. *IEEE MultiMedia 15*, 1 (2008), 78–84.
22. Lin, Y.-R., Sun, J., Cao, N., and Liu, S. Contextour: Contextual contour visual analysis on dynamic multi-relational clustering. In *SDM* (2010).
23. Pretorius, A. J., and Van Wijk, J. J. Visual inspection of multivariate graphs. In *Computer Graphics Forum*, vol. 27, Wiley Online Library (2008), 967974.
24. Rosvall, M., and Bergstrom, C. T. Maps of random walks on complex networks reveal community structure. *PNAS 105*, 4 (2008), 1118–1123.
25. Shannon, R., Holland, T., and Quigley, A. Multivariate graph drawing using parallel coordinate visualisations. *University College Dublin, School of Computer Science and Informatics, Tech. Rep 6* (2008), 2008.
26. Shi, L., Cao, N., Liu, S., Qian, W., Tan, L., Wang, G., Sun, J., and Lin, C.-Y. Himap: Adaptive visualization of large-scale online social networks. In *IEEE PacificVis*, IEEE (2009), 41–48.
27. Shi, L., Liao, Q., Tong, H., Hu, Y., Zhao, Y., and Lin, C. Hierarchical focus+context heterogeneous network visualization. In *2014 IEEE Pacific Visualization Symposium (PacificVis)* (Mar. 2014), 89–96.
28. Shneiderman, B. The eyes have it: A task by data type taxonomy for information visualizations. In *Symposium on Visual Languages*, IEEE (1996), 336–343.
29. van den Elzen, S., and van Wijk, J. Multivariate network exploration and presentation: From detail to overview via selections and aggregations. *IEEE TVCG 20*, 12 (2014), 2310–2319.
30. Wattenberg, M. Visual exploration of multivariate graphs. In *ACM SIGCHI*, ACM (2006), 811819.
31. Wong, P. C., Foote, H., Mackey, P., Chin, G., Huang, Z., and Thomas, J. A space-filling visualization technique for multivariate small-world graphs. *IEEE TVCG 18*, 5 (2012), 797–809.
32. Xu, W., Zhiquan, L., Kaili, Z., and Junying, G. Multivariate graphs representation model based on complex matrix. In *CSAE*, vol. 3, IEEE (2012), 50–54.

Trajectory Bundling for Animated Transitions

Fan Du
University of Maryland
fan@cs.umd.edu

Nan Cao
IBM Research
nan.cao@gmail.com

Jian Zhao
University of Toronto
jianzhao@cs.toronto.edu

Yu-Ru Lin
University of Pittsburgh
yurulin@pitt.edu

ABSTRACT

Animated transition has been a popular design choice for smoothly switching between different visualization views or layouts, in which movement trajectories are created as cues for tracking objects during location shifting. Tracking moving objects, however, becomes difficult when their movement paths overlap or the number of tracking targets increases. We propose a novel design to facilitate tracking moving objects in animated transitions. Instead of simply animating an object along a straight line, we create "bundled" movement trajectories for a group of objects that have spatial proximity and share similar moving directions. To study the effect of bundled trajectories, we untangle variations due to different aspects of tracking complexity in a comprehensive controlled user study. The results indicate that using bundled trajectories is particularly effective when tracking more targets (six vs. three targets) or when the object movement involves a high degree of occlusion or deformation. Based on the study, we discuss the advantages and limitations of the new technique, as well as provide design implications.

Author Keywords

Animated Transitions; Movement Trajectory Bundling; Multiple Object Tracking; Information Visualization

ACM Classification Keywords

H.5.1 Multimedia Information Systems: Animations

INTRODUCTION

Recent advances in information visualization have augmented the capacity of static graphics in understanding various aspects of data. For example, in a two-dimensional scatterplot, allowing users to switch between views with axes corresponding to different pairs of variables can help users capture the data distribution across multiple dimensions [14]. Animated transition, which generates a sequence of images to create visual continuity between changes of objects (e.g., colors, sizes, and locations), has become a popular design choice when switching between different views or layouts [8]. When the animation involves shifting the location of objects, continuous movement along the line between an object's initial and destination positions is shown to create a movement trajectory as cues

CHI 2015, April 18–23 2015, Seoul, Republic of Korea.

ACM 978-1-4503-3145-6/15/04...$15.00.
http://dx.doi.org/10.1145/2702123.2702476

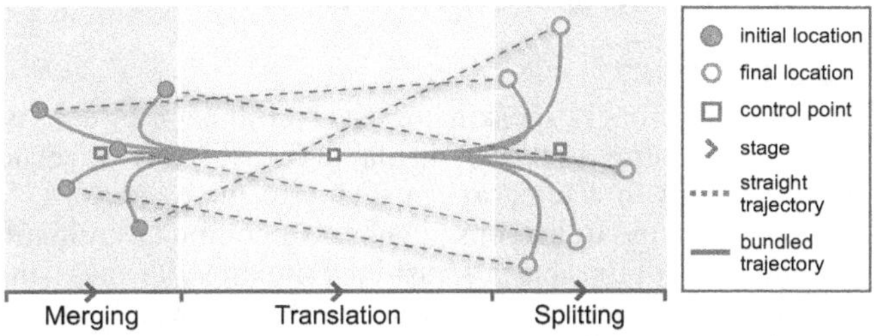

Figure 1. An illustration of the movement trajectories of five objects. Dashed and solid lines represent straight and bundled trajectories.

to help users keep track of the objects and their variations. This simple technique has been commonly used in many situations involving objects' location changes, such as updating the underlying data [2, 8, 24] or switching between different layout methods [4, 15, 29]. However, when objects' movement paths overlap, or the number of tracking targets grows, tracking moving objects becomes extremely difficult in a typical short period of animated transitions.

There has been prior work studying this issue from different perspectives of animation parameter controls, including staging [5, 14, 21], grouping [14], and timing [6]. Little has been understood about how objects' different movement trajectories affect users' ability of tracking the objects' location changes in a transition. In this paper, we take the initiative to study the effect of movement trajectories, which is a complicated problem involving the following challenges: (1) a variety of choices can be made to generate different objects' movement trajectories, but there is a lack of simple guideline that offers coherent design solutions; (2) users' perceived difficulty of tracking objects can be impacted tremendously not only by the designs of trajectories but also depending on the underlying data distribution, which is difficult to isolate in an experimental study.

In this work, we overcome these challenges by first proposing a simple yet insightful design guideline to facilitate tracking moving objects in animated transitions. Instead of simply moving an object along a straight line, we create "bundled" movement trajectories (as illustrated in Fig. 1) for a group of objects that are close to one another and share similar moving directions. Then, we design a comprehensive controlled user study to test the effect of using bundled trajectories in tracking objects in animated transitions. Using a pilot study and simulations, we decompose the complexity of tracking moving objects into factors, including trajectory lengths and number of targets, and identify three metrics—occlusion, dispersion, and deformation—which measure the tracking task complexity in terms of different spatiotemporal structures of data distribution. We conduct a controlled experiment based on these various complexity aspects. The results indicate that tracking moving objects with bundled trajectories leads to a higher tracking accuracy than simple straight trajectories when the number of targets becomes larger (six vs. three targets), or the overall moving occlusion or deformation becomes higher. Based on the study results, we discuss the advantages and disadvantages of the new technique, and provide suggestions for generating movement trajectories to effectively track objects' location changes.

BACKGROUND

Animation, broadly speaking, creates an illusion of continuous visual changes through displaying a sequence of related static images in a temporal manner. In this paper, we focus on animated transitions, a subset of computer animation techniques to turn abrupt transitions into smooth ones, thus providing a natural user experience, which is widely used in visual system designs in human-computer interaction (HCI) and information visualization (InfoVis) domains. A few general guidelines have been introduced for designing effective animations [20, 28], and the advantages and disadvantages of animations have been discussed [3, 28]. However, many of these recommendations are too general to guide the design of efficient animated transitions, especially in particular applications (e.g., InfoVis) that are concerned in this paper.

Animated transitions can be characterized by two types of parameters: temporal and spatial, i.e., parameters that govern object speed or pacing and ones that involve object trajectories. Some empirical studies about the temporal aspect of animated transitions have been conducted. For instance, Heer and Robertson [14] found that staged animations, i.e., breaking the whole animation into stages of movements, can improve a user's graphical perception for viewing statistical charts. Dragicevic et al. concluded that "slow-in, slow-out" pacing has a better object tracking performance than constant speed in animations [6]. Guilmaine et al. found advantages of using a hierarchical animation technique for tracking certain kinds of changes in tree visualizations [13]. However, such temporal approaches commonly increase the total animation time, which may not optimize users' performance. Moreover, Chevalier et al. discovered that staggering, i.e., delaying the start time of elements incrementally, actually has a negligible effect on object tracking accuracy [5].

The spatial aspect of animated transitions is related to studies on multiple object tracking (MOT) in perceptual psychology [23], since many animations usually require the user to understand which objects (e.g., points, disks, bars, etc.) move to which locations during the transitions. Results from these studies reveal key factors for people's performance in MOT tasks: speed, trajectory, and spacing. Increasing objects' moving speeds impairs tracking accuracy and decreases the maximum number of targets people can track [1,9,26], except for one case when the speed is changed by scaling the display as a whole [10]. Suganuma and Yokosawa found that the tracking accuracy is also impaired when targets share similar trajectories with distractors [27]. Object spacing can be characterized by the concept of crowding. People can track a maximum of 7 or 8 objects when there is adequate spacing, but this number drops as objects become more crowded [10].

Study results also suggest that the identities of targets tend to be lost when they are close to each other and when more distractors are introduced [22]. Despite that extensive research of this topic in psychology literature has provided a lot of empirical data and general guidelines, little has been done to propose techniques and algorithms for improving animated transitions from the spatial aspect (e.g., by carefully planning object trajectories), which is our focus here.

In InfoVis, animated transitions are usually used to smooth the switching between data views, charts, and layouts, which involves location shifting of a large number of objects. Different from general MOT tasks, elements on a visualization view often imply certain relationships among each other, that indicate different "virtual groups" of data items in a user's mental model. For example, points located close-by in a scatterplot share similar attributes, and nearby graph nodes have stronger connections in a force-directed layout [7]. To enhance the understanding and tracing of these relationships during animated transitions, results of the above empirical studies indicate that trajectory is an important cue for perceptual grouping, i.e., letting related targets move in similar trajectories and separate from distractors [27].

For static visualizations, edge bundling [16] is a common technique to reduce the number of line crossings by grouping similar edges, which has been widely applied in many visual representations including graphs, parallel coordinates, and flow maps. Nevertheless, it remains an open problem whether similar techniques can be employed in trajectory bundling in animated transitions to ease a user's tracking relevant targets across two views. Moreover, trajectories in animations have substantial differences from edges in visualizations: (1) trajectories are virtual (not visible), and (2) trajectories consist of both spatial and temporal dimensions (e.g., trajectory crossings may not result in object collisions in an animation). In summary, to the best of our knowledge, this work is the first attempt to enhance animated transitions in the spatial aspect by bundling object trajectories, and study the relevant factors and effect of this spatial approach.

TRAJECTORY BUNDLING

In this section, we introduce the design rationales and implementation of our trajectory bundling technique, which is proposed for helping users to efficiently track moving objects in animated transitions. We introduce this design based on the findings from several related studies:

- In a static display of objects, people tend to group the objects by their spatial proximity (Gestalt's proximity principle [19]). Similarly, in animated transitions, people tend to perceive objects with similar trajectories as a group [27].
- When tracking multiple objects, people are more likely to perceptually group moving objects together if visual cues of grouping are provided, and such grouping strategy can improve people's tracking performance [30].
- Distorted trajectories have minor impact on tracking single or multiple moving objects [12, 18].

Factors	Description	#	%
F1	Tracking more targets.	7	88%
F2	Increasing distance between targets.	7	88%
F3	Increasing number of occlusions.	5	63%
F4	Tracking over a longer distance.	4	50%
F5	Frequently changing target group's shape.	3	38%

Table 1. Top factors that increase the difficulty of tracking a group of moving objects reported by the pilot study users.

The first finding suggests that the objects (no matter static or moving) belonging to the same group should be placed close to each other to visually enhance their relationships. The second principle indicates providing visual cues to highlight moving objects' groups is helpful for object tracking.

We designed bundled trajectories (Fig. 1) to incorporate the above design suggestions. More precisely, we used bundled trajectories to smoothly aggregate a group of objects together during an animation, while keeping their initial and final locations unchanged. Such curved trajectories also provide visual cues of objects' group information. The third finding indicates that our design of using curved trajectories could be harmless for object tracking tasks.

We implemented the above design by using B-splines to represent the movement trajectories of a group of objects, which ensures the continuity of the movements. We computed three control points to bundle the splines together. As shown in Fig. 1, these control points are the mean locations of (1) the moving objects' initial positions, (2) the midpoints of their straight movement trajectories, and (3) their final positions. Based on these control points, we separated the transition into three stages: the merging, translating, and splitting of the group of objects. Intuitively, when compared with straight trajectories (dash lines in Fig. 1), bundled trajectories reduce moving collisions between different groups of objects, and show transition trends more clearly.

PILOT STUDY

We conducted a pilot study (8 participants) to identify factors that affect the difficulty of tracking moving objects and to collect users' feedback on our initial trajectory bundling design. During the study, we randomly generated 16 groups of 3–8 objects on a 2D plane. We ensured the objects in the same group to be closely located and move in similar directions. We showed the objects' movements to our users with either straight or bundled trajectories. We then asked the users to track a selected group of 3 or 6 targets during the animations.

This study helped us to find (1) the key factors that influence users' performance of tracking a group of moving objects and (2) the potential limitation of the proposed technique. Particularly, our pilot users commonly raised five factors as summarized in Table 1, which remarkably increased the tracking difficulty. Based on these factors, we designed a controlled study to evaluate the trajectory bundling technique under different complexity conditions. Also, most users felt the third stage ("splitting") was distracting and difficult to track. To reduce this limitation, we employed the "slow-in, slow-out" strategy in our formal study, to schedule more time for the merging and splitting stages.

STUDY DESIGN RATIONALES

In this paper, we largely borrowed the study methodologies introduced in [5, 6], since we believe the methodologies are not our focus and that reusing the state-of-the-art methods will ensure the accuracy of our experiment. However, it is nontrivial to fit those study methodologies into our problem. Many considerations have been made which will be discussed in this section, including our choices of task, test, testing environment, and complexity metrics of difficulty factors. Particularly, when compared with [5, 6], we defined a set of new complexity metrics to capture the features of a group of moving objects instead of individual ones.

Choice of Task

We focused on evaluating the effectiveness of our trajectory bundling technique at a low perceptual level. Similar with previous studies on animated transitions [5, 6], we chose to use *visual tracking tasks that require following a set of moving objects (targets), while ignoring other moving objects (distractors)*. This type of task is fundamental in animated transitions, since high-level tasks are considered to be equivalent to it, or highly depending on it, as discussed in [6].

Choice of Test

Our study focused on tracking a set of moving objects without identity, which is one type of MOT tasks [5]. At the end of such tasks, to judge the tracking accuracy, participants have to "select all/some" (i.e., select the final locations of all targets [5, 17, 25] or some of the targets [10]), or "probe one" (i.e., indicate if a particular object belongs to the target set [9, 11, 26, 30]), which are two main types of tests.

From the pilot study, we found the first test type does not fit our experiment. In our study, participants had to track up to 6 targets, where selecting all or some of the targets by using a mouse to click on each target dot was tedious and time consuming. Some pilot users complained that they forgot the answers during the selection since it cost too much time.

To avoid this problem, we borrowed the design of the "probe one" test. Particularly, we provided four sets of objects as candidate choices. Participants can review the choices by pressing the space key and make a selection by pressing the enter key; thus avoided inefficient mouse operations and ensured a quick selection. The four choices consisted of one correct answer and three distractors. We generated the distractors by randomly replacing one-third (i.e., 1 for 3-target tasks, 2 for 6-target tasks) of the targets in the correct answer with their nearest neighbors in the final frame. We conducted a series of tests with users after the pilot study to determine the proper replacing ratio that ensured a moderate task difficulty. Similar with the "probe one" test, in our design, the tracking accuracy of a test is 1 if the correct answer is selected, and 0 otherwise.

Choice of Testing Environment

To ensure participants focus on objects' movements in the study, we represented the objects as visually identical dots with the same shape, color, and size. This avoided the distraction of perceptual visual features, such as pre-attentive colors and shapes.

P	the set of data points in a dataset
$G \subset P$	a set of targets
$p, q \in P$	two data points
T	the set of sampled time points in an animation
$t \in T$	a time point
$d(p, q, t)$	the distance between p and q at time t
δ	the duration of a frame
r	the radius of a dot

Table 2. Notations used in the definition of the complexity metrics.

Also, we kept the dots relatively small to reduce occlusions during the movements. Here, we chose to control the size of the dots instead of the size of the displaying window for two reasons: (1) the window size should be fixed to ensure a precise control of movement distance, which is a key factor that influences tracking performance [10], and (2) reducing the size of visual items to reduce visual clutter is a common strategy that has been used in many visualization designs with high-density displays, such as node-link diagrams and multidimensional projections.

Finally, we conducted our study with a regular sized (15.4 inches) laptop instead of a big screen because the magnification changes of the display only have minor impact on people's object tracking performance [11].

Choice of Complexity Metrics

To better understand how the proposed trajectory bundling technique affects users' performance of tracking multiple moving objects under different conditions (such as different trajectory lengths or target numbers), we defined a set of complexity metrics (occlusion, dispersion, and deformation) based on the pilot study results for quantitatively measuring the complexity of these conditions. When compared with the existing metrics introduced in [5, 6], our new metrics focus on capturing group features of a set of related moving objects instead of the features of individual ones.

Metrics Definition

Based on the notations described in Table 2, we define our complexity metrics as follows. An illustration of these metrics is shown in Fig. 2.

Occlusion. Previous studies show that tracking accuracy is impaired when targets occlude with distractors [1, 9]. To measure the crowding between targets and distractors (i.e., how often targets occlude with distractors), we define a target crowding metric to capture the number of occlusions between targets and distractors during an animated transition:

$$occlude(G) = \frac{1}{|T|} \sum_{t \in T} \frac{\sum_{p \in G, q \notin G} overlap(p, q, t)}{|G|(|P| - |G|)} \quad (1)$$

where $overlap(p, q, t)$ is a binary function that determines whether p overlaps with q at time t. It returns 1 when an overlap occurs ($d(p, q, t) \leq 2r$); otherwise, it returns 0. $|G|$ is the number of targets, and $(|P| - |G|)$ is the number of distractors outside the target set. $|G|(|P| - |G|)$ normalizes the overall occlusions between targets and distractors at any given time t, and thus ensures the metric scores to be independent of the number of targets. At last, we compute the mean across all time points during an animation, as the final score of the occlusion metric.

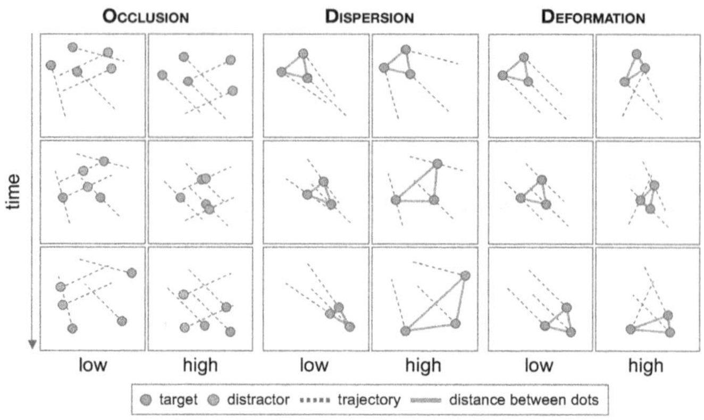

Figure 2. Illustration of the complexity metrics.

Dispersion. Animation design guidelines proposed by Heer and Robertson [14] suggest grouping similar transitions to help viewers apprehend elements undergoing the same operation. Also, Gestalt's proximity principle [19] reveals that objects near to each other are often perceived as a group. These were supported by our pilot study results. To measure the proximity of targets (i.e., how close they are to each other), we define a target dispersion metric to capture the pairwise distances of the target set during an animated transition:

$$disperse(G) = \frac{1}{|T|} \sum_{t \in T} \frac{\sum_{p_i, p_j \in G, i<j} d(p_i, p_j, t)}{\binom{|G|}{2}} \quad (2)$$

where $|G|$ is the number of targets, and $\binom{|G|}{2}$ is the number of 2-combinations of the target set G. $\binom{|G|}{2}$ normalizes the overall dispersion at any given time t, to make the metric scores independent of the number of targets. Finally, we compute the mean across all time points of an animation, as the final score of the dispersion metric.

Deformation. Previous work demonstrates that people's tracking accuracy is improved when targets' virtual shape remains constant [30]. To measure the change in targets' virtual shape (i.e., the difference of the targets' pairwise distance between two consecutive frames), we employed the metric definition proposed by [5], which captures all segments changes of the structure of a group of dots:

$$deform(G) = \frac{1}{|T|} \sum_{t \in T} \frac{\sum_{p_i, p_j \in G, i<j} |d(p_i, p_j, t) - d(p_i, p_j, t - \delta)|}{\binom{|G|}{2}} \quad (3)$$

where $|G|$ is the number of targets, and $\binom{|G|}{2}$ is the number of 2-combination of the set of targets G. $\binom{|G|}{2}$ normalizes the overall deformation between any given time t and $t - \delta$ (δ is the duration of a frame), and thus ensures the metric scores are not influenced by the amount of targets. In the end, we compute the mean across all time points of an animation, as the final score of the deformation metric.

Analysis and Discussion

Based on the above definitions, we analyzed the independence of the three complexity metrics via a correlation analysis, and explored the effect of bundled trajectories on the metric scores, when compared with straight trajectories.

Independence analysis. To analyze the independence of the proposed complexity metrics, we randomly generated 10,000 testing datasets. Each dataset contained 16 moving groups, and each moving group consisted of 3–8 moving objects. For each dataset, we randomly selected a set of 6 objects falling within the same group as the targets, and used straight trajectories for the transitions of all the objects. Based on these settings, we computed the scores of the three complexity metrics for each testing dataset, yielding 10,000 scores per metric. We then used these scores to calculate the Pearson correlation coefficients between each two metrics. The analysis results were summarized in Table 3. It shows that the proposed metrics were significantly independent of each other (p-values $< .001$), which confirmed their capability of capturing different complexity aspects of animated transitions with straight trajectories.

Metrics	Correlation (r)
occlusion / dispersion	-0.099
occlusion / deformation	-0.093
dispersion / deformation	0.090

Table 3. The pairwise Pearson correlation coefficients between each of the two complexity metrics. All have p-values less than .001.

Comparison of techniques. We compared straight and bundled trajectories based on the aforementioned complexity metrics, to see how bundled trajectories affect the scores of different metrics. To achieve this goal, we computed another set of complexity scores using bundled trajectories on the above generated testing datasets. We drew these two sets of scores (straight, bundled) in three scatter plots, one for each metric (Fig. 3). There are a total of 10,000 dots in each scatter plot, where each dot represents a testing dataset and its x and y coordinates represent the scores computed using straight and bundled trajectories, respectively. A lower score indicates a lower complexity.

In Fig. 3, we found that overall bundled trajectories reduced the occlusion and dispersion scores, and thus reduced the complexity of animated transitions from these two aspects. However, bundled trajectories increased the deformation scores, which was a reasonable finding, since curves have a higher deformation on average than straight lines. In order to further examine the theoretical results in practice, we designed a user study to compare the straight and bundled trajectories, and investigate the benefits and limitations of the trajectory bundling technique.

USER STUDY

Based on the aforementioned study design rationales, in this section, we introduce a controlled user study designed for two purposes: (1) to evaluate if the task complexity scores computed based on the three metrics are consistent with task difficulty perceived by users, and (2) to compare the effectiveness between straight and bundled trajectories.

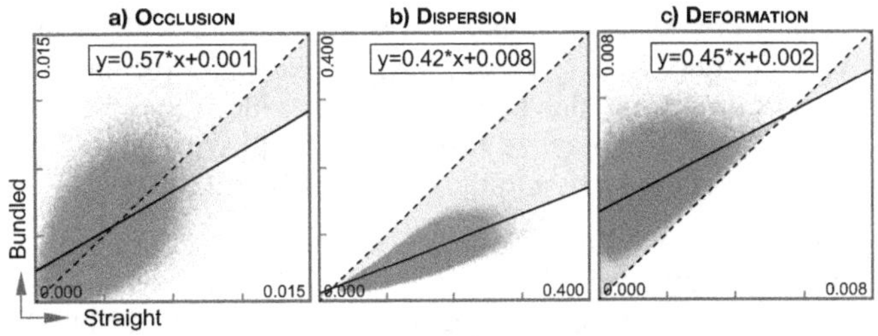

Figure 3. The comparison on computed scores between straight and bundled trajectories under each complexity metric. Predictor functions are annotated, with p-values less than .001. The dashed diagonal lines represent the equivalence of the complexity scores computed using each of the two types of trajectories. The solid lines are the linear regression results. The orange and blue areas show the decreasing and increasing of complexity scores when using bundled trajectories.

Participants and Apparatus

We recruited 16 volunteers (6 female) to participate in our study for comparing the two distinct techniques: animated transitions of moving objects with straight and bundled trajectories. All of the participants had normal vision, and were graduate students studying computer science. Their ages ranged from 23 to 33 (mean 27, $SD = 3.16$).

The study was performed on a laptop computer with a 15.4-inch display of resolution 1440$\times$900 pixels and 60 Hz refresh rate. Dots were displayed as circles of 9 pixels (0.2 cm) in radius, filled with black color. The animation window was 630$\times$630 pixels (16.8$\times$16.8 cm) in dimension, with a white background. Participants sat 55 cm from the display.

Procedure

At the beginning, we introduced the study to the participants and showed them example animations of two types of tasks: (1) tracking 3 targets moving along straight and bundled trajectories with the length of 0.5 units[1] and 0.8 units, and (2) tracking 3 and 6 targets moving along straight and bundled trajectories with the length of 0.5 units. These examples helped the participants to get familiar with our study tasks and gain some intuitions about the effect of the trajectory length and the number of targets.

Next, we gave the participants a brief lesson to teach them about using our study system to complete object tracking tasks. Particularly, in each task, users were first showed a set of dots among which targets were highlighted in red and distractors were in black. After memorizing the targets, users had to press the space key to play the animation of a study trial. Half a second before the animation started, the targets changed to black to avoid the distractions of colors. During the animation, users were asked to track the movements of the target dots. When the animation finished, users had to select the final locations of all targets based on four given choices, by pressing the space key to review the choices rotationally and pressing the enter key to make the selection.

Before the formal study, we asked the participants to finish 8 practice tasks using both techniques. Each of these tasks was at different complexity levels and had different trajectory lengths and different numbers of targets. These practice

[1]The width of the square animation window is defined as 1 unit.

tasks were designed to help users get familiar with different task complexities. We encouraged the participants to ask questions during the practice and provided them with the solutions of the practice task to ensure all participants fully understood the tasks and the two types of trajectories.

After the above preparation, we conducted the formal study. In the study, we fully randomized the order of the tasks and counterbalanced the order of using straight and bundled trajectories. For a given task, we used the same dataset with both types of trajectories to ensure a fair comparison. To avoid learning effect, we mirrored and rotated a dataset before reusing it. This approach ensured that for each of the two trajectory types in a task, the participants were tracking the same set of targets using the same dataset, but were unable to memorize the correct answer.

The tracking accuracy was recorded after each trial. After the study, the participants completed a post-study questionnaire to provide their subjective assessment of the difficulty of tasks of different factors (i.e., trajectory type, path length, and target number). We also conducted a brief informal interview to collect feedback from them. The whole study took approximately one hour per participant, during which the participant can take a break when needed.

Experimental Design and Task Generation

We employed a full-factorial within-subjects study in which each participant had to perform the following 96 study tasks twice, once for each of the two tested trajectory designs (two study blocks), yielding 3,072 (16×96×2) trials in total.

As summarized in Table 4, the three independent variables that we considered in our task design were: (1) trajectory length (0.5 units or 0.8 units), (2) target number (3 or 6), and (3) task complexity (3 metrics × 2 levels).

	2	Trajectory Length (*0.5, 0.8*)
×	2	Target Number (*3, 6*)
×	2	Occlusion (*Low, High*)
×	2	Deformation (*Low, High*)
×	2	Dispersion (*Low, High*)
×	3	repetitions
	96	tasks

Table 4. The design of study tasks.

We generated the above tasks in two steps. We first randomly computed a large number of transition datasets. Based on these datasets, we then selected the ones satisfying certain complexity requirements (e.g., low occlusion, high dispersion, and low deformation), as a task data used in the study.

Task data generation. We randomly generated 200,000 transition datasets, half of which (100,000 sets) used trajectories of 0.5 units in length and the other half used trajectories of 0.8 units in length (straight-line distance). Each dataset contained 80 moving objects represented as dots with a fixed radius of 0.014 units. We ensured that: (1) no dot overlapping existed at the initial and final frames, to avoid unnecessary confusions in users' target memorizing and answer selecting, and (2) all transitions had an equal straight-line length, to ensure objects' movements stop at the same time.

To generate data for tasks with different number of targets, we computed transition groups for each dataset, i.e., identifying groups of moving objects in which objects are close to each other at the initial frame and share similar moving directions. To achieve this goal, we extracted a feature vector (x_s, y_s, x_t, y_t) for each moving object, where (x_s, y_s) and (x_t, y_t) represent the x and y coordinates of the object's initial and final locations, respectively. This feature vector captured both the direction and location features of moving objects. We then used the K-means clustering algorithm to identify groups of objects (i.e., moving groups) based on this feature vector. In the implementation, we set $K = 16$ to make each group contain 5 objects on average. Finally, in each dataset, we randomly selected a group with exactly 3 or 6 objects as the target group of a study task.

Task selection. We selected the datasets used for study tasks from the randomly generated datasets by considering their complexity conditions. First, we computed three metric scores (occlusion, dispersion, and deformation) for each dataset and categorized each dataset into one of three complexity levels (High, Medium, and Low) based on its metric scores. Then, we sorted these datasets by the score of each metric in a descending order, yielding three ranking lists. In each list, for example, the one computed based on occlusion scores, we considered the first one third datasets as the "High" occlusion (labeled as *H*), the last one third as the "Low" occlusion (labeled as *L*), and the rest as the "Medium" occlusion (labeled as *M*). Thus, the datasets can be marked by these complexity notations. For example, the notation *LMH* represents the subset of the datasets of low occlusion, medium dispersion, and high deformation.

To obtain more sensitive results in the study, we removed datasets with *M* labels, and kept those with one of the following eight (2^3) complexity notations: *LLL, HLL, LHL, LLH, HHL, HLH, LHH* and *HHH*. For the study tasks, we randomly selected task data that satisfied this complexity requirement from the random datasets.

Task duration. Objects' moving speed is one key factor for people's tracking performance in MOT tasks [1, 9, 26]. To ensure a fair comparison, we chose to control objects' average moving speed in this study, i.e., 0.5 units per second for both types of trajectories. For transitions with straight trajectories, the durations were 1000 ms (0.5 units) and 1600 ms (0.8 units). For transitions with bundled trajectories, we set the durations based on the average curve length of the target dots to guarantee all dots move synchronously. The average curve lengths of 0.5 and 0.8 units (straight distance) were 0.64 ($SD = 0.07$) and 0.91 ($SD = 0.06$) units; thus the durations were 1280 ms and 1820 ms. Finally, we employed the "slow-in, slow-out" on both straight and bundled transitions, which did not affect the duration or the average speed.

Note that the duration of transitions with bundled trajectories was longer than those with straight trajectories. This may potentially bias the experiment results towards bundled trajectories. Studies that control the duration to be equal for both types of trajectories were left as future work.

Hypotheses

We made the following hypotheses to test in the study:

H1 For both straight and bundled trajectories, low complexity tasks in general have higher accuracy than high complexity tasks in terms of the three complexity metrics (occlusion, dispersion, and deformation), with the exception that low deformation may not be associated with high accuracy for bundled trajectories.

H2 When the number of targets increases, tracking using bundled trajectories has higher accuracy than using straight trajectories.

H3 When the trajectory length increases, tracking using bundled trajectories has higher accuracy than using straight trajectories.

H4 When task complexity increases in terms of complexity metrics (occlusion, dispersion, and deformation), tracking using bundled trajectories has higher accuracy than using straight trajectories.

Among these hypotheses, **H1** was made based on the design of our complexity metrics, and the observation that straight trajectories were significant predictors of bundled trajectories in terms of the metric scores (Fig. 3). We expected to have the exception in **H1**, since bundled trajectories increased the overall deformation in object tracking tasks (Fig. 3c). **H2** and **H3** were based on users' feedback from the pilot study, and **H4** was based on the fact that bundled trajectories reduced the overall occlusion and dispersion in object tracking tasks (Fig. 3a,b). We expected the deformation metric to be disconfirmed in **H4**, for the same reason as in **H1**.

Study Results

In this section, we describe the results of the above study. First, we validate our three complexity metrics (occlusion, dispersion, and deformation) by analyzing their correlations with users' tracking accuracy. Then, we compare straight and bundled trajectories based on the tracking accuracy of tasks with either of these two types of trajectories.

Validation of Complexity Metrics

Fig. 4 shows the mean accuracies of tasks with straight (a) and bundled (b) trajectories for each complexity level (low, high) in each metric (occlusion, dispersion, and deformation). Repeated Measures ANOVA was employed to compare the difference in mean accuracy between low and high complexity levels of each metric. Results of the ANOVA tests are annotated on the figure (significant ones at the .05 levels are highlighted with a white background).

We found significant differences in all metrics for both straight and bundled trajectories (except for deformation with bundled trajectories as we expected). Specifically, for each metric, tasks where that metric was low had significantly higher accuracy than tasks where that metric was high. This finding was consistent with **H1** and showed that our complexity metrics were highly correlated with the accuracy of the tasks. Therefore, these metrics reflected tasks' actual difficulty perceived by the participants.

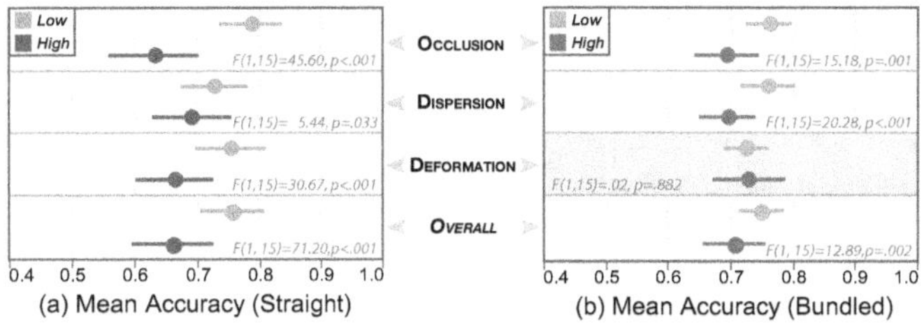

Figure 4. The mean tracking accuracies of tasks with straight (a) and bundled (b) trajectories, when each complexity metric (one per row) was low or high. Error bars are 95% confidence intervals (CIs).

Comparison between Straight and Bundled Trajectories

Fig. 5 shows the mean accuracies of 3-target tasks (a) and 6-target tasks (b), with either straight or bundled trajectories, when each complexity metric score was low or high. We conducted Repeated Measures ANOVA tests to compare the mean accuracy between tasks with straight and bundled trajectories, at each level of each metric. Test results are labeled in the figure with significant ones in a white background.

We found that the overall mean accuracy of 6-target tasks with bundled trajectories was significantly higher than with straight trajectories, which supported **H2**. Also, within 6-target tasks, for occlusion and deformation metrics, we observed that the difference of the mean accuracy between bundled trajectory tasks and straight trajectory tasks became larger and significant in high complexity levels, which partially supported **H4**. Surprisingly, this effect was not found in dispersion metric, which was not supporting **H4**.

In Fig. 6, the mean accuracies of tasks with 0.5 units (a) and 0.8 units (b) trajectories are presented, with either straight or bundled trajectories for every condition of the three complexity metrics. Repeated Measures ANOVA was conducted to compare the mean accuracy between tasks with straight and bundled trajectories, at each level of each metric (see test results labeled on the figure).

In general, tasks with bundled trajectories had higher accuracy than with straight trajectories, although there was no significant effect for comparing the overall accuracy (Fig. 6). However, significant effect was found in low and high deformation, and low dispersion conditions for 0.8 units length tasks. Moreover, for 0.8 units length tasks, when the occlusion and deformation complexities became higher, the accuracy of tasks with bundled trajectories became better than tasks with straight trajectories, which partially supported **H4**. Again, this effect was not found in dispersion metric, possibly for the same reason as discussed above.

From Fig. 5a and Fig. 6a, we found that the task accuracy difference between the straight and bundled trajectories techniques did not indicate a trend of increasing or decreasing when the complexities became higher, which seemed not supporting **H4**. However, these results were aligned with our hypotheses in **H2** and **H3**, where the benefits of bundled trajectories would be more obvious when tracking a larger number of targets in longer movement paths. Future studies are warranted to investigate these factors deeper with more levels of target numbers and trajectory lengths.

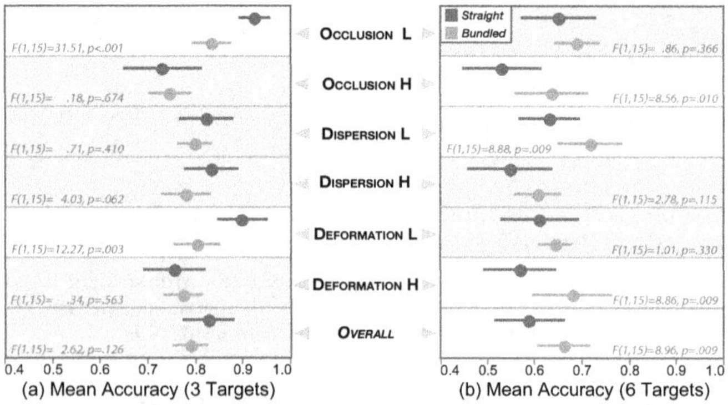

Figure 5. The mean tracking accuracies of 3-target tasks (a) and 6-target tasks (b) with either straight or bundled trajectories, when each complexity metric was low or high. Error bars are 95% CIs.

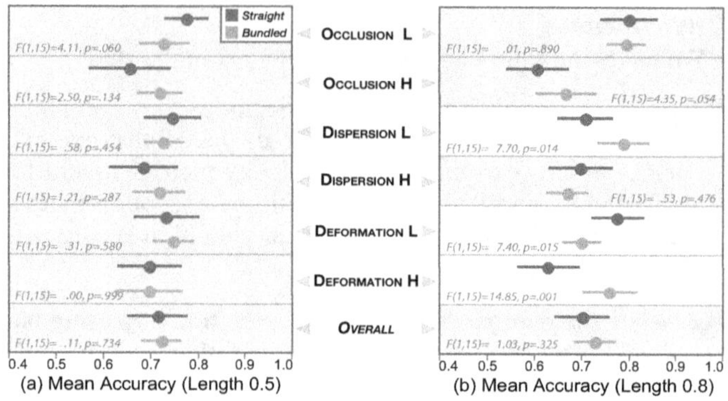

Figure 6. The mean tracking accuracies of 0.5 units trajectory (a) and 0.8 units trajectory (b) tasks, with either straight or bundled trajectories, when each complexity metric was low or high. Error bars are 95% CIs.

Questionnaire

Our study questionnaire contained eight questions to which the participants responded on a 5-point Likert scale (1=very easy, 5=very difficult). These questions compared the subjective difficulty between tasks with straight and bundled trajectories. Specifically, the comparison was based on tasks with 3 targets (Q1,Q2), 6 targets (Q3,Q4), 0.5 units trajectories (Q5,Q6), and 0.8 units trajectories (Q7,Q8). The results are shown in Fig. 7.

On average, the participants found tasks with 3 targets were easier than with 6 targets, and tasks with 0.5 units trajectories were easier than with 0.8 units trajectories. These differences were found in tasks with both straight trajectories and bundled trajectories. Comparing straight and bundled trajectories, on average, the participants found for tasks with 6 targets or with 0.8 units trajectories, bundled trajectories were easier to track than straight trajectories. However, for tasks with 3 targets or with 0.5 units trajectories, the participants' assessments of difficulty for the two types of trajectories were nearly the same.

DISCUSSION

In this section, we first introduce our findings in users' tracking strategies at each stage of animated transitions with bundled trajectories. Then, based on these findings, we explain the experiment results, and discuss the design implications.

Object Tracking Strategies

In our informal interviews after the study, we showed Fig. 1 to the users and asked them to describe their tracking strategies at each of the three transition stages (merging, translation, and splitting) when using bundled trajectories. We summarized the reported tracking strategies based on the transition stages.

Merging stage. At this stage, objects within a group move towards the first control point and are increasingly merged together. The most popular tracking strategy at this stage was "track one", i.e., following only one target, and then retrieving other targets after they become merged. This strategy reveals that at the merging stage, the movements of objects within a group are consistent and highly predictable; thus only one target has to be precisely tracked, based on which the locations of the rest can be inferred. This finding implies at this stage, the occlusions between the targets and distractors, and the deformation of the target group have minor influence on users' tracking accuracy. Moreover, the converging trajectories also reduce the dispersion of the target group, which has a tendency to improve users' tracking accuracy.

Translation stage. At this stage, objects of a group are tightly bundled together and move in a uniform direction. Users commonly developed a "grouping" strategy at this stage, i.e., perceiving and tracking the entire group of multiple objects as one single virtual object. This "grouping" strategy helped reduce the tracking difficulty as reported by our users, and can improve people's tracking accuracy as found in [30]. Moreover, at this stage, since objects within each group were tightly bundled, occlusions between targets and distractors are likely to be reduced, and the dispersion and deformation will also be minimized, thus making it a stage at which moving objects are the easiest to track.

Splitting stage. At this stage, grouped moving objects spread out to different final locations. The users had to track each one of the targets separately, i.e., using a "track all" strategy. During the splitting stage, dispersion and deformation are both increased, and occlusions between targets and distractors would cause more impairment since each target has to be followed precisely. These together make it the most difficult stage for object tracking, as declared by the users.

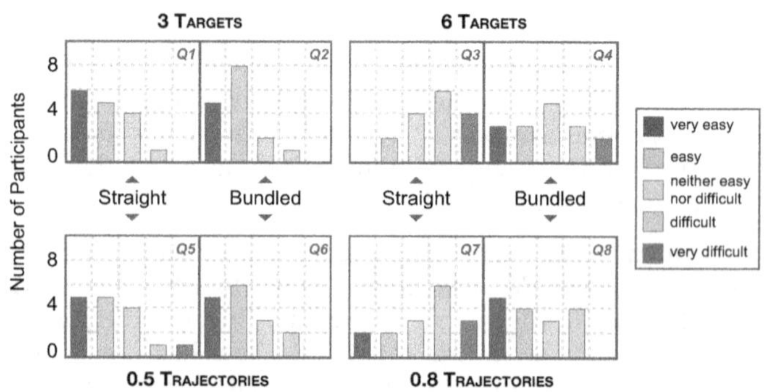

Figure 7. Results of the Likert-scale (1=very easy, 5=very difficult) questions (Q1–Q8) from the questionnaire session. A total of 16 participants responded.

Exploratory Analysis of Experiment Results

Based on the experiment results and the users' subjective feedback, we found both advantages and limitations of the proposed trajectory bundling technique. In general, bundled trajectories can help users to:

A1 Track more moving objects at a time. From the experiment, we found that for tasks of tracking 6 targets, using bundled trajectories has a significantly higher overall accuracy than using straight trajectories (Fig. 5b). In the questionnaires, users' subjective assessment of task difficulty also supported this finding (Q3,Q4 in Fig. 7). This benefit could come from the "track one" and "grouping" strategies used in the first two transition stages as discussed above. These two strategies allowed users to only track one moving object (either real or virtual), and thus significantly reduced the tracking difficulty. It implies that at the first two stages of transitions with bundled trajectories, increasing the number of targets only results in minor impairment on users' tracking performance. On the contrary, when using straight trajectories, more objects to track increases the chance of losing targets.

A2 Track moving objects with higher occlusion. In the experiment results, we found that in high occlusion condition, the accuracy of tasks with bundled trajectories was higher than with straight trajectories, and this improvement was significant in 6-target tasks (Fig. 5b). One possible reason is that bundled trajectories can reduce the overall occlusions in object tracking tasks (Fig. 3a), whereas high occlusion increases the chance of losing targets during straight-line movement transitions. Another potential reason is that, by using the "track one" and "grouping" strategies with bundled trajectories, occlusions during the merging and translation stages have less impairment on users' tracking performance, as discussed above.

A3 Track moving objects with higher deformation. From the study results, we found that (1) the tracking accuracy of tasks with bundled trajectories was nearly not impaired by high deformation (Fig. 4b), and (2) in high deformation condition, the accuracy of tasks with bundled trajectories was higher than with straight trajectories, and this improvement was significant in tasks with 6 targets (Fig. 5b) and tasks with 0.8 units trajectories (Fig. 6b). These two findings could be explained by the fact that although high deformation impairs tracking performance at the splitting stage of transitions with bundled trajectories, it has minor influence at the merging and translation stages. The finding (2) implies that this advantage is more remarkable when tracking more objects in long-distance transitions.

From the users' feedback in our informal interviews after the study, we found the major limitation of the trajectory bundling technique was caused by its splitting stage, during which individual targets have to be followed precisely. Specifically, the experiment results indicate that the trajectory bundling technique is less effective in two situations:

L1 Less effective in simple object tracking tasks. In our study, a task is considered to be simple if it satisfies any of the three criteria as follows: (1) the number of targets is small (i.e., 3-target tasks), (2) the trajectory length is short (i.e., 0.5 units trajectory tasks), or (3) any of its complexity metrics (occlusion, dispersion, and deformation) has a low score. The experiment results show simple tasks with straight trajectories achieved similar or higher accuracies than those with bundled trajectories, with only one exception for low dispersion (Fig. 5, Fig. 6). Particularly, straight trajectories significantly outperformed bundled trajectories in 3-target tasks under low occlusion or low deformation condition, and in 0.8 units trajectory tasks under low deformation condition. One explanation is that in the simple tasks, the impairment of the splitting stage outweighed the benefit of the merging and translation stage. This finding indicates the bundling technique is less effective, or even harmful, when the object tracking tasks are too simple.

L2 Less effective in high dispersion condition. Before the study, we hypothesized that in high complexity conditions, tasks with bundled trajectories would have higher accuracy than with straight trajectories (**H4**). However, the study results for the dispersion metric disconfirmed this hypothesis: bundled trajectories outperformed straight trajectories in low but not in high dispersion tasks (Fig. 5b, Fig. 6b). This could be explained by the observation that high dispersion tended to make the targets more separate at the final frame; thus intensified the weakness of the splitting stage. This finding suggests that in object tracking tasks, the trajectory bundling technique is more helpful when targets are closely distributed in the final frame and is less effective when targets are widely separated.

CONCLUSION AND FUTURE WORK

We have presented a novel trajectory bundling technique to facilitate tracking moving objects in animated transitions. Specifically, movement trajectories are "bundled" for a group of objects that are close in spatial locations and share similar moving directions. We have described a comprehensive controlled experiment to examine the effect of bundled trajectories by decomposing the complexity of object tracking tasks into different aspects. The experiment results indicate the effectiveness of using bundled trajectories when tracking more targets (six vs. three targets) or when the object movement involves a high degree of occlusion or deformation. Based on the results, we have discussed the strengths and weaknesses of our technique, and outlined design implications for generating movement trajectories to effectively track a group of objects in animated transitions.

Since our study is an initial work in InfoVis and HCI areas to propose and study bundled trajectories in animated transitions, there are a number of promising future directions to pursue. Particularly, our future work will include: (1) study of bundled trajectories in MOT tasks where moving objects have identities; (2) comparison of straight and bundled trajectories when the animation duration is controlled; (3) comparison of the trajectory bundling technique with other visual techniques that help to perceive group information in animated transitions; (4) study of the effect of "slow-in, slow-out" on object tracking with bundled trajectories.

ACKNOWLEDGMENTS

This work is partially sponsored by the U.S. Defense Advanced Research Projects Agency (DARPA) under the Social Media in Strategic Communication (SMISC) program (Agreement Number: W911NF-12-C-0028). The views and conclusions contained in this document are those of the authors and should not be interpreted as representing the official policies, either expressed or implied, of DARPA or the U.S. Government.

REFERENCES

1. Alvarez, G. A., and Franconeri, S. L. How many objects can you track? evidence for a resource-limited attentive tracking mechanism. *Journal of Vision 7*, 13 (2007), 14.1–10.
2. Bach, B., Pietriga, E., and Fekete, J.-D. Graphdiaries: Animated transitions and temporal navigation for dynamic networks. *IEEE TVCG 20*, 5 (2014), 740–754.
3. Baecker, R., and Small, I. Animation at the interface, 1990.
4. Cao, N., Gotz, D., Sun, J., and Qu, H. Dicon: Interactive visual analysis of multidimensional clusters. *IEEE TVCG 17*, 12 (2011), 2581–2590.
5. Chevalier, F., Dragicevic, P., and Franconeri, S. The not-so-staggering effect of staggered animated transitions on visual tracking. *IEEE TVCG 20*, 12 (2014), 2241–2250.
6. Dragicevic, P., Bezerianos, A., Javed, W., Elmqvist, N., and Fekete, J.-D. Temporal distortion for animated transitions. In *Proc. of SIGCHI* (2011), 2009–2018.
7. Eades, P. A heuristics for graph drawing. *Congr. Numer. 42* (1984), 146–160.
8. Elmqvist, N., Dragicevic, P., and Fekete, J.-D. Rolling the dice: Multidimensional visual exploration using scatterplot matrix navigation. *IEEE TVCG 14*, 6 (2008), 1539–1148.
9. Feria, C. S. Speed has an effect on multiple-object tracking independently of the number of close encounters between targets and distractors. *Attention, Perception & Psychophysics 75*, 1 (2013), 53–67.
10. Franconeri, S. L., Jonathan, S. V., and Scimeca, J. M. Tracking multiple objects is limited only by object spacing, not by speed, time, or capacity. *Psychological Science 21*, 7 (2010), 920–925.
11. Franconeri, S. L., Lin, J. Y., Pylyshyn, Z. W., Fisher, B., and Enns, J. T. Evidence against a speed limit in multiple-object tracking. *Psychonomic Bulletin & Review 15*, 4 (2008), 802–808.
12. Franconeri, S. L., Pylyshyn, Z. W., and Scholl, B. J. A simple proximity heuristic allows tracking of multiple objects through occlusion. *Attention, Perception & Psychophysics 74*, 4 (2012), 691–702.
13. Guilmaine, D., Viau, C., and McGuffin, M. J. Hierarchically animated transitions in visualizations of tree structures. In *Proc. of AVI* (2012), 514–521.
14. Heer, J., and Robertson, G. Animated transitions in statistical data graphics. *IEEE TVCG 13*, 6 (2007), 1240–1247.
15. Henry, N., Fekete, J.-D., and McGuffin, M. Nodetrix: a hybrid visualization of social networks. *IEEE TVCG 13*, 6 (2007), 1302–1309.
16. Holten, D. Hierarchical edge bundles: Visualization of adjacency relations in hierarchical data. *IEEE TVCG 12*, 5 (2006), 741–748.
17. Jardine, N. L., and Seiffert, A. E. Tracking objects that move where they are headed. *Attention, Perception & Psychophysics 73*, 7 (2011), 2168–2179.
18. Jolicoeur, P., Ullman, S., and Mackay, M. Curve tracing: A possible basic operation in the perception of spatial relations. *Memory & Cognition 14*, 2 (1986), 129–140.
19. Koflka, K. Principles of gestalt psychology. *New York: Har* (1935).
20. Lasseter, J. Principles of traditional animation applied to 3d computer animation. *ACM Siggraph Computer Graphics 21*, 4 (1987), 35–44.
21. Plaisant, C., Grosjean, J., and Bederson, B. B. Spacetree: Supporting exploration in large node link tree, design evolution and empirical evaluation. In *IEEE InfoVis* (2002), 57–64.
22. Pylyshyn, Z. W. Some puzzling findings in multiple object tracking: I. tracking without keeping track of object identities. *Visual Cognition 11*, 7 (2004), 801–822.
23. Pylyshyn, Z. W., and Storm, R. W. Tracking multiple independent targets: evidence for a parallel tracking mechanism. *Spatial Vision 3*, 3 (1988), 179–197.
24. Robertson, G., Fernandez, R., Fisher, D., Lee, B., and Stasko, J. Effectiveness of animation in trend visualization. *IEEE TVCG 14*, 6 (2008), 1325–1332.
25. Scholl, B. J., Pylyshyn, Z. W., and Feldman, J. What is a visual object? evidence from target merging in multiple object tracking. *Cognition 80*, 1-2 (2001), 159–177.
26. Shim, W. M., Alvarez, G. A., and Jiang, Y. V. Spatial separation between targets constrains maintenance of attention on multiple objects. *Psychonomic Bulletin & Review 15*, 2 (2008), 390–397.
27. Suganuma, M., and Yokosawa, K. Grouping and trajectory storage in multiple object tracking: impairments due to common item motions. *Perception 35*, 4 (2006), 483–495.
28. Tversky, B., Morrison, J. B., and Betrancourt, M. Animation: Can it facilitate? *International Journal of Human-Computer Studies 57*, 4 (2002), 247–262.
29. Wattenberg, M. Visual exploration of multivariate graphs. In *Proc. of SIGCHI* (2006), 811–819.
30. Yantis, S. Multielement visual tracking: Attention and perceptual organization. *Cognitive Psychology 24*, 3 (1992), 295–340.

Physical Loci: Leveraging Spatial, Object and Semantic Memory for Command Selection

Simon T. Perrault[1,2] Eric Lecolinet[2] Yoann Pascal Bourse[2] Shengdong Zhao[1] Yves Guiard[2]

[1] NUS-HCI Lab
National University of Singapore

[2] Télécom ParisTech – CNRS LTCI UMR 5141
46, rue Barrault, Paris, France

perrault.simon@gmail.com, eric.lecolinet@mines-telecom.fr, yoann.bourse@normalesup.org, zhaosd@comp.nus.edu.sg, yves.guiard@mines-telecom.fr

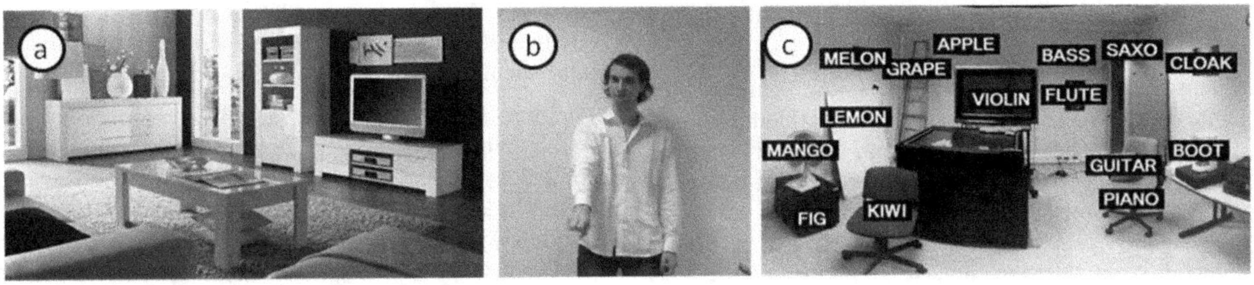

Figure 1. Principle of the Physical Loci technique: (a) The user creates associations between commands and physical objects in a room (e.g. living room), called *loci* (b) To create the associations or invoke commands, the user points at the corresponding locus; (c) actual examples of associations between commands and loci, in our experimental room setting.

ABSTRACT

Physical Loci, a technique based on an ancient memory technique, allows users to quickly learn a large command set by leveraging spatial, object and verbal/semantic memory to create a cognitive link between individual commands and nearby physical objects in a room (called *loci*). We first report on an experiment that showed that for learning 25 items Physical Loci outperformed a mid-air Marking Menu baseline. A long-term retention experiment with 48 items then showed that recall was nearly perfect one week later and, surprisingly, independent of whether the command/locus mapping was one's own choice or somebody else's. A final study suggested that recall performance is robust to alterations of the learned mapping, whether systematic or random.

Author Keywords

Spatial memory; memorization; command selection; input; association; method of loci; mnemonic device.

ACM Classification Keywords

H5.2. [User Interfaces]: Interaction Styles.

INTRODUCTION

Gestural shortcuts provide an effective way to issue commands. However, gestural shortcuts are only effective if users can easily learn and remember them. While handling a few shortcuts may be easy for most people, increasing the number of shortcuts makes the recall harder, therefore limiting the applicability and effectiveness of gestural shortcuts.

In this paper we introduce a novel way of memorizing gestural shortcuts which is inspired from the *method of loci* [36], an ancient memory technique that offers impressive learning capabilities. We also propose an implementation of this method, called *Physical Loci*, for interacting with a smart home environment, a context of use which is well suited for applying this technique.

The method of loci is a method of memory enhancement which uses images and spatial learning to organize and recall information. "Loci" refers to locations. The user of this classic technique first memorizes the layout of certain spatial structures that have a number of discrete locations, such as a building, or shops on a street, then the user mentally 'walks' through these loci and assigns an item to each by forming an image of the item and any distinguishing feature of that locus. The retrieval of items is achieved by 'walking' again through the loci, allowing them to activate the desired items. The efficacy of this technique has been well established in psychology literature [11,12]. Indeed, it has been used by memory contest champions to recall large amounts of faces, digits, and lists of words [28].

Although the effectiveness of this method is well known, it has yet to be applied to human-computer interaction. This motivated us to investigate the possibility of adapting this method for HCI use and study its effectiveness in facilitating quick memorization of an unusually large set of

CHI 2015, April 18 - 23 2015, Seoul, Republic of Korea

ACM 978-1-4503-3145-6/15/04...$15.00
http://dx.doi.org/10.1145/2702123.2702126

gesture shortcuts. In our adaptation of the method, Physical Loci (summarized in Figure 1), the users' task is easier as they are asked to associate the items to be memorized to objects and places of the surrounding physical environment, typically a room. Hence the mnemonic device involves visible, physical objects, rather than mental loci.

We conducted three experiments in which we examined learning and recall performances of Physical Loci. Experiment 1 was to validate our adaptation of the method of loci. We compared a Kinect-based implementation of Physical Loci with a mid-air Marking Menus baseline and found that Physical Loci significantly outperformed mid-air Marking Menus in facilitating memorization of shortcuts. Experiment 2 was a Wizard-of-Oz study designed to investigate two issues: whether the loci defined by one person could be used by another, and whether learned associations of 48 loci could be remembered after a day, a week, and two months. Our results indicate that loci can easily be shared among users and that retention is quite high. Our third experiment evaluated the perturbation effect of object displacement in the environment. In general recall times increased but recall rates were essentially preserved.

Overall our results suggest that Physical Loci is easy to learn, sharable among users, robust to simple environmental changes, and allows long term retention, which makes this technique promising for HCI. We also suggest scenarios where Physical Loci could be used in different contexts.

BACKGROUND AND RELATED WORK

The Classic Method of Loci

The method of loci, which dates back to the time of Aristotle, was popularized in the 1960s by Yates [36]. This method was used to remember long speeches without notes until the middle of the 17th century, and was described by Higbee [17] thusly: "Orators visualized objects that represented the topics to be covered in their speeches, and then mentally placed the objects in different locations—usually parts of a building. They then moved through this building mentally while delivering the speech, retrieving the object images from the locations as they came to them".

In the classic technique creating loci involves two steps. First, users must memorize mental images of familiar locations in some natural or logical order. Next they will associate a visual image of each item to be remembered with a location in the series. The first step is by far the most demanding but it needs to be performed only once since the same series of locations can be used for different lists of items with little interference [10].

The efficacy of this technique has been demonstrated in numerous studies since the mid-1960s [10,11,12]. Many of the studies, often conducted with students, typically were designed for remembering lists of 20, 40 or 50 words [11,12,17]. Some people have been known to achieve amazing performance, such as remembering thousands of digits in memory contests [22,28].

Practical use and application to HCI

Although efficient, the method of loci has several drawbacks. As explained above, the method of loci first requires creating and perfectly memorizing a mental representation of an ordered list of familiar locations. As one can easily verify on their own, this is a demanding and tedious task, especially for large item sets (e.g., more than 10 or 20 items). This constraint makes it difficult to apply the loci technique to HCI in its original form. A technique requiring too much initial effort is unlikely to be adopted by users. Moreover, the loci technique is purely a mental exercise. Applying it to HCI, and, more specifically, command selection, requires finding an appropriate implementation.

Personal and spatially constant mental representation

As a mnemonic device, an instance of the method of loci is created by the user, which means that people using that method can create association between any loci they are familiar with and the items they want to remember. Since places used are mental images, they rely on a spatial configuration and positioning of loci which is specific to the user. This limitation can be problematic in the context of HCI as several people may need to interact with the same system and use the same set of shortcuts. Moreover, this mental representation is not supposed to change, which means that loci are not meant to move.

Mnemonics techniques and HCI

Some mnemonics techniques inspired HCI research, such as Angesleva et al. [3], where the body image of the user serves as a mnemonic frame of reference, or Ikei et al. [18], where image annotations shown on a head-mounted display help users memorize places they visited before.

Memorization

Human memory has been extensively studied in the field of psychology (i.e., Baddeley's survey [5]). In their Working Memory model Baddeley and Hitch [5] illustrate the distinction between verbal and visuospatial information. Further, neuropsychological and neuroimaging studies distinguish between visual object and visual spatial information; we examine this distinction below [5].

Object memory involves processing features of an object or material such as texture, color, size, and orientation. In the case of the loci method, object memory plays a role in remembering precise details of the room. Yates [36] notes the importance of imagery in the method of loci because the more stunning, disturbing, or noticeable the mental images are, the better items will be memorized.

Spatial memory is another key component of the loci method as users must mentally "place" the items they want to remember in different locations. This mental place aspect increases the specificity of the loci technique, as opposed to other mnemonic devices. Spatial memory has garnered much attention in psychology [2,5,19,22] and, to a lesser extent, in HCI [4,8,29,30]. Partly because spatial learning occurs automatically, even without focused attention [2], spatial memory can help users to remember large numbers of items [5]. Maguire et al. [22] found that most of the champion memorizers they observed used a spatial learning strategy. Using functional neuroimaging, they also noted that this strategy engaged specific brain regions such as the hippocampus, which are critical for memory (and spatial memory in particular).

The utility of spatial metaphors has been shown since the development of HCI [8]. An interesting example is Data Mountain, which used a spatial 3D representation and thumbnails to help users organize, store, and retrieve 100 Web bookmarks [14,29]. This technique was shown to be faster than Internet Explorer's bookmark tree and remained effective after several months. However, this technique did not require users to recall the exact locations of bookmarks (whose names were visible on demand) but rather helped them to find their location faster. Command selection was considered in ListMaps [15], which illustrated the efficiency of grid interfaces for experts. Spatial memory was used in CommandMaps [30], in combination with hierarchy flattening, to improve GUI performance and in FastTap [16] to allow faster command selection on tablets. Finally, Virtual Shelves [21] relied on spatial awareness and kinesthetic memory for pointing accuracy, but not for the memorization of commands.

Verbal/semantic encoding also occurs in the method of loci. Items were clustered into categories in our experiments, as in most actual user interfaces. Structure is known to improve memorability [9]. Not only people recall more items if they are grouped by category [5, 23] but long-term retention increases when the structure of a set of gestural shortcuts reflects the structure of the corresponding command set [33]. Moreover, mental images used with the loci method can involve stories [36] (e.g. a painting, a place related to an historical event, etc.).

Combinations and complementary processes. Combining spatial memory with other cues has been shown to improve performance in terms of memorization [19]. According to Pavio's Dual Coding Theory [27] one can expand on learned material through verbal associations and visual imagery. Visual and verbal information are processed differently, along distinct channels, which increases the chance of remembering a given item versus the stimulus being coded one way. Moreover, imagery potentiates recall of verbal material and vice-versa, so that both channels should reinforce each other. *Elaborative encoding*, which is the process of actively relating new information to knowledge that is already in memory, may also improve long-term retention.

In conclusion, embedding memory in a detailed surrounding or context should help remembering it later and the combination of different memory channels is likely to improve memorization.

PHYSICAL LOCI

Physical Loci are a practical implementation of the loci method for gestural invocation in the context of a smart home environment. The significant difference is that this technique uses physical objects for recall (e.g. objects in the living room) and does not require the creation and memorization of an imaginary place, which is a tedious operation.

The user must first set up a mapping between a set of desired commands and loci in the room (Figure 1-a). For each command, he must point to the corresponding locus with his arm and validate to store this mapping. Commands can then be activated just by pointing to the corresponding loci and performing a validating action (Figure 1-b). Depending on the available technology, the pointing action can be done using a gesture- and location-aware remote control [34] or through free-hand interaction. While a button suffices to validate in the first case, a drawback of the second solution is that it requires a gesture delimiter, such as a quick opening of the hand [7] to distinguish command shortcuts from ordinary, everyday gestures. There is little constraint on the choice of loci except that they should be reasonably distant from one another to avoid confusion and easily identifiable by the system when the user points to them (e.g. pointing to the back wall should be avoided if using a Kinect).

Novice-to-expert transition is of particular importance in gestural interfaces. Norman [25] states a pure gestural system would make it difficult to discover its set of possibilities. We attempted to preserve the advantages of a smooth novice-to-expert transition, as in Marking Menus [20] where the user can learn expert interaction seamlessly through the force of repetition. Therefore, we provided a visual help which is displayed on demand. This visual representation, which is typically displayed on a living room TV screen, shows the locations of the loci and the corresponding commands. Figure 2 and Figure 5 illustrate different implementations of this visual cue.

EXPERIMENTS

Three experiments were conducted to investigate the following research questions.

- Exp. 1: Can Physical Loci facilitate memorization and invocation of gestural commands compared to a well-known gestural invocation method?
- Exp. 2: Once learned, how long can the loci command mapping be remembered? Can users use loci created by other people, and how does this use compare to loci created by the initial user?
- Exp. 3: How do changing object locations affect accuracy and selection times?

EXPERIMENT 1: PHYSICAL LOCI VS. MID-AIR MARKING MENUS

In this first experiment, we evaluate the ease with which gestures could be remembered with Physical Loci in comparison to a mid-air Marking Menu (mid-air MM) for in-air interaction because of its efficiency for remembering gestural shortcuts. Our implementation of marking menus was reminiscent of 2-level multi-stroke marking menus. It consisted of mid-air 2D strokes for its reliability and accuracy [37]. In essence, Physical Loci relies on pointing gestures (given location), whereas mid-air MM relies on directional gestures. In this experiment, we wanted to investigate how fast users would learn the mapping between gestures (mid-air MM) or loci (Physical Loci) with commands. Both techniques offer a smooth novice-to-expert transition, which allows measuring precisely when this transition happens.

The gestures were performed with the dominant hand. For simplicity we did not use a gestural delimiter [7] but a mouse held in the other hand. A left button press served to validate a Physical Loci pointing gesture and to mark the beginning and end of a mid-air MM gesture.

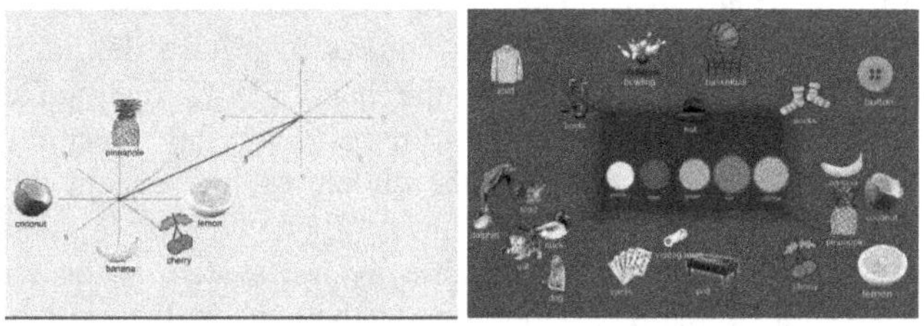

Figure 2. Visual feedback in novice mode for mid-air MM (left) and for Physical Loci (right). A virtual 3D representation of the loci on the walls was shown in this experiment.

Both techniques had a novice and an expert mode. In both cases novice mode is triggered using a click on the right button of the mouse (in a real system an appropriate gesture might serve this purpose). In a standard marking menu, the novice display normally appears after a short delay, but maintaining an extended-arm posture repeatedly in the experiment would have induced fatigue. We used a standard 2D representation for the mid-air MM novice mode (Figure 2-left) and a projected 3D representation showing the approximate location of the loci in the room for Physical Loci (Figure 2-right).

Participants and Apparatus

Participants were 3 females and 9 males aged 15-30 (average age 23); all were right-handed. The 12 participants performed a within-subjects experiment with the order of the techniques counterbalanced among participants following a Latin square. The experiment was conducted in a room (6 × 4.5 × 2.7 m) emulating a home environment (with a sofa, a table, two cupboards and posters on the walls). Participants stood 2.5m in front of a 42″ TV screen that displayed the stimuli and the visual help (Figure 2). Tasks were to first create a mapping by assigning commands to loci; then to recall the defined mappings.

Pointing, performed in the air using the dominant hand, was detected by a recognition system developed for this experiment using a Kinect for Windows 1.5. To facilitate tracking and avoid errors, loci had to be large and well-spaced from each other, were not permitted on the back wall and several loci could not be part of the same object. Participants were asked to name aloud the item they were selecting as to distinguish between recall errors and detection errors by the system.

Vocabulary and Stimuli

Experiment 1 used a vocabulary of 25 items divided into five categories of five items each (*animals*, *clothing*, *colors*, *fruits*, and *leisure activities*). We used categories to mimic realistic tasks, where commands usually belong to different categories. This 5×5 configuration also avoided penalizing the 2-level marking menu as participants could map each category to a single submenu. Stimuli were displayed on the screen as both text and image. We used a vocabulary of names that all participants would equally recognize and avoided names with an obvious relationship to loci.

Procedure

After a 10-minute familiarization stage, the mapping phase began. Participants were asked to associate a particular gestural response, either a 2-segment marking menu gesture (mid-air MM condition) or a locus in the surrounding space (Physical Loci condition), to each stimulus. For conformity, only posters could be chosen as loci in this experiment. Items were presented sequentially in a random order.

In the retrieval phase, participants were asked to first remember the particular location or gestures associated to an item and then select the item as quickly and accurately as possible. For each block, each stimulus was presented once, in a randomized order. Upon selection, users received feedback letting them know if the retrieval was correct.

Each technique was tested by participant on four blocks, for a total of 200 selections (25 items × 2 techniques × 4 blocks). In the first three blocks, the system was in expert mode by default, but the user could trigger the novice mode, if desired. In these phases, a trial would only end when the user selected the right item: in case the first selection of a trial was incorrect, the novice display would appear, forcing the user to select the correct command in novice mode. In the fourth phase, only the expert mode was available. The entire experiment lasted around one hour.

Results and Discussion

We were interested in both recall rates and system detection accuracy. We first present the results obtained from the data collected by the experimenter using mouse click data and spoken targets. Figure 3 illustrates the average number of correct selections for both techniques in expert mode only. The participants were free to interact in novice or expert mode in all but the final phase (forced expert mode).

The two learning curves are remarkably parallel except that the Physical Loci technique (PL) starts at a higher level. The difference in expert recall is a constant six items in favor of PL. Participants often felt confident enough to begin in expert mode during the first recall phase, particularly when using PL. Here, without assistance, they correctly selected more than 12 items on average. With both techniques there was a smooth and efficient novice to expert transition, with an average of 3.1 items learned in each phase. In the third phase, many Physical Loci participants felt confident enough to try the expert mode, correctly selecting ~17 items on average. In the fourth phase (compulsory expert mode), PL substantially outperformed the baseline technique. Participants recalled 22.1 items on average for Physical Loci vs. 16.4 for mid-air MM (MMM). A *t*-test for correlated samples confirmed the statistical significance of this difference ($t_{11} = 1.31$, $p<.01$). Although the experimental setup was different, and thus hard to compare, MMM results were roughly in phase with former results on memorization with similar 2D techniques (e.g., 12.9 over 16 items in [6]).

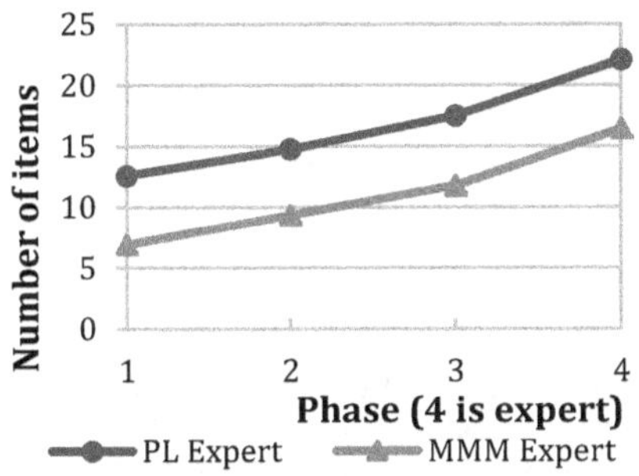

Figure 3. Average number of items remembered over time by users. Block 4 is expert-only block.

Time Performance. A *t*-test on total time (time elapsed to the user's mouse click) on the last block showed that PL was significantly faster than MMM ($t_{11}= 1.36$, $p<.01$), ending up at 3.89s against 5.27s for MMM. Reaction time was also noticeably shorter for PL (0.92s vs. 3.14s.)

System and Pointing Errors. As already mentioned, a Kinect-based system was employed to track the user's hand. In the final block, participants correctly selected an average of 14.4 items using MMM (vs. 16.4 indicated orally; thus 14.4/16.4 = 88% of these correctly recognized by Kinect) and 17.8 with PL (versus 22.1; thus 17.8/22.1 = 81%). While these results are still insufficient for real applications they are encouraging given the limited resolution of this depth camera and the pace of technological progress.

While the recall performance of the Physical Loci technique was encouragingly high, the design of the experiment did not provide data about longer-term recall; we investigated that next.

EXPERIMENT 2: TRANSFER AND LONG TERM RECALL

First, we wanted to know how the technique would perform with a *larger number of items*. Taking into account former experiments with the method of loci [11,12,17] and the fact that the experiment should not be lengthy, we chose 48 items, a rather large size relative to previous studies on expert command selection in HCI. As in the previous experiment, items were divided in categories, but of different sizes. This choice was made for the sake of external validity, as commands are generally grouped in categories of varying sizes.

Second, we added recall testing on the following day and one week later to evaluate *memory retention*. We also performed a recall test after two months with the (11 among 16) participants that were still available.

Third, while the original loci method was developed for personal use, we wanted to see whether participants could efficiently use *a mapping somebody else created*. We thus performed a between-subjects experiment with two groups: the *active* mapping group created their own mapping while the *passive* group used someone else's.

Finally, in order to release constraints about what could be a locus and still achieve sufficient precision we used a laser pointer and a Wizard-of-Oz approach. The only condition was that participants could clearly name what they were pointing to when defining loci associations in the mapping phase so that the experimenter could verify if they were pointing to the right loci during the experiment. Moreover, we improved the technique in several ways from Exp 1. During the mapping phase, all the items were presented at the same time, instead of presenting them one by one. This allowed participants to create clusters more easily. We also improved the novice mode by using a panoramic view (Figure 5) displaying loci/items associations more clearly, thus making it easier to get a global view of the mapping.

Task, Stimulus and Visual Help

For each trial, participants used the laser pointer to indicate the locus associated to the stimulus. To validate their selection they had to press a mouse button (allowing the accurate measurement of execution times). As previously, we asked participants to indicate the selected locus orally so we could distinguish pointing and mapping errors, although, ultimately no pointing errors were identified. The human wizard then clicked on the corresponding object in the experimental software. Upon selection, the system displayed the name of the selected item on the screen for three seconds, and proceeded to the next trial.

We used a neutral command vocabulary of 48 items consisting of 6 categories (*animals*, *clothing items*, *fruits*, *jobs*, *leisure activities*, and *musical instruments*). Each category had 6, 8 or 10 items. The stimulus and the visual help were displayed on a 42" TV screen at a 2.5m distance from the participant. We improved the visual help to provide a panoramic image of the room showing the name of the items associated to the loci (Figure 5). Names without icons were used to save space, avoid collision of items and hide parts of the panoramic image.

Participants

This experiment consisted of 16 new participants: 12 males and 4 females aged 22–36 (*M*=26.4). Eight participants performed the experiment in the *active* condition; eight participants in the *passive* condition.

Procedure

The experiment was divided in three sessions that consisted of training and recall blocks (Table 1). In training blocks, the visual help was delivered on user demand, after an erroneous selection, or 10 seconds after the beginning of the trial if no selection was made. In recall blocks, users could not receive help eliciting one answer per trial. As in Experiment 1, each item appeared once in each block; hence, a block was composed of 48 randomized trials.

Session (time)	Blocks
1 (*t*)	Initial phase, 1 training, 1 recall, 1 training, 1 recall block
2 (*t*+1 day)	1 recall, 1 training, 1 recall block
3 (*t*+7 days)	1 recall block

Table 1. Sessions in terms of recall or training blocks.

Initial phase in Session 1

The experiment started with a mapping phase, where participants were shown the list of items they had to remember. Then members of the *active* group were allotted up to 20 minutes (M=14.5 min) to create their own mapping. For each item, participants had to provide a short, non-ambiguous description of the locus they decided to associate with the item (e.g., "I am putting the *cat* on the *New York Poster*"). The experimenter recorded that description on the experimental software.

Using the visual help, members of the *passive* group were given a panoramic image with items already in place (Figure 5). The mapping assigned to a *passive* participant was created by the previous *active* participant. Participants had 4.5 to 5 minutes (M=4.7 min) to learn the arrangement of items and to provide a short, non-ambiguous description of each locus. At no point during this phase were the participants given additional insight about the mapping.

Design

There were two crossed factors: *mapping (active or passive)* and *block*. Recall performance was tested 5 times, twice for sessions 1 and 2; once for Session 3. Thus, each participant ran a total of 384 trials: 48×2 training blocks (TB) + 48×2 recall blocks (RB) = 192 in Session 1, followed by 48×2 RB + 48×1 TB = 144 trials in Session 2, and 48 trials in Session 3. The dependent variables were selection time (the time spent to recall the position of an item and to point at it) and the number of correct expert-mode selections in each block.

Results

To evaluate the impact of the *block* and *mapping* factors on users' performance, we ran 2-way ANOVAs with repeated measures on the *block* factor.

Active vs. passive mapping

The *mapping* factor had an effect on the number of correct recalls ($p<.001$, $F_{1,14}=21.41$): members of the *active* group remembered more items (M_{active}=47.8/48 items vs. $M_{passive}$= 46.4). Surprisingly, members of the *active* group could remember almost all items (M=47.5) at the first recall block, and all of them at the second recall block of Session 1 (Figure 4 and Table 2).

Members of the *passive* group needed more blocks to learn the mapping which explains the interaction between *block* × *mapping* factors ($p<.001$, $F_{2,28}=13.47$). However, *passive* users reached similar performance (M=47) at the second recall block. A post-hoc TukeyHSD test suggested that the gap between the two groups became insignificant ($p>.05$) after second recall block of Session 1. In Session 2, we noted no difference between the two groups of users (p=.22), and a marginal one in Session 3 (p=.07).

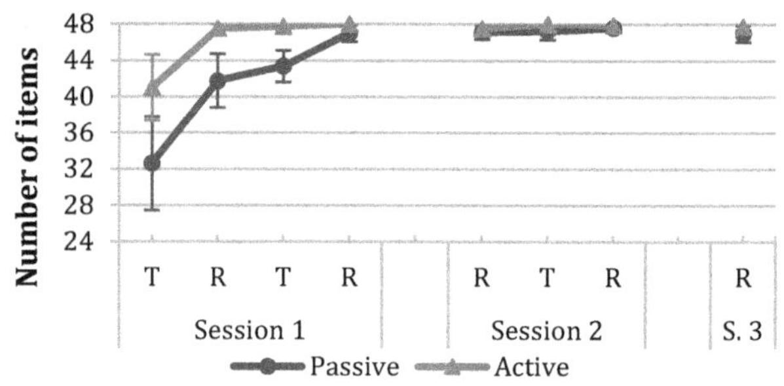

Figure 4. Mean number of items correctly recalled in expert mode for both groups. R denotes a recall block, T a training block. Error bars represent .95 confidence intervals.

Retention over time

We compared the results between the last recall block of Session 1 and first recall block in Session 2 (Table 2). For the *active* condition, we observed a marginally significant (p=.06) small decrease of performance (48 to 47.5). *Passive* condition showed a non-significant increase of performance (p=.4; 47 to 47.1 items). A comparison of the last recall block of Session 2 with Session 3 brought similar results, with a non-significant decrease of performance. Hence, performance was remarkably stable over this period.

Mapping	Session 1				Session 2			Ses. 3
Condition	T	**R**	T	**R**	**R**	T	**R**	**R**
Active	41 (0)	47.5 (5)	47.8 (6)	48 (8)	47.5 (5)	48 (8)	47.9 (7)	47.8 (6)
Passive	32.6 (0)	41.8 (0)	43.4 (1)	47 (4)	47.1 (4)	47.3 (6)	47.6 (5)	47 (4)

Table 2. Average number of items recalled over time depending on the mapping condition. Bracketed figures indicate the number of participants that managed to recall all 48 items in the block. R = recall block; T = training block.

Time Performance

We expected the task to be more demanding for members of the *passive* mapping group, and therefore to require more time. However, as shown in Figure 6, the *mapping* factor did not influence trial completion time (p=.71). Moreover, the average time decreased between sessions ($p<.001$, $F_{4,75}=11.42$). More precisely, time significantly decreased between the recall blocks within sessions (Figure 6), with a minimum of 2.9s for the last recall block of Session 2.

Figure 5. Panoramic picture of the room, with item labels placed on loci, used both for the mapping and as memory aid.

As seen above, *passive* users needed more blocks to achieve equivalent performance to *active* users. However, the initial phase was longer for *active* users (14.5 vs. 4.7 min). As memorization is known to depend on time, we compared the overall time required to achieve a nearly-perfect recall rate of 47 items or more. The values for both groups are very close: M_{active}=24.9 min for *active* users vs. $M_{passive}$=25.6 min for *passive* users. Hence, contrary to our expectation, this technique seems to have little or no dependence on whether the mapping is user-defined or not

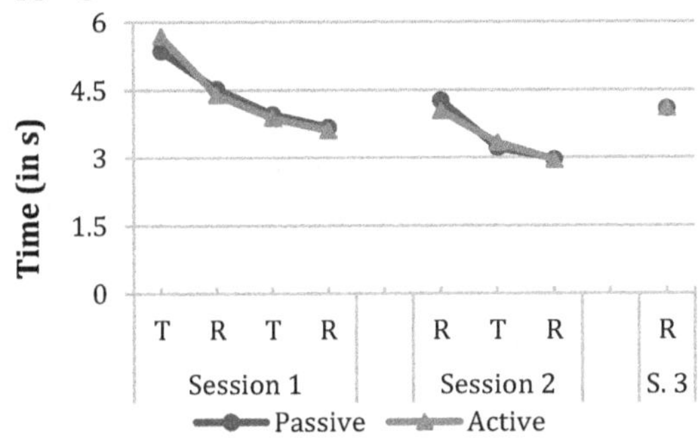

Figure 6. Average time to complete trial for each mapping condition over blocks in export mode.

Subjective results

At the end of the experiment, we asked users to rate the cognitive load on a 5-point Likert scale. A Mann-Whitney test indicated no significant differences between the two groups (M_{active}=2/5 vs. $M_{passive}$=2.2/5, p=.31). There were no reports from participants that they had trouble remembering the mapping, with no significant difference between groups (M_{active}=1.5 vs. $M_{passive}$=2.1, p=.17), suggesting no objective or subjective difference in terms of cognitive load.

We asked the participants to rate their surprise towards the results on a 5-point Likert scale. Participants were impressed by the results (3.4/5), especially those who had not previously heard about mnemonic devices and memory contests (3.9/5). This is not a surprising result as users tend to underestimate their memory capabilities [5]. More remarkable was that no difference in terms of surprise was found between the two groups (p=.42), although the passive mapping condition might seem harder.

Follow-up study two months later

We also performed a recall test 60 (+/-3) days after the experiment with the 11 participants (4 active, 7 passive) that were still present at our university at that time. A t-test on recall rates did not yield any significant differences between both populations (p=.11), with *active* participants recalling 45.5 items and *passive* participants 43 items on average. Recall times were not significantly different between the two groups (M=7.1s, p=.55), but they were quite high, especially compared to the ones observed in the sessions 1, 2 and 3 of the experiment. These results suggest that the technique is quite resilient over time, with an overall average of 43.9 items recalled after two months.

User Strategies

Active group

Although we did not give them specific cues, most participants used similar strategies during the mapping phase. They would typically start by imagining semantic links between the items and the loci, either through simple relationships ("the *peach* goes with the *red door*" – P3) or more complex associations of ideas ("the *waiter* goes with the *coffee machine* because waiters deal with coffee machines in real life, the *professor* with *books*, etc." – P7).

After a few key items were placed, participants would generally try to associate items of the same category to loci located in the same spatial area. When participants could not manage to do so (e.g. for large categories with many items) they tended to create subcategories (e.g. *wind* vs. *string* instruments). Participants also created semantic groups, e.g., by mapping all items of the *sports* category with all the *posters* of the room. Finally, participants sometimes used alphabetical ordering within a set of loci.

Participants were remarkably inventive at building up stories to link loci corresponding to the same item category ("the *dog* barks at the *cat* from the floor" – P5, who placed the cat on top of the table and the dog at the foot of the table). Altogether, these grouping strategies, using either spatial or semantic relationships through storytelling seemed to play an important role for finding the item/loci associations. For instance, when unsure about an item/locus association during the testing phase, participants would typically look at the area corresponding to this category and proceed by elimination. Moreover, as P11 said "It was easy to remember grouped items. It wasn't important how big the group was, just the sense of them being together."

Passive group

Similar strategies emerged for the passive group although the item/loci associations of these users were generally unrelated to those of the active group. For instance, while P11 (*active* participant) associated *tennis* with the *scanner printer* because it was in the same spatial area as other loci related to sports, P12 (*passive* participant using the same mapping) invented a semantic relationship between this locus and this item ("the *scanner-printer* is flat, like a *tennis* court"). Such re-interpretations occurred frequently, suggesting that participants could very easily create their own stories whatever the mapping.

Discussion
In the Background and Related work section we mentioned three components involved in memorization: object, spatial memory and semantic encoding. Previous observations suggest that spatial and semantic memory play an important role. Semantic memory was used for mapping items to loci and for creating groups of related loci. Spatial memory may be involved either globally (absolute loci positions in the room help remembering the items) or locally (relative loci positions in a group to help remembering the items).

By construction, the method of loci heavily relies on spatial organization. Practically, this could be a limitation of our technique as objects may be moved from time to time in a real-life setting. Hence, we designed a follow up study to investigate how moving loci across the room would affect recall.

FOLLOW-UP STUDY: MOVING OBJECTS
This new experiment used the same task and visual aid as the previous one but was divided into two sessions, with the spatial configuration of the room changing between sessions. The first session mirrored the previous study, with the same number of blocks. The second session was conducted the next day and consisted of two recall blocks.

Five categories of five items were used in this experiment (*animals*, *clothes*, *jobs*, *music instruments* and *sports*). The mapping phase was more constrained than in Experiment 2: five sets of 5 loci were pre-identified in the room and participants were asked to map these 5 sets with the 5 categories. This constraint allowed us to move or reorganize these 5 sets in the same way for all participants. Somehow, this constraint just operationalized what users naturally tended to do in the previous experiment.

Loci Reconfiguration
We considered *global* and *local* changes to object locations. In the first case, the set of loci is moved to another side of the room but the relative positions of the loci within the set remain the same. In the second case, only the positions of the loci within the set are changed (and remain in the same spatial area). The remaining cases were *baseline* (no change), *global+local*, and *scattered*. In the last case, the loci were scattered and relocated haphazardly in the room, breaking spatial consistency. Each of the 5 sets was moved according to one these 5 configurations. All groups were reconfigured at the same time, between the two sessions.

Participants and Design
This experience consisted of 9 participants, 7 males and 2 females aged 20–30 (M=25.8). The only factor of the experiment was *loci reconfiguration* (Figure 7). For the sake of brevity, we focus on recall rates and times on both blocks of Session 2 (next day), that show the same trends. Each participant completed a total of 150 trials: 25×2 T + 25×2 R = 100 trials in Session 1, and 25×2 = 50 trials in Session 2. We measured the selection time and the number of correct selections in each block.

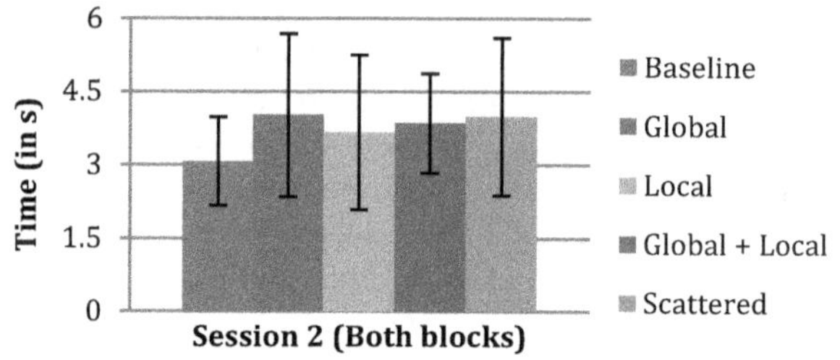

Figure 7. Mean trial times on both blocks of Session 2 for each reconfiguration. Error bars are .95 confidence intervals.

Results
An ANOVA showed no significant effect of loci reconfiguration on recall rate (p=.67) with a nearly perfect recall rate of 99.3% on Session 2, but had a significant main effect on recall times (p<.01, $F_{4,32}$=4.26). Pairwise t-tests with Bonferroni correction showed significant differences between *baseline* (M=3.07s) on one hand, and *scattered* (M=3.97s, p=.02), *global+local* (M=3.84s, p<.01) and *global* (M=4.1s, p=.03). No significant difference was found between *baseline* and *local* (M=3.66s, p=.4).

Condition	**Recall rates** (in %)			**Mean recall time** (in s)		
	B1	B2	Session	B1	B2	Session
Baseline	100	100	100	3.67	2.47	3.07
All but baseline	98.9	99.4	99.2	4.66	3.09	3.88
Global	100	100	100	4.7	3.34	4.02
Local	100	97.7	98.9	4.41	2.9	3.66
Global+Local	97.7	100	98.9	4.51	3.19	3.85
Scattered	97.7	100	98.9	5.04	2.93	3.99

Table 3. Performances for each block (B1, B2) and the session.

During Session 2, when looking for a particular object, users would usually turn around and look at the previous location of the locus, and then be puzzled when they discovered the new configuration. After that, they would perform a visual search to locate the new position of each object, explaining the differences between *baseline* and the other configurations. However, participants could gradually adapt to the new configurations. Recall times indeed decreased between blocks 1 and 2 (Table 3), and the difference between baseline and other configurations tended to decrease (from 0.99s on average to 0.62s).

Discussion
This follow-up experiment was intended to simulate a real-life situation where a few objects are moved at the same time, either globally (e.g., a cupboard consisting of several loci),

locally (e.g., a vase, books, etc. remaining in the same area), or randomly. The results suggest that users can still retrieve the corresponding items when spatial information is partly lost but that this loss of information leads to longer retrieval time (26.3% slower on average). While the number of moved items was relatively large for a realistic scenario, it is important to notice that not all spatial information was lost. For instance, results may have been different if all objects were moved randomly or the categories were larger.

GENERAL DISCUSSION

The most remarkable result of these experiments is that participants were able to efficiently learn an unusually large vocabulary of command shortcuts (48 items). With only slight exception, members of the *active mapping* group were able to correctly recall the full set of items in the first recall block: on average, they correctly recalled 47.5 items (98.9% of the set) in expert mode (2nd block of Session 1 of Experiment 2). Thus a single training block, with each item presented just once, was sufficient to learn our arbitrary vocabulary after the mapping phase. However, while impressively high, these results are in keeping with previous research on the loci technique (e.g. [12]).

Members of the *passive mapping* group achieved roughly the same result (47 correct recalls, 97.9%) by the second recall phase (4th block of Session 1). The total amount of time needed to achieve a recall rate of 47 items or more was roughly the same for both groups (M_{active}=24.9 min vs. $M_{passive}$=25.6 min). These results contrast with those of Nacenta et al. [24], who showed that user-defined gestures are easier to remember. This is probably because users were able to appropriate mappings created by others by creating new stories, as seen in the User Strategies subsection. From a practical point of view, this means that the same items/loci mapping can easily be shared among users.

Retention over time was quite high for both groups, with a recall rate of 98.9% (active group) and 98.1% (passive group) for the first block of Session 2, after one day delay. Session 3 (one week later) produced similar scores (99.5% and 97.9% correct recall). Two months later, the average recall rate of the participants still present at our lab was 91.5% (no significant difference between the two groups). Obviously, these participants did not use the system during this lapse of time, which differs from real-life, where users would relearn the mapping through continuous practice.

While our study does not precisely measure the relative contributions of the three main components involved in the memorization process (object, spatial and verbal/semantic memory) it provides some interesting hints. First, Experiment 2 showed that participants heavily relied on semantic memory for mapping items to loci and for creating imaginary relationships between loci. Participants were never out of ideas and had fun doing it. In fact, the creative process of creating stories was not only natural but enjoyable for them.

The last follow-up study clearly showed that retrieval time increases when spatial information is partly lost. However, participants could still manage to retrieve the correct items in most cases. This means that semantic and object memory could compensate for the missing information. Moreover, participants could quickly adapt to the new configurations.

APPLICATIONS

Smart home and multimedia. Smart homes offer numerous functions spanning from multiple multimedia capabilities to home security, smart energy and intelligent lighting or temperature control, etc. Remote controls have proliferated and tend to be overcrowded with buttons and confused by users. On the other hand, multi-purpose devices like smartphones or tablets often require users to select the desired appliance by searching through menus or long lists.

Physical Loci offers a simple and elegant solution to these problems. An actual system could nowadays rely on a location-aware remote control [34] or, in the near future, on an improved Kinect-like device. As in our second experiment, the system would let users create associations between loci and favorite commands by using the TV set. The user would first choose the command he wants to control (favorites TV channels, Youtube, lighting, etc.) through a conventional menu interface then point and select the desired loci with the remote control. After registration, commands would be executed by pointing on the locus and pressing the button of the remote control.

Virtual reality. As in the previous case, Physical Loci could be used in virtual environment to invoke commands without the need of displaying a menu that would interrupt the immersion of the user in the virtual world.

PCs, mobile devices. Physical Loci could serve to place invisible shortcuts at particular places on the desktop of a PC or a mobile device, thus allowing activating favorite commands very quickly. It could also serve as an unlocking mechanism for mobile devices. Instead of typing a PIN or drawing a pattern, users would select loci in a specific order to unlock the device, thus providing little visual feedback in case somebody else is watching the screen.

CONCLUSION AND FUTURE WORK

We presented Physical Loci, a selection technique reminiscent of the method of loci that leverages spatial memory, object memory and semantic associations. Results of the three experiments showed Physical Loci is easy to learn, sharable among users, robust to environmental changes, and facilitates long term retention, making it a highly promising technique for users to learn and perform spatial gestures. In further research, we plan to investigate more precisely the role of each of the components that have a role in the recall mechanism, namely spatial memory, object memory and semantic association.

ACKNOWLEDGMENT

This work was supported by the National University of Singapore Academic Research Fund R-252-000-547-112.

We also thank Joey Scarr, Gilles Bailly, Sylvain Malacria, Dong-Bach Vo and James Eagan for their suggestions.

REFERENCES

1. Anderson, F. and Bischof, W.F. Learning and performance with gesture guides. In *Proc. CHI'13*, ACM (2013), 1109–1118.
2. Andrade, J., Meudell, P. Is spatial information encoded automatically in memory? *The Quarterly Journal of Experimental Psychology 46*, 2 (1993), 365–375.
3. Angesleva, J., Oakley, I., Hughes, S., O'Modhrain, Body mnemonics: portable device interaction design concept. In *Adjunct Proc UIST'03*, ACM.
4. Ark W., Dryer, Selker T., Zhai S. Representation Matters: The Effect of 3D Objects and a Spatial Metaphor in a Graphical User Interface. In *Proc. HCI'98*, ACM (1998), 209 –219.
5. Baddeley, A.D. *Essentials of Human Memory (Classic Edition)*. Psychology Press Classic Editions, 2013.
6. Bailly, G., Lecolinet, E. and Nigay, L. Wave menus: improving the novice mode of hierarchical marking menus. In *Proc Interact 2007*, Springer, 475-488.
7. Bailly, G., Müller, J., Lecolinet, E. Design and Evaluation of Finger-Count Interaction: Combining multitouch gestures and menus. *Int. Journal of Human-Computer Studies 70*, 10 (2012), 673–689.
8. Bolt, R. A. "Put-that-there": Voice and gesture at the graphics interface. In *Proc. SIGGRAPH* '80, 262-270.
9. Bower, G. H., Clark, M.C., Lesgold, A.M., and Winzenz, D. Hierarchical retrieval schemes in recall of categorized word lists. *Journal of Verbal Learning and Verbal Behavior 8*, 3 (1969), 323–343.
10. Bower, G. Analysis of a Mnemonic Device. *American Scientist 58* (1970), 496-510.
11. Briggs, Gary G., Hawkins, Stephen; Crovitz, Herbert F. Bizarre images in artificial memory. *Psychonomic Science 19*, 6 (1970), 353-354.
12. Crovitz, Herbert F. Memory loci in artificial memory. *Psychonomic Science 16*, 2 (1969), 82-83.
13. Cloutier, J., and Neil Macrae, C. The feeling of choosing: Self-involvement and the cognitive status of things past. *Consciousness and cognition 17*, 1 (2008).
14. Czerwinski, M., Van Dantzich, M., Robertson, G., and Hoffman, H. The contribution of thumbnail image, mouse-over text and spatial location memory to web page retrieval in 3D In *Proc. Interact* (1999), 163–170.
15. Gutwin, C., Cockburn, A. Improving List Revistation with ListMaps. In *Proc. AVI'06*, ACM, (2006), 396-403.
16. Gutwin, C., Cockburn, A., Scarr, J., Malacria, S. and Olson, S. C. Faster command selection on tablets with FastTap. In *Proc. CHI '14*. ACM, 2617-2626.
17. Higbee K.L. Your Memory: How It Works and How to Improve It. Marlowe & Company, 2001.
18. Ikei Y., Otal H., and Kayahara T. Spatial Electronic Mnemonics: A Virtual Memory Interface. In Proc. *HCII'07*, LNCS 4558, Springer (2007), 30–37.
19. Jones, W., and Dumais, S.T. The Spatial Metaphor for User Interfaces: Experimental Tests of Reference by Location versus Name. *ACM Trans. Office Information Systems 4*,1 (1986), 42-63.
20. Kurtenbach, G. and Buxton, W. User Learning and Performance with Marking Menus. In *Proc. CHI'94*.
21. Li, F., Dearman, D., and Truong, K. Virtual shelves: interactions with orientation aware devices. In *Proc. UIST'09*, ACM (2009), 125–128.
22. Maguire, EA, Valentine, ER, Wilding, JM and Kapur, N. Routes to remembering: the brains behind superior memory. *Nature Neuroscience 6*, 1 (2003), 90-5.
23. Mandler, G. Organization and memory. *The psychology of learning and motivation* (1967), 381.
24. Nacenta, M.A., Kamber, Y., Qiang, Y., and Kristensson, P.O. Memorability of pre-designed and user-defined gesture sets. In Proc *CHI'13*, ACM (2013), 1099–1108.
25. Norman, D. A. Natural user interfaces are not natural. *Interactions 17*, 3 ACM (2010), 6-10.
26. Oakley, I. and Park, J. Motion marking menus: An eyes-free approach to motion input for handheld devices. *Int. J. Human-Computing Studies 67*, 6 (2009), 515-532.
27. Paivio, A. *Imagery and verbal process*. Holt, Rinehart, & Winston, 1971.
28. Raz, A., Packard, M. G., Alexander, G. M., Buhle, J. T., Zhu, H., Yu, S., Peterson, B. S. A slice of π : An exploratory neuroimaging study of digit encoding and retrieval in a superior memorist. *Neurocase 15*, 5 (2009), 361–372.
29. Robertson, G., Czerwinski, M., Larson, K., Robbins, D., Thiel, D., and Van Dantzich, M. Data mountain: using spatial memory for document management. In *Proc. CHI'98*, ACM (1998), 153–162.
30. Scarr, J., Cockburn, A., Gutwin, C. and Bunt, A. 2012. Improving command selection with CommandMaps. In *Proc. CHI'12*, ACM (2012), 257-266.
31. Scarr, J., Cockburn, A., Gutwin, G. and Malacria, S. Testing the Robustness and Performance of Spatially Consistent Interfaces. In *Proc. CHI'13*, ACM (2013).
32. Serrano, M., Lecolinet, E. and Guiard, Y. Bezel-Tap gestures: quick activation of commands from sleep mode on tablets. In *Proc. CHI'13* (2013), 3027-3036.
33. Wagner, J., Lecolinet, E., Selker, T. Multi-finger Chords for Hand-held Tablets: Recognizable and Memorable. In *Proc. CHI'14*, ACM, (2014), 2883–2892.
34. Wilson, A. and Shafer, S. XWand: UI for intelligent spaces. In *Proc. CHI'03*, ACM (2003), 545-552.
35. Wobbrock, J., Morris, M., and Wilson, A. User-defined gestures for surface computing. In *Proc. CHI'09,* ACM 1083–1092.
36. Yates, F. *The art of memory*, Random House, 1992.
37. Zhao, S., and Balakrishnan, R. Simple vs. compound mark hierarchical marking menus. In *Proc. UIST'04*, ACM (2004), 33–42.

LeviPath: Modular Acoustic Levitation for 3D Path Visualisations

Themis Omirou[1], Asier Marzo[1,2], Sue Ann Seah[1], Sriram Subramanian[1]
[1]Department of Computer Science, University of Bristol, UK.
[2]Department of Mathematics and Computer Engineering, Public University of Navarre, Spain.
{themis.omirou, s.a.seah, sriram.subramanian}@bristol.ac.uk, asier.marzo@unavarra.es

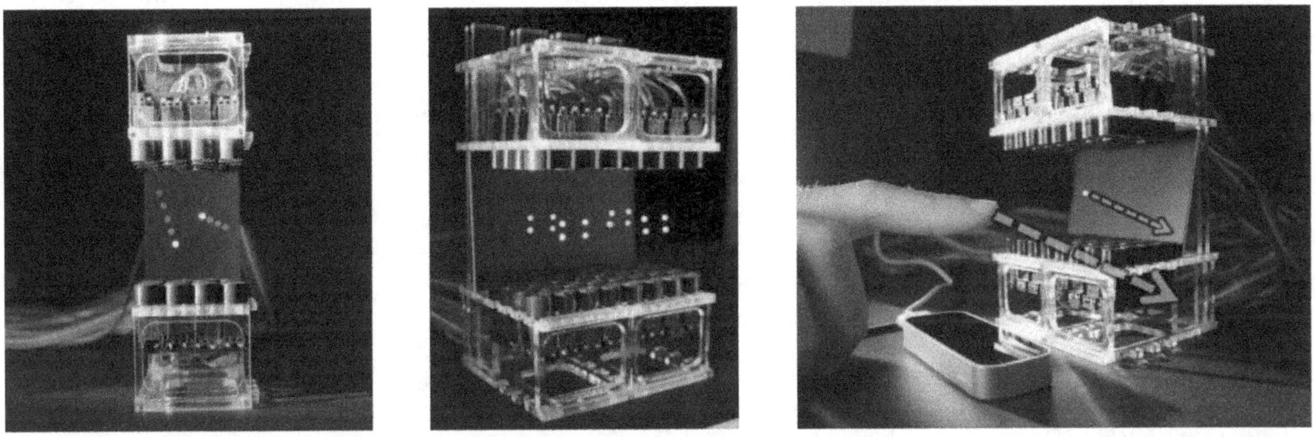

Figure 1: a) LeviPath uses two opposed arrays of transducers to levitate multiple objects across independent 3D paths; b) Interaction space can be increased by joining several LeviPaths together; c) Various devices can be used to interact with it.

ABSTRACT
LeviPath is a modular system to levitate objects across 3D paths. It consists of two opposed arrays of transducers that create a standing wave capable of suspending objects in mid-air. To control the standing wave, the system employs a novel algorithm based on combining basic patterns of movement. Our approach allows the control of multiple beads simultaneously along different 3D paths. Due to the patterns and the use of only two opposed arrays, the system is modular and can scale its interaction space by joining several LeviPaths. In this paper, we describe the hardware architecture, the basic patterns of movement and how to combine them to produce 3D path visualisations.

Author Keywords
Acoustic levitation; modular system; 3D paths; physical visualisations

ACM Classification Keywords
H.5.2. Information interfaces and presentation: User Interfaces.

CHI 2015, April 18 - 23 2015, Seoul, Republic of Korea
Copyright 2015 ACM 978-1-4503-3145-6/15/04...$15.00
http://dx.doi.org/10.1145/2702123.2702333

INTRODUCTION
Mathematicians have used physical representations of data since the 16th century. They calculated and assembled wood slices to represent and better understand 3D functions. Physical visualisations promote cognition and support visual thinking allowing humans to use an inherent skill set [8]. In a recent study Jansen et al showed that users preferred physical 3D bar charts as they were able to touch and point important parts of the chart with their fingers as well as rotate them naturally [5].

Even with the use of 3d printers and laser cutters, physical representations lack dynamicity to reflect changes in data. Shape-changing interfaces, such as inFORM [3], aim at solving this issue. inFORM consists of a 30x30 matrix of actuated columns that can individually change in height to create tangible dynamic height-fields. However, having solid columns can occlude some visualisations.

In this paper, we examine the suitability of acoustic levitation techniques to create dynamic physical visualisations. Levitation involves suspending an object in a stable position without solid physical contact. Thereby, objects can be placed in any 3D position of the interaction space enabling sturdy physical representations. Moreover, acoustic levitation offers additional advantages like direct reach-through interaction and the possibility of projecting on the object without occlusions. Several methods exist for contact-free levitation such as acoustic, optical, magnetic or quantum approaches [1]. Nonetheless, only some of them are suitable to exploit in an interactive context.

For instance, Zero-N [6] uses magnetic levitation to suspend a metallic ball and move it across the interaction space. It is possible to project on the ball and manipulate it. However, the levitated object needs to be magnetic, it is hard to scale the system for multiple objects and only the Z-axis position is controlled magnetically. The rest of the axes depend on mechanically-actuated components. Although the Universal Planar Manipulator [9] can magnetically move multiple objects, they are all resting on a table.

The use of acoustic levitation for HCI is exemplified by the system Pixie Dust [7]. In it, small objects are suspended and moved together using 4 opposed arrays of transducers employing a technique called focal lines. Although it allows several objects to be levitated, it does not enable individual control; all the objects move simultaneously in the same direction. Pixie Dust demonstrates the benefit of acoustic levitation for physical visualisations but also reveals the need for further improvements.

We present LeviPath, a modular system for levitating objects across 3D paths to represent functions, trajectories or other types of information (Figure 1). LeviPath has two main differences from previous acoustic levitation systems. Firstly, our system uses amplitude and phase manipulation to support controllable 3D levitation with only two opposed arrays of transducers. Secondly, our algorithm for controlling the position of the objects is based on the combination of basic patterns of movements. This allows to join several LeviPaths together to increase the interaction space. Additionally, different patterns can be used depending on the requirements of speed, manoeuvrability or power consumption.

LEVIPATH

LeviPath is our proposed modular system to levitate objects across a path for representing functions, trajectories or other information. LeviPath is composed of two opposed transducer arrays. Before describing the specific features of LeviPath and its working principle, it is useful to understand the principles behind acoustic levitation and the previous work in controlling a levitating object.

Principles of Acoustic Levitation

An acoustic transducer is a device capable of producing a sound wave with a certain amplitude and phase. By placing two transducers opposite to each other emitting with the same amplitude and phase, objects can be trapped and levitated in the space between, at the low pressure nodes of the standing wave. Furthermore, by changing the phase difference between the transducers the objects are moved from one transducer to the other [2]. With multiple transducers, two dimensional manipulation in air of solid or liquid particles can be achieved by either controlling the phase [10] or the amplitude of transducers [4]. Pixie Dust [7] goes further by using 4 arrays of transducers, orthogonally placed, to create three-dimensional movement.

LeviPath enables stable movement of multiple levitated objects in 3D space by manipulating both the phase and amplitude of subsequent opposed transducers. We demonstrate that only two opposing arrays are enough to levitate objects and perform all the movements needed for representing physical visualisations of 3D paths.

Movements

A pattern is the phase and amplitude of a group of transducers which are positioned above and beneath a levitating object at a specific time. These transducers create a standing wave between the top and bottom of where the object is. The transitions between several patterns move the standing wave and thus the levitated object along a 2D path contained in a plane parallel to the opposed arrays.

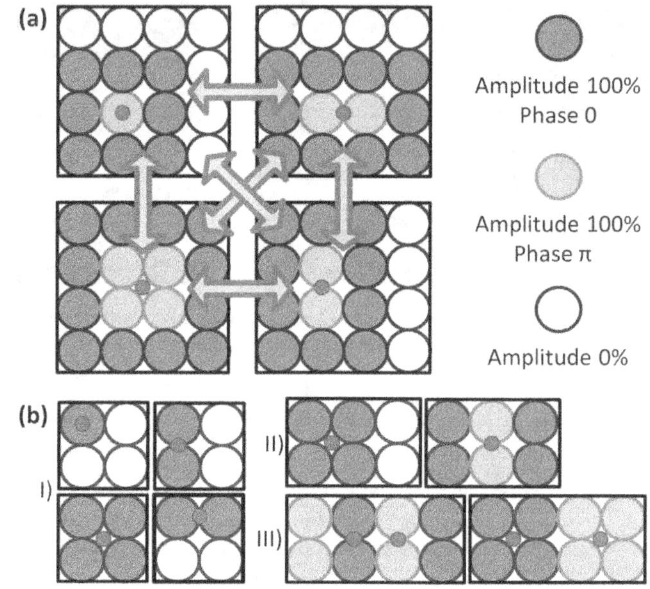

Figure 2: a) The key patterns can be interpolated between them in amplitude and phase. By doing so, the resulting position of the red levitating object also gets interpolated. b) Other patterns to levitate a single (I,II) or multiple beads (III).

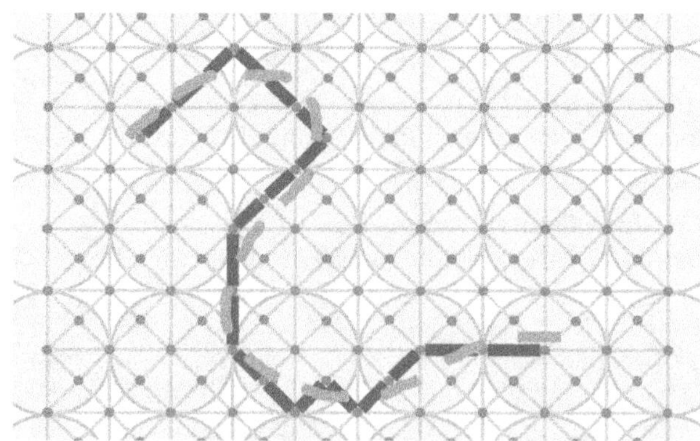

Figure 3: The red points represent the levitation points of the key patterns. Interpolating between adjacent pairs of key patterns, it is possible to move the objects along the grey lines. The desired 2D path (green) is adapted to the patterns possibilities resulting into the actual path (purple).

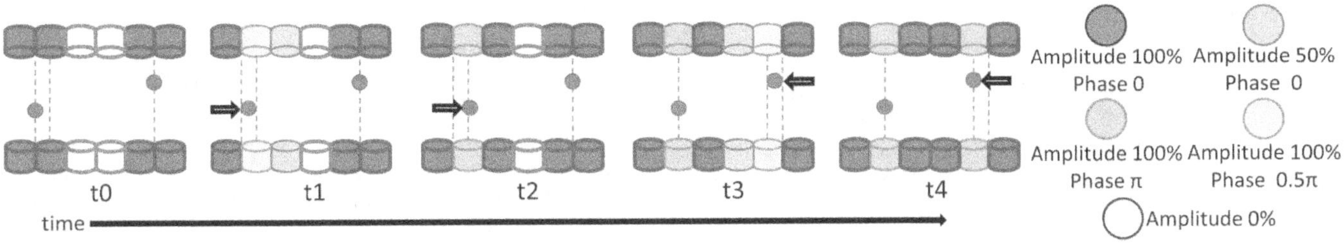

Figure 4: Individual movement of two beads in opposing directions. At time t0 both beads are stationary. At time t1, the phase of the second column of transducers increases from 0 to 0.5π and the amplitude of the third column of transducers increases from 0 to 50%; resulting in a movement of the left bead towards the centre. At time t2, a similar increase in phase and amplitude leads to continued movement for the left bead. At time t3 and t4, the same change occurs on the right side to move the second bead towards the centre. The step size in amplitude and phase determines the amount of movement.

A levitating position in the grid is more stable when the surrounding transducers have a phase difference of π with the transducers in the centre. Keeping this principle in mind, we designed our patterns to preserve this π phase difference along the required path. Consequently, we obtained improved stability resulting in faster movements of the levitated objects. The employed key patterns are illustrated in Figure 2(a). Only the status of one array is described since both top and bottom arrays use the same pattern. Figure 2(b) shows other patterns using fewer transducers, which are functional but less stable, as well as patterns for levitating multiple beads.

When we apply a constant phase difference between the top and bottom array, the bead can move perpendicularly to the arrays. Combining this 1D movement with the previous 2D movement, the levitated object can be moved across a 3D path. Given an input path, it can be decomposed into: a 2D path, controlled with the transitions between patterns (Figure 3); and a height variation, controlled with the phase difference between the top and bottom array.

LEVIPATH MODALITIES

LeviPath supports various modalities for levitating objects: single object, columns of objects and independent movement of two objects. The control of a single object has been described; however, between the top and bottom transducers, several acoustic nodes are created. Therefore, using the same approach, it is possible to place a column of beads and move them simultaneously along the same path.

Multiple levitated beads can also be moved across independent paths. As the patterns for moving one bead only occupy a certain part of the array, multiple beads can be controlled as long as the patterns do not intersect or overlap. This means that the levitated objects are always separated by at least the distance of one transducer.

In Figure 2(b), we show the key patterns that can be used to levitate two objects in different columns. By interpolating these key patterns, we can move the beads individually. As an example, in Figure 4 we illustrate a sequence of how two beads can be individually moved from the edges towards the centre with interpolations between key patterns. The step size in amplitude and phase can vary as required.

Whilst it is expected that there can be interferences from the transducers activated for levitating a second bead, their effective amplitudes decrease with distance and the patterns presented in Figure 2(a) have shown to produce stable movements.

IMPLEMENTATION

The current LeviPath system consists of two opposed arrays of transducers, a driver board and a PC (Figure 5). Each array holds 4x4 transducers (16 on top and 16 at the bottom). The MA40S4S transducers (diameter - 1cm, height - 8mm) generate a 40kHz wave with a directivity of 60° and 20 Pascals of pressure at a distance of 30cm. The separation between the two arrays was 43mm. Two LeviPaths powered at 16 volts and 0.5 amps consume a total of 8 watts.

The signals that control the transducers are generated by a custom driver board with 2 XMOS processors. This driver board transforms the information received from the PC into signals that make the transducers produce the desired amplitude and phase. The board calculates the signal for each transducer 20 times every period. Namely, it updates the signal at 800kHz giving a phase resolution of π/10 and 10 different values for the amplitude using Pulse Width Modulation.

The PC employs the algorithm described earlier to transform 3D paths into phases and amplitudes. The system also allows the control of the levitated objects with a keyboard, mouse or Leap Motion.

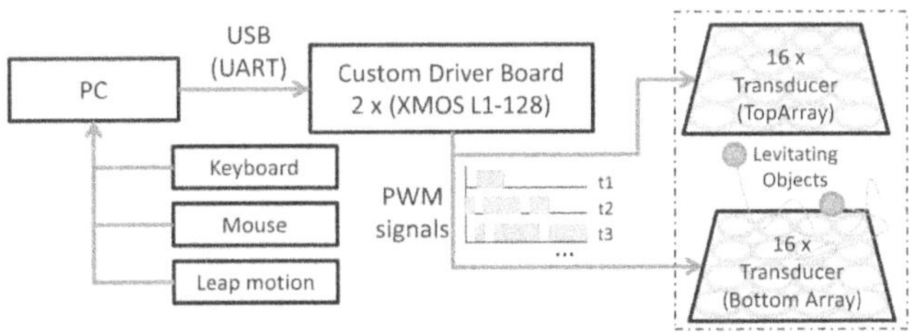

Figure 5: Hardware architecture of LeviPath. A PC issues orders to the XMOS driver board to move the bead across a 3D path. The board generates voltage signals to control the two opposed arrays.

LEVIPATH EVALUATION

Speed of the levitated objects

An experiment was conducted to measure the maximum speed of movement that can be applied to the levitated objects across two LeviPaths. We placed a different number of beads in the same column and moved them from the left side of the system to the right side (7 cm) five times. A trial consisted of moving a specific number of beads with a certain speed across the (7x5) 35 cm path. The success rate at a certain speed was measured as the number of times that all levitated beads completed the path without dropping.

The speed was controlled by a delay introduced before switching patterns. In this experiment, 10 pattern transitions represent 5mm of movement. Therefore, a delay of 1ms implies that the bead moves 5 mm in 10 ms; explicitly, 50 cm per second. Success rate for different speeds and amount of beads is shown in Figure 6. The slower the movement was, the higher the success rate. When levitating up to two beads, it is possible to maintain a success rate of 100% at a speed of 3 cm per second. We found this speed sufficient for interacting with the system comfortably.

For obtaining higher speeds, the strength of the levitating positions should be increased by using more powerful transducers or bringing the opposed arrays closer. Additionally, the algorithm should take into account inertia since the more problematic spots were the turning points. To increase position accuracy, the phase and amplitude modulation can be subdivided into more levels.

Characteristics of the Levitated Objects

With the presented hardware, we were able to levitate beads of 2 mm diameter and a density of 25 kg/m^2. The maximum weight of the levitated object is dependent on the levitation strength. The maximum size of the levitated object depends on the sound frequency; namely, the size should be smaller than half of the wavelength. Joining two LeviPaths increases the interaction space but it was always in the shape of a cuboid. However, it could be interesting to create curved paths or even joining LeviPaths in circular layouts.

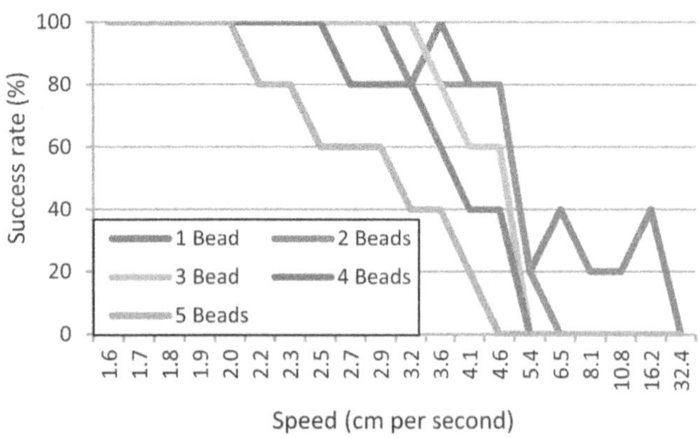

Figure 6: Success rate while moving several beads depending on the speed of movement.

CONCLUSION

A system to levitate objects across a 3D path has been described. LeviPath uses two opposed arrays of transducers and a novel algorithm to move objects based on the combination of key patterns. As a result, the system is modular since multiple devices can be joined to increase the interaction space. Additionally, multiple objects can move individually in different directions.

ACKNOWLEDGMENTS

This work has been supported by the EC within the 7th framework programme through the FET Open scheme under grant agreement no. 309191 for the GHOST (generic, highly-organic shape-changing interfaces) project and the Univeristy of Bristol. Asier Marzo is supported by the Government of Navarre through a Research Grant.

REFERENCES

1. Brandt, H. Levitation in Physics, Science, New Series, Vol. 243, No. 4889 (Jan. 20, 1989), pp. 349-355.
2. Courtney, C. R., Ong, C. K., Drinkwater, B. W., Bernassau, A. L., Wilcox, P. D. and Cumming, D. R. S. Manipulation of microparticles using phase-controllable ultrasonic standing waves, The Journal of the Acoustical Society of America, 128, EL195-EL199 (2010).
3. Follmer, S., Leithinger, D., Olwal, A., Hogge, A and Ishii, H. inFORM: dynamic physical affordances and constraints through shape and object actuation. UIST'13, 417-426.
4. Foresti, D., Nabavi, M., Klingauf, M., Ferrari, A. and Poulikakos, D. Acoustophoretic contactless transport and handling of matter in air. Proceedings of the National Academy of Sciences 110, 31 (2013), 12549-12554.
5. Jansen, Y., Dragicevic, P. and Fekete, J.D. Evaluating the efficiency of physical visualizations. SIGCHI, CHI '13, ACM (NY, USA, 2013), 2593–2602.
6. Lee, J., Post, R. and Ishii, H. 2011. ZeroN: mid-air tangible interaction enabled by computer controlled magnetic levitation. ACM UIST '11. (2011) NY, USA
7. Ochiai, Y., Hoshi, T. and Rekimoto, J. Pixie dust: graphics generated by levitated and animated objects in computational acoustic-potential field. ACM Transactions on Graphics (TOG) 33, 4 (2014), 85.
8. Moere, A.V. Beyond the tyranny of the pixel: Exploring the physicality of information visualization. In Information Visualisation. IV '08. (July 2008), 469–47.
9. Reznik, D., Moshkovich, E. and Canny, J. Building a universal planar manipulator. In Distributed Manipulation. (2000), (pp. 147-171). Springer US.
10. Seah, S., Drinkwater, B., Carter, T., Malkin, R., and Subramanian, S.. "Correspondence: Dexterous ultrasonic levitation of millimeter-sized objects in air." IEEE TUFFC 61, no. 7 (2014): 1233-1236.

Twist and Learn: Interface Learning in 3DOF Exploration of 3D Scatterplots

Mark Shovman
Yahoo Labs, Israel
marksh@yahoo-inc.com

Andrea Szymkowiak
Abertay University, UK
a.szymkowiak@abertay.ac.uk

James Bown
Abertay University, UK
j.bown@abertay.ac.uk

Kenneth C. Scott-Brown
Abertay University, UK
k.scott-brown@abertay.ac.uk

ABSTRACT
The increasing availability of 3D interfaces brings promise of improved user experience in diverse areas. Our study focuses on visual analytics, testing whether 3D interactivity improves performance in a visual data exploration task. Specifically, we compared scene rotation around vertical axis to a full 3D rotation using a InterSense IS-900 3D controller, in a task involving trivariate trend detection in a 3D scatterplot. We found that, while 3D rotation leads to slower performance, previous exposure to single-axis rotation removes that difference. This shows that an interactive 3D scatterplot can be an effective visual exploration technique for detecting trivariate patterns in the data, and highlights the role of interface learning in design and assessment of novel interfaces.

Author Keywords
3D controller; interface learning; scatterplot; visual analytics

ACM Classification Keywords
H.5.m. Information Interfaces and Presentation (e.g., HCI): Miscellaneous; H.5.2. Input devices and strategies; J.m. Visual Analytics

INTRODUCTION
2D scatterplots are ubiquitously used as the first step in exploratory data analysis, preluding formal statistical tests. Extending this visualization technique to 3D enables, in theory, discovery of complex trivariate patterns in the data, e.g., famously, the helical structure of a DNA [12]. In practice, the use of, and research on, 3D scatterplots lags behind the prevalence of trivariate patterns in science, e.g., [11] . Studies in multivariate data visualisation, e.g., [4, 7], tend to focus on 2D scatterplots, thus constraining the possible discoveries to bivariate trends.

CHI 2015, April 18 - 23 2015, Seoul, Republic of Korea

ACM 978-1-4503-3145-6/15/04$15.00
http://dx.doi.org/10.1145/2702123.2702201

Sedlmair et al.[8] find that *"interactive 3D [scatterplots] rarely helps but often hurts"* in multivariate cluster detection. In contrast, we have shown that a rotating 3D scatterplot is an efficient visualisation technique for detecting trivariate patterns [9], but not for detecting single 3D outliers [10]. We also found that limited interactivity (scene rotation around vertical axis) leads to better performance than an automated scene rotation, mostly by enabling improvement with experience [10].

In the current study, we assess the benefits of using 3D interaction devices in exploring 3D scatterplots. We hypothesise that extending interactivity, from rotation around a single vertical axis to a full 3D rotation, could improve performance.

3D interaction devices are becoming increasingly popular with the commercial success of game controllers such as Nintendo Wii or Razer Hydra [2, 6]. Using a precise 3D interaction device in a Visual Analytics task has been shown to improve performance in comparison with e.g., digital pen or voice control [3]; however the specifics of various usage scenarios are far from being thoroughly researched.

Our experimental design is a modification of [9]: in each trial, participants are presented with a 3D scatterplot composed of juxtaposed point sets that are differentiated by colour, and are asked to identify the set of points that are positioned non-randomly (i.e., exhibit a trivariate pattern). Since the pattern is only apparent in 3D, some scene rotation is required to complete the task. The overall design is a balanced within-subject block design, with one between-block variable: rotational degrees of freedom (1DOF or 3DOF); and two within-block random-order variables: number of point groups (2, 3, or 4); and number of points per group (64, 144 or 256).

METHOD

Apparatus
The experiment was run in a Virtual Environment space, lit with a consistent level of fluorescent lighting. Participants were seated 2 metres away from the midline of the 3×2 metre screen, resulting in a horizontal field of view of 74°. An IS-900 wand was used as the interaction device. Stereo projection and head tracking were available but not used, in order to make the findings applicable to commonly-available equipment. Experiment software was written in-house, in Java3D.

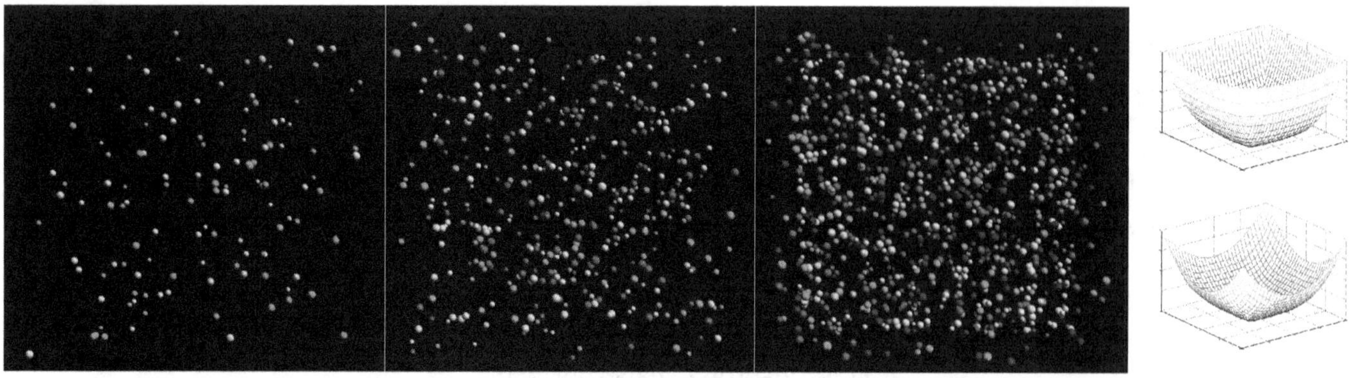

Figure 1. Stimuli; left to right: 2 × 64 points; 3 × 196 points; 4 × 256 points. Right: target shapes; top: $b = 0.1; a = 1$; bottom: $b = a = 1$.

Stimuli

A stimulus comprised a target dataset, and 1 to 3 distracter datasets (Figure 1). In distracter datasets, XYZ coordinates of points were randomly drawn from a uniform distribution in a ±1 range. In target datasets, planar (XY) coordinates were likewise random, while the depth (Z) was defined by a formula $z = a \cdot \max(x^4 + by^2, y^4 + bx^2) \cdot (1 + \xi); a = 1$ or $-1; b = 0.1, 0.4, 0.7$, or $1; \xi$ was a 10% random noise (Figure 1 right; $a = -1$ results in the same shape upside-down). The resulting depth coordinates were stretched to ±1 range. Point sizes were random, ranging from 8.3mm to 33.4mm at zero depth.

The combination of 8 target shapes, 3 data set sizes and 3 levels of number of data sets resulted in 72 stimulus sets. Eight distracter sets were also pre-generated for each dataset size. A protocol file specified, for each trial, the target set, and the number of distracter sets. The specific distracter sets, and the colours of both target and distracter sets (CIE Red, Green, Blue or Yellow) were randomly assigned during experimental runs.

Scene rotation was defined by the orientation of the IS-900 wand, sampled at 100Hz; wand position did not affect the scene. The initial view was 'directly into the cup'. In 3DOF rotation condition, pitch and yaw rotation was restricted to a square ±45° aperture[1]. Roll rotation was unrestricted since it did not change the planar image, only its orientation. In 1DOF rotation condition, only the yaw rotation, restricted to a ±45°, was available.

Procedure

The experiment was divided into a 1DOF condition block and a 3DOF condition block. Half of the participants started with 1DOF block, the other half did the 3DOF block first. Each block comprised 72 trials, i.e., all the stimulus sets, presented in random order. The blocks were broken up by ~20 minutes' break, overall taking about an hour.

[1]The restriction was added so that the participants would not be able to rotate the scatterplot completely sideways, where the target could be identified from a 2D view. We acknowledge that 3D rotation is often used to navigate to the best 2D view, however, since our focus was on detecting trivariate patterns invisible in 2D, we disabled that option.

In each trial participants were shown a stimulus until they responded by pressing a coloured button on the wand. After the response, a short auditory feedback was given: a chime for correct answer and a buzz for an incorrect one. Each 24 trials, a *'pause and rest'* screen was shown for at least 30 seconds and until button-press.

Each block was preceded by a short training exercise with the same rotation condition, repeated until the participants could reliably perform the task. Training for the first block comprised ten trials of increasing complexity. Training for the second block comprised ten trials of the same complexity as the main task, with different target shapes.

Participants

Participants were recruited via convenience sampling; most were Computer Science and Digital Arts students. They were fully briefed and debriefed, gave informed consent, and were compensated for their time. All reported having normal colour vision, which was confirmed at training stage. Data from 17 (8f/9m) out of 19 (9f/10m) participants was used for analysis (one participant did not complete the experiment while another responded with near-chance accuracy).

RESULTS

Since every stimulus set was shown to every participant twice, once in each interactivity mode, the most straightforward analysis is a direct comparison of performance, on the same stimulus set, in different interactivity modes. Only the pairs of trials with both correct responses ($n = 833$; 68% of all pairs of trials) were included. Log-mean[2] response time was 4.3 seconds for 1DOF interactivity, and 5.6 seconds for 3DOF interactivity ($t = -8.5; p < 0.001$).

A fine-grained analysis of the effects of interactivity mode is a linear regression that accounts for other parameters of the stimulus. The *ad-hoc* factors of the experiment design were: interactivity mode; number of point groups; and number of points per group. In addition, *post-hoc* ANOVAs showed that concave structures were more difficult to detect than convex structures: $F(7, 1963) = 10.4$; $p < 0.001$ for speed

[2]The distribution of response times was shown to fit a lognormal distribution; thus in all analyses, a natural logarithm of the response time for correct answers, was used as a measure of performance speed.

and $F(7, 2440) = 3.5$; $p = 0.001$ for accuracy; and that Green or Yellow target sets were more difficult to detect than Red or Blue: $F(3, 1967) = 17.9$; $p < 0.001$ for speed and $F(3, 2444) = 25.7$; $p < 0.001$ for accuracy.

The first model included the *ad-hoc* factors only. Regression analysis ($R^2 = 0.14; F(3, 1967) = 105.3$; $p < 0.001$) shows that each of the factors had a significant effect on the response time (Table 1). Note that the effect of the number of points is negative, i.e., more points lead to a faster response, while the effect of interactivity degrees of freedom is positive: increasing interactivity degrees of freedom increased the time necessary to detect the target. The effect of number of groups was positive as well: more groups lead to slower response. The residuals showed a good fit to the normal distribution.

		B	β	p
b_1	Interactivity mode	.128	.165	$< .001$
b_2	Number of Groups	.294	.308	$< .001$
b_3	Number of Points	$-.001$	$-.129$	$< .001$

Table 1. Regression coefficients for the *ad-hoc* analysis

The second model also took into account the *post-hoc* parameters: target set concavity and colour, block order, and trials order in a block. The results of the analysis ($R^2 = 0.23; F(7, 1963) = 84.8; p < 0.001$) show an R^2 higher than in the *ad-hoc* model, and, a significant effect of all parameters on the response time (Table 2). Specifically, the effect of *ad-hoc* parameters was not reduced by *post-hoc* accounting for concavity (balanced across trials) and colour (randomised across trials).

		B	β	p
b_1	Interactivity mode	.123	.158	$< .001$
b_2	Number of Groups	.300	.315	$< .001$
b_3	Number of Points	$-.001$	.130	$< .001$
b_4	Target Concavity	$-.136$	$-.175$	$< .001$
b_5	Target Colour Rating	.085	.172	$< .001$
b_6	Block Number	.262	.169	$< .001$
b_7	Trial number	.004	.104	$< .001$

Table 2. Regression coefficients for the *post-hoc* analysis

Analysing response time separately by rotation type and block order (Figure 2 right) showed a difference in performance between interactivity modes, in participants who started with the 3DOF condition. To inspect this further, the pair-wise comparison of log response times was re-run separately for participants who started with 1DOF and those who started with 3DOF mode. This analysis showed no difference for participants who started with 1DOF ($p = 0.8$), and a significant improvement in performance for participants who started with the 3DOF ($t = -12.07; p < 0.001$). Likewise, a full-factorial ANOVA of accuracy (with number of points, number of groups, block order and interactivity mode as independent variables) shows a significant interaction effect between block order and interactivity mode ($F(1, 2412) = 16.5; p < 0.001$); all other interactions were not significant.

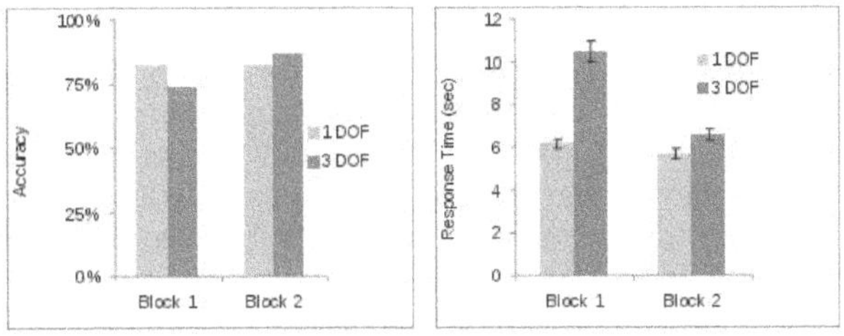

Figure 2. Accuracy and response times by rotation type and block order. Error bars for reaction time at ± 1 SEM.

An analysis of individual wand movements (Figure 3) shows that interaction in 3DOF block when it was presented first (bottom left) is more spread out than all others; also interaction in 3DOF block when it was presented second (bottom right) exhibits left-right sweeps characteristic of 1DOF interaction (top left and right).

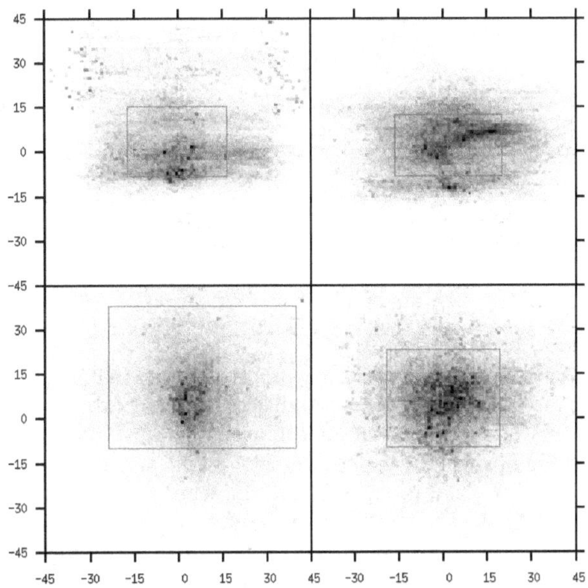

Figure 3. Wand movements in the course of experiment: a heatmap of dwell times by yaw (X axis) and pitch (Y axis); axes labeled in degrees. Red cross at mean; box at mean$\pm$1SD. Top: 1DOF; bottom: 3DOF; left: presented as 1st block; right: as 2nd block.

DISCUSSION

Contrary to our initial prediction, giving participants more control of the view did not improve performance; instead, detection in the 3DOF rotation condition was significantly slower than in the 1DOF condition, even when other parameters of the stimulus were accounted for. This is consistent with some existing literature: e.g., a classic study on the comprehension of 3D scatterplots [13] found that 3D presentation improves performance in 3D surface perception, but did not find benefits of full 3D user control of scene rotation; a more recent research of multivariate 2D scatterplot navigation [4] similarly suggests constricting rotation to a single axis at each step of the interaction.

The analysis of order effects tells a more elaborate story: 3DOF rotation took significantly longer only in the first block; when presented after a 1DOF block, 3DOF trials took approximately the same time as 1DOF trials. 1DOF trials took roughly the same time regardless of the block they were presented in. An analysis of wand movements suggests that participants who started with a 1DOF case continued to constrain their interaction to tight single-axis sweeps even when more options became available.

It is possible to conclude that full 3D interactivity is not inherently more difficult. Rather, is more difficult to master; however, exposure to a more constrained interactivity can provide transferable learning.

The learning was also apparent across the board on a smaller scale, going way beyond 'learning the task', which was amply addressed by the training sets. Order of trials in each block was a uniformly significant factor in every condition, showing gradual improvement in performance throughout the experiment. The same pattern of gradual improvement was seen in the interactive condition of our previous study [10], with participants learning to adapt the view parameters to their preference. In contrast, non-interactive trials there did not show improvement in performance over time, ruling out simple perceptual learning [5].

We believe that 'interactive interface learning' warrants further study. We plan to analyse individual wand logs in depth, for a better understanding of interface learning dynamics, and, ultimately, of the optimal usage parameters of 3D interaction devices.

Limitations

During training, several participants reported that, in some trials, the scatterplot seemed to distort instead of rotating. Such 3D reconstruction is valid if the wand is perceived as controlling the position of the camera around the scatterplot, not the scene rotation. It is overridden if the scene is assumed to have a rigid shape; however, this assumption is not natural neither for a disjoint scatterplot, nor for naturally occurring disjoint stimuli, such as falling snow or foliage. While this makes snowfalls and leaves (and perhaps 3D scatterplots) engaging to watch, it also makes their shape and movement ambiguous and difficult to parse. To resolve this ambiguity, we suggest to either add rigid anchoring objects, e.g., axes, to the scene; or use head-tracking for a scene rotation [1].

One consideration that needs to be made when constraining view control to 1D rotation is the choice of rotation axis. While any axis would in principle allow 3D reconstruction, some trivariate patterns can be conceivably much easier to detect from some orientations than from others (e.g. a helix is easier to recognise 'from the side' than 'from the top'). It is unclear how to choose the rotation axis so as to show a 'canonical' orientation of an *a priori* unknown pattern. One viable practical suggestion would be to allow both 1D and 3D rotation, perhaps making the 1D interface default, and 3D slightly harder to access (e.g., rotate and CTRL-rotate)

CONCLUSION

We show that a 3D scatterplot can be an effective for detecting trivariate patterns in the data; that restricting interactivity can lead to improved performance; and highlight the role of interface learning in design and assessment of novel interfaces.

ACKNOWLEDGMENTS

First author was supported by the University of Abertay RSSC Consortium Fund. We are grateful to Madeleine Keehner for the valuable input to this study.

REFERENCES

1. Arthur, K. W., Booth, K. S., and Ware, C. Evaluating 3D task performance for fish tank virtual worlds. *ACM Transactions on Information Systems 11*, 3 (1993), 239–265.
2. Bowman, D. A., Kruijff, E., LaViola Jr, J. J., and Poupyrev, I. *3D user interfaces: theory and practice*. Addison-Wesley, 2004.
3. Dang, N. T., Tavanti, M., Rankin, I., and Cooper, M. A comparison of different input devices for a 3D environment. *International Journal of Industrial Ergonomics 39*, 3 (2009), 554–563.
4. Elmqvist, N., Dragicevic, P., and Fekete, J.-D. Rolling the dice: Multidimensional visual exploration using scatterplot matrix navigation. *IEEE Transactions on Visualization and Computer Graphics 14*, 6 (2008), 1539–1148.
5. Gibson, E. J. *Principles of perceptual learning and development*. Appleton-Century-Crofts, 1969.
6. LaViola, J. J., and Keefe, D. F. 3D spatial interaction: applications for art, design, and science. In *ACM Siggraph 2011 Courses*, ACM (2011), 1.
7. Sanftmann, H., and Weiskopf, D. 3D scatterplot navigation. *IEEE Transactions on Visualization and Computer Graphics 18*, 11 (2012), 1969–1978.
8. Sedlmair, M., Munzner, T., and Tory, M. Empirical guidance on scatterplot and dimension reduction technique choices. *IEEE Transactions on Visualization and Computer Graphics 19*, 12 (2013), 2634–2643.
9. Shovman, M. M., Scott-Brown, K. C., Szymkowiak, A., and Bown, J. The meaning of graphs: Scatterplots as a test-bed for theories of object-hood. *Gestalt Theory 34*, 3/4 (2012).
10. Shovman, M. M., Szymkowiak, A., Bown, J. L., and Scott-Brown, K. C. Changing the view: towards the theory of visualisation comprehension. In *13th International Conference on Information Visualisation*, IEEE (2009), 135–138.
11. Tommaso, M. A trivariate model of participation, fertility and wages: the italian case. *Cambridge Journal of Economics 23*, 5 (1999), 623–640.
12. Watson, J. D., Crick, F. H., et al. Molecular structure of nucleic acids. *Nature 171*, 4356 (1953), 737–738.
13. Wickens, C. D., Merwin, D. H., and Lin, E. L. Implications of graphics enhancements for the visualization of scientific data. *Human Factors 36*, 1 (1994), 44–61.

THING: Introducing a Tablet-based Interaction Technique for Controlling 3D Hand Models

Merwan Achibet[1], Géry Casiez[2], Anatole Lécuyer[1], Maud Marchal[1,3]
[1]Inria Rennes, France [2]University of Lille, France [3]INSA, France
{merwan.achibet, gery.casiez, anatole.lecuyer, maud.marchal}@inria.fr

Figure 1: THING enables the control of 3D hand models (in blue) by sliding fingers along sliders arranged in a morphologically-consistent pattern on the tablet's screen. This creates a strong correspondence between user's input and pose of the controlled hand. Here, the user closes the virtual hand and then points the index finger.

ABSTRACT
The hands of virtual characters are highly complex 3D models that can be tedious and time-consuming to animate with current methods. This paper introduces THING, a novel tablet-based approach that leverages multi-touch interaction for a quick and precise control of a 3D hand's pose. The flexion/extension and abduction/adduction of the virtual fingers can be controlled for each finger individually or for several fingers in parallel through sliding motions on the tablet's surface. We designed two variants of THING: **(1)** MobileTHING, which maps the spatial location and orientation of the tablet to that of the virtual hand, and **(2)** DesktopTHING, which combines multi-touch controls of fingers with traditional mouse controls for the hand's global position and orientation. We compared the usability of THING against mouse-only controls and a data glove in two controlled experiments. Results show that DesktopTHING was significantly preferred by users while providing performance similar to data gloves. Together, these results could pave the way to the introduction of novel hybrid user interfaces based on tablets and computer mice in future animation pipelines.

Author Keywords
Virtual hand; multi-touch input; computer animation.

ACM Classification Keywords
H.5.2 User Interfaces: Input devices and strategies; I.3.6 Methodology and Techniques: Interaction techniques

CHI 2015, April 18–23 2015, Seoul, Republic of Korea
Copyright 2015 ACM 978-1-4503-3145-6/15/04...$15.00.
http://dx.doi.org/10.1145/2702123.2702158

INTRODUCTION
Hands are, along with the face, among the most expressive body parts, and subsequently their virtual representations are among the most difficult 3D models to animate. A realistic animation of an action as simple as grasping an object or pointing a finger requires to define numerous successive hand poses, each of which is obtained through the careful manipulation of multiple articulations, for each individual finger.

Current desktop approaches to animate these complex articulated bodies of no less than 27 degrees of freedom [26] rely on forward or inverse kinematics and require repetitive mouse-based adjustements of the individual finger joints [12]. An alternative solution consists in tracking the motion of an actor's hands using data gloves or optical tracking systems [23]. While conceptually powerful, such solutions are facing the limitations of current tracking technologies, *i.e.* their cost, complexity, or inaccuracy. As of today, it seems that there is no satisfying solution for 3D animators to achieve complex hand poses in a simple, yet effective manner.

In this work, we address these problems by contributing a novel solution that is more light-weight than motion capture, yet benefits from the flexibility and accuracy of hand-based interaction. Our approach, called THING in reference to the famous *Addams Family* character, is a tablet-based interface with which the animator controls finger configurations through multi-touch input. Each virtual finger corresponds to a slider on the tablet, that the animator manipulates to control flexion/extension and adduction/abduction. THING therefore leverages the direct mapping between the animator's own fingers and that of the virtual hand through a morphologically-consistent user interface that can be rapidly assimilated by animators. For example, a grasping motion is naturally simulated by sliding the fingertips closer together on the tablet, as illustrated on Figure 1.

Built upon THING, we present MobileTHING and DesktopTHING, two variants with different controls for the global location and orientation of the virtual hand. MobileTHING capitalizes on the mobility of the tablet and exploits it as a prop to manipulate the whole hand model by moving and tilting the device. With DesktopTHING, the hand's location and orientation are controlled with a traditional mouse. This decoupling of controls, while less direct than MobileTHING, allows for a less physically demanding manipulation and leaves one hand free for performing other tasks, such as invoking keyboard commands.

After reviewing related work we detail our contributions: **(1)** THING, a morphologically-consistent multi-touch approach for controlling a virtual hand model; **(2)** the design and implementation of two variants of THING, and their integration into a real animation tool; and **(3)** the formal evaluation of our techniques through two controlled experiments. Finally, we discuss the possible evolutions of THING before concluding.

RELATED WORK

This section reviews the traditional framework of computer animation, as well as beyond-the-desktop approaches applied to the manipulation of 3D models, including multi-touch, tangibles and motion capture.

From the 3D Mesh to the Animated Character

Before a 3D model can be animated, its mesh must be bound to a system resembling a digital skeleton, made up of joints and bones that act as "handles" that the animators manipulates to bend the model into a desired pose. This articulated system, with its degrees of freedom (DOF) and its constraints, is called a *rig*. The general framework of computer animation is based on the manipulation of such rigs that govern the pose of 3D meshes [12].

The most common approach for manually controlling rigs relies on *forward kinematic animation*, where joints are manipulated sequentially with a computer mouse [19]. For a faithful hand rig supporting all 27 DOF, this makes posing an impractical and labor-intensive task due to the highly-articulated nature of the model. Rather than controlling each joint individually, *inverse kinematics* allows animators to manipulate a *target point* at each limb's extremity, which is used to automatically guide the rest of the joints chain [28]. While it requires fewer steps than forward kinematics, individual fingers must still be manipulated one after the other. A less direct approach consists in using *drivers*, namely custom rig components (*e.g.* , finger flexion/extension) bound to UI widgets (*e.g.* sliders). Here again, the lack of parallelism remains and the decoupling of the control and model may cause the animator to split their attention. Our approach aims at providing more appropriate and parallelizable inputs by letting the animator perform the desired finger gestures herself.

Multi-touch

The use of multi-touch devices, which offer a simple and expressive way to control parameters in real time, has been explored for computer animation purposes. For instance, Kin *et al.* [9] built virtual stages for computer-generated movies with a multi-touch system. More directly related to animation, Finger Walking [16] records a two-finger "walk" on a touch surface to pantomime leg movements. Gutiérrez *et al.* used a mobile animation system to map stylus motions on a PDA to rotations of a virtual avatar joints [3]. Kipp and Nguyen [10] used two-finger input to swivel an articulated arm and position its hand. In their approach, tactile input is used to determine the hand's pose by blending between several pre-defined poses; thus, joints are not manipulated directly. However, finger configurations remain limited to variations of the reference poses. In contrast, we propose to leverage the directness of tactile input and benefits of multitouch by mapping the controls of each virtual finger to the animator's own fingers so that more manipulations can be performed simultaneously.

Tangible Interfaces

Other techniques rely on the animators manipulating tangible interfaces to control 3D models like puppeteers. Held *et al.* [4] used a depth camera to track real objects during natural toy-like interaction, but articulated objects are not supported. For articulated figures, physical armatures with flex sensors [7] or joint encoders [11] have been designed. These are generally employed for animating high-level dynamics such as gait and are not suited to finer movements like that of fingers. Jacobson *et al.* [6] developed a modular tangible interface with pluggable joints and splitters to build a variety of skeletons, including hands. However, users must use several of their own fingers to manipulate a single virtual finger so the number of DOF controllable simultaneously is reduced.

To our knowledge, no tangible interfaces are specifically tailored to hand animation. Yet, the 3D interaction field is rich in systems to control virtual hands. Tango [13] is a ball covered with pressure sensors that recognizes the pose to apply on a 3D hand depending on its pressure distribution, but it can only identify pre-recorded poses. HandNavigator [15] is a 3D mouse customized with pressure sensors under each finger. While its control scheme (*rate-control*) allows travel across long distances with only small hand motions, this type of control has been shown to hinder performance compared to position control [27]. For this reason, our system uses *position-control* for both the global hand configuration and the local finger motion. More generally, all the aforementioned methods rely on custom-made hardware while we leverage consumer-ready tablets.

Motion Capture

Actors' performance can also be recorded to be replicated on a 3D model [23]. The real-time nature and exactness of motion capture makes it an appealing solution for animation purposes. In practice though, it requires substantial hardware in the form of multi-camera or electromagnetic tracking systems, which makes it an expensive and bulky solution. Moreover, while it works effectively for whole-body tracking, highly-articulated bodies such as hands impose a dense distribution of tracking markers which creates occlusion and inaccuracy issues. As a result, such tracking solutions may be limited to only one or two fingers [21] or suffer from noise [14].

Markerless optical tracking enables hand tracking without invasive instrumentation. On the one hand, discriminative techniques determine the best match in a database of pre-defined poses according to visual observations [25, 20] — but the set of available poses is limited. On the other hand, model-based techniques minimize the discrepancy between visual data and 3D model [22, 18] — but this process is computationally demanding since it is often formulated as an optimization problem in the high-dimensional pose-space of articulated hands.

Several low-cost tracking systems specifically dedicated to hand tracking are commercially available, like the LeapMotion[1] and the CamBoard pico S[2]. While they track individual fingers for an affordable price, such devices also suffer from inaccuracies due to occlusion which makes them unfit for professional contexts requiring precision [2], such as computer animation. Kim *et al.* developed Digits [8], a wrist-worn sensor making use of low-cost infrared tracking. While the fixed position of the sensor extends the tracking space, occlusions still occur in case of overly bent or crossed fingers. Our approach prevents occlusion issues since it is not a tracking solution per se, but rather a morphologically-consistent user interface that maintains a correspondence between the motion of the animator's own fingers and the motion of the virtual fingers. Another drawback of such hardware is that they continuously track the user's hand and can potentially record unwanted motion (*e.g.* when the user moves her hand away from the tracker). In comparison, there are no ambiguities with our system since it only controls the virtual hand when the user touches the tablet's screen with her fingers.

Data gloves that measure finger flexion are tailored to hand tracking [24, 29]. Although they seem ideal for our purpose, their high cost diminishes their accessibility. More troublesomely, they do not always adapt well to different hand sizes and handedness, which makes them unusable by many users. The cumbersome nature of data gloves also interferes with other tasks, such as typing on a keyboard or using a mouse. Conversely, our approach is based on a low-cost tactile tablet, relying on multi-touch input that adapts to many morphologies and does not require any additional instrumentation of the hand.

THING

In this section, we present THING, a multi-touch technique that we developed to manipulate a hand rig with a tablet as main input device. We start by presenting the simplified hand rig that we tailored for our system before describing the associated multi-touch interface to control virtual fingers. Lastly, we present the two variants of THING that we designed to control the global position and orientation of the hand.

Hand Rig

The human hand has 27 degrees of freedom: the fingers each have 3 DOF for extension and flexion (one per phalanx) and 1 for abduction and adduction, the thumb has 5 DOF, and the wrist has 6 DOF for position and orientation. Due to physiological constraints, all these DOF cannot be controlled individually. For example finger flexion involves a close combination of each DOF of a finger. Considering these constraints, we designed a purpose-built rig with 16 DOF in order to simplify the formulation of hand poses while preserving their essential kinematics: flexion/extension, abduction/adduction and global position and orientation. Thus, we describe the pose H of our hand model with the set of parameters of Equation 1.

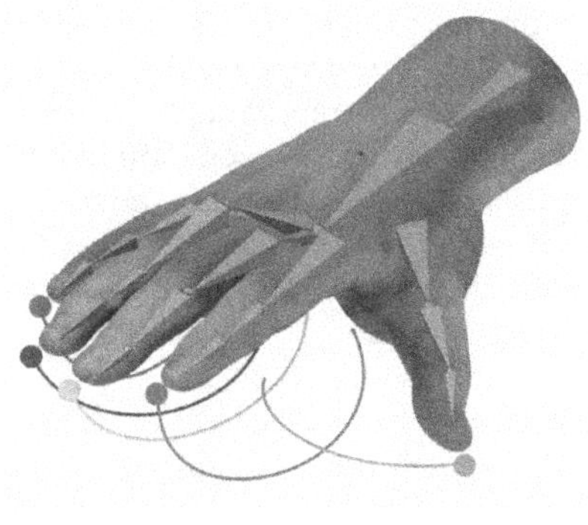

Figure 2: The rigged hand model is composed of a hand mesh, a skeletal armature (grey bones), inverse kinematics targets (colored spheres) and predefined trajectories (colored curves).

$$H = [\boldsymbol{p}, o, F_1, F_2, F_3, F_4, F_5] \qquad F_n = [f_n, a_n],\ n \in [1,5] \quad (1)$$

Position $\boldsymbol{p}$ and orientation quaternion o form the *global frame* of the hand model and encompass 6 DOF. Each parameter F_n describes the individual state of a finger, which corresponds to the *local frame* of the hand: f_n defines the flexion, where $f_n = 0$ corresponds to an extended finger and $f_n = 1$ corresponds to a fully flexed finger; a_n describes the abduction, where $a_n = 0$ means that the finger is in its neutral position, and $a_n = 1$ (resp. -1) signifies that the finger is fully abducted (resp. adducted). The local frame has thus 10 DOF.

In 3D animation, hand models are rigged with a skeletal armature consistent with human anatomy. Regarding the global frame, the skeleton root is placed at position $\boldsymbol{p}$ with orientation o. Regarding the local frame, each finger is guided by an inverse kinematics target. Editable curves define the trajectory of each target (and thus of each finger) as seen on Figure 2. Those trajectories are parametrically defined as cubic Bézier curves $B_{\boldsymbol{b}_1,\boldsymbol{c}_1,\boldsymbol{b}_2,\boldsymbol{c}_2}(x)$ with $x \in [0,1]$ ($\boldsymbol{b}_1$ and $\boldsymbol{b}_2$ are extremities, $\boldsymbol{c}_1$ and $\boldsymbol{c}_2$ are control points). Such curves are common components in 3D editors which makes them easy to use and tweak to accommodate different morphologies, from realistic hands to disproportionate cartoon hands.

Thus flexing or extending a virtual finger is a matter of moving the target guiding its motion along its constrained trajectory. If we only consider flexion then the position of a target is defined as $\boldsymbol{p}_{target}(F_n) = B(f_n)$. Abduction/adduction is realized by adding a lateral offset to the target's position, as described in Equation 2 with r_a a scalar value bounding the abduction/adduction span.

$$\boldsymbol{p}_{target}(F_n) = B(f_n) + a_n\left((\boldsymbol{c}_1 - \boldsymbol{b}_1) \times (\boldsymbol{c}_2 - \boldsymbol{b}_2)\right) r_a \quad (2)$$

[1] http://www.leapmotion.com
[2] http://www.pmdtec.com/camboardpico/

Since we constrain the fingertips along fixed trajectories, the set of reachable poses is restricted and those involving irregular joint-curling cannot be reproduced. Moreover, the thumb is defined like the other fingers even though it has more DOF, which limits its mobility. In return, however, the reduced number of DOF of the hand model can be easily mapped from multi-touch input in order to provide control over flexion and adduction through a tablet.

Multi-touch Input

Leveraging multi-touch input for animating the hand model has several benefits: **(1)** it provides efficient and natural input since users perform finger gestures themselves, **(2)** it provides parallelizable input so that all fingers can be controlled simultaneously, **(3)** it is based on low-cost and common devices and **(4)** it leverages the pre-established familiarity that users may have with tablets or other common tactile interfaces. This last point is particularly relevant for seasoned 3D artists who already use graphics tablets with similar tactile capabilities in their workflow.

Tactile surfaces provide 2 DOF per contact point (10 DOF if all fingers touch the tablet) and their inner sensors can be used to track them in space, providing six additional DOF. It is thus possible to map these 16 DOF to the 16 parameters of our hand model. Similarly, Kim *et al.* [8] mapped 2D input (depth data from a post-processed image) to finger motions with their Digits system. With THING however, multi-touch input avoid inaccuracies due to optical tracking and adapt such principle to consumer-ready hardware.

Regarding rotational tracking, most tablets embed sensors accurate enough to support real-time 3D interaction. Regarding positional tracking, current commercial tablets are not yet equipped with appropriate sensing capabilities but it is reasonable to expect that future generations of devices will provide such capability. In the meantime, we used a GameTrak[3] tracking device in our prototype.

Layout

The user interface displayed on the tablet's screen consists of five sliders, each one associated to a virtual finger. Users control the flexion and abduction of a virtual finger by sliding their own finger along and away from the slider. The morphologically-consistent layout shown on Figure 1 keeps consistency between real and virtual motions, and all virtual fingers can be controlled in parallel rather than sequentially. Additionally, the associated proprioceptive cues allow users to focus on the screen where the editor is displayed rather than looking at the multi-touch interface.

Each slider $S_n = [\boldsymbol{c_n}, \boldsymbol{s_n}]$ associated with the finger F_n goes through the 2D position $\boldsymbol{c_n}$ of the user's finger when it touches the tablet for the first time. Its direction $\boldsymbol{s_n}$ points toward a weighted barycenter of all the contacts (approximately at the center of the palm).

The first task of the user is to place her whole-hand on the tablet so that it detects handedness and associates each slider to its corresponding finger before displaying them. It is both possible to perform whole-hand input to control all virtual fingers simultaneously or to apply precise adjustments through single-finger input. For whole-hand input, users touch the tactile surface with all their fingers at the same time. This moves the sliders under their fingers. For single-finger input, they simply touch the slider associated with the desired finger.

$$\boldsymbol{d_f} = \frac{\boldsymbol{d} \cdot \boldsymbol{s}}{||\boldsymbol{s}||^2}\boldsymbol{s}$$

$$\boldsymbol{d_a} = \frac{\boldsymbol{d} \cdot \boldsymbol{s}^{\perp}}{||\boldsymbol{s}^{\perp}||^2}\boldsymbol{s}^{\perp}$$

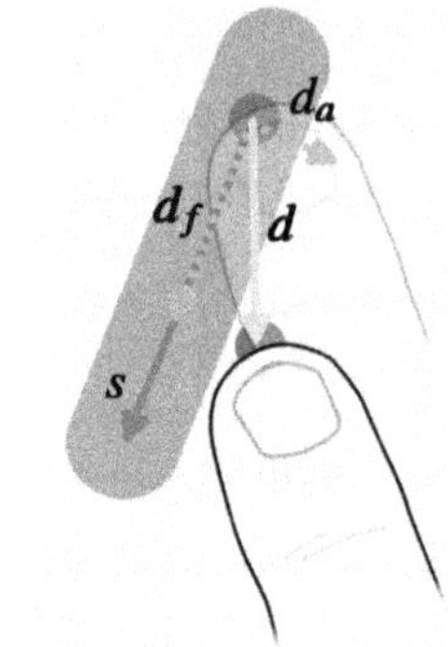

Figure 3: A motion along the slider controls the flexion of the associated virtual finger and a motion away away from the slider controls its adduction.

Each time five contacts are detected at the same time, a finger identification step is triggered. A distance-based heuristic discriminates the thumb as the finger having the greatest distance with its closest neighbor. The other fingers are then identified by ordering them according to their horizontal position. Handedness is detected by comparing the horizontal position of the thumb with respect to the other fingers.

Controls

The displacement $\boldsymbol{d}$ of a user's finger on the tablet is sampled at a high rate (50 Hz) to respectively infer finger flexion/extension and abduction/adduction.

To control the flexion of a virtual finger, we measure the displacement of the user's finger along a slider: $\boldsymbol{d}$ is projected along the slider axis $\boldsymbol{s}$ to obtain a vector $\boldsymbol{d_f}$ effectively representing a change in flexion. The direction of $\boldsymbol{d_f}$ determines the direction of the virtual finger motion (if $\boldsymbol{d_f} \cdot \boldsymbol{s} > 0$ then the virtual finger will be flexed, otherwise it will be extended).

To control the abduction of a virtual finger, we measure the distance of the user's finger to the associated slider. Similarly, the direction of $\boldsymbol{d_a}$ with respect to $\boldsymbol{s}^{\perp}$ determines if an adduction or an abduction is to occur. The magnitude of these motions is determined by the distance to the slider.

Mapping

To obtain the final f_n parameter that defines the flexion of a virtual finger, the projected vector $\boldsymbol{d_f}$ from the tactile input is modulated by a transfer function Θ with respect to the sliding speed $\boldsymbol{v_f}$ and a scaling coefficient k_f, as described in Equation 3.

$$\begin{aligned}\Delta f &= \Theta(\boldsymbol{d_f}, \boldsymbol{v_f}) \\ &= \begin{cases} 0, & \text{if } ||\boldsymbol{d_f}|| < d_{min} \\ k_f\,(||\boldsymbol{d_f}|| - d_{min})`G(\boldsymbol{v_f}), & \textit{otherwise} \end{cases}\end{aligned} \quad (3)$$

Θ thresholds the user's input so that small unintended slidings are discarded if they are less than the d_{min} threshold. It also scales the magnitude of the sliding measured in pixel on the

[3] `http://en.wikipedia.org/wiki/Gametrak`

tablet by k_f to the $[0, 1]$ range of the trajectory. Finally, it applies a gain G that modulates the resulting flexion depending on $\boldsymbol{v_f}$ (a logistic function in our prototype).

To obtain the a_n parameter that defines the abduction of the virtual finger, the projected vector $\boldsymbol{d_a}$ from the tactile input is first scaled by a scaling coefficient k_a and then fed into the abduction parameter of the virtual finger, as described in Equation 4.

$$a = \text{sign}(\boldsymbol{d_a} \cdot \boldsymbol{s}^{\perp})\ k_a\ ||\boldsymbol{d_a}|| \quad (4)$$

Two Variants

Since the motion of the virtual hand uses inputs that are separated from the motion of fingers, we distinguish two flavors of our technique:

MobileTHING All degrees of freedom are handled through the tablet, even global position and orientation.

DesktopTHING Only the fingers are controlled through the tablet. The global frame is controlled via traditional mouse input in the 3D editor.

With MobileTHING, the position $\boldsymbol{p}$ of the virtual hand is obtained from the position of the tablet: $\boldsymbol{p} = k_p\ \boldsymbol{p}_{tablet}$ with k_p a scaling coefficient increasing the virtual workspace volume. The orientation o of the virtual hand is controlled by rotating the tablet: $o = o_{tablet}^{k_o}$ with k_o a scaling coefficient. We subsequently apply a 1€ filter [1] over the obtained quaternions to reduce noise. Additionally, two buttons were placed on the tablet's screen to lock translation and/or rotation. In this way, a complex configuration can be reached and then locked so that the tablet could be rested on a desk to avoid awkward and tiring postures.

While MobileTHING is fully integrated on the multi-touch device and allows to focus on a single device for direct spatial interaction, the need to hold the tablet in the air may be detrimental to performance over long work sessions. For this reason, DesktopTHING leverages a computer mouse which is expected to reduce physical fatigue. An additional motivation for DesktopTHING is its lack of requirement for external tracking devices; especially positional tracking devices since current-generation tablets are not yet able to provide this information. Moreover, DesktopTHING allows users to keep using the keyboard along the tablet to input shortcuts in their animation software.

PROOF OF CONCEPT IMPLEMENTATION

We integrated THING in the Blender[4] 3D editor in order to demonstrate its capabilities in a real animation context.

Figure 4 features several examples of poses created with THING. On Figure 4a, frames of an animation featuring object manipulation can be seen. Figure 4b shows a use-case in which a 3D character performs gestures and object manipulation. The user simply puts either his left or right hand on the tablet to control the corresponding virtual hand.

The additional screen space offered by the tablet is a valuable feature since it displays user interface elements to help the

[4]http://www.blender.org/

(a)

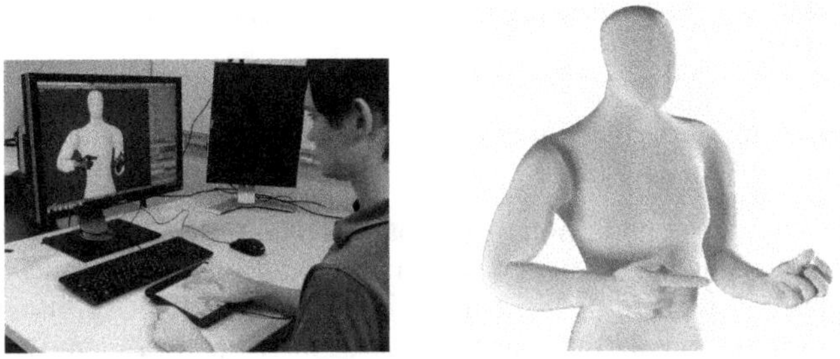

(b)

Figure 4: (a) Two frames of an animation made using THING that features juggling and object grasping (b) Use-case in which the user controls the hands of a virtual character. He controls the left and right hands of the virtual character by putting his own left and right hands of the tablet.

production of animations. In our prototype, we added several buttons to create keyframes and move in the 3D editor's timeline so that a complete animation could be crafted without leaving the tablet. More generally, the screen offers a variety of promising ways to ease hand animation; for example by adding buttons to save and load user-defined poses.

EVALUATION

We conducted two user studies to evaluate the performance of both variations of THING compared to two other input devices used for hand animation techniques: a mouse/keyboard combination and a data glove. For both studies, we measured the time to complete posing tasks with each technique and participants had to answer a subjective questionnaire.

To prevent a possible confounding learning effect between MobileTHING and DesktopTHING, we designed a first experiment comparing only MobileTHING to a data glove and mouse/keyboard. MobileTHING was chosen since it is closest to the glove technique. In a second experiment we compare the two variants of THING with a mouse/keyboard, used to cross-validate the results with the ones of the first experiment. The glove technique is expected to define an upper bound for performance to assess how our approach compares to a specialized and direct control method.

Experiment 1: MobileTHING

Apparatus

The evaluation was presented within the Blender 3D editor using Python scripting to retrieve real-time data from the various input devices used. The editor was displayed on a 24 inch monoscopic screen placed approximately 80 centimeters

(a) Mouse technique. (b) Glove technique.

Figure 5: The two techniques compared with the THING approach in the first experiment: (a) the participant uses a mouse and a standard keyboard, (b) the participant wears a data glove and additional tracking devices.

in front of participants. The realistic hand model used is part of the LibHand library [5].

In the glove condition, participants wore a right-handed 5DT glove[6] which position, orientation and finger movements were replicated onto the hand model (Figure 5b). Additional sensors tracked the global frame of their hand: a GameTrak gaming device was attached to their wrist for the position and a Trivisio Colibri inertial tracker[7] was glued to the back of the glove for the orientation. All these devices were calibrated at the beginning of each session.

In this experiment, we use MobileTHING where both the local and the global frames of the virtual hand are controlled via the multi-touch interface. Participants were given a 7" Samsung Galaxy Tab 3 tablet that was also connected to a GameTrak for positional tracking. For a fair comparison, the same rotational tracker as the data glove was used instead of the tablet's sensors.

For the control condition, participants used a computer mouse and a keyboard to control the different degrees of freedom of the hand model using standard widgets [5, p. 41] available in Blender (Figure 5a). For positioning the wrist, they could select and drag a translation widget along one of its three axes. Alternatively, they could type a keyboard shortcut triggering an unconstrained translation and drag the cursor. For orienting the wrist, they could select and drag a rotation widget around one of its three axes. Another keyboard shortcut triggered an unconstrained rotation. For controlling the finger, they could manipulate the translation widgets of the appropriate inverse kinematics target or press the translation shortcut once it was selected.

Participants

16 participants took part in the experiment. The results of 4 of these participants were discarded because they could not finish the evaluation due to issues with the data glove: the glove did not fit their hands and its sensor readings were inaccurate which made hand control very difficult. The 12 remaining participants were all right-handed males aged 22 - 31 ($M = 26$; $SD = 2.8$). Regarding their level of familiarity with Blender, 6 had no prior experience, 4 stated that they were moderately familiar with it or with similar modeling tools and 2 stated that they were familiar with it.

Procedure

Participants had control over a virtual hand and were asked to match its pose with that of a *ghost hand* displaying four predefined configurations (listed in Figure 6). These configurations were presented in increasing order of complexity: Pose #1 only required a simple flexion of the thumb, Pose #2 required a rotation around one axis and different degrees of flexion, Pose #3 required a rotation around two axes and different degrees of flexion and finally Pose #4 required a rotation around three axes and different degrees of flexion. All poses required a translation. Each pose was presented 5 times. For each trial, the hand model was reset to its initial position and orientation, with all fingers extended.

A pose was considered valid once the controlled virtual hand was superimposed with the ghost hand with a tolerance threshold. For reference, the threshold is equivalent to 10% of the distance between the wrist and the middle fingertip. Visual feedback was given by colored spheres placed at each fingertip and a larger sphere at the base of the hand. When the associated hand part was below the proximity threshold, the sphere color was modified. The editor interface was divided into four different views of the 3D scene (top, left, front and a 3/4 perspective) so that participants could complete the task without controlling a camera.

Participants were instructed to complete the task as fast as possible and they had to successfully complete the current trial before moving to the next one. We chose to control for accuracy (instead of measuring both task completion time and accuracy) to directly compare interaction techniques based on task completion times.

Experimental Design

The independent variables were the TECHNIQUE (MOUSE, GLOVE, MOBILETHING), POSE (#1, #2, #3, #4, as represented in Figure 6) and REPETITION (5 different trials). The four poses to reproduce were always presented in the same ascending level of difficulty since pre-tests showed that less experienced users would experience difficulties if they started

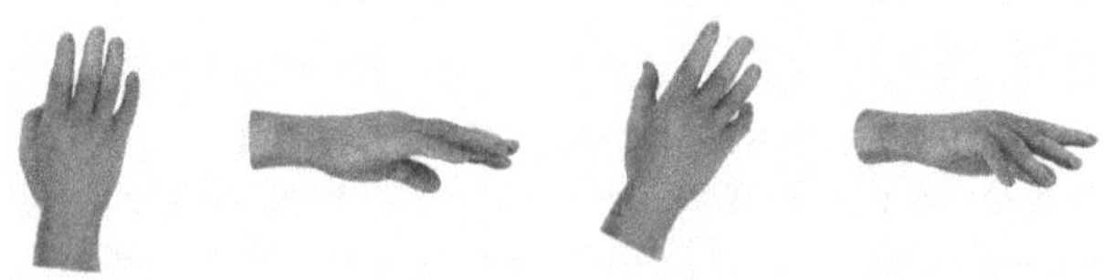

(a) Pose #1. (b) Pose #2.

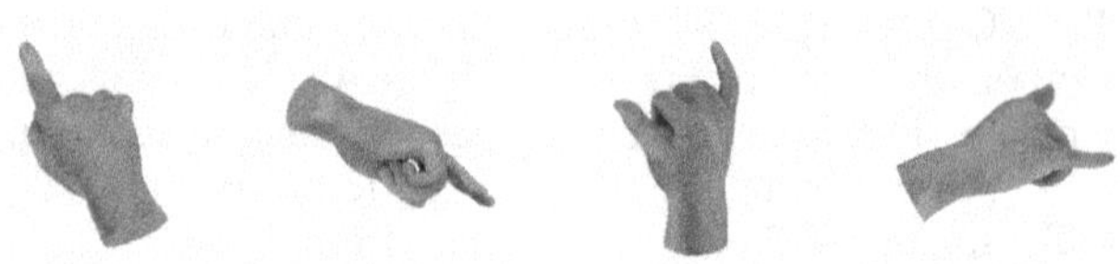

(c) Pose #3. (d) Pose #4.

Figure 6: The four poses used in the user study (top view and side view).

[5] `http://www.libhand.org`

[6] `http://www.5dt.com/products/pdataglove5u.html`

[7] `http://www.trivisio.com/trivisio-products/colibri-inertial-motion-tracker-2/`

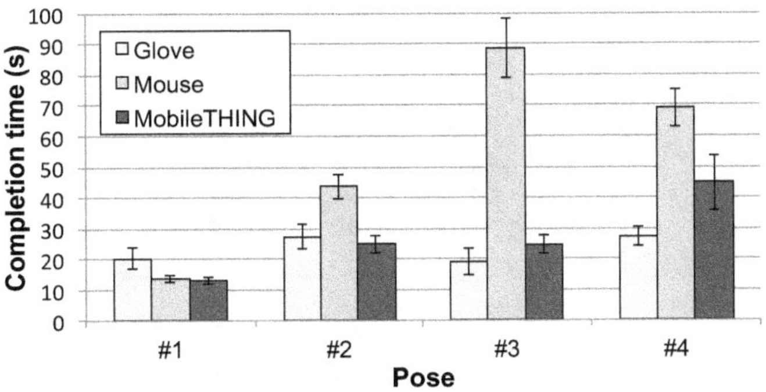

Figure 7: Completion time for TECHNIQUE and POSE, error bars representing 95% confidence interval.

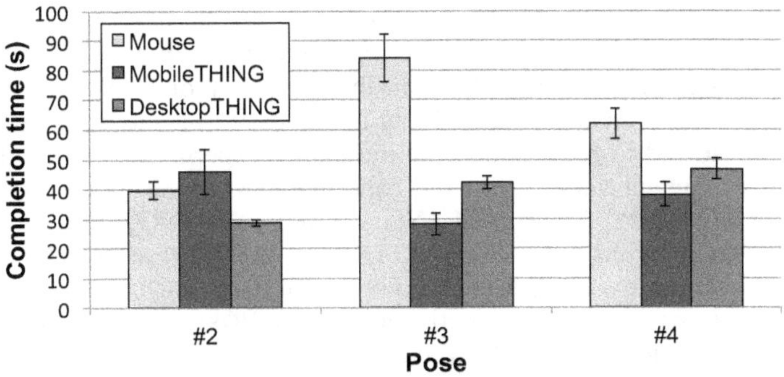

Figure 8: Completion time for TECHNIQUE and POSE, error bars representing 95% confidence interval.

directly with the more complex poses. The order of the techniques was counterbalanced among the participants using a Latin square. The total duration of the experiment was approximately 75 minutes including breaks. In total we had 12 remaining participants × 3 techniques × 4 poses × 5 repetitions = 720 total trials.

At the end of the evaluation, participants also indicated which interaction technique they preferred and filled a questionnaire to rate *ease, speed, comfort, precision* and *fatigue* using a 7-point Likert scale. A score of 7 for these criteria means a very positive rating except for *fatigue* where it means that the technique was very tiring (a rating of 1 means that it was not tiring at all).

Results

Completion time is the main dependent measure and is defined as the time taken between a three seconds countdown displayed at the beginning of each trial and the time when participants successfully matched the virtual hand with the ghost hand within the tolerance thresholds.

A repeated measures ANOVA showed a significant effect of REPETITION ($F(4,44) = 30.0$, $p < 0.0001$) on completion time, showing the presence of a learning effect. Pairwise comparisons revealed a significant difference ($p < 0.0001$) between the two first repetitions and the others (We used Bonferroni correction for all post-hoc analysis). We found no significant interaction for REPETITION. We thus removed the two first repetitions from subsequent analysis.

A repeated measures ANOVA showed a significant effect of TECHNIQUE ($F_{2,22} = 16.8$, $p < 0.0001$), POSE ($F_{3,33} = 16.3$, $p < 0.0001$) and a significant TECHNIQUE × POSE interaction ($F_{6,66} = 13.7$, $p < 0.0001$) on completion time (Figure 7). Pairwise comparisons revealed significant differences ($p < 0.002$) between MOUSE and the two other techniques (MOUSE: 53.7s, GLOVE: 23.5s, MOBILETHING: 26.8s). Pairwise comparisons showed significant differences ($p < 0.04$) between all POSE except between #3 and #4, confirming they were presented in ascending order of difficulty (#1: 15.6s, #2: 31.9s, #3: 44.1s, #4: 47.0s). Pairwise comparisons revealed no significant difference across techniques for pose #1 but MOUSE revealed to be significantly ($p < 0.02$) slower compared to GLOVE and MOBILETHING for poses #2 and #3. Pose #4 only revealed significant difference ($p = 0.001$) between GLOVE and MOUSE.

A Friedman analysis on the subjective questionnaire showed no significant effect for *global appreciation, ease, speed* and *comfort* criteria. A significant effect was found for the *precision* criterion ($\chi^2 = 2.19$, $p = 0.03$). Post-hoc analysis revealed that the MOUSE (*Median* = 6) was more precise than the GLOVE (*Median* = 4, $p = 0.03$). A significant effect was also found for the *fatigue* criterion ($\chi^2 = 2.41$, $p = 0.04$). Participants felt more fatigue when using the GLOVE (*Median* = 4) compared to the MOUSE (*Median* = 2, $p = 0.04$). No significant difference was found for MOBILETHING. Finally, when they were asked to state which technique they prefered, 2 participants chose MOBILETHING, 3 chose GLOVE and 2 chose the MOUSE technique.

Summary

As we hypothesized, the GLOVE technique performs overall very well compared to the MOUSE as it is more than twice faster than the mouse on average. However, this comes at the cost of more fatigue and less precision as highlighted by the questionnaire. The MOBILETHING technique also outperformed the MOUSE technique with an overall performance similar to that of the glove and the questionnaire did not reveal subjective differences with the other techniques.

Experiment 2: DesktopTHING

This second experiment aims at comparing the performance of the two versions of THING: DesktopTHING and MobileTHING. The experimental procedure and design are the same as the ones of the first experiment. Differences are detailed below.

For DesktopTHING, the local frame was controlled by the multi-touch interface while the global frame of the hand was controlled by a computer mouse. For controlling the global frame, the control scheme was identical to the mouse technique but participants could only manipulate the wrist and not the fingers.

Participants

Twelve participants who did not participate in the first experiment, took part in this second experiment. They were all right-handed males aged between 22 and 30 ($M = 25$; $SD = 2.4$). Regarding their level of familiarity with Blender, 4 had no prior experience, 4 were moderately familiar with it or with similar modeling tools and 4 were familiar with it.

Procedure and Experimental Design

We used the same procedure as the first experiment except we removed Pose #1 from the configuration pool since the first evaluation showed that it was easy to achieve. This allowed to reduce the duration of the experiment. The independent variables of the experiment were the TECHNIQUE (MOUSE, MOBILETHING, DESKTOPTHING), POSE (#2, #3, #4, as represented in Figure 6) and REPETITION (5 different trials). Presentation order for TECHNIQUE was counterbalanced across participants while POSE was presented in ascending order of difficulty. In summary we had 12 participants × 3 techniques × 3 poses × 5 repetitions = 540 total trials.

Results

A repeated measures ANOVA showed a significant effect of REPETITION ($F_{4,44} = 67.8$, $p < 0.0001$) on completion time, showing the presence of a learning effect. Pairwise comparisons revealed a significant difference ($p < 0.0001$) between the two first repetitions and the others. We found no significant interaction for REPETITION. We thus removed the two first repetitions from subsequent analysis.

A repeated measures ANOVA showed a significant effect of TECHNIQUE ($F_{2,22} = 8.4$, $p < 0.01$), POSE ($F_{2,22} = 4.3$, $p < 0.03$) and a significant TECHNIQUE × POSE interaction ($F_{4,44} = 9.5$, $p < 0.0001$) on completion time (Figure 8). Pairwise comparisons revealed significant differences ($p < 0.01$) between MOUSE and the two other techniques (MOUSE: 61.9s, DESKTOPTHING: 39.1s, MOBILETHING: 37.3s). Pairwise comparisons showed significant differences ($p < 0.03$) between poses #2 and #3 (#2: 38.0s, #3: 51.4s, #4: 48.9s). Pairwise comparisons revealed significant differences ($p < 0.01$) between DESKTOPTHING and MOUSE for pose #2. Significant differences ($p < 0.04$) were found between all techniques for pose #3. For pose #4, significant differences were found between MOUSE ($p < 0.03$) and the two other techniques.

A Friedman analysis on the subjective questionnaire showed a significant effect of TECHNIQUE on *global appreciation* ($\chi^2 = 3.16$, $p = 0.004$), *ease* ($\chi^2 = 2.48$, $p = 0.036$), *speed* ($\chi^2 = 2.62$, $p = 0.02$), *precision* ($\chi^2 = 2.95$, $p = 0.009$) and *fatigue* ($\chi^2 = 2.52$, $p = 0.03$) criteria. Figure 9 shows the answers to the subjective questionnaire for the significant criteria. Post-hoc analysis revealed that the DESKTOPTHING (*Median* = 7) was preferred to the MOUSE (*Median* = 5, $p = 0.004$). DESKTOPTHING (*Median* = 6.5) was also found to be easier than the MOUSE (*Median* = 5, $p = 0.035$). Post-hoc analysis revealed that DESKTOPTHING (*Median* = 6.5) was felt as being faster than the MOUSE (*Median* = 5, $p = 0.02$). In addition MOBILETHING (*Median* = 4.5) was found as less precise than DESKTOPTHING (*Median* = 7, $p = 0.009$). Participants felt more fatigue when using MOBILETHING (*Median* = 3) compared to DESKTOPTHING (*Median* = 1, $p = 0.03$). Finally, when they were asked which technique they preferred, 10 participants chose DESKTOPTHING, 2 chose MOBILETHING and none chose the MOUSE technique.

Summary

In this experiment, the MOUSE still showed much lower performance compared to the two versions of THING which are similar in terms of completion times. Compared to the first experiment, the completion times for each pose are similar, except for MOBILETHING and pose #2. We hypothesize that this may be due to a learning effect: participants started with pose #1 in experiment 1 while they started with pose #2 in this experiment.

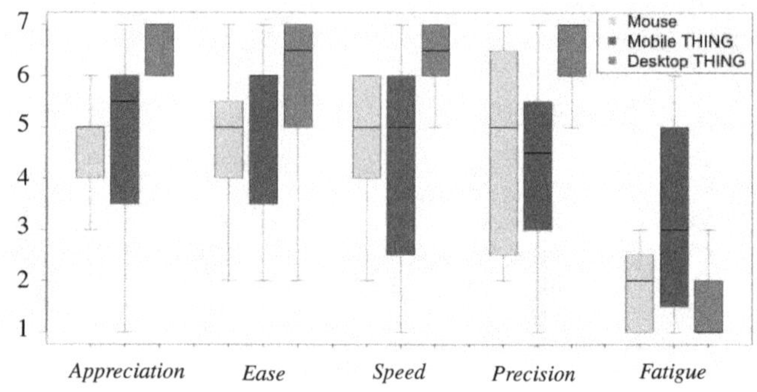

Figure 9: Boxplots for the answers to the subjective questionnaire of the second user study using a 7-point Likert scale. Each boxplot is delimited by the quartile (25 % quantile and 75% quantile) of the distribution of the effect over the individuals. The median is also represented for each Technique.

The subjective questionnaire shows an overall preference for DESKTOPTHING over the two other techniques. DESKTOPTHING was rated higher than the MOUSE in terms of *global appreciation, ease* and *speed.* DESKTOPTHING was also better rated than MOBILETHING for *precision* and *fatigue*.

DISCUSSION

Through these two experiments, the mouse technique consistently shows the lowest performance compared to the glove and the THING techniques: participants were more than 50% faster using the glove or MobileTHING in the first experiment and they were 40% faster using the THING techniques in the second one. The ability to control several degrees of freedom simultaneously with the glove and THING techniques is likely the main reason for this improved performance. Indeed, the mouse shows performance similar to those of the glove and MobileTHING with the first pose that only required the flexion of a single finger.

The first experiment revealed similar performance between the glove and the MobileTHING technique. However, THING worked consistently for all participants while the data glove was incompatible for four users (out of 16) who had smaller hands and had to stop the experiment since they could not control the hand model accurately. Additionally, several participants verbally expressed that pose #4 was difficult to replicate with the glove because they lacked the appropriate flexibility. However, they were not limited by THING since it is not dependent on the animator's own range of motion. Regarding the subjective questionnaire, participants felt significantly more tired and less precise with the glove compared to the mouse/keyboard. There was no significant effect with regards to these two criteria for THING, although some participants verbally mentioned that the tablet was heavy.

The second experiment focused on the evaluation of DesktopTHING, the variant that does not require to hold the tablet. The two versions of THING provided similar performance but participants preferred DesktopTHING. It also scored higher ratings with regards to the *ease*, *speed*, *precision* and *fatigue* criteria.

Overall, these results show that DesktopTHING is a good alternative to the mouse and keyboard in desktop environments. In scenarios requiring the user to stand up, MobileTHING appears as a potential alternative to data gloves: it shows similar performance and fits all users while the glove was incompatible with several of them. However, the tablet must be held with two hands and it is heavier than a data glove which could induce discomfort in certain configurations (*e.g.* with complex wrist rotations). Ultimately, we can imagine that users would not have to choose between MobileTHING and DesktopTHING. Instead DesktopTHING's control scheme would be used when the tablet lays on the desktop and it would switch to MobileTHING's as soon as the tablet is lifted.

Limitations and Improvements

THING controls 16 degrees of freedom of 3D hand models whereas real hands have 27 DOF. This simplification is due to the formulation of finger flexion: we reduce a chain of three joint angles to a single flexion parameter expressed with respect to a fixed trajectory. However, the real joints are not so strictly correlated and certain poses cannot be achieved using THING.

This limitation manifests itself for poses featuring uncoupled joint flexion, for example when the distal joint of a finger is extended but the others are curled. While such poses are unlikely to be necessary in free space, they occur often in the case of object manipulation when the object blocks joints or in the case of contact between fingers such as during pinching gestures. This limitation also occurs for the thumb which THING considers like the other fingers whereas it actually features 5 DOF. Thus it seems that concerning grasping motions, THING is currently capable of performing various power grasps but precision grasps requiring thumb opposition cannot be reproduced [17].

A preliminary solution to reproduce such poses is to switch back to the traditional inverse kinematics techniques since THING integrates seamlessly with the classical workflow of computer animation. In this case, users would use THING to reach a close hand configuration before using the accompanying mouse and keyboard to finely tune joints angles. A preferable solution would be to directly give control over these missing degrees of freedom on the tablet. We exploited all DOF that current tablets afford but using additional input such as force could allow users to control the fingers' trajectories. However, the low accuracy of current pressure-sensing hardware prevents from solving this issue at the moment. Another possibility is to exploit the semantic of the interaction to adjust the finger trajectories. For instance, only moving index and thumb would result in a pinch and closing the fingers around an object would adjust the trajectories to the object's shape in order to grab it in a realistic manner.

Another limitation, specific to DesktopTHING, is the need to switch from tablet to mouse to control different degrees of freedom. The homing times inherent to these transitions have a negative impact on performance. In the evaluation, participants performed on average 1.79 transitions per trial, which added on average 3.18 seconds to the task completion time. In a real applicative context, the nature of computer animation forces users to switch from the hand model to other objects in order to build sequences incrementally so these homing times are bound to occur. It would still be beneficial to reduce them for the sake of performance. One solution would be to display manipulation widgets on the tablet's screen to set the position and orientation of the virtual hand. However, this would require to frequently look at the tablet. An alternative solution would be to discard entirely the computer mouse and use the tactile surface to control the cursor on the editor's screen, similarly to a touchpad.

CONCLUSION

We introduced THING, a novel tablet-based interaction technique dedicated to the animation of 3D hand models. Our approach leverages multi-touch input to intuitively control the fingers of a virtual hand in flexion and in abduction. It also exploits spatial inputs made available by the tablet's inner sensors to place and orient the hand globally. We designed two variations of THING: **(1)** a mobile version taking advantage of all the available inputs to provide an animation system integrated in a single device and **(2)** a desktop version which delegates the control of the global frame of the hand to a computer mouse in order to reduce fatigue.

Two user studies were conducted for assessing the performance benefits granted by our technique. The first experiment compared MobileTHING to the use of a computer mouse and to motion capture via a data glove. Our approach was 50% faster than the traditional computer mouse technique. THING also demonstrated performance close to those of the most expensive data glove and it fitted all users while the glove was incompatible with several of them due to morphological variations. The second experiment compared the two variants of THING and the computer mouse to determine their relative performance and subjective user preferences. DesktopTHING was shown to provide similar performance to MobileTHING but was also considered as less tiring. Moreover, it was predominantly preferred by participants.

These results suggest that THING is a valuable interaction technique that could prove useful to 3D animators since it provides a nice alternative to traditional techniques of hand animation. THING could relieve expert users from the tediousness of traditional hand posing but it could also be relevant to non-experts since it provides a less intimidating alternative to classic forward/inverse kinematic rigs. Moreover, its barrier of entry is low compared to methods depending on less common and more expensive hardware. Its underpinning on common computer graphics primitives also makes it easily integrable into 3D editors.

Future work could first concern the consideration of a greater number of degrees of freedom in order to reach even more subtle poses. This could be achieved by exploiting other inputs, such as pressure sensing or by adding rules related to the semantic of the interaction being animated. We could also investigate the potential of THING for other applications, for instance teleoperation or gaming. Finally, THING could be generalized to other contexts for controlling virtual hands. For instance, it could find applications in virtual reality for interacting in real-time with virtual objects.

ACKNOWLEDGMENTS

We warmly thank Fanny Chevalier and Sylvain Malacria for their wise feedbacks on early versions of the paper and Daniel Vogel for the video voice over. We also thank our anonymous reviewers for their insightful comments and suggestions that helped revising the work. This work was supported by ANR (MANDARIN project, ANR-12-CORD-0011).

REFERENCES

1. Casiez, G., Roussel, N., and Vogel, D. 1 € filter: a simple speed-based low-pass filter for noisy input in interactive systems. In *Proc. of CHI* (2012), 2527–2530.
2. Guna, J., Jakus, G., Pogačnik, M., Tomažič, S., and Sodnik, J. An analysis of the precision and reliability of the Leap Motion sensor and its suitability for static and dynamic tracking. *Sensors 14*, 2 (2014), 3702–3720.
3. Gutiérrez, M., Vexo, F., and Thalmann, D. The mobile animator: Interactive character animation in collaborative virtual environment. In *Proc. of VR* (2004), 125–132.
4. Held, R., Gupta, A., Curless, B., and Agrawala, M. 3D puppetry: a Kinect-based interface for 3D animation. In *Proc. of UIST* (2012), 423–434.
5. Hess, R. *Blender Foundations: The Essential Guide to Learning Blender 2.6*. Focal Press. Elsevier, 2010.
6. Jacobson, A., Panozzo, D., Glauser, O., Pradalier, C., Hilliges, O., and Sorkine-Hornung, O. Tangible and modular input device for character articulation. *ACM Trans. Graph. 33*, 4 (2014), 82.
7. Johnson, M. P., Wilson, A. D., Blumberg, B., Kline, C., and Bobick, A. F. Sympathetic interfaces: Using a plush toy to direct synthetic characters. In *Proc. of CHI* (1999), 152–158.
8. Kim, D., Hilliges, O., Izadi, S., Butler, A., Chen, J., Oikonomidis, I., and Olivier, P. Digits: freehand 3D interactions anywhere using a wrist-worn gloveless sensor. In *Proc. of UIST* (2012), 167–176.
9. Kin, K., Miller, T., Bollensdorff, B., DeRose, T., Hartmann, B., and Agrawala, M. Eden: a professional multitouch tool for constructing virtual organic environments. In *Proc. of CHI* (2011), 1343–1352.
10. Kipp, M., and Nguyen, Q. Multitouch puppetry: creating coordinated 3D motion for an articulated arm. In *Proc. of ITS* (2010), 147–156.
11. Knep, B., Hayes, C., Sayre, R., and Williams, T. Dinosaur input device. In *Proc. of CHI* (1995), 304–309.
12. Komatsu, K. Human skin model capable of natural shape variation. *The Visual Computer 3*, 5 (1988), 265–271.
13. Kry, P. G., and Pai, D. K. Grasp recognition and manipulation with the Tango. In *Proc. of ISER* (2006), 551–559.
14. Kry, P. G., and Pai, D. K. Interaction capture and synthesis. *Trans. Graph. 25*, 3 (2006), 872–880.
15. Kry, P. G., Pihuit, A., Bernhardt, A., and Cani, M.-P. Handnavigator: hands-on interaction for desktop virtual reality. In *Proc. of VRST* (2008), 53–60.
16. Lockwood, N., and Singh, K. Finger walking: Motion editing with contact-based hand performance. In *Proc. of the Symposium on Computer Animation* (2012), 43–52.
17. Napier, J. The prehensile movements of the human hand. *The journal of bone and joint surgery 38*, 4 (1956), 902–913.
18. Oikonomidis, I., Kyriazis, N., and Argyros, A. A. Efficient model-based 3D tracking of hand articulations using Kinect. In *Proc. of BMVC* (2011), 1–11.
19. Parent, R. *Computer Animation: Algorithms and Techniques*, 3rd ed. Morgan Kaufmann Publishers Inc., 2012.
20. Romero, J., Kjellström, H., and Kragic, D. Monocular real-time 3D articulated hand pose estimation. In *Proc. of Humanoids* (2009), 87–92.
21. Sheng, J., Balakrishnan, R., and Singh, K. An interface for virtual 3D sculpting via physical proxy. In *Proc. of GRAPHITE* (2006), 213–220.
22. Stenger, B., Mendonça, P. R. S., and Cipolla, R. Model-based 3D tracking of an articulated hand. In *CVPR (2)* (2001), 310–315.
23. Sturman, D. Computer puppetry. *Computer Graphics and Applications 18*, 1 (1998), 38–45.
24. Sturman, D., and Zeltzer, D. A survey of glove-based input. *Computer Graphics and Applications 14*, 1 (1994), 30–39.
25. Wang, R. Y., and Popovic, J. Real-time hand-tracking with a color glove. *Proc. of SIGGRAPH 28*, 3 (2009).
26. Wu, Y., and Huang, T. Hand modeling, analysis and recognition. *Signal Processing Magazine 18*, 3 (2001), 51–60.
27. Zhai, S. *Human performance in six degree of freedom input control*. PhD thesis, University of Toronto, 1995.
28. Zhao, J., and Badler, N. I. Inverse kinematics positioning using nonlinear programming for highly articulated figures. *Trans. Graph. 13*, 4 (1994), 313–336.
29. Zimmerman, T. G., Lanier, J., Blanchard, C., Bryson, S., and Harvill, Y. A hand gesture interface device. In *Proc. of CHI* (1987), 189–192.

The Roly-Poly Mouse: Designing a Rolling Input Device Unifying 2D and 3D Interaction

Gary Perelman[1], Marcos Serrano[1], Mathieu Raynal[1], Celia Picard[2], Mustapha Derras[2], Emmanuel Dubois[1]

[1]University of Toulouse, IRIT
Toulouse, France
{first_name.last_name}@irit.fr

[2]LRA, Berger-Levrault
Toulouse, France
{first_name.last_name}@berger-levrault.fr

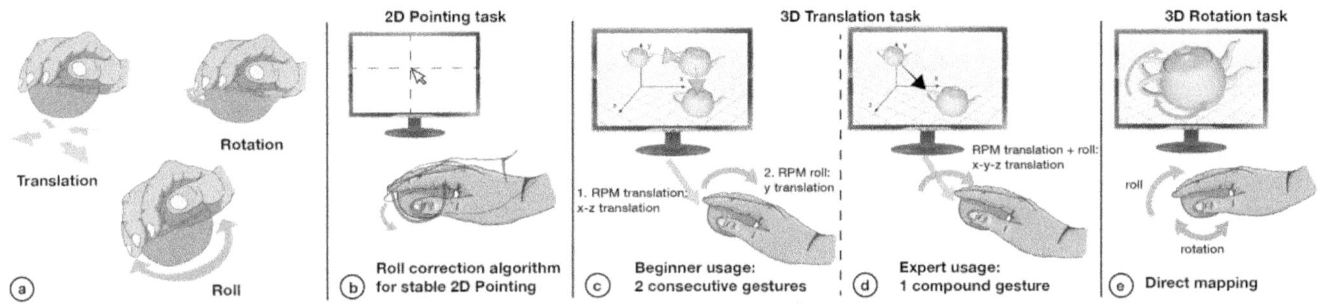

Figure 1.a) The Roly-Poly Mouse (RPM) gestures. RPM can be used for b) 2D pointing; c-d) 3D translation by combining RPM translation and roll; e) and 3D rotation by combining RPM roll and rotation.

ABSTRACT

We present the design and evaluation of the Roly-Poly Mouse (RPM), a rolling input device that combines the advantages of the mouse (position displacement) and of 3D devices (roll and rotation) to unify 2D and 3D interaction. Our first study explores RPM gesture amplitude and stability for different upper shapes (Hemispherical, Convex) and hand postures. 8 roll directions can be performed precisely and their amplitude is larger on Hemispherical RPM. As minor rolls affect translation, we propose a roll correction algorithm to support stable 2D pointing with RPM. We propose the use of compound gestures for 3D pointing and docking, and evaluate them against a commercial 3D device, the SpaceMouse. Our studies reveal that RPM performs 31% faster than the SpaceMouse for 3D pointing and equivalently for 3D rotation. Finally, we present a proof-of-concept integrated RPM prototype along with discussion on the various technical challenges to overcome to build a final integrated version of RPM.

Author Keywords

Input Device; 2D Pointing; 3D Interaction.

CHI 2015, April 18 - 23, 2015, Seoul, Republic of Korea
Copyright 2015 ACM 978-1-4503-3145-6/15/04…$15.00
http://dx.doi.org/10.1145/2702123.2702244

ACM Classification Keywords

H.5.2. Information interfaces and presentation: Interaction

INTRODUCTION

3D applications are more popular than ever with the advent of easy-to-use 3D editors (SketchUp), 3D printing and web 3D engines (Unity Web Player, Flash 3D). Affordable multi-degrees-of-freedom (DOF) devices, such as the SpaceMouse (with over a million units sold [27]), contribute to this development. However these devices are not well suited for 2D pointing in WIMP interfaces [11] (3D editor menus, web browser GUI or when switching to 2D applications). They usually work in rate control mode, less convenient for 2D pointing [36]; DOF are difficult to operate independently [11]; and some devices are bulky, or tiresome to use such as the Phantom [24]. Therefore users need to switch between the mouse and the 3D device, which is tedious and inefficient [11]. Relying only on the mouse for 3D tasks is less effective [1,9]. An all-in-one device would therefore remove device-switching costs (Homing in KLM [6]) and improve the workflow of the users of 3D applications in 2D WIMP environments.

Previous works have augmented a regular 2D mouse with additional DOF [1,13] by adding rounded edges to enable rocking gestures. These devices are limited by their initial mouse-like form factor, with a flat surface to assure the device's stability. The different DOF, i.e. mouse translation and rocking, are physically separated and the flat spot at the base of these devices physically drives the user to control only two degrees of freedom simultaneously. Besides, the rocking amplitude is limited to a rather small curved surface, thus diminishing the range of input values. In our approach, rather than providing a mouse with additional DOF, we choose to provide a rounded shape, intrinsically offering 3 DOF rotations, with capabilities for handling 2D translations.

In this paper we present the design of a rolling input device offering up to 6 DOF: the Roly-Poly Mouse (RPM). This device mimics the well-known roly-poly toy: the base of the device is hemispherical and can be rolled (2DOF), rotated (1DOF) and translated (up to 3DOF) in any direction (Figure 1).The key benefits of RPM make it a good candidate for an all-in-one device: RPM is free-moving as a mouse; has a large curved surface for rolling; and allows simultaneous and coordinated gestures to be performed by combining roll, rotation and translation. The design and usage of a symmetrical device with no stability constraint raises a number of challenges that we address in this paper: we study amplitude and precision along the different DOF; we propose a roll correction algorithm to support stable 2D pointing; and we design compound gestures for efficient 3D translation and rotation. We evaluate RPM against the SpaceMouse for 3D interaction, and results confirm that RPM is an efficient 3D device.

We build a proof-of-concept integrated prototype with a 'ring' button accessible on any device orientation and a 6DOF magnetic sensor. Using this prototype, we explore some usage scenarios that illustrate that RPM is not only interesting to unify 2D and 3D interaction, but also to extend several types of 2D applications by adding gestural control or commands.

Our contributions are 1) the design of a novel rolling input device through the experimental exploration of several design factors, 2) a novel roll-correction algorithm to support stable 2D pointing, 3) the design of a compound gesture for 3D interaction and a comparison with the SpaceMouse, and 4) a proof-of-concept wireless prototype along with usage scenarios and a discussion on technical challenges to build a final integrated version of RPM.

RELATED WORK

Mouse with multiple DOF

Prior works have augmented the regular mouse with additional DOF. Some of them added one DOF using two mouse sensors to support yawing [18,23] or a pressure sensor to control multiple levels of discrete selection modes [8, 15].These devices are however limited to 3 DOF.

Other mouse augmentations using 2 or 3 additional DOF have been proposed to allow 3D manipulations [1,13]. Rockin'Mouse [1] is a seminal input device with the shape of a regular mouse but with rounded bottom allowing the device to be tilted and thus offering two additional DOF. VideoMouse [13] is a similar device allowing for two more DOF (z-axis rotation and translation) by using a camera. These two planar multi-DOF devices derive from the mouse's form factor: they add a rounded border to the bottom but keep the flat surface on the base to preserve device stability. One limitation of this design principle is that the narrow rounded surface restricts tilting degrees (+/- 20° for the VideoMouse). Moreover even if Rockin'Mouse and VideoMouse allowed for partial compound gestures, these were limited by their form factor: the flat spot at the base of these devices physically drives the user to control only two degrees of freedom simultaneously. Studies with the Rockin'Mouse on a 3D task revealed that movements involving both planar and tilting movements occurred during the ballistic phase of the trial, while the final closed-loop phase involved one dimension at a time. Our device design is intended to increase the use of compound gestures thanks to its large hemispherical bottom that enables extended rolling and facilitates 4D gestures such as roll + translation.

The DesktopBat [28], a 5 DOF mouse, is based on the opposite approach: attaching a dome on top of a mouse, rather than below. The dome acts as an isometric input. No evaluation of this device in comparison with others has been reported so its key benefits are difficult to assess. The SpaceMouse is a 6DOF device [27] that requires dexterity as DOF are difficult to perform separately [9]: used with the non-dominant hand it is less efficient than regular mouse for 3D interaction [3]; however with the dominant hand, it has been reported to outperform the mouse [9].

Other techniques for 2D and 3D interaction

With the advent of multitouch surfaces, touch-based solutions for interacting with 3D environments have been proposed [10,12,20]. StickyTools [12] is a full 6DOF technique for rotation and translation of 3D objects. DS3 [20] is another technique based on the separation of translation and rotation that proved to be faster than StickyTools [20]. However, touch-based solutions are slower than the mouse or dedicated devices for 6D docking tasks [10]. Mid-air gestures have also been used to interact with 3D environments [24,34]. AirMouse [24] is a technique for 3D pointing in mid-air with a similar performance to that of 3D devices. 6D Hands [33] is a hand tracking system that supports bi-manual gestures for 3D manipulation. However, mid-air gestures induce fatigue and are not well suited for long interactions [24].

Round input devices

Our work is inspired by previous research on round devices [9,31,36,37]. The FingerBall (or FBall) [36] is a free-moving (isotonic) spherical device that can be held and moved in mid-air. The spherical form factor was intended to improve "precision grasp", i.e. using one's dexterity. The device showed better performance than a glove for a 6DOF docking task [37]. PALLA is a similar wireless device used to explore interaction with video games [31]. Globefish and GlobeMouse [9] are two 6DOF devices based on combining isotonic rotation with isometric translation. These devices perform well in rotation but, as with isometric devices, not in translation.

THE ROLY-POLY MOUSE (RPM)

The RPM is based on the form factor of the well-known roly-poly toy (Figure 2). The bottom is hemispherical, contains weight and its center of mass is low. When released, the device returns to its initial upright position after an inertial roll movement.

Gestures: translation, roll and rotation

The device offers up to 6 DOF with three types of simple gesture (Figure 1): translation (3 DOF), roll (2 DOF: pitch and roll) and rotation (1 DOF: yaw). In the context of desktop usage, we don't consider the z-axis translation due to fatigue: our studies explore the use of a 5 DOF RPM.

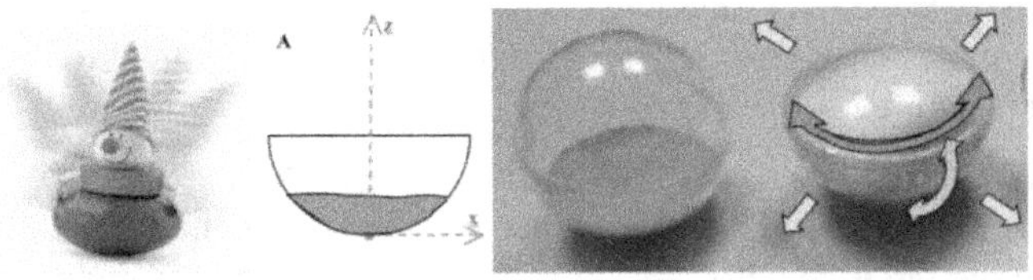

Figure 2. The roly-poly toy (a) has a low center of mass (b). Two RPM upper shapes: hemispherical and convex (c)

Key benefits

This form factor presents several key benefits that make it interesting for building an input device. As the device is **free-moving** in the x-y plane it can be used like an isotonic device such as the mouse [5]. The device contact with the surface is minimal, thus minimizing displacement friction. At the same time the device rolls and auto-repositions itself when released, **similar to an isometric device** [5]. The hemispherical bottom offers a large curved surface allowing for a wide range of possible input values. The device is symmetrical along its rotation axis (z) and thus can be used in any orientation. The three simple gestures (translation, rolling and rotation) can be combined to create **compound gestures**. For instance, effective 3D pointing with RPM is based on a compound gesture: translation + roll (Figure 1).

To sum up, this form factor combines characteristics from isotonic and isometric devices, making it a good candidate for an **all-in-one device** (Table 1 extends table in [13]). A 5 DOF device with such properties can be "very appealing to users who are reluctant to change their ways" [18].

Table 1. Comparison of sensed DOF for several multi-DOF mice (Tz can be sensed by RPM but is not used*).**

Iput DOF	Regular Mouse		Rockin' Mouse [1]		Video Mouse[13]		Space Mouse [27]		Roly-poly Mouse	
	Sensed	Rate/Pos	Sensed	Rate/ Position	Sensed	Rate/ Position	sensed	Rate/Pos	Sensed	Rate/ Position
Tx	✓	p	✓	P	✓	p	✓	r	✓	p
Ty	✓	p	✓	P	✓	p	✓	r	✓	p
Tz	×		×		✓	p	✓	r	✓	p*
Rx	×		✓	r,p	✓	r,p	✓	r	✓	r,p
Ry	×		✓	r,p	✓	r,p	✓	r	✓	r,p
Rz	×		×		✓	r	✓	r	✓	r,p
T+R	×		×		×		✓	r	✓	r,p

DEVICE DESIGN FACTORS

As a first step in the design process of RPM, we identify and analyze the various factors that affect its usage.

Radius dimension

The size of RPM is based on the average size of a regular mouse (approx. 12x6cm). We carried out informal tests with three different diameter dimensions: 6, 8 and 10 cm. The 8 cm version was the easiest to handle and translate so all our RPM prototypes are based on this dimension.

Selection mechanism

The RPM cannot hold regular front buttons that would be difficult to reach when the device rotates. Two always-available solutions are to use a 'ring' button around the device (as the one in our working prototype) or a capacitive surface. In our studies we focus on RPM gestures and shape and don't evaluate these alternatives, left for future work.

Upper shape

We considered different shapes for the upper half of the hemisphere; hereafter, they are referred to as "upper shapes". Focusing on a symmetrical form that a hand would comfortably hold, we opted for a hemisphere and varied its degree of curvature and direction (in and out). In our preliminary study we initially consider three upper shapes: hemispherical, convex (curved out) and concave (curved in).

Hand grip posture

Previous psychological and physiological studies on the grasp of tangible objects show that the type of grasp (number and position of fingers) depends on the object shape as well as on the goal [22]. Grasp postures have also been previously used as an input modality [29]. Consequently, in our preliminary study we identify the most frequently adopted hand postures and explore them in subsequent studies to evaluate their impact on RPM gesture amplitude.

Gesture amplitude

Each one of the three gestures (translation, roll and rotation) has different amplitudes. The RPM is a wireless device and thus its movement in the x-y plane is unlimited. Concerning the roll and the rotation, their amplitudes are theoretically +90/-90° for roll and unlimited for rotation. However the hand posture and biomechanical limitations of the joints involved, such as the wrist, will restrain this theoretical amplitude [19,26]. By considering different hand postures in our first study, we collect the possible range of values for each type of gesture.

DOF Integration and Separation

The different DOF of the RPM are physically integrated: when performing a displacement, there will be some rolling; when rolling or rotating, the device's center of mass probably translates. To allow for a proper separation of the DOF of the device [14], we need to know how each DOF affects the others. We study this question in the first study of the paper.

Stability: Roll correction for 2D pointing

Due to the rounded shape of the device, we noticed unintended roll when translations are done. This poses a problem: when the device rolls, the center of the device moves and thus the mouse pointer is translated (Figure 3). Note that this problem is inherent to the device and not to the tracking technique: whether we consider the center of the device or the contact point with the surface, the problem exists.

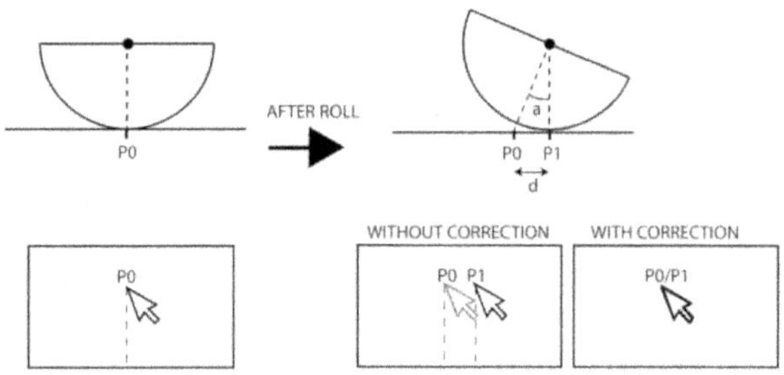

Figure 3. 2D pointing problem with a rolling device.

To solve this problem, we implemented a "roll correction" algorithm. This algorithm consists in calculating the position P0, which represents the device position upright, when the device is rolled into a position P1 (Figure 3). To calculate P0, we use the current position of the device P1, the roll and pitch angles a and p, and device radius R as follows:

$$P0.x = P1.x - \pi R * (\sin(a) + \cos(b))$$

$$P0.y = P1.y - \pi R * (\cos(a) + \sin(b))$$

In our implementation, when using the RPM as a mouse, we apply the algorithm for each frame to correct the roll deviation. We then calculate the displacement and apply the regular transfer function [7] to define the pointer position.

PRELIMINARY STUDY: UPPER SHAPES AND HAND POSTURES

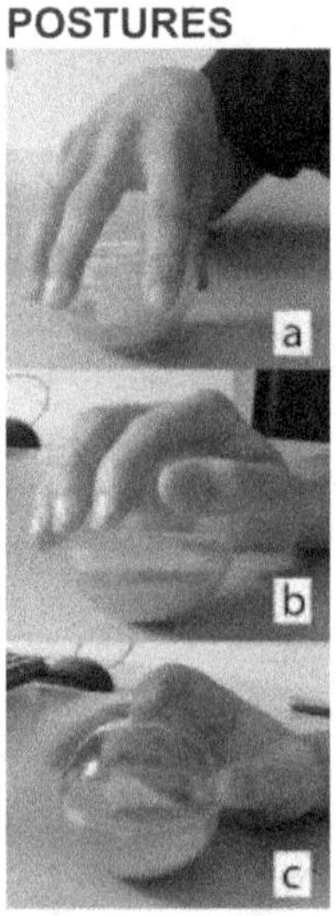

Figure 4. Most frequent hand postures.

The goal of this preliminary study was to collect most frequently used hand postures for each RPM gesture and user preference on the three considered RPM upper shapes.

Study Description

We studied 3 shapes (Concave, Convex and Hemispherical) and asked participants, for each shape, to hold the device with the dominant hand in four ways to perform four gestures: translation, roll, rotation and a compound gesture (in contact with the table). No interactive feedback was provided to participants and RPM was not tracked.

We recruited 12 participants (2 females) aged 24.8 years on average (SD=1.8). Two had previous experience with multiple DOF devices. We took 144 pictures corresponding to each hand posture (3 shapes x 4 gestures x 12 participants). We finally asked participants to order device shapes by preference. Each session lasted about 30 min.

Results

Over the 12 participants, 7 preferred Convex upper-shape, 4 Hemispherical and only 1 Concave. The Concave version of RPM was perceived to be difficult to hold and displace. In consequence we chose to remove it from the rest of our studies. Concerning the hand postures, we identified different recurrent patterns among which three were the most frequently adopted: Squeeze (Figure 4-a), Lay (Figure 4-b), and Touch (Figure 4-c). The following studies involve these three postures.

EXPERIMENTAL RPM TRACKING SETUP

In our following studies, we used the experimental tracking setup detailed below.

Tracking system

To track the translation, rotation and roll of the device we used infrared optical markers tracked by 12 OptiTrack cameras (1mm precision).The system senses the position (x, y, z) and orientation (yaw, pitch, roll) of RPM at 100Hz.

Prototype

The two RPM were weighted to be stable at rest (80gr each). Markers were placed on a support (Figure 5) to allow the cameras detect the device without impeding the user's ability to grab the device with the three selected hand postures. Informal tests had also confirmed that the marker did not limit the amplitude of comfortable rolls: the maximum possible roll of RPM given these physical markers was 70° in the marker support directions. Our tracking setup did not register contact with the underneath surface, thus we did not use clutching in our experiments.

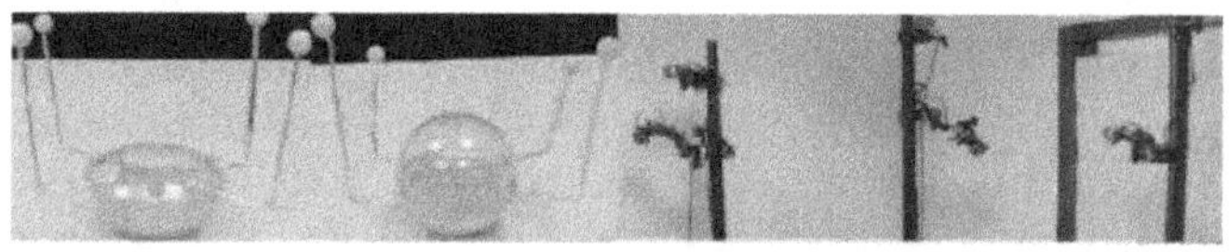

Figure 5. Experimental tracking setup.

STUDY 1: GESTURES STABILITY AND AMPLITUDE

We explore RPM gestures' stability and maximum comfortable amplitude for each upper shape, considering various hand postures

Study Description

Task and instructions

Based on the preliminary study, we decided to study gestures stability and amplitude with two upper shapes (Convex and Hemispherical) and three hand postures (Squeeze, Lay, and Touch). We chose to control hand postures to avoid any confounding effect on the results as the user's grip can have an important impact on the gesture amplitude. The task consisted in performing translations and rolls in 8 different directions and rotations in the two possible directions. We included two different distances (12 and 24 cm) for the translation task to study its effect on RPM stability. All distances and directions were drawn on the experimentation surface with circles and lines respectively (Figure 6). We asked participants to perform translations in a comfortable way from the center to the edge of the circle and back again to the center. Concerning rolls and rotation, we asked them to perform the maximum comfortable gesture. We used the tracking setup detailed in the previous section.

Figure 6. Study setup: distances and directions were drawn on the surface.

Participants

We recruited 12 participants (1 female) aged 25.7 years on average (SD=3.8). One had previous experience with multi-DOF devices and eleven took part in the pre-study session.

Design and procedure

The study follows a 2x3x4 within-subject design with Upper shape (Convex or Hemispherical), Hand posture (Squeeze, Touch or Lay) and Gesture (Short Translation, Long Translation, Rotation and Roll) as factors. We counterbalanced Upper shape and Hand posture. The study is made up of 6 blocks (each block is a combination of one Upper shape and one Hand Posture). Each block consists of 8 short translations, 8 long translations, 8 rolls and 2 rotations ordered randomly. After each trial, the device is placed in its initial position on the table.

Collected data and statistical analysis

We collected 2 devices x 3 hand postures x (16 translations + 8 rolls + 2 rotations) x 12 subjects = 1872 gestures. After each block we measured fatigue with a 6-20 Borg scale [4]. We used a Shapiro-Wilk test to determine the normality of the collected data. If the data was normal or could be normalized, we used a Univariate ANOVA test. If not, we used a Friedman test to compare more than 2 conditions and Wilcoxon tests otherwise. When we performed more than one statistical test on a particular set of data, we used the Bonferroni correction.

Results

Gestures amplitude

Rotation: We report the rotation amplitude for each direction (left and right), Hand posture and device Upper shape. A Wilcoxon test reveals no significant effect of the device upper shape on the rotation amplitude (Z=-0.98, p=0.33), thus we report mean values considering both upper shapes. A Wilcoxon test confirms a difference between left and right rotations (Z=-3.13, p=0.0017): left rotations are on average larger than right rotations (57° vs. 48°) (Figure 7-a). Results on Hand posture indicate that Squeeze allows for a larger average rotation than Touch or Lay (66° vs. 45° and 48°; $\chi^2(2)=24$, p<.001).

Roll: We report results on rolling amplitude (i.e. maximum degrees rolled in a given direction). An ANOVA test establishes a significant difference between RPM upper shapes ($F_{1,528}=34.319$, p<.001). The maximum average rolling amplitude is significantly higher with the Hemispherical RPM (39°) than with the Convex RPM (37°). Rolling amplitudes range from 27° to almost 60° depending on roll direction and hand posture (Figure 7-b,c).

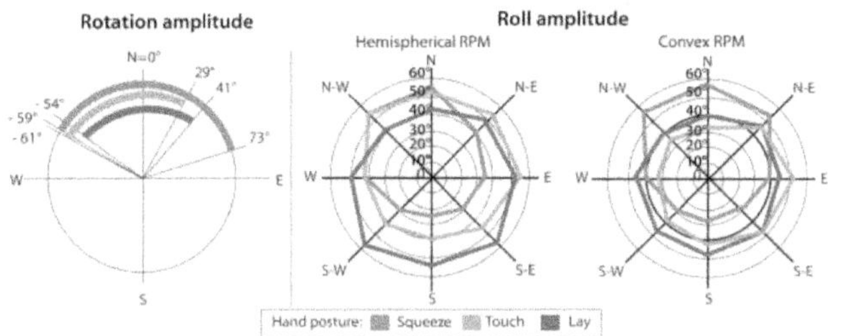

Figure 7. a) Rotation amplitude in degrees for each hand posture; b) rolling amplitude for the Hemispherical version and c) for the Convex version.

Gesture stability

Roll: Results on roll stability, i.e. deviation from the rolling direction, reveal no significant effect of the RPM Upper shape ($F_{7,528}=2.68$ p=0.09). Overall, deviation ranged from 8° to 17° for each direction (Figure 8). These results confirm that 8 directions can be reached without error, thus RPM roll can be used to interact with a Marking Menu for instance [17].

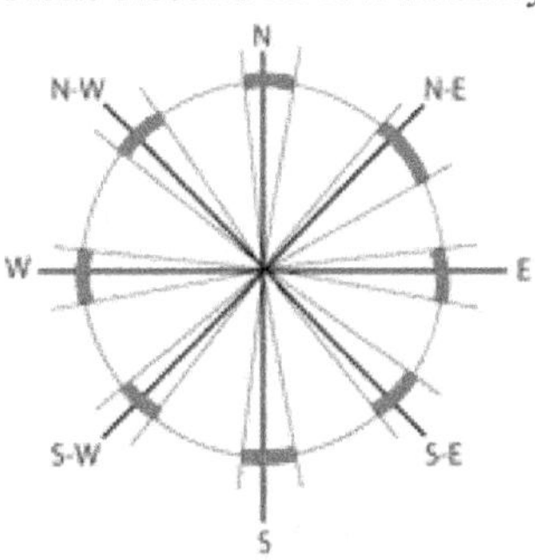

Figure 8. Rolling precision for each rolling direction

Translation: Results on translation stability, i.e. the amount of unintended rotation and roll during translations, reveal that there is on average 12° of roll and 15° of rotation while displacing RPM. There is no significant difference between Hemispherical and Convex RPM (Z=-4.29 p=0.08). While a Wilcoxon test establishes a significant difference between long and short translations (Z=-2.34, p=0.018), this difference is limited to 1° for roll. Finally no significant differences have been observed between hand postures(Z=-0.78, p=0.44).

Fatigue

The average Borg [4] score obtained is 11.72 (on a scale of 6-20). Upper shape does not significantly affect fatigue. However, fatigue measured when using the Squeeze posture is significantly higher than with other postures (Friedman $\chi^2(2)=8.46$, p=0.0144).

Summary

Our study on gesture amplitude reveals that the Hemispherical upper shape allows for the largest rolling amplitude; rotation amplitudes vary from left to right and is larger with the Squeeze hand posture. Concerning precision, roll allows for 8 precise directions; and translation stability is affected by unexpected rotation and roll. Given the fatigue results for Squeeze, we removed this posture from the following studies. From these results we define a roll threshold of 12° to avoid unintended activations and consider amplitudes up to 42° (to enable 30° rolls).

STUDY 2: 3D MANIPULATION WITH THE RPM

Taking advantage of the key benefits of RPM, we propose a technique combining RPM roll and displacement to perform 3D translations, and RPM roll and rotation to perform 3D rotation. We evaluate our solution against a dedicated commercial device, the SpaceMouse.

RPM 3D Interaction Techniques

As we use 5 DOF, applying RPM to 3D manipulation relies on a modal use: translation and rotation are performed separately. As RPM offers 2 DOF for translation, 2 DOF for roll and 1 DOF for rotation, any 3DOF task will be performed using a combination of these three gestures.

3D translation: roll & displacement

To perform 3D translation of an object, we use a position control technique: 2D physical displacement of the RPM is mapped to 2D translation of the cursor on the x-z plane in the 3D scene. The RPM front/back roll controls the elevation of the x-z plane, i.e. the y position of the plane. This technique offers the advantage to be easy to use for beginners and to support the transition to experts. Beginners can decompose a 3D translation task by performing first a 2D movement on the x-z plane, then a roll to define the y value. Advanced users can simultaneously combine displacement and roll in the same coordinated gesture to directly perform a 3D translation.

3D rotation: roll & rotation

To perform 3D rotations, two modes are possible: position control or rate control. In position control, RPM rotation and roll are directly mapped to the object 3D orientation. This mode requires clutching, as informal tests showed that to be comfortably and efficiently operated, RPM roll can be mapped to a maximum of +/- 90° rotation in the virtual scene. In rate control, the RPM roll and rotation angles are mapped to the rotation velocities of the 3D object. Informal tests revealed that position control outperformed rate control.

Study description: 3DOF pointing and docking

In this study we compare RPM with a 3D dedicated device, the SpaceMouse [27], in two separated 3D tasks: pointing and docking [21]. We do not compare with traditional mouse as it has been reported to be less efficient than the SpaceMouse for 3D interaction [9].

Tasks and instructions

We decided to conduct two sessions, each one dedicated to one 3D task: the first session consisted of performing 3D translations (3D pointing task), and the second one of 3D rotations (3D docking task). The reason we divided our experiment into two subtasks, instead of a single 6DOF docking task [21,37], is that the number of conditions for the pointing task was quite large, and combining both would make the experiment excessively long. We also wanted to study separately the performance of our device for 3D translation and for 3D rotation, and combining both would make it difficult to analyze each subtask. Previous research has proven that, even if both tasks can be carried out jointly, users usually perform them independently [21].

Figure 9. SpaceMouse device (left) and 3D environment for the 3D pointing (center) and 3D docking (right) tasks.

In the 3D pointing task, the participant is asked to reach a 3D spherical target in a 3D scene by translating a cursor (Figure 9). The target is displayed in the center of a cube delimiting the 3D environment. The cursor initial position is situated in 8 different directions (combining equal x, y and z translations) at two different distances (12.99 and 8.66) from the target. We implemented two different target sizes (0.5 and 1.7) to produce 4 Index of Difficulties (2.6, 3.11, 4.19 and 4.75 bits). In the 3D docking task, the user is asked to rotate a tetrahedral cursor until it fits the orientation of the tetrahedral target (Figure 9). The initial orientation is a non-trivial combination of two or three axis rotations giving 8 different orientations. In both tasks, the user starts a trial and validates the trial by pressing the space bar on the keyboard. To perform clutching with RPM the user presses the spacebar, as adding a second selection key for RPM would increase user's mental load. Therefore we did not measure selection errors for 3D docking since both clutching and validation used the same key. Participants were instructed to perform the task with their dominant hand as quickly and accurately as possible.

Apparatus

We use the same optical system and RPM settings as in the previous experiment. To define the gain value of the SpaceMouse rate technique, we carried out a number of tests. Some users found the regular gain too fast. We thus decided to test two gain values in our study: a gain similar to the default behavior of the device (best for most users after some training) and a smaller gain favouring precision over speed (best for most beginners). With RPM, we used a gain factor of 1:1 for translations and 1:3 for rotations and rolls. The experiment software was developed in C++ using Irrlicht 3D engine.

Participants

We recruited 12 participants (6 female), all right-handed, aged 28.5 years on average (SD=6). 5 were used to 3D interaction and 3 of them participated in previous studies.

Design

The 3D pointing session follows a 4x4 within-subjects design with Interaction Technique IT (RPM Hemispherical, RPM Convex, SpaceMouse Small-Gain and SpaceMouse Default-Gain) and Index of Difficulty ID (2.60, 3.11, 4.19 and 4.75 bits) as factors. The 3D rotation session has one within-subject factor, Interaction Technique, with the same 4 values than the previous session. Each session was divided into 4 blocks, each one corresponding to an interaction technique. Order of blocks is counterbalanced across participants by means of a 4x4 Latin Square. Cursor positions and IDs (for pointing) and orientations (for rotation) were randomly ordered inside each block.

Procedure

We performed a large training session for both tasks: users performed 30 trials/IT before the experiment, and then again 8 trials before each block. No constraints were given with respect to hand posture as we did not want to force hand posture on the SpaceMouse.

Collected data and statistical analysis

We logged all tracking data and measured completion time from stimulus onset. We also collected user preference and usability using two 5-point Likert scales to rate each interaction technique as well as fatigue using a 6-20 Borg scale. For the 3D pointing task, we collected 384 trials per user (4 IT x 8 directions x 4 IDs x 3 repetitions) x 12 users = 4608 trials in total. The session lasted about 73 min. For the 3D rotation task, we collected 192 trials per user (4 IT x 8 orientations x 6 repetitions) x 12 users = 2304 trials in total. The session lasted about 55 min. We used the same statistical analysis approach than in previous studies.

Results

3D pointing performance

Concerning completion time (Figure 10), a Friedman test reveals a significant difference between the interaction techniques ($\chi^2(3)=25.2$ $p<.001$). The two RPM versions (2.28 s) are faster than the two SpaceMouse versions (3.68 s) ($Z=-13.34$, $p<.001$). This result is true for any ID value and the difference grows with ID difficulty (29% for easier ID vs. 33% for harder ID). There is no significant difference between ITs concerning error rate, that was overall around 5% ($\chi^2(3)=0.28$ $p=0.96$).

3D docking performance

We found no significant difference between the two RPMs and the two SpaceMouse versions concerning completion time ($\chi^2(3)=2.3$ $p=0.51$).

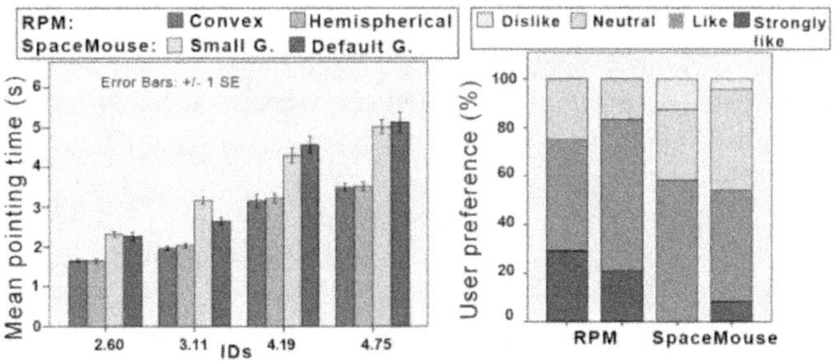

Figure 10. Mean time in s for the 3D pointing task for each IT and ID (left) and user preference (right).

User preference

There were no significant difference in terms of user preference or fatigue between both tasks; therefore we present the overall results. In terms of preference (Figure 10), 75% of the users rated Convex RPM positively (with a score of 4 or higher); 80% Hemispherical; 54% the regular SpaceMouse and 58% the slower version. In terms of usability, 75% rated Convex positively (with a score of 4 or higher); 87% Hemispherical; 45% the regular SpaceMouse and 54% the slower version. Users found that "*the SpaceMouse needs more concentration than RPM*" (p4, p9) and that "*RPM is more pleasant because I can perform the movement with a classical cursor position control*" (p6, p8, p12).

Fatigue

In terms of fatigue, there was no significant difference between the interaction techniques ($\chi^2(3)=3.50$ $p=0.32$), with an average value of 11 (6-20 Borg scale).

Summary

This study demonstrates that there is a significant difference in terms of 3D pointing time performance between the two RPM versions and the two SpaceMouse versions. RPM is 31% faster than the SpaceMouse. Concerning the 3D docking task, there is no significant difference between the different devices and SpaceMouse gains in terms of completion time. In terms of user's preference, both RPM version are considered more usable and are rated more positively than the two SpaceMouse versions. Overall, this study demonstrates that RPM can be used effectively as an input device for 3D translation and rotation and that users preferred and found RPM more usable than the SpaceMouse.

TOWARDS AN INTEGRATED VERSION OF RPM

We build on our experience in prototyping a proof-of-concept version of RPM to analyze the various technical challenges that need to be overcome to build an integrated final version of RPM.

Proof-of-concept wireless prototype

Based on our studies results, we created a working wireless Hemispherical RPM prototype with a 'ring' button all around the device. To detect the 3D displacement and rotation of RPM, we used a Polhemus Patriot Wireless tracker (7x3x2.5cm, 79.4gr.). We filtered the tracker data using a 1€ filter. To build the button we used a similar approach to the WatchIt bracelet [25]: the button consists of one resistive potentiometer (81x7.5x0.5mm) that provides up to 1024 values depending on the touch position. It is thus possible to combine the clicked position on the ring with the current RPM orientation to support multiple buttons. To interface it, we used an Arduino Fio board with a Bluetooth shield and an external battery (Figure 11). Using this prototype, we implemented two usage scenarios that we describe in the discussion section: Google StreetView and a drawing application.

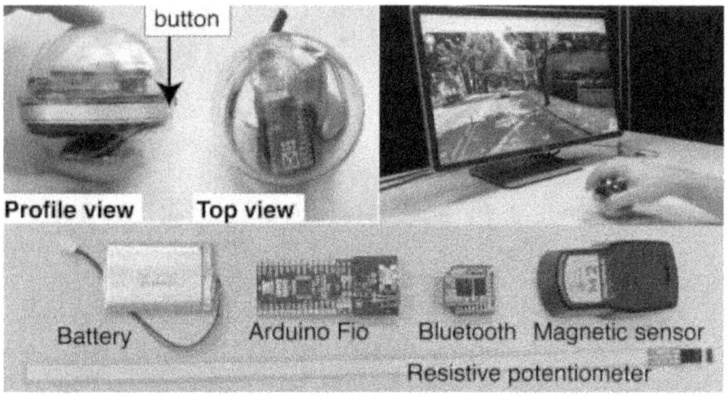

Figure 11. Proof-of-concept wireless prototype with a 'ring' button used in StreetView (top). Components (bottom).

Technical challenges

Building a final working version of RPM presents several technical challenges.

Position: to track RPM position several embedded and non-embedded solutions are possible. Embedded solutions include using magnetic sensors (although not precise enough to allow mouse-like pointing) or an embedded mini board camera similar to VideoMouse [13] (however requiring the use of a grid surface). Not-embedded solutions include using IR cameras or an underlying sensitive surface, similar to Wacom's tablets. All of these solutions would allow detecting the z-dimension at a certain level.

Orientation: to track the orientation of the device, we could use an embedded inertial measurement unit (IMU).

Contact with the underneath surface: to enable mouse-like clutching, embedded solutions include using a resistive bottom, a distance sensor or a camera as in VideoMouse [13]. This contact can be easily detected if using an underlying sensitive surface.

Hand contact: To detect when the device is held, a capacitive surface could be used. This could prevent unwanted movements of the cursor when RPM is released.

Selection mechanism: There are two main options to integrate an always-available selection mechanism invariant to rotation: an all-around 'ring' button and a capacitive surface. The 'ring' button, situated all around the device as in our working prototype, permits multi-touch input with several fingers. A more elegant solution would be to use a multi-touch surface. However, this solution would lack of haptic feedback, like on a regular button. This solution has proved to be useful for extending a traditional mouse [2,32,35] such as Apple's Magic Mouse in which it is combined with a mechanical switch. The main challenge with this solution would be to distinguish a finger touch from a palm contact or with a grasping/squeezing gesture.

Selection stability: Pressing a button could cause RPM to move. To ensure RPM stability, we should favor a selection mechanism positioned all around the device: a finger pressure would then exert perpendicularly to roll direction.

Device repositioning: even if the low center of mass of the device allows auto-repositioning, the device wobbles when released. To limit this oscillation, in particular when switching between the mouse and the keyboard, a solution based on a self-balancing mechanism coupled with the inertial measurement unit could be integrated. The main challenge would be to fit the hardware within the RPM volume.

DISCUSSION

All-in-one device

Our paper illustrates that RPM constitutes an all-in-one device capable of handling 2D and 3D tasks. Our studies demonstrate that it performs 31% faster than the SpaceMouse for 3D translation. Most users preferred the Hemispherical upper shape for 3D interaction. Our work initially explores the many other possibilities for such a novel device based on the combination of translation, roll and rotations as illustrated in the usage scenarios.

Other usage scenarios

While our main motivation to build RPM was to create an all-in-one device for 2D and 3D interaction, we explored other usage scenarios that could benefit from RPM key features. We carried out a one-hour design session with 15 participants to collect application scenarios. Many participants came up with use cases related to 3D interaction, ranging from 3D games to 3D editing. They also gave numerous ideas on a large variety of applications: in video editing; music composition; graphic drawing; web browsing; map navigation; marking menus; or exploring large datasets. For each idea, participants mapped different functions to the RPM degrees of freedom. For instance, in a map application, translation is used to translate the view and roll to adjust (rotate left/right, zoom in/out). In a drawing application, translations are mapped to drawings, rotations to the selection of the drawing colors and rolls to thickness and type of drawn lines. This design session illustrates the possible range of usage applications for RPM.

Design guidelines for rolling devices

Our studies allow us to sum up a set of design guidelines for the future adoption of rolling devices. The hemispherical upper shape has proved to be the best in terms of roll amplitude. When mapping control to roll and rotation gestures, designers should take into account the orientation as it enables different amplitudes. Roll gestures can be performed precisely in at least 8 directions and a roll threshold of 12° should be used to avoid false activations. For 3D pointing, using compound gesture is the most efficient. For 3D rotation, position control could be coupled with rate control as in [30].

Device instability

Unlike the traditional mouse or previous tilting devices such as the Rockin'Mouse, which have a flat bottom, the RPM bottom is hemispherical: the device is thus not stable. This is particularly true in two cases: when the device is released, as it wobbles, and when the device is moved, as it rolls accidentally. In the first case, a simple solution is to detect when the user is holding the device. The device can then be "turned off" when no touch is detected. In the second case, when the user moves the device on a flat surface like a mouse, an appropriate threshold must be used to avoid false positives due to unexpected roll.

Z-dimension

We did not explore this dimension in our paper as we believe it introduces the issue of fatigue. However a sporadic use is possible, for instance holding RPM on the palm during a presentation. In this context RPM could be used to perform mid-air gestures to control slides. We plan to further explore this perspective in the future.

LIMITATIONS AND FUTURE WORK

Our exploration was limited by the use of markers on RPM, by the tracking technology, by the lack of selection and clutching mechanism and by the separation of 3D tasks. The use of IR tracking allowed us to precisely measure all the gestures. As a counterpart we had to carefully place IR markers on the Roly-Poly Mouse in an unobtrusive way. Even if these markers may have had a minor effect on user's gestures, we plan to validate our findings with a wireless marker-free prototype. In addition, our experiments did not evaluate RPM in a 2D pointing task nor the use of an embedded selection and clutching mechanism. In the future we plan to compare RPM with the regular mouse for 2D pointing and evaluate different solutions as discussed above, such as the 'ring' button used in our proof-of-concept prototype. Concerning RPM size, currently based on the regular mouse size, it could be interesting to explore a smaller version of RPM where the user can manipulate it while resting the hand on the table. Finally, we plan to carry further studies on the performance of RPM for an integrated 6D-docking task to evaluate the impact of mode change.

In the future we plan to evaluate 2D pointing with RPM against a classical mouse as said earlier. A long-term study on comfort is pertinent to further explore fatigue issues. We will further explore the design space of RPM compound gestures by proposing and evaluating novel techniques for some of the aforementioned applications, for instance to manipulate graphical items orientation and position as in [16]. Finally, we plan to explore mid-air and free-roll gestures and propose novel GUIs for RPM, such as circular menus or widgets.

CONCLUSION

In this paper we present the design of a novel input device, the Roly-Poly Mouse (RPM) combining the advantages of the mouse and of 3D devices by allowing three types of gestures: translation, roll and rotation. To enable stable 2D pointing with RPM, we propose a roll correction algorithm. We identified preferred RPM upper-shapes and most frequently adopted hand postures through a preliminary study. Based on these results, a first study on gestures amplitude and stability reveals that our device allows large and precise rolls to be performed. In a second study we compare the two versions of RPM with a popular 3D device, the SpaceMouse, in two 3D tasks: pointing and docking. We propose a novel compound gesture for the 3D translation based on rolling and displacing the device. Results reveal that RPM performs 31% faster than the SpaceMouse in terms of translation time and equivalently in terms of rotation time. Users preferred Hemispherical RPM for 3D interaction. Finally, we used our experience in implementing a proof-of-concept prototype to identify the various challenges to overcome to build a final integrated version of RPM. To sum up, RPM is an all-in-one device that removes device-switching costs, improving the workflow of users.

ACKNOWLEDGEMENTS

This work was carried out as part of the research collaboration agreements IRIT-Berger Levrault (CNRS No. 099856) and LMIAMDC. The authors thank Philip D. Gray, Gilles Bailly and the members of the ELIPSE group for their useful suggestions.

REFERENCES

1. Balakrishnan, R., Baudel, T., Kurtenbach, G., and Fitzmaurice, G. 1997. The Rockin'Mouse: integral 3D manipulation on a plane. CHI '97. ACM, 311-318.
2. Benko, H., Izadi, S., Wilson, A., Cao, X., Rosenfeld, D., and Hinckley, K. 2010. Design and evaluation of interaction models for multi-touch mice. GI '10. CIPS, 253-260.
3. Bérard, F., et al. 2009. Did "Minority Report" Get It Wrong? Superiority of the Mouse over 3D Input Devices in a 3D Placement Task. INTERACT '09. Springer-Verlag, 400-414.
4. Borg, G. Borg's Perceived Exertion and Pain Scales. Human Kinetics (1998), viii 104pp.
5. Buxton, W. Lexical and pragmatic considerations of input structures. Comput. Graph., 17(1) :31-37, 1983.
6. Card, S., Moran, T., and Newell, A.1980.The keystroke-level model for user performance time with interactive systems. Commun. ACM 23, 7, 396-410.
7. Casiez, G. and Roussel, N. 2011. No more bricolage!: methods and tools to characterize, replicate and compare pointing transfer functions. UIST '11. ACM, 603-614.

8. Cechanowicz, J., Irani, P., and Subramanian, S. 2007. Augmenting the mouse with pressure sensitive input. CHI '07. ACM, 1385-1394.
9. Froehlich, B., Hochstrate, J., Skuk, V., and Huckauf, A. The globefish and the globemouse: two new six degree of freedom input devices for graphics applications. CHI'06. ACM,191-199.
10. Glesser, D., Bérard, F., and Cooperstock, J. 2013. Overcoming limitations of the trackpad for 3d docking operations. CHI EA '13. ACM, 1239-1244.
11. Hachet, M., Guitton, P., and Reuter, P. 2003. The CAT for efficient 2D and 3D interaction as an alternative to mouse adaptations. VRST '03. ACM, 225-112.
12. Hancock, M., Cate, T. T., and Carpendale, S. Sticky tools: full 6dof force-based interaction for multi-touch tables. In Proc. of ITS'09, ACM, 133-140.
13. Hinckley, K., Sinclair, M., Hanson, E., Szeliski, R., and Conway, M. 1999. The VideoMouse: a camera-based multi-degree-of-freedom input device.UIST'99.ACM,103-12.
14. Jacob, R., Sibert, L., McFarlane, D. and Preston Mullen, M. Integrality and separability of input devices. ACM TOCHI, 1, 1 (1994), 3-26.
15. Kim, S., Kim, H., Lee, B., Nam, T., and Lee, W. 2008. Inflatable mouse: volume-adjustable mouse with air-pressure-sensitive input and haptic feedback. CHI'08. ACM, 211-24.
16. Kruger, R., Carpendale, S., Scott, S., and Tang, A. 2005. Fluid integration of rotation and translation. CHI '05. ACM, 601-610.
17. Kurtenbach, G. and Buxton, W. 1993. The limits of expert performance using hierarchic marking menus. CHI '93 ACM, 482-487.
18. MacKenzie, S., Soukoreff, R., Pal C. 1997. A two-ball mouse affords three degrees of freedom. CHI-EA '97. ACM, 303-304.
19. Marteniuk, R. G., MacKenzie, C., Jeannerod, M., Athenes, S., and Dugas, C. Constraints on human arm movement trajectories. Canadian Journal of Psychology 41, 3 (1987), 365--378.
20. Martinet, A., Casiez, G., and Grisoni, L. Integrality and separability of multitouch interaction techniques in 3D manipulation tasks. IEEE Transactions on Visualization and Computer Graphics 18, 3 (2012), 369-380.
21. Masliah, M. R., and Milgram, P. Measuring the allocation of control in a 6 degree-of-freedom dockingexperiment.CHI'00, ACM, 25-32.
22. Olafsdottir, H., Tsandilas, T. and Appert, C. 2014. Prospective motor control on tabletops: planning grasp for multitouch interaction. CHI '14. ACM, 2893-2902.
23. Olwal, A, Feiner, S. 2004. Unit: modular development of distributed interaction techniques for highly interactive user interfaces. GRAPHITE '04. ACM, 131-138.
24. Ortega, M. and Nigay, L. 2009. AirMouse: Finger Gesture for 2D and 3D Interaction. INTERACT '09. Springer-Verlag, 214-227.
25. Perrault, S., Lecolinet, E., Eagan, J., and Guiard, Y. 2013. Watchit: simple gestures and eyes-free interaction for wristwatches and bracelets. CHI '13. ACM, 1451-60.
26. Rahman, M., Gustafson, S., Irani, P., and Subramanian, S. 2009. Tilt techniques: investigating the dexterity of wrist-based input. CHI '09. ACM, 1943-52.
27. SpaceMouse. Press Note March 31, 2011. http://www.3dconnexion.fr/nc/company/press-room/
28. Steed, A. and Slater, M. 1995. 3D Interaction with the Desktop Bat. In Computer Graphics Forum. Blackwell Publishers, vol 14, 97-104.
29. Taylor, B. and Bove, M. 2009. Graspables: grasp-recognition as a user interface. CHI '09. ACM, 917-926.
30. Tsandilas, T., Dubois, E., Raynal, M. 2013. Modeless Pointing with Low-Precision Wrist Movements. INTERACT 2013. Springer, p. 494-511.
31. Varesano, F. and Vernero, F. 2012. Introducing PALLA, a novel input device for leisure activities: a case study on a tangible video game for seniors. FnG '12. ACM, 35-44.
32. Villar, N., Izadi, S., Rosenfeld, D., Benko, H., Helmes, J., Westhues, J., Hodges, S., Ofek, E., Butler, A., Cao, X., and Chen, B. 2009. Mouse 2.0: multi-touch meets the mouse. UIST '09. ACM, 33-42.
33. Wang, Y., MacKenzie, C., Summers, V. and Booth, K. 1998. The structure of object transportation and orientation in human-computer interaction. CHI '98.ACM, 312-319.
34. Wang, R., Paris, S., and Popović, J. 2011. 6D hands: markerlesshand-tracking for computer aided design. UIST '11. ACM, 549-558.
35. Yang, X-D.,Mak, E., McCallum, D., Irani, P., Cao, X., and Izadi, S. 2010. LensMouse: augmenting the mouse with an interactive touch display. CHI '10. ACM, 2431-40.
36. Zhai, S. 1998. User performance in relation to 3D input device design. SIGGRAPH Comput. Graph. 32,4,50-54.
37. Zhai, S., Human Performance in Six Degree of Freedom Input Control, 1995, University of Toronto

ModelTracker: Redesigning Performance Analysis Tools for Machine Learning

Saleema Amershi, Max Chickering, Steven M. Drucker, Bongshin Lee, Patrice Simard, Jina Suh
Microsoft Research
Redmond, WA
{samershi, dmax, sdrucker, bongshin, patrice, jinsuh}@microsoft.com

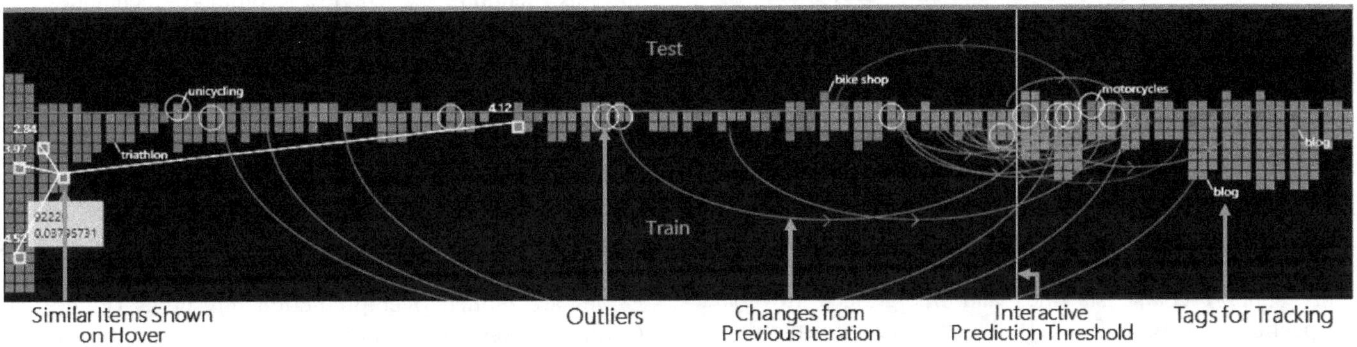

Figure 1. ModelTracker conveys overall model performance while enabling direct data inspection. Boxes represent user labeled examples and color indicates the label given (green for *positive* and red for *negative*). *Test* examples are placed at the top and *train* examples at the bottom. Examples are laid out horizontally according to the model's prediction scores, with low scoring examples to the left and high scoring examples to the right. A high performing model will have most green boxes to the right and most red boxes to the left of the display. Users can interact directly with ModelTracker to reveal additional information (e.g., hovering over an example reveals its nearest neighbors in the current feature space), inspect examples (by clicking on boxes to pull up the corresponding raw data in the display), and annotate examples for better performance tracking.

ABSTRACT

Model building in machine learning is an iterative process. The performance analysis and debugging step typically involves a disruptive cognitive switch from model building to error analysis, discouraging an informed approach to model building. We present ModelTracker, an interactive visualization that subsumes information contained in numerous traditional summary statistics and graphs while displaying example-level performance and enabling direct error examination and debugging. Usage analysis from machine learning practitioners building real models with ModelTracker over six months shows ModelTracker is used often and throughout model building. A controlled experiment focusing on ModelTracker's debugging capabilities shows participants prefer ModelTracker over traditional tools without a loss in model performance.

Author Keywords

Machine Learning; Interactive Visualization; Performance Analysis; Debugging.

CHI 2015, April 18 - 23 2015, Seoul, Republic of Korea

http://dx.doi.org/10.1145/2702123.2702509

ACM Classification Keywords

H.5.2. Information interfaces and presentation (e.g., HCI): User interfaces.

INTRODUCTION

Machine learning is an iterative process. In supervised machine learning, practitioners iteratively collect and label a sample of data, create features to represent the data, train a model with the data and features, and then inspect the model's performance to determine how to proceed in the next iteration (e.g., collecting more data, adding/editing features, experimenting with a different learning algorithm). Once a model has achieved a sufficient level of performance, typically determined by its intended use, the model can be deployed in the target application (e.g., relevance ranking, activity detection, recommendations).

The performance inspection step of the machine learning process can itself be quite involved. Performance inspection typically begins with an assessment of a model's overall ability to correctly predict labels on data, often represented with summary statistics or graphs of common metrics (e.g., accuracy values, precision-recall curves). If summary metrics indicate poor performance, a practitioner may decide to continue iterating in a trial-and-error manner or debug the model by examining its behavior and trying to diagnose problems to inform the next iteration [8,18].

Debugging model performance typically requires a disruptive cognitive switch from the primary task of building a model to the task of analyzing prediction errors (i.e., examples whose user-provided labels are predicted incorrectly by the model). For example, performance analysis may involve first locating errors within large datasets via sorting and filtering (e.g., sorting by model prediction scores, filtering by errors types) and then inspecting raw data to form hypotheses about potential causes of those errors. Many tools have also been created to facilitate deeper model analysis and error debugging (e.g., dimensionality reduction [20,7,4] and scatterplot analysis [12,6]). Such tools, however, are often more complex and heavy weight than inspecting raw data [7]. Switching between these extremes of viewing summary statistics to debugging model performance behavior can result in a loss of context and disrupts the flow of model building [18]. These disruptions can be partially mitigated with integrated environments supporting both model building and error analysis tasks. However, existing integrated environments only support coarse statistics and fine-grained raw data inspection tools (e.g., [16,21]), thereby still requiring mode switches between model building and performance analysis. In practice, therefore, performance analysis and debugging is often performed only after trial-and-error strategies fail rather than to drive subsequent iterations of model building.

In this paper, we present ModelTracker (Figure 1), an interactive visualization designed to encourage a more informed approach to model building in machine learning. ModelTracker subsumes information contained within numerous traditional summary statistics and graphs while displaying example-level performance within a single compact visualization. It also supports direct error examination and debugging, reducing disruption caused by context switching from model building to error analysis.

ModelTracker is not algorithm or data type specific, requiring only prediction scores and user labels on data to visualize performance. It can therefore support a variety of supervised machine learning tasks and algorithms. In this paper, we examine ModelTracker within the context of a general purpose machine learning environment called ICE (Interactive Classification and Extraction) [21].

This paper makes the following contributions:

- ModelTracker, a generally applicable interactive visualization supporting performance analysis during model building in supervised machine learning while enabling direct error examination and debugging.
- Usage behavior from machine learning practitioners building real models (for research and product deployments) with ModelTracker over a six month period. Observations and feedback show that practitioners interacted with ModelTracker throughout model building, indicating that ModelTracker's support for performance analysis and direct access to data helps circumvent a disruptive context switch between summary statistics and separate data inspection tools.
- A controlled experiment comparing ModelTracker's support for direct debugging of common sources of errors against traditional summary statistics and separate debugging tools, showing that participants prefer ModelTracker over traditional tools without a loss in model performance or debugging ability.

RELATED WORK

In this section, we review common techniques for conveying model performance in machine learning and related tools for debugging performance issues.

Conveying Model Performance

Summary statistics are the most common technique for conveying model performance in machine learning. Common statistics include accuracy, precision, recall, F-scores, and area under the curve (AUC). Sometimes these are plotted over model variables (e.g., precision-recall curves are plotted over prediction thresholds (Figure 2)). Confusion matrices are another popular tool for conveying model performance by contrasting user provided labels with predicted labels (using a fixed prediction threshold) in a table, displaying the frequency of examples categorized within each cell. For example, in binary classification, confusion matrices are displayed using a 2x2 grid (Figure 2) showing the number of user-model agreements along the diagonal and false positives and negatives off the diagonal. Sometimes color or shading is also used to emphasize cell counts, drawing attention to problematic categories [22].

Most popular machine learning toolkits provide built-in functionality for computing summary statistics and confusion matrices because they provide an efficient and consistent means of conveying performance over a wide variety of tasks (e.g., Weka [11], Matlab [13], R [19]). However, while summary statistics and confusion matrices can convey the presence of errors, they do not indicate severity or the potential causes of those errors. Practitioners must therefore use separate tools to locate and examine individual errors. Summary statistics therefore lend themselves well to trial-and-error, rather than an informed approach to model building [8,18]. ModelTracker bridges the gap between performance analysis and debugging, reducing disruptions caused by context switching.

Debugging Performance Issues

Debugging model performance often involves direct examination of individual prediction errors [3,18]. Errors are typically located by sorting, filtering, and grouping operations over raw data in a separate display (e.g., sorting by prediction scores, filtering by error category). Once errors are located, they can be examined and hypotheses can be generated about potential causes. This process of locating and examining individual errors can often be tedious, particularly as the size of the data set grows. In

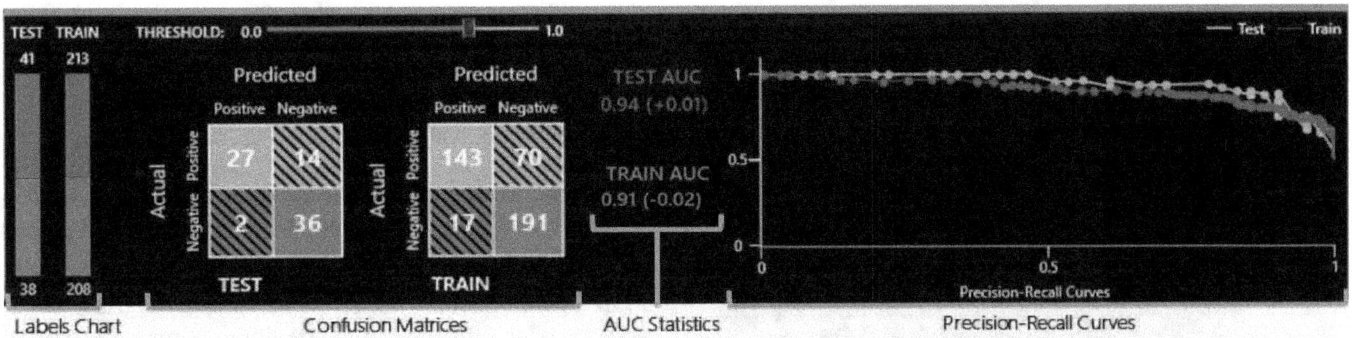

Figure 2. Common performance metrics used during model building in machine learning. Typically each metric is shown over both the *test* and *train* data. Confusion matrices contrast user labels with labels predicted by a model at a specific prediction threshold. Precision-recall curves plot precision versus recall over varying model thresholds. The area under the precision-recall curve (AUC) is often used as a summary of model performance where higher scores indicate better performance. While AUC values can be read from the corresponding curves, they are shown explicitly in the figure for emphasis. This also allows for display of change in AUC performance from one iteration of model building to the next (shown in parentheses). This figure also shows a chart illustrating the current ratio of positive and negative examples, used to encourage the user to provide balanced data.

addition, focusing on individual errors can result in a loss of context, making it difficult for users to prioritize or generalize from their observations. A similar strategy is direct *evaluation*, where users provide *new* data to the model to examine its predictions in real time (e.g., [9,10,21]). However, as with direct examination, this strategy does not facilitate prioritization or generalization of errors. In contrast, ModelTracker presents both summary and example-level performance information directly within its visualization, facilitating error identification and prioritization without the need for context switching.

Dimensionality reduction techniques such as principal components analysis, multidimensional scaling, and clustering can also be used for model debugging [20]. Dimensionality reduction projects high-dimensional data onto fewer dimensions to enable visual inspection of relationships between individual examples, often via two-dimensional scatterplots. While these techniques facilitate deeper model analysis, they can also be complex and difficult to extract insight from [7]. Multidimensional scaling, for example, requires determining a distance function to represent the similarity between data, choosing a scaling mechanism, and then interpreting results. Scatterplot analysis can itself be difficult because meaningful substructures (e.g., clusters) may not be visually salient and reduced dimensions may not correspond to real variables of the data. Projected dimensions will also typically change with each round of model building (e.g., adding new data or features), requiring reinterpretation with each iteration. In contrast, ModelTracker visualizes individual examples along consistent and real dimensions, eliminating the need to reorient and reinterpret visual dimensions after each iteration while fostering expectations about how performance should appear over time.

Many tools have been proposed to aid visual exploration of structures within projections manually (e.g., [12,14]) or semi-automatically (e.g., [7,6,4]). These tools are often complex or immersive, providing functionality to support visual data mining and knowledge discovery. In practice, therefore, cognitively demanding tools are typically only used when a deeper analysis of unexpected performance is necessary rather than to drive each iteration of model building [18]. In contrast, ModelTracker's compact visualization enables it to be always accessible for lightweight performance analysis and debugging throughout the model building process.

Scatterplots are also used for displaying other properties of the data during model building. Scatterplots and scatterplot matrices, for example, are often used to display correlations between features over the current data set [20]. This can help identify feature dependencies as well as potential clusters and outliers. However, these techniques suffer from the same issues as dimensionality reduction techniques including a significant amount of user effort in interpretation and an explicit context switching from building a model to examining properties of the model to interpret errors. In another example, Patel *et al.* [17] used a scatterplot to visualize the results of multiple models simultaneously during the machine learning process. Data points are plotted over fixed axes of entropy and incorrectness. This configuration aids detection of errors potentially caused by either mislabeled data or missing features. While this visualization can also help practitioners prioritize efforts in model debugging, unlike ModelTracker, it requires a large number of models to be trained simultaneously and does not provide an at-a-glance summary of any individual model that would eventually be exported for use in an application.

Finally, several tools have been created to help practitioners build and inspect specific types of models (e.g., decision trees [1], naïve Bayes [2], support vector machines [5], and ensemble models [22]). However, the cost of learning new tools for each type of model or machine learning task can make special purpose tools prohibitive in practice.

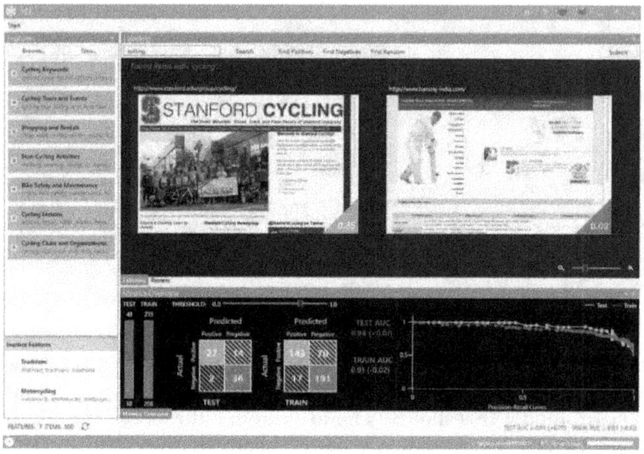

Figure 3. The ICE interface with traditional performance metrics used in machine learning (bottom panel). Users interactively label data in the labeling area (top right) and modify features in the featuring area (left). ICE automatically trains a model as a user supplies labels and features and displays its current performance in the panel at the bottom.

ModelTracker is not algorithm or data type specific, and therefore can provide a consistent means for performance analysis and debugging across a variety of supervised machine learning tasks (as discussed further in Discussion).

MODEL BUILDING REVIEW

ModelTracker was designed for use throughout model building in machine learning. While ModelTracker can be used for many supervised machine learning tasks, in the following sections we focus on its use in binary classification for ease of explanation. In this section, we briefly review the process of building a binary classifier. We then describe relevant aspects the ICE model building environment that we examined ModelTracker in [21].

Building a binary classifier typically begins with collecting and labeling data as either belonging (*positive*) or not-belonging (*negative*) to the target *class*. Next, *features* are defined to characterize relevant aspects of the data in a machine understandable representation. Features should help a classifier discriminate between the positive and negative classes as labeled by the user. Labeled data and features are then fed into a machine learning algorithm to create a model. The labeled data is typically first split into a *train* and *test* set, where the *train* set is used to fit the model and the *test* set is used to estimate model performance on new data. Sometimes a third *validation* set is also set aside for tuning model parameters. Performance is then typically displayed on both the *train* and *test* sets.

ICE is a general purpose machine learning environment for model building, supporting binary and multi-class classification as well as entity extraction. Figure 3 shows the ICE interface. Here, a user is building a binary classifier to classify web-pages as *cycling* or *non-cycling* related pages. Users find (via keyword search) and label within the main *labeling* area (top right). Users define and refine features for the classifier to use via the panel on the left of the display. For example, features that might help a classifier discriminate between *cycling* and *non-cycling* pages may be whether or not the page contains terms pertaining to *types of cycles* (e.g., "cycle" or "bicycle") or an image of a cycle. Given labels and features, ICE automatically splits the labeled data into a *train* and *test* set and then trains a model for review.

Prior to introducing ModelTracker into ICE, users would assess model performance via traditional summary statistics and graphs (Figure 2 and shown in the context of ICE at the bottom of Figure 3). These included confusion matrices, precision-recall curves, AUC statistics, and a label chart showing the balance of positive and negative labels currently provided. These metrics were computed and displayed for both the *train* and *test* sets. If performance analysis indicated problems, individual errors could be inspected by switching from *labeling* to a *review* mode. Errors could then be located via sorting and filtering and then paging through the raw data. After error inspection, users would switch back to *labeling* mode to continue (e.g., with labeling more data or adding or refining features).

MODELTRACKER

ModelTracker was iteratively designed with feedback from real users over one year to enable lightweight performance analysis and direct error examination during model building in machine learning. In this section, we explain how ModelTracker conveys model performance and how it can be used to debug common sources of errors in machine learning. Throughout this section, we also describe design decisions made based on observations and user feedback with early ModelTracker prototypes. Figure 1 shows our current version of ModelTracker (which replaces the panel of metrics in ICE, bottom panel in Figure 3) after a user has provided approximately 500 labeled examples and 7 features, and will be referenced throughout this section.

Conveying Model Performance

Each square box in ModelTracker corresponds to one user labeled example with color indicating the label given (green for *positive* and red for *negative*). Labeled examples can be shown from two sets simultaneously. In Figure 1, *test* examples are shown on top while *train* examples are shown at the bottom of the display (separated by a horizontal line). The boxes are laid out horizontally according to the model's prediction scores (e.g., ranging from 0 to 1), where examples with low scores are to the left and those with high scores are to the right. This means that a well-performing model will have most green boxes to the right and most red boxes to the left. Conversely, errors are shown by red boxes to the right and green boxes to the left. An early ModelTracker prototype displayed items as boxes in sorted order but without distributed them according to model scores. However, user feedback revealed that while ordering examples indicated relative prediction scores (and therefore relative error severity), users also wanted to understand the magnitude of separation between individual examples to better prioritize efforts in debugging errors, leading to our current display.

As labeled examples accumulate, boxes with the same prediction score are binned and stacked away from the horizontal line (e.g., examples in the top section are stacked upwards). Boxes within each bin are sorted such that examples potentially needing attention (e.g., errors) appear closer to the horizontal line. This helps keep problematic examples visible as data accumulates. Feedback from users using ModelTracker for binary classification with datasets of about 1700 examples on average confirm that this is sufficient for providing at-a-glance performance analysis while still alerting them to potential issues needing further inspection. In the Discussion section, we discuss other techniques we employ for scaling to larger number of examples (e.g., sampling for entity extraction in ICE).

ModelTracker subsumes information contained in several traditional summary statistics and graphs while also displaying more detailed, example-level performance. Confusion matrices, for example, display the number of user-model label agreements and disagreements given a specific prediction threshold. While ModelTracker does not display numerical sums, it displays agreement and disagreement via horizontal positioning of boxes according to model scores, where agreement is indicated by green boxes to the right and red boxes to the left and disagreement by red boxes to the right (false positives) and green boxes to the left (false negatives). This has the advantage of making error severity visible, in contrast to numerical sums which treat all errors equally. This also makes ModelTracker threshold independent. A vertical line in the display (Figure 1) depicts a threshold value, but functions only as a visual aid. For example, moving the line to the right emphasizes a reduction of false positives as the threshold increases (because fewer red boxes will appear to the right of the line) while potentially increasing the number of false negatives (because more green boxes may appear to the left). To display the same information using confusion matrices would require a separate matrix for *each* threshold. Moreover, to display this information over two sets (e.g., a *test* and *train* set) would require twice the number of confusion matrices.

ModelTracker also subsumes information conveyed by precision-recall curves (Figure 2). *Precision* is the number of accurately predicted positive examples over the total number of examples predicted as positive by the model, whereas *recall* represents the number of examples accurately predicted as positive by the model out of all of the examples labeled as positive by the user. Precision-recall curves plot precision values versus recall values over various prediction thresholds. Typically, the larger the area under the precision-recall curve (AUC), the better the model. Again, while ModelTracker does not display numerical precision-recall values, it depicts precision and recall via its distribution of boxes, enabling precision and recall to be visible at all thresholds simultaneously. For any given threshold value, *precision* is illustrated by the proportion of green boxes to the right of the threshold line out of all the boxes to the right of the line. Analogously, *recall* is illustrated by the proportion of green boxes that appear to the right of the line out of all the green boxes visible. In contrast, numerical values omit this important information about the distribution of data (i.e., the same numerical value may represent vastly different distributions). ModelTracker's interactive threshold line can also help to emphasize how precision and recall vary over different thresholds. For example, moving the line to the left illustrates an increase in recall (as more green boxes will appear to the right of the line) but at a cost of precision (as more red boxes will also tend to appear to the right).

Monitoring Performance during Model Building

ModelTracker automatically updates as a user iterates in model building, adding boxes as more data is provided and rearranging boxes as prediction scores change (e.g., with new data or features). This results in a spreading and accumulating effect of the green boxes to the right and the red boxes to the left over subsequent iterations, provided the performance of the model is generally improving.

ModelTracker also emphasizes prediction score *changes* on individual examples from one iteration to next to help users better understand the effects of their actions (e.g., feature modifications tend to produce larger effects than the addition of a few more labeled examples) and alert them to potentially unexpected changes. An early ModelTracker prototype illustrated changes via rotating boxes whose prediction changed from one iteration to the next. User feedback, however, suggested a need to show not only that a prediction changed, but also the magnitude of that change. The current version of ModelTracker, therefore, displays the magnitude of score changes via directed arcs from an example's previous score location to its current score location (Figure 1). Because scores on all examples tend to shift slightly from one iteration to the next, arcs are only displayed on examples whose predicted label (computed by comparing the model's prediction score to the current prediction threshold) changed from the previous iteration (e.g., on examples that went from a positive to a negative prediction). Therefore, all arcs displayed will cross the prediction threshold line.

Observations of users interacting with ModelTracker also revealed that users often inspected and then attempted to correct errors (causing an automatic update to ModelTracker's display), but were left uncertain as to whether the error was in fact corrected as a result of their actions. To aid users in monitoring and tracking examples during model building, ModelTracker supports direct annotation of examples via bookmarking or tagging. For example, a user can tag an error and then monitor if the example was in fact corrected in the next update resulting from their action by tracking the tag in the display.

Debugging Common Errors

In this section, we describe how ModelTracker supports interactive inspection and debugging of three common sources of errors in machine learning: mislabeled data, inadequate features to distinguish between concepts, and insufficient data for generalizing from existing examples. Note that these errors may manifest in different ways depending on several factors including which set the error is in (e.g., *train* or *test*), which algorithm is being used, and whether or not the model is currently over-fitted to the data. Where possible, we explain these differences. Note also that aside from correcting mislabels, attempting to correct *test* errors is typically not recommended to prevent overfitting (maintaining a model's ability to estimate performance on new data). In the Discussion section, we suggest techniques for preventing potential overfitting in ModelTracker.

Errors Caused by Mislabeled Data

Mislabeled data (often referred to as label or class noise) frequently occurs during data collection in machine learning [15] and can be resolved by locating and correcting the incorrect labels. Egregious errors in the *train* set in ModelTracker (red boxes to the far right or green boxes to the far left) tend to be candidates for mislabeled data. This is provided the model is not over-fitted to the data (in which case mislabels may appear at any location). If a user suspects a mislabel, they can click on the corresponding box to bring up the raw data in a separate viewing area (e.g., as a popup over the labeling area in ICE). Mislabels can then be corrected and resubmitted to the system.

Errors Caused by Feature Deficiencies

Another common source of error in machine learning is caused by failing to supply a model with adequate features to accurately discriminate between target concepts. For example, a model intended to recognize *cycling* from *non-cycling* pages may confuse a page about *motorcycling* as *cycling* if only given features representing terms such as "ride" or "bike" as these may appear in both pages. Correcting this type of error often requires supplying the model with additional features (e.g., the addition of features with the terms "motorcycle" or "motorbike").

Potential feature related confusion can manifest as examples that the model views as similar given the current feature space but for which the user has given different labels. This is because the ability to generalize often implies

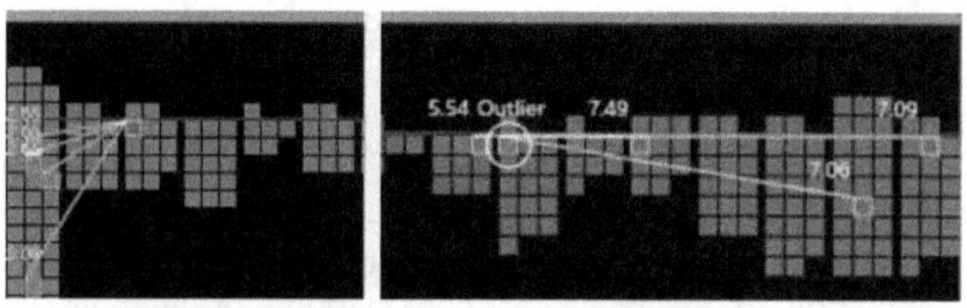

Figure 4. Connector lines showing examples considered as similar in feature space to the example hovered over. On the right, an outlier in feature space is depicted with a circle around the corresponding example.

that similar inputs (examples represented by features) have similar outputs (predicted labels). Therefore, if two examples are seen as similar by the model but different by the user (i.e., are neighbors in feature space but have different labels), this is an indication that the model is currently feature blind to some difference that the user can see. Locating such candidates for feature related errors in ModelTracker requires first hovering over errors to reveal neighboring examples (shown via connector lines between boxes, Figure 4), and then identifying neighbors with different labels (i.e., boxes with different colors connected with lines). Neighbors can be computed in many ways. We use the distance function:

$$||\boldsymbol{x} - \boldsymbol{y}||^2 = \boldsymbol{x}^T\boldsymbol{x} + \boldsymbol{y}^T\boldsymbol{y} - 2\boldsymbol{x}^T\boldsymbol{y}$$

where $\boldsymbol{x}$ and $\boldsymbol{y}$ are feature vectors representing two labeled examples. These are the same vectors supplied to the learning algorithm in ICE and therefore reflect the same information the classifier receives. For each example, we select the five nearest neighbors (i.e., with shortest distance to the target example) as the most similar and connect them with lines on hover. Clicking on boxes also brings up both the clicked example as well as the neighbors for further examination and feature ideation.

ModelTracker can also display how features are correlated with the target class as is often examined via scatterplot analysis. For example, a positive correlation is suggested if values of a particular feature are higher for the *positive* class than for the *negative* class. Correlations can reveal feature deficiencies if unexpected trends are observed (e.g., if a feature was expected to be positively correlated but has high values in both the positive and negative classes). Feature correlation is displayed on demand in ModelTracker (triggered by hovering over a feature in ICEa) and is shown via box highlighting (Figure 5) where brighter and dimmer boxes indicate larger and smaller values of the corresponding feature, respectively.

Errors Caused by Insufficient Data

Insufficient data can also result in errors. These errors are most common in the *test* or *validation* set for regions of the input space (defined by the current set of features) that are insufficiently represented in the *train* set. Depending on the details of the modeling algorithm, however, they can also

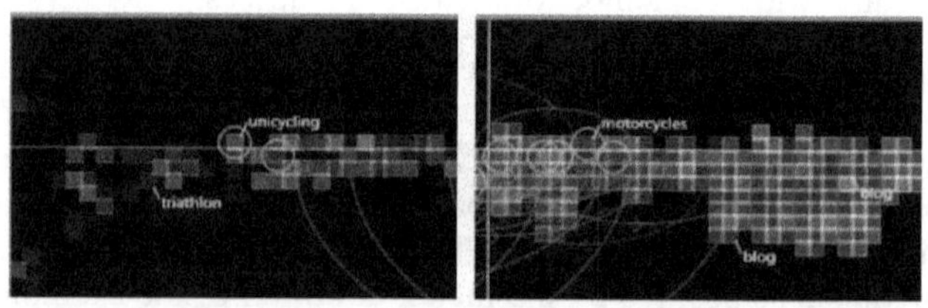

Figure 5. Correlations between features and the target class are displayed on demand via highlighting of boxes based on feature values. Brightness represents the value of the feature in the corresponding example. More bright green boxes on the right and dimmer red boxes towards the left show a feature that is highly correlated with the positive class.

occur in the *train* set when there is not yet enough examples to overcome some bias in the model (e.g., in highly-regularized linear models). Insufficient data errors often manifest as *outliers* – isolated examples distant from others in the current feature space. These errors can be corrected by providing additional data to the model.

In early ModelTracker prototypes, outliers could be identified by locating examples with distant neighbors (shown via lines between boxes). However, observations indicated that users often missed potential outliers because distance is relative to the overall distribution of examples in feature space, which is not readily apparent. To more directly draw attention to potential outliers, the current version of ModelTracker indicates outliers via circles around corresponding boxes (Figure 4).

Many techniques exist for computing outliers in statistics and machine learning. We compute outliers as examples whose nearest neighbors in feature space are greater than two standard deviations from the mean distance between all pairs of neighboring examples. By clicking on outliers, users can again inspect the corresponding example and then find additional examples similar to the outlier to supply to the model to try and correct the error.

USAGE BEHAVIOR

In this section, we report on the usage behavior of machine learning practitioners building real models (for research and product deployments) with ICE along with ModelTracker over six months to demonstrate how ModelTracker's visualization and support for direct access to data encourages frequent and regular data inspection throughout model building. We limit our analysis to binary classifiers (via logistic regression) built by people outside of our team and containing at least 400 labels. This includes 40 different models built by seven practitioners (ranging from novices to experts) over text and web page data. Example concepts these models were built to detect include *restaurant* web pages, *happy* or *angry* sentiment in text, and text containing *opinions*. These models were interactively built over an average of 5.1 hours (SD=3.8), with 1714.5 (SD=1260.2) labels and 12.1 (SD=7.7) features, and achieving final *test* AUC performances of 0.91 (SD=0.17). Note that some features such as ModelTracker's support for item tagging and identification of feature deficiencies and outliers were introduced during this period. Therefore, we only report usage statistics on features present throughout this period.

Out of the 40 sessions we examined, 35 (87.5%) involved at least one interaction with ModelTracker (i.e., one box click). If people interacted with ModelTracker, they clicked on an average of 63.3 examples (4.1% of their data) during their sessions. Figure 6 shows the average distribution of ModelTracker interactions over time, indicating that people interacted with ModelTracker throughout model building, increasing interactions as they progressed.

Interestingly, of the examples clicked in ModelTracker, only 41.6% (SD=23.6%) were in error at the time they were clicked, on average. However, because errors are computed given a specific prediction threshold, this does not necessarily capture whether people were clicking on examples that were technically correct but were still potentially problematic (e.g., negative examples with relatively high scores but still less than the threshold). Figure 7 shows the average percentage of examples clicked per score bin, indicating that users tended to click more on examples at the far ends of the display, but also still clicked on examples in the uncertain middle range.

Post-deployment interviews revealed a common usage strategy that naturally arose from unguided user interaction with ModelTracker. Practitioners explained that they often ignored ModelTracker until some initial data was collected (e.g., one participant said *"about 30 or so [initial] labels"*). Then they began inspecting errors at the far ends of the visualization, often with false positives at the far right, and then working their way inwards. They explained that these errors seemed to have "easier" and more "obvious" solutions (e.g., *"I always start with the biggest outliers [at the far ends] in part because it's a sign that the label was wrong"*), whereas errors in the middle were deemed as harder cases. During error inspection, practitioners reported trying to determine causes and actions to take including "adding features," "changing labels," or "adding labels."

Practitioners also commented on ModelTracker's visual aids and diagnostic capabilities. For example, one practitioner reported initial confusion about the connector lines showing example neighbors in feature space, suggesting the need for more instructional support. Practitioners did report that the directed arcs helped to

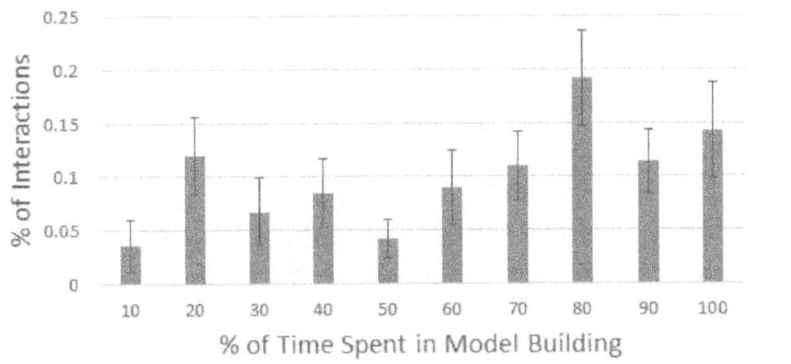

Figure 6. The average distribution of ModelTracker interactions throughout the model building process.

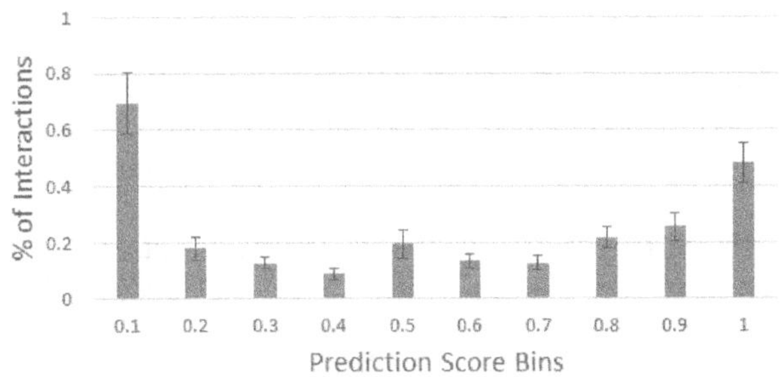

Figure 7. The average percentage of examples clicked in the ModelTracker per score bin.

verify whether an action taken resolved a suspected issue. One commented that it *"was rewarding or not [when the action did not help]."* Another commented that the arcs *"helped when it matched my expectations [about what I thought was going to happen]."* Practitioners also remarked that the arcs were less useful when there were too many of them and that the direction was sometimes hard to see.

Overall, feedback from our practitioners were positive towards ModelTracker. One practitioner commented that it is the *"most important instrument in ICE [for model building]"* and *"you can't go back [to operating without it]."* In comparing ModelTracker to summary statistics, one practitioner commented that "*[ModelTracker] gives you the complete picture. Looking at summary statistics is very good for comparing models, but I can't see what I need to do. I need to do other mini-experiments to figure that out."* However, some practitioners still desired summary statistics. One commented that *"[ModelTracker is] useful for someone new to machine learning, but I still wanted to get AUC, for people who don't use GUIs."* Interestingly, one practitioner who commented on their developed reliance on ModelTracker also requested summary statistics to help gauge improvement over time, saying "*What [the directed arcs are] getting at is a good thing, but I still want a number for whether it got better or worse overall."*

EVALUATION OF DEBUGGING CAPABILITIES

We performed a controlled experiment to examine ModelTracker's support for debugging three common errors in machine learning discussed previously (i.e., mislabeled data, feature deficiencies, and insufficient data) compared to the traditional method of using separate tools to debug. Specifically, we compared ModelTracker's interface with a *Traditional* interface, where traditional summary metrics are provided for performance analysis (Figure 2) and individual errors can then be inspected via a *review* mode. Mislabels are located via filtering by errors or error categories (false positives and negatives) and then paging through and viewing raw data. Feature deficiencies are discovered by locating errors and then clicking a button to reveal similar examples with opposite labels in the current feature space. Finally, outliers are located by filtering by outliers. Both interfaces were used within the context of ICE. The study was run using a within-subjects design, counterbalancing interface order.

Tasks

To examine debugging capabilities, we created two tasks requiring participants to fix or improve existing classifiers. These tasks occur in real scenarios such as during model maintenance (e.g., when a deployed model must be updated in light of new data) and when labels are outsourced and initial features are insufficient to model the target concept.

To create our tasks, we first built binary web-page classifiers (via logistic regression) targeting concepts related to common activities (e.g., *cooking*, *travel*). To build each classifier, we sampled data (using uncertainty-based active learning) from the Open Directory Project database (http://www.dmoz.org), an open directory of human-categorized web pages. We used the concept descriptions given in this database to guide our labeling and featuring. From these classifiers, we selected two that achieved a comparable level of performance (measured via their *test* AUC values) with 400 labels and 11 features. The classifiers we selected targeted *gardening* and *travel* related web-pages and achieved *test* AUCs of 0.95 and 0.96, respectively. We then "broke" each classifier to generate errors by first removing a random subset of 130 examples (~33% of the initial data), randomly removing 5 of the 11 features, and then randomly flipping 27 (10%) of the remaining labels. These broken *gardening* and *travel* classifiers served as the starting points for our study tasks. We also created a broken *cycling* classifier in the same way to use during the demos and practice with each condition.

Participants and Procedure

We recruited 14 participants (10 male) from a large software company including developers, test engineers, and program managers ranging in age from 23 to 53 years old. Participants self-reported as novice or proficient in machine learning, had previously built at least one model, and were familiar with precision and recall. Participants were run in groups of at most four, each working on an identical PC running Windows 8, with a 24" 1920x1200 monitor. All relevant interface actions were time-stamped and logged.

Each session began with a review of the general model building process and a hands-on tutorial of ICE (with both the *Traditional* and *ModelTracker* panels hidden). Before each condition, the experimenter gave a tutorial on the corresponding interface and then allowed participants to practice debugging the broken *cycling* classifier with it. Prior to starting each task, the experimenter walked through the target concept description. Participants were then given 20 minutes to debug and improve their broken classifiers as much as possible. Questionnaires were distributed after each condition and at the end of the study. Each session took three hours. Participants were given $30 worth of dining coupons and a $50 prize was awarded to the person with the largest classifier improvement.

Results

We analyzed classifier performance and logged data from our study using paired-samples t-tests. We analyzed performance in two ways. First, we computed the AUC improvement from the beginning to end of each task on a holdout dataset comprised of the 130 examples we removed as part of breaking each classifier. Second, we computed the number of corrected mislabels out of the 27 we introduced as part of breaking each classifier. Table 1 shows all means and standard deviations of performance and the number of labels and features included in participants' final classifiers. We found no significant

	Traditional	ModelTracker
AUC Improvement	.008 (.042)	.026 (.027)
Mislabels Corrected	8.57 (6.02)	9.86 (4.89)
Final Num Labels	327.5 (28.1)	320.9 (25.5)
Final Num Features	8.64 (1.86)	8.57 (1.34)

Table 1. Mean (SD) of performance and usage statistics.

difference in participant ability to debug or improve model performance between the two interfaces.

We analyzed our post-condition Likert-scale questions using Wilcoxon signed-rank tests. Figure 8 shows preference counts and Likert-scale question medians. 10 out of 14 participants (71.4%) preferred *ModelTracker* over the *Traditional* interface. Participants favored *ModelTracker* in terms of their perceived ease of identifying and debugging both feature deficiencies (Z=-2.49, p=.013) and insufficient data (outlier) errors (Z=-1.99, p=.046). No significant differences were found in participants' stated ability to understand their classifiers' performance or their perceived ease of identifying and debugging mislabeled data.

DISCUSSION AND FUTURE WORK

Our examination of real ModelTracker usage and our controlled experiment revealed that practitioners relied on ModelTracker throughout model building and preferred it over traditional tools without a loss in performance or debugging ability. Participants commented that ModelTracker was simpler and more intuitive than the many summary statistics and graphs required to display equivalent performance information in the traditional interface. One participant said *"I thought this UI was more intuitive... I think it is great to take such a complex concept and make it accessible."* Another said *"The single visualization captures all of the segmented version and more."* Participants also commented on the reduced overhead ModelTracker provided in terms of direct error identification and reduced mode switching: *"I liked being able to focus on the data without having to go between screen[s]," "Finding issues within the set was easy,"* and *"Very actionable information."* Of the participants who preferred the traditional interface, some commented on missing the more familiar statistics: *"[Traditional] is better if you know a bit about how classifiers work."* Some also requested a hybrid view. One participant said *"I would like to see both integrated."* Another recommended to *"have [the ModelTracker] UI default, but the ability to bring up the confusion matrix and PR curves as optional UI."*

In the ModelTracker visualization, we displayed both the *train* and *test* data to users as the ICE system provides access to both sets during model building. This has the potential to encourage overfitting by tempting users to over-engineer models to fix *test* errors. However, since overfitting only happens when users edit features or adjust model parameters (not when fixing labels), one solution may be to disable inspection of *test* examples, thereby only using the *test* area to monitor generalization performance. Another solution may be to remove the *test* altogether (or replace it with a *validation* set), and rely on summary statistics to show generalization performance in a hybrid system. Further investigation is necessary to evaluate these options for reducing the potential to overfit.

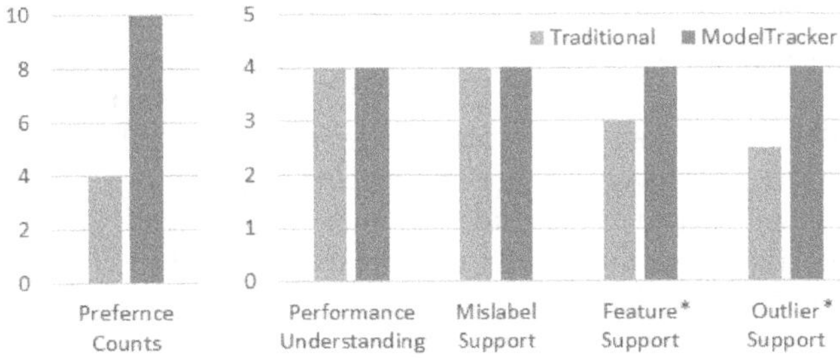

Figure 8. Overall preference counts and Likert medians. Metrics with *'s indicate significant effects were observed.

We concentrated on binary classification via logistic regression in this paper for ease of explanation. However, ModelTracker can visualize other classifiers that output probabilities (e.g., any calibrated classifier) and other supervised machine learning models. For example, within ICE [21] we also use ModelTracker for entity-extraction which uses conditional random field models to identify sequences of tokens belonging to a hierarchical set of entities (e.g., an *address* containing *street* and *city* entities). We use ModelTracker to visualize performance with respect to each entity by creating a green box for each entity (or a red box for each non-entity) labeled token or *sequence* of tokens. Prediction scores represent the relative confidence that the model assigns to these hypotheses, computed by taking the difference in probability of a parse consistent with the label and the next most likely inconsistent parse. In entity extraction, the number of boxes can grow quickly, particularly when there is one box per token. When this happens, we sample down the boxes in each score range while maintaining the same fraction of positive and negative labels.

Entity-extraction problems also have similar characteristics to multi-class classification problems, in that both can involve multiple prediction categories (hierarchical entities and multiple classes, respectively). In both cases, we can view the one-vs-remaining performance for each category in ModelTracker. An opportunity remains to integrate between-class confusability information into a single visualization to better support light-weight performance analysis and debugging in multi-class scenarios.

ModelTracker may have some benefits as a stand-alone static visualization to replace traditional performance statistics and graphs. Clearly, however, many of ModelTracker's benefits increase when it is integrated into an environment supporting an iterative process of model building and error analysis. As discussed earlier, when ModelTracker is linked back to the individual examples, mislabeled data can be quickly discovered, examples with few neighbors can be brought forward and examined, and situations where new features need to be identified can be called out. Even closer integration allows overall model performance as well as performance on individual examples to be monitored as the model is iteratively retrained. Further investigations are therefore necessary to understand the benefits of ModelTracker as a stand-alone tool.

CONCLUSION

We introduced ModelTracker, a generally applicable interactive visualization for performance analysis and debugging in machine learning. Our examination of ModelTracker usage by machine learning practitioners building real models with ModelTracker for research and product deployments over a six month period demonstrates that ModelTracker is used regularly throughout model building. Our controlled experiment further shows that ModelTracker is preferred over traditional tools for performance analysis and debugging for its simplicity and intuitiveness without a loss in model performance. This suggests that ModelTracker can replace current tools for performance analysis and debugging, encouraging a more informed approach to model building in machine learning.

REFERENCES

1. Ankerst, M., Elsen, C., Ester, M., and Kriegal, H. Visual Classification: An Interactive Approach to Decision Tree Construction. *Proc. KDD 1999,* ACM Press (1999), 392-396.
2. Becker, B., Kohavi, R., and Sommerfield, D. Visualizing the Simple Bayesian Classifier. *Information Visualization in Data Mining and Knowledge Discovery.* Fayyad, U., Grinstein, G.G., and Wierse, A. (eds). Morgan Kaufmann Publishers, 2001, 237-249.
3. Bird, S., Klein, E., and Loper, E. *Natural Language Processing with Python.* O'Reilly Media, 2009.
4. Broekens, J., Cocx, T., and Kosters, W. Object-Centered Interactive Multi-Dimensional Scaling: Ask the Expert. *Proc. BNAIC 2006*, 59-66.
5. Caragea, D., Cook, D., and Honavar, V. Gaining Insights into Support Vector Machine Pattern Classifiers Using Projection-Based Tour Methods. *Proc. KDD 2001*, ACM Press (2001), 251-256.
6. Chan, Y., Correa, C., and Ma, K-L. Flow-based Scatterplots for Sensitivity Analysis. *Proc. VAST 2010*, IEEE (2010), 43-50.
7. Choo, J., Hanseung, L., Liu, Z., Stasko, J., and Park, H. An Interactive Visual Testbed System for Dimension Reduction and Clustering of Large-Scale High-Dimensional Data. *Proc. SPIE Electronic Imaging 2013,* 865402–865402–15.
8. Domingos, P. A Few Useful Things to Know about Machine Learning. *CACM 55,* 10 (2012), 78-87.
9. Fails, J.A. and Olsen, D.R. Interactive Machine Learning. *Proc. IUI 2003,* ACM Press (2003), 39-45.
10. Fiebrink, R., Cook, P.R., and Trueman, D. Human Model Evaluation in Interactive Supervised Learning. *Proc. CHI 2011*, ACM Press (2011), 147-156.
11. Hall, M., Frank, E., Holmes, G., Pfahringer, B., Reutemann, P., and Witten, I.H. The WEKA Data Mining Software: An Update. *SIGKDD Explorations 11*, 1 (2009).
12. Hao, M.C., Dayal, U., Sharma, R.K., Keim, D.A., and Janetzko, H. Variable Binned Scatter Plots. *Information Visualization 9*, 3 (2010), 194-203.
13. MATLAB 9.0 and Statistics Toolbox Release 2014a, The MathWorks, Inc., Natick, Massachusetts, United States, http://www.mathworks.com/products/statistics, 2014.
14. Mayorga, A. and Gleicher, M. Scatterplots: Overcoming Overdraw in Scatter Plots. *IEEE TVCG 19*, 9 (2013), 1526-1538.
15. Nettleton, D. F., Orriols-Puig, A., and Fornells, A. A Study of the Effect of Different Types of Noise on the Precision of Supervised Learning Techniques. *AI Review 33*, 4 (2010), 275-306.
16. Patel, K., Bancroft, N., Drucker, S.M., Fogarty, J., Ko, A., and Landay, J.A. Gestalt: Integrated Support for Implementation and Analysis in Machine Learning Processes. *Proc. UIST 2010*, ACM Press (2010), 37-46.
17. Patel, K., Drucker, S.M., Fogarty, J., Kapoor, A., and Tan, D.S. Using Multiple Models to Understand Data *Proc. IJCAI 2011*, AAAI Press (2011), 1723-1728.
18. Patel, K., Fogarty, J., Landay, J.A., and Harrison, B. Examining Difficulties Software Developers Encounter in the Adoption of Statistical Machine Learning. *Proc. AAAI 2008*, AAAI Press (2008), 1563-1566.
19. R Core Team, "R: A Language and Environment for Statistical Computing," *R Foundation for Statistical Computing*, http://www.R-project.org, 2013.
20. Rossi, F. Visual Data Mining and Machine Learning *Proc. ESANN 2006*, 251-264.
21. Simard, P., Chickering, D., Lakshmiratan, A., Charles, D., Bottou, L., Suarez, C.G.J., Grangier, D., Amershi, S., Verwey, J., and Suh, J. ICE: Enabling Non-Experts to Build Models Interactively for Large-Scale Lopsided Problems. 2014, arXiv:1409.4814.
22. Talbot, J., Lee, B., Kapoor, A., and Tan, D. EnsembleMatrix: Interactive Visualization to Support Machine Learning with Multiple Classifiers. *Proc. CHI 2009*, ACM Press (2009), 1283-1292.

How Good is 85%? A Survey Tool to Connect Classifier Evaluation to Acceptability of Accuracy

Matthew Kay
Computer Science
& Engineering | dub,
University of Washington
mjskay@uw.edu

Shwetak N. Patel
Computer Science
& Engineering | dub,
University of Washington
shwetak@uw.edu

Julie A. Kientz
Human-Centered Design
& Engineering | dub,
University of Washington
jkientz@uw.edu

ABSTRACT

Many HCI and ubiquitous computing systems are characterized by two important properties: their output is *uncertain*—it has an associated accuracy that researchers attempt to optimize—and this uncertainty is *user-facing*—it directly affects the quality of the user experience. Novel classifiers are typically evaluated using measures like the F_1 score—but given an F-score of (e.g.) 0.85, how do we know whether this performance is good enough? Is this level of uncertainty actually tolerable to users of the intended application—and do people weight precision and recall equally? We set out to develop a survey instrument that can systematically answer such questions. We introduce a new measure, *acceptability of accuracy*, and show how to predict it based on measures of classifier accuracy. Out tool allows us to systematically select an objective function to optimize during classifier evaluation, but can also offer new insights into how to design feedback for user-facing classification systems (e.g., by combining a seemingly-low-performing classifier with appropriate feedback to make a highly usable system). It also reveals potential issues with the ubiquitous F_1-measure as applied to user-facing systems.

Author Keywords

Classifiers; accuracy; accuracy acceptability; inference; machine learning; sensors.

INTRODUCTION

As we reach the boundaries of sensing systems, we are increasingly building and deploying ubiquitous computing solutions that rely heavily on inference. This is a natural trend given that sensors have physical limitations in what they can actually sense. Often, there is also a strong desire for simple sensors to reduce cost and deployment burden. Examples include using low-cost accelerometers to track step count or sleep quality (Fitbit), using microphones for cough tracking [12] or fall detection [20], and using electrical noise and water pressure monitoring to track appliances' water and electricity use [9]. A common thread runs across these systems: they rely on inference, hence their output has *uncertainty*—it has an associated accuracy that researchers attempt to optimize—and this uncertainty is *user-facing*—it directly affects the quality of the user experience.

Consider an application that monitors energy usage of appliances to save on energy costs. Such a system is less useful—frustratingly so—if it consistently confuses two appliances such that the user cannot identify a power-hungry appliance. Patel et al. [17] introduced such a system, which uses machine learning to predict the usage of electrical appliances in the home. Their system has an overall accuracy of 85–90% in identifying individual appliances. But how we do know if 85–90% accuracy is acceptable to the users of this application? How much uncertainty is actually tolerable? Also, how sensitive are people to different types of errors—while classifiers in HCI applications are often optimized for overall measures of accuracy like F_1 score, people are often differently sensitive to false positives versus false negatives. How can we tell if people prefer higher precision or recall in this space? Also, would these tolerances change if the same sensing system were used for a different application (e.g., sensing activities of daily living for an aging parent instead of energy monitoring)?

Researchers and developers find themselves trying to extract every bit of inference performance from a system, potentially facing diminishing returns. A follow-on to Patel et al. [17] by Gupta et al. [9] improved mean accuracy to 94%, but this took several years, significant hardware updates, and identification of new features of interest. Efforts could be made to improve the accuracy even further, but at what point should one focus on the user interface over improving the accuracy of the classifier? Given the increasing prevalence of such systems, we need a systematic way to answer these questions, preferably before even starting to design or improve a classifier for a particular application.

To help researchers address these questions, we have developed a model and method for predicting how acceptable users will find the accuracy of systems that use classifiers. The primary contributions of this paper center on connecting *evaluation of classifiers* to *acceptability of accuracy*, with the aim of predicting the latter on the basis of the former. These contributions are 1) formalizing the notion of acceptability of accuracy; 2) demonstrating the association between traditional measures of classifier accuracy and acceptability of accuracy (we investigate a class of

CHI 2015, April 18–23, 2015, Seoul, Republic of Korea.

http://dx.doi.org/10.1145/2702123.2702603

weighted means of precision and recall that includes the ubiquitous F-measure and show how to use acceptability of accuracy to select which of measure to use when evaluating a classifier); and 3) devising and validating a simple survey tool developers of inference-based systems can use to help identify acceptable levels of classifier performance before expending the effort to build the systems.

As an example, imagine we are developing a smart alarm for the home that automatically identifies intruders and alerts the homeowner with a text message. While we have built a classifier for this problem, we are unsure what objective function to optimize: will our users value recall over precision, and if so, by how much? We generate a survey that describes the application and asks users how acceptable they find its accuracy to be in hypothetical scenarios with varying precision and recall (given a scenario description, the tool described in this paper generates the necessary scenarios). We deploy the survey to potential users then fit a model of acceptability of accuracy to the results. This model estimates α, a parameter from 0 to 1 describing the relative weight users place on precision versus recall: 0 means users value only recall, 1 only precision, and 0.5 each equally. The model estimates alpha at ~0.35 (some preference for recall over precision) and yields an objective function we can use to tune the classifier before we test it in a deployment. This increases the chance that our deployment is a success, as our classifier is now tuned to users' preferences for different types of errors in this application.

Our goal is not to impose further requirements for researchers to demonstrate that their good classifiers are actually good, though we believe it is possible to make such claims stronger through consideration of acceptability of accuracy. Instead, we aim to provide researchers with the tools to systematically make decisions about how to allocate resources: *e.g.,* to think about how to use a seemingly low-performing classifier to build an application with an appropriately fuzzy or broad level of feedback that users will find acceptable or to refocus resources on the user interface when the classifier is deemed "good enough".

In what follows, we outline our proposed survey instrument for assessing the acceptability of accuracy of hypothetical classifier-based applications. We describe a series of surveys in which we refined and validated our method. First, we employed this instrument to assess its face validity in four different applications drawn from the ubiquitous computing literature. Second, we deployed a refined version of the model and demonstrate its predicative validity in the domain of weather forecasting error, showing that we can estimate acceptability of accuracy to within one point on a 7-point Likert scale. We then discuss how we envision use of this tool in research and implications of this work on classifier evaluation when building systems.

RELATED WORK

A growing body of work in Human–Computer Interaction (HCI) and Ubiquitous Computing (Ubicomp) has involved investigations of the *intelligibility* of user interfaces: how transparent the reasoning or certainty of these systems are to users [14,15]. The effects of intelligibility seem to be application-dependent: displaying uncertainty sometimes has positive [1] or negative [24] effects on task performance. In a study of several hypothetical context-aware systems, Lim and Dey found that making the certainty of a system visible to users—for example, as a confidence region in location-aware systems—can improve users' perceptions of the accuracy and appropriateness of a system, so long as the accuracy is good enough [15]. However, in the context of an inference-based system, it is not clear what components of accuracy contribute to assessments of "good enough." For example, it is well-established in information retrieval literature that the unweighted F_1 score is inadequate for many applications, since users may be more concerned (for example) with precision than recall [13,22]. Yet, we still commonly use F_1 score in evaluating classifiers in many user-facing applications. In this paper, we investigate the individual effects of precision and recall on the acceptability of accuracy in inference-based applications.

In addition, given a highly intelligible system with acceptable levels of accuracy, it still behooves us to ask whether users find it to be useful. To that end, we use a variant of the Technology Acceptance Model (TAM) to validate our measure of acceptability of accuracy. TAM is a well-studied method for predicting technology acceptance, originally proposed for use in the workplace [6]. Since then, numerous variants of TAM have been proposed [27,28], and it has been applied to contexts outside the workplace, such as e-commerce [18] and consumer health technology [16]. The core constructs of TAM include perceived ease of use, perceived usefulness, and intent to use a technology, which have been shown to predict real-world use [6,18,27]. In this work, we adopt a variant of the TAM2 [27], which includes a construct called *output quality*—how well a system performs the tasks it is designed for—which we believe to be related to acceptability of accuracy in ubicomp systems.

The development of methods to evaluate ubicomp systems that use sensing and inference has been a popular topic within the last decade, and several frameworks have been proposed [2,10,25]. These frameworks aim for a holistic evaluation, whereas we explicitly look toward a method for assessing the acceptability of accuracy. Others call for evaluating ubicomp technologies through in-situ deployment studies of built systems [23]. This can be a very useful method to assess the acceptability of accuracy, and studies of applications that use sensing have been able to evaluate the acceptability of accuracy of an already built system within the context of use (e.g., [5]). These deployments are very resource-intensive, however, and thus we aim to reduce the overhead of assessing the acceptability of accuracy before such systems are built. Finally, other researchers have proposed methods of formative assessment of ubicomp systems through the concepts of sensor proxies [3] and experience sampling [4], but these methods still require in person interaction with participants, and do not provide explicit guidance on the acceptability of accuracy of inference systems. We believe our method can complement these existing approaches. In particular, by modeling acceptability of accuracy as a function of measures familiar to developers of machine learning applications—and by expressing its results as an objective function that can be optimized by learning processes—we provide a model of acceptability of accuracy that is expressed in the domain language of the experts who build these systems.

ACCEPTABILITY OF ACCURACY SURVEY INSTRUMENT

We designed a scenario-based survey instrument to systematically examine the effects of differing classifier accuracies on user's perceptions of those classifiers in the context of specific applications and user interfaces. The basic structure of the survey leads with a description of an application that makes use of a classifier; for example:

> **Electricity monitor application:** *Your residence has been outfitted with an intelligent electricity monitoring system. It is capable of keeping track of how often you use each of your appliances and how much electricity each appliance uses.*

This application description is then followed by a series of accuracy scenarios in which varying levels of performance of the classifier for that system are outlined to participants:

> *Please imagine the following:*
> - ***10 times** over a three month period, you used your clothes dryer.*
>   - ***8 of the 10 times** that you used your clothes dryer, the system (correctly) reported that you used your clothes dryer.*
>   - ***2 of the 10 times** that you used your clothes dryer, the system (incorrectly) reported that you used a different appliance.*
> - ***2 other time(s)** over the same three month period, the system (incorrectly) reported that you used your clothes dryer even though you were actually using a different appliance.*

This performance scenario lays out several properties of the classifier in bold. In order, they are:

- **Real positives (RP);** above, the total number of uses of the dryer. This is held constant.
- **True positives (TP);** above, the number of times the dryer was correctly predicted as having been used.
- **False negatives (FN);** above, the number of times the dryer was not predicted as being used even though it was.
- **False positives (FP);** above, the number of times the dryer was predicted as being used even though it was not.

These properties are expressed as frequencies rather than percentages, as work in Bayesian reasoning suggests that people's inferences are better when asked about frequencies rather than proportions [8]. The particular wording for each scenario was developed through pilots on Amazon's Mechanical Turk (http://mturk.com) and in-person.

For a given application, we generate 16 different accuracy scenarios corresponding to 4 levels of *recall* (0.5, 0.66, 0.833, 1.0) × 4 levels of *precision* (0.5, 0.66, 0.833, 1.0).[1] Note that due to the definitions of recall and precision,

$$R = \frac{TP}{TP + FN} = \frac{TP}{RP} \qquad \text{(recall)}$$

$$P = \frac{TP}{TP + FP} \qquad \text{(precision)}$$

we can calculate all the other values in the above scenarios so long as RP is known (e.g. below we fixed RP at 10).

For each accuracy scenario, we ask three 7-point Likert-item questions from *extremely unlikely* to *extremely likely*. These questions correspond to *acceptability of accuracy* (which we introduce here), *perceived usefulness*, and *intent to use* (the latter two are adapted from the TAM [6,27])[2]:

- *I would find the accuracy of this system to be acceptable.*
- *I would find this system to be useful.*
- *If available to me now, I would begin using this system sometime in the next 6 months.*

This structure allows us to generate scenarios for an application with arbitrary accuracy. Essentially, we can sample the space of possible accuracies in an application and then model how this affects acceptability of accuracy. While we have selected particular levels of accuracy here, our scenario-generating code accepts any combinations of levels.

TESTS OF FACE VALIDITY

We intend our survey to be able to answer several questions about a given application. First, we aim to model *acceptability of accuracy* based on measures of classifier accuracy. To do that, we derive several measures of accuracy from the precision and recall of each scenario (such as a weighted F-measure) and use these to predict acceptability of accuracy.

Acceptability of accuracy as we define it is intended to correspond to a measure of *output quality* in TAM2 [27], which refers to how well a system performs the tasks it is designed for (distinct from how useful someone finds those tasks to be) and has been shown to correlate with *perceived usefulness* [27]. This leads to our first test of validity:

- **T1:** *Acceptability of accuracy* and *perceived usefulness* should be highly correlated.

Further, per TAM [6,27]:

- **T2**: *Perceived usefulness* and *intent to use* should be highly correlated.

Next, we should not expect two classifiers that have the same quantitative accuracy but which are in different applications to have the same acceptability: users' sensitivity to

[1] The use of frequencies necessitates some rounding, so some scenarios have only approximately this precision/recall.

[2] Pilot versions of the survey also included *ease of use* from the TAM, but this question was confusing to users when being asked about a hypothetical system, so we omitted it.

errors will vary between applications, and our instrument should uncover this; thus:

- **T3**: Our instrument should be sensitive to *application*: classifiers with similar accuracy for different applications may have different *acceptability of accuracy*.

Finally, different types of classification error do not always incur the same cost for users (e.g., the effects of the relative weight of precision versus recall is a well-known problem in information retrieval [22], where it is more important that the top results the user sees are highly relevant than that all relevant results are returned). We should therefore expect our method to be sensitive to such differences in situations where the costs of errors differ. Thus, our fourth test:

- **T4**: When classifiers with similar accuracy for *the same* application have different levels of user burden for false positives, our test should be sensitive to this, and reflect it as a different weighting of *precision* versus *recall*.

STUDY 1: ASSESSING FACE VALIDITY

We deployed our instrument in a survey with four different hypothetical applications inspired by applications found in the ubicomp literature [9,19,29]. This variety was intended to allow us to validate T3. The applications include an *electricity monitor* (introduced above) as well as the following:

Location tracker: *Your workplace has installed a mobile application on employees' cell phones that can estimate what room at work you or your coworkers are currently in. You can use it to locate a colleague or your supervisor when you are both present at work, for example, to have a quick meeting.*

Alarm (text message): *Your residence has been outfitted with an intelligent alarm system that is capable of automatically recognizing household members when they enter, without any other interaction. For example, it does not require a password. When a stranger enters the house alone (someone that the system does not recognize), it sends you a text message.*

Alarm (police): *Your residence has been outfitted with an intelligent alarm system that is capable of automatically recognizing household members when they enter, without any other interaction. For example, it does not require a password. When a stranger enters the house alone (someone that the system does not recognize), it calls the police.*

The two variants on the alarm application are meant to explore two possible extremes of feedback: a relatively low-burden modality (text messages) and a very high-burden modality (calls to the police). These allow us to validate T4.

Survey structure for data collection

Due to the length of the survey (each application has 16 scenarios, with 3 questions per scenario), we split the survey into two branches (see Figure 1). Each participant is randomly assigned to one of two branches: the *application branch* and the *user interface branch*, corresponding to T3 and T4. Participants in the application branch are asked about the electricity monitor, location tracker, and alarm (text message) applications. Participants in the user interface branch are given the alarm (police) and alarm (text message) applications. Within survey branches, participants were shown each application in a random order. Scenario order within each application was also randomized.

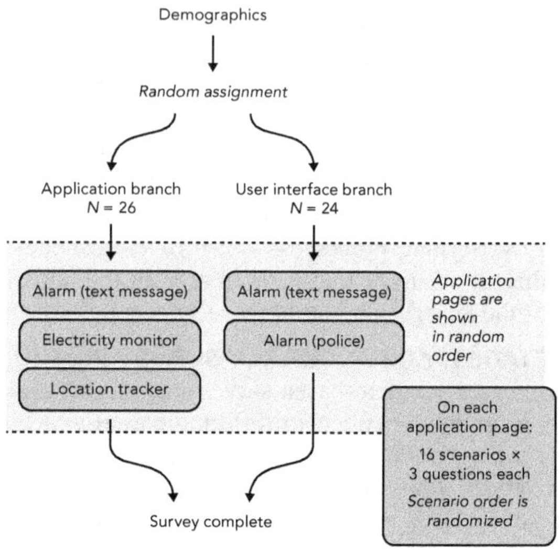

Figure 1. Survey 1 structure. Each application page (blue box) corresponds to an instance of our acceptability of accuracy survey instrument applied to a different application.

Participants

Participants were recruited via word-of-mouth, distribution on university mailing lists, and advertisements on Facebook. We had 50 participants, 26 in the application branch and 24 in the user interface branch (this was sufficient to show credible differences in model parameters due to the use of within-subjects design). Participants were entered into a raffle to win one of five Amazon.com gift cards: a $50 card or one of 4 $25 cards. Due to the length of the survey, some participants did not complete the entire survey (11 and 3 in each branch, respectively; each of these participants completed at least one application), which was expected due to its length. We used randomization of scenario order to account for this so that each application still received an adequate number of participants. We had 50% female participants, and 50% of each branch was female.

Model of acceptability of accuracy

To analyze acceptability of accuracy, we posited that acceptability of accuracy may be predicted based on some measure of classifier accuracy. In particular, because precision and recall in these applications are visible to the user, we concentrated on measures based on them. We did not consider measures that involve true negatives, as it is not clear in our scenarios that true negatives are meaningful to users. For example, what does it mean to a user that their alarm correctly did not go off whenever no one was breaking into their home? Rather, the user cares about precision: *when I actually see an alarm, how likely is it genuine?* This also offers a simpler starting point to model.

Thus, we first consider the weighted F-measure, which is equivalent to a weighted harmonic mean of precision and

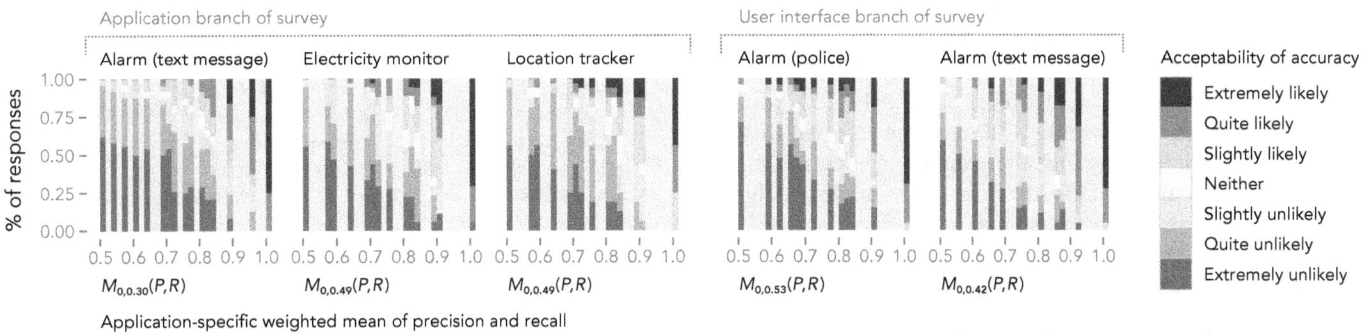

Figure 2. Acceptability of accuracy from the survey results plotted against each application's weighted geometric mean of precision and recall from our model. Optimizing this mean has the effect of also optimizing an application's acceptability of accuracy.

recall. We note that it can be considered a part of a larger class of weighted power means of precision and recall:

$$M_{p,\alpha}(P,R) = [\alpha P^p + (1-\alpha)R^p]^{\frac{1}{p}}$$

In this class, p specifies the type of mean; for example:

$$\begin{aligned} M_{-1,\alpha}(P,R) &= \left(\frac{\alpha}{P} + \frac{1-\alpha}{R}\right)^{-1} && \text{(harmonic mean)} \\ M_{0,\alpha}(P,R) &= P^\alpha R^{1-\alpha} && \text{(geometric mean)} \\ M_{1,\alpha}(P,R) &= \alpha P + (1-\alpha)R && \text{(arithmetic mean)} \end{aligned}$$

The parameter $\alpha \in [0,1]$ specifies a relative weighting of recall and precision; when $\alpha = 0.5$, both are weighted equally; when $\alpha < 0.5$, recall is weighted higher than precision; and when $\alpha > 0.5$, precision is weighted higher than recall. In this class, $M_{-1,\alpha}$ is equal to $1 - E_\alpha$ (van Rijsbergen's Effectiveness measure [22]), or the F_β-measure where $\alpha = 1/(1+\beta^2)$; thus $M_{-1,0.5}$ is the familiar F_1 score. $M_{0,\alpha}$, the geometric mean, is also known as the G-measure [21]. We consider this larger class of measures so that we have a systematic way to ask both whether harmonic mean (i.e., F measure) corresponds most closely to how people judge acceptability of accuracy for these applications (by determining p) and so that we can estimate whether for a given application, people value precision or recall more highly (by determining α for that application).

We conducted a mixed-effects Bayesian logistic regression[3] of *acceptability of accuracy* against three different weighted power means of precision and recall (harmonic, geometric, and arithmetic). Our model was as follows:

$$\begin{aligned} \text{logit}(\mu_{i,j,k}) &= \beta_{0,i} + \beta_{1,i} M_{p,\alpha_i}(P_{i,j}, R_{i,j}) + U_k \\ acceptability_{i,j,k} &\sim \text{Bernoulli}(\mu_{i,j,k}) \end{aligned}$$

For respondent k on scenario j in application i, with p drawn from a categorical distribution over (-1,0,1) corresponding to the aforementioned three types of means. Here we consider $acceptability_{i,j,k} = 1$ when a participant rates the acceptability of accuracy for that scenario as *Slightly likely* or higher and 0 otherwise. U_k is the random effect for participant k. We used the following uninformed priors:

$$\begin{aligned} \beta_{0,i}, \beta_{1,i} &\sim \text{Normal}(0,1000) \\ \alpha_i &\sim \text{Uniform}(0,1) \\ U_k &\sim \text{Normal}(0, {}^1/_\tau) \\ \tau &\sim \text{Gamma}(0.001,0.001) \\ p+2 &\sim \text{Categorical}({}^1/_3, {}^1/_3, {}^1/_3) \end{aligned}$$

This model allows us to separately estimate α_i for each application i. In addition, the posterior distribution of p will give us an estimate for how believable each type of mean is as a predictor for acceptability.

We take a Bayesian approach rather than a null-hypothesis significance testing (NHST)-based approach in modeling acceptability for several reasons. First, it yields a richer estimation of the parameters of interest: it allows us to estimate a complete posterior probability distribution of α for each application, rather than just a (point) maximum likelihood estimate. Second, as our goal is to propose methods of classifier evaluation that others can build upon, a Bayesian approach is a natural fit: posterior distributions of parameters from our model (and hopefully in the future, others') can be used to inform prior distributions in future work. We adopt Kruschke's [11] approach to Bayesian experimental statistics. In particular, we examine 95% highest-density intervals (HDIs) of posterior distributions to estimate credible differences between parameters (as opposed to an NHST approach of a 0.05 p-value threshold on the distribution of a test statistic).[5]

RESULTS

The posterior distribution of p allows us to estimate which measure best approximates acceptability of accuracy. For these applications, $p = 0$ (geometric mean) is most credible ($P(p = 0) = .81$), suggesting the G-measure may more close-

[3] While we considered using an ordinal or a multinomial logistic regression instead of a binomial regression, ultimately the question when evaluating a classifier here becomes "how many people said the accuracy was acceptable at all?", in which case this threshold would be applied after regression anyway, so the simpler model suffices while invoking fewer assumptions.

[5] Where possible we also ran similar more traditional NHST models and saw similar effects.

ly correspond to users' estimations of accuracy here. We do note that F-measure was more probable than arithmetic mean, and had only moderately less believability than G-measure ($P(p=-1)=.17$, Bayes Factor = 4.7). Figure 2 plots the proportion of people who rated the acceptability of accuracy at each level against the weighted geometric mean for that application derived from our model. Higher weighted mean is clearly associated with greater acceptability of accuracy. We break down the rest of our results based on the validity questions outlined above.

- **T3**: Our instrument should be sensitive to *application*: Classifiers with similar accuracy for different applications may have different *acceptability of accuracy*.

Confirmed. See Figure 3A: In the application branch of the survey, α for the *electricity* and *location* applications were both ~0.5, but for *alarm (text message)*, α was ~0.3. The differences between *alarm (text message)* and *electricity monitor* ($\alpha_i - \alpha_j = -.19$, 95% HDI: [–.30,–.09]) and between *alarm (text message)* and *location tracker* ($\alpha_i - \alpha_j = -.19$, 95% HDI: [–.32,–.07]) were credible on a 95% HDI, suggesting that our tool can be sensitive to differences in preferences between applications. β_1 for all applications on both branches was also credibly different from 0. While it varied, $\beta_1/100$ typically corresponded to an odds ratio of ~1.2, or a 20% increase in the odds that a person finds the accuracy of a system acceptable for every 0.01-point increase in G-measure. While their posterior distributions of α were similar, *electricity monitor* and *location tracker* had credible differences in β_1 ($\beta_{1,i} - \beta_{1,j} = 6.6$, 95% HDI: [.3,12.6]), again showing the sensitivity of the model.

- **T4**: When classifiers with similar accuracy for *the same* application have different levels of user burden for false positives, our test should be sensitive to this, and reflect it as a different weighting of *precision* versus *recall*.

Confirmed. See Figure 3C: In the user interface branch of the survey, the alarm scenario had $\alpha = 0.53$ for police compared to the much lower $\alpha = 0.42$ for alarm with text message[6], and these differences were credible on 95% HDI ($\alpha_i - \alpha_j = -.12$, 95% HDI: [–.22,–.01]). This demonstrates that the relative weighting of recall and precision for the same classifier on the same application—but with different feedback—can be quite different. Here, a more lightweight form of feedback (text messages) leads users to value recall over precision—that is, they are much more willing to tolerate false positives in order to obtain a higher true positive rate. Note also that the bulk of the posterior distribution of α (81%) for *alarm (police)* is also greater than 0.5 (although 0.5 is not outside its 95% HDI), giving

[6] While estimates of α for alarm (text message) differed between branches, a model combining both branches (Figure 3B) yields a more precise estimate of α that is consistent with the separate estimates (within their 95% HDIs) and which has all of the same credible differences with other αs as described above.

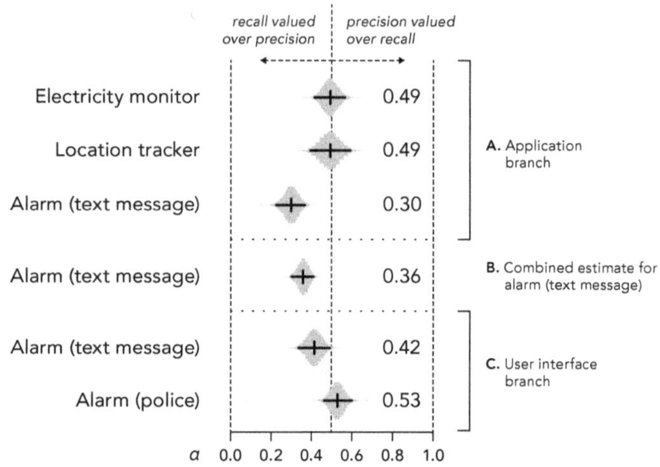

Figure 3. Posterior distributions of α for both branches of the survey. Mean and 95% HDI are indicated. Note the sensitivity of our model to different preferences of precision versus recall between applications (A) and for different feedback types (C). (B) shows a more precise estimate of α for alarm (text message) from a model combining both branches of the survey.

us some evidence that participants here valued precision over recall. This is as we would expect given the type of feedback: a false positive is costly if it results in a call to the police.

- **T1:** *Acceptability of accuracy* and *perceived usefulness* should be highly correlated.

These measures were highly correlated according to the Spearman rank correlation coefficient ($\rho = 0.89, p < 0.001$), suggesting the validity of our inclusion of *acceptability of accuracy* as a measure of output quality in the TAM.

- **T2**: *Perceived usefulness* and *intention to use* should be highly correlated.

These measures were also highly correlated ($\rho = 0.85$, $p < 0.001$).

STUDY 2: ASSESSING PREDICTIVE VALIDITY

To assess the predictive validity of our tool, we conducted a survey of perceptions of weather forecasting apps and websites. Weather prediction is a system where people are regularly exposed to the *effects* of prediction accuracy (e.g. failing to bring an umbrella when it rains) without knowing the precise accuracy of the system, as we might expect in other user-facing classification systems, making it a good candidate for validation. We obtained ground truth data of precipitation predictions from various weather forecasters in Seattle, WA, USA for the period of Sept 1, 2013–Aug 31, 2014 (http://www.forecastwatch.com/). We focused on one city, as people in deferent climates may have different preferences for precipitation accuracy. This survey had two parts:

Part 1: Existing acceptability (ground truth). We asked participants to specify which weather forecasting apps and websites they currently use and to rate each on *acceptability of accuracy* of precipitation prediction over the *last 30 days* and the *last year*. We also included *usefulness, ease of use,* and *frequency of use* questions for validating against the TAM. We again used 7-point Likert items, but used the anchors *strongly disagree/strongly agree* instead of *extremely unlikely/extremely likely*, as these statements were not predicting hypothetical use but describing existing opinions. Unlike with our survey tool, these questions do not specify the accuracy of the systems in question to participants. However, since we have the ground truth of the predictive accuracy of these systems over both time periods in question, we can model these responses in a similar manner to our hypothetical accuracy survey without the caveat that people are responding to hypothetical levels of accuracy.

Part 2: Hypothetical acceptability (our survey tool). We randomly selected one application or website from Part 1 that the participant currently uses and generated a variant of our survey instrument for that application or website. We asked them to imagine the randomly selected weather app had the accuracy described in each scenario (thus making the scenario more concrete), then to rate *acceptability of accuracy*, *usefulness*, and *intent to use*. Each scenario began, "15 days in a 30-day period, it rained" (i.e., real positives were fixed at 15). As before, we specified TP, FN, and FP (and additionally TN, as we had a fixed time interval and prevalence) using four statements like "13 of the 15 days that it rained, the weather forecast had (correctly) predicted that it would rain that day." We used the same precision and recall levels as before, but instead of giving all 16 scenarios to each participant, we gave each participant a random subset of 8 scenarios to reduce survey length.

Due to the reduced number of scenarios shown to each participant (potentially sampling over a smaller space of possible answers on the Likert scale for any individual participant), we used an ordinal regression instead of a binomial regression. Our model assumes the same latent variable representing acceptability is associated with the ordinal ratings of acceptability of accuracy in Part 1 and in Part 2.

Besides the use of ordinal instead of binomial regression, we also added two additional parameters. We added a fixed effect of *survey part* (*ground truth last 30 days, ground truth last year,* or *hypothetical*), $\beta_{2,i}$, to estimate whether people systematically over- or under-estimate their actual acceptability, as we might expect if (for example) people answering "extremely likely" are likely to give a lower rating of acceptability of accuracy when answering about a system they have experienced. We also added a scaling parameter, ζ_i, (also varied by *survey part*) to estimate whether people are more or less sensitive to changes in accuracy in real systems versus the hypothetical scenarios. By modeling these effects, we can use an individual's predictions about their own acceptability in hypothetical scenarios to estimate how acceptable they will *actually* find the accuracy of those systems to be if they used them. The model specification is:

$$\text{logit}\big(P(Y_{i,j,k} \le l)\big) = \frac{\theta_l - \beta_1 M_{p,\alpha}(P_{i,j}, R_{i,j}) - \beta_{2,i} - U_k}{e^{\zeta_i}}$$

For acceptability level l for respondent k on scenario j (or forecaster, in Part 1) in survey part i. We fix the parameters for the hypothetical part of the survey (where $i = 3$), $\beta_{2,3} = 0$ and $\zeta_3 = 0$, so the parameters from the ground truth survey parts ($\beta_{2,1}$, $\beta_{2,2}$, ζ_1, and ζ_2) can be interpreted as shifts in the location and scale of a person's hypothetical rating.

We use leave-one-participant-out cross-validation to assess the predictive validity of our model. In each fold, we fit a model with all participants' responses on Part 2 (hypothetical acceptability), but use all participants' responses except one to estimate the bias of hypothetical responses versus acceptability of known systems (Part 1). We then use the responses of the left-out participant in Part 2 to predict how they would rate the randomly-selected weather forecaster they saw in Part 2 on Part 1 of the survey based on the known accuracy of that forecasting app.

This mimics the situation where the accuracy and acceptability of an existing system is known, but the real-world acceptability of future (possibly better) systems is unknown. This scenario might arise (e.g.) if researchers in an area wish to set future targets for accuracy; such a model would provide the ability to predict acceptability levels in a population based on a combination of people's opinions of existing systems and their ratings of hypothetical systems.

Participants were recruited and compensated as in Study 1. We had 22 participants, 55% of which were female.

Results

Our model had a cross-validated mean absolute error (MAE)—the mean difference between the predicted and actual acceptability in points on the Likert scale—of 0.93, suggesting our predictions are generally within one point of the actual value on the scale. This is promising, though we note that people's ratings of actual systems were generally tightly clustered in the "acceptable" range (the MAE of using the median category as a predictor was 1.09).

This tight clustering was also reflected in our model. While weighted precision/recall had a credible effect ($\beta_1 = 13.4$, 95% HDI: [9.92,16.7]), scale parameters for the ground truth data indicated that ground truth responses were credibly less variable ($\zeta_1 = -0.437$, 95% HDI: [−0.829,−0.066]; $\zeta_2 = -0.346$, 95% HDI: [−0.673,−0.003]). These coefficients suggest that responses in the ground truth data had about 60% the variance of the hypothetical data. In other words, people were less sensitive to changes in accuracy in the systems they used than they predicted they would be in the hypothetical survey. People also tended to underestimate the acceptability of precipitation predictions in hypothetical scenarios, with ground truth responses having credibly higher ratings for the same accuracy ($\beta_{2,1} = 1.59$, 95% HDI: [1.1,2.13]; $\beta_{2,2} = 3.82$, 95% HDI: [2.94,4.8]).

We found some evidence of *wet bias* [26] in participants' preferences: the estimated α was 0.461 (95% HDI: [0.382,0.545]) with 82.3% of the distribution lying below

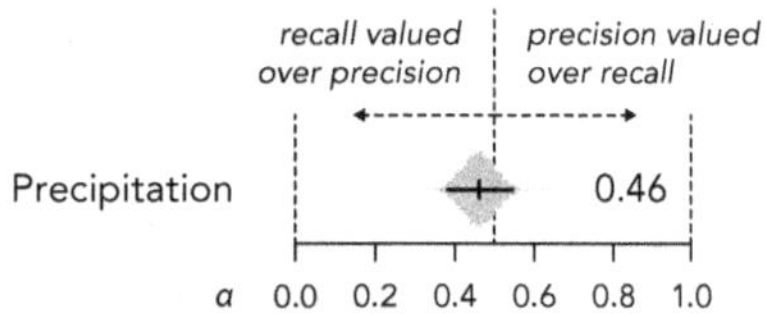

Figure 5. Posterior distributions of α for precipitation prediction. Mean and 95% HDI are indicated. Note the evidence of wet bias: 82% of the distribution lies below 0.5.

0.5 (see Figure 5). This leads some credence to the idea that people *may* weight recall higher here—desiring forecasters to catch more instances of rain in the forecast at the expense of making more false predictions of rain. We expect the prevalence of this bias to vary by climate, so make no claims to generalizability beyond the city we tested in. We note that we also asked people to state whether they thought it was worse when the forecast "does not call for rain, but it does rain" (FN) or when "calls for rain, but it doesn't rain" (FP), and 88% considered the former worse, consistent with a higher weight on recall, further validating our model.

As before, *acceptability* in the hypothetical survey was highly correlated with *usefulness* ($\rho = 0.98$, $p < 0.001$) and *usefulness* with *intent to use* ($\rho = 0.95$, $p < 0.001$). We also saw significant correlations between *acceptability of accuracy* and *usefulness* in the ground truth survey, though less strong ($\rho = 0.37$, $p < 0.001$), which is to be expected in real-world systems (where concerns like usability and convenience have additional salience over accuracy). Notably, we did not see significant correlations between *acceptability of accuracy* and *ease of use* in the ground truth ($\rho = 0.13$, $p = 0.13$), but did see moderate correlations between *ease of use* and *usefulness* ($\rho = 0.55$, $p < 0.001$)—as predicted by the TAM—suggesting that *acceptability of accuracy* is a separate construct from *ease of use* and is more related to *output quality* and *usefulness*, as we had predicted.

DISCUSSION AND IMPLICATIONS

In this section, we provide a discussion and implications for the survey instrument we have built for estimating acceptability of accuracy and its potential uses. Our research has broad implications, from deciding how to evaluate classifiers in user-facing systems, to selecting user interfaces and feedback for a new system, to allocating research resources.

What can we say absent a user interface? Selecting an objective function

Given a new classifier, typically, we might tune this classifier to optimize the F_β-measure (where β is usually 1). However, even without acceptability of accuracy ground truth, our instrument can be used to decide a more appropriate objective function to optimize during learning (e.g. an F or G measure with a particular weight). While the actual acceptability will not be known (because we cannot estimate shifts in location or scale of real-world acceptability without data from actual use), we believe that this estimated objective function will correlate with real-world acceptability of accuracy more closely than (say) F_1 score. More broadly, we believe researchers should consider whether F_1-measure truly matches their evaluation goals before employing it on user-facing systems.

Selecting a user interface to build: The potential of a low-performing classifier

As researchers in HCI and ubicomp, we often find ourselves asking, is this classifier good enough for our users? Indeed, we can recall several conversations with colleagues working on classifiers for various problems wherein someone asserted that the classifier was not good enough—and yet, the system had no user interface to speak of. If we have a classifier with (e.g.) better precision than recall, we can use our instrument to test out several hypothetical user interfaces or applications for a given classifier, and then build the application in which people weight precision as more important than recall (or vice versa, as called for by the results from our instrument). This gives us a way to increase the chances of building an acceptably accurate user-facing system given a classifier with known shortcomings. Given the potential for lower-burden, fuzzier feedback to improve the acceptability of accuracy of a system, it may be premature to rule out a weak—but adequately-performing—classifier without investigating acceptability of accuracy for potential instantiations of its user interface.

A lower performing but still acceptable classifier might also be used to preserve privacy or plausible deniability, which we believe our approach can help uncover. More simply, the lower performance classifier might be the easiest and cheapest to implement given system's computational capabilities. Knowing how accuracy trades off against acceptability would enable researchers to make these types of judgments more systematically.

Same sensor, different application: performance may not transfer

In a similar vein, a classifier that appears quite accurate for its domain may not have acceptable accuracy depending on what kind of application it is built into. For example, one might consider building many different types of systems on top of infrastructure-mediated sensing (e.g. sensors that can disaggregate energy [9] or water [7] use by appliance). The obvious example is an application for identifying high-cost appliances on a utility bill. However, a parent might also wish to use such a system to track TV usage of their child. While a certain level of false positives in tracking energy use of appliances seems unlikely to cause large discrepancies in finding high-cost devices, a few false positives in TV use may spark arguments between parents and children about TV-time quotas. We could more systematically investigate these intuitions by fitting a model of acceptability of accuracy to each of these applications. This would allow us to decide if our classifier is adequate for each use case.

Predicting future acceptability and setting targets

Given actual use of a classifier with known accuracy, acceptability ratings of that accuracy, and results from our survey instrument, we can estimate the relationship between hypothetical and actual acceptability (as with the weather data above). In this case, we can actually use hypothetical ratings to estimate the acceptability of accuracy for future classifiers that are more accurate than existing ones, and use this model to set targets for desired accuracy or to identify when we have reached a point of diminishing returns.

Training a new model: predicting when to predict

Many systems require an initial training period with a new user before they can make predictions (e.g., the Nest thermostat, Belkin Echo electricity/water monitor); such systems wait until they have built a good personalized model. But how long should training last? First impressions made by poor predictions are likely to sour users on a system. Given a model of acceptability of accuracy for an application, one could set a desired threshold of acceptability (e.g., as a percent of the user base), and use this to determine when the system should switch from training to prediction.

Expanding to other application domains

Thus far we have examined four specific application domains: electrical appliance detection, person location within an office, home alarms, and precipitation prediction. We chose applications we felt would be broadly applicable to a general audience and that we could use to validate the instrument. However, there are many other domains that can still be explored. For example, health sensing and recognition of daily activities for older adults are two popular application areas within HCI and Ubicomp. These types of applications are often only useful to certain subsets of people (e.g., someone with a specific health condition or someone caring for an older person), and thus if these domains are tested, the surveys should be targeted toward these specific populations rather than a general population (a primary reason we did not test them here). We suspect that health and older adult applications might require a higher level of accuracy, but that the user interface will again matter greatly. This is something our approach is designed to determine.

To facilitate adoption, we provide code for generating the survey based on desired precision and recall levels and fitting the model at: https://github.com/mjskay/acceptability-of-accuracy. We envision building an online repository of application examples and resulting data that can be used as guidelines to others wanting to build classifiers in a given space. For example, if someone is interested in exploring a new sleep sensor, they might look up data for similar applications in that domain and find that they need to aim for about 90% accuracy (as measured by some particular measure of accuracy, like weighted G-measure). This could also serve as a sort of "grand challenges" list for the community to help people building classifiers find interesting problems worth solving, rather than spending resources on areas with diminishing returns. At some point, resources on any given application may be better spent on improving the user interface or on another domain altogether.

Recommendations on applying the survey to research

Our experience in conducting this research leads us to make several recommendations for researchers hoping to apply a similar approach to their own applications and classifiers. We recommend presenting each user with at most 8 accuracy scenarios (as we did for the weather application), as we received feedback that the original survey (with 16 scenarios) was a bit long. We also recommend including at most two applications at a time, as our survey with three different applications had a higher rate of partial completions (11/26 compared to 3/24 in the two-application branch). Note that due to its design, a small number of participants (here, ~20-25 per application) is sufficient to achieve credible estimates of the model parameters from the survey tool.

In addition, although we used written scenarios in our example, researchers should consider other forms of representation of the system, such as visual screen mockups, storyboards, or video scenarios to help explain the intended use. Deployment on Mechanical Turk offers another approach, where each scenario could be made a single, small task.

LIMITATIONS AND FUTURE WORK

While we believe that our approach can be useful to help give researchers an easy to use method for assessing acceptable accuracy levels for a given classifier and interface, there are some limitations. First, the models are typically application-specific. However, as described in the discussion, we believe that it is straightforward to use existing classifiers in a domain to derive a model for that domain, allowing prediction of acceptability of accuracy of future classifiers. A good next step for this would be to test on more systems: for example, to simulate varying accuracies within a home electricity monitoring system and see whether people's perceptions of acceptability of accuracy can be predicted using our acceptance of accuracy survey (similar to how we validated the precipitation prediction model). We also believe that model estimates from previous, similar applications can inform future models (and here, our Bayesian approach can facilitate this). Finally, as an initial test case for our approach the survey thus far is geared toward evaluating the effect of precision and recall in binary classifiers. Further work is necessary to see how (e.g.) true negatives affect perceptions or to incorporate a broader set of classifier evaluation measures (c.f. [21]).

CONCLUSION

This work was motivated by a persistent question in HCI and ubiquitous computing research with end-user feedback based on classifiers: is my classifier good enough? We introduced a new measure, *acceptability of accuracy* and developed and validated a survey instrument that connects classifier evaluation to acceptability of accuracy. By expressing our model in the domain language of classifier designers, our approach allows us to easily adopt an evaluation method that more closely matches users' perceptions of accuracy than does the oft-used unweighted F-measure. At the same time, this method yields insight into how to build the application's feedback and whether further work on the classifier faces diminishing returns. We advocate for greater adoption of these types of evaluation methods in user-facing classifiers through the use of a community database of models of acceptability in HCI application domains.

ACKNOWLEDGEMENTS

We thank Sean Munson and Eun Kyoung Choe for their valuable feedback on this work and Cynthia Matuszek for her particular insight into the problems discussed herein. This work was funded in part by the Intel Science and Technology Center for Pervasive Computing (ISTC-PC).

REFERENCES

1. Antifakos, S., Schwaninger, A., and Schiele, B. Evaluating the Effects of Displaying Uncertainty in Context-Aware Applications. *UbiComp '04*, (2004).
2. Bellotti, V., Back, M., Edwards, W.K., Grinter, R.E., Henderson, A., and Lopes, C. Making sense of sensing systems: five questions for designers and researchers. *CHI '02*, 1 (2002), 415–422.
3. Choe, E.K., Consolvo, S., Jung, J., Harrison, B., Patel, S.N., and Kientz, J. a. Investigating receptiveness to sensing and inference in the home using sensor proxies. *UbiComp '12*, (2012), 61.
4. Consolvo, S., Chen, M.Y., Everitt, K., and Landay, J.A. Conducting in situ evaluations for and with ubiquitous computing technologies. *Int J Hum-Comput Int 22*, (2007), 103–118.
5. Consolvo, S., McDonald, D.W., Toscos, T., et al. Activity sensing in the wild: a field trial of ubifit garden. *CHI '08*, (2008), 1797–1806.
6. Davis, F.D. Perceived usefulness, perceived ease of use, and user acceptance of information technology. *MIS quarterly 13*, 3 (1989), 319–340.
7. Froehlich, J., Larson, E., Campbell, T., Haggerty, C., Fogarty, J., and Patel, S.N. HydroSense: infrastructure-mediated single-point sensing of whole-home water activity. *Ubicomp '09*, (2009).
8. Gigerenzer, G. and Hoffrage, U. How to improve Bayesian reasoning without instruction: Frequency formats. *Psychological Review 102*, 4 (1995), 684–704.
9. Gupta, S., Reynolds, M.S., and Patel, S.N. ElectriSense: single-point sensing using EMI for electrical event detection and classification in the home. *Ubicomp '10*, (2010), 139–148.
10. Koleva, B., Anastasi, R.O.B., Greenhalgh, C., et al. Expected, sensed, and desired: A framework for designing sensing-based interaction. *ACM Transactions on Computer-Human Interaction 12*, 1 (2005), 3–30.
11. Kruschke, J.K. *Doing Bayesian Data Analysis.* Elsevier Inc., 2011.
12. Larson, E.C., Lee, T., Liu, S., Rosenfeld, M., and Patel, S.N. Accurate and privacy preserving cough sensing using a low-cost microphone. *UbiComp '11*, (2011).
13. Li, X., Wang, Y.-Y., and Acero, A. Learning query intent from regularized click graphs. *SIGIR '08*, (2008), 339.
14. Lim, B.Y. and Dey, A.K. Assessing Demand for Intelligibility in Context-Aware Applications. *Ubicomp '09*, (2009), 195–204.
15. Lim, B.Y. and Dey, A.K. Investigating Intelligibility for Uncertain Context-Aware Applications. *Ubicomp '11*, (2011), 415–424.
16. Or, C.K.L. and Karsh, B.-T. A systematic review of patient acceptance of consumer health information technology. *JAMIA 16*, 4, 550–60.
17. Patel, S.N., Robertson, T., Kientz, J.A., Reynolds, M.S., and Abowd, G.D. At the Flick of a Switch: Detecting and Classifying Unique Electrical Events on the Residential Power Line. *UbiComp '07*, (2007).
18. Pavlou, P. Consumer acceptance of electronic commerce: integrating trust and risk with the technology acceptance model. *Int J Electron Comm 7*, 3 (2003).
19. Pentland, A. and Choudhury, T. Face recognition for smart environments. *Computer*, February (2000).
20. Popescu, M. and Li, Y. An acoustic fall detector system that uses sound height information to reduce the false alarm rate. *IEEE EMBS*, (2008), 4628–4631.
21. Powers, D.M.W. Evaluation: From precision, recall and F-measure to ROC, informedness, markedness & correlation. *J of Mach Lear Tech 2*, 1 (2011), 37–63.
22. Van Rijsbergen, C.J. Evaluation. In *Information Retrieval*. Butterworth & Co., 1975, 95–132.
23. Rogers, Y., Connelly, K., Tedesco, L., et al. Why it's worth the hassle: The value of in-situ studies when designing UbiComp. *UbiComp '07*, (2007), 336–353.
24. Rukzio, E., Hamard, J., Noda, C., and Luca, A. De. Visualization of Uncertainty in Context Aware Mobile Applications. (2006), 247–250.
25. Scholtz, J. and Consolvo, S. Toward a framework for evaluating ubiquitous computing applications. *IEEE Pervasive Computing 3*, 2 (2004), 82–88.
26. Silver, N. The Weatherman Is Not a Moron. *The New York Times*, 2012. www.nytimes.com/2012/09/09/magazine/the-weatherman-is-not-a-moron.html.
27. Venkatesh, V. and Davis, F.D. A theoretical extension of the Technology Acceptance Model: Four longitudinal field studies. *Manage Sci 46*, 2 (2000), 186–204.
28. Venkatesh, V., Morris, M.G., Davis, G.B., and Davis, F.D. User acceptance of information technology: Toward a unified view. *MIS quarterly 27*, 3 (2003), 425–478.
29. Ward, A., Jones, A., and Hopper, A. A new location technique for the active office. *IEEE Personal Communications*, October (1997), 42–47.

Examining the Peak-End Effects of Subjective Experience

Andy Cockburn[1] **Philip Quinn**[1] **Carl Gutwin**[2]

[1]University of Canterbury
Christchurch, New Zealand
andy@cosc.canterbury.ac.nz
philip.quinn@canterbury.ac.nz

[2]University of Saskatchewan
Saskatoon, Saskatchewan, Canada
gutwin@usask.ca

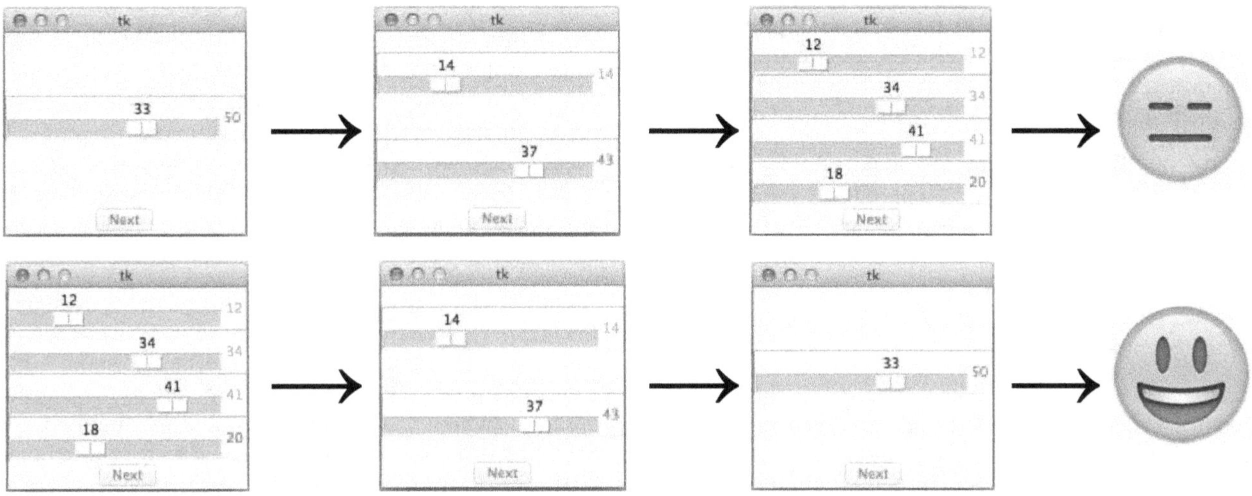

Figure 1. A characterisation of hypothetical peak-end effects on a user's subjective assessment of interactions. We hypothesise that advancing from high to low work on each page (bottom row) will be preferred to advancing from low to high work (top row).

ABSTRACT

Psychological research has shown that 'peak-end' effects influence people's retrospective evaluation of hedonic and affective experience. Rather than objectively reviewing the total amount of pleasure or pain during an experience, people's evaluation is shaped by the most intense moment (the peak) and the final moment (end). We describe an experiment demonstrating that peak-end effects can influence a user's preference for interaction sequences that are objectively identical in their overall requirements. Participants were asked to choose which of two interactive sequences of five pages they preferred. Both sequences required setting a total of 25 sliders to target values, and differed only in the distribution of the sliders across the five pages – with one sequence intended to induce positive peak-end effects, the other negative. The study found that manipulating only the peak or the end of the series did not significantly change preference, but that a combined manipulation of both peak and end did lead to significant differences in preference, even though all series had the same overall effort.

CHI 2015, April 18 - 23, 2015, Seoul, Republic of Korea

ACM 978-1-4503-3145-6/15/04…$15.00
http://dx.doi.org/10.1145/2702123.2702139

Author Keywords

Peak-end rule; subjective preferences; hedonic experience.

ACM Classification Keywords

H.5.2. [Information interfaces]: User Interfaces.

INTRODUCTION

People's willingness to use a computing system is strongly influenced by the perceived enjoyment of doing so [2, 4, 11, 17, 26]. Consequently, finding ways to manipulate and improve the hedonic and affective quality of interaction is an important and well-studied objective.

Although rarely examined in Human-Computer Interaction, peak-end effects [14] have been demonstrated to influence hedonic assessment in several settings. These include memory of pain during medical procedures [20], payment sequences and economics [16, 19], and user preferences for progress bars [7, 8]. The theory behind the effect is that the retrospective assessment of an experience is strongly dependent on the peak and ending subjective experience – in other words, our memories are substantially influenced by the most intense moment and the terminating moment.

These findings suggest that user interface experiences that finish more pleasantly may be preferred retrospectively to experiences that finish less so. Furthermore, *retrospective* assessment of experience is important because a user's willingness to repeat an interaction will be influenced by their memory of it. In short, finding ways to improve users' hedonic memory of interactions has clear utility.

We examine the presence of peak-end effects in user interfaces and their utility as a means for influencing user preferences. Specifically, we describe an empirical study that validates peak-end effects for completing a series of interactive pages. Although this represents a relatively simple interaction, it models a common interaction task (e.g., online signup forms, website checkout sequences, or setup 'wizards') where the level of enjoyment or annoyance experienced by the user is a critical factor in the application's success. For example, more than half of online transactions are abandoned by the user, and 21% of these failures are due to "the process taking too long" [24].

Our study involves presenting participants with two sequences of pages, and having them choose which page series they prefer. Both series involve exactly the same total interactive requirements from the user – moving between five pages and setting 25 sliders to target values. The page series differ only in the distribution of sliders across pages (see characterisation in Figure 1).

By varying the number of sliders on a page, the method manipulates the work required to advance between pages. As the work required on each page involves the mundane task of setting sliders, we intend that pages with few sliders will be subjectively more satisfying than pages with many. Therefore, we hypothesise that page series can be designed to induce positive and negative peak-end experiences – for example, a series that terminates with few sliders should be positive (characterised by the bottom row of Figure 1), and a series that terminates with many sliders should be negative (characterised by the top row of Figure 1). Overall, we predict that participants will prefer the page series designed to induce a positive peak-end experience (over that designed to induce a negative peak-end experience).

Experimental results confirm that peak and end effects can influence preference selections. Although only one of three conditions showed a significant effect, the results highlight subtleties in the use of workload as a method for manipulating affective experience. We discuss the design implications and identify directions for further work.

RELATED WORK

This research draws on three inter-related areas of prior work, reviewed in the following subsections: (1) peak-end effects and duration neglect, predominantly from the psychology literature; (2) HCI research on improving hedonic and affective experience; and (3) factors influencing human perception of the passage of time.

Peak-end Effects and Duration Neglect

Kahneman and colleagues introduced the peak-end rule as one of several heuristics and biases that encapsulate human deviations from objective judgment [13, 14]. They note that under a rule of *temporal monotonicity*, an objective analysis of an experience would be based on the sum of the magnitudes of its positive and negative moments, to give a total amount of pleasure or pain. However, it has been frequently observed that people instead remember experiences as momentary 'snapshots' [6], with the most intense (peak) and ending moments of positive or negative experience playing a dominant role – a *peak-end* rule. *Duration neglect* [6] is a related finding, where judgments of unpleasantness are surprisingly unaffected by their timespan. In a now famous experiment [14], participants engaged in two trials ('short' and 'long'), both of which began with immersing a hand in unpleasantly cold water (14°C) for one minute. In the 'short' trials participants then removed their hand from the water, but in the 'long' trials they kept their hand submerged for an additional 30 seconds while the water was surreptitiously warmed to a less-unpleasant 15°C. When participants were asked which trial they would prefer to repeat, 69% chose the 'long' trial: preferring the longer unpleasant experience that had a marginally less unpleasant ending – effectively choosing more pain over less.

A similar effect was observed in the retrospective reports of colonoscopy patients [20, 21], whose experience was dominated by their peak discomfort, and their discomfort at the end of the procedure – and was unrelated to the procedure's duration (which varied between 4 and 69 minutes). Similar peak-end effects have also been observed in article pricing [19] and effortful study [5]. However, the effects are sometimes subtle: for example, experiments involving purchase payment sequences [16] found that peak-end effects were not observed when participants were focused on the experimental manipulation, but that they became significant when participants were concurrently engaged in a distractor task. Experiments on gastronomic experiences [23] validated duration neglect and demonstrated preference for increasing pleasantness across courses, but failed to validate reliable effects of peak or end experience.

Hedonic and Affective Experience of Technology

The importance of fun and enjoyment in interaction is widely recognised and studied in HCI (e.g., [2, 17]). For example, in studies using word processing and graphics software, Davis et al. [4] demonstrated that motivation to use technology is positively influenced by both extrinsic factors (task usefulness) and intrinsic ones (enjoyment of use) – usefulness is the primary factor, but enjoyment is important provided task requirements are met. Other studies have analysed the subcomponents of hedonic and affective experience, seeking to model observed effects (e.g., Hassenzahl et al.'s [11] investigation of ergonomic and hedonic quality of interfaces).

Hassenzahl et al. [12] observed a recency effect of mental effort on participants' summary assessments of perceived usability – high levels of mental effort at the end of the evaluation session had a significant negative effect on perceived usability. Their analysis also showed that peak-end measures of mental workload had no effect on perceived usability.

More comprehensive reviews of affective experience in HCI are given by Venkatesh et al.'s [26] model and review of acceptance of information technology, Hartmann et al.'s [9] analysis of how users make judgments regarding user interface aesthetics and quality, and Reinecke et al.'s [22] review of how such assessments are influenced by culture.

Time Perception

Several studies have shown that time perception is subject to a variety of distortions, including:

- *Vierordt's Law* [27]: The duration of short events tends to be over-estimated, and long events under-estimated.
- *Interruption effects* [28]: People tend to overestimate the duration of interrupted simple tasks, and underestimate the duration of uninterrupted ones.
- *Rhythm effects*: The rhythm and pacing of stimuli has been found to influence time perception (e.g., [18, 25]).

In two studies of progress bars, Harrison et al. [7, 8] asked participants to observe pairs of progress bars (both 5 seconds long) and choose which appeared to pass more quickly. The first study [7] demonstrated that users perceive accelerating rates of progress (i.e., slow start, fast finish) to be faster than several alternatives, including decelerating progress. The second study demonstrated similar effects for progress bar animations [8] – increasing rates of pulsing animation were perceived as faster than decreasing rates. Harrison et al. partially attributed these findings to peak-end effects.

Agarwal [1] used the concept of 'cognitive absorption' to explain perceived usefulness and ease of use of software. Their study used factor analysis to validate five dimensions of cognitive absorption: temporal dissociation (losing track of time), focused immersion, and heightened enjoyment, control and curiosity. Their findings on temporal dissociation validate the adage "time flies when you're having fun."

These findings show bidirectional relationships between time perception and hedonic experience, motivating our experimental measurement of both.

EXPERIMENT: INTERACTION PEAK-END EFFECTS

We conducted an experiment to investigate whether peak-end effects influence users' preference for interactive tasks. The method compares user preferences and perceptions of page sequences that are identical in the total number of pages and in the total amount of work required across pages. Objectively, the total workload of the interactions is identical, with only the distribution of work across pages being varied.

The work required on each page is experimentally manipulated by varying the number of sliders that need to be set to target values (see Figure 1). Sliders are used to minimize extraneous factors that might influence other input tasks, such as errors during typed data entry. Varying the amount of work required on each page introduces two possible factors that may influence peak-end effects. First, the *workload* per page varies (e.g., a page with many sliders is more work than one with few). Second, the *tempo* of movement between pages varies, which may stimulate a rhythm effect.

The primary hypotheses are:

- **H1**: *End-effect for preference.* A page series that terminates with a low work page will be preferred to a series that terminates with a high work page.
- **H2**: *Peak-effect for preference.* A page series that includes a page with notably low work will be preferred to a series that includes a page with notably high work.
- **H3**: *Peak-and-end effect for preference.* A page series that includes an internal and terminating page with notably lower work will be preferred to a series that includes an internal and terminating page with notably higher work (a combination of **H1** and **H2**).

Pilot Study

We conducted a pilot study with 10 participants to gain initial insights into our experimental method. The pilot method asked participants to state which of two series of six pages they preferred. Each page contained a number of slider widgets that had to be set to a randomly selected value between 1 and 50, shown in red at the right-hand end of the slider (see Figure 1 for an example of the sliders). All sliders were vertically aligned and initially set to '0'. Target values turned green when correctly selected, and once all sliders on a page were correctly set a 'Next' button at the bottom of the page became active, allowing the user to move to the next page.

Both of the page series contained a total of six pages and 31 sliders, with the series differing only in the order of page presentation. The '*positive*' series used a decreasing number of sliders on each page: 10, then 8, 6, 4, 2, and 1 slider on the final page. The '*negative*' series used the opposite order, increasing from 1 through 10 page sliders. Odd numbered participants used the positive series first; even numbers used the negative series first. Before using the *positive* or *negative* series, participants were familiarized with the method using three pages with 5, 5, and 6 sliders.

After using *positive* and *negative* series, participants were asked to select their preference for the first or second series.

Pilot study results

Seven of the ten participants preferred the *positive* series, suggesting support for the peak-end prediction. The three participants who selected a preference for the *negative* series gave interesting explanations for doing so, which influenced our final experimental method.

One participant referred to 'hitting the values really easily' while using the *negative* condition. This can be interpreted as causing an unintended positive peak experience. It occurred because the randomly selected targets on one page included three occurrences of the same target value. She noted that selecting slider values was easier when a similar value was already selected because it acted as a landmark in the vertically aligned sliders. The final method balanced the

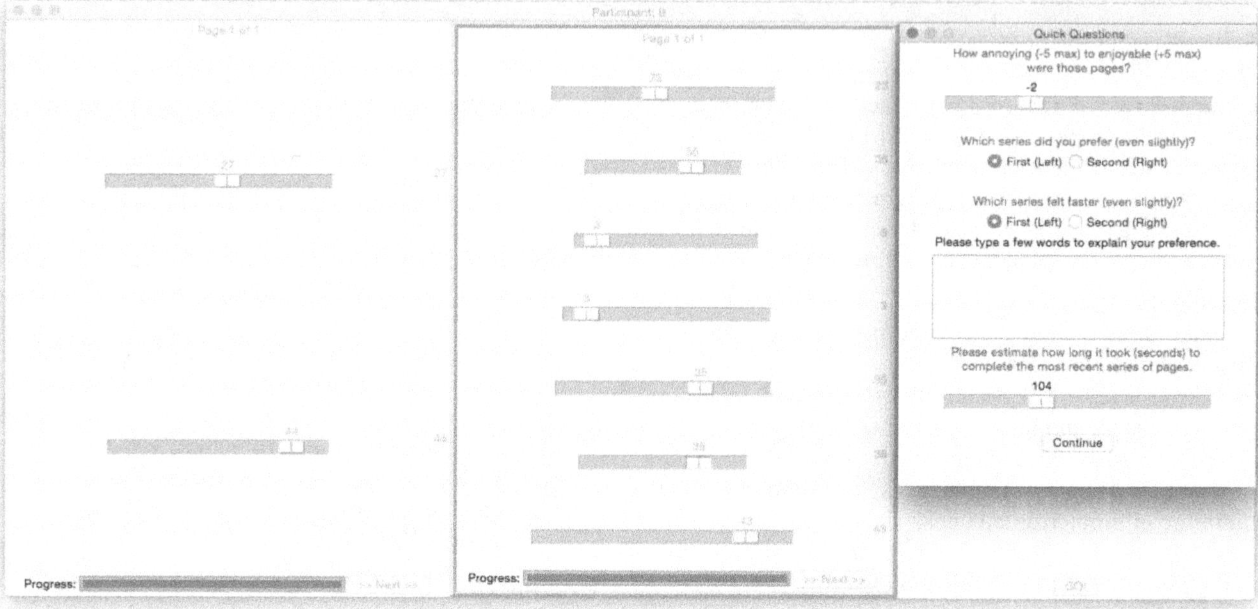

Figure 2. The experimental interface's three panes: first & second page series (left & middle); instructions & questions (right).

variance of the difficulty of selecting slider values in three ways: (1) landmark effects were reduced by randomising each slider's visual width to be between 175 and 300 pixels; (2) the sliders' initial value was 25 rather than 0 to balance the amount of slider movement required across target values; and (3) endpoint values (0 and 50) were not used as targets.

A participant who used the *positive* condition first referred to the 'shock' of the first page containing 10 sliders. We interpret this as a peak negative experience due to the failure of the practice trials to expose participants to the number of sliders used in the main trials. We remedied this by ensuring that practice included a page with as many sliders as the maximum encountered in the main conditions.

Experimental Method and Procedure

Figure 2 shows the experimental user interface, which used three panes to present a 'first' series (left), a 'second' series for comparison (middle), and instructions/questions (right).

All pages contained between one and nine sliders. Each page also contained a page counter at the top of the window (e.g., "Page 2 of 5"), a progress bar at the bottom reflecting the same proportion, and a "Next" button that was initially disabled. Sliders were vertically centred and were a random width between 175 and 300 px. They permitted selection of discrete values in the range 0 to 50 and were initially set in the centre: 25. The target value for each slider (randomly chosen in the range 1 to 49, excluding 25) was shown in red to the right of the slider, and changed to green when correctly selected. Once all page sliders were set to their target values, the "Next" button was enabled, allowing the participant to progress to the next page.

Participants initially completed a practice series of three pages containing 7, 7, and 9 sliders. They then completed three pairs of page series, with the pairs representing our manipulation of *end*, *peak*, and *peak-and-end* effects, in that order. The first sequence of each pair was presented in the left-hand pane, and the second sequence was shown in the middle pane. After each page series, participants were asked to respond to two questions concerning annoyance/enjoyment (AE) and estimated time (ET):

AE: "How annoying (-5 max) to enjoyable (+5 max) were those pages?"

ET: "Please estimate how long it took (in seconds) to complete that series of pages."

Once both page series in a pair were complete, participants answered the main experimental question on preference choice (PC) between page series, and also which series they perceived to be faster (FC).

PC: "Which series did you prefer? First (left), or Second (right)"

FC: "Which series felt faster? First (left), or Second (right)."

They were also asked to comment on their preference.

Page series design

The page series for *end, peak* and *peak-and-end* conditions were designed to test *H1-3* respectively, within the constraints of using five pages and 25 sliders in total. Table 1 shows the number of sliders in each page for the three conditions (e.g., *{a, b, c}* denotes three pages with *a, b,* and *c* number of sliders on each). The symbols '*+*' and '*–*' denote which series is intended to give an overall positive or negative subjective experience. All participants completed both series in each condition, with order counterbalanced by participant number (shown by 'Even/Odd first').

The *+end* and *–end* series focus on the final two pages of the series, and provide either an increasing or a decreasing workload: *+end* uses three then two sliders on the final pages, contrasting with *–end,* which uses five then eight.

Slider counts on the first three pages were then balanced to satisfy a total count of 25 sliders (note that the constraint of an increasing or decreasing end effect led to slightly non-symmetrical workloads in these 'non-manipulation' pages).

Condition	Even first	Odd first
end	*+{7, 7, 6, 3, 2}*	*−{4, 4, 4, 5, 8}*
peak	*−{3, 3, 9, 4, 6}*	*+{6, 6, 1, 6, 6}*
peak-and-end	*+{7, 2, 7, 6, 3}*	*−{3, 8, 4, 4, 6}*

Table 1. Paired page series used for each condition. *{1, 2, 3}* denotes 3 pages with *1*, then *2*, then *3* sliders per page; +/– denote hypothesised +ve and –ve subjective experience.

The *+peak* and *−peak* series focus on the third page, which is intended to give positive or negative peak experience in the middle of the series. *+Peak* uses one slider on the third page, contrasting with *−peak,* which uses nine. To reduce conflating divergent *end* experiences within the *peak* series, both series terminate with the same number of sliders (i.e., six – which again led to a slight asymmetry in workload for the non-manipulation pages). Slider counts were balanced across remaining pages to achieve a total of 25 sliders.

The *+peak-and-end* and *−peak-and-end* series focus on the second and final pages. The series are intended to give positive and negative peak experiences at the second page (two versus eight sliders), and also divergent ends on the final page (three versus six). Remaining pages were balanced to satisfy 25 sliders in total.

Finally, we chose to compare positive to negative manipulations, rather than positive to neutral in order to increase the strength of the effect.

Participants and Apparatus

Thirty-two undergraduate computer science students volunteered to participate (11 female; aged 18-35, mean 21). The study ran on Intel Core i7 computers running Linux Mint 14, with a wired Logitech optical mouse and a 22″ monitor at 1680×1050 px. Experimental software was written in Python, and recorded all user actions and responses.

Design

The primary dependent variable is the participants' preference choice (PC), separately analysed using binomial sign tests for each of the experimental conditions (*end, peak,* and *peak-and-end*). These analyses test hypotheses *H1-H3*. The participants' choice for which page series felt faster (FC) is also analysed using sign tests.

Paired t-tests are used for secondary analyses that are intended to characterise the participants' performance and perceptions, as described in the results section.

RESULTS

Results are separately presented for each of the experimental conditions: *end, peak,* and *peak-and-end.*

As intended, there was no significant difference between the actual times taken to complete the 5 pages and 25 sliders using the +ve and −ve page series in any of the conditions – e.g., means 81.4 s and 80.8 s respectively in the *end* condition (t_{31} = 0.33, p = .74).

Figure 3 shows the mean time taken for pages with differing numbers of sliders, ranging from 4.36 s for pages with one slider to 25.9 s for pages with nine sliders. As expected, the total time spent on each page increased linearly with the number of sliders (R^2 = *.99*). These times provide an indication of the magnitude of work required on different pages.

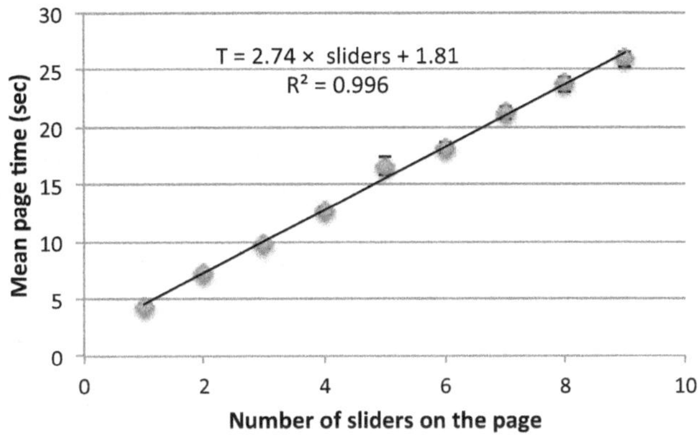

Figure 3. Mean page time across number of page sliders.

Interestingly (though unimportant for our hypotheses) an effect of Viorordt's Law was apparent: with participants in all conditions significantly underestimating the time taken to complete each series. For example, in the *end* condition the mean selected time estimation for the +ve series was 47.6 s, compared to 81 s actual time (t_{31} = 4.99, p < .001).

The following subsections present results for the main hypothesis concerning Preference Choice (PC) for each condition, followed by other measures and participant comments.

Preference Choice

End Condition

Twenty participants (62.5%) selected preference (PC) for the *+end* series, and 12 (37.5%) preferred the *−end* series. This is not statistically significant (sign test, *p*=*.21*), and we therefore reject *H1*. However, the proportion is not dissimilar to Kahneman's original study, which attained significance at 22 of 32 participants (69%).

Peak condition

Preference choices (PC) for the two peak series were evenly split, regardless of order. Seventeen participants preferred the *+peak* series and 15 preferred the *−peak* series (*p*=*.86*). We therefore reject *H2*.

Peak-and-End condition

Twenty-three participants (72%) selected the *+peak-and-end* series *{7,2,7,6,3}* as preferred over *−peak-and-end* series *{3,8,4,4,6}*, giving a significant effect (PC, p = *.02*). We therefore accept *H3*.

Order Effects and Enjoyment

Other measures provide insight into the factors that influenced participants' preference choices, as follows.

End condition

As Figure 4 indicates, series order appears to have influenced preference selections. Participants who used the ***+****end* series first were evenly split in their preference choice (8 each), whereas 12 of the 16 participants (75%) who used the ***+****end* series second selected it as preferred (p = *.07*). This may be due to the recency of the terminating positive experience when making the preference selection immediately after completing the ***+****end* series.

Nineteen participants (59%) selected the ***+****end* series as faster (FC) and twenty participants selected a shorter duration (ET) for the ***+****end* series than for the **–***end* series. However, the mean ET values were similar at 47.6 s and 50.2 s (t_{31} = 0.7, p = *.47*).Mean enjoyment ratings (AE) were also similar for the two series (0.31 for the ***+****end* series, -0.06 for the **–***end* series; t_{31} = .86, p = *.4*). Twenty-one participants (65%) rated the ***+****end* series higher than for the **–***end* series.

Peak condition

Unlike *end* conditions, order appeared to have little effect on preference choices for *peak* conditions (Figure 5). Choices for which series was perceived as faster (FC) were tied at 16 each. Means for estimated time (ET) were also tied at 49.3 s. Enjoyment ratings (AE) were -0.03 for the ***+****peak* series and -0.44 for **–***peak*, t_{31} = .9, p = *.37*).

Peak-and-End condition

Series order influenced preferences for *peak-and-end* conditions (Figure 7), with 13 of the 16 participants (81%) who used ***+****peak-and-end* first selecting it as preferred, and only 10 of 16 who used ***+****peak-and-end* second.

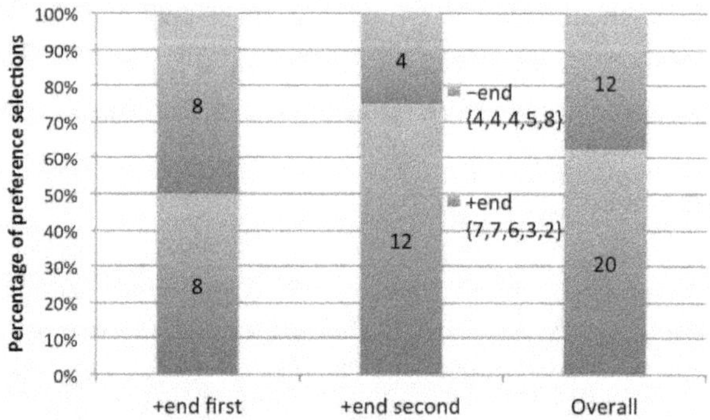

Figure 4. End condition: Proportion of preference selections for each page series (actual counts shown).

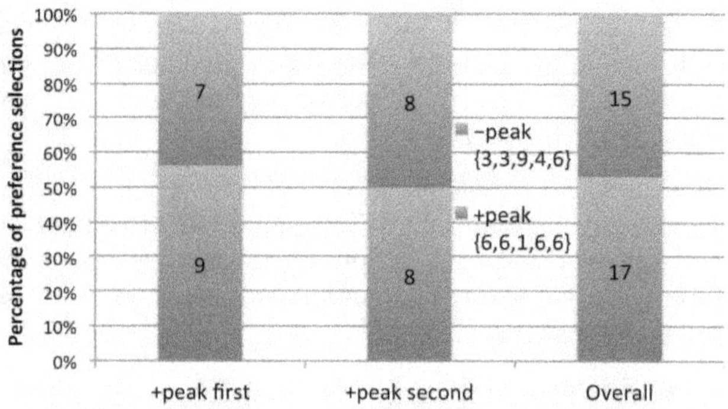

Figure 5. Peak condition: Percentage of preference selections for each page series (actual counts shown).

Twenty-one participants selected the ***+****peak-and-end* series as appearing to be faster (FC, p = *.11*). There was no significant effect of estimated time (ET, means 50.1 s and 53.3 for ***+****peak-and-end* and **–***peak-and-end*; t_{31} = 1.0, p = *.33*).

Enjoyment ratings (AE) supported the preference selections, with a significantly higher mean of 0.81 for the ***+****peak-and-end* series and 0.03 for the **–***peak-and-end* series: t_{31} = 2.18, p = *.037*. Twenty-four of the participants (75%) provided a higher AE rating for ***+****peak-and-end.*

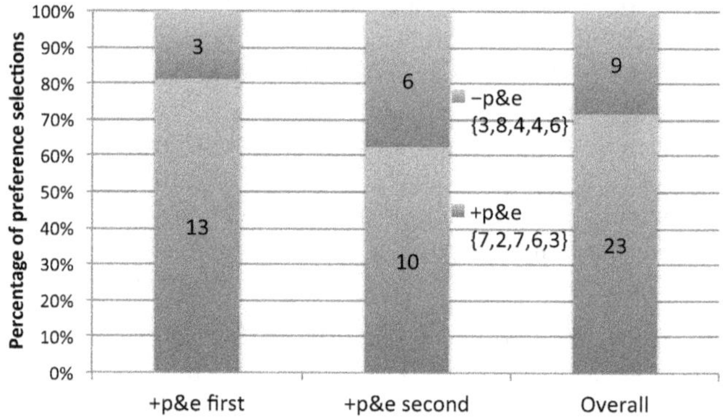

Figure 6. Peak-and-end (p&e) condition: Percentage and counts of preference selections for each page series.

In summary, for the *peak-and-end* condition we accept the primary hypothesis (**H3**) – a significant majority of participants preferred the ***+****{7,2,7,6,3}* series that was designed to induce a positive peak experience (a page with only 2 sliders) and a positive end experience (a final page with 3 sliders) over the **–***{3,8,4,4,6}* series that contained a peak negative experience (a page with 8 sliders) and a negative end experience (a final page with 6 sliders).

Participant comments

Participant comments provide interesting insight into the hypothesised effects. Participants received no instruction on the purpose of the experiment – only that it concerned their preference for user interfaces involving pages of sliders. It is therefore unsurprising that their comments refer to a variety of explanations for their preference selection. Across all conditions, participants' comments generally referred to five different categories of issues explaining their preference:

- *Page series*: variations in the number of sliders across pages (our actual manipulation).
- *Slider control:* differences in the difficulty of selecting target values (not manipulated); e.g., P16 "The bar stayed with the mouse more, so it was easier to control".
- *Visual effects:* preferences for screen certain locations.
- *Perceived time:* feeling that one condition was faster.
- *Learning effects*: practice-based improvement.

Figure 7 shows the proportion of participant comments referring to each of these preference explanations across experimental conditions. Note that nearly half of the comments explaining a preference for the *+end* series do so with respect to the actual experimental manipulation (the page series). Comments include the following:

> P10: "the number of sliders decreased on each page, so I [felt] like there was less to do overall (although it may be that the first pages just had more sliders to compensate?)."
>
> P23: "decreasing number of sliders seems quicker"
>
> P25: "smaller number of sliders to do as time went on."
>
> P27: "Fewer sliders = more enjoyable."

In contrast, only one participant explained their preference for the *−end* series with respect to the page series:

> P9: "The first lot felt like I was getting more done per page than the second one."

Instead, the majority of comments explaining preference for the *−end* series refer to differences in the difficulty of target selection (e.g., P17 "easier to get the slider on the desired point", P19 "wider sliders making it easier to select the number", P24 "easier to move the slider".) These explanations are imaginary, or due to random variance.

For the *peak* series, Figure 7 (middle) shows the proportion of comments to explain the preference choice with reference to each of the five issues described earlier. Unlike the *end* conditions, a large proportion (45%) of participants explained their preference for the *−peak* series with reference to properties of the page series, reflecting the failure of our intended manipulation of peak experiences.

Two participants referred to the unintended positive experience of having two pages with only three sliders in the *−peak* series *{3,3,9,4,6}*:

> P13: "There were a couple pages on the 2nd one with only a few sliders which was nice."
>
> P25: "...had a break where there were only a few sliders rather than heaps on one page"

Other participants explained their preference for the *−peak* series by identifying undesired features of the *+peak* series,

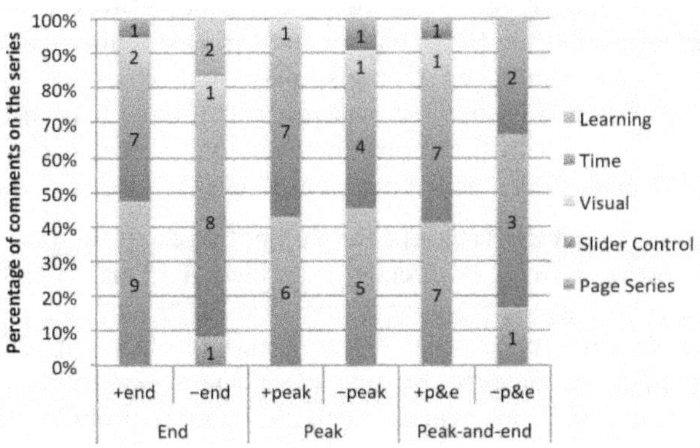

Figure 7. Percentages (and counts) of preference choice explanations referring to each of five factors.

which had six sliders on all but one page *{6,6,1,6,6}*:

> P12: "The sudden change in number of sliders in the second one [+peak] was slightly offputting."
>
> P32: "the second set [+*peak*] seemed to have more sliders on each page except one which only had one meaning that each page seemed to take longer and appeared more daunting."

However, several comments alluded to our intended manipulation. Participant 10, for instance, referred to the positive impact of the page with only one slider:

> P10: "right series [+*peak*] had some pages with very few sliders on, so seemed like fewer sliders overall."

Three participants explicitly referred to the intended negative impact of the page with nine sliders (*−peak*):

> P5: "the second with heaps of sliders was annoying."
>
> P19: "a page with lots of sliders made me feel like I was going slower."
>
> P23: "the second series felt like it was taking longer especially with the page with a large amount of sliders on it."

Figure 7 (right) shows that a relatively large proportion of comments (41%) explained preference for the *+peak-and-end* series with reference to the page series. Several attributed their preference to erroneous impressions that there were fewer sliders in the *+peak-and-end* series. Others stated that the *+peak-and-end* series had less variance in the number of sliders across pages (the inverse is true, with *+peak-and-end* having a standard deviation of 2.34 versus 2.0 for −ve series):

> P12: "The size of the list didn't seem to vary as much."
>
> P13: "It felt like there was more of an even spread."
>
> P18: "it seemed like there were less sliders."

Participant 32 explicitly referred to a peak negative experience in the *−peak-and-end* series: "one page that had a lot more sliders than the others that made it seem more time consuming." In contrast, only one participant explained their preference of the *−peak-and-end* series with respect to the page series.

DISCUSSION

Our experiment shows limited evidence that interactions which are objectively identical in total work can, in certain situations, induce different subjective experiences through manipulation of peak-end effects. Although the study found mixed results, a combined manipulation of both peak and end saw a significant change in participants' preferences. In this section, we consider explanations for our main results, discuss issues for further work, and the implications for interface design.

Explanations for Results

Of our three hypotheses, only the combination of *peak-and-end* effects is supported by the experimental data. We consider explanations for each of the main outcomes below. First, manipulation of *peak* alone did not show any overall effect, and participant comments suggest that a markedly different peak experience may not have been perceived as we intended (e.g., some participants saw the change as jarring, rather than beneficial).

Second, the lack of a significant difference for the *end* manipulations may be due to the small changes that were part of these series (e.g., a difference of only five sliders on the final page). In future studies we will test whether larger differences in the series can engender an effect. It was clear from participant comments that people regularly noticed the difference at the end of the series, and it is likely that with a larger manipulation a measurable difference will become apparent.

Third, we believe that the main reason the combined *peak-and-end* manipulation showed an effect was the added noticeability of both *peak* and *end* effects together. Even though neither individual manipulation showed a significant difference, both effects work in the same direction – and so combining them appears to provide an additive effect on people's recollection of their experience.

Methodological Issues

Rhythm effects

Our experimental method manipulated page workload (slider count) as a proxy for moment-to-moment subjective experiment (further discussed below). However, this manipulation also influences the rhythm of the user's transition between pages. Rhythm effects are known to influence user's perception of time (e.g., [18, 25]) and in HCI they have been demonstrated to influence preference for different behaviours in observed progress bars [7, 8]. Notably, however, these studies attributed some of the observed preferences to peak-end effects. In other words, even if rhythm caused or contributed to the preference choice, the explanation remains attributable to peak-end effects.

There are also questions for further work around the elements of interaction that contribute to the user's perception of rhythm. In our experiment, interaction consisted of two types of manipulation – dragging sliders and clicking the next button – and the movement between pages was the primary way in which rhythm could vary substantially. Real interactions, in contrast, are likely to include various interactive components (typing into text boxes, setting radio-buttons, selecting files, etc.) thereby creating many opportunities for the user to perceive changes in rhythm.

Influence of the terminating page

The experimental software used three interface panes to show the first series (left), second series (middle) and instructions/questions (right). Consequently, while answering questions about the two series, participants could see the terminating page of sliders for both series (e.g., Figure 2). It is therefore possible that the persistent representation of the terminating page may have influenced participants' preference selection. Although this is a legitimate concern, none of the participants commented on the issue. Furthermore, 7 of 10 participants in the pilot study preferred the positive series, using a method that did not show the terminating page of either series.

Influence of order and boredom

All participants completed the conditions in the same order: *end, peak,* and *peak-and-end* (although series order within each condition was counterbalanced). We suspect that a decrease in the level of the participants' task focus while progressing through the experiment may have contributed to their preference choices. Previous studies have noted that peak-end experiments are more sensitive when participants are engaged in a concurrent 'distractor' task, because the distractor reduces conscious deliberation on the experimental manipulation [16]. We therefore suspect that the tedium of previously setting over one hundred sliders may have led participants in the *peak-and-end* condition to be less focused on the task than those in the *end* condition.

Implications for Piecemeal Interaction

Our evaluation was modelled on collecting data through a series of discrete interactive pages. As discussed earlier, this type of interaction is common in tasks such as signup forms or checkouts, and the user experience in these simple interactions has a strong effect on successful completion. Users may abandon a transaction if they feel it is becoming annoying or taking too much time.

The results of our study are relevant for designers of these kinds of sequences. We found peak-end effects in a generic task involving slider widgets – whereas in real-world tasks where the user is personally involved in the outcome (e.g., making a purchase) there is the potential that the effects will be even greater. As a result, designers of sequence-based tasks have an opportunity to provide a better subjective experience for their users. When designing pages to gather data, designers are often relatively unconstrained regarding (1) the number of pages used to present data items, (2) the number of data items on each page, and (3) the order of pages. Other than optimising the semantic relationship within and between pages (i.e., putting related items on the same page), there is little guidance to suggest that one order might be preferable to another.

Our results suggest that designers should think carefully about peak-end effects when considering the distribution of content across pages. Doing so may improve users' subjective experience and increase their willingness to use the system again in the future; conversely, failing to consider peak-end effects may cause adverse user reactions.

Other Interface Triggers for Subjective Experience

While our method directly examined page-based interactions by varying page workload, it is likely that many interactive experiences can induce peak-end effects in diverse interactive contexts. In general, the peak-end rule is that memory for experiences (such as interactive ones) can be positively influenced by appropriately timing affective and hedonic peaks and troughs.

Interface designs for influencing hedonic experience of user interfaces are under active research in HCI. A full review is beyond the scope of this paper, but it is clear that some factors are context dependent. For example, research on 'flow' and optimal experience [3] shows the importance of balancing task challenge with the user's skill level. Our experiment used a mundane task of setting sliders to manipulate workload, but other methods for altering workload, such as task complexity, might produce divergent results for users of different skill levels – a challenging task might be positive for a skilled user, but negative for others.

Three interesting questions for further work include (1) what triggered the effects we observed; (2) what other interface features can cause related effects; and (3) how strong are the effects?

Regarding (1), while we consciously designed our tasks to influence workload, the induced effect on the user likely includes perceived tedium due to the mundane task. When designing the experiment we considered using other workload requirements, such arithmetic exercises, but we did not do so due to the lack of control for individual variance in ability (some users might find easy exercises engaging, others tedious). We intend to conduct further studies examining methods for achieving peak-end effects.

Regarding other triggers for hedonic experience (2), we are particularly interested in examining peak-end effects with gamified interaction components. Gamification [15] is under active research, and peak-end effects suggest that there may be benefits in considering the timing at which they are employed. We are also interested in examining the impact of peak-end effects in the retrospective assessment of game enjoyment.

Finally, we are interested in better understanding the strength of peak-end effects (3). Our results demonstrate significant effects on preference choice, but they do not quantify the magnitude of the positive (and negative) sensation. Reliable methods for quantifying hedonic experience are required to do so (for example, physiological sensors), and are under development [10, 29].

Workload Distribution and Subjective Experience

In varying workload across pages, the intention of our experimental method was that a page with many sliders would induce a more negative subjective experience (e.g., 'oh no, look at all these') than a page with few sliders (e.g., 'thank goodness, only two this time').

Many prior studies into peak-end effects have examined strong hedonic stimuli such as pain [6, 14]. Workload manipulation, in contrast, can be considered to be a weak stimulus for peak-end experiments, yet our results still showed significant effects. The use of workload as a manipulation does have precedent in the literature – Finn [5] described an experiment in which participants engaged in an effortful learning exercise (memorising a list of 30 complex Spanish-English word translations). Participants learned a list of 30 complex translations ('unextended') and another list that added 15 easier translations to the end of 30 complex translations ('extended'). Participants significantly preferred the extended condition (attributed to the lower terminating mental workload), despite better test performance with the unextended list.

Participant comments such as "heaps of sliders was annoying" suggest that our manipulation had the intended effect. However, there were interesting exceptions. Participant 9, for example, explained their preference for the *–end* series with reference to 'getting more done' on pages with many sliders. The subtleties of manipulating workload via number of sliders are also highlighted by the failure of the *peak* condition, in which several participants perceived the page with a single slider as abrupt.

Further empirical work is needed to better understand the interface conditions that best stimulate the positive moment-to-moment experiences on which peak-end effects depend. This includes issues concerning the granularity of the user's moment-to-moment experience – e.g., do two 'easy' pages form a stronger peak than one easy page.

CONCLUSIONS

Peak-end effects concern the substantial influence that the maximum and terminating moments of affective experience have on a person's overall memory of subjective quality. Given their prevalence in the basic teachings of psychology, there has been surprisingly little research into peak-end effects in HCI (notable exceptions were reviewed).

We presented experimental results demonstrating that, in certain conditions, peak-end effects can significantly influence user's preference for interfaces that are otherwise identical in their objective interaction requirements. Design implications of these findings suggest that simply altering the presentation order of interface components can impact remembered subjective experience. While results showed that peak-end effects *can* influence subjective preferences, they also showed substantial subtleties in their impact, suggesting fruitful opportunities for further research.

REFERENCES

1. Agarwal, R. and Karahanna, E. Time Flies When You're Having Fun: Cognitive Absorption and Beliefs about Information Technology Usage. *MIS Quarterly* 24, 4 (2000), 665-694.
2. Carroll, J. The adventure of getting to know a computer. in Baecker, R. and Buxton, W. eds. *Readings in Human-Computer Interaction: A Multidisciplinary Approach*, Morgan Kaufmann Publishers Inc., 1987, 639-648.
3. Csikszentmihalyi, M. Flow: *The Psychology of Optimal Experience*. Harper and Row, New York, 1991.
4. Davis, F.D., Bagozzi, R.P. and Warshaw, P.R. Extrinsic and Intrinsic Motivation to Use Computers in the Workplace1. *J Appl. Social Psych*. 22, 14 (1992), 1111-1132.

5. Finn, B. Ending on a High Note: Adding a Better End to Effortful Study. *J. Experimental Psychology: Learning, Memory, and Cognition* 36, 6 (2010), 1548-1553.
6. Fredrickson, B. and Kahneman, D. Duration neglect in retrospective evaluations of affective episodes. *J. Personality and Social Psychology* 65, 1 (1993), 45-55.
7. Harrison, C., Amento, B., Kuznetsov, S. and Bell, R. Rethinking the progress bar. in *Proc.UIST'07*, ACM, (2007), 115-118.
8. Harrison, C., Yeo, Z. and Hudson, S.E. Faster progress bars: manipulating perceived duration with visual augmentations. in *Proc. CHI'10*, ACM, (2010), 1545-1548.
9. Hartmann, J., Sutcliffe, A. and Angeli, A.D. Towards a theory of user judgment of aesthetics and user interface quality. *ACM ToCHI.* 15, 4 (2008), 1-30.
10. Hassenzahl, M. The Interplay of Beauty, Goodness, and Usability in Interactive Products. *Human-Computer Interaction* 19, 4 (2004), 319--349.
11. Hassenzahl, M., Platz, A., Burmester, M. and Lehner, K. Hedonic and ergonomic quality aspects determine a software's appeal. in *Proc. CHI'00*, ACM, The Hague, The Netherlands, 2000, 201-208.
12. Hassenzahl, M. and Sandweg, N. From mental effort to perceived usability: transforming experiences into summary assessments. *Extended Abstracts CHI '04*, ACM, Vienna, Austria, 2004, 1283-1286
13. Kahneman, D. *Thinking, Fast and Slow*. Farrar, Straus and Giroux, 2011.
14. Kahneman, D., Fredrickson, B., Schreiber, C. and Redelmeier, D. When More Pain Is Preferred to Less: Adding a Better End. *J. Personality and Social Psych*. 65, 1 (1993), 401-405.
15. Kapp, K. *The gamification of learning and instruction: Game-based methods and strategies for training and education*. Pfeiffer, San Francisco, 2012.
16. Langer, T., Sarin, R. and Weber, M. The retrospective evaluation of payment sequences: duration neglect and peak-and-end effects. *Journal of Economic Behavior & Organization* 58, 1 (2005), 157-175.
17. Malone, T. *What makes things fun to learn? A study of intrinsically motivating computer games*. Department of Psychology, Stanford University, Palo Alto, CA, 1980.
18. McAuley, J. *Perception of Time as Phase: Toward and Adaptive-Oscillator Model of Rhythmic Pattern Processing*. Computer Science and Cognitive Science, Indiana University, Bloomington, IN, 1995.
19. Nasiry, J. and Popescu, I. Dynamic Pricing with Loss-Averse Consumers and Peak-End Anchoring. *Operations Research* 59, 6 (2011), 1361--1368.
20. Redelmeier, D.A. and Kahneman, D. Patients' memories of painful medical treatments: real-time and retrospective evaluations of two minimally invasive procedures. *Pain* 66, 1 (1996), 3-8.
21. Redelmeier, D.A., Katz, J. and Kahneman, D. Memories of colonoscopy: a randomized trial. *Pain* 104, 1 (2003), 187-194.
22. Reinecke, K. and Bernstein, A. Improving performance, perceived usability, and aesthetics with culturally adaptive user interfaces. *ACM ToCHI.* 18, 2 (2011), 1-29.
23. Rode, E., Rozin, P. and Durlach, P. Experienced and remembered pleasure for meals: Duration neglect but minimal peak, end (recency) or primacy effects. *Appetite* 49, 1 (2007), 18-29.
24. Statistica. 2012. *Why do online shoppers leave without paying*? Retrieved September, 2014, from http://www.statista.com/statistics/232285/reasons-for-online-shopping-cart-abandonment/.
25. Treisman, M., Faulkner, A., Naish, P.L.N. and Brogan, D. The internal clock: evidence for a temporal oscillator underlying time perception with some estimates of its characteristic frequency. *Perception* 19, 6 (1990), 705-743.
26. Venkatesh, V., Morris, M.G., Davis, G.B. and Davis, F.D. User Acceptance of Information Technology: Toward a Unified View. *MIS Quart*. 27, 3 (2003), 425-478.
27. Vierordt, K. *Der Zeitsinn nach Versuchen*. Laupp, H, Tubingen, 1868.
28. Weybrew, B.B. The Zeigarnik Phenomenon Revisited: Implications for Enhancement of Morale. *Perceptual and Motor Skills* 58, 1 (1984), 223--226.
29. Zimmermann, P. *Beyond Usability – Measuring Aspects of User Experience*, Swiss Federal Institute of Technology Zurich, 2008.

Survival Analysis: Objective assessment of Wait Time in HCI

Siddhartha Asthana
Indraprastha Institute of Information Technology, Delhi
siddharthaa@iiitd.ac.in

Pushpendra Singh
Indraprastha Institute of Information Technology, Delhi
psingh@iiitd.ac.in

Parul Gupta
Indraprastha Institute of Information Technology, Delhi
parul1370@iiitd.ac.in

ABSTRACT
Waiting for the completion of a system process is an everyday experience. While waiting, a system provides feedback to the user about ongoing processes through temporal metaphors (Progress bar, Busy icons, etc.). One of the key performance requirements for temporal metaphors is to retain the user till the process completes. Researchers have evaluated these metaphors through subjective means, and objective assessment has not been well explored. In this paper, we present *survival analysis* as an objective assessment method to evaluate temporal metaphors. Through a field experiment, we demonstrate the application of survival analysis and empirically establish that auditory progress bar (a temporal metaphor for audio interfaces) works for callers of a distress helpline. To the best of our knowledge, it is the first study on distress callers. The paper further discusses the applicability of survival analysis for evaluating temporal metaphors and wait time experiments for other applications, tasks, and settings.

Author Keywords
Temporal metaphors, objective assessment, wait-time, time-perception

ACM Classification Keywords
H.5.2. Information Interfaces and Presentation (e.g. HCI): User Interfaces - Evaluation/methodology

INTRODUCTION
Waiting Time in HCI is an important aspect of system design to enhance User eXperience (UX) when the interaction between the system and its user is temporarily interrupted (e.g., loading of web page, file download, or waiting for the arrival of live agents at call centers) [27]. Literature suggests that providing feedback to a user on the system state, especially during these waiting periods, increases system usability [37]. Depending on the type of system, several temporal metaphors (visual progress bar [20], auditory progress bar [26], non-speech waiting cues [19], etc.) have been designed to provide such feedback to the user. The objective of introducing a temporal metaphor in the system is to mitigate the adverse effect of wait time so that the system can successfully hold the user until the waiting process completes. For a researcher, it is imperative to measure the effectiveness of such metaphors in holding users of the system. However, there are no standard guidelines to measure the effectiveness of a proposed metaphor. Traditionally, researchers have studied the effectiveness of these metaphors through several subjective measures including user preference [26, 13], time perception [20, 19], satisfaction [22], acceptability [13], and appropriateness [16]. At the same time, the use of objective measures has not been explored much to evaluate the effectiveness of such systems.

CHI 2015, April 18 - 23, 2015, Seoul, Republic of Korea

ACM 978-1-4503-3145-6/15/04...$15.00.
http://dx.doi.org/10.1145/2702123.2702428

In this paper, we discuss the implications of waiting time on HCI with a focus on the evaluation of temporal metaphors using objective measures. We discuss the observation that existing subjective measures are susceptible to several evaluation conditions (like cognitive load, the paradigm used for estimation [11], etc.) that can bring variations in the outcomes of the experiments. Further, there are several important objective outcomes that cannot be inferred from subjective measures like *"for what time duration can the proposed temporal metaphor hold users, on average"*. Thus, we emphasize the need for objective measures to generate objective outcomes in the study. In this paper, we study the objective assessment of temporal metaphors through a real world experiment of an auditory progress bar (*a temporal metaphor for audio interfaces*). Designing an auditory progress bar (APB) is a challenging task for researchers as the system interface does not support any visual feedback. APBs have been extensively studied in the context of *telephone hold environment*, where callers have to wait for the arrival of a live agent [26]. With the increasing use of call centers/helplines in daily life, the use of APB is becoming critical in engaging users of such systems so that they continue with the call and do not hang up. Lab studies [26] and field experiments, at bank call centers [15], have shown that APB can encourage callers to wait longer.

In this paper, we propose the use of survival analysis of actual wait time as an objective metric to evaluate temporal metaphors for holding the user. Survival analysis (or Life Testing) is an established method to deal with time-based data in the areas of medical science and reliability engineering [25]. Through Survival analysis, we fill the void of objective assessment of wait-time in HCI. We discuss the suitability of survival analysis for handling time-based data and censored observation while dealing with temporal metaphors. We demonstrate the usefulness of survival analysis to generate probabilistic estimates about a temporal metaphor's ability to hold a user for a given time and we show how to compare two or more temporal metaphors using descriptive and inferential statistics generated by survival analysis. To the best of our knowledge, it is the first study on the objective evaluation of temporal metaphors and investigating the effectiveness of APB for distress callers. Through survival analysis, the outcome of the field experiment empirically establishes that a speech based auditory progress bar can hold helpline callers for longer.

IMPLICATIONS OF WAITING TIME ON HCI

Despite technological improvements, the waiting time in interactive systems is unavoidable. Strong implications of waiting time on Human Computer Interaction has made researchers investigate acceptable waiting time, the significance of giving feedback on the waiting time to the user, and the design of temporal metaphors to provide better feedback.

Acceptable waiting time: The HCI community on acceptable waiting time has almost agreed on a 10 seconds threshold, beyond which users do not effectively focus on the task anymore [32]. In a study conducted on web users, Bouch et al., in agreement with Nielsen [32], demonstrated that 10 seconds is unsatisfactory for users [12]. The 10-second threshold holds for the systems with no visual representation (i.e. audio only) as well e.g., [16] showed that for waits more than eight seconds, users should be given speech-based delay information.

Feedback on waiting: It is now widely accepted that giving feedback on waiting time is considered satisfactory, and it increases the usability of the system [32] and the time the user is willing to wait [31, 12]. However, the temptation to give users a detailed feedback can be counterproductive. Giving a detailed feedback focuses the user's attention on the passing time, which makes the wait seem longer [13].

Temporal Metaphors: Feedback on waiting can be conveyed through several metaphors like icons [⌛], text messages [*Loading, please wait..*], audio messages [🔊 *Your Call is important to us, please wait*], progress bars [▭], etc. Among the various metaphors, progress bars [30] are dominant in current user interfaces. Research shows that, among the different types of feedback given to users, progress bars performed best in terms of acceptability for user attention and user preference [13, 19, 22]. Analogous to a visual progress bar, for interactive speech applications that lack visual display, researchers have designed auditory progress bars that include speech-based cues [29], non-speech-based cues [34, 26], etc.

EVALUATION OF WAIT TIME: SOURCE OF VARIATION

An experiment on the evaluation of waiting time involves a users' reporting about the time perceived by them (also known as subjective time). Subjective time is a complex cognitive process, and user assessment depends on several factors. Lallemand et al. have discussed the contribution of cognitive psychology to better understand subjective time [27]. Here, we discuss how these different cognitive processes and assumptions can bring variations in results and their interpretations for a waiting time experiment.

Mode of Experiment

There are two paradigms to conduct a waiting time experiment for subjective assessment, viz., prospective and retrospective paradigms. In a prospective paradigm, users are informed at the beginning of the experiment that they have to estimate the duration of a given time interval. In the retrospective approach, users are not aware of the time estimation task until the end of the experiment. Studies have shown that retrospective and prospective paradigms have opposite effects on the duration judgment [8, 9]. Block et al. have tried to investigate the reason for performance differences due to different paradigms used for subjective assessment and concluded that in prospective paradigm, a greater cognitive load on user decreases the subjective-to-objective time duration ratio whereas in retrospective paradigm a greater cognitive load increases the subjective-to-objective time duration ratio [11]. This performance difference due to the choice of paradigm used for conducting an experiment and the lack of standard methods to translate results from one paradigm to another makes it difficult to compare studies conducted in the past.

Cognitive Workload on the User

The subjective assessment of the time depends a lot on the attention given by a user on the passage of time. Thus, time is perceived as passing slowly when attention is focused primarily on time [10]. The amount of attention on temporal information is less if attention on processing non-temporal information is more, due to a high cognitive demand of a specific task [7, 40]. Thus, the subjective time judgment depends a lot on cognitive workload on the user. Further, users differ from each other in terms of cognitive capabilities, which means that for the same task, different users may perceive different cognitive loads. Thus, for the same experiment, different users report different perceived (subjective) times. Thus comparing results for performance difference of temporal metaphors based on different studies in literature is difficult, as it is not certain whether the difference in results is achieved due to a different system or different cognitive capabilities of their respective user set. One way to avoid such problems is by having a properly sampled large number of users in each experiment, but that is costly and not always feasible. Another approach may be to report cognitive load on the users during the experiment along with other experimental results. There are different psychometric scales to measure cognitive load on the user, such as the Subjective Mental Effort Questionnaire (SMEQ), also referred to as the Rating Scale for Mental Effort (RSME) [42], and NASA-TLX [21]. However, little is known about the representativeness of these scales in terms of the actual cognitive load on the users and the distribution of observed load on the user again in terms of how much is due to the system and how much is due to the difference in cognitive capabilities of a user.

Retention Delay

Retention delay is the duration of time beyond which information cannot be retained by the short-term memory of the human brain. A waiting time experiment conducted with or without retention delay may produce different results. As the human brain does not remember past events in a consistent and linear manner [1, 12], event recall happens with selectivity and bias, where it is easier to remember the first or last moments of an event than those happening in between. Initial moments are stored in long-term memory, and the last or recent moments are stored in short-term memory. Short-term memory is less stable and can be affected by a delay of more than 15-30 seconds (or retention delay); it can also be affected by an interfering activity [17]. Results for a retrospective evaluation after retention delay will solely be based on the long-term memory [27]. However, if the evaluation is done without retention delay both long-term and short-term memory affect the subjective assessment.

Psychological Models for Subjective Time

Most of the literature on waiting time is focused on explaining the distortion in subjective time perception (under or overestimation). Several models have been proposed to study the perceived time based on the existence of the internal clock [2, 14, 39].The attentional gate model proposed by Zakay et al. [41] is considered the best to explain subjective time in HCI [27]. This model consists of a pacemaker (internal clock) and an accumulator connected by a switch as described in the model proposed by Triesman [38]. Zakay's model assumes an additional gate (in comparison to Triesman's model) between the pacemaker and switch. The subjective time depends upon the way a person divides his/her attention between information encoded by a temporal information processor and non-temporal information processor. The gate takes temporal information into account and co-ordinates activation of the switch. Thus, different researchers may make use of different models to explain their results and develop different theories. For a comprehensive literature review of the models, readers are referred to [10, 18, 28].

A WAY FORWARD

The same experiment, when conducted by different researchers, may produce different results based upon different configurations that they choose for evaluation. We do not argue which one is better, but we emphasize that even when researchers explicitly mention the evaluation methodology they have chosen, it is not easy to compare the results with other experiments conducted with different evaluation methodology. As an implication of this, the literature may seem to have inconsistent findings and conflicting theories. A similar observation was made by Kortum et al. while designing an auditory progress bar (APB) for a telephonic system [26]. They mentioned that ten different studies conducted for an auditory progress bar had mixed performances (over and underestimation of time) and listener preferences. We believe that subjective analysis is a good method for understanding the attitude and preference of a user, but researchers also need to incorporate an objective analysis method for a variety of reasons. First, objective methods are less influenced by individual users, i.e., they can capture the actual behavior of a user with the system rather than user perception about the system. Second, it is less time-consuming to collect and analyze objective data for a large set of users. Third, there may be some system aspects that users cannot assess or report–for instance, *how long a system is able to hold users to wait*–and various probabilistic and statistical insights, like *the probability that a user will wait for y seconds*, cannot be assessed by users. Hence, an objective evaluation of a system needs to be integrated with the traditional subjective usability assessment methods. In this paper, we address this gap by introducing an objective evaluation technique that can generate such insights.

We propose the use of actual wait time rather than perceived wait time as an evaluation metric for objective assessment. Subjective studies were largely focused around the perceived wait time, and the use of actual wait time is limited to calculate the mis-estimation (over or underestimation) in perceived wait time [26]. In subjective studies, low perceived time is desirable which is inferred as the system can hold a user for longer. But by merely inspecting the perceived wait time, it is difficult to guess how long a user will actually wait because perceived wait time is dependent on factors other than actual wait time like the cognitive load and paradigm used (retrospective or prospective) for time estimation [11]. Hence, in our proposed objective assessment we tend to measure the actual wait time of the caller directly instead of estimating it from perceived wait time or other perceptual variables. Based on the requirement, we propose the use of survival analysis (a branch of statistics) [25] as an evaluation technique for objective assessment of the wait time in HCI. It is a statistical tool for time-based analysis and has the capability to deal with censored data. With survival analysis, we can quantify the effect of temporal metaphors, judge its statistical significance, and generate probabilistic estimates of holding a user with the passage of time.

Conceptual Foundation

Here, we describe the important terms and concepts which will showcase the appropriateness and applicability of survival analysis. For a detailed description of survival analysis, readers are referred to [25].

Time Based Events and Censored Data

A time-based event is defined as an event whose time of occurrence is the interest of study. The case in which the time of an event is known below or above an observed value but the exact time of the event is unknown is called **censored observation** [25]. For instance, in the case of temporal metaphors, the outcome of interest is to find out the tolerable wait time before a user quits or cancels an ongoing process or transaction. Here, the event to observe is the canceling or aborting of an ongoing process by the user. Different users will quit or cancel the process after waiting for a certain time, which may differ among users. The wait time of different users can be used to statistically compute the tolerable wait time for the users with respect to a temporal metaphor. However, for certain users we will not observe any event if they wait till the completion of the process. In this scenario, we know only that the user waits till a certain time but do not know exactly how long she is willing to wait. In statistical analysis, such data points are termed as the **Right censored data** as the tolerable waiting time for a user is more than the observed time by an unknown value.

There are two challenges in analyzing data pertaining to a time-based event. The first challenge is to deal with censored observations and accommodate them with normal observations in the analysis. The second challenge is that we cannot expect data to be distributed normally as with increasing wait time lesser number of users will be willing to wait.

Survival Function and Probability Estimation

Survival function is the function that relates the probability of an event with the time estimated from time-based data discussed above. Conventionally, a Survival function F(x) is defined as,

$$F(x) = Pr(X > x) \tag{1}$$

where, X is a random variable denoting the time of event occurrence and Pr(X>x) is the probability that the event will occur later than the specified time x. For estimating such survival function, we will be using Kaplan-Meir [25], a non-parametric maximum likelihood estimator, which is used in several fields of science, like medical science for estimating the life of a patient, in reliability engineering to measure the time of part failure, etc. [25]. To estimate the probability for plotting the survival function, the following procedure is followed:

- Arrange the time-based data in ascending order and denote the time value as $x_0, x_1, ..., x_n$.
- At every event, calculate the probability using following recurrence relation:

$$F(x_i) = \frac{r_i - n_i}{r_i} F(x_{i-1}) \tag{2}$$

  where r_i is the total number of events (including censored events) having time value $\geq x_i$, and n_i is the number of events (non-censored) $> x_{i-1}$ but smaller than x_i.

Size of Effect

To quantify the size of the effect of temporal metaphors on wait time behavior of users, we can calculate mean and median survival time from survival analysis (see descriptive measures of survival experience [25]).These terms are defined as:

- *Mean survival time:* It is calculated as the area under the survival curve [25]. It is one of the measurements to estimate the central tendency of the data distribution of wait time and represents how long a user waits on the system on an average.
- *Median survival time:* It is calculated as the smallest survival time for which the probability of the survival function is less than or equal to 0.5 [25]. Similar to mean, it is another factor that measures the central tendency of data distribution but is less susceptible to extreme values.

Statistical Significance

Logrank [6], a non-parametric test, is widely used in survival analysis to estimate whether the effect has statistical significance or not. It is a form of the Chi-square test and the hypothesis testing tool to compare two survival distributions. It calculates a test statistic for a null hypothesis (*survival curves for different groups are the same*) based on the following relation:

$$Statistic(Logrank) = \frac{\sum(Expected - Observed)^2}{\sigma^2(Expected - Observed)} \tag{3}$$

where $\sum(Expected - Observed)^2$ is the summation of the square of the difference between the expected number of events and observed number of events for each time point, and $\sigma^2(Expected - Observed)$ is the variance of difference between expected and observed events.

FIELD EXPERIMENT: OBJECTIVE ASSESSMENT OF AUDITORY PROGRESS BARS

In this section, we demonstrate the proposed objective evaluation technique using survivability analysis as applied on the actual wait time to generate statistical and probabilistic insight about the Auditory Progress Bar designed to handle waiting time in a telephonic queue.

Auditory Progress Bar

The Auditory Progress Bar (APB) is analogous to the Visual Progress Bar for systems with no visual representations. APB is a temporal metaphor where sound must carry the entire information load to convey temporal information. The use of the Auditory Progress Bar (APB) can be seen in telephonic queues at a call center in the form of background music, apology messages or estimated delay announcements. APBs can be broadly divided into speech based and non-speech based cues. Researchers have studied and compared various speech and non-speech based APB designs:

Non-speech cues: Peres et al. investigated building an auditory progress bar that has pleasing aesthetic and good temporal qualities [34]. In a lab study, they experimented with different audio tones like sine, cello, and songs of varying pitch and duration and measured user preference on a seven-point Likert scale and system performance based on perceived waiting time and actual waiting time. In a similar experiment, Harrison et al. explored nine different combinations of linear and non-linear tones compared against each other to determine the tone perceived as fast [19]. The study concluded that, among each pair of tones, whichever tone users encounter first is perceived as faster. Fröhlich suggested that non-speech cues must be used to replace a silent wait of short duration (four to eight seconds) [16]. The study showed that for high waiting time, continuous indication by speech cues was more pleasant and appropriate than non-speech cues.

Speech cues: Feigin conducted an experiment that announced an expected waiting time (<1 min, 1 min, 2 min, etc.) at a high level of congestion in the call center of a US bank and recommended the callers to return to IVR for self-service [15]. It was shown that approximately 1.3% of the total callers returned to IVR and the others opted to join the agent queue. The announcement resulted in the lowering of the initial high abandonment rate, maintaining the callers beyond the 70 to 80-second mark, and a new trend of abandonment around 170-180 seconds. Armony et al. have studied the equilibrium associated with the delay announcement [5]. The equilibrium exists in the sense of the cyclic dependency

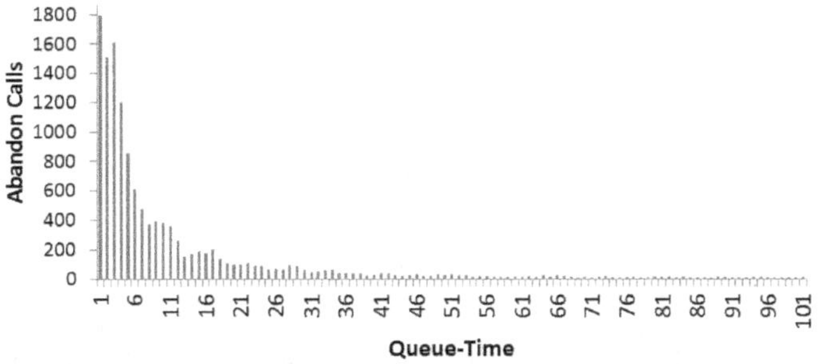

Figure 1. Distribution of Queue-time (in seconds) of abandoned call in pre-experiment data collection

of three factors, viz., the caller's response to the delay announcement, the system performance depending upon the caller's response, and the announcement depending upon system performance. Several other researchers have shown keen interest in developing ideas around delay announcements. Allon et al. have studied the impact of postponing the delay announcement in comparison to providing the delay announcement immediately [3]. They have shown that this postponement can help the call center maintain more credibility among callers and augment the resulting equilibrium in certain settings. In all the studies, the delay announcement from the call center is assumed to be of high credibility on the caller's side. However, theoretical research has also explored the effects on the queuing model if call centers provide vague and unverifiable information about delays to lure customers [4].

Speech vs. non-speech cues: Rafeli et al. explore the psychological aspects of different time fillers and their effect on the cognitive processes of the waiting caller by comparing delay announcements as a filler with two other time fillers - music and apology message [29]. Niida et al. measure the effectiveness of different time fillers on a visual display [33].

In this paper, we investigate the effect of speech-based APB on a distressed caller helpline. Next, we describe the distressed caller-helpline and our experimental design. Then we analyze the APB using survival analysis.

Helpline Background

In this section, we describe the background of the helpline to provide a better understanding of the type of callers and the context of the calls. Then, we report on the initial inspection of the data that we collected before the experiment.

181-Women in Distress Helpline

The state of Delhi is the national capital of India. To address women's concerns, the state of Delhi has etablished helplines such as 1091 (Delhi Police Women Helpline) and 23379181 (Delhi Commission for Women). Despite these helplines, however, women continue to find it difficult to gain quick access to information regarding police or other law enforcement agencies. To handle these issues, the state government of Delhi decided to start its supplementary helpline, named the *181 - Women in distress* helpline, to provide assistance to women in distress. The call center is managed by women call executives who are trained in handling women's issues and some legal advisors. The calls vary from seeking counseling over petty matters (e.g., verbal arguments within the family) to criminal assaults (dowry death, rape, etc.) as told to us by agents attending to the calls. The helpline provides advice and consultation to women and coordinates with other state agencies (police, legal aid, medical service, etc.) whenever needed for the fast resolution of women's complaints.

Helpline inspection

To understand the waiting behavior of callers, we analysed the helpline prior to experiment design. We analyzed 29,548 calls that the helpline had received in the past three months before the experiment. Out of the total calls, 13,428 were abandoned calls, i.e., calls that were not answered by any agent, and 16,120 were answered calls. We also observed that most of the callers try again, so the actual number of unanswered callers is not as high as it looks prima facie. To understand the system dynamics, in order to design our experiment better, we performed some basic analysis.

We analyzed waiting time (or queue-Time) for the abandoned calls and the answered calls separately. Figure 1 shows the distribution of abandoned calls based on queue time. For abandoned calls, we found that 95% of the calls had a queue time (waiting time) of less than 97 seconds. It shows that 95% callers on such helplines do not even wait 100 seconds, which reflects the impatience of callers due to stress. On the other hand, the waiting time in normal call centers could be as high as 40 to 50 minutes (as reported in a leading newspaper of the UK [1]). This shows that the nature of helpline callers is different from a normal call center. We want to reduce the number of abandoned calls as these calls are important for the purpose of the helpline. Though many callers return, it will still be better to serve them at the first instant. One solution is to increase the number of call executives at the time of rush hour, but due to several reasons, the number of executives cannot be increased. Thus, we would like callers to wait more so that they can talk with a helpline executive and get their problems resolved. Literature suggests that the speech based auditory progress bar announcing the estimated wait time can encourage callers to wait more in call centers of the bank [15]. However, to the best of our knowledge, this is the first study that investigates whether such approaches work for callers of helplines who may be impatient due to stress.

Research Ethics: We took the appropriate permissions from the concerned authority managing the helpline and followed ethical practices in conducting this research. Authors are familiar with US-based IRB approval. Though such approval is not required for conducting research in India, we were very much aware of the sensitivity of the data and implications of mishandling it; all the precautions were taken to ensure that the privacy of the callers remained intact. We did not access case information details, audio recordings related to the call, or any personally identifiable information about the callers. Except for the delay message, we did not change anything in the helpline setup, and our experiment did not affect the normal working of the helpline.

Experiment Design

We designed one APB that gives a periodic delay announcement and compared it with the base line system (BL).

[1]`http://www.mirror.co.uk/news/uk-news/big-six-hold-times-energy-3168050`

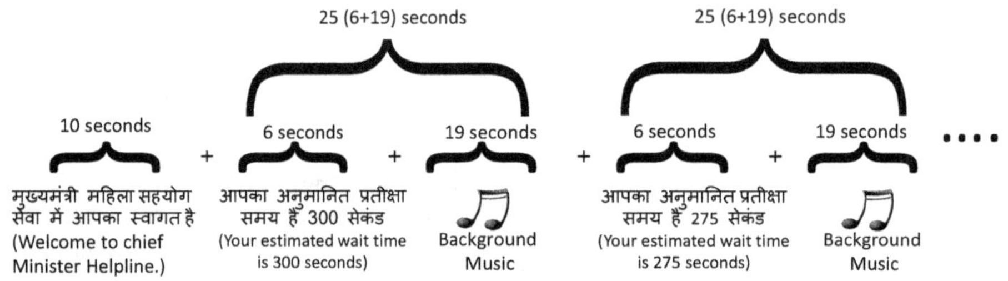

Figure 2. Functioning of APB: First callers are greeted with a 10 seconds welcome message followed by first message about an estimated delay of 300 seconds. Each message about estimated delay takes 6 seconds. Thus, a caller with Queue-time greater than 16 seconds receives at least one delay announcement. Every estimated delay message is followed by background music of 19 seconds. The repeated announcement of delay messages by subsequently deleting 25 seconds from the previous estimate continues till the estimate reaches zero. After that caller only hears the background music.

1. *Baseline (BL):* This system is the existing system of the 181 helpline, which does not provide any delay announcement to the caller. It has a pre-recorded audio message that repeatedly plays a welcome message to the caller in the Hindi language. The message translates to
"Welcome to the Chief Minister's Women Helpline!!"

2. *APB:* This is our proposed system, which announces an expected initial waiting time of 300 seconds to each caller. System keeps updating waiting time after every 25 seconds. The value of each announcement against actual wait of caller is shown in Figure 2. It is a simple system which deducts 25 seconds from the last announced time and plays it in subsequent announcements as the time left for the caller. After the 12 ($300/25 = 12$) announcements, actual wait time becomes zero and hence system stops announcing any delay. The time for duration (300 seconds) and interval (25 seconds) of APB design is based on following considerations.
   - Duration: Literature suggests to estimate the wait time for an announcement based on coverage probability (β) so that actual wait time never exceeds the announced time with probability β [24]. To ensure that the actual wait never crosses the announced wait, we would have to announce wait-time corresponding to $\beta = 1$. However, due to the exponential distribution of wait-time, the value corresponding to $\beta = 1$ will lie at infinity. We did analysis of 29,548 calls that are described in previous subsection (*Helpline inspection*) to estimate the wait time for announcement so that value of β is close to 1. The minimum value which covers sufficiently large number of callers in our system is 300 seconds ($\beta = 0.999$).
   - Interval: Choice of interval is influenced by two aspects covered in [13] and [16]. Literature suggests constant attention towards the passage of time makes the wait time perceived as longer [13]. Hence, the value of intervals between the announcements should be high as every announcement draws the caller's attention towards the passage of time. On the other side, Fröhlitch et al. indicates that the wait time greater than 30 seconds risks a potential hang-up [16]. Nah et al. quoted another study that also indicates a 30 second threshold in another context [31]. Thus, we chose a high value of interval [13] that was less than 30 seconds [16, 31] and perfectly divided the duration (300s).

We designed to route every alternate call to the same system. For each new call, the system generates a numerical call ID in an incremental fashion. We took each new call as a different call even if it came from some previous number logged in our database and assigned it to one of the systems alternatively. To preserve the privacy of the caller, the system anonymized the caller-ID (telephone number) to a different numerical ID before storing it in the database. Thus, repeated calls from the same number could be identified but reverse mapping to the phone number was not possible.

Data Collection

For the analysis, we collected data for 1 month (6th August - 5th September 2014). The system logged the following call attributes:

- Caller ID: For each call connected to our system, we logged the anonymized caller id of the telephone number.
- Time stamps: For each call, we logged the time stamps of the call's start and end.
- System allocation: For each call, we logged the system name that was allocated, i.e., BL or APB.
- Announcement Details: We logged the number of announcement messages listened to during each call and the corresponding value announced in each announcement along with the time stamp of each announcement.
- Queue Time: We explicitly logged the time spent by each caller on the system waiting for an agent to answer her calls.
- Call Status: For each call, we logged whether it was answered by an agent or abandoned by the caller.

In one month, we received a total of 8,748 calls. There was a large number of calls that got answered or disconnected with waiting time (or Queue Time) $<=$ 16 seconds and hence did not receive any delay announcement (calls with Queue Time $>=$ 16 seconds received at least one delay announcement, see Figure 2). As we want to compare the performance of the system when callers got a delay announcement to its performance when callers did not get any announcement, we removed calls with Queue Time $<=$ 16 seconds. For consistency in analysis and comparability between the systems, we removed such calls from both the systems and were left with 1,353 calls.

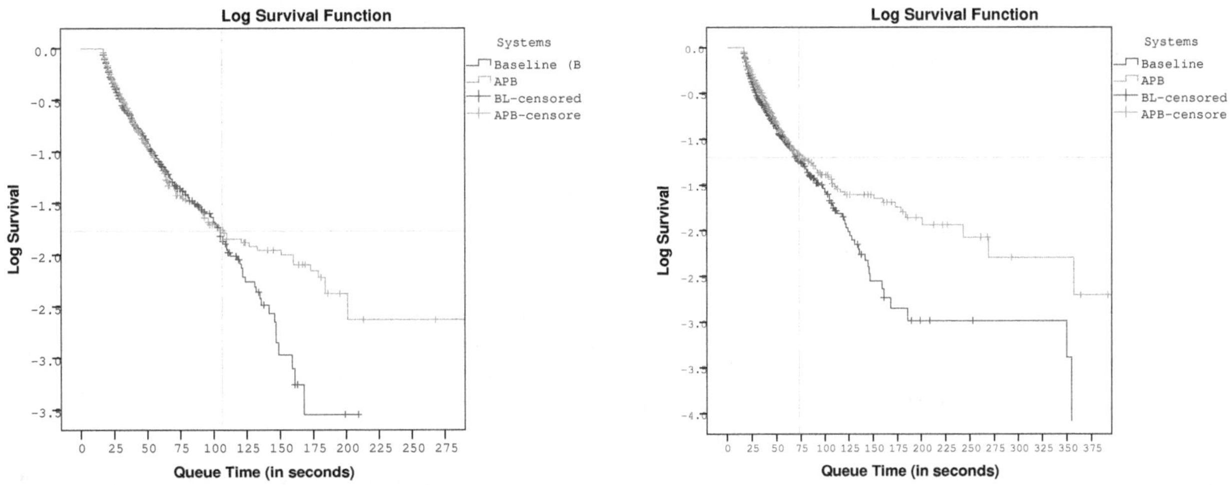

(a) Total Calls (b) First Calls

Figure 3. Survival Curve: A comparison of survivability of callers on Baseline, and APB. Markers on each curve show the corresponding censored (Answered calls) data.

Results and Analysis

Here, we present the analysis of 1,353 calls. Table 1 represents the distribution of calls between the two systems and the number of calls answered and abandoned on each system. These 1,353 calls represent the total calls from 1,082 callers, where some callers called more than once. The subsequent calls from the same caller may have a priming effect on their waiting behavior, based on their experience of the first call. To avoid any priming effect on the calls analysis, we have also presented the analysis for the data where only first call of each caller is considered. The distribution of the 1,082 remaining calls (i.e., considering only first call of each caller) is shown in Table 2. In the rest of the section, we will present the analysis for total calls and first callers separately.

System	Calls		
	Answered	Abandon	Total
Baseline	255	471	726
APB	241	386	627
Total	496	857	1353

Table 1. Total Calls

System	Calls		
	Answered	Abandon	Total
Baseline	208	383	591
APB	207	284	491
Total	415	667	1082

Table 2. First Call

Abandon Rate

A caller who waits longer has more of a chance of her call getting answered than a caller who waits for a shorter duration of time. To observe which system (APB or Baseline) can hold a caller longer, Abandon Rate is defined as the percentage of total calls that were unanswered. Hence, a better system will observe an abandon rate lower than the other system. Based on the analysis of total calls (see Table 1), the abandon rate of APB (61.56% i.e., $386/627$) is less than the Baseline (64.87% i.e. $471/726$) by approximately 3%, but results were not statistically significant ($\chi^2(1, N = 1353) = 1.59$, $p = 0.2$). On analyzing the first call only, we found the abandon rate of APB (57.8% i.e., $284/491$) was much lower than the Baseline (64.8% i.e. $383/591$) ,and the results were statistically significant ($\chi^2(1, N = 1082) = 5.5$, $p = 0.019$). This indicates that APB performed better than Baseline in holding the callers. However, a caller waiting time is just one of the factors, and there are other factors, such as congestion in the line and number of agents which also affect the abandon rate of the system. Thus, we will further analyze the system for more insights.

Survival Analysis

In this section, we demonstrate the use of survival analysis techniques as applied to wait time (Queue-Time) data collected in the experiment.

Probability Estimation

We did a survival analysis (Kaplan-Meier) to analyze the probability of callers waiting X seconds or more in the queue across different systems. In this analysis, the *queue time* is the *survival time* of the caller, *call abandonment* is the *observed event*, and *answered calls* are treated as *right censored data*[2]. We did a survival analysis of total calls and calls that were left after removing repeated calls from the same telephone number.

Figure 3a shows the estimated probability of callers waiting for a particular time (in seconds) on two different systems using total calls. The performance difference can be seen between the two systems for Queue Time > 100 seconds where the probability that callers will wait on APB is more than the Baseline. The same performance difference can be seen much earlier (around Queue Time = 60 seconds) when only first calls are considered (see Figure 3b).

[2]In this experiment, the queue time of answered calls represents right censored data as caller could have waited more than the queue time but unknown by how much.

	Mean[a]				Median			
			95% Confidence Interval				95% Confidence Interval	
	Estimate	Std. Error	Lower Bound	Upper Bound	Estimate	Std. Error	Lower Bound	Upper Bound
Baseline	63.318	4.199	55.087	71.548	39.000	2.187	34.714	43.286
APB	76.522	5.910	64.938	88.106	39.000	1.595	35.874	42.126
Overall	69.737	3.623	62.637	76.837	39.000	1.379	36.296	41.704

Table 3. Means and Medians for Survival Time based on total calls

	Mean[a]				Median			
			95% Confidence Interval				95% Confidence Interval	
	Estimate	Std. Error	Lower Bound	Upper Bound	Estimate	Std. Error	Lower Bound	Upper Bound
Baseline	74.100	7.364	59.667	88.533	40.000	2.712	34.684	45.316
APB	94.063	7.876	78.627	109.499	43.000	2.582	37.938	48.062
Overall	90.125	7.783	74.870	105.379	42.000	1.661	38.744	45.256

a. Estimation is limited to the largest survival time if it is censored.

Table 4. Means and Medians for Survival Time based on first calls

Size of Effect

We used the mean[3] and median[4] of probabilistic data generated through survival function to quantify the effect of different systems on caller waiting time. Table 3 shows the mean and median estimates of survival time for each system using total calls. The mean of APB (76.52 seconds) is approximately 13 seconds more than the Baseline (63.13 seconds). This shows that on an average, APB can hold each caller 13 seconds more than the Baseline. We observed that both the systems have the same median of 39 seconds that is evident as the left half of the survivability curve is almost the same (see Figure 3). This can also be interpreted as if the helpline has sufficient agents where the waiting time of callers is below 39 seconds, then we will not observe any performance difference between the two systems.

We did the same analysis for *first calls*, and estimated mean and median are shown in Table 4. We can see a wider gap in the performance. The mean of APB (94.06 seconds) is approximately 20 seconds more than the Baseline (74.1 seconds). Similar to the analysis on total calls, median values are close to each other.

A performance difference of 13 seconds or 20 seconds (considering only first calls) may not impact full performance difference for a normal call center, but it is a considerable improvement for helpline callers where the average waiting time is less than 64 seconds (see mean of BL in Table 3) or 75 seconds (considering first call, see mean of BL in Table 4). It is also evident from the abandon rate, which was reduced to 3-7% (see previous subsection). Further, optimization on the APB design may bring better performance.

Statistical Significance

We did further analysis to check the statistical significance of our observed performance difference through Chi-Square statistics, i.e., Logrank (Mantel-Cox). While testing total calls for statistical significance, we did not observe any difference (χ^2 (1, 1353)=0.945, p=0.33). However, on analyzing the data of first calls, we find the results are statistically significant (χ^2 (1, 1082)=5.058, $\mathbf{p<0.05}$).

[3]Mean survival time is estimated as the area under the survival curve

[4]The median survival time is calculated as the smallest survival time for which the survivor function is less than or equal to 0.5

We further analyzed the reason for not achieving statistical significance with total calls. We believe one of the reasons could be the repeated calls in the data set. We hypothesize that a caller can estimate the waiting time in subsequent calls based on one's experience of the first call. Thus, irrespective of the system, callers have sufficient information on the waiting time. To check this, we analyzed 271 repeated calls (i.e. first calls subtracted from total calls). We did not find any statistically significant differences (χ^2 (1, 271)=0.003, p>0.05) in the two systems. The repeated calls on APB had a lower mean (83.38 seconds, 95% CI[52.25, 114.51]) and median (40 seconds, 95% CI[34.47, 45.53]) than the first calls.

DISCUSSION

This section reflects on our results and discusses possible interpretations and limitations of it. We discuss how our proposed method can be generalized to other tasks, application types, and settings.

We showed that the user wait time data can be used objectively to evaluate the performance of temporal metaphors for their ability to hold callers. We showed survival analysis, a lifetime estimation technique, can be used for such purposes to generate probabilistic and statistical insights.

The first concept that we discussed is a survival curve. It is a continuous time-based evaluation of temporal metaphors. It denotes the probability a user will wait for a given time. Several insights can be drawn from this while comparing temporal metaphors. For instance, if curves are non-overlapping [] then the temporal metaphor with a curve on a higher side along ordinate (Y-axis) represents better performance. In the case of overlapping curves [], let's say intersecting at time **t** on the X-axis can be used to make a thoughtful decision on which temporal metaphor should be used based on the average wait time of task for which that temporal metaphor is employed. If average wait time of task is less than **t**, then the metaphor whose survival curve is at the higher side for wait time less than **t** should be used. Otherwise, if average wait time of task is greater than **t**, then the metaphor whose survival curve is at the higher side for wait time greater than **t** should be used. An important underlying assumption for statistical evaluation of the survival curve that overlapping curves violate is proportional hazard. If survival curves cross each other, then this is the evidence that hazards are not proportional. For such overlapping curves, the analysis should take into account the interaction effect and separate the analysis before and after the crossing. We refer the reader to [25] for hazard function and assumption of proportional hazards.

Second, we discussed quantifying the size of the effect of temporal metaphors on the wait time behavior of users. If a particular metaphor has performed well then quantifying it for the achieved difference in performance will further enhance the understanding of temporal metaphors. This may be valuable for practitioners and researchers. Such data needs to be reported with both the mean and median with their respective confidence intervals to have a better insight about the central tendency of the data. Medians may be good to report in non-Gaussian or positively skewed data (as in task time data in usability studies [36]), but sometimes due to resistance to extreme values, they do not capture the performance difference adequately. This is evident from our results where the medians are close to each other even when systems have a significant difference in performance statistically. Thus, the mean can be helpful in quantifying the effect size.

We also discussed assessing the statistical significance of the performance difference. We employed the Logrank test for this purpose, which is a form of the Chi-square test and widely used in survival analysis and life estimation techniques [6]. There are other similar tests like the Wilcoxon-test and Tarone-ware test which can be used for different applications based on the need. These tests differ in sensitivity to the survival curve and put different weights to initial events and events that are happening later in the time. For more discussion on the comparison of Logrank and other applicable tests in survival analysis and the effect of right-censoring, please refer [35].

This objective evaluation method is applicable to other application types and is well suited for large-scale, automatic usability evaluations. Along with the event of interest, user wait time behavior can be automatically logged in system and software products. Automatic system logging enables a large-scale data collection for usability assessments without relying explicitly on user response through a form or survey.

CONCLUSION AND FUTURE WORK

This paper, in which we discuss waiting time in HCI with a focus on evaluation of temporal metaphors makes a three-fold contribution. First, we identify how evaluation based on subjective measures can be influenced by contextual variables like cognitive load, retention delay, paradigm used, etc. The research on wait time has not explored objective assessment techniques. We identified the need for an objective assessment technique to minimize the influence of any contextual variables, generating objective outcomes like *How long a user will wait*. Second, we developed a method for analyzing the wait time data using survival analysis, which can be the basis for an objective assessment based user's wait time rather than perceived time. Survival analysis or other lifetime estimation techniques (like Accelerated Failure Time Model [23] and Cox regression [25]) are popular among reliability engineers and medical scientists, and we have indicated its potential use in HCI for wait time experiment. Third, we demonstrated the use of the proposed objective assessment through a field experiment. We conducted this experiment at a women's helpline where callers are more impatient than callers at a standard call center probably due to stress (as indicated by data inspection of 29,548 calls). Based on our proposed objective assessment, we showed that temporal metaphors are useful in holding the callers longer, and the results were statistically significant. One of the limitations of our findings is that the majority of callers to 181-helpline are women who live in Delhi, and may resemble callers in a similar urban demography in terms of technology exposure and familiarity with call centers. Future studies will compare our approach to how they relate to subjective measures and test with temporal metaphors other than APB.

ACKNOWLEDGMENTS

Authors will like to acknowledge the support provided by TCS Research and ITRA project, funded by DEiTY, Government of India under grant with Ref. No. ITRA/15(57)/Mobile/HumanSense/01

REFERENCES

1. Allan, L. The perception of time. *Perception & Psychophysics 26*, 5 (1979), 340–354.
2. Allan, L. G. The influence of the scalar timing model on human timing research. *Behavioural Processes 44*, 2 (1998), 101 – 117.
3. Allon, G., and Bassamboo, A. The impact of delaying the delay announcements. *Operations research 59*, 5 (2011), 1198–1210.
4. Allon, G., Bassamboo, A., and Gurvich, I. "We will be right with you": Managing customer expectations with vague promises and cheap talk. *Operations research 59*, 6 (2011), 1382–1394.
5. Armony, M., Shimkin, N., and Whitt, W. The impact of delay announcements in many-server queues with abandonment. *Operations Research 57*, 1 (2009), 66–81.
6. Bland, J. M., and Altman, D. G. The logrank test. *BMJ 328*, 7447 (2004), 1073.
7. Block, F., and Gellersen, H. The impact of cognitive load on the perception of time. In *Proc. of the 6th Nordic Conference on Human-Computer Interaction*, NordiCHI '10 (2010).
8. Block, R. Prospective and retrospective duration judgment: The role of information processing and memory. In *Time, Action and Cognition*, vol. 66. Springer, 1992, 141–152.
9. Block, R., and Zakay, D. Prospective and retrospective duration judgments: A meta-analytic review. *Psychonomic Bulletin & Review* (1997), 184–197.
10. Block, R. A. *Cognitive models of psychological time*. Psychology Press, 2014.
11. Block, R. A., Hancock, P. A., and Zakay, D. How cognitive load affects duration judgments: A meta-analytic review. *Acta Psychologica* (2010).

12. Bouch, A., Kuchinsky, A., and Bhatti, N. Quality is in the eye of the beholder: Meeting users' requirements for internet quality of service. In *Proc. of the SIGCHI Conference on Human Factors in Computing Systems*, CHI '00 (2000).
13. Branaghan, R. J., and Sanchez, C. A. Feedback preferences and impressions of waiting. *Human Factors: The Journal of the Human Factors and Ergonomics Society 51*, 4 (2009), 528–538.
14. Church, R. M., and Broadbent, H. A. Alternative representations of time, number, and rate. *Cognition 37*, 12 (1990), 55 – 81. Special Issue Animal Cognition.
15. Feigin, P. D. Analysis of customer patience in a bank call center. Tech. rep., The Technion, Haifa, Israel, 2006.
16. Fröhlich, P. Dealing with system response times in interactive speech applications. In *CHI '05 Extended Abstracts on Human Factors in Computing Systems*, CHI EA '05 (2005).
17. Gaonac'h, D., and Larigauderie, P. *Mémoire et fonctionnement cognitif: la mémoire de travail*. Armand Colin, 2000.
18. Grondin, S. Timing and time perception: a review of recent behavioral and neuroscience findings and theoretical directions. *Attention, Perception, & Psychophysics 72*, 3 (2010), 561–582.
19. Harrison, C., Amento, B., Kuznetsov, S., and Bell, R. Rethinking the progress bar. In *Proc. of the 20th Annual ACM Symposium on User Interface Software and Technology*, UIST '07 (2007).
20. Harrison, C., Yeo, Z., and Hudson, S. E. Faster progress bars: Manipulating perceived duration with visual augmentations. In *Proc. of the SIGCHI Conference on Human Factors in Computing Systems*, CHI '10 (2010).
21. Hart, S. G., and Staveland, L. E. Development of nasa-tlx (task load index): Results of empirical and theoretical research. In *Human Mental Workload*, Advances in Psychology. North-Holland, 1988.
22. Hurter, C., Cowan, B. R., Girouard, A., and Riche, N. H. Active Progress Bar: Aiding the Switch to Temporary Activities. In *Proc. of the 26th Annual BCS Interaction Specialist Group Conference on People and Computers*, British Computer Society (2012), 99–108.
23. Jin, Z., Lin, D., Wei, L., and Ying, Z. Rank-based inference for the accelerated failure time model. *Biometrika 90*, 2 (2003), 341–353.
24. Jouini, O., Akin, Z., and Dallery, Y. Call centers with delay information: Models and insights. *Manufacturing & Service Operations Management* (2011), 534–548.
25. Kleinbaum, D. G., and Klein, M. *Survival analysis*. Springer, 1996.
26. Kortum, P., Peres, S. C., and Stallmann, K. Extensible auditory progress bar design: Performance and aesthetics. *Int'l Journal of Human-Computer Interaction 27*, 9 (2011), 864–884.
27. Lallemand, C., and Gronier, G. Enhancing User eXperience During Waiting Time in HCI: Contributions of Cognitive Psychology. In *Proc. of the Designing Interactive Systems Conference*, DIS '12 (2012).
28. Lejeune, H. Switching or gating? the attentional challenge in cognitive models of psychological time. *Behavioural Processes 44*, 2 (1998), 127 – 145.
29. Munichor, N., and Rafaeli, A. Numbers or apologies? customer reactions to telephone waiting time fillers. *Journal of Applied Psychology 92*, 2 (2007), 511.
30. Myers, B. A. The importance of percent-done progress indicators for computer-human interfaces. In *Proc. of the SIGCHI Conference on Human Factors in Computing Systems*, CHI '85 (1985).
31. Nah, F. F.-H. A study on tolerable waiting time: how long are web users willing to wait? *Behaviour & Information Technology 23*, 3 (2004), 153–163.
32. Nielsen, J. *Usability Engineering*. Morgan Kaufmann Publishers Inc., 1993.
33. Niida, S., Uemura, S., Nakamura, H., and Harada, E. Field study of a waiting-time filler delivery system. In *Proc. of the 13th Int'l Conference on Human Computer Interaction with Mobile Devices and Services*, ACM (2011), 177–180.
34. Peres, S., Kortum, P., and Stallmann, K. Auditory progress bars: Preference, performance and aesthetics. In *Proc. of the International Conference on Auditory Display (ICAD2007)* (2007).
35. Peto, R., and Peto, J. Asymptotically efficient rank invariant test procedures. *Journal of the Royal Statistical Society. Series A (General)* (1972), 185–207.
36. Sauro, J., and Lewis, J. R. Average task times in usability tests: What to report? In *Proc. of the SIGCHI Conference on Human Factors in Computing Systems*, CHI '10, ACM (2010), 2347–2350.
37. Scapin, D. L., and Bastien, J. C. Ergonomic criteria for evaluating the ergonomic quality of interactive systems. *Behaviour & Information technology* (1997), 220–231.
38. Treisman, M. Temporal discrimination and the indifference interval: Implications for a model of the "internal clock". *Psychological Monographs: General and Applied 77*, 13 (1963), 1.
39. Zakay, D. Gating or switching? gating is a better model of prospective timing (a response to switching or gating? by lejeune). *Behavioural Processes 50*, 1 (2000), 1 – 7.
40. Zakay, D. Attention and duration judgment. *Psychologie Bulletin Francaise 50* (2005), 65–79.
41. Zakay, D., and Block, R. A. Temporal cognition. *Current Directions in Psychological Science* (1997), 12–16.
42. Zijlstra, F. R. H. *Efficiency in Work Behaviour: A Design Approach for Modern Tools*. Delft University Press, 1993.

Deformable Interfaces for Performing Music

Giovanni Maria Troiano, Esben Warming Pedersen, Kasper Hornbæk
Department of Computer Science, University of Copenhagen
Njalsgade 128, Build 24, 5th floor, DK-2300 Copenhagen, Denmark
{giovanni, esbenwp, kash}@di.ku.dk

ABSTRACT
Deformable interfaces offer new possibilities for gestures, some of which have been shown effective in controlled laboratory studies. Little work, however, has attempted to match deformable interfaces to a demanding domain and evaluate them out of the lab. We investigate how musicians use deformable interfaces to perform electronic music. We invited musicians to three workshops, where they explored 10 deformable objects and generated ideas on how to use these objects to perform music. Based on the results from the workshops, we implemented sensors in the five preferred objects and programmed them for controlling sounds. Next, we ran a performance study where six musicians performed music with these objects at their studios. Our results show that (1) musicians systematically map deformations to certain musical parameters, (2) musicians use deformable interfaces especially to filter and modulate sounds, and (3) musicians think that deformable interfaces embody the parameters that they control. We discuss what these results mean to research in deformable interfaces.

Author Keywords
Deformable interfaces; user interfaces; music; controller; usefulness; user study.

ACM Classification Keywords
H.5.2 [Information Interfaces and Presentation]: User Interfaces.

INTRODUCTION
Deformable interfaces are emerging in the field of HCI, for instance as elastic displays [19], bendable smartphones [5], or soft controllers [11]. Because they are made of flexible materials, deformable interfaces allow for unique gestures such as crumpling [30], squeezing [9], and stretching [29], all of which would be impossible with rigid interfaces. Yet, it is unclear how and when deformable interfaces might be advantageous compared to rigid interfaces.

Existing prototypes of deformable interfaces have been used and evaluated mainly in the lab during controlled experiments [16]. While lab studies have helped to test prototypes in a systematic way, they provided little data on users' reactions in the wild or on the usefulness of deformations in a particular domain.

CHI 2015, April 18–23, 2015, Seoul, Republic of Korea.

ACM 978-1-4503-3145-6/15/04…$15.00.
http://dx.doi.org/10.1145/2702123.2702492

The present paper argues that a study of deformable interfaces conducted out of the lab would show more realistic use and responses from users, indicating when these interfaces can be useful and how they are used. We report such a study in the context of electronic music. We chose the music domain because much earlier work have explored deformable interfaces for music [4,7,10,26,35], and because performing music is a highly challenging and expressive real-time activity. Such a study will help understand how users take advantage of different materials, shapes, and deformations to control sounds.

To investigate the use of deformable interfaces for performing music, we run three workshops borrowing techniques from participatory design [3] to receive input from musicians on how to use deformable interfaces in music. Next, we give a set of interactive deformable interfaces to professional musicians, and ask them to use those to perform music at their studios. Also, to understand how musicians would incorporate deformable interfaces with their existing equipment, we allowed them to integrate the use of non-deformable interfaces (e.g., MIDI controllers) in their performances.

The present paper makes two contributions to research on deformable interfaces. First, we contribute design implications for deformable interfaces by reporting findings from three workshops on how different materials and shapes relate to musical features. Second, we contribute findings on the use of deformable interfaces out of the lab by reporting results from a performance study where musicians used deformable interfaces to play music and commented on their experiences. Since our primary goal is not develop new musical interfaces, we discuss how the results of the workshop and the performance study extend beyond the music domain and what they mean to research on deformable interfaces.

RELATED WORK
Deformable interfaces have been proposed as elastic displays [6,18,21,34], flexible and elastic hand-held devices [7,9,20,24,31,32], bendable smartphones [1,5,12,13], sponge and foam controllers [21,23], and music controllers [4,7,10,26,35]. Studies have shown how deformations can be used as input techniques for various applications in HCI,

including depth navigation on mobile devices [5], animation [28], and 3D modeling [25]. Several studies have evaluated deformable interfaces, for instance by exploring the effect of interfaces size and materials stiffness on users' interaction [14,16], users' preferred gestures [15,17,29,32], and the use of multi-touch input on deformable surfaces [2]. However, deformable interfaces have not yet proven to suit a specific domain and possibilities for experimentation are still open. Since we evaluate deformable interfaces in music performances in the present paper, we focus the rest of this section on reviewing related work that introduces deformable interfaces to music.

Deformable Interfaces in Music

Table 1 shows a summary of the key related work on deformable interfaces used in music. We choose these papers in particular because they appeared either at NIME or CHI conferences, providing results for research on both musical interfaces and deformable interfaces. We discuss these deformable interfaces focusing on: (1) materials and deformations, (2) sensing technology, and (3) their use in relation to music.

Materials and Deformations

Deformable interfaces need to resist extreme deformations while being able to be controlled effortlessly. Therefore, materials used to build them need to be both robust and flexible. Foam is soft, robust, and affords well deformations like squeeze, push, and twist. Foam has been used to build cubic [11] and spherical [9,10] deformable music interfaces, which sometimes were also covered with fabric [35] or woolen yarn [9], so as to deliver organic feel in touch. However, foam is not very stretchable and stretch deformation, if too extreme, might feel uncomfortable or even break the material. Fabric can be more flexible than foam; for instance, materials like lycra or elastane can be allow for extreme stretching because they are very elastic. However, fabric can wear or tear with prolonged use [7]. Rubber and silicone can endure more than fabric with repeated use and have been used to build shape-retaining deformable interfaces [26,37]. They allow for easy bending or twisting, but they can be hard to stretch. Sculpton [4] used flexible metal springs and wooden spheres covered in latex to create a soft music controller in the shape of tetrahedron, allowing for squeezing, stretching, and pressing. Clay has also been used for musical interaction [33]; it is shape-retaining and can be broken and rejoined. However, the above listed materials have been presented to users only individually and no previous studies attempted to investigate how users understand or react to different shapes and materials that deform.

Paper	Materials and Deformations	Technology	Use
Sonic Banana [21]	Rubber, (bend, twist, stretch)	Bend sensor	MIDI Controller
The Embroidered Music Ball [29]	Fabric, conductive thread, (squeeze, stretch)	Pressure sensor	MIDI Controller
A Malleable Interface [11]	Conductive foam, (poke, twist, press, squeeze)	Conductive foam, copper wire	Sound Controller
A Malleable Device [18]	Paper board, rubber, wood, (press, push)	Camera sensor	Data Sonification
Clay Tone [27]	Clay, (stretch, twist, squeeze, press)	Camera sensor	Sound Controller
Zstretch [7]	Fabric, wood, (stretch, squeeze, twist)	Resistive strain gauges	Sound Controller
MARSUI [30]	Silicone, metallic wire mesh, (bend)	Bend sensor	Auditory Feedback
The Music Ball Project [10]	Sponge, (squeeze)	Microphone	Sound Controller
NoiseBear [9]	Conductive foam, woolen yarn, (stretch, squeeze, twist)	EEG electrodes, conductive thread	Sound Controller
Sculpton [4]	Wooden spheres, metal springs, latex, (squeeze, stretch, press)	Slide potentiometer, light dependent resistor (LDR)	Sound Controller

Table 1: Key related work and their main four characteristics

Sensing Technology

Sensing deformations presents various challenges. To sense deformations, a camera-based approach may be used, or materials need to be either conductive or embedded with sensors. Bend sensors were embedded in Sonic Banana [26] to sense bend and twist. However, bend sensors are fragile at their terminal part and can break with frequent use. To overcome this problem, MARSUI [37] used electrical semi-conductive tape as custom-made bend sensor. Kiefer used conductive foam to sense various degrees of pressure and squeeze [11]. NoiseBear [9] improved the robustness of Kiefer's design by adding conductive threads and cushion stuffing, so as to lower the latency of the conductive foam. Zstretch [7] used resistive strain gauges sewn at the edge of a lycra cloth in order to detect stretch. However, this approach presented problems over time, such as lowered sensitivity and the need for frequent repairs. Sculpton [4] embedded a slide potentiometer in its first version and light dependent resistor (LDR) in its second version, so as to detect when the springs are stretched. The configuration with LDR was functional but required several connections. Finally, two deformable interfaces have used a camera-based approach in order to sense deformations [19,33]. Camera-based approaches are good for prolonged use and can be effective, but deformations are sensed only when the interface is in the visual field of the camera.

Use and Evaluation

Earlier deformable interfaces for music, like Sonic Banana [22], were mostly used as MIDI controllers to manipulate sound parameters such as speed, pitch, and note duration. One quality that deformable interfaces showed in relation to music was their intuitiveness and ease of control. For instance, NoiseBear [35] supported simple squeeze interaction to control various sounds and it could be easily used by novices as well as experienced musicians. Other interfaces like Zstretch [7] showed how a stretchable controller could be used to manipulate volume, pitch, and speed in an alternative way. Sculpton [4] was used to control and generate sounds by stretching and squeezing the body of a soft tetrahedron and it was used by its creator for several live performances [39]. Kiefer used conductive foam to build a small cube-shaped interface [11] and evaluated it with eight musicians, who described Kiefer's interface as more expressive compared to regular knobs or faders. However, his study evaluated the interface only based on qualitative information, where participants were constrained to modify only specific sound parameters (i.e., phase modulation).

The deformable interfaces described above were mainly evaluated and used in the lab. Only few studies exist that are not lab-based (see [10,33]). Furthermore, users were never presented with different interfaces together, or asked how different materials and shapes affect musical interaction. Therefore, the empirical understanding of the use of deformable interfaces in music is rather one-sided in terms of methodology. To address these shortcomings, we organized three workshops to gather insights from professional and amateur musicians and a study out of the lab to investigate the use of deformable interfaces. In the next section we describe the workshops.

WORKSHOP

We conducted three workshops with nine musicians (three musicians for each workshop) on how to use deformable objects for music performances. The aim of the workshops was to inform us on how deformations could map to musical parameters and how different shapes and materials invite to musical interaction.

The structure of the workshops was based on principles of participatory design, focusing especially on activities such as experimenting with mock-ups, horizontal prototyping, thinking aloud, and brainstorming [3]. We decided to use the workshop method because it has proven to be effective when wanting users to explore and generate ideas on new technology [31]. Findings from the workshops were used for designing the deformable interfaces to be used later in the performance study.

Participants

Participants were recruited among professional and amateur musicians experienced with electronic music. We recruited a total of nine participants. Four participants were DJs, while five were performing live electronic music; all of them were experienced with music production. Furthermore, four participants were experienced with building MIDI controllers and modifying electronic music devices through circuit bending. Eight participants were male and the average age was 29.7 ($SD = 4.5$). We ran three workshops with three musicians per workshop. At the end of each workshop, participants received a small gift as a compensation for their time.

Materials

Based on related work we developed a set of 10 non-interactive mock-ups (see Figure 1). Participants used the 10 mock-ups as the main inspirational tool throughout the workshop. Table 2 indicates the similarities and differences between the mock-ups and related work.

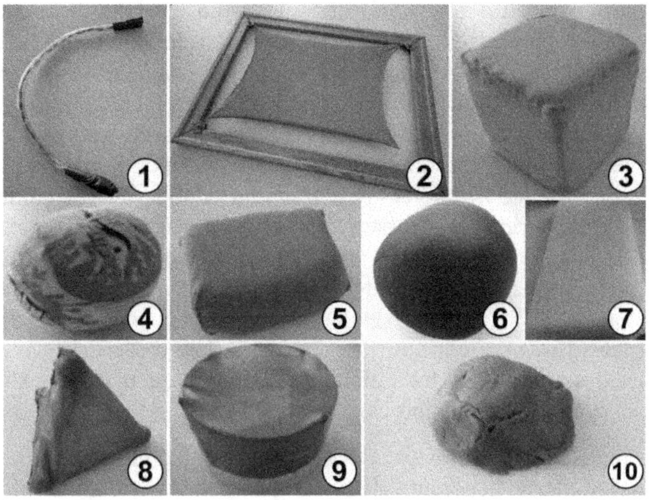

Figure 1: The object used during the workshop inspired by related work.

Workshop Set-Up

Each workshop was divided into three phases: (1) a *familiarization* phase, (2) a *simulation* phase, and (3) a *brainstorm* phase.

The *familiarization* phase was designed to introduce participants to the deformable objects. The goal of this phase was to let participants explore different materials and the deformations that they afforded. We encouraged the participants to start thinking about deformable objects as music interfaces already in this phase.

The *simulation* phase was designed to simulate possible real uses of the deformable objects for controlling sound. The goal of this phase was to receive suggestions from

No.	Paper	Original	Our Objects
1	Sonic Banana [21]	Orange rubber, 60 cm length	Transparent rubber, 60 cm length
2	Zstretch [7]	Green lycra fabric, wooden frame (36 cm length)	Blue lycra fabric, wooden frame (60 cm length)
3	A Malleable Interface [11]	Conductive foam, cube shaped, hand-sized	Foam, cube shaped, fabric covered, hand-sized
4	The Embroidered Music Ball [29]	Cushion stuffing, conductive foam, woolen yarn covered, hand-sized	Cushion stuffing, foam, fabric covered, hand-sized
5	The Music Ball Project [10]	Ball shaped sponge, rectangle shaped sponge, hand-sized	Ball shaped sponge, rectangle shaped sponge, hand-sized
6	NoiseBear [9]	Conductive Foam, Woolen Yarn	Stretch, Squeeze, Twist
7	MARSUI [30]	Blue silicone + metallic wire mesh, size N.A.	White silicone + metallic wire mesh, 18 cm
8	Sculpton [4]	Wooden spheres, metal springs, red latex, hand-sized	3D print spheres, metal springs, grey latex, hand-sized
9	A Malleable Device [18]	Paper board cylinder (16 cm radius, 7 cm height), transparent rubber, wood	Plastic cylinder (16 cm radius, 7 cm height), grey latex
10	Clay Tone [27]	Clay	Clay

Table 2: Differences and similarities between related work and our objects.

participants on how deformations could map to different musical parameters. During this phase a selection of sounds was played, which participants were asked to map to deformations. Each time a sound or an effect was played the participants picked a deformable object and suggested a potential deformation for that specific sound. Participants explained their choices by thinking aloud. The sounds played during this phase were: (1) generative sounds (keyboard, drums), (2) samples and loops, (3) sound modulations (volume, pitch, tempo, frequency), (4) filters (low pass, band pass, high pass), and (5) sound effects (delay, reverb, chorus, flanger, distortion, bit-crush). We used sounds from the default set of most electronic music software (e.g., Ableton Live®, Logic Pro®).

Finally, the *brainstorm* phase was included to let the participants generate ideas on how to use deformable objects for performing music. The goal of this phase was also to understand which of the 10 deformable objects the participants would use for real music performances. To help participants generate ideas, we used various support tools such as big paper sheets and colored post-its. We instructed participants to only generate ideas based on the 10 deformable objects used in the workshop.

Procedure

The participants were welcomed and introduced to the set-up, the workshop's purpose, and its structure. The workshop started with the *familiarization* phase, where participants could explore the deformable objects for 15 minutes. Then after a five minute break, participants went through the *simulation* phase for 50 minutes. After this, participants took another five minute break before going to the *brainstorm* phase. The *brainstorm* phase lasted 40 minutes.

Analysis

We used Microsoft Excel to code the videos recorded during the workshops. We coded each instance of deformation suggested by participants that related to musical parameters. For instance, if a participant suggested a twist deformation to apply more effect to a sound we would code this as "Twist to Increase Effect". All the instances of deformation were coded by one author and grouped into clusters, where each cluster contained identical instances of deformation-to-musical parameters.

We transcribed participants' think-aloud comments on how physical features of materials and deformations related to music (e.g., stretching the surface of a cloth would change the speed of the tempo). From those transcriptions, we identified trends and report the most interesting comments. We discuss these findings in the next section.

FINDINGS FROM THE WORKSHOPS

In this section we discuss: (1) how the participants mapped deformations to musical parameters, (2) how the participants described physical properties of deformable objects in relation to music, and (3) what deformable objects from the set the participants would use for real music performances.

Deformations to Musical Parameters

During the *familiarization* and the *simulation* phases the participants provided many suggestions on what actions to perform when playing music with deformable objects. We have identified two major trends among their suggestions, namely using simple surface contact (e.g., tap, poke, push) to generate sounds, and using object deformation (e.g., twist, stretch, bend) to modulate or applying effects to sounds..

Sound Generation

When suggesting how to play keyboard notes or drum sounds, the participants mostly tapped or poked the surface of deformable objects. Participants explained that in order to generate sounds one does not need to use complex deformations. Instead, a simple contact with the object would be enough to play a sound. Participants said that any of the objects could be used for that purpose. These results are obvious with respect to the participants' previous experience with rigid musical interfaces, in which they mostly use tapping, poking, or plucking strings to generate sounds.

Sound Manipulation

While sound generation involved mostly tapping and pushing, the participants deformed the body of the objects in many different ways when simulating sound effects and modulations. Participants generally explained that applying effects or modulating sounds has a strong analogy with sculpting or modeling physical objects.

Six participants twisted an object to increase or decrease the amount of a sound effect. According to a participant, this deformation was inspired by previous experience with knobs embedded in synthesizers and MIDI controllers. Six participants suggested stretching to modify the pitch of a sound. One participants said that pitch can be stretched to become higher or squeezed to become lower: *"I think that a stretched surface 'feels' and 'looks' like a high pitched sound, because the sound also sounds stretched"*. Two participants also showed how stretching could be used to apply reverb effect to sounds, where stretching would increase the room size or the amount of reverb.

Three participants suggested *pressing* down the body of an object to increase tempo and three participants suggested the same deformation to filter sound frequencies with high pass (HP) or low pass (LP) filters. In the case of tempo, they all explained how compressing an object should also compress the duration of a sound, thereby increasing its speed. In the case of filters, participants explained that by pressing down the body of the object they would either cutoff sound frequencies or emphasize them.

Six participants showed how *squeezing* an object in one or two hands could be used to crush or distort a sound. One participant explained the relation between squeezing and sound destruction like this: *"I can imagine that if I squeeze the object completely I will have a distorted or crushed sound. I think it's because it physically resembles the sound that I hear, because it feels like I'm destroying the sound in my hands".*

One participant showed how pushing a latex membrane upwards would emphasize certain frequencies, while pushing it downwards would cut frequencies (see Figure 2). The participant explained: "*When I push up, the latex has the shape of a peak, so I imagine this would emphasize the frequencies, whereas pushing it down should do the opposite and cut the frequencies*".

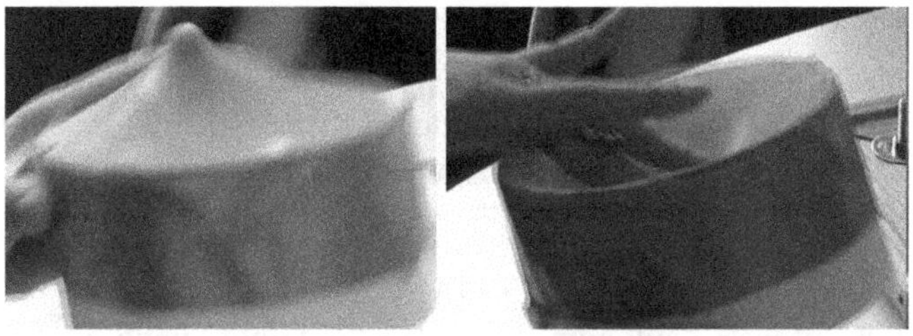

Figure 2: A participant pushing upwards and downwards on a latex membrane to manipulate sound frequencies.

We can conclude that the participants saw the deformable objects and their deformations mostly as tools for sound filtering and modulation. This suggests that a deformable interface may be useful in music performances to model and dynamically change the sonic characteristics of pre-generated sounds.

Physical Properties of Objects Related to Music

Participants were presented with both objects that retained shape and objects that did not. Participants used this property in order to simulate different musical interactions.

Non Shape-Retaining Objects

Some materials would return to their default state (shape) after being deformed. Participants explained how this property could be used to generate dynamic or automated sound events. For instance, two participants showed how non shape-retaining objects could be used to generate dynamic changes of volume. They did so by pressing on the surface of an object and explained: *"While I press down the volume is loud and we can hear the note. Then I release the surface and the faster the material goes back to its default state, the faster the volume decreases".*

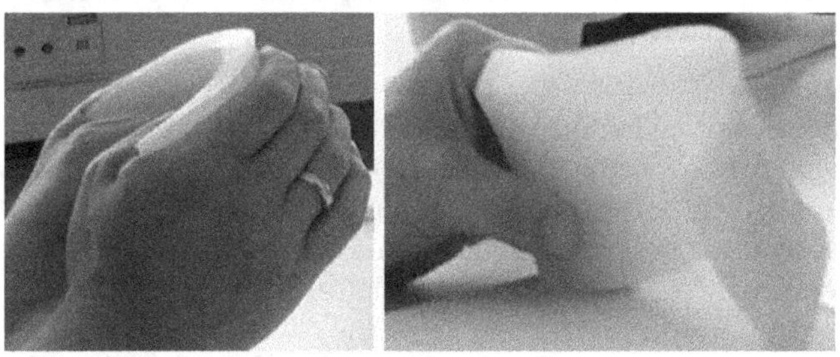

Figure 3: A participant modeling the silicone object to generate different waveforms.

Surface vibration was suggested to control dynamic sound modulations, for instance like vibrato or low frequency oscillations (LFO). One participant commented: *"I can shake the cloth and control sound oscillations in this way. But it also vibrates for a while after I touched, and somehow it feels like the surface is alive".*

Shape-Retaining Objects

Participants explained how shape-retaining objects could be used to "lock" sound parameters or to generate sound automations. For instance, one participant showed how the silicone object could be bent and locked in place to generate loops or modeling waveforms (see Figure 3).

Because clay can be torn into pieces, participants showed how this material could be used to break a sound into smaller parts (i.e., smaller sound samples). For instance, one participant showed how this feature could be used to perform what in electronic music is known as "granular synthesis".

We conclude that participants would make a distinct use between objects that retain and do not retain shape, were the former would be used to lock sound parameters, and particular types of synthesis or automated looping events, while the latter would be used for expressive control and dynamic events. However, we have noticed that participants slightly preferred non shape-retaining objects, which were mostly inspiring participant's ideas in the *brainstorm* phase.

Preferred Deformable Objects

During the *brainstorm* phase participants showed a particular interest for 5 of the 10 deformable objects, especially objects number 2, 3, 6, 7, and 8 from Figure 1. Most of the ideas produced during the brainstorm focused on these objects. Also, participants suggested what deformations would be best to use with those objects. Object 2 was preferred for stretching, while 8 was preferred for twisting. Objects 3 and 6 were preferred for pressing and squeezing, respectively. Finally, object 7 was preferred for bending. Therefore, we embedded sensors into the five objects that were preferred by the participants and made them interactive for the performance study.

PERFORMANCE STUDY

The performance study aimed to investigate how deformable interfaces are used for music performances out of the lab. Our approach to the performance study was inspired by studies of interactive interfaces in the wild [22]. We were particularly interested in how musicians perform music with deformable interfaces in a realistic environment and how they describe their experiences about using them. We asked six musicians to use five deformable interfaces in order to perform some music piece at their studios. With this study we wanted to investigate the following questions: (1) How are deformable interfaces used out of the lab to perform music? (2) What are they used for? (3) Do they change the feeling of control? (4) Are deformations systematically mapped to specific parameters? (5) Do musicians find deformable interfaces useful to play music?

Participants
Six professional musicians, all male, with an average age of 35 (*SD* = 8.8) participated in the study. Participants had between 5-25 years of experience with live performance or studio production of electronic music. None of the participants took part in the workshops or had previous experience with deformable interfaces. At the end of the session, participants received a gift to compensate for their time.

Apparatus
The set-up included interactive versions of the five preferred deformable objects (see Figure 4) as well as the musicians' own equipment (e.g., MIDI controllers, studio recording devices, laptops).

We embedded force resistive sensors (FRS) into objects 1 and 2, in order to sense when participants pressed or squeezed them. Two conductive rubber chords were sawn on the back of object 3 to sense stretch in both vertical and horizontal orientations. A single flex sensor was embedded into object 4 to sense bend deformation. Finally, we placed a rotary potentiometer inside object 5 to sense twist deformation. All the sensors were soldered to cables, plugged into a breadboard and connected to an Arduino Mega 2560, in order to send sensors' signal to the laptop. We enclosed the Arduino Mega and the breadboard in a laser cut casing.

We processed the signal coming from the Arduino Mega with the software Pure Data, using the Firmata library and Pduino, before sending the signal to the computer. In order to broadcast input from the objects as MIDI data we scaled sensors' input to values between 0 and 127 (the standard MIDI value range). In order to reduce signal noise we averaged the sensors' values over 20ms. Since we deliberately did not investigate multi-dimensional input control in the performance study, we programmed each object to sense only one type of deformation.

Procedure
The study had two primary activities: (1) mapping musical parameters to the deformations afforded by the deformable interfaces, and (2) using the mappings to perform a music piece of maximum five minutes.

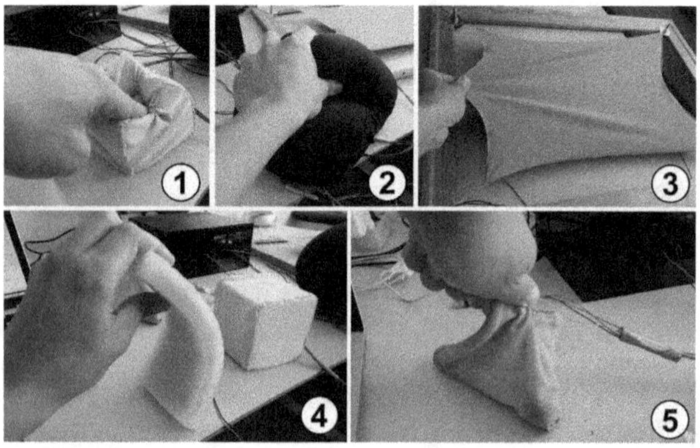

Figure 4: The deformable interfaces used during the performance study.

Before the study, participants were asked to prepare musical material for their five minutes performance and make sufficient space in their studios to use the deformable interfaces. However, we did not ask the participants to organize their performance set-up in any particular way, but rather let them choose their own space configuration. Furthermore, we instructed all the participants to download and install the software required in order to receive input from the deformable interfaces (i.e., Pure Data, Arduino and Processing).

Once at their studios, we explained to the participants the purpose of the study and introduced them to the deformable interfaces. We started by showing the participants what deformations the interfaces could support and how to control MIDI events. We guided participants through the mapping of deformations to sounds until they could handle this process autonomously. We did not impose any constraints on which musical parameters participants could choose to map. Moreover, we allowed them to use their existing studio equipment together with the deformable interfaces.

All the participants choose to control MIDI events and sounds parameters with the music software Ableton Live®. When participants were satisfied with their configuration they could start performing music. As previously said, the performance could last for a maximum time of five minutes. We imposed this time constraint to emulate the pressure of a real performance and to force the participants to perform a coherent music piece rather than randomly exploring the objects.

Once participants finished their performance, we concluded by interviewing them on their experience about using the deformable interfaces.

Data collection
We collected data for further analysis by video recording the participants' performances, as well as by storing the sensors' values in log files. Log files included timestamps (milliseconds) and streamed values from sensors sampled at a rate of 100 samples per second. Finally, we collected qualitative information from participants by video recording their interviews.

Analysis
One author coded the videos and transcribed the interviews using Microsoft Excel. From the videos we coded instances of mapping between deformations and musical parameters. Moreover, we analyzed the videos of participants' performances, focusing on how deformable interfaces were used to perform music and how they were integrated with existing instruments. Finally, we analyzed the data from the log files using MatLab, in order to investigate how long each deformable interface was used for and the how their values were controlled.

RESULTS FROM PERFORMANCE STUDY

In this section we report on (1) how participants performed music using deformable interfaces, (2) which deformations map to which parameters, (3) the time spent using each interface, and (4) how the interfaces were controlled.

Use of Deformable Interface

All participants took advantage of the haptic and tactile feedback of the deformable interfaces to quickly retrieve the sounds that they wanted to control. These observations were confirmed by the participants' comments. For instance, one participant said: *"I was looking for the low pass filter while I wanted to modify something in the program. I remembered that the filter was mapped to the squeezing ball, so I just touched the objects until I found the round shape and started to squeeze it to control the filter"* – P2.

We observed some cases where participants would use the flexibility of interfaces in a particular way. For instance, one participant mapped the pitch to bend deformation with the silicone object (Figure 4, object 4) and in order to generate a vibrato effect, he started to deform the interface with a wavelike movement. This particular use of the deformable interface supports the observation of some participants that these interfaces differ from knobs and faders present on most music controllers: *"This objects are different from faders and knobs. They make you feel like you are holding the sound in your hands and you can actually shape it"* – P3.

Because one deformable interface had springs inside and it would spring back fast if released (see Figure 4, object 5), one participant used this feature to generate quick changes in pitch; he commented like this: *"It is nice that this one springs back so fast to the center, it's dynamic and I can modulate the pitch fast. It generates an interesting conversation between the performer, the interface, and the sound"* – P1.

When we questioned participants about precision of control, they all said that it was not a concern for them during the performance, and that they rather focused on the expressive possibilities of the interfaces. We observed, however, that participants would initially monitor the sensors' values on the display. As they progressed through their performances they focused more on using the deformable interfaces and stopped looking at the display.

We observed that sometimes participants would use two or more interfaces simultaneously to modify different sounds at the same time. Five participants often used the pressing and squeezing interfaces simultaneously (Figure 4, object 1 and 2) in order to control two parameters of the same modulation or filter (e.g., the rate and the amount of a LFO). Twist and bend were also controlled together by four participants, where bend was used to modulate a sound (e.g., pitch, filter) and twist to apply effects (e.g., delay, distortion). Eventually, two participants managed to use three interfaces simultaneously, involving the use of one hand and the forearm to press and squeeze two interfaces at the same time while bending another one in the other hand.

Finally, it was interesting to notice that, even though participants were never instructed to use deformable interfaces only to control filters, effects, or modulations, they used them exclusively for those purposes. Therefore, the way participants incorporated deformable interfaces in the instrumental set-up was mainly as tools to filter or manipulate sounds, whereas the MIDI controllers and keyboards were used only when the participants wanted to trigger notes or samples.

Further Comments

All participants described the deformable interfaces as objects that embody the sounds, stressing out how the elements of a sound would be directly transposed to the interface and become physical: *"It feels like the object itself is somehow embodying the sound"* – P3.

All the participants found the deformable interfaces useful for playing music and also more inspiring and expressive than rigid interfaces. Four participants said that they would use deformable interfaces as a performative tool during live performances, while two participants would use them as creativity tools in the studio to be inspired during composition. All participants described deformable interfaces as very intuitive, easy to learn, and fun to play with. Finally, all participants described the deformable interfaces as having a more organic feel compared to rigid interfaces.

Mappings

Table 3 shows mappings between deformations and musical parameters defined by the participants. Participants mostly used the deformations to control filters and modulations.

Filters were used the most with high pass filter (HP) and low pass filter (LP), mapped overall eight times. These filters were mapped mostly to press, squeeze, and bend deformations. Participants modulated the volume and the frequency of sounds with low frequency oscillation (LFO); this modulation was mapped five times to either press or

P	Press	Squeeze	Stretch	Bend	Twist
P1	Volume (Increase)	Bit Crush (Amount)	Reverb (Amount)	Pitch (Transpose)	Pitch (Transpose)
P2	LFO (Amount)	LFO (Rate)	LP Filter (Cutoff)	LP Filter (Cutoff)	Delay (Feedback)
P3	HP Filter (Cutoff)	FM(Rate)	Beat Repeat (Note Interval)	LP Filter (Cutoff)	Delay (Feedback)
P4	LP Filter (Cutoff)	LP Filter (Cutoff)	Delay (Feedback)	Pitch (Transpose)	Distortion (Amount)
P5	LFO (Amount)	LFO (Rate)	Reverb (Amount)	Pitch (Transpose)	Panning
P6	LP Filter (Volume)	LP Filter (Cutoff)	LFO (Rate)	LP Filter (Cutoff)	Beat Repeat (Note Interval)

Table 3: Mappings between deformations and musical parameters.

squeeze deformations. The predominance of filters and modulations among the mappings confirms the idea emerging during the workshops that deformable interfaces are best for sound manipulation.

Bend was the most frequently used deformation to control pitch, while twist was used the most to control effects, such as delays, distortions, and beat-repeat. These uses also relate to findings from the workshop, where participants associated bend with pitch modulation and highlighted twist as a good deformation to control the amount of effects. Finally, stretch deformation was mostly used for effects such as reverb and delay.

Usage Time

Figure 5 shows how much each interface was used on average. This results shows that participants tend to use all the interfaces during their performance, with a slightly higher preference for pressing interaction (22.2% of the time) and less preference for stretching (15.9% of the time).

Control of Values

To understand how participants controlled the interfaces during their performances, we looked at the values registered by the embedded sensors, expressed as a percentage from not actuated (0%) to fully actuated (100%). Results showed clear trends for press, squeeze, and stretch, where most time was spent on the highest value (i.e., 100%), with respectively 9% of the time for press, 24% of the time for squeeze, and 26% of the time for stretch. These results suggest that press deformation was used less aggressively compared to squeeze and stretch.

DISCUSSION

We have collected reactions from nine musicians to 10 non-interactive objects and investigated how six musicians would use deformable interfaces to perform music. Overall, our results confirmed the usefulness of deformable interfaces in the musical context. Next, we discuss our results in detail, point to limitations of the present paper and outline future work.

Feeling of Control

One goal of our study was to investigate how deformable interfaces change the perception of control. However, few musicians commented on the precision and level of control of the deformable interfaces. Instead, musicians highlighted their ability to inspire and how they allow for serendipitous discoveries and epistemic actions [24]. The musicians also valued the haptic and tactile feedback provided by the deformable interfaces. The analysis of the log files showed that the deformable interfaces led to different interaction behaviors. For example, squeezing caused more extreme interactions than pressing. However, more studies are needed to investigate whether these implied behaviors are specific to the musical domain or to deformable interfaces in general.

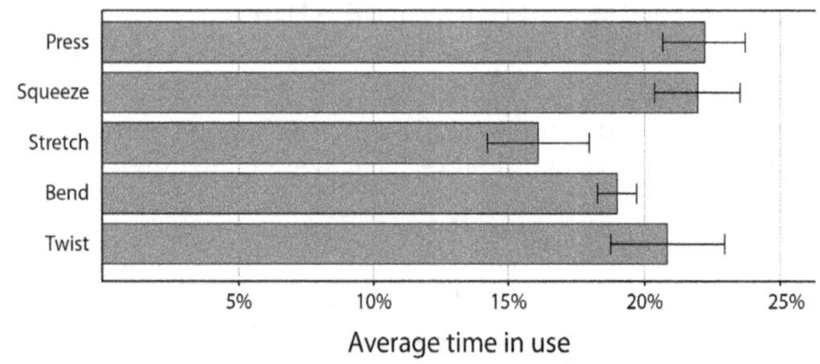

Figure 5: The average time spent by participants using each deformable interface.

Embodiment and Strong Specificness

Another important finding from the performance study is that the musicians see a stronger relation between action and effect when using the deformable interfaces than when using a regular controller. The deformable interfaces left the impression of *"having the sound in the hand"* and some musicians reported that the deformable interfaces made it easier to remember mappings than regular controls. These comments are supported by our observation of clear trends in how deformations and filters were mapped – both across individual musicians and between the workshop and the performance study. This suggests that deformable interfaces share qualities described in studies of tangible user interfaces as embodiment facilitation [24] and strong specificness [36].

Shapes, Materials, and Deformations

We found that shapes and materials played a key role for participants in both the workshop and the performance study. The haptic qualities of different materials influenced the way in which participants generated ideas on deformable interfaces and how they used them to perform music. Also, different shapes and materials implicitly suggested what deformation they would be best for. We found that these three characteristics (i.e., shapes, materials, deformations) determined how participants choose to use deformable interfaces to perform music. These results suggest that the combination of shapes, materials, and deformations are key for the design of deformable interfaces.

Limitations and Future Work

The present paper has a number of limitations, for which we aim future work to compensate. The aim of our paper was to understand differences between atomic deformations. As a consequence, the deformable interfaces were deliberately designed to support only one type of deformation. However, the capability to support many degrees of freedom is often highlighted as the prominent feature of deformable interfaces [28]. A natural next step would therefore be to merge the functionality of our five interfaces into a single deformable interface and investigate if and how this changes our findings. Second, while the performance study sought to emulate some of the pressure relating to performing music, it was still conducted in the relatively safe studio environment of the musicians. An interesting next step would be to perform a concert evaluation as Pedersen and Hornbæk [20], to investigate also how the secondary user group (i.e., the audience) experience the interfaces. Our study imposed a short time constraint (five minute) for musicians to perform with the deformable interfaces. With this approach we wanted to engage musicians in a realistic use of the interfaces rather than a random exploration. However, musical interfaces, especially if novel, may need a longer use to be assimilated by musicians. A logical next step would be to do a study where musicians train with the deformable interfaces for a longer period of time and finally go to perform live on stage with them.

CONCLUSION

Deformable interfaces afford new ways of interacting and open new possibilities for control. We have presented results from three workshops on deformable interfaces in music, and described how participants explain musical properties of shapes, materials, and deformations, and how they would use them to perform music.

With the performance study we investigated the usefulness of deformable interfaces for music performances out of the lab. We evaluated deformable interfaces with musicians performing music with a set of five deformable interfaces. The performance study showed that deformable interfaces are used mostly for sound manipulation and filtering, rather than for sound generation. They are also perceived as expressive and as embodying the sounds that they control. Finally, musicians used particular deformable interfaces for particular filters and effects.

ACKNOWLEDGMENTS

This work is part of the GHOST project founded by the EC, within the 7th framework programme through the FET Open scheme under grant agreement no. 309191.

REFERENCES

1. Ahmaniemi, T.T., Kildal, J., and Haveri, M. 2014. What is a Device Bend Gesture Really Good for? *In CHI'14. Conference on Human Factors in Computing Systems*, ACM, New York, NY, USA (2014), 3503–3512.
2. Bacim, F., Sinclair, M., and Benko, H. 2012. Challenges of Multitouch Interaction on Deformable Surfaces. *In ITS'12. Beyond Flat Displays Workshop*, ACM, Cambridge, Massachusetts, USA.
3. Bodker, K., Kensing, F., and Simonsen, J. *2004. Participatory It Design: Designing for Business and Workplace Realities.* MIT Press, Cambridge, MA, USA.
4. Boem, A. 2013. Sculpton: A malleable interface for musical expression. ACM, New York, NY, USA.
5. Burstyn, J., Banerjee, A., and Vertegaal, R. 2013. FlexView: An Evaluation of Depth Navigation on Deformable Mobile Devices. *In TEI'13. 7th International Conference on Tangible, Embedded and Embodied Interaction*, ACM, New York, NY, USA, 193–200.
6. Cassinelli, A. and Ishikawa, M. 2005. Khronos projector. *In Proc. ACM SIGGRAPH'05. Emerging technologies*, Donna Cox (Ed.). ACM, New York, NY, USA, 10.
7. Chang, A. and Ishii, H. 2007. Zstretch: A Stretchy Fabric Music Controller. *In Proc. NIME'07. 7th International Conference on New Interfaces for Musical Expression*, ACM, New York, NY, USA (2007), 46–49.
8. Gallant, D.T., Seniuk, A.G., and Vertegaal, R. 2008. Towards More Paper-like Input: Flexible Input Devices for Foldable Interaction Styles. *In Proc. UIST'08*, ACM, New York, NY, USA, 283–286.
9. Grierson, M. and Kiefer, C. 2013. NoiseBear: A wireless malleable instrument designed in participation with disabled children. *In Proc. NIME'13. International Conference on New Interfaces for Musical Expression*, KAIST, Daejeon, Korea, 122–126.
10. Jensenius, A.R. and Voldsund, A. 2012. The Music Ball Project: Concept, Design, Development, Performance. .
11. Kiefer, C. 2010. A malleable interface for sonic exploration. *In Proc. NIME'10. 10th International Conference on New Interfaces for Musical Expression*, ACM, New York, NY, USA (2010).
12. Kildal, J. and Boberg, M. 2013. Feel the Action: Dynamic Tactile Cues in the Interaction with Deformable Uis. *In CHI'13 Extended Abstracts on Human Factors in Computing Systems*, ACM, New York, NY, USA, 1563–1568.
13. Kildal, J., Lucero, A., and Boberg, M. 2013. Twisting Touch: Combining Deformation and Touch As Input Within the Same Interaction Cycle on Handheld Devices. *In Proc. MobileHCI'13. 15th International Conference on Human-computer Interaction with Mobile Devices and Services*, ACM, New York, NY, USA (2013), 237–246.
14. Kildal, J. and Wilson, G. 2012. Feeling It: The Roles of Stiffness, Deformation Range and Feedback in the Control of Deformable Ui. *In Proc. ICMI'12. 14th ACM International Conference on Multimodal Interaction*, ACM, New York, NY, USA, 393–400.
15. Lahey, B., Girouard, A., Burleson, W., and Vertegaal, R. 2011. PaperPhone: understanding the use of bend gestures in mobile devices with flexible electronic paper displays. *In Proc. CHI'11*, ACM, New York, NY, USA, 1303–1312.
16. Lee, S., Lim, Y., and Lee, K.-P. 2012. Exploring the Effects of Size on Deformable User Interfaces. *In Proc. MobileHCI'12. 14th International Conference on Human-computer Interaction with Mobile Devices and Services Companion*, ACM, New York, NY, USA, 89–94.
17. Lee, S.-S., Kim, S., Jin, B., et al. 2010. How Users Manipulate Deformable Displays As Input Devices. *In CHI'10. Conference on Human Factors in Computing Systems*, ACM, New York, NY, USA, 1647–1656.
18. Matoba, Y., Sato, T., Takahashi, N., and Koike, H. 2012. ClaytricSurface: An Interactive Surface with Dynamic

Softness Control Capability. *In Proc. ACM SIGGRAPH'12. Emerging Technologies*, ACM, New York, NY, USA, 6:1–6:1.

19. Milczynski, M., Hermann, T., Bovermann, T., and Ritter, H. 2006. A malleable device with applications to sonification-based data exploration. *In Proc. ICAD'06. 12th International Conference on Auditory Display*, London, UK, 69–76.

20. Pedersen, E.W. and Hornbaek, K. 2009. mixiTUI: A Tangible Sequencer for Electronic Live Performances. *In Proc. TEI'09. 3rd International Conference on Tangible and Embedded Interaction*, ACM, New York, NY, USA, 223–230.

21. Peschke, J., Göbel, F., Gründer, T., Keck, M., Kammer, D., and Groh, R. 2012. DepthTouch: an elastic surface for tangible computing. *In Proc. AVI'12*, Genny Tortora, Stefano Levialdi, and Maurizio Tucci (Eds.). ACM, New York, NY, USA, 770–771.

22. Rogers, Y., Connelly, K., Tedesco, L., et al. 2007. Why It's Worth the Hassle: The Value of In-situ Studies when Designing Ubicomp. *In Proc. UbiComp'07. The 9th International Conference on Ubiquitous Computing*, Springer, Berlin, Heidelberg, 336–353.

23. Schwesig, C., Poupyrev, I., and Mori, E. 2003. Gummi: User Interface for Deformable Computers. *In CHI'03 Extended Abstracts on Human Factors in Computing Systems*, ACM, New York, NY, USA, 954–955.

24. Shaer, O. and Hornecker, E. 2010. Tangible User Interfaces: Past, Present, and Future Directions. *Found. Trends Hum.-Comput. Interact.*, , 1–137.

25. Sheng, J., Balakrishnan, R., and Singh, K. 2006. An Interface for Virtual 3D Sculpting via Physical Proxy. *In Proc. GRAPHITE'06. 4th International Conference on Computer Graphics and Interactive Techniques in Australasia and Southeast Asia*, ACM, New York, NY, USA, 213–220.

26. Singer, E. 2003. Sonic Banana: A Novel Bend-sensor-based MIDI Controller. *In Proc. NIME'03. 3rd Internationl Conference on New Interfaces for Musical Expression*, National University of Singapore (2003), 220–221.

27. Smith, R.T., Thomas, B.H., and Piekarski, W. 2008. Digital Foam Interaction Techniques for 3D Modeling. *In proc VRST'08 . ACM Symposium on Virtual Reality Software and Technology*, ACM, 61–68.

28. Steimle, J., Jordt, A., and Maes, P. 2013. Flexpad: highly flexible bending interactions for projected handheld displays. *In Proc. CHI'13*, ACM, New York, NY, USA, 237–246.

29. Troiano, G.M., Pedersen, E.W., and Hornbæk, K. 2014. User-defined Gestures for Elastic, Deformable Displays. *In Proc. AVI'14 International Working Conference on Advanced Visual Interfaces*, ACM, New York, NY, USA, 1–8.

30. Vanderloock, K., Vanden Abeele, V., Suykens, J.A.K., and Geurts, L. 2013. The Skweezee System: Enabling the Design and the Programming of Squeeze Interactions. *In Proc. UIST'13. Annual ACM Symposium on User Interface Software and Technology*, ACM, New York, NY, USA, 521–530.

31. Vavoula, G.N. and Sharples, M. 2007. Future technology workshop: A collaborative method for the design of new learning technologies and activities. *2*, 4, 393–419.

32. Warren, K., Lo, J., Vadgama, V., and Girouard, A. 2013. Bending the Rules: Bend Gesture Classification for Flexible Displays. *In Proc. CHI'13. Conference on Human Factors in Computing Systems*, ACM, New York, NY, USA, 607–610.

33. Watanabe, E., Hanzawa, Y., and Inakage, M. 2007. Clay Tone: A Music System Using Clay for User Interaction. *In SIGGRAPH'07 Posters*, ACM, New York, NY, USA.

34. Watanabe, Y., Cassinelli, A., Komuro, T., and Ishikawa, M. 2008. The deformable workspace: A membrane between real and virtual space. *In Proc. TABLETOP'08. 3rd IEEE International Workshop on Horizontal Interactive Human-Computer Systems*, IEEE Computer Society, Washington, DC, USA, 145–152.

35. Weinberg, G., Orth, M., and Russo, P. 2000. The Embroidered Musical Ball: A Squeezable Instrument for Expressive Performance. *In CHI'00 Extended Abstracts on Human Factors in Computing Systems*, ACM, New York, NY, USA, 283–284.

36. Wensveen, S.A.G., Djajadiningrat, J.P., and Overbeeke, C.J. 2004. Interaction Frogger: A Design Framework to Couple Action and Function Through Feedback and Feedforward. *In Proc. DIS'04. 5th Conference on Designing Interactive Systems: Processes, Practices, Methods, and Techniques*, ACM, New York, NY, USA, 177–184.

37. Wikström, V., Overstall, S., Tahiroğlu, K., Kildal, J., and Ahmaniemi, T. 2013. MARSUI: Malleable Audio-reactive Shape-retaining User Interface. *In CHI '13 Extended Abstracts on Human Factors in Computing Systems*, ACM, New York, NY, USA, 3151–3154.

38. Ye, Z. and Khalid, H. 2010. Cobra: flexible displays for mobilegaming scenarios. *In Proc. CHI'10*, ACM, New York, NY, USA, 4363–4368.

39. sculpTon : alberto boem. http://www.albertoboem.com/index.php/project/sculpton/.

Sculpting a Mobile Musical Soundtrack

Adrian Hazzard
Mixed Reality Laboratory
University of Nottingham
Nottingham, UK, NG81BB
psxah6@nottingham.ac.uk

Steve Benford
Mixed Reality Laboratory
University of Nottingham
Nottingham, UK, NG81BB
steve.benford@nottingham.ac.uk

Gary Burnett
Human Factors Research Group
University of Nottingham
Nottingham, UK, NG81BB
gary.burnett@nottingham.ac.uk

ABSTRACT
We present an in-the-wild project to design and study a mobile musical soundtrack that enhances the experience of visiting a sculpture park. As with soundtracks for films and games, the goal was to enhance the emotional and narrative aspects of the experience while remaining in the background. We describe a compositional approach in which we first established a broad musical landscape before treating specific exhibits with detailed musical trajectories. Our study reveals how our soundtrack dramatically shaped visitors' experiences while they remained largely unaware of its operation. We distil seven experiential factors to be addressed by mobile soundtracks alongside ten compositional guidelines.

Author Keywords
Mobile; experiences; soundtracks; composition; trajectories

ACM Classification Keywords
H5.m. Information Interfaces and Presentation (e.g., HCI)

INTRODUCTION
Musical soundtracks are important features of our most powerful media experiences. They are widely used to establish context and drive a viewer's interpretation of narrative and intensify their emotional response. Moreover, soundtracks typically exert their profound influence from a subordinate position, ideally passing by largely unnoticed. This paper explores the composition of *mobile* musical soundtracks intended to accompany and enhance a variety of locative experiences. Unlike traditional media soundtracks, these utilize locative technologies to adapt the music to listeners' movements, which brings them into the realm of HCI.

Our focus on mobile soundtracks is allied to several threads of research within HCI and related fields. Prior research has revealed how people increasingly curate their own soundtracks to accompany everyday activities such as commuting or exercising by creating personalized playlists to socialize, 'astheticise' and narrate these often mundane, solitary mobile activities [6,19]. Composers have adopted mobility as a driver for creating interactive contemporary media experiences [4]. There has also been longstanding interest in HCI into how sound in general can guide movement and navigation (e.g., [20,30]).

CHI 2015, April 18 - 23, 2015, Seoul, Republic of Korea
Copyright 2015 ACM 978-1-4503-3145-6/15/04...$15.00
http://dx.doi.org/10.1145/2702123.2702236

Our focus here is somewhat different. We are interested in how composers can create meaningful music for mobile experiences where the music assumes a supporting role. What we have in mind are those formal, orchestrated mobile experiences such as cultural visiting, guided tours, and mobile games, which might benefit from having a bespoke soundtrack that reflects the activity and its environment. Consequently, our distinctive focus is to be found in music that is *deliberately composed* for an experience, *enhances emotional and narrative engagement*, and yet *remains in the background.* It is this aspect that we feel is of interest to the field of HCI, the utilization of music to actively drive mobile experiences from a secondary position.

Our goal is to establish a set of principles to guide the composers of such interactive soundtracks, helping them understand how they can subtly enhance mobile experiences and also effectively work with locative technologies, whilst maintaining a rich compositional endeavor. Here, there are two kinds of detail that a composer needs to be aware of: the mapping of music to physical space, and the experiential effects of musical accompaniments within mobile experiences. In this regard, our work builds on that of [17] which reported an experimental study into how various musical structures affected people's exploration of an empty field, proposing initial guidelines on which we extend. This following investigation presents an "in the wild" [12] design-led study in which we created a full musical soundtrack for a specific real-world experience – visiting a major sculpture park – and studied how this was experienced by visitors.

After reviewing related literature, we first describe how we developed a novel approach to composition in this real-world setting. Our subsequent study reveals how the resulting soundtrack dramatically shaped visitors' experience of the park. By reflecting on our findings, we are able to distil an understanding of the experiential factors that need to be accounted for when composing such a soundtrack and also propose specific compositional guidelines. We propose that these guidelines can support the creation of soundtracks for a variety of walking experiences – real or virtual – and thus this represents the value and contribution of this work.

RELATED WORK – FILM AND GAME SOUNDTRACKS

Our compositional approach draws its inspiration from the wider literature on media soundtracks. As this may be unfamiliar to the CHI audience, we think it is important to briefly review key related work.

Location-based music

Mobility and location are frequent drivers of contemporary music experiences, an area that has consequently witnessed a broad creative and technical exploration [4,15,35,37]. Our work concerns *placed sound* experiences [4,15,37] – normally GPS driven – where users' entry into, or exit from, geo-located trigger zones initiate playback of layers or segments of sound.

Conventions in soundtracks

Conventionally, film and computer game soundtracks serve a range of functions [5]. Wingstedt describes a set of six self-descriptive classes: *emotive; informative; descriptive; guiding; temporal;* and *rhetorical* [36]. Pauli [29] outlines three key relations between music and visual imagery: *Paraphrasing* (the music mimics the visual content), *polarization* (if the visual imagery is vague in meaning, interpretation is drawn from the character of the music) and *counterpoint* (deliberate contrast between the music and visual imagery). Meyer [27] argues, in relation to *polarization*, that music does not denote specific actions, emotions or concepts. Rather, it is the listener who forms these links, often as a result of associations built from historical exposure to other media experiences. *Paraphrasing* and *polarization* can be seen in two typical approaches to soundtrack composition, referred to as *accompaniment* and *foreshadowing* [5]. *Accompaniment*, the music is synchronized with visual events. Whereas, with *foreshadowing,* the music signposts to future events. A well-known example is found in the soundtrack to the film *Jaws*. Composer John Williams utilizes a simple theme to foreshadow the approach of the unseen shark, building tension via the expansion of instrumental layers and a graduated increase in tempo [36].

Musical treatments

We now turn to specific musical treatments employed by soundtracks. Composers of computer game soundtracks use a variety of methods to influence gameplay, such as the presentation of silence at certain locales to subtly encouraging players to move on [11], or the presentation of a salient theme or motif to indicate key events in the gameplay, often referred to as a *stinger* [13]. The latter is similar to the leitmotif – a musical motif or theme that represents a character or concept – a common device used in operas and film soundtracks alike. Lastly, we highlight musical closure, often formed from cadences, as a common device for signifying 'arrival' in western tonal music. Through repeated exposure, humans learn to anticipate such closures at key transition points within, or at the conclusion, of compositions [27]. They are also known to aid the interpretation of narrative closure in filmed events [33].

The psychology of film music

Finally, the field of music psychology research has long sought to understand the relationship between music and the perception of visual images. A consensus is held that music does alter viewers' interpretations of both the associative meaning and emotional context of images [5,8,10,27]. The level of association and congruence that a viewer perceives between music and visual imagery is considered crucial to the formation of a successful soundtrack [5,8,10]. Cohen [10] suggests that when music is temporally congruent with particular visual events, or objects, a viewer's attention is drawn to these actions. Similarly Chion [8] proposes the notion of synchrisis, where audio-visual content becomes a single modality, arguing that we *"see/hear"* films, rather than *"see and hear"* them. In addition to the affective and narrative relationships between music and visual images, music has been shown to exert an additive effect, enhancing the enjoyment of visual imagery [8,9].

COMPOSING A MOBILE MUSICAL SOUNDTRACK

In order to explore the challenges of composing *interactive locative* musical soundtracks we undertook a "in the wild" design led research engagement [12] utilizing an emergent HCI methodology – design from within [32] – where the principle researcher, who was also the composer, undertook an iterative process composition and app authoring to create a dynamic soundtrack accompaniment for a real-world cultural experience, before studying how this was experienced by visitors. This holistic approach charts all of the lessons learned throughout the process to develop the compositional principles applied here.

We produced a GPS-driven adaptive musical soundtrack to be listened to on an iPhone and headphones. The soundtrack was implemented using *Calvium AppFurnace,* which enables an author to define physical regions (zones) that start and stop audio files when a user enters or exits them (fig. 1). This technique is broadly typical of current mobile authoring tools and raised important implications for our design, as we discuss below. Pre-composed sections of music were prepared as audio files that contained either individual instrument's parts or short sections of combined parts, which were then combined and looped to form detailed musical arrangements.

We chose the Yorkshire Sculpture Park (YSP) as our wild setting, a major outdoors cultural attraction in the UK that houses a large collection of sculptures situated in 500 acres of parkland. Our choice was inspired by early visits to the park that reinforced the idea that exploring the sculptures might suit a bespoke musical accompaniment and also that it should be feasible to deliver a reasonable quality experience using current smartphones equipped with GPS. We were also inspired by Fosh *et al*'s prior research where they had designed and studied interactive trajectories through sculptures, including the use of music (albeit short and non-adaptive fragments of pre-existing, i.e. 'found', music) [14]. Our choice of musical style drew on a rich mixture of orchestral and synthesized textures to create what we intended to be an accessible soundtrack – in a nu-classical / electronica style – that we felt would be suitable for the setting and for extended listening.

Figure 1 shows a section of the YSP. The coloured areas represent distinct regions in the park, whereas the white shapes show the location of sculpture exhibits.

Figure 1: A cross-section of the YSP map

The remainder of this section introduces the distinctive approach to composition that we established over the course of the design-led iterative process. An in-depth description is found in [18]. We strongly encourage the reader to refer to the supplementary video material, as well as a fully detailed and musically annotated locale map. The videos display a POV walk-through at the park, alongside a map showing the current location and a description of the structural changes of the music.

Mapping and spotting

We visited the park on multiple occasions to map the location of exhibits, artefacts and existing boundaries and pathways. We also observed visitor behaviour including typical routes through the park and interaction with exhibits. This activity was motivated by that of *spotting* – a film production term that describes a process undertaken by a composer – the identification of scenes to be accompanied with musical cues, along with their style and relationship to the narrative [13]. This led us to develop two specific compositional techniques: *forming a musical landscape* and *composing musical trajectories*.

Forming a musical landscape

By *musical landscape* we refer to and describe the high level musical treatment of the parkland. We felt that distinct areas in the park should be accompanied by exclusive musical cues, similar to scenes from a film. Thus, we mapped out a set of regions in response to existing physical borders, distinct areas of landscaping and placement of exhibits (see fig.1). Each musical cue possessed its own character, created by a combination of unique melodic and rhythmic themes, instrumental timbres and harmonic key centres. Our map of regions led us to develop a map of musical key centres (see fig. 1 and the supplementary locale map), which enabled us to design for pleasing harmonic modulations on transitions between adjacent regions, motivated by the notion of closure [27,33]. The presentation of silence was utilized as an indicator of the outer boundary of the experience, motivated by the notion of *global attachment* outlined in [17] and the use of silence in computer games [11].

Composing musical trajectories

Given this musical landscape as a backdrop, we next turned our attention to a finer granularity of musical detail. Principally, how to accompany a visitor's trajectory into and out of interaction with the exhibits situated in the regions, thus a *musical trajectory*. We adapted the approach of [14], which encourages the designers of visiting experiences to consider the following key phases of passing through exhibits: *approaching*, *arrival, engagement* and *departure*. In designing musical treatments of each phase, we took motivation from [36] who proposes that music may have *guiding, informative, descriptive* and *temporal* effects on narrative experiences. Figure 2 illustrates a *musical trajectory*, as experienced in video example 1. First the *AppFurnace* zones are listed; the phases of the trajectory are below; this is followed by the instrument parts presented in each zone; and finally, the character symbols represent the chord progression that flows through the trajectory are presented at the bottom.

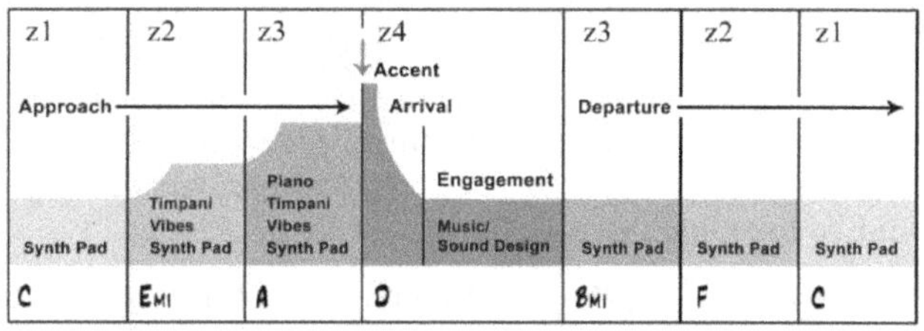

Figure 2: Musical trajectory through an exhibit

- When *approaching* an exhibit we foreshadowed the *arrival* phase (*guiding*) by increasing the musical intensity incrementally; this was achieved via the expansion of musical texture and / or a harmonic progression (see video 1 & 2).
- This intensity is then resolved at the moment of *arrival* (close proximity to an exhibit), which is punctuated by a single musical stinger (*informative*) – a simple take on a leitmotif (see video 1 & 2).
- Our musical treatment for *engagement* actually reduces musical intensity for dramatic effect and to encourage visitors to focus on the exhibits (all videos).
- Finally, we maintain a relatively low musical intensity during *departure* to prepare the visitor for moving on to the next exhibit. The inverse of *approaching* might have seemed appropriate here, but iterative testing revealed this to be incoherent as a sudden increase of intensity after *engagement* interrupted the preparation for the next *approach* phase (see video 1 & 2).

In addition to these general musical treatments, four *engagement* stages were enhanced with specific non-musical sounds, chosen to reflect the particular nature of their exhibits (*descriptive* and *paraphrasing* [29]). Examples included the sound of electricity crackling to accompany a neon sign sculpture (see video 2) or the sound of talking at an exhibit themed around conversation (video 1). These were test cases to observe how non-musical sounds might integrate into the soundtrack.

We hoped that these compositional techniques offered a fitting method to integrate a musical soundtrack into a physical experience. We anticipated that relating changes of core musical attributes (e.g. harmony, melody, timbre) sympathetically to the topology of the space, and visitor movements through it, would enable us to deliver a soundtrack congruent with the experience, thus one placed in the background. Moreover, these techniques also enabled us to compose a rich musical structure on a large-scale and with a broad harmonic, dynamic and timbral palette, thus at a level of detail typically absent from mobile musical experiences. Our final soundtrack covered 21 distinct regions housing 43 exhibits and utilized 102 original musical layers and fragments.

STUDYING OUR MOBILE MUSICAL SOUNDTRACK

We recruited twenty-two participants (11 female - 11 male) to engage in a naturalistic study of our soundtrack in use. Seventeen were aged 40+ years, three were in their twenties and the remaining two participants were aged 10 and 14 years. Three had previously visited YSP, two being regular visitors. Four happened to be trained musicians: two regular performers and two who teach music at primary school level. All participants were invited to attend the park for the purposes of the study.

We requested that they explore the site while listening to our soundtrack throughout, with removal of headphones denoting the end of the experience. No set duration was imposed although 10–90 minutes was suggested as a guide. We felt it was important to let them experience the soundtrack on their own terms, in as natural a way as possible given the constraints of research. Thus, we did not give a technical briefing about the system's dynamic functionality. All began at the same location.

Post-study interviews recorded onto a Dictaphone captured the participants' opinions of the experience. They were invited to talk freely about anything of interest and questions were posed only when required to guide the discussion and to explore various aspects of the experience, such as: what they were thinking of during the walk; appreciation of the music; routes taken; and the rationale for any key behaviors. A map of the YSP with images of the sculptures enabled participants to highlight specific exhibits during the interviews. The interviews were then transcribed from which recurring or interesting themes were highlighted.

Findings

We offer a brief overview of our data before focusing on key issues that emerged from the interviews. Visitors spent on average just over an hour walking and exploring the park, covering an average distance of 2.77km. The overwhelming majority of participants (21) described it as an enjoyable experience. Typical comments were, *"Very enjoyable"*, *"just lovely, lovely experience walking around"* and *"I've got this beautiful music going on, which enhanced the whole experience"*. Many felt that the soundtrack blended into the YSP experience, rather than functioning as a separate layer of modality, *"the whole thing seemed an experience, the music, the sculptures, where I was, everything it all seemed to be part of that experience"* (P3). However, two had some difficulty in navigating the park, which seemed to restrict the area they covered, while five experienced some technical malfunctions. Two of these were unaware of the fault – a musical fragment, which should have stopped, continued to play – but rather than disrupting their experience this appeared to extend their walk, as they continued on while the music sounded. The other three did suffer from disruption as a result of technical malfunction. The majority covered a large proportion of the soundtrack area, approaching an average of 31 exhibits each.

General reflections on the music

The vast majority of participants spoke very positively about the music, with only one expressing a dislike for it. Generally, terms such as *beautiful*, *relaxed*, *calm* and *emotional*, but also *'samey'* and *non-specific* were used to describe the music. The music was largely considered appropriate for the nature of the YSP experience. None of the participants reported any listening fatigue, although two suggested they might have stopped listening sooner had they not been taking part in the study. Prior to the walks, the investigator observed a tendency for participants to remark about the size of the headphones, or to pull a face that expressed uncertainty or embarrassment about wearing them. However, this unease was not present upon the conclusion of their walks: *"I was quite surprised that I didn't feel as self-conscious as I would normally do"*. When asked if being isolated from the ambient sound made them feel vulnerable, P3 stated, *"No, not at all. I suppose it wasn't like being on busy road or street or anything, but still there are people around you"*.

Being unaware of the operation of the soundtrack

Notably, the majority of the participants seemed unaware of the dynamic functionality of the soundtrack and some comments implied a presumption that it was a fixed linear recording: *"Like in the bit where there were more coloured sculptures you think has this been set intentionally* [changes in the music], *but then not every person is going to take the same route, so you can't say that"* (P14). This participant was describing the music matching an exhibit as though it was intentional, but they could not understand how this could be achieved. Only four participants presumed that GPS playback functionality was being used (P7,11,19,20). P11 described testing out this assumption on the boundary between two regions and following their realisation they speculated that it enhanced their appreciation of the soundtrack and the experience further. P8 (aged 14) also described testing out an arrival zone boundary at an exhibit, which contained sound design elements (see video 2). Following this account, P8 went on to state that they then proceeded to look out for other musical changes around exhibits; noting that sometimes they thought there was, but other times they could not tell.

While many appeared unaware of the adaptive nature of the music, some did describe synchronisation between the music and the wider world of the park: *"The whole experience of walking round is complete with change. Change in scenery, change in sculptures and the music seemed to reflect that quite well"* (P7) and *"You might enter a new bit and there is an evocative bit of music that goes with it and that has a bit of a 'ooh' feeling to it"* (P11). These quotes are suggestive of transitions between physical regions accompanied by new musical cues.

The stingers placed at points of *arrival* were less successful. Although noted and reported by eight participants, six of these thought they were either random musical events that were musically out of place, or felt that they signified something, but were unsure what. The remaining two identified these accent occurrences around the location of the sculptures, interpreting this to mean that they should pay attention to the local area, *"It seemed to be when I got to a more different type of sculpture, whether it was coincidence or not ... there was like a ping in the music, you'd got to look at it more carefully, look at the sculpture more carefully ... just remind yourself to look at something more intensely"* (P12).

In contrast, the four exhibits featuring impressionistic sound elements during the *engagement* phase were referred to positively by 6 participants. *"There was like a colourful Buddha. (laughs)...I think you were planning it, you got some remote control that changes the music! The music went on just one note, like a drone and I just felt really peaceful, as if he was doing his "ooommm". And I just felt like I wanted to stop there".*

Having discussed the music at length, we now turn to how this music impacted on the wider experience.

Walking alone on a winter's day

The study was undertaken during the winter months and the weather was predominately cold and wet. Furthermore, the grass was especially muddy in those well-trodden areas surrounding the exhibits. Eight participants noted, with surprise, how unyielding they were to these conditions, citing the musical accompaniment as the reason: *"I noticed lots of other people walking back because it was raining and I didn't actually feel the need to hurry"* (P1), and *"My fingers got quite cold ... normally I would look at the weather I think, "oh I'll call it a day", but no, the music, it made me feel so relaxed I just pulled my hood up and carried on"* (P3).

Eleven participants suggested the music affected their walking behaviour. Seven speculated that the music slowed down their pace, which reflects the prevalence of slow tempi throughout. In contrast, four participants singled out a particular region for discussion. This region's music was highly syncopated and at a moderately fast tempo (in comparison to the others) (see video 3). As one participant noted, *"the music was obviously getting quicker anyway, so you almost felt like you could skip through that bit"* (P14). Two participants stated that they, on occasion, felt a pull to synchronise their walking pace to the music's tempo, with one expressing frustration that the pulse of the music was ever so slight too slow, but nonetheless they adapted their walking pace to match it.

Although all participants undertook the study independently, many arrived at the YSP with family or friends. Ten participants made reference to this lone experience, as it was unusual for them to engage in this type of activity unaccompanied. Some mentioned they would not have walked as long if there had been without the music, whereas others were surprised at how much they enjoyed the solitary experience. Some went on to suggest that the music defused potential feelings of self-consciousness and isolation, for instance, *"I don't think I would have been as relaxed if I hadn't been listening to the music, especially walking round on my own" (P3).*

An enhanced emotional experience

Some commented on how the soundtrack changed the nature of the experience, typically enhancing it: *"The overwhelming thing for me was how it made it a different experience, I am so shocked, really, really shocked because it made it more than just being a visual thing ... It was almost like going to a show ... it was an experience that I would do again because I ended up having a different take on my usual visit to Yorkshire Sculpture Park" (P10).* Participant 10 has been a frequent YSP visitor for over 25 years, who also attended college at the site. Others noted how the inclusion of the soundtrack made the exhibits more engaging and enjoyable, for instance a couple reported how the music made the sculptures seem more special, even those they did not like, whereas one illustrated that the soundtrack made for a more accessible experience, *"Normally I wouldn't come to somewhere like this because I don't get a lot of where they are coming from (artists) and if you don't understand something it doesn't really float your boat, but in actual fact today wandering around on my own, I really, really enjoyed it and that must be to do with the music because the sculptures are just the same aren't they?"* (P15).

For some, this general enhancement of the sculptures spilled over into an aroused emotional state: *"I do think I have been through a range of emotions today"* (P15). Two participants highlighted how the combination of sculptures and music in a particular region created a dark and uncomfortable mood, which resulted in them wanting to leave that area: *"Sometimes it was very relative to ... how it made me feel mood wise as well ... there is one of the three men with the white faces ... walking up there looking at those ... the music became a little bit darker and it sort of made me want to move on from there"* (P6). "*There is one section where the music was quite foreboding, and it actually quite spooked me, that combined with the figures ... I've never had that kind of experience before and it got to the point where I was thinking 'I really need to get away"* (P20). Returning again to P10 (historical connection with YSP), they encountered an intense emotional reaction to the soundtrack experience, *"so immediately I put the music on and I started walking out, well I was in floods of tears because it just brought everything back, but I think it heightened it because it was the very moody music and I think it made that even more strong"*. The strength of their emotional reaction is intriguing, notwithstanding their history. The participant later implied that this type reaction was not typical of their visits to the YSP.

Focusing on the sculptures

We asked the participants where their focus of attention was during their walks. Twenty of the participants reported that their attention was firmly placed on the exhibits and parkland, *"When you look at the statues you tend to concentrate on the statues and the music just blends into the background"* (P5). Only P7, on occasion, felt that selections of particularly melodic music drew their attention away from the visual stimuli. Seventeen participants reported that the music encouraged them to view the exhibits, parkland and other artefacts with a greater intensity and for a longer duration than they would normally experience: *"It made you concentrate more on what you were looking at than if you had done it without it"* (P2); *"I'd stop and think a little bit more, probably study a bit more"* (P6); *"I think there were times when I felt the music made me more observant"* (P10). In these quotes, participants suggest that the music promoted an intense level of focus.

Others in contrast, suggested that the soundtrack masked external sound and so reduced distractions: *"Having the music on I felt cocooned and I could shut everybody else out and concentrate on what I was doing"* (P3); *"It just tended to focus my concentration more, because I had no distractions apart than what was in front of me"* (P5). Alternatively, five participants felt that the soundtrack masked their inner thoughts and dialogue, for example: *"What I was surprised about was that I'd got so much time on my own ... I thought it would make me think of work, things at home and it didn't. I didn't really have any thoughts about me at all"* (P15).

Making connections

Although participants were largely unaware of the operation of the musical soundtrack, as discussed earlier, they did note powerful, apparently serendipitous, moments when they were able to make connections between the music and the sculptures or parkland. Some of these were quite general: *"walking around sometimes it* [music] *was very relative to what I was listening to as to what I was looking at"* (P6). Others, however, were more detailed, such as the formation of connections between the colour intensity of the exhibits and changes of intensity in the music, *"I certainly liked the Buddha and the octopus, the bright ones mainly ... whether that was because some of the sculptures were blending in with the landscape, you know the lighter ones seemed to be a bit more dynamic* [music]*"* (P12), and "*there was this moment at the beginning where we were standing in the middle of ... a group of sculptures and the wind came past and blew all these yellow leaves past and the music was really atmospheric and it was just really beautiful"*.

P10 presented several very specific examples, such as connecting the melodic and rhythmic contour of a xylophone ostinato figure in a musical episode with ripple patterns they were watching on the park's lake, *"There was a tree with the light coming through from behind that was reflected onto the water, it was making the most beautiful patterns. Just at that point a xylophone was doing that repeated pattern ... if it hadn't got the xylophone pattern sort of rippling away, repeating and rippling, and the reflections on the water were very uniformed as well and I just thought 'ooh, ooh', that was a new experience anyway"*. P10 stressed that they did not intentionally seek out these connections, "*I feel sure I wasn't looking for it, it was just there"*.

DISCUSSION – EXPERIENCE AND COMPOSITION

Overall, we propose that these findings reveal our soundtrack to have provided an effective underscore for this experience. The tenor of participants' comments is that the music contributed to a distinctive experience, one in which they spent considerable time isolated, slowly moving among the sculptures, even in inclement weather, and where the music tended to focus attention on the sculptures, heighten emotional arousal and occasionally provoke moments of serendipitous reflection. And yet, the music also maintained for the most part a background role. Stylistically it integrated with the activity while technically the system mostly delivered a glitch free soundtrack, which left the majority unaware of its dynamic operation. In short, our soundtrack appears to have contributed to a cohesive, if somewhat unusual, experience while remaining in the background. Our discussion now reflects on why the experience worked as it did, drawing out lessons for practitioners and researchers. We address two broad themes: key experiential factors and compositional guidelines.

Seven experiential factors

The transcripts reveals a rich range of experiential factors that explain the distinctive qualities of our soundtrack experience. For the benefit of this discussion we address these individually referring to a broad body of literature that have had similar observations but in different settings and with different music. This enables us, with some degree of confidence to describe these factors in general terms rather than them being exclusively associated to the specific music composed for this soundtrack.

Abatement

The reported tendency for slow movement can be explained in terms of the principle of abatement. Prior research has demonstrated that humans will synchronize physical actions and movements to the tempo of music [31] and has correlated people's preferences for musical tempi with their levels of physical activity [22]. For instance, slow tempi are preferred for minimal to moderate intensity of activity. In our case the slow tempi may have encouraged an abatement of walking pace.

Accompanied solitude

Participants stressed how unusual it was for them to engage in such an activity alone, but then discussed this lone experience in a positive manner, suggesting that the music, transmitted via headphones, was the primary factor in the formation of a deeper engagement with the park and its sculptures. None expressed feeling self-conscious. This appears to mirror a stream of prior research on everyday mobile music listening [6,19], which emphases its *dissociative* function in which people immerse themselves in personalised 'soundworlds', experiencing feelings of accompanied isolation, control, self-sufficiency, an even a form of sanctuary [6].

Comfort

Participants also described a sense of detachment or comfort in the face of unpleasant weather conditions. Music has long been recognised – in the field of music therapy – for its ability to relieve pain and discomfort, whilst promoting feelings of relaxation [23,26]. Much of this work argues that stimulation of the auditory system, from listening to music, distracts attention from the body's pain sensors, and also that fast acting emotional responses to musical stimuli *"chill and thrill"* [23:152]. In our case, the musical style and timbres used, along with the largely slow tempi appears to have promoted *chill.*

Emotional enhancement

Beyond comfort, it appears that the musical soundtrack stimulated an emotional response to the YSP. Music has an historical relationship with human emotions, although the nature of this relationship remains contested [24]. A prior example of research on music's effect on emotional responses concluded that viewing pictures whilst listening to classical musical provoked strong emotional responses [3], whereas another study, which focused on human's responses to musical listening in relation to their context and setting, revealed that music listening in solitary settings led to feelings of *"calm-contentment, nostalgia-longing, and sadness-melancholy"* [21:678], both of these examples broadly reflect our experience. The additive effect that music exerts on the interpretation of visual imagery, in our case sculptures, has been accounted for in terms of *spreading activation* [9], the notion that a mood or feeling conjured from the music spreads over to any visual element experienced concurrently. Similar is Chion's concept of *conceptual resonance,* a cyclical process in which music affects a viewer's interpretation of an image, which in turn affects their impression of the music [8]. Shifting to mobile music listening, Bull and Herbert present *spreading activation* to account for how iPod's 'astheticise' their environment and in doing so improve the quality of their experience [6,19].

Increased focus

Participants reported that the music led them to focus more intently on the sculptures for longer durations than they might have otherwise. Some speculated this was due the masking of ambient noise or being free from normal social interactions, which cause distractions. This reflects Bull's [6] assertion that personal stereo listeners often control their surroundings by blocking external sound. Some visitors also reported a distraction from internal 'chatter', which is similarly reflected by Bull [6] and Herbert [19:51], who proposes the *"reduction of intensity of thought or internal dialogue"* as a primary impact that music has on humans everyday lives. Other research suggests that the music in itself may create a state of increased attention. For instance, a study of young males showed that memory and attention were enhanced whilst listening to music while their susceptibility to external distractions was reduced [28]. The core principle appears to deem that music listening initiates arousal, which then increases a listener's facility for cognitive processing, thus enhancing their attention [9]. Our 'focusing' effect is probably a combination of audio masking, solitude and musically initiated cognitive processing.

Serendipity

Some participants were open to forming connections between musical and visual events, leading to engaging serendipitous encounters. Various working definitions for serendipity have been documented including Austin who describes *happy accidents* arising from apparently unconnected events [2] and Liestman who highlights the importance of *synchronicity* [25]. Both resonate with the examples reported by our participants, including chance connections discovered along the way that were not planned by ourselves (e.g., connections between melodic ripples in the music and ripples in the water); as well as responses to our deliberately orchestrated features of the soundtrack (e.g., the sound design at the Buddha exhibit). Interestingly, moments of serendipity still occurred for the few participants who recognised the dynamic functionality of the soundtrack; presumably, as the location of musical changes and their relationship to the environment were still unknown in advance.

Congruence

For the most part, visitors considered their experiences to have been cohesive, rather than unrelated combinations of audio-visual-physical stimuli. Indeed, the majority did not even recognize the automated nature of the soundtrack. This striking finding can be explained through the concepts of *audio-visual association* and *congruence.* Several documented approaches describe the need for both temporal congruence and semantic association between music and imagery when creating audio-visual experiences that avoid distraction and divergent modalities. Two examples are Cohen's *Congruence Associationist Model (CAM)*, [5,9,10] and Chion's *Synchresis* [8]. The large majority of our visitors considered the music appropriate, thus associated to the sculpture park, while attention was principally focused on the visual artefacts (broadly reflecting the *CAM)*. That the majority did not consciously perceive the soundtrack's structural design could offer two conflicting readings: first, the music was sufficiently nondescript; second, the structure of the music was effectively associated and congruent with the structure of the park, and as such the soundtrack was not a divergent modality.

We suggest that the combination of these seven experiential factors explains the distinctive nature of this experience. Recognising these factors also raises strategies that other composers might follow to create similar experiences. First, choice of tempo is not only a musical matter, but may be used to consciously shape the pace of walking and hence of the experience as a whole, in our case slowing it down. Second, appropriate music delivered through headphones can create a particular kind of solitary visiting experience, which is comforting and can increase focus on exhibits, and may stimulate strong emotional responses. Third, with careful choice of style and alignment of its structure to that of the wider experience, composers can create congruent soundtracks in which the music soundtrack fades into the background to play a supporting role and even foster serendipity.

Some of these implications stand in contrast to previous research on interaction in museums and galleries that has emphasised the importance of supporting group visiting [34], highlighted the challenges of wearing headphones [1] and focused on the importance of collaborative displays [16]. Our experience suggests an alternative strategy, one of isolation leading to deep engagement. Not that we are suggesting that all experiences should be of this form. We recognize that many visitors seek sociable experiences. However, we suggest that isolated experiences may provide a powerful alternative for others.

Compositional guidelines

Having reflected on the broad experiential qualities of our soundtrack, we now turn back to its underlying design, revisiting our two compositional methods of a musical landscape and trajectories outlined earlier to distil a final set of compositional guidelines for mobile soundtracks. The "in the field" design led process has notably built upon and driven forward those emerging compositional techniques developed in [17], as detailed in the following.

Guidelines for musical landscapes

Our first set of guidelines address establishing the overall musical landscape within which the experience will take place. The challenge here is to create a congruent mapping between contents and layout of the environment, and thematic and harmonic structure of the music.

Define a global boundary. An explicit musical boundary should surround the area(s) of the intended experience reflecting Hazzard *et al*'s notion of *global attachment* [17]. We propose a two-layered boundary mechanism in which crossing this boundary might first be indicated by reducing the music to a background sound (a low drone in our case) and subsequently fading to silence beyond this (as several of our visitors continued to follow our drone without realizing they had crossed our global boundary).

Establish regional attachment. The overall composition can be structured around multiple regions of the physical environment that mark new areas, sub-divide larger areas, or contain artefacts of interest. Composers should encourage *regional attachment* [17] by associating each region with a different, but complementary tonal key centre and distinct timbres that contrast adjacent regions.

Compose musical transitions between regions. Harmonic modulations are recommended as coherent and effective signifiers of transitions between adjacent regions. Closely associated regions may share a common key centre and instrumentation, but achieve distinction through subtle variations to thematic and textural content.

Do not choose paths as boundaries. Although pathways appear to define natural boundaries in the physical world, composers should avoid using them as musical boundaries, as people who walk along them will tend to repeatedly retrigger modulations and musical transitions.

Guidelines for musical trajectories

The next step is to compose musical trajectories across this landscape, especially into and through key points of interest. Here we extend Fosh *et al*'s proposals for authoring trajectories through gallery and museum exhibits in terms the five key stages of *'approach, engage, experience, disengage,* and *leave'* [14], proposing that composers might adopt different musical strategies at different points along such a trajectory.

Increase intensity on approaches. Musical contours such as expanding pitch registers, layers of texture and chord progressions may foreshadow arrival at a point of interest [5]. Where chord progressions are used, the tonic chord of the region's key should be established in the outer zone of a region before the chords advance through approach zones. Added layers of instrumentation may also contain increased rhythmic content (i.e. sequences with shorter note values) to further intensify the level of textural density (see Fig. 2).

Mark arrivals. *Arrivals* may be signified by concluding any *approach* phase by climaxing and dissipating the dynamic contour, for example through harmonic resolution – via a return to the tonic chord of the region's key centre, or by way of a modulation to a new key. The addition of a musical accent or motif that signifies arrival at a specific point of interest [18] (Fig. 2) was less successful here and warrants further investigation.

Make room for engagement. Based on our experience, we suggest that the music to accompany people's *engagements* with points of interest after *arrival* should, in contrast, maintain a low dynamic level for two reasons, both of which aim to avoid interference with the wider experience. First, to shift the participant's focus towards an artifact; this might be a dramatic moment as the music fades to the background as they are confronted with an object and become more aware of the surrounding world. Second, to make space for more 'paraphrased' treatments of an artifact, for example the introduction of highly associated sounds or even a spoken word commentary.

Treat departures distinctly.
Perhaps our most unusual proposal concerns the treatment of departures from a point of interest. Here, we argue that the dynamic level of the music should stay broadly consistent with the dynamic level experienced during the *engagement* phase, rather than mirroring the *approach* music but in reverse. Some variation to the music may be desirable at this point – to present a different scene on the way out - but the music should retain the character of the region. Thus the overall musical progress through a point of interest is asymmetric, increasing in intensity on the *approach* but then dropping away during engagement and maintaining a lower level during departure (see Fig. 2).

As a final note on this topic, our experience suggests that it may be useful to begin the whole musical composition with an initial pre-canned introductory that gracefully leads the participant into the main adaptive soundtrack.

Composing for the seams in technology
Studies of location-based experiences have concluded that designers need to accommodate so-called seams in the technical infrastructure, those technical glitches caused by the unavailability or lack of precision in positioning services, wireless communications and other technologies [7]. We offer two guidelines here.

Compose for uncertain positioning. First, it is necessary to undertake detailed mapping of the setting to identify potential troublespots. Areas of high uncertainty require a coarser treatment, for example through larger zones. There should also be appropriate default music to be played when the positioning system is unavailable.

Compose for uncertain synchronization. Current location-based platforms tend to support simple discrete location triggers with little control over the fine-grained synchronization of digital media. It can, therefore, be very challenging to achieve tightly synchronized transitions between musical fragments to the level that composers might normally expect from music software. To minimize musical 'glitches', composers may wish to avoid using prominent, tightly-structured themes in favour of ambient, slowly evolving themes upon static harmonies and textures that can be easily entered and exited at any point.

CONCLUSION
We have shown how it is possible to employ current locative technologies to create a rich interactive musical soundtrack that enhances the visiting experience. Our research suggests various strategies for composers and designers, including being aware of the key experiential impacts of music, as well as guidelines for composing musical topographies and trajectories through these. It is of course necessary to recognise that the arguments in this paper are based on one example. Future research needs to explore how our findings might transfer to other settings, but the potential scope is broad: musical soundtracks of this type could accompany a whole host of walking based activities from the type described here to our daily commutes. Application in internal settings such as exhibitions and galleries is also intriguing. Especially promising in our view is the potential for use in computer games, a major market for digital technologies that routinely employs soundtracks and where there is an increasing focus on (virtual) location-based experiences. Longer-term adaptations of our guidelines might extend to dynamic music on other forms of transportation such as cars and public transport. We also see controlled studies as a possible route forward for focusing our research. We need to reiterate that we do not see such experiences as replacing other kinds of engagements, especially those that are sociable, but rather that they might form a new part of the 'armoury' for experience designers. This said we hope that our experience raises new challenges for future research.

ACKNOWLEDGMENTS
Adrian Hazzard is supported by the Horizon Doctoral Training Centre at the University of Nottingham (RCUK Grant No. EP/G037574/1) and by the RCUK's Horizon Digital Economy Research Institute (RCUK Grant No. EP/G065802/1). Steve Benford is supported the EPSRC funded Living with Digital Ubiquity project (EP/M000877/1).

REFERENCES
1. Aoki, P.M., Grinter, R.E., Hurst, A., Szymanski, M.H., Thornton, J.D., and Woodruff, A. Sotto voce: exploring the interplay of conversation and mobile audio spaces. *Proc. of CHI 2002*, ACM, 431–438.

2. Austin, J.H. *Chase, chance, and creativity: The lucky art of novelty.* Mit Press, 2003.
3. Baumgartner, T., Lutz, K., Schmidt, C.F., and Jäncke, L. The emotional power of music: How music enhances the feeling of affective pictures. *Brain Research 1075*, 1 (2006), 151–164.
4. Behrendt, F. The sound of locative media. *Convergence: The International Journal of Research into New Media Technologies 18*, 3 (2012), 283–295.
5. Boltz, M., Schulkind, M., and Kantra, S. Effects of background music on the remembering of filmed events. *Memory & Cognition 19*, 6 (1991), 593–606.
6. Bull, M. Investigating the culture of mobile listening: From Walkman to iPod. In *Consuming music together*. Springer, 2006, 131–149.
7. Chalmers, M. and Galani, A. Seamful interweaving: heterogeneity in the theory and design of interactive systems. *Proc. of DIS 2004,* ACM (2004), 243–252.
8. Chion, M., Gorbman, C., Murch, W. *Audio-vision: sound on screen.* Columbia University Press, 1994.
9. Cohen, A.J. Understanding musical soundtracks. *Empirical Studies of the Arts 8*, 2 (1990), 111–124.
10. Cohen, A.J. Associationism and musical soundtrack phenomena. *Contemporary music review 9*, 1-2 (1993), 163–178.
11. Collins, K. *Playing with sound: a theory of interacting with sound and music in video games.* MIT Press, 2013.
12. Crabtree, A., Chamberlain, A., Grinter, R.E., Jones, M., Rodden, T., and Rogers, Y. Introduction to the special issue of "The Turn to The Wild." *ACM Trans. Comput.-Hum. Interact*, 20, 3, 2013
13. Davis, R. *Complete guide to film scoring.* Berklee Press, 2010.
14. Fosh, L., Benford, S., Reeves, S., Koleva, B., and Brundell, P. See me, feel me, touch me, hear me: trajectories and interpretation in a sculpture garden. *Proc. of CHI 2013*, ACM (2013), 149–158.
15. Gaye, L., Holmquist, L.E., Behrendt, F., and Tanaka, A. Mobile music technology: Report on an emerging community. *Proc. of NIME 2006*, IRCAM—Centre Pompidou (2006), 22–25.
16. Geller, T. Interactive tabletop exhibits in museums and galleries. *Computer Graphics and Applications, IEEE 26*, 5 (2006), 6–11.
17. Hazzard, A., Benford, S., and Burnett, G. Walk this Way: Musically Guided Walking Experiences. *Proc. of CHI 2014*, ACM (2014), 605–614.
18. Hazzard, A., Benford, S., and Burnett, G. You'll Never Walk Alone: Designing a location-based soundtrack. *Proc. of NIME 2014*, (2014), 4.
19. Herbert, R. Musical and non-musical involvement in daily life: The case of absorption. *Musicae Scientiae 16*, 1 (2012), 41–66.
20. Holland, S., Morse, D.R., and Gedenryd, H. Audio GPS: spatial audio in a minimal attention interface. *environment 1*, (2001), 3.
21. Juslin, P.N., Liljeström, S., Västfjäll, D., Barradas, G., and Silva, A. An experience sampling study of emotional reactions to music: Listener, music, and situation. *Emotion 8*, 5 (2008), 668–683.
22. Karageorghis, C.I. and Terry, P.C. The psychological, psychophysical and ergogenic effects of music in sport: a review and synthesis. (2008).
23. Koenig, J., Warth, M., Oelkers-Ax, R., et al. I Need to Hear Some Sounds That Recognize the Pain in Me: An Integrative Review of a Decade of Research in the Development of Active Music Therapy Outpatient Treatment in Patients With Recurrent or Chronic Pain. *Music and Medicine 5*, 3 (2013), 150–161.
24. Konecni, V.J. Does music induce emotion? A theoretical and methodological analysis. *Psychology of Aesthetics, Creativity, and the Arts 2*, 2 (2008), 115–129.
25. Liestman, D. Chance in the midst of design: approaches to library research serendipity. *RQ*, (1992), 524–532.
26. McCaffrey, R. and Locsin, R.C. Music listening as a nursing intervention: a symphony of practice. *Holistic nursing practice 16*, 3 (2002), 70–77.
27. Meyer, L.B. *Emotion and meaning in music.* University of Chicago Press, 2008.
28. Morton, L.L., Kershner, J.R., and Siegel, L.S. The potential for therapeutic applications of music on problems related to memory and attention. *Journal of Music Therapy 27*, 4 (1990), 195–208.
29. Pauli, H. *Filmmusik, Stummfilm.* Klett-Cotta, 1981.
30. Strachan, S., Eslambolchilar, P., Murray-Smith, R., Hughes, S., and O'Modhrain, S. GpsTunes: controlling navigation via audio feedback. *Proc. of MobileHCI 2005*, ACM (2005), 275–278.
31. Styns, F., van Noorden, L., Moelants, D., and Leman, M. Walking on music. *Human Movement Science 26*, 5 (2007), 769–785.
32. Taylor, R., Schofield, G., Shearer, J., et al. Designing from within: humanaquarium. *Proc. of CHI 2011*, ACM (2011), 1855–1864.
33. Thompson, W.F., Russo, F.A., and Sinclair, D. Effects of underscoring on the perception of closure in filmed events. *Psychomusicology: A Journal of Research in Music Cognition 13*, 1-2 (1994), 9.
34. Tolmie, P., Benford, S., Greenhalgh, C., Rodden, T., and Reeves, S. Supporting group interactions in museum visiting. ACM Press (2014), 1049–1059.
35. Vawter, N.N.T. Ambient Addition: How to turn urban noise into music. 2006. http://dspace.mit.edu/handle/1721.1/36161.
36. Wingstedt, J., Brändström, S., and Berg, J. Narrative music, visuals and meaning in film. *Visual Communication 9*, 2 (2010), 193–210.
37. BLUEBRAIN. http://bluebrainmusic.blogspot.co.uk.

Walking by Drawing

Daniela K. Rosner, Hidekazu Saegusa, Jeremy Friedland, Allison Chambliss
University of Washington
{dkrosner, chgm, jsfried, achamb}@uw.edu

ABSTRACT
This paper describes a study of algorithmic living with Trace, a mobile mapping application that generates walking routes based on digital sketches people create and annotate without a map. In addition to creating walking paths, Trace enables people to send the paths to others. We designed Trace to explore the possibility of emphasizing guided wandering over precise, destination-oriented navigation. Studies of sixteen people's use of Trace over roughly one week reveal how walkers find Trace both delightful and disorienting, highlighting moments of surprise, frustration, and identification with GIS routing algorithms. We conclude by discussing how design interventions offer possibilities for understanding the work of mapping and how it might be done differently in HCI.

Author Keywords
Walking, design, geo-spatial navigation, algorithmic living.

ACM Classification Keywords
K.4.0 Computers in Society: general.

INTRODUCTION
In the 1967 artwork *A Line Made by Walking*, a field of grass presents residues of a path that artist Richard Long tracked up and down by foot [9]. Through walking, Long reshaped the environment to describe a trajectory of movement. The blades of grass bent underneath his feet to reflect the sunlight from above and produce a visible trace. In the decades since, we have seen the emergence of a different kind of path: mapping algorithms that prefigure walking routes based on Geographic Information Systems (GIS) data. Unlike the trails that came before them, GIS routes rely on algorithms to characterize and codify the physical landscape. They also share an important presupposition: walking is a destination-oriented, precise, and planned activity [5,9,13]. Whether embodied by GIS routing or fitness tracking systems, these computational traces often issue from a corpus of knowledge whose authorization and production remain hidden from the people using them [8,15].

CHI 2015, April 18 - 23 2015, Seoul, Republic of Korea

ACM 978-1-4503-3145-6/15/04···$15.00
http://dx.doi.org/10.1145/2702123.2702467

Drawing on studies of social mapping [1,11,25] and algorithmic life [6,8,15,33], we develop a complement to this technology for walking called Trace. Trace is a mobile application that transforms hand-drawn digital sketches into walking paths to share with others – thus introducing a unique form of digital communication to HCI: walking by drawing. Rather than aim for efficiency or competition, Trace relies on communication between the creators and recipients of walking paths. During field trials with sixteen people across Boston, Chicago and Seattle, Trace evoked surprising contrasts. On the one hand, people used Trace to extend their everyday interactions. They "slowed down" walking routines to encounter new features of their environment. Through the design of the routes and the accompanying annotations, they also turned walking paths into personal messages: engaging enigmatic riddles, love notes, and ruminations. On the other hand, people encountered Trace as deeply disruptive of familiar routines. Trace prompted people to explore areas they did not want to travel, sometimes revealing discriminatory behavior. Trace also obligated people to use scarce spare time and walk redundant paths — ultimately intensifying desires for efficiency and control. To reconcile these disconnects between people's perceptions and practices, the people we studied began to interrogate the procedural logics behind GIS-routing and *see* their neighborhoods through an algorithmic lens.

We use the development of Trace to examine how GIS algorithms might be done differently in the context of walking and navigation. How is GIS-supported travel achieved in practice? What do GIS algorithms translate, displace or change? What alternatives might be possible? As we describe in the paper that follows, this work has ramifications for not only design for urban mapping but also for our un-

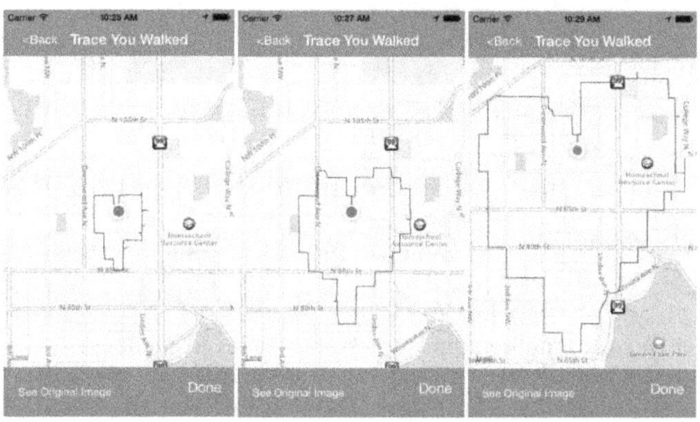

Figure 1: The Trace application enables people to sketch, annotate and send walking paths to others. The maps above illustrate a heart path adjusted for different walking durations.

derstanding of the forms of autonomy and engagement GIS systems make possible. First, it extends the spectrum of mobile navigation research to consider design for non-destination-oriented walking. In doing so, it raises the possibility of devising forms of travel independent of GIS-enabled precision and specification. Second, it operationalizes guided walking as a form of drawing to examine the social, political and communicative character of digital transport. Lastly, we contribute a study of algorithms through walking to a growing body of HCI research on algorithmic living that analyze the role of digital rules and infrastructures and their seemingly immutable form.

Our choice to study walking rather than driving or other forms of travel comes from a suspicion that the relation between walking and creative engagement can reveal important opportunities for improvisation in algorithmic life in ways that engage overlooked avenues of HCI inquiry around issues of autonomy and machine intelligence [31]. As we will see in the discussion that follows, it is by intervening in and breaking with GIS-routing practice that we may invite new recognition of the responsibilities and contingences that often challenge navigation activities more typically examined in HCI.

MAPS, ROUTES, AND WALKS

While maps have historically enabled precise and efficient movement through the world, they have equally become mechanisms for classifying and reducing it, often "reflect[ing] the maker's priorities more than those of the culture(s) they depict," maintains Rebecca Solnit, a San Francisco-based activist [25:13]. While Stamen Design's Crimespotting maps visualizing crimes in San Francisco and Oakland (http://stamen.com/projects/crimespotting), aim for civic transparency, those same maps may also deter

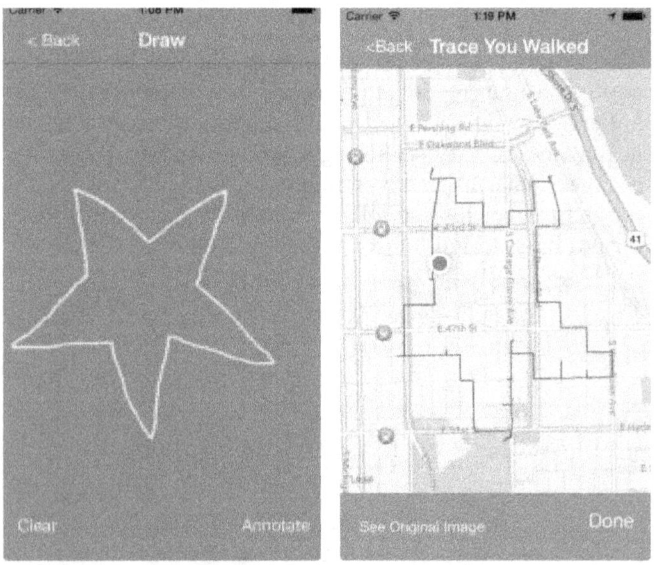

Figure 2: Plotting paths for a star introduced challenges. As one person described: "say you draw a trace for a circle it's pretty unlikely it's have you walk down the same streets but if it's the shape of star then it's more likely".

people from visiting lower income neighborhoods, reinforcing social stigmas. In their attempts to use visual representation to segregate and repress certain populations, mapping exclusions reveal power hierarchies, urban tensions and discrimination, concurrently making such practices contestable. In *Infinite City*, Solnit positions maps as invitations to alter, add, plan and otherwise manipulate "in ways that texts and pictures are not" [25:8]. A map provides entrance to a physical landscape, enacting concrete connections to the world. Solnit draws attention to the power dynamics mapping processes often conceal. Dividing North America into various 'local tribes', for example, offered colonial Spaniards a comprehensible picture of Bay Area Native American territories for museum curation [25:8]. The practices and politics of mapping continue to pervade not only civic life but also the many GIS systems that inhabit it.

This recognition of cartography as a political project resonates with an ongoing attention to psychogeographical mapping of the 1950s. French Situationalist theorist Guy Debord's [7] theory of "drifting" (or dérive) emphasized a "playful-constructive behavior" emerging from the abandonment of familiar routines and an awareness of "the attractions of the terrain." Decades later, a rich array of location-based media has drawn on this tradition to comment on the influence of mobile sensing on urbanization, spatial encounters, and processes of de-familiarization. The Broken City Lab's Drift project [3], for example, presents a mobile application that users based on randomly assembled directions. Mark Shepard's Tactical Sound Garden Toolkit similarly uses smartphones to enable people to "drift though virtual sound gardens" as they navigate urban spaces [20]. Christian Nold's [16] bio and emotion maps use wearable devices tracking galvanic skin response to offer opportunities for refection on people's relationships with geographic locations and sensing technology. Chris Speed's Walking through Time [27] mobile app allows people to view historical maps while moving through Edinburgh.

Revealing new cartographic features, several artists and cultural critics have explored the relation between mapping and human traces. British poet Iain Sinclair [23:19] imagined "templates of meaning" encoded into baroque architect Nicholas Hawksmoor's London churches, connecting the location of the churches on a map to produce an image of the Eye of Horus, an Egyptian symbol of protection. More recently, artist Jeremy Wood has pioneered a growing movement of "GPS Drawing" that explores the use of GIS to create large-scale illustrations (see Nike+, MapMyWalk www.mapmywalk.com, Strava www.ilovebicycling.com/-strava-art, and so on). Tracing paths of travel (foot, bike, car or plane) with Global Positioning Systems (GPS), the images range in diversity from marriage proposals to Internet memes. In "Surface Patterns: Walking Tours," Jen Southern [26] reproduces audio tour walks without a map to reimagine such imagery as decorative prints.

The juxtaposition of drawn traces with cartography underlies an orientation toward mapping as primarily emotional, cultural and symbolic. Geographer Denise Cosgrove has written of the "imaginative processes of discovering and denoting our place within the world, and of ordering the worlds we experience though spatial representations: graphically, pictorially, even narratively and performatively" [4:68]. The practices and politics of mapping continue to pervade not only civic life but also the many GPS-savvy citizens that inhabit it.

However, travel has only recently relied on mapping and GIS. Citing Long's walk described above, anthropologist Tim Ingold [9] recalls the practice of wayfaring, a process of retracing a path someone has travelled before. As an act of cultural reproduction, wayfaring for Ingold highlights links between walking and storytelling, wherein the line of a path or tale unfolds through space and time. Like a story one has heard before, the line has a way forward but no particular end and may ebb and flow. Walking and telling both rest on itineraries: markers that guide as opposed to specify trajectories. Contemporary examples include marches and protests such as the Million Man March in the United States. Such walks enact the values and beliefs of their members through claims to public space. Participants construe walking as social and political action.

This view of human engagement as both material and semiotic has begun to enter the HCI literature, particularly through the work of Lucy Suchman, Susan Leigh Star and Bruno Latour. These authors have emphasized the more subtle and supple relations between people and the algorithmic worlds they inhabit. Suchman [29] and Star [28] stress the influential ways "invisible work" permeate both technologists and technological (infra)structures. Latour [14:228] proposes the concept of "immutable mobiles," whereby things become transportable while remaining stabile in form, such as a projection system that "allows maps to be drawn with less deformation of shape." wherein objects like th with increasing stability as displacements through transformations. In her introduction to *Human Machine Reconfiguration*. Suchman directly connects situated action with Ingold's notion of wayfaring, foregrounding the centrality of new accountabilities and agencies. As our bodies travel through the world, we open up possibilities for becoming social and political agents as well.

This perspective has resurfaced in recent conversations on algorithmic life budding from within cultural studies and science and technology studies. Historian of science Lorraine Daston [6], for example, describes the spread of "algorithmic rules" to many disciplines through "rules of rationality [that] replaced the self-critical judgments of reasons." Media scholar Tarleton Gillespie shows how algorithms become categories of fact or truth, asking whether they can ever be 'wrong' [8]. Likewise, sociologist Scott Lash [15:71] proposes examining algorithms through their "compressed or hidden" rules to become "pathways through which capitalist power works." However, these assertions may tell us little about the critical work algorithms do as our practices change. According to science and technology studies scholar Malte Ziewitz [33], "such theorizing often ends up further mystifying the phenomena it seeks to clarify." Inspired by Harold Garfinkel's "demonstrative experiments," Ziewitz describes an ethnomethodological exploration of mapping he conducted in his Oxford 'classroom' wherein he asked students to explore the city guided by algorithms rather than maps.

Our Trace project and the concept of drawing-by-walking developed below emerged from our early engagements with these areas of theory, art practice and research. Firstly, we take up questions raised by Ingold and Suchman around improvisation and accountability in the domain of GIS technology. Secondly, we use concerns of the aforementioned locative media artists to reimagine the potential of GIS to shape and contest new algorithmic relations. And lastly, we draw together methodological tactics of Ziewitz's algorithmic walk with Wood's GPS drawing to develop drawing-by-walking as a mode of design inquiry. In drawing and walking the algorithm we reimagine the material trace [20].

DRAW TO WALK: THE TRACE DESIGN PROCESS

Our design team sought to investigate and further define this concept of walking-by-drawing through interviews examining the form and location of GIS-technology in people's walking routines. We recruited avid walkers from public online postings, including a part time dog walker and a photographer. We conducted ten semi-structured interviews lasting one to two hours. Interviews took place in person or over the phone in order to gain insight into the preexisting walking habits of the people we studied and their initial impressions of the Trace concept. We recruited participants through flyers and online ads. Interview questions focused on people's walking habits, motivation, and priorities. Based on insights we gathered from these interviews and social studies of mapping [1,11,25], we developed the following design guidelines for Trace.[1]

Travel over Transport: Non-destination-oriented Routing

The people we interviewed described several walks that accompanied a particular task, such getting to work or running errands. When the walk became time-constrained, they described seeking out the quickest route. When asked about wandering, several people expressed that they enjoy wandering in areas where they will most likely find an interesting shop or restaurant. This widespread focus on geolocatable destinations prompted us to investigate alternatives. Drawing on theories of social mapping [1,11,25], our design team built Trace to explore how GIS-supported travel could emphasize travel over transport.

[1] All participant names are pseudonyms.

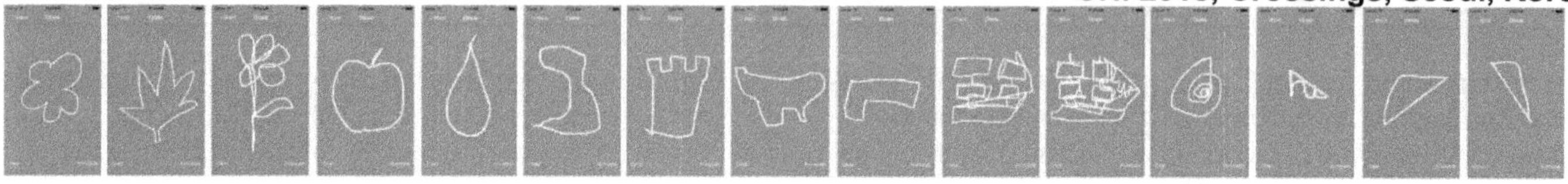

Figure 3: A selection of drawings created by people using Trace. Common themes included (left to right): objects in nature (cloud, leaf, flower, apple, raindrop); curiosities and jokes (hourglass, bigfoot, United States); seafaring (fish, sailboat); symbols (spiral, "hi"); grids for walking (triangle, triangle, "pen15").

Improvisation: Highlighting Emergent Engagements

Our interviews highlighted multiple occurrences of wandering in parks or less urban areas, as people found these walks more scenic. Sarah, an artist, related that she frequently travels with her partner and will often take the first day in a new city to wander and get acquainted with the area. She described an experience of wandering during a trip to New Orleans in which she admired the architecture: "*a lot of the buildings have wrought iron balconies that look like black lace*." To account for such moments of discovery and to explore conceptual connections between walking and improvisation [9], we designed Trace to stress emergent engagements over planned activity.

Disorientation: Embracing the Unknown through Wandering

People brought up a number of concerns for safety associated with walks. Many discussed not wanting to walk at night and not feeling safe wandering in certain neighborhoods or around busy intersections. Hailey, a university employee, described experiences of sexual harassment, such as others catcalling her and even being flashed, while walking. Revisiting theories of social mapping [1,11,25], we designed Trace to expose and engage the safety concerns that come with disorientation through wandering.

Motivation through Surprise

After hearing a brief description of Trace and viewing a demonstration of how to use the application, we asked interviewees how they might use Trace. Some people were interested in creating surprises — for example, an "*anniversary gift*": sending a partner on a walk and having her return to a special celebration. Jill, a student in Seattle, expressed the desire to create a location-specific walk for her long-distance boyfriend. She liked the idea of sending him to certain places, such a particular shop or bar, as a type of a scavenger hunt. Roger, an IT Specialist in Bellevue, expressed that he could use Trace to motivate himself and his wife to exercise. The notion of using an unexpected endpoint as inspiration for walking led us to design Trace to reveal the full path upon its completion.

THE TRACE APPLICATION

Trace is an iPhone application for *draw-to-walk* interaction: creating walking routes based on digital sketches. The application converts hand-drafted digital sketches into GIS-based routes that can be shared with others - thus enabling unique engagements through walking. The application consists of two parts: (1) Draw and (2) Walk. Using the Draw function, people can *send a Trace* in three steps:

- *Sketch*: People sketch diagrams with their finger on a blank mobile phone canvas (Figure 4b). They can tap "Annotate" to move to the next screen or "Clear" to erase and start over. Like Southern's prints discussed above, we chose to enable drawing on a clear canvas without a map to encourage alternate connotations and aesthetics, which resists a direct association with particular locations in geographic space.
- *Annotate*: People can associate digital media (images, audio, text) with any point along the line of their sketch. When their recipient later walks the Trace, they will receive the media along the path in the correlated geographic location (Figure 4c and 4d). Building on the work of Chris Speed [27] and others (*e.g.*, [3,17,26]) around location-based information and Rosner and Ryokai's [21] narrative maps depicting the geographic locations people knit, we chose to enable the appearance of annotated messages while walking.
- *Send*: People send their Trace path to one or more contacts, labeling the Trace with an optional title and description (Figure 4e). This orientation toward communication through embodied messaging builds on our prior work on communicative traces [20, 21].

Using the Walk function, people *receive a Trace* in two steps:

- *Select*: People can choose how long and which 'Trace' (the walking route) they would like to walk (Figure 5b and 5c).
- *Walk*: People view a map highlighting the upcoming segment of the journey and describing it in text. As people walk the path, they receive instructions on where to head next and annotations left by the Trace creator. People can turn off automatic routing instructions (using the phone's GPS) to move through the itinerary manually. When people finish the path, they can view the entire path and the image used to generate it (Figure 5d and 5e).

Implementation

We implemented Trace as an iOS app that can run on an iPhone 4, 4S or 5 running iOS 7 or higher. These phones feature a touch screen, a built-in GPS receiver, and Wi-Fi capabilities. We wrote the software in Objective C using the Apple Software Development Kit.

To create a Trace, people draw a closed-loop diagram and embed multi-media (text, photo or audio) annotations on the drawn Trace. The application saves the created Trace with its title and description. To retrieve a Trace, people first choose the duration they wish to walk and then select a Trace. Once they select a Trace, the application calculates a route and plots it onto the map.

The application uses the MapKit SDK to calculate a route with a three-step algorithm:

Step 1: we determine the starting and ending location (latitude and longitude coordinates) based on a person's GPS position.

Step 2: we choose a scale that adjusts the size of the drawing over the map based on the intended duration.

Step 3: we take the projected picture on the map and "snap" each point onto roads.

Each fragment of the path has a start and end point, and the end point of a path is the start of the next one. When the iPhone approaches the end point of the path, the application displays the next segment. At the end of the route, people return back to the initial starting point. While walking Traces, people also encounter annotations as they get close to a trigger point embedded in the original drawing. We save participant responses to a database on Parse.com so that we can connect dyads. During field trials, we released our prototype to people using the TestFlight application.

TRACE IN PRACTICE

After developing Trace, we used the application for three weeks to experience it ourselves and iteratively develop its design. We discovered shorter walks produce several redundant stretches (walking up and down the same block). To account for some of these hurdles, we refined the walking algorithm to include fewer (but still some) redundant stretches, introduced a manual button for moving through directions, and allowed people to see the final path and Trace. We used public online postings for recruitment in three cities: Chicago, Boston and Seattle. We chose major cities with different densities and layouts to examine the varying city landscapes and civic cultures in relation to walking.

We studied sixteen people's use of Trace over five to twenty days to create 33 walks and over 150 test Traces. Four participants made just one walk in 5 days while others engaged Trace repeatedly over a longer period of time. We made the application available to anyone who requested it (baring installation issues) and monitored use on Parse.com.

People ranged in age (21-56) and profession, including a part time dog walker, an employee for the Massachusetts Bay Transportation Authority (MBTA), and a lawyer engaging issues of rights to public space. Five people owned dogs and took regular walks with their dogs. We recruited dyads for the study through flyers and online ads, including siblings, romantic partners, and married couples. Four people used the application alone, without sending Traces to a partner. In one case, the iPhone we installed Trace on belonged to both a mother and daughter. Interview subjects differed from our study subjects; we invited all interviewees, and only three completed our field study. After introducing each person to Trace, we asked them to install the application on their own phones so that they could take walks with Trace as easily as they might use their phone or GPS. We also asked people to fill out an online diary for five days (in a Google Docs form). Diary questions included: What motivated you to create (or not create) a Trace today? How did you decide to walk this particular Trace? How did this Trace compare to other walks you've taken?

Engaging Walks as Creative Things

While designing walks for each other, the drawn walks represented a range of concerns: aesthetic, artistic prowess, the observed environment, and particular jokes or memories. For example, Lulu described aiming for humorous and delightful images that symbolized her relationship with her Trace partner and boyfriend Pablo. Lulu met Pablo at a French cultural center in Boston a few months before using Trace and decided to give him a Trace that might amuse them both. She first thought to draw a heart but wanted

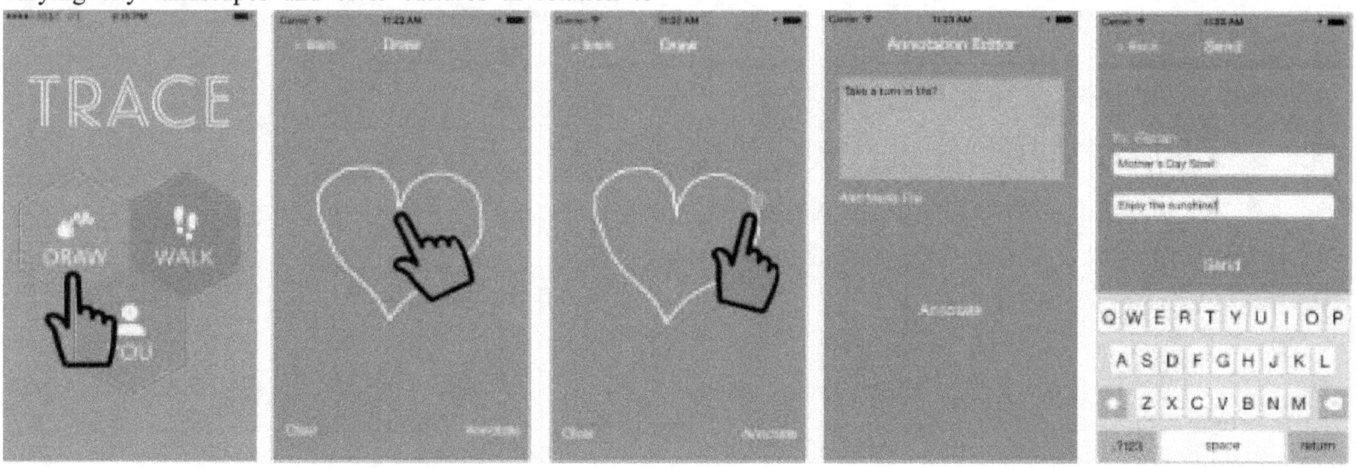

Figure 4: To draw a Trace (from left to right above): (a) touch the "DRAW" button, (b) drawn an image, (c) add one or more annotations by selecting an area of the drawing, (d) add text or media (image, audio) to your annotation, (e) provide a title and description for the Trace to send and save.

something more particular to their relationship. When she tried to draw the outline of France, she found it too difficult to recognizably sketch (or recall). Instead, she found herself drawing an outline of the United States, the country that brought them together, as Pablo came from Columbia and she grew up in the United States. To celebrate this convergence Lulu placed annotations along the outline of the States to evoke what she called "*clichéd American phrases*" such as "*best country ever*" and "*star spangled.*" She decided to walk the Trace with Pablo in downtown Boston one Sunday afternoon.

Similarly playful, Jordan, a 26 year old computer programmer living in Seattle, described wanting to give his partner of five years, Annika, "*a chuckle at the end.*" He sent Annika images of "lude" and humorous drawings such as "pen15" that Annika later described finding funny. Jordan spoke of wanting to try "*hand crafting the experience a little better.*" One aspect of this craft entailed "*place[ing] annotations along the route to give hints and as you go along and you'd have the aha moment about what this experience is about,*" he explained. After recounting her Trace walks, Annika described the application as "*the art of walking.*"

While such communication between couples prompted humor and inventive exchanges, people created a majority of walks for themselves. Many drawings described things in the world (*e.g.*, raindrops, leaves), and others detailed words or reflected visual sensibilities. Sam, an artist, described how he had "*been working with symmetry recently.*" His first Trace took advantage of this symmetry while describing a familiar object: an hourglass. Others had a particular aesthetic in mind: "*I wanted a squiggly circle.*" Often this entailed recreating the drawing more than once to produce more desirable curves, avoiding the automatically closed loop, or creating simpler paths. Sometimes people preferred abstract diagrams: patterns, textures, or simple shapes. As we will discuss, one aspect of these smooth and abstract designs was the experiences they might evoke for the walker along the way.

Perceptions of Familiarity and Safety

In designing new routes and interpreting them, people described feeling compelled to engage the unfamiliar. On Jake's walk through his own neighborhood, for example, he encountered "kooky" city dwellers he likely wouldn't have met on his own. One woman Jake called "*very unique*" he described as "*not a person that I necessarily have a model for in my head.*" Although he wandered in his own neighborhood, he came across moments he perceived to be "*a little strange.*"

This unfamiliarity could sometimes become problematic. Like most tools for generating mapping routes,'s automatic route generation did not account for "unsafe" areas of the city, raising ethical concerns for participants if the areas present real high risk of harm. One participant worked at the border of two neighborhoods in South Boston: the South End and Roxbury. "*The front of the building is in a good part of Boston and the back is in a bad part of Boston,*" she explained. During a routine walk from work at the end of the day, Trace directed her to walk in the Roxbury area. Describing this area as "*one of the scariest places in Boston,*" she chose to end her Trace. In doing so, she raised questions of territory: how GIS-enabled tools figure into the process of carving racial, ethnic, and class-based boundaries. In calling out differences between what Tara described as the "good" and "bad" neighborhood, Trace began to chart discriminatory behaviors.

While some people might not exercise the same judgment as this participant who ended her Trace, a few participants came prepared to engage and dispute issues of spatial inequality and claims to public space raised by the Trace system. A prime example is Gillian, a civil justice lawyer living in Jamaica Plain, one of the greenest and most politically active neighborhoods in Boston. Growing up in Roches-

Figure 5: To walk a Trace (from left to right above): (a) touch the "WALK" button, (b) select the duration of the walk, (c) follow directions provided on the application and use the switch to toggle off the automatically updated directions (based on GPS signal), view annotations along the way, (d) walk the Trace, and (e) view your completed walk.

ter New York to 'countercultural' parents, Gillian associated walking with civic action. On one of the Vietnam moratorium days, she led her seventh grade class out of school to join the march. As a student and later lawyer, she participated in several marches such as the first Earth Day Walk for Water and the AIDs Action Committee. Reflecting on her neighborhood today, she explained: "*Walking into Jamaica Plain is an act of making community constantly.*"

However, even in Jamaica Plain, rights to public space could be difficult to protect. Though she was now 56 and, in her words, "*of an age when I don't get harassed down the street,*" Gillian has still received recent catcalls. She was quick to point out that such experiences suggest that women's limited engagements with public space remain readily curtailed by experiences of being followed or harassed.

Gillian's walking experiences made her more reflexive on her own right to the city: "[it] *made me think about how I take for granted that the sidewalks belong to me as much as anyone else. That wherever we are, that we have a right to be there. That I belong there as much as anyone and that these spaces should be hospitable to me as much as anyone.*" Gillian cast walking as not only an opportunity for public engagement but as call for social change: a responsibility to leave the world better than how she found it. She recalled helping her parents create a 'pocket park' – a small recreational garden accessible to the public – by reclaiming land from an abandoned walkway when she was young. Now living in Jamaica Plain, she sought to fight for what urban theorist Edward Soja [24] might call 'spatial justice,' wherein human rights issues take on distinct meaning at different geographic scales and sites. Karen, who used Trace during a work trip to New York City one week, similarly described running the Boston marathon this year as "*remembrance about what happened last year.*" Walking became important for the solidarity it could enact.

'Slowing Down' and Reflecting on Desires for Efficiency and Control

Several of the people we studied described developing a capacity for noticing their surroundings while using Trace. In describing this heightened awareness they noted multiple engagements that introduced a different pace to daily routines. Jake walked four Traces in neighborhoods he usually biked or ran through but rarely walked: "*For me one of the most surprising things is we went down an alley way that was right next to our house but we hadn't been through before,*" he explained. Another participant similarly discovered a new path to a local park in her neighborhood while taking a walk with her friend one evening with Trace. Though the street she walked was only adjacent to her house, she hadn't explored the area before because she usually took paths reachable by car. Re-discovering features often overlooked in everyday environments invited unexpected surprises.

Beyond locating new paths, the unrolling of directions one segment at a time had the unexpected effect of creating breaks and therefore opportunities for engagement, or what one Seattle resident called "interesting encounters" in his neighborhood. While using Trace, a Boston resident told us she "*made it a point to walk different routes every day.*" Walking became a practice of discovery. For brothers Sam and Jake, walking a trace designed in the shape of an hourglass created unintentional pauses in their walk for "*seeing various people and just talking to them,*" Jake noted. They stopped to watch a young boy play soccer and chat with a women gardening who loved the clean Seattle air. Reflecting on the experience, Jake explained: "*there was a social element to it that we hadn't necessarily thought there would be.*" Participants not only found the pauses accommodated moments for discovering new dimensions of their environment, they also allowed for fresh encounters with the people and situations already there.

While we sought to design for walking without a destination, encoding experiential qualities of walking proved challenging, and in some cases impossible. Busy lives and routes made carving out time for a leisurely or non-'functional' walks difficult. One participant described not "expecting" the application to have considered her wellbeing. Another person explained:

> *Realize I need to not be limited by the dog - probably better to try a few out before having any limitations. Also allow myself to be more exploratory than planned as well - have to let go of known expectations of space.*

Relinquishing "known expectations" meant developing an alternate sensibility about geographic location as well as the efficiency of a route. To reproduce the sketched diagram on city streets, the application reduced the gesture of the hand to points and, in turn, a location along geographical blocks. This had the unexpected effect of prompting people to "double back," as one person noted: walking the same block(s) more than once to create single lines that resembled the drawing. Annika described this process as disorienting:

> *It feels unnatural to walk the same path. Usually people only walk down the same path if they're making mistake. So it's pretty unusual to do that on purpose. [...] I don't think I've ever turned back and walked back unless it was a mistake.*

Like moving down the same road more than once, participants also discussed the demands Trace made on their time, challenging their desire for reaching destinations. Tara, for instance, a call center employee in Boston, described her routine walks in terms of the time they took: "*walk 20 mins to and from work everyday. walk 30 mins to and from the gym everyday. walk my dog twice a day for 15-20 mins.*" Helen, a consultant and educator, described wanting to use Trace to exercise but finding few opportunities to do so. "*I had such a short period of time and it's usually relegated to rudimentary repetitive exercising*," she explained. "*Trace was more exploratory and unknown*." To make time, Helen walked her dog while using Trace but found it difficult to stick to dog friendly areas.

Without the purpose of dog walking, the people related destination-less walking to a loss of autonomy and control. After using Trace over a week, one participant compared Trace to an experience taking acid for the first time: she recalled walking around the same block with a high school friend for two hours, completely fascinated by the world around her. The process of creating a trace presented an equally distinct opportunity for taking an otherwise unusual (and at times redundant) walk.

Seeing like the Algorithm

Before beginning the study, most participants had a very different view of how Trace would utilize their drawing. Familiar with marks that *follow* their movements on digital maps, some described envisioning a process of drawing by walking (as enabled by applications such as the Fitbit). Trace, by contrast, guided people according to a drawing and revealed the path at the end of the journey. Although people received segments of the journey along the way (one to three blocks long), these small segments only hinted at the path yet to come.

This juxtaposition between the trajectories of walking and drawing led to important breakdowns in use. Initially disorienting people, Trace concealed the walking route from the person drawing. "*I didn't quite understand the sizing and how that would translate timewise and spacewise so it was challenging to walk the actual trace as planned based on the park we went to with the dog,*" Helen explained. Translation here referred to reducing the hand-drawn mark into a path that could move along blocks of a city, a process of conversion revealing the (invisible) infrastructure of mapping. After walking her partner's star-shaped Trace, another participant explained: "*I think for the more distance the lines have from one another the less likely it is to make you go down different streets. Say you draw a trace for a circle, it's pretty unlikely it'll have you walk down the same streets but if it's the shape of star then it's more likely.*" People began to follow how the conversion of diagonal lines to a path on a gridded city produced small redundant stretches (see Figure 2). For some, this meant adjusting their drawings to suit city blocks (creating rectangular shapes, for example). Other challenges developed while taking short walks that left little geographic space for an image to emerge. For example, Karen's 10-minute walk while visiting New York City enabled her to do little more than walk around a block. At other times, the GPS failed to synch with GIS satellites to accurately locate participants (particularly when people began their walks inside). Such struggles generating smooth walking routes prompted people to reflect on the (broken) functioning of the GIS algorithm and whether it could be trusted.

Taking advantage of these breakdowns, a few participants oriented their journey using what they learned of the algorithm, determined to use Trace with a destination. Jordan drew two squares that resembled the blocks he stood adjacent to. Others tried aligning Trace with a particular direction and drawing a line in the direction they sought to head (pointing the line north and drawing toward their destination, for example). While heading to the gym one day, Tara drew up in the direction she wanted to walk and then lifted her finger at the end. Since Trace created a closed loop from any drawing (ensuring the end point), she had created a loop she would only half-use. This had the unusual effect of causing her to take a meandering walk that she chose to abandon without reaching its end.

"THE ART OF WALKING"

While travelling by foot remains a central activity in the lives of the people we studied, GIS-enabled technologies have begun to complicate these experiences. Within the spaces we studied, modes of travel have transitioned from trail following to mapping and now GIS routing, introducing new and different complexities to our experience of the sites and communities through which we move. Our work has shown how the algorithmic traces of GIS technologies might present challenges to turning travel into (or returning it to) a form of communication.

Trace ultimately helped us expose these tensions as opportunities for questioning our everyday tools. Though some people found our prototype's limited instructions unfamiliar and struggled to engage its rhythms, other people began to welcome the constraints as providing a view into routing. Still others found the work presented a strange intervention into their daily walking routines. Trace opened up new experiences for participants along routine walks and prompted a return to older forms of travel without destinations. In some cases, experiences of walking unknown paths provoked participants to reconsider the place of GIS technology in their daily lives. These observations emphasize the tensions underlying design for itinerant movement and the difficulties of supporting the negotiation of agency. In the sections that follow, we discuss considerations for HCI research that emerged from these tensions.

Challenges of Design for Enchantment

Our work has surfaced challenges in developing enchantment through GIS routing technology. We found that the combination of unfolding instructions and asynchronous messaging confused people without leading them to loose interest in the path. Participants often discussed a process of defying the technology ('confusing the GPS'), and sometimes reflecting on the procedural logics devising their route. However, the redundant stretches and often mundane settings (selected based on route rather than sightlines, for example) also prompted frustration. This contrast points to the difficulties of designing for curiosity. Although people desire to remain in control of their technology, satisfaction and wonderment could emerge from allowing the (invisible) algorithm to lead the way. Participants described how reconciling these conflicting aims remained a challenge throughout their use of Trace.

Despite concerns for controlling the walk, the Trace application prompted forms of surprise and delight when participants received new Traces. Participants broadly related these experiences of being 'caught up' in moments of wonderment to the social relationship they had with a partner (a long distance relationship), the difficult circumstance of their health (for example, cancer), or their routine responsibilities (dog walking, creating labor opportunities for members of a community). These situations prompt us to consider ways of attending to the intricacies of mundane activities as opportunities for enlivening the everyday.

McCarthy and colleagues [16] have highlighted the concept of enchantment as an experience through which we become awakened to the wonder of life with and through our technologies. Yet, with few exceptions (e.g., [10]), this potential for imagining more intimate relationships with technology has remained under-examined in the design and repair of interactive systems. We found that Trace drew people in to the point of disorientation, amplifying their attention to the minutia of GIS while leaving few familiar cues for them to steady their gaze. In this sense, our work contributes to an understanding of enchantment within HCI by pointing to the challenges of developing emotional attachment to the unknown. Building on prior studies of the interplay between speculation and autonomy [31], we suggest using design interventions that probe commonplace technologies like GIS and the intimate forms of agency those technologies make possible.

The Algorithmic Wayfarer

Our work has also revealed how routing can have itinerant features that expose the always emergent nature of algorithmic life. Creating walking paths by sketching allowed participants to ignite serendipitous connections already underlying their daily interactions within their cities. For some participants this surfaced in response to shifting weather conditions (*e.g.,* drawing a raindrop, thundercloud or leaf discovered on the ground), while at other times this called on aspirational ideas (*e.g.*, the two-masted sailboat that flaunted drawing skills). Several participants relied on abstract shapes to figure out how the mapping algorithm worked for themselves before creating messages for others. Curiously, one participant noted that having access to the original drawing enabled her to see how the application "*lends itself to those kinds of paths*." Here we find an obvious but notable capacity to reexamine algorithms in daily life by considering their connections to more traditional modes of mapping through sketching. Yet, the participant's response above suggests a more nuanced view: that people may not currently live a life of algorithmic awareness, and by introducing new ways of recognizing and interacting with algorithms, we raise the possibility of not only understanding algorithms, but *identifying* with them, too.

These observations may have theoretical and material ramifications for our current understanding of algorithms in HCI. In our study we found the process of creating walking routes became less prefigured and more like the "*art of walking*," to recall Annika's phrase. This approach suggests we imagine alternative modes of mapping that could disrupt, relocate, or disorient rather than direct. Future programs of research could examine this capacity for re-engagement (and displacement) through design: using new mapping tools to trouble the necessity of a destination and invite new forms of expressivity and value. Finding less prescriptive and propositional ways to align new geographies with emergent social and civic engagements remains an important challenge for HCI.

While exposing elements of its underlying logic, the Trace application notably sparked slower experiences of walking. Odom, *et al.* [18] describe similar shifts in their recent studies of slow technology. Yet, if the application had been put to use over several months, this heightened awareness might have led to more instrumental ends. People might have responded to the ongoing misdirection, redundancy or confusion by putting down the application altogether. As other projects have sought to examine through cartographic interventions (see [5]), this project has not offered a corrective to problems proliferating from the rampant use of GPS. Rather, our study has used technological development to engender new lines of inquiry into the character of algorithmic life.

Discrimination by Design

Conventional mapping software can sometimes direct people through hazardous conditions, deteriorating roads or dangerous neighborhoods — taking people to places they may not want to go. Trace amplified this experience. Without controlling for where people walked, Trace guided people to places in the city that seemed disconnected from their daily lives and values. Although people described not wanting to visit some places in their city, for better or worse, Trace still found ways to point them there. This quality highlighted differences in the density and diversity of cities and neighborhoods. Seattle produced few "unsafe" encounters, while in Boston several people noted shifting neighborhoods on their walk and, in doing so, drawing social boundaries, both literally and figuratively. Because the Trace application was not designed for efficient routing but for wandering, people began to think less about where they wanted to go than where they were.

Furthermore, this study has asked us to consider the role GIS algorithms play in shaping our moral visions around claims to public space. As walking remains an act of public and civic engagement, we have a responsibility to continually probe and modify how GIS algorithms to accommodate and account for those who use and rely on them [32]. For example, how do GIS algorithms embody assumptions about walking speed? How do they account for safety, inaccessibility or geographical constraints? As we move forward with this work, we aim to examine opportunities for making these assumptions contestable. How they become part of people's lived experiences of public space raises important questions of pace, expressivity and autonomy for mapping technology today and in the decades to come.

ACKNOWLEDGEMENTS

Many thanks to Andrew Davidson, Nina Shahriaree, Nina Wei, Rijuta Trivedi, Sarah Fox and the adventurous walkers participating in our study.

REFERENCES

1. Alpers, S. "The Mapping Impulse in Dutch Arts," *The Art of Describing: Dutch Art in the Seventeenth Century.* University of Chicago Press, ACM Press (1983),119-168.
2. Amin, A. K., B. T. A. Kersten, O. A. Kulyk, P. H. Pelgrim, CM Wang, and P. Markopoulos. "SenseMS: a user-centered approach to enrich the messaging experience for teens by non-verbal means." In *Proc. MobileHCI*, ACM Press (2005), 161-166.
3. Broken City Project. Online at www.brokencitylab.org/projects/#drift.
4. Cosgrove, D. E. *Geography and vision: seeing, imagining and representing the world.* IB Tauris, 2008.
5. Crampton, J. W., and J. Krygier. "An introduction to critical cartography." *ACME: an International E-journal for Critical Geographies* 4, no. 1 (2006): 11-33.
6. Daston, L. J. (2013). "How Reason Became Rationality," Max Planck Institute for the History of Science website, http://www.mpiwg-berlin.mpg.de/en/research/projects/-DeptII_Daston_Reason/index_html.
7. Debord, G. "Theory of the Dérive." *Internationale Situationniste* 2 (1958): 50-54.
8. Gillespie, T. "Can an algorithm Be wrong?." *Limn* 1, no. 2 (2012).
9. Ingold, T. *Lines: a brief history*. Routledge, 2007.
10. Jackson, S. J., and L Kang. "Breakdown, obsolescence and reuse: HCI and the art of repair." In *Proc. of CHI.* ACM Press (2014), 449-458.
11. Kim, A. *Sidewalk City: Re-mapping Public Space in Ho Chi Minh City.* University of Chicago Press, (2014).
12. Komninos, A., P. Barrie, V. Stefanis, and A. Plessas. "Urban exploration using audio scents." In *Proc. MobileHCI.* ACM Press (2012), 349-358.
13. Kurgan, L. *Close Up at a Distance: Mapping, Technology and Politics*. New York: Zone (2013), 7-54, 112- 127.
14. Latour, B. *Science in action: How to follow scientists and engineers through society.* Harvard university press, (1987).
15. Lash, S. "Power after hegemony: Cultural studies in mutation?," *Theory, Culture & Society*, vol. 24, no. 3 (2007), 55-78.
16. McCarthy, J., P. Wright, J. Wallace, and A. Dearden. "The experience of enchantment in human–computer interaction." *Personal and Ubiquitous Computing* 10, no. 6 (2006), 369-378.
17. Nold, C. Bio Mapping. http://biomapping.net
18. Odom, W. T., A. J. Sellen, R. Banks, D. S. Kirk, T. Regan, M. Selby, J. L. Forlizzi, and J. Zimmerman. "Designing for slowness, anticipation and re-visitation: a long term field study of the photobox." In *Pro. of CHI.* ACM Press (2014), 1961-1970.
19. Robinson, S., M. Jones, J. Williamson, R. Murray-Smith, P. E., and M. Lindborg. "Navigation your way: from spontaneous independent exploration to dynamic social journeys." *Personal and Ubiquitous Computing* 16, no. 8 (2012), 973-985.
20. Rosner, D, K., M. Ikemiya, D, Kim, and K. Koch. "Designing with traces." In *Proc. CHI.* ACM Press (2013), 1649-1658.
21. Rosner, D. K., and K. Ryokai. "Spyn: augmenting the creative and communicative potential of craft." In *Proc. CHI*, ACM Press (2010), 2407-2416.
22. Shepard, M. *The Tactile Sound Garden.* http://www.leoalmanac.org/gallery/locative/tsg/
23. Sinclair, I. *Lud Heat: A Book of the Dead Hamlets*. Skylight Press, 2012.
24. Soja, E.. "The city and spatial justice." *Justice Spatiale/Spatial Justice* 1 (2009).
25. Solnit, R. *Infinite City: A San Francisco Atlas.* Berkeley: University of California Press, 2010, vii, 1-30.
26. Southern, J. http://www.theportable.tv/audiotours.html
27. Speed, C. Walking Through Time. Online at: http://walkingthroughtime.eca.ac.uk
28. Star, S. L., and A. Strauss. "Layers of silence, arenas of voice: The ecology of visible and invisible work." *In Proc. CSCW.* 8, no. 1-2 (1999): 9-30.
29. Suchman, L. "Making work visible." *Communications of the ACM* 38, no. 9 (1995): 56-ff.
30. Taylor, A. S., and R. Harper. "The gift of the gab?: A design oriented sociology of young people's use of mobiles." *CSCW*, no. 3 (2003): 267-296.
31. Taylor, A. S. "Machine intelligence." In *Proc. CHI.* ACM Press (2009), 2109-2118.
32. Weisman, L. K. *Discrimination by design: A feminist critique of the man-made environment.* University of Illinois Press (1994).
33. Ziewitz, M. An Algorithmic Walk. Chapter proposal for digitalSTS. 2014. Online at: http://submit.digitalsts.net.

ArtMaps: Interpreting the Spatial Footprints of Artworks

Tim Coughlan[1], Laura Carletti[1], Gabriella Giannachi[2], Steve Benford[1], Derek McAuley[1], Dominic Price[1], Cristina Locatelli[2,3], Rebecca Sinker[3] & John Stack[3]

[1]University of Nottingham, Nottingham, UK
[2]University of Exeter, Exeter, UK
[3]Tate, London, UK

timcoughlan99@gmail.com, {laura.carletti, steve.benford, derek.mcauley, dominic.price}@nottingham.ac.uk, g.giannachi@exeter.ac.uk, {cristina.locatelli,rebecca.sinker,john.stack}@tate.org.uk

ABSTRACT

Creating and utilizing simple links between items and locations in map-based systems has become a mainstream component of modern computing. In this paper, we explore support for 'art mapping', an activity that requires consideration of more complex interpretations of spatial relationships as users engage with identifying locations of relevance to artworks. Through a user study of the ArtMaps platform, and an exploratory study with professional artists, we identify diverse interpretations of spatial meaning in relation to art. We find that art mapping highlights potential for more active engagement with art through technology, but challenges existing systems for spatial representation. Through connecting our findings with work on designing for interpretation, and on space and place in HCI, we contribute new understanding of creating engagement through the spatial interpretation of art, and define potential characteristics and uses of holistic 'footprints' for artworks.

Author Keywords

Art; location; maps; interpretation; museum; geotagging

ACM Classification Keywords

H.5.m. Information interfaces and presentation (e.g., HCI): Miscellaneous.

INTRODUCTION

The tagging of items to geographical coordinates is an essential feature of online mapping, social and locative media, and photography. The meanings attached are relatively simple, such as the point a photo was taken, or the address of a business. Yet these act to bridge complex forms of human cognition and semantics for understanding the physical world, with computational requirements for defined entities and relationships to query, analyse, and usefully represent in various applications.

CHI 2015, April 18 - 23, 2015, Seoul, Republic of Korea

ACM 978-1-4503-3145-6/15/04...$15.00
http://dx.doi.org/10.1145/2702123.2702281

In enhancing these connections, future applications may demand greater nuance and diversity of spatial representation. In this paper, we explore the practice of 'art mapping' as an application of more complex interpretations of geotagging. Fundamentally, art mapping prompts people to tag artworks to locations on a map. The concept emerged for us in a project to develop novel forms of engagement with geographical data around an online art database. Through this, we have explored the complexity of interpretations that this apparently simple activity produces. Similar activities have emerged elsewhere, suggesting wider, nascent potential (e.g. [12,15] – discussed below).

In this paper, we analyse the results of a user study of a prototype platform, and to complement this from a different perspective, we analyse a study in which professional artists were asked to undertake art mapping and reflect upon it. Through this we make two contributions: Firstly, we demonstrate that art mapping presents new ways to engage with online art collections, with potential to prompt active engagement with art, artists, history, locations, and personal interpretations. This in turn has potential to elicit valuable forms of information. Secondly, art mapping activities present new opportunities and challenges in designing support for human ways of interpreting object-location relationships. This expands the application of concepts of multiple interpretation, ambiguity, space, and place, which have been highlighted as significant to HCI. Using these, we identify characteristics for systems to support novel interactions with the holistic 'footprints' of artworks.

Before introducing the project and studies, we summarise relevant trends to show how art mapping holds potential as a novel form of engagement with art and location.

Engagement through Location

Research around geotagging has highlighted that engaging the public in structured data collection can lead to valuable outcomes, such as improved geographical image search [1], or quantifying the 'aesthetic capital' of locations [21]. Art mapping may hold similar potential, but our understanding of the processes of engaging in this activity are minimal.

Relevant insights can be potentially gained from other technologically-mediated locative activities, such as geocaching - leaving items in locations for others to locate via GPS and the web. Researchers have found that geocaching holds diverse motivations, from provoking exploration of new locations, to seeing a well-known one in a new way [19]. It also provides structure through which stories and experiences can be shared [18]. Focusing on engagement with place-construction, Schaefer et al. created a collaborative authoring environment to support the use of location as an expressive element in creating narratives. While aware of the contributions of others, participant's activities did not generally involve consensus-building or collaboration around features in the environment, but instead resulted in multiple individual interpretations [22].

These 'sociolocative' practices: Social acts communicating around a physical location, have mainly focused on storytelling about authors or specified locations [8]. Art mapping extends this to include an intermediary object: an artwork, and by extension, artists, and the processes and context of the creation of the work. Activities that fit within our definition of art mapping have emerged elsewhere: Halley Docherty merged figurative paintings with Google Street View perspectives for the Guardian [12], and HistoryPin host an activity of 'Putting Art on the Map' to crowdsource locations for World War I artworks from the Imperial War Museum, UK, with over 200 'mysteries' now solved [15]. This highlights that art mapping could, like geocaching, engage and sustain interested communities.

Extending Interaction with Online Art Collections

The project was framed by trends in the museum and art gallery sector, where in many cases, digital technologies are maturing towards more central roles. Two key trends in this are engagement beyond the physical institution, and provisions to open-up authority in engaging the public.

A large number of art institutions have created online interfaces to their collection databases, with the rationale that these reach greater audiences and increase profile. Essential features include functionality to search and view images of works. Commenting, keyword tagging, and games have been used to further engage users [17]. User-generated keyword tagging and folksonomy have potential to augment professional interpretations. The type of artwork may affect how consistently people can suggest tags, but tagging has potential as an access strategy, open to personal meanings, and bridging gaps between the public and professional discourse [24]. Recent discussions of 'Open Authority' in museums argue for platforms to encourage community curation, knowledge crowdsourcing, and greater support for public use of institutional resources [20].

In summation, art mapping is a means of producing and interacting with new forms of geotagged information. It could be valuable as a means to active engagement in museums, by opening up interpretation and supporting exploration of locations in relation to art. In order to design for these qualities, we need to understand how such activities can be engaging, and define the types of relations that people interpret art as having with location. This is therefore the focus of this paper. After presenting our studies and findings, we will draw upon further literature to build implications around interpretation, space, and place.

THE ARTMAPS PROJECT

Context and Aims

Like many collecting institutions, Tate has created an online catalogue of their collection, including a web interface to digitised images of artworks, metadata, and text explanations. This in turn leads to a desire to find ways to extend online engagement beyond simple browsing or thematic tours. In this context, the ArtMaps project was conceived, aiming to find new ways to engage the public in activities that generate and reflect upon geographic information in relation to the collection, and to link work on interpretive tagging and authority in the museum space with sociolocative activities.

In contrast to the other art mapping initiatives mentioned above, we chose to take an open approach with a large, diverse collection of artworks, so as to explore the kinds of interpretations of art mapping that could be made. Our research questions were: How do people engage with, and respond to, activities involving the linking of artworks to mapping systems? And how can processes of mapping art, and the outcomes of these, be understood and designed for?

Preparing the Collection Data

ArtMaps utilizes the Tate collection database of 70,000 artworks. Of these, around 23,000 have place name tags, added by curators. Originally, these were not related directly to coordinates, indeed, over 200 relate to fictional or mythical places. Most tags are countries, cities, or landmarks (e.g. 'India', 'New York' or 'Eiffel Tower'). The automated conversion of these tags into coordinates was attempted as a starting point for the project. Tags were geocoded against databases including GeoNames [10] and Google Places [11], producing coordinates for the vast majority. This was followed by an initiative for staff and the public to locate the remaining tags. Shortcomings in accuracy and granularity were noted (e.g. works tagged with a country name would all appear at the same point), and there remained over 47,000 works that had no place tags to identify. As such, while these automated exercises provided data to initially populate the system, they also emphasised the potential value of engaging the public.

Design of the Prototype ArtMaps Platform

A website with a mobile-optimised version was developed to support art mapping with the collection. On entering the site, users are presented with a world map interface based on Google Maps, with the locations currently ascribed to artworks shown as pins. As localised knowledge is considered key, the system attempts to geo-locate users and show them the local area on entry, but users can also search for locations and explore the wider map. In addition, users can search for artists, titles, or keywords, which returns a list of relevant artworks as search results.

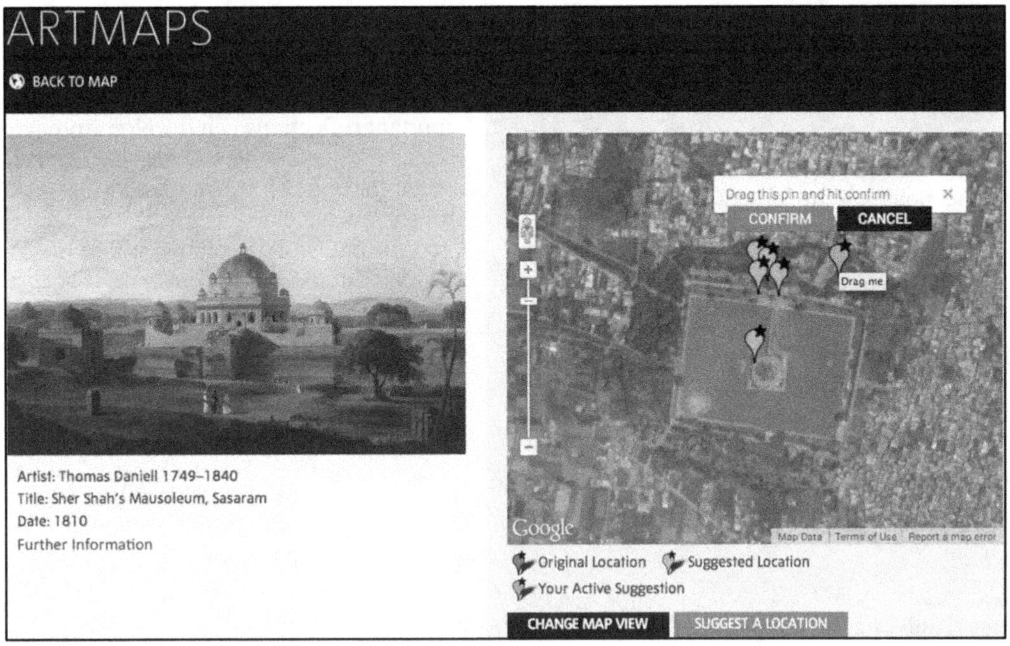

Figure 1: The ArtMaps Platform. An artwork is shown on the left - in this case, Thomas Daniell's 'Sher Shah's Mausoleum'. Users make and view suggestions through a map interface on the right. Previous suggestions from all users are shown as blue pointers.

When users select a pin or search result, the screen is split between an image of the artwork and a map of the existing location suggestions for it (see figure 1). Basic information about the artwork is provided, and a link to another page that contains more detail - commonly a text description written by curators with links to related works and information about the artist. Users are asked to make their own suggestions of locations for an artwork, and to explain these with a text comment. The meaning attributed to a suggestion is a matter for the user to decide. Multiple suggestions can be made about the same work, and these can be linked to blog entries if desired. Users can also switch between the map and a Street View perspective.

STUDIES OF ART MAPPING

In this paper we describe a user study conducted with the ArtMaps platform, where participants were recruited to use the platform and give feedback online. We also describe a study where professional artists were asked to undertake self-directed activities and reflect upon the concept. These studies were conducted in the context of a larger project, and are chosen here to provide two contrasting perspectives: interested members of the public, and makers of artworks with a high level of expertise in interpreting art.

ARTMAPS PLATFORM USER STUDY

26 participants took part in the study. We draw upon their activities and contributions, and on an online survey of open and closed questions completed afterwards by 24 of them. Participants were recruited via mailing lists and social media, and the study was conducted online to provide scope for participants from diverse locations. Geographic spread was of interest to reach beyond the vicinity of the institution, and to include a wider range of localised knowledge. In this regard, 33% of the participants reported living in a different country to the institution. The majority had an interest in arts and culture, with 63% of responses reporting a field of work or study related to heritage, arts, or libraries. 17% worked in education or research, 17% in media technology, and 4% in human resources. 67% of the study participants were male and 33% female. Ages ranged from 23–71, with a mean of 41 and 67% between 31-45.

As part of the study, suggested tasks were given to the participants, designed by the research team and experts at Tate. Participants were also encouraged to explore the platform independently. The suggested tasks had two aims: Firstly to provoke location tagging in relation to a chosen set of artworks as common foci across the participants. For this we asked participants to make suggestions on ten specific artworks, so that a concentration of suggestions around a diverse set of artworks could be studied. Secondly, we wanted to provoke varied forms of individual exploration of the collection. As such, we asked participants to suggest locations for artworks in familiar locations, and also for unfamiliar locations, and to pick an object in their environment, search for it in the collection, and suggest locations for the resulting artworks.

Participants were given up to five weeks to use the platform, with the majority taking four to five weeks before completing the exit survey. Participants received their next task when they had completed the last one. An optional final task asked participants to capture audio from their environment alongside a suggestion. This is not analysed here due to limited space.

Approach to Analysis

Our analysis examined how the location suggestions and comments made on the platform exhibited different interpretations and perspectives on the notion of mapping art (quotes from these are marked as 'platform' in the findings). Responses to survey questions provided further data from which the potential for engagement with, and challenges of, representing these different forms of interpretations could be understood (quotes marked as 'survey'). Rather than attempt to classify types of art (a complex task even for the art historian or curator), we look to identify the types of meaning users interpret the artworks to have in relation to locations. From this perspective, there are still broad distinctions to draw between – for example – suggestions given to artworks that represent an identifiable location, when compared to those that do not. However, our purpose is to identify different forms of art mapping, the processes that occur, and the support required for them.

Findings

Participants in the study made a total of 145 location suggestions and 94 comments across 80 artworks in the collection. This shows that, in addition to the ten artworks directly referenced in the tasks, participants explored further into the collection, and made contributions independently. While the participants were self-selected and the majority already held a strong interest in the arts, their feedback was encouraging for the potential of art mapping as a means to channel interest into recorded information, and support more active forms of engagement than basic browsing. Tracking down locations for artworks was, according to one participant: *"a great experience where I felt I connected more with the image than I would have done"* (P18, platform). Below we analyse characteristics of the different interpretations of how artworks could be located.

Finding the artist's perspective

The most frequent approach taken was to aim to identify the perspective taken by the artist, seen in 33 of the 80 artworks where suggestions were made. This was particular to works that figuratively depict a location. In many cases, perspective finding is engaging and potentially valuable, as even if automated tagging had accurately identified a location, perspective remains to be identified, and could be considered an equally valid or better location for a work.

Investigations of perspective were conducted through personal knowledge, various maps, Street View, or, if possible, by walking around the site. This provides a variable level of challenge: It may be non-trivial even in realistic painting or photography. For example in attempting to locate the perspective of Dennis Oppenheim's photograph: 'Reverse Processing, Cement Transplant, East River, NY'), a range of suggestions covering several kilometres of East River were given. In other cases, there is convergence, but minor variations between suggestions, because it appears impossible to identify a singular perspective with certainty (e.g. figure 2 – left).

Important reflections can develop from uncertainty. In older works, where the landscape has changed beyond clear recognition, points are suggested that fit the available data with statements clarifying a lack of accuracy. A participant noted for one work depicting a familiar location in the 18th century that *"the artist must have been situated quite a distance from the east end"* and it was *"a shame you cannot get this view anymore!"* (P14, platform) with their suggested location in the midst of a modern industrial estate. In such ways, perspective mapping provokes historical reflection, a theme that is discussed further below.

Tagging to geographic feature(s)

The tagging of geographic features was also a frequent approach, seen in response to 27 artworks (figure 2 – right). Participants enjoyed locating works in familiar places, often choosing places that they had known in the past. One stated that *"It was an enjoyable task trying to match up my memory of an area with a work"* (P2, survey). Attitudes to locating unfamiliar places were mixed, ranging from stating that *"locating artworks in places I do not know has been engaging like a treasure-hunt game"* (P6, survey), and *"I did enjoy discovering a new place through the artwork and through the maps I used to locate it"* (P14, survey) to alternatively remarks that they *"did not feel comfortable"* (P7, survey), or had *"no motivation to"* (P9, survey) locate artworks if they had no local knowledge.

Tagging to depicted features becomes more complex with artworks that contain multiple objects of interest, and in many cases these are not in realistic spatial relationships, so could not be tagged through a perspective-based approach. Take the example of David Hockney's 'Meeting the Good People'. This features several Washington D.C. landmarks, but does not present them in their natural spatial relations. An approach taken by a participant here was to individually tag the location of objects that appear in the work. A similar approach was taken in tagging pages of sketchbooks, where a single sketch may contain several locations. In this way, tagging to multiple features is a flexible approach that can overcome the non-spatial arrangements commonly found.

As the system only provided a coordinate point representation, issues arose when attempting to tag at different levels of granularity. Tagging a point is inadequate in accounting for lower fidelity depiction of features, for example to represent that *"[William] Blake's painting is definitely associated with England: the artist, the subject, the hero of the picture"* (P1, platform). It is also notable that perspective and feature-based approaches were not consistently applied by the same participant, or to the same artworks. For example in figure 1, both approaches have been used, although the perspective approach dominates.

Figure 2: Multiple suggestions tagged to the artist's perspective in relation to J.W.M Turner's 'The Colosseum, Rome, from the West' (left) and a tag for Sir William Nicholson's 'Plaza de Toros, Malaga', on the geographic feature depicted (right).

Even abstract works often take inspiration from locations, and in some cases were tagged based on their titles, such as 'Teatro Olimpico', or 'Oxford Street'. Again, investigation prompted by the request to map can lead to new discoveries and understanding. For example on Robert Delauney's 'Windows Open Simultaneously (First Part, Third Motif)', a tag was added to the Eiffel Tower with a comment that: *"I chose this object because I like the colour and abstraction.... I didn't realise it was of the Eiffel Tower until I read the blurb on the website. It was easy to map this location for the content in the image, but not sure if the mapping should only be for what we can see in the image"* (P10, platform).

Historical associations

We have already seen that perspective-based mapping can provoke historical reflections. Historical relationships with locations for both the artist (e.g. where they lived, travelled, and were inspired by) and the work (where it was painted, is, or has been, exhibited) provide further locations regularly suggested by participants (23 artworks). Unlike perspective or depicted features, they could be found for any artwork, with one participant stating that: *"there is always some locational information associated - no matter how tenuous...a picture may be painted in a location, but not be of that location. It may be by an artist who was born in X but emigrated to Y. It may be based on a literary work that was written about a location"* (P15, survey).

Carel Weight's 'Allegro Strepitoso', which depicts a somewhat fantastical scene in a zoo (figure 3), can be found via reading the description to be inspired by Regent's Park Zoo, London. E.g. *"For me the location with the strongest resonance for this picture, is Regent's Park Zoo as it has inspired the scene"* (P7, platform). Here the majority of participants suggested a location at this zoo, with several looking for a point that appeared visually similar, or checking the zoo's website to identify *"where the lions' cage is"* (P5, platform). Others noted that *"the curve of the landscaping seems to suit the content in the artwork...(but) it's hard to know what the structure of the zoo would have been like at the time"* (P10, platform) and that *"It would be interesting to discover this artwork on a visit [to the zoo] or nearby"* (P16, platform). Places of creation and host galleries were also commonly tagged in works where a geographic location was not easily identified - further tags for Allegro Strepitoso suggested both of these. Outside of the works suggested in the tasks, others such as Edouard Vuillard's domestic scene 'The Laden Table' were connected to the artist's home with a comment that *"it seems best to fall back on the original place the artist painted the work as a starting point"* (P14, platform). Contrary to the artist's intent to be ambiguous with space, the prompt to locate the work leads to investigation to find a relevant location, making visible the context and history.

Figure 3: Clustered suggestions in Regent's Park Zoo, London, made in relation to Carel Weight's 'Allegro Strepitoso'.

Archetypical representations of place

As works move away from representational depiction of specific locations, the potential for perspective and feature-based tagging reduces, but other meanings in relation to location can then come to the fore. In particular, many works represent archetypical places that viewers can connect with. In relation to Allegro Strepitoso, there is awareness that even if the work was inspired by *this* Zoo, it is purposefully ambiguous, as the artist intends to convey an archetypal notion of zoo as a place. For example statements that: *"the idea that the zoo could be an archetypical one is also appealing"* (P6, survey) and *"Another possibility is linking with an ideal "zoo", and not necessarily a real one: a place of the mind"* (P6, platform).

Personal associations

It is also clear that artworks showing archetypical places can prompt subjective responses drawing on personal memories. Julian Opie's 'Radio Wind Tyres' – an image of a generic motorway – was given as a suggested artwork in order to explore this effect. The locations suggested for it are completely divergent, covering Europe, the Middle East and North America. Participants could readily identify locations that this work reminded them of, using aspects such as *"the blue tint of the mountains in the distance"* (P11, platform) as cues to find personally meaningful locations. It was noted as *"interesting how you can locate an artwork thorough your own personal connection to it rather than where in fact it depicts, it's great that Opie as an artist includes the viewer behind his thinking"* (P18, platform), also showing the capacity to encourage reflection on the artist's work.

Here, the location tagged is clearly seen as a personal association in comments such as: *"Location obviously not 'correct', landscape doesn't even match, but it was the first road that came to mind"* (P13, platform). There were mixed impressions of engaging with this form of art mapping, with a response that *"A clear memory of mine can be associated with this work, but a memory I have never placed on a map. This was an interesting exercise"*, while also stating that they *"avoided non-topographical works"* (both P15, survey). Though less frequent (5 artworks in total), works chosen by participants also provoked these associations. For example, a participant tagged two locations for Louise Borgeouis's 'Man, Keys, Phone, Clock', reflecting personal memories of places and people.

Representational associations

A final form of place-related meaning for viewers that can be seen in the data is an association to a location for more general reasons. For example responses to Joe Tilson's 'Three Wrist Watches' tag Switzerland - due to an association with clocks and timekeeping - and Azerbaijan, as a viewer visually associated the work with the country's flag. This type of association was infrequent (3 artworks), suggesting it is not an obvious approach, but still one that could provide engagement and potentially useful data.

To conclude our findings, we focus on broader characteristics beyond the types of suggestions made.

Multiple and primary locations

Participants understood that there are multiple possible connections between an artwork and locations, but at times were seen to assume that their suggestion to the system should be singular. One stated that they *"question creating a single location for the content of the image - was the artwork created on site or in a studio in another location?"* (P10, survey) and another that *"there are potentially multiple locations that have strong and weak ties to an artist and a particular work"* (P2, platform). Multiple suggestions could be made and there are varied examples where participants did this. Participants also reflected on which they would consider most meaningful link, qualifying their suggestions with comments of the form *"(this location) seems like the best choice"*, *"if only able to suggest/record one location ... (this) has the strongest relationship"* (P14, platform), or *"the location with the strongest resonance for this picture is..."* (P13, platform).

Leaving the meaning of a suggestion open to interpretation allows choice to engage with the artwork in both artwork-appropriate and personally interesting ways. Investigations can then be intrinsically rewarding and also effective in gathering information that the system does not hold. At the same time, the ability to define the type of suggestion made is desired. Several participants wanted to clarify their type of suggestion beyond adding a comment, and one argued that: *"Location could mean many things here: provenance, production place, place depicted... without any means to indicate exactly what type of location you mean when you place a pointer I'm inclined not to do so"* (P8, platform). However, as the prior sections show, simple categorisation may not capture the nuances of a suggestion, or offer the distinct support to represent it. A further question that arises is how all suggestions for an artwork could be utilized.

Social influences

Where multiple participants made suggestions, it is possible to see elements of social influence in the comments and survey responses. Participants could be seen to be following others lead, stating for example that they chose to place their pin *"because there were other locations in the vicinity which confirmed my selection"* (P10, platform). As well as affirming that they had an appropriate location, they could follow others in the *type* of suggestion that was appropriate to make, for example stating that: *"I agree with other comment... I have suggested the (place of the) production of artwork, but it could easily be what the landscape means to the individual"* (P4, platform). In contrast, artworks without existing suggestions could be seen as an opportunity to open up the space of interpretation, e.g. in one case stating that: *"The painting didn't have any location so I am suggesting two"* (P5, platform).

A DIFFERENT PERSPECTIVE: ARTISTS REFLECTIONS

The project engaged three professional artists to capture perspectives on art mapping from artistic practice and expertise. We aimed to encourage envisioning and critical reflection around the concept, beyond what was possible in a user study of a single platform. The artists were chosen for their specific and distinct interests in using location in their work: Susan Stockwell (SS) works in a range of media and has frequently worked with maps and map-like forms. Nye Parry (NP) creates sound-based installations that utilise notions of space and place. Simon Pope (SP)'s work explores walking in the environment as a dialogic model.

The artists were commissioned to explore art mapping, produce a blog-based report, and a presentation for a public event. They were encouraged to both test the ArtMaps platform, and use other tools as desired. The blog report form allowed the freedom to integrate a range of media elements, which supported further exploration of how to represent relationships between artworks and locations. As well as viewing location as part of their practice, a serious interest is taken in other artists as inspiration and reference points. The artists showed a fluent ability to interpret art in various ways. Therefore they were akin to a demanding power user, confident to push boundaries. As part of their exploration, SS decided to make use of ArtMaps while mobile and reflected on mapping systems in relation to their own artworks. NP used both the mobile and standard web versions, and explored the existing data on artworks in the Tate online catalogue. SP produced a larger set of blog posts, using multiple media to represent explorations of art mapping with a number of chosen artworks.

Findings

The artists reflections proved valuable as they challenged the technological underpinnings of art mapping, envisioned improvements, considered the impact as a frame through which art is viewed, and acted as highly engaged users.

Challenging technological determinations

SP stated that mapping technologies made the assumption that *"'location' was our primary concern"*, that location is *"a spatial coordinate"* and that *"things that 'happen' at these coordinates are termed 'content'"*. Similarly, NP reported being *"struck by the abstract nature of the experience"* of representing artworks as points on a map, leading to thoughts about the geographical distribution of the collection, rather than a rich appreciation of artworks.

SP was drawn to find artworks that *"challenge the system's assumptions about its representation of 'place' as spatial coordinates"*, going on to argue that geo-location pushes us to a blinkered focus on being *"ever more precise"* about location. This acted as a provocation to express what is missing through trying to represent complex space/place relationships. In reference to Robert Smithson's 'Mirror Displacement' works, in which reflections of the sky and other perspectives are depicted, he asked *"Is it enough to replicate the POV or should we also calculate the location of those things represented in the mirrors, as a log of all the locations...referenced in this work?"*. For SS, it was important that *"maps can be played with"*, and are not taken as simply *"correct"*. She noted a distinction between a functional tool that told you what works were on display in nearby galleries, and her vision of art mapping tools that supported rich local relevance and the *"location of personal geographies"*. An interesting counterpoint for SP was that web hyperlinking *"confounds physical geography"*. Thus there are opportunities for overcoming geography and to *"collide"* (NP) or *"layer"* (SS) information to make visible the location-relationships found in an artwork in new ways.

Framing the experience of artworks

All of the artists envisioned ways that art mapping could provide interesting framing to the appreciation of artworks. Such presentation is of course of major concern to artists, and often at the edge of their control.

As in the user study, perspective-based activities occurred and were particularly relevant in revealing how the artist worked, which is key for the practitioner. On finding the perspective depicted in Turner's 'Thames above Waterloo Bridge', SS reported that *"being able to stand in the same place 100 years later is a strange and profound experience. It enables you to gain a deeper understanding of what the artist perceived through his own eyes"*. NP noted that a sense of place particularly emerged when using ArtMaps while mobile. They wanted to extend this to *"tell me about Turner's London, or Constable's Suffolk"*, by juxtaposing sound, historical maps, and other resources in situ. For SS, ArtMaps was a useful way to search for place in art through combinations of location and activity, such as *"artworks that are relevant to the role of tea in London life"*.

To explore the potential to represent narrative around a work, one of SP's blog posts used maps to describe the history of Richard Sierra's 'Tilted Arc', a public sculpture that was controversially removed against the wishes of the artist. Having been cut into pieces and stored in several locations, the artist considers the work destroyed, yet it still physically exists in space, and as a story. Such narratives are considered key to NP as they highlight complex relationships between place, space and art, and could *"build up a kind of biography of the artist and the painting"*.

However, as a means of framing the experience of an artwork, tools for art mapping were of concern when used in relation to works where the artist *"has so carefully constructed the narratives by which to understand his work"*. As an example, SP highlights how Richard Long's 'Two Straight Twelve Mile Walks on Dartmoor' is designed to distil experience and feed the imagination. Mapping this could therefore *"trample all over the poetry of the work"* and *"preclude other understandings or experiences"*. NP also noted that if an artist expected a cartographic framing of their work, they may try to subvert *"the experience that a literal map reading gives you"*.

DISCUSSION

Art mapping presents opportunities to expand space-based systems such that location-relevant interpretations of meaning in artworks can be represented. In applying such Geographical Information Systems (GIS) towards 'spatial humanities' research, geographers and humanities scholars have identified related opportunities and challenges to those faced here in a system for the general public: GIS are beneficial in linking diverse forms of data to locations, but were built with positivist, reductionist, and spatially-deterministic characteristics. Hence, key facets such as subjectivity and place are difficult to represent [3].

Through devising challenging applications like ArtMaps, new forms of spatial systems and activities emerge. To draw implications we focus on two themes and highlight how existing concepts in HCI link with these: Firstly, we explore mechanisms through which art mapping provokes engagement. Secondly, we identify characteristics for systems that represent and use the 'footprints' of artworks.

Interpreting Location as a Means of Engagement

Responses to art mapping suggest new forms of interaction with digital collections, with the potential for self-directed interpretation and engagement that is desired by museums and galleries [17,20,24]. Art mapping provides a frame and provocation for varied personal and shared experiences, from tracking down perspectives, investigating historical sites that are relevant to the work, or exploring associations that the viewer finds and the artist intends to provoke.

Leveraging ambiguity by requesting certainty

Broader notions of designing for interpretation have arose in HCI as part of a greater inclusion of the arts and humanities. Gaver et al. used examples of intentional ambiguity in art, such as the Mona Lisa or Guernica, to highlight the potential of ambiguity as a positive strategy in design. They argue that: *"by thwarting easy interpretation, ambiguous situations require people to participate in making meaning...the artefact or situation sets the scene...but doesn't prescribe the result"*. This can create a *"deep conceptual appropriation of the artefact"* [9].

Two tactics that Gaver et al. suggest to enhance ambiguity are *"Add incongruous functions to breach existing genres"* and *"Over-interpret data to encourage speculation"* [9]. In ArtMaps, the ambiguity present in the spatial meanings of artworks is leveraged as a means of engagement, by asking for a concrete response of specific coordinates. Giving these responses through a system for objective cartography could seem incongruous to both the study participants and artists, but it pushed them to investigate, decide, and create answers where they might otherwise remain passive.

Harnessing the capacity for multiple interpretations

Explorations of ambiguity have extended to interpreting location in mixed reality and ubiquitous computing. One theme in this has been ways in which uncertainty around location is inherent, and can be dealt with by deliberately revealing it, as users are generally adept in exploiting and approximating it [2,5]. This points to a gulf between human ways of understanding location and spatial approaches where ambiguity is excluded or considered negatively. Sengers & Gaver argue for the potential of systems that support multiple interpretations of their use and downplay the system's authority [23]. In ArtMaps, supporting users to make multiple suggestions helps them to understand that no answer need be the single correct one, and collected data could include different interpretations of spatial meaning.

Participants were led by the contributions previously made by others, and/or took their lead from our suggested tasks. Our results describe the set of observed interpretations of art mapping from these studies, but more could exist or be devised. While characteristics of the artwork may lead towards primary forms of interpretation or most-appropriate locations, users or designers could choose from a variety of foci. We may decide to investigate the artist's perspective, or interrogate the history of the work to develop a spatial narrative around it. This plurality and adaptability should be harnessed in designing art mapping systems and activities, as a means to maintain engagement and create more holistic datasets for artworks.

Supporting the Creation of Footprints for Artworks

Given our findings, we suggest that the multiple, diverse relationships between an artwork and locations could be conceptualised holistically as a 'footprint', with spatial and 'placeful' aspects. Such a data structure could be valuable in varied applications, from providing highly personal, contextualised mobile experiences, to new visualisations of the associations between an artwork, artist, or collection and its viewers. Here we summarise our findings through this and highlight value that could be drawn, both from the data produced, and the activities that produce it.

Space and place in art mapping

Prior discussions of space and place in philosophy and HCI provide a conceptual basis through which to examine the potential characteristics of a spatial footprint for an artwork. For de Certeau, place is *"the order (of whatever kind) in accordance with which elements are distributed in relationships of coexistence"*. Space *"exists when one takes into consideration vectors of direction, velocities, and time variables"* [6]. From a HCI perspective, Harrison & Dourish, consider that Space as *"the opportunity"*, is usefully distinguished from Place as: *"the understood reality"* [13]. However, a layer-cake model that deems space or place to be the pre-requisite of the other misses the complexity of this [7,14]. Instead, Harrison & Tatar identify the meaning of a place as a semantic tangle of mutually constituting resources: people, events, and loci - objects or locations that are a focus of attention [14].

It has been argued that the notion of space is detached from realities of experience [16]. Yet spatial systems underpin how online information is linked to the physical world. Brown & Perry note that a map is *"very spatial in the sense that it is both abstract and geographical"*, but also has *"platial"* characteristics, like being read in specific places, or altering how we perceive a place [4]. Dourish argues that current spatial technologies are limited by a focus on navigation, and that designers should move from asking *"how we might find our way"* to *"how, in our encounters with space, we might find **more** than our way"* [7].

To use these concepts while avoiding a layer-cake model, we suggest that certain aspects of art mapping, such as identifying a perspective, are primarily spatial as they reflect interpretations of how an artist represents space. But comments show that these activities also provoke valuable thoughts in relation to place. Other activities, still with a spatial basis, primarily focus on developing links to places, such as investigating where the artist lived or worked, or reflecting on emergent associations in viewing archetypical representations of place. All of these activities can create spatial data, and there are multiple ways in which this can enhance a sense of place. The footprint should therefore represent different relations of art and space (perspective, features), and also support further interaction around personal and contextual aspects of art-place relations (e.g. historical, archetypical). Thus we identify characteristics that would give a footprint value from each perspective:

A spatial perspective on footprints

Effective support for art mapping could make visible holistic views of relationships between artworks and locations. In envisioning support for the creation of this, we find the need to move from our existing ability to designate individual point-relationships, towards new interfaces and complex data structures. Key characteristics include:

Multiple, categorised links to locations: Interfaces to mapping systems used in web and social media systems are not currently designed to support multiple locations to be linked with a single object. Neither do they support different types of relationships, or capture how these should be interpreted. In art mapping, we identify a clear need for this. After the studies took place, a further iteration of the platform was developed to include support to categorise suggestions. Future work will explore how to adapt to different categorisations as suggested in the findings, and to then utilise these suggestions according to their categorisations. A further aspect is that particular links may be considered of primary importance by particular viewers. Hence, the capacity to foreground – generally or personally –could be useful in engagement and to produce useful data.

Advanced forms of representation: Our findings suggest potential to appropriate, and to create new forms of spatial representations. Using polygon functionality to represent areas, or making perspectives comprised of point and direction, would be useful additions, but capturing the footprints of works that take ambiguous, creative, or non-spatial approaches to their composition requires more than this. For example, to support the combination of perspective and feature mapping, we could envisage a juxtaposition of multiple coordinates and views, represented by folding relevant parts of the map onto parts of the artwork, and to *"collide"* the map and artwork as suggested by Nye Parry.

Amalgamations of links: As suggested by the above, some of the value in art mapping is a capacity to interrogate a holistic view of the relationships with locations. Beyond a map that shows all the relevant points, a footprint interface could visualise different types of links in meaningful ways. For example showing a story of the creation of the work, including locations the work was inspired by, where it was actually created, and where the artist learnt techniques used.

Identifying spatial relevance: In its simplest form, geo-location can reveal works relevant to current location, and other work in the ArtMaps project is exploring the use of the collection data in locative media experiences. Further data could be used to extend this, for example utilising a history of where a person has lived or visited, travel plans, or commonly searched locations, to reveal relevant art.

A placeful perspective on footprints

Combining narrative, art and spatial representation provides a new means to construct and appreciate places through historical and personal stories, and we find numerous examples where art mapping drew greater attention to places, in situ of a relevant location, or at a distance. The potential to support greater 'placeful' engagement with the footprints of artwork is therefore an important challenge and opportunity, with the following key characteristics:

Presencing: Further activities conducted in the project have involved walking between the galleries and locations depicted in the works on display, and combining historical tours with prompts to view relevant artworks. In this vein, and in line with the views expressed in the artist's reflections, we envision footprints supporting further 'presencing' activities – experiences designed to bring a sense of being present in a particular place. For example with the artist at the point where the work was created.

Accommodating memories and associations: Art mapping can prompt and record memories and associations around places as a particularly personalised type of engagement. With this in mind a footprint could support personal narratives intersected with artworks, and further presencing activities that share personal experiences of artworks in place. Collected data could also be used as a basis for participatory interrogation of what the artist has achieved in terms of provoking associations with place for the audience.

Identifying placeful relevance: Aside from relevance to particular locales, artworks can hold place-related meanings that are archetypal – e.g. a zoo or domestic scene. This suggests potential to relate works with all instances of a form of place. Stronger ties may be found with some instances, e.g. based on the colour used, the shape of an object, or the activity or mood depicted. Thus interfaces could broaden relevance by making visible artworks that are resonant with particular surroundings. This would constitute a novel application of Harrison & Tatar's suggestion to design *"specific places for specific people engaged in specific events in specific locations"* [14].

Concealing the spatial: Our findings suggest that in some cases an overtly spatial view can overwhelm appreciation of artworks and places, focusing attention on abstract spatial distribution or accuracy of location. In certain contexts, there may be value in covering up the spatial underpinning of art mapping, to allow placefulness to come to the fore.

CONCLUSIONS

Art is an essential form of human expression and creativity that is commonly considered antithetical to the mechanistic and rational. Art mapping takes these expressive forms, and asks us to represent them via geotagging. In this, art mapping is an unconventional activity that both utilises and challenges spatial systems. By analysing the different approaches taken in the user study, and the visions and critique of current systems by the artists, we have highlighted the potential for conceiving engagement with a broader 'footprint' of an artwork. Through this, systems could make visible human ways of understanding artworks, while maintaining the benefits of a spatial approach.

A further iteration of ArtMaps is available online at: http://artmaps.tate.org.uk, with source code available to reuse or adapt with other collections. In this iteration, we have begun to address some of the design issues raised here, such as classifying forms of suggestion. Future work will look to further challenge the singular 'dot on the map' representing most object-locations relationships.

By studying art mapping we extend geotagging, and hit limitations in functionality that suggest directions towards extending spatial representation. As well as identifying characteristics for novel systems to engage with the richly interpretable objects found in art galleries and museums, we would suggest that systems in areas such as online mapping and social media could expand the ways in which they utilise geotagging towards greater openness to multiple, user-constructed meanings. This data may need structure and categorization, but the approach has value in opening up to user-led construction of multiple interpretations of object-location relationships. In developing UbiComp and an Internet of Things, the implications of art mapping could be applied to other objects where singular forms of location tagging may actually be fundamentally insufficient.

ACKNOWLEDGEMENTS

This work was funded by RCUK through the Horizon Digital Economy Research grant (EP/G065802/1) and an RCUK Telling Tales of Engagement grant (EP/K037560/1).

REFERENCES

1. Arase, Y., Xie, X., Duan, M., Hara, T., & Nishio, S. (2009). A game based approach to assign geographical relevance to web images. Proc. WWW'09. ACM. 811-820
2. Benford, S., Anastasi, R., Flintham, M., Drozd, A., Crabtree, A., Greenhalgh, C., Tandavanitj, N., Adams, M., & Row-Farr, J. (2003). Coping with uncertainty in a location-based game. IEEE pervasive computing, 2(3), 34-41
3. Bodenhamer, D. J., Corrigan, J., and Harris, T. M., eds. (2010) Spatial Humanities : GIS and the Future of Humanities Scholarship. Indiana University Press.
4. Brown, B., & Perry, M. (2002). Of maps and guidebooks: designing geographical technologies. Proc. DIS'02. ACM. 246-254
5. Chalmers, M., & Galani, A. (2004). Seamful interweaving: heterogeneity in the theory and design of interactive systems. Proc. DIS'04. ACM. 243-252
6. De Certeau, M. (1984) The Practice of Everyday Life, tr. by S. Rendall, Berkeley California: University of California Press. 117
7. Dourish, P. (2006). Re-space-ing place: place and space ten years on. In Proc. CSCW'06. ACM. 299-308
8. Erickson, I. (2010). Documentary with ephemeral media: Curation practices in online social spaces. Bulletin. Science Technology & Society, 30(6), 387-397
9. Gaver, W., Beaver, J. & Benford, S. (2003). Ambiguity as a resource for design. Proc. CHI'03. ACM, 233-240
10. Geonames, http://www.geonames.org/
11. Google Places, https://developers.google.com/places/
12. http://www.theguardian.com/profile/halley-docherty
13. Harrison, S., & Dourish, P. (1996). Re-place-ing space: the roles of place and space in collaborative systems. Proc. CSCW'96. ACM. 67-76
14. Harrison, S., & Tatar, D. (2008). Places: people, events, loci–the relation of semantic frames in the construction of place. J. of CSCW, 17(2-3), 97-133
15. History Pin: https://www.historypin.org/projects/
16. Ingold, T. (2009). Against space: Place, movement, knowledge. In. Boundless worlds: An anthropological approach to movement, 29-43
17. Lopatovska, I., Bierlein, I., Lember, H., & Meyer, E. (2013). Exploring requirements for online art collections. Proceedings of the American Society for Information Science and Technology, 50(1), 1-4
18. Neustaedter, C., Tang, A., & Tejinder, J. K. (2010). The role of community and groupware in geocache creation and maintenance. Proc. CHI'10, ACM. 1757-1766
19. O'Hara, K. (2008). Understanding geocaching practices and motivations. Proc. CHI'08. ACM. 1177-1186
20. Phillips, L. B. (2013). The temple and the bazaar: Wikipedia as a platform for open authority in museums. Curator: The Museum Journal, 56(2), 219-235
21. Quercia, D., O'Hare, N. K., & Cramer, H. (2014). Aesthetic capital: what makes London look beautiful, quiet, and happy?. Proc. CSCW'14. ACM. 945-955
22. Schaefer, M., Tatar, D., Harrison, S., (2010) Can CSCW Technologies Help Us Re-construct Places?, Proc. CSCW'10. ACM. 567-576
23. Sengers, P., & Gaver, B. (2006). Staying open to interpretation: engaging multiple meanings in design and evaluation. Proc. DIS'06. ACM. 99-108
24. Trant, J., & the participants in the steve.museum project. (2006). Exploring the potential for social tagging and folksonomy in art museums: Proof of concept. New Review of Hypermedia and Multimedia, 12(1), 83-105

Sangeet Swara: A Community-Moderated Voice Forum in Rural India

Aditya Vashistha[†] **Edward Cutrell**[§] **Gaetano Borriello**[†] **William Thies**[§]

[†]University of Washington
{adityav, gaetano}@cs.washington.edu

[§]Microsoft Research India
{cutrell, thies}@microsoft.com

ABSTRACT
Interactive voice forums have emerged as a promising platform for people in developing regions to record and share audio messages using low-end mobile phones. However, one of the barriers to the scalability of voice forums is the process of screening and categorizing content, often done by a dedicated team of moderators. We present Sangeet Swara, a voice forum for songs and cultural content that relies on the community of callers to curate high-quality posts that are prioritized for playback to others. An 11-week deployment of Sangeet Swara found broad and impassioned usage, especially among visually impaired users. We also conducted a follow-up experiment, called Talent Hunt, that sought to reduce reliance on toll-free telephone lines. Together, our deployments span about 53,000 calls from 13,000 callers, who submitted 6,000 posts and 150,000 judgments of other content. Using a mixed-methods analysis of call logs, audio content, comparison with outside judges, and 204 automated phone surveys, we evaluate the user experience, the strengths and weaknesses of community moderation, financial sustainability, and the implications for future systems.

Author Keywords
HCI4D; ICT4D; Interactive Voice Response; IVR; India

ACM Classification Keywords
H.5.2 Information Interfaces and Presentation (e.g., HCI)

INTRODUCTION
Of the world's 7 billion mobile phone subscriptions, 78% are in developing countries [4], where phones are still used primarily for voice calls. Though smartphone penetration is growing – in India it is 10% [18], versus a mobile penetration of 73% [6] – there is still limited availability of Internet-enabled devices and bandwidth in rural contexts. Moreover, language and literacy constraints prevent usage of traditional online resources. In India, 26% of adults are illiterate [2] and 72% are illiterate with respect to English [9].

In light of these constraints, researchers have turned to *voice forums* as an inclusive means of accessing, reporting, and sharing information in rural communities. Using Interactive Voice Response (IVR), a voice forum allows users to record and listen to messages in their local language via ordinary calls on low-end mobile phones. Recent voice forums have spanned various domains, including citizen journalism [3, 13, 19], agriculture [1, 5], feedback on school meals [12], job search [30], and rural information portals [7]. Together, these forums have attracted millions of calls and hundreds of thousands of recordings.

However, one bottleneck that has prevented voice forums from rivaling the scale of large Internet websites is the process of content curation and moderation. In order to ensure respectful, accurate, and high-quality recordings, large voice forums typically employ a dedicated team of moderators, who screen recordings, offer feedback to contributors, and perform tagging, annotation, and categorization of posts. For example, both CGNet Swara [19] and Gram Vaani [3] currently employ 10-15 full-time moderators. If these platforms were to grow by orders of magnitude, it would be very difficult to manage commensurate growth of the moderator team.

In this paper, we describe Sangeet Swara[1]: a voice forum that uses *community moderation* to overcome the limitations of a dedicated moderator team. Sangeet Swara is a platform for people in rural India to share songs, poems, jokes, and other cultural content. In addition, it relies on users to rate the quality of content they hear on the system. These ratings, in turn, influence the order that recordings are played to other listeners, thereby improving the overall user experience. While community moderation has been successfully used on Internet websites, such as Reddit and StackOverflow, to date it has not been used to influence the playback priority on a voice forum. Extending community moderation to an IVR platform involves several unique challenges, including the limited affordances of the interface and users' limited experience with technology, especially in rural India.

Our primary contribution is the design and 11-week deployment of Sangeet Swara, which we evaluate along three dimensions: the engagement of users, the accuracy of community moderation, and financial sustainability. We find that users were highly engaged, with over 25,000 calls and 5,000 recordings from over 1,500 people. The service found unexpected uptake among visually impaired users, who were especially passionate about building and maintaining the community. We show that community moderation was 98% accurate in categorizing the content and gender of posts; it also made meaningful distinctions between high-quality and low-quality

[1]Sangeet Swara is a Hindi phrase meaning "musical voices."

CHI 2015, April 18–23 2015, Seoul, Republic of Korea

ACM 978-1-4503-3145-6/15/04 ... $15.00
http://dx.doi.org/10.1145/2702123.2702191

posts, and made judgments that were in 90% agreement with researchers on a sample of recordings. We also conducted an automated phone interview with 204 users, and offer qualitative findings regarding their perceptions of the service as well as the strengths and limitations of community moderation.

As a secondary contribution, we also advance the dialogue surrounding financial sustainability of voice forums in the developing world. Up until now, voice forums have relied on expensive toll-free lines in order to make them accessible to low-income callers. However, as usage scales, toll-free lines become too expensive to sustain [25]. The most direct solution to this problem is for users to pay for their own calls: an experiment that we tried in two different contexts. In Sangeet Swara, we eventually disabled the toll-free access, but found that even the most fervent rural users were unable to bear the cost of phone calls. As a follow-up experiment, we also describe Talent Hunt: an adaptation of Sangeet Swara to a higher-income context. Though Talent Hunt received considerable use, including about 27,000 phone calls from 12,000 different callers, this usage was driven mainly by a promotional contest and disappeared as soon as prizes were awarded. We discuss the lessons learned from this deployment and the implications for future voice forums.

RELATED WORK

As discussed previously, several voice forums have targeted developing regions [1, 3, 5, 7, 12, 13, 19, 30]. Most closely related to our work is a system called Gurgaon Idol, where callers to an IVR service recorded and rated audio recordings to influence eventual playback on a community radio station [15]. However, this research focused on the usability of the recording interface, the voting interface, and training of users. It did not aim to incorporate the ratings to control the playback order in a voice forum.

Prior research has demonstrated that entertainment content drives technology adoption by low-income people in the developing world [24, 27]. In fact, even voice forums that are intended for other purposes often see many recordings of songs, religious verses, and other performances [5, 13, 19]. Recognizing the appeal of entertainment, a platform called Polly allowed people to record messages, manipulate recorded messages, and forward them to friends [26]. Polly spread rapidly to many users in Pakistan and has since provided job search information as well.

The curation tasks performed by callers on Sangeet Swara are related to crowdsourcing efforts in developing regions. Jana (formerly known as txtEagle [11]), mClerk [14], and MobileWorks [21] enable users to earn money by completing small tasks on low-cost mobile phones, using either mobile Internet or SMS. We are unaware of any paid crowdsourcing platform that administers tasks via an IVR interface, as used by callers to moderate posts on Sangeet Swara.

Several news and social networking sites, including Reddit, Slashdot, StackOverflow, and others, use community votes to determine the ranking of user-generated content. There is also a mature literature on collaborative filtering and community moderation algorithms [28]. However, we are unaware of prior efforts to perform community moderation on a voice forum, which is different in several ways. For example, audio content is more difficult to skim than textual content, meaning that users may lose patience in hearing and ranking lower-ranked posts. An IVR system can also track exactly what a user listened to and what content they skipped, which is difficult to do on a webpage. Finally, the limited affordances of an IVR interface and the limited technology skills in developing regions add more constraints to our design scenario.

RESEARCH QUESTIONS

Our research goal is to create a vibrant virtual community that is inclusive of low-income users in rural India. Our success metrics are three-fold. First, do participants value their interactions with the community? Second, can the community moderate itself without outside assistance? And third, can it be financially sustainable?

In the following sections, we describe the design of Sangeet Swara, its deployment in rural India, and its evaluation using the three metrics above. We also present a follow-up experiment, Talent Hunt, that attempted to improve on financial sustainability by seeding usage in urban areas.

SANGEET SWARA DESIGN

Sangeet Swara was a voice-based platform, accessible via mobile phone, where callers could record songs, poems, jokes, and other cultural content. A key aspect of the system is that it *ranked* the recordings based on feedback from the community. The ranking aimed to order the posts according to what was most likely to be enjoyed and appreciated by listeners. There was a single, global ranking computed across all recordings and all listeners in the system. In addition to the rank order, the system calculated a separate *playback order* that determined which post a listener heard at a given time. The playback order balanced the interests of listeners (who desired to hear high-quality posts) with the interests of content contributors (who desired to have as large of an audience as possible). Both the rank order and playback order were dynamically updated based on listeners' ratings of the content. We give more details on these orderings later.

Call flow

Sangeet Swara relied on key press (DTMF) navigation: users listened to an audio menu and indicated their selection by pressing a digit. Though not as expressive as free-form speech, DTMF interactions have been shown to be robust and also preferred among users in rural India [23].

The high-level call flow is illustrated in Figure 1. The first thing that callers heard was an 8-second folk music excerpt, followed by a greeting in a male voice: "Friends, welcome to Sangeet Swara. You can record and listen to songs, poems, and jokes. Please note, it is free to call on this number." Then they were asked to select between the following options:

1. **Check on your posts.** Users who had recorded at least one post could listen to all of their recordings and also learn what rank they had obtained in the system. For users who had not recorded anything, this option was omitted.

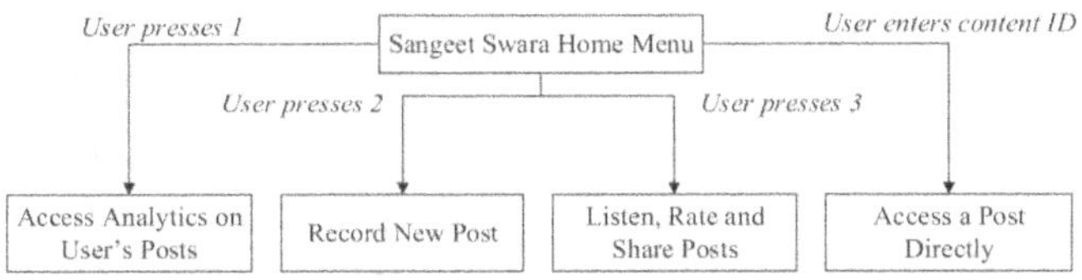

Figure 1. High-level call flow of Sangeet Swara.

2. **Record a post.** Users were encouraged to introduce themselves as part of their recording. We restricted the length of recordings to 60 seconds (plus a 10-second buffer for the introduction). After recording a post, users received an SMS with a unique five-digit numeric ID for that post. This ID could be shared and used to jump directly to the post (details below).

3. **Listen to other posts and rate them.** When users chose to listen to posts, first we played the top ranked post (introduced as "the best message on the basis of community votes"). Playing the best message first ensured that callers heard at least one high-quality recording per call. It also engendered friendly competition to be featured in the top spot. After the first post, users listened to other posts in the playback order computed by the system. In advance of playing each post, the system announced its current rank among all posts recorded to date. Since the rank order and playback order were different, users listened to an unpredictable mixture of highly-ranked and low-ranked content.

   After listening to a recording, users were required to give feedback by pressing a key for "like" or "dislike." Users could also interrupt the playback of a post to offer an early judgement, in which case the remainder of that post was skipped. Each user had only one vote to count towards a given post; if they played a post twice, they could change their vote but not increase it. Users could also press a key to receive an SMS that was suitable for sharing with friends. The SMS contained the unique ID of the post and instructions for accessing it on Sangeet Swara.

4. **Jump directly to a post.** Users could directly jump to a post by entering its ID number at the main menu. The first digit of the ID number was always different than the other options at the main menu, enabling users to make the jump immediately without navigating through any other menus.

Our design of menu prompts respected the lessons learned from prior IVR systems in low-income communities [5, 8, 16, 17]. The prompts were recorded in the local language and accent of the target area (North Indian Hindi), with slow and clear diction by the speaker (a male). Prompts explained each possible action before the corresponding key press; keys had consistent meanings across all menus; multi-digit inputs were avoided as much as possible; and invalid key presses led to explanatory error messages.

We used iterative prototyping to refine the system in advance of deployment. In a formative evaluation with our colleagues, 28 callers placed 236 calls over a period of 3 weeks. To understand usability barriers, we performed participant observation and conducted five unstructured interviews. This led to several improvements. For example, before posting a recorded message, the system played it back and asked for confirmation from the user.

Towards the end of our field deployment, we also augmented the call flow with an additional feature. We identified regular users (those who had called at least ten times) and notified them, at the beginning of the call, that they were now a "senior member" of the Sangeet Swara community. Commensurate with this distinction, we asked them to take on a new responsibility, which was to answer one pre-recorded question at the beginning of each phone call. As detailed later, we used these questions both to conduct surveys of the users and to take users' help in categorizing the content recorded by others. The survey questions solicited free-form audio responses, while the categorization questions were multiple choice. Senior members could advance to the main menu of Sangeet Swara only after answering the question posed.

Rank Order

The rank order aims to sort posts by increasing order of quality, as determined by users' upvotes and downvotes. There are two criteria that contribute to the rank ordering:

- High scores: a post with a higher ratio of upvotes to downvotes is likely to be of higher quality.
- High confidence: for comparable ratios of upvotes to downvotes, we have more confidence that a post is good if more people have voted on it.

Following Reddit's algorithm for sorting comments [20], we integrate both of these concerns by calculating the lower bound of the Wilson score confidence interval for a Bernoulli parameter:

$$\frac{\hat{u} + z_{\alpha/2}^2/2n - z_{\alpha/2} * \sqrt{[\hat{u}\,(1-\hat{u}) + z_{\alpha/2}^2/4n]/n}}{1 + z_{\alpha/2}^2/n}$$

Here, $\hat{u}$ is the fraction of upvotes, n is the total number of votes, and $z_{\alpha/2}$ is the $(1 - \alpha/2)$ quantile of a standard normal distribution. We used the lower bound of a 95% confidence interval ($\alpha = 0.05$) to compute the rank score. The post with highest score was assigned the top rank.

Playback Order

The playback order refers to the sequence in which a user listens to posts. The playback order needs to balance the following competing criteria:

- Listeners want to hear good content. This prioritizes posts with a large fraction of positive votes.
- Contributors want their posts to receive a fair ranking. This prioritizes posts with a small number of total votes (since more votes lead to a more accurate assessment of quality).

To balance these concerns, we calculate a post's playback priority according to the following formula:

$$\frac{U}{U+D} * (1 - DF)^{U+D}$$

Here, U is the number of upvotes for the post, D is the number of downvotes for the post, and DF is a discount factor that serves to balance the concerns of listeners and contributors. We used a discount factor of 0.333 after analyzing a range of values and their impact on example scenarios. We initialize posts with a single upvote to avoid division by zero.

The first term of the equation represents the priority of playback according to listeners (criterion 1), while the second term captures the priority for contributors (criterion 2). Larger numbers represent a higher priority.

When a user elects to listen to posts, the system plays the highest priority posts that the user has not yet voted on. If the user has voted on all the posts, then attention is restricted to posts the user has liked in the past, and playback proceeds in rank order instead of playback order.

Our calculation of priority is similar to other rankings that reconcile the competing metrics of quality and recency. In our context, recency corresponds to the total number of votes that a post has received to date, rather than the time elapsed since the recording.

SANGEET SWARA DEPLOYMENT

Sangeet Swara was deployed for eleven weeks. In order to lower the barriers to participation, we launched the service using a toll-free (1-800) number. However, as toll-free lines become expensive at a large scale, we also wanted to explore if users would pay for the phone calls. Thus, we moved the service to a regular number after about seven weeks.

To create awareness about Sangeet Swara in rural and small-town India, we posted a message on CGNet Swara, a voice forum for citizen journalism that has considerable reach in rural areas. The post was accessible to CGNet Swara callers for two days, during which time it was heard by 393 unique callers. Out of those, 73 people placed a call to Sangeet Swara. In order to help Sangeet Swara feel familiar to prior users of CGNet Swara, and to set the standards for the community, we seeded Sangeet Swara with fifteen songs and poems that appeared previously on CGNet Swara.

Sangeet Swara had significant uptake. As summarized in Table 1, the system received over 25,000 phone calls from over 1,500 people. There were about 5,000 posts recorded, about 200,000 playback events, and about 140,000 votes cast. Figure 2 depicts the usage over time. As detailed in the next section, usage was highest among low-income people from rural and peri-urban areas of northern and central India. Also, the service saw a high uptake among visually impaired users.

Unfortunately, usage of the system dropped dramatically when we converted the toll-free lines to regular lines. We revisit the question of financial sustainability later, both in the context of Sangeet Swara as well as a follow-up experiment.

EVALUATING THE USER EXPERIENCE

This section aims to evaluate users' experience of Sangeet Swara, including the worth they attached to the system.

Methods

We used a mixed methods approach spanning qualitative and quantitative analyses. Our primary tool was an automated phone survey, which presented a single pre-recorded question to regular users each time they called. There were nine questions about basic demographic data (sex, age, education, technology exposure, etc.) and six open-ended questions probing the background of the listener (e.g., "tell us about yourself"), their conception of Sangeet Swara (e.g., "how would you describe Sangeet Swara to a friend"), the quality of community moderation, and the strengths and weaknesses of the platform. The survey was live for ten days. All responses were provided in audio format and then translated, transcribed, and analyzed using open coding and axial coding. A total of 204 people (out of 409 regular users) answered one or more of the survey questions, and each question was answered by at least 100 people. On average, free responses were 36 words long.

	Sangeet Swara	Talent Hunt
Deployment Duration	11 weeks	22 weeks
Language of Prompts	Hindi	English
Calls	25,381	27,514
Callers	1,521	11,751
Posts	5,376	368
Contributors	516	304
Average Call Duration	4.96 mins	2.37 mins
Total Plays of Posts	198,898	42,383
Upvotes	40,590	10,832
Downvotes	99,150	3,375
Share Requests	773	251
Direct Jumps to Post ID	7,871	11,868

Table 1. Usage statistics for Sangeet Swara and Talent Hunt.

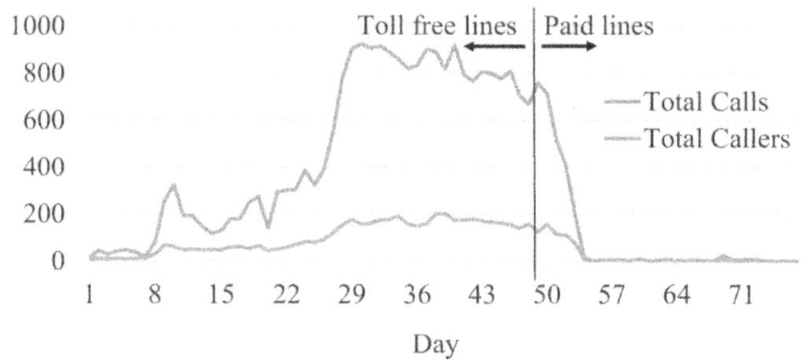

Figure 2. Call statistics for Sangeet Swara.

We performed a content analysis of 100 randomly selected posts. When we learned of the prevalence of visually impaired users, we conducted ten semi-structured telephone interviews to understand their experience in more detail. We used open coding to analyze the data obtained from the content analysis, the live interviews, and the automated interviews. We also studied call logs to understand usage patterns.

Results

Sangeet Swara led to high levels of community engagement, with users becoming devoted champions of the system. Similar to other platforms for user-generated content [22], the top 10% of callers placed 70% of total calls. The top 10% of content authors were responsible for 60% of all messages.

User Analysis[1]

Surprisingly to us, Sangeet Swara found broad and impassioned usage by visually impaired users; of those users who told us "something about themselves," 26%[2] voluntarily disclosed that they were visually impaired. The uptake by visually impaired users was organic; though voice is a natural mode of interaction for the visually impaired, we did not anticipate this usage and played no role in promoting it. Our interviews with them led to a broader study on their creation, consumption, and sharing of educational content [29].

Our users were predominately young men: 94% were male (average age=25 years) and 6% were female (average age=22 years). The youngest user was an eight year old and the oldest user was a 52 year old man. Users came from a broad range of educational backgrounds: 16% held or were pursuing a Master's degree, 40% held or were pursuing a Bachelor's degree, 24% were in high school, and 17% were in middle school. Two respondents were in primary school, and one described himself as uneducated. Our users came from a variety of vocations: 54% were students, 17% were teachers, 6% were working in private jobs, 5% were unemployed, 4% were musicians and 4% were farmers. The 42% of users who were employed reported a median annual income of USD 960 with a maximum of USD 7000. About half of users were from rural areas or small towns, while others were from larger cities.

SMS use was fairly common, with 61% reporting its use. However, most respondents had little experience with the Internet: only 16% had used an email account at least once, and the same fraction had used Facebook. Many users had never heard of Facebook; three people said: *"We don't have a Facebook account but we have an account in Bank of India."*

Content Analysis

Our open categorization of 100 randomly sampled posts found generic messages (N=36), songs (N=21), poems (N=16), users' introduction about themselves (N=6), songs played from another playback device (N=6), instrumental performances (N=4), jokes (N=3), blank messages (N=3), questions (N=3) and current news (N=2). Eighty-eight messages were recorded by males, two were recorded by females and one message was recorded by a group consisting of both males and females. We did not categorize the gender of blank messages and messages that recorded playback from other devices. Fifty-six people reported their location while recording the messages. Most of the messages came from Madhya Pradesh (N=25), Rajasthan (N=11) and Uttar Pradesh (N=8).

Songs and poems accounted for about half of the content, and were in a variety of styles. The songs spanned recognizable hits, folk music, and original pieces; solos and duets; a cappella and pieces with instruments. The top 50 posts (analyzed in a later section) are available for listening at `http://soundcloud.com/sangeet-swara/`.

The other half of posts emerged as general social media. Many messages were wishing well to the 'friends' users made on Sangeet Swara. There were greetings, good morning messages, and good night messages for other users, and responses from one user to another. Many messages were about recent topics of national or regional interest. For example, there were five messages about the 2013 North India floods. Eight users gave their phone number and encouraged others to contact them for chatting. Male users often recorded compliments for female contributors, praising their beautiful singing and sometimes requesting their phone number.

While the vast majority of posts on Sangeet Swara were respectful in tone, we found and deleted 22 posts containing abusive language or derogatory comments. As seen in prior forums such as Avaaj Otalo [5], users took an active role in policing the system, e.g., by urging others to record cultural content and to avoid abusive comments. Though we did not have time to evaluate community-based flagging and deletion of unwanted posts, this feature would be important at scale.

Value Offered to Users

Many users attributed great value to their interactions on Sangeet Swara. They recorded strong positive sentiments about the service and shared interesting anecdotes about how Sangeet Swara was impacting their lives. They considered it to be a platform where people show their creativity, voice their opinions, and record interesting content. This sentiment was often strongest among visually impaired users:

> *My mother and father are laborers. You are like my father, my god. I want to thank you again and again, this small kid wants to respect you from the bottom of my heart. I listen to abundant good content on Sangeet Swara. I never got the opportunity to hear such content elsewhere. I am in love with Sangeet Swara since the first day.*

P1 (Male, Student, Visually impaired, 18 years, Madhya Pradesh)

Visually impaired people used Sangeet Swara to showcase their talent, build social capital, and share information. Some people considered Sangeet Swara to be a platform *"to learn and understand the principles of life."* Some people considered it to be a conduit for national peace and integrity, and believed that *"it is proving the mantra of India: Unity in diversity."* One user said:

> *I am blind so I couldn't get educated. I want to thank you from the bottom of my heart because you enabled all blind people to get in touch with each other and show our talent. No matter how much I praise, it won't be enough.*

P2 (Male, Uneducated, Visually impaired, Madhya Pradesh)

Many participants thought of Sangeet Swara as a platform for promoting poor musicians from rural parts of India. They thought of it as a stage for such musicians to showcase and improve their talent, to overcome stage fright, and to step toward India-wide recognition and fame.

> *You can put your hidden talent on the forefront. People don't feel that anyone is listening and thus, they can perform without any hesitation. A performer will feel as if*

[1]Our survey targeted users who had called at least 10 times.

[2]Because different questions were answered by different numbers of users, we report the percentage of users answering a given question.

he is alone but a lot of people listen to it later on Sangeet Swara. People with stage fright can present their talent on this wonderful platform. No one can mock you. You will get to meet new people. People in far-off locations will hear you.

P3 (Male, Teacher, 26 years, Madhya Pradesh)

Many participants appreciated the voice medium, stating that it makes the process of information curation and dissemination much simpler than text-based alternatives. They considered Sangeet Swara to be an inclusive portal for low-literate people, visually impaired people, and tribal people in India.

Sangeet Swara is trying to get talent from people in villages and towns. It is a channel for talented people who never got an opportunity to show their talent. Sangeet Swara is trying to get recognition and provide a channel for such people.

P4 (Male, Musician, 22 years, New Delhi)

Sangeet Swara also helped people build self confidence. Three people reported feeling important when they use Sangeet Swara. Some people felt that Sangeet Swara was also playing a role in improving their grammar, vocabulary and communication skills.

I get a lot of knowledge by using Sangeet Swara. Some people record questions, which increases our knowledge. We get to listen to things we have never heard. We learn new vocabulary and sometimes new accents as well. I feel great when people vote for me and give me feedback, be it a good feedback or bad. I consciously think of ways to improve my messages.

P5 (Male, Student/Farmer, Uttar Pradesh)

ANALYSIS OF COMMUNITY MODERATION

Our goal in this section is to assess the usability and effectiveness of community moderation in Sangeet Swara. We start with three quantitative approaches: evaluating the accuracy of crowd categorization tasks, comparing the top 50 posts to the bottom 50 posts, and comparing the ranking of posts to an "expert" ranking. Then we consider qualitative feedback from the users.

Categorizing the Posts

Before making a judgement regarding the quality of a post, a basic task one might expect from a moderator is to categorize the content along various dimensions, such as the type of recording, gender of the contributor, language of the post, etc. Allowing listeners to search or filter content according to these metadata would be an important feature of a scalable voice forum, even though we did not implement such functionality in Sangeet Swara. Especially for Indic languages such as Hindi, it is very difficult for current speech recognition technologies to automate or assist with such tagging and categorization tasks.

As described previously, we designated regular users of Sangeet Swara as "senior members" and sometimes asked them to help categorize messages at the beginning of the phone call. Our content analysis revealed that becoming a "senior member" had a strong positive effect on users. The designation made them feel privileged, honored, and grateful. They felt more accountable for improving content quality, casting votes diligently and performing tasks:

I am now a special person on Sangeet Swara. I have to categorize posts. Please don't use any abusive language on this forum. Please don't say anything wrong because they have made me a senior member and if you do anything wrong then I will tell them.

(Post on Sangeet Swara)

Task Type	Offered	Done	Response Rate	Accuracy
Content type	1704	1551	91.0%	98%
Gender	2000	1895	94.7%	98%

Table 2. Results of categorization tasks done by community.

We asked users to categorize posts along two dimensions: content type and gender. To classify content type, users pressed a key to indicate if the recording was (1) a song, (2) a joke, (3) a poem, or (4) none of the above. To classify gender, users indicated if the speaker was (1) a male voice, (2) a female voice, or (3) they couldn't tell if it was male or female.

Senior members were asked to categorize the top 50 recordings. Whenever senior members called, one of the tasks was randomly presented to them. In total, 3704 categorization tasks were completed; for each post, we received at least 33 judgements of content type and 40 judgements of gender. The tasks were offered to 291 users, out of which 146 completed the task. The top 20% of workers performed 66% of the tasks.

For each categorization task, we aggregated the responses from the crowd and selected the majority answer as the community response. Before inspecting the community responses, a researcher categorized all the posts by the same criteria. We calculated the crowd's *accuracy* as the fraction of judgements that agreed with the researcher's and the *response rate* as the percentage of users who completed a task when it was offered to them.

The results appear in Table 2. The community showed high accuracy (98% agreement with researcher) on both content and gender classification. For each task type, only one message led to disagreement (a Bollywood hip-hop song for content type, and a muffled voice for gender). The response rate was 95% for gender, and 91% for content type. We conjecture that the gender task was easier, leading to more responses.

Many users recorded messages to share their feedback about the tasks. Some users requested more variety of tasks, while others recorded messages critiquing the recordings they categorized. Though the majority of users were excited about helping Sangeet Swara by performing tasks, two people recorded complaints. For example:

I don't want to do any tasks. I just want to listen to the content right away.

(Post on Sangeet Swara)

	Content Type				Gender			Inaudible		Language		Duration (seconds)		
	Song	Joke	Poem	Misc	Male	Female	Not Sure	Yes	No	Hindi	English	Mean	Median	Mode
Top 50	16	7	23	4	30	20	0	0	50	49	1	48	49	70
Bottom 50	10	0	2	38	46	0	4	4	46	48	2	40	35	70

Table 3. Analysis of the top 50 and bottom 50 posts.

Top 50 vs. Bottom 50 Analysis

In order to probe whether the community applied consistent criteria for desired content, we compared the top 50 messages with the bottom 50 messages (out of a total of about 5,000 messages). If community moderation was successful, the desired content would rise to the top and the poor content would sink to the bottom. We analyzed the posts on several dimensions, including content type, gender, audibility, language, content duration and the geographic region of the caller.

The results of the comparison appear in Table 3 (with the exception of geography, which is presented later). We find a significant difference in content type in the top 50 and bottom 50 posts ($\chi^2(3, N = 100) = 53.5$, $p < 0.0001$). In the top 50 posts, only four posts were in the miscellaneous category as opposed to 38 such posts in the bottom 50. Most of the posts in the bottom 50 were personal messages for another user (N=15), information about other IVR services (N=7), comments on others' posts (N=5), and blank or nonsensical messages (N=4). This demonstrates that the community was successful in promoting songs, poems and jokes to top positions, while pushing messages deviating from the intended usage of Sangeet Swara to bottom positions.

We also found a significant difference in gender between the top 50 and bottom 50 posts ($\chi^2(2, N = 100) = 27.3$, $p < 0.0001$). Of the top 50 posts, 40% were recorded by females: twenty times the fraction of female recordings in our random sample of content (2%). In contrast, the bottom 50 posts did not contain any recordings by females. This trend corroborates our user and content analyses, in which most users were male and offered special attention, flirting, and adulation to female contributors.

The top 50 and bottom 50 posts did not show significant variations in language, duration, or inaudible posts. However, it is worth noting that the bottom 50 messages contained four inaudible posts while all of the top 50 posts were audible.

We also tabulated the approximate geographical location of callers based on their caller ID[3]. The majority of content authors belonged to similar locations in the top 50 and bottom 50 posts: Rajasthan (N=10, M=14), Madhya Pradesh (N=9, M=14), Uttar Pradesh (N=10, M=7) and Delhi (N=7, M=1).

Community Ranking vs. Researcher Ranking

As an additional validation that community moderation resulted in a meaningful ranking of content, we compared the ranking of messages on Sangeet Swara to a ranking determined by a group of researchers. If these rankings differ, it does not prove that Sangeet Swara rankings are invalid, as the differences could be due to varying tastes of the demographic groups. However, if the rankings agree, it provides additional evidence that the community can perform its own moderation tasks without relying on outside assistance.

In order to compare the judgements of users and researchers, we restricted our attention to songs (the most frequent content type). Restricting attention in this way allowed a more direct comparison of quality, without conflating user preferences for one content type over another. Our experimental design asked researchers to compare a pair of songs, and to see if their preference matched the relative rank of those songs on Sangeet Swara. We prepared 20 pairs of songs from Sangeet Swara. The first ten pairs consisted of one song ranked in the top 20, and one song ranked in the middle 10. The second ten pairs consisted of one song ranked in the top 20, and one song ranked in the bottom 10. We randomized the order of the pairs, and the order of songs within pairs.

For each pair of songs, we asked three researchers (1 male, 2 female, Indian natives, average age=28 years) to select the one they liked more. Researchers were instructed to focus on the quality of the singing, doing their best to ignore any variations in language or (if the song is well known) any preference for the original version. Researchers were blind to the ranking of songs on Sangeet Swara, and rankings by each other. We used a majority vote to determine the researchers' ranking of a given pair. We compared the researchers' vote with the community ranking to measure agreement between them.

When comparing top-ranked and bottom-ranked posts, 90% of song pairs received the same ranking by researchers and Sangeet Swara users. This amount of agreement is unlikely to happen by chance (a binomial test of 10 trials, each with 50/50 chance of agreement, leading to at least 90% of judgements in either direction, yields $p = 0.02$).

When comparing the top-ranked posts and posts with middle ranking, only 60% of pairs received the same ordering from researchers and Sangeet Swara users. There are several possible interpretations of this result. The top and middle posts were more similar in quality, requiring more subtle distinctions. As song preferences are highly variable, we may have obtained a higher match if we had used a larger group of researchers. While we cannot rule out the possibility that Sangeet Swara users were less careful or less capable to compare the songs, this assertion is not supported by our other observations (such as the high accuracy on categorization tasks).

Qualitative Views of Community Moderation

To understand users' feelings about community moderation, we included a question on this topic in our automated telephone survey. The question asked, *"When you listen to posts, Sangeet Swara tells you the rank of the post. Do you feel that good posts are ranked higher on Sangeet Swara and bad posts are ranked lower?"* We received 126 responses, which were transcribed, translated, and analyzed in two different ways.

[3]In India, a phone number reveals the telecom circle in which a SIM card was purchased, but not the circle where it is currently located.

The first analysis was a coarse-grained sentiment analysis. The largest category of responses (36%) were neutral or difficult to classify. However, 35% of respondents generally agreed that good content was ranked higher and bad content was ranked lower. A slightly lesser fraction (29%) were not satisfied with the quality of community moderation.

To understand users' views with more nuance, we analyzed the transcripts using open coding and axial coding, arriving at several themes. We found that many people understood that their votes decided the rank and also influenced the playback order. These users emphasized the need to vote honestly:

> *Some messages are really good and their rank is also good. However, around 10% messages aren't good and yet they have a good rank. It is not the fault of the system. The voters should understand which message should be taken to a high level and which to a low level. I would like to tell all listeners that they should listen to messages carefully and then vote honestly. Each vote is precious.*
>
> P6 (Male, Student, 19 years, Uttar Pradesh)

Many people agreed that the quality of community moderation is good and the rank of good quality content is generally higher than the rank of bad quality content. For example:

> *The good songs are higher ranked and the bad songs are lower ranked. I am happy that you decided to rank the posts by our votes.*
>
> P7 (Male, Student, 15 years, Jharkhand)

We found some people who believed that Sangeet Swara administrators decided the rankings. They did not understand how their votes influenced the rank and playback order:

> *Whatever rank the system chooses is right. The good messages have higher rank and the bad messages have lower rank. I trust you that you will never favor anyone. You will categorize the messages properly, give good rank to good messages and will depress bad messages.*
>
> P8 (Male, Telephone operator, Visually impaired, 42 years, Madhya Pradesh)

Some people didn't agree with the ranks assigned to posts, and were unhappy with the quality of community moderation. A few people put the blame on Sangeet Swara administrators for inappropriately assigning the rank:

> *I think you don't listen to the messages. Some messages are very good but have low rank and some messages are useless but they have good rank. Either you are confused or there is some fault somewhere in your system.*
>
> P9 (Male, Student, 19 years, Uttar Pradesh)

Others felt that careless voting by users is responsible for poor quality moderation:

> *Not all the messages appear to have the right rank. I think the reason behind that is voting by the community. I think at many places people do not vote responsibly. They just want to go ahead in the playback list and they don't care whether they are pressing 1 or 2.*
>
> P10 (Male, Government servant, Uttar Pradesh)

Eight respondents demonstrated a lack of understanding between "rank" and "playback order." For example:

> *The rank which is told at Sangeet Swara, I don't understand it. Sometimes the rank is 2511, and the next message is ranked 3303 and then the next to it is 1127. Sometimes it increases and decreases and I don't understand it.*
>
> P11 (Male, Teacher, Jharkhand)

Though the distinction between rank and playback order is necessary to ensure fair playback and voting policies, there could be better and simpler ways to communicate the rankings to users. For example, instead of reading the numeric rank, a prompt could say "this is a new post, and we really need your opinion", "this post is an old favorite", "this post is liked by some people, but more input is needed", and so on.

To summarize, though community moderation demonstrated effectiveness from a quantitative standpoint, our qualitative analysis reveals that there is room to improve on how the system is understood and appreciated by users.

EVALUATION OF FINANCIAL SUSTAINABILITY

To create a voice forum that can scale and sustain without outside assistance, moderating the content is only part of the equation. The other challenge is financial sustainability. In particular, there needs to be a way to support the cost of phone calls as more and more users are calling the system.

Given how deeply many users seemed to value Sangeet Swara, we thought that a subset of users may be willing to pay for their own phone calls, thereby sustaining the system without external funding. Thus, after spending about 3,000 USD on seven weeks of toll-free support, we planned a switch to a regular line (which costed users the same as a normal phone call – 1 to 2 cents per minute, depending on their mobile plan). This required users to call a different phone number, which we announced as part of the welcome message for the five days preceding the change. We are confident that users understood the change in number, because the forum was immediately inundated with emotional requests to continue the toll-free service. For example:

> *I am very sad. Please, don't change the number. I fold my hands and request. Please consider my request. Not only me, everyone wants it to be toll-free. If it is a paid number then people won't be able to use it. Please don't reject our plea. Sorry sir. I fold my hands and pray, please don't change the number. Please cancel the announcement.*
>
> P12 (Male, Student, Visually impaired, 19 years, Uttrakhand)

Unfortunately, this student's prediction was correct. As illustrated in Figure 2, usage steeply declined without the toll-free lines. Within four weeks, it died out completely. We will say more about this result as part of our closing discussion.

FOLLOW-UP EXPERIMENT: TALENT HUNT

Though users of Sangeet Swara derived significant value and meaning from the system, they were unable to pay for their own phone calls, which limited the scale we could achieve. As a follow-up experiment, we wanted to see if similar value could be delivered to a slightly higher-income group that might be able to afford to make phone calls without toll-free lines. If successful, such an experiment could grow into a very large ecosystem, giving more opportunities for monetization and cross-subsidization of low-income users.

To explore this idea, we deployed Talent Hunt: a forum of songs, poetry, jokes, and other cultural content targeting college students in urban India. The infrastructure and call flow for Talent Hunt was almost the same as Sangeet Swara, though prompts were recorded in English (arguably the most common language for college students in India) instead of Hindi. Moreover, the biggest difference was in the financial incentives offered. Instead of using toll-free lines, we promoted participation by awarding a smartphone (Nokia Lumia 710) to authors of top-ranked posts. We made one award per week for the first six weeks. After six weeks, we still announced one winner per week (and featured winners in the main menu), but did not award any phones. Our hope was that the material prizes would be sufficient to seed interest in the forum; future participation would be sustained by social recognition and attachment to the community. We promoted Talent Hunt using posters (in college campuses), email, social media, and targeted outreach by student volunteers.

The usage of Talent Hunt over time is illustrated in Figure 3. Though it received calls from 11,751 people (7 times more than Sangeet Swara), unfortunately this usage was driven entirely by the material awards. As soon as the last phone was awarded, participation dropped to zero. We ended up spending more on the phones (USD 1517) than the users collectively spent on the airtime (USD 1305, assuming \$0.02 / min).

The award-based incentive structure also had deleterious effects on the quality of the voice forum. Despite the large number of callers, only 368 posts were recorded, which is 15 times less than on Sangeet Swara. Rather than building a supportive community of participation and sharing, users of Talent Hunt were often calling only to vote for a friend. Among ten of the top-rated posts, 99.5% of votes obtained were direct votes, in which the voter jumped directly to the post by entering its ID from the main menu: evidence that the caller was trying to support someone they knew in real life.

We also conducted semi-structured qualitative interviews with ten users who were among the top vote recipients. These users indicated that they strategically mobilized large groups of people to vote on their posts. Some of them made announcements in classrooms, on social media sites, and even at a wedding in order to gather more votes.

The quality and quantity of user engagement was also much lower than Sangeet Swara. By the standards established in Sangeet Swara, no member of Talent Hunt would have been designated a senior member. As most of the users were college students in tier 1 and tier 2 cities, they also had access to

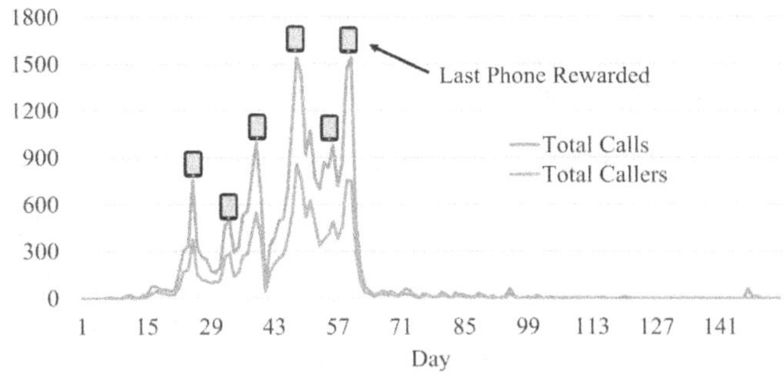

Figure 3. Call statistics for Talent Hunt.

social media platforms such as Facebook, WhatsApp, Twitter, etc. As a result, Talent Hunt offered less value to them.

To summarize, our experience with Talent Hunt showed that offering financial awards for top-ranked recordings brought several hazards to a community-moderated voice forum. Patterns of participation and voting became grossly distorted by users who sought to help their friends. Moreover, the incentive failed to seed long-term participation. Though users were able to pay for their own calls during the contest period, the usage expired as soon as the contest was over.

DISCUSSION AND CONCLUSIONS

This paper describes lessons learned from Sangeet Swara, a community-moderated voice forum in rural India. The system evoked a passionate response from users, particularly those with visual impairment, who discovered and appropriated the platform without any outreach on our part. We believe that the ability to be an equal participant (and moderator) of a voice forum was a uniquely empowering experience for these users. Our study shows that this community of untrained callers can accurately perform their own moderation tasks, including categorizing and rating posts, thereby mitigating the bottleneck of a dedicated moderation team.

For community-moderated voice forums to scale further, they also require financial sustainability, which was not achieved by either Sangeet Swara or Talent Hunt. Given that Sangeet Swara users were passionate about using the system, their reluctance to pay for the phone calls is almost akin to an "impossibility proof": for users in this demographic, it is very difficult for a voice forum to deliver sufficient benefits for users to consider paying for the calls themselves. Conversely, in the case of Talent Hunt, we believe that users were able to pay, but had lesser interest in the service, since they had access to online social media platforms.

To reduce costs in the future, one promising approach is to transfer audio content via mobile data connections (as they become available) instead of voice calls [10]. It may also be possible for callers to perform more general audio micro-tasks, similar to Mechanical Turk but administered over IVR. The revenue generated could help offset the costs of calls.

Several aspects of community moderation remain untested. Sangeet Swara focused on the domain of entertainment, where the content is relatively uncontroversial. Extending to domains such as politics and citizen journalism will require sensitivity to stronger disagreements between callers, which could impact their ratings as well as their flagging of posts for deletion. Also, 94% of Sangeet Swara users were male. It will be important to understand how to build a community that is inclusive and inviting towards women.

There are rich opportunities to broaden the scope of voice forums. Users of Sangeet Swara desired additional interactions, such as sending personal messages and listening to all posts by a given person. Generalizing a voice forum in this way could lead to a flexible social networking platform over IVR, leading to even greater uptake and engagement by rural users.

ACKNOWLEDGMENTS

We are grateful to Kalika Bali, Sankalp Chhabra, Shubhranshu Choudhary, Deepti Desai, Nakull Gupta, Dhruv Parthasarathy, Indrani Medhi Thies, Satish Sangameswaran, and Sridhar Vedantham for all of their help. We also thank the anonymous reviewers for their helpful suggestions. This work was funded in part by the Noe Professorship at the University of Washington, as well as the Catalyst Center for Sustainable Development at Microsoft Research India.

REFERENCES

1. Awaaz.de. `http://awaaz.de/`.
2. CensusInfo India 2011. `http://www.devinfolive.info/censusinfodashboard/`.
3. Gram Vaani. `http://gramvaani.org/`.
4. The World in 2014: ICT Facts and Figures. Tech. rep. `http://www.itu.int/en/ITU-D/Statistics/Documents/facts/ICTFactsFigures2014-e.pdf`.
5. Avaaj Otalo: a field study of an interactive voice forum for small farmers in rural India. In *CHI* (2010).
6. Press Release on Telecom Subscription Data as of 31st March, 2014. Tech. rep., TRAI, 2014. `http://www.trai.gov.in/Content/PressDetails/2148_0.aspx`.
7. Agarwal, S. K., Kumar, A., Nanavati, A. A., and Rajput, N. User-Generated Content Creation and Dissemination in Rural Areas. *ITID 6*, 2 (2010).
8. Chakraborty, D., Medhi, I., Cutrell, E., and Thies, W. Man Versus Machine: Evaluating IVR Versus a Live Operator for Phone Surveys in India. In *DEV* (2013).
9. Desai, S. B., Dubey, A., Joshi, B. L., Sen, M., Shariff, A., and Vanneman, R. Human Development in India: Challenges For a Society in Transition. Tech. rep., Oxford University Press, 2010.
10. D'Silva, K., Marathe, M., Vashistha, A., Borriello, G., and Thies, W. A Mobile Application for Interactive Voice Forums: Design and Pilot Deployment in Rural India. In *DEV* (2014).
11. Eagle, N. txteagle : Mobile Crowdsourcing. *Money* (2009).
12. Grover, A., and Calteaux, K. A voice service for user feedback on school meals. In *DEV* (2012).
13. Gulaid, M., and Vashistha, A. Ila Dhageyso : An Interactive Voice Forum to Foster Transparent Governance in Somaliland. In *ICTD* (2013).
14. Gupta, A., and Thies, W. mClerk: enabling mobile crowdsourcing in developing regions. In *CHI* (2012).
15. Koradia, Z., Aggarwal, P., Seth, A., and Luthra, G. Gurgaon idol: A singing competition over community radio and IVRS. In *DEV* (2013).
16. Lerer, A., Ward, M., and Amarasinghe, S. P. Evaluation of IVR data collection UIs for untrained rural users. In *DEV* (2010).
17. Medhi, I., Patnaik, S., Brunskill, E., Gautama, S. N., Thies, W., and Toyama, K. Designing mobile interfaces for novice and low-literacy users. *TOCHI 18*, 1 (2011).
18. Meeker, M. 2014 Internet Trends. Tech. rep., Kleiner Perkins Caufield Byers, 2014. `http://www.kpcb.com/internet-trends`.
19. Mudliar, P., Donner, J., and Thies, W. Emergent Practices Around CGNet Swara: A Voice Forum for Citizen Journalism in Rural India. *ITID* (2013).
20. Munroe, R. Reddit's new comment sorting system, Oct. 2009. `http://www.redditblog.com/2009/10/reddits-new-comment-sorting-system.html`.
21. Narula, P., Gutheim, P., Rolnitzky, D., Kulkarni, A., and Hartmann, B. MobileWorks : A Mobile Crowdsourcing Platform for Workers at the Bottom of the Pyramid. In *HCOMP* (2011).
22. Ochoa, X., and Duval, E. Quantitative analysis of user-generated content on the web. In *WebEvolve* (2008).
23. Patel, N., Agarwal, S., Rajput, N., Nanavati, A., Dave, P., and Parikh, T. S. A Comparative Study of Speech and Dialed Input Voice Interfaces in Rural India. In *CHI* (2009).
24. Rangaswamy, N., and Cutrell, E. Anthropology, Development and ICTs: Slums, Youth and the Mobile Internet in Urban India. In *ICTD* (2012).
25. Raza, A. A., Rosenfeld, R., Sherwani, J., Milo, C., Alster, G., Saif, U., Pervaiz, M., and Razaq, S. Viral Entertainment as Vehicle for Disseminating Speech Based Services to Low Literate Users. In *ICTD* (2012).
26. Raza, A. A., Ul Haq, F., Tariq, Z., Pervaiz, M., Razaq, S., Saif, U., and Rosenfeld, R. Job opportunities through entertainment: Virally spread speech-based services for low-literate users. In *CHI* (2013).
27. Smyth, T. N., Kumar, S., Medhi, I., and Toyama, K. Where There's a Will There's a Way: Mobile Media Sharing in Urban India. In *CHI* (2010).
28. Su, X., and Khoshgoftaar, T. M. A survey of collaborative filtering techniques. *Adv. in AI* (2009).
29. Vashistha, A., Brady, E., Thies, W., and Cutrell, E. Educational Content Creation and Sharing by Low-Income Visually Impaired People in India. In *DEV* (2014).
30. White, J., Duggirala, M., Srivastava, S., and Kummamuru, K. Designing a Voice-Based Employment Exchange for Rural India. In *ICTD* (2012).

Mobile Phones for Maternal Health in Rural India

Neha Kumar
Department of Computer Science & Engineering
University of Washington, Seattle WA 98195
neha@cs.washington.edu

Richard Anderson
Department of Computer Science & Engineering
University of Washington, Seattle WA 98195
anderson@cs.washington.edu

ABSTRACT
We present our findings from a mixed methods study of mobile phone practices of rural Indian women. We situate our study in the context of Projecting Health, a public health initiative we deployed in Uttar Pradesh (India) to target the dissemination of health information for mothers and newborns. Adopting the lens of feminist reflexivity, we reconsider our design of Projecting Health by factoring in the mobile media consumption and sharing practices of our target audience. We stress the importance of taking a community-oriented approach and show that although there are strict social conventions and patriarchal norms that constrain various practices of these women, they are able to exercise agency and mobilize help within their communities when needed.

Author Keywords
HCI4D; ICTD; Health; Information; Feminist HCI

ACM Classification Keywords
H.5.1. Information Interfaces and Presentation (e.g. HCI): Multimedia Information Systems

INTRODUCTION
The scope of HCI research has grown rapidly to include studies of technology design, adoption, and use in low-resource environments around the world, frequently categorized as HCI4D research. The 'third wave' of HCI has also brought with it an engagement with issues more social and political. This includes an interest in bringing feminist reflexivity to HCI [2, 27, 38, 21, 6]. Bardzell suggested a framework for design principles and methodologies that took inspiration from feminist theory and social sciences [2], identifying the key qualities that contribute to feminist design as pluralism, reflexivity, participation, ecology, and self-disclosure. We draw on this work as we extend HCI4D research to include an examination of women's mobile practices in rural India that we conducted to iterate on the design of an effective information dissemination model for maternal and newborn health. A Feminist HCI perspective allows us to uniquely reflect on our assumptions regarding both - the patriarchal structures in rural India that influence women's social and technological interactions and the agency these women exhibit in spite of their social limitations.

CHI 2015, April 18 - 23 2015, Seoul, Republic of Korea

ACM 978-1-4503-3145-6/15/04 ... $15.00
http://dx.doi.org/10.1145/2702123.2702258

The *Projecting Health* (PH) initiative we discuss in this paper was designed in collaboration with PATH (a health NGO) to bring globally approved health-related information to women in rural Uttar Pradesh (UP, India). By providing Accredited Social Health Activists (ASHAs) with locally crafted videos and portable projectors, PH aims to facilitate their teaching of women about ante-natal (before birth) and postpartum (after birth) health care. In this paper, we reconsider our original design using the lens of Feminist HCI. We take Muller's lead [21] to ask the "who" questions in the context of our study, using ethnographic methods to listen to the voices of our users. Although the target audience of the videos includes pregnant and lactating mothers, and target users are the ASHAs, we view the community at large as our user group, where men, women (new mothers, their mothers-in-law, ASHAs), children, project staff are *all* users to varying degrees and in varying capacities. This is in line with Rode's view of users from a "proximate" and "distal" perspective [26]. Next, we highlight in our findings how our users are not only users who can speak for themselves, but also users who can *act* for themselves. Finally, we acknowledge that we are not the "voice from nowhere" that Haraway critiques [10], but willing proponents of emancipatory action research, as Dimond [6] recognizes as a legitimate approach for Feminist HCI researchers to use, even as we attempt to observe and understand our users. Taylor questions [34] what the "better" is that we strive towards and whether we will know it when we see it. We believe we will, as we strive for women to be better informed and able to tend to their children's health to minimize the loss of health (and lives).

After presenting the body of related research within which we situate our findings, we offer background information on PH for context. We then present methodological details of our qualitative study, followed by our findings and a discussion of the prime takeaways of our work. Our goal is to make the following contributions. First, to the best of our knowledge, we offer the first detailed account of women's mobile practices in rural India, seeking also to dispel the pervasive misperception that rural Indian women operating amid severe patriarchal norms and resource constraints are unlikely to be active users of technology. Second, we strongly believe that technology use must be viewed in the context of existing social practices and we document a unique set of sociotechnical configurations that highlight the role *community* plays in aiding and facilitating media consumption, sharing, and dissemination. Third, our work also makes a novel contribution by highlighting the potential impact that existing community practices could have on development-related outcomes in an area of immense need. We consider it essential for HCI4D research (and HCI research in general) to strive for a good 'ecological fit' and our use of feminist reflexivity - with its focus on pluralism and advocacy - is aimed at demonstrating how this might be attained.

RELATED WORK

The premise for PH lies in the literature on behavior change, drawing particularly on Kumar et al.'s [17] work on behavior change for newborn survival in rural India. In this paper we also extend existing work in the areas of mHealth, mobile media practices, videos and storytelling, and feminist design, all of which are current and relevant topics of consideration for HCI research.

Mobile Health

Prior HCI research that examines the use of technology for maternal health in low-resource regions has tried to capitalize on the wide penetration and usability of mobile technology in these settings. For example, Ramachandran et al. [23] deployed short videos on mobile phones to motivate health workers and persuade village women, their goal being to attract more village women towards utilizing health services provided by the state. A related study also examined phone-based messaging between health workers and village women [24]. Fiore-Silfvast et al. [7] studied the use of mobile videos by midwives for patient education during postnatal care examinations. Molapo and Marsden [20] designed a tool to aid rural health trainers in creating mobile content for training low-literate Community Health Workers in Lesotho. Mathur et al. [19] explored the feasibility of creating and presenting digital content using a camera phone and pico projector in the domains of health care and education in a development context. Other mobile devices are also being designed for maternal health care. For instance, there is the digital PartoPen [37] that was deployed in Nairobi for early detection of maternal and fetal complications during labor. Kolko et al. [13] have discussed the design and deployment of an inexpensive ultrasound system for use by rural midwives in Uganda. We build on this work by presenting an 'in the wild' study of how mobile phones are being used - both by frontline workers and our target audience - for consumption and dissemination of health information in similarly resource-challenged settings.

Mobiles and Media

Mobile media practices in Indian settings have been a subject of study for the past 4-5 years. Smyth et al. [32] found that urban multimedia mobile users were adept at maintaining and transferring media libraries on their phone. Kumar et al. [14] studied the folk music ecology in rural and small town India, highlighting the audience that exists for consuming various forms of music on multimedia mobiles. Building on this work, Kumar and Parikh [15] and Kumar and Rangaswamy [16] discuss the growing adoption of mobile media and the informal economy that has emerged in support. All of this prior work, however, looks predominantly at male audiences. Our findings indicate that women avidly consume and share mobile media as well, but rely on a different support infrastructure due to the social and patriarchal boundaries they are subjected to. We hope to motivate future work in this area.

Local Videos and Storytelling

The 'facilitated video' approach of PH was adapted from Digital Green [9], an initiative that aims to teach farmers about better agricultural practices using locally crafted films. This approach, in turn, was inspired by Digital Study Hall's [36] work on facilitated video instruction to assist primary school teachers in Lucknow, India. Local language video and storytelling approaches to disseminating information have been adopted widely in HCI4D research. Frohlich et al. [8], Reitmaier et al. [25], and Bidwell et al. [4] have studied the creation of local mobile audio and video content for digital storytelling in rural communities of India, Kenya, and South Africa. Ladeira and Cutrell [18] highlight the instructional value of a digital storytelling approach that combines motivational content with narrative framing. Much of this work is motivated by the desire to reduce text dependence and increase audience engagement in communities where literacy rates are low. For example, Cuendet et al. [5] developed VideoKheti, a mobile interface that uses speech, graphics, and touch to help farmers locate and watch agricultural extension videos in their own dialects. In this paper, we focus additionally on the *community response* to local, storytelling-focused health videos.

Gender and a Feminist HCI Perspective

Sengers et al. [30] introduced the notion of Reflective Design, stressing the importance of reflection on unconscious values embedded in computing. We incorporate feminist reflexivity in our research as we use Bardzell's [2] framework to reflect on aspects of PH thus far, as well as to inform the design of our next iteration. Bardzell and Bardzell [3] also identify ICT4D as a potential application area in their rejection of the notion of a 'universal' design. This fits well with our ideology of situating our design in the context of local cultural practices. Shroff and Kam [31] - studying the context of Indian NGOs working to improve gender equity - have offered an in-depth analysis of the stages that women traverse on their road to empowerment. In our study, we see these stages co-occurring in the context of different women and health workers and provide a richer understanding of women's interactions with technology 'in the wild', outside an institutional context. We also draw inspiration from Dimond's [6] use of Feminist HCI in her research on a social movement organization working to end street harassment.

BACKGROUND

We deployed Projecting Health in 2012 for disseminating information regarding maternal and child health in rural Uttar Pradesh (India) with the goal of addressing local maternal and infant mortality rates that are among the highest in the country. The dissemination takes place via group screenings of locally produced short films. Our partner organizations engage video production staff and train them in storyboarding, filming, and editing. This staff is then responsible for producing films based on inputs received from the Community Advisory

Board (CAB) - a volunteer group set up by our partner organizations, comprised of community members with diverse expertise. Once the CAB approves a video storyboard, it is cast, shot, and screened. ASHAs use low-cost pico projectors to conduct group screenings. The projector acts as a 'job aid', reducing the ASHA's burden of remembering and repeating information to every mother. These films are unique in that they feature local village residents, local dialects, and local music forms.

Disseminations take place a few times a month, at most. The typical venue is a publicly accessible, closed meeting space, where a projector can be used conveniently. At the dissemination, while the women collect and seat themselves in a semicircle (some with their mothers-in-law, others with their children), the ASHA sets up the 'pico' (as it is popularly called) and tapes a white paper onto the wall if needed (see Fig 1). She begins the meeting with a recap of the video from the last meeting, asking questions to check that the women remember. She then plays the video and - taking her cue from the text in the video - stops it halfway to pose questions to her audience. The goal of these questions is to reinforce the women's learning, but they appear in the video also as an aid for the ASHA. When the screening is over, the ASHA leads a discussion of the video they just saw. The women then sit around singing local folk songs - as we observed - while some play the *dholak* or percussion. After 10-15 minutes, they disperse, returning to their household duties.

Taylor et al. [35] write that for sustained community involvement, it is important to iterate *with* community members on the design of technology interventions targeting them. Balestrini et al. [1] also discuss this in the context of their community-focused intervention in rural Argentina. In this paper, we study the community response to PH, focusing on women's technology practices and the role that mobile phones are playing in disseminating information. We view this as a process of iteration to inform our understanding of how the initiative could be developed further, factoring in ways that women are currently engaging with PH content. We adopt feminist reflexivity to do both - assess current community response and move towards a dissemination model that is receptive to emerging technology practices of women. Our next steps with PH will build on the insights that we glean from this study.

METHODOLOGY

Our IRB-approved study used a mixed methods approach, combining the results of a quantitative survey and qualitative methods such as semi-structured interviews, participant observations, and focus group sessions.

Our partner organization conducted a survey for us that included a set of questions regarding mobile penetration and the consumption of mobile videos. We asked the participants (mothers and ASHAs) if they owned a mobile phone and what they used it for. One of our main goals was to determine whether the participants had PH videos on their personal mobile devices and where they had procured these from. The results of this survey informed our approach to collecting qualitative data. Details that were difficult to capture using survey questions, e.g., the role of interrelationships in guiding women's uses of mobiles, were far easier to understand with the help of qualitative methods.

Figure 1. A Projecting Health dissemination in progress.

We conducted our qualitative study in the villages of blocks Khiro and Sareni, where the project is currently in progress. Our intention was to interview *at least* five ASHAs, five mothers, five project staff, and five men who were familiar with the films shown by PH. Some of these interviews were held one-on-one, while others quickly turned into focus group sessions as more and more village residents trickled in out of curiosity, raising our participant count to over 30. Every conversation lasted at least 45 minutes, often longer. The participants were identified based on the partner organization's knowledge and understanding of the landscape of mobile use. We also have a rich repository of data from prior visits - interviews and notes on observations - to the PH field sites. This made sure that we conducted our field work with a reasonable understanding of the field sites and their people and practices. We analyzed all our data using an iterative process of coding. This helped us in distilling the themes we discuss in this paper. Our focus in this process was on women (mothers and ASHAs) and their interactions with mobile technology. Using the lens of feminist HCI [3], we noted both the patriarchal structures that women are subjected to, and the ways in which they exhibit agency regardless.

Adopting a self-reflexive stance, we observed that although conversing fluently in Hindi (the native language of the first author) brought us closer to an 'insider' perspective [11, 33], for the participants who contributed to this study we were definitely 'outsiders'. Class and socioeconomic differences were quickly discerned, and we were received as members of an exotic species whose presence was worthy of local news articles for each day that we spent in the field.

FINDINGS

We now present the findings from our survey and qualitative study. We organize this section with the goal of highlighting two things the prevalence of mobile use in our field sites and the role played by relationships in the transfer of mobile media from one person to another. Our lens of feminist reflexivity brings us to foreground the women's perspective, the limitations they are subject to, and their agency in overcoming these limitations.

Survey

Our survey included 309 women who had seen at least three PH films and came from villages in Khiro and Sareni where PH had been deployed. Of these women, 93 percent were between ages 20 to 39, 32 percent were illiterate (unable to sign their name) and another 46 percent had a middle school education at best, and 90 percent were housewives. Almost all women said they owned a mobile. Though these were primarily used for making calls, 45 percent reported using their mobiles for listening to music and 30 percent for watching videos. Twelve percent women reported having PH videos on their own mobile or on that of a family member. A third of these women had received the videos from the ASHAs and another third from the project staff. Eight percent have watched at least one video on either their or an ASHA's mobile. Among the 32 ASHAs who were part of the survey as well, 11 had PH videos on their mobile and all of them had shown these videos (using their mobile) to other women. A third of these ASHAs said that they found it *"easier to explain using the mobile."*

We consider these survey findings significant given there was no initiative on PH's part to facilitate mobile dissemination of the videos. The percentage of women using their mobiles for consuming media was larger than we had expected, as was the percentage of ASHAs showing videos on their mobiles. This data is what motivated us to conduct our study and examine these trends from a qualitative perspective to develop a deeper understanding of the phenomenon as we proceed with PH.

Qualitative Study

The pregnant and lactating mothers in our field sites are the target audience of PH disseminations and the ASHAs are the prime actors. To understand the sociotechnical configurations that their mobile practices - the focus of our study - are embedded in, we look also at their interactions with the rest of the community. We discuss below the interactions of the women among themselves, with the men, children, and other community members, with the technology, and with the patriarchal social structures influencing their lives.

ASHAs and Mobile Phones

The public health care system instituted the role of the ASHA in 2005. ASHAs are assigned one or more villages (that is, a population of a 1,000 women) and interact regularly with the women in the assigned villages. We observed that they are commonly referred to with terms of endearment and respect as *ASHA bahu* (daughter-in-law) or *ASHA didi* (older sister). Apart from the ASHAs, there are other frontline workers who are responsible for various aspects of maternal and child health. Together, they provide health care to women before and after their pregnancy, and to children up to the age of five. There are monthly Immunization Saturdays and Village Health and Nutrition Days. The ASHAs use the pico projector to conduct back-to-back screenings of PH films for the duration of these events. Thus, PH operates not in parallel but in conjunction with this structure instituted by the state government. The ASHAs who were earlier meeting with the mothers now fulfill their duties and outreach responsibilities at *Mothers Groups* - meetings the mothers (and often, mothers-in-law/children) attend to watch projected PH films.

The state government considers the ASHAs key in promoting the health of rural women and children. The ASHAs' staying in touch with the village women and other ASHAs is evidently a priority for the government, for we learned that all ASHAs in the state of U.P. had recently been distributed Nokia mobile phones and given 100 free minutes every month to call other ASHAs. When we asked about the utility of these new phones, however, we were surprised to hear that none of our interviewees were using them. We were given two reasons. First, the SIM was from a mobile service provider that had poor coverage in the rural areas we visited. Second, these mobiles were 'basic phones' (see Fig 2) and could only be used for making calls, while the ASHAs already owned more expensive and capable multimedia-enabled mobiles. ASHA Kusum Devi[1] shared that she had inserted her new Nokia SIM into her dual-SIM multimedia device. When we asked what she had done with the Nokia, she said:

> *"I don't have any reason to use it, so it sits at home. When my phone battery goes dead and there is no electricity, then I look at it to tell the time."*

Other ASHAs shared that they had given the phone away to relatives because they had no use for a basic phone. It is clear that the state government did give some thought to the phone sets to be distributed. Having a "dust proof keypad" and a "long lasting battery" (see Fig 2) would certainly make the phone more durable in the rural setting where it will be used. It *was* designed to fit the needs of the users (the ASHAs), but from whose perspective? This draws us to the notion of ecology that Bardzell [2] has discussed. Despite the fact that the mobile was selected to suit the material limitations of the environment, we saw how its selection was designed consciously or unconsciously to limit the uses of the ASHAs. They would have liked more versatile devices that they could use in their daily practices, instead of having to carry two phones around all the time. Had these Nokia phones been multimedia-enabled, they would have given us a strong reason to explore the feasibility of mobile disseminations of PH media. However, our finding that the ASHAs are already better equipped than the state government imagined gives us even stronger reason to believe that they would be willing and able to conduct disseminations of mobile media.

Women: The Young and the Old

For a nuanced understanding of the context in which PH operates, it is necessary to understand active social norms and the inherently patriarchal family structure that persists in much of India, particularly rural parts. As Kant discusses [12], mothers-in-law have considerable influence over their daughters-in-law, who form the primary target audience of

[1] Names have been anonymized.

Figure 2. The ASHAs were given these Nokia phones by the state government. They are dust-proof and have a long battery life but they do not offer multimedia capabilities.

PH. For these young women to adopt new health practices, they must also have the cooperation of their mothers-in-law. Kant [12] describes how this authority is negotiated within households, where the pregnant daughters-in-law (or new mothers) try to resolve potential disparities between what their mothers-in-law believe and what is best from a medical/scientific perspective.

In PH, mothers-in-law are regularly included in the filming process and invited to screenings as well. For example, in one of the shootings we observed, the storyboard involved an ASHA approaching a mother-in-law of a pregnant woman and stressing the importance of institutional deliveries. As more mothers-in-law volunteer to act in these films, the general receptivity towards new health information grows. This also makes them a more engaged mobile video audience. We spoke to a few mothers-in-law who had PH videos on their phone. They showed us the files and shared that they would spend their free time at home watching these with their daughters-in-law:

> *"Once we have cooked and fed lunch to everyone, taken care of all the other household chores, and before the dinner preparations begin, we get some time to ourselves. While we are lying down, not doing anything, we go through the mobile and see what's on it. In this way, we also end up seeing the [PH] videos."*

Being able to watch the films together in this window of convenience is a crucial offering of the mobile phone. Further, when mother-in-law and daughter-in-law watch them together, one of our participants mentioned, there is lesser likelihood of disagreement between them too.

What About the Men?

Men's presence has not been solicited by PH thus far. This is not because we did not consider them to play a critical role towards the better health of their wives and children, but in response to the social conventions that make it challenging or even undesirable for them to attend disseminations. In a room full of women, the presence of men is awkward for both the men and the women, given that the primary target audience is women. As an ASHA asked, *"It is a place for women. What will the men do there?"* We have often observed, however, a few men crowding around and trying to get a peek into disseminations from outside. This is more out of sheer curiosity than a desire to partake of the information being shared. There is a general understanding among the men we interviewed that *"for them (the women) it is good"* and that "they" should watch them. Getting the men on board (if not in the dissemination) is important so that *(a)* they do not oppose their wives or daughters-in-law attending these mysterious viewings, and *(b)* they are willing to go one step further and encourage the women to do so. One of our ASHAs reasoned as follows:

> *"It is important for men also to know what is in the films. They may not be interested thinking this is for women. But when women's health suffers, then men are the ones who have to take time out from their work and go with their wife and/or child to the hospital to get the necessary treatment. The money for this treatment will go from* their *pockets."*

Though the men might 'rationally' agree with this ASHA, there are social barriers that exist between them and the information being disseminated in group screenings. Mobile media sharing practices open up new possibilities by being more inclusive of these men. Physical boundaries are relaxed and our participants claimed that it was much easier to share the media with their spouses in the confined spaces of their households. In addition to getting access to the content, it is important that they are able to watch these films in the company of their family members - wives and mothers.

Children and Youth as Helpful Intermediaries

In one of our early interviews, as we spoke to an ASHA about her engagement with her mobile phone, we found that she had multiple PH videos on it. When we asked if she had shared them with anyone, she said she had done so with several other women. However, when we asked if she knew how to transfer media from one mobile to another, she confessed that she had no knowledge of conducting mobile transfers, *"but the children will do it."* These children of varying ages who do not have their own mobile phones are adept at using them nevertheless. For them, these phones owned by their family members are among few 'toys' that they have access to, and must take apart to understand their every functionality. They make up for the ASHAs' lack of mobile expertise.

We did not initially have children on our agenda for interviews. However, as our study progressed, we found that it became increasingly relevant to consider their perspectives as well. Not only did they play a role (boys and girls both) in conducting mobile media transfers, they were also the ones to scan these mobile phones at home for content and play the media they could find. Although power dynamics could make it more complex for women to use their husbands' mobiles freely, the children appeared to have easier, freer access.

When we made visits to girls' schools, we learned that several students knew about PH. This speaks of the publicity PH has received outside of its target audience, although the schoolchildren may not be a representative group, given that we had been invited by one of their schoolteachers who was also on the Community Advisory Board and had written newspaper articles about PH. Regardless, our conversations with the girls revealed their strong desire to be of help to the women in their households - mothers, aunts, older sisters-in-law, and others. One girl stood up and said:

> *"If you want, you can give me the files, and I can make sure that every house in my village has them in a week."*

She was not the only one. Several other girls volunteered to help with disseminating these videos, willing to take on the responsibility of passing on health information to the women in their network. They claimed:

> *"If this is something that would be useful to the women in our villages, that would be good for their health, why will we not help? "*

Why indeed! Though we do not claim that these promises will all convert to action, recognizing the desire of these girls to participate aligns with our emancipatory action research agenda. Their keenness to help women in their families and villages to access information (the girls consider) valuable for their health is representative of the quality of advocacy that Bardzell [2] suggests as being a necessary component of Feminist HCI. The practice of downloading and distributing the files has also been taken on by some of the youth in the village who own a laptop[2].

Our interviews with ASHAs, other village women, schoolchildren, and village youth, all affirmed that children and youth have been regular aides for delivering mobile content to women - not just our target population, but old and young alike. This is useful not just for our current deployment, but also for future target populations - women who may become pregnant and their (present or future) mothers-in-law.

Mobile Shops for Offline Distribution

In our conversation with ASHA Durga Devi about the PH videos she had on her multimedia mobile phone, she mentioned in passing that she had taken her phone to "Vinay's shop" and asked Vinay to transfer the video files to his computer so he could download them onto the mobiles of the women who came to his shops requesting the latest songs or films as they frequently do. When we visited Vinay's shop, he confirmed that he had indeed been given the videos by Durga 5-6 months ago. There were 5 or 10 films, he said, which Durga had asked him to transfer to his customers' mobiles, telling them, *"If anyone near you is pregnant, be sure to show her these videos."* Vinay had done an average of 80-100 downloads of PH videos in the last few months but could not say how many of his customers would have seen them.

[2]These laptops were not purchased; they were distributed by the state's political leaders to those youth who attend college, promised during the campaigns for the last state assembly elections.

The nature of these mobile shops has been discussed in depth by Kumar and Parikh [15] in their analysis of mobile media landscapes in rural and small-town India. We found them to be quite as prevalent in our field sites - at one market intersection, for instance, we identified six mobile shops. These act as hubs of mobile content for the village residents - old and young, male and female. For INR 20-40 (USD 0.30-0.60), they transfer ready mixes to their customers' mobiles. We interviewed five shop-owners and asked if they knew about PH and the films that were being produced locally. Some did, some did not. They were all willing however, once equipped, to distribute these videos to their mobile media customers from the villages nearby. One of them also said:

> *"Why won't I distribute them? Of course I will distribute them. If there is content in these films that is good for our mothers and sisters and for their health, of course I will give it to my customers... of course I would try to reach out to remote audiences."*

As with the schoolgirls, we see a sense of community involvement among the shop-owners. We cannot say that their words will convert to action necessarily, but again, the desire to participate in facilitating the transfer of information for the benefit of their community's women is important to note.

Rural Women and Technology

Women in settings such as ours - rural India - are generally assumed to have limited technological expertise. This is in part due to their actual low expertise, but also because they are less visible than the men. One of the mobile shop-owners, on being asked whether women were less technologically savvy than the men, said: *"No no... they are far ahead of the men."* He went on to say that they were also more private about their mobile use, which is why it was hard to tell. In one of our focus groups, a participant showed us a video that she had recorded during the session. Based on the group's response we assume this was not a novelty. However, we saw a range of expertise levels and cannot generalize. Several young brides are confined within their households and their uses of the mobile phone are not as rich.

Figure 3. All the women in one of our focus groups show us how it's done as they play Projecting Health videos on their mobiles.

Shroff and Kam [31] point out that as women are initiated into the process of using technology, they can be seen as different users over time in terms of their confidence levels and agency, among other things. If we view our entire set of target users, we can see them as individuals occupying the different stages of that spectrum. Some are more confident, more active than others. Others are more passive consumers of content. This diversity in expertise levels is not surprising; it is to be expected. However, there is a danger in our taking an "out there" perspective [34] for it might lead us to see all rural women as identical, similarly adept or similarly inept. Taking the pluralistic perspective Feminist HCI affords us is to understand the needs and limitations of our target users, but also to seek a more nuanced understanding of the users as individuals, without a compulsion for 'difference-making.'

The women's ownership of more versatile devices than before also influenced the extent of use. As Fig 3 shows, with greater access to personal multimedia devices, the women are more likely to experiment and get to know their phones better. This also contributes to greater mobile listening and viewing. Mobile shop-owners and project staff claimed alike that a significant percentage of the women already had multimedia-enabled mobiles, as our survey also indicated. More importantly, however, we found that the local mobile shops were no longer selling mobiles without multimedia functionality (or very rarely). This implies that the next generation of women mobile owners is likely to have multimedia-enabled devices.

Not enough research highlights the engagement of women with technology in low-resource environments. Though this engagement seen in isolation may not be very illuminating - beyond providing results as in our survey section above, seeing it in the context of social, situated practices can lead to deeper insights about the potential of this technology to influence communication patterns and development outcomes.

Mobile Disseminations for Projecting Health

As mentioned, the goal of our study was to evaluate and iterate on our original PH deployment. We were interested in determining whether *(a)* existing mobile media sharing could potentially contribute to PH, and *(b)* whether mobile screenings would render projector screenings unnecessary. The above subsections address (a). We now address (b). Each time we asked whether one mode of communicating was preferable to the other, we heard a consensus that both were equally important. Though our participants sounded enthusiastic about watching PH videos on their mobiles, they wanted to continue the projector screenings as well. There are several reasons for this shared love of both. Their affordances are different but complementary, as our interviews conveyed.

PH screenings take place in closed rooms. Since we were conducting our fieldwork in the summer heat, there was a unanimous view that these spaces were uninviting and uncomfortable, in contrast to mobiles, which were portable and could be used in any setting of choice (such as *"out here on the porch"*). Further, these group screenings had limited reach. They took place 2-3 times a month at best, as opposed to mobile screenings, which could take place several times a day, as per every viewer's convenience. Another advantage of mobile viewing that was voiced by our interviewees was that the videos could be seen by various family members in the confines of their home. For instance, as we mentioned above, the men had no other access to this content. Of course, ASHAs liked mobile screenings as well since these required less effort on their part. The pico projectors have to be procured from and returned to a central location that may be several kilometers away. This requires effort and coordination, in addition to setting up and operating the projector, making sure that it is charged, and troubleshooting if needed. Though the convenience and versatility of mobile videos is undeniable, projector screenings play the invaluable role of bringing several women together socially, to a session facilitated by the ASHA (who may not always be present at mobile screenings), where the video is higher resolution and easier to watch than on a small mobile screen. These social gatherings remain indispensable, because they enable discussions between the ASHA and the mothers, allowing various questions to be raised and doubts dispelled.

Of course, mobiles are not for personal viewing alone. This addresses one of the ASHAs' use case scenarios that surfaced in our interviews. ASHA Janaki said:

> *"As you know, in rural areas, there are a lot of disputes between households. It makes more sense to do screenings for smaller sets of households, instead of one for everyone."*

Although the screen space offered is minimal, it is common for 2-3 women to collect around a mobile and watch a screen. As also captured by our survey, several screenings have taken place thus.

When we asked the ASHAs and women in our focus groups whether mobile media sharing could be useful for the distribution of PH films to increase outreach, one ASHA said thoughtfully but with determination:

> *"Yes... it could be done. I could definitely make sure that every house in the village has these videos."*

We suggested that if this seemed like too much work for her, she could also perhaps *"do a send"* of these videos to five other households and ask them to do the same. Her face immediately lit up. She said, *"that would be like a chain... I can do that right now.* The other women in the focus group animatedly discussed the feasibility of this distribution mechanism, also voicing their inclination to help in the process. This design interaction that took place with the village women and the ASHAs highlighted for us the agency of these women towards crafting their own solutions to their problems, stressing the importance of giving them a voice in the process and aligning with the principles of Feminist HCI.

DISCUSSION

Our findings above have given us clear next steps to pursue with PH for a more effective and ecologically fitting information dissemination model. We now discuss the insights we have gleaned, with the hope that they can also be applied towards other initiatives, not in the space of health care alone but for information dissemination more generally.

Community-Powered Iterative Design

Our study presents a unique combination of interventionist and interpretivist approaches by aiming to study women's mobile practices, broadly speaking, but in the larger context of a public health intervention. We were interested in studying how women were interacting with their personal devices - individually and socially - in and of themselves. Our subsequent agenda was to identify whether these practices could be leveraged towards the iterative design of PH's dissemination model. Our deeper, more nuanced understanding gained from studying the women, their technologies, and existing social structures and relations led us to conclude that mobile phones would be feasible to incorporate as an additional mechanism for disseminating PH media. Multimedia mobiles are becoming increasingly ubiquitous, intermediaries are present to support technology use and adoption, there is encouraging community support for PH, and distribution channels exist in the combined network of commercial (shops) and non-commercial (friends and family) entities. The next 'prototype' of PH, therefore, will entail using these findings to drive mobile distribution of content and supplement group disseminations. This brings us back, especially, to the qualities of participation, advocacy, and ecology discussed in [2] as we find that our community-centered approach allows us to iterate on our design by channeling the agency of the women we study in ways that can be supported by their community, socially and practically.

More than just Local

The PH model evidently supports pluralism in its localization of the films. These educational videos are not just popular because they are in the local language. They are also popular because there are no other films that are shot so close to home in language, style, or content. This content is closer to what our rural audiences desire as entertainment and includes elaborate story lines and local music forms they are familiar with. PH films thus aim to provide both entertainment and useful health information. Stories the audience can easily identify with for their cultural relevance and interspersed regional songs provide the hook that is needed to engage the viewers. Outside of a Mothers Group meeting and on a multimedia mobile device, PH films compete with various other entertainment media residing on the phone. Being local and entertaining is key to win over others in that competition.

Mobile Videos for Outreach

Prior HCI literature that focuses on videos has highlighted the value of using a storytelling or video-based approach in order to get the message across to a primarily low-literate audience. We confirm these findings but add that it is not merely the instructive value of the video that is relevant in this context, but also the fact that there exists a social and technological infrastructure for sharing them. We refer back to Sambasivan et al.'s work [28] on the viral nature of information diffusion in developing communities. In our study, we found similarly prevalent media sharing practices. Given our additional findings that multimedia mobiles are rapidly becoming ubiquitous and rendering basic handsets obsolete, there is a strong case for using videos for outreach. Additional affordances that make videos more attractive in this setting, especially in contrast to the group disseminations of PH, include the ability for unsupervised viewing, and that the files can be stored as a reference for later consultation.

Negotiating Authority within the Household

Kumar et al. [17] argue in their work that *"the locus of behavioral action is the household."* This is what we found with PH as well. The provision of accurate, globally approved health information is not sufficient. For that information to be willingly adopted towards behavior change, it is essential that existing information structures are sensitively dealt with as well. As [12] discusses, the daughters-in-law must negotiate their relationships with their mothers-in-law in order to take actions in the interest of their or their child's health. Health initiatives that target the adoption of new, scientifically informed health practices must also find a way to negotiate older practices steeped in culture. ASHAs did this by inviting mothers-in-law to video screenings, as well as making them a target for mobile dissemination. In addition, given that the support of men is important for the women to fully participate, mobile videos make it easier to access them as a peripheral audience, as stated in our findings. The mobile - equipped with PH videos - that allows for collective viewing in intimate household quarters thus takes on the embodiment of the qualities of pluralism, advocacy, and ecology all at once.

Intermediated Technology Access

The role of intermediaries in contexts such as ours has been frequently discussed in HCI4D research [29, 22]. We see in the work of Kumar and Rangaswamy [16], for instance, that when technology skills are limited, human intermediaries and mediators step in to facilitate technology use. In this study too, we found a significant presence of intermediaries helping the women with their technology use needs. Our unique finding was that these intermediaries were largely children and youth, often found in the same households as the women.

When we commenced our study, we expected the women's interactions with their mobiles to be limited. Several factors were responsible for this. These women operate within strict patriarchal structures with limited freedom. They are generally not highly educated and enjoy more restricted access to technology than the men. Doing Bluetooth exchanges of mobile media is not an activity we would have expected them to undertake. Broadening our purview to include the role of intermediaries, however, and considering other actors in the neighborhood who could help with these tasks, altered our view of the media landscape significantly. Even when the women are unable to conduct Bluetooth transfers or play videos, there are children and youth (male and female) in the household who are generally more adept with the mobile devices and readily able to help. Even the schoolgirls we spoke to expressed great enthusiasm and willingness to take on the responsibility of transferring PH videos to the mobiles of their mothers, relations, and neighbors if this would be of use to them. Notwithstanding the possibility that it was our advocacy of PH content that we saw a reflection of in them, we believe that the potential of children as change agents or 'action research assistants' is not to be underestimated.

Going Beyond User-Centered Design

An important lesson for the HCI community that our study offers is how pushing the boundaries of user-centered design and going beyond the target user can constructively impact a technology intervention. We stress the importance of looking not only at users but the context they operate within - including the technological and human elements that influence their social and cultural activities. For instance, perhaps women on their own are not aware of the full range of functions that their mobile offers, but the fact that there are children or youth around who are is important to factor in. This becomes especially relevant for societies like rural India's that have collectivist leanings. We push, therefore, for a greater focus on community- and context-centered design in HCI.

CONCLUSION

We studied mobile media practices of rural Indian women in the context of Projecting Health, a public health initiative that targets the dissemination of health information for pregnant women, lactating mothers, and their newborns using locally crafted short films. We used a Feminist HCI approach to inform the iteration of our information dissemination model, examining the potential of incorporating existing mobile media practices and taking a community-centered approach to design.We maintained our focus on the qualities of pluralism, advocacy, ecology, and participation as discussed by Bardzell [2] and showed that although there are strict social conventions and patriarchal norms that constrain various practices of these women, they are able to exercise agency and mobilize help within their communities as needed. Our next steps with Projecting Health will build on the insights we gleaned from this study.

ACKNOWLEDGMENTS

We thank PATH and our partner organizations GVS and NYST for their incredible support. We are grateful to our anonymous reviewers for their helpful suggestions and also thank Abhishek Das for his invaluable inputs and feedback. This paper is based on work supported by the National Science Foundation under grant 1111433.

REFERENCES

1. Balestrini, M., Bird, J., Marshall, P., Zaro, A., and Rogers, Y. Understanding sustained community engagement: a case study in heritage preservation in rural argentina. In *Proceedings of the 32nd annual ACM conference on Human factors in computing systems*, ACM (2014), 2675–2684.
2. Bardzell, S. Feminist hci: taking stock and outlining an agenda for design. In *Proceedings of the SIGCHI Conference on Human Factors in Computing Systems*, ACM (2010), 1301–1310.
3. Bardzell, S., and Bardzell, J. Towards a feminist hci methodology: social science, feminism, and hci. In *Proceedings of the SIGCHI Conference on Human Factors in Computing Systems*, ACM (2011), 675–684.
4. Bidwell, N. J., Reitmaier, T., Marsden, G., and Hansen, S. Designing with mobile digital storytelling in rural africa. In *Proceedings of the SIGCHI Conference on Human Factors in Computing Systems*, ACM (2010), 1593–1602.
5. Cuendet, S., Medhi, I., Bali, K., and Cutrell, E. Videokheti: making video content accessible to low-literate and novice users. In *Proceedings of the SIGCHI Conference on Human Factors in Computing Systems*, ACM (2013), 2833–2842.
6. Dimond, J. P. *Feminist HCI For Real: Designing Technology in Support of a Social Movement.* PhD thesis, Georgia Institute of Technology, 2012.
7. Fiore-Silfvast, B., Hartung, C., Iyengar, K., Iyengar, S., Israel-Ballard, K., Perin, N., and Anderson, R. Mobile video for patient education: The midwives' perspective. In *Proceedings of the 3rd ACM Symposium on Computing for Development*, ACM DEV '13, ACM (New York, NY, USA, 2013), 2:1–2:10.
8. Frohlich, D. M., Rachovides, D., Riga, K., Bhat, R., Frank, M., Edirisinghe, E., Wickramanayaka, D., Jones, M., and Harwood, W. Storybank: mobile digital storytelling in a development context. In *Proceedings of the SIGCHI Conference on Human Factors in Computing Systems*, ACM (2009), 1761–1770.
9. Gandhi, R., Veeraraghavan, R., Toyama, K., and Ramprasad, V. Digital green: Participatory video and mediated instruction for agricultural extension. *Information Technologies and International Development 5*, 1 (2009), 1 – 15.
10. Haraway, D. Situated knowledges: The science question in feminism and the privilege of partial perspective. *Turning points in qualitative research: Tying knots in a handkerchief* (2003), 21–46.
11. Hodkinson, P. 'insider research' in the study of youth cultures. *Journal of Youth Studies 8*, 2 (2005), 131–149.
12. Kant, A. Experiencing pregnancy: Negotiating cultural and biomedical knowledge. *Sociological bulletin 63*, 2 (2014).
13. Kolko, B. E., Hope, A., Brunette, W., Saville, K., Gerard, W., Kawooya, M., and Nathan, R. Adapting collaborative radiological practice to low-resource environments. In *Proceedings of the ACM 2012 conference on Computer Supported Cooperative Work*, ACM (2012), 97–106.
14. Kumar, N., Chouhan, G., and Parikh, T. Folk music goes digital in india. In *Proceedings of the SIGCHI Conference on Human Factors in Computing Systems*, ACM (2011), 1423–1432.
15. Kumar, N., and Parikh, T. S. Mobiles, music, and materiality. In *Proceedings of the SIGCHI Conference on Human Factors in Computing Systems*, ACM (2013), 2863–2872.
16. Kumar, N., and Rangaswamy, N. The mobile media actor-network in urban india. In *Proceedings of the SIGCHI Conference on Human Factors in Computing Systems*, ACM (2013), 1989–1998.

17. Kumar, V., Kumar, A., and Darmstadt, G. L. Behavior change for newborn survival in resource-poor community settings: bridging the gap between evidence and impact. In *Seminars in perinatology*, vol. 34, Elsevier (2010), 446–461.

18. Ladeira, I., and Cutrell, E. Teaching with storytelling: An investigation of narrative videos for skills training. In *Proceedings of the 4th ACM/IEEE International Conference on Information and Communication Technologies and Development*, ACM (2010), 22.

19. Mathur, A., Ramachandran, D., Cutrell, E., and Balakrishnan, R. An exploratory study on the use of camera phones and pico projectors in rural india. In *Proceedings of the 13th International Conference on Human Computer Interaction with Mobile Devices and Services*, ACM (2011), 347–356.

20. Molapo, M., and Marsden, G. Software support for creating digital health training materials in the field. In *Proceedings of the Sixth International Conference on Information and Communication Technologies and Development: Full Papers - Volume 1*, ICTD '13, ACM (New York, NY, USA, 2013), 205–214.

21. Muller, M. Feminism asks the "who" questions in hci. *Interacting with Computers 23*, 5 (2011), 447–449.

22. Parikh, T. S., and Ghosh, K. Understanding and designing for intermediated information tasks in india. *Pervasive Computing, IEEE 5*, 2 (2006), 32–39.

23. Ramachandran, D., Canny, J., Das, P. D., and Cutrell, E. Mobile-izing health workers in rural india. In *Proceedings of the SIGCHI Conference on Human Factors in Computing Systems*, ACM (2010), 1889–1898.

24. Ramachandran, D., Goswami, V., and Canny, J. Research and reality: using mobile messages to promote maternal health in rural india. In *Proceedings of the 4th ACM/IEEE International Conference on Information and Communication Technologies and Development*, ACM (2010), 35.

25. Reitmaier, T., Bidwell, N. J., and Marsden, G. Field testing mobile digital storytelling software in rural kenya. In *Proceedings of the 12th international conference on Human computer interaction with mobile devices and services*, ACM (2010), 283–286.

26. Rode, J. A. The roles that make the domestic work. In *Proceedings of the 2010 ACM conference on Computer supported cooperative work*, ACM (2010), 381–390.

27. Rode, J. A. A theoretical agenda for feminist hci. *Interacting with Computers 23*, 5 (2011), 393–400.

28. Sambasivan, N., Cutrell, E., and Toyama, K. Viralvcd: tracing information-diffusion paths with low cost media in developing communities. In *Proceedings of the SIGCHI Conference on Human Factors in Computing Systems*, ACM (2010), 2607–2610.

29. Sambasivan, N., Cutrell, E., Toyama, K., and Nardi, B. Intermediated technology use in developing communities. In *Proceedings of the SIGCHI Conference on Human Factors in Computing Systems*, ACM (2010), 2583–2592.

30. Sengers, P., Boehner, K., David, S., and Kaye, J. J. Reflective design. In *Proceedings of the 4th Decennial Conference on Critical Computing: Between Sense and Sensibility*, CC '05, ACM (New York, NY, USA, 2005), 49–58.

31. Shroff, G., and Kam, M. Towards a design model for women's empowerment in the developing world. In *Proceedings of the SIGCHI Conference on Human Factors in Computing Systems*, ACM (2011), 2867–2876.

32. Smyth, T. N., Kumar, S., Medhi, I., and Toyama, K. Where there's a will there's a way: mobile media sharing in urban india. In *Proceedings of the SIGCHI conference on Human Factors in computing systems*, ACM (2010), 753–762.

33. Song, M., and Parker, D. Commonality, difference and the dynamics of disclosure in in-depth interviewing. *Sociology 29*, 2 (1995), 241–256.

34. Taylor, A. S. Out there. In *Proceedings of the SIGCHI Conference on Human Factors in Computing Systems*, ACM (2011), 685–694.

35. Taylor, N., Cheverst, K., Wright, P., and Olivier, P. Leaving the wild: lessons from community technology handovers. In *Proceedings of the SIGCHI Conference on Human Factors in Computing Systems*, ACM (2013), 1549–1558.

36. Team, T. D. The digital studyhall. Tech. Rep. UW-CSE-07-08-01, University of Washington, 08 2007.

37. Underwood, H. M. *The PartoPen: Using digital pen technology to improve maternal labor monitoring in the developing world*. PhD thesis, University of Colorado at Boulder, 2013.

38. Van House, N. A. Feminist hci meets facebook: Performativity and social networking sites. *Interacting with Computers 23*, 5 (2011), 422–429.

Residual Mobilities: Infrastructural Displacement and Post-Colonial Computing in Bangladesh

Syed Ishtiaque Ahmed
Information Science
Cornell University, Ithaca, NY
sa738@cornell.edu

Nusrat Jahan Mim
Department of Architecture
BUET, Dhaka, Bangladesh
nusrat.mim@gmail.com

Steven J. Jackson
Information Science
Cornell University, Ithaca, NY
sjj54@cornell.edu

ABSTRACT
This paper explores discrepancies between the founding assumptions of mobile and ubiquitous computing in the western world, and the starkly different experiences of mobility and infrastructure to be found in many post-colonial environments. Based on a field study of forced mobility and technology use among populations displaced by the Hatirjheel waterfront development project in Dhaka, Bangladesh, we make two basic arguments. First, we point to the partial nature of assumptions around mobility that frame the imagination of mainstream HCI research, and argue that different and heretofore *residual* experiences of mobility must also be accounted for in post-colonial and other marginal computing environments. Second, we document four forms of infrastructural experience – dispossession, reconstitution, collaboration, and repair – that characterize real-world engagements with infrastructure in such settings. We conclude with implications for HCI research and design, and reflections on how HCI researchers might better account for such experiences in their work.

Author Keywords
Mobility; infrastructure; ethnography; development; post-colonial computing; ICTD; Bangladesh.

ACM Classification Keywords
H. 1. 2. Human Factors

INTRODUCTION
Like other sub-fields of HCI work, mobile and ubiquitous computing research is structured around assumptions. Some of these concern the technological conditions and resources available to designers, researchers, and users: stable and reliable power supplies, affordable and ubiquitous cell coverage, effective regimes of privacy and security, and most generally, technical infrastructures that simply 'work.'

CHI 2015, April 18 - 23 2015, Seoul, Republic of Korea
Copyright is held by the owner/author(s). Publication rights licensed to ACM.
ACM 978-1-4503-3145-6/15/04...$15.00
http://dx.doi.org/10.1145/2702123.2702573

Others concern the nature and experience of mobility itself, the situations from which it arises, and the kinds of actors who engage it. The modal subject of mobile computing is very often the empowered user, engaging strategically and creatively with emerging tools and systems to support new forms of mobility in their lives (or conversely, to overcome problems that mobilities voluntarily entered into create). From the standpoint of history and social science, this represents a classically liberal figure, endowed with rights, autonomy, resources, and the freedom to act and choose, including around the spatial circumstances of their lives. In this view, mobilities are, on balance, a Good Thing, and our job as HCI researchers is to find new and creative ways to support them.

In many post-colonial and economically marginal environments, however, neither of these assumptions – around infrastructure or around the liberal model of mobility – hold true. Power grids may fail or fluctuate, networks may operate sporadically (and sometimes not at all), and devices and systems of all kinds and levels may break. Even where operative, access to crucial infrastructures may be restricted by barriers of cost, literacy, availability, or social or economic standing. Nor are the conditions of mobility always as voluntary or choice-based as the liberal model would suggest. Rural-to-urban migration driven by economic need is one of the oldest themes and concerns in the development studies field [7,32] and has accelerated throughout the postwar modernization and structural adjustment eras (aided in many instances by regressive state and donor policies that have effectively hollowed out the countryside) [32]. Efforts at modernization, from dams and resettlement schemes to urban prestige projects, have displaced countless others, producing conditions of mobility that severely challenge or destroy the assumptions of the liberal model. Still others are displaced by the conditions of war and conflict: a 2013 United Nations report estimated the global population displaced by conflict, persecution, or generalized violence at 51.2 million – a figure higher than at any time since the conclusion of World War II [37].

These differences help frame the divide between HCI research attuned to the conditions of 'developing' regions (whether under the label of 'ICTD,' 'post-colonial computing,' 'computing at the margins,' etc.) and the unmarked categories of tool- or topically-framed fields of HCI work. While in developed countries, researchers are trying to incorporate affect, passion, persuasion, and other sophisticated services through smartphones, HCI researchers in post-colonial computing environments attempt to extend the reach of low-cost networks [10], build interfaces for illiterate people [21,28], and extend access to farming knowledge through agricultural support networks [23]. While mobile computing in developed parts of the world is helping users choose restaurants, music driving routes, or friends on the fly, mobile phones in developing countries are being directed towards fundamental needs and barriers around education, financial transactions, and basic health care. While 'northern' innovations in mobile computing may be focused around novel developments in hardware, software, and user interfaces, more significant and original innovations in post-colonial computing environments may be found around practices of hacking, repurposing and repair. These differences point to important contextual differences that shape and separate categories of HCI work and concern as practiced differentially across geographic and social contexts around the world. Properly acknowledged, they should also challenge and extend our core notions of infrastructure and innovation itself.

But mobile computing may also encode unrecognized assumptions around experiences of mobility that it studies and designs for. Where much HCI work in this space assumes voluntary and choice-based movement (as captured in the old Nortel Networks slogan, "Where Do You Want to Go Today?") our paper calls HCI attention to the problem of *residual mobilities*: the varied forms of involuntary migration, displacement and disruption that characterize the real-world experience of mobility for a large and growing number of people around the world – both in historically post-colonial contexts like the one studied here, but also marginal locations and experiences in what Suchman has termed the "hyperdeveloped world" [30]. Inspired by Star and Bowker's work on residual categories, and the way in which dominant systems of knowledge and assumption may render important categories of experience marginal or unthinkable, we introduce the notion of *residual mobilities* as a way of gathering and acknowledging experiences of mobility and technology use that depart, sometimes dramatically, from the choice-based assumptions of the liberal model. We argue that better attention to these forms of mobility can help combat limiting assumptions embedded in the liberal model; open new HCI insight into the often creative practices by which poor and marginal populations engage key tools and infrastructures (including computational ones); and open up new terrains for HCI impact and design.

Our claims are grounded in ethnographic fieldwork with a low-income community of approximately 1500 people in the South Begunbari neighborhood of Dhaka, Bangladesh, situated near the country's largest waterfront beautification and infrastructure development, the Hatirjheel project. The residents of Begunbari are mostly migrants from other parts of the country, and have in many instances been evicted several other times from temporary settlements and/or districts moved to make way for other commercial or public development projects. At the time of our fieldwork in spring and summer 2014, they were under threat of eviction yet again: in the second week of June 2014, the first round of bulldozers arrived to make space for the road-widening and hotel-construction projects designed to take advantage of the lake's restored natural beauty. Subsequent phases of the project will involve further eviction of Begunbari residents, including for a planned boundary wall that will limit local residents access to the project's newly developed park lands and infrastructure.

Building on interviews and participant observation with Begunbari residents, this paper pursues two basic goals. First, we seek to map one instance of the condition of residual mobility: where it comes from, how it's experienced, and how it torques and limits (rather than frees and empowers) the lives of the people who encounter it. Second, we demonstrate how people made residual under mainstream assumptions of development and infrastructure nevertheless engage strategically and creatively with the infrastructures around them, building new modes of access, support, and value. This kind of creative re-appropriation of infrastructure, we argue, is a central and underappreciated dynamic in many post-colonial and marginal computing environments, and one that HCI scholarship dedicated to other places and concerns can also learn from.

We open with a review of relevant literature in postcolonial and mobile computing, before turning to HCI and social science theories that can help us unpack the nature of mobilities and infrastructures encountered here. We then report ethnographic data around the forms of residual mobility encountered in the lives of Begunbari residents, and describe key features of our participants' interactions with technology and infrastructure. We conclude with implications for HCI research and design, and reflections on how HCI researchers might better account for such experiences in their work.

BACKGROUND AND RELATED WORK

From its earliest days, mobile computing has been built around and enshrined a basic (and we will argue *partial*) concept of mobility, its social role and desirability, and the potential role of new computational tools in supporting that. Mark Weiser, often regarded as the father of ubiquitous computing, dreamt of omnipresent and seamless computing tools and platforms that would follow and support users through a rapidly expanding mobile life. This dream – and much subsequent ubicomp work - was based on important assumptions: ubiquitous and robust core infrastructures, empowered and competent users, etc. More subtly but no less centrally, it rested on the assumption that users were in charge of their own mobility, able to enter into conditions of movement or flow on the basis of choice and desire, and able to dictate (more or less) the terms and conditions of mobility entered into – in part by adopting tools and technologies that could support or augment these choices. These assumptions worked well enough (though never perfectly) under the infrastructures, user bases, and liberal democratic and economic conditions of the 'global north' (a term of art that increasingly incorporates the wealthier sectors, locations, and peoples of 'southern' locations). In subsequent years, mobile and ubiquitous computing has flourished in the western world, proliferating an ever more imaginative range of supportive and interactive services delivered through mobile phones, tablets, wearables, and other increasingly ubiquitous devices and infrastructures.

As mobile technologies started to travel to the developing world, however, many of these basic assumptions were upset. Despite the rapid and widespread uptake of mobile phones in developing countries, important gaps and limits remained. Electricity did not reach everywhere in many developing countries, and power supplies were not stable [16]. Cellular networks rapidly blanketed urban areas, but coverage in rural and poorer regions lagged [1]. Price continued to be an important barrier to access (in particular for the higher end smart phones that northern mobile computing researchers have traditionally relied on) [25]. Digital or basic literacies posed additional barriers to use and adoption [21], and carrying and using an expensive technical device on the streets was unsafe in some contexts, and culturally frowned on in others [1]. The sum of these differences made mobile computing as practiced in many post-colonial contexts a significantly different enterprise than the better-studied forms of mobile computing characterizing 'northern' computing environments.

These absences and discrepancies have been called out most forcefully in recent HCI work around the nature and limits of post-colonial computing. Pointing out the infrastructural, cultural, and political differences that shape the entry of HCI tools and assumptions into post-colonial contexts, Irani et. al. [12] pointed to a series of *other* effects that the introduction of new computational tools, including those oriented to 'developmental' ends, might have. Computational development and reliance might further troubling and long-standing patterns of north-south dependency. The traditional 'gap' or 'lack' framing of post-colonial problems around technology might further problematic 'developmentalist' discourses that take northern conditions as the implicit goal or marker of economic and social achievement. Basic assumptions around infrastructure and development 'failures' may reflect the perspectives of northern actors and institutions, and generate new rounds of 'development projects' that fail to engage post-colonial conditions and experiences (though they may be good at sustaining the institutional machinery of the development industry). And western-centered assumptions might blind HCI researchers to what's *different* about post-colonial computing experience, ignoring sites of action and value – for example, more collaborative forms of technical agency and action [4], or the presence of robust and innovative repair networks [13]– that may differ in *positive* ways from northern computational experience. At the broadest level, HCI work on post-colonial computing has revealed the extent to which core ideas, expectations and assumptions around computing may reflect conditions and experiences specific to the 'global North,' many of which translate badly or not at all to a wider set of contemporary global realities.

Separate lines of work in sociology, geography, and urban studies have begun to open up the nature and experience of mobility itself as a complex and socially distributed space. While this work has pointed to mobility as an increasingly central and formative feature of social life (arguing in effect that societies not only *have* mobilities, they *are* mobilities), it has also pointed to extreme variations in the kinds and outcomes of mobility that members of the contemporary world practice and experience. John Urry [35] for example, has shown how the 'free' mobilities experienced through corporeal or imaginative travel in tours, games, and communication media may differ from – and are sometimes predicated on – the no-less-modern mobilities of migration, military movement, and displacement. Saskia Sassen [27] has called attention to the growing prevalence of physical and economic expulsion and displacement as central engines of economic growth and recovery. Earlier work by British geographer Doreen Massey [20] has demonstrated how the 'power-geometry' of time-space compression attached to experiences of globalization in the 1990s offered different experiences of mobilities to different social groups. These differences were defined not so much by the *fact* of mobility – both global business executives and economic refugees are mobile, after all – as by the *degree of control over the flows and movements that shape one's life*. As Massey argues,

> "Different groups have distinct relationships to this anyway differentiated mobility: some people are more in charge of it than others; some initiate flows and movements, other don't; some are more on the receiving end of it than others; some are effectively imprisoned by it". [20]

If differences in 'power-geometry' account for different experiences of mobility in the world, they also help to explain *what* and *whose* experiences are summoned easily to mind when we tell generic cultural stories about mobility (and by extension, build tools and infrastructures to support them). To have your category of experience excluded, and thus to be left out of the story and programs of design and action that build on them, is to be rendered, in Star and Bowker's term, "residual" [29].

These issues of power and residuality connect in turn to a growing body of HCI and social science work on infrastructure: roughly, the systems of physical and social support that enable, sustain, limit, and give shape to human action in the world. This includes large physical structures like road, water, electricity, and telecommunication networks. But it also includes the people, culture, and economic and social conditions that also shape the pattern and possibilities of mobility in a society. Historically, there is an essential bias in the growth of infrastructures in the uneven political landscape of developing countries. Graham and Marvin [8] have documented the emergence of new enclave networks that link privileged users of high-end infrastructures in urban areas around the globe. Larkin [17] has shown how infrastructure development in post-colonial contexts may be directed not only to technical and material purposes, but also important "performative" goals, symbolizing forms of power, control, and modernizing and/or globalizing aspiration. These studies point to the important distributional element of infrastructure, and how new infrastructure projects may be caught up in and help to reinforce unequal power relations at the local and national levels. They also suggest the existence and significance of residual mobilities, and the need to account for the distinct needs and experiences of marginal populations in our global or technical accounts of infrastructure development.

Our arguments in this paper draw on data collected through observation and interviews in South Begunbari, a marginal and low-income neighborhood in central Dhaka. Most residents of the neighborhood are migrants from other parts of the country, and have undergone numerous previous experiences of eviction, driven by development projects and/or economic or environmental need. Such forced mobilities have produced profound and challenging experiences of infrastructural displacement and uncertainty. Through processes of innovation, collaboration, and struggle, they have also built new and often creative engagements with infrastructure that have gone some distance to restoring lost services and supports. We argue that these forms of infrastructural engagement – dispossession, reconstitution, collaboration and repair – can offer theory- and design-relevant insights to HCI, and uncover important holes and opportunities in the field.

MODERNIZING DHAKA: DEVELOPMENT, DISPLACEMENT, AND RESIDUAL MOBILITIES

The urbanization of Bangladesh is interlinked with the development of Dhaka City, which has developed as the politico-administrative center of the country. Due to the concentration of both domestic and foreign investment, Dhaka has experienced massive migration from the rural areas of Bangladesh. In the last 60 years, driven by domestic and foreign investment and substantial flows of rural-to-urban migration, the population of Dhaka has increased 35 times, making it one of the world's largest and by far the most densely-populated city (ahead of such places as Sao Paolo, Delhi, London and New York) [19]. This growth has stressed or overwhelmed the city's basic infrastructures, Due to rapid urbanization and a lack of effective planning, unplanned settlements have proliferated, many in the form of slum and squatter settlements just like other developing cities as discussed in Hardoy et al [9]. Due to acute demand and high land prices, especially in the central zones and in upper class residential areas, the slums and squatter communities have moved in recent years towards the city peripheries in search of cheaper shelter, though many of the work opportunities in the informal and service economies remain concentrated in the commercial and wealthier residential districts of the city center [19]. A significant portion of the city's population lives in these slums and squatter settlements under extremely low living standards, low productivity and unemployment [34]. Because of different development projects and their associated settlements, these people are often evicted and forced to find new places to live. Paul reported the repeated experience (and constant fear) of eviction as a central challenge facing the urban poor in Dhaka, and an ongoing source of uncertainty and precariousness that undermined both general well-being and the ability to plan and organize one's life around the kinds of long-term choices and investments (education, stable employment, etc.) that might support roads out of social and economic marginality [22]. As our work below will make clear, fear of eviction was a socio-economic but also *infrastructural* concern: to be evicted was to lose not only one's dwelling, but also access to the place-based and often informal systems, services and supports that make life under conditions of urban poverty sustainable, meaningful, and sometimes good.

The community we studied is in Tejgaon, the largest industrial area of Dhaka city. Our more immediate study site of South Begunbari is surrounded by biscuit factories, metal workshops, car parts and repair shops, gas stations, truck garages, and electronic repair shops. Most residents of the community were low-literate and low-income, and worked in local factories and workshops, ran small informal businesses (tea shops, food stands, etc.), or worked as servants or occasional laborers in nearby wealthier neighborhoods. Almost all had faced multiple episodes of displacement in their life. Most had migrated from other parts of the country and had moved several times (often through eviction) within Dhaka itself. Many were under threat of eviction yet again due to the nearby Hatirjheel waterfront development project, widely hailed as one of the largest and most important Government-led modernization efforts in Dhaka in recent decades.

The Government-initiated Hatirjheel waterfront development project was launched in 2009 with the goal of beautifying the area and reducing Dhaka's notorious traffic jams by connecting important roads through bridges and widening key feeder arteries. Other objectives included rainwater retention, flood prevention, and improvement of the urban sewer system. While one side of the lake was connected to one of the city's richest neighborhoods (Gulshan, which was not affected by the project), other parts of the lakeside were occupied by low-income communities and illegal settlements. Their eviction was argued to be necessary for the beautification of the lake and purification of the lake water. Initial land acquisition and settlement removal took two years, and construction work on the bridges was completed in January 2013, with road-widening efforts (and associated evictions) continuing through the present. The project has been widely celebrated in media and tourist literatures, and the Government featured the project as an exemplary instance of modernization and urban renewal in its reelection campaign of 2014. On the other hand, the eviction process caused a massive displacement of people who used to live around Hatirjheel Lake, many of whom were dispersed to nearby Begunbari or other peripheral areas around the city.

We conducted fieldwork, interviews, and participant observation with the residents of Begunbari area. The first two authors of this paper are Bangladeshi citizens and residents, and one of them worked with the people of Begunbari for 17 months (between March 2013 and July of 2014) to construct modular and portable housing units for the displaced urban poor. Our understanding and access to the community builds largely on this extended relationship. Our participants included men and women who were evicted because of the Hatirjheel project, and others who have been migrated or forcefully displaced from other locations for a variety of other reasons. During this period of time, we observed their living conditions, social interaction places like local streets, market places, tea stalls, connecting lanes, etc. conducted interviews, took part in conversations, and took copious notes and photographs. This resulted in 200 pages of field reports and more than 300 photographs. We also conducted separate semi-structured interviews with 39 local residents, including shopkeepers, part-time domestic helpers, construction workers, rickshawpullers, garments factory workers, metal workshop laborers, vegetable vendors, etc., about the changes in their life and the role of technology in it. The interviews followed general thematic templates that were applied flexibly to accommodate informant stories and lines of concern, together with emergent issues arising in the context of interaction (per common interpretive interview techniques). These interviews ranged from 10 minutes (when interrupted by business, weather or household duties) to 2 hours, with most lasting 45 minutes to 1 hour. Bangla speaking members of the research team translated and transcribed all interviews, and developed a series of descriptive biographies across a representative range of participants. Transcripts, field notes, and biographies were reviewed by all members of the study team, analyzed and coded following grounded theory principles, and used to guide subsequent data and field collection efforts.

HATIRJHEEL AND ITS CONSEQUENCES: INFRASTRUCTURE AND RESIDUALITY

Before the Hatirjheel evictions began, Begunbari was full of single-storied bamboo and wooden structures, most built illegally on privately owned or government lands, including a variety of structures built on stilts out over the lake itself. During phase one of the eviction process, Government forces took possession of the lakeside areas, destroyed the settlements with bulldozers, and forcibly removed all illegal dwellers from the area Per frequent eviction practice in Bangladesh and other places, these steps were taken without compensation or relocation support, and sometimes little or no prior warning. Some residents displaced in these first round evictions left Begunbari and moved to other parts of the city; others shifted to adjacent portions of the same locality, also known as South Begunbari. This produced a sudden population explosion in the area, and caused a rapid shortage and densification of housing. People started to extend dwellings vertically by building 2 or 3 storied structures from wood and bamboo (participants in our study included local residents who participated in this boom as planners, carpenters, and casual laborers). Living conditions rapidly deteriorated. Housing lacked proper light and ventilation. Kitchens were dark, and the toilets were damp. The lanes between houses were narrow and muddy, and as dwellings went higher and the population increased, increasingly dark and crowded. After the construction of the bridge in Hatirjheel, Begunbari received access (in principle) to a variety of improved infrastructures which the area lacked before: well-connected road networks; water, gas, and electrical lines; satellite TV connections; etc. However, these systems included few taps or connection points available to local populations: for the most part these infrastructures ran through Begunbari without materially serving it. Government officials and private land-owners in the neighborhood justified the lack of local infrastructural investment on the grounds that most current residents were there illegally, and the entire area was likely to be redeveloped again in the next few years anyway.

Lacking infrastructural connections, Begunbari residents developed their own. Neighborhood residents built informal circulation paths to connect the community with the new government built main roads. They devised systems of plastic piping to connect households to the new water mains running past the neighborhood, and in some cases underground pipelines to connect toilets with nearby sewer mains. Some residents found ways of running lines of cooking gas to their kitchen (though many continued to burn wood or paper for cooking), either themselves or by hiring local plumbers, carpenters and handymen to complete the work.

One of the most sought after commodities in Begunbari was cheap or free electricity: almost as soon as legal supply lines were installed on poles lining the new government roads, local residents and electricians began the process of tapping and redirecting this power into Begunbari. At the household level, this was accomplished through cheap wires running through and between buildings, occasionally supported on bamboo poles. Local electricians often took responsibility for tapping the main lines (an inherently dangerous process) and for keeping this messy and failure-prone network in more or less functional form. As they reported, heavy use loads and hacked connections often caused discontinuous flow, load shedding, and fluctuations in voltage. Daily power shutdowns lasting an hour or two were regular features of Begunbari life, and often occurred two to three times per day. These hacking activities also often met with resistance. Government officials periodically came to check the lines, alternately cutting off connections or negotiating with local residents for bribes. In some cases, residents of nearby neighborhoods negatively affected by the hacks would complain (or sometimes disconnecting the illegal lines themselves). As one such resident described,

"We have always used only one light and fan for our room. But 3 or 4 months ago, we noticed an abnormal leap in our electricity bill. We paid for that month. In the next month the bill raised further up. We sensed something wrong and then discovered the illegal connections that Begunbari people made to my lines. I immediately called the electrician and disconnected them."

Figure 1. Community built lanes (left), and Water lines (right)

Similar challenges attended the neighborhood's hacked water and sewage networks. Broken or leaky pipes periodically disrupted water flow and quality, resulting in service outages and contamination of water supplies. Where breakages could be identified they were fixed, often by wrapping pipes with duct tape. In some cases, kluged networks were abandoned altogether, and residents resorted to nearby tube wells or neighborhood stores selling cheap water. Sewage blockages were similarly common, resulting in frequent and occasionally prolonged outages.

The brief account above suggests a number of important characteristics of the relationship between residual mobility and core modern infrastructures like water, power, and road systems. As we saw, the mainstream and formal infrastructures transecting Begunbari were not built with local residents in mind; indeed, the only access to them provided came from the illegal taps and informal hacks that local residents were able to work out. Because of the inherent difficulty and messiness of this work however the quality of services received was often poor and subject to repeated breakdown and disruption (though they remained for all that far better than what residents had access to before). Finally, because of their hacked and illegal nature, when core infrastructures did fail, residents were left to perform maintenance and repair on their own, either individually or through community efforts (as with the committee of neighborhood electricians charged with building and maintaining power supplies in the area). The combination of these features characterizes the complex relationship between residuality and infrastructure (both formal and informal) in Begunbari today.

ENGAGING INFRASTRUCTURE

Beyond these challenges in securing and maintaining access to basic services, residual mobilities offer an uncertain, interrupted, and challenged relationship with infrastructure and technology more generally. Stretching from uncertainties around the availability and quality of technical services to the ongoing challenge of maintaining and fixing what services they have, conditions of residuality frame different modes of technical experience and engagement than those commonly addressed in HCI scholarship. In the sections that follow we explore four of these: dispossession, reconstitution, collaboration, and repair.

i) *Dispossession*:

Dispossession of infrastructural support is a common experience in residual mobilities. Beyond their many other effects, experiences of eviction and migration detach people from key sources of material and social support. Participants in our study had recently undergone or were about to undergo exactly such processes. The uncertainty, risks, and short and long term social and economic effects of dispossession constituted an important aspect of their engagement with infrastructure.

Dispossession through eviction is often uncertain and sudden, affording little time for planning or adjustment. Notices of impending evictions are often short or non-existant. For example, one of our participants was evicted with her family from a previous dwelling at the Moghbazar Railway Slum two years ago with a one-day notice. At Moghbazar they had access to an illegal electricity line, which they used to run a couple of electric bulbs and fans, a television, a mobile phone, and a radio. After being evicted they spent five nights in the open, sleeping on roadsides, used candles and streetlights for light, and cooking on fires made from waste paper. They were also in constant fear of being moved at any time by the local Police. At that time they had no access to electricity, and hence were totally detached from all sorts of technical services. Other participants undergoing similar episodes reported keeping hand fans, charged flashlights, and supplies of candles ready in case of future similar disruptions.

Dispossession is not merely the physical detachment with material infrastructural support, but it also includes the loss of the social support that is important for people's life. This can significantly affect the access and use of technologies in the life of people affected by residual mobilities. For example, while migrating to Dhaka one of our participants left her mother in Rangpur, a district in Northern Bangladesh. Prior to a previous eviction, she maintained contact with her mother through her mobile phone, using a piece of paper with her contact numbers recorded and the help of a neighbor who knew how to use and dial the phone. Upon moving to Begunbari she lost both the paper and the neighbor, and subsequently most of the effective functionality of her phone, along with almost all her social contacts (including her mother).

Residual mobilities also often cause the dispossession of economic means, which in turn affects the use of technology in people's lives. Sudden experiences or increases in poverty often accompany eviction and migration, during which periods people may place higher priority on food, healthcare, or housing over technology. For example, when one of our participants was evicted from a previous location and migrated to Begunbari, she lost her job. Additionally she had to spend money to work out new shelter, food, and healthcare arrangements for her family. This left little money for electricity or mobile phone bills. As a result, she was detached from electrical technologies soon after her arrival in Begunbari.

ii) Reconstitution and Resistance:

The reconstitution of lost infrastructural support is an inseparable part of people's lives under conditions of residual mobility. Part of this may involve processes of reconnection to mainstream infrastructures. Other parts involve the restoration of social support, services, and contacts lost through displacement. Among its many other functions, social support is often crucial to technology use among poor and low-literate communities. After migrating to a new place, they need to redevelop social groups that will support their use of technology. Community gathering places like tea-stalls often help them rebuild this social support. A local tea-stall owner told us the following story of how new members of the community built connections and skills through conversations at his shop:

"One day a newcomer came to my tea-stall and asked for a cup of tea. At that time Mr. J was discussing how he solved a problem regarding the FNF service on his mobile phone. The newcomer asked if Mr. J could help him activate that service on his mobile phone. Mr. J agreed, and eventually we all came to know each other." (FNF is a service allowing calls to some selected contacts cheaply)

Besides developing social support for using technology, a new person in a community also needs to know the people who provide, maintain, and repair infrastructural supports. For example, all our participants in Begunbari had to know and keep a good relationship with the electricians who maintain the local power lines and fix those. Similarly, they are familiar with the plumbers, cleaners, electric repairers, and shopkeepers in the community. Newcomers need to learn these networks, for reasons of both infrastructural and sometimes social support.

People undergoing displacement also often try to maintain or re-establish communication with contacts lost through migration or displacement. Most of our participants relied on mobile phones (there own or others) to maintain contact with relatives in rural areas and sometimes to transfer money through the services provided by the phone companies. Beyond these personal and familial connections, participants also relied on social networks for other kinds of support. For example, one of our participants maintains connections with a friend from a former neighborhood through mobile contact in part because of their dependence on the friend (who works at a pharmacy) as a source of medical advice and occasionally medicine. But economic and technical barriers often hinder this reconnection process. As a 35-year-old vegetable vendor in our study explained,

"Although I miss my old friends in my village and in the places I lived before, I cannot afford calling them all. I only call people who have business with me. I saw on television that I could make cheap calls, but I do not know how."

ii) Collaboration and Sharing:

Like many other low-literate and low-income communities, Begunbari residents frequently borrow or share technical devices, and offer each other important technical assistance in basic digital literacy and operation. This matches forms of sharing and collaboration observed in other infrastructures. For example, during the period of our observations, residents were developing a new lane to connect main roads in two neighboring areas of South Begunbari. In other instances we observed neighbors collaborating to fix leaky pipes or broken sewer lines.

Again, people share their resources and help each other during the collapse of infrastructures. When water supply is broken, or when the sewerage pipes are clogged, the neighbors share their bathrooms, and toilets. Even when the gas lines break, they share their kitchen with their neighbors. However, the most common form of support is probably seen when power shuts down at nights. People were often seen to share their batteries, torchlights, and mobile phones to help each other. Also, it was very common for them to watch televisions, or listen to radios together when one's device is broken.

iii) *Hacking and Repairing*

As already reviewed above, life under conditions of residual mobility rests heavily on the ability to hack into mainstream infrastructure, and fix or restore broken technologies. Such actions become a key means by which infrastructural support is secured and maintained. Both hacking and repair activities involve many innovative and creative interventions that shape and reshape the technology to work under the conditions of residual mobility.

Illegal hacking activities are very common in Begunbari, and are indeed in many cases the only way to get access to crucial infrastructures like water and electricity. One of our participants described his recent arrival in Begunbari as follows:

"We came to Begunbari after being evicted from Mirpur slum. Although the house-owner told me there would be electricity, we did not find any. I had to call the local electrician who stretched an illegal line from the electricity wires that ran outside my window. We are still using that connection."

These hacking activities often meet resistance. Government officials periodically come to check the lines, sometimes cutting off connections and sometimes settling for bribes. Some of the hacks described above affect legal users who may also take action. As one such resident said,

"We have always been using only one light and fan for our room. But 3 or 4 months ago, we noticed an abnormal leap in our electricity bill. We paid for that month. In the next month the bill raised further up. We sensed something wrong and then discovered the illegal connections that Begunbari people made to my lines. I immediately called the electrician and disconnected those."

Similar illegal hackings are prevalent in water, gas, sewerage and satellite cable connections. One family for example who could not afford satellite channel connections solved the problem by hacking into their neighbor's satellite cable and stretching a second wire to their own television. Though the picture is not clear and often difficult to watch, they report being happy with the outcome.

Other kinds of creative technical responses can be found in repair. This includes the ubiquitous repair shops that service broken phones in and around the community, but also less formal repair knowledges, often passed around the community as tricks of the trade. We found one 40-year-old fish vendor drying his mobile phone in a bucket of rice, for example, who explained:

"I sell fish in Karwan Bazar market. Often my mobile phone falls off my pocket into the basket of fish or into the bucket of water. Then it stops working. Then I put it in the container of rice for at least one day, and my phone starts working again. I learnt this from a friend of mine."

DISCUSSION

Through the ethnographic data presented here, we have shown how the Government-led Hatirjheel waterfront project created forced mobilities in the lives of low-income residents and communities in the Begunbari area, and how those mobilities disrupted access to core infrastructures ranging from road and electricity networks to electronic and face-to-face forms of communication. We have also shown how residents pushed back, overcoming displacement and marginalization through informal hacks, fixes, and workarounds that restored or overcame (though never perfectly) the challenges and exclusions that displacement and residuality created. These findings have important implications for HCI scholarship, in ways both immediate and extended.

We begin by noting the general absence of Begunbari (or places like it) in the general stories HCI tells about mobility, computing, and the relationships between them. Stories of dispossession – and especially radical forms of dispossession like those experienced by the residents of Begunbari – are largely (though not entirely [13,22,33]) absent from HCI's general orientation to the world, which has tended to focus on moments of growth and development: the extension of core services and infrastructures, rather than their sudden and radical disruption. Asking what design can bring to such an environment poses interesting and provocative challenges. Services for timely reporting on eviction and support for short- and longer-term relocation efforts might help navigate uncertainties stemming from the sudden and multiple losses of infrastructure attached to dispossession. Real-time disaster mapping systems like *Crisismap* [38] might also be used to generate local and foreign support for the victims. Closer to home, individuals connected through social networks might leverage the benefit of extant systems to support some of the restorative or reconstitution functions described above. Our own separate research has suggested how mobile and crowd-supported systems in Bangladesh might provide support for services ranging from sexual harassment reporting [2] to distributed support for low-literacy users [3]. At the same time, research and design efforts may be extended to the infrastructure level to reduce users' detachment from services. Proper maintenance and repair of such systems might require local expert communities to sustain such technologies [13]. Both government and private sources should explore the possibilities of temporary and modular service infrastructures to address short-term needs in the areas of housing, electricity, water, gas, and sewage disposal.[1]

Beyond such implications, our study has also underlined the distinctly collaborative forms of infrastructural use and engagement that help residents navigate and ameliorate the conditions of residual mobility. These findings match prior work that has shown how technology may be shared and used collaboratively among low-literate and low-income populations across a range of post-colonial and marginal computing contexts (as reported for example by Burrell [4], Medhi et al. [21], Ahmed et al. [3], Rangaswamy et al. [24], and Sambasivan et al. [26]). The conditions of residual mobility explored here both amplify and complicate these findings. On one hand, we see how shared-access and secondary use models (where people draw on technological benefits shared through friends and networks) become even more valuable as residents navigate the uncertainties of

[1] One of the members of the project team is indeed working on a project to produce temporary, low-cost and modular housing solutions for victims of displacement.

displacement, and often lose place-based sites of gathering, information, and support (the neighborhood tea stand, relations with neighbors, etc.). On the other hand, access to technology itself may drop away, as local networks supplying access to technology or the knowledge needed to use it are dispersed. More detailed work on the relationship between infrastructural displacement and the reconfiguration of social interaction under conditions of residual mobility is an ongoing HCI need and interest.

In addition, from the uncertainty of displacement to community engagements in the hacking and fixing of infrastructure, our study raises important questions around HCI presumptions around certainty, fixity, and the (costless) longevity of systems and infrastructures. Classic HCI work by Suchman [31] has questioned the planning model at the heart of early artificial intelligence and HCI research, showing how the contingencies of place, context and situation can only ever be fully encountered and overcome in practice. This point comes through even more forcefully in worlds of residual mobility, where the presence of radical uncertainty makes 'planning' a somewhat quaint and foreign concept. If HCI is to arrive at more effective responses and interventions to the challenges confronting the residents of places like Begunbari, it may need a new set of metaphors that can live more comfortably with uncertainty – around resilience and recovery, for instance, or fixing and repair.

Our work also offers additional support to HCI themes of hacking, making, repair and other forms of creative material engagement as core and promising HCI 'moments' beyond those of design and use. Beyond their own inherent specificity and interest, post-colonial and marginal computing sites offer interesting and exemplary lessons here. Forms of innovation attached to the creative appropriation of infrastructure may open new windows of HCI work. Hacking cultures in China [18], and repair cultures in places like Bangladesh [13], Namibia [14,15], and Uganda [11] have already demonstrated distinctive and creative engagements with technologies that depart from Western norms and assumptions. The forms of infrastructural hacking and fixing woven into the everyday life and survival of people in places like Begunbari can further advance this program of work.

Finally, while our case has built from the immediate circumstances of Begunbari and the broader field of post-colonial computing, we wish to emphasize that residual mobilities and the forms of infrastructural displacement identified here are neither isolated incidents nor limited to postcolonial contexts (though they may appear in such contexts in particularly raw or 'pure' form). Millions of people around the world encounter some version of infrastructural displacement or residual mobility on an ongoing basis, whether driven by war, natural disaster, or extreme poverty attached to economic stagnation or collapse. Residual mobilities are also present in 'northern' contexts – arguably all the more so as traditional social safety nets are stripped away and the "modern infrastructural ideal" [7] splinters and decays. Here we note important parallels to HCI work addressing conditions and experiences of residual mobility and technology engagement in other seemingly very different contexts: for example, Jill Woelfer's [36] or Chris Le Dantec's [5] work on technology use and appropriation among homeless populations in Washington DC and Atlanta; or Julia Elyachar's [6] work on the forms of phatic labor that ensure ongoing social support, access and connection in Cairo. Under these conditions, understandings of residuality – and the challenges, deprivations, but also creative possibilities it encodes – become more central to HCI work and experience as a whole. Better attention to the varied forms of mobility and marginalization but also creative engagement with infrastructure occurring in places like Begunbari may further extend these lines of analysis, drawing new possibilities of comparative learning and analysis. It is also important if we are to avoid the limits of an HCI 'overfitted' to the conditions of Western social, economic and infrastructural assumptions.

CONCLUSION

This paper contributes to HCI by expanding the range and experience of mobilities the field has typically considered. We have introduced the concept of residual mobilities to better account for the technology experiences and infrastructural engagements characterizing people undergoing radical experiences of displacement. We have also pointed to the innovative and creative practices of infrastructural hacking and fixing as overlooked but potentially novel sites of HCI insight and innovation. Better accounting for such sites and experiences may help overcome the traditional limits and biases embedded in the assumptions of our field. It may also help the HCI research community develop new forms of listening and engagement in an increasingly complex and global world.

REFERENCES

1. Agar, J. *Constant Touch: A Global History of the Mobile Phone*. Icon Books, 2004.
2. Ahmed, S.I., Jackson, S.J., Ahmed, N., Ferdous, H.S., Rifat, M.R., Rizvi, A.S.M., Ahmed, S., Mansur, R.S. Protibadi: a platform for fighting sexual harassment in urban Bangladesh. In *Proc. CHI'14*, ACM (2014), 2695–2704.
3. Ahmed, S.I., Jackson, S.J., Zaber, M., Morshed, M.B., Ismail, M.H.B., and Afrose, S. Ecologies of Use and Design: Individual and Social Uses of Mobile Phones Within Low-Literate Rickshaw-Puller Communities in Urban Bangladesh. *Proc. DEV-4*, ACM (2013), 14:1–14:10.
4. Burrell, J. Evaluating Shared Access: social equality and the circulation of mobile phones in rural Uganda. *Journal of Computer Mediated Communication 15*, 2 (2010), 230–250.

5. Le Dantec, C.A. and Edwards, W.K. Designs on dignity: perceptions of technology among the homeless. *In Proc. CHI '08*, ACM (2008), 627–636.
6. Elyachar, J. Phatic labor, infrastructure, and the question of empowerment in Cairo. *American Ethnologist 37*, 3 (2010), 452–464.
7. Fields, G.S. Dualism in the Labor Market: a Perspective on the Lewis Model after Half a Century. *The Manchester School 72*, 6 (2004), 724–735.
8. Graham, S. and Marvin, S. *Splintering urbanism: networked infrastructures, technological mobilities and the urban condition.* Psychology Press, 2001.
9. Hardoy, J.E. and Satterthwaite, D. *Squatter citizen: life in the urban Third World.* Routledge, 2014.
10. Heimerl, K., Hasan, S., Ali, K., Brewer, E., and Parikh, T. Local, sustainable, small-scale cellular networks. In *Proc. ICTD'13*, ACM (2013), 2–12.
11. Houston, L. Inventive Infrastructure: An Exploration of Mobile Phone. *PhD Thesis*, Lanchaster University, 2014.
12. Irani, L., Vertesi, J., Dourish, P., Philip, K., and Grinter, R.E. Postcolonial computing: a lens on design and development. In *Proc. CHI'10*, ACM, 1311–1320.
13. Jackson, S.J., Ahmed, S.I., and Rifat, M.R. Learning, innovation, and sustainability among mobile phone repairers in Dhaka, Bangladesh. In *Proc. DIS'14*, ACM (2014), 905–914.
14. Jackson, S.J., Pompe, A., and Krieshok, G. Things fall apart: maintenance, repair, and technology for education initiatives in rural Namibia. *In Proc. iConference'11*, ACM (2012), 107–116.
15. Jackson, S.J., Pompe, A., and Krieshok, G. Repair worlds: maintenance, repair, and ICT for development in rural Namibia. In *Proc. CSCW'12*, ACM (2012), 107–116.
16. Jamasb, T. Electricity sector reform in developing countries: a survey of empirical evidence on determinants and performance. *World Bank Publications 3549*, (2005).
17. Larkin, B. The politics and poetics of infrastructure. *Annual Review of Anthropology 42*, (2013), 327–343.
18. Lindtner, S., Nardi, B., Wang, Y., Mainwaring, S., Jing, H., and Liang, W. Emerging sites of HCI innovation: hackerspaces, hardware startups and incubators. *Proc. CSCW'08*, ACM (2008), 371–382.
19. Mahbub, A.Q.M. and Islam, N. The growth of slums in Dhaka City: a spatio temporal analysis. In *SU Ahmed Eds. Dhaka Past Present Future*. Dhaka: Asiatic Society of Bangladesh, 1991, 508–521.
20. Massey, D. Power-geometry and a progressive sense of place. In *Bird, J., Curtis, B., Putnam, T., & Tickner, L. eds. Mapping the Futures: Local Cultures, Global Change*. Routledge, 2012.
21. Medhi, I., Patnaik, S., Brunskill, E., Gautama, S.N., Theis, W., and Toyama, K. Designing mobile interfaces for novice and low-literacy users. *ACM Transactions on Computer-Human Interaction 18*, 1 (2011), 2:1–2:27.
22. Palen, L., Vieweg, S., Sutton, J., Liu, S.B., and Hughes, A.L. Crisis informatics: Studying crisis in a networked world. In *Proc. e-Social Science'07*.
23. Patel, N., Chittamuru, D., Jain, A., Dave, P., and Parikh, T. Avaaj Otalo: a field study of an interactive voice forum for small farmers in rural India. *Proc. CHI'10*, ACM (2010), 733–742.
24. Rangaswamy, N. and Sambasivan, N. Cutting Chai, Jugaad, and Here Pheri: towards UbiComp for a global community. *Personal and Ubiquitous Computing 15*, 6 (2011), 553–564.
25. Rouvinen, P. Diffusion of digital mobile telephony: Are developing countries different? *Telecommunications Policy 30*, 1 (2006), 46–63.
26. Sambasivan, N., Cutrell, E., Toyama, K., and Nardi, B. Intermediated technology use in developing communities. *In Proc. CHI'10*, ACM (2010), 2583–2592.
27. Sassen, S. *Expulsions: Brutality and Complexity in the Global Economy.* Harvard University Press, 2014.
28. Sherwani, J., Ali, N., Mirza, S., et al. HealthLine: Speech-based access to health information by low-literate users. In *Proc. ICTD'07*, IEEE (2007), 1–9.
29. Star, S.L. and Bowker, G.C. Enacting silence: Residual categories as a challenge for ethics, information systems, and communication. *Ethics and Information Technology 9*, 4 (2007), 273–280.
30. Suchman, L. Practice-based design of information systems: notes from the hyperdeveloped world. *The information society 18*, 2 (2002), 139–144.
31. Suchman, L. *Human-machine reconfigurations: Plans and situated actions.* Cambridge University Press, 2007.
32. Todaro, M.P. and Smith, S. *Economic Development.* Pearson Education, 2014.
33. Tomlinson, B., Silberman, M., Patterson, D., Pan, Y., and Blevis, E. Collapse informatics: augmenting the sustainability & ICT4D discourse in HCI. In *Proc. CHI'12*, (2012), 655–664.
34. UNICEF Bangladesh. Understanding urban inequalities in Bangladesh: A prerequisite for achieving Vision 2021. 2010.
35. Urry, J. *Mobilities.* Polity, 2007.
36. Woelfer, J.P. and Hendry, D.G. Homeless young people's experiences with information systems: life and work in a community technology center. In *Proc. CHI'10*, ACM (2010), 1291–1300.
37. "War's Human Cost": World's population of displaced tops 50 million. *UN News Centre*, 2014. http://www.un.org/apps/news/story.asp?NewsID=48089
38. Crisismappers. http://crisismappers.net/.

Más Tecnología, Más Cambio? Investigating an Educational Technology Project in Rural Peru

Emeline Therias
Spotless Interactive
London
e.therias.12@alumni.ucl.ac.uk

Jon Bird
HCID Research Centre
City University London
jon.bird@city.ac.uk

Paul Marshall
UCL Interaction Centre
University College London
paul.marshall@ucl.ac.uk

ABSTRACT
Providing access to and training in ICTs is seen as key to bridging the digital divide between technology-rich communities and those with poor IT infrastructures. Several projects have focused on providing ICTs for education in developing countries, of which the best known is One Laptop Per Child (OLPC). Although, there has been significant criticism of some of these projects, in particular OLPC, due to its use of a top-down implementation strategy and the limited evidence for its educational benefits, there has been comparatively little analysis of what underlies successful approaches. We aimed to address this deficit by conducting an ethnographic study of community-based projects organised by Blue Sparrow, a small charity that donates refurbished desktop computers to schools in rural Peru, as this organisation has experienced both successes and failures when implementing its educational technology projects. The relative success of Blue Sparrow highlights the benefits of: understanding local contexts; using a bottom up approach; involving stakeholders in setting programme objectives; and empowering communities. We argue that the educational impact of such projects can be improved by: providing teacher training; integrating computers into the wider curriculum; and providing teaching materials and clear objectives for volunteers.

Author Keywords
HCI4D; One Laptop per Child; Peru; educational ICTs

ACM Classification Keywords
H.5.m. Information interfaces and presentation (e.g., HCI): Miscellaneous.

INTRODUCTION
"*Más tecnología, más cambio*" (English – "More technology, more change"): the rural Andean farmer who spoke these words was convinced that the Blue Sparrow initiative to provide his village school with computers would lead to positive changes, in particular a better education for his children. This is in keeping with the widely held view that providing Information and Communication Technologies (ICTs) can help reduce socio-economic and educational inequalities in developing or emerging contexts [33]. Some projects have focused on one-to-one computing programmes, which aim to enhance educational outcomes by providing each student with a laptop. However, these are often not very effective; for example, a study of over 300 schools in Peru found limited evidence of educational benefits for children with access to OLPC laptops [5], even though around $200M has been spent on buying 850,000 of these computers by the government [21]. However, it is not just OLPC that has found it challenging to successfully facilitate the long-term adoption of ICTs in low-resource settings: some estimates suggest that half of these projects have been total or partial failures [10]. Simply providing more technology does not inevitably lead to positive changes and Dray and colleagues deplore the practice of simply 'throwing technology' at communities to reduce the digital divide, because ignoring the deeper issues of access results in technology not being used [8]. In order to improve the effectiveness of educational technology projects it is imperative to re-consider the factors underlying both successes and failures.

The aim of this paper is to address this issue by presenting an ethnographic study of educational technology initiatives in three Andean schools in Peru that are co-ordinated by Blue Sparrow, a charity founded in 2007 through a collaboration between North American graduate students and local Peruvians. To date they have partnered with four rural and semi-rural communities in and around Huancayo, Peru. Their *Conectados* (English: 'Connected') programme donates refurbished desktop computers to schools, creates computer rooms and provides volunteers to assist with teaching computing. The main objective is to equip pupils with skills and knowledge for future employment or study. The programme has had varying levels of success in the different partner communities and we conducted an ethnographic investigation to identify key factors in the successes and failures. The contribution of this paper is a set of seven guidelines for successfully implementing educational ICT projects. Four of these focus on working with communities by: integrating local knowledge; using a

CHI 2015, April 18 - 23, 2015, Seoul, Republic of Korea
Copyright 2015 ACM 978-1-4503-3145-6/15/04…$15.00
http://dx.doi.org/10.1145/2702123.2702595

bottom-up approach; involving local stakeholders in setting programme objectives; and engaging local people as champions of the project. The other three focus on increasing the educational impact by: providing teacher training; integrating computers into the wider curriculum; and providing teaching materials and clear objectives for volunteers

BACKGROUND

Educational Technology Projects

Several projects have been predicated on the view that given the right technology children can teach themselves, even in the context of poor or non-existent educational infrastructure. Experiments have been conducted in India to test this conjecture [17]. Researchers created 'hole-in-the-wall' computer kiosks in urban slums and rural villages, where children were able to use the technology freely without adult supervision. These are reported to stimulate curiosity in the children and through their explorative use of the computers and collaborative learning, result in them teaching themselves basic computing skills as well as unfamiliar subject content [18]. However, other research has been more critical, suggesting that the children mostly used the computers to draw or play games, and community members disapprove of the lack of supervision and instruction [30].

Partly inspired by the 'hole-in-the-wall' experiments, OLPC is the highest profile educational technology project, grounded in the constructionist view that children actively create mental models of the world. Papert [23] proposed that children could teach themselves through computer use, and stated that the OLPC laptops allowed for 'natural learning' without requiring formal teaching. The aim was to bypass teacher training and curriculum reform, seen to be of limited value due to alleged teacher absenteeism and incompetence [31].

Though OLPC pilot reports typically anecdotally cite positive changes in the communities, such as increased enthusiasm and decreased absenteeism, there have been few positive formal evaluations [13]. A report on OLPC's implementation in a Uruguayan school reported positive attitudes in both students and teachers, but little evidence to support any educational impact, and the stakeholder motivation may have been influenced by the media and research attention this pilot community received [12]. OLPC is widely considered a failure [31]. While the physical design of the laptop has been hailed as innovative, many point to issues with the implementation strategy adopted [13]; OLPC has been described as adopting a 'one-size-fits-all' strategy, with a uniform top-down approach for all their target buying nations, ultimately hindering their ability to adequately meet individual stakeholder requirements [3].

Blue Sparrow is an educational charity that contrasts with OLPC in both scale and its approach to implementing educational ICT projects. It has grown from an initial partnership with a Peruvian school and now works with four schools in and around Huancayo, the capital of the Junín region and an economic centre within the central highlands of Peru. The organization's approach builds on their knowledge of the local Peruvian culture and they have built ties with community members, regularly spending time in people's homes, *"having lunch and sharing personal struggles" - Blue Sparrow Representative S.* These relationships help Blue Sparrow keep in touch with local practices and concerns about day-to-day activities such as farming. Their understanding of local contexts is particularly valuable when it comes to tailoring their programme to a specific community's needs and expectations.

Blue Sparrow set up computer labs in their partner schools, using refurbished PCs. First, the school and students create a microbusiness to provide long-term funding for the project. Then Blue Sparrow installs a brand new computer lab with an Internet connection. Volunteers, who are mainly university students from North America and Europe, provide ongoing training for students, staff, and parents in the area.

The organisation initially conducts site visits with potential partners, and first talks to school directors to understand each context before attending parent meetings. By stating that they 'partner' with the communities, Blue Sparrow positions itself in a bi-directional relationship with them, which develops over a long period: typically at least six months. The director of Blue Sparrow explained that they collaboratively *"figure out"* how they can incorporate a computer lab into a school.

In summary, there has been considerable criticism of educational technology projects, in particular OLPC, that try to reduce the digital divide but comparatively little analysis of what underlies successful approaches. We aimed to address this by studying small scale, community-based projects organized by Blue Sparrow, as this organisation has experienced both successes and failures when implementing educational technology projects.

METHODOLOGY

The first author volunteered with Blue Sparrow in 2012 and this informed the present study, conducted in the summer of 2013. This study involved data-gathering in three schools near Huancayo. Institutional ethical approval was gained prior to conducting the research and ethical considerations shaped the approach to fieldwork, due to the involvement of potentially vulnerable participants: students under the age of 18, as well as potentially illiterate adults. Careful consideration of students' needs shaped the researcher's approach to working in the schools [9]. The school directors gave consent for the research to proceed and for data gathering to be carried out on school grounds. The school directors and Blue Sparrow disseminated information about the research project to parents and teachers before the researcher's visit. Prior to any observations parents were given the opportunity for their children to opt out. In addition to the problem of illiteracy, members of a rural developing community may view forms as confusing, suspicious, or potentially threatening. For this reason, where possible written consent was obtained but alternatively an audio recording of verbal consent was collected.

Field Sites

The three schools are co-educational secondary institutions that teach students aged 11-16 (1st to 6th grades): *Rural School*, *Urban School*, and *Marginal Urban School*.

Rural School, in a mountain community, is one hour's travel by road from the city. It is the only secondary school in the village, and provides education to local inhabitants as well as villages higher in the mountains. The small number of students means that there are never more than 10 in a grade, with some classes having as few as three. Blue Sparrow inaugurated the computer lab in 2011, which was their first project in this region and the school now owns the donated computers. The regional government provided the school with 18 OLPC laptops in 2011. In total, eight hours of observation and teaching were conducted in 2nd to 5th grade computing classes.

Urban School is situated in Huancayo and a 20-minute bus ride from the city centre. The school has 20 students per class on average. It also now owns the computers donated for the computer lab by Blue Sparrow. The regional government provided the school with 26 OLPC laptops in 2011. Eleven hours of observation were conducted with 1st and 2nd grade students during their computing classes.

Marginal Urban School is also a 20-minute drive from the Huancayo centre but the surrounding area is agricultural. Class sizes average 40 students. It is in an extremely poor community. It partnered with Blue Sparrow in early 2013, and the computers are still on a retractable loan. They were provided with 66 OLPC laptops in 2011. Seven hours of observation were conducted in 1st to 4th grade computing classes, as well as during two after-school computer activities.

Data Collection

The method used was rapid ethnography, which is characterised by the use of multiple methods to gather a rich set of data in a short period [16]. The data corpus was derived from unstructured and semi-structured interviews, focus groups and informal conversations, all of which were conducted in Spanish, and participant observations.

The researcher was introduced to the school directors after initial contact had been made through email. A preliminary meeting established the best method of attending classes, as well as the scheduling constraints for each school. The researcher was presented to the teachers and students as a classroom assistant, there to observe and assist if needed. Observations in the computer labs were recorded in field notes, supported by occasional photography and videos of participants' interactions with the computers. A total of 26 hours of observations were conducted in the three schools.

Unstructured and semi-structured interviews complemented the data set gathered in 2012. The researcher interviewed the school directors in an office setting or during a tour of the school grounds. During several days of observation, the researcher progressively built a rapport with other stakeholders and conducted unstructured interviews during classroom or recess time, including several focus groups with students where the questions built on observed topics of interest (e.g. about activities conducted in class). Six interviews were recorded and transcribed. Several non-recorded interviews, and informal conversations, both inside and outside of the classroom setting, were documented in field notes. The researcher favoured note taking over audio recording, due to the unease which the latter generated in many participants. Photography was used to document the layout of the classrooms, student interactions with computers, blackboard instructions, and any other relevant information (e.g. curriculum documentation). Occasional video recording consolidated observational notes.

FINDINGS

In this section we first describe the patterns of computer usage in the three schools. Our focus is primarily on the donated Blue Sparrow machines but we also note the non-use of OLPC laptops. We then document Blue Sparrow's approach to working with local communities, which has been successful at encouraging computer use by pupils, in particular focusing on: how they empower the community; financing of Internet connections; gate keepers and local champions; and the role of volunteers. We then describe some of the key challenges faced by Blue Sparrow that restrict the educational impact of their projects: limited training; lack of consultation with students; lack of clearly defined goals; limited exposure to technology; and prevalent teaching style.

Patterns of Computer Usage

A main finding of the ethnographic study is that the desktop PCs provided by Blue Sparrow are in frequent use in schools, whereas the OLPC laptops are not used at all.

The refurbished desktop machines provided by Blue Sparrow were preferred for a number of reasons: they were perceived to be more powerful and more functional; teachers had a lack of familiarity with the operating system and applications provided on the OLPC machines, whereas they had experience of using Windows PCs; there was a lack of OLPC training available for teachers; and the PCs were more integrated into the available power and network infrastructures:

"We practically don't use them, for several reasons. One is that we don't know them well, they say it's Linux I think. There was [training] but the teacher couldn't attend I think

Figure 1: OLPC computers stored in *Rural School*

[...]. And the other is that because we have the big machines, we prefer them because it's easier, they are already installed. And a little bit as well that each [laptop] needs to be connected to a source of energy. And the other thing, they make us a bit nervous! Because the kids are playful, mischievous...they might fall or break..." - Urban Director

At the time of the study, the OLPC computers were not being used by the schools and were still in their original packaging in two of them (see Figure 1). School directors commented that teachers had attempted to use them in the past before abandoning them, and they had not been used in the previous year. This is in line with findings from evaluations reporting a decline in use, and low levels of interest after the first months of implementation [25, 32]. None of the directors felt particularly committed to the OLPC project and they did not promote it within the schools. On the contrary, both they and the teachers were concerned about liability in case the laptops might be damaged or stolen. In this way, they acted as technology 'gatekeepers', impeding their use by the students [29], and standing in the way of OLPC's goal that students should use the laptops at home. A volunteer at *Marginal Urban School* had tried previously to encourage laptop use and enable students to sign them out and take them home. The director had tentatively agreed to this initiative provided that Blue Sparrow would accept financial responsibility for any damages.

Working with Local Communities

The Blue Sparrow director stays in close contact with the schools during the initial few months to *"look for places where they're struggling and where [we] can offer additional and useful support"*. Though adopting a similar approach with all partner school communities, the organisation aims to be flexible in the way that they adapt to different needs. For instance, certain schools have made demands for volunteers to stay for a minimum period:

Yes, we've seen from experience, when the volunteers stay longer, they start knowing and working [...] also they start to plan their time, there's more stability. Two, three, four months...for example with three or four months it's better right. In one month, there's hardly time to adapt. – Urban Director

Empowering the Community

Blue Sparrow expressed a desire to hand over the running of the projects to school directors, as well as empowering the community. Blue Sparrow representatives are aware of a contradiction between wanting each computer lab to be autonomous, and placing volunteers there: they questioned whether the volunteers could become a '*crutch*' for the schools, creating a dependence on them for teaching computing classes and impeding the teachers' own development. Blue Sparrow recognises there is a critical period of time at the beginning of a project where schools need volunteers to start the computing classes; they also aim to transfer the responsibility for these classes to the schools:

"And I think the end goal of the Director should eventually be to transfer that responsibility onto the people. I don't think that that person should always hold that position, because, if the person's not there then it's gonna fail. The eventual goal would be to raise up more leaders, that he should be empowering the teachers, empowering the parents [...]. After that, it should grow, I don't think it should stay stagnant" – Blue Sparrow Representative S

"Because, on the one hand it has helped by facilitating, implementing the computer lab, which [...] is very interesting for the kids. But at the same time the project has also made us more involved.... So both those things right? One is to empower us so that we can do things ourselves, with motivation and guidance" – Urban Director

This focus on empowering communities is in line with research that suggests that to be sustainable in the long-term, community projects should ideally be locally initiated, owned and managed [1]. However Blue Sparrow representatives were also unsure how to successfully negotiate this handover of the project (cf. [27]).

Financing the Internet Connection

Blue Sparrow also aim to make projects financially independent. For example, they knew that *Rural School* would not be able to afford the cost of an Internet connection and guinea pig husbandry was chosen as a solution most suited to the community's capacities. The Blue Sparrow director explained that these animals are a lucrative product due to their status as a *"prized meat"*, and *"everybody already knows a bit about them"* in these rural communities, ensuring that there are the local knowledge and resources necessary to breed them. A micro-finance initiative was also implemented in *Urban School* where students baked and sold cakes. Blue Sparrow helped the initial start-up of the scheme through micro-loans, but they have not been involved in managing it, leaving the community to decide what the funding will be used for. At the time of the study, neither of the funding schemes were paying for an Internet connection, but they showed promise: the director of *Rural School* intended to start selling guinea pigs in the near future; in *Urban School*, any profit made was used to repay the micro-loan, with the money left over going towards buying new ingredients, but teachers expected to finance the Internet connection as soon as the loan was repaid.

Furthermore, both schemes became important as stand-alone learning experiences and were formally integrated into the school curricula:

"As long as there are resources, it's mainly for them to learn, they maintain it, they see how it all works. In the specifics, I'm not that concerned whether there is money or not. It's more about their experience" – Urban Director

The formal integration into the curriculum ensured the long-term sustainability of these ventures, and offered funding opportunities for any expenses related to the computers.

"Breeding small animals. This has its curriculum that we have to teach. [...] For example in the beginning they need to identify the different varieties of guinea pigs, gender, all that. Second grade, something else, pasture" – Rural Director

Gatekeepers and local champions

Blue Sparrow's approach is to work closely with the school director, who as a 'gatekeeper' grants access to the school as well as acting a 'champion' of the project in the school and local community. In these rural villages, the school director is a prominent figure, giving his or her opinion public visibility and sway within the community. The director's contribution to the success of the project is apparent in all partner communities: as a key figure in the rural social landscape, if the school director does not support the project then it will falter:

"And so it's hard to know, the factors that make a school successful sometimes too, because we've seen a lot of it be commissioned by the director basically. If the director can light the fire, then the teachers will follow, because they're responsible to the director and if the teachers can get on board then the kids will follow, 'cause they're responsible to...the chain of command". – Blue Sparrow Representative S

"The director seems to be the most key relationship in making the programme work. He or she has influence over the teachers and the general mood of the school. Directors have made scheduling changes on our behalf, opened up curricula to our suggestions, and encouraged teachers to incorporate volunteers or make other changes so that Conectados can be more successful. Likewise a neutral or hostile director can ruin all of those things and cause us to lose access and face aggression from the teachers". – Blue Sparrow Representative M

Indeed, initial difficulties with the Blue Sparrow project at *Rural School* stemmed from the previous director's loss of enthusiasm. The director's support appears to be a pivotal element of the Conectados project; there is a correlation with a director's commitment and computer lab usage, coordination with Blue Sparrow, success of the micro-finance scheme and volunteer satisfaction.

The directors became 'local champions' of the project when they supported and enabled it: being in a position of authority, they could set the example and promote technology use and acceptance. Committed directors who championed the project, as in *Urban* and *Rural Schools*, were crucial to its adoption and long-term use by other community members. The importance of involving local leaders who can 'champion' a project has been reported elsewhere, and might significantly affect the ultimate level of success in ICT projects [26, 30].

Teachers too appear essential to include in decision-making, due to their potential for 'gatekeeping' the technology, or showing reluctance to let students use it [3]. As Cervantes and colleagues [4, p. 953] remark "*the involvement of teachers is vital, as it is their role to facilitate learning practices*".

The role of volunteers

Warschauer [29] notes that providing computers and the Internet are only one subset of a wider range of resources that need to be made available for educational technology projects. Blue Sparrow provides additional resources, in the form of technical support and volunteers, to facilitate and maintain computer lab use. The volunteer component of the programme provides teaching assistance, facilitating integration of the technology into classroom activities. This facilitation may go a long way towards ensuring the desktop computers are actually used in schools:

If we didn't facilitate [the computers], they might end up [not used] like the [OLPC] laptops. – Blue Sparrow Representative S

By checking in regularly with each school, representatives are also able to identify and resolve technical issues: although the donated computers are officially owned by the schools after the first year and become their responsibility to maintain, a representative explained that the schools usually relied on Blue Sparrow to deal with any technical issues.

Educational impact

In this section we highlight five issues that restricted the educational impact of the Blue Sparrow initiatives: limited training; lack of consultation with students; lack of clearly defined goals; limited exposure to technology; and prevalent teaching style.

Limited training

Providing training has been shown to be important in handing over control of community technology projects, helping the users to understand the technology and use it effectively [1]. At the time of the study, three teachers had received training in computing skills: the home economics teacher in *Urban School*, and two computing teachers in *Marginal Urban School*. This training was provided independently of Blue Sparrow, and funded by the schools or regional government. Teachers identified a lack of training, both technical and pedagogical, as major barriers to the integration of computers; even teachers with technology skills and knowledge expressed a need for further support in using the computers as educational tools in the classroom.

Although Blue Sparrow attempted to provide training to teachers in *Rural School*, the initiative was unsuccessful as they repeatedly failed to show up for the sessions. Whether due to the economic constraints in their lives (e.g. many have after school jobs) or a lack of motivation to complete extra work without financial incentive, the teachers were unable or unwilling to complete training.

A lack of teacher motivation, potentially related to an increased desire for migration to the city, has been observed in many rural communities. Mitra and colleagues hypothesised that teachers' motivation might be the most important factor in determining academic achievement in schools [19].

Lack of consultation with students

The stakeholders whose expectations and requirements were least incorporated into the programme were the students: their expectations regarding technology access and use were not explicitly addressed. For example, students in *Rural School* expressed frustration about their access to the computer lab:

They always keep it closed, it should be more accessible. – Rural Student A.

Furthermore, their need to access information to help prepare for their futures was not particularly facilitated by the computer labs, although this is a primary stated aim of Blue Sparrow's organisation. It might be that in trying to meet school representatives' requirements, the organisation has been unable to prioritise this aspect of the programme's aims.

Lack of clearly defined goals

An important step for engagement with each school was to try and clearly identify success criteria. Heeks [10] points out the subjectivity of categorising success and failure in such projects, as well as the fact these criteria can change over time, and indeed all the Blue Sparrow stakeholders were hard-pressed to describe a clear vision of project success: while each stakeholder group had general expectations of the programme, they typically did not express these in terms of clearly defined and actionable goals. When asked which of the schools were considered successful in the programme, and what criteria were being used for success, Blue Sparrow representative S. struggled to define what success '*look[ed] like*':

The only one where we've seen it - we haven't really seen it be successful except for [Marginal Urban School] [...] the difference is that [Marginal Urban School] has a computing class, specifically where these teachers teach computers. [...] I would say probably [Marginal Urban School] is the most successful just because they have the teachers to back that up and to support [the programme]...because of the size of the school. – Blue Sparrow Representative S

School directors tended to characterise project success in broad terms relating to overall computer usage:

At least most of the project has taken shape...all the basic objectives yes they're helping. Of course, 'successful'...that implies that the kids as well, and the parents work together. And also on our part, the teachers, that we make better use, and have better strategies of course. But yes it has been getting better, the kids' expectations are getting realised. – Urban Director

In summary, the projects seemed driven by Blue Sparrow and the school directors' visions regarding programme structure: by facilitating their participation, the organisation partially fulfils Walton & Heeks' [28] recommendation to incorporate participation of intended end-users. Teachers' expectations were addressed to a certain extent, in cases where they coordinated with Blue Sparrow to decide class structure and organisation. An area of tension in *Marginal Urban School* concerning volunteer presence highlighted the difficulty in addressing evolving stakeholder requirements. Involving the recipient community in assessing their needs, and planning, creates more of a sense of local ownership of projects, enhancing the likelihood of long-term adoption [3, 28].

Limited exposure to technology

In *Rural School*, students' lack of exposure to computers outside of the classroom meant they were less likely to know how to use the computers in ways not explicitly taught by volunteers. Most students in *Urban School* had regular access to technology outside of class time. They were confident about using the Internet, and displayed familiarity with social media, with most owning Facebook and email accounts. While some displayed familiarity with technology, others were complete novices with the computers. A variety of levels was also evident in *Marginal Urban School*, where volunteers and Blue Sparrow spoke of a '*technology gap*'; many of the older 5th grade students were learning basic computing skills, such as how to use a mouse and keyboard, at the same time as the younger 1st graders.

Prevalent teaching style

The dominant teaching approach in Peru has been described as 'highly structured' and primarily instructive in nature [22]. Observations and reports from stakeholders confirmed this:

Copying is the primary method of teaching. – Urban Volunteer T

There is no] critical thinking, reading, or writing beyond copying what the teacher writes. – Blue Sparrow Representative M

For instance, Urban teacher M graded students at the end of each class on what they had copied into their notebooks (e.g. an Excel-generated graph, hand-drawn in the notebook). She stated that the students needed to copy otherwise the work would *"only be in the computer and nothing else"*.

The observed technology usage was focused on teaching computer skills for their own sake, rather than integrating them with other educational aims. Teachers described their objectives in terms of teaching the students to open and use the programs, without focusing on learning content. Using the computers primarily entailed 'low levels' of use, such as typing, or doing an Internet search according to a set target (c.f. [6]). In one case, Rural teacher M asked students to perform a search on 'natural resources': students typed the phrase into Google and copied and pasted content from the first links, with one even copying 64 pages of material without assessing their relevance. The teacher prioritised activity completion, paying little attention to the coherence of the information gathered.

This practice resembles the examples of 'performativity' described by Warschauer and colleagues [33], where teachers tick off 'checklists of skills' without attending to deeper issues of knowledge construction or information literacy. Volunteers and Blue Sparrow representatives were aware of this limitation. The former felt that students were not learning deeper skills relating to 'information reasoning', or identifying, accessing, understanding and contextualising reliable sources of information. Blue Sparrow representatives expressed an awareness of the importance of integrating technology use into over-arching educational aims:

It's not about using the technology, it's about using it in an effective way. – Blue Sparrow Representative M

Despite this awareness, activities trying to incorporate higher educational objectives tended to be less successful in the classroom. The 'performativity' may have been warranted by the level of computing skills: where students possessed less technology exposure and familiarity with the software, it may have been premature to focus on deeper educational objectives, such as identifying appropriate sources of information and constructing coherent arguments:

They're definitely not practicing good information searching, but at least they're using Word. – Urban Volunteer A

And you realise that projects don't work when you put way too many new elements in...we did try and do an exercise [...] but it was too many new skills, because they're not good at looking on the Internet, not very good at deciphering data...and so that was overwhelming so we changed that one. – Urban Volunteer T

The only school in which students seemed to be learning about content at the same time as using the technology was when non-computing teachers occasionally used the computer lab to teach their classes in *Urban School*:

Sometimes for example, the professor will set a topic, and the kids read, create their PowerPoint, and present. Also, sometimes the professor prepares the class and works with slides with the projector [...]. [The students] are also developing their knowledge. They are learning, to use [the computers] at the same time as developing their knowledge. Doing both at the same time. – Urban Director

The volunteers tried to incorporate what they perceived to be more creative and exploratory styles of teaching. However, the students struggled with these approaches and they tended to be hesitant in generating their own content. Urban volunteer T highlighted that the teachers *"get angry so fast at things"* when students did not exactly copy a desired output, creating a reluctance in students to do anything other than what they were shown by teachers. Urban Volunteer T explained this in terms of differences in *"the meaning of grades and progress"* between the Blue Sparrow volunteers and the local staff: the teacher *"doesn't know what [we] are looking for and what skills to build"*. The prevalent instructive teaching style may pose a significant barrier to the meaningful integration of technology in the classroom:

Teachers, especially those stuck in old and repetitive processes, can just kill [the programme]. [...] Computers open up a world of independent exploration and critical thinking, but it can also be locked down to a watch and repeat series of steps. We're trying to test whether this could be just in the form of providing a more modern dynamic curriculum to the standard teachers, or if we need to spend time with them in professional development and talk about new methods, or if it's best to just bring in volunteers who are already familiar and comfortable with creative, independent classroom styles. – Blue Sparrow Representative M

Students also considered the Blue Sparrow computers to be like "*notebooks*" and simply a new medium to copy information into:

"There you do whatever function you like, you don't have to write with pen and paper any more. It's no longer with pen and paper" – Student R

"There's Microsoft. Also to draw, there's Paint. Of course it's better than a notebook, than writing it out" – Student A

Ultimately, the value of classroom technologies lies in how they are used: if the computers are simply integrated into existing traditional teaching practices, and used as an alternative method of inputting information, they are unlikely to become 'catalysts' for change [25]. As Cuban and colleagues [6] suggest, computers in themselves do not change the quality of education; in order for them to be incorporated more effectively into the classroom and have educational impacts, they should be accompanied by deep-seated changes in teaching practice. This was something that Blue Sparrow had not yet been successful in bringing about.

DISCUSSION

Nicolas Negroponte has claimed that *"Peru's understanding of constructionist learning theories is so mature and longstanding that other countries can benefit from [the decision to use OLPC computers]. While we immediately see the difference the laptop makes in the lives of these children, we look forward to the long-term positive impact it will have on the eradication of poverty and on societies' other great challenges."* [20]

Contrary to Negroponte and the title phrase of this paper, our study has shown that 'more technology', while necessary, is not sufficient in itself to produce the positive changes needed to reduce the digital divide. In all three schools we studied, the OLPC laptops were not being used for three main reasons: they could not connect the laptops to the Internet; teachers found them unfamiliar due to a lack of training; and there were worries about the laptops getting damaged or stolen. In contrast, the schools regularly used the desktop computers provided by Blue Sparrow. Our study demonstrates how an educational technology project can succeed in getting students in low-resource settings to use computers if it is implemented appropriately. Blue Sparrow's approach focuses primarily on developing the social and technical infrastructure to support computer use in schools. Its local scale, bottom-up approach, and use of a computer lab model are more suited to the Andean school context than OLPC's global 'one size fits all', top-down approach that simply provides schools with laptops.

Blue Sparrow has an in-depth knowledge of their partner communities, ensuring the selected technology meets their needs. Furthermore, their relationship with school directors results in the latter 'championing' the technology and promoting computer use within their schools. Blue Sparrow's provision of resources to support long-term use, in the form of technical support and volunteer placement to assist teaching, helps maintain computer use in the schools. Additionally, Blue Sparrow has developed micro-finance schemes that recognise the schools' lack of resources and help them pay for their Internet connections.

Our study has identified a number of limitations of the Blue Sparrow approach. First, the organisation has encountered difficulties in negotiating the hand-over of responsibility for maintaining the computers in the long-term. Second, they do not provide teachers with any computer training and this is a significant barrier to the integration of computers into the curriculum. Third, and most significant, is that the computer use has limited educational impact. Classes appeared to focus on computing as a principal outcome rather than incorporating higher educational aims. Acquiring computing skills, while useful, should not be an end in itself, but rather should accompany over-arching learning goals [33]; computing holds little value for many pupils as a 'stand-alone subject' than when it is integrated into the wider curriculum as an educational tool to access and structure knowledge. The strengthening of teaching skills and development of more integrated curriculums, applying technology in the teaching of other subjects, would help the computer labs become an environment in which students can develop their critical thinking skills and information-seeking behaviours.

IMPLICATIONS

Based on the findings of this study, we outline seven practical implications that can potentially facilitate the long-term success and sustainability of educational ICT projects in low resource communities. We organize them into two groups: the first set is concerned with tailoring a project to meet the needs of a community; the second set focuses on how to maximise its educational impact.

Work with communities

Rather than 'throw technology' at a community, which has limited developmental impact, we propose that future projects should:

Understand local contexts. Practitioners need to understand what technology is actually needed. An understanding of the local culture helps to avoid making assumptions based on the practitioners' own culture. In the case of a larger-scale initiative, partnering with a small-scale entity (e.g. NGOs) might help facilitate access to and understanding of local culture and contexts; smaller-scale initiatives could adopt an ethnographic approach.

Use a bottom-up approach. Rather than adopting a 'one-size-fits-all' approach, educational technology projects could be formulated in collaboration with stakeholders, and programmes tailored to the specific needs of a community. This might enable practitioners to offer the most suitable ICT to a community, be flexible and adapt as requirements evolve, and also learn from any failures in order to enhance what the programme offers.

Involve stakeholders in setting programme objectives. Stakeholders have different visions of what the technology will bring to the community. It is important to make these expectations explicit by communicating with stakeholders. Involving the end-users might actually be more important than involving policy-makers. For example, getting a prominent community member to champion the technology helps to ensure that it is adopted and accepted by the community.

Empower communities. Although a certain amount of support (e.g. technical) is needed in the initial stages of an educational ICT implementation, the ultimate goal should be to empower a community so that they can self-manage and sustain it over time. Consequently, while volunteers are useful in the initial stages of a project it is important that school communities should not become dependent on them.

Focus on educational context

As demonstrated by Blue Sparrow, working closely with communities is not sufficient to ensure the educational impact of ICTs: in addition it is crucial to consider the details of how education is delivered. We therefore propose that projects should:

Provide teacher training: One aim of OLPC was to circumvent the need for teacher training and curriculum reform. However, in our study we found that teachers are the ultimate arbiters of whether educational technology is used both in their classrooms and outside of school. Therefore training not only means providing them with the skills, knowledge and ongoing support to effectively use ICTs but also crucially involves motivating them to use the technology in their lessons. As our study has shown, this can be very challenging and is a major constraint on the educational impact of ICTs. Many of the teachers in the Peruvian schools we studied had two jobs and were reluctant to attend training sessions in their own time as this would have financial implications. It may therefore be necessary to pay teaching staff to ensure their participation in training.

Integrate computers into the wider curriculum: The ultimate aim of educational ICTs is that they are used as tools to facilitate critical thinking and knowledge construction. However, our study found that the main use of Blue Sparrow technology was to teach computing skills rather than for any higher educational aims [33]. Perhaps the most effective use of the computers as educational tools was found in *Urban School* when non-computing teachers used the computer lab for some of their lessons. This suggests that training should be offered to all teachers, not just computer specialists.

Develop clear teaching materials and objectives for volunteers: Volunteers, such as the ones who work on the Blue Sparrow projects, can provide invaluable support for educational ICTs, particularly when they have wide-ranging computing skills and knowledge. However, they will rarely have training in teaching and therefore are most effective when they are provided with high quality materials and clear lesson plans. These materials have to be developed in collaboration with teachers so that there is not a clash of teaching styles.

CONCLUSION

The present study contributes to the on-going debate about the suitability of technology to enhance educational outcomes and practices. We join a body of studies evidencing the need for more formal integration of ICTs into the school systems they serve. Dray has argued that reducing the digital divide will require understanding the fit between *"technology, specific needs, and human contexts and how to negotiate the introduction and implementation of the technology"* [8]. Internal re-structuring of OLPC may see future projects committed to addressing the 'social side' of implementations [31]. Similarly, India's 'hole-in-the-wall' project has reportedly evolved from focusing on unsupervised access outside of school, to building ties with the schools and teachers [4]. This study provides a more in-depth look at the requirements of users in rural Andean communities, and provides implications for practitioners seeking to maximise educational ICT success rates in low resource contexts.

ACKNOWLEDGEMENTS

We thank Blue Sparrow and the school directors, teaching staff, pupils and their families for participating in this research.

REFERENCES

1. Balestrini, M., Bird, J., Marshall, P., Zaro, A. & Rogers, Y. 2014. Understanding sustained community engagement: A case study in heritage preservation in rural Argentina Proc. CHI'14, 2675-2684.
2. Blue Sparrow. (n.d.). Conectados. Retrieved July 19th 2013 from http://bluesparrow.org/projects/conectados/
3. Camfield, J., Kobulsky, A., Paris, J., & Vonortas, N. 2007. A report card for One Laptop Per Child. Closing the Digital Divide via ICTs and Education: Successes and Failures.http://joncamfield.com/writing/Camfield_Report_Card_for_OLPC. pdf.
4. Cervantes, R., Warschauer, M., Nardi, B., & Sambasivan, N. 2011. Infrastructures for low-cost laptop use in Mexican schools. Proc. CHI'11, 945-954.
5. Cristia, J., Ibarrarán, P., Cueto, S., Santiago, A., & Severín, E. 2012. Technology and child development: Evidence from the one laptop per child program. Inter-American Development Bank
6. Cuban, L., Kirkpatrick, H., & Peck, C. High access and low use of technologies in high school classrooms: Explaining an apparent paradox. American Educational Research Journal, 38, 4 (2001), 813-834.
7. Dangwal, R., & Kapur, P. Children's learning processes using unsupervised "hole in the wall" computers in shared public spaces. Australasian Journal of Educational Technology, 24,3 (2008), 339-354.

8. Dray, S. M., Siegel, D. A., & Kotzé, P. Indra's Net: HCI in the developing world. interactions, 10, 2 (2003), 28-37.
9. Heath, S., Charles, V., Crow, G., & Wiles, R. Informed consent, gatekeepers and go betweens: negotiating consent in child and youth orientated institutions. British Educational Research Journal, 33, 3 (2007), 403-417.
10. Heeks, R. Information systems and developing countries: Failure, success, and local improvisations. The information society, 18, 2 (2002), 101-112.
11. Heeks, R. Do information and communication technologies (ICTs) contribute to development? Journal of International Development, 22, 5 (2010), 625-640.
12. Hourcade, J. P., Beitler, D., Cormenzana, F., & Flores, P. Early OLPC experiences in a rural Uruguayan school. Proc. CHI (2008), 2503-2512.
13. Kraemer, K. L., Dedrick, J., & Sharma, P. One laptop per child: Vision vs. reality. Communications of the ACM, 52, 6 (2009), 66-73.
14. Lei, J., & Zhao, Y. One-to-one computing: what does it bring to schools? Journal of Educational Computing Research, 39, 2 (2008), 97-122.
15. Maunder, A., Marsden, G., & Harper, R. Making the link—providing mobile media for novice communities in the developing world. International Journal of Human-Computer Studies, 69, 10 (2011), 647-657.
16. Millen, D. R. Rapid ethnography: time deepening strategies for HCI field research. Proc. DIS (2000), 280-286.
17. Mitra, S. Self organising systems for mass computer literacy: Findings from the 'hole in the wall' experiments. Int. Journal of Development Issues, 4, 1(2005). 71-81.
18. Mitra, S., & Dangwal, R. Limits to self-organising systems of learning—the Kalikuppam experiment. British Journal of Educational Technology, 41, 5 (2010), 672-688.
19. Mitra, S., Dangwal, R., & Thadani, L. Effects of remoteness on the quality of education: A case study from North Indian schools. Australasian Journal of Educational Technology, 24, 2 (2008), 168-180.
20. Negroponte, N. (2006). One Laptop per Child. Retrieved June 23rd 2013 from http://www.ted.com/talks/nicholas_negroponte_on_one_laptop_per_child.html
21. OLPC. (2012) An Interview with Sandro Marcone About Peru's Una Laptop por Niño - See more at: http://www.olpcnews.com/countries/peru/english_summary_at_the_end.html#sthash.jwWNkjUe.dpuf
22. Patra, R., Pal, J., Nedevschi, S., Plauche, M., & Pawar, U. (2007). Usage models of classroom computing in developing regions. In Information and Communication Technologies and Development, International Conference on (pp. 1-10). IEEE.
23. Papert, S. (2006). Seymour Papert on USINFO. Retrieved August 29th 2013 from http://www.olpctalks.com/seymour_papert/seymour_papert_usinfo.html
24. Reitmaier, T., Bidwell, N. J., & Marsden, G. (2010). Field testing mobile digital storytelling software in rural Kenya. In Proceedings of the 12th international conference on Human computer interaction with mobile devices and services (pp. 283-286). ACM.
25. Santiago, A., Severín, E., Cristia, J., Ibarrarán, P., Thompson, J., & Cueto, S. (2010). Experimental assessment of the program 'One Laptop Per Child' in Peru. Inter-American Development Bank.
26. Schafft, K. A., Alter, T. R., & Bridger, J. C. (2006). Bringing the community along: A case study of a school district's information technology rural development initiative. Journal of Research in Rural Education, 21(8), 1-10.
27. Taylor, N., Cheverst, K., Wright, P., & Olivier, P. 2013. Leaving the wild: lessons from community technology handovers. Proc. CHI'13, 1549-1558.
28. Walton, M., & Heeks, R. (2011). Can a process approach improve ICT4D project success? Development Informatics Group.
29. Warschauer, M. 2003. Dissecting the 'digital divide': A case study in Egypt. The Information Society, 19(4), 297-304.
30. Warschauer, M. (2004). Technology and social inclusion: Rethinking the digital divide. The MIT Press.
31. Warschauer, M., & Ames, M. (2010). Can One Laptop per Child save the world's poor? Journal of International Affairs, 64(1), 33-51.
32. Warschauer, M., Cotten, S. R., & Ames, M. G. (2011). One laptop per child Birmingham: Case study of a radical experiment. International Journal of Learning, 3(2), 61-76.
33. Warschauer, M., Knobel, M., & Stone, L. (2004). Technology and equity in schooling: Deconstructing the digital divide. Educational Policy, 18(4), 562-588.

Playing the Legal Card: Using Ideation Cards to Raise Data Protection Issues within the Design Process

Ewa Luger
Microsoft Research
Cambridge, UK
a-ewluge@microsoft.com

Lachlan Urquhart, Tom Rodden & Michael Golembewski
University of Nottingham, UK
Firstname.Lastname@nottingham.ac.uk

ABSTRACT
The regulatory climate is in a process of change. Design, having been implicated for some time, is now explicitly linked to law. This paper recognises the heightened role of designers in the regulation of ambient interactive technologies. Taking account of incumbent legal requirements is difficult. Legal rules are convoluted, uncertain, and not geared towards operationalisable heuristics or development guidelines for system designers. Privacy and data protection are a particular moral, social and legal concern for technologies. This paper seeks to understand how to make emerging European data protection regulations more accessible to our community. Our approach develops and tests a series of data protection ideation cards with teams of designers. We find that, whilst wishing to protect users, regulation is viewed as a compliance issue. Subsequently we argue for the use of instruments, such as our cards, as a means to engage designers in leading a human-centered approach to regulation.

Author Keywords
Regulation, Data Protection, Ideation cards, Design

ACM Classification Keywords
H.5.m. Information interfaces and presentation (e.g., HCI): Miscellaneous

INTRODUCTION
We stand at the threshold of a major change in policy accountability around systems design. The 'designer', having played a background role in an ecosystem of products, requirements and users, is being called to the fore. International policy and transnational legal infrastructure are foregrounding the designer and highlighting a new set of legal conditions. Where once designers and systems architects were only subject to the influence of regulation at the point of product market entry, they are now being called to account from the minute pen hits paper. Privacy and security will soon be expected 'by design and by default' – and with this regulatory turn, comes a raft of responsibilities.

CHI 2015, April 18 - 23 2015, Seoul, Republic of Korea
Copyright 2015 ACM 978-1-4503-3145-6/15/04...$15.00
http://dx.doi.org/10.1145/2702123.2702142

The sphere of systems design is already clearly implicated within international policy discourse. The Organisation for Economic Cooperation and Development (OECD) privacy guidelines (2013) Part Five, call for national complementary measures. Under this section, member states have committed to consider "*the promotion of technical measures which help protect privacy*" [27]. At the same time, regulations proposed by the EU have foregrounded 'privacy by design' as the mechanism by which data protection (DP) might be assured. Whilst DP is already articulated through accepted mechanisms, such as Fair Information Practice Principles (FIPPs), these have focused solely upon the *rules* of data management and control rather than 'the system'.

The locus of responsibility, having previously rested with the user or data subject, is now being refocused. Whereas the user *was* predominately responsible for protecting their data, it is now broadly agreed that this undertaking is beyond the ability of the layperson. Instead, the weight of accountability is more firmly placed upon the data controller; in other words, those who control and are "*responsible for the keeping **and use** of personal information on a computer or in structured manual files*". Indeed, if you (a) keep/process *any* information about living people and (b) decide what personal information is to be kept, or (c) decide the purpose to which that information is to be put, you are already subject to 'serious legal responsibilities' [2]. With the advent of the coming EU General Data Protection Regulation (GDPR) however, these responsibilities are set to expand with international implications, but at what cost? As with any move to govern and control a market, so comes the fear that innovation will be stifled, lawyers will become necessary, and that subsequent costs will limit speculation, startups, and grassroots development.

However, this perspective misses a trick. If data protection is to be 'by design', surely this also presents a huge opportunity. Rather than bolting on onerous terms and conditions or parachuting in lawyers after the fact, consider the possibilities of taking a step back and asking; 'how can HCI as a community, make privacy and data protection a creative integral component of the systems we design?' What if, rather than outsourcing this knowledge and bowing to the glacial pace of the legal machine, we seek to build it into our practice? What if we were to take our human-centered skills and approaches and methodologically ply them to advance the regulatory field? In this paper we ask - how and at what stage of the design process might we engage designers with data protection regulation? Drawing upon an approach to creative engagement recognised by the design community - ideation cards - we develop a deck of cards and test these with 4 groups of designers in a workshop setting. Our study surfaced the limited ways in which designers reasoned about regulation; as a practical matter for address within a system. This both raised questions around the orientation of designers to DP, and also the need to consider the use of instruments similar to our cards in the early stages of the design process.

REGULATION AND THE ROLE OF DESIGN

'Regulation' is traditionally defined as "the sustained and focused control exercised by a public authority over activities valued by the community" [5, p.12]. From this perspective, regulation is a mechanism of state systemic control. However, changing conditions have rendered this definition less relevant, particularly within the sphere of technology where regulation includes multiple non-state actors participating in creation of technical standards, e.g. the World Wide Web Consortium (W3C) [26]. As a field of study, regulation has broadened. Technology regulation in particular is unique in that the speed of development necessitates a mixed regulatory climate, including intergovernmental treaties such as the OECD Privacy Guidelines [26], international agreements amongst private sector organisations, co-regulatory and self-regulatory arrangements, which arise from the market and often take the form of technical solutions. In this way, Internet regulation is something of *"a patchwork of different regulatory approaches in continuous flux"*[12, p.542]. Reflective of this broader conception, our study proceeds from the position that *"regulation is the sustained and focused attempt to alter the behaviour of others to standards or goals with the intention of producing a broadly identified outcome or outcomes, which may involve mechanisms of standard-setting, information gathering and behavior modification"* [6, p103]. Unlike traditional definitions, this perspective does not stipulate the source of regulation, embracing non-sate actors such as designers, whilst retaining a clear focus upon the function and intentions of regulation and the processes by which these might be achieved.

Whilst such conceptual framings are gaining ground amongst legal scholars, the extent to which HCI sees itself as part of this climate is questionable. So, if designers are currently incognisant within the regulatory machine, how can we begin the process of sensitising our community to the attending opportunities, limitations and responsibilities? One approach to encouraging thought, recognised by the design community, is that of ideation cards as a stimulus for creative endeavor.

USING IDEATION CARDS

The use of cards as a methodological design instrument is well established [15,13] as a means to "help define constrained design problems within a broader overall problem space" [15]. The use of cards as a creative stimulus has been applied to (a) the sphere of human values in the design process [13], (b) to support communication within and between families [24], (c) to encourage participants to think about security threats [30], (d) to stimulate creative methods within design practice by "representing diverse ways that design teams can understand the people they are designing for"[16], (e) to "help people explore and discuss issues around online privacy"[4], and (f) to support the exploration of design problems within a broader context [15]. Despite their different emphases, fundamental to all of these applications is the notion of cards as a mechanism to stimulate creative thought, often around subjects previously unfamiliar to the participants. Reflective of this tradition, the focus of our research was to design and test a creative method that raised awareness, amongst designers, of the intersection between their work and the proposed EU DP Legal framework. Law and policy instruments are often drafted in obtuse legalese, rendering them inaccessible to anyone other than lawyers and regulators. However, there is an increasing recognition within the legal community that, through their design decisions, technologists can play a key role in data protection. Our intention was to sensitise designers to this notion.

THE CHALLENGE OF DATA PROTECTION

Technologies already enforce regulatory norms through architecture and information management practices [20]. However, this raises important questions around the legitimacy and accountability [19,33] of such design decisions. Whilst technical solutions have been developed to protect personal data, e.g. through data anonymisation, pseudonomysation, or end-to-end data encryption, the extent to which privacy goals are considered within broader system design is less clear. The design of ambient systems that preserve privacy and respect data protection law is challenging. This is because;

(a) Ambient systems do not support established legal mechanisms such as obtaining informed user consent to data processing [8,18,21], **(b)** Human agency and control over human data processing is lessening, driven by increasingly autonomous systems with decreasing functional accountability to the user, i.e. the growth of so called 'black box' systems, **(c)** Law creates principles, rules, and sanctions, but not implementable design guidelines. Regulators advocate privacy by design approaches to data management (i.e. reflecting on and addressing privacy risks of a system during design) (EU Art 23) [9,17].

Despite these challenges, legal changes are already underway, with the 2012 proposed EU General Data Protection Regulation currently being scrutinised and altered by the legislative machinery of the European Union. If passed, the law will harmonise rights and responsibilities for data processors, controllers and subjects across 28 EU Member States, and extend to controllers outside the EU that (a) offer goods or services to EU data subjects or (b) monitoring them.

[GDPR Art 3(2)], thereby having widespread international implications.

METHODOLOGY

Our study, which brings together a multidisciplinary team, was developed in three phases:

Phase one: Consulting the legal community - We sought to identify aspects of the GDPR (EU General Data Protection Regulation 2012 Com Final 11) most likely to implicate the design community. This was achieved through deployment of a survey instrument to a small purposive sample of European data protection experts from the legal community. ***Phase two: Designing the cards*** - Having established the key principles, the second phase applied these principles to the development of a broader deck of ideation-style cards, and ***Phase three: Design workshops*** – The designed cards were tested with 21 designers through 4 structured workshops.

Phase 1- Consulting the Legal Community

In order to inform our ideation card approach, we investigated four specific areas of the GDPR. These were drawn, in part, from recommendations of the UK Information Commissioner Office, [29], on (1) *data breach notifications*; (2) *explicit informed consent*; the controversial (3) *right to be forgotten,* and (4) *privacy by design.* In order to establish the importance of these areas for systems design, we posed open questions to a highly targeted group of prominent UK data protection and privacy law experts. Seven legal academics were surveyed; primarily professors but also lecturers and doctoral researchers. The following section introduces each area and the challenges posed for designers, as highlighted by our experts.

Legal Area 1: Data Breach Notifications requirements are extended to all data processors in Article 31 GDPR. This builds on existing obligations that ISPs must notify data protection authorities, and data subjects, potentially within 24 hours when a data breach has occurred; i.e. data is accidentally or unlawfully destroyed, stolen, lost, altered, transmitted etc. [Article 2(h) PECD 2002]. Breach severity is key in determining what information should be conveyed, to whom, in what form, and how quickly [25].

The Challenge for Designers: Experts highlighted the importance of accuracy over speed of notification; i.e. proper time to investigate and inform the user of all facts in preference to frequent or incomplete warnings. Combatting 'notification fatigue' and helping users to differentiate between legitimate and fraudulent warnings were also noted challenges. The *post hoc* nature of breach notification concerned some experts. One stated: "*it's too late for autonomy after a breach has occurred*". Using reparation to coerce better security practices was also mentioned; "*the reputational harm of having to disclose a data breach should act as an incentive to improve data management*". However, relying on fines alone might result in these being seen as an acceptable 'business cost' rather than a punitive measure. Accordingly, we reflected these concerns in our card text; (a) reference to reputation damage, (b) the need for consideration of innovative approaches to notifications, and (c) ensuring breach information is accurate and within a short timeframe.

Legal area 2: Obtaining Informed Meaningful Consent is a significant challenge within Ubicomp systems [22,14]. Designing consent mechanisms that truly scaffold user understanding is a challenge which remains unaddressed by the dominant model of Terms and Conditions [21,22]. Article 4 (8) GDPR mandates a higher threshold of explicit, informed consent to data processing, requiring "any freely given specific, informed and explicit indication of... wishes ... either by a statement or by a clear affirmative action". This raises questions as to how a system might remain ambient, yet still inform and obtain this higher threshold consent.

The Challenge for Designers: Our legal experts emphasised themes (a) how to obtain meaningful informed consent, (b) how to outline risks to users properly, and (c) how to allow them to withdraw their data. Designing mechanisms to truly give choice and inform, when users may not care, was perceived to be a challenge. One expert stated: "*Consent is an important part of the matrix of protections for autonomy and dignity but it must be informed ... it is not informed consent to tick a box on a webpage or to agree to a privacy policy which you have not read.*" Many experts were critical of the nature and definition of informed legal consent as a concept, terming it 'illusory' and too 'fixed' in light of the complexity and dynamism of both the data processing landscape and human attitudes and control. It was felt that current approaches do "*not account for partial consent or revoked consent over a period of time. Often consent is not the issue, rather the lack of control re data collection is the issue.*"

Reflective of this, our cards hinted at the opportunities for creativity in addressing these requirements and stated that the form of information or delivery was not fixed, and that consent was a fluid concept requiring negotiation.

Legal area 3: The 'Right to be Forgotten'/ Right to Erasure (Article 17 GDPR) would grant a data subject rights to request the data controller stop further dissemination of data, and erase personal data relating to them, in certain conditions; e.g. when data is no longer necessary or consent is withdrawn. Here, US and EU perspectives have differed greatly. The US has voiced concerns over stifling free speech and creating censorship, whilst the EU has highlighted the importance of privacy rights [1,5]. For example, the recent European Court of Justice Google Spain Case [31] discussed balancing privacy interests of one individual against freedom of expression. In this case, Google was requested to remove website links in search results that related to an individual [23]. Other discussions focus on practical difficulties in implementation where copies may exist across different platforms and devices [11].

The Challenge for Designers: Our experts highlighted the challenge of balancing competing rights against the granularity of enforcement; e.g. the interests of archiving memories or complete and accurate records of one individual, versus the right to be forgotten of another. One expert stated *"there are approaches that make it comparatively easy to forget but they tend to overreach, causing problems for other rights. ...the worry is that over simplistic design solutions to the RTBF will overreach and harm social and political discourse."* Another expert prioritised privacy interests; *"the individual should be able to rip their data trail right off any Ubicomp system when consent is withdrawn"*. Overall, it was thought to be a valuable tool for empowering individuals. Practically however, whilst a few thought it was achievable, many wondered how it might work in reality. Reflective of this, our card text hinted at issues around balancing interests, difficulties in implementation and the technical decisions that shape this.

Legal area 4: Privacy by design (PbD) seeks to create information systems that embed privacy-enhancing solutions into the architecture. Article 23 GDPR defines this regulatory tool as the need to regard 'the *state of the art* and the *cost of implementation*...' to implement '*appropriate technical and organisational* measures and procedures in such a way that the processing will meet the requirements of *this Regulation* and *ensure the protection of the rights of the data subject*'.

The Challenge for Designers: Key design challenges from this include questions of (a) what the state of the art might be for these purposes (commercially available vs lab based technologies), (b) what an unreasonable cost of implementation (e.g. how high a percentage of overall costs) might be, and (c) what aspects of data protection/privacy should be prioritised (e.g. should there be greater focus on certain provisions depending on the context of the system, with deployment home vs public space?) Grounding such considerations through the design process is important. We sought the most detailed feedback on PbD and all experts agreed that it was an important sphere of investigation, despite a level of sematic uncertainty. Experts questioned whom the obligations are incumbent on (e.g. the designer, the manufacturer, etc.), and whilst bridging the gap between law and design is critical, one cautioned "*there is a danger to search for solely technical solutions at the expense of other measures, and to turn substantial debates about ethics and law into mere software design issues*" Experts prioritised; fair and lawful processing, purpose limitation for data use, proportionate data collection, and data subject access rights as key focus areas for ubicomp systems. These aspects were reflected within our text and divided across 2 cards. Having explained the design of our legal cards, the following section describes design of the wider deck.

Phase 2: Designing the Cards

Design of the card deck drew directly from previous work with ideation cards. As in the case of Freidman & Hendry [13] and Golembewski & Selby [15], we employed four sets of criteria, described 'suits' [15]. Taking the regulatory principles previously described, we developed a 5 card suite entitled 'Regulation'. In order to construct a deck, we added 3 factors regularly considered within the design process. These were (a) a specific system to focus group activity [30], (b) a series of user groups [30], drawn from groups from the 'edges' [10], and (c) a series of potential constraints for each system. The content of the 'constraints' and 'system' cards were generated during structured conversations with developers. The former were selected by participants to represent factors that, in their experience, typically constrained the design of data-driven systems. The latter describe systems that are, on the basis of participant input, either already in development or under discussion. Each suite featured 10 cards, making a total deck of 35. In-keeping with other card studies [13, 15] we also sought 'evocative' images, featured alongside the descriptive text.

Establishing the rules of the game

Friedman & Hendry found that a 'focused design activity' was instrumental in supporting participants to consider values. In light of this, our activity was constructed within strict parameters (temporal and systemic) to focus group attention.

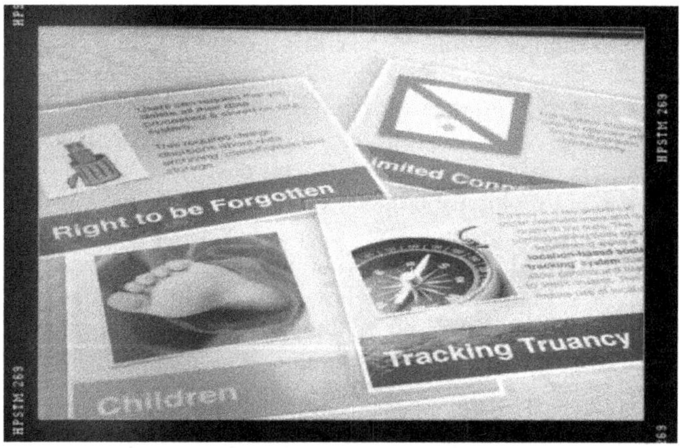

Figure 1. Examples from the four 'suits'

Creating Focus: This was established at the start of the activity with our 'System' cards. Suggesting a pre-defined system allowed us to frame and focus discussion. These cards described (a) the system function (b) the type of data to be collected, and (c) the type of organisation commissioning the work, For example: **Tracking Truancy:** *Truancy is a key problem in urban deprived areas and is costly to the state. The commissioning body (govt department) wants a location-based social 'tracking' system that will allow parents and teachers to' track' truants. This system makes use of location data.* Beyond those listed in Fig. 3, other systems included (a) a smart energy system, (b) a live biometric system for use in cinemas (c) a community-level energy monitoring system (d) a platform that allows users to sell the data generated at home, and (e) a live marketing system that provides targeted advertising on the street.

Phase 3: The Design Workshops

A series of four design workshops where held to trial the cards. The term 'designer' was used with little supporting clarification in recruitment in order to attract a broad range of participants. There were 21 participants in total, (16

Male/ 5 female). Participant specialisms included classifications of HCI, systems architects, a programmer and an engineer; years of experience ranged from a designer in the first year of his training to 16 years and system types included lab-based experiment systems to broadcast, online shopping, robotics, mobile apps, customer support, games, tracking systems, persuasive systems and databases. Participants were arranged into 4 groups.

Group 1 (G1): Most experienced, mixed specialism (predominately HCI)

Group 2 (G2): Mixed experience, mixed specialism

Group 3 (G3): Mixed experience, (predominately systems architects)

Group 4 (G4): Least experienced, mixed specialism

Groups 1 to 3 were each made up of 5 participants and group 4 including 6. Figure 2 shows the gender, years of experience of systems design, their specialism and knowledge of DP.

Ref	Gender	Yrs	Specialism	DP knowledge
G1_1	M	12	HCI	At university
G1_2	F	10	HCI	Through practice
G1_3	M	5-6	Sys Arc / HCI	At school
G1_4	F	4	HCI	Through practice
G1_5	M	16	HCI/ Sys Arc	Through practice
G2_1	M	1	HCI	Training at work
G2_2	M	9	Sys Arc /HCI	Through media
G2_3	M	10	Sys Arc	At university
G2_4	M	2-3	HCI	Through media
G2_5	M	11	Privacy expert	Expert
G3_1	M	10	Sys Arc	Training at work
G3_2	M	7	Sys Arc	At university
G3_3	M	4	Sys Arc	At university
G3_4	M	14	Sys Arc	Through practice
G3_5	M	2	Eng	Only aware
G4_1	F	4	HCI	At university
G4_2	F	2	HCI	At university
G4_3	M	5-6	Programmer	Through media
G4_4	M	2	Database	At university
G4_5	F	2	HCI	Only aware
G4_6	M	4.5	Sys Arc	Training at work

Figure 2. Participant profile

Experience of DP: Prior to the workshop, participants were asked about their DP knowledge (fig.2). We found that the majority of our participants had received only perfunctory training; 11 had experienced what they described as 'basic' awareness training at university, school, or at work. Three designers were only aware of stories in the media and 2 had only passing knowledge. Only 5 designers had a working knowledge; one participant was a DP specialist and 4 designers had developed knowledge of DP law through professional practice. Based on descriptions, DP knowledge was not systematically acquired, but rather *ad hoc*, limited or need-driven.

Cards	Group 1	Group 2	Group 3	Group 4
Syst'	Always on live wearable health device	Wearable cameras for shopping in store and home	Car that 'takes over' when sensing bad driving	Health device tied to medical records and store card
User	Everyone	Older People (65+)	Ex-offenders or those on probation	Women of all cultures and faiths
Const'	High level of user control	Limited connectivity	Low energy	Low cost
Const'	N/A	Low cost	Maximum Data	Minimal distraction
Reg	Right to be Forgotten	Data Processing	Explicit Consent	Privacy and Processing
Reg	Explicit Consent	Data Collection	Breach Notification	Breach Notification

Figure 3. Cards drawn by each group

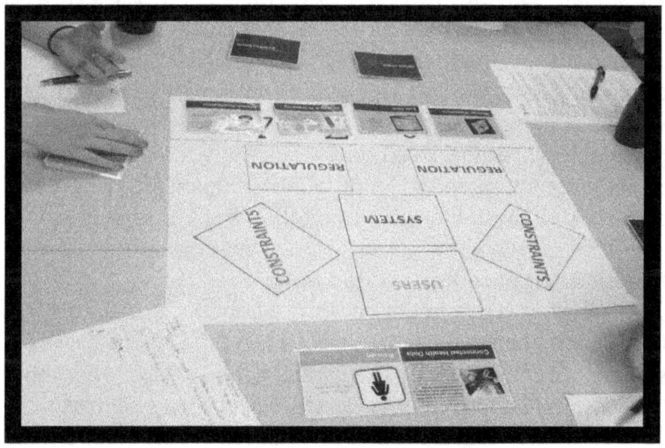

Figure 4. Card Sorting Exercise (group 4)

Workshop Schedule: The workshops began with each group drawing 6 cards, blind, from the deck (see Fig.3). Friedman & Hendry and Mackay *et al*, both emphasise the importance of time in the ideation process; e.g. authors used a 3 minute sand *timer "to both symbolise and facilitate the possibility for meaningful use in a brief amount of time"* [13 p.1146]. In order to focus participant attention, our activity was strictly timed to 30 mins and participants were told when to turn each card. Upon the start of the game, designers drew 1 System card, 1 User card, 2 Constraints cards and 2 Regulation cards, laying them face down. They were asked not to turn the cards until instructed. Timing of the game began once the system card was turned. The User card, both Constraints cards, and finally both Regulation cards were turned, each after 5 minute intervals. After the turn of the Regulation cards, participants continued their discussions for the remaining 15 minutes. With the turn of each suite, designers were asked to consider the system they were designing in light of the newly turned cards. The principle function of the cards was to prompt and encourage reflection on aspects of DP law. By turning the regulation card last ('playing the legal card') we were able to infer whether the cards stimulated DP/privacy concerns, or whether they were pre-existent. Thinking about the cards last, and therefore potentially having to rethink the nascent systems under design, primed the participants for the card-ordering task.

Card-ordering exercise: Having completed the structured activity, participants were asked to reflect upon the game overall, and the regulation cards in particular. This was catalyzed by a card-sorting activity. Participants were asked to collectively sort the cards they had worked with, in order of importance, for (a) concept, and (b) technical design. Feedback at the end of the activity for the first group suggested that it would be more realistic to have a greater number of constraints imposed upon designers. Subsequently, two cards were drawn by each remaining group.

RESULTS

Each workshop was video recorded and analysed within NVivo, using a thematic network analysis, which organised the coded text into three types of theme; (i) basic (lowest order, coded statements or beliefs that related to organising themes), (ii) organising (that cluster basic themes into organising issues) and (iii) global themes (super-ordinate themes that organise all codes into meta-groups or metaphor) [3]. Each workshop was coded separately and the resulting codes were compared to identify global themes. We give an overview of these themes in the following sections.

Not all designers are created equal

The strongest repeating theme throughout the workshops was the divide between those who classified themselves as systems architects, or programmers, and those who more closely aligned to HCI or research. The former group saw the responsibility for DP, and awareness of regulation, as unrelated to their role. From their perspective, the role of designer was to create a system aligned to its proposed function, unencumbered by external limitations such as regulation: *"When you're designing a system, at least for me, you always think of regulation as an afterthought. So, if I get what I want then I see how do I protect the user afterwards"* (G4_6).

Protection of whose interests

When engaging in the design activity, the theme of protecting interests was key. This subdivided into two categories; the interests of the user (data subject) and of whoever was responsible for the data (data controller). Groups 1, 2 and 4 began considering the protection of user data from the start of the activity – on the turn of the system card. In contrast, group 3 did not consider DP from the perspective of user protection until the turn of the regulation cards. They did, however, collectively opt to store user data locally on the system in order to protect *themselves* from any legal responsibility: *"If you know where an ex-offender is, you are in for a world of bureaucratic pain if the police come looking for that information. Whereas, if you can plausibly prove that you've no idea where they are...suddenly you are very much off the hook."* (G3_4). In this way, the turn of the regulation cards had most impact upon group 3. For example, user consent was not considered by this group until the turn of that card. Even after that point, their discussions were limited to forms of consent with which they were familiar; i.e. whilst designing a smart car they suggested that consent could occur at the point when the user sat in the driver's seat. Here, the information could be projected on the windscreen, and agreement occurring when the driver started the car. However, once the discussion developed, they became aware of the limitations of their proposed approach and began to see the need to think more creatively *"We've just designed the Ubicomp equivalent of terms and conditions haven't we?"**all laugh* (G3_3).

Where to keep the data

Designers across all groups consistently used the location of data as a mechanism for minimising risk. Equally, the role local storage as a means of augmenting user control over the data they generated was commonly employed. The rationale for this, however, varied. Again, group 3 tended towards the position that local storage enabled developers to protect themselves from liability and minimise the risk of physical harm befalling the user; e.g. if the system was allowed too much agency. Their concern did not initially extend to protection of the user from a DP perspective, though their discussions *after* the turn of the regulation cards led them to agree that such a model could also support the DP principles of breach notification and explicit consent: *"Anything to do with the command and control of the car is decided locally. But the data that it collects could be processed remotely".* (G3_02)

Conversely, groups 1 and 2 tended towards the position that local storage would (a) allow the user a greater level of control, (b) would enable them time/space to review the data, and (c) make measured decisions about exposure in order and protection. *"That sounds really nice actually. There's not enough holding on to stuff...keeping it physically near you* (G1_02)... *"so, switching the roles of the whole kind of web cloud-based bit so that your server is the thing you carry around"* (G1_05). In this way, their tendency to focus on user requirements necessarily invoked the notion of protection. Group 4, having initially conceived an ambitious system that could collect highly sensitive biometric data and update live to the cloud, were limited by the turn of the constraints cards ('low cost' and 'minimal distraction'). This drew them to review their ideas and take a more modest approach. Their redesign, again favouring local data storage, made the turn of the regulation cards ('privacy & processing' and 'breach notification') much less problematic: *"Low cost made me think of less ambitious designs. In the beginning it was going to be in your bloodstream, monitoring everything and doing stuff and sending everything to satellites and then it was oh, this just means fitbits really"* (G4_06). Group reflections at the end of the process highlighted that it was only a lack of awareness of the breadth of regulation that limited their desire or ability to incorporate such considerations at an early stage: *"That made it a bit more specific, the breach notification, the 24hr thing* (G4_1)*....Yeah, I suppose the one that would have freaked me out most would be the breach notification. I wasn't expecting it. Suddenly you'd have to design that in. That's quite scary."* (G4_2) Equally, considering DP as part of the design process, with specific users in mind, forced the groups to think in a more focused and creative way about possible solutions. For example, group 2 suggested supporting older people by automatically limiting data collection, linking it to location; so, when users entered a shop, data collection would be automatically turned on but would turn off as soon as they got home.

Revealing the user

Revealing the user card fundamentally altered the form of the system under discussion. Group 2 moved away from a permanently wearable solution to one that was wearable only during key points (such as in the store or at home) to reduce the cognitive burden and responsibility on the older user. Group 3 extended their system to include clearly defined data upload points in order to limit the liability of the company and enhance the privacy of ex-offenders and those on probation, and Group 4 sought design solutions that would enhance the ability of women of all faiths and cultures to control the flow of their data and limit access to those outside of the UK.

Group 1 was charged with designing an always on 'live' wearable health device for 'everyone'. In this case, revealing the user card elicited concerns over the possibility of designing a catchall product: *"well, you've got a failed product right there"* (G1_2)...*"designing for everyone you can't do"* (G1_5). Despite these concerns, the solution (to conceive a system that transmitted live biometric data to the cloud) elicited the most creative and complete design of all 4 groups. By having to design of everyone, Group 1 sought to envision a product that was highly customisable; a charm bracelet. This product would allow certain types of data to be transmitted, within user-defined contexts, through the physical act of clipping on components (beads). Individual beads being related to distinct data types. Their design choices were reinforced through the 'user control' constraints card and those two features (customisability and control) were applied to allow the user to indicate their explicit consent through the clipping on/off of the charms.

Everything starts from the (stereotypical) user

The default orientation of all of the HCI specialists, though not of the (single-specialism) system architects, was that user requirements should come first. All groups, except for group 3, asked whether they could turn the user card before they were asked to do so. Group 1 repeatedly stated that it made no sense to start designing a system without knowing 'who the user was'. During the card sorting exercise, groups 1 and 4 both clearly indicated that the user was as important in the conceptual design of the systems as the specification of the system itself. This was further raised during the card-sorting exercise. However, the orientation of Group 2 was somewhat different. Led by the privacy specialist, this group leaned towards the role of regulation as being to protect the user from themselves. This position was also reflected within Group 4: *"Regulations are there to protect the user from their own bad decisions. So even if the user wants something it doesn't mean they should get it just because they want it...like, you're not allowed to drive without a seatbelt even if it makes you're uncomfortable and you're an idiot. So, the government prevents you making that stupid decision through regulation."* (G4_6).

With the exception of Group 1 (who had drawn the 'everyone' user card), user requirements were seen to come first. However, when discussions of user characteristic began, highly stereotyped profiles of user traits, needs or behaviours emerged. For example, Group 2 both implied and explicated that their users (aged 65+) were frail, had poor cognitive and memory skills, were incapable of making reasoned decisions and were easily confused. *"In terms of having to turn it on and off ...They might forget and then they turn it on and they're recording their whole day and everything else."* (G2_04). Upon turning their user card (ex-offenders and those on probation), Group 3 made the assumption that such users would want to conceal their activities, would be careless of others, and that they would reoffend. In contrast, Group 4 (women of all cultures and faiths) began by focusing their system (wearable monitoring health device) on specific cultural issues. One designer drew on their own cultural experience to describe how such a device might be used as a mechanism of control, by husbands, within more repressive societies. Therefore, if the system was worn abroad, there may be grey areas in terms of DP: *"Woman...have less control over their lives. Suddenly I see this tool as a tool for controlling their lives even more so that their husband can now have access to this information"* (G4_6)

Whereas the other groups reported a natural progression of their system design with the turning of the cards, Group 1 found designing their system incredibly difficult; both self-reported and through observation. However, the key characteristic of the system they created was that it was highly individualised and customisable. By not knowing who 'the user' was, they were forced to keep their design sufficiently flexible and adaptable to suit all needs. Equally, Group 1 was the only group not to fall back upon describing existing systems. Group 1 spent far longer discussing form than any of the other groups, and expressed greater concern over whether all potential users would accept their design; leading them to seek forms with high levels of customisability. In contrast, groups 2, 3 and 4 all made assumptions as to what would be acceptable: *"If your users are going to be everyone, you've got to think about the social acceptability of it"* (G1_1)

Exhibiting regulatory behaviour

When considering the Regulation cards, four key tensions arose. These were (a) meeting DP requirements was seen as limiting to system functionality, (b) protection of the user through design was seen as distinct from conforming to regulation e.g. protection of the user was generally foregrounded, whilst DP regulation was set in the background and the relationship between the two was rarely identified, (c) securing meaningful and explicit consent was seen as incompatible with the desire for systems to remain seamless/unobtrusive from the user perspective, and (d) concerns over the necessary/required threshold of knowledge/understanding (DP competence) was repeatedly raised. It was clear that designers felt insufficiently empowered/equipped to reflect DP within their practice. However, despite this, their emergent design ideas automatically brought to bear elements of regulation though a *limiting or managing of the flow of data*. When reflecting on the commissioning body (detailed in the System cards), the majority of designers felt the need to build in control mechanisms to protect the user from external interests. The theme of control through design, as central to articulation of DP, was a dominant strand across all groups, particularly within groups 2 and 3. The concept arose in a range of contexts, such as the need (a) to design systems that directed, limited or focused user engagement or attention in particular ways, (b) for systems to enable users to be able to manage, delay and direct the flow of data from their local devices to the cloud or central system, (c) for a system to control unfettered access a company/organisation or central system might have to user data, and (d) the need to build in access control so that companies/organisations were not able to use data beyond the purposes expressly allowed by the user.

The Designer as regulator

The regulation of user behaviour was cast as a given or implicit function of design. However, when reflecting upon the role of the 'designer as regulator', the dominant feeling was that designers were currently ill-equipped to undertake that responsibility. This was attributed to low levels of awareness, skills, competence and confidence. Despite this, when ranking the importance of the cards to the design of systems, the regulation cards were positioned second in importance only to the system and user cards. This was true across all groups. The system and user cards were seen as both indivisible from each other, and of principle importance for consideration in the design process. The only group to rank the user as less important (in practice) was group 3.

Reflecting on regulation in the design process

Having completed both the 30-minute design activity, and the card sorting exercise, participants were asked to reflect upon the process. It was put to them that proposed changes in the law would locate the designer as more central to the wider regulatory landscape in the future. Groups were asked to consider their individual orientation to this statement and discuss it collectively. Overall, those groups with a more diverse spread of specialisms, and with more experienced participants (Groups 1 and 2), were more positively oriented to this proposition. They were also the groups who believed there to be a need to train/develop multidisciplinary or 'hybrid' designers who could perform the role of both concept design and systems architecture.

Discussions also raised a series of design factors that would become increasingly important for DP through design. Overall, the following suggestions were raised (a) designing for transparency of data flows but not necessarily transparency of systems, (b) a focus on data breach *detection* rather than breach notification - the focus on breach notification was seen as a weak work-around, given that the more complex and expensive issue was breach detection, (c) designing systems that meet user expectations in terms of data – e.g. not violating the context within which users expected their data to be used, (d) exploring different approaches to when and how data was released/exposed (e.g. linking DRM to personal data), (e) considering where 'windows for consent' might be designed into a system, (f) revisiting notice and how that might be redesigned for more pervasive systems, (g) designing for local data storage as default, and sharing/exposure as an exception, and (h) moving beyond the 'data dump' – e.g. beyond the simple narrative of making all data visible/accessible to the user, and instead considering how design might support individuals to make meaningful decisions about data sharing.

Engaging designers with regulation

When considering how designers might be engaged within the regulatory frame, a primary enabling theme was the need for the concept designer to have greater flexibility and control in the design process; particularly where system architecture was separated from conceptual design. It was also felt to be insufficient for DP to be a last consideration, or cast as something 'imposed upon design'. Rather, participants highlighted the need for it to be embedded in 'the institutional fabric' of the field. It was suggested that privacy and DP was currently 'under designed' due available 'off the shelf' fixes, leading designers to simply 'plug in' existing solutions rather than seeking creative alternatives. Despite recognised the value of DP through design, the idea of engaging designers in such practice was considered 'lovely in theory', but not realistic. Overall, there was felt to be a divide between the legal and design 'worlds', exacerbated by the absence of a common lexicon from which to draw. Group three was the only group not to feel the need for a closer drawing together of the fields. Instead, they preferred the model of working closely with an external legal expert, to ensure no laws were contravened. Others suggested the need for a new role - that of the 'regulation designer' who could be brought into a design team or called upon, much like an HCI specialist.

Reflecting on the cards: Overall, participants reflected positively on the cards and all felt they had been made aware of new aspects of DP. Discussions highlighted that they would be most effectively used as either an educational tool for those training to be designers, or as an ideation instrument for use within design meetings at the early, conceptual stages of the design process. Even Group 3 agreed that a greater awareness of DP at an early stage would help with the overall design process. It was noted, however, that in order to be useful as design instruments, the cards would need to include a greater level of detail. For example, groups 3 and 4 both asked the facilitator for more explicit detail about the conditions of breach notification.

DISCUSSION

Legal scholars Brownsword and Yeung describe technology as a 'regulatory tool'. From this perspective, designers not only create systems to meet explicit regulatory purposes, such as criminal justice, but also implicitly regulate by affecting users through systems which "seek to, or have the effect of, shaping behavior" [7]. As designers, our job is to direct, nudge and channel user actions through the form and function of the systems we design. By incorporating knowledge of DP law from the start of the design process, the systems we release into the world can better ensure user protection. This position is not only increasingly recognised by legal scholars, but is reflected in the way regulation is being designed; e.g through the emergent PbD agenda. Whilst our participants recognised the need for DP, they did not necessarily see themselves as instrumental within the wider regulatory system. Instead, they cast regulation as an external force, which necessitated a level of *post hoc* compliance or compromise. Regulation, and more broadly law, was seen as something to be respected through systems design but its practical implementation was cast as the province of legal professionals and DP specialists. The ideation cards allowed us to challenge the nature of this discourse. Rather than seeing regulation as external and distant, it was placed within the initial framing of design. This was well-received by designers as an awareness raising exercise, and discussions highlighted a clear need for such an instrument; both as an educational aid and means to stimulate creative thought around DP at an early stage of the design process. Despite this, key themes arising from our analysis highlight some areas that require attention.

Engagement - Designing cards for multiple interests

'Design' is a catchall term that encompasses aspects such as conceptual, aesthetic, technical and functional design. As such, when we speak of 'designers' we are in fact invoking multiple, and often hybrid, tribes. Even where system design goals are the same, each tribe brings with it a distinct perspective and, as such, any ideation card approach will need to be highly customisable to context. The approach we took worked well for HCI and creative designers, where there was some familiarity with the function of cards in the design process. However, system architects were less convinced, requiring much more detail before they could comfortably engage. Equally, early career designers exhibited very low awareness of DP regulation, suggesting that there may be a need to engage them at an earlier stage in their training. Our next steps, therefore, will be (a) to develop a more detailed educational deck, aligned to undergraduate studies, in order to create awareness and begin stimulating creative thought around designing for DP, and (b) support the development of these cards into a more dynamic instrument to be used and further developed within multiple contexts.

Promoting Human-Centered Regulation

There are currently three 'modalities of design' in support of regulation [7]. These are those that (a) encourage behavioral change, (b) ameliorate the effects of harm-generating behaviour, or (c) totally prevent harmful behaviour. Whilst such approaches regulate human behaviour, they can result in a reduction of human agency, having a negative effect on accountability, transparency and participation [7]. These modalities, however, are drawn from existing practice based upon a narrow view of regulation. If designers were to be actively engaged in the regulatory frame, and explicitly promote a human centered perspective, we are likely to see a much broader range of creative solutions such as the charm-based and location-triggered data exposure solutions beginning to emerge during our study. There is a danger that, unless designers actively and knowingly participate, their work may ultimately be coopted. Upon reflection, our participants felt there was indeed a need for closer alignment between regulation and design, though they failed to see a natural connection between user experience/requirements and DP. We would argue that, given our designers' clear focus on the user, one solution would be to embed DP within user experience heuristics. For example, designers automatically sought to enhance user control over their data by privileging local storage over the cloud and focusing on mechanisms to limit upload unless it was user-controlled. It is reasonable to imagine that traction could be gained by linking aspects of DP to existing heuristics, such as 'enhancing user control'.

Addressing the skills gap

In the same way as Lessig argued that code could be law [20], so the form that technology takes can have an effect (intentional or otherwise) on human endeavor. Currently, such regulation is limited and somewhat binary; for example what can, or cannot, be done with a product or service through DRM. However, by drawing all designers into the DP field, more nuanced and aesthetic solutions can be achieved, such as the charm bracelet suggested by Group 1. Before this can become a reality, however, there is a pressing need to raise the skills, confidence and competence of designers in respect of DP regulation. Whilst the cards were intended to sensitise participants to DP issues, it was clear that in the case of less familiar aspects, such as breach notification, what was needed was further information, guidance and support. This could be achieved through the development of guidance notes to augment the cards, or through the emergence of hybrid specialists, as suggested by participants.

CONCLUSIONS

It is clear that, as things currently stand, designers struggle to engage with regulation. There is a pressing need to draw designers into the coproduction of meaningful DP heuristics. By taking a participatory approach it is likely that, not only will translation be more effective, but it could also result in greater likelihood of ownership and buy-in from the design community. Finally, we recognise that this study privileges a

European perspective on DP. It is our intention that this research be replicated within a US context, with further international studies planned in the future. However, keeping our cards close to our chest is not the way to proceed. We hope that by making our instrument available under the Creative Commons license (see designingforprivacy.co.uk), others will develop further the work we have started.

AKNOWLEDGEMENTS

This research has been supported by the following RCUK Grant No. EP/G037574/1, EP/G065802/1 and EP/M000877/1

REFERENCES

1. Ambrose, M., Ausloos, J. The Right to be Forgotten Across the Pond. *J Inform Pol, 3*, 1-23. (2013)
2. Are you a Data Controller? At http://www.dataprotection.ie/docs/Are-you-a-Data-Controller-/43.htm
3. Attride-Stirling, J. Thematic networks: an analytic tool for qualitative research. *Qual Res. 1*, 3 (2001) 385-405
4. Barnard-Wills, D. Privacy Game. http://surveillantidentity.blogspot.co.uk/p/privacy-card-game.html
5. Bernal, P. The EU, the US and the Right to be Forgotten *In Gutwirth, S. Leenes, R. and De Hert, P. [Eds] Reloading Data Protection Multidisciplinary Insights and Contemporary Challenges*' Springer, 2014
6. Black J 'Decentring Regulation: Understanding the Role of Regulation and Self-regulation in a 'Post- Regulatory' World' (2001) 54 *Current Legal Problems* 103
7. Brownsword, R., Yeung, K. (eds), Regulating Technologies: Legal Futures, Regulatory Frames and Technological Fixes. Hart Publishing, 2008
8. Camp, J. and Connelly, K. Beyond Consent: Privacy in Ubicomp Systems in Digital Privacy: Theory, Technologies and Practices (2007)
9. Cavoukian, A, Privacy by Design: The 7 Foundational Principles, IPCO, 2011
10. Dourish, P., Bell, G. *Divining a Digital Future: Mess and Mythology in Ubiquitous Computing*. MIT Press, 2011
11. Druschel, P. The Right to Be Forgotten - Between Expectations and Promise, ENISA 2012
12. Feick, R. & Werle, R. Regulation of Cyberspace. In Baldwin, R., Cave, M., & Lodge, M. [eds] *The Oxford Handbook of Regulation*. OUP, 2010, 523-547
13. Friedman, B. & Hendry, D. The envisioning cards: a toolkit for catalyzing humanistic and technical imaginations. In *Proc. CHI'12* ACM (2012)
14. Friedman, B. Lin, P. Miller, J.K. Informed Consent by Design in Cranor, L.F. and Garfinkel, S. (Eds) Security and Usability. O'Reilly Media Inc (2005) 503-529
15. Golembewski, M. Selby, M. Ideation decks: a card-based design ideation tool. *Proc. DIS'10.* ACM Press
16. IDEO. Method Cards for IDEO: 51 Card Deck to Inspire Design. At http://www.ideo.com/work/method-cards
17. ICO on Privacy by Design, 2014 http://ico.org.uk/for_organisations/data_protection/topic_guides/privacy_by_design
18. Langheinrich, M. A Privacy Awareness System for Ubiquitous Computing Environments. In *Lecture Notes in Computer Science 2498*, Springer 237–245 (2002)
19. Leenes, R "Framing Techno-Regulation: An Exploration of State and Non-State Regulation By Technology" *Legisprudence,* 2011, Vol. 5 No. 2, 143-169
20. Lessig, L. *Code V2.0*. Basic Books, 2006
21. Luger, E. & Rodden, T. An informed view on consent for UbiComp. In *Proc. UbiComp '13*. ACM (2013), 529-538
22. Luger, E. Rodden, T. Terms of Agreement: Rethinking Consent for Pervasive Computing *Interact Comput* 25.2 (2013)
23. Lynskey, O. Rising Like a Phoenix: The Right to Be Forgotten Before the ECJ *European Law Blog (*2014)
24. Mackay, W. The Interactive Thread: Exploring Methods for Multi-disciplinary Design *In Proc. DIS'04*. ACM (2004)
25. Manson, C G. and Gorniak, S. Recommendations for a methodology of the assessment of severity of personal data breaches, ENISA, 2013
26. Mayntz, R. The Changing Governance of Large Technical Infrastructure Systems in: Mayntz, R. (ed.): Über Governance. In Stitutionen und Prozesse politischer Regelung, Schriften aus dem Max-Planck-Institut für Gesellschaftsfor-schung, Campus (2009), 121-150
27. OECD. *The OECD Privacy Framework*. OECD Publishing (2013)
28. Stahl, B.C. Responsible research and innovation: The role of privacy in an emerging framework. *Science and Public Policy*, 2013, 40 (6), pp. 708-716
29. Smith, D. One small step for EU Parliament could prove one giant leap for data protection. ICO. At. http://ico.org.uk/news/blog/2013/one-small-step-for-eu-parliament (accessed 13.03.14)
30. The Security Cards. At http://securitycards.cs.washington.edu/index.html
31. C-131/12 Google Spain v AEPD and Mario Costeja Gonzalez
32. US Federal Trade Commission, Protecting Consumer Privacy in an Era of Rapid Change: Recommendations for Businesses and Policymakers, 2012 pp. 22-32
33. Yeung K. Design for Regulation in J van Den Hoven et al (Eds) *Handbook of Ethics, Values and Technological Design*, Springer, 2014

Crowdsourced Exploration of Security Configurations

Qatrunnada Ismail[†] **Tousif Ahmed**[†] **Apu Kapadia**[†] **Michael K. Reiter**[‡]
[†]School of Informatics and Computing
Indiana University Bloomington
Bloomington, IN, USA
[‡]Department of Computer Science
University of North Carolina
Chapel Hill, NC, USA
{qismail, touahmed, kapadia}@indiana.edu, reiter@cs.unc.edu

ABSTRACT
Smartphone apps today request permission to access a multitude of sensitive resources, which users must accept completely during installation (e.g., on Android) or selectively configure after installation (e.g., on iOS, but also planned for Android). Everyday users, however, do not have the ability to make informed decisions about which permissions are essential for their usage. For enhanced privacy, we seek to leverage crowdsourcing to find minimal sets of permissions that will preserve the usability of the app for diverse users.

We advocate an efficient 'lattice-based' crowd-management strategy to explore the space of permissions sets. We conducted a user study ($N = 26$) in which participants explored different permission sets for the popular Instagram app. This study validates our efficient crowd management strategy and shows that usability scores for diverse users can be predicted accurately, enabling suitable recommendations.

Author Keywords
Android apps; crowdsourcing; permissions; privacy

ACM Classification Keywords
H.5.m Information interfaces and presentation (e.g., HCI): Miscellaneous; D.4.6 Software: Security and Protection—*Access Control*

INTRODUCTION
Users of mobile devices such as smartphones and tablets are able to install apps from online marketplaces that feature millions of apps.[1] These apps can potentially access various sensors (e.g., accelerometer, microphone, GPS, and camera) and user data (e.g., contact information and photos). In general, it is difficult for the operating system (such as Android or iOS) to ascertain whether an app is making legitimate or nefarious uses of the sensors or data. Instead, during the installation of an app, the Android operating system displays all the requested permissions, which the user either approves or denies as shown in Figure 1a. On iOS, users initially install apps and then are able to selectively enable or disable privacy sensitive permissions as shown in Figure 1b. Google has been experimenting with a similar feature ("App Ops") that allows users to selectively disable specific permissions, but it has not yet been released officially.[2]

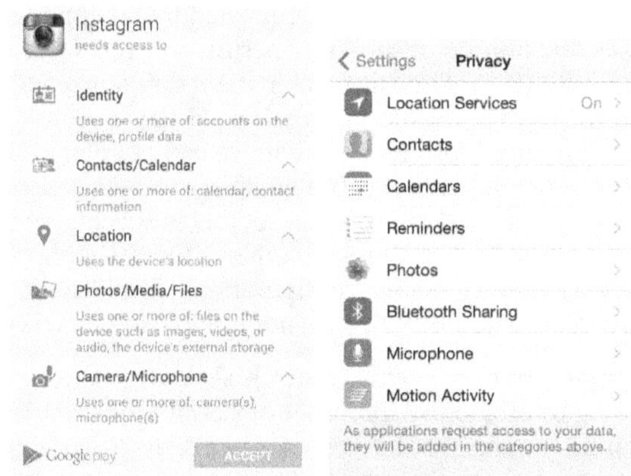

(a) Android (b) iOS

Figure 1. Control panels related to application permissions.

Ideally users would determine the fewest permissions needed for an app to support their regular usage of the app (i.e., the 'principle of least privilege' [14]). For example, Angry Birds requests access to location, but may work well for most users if access to location is disabled. While several research proposals have been made to allow more granular control or detect anomalous uses of such sensors (Bugiel et al. [2] provide a comprehensive overview of related work on Android OS security), it remains unclear how users can decide which permissions are useful for the functioning of the app. Felt et al. [4] proposed an automated technique to determine which permissions are *not* used by an app, but they did not address the relative importance of each permission that *is* used by the app. While users can provide feedback through ratings and comments on App marketplaces like Apple's App Store and the Google Play Store, no feedback or ratings are available on various *configurations* (i.e., with various combinations of

[1]`http://www.appbrain.com/stats/number-of-android-apps/, http://toucharcade.com/2014/06/02/new-ios-8-app-store-features/`

[2]`https://www.eff.org/deeplinks/2013/12/google-removes-vital-privacy-features-android-shortly-after-adding-them/`

CHI 2015, Apr 18–23, 2015, Seoul, Republic of Korea
ACM 978-1-4503-3145-6/15/04. http://dx.doi.org/10.1145/2702123.2702370

permissions disabled) of the app. Indeed, there are too many possible configurations of an app, and it is not clear if it feasible to provide meaningful feedback about all configurations.

We advocate a crowdsourced approach that leverages humans to efficiently assess various security configurations for an app and identify app configurations that strike tradeoffs between privacy and usability suitable to each user. After gaining familiarity with an app, each crowd member would volunteer to utilize a small number of configurations for that app over a test period. Based on the usability scores of configurations given by a specific user, similar crowd members would be identified and then used to recommend configurations suitable to that user. We envision that our system can be easily integrated into popular app marketplaces such as the Apple App Store and the Google Play Store. Instead of rating only one configuration of an app, smartphone users would test and rate different configurations of apps. Then our system would recommend appropriate configurations to users based on their similarities to other users in the marketplace, i.e., the crowd.

The proposed approach, however, poses challenges. First, as the number n of permissions requested by an application increases, the number of possible permission sets increases exponentially (2^n). Thus a scalable approach is needed to collaboratively explore the permission space. Second, even if these configurations can be collaboratively explored, it is not clear whether suitable recommendations can be made to a diverse set of users. A permission set that is acceptable to some users may not be acceptable to others. Finally, unobtrusively deploying and assessing configurations would benefit from measures of 'usability' that do not involve user intervention.

Research questions. This research seeks to leverage crowdsourcing to efficiently find a set of permissions for each user installing an app that strikes an acceptable balance between app usability and user privacy (by finding the permissions that are infrequently used by users or permissions that users do not mind losing). More specifically, we seek to answer the following research questions:

R1: *Can we use crowdsourcing scalably to explore security configurations of an app?* Using crowdsourcing, we seek to obtain users' perspectives on the usability of the app when certain combinations of permissions are disabled. Based on the intuition that usability scores cannot generally increase when additional permissions are removed, we develop a 'lattice-based' approach to prune the search space of permission sets and evaluate its efficacy.

R2: *Can we recommend suitable permission sets based on the crowd's ratings?* We would like to predict the suitability of various app configurations for users based on ratings obtained from the crowd (other users). In particular we explore whether collaborative filtering can be used to make such predictions effectively.

R3: *What proxies can be used to determine the usability of an app without asking users for ratings explicitly?* We seek to find if we can ascertain the 'usability' of an app in automated ways, such as measuring the time spent by a user using an app or logging any problems s/he encounters. Automated measures require fewer user interruptions and so could permit a less obtrusive exploration of the state space.

Our contributions. Before the suggested crowdsourcing strategy can be applied in general, we seek to validate our lattice-based approach and the viability of making accurate predictions of usability scores. As a first step, we perform a user study ($N = 26$) on one specific, but popular, app (Instagram). Participants tried different configurations of this app in which each configuration had specific permissions removed. Participants reported their feedback about each configuration and answered exit surveys at the end of the study.

We found that: 1) as more permissions were removed, the reported usability scores dropped (or did not increase) significantly, validating the lattice-based approach; 2) based on usability scores given by the crowd, we can predict participants' individual ratings for various subsets of permissions, and thus make suitable recommendations; and 3) to measure usability, instead of asking users for explicit feedback, other attributes such as the usage time of an app and the number of problems encountered are suitable proxies for usability.

RELATED WORK

Crowdsourcing

Crowdsourcing has been used in many studies related to Android privacy and security. Amini et al. [1] developed AppScanner, which analyzes and learns application behaviors to find privacy-related issues. In their crowdsourcing step, they ask users for their reactions to behaviors uncovered by their tool. Crowdsourcing was also used by Lin et al. [10] to capture users' expectations about privacy-related behaviors of Android applications. They used their findings to design a technique to inform Android users about the way permissions are used by an application. However, it may not be clear to users how removing certain permissions may affect the usability of the app. In our crowdsourcing step, instead of only asking users about their *expectations*, we provide them with different configurations of applications (with different permissions removed) and get users' feedback based on their *experience* with those configurations.

Studying the Effects of Permission Removal

Since users do not have fine-grained control over what specific permissions they grant apps in Android, researchers have proposed systems to give users the ability to do so. For example, Nauman et al. [12] modified Android with an advanced application installer that enables users to allow or deny each individual permission requested at installation. Rather than asking users to evaluate permissions at installation, we instead ask them to evaluate an application with selected permissions disabled. We then use their feedback as a basis for performing collaborative filtering to benefit other users. Moreover, our method of disabling permissions does not modify Android.

There are also studies about the effects on applications' performance after removing permissions. Notably, Kennedy et al. [9] proposed a system that removes permissions from Android applications to determine which removed permissions cause the app to crash. Their system, however, focuses on an automated process for evaluating the run-time effects of removing permissions and does not assess the impact on users based on real-world usage, as we do.

App Ops, a feature in Android v4.3, allowed users to selectively disable permissions for apps on their phones. However, Google removed this feature in the next update, reporting that it was experimental and could cause apps to behave in unexpected ways. For our approach, we assume the apps being explored have reasonable exception handling. We expect that App Ops-like functionality will eventually be released for Android (as it is already available in iOS) and that most apps will handle permissions restrictions gracefully.

Users' Perspectives about Permissions

Felt et al. [5, 6] and Kelly et al. [7] showed that the current way of displaying permissions is not clear to users and not effective at informing them about the potential risks of installing an app. Kelly et al. [8] thus proposed a more effective way to display the permissions and found it to be helpful for users to make better decisions with respect to their privacy. Rather than asking users directly if they think a specific permission is needed, we let users test app configurations with some permissions removed and report their feedback. We expect a combination of these approaches would be useful, whereby useful suggestions through crowdsourcing can improve information provided in the installation interface.

Collaborative Filtering

Recommender systems are used to predict ratings and to create personal recommendations in various domains. By applying statistical methods and knowledge discovery techniques, it is possible to recommend products based on user preferences [15]. Collaborative filtering is a recommendation technique that is used for predicting a user's ratings for unknown products based on the user's previous ratings and aggregating other (similar) users' ratings. Two common techniques for collaborative filtering are 'user-based' collaborative filtering and 'item-based' collaborative filtering. In user-based collaborative filtering, a user's rating for any particular item is predicted from ratings by similar users for that item [13]. In item-based collaborative filtering, ratings for an item are predicted from ratings for similar items [16]. In this paper, we incorporate the idea of user-based collaborative filtering into the mobile app privacy domain and use it for predicting the suitability of various permission sets.

APPROACH

In this section, we describe our proposed crowdsourcing approach, usability metrics, and recommender system. Moreover, we present the hypotheses that we test in our user study.

Lattice Based Approach for Crowd Management

We propose an approach whereby crowd members strategically explore the various permission sets of an app in a way that is scalable with the number of permissions requested by the app. Our main hypothesis here is that as the set of permissions removed grows, the 'usability' of the app does not increase. (We defer the discussion about how exactly we measure 'usability' to the next subsection.) Intuitively, if a set of permissions is made more restrictive, we expect the number of features of the app to also be reduced and thus result in a lower or equal rating.[3] For example, if a user thinks that a specific app is unusable when location permission is removed, s/he is likely to think the same (or worse) if the location and camera permissions are removed together. This intuition suggests an approach of a structured exploration of the permission space as we formalize next.

The permission space can be represented by a lattice structure. Consider a lattice structure as shown in Figure 2 for an app that requests four permissions. The nodes in the lattice represent the sets of *removed* permissions. The null vertex represents the original app where there are no permissions removed, so it is not shown in the figure. Each level in the lattice going upwards represents an increasing number of permissions removed. So, the first level represents nodes with one permission removed, the second level has nodes with two permissions removed, and so on.

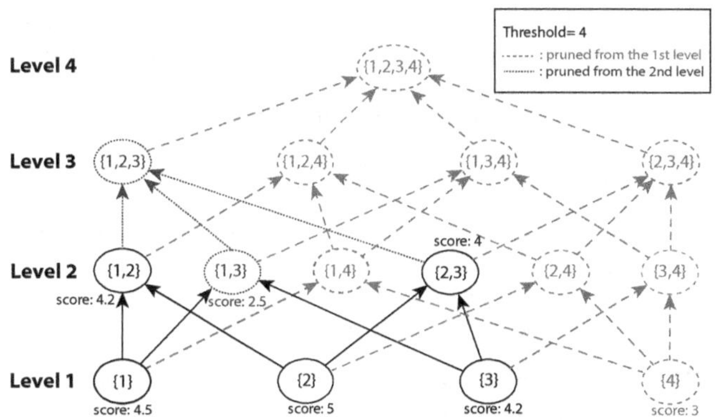

Figure 2. The lattice structure where each node represents specific permissions that are removed.

We suggest the following crowd-based exploration strategy: First, the crowd explores the first level in the lattice and the average usability score is calculated for each node. If the scores of any of these nodes fall below a certain threshold, their ancestors can be pruned and not explored because the scores are expected to be non-increasing. For example, if we consider the lattice in Figure 2, after testing all four nodes in the first level, the node $\{4\}$ has a score below the threshold. So, we prune all of this node's ancestors. This leaves us with fewer nodes to test as we proceed upwards. After testing the nodes $\{1,2\}$,$\{1,3\}$ and $\{2,3\}$, we may find that the average score for $\{1,3\}$ falls below the threshold, so we prune its ancestor $\{1,2,3\}$. This approach enables us to explore the

[3]Of course, this is not true as a rule. For example, removing one permission alone might cause the app to consistently crash, though in addition removing a second permission might prevent the app from ever attempting to use the first (and so from crashing). Though an artificial example, it shows that removing permissions need not monotonically decay the usability of the app. That said, recall that we assume apps will handle the removal of permissions gracefully; presumably this should already be true for iOS apps and will increasingly become so for Android apps once App Ops is (re)released.

permission space efficiently and find suitable configurations of permissions based on the crowd's reports, i.e., nodes {1,2} and {2,3} in our example. This technique can be more efficient than exploring the whole space, especially when the number n of permissions is large.

Before this strategy can be applied in practice, it is important to ascertain whether the presumed lattice-based relationship of usability scores holds. As a first step, we evaluate the following hypothesis for a specific application (Instagram):

H1: The usability scores of the nodes in the lattice are non-increasing as we proceed upwards in the lattice and remove more permissions.

Measuring Usability

In this paper we use the term "usability" to refer to how 'acceptable' users consider an application to be when some of its advertised functionality has been intentionally restricted. We obtain this 'ground truth' information by asking participants about their level of acceptance of using a configuration of the app (until the next major app update) with specific features disabled. We also ask them to rate the different configurations compared to the original app in which no permissions are removed. In our envisioned crowdsourcing system, we seek to measure the usability of an app indirectly without user intervention by using indirect measures that can serve as a proxy for usability. Those measures include the time spent using an app and whether there are problems found while using it.

Therefore, we have the hypotheses mentioned below. We also test whether the 'ratings' provided by users agree with the 'acceptability' scores (lending validity to using 'acceptability' as a ground-truth measure):

H2: Under the assumption that the original app is perceived as usable by users, a user's rating of a customized configuration of the app as better or worse than the original is a good predictor for the whether the user finds the customized configuration acceptable.

H3: The time spent using a customized configuration of the app can be used as a proxy to measure its usability. This means that participants who use a particular configuration longer than another configuration find the former configuration more acceptable.

H4: Whether users find problems in a customized configuration of an app can be used as a proxy to measure its usability. Participants who identify more problems in a configuration of an app will rate it as less usable than a configuration for an app where fewer problems are encountered.

Recommender System

Our goal is to leverage the crowd-based exploration of the permission subsets to recommend a suitable one for a particular user. We advocate a 'user-based collaborative filtering' approach [13] to recommend permission subsets to users based on their similarity (of ratings) to other users in the crowd.

The user-based collaborative filtering computes the predicted ratings for user $u \in U$ on all 'items' $\in I$ where the items represent permission subsets that u did not try. The algorithm first identifies the most similar users to u based on similarity in their ratings for the common items that they have tried. Those users are denoted by *k-nearest neighbors* where k is the number of those similar users. The predicted rating for user u on any item $j \in I$ is then computed as [3]:

$$p_{u,j} = \bar{r}_u + \frac{\sum_{v \in \text{Neighbors}(u)} s(u,v)(r_{v,j} - \bar{r}_v)}{\sum_{v \in \text{Neighbors}(u)} |s(u,v)|}$$

where $\bar{r}_u$ is the mean rating for user u (across all items rated by that user), Neighbors(u) is the list of u's similar users, $r_{v,j}$ is the usability rating of user v for permission set j (a positive integer in our case), and $s(u,v)$ is the 'similarity' between user u and his neighbor v. This formula calculates the difference between each neighbor v's rating for item j and v's mean rating for all items, takes the weighted mean of this difference across neighbors (using a similarity measure as the weight), and then applies this difference to u's mean rating. We give an example in the Findings section (see Table 3).

The similarity measure $s(u,v)$ can be computed, e.g., using the 'cosine similarity' of the users' rating vectors, which is shown in the formula bellow. $\mathbf{r}_u$ and $\mathbf{r}_v$ are users' u and v ratings vectors and the unknown ratings are replaced by 0.

$$s(u,v) = \frac{\mathbf{r}_u \cdot \mathbf{r}_v}{\|\mathbf{r}_u\| \, \|\mathbf{r}_v\|} = \frac{\sum_{i=1}^{n} r_{u,i} r_{v,i}}{\sqrt{\sum_{i=1}^{n} r_{u,i}^2}\sqrt{\sum_{i=1}^{n} r_{v,i}^2}}$$

We propose a specialized approach based on the lattice structure. For example, we may want to recommend as restrictive a permission set as possible (higher up in the lattice, which means enhanced privacy) as long as the usability score does not fall below a certain threshold. Furthermore, the lattice-based structure can be leveraged to improve the accuracy of our predictions given the relationship between nodes in the lattice. As hypothesized in H1, as we remove more permissions, the usability scores of the apps are non-increasing. So, if the predicted score of any node in the lattice is greater than any of its children scores, we set the predicted score for that node to the minimum score of the children nodes. For example, as we can see from the lattice depicted in Figure 2, node $\{1,2\}$ has two children $\{1\}$ and $\{2\}$. If the predicted score for node $\{1,2\}$ is 5.5, our algorithm sets it to 4.5 which is the minimum score of node $\{1\} = 4.5$ and $\{2\} = 5$. We refer to this approach as the "clamping technique", since the recommended score is clamped to the highest value allowable by the user's own scores in the lattice.

We evaluate how accurately the suggested collaborative filtering approach can be used to predict usability scores for users, and thus the viability of a crowdsourcing-based approach for identifying configurations of applications that balance usability and privacy for individual users.

STUDY METHODOLOGY

System Implementation

To answer our research questions, we conducted a user study in which we focused on Instagram, which is a popular social networking and photo/video sharing Android app. Throughout the paper, we refer to Instagram as the "test app". In the study, participants installed an Android app called "the ratings app", to provide them with different configurations of the test app and collect their feedback on each configuration.

Choice of the test app. The test app, Instagram, is a photo/video sharing and social networking app. We chose this specific app because it is one of the popular free Android apps in the Google Play store. Besides being popular, the test app requests several permissions categorized as "dangerous" (according to Android's classification),[4] providing access to sensitive user data such as their location and the camera. As permissions in Android apps are divided into four different levels depending on their risk level, we focus on the permissions in the 'dangerous' level. Permissions on this category are displayed to users upon installation of an app and need to be approved to complete the installation process [5]. In our study, we focused on four such permissions providing access to: (1) location, (2) contacts, (3) camera, and (4) microphone.

Customization of the test app for exploration. We used the Android-apktool[5] to unpack the test app's Android application package file (apk file) and access the app's manifest file. The manifest file includes the list of requested permissions. We then created different customized configurations of the test app by removing one or more permissions from the manifest file and then recompiling and repackaging the apk files. We did not have access to the the test app's code itself, and we made no modifications to the application code.

We created all possible configurations of the app by removing one or more of the four permissions listed above. This gave us a total of 15 customized configurations of the test app. The configurations are shown in Figure 4.

The ratings app. When participants installed the ratings app on their phones, they were prompted to install one of the customized configurations of the test app after they removed the original app. After installing a customized configuration of the test app, participants had two days to use it; a timer displayed the time left to request the next configuration of the test app as shown in Figure 3. Also, participants were allowed to ask for a different configuration of the test app at any time before the timer ended, but with a $0.50 deduction from their overall compensation. Moreover, the amount of money earned in the study was displayed by the ratings app as shown in Figure 3. As such, our compensation scheme (described in more detail in the Study Procedure Section) motivated participants to think carefully before requesting a new configuration.

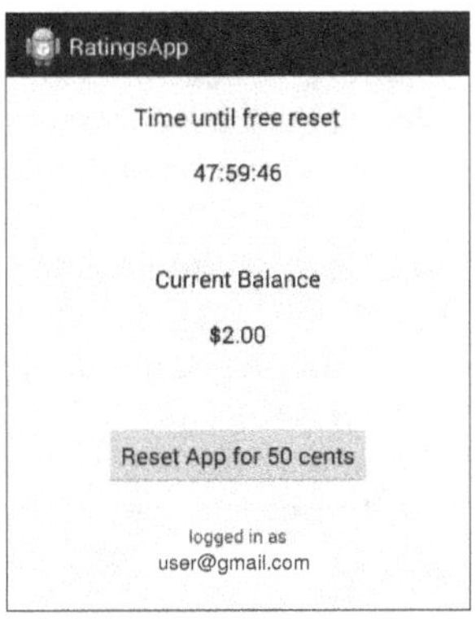

Figure 3. The ratings app home screen

[4]`http://developer.android.com/guide/topics/manifest/permission-element.html`

[5]`https://code.google.com/p/android-apktool/`

Collecting participants' feedback. At the end of the two-day period for exploring a configuration of the test app, participants received notifications to both their phones and email to remind them to visit the ratings app and request the next configuration of the test app. When participants requested a new configuration by clicking on the reset button, a survey dialog sought their feedback about the configuration that they just used. The survey questions are shown in the Appendix, which we summarize here:

Q1. We asked participants about whether they encountered problems in the configuration they just used.

Q2. We listed the disabled features (based on the removed permissions) and asked participants to rate, on a 7-point Likert scale, how acceptable they found this configuration (if they had to use it until the next major app update).

Q3. We asked participants to rate the test app's configuration compared to the original one in which there were no permissions removed.

Q4. We asked participants to estimate the amount of time they used that configuration of the test app.

After answering the questionnaire, participants were given a different configuration of the test app and the timer was reset.

Back-end. When participants asked for a different configuration of the test app, the ratings app connected to a remote server in which participants' answers to the questionnaire described above were recorded and a customized configuration of the test app was retrieved. One of the customized configurations was chosen at random while making sure that it was not previously used by the requesting participant. We also set a threshold for the number of times that each configuration was tested to make sure that we did not end up with some configurations used much more than others. Moreover, to make sure that participants actually used the provided configuration of the test app, the Ratings App kept track of whenever participants used the test app on their phones. This information was recorded at the back-end.

Design Rationale

Minimizing learning effects. The collaborative filtering approach generates recommendations by analyzing multiple ratings from each participant. Thus we needed each participant to test multiple app configurations, as they would in a real system. To minimize learning effects due to repeated exploration by the same participant, we randomized the app configurations, and their order, tested by each participant. Thus participants could not predict whether subsequent configurations would be more (or less) restrictive, and which permissions would be removed.

Managing participant workload. In collaborative filtering, more ratings from a single user generally produce better recommendations for that user (e.g., getting better movie recommendations from Netflix as the viewer watches and rates more movies). We did not want to induce fatigue in our participants (e.g., assigning too many configurations to each participant) and wanted to ensure that participants had enough time to explore each configuration to make an informed decision. Based on a pilot study with two undergraduate students, we determined that 5 configurations over 10 days was a reasonable workload to meet both goals, and we devised a compensation scheme as discussed in the next section based on this workload. We note that in our exit survey, 20 out of 26 participants said they felt they had enough time to explore each of their assigned configurations.

Study Procedure

Enrollment. Participants were required to be at least 18 years old, to have lived in the United States for at least five years, to have an Android phone with a data plan, and to already be using Instagram. Qualified participants reported to our lab to enroll in the study. They were informed of the purpose and process of the study. After consenting, participants installed the ratings app. We provided two demo configurations of the test app, allowing participants to familiarize themselves with the ratings app and the study process. We then instructed the participants to contact us after completing the study.

Ethical considerations. Our study was IRB-approved, and Indiana University's General Counsel approved our modification of Instagram's manifest file based on a 'Fair Use' analysis of its license agreement.

End of study questionnaire. At the end of the study, participants were given a questionnaire that asked for their technical backgrounds, demographics, and feedback. It also included questions related to assessing privacy attitudes.

Compensation and incentive scheme. Study participants were paid up to $25 upon the completion of the study. The study was designed to last approximately 10 days and participants earned $2 per day. However, this amount could be affected in the following situations:

- If the participant was supposed to reset the test app at the end of the two-day period but did not do so for a whole day, s/he did not earn the $2 for that day. We used this as an incentive to motivate participants to continue trying different configurations of the test app throughout the study.
- If the participant reset the test app before the end of the two-day period in which s/he was to use the test app, $0.50 was deducted from his/her overall balance. We used this penalty to make participants think twice about whether the current configuration was tolerable. So, if a participant was trying to use a feature that had been disabled, whether s/he asked for a new configuration and lost $0.50 or waited depended on how important this feature was to him/her.

At the end of the study, if no money was deducted from the participant's balance, s/he earned $20. An extra $5 was added if s/he answered the end-of-study questionnaire, which resulted in a maximum compensation of $25.

FINDINGS

Participants

We recruited our participants from Bloomington, IN, USA (a college town that is home to Indiana University) by using flyers, online university classifieds advertisements, and student mailing lists. The study lasted for two months (Feb–Mar 2014). Overall, 30 participants enrolled in our study, 4 of

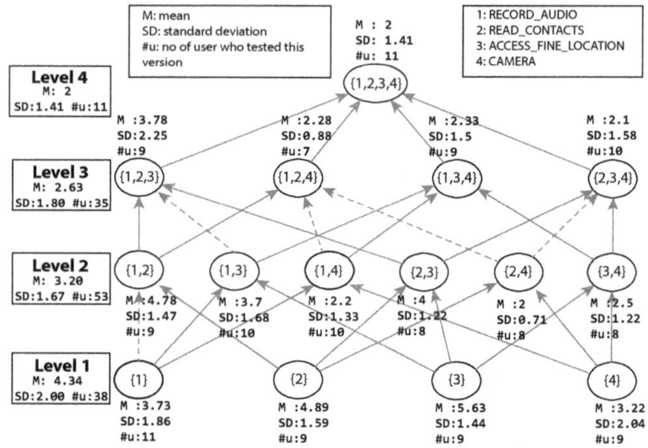

Figure 4. The lattice structure where each node represents specific removed permissions. The red arrows indicate slight increases in scores which are not statistically significant.

which did not complete the study (testing fewer than 5 configurations) so we removed their ratings. Therefore, in our analysis, we considered the 26 participants who finished the study and we ended up with a total of 137 ratings. In our sample, most of the participants (22 participants) tested 5 configurations of the test app, 3 participants tested 6 configurations and 1 participant tested 9. For the participant who tested 9, he/she repeatedly received a configuration with the camera permission removed and thus requested more configurations than most. Each configuration of the test app was rated by at least 8 participants and at most 11 participants.

Among these 26 participants, 15 were females (57.7%) and 11 were males (42.3%). All but one were students. Seven (26.9%) were Informatics or Computer Science majors, while the rest came from diverse, non-technical majors.

Analysis of the Lattice Structure

Figure 4 shows the average acceptance score (M), standard deviation (SD), and number of participants (#u) per test app configuration as well as aggregated per level in the lattice. Our main hypothesis about the acceptance scores (as a usability measure)—i.e., that they are generally not increasing as we remove more permissions—is evidenced in Figure 4.

Figure 5 also shows that as we remove more permissions, the acceptance scores tend to decrease or stay the same. The big circles in Figure 5 indicate whether the participant encountered a problem or not (Q1 in the survey).

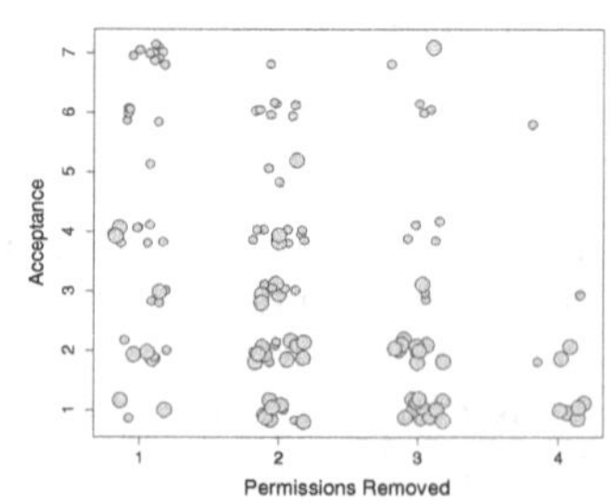

Figure 5. Scatter plot showing the effects on acceptance scores as we remove more permissions.

To test our first hypothesis (H1), we considered using a multi-level model such as the linear mixed effects model which takes into account the effects of having users contributing multiple data points. However, the homoscedasticity assumption is violated in our data because the variances of the acceptance scores of different permission subsets are not equal; therefore, we used non-parametric tests. Our conclusions hold using both the linear mixed effects model and the non-parametric tests but we report the latter because they are typically more conservative, making fewer assumptions.

We first ran a Kruskal-Wallis test, which is a non-parametric one-way (single factor) ANOVA. This test shows if there is a statistically significant difference between variables but it does not provide information about the nature of the difference (increase or decrease). To examine the difference, we ran a follow-up post hoc test. We ran the non-parametric version of the t-test called the Wilcoxon rank-sum test and since this is a post-hoc test that involves multiple comparisons, we used the Benjamini-Hochberg method to adjust the p-values from the test to control the false discovery rate. The result of Kruskal-Wallis test ($\chi^2 = 21.48$, df $= 3$, $p < 0.001$) indicates that there is significant difference in participants' acceptance scores due to the number of permissions removed. The results of the Wilcoxon rank-sum post-hoc test are shown in Table 1 where the parameter W and the p-value assess the significance of the difference (the decrease) between the variables (# of permissions removed).

Table 1 shows that as more permissions are removed, the acceptance scores decline significantly until 4 permissions are removed (at which point there is no significant difference in the scores compared to removing 3 permissions). This means that as we go from level 3 to 4, the acceptance values are neither increasing nor decreasing significantly. One reason could be that we have few data points for level 4, where we have only one node compared to the other levels. Given that the significant difference between levels indicates a significant decrease, we can reject the null hypothesis and accept our first hypothesis (H1) that the acceptance scores are non-increasing as we remove more permissions.

Comparison of # permissions removed	W	p-value	Adjusted p-value
1 vs. 2	1336.0	0.009**	0.015*
1 vs. 3	990.0	< 0.001***	0.002**
1 vs. 4	349.0	0.001**	0.002**
2 vs. 3	1143.0	0.024*	0.029*
2 vs. 4	423.5	0.017*	0.025*
3 vs. 4	233.5	0.275	0.275

Statistical significance: *** $p < 0.001$, ** $p < 0.01$, * $p < 0.05$

Table 1. Wilcoxon rank-sum results for the statistical significance of the decrease in acceptance scores as we remove more permissions.

In addition to the Kruskal-Wallis test, we performed a correlation analysis using Spearman's Rank Coefficient, which measures the tendency for two variables to increase or decrease together. While the p-value tells us the significance of the correlation between the variables, ρ tells us whether the variables are monotonically increasing or decreasing and the degree of monotonicity. Testing the acceptance score versus the number of permissions removed, we found a significant negative relationship ($\rho = -0.39$, $p < 0.001$), indicating that as more permissions are removed, the participants' acceptance scores decline; this supports the results of the previous test.

Special cases. Though we have shown that the acceptance scores are non-increasing as we move upward in the lattice, there are some exceptions in our data, shown by dashed red edges in Figure 4. However, based on Wilcoxon rank-sum tests, these increases are not significant ($p > 0.05$).

Lattice pruning approach. As this is an exploratory study, we focused on four permissions to be able to explore all subsets of permissions (all nodes in the lattice). We thus could test whether we can use the proposed pruning strategy on the lattice instead of testing all nodes in the lattice individually. Based on our questionnaire, an acceptability score of 4 can be chosen as the usability threshold, which means any node with acceptance value below 4 is not acceptable and thus its ancestors can be pruned. While we have tested only one specific app, these results point to the viability of a lattice-based approach for crowd management. This particular lattice suggests that configurations that disable access to {contacts}, {location}, and {contacts, location} are promising configurations that trade off usability and privacy for Instagram. Moreover, after the first level, only the {contacts, location} configuration would have been explored by the strategy.

Rating and Acceptance Scores

In the Methodology section, we summarized the survey questions that we asked participants after using each configuration of the test app. While in Q2 we asked about the participant's acceptance of using the app knowing that specific features were disabled, in Q3 we asked participants to rate the used configuration compared to the original app. Both questions measure, in different ways, how much participants like the app they used. Our data indicates that there is agreement between the two variables which means that the higher the rating, the higher the acceptance score. We used Spearman's Rank Correlation test to see if acceptance level (Q2) can substitute for rating (Q3) in analyses (hypothesis H2). We found a statistically significant positive relationship between the variables ($\rho = 0.84$, $p < 0.001$), and so we can accept H2.

Usability Proxies

To test our hypotheses regarding whether proxies can be used to indirectly determine the usability/acceptability of an app, we analyzed the relationships among the other variables and the acceptance score. Those variables are the time that participants reported using a specific configuration of the app and whether participants found a problem related to the disabled permissions in the app. Those variables correspond to survey questions Q4 and Q1. Figure 6a shows the relationship between the acceptance score (y-axis) and the total usage time (x-axis), and Figure 6b shows the relationship between the acceptance score (y-axis) and whether participants found a problem or not (x-axis). We can see in the figures that participants who reported using the app as much or more than the original app (total usage values 2 and 3) tended to give higher acceptance scores than those who reported using it less (total

Variable		Spearman's Rank Test		Wilcoxon Rank-Sum Test	
Dependent	Independent	ρ	p-value	W	p-value
Acceptance (Q2)	Usage (Q4)	0.47	< 0.001***	993	< 0.001***
Acceptance (Q2)	Problem (Q1)	−0.64	< 0.001***	4290	< 0.001***
Usage (Q4)	Problem (Q1)	−0.49	< 0.001***	3619	< 0.001***

Statistical significance: *** p < 0.001, ** p < 0.01, * p < 0.05

Table 2. Statistical significance results of the relationship between the other usability proxies.

usage value 1). Also, finding a problem affected the scores negatively and caused participants to give lower acceptance scores.

To test the significance of these findings, we ran both the Wilcoxon rank-sum and Spearman's Rank Coefficient tests. The results (Table 2) suggest significant relationships between the variables. The first row indicates a significant positive relationship between the usage time and acceptance score, i.e., the higher the usage time, the higher the acceptance score. The second row shows a negative relationship: whenever participants encountered problems, the acceptance scores declined. Since both relationships are statistically significant ($p < 0.001$), we can accept both H3 and H4.

Moreover, we analyzed the relationship between the usage time and finding a problem as shown in Figure 6c. We found a negative significant relationship between them as shown in the last row of Table 2. This indicates that whenever a problem was encountered, the usage time declined significantly.

Predicting User Ratings

We tested the collaborative filtering algorithm described earlier on 137 ratings from 26 participants who, on average, rated five configurations of the test app. We used the acceptance score, which was recorded on a 7-point Likert scale, as the usability measure. To calculate accuracy, we iteratively considered one of the participants' ratings as unknown and tried to predict it. Then we compared the predicted rating with the known (ground-truth) rating, specifically calculating the mean absolute error (MAE) and root mean square error (RMSE) of the collaborative filtering algorithm.

Before presenting our results, we first provide a concrete example from our dataset. Table 3 shows ratings for one participant ('active user') for whom the rating for node {1,2} is being predicted. The 'Actual' column shows the participant's actual ratings for various configurations, including the rating for {1,2} in parentheses, which is treated as the ground truth. In the 'Nearest Neighbors' column, we show the ratings of the two closest neighbors of the active user based on their cosine similarity of the rating vectors with the active user. Note that this metric normalizes participants' scores, and so Neighbor 1 is close to the active user despite having generally higher scores. The last column of Table 3 shows the predicted rating for node $\{1,2\}$. The predicted rating accounts for variations in the average ratings for individual users and in this case results in a prediction of 3.97. Applying the clamping technique, we set the prediction to 3 because 3.97 is greater than the rating value for the child node $\{1\}$ in the lattice structure. In this example clamping yields better results.

Node	Nearest Neighbors		Active User	
	Neighbor 1	Neighbor 2	Actual	Prediction
$\{1\}$	7	3	3	
$\{2\}$	6			
$\{4\}$		1		
$\{1,2\}$	6	4	? (2)	3
$\{1,3\}$	3		3	
$\{2,4\}$		2	2	
$\{3,4\}$	2			
$\{1,3,4\}$		2		
$\{2,3,4\}$			1	

Table 3. Example of the prediction algorithm

# of Nearest Neighbors	Actual		Clamping	
	MAE	RMSE	MAE	RMSE
1	1.402	2.098	1.312	1.974
2	1.375	2.072	1.301	1.987
3	1.317	1.968	1.250	1.896
4	1.301	1.925	1.236	1.845
5	1.285	1.894	1.222	1.820
6	1.273	1.872	1.207	1.794

Table 4. Accuracy of the prediction algorithm

The accuracy of our prediction is shown in Table 4. Based on our data set, we can predict the ratings using up to six nearest neighbors; for more than six neighbors the accuracy does not improve significantly. We can see that the MAE decreases as the number of neighbors increases. We anticipate that if we have larger data set then we can increase the number of nearest neighbors, which may result in better MAE and RMSE.

We compared the accuracy of our predictions with the grand average (mean of all ratings) (MAE=1.63, RMSE=2.13), and item averages (mean of each item's ratings) (MAE=1.397, RMSE=1.925). Our algorithm with the clamping technique performs better than both baselines. Thus we conclude that collaborative filtering presents a viable approach for predicting the acceptability of different permission sets for this app, and is suitable for recommending acceptable configurations to users for various privacy levels (e.g., predicting scores for this app with multiple permissions removed).

DISCUSSION AND LIMITATIONS

We now discuss the limitations of our study and directions for future work.

Sample size. Our study's size (26 participants) was adequate to test various hypotheses with statistical significance but precluded others. For example, we wanted to study whether privacy attitudes affected usability scores and could be used to improve recommendations. We hope to study such effects in a larger study, possibly by recruiting participants online.

Population. We leveraged a local population since our experiment involved an in-person visit to our lab for installation of the ratings app and training, which we thought was prudent to ensure understanding of our compensation scheme. As a re-

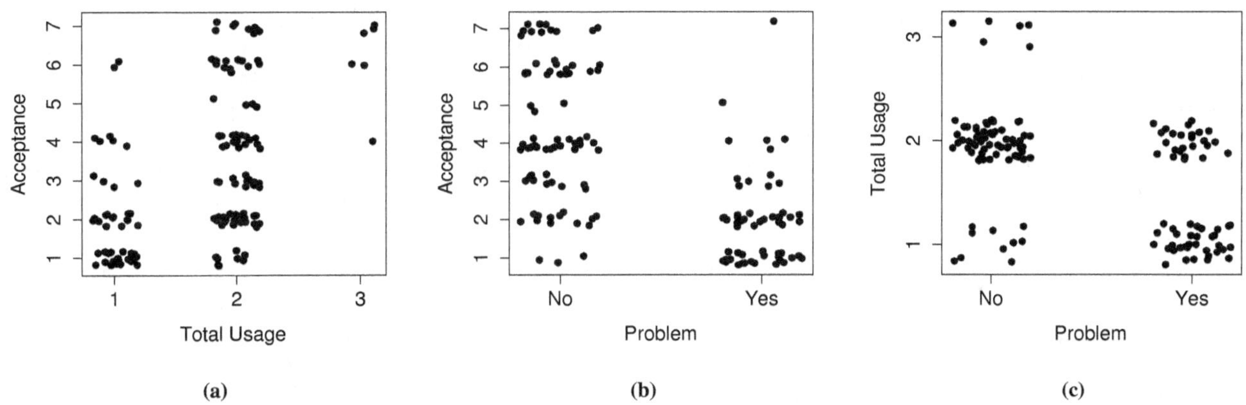

Figure 6. Scatter plots showing the relationships between the other usability proxies a) total usage time and acceptance scores, b) finding a problem in the app and acceptance scores, and c) finding a problem and total usage time.

sult, all participants but one were university students. While our results do not extend to the general population, only 25% of our participants were technical majors and thus our sample was diverse in this sense. Future work may investigate if age is an important factor and, if so, examine crowdsourced exploration based on age groups.

Scalable exploration of different apps. Our study involved only one app (Instagram), which limits the generalizability of our findings. In the future we would like to compare results across various classes of apps such as social media, games, and utilities. While we expect the general pruning strategy to work (based on H1), the lattice may be very large for some apps. To improve scalability, we may monitor which permissions are utilized by the user under normal operation (for example, using the approach by Felt et al. [4]), and then use our crowdsourced approach for subsets relevant to those permissions. Another possibility is to structure the exploration of an app based on knowledge gained from the exploration of another app. If similar users have already been identified, these users can be tasked to explore more diverse configurations, as common configurations are expected to add less information.

Installation process. On Android, users can view the permissions requested by an app during installation. Whether a participant read these permissions was unknown to us, thus possibly introducing a confound where not all participants were aware of the permission set and so were biased differently in their assessments. So, we ordered the survey questions such that participants were first asked to report any problems encountered in the app (Q1) and then informed of the removed permissions and asked to rate the app (Q2). Participants thus reflected upon their actual usage of the app immediately before rating it. Our analysis shows a strong correlation between the problems participants encountered with configurations and their ratings for those configurations, thus indicating their ratings were based largely on their experience.

Incentivizing the crowd. We envision our approach integrated into popular App marketplaces where app ratings can be enhanced to show the top recommended configurations for users. Though recruiting and motivating crowd participation to rate apps with some permissions disabled is not our focus in this paper, we expect that the reciprocal benefits that participation might offer could be a basis for doing so. Popular App marketplaces already demonstrate that users are motivated to rate apps for such reciprocal benefits.

Failure modes. Apps can behave in various ways when permissions are selectively disabled, ranging from crashes to gracefully handling errors. Our approach is primarily relevant to apps that gracefully handle any resulting errors. However, we note that combinations of permissions that render an App useless will be quickly identified by a handful of users and 'pruned' from further exploration. Thus, our approach need not inconvenience a large number of users even for apps that do not handle permission removals gracefully.

Accuracy of the recommendations. Some users may experience problems unrelated to the removed permissions. In our study we observed six such data points; removing these would have improved the MAE of our recommendations by 1.5%. In a real deployment, errors encountered by users could be analyzed for relevance to the particular configuration (e.g., by observing software exceptions). Moreover, like any other recommendation system, malicious users could provide fake ratings in favor of or against specific configurations. For example, Mukherjee et al. [11] analyzed and proposed models for detecting fake product reviews. Although detecting such ratings is out of the scope of this paper, removing those ratings would increase the accuracy of the recommendations.

CONCLUSION

Through a preliminary user study we have shown that it is feasible to apply crowdsourcing as a technique to collectively explore various security configurations of apps and find configurations that make suitable tradeoffs between privacy and usability for a diverse set of users. While others have proposed complementary techniques that rely on automated analyses or seeking opinions of permission settings from the crowd, we posit that considering opinions based on actual usage of various configurations would facilitate better recommendations to users. However, as the space of all possible permission settings grows exponentially with the number of permissions, it is imperative to follow a thoughtful crowd-management strategy; a goal of this work was to validate our lattice-based strategy for crowd management. Given our promising results, we thus advocate for further, and larger scale, research for crowd-sourced exploration of security configurations.

ACKNOWLEDGMENTS

This work was supported by grants 1228364 and 1228471 from NSF. Ismail is funded by the College of Computer and Information Sciences in King Saud University, Saudi Arabia. We thank Steven Armes for earlier work on our software; Shirin Nilizadeh for testing the software; Wesley Beaulieu and Hiroki Naganobori for assistance with statistical analysis; and Norman Su and Kelly Caine for valuable feedback.

REFERENCES

1. Amini, S., Lin, J., Hong, J. I., Lindqvist, J., and Zhang, J. Mobile application evaluation using automation and crowdsourcing. In *Workshop on Privacy Enhancing Tools* (July 2013).
2. Bugiel, S., Davi, L., Dmitrienko, A., Fischer, T., Sadeghi, A.-R., and Shastry, B. Towards taming privilege-escalation attacks on Android. In *19th Network & Distributed System Security Symposium* (Feb. 2012).
3. Ekstrand, M. D., Riedl, J. T., and Konstan, J. A. Collaborative filtering recommender systems. *Foundations and Trends in Human-Computer Interaction 4*, 2 (Feb. 2011), 81–173.
4. Felt, A. P., Chin, E., Hanna, S., Song, D., and Wagner, D. Android permissions demystified. In *18th ACM Conference on Computer and Communications Security* (2011), 627–638.
5. Felt, A. P., Greenwood, K., and Wagner, D. The effectiveness of application permissions. In *2nd USENIX Conference on Web Application Development* (2011), 75–86.
6. Felt, A. P., Ha, E., Egelman, S., Haney, A., Chin, E., and Wagner, D. Android permissions: User attention, comprehension, and behavior. In *8th Symposium on Usable Privacy and Security* (2012), 3:1–3:14.
7. Kelley, P. G., Consolvo, S., Cranor, L. F., Jung, J., Sadeh, N., and Wetherall, D. A conundrum of permissions: Installing applications on an Android smartphone. In *Financial Cryptography and Data Security*. Springer, 2012, 68–79.
8. Kelley, P. G., Cranor, L. F., and Sadeh, N. Privacy as part of the app decision-making process. In *2013 ACM Conference on Human Factors in Computing Systems* (2013), 3393–3402.
9. Kennedy, K., Gustafson, E., and Chen, H. Quantifying the effects of removing permissions from Android applications. In *IEEE Mobile Security Technologies* (2013).
10. Lin, J., Sadeh, N., Amini, S., Lindqvist, J., Hong, J. I., and Zhang, J. Expectation and purpose: Understanding users' mental models of mobile app privacy through crowdsourcing. In *2012 ACM Conference on Ubiquitous Computing* (2012), 501–510.
11. Mukherjee, A., Kumar, A., Liu, B., Wang, J., Hsu, M., Castellanos, M., and Ghosh, R. Spotting opinion spammers using behavioral footprints. In *19th ACM Conference on Knowledge Discovery and Data Mining* (2013), 632–640.
12. Nauman, M., Khan, S., and Zhang, X. Apex: Extending Android permission model and enforcement with user-defined runtime constraints. In *5th ACM Symposium on Information, Computer and Communications Security* (2010), 328–332.
13. Resnick, P., Iacovou, N., Bergstrom, M. S. P., and Riedl, J. T. GroupLens: An open architecture for collaborative filtering of netnews. In *ACM Conference on Computer Supported Collaborative Work* (1994), 175–186.
14. Saltzer, J. H., and Schroeder, M. D. The protection of information in computer systems. *Proceedings of the IEEE 63*, 9 (Sept. 1975).
15. Sarwar, B., Karypis, G., Konstan, J., and Riedl, J. Analysis of recommendation algorithms for e-commerce. In *2nd ACM Conference on Electronic Commerce* (2000), 158–167.
16. Sarwar, B., Karypis, G., Konstan, J., and Riedl, J. Item-based collaborative filtering recommendation algorithms. In *10th International Conference on World Wide Web* (2001), 285–295.

APPENDIX

Here we list the survey questions in the ratings app. In these questions, we referred to a configuration of the test app with some permissions removed as a "version" of the test app, as we feared that "configuration" might confuse participants.

Q1. Were there any features that did not appear to work in this version of the test app? • Yes • No
If (Yes), please provide examples of features that did not work (select all that apply): • Location based features • Camera based features • Microphone based features • The app could not access my contacts • Others:[ ]
Q2. The following features were removed from the test app for this version: • Camera • Location
Would you find it acceptable to use the test app with these features disabled until the next major app update from the test app- 1) Totally unacceptable 2) Unacceptable 3) Slightly unacceptable 4) Neutral 5) Slightly acceptable 6) Acceptable 7) Perfectly Acceptable
Q3. How would you rate this version of the test app compared to the original one? 1) Much worse 2) Somewhat worse 3) About the same 4) Somewhat better 5) Much better
Q4. How often did you use this version of the test app since you installed it on INSTALLATION DATE? a) Not at all b) Less than I normally use the test app c) About as much as I normally use the test app d) More than I normally use the test app

Open Book: A Socially-inspired Cloaking Technique that Uses Lexical Abstraction to Transform Messages

Eric Gilbert
School of Interactive Computing & GVU Center
Georgia Institute of Technology
gilbert@cc.gatech.edu

ABSTRACT
Both governments and corporations routinely surveil computer-mediated communication (CMC). Technologists often suggest widespread encryption as a defense mechanism, but CMC encryption schemes have historically faced significant usability and adoption problems. Here, we introduce a novel technique called *Open Book* designed to address these two problems. Inspired by how people deal with eavesdroppers offline, Open Book uses data mining and natural language processing to transform CMC messages into ones that are *vaguer* than the original. Specifically, we present: 1) a greedy Open Book algorithm that cloaks messages by transforming them to resemble the average Internet message; 2) an open-source, browser-based instantiation of it called *Read Me*, designed for Gmail; and, 3) a set of experiments showing that intended recipients can decode Open Book messages, but that unintended human- and machine-recipients cannot. Finally, we reflect on some open questions raised by this approach, such as recognizability and future side-channel attacks.

Author Keywords
cmc; social media; encryption; usable security

ACM Classification Keywords
H.5.3 [Group and Organization Interfaces]: Asynchronous interaction - Web-based interaction

INTRODUCTION
When Edward Snowden leaked news of the NSA's extensive analysis of computer-mediated communication (CMC) [17], many around the world were stunned. For others, the disclosure made visible an underlying aspect of the Internet's architecture: at many points along the way, bits pass through intermediate routers and servers *unencrypted* [4]. HTTP headers are often visible; email normally travels in plain text. Whether via under-sea cables or in Silicon Valley data centers, the prospect always loomed that a motivated and capable actor could insert themselves at points along the way, collecting and analyzing all the CMC that passed by.

CHI 2015, April 18–23, 2015, Seoul, Republic of Korea.

ACM 978-1-4503-3145-6/15/04 ...$15.00.
http://dx.doi.org/10.1145/2702123.2702295

Hey, gonna crush you and Tom in Civilization this weekend. Oh, and btw, how was your trip to Rio?!?

OPEN BOOK

1. Hey, gonna crush you and [person] in [video game] this weekend. Oh, and btw, how was your trip to [location]?!?

2. Hey, gonna crush you and somebody in Ci+ this weekend. Oh, and btw, how was your trip to the place?!?

3. Hey, gonna crush you and … in … this weekend. Oh, and btw, how was your trip to …?!?

Figure 1. An example of Open Book applied to a short interpersonal message. The words identified in orange statistically stand out from a background corpus, measured with the Google 1T dataset. The three output examples illustrate variations on generating lexical vagueness.

This kind of CMC surveillance is not, however, limited to government agencies. For at least the last decade, we have also seen widespread corporate CMC surveillance. Consider Gmail, for example. Gmail analyzes the messages you send and receive to serve better targeted ads[1]. Many companies—Facebook and Twitter among them—architect their business models surveilling and mining the CMC within their systems. It can seem nearly impossible to avoid this kind of surveillance short of opting out altogether. Recently, for example, the sociologist Janet Vertesi related her story of trying to hide her new pregnancy from this surveillance network (and the inevitable diaper ads that would follow). The project worked for nearly seven months until the news finally broke on Facebook [29].

Often technologists counter with the idea of *encryption*. The argument goes that if we encrypted everything, by default, none of this could happen. Since the discoveries of Diffie-Hellman key exchange [15] and RSA [24], we have known how to mathematically ensure that only our intended recipients read the bits we send over the Internet. Yet in the context of CMC, encryption has two seemingly insurmountable problems. First, people often simply do not understand the

[1]While not often referred to as "surveillance," it meets the criteria associated with the term.

complex mathematical transformations applied to their data—and any single slip-up can compromise the security of the entire message (or even past messages) [26, 30]. Second—we argue more importantly—CMC encryption systems face a large *social usability* challenge: everyone with whom you want to have encrypted conversations needs to have the proper software installed and configured ahead of time. This problem has dramatically affected the adoption and applicability of CMC encryption.

In this paper, we introduce a novel technique called *Open Book* designed to bridge this gap. Open Book relaxes what we mean by *encryption*, instead applying data mining and natural language processing in the service of privacy. Rather than transforming text into mathematically-generated ciphertext, such as systems like PGP do [32], Open Book looks to a social practice we often employ in the presence of eavesdroppers: *vagueness*. For example, in a recent article, danah boyd tells the story of a group of teenagers who have an extensive Facebook conversation about sex—despite the fact that many family members could potentially read it [6]. They accomplish it by 1) being vague, and 2) taking advantage of the existing common ground among the participants. Open Book realizes this practice computationally (see Figure 1). It aims to address the two major problems facing CMC encryption: 1) it works by converting words into other words, simplifying users' mental workload; 2) people can send an Open Book message without recipients needing any special software on their end. At the same time, Open Book *does not* provide the same kinds of mathematical data-protection guarantees seen in encryption algorithms such as RSA; rather, we present evidence in this paper that Open Book significantly reduces the information disclosed to eavesdroppers.

This paper's contributions are threefold. First, we present the Open Book approach and a greedy algorithm that instantiates it. At a high level, Open Book uses lexical abstraction techniques to translate messages into ones that resemble the *average Internet message*—in some sense cloaking CMC traffic in the "background noise" of the Internet. Second, we present a tool called *Read Me* that brings Open Book to Gmail. Built as an open-source browser plugin, and employing various lexical abstraction resources (e.g, Named-Entity Recognition, the Google 1T corpus, Wikipedia category hierarchies), Read Me allows Gmail users to "vague-ify" their email messages. Finally, we present the results of two experiments showing that: 1) non-experts can use Read Me to send Open Book-encrypted messages with little training; 2) Mechanical Turk workers, used here as a proxy for human analysts, cannot recover the words Open Book cloaks; and, 3) statistical machine learning algorithms have difficulty recovering topical and authorship information after the application of Open Book to an email corpus.

RELATED WORK

We primarily draw on two areas of scholarship to frame this work: common ground theory and the use of data mining on CMC. The former lays the theoretical groundwork for Open Book: that people who share common ground may be able to understand one another even in the presence of missing information. For the latter, we discuss data mining in the service of modeling users, groups and social networks. The intention is to highlight state-of-the-art results obtainable by mining CMC.

Common ground & socially-constructed meaning

In its most basic form, the theory of common ground suggests that as people interact more and more, they require less explicitly said to establish the same meaning [12]. For example, two people who just met may need to discuss (either explicitly or implicitly) their goals, values, etc. before they can ascertain the full meaning behind discourse; two old friends, on the other hand, might be able to communicate the same thing with only a well-timed nod.

Common ground theory (also known as Grounding Theory in the literature) proposes a set of mutual knowledge and referents in which speakers can *ground* their discussion, as well as the processes and conditions under which those constructs form [13, 14]. Discussants work to establish mutual knowledge through either physical co-presence, linguistic knowledge that builds up over time (e.g., referring to the abstract concept "waiter" after earlier naming the specific restaurant, thereby placing the waiter within the particular restaurant), or by relying on a set of shared norms or values. Participants in these conversations will often try to gauge what others know and act accordingly—backing off and correcting if they sense confusion. In short, common ground is shared understanding that develops over time, and has been documented in a number of conversational settings.

Originally situated in face-to-face settings, human-centered computing researchers have brought common ground theory to computer-mediated communication research. In early work, for example, theorists brought the core ideas of grounding to the development of user interfaces, the boundary through which computers and people interact, therefore requiring mutual understanding [8]. Later, researchers adopted the constructs of common ground into studies of task-oriented mediated communication (e.g., [16, 18, 20]). The original conceptualization of common ground stipulates that interference from a conversational setting—for example, difficulty decoding turn-taking [18] or interference from network latency [16] in CMC—may negatively affect group processes.

Here, we bring the ideas and findings of this line of work to bear on the construction of a new algorithm. Specifically, we situate our work on the assumption that, for many CMC correspondents, people will share enough common ground to be able to "fill in the gaps" created by Open Book transformations. We then look to investigate this assumption via experimental studies.

Data mining to model users, groups and networks

Over the last two decades, data mining has risen to both popular and academic prominence: there is a major ACM conference every year reporting the field's new findings (KDD). Covering all the important work done in this field would easily fill *the entire* 10 pages this paper permits (and more), so in this section we simply aim to visit a handful of important and seminal pieces of recent work that bear on the construction and application of Open Book. Specifically, we highlight work that showcases the extent to which you can model individual users, groups and social networks via their CMC traces.

Following less computationally-focused psychological work from a decade earlier [9], recent work has shown that CMC traces can predict future performance in the workplace [25], as well as accurately predict personality traits [10]. Moreover, recent work also documents how romantic relationships can be inferred from access to a Facebook social network alone (i.e., just its structural information), without any of the associated content [1]. (We refer back to this point later in the *Discussion*, as it bears on the purely content-based approach we pursue in this paper.)

As alluded at the beginning of the paper, clearly much of the interest surrounding data mining comes from the field of personalized advertising. For example, in a recent piece of work Groupon describes how by using a basket of data—including CMC data—the company can increase conversion rates on its group deals by presenting the "right people the right deals at the right time" [28]. Particularly germane to the experimental conditions presented in the present work, industry-based researchers have also recently reported how they use very large-scale topic models (at the level of "hundreds of millions of users") to build reliable models of large groups of people, their interests, and likelihoods of response to targeted advertisements [27, 31]. New work also reports that similar methods can even be used to understand, predict and track who will join online protest movements [21].

In the present work, we examine whether Open Book can confound this type of data mining. An assumption upon which all work like this rests is that users have little agency to cloak their data against algorithmic understanding. We investigate through a series of human and machine experiments whether applying Open Book to naturally occurring email corpora can interfere with this assumption.

OPEN BOOK

Next, we introduce the conceptual underpinnings of Open Book, highlight its advantages and disadvantages relative to existing approaches, and also discuss a greedy implementation of Open Book (see Algorithm 1). First, however, we take a very brief detour through the goals and techniques of encryption for Internet-based communication media, specifically implementations of public-key cryptography.

When an email message is transmitted from one place to another via the Internet, it transits a number of untrusted routers and servers. By default, this happens in plain text. (This is also true for HTTP transactions, etc., but here we will focus on email messages.) Therefore, a sufficiently privileged process residing on any of those routers and machines could—if it so chose—read, archive and process any email message crossing its path. A classic tactic employed against this is encryption, which at a high-level entails devising two functions, e and d such that $d(e(m)) = m$, for a message m. Usually, $e(m)$ creates a string of ciphertext that only someone who can execute $d(m)$ can understand (i.e., the intended recipient). One popular and successful form of encryption is *public-key cryptography*, a scheme that uses a public key, a private key and a mathematical procedure that is difficult in one direction as its e and d functions. For example, implementations of public-key cryptography often use prime factorization (also known as RSA [24]) as the underlying mathematical operation because while it is nearly trivial to multiply two large primes together, it is very difficult (perhaps NP-hard) to factor the resulting composite number—without access to a private key.

Systems like PGP [32] have brought public-key cryptography to email. PGP takes an email message and encrypts its body into ciphertext using RSA. (It must leave the email message's headers intact so that intervening mail servers can deliver the message properly.) As an illustration, consider the following email message taken from the Enron email corpus [22]:

```
From: keith.holst@enron.com
To: george.arvanitis@mirant.com
Subject: RE: Its all good news
Date: Wed, 31 Oct 2001 16:04:46 -0800

Nobody is better than you George!!!!!

Thanks
Keith
```

Using RSA and public-key cryptography, PGP would encrypt the message's body into ciphertext. Instead of seeing the message above, George—as well as any intervening routers and servers—would see the following email:

```
From: keith.holst@enron.com
To: george.arvanitis@mirant.com
Subject: RE: Its all good news
Date: Wed, 31 Oct 2001 16:04:46 -0800

---BEGIN PGP MESSAGE---
Version: 2.6.2

jA0EAwMC10MQsOtD0/xgyU3ZLVfnkxpeVeI4m2
aLc5aicK3L39banJ+tF0r/MQ1XMmad2SiREFzd
j0KEm5pxYFBp7IhOICzZhFHihJxSVkCpzx+QGz
21dmCdWBPylw===CGiN
---END PGP MESSAGE---
```

The ciphertext George receives represents a process of exponentiation applied to a numerical representation of Keith's original message. To decode it, George must also possess the appropriate version of PGP and the required key. With them, he clicks a button in his properly configured mail client and the ciphertext changes back into "Nobody is better than you George!!!!!" Note that for this scheme to work, Keith and George must somehow exchange public keys in a reliable and trustworthy way beforehand, something often arranged with a keyserver, either on the Internet or a private intranet.

Problems with existing approaches

However, existing approaches are not without their problems, many of which lie at the "human-level" of the stack [26, 30]. Foremost among them:

1. **PGP and similar systems present usability problems.** Imagine that you are Keith altering the message above to send to George. Upon clicking the "encrypt" button, your mail client presents you with the PGP-encrypted version of

the message, prompting you to send it to George. Did you do everything correctly? One slip-up and the encryption guarantees no longer hold. Notably, in laboratory studies people find it very difficult to use and maintain the integrity of the keys essential to these public-key schemes [30]. For example, a PGP user might easily encrypt a message with their own private key, instead of with their recipient's public key—completely defeating the protocol and rendering it vulnerable to attack. Moreover, the key exchange that two parties must complete before the first encrypted message presents difficulties. Is this truly George's key? If not, am I potentially sending a sensitive message to an attacker who can easily decrypt it?

2. **Existing systems have serious *social usability* problems.** More importantly, however, we argue that public-key schemes present serious *social usability* issues. Imagine that in the example above Keith feels strongly about encrypting his messages before they touch the public Internet. George may not feel the same way. George may not want to go through the sometimes quite long and tedious steps necessary to set up PGP so that Keith can feel safe sending a message to him. (For example, a PGP setup guide from the University of Pittsburgh contains 14 steps and takes 13 pages to print[2].) At present, Keith has no recourse but to continue lobbying George to install encryption software, even if Keith is George's only email contact who cares about encrypting messages. Or, as a recent Ars Technica article[3] put it: "E-mail encryption is not something you can impose unilaterally. To protect the contents of your account, you need to ensure that *everyone* you communicate with is in a position to handle encrypted mail—and is willing to use that ability" (emp. original).

The Open Book approach

Open Book is designed to address these two problems. As discussed earlier, Open Book borrows an idea from how people obscure their meaning from potential eavesdroppers in public places: *with vagueness*. Instead of saying, "Remember that amazing pizza we had in Chicago last February?", someone worried about eavesdroppers might translate the message into something akin to, "Remember that amazing food we ate in that city we visited a few months back?" The intended listener may be able to reconstruct the intended message, while a listener nearby probably will not. The high-level idea of Open Book is to use *lexical vaguess*—words with more abstract meanings—to conceal the specific details of any CMC message. The hypothesis is that common ground built between two people who have communicated in the past can repair the transformations done by Open Book.

Relative to the problems discussed in the previous section, this approach confers two advantages. First, addressing the single-user usability problems, Open Book has the attractive property that it simply changes words into other words. Compared to the complex mathematical representations, steps and transformations comprising systems like PGP, we hypothesize that Open Book users will more quickly and easily

Algorithm 1 Open Book (greedy)

Input: A message m to transform; a maximum number n of n-grams via which to assess distributional similarity; a background corpus distribution, $background$, against which to compare the transformed message; a tolerance ϵ for background distributional similarity; a tolerance δ for the greedy approach to altering words and phrases.

Output: A transformed version of m likely within ϵ distributional similarity of $background$.

```
function OPENBOOK(m, n, background, ε, δ)
    e ← m
    alterations ← [ ]
    for t = n, n − 1, . . . , 1 do
        if DISTSIM(e, n, background) ≥ ε then
            ng ← all t-grams of e
            for each g in ng do
                f ← FREQTABLE(g, ng, background)
                (χ², p) ← CHISQTEST(f)
                continue if p ≥ δ
                if g does not overlap a ∈ alterations then
                    v ← VAGUEIFY(g)
                    if g ≠ v then
                        e ← (e − g) + v
                        alterations ← alterations + v
                    end if
                end if
            end for
        end if
    end for
    return e
end function

function DISTSIM(t, n, background)
    ng ← (1, . . . , n)-gram representation of t
    return distributional similarity of ng and background
end function

function FREQTABLE(t, ng, background)
    f1 ← number of occurrences of t in ng
    f2 ← number of occurrences of t in background
    return (f1,LEN(ng)−f1, f2,LEN(background)−f2)
end function

function VAGUEIFY(t)
    return lexical abstraction of t, if exists, otherwise t
end function
```

understand what has happened to their message, and that unintended recipients will be less likely to understand it.

Second, and more importantly, Open Book is *unidirectional*. It only requires an encryption function; the corresponding decryption function lies in the recipient's mind. In this way, Open Book sidesteps one of the most crucial and vexing problems facing CMC encryption: convincing everyone you communicate with to use it. Rather, if Keith wants to send

[2]http://www.pitt.edu/~poole/PGP.htm
[3]http://ars.to/19mztTT

George a message, he can simply decide unilaterally to encode the message with Open Book. George need not have any special mail client, or any special software.

To direct a message away from lexical specificity and towards lexical vagueness, Open Book must have some notion of what "better" is in this context. How can it measure the improvement, if any, of a suggested change to someone's message? To solve this problem, we introduce the idea of *regressing to the mean Internet message*. In other words, while we surely cannot cloak the entirety of the message (like PGP does, for example), we can likely make the message very similar to the average Internet text—in some sense cloaking the message in the background noise of the Internet.

This has two attractive side effects. First, this process will likely confound advanced individual data mining profiles (e.g., [10]) by making it difficult to separate an individual from the average CMC user. Second, we have recently discovered that the mere act of using encryption software signals to sufficiently interested eavesdroppers that the person encrypting has something to hide, and therefore is inherently suspect. (This is the origin of the phrase "Open Book.") Simply by streaming all email traffic through a regular expression (i.e., search for "BEGIN PGP MESSAGE"), one could archive all encrypted messages. It seems unlikely, however, that an adversary could do the same with all Open Book-encrypted messages; they simply look like every other message on the Internet. We revisit this point in somewhat greater detail later in the *Discussion*.

Threat model

To be explicit, Open Book presumes its adversaries to be both human and machine analysts that can passively surveil CMC written by users. This includes platform providers (such as Google), intervening technical components (such as servers, routers, and actors siphoning off content at these points), as well as human analysts reading messages. Open Book presumes these actors to have both modern data mining techniques—as well as human intelligence—at their disposal to reverse-engineer the meaning of Open Book messages. Therefore, the goal of Open Book is to limit the amount of information available to these adversaries, while preserving usability and interpretability by intended recipients.

Greedy Open Book algorithm

Next, we discuss how we accomplish these goals technically. Specifically, we present a greedy algorithm for encrypting a message with Open Book. Algorithm 1 lists its steps; here, we will also walk through some of the scheme's key steps, as well as some of the assumptions the algorithm makes.

The algorithm consists of four main functions: OPENBOOK, DISTSIM, FREQTABLE and VAGUEIFY. The main body of the algorithmic work takes place in OPENBOOK, whereas the remaining three functions act as helpers. FREQTABLE simply constructs a frequency table for use in calculating a χ^2 statistic, while DISTSIM and VAGUEIFY remain only abstractly defined (in the software engineering sense of the word "abstract") and are expected to be overridden by particular implementations of Open Book schemes. We discuss one such implementation in the next section, but leave these

Algorithm 2 Read Me Open Book Implementation

Input: A Gmail message m to transform; the Google 1T corpus, against which to compare transformed message.

Output: An Open Book-transformed version of m likely within ϵ distributional similarity of the Google 1T corpus.

```
function README(m, google1t)
    return OPENBOOK(m, 3, google1t, 0.1, 10^-6)
end function

function DISTSIM(t, n, background)
    ng ← (1, ..., n)-gram representation of t
    return KL-DIVERGENCE(ng, background)
end function

function VAGUEIFY(t)
    if NER(t) = person then return "[person]"
    else if NER(t) = place then return "[location]"
    else if NER(t) = datetime then return "[time]"
    else if NER(t) = org then return "[organization]"
    else if NER(t) = amount then return "[amount]"
    else if POS(t) = noun then
        (cat, catmembers) ← WP-CATEGORY(t)
        (tmpl, tmplmembers) ← WP-TEMPLATE(t)
        if catmembers > 100 then return cat
        else if tmplmembers > 100 then return tmpl
        end if
        return "[thing]"
    else if POS(t) = nounplural then return "[things]"
    else if POS(t) = verb then return "[action]"
    else if LEN(t) > 6 then return SLICE(t, 0, 2) + "+"
    end if
    return t
end function

function NER(t) return t's named entity class
end function

function POS(t) return t's part-of-speech code
end function

function WP-CATEGORY(t) return t's Wikipedia category
end function

function WP-TEMPLATE(t) return t's Wikipedia template
end function
```

functions "abstract" in Algorithm 1 to illustrate the general principles of Open Book.

Open Book leaves parameterizable the number of n-grams (n-token phrases) it will consider altering in the message, with the main loop of the algorithm descending from the longest n-grams to the shortest. It also keeps track of every change it makes in the dictionary (or hash table) *alterations*, which it uses later to make sure a new proposed change does not collide with an already existing change. On every iteration of Open Book's main n-gram loop, the distributional similarity of the altered message and a background corpus is assessed:

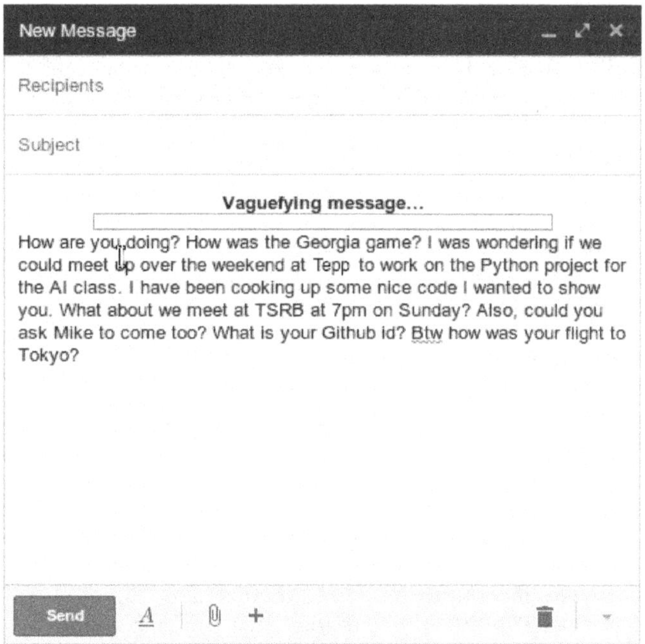

Figure 2. The Read Me application about to "vagueify" an email message at a user's request. Read Me is implemented as a Chrome and Firefox extension that detects the context where it can operate on a Gmail message. Here, the user has typed a message and instructed the system to make it "vaguer." As the transformation involves statistical machine learning, a progress bar inserted into the message updates as the transformation progresses.

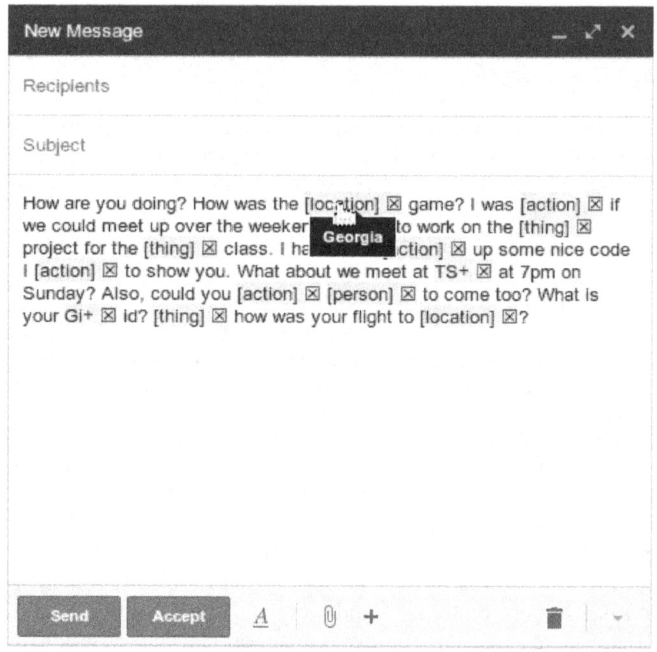

Figure 3. After a few seconds, the email on the left is transformed into this one. A new button appears next to Gmail's Send button, allowing the user to accept Read Me's changes after reviewing them and making any manual edits. Here, the user has hovered over the transformed "[location]" to reveal that the original word was "Georgia." At this point, the user can revert the change, or make manual edits by typing.

DISTSIM(e, n, $background$) $\geq \epsilon$. Particular implementations of Open Book specify the background corpus to use, as well as the parameter ϵ. When the distributional similarity of the encrypted message and the background corpus falls within ϵ, the procedure exits.

In passing through this conditional, Open Book now looks at n-grams (for a certain fixed n) and considers lexically "vagueifying" each one. It does so greedily. Looking at the frequency of a certain n-gram against its frequency in the background corpus, it calculates a χ^2 statistic: $(\chi^2, p) \leftarrow$ CHISQTEST(f). When the p-value for this test falls below a supplied parameter δ, Open Book cues the n-gram for vagueification. One way to view the χ^2 test here is as a way to isolate the distributional dissimilarity relative to the background corpus, as compared to the more omnibus computation done by DISTSIM.

Open Book then looks to make sure that the n-gram it may change does not overlap with any existing change the algorithm has made with any n-grams of equal or longer length. The reason for this is that otherwise you might see Open Book composing alterations at the phrase level (e.g., changing "New York City" into "[location] City" instead of just "[location]"). Open Book next turns to the function VAGUEIFY to supply a more lexically abstract phrase as a replacement. Note that in this section of the procedure, the algorithm assumes a very intelligent set of string and n-gram data structures: they understand their position in the parent string, can be intersected, added and subtracted. Most languages do not natively provide this functionality, but we presume it in Algorithm 1 to simplify the pseudocode.

Note that this greedy implementation of Open Book may exit without bringing the encrypted message within ϵ distributional similarity of the supplied background corpus. In the general case, this may not even be possible, for example, for arbitrarily small values of ϵ. The greedy approach presented here represents one path toward optimizing distributional similarity, but others exist. We consider some of these in the *Discussion* and also reflect on some of the limitations inherent in greedy algorithmic approaches.

READ ME: OPEN BOOK FOR GMAIL

We instantiated the Open Book algorithm in a Gmail plugin called *Read Me*. As opposed to the algorithm described above, people directly interact with Read Me. Built as an open-source Chrome and Firefox extension, the tool wraps the Open Book algorithm, supplying the necessary parameters, background corpus and overridden DISTSIM and VAGUEIFY functions. Figures 2 and 3 illustrate how people can use the tool. In this section, we describe Read Me's algorithmic implementation, as well as its user experience.

Read Me algorithmic implementation

Read Me instantiates Open Book with specific parameters, a background corpus and overridden DISTSIM and VAGUEIFY functions. Algorithm 2 lists all its steps. Read Me lets $\epsilon = 0.1$ and $\delta = 10^{-6}$, values that we discovered through inspection. (In the *Discussion*, we describe more principled methods one might use to discover these parameters.) For the background corpus, Read Me uses Google's 1T corpus [7], a large dataset documenting the frequency with which Google sees [1,2,3,4,5]-grams during its crawls of the web. While this may not perfectly capture the frequency with which some phrases appear in CMC like email, we believe it is likely to be the best resource we have documenting the frequency of n-grams on the Internet.

For its DISTSIM, Read Me uses the standard KL-DIVERGENCE metric to measure the similarity between two distributions over n-grams. To produce more lexically abstract phrase variants, Read Me populates VAGUEIFY with the output of both Named Entity Recognition and Part-of-speech taggers. Both of these methods produce lexically higher-level phrase alternatives—for example "[location]" instead of "New York City". VAGUEIFY uses the Stanford NER and POS tools to accomplish its lexical vagueness generation. We also experimented with incorporating WordNet [23] and FrameNet [2] into Read Me, as they would produce a much richer vocabulary of lexical abstraction, but they proved too slow and cumbersome for an interactive application on a single machine. We do, however, use popular Wikipedia categories and templates for noun phrases. Algorithm 2 presents one version of lexical abstraction, but users can elect from three different versions—the three that comprise the example in Figure 1. We present this particular variant in Algorithm 2 because this is the variant we used in our study.

Note that we implemented Read Me as a strictly single-user application. While a client-server model would vastly simplify installation and improve performance, it very much runs counter to the design goals of Read Me. Read Me intends to make it more difficult for eavesdroppers to snoop on your messages; sending messages off to a centralized web service for processing would completely defeat the purpose. (This does entail some design tradeoffs, such as being unable to use WordNet and FrameNet.) Read Me uses Javascript at the browser extension level to talk across local sockets to services running natural language processing toolkits in both Python and Java. In a set of benchmarks run on data from our experiment (presented next), Read Me can process a 5-sentence paragraph of English in a mean time of 2.3 seconds. (Also note that the technology stack presented here is rather cumbersome for the average user; we expect that some amount of technology "miniaturization" will need to take place before becoming widespread.)

Read Me user experience

Read Me wraps this implementation of Open Book in a Chrome/Firefox extension. After installation in the browser, the plugin and its associated software can detect when the user is composing a Gmail message. It inserts a new button in the interface, called "Vagueify" in prototypes, that permits people to execute Read Me on a message they have composed. After doing so, a progress bar labeled "Vagueifying message" keeps users updated on the underlying natural language processing (see Figure 2).

When the README function returns, the user sees the transformed version of the message (see Figure 3). Read Me highlights each individual transformation with a light gray background, allowing the user to both hover over it uncover the original word and to revert the change using the X button next to the transformed phrase. The transformed message is simply rendered as HTML, so users can directly edit the message. Read Me also populates the Gmail interface with a new "Accept" button next to the "Send" button, so that people can tell Read Me when they are happy with the altered message. Upon clicking it, Read Me strips out any of the markup highlights, bringing the message back to plain text. (Note that Read Me only stores the correspondence between transformed phrases and their originals in local main memory; that correspondence goes away upon hitting the "Accept" button.)

This constitutes a very different interaction model than what we typically see with wholly mathematical encryption schemes like PGP: people can read what changes encryption made to their message and tweak it to their liking. Some users may even view Read Me as nudges for particular phrases, changing them to flow more naturally, and running Read Me once again to check their manual edits. We discuss some of the advantages (e.g., understandability) and disadvantages (e.g., potential risk exposure) of this interaction model later.

EXPERIMENT 1: HUMAN INTERPRETABILITY

In the design of Open Book, we make two parallel and important claims: 1) intended recipients (who share common ground with the sender) can likely understand Open Book messages, despite the transformations Open Book performs; and, 2) unintended recipients cannot understand Open Book messages. Next we present the first of two experiments we conducted to assess these parallel claims.

Procedure

We recruited 10 participants from our local university community (outside the computer science research community) to participate in the study. Upon arriving in our lab, they sat at an instrumented computer running Chrome, with Read Me preinstalled. We instructed our participants to visit their Gmail Sent Mail and make a list of the five most recent personal email messages they had sent (as opposed to transactional or business email). After generating this list, participants were instructed to write each of these five people a new message consisting of between two and five paragraphs, which they would then transform with Read Me. We briefly gave our participants a high-level overview of the purpose of the system, but did not offer assistance or guidance in using the software once a session began. Our customized version of Read Me recorded locally both the original message and its transformed version for later analysis.

In this way, we snowball sampled a pool of 40 remote participants from our 10 local participants. While snowball samples can cause analytic problems [3], as samples nest within onsite participants—this model very naturally fits the context in which people would typically use Read Me. To the end of each outbound, Read Me-transformed message, we appended a survey link. The link indicated that they had received the email as part of a study and asked the recipient to reconstruct the original message in full with only access to the Read Me version. In addition, we administered NASA-TLX workload inventories [19] to both our in-person and remote participants. In our analyses, we are interested in both the number of transformations for which the remote participant can guess the original words, as well as any additional workload we place on Read Me users. We compensated local participants with a $15 gift card, but we did not compensate remote participants for completing the survey.

Analysis 1.1: Interpretability by intended recipients

19 remote participants completed the task of reconstructing the original message and the NASA-TLX inventory. In total, the reconstructed email messages comprised over 4,500 words and 521 Open Book lexical abstractions.

Intended recipients had remarkable success in reconstructing the original messages, guessing the correct underlying word or phrase in 95.2% of cases. Intended recipients felt very confident about their judgements on the whole, rating their reconstruction confidence at 6.1 on the 7-point Likert scale from the NASA-TLX. In addition, on average recipients experienced low mental workload and stress in recovering the original intent of the message, $\mu = 1.8$ and $\mu = 2.2$, respectively. The first claim appears to hold: intended recipients *can* understand Open Book messages, despite the transformations Open Book performs via lexical abstraction. As one of our participants wrote in the free-form comment section of our survey:

> I mean, you kind of have to know the person and approximately what the paragraph is about in order to guess most of the words, but it's not bad. (P12)

Analysis 1.2: Interpretability by unintended recipients

Next, we turn to assessing how well outsiders can reconstruct an Open Book-transformed message. Often in encryption papers, researchers introducing a technique will make a mathematical argument—premised on assumptions about data—and construct numerical bounds. In subsequent years, other papers appear in a sort of "cat-and-mouse game" testing the bounds and looking at side-channel attacks against the technique [5]. That traditional approach does not apply here nearly as well (i.e., Open Book is lossy and is not mathematical in nature), and so we turn to an empirical analysis of the interpretability of Open Book messages.

In particular, we turn to Mechanical Turk workers to assess the difficulty of breaking Open Book. In our opinion, Turkers represent an imperfect, but advanced adversary—perhaps resembling a human analyst who has intercepted the communication. They are imperfect because they clearly do not have access to the large side-channel attack data sources that a computationally gifted adversary would (e.g., a stream of Google search queries written by a Read Me user that might assist in decrypting any given message). On the other hand, Turkers possess the ability to understand discourse-level features of written English that far outstrip modern machine techniques. One analogy might be: Turkers may not have vast computational resources at their disposal, but can still easily break CAPTCHAS.

We recruited 5 Turkers for each of the 19 messages to perform the exact same tasks as the intended recipients: reconstruct the original message and complete a NASA-TLX inventory. We assess the same metrics: interpretability and mental workload. We paid $0.25 for each HIT and restricted the participant pool to include only those workers with a "HIT Approval Rate" above 90% to filter for reliable, well-regarded Turkers. (The HIT Approval Rate is the percentage of times a requester has marked a Turker's work as acceptable.)

Unintended recipients performed remarkably poorly in reverse-engineering the originals from Open Book messages. They successfully recovered only 12 of the 521 Open Book lexical abstractions (2.3%), not significantly different than chance. They also rated their confidence very low (predictably given their ultimate success rate) and their mental workload very high, $\mu = 1.3$ and $\mu = 5.4$, respectively. The second claim also appears to hold, given this empirical context: unintended recipients have great difficulty decrypting Open Book.

EXPERIMENT 2: MACHINE INTERPRETABILITY

In addition to using both intended and unintended human recipients to evaluate Open Book, we also wanted to understand how machines might deal with the alterations done to messages via Open Book. Therefore, we next describe a second experiment we undertook to understand how machine predictions tasks may fare in the context of Open Book.

Procedure

The message corpus we collected as part of Experiment 1 does not contain enough messages to reliably and realistically train a supervised machine learning algorithm. Therefore, we turn to the Enron email corpus [22], a well-known and established resource for naturally occurring email. First, we construct three corpora: 1) the default, unaltered Enron corpus (referred to in what follows as BASELINE); 2) the Enron corpus where a single author (chosen at random) has all of their messages transformed with Open Book (OPENBOOK); and, 3) a random baseline corpus where a single author's messages have random words deleted (RANDBASELINE). In the following two analyses, we draw from these corpora to perform structured prediction tasks, analyzing how algorithms perform on OPENBOOK relative to how they perform on BASELINE. RANDBASELINE acts as an even stronger baseline for the experiment, and also allows us to construct associated p-values via bootstrapping (explained in greater detail below).

Analysis 2.1: Predicting authors

A way to view the problem of estimating the information loss in applying Open Book is to ask: How hard is it to distinguish an individual author from the text alone? Similar to a number of existing studies profiling people, here we will try to classify whether an email belongs to a specific person or not, feeding the text alone into a machine learning classifier.

Let P represent the messages belonging to an individual person p. We consider in this analysis the classification problem of deciding whether a messages belong to P or $\overline{P}$—essentially recasting authorship classification as a binary decision problem for a given individual person. We feed all unigrams, bigrams and trigrams to a Support Vector Machine, adopting ten-fold cross-validation to evaluate the classifier's performance. Over BASELINE, we achieve an average accuracy of 71.4% in predicting an individual from text alone. Over OPENBOOK, however, this accuracy falls to 54.4% (only slightly better than chance). Adopting the bootstrapping approach introduced above, we find that a percentage difference as large as this one would be observed in only 3 out of the 10,000 cases, yielding $\frac{3}{10000} < p < \frac{4}{10000}$.

DISCUSSION

We presented the algorithmic details behind Open Book, its instantiation as the browser plugin Read Me, and two experiments probing the interpretability of Read Me's messages. Next, we reflect on some of the questions that Open Book raises, both for CMC researchers and practitioners, as well as a number of possible validity threats.

How much information is still recoverable?

Open Book (and Read Me) work on the premise of converting otherwise specific messages into ones resembling the average Internet message. At a high level, Open Book removes the most sensitive, specific information, replacing it with lexical abstractions. At the same time, we know from previous work that quite a bit of information is still recoverable from the text that an Open Book transformation would leave behind. For example, the frequency and placement of so-called function words can reveal personality traits [11]. Open Book does not consider them very important. Moreover, Open Book leaves in tact all of an email's header information (like PGP does) and therefore any attacks solely based on "meta-data" would remain viable. This would include any attacks oriented around social network analyses, for example. In short, more study is needed to analyze what information one could recover from the output of an Open Book message.

Optimization and parameter selection

We presented a greedy implementation of Open Book (see Algorithm 1). Greedy algorithmic approaches have a number of desirable properties: they are easy to understand, tend to execute quickly (especially important in interactive contexts), and relatively easy to implement. They have a number of drawbacks, as well. It seems likely that Algorithm 1 finds local optima some of the time. While outside the scope of the work we have presented in this paper, it would be worthwhile and interesting to explore more complete optimization strategies. Moreover, we found Read Me's specific parameters by inspection; grid-based parameter searches would likely improve the overall performance of the system.

Do Open Book messages have a recognizable signature?

In the Snowden documents, we learned that people who regularly use encrypted communication channels (like PGP and OTR) find themselves placed on watch lists [17]. Presumably, they have something to hide. At a technical level, this can be accomplished easily because encrypted messages have both headers proclaiming themselves as encrypted, as well character-level distributions unlike typical written English.

Do Open Book messages have recognizable signatures as well? At first blush, it appears they do not. First, since Open Book replaces words and phrases that do not occur frequently with those that do, they would look like regular written English. Second, they contain no header information denoting an encrypted message; we expect the recipient can infer (or at least recover from) the lossy lexical changes. However, this would all depend on the specific encoding scheme used by an Open Book implementation. In the one we used for our experiment, we bracketed the more lexically vague phrases to denote that we had changed them. Over time, a preponderance for brackets in email might flag a user to any interested parties. However, without the brackets, they may not stand out at all. One could imagine follow-up studies to this work that look at the identifiability of Open Book messages when embedded in a corpus of plain text messages.

Limitations

Of course, Open Book has a number of limitations. First, Open Book works on the assumption of shared common ground. It seems most immediately suited to dyadic communication, and it remains unclear if and how it might scale to groups. Intuitively, the intersecting common ground within a group of three is less than or equal to a group of four, which is less than or equal to a group of five, etc. Can Open Book work in groups of 5, 10, or 20? The experiment we present in this paper likewise limits the findings to dyads with pre-existing common ground.

Second, encryption techniques naturally go through a kind of "cat and mouse game." Researchers introduce techniques, and future researchers probe those techniques for weaknesses and vulnerabilities. As a new technique, Open Book clearly has not been subjected to this kind of scrutiny. Nor can we make firm mathematical guarantees such as RSA might. In this work, we turned to Mechanical Turk and modern machine learning techniques as attacks against Open Book. While this seems reasonable to us, it also seems reasonable that wholly computerized attacks might differ substantially from the resources available to our Turkers and topic models.

Third, and finally, while Open Book possesses a desirable *unidirectional* property, as discussed earlier, Open Book cannot deal with inbound messages. Open Book could not protect a person against Gmail learning something about them via the messages other people send. At present, we do not see a way to extend Open Book's ideas to inbound messages.

REFERENCES

1. L. Backstrom and J. Kleinberg. Romantic partnerships and the dispersion of social ties: A network analysis of relationship status on Facebook. In *Proc. CSCW*, pages 831–841, 2014.
2. C. Baker, C. Fillmore, and J. B. Lowe. The Berkeley FrameNet Project. In *Proc. COLING*, pages 86–90, 1998.
3. P. Biernacki and D. Waldorf. Snowball Sampling: Problems and Techniques of Chain Referral Sampling. *Sociological Methods & Research*, 10(2):141–163, 1981.
4. M. S. Blumenthal and D. D. Clark. Rethinking the design of the Internet: the end-to-end arguments vs. the brave new world. *ACM TOIT*, 1(1):70–109, 2001.
5. D. Boneh et al. Twenty years of attacks on the RSA cryptosystem. *Notices of the AMS*, 46(2):203–213, 1999.
6. boyd, danah and Marwick, Alice. Social Privacy in Networked Publics: Teens' Attitudes, Practices, and Strategies. In *A Decade in Internet Time: Symposium on the Dynamics of the Internet and Society*, 1999.
7. T. Brants and A. Franz. Web 1T 5-gram Version 1. *Linguistic Data Consortium, Philadelphia*, 2006.

8. S. E. Brennan. The grounding problem in conversations with and through computers. *Social and cognitive approaches to interpersonal communication*, pages 201–225, 1998.
9. R. S. Campbell and J. W. Pennebaker. The secret life of pronouns flexibility in writing style and physical health. *Psychological Science*, 14(1):60–65, 2003.
10. J. Chen, G. Hsieh, J. U. Mahmud, and J. Nichols. Understanding individuals' personal values from social media word use. In *Proc. CSCW*, pages 405–414, 2014.
11. C. Chung and J. W. Pennebaker. The psychological functions of function words. *Social communication*, pages 343–359, 2007.
12. H. H. Clark. *Using language*, volume 1996. Cambridge University Press Cambridge, 1996.
13. H. H. Clark and S. E. Brennan. Grounding in communication. *Perspectives on socially shared cognition*, 13(1991):127–149, 1991.
14. H. H. Clark and M. A. Krych. Speaking while monitoring addressees for understanding. *Journal of Memory and Language*, 50(1):62–81, 2004.
15. W. Diffie and M. E. Hellman. New directions in cryptography. *IEEE Transactions on Information Theory*, 22(6):644–654, 1976.
16. D. Gergle, R. E. Kraut, and S. R. Fussell. The impact of delayed visual feedback on collaborative performance. In *Proc. CHI*, pages 1303–1312. ACM, 2006.
17. G. Greenwald and E. MacAskill. NSA Prism program taps in to user data of Apple, Google and others. *The Guardian*, June 6, 2013.
18. J. T. Hancock and P. J. Dunham. Language use in computer-mediated communication: The role of coordination devices. *Discourse Processes*, 31(1):91–110, 2001.
19. S. G. Hart and L. E. Staveland. Development of NASA-TLX (task load index): Results of empirical and theoretical research. *Human mental workload*, 1(3):139–183, 1988.
20. P. J. Hinds and D. E. Bailey. Out of sight, out of sync: Understanding conflict in distributed teams. *Organization science*, 14(6):615–632, 2003.
21. F. Jin, R. P. Khandpur, N. Self, E. Dougherty, S. Guo, F. Chen, B. A. Prakash, and N. Ramakrishnan. Modeling Mass Protest Adoption in Social Network Communities Using Geometric Brownian Motion. In *Proc. KDD*, pages 1660–1669, 2014.
22. B. Klimt and Y. Yang. Introducing the Enron Corpus. In *CEAS*, 2004.
23. G. Miller. WordNet: A Lexical Database for English. *CACM*, 38(11):39–41, 1995.
24. R. L. Rivest, A. Shamir, and L. Adleman. A method for obtaining digital signatures and public-key cryptosystems. *CACM*, 21(2):120–126, 1978.
25. N. S. Shami, J. Nichols, and J. Chen. Social Media Participation and Performance at Work: A Longitudinal Study. In *Proc. CHI*, pages 115–118, 2014.
26. S. Sheng, L. Broderick, C. A. Koranda, and J. J. Hyland. Why Johnny still can't encrypt: evaluating the usability of email encryption software. In *Proc. SOUPS*, 2006.
27. N. Spasojevic, J. Yan, A. Rao, and P. Bhattacharyya. LASTA: Large Scale Topic Assignment on Multiple Social Networks. In *Proc. KDD*, pages 1809–1818, 2014.
28. S. Subramaniam. Frontiers in E-commerce Personalization. In *Proc. KDD*, pages 1516–1516, 2014.
29. J. Vertesi. My Experiment Opting Out of Big Data Made Me Look Like a Criminal. *Time*, May 1, 2014.
30. A. Whitten and J. D. Tygar. Why Johnny can't encrypt: A usability evaluation of PGP 5.0. In *Proceedings of the 8th USENIX Security Symposium*, 1999.
31. S.-H. Yang, A. Kolcz, A. Schlaikjer, and P. Gupta. Large-scale High-precision Topic Modeling on Twitter. In *Proc. KDD*, pages 1907–1916, 2014.
32. P. R. Zimmermann. *The official PGP user's guide*. MIT press, 1995.

Sensors Know When to Interrupt You in the Car: Detecting Driver Interruptibility Through Monitoring of Peripheral Interactions

SeungJun Kim[1], Jaemin Chun[2], and Anind K. Dey[3]
Human-Computer Interaction Institute, Carnegie Mellon University, Pittsburgh, PA 15213 USA
{sjunikim, anind}@cs.cmu.edu[1,3], and jaemchun@andrew.cmu.edu[2]

ABSTRACT
Interruptions while driving can be quite dangerous, whether these are self-interruptions or external interruptions. They increase driver workload and reduce performance on the primary driving task. Being able to identify when a driver is interruptible is critical for building systems that can mediate these interruptions. In this paper, we collect sensor and human-annotated data from 15 drivers, including vehicle motion, traffic states, physiological responses and driver motion. We demonstrate that this data can be used to build a machine learning classifier that can determine interruptibility every second with a 94% accuracy. We present both population and individual models and discuss the features that contribute to the high performance of this system. Such a classifier can be used to build systems that mediate when drivers use technology to self-interrupt and when drivers are interrupted by technology.

Author Keywords
Interruptions; Naturalistic Driving; Sensor Data Mining

ACM Classification Keywords
H.5.m. Information interfaces and presentation (e.g., HCI): Miscellaneous

INTRODUCTION
Human attention is a finite resource [25]. When interrupted while performing a task, this resource is split between two interactive tasks. People have to decide whether the benefits from the interruptive interaction will be enough to offset the loss of attention from the original task. They may choose to ignore or delay dealing with the interruption to a more convenient time. They may alternately choose to immediately address the interruption but this comes with a risk of reduced performance on the primary task or a delay in resuming their primary task [19, 22, 27].

The issue of dealing with peripheral tasks (both self-interruptions and external interruptions) is particularly critical in driving situations. Under normal driving conditions, drivers should have an appropriate following distance (ideally 2-3 seconds behind the car in front of you [*e.g.*, 12]) for safe driving. This following distance provides the driver with enough reaction time to decide whether to stop, slow down, or otherwise react to changing driving conditions.

However, driving guidelines like this assume that the driver is fully attending to the driving task. If a driver is performing peripheral tasks, those not directly related to the driving task (*e.g.*, turning off a smartphone alarm or changing the radio station), she needs to manage when to divide her attention. Depending on the frequency and duration of these additional tasks, drivers need to adapt how they apply safe driving guidelines.

Fortunately, drivers naturally adapt to changing driving conditions when dealing with peripheral tasks, *e.g.*, waiting for a red light to attend to these tasks, and not performing them in heavy traffic. They determine appropriate timings for changing the positions of their hands on the steering wheel, controlling the foot pedals, all while monitoring adjacent traffic. However, if a demand for peripheral interaction arrives at an inappropriate or unexpected time (*e.g.*, phone rings while changing lanes to exit the highway), it can lead to dangerous driving situations which may result in a driving violation, accident or even loss of life. In fact, 25% of car accidents in the U.S. are related to phone use [8].

By identifying situations or patterns when drivers are not able to attend to peripheral tasks due to their current state and driving situation, a workload manager (*e.g.*, Green [9]), may regulate the flow of information to drivers that could otherwise interfere with driving. Intelligent systems will be able to mediate the delivery of external interruptions, or even disable phone/infotainment systems to mediate self-interruptions [*e.g.*, 24], to support safer driving.

In this context, we investigate when and how drivers perform peripheral activities while driving. We identify driver and driving states and road configurations in which drivers choose to deal with interruptions.

Specifically, we explore three overarching questions:

- What are the driver and driving states in which drivers perform peripheral activities?
- What sensors and sensor features best explain the states in which drivers perform peripheral interactions?
- How quickly and accurately can systems assess opportunities for peripheral interaction?

CHI 2015, April 18 - 23 2015, Seoul, Republic of Korea

http://dx.doi.org/10.1145/2702123.2702409

Through an in-car data collection with 15 drivers, we collected a large variety of sensor data to understand driver state and driving situations including vehicle motion states, road conditions, driver motion changes, and physiological responses, while capturing driver interactions and traffic states during naturalistic driving. We demonstrate that this data can be used to build a population model that is 94% accurate at determining the interruptibility of a driver each second. We discuss the most informative features that contribute to this performance, and how such a model can be used in practice for mediating interruptions while driving. We start with an overview of background work motivating the need for sensor-based assessment of driving experiences during naturalistic driving, especially in the situations of divided attention due to in-car interruptions.

BACKGROUND WORK

Driver Experience Sampling

Traditionally, user experience has been sampled by asking people to stop mid-task and note their experience [17]. The point is for users to record *in situ* aspects of experience like mental effort or emotion, based on their own judgment. When users are engaged in naturalistic and uncontrolled real-world tasks, that approach provides low-resolution data since sampling rates need to be low to avoid disrupting the user too much, but are often too low to track dynamically varying user states [10]. This problem is especially disadvantageous in mobile contexts such as driving.

In automotive contexts, when directed to self-report experience, drivers must divert their attention from the driving task. This can diminish cognitive capabilities for the primary task by drawing attention to interruptive demands for peripheral interaction; while driving, interruptions can negatively impact primary task performance. As well, when sampling user state at the end of a driving session, *in situ* variations of that state can be blurred in relation to the overall user experience. Due to these potential issues, driver experience sampling based on self-reports has typically been explored for evaluating user interfaces (*e.g.*, dashboard designs) or within driving simulations (*e.g.*, [13],[16]) where interruptions are less dangerous.

In our work, we seek to better understand the relationship between a driver's performance of peripheral tasks and *in-situ* driver states and driving contexts. This necessitates the continuous sampling of user state while driving; therefore, we mainly explore sensor-based assessments to sample driver states. This approach provides quantifiable, fine-grained data in real-time. The feasibility of this approach has been validated in simulated driving experimentation (*e.g.*, [12], [21]), and we apply this to naturalistic driving.

Interruptions

As the physical world becomes increasingly connected with our information spaces, so too is the likelihood that information will be pushed to people during the performance of real-world tasks. At best, those interruptions may alert users to important warnings or messages, inquire about people's status (*e.g.*, affective states or health conditions for health care), or deliver information that can benefit task performance. Despite this potential value, dealing with these interruptions through peripheral interaction (interaction not directly related to the primary task) demands cognitive attention that can negatively and variably impact user experience. An improved understanding of user availability or interruptibility is necessary for mediating this impact.

Task interruptions result in a time lag before users can resume their primary task, and thus decrease primary task performance [19, 27]. Appropriate timings of interruptions can reduce the impact on users. For example, in the context of desktop computing, interruptions delivered at points of lower mental workload reduced resumption lags and minimized disruption in primary task performance compared to interruptions at points of higher mental workload [1, 6]. In an experiment in which participants were interrupted with emails about consumer products and prices [22], users who experienced deferrable interruptions during high cognitive workload tasks frequently disregarded the notifications until they reached low workload periods. The results of another experiment showed that when peripheral tasks involving reasoning, reading or arithmetic interrupt the execution of primary tasks, users require more time to complete the primary tasks, commit more errors, and become more annoyed and increasingly anxious than when those same peripheral tasks were presented at the boundary between primary tasks [2].

These studies offer important insights for designing human-centered interruptions; however, they have mostly explored static, on-screen tasks mediated with conventional computers or mobile devices (*e.g.*, the impact of call notifications for smartphone users [3]). Little research has been conducted to replicate these findings or approaches for delivering interruptions in situations in which users cannot fully divert their attention from the primary task (*e.g.*, driving cars) and in which interruption timings can critically impact the user experience. We attempt to address this in our work.

Naturalistic driving

To ensure driver safety, driving studies about dual task paradigms have mostly been conducted in simulated environments [*e.g.*, 21]. When using sensors to track drivers' eye gazes or physiological responses in these simulations, the experimental design requires special attention to achieve valid and realistic data. Due to this issue of driver safety, existing naturalistic driving datasets mostly include audiovisual records, traffic and lane information from vision-based systems [*e.g.*, 18], and researcher-estimated driver states using image processing techniques [*e.g.*, 15] on videos from multiple cameras installed in cars.

Recent advances in wearable technologies have resulted in sensors that are less intrusive and more comfortable to wear;

nevertheless little research (*e.g.*, [23]) has been performed that tracks driver body motion or physiological responses during naturalistic driving. Driver workload has been mostly evoked by imposing artificial dual-task demands (*e.g.*, auditory stimuli at pre-structured interaction times and intervals [26]). On-board diagnostic (OBD) systems or accelerometers on the steering wheel have been used to assess driver aggressiveness, driving environment and vehicle states (*e.g.*, [7, 11]). In our work, we leverage all of these sensing technologies to help us identify which sensor streams and features are most useful for tracking driver state and the performance of peripheral activities; our novelty lies in detecting driver interruptibility by continuously monitoring naturalistic driver / driving states without artificially manipulating cognitive demands.

EXPERIMENTAL SETUP

Here we describe our experimental method for collecting naturalistic driving data for the purpose of identifying situations when peripheral interactions occur.

Participants: We recruited 25 drivers (age *M*=32.0, *SD*=14.3, age range: 19 - 69, gender: 14 female and 11 male). Participants were asked to drive their own cars and were compensated with $20. The experiment took approximately two hours to complete, including about 1.25 hours of driving.

Participants had 14.5 years of driving experience on average (*SD*=13.2, range: 1 - 52 years). They self-reported that they drove on city streets 8.7 times per week (*SD*=7.1, range: 2 - 35 times) and on highways 4.5 times per week (*SD*=4.7, range: 1 - 20 times). They used familiar routes 8.8 times per week (*SD*=9.4, range: 2 - 50 times) and unfamiliar routes 1.2 times per week (*SD*=1.0, range: 0-3 times). The average driving trip duration was 30.4 minutes (*SD*=19.2, range: 10 - 100 minutes).

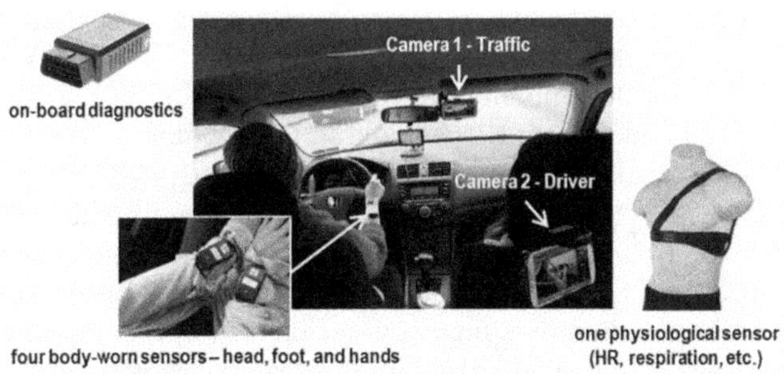

Figure 1: Experimental setup – two smartphone cameras, five body-worn sensors, and one on-board diagnostics in the cars.

Test-bed: As shown in Figure 1, we plugged an on-board diagnostics (OBD) device in study participants' cars, and they were asked to wear five body-worn sensor devices: four accelerometer sensors for capturing body motion and one chest belt sensor for tracking physiological responses. We installed two smartphones in each car - one on the front windshield and the other on the head-rest of the passenger seat. The phone cameras recorded traffic in adjacent lanes and drivers' activities in the cars. They also received information from the OBD device and body-worn sensors via Bluetooth and logged sensor data streams in real-time.

Main task: Study participants performed two sessions of naturalistic field driving. Driving routes in both sessions were selected to combine both city streets and highways. The route in the 1st session consisted mainly of highway driving to a shopping mall. Drivers were allowed to take any preferred or familiar route to get the destination (according to Google maps, the destination was 14.7 miles away). The route in the 2nd session consisted mainly of driving on city streets to a sports stadium in our city's downtown area, along with shorter lengths of highway driving compared to the previous session. In this session, drivers were asked to drive using a provided Garmin GPS to reach the destination (Google maps: 4.8 miles).

Some participants performed both driving sessions on the same day while others performed them on different days. By fixing the destinations, and in the 2nd session, the route, drivers were exposed to similar configuration of roads in terms of the number of signal lights and signs to encounter, the length of highways and streets, road curvedness, and hill gradient. By leaving flexibility about the route to take in the 1st session, we were able to collect data from driving on familiar and unfamiliar routes.

Sessions: There was a set of activities performed in each session: we installed the devices in drivers' cars and helped them wear the physiological sensors, time-synced the devices and collected baseline data, and had drivers complete a pre-questionnaire, perform the driving task, and complete a post-task questionnaire and interview.

For *syncing* the devices, experimenters shook all the wearable sensors for a period of twenty seconds, once after device setup both prior to and after completing the driving tasks. Those time-windows were used for synchronizing timestamps across data streams from the worn sensors.

For collecting *baseline measurements*, drivers were asked to grip the steering wheel at the three and nine o'clock positions, while closing their eyes after taking a deep breath. We collected sensor data streams from the body-worn sensors for 60 seconds of this "at rest" behavior.

In the *pre-questionnaire* prior to 1st driving session, we collected demographic information of study participants and information about driving frequency and patterns when performing peripheral interactions in cars.

In the *post-questionnaire* after each driving session, drivers were asked to describe situations during their just-completed session, (*e.g.*, number of passengers, familiarity to driving routes, traffics, sensor comfort, driving performance) and complete a NASA-TLX assessment.

In the *post-interview*, we sought to validate our hypothesis that the driver and driving contexts can help us determine when drivers can perform peripheral interactions. Specifically, we presented drivers with 17 images of drivers performing secondary tasks while driving (*e.g.*, eating, car radio interaction), and then asked them to comment on all the activities that they conducted during their driving session, explain what factors led them to perform those peripheral interactions, including traffic, in-car and on-road situations, and then comment on whether the moments when they chose to initiate peripheral interactions while driving would also be good for being interrupted.

Peripheral Interaction Moments Correspond to Driver Interruptibility

In regular driving situations, there are many instances of drivers engaging in peripheral interactions: actions that take place in the car, but are not related to driving the car. We believe that these instances can be used as *ground truth* of moments when the driver believes he is able to enter a situation of divided attention [5], and, therefore can better deal with interruptions. This belief needs to be validated.

For example, if a driver eats or drinks while at a red light and she usually interacts with the car radio interface searching for a particular radio station while driving at a constant speed on a street with no noticeable grade or curve in the road, these situations represent conditions in which the driver feels she is able to divide her attention. Drivers may consciously or subconsciously know about the moments in which they can perform multiple tasks at the same time. If they are not actually engaged in any peripheral interaction during such a situation, this may imply that this moment can be used to interrupt the driver with external information (*e.g.*, upcoming traffic information, text message or even advertisements), more safely than in other conditions where no peripheral interactions are ever performed (*e.g.*, during acceleration or driving on a sharp curve). It is also important to separate out interactions with activities that are performed to directly support the driving task – for example, operating blinkers for changing lanes and wipers for better visibility when raining. Moments involving these types of tasks cannot necessarily be viewed as opportunities for performing peripheral interactions or interrupting the user.

Validation: In the post interviews, all drivers described moments in which they initiated peripheral interactions during the driving session they just completed. They stated that these moments were appropriate for being interrupted.

One participant said he would perform peripheral interactions "*usually if I was at a red light or if I was stuck in traffic, also depends on the situation - if I don't have to make a turn and it's a straight road. I didn't do anything while I was making a turn or going through an intersection. I waited until it was a straight stretch of road with no places where cars would pull out and low traffic.*"

Another said "*In most cases, I chose when to have the interaction - when to turn on the wipers, when to change the radio station or adjust the volume... except when I needed more attention on driving. Wipers I turned on because there was too much stuff on the view. Radio, I changed channels when I thought it was a good time too. If I were stopped in traffic, then yes, I would think that that's also a good time to [receive interruptions].*"

TIME-SERIES DATA

Based on these interview results validating that moments in which peripheral interactions are performed are times when drivers could be interrupted, we proceeded with the analysis of the captured sensor data to automatically identify these moments. We started this process with identifying ground truth about what drivers were doing during driving sessions.

Videos and Annotation features

Camera 1: One of the two smartphone cameras was used for examining drivers' activities in cars. We manually labeled the captured videos for moments when peripheral interactions were performed and not performed. We used five labels. `DRIVING_I` includes activities that are quite central to the primary driving task (*e.g.*, changing grip positions, operating levers for blinkers or wipers, switches for opening side windows), whereas `PI` includes activities that are not directly central to the primary task (*e.g.*, eating food, manipulating the air conditioner or car radio, talking on the phone). `ONE_HAND_DRIVE_WITH_NO_PI` was used to label moments when one of the driver's hands was off the steering wheel but that hand was not performing any specific activity. `NO_HAND_DRIVE` was used for moments when both hands were off the steering wheel and not performing any peripheral activity. `STEERING_ONLY` was used for moments when both hands were on the wheel. From our interviews, moments that are labeled with `PI` or `NO_HAND_DRIVE` indicate that drivers have higher interruptibility, compared with moments of `DRIVING_I` or `STEERING_ONLY`.

Camera 2: The other smartphone camera was used for assessing the traffic around the driver. We labeled the videos for the amount of traffic visible in front of the car, to the left and right of the car, and in the oncoming lanes. The traffic labels we used were `NO_TRAFFIC`, `IGNORABLE`, `SOME`, `A_LOT` based on the approximate distance of adjacent cars and the number of cars. If the traffic in the oncoming lane was occluded by cars in the left lane or a center guardrail on a highway, we labeled it as `OCCLUDED`. We also had a label indicating the car's movement, whether it was `STOPPED` or `MOVING`.

Three experimenters, each having more than 4-years experience in psychology or human computer interaction, reviewed videos from the smartphones and labeled the kind, start time, and end time of drivers' peripheral activities, and traffic. Note that while we manually labeled the videos from both cameras, these are labels that could be automatically provided using computer vision (*e.g.*, [4]).

Six Sensors and Applied features

An *OBD device* provided information about the status of the vehicle (sampled at 1Hz) including longitude, latitude, altitude, car speed, engine RPM, throttle position, and fuel flow rate. The data were transmitted via Bluetooth to the smartphone responsible for recording traffic video.

Four *YEI 3-Space devices* were used, placed on each of the drivers' wrists, on the front of the head, and top of the foot. The devices collected information about the drivers' motions using a tri-axial gyroscope, a tri-axial accelerometer, and compass sensors, all at 4-5 Hz. The sensor data was transmitted via Bluetooth to the other smartphone. In addition, drivers wore a *BioHarness (BH) chest belt* that collected drivers' physiological data including electrocardiogram, heart rate, respiration rate, body orientation and activity at 20Hz sampling rate.

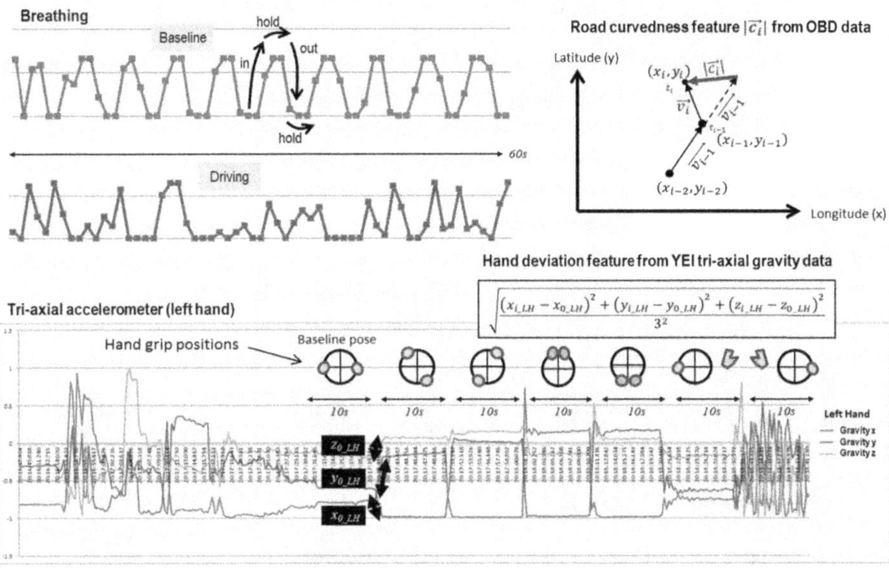

Figure 2: Examples of applied features from sensor data streams – breathing states (top-left), road curvedness (top-right), hand deviation (bottom)

After time syncing the sensors, all sensor data were aggregated, and their means (μ) and standard deviations (σ) were calculated for every 1-second segment as statistical features (referred to as '*basic*' features in this paper). In addition, we derived a series of additional features based on the basic features. For example, from the OBD data we derived *road curvedness* by tracking variations of longitude and latitude coordinates (See Figure 2 – top-right), *centrifugal forces* by combining car speed and curvedness information, types and gradient of *road slope* by using the 1st derivative of altitude data. From the YEI data, we derived motion information on how much each monitored body part moved from the baseline position (See Figure 2 – bottom). From the BH data, we quantified levels and duration of breathing-in, breathing-out, and holding-breath states (See Figure 2 – top-left). These supplementary features are referred to as '*derived*' features in this paper. In total, we had 100 basic features and 52 derived features (OBD: 72, YEI: 40, BH: 40) and 5 manually annotated features related to traffic from videos (one car driving state and four traffic states around the vehicle – front, right, left, and oncoming).

DATA COLLECTION STATUS

Of our 25 drivers, 17 drivers successfully completed both driving sessions without any loss in data. The 17 drivers drove for an average of 43m 59.2s in the first driving session (*SD* = 7m 23.5s, range: 28m 42s - 54m 14s) and 33m 18.3s in the second driving session (*SD* = 7m 42.4s, range: 25m 36s - 51m 32s) on average. For the remaining 8 drivers, most data loss came from Bluetooth disconnections either when OBD devices were accidentally dislodged by drivers' knees or when the Android data logging applications crashed. Occasionally smartphones fell from their mounts or turned enough to capture irrelevant data.

When examining the sensor data, we further excluded 2 drivers' data. Their heart rate data contained errors (higher than 200 beats per minutes during the entire driving session). This happened when the BioHarness sensor was worn too loose around the driver's torso during the driving session. We did not include data from these 10 drivers in the sensor data analysis although we did include them in the analysis of the questionnaires and interviews.

STATISTICAL ANALYSIS METHOD

With the data from our 15 remaining drivers, we examined how driver and driving states differ across our five driving state classes: `STEERING_ONLY`, `ONE_HAND_DRIVE_WITH_NO_PI`, `DRIVING_I`, `PI`, and `NO_HAND_DRIVE`.

For analyzing the continuous measures (*e.g.*, car speed), we conducted a univariate ANOVA by using a general linear model and then used either Tukey HSD or Games-Howell as *post-hoc* tests after checking the homogeneity of variances (*i.e.*, Levene Statistic), where η_p^2 was examined as effect size. For ordinal measures (*e.g.*, human-annotated data or fixed level data), we conducted the Kruskal Wallis Test followed by Mann-Whitney U test as post-hoc, where *r* was examined as effect size. In the analysis of Likert-scale rating data, Friedman tests and a Wilcoxon Signed Rank *post-hoc* test were conducted.

RESULTS

Driver Activities: Frequency and Duration

In total, 53 different activities were detected from the 15 drivers. In the remaining analysis, we focus on 22 of these activities that had a total duration of at least 90 seconds summed across multiple instances. As shown in Table 1, activities include interacting with the air conditioner or car radio, operating blinkers or windshield wipers, eating food and drinking, driving with one hand, smoking, dancing, changing hand grip, resting by removing both hands from the steering wheel, and so forth.

One-handed driving most frequently occurred (57.1 times per subject, with 6.9 instances for each 10-minute driving segment; See Table 1). When total durations were considered, summed up for each participant and summed over a 10-minute segment, it was also first (15.4 and 117.0 seconds, respectively). However, when ranking these by the duration per instance, using one's cellphone was the longest (21.7 seconds), followed by eating food or drinking, smoking, and one-handed driving.

Driver activities	Occurrence / subject	Occurrence / 10-min drive	Duration (sec) / subject	Duration (sec) / 10-min drive	Duration (sec / occurrence) M (SD)
ONE_HAND_DRIVE	**57.1**	**6.9**	**15.4**	**117.0**	**17.0 (26)**
GEAR_SHIFT	**37.1**	**4.5**	2.7	**19.0**	4.2 (6.7)
TOUCHING_SELF (e.g., face)	**24.5**	**3.0**	7.6	**28.5**	9.7 (21.5)
REST_OFF_WHEEL	**20.6**	**2.5**	**14.7**	**37.2**	**15.0 (14.1)**
L_BLINKER	**15.7**	**1.9**	3.9	8.6	4.6 (16.8)
R_BLINKER	14	1.7	4.4	9.4	5.6 (22)
CAR_RADIO	9.2	1.1	5.9	9.5	8.6 (16.7)
R_GRIP_CHANGE	8	1.0	2.9	6.3	6.6 (12.5)
HEAD_ TURNING_WAY_LEFT	7.3	0.9	4.2	4.8	5.5 (12.1)
CELLPHONE	6.7	0.8	**13.5**	**17.6**	**21.7 (26.9)**
L_GRIP_CHANGE	6.7	0.8	1.8	2.0	2.5 (3.1)
HEAD_TURNING_WAY_RIGHT	5.7	0.7	2.6	1.9	2.8 (2.7)
GPS_PORTABLE	4.5	0.5	**14.3**	6.5	12.1 (13.5)
AC_CONTROL_SWITCHES	3.1	0.4	1.8	1.0	2.5 (1.5)
BOTH_HANDS_OFF_DRIVE	2.3	0.3	2.2	3.0	11.0 (11)
FOOD_OR_DRINK	2.6	0.3	**11.6**	5.9	**18.8 (16.6)**
OTHERS_MISCELLANEOUS (e.g., shouting outside)	2.7	0.3	6.5	3.3	9.9 (10.7)
OTHERS_MUSIC	2.7	0.3	1.4	5.2	16.2 (15.3)
SMOKING	1.9	0.2	1.2	4.3	**18.3 (41.8)**
WIPER_WASHER	1.7	0.2	2.9	1.6	7.5 (12.5)
AC_AIR_VENTS	1.1	0.1	3.5	1.5	11.7 (19.2)
OTHERS_DANCE	0.1	0.0	0.7	0.2	11.0 (8.5)
Total	235.3	28.3	5.7	13.4	10.4 (19.7)

Table 1. Frequency and duration of 22 top-ranked driver activities sorted by a descending order based on occurrence per unit, in which top-five measures and activities are in bold.

For most of the driving time, drivers used both their hands (48.0%) or one hand (22.8%) for controlling the vehicle without any peripheral interaction (See STEERING_ONLY and ONE_HAND_DRIVE_WITH_NO_PI in Figure 3).

The time spent in performing a task is indicative of user workload (*e.g.*, [10]). Similarly, duration of a particular peripheral activity during driving may indicate how drivers are consciously or subconsciously estimating interaction workload for that activity. In other words, the longer the time spent on a peripheral interaction, the greater the availability for being interrupted. In this study, we found that the average duration was significantly different among the five interaction states ($F_{4,4546}$=116.2, p = .000). The pair-wise difference between each state was significant in the *post-hoc* test with the exception of the durations between ONE_HAND_DRIVE_WITH_NO_PI and NO_HAND_ DRIVE (See Figure 3 – two rightmost bars). This implies that although

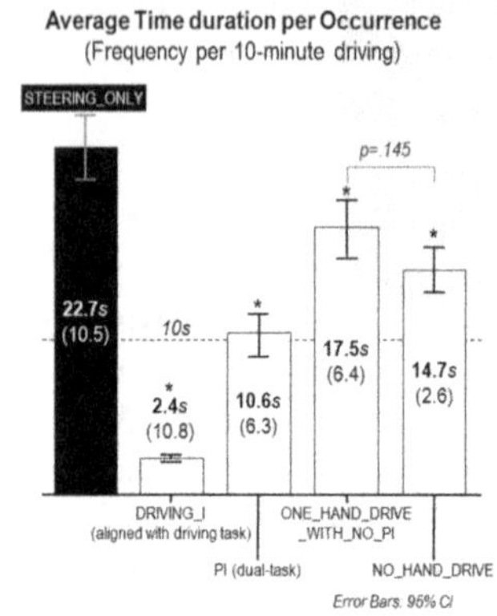

Figure 3: Average time duration of drivers' interaction states. *p<.001 compared with STEERING ONLY states.

drivers did not actually execute any peripheral activity, one handed driving is a distinct state from using both hands for steering. Similarly, there was no discernible distinction in durations between one handed and no-handed driving. We will discuss this finding later in the paper.

Driver activities that corresponded to the driving task (*e.g.*, turning on blinkers) were completed in 2.4 seconds on average, while peripheral interactions lasted for 10.6 seconds (DRIVING_I and PI in Figure 3).

Driving States: Car Speed and Road Conditions

The OBD data streams revealed that drivers significantly regulated car speed while performing peripheral activities or taking both hands off the steering wheel (See Figure 4 – the left-most bar in each group). Compared to the STEERING_ONLY state, car speed was reduced to 60% while peripheral interactions were performed (PI state in Figure 4), and almost reduced completely (slower than 3.0km/h) while driving without either hand on the steering wheel.

When drivers were in either of these two slower states, engine RPM was significantly lower and the proportion of time spent on flatter roads (*i.e.*, low grades) was significantly higher, compared to the STEERING_ONLY state. In particular, as indicated by ★ for the right-most two bars of Figure 4, drivers were on flatter and less curvy roads while driving with both hands off the steering wheel (statistically significant when compared to each of the other states). Interestingly, one-handed driving was performed at considerably high speeds, without necessarily being on flat

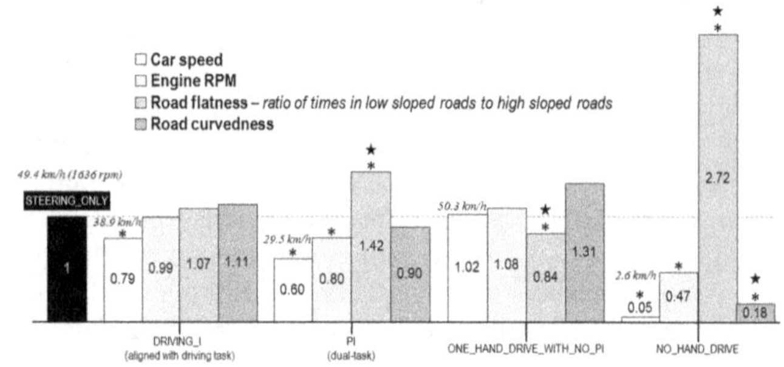

Figure 4: Driving states and road conditions. *p<.001 versus STEERING_ONLY states; ★p<.001 versus all other states.

or straight roads.

These findings imply that driving status for the PI or NO_HAND_DRIVE states are most similar. In addition, they represent the moments when the driver is likely to be more interruptible. However, we do not include one-handed driving in this group. The driving state and road conditions were different for ONE_HAND_DRIVE_WITH_NO_PI.

In addition, when examining how drivers accelerate or decelerate across the five states, we see that drivers tend to drive at more consistent speeds during PI (47.8%) or NO_HAND_DRIVE (73.7%) states than in the ONE_HAND_DRIVE_WITH_NO_PI state (24.6%) (Figure 5).

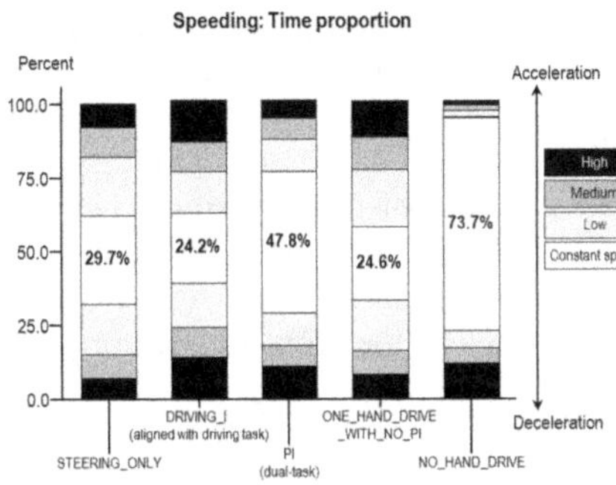

Figure 5: Time proportion of acceleration, deceleration, and constant speed across whole driving.

Driver State: Body Motion and Physiological States

The deviation of gravity measures from the STEERING_ONLY body pose were significantly different for every pair of the five states across every body element (Figure 6). In particular, the right hand movement was distinct when performing driving or peripheral activities (2nd and 3rd bars from the top). Head movement was larger when driving while taking both hands or one hand off the steering wheel without performing any peripheral activities (bottom two bars in Figure 6).

Drivers' breathing states and heart rate also significantly varied across the five interaction states ($F_{5,34693}$=6.80, p=.000 and $F_{5,36565}$ = 215.0, p=.000, respectively; Figure 7). Interestingly, for NO_HAND_DRIVE, drivers' heart rate was similarly low as the resting heart rate captured in the baseline session where no driving was performed (bottom 2 bars from Figure 7). Also, the heart rate during ONE_HAND_DRIVE_WITH_NO_PI state was similar to PI, but not to NO_HAND_DRIVE or baseline. The duration of drivers holding their breath was not statistically significant ($F_{5,4467}$=1.99, p=.075). Rather, durations for inhaling and exhaling were significantly longer for the PI or NO_HAND_DRIVE states, and similar to when resting in the baseline session.

Overall, driver physiological states for the PI and NO_HAND_DRIVE states are most similar to the resting states. We therefore confirm that from our analysis of physiological states, driving states and road conditions,

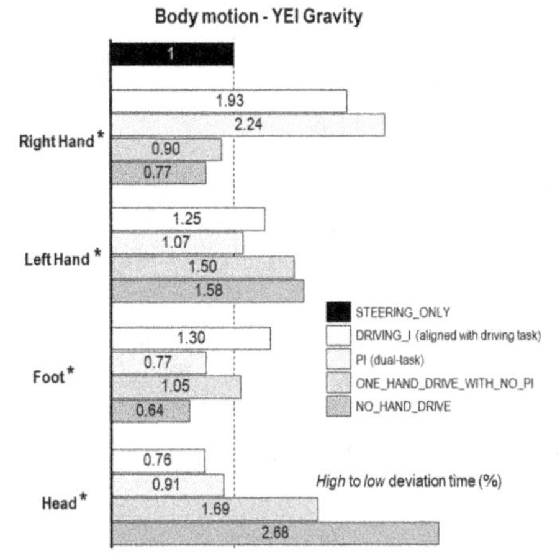

Figure 6: Driver body motion revealed in sensor data streams. * p<.01 in every pair of the five interaction states.

drivers are more interruptible than in the remaining states. However, interruptibility while one-handed driving without any peripheral interactions is still unclear since driver physiological states are similar to the two interruptible states and the baseline, but the driving states and road conditions differed significantly.

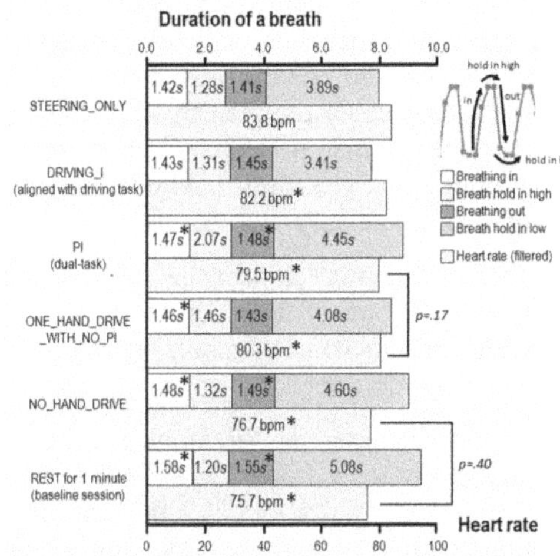

Figure 7: Drivers' physiological states revealed in sensor data streams. *p<.01 versus STEERING_ONLY states.

Identifying Opportunities for interruptions

Given the statistical differences across the five interaction states, and particularly between the more interruptible and less interruptible states, we now seek to automatically identify opportune moments for driver interruption. Specifically, we want to build a classifier that accurately detects or predicts interruptibility every second.

To build this classifier, we combined the PI and NO_HAND_DRIVE states into a single class representing instances when drivers can be interrupted (INTERRUPTIBILE). We correspondingly combined data from the remaining classes into the LESS_INTERRUPTIBLE class; note that we do not call this "Uninterruptible" since we cannot know with absolute certainty that drivers are not interruptible during these interaction states, but just that they are likely to be less so.

For this binary classification problem, we used a random forest classifier, which runs efficiently on large databases such as our sensor data. We also handled unbalanced classes using stratified 10-fold cross validation where each fold contains approximately the same percentage of samples from each target class as the complete set, and then applied different sample weights based on the ratio of samples that belong to each class. We automated this procedure for each driver and for each fold.

Our population-based classifier had an average classification accuracy of 94.3% classification accuracy across the data from all 15 drivers (*SD*=0.3%, average precision and recall: 0.94 and 0.89, respectively). From our initial list of 143 features, car speed (OBD, km/h), engine RPM, GPS bearing, centrifugal features, and the movement of the right hand deviating from the baseline position were rank-ordered as the most important features, along with two human-annotations about the car movement states (top-ranked feature) and the front traffic (7th-ranked). While we believe that these human annotations could be automated with today's image processing technologies, we built a second classifier that did not use any human annotations. The classification accuracy dropped by only 2.2% (92.1%, *SD*=0.2). This means that the binary states representing driver interruptibility can be discriminated accurately every second using sensor data only.

Next, we examined the performance of the individual models for each of our fifteen drivers, to investigate individual difference in which features were most helpful and whether such models need to be personalized.

Promisingly, the average classification accuracy of the individual models of our drivers was 94.9% on average (*SD*=2.6%, range: 90.2% from 98.2%), almost the same as the population model (94.3%) Accuracy for every driver was greater than 90% (See Figure 8).

However, the recall rate (*i.e.*, the fraction of relevant instances that are retrieved = the percentage of interruptible moments correctly classified as being interruptible) had some individual differences. Five of our drivers (driver 05, 10, 11, 21, and 23) had recall rates lower than 80%, while the precision rates (*i.e.*, the fraction of retrieved instances that are relevant = the percentage of moments identified as interruptible that were actually interruptible) were fairly consistent along with the classification accuracy across every driver.

We then focused on the top fifteen features for each driver that contributed to classification accuracy, to identify which features were commonly used in the individual models. Of the 143 features, 46 features were chosen in at least one driver's list of top fifteen features (23 from OBD device, 21 from the body-worn sensors, and 2 from the human-annotated data). Similar to the population model, engine

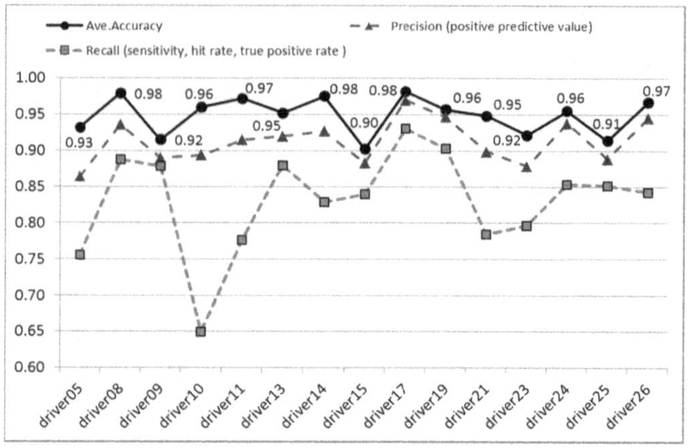

Figure 8: The classification performance of individual models for our fifteen drivers.

RPM, car speed (OBD, km/h), and car movement annotation features were identified again as important features for more than ten of our drivers. However, unlike in our group model, heart rate, foot and body trunk/torso motion were also important for five drivers, centrifugal force for seven drivers and the front traffic annotation data for only six drivers.

DICUSSION

In this section, we discuss our finding on driving states, the features that contributed to our model, and our ability to detect moments of interruptibility. We use these to point out opportunities for future research that can build on the contributions of this paper.

Driver and Driving states

Our sensor data revealed that drivers perform peripheral activities when experiencing lower workload. Similar to driving without holding the steering wheel, drivers tend to initiate peripheral interactions at a near constant car speed on fairly flat and straight roads. Further, drivers' physiological signals were similar to those during the resting states in the baseline session. This implies that drivers may defer processing peripheral tasks until they are experiencing lower mental workload, confirming findings reported in prior interruption studies (*e.g.*, [22]).

An interesting situation is when drivers use only one hand but do not perform any peripheral activity with the idle hand. In general, drivers' physiological responses during this state implied lower driver workload, closer to that of performing peripheral interaction. However, the driving states for one-handed driving were much more dynamic than when performing peripheral interactions. Drivers either accelerated or decelerated without avoiding curved roads, and more often even than when using both hands to steer. This provides an interesting hypothesis that drivers may have extra cognitive capacity to deal with peripheral interactions. It is unclear whether this "extra" capacity is actually in use for the driving task, for enjoying an idle moment without initiating peripheral activities. In our future work, we will investigate this issue.

Indicative sensor data features

The derived features used to create our classifiers had more discriminative power than the simple statistical (basic) features. For example, the centrifugal feature created with a combination of car speed and road curvedness (more precisely, the square of car velocity divided by the road curvedness feature not considering driver weight) was ranked as the 5th most important in the population model and was in the top-15 features for 7 of the drivers' individual models. If we incorporated the gravity variation coming from the road slope or the driver's seating pose, this new feature could be even more powerful.

Similarly, the derived physiological responses (*e.g.*, breathing rates) and road attributes (*e.g.*, categorized slope levels) had statistical differences between driver's interaction states. However, they did not explicitly contribute to building high performance classification models. Only two basic features, heart rate (in top-15 list for five drivers) and electrocardiography amplitude (ranked 12th in the group model) highly contributed to the classification accuracy.

To explore how to limit the obtrusiveness of our sensing system, we examined the relative values of the different sensors. For building either the group or individual models for predicting driving interruptibility, the most important features come from the cameras and vehicle movement sensors, except for the right hand motion (which could be detected via camera rather than worn sensor). For individual models, though, data from the physiological sensors was also valuable. It is possible that this body part motion could contribute to the group model as well, particularly if combined across body parts or with the car motion. We leave these refinements to future work.

Detecting Driving Interruptibility

In this study, we presented promising evidence that driving interruptibility can be accurately assessed in real-time using sensor data streams, independent of human-annotated information. Further, our results also show that accurate personalized models can be constructed from only 2 driving sessions.

However, individual models for a few drivers (*i.e.*, driver 05, 10, 11, 21, and 23) provide insufficient performance in correctly detecting driving interruptibility. Their recall was 75.3% (*SD*=6%) on average and the precision was 89.0% (*SD*=1.9%, indicating 11% false discovery rate). This (roughly) implies that one in four known opportunities for interruptions was missed. It also implies that one in ten times the driver was predicted to be interruptible, she was not. This could lead to risky driving situations, although arguably no worse than our current driving situation in which interruptions arrive unmediated to drivers. Given our finding that in a 10-minute driving window, approximately 7 and 3 minutes belong to the LESS_INTERRUPTIBLE and INTERRUPTIBLE states, respectively, this equates to drivers being interrupted when not interruptible for 42 seconds and missing opportunities for interrupting the driver for 45, over each 10 minute segment of driving. The performance of these individual models should be improved to be used in practice, but our results are already very promising. We may need longer-term data collections from these individuals or more personalized features (*e.g.*, route familiarity or habitual behaviors in the car) to improve the individual model classification accuracy.

Overall, our models performed quite well in identifying moments when the driver is in the NO_HAND_DRIVE or the PI states. While we equated this to the driver being INTERRUPTIBLE, it could be the case that drivers in one of the other states (particularly one-handed driving) could have additional opportunities for being interrupted. In the future, we would like to more thoroughly investigate driver's interruptibility in situations when they are not performing peripheral activities and not driving no-handed.

CONCLUSION

Nowadays, technology is giving us the ability to interact with information anywhere and anytime, even in the car while driving. Whether it is appropriate to interact with information depends a lot on the current driving situation and the driver state. In this paper, we sought to understand these situations and states particularly when drivers engage in peripheral interactions, actions not related to the primary task of driving the car, as they indicate opportunities to interact with information. In particular, we collected sensor and human-annotated driving data from 15 drivers and demonstrated that we could build a machine learning classifier that determined when they were interruptible with 94% accuracy. We discussed the features that contributed to this high accuracy and suggested directions for identifying features to improve on our classifier.

In continuing this work, we have a number of goals. First, we will collect additional data to confirm that our results generalize across a wider driving population and work to build models and apply features that more consistently perform across drivers and for the nuances of specific drivers. Second, with this accurate classifier, and relatively easy-to-deploy system, we can now investigate how to mediate interruptions to drivers. We plan to conduct another field study where we push interruptions at different timings to assess the real-world impact of being able to detect interruptible moments while driving. These interruptions will differ in terms of their temporal urgency, relevance to the driving tasks, and overall importance. Third, we plan to develop generalized guidelines for designing intelligent interruption systems for drivers. We will use these improved models and understanding to identify the attributes of opportune moments detected (*e.g.*, expected duration, expected level of driver engagement). For example, a relevant local advertisement should impose a short interruption during an opportune moment; if a driver has extended interruptibility, interruptions such as an alternate route/highway exit to take can be delivered.

Fourth, we plan to apply our technology to identify breakpoint moments for prompting drivers to safely participate in experience sampling while driving, which will support others doing driving-related research in naturalistic driving situations.

REFERENCES

1. Bailey, B.P., Iqbal, S.T. (2008). Understanding changes in mental workload during execution of goal-directed tasks and its application for interruption management, *ACM TOCHI*, 14 (4): 1-28.
2. Bailey, B.P., Konstan, J.A. (2006). On the need for attention-aware systems: Measuring effects of interruption on task performance, error rate, and affective state. *Computers in Human Behavior*, 22 (4): 685-708
3. Böhmer, M., Lander, C., Gehring, S., Brumby, D.P., and Krüger, A. (2014). Interrupted by a phone call: exploring designs for lowering the impact of call notifications for smartphone users. Proc. CHI '14, 3045-3054.
4. Cho, H., Rybski, P.E., Bar-Hillel, A., and Zhang, W. (2012). Real-time pedestrian detection with deformable part models. In IEEE Intelligent Vehicles Symp.: 1035–1042.
5. Curry, D., Meyer, J., and Jones, A. (2013). Driver Distraction: Are We Mistaking a Symptom for the Problem?. SAE Technical Paper 2013-01-0439.
6. Cutrell, E. B., Czerwinski, M., and Horvitz, E. (2000). Effects of instant messaging interruptions on computing tasks. Proc. CHIEA '00, 99-100.
7. Espinosa, F., Jimenez, J.A., Santiso, E., Gardel, A., Perez, D., Casanova, J. and Santos, C. (2011). Design and implementation of a portable electronic system for vehicle-driver-route activity measurement. *Measurement* 44 (2): 326-337.
8. Governors Highway Safety Association. Distracted driving: What research shows and what states can do. Technical Report. July 2011.
9. Green, P. (2004). Driver Distraction, Telematics Design, and Workload Managers: Safety Issues and Solutions in SAE publication P-387. Society of Automotive Engineers, Inc., Pennsylvania, USA, pp. 165-180
10. Haapalainen, E., Kim, S., Forlizzi, J., Dey, A. (2010). Psycho-physiological Measures for assessing Cognitive Load. In: Proc. Ubicomp '10, 301–310.
11. Hong, J., Margines, B., Dey, A.K. (2014) A Smartphone-based Sensing Platform to Model Aggressive Driving Behaviors, Proc. CHI '14, 4047-56.
12. Illinois. Rules of the Road. (2014). See Chapter 11 Safe Driving Tips for details on the "three-second rule".
13. Iqbal, S.T., Horvitz, E., Ju, Y.C., and Mathews, E. (2011). Hang on a sec!: effects of proactive mediation of phone conversations while driving. Proc. CHI '11, 463-472.
14. Kim, S., Hong, J., Li, K.A., Forlizzi, J., and Dey, A.K. (2012). Route Guidance Modality for Elder Driver Navigation. Pervasive '12 , 179-196.
15. Klauer, S.G., Guo, F., Sudweeks, J. and Dingus, T.A. (2010). An Analysis of Driver Inattention Using a Case-Crossover Approach 100-Car Data: Final Report (Report No. DOT HS 811 334). NHTSA.
16. Kun, A.L., Shyrokov, A., and Heeman, P.A. (2013). Interactions between human-human multi-threaded dialogues and driving. *Pers Ubiquit Comput.* 17(5): 825-834.
17. Larson, R., and Csikszentmihalyi, M. (1983). The experience sampling method". New Directions for Methodology of Social and Behavioral Science. 15, 41-56.
18. Lee, J. D., Moeckli, J., Brown, T. L., Roberts, S. C., Schwarz, C., Yekhshatyan, L., Nadler, E., Liang, Y., Victor, T., Marshall, D., & Davis, C. (2013). Distraction Detection and Mitigation Through Driver Feedback. (Report No. DOT HS 811 547A). NHTSA.
19. Monk, C., Trafton, J., and Boehm-Davis, D. (2008). The effect of interruption duration and demand on resuming suspended goals, *Journal of Experimental Psychology: Applied*, 14 (4): 299-313.
20. Mulligan, C. B., Schneider, B., and Wolfe, R. (2000). Time use and population representation in the Sloan Study of Adolescents. Unpublished manuscript, Alfred P. Sloan/University of Chicago Center for the Study of Working Families.
21. Riener, A., Chalfoun, P., and Claude Frasson, C. (2014). The Potential of Subliminal Information Displays to Change Driver Behavior. *Presence* 23(1): 51-70.
22. Salvucci, D.D. (2010) On reconstruction of task context after interruption. Proc. CHI '10, 89-92.
23. Schneegass, S., Pfleging, B., Broy, N., Heinrich, F., and Schmidt, A. (2013). A data set of real world driving to assess driver workload. Proc. Automotive UI '13, 150-7.
24. Sherin, K.M., Lowe, A.L., Harvey, B.J., Leiva, D.F., Malik, A., Matthews, S., Suh, R., and the ACPM Prevention Practice Committee. (2014). Preventing Texting While Driving. *Am J Prev Med.* (in press).
25. Simon, H.A. (1971). Designing organizations for an information rich world. In *Computers, Communications, and the Public Interest*: 37-72.
26. Solovey, E.T., Zec, M., Perez, E.A.G., Reimer, B. and Mehler, B. (2014). Classifying driver workload using physiological and driving performance data: two field studies. Proc. CHI '14, 4057-4066.
27. Trafton J. G., Altmann E. M., Brock D. P., and Mintz F. E. (2003). Preparing to resume an interrupted task: Effects of prospective goal encoding and retrospective rehearsal, IJHCS, 58 (5): 583-603.

LApp: A Speech Loudness Application for People with Parkinson's on Google Glass

Róisín McNaney, Ivan Poliakov, John Vines, Madeline Balaam, Pengfei Zhang, and Patrick Olivier
Culture Lab, School of Computing Science, Newcastle University, UK
{r.mcnaney; ivan.poliakov; john.vines}@ncl.ac.uk

ABSTRACT
Reduced vocal volume in Parkinson's is extremely common and can have significant social and emotional impact. We describe the development and evaluation of LApp—an application for Google Glass to help people with Parkinson's (PwP) monitor their speech volume and cue themselves to speak louder when necessary. Our findings highlight enthusiasm for using the application both at home as a volume training tool and in public social settings as a situated cueing device. We contribute insights to the literature on how eyewear technologies can provide assistance to people with health conditions and offer insights for the design of future self-monitoring and management applications on Google Glass.

Author Keywords
Parkinson's disease; Wearable technology; Google Glass; Augmented reality; Self- monitoring

ACM Classification Keywords
H.5.m. Information interfaces and presentation (e.g., HCI): Miscellaneous.

INTRODUCTION
Parkinson's is a complex neurodegenerative condition presenting in a heterogeneous range of motor and non-motor symptoms. Reduced vocal loudness is a common problem for people with Parkinson's (PwP) and is a frequently treated aspect of voice within speech and language therapy (SLT) for this group. Approximately 90% of PwP will experience a voice problem at some point. Distress, embarrassment and social isolation are highlighted as impacting factors [8] and with worldwide figures placing the prevalence of Parkinson's at around 5 million people [9], this is an issue deserving great attention. The overall aim of SLT treatment targeting loudness is to maintain a louder voice in daily life, but this can be difficult once the input of the therapist is removed. One aspect of voice loudness issues in Parkinson's that makes the maintenance of therapy gains particularly difficult is that PwP have an impaired perception of how loud they are speaking—i.e. they will feel as though they are shouting when speaking at a normal level, or speaking at a normal level when speaking quietly [10]. Lee Silverman Voice Treatment—a training program involving the intensive and constant stimulation of a loud voice through a set of simple tasks [10]—is regarded as the gold standard for treating vocal loudness problems in PwP. However, only around 20% of SLT practitioners use this treatment in the UK due to the amount of time it takes to complete [8]. Technology could prove beneficial in this context as it offers the potential to aid the self-directed monitoring and management of speech volume. For example, [5] proposed the use of a digital game to help PwP practice volume related tasks at home. While offering a home practice method, this does not address the difficulties PwP have in maintaining their volume within external settings. In this sense, the implementation of a technology to support in-situ prompting of volume, at times it is needed in everyday conversation, could prove beneficial.

CHI 2015, April 18 - 23 2015, Seoul, Republic of Korea
Copyright is held by the owner/author(s). Publication rights licensed to ACM.
ACM 978-1-4503-3145-6/15/04...$15.00
http://dx.doi.org/10.1145/2702123.2702292

Our prior research [7] highlighted how platforms like Google Glass can provide a usable and acceptable assistive device for PwP, providing opportunities to deliver discreet and in-situ cues to aid the monitoring and management of Parkinson's symptoms. We build on this prior work by describing the development and evaluation of LApp; a Glass application to aid in the monitoring and management of voice loudness issues experienced by PwP. The application was designed through workshops with 7 PwP, 6 of whom then used the application in a short field trial. We contribute to the emerging literature on how wearable technologies such as Glass can provide real-time in-situ prompts and cues related to conditions such as Parkinson's, and provide recommendations for the design of monitoring and management applications for future work to build upon.

THE STUDY
Our study was conducted in 3 stages: (i) an exploratory design workshop; (ii) iterative development of LApp and pilot testing; and (iii) real-world deployment of LApp on Glass. We describe each phase in the following sections.

Phase 1: Exploratory Design Workshop
The first phase involved an exploratory design workshop with 7 PwP (Table 1). Participants characterised the heterogeneous nature of Parkinson's in relation to their

symptoms. Our participants were aged between 60 and 81 and ranged from 5 to 15 years since diagnosis (YSD). They also had a diverse range of volume-related problems from mild to severe on the Voice Handicap Index (VHI)—a patient rated questionnaire used to gauge the emotional, physical and functional impact of voice problems [4]. We also used the Hoehn and Yahr scale [3] (H&Y)—a widely used scale for describing Parkinson's, rated by a clinical member of the research team, ranging from 0 (no signs) to 5 (needing wheelchair or bedridden)—to assess the severity of their overall condition (see Table 1). Four participants had previously engaged in a SLT program to help treat their volume and two were awaiting therapy. Our workshop lasted 3 hours and had 3 aims; (i) to discuss personal experiences of loudness issues and the impact of this has on PwP; (ii) to discuss experiences of undergoing SLT and the strategies currently being used by participants to overcome volume issues; and (iii) to scope the space for using digital technologies to help prompt loudness in daily life. The workshop was audio recorded and transcribed. We conducted an inductive thematic analysis on the transcribed data using methods outlined by [2], by coding data at the sentence to paragraph level and drawing out themes across the data set, which we summarise below.

Speech Volume, Confidence and Socialisation

Our participants expressed how significant an impact volume issues had on confidence and socialisation. Much frustration and embarrassment came from continuously being asked to speak louder by others: *"I'm constantly being got at by people telling me to speak louder"* (Michael), particularly when speaking to strangers: *"I find I have to rephrase things and I get lost and then I get embarrassed, especially if it's a strange situation"* (Robert). Gill described her experience of being dismissed by retail staff in public: *"I find that people don't think you have the intelligence to understand what they're talking about* [...] *he said "I'll just get your son to talk to me". I just couldn't get my words out for him to understand that I understood."* It is perhaps unsurprising then that participants withdrew from social situations: *"I shy away more than I used to"* (Robert).

Another concern was a feeling of being ignored. Susan explained how: *"coming over in the taxi he didn't know the way and I tried to tell him but I got no answer, I gave up in the end."* Michael also described: *"frequently during a conversation with other people I can't get myself involved, I'm just not speaking loud enough to make an impact"*. It was clear that these feelings of dismissal or invisibility had significant impacts on the motivation to interact with others. There was an overriding sense of 'giving up': *"you lose the thread of what you're trying to say, so you just shut up"*(Jerry). This was echoed by Jill: *"I try to think speak louder, but when you get into your spiel people are constantly saying speak up, so now I don't speak at all"*.

Monitoring and Managing Loudness

Participants discussed their experiences of SLT and the strategies they used to manage loudness issues, for example taking deep breaths prior to speaking, or using stock phrases to *"cue me back in"* (Robert) to a louder voice. However, it was clear that these strategies can leave individuals feeling uncomfortable: *"when you're in the pub you raise your voice because there's background noise but in a quiet place I would feel like I was shouting"* (Robert). Susan, Jill and Neil explained how they would practice their loud voice prior to speaking (e.g. when making a telephone call) but would start loudly and *"trail off"* (Neil). Three of our participants struggled with performing their SLT strategies in the first place. Robert and Neil explained how they would forget their strategies in day-to-day life, while Michael just *"didn't see the point"* of them at all.

Name	YSD	Age	VHI	H&Y
Susan	13	79	37- mild	3
Neil	7	60	41- moderate	2
Jill	6	67	32- mild	1
Michael	15	81	78- severe	4
Jerry	8	73	64- severe	3
David	5	80	27- mild	3
Robert	10	60	33- mild	2

Table 1: Participant details

For some, being able to simply monitor their volume to aid self-understanding was important: *"I don't know how to gauge the loudness of my voice, whether it's too quiet or too loud. I don't have any standard outside which is the equivalent of the people listening to me"* (Michael). Prompts were considered useful for helping to understand how volume changes over the space of a conversation: *"say I was to speak for 10 minutes, it's a long time, I start tailing off so I need something to bring me back to realise my volume"* (Robert). During the workshops different types of cues were suggested by participants (visual, haptic and auditory). There was some disagreement in relation to what would be preferred, with some suggesting audible cues that only they could hear, and others preferring visual or haptic cues they could respond to. Participants came to an agreement that cue preferences depended on context, but all felt comfortable with the idea of using a 'traffic light' style visual cue.

Phase 2: Development, Piloting and Iteration of LApp

The second phase involved the design and development of the Loudness monitoring and self-management application (LApp). Our initial design drew upon the 'traffic light' idea presented by participants in phase 1. This used a red/amber/green coloured system visualised as an orb on the Glass display which fluctuated accordingly with the speaker's vocal volume (Figure 1). The orb projected to the limits of a white line representing a conversational speaking volume (60dB (SPL)[1]). The orb was green when speech was loud enough and changed to red or amber when volume was too quiet (40dB under target) or nearing an appropriate level (20dB under target) respectively.

To test initial perceptions of this cueing method and ensure feasibility and safety we ran a small user study with 8 participants (5 males, 3 females with ages ranging from 20-

Figure 1: First (left) and second (right) iterations of LApp cue.

40) who did not have Parkinson's or volume difficulties. Participants were asked to use LApp for approximately 30 minutes while carrying out a series of social interactions of their choosing in a range of settings with varying background noise. All participants provided very similar feedback about LApp which indicated some required changes. While they found the application easy to access and use, the orb-based feedback mechanisms required too much continuous attention to monitor its size. Instead, participants advocated the use of a cue that could be monitored better with peripheral vision. To this end we redesigned the cue as a large 'thumbs up' symbol that could be more easily seen peripherally and to provide positive reinforcement that appropriate volume levels were being met. When volume reduces the symbol gradually disappears. Participants additionally had difficulty reaching the 60dB target at times, so we added a feature that allowed users to set their target volume. On reflection, we realised that it may have been difficult for PwP to reach this target and, given that the aim of our application was to promote increased vocal loudness not reach a standardised dB level, we felt that having users set their own goals that they felt comfortable with would be more appropriate for maintaining functional gains in day-to-day life.

Phase 3: Field Trial of LApp

The final stage of our study was a series of three day deployments of LApp on Glass. We aimed to explore PwP experiences of using LApp in real world contexts, to see how they familiarised themselves with and used the device, and to promote discussion related to the design of in-situ prompts to monitor and self-cue loudness in speech. We deployed the LApp on Glass with 6 of our original participants (David was unable to take part). Participants were visited in their homes and given a demonstration of how to use LApp. A researcher helped them sample a loud voice that was comfortable for them, to be used as the target volume that they would aim for when using the application. LApp was designed to support self-directed management of volume and, in this sense, participants were advised that they could make a specific decision not to raise their voice if the situation required. Participants were provided with an instruction manual for reference and were assured they could contact a researcher at any time for support. They were asked to use the application as much as possible during the period they had the system, within normal, everyday situations. At the end of the trial, each participant was interviewed in their own home for approximately 40 minutes. Each interview was transcribed and thematically analysed in the manner described in phase 1.

Name	Times Accessed	Target dB (TdB)	Above Target (AT)	Below Target (BT)
Susan	4	45	8	4
Neil	5	45	5	12
Jill	3	51	9	11
Michael	3	48	13	2
Jerry	18	55	28	5
Robert	11	52	32	6

Table 2: Averages of usage data from 3 days LApp trial

Results

Participants varied in the ways they used LApp. While Neil, Robert, Jerry and Jill took Glass out and about with them to different places, Susan and Michael preferred to use it solely at home. All participants used Glass while talking to friends at some point during the trial. Table 2 displays average figures for; number of times LApp was accessed, target dB level participants were aiming for (TdB), times voice reached above TdB but dipped before triggering the cue (AT), and times voice reached below TdB during cue presentation but increased prior to its disappearance (BT).

Being Cued by LApp – Conversing and Practicing

All of our participants engaged enthusiastically with LApp during the trial and found benefits in the feedback the system provided. Jerry immediately found that he was increasing his volume to reach the LApp target: *"it was good for getting your voice up....you had to speak up to get the* [icon] *on so I found that very good"*. All used LApp for its designed function—as a way to provide in-situ cues related to the loudness of speech. Jill found great comfort in the fact that she was able to confirm her voice was loud enough during a conversation with a friend: *"Going into the conversation, when* [friend] *said 'pardon' twice to me. I had the* [thumbs up]*, so it gave me confidence to know it wasn't me, it was him* [...] *every time that someone says pardon to you it knocks your confidence a little bit* [...] *so it gives you confidence to know that you are not always the one at fault"*. Similarly, Michael used LApp while socializing with friends, with his wife noting: *"you were speaking quite clearly when you had it on* [...] *it was lovely to hear you"*. Michael's wife noted improvements in the loudness and overall quality of his speech even just for the short period of this study. Some participants felt that the real benefit of LApp however was as a practice aid. For example, Neil explained how *"reading aloud was good practice I found"* and could see this as a benefit for him in the future: *"if I was in a situation where I was being told to repeat myself more than I liked I would go away and practice"*. However, he also reported: *"when I'm wearing it I'm conscious of the fact that I have to perform"*.

Frustrations around Feedback

As noted earlier, perceptions of vocal loudness can be impaired in PwP, leading to difficulties in registering how loud the voice actually is. During the first session, a researcher helped each individual to set a target volume on LApp which was comfortable for them to reach, yet loud enough for the researcher to hear. Despite this, several participants had difficulty reaching and maintaining the target volume once the researcher had left. Robert and Michael found that the LApp *"didn't work"* or *"just couldn't pick up my voice"* at points during the trial. Interestingly, during the final interviews (and for Robert during an additional session, where a researcher visited his home following complaints about the application *"just not working"*) LApp functioned as expected: *"when you came round and it was working, 5 minutes later it stopped working and since then I've just had a series of disasters, it just doesn't work"* (Robert). On demonstration Robert was trailing off in terms of his loudness during extended vocalisation and it was observed that, despite speaking at a sufficient volume, he was speaking in short bursts producing a disjointed voice: *"in the end I was shouting at the thing...thumbs up!...icon!"*. Considering that LApp was computing average dB over a 2 second time space his overall level was therefore not sufficient to hit his volume target (see Table 2). Since short rushes of speech are common feature in Parkinson's, this issue warrants careful consideration for a future applications aiming to support a wider range of PwP.

Problems with Glass

Finally, some of the participants experienced frustrations with Glass. While there was an appreciation of the potential of LApp, some found it difficult to set and reset their target volume. The primary issues participants faced related to tremor in their hands and arms which led to difficulties navigating Glass' menus: *"I'd touch it occasionally and set it off on a chain of events"* (Neil). However, a more immediate challenge was that the system lost battery charge very quickly. This caused particular angst on occasions when the device was being worn while out and about: *"I put them on and took them to the garden center. I felt great, didn't seem like anyone was looking at me, I felt comfortable, I could see my* [thumbs up] *and then all of a sudden it went off"* (Jill). While the participants understood that the system was a prototype, it highlighted the potential dangers of in-the-wild cueing if the technological platform is still immature.

DISCUSSION

While our ambition here was to develop LApp to be an in-situ self-management technology, we saw how being reliant on a system like this can lead to considerable frustration if things go wrong. Given the noted issues of personal distress and embarrassment associated with Parkinson's [8], this emphasizes the importance of well-tested applications and a non-trivial level of technical support (e.g. an accessible troubleshooting guide or access to a person). Researchers should also be aware that negative feedback could cause frustration with users, even if this is an accurate portrayal. To this end, having easy methods of altering settings would be beneficial. Furthermore, while there were some frustrations with using LApp out and about, some of our participants placed great value on home practice of their voice using the device. This countered our primary envisioned use-case of LApp. Taking a social shaping of technology perspective (e.g. [6]) then this should be of no surprise—in this case, the features of LApp facilitated new ways of understanding one's speech, appropriated in an unexpected (yet rather obvious) manner by PwP. As such, this highlights that tools to support the development of voice management (such as [5]) should not be entirely dismissed in favor of tools for in-situ, real time, feedback.

Furthermore, in order for Glass to be more usable to PwP there should be consideration into the sensitivity of touch gestures. The provision of longer time frames for accessing features, as well as ability to lock down Glass to a singular application could aid functionality in this sense. Our participants also had issues with battery life so future applications should consider this, particularly for systems aiming to provide continuous in-situ prompting.

CONCLUSIONS

Our study of LApp was with a small sample of PwP and over a very short trial period. However, our findings were promising and demonstrate worth in exploring the development and longer-term trial of applications to support the monitoring and management of vocal loudness through Glass. However, future work is needed to refine the application further so that it is easier to change volume settings and to improve Glass' limited battery resources through software optimisation or additional hardware.

ACKNOWLEDGEMENTS

This research was funded through the RCUK Digital Economy Program SIDE (EP/G066019/1).

REFERENCES

1. ASHA. Noise. *Audiology Information Series 7976.* (2011)
2. Braun, V, & Clarke, V. Using thematic analysis in psychology. *Qual res in psych, 3*, 2(2006), 77-101.
3. Hoehn M, & Yahr M. Parkinsonism: onset, progression and mortality. *Neurology 17*, 5 (1967), 427–42
4. Jacobson, B. H. et al. The voice handicap index (VHI) development and validation. *Am Jour Speech-Lang Path 6*, 3 (1997), 66-70.
5. Krause, M., et al. A digital game to support voice treatment for Parkinson's disease. In *Proc of CHI'13*, ACM, 445-450.
6. MacKenzie, D., and Wajcman, J. (eds.). *The social shaping of technology (2nd Ed.)*. Open University Press, Buckingham, 1999.
7. McNaney, R. et al. Exploring the acceptability of google glass as an everyday assistive device for people with Parkinson's. In *Proc of CHI 2014*, ACM, 2551-2554.
8. Miller, N., et al.National survey of speech and language therapy provision for people with Parkinson's disease in the United Kingdom: Therapists' practices. *Int Jour Lang Comm Disord*, 46, 2 (2011), 189-201
9. Olanow C. W. et al. The scientific and clinical basis for the treatment of Parkinson's disease. Neurology 72, 21 (2009), 1-136.
10. Ramig, L. et al. Intensive voice treatment (LSVT®) for patients with Parkinson's disease. *Jour Neurol, Neurosurg Psych*, 71, 4 (2001), 493-4.

Designing for and with People with Parkinson's: A Focus on Exergaming

Róisín McNaney[1], Madeline Balaam[1], Amey Holden[1], Guy Schofield[1], Dan Jackson[1], Mary Webster[1], Brook Galna[2], Gillian Barry[2], Lynn Rochester[2], Patrick Olivier[1]

[1]Culture Lab, School of Computing Science, Newcastle University, UK
{r.mcnaney; Madeline.balaam}@ncl.ac.uk

[2]Institute of Neuroscience, Newcastle University Institute for Ageing, Newcastle University, UK
Brook.galna@ncl.ac.uk

ABSTRACT

Parkinson's is a complex and multifaceted condition with a myriad of symptoms, thus, designing for and with this user group requires careful consideration. We reflect upon two studies, employing different design methodologies, relating to the design of rehabilitative exergames in Parkinson's. The first explored the concept of designing 'for' People with Parkinson's (PwP) and focused on specifications outlined by clinical stakeholders. The second used a designing 'with' approach and modified a pre-established participatory design method for use with PwP. We call attention to the importance of carrying out design work with PwP and contribute; an empathic understanding of living with Parkinson's, a set of recommendations for how to design with PwP and a set of wider considerations for developing rehabilitative exergames for PwP.

Author Keywords

Parkinson's disease; Design; Exergames; Rehabilitation;

ACM Classification Keywords

H.5.m. Information interfaces and presentation (e.g., HCI): Miscellaneous.

INTRODUCTION

There is an ongoing agenda within HCI to bring older adults and vulnerable user groups into the design process [11, 17, 18, 30] as well as focused attention on age related conditions such as dementia [27, 31]. Although the area of Parkinson's has received some attention [3, 5, 16, 19, 20, 33], there has been minimal work related to how individuals with this condition might be engaged within a design process [3, 5, 20]. Parkinson's is a particularly interesting user group for investigation due to the complex and individual nature of the condition. People with Parkinson's (PwP) can experience a vast range of physical and cognitive symptoms which can have transient periods of increased severity, as well as dealing with emotional issues relating to social stigma and embarrassment surrounding their condition [20]. A number of these socially evident factors, for example drooling, slurred speech, balance issues, and gait freezing, have the potential to be improved by well-designed technologies which could aid in the discreet and personalized provision of cues and strategies to help overcome these symptoms [e.g. 16, 19, 20, 21]. However, managing the double heterogeneity of both the condition and the individual gives rise to a variety of complexities in terms of how to design for and with such communities. In order to address this gap in the literature, we reflect on the processes we went through when designing rehabilitative exergames (digital exercise based games) with PwP and a group of clinical staff interested in the potential of using exergames to help manage issues with physical function.

CHI 2015, April 18 - 23 2015, Seoul, Republic of Korea

ACM 978-1-4503-3145-6/15/04...$15.00
http://dx.doi.org/10.1145/2702123.2702292

In this paper we describe two studies. Our first involved working closely alongside clinical staff and a small group of participants to design and develop a 'proof-of-concept' game for clinical feasibility and safety testing of the Microsoft Kinect platform for rehabilitation and exercise within Parkinson's. Our second took a more participant focused approach and worked alongside PwP, through a user-centred design process, to explore the wider design considerations for such games. We specifically define these games as rehabilitative because, although exercise based in nature, they have a particular therapeutic target. We reflect upon both processes, one which followed a designing 'for' approach and the other designing 'with' and provide an overall set of consideration for future designers wishing to work with varied groups of stakeholders in the future.

As previously mentioned, from a health perspective, the condition of Parkinson's is complex and multi-faceted, thus the process of designing with and for this user group is particularly challenging, particularly when considering the vast differences in physical ability within PwP on a day by day, or even in some cases hourly, basis due to motor fluctuations. As one of few examples of design focused work with PwP we aim to explicate the design space in three ways; 1) we provide an overview of the symptoms and experiences associated with living with Parkinson's for those seeking to enter the design space, 2) we discuss insights for design considerations that can sensitize designers to the specific needs and values of this user group, relative to exergames, and finally, 3) we provide recommendations on how to design with and for PwP.

LIVING WITH PARKINSON'S

Parkinson's is a progressive neurodegenerative disease, caused by a depletion of the neurotransmitter dopamine in the brain, which affects approximately 1 million people in the USA and 5 million worldwide [22], not to mention undiagnosed statistics from developing countries. It is estimated that approximately 60,000 Americans are diagnosed with Parkinson's each year [23]. The condition is generally associated with the ageing population, with most diagnoses occurring in those over 50, however, with an increased understanding around Parkinson's, thanks to clinical research and public awareness, more younger adults are being diagnosed with the condition - 1 in 20 new diagnoses are under 40 in the UK [25] and an estimated 4% are under 50 in the USA [23]. Parkinson's manifests itself in movement, or motor, symptoms including rigidity (stiffness), tremor (involuntary, rhythmic back and forth movement often of the hands) and bradykinesia (slowness) [6]. PwP also have difficulties with movement initiation (or hypokinesis). These symptoms have associated effects on balance; gait— wherein "freezing" episodes can occur (a feeling that the feet are stuck to the ground); arm movements and facial movements, which can cause a mask-like facial expression. Speech and voice are also typically affected making communication difficult. A range of non-motor symptoms are also common including: fatigue, compulsive behaviors— such as excessive spending or gambling, inhibition and a range of autonomic dysfunctions (e.g. impoverished temperature control; incontinence) [28]. Cognitive decline (e.g. slowing; difficulties with dual task performance) is also a common feature of Parkinson's. Longitudinal studies have found 78% eventually develop dementia [1] after experiencing motor symptoms for an average of 10 years [14]. Although the presence of anxiety and depression, alongside significant negative changes in emotional wellbeing, are identified to be highly prevalent in PwP, findings have shown that these symptoms are not systematically recognized in clinical practice [28].

EXERCISE AND REHABILITATION IN PARKINSON'S

Following the description of the myriad of symptoms which can be experienced by PwP, it is clear to see how traditional exercise methods might pose a problem. Parkinson's is generally well controlled by a medley of medications (ON times), however, with extended use of Levadopa (dopamine replacement), patients may begin to feel the effects of the medication 'wearing off' causing periods of severe symptoms (OFF times) [24]. In some cases patients can experience dramatic and unpredictable fluctuations between ON and OFF times, which can be a barrier for patients undergoing rehabilitative exercise programs. This highlights the need for a self-directed, opportunistic way of delivering exercise. Not all PwP will have the same symptoms, in fact, the scope and variability of symptoms and how they impact on function among individuals is vast, further stressing the importance of a malleable rehabilitative exercise delivery method. Technology could prove invaluable in helping to monitor and change the pace or difficulty of the exercise being delivered at home through automatic sensing, a task usually conducted by a therapist during supervised exercise.

Traditional physical therapy takes place under supervision of a trained therapist either in a clinical setting or in the patient's home. In the UK, sessions last approximately 30-60 minutes and are often delivered in blocks of sessions over the course of 6-8 weeks. The premise of these therapy sessions is to provide the patient with a set of strategies and rehabilitative exercises, to help retrain functional abilities relating to movements which are diminished due to Parkinson's. However, sessions are expensive, time consuming and must be practiced regularly to maintain any gains made. For exercises to be truly beneficial to the PwP they must learn to integrate them into their everyday movements, without the support of the clinician. Consequently, independent home practice is an important aspect of treatment. In addition, repeated and long-term training of rehabilitative exercises (i.e. high intensity of therapy) has been proven to promote neuroplasticity, reducing neurodegeneration and remapping damaged motor pathways in the brain [9]. Motivation of the patient post-therapy, to carry out home based practice of exercises, is a key barrier to generalization of therapy into everyday life. Patients are heavily supported by their therapist during the program and once it is over motivation can wane. In many cases treatment effect does not persist 6 months following discharge from a physical therapy program [12]. Having a method of providing home-based feedback and encouragement, through digital technology, could serve to better support home practice and keep motivation intact.

EXERGAMES AND THEIR ROLE IN REHABILITATION

Recent years have seen a rise in literature focusing on exercise based gaming in clinical rehabilitation. In particular several studies have focused on exergames targeting stroke rehabilitation [2, 4, 8, 15, 26]. Whilst [15] found that games such as Wii Sport can maintain and improve the physical health of stroke patients, more work was required in order to optimize the hardware and software, to ensure that a wider range of patients could engage with exergaming. [26] concluded that most clinical research reporting positive benefits, while valid, was conducted in supervised clinical settings over short time periods. They highlight the further importance of evaluating the user's experience of the games being played so that the needs of participants can be modified and adapted. [2] highlight that, without clinical supervision, patients are susceptible to carrying out compensatory movements, which can potentially impede progress or create new health problems. To overcome this, the researchers designed a motion-based video game to detect compensatory movements and teach the user how to carry out movements properly. Particularly interesting is their use of operant conditioning to shape game player behaviors, whereby correct and incorrect movements correspond to meaningful in-game indicators of success. They found this technique shaped the users' movements without decreasing the players' willingness to play games. [8] identified the importance of 'meaningful play' within rehabilitative exergames and identified how vital it is to challenge users within gameplay to ensure motivation is maintained. They highlight the benefit of using dynamic adjustment to alter difficulty within rehabilitative exergames for stroke to ensure that the needs of the individual can be effectively met. This is particularly relevant in the case of PwP due to the inevitable decline that occurs over time as a consequence of the progressive condition, as well as the variability of ability they can experience during ON/OFF fluctuations. Finally, [4] illustrated the importance of viewing each patient as an individual, each experiencing different social, emotional and practical factors within their home lives which might impact upon motivation to practice rehabilitative tasks at home. They also highlight how motivation wavers when faced with carrying out rehabilitation exercises alone in the home in comparison to clinical settings, wherein the patient is heavily supported by the therapist. This emphasizes the importance of using participatory methods to understand the user engaged in the design process. Whilst both stroke and Parkinson's share attributes in relation to physical mobility difficulties (e.g. upper limb dexterity, walking) there are clear differences between the two. Stroke is caused by a cerebrovascular incident (CVI) which causes damage to the brain which can short lived or long lasting. Rehabilitation aims to regain functional ability of paralyzed limbs to decelerate motoric decline (i.e. through underuse). In contrast, Parkinson's is a progressive degenerative condition, thus the severity picture is expected to increase. Therapeutic input therefore, whilst aiming to support increased functional ability, must account for an invariable decline as the condition progresses.

METHODS FOR DESIGN IN PARKINSON'S

Overall, the general bank of HCI literature specifically related to Parkinson's is relatively limited [e.g. 3, 5, 19, 20, 21, 33], and research related to designing for and with Parkinson's remains even more so underexplored. Both McNaney [20] and Barros [5] took a design approach modelled on [27], which focused on developing design recommendations through a set of workshops with PwP and their caregivers, using discussion around low and high fidelity prototypes to refine design ideas. Both authors took an iterative development approach to refine their design of a wrist worn cueing device to treat drooling problems [20] and a mobile based application for the day to day self-management of Parkinson's [5] respectively. Unfortunately, the authors do not reflect on the successes and challenges of their design experiences, highlighting the need for an appraisal of design methods for Parkinson's and the construction of a set of recommendations for future designers aiming to explore the design space, particularly in relation to managing contingencies which might arise within the design process around specific Parkinson's symptoms (e.g. speech, mobility). Specific to PwP, the design of rehabilitative exergames remains relatively underexplored [3, 33]. Assad et al [3] designed WuppDi!, a suite of games designed alongside PwP and a group of physical therapists, which targeted the self-directed practice of exercises to compliment physiotherapy. After researching and testing commercial games with PwP, to identify the advantages and challenges of existing game mechanics and input devices, they found that available games were too demanding for the target group. Throughout their design process the authors highlighted the importance of designing an exergame which was; simple to use, based on familiar themes, employed rhythmic music to motivate users to move and to provide auditory cues, provided feedback to support users' perceptions of their progress and provided variety to account for individual needs. Whilst these requirements offer a clear starting point for the design of exergames for PwP they focus more upon the game mechanics. Thus, there is still a gap in the literature relating to our understanding of how we might support the integration of such games into everyday life, known to be a challenge in other health related areas [4, 12], and how we might engage PwP to explore this concept.

OUR DESIGN PROCESS

The research presented in this paper encompasses two design case studies, both based around exergaming and Parkinson's. The work in case study 1, designing 'for' PwP, necessitated the development of a proof-of-concept game, with 20 minutes of gameplay, which would enable a group of clinicians to evaluate the feasibility, safety and ability of the Microsoft Kinect to detect, measure and respond to the movements of PwP appropriately. With the exception of a short scoping workshop with three PwP prior to developing the proof-of-concept game, the game was the result of a collaborative relationship between the design team and four highly experienced clinicians within the area of movement disorders. The use of our proof-of-concept game in a lab-based study enabled our clinical collaborators to confirm Microsoft Kinect could provide a feasible and safe platform for supporting PwP to exercise in the home [10]. In our second case study, designing 'with' PwP, we underwent a longer user-centred design process with PwP to understand how rehabilitative exergames could be designed to reflect the values, goals and lifestyles of our participants as well as motivate use within the home over the long term. Here, we describe these studies in detail and draw lessons learnt across the two. Within our discussion section we reflect upon the complexities of engaging PwP and relevant stakeholder in the design process and present a set of insights for future designers entering into the domain.

Case Study 1: Designing SCRUMP 'for' PwP

This study was conducted in 3 stages. We first held meetings with our clinical stakeholders to establish their requirements for the game. We then ran a short workshop with 2 PwP and 1 carer to explore how we might translate these requirements into an exergame for this user group. Drawing on insights from these initial stages we developed SCRUMP, a game to promote home practices of exercises for upper and lower limb movement. A small study to assess the game's feasibility, safety and accuracy in detecting and measuring movement in PwP was conducted and can be viewed in [10], however, for the purposes of this paper we focus on the design phases.

Establishing Game Requirements

We were approached by our clinical collaborators to develop a 'proof-of-concept' prototype, to explore the feasibility and safety of a Microsoft Kinect based game to support the practice of upper and lower limb rehabilitation exercises for PwP. Our clinical team consisted of four movement disorders professionals within a clinical ageing research unit. They saw great potential in the Kinect as a home-based platform for; a) supporting and encouraging exercise due to its ability to monitor and provide feedback on movements as they are being carried out, b) providing a safe exergaming environment due to its ability to be controlled via the body, without the need for additional hardware which could potentially pose a risk for tripping and c) offering the means for a clinician to remotely monitor patient progress and tweak exercise programs in response to the progression of an individual's symptoms.

Over five face-to-face meetings we brought both the design and clinical teams together to discuss intended specifications for our exergame. Each meeting engaged collaborators in structured discussion around; the types of exercises to target, the complexity required and how we might safely progress users of the game through gaming levels. As a result of these meetings the clinicians specified 7 physiotherapy requirements for our exergame: a) challenge balance and coordination by incorporating multi-directional stepping and reaching into the exergame, b) encourage players to take big steps and reach wide in order to support the rehabilitation of hypokinetic (smaller) movements, c) include some element of dual tasking, i.e. completing an exercise whilst completing a cognitive task at the same time, to mirror the everyday challenges of living with Parkinson's, d) not become so challenging that participants become at risk of falls, e) incorporate 20 repetitions of each activity, with more upwards and sideways reaching movements to avoid the exaggeration of slouching, randomization of activity presentation and similar repetitions of right and left movements to ensure a sufficient level of rehabilitation goals, f) begin with a shallow difficulty progression in the early stages followed by a steeper curve of progression to respond to the variance in player's ability levels and ensure all players felt a sense of achievement and g) become progressively more challenging through safe means by increasing the difficulty of stepping and reaching tasks and by performing stepping and reaching tasks concurrently.

A Scoping Workshop with PwP

Following the construction of these requirements we conducted a three-hour scoping workshop to gain early insights into how to translate clinicians' requirements into a game PwP would enjoy playing. We aimed to understand something of the gaming experiences and preferences of PwP, as well as any issues such a participant group might experience using the Kinect gaming system.

Participants were recruited through local Parkinson's UK support groups and were excluded if they had compromised mobility (i.e. unable to walk or stand unaided). We also invited carers to join the study, to add insight into the ways we might promote longer term use of the game within the home by supporting collaborative playing experiences with loved ones. We aimed to recruit 6 participants, however last minute drop-outs meant the scoping workshop consisted of 3 participants, 2 PwP and 1 carer. The workshop lasted for 3 hours and took place on Newcastle University campus. Initial discussions established how Parkinson's affected their daily lives in terms of mobility and general movement constraints, leading into discussion surrounding their general level of exercise and gameplay, what they do and who they do it with. Similar to [3], participants then had opportunity to trial the Nintendo Wii and Xbox Kinect using on the market exercise based games (e.g. Wii fit, Fitness Evolved, Just Dance). Further open discussions based on their gameplay experiences explored any usability issues for PwP, whether they envisioned playing the games at home, specific features that they liked or disliked in regards to graphics, game presentation, use of avatars etc. and any ideas they would like to see brought to life in a new game specifically for Parkinson's. Throughout the session, a researcher was collating all the ideas and design considerations being discussed by the participants. The final activity involved viewing all these ideas together and drawing up a set of final requirements that the participants would like to have in a future rehabilitative exergame.

Participants expressed enthusiasm for a Microsoft Kinect game specifically for PwP and especially one which aimed at improving function. Participants stressed the game would need to be enjoyable for them to remain motivated. Several design requirements were identified as a result of this workshop; a) participants considered strongly that the game should adapt its complexity to suit individuals at all stages of the condition- echoing our clinical collaborators, b) game content and graphics should focus on outdoor activities, especially those that were at times increasingly inaccessible to PwP as a result of their symptoms ('fantasy real life'), such as gardening, skiing and snowball fights, c) the game should use a cartoon avatar to represent their body movements to avoid a sense of feeling "silly" while playing the game and d) the game should include sound effects and rewards to motivate play and create a fun experience.

Figure 1. SCRUMP being played.

Developing SCRUMP

In response to requirements drawn from our first two phases we developed SCRUMP (figure 1) using Microsoft research's Kinect for Windows SDK. SCRUMP is a fruit picking game where the player is a farmer riding a tractor to harvest fruit. In order to encourage the player to make large stepping movements they must keep a foot on the central 'Go' button to power the tractor, while making amplified stepping to the right, left, forwards (to move the tractor up) and backwards (move it down) to steer the tractor on its path. Early levels focused only on reaching on one side, with the introduction of dual processing tasks, such as determining which type of fruit to pick with a specified hand, and using stepping sequences to drive the tractor past oncoming obstacles (sheep, high wire, bird, wasp), in later levels. The speed of the game could be manually adjusted, or set to automatically speed up or slow down dependent on an algorithm detecting the ongoing success of the player. Several sound effects were used to indicate successful (coins falling) and unsuccessful (squashing fruit) collection of fruit and obstacle avoidance (animal noise). In addition, a crowd could be heard cheering at the end of each successfully completed level and the player could visually observe the amount of fruit they had collected in a receptacle on either side of the screen.

Our study met the brief outlined by our clinical collaborators and enabled us to design an exergame which could be used safely by PwP (n=10) in supervised settings [10]. However, Galna's study [10] showed that half of the participants felt they would not be motivated to play SCRUMP if it was available to use at home. In order to probe the participants perceived value of the game, they were asked whether they would purchase the game if it was available. Only 1 participant definitively said that they would, with concerns over the cost of the game (3) and its fidelity (2) being expressed by others. The complication with focusing on clinical contributions for design is that much of our focus was around the target movements, and incorporating these into the game, and less around what motivates users to play the game in the first place. Whilst this is an extremely important element there are intricacies relating to the needs and desires of the target population, which cannot be anticipated by clinical professionals, and must be considered if we are to support and motivate longer term use of these games. In response to the knowledge gap arising from this first study we decided to undergo an in depth user-centred designing 'with' approach, to unpick the complexities of exergame requirements for Parkinson's arising from the participants themselves, without the constraints of time or clinical functionality. An 'invisible design' [7] methodology was used to probe participants' perceptions of exergaming and how it might fit into their lives.

Case Study 2: Understanding Exergaming 'with' PwP

We based our design work on the Open Architecture for Accessible Services Integration and Standardization (OASIS) approach [17], which employs the use of "invisible design" [7] through a video prompt, a method which inspires novel ideas around how a technology might look or function through ambiguous reference to a version of the technology which is never actually seen. The OASIS method involves two sessions with participants – an exploratory meeting featuring a video prompt to explore the design domain and allow participants to start articulating their own requirements and obligations, followed by low-fidelity prototyping sessions to start developing a technology based on participants' identified requirements and obligations, with a focus on aesthetic issues. OASIS was designed for use with older adults (65+) suggesting it might be an appropriate approach to take with PwP, many of whom are within this older age range. In addition, this approach places importance on "establishing an appropriate atmosphere in the meetings, to facilitate younger designers' novel insights into older people's day to day lives" [17, p.1201]. Being that we wanted to gain an empathic understanding of the lived experiences of PwP, we felt that this approach would facilitate this effectively.

Participants were recruited through local Parkinson's UK support groups. Participants of any age or disease stage were invited to join but were excluded if they had compromised mobility to the extent that they were unable to walk or stand unaided. 8 participants were recruited (6 male and 2 female) aging from 46 to 78 years old, and ranging from 1-4 on the Hoehn and Yahr scale [13] (H&Y)—a widely used scale for describing Parkinson's, rated by a clinical research team member, ranging from 0 (no signs) to 5 (needing wheelchair or bedridden)—to assess the severity of their overall condition (see Table 1). Each stage of the process was video

Participant	1	2	3	4	5	6	7	8
Age	55	68	62	78	52	69	46	65
Gender	M	M	M	M	M	M	F	F
H&Y	2	3	2	4	2	2	1	2

Table 1: Participant details

and audio recorded and underwent inductive thematic analysis to draw out themes for discussion on resultant design requirements prior to the next session. There were 2 sessions, each lasting approximately 3 hours, conducted at Newcastle University.

Session 1: Exploratory Meeting

This first session was aimed at enabling participants to get to know one another and share personal experiences. This also gave the researchers involved a chance to gain an empathic understanding of the participants' lived experiences, triumphs and difficulties surrounding their Parkinson's and their exercise and rehabilitation practices. Following this structured initial discussion, participants watched our "invisible design" video. The film created was set in the living room of a couple "Gill" and "Chris". The opening scene showed Gill finishing a phone call with a friend known as Alice. Chris was curious as to what she was talking about, which led Gill and Chris to discuss the "thing" (a digital gaming system which can be used to play games to support home practice of rehabilitative exercise) which Alice had at home, and which Gill was arranging to trial next week. The dialogue was written specifically to cover likely barriers and motivations towards exercise derived from [30]. The characters, Gill and Chris, highlighted contrasting opinions to facilitate the elicitation of positive and negative responses to the idea. The next scene, one week later, when "it" had arrived, showed Gill trying it out in their home and Chris observing. At times the film was entertaining and humorous to try to create qualities which live in the memory and promote subsequent discussion. Actors in the film did not have Parkinson's, so as to avoid making participants feel labeled with the disease or become fixated by differences between themselves and the characters. Following the film viewing, we facilitated a second discussion based around the characters in the film and their reactions to the "thing". We encouraged participants to think about why the characters had different attitudes toward the "thing" and how their use of the "thing" could be sustained over time.

Analysis of the data identified potential features, requirements for a design and potential problems with design concepts. Based on this analysis we developed several design considerations which we wanted to explore in the following workshop: methods of alerting others of your presence when playing the game (i.e. in order to engage with an online community to aid motivation), ensuring affordances can be made for the PwP during multi-player options to support playing with family members, exploring ways in which data should be captured and shared, the use of in-game notifications and feedback, and finally, how the player should be represented within the game and in what digital environment.

Session 2: Critical Evaluation of Low-Fidelity Prototypes

The OASIS method specifies that the following session should focus on the critical discussion of co-created, low-fidelity prototypes that respond to design concepts arising out of the previous workshop. In response to the reduced motor control abilities of some of our participants, which we felt would cause issues with craft based prototyping and may cause undue embarrassment in a group setting, we chose to create our prototypes digitally and use them to instead incite the critical discussion required. We developed a set of adaptation prototypes that showed how commercially available games could be adapted in relation to the themes identified in the previous workshop. This entailed demoing commercially available games to our participants through a series of promotional YouTube videos. The demoed games were carefully selected to reflect elements deemed important by our participants in the previous session (e.g. multi-player options, in-game notifications, avatar vs 'real' players). We then showed our participants an adaption layer, following each video, which was a screenshot from the game which had been adapted in different ways to support the gameplay of someone with Parkinson's, in accordance with the themes from the previous session (e.g. the provision of different kinds of feedback on progress— written, pictorial, audio, making affordances for PwP during multi-player options— hidden, notified, reaching a target). We structured conversations around each prototype to better understand the requirements identified by the participants and resolve areas of conflict. Again, analysis of the data refined our understanding of the design requirements for rehabilitative exergames for PwP.

At the end of this session we also gave participants an informal opportunity to play SCRUMP, along with several other commercially available exergames. Participants were not asked to evaluate SCRUMP in any way, instead, we used this gameplay experience to allow participants to view a concrete example of an exergame designed specifically for PwP and compare it to other games on the current market. As expected participants had difficulty with the motor skills necessary to play commercial games however, feedback for SCRUMP was very positive. All participants were keen to play the game and were able to play after a small demo and encouragement along the way due to its intuitive nature and concise instruction provided. SCRUMP did actually achieve some of the design principles established in the design sessions with this group of participants, namely its real-life fantasy theme and its dynamic adjustment making the game forgiving towards the fluctuations in Parkinson's. A full discussion of the requirements for Parkinson's that we drew from the study are described in detail below.

Exergame Requirements for Parkinson's

Below, we discuss the findings from our workshop series and reflect upon their translation to the findings we gathered in our first case study. We suggest a set of exergame considerations, specific to PwP, for future designers wishing to enter into the design space.

Through our workshop series we were able to gain deep understanding of the physical and emotional difficulties that can arise through living with Parkinson's and the social embarrassment and loss of self-confidence it can provoke: *PM1: "I am very self-conscious about almost anything I do outside of the house, even putting my coat on. I struggle to get my coat on and find that people are coming and helping me dress, which is bloody embarrassing in public. I mean, I want to be Jack the lad not the stiffy in the corner".* Building self-confidence through having a method of exercising in the privacy and comfort of the home was therefore an important factor for the participants: *PF7:"My symptoms aren't visible when my drugs are working but when they're not...social embarrassment is a massive part of Parkinson's, it erodes your self-confidence in a big, big way. So if you've got a gadget you can use at home you can exercise and you don't have to worry about anybody seeing you."* These comments echo the sentiments of PwP in [20], wherein discussion around the use of medical technologies (e.g. a falls alarm) and feelings of disability associated with them prevented their everyday use, even when alone. They also translate to the design recommendation outlined in case study 1 around using avatars to avoid feeling 'silly' during gameplay.

Grounded in Real World Activities

Participants expressed a sense of loss and *PM2: "frustration"* around activities they were no longer able to partake in due to their Parkinson's (e.g. golf, cycling, karate, swimming and cricket). One participant reported he *PM6: "wasn't able to keep up with the others"* in a line dancing class he used to attend, another reminisced about playing cricket with his grandson; *PM3: "I used to play cricket with my grandson, but I can't throw a ball anymore".* Our participants felt strongly that having an exergame which is grounded in real world activities would help them to re-connect with activities they can no longer do due to their Parkinson's. This recommendation also reflected the notion of 'real-life fantasy' that was drawn from our case study 1 workshop, wherein participants also wanted the game to represent real-life activities they were unable to do.

Establish and Maintain Community Motivation

Participants talked at length about their experiences around exercising within their Parkinson's UK group. Activities such as badminton, table tennis and dancing were among some of the exercises that they reported carrying out within their weekly group, in which PwP and family members come together to exercise within a supportive and understanding environment: *PM4: "It allows you to build up your self-confidence and the by- product of exercise is that you actually feel good...you find it's something you tend to forget with Parkinson's, just how good you feel after you've done some exercise".* Somewhat different to our clinicians' ideas for developing a single player game, the social element of the Parkinson's UK group was seen as a motivator for enabling individuals to exercise. This was carried over into discussions regarding what they would like within a rehabilitative exergame. Establishing an online community exclusive to PwP appealed to the participants as a way to expand existing social circles and reach out to others who might need help. PM1 said *"different people handle the diagnosis in different ways. Some retreat, others go for it. For those who retreat, that would be a first stepping stone for them to start going out and trying to have a life again".* Participants commented on how difficult it often was to find the time to carry out rehabilitative exercises at home and how this can be a barrier to remaining motivated: *PM2: "it's easy to fall out of the habit of doing things at home and the discipline of actually doing it. Like you're supposed to do the Conductive Education* [a structured physical rehabilitation program] *at home, the voice therapy treatment which you're supposed to do at home, and then you've got your exercises every day and then your daily routine. I mean, I'm retired now and I don't think I've ever been so busy in all my life"*

Their sentiments were reminiscent of [4] in that 'finding a balance between work, duty and fun' was important to them. They felt having an online community organized and run much like their regular meetings would be beneficial in terms of supporting and motivating one another. Participants were split in their views about whether or not there should be a competitive element to the game. They agreed the best concept for the game would be to support players in practicing and working with others towards a common goal, with the option of challenge available once they felt that they had consolidated their skills.

Don't Track Me!

Aside from the well-being and social element of exercise that they gain from their Parkinson's support group being a motivation to exercise, the participants emphasized the physiological importance of practicing exercise regularly to help manage symptoms such as stiffness and pain, however, they made reference to Wii use and feeling *PM2: "demoralized"* when returning to it after a time and *PM2: "finding that I've deteriorated, which is a disincentive to do it again".* An important point to draw from this was that participants *PF7: "don't want to track your decline, you want to stay positive!"* As a result participants wanted feedback provided by the game in terms of their achievement and progress to be forgiving of the degenerative nature of their disease. Contrasting with notions of the 'quantified self' and highly successful off-the-shelf products for encouraging exercise such as FitBit and Nike Plus, our participants didn't want quantitative data about their performance, and particularly data that they could reflect on over time. Instead, their preference was for feedback which was more abstracted, while still enabling them to still feel a sense of progress and achievement. *PM4: "as you progress through you actually put together a jigsaw. You can track your progress, your actual levels of achievement".*

Show Forgiveness of Parkinson's Symptoms

Participants articulated keenness to involve other family members in their gameplay which was impossible with current games, *PM1:"My son [...] he's too fast like most of them are. There's no point in me playing him.... Unless it was designed in a way that it could be done slowly".* Showing forgiveness within games also relates to the ability of gaming systems to create a level playing field within the game mechanics, *PM1: "with the handicap system [...] it allows more of a level playing field* [...] *if your skilled at the game but do have Parkinson's because of the symptoms you just can't reach that level. At least with the handicap system you're on a level playing field.*"

Making such measures of forgiveness visible to all players was not considered inadvisable, but instead offered opportunities to talk with family members, particularly children about the condition; *PF2: "I think it would actually help you explain say to a younger member of your family, how to explain to them that sometimes you find it more difficult.*" Finally, participants described frustrations with existing gaming systems where elements of their condition were inappropriately highlighted. *PF7: "When you do the body test on the Wii and it very nicely tells you that your left leg is shaking. The number of times I've spoken to it and said 'yeah! I've got Parkinson's!' It would be nice if it was something constructive rather than pointing out the obvious*" They wanted a system which would not only understand their symptoms (and, as such, not draw attention to them), but one that would also adapt accordingly to compensate for their symptoms as they vary. *PF7: "If your balance isn't as good or you're tremoring or have restricted movement due to the stiffness, if it could take that into account that would be better"*. Ensuring future games employ dynamic adjustment, as suggested by [8], would enable the needs of a wide range of participants to be met whilst also accounting for fluctuating ability during transient ON/OFF periods. This is, in addition, reflective of the requirement drawn out in case study 1 around adapting complexity to suit individuals at all stages of the condition.

Maintaining Privacy across Agencies

Participants raised some interesting concerns over privacy of data which could potentially be collected by the game and who their information might be shared with. The process of dynamic game play requires the game to store and respond to an individual's performance in the short term. The notion of data being stored and shared was worrying for participants. PF7 said: *"Your identity would need to be protected because there would be concerns about that information becoming available to the benefits agencies"* and PM3 noted: *"You would have to be tight on that, honest because otherwise you may well end up people actually not taking the game up. Because you'll actually get suspicious with information going missing"*. These comments were unexpected by the research team. In part, the sensitivity displayed by our participants relates to the variance in symptoms within ON/OFF periods and how this then impacts on other's understanding and acceptance of their disability. Several of our participants felt that others (i.e. the public) did not believe that they had a debilitating condition, since their symptoms were not consistently observable. As such, they worried they might be identified instead as 'shirkers' or 'benefit frauds'. In addition, because of this variance in symptoms, there was significant concern that they might be assessed on their gameplay during ON periods. Some of our participants, who were below retirement age, discussed a fear that governmental agencies might consider them well enough to return to work, especially during periods of economic decline, whilst others feared that they might have their supported physical therapy removed if they were seen to be progressing with the game.

DISCUSSION

Our paper highlights the complexities of designing with and for PwP, through a presentation of the symptoms and experiences associated with living with the condition. We have provided insights for design considerations that can sensitize designers to the very specific needs and values of this user group, in relation to the development of exergames. Aside from this, we explored the ways different stakeholders present the needs and desires of PwP within the design process. Although our findings are well motivated by the data, we recognise a limitation to our work is that we did not go on to develop and test an exergame featuring the considerations outlined in the second case study. As such, we cannot present findings which reflect whether our participants would have truly been motivated to maintain extended use of a rehabilitative exergame with their everyday lives. Further work is needed to address this issue which expands the scope of this paper.

Here we reflect upon the successes and challenges of designing exergames 'for' and 'with' PwP, addressing are gaps in the literature around understanding and managing the complexities of Parkinson's within the design process. We build upon Assad's [3] work addressing the necessities of game mechanics for exergames for PwP by highlighting the importance of engaging PwP in design, to ensure digital technologies support or improve aspects of the condition. As well as being developed in ways which avoid stigma, by responding to the community's life experiences, needs and values. The use of appropriate user-centered design methods is, in this sense, vital as it allows us, as designers, to co-design technologies with participants that solve important problems to them in ways which are appropriate.

Valuing, but Balancing Expertise

The input of clinical staff is vital in the practicalities of developing rehabilitative exergames, as they provide instruction and expertise on the specific rehabilitation exercises to be targeted. However, without the perspectives of the patients who will be playing the game, we are likely to miss crucial requirements (e.g. the desire not to track progress or the complexities of data sharing) which will be the core drivers of supporting motivation to actually use the game within a long term home environment. With our first case study, detailing the SCRUMP design process, we were working within an extremely sensitive time scale, thus we had limited time to recruit and carry out workshops with PwP to gain their insights. The game that was eventually trialed in [10] attempted to evaluate the user's experience and address the needs of participants [26]. However, the focus of this study remained within the scope of assuring the game was a safe and feasible way to deliver clinical exercises, and less around understanding the intrinsic values of the participants which that might support longer term use of SCRUMP within the home environment.

In our second case study, we wanted to gather free flowing, experience rich, qualitative accounts from PwP to fully understand how they felt exergames targeting movement rehabilitation should be designed and why. Through this process we were able to come up with a set of design considerations for designing such games 'with' PwP. These considerations, whilst matching with the first process relatively well on surface requirements such as having ways to feedback on progress and having a 'real-life fantasy' playing environment, differed significantly in terms of the depth of information we were able to collect surrounding aspects such as the importance of maintaining privacy and methods of remaining motivated through the Parkinson's community. This highlights the importance of carrying out participatory design methods, as well as involving the clinicians, when developing technology for clinical benefit. One area of interest which brings to light the differing priorities of clinicians and patients was the element of data sharing. Initial visions conveyed by our collaborators, was of a game they could tailor at distance to better suit rehabilitative needs of a patient over time. However this was in actuality an issue for our participants, who were fearful of certain types of information being shared. What we have found is that, clinicians, despite being grounded in expertise, still mainly work within a medical model of care [32] with their interests centering around providing an efficacious treatment. Whilst extremely important, this often leaves gaps in the design of rehabilitative systems which fail to take into account external factors, outside of the clinical scope, which might impact a patient's desire to engage with the technology. We report novel findings in regards to alleviating a sense of loss by designing systems grounded in real world activities, the sense of demoralisation felt by being tracked within a declining condition, the importance of dynamic adjustment to promote a sense of forgiveness of Parkinson's symptoms during fluctuations and creating assurances of data privacy.

Our findings show several value dilemmas between the clinicians and PwP we worked with. In order to truly ensure that both clinical and socio-emotional needs are being met we, as designers, must find a way to foster multidisciplinary design processes with both patients and clinicians. A seemingly simple solution to this would be to include the clinicians within the design workshops with the patients, to orientate stakeholders to the perspectives, values and ideas of one another. However, one complication that must be considered is that expertise can often influence power dynamics between stakeholders, thus our discussion with PwP may not have been as open and free-flowing had we included the clinicians within the sessions. On reflection of the conflicting values within the design process that we found, future work of this kind would benefit from an additional 'requirement validation' session including all stakeholders, wherein the design team can engage all participants in discussion points arising from both sides and facilitate the development of design solutions which meet everyone's values and needs.

Conducting Design with People with Parkinson's

As described in the 'Living with Parkinson's' section PwP can experience a multiplicity of complex symptoms. This can make the undertaking of design activities with this user group particularly difficult. Throughout our research processes we were able to draw out several experience-centered reflections around the practicalities of designing with PwP. There are a myriad of intricate sensitivities that should be taken into account when planning and undertaking the process which has not yet been reported within the literature. [17] outlines clear guidelines for conducting participatory design with older users, which we used as a framework for our own work. However, it became clear through our work that several Parkinson's specific issues were inadequately addressed by this method.

Speech: Speech problems are extremely common in PwP (around 90%) and can thus be a barrier to both the involvement of participants and the quality of data that can be collected. On reflection, our group size of 8 may have been too large to facilitate the participation of all members. Smaller groups could prove beneficial for future designers. This echoes a finding of [18] who advocated the use of smaller groups when working with older adults in design to overcome deficits and enhance participation.

General Mobility and Dexterity: Specific motor symptoms, such as freezing of gait, can make tasks such as going to the bathroom, entering a lift independently or getting in and out of a chair difficult. Being mindful of this and ensuring a team member is available to facilitate walking, as well as ensuring the workshop venue is set up using chairs with arms can mitigate these issues. Craft based resources might also pose a problem for participants due to decreased fine motor ability and tremor so alternative resources may need to be considered, as shown in modification of the prototyping activity in case Study 2.

Medication: Medication timing is key for PwP, particularly those who suffer from ON/OFF fluctuations. Clear schedules for each session should be strictly adhered to, to ensure participants know when to expect breaks. If running multiple workshops, there should be an awareness that participants might be better on one day than another. Timing workshops so that they are each held around the same time might help to combat this, although not all participants have predictable ON/OFF times.

Age Differences: We observed age disparities amongst our participants with the younger ones being more experienced in their use of technology and their readiness to adopt new technologies. While we felt that we gained useful design insights from our participants, it is possible that the ideas stemming from our invisible design activity were steered by the younger participants who were better able to associate the gaming system with current on the market systems.

CONCLUSIONS

Our process of designing SCRUMP 'for' PwP, focused mainly on the clinical requirements of the game and had minimal input from PwP. However, we produced it within a short time frame, with many of the surface requirements identified in our in-depth design process 'with' PwP. What we gained from our second process was insight into the motivating factors for supporting long-term engagement of exergames in the home. Whilst it is undeniable that clinical input is important when designing rehabilitative exergames it is equally important that users be involved heavily in the process. Future work is required to undergo long term testing of an exergame, which responds to the design requirements outlined within this study, in order to truly assess if motivation can be maintained within the home.

ACKNOWLEDGEMENTS

With special thanks to Dadirayi Mhiripiri for her hard work during this project. This research was funded through the RCUK Digital Economy Program SIDE (EP/G066019/1).

REFERENCES

1. Aarsland D et al. Prevalence, and characteristics of dementia in Parkinson disease: an 8-year prospective study. *Arch Neurol, 60*, (2003), 387–92.
2. Alankus, G., & Kelleher, C. Reducing compensatory motions in video games for stroke rehabilitation. In: *Proc of CHI'12*, Austin: USA (2012).
3. Assad, O. et al. Motion-Based Games for Parkinson's Disease Patients. In: *Proc. of Entertainment Computing–ICEC'11*, (2011), 47–58.
4. Balaam, M. et al. Motivating mobility: Designing for lived motivation in stroke rehabilitation. In: *Proc. of CHI'11*
5. Barros, AC, et al. User-centred design of a mobile self-management solution for Parkinson's disease. In *Proc. of MUM'13* (2013), 23-26.
6. Berardelli A et al. Pathophysiology of bradykinesia in Parkinson's disease. *Brain, 124, 11*, (2001) 2131-2146.
7. Briggs, P. Blythe, M. & Vines, J. Invisible design: exploring insights and ideas through ambiguous film scenarios. In: *Proc. Of CHI '12*. Austin: Texas (2012).
8. Burke, JW et al. Serious games for upper limb rehabilitation following stroke. In: *Proc. of VS-GAMES'09* (2009) 103-10.
9. Farley BG et al. Intensive amplitude-specific therapeutic approaches for Parkinson's disease. *Top Geriatr Rehabil, 24 (2)*. (2008) 99-114
10. Galna B, et al. Retraining function in people with Parkinson's disease using the Microsoft kinect: game design and pilot testing. *Jour neuroeng rehab, 11(1)*. (2014): 60.
11. Gerling, KM. et al. Exergame design for elderly users: The case study of Silverbalance. In *Proc. Of ACE '10*, (2010)
12. Green, J. et al. Physiotherapy for patients with mobility problems more than 1 year after stroke: a randomised controlled trial. *The Lancet, 359, 9302* (2002). 199-203.
13. Hoehn M, & Yahr M. Parkinsonism: onset, progression and mortality. *Neurology 17*, 5 (1967), 427–42
14. Hughes, TA et al. A 10-year study of the incidence of and factors predicting dementia in Parkinson's disease". *Neurology, 54,* (2000) 1596–602.
15. Hurkmans, HL et al. Energy expenditure in chronic stroke patients playing Wii Sports: A pilot study. *Journ NeuroEng and Rehab, 8, 38,* (2011) 1-7.
16. Krause, M. et al. A digital game to support voice treatment for Parkinson's disease. In *Proc. Of CHI'13* (2013)
17. Lindsay, S et al. Engaging older people using participatory design. In: *Proc of CHI '12*. Austin: Texas (2012)
18. Massimi, M. et al. Using participatory activities with seniors to critique, build and evaluate mobile phones. In: *Proc. Of ASSETS '07*, (2007)
19. Mazilu, S. et al. (2014, April). GaitAssist: a daily-life support and training system for parkinson's disease patients with freezing of gait. In *Proc.of CHI'14* (2014)
20. McNaney, R et al. Cueing for swallowing in Parkinson's disease. In *Proc. of CHI '11*, (2011), 619-622.
21. McNaney, R et al. Exploring the acceptability of Google Glass as an everyday assistive technology for people with Parkinson's. In *Proc. Of CHI'14*, (2014).
22. Olanow CW, et al. The scientific and clinical basis for the treatment of Parkinson disease. *Neurology. 72 (21 suppl 4):S1-S136* (2009).
23. Parkinson's Disease Foundation. *Statistics on Parkinson's*. http://www.pdf.org/en/parkinson_statistics on 03.09.2013
24. Parkinson's Disease Society. *Motor Fluctuations in Parkinson's: Information Sheet*. Parkinson's Disease Society: London (2008).
25. Parkinson's UK. *What is Parkinson's?* http://www.parkinsons.org.uk/content/what-parkinsons
26. Plow, M. A. et al. A scoping review of exergaming for adults with systemic disabling conditions. *J Bioengineer & Biomedical Sci.S1:00* (2011).
27. Robinson, L. et al. Keeping In Touch Everyday (KITE) project: developing assistive technologies with people with dementia and their carers to promote independence. *International Psychogeriatrics, 21, 3,* (2009) 494-502.
28. Shulman, LM et al. Non- recognition of depression and other non-motor symptoms in Parkinson's disease. *Parkinsonism Relat D, 8, 3,* (2002) 193-197.
29. Schutzer, KA et al. Barriers and motivations to exercise in older adults. *Prev Med, 39, 5,* (2004) 1056-1061.
30. Vines, J. et al. Questionable concepts: critique as a resource for designing with eighty somethings. In: *Proc. Of CHI '12,* (2012), 1169-1178.
31. Wallace, J. et al. A design-led enquiry into personhood in dementia. In: *Proc. Of CHI '13,* (2013) 2617-2626.
32. World Health Organization. International Classification of Functioning, Disability and Health. Geneva: WHO; (2001).
33. Yu, W et al. An interactive multimedia system for Parkinson's patient rehabilitation. In: *Proc. Of MMSys'10.* (2010). 129-137.

Being Seen: Co-Interpreting Parkinson's Patient's Movement Ability in Deep Brain Stimulation Programming

Helena M. Mentis[1], Rita Shewbridge[1], Sharon Powell[2], Paul Fishman[2], & Lisa Shulman[2]

[1]Department of Information Systems
University of Maryland, Baltimore County
Baltimore, MD 21250
{mentis, shewb1}@umbc.edu

[2]Department of Neurology
University of Maryland School of Medicine
Baltimore, MD 21201
{spowell, pfishman, lshulman}@som.umaryland.edu

ABSTRACT
The purpose of this study is to address the use of movement assessment sensors for clinical diagnosis and treatment. Eleven patients with Parkinson's disease who had undergone deep brain stimulation (DBS) surgery were observed during follow-up appointments for adjustments to the stimulation settings. We examine the ways in which the patients and clinicians assess movement ability together in the clinic and how these assessments relate to the treatment of functional disability through DBS. We have found that effective assessment of movement and treatment efficacy is a collaborative and interpretive process (co-interpretation) that relies on input from patients, clinicians, and caregivers. From these findings we describe the design directions for movement sensors to support co-interpretation of movement in a clinical context as opposed to simply movement definition.

Author Keywords
Movement; health; wearable sensors; communication; co-interpretation

ACM Classification Keywords
H.5.2 [Information Interfaces and Presentation]: User Interfaces - Interaction styles.

General Terms
Human Factors; Design; Measurement.

INTRODUCTION
With the growing ubiquity of movement sensor devices, such as the Microsoft Kinect camera or wearable accelerometers, the application of these sensors to health assessment has been a fruitful endeavor. Movement sensors have been touted as a significant advance in ongoing health care assessments through their ability to provide objective, standardized movement measurements [3, 9, 10, 16, 20, 21, 31, 36, 38]. Some have even proposed that these quantitative assessments are potentially superior to the patient history or the physical exam and that the emergence of low-cost, movement measurement devices will be able to provide clearer data to clinicians for diagnosis and treatment. However, this application of sensors to movement assessment hinges on the assumption that movement ability is not subject to interpretation, and that the impact and treatment of movement disorders can be standardized across patients and situations. This is troubling as there is a vast body of literature that discusses the highly ambiguous nature of health data and the interpretive work that one must engage in to make sense of that data and apply it to care [1, 15, 18, 19, 33].

With this paper, we report on field observations and video recordings of eleven patients with Parkinson's disease (PD) undergoing clinical assessments and treatment modifications following deep brain stimulation surgery (DBS). We present evidence that assessing a patient's motor function, the level of disability, and the efficacy of treatments are iterative and constructive acts reliant on an alignment of shared perceptions between clinician, patient, and lay caregiver – that which we term *co-interpretation.* This co-interpretation process includes the perspective of the patient and the clinician, but also can include the lay caregiver. More importantly, we show that there is a co-interpretive process in assessing the efficacy of the DBS treatments that oftentimes fails due to the difference between patient experience and clinical observation. The co-interpretive process we outline here has a significant impact on the resulting shared decision-making between the patient and the clinician, which is the hallmark of patient-centered care.

Our motivation for the study of current practices is to understand how we can use movement assessment sensors and systems in the treatment and care of patients with movement disorders. We learn that we must consider system design approaches that enable clinicians, patients, and caregivers to equally engage with and discuss the sensor data in order to integrate their interpretations towards optimum shared decision-making.

BACKGROUND
In the following section, we will review the literature that has guided us down this path. In particular, we will outline the interpretive stance that has been revealed in the expert

CHI 2015, April 18 - 23 2015, Seoul, Republic of Korea
Copyright 2015 ACM 978-1-4503-3145-6/15/04…$15.00
http://dx.doi.org/10.1145/2702123.2702342

medical gaze and how practices of 'seeing' inform that gaze. We will then discuss how the move toward a patient centered medical care model has revealed design strategies within the CHI and CSCW community for including the patient in health decision-making.

Technology's Role in Assessing Ability

The need for improved assessment of movement and mobility has resulted in growing interest in sensor technology. Ghika et al. [10] and Spieker et al. [36] were among the first investigators to explore the use of accelerometers and other sensing technology to monitor patients over extended periods of time. Recent advances in sensor features, wireless communication, signal processing, and pattern recognition have resulted in quantitative assessments of motor fluctuations [3], dyskinesia [16, 21], gait [20], and tremor [38]. And more recently, Gabel et al. [9] have used the Microsoft Kinect sensor to extract comprehensive gait information and arm kinematics for use in diagnosis, monitoring, and rehabilitation.

For PD, quantification of rigidity, bradykinesia, gait and postural stability have been studied with wearable sensors utilizing gyroscopes and accelerometers and with the use of consumer mobile technologies such as the iPad [7, 1, 22, 32, 39, 40]. Sensor systems such as the APDM Opal system (consisting of an accelerometer, gyroscope, and magnetometer) has been successfully shown to provide metrics on PD postural stability in stance, postural responses, gait initiation, gait (temporal-spatial lower and upper body coordination and dynamic equilibrium), postural transitions, freezing of gait, ankle and hip strategies for maintaining balance, and continuous monitoring of turning ability [2, 7, 1].

However, despite the wealth of systems and analytical frameworks, we still have little understanding of when and how to use these systems in clinical care and how system design can be enhanced to properly support assessment.

Interpretation in Medical Data Usage

Studies of medical information use often focus on the negotiations and interpretation of data in clinical decision-making [1, 15, 18, 19, 33]. These studies show that the information one must extract from health data is not self-evident and work must be done (alone with the data or in conjunction with others) in order to use the data in practice. Moreover seeing and assessing health is a complex process of resolving the body as it is represented through data points with what one knows from prior knowledge and what one learns through continuous interactions and explorations [27]. Thus, despite the trajectory of technological innovations to reveal more information about the health of the body, 'seeing' the body and assessing its health is still a matter of negotiation and interpretation [1, 18, 33].

For instance, in the study of atherosclerosis, Mol [28] argues that a single patient's diseased arteries become many different objects of investigation as a result of each of the different players and tests in diagnosis and assessment; all of which inform a single treatment plan. These objects come into being with the practices by which they are manipulated. Similar to the prior work we refer to at the start of this section, Mol asserts that knowledge is not understood as a matter of reference, but as one of manipulation. Knowledge is brought into being, sustained, or allowed to wither away in common, day-to-day, sociomaterial practices. Within healthcare, both patients and doctors have a perspective on the evidence of health laid before them in which they attribute meaning. This perspectivalism means that although both doctors and patients interpret the world they live in, their interpretations differ in how they are linked to past experiences, motivations, and the role of each person. Thus, neither the doctor nor the patient holds the reality of disease; all are simply interpreting it. This also includes caregiver interpretations, which can be very different from either the patient's or the clinician's [29].

Mol [28] argues that, in studying disease diagnosis and treatment, we should refrain from understanding objects as the central points of focus of different people's perspectives, and instead understand them as things manipulated in practices. Thus, if we foreground the materials, talk, and events within a healthcare context, disease and health become parts of what is done in practice. This perspective has contributed to this study's focus on the practice of interpretation of movement ability conducted in conjunction by all participating parties.

Patient-Centered Care

Within CSCW and HCI, researchers have regularly addressed the need for clear and frequent communication and engagement between patients and clinicians [6, 23], as well as the important task for patients to manage, engage with, and integrate their personal health information [5, 11, 34]. This is all in service of a patient-centered care model that has been shown to improve patient satisfaction by providing a sense of control of impairment and symptoms [14].

What is important to note for patient-centered care in movement assessment is that there is a distinction to be drawn between disability and symptoms [4]. The *measurement of symptoms* such as akinesia, tremor, rigidity, and postural abnormality tend to dominate clinical treatment. However, Brown et al. [4] showed that the severity of motor symptoms alone is of little importance in the patient's assessment of quality of life. Rather, it is the impact that these symptoms have on how the patient feels and a patient's ability to engage in activities that contributes most to quality of life.

Specifically for PD, some studies have shown that patients have a systematic bias towards overestimation of symptoms [30, 35], while other studies have shown that patients can provide accurate judgments of their disability [4, 29]. This may be because prior studies asked patients to rate clinical features of the disease (i.e. symptoms) while other studies [4] have asked patients to rate everyday abilities. For instance, a patient is likely to be able to relate how well he or she can walk without necessarily being able to rate the severity of gait disturbance. Thus, focusing on impact and relating that to symptom measures, can enhance the ability to care for the patient.

FIELDSITE: PD & DEEP BRAIN STIMULATION

This study was conducted during routine follow-up office visits of PD patients following subthalamic nuclei (STN) DBS surgery. PD is characterized by asymmetric onset of tremor, bradykinesia (extreme slowness), rigidity, and postural instability. Symptoms show individual differences, disease progression is variable, and the degree of disability can fluctuate over the course of a day. These motor fluctuations are among the most significant problems for the PD patient.

The typical pharmacologic treatment, levodopa, is very effective for reducing symptoms of PD, such as slowness of movement, stiffness, and tremor. However complications of therapy develop over long-term use (e.g. 5-10 years) including motor fluctuations, as well as longer 'wearing off' periods where the medication does not last as long as before. There are also more "on" and "off" periods that occur due to fluctuating levels of dopamine in the brain; these "on" and "off" periods occur without warning and can be more difficult to treat. DBS improves levodopa-responsive symptoms and, since stimulation is continuous, motor fluctuations are relieved.

The surgical procedure consists of the implantation of DBS leads in the brain and the implantation of a pulse generator-battery pack in the chest wall. The leads are programmed by modifying the pulse width, frequency, voltage and electrode configuration. Patients are seen initially 1-month post surgery and every 4-6 months for programming adjustments and battery monitoring.

The neurologist or DBS nurse specialist uses an external programmer device to adjust the patient's DBS settings based on the patient's history and exam. There are thousands of possible combinations of adjustments to improve patient symptoms, with certain modifications more successful for a particular symptom than others. And a clinician can make adjustments to more than one parameter in order to gain a desired effect. For instance, a clinician could reduce frequency from 160 times per second to 90 times per second and then raise the voltage so the stimulation is occurring less often but is stronger each time.

In addition, all patients have a hand-held battery-operated unit that can be used at home. Patients can control the stimulation level (based on permissions set by the clinician), including increasing or decreasing the voltage or adjusting the pulse width up or down.

DBS Follow Up Post-Surgical Assessments

The goal of the post-surgical assessment visits is to assess the patient's symptoms since the last office visit with special focus on the symptoms that may respond well to programming adjustments.

During the follow-up appointments, there are two distinct times at which Parkinson's symptoms and movement ability are assessed. The first time is at the beginning of the session utilizing United Parkinson's Disease Rating Scale (UPDRS). The UPDRS is the gold standard for assessing PD. It is a paper/pencil assessment measured on an ordinal rating scale and is based on the motor examination by the clinician and historical information from the patient. The motor examination section includes items assessing speech, facial expression, tremor, rigidity, finger taps, hand movements, leg agility, arising from a chair, posture, gait, and bradykinesia. During the DBS follow-up visits, the UPDRS is used to determine general disease severity as well as assess the patient's current state of motor function compared to their last visit.

The second time is during the DBS settings adjustments. Each adjustment needs to be assessed as to the affect it had on the patient and then recorded in the patient's medical record. These assessments focus on the symptom that the DBS settings adjustment was trying to address as well as any possible positive or negative effects the adjustment had on the patient (e.g. improved speech, worsening of tremor).

DATA COLLECTION AND ANALYSIS

The data we present here are based on an ongoing ethnographically-informed field study of DBS assessment with the intention to inform the design of movement sensors systems to support that assessment. It was conducted by a multidisciplinary team consisting of information scientists and neurologists.

The examples presented in this paper are from fieldwork performed over the course of 4 weeks at a neurology ambulatory center associated with a hospital in the Mid-Atlantic US. We obtained IRB approval from the medical center and participants consented at the beginning of their routine appointments. We did not actively recruit participants by any other means. The inclusion criteria for the study was that participants had to have been diagnosed with Parkinson's disease, have no evidence of cognitive decline, and must have undergone Deep Brain Stimulation Surgery. We employed observations and open-ended interviews, video recordings, and field notes for analysis. We also had the opportunity to ask questions of the clinicians following the assessments to further clarify and provide insight with what we observed during the clinical appointments.

A total of eleven office visits were observed including patient assessments and DBS programming, each visit was approximately 45 minutes. All visits were with the same registered nurse and attending neurologist. Table 1 describes the patient demographics. The participants we observed were primarily female. Follow-up appointments are made months in advance and it just so happened that the months we were observing in the clinic a large number of patients scheduled were female. Video recordings included discussions between patients, clinicians, and caregivers, motor assessments conducted by clinicians, and program-

	PT1	PT2	PT3	PT4	PT5	PT6	PT7*	PT8	PT9	PT10*	PT11
Age	51	52	74	56	80	57	71	61	77	43	63
Gender	Female	Female	Female	Male	Female	Female	Female	Male	Female	Male	Female
Year of Surgery	2008	2010	2007	2012	2008	2009	2014	2011	2008	2014	2008
Caregivers Present	Husband	Husband	Husband	N/A	Daughters	Husband	Friend & Daughter-in-law	Wife	Daughter	Parents	N/A

Table 2. DBS Patient Demographics (* indicates new DBS patient at 1-month follow-up)

ming adjustments to the DBS device. As a further step in data collection and validation, we employed member-checking throughout the study by discussing our interpretations with the clinicians.

We follow the analytical practice outlined in detail in [13]. An inductive, bottom-up data analysis informed by grounded theory was performed where the authors examined their field notes and videos for the key times for movement assessment. The authors transcribed the videos for iterative open-coding, generated and reviewed emerging concepts, and progressively refined and compared concepts to one another to gain internal coherency. The resulting moments of co-interpretation we observed are presented here with literature informing the discussion of our findings. The focus of this analysis was on how the clinicians, patients, and caregivers assessed motor and functional impairments based on diagnostic tests, talk, and body language.

FINDINGS

There are four times throughout each session that co-interpretation occurs: reviewing the status in the beginning of the session using the UPDRS, identifying the problem to be addressed before DBS programming, determining if the problem was addressed after DBS programming, and then determining the DBS control for the patient at the end of the session. Each of the following four sections corresponds to one of these four key co-interpretation moments.

Our motivation is to explicate the talk and action that comes together in co-interpretation – this is not achieved with one quote, but rather a series of action and talk. Thus, we present our findings as vignettes from our observed data, each illustrating key moments for the co-interpretive process of movement assessment during DBS programming. The examples provided are indicative of these interpretation moments, but are by no means the only occurrences witnessed – these four moments exist across all of the sessions we observed. PT# refers to patient and participant number in Table 1, RN to nurse, MD to neurologist, and CG to caregiver.

Vignette 1: Setting the Stage for Co-Interpretation

At the beginning of every appointment, the RN administers the UPDRS to the patient. A large portion of the questionnaire asks the patient to reflect on their experience of functional ability. Often the questions are easily answered, but sometimes the answer is not so clear.

In the following vignette, we provide an example from PT2 who had problems answering some of the questions posed in the UPDRS.

RN: "How about falling unrelated to freezing? In your worst off state, do you fall more?"
PT2: "Uh...not anymore."
RN: "OK, and how about freezing?"
PT2: [Pauses for a bit, turns to husband] "Do I freeze anymore?"
CG: "Not anymore. I haven't seen it that much."
RN: "How about walking?"
PT2: "In my worst state I shuffle walk. Small and little steps."
RN: "But you don't use a cane or a walker?"
PT2: "No."

Within the turn-taking outlined in this vignette we illustrate the need for movement assessment to take into consideration not only what can be seen within the clinic's walls but also what is occurring in the patient's day-to-day life. Communication of symptoms is critical, due to the infrequent nature of the DBS patient follow-up appointments. Patients are seen approximately every 4-6 months for DBS programming and are asked to come to their appointments 'off' their medication. This request is made so that the clinicians can get a visual understanding of how the patient appears and behaves when the medication is not in effect. However, 'off' medication at nine in the morning can be vary greatly from 'off' medication at nine at night. When the patient arrives for her appointment, she may not be 'at her worst'. A patient's worst is oftentimes at night or when under stress – and even that timing or relationship can vary widely. By asking the recall questions in the UPDRS assessment, as well as having the patient arrive off medication, the RN is attempting to co-interpret the *range* of the hold the illness has over the patient.

Identifying this range is important later in programming the DBS device. Remember that, during programming, the patient is given the ability to slightly modify parameters themselves when at home. It is an important part of co-interpretation of symptoms – when the RN, patient, and caregiver agree that the symptoms the patient is currently presenting may not be as significant as the ones the patient is experiencing during their day-to-day life. The RN will later use this information when she is determining what range of control the patient needs for the 'bad times'. We will further discuss co-interpretation during this process in Vignette 4.

It is important to remember that the subjective element of the UPDRS questionnaire tries to pinpoint the worst case symptoms by asking the patient to *recall* information of what they are like at their worst. This method of inquiry is problematic at times because the patient often does not have a proper recollection of the 'worst time'. Oftentimes a patient's worst time is best observed by the patient's caregiver. In these meetings, the caregiver's role is in providing details about ability that the patient cannot recall or about which they are unsure. Caregivers act as a third person viewing the movement issues on a daily basis and they can often remember and describe situations that were bothersome for the patient. The caregiver is the person who is most aware of the worst times due to the increased assistance they provide at home, for instance in cutting food, in dressing oneself, and in getting in and out of bed in the morning. He knows when the patient is getting tired or the medication is not working because he sees the ups and downs everyday. As we can see in this vignette, the patient turns to her caregiver – her husband in this case – and solicits his contribution to the co-interpretive practices. She knows that if she needs help, it is her husband that would have been helping her. Thus, in this case we show that co-interpretation of movement begins with the patient history gathered here through the UPDRS questionnaire device. Creating a space for all parties to begin to contribute their knowledge and understanding and converge on meaning with regards to the patient's movement ability is a first step in co-interpreting movement. And to know that what is presenting now, in that room, is not the full extent of symptoms experienced.

Vignette 2: Co-interpreting the Problem

After completing the UPDRS, the RN then attaches the programming head with tape to the outside of the patient's shirt. This is the indication that the modification of the program is to begin. At this point the RN always asks the patient, "How can I help you today?" In other words, she is asking the patient to highlight the most significant issue that a DBS adjustment might be able to address. From here on out, the modifications and assessments will focus on this stated complaint.

In the following vignette, PT6 had reporting severe rigidity as her significant complaint and the movement assessments the MD and RN rely on are manipulation of the arms and the open/close hand test (Figure 1).

MD begins to rotate the patient's wrists, moves her legs front and back, and has the patient open and close her hands on both sides.
MD: "Does medication help you at this point or are you in the same ballpark with or without?"
PT6: "Sometimes it helps and sometimes it doesn't."
MD: "So it is not like you are particularly stiff and slow first thing in the morning and you take your first medicine and it doesn't" [PT6 shakes head] "it doesn't.... You don't really feel it kick in."
PT6: "No. Kicks in in the afternoon usually."
MD: "Can you step in place?" [Patient begins to step. Neurologist turns to RN] "Is she different for left and right?" [Referring to her DBS settings for the left and right side.]
RN: "No."
MD: "So she is equal." [Manipulates patient's left wrist.]
MD: [Turning back to patient] "Do you notice any difference between your two body sides? One good side one bad side."
PT6: "Left side is bad."
MD: "Left side is worse. OK, that is what I think too."
[The neurologist then picks up the programming head for modifying the DBS setting and reduces the frequency to 120. He then begins to move PT6's left leg back and forth again.]
MD: "OK that didn't make it worse. I'm dropping frequency and I want to make sure that I'm not getting any worsening of stiffness." [Asks the patient to open and close her left hand and then step up and down with her left foot.]
RN: [Watching patient's leg] "That's actually better!"
MD: "Yeah, and now having done that, I can safely change pulse width on her left body side."
[The neurologist changes her pulse width to 180 and then moves the patient's legs front and back, has the patient open and close her hands, and then step with one foot at a time.]
MD: "Do you feel any different on your left side?"
PT6: [shakes head no]
MD: "Any better in terms of mobility?" [manipulates arm]
PT6: "No"
MD: [Turns to RN] "I'm only going to leave her pulse width at 180 because it does feel like the leg and certainly the hand are a bit looser." [Turns to patient] "So see if the medications work a little better now."

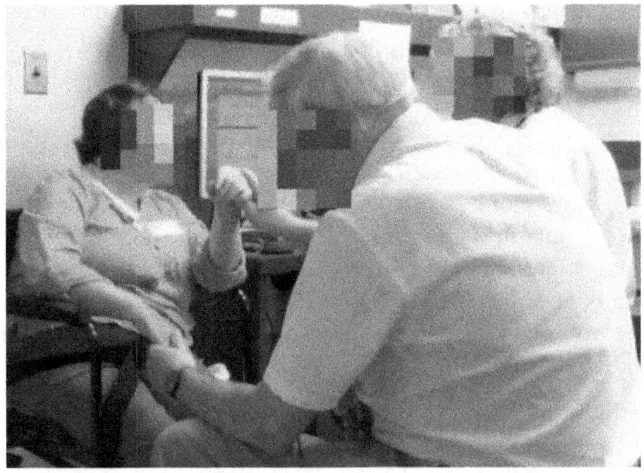

Figure 1. Bilateral Movement and Discussion

Through this vignette we see three co-interpreters of the patient's movement ability throughout DBS programming: the neurologist, the patient, and the nurse. In the beginning the neurologist's physical examination brings to his attention what he perceives as significant rigidity on the patient's left side compared to her right side. Her complaint regarding rigidity had initially not been that specific, but after further discussion, she confirms that her left side feels worse. At this point, the neurologist and patient were in agreement that her right DBS leads, which control the left side of the body, were in need of adjustment and it is clear that they are interpreting the rigidity consistently between the two of them. He notes that she is set equally on both sides at that point, which is odd as most patients do not have equal experience of symptoms. He also learns from the patient that her experience of the effect of medication is not reducing her rigidity. This is another important step in understanding how the patient is experiencing her symptoms at home. All of this data comes together to allow the neurologist and patient to co-interpret what the problem is that needs to be addressed through DBS programming.

However, as the programming is changed, we see each actor's interpretation become misaligned with the other. In this case, the neurologist chooses not to modify the programming any further. This is important to note as the identification of a problem means the neurologist has already identified his end-goal to this problem. For PT6's problem with stiffness, the neurologist's motivation was to create a basis for medication to have a better effect over the patient's symptoms. Oftentimes the DBS device itself is not the 'fix' for a particular symptom, but, in conjunction with proper medication, the DBS device allows for the medication to work more effectively for the patients. This relationship is difficult to convey to patients and, as it is unclear whether these modifications will in fact work, it creates a shaky ground for any other co-interpretive practices to carry-on. The neurologist has made a decision and the patient must wait to see if it was the right one.

Vignette 3: Co-interpreting the Efficacy of the Treatment

As we can see from Vignette 2, once a problem and a potential solution has been determined, the next step is to modify the devices programming in order to treat the problem. This is the one step that can be highly iterative – i.e. make a change, assess the effect, make a change, etc. Thus requiring a constant back and forth between the RN/MD and the patient on how the programming is doing. However, this is also the most common point of misalignment between patient and observer interpretations. As we saw in Vignette 2, the neurologist continues to make adjustments and he can feel the immediate effect of the DBS programming on the patient's leg and hand rigidity and both he and the nurse can see the effect on the rigidity through the patient's stepping ability. Both the neurologist and the nurse feel these are the signs of symptomatic relief that they are trying to achieve. The patient, however, is not satisfied with the level of change. She does not *feel* the change in rigidity. This can be a point of frustration during co-interpretation. The clinicians can feel and see the effect, but patients often do not feel the effect themselves. This oftentimes prompts additional modifications to the DBS device.

In the following vignette, PT7 is reporting problems with walking – specifically with freezing at the onset of walking. The RN determines that a change of frequency might be the solution.

RN: [Begins to reduce frequency on the right side Picks up right arm and manipulates wrist. Looks at CG and makes an expression showing satisfaction with movement.] [Says to PT7] "Tap your foot."
PT7: [Picks up and down right foot.]
RN: "That feel any different to you?"
PT7: "Not really."
RN: "OK. You don't hurt my feelings. That's OK." [all laugh]
CG: "It looked different. The way she did it."
RN: "I think it was smoother."
CG: "Yeah, usually she brings it up really stiff" [demonstrates a stiff leg picking up and down] "and this time her ankle moves" [demonstrates a flexible ankle].
RN: "Now this is the fun part." [Makes changes to the frequency on the left side. Rotates PT7's left hand. Takes PT7's right hand and asks PT7 to open and close left hand.]
RN: "The last time you did this I could hardly move this hand. Now look how loose it is. Is that good? Ok stand up." [Had her walk out of the room and down the hall.]
A little while later the neurologist enters to do his assessment and DBS adjustment. He asks PT7 to open and close her hands, and march in place. He then manually moves her legs out and back.
MD: "And you've had tremors before, right?"
CG: "Yeah, in the arms and the jaw."
MD: "And that didn't even come back when we dropped the frequency."
[Has her get up and start walking. She has a shuffling gait.]
CG: "She is doing it now."
MD: "What?"
CG: "The jaw [tremor]."
MD: "So when she walks she gets a little bit of the jaw."
CG: "Uh huh."
MD: "Is this better or worse?"[referring to gait.]
CG: "Oh much better. This is better."
MD: [Makes adjustment to frequency to 150 on the left side and 180 on the right. Asks PT7 to step in place.]
MD: [stares intently at patient's face] "And on these settings...a little bit of tremor may come back."
CG: [nodding] "But minor, though."

As we saw in Vignette 2, co-interpreting what constitutes success is a large challenge. We again see the challenge of integrating the patient's experience with the observations of the clinician and caregiver for the purpose of DBS programming. In Vignette 2, we see the clinician make a change that affects the muscle rigidity (as evidenced by ease of manipulation of joints by the clinician) while the patient reports no change. In this vignette the clinicians and caregivers are asserting their view of the patient's movement again while the patient reports no change. Much like with the previous vignette, what 'works' with DBS programming is often a try-and-see situation. And the interpretation of movement ability lies with the patient as well as the external observers. In this vignette, we also see the interpretation of the caregiver being elicited by the neurologist. Her notice of the movement improvement and returning tremor allows the neurologist to better interpret the affect of the modification he performed.

It is important to note that the DBS settings that are targeted for walking are different from the settings targeted for tremor. It is often the case that an improvement in one symptom, such as rigidity, may manifest in an increase in another symptom, such as dyskinesia. This is the case with medication as well. Thus, it is a delicate balance that the neurologist and nurse are trying to achieve between symptoms that can be affected by the DBS device as well as symptoms that can be addressed through medication. The neurologist is aware that, in general, most people consider an improvement in walking more important than a small amount of tremor. And in this vignette, the caregiver reiterates at the end that her interpretation is that a *small* amount of tremor is acceptable if the freezing gait is better addressed.

Unfortunately, patients are sometimes left out of this co-interpretive practice. We have seen that, with all of our participants, if they agree that there was an improvement, they are then in alignment with external observers; but disagreement is often relegated to the sidelines. Vignette 2 and 3 illustrate that there are several good opportunities to open up the co-interpretive space further to include all input from the patient into the discussion.

Vignette 4: Co-interpreting Settings for Patient Control

The final key moment in co-interpretation is the decision for how much of a range for modification the patient will be given. This moment is tightly tied to the first moment for co-interpretation – when the patient is remembering back to their 'worst time'. Issues that come up then must either be addressed now or it is made sure they are not made worse by changes that have been made during programming.

In the following vignette we return to the patient from our first vignette, PT2. She was most concerned with her shuffling gait. The RN had determined that a change to the pulse width was warranted and proceeds to go through a series of increases to pulse width on each side, asking the patient how she is feeling after each change. The neurologist then enters to conduct his own assessment.

RN: "What I did last time is I increased her pulse width which she said did very well and they didn't make any changes [at home]. When we have done voltage changes in the past she always undoes them by the time she gets home because she is so uncomfortable. So, I took her from 200 all the way up to 240 with improved rigidity. Took her back down to 220 because I know that she is very fragile but I'm going to give them patient control to go back up. Same thing on the other side. She was 140, I took her to 160, 180 and then took her back down to 160. And she does have improved rigidity at this higher – more was better but I didn't want to send her home with such high settings."
The neurologist begins his own exploration of pulse width setting modifications followed by foot-tapping exercises.
MD: "So, how much patient control did you give her."
RN: "I was going to give her three up and three down."
MD: "So starting on this side starting at 220 going up to 250."

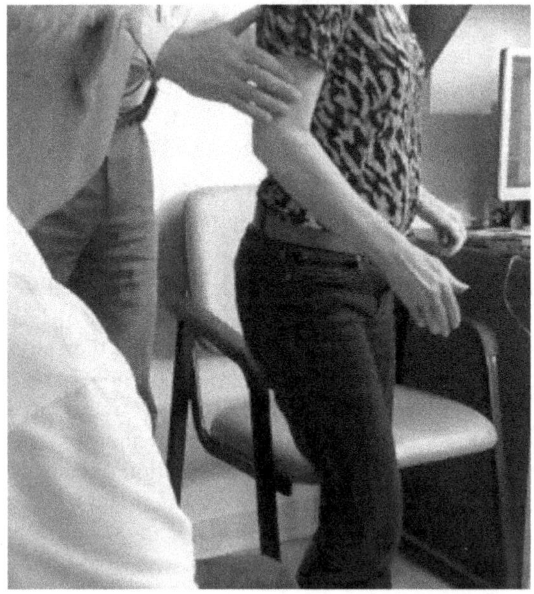

Figure 2: Checking Gait After Programming Modification

RN: "I took her to 240 and then down to 220. You've taken her up to 250?"
MD: "Yeah, and actually... I'll leave her at the lower setting but you can give her patient control. If you start her at 220 you can let her go all the way up to 250." [Turns to patient] "I think you are better at the higher. But you've got, like I said, if you feel like your feet are sticky you've got patient control to go up a good three clicks. Because it looks like when we do it on that side, if anything, it looks a little better."

Often the DBS programming will be perceived as working well in the clinic, but when the patient returns home she may experience problems or feel the settings are not addressing her symptoms as well as they were earlier. This is why the patient and caregivers are given a modicum of control over adjustments at home.

A patient does not have full control on all settings, though. The nurse specifically programs the device to provide control over one setting and for that setting, a range is defined. This setting and range has to be identified during the assessment. It is not simply enough to identify what is working during the appointment. Rather, they all must determine what options would best help the patient in enhancing quality of life outside of the clinic doors. This range is determined by a whole host of factors, including within which levels a patient can comfortably manage without demonstrating any significant side effects such as dizziness or increased cramping.

PT2 had a history of being 'sensitive' to changes to her settings – particularly with changes to voltage. Some patients are just sensitive to voltage and so clinicians must work with what they can change with little negative side effects, such as with pulse width. For every increase in pulse width, the patient showed signs of lessened rigidity and reported experiencing no negative side effects. Thus, the clinicians provided a large range for the patient to use at home. These decisions were made with the thought that there will be moments of significant rigidity at home or moments when the patient wants an improvement in smoothness of gait and so would like to bump up her pulse width settings to attain that effect.

This issue brings us full circle back to Vignette 1 where we showed that co-interpretation in DBS programming does not simply refer to interpreting movement in the clinic, but also interpreting what is occurring outside of the clinic walls and what that entails for patient control of DBS settings. Note that the patient in Vignette 4 is the same as in Vignette 1 (PT2). Remember that asking about the 'worst state' gives the clinician the insight as to how the patient is faring at home and to what extent the symptoms can interfere with every day tasks. Co-interpretation of movement is not simply because there must be an alignment *in* the clinic, but also because the patient must go home and live with these settings for the next 4-6 months.

DISCUSSION

Our motivation for the study of current practices is to understand how we can use movement assessment sensors and systems in the treatment and care of patients. In this paper, we present evidence that 'seeing' movement disorder symptoms, assessing the level of movement ability, and assessing the efficacy of treatment are co-interpreted acts reliant on an alignment of shared perceptions between clinician, patient, and caregiver. The relationship between patient and clinician for DBS programming is one of a synergistic nature that comes together during the in-clinic visit as they assess and communicate regarding movement ability. We have referred to this alignment as *co-interpretation* as the interpretive acts of all parties on the data before them is done in conjunction with one another in the exam room, which ultimately leads to shared decision-making towards treatment and care planning.

As we saw co-interpretation very much included the patient at the start of ever clinic visit, but as the session moves on, the patient is left out more and more. In Vignettes 2 and 3, we see that there is a need to better integrate the patient's interpretation into the fold with the clinicians and caregivers. We want to encourage the patient's interpretation throughout the session all the way to the end. Partnerships between patients, clinicians, and caregivers can be problematic as patient expectations pre-and-post DBS surgery may differ from the neurologist outcome measures, thereby making the assessment of movement subjective to each person's expectations [12]. However, this partnership role is at the crux of DBS programming where the patient is able to provide immediate feedback on what adjustments have been made and is able to become an active partner in the management of their care.

Design Implications

We began our paper by highlighting the design perspective that movement sensors could only better support this process by providing the clinician further data to discuss with their patients and assess whether their DBS programming modifications were having the intended effect. However, we would like to argue with this paper that movement sensors that only present processed data to clinicians could interfere with this co-interpretive process and create a greater chasm between the clinicians, the patient, and the caregivers. As we saw from our empirical work, it is not that uncommon for there to be a misalignment between patient experience and clinician determination of movement status. One could argue that what occurs in a non-sensor supported environment would continue to occur with the addition of sensors. Specifically, that interpretation of sensor data will require a shared decision-making process by the patient, caregiver, and clinician.

At this point we are reminded of work by Storni [37] who discussed the potential of unintended consequences of new health technologies. He calls upon Foucault's notion of *dispositif* to address how healthcare and medical practices are a socio-technical assemblage traditionally characterized by the centrality of a specific domain of knowledge (medicine) engendered with a set of power relations. Medical knowledge traditionally renders patients as passive and expert practices as rather disease centric. In this perspective little room is left to patients' experience and understanding, which are both often overlooked in favour of the dominant and authoritative medical discourse. This is the inequality that we, as system designers must be vigilant of in our design recommendations. Storni [37] explains how new health technologies *could* radically redefine the traditional model of care; however, they might instead run the risk of blindly reproducing traditional disease-centric assumptions and clinical knowledge power asymmetry. By allowing the machine to embody a role of uncompromising authority, Storni points out that a clinician may shift his basis for assessment from the patient's account to device-generated results. And these results translate a complex body into numbers that then guide the decision process leaving little room for interjection and contradiction by the patient. This is a similar view of those from disability studies [25, 26] – a field of critical inquiry focused on the lived experience of disability, and the societal, medical, and intellectual policies and rhetoric surrounding it. Most applicable here is the concern with the technological outcomes of such social forces in light of the lived experiences of individuals with disability. Namely, that the person designing a piece of software is, in some sense, defining who is disabled with respect to that software, thus typically reinforcing the medical models characterized by *fixing* an impairment.

Thus, the role of movement sensors in healthcare is also at risk to blindly reproduce traditional disease-centric assumptions and power asymmetry that do not always make room for patient perspectives. Storni's [37] suggestion to combat this is a model of co-construction of knowledge where different domains of knowledge can integrate without being in conflict and the contribution of a non-specialist (e.g. a patient or caregiver) is of vital importance. And the disability studies domain advocate for a shift of the conversation to one in which patients lead the definition of their health status and the management of their own health trajectory.

Alternative ways to present and visualize data need to be considered in the design of movement sensors in order to enable clinicians, patients, and caregivers to observe and interpret together. This is not a particularly new direction. There have been researchers within the HCI and CSCW fields that have tried to address the presentation of health data in a less intimidating manner in order to encourage patient engagement [8, 24]. What we are proposing is the visualization of movement sensor data to be displayed within the context of the clinical activity for co-interpretation. Furthermore, we argue that the visualizations should frame movement sensor data as not self-evident or definitive, and allow for the open discussion of that data by all parties equally. This would allow movement sensors to align with the clinical practices focused on patient centered care. Our goal should be to design movement sensor systems with the aim to promote a patient-centric perspective and to make room for the patient's understanding and point of view. We have begun to do just that through the presentation of hand movement data during DBS programming sessions. We capture before and after DBS programming of the hand open/close test and then present graphs of the data (i.e. not a UPDRS rating) on tablet computers (i.e. not the clinician's desktop computer) in order for all to gather around and co-interpret the graphs. As we move forward, we hope that this will present us with evidence of the benefit of the integration of movement sensors within an ecosystem of co-interpretation.

Conclusion

Our findings inform the importance of data visualization based on movement sensors for co-interpretation of movement disorder symptoms and shared decision-making. Sensors can provide much needed standardization across time, location, and people, to improve clinician understanding but sensors can also intrude on the important co-interpretive process of managing symptoms and improving quality of life. There are a number of fundamental questions that must be further explored in order to unpack the implications of movement sensors in a clinical decision-making environment. For instance, how does the perceived fidelity of movement sensors influence the co-interpretive process of movement assessment? And how do representations of movement symptomatic data influence the shared decision-making process? Further exploring mechanisms for co-interpreting 'objective' data could be applicable across diverse sensors/devices and health contexts to support patient empowerment and patient-centered care.

ACKNOWLEDGMENTS

Thank you to Courtney Pharr (Clark University) for her help in data collection and transcription.

REFERENCES

1. Alač, M. (2008). Working with brain scans: Digital images and gestural interaction in fMRI laboratory. *Social Studies of Science, 38*(4), 483-508.
2. Baston, C., Mancini, M., Schoneburg, B., Horak, F., & Rocchi, L. (2014). Postural strategies assessed with inertial sensors in healthy and parkinsonian subjects. *Gait & posture, 40*(1), 70-5.
3. Bonato, P., Sherrill, D. M., Standaert, D. G., Salles, S. S. & Akay, M. (2004). Data mining techniques to detect motor fluctuations in Parkinson's disease. *Proc. Conf. IEEE Eng. Med. Biol. Soc., 7*, 4766–9.
4. Brown, R.G., MacCarthy, B., Jahanshahi, M., Marsden, C.D. (1989). Accuracy of self-reported disability in patients with Parkinsonism. *Arch Neurol., 46*, 955-9.
5. Chen, Y. (2011). Health information use in chronic care cycles. In *Proc. CSCW*, 485-8.
6. Coovert, S. A., Ducey, A., Grichanik, M., Coovert, M. D., & Nelson, R. (2012). Hey doc, is that your stethoscope?: increasing engagement in medical education and training with iPads. In *Proc of CSCW,* 71-4.
7. El-Gohary, M., Pearson, S., Mcnames, J., Mancini, M., Horak, F., Mellone, S., and Chiari. L. (2014). Continuous Monitoring of Turning in Patients with Movement Disability. *Sensors,* 14(1), 356-69.
8. Frost, J., & Smith, B. (2002). Visualizing health practice to treat diabetes. *In CHI'02 Extended Abstracts*, 606-7.
9. Gabel M., Renshaw E., Schuster A., & Gilad-Bachrach R. (2012). Full Body Gait Analysis with Kinect. *Annual International Conference of the IEEE Engineering in Medicine and Biology Society.*
10. Ghika, J., Wiegner, A. W., Fang, J. J., Davies, L. , Young, R. R. & Growdon, J. H. (1993). Portable system for quantifying motor abnormalities in Parkinson's disease. *IEEE Trans. Biomed. Eng., 40*(3), 276–83.
11. Grimes, A., Landry, B. M., & Grinter, R. E. (2010). Characteristics of shared health reflections in a local community. In *Proc of CSCW,* 435-44.
12. Hasegawa, H., Samuel, M., Douiri, A., Ashkan, K. (2014). Patients' Expectations in Subthalamic Nucleus Deep Brain Stimulation Surgery for Parkinson Disease. *World Federation of Neurosurgical Societies.*
13. Heath, C., Hindmarsh, J., & Luff, P. (2010). *Video in qualitative research.* Sage Publications.
14. Higginson IJ, Astin P., Dolan S. (1998). Where do cancer patients die? Ten-year trends in the place of death of cancer patients in England. *Pall. Med., 12*, 353–63.
15. Hirschauer, S. (1991). The manufacture of bodies in surgery. *Social Studies of Science, 21*(2), 279-319.
16. Hoff, J.I., van den Plas, A.A., Wagemans, E.A., & van Hilten, J.J. (2001). Accelerometric assessment of levo-

dopa-induced dyskinesias in Parkinson's disease. *Move. Dis., 16*, 58–61.

17. Horak, F. B., & Mancini, M. (2013). Objective biomarkers of balance and gait for Parkinson's disease using body-worn sensors. *Move. Dis., 28*(11), 1544-51.

18. Joyce, K. (2005). Appealing images: Magnetic resonance imaging and the production of authoritative knowledge. *Social Studies of Science, 35*(3), 437-462.

19. Kaplan, B. (1995). Objectification and negotiation in interpreting clinical images: Implications for computer-based patient records. *Art. Intell. in Med., 7*, 439-54.

20. Keijsers, N. L., Horstink, M.W. & Gielen, S. C. (2006). Ambulatory motor assessment in Parkinson's disease. *Move. Dis., 21*, 34–44.

21. Keijsers, N.L., Horstink, M.W., van Hilten, J.J., Hoff, J.I. & Gielen, C.C. (2000). Detection and assessment of the severity of levodopa-induced dyskinesia in patients with Parkinson's disease by neural networks. *Move. Dis., 15*, 1104–11.

22. Kim, J.W., Lee, J.H., Kwon, Y., Kim, C.S., Eom, G.M., Koh, S.B., … & Park, K.W. (2010). Quantification of bradykinesia during clinical finger taps using a gyrosensor in patient's with Parkinson's disease. *Med. & Bio. Engin. & Comp., 49*, 365–71.

23. Liu, L. S., Hirano, S. H., Tentori, M., Cheng, K. G., George, S., Park, S. Y., & Hayes, G. R. (2011). Improving communication and social support for caregivers of high-risk infants through mobile technologies. In *Proc CSCW*, 475-84.

24. Mamykina, L., & Mynatt, E. (2009). Interpreting Health and Wellness Information. Symonds, J. et al. (eds.) *Auto-identification and Ubiquitous Computing Applications*, Idea Group Inc.

25. Mankoff, J., Hayes, G. R., & Kasnitz, D. (2010). Disability studies as a source of critical inquiry for the field of assistive technology. In *Proc of ASSETS*, 3-10.

26. Meekosha, H., & Shuttleworth, R. (2009). What's so'critical'about critical disability studies?. *Australian Journal of Human Rights, 15*(1), 47.

27. Mentis, H.M. & Taylor, A. (2013). Imaging the Body: Embodied Vision in Minimally Invasive Surgery. *Proc. of CHI*, 1479-88.

28. Mol, A. (2002). *The body multiple: Ontology in medical practice*. Duke University Press.

29. Morrow, C. D., Smentkowski, K., Schwartz, S., Armstrong, M. J., Gruber-Baldini, A. L., Anderson, K. E., … & Shulman, L. M. (2014). Does spouse participation influence quality of life reporting in patients with Parkinson's disease? *Quality of Life Research*, 1-5.

30. Pareés, I., Saifee, T.A., Kassavetis, P., Kojovic, M., Rubio-Agusti, I., Rothwell, J.C., … & Edwards, M.J. (2012). Believing is perceiving: Mismatch between self-report and actigraphy in psychogenic tremor. *Brain, 135*(1), 117-23.

31. Patel, S., Lorincz, K., Hughes, R., Huggins, N. (2009). Monitoring motor fluctuations in patients with Parkinson's disease using wearable sensors. *IEEE Trans. on Information Technology in Biomedicine, 13*(6), 864-73.

32. Patrick, S.K., Denington, A.A., Gauthier, M.J.A., Gillard, D.M., and Prochazka, A. (2001). Quantification of the UPDRS rigidity scale. *IEEE Trans. on Neural Systems and Rehabilitation Engineering*, 9(1), 31-41.

33. Prasad, A. (2005). Making images/making bodies: Visibilizing and disciplining through magnetic resonance imaging. *Science, Technology & Human Values, 30*(2), 291-316.

34. Pratt, W., Unruh, K., Civan, A., & Skeels, M. (2006). Personal Health Information Management. *CACM, 49*(1), p51-55.

35. Shulman, L. M., Gruber-Baldini, A. L., Anderson, K. E., Vaughan, C. G., Reich, S. G., Fishman, P. S., & Weiner, W. J. (2008). The evolution of disability in Parkinson disease. *Movement Disorders, 23*(6), 790-796.

36. Spieker, S., Jentgens, C., Boose, A. & Dichgans, J. (1995). Reliability, specificity and sensitivity of long-term tremor recordings. *Electroencephalography & Clinical Neurophysiology, 97*, 326–331.

37. Storni, C. (2009). The politics of design in Socio-technical dispositif. Reconciling Healthcare toward a future patient-centric perspective. Proc. of *Interact*.

38. Thielgen, T., Foerster, F., Fuchs, G., Hornig, A., & Fahrenberg, J. (2004). Tremor in Parkinson's disease: 24-hr monitoring with calibrated accelerometry. *Electromyography and Clinical Neurophysiology, 44*, 137–146.

39. Weiss, A., Herman, T., Giladi, N., & Hausdorff, J. M. (2014). Objective Assessment of Fall Risk in Parkinson's Disease Using a Body-Fixed Sensor Worn for 3 Days. *PloS one, 9*(5), e96675.

40. Weiss, A., Herman, T., Plotnik, M., Brozgol, M., Maidan, I., Giladi, N., ... & Hausdorff, J. M. (2010). Can an accelerometer enhance the utility of the Timed Up & Go Test when evaluating patients with Parkinson's disease?. *Medical engineering & physics, 32*(2), 119-125.

The Virtual Meditative Walk: Virtual Reality Therapy for Chronic Pain Management

Diane Gromala[1], Xin Tong[1], Amber Choo[1], Mehdi Karamnejad[1], Chris D. Shaw[1]
[1]Simon Fraser University
[1]250 -13450 102 Avenue
[1]Surrey, BC V3T 0A3 CANADA
{gromala, tongxint, achoo, mehdi_karamnejad, shaw}@sfu.ca

ABSTRACT
Because the nature of chronic pain is complex, pharmacological analgesics are often not enough to achieve an ideal treatment plan. Virtual Reality (VR) technologies have emerged within medical research in recent years for treating acute pain, and proved to be an effective strategy based on pain distraction. This paper describes a VR system designed for chronic pain patients. The system incorporates biofeedback sensors, an immersive virtual environment, and stereoscopic sound titled the "Virtual Meditative Walk" (VMW). It was designed to enable chronic pain patients to learn Mindfulness-based stress reduction (MBSR), a form of meditation. By providing real-time visual and sonic feedback, VMW enables patients to learn how to manage their pain. A proof-of-concept user study was conducted to investigate the effectiveness of the VR system with chronic pain patients in clinical settings. Results show that the VMW was more effective in reducing perceived pain compared to the non-VR control condition.

Author Keywords
Virtual Reality; Chronic Pain; Biofeedback; Mindfulness Meditation.

INTRODUCTION
An estimated 20% of people in North America [1] and 15-20% in industrialized nations [2] suffer from chronic pain. Chronic pain is defined as pain that lasts more than 6 months and persists beyond the healing of its putative cause. The complexity of this condition involves neurobiological, psychological and social dimensions, and as such, no universal treatment exists [3]. Although pharmacological approaches are the most common treatment method, they cannot address all aspects of the condition. Moreover, analgesics such as opioids can have serious side effects, including dependency and addictive tendencies [4], and misuse of opioids is a fast-growing problem among certain patient demographics [5].

CHI 2015, April 18–23, 2015, Seoul, Republic of Korea.

http://dx.doi.org/10.1145/2702123.2702344

One of the standard supplementary or adjuvant approaches to managing chronic pain is MBSR. The primary goal of MBSR is to enable patients to reduce stress and improve their health via improvements in the maintenance of their psychological states [6]. This is particularly important for chronic pain patients, as the persistence of pain itself is stress-inducing. Moreover, because there is currenty no known cure, and because current treatments present limitations, many patients are left with a sense of hopelessness [2].

Hoffman et al. convincingly demonstrated that immersive Virtual Reality (VR) is an effective way to manage attention in computer-generated virtual places as a form of pain distraction [7]. Thus, VR can be used as a powerful pain control technique and tool for patients to manage and alleviate their acute or short-term pain [8]. However, it is not yet known if the analgesic effects of VR persist beyond the VR sessions. No peer reviewed user studies have yet been published to investigate whether VR is helpful for managing chronic pain on a long-term scale.

This paper outlines a novel approach constructed for managing chronic pain using VR, biofeedback technology and the MBSR technique. The results of this research suggest that learning MBSR while immersed in a virtual environment can lead to further decreases in perceived pain in contrast to learning MBSR without VR.

RELATED WORK
While treatment of severe chronic pain solely by pharmacological approaches is limited and problematic [9], there are alternatives and adjuvant approaches that help patients manage their long-term pain and reduce its intensity.

Medical applications of VR have begun to emerge over the past decade, including rehabilitation, surgical simulators, and telepresence surgery [10]. In 2003, researchers at the Georgia Institute of Technology designed an immersive virtual environment (VE) — the Meditation Chamber — to train participants to reduce their stress [10]. The researchers used biofeedback sensors to monitor arousal; this data in turn affected the visual assets in the VE. Participants were able to successfully reduce their stress levels while observing the VE's continuously changing visual feedback, and the VE was more effective than biofeedback alone.

VR has also proven to be an effective method to reduce perceived pain during burn wound care [12]. Hoffman et al. designed a series of distraction-based VR studies in which patients reported up to 50% reduction in perceived pain. Although these studies were small, they have been replicated and extended since 1999. Several other VR applications not built upon pain distraction were developed to mitigate pain. Drawing upon the well-known "mirror therapy" espoused by neuroscientist V.S. Ramachandran, Murray et al. deployed VR as a solution to treat phantom limb pain [11]. Although this study was preliminary, the users reported they felt sensation in their phantom limb and reported a decrease in phantom pain.

In 2013, Shiri et al. created a VE and biofeedback system to treat pediatric headaches [12]. They obtained galvanic skin response (GSR) levels of patients with chronic headaches over ten sessions, each lasting 30 minutes. The GSR data was processed and used to affect the VE that the users were exposed to. The users were instructed to perform relaxation techniques; as they became more relaxed, the VE showed a happier picture of them. The researchers reported that during the intervention, patients with migraines experienced a significant decrease in headache pain using Visual Analog Scale [13]. E. Hudlicka also designed and evaluated a virtual mindfulness coach for patient education and health behavior training. Results suggested that coach-based training was more effective compared to self-administered approaches for mindfulness practices [14].

These works indicate that VR has been effective for treating acute pain; however, such VEs present limitations for managing chronic pain. We must consider the inherent approach in the use of VR for acute pain is based on pain distraction. It is impossible to distract chronic pain patients in a VE for significant and frequent periods of time, or whenever their pain begins to flare. Thus, our research focuses on utilizing VR as a therapeutic intervention to teach MBSR, a well-established pain management technique, which in turn may enable patients to more easily develop an effective long-term pain management tool.

VIRTUAL MEDITATIVE WALK: USER STUDY DESIGN AND METHOD

Virtual Meditative Walk

MBSR, a form of mindfulness meditation, is a technique that takes time and effort to learn. Initially, it requires a focus on one's internal states, rather than on the world. The design of the Virtual Meditative Walk (VMW) provides a peaceful, non-distracting and safe environment for users to immerse themselves in as they learn to achieve a stable meditative practice as they learn to control (or exert agency over) the physiological aspects that are necessary to achieve the positive effects of MBSR. The VMW is a VE where participants immersed in the virtual reality find themselves "walking" in a beautiful forest composed primarily of a deciduous forest and undergrowth. The surrounding area is relatively mountainous, reminiscent of the trails found along the northwest coast of North America. The camera slowly moves along a worn dirt pathway, as if the user is walking. This allows patients to explore the forest without requiring physical distractions or attention in order to achieve further passage. (Figure 1.)

The GSR sensors continuously track the patient's changing arousal levels, and in turn modify the VMW's weather. The light fog in the forest, for example, recedes as a patient's GSR levels start to stabilize in favor of a mindful state. Alternatively, the fog thickens and draws closer when the patient's arousal levels increase. This serves as seamless visual feedback for patients immersed in the VMW. Figure 2 shows how the VE changes according to variabile changes in the patients' biofeedback data.

Figure 1. Path design in VMW virtual environment.

Figure 2. As patients approach an inferred meditative state, the fog begins to dissipate (left to right), and sounds become more audible and spatial.

Study Intent

This proof-of-concept study was designed to determine if a Virtual Environment, combined with MBSR training and biofeedback, helps pain patients better manage their long-term chronic pain, given the limitations of VR pain distraction. Will patients fare better using the VMW to learn MBSR, compared to patients who learn MBSR without immersive VR? If such a VR intervention is able to reduce perceived pain levels among chronic pain patients in a clinical setting, it may be possible that the *long-term* benefits for patients learning MBSR to better manage their long-term persistent pain could be significantly improved.

Our focus groups and participatory design sessions made it clear that the use of VR itself may impose limitations that require greater investigation. For example, we found that some patients cannot sit for more than 20 minutes, that others cannot tolerate the weight or pressure of a head-mounted display (HMD) like the Oculus Rift, and that the planned use of a treadmill was too problematic to use in this initial stage. And so the study not only served as a proof-of-concept experiment, but it provided us further insight into how future studies can be better designed to accommodate customized patient needs.

Participants & Procedures

Initially, the study included twenty participants. However, because seven participants refused to fill out the pain assessment forms, their data was excluded. The participants who were included comprised thirteen patients from the Greater Vancouver area, ranging from 35 to 55 years of age (mean = 49, SD = 8.2); each had a diagnosis of chronic pain. Six participants (3 male, 3 female) were randomly assigned to the control group, and the other seven (3 male, 4 female) were assigned to the VR group. The experimenter introduced each participant to the study, and then attached the GSR sensors. Participants in the control group were required to listen to the MBSR training audio track. Participants in the VR group listened to the same MBSR training audio track while immersed in the VMW. Firsthand Technology's DeepStream VR viewer was used. Patients in both groups participated in the MBSR training for twelve minutes.

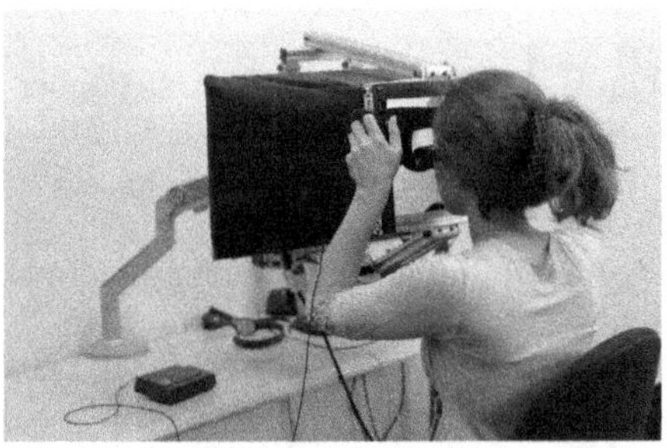

Figure 3. A participant in the VMW study using the DeepStream stereoscopic viewer.

Apparatus

The construction of the physical setup for the VMW required the use of the DeepStream VR viewer, which was installed in a room in a pain clinic for the study. The DeepStream is a stereoscopic VR viewer compatible with PC or Mac computers; it is mounted on a movable arm to ensure flexibility and to maximize patient comfort. The DeepStream rests directly in front of the participant's eyes and does not grip the head, unlike HMDs such as the Oculus Rift, which may cause unnecessary discomfort or pain with this particular participant demographic. The GSR sensors, which are small clips, were gently put onto two of the patient's fingertips; none of the participants reported discomfort from their use.

Instruments

A simple statistical analysis was conducted before and after the study session in order to compare perceived reported pain levels. Study investigators used an 11-point Numerical Rating Scale (NRS) in which patients self-report their pain levels between the numerical values 0 and 10; 10 equates to the worst pain possible and 0 equates to no pain felt. The NRS instrument was chosen because of its simplicity of understanding and ease of use, and because the investigators wanted to avoid distressing the pain patients with complex and lengthy questionnaires. Prior experience taught us that these participants, who may already be feeling some discomfort, end studies prematurely when confronted with the same lengthy questionnaires that they are compelled to fill out for most of their clinical visits.

RESULTS AND ANALYSIS

In this study, time and condition were two independent variables. Time was a within-subjects factor, as every participant was measured before and after their MBSR experience. The study used a between-subjects design; a participant either belonged to the VR group or to the control group. Therefore, a two-way mixed ANOVA was run to analyze the collected data. We found a significant main effect of Time, $F(1, 11) = 10.44$, $p < .01$, $r = .61$. The main effect of Condition was not significant, $F(1, 11) = 1.53$, $p > .05$, $r = .25$. This indicated that when the time at which NRS was measured is ignored, the initial pain level in the VR group was not significantly different than that in the control group. There was a significant Time x Condition interaction (as shown in Figure 4), $F(1, 11) = 8.16$, $p < .05$, $r = .54$, indicating that the changes in the pain level in the VR group were significantly different compared to the change in the control group. Specifically, there was a significant drop in NRS ratings in the VR group, $t(6) = 2.86$, $p < .05$, $r = .57$, but a very weak drop in the control group, $t(5) = 1.24$, $p > .05$, $r = .26$. These findings indicate that the VMW (VR paired with biofeedback for MBSR training) was significantly more effective than MBSR alone at reducing reported pain levels among participants. LS Means test results are shown in Figure 4.

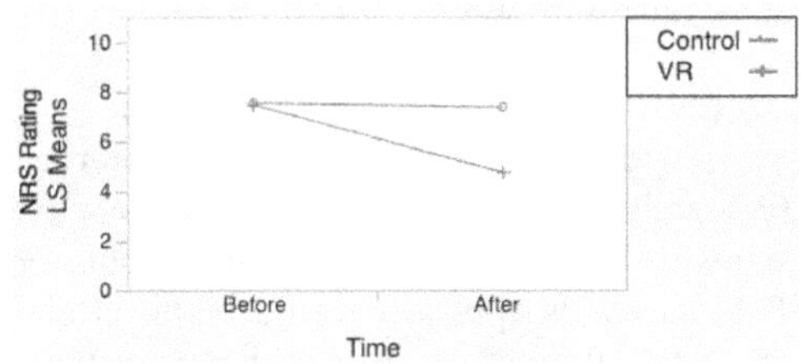

Figure 4. VR and Control Groups NRS Rating LS mean value before and after experiment

DISCUSSION

It is promising to examine the pain reduction reported by participants in the VMW study, as the impact the VR had on chronic pain patients occurred after such a short amount of time. Compared to the control group, the VR group experienced a reduction of pain, on average, equalling 2.6 on the NRS scale. One must also consider that the patients themselves were only immersed in the VR for twelve minutes, which is a short amount of time for an MBSR session. Future studies with longer immersion times and a focus on how long the analgesic effect may linger after the meditative session is the natural next step in continuing this line of inquiry. The introduction of more detailed reporting methods of perceived pain, such as the use of the McGill

Pain Questionnaire, could also yield new insights into the details surrounding perceived reported pain after the VR intervention. This will require greater effort put towards the understanding of pain patient experience within the context of the clinic to ensure their comfort and stamina are not negatively impacted.

Although the single trial outlined does not speak to the effectiveness of potential long-term capabilities for VR chronic pain management, the VMW enables chronic pain patients to consider that their pain experiences could be further managed through MBSR practiced over the long-term. By multiple training sessions and regularized practice, patients can learn to more easily situate the psychophysical mediation of their internal experiences into everyday life. The pain reduction reported by the NRS data is an early step in proving that VR and biofeedback systems may be an effective first step in promoting this behavioural change.

The VMW was designed using a cross-platform game engine that enables researchers or patients to run the VMW on a wide variety of devices, including handheld phones and tablets. These could enable patients to enhance their MBSR skills in a more easily accessible manner outside of clinical settings. This would also allow researchers and health practitioners to extend the use of VR technology from research and clinical settings to patient homes. To achieve this goal, a key approach would be to migrate the current VE to devices patients already own. Smaller, portable stereoscopic viewers could also be used with mobile devices such as Google Cardboard or the FOV2GO, both of which are low-budget stereoscopic viewing devices; this approach is currently being investigated by the study investigators for future work.

CONCLUSION

In this paper, we discussed how a VR intervention, in conjunction with MBSR and biofeedback, was better able to invoke positive results in chronic pain patients, compared to MBSR alone. This approach could be an effective non-pharmacological alternative or supplementary method to existing pain management strategies. By teaching mindfulness meditation to patients in this context, we believe that pain patient health may be improved over time.

REFERENCES

1. Macfarlane G. J., McBeth J., and Silman A. J., Widespread body pain and mortality: prospective population based study. *BMJ*, 323 (2001), 662–665.
2. Gatchel R. J., Peng Y. B., Peters M. L., Fuchs P. N., and Turk D. C., The biopsychosocial approach to chronic pain: scientific advances and future directions. *Psychol. Bull.*, 133 (2007), 581–624.
3. Fishbain D. A., Cole B., Lewis J., Rosomoff H. L., and Rosomoff R. S., What percentage of chronic nonmalignant pain patients exposed to chronic opioid analgesic therapy develop abuse/addiction and/or aberrant drug-related behaviors? A structured evidence-based review. *Pain Med. Malden Mass*, 9 (2008), 444–459.
4. Jamison R. N., Ross E. L., Michna E., Chen L. Q., Holcomb C., and Wasan A. D., Substance misuse treatment for high-risk chronic pain patients on opioid therapy: a randomized trial. *Pain*, 150 (2010), 390–400.
5. Reibel D. K., Greeson J. M., Brainard G. C., and Rosenzweig S., Mindfulness-based stress reduction and health-related quality of life in a heterogeneous patient population. *Gen. Hosp. Psychiatry*, 23 (2001), 183–192.
6. Hoffman H. G., Chambers G. T., Meyer W. J., Arceneaux L. L., Russell W. J., Seibel E. J., Richards T. L., Sharar S. R., and Patterson D. R., Virtual reality as an adjunctive non-pharmacologic analgesic for acute burn pain during medical procedures. *Ann. Behav. Med. Publ. Soc. Behav. Med.*, 41 (2011), 183–191.
7. Hoffman H. G., Patterson D. R., Carrougher G. J., and Sharar S. R., Effectiveness of virtual reality-based pain control with multiple treatments. *Clin. J. Pain*, 17 (2001), 229–235.
8. Baer R. A., Mindfulness Training as a Clinical Intervention: A Conceptual and Empirical Review. *Clin. Psychol. Sci. Pract.*, 10 (2003), 125–143.
9. Satava R. M., Surgical robotics: the early chronicles: a personal historical perspective. *Surg. Laparosc. Endosc. Percutan. Tech.*, 12 (2002), 6–16, Feb.2002.
10. Shaw C., Gromala D., and Song M., The Meditation Chamber: Towards Self-Modulation. *Proc. ENACTIVE (2007)*, 121–133.
11. Murray C. D., Pettifer S., Howard T., Patchick E. L., Caillette F., Kulkarni J., and Bamford C., The treatment of phantom limb pain using immersive virtual reality: three case studies. *Disabil. Rehabil.*, 29 (2007), 1465–1469.
12. Shiri S., Feintuch U., Weiss N., Pustilnik A., Geffen T., Kay B., Meiner Z., and Berger I., A virtual reality system combined with biofeedback for treating pediatric chronic headache--a pilot study. *Pain Med. Malden Mass*, 14 (2013), 621–627.
13. Varni J. W., Seid M., and Rode C. A., The PedsQL: measurement model for the pediatric quality of life inventory. *Med. Care*, 37 (1999), 126–139.
14. Hudlicka E., Virtual training and coaching of health behavior: example from mindfulness meditation training. *Patient Education and Counseling*, 92 (2013), 160-166.

Sharing is Caring: Assistive Technology Designs on Thingiverse

Erin Buehler[1], Stacy Branham[1], Abdullah Ali[1], Jeremy J. Chang[1], Megan Kelly Hofmann[2], Amy Hurst[1], Shaun K. Kane[3]

University of Maryland, Baltimore County
Information Systems Department
{eri4, sbranham, aali6, c86, amyhurst}@umbc.edu

Colorado State University, Fort Collins
Computer Science Department
hofmann.megan@gmail.com

University of Colorado, Boulder
Department of Computer Science
shaun.kane@colorado.edu

ABSTRACT

An increasing number of online communities support the open-source sharing of designs that can be built using rapid prototyping to construct physical objects. In this paper, we examine the designs and motivations for assistive technology found on Thingiverse.com, the largest of these communities at the time of this writing. We present results from a survey of all assistive technology that has been posted to Thingiverse since 2008 and a questionnaire distributed to the designers exploring their relationship with assistive technology and the motivation for creating these designs. The majority of these designs are intended to be manufactured on a 3D printer and include assistive devices and modifications for individuals with disabilities, older adults, and medication management. Many of these designs are created by the end-users themselves or on behalf of friends and loved ones. These designers frequently have no formal training or expertise in the creation of assistive technology. This paper discusses trends within this community as well as future opportunities and challenges.

Author Keywords

Assistive technology; design; disability; open-source; personal-scale fabrication; prototyping; 3D printing.

ACM Classification Keywords

K.4.2 [**Computers and Society**]: Social Issues – *assistive technologies for persons with disabilities.*

INTRODUCTION

Personal-scale fabrication tools such as 3D printers can enable the rapid development of low-cost, highly customized physical objects. These features are particularly beneficial to the creation of assistive technologies. An assistive technology (AT) is any item that enables a person with a disability to complete a task that they would otherwise be unable to do. Commercially available AT devices are frequently costly and available in a limited selection. The use of personal-scale fabrication tools to make modifications to existing AT devices and create novel designs is a growing area of interest (Figure 1). This technology affords not only the ability to reduce costs and personalize devices, it can also empower caregivers and end-users of AT to create their own assistive solutions.

CHI 2015, April 18 - 23 2015, Seoul, Republic of Korea.
Copyright 2015 ACM 978-1-4503-3145-6/15/04...$15.00.
http://dx.doi.org/10.1145/2702123.2702525

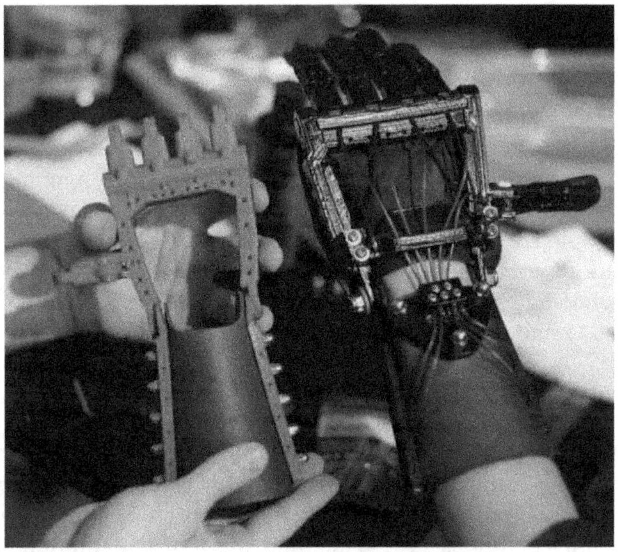

Figure 1. An example of a 3D-printable prosthetic hand, a popular type of assistive technology featured on Thingiverse.com. (Thing # 229620)

Online communities and open-sourced websites have been evolving concurrently with personal-scale manufacturing tools to share models and files. These sites encourage the free and open sharing of 3D-printable designs, allowing for the widespread dissemination of ideas and objects. For this study, we chose to examine Thingiverse.com, a popular open-source design repository and community affiliated with MakerBot, a consumer 3D printer manufacturer. Thingiverse enables anyone to freely download source files and registered users can comment on and favorite designs. While Thingiverse supports a variety of file formats that can be used for many types of personal-scale manufacturing (including laser cutting and milling), the majority of the designs are intended for 3D printing.

Our research examines this open design community structure and its impact on do-it-yourself (DIY), or self-designed, assistive devices. This two-part study looks at the existing landscape of AT designs in Thingiverse and looks further into the motivations of these AT designers. We conduct a survey of existing AT designs and present an overview of the variety of AT designs, the disabilities they serve, and the differing complexity involved in fabrication. We explore the motivations, perceptions, and skills of the designers of these items through an online questionnaire. We close with a discussion of the future shape of this community and the challenges posed to technologists to support a successful and more diverse AT-maker landscape.

RELATED WORK

This paper presents a case study of one online community, Thingiverse, and its members' creation and dissemination of assistive technology. The work sits at the intersection of and contributes to the following research areas: assistive technology, personal fabrication of assistive technology, and online maker communities.

Assistive Technology Design and Challenges

For the purposes of this paper, we define *assistive technology* as any piece of technology that is designed to increase, maintain, or improve the functional capabilities of people with disabilities, older adults, or people with chronic health conditions [10]. Adopting this broad definition of accessibility allows us to analyze a range of both mainstream and novel assistive technology designs.

While assistive technology has the potential to improve people's lives, gaining access to the appropriate assistive technology can be difficult. Many traditional assistive technology products are expensive and may not adequately meet a user's unique needs [3,14]. Even if an appropriate, affordable assistive technology exists, a user may choose not to use it due to perceptions of stigma or issues of personal identity [16].

Personal Fabrication of Assistive Technology

Because assistive technology must often be customized to individual needs, "do-it-yourself" is not an unfamiliar practice in this area. In some cases, assistive technology products are designed by the users themselves or by family members. Examples popularized by media include Hugh Herr [1], a biophysicist and engineer whose limb loss in a climbing accident led to his advanced research in leg prostheses and orthoses; and Samuel Farber [4,13], founder of the universally designed household brand OXO[1] who identified the need for accessible kitchenware after observing his wife's struggles with arthritis. More recently, personal fabrication has been popularized through the development and availability of user-friendly, low-cost fabrication tools such as 3D printers [5]. DIY or self-designed AT can address several of the pitfalls of traditional or off-the-shelf AT. Devices and modifications can be tailor-made in a way that is often unavailable or pricey for standard AT fittings, end-user involvement can increase buy-in and reduce user abandonment, and some DIY solutions can be made with inexpensive materials that are equal or near equal in robustness to their costly, commercial counterparts.

The potential for personal fabrication to revolutionize assistive technology has been highlighted by several high-profile projects, such as the Open Prosthetics Project[2] and e-NABLE[3]. Despite this potential, few studies have examined the use of modern personal fabrication technologies, such as 3D printers, for creating assistive devices. Hurst and Tobias [9] explored motivations for creating DIY assistive technology. Buehler et al. [2] examined how organizations that served people with disabilities used personal fabrication tools such as 3D printers. Hook et al. [7] have also begun exploring the role of 3D printing as a means to DIY assistive technologies, in particular looking at children with disabilities as designers [6]. Our investigation presents a systematic evaluation of assistive technology creation and dissemination in an online community of assistive technology makers on Thingiverse.

Communities Supporting Making and Fabrication

Many online and local communities have formed around maker practices. In some cases, these communities form "maker spaces" to pool resources and gain access to more expensive equipment [5]. These communities also provide feedback and support for designers and makers. Maker spaces may exist both in the physical world and online. Tanenbaum et al. [17] and Lindtner et al. [12] have studied maker spaces and the interactions around them. Tseng and Resnick [19] studied the design, documentation, and use of designs in the Instructables community and Rosner et al. [15] examined online interactions involving the sharing of design instructions for various DIY projects in the IKEA hacking community. Kuznetsov and Palos [11] conducted a study of six DIY/maker communities (Instructables, Dorkbot, Adafruit, Ravelry, Craftster, and Etsy) and identified structures in the communities that promote sharing, creativity, and independent skill building. Our study is among the first to study an online community with a focus on the creation of assistive technology.

[1] http://www.oxo.com/AboutOXO.aspx

[2] http://openprosthetics.org/

[3] http://enablingthefuture.org/

There are a multitude of fabrication, design, and assistive-technology communities online. In searching for assistive creations in fabrication communities, we identified certain structures, such as design repositories, tutorial sites, and member-focused or forum formats. We also saw open-source and purchase-format design-sharing sites. In tutorial and forum-based communities, we were able to find sites specific to assistive technology and/or personal ability.

We studied the Thingiverse community because it is currently the largest open-source repository, with over 100,000 user-submitted designs for 3D printed, laser cut, or milled objects[4]. Its size and popularity make it a useful lens to investigate the degree to which AT is supported in the mainstream maker movement. It also includes a customizer tool that allows users to "remix," or edit, a previously posted design to improve upon or personalize them, and then share those modifications.

SURVEY OF ASSISTIVE TECHNOLOGY CURRENTLY AVAILABLE ON THINGIVERSE

We completed a survey of existing AT designs shared on Thingiverse. This included manually finding and strictly classifying AT designs. Below, we present our methods of searching and sorting designs to create this dataset.

Search Terms and Procedures

We collaboratively derived a set of key terms related to assistive technology and healthcare needs (Table 1) that included field-specific terms from the literature and colloquial terms to surface as many relevant designs as possible. We then queried the Thingiverse search engine with each term using a desktop browser. Multi-word searches were placed within quotation marks to obtain exact string matches.

We refined our key term list after preliminary searches to ensure coverage. We then added any terms that we did not initially include, but appeared in design descriptions or comments (e.g., "handicap"). Our final list included 173 terms, with 115 yielding appropriate results and 58 yielding none. Search terms not yielding results included "hearing impaired," "motor impairment," "cognitive disability," "paraplegic," "quadriplegic," "Parkinson's," and "Alzheimer's" despite there being numerous designs that might be described by these keywords.

We manually evaluated our search results, totaling over 25,000 "things," for relevance and created a master list of AT designs. For each design, we gathered the "thing" number (a unique ID given to designs on Thingiverse.com), title, designer handle, and the number of likes, makes, and remixes (Figure 3). We categorized each list item according to a set of formal inclusion criteria (Figure 2).

[4] MakerBot, host of Thingiverse, claims it passed the 100,000 mark on June 8, 2013.

Keyword	Frequency
pill (58), pill box (18), pillbox (14)	90
prosthetic (44), prosthesis (17)	61
disabled (14), disability (12), disabilities (10), impaired (1), impair (1), handicapped (3), handicap (1)	42
visual (25), visually impaired (7), visual impairment (1)	33
enable	25
tactile (19), tactile graphic (3)	22
assistive device (11), assistive (9), assistive technology (2)	22
Braille	18
grip	18
wheelchair	17
access (11), accessibility (6)	17
amputee	15
medicine	12
elderly (4), old (3), senior (3), aged (1)	11
cane	10

Table 1. Top 15 keywords that appeared in the complete set of 3D models identified as assistive designs.

IC 1. *Traditional assistive technology products currently available as products or made by therapists:* tools for activities of daily living or math manipulatives for people with cognitive disabilities (6% of designs).

IC 2. *Accessible media:* including tactile graphics with Braille that modeled DNA, atoms, or buildings (11%).

IC 3. *Accessories for assistive devices:* aesthetic toppers for canes, power wheelchair joysticks, or game controller joysticks for people with physical disabilities (8%).

IC 4. *Concept designs and prototypes for assistive technologies:* creative solutions to accessibility challenges or needs that aren't currently addressed by existing products, such as a visionary design of a non-surgical cochlear implant for the profoundly deaf or severely hard of hearing, or a heat-based display (4%).

IC 5. *Prosthetic limbs:* prosthetic hands, fingers, or partial fingers for amputees (17%).

IC 6. *Tools for medication management:* pill-cutting guides or containers for sugar cubes for older adults and people with diabetes (36%).

IC 7. *Other design explicitly intended for disabled or senior users:* spinner rings for people with ADHD (18%).

Figure 2. Example designs from our inclusion criteria (IC). IC 1) Right angle spoon for people with limited dexterity. IC 2) Tactile graphic of Yankee stadium. IC 3) Wheelchair mounted environment controller. IC 4) Prototype to convert images to heat for people with vision impairment. IC 5) Prosthetic hand for users with a functional thumb. IC 6) Pill bottle lid with daily reminder label. IC 7) Ironing guide for individuals with vision impairments.

We categorized the first 100 items collaboratively and the remaining independently. If categorization for an item was unclear, it was discussed with the group. We achieved agreement, often by removing items whose descriptions did not explicitly indicate intended use by people with disabilities or the aging population. The final list contained 363 unique designs uploaded by 273 designers.

Limitations

Despite efforts to cast a wide net, there are limitations to our search approach. We did not conduct an exhaustive search of all Thingiverse designs, but instead chose to search based on a key term criteria. There were also limitations to the website itself, including a search result bug limiting us to viewing only the first 1,032 results of a search regardless of the number of hits. Additionally, the Thingiverse search feature does not include the text found in comments, which might have provided us with more context clues about which designs were intended for assistive use. With any user-generated content, there is the possibility of missed search results due to vague, misspelled, or missing descriptions and keyword tagging by the contributors themselves. Some objects that are assistive tools, like a toothpaste tube key, were excluded from our list because they fell on the edge of our inclusion criteria (thing 35064).

Statistics About Designs

Our search process identified a variety of designs to solve accessibility challenges (Figure 2). The category with the most designs was IC 6, tools for medication management, which had 130 things of the total 363 and was dominated by pill boxes, bottles, dispensers and accessories like tops and dividers (107 things). The category with the second most designs was IC 5, "prosthetic limbs," which had 61 things and was dominated by prosthetic hands, hooks, and related parts (41 things).

The majority of designs either mimicked or replaced devices that are already available on the commercial market, such as splints, tactile graphics, prosthetics, and pillboxes. Many of these came at lower cost (e.g., prosthetic prints run in the hundreds of dollars instead of in the thousands). But for other items, cost savings are not so clear (e.g., pill boxes, which can cost less than $10 on the commercial market).

Many items were highly specialized, thus not commercially available, enabling people to have more control over inaccessible environments or inadequate medical care. For example, one designer created an adapter to fit their child's preferred Vortex inhaler mask to an incompatible PARI JuniorBoy SX compressor (thing 237169). At least one item was designed because its commercial vendor had gone out of business and was no longer available to consumers (Trautman Hook, things 2194 and 2114).

As we discuss in greater detail in following sections, the value of creating these designs extended beyond the utility of the thing itself. For example, on design profiles, we found that some designers expressed enjoyment in the process of invention (e.g., "I love to invent," thing 324072) or pride in who made the item (e.g., "Designed by two dyslexic students. :) :)", thing 186338).

In Figure 3, we highlight several designs with high numbers of likes, makes, and remixes. While these metrics are not an explicit statement of the popularity of an item, it is one way to discern if a design is receiving attention within the Thingiverse community. Prostheses dominated our list in terms of likes, with four (things 261462, 242639, 92937, and 380665) of the top five most liked AT designs being variations on prosthetic hands, but made up less than 17% of the total AT designs. Despite being relatively complex prints, the prosthetic hands were also printed several times as indicated by their high number of makes.

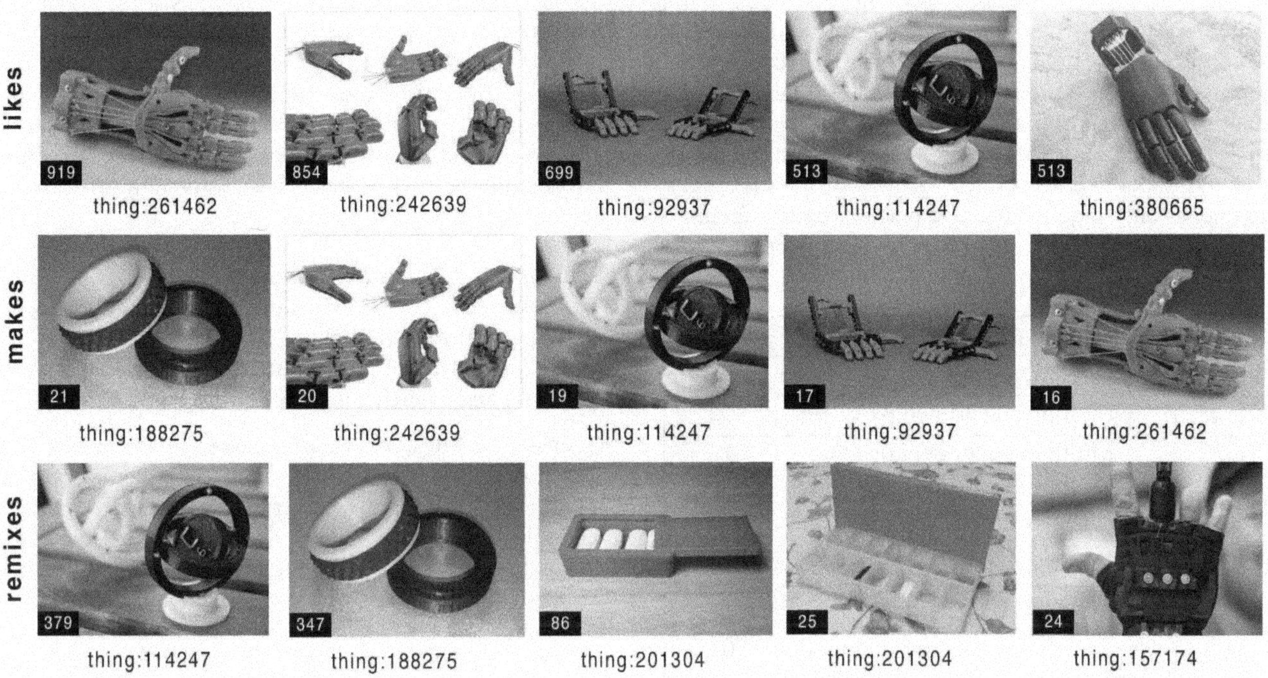

Figure 3. Overview of the top 5 items with respect to likes (top row), makes (middle row), and remixes (bottom row) among the 363 AT designs identified. Likes accrue when account holders click the "Like" button on a design profile. Makes accrue when an account holder clicks the "I made one" button on the design profile to indicate having made a copy. Remixes accrue when account holders click the "Remix it" button on a design profile. This figure illustrates the popularity of prosthetic hands and pillboxes in our dataset. All counts are publicly viewable on Thingiverse.com and were gathered August 2014.

This perceived popularity may be due in part to media coverage of open-sourced prosthetics resources.

Designs like the spinning ring fidget (thing 188275) and the pill boxes (things 201304 and 273754) also received a high number of makes, which might be linked to their universal appeal as everyday items (i.e., the fidget is intended for sensory or attention issues and pill boxes are for medication, but both items can be used by anyone for other reasons). The most remixed item, a model of an atom with tactile information on the surface (thing 114247) includes an accessible version with Braille labels, but it may be among the most remixes and makes due its versatility as an instructional aid (i.e., the design offers the ability to print a model of any atomic element with the correct information about each already programmed into the remix options).

Publically Available Designer Information

We surveyed the publically available information about the designers in order to understand more about them. Of the 363 models that matched our inclusion criteria, 273 were created by unique designers. According to each designer's profile, 258 of these designers are individuals, and 15 belong to groups or organizations. Most designers (215), only uploaded a single design, 33 designers uploaded 2, and the most active designer uploaded 13. Of the 166 designers who disclosed their location in their profile, 93 were in the United States.

To help users manage objects they find interesting, Thingiverse allows users to create collections on their profiles. A collection is a group of related models either created by the owner of the profile or by other designers. 104 designers had a collection of models that met our inclusion criteria as assistive technology. While this survey was helpful, we had many remaining questions about designers that we investigated with a questionnaire.

Construction Requirements

We observed a diverse range of construction requirements for items in our dataset in terms of the amount of assembly required prior to use, what tools were used to manufacture the part, and whether or not the object required extra parts (i.e. string, bolts, or rubber bands). 98% of all items in our dataset were designed to be 3D printed, 30% do not require any assembly prior to use, and almost 28% require assembly and additional parts (Table 2).

Construction requirements are an important consideration for adoption as these can impact the cost, difficulty, and time required to build the technology. For example, single-part designs are likely faster and less expensive to produce than designs consisting of multiple parts, and can be manufactured using only one machine. Single part designs are also attractive, as they only require the end user to control the fabrication machine, increasing the likelihood that those with limited abilities will engage in making AT.

While designs that require assembly and additional parts may be more technically complex, the effort and materials required for assembly may deter some individuals from attempting to make them. For example, many of the prosthetic hands require significant assembly and specific external parts that may reduce the likelihood that the target user would undertake this project. However, the fact that a bottle opener only requires a single part to be manufactured and that it is "ready to go" after printing increases the chance that an end user would make it (Figure 4).

No assembly required	One 3D printed part	29.8%
	One laser cut part	0.3%
Some assembly required	Multiple 3D printed parts	40.5%
	Multiple laser cut parts	1.3%
	Multiple 3D printed and laser cut parts	0.3%
Some assembly required and extra parts	3D printed parts	27.5%
	Laser cut parts	0.3%
	3D printed and laser cut parts	0.0%

Table 2. Summary of assistive technology items currently on Thingiverse broken down by construction requirements.

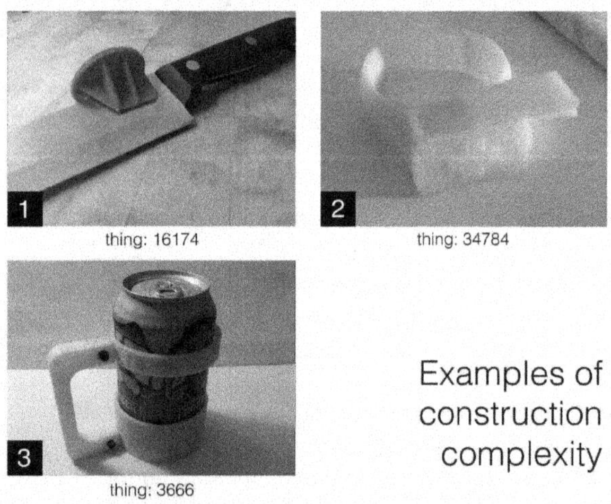

Figure 4. Example items with different construction requirements: 1) knife assistant for limited dexterity (no assembly required); 2) a wearable pill box (some assembly); and 3) cup holder (assembly and extra parts).

QUESTIONNAIRE TO UNDERSTAND WHY PEOPLE DESIGN ASSISTIVE TECHNOLOGY

While the Thingiverse website encourages designers to include stories about the objects, we could not find much information about the motivations for designing these objects. In order to gain a deeper understanding of why these objects were being designed, we invited these designers to complete an online questionnaire. We contacted all 273 designers to participate in our questionnaire and received 70 responses (25.6% response rate) over a two-week period. Participants were added to a raffle for a $100 gift card as compensation for their efforts. The questionnaire took approximately 15 minutes to complete and contained both closed and open-ended questions. Respondents were asked to provide demographic information and to describe the motivation, process, tools, and outcomes of their designs.

Self-reported Designer Demographics

We asked designers for more details about themselves, including information about any disabilities they might have (Table 3), age, occupation, and experiences with 3D modeling and assistive technologies.

Over 48% of designers had a career in a STEM (Science, Technology, Engineering, and Mathematics) field, including engineers, programmers, and information technology specialists. Fewer than 13% reported health care occupations, such as neurologist or dentist. Students made up approximately 14% of the respondents, and less than 3% of respondents indicated 3D printing expertise as their career. The remaining 14% included a wide range of careers, such as an artist, a realtor, business professionals, and teachers.

The designers reported ages between 18 and 71 with the mean age 37 and 18.8% being over the age of 50. The majority of designers (>76%) reported that they had no disability. The top three reported personal uses for AT were medication management, physical or motor impairments, and learning disabilities (all fewer than 1% of our sample).

Design and Printing Process

To better understand the history and use of these models, we asked about the process of designing and printing their objects. We found the majority of users (59%) reported that it took a day or less to create and finalize their designs. Most respondents reported building their designs on a personal 3D printer, as opposed to in an office or at a public maker space. All but 9 designs were successfully printed at least once, 46 were printed more than once, and none of them were printed more than 5 times. Of the designs that weren't printed, all respondents reported that they did not have access to a 3D printer. Several users indicated that their design was novel, in part or in whole. Often users had submitted designs that closely resembled other designs on Thingiverse or objects outside of Thingiverse such as in an AT catalog. In most cases, we could not discern if users were unaware of the existence of the other objects or if they merely perceived their own design to be truly unique.

Motivation for Designs

In order to understand the motivation for designing these objects, we asked questions about why and for whom designs were created. These open-ended question asked respondents to describe the motivation behind their designs in their own words.

We analyzed these responses using open coding with six categories. To further differentiate between these motivation categories we provide brief descriptions of each, along with a quote from one of the respondents.

	Target User	Designer
Allergies	1	0
Cognitive	7	1
Coma	1	0
Dexterity	15	1
Elderly	11	2
Learning	2	2
Medication Users	14	6
Physical / motor	23	5
Reading	0	1
Sensory	6	0
Temporary injury	3	1
Visual	11	1
None	**9**	**53**
Declined to Answer	**8**	**4**
Multiple Answers	**42**	**8**

Table 3. Self-reported respondent and target-user abilities.

I Made This for Myself

"I have tendonitis and ulnar nerve damage (repetitive stress injury) and was curious if I could improve the ergonomics of my Magic Trackpad by changing its angle similar to how 'vertical' mice help traditional mouse users with similar wrist/hand problems."

The ability to self-design assistive technology is highly empowering. Our questionnaire found that 13 designers created AT designs for their own use. This is particularly significant when considering the high rate of user abandonment in AT, which may be reduced if the end-user has a direct role in the design and creation of their AT [9]. While we were encouraged to see some self-designers, this was not as common as we had hoped. Increasing the number of self-designers might be accomplished in the future by increasing awareness of making assistive technology or by providing more accessible software and hardware tools for the creation of these designs [8].

I Made This for Someone I Know

"My aunt came to me for help, because she was having difficulty moving my uncle around whenever he had mini seizures. Since he had a walker anyway, she needed a way to push him around when he can't help himself."

Making an object for someone the respondent knew was the most common response with 24 designers indicating that they created AT designs for friends, family members, and other acquaintances. This included designs for aging parents, partners with disabilities, and children. Given the range of disabilities reported, it is difficult to say with confidence why more disabled users were not self-designing. Possible reasons could be the perceived difficulty of 3D modeling and fabrication, leading end-users to approach friends or family members with existing engineering or computer skills. Depending on ability, end-users may not have accessible design tools to create designs, but we did not fully explore this in our questions.

A close relationship with the end-user enables these designers to have a discourse. The designers would, in theory, be familiar with the user, task and environment. These are key factors in creating a positive user experience. A dialogue with the intended user has the potential to design for the individualized needs of specific disabilities. Ways to promote this dialogue could include community efforts to pair designers with end-users or finding ways to support this connection through the design sharing web sites more implicitly.

This Was a Personal Challenge

"I want to create useful objects. This bracelet I've designed, can contain medications, a note with dangerous allergens, or emergency phone numbers for elderly ill people."

13 respondents reported their motivation to create the design as wanting a personal challenge. They described wanting either a test of their ability as a 3D designer or they simply identified what they perceived as a need and created an object to fill that need. These respondents likely did not talk to anyone with the disability they were attempting to address, and had to guess preferences. This begs the question, should these types of AT designs be encouraged and/or dispersed? With little or no AT training and no contact with the end-users, it is difficult to say what if any value these items have to the disability community at large.

This Was Required for a Class or Competition

"I created this design for an undergraduate course I was taking in engineering design. The concept was to create a pillbox that could keep track of medication usage throughout a week (or weeks)."

Only five respondents indicated that they created and uploaded their designs as part of a contest or as required by a classroom assignment. The pitfalls of the previous category apply here, as well. As with the designers creating items for others, for these projects to have any impact it might be more appropriate to pair contestants and students with individuals with disabilities or related support organizations. In this way, students and contestants can still tackle interesting design challenges, while bolstering the applied outcome of their projects. This might improve designs and increases visibility for accessibility issues.

This Was Part of a Research Project
"I did my Masters thesis designing and printing objects for two children with blindness to help them in school and see if having a 3D printer in school is a good resource."

Only six respondents indicated that they participated in research and/or development as their occupation and that this was the motivating factor in the creation of their design. Open source sites like Thingiverse present an excellent opportunity to the academic and research community to share their work, as these respondents have. We hope to see more research labs creating and open-sourcing their designs in the future to help spread awareness of the possibilities of building AT and to advance these designs with end-user input.

This Isn't Intended for a Disability
"Creating adapters to join different products that fulfill the same use, but utilize proprietary measures."

Despite keywords, descriptions, and our inclusion criteria, eight respondents indicated that they did not perceive their design as targeted to a person with a disability. Examples of this perception included the appropriation of pillboxes as anything-goes storage containers or understating a dexterity aid as simply "useful". These examples are an interesting mix of universal design issues and "Accidentally AT" objects, a concept we describe in the next section. This may be indicative of an issue of the visibility of disabilities in the maker community at large.

DISCUSSION AND FUTURE CHALLENGES

In this section we extrapolate from our findings and contemplate the deeper meanings and future exploration of open-sourced AT designs.

Diversifying the Designer Population

More than half of our respondents reported that they had no formal training in 3D modeling and personal fabrication tools. Given that the current wave of these tools, especially 3D printers, are targeted to novice users, this finding did not surprise us. Several respondents described themselves as self-taught, learning techniques such as 3D modeling by watching videos on youtube.com and experimenting with open-source design tools. While this finding suggests these activities are not just for professionals, we observed that the average designer has a technical background.

The majority of respondents were members of the STEM and health care community, with fewer than 36% reporting occupations outside of hard science or technology fields. While many of these designers claimed no previous experience with modeling tools, it is important to recognize that 3D modeling, 3D printing, and personal fabrication have roots in engineering and that the formal skills of an engineer may supplement their informal use of these tools. This might indicate a need to encourage a wider variety of people with differing skills to utilize rapid prototyping.

Out of a group of 69 designers creating assistive designs, more than 76% of the designers reported that they had no disability themselves and less than 1% had any formal training in assistive technologies. While this might be alarming for a trained accessible technologist, we consider it an opportunity. There is clearly room to extend more support to alternative users, both in creating accessible tools and helping to democratize this technology for a more heterogeneous group of end-users.

As we discussed earlier, the ability to create customized and inexpensive assistive devices is a tremendous benefit to persons with disabilities, yet judging from the distribution of designers in our study, this group is not completely represented in the current make-up of 3D designers and makers. This is not to say that the engineers and technologists lending their skills to the AT cause are unwelcome. Instead, we pose the question, how do we diversify these designers and create more opportunities for designers with disabilities to self-design and become further incorporated into the making movement? Does this call for changes to fabrication tools or design repositories or both?

Actionable steps to support this goal might include simplifying tools, creating alternative design interfaces, or providing a new delivery system for tutorial information. Technologists should consider the abilities and goals of these potential AT-makers and work with them to uncover best practices for fabrication tool design.

Finding Assistive Technology On Thingiverse

Accidentally Assistive Technology
In classifying items using our inclusion criteria by assistive technology type or target user ability, we created the "Accidentally AT" subcategory. These had incidental keywords or were not perceived or intended as assistive objects by their designers. An example of an item in this category was a handle for soda cans, which enables a user with limited hand mobility or dexterity to grasp a cylindrical cup. The design description contains no language or keywords related to disability or being an assistive device. The reason we found this object was because our search term "old" was a substring within the word "holder". Nothing about the description indicates that this is an assistive device, but drinking aids are a very common tool used by persons with motor or dexterity impairments. Conversely, there is a similar cup-holding Thingiverse design with explicit disability keywords such as "tremor" and "handicap".

We saw multiple examples of objects in this category with information that would assist an individual with a visual impairment, however these were not designed with this audience in mind. For example, we found a special gaming die with custom tactile markers for eyes-free verification of a role.

From our analysis, the language used to describe objects is important. We feel these examples beg the larger question of whether or not items on Thingiverse should be tagged in a consistent way to indicate they are intended as or have been used as an assistive technology. Is this simply a matter of visibility or can a greater argument be made for universal design? A keyword from the non-AT cup holder was "useful", perhaps indicating support for more inclusive designs benefiting a range of end-user populations. There is a unique balance between highly personalized and universally useful AT design. A prosthetic limb may require careful customization to be both useful and comfortable for the wearer; meanwhile, a cup holder need only be scaled to fit the right beverage and/or hand size to be used by a variety of people. In both cases the base design can be shared, modified, and recreated to benefit others. Labeling one as assistive and the other as useful could be seen as arbitrary or even exclusionary. This is a sensitive subject as there may be negative stigma attached to tagging items as assistive technologies.

How Are Models Different from Tactile Graphics?

In deciding how to define and categorize assistive designs, we struggled to define what constituted a tactile graphic. There exist official guidelines for when and why to provide a tactile graphic [18], but in this domain, there is no clear distinction between a tactile graphic and any other 3D model. For example, is a model of the Sphinx a tactile graphic or "just" a model? If a model of a famous monument is a tactile graphic, then is a 3D bust of a stranger also a tactile graphic? With these questions in mind, we opted to exclude many 3D models that could have been considered tactile graphics using our inclusion criteria. Without printing and testing each item, we had no way to confirm what information could be conveyed by these designs in tactile form, and thus excluded models that did not explicitly state that they were for a population with a disability (such as a visual impairment or a learning disability that benefits from tangible interactions).

Filtering Spam Generated by Thingiverse's Customizer

The Thingiverse tool Customizer offers designers the ability to quickly and easily modify an existing design. By providing modifiable parameters with an existing design, any Thingiverse user can create a customized ("remixed") design with a few clicks. While helpful for customization, this tool generated a lot of duplicate objects creating a "spam" effect. Users frequently made indistinguishable duplicates of objects from Customizer. For example, we found over 100 pillbox designs that are almost all remixes of one or two basic seven-day pillboxes. These identical objects were created by users who made a copy of the original design and then saved their copied creation without making any changes. Only a handful of users made significant modifications to these designs. We still included pillbox designs in our findings, as they are a form of medication management, but it is important to note how this scenario can create remix bloating.

Another trend we felt added noise to the AT collection was adding Braille to objects without any apparent discretion. The Customizer allows designers to engrave or emboss text onto designs from a selection of fonts, including a Braille font. This generated several objects with Braille added seemingly at random with no particular benefit to a visually impaired end-user. One example was a bracelet with Braille text around the outside. While this may have value as a means to express oneself in Braille, it is unclear how this would be considered as an assistive technology. This complements our earlier finding that the vast majority of AT designers in this space had little or no training in assistive technology.

The Customizer offers valuable modification features, but it can create noise that overwhelms search results. This spam may frustrate users and prevent the discovery of beneficial designs and design modifications. As the Thingiverse community continues to grow, it is important to consider the impact of this tool to ensure quality designs that are easy for end-users to find. Technologists could consider this a special case search, in which searching fabrication designs for a subset of assistive designs may differ from other search behaviors or repository structures.

Measuring the Impact of Designs On Thingiverse

We feel the presence of these AT designs on Thingiverse speaks to a potential for more empowered end-users self-designing assistive solutions, there are also questions to be asked about the visibility and perception of making AT. With over 100,000 designs on Thingiverse, the 363 designs we identified make up less than 0.004% of the total designs available for download. Within our AT design set, there are several items that go unsung while others receive phenomenal attention. One of the more advanced prosthetic hand designs was prominently featured by the Thingiverse site during our initial design audit. It garnered hundreds of likes and over a dozen reported makes. Other items, such as exaggerated bottle openers to help persons with limited dexterity, may only have a handful of likes and no makes. This is especially interesting when considering the complexity of the prosthetics (multiple prints and external hardware) when contrasted against a bottle opener designed for users with limited dexterity (single print ready without modification or additional hardware) that can be printed in a short window of time and can be adopted for a variety of persons and abilities.

While the measures we describe give us a sense of the popularity of these designs with Thingiverse members, we are unable to measure the ultimate impact these AT designs had for their target users. Thingiverse supports comments on designs, but there were no end-user testimonials rating or discussing the designs.

Without this information, it is unclear if these designs made any significant or lasting impact. We feel testimonials and user experiences with these designs is crucial to further cultivate a community resource for assistive technologies, as this feedback will likely encourage users to try this technology.

CONCLUSION

In this study, we explored the existing community of assistive technology designers within Thingiverse.com. We found several AT-related designs spanning a range of ability and that the majority of the AT designers do not themselves have disabilities, nor do they have any training in assistive technology. We discussed strategies for diversifying the designer population and identified areas where open source AT on Thingiverse might be improved. We also discussed the current and potential impact of designing AT objects and sharing their designs freely online. Our suggestions included creating more communication between existing designers and the community of users with disabilities, promoting more visibility of AT designs with appropriate keywords and features for open-sourced sites, and the creation of accessible tools for users with disabilities to self-design assistive solutions. We believe there is a future in open-sourced designs to become a valuable source of solutions to persons with disabilities. We hope the technology community provides more access and support to persons with disabilities and to see this community grow.

ACKNOWLEDGMENTS

We wish to thank the Thingiverse community and all of our respondents for their contributions. This material is based upon work supported by the National Science Foundation under Grant No. EEEC-0540865.

REFERENCES

1. Adelson, E. Best Foot Forward. *Boston Magazine*, 2009. http://www.bostonmagazine.com/2009/02/best-foot-forward-february/.
2. Buehler, E., Kane, S.K., and Hurst, A. ABC and 3D: Opportunities and Obstacles to 3D Printing in Special Education Environments. *Proceedings of ASSETS '14*, (2014).
3. Dawe, M. Desperately Seeking Simplicity: How Young Adults with Cognitive Disabilities and Their Families Adopt Assistive Technologies. *Proceedings of CHI '06*, (2006), 1143–1152.
4. Fox, M. Sam Farber, Creator of Oxo Utensils, Dies at 88. *NYTimes.com*, 2013. http://www.nytimes.com/2013/06/22/business/sam-farber-creator-of-oxo-utensils-dies-at-88.html.
5. Greshenfeld, N. *Fab: The Coming REvolution on Your Desktop--From Personal Comptuers to Personal Fabrication*. Basic Books, New York, 2005.
6. Hook, J., Verbaan, S., Durrant, A., Olivier, P., and Wright, P. A study of the challenges related to DIY assistive technology in the context of children with disabilities. *Proceedings of DIS '14*, (2014), 597–606.
7. Hook, J., Verbaan, S., Wright, P., and Olivier, P. Exploring the Design of technologies and services that support do-it-yourself assistive technology practice. *Proceedings of DE '2013*, (2013).
8. Hurst, A. and Kane, S. Making "Making" Accessible. *Proceedings of IDC '13*, (2013), 635–638.
9. Hurst, A. and Tobias, J. Empowering Individuals with Do-It-Yourself Assistive Technology. *Proceedings of ASSETS '11*, (2011), 11–18.
10. IT Accessibility Workforce. Assistive Technology Act of 1998. 1998. http://www.section508.gov/assistive-technology-act-1998.
11. Kuznetsov, S. and Paulos, E. Rise of the expert amateur. *Proceedings of NordiCHI '10*, (2010), 295.
12. Lindtner, S., Hertz, G.D., and Dourish, P. Emerging sites of HCI innovation. *Proceedings of CHI '14*, (2014), 439–448.
13. OXO Consumer Services. About Us - XO - Thoughtfully Yours. 2014. http://www.oxo.com/AboutOXO.aspx.
14. Phillips, B. and Zhao, H. Predictors of Assistive Technology Abandonment. *Assistive Technology 5*, 1 (1993), 36–45.
15. Rosner, D. and Bean, J. Learning from IKEA hacking. *Proceedings of CHI '09*, (2009), 419.
16. Shinohara, K. and Wobbrock, J.O. In the Shadow of Misperception : Assistive Technology Use and Social Interactions. *Proceedings of CHI '11*, (2011), 705–714.
17. Tanenbaum, J.G., Williams, A.M., Desjardins, A., and Tanenbaum, K. Democratizing technology. *Proceedings of CHI '13*, (2013), 2603.
18. The Braille Authority of North America. Guidelines and Standards for Tactile Graphics, 2010. 2014. http://www.brailleauthority.org/tg/web-manual/index.html.
19. Tseng, T. and Resnick, M. Product versus process. *Proceedings of DIS '14*, (2014), 425–428.

Understanding the Role of Community in Online Dating

Christina Masden and W. Keith Edwards
GVU Center and School of Interactive Computing
Georgia Institute of Technology
Atlanta, GA USA
{christinamasden, keith}@cc.gatech.edu

ABSTRACT
Online dating sites have become a common means of finding a romantic partner. And yet, these sites differ greatly from many other socially oriented websites: perhaps most notably, the pairwise style of interaction afforded by these sites prevents a robust online community from forming. Users, however, have taken matters into their own hands by creating thriving external forums for discussion of specific dating sites. We report on a multiple methods study of two online dating services, via observation and interviews with users of the forums associated with these sites. Our findings suggest that these forums play an essential role in creating an "outsourced community" for the dating sites, and also reveal practices around how some users "game the system" in online dating, the prevalence of harassment in online dating, and users' frustrations with current dating sites. We conclude with a number of recommendations for system design.

Author Keywords
Social computing; online dating; legitimate peripheral participation; online communities.

ACM Classification Keywords
H.3.5 [Online Information Services]: Web-based services

INTRODUCTION
Increasingly, online dating has become an accepted and even commonplace way to search for a partner. Recent surveys from the Pew Internet & American Life Project, for instance, indicate that 11% of American adults have used either an online dating website or mobile phone-based app; further, of those currently "single and looking," this number rises to 38% [41]. 29% of Americans know somebody who has used online dating to find a spouse or long-term partner; for college graduates, this increases to 41% [41]. And, as of 2013, the online dating industry generated around $2 billion USD in revenue [36].

ACM 978-1-4503-3145-6/15/04 $15.00
http://dx.doi.org/10.1145/2702123.2702417

Part of the appeal of these sites is that, divorced from face-to-face indicators of attraction, both parties are free to present themselves in an idealized manner. Online dating offers a way to find potential partners you wouldn't ordinarily meet, freer of context than in real life. Further, the online interaction is always between two individuals. In other words, while profiles are viewable by many, messages or chats are only sent from one person to another, and are not viewable by any other members of the site. This affords a privacy not easily experienced in real world contexts, where friends, family, acquaintances, and even strangers in public are often privy to the details of romantic encounters, whether firsthand or through the grapevine.

This pairwise interaction between two individuals means that dating websites are perhaps unique among socially oriented websites: unlike in other, more open, online communities, in which many people can see each others' posts, interaction on dating sites is viewable only by the two involved parties. Further, even visibility of profiles may be restricted. For example, in heterosexual dating dynamics, absent putting forth effort to use the site in an unintended way, a user will only see profiles of the opposite gender—information that may not necessarily help that user understand how to better present his or her own profile on the site. This lack of visibility raises a number of questions: how are users learning to use these sites, and making the transition to "experts"? Are there norms that develop on particular sites, despite the fact that users cannot see a wide cross-section of behavior there? What impact does this lack of visibility have on participation on these sites?

One interesting effect of this lack of visibility is that entire "third party" user-created forums have arisen that are dedicated to providing an online community to users of specific dating sites. These forums—many of which have tens of thousands of members—facilitate sharing stories, critiquing profiles, and offering advice for success.

We were interested in both exploring the role these forums played in the culture of online dating, and in using them as a lens into behavior and practices of the dating sites—which may not have been directly visible on the dating sites themselves. In this paper we report on a multiple methods study of online dating users, involving observation of community forums focused on two popular online dating sites, as well as interviews with users of these sites. We set out to understand:

- How lack of visibility into interactions shapes behavior, and how users move from novice to expert in online dating websites
- What social practices and norms exist around online dating, and how they are established and shared
- What design opportunities might exist for enhancing the experience of online dating

RELATED WORK

In this section, we review relevant prior work in the areas of online dating (and the design of online dating services), online communities and social networks more generally.

Self-Presentation in Online Dating

As noted in the introduction, one of the advantages of online dating sites is that they allow members to construct a carefully crafted persona to expose to potential partners. In fact, advice on "presenting your best self" has been seen as an important aspect of online dating since the earliest days of computer-mediated personals: for example, an early Usenet FAQ on online dating profiles both spoke of the benefits of being able to present one's self to potential partners without needing to address physical attractiveness, location, or community, and tips on how to write the most advantageous profile for getting responses [6].

Dating site users appear to be well aware of the importance of self-presentation—and the role of the profile in conveying that self-presentation—in attracting potential matches [23, 44], and prior work has explored the role that deception plays in "fudging" quantifiable metrics like height and weight [42]. Physical attractiveness is also an important aspect in choosing a mate, and thus the photographs of members are highly salient to potential matches. However, previous studies have shown that around a third of photographs are rated as being "inaccurate" in their depiction of the member—and this deception is often a result of users' desires to mediate, control, and enhance their self-presentation [25, 42].

Given the importance of the profile, it is perhaps unsurprising that roughly a quarter of online daters have been reported to have asked for outside help in creating their profile; there is, however, little data to suggest how this process works [26]. Given the widespread use of external help in crafting one's self-presentation, we were interested in better understanding exactly how online dating site users were determining what information to present on their profiles. What affordances, if any, led to the discovery of methods to improve a profile? Additionally, we were interested to see if more sophisticated forms of deception had evolved since previous explorations in this area.

Online Dating Design

Other work has explored the designs of online dating sites, and the features that these systems provide. In a few cases, work has explored the possibility of creating more "experiential" systems with rich interaction modalities. For example, rather than focusing on text descriptions and searchable traits, some of these systems strive to create a virtual date experience [20]. Games like World of Warcraft have been appropriated to provide an immersive gaming medium for experiential online dating, for instance [43].

Much prior work has focused how online daters select potential mates, and which characteristics matter the most to them. For example, earlier studies have demonstrated the importance of homophily to online daters: most users of dating sites are generally interested in potential partners who are similar to themselves in many regards [18]. For example, similarity in education level was found to be of high importance when selecting a mate [26]. Areas of difference do exist, however. Studies and data analysis have shown that heterosexual men and women both prefer different attributes in a mate [39], with men choosing to date slightly younger women and rating attractiveness and youth as primary desirable characteristics; and women dating slightly older and preferring height and higher income as primary desirable characteristics (although men, when offered a choice, choose a mate with higher income as well) [26]. Thus, many current dating sites provide options for filtering potential mates based off attributes such as height, income, age, and so forth.

However, despite the prevalence of these mechanisms, many studies have demonstrated the shortcomings of matching and profile systems [17], and how the filtering approaches commonly used by dating sites today can be ineffectual, at least when measured by metrics such as retaining users. Current systems have poor return rates and seem to favor a male-initiated approach. Men initiate most conversations, sending 73.3% of messages; and yet 78.2% of these messages are not returned [18].

Given this body of existing work, we felt that examining a matching-based site with "open market messaging" (OkCupid) as well as a system with restricted messaging (Tinder) might lend insight into how online dating site design mediates messaging dynamics. The specifics of these particular websites and further reasons for their selection will be expanded on in "Study Design".

The Role of Communities

The goal of online dating is, ultimately, to connect individuals in person. And, despite the concern that online dating might separate people from their real world communities and existing social networks [37], prior work has demonstrated that this may not be the case. Online dating is deeply tied to the physical world, as people use their non-dating social networks as a method to find potential partners [15, 33], and also share their profiles with real world friends [41].

However, the virtual, online communities created by the third party forums we observed clearly played an important role that was not tied to physical place, real world communities, or users' local social networks. Prior work has explored how robust online communities can promote shared understanding and innovation [13, 28, 32]. They can also serve as virtual third places [35] for wide-ranging discussions.

Thus, we were interested in understanding the role that user-created forums played in creating a virtual community of online dating users, and what purposes these sites served to their members. These sites fostered discussion at times seemingly divorced from the objective of finding a partner, and with lively participation in their own right (one community even organized offline meetups for its members, for instance).

STUDY DESIGN

To better understand the use of online dating sites and the role that external forums play in such sites, we undertook a multiple methods study, primarily focusing on third party Reddit forums associated with two specific dating sites, OkCupid and Tinder. Our insight into the importance of these third party Reddit forums came during our initial explorations into online dating: OkCupid's Terms of Service prohibit research-related activity, and while searching for alternate ways to recruit participants, we discovered that these third party forums provided a window into the dynamics of the online dating websites that would otherwise be impossible to observe.

We selected OkCupid and Tinder because they are both large, global sites, but are also fundamentally quite different. OkCupid, launched in 2004, is a matching-based online dating site. Profiles—complete with text, photographs, and a "match percentage" (which compares the compatibility of two users)—are the primary way that a user selects a potential romantic partner. Users are free to message anyone they wish.

Tinder, launched in 2012, is a location-based phone application. Profiles have photographs and a very short list of personal information. Tinder is connected to a user's Facebook profile, and shows "friends in common." Users swipe left to dislike an individual and swipe right to like. If both users swipe right, they are matched and are permitted to communicate with each other. This contrasts greatly with OkCupid's model of allowing any user to message any other user.

The forums we focused on were hosted on Reddit, a widely used site that allows registered members to submit content, which can then be up-voted or down-voted; content is publically viewable, but may only be posted by members. Content is organized into "subreddits" focused on particular topics. The subreddits for discussion of our target dating sites—called /r/OkCupid and /r/Tinder—were large and active, with the OkCupid-focused subreddit having over 60,000 members and the Tinder-focused subreddit having over 35,000 [1, 3]

The first phase of our study used observation of these sites. A member of our research team observed public content in multiple threads over a period of approximately four months, collecting field notes and forming preliminary categories of the discourse there. /r/OkCupid is highly active—100 new threads per day with 1000 new comments among them would not be uncommon. /r/Tinder is quite active as well: 75 threads per day with 400 comments among them would not be uncommon. This period of observation allowed us to get a sense of the breadth of discussion on the sites, and to formulate a targeted interview guide for use in the second phase of the study.

In the second phase, we recruited nine participants from these subreddits (one from a thread on online dating advice on another subreddit), administered a questionnaire focused on demographic and site usage information, and conducted a semi-structured interview with participants exploring their usage and experiences with online dating. Interviews lasted approximately 30-60 minutes, and were conducted via Skype or Google Voice. Average length was ~36 minutes, and median length was ~33 minutes. Study participants were not compensated.

Following this, interviews were transcribed and the research team conducted an inductive thematic analysis [8], and merged the themes from the interviews with themes from the observational period of the study.

The age range of those interviewed was 22-45, with median of 26. Three were female, and six male. Five participants were from the United States, two from Canada, and one from Norway. All nine participants were either current or former OkCupid users, and five were current or former Tinder users.

Our interview sample was ~66% male, which may partially be due to Reddit itself: Reddit has a high proportion of male posters, so our pool of possible participants was drawn from a population that skews 74% male sitewide. Additionally, recruitment posed a number of challenges that became visible to us through observation of the subreddits. For example, despite not responding directly to recruitment requests, we observed that some users we reached out to had created threads with discussion about whether participating in the study would be worth the effort, with community members explaining that they had gotten our requests, but didn't feel it would be interesting, worthwhile, or pleasant for them to speak about their experiences.

RESULTS

Through participant interviews and forum observation, we were able to form a clearer picture of aspects of user behavior on dating sites. It became apparent that participants were using these third party forums to construct a better understanding of online dating, both generally and site-specific, and also revealed aspects of user behavior on the dating sites themselves.

Our findings can be broken down into four categories:

- The role of forums in establishing community
- Strategies and gaming
- Anti-social behavior in online dating
- Frustrations with the experience of online dating

In the sections that follow, we present our findings organized along these themes. Throughout, we present quotes from our interviews with participants that are illustrative of the data gathered both from interviews and our forum observations.

The Role of Forums in Establishing Community

First, we consider the role that the third-party forums play in establishing the norms and culture of online dating sites, and facilitating users becoming more "expert" on these sites. As noted in the introduction, the lack of open interaction on the dating sites—set against members' desires to learn how to most effectively participate in these sites—drove members to the third party forums. Of course, the very existence of the thriving forums we studied attests to this need, but we set out to highlight specifically what members sought from these online communities on Reddit, and what gaps in knowledge existed. We found that participants used these forums to share experience and to offer advice, and the forums played a major role in shaping how participants used the dating sites.

P3 (male, OkCupid and Tinder user) describes his first post on a third party forum asking for help due to a lack of response on Tinder:

> *"... I...[posted asking for help]...once because I was so frustrated ... [that was] the day I genuinely gave up on Tinder because... [I had just been] liking everything for ...hours and hours and hours and just nothing..."* –P3

Sharing of information and best practices frequently were framed as what *not* to do. P3, for instance, references subreddits dedicated to "cringe-worthy" or "creepy" personal pictures or personal messages (called PMs) encountered on dating sites; these were instructive as cautionary examples not to be followed:

> *"I'm also a frequent viewer of Cringepics and Creepy PMs, whichever, do you know that Reddit?...It's a good indication of what not to type to women online, and it's a good reference to keeping [...] your head in the game. Luckily I haven't been doing any of those mistakes."* –P3

The forums provided a backchannel, allowing members to share examples of introductions received that were considered inappropriate or unappealing, allowing others to learn from their mistakes:

> *"On the Reddit subforum on Tinder [...] a lot of people have those stupid kind of dorky introduction lines. I don't do that, I just do the general hows it going kind of thing, and that seems to be working pretty well..."* -P4

Participants also shared guidance on how to structure a profile for maximum appeal. Many users, such as P5 (male, OkCupid and Tinder user), explicitly noted how the lack of visible interaction was problematic in crafting a profile. On some heterosexual dating sites, for example, one may not have access to the profiles of one's own gender. Even when others' profiles are visible, the "effectiveness" of those profiles is not:

> *"I think it's been interesting because...most of the people that are posting on there are guys, so looking at the other guys profiles has just...seeing what other guys are doing because I wouldn't know otherwise."* –P5

Surprisingly to us, some participants made commitments to the forums that sometimes outlasted—or even predated—their commitments to the dating sites themselves. One such user was P2 (male, OkCupid user), who might be considered a "success" and an "advanced user" of OkCupid. P2 maintained two long-term relationships and went on between 20-30 dates that resulted from connections made on the site. P2 became a user of the OkCupid subreddit *before* becoming a user of OkCupid itself:

> *"I think probably two and a half years ago, when I was not single, when I hadn't used OkCupid yet I was really fascinated with the idea of it...I just liked the concept of online dating in general, and so I found this subreddit for it and I just started reading it and [was] pretty interested to read people's experiences through it...that subreddit is... a lot of people feel very open, and talk about their experiences, they're very interesting to read about."* –P2

At the time of our interview, P2 was no longer an active OkCupid user, but still regularly read the OkCupid subreddit and used it to offer advice to others:

> *"I would say giving advice, I would say, um, posting responses to stories or just, like if I find [...] some discrepancy or something nifty..."* –P2

> *"Well I haven't logged onto it [his OkCupid account] in the past three months, and...I mostly...just use and help my friends with OkCupid profiles at this point,...I would say I'm not shy talking about it just because I feel like I've kind of figured out a lot about it and I think my friends can testify."* –P2

When he spoke of *how* he achieved the knowledge, the subreddit forum clearly played a strong role. This came in the form of messaging men who had posted on the OkCupid subreddit:

> *"[...]a lot of times they would be on the...OkCupid subreddit and I just messaged them and asked them why they chose to do things a certain way, and, I think a lot*

> *of guys would be scared to do that [...]I think that most people are very, very happy talking about themselves [...] most guys were actually very open, oh yeah I did this, I read this here, yeah, I had a girlfriend that told me this." -P2*

For some users, the discovery of a forum for sharing tips about particular dating sites made the difference in whether they used the site or not. For example, P4 (male, OkCupid and Tinder user) found the Tinder subreddit in conjunction with beginning to use the smart phone app:

> *"Not long. I only discovered Reddit after her and I broke up, so let's say, probably in mid-July, so a month and a half, almost two months."* –P4

He articulates a style of forum participation experienced by many participants, described as engagement by reading anecdotes and participating in critique. Many participants mentioned this style of engagement, as the long periods of time spent on dating websites led to downtime between profile improvements:

> *"I usually more of like the comedic side, like, what was your worst date, what was your most awkward sexual encounter... stuff that's just kinda gonna cheer me up and make me laugh a little bit more. [...] I do go on the Tinder one, like, help my profile, what do you do, what's a good first introduction, like I'm really interested in meeting this girl, blah blah, stuff like that, but it's usually more of the comedic side that I'm into." –P4*

He also gleaned information on improving his Tinder profile and implemented changes based on this information:

> *"I guess I did add my height on my profile [...] people were saying that that does help, I haven't noticed an increase in traffic or whatever on that, but then, but I'm not, again, I'm not super super tall."* –P4

This critical examination and exchange was not without tension, however. Critique observed on both subreddits varied from simple profile adjustments to suggesting that the person was simply not attractive enough to have success. Often this exchange would result in arguments between the user who had initially asked for critique and other users that had offered advice. P7 (female, OkCupid and Tinder user) speaks of how she felt uncomfortable with the advice offered by other /r/OkCupid members:

> *"I think I did, like, once or twice but when it's like very glaring, when its, you know, maybe that's not super flattering or... something that's easy to fix. [...] It's like if they say something that's very generic language, maybe use an anecdote, but I think it's a little presumptuous to give the kind of detailed critiques like some of the other users do,' cause when I would take that advice I would like, attract a certain kind of demographic that I didn't want to."* –P7

Strategies and Gaming

Our interviews and observations of forum participants also revealed important aspects of how they interacted on the dating sites, many of which would have been hidden or hard to detect from the sites themselves. For example, participants frequently spoke of strategizing their techniques to obtain the best chances of getting a response or date. A common phrase used was that online dating was "a numbers game." P2 speaks of a feature on OkCupid, where rating a user as 4 or 5 stars notifies them that you've rated them highly.

> *"I figured out that one of the key ways to improve exposure is to five star literally hundreds of people... literally hundreds of people's profiles,* [...] *and from that I think I got anywhere between, I would say, probably, 50 to 60 new messages each week."* –P2

Users exploited the mechanics of the sites to find ways around the visibility restrictions they imposed, and to provide "plausible deniability" for unwanted social interactions. P1 (male, OkCupid user), for instance, created a fake OkCupid profile to allow him to view others' profiles without them knowing his identity, and to avoid the perceived need to respond to unwanted, unsolicited messages:

> *"I realized at a certain point in the last couple of years that [a fake profile the user had created] technically was still active... so I will usually use that to you know, look at other peoples' profiles when I don't want them to know that I've done so, and I think that's sometimes something I do when I get an unsolicited message I'm not going to respond to..."* - P1

P8 (female, OkCupid user) spoke of searching for women on OkCupid to "view the competition," but declining to visit their profiles to prevent the impression that she was taking an interest (OkCupid has an option to allow users visibility of who has visited their profile):

> *"I just did a search, a cursory one to see who my competition is... I just didn't want them to think that I was checking them out! So I just looked at the photos."* –P8

Participants actively rated themselves in terms of numbers of responses to their messages. Further, calculating the "response rate" allowed participants to assess the effectiveness of their strategies, such as what information to request in a message. This was such an established practice that posts in /r/OkCupid asking for advice were frequently accompanied with a numerical response rate:

> *"...I was interested too, so I [...] was doing the math and I'm pretty sure it's [...] at 10 percent response rate, so... yeah, every ten messages I send I get like one response."* –P5

> *"I would say that everybody I've asked for a phone number I've gotten it and that would probably be [...] over 20, but actually once I get the phone number then [asked to meet them], it's dropped off significantly, so of...let's say 25 for example, I've met [...] maybe 6 tops..."* –P4

Users appropriated features in the designs of these sites as a way to target specific users, sometimes for unexpected purposes. For example, OkCupid has a visual indicator of how often a given person responds to personal messages: green encodes a high response rate, red a low rate, and yellow in the middle. It's typical for most women to have red indicators and men to have green. Members used this feature in a number of ways. For example, in forum posts on /r/OkCupid, users spoke of using the color dot system as a metric for dating value, asking if a woman with a green or yellow dot is less "valuable" to pursue than a woman with a red dot. P2 describes his attempt to understand how to improve his profile by viewing the profiles of other males with "red dots," as their low response rate meant an unusually high level of unresponded-to female contact:

> *"Guys who are red dotted on OkCupid are pretty rare, and so what I did is I just went and I looked at all their profiles."* –P2

Tinder's design has also created a common way for men to game the system. Tinder only allows for a "match" to occur if both parties have "liked" or "swiped" the other's profile. This is meant to give an indicator of mutual attraction. However, male participants spoke of simply swiping on *all* the profiles, and then going to look at any women who had matched with them.

> *"So everybody in...I think it's 70 kilometers...[gets] liked automatically. Um, and then after that, once I get matched with them, then I do look at their pictures, their profile."* –P4

One /r/Tinder user even built a mechanical robot for this purpose, called Tinder-o-Matic, which uses a stylus to swipe profiles on the Tinder application on a smart phone [5]. This robot was described by P3 (not the builder):

> *"I've also seen like, have you seen the machine that's like, a finger that just automatically clicks like? That like, a robot they made, did you see that one?"* –P3

Users in our observation reported manipulating the location-based features of Tinder. Members spoke of spoofing their location to both find users slightly outside of their maximum area, and to see if they would be considered as attractive in other locations.

In general, /r/Tinder members had a highly developed culture of experimentation and data collection. This included running structured experiments to see which profile photos fared the best. The results of this experimentation were often presented in strikingly sophisticated ways, readily using statistics, developing categories, and testing their theories many times.

Anti-Social Behavior in Online Dating

Aspects of the culture of online dating sites revealed themselves through interviews and our observational data. These aspects included the prevalence of harassment and other anti-social behavior, as well as the role that the forums played in exposing it.

> *"Sometimes it's easier for me to not respond than it is for me to like, hi, thanks for the message, I'm not interested."* –P1

> *"I've felt uncomfortable... I'm a minority, I'm an Indian woman, and I'm overweight, so there's some comments about that that I like really, really don't appreciate."* –P7

Although this behavior is visible only to the recipients on the dating sites, /r/OkCupid and /r/Tinder are filled with posts calling out this behavior. These forums provide a place to share and expose harassment to others via screenshots and text dumps. Upon experiencing harassment, P8 turned to /r/OkCupid to understand more about community norms and how to prevent that behavior in the future.

> *"I just wanted to get etiquette [...] to see what...I should do first about responding to people who...I wasn't interested in and I know that they have F.A.Q.s on the sub [...] so I decided to post the interaction that I had, the screenshot of the interaction I had with a rude guy that made a message and then I asked people in the sub, like, is this common?" –P8*

P8 speaks about the responses she got to her query:

> *"It seemed like the overwhelming majority said just don't bother responding, if you don't like somebody, just don't bother. [...] They also said that it's okay for a sender to expect like the first person who is initiating contact expect that they won't get any confirmation of whether or not the other person is interested." –P8*

P8 also spoke of being nervous and shocked by negative interactions. Her fear of harassment and retribution was echoed by others on /r/OkCupid. Posts spoke of techniques to prevent stalking, such as never using photographs that are present on another social networking site, so that potential stalkers could not make a connection between one's online dating profile and one's real identity. P8 feared personal damage from rebuffed suitors:

> *"I don't like that they can see my profile when I've blocked them."* –P8

> *"I just have pictures on there, and I don't know how [...] messed up these people are, but what if they download it and do something with it and then post it on my Twitter? [In] this situation you have somebody*

who is personally hurt and they can really mess things up for you if they wanted to…" –P8

While every participant spoke of the significant harassment issues faced by women on online dating sites, male participants also reported experiencing harassment. These harassment cases were generally instigated by a solitary rebuffed individual. These negative experiences are confirmed in the literature–28% of online daters have said that they've been contacted in a way that made them feel uncomfortable or harassed, with a far greater proportion of females than males experiencing discomfort [41].

Frustrations with the Experience of Online Dating

Participants expressed common themes of frustration with the experience of online dating (and dating in general). These often held across OkCupid and Tinder.

Lack of novelty and lack of spontaneity in conversation came up quite often. First dates seemed stilted, and connections were difficult to make. Personal profiles were often seen as tired, clichéd, or uninformative:

> *"I wish there was some way to make it… before you ask them out on a date, that there was a way to just tell who someone was online without having them describe themselves, because people are not very good at describing themselves. Everyone's always fun-loving, loves to laugh, loves to travel, um, loves to hang out with friends, loves to watch Netflix or go out to the bar, […] I wish there was some better way to get descriptions of people."* –P2

A practice called catfishing, the act of using false photos to deceptively engage with site users, was also a concern. Often, this behavior went beyond the minor deception of exaggerating height or attractiveness. /r/OkCupid threads ask for advice on identifying catfish and share stories and screenshots of possible catfish. Participants mentioned using techniques like Google Reverse Image Search to determine if a profile was genuine. P3 speaks of an experience he had with a catfish profile:

> *"It was probably like a fake account or what they call a catfish […] somebody posing to be someone else. […] She was [a] really pretty girl and we had like a lot in common… [but] it was basically a joking profile, she was just fucking with people and wasting people's time…"* –P3

Men also spoke of frustration at the unclear reasons why they were not receiving responses:

> *"So it's a lot of like… you send out a message and you never get a reply…which doesn't happen in real life, I mean, if I go to a bar and I ask a girl she will answer me regardless of what I say in some forms."* –P3

> *"I don't know if […] I'm really getting drowned out, like, somebody just can't even see my message cuz they're getting so many, but it also can be like, you know, people are just getting all these like really weird messages and they get burnt out on the whole thing and they're like, ugh, here's another one, I don't want to read that one either, so I don't know."* –P5

One common frustration noted by participants and /r/OkCupid posters was termed "the fade." The fade described when a potential romantic partner slowly stops responding to messages.

> *"I mean, you can [….] hear about people talk about the fade […] you know, I saw they posted something on Facebook or I saw them on online dating, so I know they're not dead…" –P1*

Bots, or fake automated profiles, were also a common annoyance for users of both websites.

> *"I think I remember the very first time I logged in, um, like somebody sent me a message but then it became really apparent that they were just another spambot."* –P5

DISCUSSION

Initially, we set out to understand how online dating users were making sense of the norms and practices that worked well. While investigating this research question, we noted that online dating users do not have the privilege of being able to observe the actions of others. Messaging on these sites is hidden from all except the participants, which obscures and prevents the learning and establishment of norms that occur in robust online communities.

Much research has focused on how online communities grow in the presence of visible feedback and visible social norms. For example, Bryant, et. al. described the process of "becoming Wikipedian" through the lenses of Activity Theory and Legitimate Peripheral Participation [11]. Newcomers became advanced users by initially making small edits to articles that they had expertise in, and gradually began to view themselves as part of the Wikipedia community. Their relation to Wikipedia changed as they participated, and their as expertise increased users began to perform in managerial roles in the Wikipedia ecosystem.

Wikipedia novices learn community norms, practices, and gain expertise through clearly written instruction, policy, and through community members reverting edits. This runs in clear contrast to online dating site novices, where instructions are limited to explaining where to upload a photograph, and thus there is little room for Legitimate Peripheral Participation to play out.

And, although previous research has shown that feedback and moderation greatly influence likelihood to continue participating on a website [30], new members of online dating websites are mostly unable to receive true feedback on their actions. The only indicator of whether a profile is appropriately designed, or whether a message is cleverly crafted, lies in the hands of another individual. A received message provides a form of feedback; a reply from a potential partner one has reached out to provides another form of feedback; if both people like each other on Tinder, the "match" provides feedback [30]. But in all of these cases, the feedback is intermittent and specific to the individual with whom the user is wishing to engage. Additionally, this "feedback" could be based on any number of factors unrelated to actual physical attractiveness: profile quality, photograph styles, message quality, and so on.

The third party forums clearly play a role here, providing a more open online community in which members can learn from one another and become socialized in the norms of the sites. Essentially, the normalizing and learning functions of a robust online community [13] are absent in online dating sites, but have been outsourced to third party forums.

With this understanding, we were able to find common ground in existing work. This "outsourcing of a community" runs parallel to Turkopticon, where Mechanical Turkers are offered an opportunity to voice their experiences with requesters [27]. Mechanical Turk is, in many ways, similar to online dating websites in terms of lack of visibility in interactions. By giving Turkers the ability to expose "good" and "bad" requesters, a community was created surrounding actions previously obfuscated.

Other "outsourced communities" exist around real-world interactions. Hollaback, a website that allows those who have been victims of street harassment to upload their stories and tag them on a map, provides a similar form of community for those whose shared experience would otherwise be hidden. Interaction between a street harasser with a harassee also lacks visibility and accountability; shifting the conversation to Hollaback both created a community where none existed before, and allowed community members to understand the harassment in a way that hadn't been possible previously [14][7].

DESIGN IMPLICATIONS

In 2004, Fiore & Donath spoke of how technological limitations hampered the development of novel social dating systems [17]. As it is now a decade later, and there have been great advances in technology, we feel that it is time to revisit this area. The findings from our study suggest several areas in which we believe the experience of online dating might be improved. We position these by threading the relevant themes (the importance of community forums, strategies and gaming, anti-social behavior, and frustrations) through each design suggestion.

One possibility is the reintegration of the outsourced community back into the dating sites themselves. Our participants clearly expressed a need for learning best practices and normative behavior around online dating, and a forum integrated directly into the dating site might provide the elements of community missing currently. Such a function might also afford moderation by the dating site, potentially reducing discussions of "gaming" the site (although such discussions might be merely driven elsewhere). Some dating sites have taken steps in this direction, but they are limited: for example, although OkCupid does have a community forum, newer accounts are prohibited from posting in or viewing them. Our study suggests, however, that a key question is how strongly such a feature should tie to users' identities and profiles elsewhere on the site. By foregrounding the previously "backchannel" communication of the subreddits, we break the carefully crafted "front stage" personas visible through site profiles [21].

To address the perceived lack of "novelty" in online dating—and potentially also tackle issues of gaming the system—fruitful paths to explore might take advantage of media other than text to facilitate interaction, particularly the initial introductions between two members. Participants frequently spoke of the lack of clever, fun ways to contact matches, mentioning the stilted conversations, lengthy "letter-like" messages, and boring introductions. Online dating forum users cited a desire for fun, games, and socialization, and go to great lengths to understand the specifics of online dating systems. Games might provide a more immersive, less filtered form of dating [20, 43].

Users also spoke of putting enormous effort into messaging potential partners for very low return rates, and noted the frustration of this approach. In opposition to this *active* approach, there may be an opportunity to provide a more *calm, passive* method of connecting potential matches. As many people maintain an active presence on other social networks that are unrelated to online dating, one possibility would be to explore using these existing social networks to suggest and communicate potential matches. For example, a particularly good match might appear as a tweet in a Twitter feed. If the actual profile of the match were visible (rather than an external link to an online dating site profile) this might offer the additional benefit of painting a more complete picture of the individuals, since the connection would be with a user's general social media profile, rather than a profile specifically created for the purpose of maximizing dating "hit rate" [22]. A tension exists here, however: connecting with users' social media profiles is a privacy concern, especially given the prevalence of anti-social behaviors exhibited in our forum observations. Anti-social concerns might be averted by only offering this service with a "real name" or address verification system; reputation systems have been successfully used on social networks connecting strangers in face-to-face interactions [31, 34].

Crowdsourcing may also provide untapped mechanisms to provide more accurate assessments of a potential match's personality. Prior research has shown that crowdworkers are able to discern facets of personality from social media [9]. A common tension raised by participants was that online dating profiles did not represent the user in an accurate way. Crowdworkers might be able to review a social media profile and then determine if that person's online dating profile matched their impression of personality. Although participants spoke of asking real-world friends and family for advice on profiles, it is possible that wholly impartial parties would be superior in this area. It may also be possible to use online dating site users as crowdworkers; the ingenuity, cleverness, and motivation to "figure it out" that we observed in the behaviors of online dating forum users suggests that creative uses of this untapped resource may exist.

Gender dynamics clearly presented a huge issue in our study, not only in terms of the differential experiences between men and women, but also in the levels of harassment and anti-social behavior experienced by women. Every participant interviewed who had used OkCupid spoke of the substantially higher message receive rate for women versus men. This suggests to us that there is much more room to explore design choices with respect to messaging allowances and "the sexual marketplace." For example, these might take the form of a points system in which users earn the ability to message by exhibiting pro-social behaviors. Such allowances might reduce the prevalence of some of the gaming behaviors we observed and also help to establish better norms for interaction.

Finally, one possibility is to foster an online version of real world "matchmakers"—friends and acquaintances who serve an introductory role in the early stages of a relationship. We know that friends meet partners through friends [41], and there is the possibility to build digital systems that facilitate this pattern of interaction. Some existing systems come close to this. For example, Tinder utilizes a user's Facebook friend network to present potential matches. However, this information is used exclusively to visualize ties in common, and the two parties still interact directly with each other. Couplet [2] comes closer still, allowing a Facebook user to match two of their friends together for a date. A further extension of such a system may facilitate friends vetting the profiles of strangers, or people more distant in their networks, as potential matches. Finally, the matchmaking service might also be drawn from community forums: who better to give advice than those already invested into giving feedback?

CONCLUSION

Online dating sites have become an increasingly common means of finding a romantic partner, and yet these sites differ greatly from the online communities that have been well studied in our research field. By focusing on an "outsourced" community of the users of these sites, we gained insight into the need for the sorts of learning and establishment of social norms that exist in online dating. Further, we have shed light on some of the practices that exist in online dating—ranging from the ways in which users attempt to game the system, the prevalence of widespread anti-social behavior, and users' frustrations with the sites. We believe that these findings suggest a rich lode of opportunity for future system design work to enhance the experience of online dating.

ACKNOWLEDGMENTS

This material is based upon work supported by the National Science Foundation Graduate Research Fellowship under Grant No. DGE-1148903 and NSF Grant No. IIS-0904431.

REFERENCES

1. *Best of Tinder • /r/Tinder.* 14 Sept 2014. https://reddit.com/r/tinder.
2. *Georgia Institute of Technology.* 22 Sept 2014. http://www.news.gatech.edu/2014/02/17/couplet-love-story.
3. *OkCupid on Reddit • /r/OkCupid.* 14. Sept 2014. Available from: https://reddit.com/r/okcupid.
4. *Terms | OkCupid.* 12. Sept 2014. http://www.okcupid.com/legal/terms.
5. *The Tinder-O-Matic. Sink Hacks.* 22 Sept 2014. http://sinkhacks.com/tinder-o-matic/.
6. *Usenet Personals: Advice for Straights FAQ (1/3.* 14 Sept 2014. http://www.faqs.org/faqs/personals/straightfaq/part1
7. Bardzell, S. and J. Bardzell. *Towards a Feminist HCI Methodology: Social science, Feminism, and HCI.* In *Proceedings of the SIGCHI Conference on Human Factors in Computing Systems.* 2011. ACM.
8. Bernard, H.H.R. et. al, *Analyzing Qualitative Data: Systematic Approaches.* 2009: SAGE publications.
9. Biel, J. and D. Gatica-Perez, *The Youtube Lens: Crowdsourced Personality Impressions and Audiovisual Analysis of Vlogs.* Multimedia, IEEE Transactions on, 2013. 15(1): p. 41-55.
10. Bruckman, A., et al. *Managing Deviant Behavior in Online Communities.* In *CHI'06 Extended Abstracts on Human Factors in Computing Systems.* 2006. ACM.
11. Bryant, S.L. et al. *Becoming Wikipedian: Transformation of Participation in a Collaborative Online Encyclopedia.* In *Proceedings of the 2005 international ACM SIGGROUP conference on Supporting group work.* 2005. ACM
12. Collins, S.A., C. Missing, *Vocal and Visual Attractiveness are Related in Women.* Animal behaviour, 2003. 65(5): p. 997-1004.
13. DeSanctis, G., et al., *Learning in Online Forums.* European Management Journal, 2003. 21(5): p. 565-577.
14. Dimond, J.P., et al. *Hollaback!: The Role of Storytelling Online in a Social Movement Organization.* CSCW 2013. ACM.

15. Ellison, N.B., *Social Network Sites: Definition, History, and Scholarship.* Journal of Computer-Mediated Communication, 2007. 13(1): p. 210-230.

16. Finkel, E.J., et al., *Online Dating A Critical Analysis From the Perspective of Psychological Science.* Psychological Science in the Public Interest, 2012. 13(1): p. 3-66.

17. Fiore, A.T. et al., *Online Personals: An Overview.* In *CHI'04 Extended Abstracts on Human Factors in Computing Systems.* 2004. ACM.

18. Fiore, A.T. , J.S. Donath. *Homophily in Online Dating: When Do You Like Someone Like Yourself?* In *CHI'05 Extended Abstracts on Human Factors in Computing Systems.* 2005. ACM.

19. Fiore, A.T., et al. *Assessing Attractiveness in Online Dating Profiles.* CHI 2008. ACM.

20. Frost, J.H., et al., *People are Experience Goods: Improving Online Dating with Virtual Dates.* Journal of Interactive Marketing, 2008. 22(1): p. 51-61.

21. Goffman, E., *The Presentation of Self in Everyday Life.* 1959.

22. Golbeck, J., C. Robles, and K. Turner. *Predicting Personality with Social Media.* In *CHI'11 Extended Abstracts on Human Factors in Computing Systems.* 2011. ACM.

23. Hall, J.A., et al., *Strategic misrepresentation in online dating: The effects of gender, self-monitoring, and personality traits.* Journal of Social and Personal Relationships, 2010. 27(1): p. 117-135.

24. Hancock, J.T., C. Toma, and N. Ellison. *The Truth About Lying in Online Dating Profiles.* CHI 2007. ACM.

25. Hancock, J.T. and C.L. Toma, *Putting Your Best Face Forward: The Accuracy of Online Dating Photographs.* Journal of Communication, 2009. 59(2): p. 367-386.

26. Hitsch, G.J. et al. *What Makes You Click?—Mate Preferences in Online Dating.* Quantitative Marketing and Economics, 2010. 8(4): p. 393-427.

27. Irani, L.C. and M. Silberman. *Turkopticon: Interrupting Worker Invisibility in Amazon Mechanical Turk.* CHI 2013. ACM.

28. Jones, Q., *Virtual-Communities, Virtual Settlements & Cyber-Archaeology: A Theoretical Outline.* Journal of Computer-Mediated Communication, 1997. 3(3).

29. Kosinski, M., D. Stillwell, and T. Graepel, *Private traits and attributes are predictable from digital records of human behavior.* Proceedings of the National Academy of Sciences, 2013. 110(15): p. 5802-5805.

30. Lampe, C. and E. Johnston. *Follow the (Slash) dot: Effects of Feedback on New Members in an Online Community.* SIGGROUP 2005. ACM.

31. Lauterbach, D., et al. *Surfing a Web of Trust: Reputation and Reciprocity on Couchsurfing.com.* CSE'09. IEEE.

32. Lave, J. and E. Wenger, *Situated Learning: Legitimate Peripheral Participation.* 1991: Cambridge university press.

33. Lee, A.Y. and A.S. Bruckman. *Judging You by the Company You Keep: Dating on Social Networking Sites.* CSCW 2007. ACM.

34. Masden, C.A., et al. *Tensions in Scaling-up Community Social Media: A Multi-Neighborhood Study of Nextdoor.* CHI 2014. ACM.

35. Oldenburg, R., *The Great Good Place: Cafes, Coffee Shops, Bookstores, Bars, Hair Salons, and Other Hangouts at the Heart of a Community.* 1999: Marlowe New York.

36. PRWeb. *Dating Services in the US Industry Market Research Report from IBISWorld Has Been Updated.* 2013 16 Mar. 2013; Available from: http://www.prweb.com/releases/2013/3/prweb10537905.htm.

37. Putnam, R.D., *The Strange Disappearance of Civic America.* American Prospect, 1996: p. 34-49.

38. Rosen, L.D., et al., *The Impact of Emotionality and Self-Disclosure on Online Dating Versus Traditional Dating.* Computers in Human Behavior, 2008. 24(5): p. 2124-215&.

39. Rudder, C., *Dataclysm: Who We Are (When We Think No One's Looking).* 2014: Random House LLC.

40. Skopek, J. et al. *Who Contacts Whom? Educational Homophily in Online Mate Selection.* European Sociological Review, 2010: p. jcp068

41. Smith, A., M. Duggan. *Online Dating & Relationships.* Pew Internet & American Life Project, 2013.

42. Toma, C.L. et al., *Separating Fact From Fiction: An Examination of Deceptive Self-Presentation in Online Dating Profiles.* Personality and Social Psychology Bulletin, 2008. 34(8): p. 1023-1036

43. Yee, N., et al. *Introverted Elves & Conscientious Gnomes: The Expression of Personality in World of Warcraft.* In *Proceedings of the SIGCHI Conference on Human Factors in Computing Systems.* 2011. ACM.

44. Zytko, D. et al., *Impression Management Through Communication in Online Dating.* In *Proceedings of the Companion Publication of the 17th ACM Conference on Computer Supported Cooperative Work and Social Computing.* 2014. ACM.

Making Social Matching Context-Aware — Design Concepts and Open Challenges

Julia M. Mayer
New Jersey Institute of Technology, USA
jam45@njit.edu

Starr Roxanne Hiltz
New Jersey Institute of Technology, USA
hiltz@adm.njit.edu

Quentin Jones
New Jersey Institute of Technology, USA
qgjones@acm.org

ABSTRACT
Social matching systems recommend people to people. In an ideal world, such systems could be *context-aware,* in that they would introduce users to each other in situations where they are mutually interested, available and open to meeting (i.e., facilitate a *valuable encounter*). Unfortunately, today's systems primarily match individuals based on simple similarity and proximity metrics. This paper explores how contextual information available on today's mobile phones could be used to identify opportunities for people to make valuable new connections. Three types of context that are relevant for this work are: *relational, social* and *personal.* We present insights gained from several iterations of semi-structured interviewing (N=58) exploring these three types of contexts and propose novel context-aware social matching concepts such as: *sociability of others* as an indicator of opportune social context; *activity involvement* as an indicator of opportune personal context; and *contextual rarity* as an indicator of opportune relational context.

Author Keywords
Context-aware social matching; introduction systems; chance encounters; social recommender systems

ACM Classification Keywords
H.1.2 [Information Systems]: User/Machine Systems.

INTRODUCTION
Chance encounters, the unintended meetings between people unfamiliar with each other, help people to create new social ties, such as making new friends, advancing one's career or finding an activity partner [2]. Every day we cross paths with numerous strangers, who might just be that tennis partner we have been looking for, the ideal partner for a political discussion, or the Spanish tutor we need so desperately. While we may not be aware of these nearby individuals, our smartphone could be. Social matching systems aim at supporting the creation of new social ties by recommending people to people [36]. While social matching is often considered to be synonymous with online dating (*Match.com, OKCupid, eHarmony*, etc.), it also supports a broader range of social needs, such as professional networking (e.g., *LinkedIn* people recommendations) or the formation of new friendships through mobile people discovery apps (e.g., *Highlight, MeetMe*).

The problem is that the matching supported by current mobile social applications is overly simplistic. Systems tend to assume that one's listed profile attributes and interests are always relevant which can lead to overwhelming amounts of irrelevant matches. For example, a user who sits in a coffee shop in New York is unlikely to be interested in a match notification informing him that someone nearby is also from New York and likes coffee. Unfortunately, beyond simple notions of similarity, proximity and social ties, we have limited knowledge about how systems could facilitate valuable chance encounters in socially intelligent ways. Therefore, this paper investigates what constitutes an opportune context for chance encounters, the impact of mobility on people's interest in meeting others, and how mobile systems could utilize contextual data to identify opportunities for valuable chance encounters. The contribution of this paper is a framework of contextual factors that should be taken into account when designing context-aware mobile social matching systems.

We begin with a review of the background literature, systems and theories of prior work and an examination of how they could inform the design of context-aware social matching systems. We then outline our theoretical framework that categorizes aspects that are relevant for this work into *social, personal, and relational context.* Our research questions further explore how these three types of context can be used to identify opportunities for valuable encounters. We present findings from a semi-structured interview study (N=58) and conclude by discussing the design implications of our findings as well as proposing novel context-aware social matching concepts that could enable systems to facilitate valuable mobile encounters.

CHI 2015, April 18 - 23 2015, Seoul, Republic of Korea
Copyright 2015 ACM 978-1-4503-3145-6/15/04...$15.00
http://dx.doi.org/10.1145/2702123.2702343

BACKGROUND

Below we present a summary of prior mobile systems that aim to introduce people to people. We then turn to context-aware computing research and its notion of 'context'. Finally, we review the notion of place and articulate our work through the lens of proxemics, which posits that the physical and social environment and distance between people have a strong impact on social interaction.

Prior Systems

People tend to seek out others who are just like them (*similarity-attraction effect*, i.e., "Birds of a feather flock together") [24]. Early research on mobile social matching aimed at building prototypes with a focus on proximity and similarity, rather than trying to get a more nuanced understanding of what users desire when being introduced on the go. One of the first systems, *Nokia Sensor* [30], relied on Bluetooth beacons to discover nearby people and to communicate with them. *Social Net* [35] used explicit social network information and RF-based devices to introduce people located in proximity to one another using a common friend. *Social Serendipity* [6] used Bluetooth and a database of user profiles to recommend face-to-face interactions between nearby users who share common preferences. *WhozThat?* [3] shared social networking IDs locally to help users find others with common interests.

Mobile social matching systems have gained wide popularity in the online dating space and a majority of online dating sites now offer mobile applications that help find dating partners in the users' vicinity (e.g., *OkCupid Mobile, eHarmony Mobile*). While some matchmaking algorithms are very complex in that they attempt to find *the perfect match* based on numerous personality traits and lengthy questionnaires, mobile apps like *Tinder* and *Grindr* have gained significant popularity by using a much simpler approach. In *Tinder*, the user is shown a series of photos of people who meet certain age, gender, and location criteria and users can simply indicate who they like (swipe right) and who they do not like (swipe left). Only if both users indicate interest in each other are they able to message each other. In this case, mutual interest and availability based on location is all the system uses for social matching.

Context-awareness

Context-aware computing is a computing paradigm that aims at understanding the user's current context and treating it as an input to allow computational systems to be sensitive to the situation in which the user is immersed [1,4,5]. Even though we intuitively understand what "context" is, it is hard to elucidate, and even harder to make a computer system understand it. Context has been defined as "*location, identities of nearby people and objects, and changes to those objects*" [32] and further specified as "*any information that can be used to characterize the situation of an entity where an entity could be a person, place, or object that is considered relevant to the interaction between a user and an application, including the user and applications themselves*" [1]. Of particular relevance to this work is Dourish's notion of context as a *relational property* between objects or activities that defines if something is contextually relevant to some particular activity [5]. Relational context requires constant in situ negotiation of meaning of place and action. The notion of relational context was also used when studying human interruptability, where relational context referred to who the interruption was from and what it was about [10].

While mobile phones are able to collect increasing amounts of information using various sensors, such as user location, user movement, environmental noise, temperature, and people nearby, its availability along with the lack of uniform methods to define, acquire and process contextual data has created new challenges in context-aware computing. Social matching can greatly benefit from contextual information, particularly the relational context between people. Prior work found that the rarer shared attributes of users in the current context are, the more desirable a social match based on these contextually rare shared attributes is (*contextual rarity* [22]). For example, being matched with somebody because they are a fellow HCI researcher at CHI is less desired than when the two individuals are both attending a large handball tournament (where the attribute "HCI researcher" is assumed to be rather rare). However, we need to gain a deeper understanding of what contextual aspects define an opportunity for a valuable encounter in order to design context-aware social matching systems.

The Notion of Place

From sociology and psychology research we know that people's current environment influences social interaction between strangers [5,14]. A place is "a space, which is *invested with understandings* of behavioral appropriateness, cultural expectations" [15] and places - just like individuals - have their own personalities and act as "social" filters; different types of places attract certain people. For example, social norms at places or events might prescribe certain behavior regardless of the fact that those present are strangers, e.g., dinner parties, work, summer camps and conferences [9,33]. Prior work found that individuals are interested in knowing about others nearby in places designed for socializing, such as pubs and diners, or in places where people have long waiting periods, such as airports and train stations [11,18].

Urban overload and population density might negatively impact interaction between strangers and increase social barriers [26]. Levine [20] explored local and environmental variations in people's willingness to help a stranger and found that the characteristics of the local environment are the main predictor. For example, people in more crowded cities were much less likely to take the time to help. This shows that an understanding of place - not only in terms of physical space but also its meaning, its activities, its crowdedness, etc. - could potentially be used to infer how opportune the moment is for a social match.

Proxemics

Proxemics provides another perspective on how culture affects the way people understand the space around them and how proximity between people is interpreted and used to mediate interactions with others [14]. Perception of space is dynamic because it is related to action (i.e., what can be done here) rather than what is seen by passive viewing. Hall [14] distinguishes between *personal space* (immediate space surrounding a person) and *territory* (claimed area to defend against others). To assess and understand the effect of distance on communication, personal space can be divided into (1) *intimate distance* for embracing, touching or whispering, (2) *personal distance* for interactions among good friends or family members, (3) *social distance* for interactions among acquaintances, and (4) *public distance* used for public speaking [14]. In applying proxemics to ubiquitous computing, Greenberg et. al. [13] suggest that the dimensions of *distance, orientation* (e.g., facing toward or away from), *identity* (e.g., entity type), *movement,* and *location* (e.g., a particular room and its characteristics) be taken into account.

Research has shown that physical proximity and the resulting opportunity to interact increases attraction (*mere-exposure-effect*) [17] and that proximity further provides the occasion for the discovery of common attitudes [28]. The probability of face-to-face contact between two people decreases exponentially as the physical distance increases because distance increases effort [7,34]. Co-location traces have been used to identify groups and their associated places and predict the probability of contact between two users [21]. Further, it was found that people who have regularly seen each other before but never directly interacted (i.e. *familiar strangers* [26]) are more likely to introduce themselves in an unfamiliar setting, for example while travelling, than perfect strangers, as they have a background of shared experiences [29].

THEORETICAL FRAMING

Our review of background literature highlights some of the complex social dynamics of meeting new people in various contexts. The concept of *context-awareness* has not been explored deeply from a social-matching perspective. In order to build *context-aware* social matching systems, we need to understand how we could identify situations in which people want to meet new people, i.e., when are good opportunities for a system to introduce users to each other. We define *opportunities for valuable (mobile) encounters* as situations in which two or more people are mutually open to and interested in computer-mediated introductions. We believe such *opportunities* exist when two people are (1) interesting or relevant to each other in their current situation (*opportune relational context*), and/or (2) are in a situation where they are willing/able to act on the

a)

b)

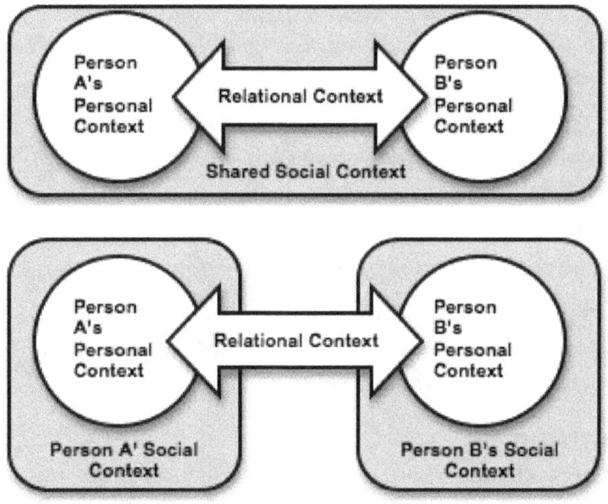

Figure 1. Relevant aspects of context for identifying opportunities for valuable encounters between people in a) the same social context or in b) distinct social context

introduction and start interacting (*opportune social context & personal context*). We propose a theoretical framework outlining *social, personal,* and *relational context* as relevant when identifying opportunities for valuable encounters:

Social Context: External factors of the place, such as the place type, activities offered, the people present within that place and their intentions, associated social norms, reputation, safety, etc.

Personal Context: Individual factors affecting people's state of mind, their attitude, ability and willingness to engage in a mobile encounter, e.g., based on current involvement in an activity.

Relational Context: Factors affecting the nature of the relationship between people (i.e., affinities, reason for match), including information about similarities, shared social ties, proximity, etc.

Figure 1a) and b) illustrate that while relational context depends on the relationship between person A and person B, personal context is an individual attribute. Person A and B could be either in the same social context, same place and time (Figure 1a) or they could be in different social contexts, e.g. different places or time (Figure 1b). Formalizing these constructs allows us to map out the design space of context-aware social matching systems.

This framework was informed by prior literature and further refined by insights from the iterative interview process presented later in this paper. Thus, while the framework was used to structure the interviews, our insights from the interviews also further refined the framework.

RESEARCH QUESTIONS

In order to gain a deeper understanding of these constructs, we need to answer the following research questions:

RQ1: What external factors define situations where people are interested in meeting new people? (Opportune social context)

RQ2: What individual factors define situations where people are interested in meeting new people? (Opportune personal context)

RQ3: What relational factors define who people are interested in meeting? (Opportune relational context)

RQ4: How do these factors - social, personal, and relational context - interrelate in defining who people are interested in meeting?

METHOD

We conducted short semi-structured interviews in various locations to investigate the proposed research questions. A total of 58 interviews were completed which lasted on average 15 minutes. The relatively short interviews were necessary because we stopped people in the midst of their daily activities, without an appointment, in order to take their current situation into account. All procedures were approved by an Institutional Review Board.

Participants and Places

The research involved several rounds of interviews, data analysis and refinement of our interview guide. The characteristics of the setting / "place" and the activities occurring there were observed and noted before beginning interviews. The initial interviews were conducted with students on an urban university campus with approximately 10,000 students during Fall 2013. These were complimented by two rounds of interviews with people in various public places in Manhattan, NYC (Spring 2014).

The focus of the early interviews with students was to get an initial understanding of the research space, to iterate quickly on findings and refine interview questions. College students are at a point in their lives where they are actively looking to build their social networks and an urban university campus in theory provides an environment that offers numerous opportunities for people to make new connections. Therefore, studying students within this larger urban environment provided a good starting point for learning about people's habits, patterns, and expectations in regards to meeting new people.

Students were randomly selected at different places around campus and asked to participate in a short interview (no incentive offered), similar to market research street intercepts. This approach allowed for the exploration of a variety of locations and quick necessary iterations in our interviews as the study progressed. Most students were willing to be interviewed, with only six out of 52 approached people declining participation in the study, resulting in 46 completed interviews. The average participant age was 21 years old with a range of 18-32. Females made up 28% of participants, consistent with the population of the predominantly male university. Participants had a variety of majors (business management, biology, mechanical engineering, computer science, digital design, etc.) and about one third of the participants lived on campus while the rest were commuters.

Interviews were conducted both indoors and outdoors, at locations with defined activities (15 at racquetball courts, soccer field, etc.), social settings (18 at student lounges), and non-social settings (13 at library/academic buildings). The soccer field was described as being used for games of pick-up soccer, but also for cricket, track practice, baseball, etc. Student lounges often provided us with students relaxing with other friends, groups working on assignments, or study sessions. At the library and academic buildings, we interviewed mostly solitary individuals studying or waiting for the next class to start, rather than groups of friends.

After five iterations of interviewing, initial analysis [16], and interview guide refining, we conducted in-depth open coding, employing emergent theme analysis of the data collected [8] from our campus based interviews. To reflect on emerged themes and patterns and see if they also held with a more general population and more diverse places we conducted a final round of interviews with 12 people in public places around Manhattan, NY, over two days (again, no incentive offered). Here the average participant age was 32.8, ranging from 22-48 with 50% being female. Interviewees had a diverse professional background (e.g., artist, medical doctor, office worker, film producer, software engineer, etc.). People were interviewed in six different public places around Manhattan, NY: Park (3), train station (3), Ground Zero (3), cafe (2), bar (1). All interviewees were alone except one man was with his wife.

Two slightly different sampling strategies were applied on the two days. The first day, the interviewer approached only people that appeared to be available and potentially open to be interviewed based on observed activity, being alone, and not glued to his/her phone. This resulted in all 6 approached people agreeing to be interviewed. On the second day, the sampling strategy was slightly modified and people were approached at random (i.e., no matter if they looked busy or available) and interrupted to ask if they would be willing to participate in a short interview. This resulted in 9 of 15 approached people declining to be interviewed. Most people who declined were walking somewhere, said they had to be somewhere or said they "didn't feel like it."

We acknowledge that differences between students and general public could have potentially biased our findings. However, we did not see strong differences between the two groups regarding their interest in meeting others. While strength of effects cannot be determined from qualitative studies, we did observe that people from the general public who were married and/or had a stable social circle seemed less interested in meeting new people when in their usual surrounding. Yet, when not in their usual surrounding (e.g., traveling, at a conference), their reasons and motivations for meeting new people were aligned with those of students.

Interview Process

Before we started the interviews, we recorded characteristics of the current situation of a potential interviewee from observation (location, place type, crowdedness, typical activity, etc.). After agreeing to be interviewed, we asked participants questions about their specific situation (what they were doing, how often they were here, who they were with, etc.). Then we delved deeper into their current as well as general interest in meeting new people. We encouraged storytelling by asking about specific past experiences of meeting new people at this or other places and specifically probed for situations where they liked/disliked meeting new people, where they found meeting new people particularly hard/easy and where they faced challenges and frustrations with finding interesting new people to talk to. We further asked them to elaborate on their motivations for interacting with new people and questioned them about their thoughts on being introduced to someone nearby by a mobile app. All interviews were recorded, with the permission of the participant, for later transcription and analysis.

FINDINGS

We recorded 926 minutes of semi-structured interviews, which we transcribed. For our analysis we followed a Grounded Theory approach [8] and used open-coding with two independent coders coding the transcripts to look for emerging themes around our three research questions. We discuss our findings below, which are illustrated through representative quotes with names changed to preserve participants' anonymity. The place of the interview is added to the quote when relevant.

Opportune Social Context

Participants generally identified places or situations where they felt it was "okay" to socialize as: bars, parties, conferences, organized trips, fraternities, and student clubs. While it may seem obvious to us that a bar is *more social* than a library, it is still difficult for systems to understand and identify opportune social contexts. From interviews we identified *sociability of people nearby, the familiarity with place and people, perceived safety,* and *jointly attended events/activities* as factors that influence how opportune the current social context for a mobile encounter is.

Sociability of People Nearby

A theme that emerged as important when meeting new people was a sense of other people's openness for socializing in the current context. Knowing if other people around them were open to meet new people influenced participants' openness, too. As Jenny put it, *"It's easy to strike up a conversation with someone when the other person seems open* Several participants expressed fear of rejection, e.g.: *"I'm always scared of bothering someone so that's like a reason why I wouldn't talk to someone in the park because people go there to read a book."* (Nicole at Union Square Park, NYC)

Participants illustrated how they assess not only their own but others' availability when thinking about meeting new people. Mark told us: *"At the beginning of the semester everyone is looking to meet new people with the influx of freshman...it sort of sets the expectation of meeting new people."* People seem to have a general idea of how open others around them are for socializing (which may not always be true, e.g., *pluralistic ignorance* [25]). Interestingly, openness to socializing seems to be 'contagious'. When people assume that others are not open to socialize then they will not socialize either. When people assume others are open to socialize, they are open, too.

Familiarity with Place and People

Familiarity with the people nearby as well as with the current place influenced people's interest in meeting others. Arnold told us, *"When my friends and I went snowboarding, I didn't really talk to anyone new because I was with a group of friends."* Participants were more motivated to meet new people when alone instead of with friends. Being in a new unknown place (e.g., while traveling) may also influence interest in meeting others. As John told us: *"I was at a bar in Hong Kong. I don't normally go up to others at bars but saw he was watching a soccer match and was traveling alone, so I started a conversation."*

Perceived Safety

We repeatedly heard that people are less open to meet new people when they feel unsafe in their environment. Maria told us *"I wouldn't want to meet someone in [an unsafe neighborhood] but on campus we're all students. I would be ok with other students coming up to me."* Here, the affiliation to a certain place (students on their campus in our case, or being a member of a church or gym) influences this feeling of safety towards meeting others. Other factors like time of the day, crime history, crowdedness, and reputation of a place also seemed to influence perception of safety.

Jointly Attended Events or Activities

Interview findings show how knowing about others who are at a place for the same reason (event or activity) helps people to connect with each other. Mark told us, *"It's easy to make new friends at certain organized hangouts, and things like different events. [...] Most of the awkwardness of actually making new friends is taken care of by the structure of the club."* Shared experiences makes connecting to new people easier, as Norbert told us: *"I once went bungee jumping in Switzerland and met people on the way to do that. [...] We all kinda bonded, I think because in these moments of fear, these extreme situations make you bond."* This illustrates how opportune social context could be derived from information about organized events or activities, such as conferences, concerts or clubs.

Opportune Personal Context

Exploring individuals' state of mind, their attitude, ability and willingness to engage in a mobile encounter, we found that involvement in an activity is the strongest predictor of how opportune current personal context is. For example, people in a hurry or busy with something else are rarely willing to meet new people. We talked to Angela in a train station and she said: *"I don't think you meet many people here, because everybody is hurrying somewhere, everyone is going somewhere, people don't have time to stop and chat with you."* During interviews, people repeatedly told us that they would not want to be introduced to new people when they are busy with something else: *"Anytime that I'm really sort of busy and focusing on something I'm not up to meeting someone new. If I'm in studio, working on something and somebody comes in, my desires to keep on working won't allow my concentration to be broken, more so than to meet them, to get to know them."*(Marcel)

Compared to that, it seems easier to meet new people while waiting somewhere. As Natasha said, *"Meeting people is easier, for example in a waiting room where there isn't so much outside distraction and it's just they waiting for someone, there is someone who has the same intention as you have, wait for something."*

We derived another strong indicator of people being less open when busy from our experience with finding participants to interview for this study. Students tended to be less likely agree to an interview at times between classes, as most students were focused on getting to their next class. Similarly, the majority of our declined interviews on campus (5 out of 6) occurred soon before the end of the semester with students citing the need to study as a reason for not participating in the interview. In Manhattan, people who declined an interview (9 out of 15) seemed to be in a hurry, or excused themselves with the reason that they had to be somewhere.

Opportune Relational Context

From our interviews, we found that people's reasons and motivations for meeting certain people vary strongly across contexts. In line with the similarity-attraction effect [24,27], *having something in common with another person* was one of the most mentioned reasons for connecting to a person. Delving deeper into what made these people interesting or relevant to participants, we found that *contextually rare shared attributes, contextually rare, but not shared attributes,* and *activity partnering* were the most prominent themes emerging around relational context.

Contextually Rare Shared Attributes

Prior research briefly explored the idea of contextually rare shared attributes used for matching [22]. We also repeatedly heard that people typically were interested in others with whom they share *something rare* in the current context. When delving deeper, we found that contextually rare shared attributes often are nationality, ethnic minority, religion or extraordinary hobbies. For example, Alyssa from Nigeria told us of the importance of meeting other Nigerians while on her current campus in the United States, *"I found out that [this other person] was also Nigerian, so I introduced myself with that [...] and made friends with him because of that. I kind of know all the Nigerians on campus. So I was kind of interested that there was another Nigerian that I didn't know."* Because being Nigerian on an American campus was something unusual to Alyssa, she was interested in meeting any other Nigerian in this context.

Similarly, Scott, who is very religious, explained how his interest in meeting others from his religion varies based on where he is and how common his religion is in that place: *"In my town [my religion] is all over. But here [on campus] it's a lot rarer. Most of my friends from that religion go to [other colleges]."* When asked if he would like to meet others from his religion on campus, he said *"Yeah of course, there are always surprises around. That would be cool."*

We repeatedly heard from participants that they would be interested in meeting others that have a certain sought-after skill or interest; usually something that none of their current contacts does or have. Jenny, for example, told us: *"I would totally want to meet somebody right now who does 'international education'. I currently don't know anyone who does that, so I would make the time to have a conversation, definitely. It's what I wanna do next, it's a big career move for me."*

Contextually Rare but Not Shared Attributes

We found that in some situations people are interested in others because they are both in some way different than the rest of the crowd at a place, i.e., have a contextually rare but not shared attribute. In other words, rather than being "birds of a feather" they are the "odd ducks". For example, Arnold, who was at a dinner party with his girlfriend where everybody was an artist, told us: *"I felt like an outsider because I was the only one there who wasn't an artist. But then I found this other guy who also wasn't an artist and we immediately bonded."* Similarly, another participant told of a recent internship she had in Wisconsin. She described the formation of a close friendship with the other external student based solely on the fact that neither of them was from Wisconsin. Pam said, *"When we found out we both weren't from Wisconsin, there was something for us to talk about. Eventually we got to know everyone else who was part of the internship but it was much easier for me to connect with [the other person who wasn't from Wisconsin]."* This illustrates that people do not necessarily have to have a specific attribute in common. Instead, interest in a match may result from both ***not*** possessing a common attribute that everyone else possesses (i.e., everyone was an artist except Arnold, everyone else was from Wisconsin except Pam).

Activity Partnering

People often were interested in meeting others with whom to do an activity of interest. Sue, who enjoys dancing salsa, told us: *"I have a friend who comes with me all the time but she's a girl and it doesn't work because you have to have a guy partner for salsa. We go together but we don't dance together. I would like to meet others who dance salsa, especially if they do it here [on campus]."* Currently, activity partners are generally sought at places where the activity can be done, e.g., finding tennis partners by the tennis courts. People mentioned how they intentionally go to certain places that imply a certain activity or interest to meet likeminded people there and/or do activities together: *"I go down to the game room whenever I have time, you know you play with others and that's how you make friends. [...] Most of the people I know are from there"* (Scott). Participants identified locations where they went to meet others for specific activities: the soccer field, racquetball courts, church, game room, bars, and classrooms.

However, in many cases such attempts were problematic and unsuccessful due to lack of knowledge about who nearby might also be interested in doing a certain activity. Sue told us when talking about her interest in salsa: *"I'm sure there are a lot of people who do this around [this university] but I don't know, I don't know them. You can't ask someone, 'Oh, do you do salsa?' You can't just go up to somebody and ask. But if I knew someone was interested, I would talk to them about it."* This also illustrates the general challenge people have to discover and connect to interesting or relevant people nearby.

Interdependencies between Social, Personal, and Relational Context

We further examined how social, personal, and relational context may jointly define the extent to which an encounter represents a valuable opportunity.

Opportune Relational Context Trumps Inopportune Personal or Social Context

From the interviews we found that in some cases, even if people are busy they want to know about specific interesting people nearby. For example, in the rare case of another person from El Salvador nearby, Aaron would always want to be introduced, no matter how busy: *"I wouldn't consider it an interruption; I can choose to continue the introduction. I'd still like to know I had the chance of meeting another person from El Salvador."* This suggests that while opportune relational context provides the basis for a valuable encounter, social and personal context are mediators either improving or impairing the encounter opportunity.

Compatibility and Conflicts between Relational and Social Context

We further found that in a situation where the reason for the match (relational context) and their current situation or activity (social context) would be compatible, participants were more open to introductions, even when busy. Initially, Eugene said, *"I [wouldn't want to meet new people at] the library. Because I'm there to study and I'm usually there by myself trying to keep focus and I wouldn't want people, even like my friends, disturbing me."* But later he admitted, *"It all comes down to what I'm doing. If I'm studying for an exam, [I wouldn't want to be interrupted], unless that person wants to study the same thing that I'm studying, then I would take the time to talk to that person."*

In a different case, a participant told us of not wanting to meet new people when the reason for the match (relational context) conflicts with the current activity (social context). Scott, who is religious and generally interested in meeting others from his religion, said *"I mean I don't want to meet people from my religion if I'm at a party, when I'm doing something I'm not supposed to be doing ... You know, I mean I'm human. I do stuff."* This suggests that the compatibility or conflict between relational context and users' current social context influences whether a mobile encounter is considered valuable and wanted.

DISCUSSION & DESIGN IMPLICATIONS

While some of our findings reflect what can be found in sociology and psychology literature, no prior work has explored how context-aware social matching systems could be designed accordingly. In order to map out the design space for context-aware social matching systems, we discuss our findings in the light of what they mean for system design. In particular we outline how opportune social, personal, and relational contexts could be identified based on contextual user information that currently is, or soon will be available on mobile devices (Table 1). Several open challenges regarding how systems could obtain an understanding of how opportune a user's current context is, are pointed out along the way.

Social Context	Personal Context	Relational Context
Contextual Sociability - Place type - Crowdedness - Typical activity at place - Time / season - No. of people new to place - No. of new connections made at the place - Self-reported openness *Contextual Familiarity* - No. of friends in close proximity - No. of prior visits to place	*Contextual Engagement* - Current Activity - Scheduled upcoming events - Speed of moving - Self-reported busyness	*Contextual Rarity* *Contextual Oddity* *Contextual Activity Partnering*

Table 1. Potential Indicators of Opportune Social, Personal and Relational Context

Identifying Opportune Social Context

Interview findings suggest that *sociability of others nearby* influences whether people are interested in meeting others. For systems to get an understanding how sociable people at a certain place are, several factors could be considered, such as place type, crowdedness, and typical activity. In some situations, the time (e.g., beginning of the semester) and the amount of people new to a place (e.g., lots of freshmen) can be indicators of how open people generally are. A direct measure of *sociability of others* could also be collected directly from users through unobtrusive user interfaces allowing users to input their openness to meeting others in a quick and easy way in various settings. Another more indirect measure of sociability of people at a place may be the *number of new connections between people* made at a place. This could be computed based on total connections over an extended time period, seasonally adjusted (e.g. start of each fall semester), or relative to a given point in time (e.g. tonight).

The interviews also showed that *familiarity with place and people* influence how opportune the social context is. This could be inferred by systems based on the number of friends (or otherwise known people) in close proximity, as well as a measure of how often a user has been to a place before, to decide if the social context is opportune.

Identifying Opportune Personal Context

We learned from interviews that *involvement in an activity* defines how opportune an individual's personal context is. Contextual cues informing us about a users' busyness could be derived from scheduled upcoming events in the user's calendar or at a place (e.g., a class or a meeting) and/or the speed at which people move (hurrying somewhere). Furthermore, the current place (library) and current activity (study) can provide hints about a users' busyness.

Identifying Opportune Relational Context

As pointed out earlier, an opportune relational context is the basis of all valuable encounters between people. We propose three concepts that could be used to infer opportune relational context: *shared contextual rarity, contextual oddity* and *contextual activity partnering*.

Our findings dictate that the rarity of a user's attribute in the current relational context is a powerful predictor of how opportune the relational context is. The underlying logic of *shared contextual rarity* is: the rarer a shared user attribute is in the current context, the more interested the user is in meeting another person who shares this contextually rare attribute [22]. Systems can calculate the prevalence P_a of an attribute a by dividing the number of occurrences of the attribute n_a by the size of the population N. While this concept has been previously explored through a survey study [22,23], there are still many open challenges related to the size of the population to take into account (a room, a building, a neighborhood, a town, etc.) and the granularity of the user attributes to be considered.

Contextual oddity could be used in the specific case of not shared contextually common attributes to match outsiders. Our findings illustrate how people who do not necessarily have anything in common but are different than the general crowd in the current situation tend to bond more easily. Systems could identify such outsiders in situations where a very high proportion of people share a certain attribute by identifying people who do not possess this common attribute. To achieve this computationally, further research into the dynamics of outsiders in mostly homogenous groups and how systems can identify them is needed. This approach presents new opportunities to connect people who are not alike, which is valuable for learning from different people, being exposed to different opinions and mindsets [12], and building "bridging" social capital [31].

Furthermore, the concept *contextual activity partnering* could be used to match people for activities that are relevant, interesting and available to them in the moment or in the near future. Contextual information regarding the typical activity at the current place as well as users' current activity in addition to users' activity interests could be used to identify and match activity partners near a location where the activity is offered.

Identifying Interdependencies

Study findings also suggest that there are interdependencies between social, personal and relational context. When there is a very strong relational motivation for a match, social and personal context seems to play a less significant role. However, when the relational motivators are lower, opportune social and personal contexts are required. This should be considered by system design.

Furthermore, *contextual compatibility or conflict* could be considered by systems to infer opportune and inopportune social context to introduce people. While a social match might be possible in one situation it may not be acceptable or appropriate. Reducing the likelihood of matches on religion in a wild party environment, or romantic introductions in a workplace setting, may seem obvious but is not addressed by existing matching systems. Similarly, if the reason for the match (taking the same class) and the current activity (studying for that class) are compatible, an encounter opportunity is even more valuable.

Mediating the Introduction Once an Opportunity is Identified

While this paper mostly focuses on identifying opportunities for valuable encounters, we also want to briefly discuss how context-aware social matching systems could mediate an introduction between two people. Once an opportunity is identified as being valuable enough to inform the user about it, an introduction is triggered. The matched parties get informed about the opportunity and get provided with tools to connect with each other (e.g., messaging, profile exchange). The most crucial part of the introduction is the amount and kind of information that comes with the initial match notification. Enough information to make the value of the encounter obvious has to be revealed but at the same time user privacy has to be ensured. This means that the reason for the match (relational context) should ideally be revealed to the parties concerned to help the introduction process. Furthermore, specific information about the social and personal context that contributes to the encounter opportunity being valuable should be conveyed. For example, our interview findings showed how important it is for people to know that others, and in particular the matched person, is currently open to meeting new people. We believe that conveying this information through the app can increase successful introductions.

We understand that computer-mediated mobile encounters are changing the nature of the interaction and are not exactly the same as chance encounters between people without a system mediating. Future work testing an instantiation of a mobile social matching application will explore how such a system itself influences people's perception of the value of encounter opportunities in varying contexts.

LIMITATIONS

This qualitative research was exploratory, aimed at developing an initial understanding of the problem of developing a system to identify potentially valuable mobile encounter opportunities. We used semi-structured interviews to uncover underlying motivations that influence people's interest in meeting new people across different situations. Our contribution is to better understand the interaction of a number of factors that influence mobile encounter opportunities. At this stage, we do not present computational aspects of the proposed concepts but instead aim at theory construction and raising important issues.

Only a limited number of subjects were interviewed, in two locations, a college campus in the Northeast USA and in Manhattan public places. Openness to meeting new people may vary in different geographic locales, such as small towns, different regions of the USA, and other countries.

We are aware of a certain self-selection bias since we only talked to people who currently were open to be interviewed. We did note where, when and why people declined to interview with us, if a reason for refusal was volunteered.

CONCLUSION

This paper explored the nature of situations in which opportunities exist for valuable mobile encounters. We present a theoretical framework of social, personal, and relational context as important aspects for identifying such opportunities. Insights gained from an interview study suggest that opportune social context relates to sociability of people nearby, familiarity with place and people, perceived safety of the location and jointly attended events and activities. Moreover, opportune personal context is mostly reliant on people's current activity and how busy they are. Finally and most importantly, opportune relational context can be identified based on contextually rare shared and not shared attributes, as well as activity partnering. From these findings we derive novel design concepts to identify valuable mobile encounter opportunities based on social, personal, and relational context. These are instrumental in the implementation of context-aware social matching applications.

Moreover, social matching systems rely on the fact that users are willing to share personal information with others. The collection of personal and contextual information requires a thorough understanding of users' privacy concerns. While this study did not directly examine privacy concerns, we do recognize that it is an important issue. Privacy safeguards to protect users will be considered as part of future work.

As a next step, we are planning to conduct a quantitative Experience Sampling Method (ESM) [19] study with a larger sample of random participants to explore how social, personal and relational context could be operationalized to identify valuable mobile encounter opportunities. Expanding our understanding of these concepts will produce entirely new possibilities for social navigation enabling people to create new, valuable, unexpected relationships on the go.

ACKNOWLEDGMENTS

This research is partially supported by a grant from the National Science Foundation 1422696.

REFERENCES

1. Abowd, G.D., Dey, A.K., Brown, P.J., Davies, N., Smith, M., and Steggles, P. Towards a Better Understanding of Context and Context-Awareness. In H.-W. Gellersen, ed., *Handheld and Ubiquitous Computing*. Springer Berlin Heidelberg, 1999, 304–307.
2. Bandura, A. The psychology of chance encounters and life paths. *American Psychologist 37*, 7 (1982), 747–755.
3. Beach, A., Gartrell, M., Akkala, S., et al. WhozThat? evolving an ecosystem for context-aware mobile social networks. *IEEE Network 22*, 4 (2008), 50–55.
4. Dey, A.K. Understanding and Using Context. *Personal Ubiquitous Comput. 5*, 1 (2001), 4–7.
5. Dourish, P. What We Talk About when We Talk About Context. *Personal Ubiquitous Comput. 8*, 1 (2004), 19–30.
6. Eagle, N. and Pentland, A. Social serendipity: mobilizing social software. *IEEE Pervasive Computing 4*, 2 (2005), 28 – 34.
7. Festinger, L., Back, K.W., and Schachter, S. *Social Pressures in Informal Groups: A Study of Human Factors in Housing*. Stanford University Press, 1950.

8. Glaser, B. and Strauss, A. *The Discovery of Grounded Theory: Strategies for Qualitative Research.* Aldine Transaction, 1967.
9. Goffman, E. *Behavior in Public Places.* Simon and Schuster, 1966.
10. Grandhi, S. and Jones, Q. Technology-mediated interruption management. *International Journal of Human-Computer Studies 68*, 5 (2010), 288–306.
11. Grandhi, S.A., Jones, Q., and Karam, S. Sharing the big apple: a survey study of people, place and locatability. *CHI '05 Extended Abstracts on Human Factors in Computing Systems*, ACM (2005), 1407–1410.
12. Granovetter, M.S. The Strength of Weak Ties. *American Journal of Sociology 78*, 6 (1973), 1360–1380.
13. Greenberg, S., Marquardt, N., Ballendat, T., Diaz-Marino, R., and Wang, M. Proxemic Interactions: The New Ubicomp? *interactions 18*, 1 (2011), 42–50.
14. Hall, E.T. *The Hidden Dimension.* Anchor, New York, 1990.
15. Harrison, S. and Dourish, P. Re-place-ing space: the roles of place and space in collaborative systems. *Proceedings of the 1996 ACM conference on Computer supported cooperative work*, ACM (1996), 67–76.
16. Hughes, J., King, V., Rodden, T., and Andersen, H. Moving out from the control room: ethnography in system design. *Proceedings of the 1994 ACM conference on Computer supported cooperative work*, ACM (1994), 429–439.
17. Insko, C.A. and Wilson, M. Interpersonal attraction as a function of social interaction. *Journal of Personality and Social Psychology 35*, 12 (1977), 903–911.
18. Jones, Q., Grandhi, S.A., Whittaker, S., Chivakula, K., and Terveen, L. Putting systems into place: a qualitative study of design requirements for location-aware community systems. ACM (2004), 202–211.
19. Larson, R. and Csikszentmihalyi, M. The Experience Sampling Method. *New Directions for Methodology of Social & Behavioral Science 15*, (1983), 41–56.
20. Levine, R.V. The Kindness of Strangers: People's Willingness to help somone during a chance encounter on a city street varies considerably around the world. *American Scientist 91*, 3 (2003), 226–233.
21. Mardenfeld, S., Boston, D., Pan, S.J., Jones, Q., Iamntichi, A., and Borcea, C. GDC: Group Discovery Using Co-location Traces. *2010 IEEE Second International Conference on Social Computing (SocialCom)*, (2010), 641–648.
22. Mayer, J.M., Motahari, S., Schuler, R.P., and Jones, Q. Common attributes in an unusual context: predicting the desirability of a social match. *Proceedings of the 4th ACM Conference on Recommender Systems*, ACM (2010), 337–340.
23. Mayer, J.M., Schuler, R.P., and Jones, Q. Towards an understanding of social inference opportunities in social computing. *Proceedings of the 17th ACM intl. Conference on Supporting Group Work*, ACM (2012), 239–248.
24. McPherson, M., Smith-Lovin, L., and Cook, J.M. Birds of a Feather: Homophily in Social Networks. *Annual Review of Sociology 27*, (2001), 415–444.
25. Merton, R.K. *Social Theory and Social Structure.* Simon and Schuster, 1968.
26. Milgram, S. The Familiar Stranger: An Aspect of Urban Anonymity. In *The Individual in a Social World: Essays and Experiments.* MA: Addison-Wesley, 1977, 51–53.
27. Morry, M.M., Kito, M., and Ortiz, L. The attraction–similarity model and dating couples: Projection, perceived similarity, and psychological benefits. *Personal Relationships 18*, 1 (2011), 125–143.
28. Newcomb, T.M. The Prediction of Interpersonal Attraction. *American Psychologist 11*, 11 (1956), 575–586.
29. Paulos, E. and Goodman, E. The familiar stranger: anxiety, comfort, and play in public places. *Proceedings of the SIGCHI Conference on Human Factors in Computing Systems*, ACM (2004), 223–230.
30. Persson, P. and Jung, Y. Nokia sensor: from research to product. *Proceedings of the 2005 conference on Designing for User eXperience*, AIGA: American Institute of Graphic Arts (2005).
31. Putnam, R.D. *Bowling Alone: The Collapse and Revival of American Community.* Simon and Schuster, 2000.
32. Schilit, B.N. and Theimer, M.M. Disseminating active map information to mobile hosts. *IEEE Network 8*, 5 (1994), 22–32.
33. Shimanoff, S.B. *Communication rules: Theory and research.* Sage Publications, Beverly Hills, CA, 1980.
34. Sykes, R.E. Initial Interaction between Strangers and Acquaintances: A Multivariate Analysis of Factors Affecting Choice of Communication Partners. *Human Communication Research 10*, 1 (1983), 27–53.
35. Terry, M. and Mynatt, E.D. Social Net: Using Patterns of Physical Proximity Over Time to Infer Shared Interests. *In Proceedings of Human Factors in Computing Systems (CHI 2002*, ACM Press (2002), 816–817.
36. Terveen, L. and McDonald, D.W. Social matching: A framework and research agenda. *ACM Transactions on Computer-Human Interactions 12*, 3 (2005), 401–434.

The Known Stranger: Supporting Conversations between Strangers with Personalized Topic Suggestions

Tien T. Nguyen[1], Duyen T. Nguyen[2], Shamsi T. Iqbal[3], and Eyal Ofek[3]

[1]University of Minnesota
Minneapolis, MN, 55455 USA
tien@cs.umn.edu

[2]Carnegie Mellon University
Pittsburgh, PA, 15213, USA
tdnguyen@cs.cmu.edu

[3] Microsoft Research
Redmond, WA 98052 USA
{shamsi,eyalofek}@microsoft.com

ABSTRACT
Striking up a good conversation with new acquaintances is often difficult. In this paper we introduce a system that uses a ranking recommendation algorithm to generate real-time personalized topic suggestions during a conversation. The system then delivers the suggestions via Google Glass. We conducted a study with 38 pairs of strangers, who received such suggestions while conversing with a person they met for the first time. Participants found the suggestions to be helpful, but only at the right moments, and for certain types of speakers. Our results contribute to the understanding of how communication interventions influence people's experience and behaviors, and enhance interpersonal interactions. Our study also presents design implications for applications on wearable devices to facilitate conversations between strangers.

Author Keywords
Conversations, strangers, personalization, topic suggestion

ACM Classification Keywords
H.4.3. Information systems applications: Communication Applications

INTRODUCTION
Meeting new people and making new friends is an important part of everyday life. Pleasant interaction with friends helps relieve stress and reduce feelings of loneliness [27]. Casual acquaintances or weak social ties can provide resources for various tasks such as job hunting, information searching, or expanding one's social network [8]. The first conversation with a new acquaintance is crucial for the establishment of a relationship [21]. However, maintaining a good first conversation with a stranger after the ice-breaking phase is often difficult.

Various studies have investigated how technologies could improve social interactions between strangers or casual acquaintances. Social games such as FishPong [30] or Table Tilt [17] are expected to encourage spontaneous social interaction among coffeehouse patrons and academic conference attendees. These games, however, were not designed to enhance the conversational experience beyond the ice-breaking phase. McCathy [11] introduced a system that displayed suggestions for conversation when two coworkers approached the system.

CHI 2015, April 18 - 23 2015, Seoul, Republic of Korea Copyright is held by the owner/author(s). Publication rights licensed to ACM. ACM 978-1-4503-3145-6/15/04...$15.00 http://dx.doi.org/10.1145/2702123.2702411

In this study, we introduced a new technique to help strangers have engaging first conversations. Strangers who share little common knowledge about each other often have difficulties finding good topics for discussion [22]. Our goal was to explore if unobtrusively providing personalized suggestions to collocutors about what to discuss in their first conversation will improve their experience.

Towards this goal, we conducted a study with 38 pairs of strangers where a background system delivers potential conversation topics of mutual interest to the participants during a face-to-face conversation. The system collects preferred topics of discussion from participants a priori and uses techniques in recommender systems to determine a list of conversation topics that would be of interest to both parties. We studied how often participants used the suggestions, how the suggestion impacted the nature of the conversation and how participants perceived the quality of the conversation compared to having no suggestions. We found that suggestions improved conversation experience but only when delivered at the right time. Our results contribute to the understanding of how communication interventions and wearable technologies can enhance interpersonal interactions, and has design implications for systems to facilitate conversations between strangers.

RELATED WORK

How strangers converse
Previous studies have analyzed how two strangers develop conversational topics during the first encounter. Initiating conversation with a stranger involves taking certain risks. Speakers do not want to appear impolite, offensive, or intrusive [22]. Therefore, they tend to start with neutral, non-threatening, safe topics such as the weather, or topics derived from known common contexts [22, 7]. These "setting topics" [22, p. 240] however can only serve as a transition step to deeper, extended conversations. They do not contribute much to familiarity, and are often quickly exhausted, or abandoned [22].

Successful transition steps with the "setting topics" enables strangers to escalate from exchanging non-intimate content (e.g. name, job, hometown, etc.) to highly intimate information on a broader range of topics (e.g. romantic relationships, sexual orientation, etc.), which Svennevig called "encyclopedic topics" [22, p. 240]. Such extended self-disclosure is the key to relationship development [1]. Various studies demonstrated that disclosure of personally relevant information, thoughts and feelings facilitates understanding, increase liking, and invite reciprocation between conversation partners [1]. But if the transition steps are not successful, the conversation becomes non-rewarding and relationships cannot develop further.

During the transition from "setting topics" to "encyclopedic topics", speakers use the personal information they obtain about each other to compute which topics are rewarding and which are not [22]. For two strangers in their first meeting, finding rewarding topics is difficult [22]. One reason for such difficulty is the lack of information about the partners' topic preferences [22]. Various studies suggest that common ground, which is the shared knowledge between two speakers, is important for maintaining the content and flow of a conversation [4]. Clark et al. [5] stated that two people could not even begin to coordinate on the content of their conversation without assuming some common ground between them. Yuan et al. [31] found that lack of common ground was among the factors preventing non-native English speakers at an American institution from engaging in informal conversations with native English speakers. Without knowledge about the partners' interests, speakers cannot predict the partners' reactions to different topics in order to choose what to say or ask [7, 8]. On the other hand, speakers may not have a good response to, or lack knowledge and interest to follow a topic that the partners suggest [22]. The lack of relationship between strangers prevents them from too much self-disclosure, thus shortening their engagement on certain topics [7, 22].

Facilitating conversation between strangers

Social games like FishPong [30] and Table Tilt [17] aim to encourage spontaneous interaction with strangers at coffee shops or conferences. However, these systems are not designed to influence the conversations content. McCathy developed GroupCast [11], a display in public areas to support conversations among people who passed by it by showing their mutual interests. However, suggestions from GroupCast might not be personalized to the preferences of each speaker. Furthermore, how suggestions affect the conversations between strangers was not evaluated.

We extend previous work to support conversation between strangers by providing suggestions that are personalized at both the individual level and pair level. To go beyond the 'setting topics', we collected information about the speaker's interests, expertise, hobbies, and other personal details with their consent, and applied recommendation techniques to extract their preferences for conversation topics, and generate suggestions that they are most likely to use.

Developing topics for conversations

To foster rewarding first conversations beyond the initial ice-breaking phase, strangers need information about each other's interests and preferences for "encyclopedic topics". Svennevig proposed that knowing areas of common expertise or interest may have strong affiliative effects, as it helps speakers establish extended common ground, and contributes to emotional bonding through common involvement in the discussion [22]. In this study we design a way to help strangers know about each other's interests to find engaging conversation topics.

Rhodes [19] proposed a system design called *Remembrance Agent,* which retrieved relevant information and delivered it to users. Our system design is similar to *Remembrance Agent,* except we use recommender systems techniques to generate a list of recommendations for a pair of strangers.

Recommender systems research shows that understanding user interests and providing viable suggestions successfully assists users in their daily tasks. These tasks range from individual level tasks (such as finding articles to read [18] or movies to watch [25]) to group level ones, such as forming a community of the same interests or building relationships on Twitter [9]). Public digital information, made available today by various online networking services, can be harnessed to extract user interests and preferences implicitly. For example, Hannon et al. [9] used tweets to infer user preferences, and subsequently were able to recommend other users they should follow. User interests and preferences can also be extracted explicitly. Nguyen et al. [13] showed that enhanced rating interfaces could improve suggestion quality. Using techniques found in recommendation system research, we generate a list of viable suggestions tuned to the preferences of both speakers (as a pair) to support first conversations.

THE CURRENT STUDY

To understand how topic suggestions during a first conversation between two strangers may help improve the strangers' communication experience, we conducted a study examining the following three research questions:

RQ1. How useful do strangers talking to each other for the first time perceive the topic suggestions to be?

RQ2. How do suggestions affect the conversational experience (regardless of whether participants use the suggestions)?

RQ3: How do participants use the suggestions they receive? Does the number of suggestions used impact the conversation experiences between these participants?

Conversation experience was measured in terms of self-reported 'liking' of the conversation, number of silences during the conversation, perceived quality of the conversation and feeling of closeness and connection with

Figure 1. A participant saw at most three suggestions via the Google Glass screen

their partner at the end of the conversation. We expect that the personalized suggestions for each participant and each pair will have positive effects on their conversations.

METHOD

We conducted a lab experiment with 38 pairs of strangers. The manipulation is the presence (or lack thereof) of topic suggestions. Each pair conversed for a total of 30 minutes, divided into two 15-minute conversation sessions. During one of the two 15-minute sessions, both participants in the pair received topic suggestions. In the other session, neither of the participants received suggestions. The order in which participants received suggestions was counterbalanced. 20 pairs received suggestions in the first session, 18 pairs received suggestions in the second session. When suggestions were delivered, participants were told that it was up to them to use the suggestions as conversation topics or ignore if not useful or desired.

Participants

41[1] pairs of English speaking participants (55 males, 31 females, aged 15 to 58, average age 27) who did not know each other were recruited for the study using a corporate recruiting service and word of mouth.

Materials

Website to collect information about participants

A pilot study with 4 participants showed that when talking to strangers, people tend to talk about six areas: 1) their interests and hobbies, 2) jobs, 3) schools, 4) skills, 5) spoken languages, and 6) cities they visited or wished to visit. Prior to the experiment, we built a website to collect[2] public data regarding jobs, schools, skills, languages, which are available in their LinkedIn profile. Participants were also asked to fill out a personal information questionnaire about their hobbies, favorite cities and personalities.

Algorithm to generate suggestions

We built a ranking recommendation algorithm to generate personalized suggestions that would be of mutual interests to both participants, or of the interests of each participant in the pair. Thus, the suggestions that were ranked highest were shown first.

First, based on the information we collected about each participant from the website, we generated a list of words or phrases as topic suggestions. We then classified the suggestions into the six aforementioned areas. For each pair of participants, based on how comfortable both participants were with each area of conversation topics, we computed a score representing how likely the pair would use each suggestion. If a suggestion is common to both participants (e.g., a mutual interest or hobby), then this score is the product of the topic preference scores of both participants. Otherwise, we performed a greedy search using Stanford's NLP library [10] and the WordNet Similarity[3] with WUP [28] semantic relatedness score to find the topics of conversation both participants wanted to discuss[4]. The score is then computed as the product of the value returned by the greedy search and the topic preference scores. Suggestions with zeros score are discarded. Finally, we manually checked the list of suggestions for each pair and removed all meaningless suggestions (such as stop words).

Delivering suggestions

To avoid interfering with the natural interactions between participants, suggestions are delivered as subtly as possible. Prior research has suggested that dyads in face-to-face conversations are able to process information subtly if delivered visually around the direction of eye gaze [15]. Thus, we used Google Glass to deliver suggestions while keeping the interference with natural eye contact to a minimum. Moreover, the Google Glass screen is only viewable by the participant wearing it. Thus we could avoid revealing the occurrence or content of suggestions to their partners. Participants could also discretely ignore or take suggestions. Figure 1 shows how the suggestions appear on Google Glass screen from the point of view of the participant wearing it.

Figure 2. Participants wore Google Glasses with some suggestions on the screen.

[1] 3 pairs were removed from the analyses due to technical problems

[2] with participant consent

[3] http://wn-similarity.sourceforge.net/

[4] We also implemented an overwritten mechanism in case we found a pair of words has higher semantic meaning than the WUP relatedness score.

Previous work [15] has shown that users are able to maintain continuity of conversations while simultaneously looking at three short phrases on a screen and while listening (not talking) to their conversation partner. Based on this, the system delivers at most three suggestions at a time, every two and a half minutes on average. Participants did not receive suggestions at the same time, and did not receive the same set of suggestions. For most pairs, we allowed approximately equal time between any two subsequent sets of suggestions. Additionally, whenever a participant seemed to be distracted, bored or out of topics for the conversation, s/he also received suggestions.

In summary, the system consists of a recommendation algorithm to pre-compute topic suggestions, a database to store the suggestions, and an interface for the experimenter to deliver the suggestions to the Google Glass.

Communication task

Participants were asked to talk to their partners about anything they wanted except topics related the current study, such as the lab location or equipment. They were also asked to not tell their partners when they receive suggestions.

Post conversation questionnaire

A paper-and-pencil post-conversation questionnaire was presented right after each conversation session to measure participants' experience during the session.

Procedure

Two participants were randomly paired up and invited to a lab experiment. The experimenter ensured that they did not know each other. Participants were asked to sit facing each other, wearing Google Glasses (Figure 2), and were instructed not to chat before the experiment started.

The experiment consisted of two conversation sessions, during only one of which they received topic suggestions. The second sessions represented what we intended to be conversations between strangers after the initial ice-breaking phase. Each conversation session lasted 15 minutes and was followed by the post conversation questionnaire. Participants wore the Glasses throughout the study. The entire experiment was video recorded. After the experiment, participants were thanked and rewarded.

Measures

Participant's personality

In the personal information questionnaire, participants answered a 10-item Big-Five personality survey measuring extraversion, emotional stability, agreeableness, conscientiousness, and openness to new experience from

Gosling et al. [6]. Following Gosling et al. [6] we average participants' answers to get the measurement for each of these 5 personalities. For easy interpretation of the results, we reverse-coded the items measuring extraversion, and averaged these items to get the measurement for introversion.

Measure	Items
Conversation Quality Cronbach's $\alpha = .78$	I enjoyed the conversation with my partner.
	The conversation was interesting.
	I was able to express my opinions.
	Finding topics of mutual interest was easy.
	I want to talk with my partner again.
Closeness to the partner Cronbach's $\alpha = .70$	I was emotional in the conversation.
	During the conversation, I connected with my partner easily.
	The conversation I just had was intimate.
Privacy concern	I am concerned about my privacy (regarding the information the system collects about me).
Knowledge of partner	I feel that know my partner as a person
Suggestion usefulness	I think the suggestions were useful
Liking of session	I like this conversation session.

Table 1. Survey items to measure participants' thoughts and feelings during conversations

Use of suggestions in each conversation session

During the conversation session in which suggestions were shown, the experimenter marked delivered suggestions that were used by participants in the conversation afterwards. We then calculated the percentage of suggestions that were adopted by the participants.

For pairs where suggestions were displayed during the first session, we counted any topics mentioned during the second session that are related to the suggestions showed during the first session. E.g., if we showed the word "eating" during the first session, and participant discussed different dining places and food during the second session, this was considered to be a valid use of a given suggestion.

Counts of silences

Following McLaughlin et al. [12] a silence in a conversation was defined to be a noticeable pause in the conversation, often after concluding an ongoing topic, accompanied by filler words such as 'umm' or 'uh', and usually followed by a new topic. The researchers listened to audio recordings of the conversations to count the silences.

Self-reported reactions towards the conversation sessions

The post conversation questionnaire consisted of 12 questions used to measure participants' subjective thoughts and feelings towards the conversation. We asked 5 questions to measure general conversation quality [3], 3 questions measuring feelings of closeness towards the partner [3], 1 question on knowledge of the partner, 1 question about liking of the session, 1 question about perceived suggestion usefulness. As privacy concern is one of the main difficulties in implementing ubiquitous computing devices (Rhodes et al [20]), we ask 1 question about their privacy concern. All questions (Table 1) used a scale of 1 (Strongly Disagree) to 7 (Strongly Agree).

RESULTS

We report the results in three main parts according to our three research questions. Table 3 provides a summary of our main findings.

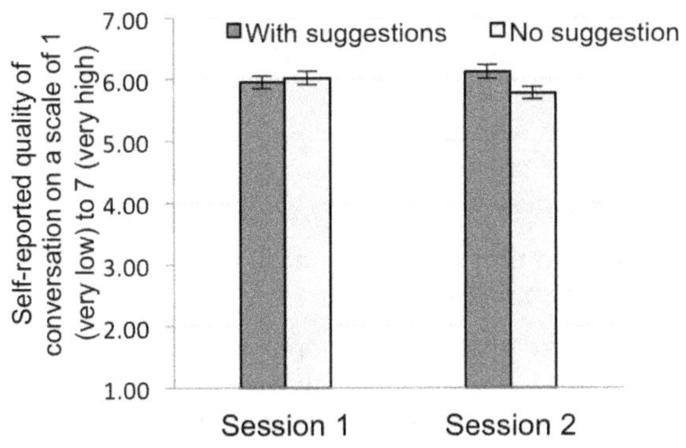

Figure 3. Participants' reported quality of conversation in two conditions, during the 1st and 2nd sessions.

RQ1: Perceived usefulness of the suggestions

First, to answer RQ1, we analyzed how useful the participants found the suggestions delivered to them. The mean rating of perceived usefulness of the suggestions was 4.68 (N = 76, SD = 1.52). A one sample t-test showed that this mean rating was significantly higher than the middle neutral point of 4 (t[75] = 3.91, p <.001), suggesting that participants found the suggestions to be somewhat useful.

Furthermore, the mean rating of perceived privacy concern regarding the information our system collected to generate the suggestions was 2.76 (N = 76, SD = 1.77). A one sample t-test showed that this mean rating was significantly smaller than the middle point of 4 (t[75] = -6.08, p <.001). So participants were not concerned about the information we collected from them for the study.

RQ2: Effects of suggestions on conversational experience

RQ2 asked how the participants' conversation experience differed if they received suggestions and if they did not. To answer this question, we compared the self-reported reaction towards the conversation sessions where participants received suggestions, and conversation session where they did not. We also compared the number of silences that we counted during each session where pairs received suggestions, and where they did not. We conducted mixed-effect ANOVAs on the self-reported liking of the session, perceived conversation quality, closeness and connection with partner during the two sessions, with suggestion conditions, the session order, and the interaction of the two as the fixed factor, and pairs and participants nested in pairs as the random factor.

Liking of the session. We did not find any significant main effect of suggestions (F[1, 74]=.14, n.s.) or session order (F[1,36]=2.34, p=.23). We also did not find any significant interaction effect (F[1, 74]=2.22, p=.14).

Perceived conversation quality. We found no significant main effect of either suggestions (F[1, 74]=.26, n.s.) or session order (F[1, 36]=2.20, p=.14), but a significant interaction effect of session order and suggestion condition (F[1, 74] = 4.42, p=.03). This means that the effect of suggestions on perceived conversation quality in the first session was different from the second session.

Hence, we analyzed the data in the first session separately from the data in the second session. We conducted mixed effect linear regressions on the participants' self-reported liking of the conversation during the first session. We included in these mixed-effect regressions the random effect of the pairs. The fixed effects are the suggestion condition (with or without suggestion), the participants' personalities, and their interaction. There was no significant difference in conversation quality between those sessions with suggestions, and those without (F [1, 36] < 1, n.s.). With data from the second session, to account for the effects of the participants' feelings during the first session, we added the fixed effects of perceived conversation quality, closeness, and knowledge of partners during the first session. Participants reported significantly higher conversation quality when they received suggestions (M = 6.12, SE = .08) than when they did not (M = 5.78, SE = .08, F [1, 35.96] = 6.76, p = .01) (Figure 3).

For only the second session, we also found a significant interaction effect of suggestion condition and participants' introversion on the reported conversation quality (N= 76, β [with suggestion] = -.01, SE = .01, 95% CI [-.03, .009], F [1, 62.5] = 5.88, p = .01). We also found a negative main effect of introversion on the reported quality of conversation (β = -.08, SE = .04, 95% CI [-.15, -.002], F [1, 62.5] = 5.88, p = .01). Figure 4 shows the relationships between introversion and self-reported conversation quality in two conditions: when participants received suggestions, and when they did not during the second session. When participants did not receive suggestions during the second session, the more introverted the participants, the lower the reported conversation quality. When they received suggestions, however, the reverse relationship emerged: the more introverted the participants, the higher the reported conversation quality.

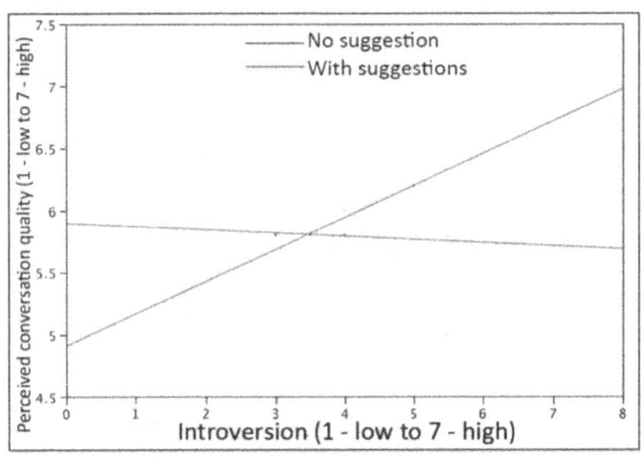

Figure 4. Relationship between self-reported conversation quality and introversion in two conditions in the 2nd session.

Perceived closeness with partner. We did not find any significant main effect of suggestions (F[1, 74]=1.24, p=.45) or session order (F[1, 36]=1.64, p=.21). But the interaction effect of suggestion and session order was significant (F [1, 74]=19.49, p<.001). This means suggestions had different effects on perceived closeness to partner in the first session and in the second session.

During the first session, there was no significant difference in perceived closeness for participants who received suggestions and for those who did not (F [1, 36] < 1, n.s.). However, during the second session, participants reported significantly higher closeness if they received suggestions (M = 4.76, SE = .15) than if they did not (M = 3.67, SE = .15, F [1, 37.86] = 23.72, p < .01) (Figure 5).

Knowledge about partner. We found a significant main effect of suggestion condition (F[1, 74]=16.85, p<.001), and a significant interaction effect of suggestion condition and session order (F [1, 74]= 29.75, p<.001). The main effect of feed order was not significant (F[1, 36]=1.23, p=.45). This also means that the effect of suggestions on self-reported knowledge about the partner differed from the first session to the second one.

During the first session, there was no significant effect of condition on the perceived knowledge about the partners (F [1, 36] = 2.82, p = .10). However, the effect of condition was significant during the second session (F [1, 37.5] = 21.98, p < .01). Participants reported knowing their partners more if they received suggestions (M = 6.11, SE = .16) than if they did not (M = 5.30, SE = .15) (Figure 6).

Number of silences. The number of silences for each pair in each 15-minute conversation session was negatively skewed and zero-inflated, with mean 1.053 (N=76, SD = 1.83, Min = 0, Median = 0, 90th percentile = 3, Max = 11). We conducted a mixed-effect general linear regression for Poisson distributions on the number of silences counted for each pair during each session, with the suggestion condition as the fixed effect, and the pair as the random effect. For the first session, we found that there were significantly more silences if participants received suggestions (M = 2.10, SD = 2.78, Min = 0, Median = 1, 90th percentile = 5.10, Max = 11) than if they didn't (M = .50, SD = .85, Min = 0, Median = 0, 90th percentile = 1.30, Max = 3, β [suggestion condition] = 1.28, SE = .53, 95% CI [.37, 1.75], z = 2.39, p = .01). For the second session, there was no difference in the number of silences between the suggestion condition and the no suggestion condition (z = 1.10, p = .28).

RQ3: Suggestion usage and its influence on conversation experience

Participants' use of the suggestions during conversations

For sessions during which participants received suggestions, how did they use these suggestions in their conversations? Each participant received an average of 15 suggestions during a 15-minute conversation session (SD = 6.34, Min = 6, Median = 15, 90th percentile = 24, Max = 31). On average, in sessions where suggestions were delivered, we found that participants used on average 3.46 suggestions, or 23% of the suggested topics (SD = .21, Min = 0, Median = .18, 90th percentile = .58, Max = .82). Half of the pairs received suggestions only in the first session. , In these pairs, during the second session, participants reused on average 1.68 suggestions or 12% of the suggestions they got in the first session (SD = .14, Min = 0, Median = .07, 90th percentile = .33, Max = .50).

We compared the percentage of delivered suggestions that were adopted by participants afterwards during the first session (when two speakers are complete strangers) and the second conversation session (after they have gone through the initial icebreaking phase). We used a mixed effect general linear regression of Poisson distribution, with the session order (first or second) as the fixed effect, and the pair as the random effect. We conducted this analysis only on the data from sessions during which participants received suggestions (N = 76). We found that participants adopted a significantly higher (z = 2.50, p = .01) percentage of the suggestions in the first session (M = .21, SE = .22) than in the second session (M = .10, SE = .14).

Effects of number of used suggestions on conversation experience

We conducted a mixed-effect linear regression on the self-

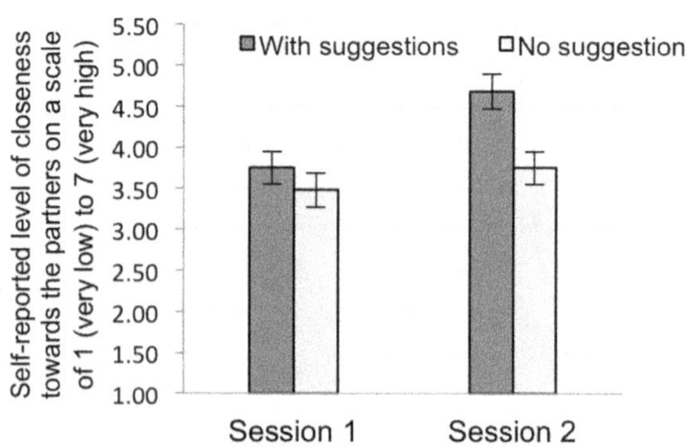

Figure 5. Participants' reported level of closeness to their partners in two conditions during the 1st and the 2nd

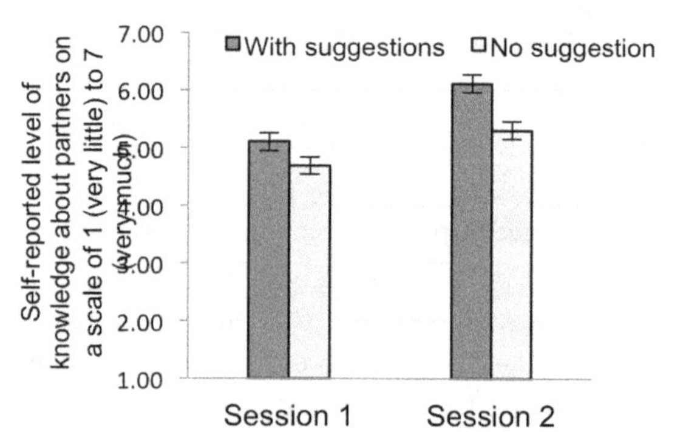

Figure 6. Participants' reported level of knowledge about their partners in two conditions, during the 1st and 2nd sessions.

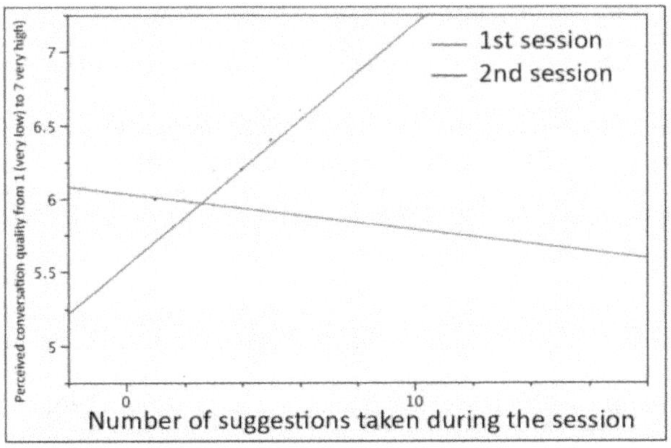

Figure 7. Perceived conversation quality as a function of the number of suggestions taken during the 1st and 2nd

reported level of liking for the session, perceived conversational quality, closeness to the partners, and knowledge about the partners as a person. We included as the fixed effects the order of the session (first or second), the number of suggestions that participants took, and the interaction between the two. The random factor is the pairs.

While we did not find any significant effect of the number of suggestions used on the level of liking of the session, perceived closeness to the partners, and knowledge of the partners as a person, we found a significant positive effect of the number of suggestions taken on the perceived quality of the conversation ($\beta = 1.06$, SE = .35, 95% CI [.37, 1.75], $F[1, 64.97] = 8.84$, $p < .01$). The more suggestions participants took, the better the quality of the conversation they reported having. Moreover, we also found a significant interaction effect of the session order, and the number of suggestion taken (β [for first session] = -1.16, SE = .35, 95% CI [-1.85, -.47], $F[1, 64.97] = 10.59$, $p < .01$). Figure 7 shows that those who received suggestions in the second session perceived the conversation quality to be better with more suggestions. However, those who received suggestions in the first session did not perceive the quality to change significantly with the number of suggestions.

Indeed, a mixed effect linear regression on the data from only the first session revealed no significant effect of the number of suggestions taken on the perceived quality of the conversation in the first session ($F[1,39] < 1$, n.s). On the other hand, a mixed effect linear regression on the data from only the second session, controlling for the perceived conversation quality reported in the first session, showed that the number of suggestions taken had a significant positive effect on the perceived quality of the conversation in the second session ($\beta = .16$, SE = .04, 95% CI [.08, .23], $F[1, 34] = 19.69$, $p < .001$) (see Figure 7). The more suggestions participants used during the second session, the higher the reported conversation quality.

Comments from the participants about the suggestions

Participants left comments about the suggestions that they received during their conversations. These comments reflected what we found with our quantitative analyses. Three main findings emerged from these comments. First, participants found the suggestions useful, and that the suggestions helped them find discussion topics when they ran out of subjects during the 2nd session. Second, participants found the equipment and the suggestions distracting at times. Third, many participants thought the suggestions were useful for introverts but not extroverts. We presented the findings and comments in Table 2.

DISCUSSION

The effect of topics suggestions on conversations between strangers

Although participants thought topic suggestions were helpful, their communication behaviors, self-reported conversation experience, and the comments they left present a more complex story. First, we found that participants adopted more suggestions during the first 15-minute conversation session when both participants knew little of each other than during the second session. As the suggestions provided topics both of them might be interested in, participants might have used the suggestions to support the process of developing mutual knowledge about each other, and laying the groundwork for further conversation contents, as suggested by Clark et al. [5]. The comments from the participants also illustrated how the suggestions "guided" them "to sub-conversations", and helped them know each other better. In contrast, we found that during the first session, participants who received suggestions did not report a better experience than those who did not receive suggestions. Perhaps during the first session, participants were able to navigate the ice-breaking phase on their own with safe "setting topics" [22]. Suggestions might have created additional pressure and awkwardness over the natural pressure of a first meeting, as participants might feel compelled to use suggestions when they appeared. Additionally, as some of them commented, it felt awkward to lose eye contact and glance at the suggestions while trying to maintain a fluid conversation. This reflects the challenges when designing technologies to foster conversations, as mobile, wearable devices have been found to create disruptions in human interactions [24].

On the other hand, in the second session, participants who received suggestions reported a better experience than those who did not. After some time familiarizing with the partners, participants might have been able to use the suggestions more selectively to start interesting discussions with less awkwardness than the first session. Some participants commented that in the second sessions the suggestions helped them find new things to talk about when they ran out of topics. This finding is also consistent with the result that during the second session, the more suggestions participants used, the better the conversation qualities they reported. An alternative explanation for our finding may be that participants felt compelled to use the suggestions and thought the conversations to be better with suggestions because they knew they and their partners would receive suggestions. However, this alternative

Themes	Example comments from participants
Suggestions were useful.	• *It is good to have something to fall back on when other conversational gambits might fail.* **(P94, suggestions during the 2nd session)** • *I think the system did help introduce common interests, especially when [we ran out of topics during the previous conversations]. Overall, the second session was easier because of it.* **(P119, suggestions during the 2nd session)**
Equipment and suggestions created distractions.	• *I think the suggestions were helpful, but maybe too 'invasive'? I felt like I needed to use them & changed topic more often than I wanted.* **(P55)** • *The suggestions need to take into account the current conversation & content. I found the suggestions were not related and using them would break the flow.* **(P96)** • *The biggest drawback to the google glass was that [my partner] was looking at the Glass sometimes instead of me, so it's feels more awkward.* **(P132)** • *While it was beneficial to have the [suggestions], it felt unnatural having to avert eye contact to look at them.* **(P106)**
Introverts would benefit from suggestions, but not extroverts.	• *For people more introverted, I think something like this could be very helpful.* **(P117)** • *In situations where two people feel shy, somewhat awkward or nervous, topics of mutual interest can encourage fluid dialogue and a more natural conversation.* **(P80)** • *The glass could be helpful for people who are not social. But for social people, glasses are distracting and bothersome.* **(P102)** • *I prefer without suggestions as I am relatively outgoing, but I can see how they would be helpful for people who have difficulties the first time they meet someone.* **(P105)**

Table 2: Summary of comments from participants

explanation cannot account for the findings that more suggestions were used in the first session than the second session, and that in the first session the suggestions did not make any difference in conversational experience.

Our study tested how the system performed both in the first and second sessions, i.e. during and after the ice-breaking phase. This sets our study apart from previous studies [e.g.,11] about systems to help strangers initiate conversations, in other words, only during the ice-breaking phase. In fact, the focus of our system is to foster conversational experience not during, but after ice breaking. Our results showed that the system achieved this goal in several aspects.

Our results thus provide preliminary evidence that the suggestions may be helpful for strangers to continue having interesting conversations after the initial ice-breaking phase. However, our results also cautioned about the awkwardness and disruptions that suggestions might cause when delivered in certain ways at certain points of time during the conversation. When two strangers first meet, most go through a typical getting-to-know-you exchange, asking familiar, almost routine questions about location, family, or work (as one participant remarked) [22]; and they can do this naturally without suggestions. Introducing suggestions in this phase, especially suggestions that require occasional averting of eye contact from the partners could interfere with the normal conversational flow and have an adverse effect on speakers' experience.

Effects of suggestions on introverts and extroverts

Another interesting result was the difference in the effect of suggestions on introverts and extroverts. When participants received suggestions, participants who scored higher on the introversion scale reported a higher perceived conversation quality. The reverse relationship was true when there was no suggestion. So the suggestion seemed to have helped introverted participants enjoy the conversation more, perhaps by encouraging exploration of a diverse array of conversational topics, as introverts tended to shy away from deeper topics after the initial ice-breaking phase. This is consistent with the comments our participants provided.

But as the introversion scale is the inverse of the extroversion scale, this result also suggests that the more extroverted the participant, the lower the perceived conversation quality. Extroverts, who naturally enjoy interactions with others, are probably able (and may even prefer) to direct the conversation on their own [23]. They may find the suggestions distracting and bothersome as our participants commented.

In summary, our results contribute to the understanding of how conversational interventions such as providing topic suggestions influence the behaviors and experience of the speakers. Our study calls attention to not only the benefits of conversational interventions, but also the drawbacks of these techniques, and the various factors such as speakers' personalities and interface design that influence the usability of these interventions.

LIMITATIONS & FUTURE DIRECTIONS

Our study is not without limitation. Our sample was limited to those who had LinkedIn profiles because we had to collect LinkedIn user data. The constraint about the topics they couldn't discuss was somewhat unnatural for the first conversation, but was necessary to examine the effects of the suggestions.

For the next steps, we hope to develop a detailed coding scheme for the transcripts of the conversations and analyze the topics discussed when the pairs received suggestions, and when they did not. We also want to analyze the non-

	Research Questions	Findings
1	Did participants find the suggestions useful?	Somewhat useful. Participants were not concerned about the information we collected from them for the study.
2	How do suggestions affect the conversational experience (regardless of whether participants use the suggestions)?	Positive effects on conversational experience but only during 2nd session: Significantly higher perceived conversation quality, closeness to partners, and knowledge of partners with suggestions than without.. Introverted participants benefited from the suggestions, but extroverted participants did not.
3	How did participants use the suggestions they received?	Participants adopted a significantly higher percentage of the suggestions in the 1st session than in the 2nd.
	Does the number of suggestions used matter?	Those who received suggestions in the 2nd session perceived the conversation quality to be better with more suggestions. However, those who received suggestions in the 1st session did not perceive the quality to change significantly with the number of suggestions.

Table 3: Summary of main findings.

verbal behaviors of the participants from the video recordings of the conversations. In future studies, we would like to conduct the study in more natural settings such as at coffee shops, parties or conferences, and where participants may not be aware that their partners receive suggestions. We also wonder if topic suggestions in the form of images instead of text, similar to IdeaExpander [26], could help improve participants' experience and how. Lastly, the current system delivered the best suggestions first. We did not test how such order of delivery influenced the conversations. Thus, it may be interesting to explore the optimal order of suggestions.

DESIGN IMPLICATIONS

First, our results demonstrate the benefits of a system that provides personalized suggestions during conversations between strangers. Such systems can make use of personal details about each person that can be collected easily from simple pre-questionnaires, or from public profiles on social network sites such as LinkedIn, and apply well-known techniques from recommender systems. These systems may be useful, especially for people who are shy and reserved, to make friends in informal contexts, such as at academic conferences, social events, or after moving to a new place.

However, our results also show that topic suggestions were only beneficial when shown at the right moment, and could even backfire by creating distractions and disruptions in the current conversational flow. Thus, a topic suggestion system should also be able to closely monitor the ongoing conversation to detect when to intervene (e.g. when both speakers run out of things to discuss and silences emerge). Previous studies ([14]) show that it is possible to detect speakers' engagement in conversations based on the conversational content. There have been several systems that monitor the emotions and behaviors of speakers in a conversation ([29, 2]). The topic suggestion mechanism can be integrated with these systems to support more rewarding interaction between strangers. Speakers could even train the system to recognize their conversation style by turning on or off suggestions as they please.

Although our participants found the topic suggestions useful, they disliked that these suggestions were not in sync with the ongoing content of the conversations, resulting in distractions. To reduce the invasiveness, and increase the benefits of suggestions, systems should propose topics to speakers related to the current flow the conversation. Dynamic suggestions, intelligently adapted to ongoing the conversational content, may even spark new ideas for speakers and broaden their conversation [26]. Moreover, systems should display suggestions according to the quality of the conversation. If the conversation is flowing without suggestion, there is no need for intervention.

Our results also cautioned about the different, even opposite, effects of suggestions on different types of speakers' personalities. Extroverts felt the suggestions were bothersome and distracting, while introverts were more receptive towards them and found them useful. So topic suggestion systems should learn the speakers' personalities to decide whether and when to deliver suggestions. Another possibility is to allow users to disable the topic suggestions if they want. Our study calls attention to the important role of collocutors' personalities in the design and use conversation interventions.

Lastly, wearable technologies enable people to receive multiple channels of information during a conversation in an unobtrusive manner. However, we found that some participants felt uncomfortable diverting their eyes to look at the device, or seeing their partners looking at the device instead of them. We wonder if other wearable technologies that are less invasive to one-on-one conversation, such as smart contact lens [16], could help ease the uncomfortable feelings and improve the conversation experience.

ACKNOWLEDGMENTS

We thank all the reviewers, our participants, members of the Natural Interaction group at Microsoft Research, & Kenny Shores for their valuable feedback.

REFERENCES

1. Altman, I., & Taylor, D. A. (1973). *Social penetration: The development of interpersonal relationships.*, Oxford: Holt, Rinehart & Winston.

2. Bergstrom, T., & Karahalios, K. (2007). Conversation Clock: Visualizing audio patterns in co-located groups. *Proc. HICSS '07,* 78-78.
3. Burgoon, J. K., & Hale, J. L. (1987). Validation and measurement of the fundamental themes of relational communication. *Communication Monographs, 54, 1,* 19-41.
4. Clark, H. (1992). *Arenas of Language Use*. Chicago: The University of Chicago Press & CSLI.
5. Clark, H. H., & Brennan, S. E. (1991). Grounding in communication. *Perspectives on socially shared cognition, 13*, 127-149.
6. Gosling, S. D., Rentfrow, P. J., & Swann Jr, W. B. (2003). A very brief measure of the Big-Five personality domains. *Journal of Research in personality, 37*, 6, 504-528.
7. Goffman, E. (1967). On face-work. In *Interaction Ritual: Essays on Face-to-Face Behavior*, 5–46. New York: Pantheon.
8. Granovetter, M. S. (1973). The strength of weak ties. *American Journal of Sociology*, 1360-1380.
9. Hannon, J., Bennett, M., & Smyth, B. (2010). Recommending twitter users to follow using content and collaborative filtering approaches. *Proc. RecSys '12*, 199-206.
10. Manning, C. D., Surdeanu, M., Bauer, J., Finkel, J., Bethard, S. J., & McClosky, D. (2014). The Stanford CoreNLP Natural Language Processing Toolkit. *Proc. ALC'14*, 55-60.
11. McCarthy, J. (2002). Using public displays to create conversation opportunities. *Proc. CSCW'02 Workshop.*
12. McLaughlin, M. L., & Cody, M. J. (1982). Awkward silences: Behavioral antecedents and consequences of the conversational lapse. *Human Communication Research, 8, 4,* 299-316.
13. Nguyen, T. T., Kluver, D., Wang, T. Y., Hui, P. M., Ekstrand, M. D., Willemsen, M. C., & Riedl, J. (2013). Rating support interfaces to improve user experience and recommender accuracy. *Proc. RecSys '13*, 149-156.
14. Nguyen, D. T., & Fussell, S. R. (2014). Lexical Cues of Interaction Involvement in Dyadic Instant Messaging Conversations. *Discourse Processes, 51*, 468-493.
15. Ofek, E., Iqbal, S. T., Strauss. K. (2013). Reducing Disruption from Subtle Information Delivery during a Conversation: Mode and Bandwidth Investigation. *Proc. CHI'13*, 3111-3120.
16. Parviz, B., Tan, D. (2011). Functional Contact Lens Monitors Blood Sugar Without Needles http://research.microsoft.com/en-us/collaboration/stories/nui_contactlens_cs.pdf, retrieved 2014-09-17.
17. Powell, E., Brinkman, R., Barnes, T., & Catete, V. (2012). Table tilt: making friends fast. *Proc. FDG'12,* 242-245.
18. Resnick, P., Iacovou, N., Suchak, M., Bergstrom, P., & Riedl, J. (1994, October). GroupLens: an open architecture for collaborative filtering of netnews. *Proc. CSCW 94*, 175-186.
19. Rhodes, B. J. (1997). The wearable remembrance agent: A system for augmented memory. *Personal Technologies, 1, 4*, 218-224.
20. Rhodes, B. J., Minar, N., & Weaver, J. (1999). Wearable computing meets ubiquitous computing: Reaping the best of both worlds. Procs. of the 3rd International Symposium on Wearable Computers, 141-149.
21. Sunnafrank, M. J., & Miller, G. R. (1981). The role of initial conversations in determining attraction to similar and dissimilar strangers. *Human Communication Research, 8*, 16-25.
22. Svennevig, J. (2000). *Getting acquainted in conversation: a study of initial interactions (Vol. 64)*. Amsterdam: John Benjamins Publishing.
23. Thorne, A. The press of personality: A study of conversations between introverts and extraverts. *Journal of Personality and Social Psychology, 53,* 718-726.
24. Tolmie, P., Crabtree, A., Rodden, T., & Benford. S. (2008). "Are you watching this film or what?": interruption and the juggling of cohorts. *Procs. CSCW '08*, 257-266.
25. Vig, J., Sen, S., & Riedl, J. (2012). The tag genome: Encoding community knowledge to support novel interaction. *Proc. TIIS, 2,* 13.
26. Wang, H. C., Cosley, D., & Fussell, S. R. (2010, February). Idea Expander: Supporting group brainstorming with conversationally triggered visual thinking stimuli. *Proc. CSCW '10*, 103-106.
27. Weiss, R. S. (1973). Loneliness: The experience of emotional and social isolation. Cambridge: MIT Press.
28. Wu, Z., & Palmer, M. (1994). Verbs semantics and lexical selection. *Proc. ACL' 94*, 133-138.
29. Yeo, Z. (2008). Emotional instant messaging with KIM. *CHI'08 Extended Abstracts, 3729-3734.*
30. Yoon, J., Oishi, J., Nawyn, J., Kobayashi, K., Gupta, N. (2004). FishPong: encouraging human-to-human interaction in informal social environments. *Proc. CSCW '04*, 374-377.
31. Yuan, C. W., Setlock, L. D., Cosley, D., & Fussell, S. R. (2013). Understanding informal communication in multilingual contexts. *Proc. CSCW '13*, 909-92

Augmenting Social Interactions: Realtime Behavioural Feedback using Social Signal Processing Techniques

Ionut Damian*, Chiew Seng Sean Tan‡, Tobias Baur*, Johannes Schöning‡, Kris Luyten‡, Elisabeth André*
*Human Centered Multimedia, Augsburg University, Germany
‡Expertise Center for Digital Media, Hasselt University - tUL - iMinds, Belgium
{damian, baur, andre}@hcm-lab.de, {sean.tan, johannes.schoening, kris.luyten}@uhasselt.be

Figure 1. Concept of the *Logue* system: A user wearing an HMD while giving a public speech (left). Using various sensors and social signal processing techniques (not illustrated), the user receives realtime feedback on his own behaviour superimposed on field of view (right).

ABSTRACT

Nonverbal and unconscious behaviour is an important component of daily human-human interaction. This is especially true in situations such as public speaking, job interviews or information sensitive conversations, where researchers have shown that an increased awareness of one's behaviour can improve the outcome of the interaction. With wearable technology, such as Google Glass, we now have the opportunity to augment social interactions and provide realtime feedback on one's behaviour in an unobtrusive way. In this paper we present *Logue*, a system that provides realtime feedback on the presenters' openness, body energy and speech rate during public speaking. The system analyses the user's nonverbal behaviour using social signal processing techniques and gives visual feedback on a head-mounted display. We conducted two user studies with a staged and a real presentation scenario which yielded that *Logue*'s feedback was perceived helpful and had a positive impact on the speaker's performance.

Author Keywords

Computer-Enhanced Interaction; Behaviour Analysis; Peripheral Feedback; Social Signal Processing

CHI 2015, April 18 - 23 2015, Seoul, Republic of Korea

ACM 978-1-4503-3145-6/15/04$15.00
http://dx.doi.org/10.1145/2702123.2702314

ACM Classification Keywords

H.5.m. Information Interfaces and Presentation (e.g. HCI): Miscellaneous

INTRODUCTION & MOTIVATION

When communicating with others we tend to use several modalities simultaneously. The most obvious way of communication is speaking to each other (verbal communication). However, our body also plays a very important role during direct communication. It communicates subtleties and emotions to others related to what we are talking about and in which context we are addressing others. In the last decades other researchers have shown that nonverbal behaviours, such as gestures, facial expressions or the way we use our voice, play a more significant role during an interaction than its verbal counterpart [5, 17, 26]. To become an efficient communicator, mastering appropriate usage of both verbal and nonverbal communication is essential.

For particular situations such as a public speech, a sales conversation or a job interview, people often need to train and practice both their verbal and nonverbal communication skills, because they can substantially contribute to reaching the set targets, e.g. getting hired [9, 12, 18]. Traditionally, training is done off-line in practice sessions with experts that provide feedback. One well-known approach is using role-plays with a coach that are recorded on video, with the recordings being analysed and discussed afterwards.

We present *Logue*, a system designed to provide in-situ and realtime feedback on a speaker's nonverbal communication unobtrusively during a public speaking scenario using a wearable display (Figure 1). The feedback aims to increase the

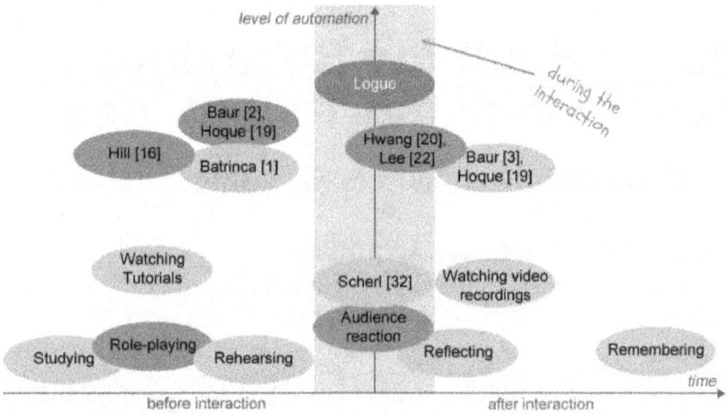

Figure 2. ***Logue*** **put in relation to current training practices and related work.**

users' awareness of their own nonverbal behaviour, as well as inform of the behaviour's appropriateness in the given scenario. *Logue* employs social signal processing techniques to analyse the speaker's performance using data from a microphone and a depth camera. Based on this processing, we can then inform the user on the speech rate, body energy and openness in realtime using an HMD.

We also discuss the challenges that arise from augmenting social interactions and use these as drivers for the design of our system. Specifically, we focus on how to provide the users with an additional information channel (behavioural feedback) without distracting them from their main task. Over the course of two user studies, we evaluate the effect of *Logue* on the user's behaviours as it is measured (A) by the system using signal processing, (B) by other persons and also (C) by the users themselves using surveying techniques. We show that *Logue* has a positive effect on the performance of the users, enabling them to adapt their behaviour in realtime.

RELATED WORK

Progress made in the area of social signal processing has enabled the development of novel tools for training social skills. These tools record and automatically analyse social and emotional signals while human learners engage in a social interaction. Popular scenarios for training social and emotional skills include job interviews [2, 19], public speeches [1, 23], military scenarios [16] or for social anxiety [28] or stress training [24]. In many cases, the analysis of social and emotional signals is done in realtime, for example, to enable the virtual character that simulates a human interlocutor to immediately respond to it. However, the human learner is usually not given any explicit feedback on her or his performance before the end of the interaction. For instance, the TARDIS system [3] enables the learners to inspect previous interactions conducted with a virtual character serving as a recruiter in a job interview. In this paper, we present an approach that provides realtime feedback on social behaviours: directives are automatically generated by a computer system while the user is engaging in a social interaction.

Live feedback has already been successfully employed in psychotherapeutic training sessions. Various devices, such as ear phones and teleprompters, have been explored to present conversational aids selected by a human supervisor. An example of such a training scenario is presented by Scherl and Haley [32]. While a trainee therapist is talking to a patient, he or she is provided with directives from a human supervisor that are displayed on a computer monitor. An evaluation revealed that computer-supported live feedback can be provided effectively during conversations between trainee therapists and their patients as long as the directives from the human supervisor are clearly formulated and kept short. However, the conversational aids are manually produced by a human coach. In contrast, our work presents an approach that generates directives automatically, drawing on the concept of augmented social interaction.

Figure 2 places our proposed concept in relation to known training practices and related work. The horizontal axis describes the timing of the training relative to the interaction itself whereas the vertical axis categorizes the methods based on their level of automation.

AUGMENTING SOCIAL INTERACTIONS

Starting from Engelbart's framework for augmenting human intellect [13], Xia and Maes [38] identify new cognitive domains for personal augmentation including memory, motivation, decision making, and mood. In our work, we propose social augmentation as a novel domain based on the consideration that social behaviour is at the core of human intellect. Social augmentation includes the use of physical items, such as miniaturized sensors and light-weight displays, to provide users with automatically generated realtime feedback on their nonverbal behaviours.

Earlier studies by Scherl and Haley [32] have shown that the display of conversational aids during social interactions may improve communication. Furthermore, studies by Ofek and colleagues [27] seem to indicate that secondary information can be consumed by users during a conversation without the interlocutors noticing it. Despite encouraging findings, there are also qualified concerns that social communication might be impaired by secondary information that interferes with it.

A particular challenge is the dual-purpose use of modalities. On the one hand, gestures may be employed to control the social augmentation interface. On the other hand, they may serve to accompany speech in social interactions. To avoid disruptions resulting from the dual-purpose use of modalities, interactions to control the interface have to be kept at a minimum or even avoided completely.

Similarly, eye gaze is also susceptible to problems regarding dual-purpose use of modalities. More precisely, there is a risk that wearable displays lead to reduced gaze contact because the user needs to split her or his attention between the display and the social interlocutor. Studies by McAtameny and Parker [25] point out some of the issues arising from the use of a head-mounted display during social interactions. While wearing a non-activated head-mounted display does not seem to influence how others perceive the user, an activated display may have a negative impact on the social interaction.

To solve these issues, a number of techniques have been developed to provide secondary information in a way that does not disrupt social interaction. Ofek and colleagues [27] conducted various experiments to derive design guidelines for the presentation of secondary information on a head-up display. They found that users can process information better when it's delivered in batches rather than sequential. Furthermore, they strongly advise against the use of auditory cues while the user is speaking. Experiments by deVaul and colleagues [11] demonstrated the potential of subliminal cues as a way to present memory aids in a non-distracting manner.

Our paper extends previous research by combing techniques for social signal processing with techniques for personal augmentation in order to provide people with live visual feedback on their social behaviour. While users are engaged in a social interaction with others, social communication aids are projected as overlays in their field of view. There are a number of options that might be taken into account to provide sociometric feedback. We excluded audio feedback because it might disturb users if they are producing sounds themselves (e.g. speaking), as noted by [36, 27]. Vibrotactile feedback has been successfully employed for teaching sensory-motor skills, for example, when playing a musical instrument [36]. However, for our purpose, haptic feedback seems less appropriate since speakers might have problems to relate a larger variety of haptic signals to specific conversational features. A number of systems that aimed to give feedback on communicative behaviours made use of mobile phones, for example, to support communication in face-to-face conversation [22], group meetings [21], during public speeches [31] or to help children with language delay [20]. Social augmentation techniques have also been explored in video conferencing settings [35] using normal desktop monitors. We decided to make use of head-mounted displays which bear the advantage that they do not require speakers to switch back and forth between the device and the interlocutor(s). Augmentation cues can be proactively provided to the users without requiring them to deliberately focus on the device. Furthermore, such devices are more suitable to provide personal information, such as feedback on the user's presentation behaviour, than external displays. External monitors might cause privacy problems as the feedback would be viewable by other persons as well. HMD's also allow the user to receive feedback while still looking in the direction of the interlocutor, which is of particular importance during social interactions. In this manner, we hope to keep the disruption of the social interaction as low as possible while giving guidance to users.

SCENARIOS

In this section we will present the reader with three concrete scenarios where social augmentation is feasible and discuss how it can benefit the users.

Job Interview

Job interviews, as a type of human-human interaction, rely on the ability of the interlocutors to read each other's behaviour and emotion. For the recruiter, the goal is to determine whether the interviewee is adequate for a specific job [30]. In this scenario, it is expected from the interviewee to remain cool and composed and not show extreme emotions [33]. More precisely, behaviours such as body expressivity (e.g. gestures, postures or facial expressions), vocal quality (e.g. speech rate, loudness, etc.) and eye gaze behaviour have been found to be problematic during job interviews [18, 8]. Considering this, the interviewee's nonverbal behaviour is a crucial element in the outcome of the whole interview and an increased awareness would only benefit this outcome.

The main challenge of this scenario is related to sensor choice. Considering the fact that a user attends job interviews in different locations, there is need for a fully wearable system that also ensures the full privacy of the applicant. To this end, sensors such as clothing embedded IMUs (inertial measurement units) or eye tracking glasses are preferable to remote sensing devices.

Information-sensitive conversation

During information-sensitive conversations, such as physician-patient conversations, ensuring sufficient behavioural awareness can be advantageous to the interaction goals. Blanch et al. [6] showed that the quality of nonverbal skills impacts how the physician is perceived by the patient. If we take the physician-patient conversation as an example, interaction augmentation can assist the physician with the delivery of sensitive information. For example, the system could remind the physician to use pauses to allow the patient to process the information, or provide feedback to increase vocal quality (e.g. speech rate, loudness) to boost the likelihood of the patient correctly understanding the message. Furthermore, an appropriate display of facial expression can also help avoid misunderstandings.

In order to allow the physician to be mobile and have consultations in different locations, body worn sensors are more appropriate than remote sensors. For instance, a microphone could be used for the speech and turn-related features and a head worn sensor, for example attached to a glass frame (or HMD), would allow the analysis of facial expressions [14].

Public Speaking

Public speakers need not only deliver a convincing message to their audience, but also inspire and generate enthusiasm at the same time. Thus, public speaking is a particularly stressful situation as the speakers need to master both their verbal and especially their nonverbal behaviour. For example, even a highly interesting message, if delivered with a reduced speech rate may cause boredom. Similarly, if the speech rate is too high, people might have difficulty understanding the message at all. The key lies in the balance.

In light of this, providing the user with feedback on nonverbal behaviour may help maintain this behavioural balance. For instance, feedback on speech rate and body energy would help the user to better convey excitement and enthusiasm, whereas increasing awareness on posture and gesture display can make the speaker appear friendlier and more approachable [29].

Unlike the other scenarios, remote sensors (e.g. video camera, depth camera, room microphone) are feasible for public

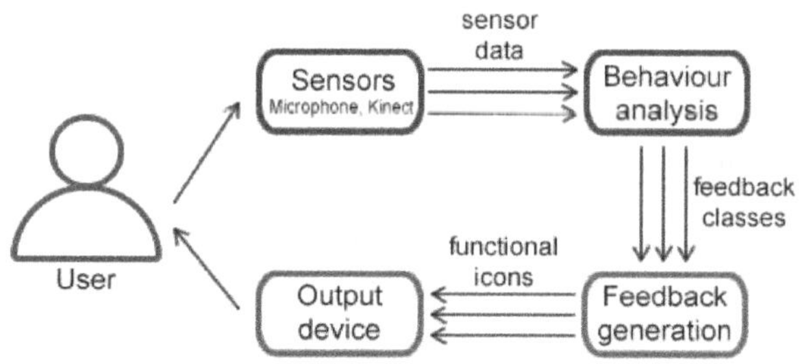

Figure 3. Structure of *Logue* showing the two main components, behaviour analysis and feedback generation, and the information loop.

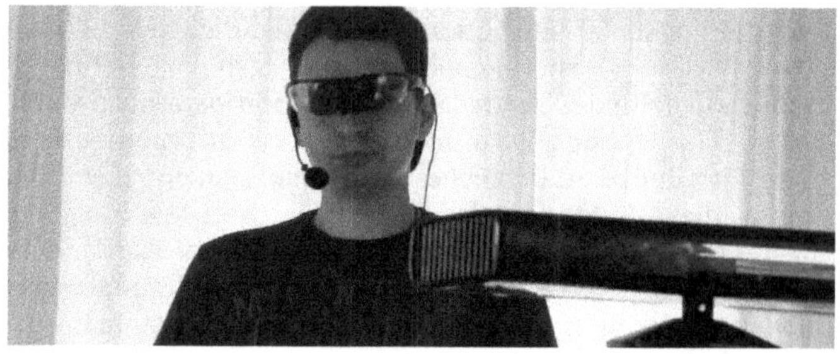

Figure 4. System setup: user wearing the HMD and microphone (far plane), and a Microsoft Kinect oriented towards him (near plane).

speaking and do not suffer from the increased intrusion level associated with body worn sensors.

THE LOGUE APPLICATION

In order to get a better understanding of the feasibility of augmenting social interaction, we implemented the *Logue* system for the scenario of public speaking. *Logue* augments public speakers by providing them with realtime feedback on their nonverbal behaviour. The aim of the system is to increase the user's awareness of her or his own body language as well as provide guidance towards improving it. Figure 3 gives an overview of the system components as well as the information loop.

Logue consists of two main components. First, the behavioural analysis component is responsible for perceiving, processing and classifying the user's nonverbal behaviour using various sensors. The resulting analysis is then sent to the feedback generation component where it is converted to functional icons, which are then displayed on the HMD.

Behaviour Analysis

In the scenario of public speaking, body expressivity and vocal quality are good features to measure the quality of the nonverbal behaviour of a speaker. Since the main goal of the system is to improve the user's awareness of her or his own nonverbal behaviour, we explicitly avoided any presentation-related features (e.g. total time, time-per-slide). Furthermore, using small-scale in-lab pretests, we narrowed down the feature set to features that are technically feasible to be recognized robustly in realtime. For example, while vocal clearness and loudness are good candidates, pretests showed that the analysis is very susceptible to environmental noise, the position of the microphone and non-vocal sounds (throat clearing, coughing). We ended up with three features (feedback classes) that provide the speaker with feedback on speech rate, body energy and openness.

To measure these three features, we use the Microsoft Kinect depth camera and the SHURE WH20 close-talk microphone paired to a TASCAM US 322 audio interface (Figure 4). The sensors' signals are processed by the SSI framework [37]. The SSI framework is an open-source project that supports the synchronized recording, processing and classification of sensor data in realtime. Its plugin-based architecture enabled us to easily expand SSI with new processing and classification plugins and build the signal processing pipeline required for *Logue*.

To compute the speech rate in realtime, we rely on work done by Jong and Wempe [10] to split voiced audio segments into syllables. The number of syllables is then divided by the length of the utterance to yield the speech rate.

Body energy is measured from the tracked positions of the user's hands in accordance with related literature [3, 7]. More precisely, we use the position of the wrist joints (as these are more robustly tracked by the Kinect than the hands) relative to the neck joint to compute the spatial displacement over the course of 5 seconds. The displacement is normalized using the arm span of the user to make the measurement user independent.

Openness is computed in a similar way. The difference is that instead of measuring the spatial displacement, we compute the Euclidean distance between the hands. However, unlike spatial extent [3], openness can also be negative if the arms cross.

Before forwarding the analysis results to the feedback component, we apply a final moving average filter to each feedback class with a window of five utterances (speech rate), 50 seconds (energy) and 30 seconds (openness). The goal here is to analyse the behaviour of the user as a whole rather than focus on fluctuations during the interaction. After this final processing step, the results of the behaviour analysis are forwarded asynchronously to the feedback generation module. In this manner, we achieve an effective update rate of one sample/utterance for speech rate and 30 samples/second for energy and openness.

Feedback Generation

The results of the behaviour analysis are converted into functional icons by the feedback generation module. Each feedback class is presented to the user using a different functional icon. A functional icon is able to express multiple intensities as well as provide information on whether the behaviour's current state is appropriate for the scenario.

For each feedback class, two thresholds (a lower and an upper threshold) determine how the behaviour state is mapped onto the intensities of the functional icons (low, medium or high). The thresholds also generate an appropriateness corridor, with behaviours within this corridor being marked appropriate and those outside inappropriate.

These thresholds were configured beforehand in a small-scale study during which, three users purposely performed well and

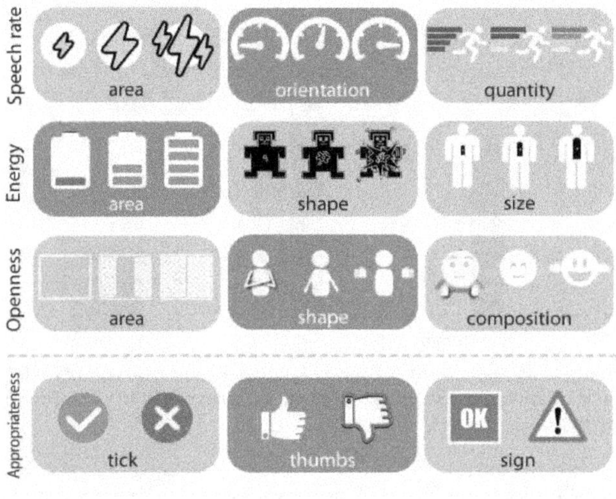

Figure 5. Initial icon set categorized by feedback classes and theme. Highlighted icon groups have been found to be most representative of their particular feedback class.

bad for each of the feedback classes. The resulting data was averaged across all participants and used to compute the two thresholds for each class. While these thresholds are meant to describe normal speaking behaviour, one could also choose other thresholds for very specific situations, e.g. to lead a presenter to perform in a highly energetic way using a loud voice.

The appropriateness of a behaviour is represented using a small symbol positioned beneath the main symbol. The main reason for separating the appropriateness from the intensity was to have both channels encoded in both shape and colour to ensure correct and fast recognition on see-through displays. Such displays are notorious for causing colour perception difficulties in uncontrolled environments [15].

Feedback Icon Selection

For *Logue* it is important that the feedback icons do not distract the users from their primary task, i.e. the social interaction itself, while still generating awareness and providing guidance. Therefore we created an initial set of 33 icons (Figure 5), designed to be understandable at a glance when viewed on a see-through HMD and to require only minimal attention for information extraction. These span our feedback classes, i.e. *speech rate*, *energy* and *openness*, and six intensity themes inspired by [4, 34] (shape, area, orientation, size, composition and quantity). The set also includes six additional icons covering the two appropriateness classes *positive* and *negative*.

Once the initial set was completed, we conducted a user study to help us select the most appropriate icons for each feedback class. For this, we split the icons into groups, each representing a single feedback class (as shown in Figure 5), and asked 25 students (4 female, 21 male; mean age of 22.4) from our university to rate on a scale from 1 (worst) to 7 (best) how representative of the feedback class each icon is.

The best rated icon groups (highlighted in Figure 5 with a dark grey background) for each feedback class have been implemented in the system. The functional icons are positioned in the upper right corner of the user's field of view to minimize distraction. The icons are shown persistently on the HMD in order to avoid unintentional jumps in gaze due to the appearance and disappearance of icons. For the visualization, we use a Vuzix STAR 1200 optical see-through HMD. It features a 1280x720 resolution spanned over two see-through displays, which offer a 23" diagonal field of view. Our system can be easily adapted to work on different HMDs, such as Google Glass.

EVALUATION

To ascertain the feasibility of the *Logue* application, we conducted two user studies using the public speaking scenario described above. For the first study, a mixed group of participants were recruited from the university to use the system in a controlled environment. They were given the task of presenting an "elevator pitch" speech to a small, targeted audience. The goal of their talks was to convince the targeted audience, which played the role of potential investors, to invest in their projects. The study aimed to quantitatively determine the impact of *Logue* on the participants' presentation performance.

For the second study, we asked senior PhD students to test *Logue* during a presentation that had to be given to peers and supervising professors at an annually organized PhD workshop. The goal of this study was to understand qualitatively the usage of *Logue* in a real setting that was not staged for the purpose of the study.

Study One: Quantitative Evaluation

The first study focuses on the collection of questionnaire data and measurement of the social signals of the participants. This allowed us to compute both subjective and objective measurements of the participants' performance.

Participants and Apparatus

We recruited a total of 15 computer science undergrad and recently graduated students (13 male and 2 female) with an average age of 26.13 (henceforth referred to as P1, $\cdots$ P15). On a 7-point Likert scale (1 = worst, 7 = very good), the participants rated themselves 3.33 for frequency of holding presentations and 4.07 on how skilful they think they are. Two employers of the institute (aged 28 and 35) were recruited to act as observers during the whole study.

The study was held in a typical conference room with the participant standing at the front of the room facing two observers at a distance of 3 m. The observers were instructed to pay attention to the nonverbal behaviour of the participants. Each participant wore the Vuzix HMD and a head-worn microphone. The Kinect was positioned in a way that did not obstruct the observers' view of the participant (Figure 6).

Task and Procedure

The participants were asked to perform two public speeches for two conditions (control and experimental) in a within subject design, i.e. one speech for each condition. In the control condition (CC) the users wore the entirety of the system setup but the feedback visualisation was deactivated. This condition provides a baseline for quantitative comparison as

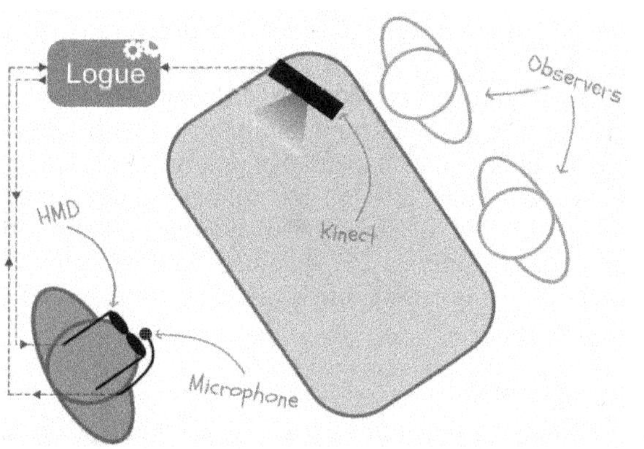

Figure 6. Evaluation setup showing the participant facing two observers while wearing the HMD and microphone. The Microsoft Kinect was positioned on the conference table between the participant and observers, and was oriented towards the participant.

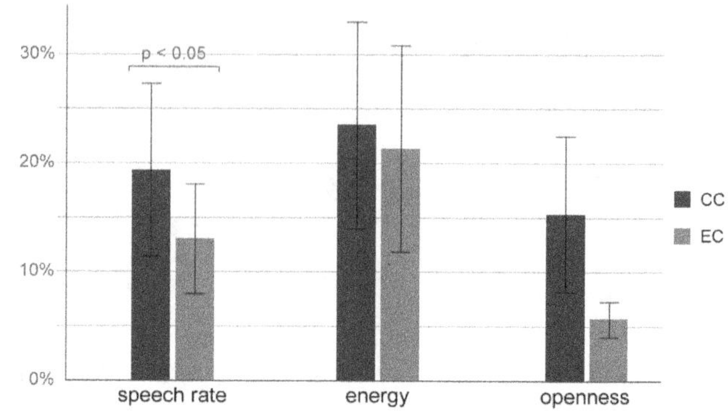

Figure 7. Percentage of inappropriate behaviour (y-axis) for each feedback class across conditions (control vs. experimental). Lower values are better.

no feedback was presented to the participants. In the experimental condition (EC) the participants received feedback on their nonverbal behaviour using the proposed *Logue* system. The observers were blind to how the conditions were assigned to the participants. To minimize learning effect, the two sessions were scheduled to be roughly two weeks apart and the order of the conditions was randomized. The topics of the speeches were various software projects on which the participants worked in the past half year. Each talk was expected to last approximately five minutes and no supportive materials (e.g. slides) were allowed. The participants were told to act as if the observers were potential investors, who might be interested in investing in their projects.

Prior to each session, participants filled out a questionnaire about their experience with regards to public speeches.[1] The participants were then given instructions on how to use the *Logue* system and the feedback mechanism was explained in detail. Emphasis was placed on making sure that each student had fully understood the correlation between her or his behaviour and the feedback icons. Afterwards, the participants were allowed five minutes to familiarize themselves with the system and ask any questions to the experimenters.

After each session, both the participant and the observers filled out a second questionnaire meant to elicit data regarding the participant's performance as a public speaker[1] and perceived user experience.[1] Lastly, a semi-structured interview with the user to gather general feedback about the system was conducted.

Results

We recorded video, audio, depth and social signal data from a total of 30 sessions in addition to the questionnaire data. The average length of each session was 4 minutes and 18 seconds. The audio recording from one participant had to be excluded from the analysis due to a medical condition that caused frequent throat clearings and interfered with the audio analysis. Similarly, the recording of one participant was omitted from the energy and openness analysis due to skeleton tracking problems.

[1] `http://hcm-lab.de/downloads/chi15`

(A) Impact on objective measurements. We processed the recorded data for each feedback class by computing how many of the participants' vocal segments ("utterances") measured speech rates outside of the thresholds. We normalized this value by the total amount of utterances of the session and averaged it over all participants to get a measure of the speech rate inappropriateness for each condition. We proceeded in an analogue way for energy and openness. However, since the energy and openness are computed continuously (unlike the speech rate), we used the normalized duration in seconds of the time spent outside of the thresholds instead of the number of utterances.

The resulting values can be seen in Figure 7. A One-Way Repeated Measure MANOVA revealed by trend a multivariate effect of social augmentation on the amount of inappropriate behaviour for speech rate, energy and openness, $F(3, 11) = 3.215$, $p = .065$. When looking at the feedback classes individually, a Wilcoxon signed rank test showed significant differences between the conditions for speech rate with $p = 0.033$, $Z = -2.134$. There was no significant effect for energy and openness though. As Figure 7 illustrates, we measured increased standard errors of the mean for all feedback classes. These were caused by the participants who never crossed the thresholds and thus yielded zero amount of inappropriate behaviour.

When taking a closer look at the data we can observe how the participants reacted to the feedback. Figure 8 shows P13's openness over time and how it was affected by the behavioural feedback (symbolized by the vertical lines). As can be seen in the figure, P13 immediately reacted on the systems feedback by performing more open gestures.

(B) Impact on observer's perception. The observers rated the participants as significantly more open ($F(1, 14) = 3.333$, $p = 0.045$) when the social augmentation mode was activated than when it was not. This suggests that the social augmentation mode had an observable impact on the participants' behaviour. However, we did not find any significant differences for the other dimensions of the observers' questionnaire.

(C) Impact on self perception. T-tests for one sample revealed that the participants' subjective ratings of the social augmentation mode were significantly above the neutral value of 4.0

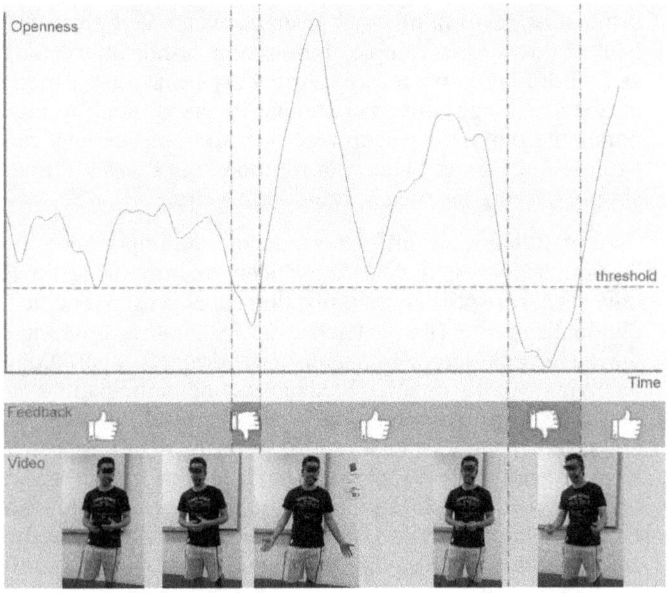

Figure 8. Example of participant's openness over the course of a session in the experimental condition.

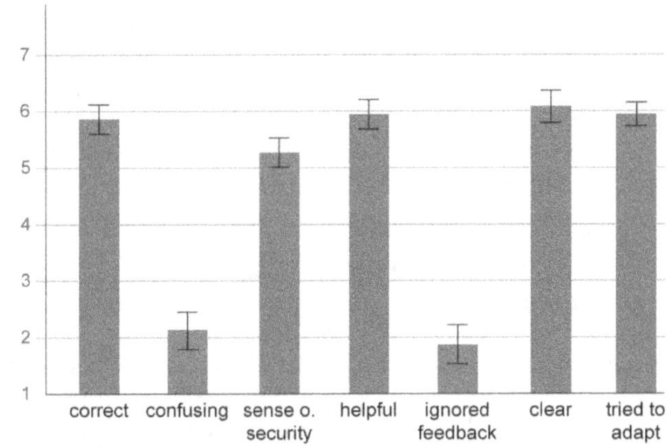

Figure 9. Results of the user experience questionnaire showing means on a 7-point Likert scale (1 = worst, 7 = very good). Two items (*confusing* and *ignored feedback*) are reverse-scored.

(Figure 9). The participants thought the feedback was correct ($t(13) = 6.77$, $p < .0005$), helpful ($t(14) = 7.25$, $p < .0005$) and not confusing ($t(14) = -5.332$, $p < .0005$). The feedback also gave them a sense of security ($t(14) = 4.75$, $p < .0005$) and they said that they did not try to ignore the feedback ($t(14) = -6.094$, $p < .0005$). A comparison between the conditions yielded no evidence that the participants felt distracted by the social augmentation mode or that the social augmentation mode increased the difficulty of the main task.

Study Two: Qualitative evaluation in a real setting

Following our first study, where we made use of an enacted scenario, we conducted a second study in order to test *Logue* in a real presentation setting. To this end, we recruited speakers from an annual doctoral workshop who volunteered to make use of *Logue* during their presentation. The workshop gives computer science PhD students the opportunity to present the current state of their work to their peers and supervisors. The experimental setting did not only expose the participants to more realistic conditions, but the quality of the presentation also had an impact on the participants' standing within the laboratory. Apart from the fact that some people made use of *Logue* during their presentation, the workshop was held in a similar manner as the years before.

Participants and Apparatus

For the second study, three senior computer science PhD students (P16, P17 and P18) were recruited. Similar to the other workshop participants, they had to give a prepared presentation on their PhD topics. The talks took place in a seminar room, with the participant standing at the front of the room and facing the audience, which consisted of 13 peers and two supervising professors. All speakers made use of slides to accompany their presentation. The presentations lasted about 30 minutes and typically included ten minutes of discussion.

Task and Procedure

After the talk and the scientific discussion, an open discussion on the style of presentation followed. The audience was asked questions regarding the perceived quality of the talk as well as whether they felt the proposed system had influenced the quality of the presentation in a positive or negative manner. Later, we conducted a semi-structured interview with each participant to elicit her or his impression of the system.

Results

We highlight three outcomes of the semi-structured interviews regarding *Logue*'s impact on behaviour, its level of distraction and its usefulness.

Did you adapt your behaviour? Speaker 1 (P16) stated "One time during the presentation I felt I was talking too fast and then I remembered I had this thing on my nose so I looked at the feedback and this was actually the case. I then tried to talk slower." We then asked the audience what they thought about the speech rate. One observer said "[the speech rate] was not actually disturbing, but it would have helped if he would have talked slower," indicating that there were indeed issues with the speaker's speech rate. P17, who told us prior to the study that he is aware he talks really fast, explained: "I was surprised that the speech rate did not become red sooner [...] once I saw the feedback that I was talking too fast, I tried too adapt." Hence, *Logue* had an effect on their presentation and they tried to adapt their behaviour as suggested by the system.

Was the system distracting? All participants complained about the bulkiness of the HMD. Despite this, P16 added "it is a very interesting concept, most of the time I did not perceive the system, only when I consciously looked at the feedback. It would be interesting to try it out for a longer period of time, for example to use it when teaching a class ... but with the Google Glass." P17 also said "the system was unobtrusive [...] I consciously looked at the feedback from time to time." We take this as a positive sign that *Logue* does not pose an unacceptable distraction for the speakers.

Would you use it? When asked whether they would use the system, all were positive. P16 said: "I would use it during real presentations or while teaching a class. Or to train for a presentation;" P17 was more reserved and said "If you used it regularly you would get a feeling for what's good or bad so that you might not need it any more after a while." These statements are encouraging, suggesting that *Logue* provides sufficient value to warrant its regular use, for example during lectures.

Discussion

Impact on behaviour

The results from the first study suggest that the system has an impact on the behaviour of the participants. For all three feedback classes, we were able to measure improvements over the control condition in terms of amount of appropriate behaviour as measured by the system, with significant effects for the speech rate.

To get a better understanding of how the system impacted the behaviour of a speaker, we refer to Figure 8. It shows how P13 adapted his openness after the feedback changed, but also how it slowly degraded over time until another correction was needed. This effect further strengthens the potential of the proposed approach, as it acts similar to a reinforcement technique, repeatedly reminding the users to adapt their behaviours. This effect was found among multiple participants and is backed up by statements from the semi-structured interviews from both studies. For instance, P1 stated "I think the system helped me a lot as it reminded me to talk slower. This is a problem many people pointed out to me after I hold a presentation and it felt good to get the feedback during the talk."

In some cases we found evidence of a longer term effect on the participants. During his second session (CC), P10 used very broad gestures when describing his project's composition. When confronted, he admitted to remembering the feedback from the first session (EC) despite them being two weeks apart. While this effect may have had a negative impact on the actual goal of the first user study, it is nevertheless encouraging for the scope of the project and we plan to investigate this as part of our future work.

Need for personalization

It is interesting to note that some participants did not cross the thresholds at all. Furthermore, participants seemed to react differently to the feedback. Some adapted the behaviour instantly, others gradually and a few participants ignored it. This can be explained by a heterogeneous distribution of presentation skill among the participants. If we classify the participants into experts and novices based on their answers from the demographics questionnaire, we notice some interesting trends. Novice users improved their speech rate more than experts (mean decrease in amount of inappropriate behaviour $\Delta = 9.3\%$ versus $\Delta = 0.9\%$). This shows that experts are already speaking at an optimal speech rate. Remarkably, when looking at the openness dimension, the effect is reversed. The experts managed to improve more ($\Delta = 31.5\%$) than the novices ($\Delta = 1.2\%$). A possible explanation for this is that the participants who rated themselves bad at public speaking (i.e. the novices) appeared to be more introverted and thus had difficulties performing open gestures even when given feedback to do so. For example, during the post-hoc interview, P1 said "I did not know how to correct my behaviour. I tried to perform more gestures, but I found it very difficult to incorporate these into my performance." A similar statement came from P15: "I knew I had to move more, but I was afraid that simply moving my hands would look weird."

We argue that these differences denote the importance for a customizable system. More precisely, there is need for not only scenario-specific customization but also user-specific individualization. This is backed up by another observation during the post-interaction interviews: despite all participants receiving equally detailed feedback, some participants stated that they were overwhelmed by the feedback whereas others asked if we can increase the level of detail on the behaviour analysis. We received similar feedback from the second study, with P16 stating: "It would be good to know how far above the threshold I am." P17 also noticed the need for customization when saying that in its current state, *Logue* "is good for newbies" but "probably not accurate enough for professionals."

Participants also stated that they can envision themselves using the system as preparation for stressful social situations such as public speeches. In such training environments, an increased level of detail for the peripheral feedback would be feasible, as the primary task is no longer the actual interaction, but the training itself. We intend to investigate this aspect in future evaluations.

Not a distraction

When asked whether the system distracted them from the act of giving a talk, the participants assured us that the impact was minimal. P15 stated "It felt distracting at first, but then I noticed that I can look through the displayed feedback. Once this was clear, I only glanced at the feedback from time to time to see whether anything has changed." Other participants, including the senior PhD students from the second study, made similar statements, saying that they were checking on the behaviour during speech or thinking pauses to see if something had changed. These results support our initial design choices, in particular the use of persistent visual feedback. We argue that in this manner, the participant is able to decide when to access the information, thus minimizing the impact on the primary task. We aim at a more in depth analysis of this aspect in future work. We are especially keen on comparing different feedback delivery methods and modalities.

Sense of security

The semi-structured interviews also revealed an increased sense of security for the participants in the experimental condition. This was even the case for participants who behaved appropriately the whole time. P6 expressed: "I would look at the icons from time to time and seeing them green made me feel better about my performance." The participants who did the control condition after the experimental condition even stated that they "missed" the system as they were unsure of the appropriateness of their behaviour. We received similar statements from the three senior PhD students in the second study, who can be regarded as more experienced speakers. Both P17 and P18 mentioned an increased sense of security, with P18 saying "It was a good feeling seeing everything green ... it's like applause, or as if someone looks at you and nods. However, the green lasts longer than a nod [laughs]." P17 was more cautious: "it could help with feeling more secure [...] if you are untrained and get cold feet."

Social acceptability

During the second study we also asked the audience after every presentation for their thoughts and feelings on the system. Overall, they mentioned that the system appeared odd to them in the beginning because of the bulkiness of the HMD. However, they soon got used to it and it did not distract them from the actual presentation. It is very likely that a lighter HMD would increase the acceptability in the eyes of the audience. No privacy-related concerns were raised by the audience or the speakers themselves. However, this is most likely due to the study setup and the technical affinity of the participants. Nevertheless, we argue that as long as the system only analyses the user's own behaviour, *Logue* does not violate the privacy of surrounding persons.

Limitations

A major limitation of this initial implementation of augmented social interaction was the HMD, as almost all participants complained about its weight and size. However, these issues will be mitigated when transitioning to a lighter HMD, such as Google Glass.

Although the system had a positive effect on the participants' behaviour as measured by the system, no major effects were noticeable on the perception of the observers. One possible explanation for this is that accurately assessing another person's behaviour is very difficult. Furthermore, the quality of a presentation is also a very subjective measure making the search for an objective definition of a perfect presentation futile. Most of us have witnessed good talks, but which were nothing alike. Considering this, it is possible that for our observers, different feedback classes and thresholds might have had a larger effect on their perception of the talks. The fact that we only had two observers (the objective sensor measurements were the study's main focus) is also likely to have contributed. In future studies we would like to employ a larger number of observers in the hope of getting a better assessment of the audience's perception.

CONCLUSION AND FUTURE WORK

The aim of augmented social interaction is to inform the user of shortcomings in the nonverbal behaviour and thus, enable her or him to adapt the behaviour in an attempt to improve the outcome of the interaction. To get a better understanding of how this would translate to an actual system, we implemented *Logue*, a system that augments public speakers using a head-mounted display and various sensors. *Logue* provides the user with behavioural feedback on two levels. First, it informs the user of the current state of her or his speech rate (How fast am I talking?), body energy (How much do I gesticulate?) and openness (How open is my posture?). Secondly, the system indicates the quality of each of these three behavioural cues in relation to the public speaking context. For example, a high speech rate would be marked as inappropriate as it may impact the listeners' ability to follow the talk. We evaluated *Logue* not only in a staged, but also in a real presentation setting to see how it impacts the behaviour of the user. Both studies yielded promising results, with users being positive about the effect the system has on one's performance and mental state while not distracting from the main task. In the first study we also collected objective data from the behaviour analysis component. Here we found evidence for improvements across all three dimensions, i.e. speech rate, body energy and openness, when using *Logue*.

The main contribution of the paper lies in the design and implementation of a new form of realtime nonverbal behaviour feedback during social interactions using wearable devices and sensors. To achieve this, multiple software components have been designed and integrated into one coherent system. The system is open source and available for download.[2]

Overall, we find it highly motivating to see how well this initial prototype was received. Its mix of peripheral feedback and social signal processing enabled users to adapt their nonverbal behaviour during the actual interaction without degrading the primary task. Work is still required on the scenario level, especially when it comes to choosing feedback classes and setting thresholds. Here, we would like to conduct more in-depth studies to accurately determine which configuration of feedback classes and thresholds are representative for good and which for bad public speaking behaviour.

Acknowledgements. This work was partially funded by the EC within FP7-ICT-2011-7 (288578 - TARDIS)

REFERENCES

1. Batrinca, L., Stratou, G., Shapiro, A., Morency, L.-P., and Scherer, S. Cicero - towards a multimodal virtual audience platform for public speaking training. In *Proc. IVA*, vol. 8108. Springer, 2013, 116–128.

2. Baur, T., Damian, I., Gebhard, P., Porayska-Pomsta, K., and André, E. A job interview simulation: Social cue-based interaction with a virtual character. In *Proc. SocialCom*. IEEE, 2013, 220–227.

3. Baur, T., Damian, I., Lingenfelser, F., Wagner, J., and André, E. Nova: Automated analysis of nonverbal signals in social interactions. In *Human Behavior Understanding*, vol. 8212 of *LNCS*. Springer, 2013.

4. Bertin, J. *Semiology of graphics: diagrams, networks, maps*. University of Wisconsin press, 1983.

5. Birdwhistell, R. L. *Kinesics and context: Essays on body motion communication*. University of Pennsylvania press, 2011.

6. Blanch, D. C., Hall, J. A., Roter, D. L., and Frankel, R. M. Is it good to express uncertainty to a patient? correlates and consequences for medical students in a standardized patient visit. In *Proc. EACH*, vol. 76 (2009), 300 – 306.

[2] `http://goo.gl/QXGyRG`

7. Caridakis, G., Raouzaiou, A., Karpouzis, K., and Kollias, S. Synthesizing gesture expressivity based on real sequences. *Multimodal Corpora* (2006).

8. Carl, H. Nonverbal communication during the employment interview. *ABCA Bulletin 44*, 4 (1980).

9. Cohen, B. M., and Etheredge, J. M. Recruiting's main ingredient. *Journal of College Placement* (1975).

10. de Jong, N. H., and Wempe, T. Praat script to detect syllable nuclei and measure speech rate automatically. *Behavior Research Methods 41*, 2 (2009), 385–390.

11. DeVaul, R. W., Pentland, A. S., and Corey, V. R. The memory glasses: Subliminal vs. overt memory support with imperfect information. In *Proc. ISWC* (2003).

12. Drake, L. R., et al. How do employers value the interview?. *Journal of College Placement 32*, 3 (1972).

13. Engelbart, D. C. Augmenting human intellect: A conceptual framework. Air Force Office of Scientific Research, AFOSR-3233, 1962.

14. Fukumoto, K., Terada, T., and Tsukamoto, M. A smile/laughter recognition mechanism for smile-based life logging. In *Proc. AH*, ACM (2013), 213–220.

15. Gabbard, J. L., Swan, J. E., Zedlitz, J., and Winchester, W. W. More than meets the eye: An engineering study to empirically examine the blending of real and virtual color spaces. In *Proc. VR*, IEEE (2010), 79–86.

16. Hill J, R. W., Gratch, J., Marsella, S., Rickel, J., Swartout, W. R., and Traum, D. R. Virtual humans in the mission rehearsal exercise system. *KI 17*, 4 (2003), 5.

17. Hogan, K. *Can't Get Through: Eight Barriers to Communication*. Pelican Publishing, 2003.

18. Hollandsworth, J. G., Kazelskis, R., Stevens, J., and Dressel, M. E. Relative contributions of verbal, articulative, and nonverbal communication to employment decisions in the job interview setting. *Personnel Psychology 32*, 2 (1979), 359–367.

19. Hoque, M. E., Courgeon, M., Martin, J., Mutlu, B., and Picard, R. W. Mach: My automated conversation coach. In *Proc. UbiComp* (2013).

20. Hwang, I., Yoo, C., Hwang, C., Yim, D., Lee, Y., Min, C., Kim, J., and Song, J. Talkbetter: Family-driven mobile intervention care for children with language delay. In *Proc. CSCW*, ACM (2014), 1283–1296.

21. Kim, T., Chang, A., Holland, L., and Pentland, A. S. Meeting mediator: Enhancing group collaborationusing sociometric feedback. In *Proc. CSCW*, ACM (2008).

22. Lee, Y., Min, C., Hwang, C., Lee, J., Hwang, I., Ju, Y., Yoo, C., Moon, M., Lee, U., and Song, J. Sociophone: Everyday face-to-face interaction monitoring platform using multi-phone sensor fusion. In *Proc. MobiSys*, ACM (2013), 375–388.

23. Li, X., and Rekimoto, J. Smartvoice: a presentation support system for overcoming the language barrier. In *Proc. CHI*, ACM (2014), 1563–1570.

24. Lu, H., Frauendorfer, D., Rabbi, M., Mast, M. S., Chittaranjan, G. T., Campbell, A. T., Gatica-Perez, D., and Choudhury, T. Stresssense: Detecting stress in unconstrained acoustic environments using smartphones. In *Proc. UbiComp*, ACM (2012), 351–360.

25. McAtamney, G., and Parker, C. An examination of the effects of a wearable display on informal face-to-face communication. In *Proc. CHI*, ACM (2006), 45–54.

26. Mehrabian, A. *Silent messages: Implicit Communication of Emotions and Attitudes*. Wadsworth Publishing Co Inc, Belmont, 1981.

27. Ofek, E., Iqbal, S. T., and Strauss, K. Reducing disruption from subtle information delivery during a conversation: Mode and bandwidth investigation. In *Proc. CHI*, ACM (2013), 3111–3120.

28. Pan, X., Gillies, M., Barker, Clark, D. M. C. M., and Slater, M. Socially anxious and confident men interact with a forward virtual woman: An experiment study. *PLoS ONE 7*, 4 (2012), e32931.

29. Pease, A. *Body Language*. Sheldon Press, London, 1988.

30. Posthuma, R. A., Morgeson, F. P., and Campion, M. A. Beyond employment interview validity: A comprehensive narrative review of recent research and trends over time. *Personnel Psychology 55*, 1 (2002).

31. Saket, B., Yang, S., Tan, H., Yatani, K., and Edge, D. Talkzones: Section-based time support for presentations. In *Proc. MobileHCI*, ACM (2014), 263–272.

32. Scherl, C. R., and Haley, J. Computer monitor supervision: A clinical note. *The American Journal of Family Therapy 28*, 3 (2000), 275–282.

33. Sieverding, M. be cool!: Emotional costs of hiding feelings in a job interview. *International Journal of Selection and Assessment 17*, 4 (2009), 391–401.

34. Szczerba, J., Hersberger, R., and Riegelman, A. Design and evaluation of a differential speedometer. In *Proc. HFES Meeting*, vol. 56 (2012), 1629–1633.

35. Tan, C. S. S., Schöning, J., Luyten, K., and Coninx, K. Investigating the effects of using biofeedback as visual stress indicator during video-mediated collaboration. In *Proc. CHI*, ACM (2014), 71–80.

36. van der Linden, J., Johnson, R., Bird, J., Rogers, Y., and Schoonderwaldt, E. Buzzing to play: Lessons learned from an in the wild study of real-time vibrotactile feedback. In *Proc. CHI*, ACM (2011), 533–542.

37. Wagner, J., Lingenfelser, F., Baur, T., Damian, I., Kistler, F., and André, E. The social signal interpretation (ssi) framework - multimodal signal processing and recognition in real-time. In *Proc. ACM MM* (2013).

38. Xia, C., and Maes, P. The design of artifacts for augmenting intellect. In *Proc. AH*, ACM (2013).

Understanding Long-Term Interactions with a Slow Technology: An Investigation of Experiences with FutureMe

William Odom
School of Interactive Arts and Technology
Simon Fraser University
Surrey, BC, Canada
wodom@sfu.ca

ABSTRACT
Emerging over a decade ago, *slow technology* is a design philosophy aimed at supporting experiences of reflection through and on technology in everyday life. Recent research has suggested that slow technologies can open up new forms of interaction with digital content that support self-reflection and re-visitation of the past. However, little work has investigated people's long-term interactions with systems that embody this design strategy. To investigate, a qualitative study with 31 participants was conducted to understand their long-term experiences with FutureMe—a slow technology that has been in use for over twelve years by more than one million people. Findings reveal that, despite its simplicity, FutureMe produced a range of outcomes—from profound reminiscence to unsettling encounters. Findings are interpreted to present opportunities and implications for future research and practice initiatives.

Author Keywords
Slow Technology; Temporality; Reflection; Memories.

ACM Classification Keywords
H.5.m. Information interfaces and presentation (e.g., HCI): Miscellaneous.

INTRODUCTION
The growing presence of social, cloud and mobile computing has created a world in which people generate, manipulate, and share digital content at larger scales and faster rates than ever before. These new technologies have enabled people to create vast collections of digital materials that capture their life experiences—a valuable resource for connecting with others and reflecting on one's own life [5,16,18,30]. People also now exchange digital content nearly instantaneously across vast distances, generating a sense of social presence and closeness with others no matter their physical location [15,25,36].

CHI 2015, April 18 - 23 2015, Seoul, Republic of Korea

978-1-4503-3145-6/15/04···$15.00
http://dx.doi.org/10.1145/2702123.2702221

These technological trends have opened up many opportunities to support people in nurturing social relationships as well as contemplating their life experiences. Yet there are growing concerns in the HCI community over how the rapid acceleration of personal digital content production and accumulation might complicate the longer-term significance of these materials. As digital archives grow larger, it becomes increasingly difficult to get a grasp on just how big they are and what is captured within them [33,37]. People's personal digital content is also becoming fragmented across many different systems leading to losses in control over and awareness of these things [27]. These effects can lead to people feeling progressively less interested in engaging with their digital collections, which limits their ability to be meaningful resources for reflection and social connection in the future [18,27,37].

In parallel to these emerging issues, there has been growing interest in how designing for slowness and reflection [9,11,19,20,34] can open up new and radically different ways of engaging with technology in everyday life. Several recent studies have begun to suggest that *slow technologies* can open up meaningful forms of interaction with digital content that support experiences of self-reflection and re-visitation of the past [14,26,35]. However, little work to date has investigated people's actual *long-term* experiences with interactive systems that embody this design strategy.

To investigate these issues, we conducted in depth interviews with 31 participants to understand their long-term experiences with FutureMe—a slow technology that has been in use for over twelve years by more than one million users (www.futureme.org). FutureMe enables people to send emails and photos delayed by to 60 years to their 'future self' or to others. Despite its relative simplicity, findings revealed a range of outcomes emerged across our participants' long-term interactions with FutureMe. This included experiences of reminiscence to leveraging slowness to work through difficult social circumstances to unexpected and disturbing encounters.

This paper makes two contributions. First, it provides rich descriptions of people's long-term experiences with a slow technology. Second, it describes considerations for future research and practice initiatives in the HCI community with an eye toward framing interactions with personal digital content within an expanded temporal framing.

BACKGROUND AND RELATED WORK

Material possessions play important roles as triggers for personal and shared memories; they capture and signify our evolving sense of self and social relationships with others over time. Csikszentmihalyi and Rochberg-Halton [6] articulate the complex ways material things represent the development of life goals and achievements. Belk [3] offers a framework for understanding how people *extend* their sense of self through their things, in part by drawing on them as resources for self-reflection. In parallel to Belk's theorization, McAdams characterizes identity construction as the development of a coherent *life story*—a synthesis of stories uniting events from the past and present interwoven with aspirations for the future [21]. Here, possessions play central roles in pointing back to the past, capturing a current sense of self, and projecting desired futures. More broadly, many others across the social sciences and humanities have investigated the complex roles material artifacts play in supporting memory, reflection, and reminiscence.

Within the HCI community, a growing body of research continues to emerge that focuses on how experiences of reflection and reminiscence can be better supported by interactive systems. Researchers [16,18,30] have presented values-oriented approaches to designing tools to support the archiving of cherished digital content. Several projects have implemented novel ways of embodying and interacting with sentimental digital content [e.g., 10,31]. Recent studies have expanded focus to online environments, illustrating how the generation of digital content through various services can produce meaningful resources for self-reflection and exploration of social relationships [1,5,38].

However, there are growing concerns in the HCI community over the rapid accumulation of digital content and how this trend might complicate the longer-term value of these materials. As digital collections swell in size, it makes it difficult for people to gauge an accurate sense of their size and the memories captured within them [18,29,33,37]. This can make people feel progressively less interested in curating their collections, diminishing their ability to function as resources for identity exploration, self-presentation and reflection over time [e.g., 27]. The proliferation of digital content is also leading to lead to experiences of over-connection [12] and, in some cases, migration away from interactive systems entirely [2].

In parallel to these issues and, in some cases motivated by them, there has been a resurgence of interest in the HCI community in slow [9,11,17,19,20] and reflective [34] design strategies. Here, slow and reflective design share similar aims in their agenda to provoke reflection on one's life and the role of technology in it. On a deeper level, these design strategies present an alternative reconfiguration of human interaction with technology that brings temporality into focus and foregrounds how human-technology relations can evolve over time in rich and complex ways.

Inspired by these design strategies, several recent studies have explored how enforcing longer time periods between the use and non-use of personal digital content may open up new opportunities for reflection and reminiscence. Postulator [14] is an online application that enables people to send annotated images or videos to one's self or others at any point in the future. The Postulator system shares similar ambitions of FutureMe, but to date has yet to be formally evaluated. The Reflexive Printer [35] explores technology-mediated reminiscence by, once per day, selecting one photo from its user's smartphone, physically printing it, and then provoking the user consider whether the digital photo should be deleted or saved. This prototype was deployed in a pilot study with two users over a three-week period where initial findings suggested that the daily material emergence of photos could be successful at supporting reminiscence. The Photobox [26] is a slow technology embodied in the form of a wooden chest that randomly selects and prints a digital photo from its owner's Flickr archive four or five times per month. Three Photoboxes were deployed in three households respectively over a fourteen-month period. Findings revealed a shift in people's attitude from frustration to appreciation as the slow interaction pattern helped build anticipation around when another photo would print and what memories it might contain. These studies are promising; however, they remain small in scope in terms the number of participants engaged and the duration of time people experienced the respective design artifacts.

Collectively, these strands of research have made important contributions to understanding the growing presence of digital content in people's everyday lives. They also reveal that new problems are emerging as the rapid proliferation of digital content threatens its ability to function as a valuable resource for reflection. Nascent research has shown slow technology could be an intriguing approach to mediate and support experiences of self-reflection, contemplation, and social connection. However, virtually no work to date has explored the effect of this design strategy on people's experiences over a long-term timescale. In this paper, we take a step toward addressing this gap by (i) contributing a rich, descriptive understanding of people's long-term experiences of a slow technology aimed at supporting self-reflection and re-visitation of social relationships and (ii) interpreting these findings to frame future research and practice initiatives in the HCI community.

METHOD AND PARTICIPANTS

FutureMe (www.futureme.org) is an online application that enables people to send emails and photos delayed by potentially long periods of time (from one day to sixty years) to their own email address or the addresses of others participating in the service. After an email is sent, it can never be viewed again until the intended recipient receives it, although the sender retains the option of deleting it up until it is received. FutureMe has operated since December 2002; the photo feature was added in 2011. At the writing of this paper, over three million messages have been sent by approximately one million users. While other applications targeting slow delivery of digital content exist, none have been used as extensively nor as long as FutureMe. Its widespread use of over the past twelve years presents an unusually rare opportunity to better understand the long-term effects of a much slower approach to experiencing, reflecting on, and sharing digital content.

However, there are a few important things to note about FutureMe. First, it is designed with the intention of supporting the re-experience of digital memories. Thus, our study participants likely already had some interest in engaging in these kinds of activities when they decided to use the service. Second, FutureMe did not support 16-bit character encodings for its first seven years; this largely restricted users desiring to write in Asian languages from participating. Since 2011 access to the service has been blocked in China. Third, users have the option of making their messages public on the FutureMe website where any user of FutureMe can view them. We excluded participants that used this option as it could have interfered with our aim of exploring encounters with digital content from the past that may be highly sensitive, intimate, or idiosyncratic.

A diverse sample of people were recruited for this study to elicit a wide range of rich descriptions of sending and receiving digital content with long periods of non-use in between. This approach does present limitations; for example, it makes it hard to generalize findings to any particular population of people. However, considering the lack of work in this area, it seemed prudent to begin with a diverse group to gain a rich, descriptive understanding of the space as a whole to inform what might be salient issues for future HCI research and practice.

With that in mind, a total of 31 participants (17 female and 14 male) were recruited via online advertisements linked primarily through FutureMe's online forum and its social media feeds (e.g., Facebook). To support our goal of understanding long-term experiences, we required participants to have used FutureMe in some capacity for at least three years. We also required them to have sent or received at least one message delayed by at least one year (although we did not stipulate any requirements beyond this in terms of usage patterns or experience). In this paper, we report on findings related to participants' experiences with digital content that had been delayed by at least one year.

Our resulting sample represented people at different life stages, in many different occupations, and from several different countries. Our youngest participant was aged 23 and our oldest 75 years old (mean=38.8). Occupations included store clerk, schoolteacher, graphic designer, landscaper, retired pharmacist, and university student. Participants hailed from the following countries: 3 Australia, 6 Canada, 2 Mexico, 1 India, 11 US, and 8 UK. All owned personal computers. Participants' computing expertise and practices varied. The majority reported using email and social media frequently; however, several had much less routine practices of sharing digital content.

Participants were first provided with a brief online survey to gauge their general usage patterns and probe experiences over time through open-ended responses. After reviewing survey responses, we then scheduled and conducted semi-structured interviews with participants, which lasted between 40-65 minutes. All interviews were conducted over video chat in English (with the exception of 3 which were conducted through an Instant Messaging system). Interviews aimed to develop an understanding of each participant's orientations toward a wide range of issues, some of which included their motivations for sending emails, reactions to receiving emails, reflections on the digital content experienced through FutureMe, and potential issues that may have emerged over time. We also probed how their experience of the system may have shifted over time and if interactions with FutureMe motivated any actions or behaviors outside of the application.

All interviews were audio-recorded, which produced 30+ hours of content. Relevant segments of from each recording were transcribed. Notes were also taken during each interview. These notes were reviewed immediately following each interview, and tentative insights were logged in reflective memos [8]. Analysis of the data was an ongoing process. This included repeatedly reviewing notes and tentative insights in an ongoing process to surface underlying themes [24]. Affinity diagrams were also created to reveal connections across participants. Textual documents were then coded using themes. Data were then organized into concrete themes.

FINDINGS

Through preliminary surveys, participants reported using FutureMe for an average of 6.7 years (min=3, max=11); 5 participants used the system for over a decade. Participants reported sending an average of 18 total messages (min=3, max=67) and received an average 12 total messages (min=3, max=59). All reported sending at least 1 photo since this feature was introduced in 2011.

In the following sections, we present examples and descriptions that help best capture the core themes that emerged in interviews with participants. In this, we refer to each participant with a pseudonym, followed by her or his age and nationality. We begin by describing the various motivations guiding participants' use of FutureMe, from capturing and sharing digital memories to attempts to augment experiences in the future from the past. We then highlight how some participants uniquely leveraged the quality of slowness to work through sensitive personal situations. Following this, we detail difficult to resolve encounters that emerged, which often owed to accounts on FutureMe transcending the lifespan of their owners. Finally, we articulate how, in some cases, FutureMe provoked reflection on the relative state of participants' own digital collections and the timescales that contemporary digital technologies tend to embody and operate in.

General orientations and sensitivities to FutureMe

While on a general level participants tended to value the way FutureMe operated, many reported experiencing an initial adjustment period to its pacing: "*When I sent my first few* [messages], *I sat there like 'ok what now'. ...Even though I knew how it's supposed to work, I was still expecting something to happen. At that moment I realized how different it is. ...to have to wait for years pass to get feedback from a computer is not a familiar feeling. ...I didn't see the value at first. Later down the line it's become captivating*" (Jackie-36-US).

Participants also commented on how the constraints of the system prompted them to create digital content with a deeper sense of consideration and intention. For example, one of our oldest participants connected her experience to the pre-digital era she grew up in: "*Back in my day, people could only write letters. ...You're writing by hand, so you have to slow down and think and let your thoughts out. You can feel that when you read* [a letter]. *...that person is alive with you in the room. Emails and texts don't hold up the same way. No one devotes the time to be thoughtful. ...This* [FutureMe] *isn't like that. If I'm sending it to myself or someone, I know that once it's sent, it's 'out there' on its way and I'm not going to be able to change it. So, I'd better think good and hard about what's going into it*" (Bridget-75-UK). In other cases, participants contrasted FutureMe with contemporary digital technologies and services: "*It's like heaps of* [digital] *stuff is zooming around us, isn't it. I get tagged in stuff from parties and shows on Facebook. I don't see half of it. ...there's not so much meaning in it, is there. ...I'd say* [FutureMe] *is different ...not just cause stuff's way more slow. But because there's more of a sense of intention behind them* [messages]" (Liam-28-Australia).

Collectively, these quotes help illustrate several ways participants characterized their general orientations toward FutureMe and the effects of its operation on a wider timescale. However, despite FutureMe's relatively simple characteristics, participants' uses and experiences of it over time were complex, diverse, and sometimes surprising.

Slow digital content from and to one's self

The motivations for crafting digital content to send to one's self in the future centered on two general themes. First, to generate specific records of life experiences or lessons to reencounter years later. Second, to influence future events or behaviors related to one's life. Unexpected instances also occurred as interactions with FutureMe caused participants to consider their own mortality or they reencountered digital content that had no memory of sending.

Crafting and re-visiting digital records of life experiences

Participants reported proactively capturing a range of life experiences through digital content to re-visit in the future. One theme centered on recording events related to professional advancements in the service of generating celebratory reminders of past achievements (e.g., finishing graduate school, receiving a hard earned professional certification). Participants also captured momentous events that were viewed as symbols of personal growth or milestones (e.g., birth of a child, 40th birthday). A smaller, yet consistent theme centered on the capture of mundane experiences, such as a record of one's activities over a given day. Participants speculated that, while ordinary now, this digital content could be a valuable record of everyday life when reencountered in the future.

All but two of our participants had received emails or photos from their past self, and many remarked on their value. For example, Simon-51-US, reflects on receiving 4 emails and 2 photos from himself over the past 7 years: "*I send them* [slowed by] *2 to 4 years. ...with that much time any anticipation fades away. That's how they become remarkable. ...It's significant to get one. ...In those moments I dive back into life. ...*[I] *figure out how I somehow ended up 'here' today.*" In other cases, participants drew distinctions between the digital content they received through FutureMe and their other digital stuff. Tim-39-US, whom had used FutureMe for 10 years, described annually writing a 'life synopsis' of the year's events and sent it slowed by 1 year. He reflects on the 9 emails he now possesses: "*They've grown to become an interesting portrait of who I was and what I was trying to do. None are exceptionally long, but they each speak to different parts of me. ...there are so many photos, posts, feeds... the list goes on. ...but it's still easy to lose track of how much things change in one year because we're so focused on what happened today or last weekend. ...These emails are way more valuable to me than 9,000 photos documenting everything that happened in between them.*"

Collectively, these examples help illustrate how the creation, forced non-use, and eventual reencounter of digital content supported experiences of self-reflection. They also reveal how a slower interaction pacing provoked mindful consideration of broader themes within participants' lives and, in some cases, in ways that starkly contrasted other digital stuff they accumulated over time.

Attempting to influence one's future life

Participants also described leveraging the slowed delivery of digital content in concerted attempts to influence future events, experiences or behaviors. The rationale for engaging in this practice varied from the mundane to the extraordinary. In some cases, participants described attempts to positively shape their future mood: "*When I'd be feeling really happy, I'd write down why and send myself 'a smile' ...to some random point* [in the future]. *...funny enough* [getting them] *feels pretty natural. ...like how a smell can vividly remind you of a place that lingers for a little while*" (Jessica-27-Canada).

However, we encountered several other cases in which participants' goals had a more serious tone. These instances often centered on providing support for remaining committed to a lifestyle change (e.g., adopting a healthier diet, quitting smoking) or to get through difficult physical or emotional situations (e.g., battling a long-term disease, beating drug addiction). Shannon-29-UK reflects back on many emails she sent in the past (starting 3 years prior, each staggered by 6 months) while in the grips of battling drug addiction: "*Writing those* [emails] *helped keep me going. When I'd get one, I'd think, 'I can make it to the next one' ...I* [still] *get them twice a year. ...It's a stinging reminder, but it's good. I don't ever want to be back there again.*"

In other cases, participants sent themselves supportive photos or emails that were targeted at a specific future event that they anticipated would be challenging or difficult to overcome. Dylan-26-USA describes receiving an email aimed at summoning courage in his future self to go skydiving and face his fear of heights: "*I listed all the reasons why I needed to do it and sent it so it'd arrive the day before my birthday. ...Sure enough* [a year later] *I'd been having second thoughts. ...It reminded me why I felt so strongly in the first place. ...I went on with it and I'm glad. ...to me it represents that I'm going to do something if I have a good reason, no matter what.*"

Unanticipated effects of sending slow content to one's self

The examples directly above highlight unique and deliberate ways participants drew on FutureMe as a resource to shape experiences in the future—from simply boosting one's mood, to fashioning an ongoing support system dedicated to keeping one grounded. However, in a few cases participants reported unexpected or unsettling experiences emerged from receiving digital content from their past self. The most striking example was Doug-26-US's experience of receiving an email from when he was heavily entrenched in drug and alcohol abuse: "*So, I got it out of the blue. Had no memory of writing it. But I could tell it was me. Didn't make much sense. Only thing that was certain was I was fucked up. ...At first I thought maybe I'd search for some meaning in it, you know like with a dream. ...it was stupid. ...that whole time in my life was meaningless. It was depressing.*" In a handful of other instances, participants reported reencountering digital content from their past self associated with life goals that were unattained or had become impossible; most of these instances were deemed undesirable.

Finally, in our interviews, several participants responded with a sense of hesitation when we probed into whether they had sent themselves digital content far into the future. These tensions centered on a general shared perception that sending digital content fifty years into the future can raise an unfamiliar set of concerns: "*It's an amount of time that's hard to get my head around. I mean how would I know I'd even remember it? What if I didn't? What if I'm already dead? Where is it going to go then? I don't think I'd want it to live on somewhere without me*" (Alex-27-US). Alex's statement makes a salient point: even though FutureMe has been used for over a decade, this is relatively little time in the lifespan of a person and it is unclear what could result from encountering digital residue from a time in one's life long forgotten, or for it to transcend one's life entirely.

Sharing and receiving slow digital content with others

Participants reported sending slowed digital content to, or receiving it from, relatives, close friends, significant others, and, to a smaller extent, people they no longer have close social relationships with. Three main themes emerged that broadly characterize these experiences, which are described in combined sections below.

Sharing memories of major or mundane life experiences

The most common factor that motivated participants to send digital content to someone else was to capture shared social experiences. These kinds of experiences frequently related to major life events (e.g., college graduation, a long awaited marriage) or annual festive events (e.g., Christmas, Seder, a birthday). Emails often aimed to communicate personally significant aspects of events and, at times, to preserve them from being lost over time. Dale-31-US describes sending an email delayed by 5 years to his Dad after attending his parent's 20th anniversary party: "*There was this look in his eyes, not just happiness but contentment. I hadn't seen that in a long long time. ...It's something that wouldn't be recognizable in a photograph. ...I didn't want that memory of the way he felt at that exact moment to fade away over time. I wrote him about how he looked and how it made me feel. He should get it right before his 25th anniversary.*" (Dale-31-US). Participants also commonly described the reminiscent quality of this kind of digital content, which, Samuel-54-Australia characterized as "*well-aged bits that unexpectedly pop in my inbox and take me way back to a time and place that I wish I was in.*"

In other cases, FutureMe was used to nurture and signify an intimate social bond between two people. Debbie-45-US, whom had used FutureMe for nearly 10 years, described receiving a message from her sister 8 years ago (which had been written one year prior) that detailed their comically disastrous attempt at painting a house together. She and her sister had since taken to occasionally writing each other 1-3 year delayed emails about other mishaps in their lives: "*it's a truly lovely record of our lives together and apart, richer than any photo album or relic of the past.*" In further reflecting on the emergent value of these digital materials, she noted: "*if an archeologist were to find them, I'm sure they'd seem pretty ordinary. ...they represent changes in our lives, but in ways only we'd probably understand.*"

However, messages did not always hold the value reflected in the statements above and they sometimes resulted in tensions when events were remembered differently: "[My cousin] *sent me his memory of a camping weekend our families have* [each year]. *I was like cool, but there was this part about how I let our campfire go out one night. But I'm sure he let it go out! I thought he was joking but it turned out he wasn't. It's made me wonder if I'm crazy. ...We still disagree about it*" (Javier-Mexico-29). Several other participants described feeling dismayed, confused, and, in one case, confrontational after finding other people's recollections of the past that did not match their own.

Leveraging slowness to work through issues that 'need time'
Participants also described desires to capture feelings tied to a social relationship or experience in the present, specifically with the intention of revealing it at a later point in time. The largest set of participant responses centered on the need to communicate feelings to a person they were no longer in a close relationship with. For example, Amanda-24-US describes the relief she felt after sending an email delayed by 2-years to her ex-partner: "*I wanted to wish him well, but whenever I saw him, even if he was just coming online, I was filled with feelings of sadness and contempt. ...It was only going to change with time, and time wasn't moving fast enough. ...I wrote a message that that focused on the positive parts* [of our relationship]. *...I sent it knowing he'd get it in a few years, after things mellowed out. ...It was a huge relief. A big step for me.*"

A handful of participants also described how they leveraged the application to push themselves to work through disclosing sensitive information to others. The most compelling example emerged in Arnold-33-US's description of sending a 2-year delayed message to his parents in which he revealed he is homosexual. "*I had been planning to tell them for years but kept backing off. By the time I turned 28 I was like it's now or never. ...I still felt hesitant. ...I never intended to use* [FutureMe] *to tell my parents I'm gay, but sitting down and writing that message and sending it and knowing they're gonna get it gave me the motivation to finally do it. ...It actually went well. ...I didn't tell them about* [the message] *and they were pretty touched when they got it.*"

A few cases also emerged in which participants described receiving digital content that provided the impetus to re-attempt working through a troubled relationship: "*When I got divorced, my son and I didn't talk for a long time. I felt like he refused to understand or accept why I couldn't be happy in that marriage. ...I got a message from him. He wrote it 3 years earlier. Reading his perspective on things back then made me see I didn't do a good job communicating. But at that time there's no way I would've been receptive to hearing that. ...It ended up being a step toward us reconnecting*" (Roger-49-Canada).

Collectively, these reflections help highlight how participants leveraged the slow, deliberate nature of FutureMe as a resource to mediate intimate and difficult interactions with other people in unique and, ultimately, productive ways. It was clear in our interviews that considerable reflection and work went into crafting the digital content that was sent or received in these instances. Several other examples did emerge in which other participants described sending time-delayed digital content in the in the heat of a moment. In many of these cases they returned later to delete them and, in a couple instances, regretted that they had been sent.

Communicating beyond one's own lifetime
A third thematic issue characterizing experiences of slowed shared digital content centered on the capability to deliver information or materials to others beyond one's own lifetime. These examples ranged from profoundly moving experiences to instances that were troubling and difficult to resolve. The majority of participants reported that at some point they had considered sending emails to others that would be received after they had passed away. During these discussions, participants commonly (and often without prompts) reflected on what it might mean to have some sense of digital agency in the afterlife: "*it's attractive to think about, but also very strange. ...to digitally defy time, plan for things to happen after I'm gone*" (Selvin-42-India).

The ambivalence reflected in Selvin's statement manifested in several instances participants described in which they had initially created digital content to be posthumously delivered, but later deleted it. The issues that motivated these decisions owed to three main reasons. First, as time progressed, some participants forgot exactly what the digital content they had sent revealed about them. Second, events transpired after the digital content was sent that explicitly made it no longer representative of the sender's perspective. Third, a few participants encountered a negative digitally-mediated experience related to a departed loved one, which caused them reconsider sending posthumously delivered digital content (e.g., a Facebook notification to reconnect with a departed friend).

Nonetheless, a handful of participants had received posthumous digital content, which had since become deeply cherished. For example, Barbara-55-US described receiving a humorous email and photo from a close friend 2.5 years after he passed: "*He used to run races in little skimpy pink shorts. That tickled me and he knew it. ...he sent a photo where he's in those shorts with a goofy grin. ...*[He] *wrote that he's still wearing them in heaven even if it's against the 'dress code.' Ha! what a wonderful reminder of him and his character.*" In another case, Jenny-27-Canada, reflected on a touching email she received from her father 5 years after his death: "*It brought up a lot of emotions ...He mostly wanted to make sure I knew he's still watching over me ...Getting it after such a long time made me cherish the memories of him even more. It's one of the most special things I have from him.*"

However, receiving posthumous digital content could also lead to confusing and, at times, troubling experiences. Deena-49-UK described receiving a series of images over the course of a few years from her departed uncle that she struggled to make sense of, and which ultimately motivated her decision to leave the FutureMe service entirely: "*About a year after he died I started getting these photos. Nothing written. They'd be people I didn't know or some place I'd never been. Drove me bonkers. ...Why'd he send'em? Were they for me? It was right stressful. So I packed up* [using it] *for good.*" Shelly-37-US also encountered an unpredictable series of emails from her departed younger sister that became increasingly difficult to deal with: "*Some were about her regrets. Others didn't make any sense. ...and they keep coming. It's not like she left a note. It's haunting. I want to know why she doesn't want to let things be.*"

Collectively, these two examples highlight the complex effects that receiving digital content delayed over varying periods of time can produce, especially when the senders' intentions are ambiguous. The unpredictable, continued emergence of new digital materials from departed ones that Deena and Shelly experienced produced unsettling ongoing tensions that left them with little choice other than to abandon using their accounts entirely or continue wrestling with 'haunting' uncertainty.

Broader emergent reflections and actions over time

Encountering slow digital content also prompted a range of actions, behavior and reflections more broadly within participants' everyday lives. Participants frequently described socially reconnecting with people tied to the memories triggered by FutureMe (e.g., through SMS, phone or video chats, face-to-face meetings). It was also common for participants to revisit physical or digital materials tied to past life experiences or social relationships, which they often had not interacted with in years. While these interactions could be highly meaningful, several participants described unexpected emergent complications, which nearly always owed to their inability to locate the materials they desired. While instances did emerge with physical artifacts, the vast majority centered on their digital content and collections. In some cases, these experiences left participants dismayed at the size and state of their personal digital archives: "*I got this wonderful email my friend wrote right after we graduated college.... I wanted to look at photos from then. ...I couldn't believe how hard it was. ...some on my laptop, some on my old computer in the basement. ...I remembered someone posting old photos of us on Facebook but I couldn't find those either. ...It was a sobering experience. I realized the organization of my digital life is completely out of control.*" (Jane-29-US).

Additionally, Deb-50-US reflects on insights triggered by a series of slow emails received from her son: "*I was thinking about them* [emails] *while looking through* [physical] *photo albums I made as he grew up. ...It dawned on me how they are good markers of points in his life, kind of like how a photo album is. But, you know, they're still just an email, only one thing. They don't have the depth like an album does. ...Then I got thinking about how I don't even have the digital photos that would provide that same kind of experience. ...they're all over. ...I'd have to dig through old folders and that's just the beginning.*"

Despite these issues, most participants reported highly meaningful experiences emerging from interactions with FutureMe. Interestingly, however, when probing deeper in the interviews, perceptions differed to some extent over having what was often regarded as extraordinary digital content embodied and stored within an email: "*Email is extremely useful. It's also bland and unexpressive. ...so when I think about having things that I treasure, ...things I want to have forever. I feel like I need a different format.*" (Alex-27-US). Similarly, Samantha-UK-34 noted: "*they are gems, they are, really, but my email [account] is a rubbish dump, and that doesn't feel quite right at the end of the day*" (Samantha-UK-34). Interestingly, a handful of participants reported explicitly valuing having their slow digital content become introduced into their email stream: "*I don't mind, it's how memories work. They're all fleeting. ...Of course I enjoy engaging with them but then more* [emails] *pile up, they get buried, slowly disappear.*" (Jessica-27-Canada). Kate-37-US desired to have even more control over her digital content fading away: "*If I can decide when it's delivered in the future, I should also be able to decide when it will vanish for good. ...Even though it'd be gone, it might still stay with me or it might not. Having that impermanence would be meaningful.*"

Finally, several discussions emerged in which participants reflected more broadly on the quality of their long-term interactions with FutureMe. For example, Terry-44-US reflected on the trajectory of his decade-long experience: "*The world was such a different place when I started using it. ...No Facebook. No Twitter. Things were busy, but they didn't feel as fast moving. ...*[FutureMe] *is so simple. It doesn't ask anything of me. I can leave for it a year or two or longer and come back to it. ...That's why it still feels relevant and authentic. These are hard to find qualities in the digital world these days.*" Dale-31-US similarly perceived value in the slower, yet deliberate way FutureMe operates and it's long-term potential: "*I barely 'use' it, but at the same time I don't feel like letting it go. I want it for the rest of my life ...because it's working in a timeframe that's on a whole other level. It's one that technology doesn't engage much but I think there's benefits to having something focusing on the long-haul and having to think about things in that way.*"

DISCUSSION

It is clear that creating, re-encountering or experiencing digital content through a slow technology can produce complex effects. A key contribution of this study is to present rich descriptions of what these effects are and how they shaped people's experiences over time. While its functionality was both limited and simple, participants drew on FutureMe for a range of purposes—to generate unique resources for self-reflection, to influence events in the future, and to nurture, work through, or reflect on intimate social relationships. Interactions with FutureMe led to a range of unexpected experiences, and catalyzed reflections and actions beyond the digital content it delivered. Ultimately, FutureMe was capable of triggering a spectrum of experiences—from poignant moments of beauty and epiphany to humorous flashes to unsettling encounters.

Collectively, this diverse collection of accounts builds on and extends prior works by providing new insights into the potential benefits and tradeoffs bound to the long-term use of a socially situated slow technology. Prior slow technology systems aimed at reflection and reminiscence, such as the Photobox [26] and Reflexive Printer [35], operated completely autonomously, re-presenting users with photos from their past. In both cases, these design artifacts enforced periods of non-use between each photo—ranging from one day to several weeks—in the service of slowing interaction patterns and building anticipation around what might be encountered next. In contrast, the much longer enforced timespan we explored in FutureMe—where messages were delivered at minimum one year from when they were sent—caused participants' anticipated future experience of the system to fade away entirely. It became clear that this effect created an added sense of gravity to the experience of receiving a message. In several cases participants reported that this long time lapse led them to attribute an extraordinary or remarkable quality to the digital content they received. More broadly, the seldom yet persistent emergence of messages paired with the intentional, targeted nature of digital content crafted through FutureMe appeared to further amplify experiences of surprise and mindfulness of the past in ways that could trigger deep contemplation or simply linger momentarily.

However, these qualities also led to instances in which people's recollections of past events deviated from the digital content sent through FutureMe in strange and curious, if not unsettling, ways. These instances parallel earlier research describing how re-encountering unexpected digital materials from one's past can trigger a sense of re-accountability over experiences that had been reconciled and put to rest [13]. Our work further reveals tensions that can emerge when the agency to unpredictably introduce 'well-aged' digital traces into one's life is extended to other people. These tensions were especially amplified in cases where participants were burdened by receiving confusing or ambiguous digital content from departed loved ones. These instances exemplify the *asymmetrical* nature of posthumous exchanges of digital content where people can be left with an unsettling responsibility to come to terms with things communicated to them from the departed, despite having no clear way of resolving them [22,29]. As slow technology systems continue to emerge, there is a clear need to develop strategies for striking a balance between offering better methods to contextualize digital exchanges over long time periods, while also avoiding over-complicating the value and richness that often emerged from crafting messages the relatively simple way FutureMe operated.

On a broader level, FutureMe emerged as a unique example of a slow technology that resonated with earlier articulations of this interaction design philosophy [11]. Its functionality and design qualities enabled it to easily fade in and out of perceptual view over considerable amounts of time. Interactions with the system provoked mindful consideration of participants' lives, their technological habits, and even their relations to other contemporary domestic technologies. And, as experiences slowly accumulated around FutureMe, the uniqueness and character of people's relation to the system manifested through its temporal form [20]. Taken as a whole, findings from our study of FutureMe suggests further design considerations that can guide future research and practice initiatives in the HCI community, which we turn to next.

DESIGN CONSIDERATIONS

Exploring divergent design strategies for supporting reminiscence through slow technologies—Interactions with FutureMe catalyzed various rich moments of reflection, which, in several cases, triggered participants to search for other physical and digital materials related to particular memories captured in the digital content they received. In many of these cases, participants encountered complications, often becoming overwhelmed (and at times surprised) by the vast unstructured and fragmented nature of their personal digital collections. These tensions are reflective of growing concerns in the HCI community over people's increasing loss of control over and awareness of their digital content, and the critical implications this suggests for its long-term significance [27,33,37].

However, design strategies for productively engaging with these growing problems are sparse and underdeveloped. One key reason owes to the complexity of separating and collating people's meaningful (and often highly idiosyncratic) digital materials from their trivial things [18]. While not explicitly designed for this use, the nature of digital content generated through FutureMe tended to provide a unique index (or "good marker" as Deb-50-US noted) of significant points in people's life (whether mundane or extraordinary). While it is not our intention to suggest slow technologies like FutureMe ought to be augmented per se, the information or metadata captured through their use could be leveraged outside of the system to index, collate, combine, and re-form various other kinds of digital content (e.g., photos, music, video, audio, messages) related to a particular life experience, period in a social relationship, or otherwise memorable event. These assemblies of digital content themselves could emerge slowly over time, potentially forming into rich digital representations of one's life. This design direction could potentially alleviate some of the conflicting tensions participants experienced that centered on having deeply cherished, digital content embodied and often stored in the banal form of an email. Emerging research exploring the convergence of online and offline digital content could be leveraged in support of this direction [e.g., 27,38], as could work exploring the embodiment of sentimental digital content in radically new and engaging forms [28,31].

Nonetheless, it seems crucial that this approach is handled cautiously. It was evident that participants did not always desire to re-encounter digital content from the past (even if they themselves produced it). Participants also held differing perspectives on the appropriate treatment of digital content they received. Some found its placement (and eventual 'fading away') in their ever-expanding email archive was suitable, while others desired for more expressive and deliberate ways of instilling a sense of impermanence in these digital materials. These instances highlight the importance of supporting a wide range of perspectives and desires when designing slow technologies and, more generally, social media systems. Emerging research that proposes decay as a metaphor for design [10] as well as new approaches to digital file dispossession [23, 32] could guide future research aligned with this direction.

Envisioning the long-term role of interactive systems in mediating intimacy—This study also revealed various ways participants leveraged FutureMe to mediate intimate interactions with others. As messages or photos accumulated over time, deeply valued digital records of one-to-one relationships surfaced. Participants also leveraged slowness to work through social relationships that "needed time." While subtle, this emergent use of the enforced timespan of non-use afforded by FutureMe provided a crucial support mechanism to give participants the inertia needed to move on from difficult situations. In this, it led to experiences of personal growth and catalyzed slow steps toward resolving a troubled relationship.

However, intimate exchanges with loved ones could also be disrupted through FutureMe. As noted, this was most evident in cases where departed loved ones were, in a sense, digitally re-animated by the system and participants continued to receive ambiguous, difficult to resolve posthumously sent messages. One pre-emptive strategy to address these tensions could be to design subtle features into future applications that enable people to inscribe short annotations to clarify or contextualize their reasons for sending a time-delayed message. This intervention could help support the sender in remembering what was sealed away in a message written long ago. More importantly, it could help clarify the intentionality behind why a message or series of messages were sent. It could also be beneficial to complement this approach with an intervention that enabled the receiver of unsettling messages to 'mute' or opt out of receiving further correspondence from a particular sender. We see this combined direction as paralleling efforts to develop sensitive, values-oriented approaches to dealing with the digital detritus left behind by people as the longevity of their digital accounts supersedes their own lifetimes [4,7,22,29].

On a higher level, our findings present diverse and, at times, unexpected ways FutureMe opened up intimate interactions along a wider temporal framing. The HCI community has long explored the design of technologies that compress space to mediate a sense of social intimacy with others. This body of work has adopted a wide range of materials and modalities, from the direct and synchronous [25] to the tactile [36] to the indirect and minimal [15]. However, virtually no work has explored the issue of designing technologies to mediate long-term intimate interactions. The rich descriptions from our study arguably give more weight to questions that have to date only been explored on conceptual or speculative levels in HCI. For example, what kinds of experiences could unfold if one was to re-encounter a 'haptic kiss' recorded and sent from a loved one (or an ex-lover) 20 years in the past? What if it could only be experienced once? Or, a different kind of digital assemblage followed it at some point in the future? What is clear is that the time has come to more critically consider the actuality of these interactions and the implications that they suggest for the field of HCI. They do, after all, represent major opportunities, issues and consequences that the HCI community will inevitably have to face.

CONCLUSION

This paper has reported findings from in depth interviews aimed at understanding participants' long-term interactions with FutureMe—a rare example of a slow technology that has been widely used over an unusually long time period. Findings revealed that, despite this technology's limited functionality, it produced a spectrum of experiences and effects. Based on these findings, we have discussed and outlined several considerations for future research and practice initiatives. This paper presents one of what are many approaches needed to unpack the complex and profound implications that result from people's long-term interactions with interactive technologies. We hope this research will be a step toward influencing future initiatives in the HCI community that bring the subject of human relations with technology over time more seriously into focus, now and long into the future.

ACKNOWLEDGEMENTS

Many thanks to the participants for their time, the reviewers for their thoughtful comments on this paper, and the Everyday Design Studio for much inspiration and support. This work is supported in part by a Banting fellowship through the Social Sciences and Humanities Research Council of Canada.

REFERENCES

1. Bae, J., Lim, Y., Bang, J., Kim, M. 2014. Ripening Room: Designing Social Media for Self-Reflection in Self-expression. *Proc. of DIS '14*, 103-112.
2. Baumer, E., Adams, P., Khovanskaya, V., Liao, T., Smith, M., Schwanda, V., Williams, K. 2013. Limiting, leaving,

and (re)lapsing: an exploration of facebook non-use practices and experiences. *Proc. of CHI '13*, 3257-3266.

3. Belk, R., 1988. Possessions and the Extended Self. *Journal of Consumer Research,* 15, 2, 139-168.
4. Brubaker, J., Dombrowski, L., Gilbert, A., Kusumakaulika, N., Hayes, G. 2014. Stewarding a Legacy: Responsibilities and Relationships in the Management of Post-mortem Data. *Proc. of CHI '14*, 4157-4166.
5. Cosley, D., Sosik, V., Schultz, J., Pessapati, S., Lee, S. 2012. Experiences with Designing Tools for Everyday Reminiscing, *Human-Computer Interaction*, 27.
6. Csikszenthmihalyi, M., Rochberg-Halton, E. 1981. *The Meaning of Things: Domestic Symbols and the Self.* Cambridge University Press.
7. Friedman, B., Nathan, L. 2010. Multi-Lifespan Information System Design: A Research Initiative for the HCI community. *Proc. of CHI '10*, 2243-2246.
8. Glaser, B., Strauss, A. 1967. *Discovery of grounded theory: strategies for qualitative research.* Sociology press.
9. Grosse-Hering, B., Mason, J., Aliakseyeu, D., Bakker, C., Desmet, P. 2013. Slow design for meaningful interactions. *Proc. of CHI '13*, 3431-3440.
10. Gulotta, R., Odom, W., Faste, H., Forlizzi. J. 2013. Digital Artifacts as Legacy: Exploring the Lifespan and Value of Digital Data. *Proc. of CHI '13*, 1831-1840.
11. Hallnas, L., Redstrom, J. 2001. Slow Technology: Designing for Reflection. *P. Ubi. Comput. 5*, 201-212.
12. Harmon, E., Mazmanian, M. 2013. Stories of the Smartphone in everyday discourse: conflict, tension & instability. *Proc. of CHI '13*, 1051-1060.
13. Harper, R., Randal, D., Smyth, N., Evans, C., Heledd, L., Moore, R. 2008. The Past is a Different Place: They Do Things Differently There. *Proc. of DIS '08*, 271-280.
14. Hawkins, D., Procyk, J., Neustaedter, C. 2014. Postulater: slowing the pace of media sharing. In *Adjunct Proc. of DIS '14*. 89-92.
15. Kaye, J. 2006. I just clicked to say I love you: rich evaluations of minimal communication. *CHI EA '06*, 363-368.
16. Kaye, J., et al. 2006. To have and to hold: exploring the personal archive. *Proc of CHI '06*, 275-284.
17. King, S., Forlizzi, J. 2007. Slow messaging: intimate communication for couples living at a distance. *Proc. of DPPI 07*, 451-454.
18. Kirk, D., Sellen, A. 2010. On human remains: Values and practice in the home archiving of cherished objects. *ACM TOCHI* 17, 3, Article 10 (July 2010).
19. Leshed, G. 2012. Slowing down with personal productivity tools. *interactions* 19, 1, 58-63.
20. Mazé, R., Redström, J. 2005. Form and the Computational Object. *Digital Creativity,* 16(1).
21. McAdams, D. P. 2001. The Psychology of Life Stories. *Review of General Psychology*, 5, 2, 100-122.
22. Massimi, M., Odom, W., Banks, R., Kirk, D. 2011. Matters of Life and Death: Locating the end of life in lifespan-oriented HCI research. *Proc. of CHI' 11*, 987-996.
23. Mayer-Schonberger, V. 2009. *Delete: The Virtue of Forgetting in the Digital Age*. Princeton University.
24. Miles, M. B., Huberman, A., M. 1994. *Qualitative Data Analysis.* Thousand Oaks, CA: Sage.
25. Neustaedter, C., Greenberg, S. 2012. Intimacy in long-distance relationships over video chat. *Proc. of CHI '12*.
26. Odom, W., Sellen, A., Banks, R., Kirk, D., Regan, T., Selby, M., Forlizzi, J., Zimmerman, J. 2014. Designing for Slowness, Anticipation and Re-visitation: A Long Term Field Study of the Photobox. *Proc. of CHI '14*, 1961-1970.
27. Odom, W. et al. 2013. Fragmentation and Transition: Understanding Perceptions of Virtual Possessions among Young Adults in South Korea, Spain and the United States. *Proc. of CHI '13,* 1833-1842.
28. Odom, W. Banks, R., Kirk, D., Harper, R., Lindley, S., Sellen, A. 2012. Technology Heirlooms? Considerations for passing down and inheriting digital materials. *Proc. of CHI '12*, 337-346.
29. Odom, W., Harper, R., Sellen, A., Kirk, D., Banks, R. 2010. Passing On and Putting To Rest: Understanding Bereavement in the Context of Interactive Technologies. *Proc. of CHI '10*, 1831-1840.
30. Petrelli, D., van den Hoven, E., Whittaker, S. 2009. Making history: intentional capture of future memories. *Proc. of CHI '09*, 1723-1732.
31. Petrelli, D., Villar, N., Kalnikaite, V., Dib, L., Whittaker, S. 2010. FM radio: family interplay with sonic mementos. *Proc of CHI '10*, 2371-2380.
32. Sas, C., Whittaker, S. 2013. Design for forgetting: disposing of digital possessions after a breakup. *Proc. of CHI '13*, 1823-1832.
33. Sellen, A., Fogg, A., Aitken, M., Hodges, S., Rother, C., Wood, K. 2007. Do life-logging technologies support memory for the past?: an experimental study using sensecam. *Proc. of CHI '07*, 81-90.
34. Sengers, P., Boehner, K., David, S., Kaye, J. 2005. Reflective Design. *Proc. of CC '05*, 49-58.
35. Tsai, W., Wang, P., Lee, H., Liang, R., Hsu, J. 2014. The reflexive printer: toward making sense of perceived drawbacks in technology-mediated reminiscence. *Proc. of DIS '14*. 995-1004.
36. Vetere, F., Gibbs, M., Kjeldskov, J., Howard, S., Mueller, F., Pedell, S., et al. 2005. Mediating intimacy: Supporting Strong-Tie Relationships. *Proc. of CHI '05*, 471-480.
37. Whittaker, S., Bergman, O., Clough, P. 2010. Easy on that trigger dad: a study of long term family photo retrieval. *Personal Ubiquitous Comput.* 14, 1, 31-43.
38. Zhao, X., Lindley, S. 2014. Curation through Use: Understanding the Personal Value of Social Media. *Proc. of CHI '14*, 2431-2440.

Reflective Informatics: Conceptual Dimensions for Designing Technologies of Reflection

Eric P. S. Baumer
Communication Department and Information Science Department
118 Gates Hall, Ithaca, NY 14853, USA
Cornell University
ericpsb@cornell.edu

ABSTRACT
Despite demonstrated interest in designing for reflection, relatively little work provides a detailed explication of what exactly is meant by reflection or how to design around it. This paper fills that gap by reviewing and engaging with conceptual and theoretical models of reflection, organized by the disciplinary and epistemological perspectives each embodies. Synthesizing across this theoretical background, the paper identifies three dimensions of reflection: breakdown, inquiry, and transformation. Together, these dimensions serve as the foundation for *reflective informatics*, a conceptual approach that helps bring clarity and guidance to the discussion of designing for reflection. The paper distinguishes reflective informatics by demonstrating how it both differs from and complements existing related work. Finally, the paper provides a critically reflexive consideration of its own latent assumptions, especially about the value of reflection, and how they might impact work on designing for reflection.

Author Keywords
Reflection; reflective informatics; design; reflective HCI.

ACM Classification Keywords
H.5.m. Information interfaces and presentation (e.g., HCI): Miscellaneous.

INTRODUCTION
"Without [reflection] no judgment of experience would be possible at all." [25]

Researchers in HCI have demonstrated significant interest in designing technologies to support reflection [6,15,31,42]. While it provides an exciting and challenging application area, there persists a certain "fuzziness in which the term 'reflection' is used within the HCI community" [15:221]. Indeed, few of the papers describing systems purported to support reflection provide more than a one- or two-sentence definition of the concept [6,15]. Work in this area may benefit from a more explicit discussion of what we mean when talking about reflection.

Part of the issue may arise from the diverse auspices under which prior work has been conducted. As mentioned above, substantial work has already been undertaken in designing technologies of reflection [6], so reflection *per se* is not necessarily novel. However, much of this work remains somewhat disjoint, spanning applications from health to education to personal informatics to design support tools [15]. Articulating a larger conceptual umbrella under which this work operates may facilitate engagement with foundational concepts and theories of reflection.

This paper, then, seeks to provide such a conceptual grounding, one that can be relevant to and shared by the disparate strands of work around designing for reflection. After reviewing previous approaches to reflection in HCI, it considers several theoretical approaches, organized under the various disciplinary and epistemological perspectives they embody, that might prove useful in conceptualizing what exactly we mean by reflection. Synthesizing across these theories, the paper proposes the term *reflective informatics* and offers three dimensions along which computational and information technologies may be designed to promote, foster, encourage, or support reflection. These dimensions are explicated both through grounding in the theoretical literature on reflection and through comparison with prior instances of designing for reflection. The paper concludes by taking a critical, reflexive turn, considering its own underlying commitments and latent assumptions about reflection as well as some of the tensions inherent in designing, and evaluating, technologies of reflection.

Crucially, it would be deleterious to use "reflective informatics" as a keyword or silo to set reflection-oriented papers apart from other, ostensibly non-reflection-oriented work. Rather, the term represents a sensibility toward the relationship between computational technology and reflective thought in such a way that highlights its permeation though and relevance in numerous different contexts. Indeed, reflection cannot and should not be isolated as its own subfield within HCI. Instead, this paper works toward providing underpinning concepts and unifying concerns that may be readily applied to a variety

CHI 2015, April 18 - 23 2015, Seoul, Republic of Korea

ACM 978-1-4503-3145-6/15/04…$15.00
http://dx.doi.org/10.1145/2702123.2702234

of domains, from health to education to personal informatics. Furthermore, it also aims to elucidate both how endeavors to support reflection in those disparate areas might share commonalities and how they might mutually benefit from each others' insights.

The paper thus makes two primary contributions. First, by reviewing work on reflection from a variety of disciplines, it provides needed [6,15] conceptual and theoretical grounding for reflection in HCI. Second, by synthesizing across that work, it suggests three specific dimensions for applying these concepts and theories in technology design.

RELATED WORK

This section both demonstrates reflection as a topic of interest in HCI and considers some of the ways in which prior work has engaged with the concept. Such work can be grouped into two broad, partially overlapping strands.

The first strand acknowledges the importance of reflection in the design process. For example, Schön's descriptions of reflective practice [43] and of design as a reflective conversation with materials [44] have been applied to improving the quality of interaction design [33]. Value sensitive design [18] emphasizes designers' capacity for reflection on the value commitments embedded in (a) design. Numerous approaches have been taken to facilitating reflection in the design process, including (perhaps somewhat reflexively) designing tools to help designers reflect [see 6 for a review].

A second strand of work, more directly relevant here, deals with reflection among users. This section reviews three approaches that explicitly discuss reflection among technology users. For each, we argue that the dimensions articulated below help fill a gap by providing the theoretical grounding and conceptual language necessary to engage with, and design for, reflection [6,15].

Personal Informatics

Reflection plays a central role in the conceptualization of personal informatics. Li et al. define personal informatics as systems that "help people collect personally relevant information for the purpose of *self-reflection* and gaining self-knowledge" [31:558, emphasis added]. In addition to giving reflection a central place in its definition, their model of personal informatics includes reflection as one of five stages. An individual who (1) has the *motivation* to examine her or his personal information, (2) has *collected* that information, and (3) has *integrated* it into a meaningful form(at) can then (4) *reflect* on her or his data. This reflection leads to subsequent (5) *action* wherein the individual changes her or his behavior (or perhaps not) based on reflections about her or his data and the resultant increase in self-knowledge.

Reflection, then, functions as the impetus in personal informatics that moves the individual from examinations of her or his data to action. Despite this central importance, work on personal informatics provides relatively little detailed explication of what actually constitutes reflection. For Li et al., "looking at lists of collected personal information or exploring or interacting with information visualizations" [31:562] is constitutive of reflection. A colloquial definition such as this, rather than one based in previous theoretical work on reflection, is not itself a weakness. However, this definition provides relatively little guidance in terms of how we might go about designing for reflection. The dimensions of reflective informatics presented below provide needed conceptual and theoretical grounding, along with design strategies for each identified dimension of reflection. Thus, this paper supplies both a working definition of what constitutes reflection and guidance as to how we might design for it.

Reflective Design

Reflective Design [45] applies Agre's notion of critical technical practice [1] to HCI. In so doing it brings "unconscious aspects of experience to conscious attention, thereby making them available for conscious choice" [45:50]. This approach involves designers identifying "attitudes, practices, values, and identities" [45:50] on which existing, norm-reinforcing designs are often predicated and instead designing based on alternative assumptions. As one of the few lines of prior work to provide theoretical grounding, Sengers et al. define reflection by drawing on "a Western tradition of critical reflection [in] Marxism, feminism, racial and ethnic studies, media studies and psychoanalysis" [45:53]. For example, in considering the design of technology for a museum, Boehner et al. [9] identified one-way transfer of information, from curators to visitors, as the dominant paradigm in existing designs. Using reflective design led to developing alternative technologies that allowed "visitors to add their own voice to the curator's voice" [45:53]. The influence of critical theory, and a resonance with critical design [14] (described further below), can be seen here in how this design challenges and shifts the power relations between visitors and curators.

While they chiefly emphasize the importance of reflection among designers, Sengers et al. [45] also mention and discuss the importance of promoting reflection among users as part of reflective design. However, of the six principles of reflective design, only two explicitly focus on users: "designers should support users in reflecting on their lives" and "dialogic engagement between designers and users through technology" [45:55–56]. These principles acknowledge users primarily in terms of their relationships with designers. Moreover, they provide little in the way of practical guidance for designers. Thus, an approach that provides explicit dimensions of reflection and concomitant strategies for designing around those dimensions represents an important complement to this previous work.

Slow Technology

Much technology is designed in service of enabling

efficient work, wherein speed and productivity are lauded above almost all else. Hallnäs and Redström [20] explore an alternative. Drawing an analogy from the distinction between fast food and a gourmet meal, they suggest countering existing "fast" technology by designing "slow" technology. For example, consider "an electronic doorbell that plays short fragments of a very long melody" [20:202] with each ring. The doorbell cannot be fully understood after one use. Doing so takes time, both in terms of repeated use and in terms of pausing to consider the relationships among the melodic pieces. Another example, the ChatterBox, is described below. Such designs, they suggest, help make space for reflection.

Slow technology provides a certain design sensibility that uses slowness to make space for reflection, making it complementary to but distinct from the dimensions of reflection articulated here. Furthermore, Hallnäs and Redström [20] remain somewhat vague as to what constitutes reflection. This vagueness is not necessarily a limitation; they may have intentionally avoided constraining the possible design space of slow technology. However, this vagueness also opens an opportunity to articulate more fully what we mean by reflection, as is done is this paper.

THEORETICAL BACKGROUND

To provide more grounded explication of how we might approach reflection in interaction design, this section describes a variety of conceptual and theoretical approaches to reflection. An exhaustive review of such work far exceeds the scope and space constraints of this paper [see, e.g., 16,34]. Instead, this section revolves around various disciplinary-epistemological approaches to reflection. Researchers in a range of disciplines—from philosophy to psychology to education—have provided a variety of conceptual and theoretical tools for thinking about and analyzing reflection. Organizing this work in terms of discipline and epistemology helps us see not only commonalities but also differences among these various approaches.

Note that this paper does not argue that any single conceptualization of, epistemological approach to, or theoretical framework for reflection *should* be used as an underpinning to designing for reflection. Indeed, each of the following have strengths and limitations in terms of guiding design. Rather than championing one approach or another, this paper instead suggests that greater insight with respect to informing design can be gleaned by identifying differences between and, moreover, commonalities among these theoretical approaches.

Philosophical

One of the original considerations of reflection in Western philosophy comes from Kant [25]. He begins his philosophical investigations by arguing for the existence of two types of mental faculties. The first, Understanding, involves comprehension of and reasoning about (or as Kant calls it "legislating") the domain of the natural world. The primary role of understanding is the identification and application of natural laws that necessitate how the world works. The second mental faculty, Reason, has the moral world as its legislative domain. Reason involves the identification and application of moral laws based on what freedoms of action are and are not possible with respect to human desire. Later, Kant extended this framework to include a third faculty of Judgment that mediates between nature and morality, between the natural world and the world of human desire. It is our faculty of judgment, he argues, that enables notions of aesthetics and beauty, i.e., the application of human desire to the natural world.

"The power of judgment in general is the faculty for thinking of the particular as contained under the universal" [25:Intro. IV, 5:179]. Of this faculty of judgment, Kant describes two kinds. In instances where the universal (e.g., a law) is given, then the judgment that operates to subsume particular instances under that universal is referred to as determining or as "determinant judgment." "If, however, only the particular is given, for which the universal is to be found, then the power of judgment is merely reflecting" [25:Intro. IV, 5:179] or "reflective judgment." Universals arising thusly do not derive directly from nature, otherwise they would be considered given. Rather, the reflecting power of judgment itself generates and gives rise to such universals. Kant places great significance on this capacity, suggesting at one point that all empirical concepts derive from it and that "without [this reflecting power] no judgment of experience would be possible at all" [25:FI V 20:212].

Another example comes from Dewey's [12] discussion of reflective thought, which places significant importance on reflection as a fundamentally important type of thinking. He defines reflective thought as "active, persistent, and careful consideration of any belief or supposed form of knowledge in the light of the grounds that support it, and the further conclusions to which it tends" [12:6].

This type of thought occurs through five distinct steps. First, it begins with "the inherently doubtful—with the confusing, obscure, or conflictual situation" [12:121]. The second step, identifying and defining the nature of the perplexing situation, may coincide with the first step. The third step involves suggestion of possible explanations. In the fourth step, the implications or consequences of each potential explanation are generated and considered. The fifth and final step compares these implications with the troubling situation to verify which, if any, of the potential explanation can account for it.

Dewey describes this puzzle-testing process occurring in even the most quotidian of situations, from navigating a city in order to arrive at an appointment on time ("I was down on 16th St. [at 12:20 and] I had an engagement at 124th St., at one o'clock" [12:69] p. 69), to puzzling out why bubbles form on the outsides of freshly washed glass tumblers placed upside-down ("Air from outside must have been expanded by the heat of the tumbler" [12:71]). Dewey devotes much focus to the training of (reflective) thought, especially the conduct and goals of education, which accounts for his influence in scholarship on the role of reflection in education [e.g., 17,36], to which we return below.

Cognitive

Another series of approaches to reflection comes from cognitive and developmental psychology. From this perspective, reflection is seen as a particular type of cognition, differentiated from others by its non-automatic character. Many dual-process models [24] describe two general modes of thought. The first, the automatic system, is responsible for quick, instinctive, or reactive decisions in our everyday activities. Indeed, drawing on prospect theory [23], Thaler and Sunstein [48] acknowledge that much of the thought conducted by this system is more likely to be seen as instinct than as "thinking." In contrast, decisions made by the reflective system occur slowly, with much deliberation and conscious intentionality. Thaler and Sunstein, though, focus primarily on using "nudges" to influence decisions made by people's automatic system, making their work not as directly relevant here.

In a similar example, Norman [38] differentiates between what he calls experiential cognition and reflective cognition. The former deals with "a state in which we perceive and react to the events around us efficiently and effortlessly" [38:16]. Reflective cognition, on the other hand, deals with intentional thought, decision making, and, crucially, "new ideas [and] novel responses" [ibid.]. While he acknowledges this bipartite treatment of cognition as an oversimplification, Norman goes on to suggest that much work in technology design focuses too greatly on experiential cognition. Incorporating a greater balance of support for reflective cognition, he suggests, can facilitate the design of technologies that better draw out humanity's creative capacity.

Other cognitive approaches are more fine-grained. King and Kitchener [26] developed a stage-based model of what they call reflective judgment describing how people come to be (more) reflective (without explicit invocation of Kant's [25] notion of reflective judgment described above). Rather than two modes, reflective and non-reflective, their model consists of seven stages. In the pre-reflective stages, "knowledge is assumed to exist absolutely and concretely" [26:48] in the world and thus needs to justification. More reflective stages are characterized by an acknowledgment of the contingency of knowledge. Knowledge is rarely seen as absolutely right or wrong but rather more or less reasonable, based on the arguments made and evidence available.

Reflective judgment, King and Kitchener [26] suggest, provides greatest value in situations of ill-structured problems involving significant uncertainty. For such problems, solutions cannot be "described with a high degree of completeness," nor can the problem be "resolved with a high degree of certainty" [26:11]. For example, the question of whether or not the ancient Egyptians had the mathematical knowledge, the necessary tools, and adequate power sources to build the pyramids can be seen as ill-structured. A non-reflective response would indicate that, because the pyramids are in Egypt, the Egyptians must have built the pyramids. A more reflective response might acknowledge, as one participant did, that "right and wrong are not comfortable categories [here...] it's more or less likely or reasonable, more or less in keeping with what the facts seem to be" [26:72]. Thus, in this view, reflection enables reasonable, evidence-based decision making, even in the face of uncertainty.

Educational

The potential relationship between education and reflection can be seen in some of the work above. Dewey [12] specifically describes the importance of reflective thought in education. Norman [38] suggests that education functions best when combining a balance of experiential cognition and reflective cognition. Much of King and Kitchener's [26] empirical work examines how reflective judgment develops as individuals move from primary and secondary education through university and into post graduate education. Indeed, several other scholars articulate deep connections between education and reflection [e.g., 17,27,36,37,43], two of which are described here.

For Moon, "reflection is intimately linked with the process of learning" [37:100]. She describes reflection as a mental process or, at times, a mental function, taking as inputs things that are already known to the individual and producing as output greater understanding. Thus, "reflection [is] a secondary action on already learnt material" [37:159], a reprocessing of knowledge or theories that may itself produce further knowledge or theories. In this way, reflection represents a form of deeper learning, involved not only in making meaning but in what Moon calls "working with meaning." Thus, reflection is integral to what Kolb [27] calls "deep learning," i.e., learning that transforms experience into knowledge.

Focusing more on the informal education of professionals and professionalization, Schön's [43] investigation of reflection studies how professionals think. His interests lie in what he refers to as "the epistemology of practice" [43:vii], that is, the kinds of knowing that professionals evidence through the conduct of their practice. In many ways, this focus resembles tacit knowledge, when there are things we know but "we cannot say what it is that we know" [43:49]. This knowledge is not abstract but is knowledge in doing, or, as Schön puts it, "knowing-in-action."

Schön describes a number of examples, ranging from professional baseball pitchers "finding the groove [...]

studying [their] winning habits and trying to repeat them every time [they] perform" [43:54], to an investment banker who acknowledges that operating numbers "allow him to calculate 'only 20 to 30 percent of the risk in investment'" [43:63]. Situations of reflection are often precipitated by the unexpected, and such "reflection tends to focus interactively on the outcomes of action, the action itself, and the intuitive knowing implicit in the action" [43:56]. This conception creates an inextricable, dialogic link between reflection and action; reflection is not an abstract, heady activity but is intimately intertwined with the performance of action. This kind of reflection-in-action, Schön argues, moves beyond positivist-based technical rationality to grapple with "situations of uncertainty, instability, uniqueness, and value conflict" [43:49].

Critical

Work in a fourth epistemological paradigm does not always use the term "reflection" but nonetheless shares many goals and sensibilities with other work reviewed here. Critical design "asks carefully crafted questions and makes us think, [...] its purpose is to stimulate discussion and debate" [14:58]. Put another way, "critical design [means] things that make you think" [8:501].

The epistemological paradigm underlying critical design derives largely from critical theory. This perspective neither sees knowledge as externally existent and objectively knowable in the style of positivist epistemology, nor does it see knowledge as a fully intersubjective social construction in the style of interpretivist epistemology. Instead, critical approaches consider knowledge as contingent upon, and in many ways arising from, the particular historical circumstances and power structures in which that knowledge is created [39]. While a detailed explication of critical theory exceeds this paper's scope, the application of critical perspectives in design [cf. 3,4] bears relevance to reflection. Specifically, critical design represents a means of drawing attention to, and arguably encouraging reflection on, the power dynamics and historical contingencies on which knowledge is predicated.

The influence of critical approaches can be seen in recent developments in HCI [e.g., 3,4,20,22,45]. However, critical designers do not always use the term "reflection" to describe the experiences they hope to evoke. Indeed, a recent review of reflection in HCI found few, if any, critical design papers that self-identified as pertaining to reflection [6]. Nonetheless, we include critical approaches here for two reasons. First, they provide an important epistemological alternative to other approaches dominant in HCI [cf. 39]. Second, they demonstrate that interest in the phenomena of reflection exist in HCI beyond work that self-identifies as being about reflection.

Summary Notes

Before moving on to consider how these theoretical approaches can be leveraged to inform design, it is valuable to note some comparisons and contrasts enabled by the epistemological grouping used here.

First, in both the philosophical and cognitive approaches, reflection is seen as a largely mental, almost exclusively individual activity. Dewey's [12] descriptions in his examples of reflective thought foreground vividly the individual, internal aspects. Likewise, Kant's [25] discussion of reflection arises during an explicit focus on mental faculties. This focus also appears salient in cognitive frameworks that emphasize the role reflection plays (or at times does not play) in individual decision making [48]. Similarly, King and Kitchener's [26] model describes individual cognitive development.

In contrast, educational approaches at least mention, if not emphasize, social (inter)action. For example, Schön's [43] case study of town planners shows that they do not work in isolation; rather, their reflection is embedded in a complex milieux of regulatory systems, advocacy groups, etc. Furthermore, these practitioners' reflection occurs not primarily through internal mental activities but "in action," in the conduct of their work. For Freire [17], the sociopolitical contexts give reflection not only its shape but also its purpose. Similarly, "critical design takes as its medium social, psychological, cultural, technical and economic values, in an effort to push the limits of lived experience" [14:58].

Second, these approaches differ in the value judgments they make about reflection. Cognitive approaches clearly imply reflective thought as often preferable to or even superior to "automatic" [48] or "pre-reflective" [26] thinking. Simultaneously, though, they acknowledge both the value of the rapid decision making that comes with such automatic thought and the impossibility of constantly engaging in reflective thought [38,48]. Critical approaches also value reflection for its potential to challenge existing sociocultural norms.

In contrast, philosophical approaches do not make such expressly clear value judgments about the preferability of reflective thought. For Kant [25], reflective judgment represents one mode of being, one particular way in which an individual experiences and interacts with the world that accounts for the ability to navigate relationships between abstract generalizations and particular concrete instantiations. Despite the importance Kant places on reflective judgment, he does not suggest that individuals should (or perhaps even could) be "more" reflective.

SOME DIMENSIONS OF REFLECTIVE INFORMATICS

Rather than arguing for or against the use of any one of these theoretical approaches or conceptual models, this section moves from contrasts to consider commonalities. In some ways, this strategy resembles that of Fleck and Fitzpatrick [15], who review literature on reflection to enumerate five levels of increasing reflectivity. However, rather than suggest means of designing for more reflection, this section synthesizes across the different perspectives reviewed above to distill several common elements. These commonalities serve as dimensions that can help guide the design of technologies for reflection.

These dimensions are not intended as prescriptive, i.e., they do not tell designers what to do. Nor do the dimensions constitute a phase- or stage-based model of reflection; the reflecting individual need not necessarily progress linearly from each dimension to the next. However, they are not totally independent of one another, either, as described further below. Finally, this section articulates *some* dimensions of reflective informatics. Future work, especially both design work and empirical studies of reflection, may identify valuable revisions, limitations, or alternatives to these dimensions. Rather, these dimensions provide a series of generative conceptual tools that can help inform or perhaps inspire design. In addition to grounding each dimension in the theoretical work reviewed above, this section also provides examples of previous work on designing for reflection. These examples both demonstrate how each dimension may play out in practice and provide design strategies for addressing each dimension. Ultimately, these dimensions helps establish common ground, advancing the discussion both of what exactly we mean by reflection and of how to design for it.

Breakdown

Instances of reflection are often precipitated by various types of breakdowns. Dewey [12] emphasizes doubtful or puzzling situations. Schön considers situations of surprise, uncertainty, or conflict where "there is some puzzling, or troubling, or interesting phenomenon" [43:50]. Making an analogy to Kuhn's notion of paradigm shifts [29], Mezirow [36] focuses on "disturbing anomalies" that do not fit with an individual's current meaning perspectives.

Why are breakdowns important moments with respect to reflection? The importance of breakdowns in other intellectual traditions provides some suggestions. Ethnomethodology [19], for example, focuses on breakdown and repair as moments when the tacit, implicit social structuring of interaction must be explicated by its interactors. Similar resonance can be seen with the phenomenological distinction between ready-to-hand, wherein a tool is used so unconsciously as to feel like an extension of the self, and present-at-hand, wherein a tool is examined consciously for its own properties [21]. Such changes from ready-to-hand to present-at-hand are often precipitated by moments when the tool ceases to function normally. Such conscious and explicit consideration of that which was previously unconscious and implicit, similar to the reflective modes in dual process models of cognition [23,24,38,48], acts to provide opportunities for reflection.

Taking breakdowns into account when designing may mean at least two things. First, as noted elsewhere e.g., [13,46], providing support for breakdowns can help technological tools better align with human practices. In some instances, such support may also help facilitate reflection. Second, perhaps somewhat more provocatively, drawing attention to or even inducing breakdowns may provide opportunities for moments of reflection. "Unless there is something doubtful, the situation is read off at a glance" [12:102]. Critical design takes a similar, if more measured, approach to breakdown by striving for a "slight strangeness [...] too weird and [designs] are instantly dismissed, not strange enough and they're absorbed into everyday reality" [14:63]. Thus, drawing attention to or even creating moments of perplexity and doubt may prove a useful design strategy.

Examples

While breakdown plays a central role in several conceptual and theoretical approaches to HCI design [e.g., 13], designing explicitly for breakdown in support of reflection occurs less often. As one example, some of the work in personal informatics [31] is predicated on breakdowns, often via comparison either with a user's own past data, such as task performance [e.g., 35], or data from other users, such as related search queries [e.g., 5]. Such breakdowns resonate primarily with the cognitive and educational perspectives reviewed above. Another example, ShoddyPop [32], randomly delays the delivery of email messages. Doing so arguably alleviates the onus to respond quickly, since the recipient will not receive the reply immediately, thus making time and space for reflection [cf. 20] on the content of the exchange. This example aligns more closely with philosophical and, to some extent, critical accounts of reflection.

All these examples work by violating expectations. That is, the designer identifies an expectation the user is likely to hold. The system then renders that expectation inaccurate, either by suggesting that the expectation does not hold or by intentionally violating the expectation. Doing so implicitly suggests that the expectation warrants closer examination.

Inquiry

Another important aspect in many frameworks of reflection is the process of conscious, intentional inquiry. Such processes figure prominently in both Kant's [25] notion of reflective judgment and Dewey's [12] description of reflective thought. The whole process he describes of examining why fog forms on freshly washed glass tumblers [12:71] exemplifies a process of inquiry, of generating, testing, revising, and further testing hypotheses. Indeed, Dewey at times refers to his conceptualization of reflection as a process of inquiry.

Inquiry plays a similarly important role in educational approaches to reflection. In Moon's [37] description, reflection involves re-examination of things—concepts, ideas, theories, etc.—already learned, i.e., inquiry on existing knowledge. Inquiry also takes a central place for Freire [17], though for him inquiry focuses on the political, social, and cultural contexts of learning.

Among cognitive approaches, this idea of inquiry occurs

most saliently in King and Kitchener's [26] work. In particular, their emphasis on the nature of knowledge and the basis of justification for that knowledge essentially represents a particular type of inquiry. In contrast to Thaler and Sunstein's [48] reflective mode or Norman's [38] reflective cognition, inquiry for King and Kitchener examines not knowledge itself but the origins thereof, i.e., epistemological inquiry.

Critical approaches often spur inquiry into the values underlying design. Indeed, critical design often employs "value fictions" wherein dominant values are subverted, for example, challenging the masculine-dominant gender norms of a gym [4]. Such subversions can (though not always do) provoke inquiry into the normative values being challenged.

Thus, designing for reflection means creating opportunities for, as well as supporting, inquiry. Doing so could take many forms. Taking after Dewey [12], a design could enable and encourage a process of iterative hypothesis testing and refinement. Resembling Moon [37], a design might focus on the explication of what a user already knows to encourage reflective re-examination of that knowledge. Bardzell et al. [4] suggest that inquiry may result less from the design *per se* and more from dialog between participants and researchers. Drawing on King and Kitchener [26], a design could emphasize inquiry into the origins of knowledge and the evidence provided therefor. Keeping in mind Schön's notion of reflection-in-action [43], such inquiry need not be entirely abstract or cognitive but may occur tacitly in the process of interacting with the system.

Examples

Prior approaches to inquiry become most apparent in work that focuses on reviewing (and reflecting on) past experience(s). For example, Wandering Mind [40] attempts to promote reflection by encouraging exploration of old journal entries. The personal informatics systems mentioned above as triggering breakdown often subsequently allow or encourage users' inquiry into their data, demonstrating the interdependence among dimensions. Inquiry becomes especially notable in work involving group discussion. For example, Prilla et al. [41] describe a system that supports stroke ward staff in reflecting on conversations with family members of patients. The design focuses on users (re)examining notes about their experiences, as well as subsequent group discussion. Arias et al. describe a system for collaborative civic design that explicitly includes a reflection space for "present[ing] information related to the problem at hand for exploration and extension" [2:95]. Thus, the design designates a separate space specifically for inquiry. ConsiderIt [28] similarly distinguishes between statements either supporting or opposing state ballot measures and the arguments to support those statements. Doing so allows for further investigation or examination of the arguments and the statements they support.

From these, we can draw out three design strategies for supporting inquiry. First, a design may incorporate review of past experiences. Second, a design can designate a particular space for inquiry separate from the primary activities to which that inquiry pertains. Third, group discussions may prove an effective means of promoting reflective inquiry.

Transformation

Reflection ultimately involves change. It is not only about examining the current state of the world or one's self but also about envisioning alternatives.

For educational scholars [10,27,37], reflection transforms experience into learning. Especially for Moon, reflection is a process of refining previous learning, that is, transforming understanding. For Kant, reflective judgment is that which reorders our conceptual schema. Reflection occurs precisely when our existing conceptual schema do not apply (or do not apply well) and thus we need to reschematize nature in order to come to a (better) understanding of it.

Schön's reflective practitioners often transform their understanding of a situation. For example, an investment banker found himself leery of an opportunity with a large Latin American bank where "the bank's operating numbers seemed satisfactory" [43:63] but he still felt an unease. The investor realized that "he had been treated with a degree of deference out of all proportion with his actual position" [43:64]. This reflection altered his understanding of the situation, and he chose to forgo any new investments with that bank. "Some months later, the bank went through the biggest bankruptcy ever in Latin America" [43:64].

Cognitive approaches that contrast reflection with more automatic thought processes grant reflection the ability to change the rules by which the automatic systems act. For example, heuristic decisions often function based on loss aversion [23], a preference for avoiding losses over seeking gains. Reflective decision making, however, enables decision making that is not subject to such biases [24].

Critical approaches involve not only questioning fundamental assumptions but exploring alternatives. Value fictions [14] represent one type of transformation enabled by critical design. Transformational products "attempt to actively shape their users' attitudes" [30]. An emphasis on transformation is also evident in Freire's [17] arguments about social change based on critical reflection.

Examples

Of the dimensions described here, transformation likely poses the most difficult challenge to designers. Transformation involves change to the fundamental, basic conceptualization of a situation, such as in Kant's reschamitization [25] or critical design's value fictions [14]. A design, however, often embodies a particular (i.e., single) stance or conceptualization of a situation. Designing for transformation, then, requires that the design be at least comprehensible (and perhaps usable and/or useful) when approached with different conceptualizations.

Consider Hallnäs and Redström's ChatterBox [20]. The system randomly concatenates snippets of text mined from office emails and displays them as isolated statements, e.g., "To participate in the burglar it will be necessary to register for the i3 Annual," or, somewhat more intriguingly, "Who else is to?" If approached as a tool to increase efficiency and productivity, i.e., as "fast" technology, the ChatterBox seems nearly incomprehensible. Instead, the system requires a transformation of the user's perspective to one that allows for slow technologies, that is, it requires "slowness in learning, understanding and presence [giving] people time to think and reflect" [20:203]. Importantly, such transformation could not occur without breakdowns triggered by the system's inscrutable sentences, again illustrating interconnections among the dimensions. In a related vein, Cheng et al. apply a similar stance on slowness and reflection in the design of GoSlow [11], mobile application that encourages moments of solitary contemplation. Their evaluation of the system, however, suggests that a gap may exist between simply pausing, i.e., going slow, and fundamental transformation.

Similarly, the lens of transformation provides for multiple interpretations of ChatterBox. On the one hand, one could see ChatterBox as designed for transformation in that in requires a transformation from the normative approach to technology in order to make sense of it. On the other, one could argue that ChatterBox does not support transformation in that it requires users take one particular approach rather than supporting the user as s/he moves through the experience of transformation.

DISCUSSION AND FUTURE

In the spirit of reflection, this section takes a reflexive turn on the paper itself. That is, it calls out some of the assumptions underlying the paper (i.e., it incites breakdown), examines the implications thereof (i.e., it conducts inquiries), and considers potential alternatives (i.e., it proposes transformation). Doing so does not cause the paper to undermine itself; rather it ensures that the ideas herein are presented with a degree of humility, acknowledges the paper's underlying value commitments, and suggests important areas for future investigation.

Reflection as Valuable – First and foremost, this paper is predicated on the assumption that reflection is valuable and that engaging in it is desirable. Given the extent of work on reflection in both interaction design [6,15,42] and other areas [16,34], this assumption seems hardly exceptional. However, considering its ramifications and alternative guiding assumptions may be illuminating. Situations may exist in which reflection is less valuable or perhaps even harmful. A doctor at the operating table, for example, might benefit from reflection-in-action [43] related to the procedures s/he is conducting, but s/he may become distracted from the task at hand by reflection on the economic and sociopolitical inequalities perpetuated by her or his country's health care system. One could even imagine a sort of "paralysis by analysis" in which an individual or group becomes so consumed by reflecting—on their assumptions, value commitments, biases, etc.—that it becomes difficult if not impossible for them to come to a meaningful resolution. Granted, given the close linkages between reflection and action argued for by some [17,43], such situations may be unlikely. Other conceptualizations of reflection [e.g., 12] may certainly allow such paralysis by analysis as a possibility.

Power and Privilege – This paper also does not explicitly address questions about the potentially privileged position of reflection. Who is granted the opportunity to reflect, by whom, and under what conditions? The critical approaches reviewed here speak to some of these concerns [14,17,45]. For Freire [17], the capacity for reflection does not necessarily derive solely from positions of power. Rather, given an appropriate pedagogical approach, reflection, particularly critical reflection on the power dynamics between oppressors and the oppressed, can become a tool for and means of empowerment. While fully addressing these issues exceeds this paper's scope, such sociopolitical concerns should remain central to work on designing for reflection.

Evaluation – Finally, evaluation poses a highly complex challenge. How does one evaluate technologies of reflection? Trying to determine when an individual (or group) is being "more reflective" seems at best a misconstrual of the value of reflection and at worst a harmful and deleterious reduction of an incredibly intricate phenomenon [cf. 47]. Instead, this paper suggests three approaches that may prove more suitable.

First, rather than trying to determine *how much* reflection a person is demonstrating, we might instead ask *in what ways* an individual (or group) is reflecting (or not reflecting). Aspects of either King and Kitchener's [26] or Fleck and Fitzpatrick's [15] frameworks could be used to describe which types of reflective thought occur in what contexts. In both cases, though, it would be difficult to avoid the temptation of seeing a technology of reflection as more effective because users engaged in styles of reflection associated with higher stages in the model. Alternatively, one could hinge such an evaluation on the dimensions articulated here. Perhaps, for example, experiences with a technology provide strong evidence for acknowledging breakdowns but less evidence of inquiry. Moving thusly from quantification to qualification may help grapple with reflection's complexity. Furthermore, doing so may provide valuable revisions to or extensions of the dimensions articulated here.

Second, rather than attempting to assess reflection *per se*, one could instead ask what role reflection plays in the broader contexts in which it occurs. The question, then, may become what benefits reflection provides. Carrying this approach too far, however, risks a displacement, wherein reflection is linked with some desired outcome (e.g., increased learning, improved performance), and assessment of that outcome is taken as evidence that reflection occurred [6]. Making a comparison between evaluating reflection and evaluating art, Hallnäs and Redström suggest that "one cannot explain what a symphony by Beethoven is [...] by empirical studies of a collection of concert visitors" [20:209]. Similarly, formal methods and traditional user studies of people interacting with technologies of reflection may provide poor accounts of that reflection. Instead, novel evaluation methods may need be necessary to grapple with the broader contextual ramifications of reflection.

Finally, HCI evaluation generally attempts to ascertain the impacts of design, often asking the question, "Did it work?" In the context of reflection, focusing on this question may limit the potential impact our studies of such technologies can have. Instead, we might considering using the design as a means of deepening our understanding of reflection itself. Rather than trying to design systems to make people more reflective, we can seek to understand how different interventions alter the nature of reflective thought. This approach suggests a move from seeing reflection as a problem area in need of a solution to seeing reflection as a complex situation in which we can pose various design interventions [cf. 7]. Thus, avoiding an insistence on demonstrating that our design "works" may open up opportunities to understand more fully both the nature of reflection and the potential impacts of our interventions.

CONCLUSION

Designing for reflection does not represent an entirely novel endeavor [6,15,31,42]. While important prior work has pioneered this area, it lacks a strong conceptual and theoretical grounding [6,15]. Designers of technologies for reflection need a common vocabulary for talking about (1) what reflection is (and, implicitly, what it is not) and (2) how we might go about designing for reflection.

This paper addresses that gap, reviewing a range of literature on reflection from a variety of disciplinary and epistemological perspectives. Focusing on commonalities among these theories, the paper proposes three dimensions of *reflective informatics*, which help articulate how design may support reflection. To help ground the discussion, each dimension is explicated with examples from existing systems and design interventions. These examples demonstrate that the dimensions map well onto and help us understand better existing design practice. Furthermore, comparisons with related approaches show how these dimensions fill a gap in our existing approaches. Thus, this paper provides an important contribution toward drawing work on designing for reflection under a shared conceptual umbrella, as well as giving that work a common conceptual language to discuss the unique challenges in designing for reflection.

Ultimately, this paper not only to provides a scaffold for designing for reflection, it also seeks to provoke conversation about and deeper engagement with the conceptual definition and theoretical grounding of reflection in technology design. That is, the theoretical grounding of reflection should not be seen as a "solved" problem. Indeed, future work should explicitly engage with multiple definitions of, theories of, and frameworks for reflection in design. Only through such practical application can we hope to understand how best to design for reflection.

ACKNOWLEDGMENTS

This material is based in part upon work supported by the NSF under Grant No. IIS-1110932. Thanks to Vera Khovanskaya, Phoebe Sengers, Geri Gay, and the anonymous reviewers for comments on earlier drafts.

REFERENCES

1. Agre, P.E. *Computation and Human Experience.* Cambridge University Press, Cambridge, 1997.
2. Arias, E., Eden, H., Fischer, G., Gorman, A., and Scharff, E. Transcending the Individual Human Mind - Creating Shared Understanding through Collaborative Design. *ACM ToCHI 7*, 1 (2000), 84–113.
3. Bardzell, J. and Bardzell, S. What is "critical" about critical design?. *Proc CHI*, ACM Press (2013), 3297–3306.
4. Bardzell, S., Bardzell, J., Forlizzi, J., Zimmerman, J., and Antanitis, J. Critical Design and Critical Theory: The Challenge of Designing for Provocation. *Proc DIS*, (2012), 288–297.
5. Bateman, S., Teevan, J., and White, R.W. The Search Dashboard: How Reflection and Comparison Impact Search Behavior. *Proc CHI*, (2012), 1785–1794.
6. Baumer, E.P.S., Khovanskaya, V., Matthews, M., Reynolds, L., Sosik, V.S., and Gay, G. Reviewing Reflection: On the Use of Reflection in Interactive System Design. *Proc DIS*, (2014), 93–102.
7. Baumer, E.P.S. and Silberman, M.S. When the Implication Is Not to Design (Technology). *Proc CHI*, (2011), 2271–2274.
8. Blevis, E. Stillness and Motion, Meaning and Form. *Proc DIS*, (2014), 493–502.
9. Boehner, K., Gay, G., and Larkin, C. Drawing evaluation into design for mobile computing: a case study of the Renwick Gallery's Hand Held Education Project. *J of Digital Libraries 5*, 3 (2005), 219–230.
10. Boud, D., Keogh, R., and Walker, D., eds. *Reflection: Turning Experience into Learning.* Kogan Page, London, 1985.
11. Cheng, J., Bapat, A., Thomas, G., et al. GoSlow: Designing for Slowness, Reflection and Solitude. *Proc CHI Ext. Abst.*, (2011), 429–438.

12. Dewey, J. *How We Think. A restatement of the relation of reflective thinking to the educative process.* D. C. Heath, Boston, 1933.
13. Dourish, P. and Button, G. On Technomethodology: Foundational Relationships between Ethnomethodology and System Design. *Human-Computer Interaction 13*, 4 (1998), 395 – 432.
14. Dunne, T. and Raby, F. *Design Noir: The Secret Life of Electronic Objects.* Birkhäuser, Berlin, 2001.
15. Fleck, R. and Fitzpatrick, G. Reflecting on Reflection: Framing a Design Landscape. *Proc OZCHI*, (2010), 216–223.
16. Fook, J., White, S., and Gardner, F. Critical reflection: a review of contemporary literature and understandings. In S. White, J. Fook and F. Gardner, eds., *Critical reflection in health and social care*. Open University Press, Maidenhead, 2006, 3–20.
17. Freire, P. *The Pedagogy of the Oppressed.* Seabury, New York, 1970.
18. Friedman, B., Kahn, P.H., and Borning, A. Value Sensitive Design and Information Systems. In P. Zhang and D. Galletta, eds., *Human-Comput Interact in Mgmt Info Sys*. M. E. Sharpe, London, 2003, 348–372.
19. Garfinkel, H. *Studies in Ethnomethodology.* Prentice-Hall, Englewood-Cliffs, NJ, 1967.
20. Hallnäs, L. and Redström, J. Slow Technology – Designing for Reflection. *Personal and Ubiquitous Computing 5*, 3 (2001), 201–212.
21. Heidegger, M. *Being and Time.* Harper & Row, 1927.
22. Irani, L., Vertesi, J., Dourish, P., Philip, K., and Grinter, R.E. Postcolonial computing: a lens on design and development. *Proc CHI*, ACM (2010), 1311–1320.
23. Kahneman, D. and Tversky, A. Prospect Theory: An Analysis of Decision Under Risk. *Econometrica 47*, 2 (1979), 263–292.
24. Kahneman, D. *Thinking, Fast and Slow.* Farrar, Straus and Giroux, New York, 2011.
25. Kant, I. *Critique of the Power of Judgment.* Cambridge University Press, Cambridge, 1790.
26. King, P.M. and Kitchener, K.S. *Developing Reflective Judgment.* Jossey-Bass, San Francisco, 1994.
27. Kolb, D. *Experiential Learning: Experience as the source of learning and development.* Prentice-Hall, Englewood Cliffs, NJ, 1984.
28. Kriplean, T., Morgan, J., Freelon, D., Borning, A., and Bennett, L. Supporting Reflective Public Thought with ConsiderIt. *Proc CSCW*, (2012), 265–274.
29. Kuhn, T.S. *The Structure of Scientific Revolutions.* University of Chicago Press, Chicago, 1962.
30. Laschke, M., Hassenzahl, M., and Diefenbach, S. Things with attitude: Transformational Products. *Create Symposium*, (2011).
31. Li, I., Dey, A., and Forlizzi, J. A Stage-Based Model of Personal Informatics Systems. *Proc CHI*, (2010), 557–566.
32. Lindley, S.E., Harper, R., and Sellen, A. Desiring to be in Touch in a Changing Communications Landscape: Attitudes of Older Adults. *Proc CHI*, (2009), 1693–1702.
33. Löwgren, J. and Stolterman, E. *Thoughtful Interaction Design.* MIT Press, Cambridge, MA, 2004.
34. Lyons, N., ed. *Handbook of Reflection and Reflective Inquiry.* Springer, New York, 2010.
35. Malacria, S., Scarr, J., Cockburn, A., Gutwin, C., and Grossman, T. Skillometers: Reflective Widgets that Motivate and Help Users to Improve Performance. *Proc UIST*, (2013), 321–330.
36. Mezirow, J. How Critical Reflection Triggers Transformative Learning. In J. Mezirow, ed., *Fostering Critical Reflection in Adulthood*. Jossey-Bass, San Francisco, 1990, 1–20.
37. Moon, J. *Reflection in Learning & Professional Development.* RoutledgeFalmer, Abingdon, Oxon, 1999.
38. Norman, D.A. *Things That Make Us Smart.* Perseus Group, New York, 1993.
39. Orlikowski, W.J. and Baroudi, J.J. Studying Information Technology in Organizations: Research Approaches and Assumptions. *Info Sys Research 2*, 1 (1991), 1–28.
40. Pirzadeh, A., He, L., and Stolterman, E. Personal Informatics and Reflection: A Critical Examination of the Nature. *Proc CHI Ext. Abst.*, (2013), 1979–1988.
41. Prilla, M., Degeling, M., and Herrmann, T. Collaborative Reflection at Work: Supporting Informal Learning at a Healthcare Workplace. *Proc GROUP*, (2012), 55–64.
42. Sas, C. and Dix, A. Designing for reflection on experience. *Proc CHI Ext. Abst.*, (2009), 4741–4744.
43. Schön, D.A. *The Reflective Practitioner.* Basic Books, New York, 1983.
44. Schön, D.A. Designing as reflective conversation with the materials of a design situation. *Research in Engineering Design 3*, 3 (1992), 131–147.
45. Sengers, P., Boehner, K., David, S., and Kaye, J. "Jofish." Reflective Design. *Proc Critical Computing*, (2005), 49–58.
46. Suchman, L.A. *Plans and Situated Actions.* Cambridge University Press, Cambridge, 1987.
47. Sumison, J. and Fleet, A. Reflection: can we assess it? Should we assess it? *Assessment & Evaluation in Higher Education 21*, 2 (1996), 121–130.
48. Thaler, R.H. and Sunstein, C.R. *Nudge.* Yale University Press, New Haven, CT, 2008.

Stock Lamp: An Engagement-Versatile Visualization Design

Yuzuru Tanahashi
University of California, Davis
ytanahashi@ucdavis.edu

Kwan-Liu Ma
University of California, Davis
ma@cs.ucdavis.edu

ABSTRACT

Design methodologies for information visualizations are typically based on the assumption that the users will be fully engaged in the visual exploration of the displayed information. However, recent research suggests that there is an increasing diversity in *how* users engage with modern visualizations, and that the traditional design theories do not always satisfy the varied users needs. In this paper, we present a new design concept, engagement-versatile design, for visualizations that target users with a variety of engagement styles. Without losing generality, we demonstrate the feasibility of this concept through the designing of a system called Stock Lamp, an engagement-versatile visualization that helps users keep track of the stock market in real-time. This design process includes identifying different modes of engagement, deriving design implications from each engagement-mode, and applying them to the visualization's design. Our user study shows that Stock Lamp is able to consistently relay market information even when the users are multi-tasking. We believe this study establishes a new concept that promotes a systematic design approach that leverages both theoretical and empirical design methodologies for future visualization development.

Author Keywords

Design concept; visualization usability; user engagement;

ACM Classification Keywords

H.5.m. Information Interfaces and Presentation (e.g. HCI): Miscellaneous

INTRODUCTION

Information visualization has grown into a ubiquitous technology with various application scenarios. Recent visualizations are no longer limited to the traditional settings that used to focus on single users, advanced data analytics, and desktop monitors. These diverse application scenarios have inspired many studies on new design guidelines for visualizations that exceed the traditional use case scenarios. For example, visualization systems that allow multiple users to conduct collaborative data analyses require various new design guidelines regarding how the collaboration is supported by the system [18, 19]. Visualizations that target public users also often require additional design considerations in order to aid average computer user's limited domain knowledge and to help individual users achieve their personal goals [29, 32]. There are also unique design guidelines for visualizations that are intended for unconventional display settings from mobile displays [11] to wall-sized displays [6]. These studies have provided developers extensive guidance on what elements to consider when designing non-traditional visualizations.

CHI 2015, April 18 - 23 2015, Seoul, Republic of Korea
Copyright 2015 ACM 978-1-4503-3145-6/15/04 $15.00
http://dx.doi.org/10.1145/2702123.2702323

Correspondingly, designing visualizations for real-world applications requires further design consideration with respect to *how* users interact with visualizations in real-world settings. One of the key elements to consider is the varied engagement styles the users exhibit towards visualizations. Visualizations in real-world settings do not always receive the user's full attention or active interaction. Therefore, these visualization system cannot base its design under the assumption that its users will be fully engaged in the visual analytics/exploration of the displayed information (e.g., [8, 26]).

In this paper, we present a new design concept, engagement-versatile design, for visualizations that serve users with a variety of engagement styles. First, we present a simple taxonomy of user engagement styles based on our observation on how users interact with desktop visualizations and discuss how the unique characteristics of each engagement style influences the visualization design. We then apply this new design concept to the construction of a system called Stock Lamp, a visualization system that helps part-time investors to keep track of the stock market in real-time. The results of our user study show that Stock Lamp can effectively relay information to users in different modes of engagement. We believe this study establishes a new systematic approach for deriving visualization designs from a range of engagement styles and will provide future developers with a new perspective for understanding visualization usability in real-world settings.

RELATED WORK

Basing the visualization design on the characteristics of *how* users engage with the system is not a new concept. Ambient display is a type of information visualization specifically designed to reside in the user's peripheral vision. In order to relay information to users who are not actively engaging with the system, ambient displays often require a different set of design considerations from traditional visualizations [28]. There has been extensive research on ambient display designs and their potential effects on users [20, 30]. Based on the absence of user's focused attention and active interaction, ambient displays, in general, need to be unobtrusive to user's daily activities, able to effectively notify users when urgent events arise, and aesthetically pleasing to users. These studies identify ambient displays as a unique type of information visualization which is intended for a particular setting where the users exhibit low-level of engagement towards the system.

Moreover, recent research suggests that there are different phases in how users engage with visualizations, and that visualizations in real-world settings tend to take different roles from ambient displays to interactive visualization systems depending on the user's level of engagement. Brignull and Rogers [10] made an observation that there are three stages of user activity between users and interactive public displays. Based on these different user activity stages, they discussed the design considerations to encourage users to interact with the displays. Vogel and Balakrishnan [33] pointed out that visualizations' application contexts change based on different phases of user interaction and presented a prototype system that allows users to smoothly transition between different interaction phases by taking the characteristics of each interaction phase into the design considerations. Both of these studies recognized the existence of a multi-modal engagement style and discussed the importance of taking each mode of engagement into the visualization's design consideration.

We extend these studies by establishing a clear concept of a design approach for visualizations whose users exhibit a wide range of different engagement styles. Since different visualization systems target different users in different environments and have different goals, how users engage with these different visualizations also vary case by case. Therefore, we do not expect that the different modes of engagement discussed in this paper will directly apply to all visualization systems. Instead, we believe that our design process of extracting distinct modes of engagement through observation and deriving design implications from the characteristics of each engagement style will provide future developers a systematic approach to design visualizations for their intended settings and for understanding visualization usability from perspectives of different user engagement styles.

ENGAGEMENT-VERSATILE DESIGN

Engagement-versatile design is a new design concept for visualization systems that target audiences who exhibit different styles of engagement towards the visualization. Current visualization systems are typically designed under the assumption that the users are fully engaged in the visual exploration of the data. However, recent studies (e.g., [26, 33]) have shown that this assumption does not always align with how users actually interact with visualization systems in the real-world. One of the challenging issues of designing these types of visualizations that exceed the typical assumption is that there is no concrete design guidelines for them since how users engage with these visualizations differ case by case depending on their target audiences, deployed environments, and intended goals among other attributes. The engagement-versatile design concept promotes the development of visualization systems that can effectively relay information to users in various situations by focusing on matching the visualization's utility to each distinct mode of user engagement.

Engagement Modes

Engagement modes refer to the distinct styles in how users engage with the visualization. Identifying different engagement modes from how users interact with the visualization in its intended application context helps developers understand what type of utility is expected by the users. Therefore, by deriving a variation of design implications from each distinct engagement mode and incorporating them into the visualization's design helps the visualization to achieve the versatility necessary to maximize its utility in different situations.

In this study, we consider two attributes, *attention* and *participation*, based on our observation of how users interact with desktop visualizations, to determine the user's engagement mode. Each of these attributes encompasses two statuses. (1) The attention attribute indicates the status of a user's attention towards the visualization, and it is assigned a status of either *peripheral* or *focus*. Peripheral attention suggests that the visualization resides in the user's peripheral vision and is not given full attention. Focus attention suggests that the visualization is observed by the user, and it is given full attention. (2) The participation attribute indicates the status of a user's participation in the visual data exploration, and it is assigned a status of either *passive* or *active*. Passive participation suggests that the user is simply gazing at the visualization and not interacting with its user interfaces to actively explore the data. Active participation suggests that the user is utilizing the user interfaces to actively explore the data.

Based on these attention and participation statuses, we derive three distinct engagement modes relevant to the visualization.

- Periphery-Passive mode
- Focus-Passive mode
- Focus-Active mode

Periphery-Active mode is not included because it is a mode that is not feasible; actively interacting with systems that are in the periphery is not commonly practiced. Each of the three engagement modes we consider defines a unique interaction style and the expected role of the visualization. These modes allow us to accommodate users in different work settings with different degrees of interest.

Periphery-Passive Mode

Periphery-Passive mode describes a situation where the visualization is neither in the user's direct line of sight nor given much attention (it is in the user's periphery). In addition, the users are also not actively interacting with the visualization (passive interaction). In this situation, the users are not particularly interested in gaining specific information. Instead, the users prefer to quickly check data updates by glancing at the visualization without breaking concentration towards their main tasks. Therefore, the visualization in Periphery-Passive mode takes a role similar to an ambient display [28].

Focus-Passive Mode

Focus-Passive mode describes a situation where the visualization is in the user's direct line of sight and is given full attention (focus). However, the users are not interacting with the visualization to explore the data and are only gazing at the visualization (passive interaction). In this situation, the users are interested in gaining information from the visualization, but they have no particular objective or information on which they want to focus. Hence, the users are only interested in receiving information and are not particularly motivated in retrieving specific information. Therefore, the visualization in Focus-Passive mode takes a role similar to a static or an animated visualization system.

Focus-Active Mode

Focus-Active mode describes a situation where the visualization is in the user's direct line of sight and given full attention (focus), and where the user is interacting with the visualization to explore and investigate the data (active interaction). In this situation, the users are not only interested in gaining information from the visualization, but are also motivated to retrieve information based on specific interests. Therefore, the visualization in Focus-Active mode takes the role of a typical interactive visualization system, which facilitates extensive exploration and in-depth data analysis.

Design Approach

The three situations described above reflect the everyday circumstances under which most users interact with visualization systems. Therefore, leaving out any one of these engagement modes from the design consideration confines the types of users that the visualization can support and consequently limits the practical value of the visualization [15].

Engagement-versatile design allows visualizations to encompass all types of users by incorporating the design guidelines suggested by different visualization categories and associating these guidelines to the respective engagement mode into the construction of the visualization.

Our design approach for constructing an engagement-versatile visualization is as follows. For each visual component of the visualization, we identify the engagement modes to support. Then, we make our design decisions for each of these visual components based on the design guidelines appropriate to the engagement modes. By employing the engagement-versatile design concept, the visualization will be able to not only serve a wider range of users but also provide valuable information to the users in different situations.

STOCK LAMP

To demonstrate the feasibility of engagement-versatile design, we created Stock Lamp. Stock Lamp is a real-time visualization system of stock market data and online news feeds that targets the part-time investor demographic. This visualization system incorporates the unique feature of engagement-versatile design to help part-time investors in different situations keep track of market information, ongoing news, and social comments regarding a set of stocks.

We chose stock data for this case study for two reasons. First, stock information is neutral against personal preference. Most investors have a clear goal, which is to maximize capital gain. This consistency in user objective allows us to ask questions with well-defined answers for our user study. Second, there already exists a large population of part-time investors ranging from college students, office workers, to house wives who have limited time to engage with their investing activities. These potential users allowed us to gather valuable feedback throughout the development of Stock Lamp and also suggests the system's prospective real-world application.

Data Processing

The data used in Stock Lamp was collected from two online sources: Google Finance [1] and Twitter [3]. Google Finance provides market information, including price, transaction volume, related companies, and relevant news about the stocks. Twitter provides social comments relevant to the stock companies. In order to maintain this study's focus on its visual presentation method, we did not apply further data processing to derive additional information about the collected data.

Visual Components

Stock Lamp is equipped with two views, *lamp-view* (see Figure 1) and *info-view* (see Figure 3), and it displays either one of them based on the user's interest or engagement mode. Lamp-view displays market information and social attention on each stock through a figurative visual representation of the data. In lamp-view, users can view abstract information about stocks (e.g., whether the stock price is rising or dropping, and whether the companies are mentioned much on Twitter). However, the users in lamp-view cannot see detailed information (e.g., how much growth in price, what type of tweets are currently trending) about the individual stocks. Info-view complements lamp-view by providing users with detailed information in a descriptive fashion using texts and charts.

Lamp-View

Lamp-view employs a design model refered to as organic visualizations that is often considered to be aesthetically pleasing and to attract people's curiosity [25, 27]. In addition to employing organic visualization design, we also pay extra attention to the speeds of moving entities and color transitions in the lamp-view to ensure that the visualization maintains its unobtrusiveness as new data arrives. These design decisions were made to incorporate design guidelines for ambient displays and therefore support users in Periphery-Passive mode.

The inspiration of lamp-view is derived from lava lamps, a popular decorative ornament from the 1960s [2]. We chose lava lamps as a source of inspiration based on its decorative characteristics. Lava lamps have been a popular item for decorating various indoor environments. The liquid wax in lava lamps form various shapes and are constantly moving around, yet lava lamps are not considered distracting. Instead, they are often characterized as relaxing and fun to watch. Therefore, by virtually emulating a lava lamp, we believed that we could attain some of the product's core values: aesthetically pleasing, entertaining, soothing etc. These values are important in order to attract the attention of the uses in Periphery-Passive mode without being conceived as disturbing.

Figure 1 shows a screenshot of lamp-view. In lamp-view, Stock Lamp visualizes a set of stocks as jelly-like blobs[1] whose size, position, color, and brightness conveys information about their respective stocks. The lamp-view also includes a retractable side-panel that displays more detailed information about a featured stock to provide users with further information on stocks of their interest.

Figure 2 illustrates lamp-view's visual encodings. The size of the blob indicates the size of the stock's transaction volume over the last 20 seconds compared to its average volume. The vertical positions of the blobs depict the distribution of the price growth rate among the visualized stocks. The color of the blob indicates the price growth rate of the stock following the conventional practice for stock price indicators. The

[1]Each blob is generated by 20 metaballs [7] that randomly move within a certain radius from the core position of the topic.

brightness of the blob indicates the social attention towards the stock based on Twitter data. The horizontal positions of the blobs were fixed in order to help users maintain orientation in the visualization during their absence. By restricting the blobs from migrating horizontally, lamp-view allows users to quickly spot the blob representing the stock of their interest without needing to search the whole screen. These design decisions were made based on considerations in how people tend to interpret visual representations [13] and the feedback gathered from our pilot users[2].

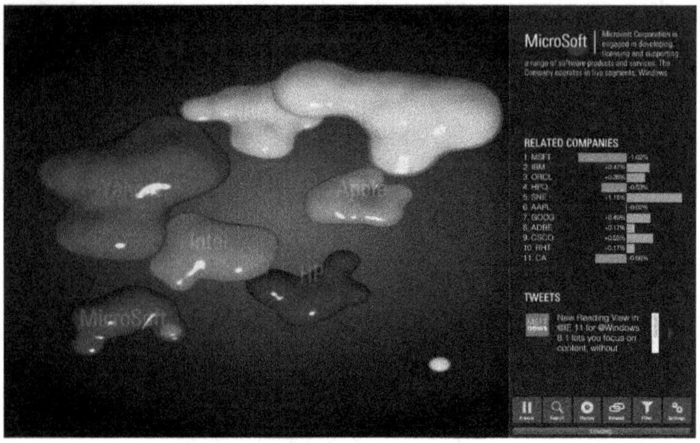

Figure 1: A screenshot of lamp-view.

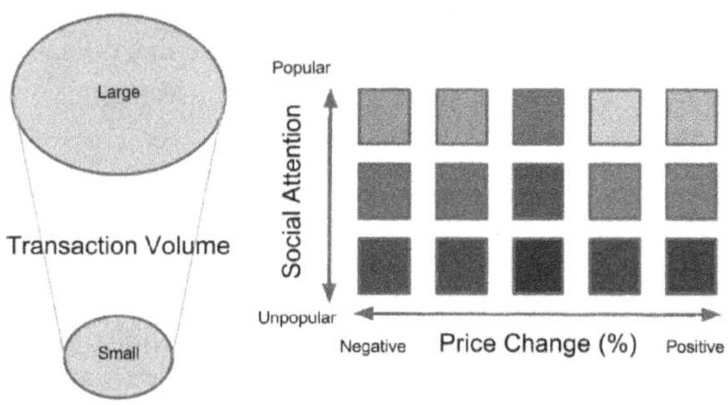

Figure 2: The visual encoding of stock data in lamp-view.

The retractable side-panel displays small pieces of textual information about a featured stock to supplement the figurative lava lamp metaphor. This side-panel consists of four components: description, related, tweets, and controller. The description component displays the featured company's name and its description. The related component displays the stock information of the companies that are related to the featured company. The tweets component displays tweets that contain content associated with the featured company. The controller component provides a simple user interface for controlling animation settings and customizing the content displayed in the side panel. These pieces of information are based on what other web sites (e.g., [1, 5]) display for individual stock.

Since the contents displayed in this side panel are descriptive and require the user's full attention, the side-panel is hidden by default when users are in Periphery-Passive mode. This helps the lamp-view to maintain a simple view allowing users to appreciate the visualization's artistic aesthetics without feeling the need to analyze the information when they glance at the display while working. The side-panel appears when the system detects that the users are in Focus-Passive or Focus-Active mode. The featured company is randomly selected by the system for the users in Focus-Passive mode, or manually selected by the users in Focus-Active mode.

In order to warn users the occasional sudden changes in stock market, the blobs in lamp-view would also jiggle rapidly and emit pulsing lights to catch the user's attention when certain data values exceeded some threshold set by the user.

Info-View

Info-view presents detailed information about a specific company through a series of infographics-like visualizations. Figure 3(a) shows a screenshot of info-view. After selecting a particular company, the info-view displays a set of visualizations that show different aspects of the company's data.

There are four types of information available in the Stock Lamp's info-view: history, related companies, news, and people. These different aspects of the company are presented to the users in small widgets referred to as info-cards. Each info-card portrays one aspect of the specified company based on the most recent data.

Figure 3 shows the four different types of info-cards: history-card, related-card, news-card, and people-card. History-card portrays the history of the company's stock and important news published over the last three months. In this card, the line chart depicts the temporal history of the stock's price and the flags in the chart link the past news articles that are considered to have had an effect on the stock prices listed on the right. To provide users with an idea of the content of the news article, this list includes the headline of the news article and users can click on the text to review the full article. Related-card displays a set of companies that are related to the company and the current stock prices of those companies. News-card displays a list of the most recent online news articles relevant to the company. This card also provides access to the full article by clicking on the listed items. People-card presents a summary of the tweets associated with the company by listing the top ranking Twitter users (with the most favorited/re-tweeted tweets) and their most popular tweets.

In info-view, these four types of info-cards are generated per company and are individually displayed on the screen. The number of info-cards visible to the users depends on the screen real estate and the user settings. In our example of Stock Lamp, info-view displays two info-cards simultaneously (see Figure 3). To explore other info-cards, users can either scroll to the info-card of their interest or call it out by specifying the company and the card type in the control-panel on the right. This control-panel also allows users to return to lamp-view by clicking on the snapshot of the blobs at the top.

Since these info-cards all contain pieces of information that are more contextual than abstract, the visualizations in info-view are more descriptive than figurative and tend to require the user's full attention. Thus, info-view mainly targets users

[2]Three university employees: a data-specialist, a visualization developer, and a graphics designer volunteered as pilot users for this research. All three were familiar with the data, and two had experience in part-time stock investment.

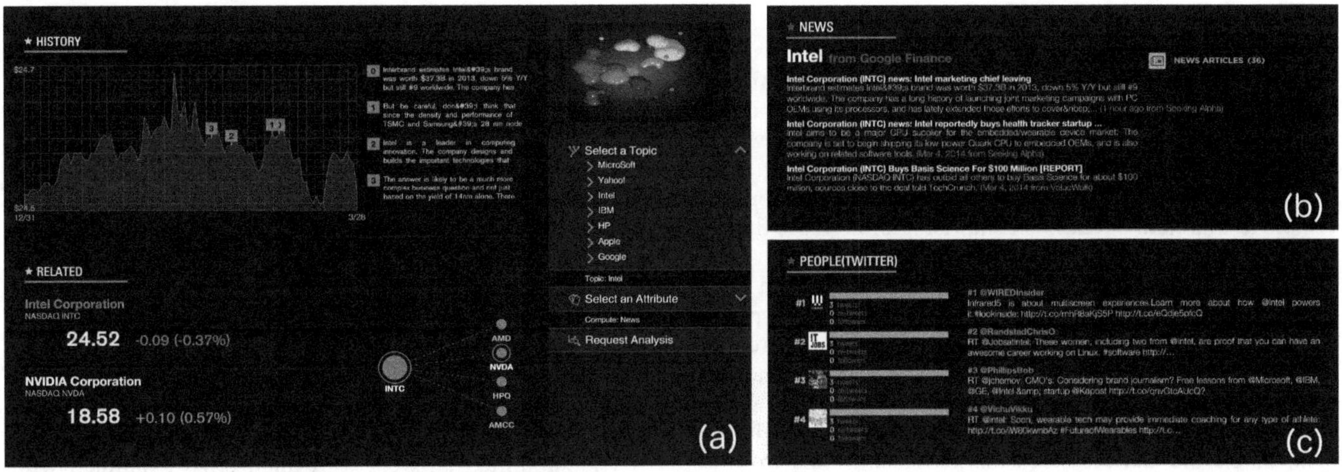

Figure 3: (a): A screenshot of info-view. The displayed info-cards are (top) history-card and (bottom) related-card. (b): An example of news-card. (c): An example of people-card.

in Focus-Passive and Focus-Active modes. In order to keep providing all users with fresh and updated information, the info-view scrolls a new info-card into view automatically after a set period of time when the users are in Focus-Passive mode. Otherwise, it will wait for input from the user.

Implementation

The implementation of the visual components for Stock Lamp uses two web-based graphics programming technologies, WebGL [4] and D3 [9]. We chose WebGL over other web-based graphics because it was the only graphics language that could take advantage of the GPU and maintain a frame rate for smooth animation without compromising graphical resolution. We used D3 for implementing the visualizations seen in info-view. We chose D3 for generating the info-cards because D3 is one of the most simple graphics languages and has a great built-in library for managing user interactions with visual entities. This simplicity helped us design and develop a variety of info-card templates for testing on pilot users, and also allowed us to easily add new info-card designs as new data attributes are introduced to the data.

For detecting the user's engagement mode, Stock Lamp combines two pieces of information: the user's attention (derived by a simple eye detection/tracking system [23] using the webcam video stream) and interaction (based on the use of the mouse or touchscreen). Any sort of interaction with the system indicated that the user was in Focus-Active mode. Otherwise, Focus-Passive mode or Periphery-Passive mode was determined based on whether the user's eyes were directed to the visualization or not. This simple engagement detection mechanism worked well for our simple case study. However, we believe that future engagement detection mechanisms will need to be modified and designed accordingly to the system's deployed environment and to its target audiences.

USER STUDY

In order to evaluate Stock Lamp for its usability with respect to the three user engagement modes, we conducted a user study consisting of three tests, one for each engagement-mode. Each test contained a unique set of tasks specifically designed to simulate situations that would prescribe the respective engagement-mode to the users. Participants in the user study were asked to take all three tests twice: once using Stock Lamp, and once using *Dashboard*. In order to avoid any learning effects, half of the participants were asked to test Stock Lamp first and Dashboard next, and the other half were asked to test in the reversed order.

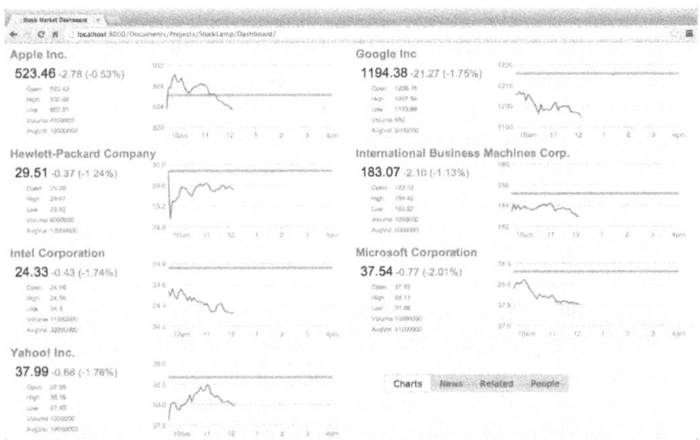

Figure 4: A screenshot of Dashboard showing the stocks' history data. Each widget contains basic market information, including price, transaction volume, and a market price chart.

Dashboard is another real-time visualization system we developed that emulates a more traditional stock visualization style. The data used in Dashboard is exactly the same data as in Stock Lamp, and the difference between these two systems is solely based on their styles of presentation. Dashboard displays a set of widgets portraying a company's data based on one of four attributes: history, related companies, news, and people. Figure 4 shows a screenshot of Dashboard displaying the history attribute. Users can switch the displayed information to a different attribute using the buttons in the bottom right corner. Dashboard's visual design is based on a more traditional presentation style for stock data, and its visual elements are mostly borrowed directly from major web-sites that provide real-time stock data [1, 5].

The data used in this user study was pre-collected for 5 consecutive weekdays, from March 2 to 7 2014, at 20-second intervals during the stock market's open hours. This collected data consisted of seven stocks whose stock symbols are AAPL, GOOG, HPQ, INTL, YHOO, MSFT, and IBM. The number of stocks to display was determined based on a series of financial articles which recommended non-professional investors to maintain portfolios comprising of no more than 10 stocks [14, 24]. In addition to this recommendation, we also believe that seven is a suitable number to visualize on Stock Lamp considering the lamp-view's scalability with respect to the number of blobs that can fit in the limited display real estate and be viewed effortlessly within the people's attention capacity [16]. We used pre-collected data instead of real-time data for this user study in order to prevent the participant's local time zone and the stock market closing time from affecting the user experience while taking the tests.

Procedure

All participants of in the user study were asked to follow a specific procedure consisting of four steps.

Step-1: Introductory Tutorial

Step-2: Focus-Passive Test Session

Step-3: Periphery-Passive Test Session

Step-4: Focus-Active Test Session

Each test session contained two tests with the exact same tasks. The first round using Stock Lamp, and the second round using Dashboard. The order of the three test sessions were determined based on the complexity of the tasks requested in the test sessions. By assigning the test sessions with simpler tasks to earlier steps, the users were able to gain enough experience in both visualization systems to carry out complex tasks in the later steps.

Introductory Tutorial

In the introductory tutorial, users were given an online presentation which introduced the two visualization system, Stock Lamp and Dashboard. The presentation explained the basic concept and how to visually interpret the displayed information in these two systems. Once the users were done with the presentation, the tutorial gave a quick comprehension check by prompting a set of simple questions, each coupled with a screenshot of a visualization. Overall, the introductory tutorial took users approximately 5 minutes.

Focus-Passive Test Session

In the first test session, the users were asked to analyze the displayed information by gazing at the visualization system without any interaction. The task for this test was to identify the four companies that answer the following four questions:

Q-FP-1: Which company had the best price growth rate?

Q-FP-2: Which company had the worst price growth rate?

Q-FP-3: Which company had the largest transaction volume?

Q-FP-4: Which company had the least transaction volume?

Here, the price growth rate indicated the percentile growth of the stock price, and the transaction volume indicated the current transaction volume relative to the respective company's daily average transaction volume. For all four questions, the users were prompted to select one response out of eight options. The options consisted of the seven company names and an additional answer "Not sure" for participants who were not sure of the correct answer.

After establishing the task objective, the users were shown the respective visualization system (Stock Lamp or Dashboard) for 1 minute. In order to test a range of different stock market situations, the data displayed in the system was selected from a random timestamp for each test. In this test, Stock Lamp was fixed to display lamp-view with the side-panel visible, and Dashboard was fixed to display the history data as seen in Figure 4. After the 1 minute was up, the visualization was blacked out and the participants were asked to submit their responses to the four questions.

The submitted answers were then cross-examined with the data presented to the participant and were each converted into points (from -3 to 3) based on its correctness. The correctness of an answer was measured by how closely the answered company ranked to the correct answer (higher points for closer answers; 3 points for correct answer). The answer "Not sure" was worth 0 points. By measuring the correctness using a range of scores instead of employing an all-or-nothing type of scoring system, we aimed to mitigate the effects of the different displayed data on the user's performances. These four points were compiled into one correctness score (ranging from -12 to 12 with an expected value of 0), which represented how well the user performed in the task.

Periphery-Passive Test Session

In the second test session, the users were asked to analyze the information displayed in the visualization while playing a game. The task for this test was to identify the four companies that answer the same four questions (Q-FP-1–4) as in Focus-Passive test with an additional request. The additional request was to aim for a high-score in the game.

The game we used was an online Whack-a-Mole [22] where each mouse click on the correct target was awarded one point. Achieving a high-score in this game requires the user's full attention to quickly assess and react to the moving targets. Therefore, it allows us to effectively simulate a situation where the participant's engagement towards the visualization system is Periphery-Passive [31]. In order to prevent the testing order from affecting the game scores, all participants went through one trial of the game before taking this test.

After establishing the task objective, the users were asked to start playing the game for 2 minutes on their primary monitor with the respective visualization system (Stock Lamp or Dashboard) for two minutes on their secondary monitor. In order to test a range of different stock market situations, the data displayed in the system was also selected from a random timestamp for each test. In this test, Stock Lamp was fixed to display lamp-view with the side-panel retracted, and Dashboard was fixed to display the history data. After the 2 minutes elapsed, the visualization was blacked out and the participants were asked to submit their responses to the four questions and record their game scores. The four responses to the questions were then compiled into one correctness score in the same fashion as in the Focus-Passive test session.

Table 1: Test Results Summary: Mean and (Standard Deviation)

	Focus-Passive (31)	Periphery-Passive (27)		Focus-Active (31)					
	Correctness	Correctness	Game	MD	PD	TD	Ef	Pe	Fr
Stock Lamp	8.48(2.82)	8.81(2.72)	30.70(13.93)	5.77(2.35)	3.77(2.42)	4.48(2.17)	5.48(2.46)	5.13(2.42)	4.94(2.42)
Dashboard	7.30(3.31)	4.52(3.76)	26.63(12.20)	6.50(2.39)	4.20(2.78)	5.17(2.70)	6.17(2.04)	5.40(2.18)	5.47(2.43)

The reason Focus-Passive tests and Periphery-Passive tests have different durations is based on the feedback we got from the pilot users (who at this point were familiar with both visualizations). The feedback regarding Focus-Passive tests suggested that gazing at the same information for 2 minutes is too long and that the users would become bored. On the other hand, for the Periphery-Passive tests, users feel extremely hurried if they are asked to effectively execute the task while multi-tasking within 1 minute. Therefore, to allow users to comfortably execute the requested tasks, we assigned a 1 minute gazing time for the Focus-Passive test and a 2 minute multi-tasking time for the Periphery-Passive test.

Focus-Active Test Session

In the third test session, the users were asked to freely explore the data using the visualization system to make their own future investment decisions. The task for this test was to analyze the presented data and decide on one stock to sell and another stock to invest in exchange.

After establishing the task objective, the users were shown the respective visualization system visualizing data from a randomly selected timestamp for 3 minutes. In this test, all interactions and views for both Stock Lamp and Dashboard were accessible to the participants. After the 3 minutes was up, the visualization was blacked out and the participants were asked to submit two forms.

The first form contained four questions regarding the task:1.) Which stocks would you sell? 2.) What information helped decide on selling this stock? 3.) Which stocks would you buy more? 4.) What information helped decide on buying this stock? These questions were asked mainly to later confirm that the user was able to execute the requested task.

The second form contained six questions that asked about different aspects of the user experience while carrying out the task. The six questions were based on the NASA Task Load Index (TLX) [17]: Mental Demand (MD), Physical Demand (PD), Temporal Demand (TD), Effort (Ef), Performance (Pe), and Frustration (Fr). The first three questions asked how mentally, physically, and temporally challenging the task was using the visualization. The next three questions asked the user's experience in executing the task using the visualization with respect to their required effort, achieved performance, and perceived degree of frustration/stress. The responses for all six questions were based on a scale from 1 to 10, where 1 indicating low and 10 indicating high. (For performance, 1 indicates good and 10 indicates poor). Intuitively, the lower value indicates that the user considered the task was easier to accomplish.

Results

A total of 31 users (6 females) consisting of students, office workers, and house wives, ranging from age 23 to 34 participated in the study. Since experienced stock investors tend to have extensive training and are often familiar with the traditional style of stock visualization, we chose participants that have little to no experience or training in stock investments. All three test sessions were conducted online and the participants were asked to take the tests in their own personal settings. Four users were not able to conduct the Periphery-Passive test session due to its system requirement (a minimum of 2 monitors). These four users were excluded from the all analyses unless specified otherwise.

Table 1 shows a summary of the collected results. The two values in each cell correspond to the mean (μ) and the standard deviation (σ) for all users who participated in the test session. The numbers of users in these test sessions are shown in the parentheses accompanying each test session's name.

First, we used these results to examine if there were statistically sound effects on the users' performances based on the difference in visualizations (system) and engagement modes (e-mode). For this analysis, we applied two-way analysis of variance (ANOVA) to the correctness score of 27 users who took both Focus-Passive and Periphery-Passive test sessions. Table 2 shows the results of this analysis. These results indicate that both the visualization system and the engagement mode individually have an effect on the user's performance. At the same time, the combination of these two attributes also shows statistical significe suggesting that the effects of the engagement mode to the user's performance are not consistent for Stock Lamp and Dashboard.

Table 2: Two-way ANOVA

	Sum of Square	df	Mean Square	F	p
System	202.81	1	202.81	20.07	$> .0001^{***}$
E-mode	40.33	1	40.33	3.99	$.0484^{*}$
System:E-mode	65.34	1	65.34	4.10	$.0125^{*}$
Error	1051.19	104	10.11		
Total	1359.67	107			

Note: The symbol * on p indicates a .01 significance level and *** indicates a .001 significance level.

To gain a deeper insight into these suggested effects, we extended our analysis by applying pairwise comparison for correlated observations to the same correctness scores. Table 3 shows the results of this pairwise comparison. Here, we denote each test by hyphenating the abbreviations of the respective visualization system (SL for Stock Lamp and D for Dashboard) and the engagement mode (FP for Focus-Passive and PP for Periphery-Passive). In this pairwise comparison, the Bonferroni per-comparison error suggests that p values need to be below .0083 to achieve the conventional .05 significance and below .0017 to achieve .01 significance level.

Based on these pairwise comparison results, we can further analyze the data and isolate what is causing the differences in the user's performance. Among these six comparisons,

Table 3: Pairwise Comparison of correctness Scores

Comparison			μ	σ	σ_{err}	$t(26)$	p
SL-FP	–	D-FP	1.19	4.05	0.78	1.52	.1403
SL-FP	–	SL-PP	-0.33	3.37	0.65	-0.51	.6121
SL-FP	–	D-PP	3.96	5.03	0.97	4.10	.0004**
D-FP	–	SL-PP	-1.52	4.72	0.91	-1.67	.1064
D-FP	–	D-PP	2.78	3.48	0.67	4.15	.0003**
SL-PP	–	D-PP	4.30	5.12	0.99	4.36	.0002**

Note: Taking Bonferroni per-comparison error into consideration, the symbol ** on p indicates a .01 significance level.

all three comparisons that contain the Periphery-Passive test using Dashboard (D-PP) show that there is a drop in the user's correctness score with significance at the .01 level. On the other hand, the comparisons that contain the Periphery-Passive test using Stock Lamp (SL-PP) show no significant evidence to indicate a decline in the user's performance. These observations suggest that Stock Lamp has a significant advantage over Dashboard in presenting information to the users who are multi-tasking. We further confirmed this hypothesis by conducting a paired two-tailed t-test on the user's Periphery-Passive test session's game scores. The results of this t-test indicated users were able to score 3.46 more in average using Stock Lamp at the significance of .05 level.

Another interesting comparison is between Stock Lamp and Dashboard in Focus-Passive mode (SL-FP—D-FP). Although our two-way ANOVA indicated that there is a relationship between system and user performance, the pairwise comparison for the Focus-Passive test session was not able to provide sufficient evidence to corroborate the ANOVA's results. This suggests that if the visualization has the user's full attention, then there might not actually be a significant difference between Stock Lamp and Dashboard. We believe this result is related to the difference in personal preferences for information presentation styles, and discuss this idea further below.

Next, using the self-reported workload measurements from the Focus-Active test session, we examined whether one visualization system was perceived as easier to use than the other by the users. For this analysis, we applied the Wilcoxon signed-rank test to each set of task load index scores. We chose the Wilcoxon signed-rank test for comparing these scores because these scores are strongly affected by each individual user's subjective interpretation of the scoring measurements. Therefore, these scores needed to be treated on an ordinal scale and paired with the score for the other visualization before comparing between users.

Table 4: Wilcoxon Signed-Rank Test of NASA TLX Scores

Question	W	N_r	z	p
Mental Demand	101	27	1.21	0.23
Physical Demand	17	19	0.33	0.74
Temporal Demand	53	24	0.75	0.45
Effort	107	26	1.35	0.18
Performance	25	27	0.29	0.77
Frustration	92	30	0.94	0.35

Table 4 shows the results of the Wilcoxon signed-rank test. These results indicate that the data showed no statistical significance; neither visualization system were perceived easier than the other to carry out task. However, as we had proposed in the case of the pairwise comparison of the Focus-Passive test session, the absence of the statistical significance in this task load feedback might have been due to the differences in personal preferences among the participating users. In other words, within the participating users, there might have been a group of users who prefer Stock Lamp over Dashboard who can score better in the Focus-Passive test session and who also consider the workload of analyzing data to be easier using Stock Lamp, and another group with the opposite preference.

To examine this hypothesis, we conducted another Wilcoxon signed-rank test on the self-reported workload measurements collected from two different groups, Group-SL and Group-D. These groups were separated based on their correctness score in the Focus-Passive test session. Group-SL consisted of 19 participants that were able to score more points using Stock Lamp, and Group-D consisted of 15 participants that were able to score more points using Dashboard. There were 3 participants that scored the same points using Stock Lamp and Dashboard. These participants were put into both groups.

Table 5: Wilcoxon Signed-Rank Test for Group-SL and -D

	Group-SL				Group-D			
	W	N_r	z	p	W	N_r	z	p
MD	85	17	2.00	.04*	-11	12	-0.41	.68
PD	25	11	1.09	.28	-17	10	-0.84	.40
TD	65	13	2.25	.02*	-26	14	0.80	.42
Ef	52	15	1.46	.14	15	13	0.51	.61
Pe	20	16	0.50	.62	5	12	0.18	.86
Fr	111	18	2.41	.02*	-35	15	-0.98	.33

Note: The symbol * on p indicates a .05 significance level.

Table 5 shows the results of Wilcoxon signed-rank test for the two groups. These results show that participants who belong to Group-SL provide sufficient evidence to conclude that the distribution of their responses regarding Mental Demand, Temporal Demand, and Frustration all shift right when using Dashboard for Focus-Active test at $p < .05$ significance. In other words, these results suggest that users who can score better in Focus-Passive test using Stock Lamp also tend to find Stock Lamp easier to use than Dashboard when analyzing stock data. On the other hand, the participants who belong to Group-D do not indicate that the opposite direction of the preference is true. That is, users who were able to score better in Focus-Passive test using Dashboard do not necessarily find Dashboard easier to analyze stock data.

In summary, we were able to draw two conclusions from our user study.

- Stock Lamp is an effective system for presenting information to users who are multi-tasking.
- Users who are able to effectively interpret the data presented by Stock Lamp also tend to find Stock Lamp easy to use for exploring and analyzing stock data.

These findings imply that our consideration towards engagement-versatile design was successful in allowing Stock Lamp to encompass users with limited attention without compromising the user experience in other engagement modes. Furthermore, the users who found that Stock Lamp intuitive and effective for making investment decisions in a limited time prove that Stock Lamp indeed has the potential of becoming a practical supplementary tool for monitoring the stock market.

In addition to these functional aspects, we also received many positive comments from the users regarding the Stock Lamp's entertaining visual aesthetics. One of the users thought that Stock Lamp would be a great visualization to display in a company's lobby to show its stocks in comparison to that of its competing companies to promote awareness to the employees. Another user said that the figurative representation of the stock data is less obvious and would be a nice camouflage for part-time investors who want to use it while working.

DISCUSSION

Stock Lamp presents certain advantages over traditional visualizations as shown by the user study. However, predicting future market trends requires comprehensive analyses, taking into account not only company performance and stock price history, but also relevant news articles, state policies, and public opinions. While we do not expect traditional visualizations to be replaced by Stock Lamp, we do anticipate Stock Lamp to be used as a supplementary tool by part-time investors. Most visualization tools need to be utilized in conjunction with other tools to provide the users with multi-faceted views. Based on our findings, Stock Lamp can serve these investors as a great auxiliary source of information to maintain market awareness and conduct quick checks on data relevant to their stock portfolios.

Moreover, Stock Lamp is a simple demonstration of a grander concept: engagement-versatile design. The visual components of Stock Lamp – lamp-view and info-view – can be utilized as templates for constructing engagement-versatile visualization systems and applied to different datasets. For example, we have also been developing:

- News Lamp: A visualization that displays trending online news topics. This system aims to provide users with an online news portal where users can access news articles, blog posts, and social comments on a topic of their interest.
- Access Lamp: A visualization that displays server access information. This system aims to help system administrators monitor server access and identify potential threats.

Similarly, these engagement-versatile visualizations do not require users constant attention. This study provides an initial discussion towards categorizing engagement styles between users and visualizations. We considered two attributes, attention and participation, as preliminary components for developing the partitioning of distinct engagement styles. We anticipate the future expansion of engagement style categories by the addition of newly identified attributes. In particular, we believe that visualizations operated in environments beyond the conventional desktop settings may suggest new attributes, leading to the establishment of more engagement style categories, similar to the efforts of Jansen and Dragicevic [21].

CONCLUSION AND FUTURE WORK

In this paper, we introduce a new design concept, engagement-versatile design, for constructing visualization systems that target a wide range of users with different engagement styles. We first identify three unique modes of engagement between users and desktop visualizations, and then discuss how each mode helps derive design guidelines for constructing a visualization that can serve users with different engagement modes. We then demonstrate the feasibility of this design concept by constructing a real-time stock market visualization system called Stock Lamp.

Through an extensive comparative user study, we show that the system can effectively present market information to its users. In particular, when users are asked to multi-task, Stock Lamp was able to present information more effectively than a traditional visualization, validating the benefits of applying engagement-versatile design.

To the best of our knowledge, this study is one of the first to to establish a design concept for addressing the diverse styles of user engagement and applying them to enhance the visualization's utility – all in a systematic manner. We believe that this study will help future developers design practical visualization systems that target broader audiences, going beyond conventional application scenarios that are commonly limited to domain experts and their analyses of data.

Our future research will attempt to extend our understanding of engagement-versatile design in two different directions. One direction is to measure the success of the integration of engagement-versatile visualizations into users' daily lives. We plan to do this by opening our engagement-versatile visualization systems (including Stock Lamp) to the public and conducting a long-term user study observing user activities for an extensive period of time. Another direction is to extend our simple attention/participation engagement model to a more comprehensive taxonomy of engagement modes. We plan to do this by reviewing the variety of engagement styles users exhibit toward different systems. For example, systems with wall-sized displays, tangible interfaces, and augmented reality applications all potentially influence users' engagement styles, thus presenting potential other modes of engagement (e.g., [12]). A thorough review of existing systems and their user engagement scenarios would help us establish a rich taxonomy of engagement modes, ultimately assisting the design of practical visualizations for different audiences and situations.

ACKNOWLEDGMENTS

This research was sponsored in part by the National Science Foundation through grants DRL-1323214 and IIS-1320229 and the UC Davis RISE Program.

REFERENCES

1. Google Finance. `https://www.google.com/finance`.
2. Lava lamp. `http://lavalamp.com/`.
3. Twitter. `https://twitter.com/`.
4. WebGL. `http://get.webgl.org/`.
5. Yahoo! Finance. `http://finance.yahoo.com/`.
6. Andrews, C., Endert, A., Yost, B., and North, C. Information visualization on large, high-resolution

displays: Issues, challenges, and opportunities. *Information Visualization 10*, 4 (2011), 341–355.

7. Blinn, J. A generalization of algebraic surface drawing. *ACM Transactions of Graphics* (1982), 235–256.
8. Block, F., Horn, M., Phillips, B., Diamond, J., Evans, E., and Shen, C. The deeptree exhibit: Visualizing the tree of life to facilitate informal learning. *IEEE Transactions on Visualization and Computer Graphics* (2012), 2789–2798.
9. Bostock, M., Ogievetsky, V., and Heer, J. D3: Data driven documents. *IEEE Transactions on Visualization and Computer Graphics* (2011), 2301–2309.
10. Brignull, H., and Rogers, Y. Enticing people to interact with large public displays in public spaces. In *Proceedings of the IFIP International Conference on Human-Computer Interaction* (2003), 17–24.
11. Chittaro, L. Visualizing information on mobile devices. *Computer 39*, 3 (2006), 40–45.
12. Edge, D., and Blackwell, A. F. Peripheral tangible interaction by analytic design. In *Proceedings of the 3rd ACM International Conference on Tangible and Embedded Interaction* (2009), 69–76.
13. Elby, A. What students' learning of representations tells us about constructivism. *The Journal of Mathematical Behavior 19*, 4 (2000), 481 – 502.
14. Evans, J. L., and Archer, S. H. Diversification and the reduction of dispersion: An empirical analysis. *The Journal of Finance 23*, 5 (1968), 761–767.
15. Fekete, J.-D., Wijk, J. J., Stasko, J. T., and North, C. The value of information visualization. In *Information Visualization*. Springer-Verlag, 2008, 1–18.
16. Haroz, S., and Whitney, D. How capacity limits of attention influence information visualization effectiveness. *IEEE Transactions on Visualization and Computer Graphics 18*, 12 (2012), 2402–2410.
17. Hart, S. G., and Staveland, L. E. Development of nasa-tlx (task load index): Results of empirical and theoretical research. *Advances in psychology 52* (1988), 139–183.
18. Heer, J., and Agrawala, M. Design considerations for collaborative visual analytics. In *IEEE Symposium on Visual Analytics Science and Technology* (2007), 171–178.
19. Isenberg, P., Elmqvist, N., Scholtz, J., Cernea, D., Ma, K.-L., and Hagen, H. Collaborative visualization: Definition, challenges, and research agenda. *Information Visualization 10*, 4 (2011), 310–326.
20. Jafarinaimi, N., Forlizzi, J., Hurst, A., and Zimmerman, J. Breakaway: an ambient display designed to change human behavior. In *Proceedings of ACM Extended Abstracts on Human Factors in Computing Systems* (2005), 1945–1948.
21. Jansen, Y., and Dragicevic, P. An interaction model for visualizations beyond the desktop. *IEEE Transactions on Visualization and Computer Graphics 19*, 12 (2013), 2396–2405.
22. Jim Barrett. Whack A Mole. `http://www.ictgames.com/whackAMole/`.
23. Kawato, S., and Ohya, J. Two-step approach for real-time eye tracking with a new filtering technique. In *IEEE International Conference on Systems, Man, and Cybernetics*, vol. 2 (2000), 1366–1371.
24. Lee Brodie. How many stocks should you own at one time? `http://www.cnbc.com/`, 2014.
25. Levin, G., and Lieberman, Z. In-situ speech visualization in real-time interactive installation and performance. In *Proceedings of the 3rd International Symposium on Non-photorealistic Animation and Rendering* (2004), 7–14.
26. Ma, J., Liao, I., Ma, K.-L., and Frazier, J. Living liquid: Design and evaluation of an exploratory visualization tool for museum visitors. *IEEE Transactions on Visualization and Computer Graphics* (2012), 2799 –2808.
27. Ogawa, M., and Ma, K.-L. code_swarm: A design study in organic software visualization. *IEEE Transactions on Visualization and Computer Graphics* (2009), 1097–1104.
28. Pousman, Z., and Stasko, J. A taxonomy of ambient information systems: four patterns of design. In *Proceedings of ACM working conference on Advanced visual interfaces* (2006), 67–74.
29. Pousman, Z., Stasko, J., and Mateas, M. Casual information visualization: Depictions of data in everyday life. *IEEE Transactions on Visualization and Computer Graphics* (2007), 1145–1152.
30. Skog, T., Ljungblad, S., and Holmquist, L. Between aesthetics and utility: designing ambient information visualizations. In *Proceedings of IEEE Symposium on Information Visualization.* (2003), 233–240.
31. Somervell, J., McCrickard, D. S., North, C., and Shukla, M. An evaluation of information visualization in attention-limited environments. In *Proceedings of the Eurographics - IEEE TCVG Symposium on Data Visualisation* (2002), 211–216.
32. Sprague, D., and Tory, M. Motivation and procrastination: Methods for evaluating pragmatic casual information visualizations. *IEEE Transactions on Computer Graphics and Applications* (2009), 86–91.
33. Vogel, D., and Balakrishnan, R. Interactive public ambient displays: Transitioning from implicit to explicit, public to personal, interaction with multiple users. In *Proceedings of the 17th Annual ACM Symposium on User Interface Software and Technology* (2004), 137–146.

Real-Time Representation Versus Response Elicitation in Biosensor Data

Mark Matthews, Jaime Snyder, Lindsay Reynolds, Jacqueline T. Chien, Adam Shih, Jonathan W. Lee, Geri Gay
Cornell University, Department of Information Science
{mjm672, js2829, jtc229, as986,jwl274, gkg1} @cornell.edu

ABSTRACT
Recognized stress management techniques include cultivating mindfulness, breathing exercises, and meditation. While these approaches have been shown to mitigate the negative effects of stress, they can be difficult to learn or consistently apply. To support these techniques, we developed MoodLight, a playful system that uses ambient colored light to provide feedback regarding an individual's current arousal levels. Like many affective computing systems, MoodLight was designed to help users observe their internal state and learn to relax. However, our findings indicate that prompting or leading feedback can be more effective than real time feedback in helping users relax. This work contributes to affective computing by suggesting alternative approaches to designing biofeedback systems for stress management.

Author Keywords
Affective computing; stress management; biosensors

ACM Classification Keywords
H.5.m. Information interfaces and presentation (e.g., HCI): Miscellaneous.

INTRODUCTION
Stress is becoming a public health crisis [2], with most Americans suffering from moderate to high stress and nearly half reporting increased levels over the last 5 years, costing the US economy $300 billion a year in reduced productivity and absenteeism [3]. Avoidance behavior, a by-product of stress, is any activity a person engages in to avoid facing the source of stress, resulting in a negative impact on everyday life. Examples include gambling, watching television, and playing computer games. Given increasing evidence that, at least for some, technology is a significant source of stress and increasingly a pathway to unhealthy stress avoidance behaviors [6; 16], there is a need for novel approaches to support effective relaxation management outside of these established pathways.

CHI 2015, April 18 - 23 2015, Seoul, Republic of Korea
Copyright 2015 ACM 978-1-4503-3145-6/15/04<$15.00
http://dx.doi.org/10.1145/2702123.2702485

MoodLight is an interactive lighting system that provides an ambient visual representation of momentary experiences of arousal, a commonly used measure of stress or relaxation. Electro-dermal activity (EDA) sensors collect biometric data about an individual's current arousal level; this information is fed into a programmable lighting system and fluctuations in arousal level are represented as changing colored light. Like many other affective computing systems, MoodLight was designed based on the premise that increasing awareness of one's internal states can have a positive effect on health.

The study described here was originally designed to explore contextual issues related to receiving biosensor feedback in solitary versus social conditions. In establishing a baseline for this work, we examined the effect of receiving feedback based on one's current level of physiological relaxation ("real-time feedback") compared to receiving feedback that displays systematic progress towards relaxation regardless of the users' level of physiological relaxation ("leading feedback"). We discovered that leading feedback can influence relaxation more than real-time feedback.

BACKGROUND

Stress Interventions
Much affective computing research focuses on technology-based interventions to support relaxation and reflection; these systems typically detect a person's emotional state via physiological markers and provide feedback. Biofeedback is one method to do this. It is a process by which people can monitor their physiological symptoms using sensor technologies, providing opportunities to observe changes in signals like heart rate, skin conductance and brain activity. For example, AffectAura measures head position, posture, voice activity, electrodermal activity, and GPS to provide users with an interactive visualization of their predicted affective state [9].

For many decades, biofeedback has been used clinically to support relaxation skills training and to help reduce stress-related symptoms [4]. These systems typically combine wired sensors with very simple onscreen feedback. In the last decade more immersive displays have been developed, such as Relax2Win, an "affective" computer game designed to help children overcome anxiety problems in clinical settings [11]. In this racing game the player's EDA levels control a game character in a race; the more relaxed the player becomes the faster their game character goes.

The Current Study

Although cultivating a greater sense of awareness has been shown to have a positive influence on mental health, people report finding mindful practices such as meditation difficult to learn and apply in daily life [5]. With MoodLight, we bridge areas of personal informatics and affective computing by designing a system that supports affective ambient feedback based on personal biometric data. As described above, there are a variety of approaches to technological relaxation interventions. For this study, we hypothesized that participants would relax more quickly when viewing real-time feedback about their level of relaxation than when exposed to generic leading feedback that reflects a general trend toward a relaxed state but does not actually reflect the user's current state.

METHOD

System Description

The MoodLight system consists of EDA sensors (Figure 1, left), an android device, a HUE brand programmable light bulb, and a desk lamp. Using this setup, it is possible to change the color of light in a room in response to an individual's relative arousal level (discussed below).

The Personal Input Pod (PiP; https://thepip.com), a commercial sensor held between one's fingers (Figure 1), is used to detect changes in an individual's arousal levels associated with the autonomic nervous system. Compared to other sensors, PiPs are easy to use and non-invasive, allowing for conditions that could more easily be adapted to personal use in future work.

Arousal is a commonly used measure of stress, yet while EDA sensors can detect a heightening response to stimuli, they cannot disambiguate whether an individual perceives that sensation as positive or negative. For example, high physiological arousal could be caused by exciting good news (positive) or by some sudden shocking news (negative). The amplitude and rise time of EDA pulses vary between individuals, making direct comparisons challenging. The algorithm for assessing changes in individual EDA levels takes this into account by applying Least Means Squares (LMS) on successive windows of data to determine the slope of the EDA curve, and also uses a threshold up/down counter to reject spurious peaks/troughs. In this way, the EDA reading is used to create a relative representation of an individual's arousal level based on fluctuations in their readings over a period of time. For this study, the system relied on a generic profile for interpretation of EDA data.

Procedure

We used a within-subjects experimental design to test our hypothesis. After completing a consent form, participants were introduced to the study, then completed a series of questions about their demographics, state and trait anxiety, and current stress levels.

Following that, participants completed the experimental trials of Moodlight. Each participant completed one trial of each condition, the order of which was randomized. Participants were asked to complete each trial by changing the color of the light from a deep red to a deep blue as quickly as possible by relaxing. Design choices related to color display were informed by the work of Walters et al. [15] which showed that people exhibited a tendency for long-wavelength colors (towards the red end of the spectrum) to induce feelings of high arousal and short-wavelength colors (towards blue) to induce feelings of low arousal.

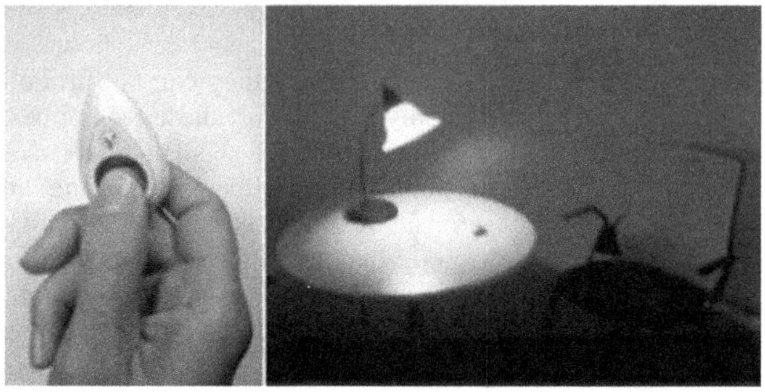

Figure 1. EDA sensor (left) and room configuration (right)

Participants were notified of the trial's completion by a soft chime, at which point the experimenter entered the room and shut off the application. After each trial, participants completed a short questionnaire about their perceptions of the system. These questions focused on whether participants believed they could control the output of the lights, the degree to which MoodLight engaged them, and their level of enjoyment; subjective arousal was measured using Taylor's 5-item momentary stress measure [10]. After the trials were complete, participants were debriefed, allowed to ask questions, and offered the opportunity to participate in an optional follow-up interview. The qualitative analyses of these interviews are reported elsewhere [13].

Experimental Conditions

In the *real-time-feedback* condition, participants were in a room by themselves and were asked to relax in order to change the color of their lights from red to blue as quickly as possible. Their EDA output was used to influence the color of the light, providing real-time feedback.

The *leading-feedback* condition was similar, in that participants were given the same instructions (i.e., to relax in order to change the color of their lights from red to blue as quickly as possible,) except that unbeknownst to them, in this condition the color of the light was not influenced by their EDA output. Instead, participants were shown a pre-recorded light output that lasted 179 seconds and progressed to the full deep blue color. Participants' actual EDA output was recorded to allow for analysis of their relaxation speed.

Participants were not aroused between trials, instead they were brought to baseline before each trial by completing a distractor task involving writing a short response to a neutral prompt (e.g., giving directions to the campus bookstore, describing the furniture in their bedroom).

Participants also completed 2 additional conditions that will not be reported in this paper: a cooperative condition where they relaxed with another participant to change the light from red to blue as quickly as possible, and a competitive condition where participants competed against a partner to be the first to reach a relative relaxed state.

Setup

The study was conducted in two identical experiment rooms in an academic department. There were no personal or decorative items in the rooms; each space contained a small table and two chairs. The rooms were set up with one desk lamp containing a HUE bulb and an android phone to control the system (Figure 1, right.)

Participants

There were 62 participants in the study, of whom 39 were female. All were students at a large US university. Students were recruited via an on-campus web-based recruitment system, and received either $5 cash or course credit for their participation. Participants ranged from 18 to 29 years of age. We measured participants' baseline state (M=3.45 of 5, SD=2.30) and trait (M=3.60, SD=2.48) anxiety levels at the beginning of the experiment [14].

Data Collection and Analysis

Performance was measured by the number of seconds between the beginning of the session and the participant reaching the score associated with the maximum blue state. However, there were instances in which participants did not fully complete one of the trials (i.e., those that were relaxing far less quickly than the prerecorded session). Instead of discarding this data, we compared relative progress as follows. Fourteen participants did not complete the leading feedback condition. Their sessions were truncated to the lowest score achieved and the time to completion to that score was used for analysis to prevent a bias toward the leading feedback condition. There was no difference in the stress to relaxation ratio of the truncated parts (M=.53, SD=.82) and the parts used for analysis (M=.58, SD=.52), $t(1,27) = .49$, *n.s.*

RESULTS

Linear Mixed Model Analysis was performed on data gathered from trial times and questionnaires, with trials nested within participants nested within pairs. For both models, condition, trial order, age, gender, state anxiety and trait anxiety were set as random variables. None of these variables had a statistically significant effect. Note that the denominator degrees of freedom in these models are estimated using a Satterthwaite's approximation, which can yield non-integer degrees of freedom [1].

We hypothesized that participants would relax more quickly in the solo condition than in the leading feedback condition. Overall, the model indicated a significant effect for trial type, $F[3, 81.02] = 2.93, p = .039$. Post-hoc comparisons revealed that, contrary to our hypothesis, participants actually completed the leading feedback trial more quickly (M=144.13 seconds, SE=8.51) than the solo trial (M=173.67, SE=8.52), $F[81.163] = -29.55, p = .025$. There were no significant differences in any other combination of conditions. This indicates that participants relaxed more quickly when presented with non-representative feedback that modeled steady progression toward relaxation than when presented with representative real-time feedback about their current emotional state.

Following each of the trials we asked participants questions about the system, including "How much did you feel like you could control the output of the lights?" There was no difference in participants' responses following the leading feedback condition (M=2.74 out of 5, SE=.29) than in the solo condition (M= 2.67, SE=.29), $F[81.438] = -.07$, *n.s.* This indicates that, overall, participants were not aware that they were unable to control the lights in the leading feedback condition, and consequently reduces the likelihood that the differences in performance were due to participants catching on to the ruse and relaxing more easily under the belief that they were not being evaluated.

DISCUSSION

In designing the MoodLight system, we were motivated by a belief that cultivating self-awareness is one of the most important potential contributions of affective computing to the problem of stress management. While mindfulness and awareness of one's level of relaxation certainly has benefits [8], this study finds that in the contexts of performing exercises to actively reduce stress, it is more beneficial to be exposed to stimuli that suggest progress, even if that stimuli does not authentically represent a person's current state. We discovered that the possibility of using leading or prompting feedback in conjunction with real-time output could offer new possibilities for using biofeedback as a form of clinical intervention. This finding challenges current affective computing trends that focus on real-time representation of internal emotional states.

One of the challenges in designing a system that seeks to both represent the self and instigate change in the self lies in evaluating performance. While on a day-to-day basis our experience of affect and emotion is far from static, protocols and expectations for affective system design often require us to make clear distinctions between states, actions and outcomes. The results reported here draw attention to ambiguities among these factors and suggest alternative approaches for representing state and change in these systems.

The power of visualizing positive change is not a new concept in clinical psychology and self-help literature [12]. Recent HCI research has explored representation of the self through a range of visual metaphors such as blossoming flowers [7]. Most of these systems model positive change as it unfolds in real-time. Our study shows that using an affective system to model positive change as an aspirational target while at the same time tracking real-time biosensor data regarding real time progress towards a relaxation goal can provide a beneficial experience to users. Based on this work, we believe that there is value to exploring the intentional integration of self-representation and aspirational provocation in affective systems.

One topic for future research in this area is to determine whether the effect we observed holds true for non-light types of therapeutic stimuli such as sound, or screen based tools and whether the effects observed here are maintained over longer periods of time. Another area for research work concerns the ethical implications of this study. While effectively misleading individuals about their current arousal levels may be more effective in promoting physiological relaxation, this may be an ethically troubling design feature to implement in a therapeutic tool designed for naturalistic use if not carefully considered and used sparingly (e.g., to disrupt a negative feedback loop in which individuals become increasingly stressed about their inability to relax).

There are some limitations that should be considered when interpreting these findings. Like many other studies of this nature, this study relied on a student sample and these results may not extend to other populations. Additionally, this study used an experimental method in which participants were aware of being evaluated, and the effect seen here may not be generalizable to more natural patterns of stress and relaxation.

CONCLUSION

We developed the MoodLight system to assist with relaxation techniques through the cultivation of awareness of one's current state, with the belief that such awareness helps further promote relaxation. However, results from the current study indicate that such a belief may be inaccurate, as participants relaxed more quickly when presented with inauthentic feedback that showed a steady progression toward relaxation than when presented with real-time feedback about their current state. We believe this provides an opportunity to further explore providing aspirational feedback in such systems.

ACKNOWLEDGMENTS

Mark Matthews' work was supported by a Marie Curie Fellowship (Project Number: 302530).

REFERENCES

[1] SPSS Technical Report - Linear Effects Mixed Modeling.

[2] Anderson, N.B., Johnson, S.N., Belar, C.D., Breckler, S.J., and Nordal, K.C., 2012. *Stress in America: Our health at risk.* Amer Psychological Assoc.

[3] APA, Psychologically healthy workplace program: Creating a psychologically healthy workplace.

[4] Bouchard, S., Bernier, F., Boivin, E., Morin, B., and Robillard, G., 2012. Using biofeedback while immersed in a stressful videogame increases the effectivess of stress management skills in soldiers. *PloS one 7*, 4, e36169.

[5] Carmody, J. and Baer, R.A., 2009. How long does a mindfulness□based stress reduction program need to be? A review of class contact hours and effect sizes for psychological distress. *J clin psych 65*, 6, 627-638.

[6] Chak, K. and Leung, L., 2004. Shyness and locus of control as predictors of internet addiction and internet use. *CyberPsych & Behav 7*, 5, 559-570.

[7] Consolvo, S., Mcdonald, D.W., Toscos, T., Chen, M.Y., Froehlich, J., Harrison, B., Klasnja, P., Lamarca, A., Legrand, L., Libby, R., Smith, I., and Landay, J.A., 2008. Activity sensing in the wild: a trial of UbiFit Garden. *Proc CHI*, 1797-1806.

[8] Grossman, P., Niemann, L., Schmidt, S., and Walach, H., 2004. Mindfulness-based stress reduction and health benefits: A meta-analysis. *J psychosomatic research 57*, 1, 35-43.

[9] Mcduff, D., Karlson, A., Kapoor, A., Roseway, A., and Czerwinski, M., 2012. AffectAura: an intelligent system for emotional memory. *Proc CHI*, 849-858.

[10] Russell, J.A., Weiss, A., and Mendelsohn, G. A., Affect Grid: A Single-Item Scale of Pleasure and Arousal. *J Personality and Social Pscyh*, 57, 3 (1989), 493-502.,

[11] Sharry, J., McDermott, M., and Condron, J. 2003. Relax To Win: Treating children with anxiety problems with a biofeedback video game. *Eisteach*, 2, 22-26.

[12] Sheldon, K.M. and Lyumbomirsky, S., 2006. How to increase and sustain positive emotion: The effects of visualizing best possible selves. *J Pos Psych 1*, 2, 73-82.

[13] Snyder, J., Matthews, M., Chien, J., Chang, P., Sun, E., Abdullah, S & Gay, G. 2015. MoodLight: Exploring Personal and Social Implications of Ambient Display of Biosensor Data. To appear in *Proc CSCW*. 2015. ACM.

[14] Spielberger, C.D., 2010. *State-Trait Anxiety Inventory. State-Trait Anxiety Inventory*. John Wiley & Sons, Inc.

[15] Walters, J., Apter, M.J., and Svebak, S., 1982. Color preference, arousal, and the theory of psychological reversals. *Motivation and Emotion 6*, 3, 193-215.

[16] Yuen, C.N. and Lavin, M.J., 2004. Internet dependence in the collegiate population: the role of shyness. *CyberPsychology & Behavior 7*, 4, 379-383.

Tutorial Authorship and Hybrid Designers: The Joy (and Frustration) of DIY Tutorials

Ron Wakkary[1,2], Markus Lorenz Schilling[1], Matthew A. Dalton[1], Sabrina Hauser[1], Audrey Desjardins[1], Xiao Zhang[1], Henry W.J. Lin[1]
[1] Simon Fraser University, Surrey, British Columbia, Canada
[2] Eindhoven University of Technology, Eindhoven, Netherlands
{rwakkary, mschilli, mdalton, shauser, adesjard, xza57, hwlin}@sfu.ca

ABSTRACT
Tutorials are critical to the success and vitality of DIY practices. In this paper, we elevate the importance of tutorial authorship as one way to maintain and improve the quality of tutorials in DIY. We discuss the role interaction designers can play as *hybrid designers,* mediating between author and audience to contribute to the improvement of practices of tutorial authorship in DIY. We examine the quality of tutorials through the building and analysis of ten DIY projects and tutorials. We analyze key issues across three categories: 1) competences, components and tools, 2) sequencing, 3) and communication. We offer findings that are both practical guidelines for detailed improvements of tutorials and structural themes for improving tutorial authorship including the themes of *accurate information*, *competences and tools*, and *tutorial format*. In conclusion, we discuss the potential for interaction designers to simultaneously mediate and shape tutorials and tools in a form of hybrid design.

Author Keywords
DIY; Tutorials; Interaction Design; Making Culture; Authorship; Hybrid Designer.

ACM Classification Keywords
H.5.m. Information interfaces and presentation (e.g., HCI): Miscellaneous.

INTRODUCTION
The emergence of Do-it-yourself (DIY) practices has disrupted how we produce and who produces designed artifacts and technologies. At the center of DIY practices are the decentralization of design and production and the wide scale empowerment of amateurs and hobbyists to become designers and producers. Key to this paradigmatic shift of empowering a new class of producers is the learning and sharing of DIY projects through the means of online tutorials. Tutorials explain the components, tools, and processes required to make DIY projects. The practice of writing and sharing DIY tutorials is at the heart of the distributed production and creativity of DIY. Tutorials not only provide tutorship of particular projects, they also develop the skills and competences of those involved in DIY and, in doing so, expand the culture and practices of DIY. It is fair to say that the vitality of DIY practices relies on the effectiveness and quality of tutorials. Additionally, we see a role for interaction designers to help improve upon the practice of tutorials in DIY. Hence, in this paper, we ask two questions: 1) What is the quality of a typical DIY tutorial? 2) What role can interaction designers play in supporting and enhancing the quality of tutorials in the practices of DIY?

With the first question in mind, we set out to examine tutorials of DIY projects. We created a sample of ten projects from a variety of known DIY sources. With a systematic process of analysis, we attempted to make each of the projects following the instructions of the tutorials. In this paper, we report on our findings that examined tutorials across three categories: 1) competences, components and tools, 2) sequencing, 3) and communication. In our findings, we provide practical guidance to improve tutorials and describe the key issues organized under the themes of accurate information, competences and tools, and tutorial format.

To answer the second question, we critically explore the current and past practices of DIY tutorial authorship. We begin with a review of relevant past practices in tutorials including print DIY, the Whole Earth Catalog, cookbook practices, and Braun's Lectron kit. This inspired us together with findings from our study to propose that interaction designers can constructively influence DIY practices as a *hybrid designer*. In the context of DIY, hybrid design mediates through design the role of tutorial authors and the audiences. The idea of designing resources to support everyday practices like DIY is influenced by theories of social practice [16]. In a separate paper [22], we discuss the relations of social practices and interaction design more fully as "practice-oriented" design that includes the idea of a hybrid designer.

We begin the paper with a discussion of tutorials and technical writing. This is followed by a review of literature

CHI 2015, April 18 - 23, 2015, Seoul, Republic of Korea.

ACM 978-1-4503-3145-6/15/04 $15.00.
http://dx.doi.org/10.1145/2702123.2702550

in HCI related to DIY practices. We then review practices of tutorial authorship as a last part of related works. Following that, we present our study and data analysis examining the quality of DIY. We conclude with practical guidelines and by emphasizing the importance of tutorial authorship. This leads to our central argument that interaction design can support DIY practices in a form of hybrid design that simultaneously mediates matters of and shapes tutorials and tools.

Our approach in this paper is both empirical and analytical. We encapsulate an auto-ethnographic study within a critical argument. The argument begins with the antecedents to DIY that reveal the importance of tutorials to a practice but especially how designers can positively shape DIY practices. The argument continues with an analytical reading of the study findings of DIY tutorial to link these to our discussion of antecedents. The critical argument concludes by drawing on the analysis of historical antecedents and study findings to make the claim of a hybrid design role for interaction designers.

TUTORIALS AND TECHNICAL WRITING

Today, with developments in information technology, the Internet, help systems, and distance learning, tutorials have reached an unprecedented level of popularity [7,13]. This change fostered more self-directed tutorials rather than the interactive facilitation of traditional in-person tutorials [1]. In DIY, the self-directed nature of online tutorials can make it a challenge to balance independent learning with detailed and responsive guidance. However in our study we found a related but more pressing issue to be increasing the quality of DIY tutorials.

Technical writing can be described as a style of writing that allows any user to read and clearly understand a textual and/or visual medium that informs the reader about a technology, service or product regardless of his knowledge. Technical writing needs to fulfill several requirements like accuracy, understandability, and accessibility [8]. The Society for Technical Communication (STC) originating in 1953, is the oldest professional association for technical communication and reaches across every industry and continent (see http://www.stc.org). However, despite this longstanding professional discipline, there is virtually no interaction between DIY practices and the professional practices of technical writing. While the quality of DIY tutorials would benefit from the expertise of technical writing it is typical of an everyday practice like DIY to see itself as distinct if not in contradiction to professional organizations and practices and thus not seek professional input [6].

DIY and HCI

In the past years, the HCI field has shown increasing interest in DIY communities and practices. Buechley et al. held a seminal workshop at CHI 2009 [3]. The discussions ranged from practical aspects such as the tools and materials to the broader political, economic, and social implications of DIY practices. Some of these broader issues have been taken up by researchers to provide more insights into the impact of DIY communities and practices. Some researchers argue DIY communities exemplify alternative ways to engage with everyday objects and technologies [2]. Relatedly, others argue that DIY practitioners aim to fit DIY to their own cultural identity [17]. Lindtner et al. [10] found DIY practices are evolving and transformative, becoming new forms of industrial innovation and manufacture that extended these practices beyond hobbies.

Related to our focus on tutorials, researchers have also worked at creating guidelines and tools to support them. For example, De Roeck et al. [14] provided thirteen design rubrics to help designers envision and design systems that enable people to program computers more easily. One strand of research on DIY practices has focused on craft knowledge creation, communication, and consumption. Torrey et al. [19] observed the engagement of electronics and computer hobbyists in the generating process of online How-to pages. They presented this process in three stages: the *project* (making the project itself), the *story* (documenting the story of making), and the *contribution* (broadcasting the How-To). They argued that, at each step, the nature of the work conducted by the hobbyists changed and that a translation process took place from the physical actions to the written and visual instructions. Torrey et al. [18] also explored the online knowledge seeking strategies among crafters and presented the limitations of utilizing these strategies. Kuznetsov and Paulos [9] investigated the motivations and means of DIY amateurs participating in and contributing to online knowledge sharing. Tseng and Resnick [20] examined the challenges project authors encounter when documenting a DIY project and the varied ways in which these authors translated their documentations into “a sharable format” [p.425]. Dalton et al. [5] presented an experimentation of transforming two existing DIY tutorials into a cookbook recipe format. They argued that the maturation process of cookbooks is a good reference for the evolution of DIY tutorials, particularly with regard to formatting tutorials. Together, this research demonstrates that the open sharing of knowledge is an important element of DIY culture and embodies a vital value of DIY practices. However, we see a gap in the research investigating the quality of DIY tutorials, which we argue is the basis for successful knowledge transfer.

Our work is different from this previous research in the sense that instead of exploring DIY practices through looking at what DIY enthusiasts do, we examine what makes up a quality DIY tutorial by *acting the role* of enthusiasts—following the existing DIY projects' instructions to recreate the projects—and directly experiencing the challenges and issues. Further, we aim to critically suggest a practice-oriented role for interaction designers as hybrid designers to support DIY practices.

PRACTICES OF TUTORIAL AUTHORSHIP

We present in this section related previous practices of DIY tutorials to help establish the importance of tutorial authorship and initiate our argument that links historical relations between design and early DIY as means to improve DIY practices. We explore print DIY, namely the Whole Earth Catalog, the practice of cookbooks, and Braun's Lectron. We later draw on these antecedents and incorporate them in our discussion of findings.

Print DIY and the Whole Earth Catalog

The era of printed DIY or instructional tutorials are key antecedents to current DIY practices. From the earliest DIY instructional tutorials in Popular Mechanics to the rise of car repair and especially home renovations that remains very popular, print DIY had evolved into a strong practice. The boom in the 1970s of early DIY can in large part be attributed to Stewart Brand's Whole Earth Catalog, which was founded in 1968 and represented the convergence of counter-culture and systems thinking [12,21].

The Whole Earth Catalog, as mentioned above, was a watershed moment in print DIY, that in ethos holds much in common with today's DIY movement. Founder Stewart Brand saw in print the power to bring together "counterculture communities, back-to-the-land households, and innovators in the fields of technology, design, and architecture" [12] to both foster and celebrate individual creativity and invention in the service of community building (see also [21]).

The relevance of the Whole Earth Catalog to our exploration is that it demonstrates that tutorial authorship goes well beyond the goal of instruction toward caring for and guiding a practice that has implications that can lead to far reaching change. The Whole Earth Catalog and Brand can be seen as an early example of a hybrid design in DIY. Brand in most cases did not author the tutorials but formatted and produced them in the Whole Earth Catalog. He was careful to lead and cultivate credibility through the communication and dissemination of quality tutorials [23].

Cookbooks

We see cookbooks as another form of instructional genre that contributes to the idea of tutorial authorship. The evolution of the modern cookbook began with the communication of the competences and skills of the professional cook only to later give way to cookbooks that positioned themselves as a dialogue and exchange between homemakers and amateur cooks. This gave rise to the importance of the cookbook author over or equal to the professional chef. The practice of amateur cooking relied more on the skills of a good tutorial author than a skilled chef who cannot share their knowledge. Commensurate with the rise of the tutorial author, cookbooks evolved to consider instructions that addressed building on the competences of the amateur cook, clear and precise formatting of recipes, and local translations in sourcing ingredients.

For example, the first classical modern cookbook, *Mastering the Art of French Cooking* [4] by classically trained Julia Child and co-authors, devoted attention to making the traditions of French cooking accessible to the American market by translating the ingredients list to those that can be sourced at the American grocery stores and to train a largely untrained audience in the basic skills and techniques of professional cooking. The competences development included tutorials on basic skills like cutting vegetables, necessary kitchen tools, and basic but essential knowledge of wines [4]. Erica Rombauer, an amateur cook and author of the most successful commercial cookbook, *Joy of Cooking* [15], similarly translated skills and knowhow to her fellow amateur cooks. Most importantly, Rombauer progressed the format and tone for cookbook instruction that became normalized to ensure brevity, clarity, accuracy, and adequate preparation and timing.

Popular cookbook authors like Nigella Lawson and online bloggers like Deb Perelman (http://smittenkitchen.com) are more known as authors and food enthusiasts then professionally trained chefs, which they are not. Rombauer's background as an amateur opened cookbook authoring to amateur experts and peer-to-peer sharing, which relates back to the essentials of DIY tutorials.

Braun's Lectron

An early example of how design abilities and knowledge can better support learning is Lectron, a system and toolkit for experimenting with and learning about electricity. Lectron was invented in 1966 by Georg Franz Greger and directed towards younger hobbyists but initially had little success. In 1967, Braun bought Lectron, recognizing the systems potential to play a significant role in teaching electronics. A significant contribution to the subsequent success of Lectron as an educational system came from the Braun design team under the lead of Dieter Rams. They not only re-designed the packaging but also invented new models (see figure 1). A bestselling model called Buchlabor (translates to booklab) included an award winning instruction book, which was translated in multiple languages (see http://www.lectron.info). Through the design efforts to support the new direction, the product became a national and international success and reached a wider audience including a young Massimo Banzi (founder of Arduino) who shared his experience with Lectron:

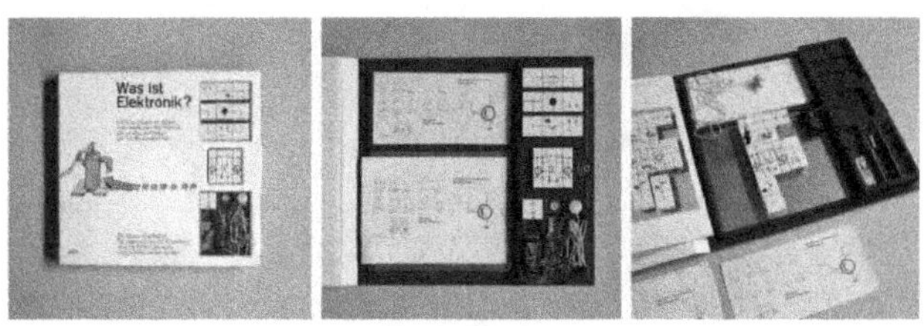

Figure 1 Lectron, a teaching tool to experiment with and learn about electronics.

This is the "toy" I used to learn electronics when I was a kid. It had a huge impact on me as it made me interested in electronics and design. The manual that came with it also influenced the way I teach [11].

The example of Lectron shows how design can positively shape a learning system and support its educational intent. Translating complex structures into simple, concrete, easy to follow entities are critical skills and part of the benefits of design that can also serve to improve DIY tutorials.

The aim of this section is to begin our argument for how designers can positively support DIY practices by revealing the relationship between design and prior tutorial authorship practices. We will return to this critical argumentation by drawing it into our discussion of findings. However, next we shift to the empirical study that links past practices to current practices and issues in DIY tutorials. In the following section we report on the methods and findings of our study of building ten DIY projects.

OUR STUDY

Aiming to examine the quality of DIY tutorials, we put ourselves in the position of DIY enthusiasts, attempting to build ten DIY projects by following their tutorials. We documented this process and analyzed our experiences and observations. In the context of our study, we believe that the process of following the tutorials ourselves is a straightforward way to investigate the challenges and opportunities of DIY instructions.

Selection

We carefully selected our sample of DIY project tutorials making sure they were from different sources and of various difficulty levels, required a variety of technical expertise, and used different instructional formats such as video, text, and text/image combinations. In order to cover a range of skills and competences involved, we previously categorized twenty-two DIY projects into three difficulty levels - easy, medium, and hard - based on our experiences. We further reduced this to ten projects covering each difficulty levels (see table 1) based on which projects were new to researchers and those they were most interested in making. If we happened to come across a tutorial with an existing rating scale (for example the Wii Nunchuck Mouse) we found that our assessment coincided with the tutorials prescribed difficulty.

We used various criteria such as user reviews and online expert selection to confirm our tutorials were tested and accepted within the DIY communities. Some of our chosen sources such as Instructables (http://instructables.com) and Thingiverse (http://thingiverse.com) are a repository for tutorials from individuals around the world. Both have internal user rating systems, as well as systems that allow staff to feature quality tutorials. In these cases, we chose highly rated or featured tutorials. We further chose tutorials from Make Magazine (http://makezine.com), a quarterly magazine that handpicks, edits, and presents DIY tutorials to the public; from Fattelo (http://fattelo.com), an Italian design company whose DIY project was featured by many design blogs and websites; and from Jdeboi (http://jdeboi.com), a personal website of Jenna deBoisblanc, whose tutorial was featured on several well-known blogs including Lifehacker (http://lifehacker.com), TreeHugger (http://treehugger.com), Bike Hugger (http://bikehugger.com), and Adafruit (http://adafruit.com). Furthermore, we chose a tutorial released by MIT Media Labs High-Low Tech department, featured on several tech blogs including Boing Boing (http://boingboing.net) and Hackedgadgets (http://hackedgadgets.com) that was made into a featured tutorial on Instructables by the original author. We also included two tutorial kits, which are fully assembled and packaged projects that come with all of the materials, components, and instructions. We chose the TV-B-Gone kit tutorial from Mitch Altman (Cornfield Electronics (http://cornfieldelectronics.com), which has

Cardboard Desk Lamp	Gear O'Clock	TV-B-Gone Kit	Wii Nunchuk Mouse	Biped Walking Robot Kit	pimpMyBike	Sleek Word Clock	Solar Shrub	DIY Cellphone	Google Play Radio
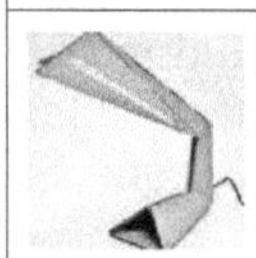	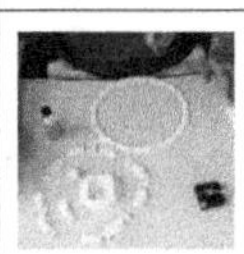		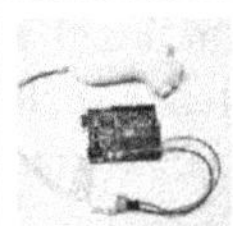		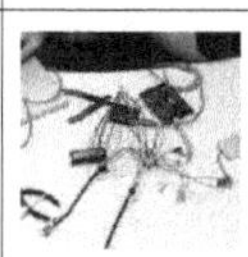				
Fattelo	Thingiverse	Cornfield Electronics	Make Magazine	Gakken	Jenna deBoisblanc	Instructables	Instructables	MIT Media Labs	Instructables
Computer desk lamp built out of cardboard	3D Printed mechanical clock using two gears	Universal remote to turn off and on almost any TV	Control your mouse cursor with a Wii Nunchuck	Mechanical robot that walks toward a wind source	Bike light system built with an Arduino	A clock that tells the time by highlight-ing words	Solar Plant to charge your electronic device via USB	Cellphone built from electronic components	Streaming radio built around a Raspberry Pi
Easy	Easy	Easy	Easy	Medium	Medium	Medium	Meduim	Hard	Hard

Table 1 List of projects, including their source, description and level of difficulty (Photos by Henry Lin)

Figure 2 Still from time-lapse documentation of the Solar Shrub build

been revised several times and a kit from Gakken (http://ghd.gakken.co.jp/english), a Japanese company whose educational kits are widely popular.

Our Technical Backgrounds

Six members of our design research studio were involved in completing the tutorials. Our competences, tools and building environment were more than sufficient to complete the selected projects with adequate instructions. We identify ourselves as DIY enthusiasts, with different degrees of involvement in the community. Personal projects from the members of our design studio include making a CNC machine, renovating a house, converting a van into a camper, making simple electronic devices and more. Each member brings a unique skill set including knowledge of working with electronics, reading schematics, soldering, or building skills. In addition, our studio has a wide range of equipment and tools including soldering irons, multimeters, a 3D printer, and a laser cutter.

Build and Process Documentation

All tutorial builds were conducted by a minimum of the same two researchers from our group. During each build, one of them took charge of building, while the other one took charge of observation and documentation. Other builders alternated among the builds. This system ensured we had two separate individuals who could provide a frame of reference across all tutorials for how well or poorly written individual steps or entire tutorials were written. The other four participants provided help in building, data gathering and analysis. Whilst building, we annotated tutorials and a stationary camera was set up to take pictures every five seconds of the build, which allowed us to create a time-lapse video of every project build (See figure 2). These images, videos, and annotations helped us analyze the building process further.

Study Data

Attempting to build the chosen ten projects, we ended up with different outcomes. Despite challenges with instructions, some projects were finished within a short period of time, whereas other projects were complicated and overly time consuming due to the complexity of the builds and poor instructions. Some projects were impossible to follow or complete based on the tutorials. While we were able to build all of the easy projects, one medium and one hard project were not completed.

After the build, we catalogued several elements of the tutorial's quality in a spreadsheet including but not limited to sequences, procedures, materials, tools, skills, preparation, sourcing of materials, costs, text/images, and outcome. We began our analysis by discussing each project individually, in terms of the positive and negative aspects of the different catalogued elements. Following that, we created a higher-level thematic analysis combining data from all projects, which we ultimately organized across three categories: 1) competences, components and tools; 2) sequencing, 3) and communication. In what immediately follows, we present this analysis from our examination of DIY tutorials in detail.

ANALYSIS

There are different aspects to following a tutorial and these aspects are largely interdependent. In our analysis, we broke this process down into three categories: 1) competences, components and tools, 2) sequencing, 3) and communication. Note that these categories are not mutually exclusive. We should mention that we encountered various issues in sourcing components; however, we have omitted those findings for reasons of space and to focus specifically on the content and form of tutorials.

Additionally, the issue of accuracy affects all aspects of the tutorial and can be considered as an orthogonal concern to our three categories. More specifically, a tutorial that communicates false information albeit well is still flawed. It is a fundamental value of DIY tutorials to pass on accurate knowledge and know-how on a specific project. In our analysis, we made the assumption (like others relying on tutorials) that the knowledge communicated in our sample tutorials would be accurate and credible. However, many, if not all, tutorials fell short in accuracy. This happened most commonly through omission or leaving out details, which often led to confusion or errors. For example, in the instructions for the Sleek Word Clock the author does not describe which sets of LED strings need to be soldered onto a single male pin header. This determines which LEDs and therefore which words are displayed to show the correct time. In another critical flaw, a missing detail led to our failed build of the Gear O'Clock. The instructions do not mention to glue the numbers for the clock counter-clockwise onto the outer gear. Attaching the numbers clockwise onto the outer gear (what we did) resulted in our clock's display running in the reverse direction – counter-clockwise.

Competences, Components and Tools

The required competences, components, and tools to successfully complete a tutorial are a complex interrelated set of issues unto themselves. A tool is only as useful as the builder's competences to use it properly, which will lead to the successful or failed integration of components. For example, a component that requires soldering to a circuit board necessitates a soldering iron and the appropriate skills. The challenge for any tutorial is that a breakdown, omission, or inaccuracy anywhere along this chain can lead to confusion or an error. Adding to the challenge, the required and available tools and competences of the builder can be difficult to predict and fully understand.

Our tutorials were inconsistent and unclear on how to present the related aspects of competences, components, and tools. Each tried various strategies from listing materials and tools separately to embedding the information throughout the tutorial.

Common issues with our tutorials were that information on tools and components were difficult to find in the tutorials, and necessary tools and materials were often omitted. These issues compounded each other depending on the format the tutorial authors used. For example, information on tools and competences that were embedded in the sequence of the tutorial were easy to find at the relevant step but difficult to find at the outset during preparation for a build. This was the case with the Sleek Word Clock. In other instances, components and tools were presented as a list at the beginning of the tutorial, however in these cases when a particular step was confusing it could be difficult to determine if this was due to an omission or to the inaccuracy in the components and tools list. Yet, this approach allowed for adequate preparation at the outset of the build, if the lists were accurate.

Beyond components and tools, competences are a more challenging aspect of DIY tutorials. In essence, it is a matter of authors targeting a project at a particular skill and knowledge level of the builder. However, anticipating a level of expertise can be difficult and it is a challenge to assume what competences constitute a level of expertise, especially since our DIY builds required a wide range of skills and knowledge from crafts to electronics. For example, a builder can have advanced electronics skills but little knowledge of physical construction.

A small minority of our tutorials explicitly stated the expected skill level of a potential builder like the Wii Nunchuck Mouse; the majority of our tutorials did not. Yet, existing competences of a builder are inevitably assumed, which is not without problems. Especially, two of our tutorials stretched the presumptions of builder competences too far. In pimpMyBike, the expectation of the tutorial was that builders could pull together discrete builds into a complete project but the gaps between the builds were simply too great for us and we were not able to complete the project. With the Google Play Internet Radio, the author states that the components list is incomplete since it is difficult to manage a list of parts for a project of this complexity. The tutorial restricts itself to listing the six most important components with the expectation that the builder has the competence to determine the necessary missing components and how to integrate these. Despite our advanced competences, we were not able to build this project.

An additional strategy to address competences are tutorials that aim to complement existing skills and know-how of a potential builder with explicit guidance on specialized skills or learning new competences in order to complete the project. Despite the challenges of the pimpMyBike tutorial, it was successful at providing links to other tutorials on specific skills and knowledge needed such as soldering. In another example, the DIY Cellphone required having circuit boards printed by a fabrication service. The author provided the reader with several online companies to print circuit boards. He also explained how the builder could ensure that they receive a properly printed circuit board from the service. In this case, when required competences were too high, the author provided clear alternatives to overcome the challenge.

Sequencing

Sequencing refers to the completion of tasks within a tutorial in the right order. We expected tutorials to be successful at this since essentially, tutorials tell a story of how to build something from beginning to end, and the tutorials in our study generally were. In one particular case, the TV-B-Gone, the authors took the additional effort to organize the tutorial into sections of sub-tasks that made managing the process simpler. For example, the tutorial was separated into nine sections including an overview, F.A.Q, Make It, Testing, Using, Design Notes, Download, Buy Kit, and Forums. When required, individual sections were very detailed. The section 'Make It' for instance had three sub-sections: for preparation, for the parts list, and for soldering.

However, we also found several sequencing issues within our tutorials. These included large gaps between single tasks, tasks that describe too much information at once, and tasks that require information external to the tutorial. For example, in the Google Play Radio, the gaps between the tasks were too large to bridge without more information. This created a sequence that failed to clearly link a current task to actions of the next or previous tasks. Independent tasks were accurate but it was very challenging to see how steps were interrelated and how progress was made towards the whole build.

The instructions for the Biped Walking Robot included too much information within a description of a single task. The tutorial utilizes graphics and pictures to show a snapshot of the current build with an illustration at each step or task. This is a helpful idea yet the builder is required to attach too many parts within a single step such that the mapping of the sequence to the illustrations becomes difficult to follow.

In the section on Competences, Components and Tools, we referred to the pimpMyBike as a good example of complementing anticipated competences of the builder with new competences through linking to other tutorials.

Conceptually this is a good idea; however, in this case the tutorial often linked too many supplementary videos for the number of tasks. Moreover, the greater issue was that the external tutorials delivered information and know-how in a different style, with different terminology, and within a different context or even project. This disrupted the sequencing of the tutorial making for a fragmented and cumbersome process.

Communication

The communication of a project refers to the use of text, images, and videos in the tutorial. We previously discussed the difficulties of inconsistent video presentation in the tutorial for the pimpMyBike (see Sequencing). In addition to poor video consistency, poorly displayed text can be difficult to follow. For example, the tutorial for the Gear O'Clock is exclusively text. Aside from an online gallery of finished builds there are no images to help with instruction. The build process for this particular project is very spatial, requiring 3D printed parts, and assembly and manipulation of clock mechanisms. Illustrations would definitely help visualize the required tasks.

While mostly helpful, when used poorly, images can make following tutorials difficult. For example, the images in the tutorial for the Solar Shrub are well photographed but the inconsistent orientation and lack of annotations makes it difficult to understand the purpose of the images. In addition, the images need to be in sequence. In the TV-B-Gone, a photo shows parts soldered onto the circuit board despite that step not having yet been completed in the tutorial. This led to confusion and the feeling that we missed a step.

Despite this misstep in the TV-B-Gone tutorial, the tutorial, like others in our sample, managed the proximity of images to textual descriptions of tasks well. In this particular case, two columns and rows were used for formatting so that each step was accompanied by an image in the same row. Annotations and numbering of images can help with communication. For example, the author of the Sleek Word Clock made use of annotations within his instructions and each picture was numbered allowing images to be cited in the text descriptions.

FINDINGS

Based on our analysis we provide practical guidance and identified three themes that highlight in more detail and complexity issues with DIY tutorials: accurate information, competences and tools, and tutorial format. Our practical findings are straightforward recommendations drawn from our analysis:

- Ensure information is accurate;
- Do not omit necessary tools and components;
- Clearly identify necessary tools and components;
- Identify prerequisite and necessary competences;
- Clearly sequence tasks and required information;
- Divide tasks into manageable steps;
- Communicate through texts <u>and</u> images in proximity to each other and relevant tasks;
- Provide quality images with consistent orientation.

Other issues emerged in our study such as considerations of global DIY related to sourcing and the role of localizing tutorial authorship; however, for considerations of space we maintain our focus here on tutorials and tutorial authoring. In what follows, we return to our discussion of past practices of tutorial authorship, presented in previous sections, for improving the current practice of DIY tutorial authorship. Our aim here is to link our study with our larger argument of what role interaction design can play in supporting the practices of DIY. In each theme below we integrate our findings with what we learned from past practices to connect together past and current practices and establish a basis for the argument of supporting future DIY practice through hybrid design.

Accurate information

As we discussed in the analysis, we found that accuracy was an orthogonal issue that covers aspects of competences, components and tools, sequencing, and sourcing. Incomplete or misleading information was part of many of our tutorials. For instance, it happened that all or some tools or components required for a given project were not mentioned in the related tutorial. This inaccuracy often led to confusion, time delays, or failure. From all ten projects, we did not find one tutorial that accurately presented required components, tools, sourcing or sequencing.

Accuracy is a measure of the quality of DIY tutorial practices. Similar to cooking, the practice of authoring cookbooks is as important a practice to peer-to-peer cooking as is cooking itself. Without accurate and accessible DIY tutorials, the practice of DIY would be at risk. In part, the understanding of tutorial authorship as a practice makes explicit the need for accuracy and shifts the factor of credibility to the tutorial author whose success is dependent on consistently producing accurate tutorials. In the antecedent practice of the Whole Earth Catalog, the simple criteria of quality and accuracy were established by the criterion that the catalog 'be useful as a tool'. This authorial promise needed to be kept. Inaccuracies diminish the quality and usefulness of DIY tutorials and the credibility and success of the tutorial author.

Competences and tools

In building our DIY projects we observed a wide range of tools and competences tutorial authors expected the builders to have. Those expectations varied across the tutorials and were often not explicitly presented. This highlights the gap between the level of competences of the author and the different types of builders that could be interested in any given project. The low barrier to entry to DIY tutorial sites widens the range of skills makers can have when firstly approaching a project [9] . This raised not only the issue of explicitly identifying the intended audience for a project but considering a potential builder's capacity to augment and complement existing skills and know-how by learning new abilities. We also raised the problem that competences, components, and tools form a related chain of issues in which a component that requires a complex tool like a laser cutter assumes the competence to operate the tool. In general, we did not see tutorial authors who clearly identified their audience (or multiple audiences) and who fully understood the interrelated nature of competences and tools.

The set of competences, component and tools is a complex matter that needs to make itself more evident as a critical factor in tutorial authorship. A first step is a fuller acknowledgment and explicit addressing of the audience in tutorials. Anticipating competences is a challenge and we are not suggesting that there is one way to address this; in fact, DIY projects with similar ends but a varied range of required competences, components, and tools are what is emerging in the DIY community. The re-alignment of the Lectron product line offers another example of understanding an audience's competences. Braun realized that the system was too expensive to be a children's toy. Parents could hardly afford the system and therefore Braun designed new, cheaper and simpler models to target the toys market but also promoted the more expensive system to vocational schools.

DIY is rooted in an everyday practice such that it is unlikely that basic knowledge and principles would ever make sense to be learned in the abstract. Competences and skills are rarely separated from the project at hand. This is reflected in the fact that sites like Instructables maintain a flat structure with little separation between a tutorial on soldering and tutorials on complex projects. In this sense, it is incumbent on tutorials to take on the role of tutoring competences as well as direct making. As we discussed in the Cookbooks section, early cookbooks used the first chapter to cover a vocabulary of cooking skills that would be referred to later in the recipes. The Whole Earth Catalog established itself as a platform for learning that advocated independent education, meaning the ability to cumulatively develop skills and know-how. This holistic approach fits the view of an ecology of learning in which tutorials are connected to other tutorials and resources.

Format

Our findings show that our tutorials were inconsistent in the quality of their communication and presentation of content. This ranged from poor images, poor text formatting or text intensive tutorials, to linking incompatible videos. In addition, it was not clear if listing components, tools and techniques at the outset of a tutorial in comparison to embedding this information at the step or task required was better, each approach having its own benefits and tradeoffs.

In cooking, format and presentation of recipes evolved as the practice of peer-to-peer home cooking progressed. Arguably, recipes are variations of a simple format that makes them clear and legible. For example, in *The Joy of Cooking* [15], the authors codified the recipe format to follow simple criteria such as clearly identify all necessary ingredients in sequence; explicitly state required techniques in the correct sequence; and specify the outcome in terms of quantity or appearance. For Braun the design and presentation of Lectron was a critical point towards its success.

Summary of findings

In our study and analysis on DIY tutorials, we have discussed detailed issues and problems we encountered and provided practical guidance for improvement of tutorials. We also stressed the importance of tutorial authorship as a practice, providing a structural focus and detailing three themes to improve the practices of DIY. In particular, good practices would address accuracy as a matter of credibility, competences and tools would be at the right level by knowing the audience; and targeting specific audiences and sharing clear formatting criteria would improve communication. We have argued that raising the importance of tutorial authorship will lead to better DIY practices. In the next section, we discuss what role interaction designers can play, and we describe this role as the one of *hybrid designers* who support and enhance the quality of tutorials through the combined expertise of DIY tutorial authorship and design.

DISCUSSION: THE ROLE OF INTERACTION DESIGNERS

While DIY practices exist broadly in the real and virtual worlds, DIY tutorial authorship has largely become an online and computer technology related practice. Given this, interaction design has a critical and significant role in improving tutorial authorship in DIY practices. We see opportunities for interaction design to create better tutorial tools and tutorial generation tools. These tools not only make it easier for authors to create and assemble content but foster better practices of tutorial authoring by the design of good tools. Our practical guidelines can help with considerations for designing tools and as we discussed previously, better tools has been a focus of HCI research in DIY [9,14,19].

However, in addition to a level of technical and design support for DIY practices, in this paper we take the opportunity to build on the structural approach of our findings and articulate a potentially deeper relationship between DIY and interaction design practices in what we term *hybrid design*. The key distinction with hybrid design from typical interaction design is that the outcome of the process is on *resources* for further actions like tutorials rather then finished outcomes like systems or artifacts. A structural relationship between DIY tutorial authorship and interaction design would be built upon essential competences of interaction design practice: the skills and knowledge to design with technology as a medium; the in-depth analytical focus on users of designed systems; and the trained ability to co-design and mediate designs with other experts.

These essential competences would be at the center of a hybrid design approach. As such, a hybrid designer in the context of DIY might focus on tutorials, tools, materials, or processes to mediate between the creator of the content of tutorials and the targeted audience. More specifically, the interaction designer utilizes design to *shape* the content, form, and reception of tutorials. Reception in this sense means the way in which a tutorial is read and utilized which in interaction design terms would foreground interaction. In a hybrid fashion, an interaction designer may work alongside a tutorial author or become an author herself.

Our notion of a hybrid design in the DIY context is inspired by the work of Dieter Rams and Braun on Lectron and Stewart Brand's work on the Whole Earth Catalog. We understand Rams and Brand's contribution as making DIY knowledge widely accessible to many diverse communities – thus becoming translators between two worlds. This emphasis of translation over creation is why we refer to the designer as a hybrid. In addition to Rams and Brand, a contemporary example of a hybrid designer, described by [22], illustrating how a professional designer, Antonio Scarponi from Conceptual Devices, designed a tutorial for an aquaponics system named *Malthus*. Additionnally to sourcing the parts and creating the build process, as a designer Scarponi invested heavily in the tutorial *shaping the content, the form, and the reception.* Notwithstanding that Scarponi is not an interaction designer, it is a good example of how designers can leverage expertise in mediating between practices or domains of knowledge, and in the case of hybrid design produce a resulting form that is the mediation or tutorial and not the outcome or DIY build.

Interaction designers' trained ability to co-design and mediate designs with other experts is essential to being a good hybrid designer. Working with and for the DIY community needs a deep understanding of DIY 'language', practices, tools, materials, and motivations on the one hand and deep design understanding and skills on the other. Not unlike participatory design, the shared matter of concern between designers and DIY enthusiasts, in this case the tutorial, becomes a design situation. Informed by DIY expertise, design is utilized to address the inherent complexities of producing a tutorial. Furthermore, tutorials as a whole become a design opportunity that allows tutorial authors to look beyond the immediate situation to advance the practices of DIY. For example, tutorials can help improve the competences and skill levels of builders.

Interaction designers are trained to apply in-depth analytical attention to users of designed systems. In the context of hybrid design in DIY, keeping attention on the audience of tutorials throughout the design process would vastly improve tutorials. We suggested in our findings that the ability to know the audience would help tutorial authors address complex issues like competences, tools, and communication. Not unlike HCI and learning, we know from experience that interaction designers can design with the relationship between interaction and learning foremost in the designer and tutorial author's minds. Understanding the style of interactions that are beneficial and which competences can best be leveraged is part of knowing the audience in a design sense that would advance the practice of DIY tutorials.

A fundamental quality of an interaction designer is to have the skills and knowledge to design with technology as a medium. Interaction designers understand that in designing with technology, the elements of content, form, interaction, and technology must be an integrated problem and a holistic solution. Given this, we argue that a hybrid designer (on her own or alongside a DIY practitioner) goes beyond designing DIY tools or technologies, to operate at a deeper level in which the creation and designing of a tutorial involves questions of form, technologies, and interaction that incorporate tool making alongside tutorial making. In other words, interaction designers simultaneously generate content and form, or in DIY terms: instructions and instructional media. Arguably there are traces of this approach at the platform level where content and form is integrated in DIY platforms like Instructables, Make: magazine, YouTube, and discussion forums. Yet we see much value in hybrid designers leveraging and progressing this idea at the level of individual authors rather than at the organizational and commercial level that currently exists since DIY is fundamentally a peer-to-peer practice. However this difference between organizational and individual level hybrid design needs further research. Alongside DIY practitioners or on their own, hybrid designers can design tutorials and tutorial tools as a synthesized practice that more fully realizes the potential DIY tutorials and their relations to technologies.

In summary, we discussed how interaction designers in a form of hybrid design can potentially contribute to supporting and enhancing the quality of tutorials and hence DIY practices. A hybrid designer working with or as a DIY practitioner translates between worlds and approaches tutorials as a design situation and tutorial authorship as a design opportunity to advance DIY practices. A hybrid designer leverages interaction design's attention to knowing the audience that would help tutorial authors address complex issues like competences, tools, and communication. Moreover, interaction designers approach tutorials by simultaneously *shaping the content, form, and reception* such that the practice of tutorial authorship integrates the concerns of the tutorial content, technologies, and interaction. We presented examples that inspired us to address the findings of our study, and furthermore, the questions the examples raise point to opportunities for the HCI community to contribute to improving tutorial authorship in DIY practices.

LIMITATIONS

We offer our discussion of interaction designers as hybrid designers as one possibility of many in ways to support DIY practices in a complementary fashion. We are not recommending that interaction designers "take over" DIY practices nor see that as remotely possible. Rather we offer this as a challenge to HCI, one being grounded in our empirical analytical findings to find ways to learn from and support everyday practices like DIY.

Additionally, we are aware that tutorials are very rarely used in a vacuum and that they are in fact part of an ongoing complex of practices of learning and making; an ecology of learning, that includes a collection of tutorials often addressing similar projects as well as discussions and exchanges between the tutorial author and builders or between builders. Lastly, our study did not include emerging forms of DIY tutorials such as annotated single images as those found on Reddit (reddit.com) and Pinterest (pinterest.com), which may offer a different approach.

CONCLUSION

In conclusion, we analyzed ten DIY projects for the quality and effectiveness of the tutorials. Our findings are organized and presented with respect to accurate information, competences and tools, and tutorial format. This work advances the understanding of DIY tutorials by providing an analysis of the quality of tutorials, guidelines for improvement and raising the importance of DIY tutorial authorship as a practice in its own right. Inspired by Lectron, cooking practices, and the Whole Earth Catalog we see room for interaction designers in the role of hybrid designers to contribute to improving tutorial authorship and DIY.

ACKNOWLEDGMENTS

We would like to acknowledge the support of the Natural Sciences and Engineering Research Council (NSERC) of Canada and the various tutorial authors who generously responded to our many questions.

REFERENCES

1. Anderson, C. Enabling and Shaping Understanding through Tutorials. In *The Experience of Learning: Implications for Teaching and Studying in Higher Education*. Scottish Academic Press, 1997, 184–197.
2. Bardzell, J., Bardzell, S., and Toombs, A. "Now That's Definitely a Proper Hack": Self-made Tools in Hackerspaces. In *Proc. CHI'14*, ACM Press (2014), 473–476.
3. Buechley, L., Rosner, D.K., Paulos, E., and Williams, A. DIY for CHI: methods, communities, and values of reuse and customization. *Ext. Abstracts CHI'09*, ACM Press (2009), 4823–4826.
4. Child, J., Bertholle, L., and Beck, S. *Mastering the art of French cooking. Volume one Volume one*. Knopf, New York, 1961.
5. Dalton, M.A., Desjardins, A., and Wakkary, R. From DIY Tutorials to DIY Recipes. *Ext. Abstracts CHI'14*, ACM Press (2014), 1405–1410.
6. Desjardins, A. and Wakkary, R. Manifestations of Everyday Design: Guiding Goals and Motivations. In *Proc. C&C'13*, ACM Press (2013), 253–262.
7. Fernquist, J., Grossman, T., and Fitzmaurice, G. Sketch-sketch Revolution: An Engaging Tutorial System for Guided Sketching and Application Learning. In *Proc. UIST'11,* ACM Press (2011), 373–382.
8. Jayaprakash, S. *Technical Writing*. Himalaya Publishing House, Mumbai, 2008.
9. Kuznetsov, S. and Paulos, E. Rise of the expert amateur: DIY projects, communities, and cultures. In *Proc. NordiCHI'10*, ACM Press (2010), 295–304.
10. Lindtner, S., Hertz, G.D., and Dourish, P. Emerging Sites of HCI Innovation: Hackerspaces, Hardware Startups & Incubators. In *Proc. CHI'14*, ACM Press (2014), 439–448.
11. Museum of Modern Art. Talk to Me. 2011. http://www.moma.org/interactives/exhibitions/2011/talktome/.
12. Museum of Modern Art. Access to Tools: Publications from the Whole Earth Catalog, 1968-1974, 2011 -. http://www.moma.org/interactives/exhibitions/2011/AccesstoTools/.
13. Neal, L. Distance Learning (Tutorial). In *Proc. SIGCPR'98*, ACM Press (1998), 307–308.
14. De Roeck, D., Slegers, K., Criel, J., et al. I Would DiYSE for It!: A Manifesto for Do-it-yourself Internet-of-things Creation. In *Proc. NordiCHI'12*, ACM Press (2012), 170–179.
15. Rombauer, I. von S. and Becker, M.R. *Joy of cooking*. Bobbs-Merrill, Indianapolis, 1975.
16. Shove, E., Watson, M., and Ingram, J. *The Design of Everyday Life*. Berg Publishers, Oxford, GBR, 2007.
17. Spencer, A. *DIY: The Rise of Lo-fi Culture*. Marion Boyars Publishers, London, 2005.
18. Torrey, C., Churchill, E.F., and McDonald, D.W. Learning How: The Search for Craft Knowledge on the Internet. In *Proc. CHI'09*, ACM Press (2009), 1371–1380.
19. Torrey, C., McDonald, D.W., Schilit, B.N., and Bly, S. How-To pages: Informal systems of expertise sharing. In L.J. Bannon, I. Wagner, C. Gutwin, R.H.R. Harper and K. Schmidt, eds., *ECSCW 2007*. Springer London, 2007, 391–410.
20. Tseng, T. and Resnick, M. Product Versus Process: Representing and Appropriating DIY Projects Online. In *Proc. DIS'14*, ACM Press (2014), 425–428.
21. Turner, F. *From counterculture to cyberculture: Stewart Brand, the Whole Earth Network, and the rise of digital utopianism*. University of Chicago Press, Chicago, 2006.
22. Wakkary, R., Desjardins, A., Hauser, S., and Maestri, L. A Sustainable Design Fiction: Green Practices. *ACM TOCHI 20*, 4 (2013), 23:1–23:34.
23. Whole Earth Catalog. *Stewart Brand*, 1969.

Hybrid Practice in the Kalahari: Design Collaboration through Digital Tools and Hunter-Gatherer Craft

Jennifer Jacobs
MIT Media Lab
jacobsj@media.mit.edu

Amit Zoran
MIT Media Lab & The Hebrew University
zoran@cs.huji.ac.il

ABSTRACT
People have been making things for a long time, yet digital making has developed mostly within an industrial context. We question how non-digital craft cultures can inform the design of digital tools. Furthermore, what methods can help us understand these cultures in ways that are relevant to digital practice? As makers ourselves, we see potential for collaborative making to mitigate barriers in communication and provide insight into non-digital practices and values. To evaluate this approach, we visited a hunter-gatherer community that preserves an ancient craft, bringing with us digital design and fabrication tools. Working together, we merged digital tools with ostrich eggshell jewelry craft. We use this experience to draw conclusions about making as a form of communication, the importance of supporting appropriation and immediacy in collaborations, the challenge of combining abstract design tools with concrete approaches, and the value of incorporating design and making into communal life.

Author Keywords
Design; Collaboration; Hunter-Gatherers; Craft; Digital Fabrication; Hybrid; Computer-Aided Design (CAD).

ACM Classification Keywords
H.5.2. User Interfaces: User-centered design.

INTRODUCTION
Digital technology continues to open new pathways for creation, but people have been making things long before computers existed. We wonder what elements of traditional making are absent in the use of emerging technology and what is required to blend technologically supported making practices with traditional ones. We believe that the dialog on technologically supported making can be enhanced through a better understanding of making practices in traditional indigenous cultures. Anthropology offers one approach to studying indigenous societies; however we are human computer interaction (HCI) researchers, not anthropologists. Therefore we approach these questions through our role as digital makers. Our hypothesis is that by engaging with non-digital crafting societies *through the mechanism of collaborative making,* we can bridge differences in communication, resulting in an enhanced understanding of the making practices of these cultures. Further, we posit that by incorporating digital tools in collaboration with a non-digital, non-industrial culture, we can gain new insight into the affordances and limitations of this technology. To examine this hypothesis, we apply digital design and fabrication technology to the craft of a people with a unique worldview: hunter-gatherer societies.

Figure 1: (a-b) Ju/'hoansi workshop participants, (c-d) traditional ostrich eggshell bead jewelry, and hybrid designs made with traditional materials and (e) CNC or (f) 3D printing.

Because they maintain elements of a lifestyle that dates back thousands of years in the past [12], sub-Saharan hunter-gatherers provide a connection to early forms of human craft. The Ju/'hoansi[1] are a small group of (former) hunter-gatherers in southern Africa who practice a form of

[1] The Ju/'hoansi speak a click based language. Symbols (!, /, and ≠) are used to denote different click sounds of their language.

CHI 2015, April 18 – 23, 2015, Seoul, Republic of Korea

ACM 978-1-4503-3145-6/15/04···$15.00
http://dx.doi.org/10.1145/2702123.2702362

Figure 2: The workshop - (a) our car and the working environment; (b) Roland Modela MDX 15; (c) demonstrating the Modela's operation to Ju/'hoan men; (d) Ju/'hoan woman working on a piece of jewelry; (e) collaborative practice and design discussion.

decorative jewelry craft using ostrich eggshell (OES) beads (Figure 1). In this research, we juxtaposed digital making with Ju/'hoan craft practices in two forms. First, as digital designers, we applied our tools to the design and machining of traditional Ju/'hoan craft materials into finished artifacts. Second, we conducted a collaborative design workshop with a Ju/'hoan community in Namibia, where together we created artifacts through a combination of digital and traditional techniques. Our contribution was also twofold: We outline our approach in applying modern technology to ancient practice, and used the analysis of this process to advocate for new approaches to technological design and development. Further, we detailed the challenges and successes of this collaboration, and used this experience to motivate general strategies for engaging greater diversity and participation in making in our own society.

The paper is structured around a presentation of the workshop we conducted in Namibia in May 2014 (Figure 2). In the next section, we introduce the Ju/'hoan culture, reinforcing our motivation for working with this specific group. In *Related Work* we summarize the current trends in digital design and fabrication studies, before presenting the *Technology and Techniques* (both traditional and digital) that were used in this collaboration. The *Workshop* section describes the collaborative experience, followed by the conceptual discussion and conclusions.

THE JU/'HOANSI CULTURE AND CRAFT

The Ju/'hoansi are a small foraging society living in Namibia and Botswana. They maintained their traditional nomadic way of life until the second half of the twentieth century, hunting and gathering in the central Kalahari Desert. Modernization has forced the Ju/'hoansi to permanently settle and adapt a new way of life [3]. The Ju/'hoansi have minimal notions of ownership, hierarchy, and division of labor when compared with agricultural societies. All adult members participate in making activities, with specific activities for each gender.

The Ju/'hoan symbolic system is difficult to document [13]. Because the Ju/'hoansi come from a foraging tradition, their material culture emphasizes immediate applications. They invest in social ties rather than material storage, and their symbolic culture does not embody long-term principles [2, 12]. Their aesthetic preferences are driven by personal desire and rarely described in abstract terms. Creativity and individualism are welcomed, but communities favor modesty and equality. Individual pride or exceptional differences in style are disapproved. The prototypical example Ju/'Hoansi symbolic design is their OES craft.

Historically as well as today, OES jewelry craft is relegated to women, with a few exceptions. Traditionally, Ju/'hoansi used OES beads as a raw material for jewelry making, for personal uses or as part of *hxaro*, a gift exchange ritual. Through hxaro networks, artifacts swapped hands, serving as a channel of symbolic communication between communities. Wiessner [20] proposed that individual style preference serves to express identity within the community.

With permanent settlements, the Ju/'hoansi can no longer depend exclusively on foraging, and have sought alternative ways to make a living. A number of Ju/'hoan villages welcome visitors and demonstrate traditional practices for a fee. Ju/'hoan OES craft also provides a source of income in the African curios market. Although commoditized, Ju/'hoan craft remains an important community practice and form of creative expression. Moreover, many Ju/'hoan communities attempt to preserve other elements of their traditional way of life. Although no longer the primary food-source, some Ju/'hoansi still forage, and many still speak their traditional language with click consonants. The villages we visited only had one or two English speakers to translate. Even communicating through a translator proves challenging because of the linguistic divide between western and Ju/'hoan languages.

The Ju/'hoansi are professional makers and create products for contemporary markets, but possess a fundamentally different attitude than that of any industrial or digital society. Their OES craft is a product of their distinct culture. Because they are craft professionals that strongly differ from professionals in post-industrial cultures, the Ju/'hoansi are ideal collaborators in a comparison of traditional and digital practices.

RELATED WORK

Recently, digital design and fabrication has evolved into a mainstream topic within HCI and computer-graphics communities. Current research trends focus on improving interactions with digital fabrication tools [7] or seeking real-time integration of design and fabrication [23]. New technologies affect the design process, directly changing the aesthetics of the resultant artifacts. Tools and techniques including parametric design [16], modular design and assembly [8], digitally made connectors and flexible manifolds [18], or digitally fabricated moving parts [17] are enriching the digital making culture with new capabilities and aesthetics.

Lately, researchers have proposed hybridizing design and fabrication processes for efficiency [14]. We seek a fusion that goes beyond optimization. Zoran et al. outlined the limitations of 3D printing compared to manual craft by describing how digitally designed artifacts are intrinsically reproducible. They combined digital fabrication and craft in a work involving broken ceramics restored with 3D-printed elements, to create objects that function as memorials [22]. *Hybrid Basketry* [21] presented 3D-printed structures that allow the growth and development of hand-woven organic fibers. Others have sought to support new audiences in technological making. Buechley et al. conducted workshops [4] where electronic components were integrated with traditional practice, demonstrating how re-contextualizing existing technology empowers new communities and emphasizes different values. Jacobs et al. conducted several workshops with North American novices using a custom procedural design software, called *DressCode*, and other tools to produce fashion accessories through procedural design, digital fabrication, and manual craft activities [10, 11]. In our work, we applied a similar approach (including a use of DressCode), but worked with makers from an indigenous culture who, although new to digital technology, were professional rather than amateur designers.

Efforts to introduce advanced technologies to traditional societies are not new. Non-profit initiatives like the FabLab program [6] introduce digital tools in developing countries to address local problems. HCI for development focuses on empowering users in underserved populations and applying technological innovations to address challenges in these communities [5]. We are distinguished from these approaches by evaluating practices and tools from our own culture rather than building solutions for developing countries. HCI participatory research strategies seek to involve the user in the process of designing tools and generating solutions for their problems [9]. We seek to work with traditional communities as peers rather than users. Bardzell et al. observed western and non-western craft traditions to provide insight into alternate design objectives for technology [1]. We also wished to evaluate our technology from a culturally distinct perspective, but desired to go beyond observation into collaboration.

In recent years, the industrialized world has experienced a resurgence in DIY (do-it-yourself), popularly termed the Maker Movement. Tanenbaum et. al. describe how making offers the opportunity to democratize design and manufacturing. While pleasure and expressivity are important values in hobbyist making, they coexist with utilitarian objectives [19]. We recognize that our perspectives on making are influenced by maker culture and

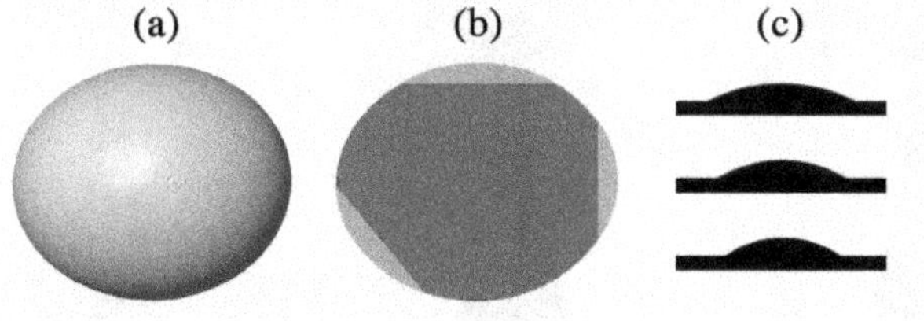

Figure 4: (a) 3D scanned ostrich egg. (b) Cross-sections (in orange) of curvatures from the egg used to prepare three 3D-printed jigs (c) for milling the eggshells.

seek to interrogate this perspective in our collaboration with the Ju/'hoansi.

TECHNOLOGY AND TECHNIQUES

We initiated the research by applying digital tools to Ju/'hoan craft. We based our approach on observations from two prior visits to Ju/'hoan communities. Here we outline the Ju/'hoan OES technique in detail, and describe our methodology in applying digital fabrication to their practice.

Traditional and Manual Technologies

Traditionally, Ju/'hoan makers break whole OES, which have an average thickness of 2.5 mm, into small fragments. Then they manually drill holes in the center of each piece using a long wooden stick with a metal nail. Once drilled, the beads are strung together and sanded. Frequently, beads are dyed or baked to give them a darker color. The beads are manually assembled into necklaces and bracelets, ranging from single strands to complex matrixes and interwoven patterns (Figure 1, c and d). When assembling jewelry, some makers intersperse OES beads with beads made of wood, seeds or nuts, or with purchased glass beads.

Computational Technologies

We explored the hybridization of Ju/'hoan craft with computer-aided design and digital fabrication by creating our own jewelry. This exploration produced a set of sample artifacts (see Figure 1, e and g), as well as a set of digital techniques, which we theorized could be applied to real-time collaboration with the Ju/'hoansi. Our objective was to contribute techniques that brought new forms and aesthetics to traditional OES creation, rather than to render traditional skills obsolete with digital means.

CNC Milling

Computer numerical control (CNC) milling enabled unskilled carvers such as us to create complex forms from OES. We developed a technique to mill OES using a Roland Modela MDX 15, a small and portable 3-axis CNC milling machine with a working area of 152 x 101 mm. We used 1/64" ball-nose and 1/32" square carbide endmills for all the OES milling. The curvature, fragility and irregularity of OES material required a custom technique to effectively mill. We used curved, custom 3D-printed Nylon12 jigs (each 100x75x40 mm) to affix eggshell fragments to the surface of the Modela. We produced the jigs by scanning an intact ostrich egg and extracting several manifolds from the data (Figure 4).

Figure 5: Hybrid designs with traditional elements and 3D printed pendants from //Xaoba (a-e) and from Grashoek (f-j).

Small eggshell fragments (beads and modular parts, below 10x10 mm) could be cut without changing the height of the milling bit (with an average milling time of 5 min). However, larger fragments (up to 50x50 mm) with a significant height difference between their center and edges required a 3D tool path to match the curvature. A custom procedural script in Grasshopper automated the conversion between 2D vector drawings to 3D toolpaths. This workflow required 30-60 min of machining per piece, depending on the complexity of the design.

Additive Fabrication

We explored 3D printing as a way to introduce new materials and mechanical affordances into Ju/'hoan craft. Using computer-aided design (CAD), we created and 3D-printed a series of components to be used in the workshop, referencing traditional Ju/'hoan designs in the process. We sought to amplify the relative advantages of 3D printing (such as enabling the creation of overhanging structures and holes that are infeasible to create through 3-axis milling). We developed three different types of Selective-Laser Sintering (SLS) objects: protective *frames*, 3D-printed *connectors*, and stand-alone *pendants*.

Frames Large milled eggshell pieces were extremely fragile and required reinforcement to make them wearable. In addition to a few milled wooden enclosures, most of the milled pendant designs presented later (Figures 6, 7, and 8) use 3D-printed frames for protection. This series of round, lightweight frames had three flexible struts protruding into the center, which affixed to the back of an eggshell with epoxy, supporting pendants at a range of shapes and sizes. The frames were designed with holes for connecting twine to facilitate their incorporation into jewelry.

Connectors As modularity and assembly are fundamental to digital design practice, we attempted to design modular components that were compatible with OES fragments. We created 3D-printed press-fit connectors that could join 2, 3 or 4 OES fragments, all on the same spatial plain (Figure 9, c). The connectors included small arms with pins, requiring 1mm holes to be milled in the OES, 1.8mm from its edge.

Pendants Additive fabrication enabled the creation of intricate interconnected forms and moving parts not possible through any other form of fabrication. We produced SLS Nylon12 and DMLS (Direct Metal Laser Sintering) steel standalone components, carefully considering the Ju/'hoan traditional jewelry designs, while using a digital design language and 3D printing affordances (synthetic materials and interconnected parts) to highlight the difference in practices (Figure 5).

COLLABORATION METHODOLOGY

Our goal of collaboration with Ju/'hoan makers required us to prepare the techniques we developed in the lab for deployment in Ju/'Hoan communities in Namibia. In practical terms, this necessitated that our techniques were **mobile** (we rented a 4WD pickup truck for the workshop and powered the Modela via the car battery), **robust** (we refined the milling technique to the point that we could repeat it more-or-less without error, and brought 3D printed pendants not dependent on milling), and **open-ended** (we attempted to create a variety of approaches, that could suggest different creative possibilities). We had no means to contact the Ju/'hoan villages in advance, so the only way for us to propose a workshop was to ask in person.

We estimated that our greatest challenge would be in effectively communicating our intent given the cultural and

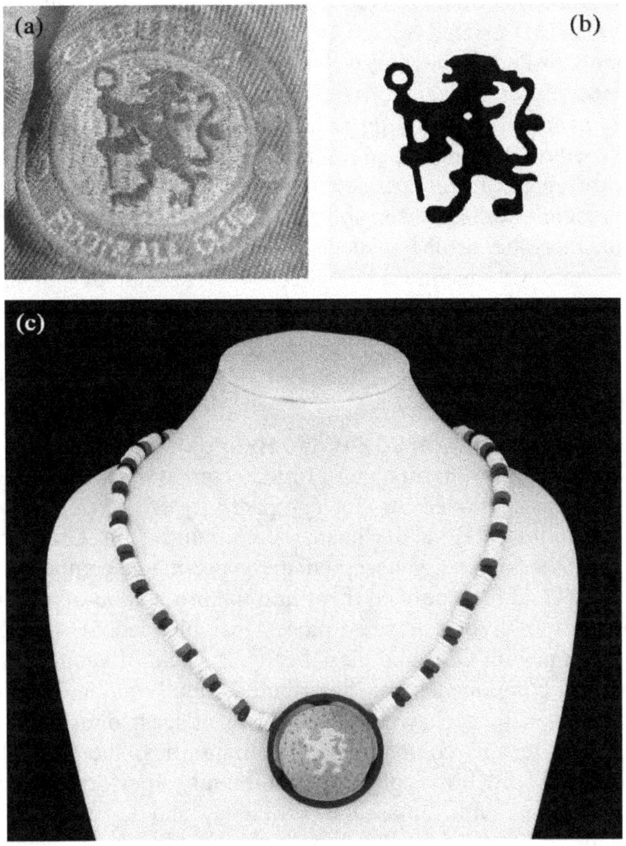

Figure 6: Digitized Iconography: digitizing a particular symbol (a, b) before engraving it on the dyed OES (c).

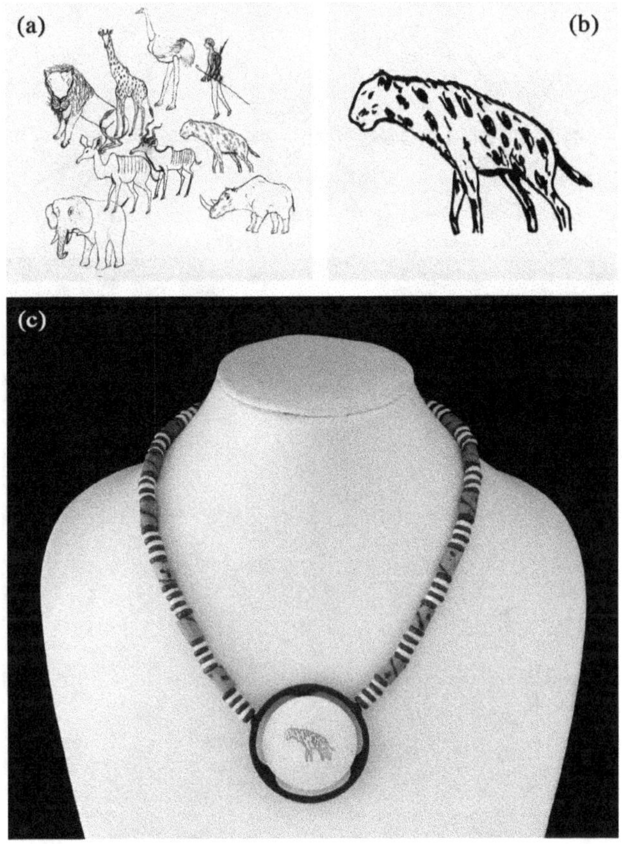

Figure 7: (a) Boo's drawings; (b) a digitally duplicated hyena; and (c) a digitally engraved and dyed hyena on an OES.

language barriers. We planned a variety of introductory acts with the hope that one would provide an entry point into the collaboration. We shared the OES sample artifacts we had created in our lab and described the tools we used to create them. We also shared personal artifacts that we had created outside of this project to attempt to give context to our work as makers prior to our interest in OES craft. Because the Ju/'hoansi have a strong culture of gift giving, we brought gifts with us as another form of initial engagement. The gifts ranged from edibles (tea and tobacco), commercially made jewelry components and tools (glass beads, sand paper, twine and connectors), and artifacts we designed in advance (3D-printed pendants and beads). Following these "icebreakers," we explained that we had brought our tools (a CNC mill and computers running CAD software) with us, and if they were interested, we would like to return, share our techniques, learn from them, and make jewelry together.

This work was not without some risk, such as the potential for miscommunication or unintentional exploitation as a result of the economic divide between us and the Ju/'hoansi. We attempted to mitigate this risk through transparency in our intentions. When proposing the collaboration, we explained that we were interested in sharing Ju/'hoan craft with people in our community. We asked permission to take photos of the artifacts that were created to aid in telling the story of how Ju/'hoan craft could connect with our way of making. Because the Ju/'hoansi have a commercial interest in selling jewelry, we offered to buy any artifacts they produced in the workshop *only* if they were interested in selling them. Although we support advocacy and aid efforts on behalf of the Ju/'hoansi, our goal was to broaden perspectives on digital design. Therefore we approached the Ju/'hoansi as creative peers and design professionals Despite our preparations, there was no precedent for which to base this collaboration. This made it difficult to predict how the Ju/'hoansi would react to the idea of a collaborative workshop, and what they might consider the benefits of such an interaction.

WORKSHOP

We ended up working with two communities of Ju/'Hoansi makers in Namibia, in the villages of Grashoek and //Xaoba. Both villages had opened living museums to the public and one or two English speakers. We began with single day visits to both villages. Showing our prior work provided an entry point into the collaboration. The Ju/'hoansi were curious about the materials and techniques we used (CNC'd wood, plastic and leather), which in-turn,

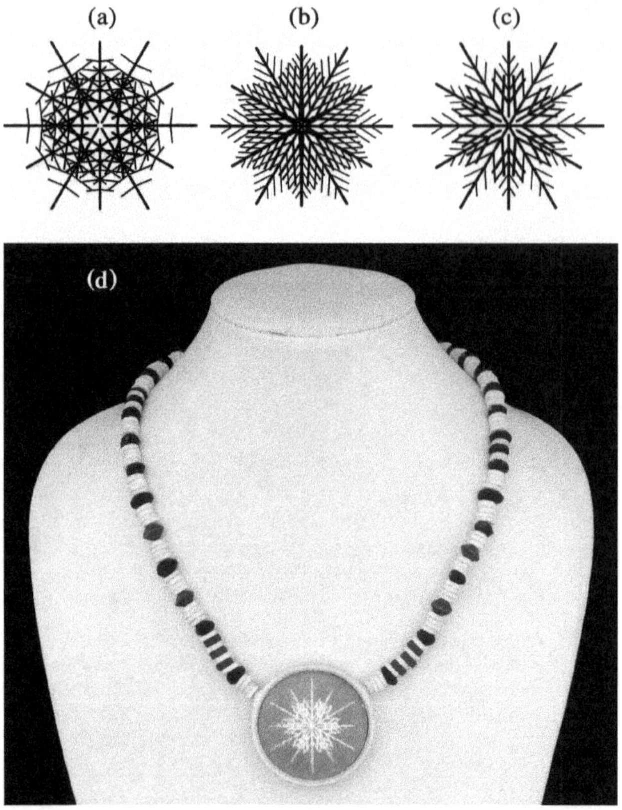

Figure 8: (a-c) Parametrically designed snowflakes and (d) the final design engraved on a dyed ostrich eggshell.

allowed us to describe our interest in their materials and techniques by showing them the OES jewelry we had created. We also gave a collection of 3D-printed beads and pendants to each community.

We received positive reactions from both communities about the possibility of a multiple-day workshop. //Xaoba was more remote than Grashoek and received less tourist traffic, so we began our long-term collaboration there, setting up camp next to the village a day after our initial visit. On the first day of camping, we demonstrated the process of CNC milling with a supply of OES we had purchased beforehand. Immediately the makers of //Xaoba gathered their tools (blankets, drills sanding stones and twine), put forth ideas for designs to create on the mill, and began crafting beads nearby. In total, we spent five days in //Xaoba, working six to eight hours a day with ten women. This time was interspersed with a three-day hiatus to restock our food and materials, and iterate on our collaborative strategies. Following time in //Xaoba, we returned to Grashoek for a single-day visit, enabling us to compare different approaches with the 3D-printed components between the two communities. All the makers in our collaboration were women. The men participated by contributing ideas and company, and often worked on other crafts simultaneously, such as crafting arrows and axes.

Overall, we collaboratively created roughly 60 artifacts (30 hybrid 3D-printed pieces, 8 milled pendants, and some small milled pieces). We detailed the process of creating these pieces by categorizing them by style and approach: *3D-printed hybrids*, *digitized iconography*, and *modular assembly*. We developed a set of criteria to aid in reflection with regards to the artifacts: Do the artifacts appeal to our personal stylistic sensibilities? Do our collaborators consider the artifacts successful? Do the artifacts show evidence of meaningful application of digital design and fabrication? Are the artifacts stylistically distinct from prior examples of Ju/'hoan craft? Do the artifacts demonstrate successful combinations of our techniques and Ju/'hoan techniques?

Style Diversity with 3D-Printed Hybrids

The ease of sharing 3D-printed components with the Ju/'hoansi enabled us to compare styles between two communities. Both Ju/'hoansi communities in Grashoek and //Xaoba readily accepted these pre-made components as gifts and incorporated them into the production of a large number of hybrid jewelry pieces that blended 3D-printed elements with OES and glass beads. In each village the 3D-printed components were distributed equally among all the makers, with each woman receiving at least one bead of each style and color. In both communities, the English-speaking member of the community performed the distribution with remarkable efficiency and fairness. As a result, the hybrid jewelry generally contained one central 3D-printed element, surrounded by handmade or glass beads or both. This approach differed from our intuition in using the beads ourselves (i.e. using multiple 3D-printed beads that matched in color and style in a single piece of jewelry).

Although we observed similar communal practices between Grashoek and //Xaoba, the styles of the artifacts were markedly different (Figure 5). Whereas the makers in Grashoek used a single 3D-printed component per necklace, they balanced the design by OES, wooden beads, or seed that directly complimented the color or shape of the 3D-printed component. Alternatively, they created a coherent composition by augmenting the 3D-printed part with handmade beads. The //Xaoba makers took a different, free-form approach in integrating the 3D-printed components, by breaking some of them apart into smaller beads and situating them with similarly colored pendants.

Whereas we observed evidence of different styles between individuals, these differences were subtle, and deferred to the overall style of the community. The existence of personal style encompassed by community style lended credence to our objective of a collaborative design process with the Ju/'hoansi makers. It demonstrated that despite differences in our symbolic worldview and use of technology, we were engaging in design practices with comparable levels of sophistication, with an awareness of individual style and community norms.

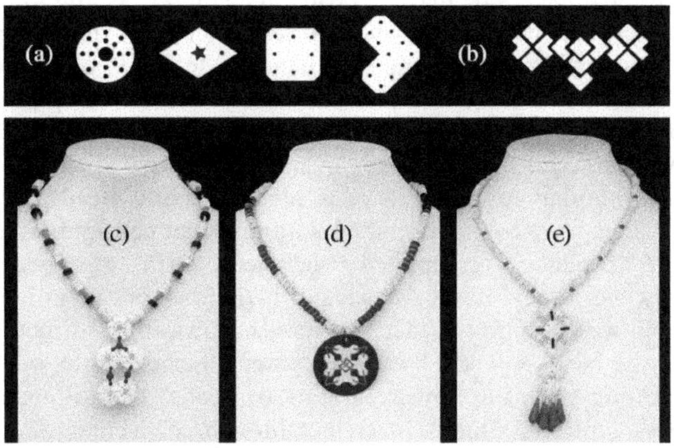

Figure 9: Modular Assembly. (a) Digital designs of modular beads, and (b) a pattern demonstrating design possibilities, using two modules. (c-e) Examples of different design configurations.

Digitized Iconography

One primary affordance of digital practice is the systematic reproduction of a motif with variations in scale and physical medium. The makers of //Xaoba readily took advantage of this, resulting in a series of graphic pendants in the form of large, dyed eggshell pendants inscribed with a motif. Both men and women in the village dictated the designs for the pendants by either drawing on the sand or sketching on paper. We digitally duplicated the drawings, and following the pendant's completion, one of the women (either the woman who designed it, or a female relative of the male designer) assembled the pendant into a complete necklace.

Very few of these designs corresponded with traditional Ju/'hoansi motifs. In the most extreme example of this, several people requested designs by referencing of images on their clothing. The village healer requested a lion, using his Chelsea Football Club hat as a source (Figure 6), and another man requested a snowflake, by referencing the design on his knitted cap. In these cases, the people selecting the designs were unfamiliar with their original meanings; the man who selected the snowflake was unaware that the graphic referenced actual snow.

During the last days of our stay, we collaborated with a skilled illustrator named Boo to produce an additional series of graphic pendants. Boo's subject matter corresponded with traditional conceptions of Ju/'hoansi culture. From his illustrations, members of the village selected specific drawings to be translated to pendants (Figure 7). In several cases (such as the snowflake), the style of the designs provided by the Ju/'hoansi makers was highly procedural in nature. In these cases, we employed parametric modeling to provide another means of collaboration: we used DressCode to create a parametric model of their original design, presenting variations to the local maker (Figure 8). Although the Ju/'hoansi were impressed with parametric tools and appreciated the motifs they produced, they did not show interest in using them to explore new designs.

The graphic pendants represent a successful collaboration. Together with the Ju/'hoansi we were able to systematically apply iconography defined in a variety of formats and translate it at a smaller scale to a different material with high fidelity. Although we provided the tools for this process, both the iconography, and the approach (take a specific image from a different context and apply it to the eggshell) were dictated by the Ju/'hoan makers. Although they had a novel aesthetic, the pendants preserved qualities of the style and character of the //Xaoba makers. The primary limitation of the pendants was that they were restricted to one application of digital fabrication (translating a digital design to a new physical context). We therefore attempted to explore other affordances of digital fabrication that could be integrated with Ju/'hoan practices.

Modularity and Precision

Beaded jewelry making can be described as a form of modular design wherein a variety of modules can be assembled into varying configurations. Well-crafted modules are highly reconfigurable, enabling an exploratory design process. We observed modular design among the Ju/hoansi; designers would distribute all of their beads on a blanket in front of them, select groupings of 2-5 beads, and thread them in sequence onto a necklace. After several iterations, the Ju/'hoan designers evaluated their progress, removed beads and begin again with an altered sequence, while consulting others for suggestions. Frequently, necklaces were re-assembled 4- times before completion.

Digital fabrication supports the rapid and precise production of small volumes of compatible parts, making it an excellent tool for prototyping modular systems. We attempted to exploit this these affordances in several different ways with respect to Ju/'hoansi practice:

Multi-part standalone configurations dependent on precision: This included a press-fit working gear pendant (Figure 12), a press-fit wood and eggshell pendant (Figure 9, d) and a gradient consisting a series of beads, which when strung in order of size produced a transition between a circle and star pattern (Figure 10).

Modular bead systems: These consisted of OES sets with multiple connection points that could be combined in multiple configurations by hand with handmade and glass beads by the Ju/'hoansi to produce different patterns (Figure 9, a and b). Several of these reconfigurable designs were compatible with 3D-printed press-fit connectors, that could be snapped together to create different arrangements (Figure 9, c).

Modular systems comprised of press-fit components: Combining the two approaches above, we created a series of press-fit cube "beads" out of OES (figure 11). In this case, the press-fit components that comprised the beads themselves were modular, and the assembled beads were also re-configurable and could be assembled with other types of beads.

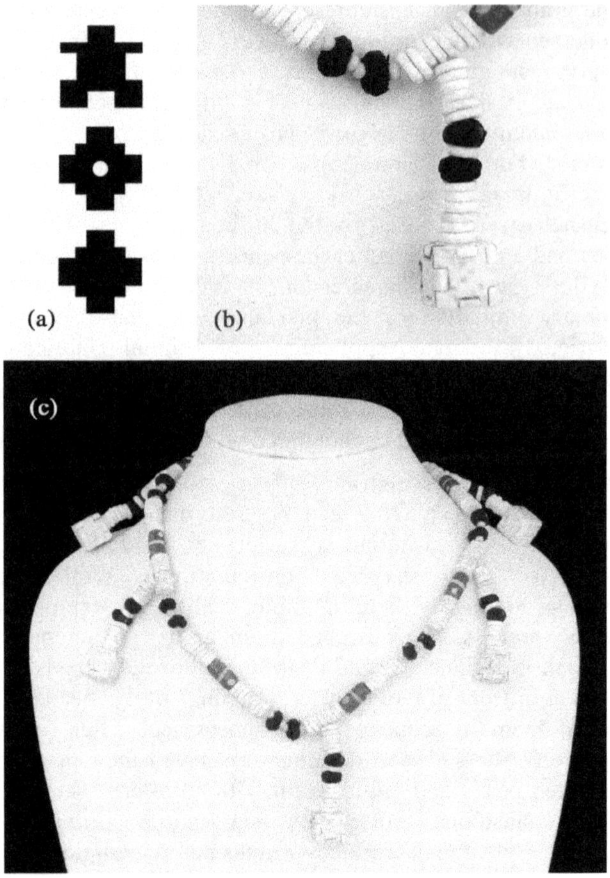

Figure 11: Press-fit cubes, a common technique in digital fabrication. (a) The cube components; (b) an assembled cube; and (c) the final jewelry designed and assembled by a Ju/'hoansi maker.

Figure 12: Design of a working gear mechanism (a), and the final assembly of the jewelry (b). We designed the gear-pendent and Ju/'hoansi integrated our work inside the necklace.

Our objective in developing these examples was to communicate the modular affordances of the digital tools to the //Xaoba makers, thereby enabling them to offer suggestions for effective modular beads. In this case, our intentions for Ju/'hoansi-prompted iterations did not come to pass. For the press-fit cubes and gear mechanism, the //Xaoba makers treated the beads in a similar fashion to the 3D-printed beads; they incorporated them into necklaces, and complemented them with hand-made beads of similar colors. Despite our explanation that, unlike the 3D-printed beads, we possessed the means to make additional variants of this style, the //Xaoba makers never pursued this. We saw similar results with the reconfigurable beads. The //Xaoba makers experimented with different configurations, and produced completed necklaces with the beads; however, they never requested variations or alterations. This was despite the fact that design flaws in the structure of the beads quickly became apparent. For example, when creating intricate woven patterns of beads, the Ju/'hoansi pass multiple strands of twine through the center of the beads; however, the holes on the milled beads were too narrow to accommodate this technique.

DISCUSSION

We began this work with the goal of understanding how digital practices could be reconciled with traditional making, and how making could enable symbolic communication. We discovered that immediacy and appropriation in digital design can support the ideation and iteration, even in a society that is new to digital affordances. We also identified limitations of digital technology in non-digital cultures: the abstractions of digital tools conflict with the concrete design practices of the Ju/'hoansi, and the design of the digital tools themselves conflict with the social aspects of Ju/'hoansi making. We succeeded in using making as a method of communication, insofar as it provided a method to overcome significant differences in language and culture, resulting in a prolific collaboration. Through making, we gained an understanding of how the social craft activities of the Ju/'hoansi strengthen community ties and reflect on how this compares to the role of making in our own culture.

Making as a Form of Cross-Cultural Communication

Language and cultural differences can pose severe barriers in collaborative settings. We found that engaging in collaborative making indeed enabled us to bridge many of these barriers, as evidenced both by the significant number of artifacts we produced together, the fact that the Ju/'hoansi's valued the artifacts, and that they expressed great interest in pursuing similar collaborations.. When attempting to collaborate with people of different cultures, sharing prior artifacts that communicate one's personal approaches and aesthetics can assist in communicating values and ideas. Preparing a diversity of avenues for creation allows for people to explore alternatives, when some efforts prove infeasible. Finally, the process of making itself offers a form of practical communication (for example showing an example sequence of beads, or drawing a pattern), when verbal language is not an option.

Joint Affordances in Digital and Traditional Tools

Chiefly, we saw compatibility between digital and traditional tools in mechanisms for appropriation. Ju/'hoansi makers are extremely skilled in working with

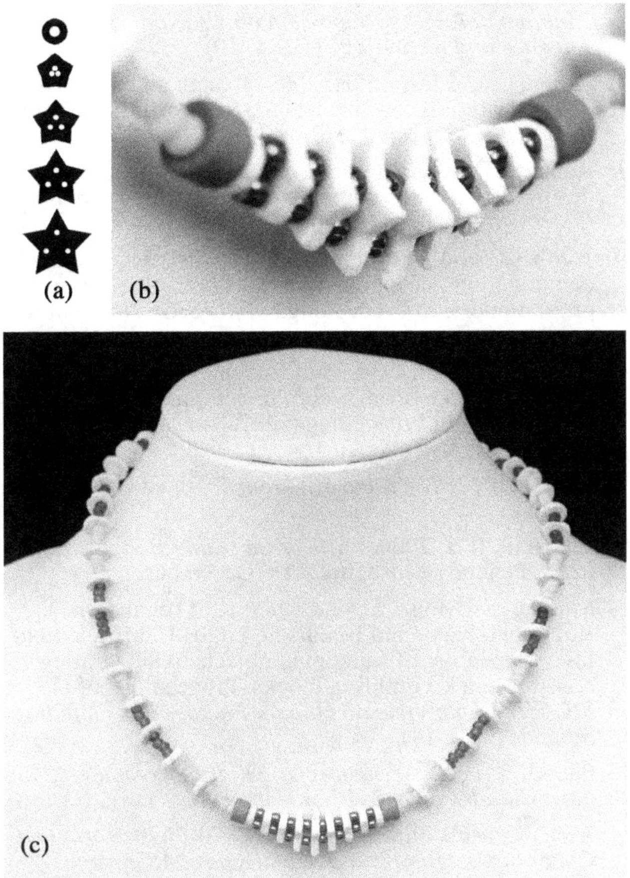

Figure 10: Configuration through transformation, morphing two geometries together (a) to achieve an OES design that is digital by nature (b-c).

available components to suit their design. The breaking of 3D printed components to create unified compositions in //Xaoba is a testament to this appropriation. One of the powerful aspects of digital design tools, is that they enable creators to pull pieces of content from other places, reshape those pieces, and add them to new creations. The iconographic pendants represent a successful hybridization of Ju/'hoansi approach to appropriation (applying foreign symbols from their clothing to a their own contexts), together with our own digital approach. The milling workflow aligned with the immediacy of Ju/'hoansi practice: they dictated an idea; we translated it to a pendant; and within one hour they could begin assembling a piece. This immediacy translated into a rapid set of successive ideas on variations on the process (drawing in the sand; selecting icons on one's clothing; drawing icons by a skilled illustrator). Research into interactive fabrication often has a similar goal in aiding iterative design by reducing the amount of time between ideation and realization. In reconciling digital tools with tradition, we argue that supporting immediacy and appropriation is essential.

Barriers Between Abstract and Concrete Practices

A significant barrier we observed in our collaborative practice involved the incompatibility between digital and non-digital mechanisms for iteration, highlighted by our failed attempts to collaboratively make new modules with new affordances. In digital practice, designers must translate design ideas, including variations to an existing design, to a systematic sequence of software operations. This process requires an abstracted conception of the functionality of the software. Conversely, the Ju/'hoansi identify with immediate concepts and their making practices are dictated by the concrete. Specifically, they explore variations by iterating over available physical components in view in front of them on a blanket. Thus, many of our attempts to encourage conceptual-design discourse through demonstration of new digital solutions were rejected. The Ju/'hoansi makers used the parts we generated with CNC techniques as unalterable beads rather than as templates for iteration. Conversely, when provided with concrete components like the 3D-printed pieces that afforded variation (albeit unexpectedly), the Ju/'hoansi modified them to suit different functional and aesthetic purposes.

In seeking ways to make digital tools that better facilitate exploratory modular practices, one approach is to design domain-specific CAD tools that enable designers to reconfigure virtual and physical modular parts through a small number of operations that are derived from the topology of the parts themselves. This may serve as an alternative to current tools that require designers to work from an expansive set of operations to generate custom forms. Tools like this could be relevant to non-digital cultures; however, they may also assist in broadening participation in digital design and fabrication in our culture.

Reinforcing Community Through Making

Our collaboration with the Ju/'hoansi enabled us to develop an understanding of the communal role of making. Despite the fact that the Ju/'hoansi are professional designers, craft is not merely a professional practice. Within the communities we observed, the act of making is imbedded within the other elements of daily life. The Ju/'hoansi also exhibit a lack of hierarchy in making. While there are different levels of skill and expertise among different craftspeople, *all* Ju/'hoansi participate in making. Collective making is important, not only as a recreational activity or a source of income, but as a mechanism for sustaining community bonds. Conversely, in our culture, craft is often either practiced by experts in a professional setting or a hobby for amateurs in their leisure time. In either case, craft is performed in a specialized setting and frequently among individuals of comparable skill. Papert argued for creating educational environments that are embedded in rich cultural-social experiences as a mechanism for encouraging meaningful participation [15]. Similarly our experience with the Ju/'hoansi suggests that if we wish to broaden meaningful creative participation in our own culture, we should seek to incorporate making more closely with our daily lives. Part of this approach involves continuing to design digital tools that encourage working collectively rather than individually. The greater challenge perhaps, is to create environments where experts and novices, young and old, can make together as colleagues.

CONCLUSION

By conducting a workshop with makers from a non-digital culture and practice, we demonstrate the opportunities and limitations of collaborative making as a mechanism for cross-cultural creative dialog. In the face of severe communication challenges, collaborative making can convey one's objectives and approaches. It offers the opportunity to examine our own tools and practices from a different worldview, resulting in new avenues for technology design.

As a final note, we add a personal, important reflection: *The value of a communal working atmosphere should not be underestimated.* Working with Ju/'hoan makers, we experienced intangible qualities in the environment. Ju/'hoan makers readily share resources and ideas without individual pride. They invest long working hours to learn from foreigners while seamlessly maintaining the flow of daily life. In the interest of creatively empowering entire communities within our own culture, we feel strongly about the need find ways to incorporate these qualities back into to digital practice.

ACKNOWLEDGMENTS

We deeply thank all the Ju/'hoansi makers that participated in this collaboration. Special thanks to M. Biesele and the Kalahari Peoples Fund; K. le Roux from OMBA trust; P. Wiessner; and J. Ito (director of the MIT Media Lab). We would also like to thank T. Rucham, A. Aksamija, S. Follmer, J. Brandt, D. Mellis and M. Resnick.

REFERENCES

1. Bardzell, S., Rosner, D. K., and Bardzell, J. 2012. Crafting quality in design: integrity, creativity, and public sensibility. Proceedings of *the Designing Interactive Systems Conference*, June 11-15.
2. Biesele, M. 1996. *Women Like Meat: The Folklore and Foraging Ideology of the Kalahari Ju/'Hoan*. Wits University Press, January.
3. Biesele, M. and Robert K. H. 2013. *The Ju/'Hoan San of Nyae Nyae and Namibian Independence: Development, Democracy, and Indigenous Voices in Southern Africa.* Berghahn Books; Reprint edition, February.
4. Buechley. L., and Perner-Wilson, H. 2012. Crafting technology: Reimagining the processes, materials, and cultures of electronics. ACM *Trans. Comput.-Hum. Interact.* 19, 3, Article 21, October, 21 pages.
5. Dray, S. M., Siegel, D. A., and Kotzé, P. 2003. Indra's Net: HCI in the developing world. *Interactions* 10(2): 28-37.
6. Fab Foundation. http://www.fabfoundation.org/fab-labs/ Last accessed July 23, 2014.
7. Follmer, S., Carr D., Lovell, E., and Ishii, H. 2010. CopyCAD: remixing physical objects with copy and paste from the real world. In Adjunct proceedings of *the 23nd annual ACM symposium on User interface software and technology* (UIST '10).
8. Hiller, J., and Lipson, H. 2009. Design and analysis of digital materials for physical 3D voxel printing. *Rapid Prototyping Journal*, 15/2, 137–149. Emerald.
9. Kensing, F. and Blomberg, J. 1998. Participatory design: Issues and concerns. *Computer Supported Cooperative Work* (CSCW).
10. Jacobs, J., and Buechley, L. 2013. Codeable objects: computational design and digital fabrication for novice programmers. In Proceedings *of the SIGCHI Conference on Human Factors in Computing Systems* (CHI '13).
11. Jacobs, J., Resnick, M., and Buechley, L. 2014. Dresscode: supporting youth in computational design and making. In Proceedings of *Constructionism 2014 Conference*. Vienna, Austria.
12. Lee, R. 2012. *The dobe Ju/'hoansi*, 4th ed. Thomson learning.
13. Marshall, L. J. 2004. *Nyae Nyae !Kung Beliefs and Rites*. Peabody Museum Press, December.
14. Mueller, S., Mohr, T., Guenther, K., Frohnhofen, J., Rollmann, K.A., and Baudisch, P. 2014. faBrickation: fast 3D printing of functional objects by integrating construction kit building blocks. Proceedings of *the SIGCHI Conference on Human Factors in Computing Systems* (CHI '14).
15. Papert, S. 1980. *Mindstorms: children, computers, and powerful ideas*. Basic Books, Inc., New York, NY.
16. Reas, C., McWilliams, C., and LUST. 2010. *Form and Code: In Design, Art and Architecture, A Guide to Computational Aesthetics.* Princeton Architectural Press.
17. Schmitt, P. and Seitinger, S. 2009. Plywood punk: a holistic approach to designing animated artifacts. In Proceedings of *the 3rd International Conference on Tangible and Embedded Interaction* (TEI '09). ACM.
18. Schneegass, S., Shirazi, A. S., Döring, T., Schmid, D., and Schmidt, A. 2014. NatCut: an interactive tangible editor for physical object fabrication. In *CHI '14 Extended Abstracts on Human Factors in Computing Systems* (CHI EA '14).
19. Tanenbaum, J., Williams, A., Desjardins, A., and Tanenbaum, K. 2013. Democratizing technology: pleasure, utility and expressiveness in DIY and maker practice. *In Proceedings of the SIGCHI Conference on Human Factors in Computing Systems* (CHI '13).
20. Wiessner, P. 1997. *Seeking Guidelines through an Evolutionary Approach: Style Revisited among the !Kung San (Ju/'hoansi) of the 1990s*. Archeological Papers of the American Anthropological Association.
21. Zoran, A. 2013. Hybrid Basketry: Interweaving digital practice within contemporary craft. In ACM SIGGRAPH 2013 Art Gallery.
22. Zoran, A. and Buechley, L. 2013. Hybrid reAssemblage: An Exploration of Craft, Digital Fabrication and Artifact Uniqueness. *Leonardo, Journal of Arts, Sciences and Technology*, volume 46, issue 1, February 2013.
23. Zoran, A., Shilkrot R., and Paradiso, J. A. 2013. Human computer Interaction for Hybrid Carving. *The 26th annual ACM symposium on User interface software and technology* (UIST '13).

The Proper Care and Feeding of Hackerspaces: Care Ethics and Cultures of Making

Austin L. Toombs
Indiana University
919 E 10th Street, Bloomington
IN 47408
altoombs@indiana.edu

Shaowen Bardzell
Indiana University
919 E 10th Street, Bloomington
IN 47408
selu@indiana.edu

Jeffrey Bardzell
Indiana University
919 E 10th Street, Bloomington
IN 47408
jbardzel@indiana.edu

ABSTRACT

Communities of making have been at the center of attention in popular, business, political, and academic research circles in recent years. In HCI, they seem to carry the promise of new forms of computer use, education, innovation, and even ways of life. In the West in particular, the maker manifestos of these communities have shown strong elements of a neoliberal ethos, one that prizes self-determination, tech-savvy, independence, freedom from government, suspicion of authority, and so forth. Yet such communities, to function as communities, also require values of collaboration, cooperation, interpersonal support—in a word, *care*. In this ethnographic study, we studied and participated as members of a hackerspace for 19 months, focusing in particular not on their technical achievements, innovations, or for glimmers of a more sustainable future, but rather to make visible and to analyze the community maintenance labor that helps the hackerspace support the practices that its members, society, and HCI research are so interested in. We found that the maker ethic entails a complex negotiation of both a neoliberal libertarian ethos and a care ethos.

Author Keywords

Care; care ethics; ethnography; hackerspace; HCI

ACM Classification Keywords

H.5.m. Information interfaces and presentation (e.g., HCI): Miscellaneous.

INTRODUCTION

HCI—along with related fields such as Science and Technology Studies (STS) and Computer-Supported Cooperative Work (CSCW)—has shown an interest in understanding behaviors, identities, and communities of making [4]. This work has led to an understanding of cultures of making as able to revolutionize industries, teach people computational thinking, and help people live more sustainable lives. In HCI specifically, maker culture research has focused on the individual creativity and appropriation skills of makers [33,34,39,40]; maker communities as sites where people are taking up and working on visions of the future through HCI [22]; the expert-amateur and empowered statuses enjoyed by individual makers [2,12,18,29]; making as an educational initiative [7,9,24]; the sophistication of the material engagement required for making activities [6,15]; and the specific tools or methods used by makers [3,25,26]. Common throughout much of the work on making in HCI is an implicit focus on individual makers and their skills. While this focus is in line with the espoused neoliberal libertarian ideology of individualism and self-reliance often found in maker culture [23], which we discuss in a later section, it cannot explain the everyday, mundane labor required for a *community* of makers to persist.

CHI 2015, April 18 - 23 2015, Seoul, Republic of Korea.

http://dx.doi.org/10.1145/2702123.2702400

We contribute to research on cultures of making by addressing this gap and demonstrating how an ethnographic analysis through the lens of care ethics can provide a fuller understanding of the sociality of hackerspaces. We begin this work here by describing the makers we studied both as individuals who practice care, and as members of a social community built around a productively negotiated ideology between a traditional "hacker ethic," foregrounding autonomy, and care, foregrounding interdependence. We incorporate a discussion of care to make sense of this tension as well as to characterize the hackerspace as not merely a physical location where makers happen to work but as a representation of the sociality of their community, one that plays a vital role in its maintenance.

A focus on care has allowed researchers in HCI and analogous fields (e.g., STS [30]) to explore how people in communities relate to one another, and how care is a productive lens to develop a richer understanding about what is happening *on the ground* in those communities. In this paper, we present our findings from an ethnographic study of a hackerspace, a study that was conceptually informed by care ethics as developed in [17], and methodologically based on Carspecken's critical ethnography [8]. Specifically, we will demonstrate that care is a productive research framing for accounting for the community maintenance work in making spaces. Broadly, we will show that investigating the ethics of care in technology-mediated social spaces can help HCI researchers and designers uncover how these communities are successfully maintained over time.

BACKGROUND

The research on making in HCI in recent years represents an agenda dedicated to developing an understanding of maker culture as a sociotechnical practice and user experience. These include the exploration of the process of becoming a "maker," the expression of that subjectivity through interaction with materials and participation in a situated maker community, as well as the role of a more generalized maker ethic rooted in the movement's history. We contribute to ongoing research in HCI on making culture by employing care and care ethics in a generative way to reveal the often-neglected care labor and maintenance work that is inextricably a part of what it means to participate in such a community. We begin by summarizing the state of the art of making research in HCI and then by introducing care ethics.

Making and HCI

The espoused ethic of so-called maker culture is one of a drive toward independence through self-empowerment. This culture is sometimes discussed as a monolithic entity that contains within it any act, identity, or community that can be loosely tied to any of a number of activities from hacking, tinkering, repair, construction, and sometimes even design. Scholarship on cultures of making is beginning to address concerns of the *actual* inclusivity of these cultures, as well as the plurality of maker subjectivities and participation [1]. Studies of many such local contexts have taken place in the past few years [1,3,12,15,22,33,36]. These pluralities supplement the generalized, national-level understanding we currently have about what it means to be a "maker" by providing an account of how making is performed by individuals in specific contexts.

Related work in CSCW on community workspaces has also addressed how these cultures of making "shape collaboration and the social organization of work" [32] as well as how making infrastructures play a role in repair work [31]. There is also research on peer production, a body of work related to the study of making in HCI, which explores the process of becoming a maker as a member of a hackerspace [36], and the situatedness of individual maker communities [16]. HCI research benefits from this work through a deeper understanding of cultures of making, contributing to the discussion of the plurality of maker subjectivities as well as opening up the conversation to how maker communities and maker cultures are sustained.

Our work presented here continues this agenda by investigating the maintenance work needed to run and support such communities. Specifically, we argue that a care ethics perspective can augment ethnographic and other observational methodologies to render visible and to help us analyze community maintenance practices, which we define as actions that are teleologically oriented toward the success of the hackerspace as a social group.

Care and Care Ethics

This work presents an analysis that was conducted in two stages. In the first stage, ethnographic data was categorized using Korth's [17] three-part typology of care, which we introduce below. Once data was collected under each of these three types, we used concepts from care ethics, as developed in ethics and feminist philosophy, as an interpretative lens to explicate the actions within each type.

Care ethics engages with the ethical, moral, and value implications of care. Care ethics was introduced to the study of ethics through a series of debates now known as the Kohlberg-Gilligan controversy [27]. Kohlberg's theory of moral development claimed to demonstrate a lower capacity of morality in women, which Gilligan instead attributed to a reliance on a male-biased perspective of ethical behavior. Gilligan regards care ethics as the alternative ethical standpoint toward which women are socialized, contrasted with the abstract and universalized principles of morality and justice toward which men are socialized. She has since expanded on care ethics, along with other feminist care ethicists such as Nel Noddings, to describe an epistemological angle on ethics that focuses on empathy and the interrelatedness of people [11,28]. Fisher and Tronto, two prominent care ethicists, define care as:

a species activity that includes everything that we do to maintain, continue, and repair our 'world' so that we can live in it as well as possible. That world includes our bodies, our selves, and our environment, all of which we seek to interweave in a complex, life-sustaining web [10].

Care for Fisher and Tronto is an important and universal part of everyday life. Tronto further expands the notion of care beyond its previous position as merely a social or private virtue to encompass important social and political implications [38]. Tronto does not position care as superior to—or a substitute for—traditional moral concerns, but instead claims that a commitment to care is an integral piece of a democratic ideal of citizenship [13]. This understanding of care helps us explore the broader impacts of the everyday care in the hackerspace and speculate more broadly on the roles of care in HCI design.

STS scholar Puig de la Bellacasa argues that engaging with care requires a speculative commitment to neglected things and encourages an ethos of care within the study of science and technology. To her, care is something we *do* and is ethically and politically charged [17,30,37]. Research on care ethics has also begun to filter into HCI. In a commentary on the work by feminist political theorist and philosopher Seyla Benhabib, Bardzell [5] argues for a care ethics-based, emancipatory, and utopian view of ubiquitous domestic computing, inspired by Benhabib's notion of "discourse ethics," which combines the strengths of both justice and care ethics. Similarly, Light and Akama discuss the politics of care within the context of participatory design and the role of participatory designers as "custodians of care" [21]. They present interventions within participatory design as capable of social change and altering social relations (though not to be taken as far as social engineering).

In all of these cases, care is a responsibility of designers, who are increasingly creating the means through which we enact our sociality as interdependent beings in specific contexts. We further this line of research by studying care as it is empirically enacted using the typology of care developed by Barbara Korth [17], whose work is based on the social interactions between groups of friends and between educators and students. Many of Korth's insights about care are directly relevant to our study on this particular hackerspace in that it serves both as a social group and as an educational space. Korth's typology of care will be introduced as we use it in a later section.

RESEARCH APPROACH

This work reports the findings of a 19-month ethnography (10/2012-05/2014) of a Midwestern U.S. college town hackerspace (hereafter Null Alpha), analyzed through the lens of care and care ethics. This fieldwork includes approximately 250 total hours of direct contact with participants in Null Alpha, and over 15 hours of targeted interviews with members. The data this ethnography has generated are in the form of jottings, field notes, photos, and recordings of notable events. All participants' names have been changed. Null Alpha was chosen based on several factors: 1) the community was relatively young and expanding its member base, allowing us to observe how new members learned how to become part of the community; 2) the members explicitly and consistently relied on a "flat hierarchy" as their primary means of governance, the success of which members attributed to the closeness of their community; and 3) its proximal convenience, which allowed the researchers to engage in a long-term immersion.

Null Alpha began in 2010 with a group of friends in a basement working on projects together, sharing their tools and know-how. As community interest in making grew, the group moved through several spaces, with each subsequent space making room for more members and more machines. For the majority of the duration of this study, the space has had approximately 30 dues-paying members (all Caucasian between 19 and 50 of age, including 2 females, one of whom is a founding member) and a handful of regular visitors sharing 1,400 square feet of space and various donated and/or purchased tools. The 19-month ethnography took place on site at Null Alpha and off-site during workshops or other events. One member of the research team hacked and tinkered alongside other members.

The ethnography was conducted through the critical ethnographic approach developed by Carspecken [8], which includes a specialized set of empirically validated tools that enable the researcher to reconstruct qualitative data to explore meaning within illocutionary spaces. This approach has a metatheoretical basis in Habermas' Theory of Communicative Action and a pragmatic modification of Mead's intersubjectivity. Very briefly, this metatheoretical background situates *mutual understanding* as obtained through communicative acts and as possessing linguistic structures. The meanings behind these communicative acts are always intersubjective; that is, they can be thought of as a dialogue between the communicator and an external other, which can range from an actual interlocutor to an imagined potential other. By positioning these meaning making structures as inherently intersubjective, we can begin to reconstruct the meaning of an action through a pragmatic horizon. In other words, we can reconstruct different levels of meaning by exploring the bounded set of potential messages communicatively transmitted. Reconstructing the meaning of an act requires a deep level of familiarity with the interlocutors in question. In this case, that familiarity is built through long-term engagement in the field.

This metatheoretical framework allows us to enumerate the possible meanings behind intersubjective acts and, through those possible meanings, describe the care performed in this social group. Barbara Korth, a student of Carspecken's, developed a typology of care that aligns specifically with the metatheoretical framework employed in Carspecken's critical ethnographic approach, and represents one of the only operationalized frameworks available for an empirical study of care-in-action. We rely on Korth's typology of care-in-action to find patterns in the acts of care we reconstructed, enabling us to then uncover the normative system structures in place that make some acts of care possible, while preventing others [17]. Korth, discusses the relationship between care and her work in this way:

A critical, qualitative approach to care is capable of articulating both the particularistic and the more general features of care-in-action precisely because the approach is about meaning and meaning often entails grasping, at least tacitly, both the particularistic and the general features of meaningful acts. Meaningful acts are always reconstructively understood from within their sociocultural milieu and not in isolation from that context. [17]

Care ethics thus shares critical ethnography's methodological commitment to an on-the-ground understanding of participants in/and their contexts, shifting the "focus from abstract individuals and their actions to concrete, situated people with feelings, friends, and dreams—persons who can be cared about" [14]. For these reasons, we argue that a care ethics perspective is appropriate towards developing an account of hackerspace community maintenance, and that Korth's care-in-action typology is a methodological fit for the critical ethnographic methodology we have deployed.

CARE IN THE HACKERSPACE

We now present and discuss the care work we have seen in Null Alpha. We identify intersubjectively valid acts (that is, acts that are recognizable by members of this community) of care, guided by our experience as participants in this particular community of practice. We then analyze the data using a deductive approach [19] guided by Korth's typology of care: overt-explicit care-in-action, overt-implicit care-in-action, and covert-implicit care-in-action [17]. This 3-part typology of care helps to uncover the normative structures behind these enactments of care. The first qualifier, which distinguishes between "overt" and "covert" care, describes the extent to which participants recognize the communicative act as care in a direct sense. The second qualifier, "explicit" or "implicit," refers to the meaning-imparting strategies of the enacted care. The first, *Overt-Explicit Care*, is immediately recognized as care and responded to accordingly, such as when one holds the door open for someone whose hands are full, and that person then responds with a smile, nod, or a "thank you." The second, *Overt-Implicit Care*, describes caring actions where the fact that these are acts of care is not foregrounded in the interaction. An example of this is joking with a loved one after an argument, where the primary purpose of the joke might actually be to establish mutual forgiveness. Finally, *Covert-Implicit Care* is care that would be undermined if it were to be immediately recognizable as care by the care receiver. Letting a child win at a game is an example of this, where the actor and others recognize this action as one motivated by care for the child, but were the child to recognize this care, its intention would be undermined.

Overt-Explicit Care-In-Action

Overt-Explicit care is recognizable by the participants present for its enactment. The majority of the overt-explicit acts of care in Null Alpha involve donating personal resources (e.g., time, money, bodies, and skills, etc.), teaching others how to use a specific tool, or attempting to "reward" individuals for doing other kinds of care work. This hackerspace regularly organizes workshops that are open to the broader community. These workshops are primarily useful for Null Alpha in further promoting its image and encouraging more people to show up, get involved and interested, and hopefully sign up as dues-paying members. The more dues-paying members Null Alpha has, the more rent it can afford, with leftover money being used to purchase more equipment for the space. The workshops also sometimes have a cost associated with them, and when the cost covers more than the price of the materials consumed, the extra money goes directly into Null Alpha's account. When members volunteer to organize a workshop for the space or to help run a workshop organized by another member, they are donating their resources toward maintaining the space and helping it remain afloat.

This motivation extends to other forms of voluntary work as well: cleaning the space when it gets cluttered or dirty; scouting for larger locations for the space; leading and assisting with the physical construction of walls when the new location is acquired; assisting with the transfer of thousands of pounds of tools; etc. As with leading a workshop, members perform these tasks to maintain the community. Others recognize these acts as donations as well, and members endeavor to remind each other that such donations are not mandatory, and so are especially appreciated.

Attempts have even been made to establish tangible systems through which these acts of care can be "rewarded" through gamification strategies, such as virtual badges. One of the authors, for instance, earned the "event volunteer" and "support crew" badges for various efforts around the space. The "support crew" badge is particularly interesting because it tries to turn ownership of shared chores in the space into an achievement. Its description reads:

Awarded to people (both members and non-members) who regularly take ownership of chores in the space. From taking out the trash & recyclables, cleaning the toilet, to maintaining the RFID system, asset tagging system, and other technical infrastructure. Can also apply to people who maintain a shared tool like a 3D printer or the Mill or an 'area' like the ham radio table.

Awarding these badges is its own kind of overt-explicit care, and is meant to signify the appreciation of another's actions. However, these badges did not catch on and were eventually ignored. Had they continued, it would have been interesting to see how they affected the way Null Alpha members viewed the acts of care for which they were being rewarded. Would the badges eventually cheapen these activities by turning them into achievements? Would chores and other caring activities not included in the badge system, such as covert acts of care or care enacted implicitly, be left to the wayside?

Beyond actions motivated by the advancement of the hackerspace as a community, we also found instances of overt-explicit care-in-action directed toward individual members or visitors. As Null Alpha is a potentially dangerous environment, this sometimes takes the form of concern for bodily wellbeing, such as when one of the authors attempted to assist Greg (31, male, software developer, Caucasian) when he sliced his finger on a milling machine (to which he replied "I'll just put some superglue on it"). However, the majority of the overt-explicit care in this space takes the form of a member showing someone else how to use a specific tool. In previous work, we have shown how the use of a tool can become a part of hackerspace members' identities [3]. The members who are most closely identified with a particular tool are often designated as the instructors for its use. When a member or visitor asks for assistance with that tool, others delegate to the particular member "in charge" of that tool. That member often does not see taking on this instruction as a chore. By passing on their skills to another person, they are able to simultaneously perform care and reinforce their identity as both a benevolent person and as a person skilled with that particular tool. Andrew (mid-30s, male, system administrator, Caucasian), one of the founding members of Null Alpha, said this about getting to help people:

I really like to see someone be able to work on their own after I've helped them, and so I'm still on the phase of trying to do that. I don't know, I mean, I think I'm just kind of a run-of-the-mill geek. I know a little bit about a lot of things but not a lot except my certain specialty areas. I'm very glad that I've been able to be helpful to a lot of people in a lot of different areas.

For Andrew, helping others become more independent falls in line with the ideals of what a hackerspace should be. Sharing their skills with others is one way that hackerspace members explicitly care for individuals, and thereby further the ethos of care in Null Alpha. In this space, overt care that is explicitly enacted is acceptable when it is motivated by a desire to teach, to learn, or to participate in activities that directly benefit the community. These caring acts demonstrate the responsibility of hackerspace members to care for each other and for visitors, and also highlight the difference in competence to enact care between members. It is less common to see overt care that explicitly addresses one's identity as a maker, or one's subjective state. These caring activities are more commonly enacted through implicit meaning structures.

Overt-Implicit Care-In-Action

Overt-implicit care-in-action refers to "the caring act that is clear and recognizable among participants, but the mechanism through which the care is enacted is implicit" [17]. In other words, the act is not directly pointed out as care, but others can recognize it as care. This type of care is most evident in how the members welcome visitors to the space, and in the community's political structure.

In welcoming visitors to the space, the act is recognizable as care by both parties, but the fact that this is a caring act is not foregrounded in the interaction. When people look unfamiliar, members will often go out of their way to welcome them and show them around, or will at least make sure the unfamiliar faces are directed toward someone who can give them a few minutes of their time to help them feel welcome. The space is open once a week to the public, but there is no formal way to schedule visits or tours, so it is up to the members to recognize when a tour is appropriate. Helping visitors feel welcome is important for Null Alpha for several reasons: first, because visitors can eventually become dues-paying members who help sustain the community financially; second, because visitors who feel comfortable will invite their friends, will stick around and hang out, and will open up and talk about their projects, skills, strengths, and weaknesses. These welcoming acts become especially apparent when visitors appear to be particularly uncomfortable or might feel out of place. Every member of this space is Caucasian, and all but a handful are male, middle-class, educated, and proud of their identities as "nerds." Every once in a while, someone who does not fit that description will show up, and in those instances members will go above and beyond to show them around the space and make sure someone is talking to them at all times. In one particular instance Frank (mid 40s, male, electrical engineer, Caucasian) devoted an entire Wednesday public meeting night, which he usually spends catching up with his friends, chaperoning a middle-aged PhD student from Taiwan and making sure that she became familiar with the space and was introduced to all of the other members. In regular meetings at Null Alpha, members address their lack of diversity and always come to the same solution: to try to treat everyone equally, and to be especially welcoming to new faces. This is problematic in its own ways, but it shows that the members recognize their diversity problem, and actively take steps to address it.

Overt-implicit care-in-action is an important part of helping members feel like they fit in with the community. This sometimes comes in the form of complimenting or legitimating another's projects, usually by calling it "badass" or "a proper hack." This is especially apparent for projects created for the space, like when Dennis (mid-30s, male, web developer, Caucasian) made badges with functioning gears with the laser cutter to improve on the marketing of the space during a maker conference they organized, or when Andrew hacked a network cable to connect two projects in the space that greeted members as they came in. These encouragements help support maker identities, and encourage members to believe in the legitimacy of their projects. Without even these bland encouragements, it would be easy to become self-critical of one's projects and start to disconnect with the maker community.

These acts of care do not necessarily center on activities specific to Null Alpha. Other examples include helping members feel like they are funny by laughing at their jokes or participating in sharing funny stories; being playful with each other, such as calling each other deliberately by the wrong name (which has become a running inside joke in this space); and discussing issues from work or home that do not directly relate to Null Alpha or the activities taking place there. These types of activities help people feel like they fit in with a social group that just so happens to build, tinker, and hack things.

The political and organizational structures of Null Alpha also work to help members feel a legitimate stake in the social group. Politically, Null Alpha has a flat hierarchical structure and is emphatically a consensus organization. Members of the board are quick to note that board duties are more of a chore, and that they do not have—and do not want—more power over how the space is used than anyone else. In the espoused organizational philosophy of the space, all dues-paying members have an equal say in how the space is used. Although it is not hard to find instances when some members really do have more power than others, they do work to sustain an egalitarian atmosphere. When a topic for discussion is large enough to impact how the space is run, such as when searching for a new location, the members are called in for a vote. Each time a vote is held, members are reminded that this hackerspace is not a democracy but is a consensus organization, and all members must agree before the space can move forward with a decision. Just after one such meeting, Karen (mid-30s, female, system administrator, Caucasian), Mike (early-40s, male, software developer, Caucasian), and Ben (late-20s, male, freelance programmer, Caucasian) were discussing just how hard it is to keep a group going this long as a consensus organization without falling back on other political structures:

Karen [to Ben]: you don't realize how hard it is to run a consensus organization, and we do it so well. So many [other consensus organizations] fail early.

Mike [to Ben]: And we've had a couple of tough votes too, [we] haven't just been coasting!

The focus on consensus in this social group creates a systemically enforced level of respect and care among members and between members and Null Alpha as an institution. To reach consensus, as opposed to unanimity or majority agreement, the members have to be willing to put aside selfish motivations they might have in order to benefit the collective.

The physical organization of the space also systemizes care. The way the tools in the space are made available to members helps promote a feeling of collectivity. In this hackerspace, very few tools are actually owned by the space itself. Instead, members donate their tools, which are organized through Null Alpha's asset tracking system. In hackerspaces where the organization owns the majority of the tools, becoming a member can feel like buying into a service. With this hackerspace's collection of tools that belong to individual members, it feels more like buying into a community of sharing.

These overt-implicit acts of care are often used to solidify a feeling of belonging or a welcoming atmosphere. They are recognizable as caring situations, but if they were made more explicit they would be less effective. It would feel insincere, or even creepy, if a member approached a visitor and told them "I am going to show you around the space so that you will feel comfortable here." But the action itself is recognizable by others as an implicit form of care. To recognize when these acts are most appropriate requires at least some level of attentiveness. In the next section, we discuss care-in-action that is backgrounded even further.

Covert-Implicit Care-In-Action

With covert-implicit care, caring acts "must hide in the discourse in order to avoid undermining [their] own caring potential. Covert Care-in-Action works off the same pragmatic structures as Overt-Implicit Care-in-Action, but its caring interpretation is masked or left unsaid" [17]. These acts of care are only known to the care-giver, and not by the care-receiver. If the care-receiver were to recognize such an act, it would diminish its effectiveness. In this social group, these forms of care were evident in interpersonal communication among members, and in the physical environment.

A large part of being a member in this hackerspace involves listening to other members "geek out" about their pet projects or favorite topics. This type of listening, even when interlocutors offer nothing more than bland encouragements and feigned interest, helps validate one's interests and hobbies. This legitimation of interests then establishes a sense of belonging and fitting in to Null Alpha, and sets it up as a worthwhile social endeavor. The style of active listening we have observed in Null Alpha seems to be uncharacteristic of what one would expect in such an environment so steeped in "geek" culture. When discussing what it is like to be a new member to the space who is still feeling out the social interactions there, Justin (mid-30s, male, stay at home dad, Caucasian) shared a few thoughts on what makes the space feel surprisingly welcoming:

I've been impressed, and this has come to mind a couple times, [with] how many questions I'm able to ask, and some of them seem very very simple, and I've yet to have someone look at me, like 'you don't know what that is?'...Everyone has been so willing to share what they know or help me figure out how to find the answer that I'm looking for without going 'oh, you don't know that?' or 'you have never done that?' it's so, I do see it as it's a support and its also kind of inspiring.

This same subject came up in a separate interview with Mike, one of the founding members:

It can be a little intimidating because, you know, geeks aren't always socially sensitive. So you might occasionally have a situation [...] where people don't mean to offend you, and be like 'oh you don't know that?' but I haven't really seen that much here, I think people are pretty nice.

It is important to create an atmosphere where members can feel safe being vulnerable and exposing their weaknesses and the gaps in their knowledge. Covert-implicit acts of care enable this kind of vulnerability among members by being accommodating and helpful without calling attention to that vulnerability.

A related example of covert-implicit care-in-action we recognized was in how the members often downplayed their own expertise or their own achieved levels of skill by presenting almost any activity as one that "anybody can do." This typical interaction seems to be in conflict with a desire to show off one's skills and abilities, which would be more appropriate for a social situation actually governed through a libertarian ideology. Central to this tension is a desire to care for one's interlocutors, students, and co-hackers. On the one hand, hacking should be impressive because for some individuals that is what makes it an endeavor worth pursuing. On the other hand, hacking cannot seem too difficult or one risks alienating potential members. Andrew and

Karen, two of the founding members, are constantly downplaying their own expertise. This helps make them more approachable and inspires visitors and new members to take on more challenging projects, while also feeling like they are not surrounded by a group of people who are elite.

The physical atmosphere of Null Alpha also contributes to this sense of community through covert-implicit acts of care on the system level. The space has few doors that lock, other than the front door and the donation boxes. The refrigerator, which is often stocked with soda, beer, and bottled water, as well as a stash of chips and candy, are left unattended and subject to the "honor system," where members are asked to donate a nominal amount of money to help keep the refreshments stocked. This assumption that visitors can be trusted in the space helps people *feel* trusted, and helps further establish to members the collective ownership of the space. This does not even begin to cover the expensive computers, tools, and parts in the space that could potentially be taken, and that can be used freely and without supervision except when safety is a concern.

These covert-implicit acts of care are often employed to reassert and establish the maker identity claims of other members, even when it might require downplaying one's own identity claims as a skilled hacker. By actively listening to other members when they share their interests, and by cultivating an atmosphere where nobody has to feel less intelligent for not knowing a particular fact or for not understanding something, members lower the bar to the maker identity and encourage others to adopt it. Covert-implicit care-in-action requires a more sophisticated internalization of attentiveness for the caregivers, and ability to recognize the responsiveness of the care-receivers.

Throughout this section we have discussed the care that we have observed in Null Alpha. We do not simply claim that the members care about each other and about the hackerspace as an institution. Rather, what we hope to have demonstrated is how their caring acts show a deeper relationship between their specific hacker community, cultures of making more generally, the broader community in which they are situated, and their ability to identify as participants in these contexts. Their relationships with each context rely heavily on the interdependence and caring relationships developed among participants, which appears paradoxical for a community whose espoused ideal participant is one who is self-sufficient and independent.

DISCUSSION

We have shown a range of caring actions that we observed in this particular hackerspace. In this section, we first discuss how these caring actions exist in tension with one of the dominant underlying ideologies of this and many other hackerspaces: libertarian egalitarianism. We then deconstruct several context-specific examples that demonstrate this tension.

Hacker Libertarianism and ... Care?

Existing literature on hackerspaces, hacking, and making culture reveals much about the ideology and ethical stance behind the maker cultures. Hacker ethics have been described in various accounts ranging from radical hacker activists with a mistrust of authority, a need to free all information, and a devotion to self-reliance [20] to communities of interest seeking to democratize technological practice in more peaceful ways [35].

These ethics, in their various forms, are visible in mainstream writings on maker culture. The *Hackerspace Design Patterns* presented on hackerspaces.org are meant to describe what it takes to create and successfully run a hackerspace. The initial construction of these patterns can be traced back to the 24th Chaos Communication Congress, also known as "the European Hacker Conference." Their descriptions are geared toward maximizing individual anti-authoritarian interests, with only small nods—focusing primarily on infrastructure or collecting strong personalities—toward serious discussion of what it takes to build and maintain a community. Instead they prescribe simplistic methods for resolving conflict, such as commanding others to take care of certain actions like taking out the trash, or throwing away other's belongings that are in the way, and they diminish the concerns of others by calling out what is or is not "pointless discussion." Another mainstream publication on maker culture, *Fab*, is a book by Neil Gershenfeld on the emergence of FabLabs and the role he played in helping to democratize the manufacturing process for individuals in select communities around the world. *Fab* has also been criticized for focusing too heavily on the tools and materials of these FabLabs, and not enough on the nature of the community involvement required for them to be successful [16].

Taken together, these accounts and others like them portray an ideology in hacker culture closely associated with libertarian autonomy. This ideology was visible to us throughout this ethnography, such as when members discussed issues of diversity and equality. When asked about the poor representation of women in Null Alpha, leaders Karen and Andrew typically responded as follows: "our door is always open to anyone who wants to come." When the topic was discussed in a members' meeting, the consensus was that "all we can do is make sure everyone feels equally welcome here. If you hear of anyone feeling unwelcomed please bring it up so we can address it." In this hackerspace, making sure everyone felt welcomed meant treating everyone the same. This is demonstrative of a libertarian stance toward equality, which involves assuming a universalized position toward such social and systemic issues, concomitant with an espoused blindness toward gender, race, sexuality, and other differences.

But one of the core contributions of this research is that even though there are clear signs of this libertarian influence, we have seen that the members do not, and cannot, enact this espoused ideology completely; the actual enacted philosophy of the hackerspace relies much more heavily on interdependence of members, on social connections, and on caring about and for each other than their explicitly embraced ideology would seem to allow. On a micro-interactional level, community members depend on each other for support, both in their projects and emotionally as fellow human beings. On a larger scale, Null Alpha has very strong ties with the surrounding city, both in receiving and in generating support.

In their article on MIT-Fablab Norway, Kohtala and Bosqué discuss the individuality of a particular space in the FabLab network, and explain, "it is the people and their individual strengths and curiosities that have formed the Fab Lab movement and will continue its trajectory" [16]. We take this insight a step further and add that the member's abilities to *care* for one another is also a crucial aspect of the continued success of these communities. Many of their actions are not covered in the hackerspace design patterns, are ignored in Gershenfeld's Fab, and are often also neglected in the current literature surrounding maker culture and hackerspaces more specifically.

We are concerned that some HCI research on making inadequately explores the nature and significances of maintenance work, focusing on the hacking, making, repairing and other forms of collaborative work, but complicitly following the hackerspaces themselves in obfuscating the ways that interpersonal care is as constitutive of the maker identity as other key components (e.g., forms of labor and practice; attitudes towards authority, information, and materials). Our exploration of this maintenance work has begun to reveal the ethic in place at this particular hackerspace—and likely others—as a *negotiated* ethic. This ethic complexly includes both the espoused libertarian ideals of individualism and independence that underlies hackers' self-image *and* the hidden-yet-enacted care ethic ideals of interdependence, support, and community.

Caring—But Still a Hacker

Obviously, care is common in any community of practice. However, what makes the study of care in maker communities particularly interesting is how the tension between the espoused libertarian hacker ideology and the need for community maintenance and interdependent care plays out on an everyday basis. A few examples serve to highlight the roles that this tension plays.

Earlier, we referenced the failed digital badge implementation to reward members for doing chores around Null Alpha, such as cleaning the bathroom, tidying up, and taking out the trash. This project seemed like a good idea: by providing extrinsic motivation in the form of hacker-made badges signifying the social capital that one has accrued as a result of doing chores, the plan seemed to capture the libertarian hacker ethos, with its notions of making (a self-made currency, no less), individualism, competition, and the entrepreneurial spirit of accruing capital. Yet as we saw, the experiment failed. Hackerspace members did indeed do chores around the space, but no one seemed interested in collecting the badges. Care ethics theorists note that care is built into our bodies, our natures, and our social mores. Perhaps the desire to keep the space clean for oneself and everyone else is, in the collective consciousness of the hackerspace, sufficiently deep and automatic that it does not need the extrinsic motivation of a gamified system to set it into motion.

If the failed badge experiment suggested an instance of care winning out over libertarian ideals, evidence of the opposite also presented itself. We refer to the ethos of empowerment so central to the rhetoric of hacking, in hackerspaces themselves, mainstream journalism, and many academic research papers alike. In our hackerspace, this was expressed in the ubiquitous refrain "anyone can be a maker." This ethos is, in turn, backed up by a number of tactics to support it, as we saw. These include the willingness to help others, the nearly infinite patience in the face of "stupid" questions, and leaders' habit of playing down their own expertise to build up the confidence of less experienced members. In many ways, these are all tactics of care.

Yet for several reasons they can also be read as a libertarian ethos "colonizing" care. One reason is that these acts of care are instrumentally understood to contribute to the health of Null Alpha, an institution—and egalitarian co-op legally incorporated as a non-profit—that its (non-)leaders are eager to build. These care tactics are good for business: they encourage prospective visitors to visit; one-time visitors to become regular visitors; and regular visitors to become dues-paying members.

More deeply, the ethos that "anyone can be a maker" obscures the fact that *not* everyone can be a maker. A single mother with three part-time jobs and no car probably cannot be a maker—not, at least, in the sense that "being a maker" is specifically understood in this and other hackerspaces. Such an individual becomes literally invisible in the maker ethos, thus redefining "everybody" down to a certain social class; it is presumably not a coincidence that the majority of dues-paying members are men in their thirties with professional careers, many of which are in IT. Likewise, the well-intentioned blindness to gender, race, social class and so forth has no traction to take on *structural* problems that affect Null Alpha, such as gender inequality. We saw in our data that the hackers clearly hope that they can *individually* woo women and other non-traditional participants who self-select their way into Null Alpha—certainly a laudable intention. But for every such participant who does wind up in the space, how many others don't show up at all? The open-door policy and special attention to special visitors tactic cannot reach these prospective participants. For these reasons, we argue that in some ways care can be seen to be subordinated to and in service of the more traditional neoliberal values of the hackerspace.

On the more micro-scale of interpersonal interactions, the tension between the care ethos and the libertarian is expressed in subtle ways. We saw earlier that most of the overt or direct care deals with working on projects together or using each other's tools, while more implicit forms of care tend to be the care that supports identity formation and feelings of inclusion. One reason these are implicit is because if they were explicit the participants would have to engage directly with how these moments of support conflict with the espoused hacker ethic and ideals of self-sufficiency and independence. This points to a tension in the participants' identities as hackerspace members: one where they have to choose between being "real" hackers and being supportive community participants. Many of the members have found ways to negotiate this tension: Greg often acts as though he is not excited about a project, acting instead through a veil of detachment, but he is often the quickest to provide support; similarly, Karen uses sarcasm and irony to ease the tension of a situation or to help outsiders feel included and familiar; and several members, notably Andrew and Dennis, rely on constructing instructional scenarios that demonstrate care in a maker-sanctioned mode of expression. Members might not feel like they have the space to explicitly address each others' subjective states, but are instead more comfortable enacting care through these more covert means.

CONCLUSION

Ultimately this hackerspace relies heavily on care and on community involvement and engagement, which care ethics literature and care theory can help us understand. Extending more broadly, current literature on making cultures often discusses how the barrier of entry to these communities and practices can be lowered. It is easy to conceive of this barrier as comprising knowledge or skill requirements, or difficulty *understanding* or figuring out how to physically get started. It is more difficult, but perhaps more accurate, to conceive of these barriers as sociological; who is or is not able to participate in these activities might have less to do with their skills and more to do with their ability to fit in with these communities of interest. An analysis of the care and care ethics involved in these communities can help uncover how they actually operate on the ground.

As making and hacking become boundary objects around which communities form, their underlying norms and ethics have to adapt to accommodate the inherent everyday sociality of what it means to become part of a community. This adoption can lead to tensions between the old and new ethics. By critically engaging with care theory and care ethics, we are able to see where those types of tensions reside and can discuss how the mundane interactions in these social situations are playing out. In the case of this hackerspace, critically investigating the care enacted in these social situations reveals certain vulnerabilities that accompany the adoption of a maker identity, such as the tension between being a "real" maker and being a good community member, or the confusion associated with acknowledging or rewarding explicit acts of care.

We see at least two ways to think about care in future HCI research: as an analytical lens to inform ethnographic and other studies of such communities and their practices (which is what we have done here); and as means of influencing interventions that might bring about changes that are beneficial both in ethical terms (e.g., evening out gender imbalances) and in more entrepreneurial terms (e.g., establishing and maintaining a community sufficient to support a hackerspace durably). As hacking continues to become increasingly politically active—with civic forms of hacking, White House-sponsored National Days of Civic Hacking, and notions of hacking as a mode of citizenship—it would be constructive to develop a clearer delineation of the relationships between the hacker, understood as a practitioner of information and both physical and digital materials, and the hacker understood as a citizen who contributes to the social good and who thereby embodies hacker-care.

ACKNOWLEDGMENTS

This research was funded by NSF IIS Creative IT (#1002772) and the Intel Science and Technology Center for Social Computing. We are grateful for the feedback from our anonymous reviewers and Colin Gray.

REFERENCES

1. Ames, M. G., Bardzell, J., Bardzell, S., Lindtner, S., Mellis, D. A., and Rosner, D. K. (2014). Making Cultures: Empowerment, Participation, and Democracy - or not? In *Proc. of CHI2014 EA*. ACM Press.
2. Bardzell, J. (2007). Creativity in Amateur Multimedia: Popular Culture, Critical Theory, and HCI. *Human Technology*, 3 (1), 12-33.
3. Bardzell, J., Bardzell, S., and Toombs, A. (2014). "Now that's definitely a proper hack": Self-made Tools in Hackerspaces. In *Proc. of CHI2014*. ACM Press.
4. Bardzell, J., Bardzell, S., DiSalvo, C., Light, A., D. K. Rosner. (2014). "Making Cultures" Spotlight.
5. Bardzell, S. (in press). Through the "Cracks and Fissures" in the Smart Home to Ubiquitous Utopia. In Bardzell, J., Bardzell, S., and Blythe, M. (eds.). *Critical Theory and Interaction Design.* MIT Press.
6. Bardzell, S., Rosner, D. K., and Bardzell, J. (2012). Crafting quality in design: Integrity, creativity, and public sensibility. In *Proc. of DIS2012*. ACM Press.
7. Buechley, L. (2010). LilyPad Arduino: Rethinking the Materials and Cultures of Educational Technology. In *Proc. of ICLS2010*, International Society of the Learning Sciences, pp. 127-128.
8. Carspecken, P. F. (1996). *Critical ethnography in educational research: A theoretical and practical guide.* Psychology Press

9. DiSalvo, C., Nourbakhsh, I., Holstius, D., Akin, A. and Louw M. (2008). The Neighborhood Networks Project: A Case Study of Critical Engagement and Creative Expression through Participatory Design. In *Proc. of PDC2008.*
10. Fisher, B., and Tronto, J. (1990). Toward a Feminist Theory of Caring. In *Circles of care: Work and identity in women's lives*, pp. 35-62.
11. Gilligan, C. (1982). *In a Different Voice*. Harvard University Press.
12. Grimme, S., Bardzell, J., and Bardzell, S. (2014, accepted). "We've conquered dark": Shedding a light on empowerment in critical making. *Proc. of NordiCHI2014.* ACM Press.
13. Hamington, M., and Miller, D. C. (2006). Introduction: A Modern Moral Imperative. In Hamington, M., and Miller, D. C. (eds.) *Socializing care: Feminist ethics and public issues.* Rowman & Littlefield Publishers.
14. Hamington, M. (Ed.). (2010). *Feminist Interpretations of Jane Addams*. Penn State Press.
15. Jackson, S. J., and Kang, L. (2014). Breakdown, Obsolescence and Reuse: HCI and the Art of Repair. In *Proc. of CHI2014.* ACM Press.
16. Kohtala, C., and Bosqué, C. (2014, in press). The Story of MIT-Fablab Norway: Community Embedding of Peer Production. *Journal of Peer Production.*
17. Korth, B. (2003). A critical reconstruction of care-in-action. *The Qualitative Report*, *8*(3), 487-512
18. Kuznetsov, S., and Paulos, E. (2010). Rise of the Expert Amateur: DIY Projects, Communities, and Cultures. In *Proc. of NORDICHI2010.* ACM Press.
19. Lecompte, M. and Schensul, J. (1999). *Analyzing and Interpreting Ethnographic Data.* AltaMira Press.
20. Levy, S. (2001). *Hackers: Heroes of the Computer Revolution.* Penguin Books.
21. Light, A. and Akama, Y. (2014, to appear). Structuring Future Social Relations: The Politics of Care in Participatory Practice. *Proc. of PDC2014.*
22. Lindtner, S., Hertz, G. D., and Dourish, P. (2014). Emerging sites of HCI innovation: Hackerspaces, hardware startups & incubators. In *Proc. of CHI2014.* ACM Press.
23. Maxigas. (2012). Hacklabs and Hackerspaces - Tracing Two Genealogies. *Journal of Peer Production (2)*: n. pag.
24. Mellis, D. A. and Buechley, L. (2012). Case Studies in the Personal Fabrication of Electronic Products. In *Proc. of DIS2012.* ACM Press.
25. Mellis, D., Follmer, S., Hartmann, B., Buechley, L., and Gross, M. D. (2013). FAB at CHI: Digital Fabrication Tools, Design, and Community. In *Proc. of CHI2013 EA.* ACM Press.
26. Mota, C. (2011). The Rise of Personal Fabrication. In *Proc. of Creativity and Cognition 2011.* ACM Press.
27. Murphy, J., and Gilligan, C. Moral development in late adolescence and adulthood: A critique and reconstruction of Kohlberg's theory. *Human Development, 23* (1980), 77-104.
28. Noddings, Nel. (1982). *Caring: A Feminine Approach to Ethics and Moral Education.* University of CA Press.
29. Pace, T., Toombs, A., Gross, S., Pattin, T., Bardzell, J., and Bardzell, S. (2013). A tribute to Mad Skill: Expert Amateur Visuality and World of Warcraft Machinima. In *Proc. of CHI2013.* ACM Press.
30. Puig de la Bellacasa, M. (2011). Matters of Care in Technoscience: Assembling Neglected Things. *Social Studies of Science, 41* (1): 85-106.
31. Rosner, D. K., and Ames, M. (2014). Designing for Repair?: Infrastructures and Materialities of Breakdown. In *Proc. of CSCW2014.* ACM Press.
32. Rosner, D. K., Lindtner, S., Erickson, I., Forlano, L., Jackson, S. J., and Kolko, B. (2014). Making Cultures: Building Things & Building Communities. In *Proc. of CSCW2014.* ACM Press.
33. Rosner, D., and Bean, J. (2009). Learning from IKEA Hacking: I'm Not One to Decoupage a Tabletop and Call it a Day. In *Proc. of CHI2009.* ACM Press.
34. Tanenbaum, J., Tanenbaum, K. and Wakkary, R. (2012). Steampunk as Design Fiction. In *Proc. of CHI2012.* ACM Press.
35. Tanenbaum, J., Williams, A. M., Desjardins, A., and Tanenbaum, K. (2013). Democratizing Technology: Pleasure, Utility and Expressiveness in DIY and Maker Practice. *In Proc. of CHI2013.* ACM Press.
36. Toombs, A., Bardzell, S., and Bardzell, J. (2014, in press). Becoming Makers: Hackerspace Member Habits, Values, and Identities. *Journal of Peer Production.*
37. Tronto, J. C. (1993). *Moral boundaries: A political argument for an ethic of care.* Psychology Pres
38. Tronto, J. C. (2006). Vicious Circles of Privatized Caring. In Hamington, M., and Miller, D. C. (eds.) *Socializing care: Feminist ethics and public issues.* Rowman & Littlefield Publishers.
39. Wakkary, R., and Maestri, L. (2007). The resourcefulness of Everyday Design. In *Proc. of Creativity and Cognition.* ACM Press.

Wakkary, R. and Maestri, L. (2008). Aspects of Everyday Design: Resourcefulness, Adaptation, and Emergence. *International Journal of Human-Computer Interaction*, vol. 24, no. 5, pp. 478-491

Patterns of Physical Design Remixing in Online Maker Communities

Lora Oehlberg
Inria
lora.oehlberg@gmail.com

Wesley Willett
Inria / University of Calgary
wesley.willett@ucalgary.ca

Wendy E. Mackay
Inria
wendy.mackay@inria.fr

ABSTRACT
Makers participate in remixing culture by drawing inspiration from, combining, and adapting designs for physical objects. To examine how makers remix each others' designs on a community scale, we analyzed metadata from over 175,000 digital designs from Thingiverse, the largest online design community for digital fabrication. Remixed designs on Thingiverse are predominantly generated designs from Customizer– a built-in web app for adjusting parametric designs. However, we find that these designs do not elicit subsequent user activity and the authors who generate them tend not to contribute additional content to Thingiverse. Outside of Customizer, influential sources of remixing include complex assemblies and design primitives, as well as non-physical resources posing as physical designs. Building on our findings, we discuss ways in which online maker communities could become more than just design repositories and better support collaborative remixing.

Author Keywords
Hacking; Maker Communities; Customization; Remixing; User Innovation; Collaboration

ACM Classification Keywords
H.5.m: Information interfaces and presentation (e.g., HCI): Miscellaneous

INTRODUCTION
Lawrence Lessig [11] argues that we have moved from a "read-only" culture to a "read/write" culture: instead of passively consuming information or products, users now actively participate in creating their own, personalized objects. The Internet and social media has led to an explosion of "remix culture"[6], but until recently, remixing was mostly limited to media content like songs, images, and videos. However, the advent of inexpensive fabrication machines including 3D printers and laser cutters has enabled more consumers to design, create, and remix physical objects that previously required mass manufacture.

CHI 2015, April 18 - 23, 2015, Seoul, Republic of Korea
Copyright 2015 ACM 978-1-4503-3145-6/15/04...$15.00
http://dx.doi.org/10.1145/2702123.2702175

The maker movement [5], an extension of Do-It-Yourself (DIY) culture, has largely grown out of environments like Hackerspaces and FabLabs where hobbyists can create and share their designs. Creating physical objects can require many different kinds of expert knowledge, including how to prepare digital designs for fabrication or operate a fabrication machine. *Makers* are thus encouraged to borrow and adapt (or *remix*) each others' designs. Online communities, such as Thingiverse[1], Youmagine[2], and Ravelry[3], form an important piece of this ecosystem, allowing geographically distributed makers to share designs with each other. Visitors to these sites can download publicly available design files and reproduce them using their local fabrication equipment. Some of these communities also record the provenance of remixes, allowing makers to link their work to the earlier designs that inspired them. In *Makers*, Chris Anderson [1] celebrates the promise of remixing:

> *The ability to easily "remix" digital files is the engine that drives community. What it offers is an invitation to participate. You don't need to invent something from scratch or have an original idea. Instead, you can participate in a collaborative improvement of existing ideas or designs (p. 74).*

In this idealized view of collaboration, makers collectively contribute to the development of new designs by iteratively remixing and refining one another's work. Moreover, this view assumes that remixing serves as an entry point for new makers, who can dissect and build on top of the work of others to bootstrap their own making practice.

While previous examinations of maker communities have looked at remixing anecdotally [20], the rapid growth of online maker communities provides an opportunity to analyze this behavior at a much broader scale. By examining how tens of thousands of makers are actively engaging in remixing on community sites, we can build a more grounded understanding of the impact of remixing on maker communities.

In this paper we investigate how makers remix digital designs for physical objects on *Thingiverse,* a well-established online 3D printing community. We chose to

[1] *http://www.thingiverse.com*
[2] *http://www.youmagine.com*
[3] *http://www.ravelry.com*

focus specifically on Thingiverse–which calls itself "the world's largest 3D printing community"–because detailed metadata about remixing and authorship is available for most of the objects shared on the site since its inception in 2008.

We begin with a review of related work and then present findings from a quantitative analysis of five years of metadata. We examine the impact of Customizer–a parametric design tool within Thingiverse–and also examine non-Customizer designs to explore how users interpret remixing. We identify genres of designs whose remixing behavior manifests itself in unexpected ways. We conclude with specific suggestions for online design repositories and design software that provide better support for remixing and build stronger online maker communities.

RELATED WORK

This paper examines how a specific online maker community, Thingiverse, supports remixing of physical designs. Our investigation relies on prior studies of *maker culture*, which provide context for understanding maker behavior and motivations. We also build on prior examinations of *remixing* practice in other disciplines.

Maker Culture

Research into maker culture has focused primarily on qualitative studies of individuals' experiences as they participate in maker communities, including their motivations for participation [10], and how being a maker influenced their interactions with materiality [7] and changed their involvement in consumerism [15]. Makers' main motivations for contributing to communities include finding inspiration for future projects, learning new concepts, and receiving feedback on projects [10]. Researchers have profiled specific maker communities and do-it-yourself (DIY) practices, such as IKEA Hacking [18] and Steampunk [19]. These researchers have advocated for the development of new creative tools that "celebrate skilled, creative reuse and customization" [18] or attract "users who are not content to consume but wish to customize, remix, and design for themselves" [19]. Online maker communities already offer basic support for sharing and downloading files for remixing, recording the provenance of design inspirations, and even platforms for easy customization. Most of this previous research has been qualitative, capturing individuals' experiences and motivations for participation, but has yet to provide a community-scale understanding of how makers share and build on one another's ideas.

Remixing

Not just makers remix; everyday users consistently reuse and re-appropriate mass-produced designs [21]. By remixing others' work, individual makers can learn from others' ideas and more quickly create improved, tailored, or innovative designs. This idea has been explored in previous work by Mota [15], who argues that remixing satisfies a maker's needs for new, creative, or personalized objects. Moreover, digital content creators are often quite open about borrowing and remixing. In a study of users of how-to pages, Torrey *et al.* [20] found that users "freely acknowledge their use of ideas they had first seen in other people's projects". By extracting valuable sub-components from existent designs and hacking them together, makers are engaging in design–despite the lack of refinement [8].

Remixing behavior has also been examined in the context of peer-produced resources including code [2,9], software configurations [6,13,14], and community-authored web content such as WikiBooks [12]. However, in many ways these peer-produced resources are more straightforward than collaborating around physical products. When users share software configurations, they all configure the same interface; community-authored web content has more explicit, communal goals than the maker community; it is easier to borrow from and trace the origins of written lines of code, whereas physical features are far more difficult to specify and isolate.

Perhaps the most similar approach to ours is Cheliotis and Yew's analysis of the social structure of ccMixter [4], an online community of musicians who sample and remix each others' tracks. By analyzing the social network of remixing links between samples, Cheliotis and Yew found that merging motifs (several samples being resolved into one track) were less common than branching motifs (one track inspiring many other designs), and that site contests did not necessarily attract new users who later contributed content or remixes to the community. We use this analysis as a point of comparison with a digital media remixing network.

Finally, a few initial research efforts have started to examine peer production on Thingiverse. In particular, Papadimitriou and Paplexakis used Thingiverse metadata in the period leading up to February 2013 to look for predictive relationships between metadata features, including number of views, links, and makes [17]. They also built an interactive visualization of Thingiverse remixing[4]. We focus more specifically on remixing within Thingiverse, and also examine the impacts of major changes to the site in the year and a half since their analysis–including a more than 5-fold increase in the size of the site as well as the introduction of new parametric remixing tools.

AN INTRODUCTION TO THINGIVERSE

Thingiverse was founded in November 2008 by MakerBot[5], a major manufacturer of consumer 3D printers. The site is intended to serve as a design repository and social network for hobbyist digital fabrication where community members can submit designs and share them with others. Perhaps unsurprisingly, the majority of the designs shared on the site are 3D models intended to be fabricated using a 3D

[4] *http://bitquill.net/make/remix/*
[5] *http://www.makerbot.com*

Figure 1: Things include: a) 3D designs for fabrication (3D-printed mug handle, Thing 310961, by LeFabShop); b) 2D designs for fabrication (laser-cut 6-pack holder, Thing 16643 by BrianEnigma); c) 2D designs for etching (etching on a glass vase, Thing 93972 by YourLaser, illustration by Leo Blanchette).

printer. However 2D designs for laser cutters or CNC Mills are also fairly common. The site also serves as a social network on which users can post comments, photos, and other social content.

Although many users visit the Thingiverse site, we are primarily interested in *authors*, i.e. those who post content under a unique username. The primary means by which authors contribute to Thingiverse is by creating *Things*–design projects which typically include 3D or 2D design files for fabrication or etching (see Figure 1) as well images of the design and instructions for creating it. Each Thing can also include references to *sources*–other Things that a design is "inspired by, derived from, or a remix of". Throughout this paper, we refer to these referenced Things as *sources* and resulting Things as *remixes*.

Every Thing is assigned a unique sequential ID number when it is created and can be accessed by a unique URL that includes that ID. For example, Thing "16369" can be found at http://www.thingiverse.com/thing:16369. While they are being created, Things are *private*. However, once published, Things are *public* and are visible on the site. Authors can also delete Things and Thingiverse administrators occasionally block Things for violating the site's terms-of-service, hiding them from the site. Each public Thing page includes a range of metadata: the Thing name; the author's username; publication date; the number of times other users have liked, collected, commented, made, or remixed the design. For example, Figure 2 shows a Thing page for a "Customized Atom Deluxe" design, which can be downloaded and 3D printed.

While most Things specify a single design, some authors provide parametric models–3D designs in which some design parameters can be easily changed to generate variations of the design. During the first four years of Thingiverse, most parametric designs were shared as files from OpenSCAD[6], a computer-assisted design (CAD) programming language. However, generating design variations from a parametric model required modifying the design directly in OpenSCAD.

On 15 January 2013, Thingiverse introduced *Customizer*[7], a built-in web app that lets authors upload parametric models from OpenSCAD. Other users can then modify and generate variations directly on Thingiverse and download a customized, ready-to-print file (see Figure 3). This allows non-expert users to create new, custom designs without using code or CAD software–but this customization is limited to the parameters exposed by the original author. Customizer provides live previews of the generated design, allowing users to iterate and refine their modifications. For example, in Figure 3 a user can create a customized model atom by using a menu to select a custom typeface and using sliders to specify the size and spacing of the electron rings. Each time a user exports a generated design, it is automatically added as a new Thing with pre-populated metadata, including a name and description, instructions

Figure 2: Customizable Atom (Thing 114247 by Roman Hegglin). Metadata includes:
a) Thing name, author's user name, publication date,
b) description, instructions, and uploaded files
c) user activity (liked, collected, commented, made, remixed)
d) link to Customizer.

[6] *http://www.openscad.org*

[7] *http://www.thingiverse.com/apps/customizer*

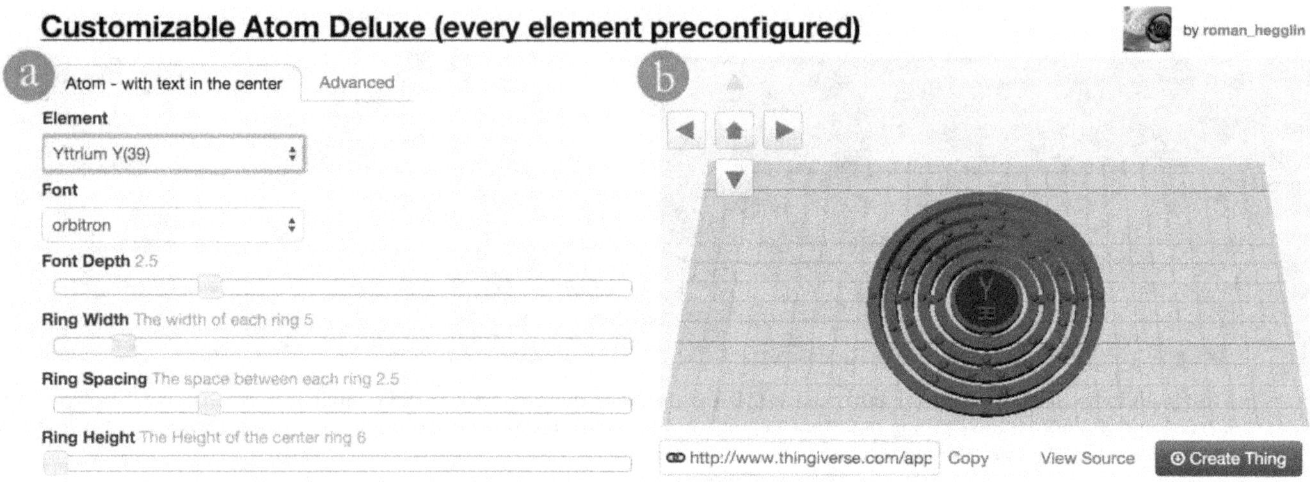

Figure 3: The Customizer App for a Customizable Atom (Thing 114247 by Roman Hegglin) allows users to a) specify font and ring characteristics, and b) preview the resulting design on a virtual model.

that contain the customization parameters, and a "customized" tag. The original parametric design is listed a *source* for the generated remix.

Note that all Thingiverse behavior is voluntary. Users may download and modify a design without uploading their remix to Thingiverse. Even if they do upload a remix design, they may or may not indicate the original Thing as a source. More generally, authors are free to define what constitutes a source or a remix as they create content.

RESEARCH QUESTIONS

The advent of low-cost, consumer-grade fabrication equipment has introduced an entirely new domain for remixing–specifically, the remixing of digital designs intended for physical fabrication. By examining online maker communities like Thingiverse, we can now explore this remixing behavior at a community scale. In our study we focus on the following questions:

R1. How does remixing physical designs in an online maker community differ from the remixing of other electronic media?

R2. How do parametric design tools influence authors' contribution to, and participation in online maker communities?

R3. What kinds of designs are the most influential and how can digital authoring and sharing tools foster these sorts of productive designs?

To answer these questions, we examine patterns of remixing on Thingiverse and contrast it to patterns observed in other communities, such as the audio remix site ccMixter [4]. In particular, we investigate the adoption of Customizer and how generated designs affect community behavior on Thingiverse. Finally, we analyze sources that both directly and indirectly inspire large numbers of remixes on Thingiverse and identify qualities that make them well suited for remixing.

METHODOLOGY

We conducted a quantitative analysis of Things on Thingiverse. Over the course of several days in July and August 2014, we downloaded the complete web pages for 350,354 unique Things. This corpus covers all Things published in the period from the launch of Thingiverse in 2008 until 22 July 2014, and includes data from both before and after the introduction of Customizer in January 2013. Because we collected all public Things on Thingiverse since the founding of the site, we are able to examine the evolution of how users publish and remix.

We parsed each Thing page to gather metadata about the design, including its title, author, publication date, and tags, as well as the number and types of files available for download. We also gathered information about social activity around the Thing, including the number of times that users viewed, liked, commented, downloaded, and made the Thing. Finally, we gathered a list of any source Things that the design was remixed from, and counted the number of times the design itself had been remixed. These relationships allowed us to reconstruct the complete graph of remixing on Thingiverse.

We used the NetworkX[8] Python library and GraphViz[9] to analyze and visualize the *remixing graph*—links between sources and remixes that primarily exhibit a tree-like inheritance structure. We also used this data to identify particularly influential and surprising Things, which we examined via qualitative case studies.

RESULTS & DISCUSSION

Of the 350,354 Things we collected, about half (176,142 Things) are *public* with open metadata while the other half (174,212 Things) are *private* or *under moderation* and include no metadata. This data set is several orders of

[8] *http://networkx.github.io*
[9] *http://www.graphviz.org*

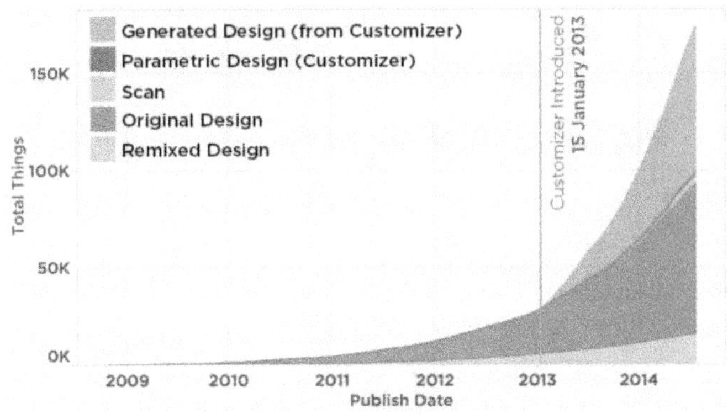

Figure 4: Total Things in Thingiverse.

magnitude larger than the content network of ccMixter which contained only 9,300 works [4]. Figure 4 shows the growth in the total number of Things in Thingiverse since its inception. This graph highlights the impact of Customizer, whose introduction in January 2013 corresponds with a huge jump in activity. The total number of Things on the site nearly tripled in the following year, and generated designs from Customizer now represent an increasingly large fraction of total designs.

Authorship

Since the introduction of Customizer, the number of authors contributing content to Thingiverse has grown by almost 600%, from 7,230 authors on 15 January 2013 to 42,957 by 22 July 2014. Most authors (39,722 or 92%) publish fewer than 10 Things (median = 2, average = 4), and 19,357 authors (45%) published only one Thing. On average, authors with more than one Thing were active for 144 days (median = 39 days). We divided authors into three groups, based on when they were active on Thingiverse:

- Authors who were only active *before* the introduction of Customizer (4,678 authors or 11%).
- Authors who are active both before *and* after the introduction of Customizer (2,531 authors or 6%).
- Authors who are only active *after* the introduction of Customizer (35,749 authors or 83%).

While many authors who contribute Things were never involved in remixing (13,500 or 31%), we are most interested in the 29,458 authors (69%) who contributed either sources or remixes. This fraction is lower than the number of authors (79%) who were involved in remixing on ccMixter in Cheliotis and Yew's analysis [4]. One possible explanation is that Thingiverse places more emphasis on sharing content for fabrication, while ccMixter is expressly focused on remixing.

Of the authors who were involved in remixing, the majority (24,382 or 83%) only remixed others' work and their work never served as the source for a remix. A smaller number (3,285 or 11%) both created remixes *and* had their work remixed by others, while an even smaller minority (1,791 or 6%) had their work remixed by others but did not create remixes themselves.

Remixing Graph

We created a directed graph of remixing relationships between Things, where vertices represent the 98,766 Things involved in remixing. Edges in the graph represent remix relationships and point from source Things to the Things that remix them. This created a number of tree-like subgraphs in which the provenance of each Thing can be traced back over multiple generations of prior remixes. We measured the *generation* of each remixed Thing by counting the path length between it and its most distant ancestor.

Many of the motifs (see Figure 5) identified by Cheliotis and Yew [4] in music remixing also appear in our graph and correspond with common design activities. For example, *branching* out from a source indicates divergent ideation of new designs, while *merging* integrates multiple sources of inspiration into one remix design.

The entire remixing graph consists of 6,536 independent subgraphs. The majority of these subgraphs (5,187 or 79%) only include one generation of remixing. Most subgraphs (3,760 or 58%) are *pairs*–one isolated source with a single remix. Many other subgraphs (1,427 or 22%) are simple examples of branching and merging patterns. For example, 1,297 subgraphs are *source stars* (average # remixes = 12; median = 3, max = 832), in which one generation of remixes emanates from a single source Thing. The majority of these source stars (724 subgraphs or 55%) were created from Customizer. Meanwhile, 130 subgraphs are *remix stars* (average # sources = 2; median = 2; max = 13) in which one generation of sources are combined in a single remix. In total, 16,860 Things (17% of the remixing graph) were sources or remixes in star structures.

However, as in electronic media remixing, remixing in Thingiverse also exhibits a variety of more complex patterns. Over 20% of subgraphs (1349 of 6,536), comprising 74,386 nodes, contain complex combinations remixing patterns. In these remaining subgraphs, we saw a number of anomalous motifs such as *mutual citation dyads* (114 occurrences), *feed-forward loops* (1,713 occurrences), and even one *self-loop* (see Figure 5). These often appear to be evidence of a lack of support for more nuanced tracking of versions and relationships among Things. For example, Thing 13710 referenced itself as its own source, creating a *self-loop*. In fact, the author edited this Thing to post an updated version of his or her original design, noting "version 2 of the original logo" in the description.

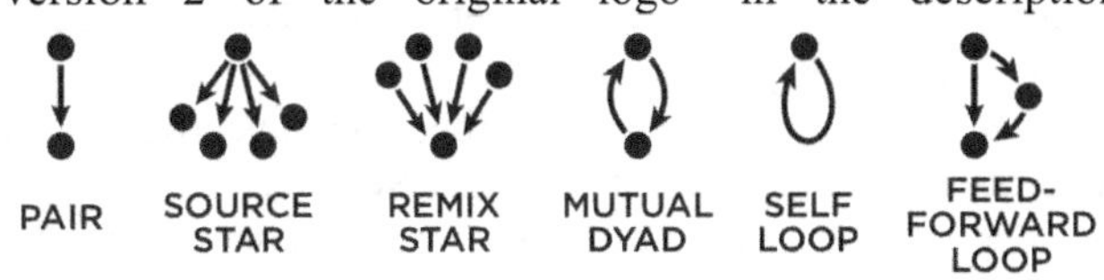

Figure 5: Common network motifs in Remixing Graph.

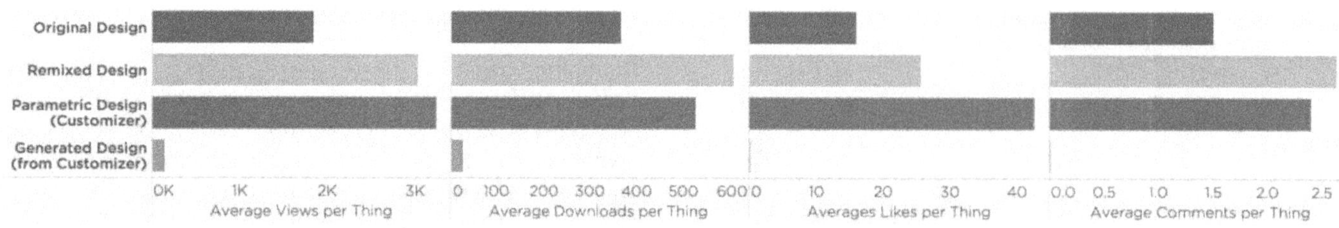

Figure 6: Average User Activity level (Views, Downloads, Likes, and Comments) by Thing Category. Very few generated designs from Customizer elicit subsequent user activity, in contrast to all other types of Things.

Ultimately, Things can be remixed in highly diverse ways and there is no single archetypal pattern. The one clear exception, however, is *Customizer*, where remixing manifests itself very differently.

Parametric Design Tools & Customization

The number of Things in Thingiverse has risen steeply since the introduction of Customizer (see Figure 4). As of July 2014, the site contains 1,692 parametric designs that are configured for use with Customizer. These make up only 2% of the remixing graph and fewer than 1% of all Things on the site. However, authors have used Customizer to generate 74,949 new Things from these parametric designs. These generated Things now make up 74% of the remixing graph and 42% of *all* public Things on the site. Thus the majority of remixed Things are derived directly from a very small number of parametric designs. In fact, the top 120 most-remixed Things are all parametric designs from Customizer, each of which has been used to produce hundreds or thousands of generated designs. The most popular Customizer designs (including 9 of the top 10 most-remixed Things) allow users to add or change aesthetic features–primarily by adding text or images to an existing object. These aesthetic parametric models are classic examples of mass-customization and personalization but they provide few opportunities to tailor designs to new contexts or improve their functionality.

Although designs generated from Customizer make up the majority of the remixing graph, they are mostly dead-ends and do not inspire subsequent user engagement. Of the 74,958 generated Things, only 59 are sources with remixes of their own! Generated designs also prompt almost no additional user activity and–as Figure 6 shows–they are rarely viewed, downloaded, liked, or discussed.

Generated designs themselves do not seem to contribute to the broader Thingiverse community. However, one hypothesis might be that creating generated designs can still inspire authors to participate more broadly and eventually create other remixes or original designs. To test this, we calculated the proportion of authors' total things that were generated using Customizer, focusing specifically on authors who started using Thingiverse after Customizer's introduction. We then sorted authors who had created at least two Things into one of three categories: those who *only* created generated designs with Customizer, those who *never* used Customizer, and those who both used Customizer and created remixed or original Things.

Figure 7 shows that 49% (9,101) of these authors *only* generated designs using Customizer, while a similar number (6,397 or 39%) *never* used Customizer. Surprisingly, only 17% (3,199) of these authors generated designs in Customizer *and* created outside of Customizer.

While this split is influenced by the fact that the majority of authors on Thingiverse (35,527 or 83%) have created less than 5 things, a divide persists even among much more active authors. For example, among the 148 authors with 25–29 Things, 42% (63 authors) still exclusively generated designs using Customizer, and 28% (42 authors) had never used it. This divide suggests that Customizer may have attracted a large, new group of authors to Thingiverse, but that few of these authors transition from using Customizer to creating their own designs or remixing without the support of parametric designs. Meanwhile, a separate large group of authors avoid Customizer completely.

Successful Sources of Remixing

We argue that generating a design by simply manipulating prescribed parameters does not fit with the more experimental and creative vision of remixing. To seek out remixing behavior that more closely resembles this vision, we delved deeper into the 23% of the remixing graph (23,125 Things, 13% of all public Things) that do not involve Customizer. In particular, we wanted to identify what common types of source Things successfully inspire new and different designs or have lasting impact.

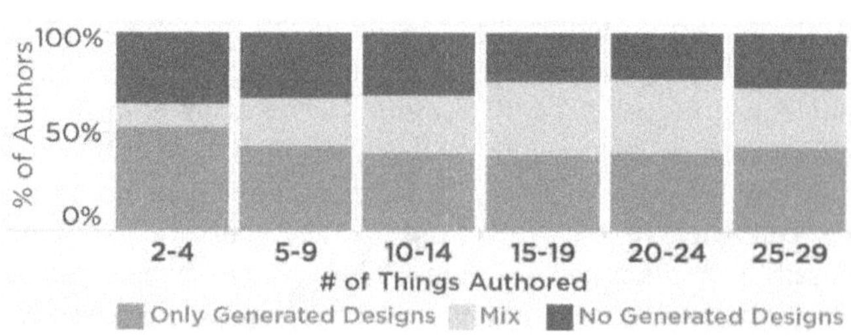

Figure 7: Percent of authors who have only generated designs from Customizer (orange-bottom), who have no Customizer-generated designs (blue-top), and who have a mix (yellow-middle), by the author's total number of Things. Only includes authors who started using Thingiverse after the introduction of Customizer.

To identify successful sources, we excluded all Things generated with Customizer from our dataset and calculated three measures of influence: number of remixes, number of descendants, and generations of influence. We then manually examined the 40 sources with the most remixes, the 40 sources with the most descendants, and the 40 longest remix chains. We thematically clustered these Things and chains to identify characteristics that may lead Things to become influential sources. We identified four genres of successful Things:

Assemblies and their Components: Many authors post complex assemblies of parts. Sometimes assemblies are posted as a single Thing, while other times individual parts are posted separately. Both assemblies and their components are influential in the remixing graph, with authors often borrowing pieces from a source or combining individual sources into assemblies. Assemblies often correspond to directed or well-defined projects. For example, the DIY 3D Printer community dominates most measures of successful remixing with 27 of the most-remixed sources and 32 of the sources with the most descendants. It is also the subject of 14 of the longest remix chains. Another example of a successful assembly is flying quadcopters, with 2 of the most-remixed sources. These directed projects attract a wide range of contributors–full assemblies of the Rostock (Thing 17175) and MendelMax (Thing 20355) DIY 3D printers each had over 60 remixes from 41 unique authors. These examples clearly illustrate the type of remixing advocated by Anderson [1], in which a group of authors collaborate and iterate on each others' designs.

Primitive Mechanisms and Forms. Some influential Things are primitive mechanisms (2 of the most-remixed sources and 6 of the sources with the most descendants) or primitive forms (7 of the most-remixed sources and 9 of the sources with the most descendants). Successful primitive mechanisms such as screws (Thing 8796; Thing 8793) or pin connectors (Thing 10541) are applicable in many domains. These primitives are usually remixed to add a specific functionality or aesthetic properties to an object.

Meanwhile, successful primitive forms range from basic shapes like a 3D heart (Thing 6190) to small sculptural figurines that can easily be fused or attached to other models. Many of these forms, including a "Gangsta" figurine (Thing 5367), "Beefy Arms" (Thing 217849,), a Cute Octopus (Thing 7900), and a scanned bust of comedian Stephen Colbert (Thing 9104) have become memes on Thingiverse and are often remixed as in-jokes within the community.

Sets of Things: Some Things appear influential because they are representative of a set–a group of independent Things that are thematically related. For example Thingiverse contains at least 33 different pieces that can be printed and combined to build marble runs. All of these pieces are posted as separate Things, but are listed as

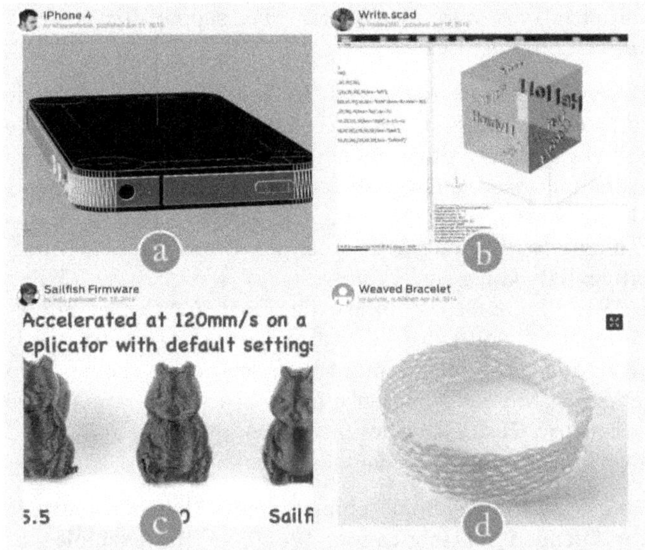

Figure 8: Non-physical Things include: (a) a reference model for making iPhone accessories (Thing 3392 by whosawhatsis), (b) software library for a CAD tool (Thing 16193 by HarlanDMii), (c) firmware that improves 3D print quality (Thing 32084 by jetty), and (d) novel fabrication technique demonstrated with a simple aesthetic example (Thing 309548 by gcoder).

remixes of the same original piece (Thing 62314). This remixing relationship is the main indicator that identifies them as a set. Unlike assemblies, Things in a set tend to be remixed by the author of the original source. In fact, three out of four sets in our sample were exclusively remixed by the source author.

Accessories: Another influential class of sources is after-market accessories for consumer products. Remixing here may be useful because accessories require careful physical fit with an existing, often mass-produced object. For example, two of the most-remixed sources in our sample are both enclosures for a Raspberry Pi computer (Thing 16104; Thing 24461). Starting from designs allows remix authors to keep the geometry that interfaced with the computer itself while tailoring the case to their own needs. We also observed chains of remixes that modify Things designed to work with one type of device to fit another. For example, in one remix chain, a mount protector designed for an SLR camera (Thing 11780) is remixed over several generations to hold a GPS, fit a different camera, and ultimately interface with a GoPro.

Non-Things: Tools & Techniques

Thingiverse's guidelines specify that "designs must represent a real, physical object that can be made." However, while exploring influential sources, we noticed that many source Things do not represent physical objects at all. To more deeply examine the role of non-physical Things in Thingiverse, we used snowball sampling to gather a set of 55 examples. We clustered these Things according to their roles and discovered that most represent various *Tools and Techniques* that support design and fabrication processes:

Design Software. We found 16 examples of standalone software and plug-ins for CAD tools. These software tools address a variety of computational needs, including giving users increased control over surfaces in digital models (Thing 8786) and converting 2D shapes into 3D forms (Thing 24639, Thing 25036). By most measures, the most influential Thing in Thingiverse is *Write.scad()* (Thing 16193, Figure 8b)–a library for OpenSCAD that allows designers to add extruded text to models. This library has been directly remixed more than any other Thing (105 remixes). Moreover, because many of its total remixes are parametric Customizer designs it has ultimately influenced a very large number of total descendants (14,276).

Reference Models. Some Things contain 3D models but are not intended for fabrication. We found 13 examples of reference models whose geometry provides accurate measurements for a design. Our sample of reference models primarily consists of popular consumer electronics (e.g., mobile phones, cameras) and kit electronics (e.g., Raspberry Pi, Arduino, Adafruit Flora) and can be used to build accessories for them. For example, Figure 8a (Thing 12879) shows a precise model of an iPhone based on published specifications from Apple. Comments on these models indicate that authors use them to ensure correct fit–either by using the model in CAD software or, in rare cases, by printing the model to physically test it.

Design Workflows. We also found 7 examples of workflows that explain processes for connecting existing design software in order to produce new designs. For example, "Huge Yosemite Model" (Thing 351271) offers workflow instructions on how to create 3D models from LIDAR data. These workflows offer step-by-step instructions more commonly found in how-to pages [20].

Fabrication Firmware. Makers can augment their fabrication machines by adapting or improving the firmware that drives them. We found 9 different firmware packages, the most popular of which was Sailfish (Thing 32084, Figure 8c) a 3D printer firmware that offers finer resolution and better quality output.

Fabrication Techniques. Makers can use low-level programming languages to control specific fabrication parameters. For example, GCode scripts can control tool paths, extrusion temperatures, and feed rates for 3D printers. These scripts allow makers to invent new ways of manipulating material to create forms and structures. We found 10 examples, including the Weaved Bracelet (Thing 309548, see Figure 8d)–a GCode script that creates a bracelet "woven" by a 3D printer. In another example, Laser Origami (Thing 180990) replicates a fabrication technique originally introduced by Mueller *et al.* [16]. While fabrication techniques sometimes appear as independent non-physical Things, they are often presented

Figure 9: The a) Folding Wood Booklet (Thing 12707 by snijlab) shows a novel hinge technique from laser-cut plywood. It was remixed into a b) Business card holder (Thing 15845 by Guy Dickinson) as well as c) Test pieces for exploring forms made possible with this technique (Thing 12859 by Beehive).

in the context of an example application. Subsequent remixes may abstract the technique to help others apply it for new designs.

Remixing Non-Physical Things

Authors may remix tools and techniques either to *improve* or *apply* them. Improved versions of tools may be more efficient than the original source, add new functionality, or update the original to work with more recent physical objects, fabrication machines, or software. For example, the Folding Wood Booklet (Thing 12707, Figure 9a) presents a laser-cut integrated living hinge, and has been remixed in multiple ways. Some remixes (e.g., Thing 12859, Figure 9c) improve and extend the technique itself by creating test shapes that explore the range of flexible forms. Alternatively, the same tools or techniques can be applied to create specific designs (e.g., Thing 15845, Figure 9b).

Others may *appropriate* the tool or technique in unintended or unexpected ways. For example, we found a series of Things (e.g., Thing 13620) that use GCode to control the motors in a 3D printer and create musical sound patterns. By applying the tool in a radically different way, authors who appropriate introduce new possible functionalities to the tool, without modifying the tool itself.

Other examples represent the creative reframing of the concept of a Thing as a *performance of making* that can be recreated, shared and appropriated by others in the maker community. For example, Thing 40770 provides not only the design of a new cup, but also the concept of creating a new cup design every week. Each week the author created a new cup but marked it as a remix of the original cup. This link connected subsequent designs to the routine that produced them. In cases like this, the source does not provide any reference geometry, but inspiration on how to perform making on a regular basis.

IMPLICATIONS FOR DESIGN

Based on our examination of Thingiverse, it is clear that previous notions of remixing in maker communities are incomplete. While parametric tools like Customizer allow more users to generate personalized objects, these designs end up isolated from the rest of Thingiverse. Moreover the most influential sources for remixing include both physical things like assemblies, primitive forms, and mechanisms and non-physical things–tools and techniques that aid design and fabrication. Building on these findings we identify opportunities for online maker communities to foster better remixing practices.

Tracking Versions and Assemblies

Version tracking and support for specifying assembly relationships between parts are both already found in PDM systems such as Autodesk Vault[10]. However, on Thingiverse remixing is the *only* systematic way of indicating a relationship between things. Adding version tracking and assembly support features to an online maker community could allow makers to collaborate on more complex assemblies and avoid the confusion caused by multiple versions of the same design.

Making the Remixing Graph More Accessible

In our experience as researchers, our visual representations of the remixing graph immediately clarified how specific Things related to and influenced each other. Currently, navigating the graph of remixed and related designs on sites like Thingiverse tends to be linear and tedious, with only one generation of designs visible at a time. Makers could benefit from browsing and search tools that allow them to more fluidly traverse the remixing graph to find influential or readily remixable sources. By exploring families of related designs, authors could better understand the relationships between designs and select the best sources for their own remixes.

Providing Reference Models for Consumer Products

Accessories for consumer products are popular on Thingiverse because they allow makers to personalize or extend the utility of their existing devices. Despite this enthusiasm, makers manually create almost all reference models for devices or attachment points. Companies and standards bodies could support user engagement by systematically posting reference models of products and standard parts to online maker communities–actively encouraging users to build accessories that enhance consumer products. Remixes that utilize these models would presumably be more reliable because they are based on accurate, verified geometry. Moreover, authors could easily locate accessories for an object by looking for designs that utilize its reference model.

[10] *http://www.autodesk.com/vault*

Highlighting Tools & Techniques

While Thingiverse requests that new Things "real, physical object that can be made", non-physical tools and techniques offer unique value to users as they are remixed and applied to new designs. Online maker communities need to highlight non-physical tools and techniques so that authors can more quickly and creatively develop, adapt, or customize their designs.

Learning Design through Parametric Models

A large number of authors on Thingiverse only produce generated designs using Customizer and never contribute other content. One possible reason for this is that many authors lack the technical expertise necessary to modify designs using CAD tools. One way to bridge this gap might be to allow authors to open parametric designs like those used in Customizer in beginner-friendly CAD tools, and generate designs from there. This could provide a less intimidating entry point for CAD where users could continue to interact with and refine designs according to its predefined parameters. These tools could help scaffold users by showing them alternative ways of making the same changes to models using the CAD interface. Over time, as users become more familiar with CAD, they could not only adjust parameters but also begin to add new features, creating richer remixes and building their expertise. Ultimately this could scaffold users' development as designers, using an approach similar to Carle's Virtual Design Apprenticeship model [3]: *adopt, adapt, combine,* and *create*.

Aggregating Users' Experiences

When authors generate designs using Customizer, they typically have little or no information about which parameterized settings are good or effective combinations. This is true, even if hundreds or thousands of others have attempted to generate the same design. Online maker communities with parametric design tools could improve this experience by tracking how the community uses these tools, and displaying this data back to authors. For example, tools like Customizer could summarize previous users' choices using small charts integrated into the dropdowns and sliders used to specify parameters [22]. These social cues could help authors identify and replicate common configurations or produce new unique designs.

A similar approach could be used to share successful or unsuccessful fabrication experiences. When producing a design, authors often have little information about whether or not it will work with their fabrication equipment, materials, or machine settings. Online maker communities could help fill this gap by rewarding authors who document their experience of fabricating a design and contribute information about the configuration they used. This information could highlight tested fabrication setups and discourage authors from repeating others' failed attempts.

CONCLUSION AND FUTURE WORK

This paper provides the first community-scale analysis of remixing behavior in online maker communities. Our analysis shows that authors of 3D designs on Thingiverse do not remix as frequently or draw from as many sources as those in online audio communities like ccMixter. We also characterized the impact of parametric design tools like Customizer, which provide lightweight ways of producing generated designs. We find that Customizer falls short of traditional definitions of remixing, in that generated designs do not elicit subsequent user activity and relatively few authors create both generated designs and original ones.

Outside of Customizer, we do find examples of productive, influential sources of remixing in the form of complex assemblies, accessories, primitive mechanisms, and primitive forms. However, some non-physical things are also influential sources of remixing. In fact, we found numerous examples of non-physical Things that support design and fabrication process by providing reusable tools and techniques.

Ultimately, online maker communities document the performance of making, and allow authors to recreate or find inspiration in others' making experiences. Thingiverse is by no means the only online maker community that supports remixing. Other sites like Ravelry and Autodesk's 123D Circuits[11] formalize remixing using different (and sometimes more expressive) mechanisms and may provide a useful counterpoint. Thus, comparing remixing behavior across these sites could help us even better understand how the design of maker communities impacts creative output.

ACKNOWLEDGMENTS

We would like to thank the Thingiverse authors who gave permission to use images, and Jarkko Moilanen. This research was supported by the European Research Council under grant ERC-2012-AdG #321135 CREATIV.

REFERENCES

1. Anderson, C. *Makers: The New Industrial Revolution.* Crown Business, New York, 2012.
2. Biazzini, M. and Baudry, B. "May the Fork Be with You": Novel Metrics to Analyze Collaboration on GitHub. *Proc. of International Workshop on Emerging Trends in Software Metrics*, ACM (2014), 37–43.
3. Carle, A. Promoting Learning of Instructional Design via Overlay Design Tools. 2012. http://www.eecs.berkeley.edu/Pubs/TechRpts/2012/EECS-2012-246.pdf.
4. Cheliotis, G. and Yew, J. An Analysis of the Social Structure of Remix Culture. *Proc. of Conference on Communities & Technologies*, ACM (2009), 165–174.
5. Dougherty, D. The Maker Movement. *Innovations: Technology, Governance, Globalization 7*, 3 (2012), 11–14.
6. Gantt, M. and Nardi, B.A. Gardeners and Gurus: Patterns of Cooperation Among CAD Users. *Proc. of CHI 1992*, ACM (1992), 107–117.
7. Goodman, E. and Rosner, D. From Garments to Gardens: Negotiating Material Relationships Online and 'by Hand.' *Proc. of CHI 2011*, ACM (2011), 2257–2266.
8. Hartmann, B., Doorley, S., and Klemmer, S.R. Hacking, Mashing, Gluing: Understanding Opportunistic Design. *IEEE Pervasive Computing 7*, 3 (2008), 46–54.
9. Hill, B.M. and Monroy-Hernández, A. The Cost of Collaboration for Code and Art: Evidence from a Remixing Community. *Proc. of CSCW 2013*, ACM (2013), 1035–1046.
10. Kuznetsov, S. and Paulos, E. Rise of the Expert Amateur: DIY Projects, Communities, and Cultures. *Proc. of NordiCHI*, ACM (2010), 295–304.
11. Lessig, L. *Remix: Making Art and Commerce Thrive in the Hybrid Economy.* Penguin Books, New York, 2009.
12. Liccardi, I., Chapuis, O., Yeung, C.-M.A., and Mackay, W. Redundancy and Collaboration in Wikibooks. In P. Campos, N. Graham, J. Jorge, N. Nunes, P. Palanque and M. Winckler, eds., *Human-Computer Interaction – INTERACT 2011.* Springer Berlin Heidelberg, 2011, 215–232.
13. Mackay, W.E. Patterns of Sharing Customizable Software. *Proc. of CSCW 1990*, ACM (1990), 209–221.
14. Mackay, W.E. Triggers and Barriers to Customizing Software. *Proc. of CHI 1991*, ACM (1991), 153–160.
15. Mota, C. The rise of personal fabrication. *Proc. Creativity & Cognition 2011*, ACM (2011), 279–288.
16. Mueller, S., Kruck, B., and Baudisch, P. LaserOrigami: Laser-cutting 3D Objects. *Proc. of CHI 2013*, ACM (2013), 2585–2592.
17. Papadimitriou, S. and Papalexakis, E.E. Towards Laws of the 3D-printable Design Web. *Proc. of ACM Web Science*, ACM (2014), 255–256.
18. Rosner, D. and Bean, J. Learning from IKEA Hacking: I'm Not One to Decoupage a Tabletop and Call It a Day. *Proc. of CHI 2009*, ACM (2009), 419–422.
19. Tanenbaum, J.G., Williams, A.M., Desjardins, A., and Tanenbaum, K. Democratizing Technology: Pleasure, Utility and Expressiveness in DIY and Maker Practice. *Proc. of CHI 2013*, ACM (2013), 2603–2612.
20. Torrey, C., McDonald, D.W., Schilit, B.N., and Bly, S. How-To pages: Informal systems of expertise sharing. In L.J. Bannon, I. Wagner, C. Gutwin, R.H.R. Harper and K. Schmidt, eds., *ECSCW 2007.* Springer London, 2007, 391–410.
21. Wakkary, R. and Maestri, L. The Resourcefulness of Everyday Design. *Proc. of Creativity & Cognition 2007*, ACM (2007), 163–172.
22. Willett, W., Heer, J., and Agrawala, M. Scented Widgets: Improving Navigation Cues with Embedded Visualizations. *IEEE Transactions on Visualization and Computer Graphics 13*, 6 (2007), 1129–1136.

[11] *http://123d.circuits.io*

Effects of Language Modeling and its Personalization on Touchscreen Typing Performance

Andrew Fowler*
Oregon Health & Science University
Portland, OR
fowlera@ohsu.edu

Kurt Partridge, Ciprian Chelba, Xiaojun Bi, Tom Ouyang, and Shumin Zhai
Google, Inc.
Mountain View, CA
{kep,ciprianchelba,bxj,ouyang,zhai}@google.com

ABSTRACT
Modern smartphones correct typing errors and learn user-specific words (such as proper names). Both techniques are useful, yet little has been published about their technical specifics and concrete benefits.

One reason is that typing *accuracy* is difficult to measure empirically on a large scale. We describe a closed-loop, smart touch keyboard (STK) evaluation system that we have implemented to solve this problem. It includes a principled typing simulator for generating human-like noisy touch input, a simple-yet-effective decoder for reconstructing typed words from such spatial data, a large web-scale background language model (LM), and a method for incorporating LM personalization. Using the Enron email corpus as a personalization test set, we show for the first time at this scale that a combined spatial/language model reduces word error rate from a pre-model baseline of 38.4% down to 5.7%, and that LM personalization can improve this further to 4.6%.

Author Keywords
Mobile text entry; keyboard error correction; language modeling

ACM Classification Keywords
H.5.2. User Interfaces: Input devices and strategies

INTRODUCTION
Text input methods have often been key features in shaping the paradigm shifts in mobile computing in the last decades. For example, handwriting with a modified character set (Graffiti) was central to the Palm Pilot era of PDAs. Miniature thumb keyboards dominated the design of BlackBerry and similar devices. Smart touch keyboards (STK) enabled the current generation of full touchscreen mobile devices.

STK products rely on language models, or least a dictionary, to correct touch errors, autocomplete partial letter strings to complete words, and predict what the user will type next. Surprisingly (and for methodological reasons discussed later) the quantitative effects of applying language modeling to touch-based STKs have never been formally reported in the research literature. In fact many recent studies of touch screen typing do not involve LMs at all (e.g. [10]). Our concern is that in many cases, evaluation without language-model based correction may lead to incorrect conclusions about the benefits of a particular technique. For example, [34] found that improvements in spatial error modeling had little effect in practice since LM-based correction compensated for such spatial errors. For this reason, quantitatively benchmarking the effects of a standard LM to STK is one of the goals of this paper.

Conversely, traditional metrics of language models in isolation may not accurately reflect how they perform in a deployed decoder. A model-intrinsic measure like per-word perplexity, though commonly used to compare LMs, can correlate poorly with downstream metrics, as is the case with word error rate in speech recognition [6]. *Extrinsic* evaluations like typing accuracy, which more closely reflect the experience of an actual user, can only be evaluated if the user's role in the decoding process is considered.

An especially relevant language modeling technique for mobile text entry, and one that is also difficult to measure, is *LM personalization*, in which a language model's lexicon and probabilities are made flexible and adaptive to the user. A natural way to accomplish this is to utilize a user's written history, since it best reflects that person's usage of language. However, scientific understanding of text input LM personalization is limited. The most detailed work dates from 2006, and studies previous-generation mobile devices with physical keyboards [30]. Modern soft keyboards, with more fuzzy input on touchscreens, may rely more heavily on LMs, and therefore are more likely to benefit when personalization works, or suffer when it does not.

In this paper, we contribute the first large-scale longitudinal simulation study of the effects of language modeling, with and without personalization, on finger-touch-based soft keyboards. As a methodological contribution, we created a novel integrated framework (dubbed Sketch Jr.) for testing input *accuracy*, which differs from intrinsic measures such as LM perplexity and keystroke savings, which are typically computed in isolation of the input problem. Our method allows for *extrinsic evaluation* of our models by incorporating large-scale simulation of human-like inputs. We evaluate our LMs in connection with sloppy user input based on empirical data, using a principled error correction and word completion model (decoder). We use the longitudinal real-world text-writing history of a large group of individuals (the Enron Corpus). Through this human simulation, we show that a background LM can reduce typing word error rate (WER)

*This work was done while Andrew Fowler was an intern at Google Inc.

CHI 2015, April 18–23, 2015, Seoul, Republic of Korea
ACM 978-1-4503-3145-6/15/04
http://dx.doi.org/10.1145/2702123.2702503

from 38.4% to 5.7%, and that personalized LMs further reduce this error to 4.6% (a 19.3% relative change compared to the non-adapted model). We also examine personalization methods based on the idea of an exponentially-decaying cache, and find that a decay time in months is optimal, but that the decay curve has little effect on the overall performance result. This work is also, as far as we know, the first to study and quantify the tradeoff between the overall error rate and *false corrections*, a subclass of errors highly visible to end-users.

RELATED WORK

Language Models for Text Entry

In the broad sense, language models have long been used in text input. The simplest LM is a lexicon, i.e. a list of permissible words. A lexicon can already provide quite powerful constraints in, for example, decoding ambiguous 12-button-based dialpad input found on traditional phones, which dates back to the early 1970's [28]. Since entering logographic text such as Chinese with a Roman alphabet is highly ambiguous, applying some form of model that maps Roman letter-based phonetic input to logographic characters has also been necessary and common in East Asian countries for a long time [30]. Innovations such as word-gesture typing, or shape writing [36, 37], also leverage language regularities in the form of a lexicon that could further be adapted to the individual user by extracting a vocabulary from the user's past documents [22], or by moving passive words into an in-use active vocabulary [23]. Goodman and colleagues [11] drew inspiration from speech recognition for stylus keyboard tapping and applied a character n-gram model to correct stylus taps[1], achieving a reduction in *character-level* error rate from 2.40% to 1.39%. Klarlund and Riley [17] applied N-gram language modeling to a cluster keyboard (i.e. a keyboard with reduced number of keys), and showed large improvements over unigram frequency models. Tanaka-Ishii [30] presented a very comprehensive and systematic study of four types of LMs, namely unigram, co-occurrence, MTF (move to front, which gives higher priority to recent words), and PPM (prediction by partial match), and studied their use in adaptation for text input. These were applied in English with reduced keyboards, in Japanese with kana, and in Thai also with ambiguity but not errors. It was found that PPM outperformed other techniques in ranking prediction candidates. The PPM model used was an interpolation between a unigram model trained on a 30M Wall Street Journal news corpus (for English) and a n-gram model trained on a small user corpus. The average rank improvement with adaptation depended on the user corpus size. For example when the size of the user corpus increased from 0 to 50,000 words, the PPM prediction average rank of the intended word improved from 1.3 to 1.09.

Language Model Adaptation

The essential problem that LM adaptation seeks to solve is the problem of *domain mismatch*. LMs can be trained on enormous text corpora, but those corpora rarely match the domain of the target text one wishes to model. In-domain text is usually small in quantity and not enough to build a robust model.

[1]Since Goodman et al. involved *small-scale* observations with a *stylus* input using *character-level* evaluations/LM, it differs significantly from our work, in particular because their baseline tapping error rate is one fifth of ours.

LM adaptation algorithms attempt to combine the benefits of a large, out-of-domain model with a small in-domain model. *Personalization* can be seen as the ultimate adaptation problem, since one is adapting to a single individual (for which in-domain text is almost certainly limited). LM adaptation has been studied extensively. An excellent review of various algorithms can be found in [2] and [9].

Cache-based LM adaptation keeps a continuously-updated cache of words, and use this cache to build the adaptation/personalization model. In the context of model adaptation, the model generated from the cache is the in-domain model. A cache varies slightly from other adaptation techniques in two ways: First, the adaptation model must be updated on the fly because new words are typed continuously (the technique is commonly called dynamic cache-based adaptation to reflect this fact). Second, the user cache may begin in a completely empty state, or be primed with a small amount of in-domain text (in our case, we primed with 30 days of user emails). Cache-based LM adaptation was used by [24] to improve the performance of a speech recognition system.

Cache-based LMs are further explored in [8], which describes a method in which the relative weights of words in the cache are made to decay exponentially, with "older" words having lower weights. This reflects the common-sense notion of *recency*, which suggests that, in general, more recently-used words in a text will re-occur with higher probability than words used in the more distant past. The results of [8] indicate that using an exponentially-decaying cache results in improvements in perplexity, but as shown later, our extrinsic evaluation of text entry appears to indicate that these gains are negligible in our application.

RESEARCH METHODOLOGY

Two crucial questions in our experimental design were whether to primarily rely on modeling and simulation or human subjects directly, and whether to collect text from users or use an existing corpus. We decided to simulate using a large real world text corpus (Enron) for all experiments, for the following reasons:

- **Practicality and Scale:** Scale is important to language modeling evaluation, particularly with personalization. Variances and nuances in language use can only be revealed with longitudinal data. Further, as we later confirmed, large user-to-user variance is possible and many users are needed to give meaningful results. Collecting this amount of data from individual users is possible, but impractical. In addition, we required a large development set in order to empirically optimize various system parameters. Large-scale parameter optimization of this kind without simulation is infeasible.
- **Privacy and Reproducibility:** Another problem with collecting native text from individuals is that they would have a reasonable expectation of privacy. The Enron Corpus largely avoids this issue, and its widespread availability allows for experiments that are vastly more reproducible.
- **Availability of Foundational HCI Research:** Recent HCI research has measured crucial parameters of human motor control for text entry tasks. It has been shown that tapping on key targets may be modeled by a Gaussian distribution

model whose parameters depend on hand posture (finger, thumb, or two thumbs), the portion of the keyboard (left, right, top, or bottom), and the individual user [10, 1, 3].

We do not wish to discount the advantages of human tests, which would provide valuable information not available to simulation, such as how users respond to personalized text input and what strategies are used to correct errors. Human tests would also validate our simulation approach. We reserve these questions as important avenues for future work; for the present work, however, we assert that combining human input models established from users' natural typing data and longitudinal real world text writing records captures the essence of smart touch keyboard evaluation and reveals the effects of language modeling at a large scale.

DATA

Background Language Model

Our background model was a Katz-smoothed [16] bigram LM trained on 114 billion words scraped from the publicly-accessible web in English. We pruned the model size using entropy pruning [29], a technique for decreasing the size of a backoff LM. The basic method involves selecting n-grams for removal from the model by measuring the relative entropy of models with and without that n-gram. A threshold is set for excluding n-grams by this criterion. The choice of Katz over the more popular Kneser-Ney [19] for smoothing was dictated by the small memory footprint available for the LM on a mobile device, and the reduced difference between the two approaches after entropy pruning [5]. The final pruned model contained about 8.5 million n-grams (8.4M bigrams and 168K unigrams).

Enron Corpus as an Evaluation Set

The Enron Corpus [18] is a large set of emails that were collected by the Federal Regulatory Commission when the Enron Corporation was under investigation in late 2001. This corpus was made public in 2003, and consists of over 600,000 individual email messages from multiple years (1998 to 2002). It is one of the largest collections of email publicly available, and is a valuable and widely-used resource for natural language research.

In the field of text entry, Enron data has been used for the creation and comparison of phrase sets to be used in other text entry experiments [20, 21, 31] . In [26], Enron data was compared to data from Facebook and Twitter in an information-theoretic manner, with the goal of judging how "representative" various phrases are. Enron has also been used for domain adaptation in tasks other than language modeling [7, 27, 35].

The Enron Corpus is well suited for text entry research for three reasons: First, it consists of human communication, making it a better match to text input applications. Second, it consists of a relatively large body of real-world usage of text communication (as opposed to news corpora [4] or fiction writing [32]). Third, the corpus preserves a long history of communication by user with minimal privacy concerns, allowing for more in-depth research into personalization techniques.

However we found the Enron corpus to be inadequate in its raw form. Our preprocessing of the corpus was extensive, and included deduplication, signature text removal, name canonicalization, and attached text removal. Because our goal was LM personalization, the driving idea of these preprocessing steps was a desire to have clean text for each user that was strongly linked to that user, i.e. not generated automatically or typed by somebody else. This is particularly important when modeling for text entry, since URLs and attached messages are very unlikely to have been typed by the person doing the text entry. We found that extracting clean, human-generated text from the Enron Corpus is surprisingly nontrivial, so we have made the details of our preprocessing available as an auxiliary document to this paper.

Development and Test Sets

The next step was to divide the Enron emails into test sets. We selected 90 Enron users, each with more than 1500 total words in their collected sent emails. We defined a minimum word count per user for two reasons: First, we wanted a large enough volume of text to perform adaptation experiments that involved learning user words and adapting a model to them. Second, we wanted to avoid sparsity issues. We divided these 90 users into development and test sets of 45 users apiece, with a similar distribution of per-user word counts in each set. The development set contained 38,114 messages and 1,355,266 words, and the test set contained 31,740 messages and 1,214,403 words. Since our models are based on caching, there is no Enron training set per se; user models are trained dynamically as one proceeds through each user's portion of the test set.

SIMULATION

The basic workflow of our system is to generate simulated keyboard taps for a given text, use a decoder to reconstruct the text from those noisy taps in the presence of various LMs, then evaluate the output.

Simulated Smart Touch Keyboard Typing

We have discussed the benefits of human simulation as a general research method in LM personalization. Here we provide critical details needed to making such simulation meaningful to text input. We also point out aspects of typing not simulated in the current work.

In order to study the impact of LM personalization in STK applications, we simulated each Enron user typing his or her test set in chronological order using a simple STK decoder, to be described shortly. We used the key layout from the specifications of the Nexus 5 QWERTY keyboard, which has a single-key width of 6.16 mm and a key height of 9.42 mm. We assumed that the user was perfect in *intent*; in other words, the user's target word is always the actual target word[2]. Additionally, if the decoder fails to produce the target word, it is simply counted towards the error rate but we do not simulate any attempt on the part of the user to correct such errors with backspace or other methods.

To evaluate the power of LMs and personalized LMs in error correction, we introduced human errors in the simulated input process that reflected the main source of error in touch

[2]This does not exclude the possibility of spelling errors in the Enron Corpus; in this case, we simply assume that the typo is the correct target, and judge it accordingly.

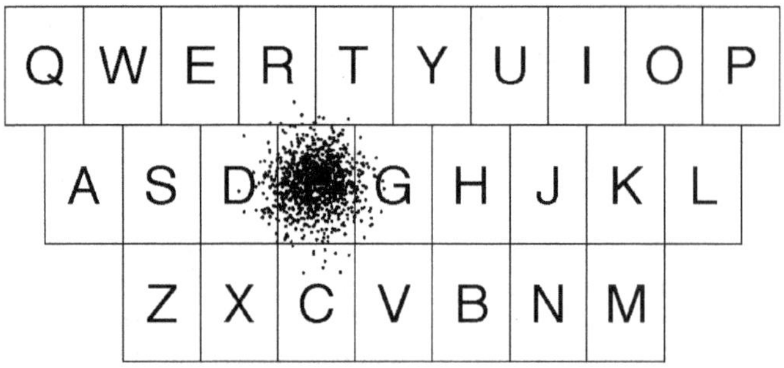

Figure 1. Our keyboard layout with 1000 randomly sampled taps on the "F" key

screen keyboards. We incorporated spatial noise in the tapping/typing signal by sampling randomly from a 2D Gaussian distribution. The mean of the distribution for each tap was the center of the intended key, and the standard deviations were set to be 1.97 mm in the x direction and 1.88 mm in the y direction, as illustrated in Figure 1. These values were based on [1], which determined the 2D Gaussian distribution to be representative of actual human tapping, and described typical variances. Taps landing outside of the border of the intended key and inside another key were given the identity of the new key in the literal string output (a typing error). Taps outside the border of *every* key were discarded and resampled. We found that these settings result in a per-tap error rate of 12.8%, which translates to 38.4% of words in the test set containing at least one key error. In practice, the actual amount of spatial errors follows a speed-accuracy trade off model. The faster one types, the more errors one would make. See "FFitts law" [3] for an in depth exploration of the speed-accuracy model of touch screen target acquisition containing both relative and absolute precision errors.

We deliberately chose the 2D Gaussian for modeling spatial touch, for multiple reasons: First, we desired a simple, principled model (in the spirit of "Occam's razor") that still captured the spatial variance needed to test LM contribution to decoding noisy touchscreen input. Second, 2D Gaussian is at the core of spatial models used in commercial level keyboards such as the Android Open Source Project (AOSP) keyboard. Third, while more complex models of touch have been explored in the literature (Holz et al. [13], Azenkot & Zhai [1], and others highlight additional phenomena involved with finger touches, in particular spatial offsets that depend on finger position, visual cues, and hand posture), it is quite hard to put these models in practice because of issues such as sensor requirements. Fourth, Yin et al. [34] showed that if a more complex hierarchical backoff model (with hand posture and key location dependencies) is used, the gain is large when considering individual letters only but small (diminishes) when connected with an LM. We believe further gains can still be made in the future with improved spatial modeling, but a simple Gaussian model reflects the state of the art and is sufficient in testing LM contribution.

We made three further simplifying assumptions about the test data and the simulated user. First, since the simulated STK contains only the symbols a–z, the typing simulation only considers those letters. We stripped out other non-space symbols before testing. Second, the simulated user always taps the space bar correctly, i.e. always taps it when intended and never taps it when not intended. Third, the input process is case-insensitive.

We chose to focus on 2D spatial noise exclusively as a source of error in the tapping signal. There are other potential error sources, many of which fall under the category of *cognitive error*. An example of a cognitive error would be the user misspelling a word because they do not know the correct spelling. In such a scenario, an incorrect string is created, but it is not due to an error of typing; the user intended the string, whether or not it was correct. For instance, typing `forword` instead of `forward` would constitute a cognitive error, while `forqard` would likely be a spatial error. Other cognitive errors include selecting the wrong word from the suggestion list, or failing to tap the correct word when it appears in the selection list. Because modeling cognitive error is subtle and because we wish to be able to interpret our results more straightforwardly, we exclude it from our experiments. Similarly, we exclude errors involving inserted and deleted characters. Overall, our goal was to introduce a predominant type of error in sufficient and representative quantity to test the LM personalization effect in correcting that error type. Other types of errors may follow the same pattern, but should be further researched in the future.

A Simple Model Decoder

Once our simulator had generated a sequence of taps, we next applied a simple model decoder to represent the core function of a STK. The general idea of combining a spatial model of touchscreen behavior with language modeling for text entry has previously appeared in the literature. For example, Weir et al. [33] applied user-customized spatial models and used touch pressure as a signal to increase the spatial model weight relative their LM weight. Our work differs from Weir et al. in our use of longitudinal user data, the large scale of our simulations, and the fact that we personalized our LMs rather than our spatial model. For the purpose of systematically evaluating the impact of LM adaptation in mobile text input applications, our decoder was not designed to be optimal, complete, or computationally efficient. Instead it was meant to be as simple as possible but still able to take advantage of a language model and effectively correct imprecise spatial input.

Suppose we have a tap sequence $T = t_1, t_2, ..., t_n$, where the t_i values are the coordinates of each tap, and a potential word $w{=}l_1, l_2, ..., l_m$, where the l_i values are the letters that make up that word. Note that any predicted word must have at least n letters, so we require that $m \geq n$. We define the spatial score $S(w|T)$ as

$$S(w|T) = \sum_{i=1}^{n}((t_{ix} - l_{ix})^2 + (t_{iy} - l_{iy})^2), \quad (1)$$

where t_{ix} and t_{iy} are the x and y coordinates of the tap t_i, and l_{ix} and l_{iy} represent the x and y coordinates of the key center of the letter l_i.

We further let $L_{LM}(w|c)$ be the negative logarithm of the LM probability of the word w given context c. The combined score $B(w|c,T)$ is equal to

$$B(w|c,T) = L_{LM}(w|c) - \gamma S(w|T), \quad (2)$$

where γ is the spatial model weight. The best-scoring word w_{best} under the combined model is therefore

$$w_{best} = \arg\max_{w} B(w|c, T). \qquad (3)$$

We found through experiments on our development set that the optimal spatial model weight γ for our task is 0.00022[3].

Algorithm 1 Procedure for generating possible words matching a tap sequence

```
procedure GETPOTENTIALWORDS(T, d)
    input: list T of n taps; distance threshold d
    wordlist ← []
    for t_i in T do
        generate set S_i of all letters on keyboard with centers
        within distance d of t_i
    for w_p in lexicon L with ≥n letters do
        for letter l_i in w_p, 1 ≤ i ≤ n do
            if l_i ∈ S_i then
                continue
            else
                break (word contains too-distant letter)
        append w_p to wordlist
    return wordlist
```

An important parameter in our spatial decoding technique is a pruning criterion, used to decrease the size of the search space by limiting potential keys for each tap. Any key with a center within a specific radius from the tap may be a potential letter. Given the geometry of our simulated keyboard, this allows for between one and five potential keys for each tap. The search algorithm then recursively traverses the tree of possible words and word prefixes given these potential keys, and filters out all prefixes that do not match a known word in our LM lexicon. This is demonstrated in the procedure GETPOTENTIALWORDS in Algorithm 1. We found using the development set that the pruning radius of 7.99 mm resulted in fast simulation without degrading model performance.

Figure 2 and Table 1 illustrate a simple example of the combined decoder at work. The spatial decoder has no notion of word probabilities in language therefore alone can only function as a naive keyboard. It favors the spatially-closest words. The LM has no spatial data (other than what set of keys is nearby each tap), so it simply gives the most probable words possible given the pruning radius. The combined model synthesizes these two sources of information to generate a better word list. Note that all three models, *even the spatial model*, are constrained by the lexicon; the word '`bs`' is absent from Table 1 because it is not in the lexicon, despite the fact that it is the typed literal string. The top word in the spatial model, '`ba`,' is the word in the lexicon (albeit rare) with the highest spatial score. (As mentioned elsewhere, our decoding procedure has a method for including the actually-typed sequence in the suggested words list, but this is a separate process.)

[3]The small value of γ is a consequence of our spatial model outputting much larger absolute values than our LM, ultimately because the spatial model uses pixel widths as a distance unit.

Algorithm 2 Procedures for typing simulation and evaluation

```
procedure CALCULATEACCURACY(w, n, c, d)
    input: target word w of length n, previous context c
    input: pruning threshold d, autocorrect threshold φ
    T ← []
    for letter l_i in w do
        t_i ← sample from 2D Gaussian centered at l_i
        add t_i to T
    wordlist ← GETPOTENTIALWORDS(T, d)
    lit ← string of actual keys tapped by taps in T
    if wordlist is not empty then
        for w_p in wordlist do
            calculate score B(w_p|c, T) given T and c
        if highest score > φ then
            w_best ← w_p with highest model score
        else (best word not good enough; use lit. string)
            w_best ← lit
    else (no suggestions; use literal string)
        w_best ← lit
    if w_best = w then
        return success
    else
        return failure
procedure CALCULATEEFFICIENCY(w, n, c)
    input: target word w of length n, previous context c
    T ← []
    for i in 0 ... n do (iterate over number of taps)
        if i > 0 then
            l_i ← i^th letter of w
            t_i ← key center of l_i
            add t_i to T
        wordlist ← GETPOTENTIALWORDS(T, 0)
        lit ← string of actual keys tapped by taps in T
        if wordlist is not empty then
            for w_p in wordlist do
                calculate score B(w_p|c, T) given T and c
            w_bestset ← three w_p with highest model score
        else (no suggestions; use literal string)
            w_bestset ← lit
        if lit ∉ w_bestset then
            if w_bestset contains less than three words then
                append lit to end of w_bestset
            else
                replace 3^rd word in w_bestset with lit
        if w ∈ w_bestset then
            return i + 1 (count of taps needed to type w)
```

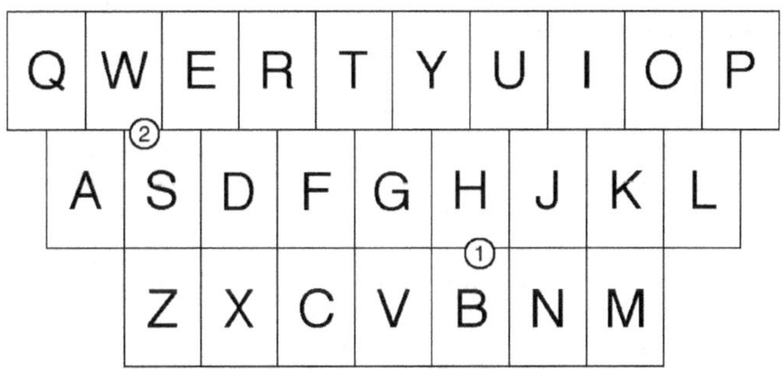

Figure 2. Two example taps on the simulated keyboard.

	Decoding Method		
Rank	Spatial Model	Language Model	Combined
1	ba	be	be
2	ha	he	best
3	be	had	bad
4	he	best	he
5	bad	bad	had

Table 1. Top potential words given the taps in Figure 2, under the spatial model only, language model only, and combined decoder.

EVALUATION METRICS

Language models are often evaluated using the *per-word perplexity* metric across a test set [15]. It is an information-theoretic measure of how well a statistical model predicts a sample. In theory, a language model better suited to the test data will result in a lower perplexity value. Many LM adaptation techniques are evaluated in this way, and report a decrease in observed perplexity as evidence of an improved model. In practice, however, even significant improvements in perplexity do not necessarily correlate with commensurate improvements in extrinsic objectives, particularly in speech recognition research, where WER is the dominant evaluation metric [6, 12]. Further, perplexity is often difficult to compare across tests, because it is lexicon-dependent, i.e. the models involved must use the same word list. This is not easy to accomplish in an adaptation/personalization setting, where adding new words to a model is of central importance.

One response to the shortcomings of perplexity and other LM-intrinsic metrics is to use LM-extrinsic evaluation, a research philosophy outlined in [14]. In our case, the extrinsic evaluation metrics are keystroke savings and WER. Keystroke savings (see Equation 4) is the de-facto evaluation standard for text entry efficiency measurement [25]. WER is a standard way of measuring the accuracy of a word-based decoding task, and is widely used in speech recognition.

Importantly, an LM's extrinsic power in error correction (i.e. word-level accuracy) can *only* be measured in the presence of noise and a complete closed-loop system that includes a decoder and erroneous input. The development of such a system, and the ability it affords to measure error correction, are key contributions of our research. In ASR it was only when a reference recognizer was applied that language modeling studies could move from intrinsic measures such as perplexity to extrinsic measures such as WER [6]. Since "fat" finger imprecision is the main source of noise in finger-operated touch keyboard [1], the simple model decoder as described earlier together with the spatial noise model and the real world personal history data set of Enron emails enabled us to measure the extrinsic power of the LM and its adaptation.

Simulating Word Correction

When simulating word *correction*, we proceed one word at a time. The simulator samples one tap (with spatial noise) for *every letter* in the target word, then returns the single most probable word from the decoder. If this word has a probability above a certain *autocorrect threshold*, the word is typed, followed by a space. If not, the uncorrected *literal string* is typed (the literal string is the sequence of visual keys tapped; in the case of Figure 2, the literal string is '`bs`'). A threshold value 0.7 was used for all of our accuracy experiments, for reasons explained in the Results section below. This is demonstrated in the procedure CALCULATEACCURACY in Algorithm 2. The evaluation metric for word correction is word error rate. WER is calculated by dividing the number of incorrectly-decoded words by the total number of words.

Simulating Word Prediction

When simulating word *prediction*, we also proceed one word at a time, but there are two important differences. First, we provide the simulated user with a list of three word suggestions after each tap, potentially saving keystrokes. Second, in order to isolate the prediction effect, we exclude spatial noise.

The following is demonstrated in the procedure CALCULATEEFFICIENCY in Algorithm 2. For each word, we incrementally simulate perfect input for each letter, starting with zero taps. At each point, the LM (no spatial model or decoding) generates the three most probable words given the letters so far (including the case where there are not yet letters typed). If the literal string is not among these three, the third-most-probable word is removed and replaced with the literal string. Otherwise, the list remains unchanged. We assume that the simulated user will notice immediately if the target word is among these top three. If so, we count one keystroke for selecting the word. If not, we make another simulated tap and generate a new suggestion list. (Note that, in word-initial position, no taps have occurred, and all words in the LM are possible.) In the case where all n taps are needed to type an n-letter word, the simulated user makes one last check for the target word in the top-three word prediction list. If the target is there, it is selected. If not, a space key is typed. When the space key is tapped, the single most probable word in the prediction list is entered. This is the reason the literal string is always included in the list. Without the literal string the user has no way of entering words that are not in the LM lexicon.

The evaluation metric for word prediction is keystroke savings, as defined in Equation 4. Because we assume no spatial noise when measuring word prediction, accuracy is always 100%.

$$ks = 1 - \frac{total\ taps\ required}{total\ characters\ in\ test\ set} \tag{4}$$

Note that, when simulating either correction or prediction, each word requires a minimum of one keystroke, since either space or select-suggestion must be tapped to move to the next word.

Since our LM is a bigram model, its probabilities are conditioned on the previous word in each context. At the beginning of each line (every line in the test set is a sentence), the model is primed with the start-sentence symbol `<S>`. After each word is entered, that word becomes the previous word, *even if the typed word is incorrect and does not match the true string*. The latter scenario matches real-world use, since the typed word is all any typing system has access to, even if it is not correct. In the case of words not in the LM lexicon, the previous word is set to the unknown symbol `<UNK>`.

LANGUAGE MODEL PERSONALIZATION

We implemented two basic types of cache-based language models: Uniform and exponentially-decaying. The uniform cache considered a sliding window of words stretching back as far as available in the user's test data, and consisted of an unsmoothed unigram LM from the words in that window. It was continuously updated with each individual user's writing history as simulation progressed. We used linear interpolation to combine the background model with this in-domain cache model[4]. Linear interpolation is a simple technique for LM adaptation. Equation 5 (adapted from [2]) illustrates the basic interpolation method, where $P(w|c)$ is the conditional probability of word w given context c, P_A is the adaptation model, P_B is the background model, and λ represents the relative weight of the background model.

$$P(w|c) = (1-\lambda)P_A(w|c) + \lambda P_B(w|c) \quad (5)$$

We found through experiments on held-out data that the optimal window size is infinite, i.e. all words in the user's history should be kept in the cache. Further, we found the optimal λ value to be 0.8.

The exponentially-decaying cache was derived from [8], which first described the technique. It used an unsmoothed unigram model like the uniform cache, but instead of counting words directly we modified the weights according to how far back they were in the cache. This captured the recency effect. Equation 6 (adapted from [8]) illustrates the basic method, where P_{cache} is the conditional probability of word w_i given the cache w_1 through w_{i-1}, and I is a binary function such that $I(A) = 1$ if A is true, and 0 otherwise. The decay rate α describes how quickly word weights decay in the cache, and β is a normalizing constant:

$$P_{cache}(w_i|w_1, w_2, ..., w_{i-1}) = \beta \sum_{j=1}^{i-1} I(w_i = w_j) e^{-\alpha(i-j)} \quad (6)$$

We used a grid search on held-out data to find that the optimal decay rate α is 0.0003, which is a slow rate of decay but consistent with the values determined in [8]. An α value of 0.0003 means that it takes roughly 2300 words of history before the adjusted weight decreases to half of its initial value. Since most users in the test set generate between 1000 and 2000 words per month, this decay rate can be said to take months to take effect. Note, however, that this formulation is based on word positions rather than elapsed time. A word located at position $i - 100$ may have been typed at any point in the past, depending on the user. As with the uniform cache method, we combined the cache model with the background model using linear interpolation, as in Equation 5. We again found the optimal λ value to be 0.8.

For both cache methods, we primed the cache with the first 30 days of email from each of the 45 individuals in the test set. Messages sent during this period were used only to fill the personalization cache, and not simulated for evaluation purposes. The choice of 30 days was based on an empirical study on the development set, which showed that 30 days generally provides a reasonable initial cache size. The mean size of this priming cache in the test set was 1429 words. Both cache models were updated from the 31st day onward till the end of each individual's text available in Enron.

[4]Note that since a LM requires large quantities of text, using the cache model alone would not be effective; even users with large text histories do not have enough text to build a useful LM without sparsity issues.

Model	WER %	OOV %
No Language Model	38.4	n/a
Background LM Only	5.7	1.6
Uniform Cache Adaptation	4.6	0.9
Decaying Cache Adaptation	4.6	0.9

Table 2. Word error rates for various model setups, averaged across all simulated Enron users.

We define the model lexicon at any given time to be all words in *either* the background model unigram list or the cache. When a word was absent from one of these two models, it received a probability of zero in that model before the interpolation defined by Equation 5 took place. Though the background model did contain an <UNK> symbol, we normalized it out when calculating word probabilities[5]. We also make no attempt to estimate probabilities of words not in either model, i.e. entirely absent from the model lexicon (though we do preserve the literal string, which can sometimes be absent from both models).

RESULTS

By replicating and simulating users' natural finger touch input behavior, multi-user and longitudinal writing records, and the primary functions keyboard decoding, we are able to reveal what simple human subjects lab experiments could not do—quantitatively benchmarking the effects of language modeling with and without personalization at scale.

Word Correction

Table 2 shows WER results for the accuracy experiments. The first row represents the value of a naive keyboard without any language modeling and takes the literal string only, which is equivalent to decoding touch input according to its closest key centers. The word error rate of such a naive keyboard is 38.4%.

With a background LM combined with the simple decoder, both as described earlier, the error rate is drastically reduced to 5.7%. This is at the 0.7 autocorrect threshold operating point, as explained below. LM personalization further improves the error rate to 4.6%, a relative decrease of 19.3%. The exponentially-decaying cache method did not outperform the uniform cache method.

The OOV rate is calculated on a per-word basis as the human simulation progresses through the test set. In the case of cache-based models, a given word is considered OOV if it did not exist in the background model or the cache (though since all OOVs are added to the cache immediately, no word can be an OOV twice for the same user). The cache is emptied before moving to a new user in the test set.

False Corrections and the Autocorrect Threshold

In our word correction experiments, we considered one type of failure to be worse than the others. If the literal string is correct, but the autocorrect mechanism changes it to a word that is incorrect, we call this a *false correction*. The rationale for setting apart these failures is this: Suppose a user carefully types a word such that all taps in that word fall inside their respective target key boundaries. The user likely has a strong

[5]We still use <UNK> for n-gram contexts; see earlier paragraph on LM conditioning.

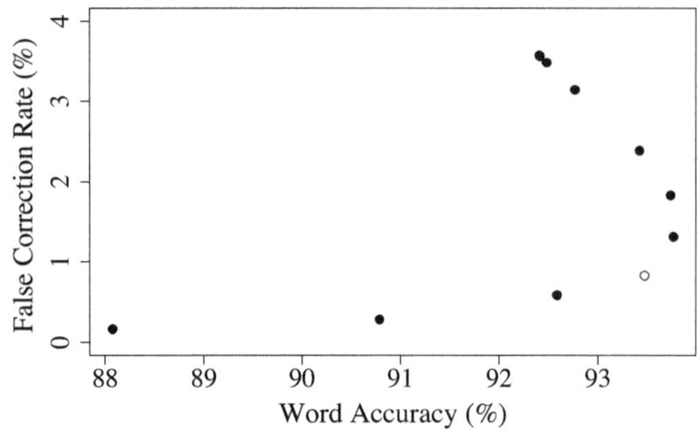

Figure 3. Tradeoff between overall word accuracy and false correction rate, managed by varying the autocorrect threshold from 0.0 (upper right) to 0.95 (lower left). The rightmost dot is optimal from an overall word accuracy standpoint, but we chose the white dot as an operating point to bring the false correction rate below 1%.

expectation that the STK will output the literal string, and autocorrecting to another string is particularly undesirable. We therefore may wish to decrease the rate of false corrections, even at the cost of a slight increase in overall word error rate.

We found that this tradeoff can be managed by introducing an *autocorrect threshold* parameter to our model. It operates as follows: If the top-scoring word is not equal to the literal string, *and* its probability[6] is below the autocorrect threshold, we prevent the decoder from performing a correction and simply *use the literal string*.

Figure 3 illustrates the tradeoff, calculated on a subset of the development set. It turns out that allowing the decoder to *always* perform correction, i.e. an autocorrect threshold of 0.0, results in a high rate of false corrections, more than 3.5%. This amounts to nearly half of all failures for this test. The optimal autocorrect threshold value for maximizing *overall* accuracy is roughly 0.6, which corresponds to the typical accuracy of any given literal string[7]. We selected 0.7 as the operating point for the autocorrect threshold in all of our accuracy experiments. This choice caused a slight decrease in overall accuracy, but it brought the false correction rate below 1%. On the test data, the false correction rate was 0.70% for the baseline model and 0.39% for the uniform cache mixture model, representing an even larger relative WER improvement than we observed for overall failures.

Precision and Recall

Another way to think about the performance of the word completion model is as a tradeoff between precision and recall. In our case, precision is defined as the proportion of autocorrected words that were changed to the true word. Recall is defined as the proportion of words needing correction (i.e. with incorrect literal strings) that were autocorrected to the true word. Figure 4 shows the precision vs. recall curve. Note that, under the conditions of our model, 100% recall is not possible. This is due to the fact that sometimes a literal string (with an error) is the only word in the predicted word list. This can happen when the decoder fails to generate any candidates because the tap sequence is too far from any known word. In this situation, correction cannot occur in our model (not even a false correction), because no candidates exist.

[6]We converted the log-space model scores to probabilities and normalized to make this calculation.

[7]This is just the accuracy of a word in the no-model scenario, or $1.0 - 0.384$.

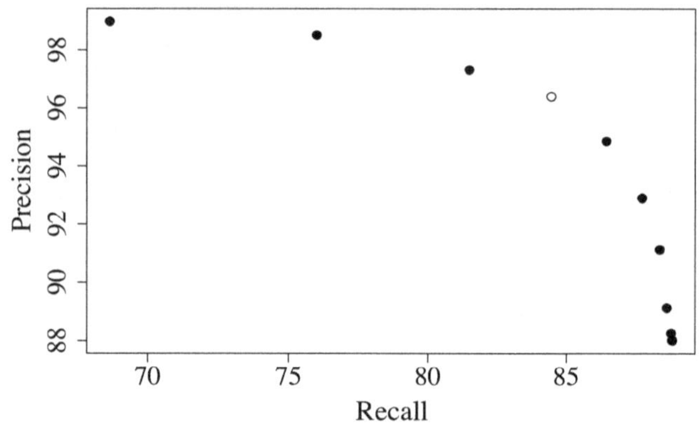

Figure 4. Precision vs. recall in word correction, generated by varying autocorrect threshold from 0.0 (lower right) to 0.95 (upper left). Operating point is white dot, equivalent to Figure 3.

Model	Keystroke Savings %
Background LM Only	42.1
Uniform Cache Adaptation	45.7
Exponential Cache Adaptation	45.8

Table 3. Keystroke savings for various model setups, averaged across all simulated Enron users. See Equation 4 for definition of keystroke savings.

Word Prediction

Table 3 shows keystroke savings results for our efficiency experiments. Without any language modeling (not even a lexicon), keystroke savings would not be possible. The background LM increased (potential) keystroke savings from 0% to 42.1%. When using a cache model for LM personalization, this number was further increased to 45.7%, a relative gain of 8.6%. As before, the uniform cache method performed comparably to the exponentially-decaying cache method.

Results by User

The results in Tables 2 and 3 represent averages over all users in the test set, but LM personalization had different effects on different users. Of the 45 users in the test set, 42 exhibited improved typing accuracy under the uniform cache adaptation method. This relative improvement in WER ranged widely, from 2.9% to 30.9%. Of the three users whose accuracy got worse, one had accuracy decrease from 91.4% to 89.3%, one decreased from 91.5% to 91.1%, and one decreased from 92.9% to 92.7%. All three with decreased performance had fewer than 1500 words in their priming emails, which suggests that it may be prudent to delay the application of cache-based adaptation until a sufficient amount of user text has been collected.

CONCLUSION AND DISCUSSION

Through research methodology innovation and evaluation system development, we have investigated the effects of language models, with and without personalization, for improved accuracy and efficiency of contemporary touch screen keyboards operated with sloppy finger touches. In our benchmark tests, we demonstrated that it was possible to decrease word error rate due to imprecise finger touch tapping from 38.4% to 5.7% using a simple decoder and a background language model. LM personalization further improved this result to 4.6%. Language modeling also improved prediction efficiency to 42.1% (without personalization) and 45.7% (with personalization). The OOV rate of the test set improved from 1.6% to 0.9% using a personalized model. We also showed how raising the autocorrect threshold could lower the false correction rate from 3.5% to 0.7% without significantly affecting overall model performance.

These results were only observable and tuneable because of our novel evaluation methodology. First, we leveraged web-scale data training and entropy pruning to produce a state-of-the-art background LM. Second, the adoption of the Enron Corpus with long-term individual history enabled us to study personalization effects with real-world language use fidelity. Third, we developed a simple yet effective model decoder, which enabled us to measure extrinsic power in an integrated closed loop evaluation system. Fourth, we introduced human-like noisy spatial input in the evaluation based on empirical findings previously reported in the literature. Taken together, these methodological innovations allowed us to efficiently conduct computational experiments over two million words of text, which otherwise would have taken months or years of calendar time to perform. Crucially, this combined closed-loop system also allowed us to report *accuracy* on a large scale (whereas efficiency has been a typical metric in text entry research). We additionally found, somewhat counter-intuitively (but consistent with [30]), that the exponential decay cache model did not outperform the simple uniform cache.

All of these methodological innovations have limitations, as is true of any research methodology. Although we based both the spatial input and the language content on human generated data from [1] and Enron respectively, they were nonetheless simplified to a degree that efficient experiments could be run. Future work needs to replicate and expand these results.

Another opportunity for future work is to study how cognitive errors, particularly spelling errors, affect decoding performance. This would clarify whether the gains we have observed via LM personalization with spatial noise can be observed in a more general error framework. Along this same lines, although we found that adding OOV words to the cache is always desirable in our system, cognitive error would likely introduce the problem of learning misspellings, which may require separate techniques to manage. Other ideas, such as varying the amount of spatial noise, expanding to input methods other than QWERTY, and applying our techniques to gesture typing, are all interesting avenues for future work.

ACKNOWLEDGMENTS

This paper is based on work supported by the National of Institutes of Health under grant R01 DC009834. Any opinions, findings, and conclusions or recommendations expressed in this paper are those of the authors and do not necessarily reflect those of the National Institutes of Health or the authors affiliations.

REFERENCES

1. Azenkot, S., and Zhai, S. Touch behavior with different postures on soft smartphone keyboards. In *Proceedings of the International Conference on Human Computer Interaction with Mobile Devices and Services*, MobileHCI '12, ACM (2012), 251–260.
2. Bellegarda, J. R. Statistical language model adaptation: review and perspectives. *Speech Communication 42* (2004), 93–108.
3. Bi, X., Ouyang, T., and Zhai, S. Both complete and correct? multi-objective optimization of touchscreen keyboard. In *Proceedings of the SIGCHI Conference on Human Factors in Computing Systems*, CHI '14, ACM (2014).
4. Charniak, E., Blaheta, D., Ge, N., Hall, K., Hale, J., and Johnson, M. BLLIP 1987-89 Wall Street Journal Corpus Release 1.
5. Chelba, C., Brants, T., Neveitt, W., and Xu, P. Study on Interaction between Entropy Pruning and Kneser-Ney Smoothing. In *Proc. Interspeech*, ISCA (Makuhari, Japan, 2010), 2242–2245.
6. Chen, S. F., Beeferman, D., and Rosenfield, R. Evaluation metrics for language models. Tech. rep., Carnegie Mellon University, 1998.
7. Chiticariu, L., Krishnamurthy, R., Li, Y., Reiss, F., and Vaithyanathan, S. Domain adaptation of rule-based annotators for named-entity recognition tasks. In *Proceedings of the Conference on Empirical Methods in Natural Language Processing*, EMNLP '10, Association for Computational Linguistics (2010), 1002–1012.
8. Clarkson, P. R., and Robinson, A. J. Language model adaptation using mixtures and an exponentially decaying cache. In *Proceedings of the International Conference on Acoustics, Speech and Signal Processing*, vol. 2 of *ICASSP '97*, IEEE (1997), 799–802.
9. DeMori, R., and Federico, M. Language model adaptation. In *Computational models of speech pattern processing*. Springer, 1999, 280–303.
10. Findlater, L., Wobbrock, J. O., and Wigdor, D. Typing on flat glass: examining ten-finger expert typing patterns on touch surfaces. In *Proceedings of the SIGCHI Conference on Human Factors in Computing Systems*, CHI '11, ACM (2011), 2453–2462.
11. Goodman, J., Venolia, G., Steury, K., and Parker, C. Language modeling for soft keyboards. In *Proceedings of the International Conference on Intelligent User Interfaces*, IUI '02, ACM (New York, NY, USA, 2002), 194–195.
12. Goodman, J. T. A bit of progress in language modeling. *Computer Speech & Language 15*, 4 (2001), 403–434.
13. Holz, C., and Baudisch, P. Understanding touch. In *Proceedings of the SIGCHI Conference on Human Factors in Computing Systems*, CHI '11, ACM (2011), 2501–2510.

14. Jones, K. S. Towards better NLP system evaluation. In *Proceedings of the Workshop on Human Language Technology*, Association for Computational Linguistics (1994), 102–107.

15. Jurafsky, D., and Martin, J. H. *Speech & Language Processing*, second ed. Prentice Hall, 2008.

16. Katz, S. Estimation of probabilities from sparse data for the language model component of a speech recognizer. In *Proceedings of the International Conference on Acoustics, Speech and Signal Processing*, vol. 35 number 3 of *ICASSP '87*, IEEE (1987), 400–01.

17. Klarlund, N., and Riley, M. Word n-grams for cluster keyboards. In *Proceedings of the EACL Workshop on Language Modeling for Text Entry Methods*, TextEntry '03, Association for Computational Linguistics (Stroudsburg, PA, USA, 2003), 51–58.

18. Klimt, B., and Yang, Y. Introducing the Enron corpus. In *Proceedings of the Conference on Email and Anti-Spam*, CEAS '04 (2004).

19. Kneser, R., and Ney, H. Improved backing-off for m-gram language modeling. In *Proceedings of the International Conference on Acoustics, Speech and Signal Processing*, vol. 1 of *ICASSP '95*, IEEE (1995), 181–184.

20. Kristensson, P. O., and Vertanen, K. Asynchronous multimodal text entry using speech and gesture keyboards. In *Proc. Interspeech* (2011), 581–584.

21. Kristensson, P. O., and Vertanen, K. Performance comparisons of phrase sets and presentation styles for text entry evaluations. In *Proceedings of the International Conference on Intelligent User Interfaces*, IUI '12, ACM (2012), 29–32.

22. Kristensson, P. O., and Zhai, S. SHARK2: A large vocabulary shorthand writing system for pen-based computers. In *Proceedings of the ACM Symposium on User Interface Software and Technology*, UIST '04, ACM (New York, NY, USA, 2004), 43–52.

23. Kristensson, P. O., and Zhai, S. Improving word-recognizers using an interactive lexicon with active and passive words. In *Proceedings of the International Conference on Intelligent User Interfaces*, IUI '08, ACM (2008), 353–356.

24. Kuhn, R., and De Mori, R. A cache-based natural language model for speech recognition. *Pattern Analysis and Machine Intelligence, IEEE Transactions on 12*, 6 (1990), 570–583.

25. MacKenzie, I. S., and Soukoreff, R. W. Text entry for mobile computing: Models and methods, theory and practice. *Human–Computer Interaction 17*, 2-3 (2002), 147–198.

26. Paek, T., and Hsu, B.-J. P. Sampling representative phrase sets for text entry experiments: a procedure and public resource. In *Proceedings of the SIGCHI Conference on Human Factors in Computing Systems*, CHI '11, ACM (2011), 2477–2480.

27. Sandu, O., Carenini, G., Murray, G., and Ng, R. Domain adaptation to summarize human conversations. In *Proceedings of the Workshop on Domain Adaptation for Natural Language Processing*, Association for Computational Linguistics (2010), 16–22.

28. Smith, S. L., and Goodwin, N. C. Alphabetic data entry via the Touch-Tone pad: A comment. *Human Factors: The Journal of the Human Factors and Ergonomics Society 13*, 2 (1971), 189–190.

29. Stolcke, A. Entropy-based pruning of back-off language models. In *Proceedings of News Transcription and Understanding Workshop*, DARPA (Lansdowne, VA, 1998), 270–274.

30. Tanaka-Ishii, K. Word-based predictive text entry using adaptive language models. *Natural Language Engineering 13* (2 2007), 51–74.

31. Vertanen, K., and Kristensson, P. O. A versatile dataset for text entry evaluations based on genuine mobile emails. In *Proceedings of the International Conference on Human-Computer Interaction with Mobile Devices and Services*, MobileHCI '11 (August 2011).

32. Ward, D. J., Blackwell, A. F., and MacKay, D. J. Dashera data entry interface using continuous gestures and language models. In *Proceedings of the ACM Symposium on User Interface Software and Technology*, UIST '00, ACM (2000), 129–137.

33. Weir, D., Pohl, H., Rogers, S., Vertanen, K., and Kristensson, P. O. Uncertain text entry on mobile devices. In *Proceedings of the SIGCHI Conference on Human Factors in Computing Systems*, CHI '14 (April 2014), 2307–2316.

34. Yin, Y., Ouyang, T. Y., Partridge, K., and Zhai, S. Making touchscreen keyboards adaptive to keys, hand postures, and individuals: a hierarchical spatial backoff model approach. In *Proceedings of the SIGCHI Conference on Human Factors in Computing Systems*, CHI '13, ACM (2013), 2775–2784.

35. Zajic, D. M., Dorr, B. J., and Lin, J. Single-document and multi-document summarization techniques for email threads using sentence compression. *Information Processing & Management 44*, 4 (2008), 1600–1610.

36. Zhai, S., and Kristensson, P. O. Shorthand writing on stylus keyboard. In *Proceedings of the SIGCHI Conference on Human Factors in Computing Systems*, CHI '03, ACM (New York, NY, USA, 2003), 97–104.

37. Zhai, S., and Kristensson, P. O. The word-gesture keyboard: reimagining keyboard interaction. *Commun. ACM 55*, 9 (Sept. 2012), 91–101.

VelociTap: Investigating Fast Mobile Text Entry using Sentence-Based Decoding of Touchscreen Keyboard Input

Keith Vertanen[1], Haythem Memmi[1], Justin Emge[1], Shyam Reyal[2], Per Ola Kristensson[2,3]
[1]Montana Tech, USA, [2]University of St Andrews, UK, [3]University of Cambridge, UK
{kvertanen | hbmemmi | jemge}@mtech.edu, smr20@st-andrews.ac.uk, pok21@cam.ac.uk

ABSTRACT
We present VelociTap: a state-of-the-art touchscreen keyboard decoder that supports a sentence-based text entry approach. VelociTap enables users to seamlessly choose from three word-delimiter actions: pushing a space key, swiping to the right, or simply omitting the space key and letting the decoder infer spaces automatically. We demonstrate that VelociTap has a significantly lower error rate than Google's keyboard while retaining the same entry rate. We show that intermediate visual feedback does not significantly affect entry or error rates and we find that using the space key results in the most accurate results. We also demonstrate that enabling flexible word-delimiter options does not incur an error rate penalty. Finally, we investigate how small we can make the keyboard when using VelociTap. We show that novice users can reach a mean entry rate of 41 wpm on a 40 mm wide smartwatch-sized keyboard at a 3% character error rate.

Author Keywords
Mobile text entry; touchscreen keyboard; sentence decoding

ACM Classification Keywords
H.5.2. Information Interfaces and Presentation: User Interfaces—*Input devices and strategies*

INTRODUCTION
A common text entry method on touchscreen mobile devices is an on-screen keyboard. Several solutions have been proposed to improve mobile touchscreen typing. One approach is to partially or completely redesign the standard QWERTY touchscreen typing experience. Examples include gesture keyboards [13], optimized keyboards such as ATOMIK [23], interlaced QWERTY [22], the quasi-Qwerty optimized keyboard [2], multidimensional Pareto keyboard optimization [5], multilingual keyboard optimization [3], KALQ [17], and systems that adapt to user input or sensor data (e.g. [4, 6]).

Another approach is to keep the QWERTY touchscreen keyboard but assist users by offering predictions and automatic typing correction. Goodman et al. [9] were the first to propose correcting touchscreen typing errors by combining a probabilistic touch model and a character language model. Their system corrects errors on a character-by-character basis. Kristensson and Zhai [14] propose a dictionary-based word-level correction system based on geometric pattern matching. Recently, several touchscreen typing systems have leveraged additional information, such as activity (walking versus standing) [7], or hand posture [8]. Other recent improvements include using pressure information and Gaussian Process regression within a probabilistic decoder [21], and the development of an algorithm that simultaneously accommodates both completions and corrections [1].

Commercial systems, such as SwiftKey, Fleksy, and the built-in Android and iOS keyboards, perform automatic error correction on a letter-by-letter and word-basis. Some, such as the built-in Android keyboard, support sentence-based entry by allowing the entry of words without spaces and then performing separation and autocorrection when the user hits the space key. To our knowledge, no work has explored the performance and design aspects of such sentence-based entry.

In this work, we explore the performance potential of *sentence-based decoding*: delaying automatic typing correction until after an entire sentence has been entered. We have developed a state-of-the-art touchscreen keyboard decoder called VelociTap that supports sentence-based decoding. VelociTap enables users to seamlessly choose from three word-delimiter actions: pushing a space key, swiping to the right, or simply omitting the space key and letting the decoder infer spaces automatically. VelociTap was iteratively designed based on two pilot studies. The pilots established users could actuate taps quickly even without recognition feedback after each word. Further, despite the noisy input resulting from users aiming for speed instead of accuracy, we could still accurately recognize the input.

Given the promising performance seen in the pilots, we investigated three design aspects we suspected could further increase the speed and utility of the approach: intermediate visual feedback, word-delimiter action, and effective keyboard size. We show that intermediate visual feedback does not significantly affect entry or error rate. We find that using the space key to delimit words provides the best accuracy. We also show we can offer users flexibility in word-delimiter actions without impacting accuracy. Finally, we investigate how small we can make the keyboard. VelociTap enables novice users to reach a mean entry rate of 41 wpm on a 40 mm smartwatch-sized keyboard at a 3% character error rate.

CHI 2015, April 18 - 23 2015, Seoul, Republic of Korea

http://dx.doi.org/10.1145/2702123.2702135

VELOCITAP DECODER

Our decoder takes a sequence of noisy touch events and searches for the most probable sentence given that sequence of touches. The decoder uses a probabilistic keyboard model, a character language model, and a word language model.

We assume the user is entering the letters A–Z plus space and only consider lowercase text. For each touchscreen tap, the keyboard model produces a likelihood for each of the 27 characters. Similar to previous work [9], the likelihood of each key is given by a two-dimensional Gaussian distribution centered at each key. The x- and y-variance of a key's Gaussian distribution is computed by multiplying the x- and y-size of each key in pixels by an x- and y-scale factor. We use the same two scale factors for every key. We use the first (x, y) coordinate in a touch event to calculate the key likelihoods.

We combine the keyboard likelihood with a prior probability from the language model. This is done by adding the keyboard model log probability to the language model log probability multiplied by a scaling factor. The scaling factor controls the relative contribution of the keyboard model and the language model. Log probabilities are used to prevent underflow. During the decoder's initial search, we use a 12-gram language model that bases the probability of the next character on the previous 11 characters (including space).

Our initial search finds a list of up to the 50-best sentence hypotheses. After the search completes, we add to each hypothesis the log probability of the sentence under a word language model. We used a 4-gram language model that bases the probability of the next word on the three previous words.

We trained our language models on billions of words from blog, social media, and Usenet data. We optimized our models for mobile text using cross-entropy difference selection [15]. In this method, only sentences well-matched to an in-domain language model are used in training. We created the in-domain model from email sentences with 1–12 words from the W3C email corpus and the non-spam messages in the TREC 2005 corpus. We trained a separate language model on each corpus and then created a mixture model using linear interpolation with weights optimized on held-out text.

Our 12-gram character language model had 103 M N-grams and a compressed size of 1.1 GB. Our 4-gram word model was trained with an unknown word and had 194 M N-grams and a compressed size of 2.0 GB. The word model's vocabulary consisted of the most frequent 64 K words in our training data that were also in a list of 330 K words compiled from human-edited dictionaries[1]. We used BerkeleyLM [18] for language model probability lookups.

A very common type of touchscreen typing error is substituting one letter for another. This is due to the difficulty of precisely tapping small buttons with a large finger. But users may also occasionally tap an extra key or skip a key altogether. To handle this, at each position in the tap sequence, our decoder adds a deletion hypothesis and a set of insertion hypotheses.

[1]Compiled from Wiktionary, Project Gutenberg Webster's dictionary, CMU pronouncing dictionary, and GNU aspell.

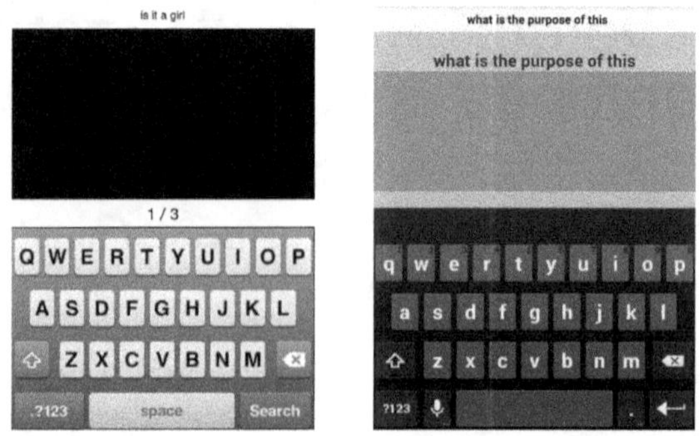

Figure 1. Interfaces in the first pilot (left) and second pilot (right).

The deletion hypothesis drops the current tap without generating any text. The insertion hypotheses add all possible characters (including space) before the next observed tap.

Our decoder searches the hypothesis space of all possible character sequences given a sequence of taps. In order to keep the search tractable, we employ beam pruning. We prune any hypothesis that becomes too improbable compared to the best previous hypothesis at a given position in the tap sequence. By varying the beam width, we can control the tradeoff between speed and accuracy. In our first two pilot studies, we will use a decoder that searches via a recursive depth-first algorithm. The algorithm operates on a single thread, exploring hypotheses in probability-ranked order during its descent.

The decoder's free parameters consist of the x- and y-keyboard variance factors, character and word language model scale factors, and penalties for insertions and deletions. As we will describe later in this paper, we optimized these parameters on development data.

VelociTap can operate either offline on recorded traces or online performing real-time recognition. Real-time recognition can be performed either on the mobile device or proxied to a remote server. In this work we are interested in the performance potential independent of device resource constraints. As such, we used a remote server for all recognition.

PERFORMANCE PILOT 1

The goals of this pilot study were to explore the performance potential of VelociTap and to investigate if users could effectively tap out sentences without feedback from the interface.

We developed a data collection app for 4th generation iPhones. Our app displayed an image of the standard iPhone QWERTY keyboard in portrait configuration (Figure 1, left). Our app displayed stimuli sentences at the top and recorded touch events. No actual recognition took place on the device. While typing, participants received no audio, visual, or tactile feedback. After completing a sentence, the app displayed the entry rate in words-per-minute. Since no recognition result was available during the pilot, this entry rate was based on the number of characters in the corresponding stimulus.

We recruited 45 participants who were aged 18–57 (mean = 24). 26% were female, and 73% were university students. Participants were not paid, rather we offered a prize of a Nexus 7 tablet to whoever had the highest entry rate subject

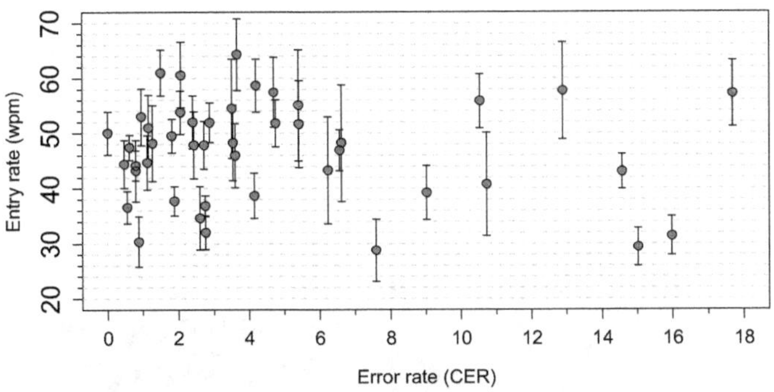

Figure 2. The error and entry rate of each participant in the first pilot. Vertical whiskers show one standard deviation.

to a maximum recognition character error rate of 10% (determined later in offline recognition experiments).

Participants were allowed to practice on three sentences. Participants in this pilot, as well as all other studies in this paper, were instructed to hold the device in their non-dominant hand and use a single finger of their dominant hand to type. Participants then entered 20 short sentences (3–8 words) taken at random from memorable sentences written by Enron employees on their Blackberry mobile devices [19]. Afterwards, participants completed a short questionnaire.

We conducted offline experiments on the logged data. Our decoder's parameters were optimized with respect to 400 sentences typed by two of the authors. We measured the entry rate in words-per-minute (wpm), with a word defined as five characters including spaces. The number of characters was based on the recognition result. We timed entries from a sentence's first tap until the user moved to the next sentence by tapping with two fingers. Participants' average entry rate was 46.8 wpm (sd = 4.7, min = 28.7, max = 64.3).

We measured error rate using character error rate (CER). CER is the number of insertion, substitution and deletions required to turn the recognized text into the reference text, divided by the number of characters in the reference text. Despite receiving no feedback during typing, participants' error rates were low with an average CER of 4.7% (sd = 4.6, min = 0.0, max = 17.7). We found that nearly two-thirds of sentences were decoded with no recognition errors. A good language model was critical for decoding. Simply using the key closest to each tap resulted in a high average CER of 20.2%.

As shown in Figure 2, each participant operated at different points in the error and entry rate envelope. Notably, 31 of the 45 participants had error rates of less than 5% CER. They did so while entering text at 30–64 wpm. This shows that novice users can quickly adapt to writing entire sentences without intermediate feedback. While the participants in the first pilot did not see any recognition results, they still provided tap data that could be decoded with a high degree of accuracy.

A sentence-based decoder may have an advantage in that it can search for the best text given all the data. Touchscreen keyboards typically perform auto-correction only on the previous word. To investigate the impact of sentence-based decoding, we modified our decoder to limit its search to a window of the last N characters. So for example, at a window

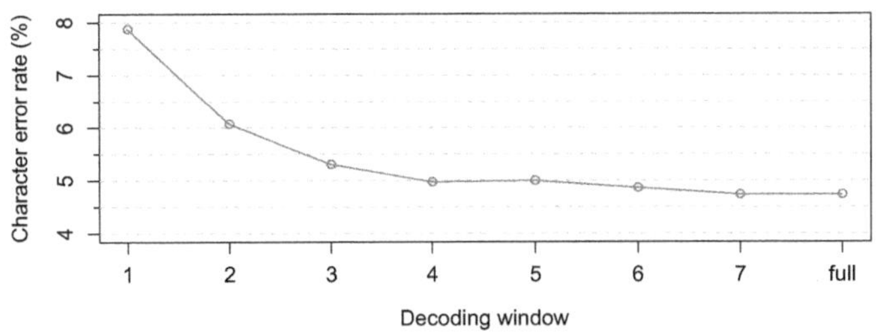

Figure 3. Error rate in the first pilot, varying how many previous characters the decoder was allowed to change. The label "full" indicates decoding over the entire sentence.

size of 1, the decoder found the next best character given the current observation but with all prior characters fixed.

As shown in Figure 3, increasing the freedom of the recognizer to change past characters improved accuracy. Gains were small beyond a window size of five. Assuming a word length of five, this suggests existing interfaces based on auto-correction of only the last word are providing accuracy similar to full-sentence decoding. However, as previously mentioned, sentence-based decoding may still have an advantage in that it avoids distracting users while they enter text.

PERFORMANCE PILOT 2

For our second pilot, we designed an app to provide real-time sentence-based decoding of taps entered on a mobile device. The goals of this pilot were to investigate how practice and real-time feedback of recognition results affects performance.

We used a client/server setup in which the user interacted with the mobile device and recognition was performed on a 3.6 GHz 8-core server. We used an Android Nexus 4 mobile device which has a screen measuring 101 mm × 60 mm. Our interface used an image of the Google keyboard in portrait orientation (Figure 1, right). Taps played a click sound and vibrated the device. Our decoder's parameters were optimized with respect to 251 sentences typed by two of the authors plus four users who had taken part in the first pilot. These four users did not take part in this pilot.

We called back six participants who had taken part in the first pilot. The six participants were the first to respond to our request for participation in the follow-up pilot. They were aged 21–29 (mean = 24), one was female, and five were university students. They were paid $20 and told the fastest participant with a CER below 5% would receive a $20 bonus.

In this study, participants received real-time feedback of the recognized sentence along with the entry and error rate based on the recognition. Participants entered 12 blocks of 20 sentences in a 2-hour session. The 240 sentences were taken from the Enron mobile test set [19]. We chose sentences with 5–10 words that had been memorized correctly by at least 6 out of 10 workers in [19]. Sentence order was randomized.

Before the first block, participants were allowed to practice on a set of three sentences. After each block, the app showed the average entry and error rate for that block. Participants took a short break between blocks. After the sixth block, participants took a longer break of about 10 minutes.

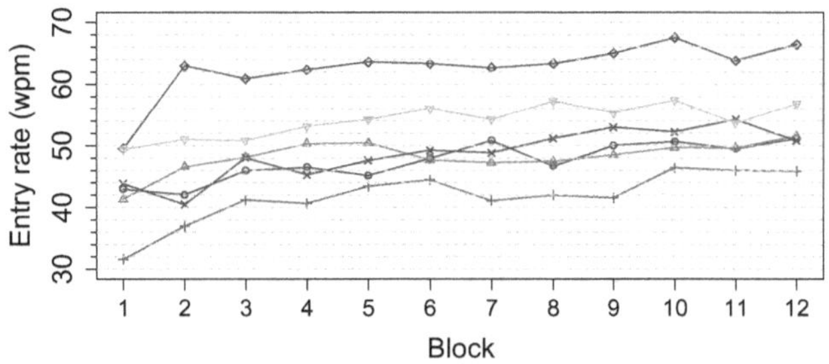

Figure 4. Entry rate on each block of 20 sentences in the second pilot. Each line is a single participant.

The entry rate was measured from a sentence's first tap until the recognition result was displayed. Recognition was performed after the user typed an entire sentence and then touched a large orange area with two fingers. The delay between a user's double-touch and the display of the recognition result averaged 0.17 s per sentence. This delay included both network latency and decoding time.

As shown in Figure 4, participants' entry rates were fast with an average per-participant entry rate of 50.5 wpm. The entry rate increased from 43.1 wpm in the first block to 53.8 wpm in the final block. Repeated measures analysis of variance showed a statistically significant main effect for block ($F_{1,5} = 13.894, \eta_p^2 = 0.735, p < 0.001$). Our fastest participant had an entry rate of 62.6 wpm with a CER of 2.5%.

Error rates were low with an average CER of 4.5%. Repeated measures analysis of variance showed that error rates did not significantly vary across the blocks ($F_{1,5} = 1.872, \eta_p^2 = 0.272, p = 0.064$).

IMPROVED DECODER

Based on the decoder's performance in our pilot studies, and in order to support our planned experiments, we made a variety of improvements to VelociTap. We enhanced our ability to automatically insert spaces. This was done by first introducing a space insertion penalty separate from the general insertion penalty (which inserts all possible characters). By setting a smaller penalty for space insertions, the decoder can more readily infer spaces when users omit spaces altogether.

Our single-threaded recursive depth-first algorithm was too slow when numerous space insertions were needed. We replaced our search algorithm with a multi-threaded algorithm. In the new algorithm, threads first choose a random partial hypothesis, each consisting of its position within the observation sequence, its previously generated text, and its accumulated log probability. A thread extends a partial hypothesis by one observation, creating a set of new partial hypotheses. By proceeding in this way, the search is able to quickly find hypotheses requiring the insertion of many spaces.

Previously, we applied a word language model only after completing a sentence hypothesis. We modified the decoder to assess word language model probabilities during its search. Additionally, we added an out-of-vocabulary (OOV) penalty based on whether a word was in a list of 64 K frequent words. This allows explicit adjustment of the penalty incurred by OOV words independent of what would result by just using the character and word language models.

Figure 5. Google (left) and VelociTap interfaces (right) in Experiment 1. The user is tapping "m" and this key's popup is being shown.

We added support for a backspace key that deletes the previous tap event. Currently we treat the backspace key deterministically: a tap is considered a backspace if its location is closer to the backspace key than any other key. We also added support for right and left swipe gestures. A swipe is detected based on a gesture's distance and angle. Such gestures will be used to enter spaces or to delete a previous tap.

EXPERIMENT 1: VISUAL FEEDBACK

Our pilot studies explored the performance potential of sentence-based entry. We conjectured the lack of visual feedback in the pilot studies contributed to the fast entry rates. The goal of Experiment 1 was to determine whether this was in fact the case. Since a user can enter text arbitrarily fast by ignoring accuracy, we also compare our accuracy against that of a commercial state-of-the-art error-correcting keyboard.

Study Design, Apparatus, and Procedure

We used a within-subject design with three conditions:

- **GOOGLEFEEDBACK** – Participants entered text using the Google keyboard (Figure 5, left). Google's keyboard performs sentence decoding if a user enters a sequence of words without spaces (e.g. "thecatsat"). For each tap, the nearest character was added to a text area below the stimulus sentence. Tapping the backspace key deleted the last character. Upon hitting the space key, the entry was decoded and the recognition result replaced the nearest character text. Swiping up moved to the next sentence and displayed the error and entry rate for the previous sentence.

  We configured the Google keyboard to vibrate for 8 ms, to make the standard keyboard click sound, and to show popups on each key press. We set the auto-correction level to "very aggressive". We disabled correction suggestions, gesture typing, and auto-capitalization.
- **VTFEEDBACK** – Participants entered text using VelociTap (Figure 5, right). Taps caused an 8 ms vibration, made a click sound, and displayed a key popup. For each tap, the nearest character to the tap was added to a text area below the stimulus sentence. Tapping the backspace key deleted the last character. Participants swiped up to perform recognition. The recognition result replaced the nearest character text and displayed the error and entry for that sentence. Swiping up again moved to the next sentence.

	Entry rate (wpm)	Error rate (CER %)	Backspaces per sentence
GOOGLEFEEDBACK	43.4 ± 8.7 [28.9, 59.7]	5.2 ± 5.8 [0.8, 28.8]	0.23 ± 0.30 [0.00, 1.30]
VTFEEDBACK	41.9 ± 8.9 [26.8, 65.3]	**1.8** ± 2.3 [0.0, 11.3]	0.18 ± 0.28 [0.00, 1.20]
VTNOFEEDBACK	**43.5** ± 8.0 [29.5, 62.2]	2.7 ± 3.5 [0.0, 15.9]	**0.09** ± 0.17 [0.00, 0.80]
Omnibus test	$F_{2,46} = 2.256$, $\eta_p^2 = 0.089$, $p = 0.116$	$F_{2,46} = 16.169$, $\eta_p^2 = 0.413$, $p < 0.0001$	$F_{2,46} = 3.313$, $\eta_p^2 = 0.126$, $p < 0.05$
Significant pairs	n/a	GOOGLEFEED > VTFEED, $p < 0.01$ GOOGLEFEED > VTNOFEED, $p < 0.01$ GOOGLEFEED ≈ VTNOFEED, $p = 0.074$	None significant, $p > 0.09$

Table 1. Statistics from Experiment 1. Results are formatted as: mean ± sd [min, max].

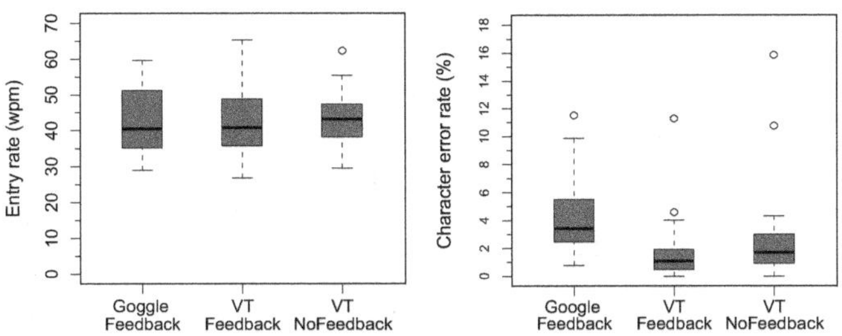

Figure 6. Entry rate (left) and error rate (right) in Experiment 1.

- **VTNOFEEDBACK** – This was similar to the previous condition but without visual feedback during entry. There were no key popups and no text was displayed until after recognition was performed. Participants could still type a backspace, but there was no indication of its effect.

The decoder's parameters were optimized on development data recorded by three of the authors. This data consisted of each author tapping 100 sentences without spaces.

We used a Nexus 4 mobile device in portrait orientation. In all conditions, the keyboard appeared on the bottom section of the screen. The keyboard measured 60 mm × 35 mm with each letter key measuring 5 mm × 6 mm.

We recruited 24 participants via convenience sampling. Participants were paid £5 for taking part in a one-hour session. None of the participants had participated in previous experiments. Participants were aged 18–32 (mean = 25), 75% were male, 88% were computer science majors, and 67% were native English speakers. On a 7-point Likert scale where 7 = strongly agree, participants rated the statement "I consider myself a fluent speaker of English" from 5–7 (mean = 6.4).

For each participant, we drew a random subset of 60 sentences from the set of 240 sentences used in the second pilot. Participants typed 20 sentences in each condition. The order of conditions was balanced. After completing all conditions, participants filled out a paper questionnaire.

The study was conducted in the UK. In the GOOGLEFEEDBACK condition, recognition was performed on the Nexus 4. In the VTFEEDBACK and VTNOFEEDBACK conditions, recognition took place on a 3.2 GHz 6-core US-based server.

Results

Unless otherwise noted, we tested for significance using a repeated measures analysis of variance. For significant main effects, we used Bonferroni corrected post-hoc tests.

Entry rate was measured from a user's first tap until the recognition was displayed. VelociTap took 0.92 s to return a result

"I consider visual feedback an important factor in improving accuracy"
"nice to have a bit of feedback with each keypress"
"more comfortable for a first time user"
"if I lose my focus while typing I can find my place again"
"in the real world I would prefer visual feedback to avoid too much stress"
"seeing what I type gives a better idea of what I am writing"
"I preferred having feedback to keep track of my progress"

Table 2. Comments supporting feedback in Experiment 1.

(80% due to network latency). The Google keyboard returned results nearly instantly. As shown in Figure 6 (left), average entry rates were similar: GOOGLEFEEDBACK 43.4 wpm, VTFEEDBACK 41.9 wpm, and VTNOFEEDBACK 43.5 wpm. These differences were not significant (Table 1, left).

Error rate was measured by computing the CER of the recognition against the stimulus. As shown in Figure 6 (right), participants' average error rate was higher in GOOGLEFEEDBACK 5.2%, compared to VTFEEDBACK 1.8%, and VTNOFEEDBACK 2.7%. The higher error rate in GOOGLEFEEDBACK was statistically significant (Table 1, center).

In 10 sentences out of 480 in GOOGLEFEEDBACK participants hit the space key more than once. This triggers multiple decodes, potentially making accurate recognition more difficult. Additionally, we observed the Google keyboard failed to perform any decoding on 29 sentences. Google's keyboard strictly speaking has a harder job as it does not know whether sentence-based decoding is desired or not. Removing these 39 sentences from the data, the error rate in GOOGLEFEEDBACK was still 2.8%. Thus even under these generous assumptions, VelociTap compares favorably in accuracy. We are however using substantially more computational resources than Google's on-device decoder. But from a research standpoint, this frees us to explore future-looking designs that might not be currently possible on-device.

Users could hit the backspace key to erase the last tap. The average backspaces per sentence were: GOOGLEFEEDBACK 0.23, VTFEEDBACK 0.18, and VTNOFEEDBACK 0.09. No pairwise differences were significant (Table 1, right).

We asked participants which of the three interfaces they would choose if they could have only one on their mobile device. 11 participants preferred VTFEEDBACK, 8 preferred VTNOFEEDBACK, and 5 preferred GOOGLEFEEDBACK. As shown in Table 2 and 3, participants' open comments also reflect this mixed preference about visual feedback.

EXPERIMENT 2: WORD-DELIMITER ACTIONS

Our previous experiment showed that while omitting intermediate visual feedback during entry might have slightly increased entry rate, it might have also slightly increased error

	Entry rate (wpm)	Error rate (CER %)	Backspaces per sentence
NoSpace	**31.6** ± 8.6 [21.1, 52.8]	6.6 ± 6.3 [0.0, 18.1]	**0.46** ± 0.44 [0.05, 1.55]
Space	30.2 ± 7.2 [19.2, 46.5]	**1.1** ± 1.0 [0.0, 4.0]	0.89 ± 0.92 [0.00, 3.65]
Swipe	26.8 ± 5.8 [20.1, 41.3]	1.8 ± 2.1 [0.0, 7.1]	0.79 ± 0.83 [0.05, 3.10]
Omnibus test	$F_{2,46} = 15.342$, $\eta_p^2 = 0.400$, $p < 0.0001$	$F_{2,46} = 14.949$, $\eta_p^2 = 0.394$, $p < 0.0001$	$F_{2,46} = 4.957$, $\eta_p^2 = 0.177$, $p < 0.05$
Significant pairs	Swipe < Space, NoSpace, $p < 0.01$	NoSpace > Space, Swipe, $p < 0.01$	NoSpace < Space, Swipe, $p < 0.05$
	NoSpace ≈ Space, $p = 0.524$	Space ≈ Swipe, $p = 0.399$	Space ≈ Swipe, $p = 1.0$

Table 4. Statistics from Experiment 2. Results are formatted as: mean ± sd [min, max].

"allowed me to concentrate on typing and not what I had already typed"
"a hindrance, when walking and texting I am unlikely to check"
"without it I felt more free to go for speed and trust the autocorrection"
"having feedback slowed me down"
"trusting the algorithm I typed faster and focused more on the keyboard"
"noticing a mistake while typing delays typing"
"visual feedback was more distracting even though I didn't look at it"
"focus more on placing taps faster and more accurately"

Table 3. Comments supporting no feedback in Experiment 1.

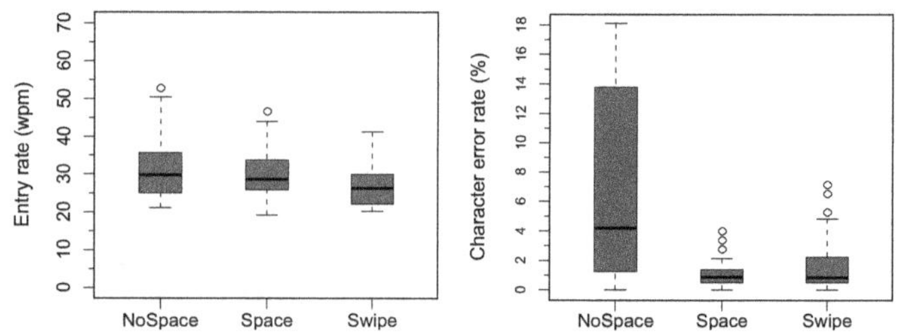

Figure 7. Entry rate (left) and error rate (right) in Experiment 2.

rate. Given that users have come to expect visual feedback as they type, we opted to use visual feedback in Experiment 2.

The Google keyboard uses spaceless entry in its sentence-based decoding approach. This design choice allows users to switch between more typical word-at-a-time entry and sentence-based entry. However, such spaceless entry is only one possible design choice. The goal of Experiment 2 was to investigate the impact of different actions users could take to delimit words. Our hypothesis was that providing no spaces during entry would be faster but cause more recognition errors than explicitly tapping a space key. Further, we conjectured that using a swiping gesture in lieu of tapping a space key [13] would provide a further reduction in errors.

Study Design, Apparatus, and Procedure

We used a within-subject design with three conditions:

- **NoSpace** – Participants typed all the letters of a sentence with no explicit separator between words. This is similar to how current commercial keyboards such as Google and SwiftKey support sentence-based entry. In this condition, the decoder investigated space insertions between all taps. The tap observations themselves were not allowed to generate a space (i.e. even a tap on the space key was considered to be a nearby letter and not a space).
- **Space** – Participants tapped the space key between words. In this condition, the decoder's keyboard model treated spaces probabilistically just like any other character on the keyboard (i.e. the probability of a character was determined by the distance to the center of the key).
- **Swipe** – Participants made a right swipe gesture anywhere on the screen between words. A swipe was considered any touch trace with a horizontal width above a configurable threshold. Upon detecting a swipe, the interface played a "whooshing" sound. Swipes were treated deterministically during the decoder search (i.e. a swipe had to be a space and taps were never considered to be spaces).

The decoder's parameters for each condition were optimized with respect to development data recorded by three of the authors. This data consisted of 100 sentences entered by each of the authors using the three different word-delimiter actions.

We used a Nexus 4 mobile device with recognition taking place on a 3.6 GHz 8-core server. The Nexus 4 and server were connected to the same Wi-Fi access point. Users could tap the backspace key to delete the previous character. The displayed keyboard was identical between conditions. In the NoSpace and Swipe conditions, participants were instructed not to tap the space key even though it was visible.

We recruited 24 participants via convenience sampling. Participants were paid $10 for taking part in a one-hour session. None of the participants had participated in previous experiments. Participants were aged from 18–46 (mean = 26), 83% were male, 29% were computer science majors, and 64% were native English speakers. On a 7-point Likert scale where 7 = strongly agree, participants rated the statement "I consider myself a fluent speaker of English" from 5–7 (mean = 6.6).

For each participant, we drew a random subset of 60 sentences from the set of 240 sentences used in the second pilot. Participants typed 20 sentences in each condition. The order of conditions was balanced. After completing all conditions, participants filled out a paper questionnaire.

Results

Entry rate was measured from a user's first tap until the recognition was displayed. VelociTap took about 0.26 s to return a result. As shown in Figure 7 (left), NoSpace had the fastest average entry rate of 31.6 wpm, followed by Space at 30.2 wpm, and Swipe at 26.8 wpm. Swipe was significantly slower (Table 4, left).

Error rate was measured by computing the CER of the recognition against the stimulus. As shown in Figure 7 (right), participants' average error rate was highest in NoSpace at 6.6%, followed by Swipe at 1.8%, and Space at 1.1%. NoSpace had a significantly higher error rate (Table 4, center).

Error rates in NoSpace were highly variable (Figure 8). For some users, the decoder frequently failed to insert spaces between words (a failure we also saw with the Google keyboard in Experiment 1). As we will discuss, tuning on more spaceless data and a wider beam width eliminated this problem.

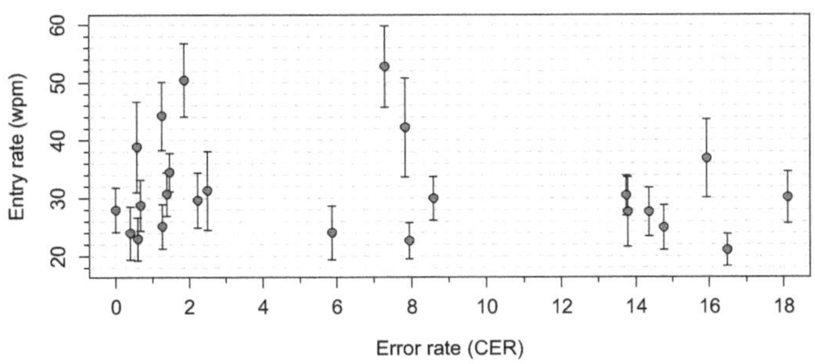

Figure 8. Error and entry rate of participants in NOSPACE condition of Experiment 2. Vertical whiskers show one standard deviation.

Users could hit the backspace key to erase the last tap. Participants' average backspaces per sentence were: NOSPACE 0.46, SPACE 0.89, and SWIPE 0.79. NOSPACE resulted in significantly fewer backspaces (Table 4, right).

At the end of the experiment, participants were asked which of the three spacing strategies they preferred. 13 participants preferred SPACE, 7 preferred SWIPE, and 3 preferred NOSPACE (one participant failed to complete the question).

Comments from those preferring SPACE focused on its familiarity: "aversion to change", "more intuitive", "I am used to this", "well adjusted to the spacebar...I don't have to make any extra movement", "more familiar with it", "more natural, programmed into muscle memory", "the only method I have used all my life", "the default in my brain will always be to hit the spacebar", "like computer typing", and "more normal".

Those preferring SWIPE commented on the accuracy and feel: "Because I hit other letters when I press the spacebar", "it was new and easy to pick up", "intuitive and functional", and "allowed for more accuracy...I liked the feel...allowed me to look at key display".

Those preferring NOSPACE commented mostly on the speed advantage: "typed faster...was very accurate", "faster to type out sentences", and "I type the fastest with this interface...very easy, natural adjustment to omit spaces".

Offline Experiments and Combining Actions

Prior to Experiment 2, we had limited data to tune for each word-delimiter action. We used the data from the first 12 participants in Experiment 2 to tune a set of parameters for each action (skipping spaces, hitting the space key, or swiping right). We also combined data from all actions, creating a setup supporting any of the three actions. We tested each of the four setups against subsets of the unseen data from the second 12 participants in Experiment 2. Additionally, we widened the beam width in hopes of reducing errors.

Table 5 shows that using a setup matched to the test set provided low error rates in all cases. More importantly, a setup combining all actions performed well regardless of the test set. Even with a wider beam width, the combined setup recognized traces in the combined test set in about 0.04 s (sd = 0.025, min = 0.01, max = 0.44). Thus it appears possible to support all actions within the same setup, allowing users the flexibility to delimit words however they like.

Decoder setup	Test set			
	NOSPACE	SPACE	SWIPE	COMBO
NOSPACE	**1.4**	2.1	10.8	4.8
SPACE	4.3	1.3	13.7	6.5
SWIPE	27.3	26.2	2.4	18.6
COMBO	2.1	**1.2**	**2.0**	**1.8**

Table 5. Error rates on different test sets using different decoder setups.

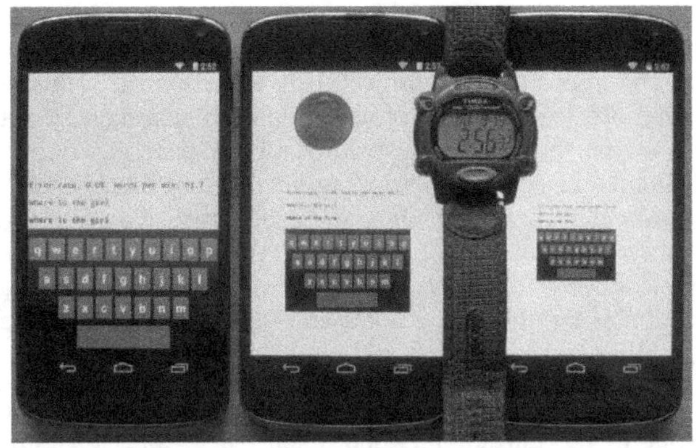

Figure 9. The three keyboard layouts used in Experiment 3 running on Nexus 4 devices. A penny and Timex Expedition watch added for scale.

EXPERIMENT 3: KEYBOARD SIZE

Experiments 1 and 2 showed that sentence-based decoding was fast and accurate on a full-sized portrait keyboard. Based on these experiments, we arrived at a very accurate decoder setup (1.8% CER) allowing flexible word-delimiter actions. The purpose of Experiment 3 was to investigate if this setup could enable users to type on smaller keyboards while retaining their existing typing behavior (i.e. tapping on an unmodified QWERTY keyboard). Smaller keyboards may be useful on normal-sized devices in order to reduce occlusion, reduce motor demands, or to allow one-handed entry. They may also be useful on wearable devices such as smartwatches.

Study Design, Apparatus, and Procedure

We used a within-subject design with three conditions:

- **NORMAL** – Participants used a full-sized portrait keyboard measuring 60 mm × 40 mm with letters measuring 5.2 mm × 7.0 mm.
- **SMALL** – Participants used a keyboard measuring 40 mm × 26 mm with letters measuring 3.4 mm × 4.5 mm. This keyboard's width is slightly smaller than the screen of a Sony SmartWatch 2 (42 mm).
- **TINY** – Participants used a keyboard measuring 25 mm × 16 mm with letters measuring 2.0 mm × 2.8 mm. This keyboard's width is slightly smaller than the screen of a Samsung Gear 2 watch (30 mm).

The decoder's free parameters were optimized with respect to 2412 traces recorded in previous experiments (an equal number in each of the three spacing strategies). However, as this data was exclusively from a full-sized portrait keyboard layout, we increased the keyboard model's x- and y-variance parameters for the SMALL and TINY keyboards. These variance parameters were tuned with respect to 80 traces recorded in each of the two layouts by three of the authors.

	Entry rate (wpm)	Error rate (CER %)	Left swipes per sentence
NORMAL	**40.6** ± 8.4 [23.8, 57.5]	**3.0** ± 1.7 [0.6, 6.1]	**0.25** ± 0.50 [0.0, 1.7]
SMALL	38.2 ± 7.8 [22.1, 50.0]	4.0 ± 1.9 [1.7, 7.6]	0.31 ± 0.65 [0.0, 2.1]
TINY	34.9 ± 12.2 [13.4, 54.2]	10.7 ± 6.9 [5.4, 30.0]	0.29 ± 0.66 [0.0, 2.2]
Omnibus test	$F_{2,22} = 4.343$, $\eta_p^2 = 0.283$, $p < 0.05$	$F_{2,22} = 13.494$, $\eta_p^2 = 0.551$, $p < 0.0001$	$F_{2,22} = 0.179$, $\eta_p^2 = 0.016$, $p = 0.837$
Significant pairs	None significant, $p > 0.05$	TINY > SMALL, NORMAL, $p < 0.05$ SMALL ≈ NORMAL, $p = 0.470$	n/a

Table 6. Statistics from Experiment 3. Results are formatted as: mean ± sd [min, max].

We used a Nexus 4 mobile device with recognition taking place on a 3.6 GHz 8-core server. The Nexus 4 and server were connected to the same Wi-Fi access point. Users could swipe left to delete the previous entered character. We used left swipe for deletion instead of a backspace key due to the difficulty in accurately tapping such a key on a small keyboard. The keyboard only displayed the keys A–Z plus a spacebar (Figure 9). Taps outside the rectangular keyboard were ignored (i.e. they did not provide audio or vibration feedback and they were not used in the recognition process).

We recruited 12 participants via convenience sampling. Participants were paid $20 for taking part in a two-hour session. None of the participants had taken part in previous studies. Participants were aged from 18–35 (mean = 21.8), 67% were male, 58% were computer science majors, and 75% were native English speakers. On a 7-point Likert scale where 7 = strongly agree, participants rated the statement "I consider myself a fluent speaker of English" from 5–7 (mean = 6.8).

Each participant wrote a total of 240 sentences taken from the Enron Mobile data set [19]. We chose sentences with four or more words that also had a length of 40 characters or less (so as to fit on a single line on the device). These sentences had not been used in any previous user trials or development data collections. Throughout entry, the stimulus sentence was shown directly above the keyboard (Figure 9). As a participant typed, the nearest key to each tap was displayed directly below the stimulus sentence. After swiping up, the intermediate feedback text was replaced with the recognition result.

In each condition, participants wrote six practice sentences. In order to remind participants of the spacing options, we asked participants to write two sentences using the space key, two without any spaces, and two with a swipe for space. Participants then wrote four blocks of 20 sentences with a short break between blocks. Each participant received sentences in a randomized order. The order of conditions was balanced.

After each condition, participants completed a questionnaire asking how they performed spacing in that condition. Open comments were also solicited. Participants then completed a raw NASA-TLX task load survey [10].

Results

Entry rate was measured from a user's first tap until the recognition was displayed. VelociTap took about 0.26 s to return a result. As shown in Figure 10 (left), participants' average entry rate decreased as keyboard size decreased: NORMAL 40.6 wpm, SMALL 38.2 wpm, and TINY 34.9 wpm. None of the pairwise differences were significant (Table 6, left).

Error rate was measured by computing the CER of the recognition against the stimulus. As shown in Figure 10 (right),

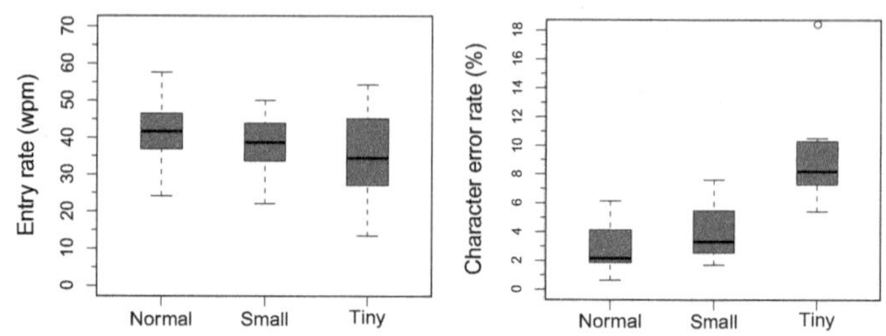

Figure 10. Entry rate (left) and error rate (right) in Experiment 3.

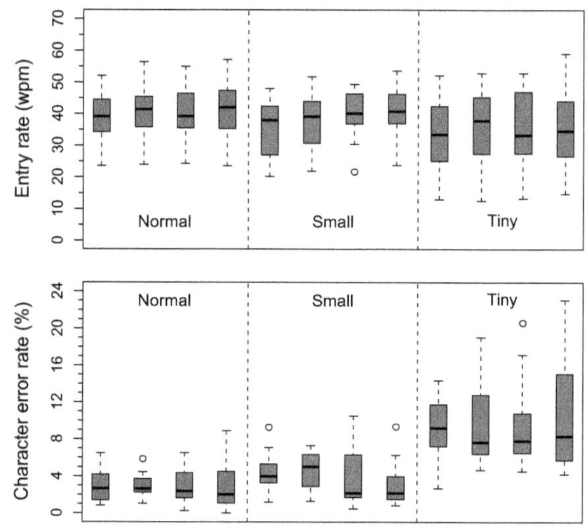

Figure 11. Entry rate (top) and error rate (bottom) in the four blocks of sentences in each keyboard size in Experiment 3.

participants' average error rate increased as keyboard size decreased: NORMAL 3.0%, SMALL 4.0%, and TINY 10.7%. TINY had a significantly higher error rate (Table 6, center).

Users could swipe to the left to delete the last character. Participants' average left swipes per sentence were: NORMAL 0.25, SMALL 0.31, and TINY 0.29. These differences were not significant (Table 6, right).

We were curious if participants' performance improved with practice. Figure 11 shows entry and error rates in each block of each condition. In the NORMAL keyboard, participants' average entry rate increased from 39.4 wpm in block 1 to 41.4 wpm in block 4. Average error rates were similar, 2.9% in block 1 and 3.0% in block 4. In the SMALL keyboard, entry rate increased from 35.2 wpm in block 1 to 40.5 wpm in block 4. Error rate decreased from 4.5% in block 1 to 3.1% in block 4. In the TINY keyboard, entry rate increased from 33.5 wpm in block 1 to 35.6 wpm in block 4. Error rate decreased from 12.3% in block 1 to 11.3% in block 4.

Subjective task load was measured by a raw NASA-TLX which is on a scale from 0–100. Participants' overall task load

	Mental	Physical	Temporal	Performance	Effort	Frustration	Overall
NORMAL	**37.5** ± 23.2	40.8 ± 27.0	**37.1** ± 24.8	**25.0** ± 20.2	**34.6** ± 21.6	**20.0** ± 19.1	**32.6** ± 17.0
SMALL	42.9 ± 26.8	**39.6** ± 30.9	49.6 ± 27.1	28.3 ± 23.3	49.6 ± 25.4	33.8 ± 22.2	40.6 ± 19.7
TINY	72.5 ± 23.9	68.8 ± 28.5	66.3 ± 30.1	47.9 ± 35.6	66.3 ± 28.9	56.3 ± 34.1	63.0 ± 24.2
Significant pairs	TINY > SMALL TINY > NORMAL	n/a	TINY > SMALL	n/a	TINY > NORMAL	TINY > SMALL TINY > NORMAL	TINY > SMALL TINY > NORMAL

Table 7. Results from the NASA-TLX task load survey in Experiment 3. Significant omnibus χ^2 tests at $p < 0.05$ were checked for significant pairs via Bonferroni corrected Wilcoxon signed-rank tests. Statistical test details have been omitted for clarity. Significant pairs all had $p < 0.01$.

Participant(s)	Keyboard size		
	NORMAL	SMALL	TINY
1, 3	NOSPACE	NOSPACE	NOSPACE
2, 4, 6, 8	SPACE	SPACE	SPACE
11	SWIPE	SWIPE	SWIPE
5	NOSPACE	NOSPACE	SWIPE
7	SPACE	SPACE	NOSPACE
9	SPACE	SPACE	NOSPACE
10	MIX†	MIX†	MIX†
12	SPACE	NOSPACE	SPACE

Table 8. The space strategy adopted by participants in each condition in Experiment 5. †Mixture of SWIPE and SPACE.

index increased as keyboard size decreased: NORMAL 32.6, SMALL 40.6, and TINY 63.0. As shown in Table 7, TINY had significantly higher overall task load as well as higher mental, temporal, effort, and frustration scores.

We measured how many right swipe gestures each participant did per sentence. We also measured how often the space key was judged the most probable key for the taps comprising a sentence. We used these two measures to classify a participant's strategy using the following rules: SWIPE if a user averaged more than two right swipes per sentence, SPACE if a user averaged more than two space taps per sentence, and NOSPACE if both measures were less than 0.5. Table 8 shows the strategy adopted by participants. For all keyboard sizes, the conventional SPACE strategy was the most popular.

At the end of the experiment, we asked participants to rank the keyboard sizes in terms of speed and accuracy. NORMAL and SMALL tied as the fastest, with 4.5 participants ranking it as the fastest (one participant ranked NORMAL and SMALL equally). NORMAL was ranked as the most accurate by eight participants, with SMALL coming in second with three votes.

Participants' comments were critical of the TINY keyboard: "very difficult and inaccurate", "incredibly difficult to use accurately", "hard to feel like you hit the right key", "awful and very difficult to use", "a nightmare", and "not something I would tolerate". Participants were more enthusiastic about the SMALL keyboard: "high accuracy with great speed", and "felt very good, allowed for near normal texting".

Small Keyboard Potential

The TINY keyboard had a high error rate of 10.7%. Since we had little data from the small keyboard prior to Experiment 3, we first explored whether better decoder parameters would improve accuracy. We split the data from Experiment 3 into two halves, optimizing parameters on users 1–6 and testing on the data from users 7–12. We also widened the search width, increasing recognition time from 0.11 s to 0.31 s. The improved setup had a CER of 6.4% on the test data.

To further demonstrate the potential of the smallest keyboard, the first author practiced with the TINY keyboard for an hour. After the hour, the author wrote all 240 sentences from Experiment 3 using a right swipe for spaces. His entry rate was 37.5 wpm (sd = 4.6) with a CER of 3.6% (sd = 7.8).

DISCUSSION

Despite receiving no feedback during sentence entry, novices in our first pilot were able to achieve very fast entry rates of 47 wpm. After two hours of practice, experts in our second pilot were able to write at 54 wpm. Both novices and experts had error rates below 5%. In Experiment 1 we showed that the high text entry performance in the pilots generalize in a controlled experiment with participants reaching between 41.9 and 43.5 wpm on average. Further, the VelociTap decoder resulted in a significantly lower error rate compared to the Google keyboard while retaining a similar entry rate.

Our three experiments provide design implications for text entry methods that use sentence-based decoding. Experiment 1 showed that intermediate visual feedback does not significantly affect entry or error rates. Experiment 2 revealed that pushing the space key is the most reliable word-delimiter strategy. Offline experiments using data from Experiment 2 showed that it is possible to provide a flexible choice of word-delimiter actions without sacrificing accuracy. Experiment 3 showed that sentence-based decoding enables users to reach a mean entry rate of 41 wpm on a 40 mm wide smartwatch-sized keyboard at a 3% character error rate. Sentence-based decoding allowed users to reach about the same text entry performance using a 60 mm and a 40 mm wide keyboard. However, the 25 mm wide keyboard was difficult for novice users, which suggests that while sentence-based decoding allows a relatively small keyboard, it is likely more useful on larger smartwatches, such as the 42 mm wide Sony SmartWatch 2.

We see several avenues for future work. First, not tapping space between words should result in faster text entry, assuming accurate decoding. However, not pushing space also makes it hard for users to track where they are in their entry. Further, we observed many users habitually tapped spaces. Thus some user training might make the no space word delimitation policy more effective. Another interesting comparison would be to compare sentence-based entry against a word-at-a-time approach and to investigate two-thumb typing.

In Experiment 3, all keyboard sizes were evaluated on a Nexus 4 phone. This was done to ensure we could reliably control the keyboard-size independent variable. A natural follow-up is to test VelociTap on an actual watch-sized device, investigating the influence of factors such as mobility and encumbrance. Further, participants were using keyboards down to 25 mm in width. We suspect performance on such small keyboards is related to the size of a user's hands. While our recognition-based approach may work at such sizes for some users, it may be difficult for all users to obtain satisfactory performance. Such users may need a letter-by-letter approach using multi-step selection (e.g. Zoomboard [16]) or larger ambiguous keys (e.g. [11]). An interesting challenge is whether a hybrid system could allow seamlessly switching between sentence-based decoding and other approaches.

Finally, all studies in this paper used a text transcription task. It is also possible to use composition in text entry studies [20]. It would be interesting to see how sentence-based decoding, and other methods that rely heavily on language models, tackle users composing their own text, which may involve rare or novel words. User performance and preference with regards to visual feedback may also differ when composing novel text rather than transcribing provided text.

CONCLUSIONS

Touchscreen keyboards typically encourage users to enter text one letter or one word at a time. In this paper, we have presented the VelociTap decoder that enables a sentence-at-a-time approach. We have evaluated this approach in two pilot studies and three experiments and presented design implications for text entry using sentence-based decoding.

It was recently argued that mobile text entry needs to focus on surpassing the inviscid entry rate: the point at which a user's creativity is the bottleneck rather than the text entry method [12]. This point is currently estimated at 67 wpm and most entry methods are below 35 wpm [12]. Our work highlights the high entry rates and low error rates achievable by simply throwing noisy touchscreen typing data at a probabilistic decoder with a well-trained language model. Therefore, we believe sentence-based decoding may serve as a foundation to help achieve a viably inviscid mobile text entry method.

REFERENCES

1. Bi, X., Ouyang, T., and Zhai, S. Both complete and correct?: multi-objective optimization of touchscreen keyboard. In *Proc. CHI* (2014), 2297–2306.
2. Bi, X., Smith, B. A., and Zhai, S. Quasi-Qwerty soft keyboard optimization. In *Proc. CHI* (2010), 283–286.
3. Bi, X., Smith, B. A., and Zhai, S. Multilingual touchscreen keyboard design and optimization. *Human-Computer Interaction 27*, 4 (2012), 352–382.
4. Cheng, L.-P., Liang, H.-S., Wu, C.-Y., and Chen, M. Y. iGrasp: grasp-based adaptive keyboard for mobile devices. In *Proc. CHI* (2013), 3037–3046.
5. Dunlop, M. D., and Levine, J. Multidimensional Pareto optimization of touchscreen keyboards for speed, familiarity and improved spell checking. In *Proc. CHI* (2012), 2669–2678.
6. Findlater, L., and Wobbrock, J. Personalized input: improving ten-finger touchscreen typing through automatic adaptation. In *Proc. CHI* (2012), 815–824.
7. Goel, M., Findlater, L., and Wobbrock, J. WalkType: using accelerometer data to accomodate situational impairments in mobile touch screen text entry. In *Proc. CHI* (2012), 2687–2696.
8. Goel, M., Jansen, A., Mandel, T., Patel, S. N., and Wobbrock, J. O. ContextType: using hand posture information to improve mobile touch screen text entry. In *Proc. CHI* (2013), 2795–2798.
9. Goodman, J., Venolia, G., Steury, K., and Parker, C. Language modeling for soft keyboards. In *Proc. AAAI* (2002), 419–424.
10. Hart, S. G. NASA-task load index (NASA-TLX); 20 years later. *Proc. Human Factors and Ergonomics Society Annual Meeting 50*, 9 (2006), 904–908.
11. Komninos, A., and Dunlop, M. Text input on a smart watch. *Pervasive Computing, IEEE 13*, 4 (2014), 50–58.
12. Kristensson, P. O., and Vertanen, K. The inviscid text entry rate and its application as a grand goal for mobile text entry. In *Proc. MobileHCI* (2014), 335–338.
13. Kristensson, P. O., and Zhai, S. SHARK^2: a large vocabulary shorthand writing system for pen-based computers. In *Proc. UIST 2004* (2004), 43–52.
14. Kristensson, P. O., and Zhai, S. Relaxing stylus typing precision by geometric pattern matching. In *Proc. IUI* (2005), 151–158.
15. Moore, R. C., and Lewis, W. Intelligent selection of language model training data. In *Proc. ACL* (2010), 220–224.
16. Oney, S., Harrison, C., Ogan, A., and Wiese, J. ZoomBoard: A diminutive Qwerty soft keyboard using iterative zooming for ultra-small devices. In *Proc. CHI* (2013), 2799–2802.
17. Oulasvirta, A., Reichel, A., Li, W., Zhang, Y., Bachynskyi, M., Vertanen, K., and Kristensson, P. O. Improving two-thumb text entry on touchscreen devices. In *Proc. CHI* (2013), 2765–2774.
18. Pauls, A., and Klein, D. Faster and smaller N-gram language models. In *Proc. HLT* (2011), 258–267.
19. Vertanen, K., and Kristensson, P. O. A versatile dataset for text entry evaluations based on genuine mobile emails. In *Proc. MobileHCI* (2011), 295–298.
20. Vertanen, K., and Kristensson, P. O. Complementing text entry evaluations with a composition task. *ACM Transactions of Computer Human Interaction 21*, 2 (Feb. 2014), Article No. 8.
21. Weir, D., Pohl, H., Rogers, S., Vertanen, K., and Kristensson, P. O. Uncertain text entry on mobile devices. In *Proc. CHI* (2014), 2307–2316.
22. Zhai, S., and Kristensson, P. O. Interlaced QWERTY: accommodating ease of visual search and input flexibility in shape writing. In *Proc. CHI* (2008), 593–596.
23. Zhai, S., Sue, A., and Accot, J. Movement model, hits distribution and learning in virtual keyboarding. In *Proc. CHI* (2002), 17–24.

Text Entry on Tiny QWERTY Soft Keyboards

Luis A. Leiva[1,*] Alireza Sahami[2] Alejandro Catalá[3] Niels Henze[2] Albrecht Schmidt[2]
[1]PRHLT Research Center [2]hciLab [3]ISSI-DSIC
[1,3]Universitat Politècnica de València [2]Universität Stuttgart
[1]llt@acm.org [2]{name.surname}@vis.uni-stuttgart.de [3]acatala@dsic.upv.es

ABSTRACT

The advent of wearables (e.g., smartwatches, smartglasses, and digital jewelry) anticipates the need for text entry methods on very small devices. We conduct fundamental research on this topic using 3 qwerty-based soft keyboards for 3 different screen sizes, motivated by the extensive training that users have with qwerty keyboards. In addition to ZoomBoard (a soft keyboard for diminutive screens), we propose a callout-based soft keyboard and ZShift, a novel extension of the Shift pointing technique. We conducted a comprehensive user study followed by extensive analyses on performance, usability, and short-term learning. Our results show that different small screen sizes demand different types of assistance. In general, manufacturers can benefit from these findings by selecting an appropriate qwerty soft keyboard for their devices. Ultimately, this work provides designers, researchers, and practitioners with new understanding of qwerty soft keyboard design space and its scalability for tiny touchscreens.

Author Keywords

Text Entry; Small Screens; Small Devices; QWERTY

ACM Classification Keywords

H.5.2 User Interfaces: Prototyping; Screen design

INTRODUCTION

With the ongoing breakthrough of wearables, such as smartwatches or digital jewelry, text entry on devices with very small screens (1" wide or less) becomes increasingly relevant and a challenging issue, simply because space is at a premium. A number of approaches have been proposed to enter text on such devices. However, today every text entry technique or keyboard layout based on a touchscreen has to compete with qwerty.[1] Users are only willing to switch and use a different keyboard if the technique is easy to use or learn. The low startup speed, at least partially, precludes the success of a number of text entry techniques that offered high-speed performance after intensive training; e.g., [24, 30]. Compared to gesture-based entry techniques [41] or multi-chord keyboards [24], qwerty keyboards have the advantage that users are already familiarized with the layout and the input technique is easy to understand.

Based on the assumption that standard qwerty soft keyboards are impractical on very small screens, Oney *et al.* [29] proposed ZoomBoard, a qwerty-based multi-tap soft keyboard. Initially, a qwerty keyboard is displayed onscreen. When the user taps on the keyboard, it zooms in and shows an enlarged version of the tapped region. The user can then select a character with an additional tap on the enlarged keyboard region. Oney *et al.* conducted a preliminary evaluation on a 16 mm wide (roughly 0.5") keyboard, and observed that ZoomBoard outperforms a same-sized qwerty soft keyboard that provides no additional assistance for the user. However, the inherent need of using multiple taps to enter a single character makes it unlikely that ZoomBoard would perform as well on larger soft keyboards.

A number of commercial devices with small touchscreens are actually wider than 0.5" (or 0.7" diagonal); e.g. the Sony SmartWatch (1.3"), the i'm S.p.A. watch (1.54"), the Samsung Galaxy Gear (1.63"), or the iPod Nano (available at 1.5" and 2.5"). It is therefore unclear up to which size a zooming approach provides an actual benefit and at which point it will be outperformed by a single-tap approach. In addition, even current standard implementations of qwerty soft keyboards provide different types of assistance for the user. Callouts above the key that are displayed when the finger lands on a key, for example, aim to address the occlusion problem ("fat-finger") and increase user performance. Therefore, different types of assistance for small qwerty soft keyboards still remain largely unexplored.

We investigate the scalability of 3 qwerty-based text entry techniques for 3 diminutive screen sizes, by using 16 mm, 21.3 mm, and 28.4 mm wide soft keyboards. In addition to ZoomBoard, we implemented a qwerty soft keyboard that presents the currently selected character above the keyboard, similar to the callouts provided by current smartphone keyboards. We also implemented ZShift, an extension of the Shift pointing technique [39] that we have adapted for text entry. We show that different screen sizes demand different keyboard techniques. For instance, ZoomBoard performs well on the smallest screen size whereas ZShift scales better to larger screen sizes. We found that the three keyboards approach reasonable entry speeds along with competitive accuracy. We also observed that users got quickly familiarized with all keyboards after entering just 5 sentences with each keyboard-screen combination within a single session. In general, manufacturers can benefit from these findings by selecting an appropriate qwerty soft keyboard for their devices. Ultimately, this work provides designers, researchers, and practitioners with new understanding of qwerty soft keyboard design space and its scalability for tiny touchscreens.

*Work done while visiting the hciLab in Stuttgart.

[1]We use QWERTY in lowercase form to improve typesetting.

CHI 2015, April 18–23, 2015, Seoul, Republic of Korea.

ACM 978-1-4503-3145-6/15/04 ...$15.00.
http://dx.doi.org/10.1145/2702123.2702388

RELATED WORK

The concept of very small interactive mobile devices has recently sparked interest well beyond HCI research. In particular, wearables such as smartwatches, smartglasses, and digital jewelry are becoming widely available to consumers. Interestingly, these devices can receive notifications in many forms but there is usually no direct way of replying [19].

Speech input seems to be an obvious choice to enter short messages, names, or addresses on very small devices. However, there are situations where it is too noisy or inappropriate to use; e.g., asking for personal data on an overcrowded environment. Researchers have proposed to use handwriting to enter text on mobile devices [17, 45], though it is difficult for the user to see what is currently being written on very small screens. In addition, handwritten text (much like voice) is prone to recognition errors. Alternatively, the rear of the device can be used for interaction [1], though it is typically unavailable on consumer devices. Another possibility are wrist-worn devices like Facet [23], a circular bracelet of multi touch displays, although their form factor is too big to be practical.

Soft Keyboard Layouts

In general, physical qwerty keyboards are commonplace and the first text entry device for most users. Thus, other techniques and keyboard layouts have to compete with it. Even soft keyboard layouts optimized for movement efficiency following Fitts' law and character frequencies such as OPTI [28] or ATOMIK [44] showed that users need to invest non-negligible time until the qwerty layout is eventually outperformed. Most users are not willing to switch to a different input technique or even a different layout if it does not provide a similar startup speed. In fact this is the dominant factor for adoption of text entry techniques [6]. A prominent high-performance example is Twiddler, a one-handed chording keyboard [24] that allows users to achieve up to 60 WPM—comparable to a physical qwerty keyboard [34], but only after months of training.

Currently, qwerty-based text entry predates other alternatives. Due to the proliferation of touchscreen devices, different approaches have been developed to improve qwerty soft keyboards, from subtle changes to the internal processing of touch input [10, 12] to slight changes of the button layout [4]. Himberg *et al.* [13] developed an adaptive numerical soft keyboard that observes where the user is touching and adapt the shape of the virtual keys to reduce the error rate. Similar work by Kristensson and Zhai [20] uses geometric pattern matching to reduce the error rate for stylus-based text entry. Gunawardana *et al.* [10] developed an anchored keyboard adaptation, and a user-simulated study suggested that it may reduce the error rate. Using these techniques on small devices might not be practical due to the number of keys involved and the fat-finger problem. While previous works have explored multi-tap and predictive alternatives [5, 14, 16, 19], researchers still tried to shrink down a qwerty keyboard to fit on very small touchscreen. For instance, Kim *et al.* [18] used one key for interaction, Minuum[2] compressed the qwerty layout to one line, and Oney *et al.* [29] used iterative zooming to enlarge the keys.

[2]`http://minuum.com`

Interaction Techniques for Text Entry

Several interaction techniques using different sensors show promise for entering text on very small devices; e.g., using magnetometers [11], tilting a wrist-worn device [31, 36], or combining physical pan, twist, tilt, and clicks [42]. Such techniques remain to be further explored, but also remain difficult to deploy in practice.

Gesture-based text entry techniques such as EdgeWrite [41] or Quikwriting [32] became common on mobile devices that required a stylus as input. Reducing the input space to well-delimited zones simplified recognition accuracy, which was an issue in former approaches such as Graffiti [27] or Unistroke [9]. Other works pursued a minimal set of 4 keys, or interaction zones if used in gesture-based systems, that would allow efficient text entry such as MDITIM [15], LURD [7], and H4-Writer [26]. The key problem of these gesture-based input techniques is that an additional stylus is required, and thus yet another device that might be even larger than the actual device the user interacts with. On the other hand, using the finger in lieu of a stylus leads to the fat-finger problem that is particularly severe on very small screens.

Small Target Acquisition Techniques

Another strand of research focuses on techniques to select small targets with a finger without changing the size of the target while achieving an acceptable error rate. In Shift [39] target selection is approached through callouts showing a copy of the area occluded by the finger in a non-occluded area. In TapTap [35] the occluded area is magnified and the user has to touch the desired target with a second touch, similar to ZoomBoard. In Escape [43] targets are visually enhanced with arrows that indicate the direction in which the user has to drag the finger after touching a target. Those interaction techniques are not very well suited for text entry since additional interactions are required, which in turn require more time and higher mental effort compared with a simple touch. Nevertheless they can play a relevant role if they are properly combined in new scenarios on small touchscreens, where target selection can be specially challenging and special needs are therefore required [33]. For instance, Swipeboard [3] allows users to enter text with two swipes: the first swipe specifies the region where the character is located, and the second swipe specifies the character within that region. This approach is target-agnostic and so after some training users can perform eyes-free, shorthand input.

In sum, a significant body of research has investigated text entry for small devices. While diverse alternatives to qwerty-based text entry have been proposed, the comparatively high usability of qwerty keyboards suggests that these keyboards will play a major role for small touchscreen-capable devices that currently hit the market. ZoomBoard is the most recent approach that has been especifically designed to address this issue on diminutive screens. For larger screen sizes, however, callout-based techniques can be used instead. Furthermore, it remains unclear how these approaches actually perform in comparison. In particular, it is unclear how each technique scales and which technique is appropriate for which device size. Our work is the first to address this choice.

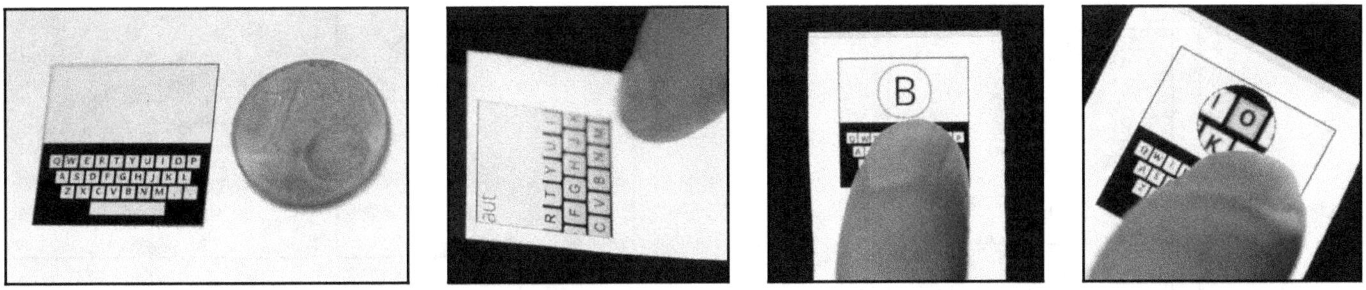

(a) Reference scale (b) ZoomBoard (c) Callout (d) ZShift

Figure 1: Our three prototypes. As a reference, a 1 cent Euro coin (16 mm, or 0.6", 3 mm smaller than a US penny) is shown in (a).

THREE TINY QWERTY SOFT KEYBOARDS

To date, ZoomBoard is the only qwerty soft keyboard that has been specifically designed to enter text on tiny touchscreens. However, we propose two alternatives to this technique, motivated by the following considerations:

1. A qwerty keyboard layout, due to its 2:1 (or higher) aspect ratio, typically takes up only half of the screen space. Therefore, the remaining space can be available to display information related to text entry.
2. Tiny touchscreen sizes may range from "very small" (less than 1") to "moderately large" (e.g., 2.5" for the newest iPod Nano). Thus, different text entry techniques may perform differently depending on the available space onscreen.

Figure 1 shows the three prototypes we have studied. All prototypes are web-based and have been tested on different browsers, including mobile and desktop computers. The prototypes are released as open source software, so that anyone can contribute to improving them or build alternatives by reusing parts of the code.[3]

ZoomBoard Keyboard

To increase the accuracy with which a key can be acquired, instead of immediate selection, the keyboard zooms in (Figure 1b). Specifically, when the user taps on a key, the keyboard iteratively zooms in (visual magnification) until reaching a certain level of zoom. Then, the user can enter a character with an additional tap. Afterward, the keyboard goes back to the initial zoom level. As the keyboard layout is visible to the user after each tap, less typing errors are likely to occur compared to a non-zooming qwerty soft keyboard, which may suffer from severe occlusion problems on tiny screens.

Callout Keyboard

The Callout keyboard is inspired by the soft keyboards used on current smartphones. When the user touches a key, a callout showing the character that is about to be entered is created in a non-occluded location (the upper part of the screen, Figure 1c). The user can refine the key to be entered by slightly moving the finger on the keyboard, and then enter the character by lifting up the finger. This technique allows the user to enter one character per tap, which might be more efficient than ZoomBoard.

[3] `http://personales.upv.es/luileito/tinyqwerty/`

ZShift Keyboard

The Callout keyboard has the drawback that once the finger has landed on the touchscreen, it occludes most (if not all) of the keyboard. Therefore, if the user wants to refine key selection, she must rely on her spatial memory to know how keys are exactly arranged. Thus, we provide the user with a stronger hint about where each key is located. We applied the Shift pointing technique [39], which was designed to ease target acquisition but we have extended for text entry. Shift creates a callout showing a copy of the occluded screen area (motor magnification). Using this visual feedback, users might be more accurate while entering text. However, for small keyboards we believe that Shift alone is not sufficient. Thus, we enhance the callout area with one level of zoom over the occluded area, providing also visual feedback of the touched key (Figure 1d), yielding a *Zoomed* Shift technique (ZShift).

Common Features

Following previous keyboard designs that already used swipe gestures to replace touchscreens buttons [8, 22, 29], we apply these gestures to the following functions. On each keyboard prototype, the user can enter a space either by tapping on the space bar or by swiping to the right over the keyboard. To delete text, the user must swipe to the left. To load different keyboard layouts (e.g., one for symbols and numbers, other for punctuation or currency symbols, etc.) the user can swipe either up or down, following a carousel metaphor, allowing thus a continuous, circular navigation through all available keyboard layouts. To submit the entered text, the user must tap on the upper part of the screen (see Figure 2).

EVALUATION

We conducted a controlled user study to compare the three keyboard alternatives using text-copy tasks, as usual in text entry experiments. We tested the 3 keyboards with 3 different sizes (see Figure 2), 9 conditions in total. We simulated a smartwatch using a touch-capable smartphone, in order to eliminate a potential evaluation bias. It must be noted that using actual smartwatches would require a different model for each screen size, resulting in different form factors, touch responsiveness, and screen resolutions. Instead, using the same device for all participants eliminates these undesirable effects. Our evaluation is thus general enough so as to illustrate how text entry would perform on wearables featuring tiny qwerty soft keyboards.

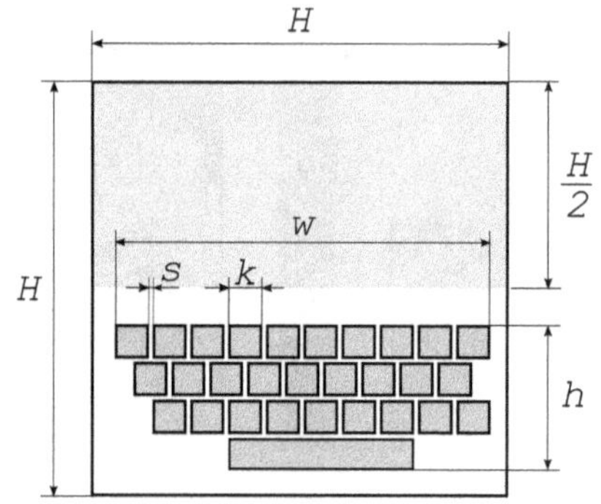

Screen	*H*	*w*	*h*	*k*	*s*
Small	18	16.0	6.5	1.5	0.3
Medium	24	21.3	8.6	2.0	0.4
Large	32	28.4	11.4	2.6	0.5

Figure 2: Keyboard definition and the values used for each of the screen sizes. All dimensions are given in millimeters.

Apparatus
We used a Samsung Nexus S mobile phone running Android 4.1 with a 4" display (233 dpi). The phone was attached in landscape orientation to the non-dominant arm with two wide black strips; see Figure 3b. The strips, in addition to fasten the phone, simulate the edges of a watch and cover the screen in such a way that only the simulated screen width is visible to the user.

The layout of the tested keyboard prototypes are accurately defined in Figure 2, each one being one third larger than its predecessor. It can observed that "small" (18 mm), "medium" (24 mm), and "large" (32 mm) screen sizes are actually all very small compared to current smartphone keyboards. Since our prototypes were written in JavaScript, we used the Firefox web browser for Android. The browser was launched in fullscreen mode, so the ribbon at the top of the browser, which also includes the URL box, was not visible to the participants. Similar to the study conducted by Oney *et al.* [29], ZoomBoard was configured to work with one level of animated zoom, so that each character was entered with 2 taps.

Design
We considered two independent factors: *Keyboard* method (3 levels: ZoomBoard, Callout, ZShift) and *Screen* size (3 levels: small, medium, large). We further used 8 dependent variables: 6 performance-related (described in Analysis of Text Entry Performance) and 2 usability-related factors (described in Analysis of Usability and Workload). We also investigated how each condition performed at the phrase level, to obtain a holistic overview about the different keyboard layouts.

We used a repeated measures within-subjects design, i.e., participants were assigned to all treatment levels of every factor combination. The Latin square design was adopted to counterbalance the order of the conditions, i.e., we generated a 9x9 assignments matrix were every single condition followed every other condition only once [2], and each participant followed one of the rows of the assignments matrix. The data were analyzed using a two-way multivariate analysis of variance (MANOVA), since there is more than one dependent variable as main outcome, followed by a series of ANOVAs and post-hoc comparisons per each screen size group, where applicable.

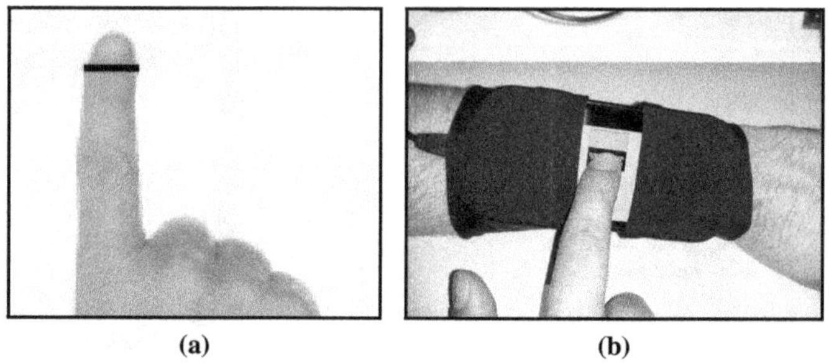

Figure 3: Measuring index finger's width (3a, black strip) and detail of the evaluation setup (3b).

Participants
We recruited 20 participants (5 female) aged 21–29 (*M*=24.7, *SD*=2.2) using our University's mailing lists. We intentionally wanted a rather broad sample and recruited participants with many different backgrounds; e.g. Mechanical Engineering, Informatics, or Physics. All participants regularly used PC keyboards. Thirteen participants stated that they could perform blind-typing on a PC keyboard. Seventeen participants were right-handed and 17 owned touchscreen smartphones. Each participant was paid 10€ at the end of the evaluation.

Procedure
We conducted the study in a calm office environment. Participants were seated during the whole study, as we anticipated that it would take about one hour per participant. Each participant was briefly described the purpose of the study to begin with. We measured the width of their dominant hand's index finger with a digital caliper, for which it was aligned with the distal interphalangeal joint (see Figure 3a). The average size of the index finger was 16.1 mm (*SD*=1.4). This gives an approximate idea of how much of a very small screen is occluded by the finger.

Participants started the study by signing in a consent form and answering a demographics questionnaire. Next, the phone was attached to the non-dominant arm. Through a short guided demo, the three keyboards were presented and explained to each participant. People were asked to type their full name using each keyboard design on the medium-size keyboard. They were told to use the index finger of the dominant hand for entering text during the whole study. This warm-up session took approximately 1–2 minutes on average per condition. Afterward, the actual evaluation began.

Each participant had to enter 5 phrases for each of the 9 different keyboard-screen combinations, resulting in 45 phrases submitted per participant, 900 phrases in total. As previously commented, we used a Latin square design to counterbalance the order of the conditions. This procedure reduces learning effects as well as asymmetrical skill transfer across conditions.

Phrases were picked at random from the MacKenzie and Soukoreff phrase set [25], which is a well-known standard dataset to conduct text entry experiments. All phrases had neither punctuation symbols or numbers, and were lowercased in order to let participants easily focus on each keyboard technique. A phrase was shown at a time above each keyboard, and we ensured that all phrases were different for each participant and condition; in fact no phrase was entered twice in any of the conditions. Participants were asked to enter the presented text as quickly and accurately as possible. They were allowed to correct mistakes as they went, for which they would use the left swipe gesture to delete the last character. Each phrase was permanently shown to the participants until they submitted it, in order to avoid memorability bias.

Participants were able to practice and get accustomed to the keyboard-screen combination used in each condition before actually evaluating it. These attempts took between 2 and 5 minutes per participant. After finishing typing a phrase, participants had to tap on the upper part of the soft keyboard to submit the phrase and load a new one. When each condition finished, participants were asked to answer the SUS and NASA-TLX questionnaires on a nearby desktop computer.

RESULTS

In our prototypes, for pragmatic reasons, a phrase was submitted by tapping on the upper part of the screen. It turned out that in 12 cases participants accidentally tapped on that part when tried to reach a key from the first row of the keyboards. To remove the accidentally submitted phrases, we only considered those phrases that were transcribed at least by 50%. This resulted in 888 phrases for analysis, which anecdotally correspond to 12.3 hours of typing data.

A MANOVA test was first performed to take into account the interaction effects between variables and protect against inflating the Type 1 error in follow-up ANOVAs and post-hoc comparisons, whether appropriate. Prior to conducting the MANOVA, a series of Pearson correlations were performed in order to test the MANOVA assumption that the dependent variables would be correlated with each other. Table 1 summarizes these correlations. A non-significant result after the Box's M test ($p > .05$) indicated a lack of evidence that the homogeneity of variance-covariance matrix assumption was violated. No univariate or multivariate outliers were evident and MANOVA was considered thus to be an appropriate analysis technique.

	KSPC	WPM	CER	Nerr	Cerr	Ceff	SUS	TLX
KSPC	—							
WPM	**-0.21**	—						
CER	0.08	**-0.14**	—					
Nerr	0.05	-0.06	**0.95**	—				
Cerr	**0.33**	**-0.35**	0.06	-0.06	—			
Ceff	**0.19**	-0.10	0.07	0.01	**0.06**	—		
SUS	**-0.04**	**0.39**	**-0.15**	**-0.09**	**-0.03**	**-0.20**	—	
TLX	**0.06**	**-0.36**	**0.24**	**0.15**	**0.02**	**0.17**	**-0.04**	—

Table 1: Pearson's r correlation between all dependent variables. Statistical significance ($p < .05$) is denoted in bold typeface.

MANOVA tested the hypothesis that there was one or multiple differences of the mean between *Keyboard* levels (ZoomBoard, Callout, ZShift) and screen *Size* levels (small, medium, large). Significant multivariate effects were found among the 9 conditions, both regarding *Keyboard* [$F_{2,171} = 23.69$, $p < .0001, \eta_p^2 = 0.53$] and *Size* [$F_{2,171} = 8.49$, $p < .0001, \eta_p^2 = 0.29$]. In addition, a significant *Keyboard*Size* interaction was found [$F_{4,171} = 1.55$, $p = .028, \eta_p^2 = 0.13$]. We therefore split the dataset by screen size and performed univariate ANOVAs, with appropriately adjusted significance levels to guard against the risk of over-testing the data. All comparisons used the Holm-Bonferroni correction.

The following analysis includes four parts. First, we investigate text entry performance using all keyboard-screen combinations. Next, we assess usability and workload through the analysis of the SUS and NASA-TLX questionnaires. We also provide anecdotal evidence of the typing errors commited by the participants. Finally, we assess user's short-term learning on a per-trial basis.

Analysis of Text Entry Performance

We assesed text entry performance using the following measures. Certainly there are more conceivable measures that could be used, but for brevity's sake we report the most relevant and well-established measures in the literature.

Analysis of Words Per Minute and Key Stroke Per Character

Words Per Minute (WPM) and Key Stroke Per Character (KSPC) are widely used measures of input speed. For standardization purposes, in WPM a word is defined as five consecutively entered characters, including spaces. KSPC is the number of interactions (e.g., taps, swipes) required to enter a character, including backspaces. KSPC is device-dependent, and thus ZoomBoard has a theoretical lower bound of 2.0, though this can be lowered down to 1.84 if the swipe gesture is used for entering spaces [29].

	ANOVA			Keyboard		
Screen	$F_{2,57}$	p-value	η_p^2	ZoomBoard	Callout	ZShift
Small	6.89	.002	0.19	6.0 (1.4)	4.3 (1.7)	5.4 (1.2)
Medium	0.70	.498	0.02	7.8 (1.2)	7.1 (2.0)	7.2 (2.3)
Large	0.96	.386	0.03	8.2 (1.2)	8.3 (2.3)	9.1 (2.9)

Table 2: WPM results (higher is better). Mean values are shown in the Keyboard column. SDs are denoted in parentheses.

As shown in Table 2, WPM differences were found to be statistically significant only for the small screen. Post-hoc pairwise comparisons using the t-test (Holm-Bonferroni corrected) revealed that the Callout keyboard performed worse than the other alternatives.

As shown in Table 3, KSPC differences were found to be statistically significant for all screen sizes. Post-hoc pairwise comparisons using the t-test (Holm-Bonferroni corrected) revealed that ZoomBoard required more KSPC than the other alternatives for all screen sizes. ZShift was the best performer overall. For medium and large sizes, there were no significant differences between ZShift and Callout.

	ANOVA			Keyboard		
Screen	$F_{2,57}$	p-value	η_p^2	ZoomBoard	Callout	ZShift
Small	36.88	<.0001	0.56	2.7 (0.5)	1.8 (0.4)	1.5 (0.2)
Medium	50.11	<.0001	0.63	2.2 (0.2)	1.5 (0.2)	1.4 (0.2)
Large	112.68	<.0001	0.79	2.1 (0.1)	1.4 (0.1)	1.3 (0.2)

Table 3: KSPC results (lower is better). Mean values are shown in the Keyboard column. SDs are denoted in parentheses.

Analysis of Character Error Rate

Character Error Rate (CER) is the most widely used measure of accuracy. CER is computed as the Damerau-Levenshtein distance between the submitted text and the reference text, normalized by the number of characters in the reference text.

	ANOVA			Keyboard		
Screen	$F_{2,57}$	p-value	η_p^2	ZoomBoard	Callout	ZShift
Small	4.41	.016	0.13	1.1 (1.3)	2.6 (2.1)	1.3 (1.3)
Medium	0.51	.603	0.01	1.2 (2.1)	0.8 (1.0)	1.3 (1.8)
Large	0.97	.383	0.03	1.4 (2.3)	0.7 (0.9)	0.9 (1.3)

Table 4: CER results (lower is better). Mean values are shown in the Keyboard column. SDs are denoted in parentheses.

As shown in Table 4, CER differences were found to be statistically significant for the small screen size. Post-hoc pairwise comparisons using the t-test (Holm-Bonferroni corrected) revealed that Callout performed worse than the other alternatives. No significant differences between ZoomBoard and ZShift were found.

Analysis of Device-independent Performance Measures

CER is an incomplete accuracy measure, in the sense that it cannot differentiate among the errors that were *corrected* by the user, yet these are an important aspect of text entry. Also, KSPC does not differentiate between the cost of committing errors and the cost to fix them. For these reasons, here we use measures that consider the *input stream* [37]. The input stream contains information about all text that has been entered and erased. Thus it is both device- and method-independent [40].

Corrected Error Rate (Cerr) provides an equivalent for the KSPC (the cost of typing and fixing errors). Some authors suggest to break down Cerr in 2 sub-metrics [38], but this fine-grained distinction provides little insights when there is no "pathologic error correction",[4] as in our data. Second, Non-corrected Error Rate (Nerr) is analogous to CER (a measure of the errors remaining in the transcribed text). Nerr and Cerr together account for the Total error rate (Terr), which will not be reported here for brevity's sake. Finally, Correction Efficiency (Ceff) measures the ease with which the user performed error corrections.

Differences were found to be statistically significant in terms of Cerr for medium and large screen sizes (Table 5), in terms of Nerr for small screen size (Table 6), and in terms of Ceff for medium screen size (Table 7). Post-hoc pairwise comparisons using the t-test (Holm-Bonferroni corrected) revealed statistical significance.

[4] The user notices he has committed an error and goes backspacing destructively to the error and re-enters the correct text.

	ANOVA			Keyboard		
Screen	$F_{2,57}$	p-value	η_p^2	ZoomBoard	Callout	ZShift
Small	1.63	.203	0.05	14.2 (6.2)	17.3 (5.9)	14.1 (6.7)
Medium	10.77	.0001	0.37	6.8 (4.8)	14.0 (5.1)	12.6 (5.5)
Large	12.32	.0001	0.43	5.9 (3.2)	11.7 (3.4)	11.4 (5.4)

Table 5: Cerr results (lower is better). Mean values are shown in the Keyboard column. SDs are denoted in parentheses.

	ANOVA			Keyboard		
Screen	$F_{2,57}$	p-value	η_p^2	ZoomBoard	Callout	ZShift
Small	3.48	.037	0.10	0.8 (1.0)	1.8 (1.6)	0.9 (1.1)
Medium	0.72	.490	0.02	1.0 (1.7)	0.5 (0.6)	0.9 (1.1)
Large	1.91	.157	0.06	1.5 (2.7)	0.5 (0.6)	0.7 (1.0)

Table 6: Nerr results (lower is better). Mean values are shown in the Keyboard column. SDs are denoted in parentheses.

	ANOVA			Keyboard		
Screen	$F_{2,57}$	p-value	η_p^2	ZoomBoard	Callout	ZShift
Small	1.05	.356	0.03	93.0 (13.4)	92.7 (13.7)	85.7 (24.4)
Medium	6.11	.003	0.17	72.2 (32.9)	94.0 (14.6)	93.0 (13.4)
Large	1.61	.207	0.05	78.0 (19.3)	88.0 (16.4)	85.0 (18.2)

Table 7: Ceff results (higher is better). Mean values are shown in the Keyboard column. SDs are denoted in parentheses.

Analysis of Usability and Workload

We measured usability through the System Usability Scale (SUS) and perceived workload through the NASA Task Load Index (TLX). SUS comprises 10 questions assessed in a 1–5 Likert scale, giving a global view of subjective assessments of usability. The overall SUS score ranges from 0 to 100 (the higher the better). TLX comprises 6 questions assessed in a 1–10 scale, each question related to one of the following dimensions: mental demand, physical demand, temporal demand, performance, effort, and frustration. The overall TLX score ranges from 0 to 100 (the lower the better).

Differences in SUS (Table 8) and TLX (Table 9) were found to be statistically significant for the small size. This was also true regarding TLX differences for the medium size. All other ANOVAs did not reveal statistically significant differences.

	ANOVA			Keyboard		
Screen	$F_{2,57}$	p-value	η_p^2	ZoomBoard	Callout	ZShift
Small	6.25	.003	0.17	67.8 (13.1)	51.1 (11.5)	59.7 (19.1)
Medium	1.22	.300	0.04	75.2 (14.4)	68.1 (15.0)	73.8 (16.2)
Large	2.56	.087	0.08	83.5 (11.4)	77.1 (15.2)	85.6 (9.8)

Table 8: SUS results (higher is better). Mean values are shown in the Keyboard column. SDs are denoted in parentheses.

Post-hoc comparisons (Holm-Bonferroni corrected) of SUS and TLX for the small size revealed that the Callout keyboard was perceived as significantly worse than the other alternatives,

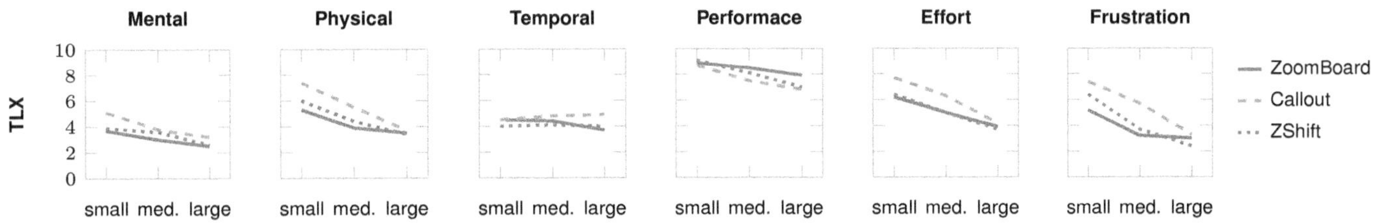

Figure 4: Scores for each of the 6 TLX dimensions (lower is better). Performance measures "how difficult was to enter text."

	ANOVA			Keyboard		
Screen	$F_{2,57}$	p-value	η_p^2	ZoomBoard	Callout	ZShift
Small	4.91	.010	0.14	21.9 (4.2)	26.0 (4.3)	22.5 (4.8)
Medium	3.97	.024	0.12	18.8 (4.4)	22.5 (5.3)	19.4 (3.7)
Large	1.24	.294	0.04	17.2 (3.9)	18.7 (4.4)	16.9 (3.6)

Table 9: TLX results (lower is better). Mean values are shown in the Keyboard column. SDs are denoted in parentheses.

and ZoomBoard was perceived better in terms of SUS than ZShift but not in terms of TLX. Regarding TLX for medium screen size, the Callout keyboard scored significantly higher than ZoomBoard and ZShift, and no statistically significant differences were found between ZoomBoard and ZShift. Since all other ANOVAs did not reveal statistically significant differences between conditions in the remaining screen sizes (both for SUS and TLX), no further post-hoc tests were performed.

Analysis of Typing Errors

We observed that 160 phrases had some transcription errors, either because of typos (*Typo*, 110 cases), because a different word—although grammatically correct—was entered (*Diff*, 69), or because fewer words (*Less*, 31) or more words (*More*, 15) than the reference phrase were entered. Figure 5 shows a histogram of the error distribution. As observed, most of the submitted phrases were error-free, and at most 4 phrases had 3 transcription errors. Table 10 shows some examples of the errors committed by the users.

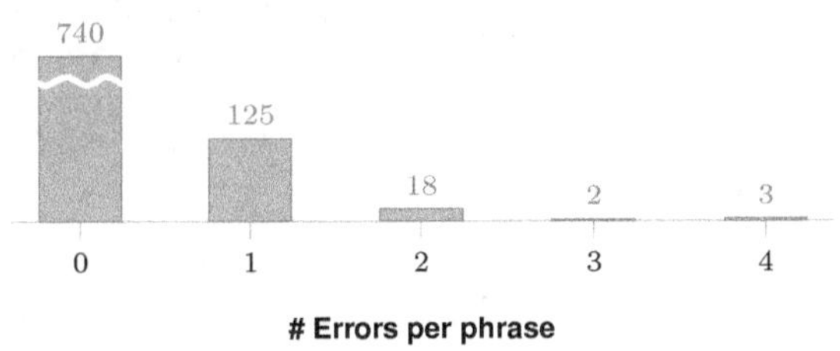

Figure 5: Histogram of phrases containing transcription errors. Most of the submitted phrases were error-free.

Analysis of Short-term Learning

We analyzed the collected data to determine improvements (or the lack thereof) throughout each condition. The measures were averaged on a per-trials basis, so that there were 5 observations or "data points" for each of the 9 tested conditions.

As shown in Figure 6, participants performed consistently better while entering the fifth phrase in all conditions. In

Error type	Example (reference text above transcribed phrase)
Typo	an occasional taste of chocolate **an occasional taste of chpcolate**
Diff	this mission statement is baloney **the mission statement is baloney**
Less	the back yard of our house **the backyard of our house**
More	i hate baking pies **i hate baking and pies**

Table 10: Examples of transcription errors (underlined).

addition, we observed that performance improved as screen size increased. This was so for all measures, though we report results about WPM and KSPC by way of illustrative examples. A simple linear regression analysis for each condition revealed that all fits were statistically significant ($R^2 > 0.8, p < .001$).

DISCUSSION

This work provides valuable new knowledge for text entry researchers, and for interaction designers that want to incorporate text entry methods on very small screens. In the following we comment on the main findings derived from our study.

Findings

Overall, participants liked ZoomBoard and ZShift the most. A frequent observation was that, on medium and large screens, participants complained about having to issue 2 taps with ZoomBoard to enter each character. One participant stated that *"ZoomBoard was especially irritating on the larger screen"*, who found ZShift to be the most likable alternative.

For the small screen (16 mm), our results show that ZoomBoard provides the highest WPM (6.04) followed by ZShift (5.41), though this difference is not statistically significant. Further, ZoomBoard's KSPC is almost twice higher than ZShift, this difference being statistically significant. On the other hand, there is no significant CER differences between ZoomBoard and ZShift. This suggests that both ZoomBoard and ZShift are less error-prone than Callout on the small screen. It was interesting to notice that all entry speeds are very slow compared with current smartphones, where WPM is typically about five times higher. Furthermore, Callout was significantly slower than the other keyboards, especially on the small screen. This suggests that current soft keyboards are not appropriate for use on very small screens, and that other alternatives should be devised, such as ZoomBoard or ZShift.

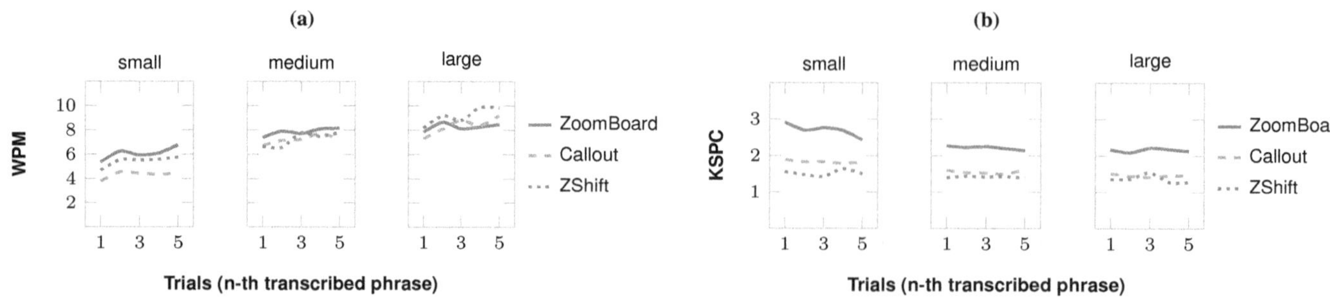

Figure 6: Evolution of performance in terms of WPM (a) and KSPC (b) for all combinations of screen size and keyboard.

For the medium (24 mm) and large (32 mm) screens, no statistically significant differences were found between the keyboards both in terms of WPM and CER, but it was so in terms of KSPC. Thus, all keyboards are usable on the medium and large screens. Using ZShift indeed leads to the lowest KSPC. For the medium screen, however, using the Callout technique requires a higher mental workload and its usability was perceived to be lower than the other techniques. On the other hand, mental workload was not found to be significantly different on the larger screen. Specifically, ZShift usability was perceived to be higher than the other keyboards.

The analysis of TLX dimensions suggests that users are geared toward text entry techniques that do just require 1-step interaction, without lifting the finger from the touchscreen. For instance, temporal demand, effort, and frustration scores were the lowest in ZShift for the large screen, and Callout performed the best for the medium screen. Therefore, having to issue two taps to enter one character seems to be questionable for medium and large screens. In fact, the qualitative comments of our participants indeed reveal the inconvenience of issuing two taps to enter a single character. This was especially mentioned for the larger screen.

Implications for Design

Our findings and related results provide estimates of the advantages and drawbacks attributed to different soft keyboard design choices. Thus, where to use any of the approaches we have studied can be an informed choice depending on the available space onscreen. In the following we summarize the main implications derived from our findings.

The larger the tiny screen, the better

We observed that performance improved as screen size increased. Of special importance is the case of the larger screen, where Callout and ZShift achieved 10 WPM. Interestingly, it was observed that all participants systematically perceived the three keyboards being more usable as screen size increased (Table 9). A detailed analysis of each TLX dimension revealed that this behavior was surprisingly consistent for all keyboard-screen combinations (Figure 4). This puts forward the fact that a few millimeters can make a difference.

Text entry on tiny qwerty keyboards is feasible

The short-term learning analysis suggests that the tested keyboards provide reasonable entry speeds on very small screens along with competitive accuracy. Interestingly, in terms of KSPC, both Callout and ZShift keyboards stabilized around 1.5 on all screen sizes, which means that transcription errors were systematically committed from time to time (Figure 6b). Meanwhile, ZoomBoard approached its innate value of 2.0 when entering the fifth phrase on all conditions. This suggests that our participants were more accurate with ZoomBoard.

Text entry on tiny qwerty keyboards is not so error-prone

Participants were told to type as fast and accurate as possible, and were able to correct errors as they went. Unsurprisingly, the smallest screen was the most error-prone overall, where ZoomBoard and ZShift outperformed Callout. This is so because they provide mechanisms based on zooming and visual context that allows users to deal with the inaccuracy of finger-based input. With Callout, users can still move their finger before lifting it up, however we found that it was not enough to achieve competitive accuracy on diminutive screens. For the larger screen these differences faded away. In the end, we observed that 20% of the submitted phrases had one or more transcription errors. Most of them were typos, therefore incorporating error correcting mechanisms would be plausible and very useful to improve all keyboard alternatives.

Submitting text on tiny screens can be tricky

We observed that simply tapping on the upper part of the screen to submit text can become a trouble, as users could accidentally submit when actually trying to enter a character. Hence, when designing a "submit text" interaction for tiny touchscreens, a more elaborated interaction should be considered; e.g., by issuing a double tap.

Cognitive aspects of text entry on tiny qwerty keyboards

Callout and ZShift require the user to relocate the focus of attention; i.e., she has to look first in which key her finger has landed, then she has to move eyesight to the upper part of the screen to verify it, as the finger is occluding most of the keyboard. Conversely, participants got immediately familiarized with ZoomBoard, since tap+zoom interactions are simple to perform, easy to understand, and do not occlude the keyboard because of the first tap. Therefore, the other techniques are cognitively inferior to begin with and may require a little practice for the very first time. Nevertheless our data shows that ZShift performs similar to ZoomBoard on small and medium screens, and that both ZShift and Callout outperform ZoomBoard on the larger screen.

One qwerty keyboard for one tiny screen
ZoomBoard was evaluated with a fairly small user sample (4 females, 2 males). We can now corroborate that Oney *et al.*'s findings still hold in a more general setting with a broader user sample. In sum, ZoomBoard is a reliable solution for entering text on diminutive screens. Considering that it was outperformed by ZShift on the larger screen, we would probably recommend ZoomBoard for really small devices such as necklaces or earrings, and ZShift for mid-sized devices such as smartwatches or bracelets.

Limitations

Apart from the "usual suspects" in lab-based studies (number of participants, age, etc.), we should mention that we used a relatively small number of phrases for each condition, and they were all different in each condition, for all participants. This may have made true differences between conditions difficult to detect. Nevertheless, all phrases have similar complexity, are moderate in length, easy to remember, and representative of written English [25]. Moreover, each participant tested each keyboard-screen combination for around 10 minutes, so special consideration was put into balancing user effort and data granularity. We hypothesize that a longitudinal between-subjects learnability study (i.e., only 1 keyboard-screen condition per participant instead of 9 conditions) would clearly reveal the actual benefit of using each keyboard over time, because carryover and fatigue effects would had little influence.

Modern soft keyboards use word prediction and error auto-correction mechanisms, and for tiny screens it is plausible that these would be very useful. However, we did not test this effect because it would have introduced another factor that would have compromised the internal validity of the experiment. This actually brings us to the following discussion.

Our study was conducted in a controlled environment, with users performing copy-text tasks. Although it may seem more natural to have users enter free text on an actual wearable device and increase thus the external validity of the experiment, it is critical to make the text entry method the only independent variable in the experiment, and increase thus its internal validity [21]. Indeed, if users were just asked to type "anything as fast and accurately as possible" they would introduce rather biased text. Therefore, we are confident that the observed effects between keyboards and screen sizes are, to a large extent, due to the test conditions.

CONCLUSION AND FUTURE WORK

We investigated the scalability of 3 qwerty-based soft keyboards for 3 small screen sizes. Text entry on tiny touchscreen devices might typically be limited to simple tasks such as writing names, addresses, calendar events, or short messages. However, until now text entry alternatives for such devices were scarce. Our research is based on the existing familiarity that computer users have with qwerty keyboards, a well-established property that every soft keyboard has to compete with, for better or worse.

Through a comprehensive study, we showed that different screen sizes demand different types of assistance. Our results reveal that users subjectively perceive ZoomBoard to be the best choice for the smallest screen (16 mm wide). However, ZShift achieves similar performance—all metrics are statistically comparable, excepting KSPC that is innately higher for ZoomBoard. For the other screen sizes (24 and 32 mm wide) ZShift is the best performer overall. It was interesting to observe that users got quickly familiarized with all text entry techniques.

Overall, the three keyboards we studied approach reasonable entry speeds along with competitive accuracy for entering text on tiny touchscreens. Broadly speaking, a technique like ZoomBoard, which relies on tap+zoom interactions and deals with occlusion by forcing users to lift up their fingers, is competitive for diminutive touchscreens. Nevertheless, more advanced approaches like ZShift, that provide visual feedback through a zoomed callout, may achieve better performance.

Finally, we believe there are 3 research avenues worth following for future work. First, to explore if there are any gender differences in performance. We suspect that female users, who typically have smaller fingers, might perform better. Second, to study fined-grained interactions related to usage patterns in the ZShift and Callout keyboards. For instance, do users initially touch some keys adjacent to their target? If so, do they succeed in correcting such mistake? Third, to incorporate some error correcting and/or prediction mechanisms. As previously discussed, these are used in modern soft keyboards, and for tiny screens it is plausible that they would be very useful.

Looking forward, we believe our work provides valuable research opportunities in text entry on very small screens. In general, manufacturers can benefit from this paper by selecting the most appropriate qwerty soft keyboard for their devices. Ultimately, this work provides designers, researchers, and practitioners with new understanding of qwerty soft keyboard design space and its scalability for tiny touchscreens.

ACKNOWLEDGMENTS

We thank our participants and the anonymous CHI reviewers. This work is part of the Valorization and I+D+i Resources program of VLC/CAMPUS and has been funded by the Spanish MECD as part of the International Excellence Campus program. This work has also been partially supported by the Spanish MINECO (TIN2014-37475 and TIN2010-20488) and the GVA VALi+d program (APOSTD/2013/013).

REFERENCES

1. Baudisch, P., and Chu, G. Back-of-device interaction allows creating very small touch devices. *Proc. CHI* (2009).
2. Bradley, J. V. Complete counterbalancing of immediate sequential effects in a Latin square design. *J. Amer. Statist. Ass. 53* (1958).
3. Chen, X., Grossman, T., and Fitzmaurice, G. Swipeboard: A text entry technique for ultra-small interfaces that supports novice to expert transitions. *Proc. UIST* (2014).
4. Dunlop, M., and Levine, J. Multidimensional pareto optimization of touchscreen keyboards for speed, familiarity and improved spell checking. *Proc. CHI* (2012).

5. Dunlop, M. D., and Crossan, A. Predictive text entry methods for mobile phones. *Personal Technologies 4*, 2–3 (2000).
6. Dunlop, M. D., and Masters, M. M. Pickup usability dominates: A brief history of mobile text entry research and adoption. *Int. J. Mobile Hum-Comput. Int. 1*, 1 (2009).
7. Felzer, T., and Nordmann, R. Alternative text entry using different input methods. *Proc. ASSETS* (2006).
8. Findlater, L., Wobbrock, J. O., and Wigdor, D. Typing on flat glass: examining ten-finger expert typing patterns on touch surfaces. *Proc. CHI* (2011).
9. Goldberg, D., and Richardson, C. Touch-typing with a stylus. *Proc. CHI* (1993).
10. Gunawardana, A., Paek, T., and Meek, C. Usability guided key-target resizing for soft keyboards. *Proc. IUI* (2010).
11. Harrison, C., and Hudson, S. E. Abracadabra: wireless, high-precision, and unpowered finger input for very small mobile devices. *Proc. UIST* (2009).
12. Henze, N., Rukzio, E., and Boll, S. Observational and experimental investigation of typing behaviour using virtual keyboards for mobile devices. *Proc. CHI* (2012).
13. Himberg, J., Häkkilä, J., Kangas, P., and Mäntyjärvi, J. On-line personalization of a touch screen based keyboard. *Proc. IUI* (2003).
14. Ingmarsson, M., Dinka, D., and Zhai, S. TNT: a numeric keypad based text input method. *Proc. CHI* (2004).
15. Isokoski, P., and Raisamo, R. Device independent text input: a rationale and an example. *Proc. AVI* (2000).
16. James, C. L., and Reischel, K. M. Text input for mobile devices: comparing model prediction to actual performance. *Proc. CHI* (2001).
17. Kienzle, W., and Hinckley, K. Writing handwritten messages on a small touchscreen. *Proc. MobileHCI* (2013).
18. Kim, S., Sohn, M., Pak, J., and Lee, W. One-key keyboard: a very small QWERTY keyboard supporting text entry for wearable computing. *Proc. OZCHI* (2006).
19. Komninos, A., and Dunlop, M. Text input on a smart watch. *Pervasive Computing 13*, 4 (2014).
20. Kristensson, P. O., and Zhai, S. Relaxing stylus typing precision by geometric pattern matching. *Proc. IUI* (2005).
21. Leiva, L. A., and Sanchis-Trilles, G. Representatively memorable: Sampling the right phrase set to get the text entry experiment right. *Proc. CHI* (2014).
22. Li, F. C. Y., Guy, R. T., Yatani, K., and Truong, K. N. The 1line keyboard: a QWERTY layout in a single line. *Proc. UIST* (2011).
23. Lyons, K., Nguyen, D., Ashbrook, D., and White, S. Facet: a multi-segment wrist worn system. *Proc. UIST* (2012).
24. Lyons, K., Starner, T., Plaisted, D., Fusia, J., Lyons, A., Drew, A., and Looney, E. Twiddler typing: One-handed chording text entry for mobile phones. *Proc. CHI* (2004).
25. MacKenzie, I. S., and Soukoreff, R. W. Phrase sets for evaluating text entry techniques. *Proc. CHI EA* (2003).
26. MacKenzie, I. S., Soukoreff, R. W., and Helga, J. 1 thumb, 4 buttons, 20 words per minute: design and evaluation of H4-writer. *Proc. UIST* (2011).
27. MacKenzie, I. S., and Zhang, S. X. The immediate usability of graffiti. *Proc. GI* (1997).
28. MacKenzie, I. S., and Zhang, S. X. The design and evaluation of a high-performance soft keyboard. *Proc. CHI* (1999).
29. Oney, S., Harrison, C., Ogan, A., and Wiese, J. ZoomBoard: a diminutive QWERTY soft keyboard using iterative zooming for ultra-small devices. *Proc. CHI* (2013).
30. Oulasvirta, A., Reichel, A., Li, W., Zhang, Y., Bachynskyi, M., Vertanen, K., and Kristensson, P. O. Improving two-thumb text entry on touchscreen devices. *Proc. CHI* (2013).
31. Partridge, K., Chatterjee, S., Sazawal, V., Borriello, G., and Want, R. TiltType: accelerometer-supported text entry for very small devices. *Proc. UIST* (2002).
32. Perlin, K. Quikwriting: continuous stylus-based text entry. *Proc. UIST* (1998).
33. Ren, X., and Moriya, S. Improving selection performance on pen-based systems: a study of pen-based interaction for selection tasks. *ACM TOCHI 7*, 3 (2000).
34. Roeber, H., Bacus, J., and Tomasi, C. Typing in thin air: the canesta projection keyboard – a new method of interaction with electronic devices. *Proc. CHI EA* (2003).
35. Roudaut, A., Huot, S., and Lecolinet, E. TapTap and MagStick: improving one-handed target acquisition on small touch-screens. *Proc. AVI* (2008).
36. Sazawal, V., Want, R., and Borriello, G. The unigesture approach one-handed text entry for small devices. *Proc. MobileHCI* (2002).
37. Soukoreff, R. W., and MacKenzie, I. S. Metrics for text entry research: An evaluation of MSD and KSPC, and a new unified error metric. *Proc. CHI* (2003).
38. Soukoreff, R. W., and MacKenzie, I. S. Recent developments in text-entry error rate measurement. *Proc. CHI* (2004).
39. Vogel, D., and Baudisch, P. Shift: A technique for operating pen-based interfaces using touch. *Proc. CHI* (2007).
40. Wobbrock, J. O., and Myers, B. A. Analyzing the input stream for character-level errors in unconstrained text entry evaluations. *ACM TOCHI 13*, 4 (2006).
41. Wobbrock, J. O., Myers, B. A., and Kembel, J. A. EdgeWrite: a stylus-based text entry method designed for high accuracy and stability of motion. *Proc. UIST* (2003).
42. Xiao, R., Laput, G., and Harrison, C. Expanding the input expressivity of smartwatches with mechanical pan, twist, tilt and click. *Proc. CHI* (2014).
43. Yatani, K., Partridge, K., Bern, M., and Newman, M. Escape: a target selection technique using visually-cued gestures. *Proc. CHI* (2008).
44. Zhai, S., Hunter, M., and Smith, B. A. Performance optimization of virtual keyboards. *Hum-Comput. Interact.* (2002).
45. Zou, Y., Liu, Y., Liu, Y., and Wang, K. Overlapped handwriting input on mobile phones. *Proc. ICDAR* (2011).

Performance and User Experience of Touchscreen and Gesture Keyboards in a Lab Setting and in the Wild

Shyam Reyal[1]
[1]School of Computer Science
University of St Andrews, UK
smr20@st-andrews.ac.uk

Shumin Zhai[2]
[2]Google Inc
Mountain View, California, USA
shumin.zhai@google.com

Per Ola Kristensson[1,3]
[3]Department of Engineering
University of Cambridge, UK
pok21@cam.ac.uk

ABSTRACT
We study the performance and user experience of two popular mainstream mobile text entry methods: the Smart Touch Keyboard (STK) and the Smart Gesture Keyboard (SGK). Our first study is a lab-based ten-session text entry experiment. In our second study we use a new text entry evaluation methodology based on the experience sampling method (ESM). In the ESM study, participants installed an Android app on their own mobile phones that periodically sampled their text entry performance and user experience amid their everyday activities for four weeks. The studies show that text can be entered at an average speed of 28 to 39 WPM, depending on the method and the user's experience, with 1.0% to 3.6% character error rates remaining. Error rates of touchscreen input, particularly with SGK, are a major challenge; and reducing out-of-vocabulary errors is particularly important. Both SGK and STK have strengths, weaknesses, and different individual awareness and preferences. Two-thumb touch typing in a focused setting is particularly effective on STK, whereas one-handed SGK typing with the thumb is particularly effective in more mobile situations. When exposed to both, users tend to migrate from STK to SGK. We also conclude that studies in the lab and in the wild can both be informative to reveal different aspects of keyboard experience, but used in conjunction is more reliable in comprehensively assessing input technologies of current and future generations.

Author Keywords
Mobile text entry; gesture keyboard; experience sampling

ACM Classification Keywords
H.5.2: User Interfaces—*Input devices and strategies.*

INTRODUCTION
Mobile text entry has been a topic of intense research for over two decades (see [6, 12, 13, 19, 20, 27] for surveys and overviews). Text entry on touchscreen mobile devices is typically carried out using one of two intelligent text entry methods [12]. The first involves typing using a single finger or two thumbs on a touch tapping QWERTY keyboard. In this paper we will call this method Smart Touch Keyboard (STK). Modern STKs perform automatic typing correction (e.g. [10, 16]) and allow users to choose among word predictions. In the research literature, STKs automatic typing correction algorithms have been further refined by considering users' posture [9], whether users are walking or standing still [8], finger pressure and Gaussian Process regression of touch locations [24], and by simultaneously supporting both word completions and automatic typing correction [2].

CHI 2015, Apr 18-23, 2015, Seoul, Republic of Korea
ACM 978-1-4503-3145-6/15/04.
http://dx.doi.org/10.1145/2702123.2702597

An alternative dominant text entry method is the Smart Gesture Keyboard (SGK) [15, 25, 26]. To write on a SGK a user slides a finger across the touchscreen keyboard. For example, to write the word "the" the user may land on the *T* key, slide to the *H* key, continue to the *E* key, and then lift up the finger. This produces a gesture that is recognized by the system and is pattern matched to find the word whose trace on the keyboard most resembles the user entered gesture. This gesture keyboard paradigm has appeared in products such as ShapeWriter, Swype, T9 Trace, Flext9, SlideIT, TouchPal and Google Keyboard on Android or iOS. The SGK paradigm has also been expanded into applications such as command entry (for example, *Cut*, *Copy*) [17], SGK layout designs [22], an algorithm for combining SGK input and speech recognition [14], and a bi-manual SGK [1].

Empirical studies of the performance, or experience, of writing using the SGK are generally difficult to conduct because text entry is a complex form of interaction involving motor skills, memory, learning and other cognitive aspects of human behavior. These factors may change from the laboratory to real world everyday use environments. For STKs the topic is even more complicated because inevitably the empirical results are to a large degree dependent on the algorithms, parameters, and the sizes of the keyboard vocabulary, and product design in general at the time of the study. Nonetheless, not having any in-depth empirical studies is not acceptable for the HCI field. Continued progress and innovation in the text entry field cannot have a solid empirical footing if we do not even know how well current technologies work for users.

In this paper we first report the results of a multi-session empirical experiment that investigates STK and SGK performance in the lab. Thereafter we introduce our Experience Sampling Method (ESM)-based text entry evaluation tool and methodology and present the results of a STK and SGK study in the wild in which we sampled participants' STK and a SGK performance and user experience for four weeks. We provide a comprehensive analysis of entry and error rates, out-of-vocabulary (OOV) issues, users' preferred hand postures, users' preferences and open comments, and contrast and compare both the relative performance of STK and SGK and the effect of the study design on the collected data.

RELATED WORK

Despite the prevalence of STKs and SGKs there is a lack of in-depth studies about their text entry performance, in particular outside a lab environment.

Goel et al. [8] evaluated their WalkType system with 16 participants in sitting and walking conditions in a single 45-minute session. The entry rate for STK was 31.1 WPM in the walking condition and 28.3 WPM in the sitting condition. Goel et al. [9] also evaluated their ContextType STK with 16 participants in a single one-hour session. The entry rate for the ContextType STK was 27.5 WPM and the corrected error rate was 4.86%. The baseline condition was a standard (non-correcting) touchscreen keyboard which resulted in a corrected error rate of 6.49%. Weir et al., [24] evaluated their pressure-sensitive STK with 16 participants in a single session and reported an average entry rate of 19.23 WPM. Dunlop and Levine [5] evaluated two touchscreen keyboards based on Pareto optimization techniques, with 10 participants and four 45 minute trial sessions each. The entry rate on the regular QWERTY STK was 21.3 WPM.

A previous evaluation compared the performance of an SGK running on a pen-based computer with a physical two-thumb keyboard [11]. It found that the SGK resulted in 25 WPM average speed after 25 minutes of writing. In a second study, participants wrote text at 40 WPM on average, although it is important to note that in that study participants were repeatedly writing the same phrases in order to accelerate motor memory [11]. A brief SGK study was also included in conjunction with the presentation of a text entry experiment tool for Android devices [3]. This study involved six participants using an SGK for 20 minutes. The final entry rate for SGK was 20 WPM. Finally, another small SGK study involved 14 participants writing using the SGK for five minutes on a Windows 7 tablet [21]. The entry rate for the SGK was 12 WPM.

EXPERIMENT 1: LAB EXPERIMENT

This was a multi-session within-subjects experiment, in which we compared the performance of STK and SGK using the transcription task in a lab environment. The primary dependent variables were entry rate (WPM) and error rate, measured as character error rate (CER).

Method

Participants

We recruited 12 volunteers from the University of St Andrews campus, an equal number of males and females. Their ages ranged from 21–34 (mean = 25, SD = 4). Four of them were native English speakers while the rest spoke English as their second language. Five were Android smartphone or tablet users, three were iPhone or iPod users, one was a Nokia Lumia Windows Phone user, two were BlackBerry users, and two did not use a smartphone. Ten had used an STK before and three had used an SGK before. Each participant was required to attend ten sessions lasting just under an hour. They received a £5 Amazon voucher per session.

Apparatus and Material

We used two identical LG Nexus 4 mobile devices running Android 4.3. The 4.7" Corning Gorilla Glass 2 touch screen had a resolution of 1280 × 768 pixels at 320 pixels per inch. The physical devices measured 133.9 × 68.7 × 9.1 mm. We used the Google keyboard, which was shipped with the device, with all default settings. The Google keyboard has a state-of-the-art STK and a state-of-the-art SGK built in.

Procedure

The experiment consisted of ten sessions split into five sessions for STK and five sessions for SGK. We divided the participants into two equal groups. Participants in the first group completed their first five sessions using the STK and the last five sessions using the SGK. The other group had the opposite order.

Before commencing the first and the sixth sessions, participants were given time to familiarize themselves with the new text entry method if they hadn't used it in the past. The sessions were spaced at least four hours apart and were maximally separated by two days. Each session consisted of five 10-minute-long typing runs followed by two-minute-long breaks.

We used the Enron mobile email dataset [7] as our phrase set. We pruned this dataset for sentences containing no numbers, no punctuation, no words with spelling errors, and no special characters. From this set, we extracted sentences that were no longer than 60 characters in length with spaces. This gave us a total of 1,008 sentences for our stimuli. We counted 1,457 unique words in this test set.

We compared all the words in the test set against a standard lexicon (64K common words used in the English language). The words that weren't in the lexicon were each entered carefully on the Google keyboard, by tapping the center of each key on the STK and by gesturing from the center to center of each key on the SGK. We noted that the same 44 words were out of vocabulary (OOV) words for both the STK and SGK. These OOVs appeared in 45 sentences (4.46% of 1,008) in the stimuli set, and were marked as sentences with OOV words. These OOV sentences were analyzed in post-hoc analyses after the experiment.

The experiment used a transcription task where participants were shown a phrase from the dataset and asked to copy it. We encouraged participants to focus on both speed and accuracy by providing an additional £15 Amazon voucher as an incentive to the fastest and the most accurate participants. Whilst being encouraged to use the Google keyboard's suggested words for correction, we discouraged participants to use the backspace and to correct words that were already entered. Participants were seated during the experiment, with no distractions from the environment. Our experiment app recorded the stimulus (test) phrases and the response text using millisecond timestamps when the user entered the first character and when the user pressed NEXT.

Participants rated their previous experience with software keyboards (STK and SGK) on mobile devices, and self-rated themselves on how fast and accurate they thought they were. During each two-minute break, they were asked to rate the speed, accuracy, preference, and ease of use of the currently used text entry method. Answers were recorded on a 1–7 Likert scale.

We intentionally did not control hand posture. Instead we asked participants to use their preferred posture and report it at the end of each session. The choices were single thumb, single finger and two thumbs.

At the end, participants were asked to write descriptive and open comments about what they liked and/or disliked about each text entry method.

Results

In total we collected 100 hours of data (50 minutes of writing per session (excluding breaks) × 120 sessions). Using STK, participants entered an average of 1393 sentences (SD = 275) during each session totaling 13,927 data points. 211 of these were filtered out as outliers since they were determined to be more than three standard deviations away from the mean. Using SGK, participants entered an average of 1,282 sentences per session (SD = 225), which totaled 12,816 data points; out of which 278 points were discarded as outliers.

All statistical analyses were done using repeated-measures analysis of variance at significance level $\alpha = 0.05$. Bonferroni corrections were used to adjust the significance levels for post-hoc analyses. We report the majority of the statistical results in tables. In the tables m is the sample mean, S1 is the first session in a condition, S5 is the 5th (last) session in a condition, 95% CI means the 95% confidence interval (Z-scores).

Entry Rate

Entry rate was measured in words-per-minute (WPM), with a word defined as five consecutive characters including spaces. STK was significantly faster than SGK (Figure 1 and Table 1). Also participants improved significantly with practice (Figure 1).

Character Error Rate

Character Error Rate (CER) was calculated as the minimum edit distance between the stimulus phrase and the response text, divided by the number of characters in the stimulus phrase. Error rates were "corrected error rates" as the error rates are measured after either the user or autocorrect had corrected the response text. SGK resulted in a significantly higher error rate (2.04–2.34% CER) than STK (1.09–1.11% CER); see Table 2.

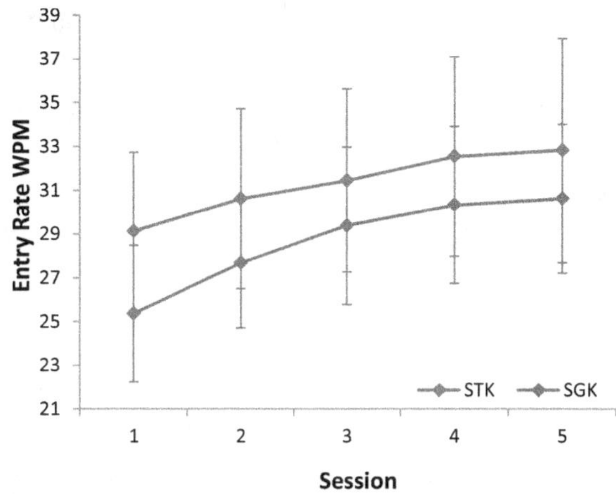

Figure 1. Mean entry rate (wpm) and 95% confidence intervals as a function of session in the lab study.

WPM	m S1	95% CI S1	m S5	95% CI S5
STK	29.1	25.5 - 32.7	32.8	27.7 - 37.9
SGK	25.4	22.2 - 28.5	30.6	27.2 - 34.0
ANOVA	F_{df}	df	η_p^2	p
Input Type	5.406	1,11	.330	**.040***
Session	22.036	4,44	.667	**.000***
Input × Session	0.818	4,44	.069	.521

Table 1. Entry rate analysis in the lab study

CER	m S1	95% CI S1	m S5	95% CI S5
STK	1.09	0.38 - 1.79	1.11	0.25 - 1.97
SGK	2.34	1.49 - 3.18	2.04	0.89 - 3.18
ANOVA	F_{df}	df	η_p^2	p
Input Type	17.267	1,11	.611	**.002***
Session	0.397	4,44	.035	.810
Input × Session	0.669	4,44	.057	.617

Table 2. Error rate analysis in the lab study

Word Error Rate

Word error rate or WER is analogous to CER, but using whole words instead of characters. The word error rate followed a very similar pattern to the CER. Thus we do not include it in subsequent analyses.

Excluding Sentences with OOV Words

We identified 1,131 data points containing OOV sentences (4.31% of 26,254). Recall that all the OOVs in the study affect both STK and SGK. Excluding OOV sentences results in a narrowing of the entry rate of STK and SGK and the difference is no longer significant (Table 3). CER also dropped slightly but the difference between STK and SGK is less marked (Table 4).

WPM	m S1	95% CI S1	m S5	95% CI S5
STK	29.4	25.7 - 33	33.1	27.9 - 38.3
SGK	25.8	22.7 - 28.9	31.2	27.8 - 34.6
ANOVA	F_{df}	df	η_p^2	p
Input Type	3.946	1,11	.264	.072
Session	22.376	4,44	.670	**.000***
Input × Session	1.071	4,44	.089	.382

Table 3. Entry rate analysis in the lab study excluding sentences with OOV words

CER	m S1	95% CI S1	m S5	95% CI S5
STK	1.05	0.35 - 1.76	1.09	0.2 - 1.98
SGK	2.18	1.32 - 3.03	1.90	0.76 - 3.04
ANOVA	F_{df}	df	η_p^2	p
Input Type	12.429	1,11	.530	**.030***
Session	0.343	4,44	.030	.848
Input × Session	0.572	4,44	.049	.685

Table 4. Error rate analysis in the lab study excluding sentences with OOV words

Only Investigating Sentences with OOV Words

We investigated the previously excluded 1,131 data points, which consisted only of OOV sentences. The STK was significantly faster than SGK when participants entered sentences with OOVs (Table 5). While both conditions have been affected by OOVs, SGK was penalized more.

As expected, very high error rates are reported in both conditions, but they are significantly higher in SGK (Table 6). Overall OOVs present more challenges to SGK than STK. We will return to this point later in the discussion.

WPM	m S1	95% CI S1	m S5	95% CI S5
STK	25.2	21.7 - 28.7	28.9	24.6 - 33.2
SGK	18.8	15.5 - 22.2	22.6	18.6 - 26.7
ANOVA	F_{df}	df	η_p^2	p
Input Type	35.929	1,11	.766	**.000***
Session	6.132	4,44	.358	**.001***
Input × Session	0.303	4,44	.027	.874

Table 5. Entry rate analysis for the lab study: only sentences with OOV words.

CER	m S1	95% CI S1	m S5	95% CI S5
STK	1.68	0.78 - 2.57	1.41	0.7 - 2.13
SGK	5.80	4.23 - 7.36	4.86	3.14 - 6.57
ANOVA	F_{df}	df	η_p^2	p
Input Type	48.2	1,11	.814	**.000***
Session	0.955	4,44	.080	.441
Input × Session	1.055	4,44	.087	.390

Table 6. Error rate analysis for the lab study – only sentences with OOV words

Figure 2 indicates that two-thumb STK was the fastest, closely followed by single finger SGK. The difference in error rate between the different hand postures within STK was complex (Figure 3). Within SGK, single finger SGK produced lower error rates than single-thumb SGK (Figure 3). These results are indicative only, as a) hand postures were not controlled in the experiment, b) hand postures were self-reported by the participants, and c) some participants varied their hand postures across sessions. For these reasons, we do not report results of statistical analyses for hand postures. However, the data suggest hand posture might be an important factor for complete understanding of STK and SGK performance. Moreover, our data indicates that hand postures might have different effects on STK and SGK.

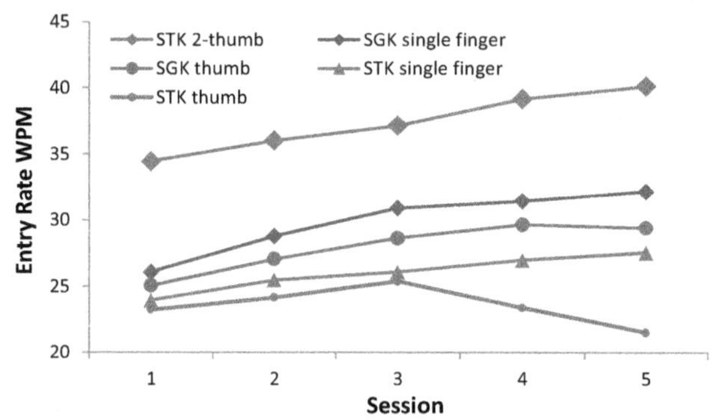

Figure 2. Mean entry rate as a function of session in the lab study, for different hand postures.

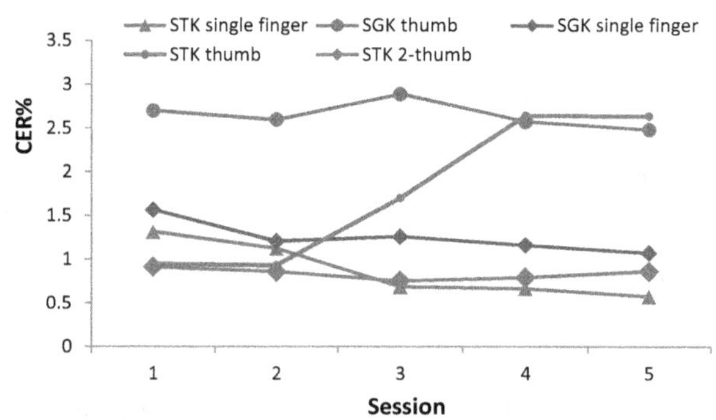

Figure 3. Mean character error rate as a function of session in the lab study, for different hand postures.

User Ratings

We calculated the median Likert-scale ratings from the participants' subjective ratings provided during their two-minute breaks between typing runs.

User Rating	STK		SGK	
	$\chi2(4)$	p	$\chi2(4)$	p
Input Speed	2.069	.723	15.584	**.004***
Accuracy	7.948	.093	13.083	**.011***
Ease of use	6.450	.168	14.530	**.007***
Preference	6.996	.136	14.231	**.006***

Table 7. Friedman's test results for session in the lab study

Friedman's test revealed that across sessions participants felt their text entry experience became faster, more accurate, easier and more preferable with SGK over the sessions (Figure 4, Table 7). This was not the case with STK, whose plots were more flat. Users rated STK as significantly faster, easier to use and more preferred over SGK. However, they didn't find it significantly more accurate (Table 8).

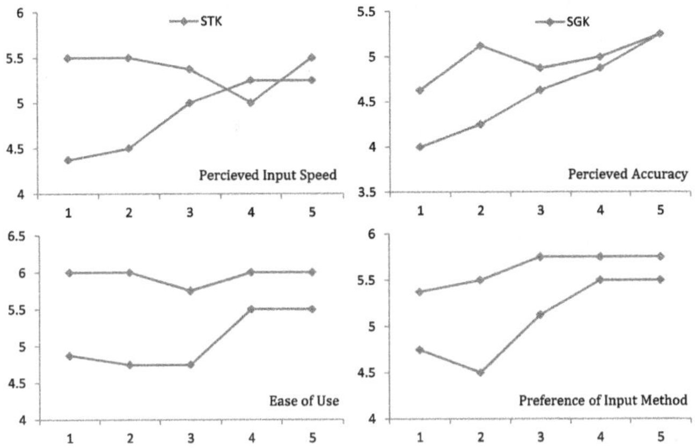

Figure 4. Users' subjective ratings during the lab study. *x*-axis: session; *y*-axis: Likert scale rating (1–7).

User Rating	Median		Friedman's Test Statistics	
	STK	SGK	$\chi 2(1)$	p
Input Speed	5.5	5	6.231	**.013***
Accuracy	5	4.75	2.200	.138
Ease of use	6	5	5.453	**.020***
Preference	5.5	5	7.681	**.006***

Table 8. Statistics for user ratings in the lab study

Open Comments

Participants also contributed open comments on what they liked and disliked about each input method. Five representative comments for and against each text entry method are as shown in Table 9. A few participants added general comments such as: "Speed and accuracy depends upon how tired you are and your mental state" and "Started to use gesture input on a daily basis".

EXPERIMENT 2: AN ESM TEXT ENTRY STUDY

While a lab experiment is the de-facto standard text entry evaluation methodology, we were curious to see how people use STK and SGK on their own mobile devices outside the lab amid their everyday activities. We therefore set out to conduct a text entry evaluation based on the Experience Sampling Method (ESM), in particular the way it has been used in ubiquitous computing [4]. To the best of our knowledge, ESM has not been used to compare two text entry methods before. We decided to compare the text entry performance and perceived user experience of STK and SGK "in the wild" in a study in which participants performed transcription tasks whilst attending to their daily tasks. As in our previous study, the primary dependent variables were entry rate, and the character and word error rates. For this purpose we developed a new Android app that enables researchers to carry out ESM text entry experiments in the wild. The app is open source and can be obtained by contacting the authors.

STK Positives	STK Negatives
"easier to input names, slang, abbreviations, and possible to change manually" "faster, and gives more control over what is been typed" "much less fatigue than gesture keyboard" "more convenient as can use two thumbs or fingers to type" "easier to correct errors"	"short words are repeatedly mistaken" "time taken to type a long word is annoying" "accidently pressed space a lot of times instead of bottom row keys" "I sometimes press the dot instead of the space" "backspace button hit when trying to press L"
SGK Positives	**SGK Negatives**
"new experience for me, really liked it" "enjoyable for me to slide my finger instead of tapping" "gives spaces between words automatically" "requires less movement of fingers, a smooth curve instead of several tappings" "words quickly become committed to muscle memory"	"difficult and time consuming to correct simple errors" "if a single motion is incorrect, it will never guess the correct word" "impossible to input a word not in the dictionary" "fatigue when typing for long hours" "fingers get tired quickly, and if your hands are wet, gets even more difficult"

Table 9. Open comments by users in the lab study

Participants

We recruited 12 volunteers from the university campus. These too were a broad sample as they came from various schools and departments. 7 were male ages were 21–42 (mean = 27, SD = 6). Three had English as their first language and the others spoke English as their second language. None of the participants in the ESM study had participated in the lab-based study.

Method

Participants installed our custom ESM-inspired app on their own Android mobile devices and use it for 4 weeks. They were compensated with a £50 Amazon voucher. We encouraged participants to focus on both speed and accuracy by providing an additional £15 Amazon voucher as an incentive to the fastest and the most accurate participants. The only prerequisite of participation was that they used an Android device that they could download Google keyboard and install the ESM app on it.

Apparatus and Material

The apparatus used by the participants were their own android mobile devices. The devices used by the twelve participants were five Galaxy S3's (display size 4.8"), one Galaxy S4 (5.0"), one Galaxy Note (5.3"), one Galaxy S2

(4.3"), one Nexus 4 (4.7"), one Lenovo S720 (4.5"), one HTC Desire (3.7"), and HTC One S (4.3"). All the devices ran Android 4.0 or later and supported the Google Keyboard. Each participant downloaded Google keyboard from the Google Play Store and set it as their default input method on their mobile device before starting the study.

Procedure

The app was configured to give each participant 300 tasks over the full duration of the experiment, which was about 10 tasks per day, evenly spread during times the participants could be expected to be awake (the exact times were determined specifically for each individual study participant). Each sample required users to transcribe three phrases, thus collecting around 900 data points from each participant. We used the same Enron mobile phrase set as in the previous study.

The goals were to capture text input performance in a variety of everyday environments and mobility settings. The participants could defer a sampling prompt if it were inopportune. In practice they accepted prompts when they were standing, walking, using the computer, during lectures, while cooking, while travelling in moving vehicles and whilst lying on the bed.

Half of the participants used STK for the first two weeks and half of them used SGK. After two weeks the participants switched to the other text entry method.

Results

Each participant entered an average of 469 (SD = 13) phrases on STK, and 447 (SD = 45) phrases on SGK. This resulted in 5,623 and 5,363 data points for STK and SGK respectively. We discarded 97 and 120 data points as outliers based on the same filtering criteria as in the previous lab study. After filtering we ended up with 5,526 and 5,243 valid data points for STK and SGK. We split these data points into nine blocks, such that each block contained around 50 ordered data points.

Entry Rate

SGK was significantly faster than STK, and participants improved more with SGK than with STK with practice (Figure 5 and Table 10).

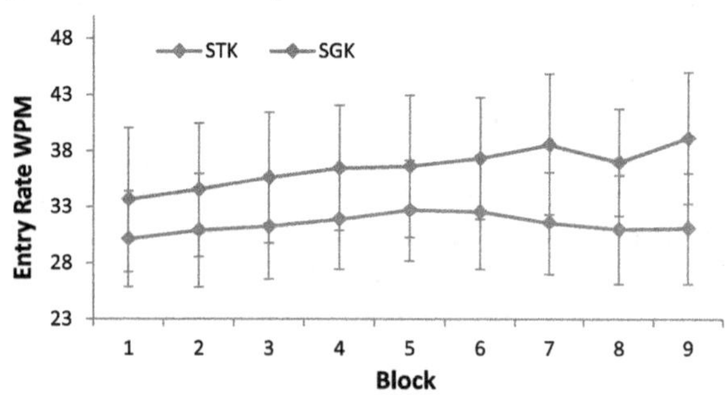

Figure 5. Mean entry rate and 95% confidence intervals as a function of block in the ESM study.

There is a striking difference in speed patterns between Experiment 1 and Experiment 2 (cf. Table 1 and Table 10). While the STK results are quite similar, the SGK results in the ESM experiment started much faster and grew even higher in speed as the study progressed (Figure 5).

WPM	*m* S1	95% CI S1	*m* S9	95% CI S9
STK	30.1	25.9 - 34.4	31.1	26.1 - 36
SGK	33.6	27.2 - 40	39.1	33.3 - 45
ANOVA	F_{df}	df	η_p^2	p
Input Type	5.965	1,11	.352	**.033***
Session	3.818	4,44	.258	**.001***
Input × Session	1.094	4,44	.090	.375

Table 10. Entry rate statistics in the ESM study.

Character Error Rate

SGK produced significantly higher CER than STK, which was similar to the lab study, but with higher values in both conditions (Figure 6, and Table 11).

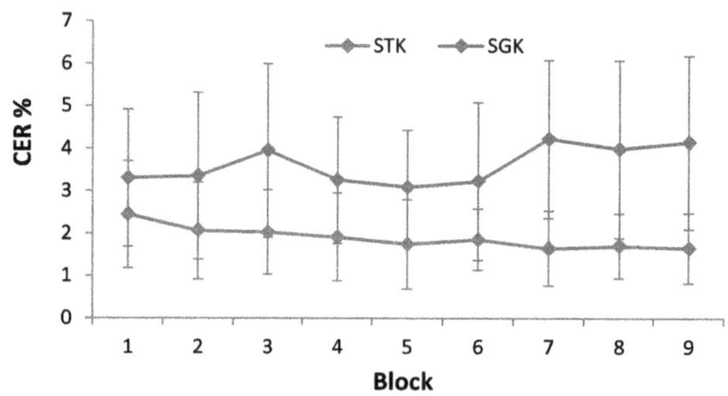

Figure 6. Mean error rate and 95% confidence intervals as a function of session number in the ESM study.

CER%	*m* S1	95% CI S1	*m* S9	95% CI S9
STK	2.44	1.18 - 3.71	1.65	0.82 - 2.48
SGK	3.30	1.69 - 4.92	4.14	2.1 - 6.18
ANOVA	F_{df}	df	η_p^2	p
Input Type	10.552	1,11	.490	**.008***
Session	1.375	4,44	.111	.219
Input × Session	1.559	4,44	.124	.149

Table 11. CER statistics in the ESM study

Exclusion of Sentences with OOV words

As in the lab study, we excluded 465 (4.31% of 10,769) data points which contained the identified OOV sentences. SGK was still significantly faster, produced significantly more errors, and participants improved over the sessions.

WPM	*m* S1	95% CI S1	*m* S9	95% CI S9
STK	30.3	26 - 34.7	31.3	26.4 - 36.1
SGK	34.3	27.7 - 40.8	39.3	33.5 - 45
ANOVA	F_{df}	df	η_p^2	p
Input Type	7.015	1,11	.389	**.023***
Session	3.376	4,44	.235	**.002***
Input × Session	1.083	4,44	.090	.382

Table 12. Entry rate statistics in the ESM study excluding OOVs

CER	m S1	95% CI S1	m S9	95% CI S9
STK	2.40	1.15 - 3.66	1.64	0.78 - 2.49
SGK	3.29	1.69 - 4.88	3.93	1.89 - 5.96
ANOVA	F_{df}	df	η_p^2	p
Input Type	8.298	1,11	.430	**.015***
Session	1.329	4,44	.108	.240
Input × Session	1.403	4,44	.113	.206

Table 13. Error rate analysis in the ESM study, excluding OOVs.

Sentences with OOV words

As in the lab study, we investigated those sentences containing OOV words. This was particularly interesting as the entry rate for SGK dropped so low that it was no longer faster than STK as before (cf. Figure 7 and Table 14 with Figure 5 and Table 10). This is also similar to what we noted in the lab study; OOV's greatly impact the entry rate of SGK.

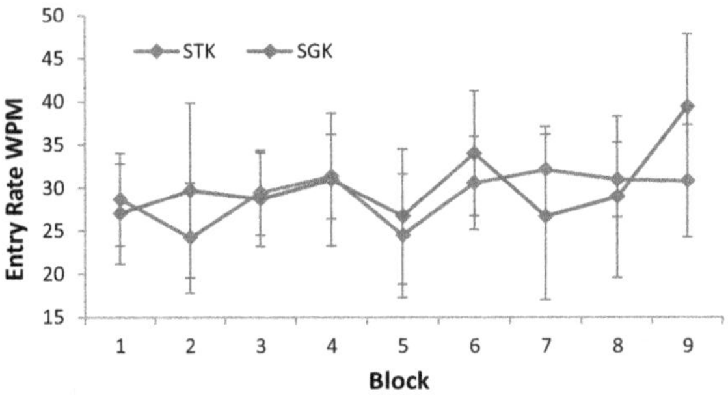

Figure 7. Mean entry rate and 95% confidence intervals as a function of session number in the ESM study: only sentences with OOV words.

WPM	m S1	95% CI S1	m S9	95% CI S9
STK	28.6	23.3 - 34	30.8	24.3 - 37.3
SGK	27.0	21.2 - 32.8	39.4	30.9 - 47.8
ANOVA	F_{df}	df	η_p^2	p
Input Type	0.135	1,11	.012	.720
Session	2.822	4,44	.205	**.008***
Input × Session	1.588	4,44	.126	.140

Table 14. Entry rate analysis in the ESM study with OOVs.

SGK produced much higher CER than STK and there was a significant change in the error rates across the blocks (Table 15).

CER	m S1	95% CI S1	m S9	95% CI S9
STK	3.39	1.48 - 5.31	2.11	0.67 - 3.55
SGK	3.46	1.42 - 5.51	7.98	4.43 - 11.54
ANOVA	F_{df}	df	η_p^2	p
Input Type	51.018	1,11	.831	**.000***
Session	2.718	4,44	.198	**.010***
Input × Session	1.635	4,44	.129	.126

Table 15. CER statistics in the ESM study with OOVs

Hand Posture

When using STK, eight participants mostly used two thumbs to type (3,686 data points) and four participants mostly used a single finger (1,843 data points). When using SGK, nine participants used single finger (4,057 data points) while three users used single thumb (1,186 data points). No participants opted for neither bi-manual gesture input on SGK or single thumb on STK. The number of participants who used the same hand posture is quite similar in both the studies; therefore we can quantitatively compare the results. In the ESM study, single thumb SGK was the fastest, followed by single finger SGK and two-thumb STK (Figure 8).

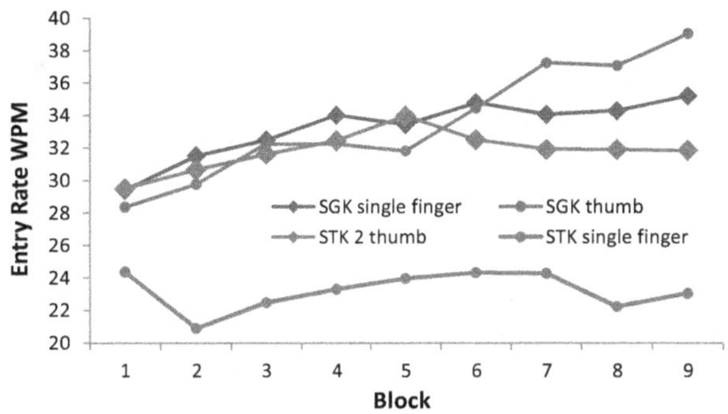

Figure 8. Mean entry rate (wpm) as a function of block in the ESM study for each hand posture.

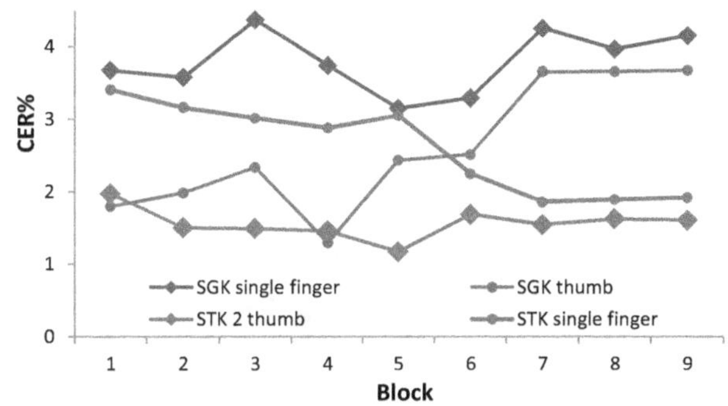

Figure 9. Mean character rate as a function of block in the ESM study for each hand posture.

Compared to Experiment 1 (Figure 2) it can be seen immediately that the entry rate is lower for STK and higher for SGK. Two-thumb STK is not the fastest text entry method/posture in Experiment 2, a position taken over by single-thumb-SGK. Also, while the single finger input was faster in SGK in Experiment 1, single thumb is faster in Experiment 2. However, within STK, the two-thumb posture still outperforms STK with a single finger. Two-thumb STK produced the lowest CER, followed by single thumb SGK (Figure 9). As in Experiment 1, the hand posture results should be interpreted as indicative.

When comparing error rates across the two experiments, the ESM study has higher values. The two-thumb STK produces the lowest error rate across both studies. In

Experiment 1, within SGK, single finger input resulted in a lower error rate, but in Experiment 2 this position is taken over by single thumb. Also, in Experiment 1, all STK hand postures had lower error rates than SGK hand postures, but in Experiment 2 the ranking is more mixed.

Subjective Ratings

The participants provided ratings on how the study affected their regular text input practices. At the beginning and end of the study, we collected ratings about the users' SGK usage level outside the experiment; with 1 meaning they only used STK, and 7 meaning they only used SGK.

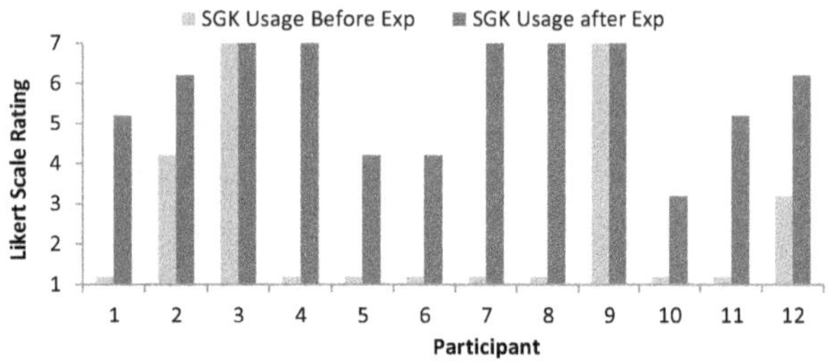

Figure 10. Level of SGK usage of participants outside the experiment, before and after the ESM study. 1 = no use (only STK), 7 = full use (only SGK).

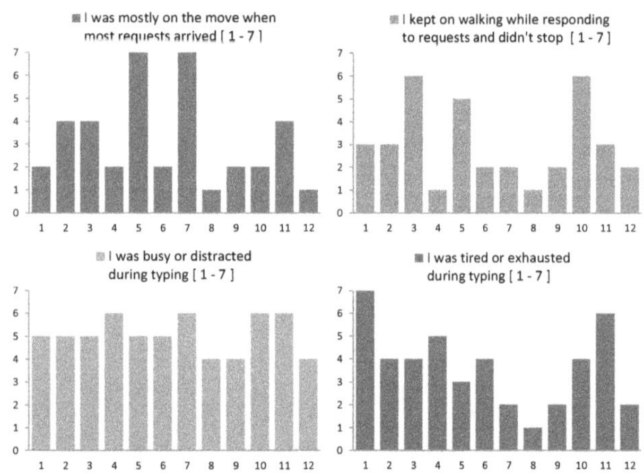

Figure 11. Movement, distraction and tiredness level of participants while typing in the ESM Study. x-axis: participant, y-axis: Likert Scale rating (1-7).

Figure 10 shows that at the beginning of the study eight participants were not using SGK outside the experiment at all. But at the end of the study, three participants within that set of eight participants had completely converted to using SGK as their main text entry method outside the experiment, with the other five participants reaching at least a halfway point (50/50 usage of STK and SGK). Two users have always used SGK, and the study had not affected their preference. Two other users had used both STK and SGK at the beginning of the experiment, and towards the end they had also shown a shift towards using the SGK more. It is remarkable that all users who only used STK prior to participating in the experiment were affected by this study.

Figure 11 shows the users' subjective ratings on their experience during the random times they were requested to participate in the study. The top two plots show that some participants were on the move when the ESM app requested them to type on their phones, and some of them continued to walk while typing instead of stopping. The bottom two plots show how busy, distracted or tired they were when actually typing texts. This is particularly useful in understanding how different the environment was when compared to the lab based Experiment 1, where the users were seated in a quiet environment, rested, and fully focused on the experiment task.

Open Comments

Five representative comments for and against each text entry method are as shown in Table 16. Participants in the ESM study also provided general comments, such as:

"I learned to use Gesture Keyboard and I'm currently using it. I also learnt about Google keyboard and it is now my default method of input"

"I will use gesture as much as I can for typing and also will introduce it to my friends"

"I will continue to use Google keyboard, both its tapping and gesture functions feel more user friendly than the Samsung keyboard"

"It's the first time I learnt this method and will definitely continue using it over tapping for my everyday use" – here "this method" refers to SGK

(a) STK Positives	(b) STK Negatives
"not restricted by the words suggested by autocorrect"	"difficult to have both speed and accuracy"
"ability to correct mistakes instantly"	"difficult to type while in motion, moving or walking"
"haptic feedback is also useful as a way of confirming you typed the correct number of letters"	"keys are quite small and very easy to make mistakes"
"could use two thumbs instead of one so one hand doesn't get tired"	"never could type as fast as the QWERTY on blackberry"
"More flexibility over what I type"	"boring"
(c) SGK Positives	**(d) SGK Negatives**
"easier to use with one hand"	"thumb gets tired quickly"
"feels natural and takes less effort"	"limited to words provided by the dictionary, have to go back and tap to get the required words"
"automatically adds a space to my words"	"sometimes breaks a single word into two"
"you don't have to be very accurate as it can recognize the intended word"	"cannot correct one or two letters, have to start from the beginning"
"can learn and get used to it easily"	"when typing a really long word, I sometimes get confused and move in the wrong direction"

Table 16. Open comments for and against each input method.

DISCUSSION

The lab study revealed that STK, in the two thumb tapping condition, was significantly faster than SGK (of both finger and thumb conditions, Figure 2). The ESM-study in Experiment 2 showed that SGK (of both finger and thumb conditions) was significantly faster than STK. Three factors might explain this discrepancy. First, in the ESM study participants used their own mobile devices, which they were already familiar with. It is possible this would benefit SGK more, particularly for the unique one handed thumb gesturing condition which required a good grasp of the device and making gestures with the same hand. Second, the lab-based test environment might have benefitted STK. In the lab study, participants were seated, fully focused on the task, and not distracted by any other simultaneous task. This situation benefitted participants using an STK with two thumbs, which was the only posture in which participants in Experiment 1 were faster with STK than SGK. In the ESM-study, when randomly requested to sample their text input performance, the participants were most likely busy with other activities, such as being on the move. Here the STK with two thumbs performed similar to SGK initially, but became less fast than SGK when the users gained more experience (Figure 8). Third, perhaps most importantly, SGK is a more novel typing method than STK. The ESM-study exposed such a novel method to the participants and enabled them to use it outside of the study (Figure 10) on their own device and hence realized SGK's greater potential in later sessions (Figure 8).

The experiments revealed that the SGK results in significantly higher error rates than STK. Participants' open comments provided for each input method included remarks such as stating instances where they could enter non-dictionary words in STK, while using the SGK the option wasn't available. This problem of OOV errors is shared among some other intelligent text entry methods that operate on word units, such as speech recognition [12].

Overall we find error is still a major challenge for text input and SGK suffers higher error rates than STK. A particular source of error is OOV. Our post-hoc analyses show that having to type sentences with OOVs impacts the entry rate in general, but the effect is stronger for SGK. As has been previously observed [18], there are two categories of errors in word-recognizers: confusion errors and OOV errors. An SGK user must know or infer whether a word is in the SGK vocabulary in order to be able to distinguish between these two error categories. If the user cannot accurately categorize the error, the user risks repeatedly trying to articulate the gesture for a word that is OOV. We propose mitigating this problem by either using generative OOV models that can predict words not in the vocabulary, such as the joint multigram models used in speech recognition, or by employing an interactive lexicon technique with active and passive words [18].

Our lab-study and ESM-study used different methodologies and it is therefore unsurprising they yielded different results. The discrepancies in the results suggest that future text entry studies need to carefully consider both internal and external validity. The ESM-methodology for text entry we introduced in this paper tests user performance of different text entry methods in situations that are more representative of everyday mobile phone use. Its results may therefore better support external validity.

Finally, our studies also revealed how users' preferences changed over time. We found that the participants demonstrated a definite trend towards moving to SGK, a still relatively novel method to many mobile users (as is illustrated in Figure 10). This is perhaps the strongest empirical finding in favor of the SGK method to date—when exposed to this new method (to many of them for the first time) the participants "voted with their feet" by using it more often. Importantly such a shift was based on the entire experience including (and beyond) speed and accuracy. To paraphrase the feedback from one of the participants: this experiment may have changed a few lives.

LIMITATIONS AND FUTURE WORK

We found that hand posture is a potentially important factor on STK and SGK performance, but hand posture was not explicitly controlled in our experiments and therefore our conclusions on hand posture's role are limited. A follow-up study which controls for hand posture would be able to state more definitive conclusions. We also did not control for device type in the ESM-study and we did not record participants' typing outside the sampling points in the ESM-study (in order to protect participants' privacy). Finally, in both our studies we used the standard transcription task. Complementary data might be gained by also using a composition task [23], which is able to more accurately model actual text entry activities.

CONCLUSIONS

Smart text input on mobile and touchscreen devices has been an active area of innovation both in the research literature and in the commercial world. However, as we noted in the introduction and related work, empirical research has been limited in scope, size, and technology form factor. Most reported text entry research has also been based on research prototypes. This paper reports the results of two systematic studies, in the largest scale in text input that we are aware of, using a widely deployed, publically available product with both STK and SGK capabilities from the same developer, establishing a set of empirical findings useful for further advancement of the field. First, we found that text can be entered at an average speed of 28 to 39 WPM, depending on the method and the user's experience, with 1.0% to 3.6% character error rates remaining. Second, error rates of touchscreen input, particularly with SGK, are still quite high; further advancements in the field need to focus on error tolerance and error correction. Reducing OOV errors are particularly important. Third, SGK and

STK both have strengths, weaknesses, and different individual awareness and preferences. Two-thumb touch typing in a focused setting seems particularly effective on STK, whereas one handed SGK typing with the thumb seems particularly effective in more mobile situations. This research shows that when exposed to SGK, users tend to migrate from STK to SGK. This constitutes perhaps the strongest empirical evidence of SGK's strength. Fourth, research methodology matters; studies in the lab and in the wild both can be informative to different aspects of keyboard experience, but used in conjunction is more reliable in comprehensively assessing input technologies of current and future generations.

REFERENCES

1. Bi, X., Chelba, C., Ouyang, T., Partridge, K. and Zhai, S. 2012. Bimanual gesture keyboard. In Proc. UIST 2012. ACM Press: 137–146.
2. Bi, X., Ouyang, T., and Zhai, S. Both complete and correct?: multi-objective optimization of touchscreen keyboard. In Proc. CHI (2014), 2297–2306.
3. Castellucci, S.J. and MacKenzie, S. 2011. Gathering text entry metrics on android devices. In Extended Abstracts CHI 2011. ACM Press: 1507–1512.
4. Consolvo, S. and Walker, M. 2003. Using the Experience Sampling Method to Evaluate Ubicomp Applications, IEEE Pervasive Computing 2(2): 24–31.
5. Dunlop, M.D. and Levine, J. 2012. Multidimensional pareto optimization of touchscreen keyboards for speed, familiarity and improved spell checking. In Proc. CHI 2012. ACM Press: 2669–2678.
6. Dunlop, M.D. and Masters, M.M. 2009. Pickup usability dominates: a brief history of mobile text entry research and adoption. International Journal of Mobile Human Computer Interaction 1(1): 42-59.
7. Enron Mobile Email Dataset http://keithv.com/software/enronmobile/
8. Goel, M., Findlater, L., and Wobbrock, J. WalkType: using accelerometer data to accomodate situational impairments in mobile touch screen text entry. In Proc. CHI (2012), 2687–2696.
9. Goel, M., Jansen, A., Mandel, T., Patel, S. N., and Wobbrock, J. O. ContextType: using hand posture information to improve mobile touch screen text entry. In Proc. CHI (2013), 2795–2798.
10. Goodman, J., Venolia, G., Steury, K. and Parker, C. 2002. Language Models for Soft Keyboards. In Proc. The Eighteenth National Conference on Artificial Intelligence, 419–424.
11. Kristensson, P.O. 2007. Discrete and Continuous Shape Writing for Text Entry and Control. Doctoral dissertation, Linköping University, Sweden.
12. Kristensson, P.O. 2009. Five challenges for intelligent text entry methods. AI Magazine 30(4): 85–94.
13. Kristensson, P.O. 2014. From wax tablets to touchscreens: an introduction to text entry research. ACM XRDS 21(1): 28–33.
14. Kristensson, P.O. and Vertanen, K. 2011. Asynchronous multimodal text entry using speech and gesture keyboards. In Proc. Interspeech 2011. ISCA: 581–584.
15. Kristensson, P.O. and Zhai, S. 2004. SHARK^2: a large vocabulary shorthand writing system for pen-based computers. In Proc. UIST 2004. ACM Press: 43–52
16. Kristensson, P.O. and Zhai, S. 2005. Relaxing stylus typing precision by geometric pattern matching. In Proc. IUI 2005. ACM Press: 151–158.
17. Kristensson, P.O. and Zhai, S. 2007. Command strokes with and without preview: using pen gestures on keyboard for command selection. In Proc. CHI 2007. ACM Press: 1137–1146.
18. Kristensson, P.O. and Zhai, S. 2008. Improving word-recognizers using an interactive lexicon with active and passive words. In Proc. IUI 2008. 353–356.
19. MacKenzie, I.S. and Soukoreff, R.W. 2002. Text entry for mobile computing: models and methods, theory and practice. Human-Computer Interaction 17(2): 147–198.
20. MacKenzie, I.S. and Tanaka-Ishii, K. (Eds.). 2007. Text Entry Systems. San Francisco: Morgan Kauffman, 139-158.
21. Nguyen, H. and Bartha, M.C. 2012. Shape Writing on Tablets: Better Performance or Better Experience? In Proc. The Human Factors and Ergonomics Society Annual Meeting 2012. SAGE: 1591–1593.
22. Rick, J. 2010. Performance optimizations of virtual keyboards for stroke-based text entry on a touch-based tabletop. In Proc. UIST 2010. ACM Press: 77–86.
23. Vertanen, K. and Kristensson, P.O. 2014. Complementing text entry evaluations with a composition task. ACM Transactions on Computer-Human Interaction 21(2): Article No. 8.
24. Weir, D., Pohl, H., Rogers, S., Vertanen, K., and Kristensson, P. O. Uncertain text entry on mobile devices. In Proc. CHI (2014), 2307–2316.
25. Zhai, S. and Kristensson, P.O. 2003. Shorthand writing on stylus keyboard. In Proc. CHI 2003. ACM Press: 97–104.
26. Zhai, S. and Kristensson, P.O. 2012. The word-gesture keyboard: reimagining keyboard interaction. Communications of the ACM 55(9): 91–101.
27. Zhai, S., Kristensson, P.O. and Smith, B.A. 2005. In search of effective text input interfaces for off the desktop computing. Interacting with Computers 17(3): 229–250.

Using Time-Anchored Peer Comments to Enhance Social Interaction in Online Educational Videos

Yi-Chieh Lee[1], Wen-Chieh Lin[1], Fu-Yin Cherng[1], Hao-Chuan Wang[2], Ching-Ying Sung[1], Jung-Tai King[1]
[1]National Chiao Tung University, Taiwan, [2]National Tsing Hua University, Taiwan
be341341@gmail.com, wclin@cs.nctu.edu.tw, fufu22710@gmail.com, haochuan@cs.nthu.edu.tw, {jtchin2, eva350053}@gmail.com

ABSTRACT
Online learning is increasingly prevalent as an option for self-learning and as a resource for instructional design. Prerecorded video is currently the main medium of online education content delivery and instruction; this affords asynchronicity and flexibility, and enables the dissemination of lecture content in a distributed and scalable manner. However, the same properties may impede learners' engagement due to the lack of social interaction and peer support. In this paper, we propose a time-anchored commenting interface to allow online learners who watch the same video clips to exchange comments on them. Comments left by previous learners at specific time points of a video are displayed to new learners when they watch the same video and reach those time points. We investigated how the display of time-anchored comments (dynamic or static) and type of comments (content-related or social-oriented) influenced users' perceived engagement, perceived social interactivity, and learning outcomes. Our results show that dynamically displaying time-anchored comments can indeed enhance learners' perceived social interactivity. Moreover, the content of comments would further affect learners' intention of commenting. Based on our findings, we make various recommendations for the improvement of social interaction and learning experience in online education.

Author Keywords
Online Educational Interface; E-learning; Synchronous Communication; Asynchronous Communication.

ACM Classification Keywords
K.3.1. Computer and Education: Computer Uses in Education, Distance Learning.

INTRODUCTION
Online learning has become one of the most influential media of instruction. Online courses not only provide a new approach for self-education but also show potential in transforming education, such as the introduction of flipped classrooms, where students are expected to learn from a combination of prerecorded video lectures and in-class non-lecture activities.

Online course platforms such as Massive Open Online Courses (MOOCs) and Open Course Ware (OCW) are now widely used, with the proliferation of diverse curricula attracting hundreds of thousands of learners to join them. Online educational platforms provide course materials to learners using a variety of methods. However, prerecorded online videos appear to be the universal main medium for content and instruction delivery across all online learning systems.

While it is widely agreed that the quality of video content is an important factor in the quality of online education, existing analytics seem to suggest that videos with high-quality content alone are insufficient to ensure this. Some studies [8, 10] have explored online learners' learning outcome and engagement with videos in MOOCs [15], but there is still limited clue showing that videos alone are the only best design choice in the design space of online education. In fact, previous studies indicated that many online learners reported the sense of isolation and that can hinder their ability and performance of learning [21]. It is especially noteworthy that there are seldom works focusing on supporting social interaction in online education.

Social interaction, such as asking and answering questions or collaboration among peers, may have not only important cognitive consequences, but also the potential to enhance learners' engagement with online courses. Previous work [10, 15] has indicated that engagement is one of the most important components of effective learning; Dixson [10] further suggests that rich communication using multi-modal interactions may be related to higher engagement, with learners spending more time on the topics at hand and being more motivated to learn about them [1, 27]. Moreover, highly interactive communications provide online course attendees with opportunities to practice different aspects of content processing and learning, such as remembering and retrieving the course content, which could also help online course attendees to construct their knowledge more efficiently [1]. Although there is a consensus in the learning science literature that social interactions are crucial to meaningful and productive learning [1,

CHI 2015, April 18-23 2015, Seoul, Republic of Korea.
Copyright © 2015 ACM 978-1-4503-3145-6/15/04..$15.00.
http://dx.doi.org/10.1145/2702123.2702349

27], it remains unclear how to effectively support and leverage social interactions to enhance online learning.

Existing designs for communication in online education systems can be categorized into two distinct types: synchronous and asynchronous. Asynchronous communication, such as the discussion forums that are often integrated with online course platforms, can better afford in-depth and more thoughtful discussion [20]; however, prior research [4, 20] also indicated some limitations of asynchronous designs, e.g., a lack of immediate feedback, and learners' perception of social disconnection etc. Huang et al. [18] indicated there are very few learners engaged in forums, and only about 5% of registered users contribute to the discussions in forums. Synchronous communication such as live chat affords immediate information exchange and discussion, with learners typically producing a greater volume of messages [20]; social presence is also much better supported by this mode of communication [26]. However, synchronous communication also has various drawbacks. Two major constraints, in the context of MOOCs, are that it can be technically very difficult to mediate and support large-scale conversations, and that online learners may not have enough time for deep reflection when interacting with others via synchronous communication [4]. Besides these technical difficulties, the global learner population from various time zones is also a challenge to synchronous communication.

To address these problems, we propose a design that allows shared commenting and annotation of video content, namely *time-anchored commenting* to support comment exchange and social interaction for online course videos. The time-anchored commenting design combines certain characteristics of both synchronous and asynchronous communication technologies. It partially resembles asynchronous discussion forums, in that users can leave their comments when watching a course video, but in addition to its content, each comment is time-stamped with the corresponding playing time of the video that users were watching. In other words, the proposed design will explicitly connect or anchor the content of the comment to the content of the video along its timeline. As a result, when other learners subsequently watch the same course material, existing comments can be displayed dynamically when the playback time matches the time of annotation. In this way, the system provides learners a way to exchange information and interact with previous learners around the video content, despite that learners reading and writing the comments are neither co-present nor watching the video at the same time.

Previous work [12, 14] in a different context also proposed similar techniques. The time-anchored design can be used to synchronize comments around a specific event in the video, allowing audiences to follow it more easily. However, similar techniques have mostly been evaluated in the context of digital entertainment and there is still a gap in our understanding of how these techniques might influence online learning.

This paper intends to make three contributions: (1) To build a prototype system for time-anchored commenting and demonstrate how it can be integrated with online educational videos; (2) To conduct a lab experiment to determine whether and how the time-anchored design influences learners' perceived engagement, perceived social interactivity, and learning outcomes in the context of online learning; and (3) To examine the influence of comment type (content-related or social-oriented) on users' learning and interactions, by performing an initial content analysis of comments.

RELATED WORKS

The number of users of online courses has increased dramatically in recent years. Some online course platforms even provide verified certificates to learners who fulfill course requirements; as such, online learning has become a significant instructional avenue. Online course platforms supply various curricula and are intended to improve users' learning outcomes and engagement [15]. One of the important issues confronting online learning is social interaction, in particular learner-learner social interaction, which has been understated. Vygotsky [29] has implied that learners can work together to create knowledge collaboratively and support one another's learning, while Johnson [20] points out that learner-learner or learner-instructor interactions are prerequisites for course satisfaction. Currently, online learning platforms' major social-interaction approaches comprise discussion forums (asynchronous) and chatrooms (synchronous). We discuss their advantages and disadvantages in the following sections.

Asynchronous Communication

The effects of the use of asynchronous discussion in online learning have been investigated extensively [4, 8, 26, 28, 16]. Some studies [19, 22] have compared face-to-face discussion with online discussion to examine the latter's effectiveness as an aid to learning, and the results indicate that online discussion could be superior to face-to-face discussion in some cases. In addition, Koory [22] found that learners reported higher levels of course satisfaction when online discussions were used, and that the text-based communication in online courses reinforced learners' literacy skills. Other previous studies [8, 2] also found that integrating a reputation system with MOOC forum could increase the forum engagement [2] or induce more responses, but it had no impact on the users' sense of community [8]. A number of studies [19, 20] state that asynchronous communication in online courses enriches users' learning experiences [30] and increases the number of comments with high-quality contents. However, a clear limitation of asynchronous discussion is its lack of immediate social interaction, with one prior study [20] noting specifically that asynchronous postings were slow and emotionless.

Synchronous Communication

Chatrooms are less frequently adopted in online courses than discussion forums, because the former are seen as essentially recreational, and therefore likely to distract users from their learning tasks [6]. Nevertheless, Coetzee et al. [7] compared the influence of chat-tab interfaces (dedicated pages for chat) with that of embedded-chat interfaces (chatrooms placed in every pages) on a MOOC platform. They found no evidence that chat adversely impacts online learning. Other research [11, 20] has suggested that synchronous online discussion can develop a sense of community among learners.

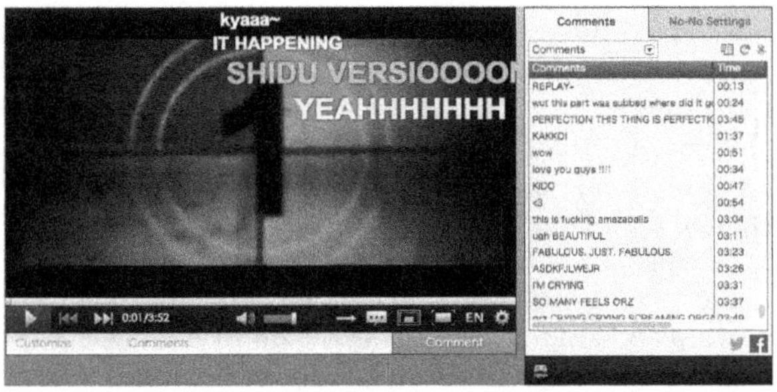

Figure 1. The interface of *niconico*

Conversation is one of life's enjoyable experiences [31], and integrating real-time communication with online video-watching can make users feel they are together despite being physically dispersed. Weisz et al. [31] found that chat during video viewing has a positive influence on social relationships and mutual engagement. However, real-time chat encounters problems when the number of active users becomes large [17]. Hamilton et al.'s study [17] using live streams of video indicated that users can become frustrated due to the difficulty of interacting with an over-abundance of streams. A similar problem also exists in MOOCs [20, 4].

Other Interaction Methods for Online Videos

Online courses attract large numbers of learners every day [23]. This characteristic can help teachers improve the quality of online course videos as well as teaching strategies, and learners can potentially obtain help from other learners online [9]. Cross et al. [9] proposed an online platform to help improve online courses' presentation quality, operating on similar lines to Wikipedia. Some other recent researches [12, 14] proposed annotation systems to enrich online videos, either by annotating specific object [12] or text-based comments [14] on a video, thus helping users share their comments with other audience members and motivating social interaction.

The video-sharing website *niconico* allows users to leave text-based comments in online videos (Figure 1). An important feature of *niconico* is that users' comments will be dynamically displayed on videos. These comments are shown on the top half of each video according to the playing time. This interface design enables the user to easily realize which events in the video have been focused on by other viewers, and thus has the potential to enhance social interaction.

Online learning videos can be accessed worldwide, which makes it relatively convenient for learners to revisit specific parts of an online course, and to receive feedback from other learners. Nevertheless, the methods of learner-learner interaction in current online learning are probably too limited to be effectively exploited. Inspired by *niconico*, this paper introduces a time-anchored commenting method and examines its effect on a selection of online learning videos. Given a sufficiently strong connection with the video content, we anticipate that this approach to learner-learner communication will bring significant benefits to online learning.

Although both *niconico* and our method align comments with the video time, we do not directly embed/overlap comments in the lecture video like *niconico* does. We display comments beside the video (Figure 2CD). Our design could avoid distracting the learners. Besides, the display style in *niconico* is also more diversified and sometimes exaggerated. Besides introducing a new interaction design for online educational videos, this paper focuses on exploring the influences of time-anchored commenting on learners. As *niconico* has never been applied to online educational videos, our study is critical for understanding the impact of time-anchored commenting in this domain.

RESEARCH HYPOTHESES

To explore the effects of the integration of time-anchored commenting into online course videos, we developed a communication platform broadly similar to the annotation systems in *niconico*. We then conducted an experiment and face-to-face interviews to investigate how learners interacted with others on this new platform, and measured its influence on perceived engagement, perceived social interactivity, and learning outcomes.

Engagement and social interaction play important roles in any online learning environment, motivating learners to keep learning online and engaging them with course content. As time-anchored commenting directly connects learner-generated comments with video course content, it seems likely that peers' comments could influence a learner's perspective and social interactions. Due to social interactions, learners will probably leave not only content-related comments but also social-oriented comments such as off-topic chats and jokes. However, as the number of peer-generated, content-related comments increases, we expect that online learners would become more engaged in the content of their course. Therefore, our first research hypothesis is:

H1. Time-anchored commenting will enhance online learners' perceived engagement with their course, and this effect will be more marked as the number of content-related comments increases.

As we mentioned that one of important capabilities of time-anchored commenting is dynamically displaying users' comments, thus, how to display the collected comments is a crucial issue. If comments left by previous learners are displayed dynamically when the current playback time matches the playback time at which they were added, it will result in an immediate impact on how learners interact with others' feedback. Indeed, this may make learners feel as if they are viewing the video synchronously. Consequently, we hypothesize that dynamically displaying peers' time-anchored comments would motivate (perceived) social interactivity and probably encourage learners to write comments in the same clip. Thus, our next two hypotheses are:

H2. Dynamically displaying time-anchored comments will enhance learners perceived social interactivity.

H3. Dynamically displaying time-anchored comments will encourage learners to leave more comments.

Finally, when introducing any new technology into learning environments, it is essential to assess its effect on learning

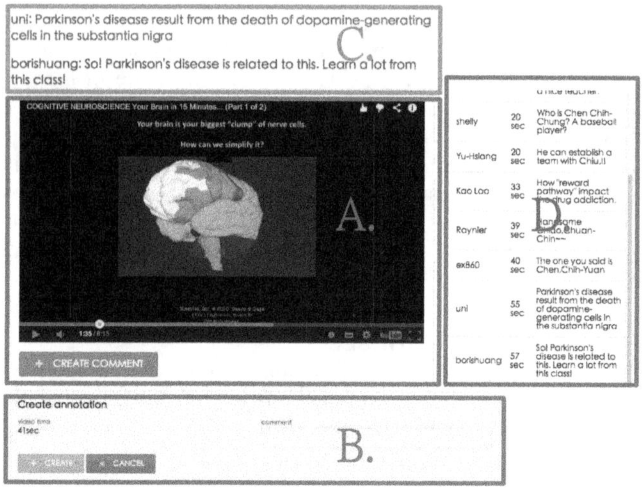

Figure 2. The interface of our system used in the experiment.

outcomes. As comments left by previous learners may include both content-related and social-oriented comments, we assume that content-related comments would provide subsequent learners with useful supplementary ideas and information that may improve their learning outcomes. Our final research hypothesis is therefore,

H4. Content-related comments will help achieve better learning outcomes in online courses than social-oriented comments.

METHOD

Interface Deployment

We embedded an online video player in the interface (Figure 2A). Participants could use the video player to control the course videos, and press the 'CREATE COMMENT' button shown in Figure 2A to leave their comments. When the button was pressed, the course video would be paused automatically and the participants were allowed to leave their comments (Figure 2B). The system also recorded the timestamp of the video. After the participants pressed the 'CREATE' button shown in Figure 2B, or 'Enter' on the keyboard, their comments would be added to the area shown in Figure 2D, which statically displayed all the time-anchored comments collected from other participants. If participants wanted to browse other comments, they could scroll the bar manually. Figure 2C indicates the area that showed all time-anchored comments dynamically along with the playing of the video.

Experimental Design

Stage A

The main purpose of this stage was to collect learners' comments. Although many comments can be found on online learning websites, these sources were not deemed appropriate for our experiments, because few, if any, online courses offered to date have recorded users' comments using a time-anchored method. Thus, it was necessary as part of our experiment to collect users' comments in a time-anchored way.

We selected three online courses from online learning websites. In order to reduce the subject bias, we chose them from three different fields: neural science, economics, and philosophy. Each offered a basic curriculum aimed at undergraduates or novices; this made it less likely that participants would abandon their courses due to the difficulty of the subject matter. We chose a video clip, with a length of approximately 15 minutes, from each course video. The neural science video "Reward and Addiction" was obtained from the OCW of National Tsing Hua University; The economics video "Introduction to Economics" was obtained from the OCW of National Chiao Tung University; The philosophy video "Understanding the Greek Philosophy" was from the Coursera at National Taiwan University.

Participants enrolled in Stage A watched all three video clips and were allowed to leave comments in our system. We recorded the comments and their corresponding time stamps in the videos. Each participant's comments were added to the database immediately, so that at any given point in the experiment, all comments made by previous participants could be seen by those who followed them.

Stage B

In this stage we examined two factors, display method and comment type, to investigate our research hypotheses. Dynamically displaying users' comments is an important capability of time-anchored commenting, thus, we examined two display methods in our experiments. The first was time-anchored dynamic display, in which each comment appeared in Figure 2C at the time its time stamp indicated until the following comments appeared. The second method (Figure 2D) displayed the same time-anchored comments, but the participants had to scroll down the bar and correlate the comments' timing with the video themselves.

In order to explore how the characteristics of comments influenced users' learning and social behaviors, we categorized the comments collected in Stage A into two groups, content-related and social-oriented comments. The former group consisted of those comments deemed relevant to the curriculum content of the course videos. For example, learners might summarize what they saw as the important parts of course videos, leave their opinions of the course content, or ask questions about it, such as "*Law of demand: There is an inverse relationship between quantity demand and its price.*" (economics course); "*According to these three properties, I think that Pre-Socratic philosophy was concerned with the features of objects on earth.*" (philosophy course); "*Was bipolar disorder caused by an excess of dopamine? I thought it would make people feel happier.*" (neural science course).

In contrast, comments comprising jokes, off-topic conversation, and other matters irrelevant to the curriculum were classified as social-oriented comments. For example, "*It's a lively description which is easy to remember! However, I still got a bad score on the test. XDD*" (economics course); "*The teacher could speak slowly. He usually makes slips of tongue!*" (neural science course)

Based on the two factors investigated in this work, we probed

2 (dynamic or static) × 2 (content-related or social-oriented) experimental conditions in this stage. We added an additional condition, which did not include any comments, as the baseline. Consequently, there were a total of five experimental conditions (C0-C4) in Stage B:

Condition 0 (C0): Baseline, No Comments. This condition was a control group, so there were no previous users' comments shown on the web page. However, the participants could still leave their own comments as they watched the online course content.

Condition 1 (C1): Dynamic and Content-related Comments. This condition primarily included comments from the content-related group. To avoid making the participants feel the comments were unnatural, we manipulated the proportion of comments of each type, as 80% content-related and 20% social-oriented. The system dynamically displayed these time-anchored comments as the video was played.

Condition 2 (C2): Dynamic and Social-oriented Comments. The interface and the method used to display the comments in this condition were the same as those of C1. However, the proportions of the two comment types were reversed, with content-related comments making up 20% of the total and social-oriented comments, 80%.

Condition 3 (C3): Static and Content-related Comments. In this condition, we removed the function of the time-anchored dynamic display. The participants could see each comment as well as the time-stamp relating it to the video, but they needed to map the time of each comment themselves vis-à-vis the videos. Content-related comments accounted for 80% of the total, and social-oriented comments for 20% in this condition.

Condition 4 (C4): Static and Social-oriented Comments. The methods for displaying the comments in this condition were the same as those of C3, but the proportion of content-related comments was 20% and of social-oriented comments was 80% in this condition.

Participants

Stage A

A total of 50 participants (21 females) were involved in the experiment in Stage A. All participants were undergraduate or graduate students (M=20.6 years old). In this stage, participants enrolled in the three selected online courses, and were required to complete all of them.

Stage B

There were 52 participants (16 females) who participated in stage B. All of them were undergraduate or graduate students (M=21.3 years old). None of them had taken part in Stage A. In this stage, all participants took part in the experiments in our laboratory and were interviewed afterwards.

Procedure

In Stage A, participants were required to watch a three-minute tutorial video before initiating the main tasks. The video introduced the basic rules of the experiment and demonstrated how to use our system to leave comments on online course videos. Each participant was given three Internet links for the three selected online courses and asked to complete all of them within 20 days after receiving the links. Participants could take the same course as many times as they wished within the 20-day time limit. After collecting the participants' comments in Stage A, we invited three experts separately to categorize them into content-related comments and social-oriented comments, as required by the experimental factors in stage B. If a comment could not be classified conformably, three experts would discuss to find the category that they were all agree for the comment. While the comment still could not be classified, it was discarded from the experiment.

Stage B was a lab-based experiment. Participants needed to complete a pretest before watching the online courses. The purpose of pretesting was to examine the background knowledge of each participant. They were also required to fill in posttests after finishing each online course. The participants were informed that they would sequentially watch three online course videos, and take a survey as well as a posttest at the end of each course video. The three videos were the same as those in Stage A, and the order in which they were watched was randomly assigned to each participant. The five experimental conditions described above (C0-C4) were randomly deployed with equal probability; in other words, every participant watched three online courses with three different conditions. We had 24, 34, 33, 33, and 32 participants in C0, C1, C2, C3, and C4, respectively.

We introduced the components of the two different interfaces at the beginning of each course without informing participants that the displayed comments had been edited. Participants could also leave comments of their own in this stage. The lengths of all course videos were about 15 minutes. Participants were asked to finish studying and commenting on the online course videos within 25 minutes, and were allowed to rewind and replay parts of the videos as many times as they wanted within the overall time limit.

Measure

Survey

After watching each course video, the participants were required to fill in surveys. Each survey contained a total of 11 items, and used 5-point Likert scales (1-strongly disagree, 5-strongly agree). The items measuring perceived engagement were modified from [24, 25] and the items measuring perceived social interactivity were adopted from [13, 32].

Learning Outcomes

To investigate the influence of the different experimental conditions on learners' performance, we used the knowledge-oriented recall test as measures and used pretest and posttest scores to evaluate participants' learning outcomes. Although both tests were almost the same, the order and wording of the questions were modified. We designed the tests based on the course slides and other course content, such that participants should have been able to answer these questions if they had focused on the online material. Some example questions of test are: "*What is Reward System? Please give a brief explanation.*" (neural science course); "*What is Pre-Socratic philosophy and its alias?*" (philosophy course).

Course	Total Number of Comments	Content-related	Social-oriented
Neural Science	430	40%	60%
Economics	420	50%	50%
Philosophy	427	40%	60%

Table 1. The number of classifiable comments collected in Stage A

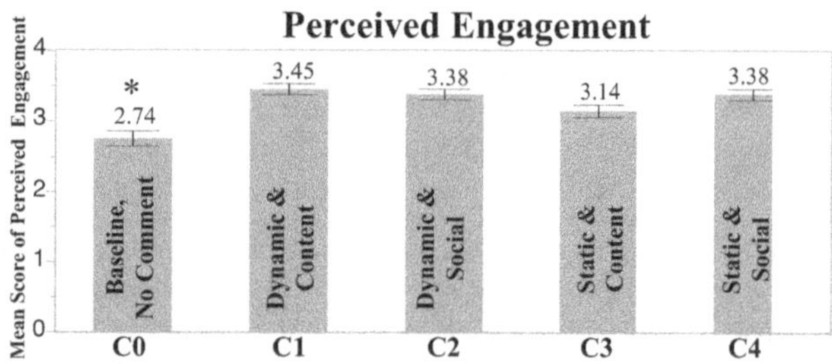

Figure 3. The result of perceived engagement. Error bars denote one standard error.

Interview

To supplement quantitative analysis, we conducted face-to-face interviews to help us understand each participant's learning experiences on the online courses. These interviews took place after each participant had completed the Stage B experiments. Each interview lasted about 20 minutes. Interviews were audio-recorded and transcribed before analysis. The questions asked in the interviews addressed three issues: 1) the influence of others' comments on the interviewee's own, 2) user experiences with the different interfaces in our system, and 3) the participants' past experiences of using online learning websites.

RESULTS

Comment Collection

After excluding comments that could not be successfully classified by the three experts, there were total of 1,277 comments classified as either social-oriented or content-related (Table 1), as previously explained; and these two categories were used in Stage B to explore effects on perceived engagement, perceived social interactivity, and learning outcomes, as detailed in the sections that follow.

Perceived Engagement

We computed a one-way ANOVA with condition (C0-C4) as the independent variable. The dependent variable was the perceived engagement score derived from the survey. The user ID was set as the random variable. A Tukey HSD test was used for post-hoc analysis. Figure 3 shows the results for perceived engagement in each condition.

There was a main effect of experimental conditions on perceived engagement ($F(4, 124.3)$=8.16, p<.0001, η^2=.20). Furthermore, C0 (M=2.74, SD=.43) had a significantly lower perceived engagement score (p<0.05) than all the other conditions (C1:M=3.45, SD=.43; C2:M=3.38, SD=.42; C3:M=3.14, SD=.49; C4:M=3.38, SD=.43). Although C3 had a notably smaller mean score than C1, C2, and C4, this difference was not statistically significant. These findings indicate that the time-anchored commenting system we devised could enhance learners' perceived engagement with the online courses, regardless of the method of display or the type of comment.

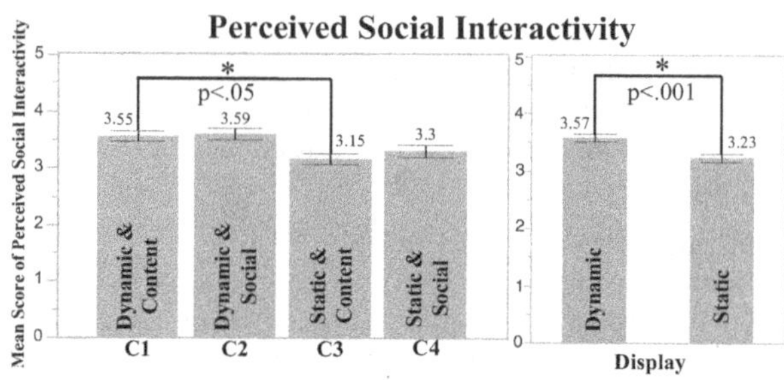

Figure 4. The result of perceived social interactivity

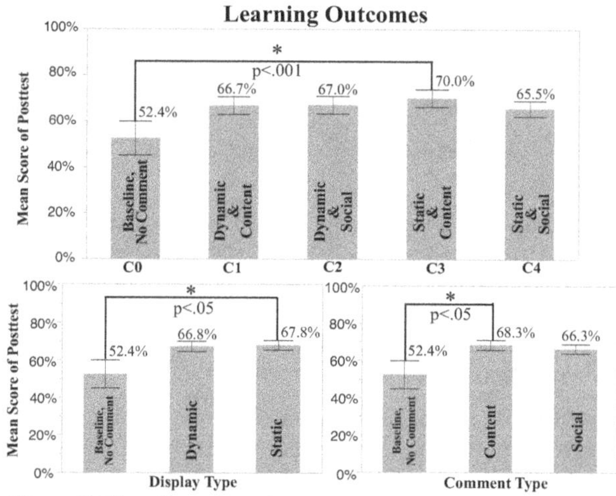

Figure 5. The adjusted results of the posttest of learning outcomes

Perceived Social Interactivity

Because no comments were presented in C0 condition, the C0 condition was excluded and a two-way ANOVA (2 types of display $\times$ 2 types of comments) was used to analyze the scores for perceived social interactivity. User ID was set as the random variable. A Tukey HSD was used to analyze the relationships between the conditions.

All results are shown in Figure 4, where error bars represent one standard error. The type of comments was non-significant ($F(1, 85.56)$=.36, p=.55, η^2=.01). However, there was a main effect of the methods of display ($F(1, 128)$=12.07, p<.001, η^2=.10). These results reflect that the display method influenced participants' perceived social interactivity. We also found that the score of perceived social interactivity in C3 (M=3.15, SD=.52) was significantly lower than that in C1 (M=3.55, SD=.50, p<.05). In other words, it seems that dynamic display significantly enhanced the level of perceived social interactivity associated with content-related comments. Although C2 (M=3.59) had a higher mean score than C4 (M=3.3), there was no statistically significant difference between them. This implies that, in the case of social-oriented comments, the effect of display method to the learners' perceived social interactivity would not be as significant as that for content-related comments.

Learning Outcomes

We used mixed-model ANCOVA to examine the effects of different conditions on learning. We used ANCOVA here in order to treat pre-test scores as a covariate and to reveal the real impact of our conditions on post-test scores and thus learning. To analyze the data, we treated user as a random variable, experimental condition and course as fixed variables, pretest score as a covariate, and posttest score as the dependent variable. A Tukey HSD was used to analyze the relationships between the conditions.

The mean accuracy of posttests in each condition is shown in Figure 5. The main effect for condition was non-significant ($F(4, 122.2)$=2.056, p=.08, η^2=.04). Further post-hoc analyses using Tukey HSD show that C3 had a significantly better learning outcome than C0 (p<.001). We also analyzed the effects of display method and comment type with the same method, respectively. A significant main effect for display method was found ($F(2, 128)$=3.52, p<.05, η^2=.03). The static display method (C3 and C4) resulted in a significantly higher posttest score than C0, but the dynamic display method (C1 and C2) did not. In addition, we found a significant main effect for comment type ($F(2, 127.7)$=3.30, p<.05, η^2=.03). The content-related comments (C1 and C3) led to significantly better posttest score than C0, but no significant difference was found between social-oriented comments (C2 and C4) and C0. These findings suggest that statically displaying prior users' content-related comments might enhance learning outcomes.

Effect of Comments

To further explore the effects of comment types, we investigated the impact of comments from the qualitative data. More than half (51%) of the participants reported that they preferred the content-related comments when learning on our platform, while 42% of them liked the social-oriented comments more. The remaining 7% of participants did not like any type of comment to be displayed when they were learning. Two of the interviewees who preferred the content-related comments described their experience as follows:

"Some users noted the important or complex contents of the courses, and I can read these notes after watching the course video." (S2)

"There were several technical terms in the neural science course and philosophy course. I noticed that some learners kindly commented the detailed information about those terms." (S23)

A participant who liked the social-oriented comments reported his experience as follows:

"There are lots of interesting comments in the video. I'd like to read and respond to those comments when I feel something is boring in the courses. And I thought those interesting comments can help me revive." (S15)

Finally, those participants who did not like any comments had a fairly consistent reason:

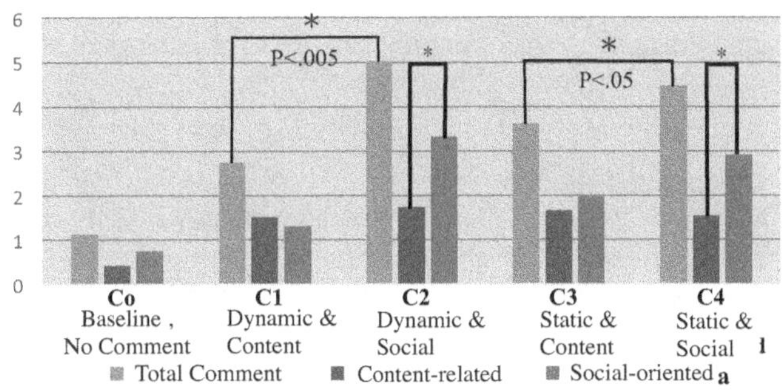

Figure 6. The quantity of comments in five different experimental conditions. The unit is the average number of comments for each participant in different conditions

"Reading those comments with a course video would distract me, and I thought I am used to focusing on the courses." (S43)

According to the interviews, the 93% of participants who preferred displaying the comments wanted to find facilitating information or interesting comments to help them engage with the video courses. In contrast, those participants who did not like the online comments thought that these would distract them from learning the content of the video itself.

Quantity of Comments in Stage B

Figure 6 shows the average number of comments posted by each participant in each experimental condition, and indicates that C2 and C4 yielded the largest number of comments, trailed by C3 and C1, and lastly by C0. This result indicates that the participants would not necessarily leave more comments in the conditions that feature dynamic display.

This finding could be explained by the participants' responses to the two of the questions that we summarized from the interviews. The first was "Do you perceive more social interaction with others when their comments are replayed dynamically?", to which 80% of participants reported "Yes", and 20% said "No". The second question was "Does the dynamic display motivate you to leave your own comments?", to which 37% of participants said "Yes", while the other 63% said "No". One of interviewees made the following remark:

"The factor that motivated me to leave a comment is the contents of comments such as questions and interesting topics." (S18)

A one-way ANOVA was performed and the result indicated a significant main effect for experimental condition ($F(4, 109.77)$=5.155, p<.005, η^2=.06). As can be seen from Figure 6, C4 yielded more comments than C3 (p<.05), while C2 generated more comments than C1 (p<.005). Therefore, it appears that social-oriented comments tended to increase learners' intentions to leave comments. It can also be seen that approximately half of the comments were content-related in C1 and C3, whereas in C2 (p<.005) and C4 (p<.05), social-oriented comments outnumbered content-related comments by approximately double. We can also observe from Figure 6 that the quantity of content-related comments was about the same in four conditions (C1, C2, C3, and C4).

These findings imply that social-oriented comments might encourage subsequent participants to leave additional social-oriented comments of their own.

DISCUSSIONS

We summarize the findings and contributions of the study, and then discuss the implications to design and research as well as the limitations of the current study as following.

Summary of Findings

From the results of the study, we confirmed that online learners experienced higher perceived engagement and left more comments when prior learners' time-anchored comments were displayed (H1 supported). This matched the findings in previous studies [3, 5] suggesting that peers could supply excellent feedback, and demonstrating that the content of this feedback could prompt learners to actively engage in learning and reflect on their learning processes. In addition, dynamically displaying the time-anchored comments tended to make learners perceive more social interactivity, as compared to static display of the comments; and this difference was especially salient in the case of content-related comments (H2 supported).

Also, dynamically displaying the time-anchored comments might not always encourage learners to leave more comments than displaying them statically (H3 rejected). This finding indicated that higher levels of perceived social interactivity do not imply that users would definitely or necessarily engage more in commenting behavior. It is necessary to treat the perception of social interactivity and commenting behavior separately, which will need further analyses in the future to understand the underlying mechanisms.

In terms of learning achievement, we found that content-related comments could enhance learners' learning outcomes relative to the baseline, but did not reach a significantly better level than social-oriented comments (H4 rejected). Our results also indicated that time-anchored commenting did not degrade learning outcomes when compared with the baseline condition (in which new comments could be made, but no prior users' comments were displayed). These findings appeared to be consistent with prior research [7] that suggested embedding chatrooms in online course material would not adversely affect learning outcomes. Moreover, users' learning outcomes were actually enhanced under the condition of statically displayed content-related comments. This is in keeping with a prior finding [5] that collaborative experiences help learners understand complex systems and concepts. Learners are given the opportunity to interact with the comments both to gain information they need, and to receive guidance that may improve their learning and reasoning.

We also noted that social-oriented comments could stimulate learners to leave more comments while maintaining the same level of participation in content-related discussion. Figure 6 shows that all of the experimental conditions with time-anchored comments (C1-C4) collected more learner comments than the baseline condition (C0). This suggests that time-anchored commenting in general could encourage learners to participate in more course-related discussions. Moreover, we found that the numbers of content-related comments in the content-related conditions (C1 and C3) and social-oriented conditions (C2 and C4) were similar. This is a particularly interesting finding because one might think that social-oriented comments could distract learners, and/or prompt them to leave fewer content-related comments. However, we found that although the proportion of social-oriented comments increased in the conditions with social-oriented comments, the learners still left a similar amount of content-related comments in these conditions.

Design Implications

Time-anchored commenting retains the flexibility of asynchronous communication that is commonly adopted in online education (e.g., web forum), while at the same time increases indirect information exchange and interactivity between peer learners. Although similar techniques have been used in the design of *niconico* and other video streaming sites, the use of the method in the context of online education for enhancing engagement and interactivity is still limited. Our study represents an initial step toward this direction. Below we present a number of design implications for instructors and researchers interested in incorporating time-anchored commenting in online courses and education.

1. Dynamic display tends to work better than statistic display. Our findings indicate that neither a dynamic nor a static display method would decrease participants' learning outcomes, but participants perceived more social interactivity when the comments were dynamically displayed. Hence, we suggest that designers consider displaying time-anchored comments dynamically to improve learners' perceived social interactivity; however, it is also beneficial to consider individual differences in preference and learning style, and provide different display options for them, since some interviewees reported feeling slightly annoyed when comments were actively shown on the screen. Furthermore, the dynamic display method could particularly enhance perceived interactivity of content-related comments. Because the content-related comments are usually more intense than social-oriented comments and are often time-sensitive, showing these time-anchored comments at the correct time points could be more beneficial to the learners.

2. Social-oriented comments are desirable. If there are more social-oriented comments to start with, our results show that the number of new social-oriented comments would increase but new content-related comments would not be inhibited. It should be borne in mind, however, that content-related comments could provide supplemental information for learners and probably enhance their learning outcomes. Therefore, depending on the purposes of the online courses, instructors may find it useful to modulate the proportion of content-related and social-oriented comments to channel the direction of learners' discussions online. If we could further detect learners' status in an online course, this method could also be used to automatically modulate the constitution of comments: for example, we may choose to decrease the proportion of content-related comments relative to social-oriented comments if we detect that learners' perceived social interactivity or perceived engagement is falling.

3. Video-centered, time-anchored comment exchange supports collaborative learning. The biggest difference between this time-anchored design and regular chatrooms is the connection with video. Learners can leave their comments at the exact moment the course content confuses them, making it easier for peer learners to help them. Several interviewees mentioned in the post-study interviews that seeing other learners noting the important or complex contents of the online courses helped their own learning. The design allows learners to use a large body of auxiliary messages generated by the learning community to understand difficult information and form collaborative relationships with their peers. There is a potential to extend the time-anchored commenting method as a full-fledged design for large-scale collaborative learning in the future.

LIMITATIONS AND FUTURE WORK

This study has some limitations. First, our experiments conducted in a lab setting cannot account for contextual factors, which are certainly important for the research of online learning, e.g., characteristics of learners, number of learners, and length of study. The current results are more adequate for applications of online learning videos where the number of learners watching the same video and characteristics of the learners would approximately match the structure of the current study, such as flipped classrooms.

As a lab study, the number of sample learners examined is smaller than the number of learners present in a regular MOOC course. The current study is intended to explore the utilities of the time-anchored peer commenting mechanism, and thus it is reasonable to test our hypotheses with the experimental design and the sample size. In addition, the impact of the design on learning was evaluated in a short period of time. We also need a solution to deal with hundreds or thousands of comments present in real MOOCs, which may involve automatic analyses of language content and personalized sampling of comments.

To generalize our findings and to increase the external validity of the time-anchored method, it would be complementary to scale up the work, conducting deployment studies to understand the impact of the method on actual online learners, especially given that the current study has obtained promising results.

Second, our findings suggest that dynamically displaying time-anchored comments can enhance learners' perceived engagement and perceived social interactivity. The design therefore may be able to improve the completion rates of online courses, which is known to be one major challenge to MOOCs. A future deployment study with real usage data will help verify this possible benefit.

Third, in terms of data analytics, we decided to treat the course as a fixed effect in the linear model analysis of learning outcomes. The decision of treating the course either as a random or fixed effect will lead to different interpretations. Because we plan to replicate the study with other courses in the future, we see the feasibility to treat course as a fixed effect, and replications will help generalize the results.

Fourth, instructors also play an important role in the learning process and social interaction, regardless of whether the course is delivered in face-to-face or online settings. Kizlicec et al. [21] investigated how adding the instructor's face to a learning video affects learners. They found whether showing or hiding the instructor's face did not affect recall ability. Our result, on the other hand, shows that utilizing the learners' social-oriented comments could increase their learning outcomes. It is worth further exploring the effects of different types of social interactions and social cues. The contributions that may be made by instructors are also worth considering in future work.

CONCLUSION

In this study, we have presented a time-anchored commenting method for online educational videos, along with the results of an experiment we conducted to investigate the impact of this method on learners. We focused on two main factors, display methods and comment types, and their respective influences on learners' perceived engagement, perceived social interactivity, and learning outcomes in video-based learning. Based on the findings of the experiments, we found that dynamically displaying time-anchored comments enhanced learners' perceived social interactivity. Moreover, previous learners' comments had positive influences on later learners' perceived engagement. We hope this work provides some new perspectives that will help improve social interaction and learning experiences in online video-based education.

ACKNOWLEDGMENTS

We thank the anonymous reviewers for their insightful comments. This work was supported in part by Taiwan Ministry of Science and Technology (MOST) under grants 101-2628-E-009-021-MY3, 102-2221-E-009-082-MY3, 102-2221-E-007-073-MY3, and UST-UCSD International Center of Excellence in Advanced Bioengineering sponsored by Taiwan MOST I-RiCE Program under grant 103-2911-I-009-101.

REFERENCES

1. Abrami, P. C., Bernard, R. M., Bures, E. M., Borokhovski, E., and Tamim, R. M. Interaction in distance education and online learning: Using evidence and theory to improve practice. *Journal of Computing in Higher Education 23*, 2-3 (2011), 82–103.

2. Anderson, A., Huttenlocher, D., Kleinberg, J., and Leskovec, J. Engaging with massive online courses. In *WWW'14* (2014), 687–698.

3. Anderson, T., and Elloumi, F. *The theory and practice of online learning*. Athabasca University Press, 2008.

4. Branon, R. F., and Essex, C. Synchronous and asynchronous communication tools in distance education. *TechTrends 45*, 1 (2001), 36–36.

5. Bransford, J. D., Brown, A. L., and Cocking, R. R. *How People Learn: Brain, Mind, Experience, and School.* The National Academies Press, 2000.
6. Burnett, C. Learning to chat: Tutor participation in synchronous online chat. *Teaching in higher education 8*, 2 (2003), 247–261.
7. Coetzee, D., Fox, A., Hearst, M. A., and Hartmann, B. Chatrooms in MOOCs: All talk and no action. In *L@S* (2014).
8. Coetzee, D., Fox, A., Hearst, M. A., and Hartmann, B. Should your MOOC forum use a reputation system? In *CSCW* (2014), 1176–1187.
9. Cross, A., Bayyapunedi, M., Ravindran, D., Cutrell, E., and Thies, W. VidWiki: Enabling the crowd to improve the legibility of online educational videos. In *CSCW* (2014).
10. Dixson, M. D. Creating effective student engagement in online courses: What do students find engaging? *JoSoTL 10*, 2 (2010).
11. Duemer, L., Fontenot, D., Gumfory, K., Kallus, M., Larsen, J., Schafer, S., and Shaw, B. The use of online synchronous discussion groups to enhance community formation and professional identity development. *Journal of Interactive Online Learning 1*, 2 (2002), 1–12.
12. Goldman, D. B., Gonterman, C., Curless, B., Salesin, D., and Seitz, S. M. Video object annotation, navigation, and composition. In *UIST* (2008), 3–12.
13. Granovetter, M. The strength of weak ties: A network theory revisited. *Sociological theory 1* (1983), 201–233.
14. Guimarães, R. L., Cesar, P., and Bulterman, D. C. Let me comment on your video: Supporting personalized end-user comments within third-party online videos. In *Proceedings of the 18th Brazilian symposium on Multimedia and the web* (2012), 253–260.
15. Guo, P. J., Kim, J., and Rubin, R. How video production affects student engagement: An empirical study of mooc videos. In *L@S* (2014), 41–50.
16. Guzdial, M., and Turns, J. Effective discussion through a computer-mediated anchored forum. *The journal of the learning sciences 9*, 4 (2000), 437–469.
17. Hamilton, W., Garretson, O., and Kerne, A. Streaming on twitch: Fostering participatory communities of play within live mixed media. In *CHI* (2014).
18. Huang, J., Dasgupta, A., Ghosh, A., Manning, J., and Sanders, M. Superposter behavior in mooc forums. In *L@S* (2014), 117–126.
19. Johnson, G., and Howell, A. Attitude toward instructional technology following required versus optional WebCT usage. *Journal of Technology and Teacher Education 13*, 4 (2005), 643–654.
20. Johnson, G. M. Synchronous and asynchronous text-based CMC in educational contexts: A review of recent research. *TechTrends 50*, 4 (2006), 46–53.
21. Kizilcec, R. F., Papadopoulos, K., and Sritanyaratana, L. Showing face in video instruction: effects on information retention, visual attention, and affect. In *CHI* (2014).
22. Koory, M. A. Differences in learning outcomes for the online and F2F versions of "an introduction to shakespeare". *Journal of Asynchronous Learning Networks 7*, 2 (2003), 18–35.
23. Martin, F. G. Will massive open online courses change how we teach? *Commun. ACM 55*, 8 (2012), 26–28.
24. O'Brien, H. L., and Toms, E. G. The development and evaluation of a survey to measure user engagement. *Journal of the American Society for Information Science and Technology 61*, 1 (2010), 50–69.
25. O'Brien, H. L., and Toms, E. G. Is there a universal instrument for measuring interactive information retrieval?: the case of the user engagement scale. In *Proceedings of the third symposium on Information interaction in context* (2010), 335–340.
26. Oztok, M., Zingaro, D., Brett, C., and Hewitt, J. Exploring asynchronous and synchronous tool use in online courses. *Computers & Education 60*, 1 (2013), 87–94.
27. Romiszowski, A., and Mason, R. *Handbook of research for educational communications and technology*, 2 ed. Taylor & Francis, 2004, ch. Computer mediated communication, 397–431.
28. van der Pol, J., Admiraal, W., and Simons, P. R.-J. The affordance of anchored discussion for the collaborative processing of academic texts. *International Journal of Computer-Supported Collaborative Learning 1*, 3 (2006), 339–357.
29. Vygotsky, L. S. *Mind in society: The development of higher psychological processes.* Harvard university press, 1980.
30. Walker, R., and Arnold, I. Introducing group-based asynchronous learning to business education. reflections on effective course design and delivery. *Educational media international 41*, 3 (2004), 253–265.
31. Weisz, J. D., Kiesler, S., Zhang, H., Ren, Y., Kraut, R. E., and Konstan, J. A. Watching together: integrating text chat with video. In *CHI* (2007), 877–886.
32. Zhang, S., Jiang, H., and Carroll, J. M. Integrating online and offline community through facebook. In *IEEE International Conference on Collaboration Technologies and Systems* (2011), 569–578.

Designing a Physical Aid to Support Active Reading on Tablets

Andrea Bianchi
Sungkyunkwan University
Suwon, Korea
andrea.whites@gmail.com

So-Ryang Ban
Sungkyunkwan University
Suwon, Korea
thdid48@gmail.com

Ian Oakley
Dept of Human & Systems Eng.
UNIST, Ulsan, Korea
ian.r.oakley@gmail.com

ABSTRACT

Tablet computers and portable eReaders are gradually becoming the preferred platform for the consumption of textual materials. However, although these technologies are powerful, it is widely acknowledged that print documents better support the advanced *active reading* tasks necessary to gain a deep understanding of a text. While prior work to address this issue has aimed improve digital eReaders by either leveraging familiar physical affordances or by extending paper's capabilities with digital tools, in this paper we propose a juncture of these two approaches. We first present a formative study that captures the needs and requirements of users during active reading tasks with tablets. We instantiate the findings in the design of a simple physical aid to support active reading: a smart bookmark. We then define an interaction space for this device, describe a set of interfaces designed to facilitate active reading and close with a user study that assesses the potential of the bookmark device and interaction techniques.

Author Keywords

eReader; active reading; tangible; tablet; bookmark; eTab.

ACM Classification Keywords

H.5.2 Information Interfaces and Presentation: Input.

INTRODUCTION

Reading is becoming digital. In today's information dense world, absorbing, processing and understanding increasing amounts of written content is a core skill for knowledge workers. Digital technologies such as eReaders and tablets are facilitating reading activities by making this wealth of material available to users in convenient, lightweight, connected and readily accessible form factors. However, while powerful, these devices are not well suited to Active Reading [19] tasks, a term referring to a broad set of cognitive skills and activities, such as thinking, learning, note taking, annotations, searching and skimming, that enable an individual to achieve a deep level of comprehension of a document. For example, it is the process that academics engage in when performing a close reading of a research article.

CHI 2015, April 18 – 23, 2015, Seoul, Republic of Korea.
Copyright 2015 ACM 978-1-4503-3145-6/15/04...$15.00.
http://dx.doi.org/10.1145/2702123.2702303

In fact, it has long been reported that people prefer to perform active reading with physical paper rather than on personal computers [24] and recent updates to this literature indicate the same holds true for tablet computers [19, 27]. Recognizing these problems as a design opportunity, many authors have investigated how technology can be improved to better support active reading. In early work on the topic, O'Hara and Sellen [21] suggest that design efforts should be directed towards aiding three key tasks: annotation, effortless navigation, and flexible spatial layout. Instantiating such recommendations, pioneering work such as XLibris [25], an active reading system based on a pen tablet and paper-like user interface, attempted to surpass the traditional reading experience by pushing its design in two ways. On one hand it augmented reading by integrating novel digital tools and functions such as search and indexing. On the other, it enabled users to transfer their normal reading practices from the physical world to the digital by its reliance on a pen and slate format device.

Most subsequent work can be broadly categorized as developing these two themes, creating either advanced software interfaces to improve tasks such as page navigation [28], copy/paste [29], annotations [14] and information gathering [12], or sophisticated hardware systems that mimic the properties of structure of physical paper books (e.g., dual screen readers [13] and foldable [7] or flexible [3] displays). While both approaches have value, purely software based solutions lack the vaunted (and valued) physicality of books while, practically, current hardware based approaches suffer from the complexity of the prototypes produced. These often require additional fixed hardware infrastructure such as cameras and projectors [8, 10], multitouch-tables [12, 14], or propose substantial alternations and modifications to the slate style tablet computer [3, 7, 11]. As such, while these approaches are novel, its unclear they are well matched to real eReading scenarios for tablets which place value on qualities such as portability, mobility, reliability, convenience and robustness [6, 7, 27].

The work in this article seeks to define a space at the juncture of these two approaches. It aims to combine the benefits of a physical user interface with the power and flexibility of digital representations in a lightweight and unobtrusive design for currently available eReading platforms. It does this by proposing a novel active reading system for tablet computers based on augmenting a familiar physical tool: a bookmark. The paper presents a formative study that captures user needs and requirements for such a tool. Using the insights gained from this process we designed and developed a functional prototype on a tablet computer and performed a study to capture user reactions. The contributions of this work are 1) extending the literature on understanding user needs in active reading tasks on tablets, 2) explicitly considering the role that a physical tool could play in mediating the digital reading experience, and 3) instantiating this knowledge in the design of a functioning prototype.

RELATED WORK

Active Reading combines activities such as thinking, learning, note taking, annotations, searching or skimming to gain a deep understanding of a written text [21, 25, 27]. Prior work in HCI has comprehensively contrasted how individuals perform active reading on paper versus on personal computers [19, 21] or tablets [6]. Accordingly, the review in this article focuses on two specific and relevant topics: readers that use physical interfaces to mimic the affordances of paper and those that use software interfaces to provide novel features and functions.

Physical interfaces leveraging on book affordances

Numerous authors have, through the construction of elaborate hardware, mimicked specific qualities of paper books in custom digital devices, typically with the goal of transferring the affordances of paper to the digital domain. For example, Chen et al. [7] presented a hinged dual-display system that creates a pair of display surfaces that can be opened and closed like a traditional book. They explored interactions such as content navigation or marking pages. Codex [13], a broadly similar system, extended these ideas by adding a stylus and investigating how coupled screens could aid tasks such as reading and note-taking. Other authors have explored squeezable or flexible systems that mirror aspects of the deformability of paper. Both gBook [3] and BendFlip [33], for example, sense forces and deformations to their surfaces to control navigation – simulating actions such as flipping rapidly through the pages of a book by bending it between finger and thumb. This work provides compelling design exemplars and motivates our research in that it convincingly demonstrates that physical aspects of the reading experience – the multiple surfaces available and the hand manipulations that can be performed – are important, valuable and worth conserving in the digital domain.

New features for digital content

Researchers have also explored new ways of working with text enabled by digitization. Hinckley et al. [12], for example, extended the vocabulary of actions that can be performed during an active reading task by introducing "pockets", virtual locations where users can temporarily stow notes, reminders or bookmarks and the idea of two-way cross-referenced notes that are dynamically linked to the text. Building on these ideas, LiquidText [28] further explored mechanisms for linking and referring to notes. The system allows users to create notes and excerpts of text, displayed in a separate area, that are flexibly linked to the source material and can be dynamically manipulated.

Indeed, note taking has been the focus of much research. The importance of physical paper in such processes is well acknowledged [24] and reflected in HCI projects. For example, Mackay et al. [18] presented prototypes to support note-taking scenarios among scientists based on the combination of a physical notebook, a graphics tablet, pens that can write on these surfaces and a magic lens [2, 26] that mediates between the physical and digital representations. Similarly, PapierCraft [17] and S-Notebook [22] use the Anoto pen system to issue commands or establish links between paper-based and digital contents. Hinchley et al. [14] extend these ideas by exploring rich bimanual input combining a digital stylus and multi-touch. Proposed interactions such as using a touch to mark a location in a book, then flipping to another page and writing a note with a pen before returning to the marked page highlight the power and potential of rich physical interactions coupled with digital annotations. Physical metaphors for bookmarks and eReaders have also been explored. NoteDrop [29], for instance, uses a special wearable bracelet to allow users to physically "pick up" words from a document by placing a physical object on a multi-touch screen. These words can then be physically dropped into zones on the side of the device to trigger actions such as copying or searching.

This literature presents a compelling case for the benefits that digital tools bring to the reading experience. The research in this paper aims to combine these advantages with the power and familiarity of a physical, tangible reading aid to provide readers with seamless, direct interaction with digital tools and content.

Tools and techniques for interacting with digital content

This work also builds on a set of well known techniques for tangible interaction with digital content and for sensing, visualizing and interacting on and with transparent devices such as magic lenses [e.g., 2, 10, 11]. In particular our work is inspired by the idea of manipulating physical widgets and tiles to seamlessly interact with digital content – concepts that originate with metaDesk [30] and have been extended in influential systems such as DataTiles [23], Tangible Tiles [31], paper GUI palettes [8], and explored commercially in products such as Adobe's Ink & Slide [1], a device designed to aid sketching on tablets. Our work also builds on prior systems that have presented transparent physical widgets that enable interaction with content displayed directly beneath their surface. Prominent work in this area includes SLAP widgets [32], the tPad [11] and cAR [10].

While SLAP widgets are tracked using visual markers in a tabletop system, tPad and cAR rely on a custom semi-transparent capacitive screen tracked by an external camera or situated over a tabletop. cAR is particularly relevant to our work as it explores how transparent physical widgets could be applied to reading tasks. However, cAR differs from the current paper in its focus on the technical realization of sensing solutions and its reliance on a large-scale computing platform. Indeed, cAR presents interaction techniques for Active Reading (based on actions such as moving or drawing on the display) only briefly and there is little discussion of the motivations underpinning their design. Finally, specific magic lens techniques that influenced our work include those that sense and react to touch input and gestures over their surface [2, 16, 26].

In sum, the goal of this paper is to combine these powerful interface and interaction ideas from literature into a novel, concrete and practically feasible (e.g. unpowered and compatible with current tablet platforms) design-led prototype that can support active reading tasks.

FORMATIVE STUDY

To inform the design of a tangible interface for active reading, we conducted a formative study using the speed-dating technique [9] to capture user needs and requirements. Speed-dating is a concept validation technique in which users are presented with storyboards depicting a range of possible usage scenarios describing tasks and activities, with the goal of conveying a rich set of possibilities and stimulating a detailed discussion about a targeted design space. It is expressly intended to help designers choose to *make the right thing* during the early stages of project conceptualization. The comments, reactions and opinions of participants are captured. Designers then synthesize this information with the aim of expressing user needs and the validity and value of specific design directions and concepts.

Participants and method

We recruited 10 users (age 25-27, four female, all engaged in, or recently completed, graduate studies) who regularly perform active reading of academic papers. They were compensated with 10 USD. All participants owned an eReader device, tablet or smartphone that they used for reading books and articles (40% academic material, 10% fiction, 50% non-fiction) from various locations (70% home or workplace, 30% traveling and commuting). Half of participants preferred physical books over eReaders for affective reasons such as feeling genuine ownership of print material or enjoying the material texture of paper. Those who preferred eReaders reported appreciating the portability benefits of storing multiple articles on a single device.

Method and material

The user study was carried out in a quiet lab area and took approximately 1 hour and 20 minutes per participant. On

Skimming. Paul needs to summarize a set of articles. He loads them on his bookmark and taps on each to browse the abstracts, delete irrelevant papers and skim through the different paper sections. He uses his bookmark to review the articles before presenting a summary.

Reminders. Jay is reading a textbook. He uses his bookmark to schedule his reading activities, receiving prompts and reminders to stick to his plan. Whilst reading, he stores notes and annotations by drawing on his bookmark.

Graphics. Sara's client shows pictures of how she wants to remodel her home on her tablet. Sara uses her bookmark to grab a copy and then makes notes around them. Later, she uses her bookmark to make precise measurements and consolidate, tag and organize her notes.

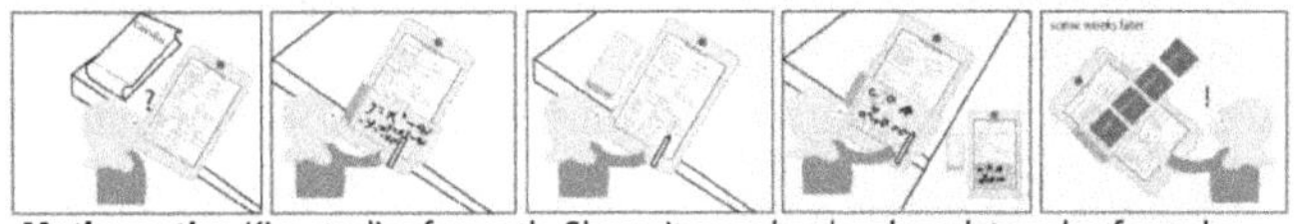

Mathematics. Kim studies for math. She writes on her bookmark to solve formulae then removes it from the screen to hide her workings and see the original content clearly. She also makes some permanent memos about key concepts. During revision, she reviews a list of these notes.

Review. Liza reviews an academic paper. She uses her bookmark to look through the pages and check citations whilst reading. She stores a copy of an important figure so she can examine it throughout her read. She also makes notes to help organize her review.

Traveling. Quentin is on a flight, reviewing his travel guide. He uses his bookmark to save info on tourist sites and control the brightness and text size of his tablet. Upon arrival, he reviews his saved travel plans.

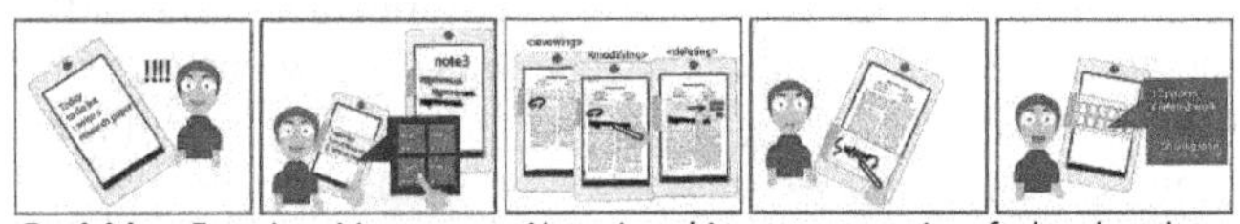

Revisiting. Faraz is writing a paper. He reviews his past summaries of related work, perusing and editing his notes. He uses his bookmark to obscure irrelevant parts of the text. Finally, he compiles a set of relevant articles on his bookmark and sends it to his co-authors.

Figure 1. The storyboard/scenarios used in the formative study. The captions shown are translated summaries.

arrival, participants were briefed about the experiment and their demographics were collected. The interviewer presented seven scenarios/storyboards (see next section) and, after clarifications, collected user opinions, elaborations and reflection on each one for ten minutes. The session closed with time for open comments, reflections and suggestions from participants.

One prominent theme in the storyboards was examining academic research – a complex, challenging activity that requires training, skill and practice [15]. The storyboards were also inspired by prior research on active reading [12, 27] and Keshav's [15] three-pass model of reading which highlights key processes of skimming, in depth reading and reviewing. Ultimately, we produced seven storyboards (Figure 1), redundantly depicting a broad set of tasks, features and situations in the following scenarios.

Skimming. A student is asked by his supervisor to perform a literature review of several articles. This scenario explores page-to-page navigation, paper management and the saving and review of collections of articles.

Reminders. A user tasked with reading a book in a set period of time defines a reading schedule. The scenario explores notifications, highlighting text and taking notes.

Graphics. A user reviews a paper with rich and detailed graphics. This scenario covers pen annotations, note management and physically measuring angle and length.

Mathematics. A user reads a textbook containing many mathematical equations. This scenario explores annotations in the form of processing material (e.g. working out an equation) and making comments for later reference.

Review. A user reviews an article for a journal or conference. This scenario explores techniques for comparing and cross-referencing among parts of a document and reviewing notes and annotations.

Traveling. This scenario explores reading during travel. It explores managing content for future reference and tools to increase the legibility of text in distracting environments.

Revisiting. A user returns to a paper, reviewing their previous annotations and saved contents and uses tools to focus their attention of specific parts of the text.

Results

We processed the outcomes of the study by conducting an affinity process on user feedback. This focused on identifying the subset of tasks and activities presented in the scenarios that users reported to be valuable, interesting and useful, then clustering these together into meaningful groups. Ultimately, we arrived at two-dimensional structure that showed how three common readings tasks were supported by three different classes of activity. We termed the three tasks *skimming*, or rapid scanning with the goal of gaining an overview of a document, *understanding*, with the goal of achieving comprehension of a text, and *discussing*, or the deep reading required to be able to analyze or criticize an article. In formulating this structure, we drew on Keshav's [15] three-pass reading approach as a mechanism for understanding and interpreting user comments; the three tasks we propose reflect those he describes. The three kinds of activities are *managing*, *annotating & extracting*, and *exploring*, activities similar to those suggested by O'Hara and Sellen [21]. These activities were derived by synthesizing the features and abilities our participants reported to be of most interest and value. Managing activities correspond to navigating around, adding, deleting or re-ordering sets of pages, documents, notes or other material. Annotating and extracting activities relate to creating and linking notes to content and capturing or retrieving content for subsequent (potentially external) sharing or use. Finally, exploring activities entail visualizing, searching or comparing different parts the document in order to better understand particular points or extract key information. We discuss these activities in more detail below and they are summarized in Table 1.

In terms of the management activity, *navigation* came across strongly as a core reading activity. This has featured prominently in prior work [12, 28] and our participants once again highlighted its importance. Efficiency and flexibility were particularly valued properties. Beyond easy sequential navigation, users also favored rapid access to document overviews that would enable them to quickly jump to specific pages to support skimming style reading. They also reported a desire to mark or store particular pages for later reference, such as during subsequent viewing for clarifying or discussing content. When considering both sets of documents and their own comments or annotations they made similar observations relating to the importance of ordering, highlighting or otherwise prioritizing particular elements or articles. Marking (for subsequent viewing) the perceived relevance and importance of particular content was viewed as a vital task for achieving deep comprehension.

The *annotating and extracting* activity relates closely to note taking features that appear in prior work [e.g., 13, 14, 18]. Users valued annotations for all three of the reading processes we identified. During skimming, notes serve as quick reminders. During understanding readings, notes link to and are used to clarify contents. In discussion readings, notes are collated, sorted, categorized and potentially shared with others. Users also identified two broadly different classes of notes – those that refer to particular content specifically (and typically are written directly over that content) and over-arching comments that refer to a document in a general sense, rather than any specific point, region or section (a distinction previously characterized as inter-page versus intra-page annotations [27]). Users also raised concerns about clutter. There were two main issues. Firstly, users were concerned that notes might obscure the original content, making it hard to view or access. Secondly, revision of notes was viewed as essential to their effective use – editing, sorting, deleting and reordering were important in ensuring notes were useful as opposed to simply overwhelming and profligate. Finally, users were very positive about using styli to create hand written (rather than typed) notes, as this would allow integration of content such as drawings, expressions (e.g. exclamation marks, emoticons) and spatial information (e.g. arrows).

	Managing content	Annotations & Extractions	Exploring
Skimming	1 Quick navigation among pages. View document overviews.	2 Add/delete memo-style notes. Notes that link to source material.	3 Rapid access to content on other document pages.
Understanding	4 Organize content by priority. Store and manage content.	5 Capture excerpts for reference. Writing annotations on original file and control its visibility.	6 Highlighting text. Tools to analyze content (e.g. measure, isolate or increase prominence).
Discussing	7 Categorize annotations automatically (e.g. time) & manually (e.g. tagging). Easy sharing of notes.	8 Show and hide notes. Manage captured excerpts and notes.	9 Flexibly make, show and hide highlights and text.

Table 1. Results of the formative study. Three common reading tasks (skimming, understanding and discussing) supported by three activity types (content management, annotation & extraction, and exploring). Table cells show specific examples in each area. The results are derived from an affinity process conducted over user feedback received during the study.

Regarding the *exploring* activity, users commented very positively on ideas about displaying and manipulating alternative content on a reading aid, describing these kinds of feature as "like a small dual screen". They saw value in using this kind of capability to rapidly examine or contrast text or image excerpts from other pages or documents with currently displayed content. These results match previous authors' focus on supporting text extraction for quick cross-comparison [10, 14, 28]. However, moving beyond the approaches proposed in these prior systems, users also emphasized the importance of accessing captured material while remaining in the context of the current document and without disrupting the flow of reading. Different participants also stressed that different forms of content might be useful – their notes, content from other pages in a document, particularly important charts or images and even material from an entirely different, but related, documents. They also indicated that, typically, cross-referencing tasks involve viewing multiple pieces of information from a range of sources and that tools should support a variety of display, navigation, access, search and view options.

Users also made comments about the use of a physical aid as a practical tool to support examining a document. They saw value in using the tool physically – to highlight particular parts of text, or to establish the relationships of particular elements in complex figures. They were negative on its use to control or deal what were perceived as digital aspects of the system: font sizes, screen brightness, alarms and reminders. This kind of functionality was viewed as redundant with the basic tablet UI or, in the case of reminders, "annoying" and superfluous.

Finally, users also advanced opinions and comments about viable form factors for a physical bookmark object. The idea of a rectangular window with a handle at one end was prominent. Opinions as to an optimal size of the object varied considerably. One group of users indicated a large bookmark, capable of covering the width of the tablet would best support annotation and visualization activities. Others were more concerned about portability and suggested much smaller, easier to carry, sizes. Some suggested the idea of integrating the bookmark into a pocket in a tablet cover or case, an already common type of accessory. A final practical concern is that users almost universally and strongly disliked the idea of having to charge an additional device – any reading aid should either be unpowered or capable of operating without recharge for substantial periods of times, ideally in the order of several weeks or longer.

Selection of features for design

Extending the affinity process that led to Table 1, we isolated a subset of the activities in the study scenarios that users found valuable (e.g. those relating to content management, annotation and visualization) and discarded those that received negative comments or a lack of interest (e.g. reminders, or controlling display settings). These activities appear as the examples in Table 1 (shown in cells one through nine). To move towards designing applications based on these findings, we further reduced the examples to a set of five cross-cutting interface features termed: *page navigation*; *content capture*; *annotation*; *magic lens* and; *visual aids*. The *navigation* feature drew on activities shown in Table 1 such as moving between pages, storing content and providing overviews (shown in cells 1 and 4). Similarly, *content capture* reflected ideas about storing and managing images extracted from on-screen contents (cells 5 and 8). The *annotation* feature consisted of techniques to make, save, edit and organize inter-page and intra-page annotations [27] (cells 2, 5, 7 and 8) while the *magic lens* collected issues relating to exploring and cross-checking other document contents whilst reading a page (cell 3). Finally, the *visual aid* feature related to processing the physical qualities of documents – obscuring or highlighting specific content areas and measuring qualities such as length or angle (cells 6 and 9). These interface features became the targets for our subsequent interaction design process.

In conclusion, the formative study clearly shows that the tasks performed during active reading vary considerably depending on the desired level of understanding of the text. Moreover, the activities to support these tasks are not necessarily similar (e.g., annotation versus bookmarking), suggesting that designers should strive for a diversification of approaches (e.g., developing multiple distinct tools) instead of proposing single unified solutions. Finally, the study emphasized that users involved in a reading task see considerable value in the simplicity and directness of a physical tool and physical interaction over an elaborate graphical user interface.

INTERACTION SPACE

Reflecting the conclusions from the formative study, this paper proposes an active reading aid in the form of a smart bookmark: the eTab. It takes the form of a transparent physical object that requires no batteries and that can be placed on the surface of a tablet computer [10, 32] and its presence sensed by the device's capacitive screen [5]. With this setup it is possible to use it as a display surface for alternative or augmented content. The bookmark is also sufficiently thin that touches and gestures on its surface are detected by the tablet multi-touch screen underneath it. The design space enabled by this setup results in a novel combination of both display and interaction possibilities. We isolate the most important features in Figure 2:

Looking. Similar to a magic lens [2, 16, 26], the bookmark allows users to simultaneously view two separate information spaces, one on the main tablet screen and one through the bookmark. These spaces can be adjusted as the tool can be freely moved around the surface and the content can be updated to reflect its location.

Interacting. As with SLAP widgets [32], touches and gestures (single tap, double tap, swipe, pinch, drag) on and off the bookmark can be discriminated and mapped to different interface actions (a vocabulary of gestures comparable or larger than that of similar systems [10, 11]). For example, swiping on the bookmark can be used to navigate between documents, while swiping on the tablet could be used to navigate within the current document.

Transitions. The presence of two separate information spaces also inherently supports interaction between these zones. Touch or strokes can be used to move, or otherwise associate, content from one interaction space to the other. This functionality can provide the advantages of dual-screen setups such as Codex [13] and the rich two-way linking present in LiquidText [28].

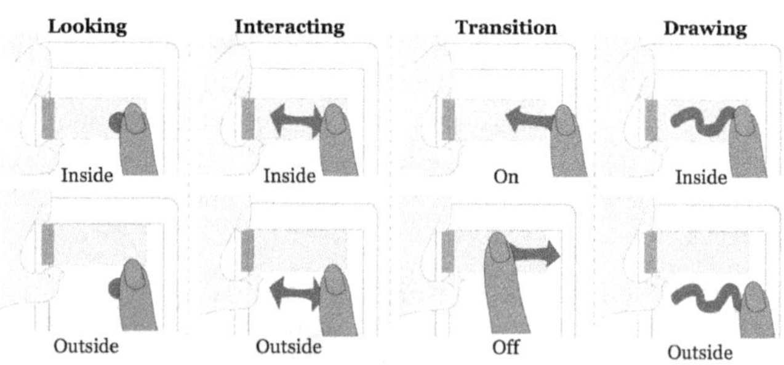

Figure 2. The two interaction spaces available with the eTab. Interaction can be separated based on whether it takes place on or off the transparent region of the bookmark. Interactions include looking at different content, interacting with gestures or taps, dragging from one space to the other, and drawing or writing using either or both the spaces.

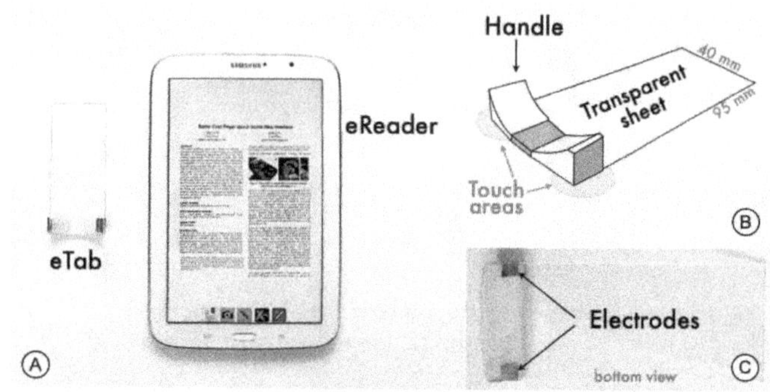

Figure 3. System overview (A); a sketch of the eTab highlighting the touch areas and transparent sheet (B); bottom view of the eTab prototype (C).

Drawing. Similarly, annotations, sketches and other drawn content can be entered both on and off the bookmark surface, allowing user entered content to be treated differently. For example, each space could be used to store different types of annotation, or one space could be used for annotations and the other for gestural input, potentially enabling a rich set of bimanual interactions [8, 14].

PROTOTYPE

The prototype (Figure 3) consists of a physical bookmark-like object and an eReader application developed for Android, running on a Samsung Galaxy Note 8.0 tablet. The physical bookmark (Figure 3.B) is composed of a 40 mm wide x 95 mm long x 0.5 mm thick transparent plastic body with a low-profile 3D printed handle. Similar to DataTiles [23] and SLAP widgets [32], the use of a thin transparent sheet allows the tablet touchscreen to precisely register input to bookmark's surface. Moreover, it serves to clearly and physically depict the size of the virtual bookmark region. The upper surface of the bookmark's handle is covered with a thin copper sheet which is connected to a pair of 0.5 cm square copper coated regions on its base (Figure 3.C). Due to the conductivity of the metal sheet, placing the bookmark on a multi-touch capacitive screen and touching the handle causes a recognizable pair of touch points to appear, a well documented technique for tracking physical objects on a tablet computer [1].

The eReader application is based on a standard portrait format viewer that allows users to navigate to different pages of a document by tapping on the sides of the screen, to zoom with pinch gestures and to pan with single finger movements. When the bookmark is placed on the screen its presence is registered based on the two capacitive points it produces. However, it remains inactive until a user taps on its transparent body. When this occurs, the currently selected bookmark view is activated and remains on until the bookmark is removed from the tablet screen. Whilst on-screen users can view and interact with the bookmark using the interaction space we define above: by repositioning it, looking at the contents displayed on its body and tapping, drawing or gesturing on, around or between this region and the surrounding screen area (Figure 2). Using this setup and

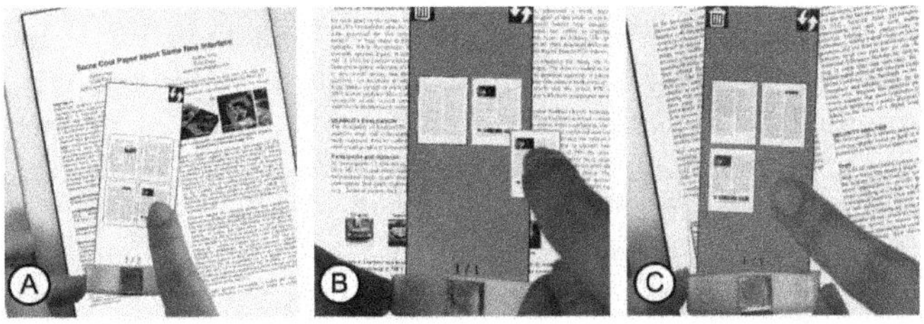

Figure 4. Navigation to pages by tapping on thumbnails (A), bookmarking custom pages by dragging them on to the eTab (B), and deleting pages by selecting them (C).

the features for design previously selected, we instantiated the results of the formative study into five different tools. The individual modes are selected from a row of five icons docked at the bottom of the tablet, each corresponding to a specific bookmark mode. The icons appear only before the eTab is activated (e.g. before placing it on the screen). This switching mechanism was inspired by common GUI designs (e.g. OSX dock).

Page Navigation

Navigation and marking pages for reference is a core feature for active reading. As such we developed page navigation functions (Figure 4) that enable users to quickly select and move to any page in a document. This is achieved by placing the eTab on the screen. Underneath its transparent body, thumbnails of all the document pages in groups of four are displayed, with the current page shown on the main display highlighted. Users can tap on a page to navigate to it and move to previous or subsequent sets of page thumbnails by swiping across the eTab.

A button located at the tip of the eTab toggles to a mode in which users can view and manage thumbnails of a set of saved pages. Pages are added to the set by tapping on the main tablet screen and dragging onto the eTab (a feature that resembles the pockets in Hinckley et al's GatherReader system [12]) and removed by tapping on the thumbnail and dragging off the eTab (Figure 4.B). Saved pages can be viewed by tapping on the thumbnail. Finally, there is also an explicit delete button for fast deletion of bookmarked pages (Figure 4.C).

Screen Capture

Taking advantage of the ease with which the eTab can be moved around, we designed a screen capture tool (Figure 5) to support saving, comparing and cross-referencing content. In this mode, once the eTab is positioned on the page, it acts as a camera. Tapping on the eTab takes and stores a screenshot of the content underneath its transparent body (a feature similar to one proposed in cAR [10]). Multiple screenshots can be taken and a user can tap a button to review the captured contents. These are displayed on the eTab body and are stored permanently on the tablet, making them available as a reader moves to other pages and, indeed, other documents. Swiping across the body of the eTab navigates through the set of stored screenshots and they can be deleted in the same way as the page thumbnails described above. The images are also stored in public

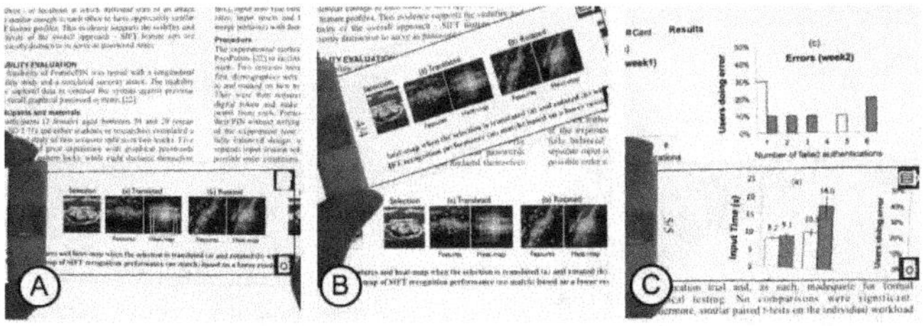

Figure 5. Screen-capture portions of the screen by tapping on the eTab (A, B). Screen-captures are saved and can be viewed (and navigated among) by swiping on the eTab surface (C).

folders on the tablet (and potentially on the clipboard), making them easily available to other applications, a feature explicitly requested by users.

Notes and Annotations

The ability for users to take notes and otherwise annotate material is a critical to active reading [27]. Accordingly, this issue has received considerable attention in the research community [e.g. 8, 14, 18, 28]. Similarly, the participants of our formative study repeatedly highlighted the importance of different kinds of notes. Specifically they strongly valued the ability to write notes that summarize comments referring or relating to the document as a whole, as well as notes directly linked to (and typically written over) specific portions of text in the document.

In line with these comments, we developed two different note formats. In the first (Figure 6.A), users write notes directly on the transparent body of the eTab, as they would write a post-it note in a real document. As with the screen capture application they can navigate through a set of notes by swiping across the eTab, delete notes via a trashcan icon, or modify the current note by simply writing or drawing additional content. These notes can be accessed from any page or document in the reader and can also be saved and copied for use and integration with external applications. In the second annotation format (Figure 6.B and C), users write and draw on the page around the eTab, directly on the displayed contents. These annotations are displayed only in the document locations in which they were original made, scaled in accordance with the main text, and are shown only when the eTab is placed on the screen. This ensures the marks do not permanently clutter or obscure the original contents. Whilst in this mode, the eTab displays a palette of colors and brush options (similar to [8]) that users can tap to select and control the format and style of their annotations (Figure 6.B).

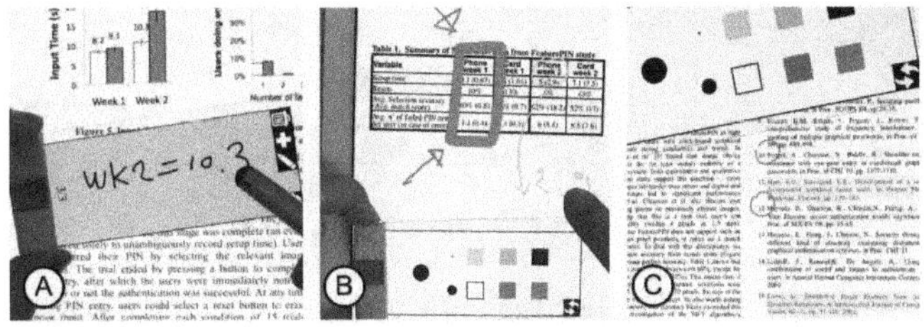

Figure 6. Two note styles are implemented. Post-it notes (A) and in-text annotations (B and C). With annotations, the eTab serves as a palette for colors and pen sizes (B).

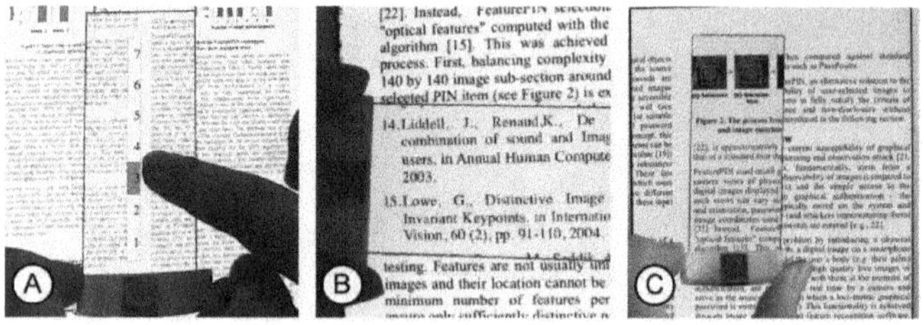

Figure 7. The X-Ray magic lens allows users to select a different document page (A) that will be visualized inside the eTab for reference or comparison with current contents (B, C).

X-Ray magic lens

Inspired by the work on magic lenses and contextual information displays [2, 16, 26], we designed an X-Ray tool that allows users to view the content on any page in a document in a window delimited by the eTab's transparent body (Figure 7). This system allows a user to quickly glance through the document to retrieve information present in another location. For example, a user could review or clarify a passage on a previous page (Figure 7.C), cross-reference a figure or check a citation (Figure 7.B) by looking through the X-Ray tool instead of flipping to the relevant page. In this way, the X-Ray tool offers ready access to other pages (scaled and panned with the current page) in order to support comparison and cross-referencing tasks.

Visual helpers

In the formative study, users reported challenges in following prose in dense writing on screen. To address these issues, we developed simple visual aids that allow users to underline an area of text (Figure 8.A), or to selectively obscure the content of lines above and below one of particular interest (Figure 8.B). These tools are designed to help users focus on a specific portion of text or minimize peripheral distractors. Extending these ideas we also created a ruler tool (Figure 8.C) that can be used to measure the length and angle between on-screen objects. This function is particularly intended for tasks such as examining maps, floor plans and images with scales. Users can rely on an accurate physical ruler integrated with the digital system and not have to physically print off articles in order to take measurements with traditional off-line tools.

USABILITY STUDY

We conducted an informal usability evaluation using the 10 participants who completed the formative study. They were first introduced to the eTab features and then given the opportunity to try them out. Comments and opinions were solicited throughout and the study took about 20 minutes per participant. Overall, users reported the bookmarking, annotations, screen-capture and the X-Ray magic lens functions to be both useful and usable. Comments included P5's appreciation of the ease with which pages could be added or removed from custom sets of bookmarks. P4 was positive about hiding all in-text annotations when the eTab is off the screen as it enabled him to "quickly see the original paper" while P10 appreciated the X-Ray tool as it was "more convenient than page jumping" when checking material in other pages. Finally, P2 regarded the screen-capture tool as very "familiar".

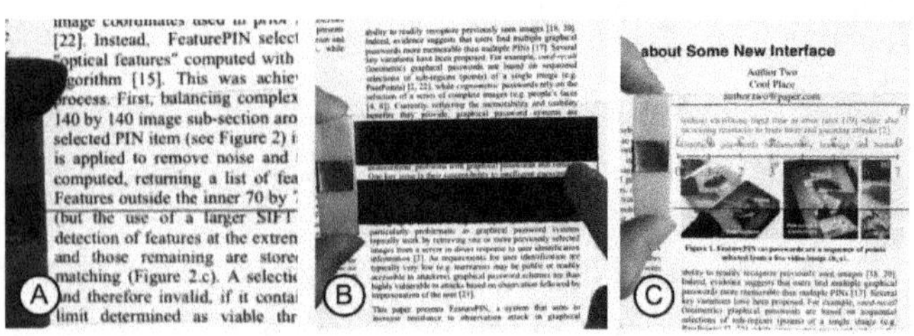

Figure 8. Visualization tools: an underline (A) and a visual band (B) to help users read dense text. A ruler tool (C) to measure length and angles of on-screen content.

Other tools received mixed comments. For example, P3 and P9 indicating that the line and the band tools are simple to use, but have limited applicability. P6 saw value in combining the navigation tool with the post-it notes, but P7 and P8 remarked that the eTab is small and would limit the usefulness and depth of the notes they could make. The small size of the eTab was also mentioned for the screen-capture (P2). These comments highlight a key recurring trade-off between the need for a portable physical tool and a large surface for rich interaction. One way to alleviate this concern would be to allow users to virtually expand the bookmark in specific circumstances – for example, during note taking, they could use a magnifying widget to expand the available drawing canvas. Finally, while some participants appreciated the consistency between the different applications (P10: "all eTab interaction methods are similar, so it is easy"), others commented that some of the interactions, such as dragging a page of the surface of the eTab to delete it, have poor affordances – there are few cues to indicate what can be done. We note this is a common problem with gestural style UIs [20].

DISCUSSION

Exploring multiple diverse ideas is a powerful way to gain insights into new input modalities and technologies [14]. For this reason we designed the eTab to cover a range of topics and to function not as a single monolithic system, but as a set of five different applications with complementary features designed to work together rapidly and seamlessly – users can simply lift and replace the eTab to switch modes. We argue this perspective is well suited to complex and varied tasks involved in active reading. For example, as illustrated in Figure 9, a typical active reading scenario with the eTab might involve a user studying a paper and quickly looking up a reference using the X-Ray functionality, then switching to annotate, comment on or highlight some text directly on the screen using a stylus. As reading continues, they navigate around the page by zooming or panning and then make a post-it note comment for later reference. This complex sequence of actions can occur rapidly and fluidly based on the rich bi-manual input [14] enabled by combining the physical tools of the eTab and a standard stylus with finger touches. As in previous work [14] and, as

Figure 9. The flow of interactions across a series of interrelated subtasks using hands, stylus and the eTab.

exemplified in Figure 9, the real value of the eTab system lies in the way it supports a rapid flow between the different interaction styles required for a series of closely interrelated subtasks. It serves as a mechanism to mediate between activities without disrupting focus and the flow of work.

Ultimately, the novel aspects of this work, compared to previous systems with similar design intentions [10, 14], is that it further expands the vocabulary of actions and the set of tools involved in the interactions that support active reading tasks. It also specifically focuses on the design of tools that operate with current available portable eReader devices (such as tablet computers). While Hinckley et al. [13, 14] made a case for the benefits of simultaneous use of touch and pen input, in this paper we extend this argument to explore the value that the eTab, a physical tool with very different physical properties and affordances, can bring to the active reading task. We design, present and discuss the novel interactions enabled by this tool, and show how they can co-exist in the ecosystem of interactions based on the more standard input techniques of pen and touch. Ultimately we believe that physical tools have much to offer to the digital reading experience and that the eTab represents a novel interactive design that showcases key aspects of this potential.

LIMITATIONS, FUTURE WORK AND CONCLUSION

This paper has presented the eTab, a simple physical aid for active reading on a tablet computer that works with currently available tablet devices and without batteries. The design of the system was motivated by prior literature and a formative study in which we exposed participants to scenarios depicting the potential of such a tool. We instantiated their feedback in the design of the eTab software in order to support activities such as rapid navigation, flexible note-taking and easy capture, manipulation and comparison of content. Finally, we validated our designs in a qualitative user study.

There are also limitations to this work. Perhaps the most serious is that the qualitative study, whilst informative, was brief and lab-based. As such, it does not allow us to comment on how the system would be used during real reading experiences – whether positive commentary on novel features such as the screen capture or X-Ray would actually lead to integration into real world reading practices. Given the simplicity, portability and robustness of our hardware, a more naturalistic field study is an obvious next step for this work.

There are also many further opportunities for future work. In terms of developing the prototype, we plan to explore different physical form factors. The formative study showed users had diverse preferences regarding the size of a prospective digital reading aid – either small and portable or large and with a substantial viewing/interaction space – and we are interested in exploring the potential of such variations. It is also clear that users manipulate the eTab (and devices in closely related systems [10, 11]) in a typical bimanual way: the device is fixed in place with non-dominant hand and interaction occurs with the dominant hand. This provides some guidance as to effective minimum sizes for the eTab – it must be sufficiently large to comfortably support this bimanual interaction style. To deal with the range of size recommendations, we are also interested in developing software or hardware prototypes than might expand and contract (virtually via an on-screen widget or physical via a mechanical mechanism) to provide users with differently sized eTab devices that can best cater to their preferences and needs.

Future versions of the eTab software should also improve the integration between the eTab modes – currently switching modes requires removing and replacing the eTab on the screen, an action that might become overly laborious if frequently performed. We are also interested in designing interfaces based on text-extraction functionality to support search, translation and text mining. Finally, in terms of the empirical work, a more substantial and longer-term usability study would improve the scope and validity of the findings from the second experiment in this article.

Ultimately, despite the advantages of paper, we believe that the convenience of digital reading platforms (such as tablet computers and eBook readers) will make them the dominant format for consumption of textual material. The eTab, by merging key aspects of the physical experience with the process of digital reading, represents a feasible and practical step towards combining the best of both these worlds – the expressiveness and rich affordances of physical objects with the flexibility and power of digital contents.

ACKNOWLEDGMENTS

This paper was supported by Samsung Research Fund, Sungkyunkwan University, 2014, and by Basic Science Research Program through the National Research Foundation of Korea (NRF) funded by the Ministry of Science, ICT and Future Planning (2014R1A1A1002223).

REFERENCES

1. Adobe Ink & Slide: http://www.adobe.com/products/ink-and-slide.html [Last access: January 2015].
2. Bier, E.A., Stone, M.C., Pier, K., Buxton, W., DeRose, T.D.: Toolglass and magic lenses: the see-through interface. In SIGGRAPH'93, 73-80.

3. Burstyn, J., Herriotts, M.A.: gBook: an e-book reader with physical document navigation techniques. In CHI EA'10, 4369-4374.
4. Büschel, W., Kister, U., Frisch, M., Dachselt, R.: T4 - transparent and translucent tangibles on tabletops. In AVI '14, 81-88.
5. Chan, L., Müller, S., Roudaut, A., Baudisch, P.: CapStones and ZebraWidgets: sensing stacks of building blocks, dials and sliders on capacitive touch screens. In CHI'12, 2189-2192.
6. Chen, G., Cheng, W., Chang, T., Zheng, X., Huang, R.: A comparison of reading comprehension across paper, computer screens, and tablets: Does tablet familiarity matter? In Journal of Computers in Education, 1-13.
7. Chen, N., Guimbretiere, F., Dixon, M., Lewis, C., Agrawala, M.: Navigation techniques for dual-display e-book readers. In CHI'08, 1779-1788.
8. Dachselt, R. and Al-Saiegh,S.: Interacting with Printed Books Using Digital Pens and Smart Mobile Projection. In CHI EA'11, 21-23.
9. Davidoff, S., Lee, M.K., Dey, A.K., Zimmerman, J.: Rapidly Exploring Application Design Through Speed Dating. In UbiComp'07, 429-446.
10. Hincapié-Ramos, J.D, Roscher, S., Büschel, W., Kister, U., Dachselt, R., Irani, P.: cAR: Contact Augmented Reality with Transparent-Display Mobile Devices.In PerDis '14, 80-85.
11. Hincapié-Ramos, J.D, Roscher, S., Büschel, W., Kister, U., Dachselt, R., Irani, P.: tPad: designing transparent-display mobile interactions. In DIS '14, 161-170.
12. Hinckley, K., Bi, X., Pahud, M., Buxton, B.: Informal information gathering techniques for active reading. In CHI'12, 1893-1896.
13. Hinckley, K., Dixon, M., Sarin, R., Guimbretiere, F., Balakrishnan, R.: Codex: a dual screen tablet computer. In CHI'09, 1933-1942.
14. Hinckley, K., Yatani, K., Pahud, M., Coddington, N., Rodenhouse, J., Wilson, A., Benko, H., Buxton, B.: Pen + touch = new tools. In UIST'10, 27-36.
15. Keshav, S.: How to read a paper. SIGCOMM Comput. Commun. Rev. 37, 3 (July 2007), 83-84.
16. Kim, K.T. and Elmqvist, N.: Embodied Lenses for Collaborative Visual Queries on Tabletop Displays. In Information Visualization, 11(4): 336-355, 2012.
17. Liao, C., Guimbretière, F., Hinckley, K., Hollan, J.: Papiercraft: A gesture-based command system for interactive paper. In TOCHI. 14, 4, Article 18, 27 pp.
18. Mackay, W.E., Pothier, G., Letondal, C., Bøegh, K., Sørensen, H.E.: The missing link: augmenting biology laboratory notebooks. In UIST'02, 41-50.
19. Morris, M.R., Bernheim Brush, A.J., Meyers, B.R.: Reading Revisited: Evaluating the Usability of Digital Display Surfaces for Active Reading Tasks. In TABLETOP'07, 79-86.
20. Norman, D.A.: Natural user interfaces are not natural. In Interactions 17, 3 (May 2010), 6-10.
21. O'Hara, K. and Sellen, A.: A comparison of reading paper and on-line documents. In CHI'97, 335-342.
22. Pietrzak, T., Malacria, S., Lecolinet, E.: S-Notebook: augmenting mobile devices with interactive paper for data management. In AVI'12, 733-736.
23. Rekimoto, J., Ullmer, B., Oba, H., DataTiles: a modular platform for mixed physical and graphical interactions. In CHI'01, 269-276.
24. Sellen, A. J. and R. H. R. Harper, The Myth of the Paperless Office, 2003, pp. 242.
25. Schilit, B.N., Golovchinsky, G., Price, M.N.: Beyond paper: supporting active reading with free form digital ink annotations. In CHI'98, 249-256.
26. Spindler, M., Tominski, C., Schumann, H., Dachselt, R.: Tangible views for information visualization. In ITS'10.
27. Tashman, C.S. and Edwards, W.K.: Active reading and its discontents: the situations, problems and ideas of readers. In CHI'11, 2927-2936.
28. Tashman, C.S. and Edwards, W.K.: LiquidText: a flexible, multitouch environment to support active reading. In CHI'11, 3285-3294.
29. Thom, E. and Jones, M.: Holding onto the magic: lightweight augmentation of digital reading devices. In DIS'12, 510-513.
30. Ullmer, B. and Ishii, H.: The metaDESK: models and prototypes for tangible user interfaces. In UIST'97.
31. Waldner, M., Hauber, J., Zauner, J., Haller, M., Billinghurst, M.: Tangible tiles: design and evaluation of a tangible user interface in a collaborative tabletop setup. In OZCHI'06, 151-158.
32. Weiss, M., Wagner, J., Jansen, Y., Jennings, R., Khoshabeh, R., Hollan, J.D., Borchers, J.: SLAP widgets: bridging the gap between virtual and physical controls on tabletops. In CHI'09, 481-490.
33. Wightman, D., Ginn, T., Vertegaal, R.: BendFlip: Examining Input Techniques for Electronic Book Readers with Flexible Form Factors. In INTERACT'11, 117-133.
34. Zeleznik, R., Bragdon, A., Adeputra,F., Ko, K.: Hands-on math: a page-based multi-touch and pen desktop for technical work and problem solving. In UIST'10, 17-26.

Couples' Communication Channels: What, When & Why?

Henriette Cramer
Yahoo Labs
Sunnyvale, CA
henriette@yahoo-inc.com

Maia Jacobs
Georgia Institute of Technology
Atlanta, GA
mjacobs30@gatech.edu

ABSTRACT
An overwhelming variety of communication channels are available to consumers. Here, we present an overview of the aspects that need to be accounted for when intimate partners select a communication channel. We present interviews with 10 cohabiting couples (20 participants) and an 8-day diary study of communication and coordination. Using reported instances of within-couple communication, triggered by relationship-oriented or practical household needs, we identify why particular channels are chosen or sequenced. Extending media richness critiques, we identify additional factors that influence communication choice such as intimate knowledge of the others' habits, possibilities to add emotional meaning, and couples' shared needs as an identifiable unit. We also extend the notion of network effects on channel choice, and discuss the ecology of channel, networks, devices and device settings involved between partners. Finally, channel choice is not an all-or-nothing game; multiple channels can, and must, co-exist.

INTRODUCTION
The number of communication channels and services available on computers as well as mobile devices is enormous. For instance, in a sample of Android app usage with 4,145 users between Aug 2010 and Jan 2011, Böhmer et al. [1] found 881 communication apps in active use. McGregor et al. found similar variety and sequential usage of communication apps in a qualitative iPhone screen capture study [5]. These findings raise the long-standing question of how users pick and choose between the communication channels that they have available to them [3,4,6].

Using interviews and a diary study with 10 cohabiting couples (20 individual interviews, 127 diary entries from 19 participants over 8-days), we discuss the intricacies in channel and app choice when the sender and recipient have intimate knowledge of each other. We describe which channels they reported using, and the factors that influenced channel selection when communicating with each other when apart. We found that all couples used a variety of channels to communicate with each other. We provide evidence that a multitude of factors, beyond characteristics discussed in the literature, influence why couples pick a particular channel. We extend the notion of media characteristics to allow for consideration of the ecosystem of the networks, devices and the particular apps involved in a communication sequence. We focus on the influence of their affective bond and needs to communicate and reciprocate affective value; their adaptation to intimate knowledge of habits and preferences, and to context changes to avoid issues. We further elaborate on especially the relationship and affect-oriented aspects of channel choice within this context and channel switching.

CHI 2015, April 18–23, 2015, Seoul, Republic of Korea.

ACM 978-1-4503-3145-6/15/04...$15.00.
http://dx.doi.org/10.1145/2702123.2702356

RELATED WORK
Relationships are maintained through communication via a multitude of channels. O'Hara et al. [7] describe how relationships are performed using small, continuous narratives, mediated by the features of messaging platforms. Channel properties alone, such as media richness, however poorly predict channel *choice* and neglect social influence and preferences [3,4]. Even when a service is supposedly designed for a specific purpose, users may not necessarily choose it over other channels. For example, while complex coordination tools exist, people often use more open channels (texting, calls, emails) as they do not curb the conversational process [8].

Media synchronicity theory [3] posits that channel capabilities should match individuals' needs to both *convey* information and to *converge* into shared meaning. It identifies five media capabilities: symbol sets (e.g. text, visual), parallelism (simultaneous transmission), transmission velocity, rehearsability (e.g. fine-tuning), and reprocessability. The theory predicts that combining multiple media likely improves communication. It however focuses most on fit of a type of channel for the task completion process, not finer-grained choice between, for example, different types of textual messaging. Loyalty to a specific platform is affected by its user experience as well as network externalities [10]. In addition, Church and Oliveira [2] find tradeoffs, for example WhatsApp's perceived benefits included low cost, sense of community and immediacy, but SMS was seen as more reliable and privacy preserving. We however will illustrate the necessity to extend such channel characteristics perspectives in light of the more complex ecosystems of type of channel, specific app(s), device platforms and individuals' device settings; but also the affective needs in intimate settings.

Using a case study of three professionals, and their use of email in specific, Jung and Lyytinen [6] propose further work from an 'ecological' perspective in which users make a channel choice through a process of exploring their surroundings, and then picking the medium which affords achieving a particular communication goal. They distinguish the dimensions of media characteristics, social influence, and communication context. Here, we further extend their perspective by focusing on relational and affective aspects. We use a relationship-oriented rather than a work task setting, and provide an overview of those factors we encountered within a sample of couples such as focus on relationship, emotional meaning, couple's shared identity and habits. This relationship-oriented approach may help to provide better communication tools for couples in the future that consider their unique, shared and individual, contextual needs. Rather than focusing on couples' conflicts as in [9], we explore how different channels support couples' needs in a broader light.

METHOD

Ten couples (20 participants) from the San Francisco Bay Area were recruited through Craigslist and social media. 7 Female/Male couples participated, 1 F/F, 2 M/M. All were cohabiting, some lived with children, family or roommates. They had been together from <1 to 10+ years. Ages ranged from 19-60, with varied socio-economic backgrounds. They ranged from tech-enthusiasts to those who resisted buying a smartphone. As a qualitative study, this sample is not meant to be 'representative' but to provide insight into varied practices.

Interviews were individual (1.5-2 hours per person) and transcribed. Interviews focused on devices and services used, daily routines, and sharing between the couple. Here, we focus on why certain communication channels or services were used. The couples also took part in a follow-up 8-day diary study, asking for both instances of communication and coordination that day between the couple and reasons why they picked a particular channel. Participants were compensated $10 per diary entry. 19/20 participants provided diary entries (3-8 per person, mdn=7, M=6.2). In total the 125 diary entries provided 65 instances related to coordination, and 107 other communications. Over 500 interview fragments from the first 10 interviews were inductively categorized by the authors until full agreement was reached. The other interviews and the diary entries were used for validation to see whether further extension would be necessary. The clusters related to channel selection were compared with related work.

RESULTS

We first outline the variety of channels used, and the triggers for in-couple communication. We then elaborate on the reasons why the couples picked particular channels.

Channels used

The 20 couples used a variety of channels, including face-to-face, calls, text/iMessage, Google HangOuts, various email services, Skype (messaging, calls) Facetime, Facebook (Messenger, posts, tagging), Snapchat, Instagram, Twitter, WhatsApp, WeChat, Groupme, physical notes/post-its, Calendars, Life360, Evernote, Grocery lists apps, Yo (justyo.com), GroupMessage, and Dropbox.

In line with media synchronicity [3], single goals were sometimes reached through a multitude of channels *"On Friday [Partner] did a quick lunchtime stop at the store and took pictures, which she attached to an MMS. We then chatted using Google Chat (she was at her workplace) then when I arrived I used FB [Facebook] chat to let her know her I was there (because FB chat is what we use everywhere else). When we were there we referred to our Evernote [shopping] list"*-P12

Automatic & low effort channels

Underexposed in earlier media choice work, systems sometimes perform pre-set actions on users' behalf. One participant for example used Life360, a family locating and messaging app, to automatically send her partner notices of departure/arrival. This presents a promising avenue for systems that integrate or pick channels on behalf of users – as well as the interpretation of what these automatic messages mean to the 'sender' and receiver. This is related, but contrasted from, low-effort, but still active effort by for example sending a Yo [mobile app, only sends the word 'Yo']: *"Because I was exhausted and didn't even feel like communicating explicitly."*-P11. The Yo has to be interpreted by the receiver, but also expresses active 'thinking about you'.

Communication triggers and needs

The communication cases could roughly be divided into relationship, affect-oriented communication and fulfilling practical (household) purposes.

Relationship/emotionally-salient instances included 1) 'Just for you' cute or silly content that was considered inappropriate for others: *"a lot of things I send her is like bold and funny and they're just for her only"*-P8. 2) Emotionally salient moments they wanted to share with their intimate partner, either big events: *"I got this award in my class [...], where I can't even hold it in, I have to tell him"*-P1, or more mundane occurrences: *"... it was so cute, [baby] been sucking on his thumb, [...] I would take a picture of that and send it to him"*-P5. For these instances, preserving a sense of private, intimate or playful conversation appeared most important when picking a channel.

Practical needs-oriented instances focused on coordination 1) Planning, routines, deviations and general situational awareness *"Checking on each other's location when we were shopping in Ikea"*-P17, or ritual, habitual calls at for example the end of the workday. 2) Household goals: *"now* *we're looking at houses we'll send each other house...we liked"*-P9.

Quite interesting were mixtures of practical and emotional needs: 3) Safety *"I went out and I was home really late and I got very drunk and I was really scared [...] so I Skyped him"*-P9. For these instances, reaching their partner in a timely, reliable manner was crucial – but just as important is inspiring confidence in a partner from afar and feeling safe to communicate in a sensitive and private situation.

Representation as a couple For external communications, however, channels had to fulfill an additional need. Couples wanted to send messages that appeared to originate from them together as one unit (e.g. invitations), but also sometimes 'pretended' to be their partner when tasked to deal with a household issue (e.g. emails on orders in one name). In some cases, one partner was, whether or not by personal choice, the custodian of a channel *"he refuses to be on facebook, so I show him funny things that his sister puts on facebook a lot"* –P1.

Channel choice

Not surprisingly, as cohabiting couples, most participants preferred face-to-face communication. Tools were however used at home too, for convenience: *"I'm usually up here [...]When I'm not down there relaxing or family time [...], she will text me. That's our main communication, rather than her trudging up here or yelling"* –P6.

For communication while apart, our couples considered the channels they had available to them in the current context of both themselves as sender and their partner as recipient. Senders made tradeoffs between their needs, channel properties with the message to be conveyed, their own context, and their perception of the other's contextual preferences. However, especially apparent in this setting of intimate partners were the needs in communicating and reciprocating affective value, adapting to intimate knowledge of the other, and anticipating changes that would make combining or switching channels more appropriate.

Affective value

For couples, the emotional value of a channel was more salient than discussed in earlier work in other contexts. When we take the channel properties from existing work such as media synchronicity [3], we see commonalities, but also necessary extensions to account for nuances not previously identified. The possibilities to change content's affective meaning by using a particular app played a role much beyond symbol sets and reprocessability as identified in media synchronicity [3]: *"I would Snapchat her like if I had a photo and I make it funny, then I'd send it to her. Snapchat's really easy to make it a funny drawing"*-P8

Knowing that one's partner was engaged and moved by a message was important to our participants. Couples were specifically interested in not just sharing a particular type of content, but even more so in their partner's affective reaction: *"I want the reaction of him being entertained by [funny content]"* -P1. Shared traditions emerge and one couple, for example, had the habit of sharing hand-written notes or drawings, *"its more like, touching. It hits you harder"*-P10. This extends social influence as discussed in [6], and also adds a useful distinction to be made between social-emotional meaning within and outside the couple. Perceived content quality and social standing would influence whether any communication visible to the outside world (e.g. Facebook posts) would be appropriate.

Intimate knowledge of the other

Understanding each others' context and needs was crucial. Our couples tried to empathize with recipients' known preferences and context, but individual preferences can be trumped by urgency. For example, *"Texting is actually more immediate, or more, 'I really need your attention right now' [...] **I** hate texting so **we** don't do it that often"*-P1. Knowing each others' habits, in terms of the partner's activities at a particular time of day and the constraints at their expected location (e.g. workplace rules): *"Our understanding is we use google hangout during work hours since I can't access FB at work, but I do have access to Google"*-P11

Participants dealt with each others' 'known imperfections' and, for example, used multiple channels to reinforce messages: *"he forget so I'll just be like, 'I'm going to call you and I'll tell you and then I'm going to send it to you because I don't trust you for finding the correct brand of brownies'"* –P9

Changing & combining channels

Knowledge of the other also influenced sequencing of channels, as outlined below. Something not yet adequately addressed in work focusing on media properties are the intertwined effects of the ecosystem of apps, combined devices, and network involved**.** This went beyond effects of network externalities as addressed in [10]; participants also considered sender-receiver platform combinations within the changing context of the other. Focusing on couple conflict, Scissors and Gergle [9] found that couples switched channels for reasons such as conflict escalation, managing one's emotions, and resolution attempts. In our non-conflict setting, switching mainly occurred for more practical reasons:

- Reinforcing, such as in the brownie example above
- Resolving channel issues together: "[We] *Chatted in Google hangouts, figured out what was wrong with Yo", "We figured out that Yo has been working fine and that [partner] had all app notifications other tha[n] Facebook turned off on her phone. So we may use Yo more now"*-P12.
- Avoiding issues or potential conflict, dealing with (anticipated) contextual changes. Sometimes things would have to wait to avoid annoyances: *"it's just too much [...], I can't do it in a text, so I called her. There*

was one piece that was urgent but the rest waited until I got home"-P6 or had to be escalated before issues arise, often due to urgency/non-response: *"he's really busy at work, so he didn't email me back so then I call him [...] I think I gave him an hour. Normally if he's going to respond, then he'll do it quickly"* -P4

Note that couples didn't necessarily prefer to sequence multiple channels: *"It was weird to move between MMS, google chat, and Facebook chat. [...] my phone deals with all [...] equally well, but it would be best if there was one service that supported images and text reliably and was not blocked at [her] workplace."*-P12. However, sometimes (but certainly not always) the combination of channels in itself communicated importance and, as such, added meaning.

DISCUSSION & CONCLUSION

Users can pick from an overwhelming amount of channels. Our couples considered many tradeoffs while deciding which channel(s) would best support their communication needs, and moved between channels. While models of channel choice exist, they did not capture all patterns that emerged in the instances shared by our couples. Jung and Lyytinen [6] mention the role of social influence and context, but it is useful to distinguish between senders' experience of their own context, and their consideration of the recipient. Couples were especially sensitive to affective effects they had on their partner, and considered their intimate knowledge of the other's context in a more elaborate manner than expected from task-oriented models that focus on channel fit [3] rather than choice. Couples also shared types of communication reserved for their partner alone that had to be especially safe, immediate as well as intimate, illustrating the importance of using varied, specific research settings such as couples in this work. We also show that couples' channel switching in conflict situations [9] is motivated differently than switches in the non-conflict situations addressed in this study.

Our findings focused on channel properties, build on the notion of assessing capabilities rather than services as a whole [3] and consideration of network externalities [10], but adds that we should rather focus on the intertwined effects of network, apps' features, device platforms and settings on both sender and recipient's ends – as well as the knowledge that sender and receiver have of each other.

Channel choice is not necessarily an all-or-nothing game. It is crucial to note that using multiple channels can also add meaning, and emphasize urgency or importance. Developers can tweak their services to ensure that a specific type of channel works for a diversity of content, and devices, to be a good fit for specific situations. They however cannot control contextual externalities, couple's traditions, nor another app simply already being open on the screen. The intimate context of couples provides opportunities for more playful and affect-focused channel design – especially in communicating emotions, care, and allowing a richer reciprocal understanding of the other's emotional engagement with, and appreciation of, your message. New apps should not focus on being the end-all of communication, but rather understand how they can add to, the myriad of options that users already have within their social context.

ACKNOWLEDGMENTS

Big thanks to our couples, and Yahoo colleagues Kevin Cheng, Sukhada Jog and Yi Huang for their help and contributions.

REFERENCES

1. Böhmer, M. Hecht, B. Schöning, J., Krüger, A., Bauer, G. Falling asleep with Angry Birds, Facebook and Kindle. *Proc. MobileHCI'11* (2011), 47-56.
2. Church, K., De Oliveira, R. WhatsUp With WhatsApp? Comparing Mobile Instant Messaging Behaviors with Traditional SMS, *Proc. MobileHCI'13* (2013).
3. Dennis, A., Fuller, R., Valacich, J. Media, Tasks and Communication Processes: A Theory of Media Synchronicity, *MIS Quarterly* 32, 2 (2008), 575-600.
4. El-Shinnaway, M., Markus, M. (1997). The poverty of media richness theory: explaining people's choice of electronic mail vs. voice mail. *IJHCS*, 46, 443–467.
5. McGregor, M., Brown, B., McMillan, D. 100 days of iPhone use: mobile recording in the wild. *CHI'14 Extended Abstracts* (2014), 2335-2340.
6. Jung, Y., Lyytinen, K. Towards an ecological account of media choice: a case study on pluralistic reasoning while choosing email. *Information Systems Journal*, 24, 3 (2014), 271-293.
7. O'Hara, K., Massimi, M., Harper, R., Rubens, S., Morris. J., 2014. Everyday dwelling with WhatsApp. *Proc. CSCW'14* (2014), 1131-1143.
8. Schuler, R., Grandhi, S., Mayer, J., Ricken, S., Jones, Q. The doing of doing stuff: understanding the coordination of social group-activities. *Proc. CHI'14* (2014),119-128.
9. Scissors, L. Gergle, D. "Back and forth, back and forth": channel switching in romantic couple conflict. *Proc. CSCW'13* (2013), 237-248.
10. Zhou, T., Lu, Y. Examining mobile instant messaging user loyalty from the perspectives of network externalities and flow experience. *Computers in Human Behavior*, 27 (2011), 883-889.

The Messaging Kettle: Prototyping Connection over a Distance between Adult Children and Older Parents

Margot Brereton, Alessandro Soro, Kate Vaisutis, Paul Roe
Electrical Engineering and Computer Science, Queensland University of Technology
2 George St, Brisbane, QLD 4000, Australia
[m.brereton, alessandro.soro, k.vaisutis, p.roe]@qut.edu.au

ABSTRACT
A prototype "messaging kettle" is described. The connected kettle aims to foster communication and engagement with an older friend or relative who lives remotely, during the routine of boiling the kettle. We describe preliminary encounters and findings from demonstrating a working prototype in morning tea gatherings of people in their 50s-late 70s and from introducing it into the homes of two people in their 80s who live on another continent. Key findings are that: The concept of keeping in touch around a "habituated object" such as a kettle was well received; Simple and varied interaction modalities that allow asymmetric forms of communication are needed; Designing for use across different time zones requires attention; And, that even when augmenting a habituated object, the process of introduction, appropriation and habituation still needs significant attention and investigation.

Author Keywords
Habituation; Elderly; Internet of Things

ACM Classification Keywords
H5.3. Group and Organization Interfaces

INTRODUCTION
Ageing healthily is associated with maintaining social connection and an active, healthy lifestyle. In this note we examine how technology might assist social connection with an elderly friend or relative who lives some distance away. While attention has been paid to "monitoring the elderly," often with intrusive unfamiliar technology, relatively little technology push research outside of HCI has considered social engagement, which is far more important than monitoring, being based upon feelings and empathy rather than just location and movement.

CHI 2015, April 18 - 23, 2015, Seoul, Republic of Korea

ACM978-1-4503-3145-6/15/04…$15.00.
http://dx.doi.org/10.1145/2702123.2702462

The lives of two people who wish to maintain a connection at a distance may be different in their routines, inclinations to use technology, levels of busyness and social roles. These asymmetries come into play in design of technology to support engagement of older people. [5, 9] Since older people often express difficulty in keeping up with new technologies, our approach focuses on augmenting "habituated" objects, ones that older people already use routinely, with simple expressive forms of communication.

Our design approach seeks to understand and augment existing routines and relationships in places that people already inhabit [10]. The approach recognizes that technology is something that we dwell with, that becomes part of the fabric of our practices and lives [2]. When a new technology is introduced, it enters a network of relations that make its use possible [13]. Design continues in use and a process of design after design begins [6], where people begin to invent how they will adopt, accommodate and shape a technology to their needs and habits and how their habits will in turn be shaped by the technology.

This research aimed to investigate remote connection and communication with elders by augmenting an existing comfort routine of boiling the kettle to make tea. We describe the initial phase of research in which we built and demonstrated a functioning prototype "messaging kettle" in order to (1) get feedback from prospective users about the concept, (2) understand their willingness to take part in home trials, (3) explore preferred interaction modalities, and (4) expose deployment details in order to refine the design and thus maximise the success of home trials. In addition to a novel means of connection, we contribute further exposure of thorny issues that arise when deploying technology in the home, particularly for older adults.

RELATED WORK
Many CHI research projects have investigated intimacy at a distance, informing this work. Strong and Gaver, [14] in "Feather, scent and shaker" presented forms of minimal intimate, expressive communication, moving first steps into emotive and non-informational communication. In the seminal technology probes paper [7], digital post-it notes and images displayed in frames were used between families to

send notes, images, and greetings, supporting both playful exchange and explicit communication.

Intergenerational connection across distance has been investigated using a variety of approaches, notably through sharing photos [5, 12] through connecting into social networking sites, *Tlatoque* [4], through playing cards [8], through connecting furniture [11] and using gesture and video through a physical proxy designed to look like a fabric covered wooden lamp, *Homeproxy* [15]. The concept of connection around particular places used by families has been explored, notably using the fridge and the family clock [16]. While these projects have inspired this work, none is based around a particular habitual everyday comfort routine such as boiling the kettle to make tea. Ten Bhömer beautifully explored interaction through connected teapots, but they were non-functional [17]. Chung developed a shared synchronous drinking interaction concept, *Lover's Cups*, that was implemented, but not, to our knowledge discussed or trialled with prospective users in homes [3].

Lindley et als review of literature from gerontology, HCI and human factors [9] found that adult children wanted peace of mind about their parents welfare through technology and that older people were interested to derive details about their children's lives through technology, however their desires for connection may be asymmetric.

Our work contributes by (1) Intertwining communication with habitual use of objects in social comfort routines; (2) Supporting asymmetries of desire for connection; and (3) exploring issues of deployment in homes. We investigated use of a messaging kettle to connect adult children in their 50s-60s with their parents in their 70s-80s.

THE MESSAGING KETTLE

The messaging kettle was designed to support a feeling of connection at a distance around the routine of boiling the kettle. The concept was derived from our prior work [1,18], in which we undertook contextual interviews with older people in their homes, asking about objects of significance to them, both emotionally and practically, and methods of communication with friends and relatives. The possibility of communicating through things was explored [18]. Although users of technologies such as email and mobile phones, many older people expressed that they found new technologies such as Skype difficult to configure and use [18]. This led us to consider how favourite objects might be augmented to help older people keep in touch. Participants were interested, but found this notion hard to grasp. Hence we decided to build a prototype. We based the prototype on the kettle as it had been identified in several interviews as being part of enjoyable comfort-inducing social routines.

Particularly when living apart and in different time zones, close friends and relatives miss everyday interactions with each other. The core idea was that two kettles could indicate to each other when they were switched on, showing use at the remote location. One might leave a small message during the routine of boiling the kettle, such as "just got back from the shops" or "terrible weather" to keep connected, but without making communication a burden.

Figure 1 The Kettle Mate and Tea Box. When the connected remote kettle (in another house) is switched on, the kettle mate displays a dynamic orange/red show of lights as shown.

The requirements for the Messaging Kettle were that it be easy to use and safe. It should provide a simple direct private connection to a particular person via their kettle – somewhat like a presidential hotline. It should indicate when the other kettle is in use, so that the user can know that their relative or friend is boiling the kettle and that their own boiling activity is being displayed remotely. The display should fade gradually as the kettle cools, giving a vague indication of when it was last used, and allowing for not seeing the actual boiling event. It should also have the capability to send a simple message. The resulting design consisted of two complementary pieces, a kettle mate and tea box, that are interconnected, but capable of functioning independently from one another. The two pieces allowed us to explore different form factors and interface modalities and allowed for asymmetric communication preferences.

The *Kettle Mate* (Figure 1) is a kettle shaped device meant to sit close to any actual kettle or teapot and augment its functionalities without interfering with its original and primary uses, thus allowing people to use their own kettle. It is controlled by an Arduino and houses a contact-less infra-red temperature sensor in its "spout" to recognize the state of use of the local kettle (for example when it is switched on, boiling, or cooling down). It shows the remote kettle's state of use through an animated display of orange/red and blue lights. It provides voice messaging by means of a microphone and speaker operated through a minimalistic user interface, a red button to record/send a message and a green one to play incoming messages.

The KettleMate connects by Bluetooth to an Android tablet embedded in a hardwood tea box. The tea box provides scribbling and message archive abilities. An embedded GSM (phone) chip is used so that no home network is needed. As some older adults have difficulty with hearing and others with vision, we incorporated both audio and visual communication: when switched on, The smart *Tea Box* (Figure 1, 2) opens a dedicated application that allows scribbling using a stylus, as well as scrolling through previous messages. A simple interface for choosing ink color, erasing errors, and posting a message is displayed on screen. A blue light on the Kettle Mate indicates when a new scribble is left in the Tea Box.

Figure 2 Tea Box during in-home demonstrations showing a message sent from another continent.

A Messaging Kettle is coupled to an identical companion, possibly several time zones away. The two devices are meant to virtually act as a wormhole between two places, making the act of boiling each kettle visible at the remote end, and relaying messages and scribbles as desired, forming a communication habit around kettle routines.

MORNING TEAS AND IN-HOME EVALUATIONS

Having built a fully functional working prototype, our goal was to test and demonstrate the concept before refining the interaction design, so that we could learn from user feedback and from setup in different kitchens, *design in use*. The kettle mate is twice its intended size, due to the electronics being implemented on an evaluation board rather than as a printed circuit. It is cut in the form of a kettle from Medium Density Fibreboard (MDF), although a prototype for prolonged testing will be made in a more refined form and material.

We undertook two "morning teas" and two in-home demonstrations. The "morning teas" consisted of asking people to come for morning tea or coffee, a tradition in our country, where they would learn about and discuss a proposed new technology. At morning tea we discussed the experiences and challenges of staying connected with an older parent or with adult children and then provided a demonstration of the messaging kettle. Following the demonstration, participants tried out the prototype, sending and receiving messages and boiling events. We asked for feedback, suggestions and likely use scenarios.

Morning Teas: One morning tea was held with 5 people in their 50s-60s all of whom had an older parent in their 80s. Another was held with 6 people in their late 70s accompanied by two adult children in their 40s and 50s (who came primarily to provide transport, and did not appear to influence proceedings). Participants were recruited through personal contact and snowballing, but were not relatives or close friends of ours. They came largely from households in middle income suburbs. **In Home Demonstrations**: The prototype was demonstrated in the home of an older relative (mid 80s) of one of the research team and also in the home of one of her friends. In home demos lasted 25 minutes. Participants were in the UK and tried the kettle, communicating with a researcher in Australia. **Analysis:** Morning teas and demonstrations were videoed and thematic analysis was undertaken.

FINDINGS

The Concept: Adult children in their 50s and 60s were all enthusiastic about the messaging kettle and expressed appreciation for technology that considered their elderly parents. Each described personal scenarios of use. They liked the idea of having a way to see that their parents were up and active. Some of their elderly parents had a neighbor that checked in on them, one just checking to see if the blinds opened each day. The adult children liked the dual modalities of voice and scribble messaging as some had parents with poor hearing and others with poor vision. They felt that being able to write or record a message was a good daily activity for their parents, and they liked the thought of keeping their parents in contact in a more active way, using their motor and cognitive skills.

Six morning tea participants in their 70s discussed keeping in touch with technologies prior to the messaging demonstration. They expressed that: (1) It was difficult to find good times and ways to connect, especially across time zones; *"They're always busy, I'd love to speak that one now but it's the wrong time;"* (2) A common sentiment was being out of sight and out of mind; *"When you don't see a person often you tend not to think about them and it takes more effort to keep in touch;"* (3) They preferred more traditional forms of voice and face to face communication; *"The new way is to text etc. but I like to talk on the phone." "Messages can be received the wrong way if you can't see or hear the person."* (4) They found it difficult to keep up with and configure new technologies, and often relied on adult children for help.

They showed a lot of interest in the messaging kettle demonstration, liking the display lights and message screen as easy to use and see. They emphasized the importance of simplicity and cost, appreciating these aspects of the design. They felt it would augment but not replace the other communication. However, only three of the six workshop participants were keen to try the kettle in a longer trial. For the three who were ambivalent or not keen, it was hard to elicit whether they did not like the idea of the interaction itself, or whether they could not envisage a relationship into which the technology would fit, or both. One man, was keen to have connected boiling events, but did not think he would send messages. Another man who was ambivalent expressed interest in possibly connecting a different object.

Ways to Keep in Touch: Having seen and tried the messaging kettle, participants felt that interaction around routine activities could possibly create good communication habits with less effort. One woman in her late 70s commented she would like to use it to keep in touch with an old friend who lived in another continent, but that *"you would have to take it there and show her how to use it. She won't email."* A common observation was that some older people are reluctant to try even a simple new technology, may need showing, and may not eventually adopt. They expressed interest in keeping in touch with more than one person through the kettle including friends and family.

Managing Time: There were different opinions about managing aspects of time. Some felt an explicit indication of the time that the kettle last boiled would be good. There was debate about showing times in local time, remote time or both. Others simply wanted to know if their friend had had a cup of tea. There was concern that a light display or message could wake them at night, indicating the need to consider use across time zones.

Where to Put It: In-home demonstrations with two women in their 80s, both email users, revealed issues about how the new technology might be made at home. One had a small kitchen with every surface in use, in particular because all her items needed to be easily reached. With limited electric sockets there was the simple issue of where to plug it in and find a space for it. Both women liked the concept, and were excited to see boiling displays and messages from afar, but it needed tailoring to their circumstances. One had multiple kettles *"I use the bedroom one upstairs in the morning and this one in the kitchen during the day."* This participant asked for a wall mounted teabox, as was also suggested by the older morning tea participants - easy to see and not in the way. The second woman had plenty of room in her kitchen and was enthusiastic, also proposing connecting wine glasses to share a drink with her daughter overseas.

CONCLUSIONS

Our preliminary investigation with the messaging kettle prototype in a very small sample revealed that adult children and some (approx 50%) of their older parents liked the idea of keeping in touch with a habituated object such as a kettle. It supports asymmetric communication preferences and ambient and whimsical connection as well as explicit communication during the everyday routine of using the kettle. However, the need for *design in use* to refine deployment details and to support uptake and habituation for older people was strongly felt. The need to deploy in homes for longer periods to explore uptake, use, interface, appropriation and habituation was confirmed.

ACKNOWLEDGMENTS

We thank our participants and the Australian Research Council for Discovery grant DP150104001.

REFERENCES

1. Brereton, M. Habituated Objects: Everyday Tangibles That Foster the Independent Living of an Elderly Woman. *Interactions 20*, 4 (2013), 20–24.
2. Brown, B. and Randell, R. Building a context sensitive telephone. *Computer Supported Cooperative Work (CSCW), 13*(3-4), (2004) 329-345.
3. Chung, H., Lee, C. H. J., & Selker, T. Lover's cups: drinking interfaces as new communication channels. *Proc.CHI'06 extended abstracts. ACM (2006),* 375-380.
4. Cornejo, R., Tentori, M., & Favela, J.. Ambient Awareness to Strengthen the Family Social Network of Older Adults. (CSCW), 22(2-3), (2013), 309–344.
5. Davis, H., Vetere, F., Gibbs, M., and Francis, P. Come play with me: designing technologies for inter generational play. *Universal Access in the Information Society, 11*(1), (2012), 17-29.
6. Ehn, P. Participation in design things. *Proceedings of the Tenth Anniversary Conference on Participatory Design 2008*, Indiana University (2008), 92–101.
7 Hutchinson, H., Mackay, W., Westerlund, B., et al. Technology Probes: Inspiring Design for and with Families. *Proc. CHI*, ACM (2003), 17–24.
8. Kerne, A., Hamilton, W. A., & Toups, Z. O. (2012). Culturally Based Design: Embodying Trans-surface Interaction in Rummy. In Proc. Conf on CSCW, New York, NY, ACM Press (2012), 509–518.
9. Lindley, S.E., Harper, R., and Sellen, A. Designing for Elders: Exploring the Complexity of Relationships in Later Life. *Proc 22nd British HCI:* BCS (2008), 77–86.
10. Nansen, B., Vetere, F., et al. Reciprocal Habituation: A Study of Older People and the Kinect. *ACM Transactions on CHI 21*, 3 (2014), 18:1–18:20.
11. Patel, D. & Agamanolis, S. Habitat: awareness of life rhythms over a distance using networked furniture. *Adjunct Proceedings. UbiComp*, Seattle, 2003
12 Rowan, J., & Mynatt, E. D. Digital Family Portrait Field Trial: Support for Aging in Place, In *Proc.CHI 2005* New York, NY, ACM Press.(2005) 521–530.
13. Suchman, L. A. Practice-based design of information systems: *The information society* 18.2 (2002): 139-144
14. Strong, Rob, and Bill Gaver. Feather, scent and shaker: supporting simple intimacy. *Proc CSCW*, (1996), 29-30.
15. Tang, J.C., Xiao, R., Hoff,et al HomeProxy: Exploring a Physical Proxy for Video Communication in the Home. *Proc. CHI 2013* ACM Press (2013), 1339–1342.
16. Taylor, A., Harper R et al Homes that make us smart. *Personal & Ubiquitous Computing 11*,5(2006),383–393.
17. ten Bhömer, Martijn, Communicating Teapot, http://youtu.be/oKXpvNXh9Wo
18. Vaisutis, K., Brereton, M., et al. Invisible Connections: Investigating Older People's Emotions and Relations around Objects. *Proc.CHI 2014* (2014), 1937–1940

The Effect of Signal Expense and Dependability on Family Communication in Rural and Northern Canada

Roberta M. Melvin[1], Andrea Bunt[1], Erick Oduor[2], Carman Neustaedter[2]

Department of Computer Science
University of Manitoba
Winnipeg, Manitoba, Canada
melvin@umanitoba.ca, bunt@cs.umanitoba.ca

School of Interactive Arts & Technology
Simon Fraser University
Surrey, British Columbia, Canada
{eoduor, carman}@sfu.ca

ABSTRACT

Family communication and technology designed to support it is a widely studied topic. However, most research that focuses on family communication in North America tends to assume high degrees of connectivity and Internet access. We present a study of family communication practices in rural and northern areas of Manitoba, Canada where Internet connectivity is intermittent or severely limited in some communities. Our results show the ways in which individuals stay connected with outside relatives can be hampered by communication infrastructure challenges. In particular, these challenges can dictate how, where and how often conversations with loved ones take place. Our results also indicate that these experiences, many of which are negative, can create lasting impressions that may be difficult to alter as infrastructure improves. This suggests opportunities for designing family communication technologies for outdoor locations with better connectivity, scheduling communication during times with better connectivity, and combating social isolation.

ACM Classification Keywords

H.5.3. Information interfaces and presentation: Computer Supported Cooperative Work; H.4.3 Communication Applications

Author Keywords

awareness; family communication; ict4d; mobile devices; rural environment

INTRODUCTION

Family members have a natural desire to stay in touch with one another when they are separated by distance [23, 31, 33]. This allows them to stay aware of what others in their family are up to, coordinate shared activities, and, feel close and connected to one another [23, 33]. We also see systems being designed to support family communication, including video communication systems [1, 17, 18, 19, 38], photo-sharing applications [4, 22], and messaging systems [11, 14]. Yet the reality is that most of this research focuses on family communication practices and technology design in areas of the world that contain rich technological infrastructures. This means that family members can typically easily stay 'connected,' if they so desire.

There also exists a growing amount of research on communication practices in developing countries where technology and connectivity is more limited. This research shows the ways in which family members still manage to stay connected with one another using only 'basic' forms of technology available. For example, research shows a heavy reliance on mobile devices, phone sharing, and the use of intermediary family members to pass on messages (e.g., [26, 27, 35, 36]).

In contrast to these two settings, our work focuses on family communication in rural communities *within* a developed country—in our case, Canada. Specifically, we investigate family communication practices in rural and northern regions of the province of Manitoba that are relatively 'unconnected' with the rest of the country because of a lack of technological infrastructure and, in some cases, their more isolated location.

We conducted an exploratory study involving in-depth semi-structured interviews with people living in these areas. Our goal was to learn about the communication practices of families with an emphasis on understanding how the difference in technological infrastructure affected communication practices. We also wanted to understand how family communication routines in this area differed from more developed regions of the country that contain nearly instant access to technology and connectivity.

To foreshadow, our results show that families in the rural and Northern communities we studied have a strong desire to maintain relationships with their geographically distributed relatives, with an emphasis on staying current with each others' general well being. Participants' choice of communication tool, however, was rarely based solely on preference. Participants frequently considered anticipated incurred costs, either for themselves or their family members, and reported having to work around poor connectivity by changing the location, communication frequency and conversation format (e.g., often having to

CHI 2015, April 18 - 23 2015, Seoul, Republic of Korea

ACM 978-1-4503-3145-6/15/04...$15.00
http://dx.doi.org/10.1145/2702123.2702301

rely on short text messages). At times, these struggles led to diminished contact and closeness with family members, and created lasting negative impressions of media-rich tools. Together, these results suggest future design directions that are aware of and help families mitigate connectivity challenges, as well as those that foster closeness when only low-bandwidth communications are possible.

RELATED WORK

Family Communication in Developed Countries

Research in HCI has a strong history of studies on families, their domestic routines, and how family members communicate with one another over distance. Research on family communication practices in technologically-developed areas of Canada found a strong need to stay connected with family members, but the level of connection varied based on the closeness of the relationships [23]. Regardless of the relationship, people wanted an awareness of the location, activities, and well-being of the person [23]. Thus, conversations were often tied to details about 'how one was doing,' sometimes in a very casual manner [23]. When technology was used to mediate relationship and enable communication over distance, people were very good about knowing which technology to use to most easily reach a friend or family member [23].

Tee *et al.* [33] conducted a similar study of family members in the United States and found that some people desired to have more contact with certain family members than they were able to achieve. This was because of busy schedules or the lack of technology usage by some extended family members [33]. People also did not want to feel obligated to contact family members if they were already too busy [33]. Romero *et al.* [31] studied family communication in the Netherlands and found that people disliked feeling obligated to communicate and had a preference for targeted, in-the-moment communication.

Research has also explored technologies that families use to aid communication. A general trend is to try and connect people with increasingly higher-fidelity mediums (e.g., video chat) and increased bandwidth [1, 17, 18, 19]. This is because family members typically feel closer to their remote loved ones when they can actually see them over systems like video chat [1, 17, 18, 19]. Young children are also more likely to understand communication mediums such as video chat, since the medium is most similar to face-to-face situations [3, 10]. Other technologies like the telephone can be challenging for them to use [3, 10].

We also know that synchronous communication exchanges are not without their challenges. Families often have difficulty scheduling video-chat calls, especially when time zones come into play, and must instead rely on asynchronous communication technologies at times [6]. In cases of health issues, people sometimes prefer simply talking on the phone [29]. This reflects the connection felt by hearing someone's voice, and also a desire to hide one's appearance if in diminished health [29]. Social media sites such as Facebook are also increasingly being used by people to connect with a broad range of family members and friends [5, 15]. This allows them to 'keep up' with the happenings of others [15] and strengthen their relationships [5]. Prior research has also examined infrastructure-related challenges that families in urban centres can face when communicating with video-based technologies, such as video distortion (e.g., [1, 30]).

Other research looks at the design of research prototypes to support family communication. The aim of these systems is to promote awareness and connectedness between distributed family members [11, 18, 20, 22]. These systems typically focus on the exchange of pictures or textual messages between family members via mobile devices [24, 31] or special-purpose digital frames [18, 20, 22]. Systems have focused on a variety of family relationships ranging from parent-child interaction over distance [38], to the connection of adult children with their elderly parents [22]. There have also been systems designed to provide next-generation video connections between family members [17, 38] where video links can be left going for extended periods of time, if desired. Finally, there is a desire to make family communication 'fun' by encouraging playful interactions [20]. Again, all of these systems rely on nearly instantaneous access to the Internet where people can share information with family members in-the-moment. Little consideration is paid to situations where Internet connectivity may be intermittent or non-existing.

Melvin and Bunt [21] studied the use of communications technology in the same region of rural Canada as reported in this paper. The focus was on workplace communication, however, many people intertwined work and family life. Findings showed that people often needed Internet access for work activities in areas outside of work offices and work hours. They developed unique workarounds for gaining connectivity, including driving out of one's way for cellular service and choosing asynchronous technologies instead of synchronous ones. The authors suggest designing tools that provide feedback and awareness of connectivity levels.

Family Communication in Developing Countries

Research has also explored family communication in developing countries where technology and connectivity is less prevalent. Studies of developing countries have shown heavy reliance on mobile phones for connecting with family members given their low cost [13, 26, 27, 35]. For example, in studies of family life in Jamaica, researchers found that people communicated with clusters or small groups of family members using mobile phones [12]. A large focus was on communication around familial support for economic activities [13]. In El Salvador, mobile phones were shown to be used by family members to exchange information and advice about kinship [34].

Studies of technology usage in Kenya, Africa, again, illustrate a focus on mobile phone usage when it comes to family communication using technology [26, 27, 35]. Here

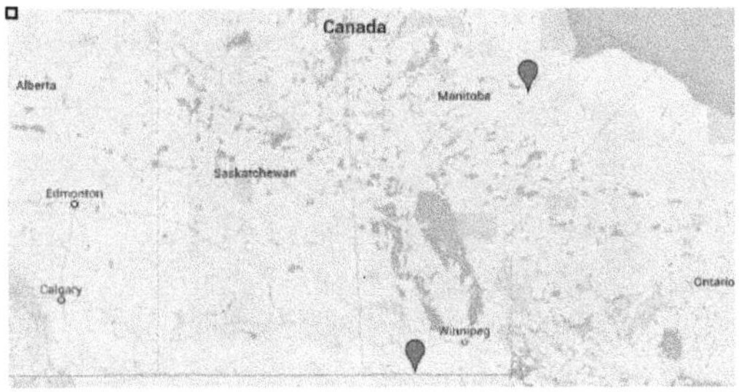

Figure 1. A partial map of Canada illustrating the two locations in our study. The North-most marker represents Gillam, whereas the Southern marker represents RM Roblin.

we learn that technology-based family communication often focuses around discussing support for economic activities [26, 27, 35], providing life guidance, and coordinating everyday activities [26, 27]. Technology usage is affected, however, by a lack of electricity, the costs of calling, gender, and whether or not one is an eldest child in the family [26, 27]. Mobile phones are often shared amongst family members who live in the same village setting [27]. To reduce communication costs, communications may be pre-planned [37] and activities such as 'beeping' are used [35]. We also know that despite the limited technologies available in countries like Kenya, many companies continue to design for 'advanced smartphones' [36].

Of course, we recognize that there are large differences in culture and the level of development between the regions we have studied as compared to that of many developing countries. Canada is considered a first world country (despite many rural regions experiencing infrastructure challenges) whereas many of the developing countries described above would still be considered 'third world countries.' Despite this, we feel findings from prior work in developing regions present an interesting backdrop for understanding technology usage in areas of Canada that are also struggling with limited connectivity.

In summary, we see a wealth of research on family communication practices and technology usage in both developed and developing countries. While valuable, none of these studies have explored family communication in *developing regions* of a *developed country* like Canada. This is the focus of our study, discussed next.

STUDY METHODOLOGY

We conducted an interview-based study within rural and northern Manitoba to understand family communication practices in areas that have much more impoverished communication infrastructure than what is typically found in urban areas. In the next section we describe the two communities included in our sample and how their Internet access differs from what is typical in urban areas of Canada.

Communities, Participants and Recruitment

We recruited fifteen participants (nine female) from two primary communities within Manitoba, Canada, marked on the partial Canadian map shown in Figure 1. The locations were selected as previous work suggested they face connectivity issues [21]. Recruiting started with the first author's personal connections and we grew our sample by networking in the communities.

Our first group of participants (P1-P9) came from rural areas in southwestern Manitoba shown at the bottom of Figure 1. This region is located approximately 200 kms from a major city (Winnipeg). We included seven people from the Rural Municipality of Roblin (RM Roblin), whose population is around 1000 people. RM Roblin is primarily a farming community (see Figure 2), and the local geography attracts a number of tourists who come to hunt or fish. We also had two participants from the Rural Municipality of Louise (RM Louise) a municipality adjacent to RM Roblin with the same economic base and geography. This area includes large regions where hardwired unlimited Internet is not available so these municipalities are heavily dependent on wireless technologies for access to Broadband Internet. Dependence on wireless technology to access Broadband Internet means that network access is frequently disrupted by geography, foliage, wind and cloud cover [21]. For example, cellular and wireless signals cannot reach into the local river valley and portions of the municipality are outside the reach of the signals from the nearest cellular towers.

Residents in this area of the province have only two (Internet Service Provider) ISP options, both of which involve data caps, resulting in \$135 to \$275 per month fees for data transfer of 125G. Download rates in these regions are frequently less than 5 Mbps [8]. In contrast, in Winnipeg, Manitoba's largest urban center, there is a choice of four ISPs, with costs between \$43 and \$63 per month for 50Mbps or more [8], often with unlimited data caps. Given a median income level of 26K (compared to \$32,000 in Manitoba's urban centres [32]), Internet represents a significant expense for residents in these rural communities.

Figure 2. A farmyard in the RM Roblin/RM Louise area.

Figure 3. The edge of Gillam, Manitoba, where the town meets the forest. This is at the 56 parallel, just south of where permafrost begins.

Our second group, comprised of six participants (P10-P15), came from Gillam, a community in Northern Manitoba, located approximately 1000 km from Winnipeg. Gillam, whose population is around 1,100, is one of the north-most Manitoban communities accessible by car. Its major industries include rail, tourism, and construction. The most predominant employer is the provincial utility company, which maintains a number of Hydro Electric damn sites in the region and is constructing more. The Fox Lake Cree Nation maintains Aboriginal reserve sites near to Gillam in addition to band members living in the town itself. Figure 3 provides an aerial view of Gillam and the surrounding, whereas Figure 4 depicts a typical street within the town.

In this second region in our study, only the highest density communities have access to reasonably priced communications. Within Gillam, high speed, unlimited data can be accessed via one available provider for \$55/month. Outside the main community, the cost of 125G of data with upload speeds of 1Mbps quickly rises to \$275/month.

Across both regions, participant ages ranged from their 20s to 60s. Occupations included farmers, store owners, administrators, child care workers, hunters, and mechanics. Three participants were unemployed. Eleven participants had some level of secondary school education, while the remaining four had completed or taken portions of high school.

Participants were provided with a 15\$ honourariam in appreciation for their time.

Semi-Structured Interviews

We conducted a semi-structured interview with each participant that lasted approximately 30-45 minutes. We began each interview by asking the participant to draw his/her family communication network on a piece of paper and to indicate the closeness of these relationships (see Figure 5 for an example); this is similar to other studies on family communication [23, 27, 33]. We then used these drawings to ground discussions in the remainder of the interview, which focused on how often participants communicated with each family member, what they communicated about and what technologies they used. Questions included, for example, "*What is your usual method of communicating with [family member X]?*" and "*Can you tell me about the last conversation you had?*"

Figure 4. A typical street within the town of Gilliam.

Throughout the interview, we were particularly interested in how the participant's location and that of their family or friends affected communication. We wanted to understand if the availability and cost of accessing and using technology in that location played a role in what technology was used, what was talked about, and who was talked to. We also investigated situations where technological issues meant that particular family and friends were not part of regular communication practices, e.g., it was too hard to reach them so communication dropped off. Thus, our interviews focused on family communication and also a *lack of* communication where we explored technology access, infrastructure, and social barriers.

Data Collection & Analysis

We recorded audio of all interviews, which were later transcribed in full, and took notes and pictures of the communities and participants' homes. We then performed a thematic analysis of the interview transcripts and our notes. Photos and family network diagrams aided our analysis of the transcripts by providing additional details.

Our analysis revealed several main themes that we report on next in our results. First, we describe the focus of communication and which technologies participants chose to use with their family members when communicating over distance. These findings are similar to findings from previous work on family communication in developed countries. Yet what stood out as a large contrast to other regions in North America that face less infrastructure challenges were the ways in which availability of a cellular signal and the cost of services influenced how, where, and when families communicated using technology. We detail this second. Finally, we document the attitudes towards technology that our participants expressed, which reflect

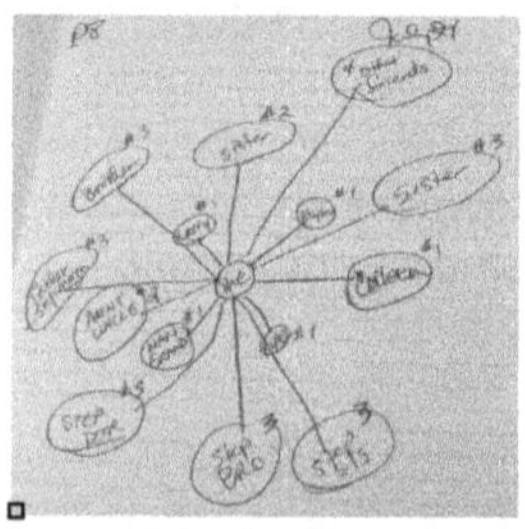

Figure 5. An example family network diagram.

their longstanding 'battle' with poor technical infrastructures due to their location in rural Canada.

COMMUNICATION ROUTINES AND CONTENT

Family Communication Networks

Participants told us that their family communication routines focused around conversations with a range of family members, including immediate family (e.g., siblings, parents), extended family (e.g., cousins, aunts, uncles), and a mixture of friends with varying relationship levels. This is similar to studies of other developed and developing regions of the world [23, 27, 31, 33].

Yet participants also talked about how the availability of technology infrastructures (e.g., cellular tower, Internet connections) played a role in terms of who they talked to and how often. Participants found it easier to maintain relationships with those people who had better access to technology. Family and friends who could not afford robust phone plans, or for whom there was a lack of signal, were more difficult to maintain an up-to-date relationship with. Communication was more challenging and less frequent in these cases. For example, P2's adult grandchildren lived several hours away from her. They had tight budgets and, as a result, they would ration their mobile phone conversations.

> *"He doesn't call because it costs him. ... Well, I'd like to talk at least once a week with them all." –P2*

Similarly, P4 would like to talk with her sister more often. If cost was not a concern they would speak to each other much more often. Instead, she relied on hearing about other family members through an intermediary, her mother.

> *"Probably once a week, we're talking probably once a month right now, everything is through my Mom." –P4*

Participants who were faced with limited technology infrastructures described having had much weaker ties with their relatives that lived far away when compared to our other participants. For example, P10 lives near Gillam and has family that live in a community accessible only by winter roads (i.e., frozen bodies of water turned into roads for the winter) and airplane, where only satellite Internet and no cellular signal is available. Maintaining a relationship with these relatives was especially challenging because she had next to no opportunities to see them in person.

> *"Two older sisters live far away from me, but they live in [the distant community]. I got relatives that live [there]. I don't even know half of them." –P10*

Communication Content

Most communication with friends and family was described as general discussion around topics of everyday life. This included jokes, gossip, and descriptions of one's activities and happenings. Again, this reflects family communication patterns in developed countries. In contrast to developing regions of the world [27, 35], we did not see a heavy emphasis on discussions of finances and economic activities. Thus, this region did not face the same level of economic hardships as is found in many developing countries. As such, conversation could easily focus on 'less pressing' topics about daily life. Our participants described their conversations as occurring whenever it was convenient, sometimes limited by connectivity and cost (described more later). Other conversations were more urgent, needing to take place somewhat immediately.

Communication about health situations was ubiquitous in our interviews. Participants talked about keeping track of family members' medical situations, and about notifying distant relatives of deaths in the community. For example, P4 lives and works in the RM Louise. While P4's siblings are spread out over the province (spanning approximately 80000 square kms), she depends on her sister, a nurse, for healthcare advice about her child on a regular basis.

Technologies Used

Families made significant use of technology as a part of their family communication practices, using different tools for different situations and people. Similar to other research this included the telephone, text messaging, email, video chat [1, 19, 24, 31, 33], and social media [5].

All technologies were used for targeted communication with a particular family member, while social media naturally lent itself to communicating with a large number of family members all at once, via status updates. For example, participants described accessing Facebook on a daily basis to see what was going on in family members' lives in an asynchronous fashion. Participants also talked about migrating between technologies depending on the nature of conversations. For example, when a conversation became more involved, participants described moving from Facebook messaging to a phone conversation, which they felt was a richer method for communicating.

While the choice of tools was often based on communication content (e.g., emotional conversations vs. short discussions about everyday life activities), the availability of a consistent signal played a more dominant role as did the cost of the technology. In the following sections, we detail how these aspects affected communication and technology choice.

THE SIGNIFICANCE OF COST

Our participants often cited the cost of technology as a strong reason for choosing one type of technology over another when communicating with their family members. Thus, even though they typically knew what technologies were most likely to reach their family members, they had to first ensure that it was affordable for themselves and for the recipient. In this way, technology selection reflected their knowledge of their family members' financial situation, as well as their own.

As described in our method section, the options and costs available differed significantly between densely populated and sparsely populated communities, where income levels also tend to be lower. This sharp contrast in cost gives residents additional concerns to consider when planning

Figure 6. A participant's communication station in his living room, dominated by a large screen for VoIP and video calls.

communication with family members spread out across the province.

For example, many family members of participants, particularly the younger adults, had forgone having a landline phone in order to afford a mobile phone. Mobile phones were seen as ways to make themselves more accessible to family and friends, despite infrastructure challenges (described in the next section). They also represented additional levels of safety, e.g., if an emergency situation arose while out, they could easily call others. Family members were very conscious of the cost of using mobile phones, in particular for the recipient of calls. For example, in the quote below, concerns over the cost of phoning a family member lead to communication happening through an intermediary person:

> *"[We communicate via] Text, [my sister] doesn't have a landline, and her cellphone only accepts phone calls at certain times, she can't afford a full phone. [...] 99% of it is funneled through my Mom, Mom talks to her at least once a day." –P4*

As an alternative to either landlines or cellphones, participants also used online voice and video tools to reduce costs. Some participants had unlimited data access through their home Internet service leading this to be an affordable choice.

> *"And it's the cost, the price is right [with Skype]" -P5*

For them, online tools were seen as particularly helpful for contacting friends and relatives outside of Canada, since the cost of phone calls increases significantly for out-of-country calls. As an example, P14 lives in Gillam for work reasons. He lives alone, and owing to his desire to keep in close contact with family members, his communication workstation dominates his living space as shown in Figure 6. P14, who has access to high speed Internet with unlimited data downloads, found the long distance charges on his cellphone to be too expensive and so he prefers to pay a flat rate for calling anywhere in North America using a 'Voice over IP' (VoIP) tool.

> *"Mainly the Internet now, used to be phone. .... [now]...I have a magic jack because it's cheaper to use. I can phone anywhere in North America for a flat rate." –P14*

The cost of using online tools like Skype and VoIP can vary considerably in the rural areas we studied when compared to urban centres. Service providers put caps on data usage, which are often lower near the edges of the network's coverage area. This was often where our participants resided, and going beyond data caps was very costly. Since video conferencing involves the transfer of large amounts of data, it could, at times, be too expensive for the residents in these areas to use. For example, P8's family lived in northern Canada for a number of years where she worked as a nurse, while their extended family remained in Southern Manitoba. Video tools were helpful for communication, but eventually the cost became prohibitive as large data downloads carried significant additional costs. Eventually, P8 had to restrict the types of tools they used to keep in touch their extended family.

> *"In Iqaluit... the Skype was used too much, it used up too much of our Internet, like you couldn't get a high enough setting for your monthly usage ... It ended up being very expensive, and had to tell him to stop calling me." –P8*

Thus Internet affordability in rural communities, which is generally higher than in urban centres, can affect both the frequency and format of family communication.

SIGNAL PREDICTABILITY AND LOCATION

For participants in both rural Southern Manitoba and Northern Manitoba, stability and availability of cellular signal was an issue and had a strong effect on when and where one could contact family members. Some participants could not get a signal at all in their local area, and others had to find just the right location to make a call. Sometimes this required driving into nearby towns, which would take between 10 and 30 minutes.

> *"Cellphones don't work there, so she had to go into town and use the [landline] phone." –P6*

For example, P6 did not use a cellphone for communication when traveling in rural Manitoba owing to a lack of consistent signal. Instead, she found a workaround: She subscribed to the OnStar auto security service. Normally this service is subscribed to by people so that they can call for help when an emergency situation arises, e.g., when a person's car breaks downs. As such, it maintains a strong level of reception even in remote areas. P6 used a somewhat unknown feature of this service where she would prepay for calling minutes and then contact people through the service in her vehicle. P6 was always able to get a signal.

> *"Its fabulous because it does have really good reception, everywhere [...] I don't carry a cell phone for that reason." – P6*

Another example comes from P9 who lives and works just past the edge of the local cellular towers' signal reach. He described using his cell phone at these locations as something of an exercise in patience. Here he had to be in just the right location and angle.

> *"I can't send anything until I open the door and face [my cell phone] towards [local tower]. I go to the house, you cannot send anything unless we point it to the window outside, send it in that direction to [local tower]." –P9*

Figure 7. A rural road in the winter months, illustrating that travelling to areas with better connectivity can be difficult.

Besides being generally cumbersome, any type of signal availability workaround involving the outdoors has an additional challenge related to the weather in the region. The winter season typically lasts five or six months, with normal temperatures in the -15°C to -30°C range (with the wind chill making these temperatures feel significantly colder). Figure 7 shows a Manitoba highway in winter. Travel at this time of year is more challenging making technology mediated communication that much more desirable.

RM Roblin is on the edge of two local cell signal 'bubbles'. Other participants in this area, like P9, described similar issues where signals were only possible if there were not trees between them and the cellular tower. By comparison, in the town of Gillam, the signal can be quite strong. However, we observed it dropping to nothing without any explanation as to the reason. Participants confirmed that this was a common occurrence in the area. They also talked about the speculations amongst residence as to the reason for the unpredictable service, including alleged politics between two cellular service providers, Rogers and Manitoba Telecom Services (MTS).

> *"It will go from full service to no service. No cell service... its very choppy up here. Apparently a lot of it is Rogers was on the MTS tower and so MTS took them off, so Rogers didn't work up here at all for a few days, it's very... a lot of drama." - P15*

For people with cellphones, text messaging was often the most economical and reliable option for communication. When signals were poor as described above, a short text message was likely to get to a recipient eventually, while communicating via a voice call could be much more challenging. Thus, participants often favored asynchronous communication over synchronous communication because of the reliability of the technology. This superseded their desire to have conversations that were more 'natural' and similar to face-to-face situations, as would occur over the phone.

> *"Text will go through better than a call ... and we did lots of little voice messages." – P6*

> *"It cuts in and out and then you're fighting to get communication and such." - P4*

> *"He's in southeastern portion of Manitoba, there's absolutely zero reception there, and we text or email." –P9*

ATTITUDES AROUND TECHNOLOGIES

Like most people, participants wanted their experience of using technology to be as straightforward as possible. Tools that provided 'one click' access to communication were favored over anything that required additional setup or maintenance. Once a system was understood and used, participants said that they were especially reluctant to move on to new and possibly better systems. This reflected their past experiences in 'fighting' with technology and a lack of bandwidth and connectivity, and often giving up on 'newer' technologies because of such issues.

The strongest example of this comes from video conferencing technologies, e.g., Skype, FaceTime. These systems were very attractive tools for families because they offered communication that was most similar to face-to-face situations. When distance precluded face-to-face communication, most participants tried using video communication tools as a stand-in. These were usually reserved for the types of conversations where visual feedback had the most impact, often this involved children.

Unfortunately, there was variability in the reliability of video conferencing systems and this had lasting effects on the attitudes of our participants towards so-called new and improved technologies. For example, P3 was able to use Apple's FaceTime to converse with a relative. It worked well and so she wanted to use it to see her grandchildren. However, to date, this has not happened because the family continues to face issues in getting the system to work. Because of their consistent struggle with cellular and Internet infrastructures and technology access (Wi-Max Internet and booster required to access cellular signal), they felt this was likely a result of poor cellular or Internet services (which may or may not be the actual case).

> *"Yeah, it is very strange. ... he's trying to figure it out. He's got an iphone and an ipad, I have an iphone and an ipad... and we can't get it to work." –P3*

Another example comes from P6 who told us about how she reached out for help when her experience using a video communication system was unsatisfactory. After talking to the customer service people for the software and to her Internet service provider, she was left in a deadlock. Each blamed the other for her experience problems.

> *"Our help desk had suggested that they update the router, and then [Manitoba Telecom Services (MTS)] came in to see it and said its absolutely fine. So you know you're between a rock and a hard place, you phone a help desk and they say this is an MTS issue, and you phone MTS and they say everything is [ok on their end]" - P6*

Following these frustrating experiences, P3 and P6 said they were reluctant to go back to using video chat and similar technologies. Without knowing what was causing the problem, participants had little faith in a better experience next time.

DISCUSSION

Participants in our study live in a country with established and high-functioning technology infrastructures. However, in their particular geographical locations, the infrastructure is still "developing", in the sense that it lags significantly behind that found in urban areas of the country. Our findings, therefore, provide a unique compliment to two existing, well-established threads of research: studies of family communication within regions with robust and mature technical communication infrastructures, and studies of areas of the world that are as a whole still developing. In this section, we contrast our findings to prior work, and discuss a number of challenges and opportunities that our findings highlight for designers moving forward.

Communication Information

In comparison to studies in similarly developed countries, we find the general communication goals and intents to be similar in both environments. That is, people want to stay in touch with family members such that they can share knowledge of their activities, location, and well being, including health-related information [23, 31, 33]. The reliability and consistency of connectivity in the areas we studied had less in common with issues reported in prior work. While other researchers have found connectivity issues in studies of Skype (e.g., [1, 30]) these are of a different magnitude than that found in our study. In these studies, it is about bouncing connections, reduced fidelity, distortions, etc. where a person can get a connection in their home at some point. In our study it is about a complete lack of connection, a connection at only certain times, or a connection in obscure locations such as driving to a remote area, going outside of one's home, or being in one's car. Despite the limited connectivity at varying points in time, our participants tend to achieve enough communication that their basic goals can be met albeit often with considerable difficulty or on an alternate timeline.

The implication of these findings is that the functional requirements of family communication technologies for rural areas such as those in our study should be very similar to that of regions that have a more developed infrastructure. In other words, the functionality provided in systems such as email, Facebook, and video chat systems (e.g., Skype, FaceTime) is still that which people need and want in these regions. The difference lies in people's ability to use such tools because of limitations in technology infrastructures. Thus, instead of designing to support the exchange of different types of information, communication technologies for these regions should focus on ways to share the same information but at a lower bandwidth, or in creative ways that get around infrastructure challenges.

Communication Systems

Like most people in developed areas of the world, participants in our study also shared a preference for communication tools that could help simulate the experience of being face-to-face, but at a distance, e.g., telephone conversations, or video-chat sessions. However, for our participants, both economics and infrastructure, as well as the interplay between the two, often made using these preferred tools difficult. While participants spoke of the advantages of multi-media and synchronous conversations, cost and signal predictability made the asynchronous text-message format popular. More in-depth communications often involved a location change, which could mean driving to areas of better reception, communicating through a service that was only available within a car, or moving outdoors, a less than practical solution in the cold (e.g., -30°C) winter months.

Improving the infrastructure will take years and is largely out of the control of system designers. In the meantime, there are opportunities to design technologies that aide users in understanding existing (and ever changing) connectivity levels to enable them to make more efficient use of current infrastructure. As an example of research in this direction, Chetty et al.'s Kermit [7] visualizes real-time local speed and network usage. For wider networks, crowdsourced maps of available connectivity are increasingly available [28]. Integrating such data into communication tools could improve efficiency and user attitude towards them.

We also see design opportunities for researchers and practitioners to rethink the places and locations that family communication technologies are to be used in. For example, video-chat systems are commonly designed to be used on a laptop or smartphone, especially in an indoor setting like a house. In the contexts we have studied, designers would find fruitful opportunities to design communication technologies for the locations where people are likely to get connectivity. For example, this might include a cold outdoor environment or a parked vehicle (after driving to find a cellular signal).

Scheduling Communication

Another design opportunity lies in scheduling tools to help families find reliable times and locations for communication when faced with instable connections. Finding times to communicate with distant family members is challenging at the best of times, but even more so if one has to factor in additional constraints known to affect signal quality like location and cloud cover. For example, designers might think about ways for systems to explore weather forecasts and propose communication times to family members that will be likely to have a strong cellular connection. This could be incorporated into calendar applications that allow one to 'negotiate' communication times between family members in different locations based on weather patterns.

In our study, we also found that asynchronous, text-based communication was considered the most reliable, and often only option for casual family communication. This was because messages sent by family members could be delayed if a cellular connection was poor. Designers may find value in rethinking how the types of rich media found in synchronous tools such as video chat and audio phone calls may be designed for asynchronous communication exchanges. For example, video chat might be more readily accessible to people in rural areas of Manitoba if information exchange was done with low bandwidth video snapshots (as opposed to high fidelity video). Alternatively, residents in these areas might welcome communication via asynchronous video threads, somewhat akin to the 'video messaging' supported by tools like Skype, Qik, and WhatsApp [25].

Social Isolation

Our study also surfaces knowledge related to social isolation and a lack of relationships with others. Related research has found that older adults in care homes and hospice face challenges related to diminished contact with family members [2, 9]. Our results show that family members in rural areas of Manitoba begin to lose contact with their loved ones because of infrastructure challenges. That is, those who live in regions where connectivity is low or close to non-existent see diminished communication with family and friends because of their poor connectivity. We also saw that people make fewer efforts to communicate with these individuals. Together, this suggests a design opportunity for family communication technologies to focus on ways to connect individuals with very limited connectivity. Such technologies should focus on providing basic pieces of information, even as if to say, "I am still around."

Perceptions of Technology

As infrastructure improves, which is likely to be a slow process due to the economics of servicing these difficult-to-reach and low-population density regions [20], designers face the additional challenge of existing perceptions of communication technologies that have been formed through years of frustrating experiences in the minds of rural Manitobans. Our findings indicate that users may be quick to dismiss media-rich tools as simply not being suitable for their environments, particularly if they have any difficulty with initial setups. Because of this, designers must think about how to alter the perceptions of users within their designs. This may mean designing for 'relationship building' between people and the technology so that they can develop a sense of trust that it will work. How one does this specifically is a certainly an open design question.

This issue also suggests that new technologies should be designed with 'fail safe' mechanisms such that users do not realize their worst fears: that the technology indeed does not work for them, just like the previous technology. In this case, designers could think about ways of providing services of a lesser quality within the same tool, if the highest quality of service fails. Using video chat as an example, one might imagine a system initially trying to send high fidelity video. Yet, if this turns out to not be possible because of infrastructure issues, the system could gracefully downgrade its interaction capabilities to asynchronous video messages while alerting the user to the issue and providing an understanding of why the change in functionality has occurred.

CONCLUSION

In studying rural and northern communities in Canada, we have highlighted the unique challenges that families face when trying to stay connected with their geographically distributed family members. While we sampled from only two communities within a single province in Canada, there is reason to be optimistic that our results will generalize to other similar communities, whose communication infrastructure lags significantly behind the rest of the country, particularly in communities with similar primary industries (e.g., farming) and income levels. Consequently, our findings suggest that designers of family communication technologies should continue to consider lower-bandwidth and asynchronous technology alternatives, even though such considerations are no longer as important in urban centres.

ACKNOWLEDGEMENTS

This work was supported by the GRAND Network Centre of Excellence and the Natural Sciences and Engineering Research Council (NSERC).

REFERENCES

1. Ames, M., Go, J., Kaye, J., and Spasojevic, M. Making Love in the Network Closet: The Benefits and Work of Family Videochat. *Proc. CSCW*, (2010), 145-154.
2. Baecker, R., Moffatt, K., and Massimi, M. Technologies for Aging Gracefully, *Interactions*, 19(3), (2012), 32-36.
3. Ballagas, R., Kaye, J., Ames, M., Go, J., and Raffle, H. Family Communication: Phone Conversations with Children. *Proc. IDC* (2009), 321-324.
4. Brush, A.J., Inkpen, K.M., and Kimberly, T. SPARCS: Exploring Sharing Suggestions to Enhance Family Connectedness, *Proc. CSCW,* (2008), 629-638.
5. Burke, M. and Kraut, R. Growing Closer on Facebook: Changes in Tie Strength through Social Network Site Use, *Proc. CHI,* (2014), 4187-4196.
6. Cao, X., Sellen, A., Brush, A. J. B., Kirk, D., Edge, D., and Ding, X. Understanding Family Communication Across Time Zones. *Proc. CSCW, (2010)*, 155-158.
7. Chetty, M., Halslem, D. Baird, A. , Ofoha, U., Sumner, B., and Grinter, R Why is my Internet Slow?: making network spepds visible. *Proc CHI (2011)*, 1889-1898
8. CRTC, Communications Monitoring Report 2014 http://www.crtc.gc.ca/eng/publications/reports/PolicyMonitoring/2014/cmr.pdf (Accessed January 2015)
9. David, J., Benjamin, A., Baecker, R., Gromala, D., and Birnholtz, J. Living with Pain, Staying in Touch: Exploring the Communication Needs of Older Adults with Chronic Pain, *Extended Proc. CHI,* (2011).
10. Forghani, A. and Neustaedter, C. The Routines and Needs of Grandparents and Parents for Grandparent-

Grandchild Conversations Over Distance, *Proc. CHI,* (2014), 4177-4186.

11. Hindus, D. Mainwaring, S.D., Leduc, N., Hagström, A.E., Bayley, O. Casablanca: Designing Social Communication Devices for the Home, *Proc. CHI*, (2014), 325-332.

12. Horst, H. Blessings and Burdens of Communication: Cell Phones in Jamaican Transnational Social Fields, *Global Networks*, 6(2), (2006), 143-159.

13. Horst, H. and Miller, D. From Kinship to Link-up: Cell Phones and Social Networking in Jamaica, *Current Anthropology*, 46(5), (2005), 755-778.

14. Hutchinson, H., Mackay, W., Westerlund, B., Bederson, B., Druin, A., Plaisant, C., Beauduin, M., Conversy, S., Evans, H., Hansen, H., Roussel, N., Eiderback, B., Lindquist, S. and Sundbad, Y. Technology Probes: Inspiring Design for and with Families, *Proc. CHI,* (2003), 17-24.

15. Inkpen, K., Du, H., Roseway, A., Hoff, A., & Johns, P.. Video kids: augmenting close friendships with asynchronous video conversations in videopal. Proc CHI (2010), ACM, 2387-2396.

16. Joinson, A., 'Looking at', 'Looking up' or 'Keeping up with' People? Motives and Uses of Facebook, *Proc. CHI*, (2008), 1027-1036.

17. Judge, T.K., and Neustaedter, C. Sharing Conversation and Sharing Life: Video Conferencing in the Home, *Proc. CHI,* (2010), 655-658.

18. Judge, T.K., Neustaedter, C., and Kurtz, A.F. The Family Window: The Design and Evaluation of a Domestic Media Space, *Proc. CHI,* (2010), 2361-2370.

19. Kirk, D., Sellen, A., & Xianc, A. Home Video Communication: Mediating Closeness, *Proc. CSCW,* (2010), 135-144.

20. Lindley, S., Harper, R., and Sellen, A. Designing a Technological Playground: A Field Study of the Emergence of Play in Household Messaging, *Proc. CHI*, (2010), 2351-2360

21. Melvin, R. and Bunt, A. Designed for Work, But Not From Here: Rural and Remote Perspectives on Networked Technology, *Proc. DIS,* (2012), 176-185.

22. Mynatt, E.D., Rowan, J., Jacobs, A., and Craighill, S. Digital Family Portraits: Supporting Peace of Mind for Extended Family Members, *Proc. CHI,* (2001), 333-340.

23. Neustaedter, C., Elliot, K., and Greenberg, S., Interpersonal Awareness in the Domestic Realm, *Proc. OzCHI,* (2006), 15-22.

24. Neustaedter, C., and Judge, T.K. Peek-A Boo: The Design of a Mobile Family Media Space Video, *Proc. Ubicomp,* (2010), 449-450.

25. O'Hara, K., Massimi, M., Harper, R., Rubens, S., and Morris, J., 2014. Everyday dwelling with WhatsApp., *Proc CSCW(2014)*. ACM,1131-1143.

26. Oduor, E., Neustaedter, C., Hillman, S., and Pang, C. Family Communication in Rural and Slum Regions of Kenya, *Proc. CHI Extended Abstracts,* (2013).

27. Oduor, E., Neustaedter, C., Judge, T.K. Hennessy, K., Pang, C., and Hillman, S. How Technology Supports Family Communication in Rural, Suburban, and Urban Kenya, *Proc. CHI,* (2014), 2705-2714.

28. Open Signal Maps crowd sourcing connectivity map. http://opensignal.com/,(accessed January 2014)

29. Pang, C., Neustaedter, C., Riecke, B. E., Oduor E., Hillman, S. Technology Preferences and Routines for Sharing Health Information during the Treatment of a Chronic Illness, *Proc. CHI*, (2013), 1759-1768.

30. Rintel, S. . Video calling in long-distance relationships: The opportunistic use of audio/video distortions as a relational resource. Electronic Journal Of Communication, 22 (4) (2013), 23.

31. Romero, N., Markopoulos, P., van Baren, J., de Ruyter, B, Jsselsteijn, W., and Farshchian, B. Connecting the Family with Awareness Systems, *Personal and Ubiquitous Computing*, 11(4), Springer-Verlag (2006), 299-312

32. Statistics Canada. Neighbourhood income and demographics, taxfilers and dependents with income by total income, sex, and age group (2012) http://www5.statcan.gc.ca/cansim/a05 (Accessed September 2014)

33. Tee, K., Brush, A.J.B. and Inkpen, K.M., Exploring Communication and Sharing Between Extended Families, *International Journal of Human-Computer Studies*, 67(2), (2009), 128-138.

34. Vertovec, S. Cheap Calls: The Social Glue of Migrant Transnationalism. *Global Networks,* 4(2), (2004), 219-224.

35. Wyche, S. and Grinter, R. "This is How We Do it in My Country": A Study of Computer-Mediated Family Communication Among Kenyan Migrants in the United States, *Proc. CSCW,* (2012), 87-96.

36. Wyche, S. and Murphy, L. "Dead China-Make'' Phones Off the Grid: Investigating and Designing for Mobile Phone Use in Rural Africa, *Proc. DIS,* (2012), 186-195.

37. Wyche, S.P., Smyth, T.N., Chetty, M., Aoki, P.M. and Grinter, R.E., Deliberate Interactions: Characterizing Technology Use in Nairobi, Kenya, *Proc. CHI,* (2010), 2593-2602.

38. Yarosh, S., Cuzzort, S., Müller, H., and Abowd, G.D. Developing a Media Space for Remote Synchronous Parent-Child Interaction, *Proc. IDC*, (2009), 97-105.

Texting while Parenting: How Adults Use Mobile Phones while Caring for Children at the Playground

Alexis Hiniker, Kiley Sobel, Hyewon Suh, Yi-Chen Sung, Charlotte P. Lee, Julie A. Kientz
Human Centered Design and Engineering
University of Washington
{alexisr, ksobel, hyewon25, ycsung, cplee, jkientz}@uw.edu

ABSTRACT

Child development research suggests that using phones while caring for children can be problematic, but limited prior work in this space makes defining appropriate use challenging. We conducted the first exploration of whether adults feel pressure to limit phone use in this context and whether they choose to do so. Through mixed methods, we collected data from 466 adult caregivers at playgrounds. We found that phone use was a small part of playground time, yet a notable source of guilt. Adults engaged in systematic and specific phone-use and phone-non-use behaviors in order to prioritize their children above themselves. Our results indicate that caregiver values and self-control together predict behavior and can be used to model phone use in this context. Users' mixed success with engaging in intentional periods of non-use suggests that a design agenda which prioritizes cycles of engagement, disengagement, and re-engagement may be of value to this group.

Author Keywords

Children; Parents; Families; Mobile Phones; Mindfulness; Non-Use

ACM Classification Keywords

K.4.2. Social Issues

INTRODUCTION

Today's mobile phone users have near-continual opportunities to engage with devices and, as a result, are faced with constant decisions regarding the way in which they integrate phone use into their current context. While this has resulted in individuals beneficially incorporating phone use into many aspects of daily life, it has also given rise to broad "pushback" against technology [21] and decisions to limit use of particular technologies or use in particular settings. Understanding users' decisions around technology integration and contextualized use and non-use is a growing area of HCI research [2].

CHI 2015, April 18 - 23 2015, Seoul, Republic of Korea

ACM 978-1-4503-3145-6/15/04...$15.00
http://dx.doi.org/10.1145/2702123.2702199

Previous work has identified adults caring for children as a distinct user group with common non-use motivations [9]. Here we examine the ways in which adults use their phones when they have children in their care and their perspectives on the appropriateness of phone use in this context. A limited amount of child development research suggests that caregiver phone use may be detrimental to children [24, 28, 31], and the mainstream media has used this as fuel for an emotionally charged debate [19, 23, 33]. Given these potential sources of pressure, we chose to investigate caregivers' values about their own phone use in caregiving contexts, and how such values translate into emotions and behaviors.

We chose to conduct this investigation at playgrounds, a space where adults and children play together, children play independently, children encounter modestly risky situations [22], and adults enjoy time to themselves – thus providing a variety of social contexts for phone use and non-use. The playground's informal public atmosphere also gave us the opportunity to unobtrusively collect rich, naturalistic data on caregivers' behaviors and phone-use practices. In pursuing this investigation we asked the following research question: How and why do adult caregivers use their phones when caring for children at the playground?

This work provides necessary empirical data for value-sensitive design [10] for a user group that must integrate personal needs with constraints and desires driven by their role as caregivers. The contribution of this work is foremost to sensitize designers to the unique needs of children's caregivers by documenting common habits, beliefs, and concerns related to device-use in caregiving contexts. Our data also reveal distinct subgroups of caregivers and suggest several avenues for creating differentiated technical supports for each. Finally, our results reveal predictive relationships among beliefs about the appropriateness of phone use, patterns of use, reported self-control, and feelings of guilt. These stable relationships across our large sample offer to inform predictive models of user behavior and provide formative work for building new sociotechnical theory.

RELATED WORK

Phone Use While Caring for Children

One body of prior work describes adult phone use when caring for children as detrimental to the children in care [28, 31]. The child development research community has been a forerunner in investigating this space and reported uniformly discouraging findings. Radesky and colleagues collected observational data from 55 families eating together at fast food restaurants. They documented the ramifications of adults' constant connectivity, uncovering thematic distractibility, irritability, and inability to be interrupted among those using phones [24]. Other work has reported that adults respond inappropriately to children when they are distracted by devices [31] and that children experience adults' phone distraction as alienating and emotionally dissatisfying [28].

Researchers have expressed concern that adults' phone use while caring for children is displacing play-based adult-child interactions [28]. As play and face-to-face interactions are the bedrock of young children's social learning and language acquisition [5, 11], adults' phone-use practices are potentially disruptive to critical elements of children's early learning environments. Despite these early investigations, work in this area is still in its infancy [24], and many of these concerns remain speculative. To date, no authoritative body has published specific recommendations or evidence-based guidance for parents on this topic.

Our work builds on these investigations by presenting data on the extent to which adult caregivers are aware of these concerns and investigates adults' behaviors and the motivations behind them. We provide the first data on caregivers' experience of navigating social pressures to put devices aside while caring for children.

Phone Use and Parenting Ideology

A second body of work documents a cultural trend to make unproductive extrapolations from the scoped findings of child development research. In Western culture, the dominant modern parenting ideology, known as "intensive parenting," emphasizes the responsibility of parents and other caregivers to craft an environment for children that is rich with stimulating, caregiver-facilitated activities and interactions, intentionally designed to promote ideal development [14]. Beginning in the middle of the last century and intensifying in the 1990s, this school of thought posits that the agentic and self-reliant caregiver has the capacity to directly shape the cognitive development of the child in care [32]. Parents who are not oriented toward such goals are seen as needing education and improved parenting skills [25].

Critics of intensive parenting have documented that parents experience its standards as unattainable, overly idealized, and disempowering [25, 32]. Past research has suggested that there is little support for the idea that such "concerted cultivation," above a baseline of what children in middle-class, Western society might experience in daily life, improves children's long-term outcomes or increases intellectual ability [3, 32]. On the contrary, prior work shows that intensive parenting limits children's necessary opportunities for free-play, developmentally appropriate risk-taking, and self-entertainment [3, 16, 17].

As prior work has positioned adult phone use as potentially detrimental to children, it is a natural candidate for intensive parenting debate. Given that conversations influenced by intensive parenting standards, such as debates about breastfeeding [18] or mothers working outside the home [6], have led to guilt, confusion, and lack of self-efficacy in parents [30], it is plausible that adults experience negative emotions when reflecting on phone use or non-use in caregiving contexts. Our work provides the first investigation of caregivers' perspectives on this topic.

Designing for Families, Designing for Non-Use

While the CHI community has long designed for families, systematic analysis of this design space [15] shows that the resulting tools typically facilitate communication, coordination, family togetherness, and entertainment. Hashish and colleagues created a prototype technology to help children and parents collaboratively filter content on tablets [13], but research on supports for families which enable reflecting on or limiting technology use are rare.

However, prior work has investigated users' reflections on desired use and their non-use behaviors in other contexts. Prior work documents users' decisions to give up Twitter for Lent [27], resist constant connectivity [20], and respond to social pressure to reduce smartphone dependence [12]. Ames reports that college students experience guilt and anxiety in response to expectations to be continually present with both those they are with physically and those they are connected to through devices [1]. Satchell and Dourish explore the design implications of resistance to phone use and call on the CHI community to consider "the non-user" with the same rigor given to consideration of "the user" [26].

Our work sits at the intersection of understanding families and understanding how individuals integrate technology use and non-use. While each of these areas boasts a sizable body of literature, no prior work has examined the systematic ways in which parents and other caregivers manage their technology habits while caring for children. Our findings lay the groundwork for understanding this design space and supporting these individuals in being users or non-users when, where, and how they see fit.

SITE DESCRIPTION AND METHODS

To understand how adult caregivers use their mobile phones at the playground, we conducted: 1) covert nonparticipant observations, 2) semi-structured interviews, and 3) an online survey, all targeting adults who supervise children at playgrounds in north Seattle. We collected data from 466 adult participants during the spring and summer of 2014.

Study Sites and Participants

We performed observations and interviews at seven different playgrounds in the north Seattle area. Although we collected data from a diverse set of neighborhoods, this sampling was not intended to be representative of the general population. We included only caregivers who were supervising at least one child who appeared to be less than 10 years old. There were no exclusion criteria based on caregiver characteristics, and we observed a variety of adult caregivers including parents, grandparents, and nannies.

Total Respondents = 154	
Gender	Female (79%), Male (21%)
Relationship	Parent (93%), Nanny (6%), Other (1%)
Household Income	<$50K (6%), $50K-$75K (8%), $75K-$100K (14%), >$100K (60%), No Response (12%)
Race/Ethnicity	Non-Hispanic white (87%), Hispanic (6%), Asian (3%), Mixed race (1%), No response (3%)

Table 1. Demographic information for survey participants

We took notes on 171 adult caregivers during our qualitative observations (69% female). We timed the phone use of a separate 111 adults (68% female). We were unable to judge other demographic information about these individuals with certainty. We interviewed 25 adults (84% female). Of interviewees, 18 (69%) were parents; 5 (19%) were nannies; and 3 (12%) were other family members. Demographic information for survey participants is shown in Table 1.

Observations of Caregiver Behavior

Over three months, researchers individually visited seven playgrounds in north Seattle. Site visits were spread over all days of the week between 8 a.m. and 7 p.m. Across 22 visits we collected a total of 33 hours of observational data. Because we could not always observe all individuals simultaneously, researchers chose a subset of caregivers to observe based on their location within the playground and their arrival time. Once the researcher began observing a caregiver, she continued observing him or her until the caregiver left the playground. We documented field data in jottings which were later used to develop ethnographic fieldnotes [8].

Quantitative Observations of Phone Usage

During an independent set of visits to the same field sites, we observed an additional 111 participants without taking jottings. Instead we timed participants' phone usage precisely (in seconds) in order to quantify the frequency and duration of phone usage at the playground. Again, we assigned field sites to random days of the week and times of day, and we selected a subset of caregivers based on their locations and arrival times. Together across both types of observations, we observed 41.4 hours of playground time and recorded data on 282 caregivers.

Interviews with Caregivers

As adult caregivers' perspectives and experiences related to phone use at the playground were not accessible through observation alone, we conducted semi-structured interviews with an additional 25 participants. We approached and recruited participants at the same playground field sites using the same inclusion criteria as our observations. Given that caregivers were supervising children when we solicited interviews, our interview was intended to last no more than 15 minutes. We gave interviewees freedom to attend to their children and supported interruptions during the interview. Some participants generously spent 40 minutes or more elaborating on their responses.

Our interview protocol was shaped by early findings from our observations and was designed to elicit caregivers' self-reports describing their phone-use behaviors, motivations for phone use, and values and beliefs about phone use at the playground more broadly. Example questions included *"How have you used your phone while you've been at the playground today?"* and *"Do you have any particular strategies for keeping an eye on your child when you're using your phone?"*

After completing the interview, participants were given a $10 gift card as a thank-you for their participation. The total combined length of all interviews was 247 minutes (mean = 9.88, SD = 7.17). All interviews were audio recorded and transcribed by the research team.

Survey of Caregivers

Based on findings from our interviews, we developed a survey protocol to determine whether interview themes would be corroborated by a larger sample of the same community. In order to draw from the same population, we advertised to online groups and mailing lists that 1) restricted membership to either parents or to nannies and 2) had residency requirements limiting membership to those living in the areas surrounding our field sites. We asked caregivers to report on their mobile phone use at the playground, desired mobile phone use at the playground, motivations for choosing to use or avoid using mobile phones at the playground, strategies for integrating phone use into playground experiences, and beliefs about appropriate phone use, among other topics. As a thank-you for their participation, respondents had the opportunity to enter a raffle for $15 gift cards (with 1 in 10 odds of winning). We received complete responses from 154 caregivers who routinely visit playgrounds in north Seattle. Of the 47 survey questions, 9 were open-ended. Two researchers coded open-ended questions for 14 codes spread evenly across 6 categories. Average agreement (Cohen's κ) on a random 10% of the data was .873 with all values of κ > .71. Disagreements on codes were discussed until they reached consensus.

Qualitative Analysis

Using a grounded theory approach [4], we iteratively reviewed and coded field notes, interview transcripts, and open-ended survey questions for themes. Data collection and analysis were interwoven, such that themes from early observations were used to develop our interview protocol, and themes that emerged from interviews formed the basis of our survey development. Data analysis was continual throughout our data-collection process. Each researcher reviewed her own data independently and the team collaboratively created a codebook capturing salient themes. Field-note codes from observations covered nine areas: child-caregiver interaction, children's attempts to interrupt adults, caregiver position, supervision style, phone activities, non-phone activities, balancing phone use with child needs, behavior just before and after phone use, and children's activity during phone use. Code categories drawn from interview data included: beliefs about the purpose of the playground, parenting style, concerns about phone use while caring for children, and benefits of phone use. After finalizing the codebook, each researcher independently coded the same randomly selected field note. Codings were reviewed as a group to ensure consensus. Using data from fieldnotes, we drafted analytical memos to develop themes. The memoing process was repeated for data collected from interviews and open-ended survey questions.

Ethics Statement

In undertaking this research, we considered the ethics of conducting observations of public behavior without participants' knowledge or consent. We felt that informing those we observed would potentially alter their behaviors (raising concerns about the validity of the data) and detract from their experience at the playground. It would also have been prohibitive to broadly solicit consent from all playground-goers. As we did not collect identifiable or sensitive data, and participants had no reasonable expectation of privacy, we chose to observe unannounced. This is consistent with the limited prior work investigating caregiver behaviors in this space [4]. The Institutional Review Board at the University of Washington deemed this study exempt from review per federal exempt category 2 for surveys, interviews, and observations of public behavior.

RESULTS AND ANALYSIS

Description of Phone Use

The Amount of Time Adults Spend Using Phones

For the majority of our participants, phone use was a non-dominant part of their time at the park. This was consistent across all behavioral observations and corroborated by our quantitative observations. Nearly two-thirds of our participants spent less than 5% of their time at the park using a phone, including 41% who did not use a phone at all (see Figure 1). When adults were using a phone it was often for a short period of time. Nearly 30% of all uses were less than 10 seconds long and more than half were less than one minute (see Figure 1). Phone use via voice calls was far less common than phone use via touch interaction and comprised roughly 5% of all instances of use. We found no significant effect of gender on the percentage of playground

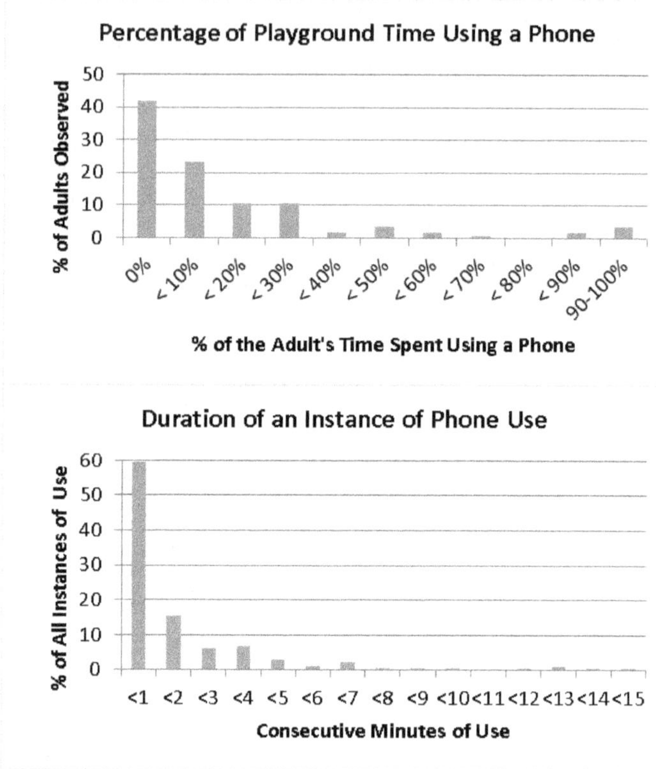

Figure 1: Top – Amount of time spent on the phone Bottom – Duration of phone uses

time spent on the phone, average duration of an instance of phone use, percentage of phone time spent making voice calls, or total number of instances of phone use.

What Adults do on Phones and Why

Interviewees reported using their phones for texting (48%) and calling (48%), followed by email (38%), picture-taking (38%), and Facebook (20%). A small minority of interviewees mentioned other online activities and checking the time, and one interviewee reported playing casual games on her phone. These reports were consistent with our survey data, though survey respondents reported each of these uses with higher frequency. This may be reflective of the fixed set of options provided to those surveyed, in contrast to our interview protocol, which asked participants for a free recall of the ways they use their phones. Table 2 reports the frequency with which survey respondents use these and other technologies at the playground.

The end-goals behind this technology use were varied (see Table 2). Tasks potentially related to childcare, such as checking the time, coordinating with others, and taking pictures, were reported more than twice as often as parent-centric tasks such as socializing, doing work, or viewing entertaining content.

In addition to describing the purpose of their phone use, we asked survey participants to report the type of situations that lead them to use the phone at the playground. The most frequently cited trigger for phone use was boredom, reported by 40% of those surveyed. We also asked participants to report situations that cause them put down the phone. A majority reported at times choosing not to use their phone because they felt it would compromise child safety (57%), make it hard to be responsive to their child (65%), or model behavior that they do not want their child to emulate (52%).

Absorption when Using Phones

Adults' Responses to Children with and without Phones
As prior work has tied adult phone use to a lack of responsiveness to children [24, 28, 31], we compared participants' responsiveness when they were and were not using phones. We observed 32 instances in which a child attempted to interrupt or gain the attention of an adult using a phone. In 18 cases (56%), the adult did not respond to the child at all, (did not speak and did not look away from the phone).

By comparison, we observed 70 instances in which a child attempted to interrupt or gain the attention of an adult who was *not* using a phone. In these cases – when the adult was tending to the needs of another child, engaged in conversation with another adult, or simply removed from the play area and staring into space – children's bids for attention were usually met with a prompt reply. There were 8 instances (11%) in which an adult without a phone did not respond in any way to a child's request.

Thus we saw a notable difference in adults' ability to be interrupted when they were and were not using phones. Interrupted adults did not always provide responses that satisfied children, for example, we observed an interaction in which: "The boy says, 'Mom, look!' 'Mom, look!' And asks if she will play with him. She says, 'I have to stay with the dog…there are other people you could play with'" (Field Observation). But it was rare for an adult to remain silent unless he or she was using a phone.

To contextualize this absorption, we saw these 102 total interruptions across 33 hours of observation, always observing multiple children at once. That is, across several child-adult groups we saw one interruption roughly every 20 minutes. The majority of playground time was dominated by adults sitting and watching as children played independently and by adult-child interaction.

Adults' Experiences with Absorption
We investigated adults' awareness of and feelings about the absorption we observed in phone users. The majority of our interview participants (22 of 25) spontaneously mentioned that either they or phone users generally pay less attention to their physical surroundings when using phones. However, our interviewees also expressed confidence that when they use phones they consistently monitor for children's requests. We asked interviewees who had used a phone at the playground that day to report what their child had been doing during phone use. In response, we received a variety of vague and sometimes defensive answers, such as:

Technology	%
Texting	85
Camera	85
Email	64
Voice calls	57
Clock	49
Social media	48
Browser	28
Games	5
Reading app	3
Video calls	1
None	2

Purpose	%
Picture-Taking	88
Coordination	79
Check the Time	75
Available: Emergency	71
Available: Family	71
Sharing Pictures	47
Information	41
Available: Work	41
Socialization	30
Do Work	28
Entertainment	21

Table 2: What survey respondents do on phones and why

"Yeah, so either climbing on some structure or playing. I kind of try to watch obviously." – P23

"I did those things very quickly. They just kept doing whatever they were doing" – P20

"Um, pretty much what he's doing now?" – P11

Collectively, our interviewees reported that they believe phone use dilutes their attention to the physical world, but also that their children's requests draw them back to the present moment on demand, an opinion that was at odds with the behavior we observed.

Survey participants agreed with interviewees; more than 80% of respondents reported that it is more difficult for them to pay attention to their children when using a phone (Figure 2). Like interviewees, survey participants were less likely to agree that phone use makes it harder to respond to child requests. Participants reported feeling significantly more confident that their child can get their attention when requested than confident that they are proactively paying attention to their child ($t = -8.96, p < .001$) (Figure 2). Thus, while adults generally believe that they are absorbed when using phones, many still believe that their absorption does not hinder their ability to be available upon request.

Values and Beliefs about Using the Phone

Through qualitative analysis, we found that both interview-

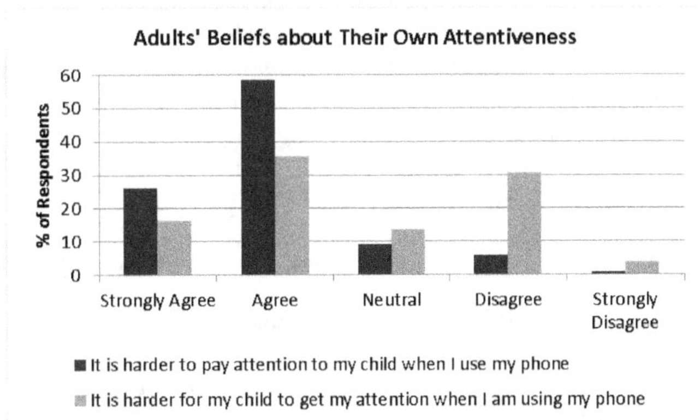

Figure 2: Adults believe they are absorbed by phone use but many feel they remain as available to their children as when they are not using phones

ees and survey respondents fell into three distinct categories based on self-reported values regarding phone use: 1) caregivers who believe it is appropriate for adults to use their phones whenever their children are safe and occupied, 2) caregivers who believe phone use should be minimized but that they are unable to live up to this ideal, and 3) caregivers who believe phone use should be minimized and that they successfully achieve this ideal minimization. These were not categories that the research team had preconceived and we did not describe or prompt participants to identify with any of these profiles.

Profile 1: Confident Users

A sizeable minority of interviewees (28%) expressed the belief that within certain bounds – typically, when children are safe and occupied – phone use of any kind is appropriate. These interviewees unapologetically described instances where they were *"just, like, sitting there on Facebook or texting somebody,"* (P16), *"online checking grades,"* (P15), or *"checking Facebook or work email, basically. Sometimes I read the New York Times on my phone"* (P23). As one father explained: *"As long as I can see him I'm comfortable [using the phone]"* (P4). These users expressed no reservations about using their phones at the playground and no desire to regulate their phone use in any way, provided that their child was safely and independently occupied.

Like interviewees, a non-trivial minority (18%) of survey respondents expressed beliefs consistent with this profile. These individuals reported feeling comfortable using their phones without restrictions, though again adding the disclaimer that their child must be safe and happy. As one survey participant explained: *"If my child is playing independently and is in a safe situation, I see no reason not to do my own thing."*

Profile 2: Users Who Would Like to Increase Non-Use

Nearly half of all interviewees (44%) reported both that they believe phone use should either be completely minimized or restricted to specific playground-appropriate tasks (such as taking pictures of children, checking the time, or managing essential coordination) and also that they struggle to live up to this self-imposed standard. These participants used the word "try" when describing their efforts to avoid phone use, such as: "*I try very hard not to check email or do Facebook,"* (P1) *"I try not to be on it if I don't have to,"* (P19), or *"I tried to leave it [at home]"* (P10). Despite their reported attempts to disengage, these participants described struggling to resist the desire to use the phone. While many felt they were doing a good job of working toward this goal, all reported that they would like to use the phone even less.

Similarly, 40% of survey participants reported simultaneously that they believe phone use should be limited and that they would like to make further progress toward this ideal. As participants explained:

"At the park, I want to use my phone less...The more I keep my own promises regarding my phone use, the better I feel."

"I don't want to be addicted to my phone... The less she sees me holding it, the better... I use my phone more than I would like."

"I want to use it less, but bad habits are hard to break!"

These caregivers described themselves when using the phone in front of their child as: *"not as attentive," "not as responsive," "ignoring," "not a good role model," "a slave to my phone," "absorbed in the device,"* or *"set[ting] a bad example."*

Profile 3: Confident Non-Users

A third group of participants expressed the belief that phone use in this context should be minimal, and they have successfully achieved this. These participants made strong statements about consistently living up to the standards they hold for themselves around phone use. 24% of interviewees fell into this category and described their phone use with statements such as: *"Everybody who knows me knows that I don't answer the phone [when caring for children]"* (P5).

This category emerged naturally among the larger sample of survey participants as well. Of those surveyed, 36% felt that phone use should be kept to a minimum and that they successfully achieve this standard. One participant described her own behavior saying: *"I typically don't have trouble leaving my phone in my pocket for an hour and I regularly can go for a whole playground visit without pulling it out. This is about the way I want it to be."*

Implications of Caregiver Profiles

We found that caregiver profile was a significant predictor of feelings of guilt. A Kruskal-Wallis H test showed that the effect of caregiver-type on the extent to which participants agreed with the statement *"I feel guilty when I use my phone at the playground"* was significant ($X^2(2, 137) = 25.29$, $p < .001$). Post hoc analysis using the Tukey HSD test indicated that 1) caregivers who believe they have successfully minimized their use feel significantly less guilt than phone users who would like to further reduce their use ($p < .05$) and 2) that caregivers who believe phone use is appropriate whenever children are safe feel less guilt than caregivers who believe all phone use should be minimized ($p < .05$).

Surprisingly, it also showed that confident non-users feel significantly more guilt than caregivers who believe phone use is appropriate whenever children are safe ($p < .05$). One might expect that users who feel fully satisfied with the way they use their phones would feel no more guilt than those who believe all phone use is appropriate. But for our participants, valuing minimal phone use was associated with increased feelings of guilt regardless of how effectively users' felt they controlled their behavior.

Perceptions and Judgments of Self versus Others

Our investigation was motivated in part by social commentary on using phones while caring for children, and we explored the extent to which caregivers feel judged for their phone use and the extent to which they judge others. Only two of our 25 interviewees were primarily critical of other caregivers' phone use at the playground. Nearly all interviewees were primarily agnostic toward other adults' use, with a subset going further and making statements of support, explaining that what they see from others *"feels good,"* (P22), that they are *"impressed"* by other caregivers (P19), and that *"people are pretty attentive to their kids"* (P23).

While some interviewees explained that they "worry" about other adults not giving children high quality attention (P8) or feel that others should "temper [their use] a little bit" (P12), in these instances, interviewees explained that they are equally concerned about their own behaviors. Further, interviewees who held themselves to a standard of minimal or no phone use while caring for children held more relaxed standards for other caregivers. Many interviewees expressed discomfort with the idea of judging others, explaining *"I'm one of those connected people so obviously I can't judge,"* (P23) or *"it's easy to judge...but I try not to"* (P22).

27% of participants reported feeling judged, suggesting that feelings of judgment may be a minor theme. Despite participants' reluctance to judge others, we found significant differences between adults' perceptions of their own behaviors and their perceptions of the behaviors of others. A paired-samples t-test revealed that participants were more likely to agree with the statement *"the way I use my phone at the playground is appropriate"* (mean = 2.21, sd = 0.75) than the statement *"the way other adults use their phones at the playground is appropriate"* (mean = 3.14, sd = 0.70, $t = 4.10$, $p < .001$). Response options ranged from *"1: Strongly Agree"* to *"5: Strongly Disagree."* Participants were also significantly more likely to agree that others should reduce their phone use (mean = 2.55, sd = 0.86) than that they should do so themselves (mean = 2.87, sd = 0.96, $t = -11.95$, $p < .001$).

Thus, despite commentary reflecting reservations about passing judgment, participants feel that their behavior is both more restrained and more appropriate than that of their peers. These results are consistent with the gap between perceptions of self and others observed in other domains, such as the classic example of 90% of drivers believing they are more cautious than the average driver [7, 29].

Adults' Interest in Technology Support

Given that 40% of interviewees and 44% of those surveyed reported a desire to change their current phone use habits (either by reducing the total time they spend with the phone or by cutting down on particular behaviors), there may be a design opportunity in this space to support adults in achieving their desired phone use. However, when we asked survey participants whether they would be interested in a tool to *"help monitor [their] phone use and achieve [their] desired phone use,"* the response was negative. 74% of all participants and 60% of those who wanted to change their behavior were firmly against the idea of using such a tool, while only 16% of all users and 26% of those looking to change expressed enthusiastic interest. Negative responses reflected thematic resistance based on: satisfaction with their current behavior (41%), valuing self-monitoring (21%), the oxymoron of using technology to reduce technology use (17%), and general technology fatigue (9%).

Two of these themes, valuing self-monitoring and the belief that technology to manage technology use is problematic, may pose unique barriers to designing to support this goal. Many respondents who expressed a desire to reduce phone use were resistant to the idea of leaning on supports and felt they should be able to change their behaviors themselves. They explained: *"I really should just limit my own usage and not be so addicted that I need an app,"* and *"Apps like these are for weak-minded people with no self-control...I will strive harder next time."* This category of comments suggests that designing to support adults who wish to reign in their phone use at the playground will require consideration of their potentially competing desire for self-sufficiency.

A second design barrier may be the fact that so many of our participants viewed technology as an inherently unproductive vehicle for delivering solutions to support intentional technology use. As one respondent explained: *"An app to cut down on apps? It feels like it feeds in[to] cell phone dependency."* Though many respondents who expressed this opinion wanted to adjust their usage, they felt that technological supports were as concerning as the technologies they want to avoid. This category of comments suggests that designing to support adults in achieving this goal will require consideration of the fact that new technologies may be rejected and solutions may need to be invisibly embedded in adults' current experiences on the phone. This value and thus this design barrier may extend to other groups of users trying to resist technology and to other non-use contexts.

Respondents who were unequivocally interested in trying out such a tool (16%) hoped that it would help them *"see perception vs. reality"* in the amount of time they spend on the phone. Respondents most frequently reported that reminders to put down the phone or data documenting their actual use would be most helpful.

Practices for Integrating Phone Use at the Playground

In absence of tools to support caregivers in achieving their ideal phone use, we observed that participants engaged in five thematic practices when using their phones at the playground, which appeared to serve as attempts to mitigate the impact of phone use on children. We probed this topic with interviewees and learned that some of these are conscious strategies intended to mitigate phone absorption.

Using the Phone in Short Bursts

Adults commonly used their phones at the playground for very short periods of time: taking out the phone, looking at the screen momentarily, putting it away, and then returning to attending to their children. Although we observed some caregivers who used their phones for extended periods of time, most instances of adult phone use were very brief. This was corroborated by our quantitative observations of phone use in which 40% of phone uses were 30 seconds or less. 36% of survey participants reported that they intentionally practice this strategy of short-burst phone use. Interviewees described using this strategy as well; as one explained: *"When I use it, it's usually **quick things** like messaging or I don't really have time to read long article or like that. So that's my strategy – **short quick things**"* (P11).

Glancing Back and Forth between Phone and Child

We also observed that adult phone users frequently glance back and forth between their phone and their child, often shifting their gaze as frequently as every few seconds. 37% of survey participants reported that they do this regularly and several interviewees spontaneously described glancing between phone and child. When asked how she used her phone, one interviewee said she would *"look at it and then... fiddle around with something, like email or texts, and then **glance up and then go back**"* (P16).

Waiting until the Child is Safe and Occupied

Adults systematically used their phones when their children were safe and occupied, for example, waiting until children were playing in a contained area like a sandbox or using the phone when children were playing cooperatively with others. The majority of interviewees reported that they tactically use phones once children are in *"safe"* situations, as did 58% of survey participants.

An exemplar of this strategy is phone use while young children are in swings. We frequently observed adults using their phones while their children were in bucket swings with leg holes and a safety belt intended to keep young children in the seat. Toddler swings restrain and protect the youngest children at the playground in a way that no other playground equipment does. Adults concurrently attended to their phones and their children by pushing them on the swings with one hand and holding, scrolling, tapping, and looking at their phone in the other hand. This was corroborated by interviewees as a conscious strategy.

Post-Phone Adult-Initiated Engagement

We observed adults initiating enthusiastic interactions with their children immediately after phone use. Though no interviewees commented on this explicitly, in our behavioral observations we noticed an ebb and flow of adult engagement with children such that during phone use adults typically did not engage with their children but proactively initiated interaction immediately after putting the phone away.

For example, one participant used his phone for about fifteen minutes. After putting his phone back in his pocket, he walked up to two boys playing in the sandbox, *"hold[ing] up his hands and curl[ing] his fingers to make monster claws and growl[ing]"* (Field Observation). In these instances, adults' engagement with children 1) followed a period of focused phone engagement, and 2) was adult-initiated rather than in response to a child request or interruption.

Avoiding Phone Use

To mitigate potential effects of phone use on children, interviewees reported deliberately making their phones inaccessible as a means of avoiding phone use altogether at the playground. One interviewee (P10) explained that she was not tempted to use her phone that day because she intentionally did not bring it to the playground. Three other interviewees (P12, P14, and P5) reported leaving their phones in their bags, so that phones were available but more easily ignored. Survey respondents also reported an inaccessibility-as-avoidance strategy and described leaving their phones in the car or using flip phones instead of smartphones to minimize features and potential distractions.

DISCUSSION & CONCLUSION

Our results provide extensive empirical data on phone-use decisions within a specific group of users with a common potential motivator for pushing back against technology. Our findings indicate that, for the majority of our participants, phone use occupies a small fraction of their time with their children and that this limited use is intentional. A small set of common, child-centric concerns – the need to 1) supervise, 2) be responsive, and 3) act as a role model – drive this intentional non-use. Though no formal, expert guidance suggests they do so, the majority of our participants (68% of interviewees, 76% of survey respondents) attempt to minimize their phone use and report negative emotional experiences of engaging with technology while children are in their care. Further work remains to tease apart the extent to which these negative feelings arise from their personal experiences with phone use and the extent to which they arise from a social climate that is critical of phone use by caregivers.

Relatedly, participants found their phone use to be more acceptable when it either involved the child (taking pictures) or directly related to the child's needs (coordination with others, setting a timer). Even participants who believe phone use should be minimal usually felt comfortable engaging with the phone for child-related reasons. These results suggest that for many caregivers, playground time centers on child needs and phone use is appropriate only in service of these needs. Desired patterns of use and non-use for these caregivers arises from their perceptions of what is best for their children rather than what is best for themselves.

For a large subgroup (nearly half of participants), a gap exists between desired and actual patterns of use and non-use, and this delta is a source of guilt. These participants report wanting to change their behavior and feeling unable to do so. Given the success of self-monitoring tools in a variety of other domains, this space appears to be a promising target for data-tracking and goal-setting applications. As participants both underestimated the extent of their unresponsiveness and felt notable guilt even when their overall phone use was minimal, providing these individuals with accurate behavioral data may be valuable. Capturing and reporting such data could potentially support caregivers in better achieving their expressed values (e.g., improving responsiveness) and assuage unnecessary guilt (e.g., by showing that their usage is minimal). However, participants' resistance to new technologies also suggests that the experience of collecting and viewing such data would only be acceptable if embedded seamlessly into their current digital experiences. These data also suggest that altering existing applications to be less tempting and more respectful of non-use desires would also be of value.

Our findings further reveal that while this device-resistance is prevalent, it is not universal. A distinct subgroup of caregivers expressed that unlimited adult phone use is appropriate and that they have no desire or intention to limit their time with the phone. Thus the larger user-group of those caring for children is not monolithic; use and non-use intentions and behaviors are better predicted by caregiver profile than by general status as a caregiver. Supporting and designing for caregivers who value unlimited use will likely look very different from supporting and designing for caregivers who value minimal use. Our results suggest that to best understand this user group, value-sensitive design for caregivers should probe whether or not an individual values minimal use in caregiving contexts, as well as the individual's perceptions of his or her own behavioral control.

Finally, the subgroups of caregivers that emerged from our data and their associations with specific emotional experiences related to phone use suggests that these categories offer predictive utility. Concerns about supervision, responsiveness, and modeling appear to predict feelings about phone use. Feelings about phone use, purpose of phone use, and perceptions of behavioral control in turn appear to predict phone-use behavior in this context. Participants reported that their values about phone use at the playground are similar to their values about phone use when caring for children in other contexts, thus the relationships we document here may be useful for modeling caregivers' desires and behaviors across a variety of contexts and technologies. Further work remains to develop and assess this theoretical model.

Nearly every interviewee and survey respondent reported having thoughts about phone use in caregiving contexts. Caregivers' consistent ability to articulate their desired phone use suggests this is a salient topic for these users. Within this community, the majority of caregivers appear to think about this, value minimal use, and translate this belief into behavior. These include common patterns of use (e.g., using a phone only after securing a child in a swing) and common patterns of non-use (e.g., locking the phone in the car). While these use and non-use behaviors are superficially different, they are enacted to achieve the same end-goal of enabling caregivers to put child needs first.

Our findings show that the need to prioritize child-centered concerns is fundamental across diverse members of this user group and should not be ignored. Today's technologies support this need with mixed success. Mobile phones give our "confident users" the freedom to first provide their child with outdoor free-play and then engage with technology. Caregivers of all types appreciate the phone's ability to take pictures of children and facilitate real-time coordination while they are at the playground. But our "users who would like to increase non-use" report frustration with their phone-engagement. These reported positive and negative experiences are both consistent with a world in which designers focus on engagement with minimal consideration of disengagement. Our results suggest that designing to support user-driven disengagement and re-engagement would be of value to this group. In absence of this, caregivers who feel their phone use inhibits their ability to prioritize child needs express a significant guilt burden, take measures to restrain their own behaviors, and in some cases abandon their devices altogether.

Our sample, and the Seattle metropolitan area, is less racially diverse, has a higher educational attainment, and higher household income than the American average. Patterns of phone use, technology access, caregiving attitudes, and family resources are likely to differ between the communities we studied and other areas. Future work remains to understand the extent to which our findings generalize to other populations. While participants reported that their values and behaviors at the playground are consistent with their values and behaviors in other caregiving situations (and thus may generalize beyond the playground), our sample was restricted to adults who bring their children to the playground in the first place. Future work is needed to understand whether these patterns hold among caregivers who are less likely to provide playground opportunities.

Parenting is a challenge in many ways, and the HCI research community has long investigated opportunities to support parents through technology. Our data provide new understanding of the needs of parents and other caregivers and offer to inform new models of caregiver behaviors in sociotechnical contexts. Such an understanding opens many new design possibilities including extracting design principles from the values we document here; designing for cycles of engagement, disengagement, and re-engagement; and examining caregiver guilt as a design target. We look forward to future contributions and discussion in this space.

ACKNOWLEDGMENTS

We gratefully acknowledge the contributions of our participants. We wish to thank Dharma Dailey for her help with this research.

REFERENCES

[1] Ames, M. (2013). Managing mobile multitasking: the culture of iPhones on Stanford campus. *CSCW'13*, (pp. 1487–1498).

[2] Baumer, E.P.S. et al. (2014). Refusing, limiting, departing: why we should study technology non-use. *Ext. Abstracts CHI'14*, (pp. 65–68).

[3] Brussoni, M., Olsen, L.L., Pike, I., & Sleet, D.A. (2012). Risky play and children's safety: Balancing priorities for optimal child development. *Int J Environ Res Publ Health, 9*(9), 3134-3148.

[4] Charmaz, K. (2006). *Constructing grounded theory: a practical guide through qualitative analysis*.

[5] Christakis, D.A. (2009). The effects of infant media usage: what do we know and what should we learn?. *Acta Paediatrica*, *98*(1), 8-16.

[6] Christopher, K. (2012). Extensive mothering: Employed mothers' constructions of the good mother. *Gender & Society, 26*(1), 73-96.

[7] Codol, J.P. (1975). On the so-called "superior conformity of the self" behavior: Twenty experimental investigations. *European Journal of Social Psychology*, *5*(4), 457–501.

[8] Emerson, R.M., Fretz, R.I., & Shaw, L.L. (2011). *Writing ethnographic fieldnotes*. University of Chicago Press.

[9] Foot, K.A. (2014). The Online Emergence of Pushback on Social Media in the United States: A Historical Discourse Analysis. *Int J Comm, 8,* 30.

[10] Friedman, B. et al. (2009). Value Sensitive Design and Information Systems. *The Handbook of Information and Computer Ethics*. John Wiley & Sons, Inc., 69–101.

[11] Ginsburg, K.R. (2007). The importance of play in promoting healthy child development and maintaining strong parent-child bonds. *Pediatrics*. *119*(1), 182–191.

[12] Harmon, E., & Mazmanian, M. (2013). Stories of the smartphone in everyday discourse: Conflict, tension & instability. *CHI'13* (pp. 1051–1060).

[13] Hashish, Y. et al. (2014). Involving children in content control: A collaborative and education-oriented content filtering approach. *CHI'14* (pp. 1797–1806)

[14] Hays, S. (1996). *The cultural contradictions of motherhood*. Yale University Press.

[15] Isola, S., & Fails, J. (2012). Family and design in the IDC and CHI communities. *IDC'12* (pp. 40–49).

[16] Lareau, A. (2002). Invisible Inequality: Social Class and Childrearing in Black Families and White Families. *American Sociological Review*.

[17] Lareau, A. (2010). Unequal Childhoods. *Race, Class and Gender: An Anthology*, 343–351.

[18] Lee, E.J. (2008). Living with risk in the age of 'intensive motherhood': Maternal identity & infant feeding. *Health, Risk & Society*, *10*(5), 467-477.

[19] Manjoo, F. (2014). You don't have to feel very guilty about using your smartphone while parenting. *The New York Times*.

[20] Mazmanian, M. (2012). Avoiding the trap of constant connectivity: When congruent frames allow for heterogeneous practices. *AMJ*.

[21] Morrison, S., & Gomez, R. (2013). Pushback : The growth of expressions of resistance to constant online connectivity. *iConference* (pp. 1–15).

[22] Morrongiello, B.A., & Dawber, T. (2000). Mothers' responses to sons and daughters engaging in injury-risk behaviors on a playground: implications for sex differences in injury rates. *J Exp Child Psychol*, *76*(2), 89–103.

[23] Park, A. 2014. Don't Text While Parenting - It Will Make You Cranky. *Time Magazine*.

[24] Radesky, J.S. et al. 2014. Patterns of mobile device use by caregivers and children during meals in fast food restaurants. *Pediatrics*, *133*(4), 843–9.

[25] Romagnoli, A. & Wall, G. (2012). "I know I'm a good mom": Young, low-income mothers' experiences with risk perception, intensive parenting ideology and parenting education programmes. *Health, Risk & Society*, *14*(3), 273-289.

[26] Satchell, C. & Dourish, P. (2009). Beyond the user: use and non-use in HCI. *OzCHI'09* (pp. 9–16).

[27] Schoenebeck, S.Y. (2014). Giving up Twitter for Lent : How and why we take breaks from social media. *CHI'14* (pp. 773–782).

[28] Steiner-Adair, C. & Barker, T.H. (2013). *The big disconnect: Protecting childhood and family relationships in the digital age*. Harper Business.

[29] Svenson, O. (1981). Are we all less risky and more skillful than our fellow drivers? *Acta Psychologica, 47*(2), 143-148.

[30] Tummala-Narra, P. (2009). Contemporary impingements on mothering. *The American Journal of Psychoanalysis*, *69*, 4–21.

[31] Turkle, S. (2011). *Alone Together: Why We Expect More from Technology and Less from Each Other*. Basic books.

[32] Wall, G. (2010). Mothers' experiences with intensive parenting and brain development discourse. *Womens Stud Int Forum*, *33*(3), 253-263.

[33] Worthen, B. (2012). The Perils of Texting While Parenting. *The Wall Street Journal*.

Exploring Time-Dependent Concerns about Pregnancy and Childbirth from Search Logs

Adam Fourney[1,2], Ryen W. White[2], Eric Horvitz[2]
[1]University of Waterloo, Waterloo, ON, Canada
[2]Microsoft Research, Redmond, WA, USA
afourney@cs.uwaterloo.ca, ryenw@microsoft.com, horvitz@microsoft.com

ABSTRACT
We study time-dependent patterns of information seeking about pregnancy, birth, and the first several weeks of caring for newborns via analyses of queries drawn from anonymized search engine logs. We show how we can detect and align web search behavior for a population of searchers with the natural clock of gestational physiology via proxies for ground truth based on searchers' self-report queries (e.g., [I am 30 weeks pregnant and my baby is moving a lot]). Then, we present a methodology for performing additional alignments, that are valuable for learning about the concerns, curiosities, and needs that arise over time with pregnancy and early parenting. Our findings have implications for learning about the temporal dynamics of pregnancy-related interests and concerns, and also for the design of systems that tailor their responses to point estimates of each searcher's current stage in pregnancy.

Author Keywords
Health; search; pregnancy; childbirth; temporal processes

ACM Classification Keywords
H.5.m. Information interfaces and presentation (e.g., HCI): Miscellaneous.

INTRODUCTION
Contemporary search engines often employ personalization methods, tailoring results to searchers' individual information needs. Searcher interests and preferences may be inferred from long-term query histories and interactions [4,29]. Our lives, however, are punctuated by major events such as graduation, marriage, the birth of a child, and death of a loved one. These life events often precipitate changes in our interests, preferences, and priorities [12], and the changes may evolve over the course of weeks or months (e.g., when buying a house [20]). In these periods, a person's continually evolving information needs may be poorly reflected by their prior history of search queries. However, many life events unfold along a predictable trajectory and sequence – as if following a predetermined script or schedule. If information systems can learn these schemas, and can detect when they apply, then they may better serve their users during time-dependent episodes.

CHI 2015, April 18 - 23 2015, Seoul, Republic of Korea
Copyright 2015 ACM 978-1-4503-3145-6/15/04...$15.00
http://dx.doi.org/10.1145/2702123.2702427

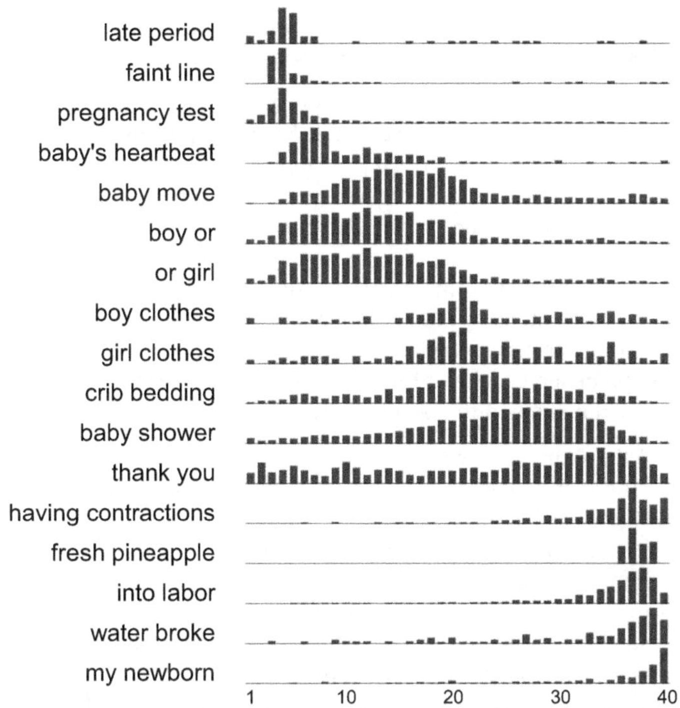

Figure 1: Histograms of query bigrams over 40 weeks of gestation. Time-dependent query volumes of each bigram (left) are displayed by gestational week for searchers who self-identified as pregnant (n=13,030 searchers). Each bar represents the proportion of searchers who searched at least once for bigram of interest in the corresponding gestational week. Histograms are normalized with respect to the maxima of each bigram.

We explore pregnancy and childbirth–hallmark examples of life events with well-characterized temporal dynamics. With pregnancy and childbirth, physiological processes and cultural practices (e.g., ultrasound exams, lab tests, baby showers, naming, birth announcements, etc.), conspire to stimulate curiosities, concerns, and information needs on a schedule. We demonstrate how search query logs can be leveraged to learn a detailed model of this phenomenon. Specifically, we present methods for aligning search queries with the 40 gestational weeks of pregnancy, and show, through detailed log analyses, that information needs of new and expectant mothers wax and wane in predictable patterns over the course of the weeks of pregnancy and beyond.

Figure 1 illustrates the temporal dynamics of pregnancy-related query bigrams over time. As an example, gender prediction queries (e.g., [does carrying low mean a boy or a girl]) taper off around the 20th week of pregnancy. In the same gestational week, we observe a short-lived increase in interest for gender-specific baby clothing. The timing of these events coincides with that of the mid-pregnancy ultrasound—a screening procedure where many parents first learn of the likely gender of their child [25].

Search logs provide some more surprising signals about searcher interests. For example, Figure 1 reveals a sudden rise in searches for *"fresh pineapple"* in the final weeks of pregnancy. Pineapple contains the enzyme bromaline, which is believed to induce labor [30], but is also destroyed by food processing procedures (e.g., canning or juicing). The timing and specificity of this query activity could be interpreted as showing intent to induce labor in the final weeks of pregnancy. Per these examples, date-aligned query logs afford an unprecedented view of pregnancy and childbirth, as experienced by tens of thousands of people.

In the short-term, we envision leveraging these temporal patterns to anticipate the queries of new parents, allowing search engines to better meet the information needs of this population through methods such as personalization [4]. In the medium-to-long-term, we envision leveraging this resource to investigate public health concerns (e.g., postpartum depression, gestational diabetes, spontaneous preterm labor, pregnancy related hypertension, drug abuse in pregnancy, etc.). Also, such studies frame questions about the ethics of large-scale data analyses by bringing to light potential inferences that can be made about people—even when using anonymized logs. Thus, this work can bring to the fore important discussions about privacy.

A key insight that we leverage is that a small percentage of searchers will make unambiguous statements via their queries about the nature and timing of their experiences. Though sparse, these special queries serve as crisp entries on the timeline of a well-characterized process, such as the physiology of pregnancy and childbirth. The unambiguous entries enable a large number of other queries to be synchronized, and such data, at the population level, can be leveraged to construct more general recognizers with the ability to identify and embed more common querying behavior on the timeline.

Our primary contributions with this research are as follows:

- We present and validate a set of *self-report* query templates that can be used to identify a cohort of searchers who we strongly believe are pregnant or to have recently given birth.
- We align the query histories of these searchers to the gestational weeks of pregnancy, and we characterize how their information needs evolve over time.
- We demonstrate how the temporal characterization of pregnancy-related searches can be leveraged to detect additional pregnancies in the query logs, beyond the original set of self-reporting searchers.
- We leverage the expanded dataset to characterize differences in the information needs of first-time mothers (primipara) and those of more experienced mothers (multipara). We tailor the temporal models accordingly, affording additional opportunities for personalization.

The remainder of this paper is structured as follows: We next present related work. Then, we describe data used in our studies. We describe methods for identifying an initial set of new and expectant parents, and how due dates or delivery dates may be estimated from search histories. We characterize how searchers' information needs evolve over the gestational weeks of pregnancy. Then, we describe how these temporal patterns can be leveraged to more generally detect and classify additional searchers. Finally, we compare and contrast the information needs of primipara and multipara. We conclude with a discussion of applications, implications, and potential concerns raised by this work.

BACKGROUND AND RELATED WORK

Recent work has demonstrated the value of performing time-series analysis on large-scale search query logs. For example, Choi and Varian demonstrated how such analyses can be leveraged to estimate economic indicators such as consumer confidence or the unemployment rate [7]. Likewise, Shokouhi demonstrated how time-series analysis can be used to identify topics of periodic or seasonal interest [26]. In this paper, we are particularly interested in applications of these types of analyses to public health research. Here, Ginsberg et al., demonstrated how query data can be used to estimate the prevalence of seasonal influenza in a population [14]. White et al. developed methods to detect adverse drug interactions by monitoring a population's medication and symptom-related search queries [32,33]. West et al. leveraged query data to investigate nutrition, including exploration of a potential association between dietary sodium and rates of hospital admissions for congestive heart failure [31]. In other work, Cooper et al. characterized correlates between cancer-related search activity and: cancer incidence rates, mortality rates, as well as mentions of cancer in the media [8]. Each of these examples highlights the richness and ecological validity of query log data for characterizing phenomena relative to a public time reference (e.g., the calendar date, or the date of a news article). Our work extends this research to phenomena that have well-characterized temporal dynamics, but that are experienced at different times by different individuals. In this sense, our work more closely aligns with, and extends, Richardson's vision for long-term query log analysis [20].

Early work examining health-related web search identified pregnancy as a primary topic of interest [27]. A decade later, pregnancy continues to top the list of health-related search topics [11,34]. In the intervening ten years, much has been written about how new and expectant parents leverage this important online resource [1,5,13,21,28]. However, query data is difficult to come by, and academics have typically relied on surveys [1], focus groups [5], or in-situ interviews [13] to learn about this phenomenon. These methods provide valuable insights into the motivations, opinions, and search strategies of expectant mothers. We complement this work by examining how pregnancy-related searches are manifest in the logs of a major contemporary search engine. This affords significant insight into how people pursue pregnancy related searches in naturalistic search settings.

Beyond logs of search queries, recent work has leveraged social media interactions to investigate aspects of pregnancy and childbirth. De Choudhury et al. characterized postpartum behavioral changes apparent in Twitter [9] and Facebook [10] postings. The work includes the construction of models that predict likely postpartum changes before the birth of the baby. Morris investigated how new mothers use social networking sites following the birth of their children [17]. Relevant to this work, Morris described typical parenting-related questions posted to these networks, and characterized how a mother's postings evolve over the months following a birth. Query log analyses serve as valuable complements to studies with social media—especially in light of recent research showing significant differences in health questions that people pose to their social networks versus in search [11].

Finally, reports appearing in the press have described how pregnancy-related searches are manifest in the query logs of major search engines [21,28]. Stephens-Davidowitz recently authored an opinion piece for the New York Times in which he compares pregnancy-related searches across 20 countries [28]. Closest to our work is a recent Google report targeted at marketers and advertisers [21]. In this work, Rost et al. leverage query log data to characterize broad trends in the information needs of new and expectant parents. Three distinct phases of parenthood are considered: pregnancy, caring for newborns, and caring for toddlers. Our research fills in many missing details by investigating the week-to-week information needs of this population.

DATA AND METHODS

We seek to characterize how information needs of new and expectant parents evolve during pregnancy. We shall first describe the general query log dataset. Then, we present a methodology for building a set of searchers who present strong evidence suggesting that they are pregnant. Finally, we describe how users' query histories are aligned with the gestational weeks of pregnancy.

Query Log Dataset

We rely exclusively on an existing proprietary dataset consisting of search queries posed to the Microsoft Bing web search engine over an 18-month period between June 2012 and December 2013. We restrict the analysis to English queries that were issued from searchers within the United States geographic locale. The resulting set consists of billions of queries, posed by tens of millions of anonymous searchers. Given the terms of use under which the data were collected, we rely only on anonymous numerical identifiers to associate queries with individual search histories.

We note that the query log dataset captures a dynamic population of searchers. Over the 18 months of data collection, new users arrived to the search engine, existing searchers departed, and anonymous user identifiers were occasionally reset. Examples of such reset events include searchers updating their Web browser or clearing their browser cookies. Users in our dataset have a median of 12 weeks of historical data.

Establishing a Set of New and Expectant Mothers

Although the query log dataset includes tens of millions of searchers, we expect only a small fraction of these individuals to be pregnant or to have had a recent childbirth during the timeframe of data collection. Limiting factors include the general fertility rate of the population, and the specific demographic of the search engine. Our study of pregnancy and childbirth requires that we identify, with high confidence, a subset of searchers whose query histories coincide with their pregnancy and childbirth experiences.

To identify searchers who may be experiencing pregnancy, we focused on individuals who had performed at least one search containing the first-person declaration of pregnancy: [I am *N* weeks pregnant]. Here, *N* is a placeholder for any integer ranging between 4 and 42 weeks. A lower limit of 4 weeks was chosen to match the time when a mother's human chorionic gonadotropic (hCG) hormone levels are sufficient to yield reliable home pregnancy test results [6]. An upper limit of 42 weeks was chosen because 97% of births occur before the 43rd week of pregnancy [16].

We removed from consideration queries containing additional qualifiers. For example, we excluded queries such as: [I think I am *N* weeks pregnant], and [when I am *N* weeks pregnant]. We considered the remaining unqualified queries as self-reports about the searchers' situations at particular times. We argue that these clear unambiguous statements are at least as reliable as survey responses, given that they are unprompted. Per these definitions, 13,030 individuals self-report as pregnant in the dataset.

Since children may be born in different gestational weeks, prenatal self-report statements are insufficient for reasoning about the timing of postpartum queries. To investigate information needs in the weeks following births, we identify searchers who self-report as having recently given birth. We focused on individuals searching with variations of the phrase [my *N* week old DEPENDANT]. Again, *N* is a placeholder for an integer, this time ranging from 1 to 24. Likewise *DEPENDANT* is a placeholder for such terms as: "son", "daughter", "newborn", "infant", "baby" or "child". Applying this methodology on our dataset yielded a set of 8,535 individuals who issued self-report queries in this way.

Alignment of Queries to Gestational Week

By design, the queries we used to construct the self-report sets each serves as a point of reference that can be used to align a searcher's entire search history with the gestational weeks of pregnancy, or with the weeks postpartum. For example, if a woman queries [I am 34 weeks pregnant and am having trouble sleeping], then we know that queries issued two weeks prior occurred in week 32 of pregnancy. Likewise, if a parent queries [how much should my 6 week old baby sleep], then we can compute the child's birth week by looking six weeks prior to the time that the query was issued.

EVOLUTION OF INFORMATION NEEDS OVER TIME

In the previous section, we described how web search queries of 13,030 self-reported expectant mothers can be aligned with the 40 weeks of gestation. Likewise, the searches of 8,535 self-reported new parents can be aligned with the weeks postpartum. In both cases, the data can be aggregated, yielding a characterization of pregnancy-related concerns unprecedented in scale. We now explore how the information needs of new and expectant parents evolve longitudinally. Potential applications include personalized search and analyses for clinical and public health.

Ebb and Flow of Pregnancy-Related Query Topics

Figure 1 detailed how interest in a set of phrases, captured as bigrams, varies over the 40 gestational weeks of pregnancy. Figure 2 presents similar information, but for queries issued over the first 24 weeks postpartum. In both figures, histogram bars correspond to weeks, and bar heights express the proportion of self-reported new and expectant mothers who issued a query containing the bigram of interest during the corresponding week. We normalize bars by dividing each entry by its histogram's maximum value.

As illustrated in Figures 1 and 2, concerns evolve throughout pregnancy, and into the weeks following the birth of a child. In early pregnancy (Figure 1), we see a continuous shift in interests, transitioning from one phase of pregnancy to the next: e.g., missing a period, taking a pregnancy test, experiencing morning sickness, detecting the baby's heartbeat on an ultrasound, and feeling the first signs of baby movement. Likewise, queries during the postpartum period (Figure 2) capture a predictable pattern of interest in newborn development, from smiling for the first time, to eating solid foods.

Beyond identifying interests linked with well-known milestones, aligning time-dependent patterns of queries across a large population may yield new insights. Figure 3 shows regularities in how expectant mothers search on pain or discomfort over 40 weeks of pregnancy. Figure 4 characterizes regularities in distributions of words about emotional states during the same timeframe. We see that queries about "*back pain*" occur more often in the first and third trimesters than in the second trimester. Likewise, occurrences of the query terms "*worried*", "*scared*" and "*terrified*" all peak at around the fifth gestational week—around the time women test positive for a pregnancy. These examples highlight the scope and personal nature of concerns expressed via queries.

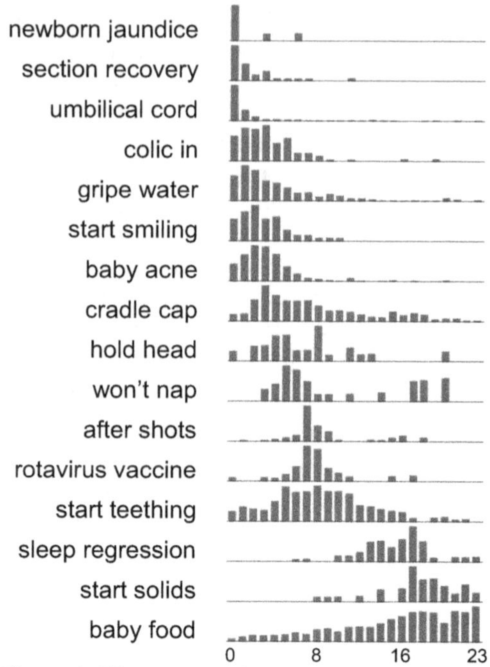

Figure 2: Histograms of query bigrams for the 24 weeks following inferred birth dates. Histograms show time-dependent query volume of bigrams for searchers who self-identified as new parents (*n*=8,535 searchers). Bars show the proportion of searchers who searched at least once for the bigram of interest within the associated week. Histograms are normalized with respect to the maxima for each bigram across the 24 weeks.

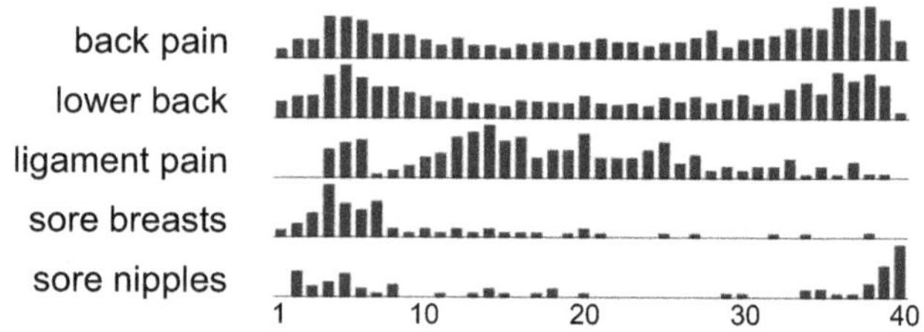

Figure 3: Histograms of pain-related bigrams over 40 gestational weeks. Columns correspond to gestational week. Histograms are normalized w.r.t. the maxima of each bigram.

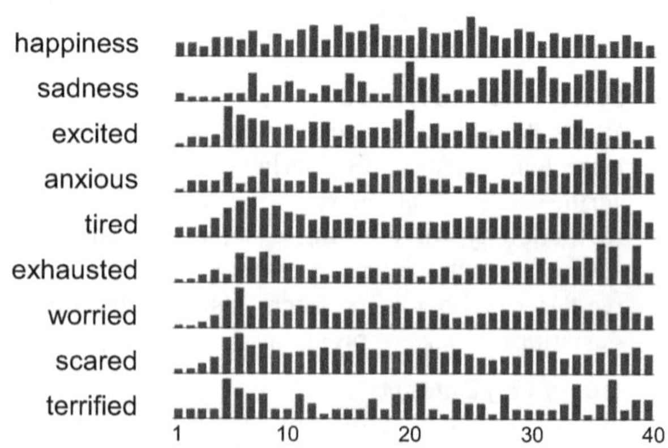

Figure 4: Histograms for terms in queries reflecting potential emotional state over the 40 gestational weeks of pregnancy. Histograms are normalized w.r.t. the maxima of each bigram.

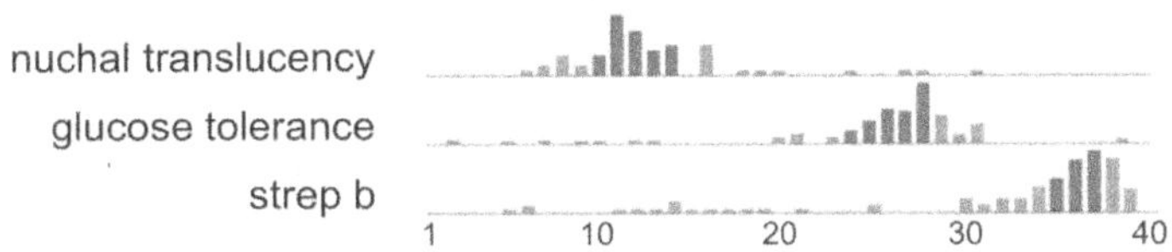

Figure 5: Histograms detail about how interest in three standard prenatal screening procedures vary over 40 gestational weeks. Bars show the proportion of searchers who have searched at least once for the bigram of interest in the associated week. Red bars report weeks in which each test is typically performed, as reported in [2], [18], and [24] respectively.

Validation of Temporal Alignment

Compelling examples of phrases exhibiting temporal regularities include bigrams associated with prenatal screening procedures (Figure 5). These screening procedures are performed at very specific times during pregnancy [2,18,24], and afford an opportunity to validate our alignment of query histories to the gestational weeks of pregnancy. For example, we note that fetal nuchal translucency is typically measured between the 10th and 14th week of pregnancy, as part of a standard screening procedure for Down syndrome [18]. In our dataset, searches including the phrase "*nuchal translucency*" align well within this range (highlighted in red in Figure 5). Likewise, interest in both the glucose tolerance test, and the test for the group B streptococcus bacteria also align well with the periods in which these tests are typically performed (weeks 24-28 in the former case [24], and weeks 35-37 in the latter [2]). These findings strongly argue for the veracity of the self-report statements, and support our query-history alignment methodology.

Implications for the Design of Personalized Systems

Temporal trends can present opportunities and challenges for personalized search [4,29]. The opportunity is afforded by recognizing that the information needs of new and expectant parents evolve along a predictable time-dependent trajectory that may be anticipated by a personalized search engine. One identified challenge is that many topics are relevant for only a short window of time during pregnancy. For personalized search engines to fully leverage such time-dependence, accurate detection of the current gestational age is required. In the next section, we present a more general methodology for both detecting pregnant searchers in the query logs and predicting gestational age.

MODEL

So far, we have characterized how information needs of new and expectant mothers evolve over the course of pregnancy. Some interests, such as those relating to medical screening procedures, arise in specific gestational weeks. In this section, we demonstrate how topics of transient interest can be leveraged to detect and align pregnancies beyond the 13,030 expectant mothers who we identified from search logs via first-person self-reporting queries.

Classification and Prediction

Mirroring our prior use of self-report templates (e.g., [I am *N* weeks pregnant]), we seek to construct a model that can: (1) classify searchers as pregnant or as not pregnant, and (2) can align their histories with the gestational weeks of pregnancy. The latter is equivalent to estimating due dates. Likewise, we would like a model that can (3) classify searchers as having recently given birth, and can (4) estimate the date of delivery when appropriate. While many solutions are possible, we achieve strong performance using a simple heuristic method employing linear regression. Our approach is motivated by a fictitious, but representative example. Suppose Alice's query history includes the following searches:

- [positive pregnancy test] on April 2, 2012
- [glucose tolerance test] on September 20, 2012
- [2 cm dilated] on November 28, 2012

With limited uncertainty, we may treat each of these queries as independent estimates of Alice's gestational age. In this case, the query [positive pregnancy test] suggests that Alice is 4 weeks pregnant on April 2nd. The query [glucose tolerance test] suggests that Alice is 28 weeks pregnant on September 20th, and so on. These estimates can be fit to a linear model. In this case, when both the dependent and independent variables are expressed in weeks, the line of best fit (via least squares) is found to exhibit a slope of 1.017. Alice appears to be gaining approximately one gestational week per week of time elapsed, thus we consider Alice's query behavior to be consistent with pregnancy. Since the slope is within a narrow threshold of acceptable values, we classify her as pregnant, and we use the regression line to align her complete query history with the inferred gestational weeks of pregnancy.

When performing linear regression on query data, we have found that ordinary least squares performs quite poorly. Inspecting errors reveals two common problems: First, searchers occasionally make typographical errors. For example, a user may type [4 weeks pregnant], and then quickly correct the query to read [24 weeks pregnant]. Second, we have observed that newly pregnant mothers often search ahead, e.g., researching later stages of pregnancy while in the first few weeks of gestation. In both cases, large residuals profoundly corrupt parameter estimates. We address this problem by adopting the Theil-Sen estimator, a non-parametric approach to robust linear regression. With the Thiel-Sen estimator, up to ~30% of the data can be corrupted, and the estimator will still provide reliable results [22].

Feature Selection and Parameter Values

When implementing this strategy we must make two choices. First, we need to decide on a threshold, $[1-\beta, 1+\beta]$ for the slope of the regression line. Second, we must select a set of query phrases to generate the pointwise estimates of the gestational week. For this, we desire phrases that (1) are associated with pregnancy, and (2) occur within a narrow range of gestational weeks. Intuitively, a good phrase will be one whose occurrences are difficult to predict prior to learning that user is pregnant, but easy to predict when we obtain knowledge of her gestational week. This tradeoff can be expressed mathematically as information gain [23], which we estimate as reduction in entropy H, as follows:

$$\boldsymbol{IG}[\![f]\!] = \boldsymbol{H}[\![p(w_{year} | f)]\!] - \boldsymbol{H}[\![p(w_{gestation} | f)]\!] \quad (1)$$

Here, the conditional distribution $p(w_{year} | f)$ characterizes how occurrences of the phrase f are distributed over the 52 weeks of a calendar year. Likewise, $p(w_{gestation} | f)$ characterizes how occurrences of the phrase f are distributed over the 40 weeks of gestation. In both terms, $\boldsymbol{H}[p(x)]$ corresponds to the usual entropy function:

$$\boldsymbol{H}[\![p(x)]\!] = -\sum_x p(x) \log p(x) \quad (2)$$

Our model selects the set of phrases from which to generate pointwise estimates by choosing the top η trigrams sorted by information gain, as defined in (1). This parameterization of phrase selection yields a model with two numeric parameters: β and η. Using a systematic parameter sweep, we explored a range of possible parameter values. We found that setting η=300, and β=0.15 achieves a good tradeoff between detecting a large number of expectant or new mothers, while achieving low average error in due date / delivery date prediction. We describe these evaluations in the next section.

Evaluation

Linear regression is used to simultaneously classify searchers as pregnant or not pregnant, and to align a searcher's query history to gestational weeks. The latter is equivalent to estimating a searcher's due date. We present an evaluation of both date prediction and classification. When working only with query log data, evaluation of model performance is challenging. The primary complication arises from the lack of ground-truth labels for searchers beyond those who unambiguously self-report their pregnancy or postpartum statuses. For this reason, we employ a range of evaluation methods, each testing a different aspect of the model.

Prediction Accuracy for Due Dates and Delivery Dates

Self-report data can be used to evaluate the accuracy of due date prediction. Evaluation is performed by learning a model from one set of self-report searchers, and then employing the model to estimate the due dates of the remaining self-report users. Results are cross-validated by repeating the procedure K=16 times, on K distinct data partitions.

Unfortunately, a complication persists even when performing cross-validation: under the above protocol, training and test data are both drawn from self-report searchers. Each of these searchers is guaranteed to have issued the query [I am N weeks pregnant]. This is an excellent feature for estimating gestational age. To mitigate this confound, we remove from consideration all queries containing self-report statements.

Taking all aforementioned factors into consideration, we found that the regression model predicts a searcher's due date to within ±0.685 weeks on average (median: 0 weeks). Predictions of delivery date based on postpartum queries (looking back in time) perform only slightly worse, achieving an average error of ±0.787 weeks (median: 0 weeks).

Estimating Classification Precision

The evaluation demonstrates that due dates and delivery dates can be accurately predicted, provided that we have information via self-reports that the searcher is pregnant, or that they have recently given birth. We also proposed applying a threshold on the slope of the regression line as a heuristic for detecting new or expectant mothers. To investigate the performance of this approach, we ran the classifier on the full 18-month query log dataset. In total, 93,463 searchers were classified as having experienced pregnancy during this timeframe, as compared to the 13,030 users in our self-report dataset. To verify the accuracy of the classification, we randomly sampled 100 of the searchers who were found using this method, omitting individuals who were part of the self-report dataset. Two researchers involved in this study then independently examined the query histories of these users, to make a determination of classification accuracy. Each rater labeled 99 searchers as having experienced pregnancy, and only one searcher who probably was not pregnant during this time. Moreover, the two raters were in perfect agreement about which searcher was falsely returned—an individual who was posing questions about their pregnant pet Rottweiler dog. We can therefore estimate that the classification heuristic achieves high precision when detecting pregnancy.

When applied to the problem of detecting mothers who had recently given birth, the classifier returned 42,548 searchers for whom delivery dates could be estimated. This represents a large increase over the 8,454 searchers appearing in the self-report dataset. The evaluation procedure was repeated. In this case, 97 searchers were labeled as having recently given birth. We again estimate that the classification heuristic achieves high precision when detecting recent childbirths. Unfortunately, recall performance cannot be easily measured in the same way. The difficulty arises from our inability to discern true negatives from false negatives without ground truth data (i.e., a person *not* searching about pregnancy may still be pregnant, and there is no way to determine this from the query logs alone).

Correlation with CDC Birth Data

As a final method to validate the model, we consider the 1,892 women whose query histories contain sufficient data to perform regression for both gestational and postpartum week alignment. In these cases, we can compute the gestational week in which each mother gave birth, by using the postpartum model to determine in which week of the year the birth took place—and then consulting the prenatal model to map this calendar week to a gestational week.

Figure 6 shows the distribution of births by gestational week, as estimated by our model (blue/solid curve). When compared to data compiled for the same span of time [16] by the Center of Disease Control (Figure 6, green/dashed curve), we find a Pearson correlation of $r = 0.97$ ($p < 0.0001$). While this measure is extremely encouraging, we note that predictions

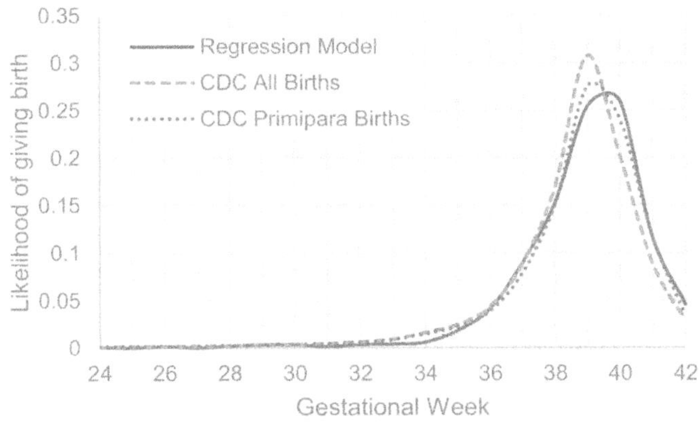

Figure 6: Distribution of birth events by gestational week (United States, 2012). The green/dashed curve represents *all* live births, as recorded in [16]. The red/dotted curve represents births to *first-time* mothers. The blue/solid curve represents the value computed by our model, using only search log data. Our model correlates well with both CDC curves (Pearson $r = 0.97$, $p < 0.0001$ for all births, and $r = 0.995$, $p < 0.0001$ for births to first-time mothers).

made by our model skew slightly toward later gestational weeks. There are a number of possible explanations for this skew. For example, we cannot rule out systematic noise in the data. Systematic noise could arise from the already noted tendency for some searchers to search ahead in early pregnancy. It is possible that our regression technique does not completely correct for this phenomenon.

The skew towards later weeks could also arise if the user population is biased towards *primipara* (first-time mothers), as primipara tend to give birth later in pregnancy than *multipara* (mothers with at least one prior live birth) [16]. This explanation is compelling: when the CDC data is filtered to include only first-time mothers (Figure 6, red/dotted curve), we find a Pearson correlation of $r = 0.995$ ($p < 0.0001$). A bias towards primipara could arise if the query logs skew towards a younger population with people who have had fewer childbearing years. Alternatively, first-time mothers may issue more queries, and are thus more likely to be detected by our model. This latter hypothesis motivates a more detailed comparison of primipara and multipara in the search logs. We explore this topic in the next section.

INFORMATION NEEDS OF PRIMIPARA VS. MULTIPARA

We now explore differences in the information needs of primipara and multipara births. We conjecture that these two groups have different needs and interests when searching for information related to pregnancy.

Establishing Primiparous and Multiparous Searchers

To identify primipara in the query logs, one author sampled 2000 queries containing the phrase "*first pregnancy*", then identified queries that suggest a searcher's primiparous status. For example, the query [length of labor first pregnancy] meets this criteria while the query [first pregnancy appointment] does not. In total, 1180 queries were found to unambiguously identify 1678 searchers as first-time mothers (queries may be searched by more than one individual). To assess the reliability of the inclusion criteria, a second researcher examined 200 of the 2000 sampled queries. A high inter-rater reliability was observed between the two judges (Cohen's Kappa of $\kappa = 0.9389$).

The procedure was repeated to identify multipara, this time sampling queries containing the phrases "*Nth pregnancy*", or "*previous pregnancy*" (where N is any integer greater than 1). In total, 1594 queries were found to unambiguously identify 1709 searchers as multipara. Again, a second researcher examined 200 of the 2000 queries, and again high inter-rater reliably was attained (Cohen's Kappa of $\kappa = 0.9386$).

Top Primipara Bigrams	Top Multipara Bigrams
baby shower	for kids
baby clothes	for toddlers
baby registry	year old
baby cribs	pregnancy showing
baby furniture	birthday party
nursery ideas	2 year
shower invitations	in children
baby nursery	year olds
stretch marks	in toddlers
birthing classes	double stroller

Table 1: Top 20 bigrams (excluding bigrams stating live birth order) for distinguishing primipara from multipara.

Distinctiveness of Needs of Primipara and Multipara

As a first step we identified information needs discriminating primipara and multipara. To do this, we examined larger search histories of primiparous and multiparous searchers, and computed normalized information gain [23] for each bigram or trigram encountered in their respective query streams.

Table 1 presents the top 10 most discriminative bigrams for each class, excluding bigrams that explicitly mention live birth order (e.g., "*first pregnancy*", "*second pregnancy*", etc.). The resultant features appeal to our intuition, and strongly suggest that our sets of primipara and multipara are indeed capturing real phenomena. Primipara are more likely than multipara to: plan baby showers, decorate nurseries, attend childbirth classes and worry about stretch marks. Conversely, multipara are more likely to search about: toddlers, birthday parties, and double strollers.

Time-Dependent Differences in Information Needs

Having identified small populations of multipara and primipara in the query data, it is possible to compare and contrast the evolution of information needs for the groups. Figure 7 presents how a set of trigrams are manifest in both populations. As before, the horizontal axis denotes the gestational week of pregnancy and the vertical axis denotes the proportion of the population issuing at least one query containing the trigram of interest in a given week. In the first three examples, the differences between primipara and multipara are chiefly ones of magnitude: assumed first-time mothers are more likely to ask which foods to eat when pregnant, or to ask if a particular experience is normal, and multipara are more likely to search for a "*due date calculator*". We hypothesize that multipara are more likely to be familiar with the terminology generally used to describe these tools, or to even know that such tools exist online.

The three examples at the bottom of Figure 7 characterize query phrases where the differences between primipara and multipara are chiefly those of timing. For example, while both groups appear to begin asking when will they "*start to show*" nearly immediately after learning of pregnancy, multipara stop asking approximately four weeks before primipara. This agrees with the belief that multipara will begin to show earlier in pregnancy than primipara [35]. Likewise, occurrences of the phrase "*feel the baby*" rise and fall earlier for multipara than for primipara. This agrees with the observation that quickening (first perception of fetal movement) occurs several weeks earlier for multipara than for primipara [15]. These examples should not be misinterpreted as confirmations of these presumed phenomena; that these are beliefs are popular is a significant confound, and may themselves explain patterns in observed querying behavior.

Finally, query activity including the trigram "*signs of labor*" is nearly identical for primipara and multipara. However, the curve for multipara is slightly shifted towards earlier gestational weeks, agreeing with the observed phenomenon that multipara give birth slightly earlier than primipara [16].

These examples demonstrate that, in the case of pregnancy, temporal models can be refined and tailored to reflect differences between subpopulations of users. These refined models may afford additional or improved opportunities for search personalization, and may yield additional insight when leveraging the query logs to pursue other questions of scientific interest.

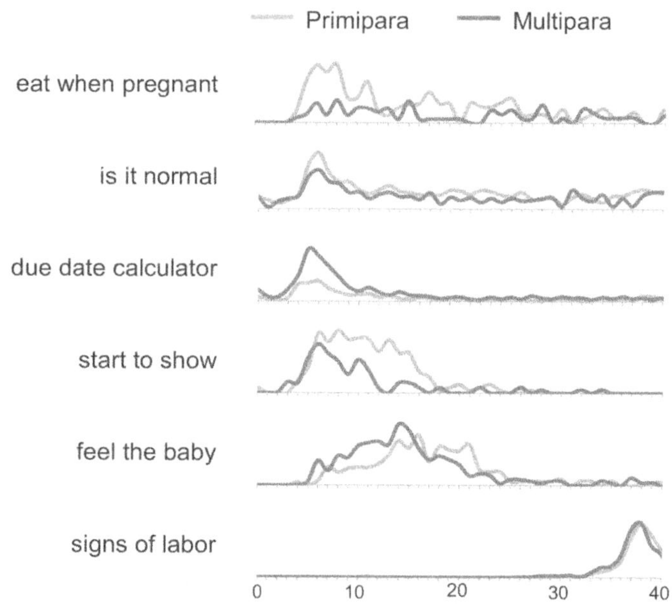

Figure 7: Graphs characterizing the differences between the search behavior of primipara (blue) and multipara (red) for a range of trigrams. Curves report temporal changes in the proportion of primipara or multipara searching with the trigram over the gestational weeks of pregnancy. The top three graphs exemplify differences in query volume. The bottom three graphs exemplify differences of timing.

APPLICATIONS

A central thesis of this research is that a new or expectant mother's information needs depend on many factors including her gestational week at time of query, and her previous experience with childbirth. In many cases, these details can be inferred from a searcher's query history. This affords the possibility of constructing information interfaces that tailor results to the searcher's specific situation. We outline some of these possibilities below, then describe how these models could be applied to investigate topics of public health.

Supporting Mothers through Personalized Search

For example, Figure 3 reports that expectant mothers issue many queries with the term "*exhausted*" in both early and late pregnancy. Fatigue in early pregnancy has been linked to hormonal changes, while fatigue in late pregnancy has been linked to iron deficiencies and trouble sleeping [3]. Search engines could leverage temporal information about these searches to tailor relevance rankings of fatigue-related pages in cases where the searcher's stage of pregnancy is known.

Our research also raises the possibility for personalized search to take a more direct role in advising new and expectant mothers. For example, if an expectant mother searches for airline tickets in a vertical search engine, the flights returned could each include a brief description of the airline's policy on flying while pregnant. This is particularly important during the later stages of pregnancy when there may be more restrictions over whether expectant mothers can fly. Likewise, if a new mother searches for information about high fevers in children, and it is known that her child is less than two months old, the search engine could advise the searcher of a potential medical emergency and the need to seek professional medical attention.

Supporting New and Expectant Mothers through Aggregation of Pregnancy Experiences

Online pregnancy resources often serve as community support [13] to reassure expectant mothers that physical discomfort (e.g., morning sickness, soreness, back pain), and emotional stressors (e.g., worry and fatigue), are temporary experiences. Query logs provide quantifiable data to support these assertions, and could serve a role in supporting mothers in times of discomfort or stress. For example, women searching for information about back pain in early pregnancy might be comforted to know that: (1) many expectant mothers have issued similar queries at the same stage of pregnancy, and (2) the queries do not tend to persist into the second trimester.

Applications for Public Health Research
In the medium-to-long-term, we envision leveraging this resource to investigate matters of public health concern (e.g., postpartum depression, gestational diabetes, spontaneous preterm labor, drug abuse in pregnancy, neonatal jaundice, etc.) As an example, we consider the topic of self-induced labor. Figure 8 characterizes when different herbal or homeopathic methods of labor induction are most commonly searched. Interest in these methods experiences an uptick in week 36 and peaks in weeks 37 or 38. Whether such methods work as may be believed, this finding is troubling: medical practitioners caution against inducing labor prior to week 39 of pregnancy [19]. The primary concern with earlier induction of labor is that, while a child born in week 37 is not premature, there may be dating inaccuracies. Consequently, early induction raises the risk of complications resembling those experienced with premature births. Query logs alone may not be sufficient to determine if women are following through with their intention to induce labor, or if common methods are effective. Nevertheless, this could justify further studies investigating the impact of this phenomenon.

ETHICS AND PRIVACY
All data access and analysis performed for this research was done in accordance with Bing's published end-user license agreement, which specifies that user data may be used for research purposes and to improve the search experience. Our work was conducted offline, on data collected to support existing business operations, and did not influence the presentation of search results or other aspects of the user experience. All data were anonymized prior to analyses. The Ethics Advisory Committee at Microsoft Research considers these precautions sufficient for triggering the Common Rule, exempting this work from detailed ethics review.

Nevertheless, important ethical questions come to the fore with research that shows how inferences can be made about people based on their activities with online services. We realize that many may view pregnancy and childbirth as sensitive subjects. The results reported in this paper are aggregates of many searchers, and characterize positive or unexceptional aspects of experiences with pregnancy and newborns. However, search logs contain a broad spectrum of pregnancy-related topics. They capture the concerns of those who are struggling to conceive a child and those who have experienced a loss. They include questions about paternity and about abortion. And, they provide evidence of behaviors that may place children at risk (e.g., abuse of recreational drugs while pregnant). Studying these and other sensitive phenomena can advance research in clinical medicine, public health, psychology, and sociology. However, we need to reflect with the broader research community and with the public at large about the ethical and privacy implications of the research. We hope that studies like this one will help to frame the discussion about acceptable or expected uses of large-scale behavioral data when seeking deeper insights about human behavior, whether the data is acquired via search services or via publicly-visible posts, such as those made to Twitter [9].

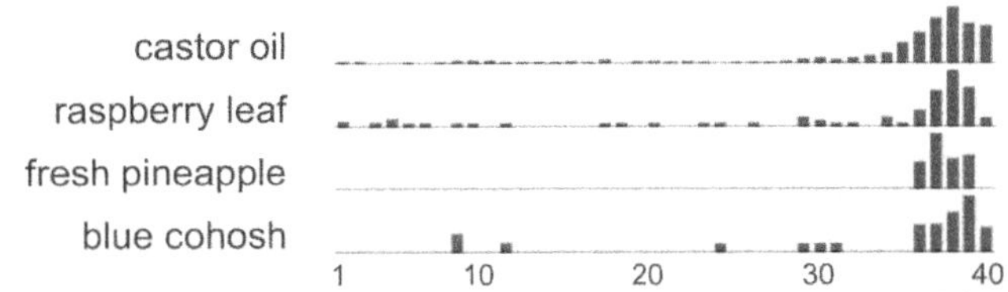

Figure 8: Histograms characterizing how the interest in self-induction of labor, varies over the 40 gestational weeks of pregnancy. Activity begins to rise in week 36 and peaks around week 38. Induction before week 39 is not recommended.

DISCUSSION AND CONCLUSIONS
Pregnancy and childbirth have profound impact on the lives of expectant and new mothers, and information seeking leaves a clear signature in logs of their search activity. We presented methods for characterizing these dynamic processes via retrospective analyses of logged search engine queries. We also performed additional alignments to refine our understanding of these phenomena.

The analysis is limited in several ways. Our method considers the appearance of special first-person queries as strong evidence of pregnancy. However, we could not contact participants directly. Thus, we had no way to verify that they were in fact pregnant. Follow-on studies with new and expectant mothers are required to validate our approach. Our study also focuses only on search activity in the United States. Pregnancy is treated differently in other countries [28] and further analysis of related search activity in different geographic regions is needed to understand the generalizability of our methods to different countries and cultures.

Pregnancy is an important topic and our study demonstrates the value of logs as a broad lens on relevant interests and concerns. Our findings have implications for learning about the temporal dynamics of pregnancy-related interests and concerns, and also for the design of systems that tailor their responses to point estimates of searchers' current stage in pregnancy. While our work focuses on pregnancy and childbirth, the methods presented in this paper will generalize to other life events, such as the treatment of a chronic disease, where well-characterized temporal dynamics of physiology or other processes can be synchronized with search queries.

REFERENCES
1. Allen, K. Parents online. *Pew research center's internet & American life project*, 2002. http://www.pewinternet.org/2002/11/17/parents-online/.

2. American Congress of Obstetricians and Gynecologists. Group B streptococcus and pregnancy. 2011. http://www.acog.org/Patients/FAQs/Group-B-Streptococcus-and-Pregnancy.

3. Amy, F. First trimester fatigue. *University of Rochester medical center: health encyclopedia*, 2014. http://www.urmc.rochester.edu/encyclopedia/content.aspx?ContentTypeID=134&ContentID=4.

4. Bennett, P.N., White, R.W., Chu, W., et al. Modeling the impact of short- and long-term behavior on search personalization. In *Proc. SIGIR '12*, ACM (2012), 185–194.

5. Bernhardt, J.M. and Felter, E.M. Online pediatric information seeking among mothers of young children: results from a qualitative study using focus groups. *Journal of Medical Internet Research 6*, 1 (2004).

6. Butler, S.A., Khanlian, S.A., and Cole, L.A. Detection of early pregnancy forms of human chorionic gonadotropin by home pregnancy test devices. *Clinical Chemistry 47*, 12 (2001), 2131–2136.

7. Choi, H. and Varian, H. Predicting the present with google trends. *Economic Record 88*, s1, (2012), 2–9.

8. Cooper, P.C., Mallon, P.K., Leadbetter, S., et al. Cancer internet search activity on a major search engine, United States 2001-2003. *J Med Internet Res 7*, 3 (2005), e36.

9. De Choudhury, M., Counts, S., and Horvitz, E. Predicting postpartum changes in emotion and behavior via social media. In *Proc. CHI '13*, ACM (2013), 3267–3276.

10. De Choudhury, M., Counts, S., Horvitz, E.J., and Hoff, A. Characterizing and predicting postpartum depression from shared Facebook data. In *Proc. CSCW '14*, ACM (2014), 626–638.

11. De Choudhury, M., Morris, M.R., and White, R.W. Seeking and sharing health information online: comparing search engines and social media. In *Proc. CHI '14*, ACM (2014), 1365–1376.

12. Duhigg, C. How companies learn your secrets. *The New York Times*, 2012. http://www.nytimes.com/2012/02/19/magazine/shopping-habits.html.

13. Gibson, L. and Hanson, V.L. Digital motherhood: how does technology help new mothers? In *Proc. CHI '13*, ACM (2013), 313–322.

14. Ginsberg, J., Mohebbi, M.H., Patel, R.S., Brammer, L., Smolinski, M.S., and Brilliant, L. Detecting influenza epidemics using search engine query data. *Nature 457*, (2009), 1012–1014.

15. Levene, M.I., Tudehope, D.I., and Thearle, M.J. Definitions and terminology. In *Essentials of Neonatal Medicine*. Wiley, 2000, 9.

16. Martin, J.A., Hamilton, B.E., Osterman, M.J., Curtin, S.C., and Mathews, T. Births: final data for 2012. *National Vital Statistics Report 62*, 9 (2013), 1–87.

17. Morris, M.R. Social networking site use by mothers of young children. In *Proc. CSCW '14*, ACM (2014), 1272–1282.

18. Nicolaides, K.H., Azar, G., Byrne, D., Mansur, C., and Marks, K. Fetal nuchal translucency: ultrasound screening for chromosomal defects in first trimester of pregnancy. *BMJ : British Medical Journal 304*, 6831 (1992), 867–869.

19. Oshiro, B.T., Henry, E., Wilson, J., Branch, D.W., and Varner, M.W. Decreasing elective deliveries before 39 weeks of gestation in an integrated health care system: *Obstetrics & Gynecology 113*, 4 (2009), 804–811.

20. Richardson, M. Learning about the world through long-term query logs. *ACM Trans. Web 2*, 4 (2008).

21. Rost, J., Johnsmeyer, B., and Mooney, A. Diapers to diplomas: what's on the minds of new parents. *Think with Google*, 2014. http://www.thinkwithgoogle.com/articles/new-parents.html.

22. Rousseeuw, P.J. and Leroy, A.M. Other techniques for simple regression. In *Robust Regression and Outlier Detection*. John Wiley & Sons, 2003, 67–78.

23. Russell, S. and Norvig, P. Choosing attribute tests. In *Artificial Intelligence a Modern Approach*. Prentice Hall, 2003, 660.

24. Sacks, D.A., Greenspoon, J.S., Abu-Fadil, S., Henry, H.M., Wolde-Tsadik, G., and Yao, J.F.F. Toward universal criteria for gestational diabetes: The 75-gram glucose tolerance test in pregnancy. *American Journal of Obstetrics and Gynecology 172*, 2, Part 1 (1995), 607–614.

25. Salomon, L.J., Alfirevic, Z., Berghella, V., et al. Practice guidelines for performance of the routine mid-trimester fetal ultrasound scan. *Ultrasound in Obstetrics & Gynecology 37*, 1 (2011), 116–126.

26. Shokouhi, M., and Radinsky, K. Time-sensitive query auto-completion. In *Proc. SIGIR '12*, ACM (2012), 601–610.

27. Spink, A., Yang, Y., Jansen, J., et al. A study of medical and health queries to web search engines. *Health Information & Libraries Journal 21*, 1 (2004), 44–51.

28. Stephens-davidowitz, S. What do pregnant women want? *The New York Times*, 2014. http://www.nytimes.com/2014/05/18/opinion/sunday/what-do-pregnant-women-want.html.

29. Teevan, J., Dumais, S.T., and Horvitz, E. Personalizing search via automated analysis of interests and activities. In *Proc. SIGIR '05*, ACM (2005), 449–456.

30. Tiran, D. Complementary therapies: your questions answered. Use of pineapple for induction of labour. *Pract Midwife 12*, 9 (2009), 33–4.

31. West, R., White, R.W., and Horvitz, E. From cookies to cooks: insights on dietary patterns via analysis of web usage logs. In *Proc. WWW '13* (2013), 1399–1410.

32. White, R.W., Harpaz, R., Shah, N.H., DuMouchel, W., and Horvitz, E. Toward enhanced pharmacovigilance using patient-generated data on the Internet. *Clinical Pharmacology & Therapeutics 96*, 2 (2014), 239–246.

33. White, R.W., Tatonetti, N.P., Shah, N.H., Altman, R.B., and Horvitz, E. Web-scale pharmacovigilance: listening to signals from the crowd. *Journal of the American Medical Informatics Association, 20*, 3 (2013), 404–408.

34. Google's top health searches for 2012: cancer, pregnancy symptoms and ... hemorrhoid? *MedCity news*. http://medcitynews.com/2012/12/googles-top-health-searches-for-2012-cancer-pregnancy-symptoms-and-hemorrhoid/.

35. Pregnant again: What to expect this time around. *BabyCenter*. http://www.babycenter.com/0_pregnant-again-what-to-expect-this-time-around_10305185.bc

Run Spot Run: Capturing and Tagging Footage of a Race by Crowds of Spectators

Martin D Flintham, Raphael Velt, Max L Wilson, Edward J Anstead, Steve Benford, Anthony Brown, Timothy Pearce, Dominic Price, James Sprinks
Mixed Reality Lab, School of Computer Science
University of Nottingham, UK
{martin.flintham, raphael.velt, max.wilson, edward.anstead, steve.benford, anthony.brown, timothy.pearce, dominic.price, james.sprinks}@nottingham.ac.uk

ABSTRACT
There has been a massive growth in the number of people who film and upload amateur footage of events to services such as Facebook and Youtube, or even stream live to services such as LiveStream. We present an exploratory study that investigates the potential of these spectators in creating footage en masse; in this case, during a live trial at a local marathon. We deployed a prototype app, RunSpotRun, as a technology probe to see what kinds of footage spectators would produce. We present an analysis of this footage in terms of its coverage, quality, and contents, and also discuss the implications for a) spectators enjoying the race, and b) extracting the stories of individual runners throughout the race. We conclude with a discussion of the challenges that remain for deploying such technology at a larger scale.

Author Keywords
Video; public settings; marathon; crowd sourcing; tagging; story telling.

ACM Classification Keywords
H.5.m. Information interfaces and presentation (e.g., HCI): Miscellaneous.

INTRODUCTION
There has been a massive growth in amateur video capture and sharing by spectators at public events, ranging from marathons and cycle races, to music festivals and gigs, and even marches and protests. This has been fuelled by the increased ownership and sophistication of smartphones that enable spectators to capture videos in the first place, coupled with the emergence of social media services such as YouTube and Facebook that allow them to subsequently share and tag them. This emerging practice is now being further driven through a new generation of streaming services such as Bambuser, LiveStream and UStream that allow spectators to broadcast live video footage across low-bandwidth mobile internet connections such as 3G [10]. Consequently, capturing and sharing video documentation is fast becoming an integral part of attending events [1].

Our interest here lies in how we might better support this emerging practice by enabling spectators to more actively and systematically capture video from public events. We seek to do this in a way that delivers a video corpus with sufficiently broad coverage, quality and structure to facilitate the telling of various stories after the event.

This both draws on and contributes to a growing interest in HCI in crowdsourcing documentary media, including previous research addressing the optimization of groups capturing video on the ground [17] and the post-hoc integration of user-generated content into multimedia archives, either automatically (using audio features) or through additional contextual metadata such as location and time [22,23]. Our interest also relates to previous research into the generation of souvenirs and stories from everyday experiences, including creating multimedia photostories from a theme park visit [6], collaborative collection of photos of a rally competition [18], and supporting everyday storytellers with lightweight approximations of professional broadcast editing [3].

This focus of this paper, however, is on driving the systematic and widespread *capture* of video by spectators *during an event*. We describe how the deployment of a prototype system called RunSpotRun 'in the wild' at a public marathon enabled spectators to generate a corpus of tagged videos of runners. We then present an analysis of this corpus from the point of view of coverage, quality and content and show how it might underpin the generation of various stories from the race. This enables us to:

- Determine whether it is feasible for spectators to generate a video corpus that offers good coverage of a race, geographically, temporally and of individuals;
- Reveal the nature of the videos that spectators capture in terms of their content and quality;
- Understand how this video capture and tagging affects the experience of spectating;

CHI 2015, April 18–23, 2015, Seoul, Republic of Korea.

http://dx.doi.org/10.1145/2702123.2702463

- Discuss opportunities and challenges for scaling-up this approach in the future.

TELLING STORIES FROM MARATHONS

We have chosen marathon races as suitable target for exploring how spectators can crowd-source video for several reasons. First, their distributed nature makes them difficult to capture in detail using conventional means. Second, they involve large crowds of active spectators who line the streets at many different vantage points along the course. Third, we suggest that there is a strong desire for participants to tell their personal stories to family, friends and to sponsors; indeed the proliferation of race-souvenir photography is perhaps evidence of this, as is the use of live meta-data to increase engagement with spectators [5]. We therefore begin by briefly considering some of the ways in which this is currently achieved and how these have motivated our own approach.

Marathon photo and video souvenir services

Various companies have been springing up to capture photos and more recently videos from marathons, using additional technologies to record the positions of runners at key locations in order to index into and subsequently identify runners in the captured media. Many marathons use systems such as ChronoTrack (www.chronotrack.com) or Ultra (rfidtiming.com/ultra-2/) which time runners using RFID tags attached to the their shoelaces and reader-gates deployed at the start, end or other strategic locations. This technology was used [21,24] by Asics at the New York Marathon to publish the progress of runners online and to allow friends and family to send messages of support to screens around the course via social media (www.supportyourmarathoner.com). Marathon Photos, on the other hand, (www.marathon-photos.com) provides a commercial photography service for international long distance running events. Entering the name of the event and runner name or number extracts a set of professionally generated photos and videos of their race captured at the finish line. The service also allows the user to locate additional footage by sorting their multimedia dataset by time, location, runner gender and runner clothing.

However, the collective use of these systems to create navigable corpuses of video is still in its infancy, and many problems remain to be solved. Tracking technologies such as RFID have a limited granularity, and at smaller events this technology is likely to have gates only at the start and the end of the race. Similarly the amount and variety of complimentary professional footage is limited, typically being captured from a small number of locations.

Television coverage of marathons

There is also a longstanding tradition of professional outside broadcasting of marathons. However broadcasters face two key challenges: they cannot be at every event and they typically can only offer very limited coverage when they are present. Recent coverage of an event such as the London Marathon required 51 HD cameras [20] to deliver live coverage that, necessarily, focused on a relatively small proportion of the runners taking part. While the relatively few elite athletes provide a natural focus for broadcasters, there is an increasing interest in reporting the stories of the swathes other amateur and charity runners who take part. Perhaps the bigger challenge lies in the many thousands of other races at which broadcasters simply cannot be present, from small fun-runs to large annual city-based marathon events involving thousands of participants, many of whom run for charitable causes, and which also attract large crowds of spectators to support them. One solution for documenting these events may lie in amateur video footage, and leveraging the ad-hoc and informal video capture using mobile phones that is increasingly a ubiquitous part of the spectator experience [12]. Indeed, some amateurs already systematically organize themselves to capture and curate collections of video, particularly from music gigs [16,19].

APPROACH

We undertook a study to explore how spectators at a marathon might collectively generate a video corpus that covered the event. Our study unfolded in three stages: capturing a video corpus, interviewing spectators about their experiences, and visualizing and analyzing the footage that they captured.

Capturing and live-tagging a video corpus

We designed and implemented RunSpotRun primarily to crowd-source short video clips of a live marathon via consumer smart phones used by spectators while watching the race. At the same time the system also collects both automatic and spectator entered meta-data regarding clips and the runners in the race to aid future indexing and navigation. The system comprises an Android client application that captures video, tags of runners as entered by spectators, and the reported position of the spectator.

The RunSpotRun Android application, shown in figure 1, presents a camera preview to spectators, and that is locked to always display in landscape mode in order to consistently capture video in this format. A large button enables users to begin recording video and audio using the built-in camera and microphone and this is then stored locally. The maximum length of an individual video clip is limited by the underlying storage on the phone; so that spectators can either collect a large number of individual clips by starting and stopping broadcasting, or can continually record for long periods of time.

The application presents a simple numeric keypad overlaid upon the camera preview which can be used to manually enter the official (unique) runner numbers that are displayed on their bibs as they are observed passing through the shot, essentially live-tagging runners while filming. Multiple runner numbers can be entered for a single video clip. We opted for manual live-tagging of runners as being the simplest – and we hoped most reliable – baseline for noting the presence of interesting runners in video clips, given that significant occlusion of numbers was likely to be an issue.

On entry of a runner number the application updates a local tag document with the runner number, a unique identifier for this spectator, the spectator's position as reported by GPS, a unique identifier for the current video clip and current time-stamp. The application also periodically logs and reports the spectator's GPS position even when they are not tagging. In the study, this metadata was synchronized with a master server whenever the network allowed, while video files were stored locally and manually recovered after the event. The current version of the app allows spectators to choose to upload videos at their convenience.

Figure 1: The RunSpotRun capturing interface

Deploying RunSpotRun

We conducted a full field trial of RunSpotRun at our local city marathon in September 2013. This annual race consists of a full marathon (26 miles), a half marathon (13 miles) and a junior mini marathon. Over 8000 entrants attempted the 2013 event across these disciplines, and in our trial we focused on the half marathon as the most popular event with over 6500 runners [15]. The course of each race starts and ends at an embankment next to the river, to the south of the city centre. While completing the course runners get to take in several of the city's major landmarks, running on a mixture of temporarily closed public roads and thoroughfares, and private land. In the past the race has attracted over 10,000 spectators [14].

Participants

For this trial, we recruited spectators to attend the marathon and use RunSpotRun while watching the race at various points along the course. These participants were recruited through mailing lists and through the recommendation of participating runners who knew of friends or family who would be attending to spectate. Some had planned to attend as spectators anyway as part of a planned day out. Overall, participants consisted of one family group, 4 pairs, and 8 individuals. Spectators were allowed to move around the course and to film and tag freely; however on occasion during the trial we sent messages through the application notifying them of ongoing race information so that they could plan their activities.

Spectators were briefed on their participation one or two days before the marathon, and loaned an Android smartphone with the application preloaded. We conducted these sessions in advance of the marathon to ensure that the spectators underwent their usual 'spectating activity', as far as possible, situating themselves along the course at a location of their choosing rather than the nearest section to the briefing site. Spectators were not given a prescribed location from which to view the marathon, nor were they given particular directions as to the duration or manner of videos that they might capture. However we did require them to spend at least 90 minutes attending the marathon, during which they were asked to both use the application but also to move around the course and act as normal spectators as much as dedicated camera operators.

Interviewing the spectators

Our recruited spectators were interviewed about their experience after the marathon. Interviews were semi-structured and focused on asking spectators about the location they chose to spectate from and their rationale for choosing these, any other locations they subsequently moved to, the videos they captured, the runners they tagged, their experience using the application and their overall experience of attending the event.

Post-race tagging of the video corpus

After the event, we undertook two further tagging exercises in order to better classify and understand the content that has been captured. To support this, we developed a browser-based tagging interface that presented a user with a two-minute segment of video footage and allowed them to enter tags, either for a moment in time or for a configurable duration. First, we used this browser to comprehensively categorise all footage according to four key dimensions so as to help us understand the overall, nature and quality of the captured video material:

- **Runner density**: none, sparse, average, many, dense
- **Type of camera shot**: non footage, blurry, walking with camera, still shots, tracking shots
- **Elements of the race,** including: race, off-race, start line, finish line and incidental footage or scenery
- **Area of the race**: urban or countryside

The second exercise involved extending this broad analysis with richer metadata that might reveal more noteworthy or esoteric elements of the video content. We selected a random sample of footage and subjectively tagged the content of the footage for features of likely interest to potential viewers. From these tags we created a schema involving 6 dimensions; types of runners, type of footage, types of terrain, elements of the race, and types of captured audio. Next, we recruited a group of researchers not connected to the project to apply the schema to the broader video corpus, or adding additional tags by free text.

Visualising and exploring the corpus

We then developed an interactive visualization to enable us to explore our tagged video corpus in greater depth. This involved two further steps that we briefly note before presenting our findings. First, we developed a simple technique for translating the reported GPS positions of spectators into a distance along the half-marathon course. Second, we used this as the basis for the more complex task of inferring the runners' positions throughout the race at different times. We obtained public data giving each runner's official start and finish time as they crossed the start and finish gates published by the race organisers after the event. We then worked out a series of further positions/times for each occasion they had been tagged by a spectator (with a known position). This allowed us to estimate their path as being a series of linear segments connecting their official start point, any subsequent points at which they were tagged, and their final end point.

FINDINGS

Our 17 participants recorded a total of 412 videos, totaling 11 hours 29 minutes of footage. The videos range in duration from 2 seconds to 31 minutes 10 seconds with an average length of 1 minute 48 seconds. Spectators produced a mean of 31.8 videos each, with one uploading as many as 64. In total spectators entered 3108 live-tags of runners during the race. Of the total amount of footage, 33 minutes was excluded from the corpus, due to being damaged or infringing on ethical and privacy issues (e.g., due to children being without filmed with parental permission). This left 10 hours and 56 minutes of footage that was tagged and analysed. We categorized all of the video using our schema, and subsequently a sample of (55% of the footage, or ~200 videos) was free tagged, applying a total of 486 unique tags.

Overall coverage

Figure 2 visualises the overall spatial and temporal coverage of our video corpus. The horizontal axis shows distance along the half-marathon course while the vertical axis shows time running downwards from 09:30 when the race began until sometime after 12:30 when it finished. Each blue line describes the trajectory of an individual runner as a simple linear interpolation between start and end times. Brown rectangles show the locations and times of captured videos while blue circles show individual tags of runners. The combination of all runner trajectories generates a quadrilateral shape whose vertices are, at the top left, the moment the starting gun was fired, at the bottom left, the latest crossing of the start line, and at the right, the moments when the fastest and the slowest runners crossed the finishing line. The visualization shows that there was good temporal coverage of the event. For example, videos located between 8.5 and 10.5km appear to cover 87% of the time frame within which the race passes through this region. Spatial coverage was patchy however, with spectators tending to remain in one place, except for a few who moved along the course.

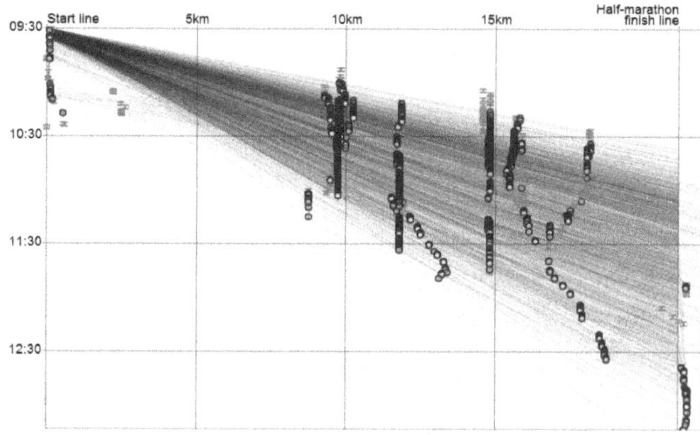

Figure 2: Race visualization

Geographic coverage

Figure 3 sheds further light on the geographic distribution of the videos by plotting them on a map of the racecourse.

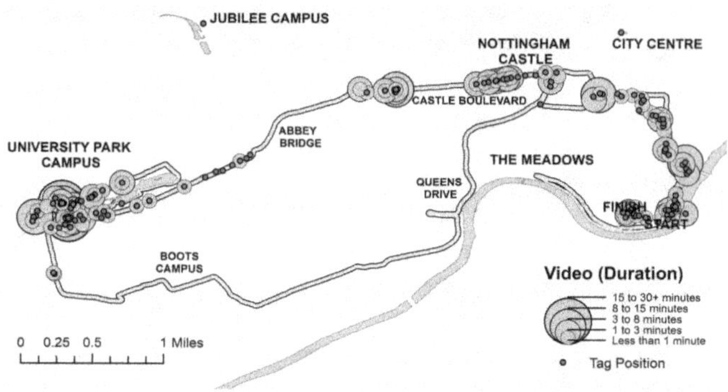

Figure 3: Geospatial video coverage of the course

This reveals how notable geographic properties of the route affected capture. The start and finish line of the route are close to one another, enabling a spectator to watch the start of the race, then move a short distance to observe runners returning and crossing the finish line. There is also a very tight switchback, where a few metres away runners move in the opposite direction to those who started earlier. Similarly the route includes a much larger switchback around a park area, allowing spectators to see the runners more than once.

As can be seen, there are two areas where the majority of video capture and tagging takes place, the eastern part of the route between the city centre and the start / finish line and the western part of the route around the university campus, and these correspond to spectators' own reports of pleasant and interesting places to view from. Sporadic coverage can be seen along one of the main thoroughfares, but there is little coverage along the south leg of the route that passes through a relatively inaccessible private industrial estate. Of the 11 hours of footage, 69.8% of the footage was of urban sections of the race, while 30.2% was of countryside and park areas. While we might expect the start and finish lines to be popular viewpoints, they received little coverage at 2.5% and 5.1% respectively, perhaps because they are crowded with runners and officials.

Spectators discussed their own "starting location", or the point on the marathon route that they chose to begin spectating. Reasons for selecting a starting location were varied. Half of the interviewed participants commented on the fact that they chose their starting location as being conveniently close to where they live. Other participants appeared to choose their location either based on prior knowledge of good vantage points, e.g. "*we stood near the west entrance…my brother was running and that's where I stood last year to see him*", or based on being in search of a good atmosphere, e.g. "*The embankment, the start line, we thought it was the busiest…the more exciting, where all the atmosphere was…a good place to spot people.*"

While some spectators tended to remain in a single location for the duration of their spectating, particularly the pairs and the family group who remained in the relatively pleasant environs of the park, others moved to a new location during the event. Some spectators commented that they changed location in order to capture a variety of footage; one spectator noted how they stayed on "*[ ] mainly…different sides of the road, different angles…We ended up at the finish line eventually. But that was later.*" Another spectator stated how they slowly walked alongside the route: "*Started from the station, followed the marathon down the river… arrived at the finish line. Stayed at the finish line for a while…then walked back along the river… I went quite late, so I tried to… not film the best ones, but the last ones in a way.*"

Coverage of tags

We now turn our attention to the coverage of tagging. Of the 412 videos captured, 212 were explicitly tagged with runner numbers at least once. Spectators entered 3108 live-tags in total, generating on average 164 tags each, with one prolific spectator managing 561 during the event, while conversely two of the spectators managed less than 10. 2140 distinct runner numbers were entered, of which 1805 exist in the official results. 25% of all runners taking part in the marathon were tagged at least once, and of these runners spectators generated an average of 1.4 tags of each.

Video content

According to the tags generated during our post-hoc tagging exercise, 10.8% of our corpus was footage of very dense periods of runners passing, 34.6% was of 'many' runners; 32.9% was of an average number of runners, and 19.2% was of areas of the course with sparse numbers of runners. 72.1% of the video was footage that also included other spectators, while only 1.3% was of the scenery, and wider environment around the race, rather than of the race itself. As shown in figure 4 the most sparsely populated footage is of the fastest and slowest racers, whilst the denser footage is from around the start line or featuring the majority of middle-speed racers. This allows us to filter the footage to show just professional runners, or instead just the main body of fun runners.

Some tags and videos appear to be outside of the normal envelope, for example near the start line and more than half an hour after the official start. A closer look at the videos in this cluster reveals that these tags correspond to children participating in the 2.5km-long mini-marathon, which started later, from the same location. When comparing the official results for the mini-marathon and the half-marathon, it appears that bib numbers are not unique between races and that these tags have been erroneously attributed to adult runners. Similarly a cluster of videos past the finish line, and after the apparent finish time, show how spectators have captured videos of runners cooling down after the race. Interestingly, one of the spectators spoke about filming these aspects of the race other than runners just passing by "*I did enjoy the social aspects which I could film at the finish line…people who had arrived, who had their families, who were laying down near the river. I enjoyed all the atmosphere of an event, a happy event.*"

Unsurprisingly, spectators reported that it was difficult to tag all runners in shot when the race was at is most densely packed. They therefore developed strategies for prioritizing: "*I tried to tag some people, especially ones…that were very happy, or were interacting with other people, some were wearing really funny clothes.*" Some spoke about runners who stood out as warranting tagging" "*People with fancy dresses, like Robin Hood, like Santa Claus. Other people were dressed up like hospital doctors.*"

Our collection of free-text post-tags provided more specific and descriptive labels, referring to notable features such as types of scenery – "lake", "grass section", features of individual runners – "green wig", "sickbed on wheels", "pace setter", or elements surround the race – "police", "background music", "balloons".

Camera-work and video quality

According to our post-hoc analysis, 87% or 9.5 hours of footage comprised close range shots taken from a vantage point immediately adjacent to the course, while only 7% was from a distance. Both of these, however, included mixed quality footage. 6.8% was considered 'non-footage' captured accidentally, often of spectators feet or the inside of pockets. A further 2.4% was considered blurry footage. From the free-tagged footage, a total of 5% of the footage was tagged as 'shaky', and 4.5%, was tagged as being considered unusable 'Junk footage'. Interestingly, one spectator consistently produced this junk footage.

The vast majority of the footage, 83.1%, was still-shot footage where the spectator was (shakiness aside) keeping the camera focused in a fixed direction. Combined, 70.8% was both still shot and close range footage of the race. Only

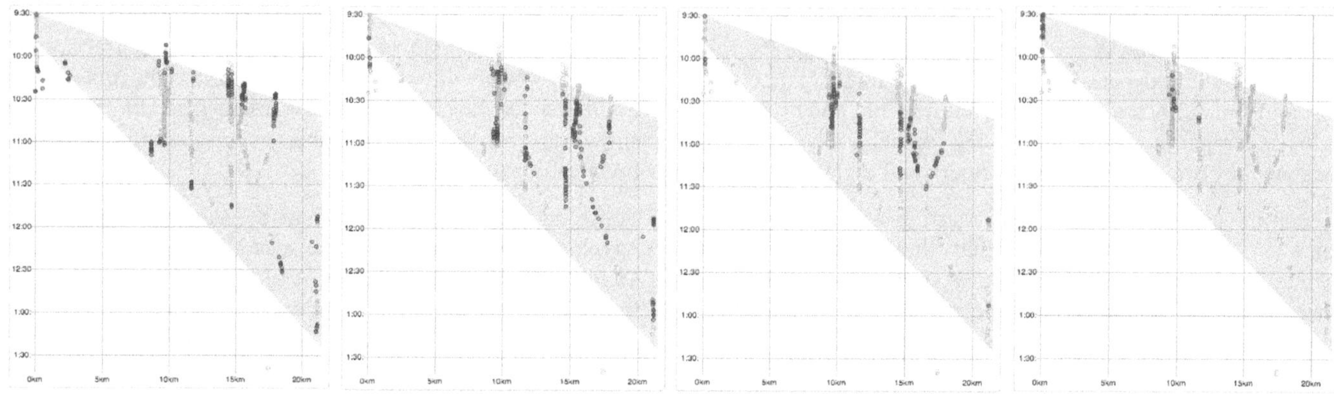

Figure 4: Videos of the race that included (from left to right): sparse, average, many, and dense populations of runners

5.9% of the footage appeared to be tracking specific targets (classified as a 'tracking shot'). 10.4% of the footage was captured while the spectator was walking alongside the route whilst filming. One spectator described their strategy for choosing how to film - to treat the event as if they were recording official race footage. They said, "*I was thinking as a professional video man. I was trying to make as many different recordings as possible from different angles and different points of view, just to have a variety of footage.*"

Inappropriate videos

Given the uncontrolled nature of the filming, some potentially inappropriate footage was recorded and highlighted with post-tagging. In our dataset, 8 tags were assigned using the word 'toilet', and highlight runners entering the toilets adjacent to the course. 31 segments of video were also tagged as featuring 'children', while only 4 were of the children's race itself. Some videos also clearly show car registration plates driving behavior, and audio of a phone call captured from the companion of one spectator.

Similarly, the video contained footage that runners or spectator might potentially prefer not be published. 3 post-tags were used to tag tired runners. Similarly tags like 'Slow Coaches' and 'Really slow people' were used. Others include footage of 'cramp' and 'encouragement of a failing'. Some tags may be inconsiderate, such as 'ridiculous shorts'. One spectator highlighted the unnatural feeling of videoing and live-tagging strangers in public, "*Pulling out a phone and shooting video in public, really not my thing...you could feel quite self conscious about it.*", however this contrasts with our observations of spectators filming the event in order to capture friends and family.

Creating video stories of the race

We now drill deeper into our data to show how it is possible to search the corpus in order to reveal stories of individual runners or of the event as a whole.

We begin by using our visualization to demonstrate how we might tell the story of a typical runner. In figure 5 we have isolated the trajectory of one runner, bib number 1134, who was live-tagged on 4 occasions by our spectators. We used this to cue up a video playlist of the specific times within these videos at which they had been tagged. Figure 6 (top left) shows that the runner, wearing an orange top, is clearly visible as the videos play out. Next, we can extract other videos that intersect this runner's traectory, but in which they were not explicitly tagged. Inspecting these *implicated* videos reveals that the runner is clearly visible in four of them, for example as shown in figure 6 (top right), including a video where the density of runners was far too great for our spectators to tag all of those passing by, and runner 1134 is only partially visible in the shot, but recognizable by their orange top. In total, we have extracted a playlist of 8 videos of runner 1134, each with a segment showing them entering and running through the shot.

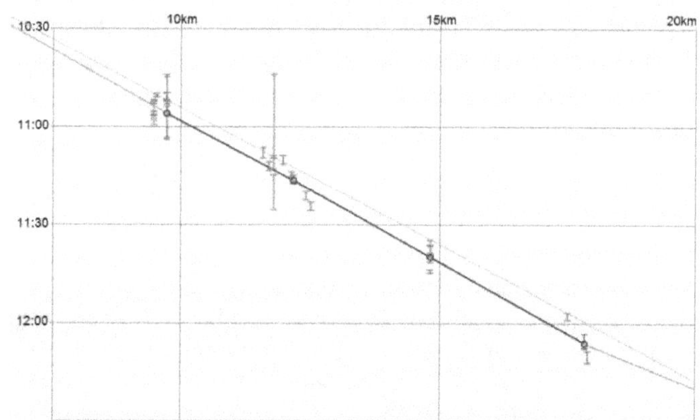

Figure 5: Visualizing the progress of runner 1134

Next we use a combination of live-tags and post-tags to construct a story of one of the many costumed fun runners taking part in the race (often running for charity). Runner 2574 shown in figure 6 (lower left) is dressed as the children's television character "cookie monster" and has been live-tagged in 3 times in our corpus. However, their highly visible costume has also resulted with them being further post-tagged multiple times as "cookie monster" and also with the more general "costume" and "fun runner" tags. These tags allow us to identify 6 more videos in which the same runner can be seen.

Finally, we use our tags to create playlists of videos that tell broader stories of the marathon as an event, rather than

Figure 6: (top left) Videos of runner 1134 explicitly tagged (top right) identified by trajectory (lower left) cookie monster by tag (lower middle) by bib number (lower right) Robin Hoods in costume

focusing on an individual runner. Many runners dressed as the popular hero Robin Hood. The collection of post-tags contains 60 tags of Robin Hood across all videos, allowing us to create playlist highlighting this unique feature of the race from a larger set of runners (e.g., figure 6, lower right).

Spectating and filming

We end by drawing on the interviews with spectators to understand some key aspects of their experience, both as spectators of the marathon, and as active spectators engaged in using RunSpotRun.

Live-tagging of runners' bib numbers at such a high-density event produced some interesting user feedback. One spectator noted *"It was hard sometimes, if you were trying to read numbers on the vest... whilst typing at the same time. You didn't have time to concentrate as much on the runners,"* similarly, another participant said *"They were just such a big crowd, very close to each other...I keyed in as many numbers as possible"*. The family group acted as a team to collaboratively tag, with one member reading out the runner numbers as they passed, while another typed the numbers in while filming. One spectator indicated how the density of runners made them select a certain filming and tagging strategy; *"When we eventually went from a trickle of people to thousands of people, non stop....it made more sense to pick a spot, turn on the broadcasting...and occasionally tag when I could."*

Spectators did not spend the entirety of their time filming, and this is revealed by the data. However RunSpotRun did have some impact on the normal spectator experience, with one spectator noting how using the mobile phone affected their ability to clap runners along, "*Because I'm holding the phone in my hands, I can't do anything else...you cannot clap and do anything*". Another similarly noted that their obligations as a spectating friend took priority over using the application, in that when they did see a runner they knew they clapped and cheered rather than tagged the runner, and when they had passed were unable to then tag them as their number was only visible from the front, despite having videoed them. Spectators provided important insights into the difficulty of attempting to spot a particular runner in the crowd. One spectator stated "*you were very much sort of looking for that person, that made you stop recording and tagging everyone – you kind of just thought, well I'll wait and see if I can see this person coming.*"

Conversely, spectators commented on the potential value of the corpus of videos as a motivation for engaging with the application. One spectator commented *"It was a really good atmosphere, I'm really glad I took part. It's just a really good experience...if I tag a lot of people, maybe they can log in somewhere... and have their own little video of them running the marathon."* Similarly, another spectator said, *"I think if we could use this properly, they can get more photos of themselves, and that could be a very good thing."* Finally, a spectator commented that they introduced their own element of competition into the tagging activity - *"it was to try and beat other people that motivated me."*

DISCUSSION

Our findings suggest that the approach of crowdsourcing videos at a marathon is feasible. Even a small proportion of spectators were able to film and tag a good proportion of runners (though many were not tagged). Our corpus showed good temporal coverage but more patchy geographic coverage. Many of the videos were deemed to be of a usable quality and we have shown that it is possible to mine the corpus to extract stories of individuals and the wider race. We saw how spectators naturally cluster around key areas, including loops and switchbacks that afford good vantage points for capturing the race. We revealed that while they are able to film and tag spectators, this becomes difficult when the race is crowded and when they need to clap and cheer people they know (who may be key targets). We now consider how this approach can enable various forms of storytelling and the challenges of going public.

Enabling Storytelling

The associated metadata generated by our spectators and our tagging exercises makes this video material inherently searchable and therefore open to flexible future uses. Our visualizations and resulting playlists of video segments are generated from a corpus of data that is searchable by runner, spectator, location, time and tags, and we have seen that the video content is of sufficient quality and detail that it is possible to drill into the corpus to extract several videos of particular runners that can be used to begin to tell individual and broader stories of the marathon experience.

This approach could extend existing television broadcasting approaches by providing complementary, concurrent and navigable footage. For example, broadcasters might draw on this material during a TV broadcast, or as part of a "red button" (interactive UK digital television) service or companion application that allows viewers to explore it for themselves. Similarly our ad-hoc individual runner stories could sit alongside official finish-line photography that also allows imagery and footage to be identified by runner number. However, we also note the potential for online and social media, where people could search out clips of themselves or chosen runners and construct short individual video montages as souvenirs of the marathon experience. Many runners participate to raise money for charity, and ultimately generating documentary videos may form a key support and possibly important motivator of this activity.

Improving coverage

However, future applications such as these may require greater coverage, especially of runners, but perhaps also geographically. We might assume a larger number of spectators using RunSpotRun would equate to an equivalent increase in coverage of a race. However, our study suggests that this cannot be taken for granted, as spectators tend to gather around certain locations, and factors such as the density of runners at any given point affects tagging activity, and our subsequent ability to explore the corpus. One implication is that we need to investigate techniques to optimize and balance coverage along the route.

Strategies might include directing spectators using messaging, or encouraging them to tag in particularly niche locations using gamification. It may also be the case that spectators tend to congregate at vantage points that lend themselves to particularly interesting footage, and instead resources should be concentrated at these points to maximize the available footage. Our study suggests that it may help to be able to profile the spectators so as to understand their preferred behavior better, for example a family spectating the marathon may stay in a park environment that is convenient for travelling to the event, whereas a singleton who sees themselves more as a dedicated camera operator may be more willing to move.

Overall we have found that our video corpus largely consists of usable and engaging footage, however this is intermittently compromised by errors in camera work from filming the floor or towards the sun, or with a finger in the shot, and also with appropriately captured but inappropriate content. Here there are challenges at many levels both individually and across all spectators, for example in how to train spectators on the fly in basic camera work to capture default wide and tracking shots, and capturing a broad range of footage that covers the race in progress, shots of the pre-race build up, post-finish line celebrations, and the associated mini-marathon. This might be enabled by reward structures that favour high quality or desired footage, or even high-level orchestration by a professional director.

Finally, we need to ensure that capturing and tagging integrates with the normal spectator experience, adding to the experience during downtime rather than detracting from it at key moments. Again this may depend on who spectators are and their motivations for attending the event, but the most obvious issue that we have observed is the tension between cheering and applauding whilst filming, ironically of runners that spectators are most interested in. Our study suggests that the system could be used to scaffold the normal spectator activity, perhaps by making use of incoming tags from further up the course and our understanding of the expected trajectory of a runner to give an indication that a particular runner might be expected to be visible in a certain time frame. Our interface might include more detailed runner profiles, or hot-keys that allow easy tagging of predicted runners when they are eventually seen, or to include photographs akin to a "spotters guide".

Going Public

While deploying RunSpotRun at scale, perhaps involving hundreds of the many spectators present, might deliver greatly enhanced video coverage, there are a number of further challenges that need to be met to realize this.

Motivation

The spectators who took part in our study may have been highly motivated to engage with the capture and tagging activity due to the fact that they were explicitly asked to do so. We are aware that the majority of normal spectators at the marathon may be less so, and are likely to behave differently; as with all crowdsourcing activities there is a significant challenge in understanding how to motivate a large number of participants.

One solution may lie in social media, and in making the capturing activity a social and collaborative task by having runners solicit spectators in capturing video of them by indicating in advance why they will be running and what they will be wearing. Spectators may be willing to engage with activity due to their involvement or engagement with the event and its participants for purely intrinsic reasons [1], however it is important to do so without taking them away from the default spectating experience [7]. Previous research [2][26] on tagging multimedia collections has identified that one category of motivation is "social organisation", that individuals may be happy to take the time to tag because it helps to enrich and document the mutual experience so it can be more easily shared. Another solution may lie in the fact that many runners take part in marathons to raise money for charity, and capturing video might even become tied into charitable giving. However, a more realistic view might be to consider a stratified approach in which many spectators film a little, perhaps looking for family members or other key individuals, while a few might be motivated to film much more extensively.

Indexing the video corpus

There are further challenges regarding our capturing and tagging methodology. As above, we might attempt to automatically detect and reduce instances of poor quality, for example by detecting shaky or blurred shots, or more proactively directing shots to avoid duplicate content [17]. Our visualization interface helps to identify and remove some obvious errors, such as the reuse of runner numbers in the children's race, however further development of the mobile interface could also help prevent other keying errors. We also recognize the significant potential to integrate the tagging data with other existing runner tracking systems, for example RFID gates and self-logged runner GPS data. While we saw no evidence that the live-tagging interface adversely affected the quality of the footage, in the longer term image-processing technologies bring the potential to automatically tag runners, both live and post-hoc. However, the crowded nature of races may make this a challenge for automated systems (as for humans) and an outcome of our study is a dataset that can help drive forward the development of such approaches.

The addition of rich post-tagging of the video corpus may require a different approach to operate at scale with many hours more footage than we tagged in our study. Again, a computer vision approach could aid some aspects such as classifying the density of runners and quality of camera work. However, a useful and complementary approach may lie in crowdsourcing. We have seen how it is possible to predict videos in which runners may appear from estimates of their race trajectories. This suggests extending our post-tagging interface to enable online viewers to not only search for videos of specific runners, but also to retag them when they find them. In turn, further tagging might improve estimated trajectories and so make it easier to predict likely videos, which in turn would drive further tagging. However, any approach that opens up the corpus to a wider audience must be sensitively structured to take account of issues of consent and to deal with undesirable footage, perhaps by requiring runners to specifically opt into being tagged themselves in advance, or approving content.

Direction and Slow Search

One final discussion point concerns a potential longer-tem consequence of success. If we solve the problems of large-scale motivation and tagging by many spectators then we could potentially generate very large corpuses of video. A particular challenge in the future may arise from flooding mobile networks with data, especially at crowded public events where an unusually large number of people occupy a small number of mobile network cells. The ability to upload video would be severely compromised. A potential solution may be to continue with our strategy of transmitting meta-data (tags, locations) as near to real time as possible in order to support direction of capture, social coordination and motivational activities, but to intelligently upload videos selectively with a view to minimizing network congestion, to provide an engaging online view.

The rapid publishing of metadata followed by actual videos sometime later, opens up a novel space of possibilities for constructing slow-search [25] viewing interfaces. We might enable online viewers to search for footage of particular runners based on the currently available metadata and show estimates of when the actual videos might be available if they are prepared to wait for them to be uploaded. Indeed, upload of selected videos might be prioritized or negotiated based on demand – who wants them when – or coverage – if they are of unusual or sparsely covered locations.

CONCLUSIONS

We have explored the use of a prototype video crowdsourcing system to provide a rich corpus of videos that document a marathon race. Our methodology has shown that a small number of spectators acting freely around the marathon route can capture a significant amount of video and also concurrently index it with tags. Further post-tagging and inspection of the video corpus has subsequently allowed us to extract and construct short video souvenirs of individual runners and the broader event. We conclude that our approach is promising, but we have also highlighted specific challenges that remain, particularly regarding how RunSpotRun can be deployed to large numbers of spectators. We believe that our approach is also applicable to other sporting events that involve crowds of spectators lining a linear, geographically distributed course, for example cycling or rallying events, and perhaps to other kinds of public events beyond these.

ACKNOWLEDGMENTS

We gratefully acknowledge the support of the Horizon Centre for Doctoral Training (EP/G037574/1). This work was also supported by a Google Research Award.

REFERENCES

1. Ames, M., Eckles, D., Naaman, M., Spasojevic, M., and House, N. 2010. Requirements for mobile photoware. Personal Ubiquitous Computing.14, 2, 95-109
2. Ames, M. and Naaman, M., 2007. Why we tag. In Proc. Of CHI '07. ACM, NY.
3. Bartindale, T., Hook, J., and Olivier, P. 2009. Media Crate: tangible live media production interface. In Proc of TEI '09. ACM, New York, NY, USA, 255-262.
4. Ben-Ami, I., Basha, T. and Avidan, S., 2012. Racing Bib Numbers Recognition. In Proc of British Machine Vision Conference 2012. 19.1-19.10.
5. Curmi, F., et al. 2013. HeartLink: open broadcast of live biometric data to social networks. In Proc. of CHI '13. ACM, New York, NY, USA, 1749-1758
6. Durrant, A., et al. 2011. Automics: souvenir generating photoware for theme parks. In Proc. Of CHI. ACM, NY, 1767-1776
7. Engström, A., Perry, M., and Juhlin, O. 2012. Amateur vision and recreational orientation:: creating live video together. In Proc of CSCW '12. ACM, New York, NY, USA, 651-660
8. Esbjörnsson, M. et al., 2006. Watching the cars go round and round. In Proc. Of CHI '06. ACM, NY.
9. Jacucci, G. et al., 2007. Comedia. In Proc. Of CHI '07 ACM, NY.
10. Juhlin, O., Engström, A. and Reponen, E., 2010. Mobile broadcasting: the whats and hows of live video as a social medium. In Proc. of MobileHCI '10. ACM, NY
11. Kennedy, L. and Naaman, M.. 2009. Less talk, more rock: automated organization of community-contributed collections of concert videos. In Proc of WWW '09. ACM, New York, NY, USA, 311-320.
12. Laibowitz, M.,et al. 2010. Multimedia content creation using societal-scale ubiquitous camera networks and human-centric wearable sensing. In Proc. of Multimedia '10. ACM, New York, NY, USA, 571-580
13. Ludvigsen, M. and Veerasawmy, R., 2010. Designing technology for active spectator experiences at sporting events. In Proc. of OZCHI '10. ACM, NY
14. Nottingham Evening Post Article. 2012. http://www.nottinghampost.com/guide-Nottingham-s-Robin-Hood-Half-Marathon/story-17004302-detail/story.html
15. Nottingham Marathon Results. 2013. http://robinhoodhalfmarathon.co.uk/
16. Radiohead Prague. 2009. http://radiohead-prague.nataly.fr/. Retrieved 09/14
17. De Sá, M., Shamma, D., and Churchill, E. 2014. Live mobile collaboration for video production: design, guidelines, and requirements. Personal Ubiquitous Computing. 18, 3 (March 2014), 693-707.
18. Salovaara, et al. 2006. Collective creation and sense-making of mobile media. In Proc. of CHI '06. ACM, NY, 1211-1220
19. Shrestha, P., et al 2010. Automatic mashup generation from multiple-camera concert recordings. In Proc. of Multimedia '10. ACM, New York, NY, USA, 541-550.
20. SiSLive, 2011. Case Study: London Marathon 2012, Available at: http://www.sislive.tv/case-studies/LondonMarathon.pdf
21. Sniderman, Z., 2011. New York Marathon Runners Getting Digital Love from RFID Chips. 28/10/2011. Available at: http://mashable.com/2011/10/27/marathon-runners-rfid-chips/
22. Snoek, C., et al. 2010. Crowdsourcing rock n' roll multimedia retrieval. In Proc. of Multimedia '10. ACM, New York, NY, USA, 1535-1538
23. Sundaram, H. and Campbell, M., 2008. Event Mining in Multimedia Streams. Proceedings of the IEEE, 96(4), pp.623–647.
24. Swedberg, C., 2011. New York City Marathon Offers Enhanced RFID-enabled Apps. RFID Journal.
25. Teevan, J., Collins-Thompson, K., White, R., and Dumais, S. 2014. Slow search. *Commun. ACM* 57, 8 (August 2014), 36-38.
26. Van Velsen, L. and Melenhorst, M. 2009. Incorporating user motivations to design for video tagging. Interacting with Computers, 21(3), pp.221–228
27. Vihavainen, S., et al. 2011. We want more: human-computer collaboration in mobile social video remixing of music concerts. In Proc of CHI '11. ACM, New York, NY, USA, 287-296

Crowdsourcing Synchronous Spectator Support: (go on, go on, you're the best)$^{n-1}$

Franco Curmi
HighWire DTC,
Lancaster University,
Lancaster,
United Kingdom
f.curmi@lancaster.ac.uk

Maria Angela Ferrario
Lancaster University
Management School,
Lancaster University,
Lancaster,
United Kingdom
m.a.ferrario@lancaster.ac.uk

Jon Whittle
School of Computing
and Communications,
Lancaster University,
Lancaster,
United Kingdom
j.n.whittle@lancaster.ac.uk

Florian 'Floyd' Mueller
Exertion Games Lab,
RMIT University,
Melbourne,
Australia
floyd@exertiongameslab.org

ABSTRACT

Many studies have shown that crowd-support, such as cheering during sport events, can have a positive impact on athletes' performance. However, up until recently this support was only possible if the supporters and the athletes were geographically co-located. Can cheering be done remotely and would this be effective? In this paper we investigate the effect and possibilities of live remote cheering on co-located athletes and online supporting crowds that have a weak social tie and no social tie with the athlete. We recruit 140 online spectators and 5 athletes for an ad-hoc 5km road race. Results indicate that crowds socially closer to the athletes are significantly more engaged in the support. The athletes were excited by live remote cheering from friendsourced spectators and cheering from unknown crowdsourced participants indicating that remote friends and outsourced spectators could be an important source of support.

Author Keywords

Crowdsourcing; Friendsourcing; Spectator Support; Social Networks; Sports; Spectators; Broadcast; Cheering; Human Behavior.

ACM Classification Keywords

H.5.m. [**Information interfaces and presentation**]: Miscellaneous; H.5.3 [**Group and organizational interfaces**]: Synchronous interaction; J.4 [**Social and behavioral science**]: Psychology

INTRODUCTION

The Facebook 'Like' button was a revolutionary tool in digitizing a tiny yet significant piece of human communication within social networks. Receiving 'Likes' can have a positive effect on the emotions of the social network user receiving them and in the context of behavior change, this is often used as a source of motivation for people trying to attain new goals [18]. However while this type of support is very applicable in scenarios of behavior change that have longitudinal measures [24, 27], such as in motivating persons who are trying to become more physically fit [9] or cease smoking [25], it might not be as practical for situations where motivation is needed in real-time and in sync with the activity that is being conducted such as cheering athletes during a race. Current social networks were primarily designed for asynchronous communication. While this has many advantages, for instance, the message receivers do not need to be online to receive the messages, it may be inapt for situations where support from one's network needs to be in sync with its demand. Currently, athletes who share information about their events through online social networks, often receive encouraging 'Likes' and posts in support. However, athletes typically see these posts only when the activity is completed. Consequently, any motivation created through the perceived social value of accumulating 'Likes', does not translate into support during the activity and has no influence on the outcome.

To start exploring synchronous social network support we use sports. Sports was chosen because many studies have already showed that cheering co-located spectators (e.g. on a race course) can have a direct impact on the performance of the athletes [8, 14]; but can this be done remotely? This could have a huge impact yet there has been negligible HCI or CSCW work that explores ways of digitizing synchronous crowd support in this context. Possible benefits may include 1) allowing fans that don't afford to be physically present at the event's location to support the athlete, 2) allowing non-famous athletes to recruit support from their personal social networks or 3) potentially harnessing the support from globally crowdsourced participants through platforms like Amazon Mechanical Turk. Is this support possible and does the nature of the online crowd matter? Put in another way, are athletes more motivated by friends or is the support of strangers just as effective, if any?

CHI 2015, April 18 - 23 2015, Seoul, Republic of Korea Copyright is held by the owner/author(s). Publication rights licensed to ACM. ACM 978-1-4503-3145-6/15/04...$15.00 http://dx.doi.org/10.1145/2702123.2702338.

We implement a system where long distance runners broadcast location and heart rate data to online spectators. The spectators can then cheer the athletes by pressing a 'Cheer' button. This sends an immediate alert to the selected athletes thus making the athletes aware that a crowd is following their activity. In the study we use a crowd made up of two groups. 1) Friendsourced volunteers. Based on Bernstein et al.'s proposition, we express friendsourcing as "collecting resources from a socially-connected group of individuals" [6]. 2) A paid crowd that was recruited through Crowdflower; a crowdsourcing platform. We then analyzed the effects on both spectator groups and the athletes (being cheered on).

The data showed that friendsourced participants were more engaged with the system than outsourced spectators. We found that the athletes showed mild excitement when receiving real-time haptic and audible cheers but were particularly excited by knowing the number of cheers submitted and the number of people following the activity (logged in and not necessarily cheering) during the event.

RELATED WORK

Up until a few years ago an athlete's performance was often broadcast only if the athlete was famous enough to merit television broadcast. In recent years as social networks became increasingly ubiquitous it became possible for almost any athlete with Internet access, to broadcast their participation in sport events. Freely available mobile applications like Runkeeper, Runtastic and Azumio allow users to share locative and physiological data, with selected friends or even publicly. These commercial implementations were preceded by a number of studies within academia that studied the effect on the athletes and spectators when sharing real-time data during sport events [17, 19, 23]. Sport applications such as Runtastic more recently implemented feedback features by which athletes can not only share live data but also receive live cheers from friends during the activity. After the event, the athletes can then look into who sent them cheers over a web interface. These commercial applications however do not provide much scientific insight on the social network effect of sharing live data and the impact that real-time spectator-support may have on athletes, if any.

Curmi et al. explored work in the area of real-time spectator support in 2012 through the HeartLink project [11]. In this work athletes shared heart rate data online and friends encouraged the athletes remotely. The HeartLink project consisted of two pilot studies and focused on the design and implementation of such systems. The study presented here follows the recommendations for future work that was suggested in this work namely: A) A need to validate results with a larger population. Thus spectator population was increased from 9 to 140. B) Test a new fully independent system (BioShare) and observe whether HeartLink's outcomes were influenced by issues raised from relying on distributed 3rd party systems. C) More importantly, compare and contrast the engagement of friends vs. unknown crowds by having different groups under observation concurrently. Additionally, we observe whether spectators are influenced by the social connectedness between the person cheering and the participant receiving the cheers. We also explore the effect on the athletes from being remotely cheered and whether the nature of the online cheering crowd matters - are athletes more motivated when supported by known crowds in contrast to unknown crowds?

Supporting crowds that are made up of unknown spectators are typical in sport events. On the other hand, the use of crowdsourced participants for user support is also not new and in recent years, through online crowdsourcing platforms, many innovative applications were developed such as summarizing academic papers [5] or deciphering blurred text [21]. But can crowd support and crowdsourcing be combined effectively in a real-time context?

Real-time Factor

The real-time context is particularly challenging in crowdsourcing. Most crowdsourcing platforms are not designed for recruiting workers as a just-in-time workforce. Typical crowdsourced jobs, such as online surveys, are posted on crowdsourcing platforms and workers would complete the tasks when they please. In the cheering case however, the support has to happen at a specific time and workers have to 'sync' with the event rather then vice versa. Related work is found in studies on crowd-powered interfaces with highly innovative techniques for crowdsourcing just-in-time work such as VizWiz - a system for crowdsourcing near real-time support for vision impaired [7], Lasecki et al.'s ingenious work for captioning live speech [20] and Bernstein et al.'s work on queuing workers using multiple queuing models [4]. However, with the exception of Morris et al.'s work on 'Crowdsourcing Collective Emotional Intelligence' [22], there is very little knowledge on crowdsourcing spectator support.

STUDY DESIGN

In the initial stages of the study that is presented in this paper, two design approaches for digitizing cheering during sport event were considered. The first was that of studying current cheering practices ethnographically and then finding ways to replicate as best as we can the cheering process digitally. The second was that of identifying radically new ways by focusing on the core objective (i.e. motivating the athletes) and designing new systems around this. While both approaches are pertinent, the second approach was adopted. In the first approach it is more likely to omit possible radical new ways of reaching equal or better outcomes for supporting the athletes. Through emerging digital tools, new approaches to cheering might now be possible but are not present in the 'traditional' co-located cheering processes. Consequently design started with a bottom up approach and a series of tests with different prototype configurations.

The preliminary tests were conducted during a range of events that included running, mountain running and cycling, and were intended to 1) test the data broadcasting system, 2) explore the study dynamics within simpler scenarios than those described in this paper and 3) gather insights on the user experience of both the athlete and the spectators. The insights gained from these pretests were then used to develop the research questions and the design of the exploratory deployment here described.

For this study we organized an ad-hoc 5 km race with co-located athletes and an online crowd of spectators. The race selection was based such that there will be enough time for the spectators to log in and understand the interface while at the same time make sure the race was not too long, so as not to increase the complexity of managing the online crowd. Additionally, the selection of the race course ensured that the event would have mobile network coverage on a selected service provider for at least 70% of the course.

Data sharing infrastructure

The data broadcast system was implemented using BioShare [10]. BioShare is an open source application that was designed for broadcasting data during day-to-day activities through a smartphone app and a web portal for visualizing the broadcasted data in real-time. The mobile application runs on Android devices and allows users to collect data through Bluetooth-connected sensors. This data is then shared with an online crowd that can interact with the data-sharing users through multiple modalities.

BioShare was specifically designed for researchers and as such, it also logs user interaction for post event analysis. The system was configured as illustrated in Figure 1. We re-configured the default settings in BioShare such that data is broadcast to those who log through a login process that will be described in the next sections.

In the pre-event tests we found that during synchronous studies that involve online crowds, a communication channel between the researchers and the crowd is essential. The real-time factor makes this work challenging particularly because it is difficult to predict all possible failure modes in such live activities at design stage. Additionally, unlike an in-the-lab study, the researchers have very limited feedback on what is happening within the distributed crowd (and no feedback from facial expressions and body language that may help in adjusting the study accordingly). In this light, a feature that allowed the researchers to broadcast messages on the spectators' interface was also implemented. This was used to inform the spectators of any technical issues that might occur during the live event.

Athlete Participants

We recruited 5 athletes form a university running club who 1) were happy to participate in the study, 2) train regularly for competitive running and 3) had a detailed log of performance records in 5k races. In return of participating, a

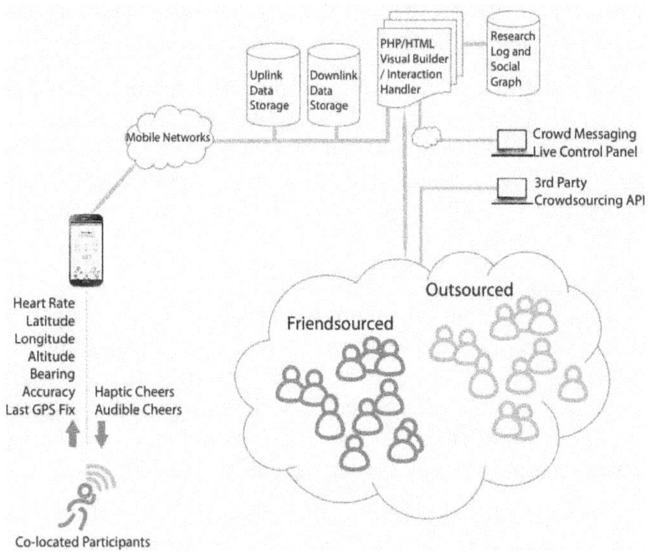

Figure 1: The system infrastructure.

donation was given to the running club. The researchers did not know the athletes prior to this work and met them for the first time just before the race. None of the participants had used smart phones or any other device to track their performance during previous races so the participants had little predefined expectations of the technology or the user experience of carrying extra devices during the event.

Before starting the race the athletes were each given a Nexus 5 phone that was preconfigured with the customized BioShare application, an armband, a mobile data connection and a Polar WearLink heart rate chest strap that was connected to the phones via Bluetooth. The heart rate data type was used as it is a physiological parameter that is easy to measure in unobtrusive ways and because heart-rate measuring sensors are becoming very popular in emerging smartphones and wearable devices. Additionally the heart rate can indicate the fitness levels of individuals and the effort exerted during an activity. To ensure consistency, the phones were preconfigured and positioned by the researchers. The armbands were color-coded and this coding was used for identification of the participants on location.

Crowd Participants

In parallel with recruiting the athletes, 140 online spectators were recruited for the live event. 76 of these participants were recruited from CrowdFlower - an online crowd-sourcing platform with a global distribution of active workers. Unlike Amazon Mechanical Turk, CrowdFlower supports European requestors at the time of writing. Crowdsourcing through an independent platform minimized the probability of having participants within this group that are socially connected with the athletes. These spectators were first introduced to the interface. They were then asked to follow the running athletes online for as long as they wish to and support them in the best way they could. At the end, they were presented with an 8-question survey.

A second group of spectators (n=64) were recruited through social networks at the athletes' university. Communication requesting participants to support the athletes was sent to the athlete's running club Facebook group and their departments' mailing lists. In this paper we refer to this group as 'Friendsourced'.

Procedure

During the event each of the devices carried by the participants collected and broadcasted live data as shown in Figure 2. Online spectators could visualize the live data through any Internet connected web browser after logging in through a Facebook app. The participants were also given the option to log in anonymously.

Following this, spectators were presented with live data visuals from each athlete consisting of heart rate, average heart rate during the event, a line chart with the heart rate, event duration in minutes, percentage of the task completed, meters covered, speed, pace and a chart with the running course overlaid on a map. All the data was dynamically updated every 2 seconds, on average, thus giving a "real-time" feel.

Spectators in both groups could change the athlete that was being followed at any time. This was done to observe how the crowd reacts to different athletes' performance. Just before the race the athletes were assigned as Participant 1 to 5 and this naming was used in the spectators' interface. Thus during the live event, none of the spectators knew who is, say, 'Participant 1'. However, the friendsourced crowd knew that the athletes were from their same department or running club. This approach was adopted to limit the range of tie strength within the group and ethical data sharing issues. In this study we consider these actors as having weak ties [16] with the athletes. The participants who were outsourced through the global crowdsourcing platform were considered as having no ties.

Interaction modality

Spectators could 'Cheer' the selected athlete by clicking a Cheer button. This button sent a small vibration to the device carried by the selected athlete. If the cheering spectator logged in through the Facebook application, then the athlete also heard the name of the person who cheered through the device's speaker and a speech synthesizer; otherwise the athlete heard 'Guest'. The interface presented also allowed all the spectators to post comments through a Facebook frame. By default the posts submitted by the spectators did not go on their personal Facebook profile but were only visible on the spectators' interface. To ensure that the data is not contaminated with crosstalk between the groups, each spectator only saw comments that were posted by those in the same group and following the same athlete.

The data broadcasting app (Figure 3) was designed in such a way that the users do not need to interact with it through

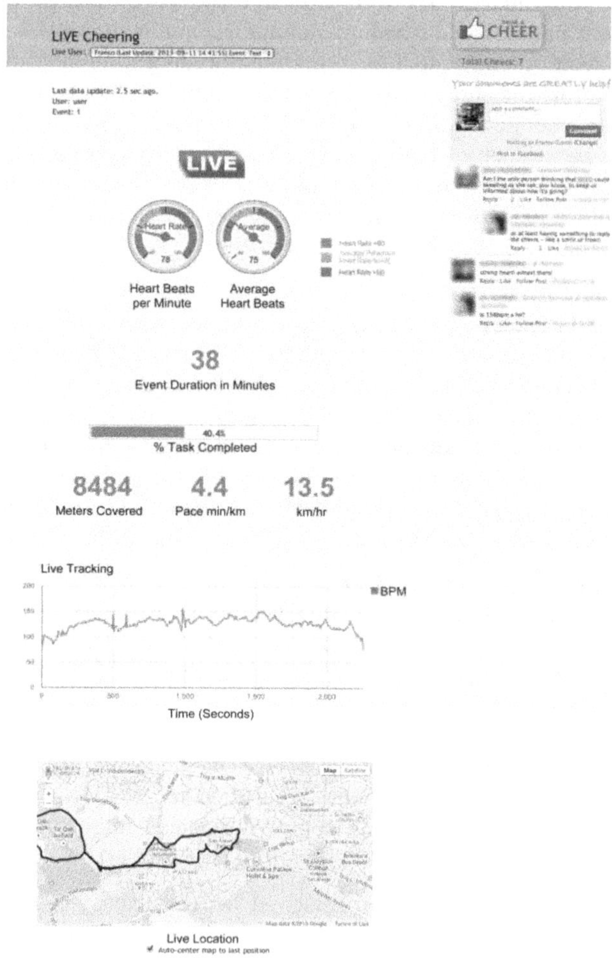

Figure 2: Sample spectator interface.

touch during the activity. Before starting the event, the athletes were briefed on how the system works and what the haptic and audible feedback represents. The pre-event tests showed that the sound level is a key part of the user experience and a too low volume makes understanding difficult while a too high volume, particularly in public areas, makes the system awkward. For health and safety reasons the design intentionally avoided any use of headphones to hear the audible feedback so sound was generated through the device's speaker. At an ambient noise of 70db, the loudness of the devices was set to produce 76db at 30cm for 6db above ambient. 30cm was calculated as the average distance between the sound output of the device inside the armband and the nearest participant's ear. The ambient noise was calculated in pre-event trials using a Phonic audio analyzer PAA3.

Data collection

During the race data was intermittent for 40% of the race due to lack of mobile reception coverage and interference on the Bluetooth communication channels. Any intermitted data was identical for all conditions. The broadcast was time stamped and logged together with the interaction that

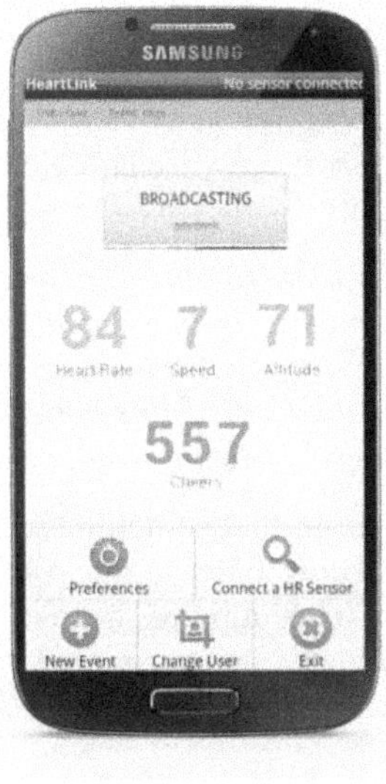

Figure 3: Customized BioShare research application running on athlete's devices.

spectators had with their interface including the cheers submitted, the comments posted and the duration of each participant following the data.

Additionally, when a spectator changed the athlete that was being followed, a modal form containing four questions was presented after 5 seconds. The 5 seconds delay was set to filter out any quick changes in athlete selection. This form collected information on the social network ties among participants, the spectator's age and allowed the spectators to leave comments. Qualitative data was collected from the athletes immediately after the race through a focus group. We felt that a focus group would generate more ideas through cross-pollination among the group in contrast to one-to-one interviews. This post-event focus group was made up of the 5 participating athletes, 3 co-located spectators (2 of these were also members of the

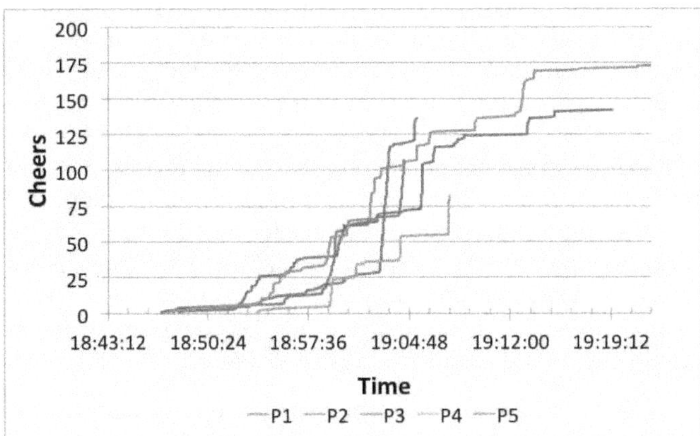

Figure 4: Cumulative live cheers submitted to the athletes.

running club but were injured on the day) and 1 interviewer. In the next section we present insights collected from the study, focusing particularly on the athletes' reactions to the spectator support and the spectators' interaction with the system in terms of the cheers submitted, posts submitted and spectator duration.

FINDINGS

Cheers submitted and crowd duration

The athletes (A) received a total of 727 cheers (A1: 118, A2: 150, A3: 155, A4: 85, A5: 219). Figure 4 represents the distribution of the cheers submitted for each participant. This data shows similar results to previous work [11] where spectators devised strategies to maximize the effectiveness of their cheers. This included holding back from submitting cheers at the beginning to then use the cheers when they feel the athletes need them most. Post event analysis showed that this repetitively resulted in an s-curve cumulative cheering distribution both for individual athletes as well as in aggregate. We note that the spectators had no limit on the number of cheers submitted. Only cheers that were submitted from five minutes before the start of the activity and up to five minutes after the completion of the activity for individual participants are represented in Figure 4. The aggregate number of cheers represented is 645.

Figure 5 shows the time spent online by distribution density for each spectator group. Participants who were friendsourced spent significantly more time on the site (mean 14min. 24sec.; SD 21min. 45sec.) than paid outsourced spectators (mean 7min. 26sec.; SD 8min 48sec). They were also more diverse in engagement then the outsourced spectators.

Post-event focus group with athletes

The insights gained from the post-event focus group complemented this data and contributed to contrast 1) the type of support that was provided (e.g. cheering modalities and motivators wrapping the live cheers), 2) the source of support (e.g. the contrast between the support from friendsourced and outsourced crowds on the participants), and 3) directions for future work in system design. These will be discussed next.

1. Type of support provided

We found that the participants were excited when they received live cheers during the race however other motivational factors that were not intentionally designed emerged during these interviews. Namely, the total number of cheers that each athlete receives and the number of spectators that are currently following their performance live on the portal (even though they might not necessarily cheer) could be a source of motivation. Whenever an athlete (A) arrived at the finish line, the interviewer (I) collected the devices and sensors. The interviewer then informed the arriving athlete the total number of cheers that the athlete received up until then and this resulted in high excitement from the athletes receiving the information. During the race,

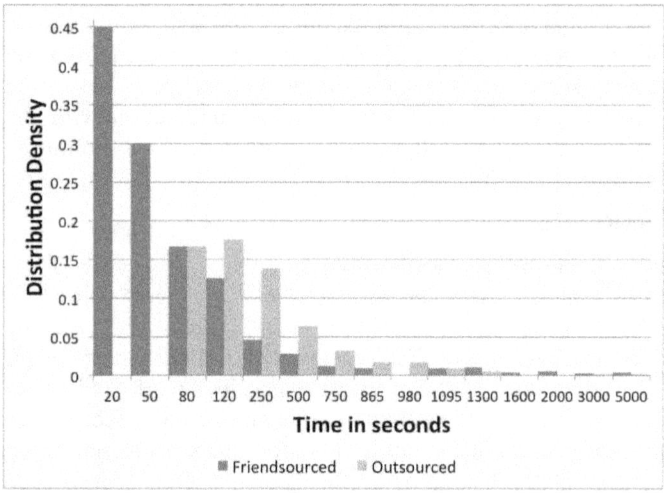

Figure 5: Friendsourced and outsourced crowd duration.

the athletes were only receiving aggregate cheers at a minimum of one vibration every 10 seconds (if cheers were sent within those 10 seconds) but they were not aware of the actual total number of cheers up until that point.

I: yours is 137 cheers.
A2: 137 cheers? all for one persons! 137?
[excitement/laughing] quite a lot.
[A2 some time later; asking A1] Is that the most cheers?
A1 what's the cheer count you've got?...
[later] Co-located spectator 1: how much have you got?
A2: a 137 cheers apparently
Non participating athlete: you're a popular man.
A2: 137? that can't be right; a 137 in all? in total?
I: no no, just for you
A2: just for me? What!
Race Organizer [teasingly]: oh we're getting insane there.
I don't know who said I don't want my arm to be cheered (before the race).

Not only receiving the cheers during the race excited the athletes but even simply getting to know the total number of cheers that were submitted. This, become a matter of competitive comparison more than the race timings themselves. All the participants agreed that the 10 seconds interval was fine otherwise "it might become a bit annoying." [A5]

Asked about the sound level of the devices, during the race the participants felt it was *"all right actually, I could hear the names and that was an all right noise, you don't want it really loud. If there were a lot of people on the way then you might need it a bit louder."* [A2] Three of the participants commented that they did not feel the vibrations. We found that the typical smartphone vibration is not a reliable communication modality when strapped on the arm in a running context. The strength of the haptic feedback was weak particularly since the armbands suppressed the vibrations. The audible feedback, calibrated as listed earlier, proofed to be more reliable in this context.

2. Source of the provided support

The athletes were asked a series of questions that were intended to identify whether the support from people they know was found more relevant then the support that was received from unknown crowds. Three of the athletes agree that both are relevant:

A3: ...it's already nice to know people you know [are there]. A lot of numbers, is like when we go to big races and there are loads of crowds cheering you, and you don't know anyone... we always find this better - that is - with the volume of people there, cheering you on.

R5 partly agrees stating that sometimes it is "*better to have people you don't know cheering... you don't want your mum dominating*". The athletes were not bothered when they heard other athletes being cheered claiming that "*it is how it works in real-life, you hear all cheers around you*" A4.

3. Considerations for future designs

We observe that the athletes' suggestions for future design were particularly focused around new cheering modalities and means of aggregating the collective support. A3 suggests having features that allow the spectators to "*record their name*" as this is expected to communicate emotions better then a text to speech synthesizer. In this case, the athletes are likely to recognize the voices even if names are not narrated. A2 agrees: *"I don't think there is much more you could feel, because anything longer than that could be annoying. ... we though of if people online could record something, say it would come up with their voice, say 'go on go on, you're the best' [clapping - excited] and it is in their voice."* Similar remarks were made by A4 and A5. When we aggregate the suggestions that emerged from the athletes we observe that, unknowingly and indirectly, the athletes were encouraging more synchronous social interaction within the system and from the crowd.

The modality of aggregating and communicating the support seems key for motivating the athletes. During the event the athletes received a haptic and audible cheer at most every 10 seconds if there were any cheers submitted in the previous 10 seconds – irrespective of the number of cheers submitted. The athletes, as quoted in previous sections, positively commented on this as a way of limiting the number of 'alerts'. However, this approach tells the athletes nothing about the number of spectators that are actually cheering. Non-participating athlete A7 suggested varying the sound level of the cheers based on the size of the cheering crowd, *"...say, every 10 seconds if there are more cheers than the previous [10 seconds] you get a louder noise."* This approach would be congruent to the s-curve cheering distribution presented earlier.

A major issue for all the participants except for one was the device form factor, claiming that they would not carry the device during competitive races due to the size and weight that they would have to carry. A3 states *"it has to be a less clunky device for me. I could never run with something as big as that on my arm. I know that you can't at the moment but if you could put it into your Garmin [watch]...".* A4 suggest that a device on the waist would be less annoying than on the arm. Similarly A3 comments: *...people that are racing wouldn't do it; they want as little weight as possible... I really don't like it [carrying that device].* The only athlete who did not mind carrying the device had significantly bigger arms then the other athletes. This suggests that if such technology is designed for mass diffusion, then the size and weight of the device are critical design factors and that the current smartphone form factor is still not small enough for using it during competitive races.

From a spectator-support perspective, all the (competitive) athletes agreed that cheering would be more effective for non-competitive athletes such as the occasional amateur marathon runners "*because they are struggling to finish the race unlike people who train regularly*" and "*knowing that people are supporting you at that moment in time could be a source of encouragement*".

Facebook comments

Figure 6 shows the distribution of posts send by the spectators during the event. Posts can be grouped into those that were directed to the athletes and those directed to the community on the site. The latter were instigated either because of intermittent data or because one or more spectators wanted clarifications on the system itself. The spectators posted a total of 60 comments. 28 comments were posted in the landing page and 32 were posted in the athlete's respective visualizations.

The athletes' demands for increase in social interaction that were exhibited during the focus group were also reflected in the comments posted by the crowd. For example, as athletes proposed that future implementations should allow spectators to send them live or recorded voice messages, many of the spectators were already posting text formatted as if the athlete would hear them, even though the spectators knew that the text messages will not be received by the athletes up until after the race. Posts like "Keep going (you aren't running as fast as you can)!" and "ALMOST THERE!" were typical. We observe that these are quite distinctive from the classical social network posts where athlete's friends often congratulate the athlete upon successfully completing an event - thus using the past tense rather then the present.

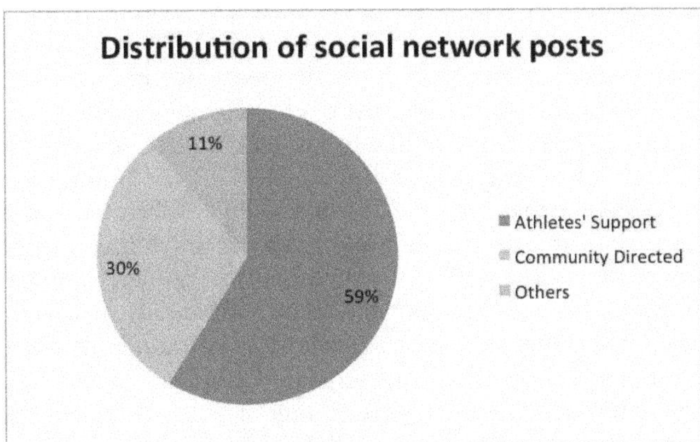

Figure 6: Distribution of social network posts submitted by the spectators.

DISCUSSION AND LESSONS LEARNT

These results have both academic and commercial implications. The design of real-time systems for supporting athletes from remote crowds received negligible attention up until now as little research was done around real-time interaction between co-located and distributed crowds in sport events. We expect that similar studies that involve complex real-time structures will increase in the near future. With the rapidly advancing social networking and communication technologies, the implementation of such systems is becoming more feasible. These results also indicate that real-time spectator support could have high impact for many stakeholders that are directly and indirectly involved in the cheering process. Athletes feel more supported and the cheering process can increase spectator engagement. This process could be very attractive for indirect stakeholders such as marketing strategists who seek tools that facilitate social network diffusion through innovative sports-based communication channels. Additionally, having spectator support that is received 'just-in-time' when it is needed, is expected to augment the social support models that are used on existing social networks. Next we summarize the key lessons learnt around the effect of synchronous spectator support on the athletes, the spectators, and the limitations in the tested design.

Athletes' motivation

The motivation instilled in the athletes through live cheering could be explained through theories of expectations management [1] and self-determination theory (SDT) [13]. In the work presented in this paper, the participants had more online supporters then they expected. This difference between their 'expectations' and 'actual' support, created the excitement that was reported earlier. It will be interesting to analyze if the inverse effect would happen should the athletes not receive any cheering when they are expecting to be cheered. We believe that this would have a negative effect on the athletes that translates into a demotivating factor with similar effect to that of receiving jeers rather then cheers [14].

As regards motivation, sport athletes' 'intrinsic motivation' arises from values within the activity itself - for example, they may enjoy running, or satisfy a need to seek attention, or simply feel physiologically better. The motivators that are not intrinsically part of the activity such as receiving medals or as in the case of this study, receiving 'digital cheers', are 'extrinsic motivators'. Based on the motivational synergy model [2], these can fall in one of two states: 'synergistic' (in which case these support the intrinsic motivators thus augmenting the satisfaction and performance improvement from the intrinsic motivators) or 'non-synergistic' (in which case they undermine the intrinsic motivation). For example an athlete's intrinsic motivation for participating in running events may be attention seeking. In this case, the cheering process presented, is expected to increase the athlete's motivation should this make the athlete aware that an even larger crowd is following the performance. Inversely, the cheering becomes non-synergistic should this distract the athlete from the core intrinsic motivators, say, when the cheering device makes a bothering loud noise in public.

Deci and Ryan provide a more detailed approach to classifying extrinsic motivation over five classifications in the organismic integration theory as a subclass of SDT [26]. In this regard, our observations of the athletes' reactions brings us to highlight the psychological need of '*relatedness*' where through remote cheering the athletes feel connected to others and build a sense of belonging. Further research that looks into how the cheering process can be designed in ways that make this support synergistic to the athlete's intrinsic motivators is needed. Such design must take into account individual personalities and traits as different athletes have different motivators individually, which are different across time.

While paying crowds might not pertain to an applied research perspective, in hindsight, the predicted effectiveness went beyond our expectations. Both groups motivated the athletes (including paid participants) particularly because paid participants could freely cheer any athlete, so the athletes were motivated by the fact that the crowd was cheering 'them' vs. 'others' (rather than whether it was a friend or a paid supporter). It seems that in the proposed model, supporters' pay did not distract the intrinsic motivation of the athletes [12].

Spectators' engagement

The results confirm that the spectators' engagement is influenced by **1) the social tie strength** between the supporter and the athlete. This is not all encompassing and other unaccounted factors may be present. **2)** The **type of data visualized** is also expected to influence engagement as shown in Figure 4. Additionally, when comparing the event discussed in this paper to the work done in the HeartLink pilot studies [11], through content analysis of the spectators' posts in the two settings, we observe that the cheering crowd was much more enthusiastic in HeartLink. We believe that this effect was due to the 'charity' nature of the HeartLink event; the charity element seems to inject an obligation of making social good and encourage athlete-support. Thus another influencing factor is expected to be **3) the perceived athlete's motivation to do the activity** as in the theory of mind [3] – this perceived motivation ranges from self-centered (e.g. a competitive event) to altruistic (e.g. supporting the charity run's cause through the perceived value of supporting the athlete). In this light, the fact that the race in this study was specifically organized for a research purpose (in contrast to a public event) may have also influenced the intrinsic motivation of both the participating athletes and the spectators. Finally, **4) the spectator's incentive for recruitment** (e.g. being paid vs. voluntary support) is another influencing factor of spectator engagement that is worth further exploring through crowding theory [15].

In this work we did not account for the effect of paid vs. unpaid crowds. Future work is expected to single out these conditions across groups of equal social ties and pay. To decrease the workers' time-to-recruitment, we paid twice the value that was suggested by the platform for each worker thus making the task more compelling for the job-seeking workers. The job was posted 15 minutes before starting the event and any data from workers who started the 'task' after race completion were removed from the dataset. 0.20$ were paid to each worker for taking part in the task that was estimated to be fun and lasting few minutes on average. Participants were not instructed on how long they should watch the event for. They could spend just a minute but they were also free to stay online for longer if they wished to do so. Thus, a payment strategy was set such that pay was large enough to trigger an initial engagement from participants but low enough to allow us to observe if the initial paid engagement becomes intrinsic once spectators log in (i.e. would spectators freely stay online beyond what they are paid for by current crowdsourcing norms?). Based on the crowdsourcing platform's independent post-activity survey, through this approach the assigned task scored high on "contributor satisfaction" (4.3/5 n=41) and "pay" (4.3/5; n=41).

Issues, limitations and critical reflection

In conducting this exploratory deployment the authors faced a number of challenges arising from the quite unusual combination of interaction contexts that were involved. Namely, 1) being in-the-wild, 2) having co-located participants in combination with 3) a geographically distributed crowd that was recruited through social networks, 4) an outsourced crowd and 5) all necessitating synchronous interaction. Each of these factors augmented the complexity of running the deployment. The intermittent data broadcast that was due to the lack of mobile reception in parts of the racecourse was equal to all conditions yet it may have impacted some of the results. When an athlete enters a temporary 'blind spot', spectators following that athlete seem prompted to switch and follow other athletes. In this light we refrained from reporting results that would have had direct influence from this. For example, it would have been interesting to link the cheering patterns of spectators to the athletes' positions in the race but further tests are needed. Data indicated that athletes who ran slower received most cheers however this was not due to social network effects but was likely due to broadcasting for a longer timeframe thus giving the spectators more time to cheer. We do encourage future research to look deeper into this interesting area of human behavior with questions such as: 'During a challenging task, do crowds support the weakest or the strongest, and how is the distribution effected by the social tie strength between the supporter and the supported?' Our generalized hypotheses, based on athlete's feedback in this study, is that while the supported might appreciate support from both strong and no tie, the weak ties might be the most effective.

Future work

In addition to the future work suggested above, experimenting with different cheering modalities is an avenue worth pursuing. This should look at 1) **ways to aggregate and communicate** the support (e.g. using spacialized audio, modulating the audio amplitude based on crowd size or using different haptic feedback positioning). Another important factor is 2) the **type of support** that is communicated (e.g. communicating the number of persons following online, number of cheers, or using a recommender system to compute and present the most motivating comments to the athletes in near real-time).

In hindsight, in future we would modify three key design decisions taken; 1) presenting the data of one participant at a time in the interface, 2) allowing users to switch athletes and 3) presenting anonymized participants:

1) *Presenting collective vs. individual athlete data*: Our observations of the event dynamics indicated that if the spectators were presented with athletes' aggregate data, like for example a map that represents the location of all the athletes, then the crowd might have taken different cheering strategies. Presenting the spectators with individual athlete's data was a research driven design decision. From pilot studies we learned that presenting the data of all the athletes in one interface makes it difficult to link spectator comments with the data that prompted those comments. However, presenting multiple athletes in one interface would help spectators follow athletes' relative performance. This would let us observe the distribution of spectator-support from human crowds across the weakest and the strongest athlete.

2) *Switching athletes*: Additionally, if spectators were locked into selecting one athlete at the start of the event, rather than being allowed to change athletes throughout the event, we envisage that the spectators would have been more captivated in having 'their' athlete do better thus increasing engagement through gamification dynamics.

3) *Anonymizing participants*: We believe that there is significant room for improvement in terms of spectator engagement particularly by designing interaction around spectators' intrinsic motivation to follow such events. The increase in engagement of the friendsourced and outsourced spectators shows that the bond between the spectators and the athlete is a key element of spectators' engagement. The anonymization of athletes within the spectators' interface was a design decision taken to minimize ethical concerns when sharing data, however, if the athletes were presented with their real names, we believe that the spectators would have experienced a more 'personal' connection. The decision to anonymise athletes was driven by the researchers not the athletes. Since this work was a first deployment of its kind in a research setting that includes very personal data sharing such as heart rate, we felt that it would be appropriate to use anonymity in this case. This decision was also supported by earlier interviews conducted with experts in this area [10]. Although future deployments of the system will not anonymise athletes for reasons specified earlier, the anonymisation of athletes in this context had research benefits, namely, that the cheering decisions (as perceived by the athletes) were based on athletic performance.

As findings show, a few more years of technological advancements are needed until easier and less obtrusive solutions are widely available. The smartphones' form factor and the unpredictability of mobile-data communication infrastructures are key issues. The availability and quality of mobile data connections are dependent on the number of users using the system at one time and the (typically) unknown operator's data vs. voice bandwidth policies at the connected nodes. This nulls the relevance of testing the mobile data connection across the course before events since the actual scenario during the race, particularly if it involves more than a handful of participants, may change drastically during the event. Predictability is critical if such systems are scaled up for larger crowds during popular city marathons. Interestingly, technology has evolved in such a way that aggregating and broadcasting data from large crows that are distributed across the globe may be easier than aggregating data from co-located in-the-wild participants.

In the longer term, further studies could precisely indicate how humans seek spectator support and socially support others. In specific contexts of human behavior, would we cheer the best or the weakest? Having enough data for a specific scenario, can we build a model that takes into consideration the data presented to spectators, the real-time performance and the social connectedness, to predict cheering patterns? Having such a model, could we influence the cheering patterns and maximize the athletes' performance - for example by encouraging cheering just when the athletes need them most?

CONCLUSION

The innovativeness of the work presented in this paper is the crowdsourcing of real-time spectator support through friendsourced and outsourced crowds. In this paper we have presented the results and insights gained from the study with 5 co-located athletes and an online crowd of 140 distributed spectators that were recruited from community networks and a crowdsourcing platform. The results showed that the social ties between the spectators and the athletes influence the engagement of spectators. More importantly, as in co-located cheering, the athletes were excited with both the support received from known crowds as well as support that was received from unknown crowds. This indicates that in spectator support, within the context that is presented in this paper, outsourced spectators could be a valuable source of support. We hope that this first step in crowdsourcing just-in-time support will help other researchers and more importantly stimulate new research in this very promising area.

ACKNOWLEDGMENTS

This research was supported by HighWire, a post-disciplinary programme at Lancaster University funded by the UK Digital Economy Programme (EP/G037582/1). This work also received support from the UK Research Council through the Catalyst project, (EP/I033017/1).

REFERENCES

1. Adam Mahmood, M.O., Burn, J.M., Gemoets, L.A., and Jacquez, C. Variables affecting information technology end-user satisfaction: a meta-analysis of the empirical literature. *International Journal of Human-Computer Studies 52*, 4 (2000), 751–771.
2. Amabile, T.M. Motivational synergy: Toward new conceptualizations of intrinsic and extrinsic motivation in the workplace. *Human Resource Management Review 3*, 3 (1993), 185–201.
3. Bae, S., Jang, J., and Kim, J. Good Samaritans on social network services: Effects of shared context information on social supports for strangers. *International Journal of Human-Computer Studies 71*, 9 (2013), 900–918.
4. Bernstein, M.S., Brandt, J., Miller, R.C., and Karger, D.R. Crowds in two seconds: Enabling realtime crowd-powered interfaces. *Proc. UIST'11,* ACM Press (2011), 33–42.
5. Bernstein, M.S., Little, G., Miller, R.C., et al. Soylent: A Word Processor with a Crowd Inside. *Proc. UIST'10,* ACM Press (2010), 313–322.
6. Bernstein, M.S., Tan, D., Smith, G., Czerwinski, M., and Horvitz, E. Personalization via friendsourcing. *Transactions on Computer-Human Interaction 17*, 2 (2010), 6:1–28.
7. Bigham, J.P., Jayant, C., Ji, H., et al. VizWiz: nearly real-time answers to visual questions. *Proc. UIST'10,* ACM Press (2010), 333–342.
8. Carron, A.V., Loughhead, T.M., and Bray, S.R. The home advantage in sport competitions: Courneya and Carron's (1992) conceptual framework a decade later. *Journal of sports sciences* 23, 4 (2005), 395–407.
9. Consolvo, S., Klasnja, P., McDonald, D.W., and Landay, J.A. Goal-setting considerations for persuasive technologies that encourage physical activity. *Proc. Persuasive'09,* (2009), 1–8.
10. Curmi, F., Ferrario, M.A., and Whittle, J. Sharing real-time biometric data across social networks: requirements for research experiments. *Proc. DIS'14,* ACM Press (2014), 657–666.
11. Curmi, F., Ferrario, M.A., Southern, J., and Whittle, J. HeartLink: open broadcast of live biometric data to social networks. *Proc. CHI'13,* ACM Press (2013), 1749–1758.
12. Deci, E.L. Effects of Externally Mediated Rewards on Intrinsic Motivation. *Journal of personality and social psychology 18*, 1 (1971), 105–115.
13. Deci, E.L. and Ryan, R.M. Cognitive Evaluation Theory. In *Intrinsic motivation and self-determination in human behavior*. Springer US, Boston, MA, 1985, 43–85.
14. Epting, L.K., Riggs, K.N., and Knowles, J.D. Cheers vs. Jeers: Effects of Audience Feedback on Individual Athletic Performance. *American Journal of Psychology,* 13, 2 (2011), 299-312.
15. Frey, B.S. and Jegen, R. Motivation crowding theory. *Journal of economic surveys 15*, 5 (2001), 589–611.
16. Granovetter, M. The strength of weak ties: A network theory revisited. *Sociological theory 1*, (1983), 201–233.
17. Hallberg, J., Svensson, S., Ostmark, A., Lindgren, P., and Synnes, K. Enriched media-experience of sport events. *Sixth IEEE Workshop on Mobile Computing Systems and Applications*, (2004), 1-8.
18. Joinson, A.N. Looking at, looking up or keeping up with people? *Proc. CHI'08,* ACM Press (2008), 1027–1036.
19. Kurvinen, E., Lähteenmäki, M., Salovaara, A., and Lopez, F. Are You Alive? Sensor data as a resource for social interaction. *Knowledge, Technology & Policy 20*, 1 (2007), 39–49.
20. Lasecki, W.S., Miller, C.D., and Bigham, J.P. Warping time for more effective real-time crowdsourcing. *Proc. CHI'13,* ACM Press (2013), 2033–2036.
21. Little, G., Chilton, L.B., Goldman, M., and Miller, R.C. Exploring iterative and parallel human computation processes. *Proc. KDD-HCOMP'10,* ACM Press (2010), 68–76.
22. Morris, R.R. and Picard, R. Crowdsourcing Collective Emotional Intelligence. *arXiv.org*, 1204.3481, (2012).
23. Mueller, F., Vetere, F., Gibbs, M.R., Edge, D., Agamanolis, S., and Sheridan, J.G. Jogging over a distance between Europe and Australia. *Proc. UIST'10,* ACM Press (2010), 189–198.
24. Munson, S.A. and Consolvo, S. Exploring goal-setting, rewards, self-monitoring, and sharing to motivate physical activity. *Proc. Pervasive Health*, (2012), 25–32.
25. Ploderer, B., Smith, W., Howard, S., Pearce, J., and Borland, R. Patterns of support in an online community for smoking cessation. *Proc. C&T'13*, ACM Press (2013), 26-35.
26. Ryan, R.M. and Deci, E.L. Self-determination theory and the facilitation of intrinsic motivation, social development, and well-being. *American psychologist 55*, 1 (2000), 68–78.
27. Skeels, M.M., Unruh, K.T., Powell, C., and Pratt, W. Catalyzing social support for breast cancer patients. *Proc. CHI'10*, ACM Press (2010), 173–182.

Bootlegger: Turning Fans into Film Crew

Guy Schofield, Tom Bartindale, Peter Wright
Culture Lab, Newcastle University, Newcastle Upon Tyne, United Kingdom
g.p.schofield@ncl.ac.uk, tom@bartindale.com, p.c.wright@ncl.ac.uk

ABSTRACT
Bootlegger is a system for creating multi-camera films of live music events using mobile devices. Using readily available technology and a synthesis of film-making conventions, the system coordinates music fans at live shows into an improvised film crew, suggesting shots, collating footage and generating rich metadata in real time. Bootlegger is part of a research project exploring adapting professional media workflows to amateur contexts in order to lower the bar to entry for media production. By enabling concert-goers to contribute to high-quality concert films, the system leverages mobile phone 'bootlegging' practices to support emerging musicians.

Author Keywords
Mobile, DIY, bootlegging, user-generated content, amateur video, digital video

ACM Classification Keywords
H.5.m. Information interfaces and presentation (e.g., HCI): Miscellaneous;

INTRODUCTION
SiDE (Social Inclusion through the Digital Economy) Creative Media is a research project exploring how technology can be used to empower communities to tell their own stories via professional-quality but amateur-led media production. The project is especially dedicated to developing frameworks that enable young people to learn digital skills and engage with the creative industries.

In this paper we describe Bootlegger: a system that supports musicians and their fans in creating high-quality multi-camera concert videos using their own mobile devices. The system leverages 'bootlegging'; the growing phenomenon of music fans recording mobile phone clips at live music events. It connects fans with their favourite artists by establishing a collaborative video production workflow around a live concert, the results of which can then be edited by the artist and used to promote their practice.

In recent years, developments in digital music technology have meant that emerging musicians have become increasingly able to produce, record and promote music themselves, without financial and logistical support from studios, promoters or record labels [1]. The ease of use and availability of laptop recording software has led to an unprecedented democratization of music production, a domain once almost entirely controlled by record companies [2]. This revolution in digital music production has been mirrored by similar developments in photography and video technology; consequently, the technical means are becoming available for emerging musicians to produce professional-quality visuals to support their music.

Videos of live performances are considered particularly desirable artefacts [3]. Consumed by fans as an entertaining aesthetic experience in themselves, on similar terms to an artist's musical recordings [4], they can also form a documentary and promotional role, testifying to a performing artist's capabilities, demonstrating their stagecraft and ability to engage audiences.

Bootlegger explores whether mobile technology can assist non-professional film makers to make high quality concert videos by enabling them to adopt workflows and conventions from professional film and TV practice. Deployed on concert-goers' mobile phones, Bootlegger acts as an automatic director/producer, coordinating music fans into a tightly-organized production team. During a live show, the system supports and instructs audience members in capturing a range of shots. These shots are assigned according to a scheme that prioritizes coverage and visual consistency: as one user is asked to shoot the lead singer in close-up, another might be asked to cover the entire stage, while a third might be tasked with capturing detail shots. At the end of the event, footage is uploaded to the cloud and is accessible directly by the artist or band for editing. In this way, fans are rewarded for their time and effort by being able to take a genuine and active part in their favourite artists' work.

CONTEXT
Using the internet, musicians are also now able to distribute their own music via subscription services such as Spotify or download sites like iTunes [5, 6]. Without the need to raise capital to press records or CDs, musicians whose practices generate little or no income can sell their work alongside multi-million pound media companies [1]. This shift in business models has led to an explosion of creativity in the music industry, with more musicians than ever before able to market their music to an increasingly global audience. Over 20 million tracks are available through Spotify alone,

CHI 2015, April 18 - 23 2015, Seoul, Republic of Korea

ACM 978-1-4503-3145-6/15/04...$15.00
http://dx.doi.org/10.1145/2702123.2702229.

many of which are submitted by musicians without record company support [6].

The world-wide web now accounts for the majority of global music sales and live event promotion [1]. Online platforms such as Reverbnation [7] and Bandcamp [8] offer elaborate web platforms geared specifically towards musicians with integrated downloads, media streaming and e-commerce facilities to support promotion, sales and audience recruitment. These sites effectively combine the roles of record company and record shop in enabling musicians to bring their work to audiences.

Despite these developments, audience numbers have not swelled to match the volume of music now being produced, and artists face increasing competition for listeners [1]. As a consequence, there is a rise in the professionalization of music at grass-roots level, where musicians increasingly attempt to distinguish themselves from their peers through promotion with high-quality images and videos [2]. Electronic Press Kits (EPKs) are becoming an increasingly popular tool for dealing with venues, promoters and booking agents, containing press-releases, high quality photography and video clips.

Planning, shooting and editing a coherent and visually striking music video is a complex task. Not only does it require a detailed knowledge of camera operation and the conventions of TV and cinema but it also necessitates planning and resources. Even live music videos shot at a single venue require substantial organisation, generally requiring a crew of trained camera operators and specialist equipment. Commissioning this type of production is expensive and beyond the resources of most emerging musicians. However: the rise of music and video streaming services has also resulted in a huge surge in another form of music video: the unauthorised fan recording, or 'bootleg'. Millions of music fans every year upload clips of their favourite artists, captured using mobile phones taken at live concerts. This phenomenon is usually spontaneous and rarely coordinated [9].

Unauthorised recording is hugely controversial among established successful artists, with a number of high-profile musicians claiming that illegal recording damages their reputation, infringes their copyright and affects their income. Kate Bush, during a recent series of concerts asked concert goers to refrain from recording clips of her performances, apparently concerned that poor-quality recordings would undermine the promotion of her shows [10]. Other artists have expressed concern that the phenomenon of fan-recording damages the concert-going experience, as concert-goers block the view of others with mobile devices. Among emerging artists however, who have yet to establish income from their music, financial impact is close to non-existent and many grass-roots musicians recognise that online clips can be a valuable source of free promotion and publicity [11].

Several online services have already begun to leverage mobile phone bootlegging practices, in order to both encourage fans to support their favourite artists and to make available an inexpensive source of video footage that musicians might use themselves. Some of these services attempt to overcome the problem of low-quality sound while co-opting fans as a source of footage for musicians' concert videos. FanFootage.com [12] (formerly 45sound) provides users with the opportunity to upload footage of live shows, which is then automatically synchronised with high-quality sound recordings provided by the artist. The resulting video can then be viewed on the artist's Fanfootage page. Similarly, Vyclone [13] uses basic synchronisation to enable small numbers of mobile phone users to make multi-camera films from aggregated content, via a simple online editing system.

Some musicians and bands have directly leveraged bootlegging activity to engage fans and generate novel video content. *Awesome, I fuckin' Shot That* was an experiment by the Beastie Boys in which 50 DV camcorders were loaned to members of the audience during a show at New York's Madison Square Garden [14]. The band Nine Inch Nails applied a similar strategy to the editing of live concert footage in their project *Another Version of the Truth* [15] in which professionally shot footage was made available to fans through the internet. The resulting amateur edits were then packaged and marketed by the band.

Services like Fanfootage and projects like *Awesome* suggest ways in which musicians can draw upon the creativity of their fans, however this engagement is limited, occurring only at the point that the video is shared. While the musician has no say in the specifics of what is recorded (beyond the broad context of the concert), neither does the fan have any idea if what he or she is recording is of use. An artist soliciting footage from fans with no video training has no guarantee that the result will be aesthetically acceptable in terms of framing and composition. Without radio equipment, communication between fans across a venue during an event is practically impossible; consequently there is also no way of ensuring that a sufficiently complete range of angles will be captured. Without a unified scheme for logging shots, collating a body of fan footage remains a time-consuming manual process. A number of HCI projects have provided insight into sharing media via mobile devices. Esbjornsson et al. [16] developed a mobile application for motorsport fans to exchange live images and information about rally events, in order to more fully connect spectators to the action. Flintham, Reeves and Durrant [17] developed a system enabling spectators to share live video of marathon events to augment traditional broadcast media, or in the case of small-scale events where TV coverage was inappropriate, replace it altogether. Once again, however neither of these projects dealt with the aesthetic quality of the resulting footage.

In developing Bootlegger, we propose that a more effective method of engaging fans in recording an event is to take a directorial approach: where fans are coordinated centrally on a moment-to-moment basis as they use their mobile devices. Moreover, by incorporating some basic tuition in cinematography into Bootlegger, we ensure that a range of well-composed, aesthetically coherent shots are captured.

Other research in HCI has suggested strategies for integrating cinematic conventions into multi-camera movie making. Lino et al. [18] have developed a number of applications that apply cinematic conventions to the control of virtual cameras. Lino et al.'s Director's Lens project also tutors users in shooting virtual dramas through suggesting various shots according to templates [19]. In terms of parameterising the overall structure of a video, The *documatic* project [20] involved automatic generation of the entire structure of a video via similar generic means while the *Cinejack* project [21] investigated automatically controlling the narrative arc of a video via interactive editing. Lastly, Engström, Esbjörnsson, and Juhlin [22] suggest ways to coordinate of multiple mobile devices in live music environments.

Concert videos have been a popular documentary form since the 1960s and tend to conform to genre conventions in both style and content. Many of these, such as how to frame the human body are common to cinema in general and are detailed at length in film-making texts [23]. Others are peculiar to the genre and extend from choice of subject and type of shot to the overall structure of the film. As part of a project on video indexing, Snoek, Worring, Smeulders and Freiburg [4] identified a small range of common shots common in concert videos and attempted to use these to classify over 100 videos shot by shot.

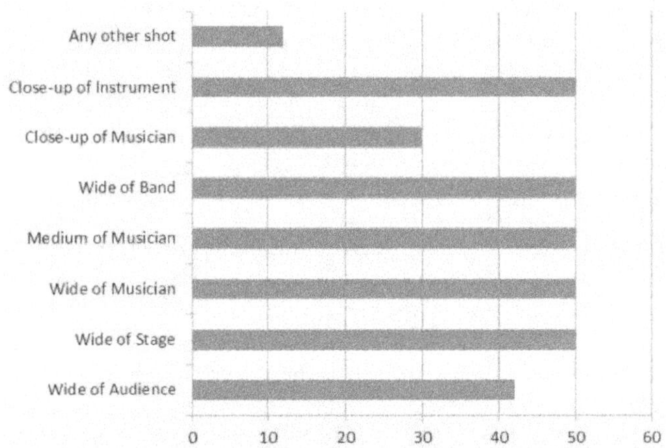

Figure 1. Shots included in the 50 videos surveyed.

In planning Bootlegger, we built upon this approach, conducting our own survey of over 50 concert videos across a number of genres, including rock, country, folk, hip-hop and metal. These videos were selected as representing the broadest possible range of directorial approaches, incorporating differences in venue size and type, context (e.g. festival, TV live set, and individual concert), production values and type of ensemble. In each of these videos we noted each shot type that occurred, resulting in an exhaustive list of standard shot types.

We found a remarkable similarity in directorial style across all these videos, with more than 38 being composed exclusively from 7 types of shot and only 12 containing shots other than these (see figure 1). This suggested that a generic music video template might be relatively simple to compose. This list of shots became the basis for designing the Bootlegger direction system.

DESIGNING BOOTLEGGER

Bootlegger explores how technology can be used to enable non-professional film-makers to make professional quality concert videos. Drawing on the authors' experience and prior work [24, 25] in working with live production crews, we adapted workflows and conventions used by professional film and TV to organise concert-goers into ad-hoc production teams.

In a traditional video production team, camera operators are typically led by a director who has an overview of what each crew member is able to capture. In ideal circumstances, such as in a dedicated TV studio, a director shooting a live event has both an overview of what each camera is capturing (usually via a set of monitors) and moment to moment contact between crew members, often via radio. Bootlegger was designed to fulfil this directorial role, assigning different shots and subjects to each camera-operator by monitoring their current availability in order to provide possibilities for the editor.

Typically, the role of a camera operator is to apply their own knowledge according to the director's brief in capturing the subject. As both director and camera crew have a shared technical knowledge of film-making convention, this brief can often be as concise as 'get a close-up of the singer'. The camera operator, from training and experience, knows exactly how to compose each shot and what position they need to be in and needs no further information. In organising non-expert mobile phone users into a production team, it could not be assumed that the camera operators would know how to compose each shot. Bootlegger was therefore designed to guide camera operators by displaying generic compositions alongside each set of instructions.

To ensure that the design of the system would be appropriate to its users, we also collaborated with a number of early-career musicians throughout the project. Bootlegger's development team used discussions with these artists to design the system, which was then tested and evaluated incrementally at the artists' live shows. We also asked the participating musicians for their views on concert videos, in particular, what a concert video should seek to achieve, what types of shots to include in the system and what they might use the resulting videos for. We found from these discussions that the artists' chief source of anxiety over audience members bootlegging their work was not copyright infringement or loss of revenue but quality and control over footage. One musician posed the question,

"I think the main concern, I'd say, from an artistic point of view, would be: what if they do a bad gig, and you get this footage of a bad gig?"- Musician

Sound quality was a particular concern as mobile phone microphones are often unable to cope with the high audio levels at amplified concerts.

In summary, the Bootlegger system needed to be enjoyable and simple to use, requiring little conscious control or organisation on the part of the user. Shooting live music events presents unique challenges to the film-maker. Live music shows invariably feature low light, wildly varying sound levels, crowded environments and unpredictable subjects. It was imperative therefore that Bootlegger be easy to use in a confusing, noisy environment. The system would need to be able to handle the moment-to-moment complexity of maintaining visual consistency and total coverage while providing enough variety in its tasks to prevent users becoming bored. An uncluttered UI and simple controls were necessary, as were a minimum number of steps in the login and start-up procedures. As live music events take place in a wide range of venues, it was also necessary that Bootlegger be agnostic to the varying availability of mobile network infrastructure.

The design priorities behind the system could be summarised as follows:

1. To ensure the aesthetic quality of footage on a per shot basis.
2. To maintain maximum coverage of all subjects across all cameras.
3. To streamline the editing process by producing metadata for each video clip shot.
4. To ensure that using the system would increase, not diminish users' enjoyment of the concert, through an increased engagement with the artists.

IMPLEMENTATION

Bootlegger is implemented as a client-server infrastructure. A central server-based node.js Sails MVC application backed by a no-SQL Mongo-DB data store and Amazon S3 file store server acts as the event camera director maintaining all real-time shot allocation logic and event metadata. This application can be horizontally scaled to meet the size or volume constraints of current events. Bootlegger users becoming members of the film crew download a native mobile application written in the cross-platform Xamarin framework. This application sets up a consistent and robust real-time bi-directional communication link via a web-socket to the server API. As consistent network signal cannot be guaranteed in live music venues, only small JSON control messages are sent between the server and mobile device, reducing the bandwidth requirements and latency for directorial decisions.

Event Template

Bootlegger's design relies largely on abstracting the conventional structure and production practices of live concert video production into configurable parameters. In Bootlegger, the genre and cinematographic conventions of each type of live event are defined in an *event template* (e.g. live concert). The template defines parameters generic to music events that can be edited by the event organiser (see Figure 2), such the names of performers and their approximate location on stage, which are automatically included in instructions to the camera operators (see Figure 5).

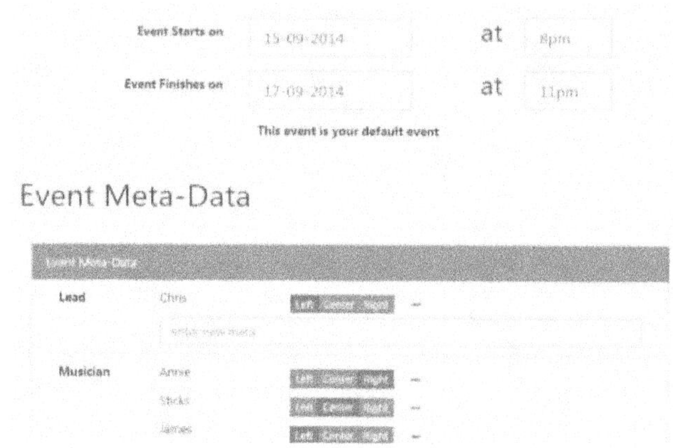

Figure 2. Setting up an event in the web application.

The template defines a hierarchy of 3 key parameters, *roles, subject classes* and *shots* (see Figure 3). Roles describe possible camera positions of a crew member in the venue and a list of shots that could be taken from this position. Upon choosing an event, users are asked to select a rough physical position which matches their location: close to the stage, in the middle of the audience or at the back of the venue. This position determines which shots are included in a palette of possible allocations. Users taking the close role are mainly asked to capture close-up and detail shots, whereas wide shots are allocated to users furthest from the stage.

This selection is deliberately broad, taking into account that both musicians and fans might move around during the show and that stages might be configured in very different ways: the approach works with any configuration where the musicians are located in the same space, regardless of the size or layout of the venue. More precise electronic location of either users or musicians is not attempted, again due to the likelihood of poor network infrastructure at music venues. To add context to the resulting videos, roles are also available which include the outside of the venue (to cover audience or band members arriving) and backstage areas (requesting contextual shots of musicians preparing to perform).

The percentage of total shots that should be devoted to each *subject class* is also defined in the event template. Subject classes describe the subject of each shot: lead musician, supporting musician, detail or audience. In the live music event template, generic rules are applied: for example, the majority of shots should be of the band, of which more than 50% should be depict the lead musician, while only 5% should be shots of the audience.

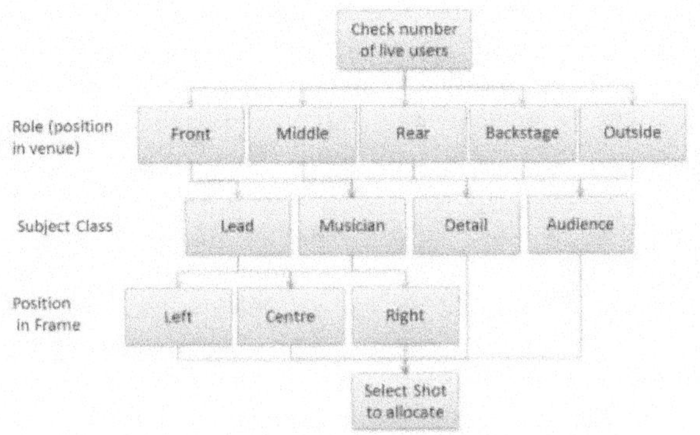

Figure 3. Shot allocation logic in Bootlegger

The *shot* definition describes each individual clip requested and references a semi-transparent image overlay (see Figure 4), and a text instruction which is displayed in the camera view of the mobile application. Each overlay and description demonstrates to the user a conventional framing that might be included in a professionally-shot live concert video. In order to ensure a spatially coherent series of shots, the shot type definition also references how the subject should be framed in every shot: whether to the left, the right or the centre of the frame. Consistency of framing is a key factor in maintaining spatial legibility across the whole film.

Auto-Director

During the event, the server timing algorithm uses the information in the event template and the current state of each user to constantly assess who is live, which shots have already been allocated to which user and how long they have left to record, (see Figure 6).

Figure 4. A selection of overlays for different shots

If only one operator is left it asks that they record continuously, in order to avoid gaps in coverage. After each recording, a thumbnail and all associated metadata is uploaded to the server allowing the shot allocation logic to maintain an accurate overview of available footage and crew availability.

After the event the user uploads their footage over WiFi at their leisure. Crucially, the footage is uploaded to the event organiser's account and then removed from the phone, enabling the user to contribute their footage to the event, whilst allowing the organiser (usually the artist) to maintain control of the video.

Mobile Application

The mobile application is designed to be lightweight and agnostic to both events and shot allocation logic. On connecting to an event, all shot overlay assets are automatically downloaded to the local device (to save bandwidth). Any member of the team hitting a start button triggers the event system to start, at which the Bootlegger auto-director begins assigning shots, according to each user's role and current status. After selecting a shot, the user is counted in (over 5 seconds) and a fixed recording period is initiated (around 25 seconds per shot). Recording is initiated remotely in staggered phases across the user group to guarantee maximum coverage. After each recording phase ends, the auto-director immediately offers another shot, waits for a few seconds for the user to accept or reject it and then begins the recording cycle once more.

Besides the overlay (which can be turned off if the user desires), the camera interface is superficially similar to standard mobile camera applications and is designed to help users obtain a clear unobstructed view of the capture target. Digital zoom is restricted to 2x, to retain as much image quality as possible, while a tilt indicator appears on screen if the camera is rotated away from the horizontal. Users are informed via an on-screen message whenever new operators join or leave the crew.

Figure 5. Bootlegger's UI, showing an overlay.

Event Administration

The server's HTML5 web application allows event organisers to monitor a production in real-time. Figure 6 shows the interface for the application. Moving coloured bars show the state of each camera (recording, allocating a shot or waiting). As each clip is captured, a thumbnail and corollary data become available to view.

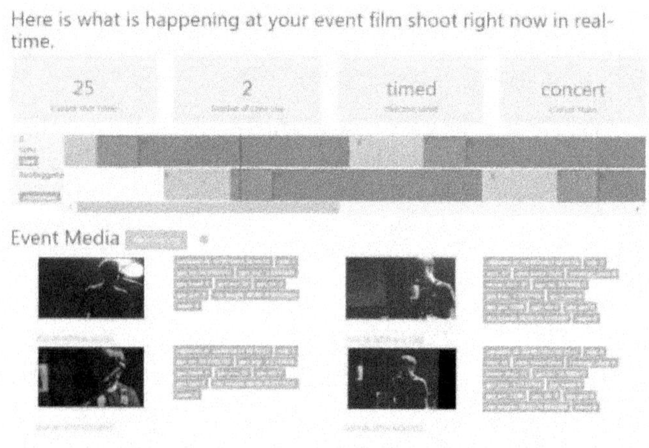

Figure 6. A show in progress, showing current state of each user and incoming metadata

An advantage of using smart phones over conventional video cameras is the potential for appending metadata to the footage, to aid navigation of the clips and streamline the editing process. During capture, each clip is tagged with the identity of the current user, their role, the shot type and subject requested by the auto-director, zoom level, rotation of the device, clip length, timestamp and any available location information. This information is aggregated by the server and can be downloaded as a detailed shot-list with thumbnails of each clip to aid logging and editing, or as an approximated Final Cut Pro XML Edit Description List (EDL), which can be loaded into FCP or Adobe Premiere. The editor is presented with each clip and its associated audio, arranged track by track in temporal order, simplifying a normally time-consuming manual process.

Audio Synchronisation

Although smartphone camera technology has advanced considerably in recent years, microphones in mobile devices and video cameras are often not suitable for recording live music. As sound quality is an important factor in concert films, it is envisaged that Bootlegger event organisers would take a separate audio recording of the event, either from microphones in the venue, through the event's Public Address system, or ideally a combination of the two. As precise audio synchronisation can be a difficult and time consuming task, Bootlegger's server application enables the user to upload a high-quality audio recording of the event as a synchronisation reference against which each video clip is checked and assigned a precise start time. This processing step, building on an approach by Orfanidis [26], can be used to generate a far more precise EDL in which all clips are synchronised exactly.

DEVELOPMENT IN THE WILD

As a system designed for chaotic environments, Bootlegger was developed as much as possible 'in the wild' with each design iteration tested at real music events. The design of Bootlegger, from a basic specification drawn up through discussion with the participant musicians, was developed over several phases, each of which was tested at their own music shows by volunteers and friends of the bands. This approach, suggested by Rogers et al. [27] and Taylor et al. [28] was used to ensure that at every stage, the system could support users to capture high-quality footage under real-world conditions.

This iterative design cycle relied on developing fully functional prototypes which could be used by concert-goers. Choosing to test each version of the system at live music events meant that we had no control over the layout, lighting and atmosphere of venues, behaviour of the bands and audiences or characteristics of the sound. As all the test events were at small venues ranging in capacity from 50 to 300 people, this usually meant coping with poor lighting, unusual stage layouts and a lack of space for camera operators to stand. The unrepeatable nature of each event coupled with the necessity for uninterrupted coverage of each track meant that failure of the system, even for a moment would render even well-shot aesthetically pleasing footage unusable. Stability and robustness of the system was therefore paramount at each stage.

'Camera crews' were recruited largely by the musicians and were shown the system for the first time in the hours before the test event. At each show, the fans were asked to record the entire show if they could: a task that would both test the system as thoroughly as possible and would also generate the maximum amount of test data and video footage. After each show, the 'camera crew' were interviewed and the footage manually edited by the authors into a music video. These videos were then used as a focal point for discussion with the musicians who were asked specific questions relating both to the quality and variety of the output. The resulting information was then fed into the next version of the system.

At each event we used a range of Android mobile devices with all with different HD cameras and technical characteristics. We also deployed 2 entry-level MP3 recorders; to record ambient sound and the direct feed from the venue PA system. A mix of these two recordings was used for the audio of each video project, with audio from mobile devices used only for synching clips to the edit.

The first of the test events involved a country/folk band at a local bar venue. 5 users were given phones running the application immediately before the show. After a short explanation by the development team, they were asked to film the band's entire 25 minute set, focussing particularly on 3 tracks that the band were keen to have featured in live videos. Discussions around the resulting video prompted several further developments to the system. Although Bootlegger was designed to avoid the need for a high-bandwidth network connection, a weak 3G signal is necessary to maintain connections between each phone and the server. Poor 3G coverage at the event (the show was in a thick-walled basement venue in an industrial building) led to minimising even further the system's reliance on network infrastructure. A high stage meant that close shots were difficult to attain, necessitating an increase in the allowed range of digital zoom. One operator filmed the entire set with the phone held upright, suggesting that the system should sense the device's orientation and prompt users if they were making this basic error.

Further testing was carried out at a local music festival, with 6 volunteers covering sets by an indie-rock band and an electronic act in two different venues. Once again, both sets were filmed in their entirety, with a particular focus on 3 tracks, identified by the musicians as candidates for editing. Analysis of the resulting videos led to the addition of several more features including a control to turn on the phone's LED light in low-light conditions (the lighting was extremely low in both venues) and the addition of shots suitable for bands who used live projections. As one venue was very small, a number of nearly identical shots were captured by different operators at the same time. These duplicate shots violated the '30 degree' rule of film-making; where cuts from similar but not identical camera angles are read as a jarring jump-cut. The auto-director's logic was therefore changed to ensure that different operators would never receive the same shot request at the same time.

Figure 7. Difficult lighting was common at test events. Here, the stage lights had been turned off in favour of projections.

Two more shows were filmed, 1 month apart, with minor adjustments made to the auto-director logic and improvements made to the login system, both with 4-6 volunteers filming indie-rock bands in small bar venues. Once again, videos were edited from the resulting rushes and the musicians were interviewed. Further changes to the system included increased support for editors through minor revisions in formatting the metadata and a tightening of the auto-director's scheduling, reducing the length of shots that operators are asked to shoot.

EVALUATION

To date, Bootlegger has been deployed at 5 concerts by 4 bands to film over 40 tracks of which 6 have been edited into videos. After finishing Bootlegger's development, we subjected the footage and videos from later versions of the system to a multi-stage analysis to take in both straightforward dimensions relating to the quality of the system's results and more complex experiential factors concerning Bootleggers use.

We focussed first on the aesthetic qualities of footage captured at the test events, with particular reference to image quality, composition and coverage. As discussed, mobile devices often perform poorly compared to cameras with larger lenses or sensors in low-light, high contrast situations. In editing the trial clips into videos, each project was subjected to a conventional colour-grading process using Adobe Premiere's built in filters. Substantially more video noise was visible in the resulting films than might be expected from footage shot using professional cameras, however many of the musicians were enthusiastic about this quality. Although one musician commented that the slightly grainy image chimed better with his band's aesthetic than a more polished video might, this might not be appropriate for all musicians and represents a limitation of the system when used with older or low-specification phones. We anticipate however that as mobile phone cameras continue to improve, this problem may become less common.

Not only are mobile phones lighter than most professional cameras but their design necessitates holding them at arm's length in order to see the viewfinder. As concert-goers were unlikely to have access to any means of stabilising their devices, camera shake was a concern. Once again however, we were pleasantly surprised by how few shots had to be discarded due to excessive camera-shake. Several musicians actually highlighted camera-shake as a positive feature of their video.

"...you see these really slick, live videos that people have put together and while they can be very beautiful I don't necessarily feel any energy from the performance coming through". - Musician

In some concerts, especially those with moving lights or projections, the phone sometimes struggled to establish focus. This suggests that a manual or fixed focus setting might be appropriate in future versions of Bootlegger.

Bootlegger's shot descriptions and overlay images were designed to ensure coherency and quality in composition and visual style: however, they rely on users correctly interpreting them and having both the desire and ability to compose a similar shot. During recording, Bootlegger clips are tagged with information about the operator's role, the subject and the type of shot requested. To evaluate how closely users followed the shot allocations, we checked each clip manually to determine that its description matched its contents and noted the results.

We found that over 80% of shots were accurately tagged. Only one particular type of shot, *close-ups of musicians,* was often tagged incorrectly, as musicians struggled to capture them due to the phones' wide field of view. One audience member commented that,

"It was hard, you would have had to be right up in their face." - Audience Member

Overcoming this problem with current mobile phones is a challenge, as phone lenses are rarely interchangeable. At one concert we experimented with inexpensive clip-on lenses which allowed for tighter fields of view, at the expense of some image quality. Once again however, some newer mobile devices are now available with optical zoom which would eliminate this problem altogether.

In assessing how well the auto-director algorithm managed coverage of the events, we looked first at how many choices of subject it offered the editor at any moment. In the most recent test (see figure 9), with 5 cameras, the system was able to offer a minimum of 3 different subjects at any moment during a 40 minute live show, ranging from individual shots of musicians to detail shots and wide shots of the stage and audience. The differences in roles can be seen clearly in Figure 9: Users A and C were at the rear of the venue, while Users B and D were at the front. User E was in the middle, resulting in very different shot allocations. The shot allocations from one event (5 crew producing 107 shots) demonstrate how the auto-director requested shots clearly within the governing rules for the event *Subject Category (actual, requested), Lead: (49%, 50%), Musician: (40.1%, 40%), Audience: (3.7%,5%), Detail: (3.7%, 5%).*

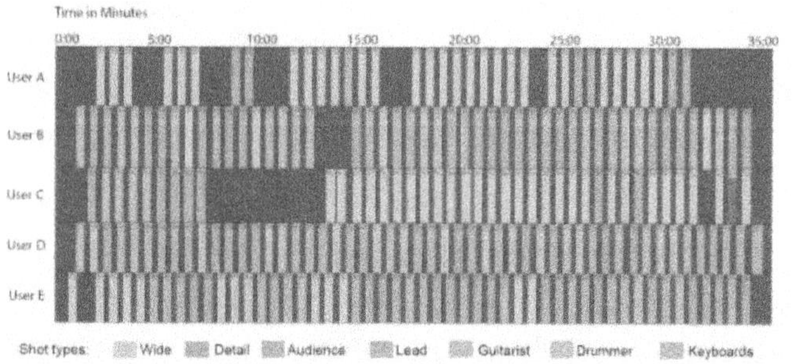

Figure 9. False-coloured shots captured during a 40 minute set laid out in a video editor.

As mobile phone recording at live events is a controversial activity, in developing Bootlegger we were particularly interested in how users felt about being co-opted into a camera crew, whether this increased or decreased their enjoyment of the event and whether they felt comfortable shooting for relatively long periods of time.

In general, all our volunteers reported that the experience was enjoyable and few reported feeling uncomfortable, even in approaching the band for close-ups. This was despite the extreme conditions of our tests, where users were asked to record for the whole duration of the set, rather than at certain moments. An exception to this was shooting members of the audience, which was distinctly unpopular with a number of users, partly because of social anxieties and partly because users felt that small audience numbers reflected badly on the artists.

"I felt self-conscious about the audience shot...I just didn't really do it, just because there was us filming and then a lot of people just looking miserable. I didn't want to film them."- Audience Member

To ameliorate this, early shots requesting close-ups of audience members were later removed leaving only a request to capture a brief wide shot of the audience. On one occasion, we did observe an operator apparently losing interest in shooting the event and beginning to exploring different features of the application however this only occurred in the final moments of one particular gig.

DISCUSSION

Bootlegger's development 'in the wild' and the discussions with artists surrounding it were productive, not just in building and testing the system but in providing a focus for discussion about the effect of technology on grass-roots music and the phenomenon of fan recording. Working with emerging musicians at small-scale shows was not however without its challenges. Often, the deciding factor in the success or failure of a video was not Bootlegger's performance but the aesthetics of the venue and stage and in some cases how well the musicians felt they had played. One edit which the research team thought was particularly successful was rejected by the artists immediately,

"I actually prefer the edit but we just made too many mistakes for us to use it." - Musician

Despite these challenges, the artists said that they would be able to use 4 out of 6 of the videos shot during the project, with only 2 early pieces rejected: one due to the artist's reservations about their own performance and one because of a lack of close shots.

A theme which recurred throughout our interactions with the artists was the importance of reciprocity and collaboration between artists, promoters and other figures in the music scene such as promoters and journalists. In a domain which generates little revenue, many of our musicians used publicity and recommendation as currency, often actively promoting other musicians' shows and releases over social media. When asked how often this promotion was reciprocated, one musician said,

"Always. I don't think we've ever had a band we've tweeted not retweet something of ours."- Musician

Bootlegger integrated well with this ethos and several of the musicians commented on particularly enjoying the collaborative aspect of the system, feeling grateful to their fans for taking the time to contribute to their work. One band asked that their friends be credited in the videos and that a Bootlegger logo be added to the end of the piece, wanting to acknowledge our support for their work.

Similarly, many of the volunteers at our deployments were either friends of the musicians or had already been to previous shows and were excited to be actively involved in supporting the musicians and contributing to their practice.

Many had suggestions for adding features to Bootlegger which supported this further, such as auto-generating credits or monitoring who had shot the most footage or captured the best shots.

One user commented that any discomfort he might have felt in using his phone camera at an event was greatly reduced by a sense of permission gained through contributing to the band's work. Having described his previous uses of camera phones at music events as *'for bragging rights'*, he stated that the experience of contributing to a greater project and working as part of an improvised team had felt far more positive and productive.

'There was a sense of belonging and I felt I was doing something important and those two things went together.", -Audience Member

Several users commented that Bootlegger's continual requests for shots caused them some stress, leaving them feeling unsure whether they were allowed to leave the room, or stop recording. This may have been due to the extreme circumstances of the test events where fans shot an entire live set, rather than one or two tracks. A possible solution to this problem might be simply to include reassurances in Bootlegger's introduction that constant recording is not advised.

During discussions with musicians, we repeatedly asked whether they worried that fans were infringing their copyright through YouTube postings. In all cases the musicians enthusiastically replied in the negative, agreeing that if the video was a good document of the event, it represented a useful source of promotion.

POSSIBILITIES FOR OTHER DOMAINS

Bootlegger opens up a wealth of possibilities for exploring participatory camera orchestration and video production. Bootlegger's flexible architecture and event agnostic implementation suggest its possible use at other genres and types of live event, including sporting events, arts festivals, protests and rallies. Early prototypes are being deployed at real-world events with one version successfully trialled with over 30 volunteers at a UK half-marathon, the Great North Run. In parallel, alternative event templates and direction approaches are being developed to take into account differences in the format and structure of these events.

Some of these formats might well necessitate a more detailed approach to the way Bootlegger deals with the temporal structure of events. Currently, due to the often chaotic schedules prevalent in grass-roots music events, Bootlegger makes no attempt to distinguish between different parts of a concert set. In longer events (for example festivals or sports events taking place over several days), it may be necessary to incorporate automatic or manual switching between different phases to account for different types of subject becoming available at different times.

Bootlegger has the capability to orchestrate much large production teams, but we have yet to trial an event with large numbers of users and without briefing fans before the show. As Bootlegger is still in development, the study described here is relatively small scale and we have yet to determine how the approach will cope with more casual participants who might only take part in filming a small segment of the set. We speculate that the greater the number of participants the less likely this problem is to occur, however this hypothesis has yet to be tested.

We will continue to maintain the Bootlegger system, distributing and promoting the mobile application through Google's play store. This approach will enable us to deploy Bootlegger to a larger number of participants and bands and on a larger scale to investigate how participation in these contexts changes.

CONCLUSIONS

Using Bootlegger as both an automatic director and a basic camera tutor has enabled fans with little or no video experience to capture enough good-quality footage to provide an editor the material needed to create compelling videos. In our trials, Bootlegger performed well, effectively producing a variety of useable footage that our participant musicians have begun to use in their publicity material.

The musicians' enthusiasm for publicising their friends' and contributions and for promoting Bootlegger suggested that technologies that support community building for musicians can be valuable, potentially unlocking opportunities and resources in a domain where publicity and recommendation are valuable currency. It is of course possible that there may be unforeseen negative outcomes to this professionalization of user generated content. In designing Bootlegger we are attempting to harness the dynamism of fan footage, however it remains to be seen whether through instructing fans in cinematography, some of this dynamism might be lost. We suggest that supporting this type of activity using readily available and relatively inexpensive technology represents a useful and cost-effective way for musicians to promote themselves and each other. Moreover, using digital technology to 'professionalize' amateur media production can be both useful and rewarding for musicians and their fans.

Concerns over intellectual property and audience experience have led many established musicians to criticise or ban outright the use of mobile devices at music events. As this contrasts with the views of the emerging musicians we worked with, it is apparent that there is a point at which fan recording becomes detrimental to musicians' practices. We suggest that leveraging fan's desire to record their artist's shows and using systems like Bootlegger to ensure quality and control of IP might be a constructive solution to some of these issues.

Bootlegger has proved that orchestration of multiple cameras can be achieved through a relatively simple synthesis of cinematography conventions and readily available technology. By combining elementary tuition in cinematography, a real-time directorial engine and a stream-lined system for logging and collecting footage, Bootlegger has demonstrated that mobile phones can be used to enable non-professional camera operators to contribute to a professional video workflow. Besides the potential benefit to musicians and other communities of practice described in this paper, these findings contribute to a growing body of knowledge around the integration of user-generated content with professional media practice. As the quality of mobile phone cameras continues to improve, we anticipate that systems like Bootlegger will increasingly blur the boundaries between professional and amateur media production.

ACKNOWLEDGEMENTS

This work was supported by the RCUK Digital Economy Programme [grant number EP/G066019/1 - SIDE: Social Inclusion through the Digital Economy]

REFERENCES

1. Panay, P. "Rethinking music: The future of making money as a performing musician. *Rethinking Music* (2011), 57
2. Palfrey, J., and Gasser, U. *Born digital: Understanding the first generation of digital natives*. (2013), 125
3. Farber, J. 'Director's view: creativity and innovation harder to come by in '88; MTV, labels, music itself to blame', *Billboard*, 12 November (1988) pp. V3, V8
4. Snoek, C. G., Worring, M., Smeulders, A. W., & Freiburg, B. The role of visual content and style for concert video indexing. In *IEEE International Conference on Multimedia and Expo* (2007) 252-255
5. Spotify. Retrieved September 8th 2014. http://www.spotify.com
6. iTunes. Retrieved September 8th 2014 http://itunes.com
7. Reverbnation. Retrieved September 8th 2014. http://www.reverbnation.com
8. Bandcamp. Retreived September 8th 2014 from. http://bandcamp.com
9. Lingel, J., & Naaman, M. You should have been there, man: Live music, DIY content and online communities. *New Media & Society*, 14(2) (2012), 332-349.
10. Guardian Online. Report on Kate Bush Concert. Retrieved September 20th 2014. http://www.theguardian.com/music/2014/aug/19/kate-bush-asks-fans-no-phones-tablets-london-gigs
11. Generator (personal communication) (May 2014)
12. Fanfootage. Retrieved September 20th 2014 from http://fanfootage.com.
13. Vyvlone. Retrieved September 20th 2014. http://vyclone.com
14. *Beastie Boys Starring in Awesome: I Fuckin' Shot That!*. Polyband, (2007).
15. This One Is On Us. Retrieved September 20th 2014. http://toiou.org/
16. Esbjörnsson, M., Brown, B., Juhlin, O., Normark, D., Östergren, M., & Laurier, E. Watching the cars go round and round: designing for active spectating. In *Proc. CHI '06*, ACM Press (2006), 1221-1224.
17. Flintham, M., Reeves, S., & Durrant, A. Creating an Outside Broadcast of a Marathon.
18. Lino, C., Christie, M., Lamarche, F., Schofield, G., & Olivier, P. A real-time cinematography system for interactive 3d environments. In *Proc. SIGGRAPH '10* (2010), 139-148.
19. Lino, C., Christie, M., Ranon, R., & Bares, W. The director's lens: an intelligent assistant for virtual cinematography. In *Proc. ACMMM '11*. ACM (2011), 323-332.
20. Quitmeyer, A., & Nitsche, M. Documatic: participatory, mobile shooting assistant, pre-editor, and groundwork for semi-automatic filmmaking. In *Proc. EuroITV '12* (2012), 135-138.
21. Schofield, G., Green, D., Smith, T., Wright, P., & Olivier, P. Cinejack: using live music to control narrative visuals. In *Proc. DIS '14* ACM (2014), 209-218
22. Engström, A., Esbjörnsson, M., & Juhlin, O. Mobile collaborative live video mixing. In *Proc. MobileHCI '08*. ACM (2008), 157-166.
23. Arijon, D. Grammar of the film language (pp. 12-177). London: Focal Press. (1976).
24. Bartindale, T., Schofield, G., Olivier, P., & Wright, P. Supporting Participatory Media Production through new Interaction Technologies. Digital Economy 2013, (2013).
25. Broth, M. The Production of a live TV-interview through mediated interaction. Logic and Methodology. Retrieved from http://konference.fdvinfo.net /rc33/2004/Data/PDF/stream_02-07.pdf (2004).
26. Orfanidis, S. J. Optimum signal processing: an introduction (1985).
27. Rogers, Y., Connelly, K., Tedesco, L., Hazlewood, W., Kurtz, A., Hall, R. E., & Toscos, T. *Why it's worth the hassle: The value of in-situ studies when designing UbiComp* Springer (2007), 336-353.
28. Taylor, R., Schofield, G., Shearer, J., Wallace, J., Wright, P., Boulanger, P., & Olivier, P. Designing from within: humanaquarium. In *Proc. CHI '11* ACM (2011), 1855-1864.

In-group Questions and Out-group Answers: Crowdsourcing Daily Living Advice for Individuals with Autism

Hwajung Hong, Eric Gilbert, Gregory D. Abowd, Rosa I. Arriaga
School of Interactive Computing and GVU Center
Georgia Institute of Technology
Atlanta, GA USA
{hwajung, abowd}@gatech.edu, {gilbert, arriaga}@cc.gatech.edu

ABSTRACT
Difficulty in navigating daily life can lead to frustration and decrease independence for people with autism. While they turn to online autism communities for information and advice for coping with everyday challenges, these communities may present only a limited perspective because of their *in-group* nature. Obtaining support from *out-group* sources beyond the in-group community may prove valuable in dealing with challenging situations such as public anxiety and workplace conflicts. In this paper, we explore the value of supplementary out-group support from crowdsourced responders added to in-group support from a community of members. We find that out-group sources provide relatively rapid, concise responses with direct and structured information, socially appropriate coping strategies without compromising emotional value. Using an autism community as a motivating example, we conclude by providing design implications for combining in-group and out-group resources that may enhance the question-and-answer experience.

Author Keywords
Autism; social support; online community; crowdsourcing; Q&A; in-group, out-group;

ACM Classification Keywords
H.5.3. Information Interfaces and Presentation: Group and Organization Interfaces: Computer-supported cooperative work, Web-based interaction

INTRODUCTION
People living with autism[1] encounter a variety of difficult social situations throughout their daily lives [27], such as preparing for an upcoming phone interview, handling extreme anxiety at a crowded school dance party, or dealing with a noisy neighbor. The unwritten rules of a complex social world create barriers for people with autism [16]. Seeking clarification or advice about these social challenges is key to navigating everyday life more effectively [20].

http://dx.doi.org/10.1145/2702123.2702402

An available social support network provides an important source for such advice. Physical support networks, comprised of immediate family, friends, and caretakers, can provide guidance for performing basic daily activities, but it is unrealistic and undesirable for them to be an individual's only resource, and they are not always available when needed. Fortunately, our increasingly Internet-connected society has created virtual social networks, increasing the pool of people who might supplement the advice provided by a local support network. Many literate individuals with autism have access to a virtual network of people via a variety of online communities, allowing them to satisfy their informational and emotional support needs by engaging in question–and-answer (Q&A) interactions [2].

Online communities have emerged as social platforms for people on the autism spectrum to self-disclose, vent, and share [17]. These *in-group* [22] communities provide a key benefit by forming communicative relationships with online peer groups and allowing members to share similar experiences or information to address other members' concerns [13]. However, the members of these communities may lack certain social skills themselves, which, in turn, may affect the nature of their advice.

Crowdsourcing is a common approach for recruiting a diverse set of people to provide information and advice online [10,14]. Prior research shows perspective-taking through interactions beyond autism peer groups is critical to improve interpersonal relationships and obtain socially appropriate knowledge [8,18]. Using crowdsourcing to generate *out-group* answers may compensate for the limited perspective of in-group members and may augment the existing in-group support for people living with autism.

In this paper, we seek to explore the potential of a crowdsourcing approach to enable individuals with autism to garner wider and more varied social support from out-group workers in order to cope with everyday issues and frustrations. We begin by following up on a preliminary content analysis of threads in a large online autism community in order to characterize common in-group questions. Our findings indicate that the community's in-group members either explicitly or implicitly solicit support to deal with a wide array of everyday problems, ranging from tips to partake in small talk at a hair salon to requests for financial planning advice.

[1] Throughout this paper, we use the term autism to refer to conditions related to both a medical diagnosis on the autism spectrum, including Asperger's Syndrome, as well as the social definition used by those who identify with the autistic life experience.

We examine whether valuable out-group answers to these in-group questions can be generated by a crowdsourcing approach using Amazon Mechanical Turk (MTurk). We present quantitative and qualitative findings about the differing characteristics and values in answers between groups, including the speed, relative directness, conciseness, informational and emotional support, and perceived helpfulness provided. Our results suggest that crowd workers rapidly provide concise and direct answers offering a broader out-group perspective without loss of emotional support than those obtained solely within the community itself. Building upon these findings, we suggest design opportunities that improve existing in-group communities by including user-initiated features to seek responses from an out-group. The features we propose include a tool that helps users identify better answer source based on the support-seeking context.

The contributions of this work include:

- A content analysis of 1,935 conversation threads from a large existing online autism community, aimed at characterizing in-group question-asking and support-seeking behaviors that reflect everyday concerns of this population.
- An empirical study to crowdsource out-group answers to questions generated in the online autism community, with quantitative and qualitative analysis to identify if out-group answers can provide added value to in-group support.

RELATED WORK

In-group Online Communities

Individuals with autism are known to have cognitive and social skills deficits that lead them to require support to cope with challenges in navigating daily life [27]. Many users with autism go to autism-specific communities to gather advice and foster self-advocacy from others with similar concerns and difficulties. We characterize the community as *in-group* as defined by Tajfel [22]. In-group is a social group to which an individual psychologically identifies as being a member based on the following one's cognition and value: 1) a sense of awareness to similarities and differences, 2) a perceived value connotations as being a member, and 3) a willingness to provide emotional comfort and support to its members. The conceptual in-group membership has been instantiated by computer-mediated communication (CMC) technologies, such as online communities dedicated to a particular group concerned with a range of issues, for example breast cancer [26], motherhood [21], and chronic disease [9].

Previous research has largely focused on how people fulfill their various social support needs by disclosing personal experiences to people with similar conditions in these specialized online communities. According to a breast cancer community study, both informational and emotional forms of support are critical to a support-seeker's satisfaction [24]. A study of CMC technology used by adults with autism revealed that these in-group online communities offer greater emotional support through the sharing of feelings which lead to a perceived increase in quality of life [5]. Thus, an online autism community is a place where myriads of conversations have been generated to meet emotional and socialization needs for increasing self-esteem and self-confidence of the users.

Indeed, not only do users of in-group communities seek emotional support from its members, but they also request information or advice in the form of an explicit question [24]. Requests or questions posted to an in-group community, in turn, can provide a lens for analyzing various types of social support sought by members of the special group. We focus on support-seeking threads in an online autism community to identify current needs and concerns of the members. We also investigate how their requests are addressed by the responses of others. While a large body of research has explored the emotional impact of responses provided to a requester, less is known about the practical value of responses from in-group who are likely struggling with similar concerns. Thus, we investigate the characteristics of autism community responses as well as the responses from outside of the community.

Crowdsourcing Advice from Out-Group Individuals

Soliciting online advice on daily living from both strong-ties as well as weak-ties is called *friendsourcing* and is a common information-seeking behavior [15]. One recent study explored a social media-based remote assistance for adolescents with autism [8]. The study revealed that obtaining ideas and perspectives from one's weak-ties beyond an immediate caregiver could improve their independence. Building upon the prior work, we seek to determine whether people outside of an in-group autism community could be leveraged to provide a wider perspective of everyday life.

Researchers are increasingly beginning to consider *crowdsourcing* approaches to exploiting non-ties, the crowd workers, to support information seeking in one's everyday life [10,14]. Crowd workers—belonging to what Tajfel calls an *out-group* when compared to a specific online community made up of self-selected members [22]—individually come and go, but the pool of workers is available to perform tasks at any moment. The notable example of taking advantage of crowdsourcing for seeking support in daily living is VizWiz [3], which assists visually impaired individuals with providing on-demand answers for performing everyday activities, such as providing subjective fashion advice [6]. Jeong et al. studied whether crowd workers could provide answers to everyday questions on Twitter, such as "about to get my nails done. What colour shall I get?" [10]. They found that the overall quality of crowdsourced answers was similar to the quality of friendsourced answers. Receiving answers from strangers can be a positive experience for some, as strangers could be more honest and provide a wider variety of responses while challenges associated with too many differing opinions and a decoupling from important context remain [14].

Not only does crowdsourcing provide useful information to the general population, but it also supports specialized communities. Crowd workers on Amazon Mechanical Turk (MTurk) have been used to provide helpful information to caregivers of individuals with autism [4]. However, it has not been investigated whether the crowd workers can directly benefit individuals with autism. We, therefore, hope to further clarify those benefits and identify an opportunity to improve upon the in-group discussion through the introduction of out-group answers.

METHOD

We describe the 6 steps of data collection and our analysis methods below. Our study starts with the selection of everyday life Q&A threads in a specific online autism community and ends with the evaluation of responses provide by both in-group and out-group members along a number of quality dimensions.

Research Site and Study Demographics

This study investigated threads from the public discussion boards of a large online autism community with more than 6,000 registered members and 19 discussion boards organized by such criteria as users (e.g., family and friends), topics of concern (e.g., love, relationship and dating), and interests (e.g., technology). In these boards, individuals that self-identify as being on the autism spectrum post questions, self-disclose personal stories, and impart health-related information (e.g., diagnosis, treatment). Thus, this discussion board platform is a rich environment for studying what kinds of support individuals with autism seek.

Individuals with autism can vary widely in their level of social and cognitive functioning. The present study focuses on individuals on the high-functioning end of the autism spectrum who are able to use an online community to seek social support. Members of the community do not necessarily have an official diagnosis of autism though the community's name suggested that they might have Asperger's syndrome. Neurotypical individuals (people who are not on the autism spectrum) are also allowed to participate in the community. Upon registering, the user is asked to generate a profile with a pseudonym and indicate his or her diagnostic status. Because of the level of privacy safeguards, it is virtually impossible to confirm the demographics of individual members. Our observations on the site suggest that its user base appears to consist largely of individuals with autism, but some are also family members, friends, or spouses of individuals with autism.

Data Collection and Analysis

As of September 2014, the community hosted 8,094 threads, and 145,865 individual posts. While various types of conversations have occurred in the community, we focused on the practice of asking for support. Thus, we wanted to analyze threads that either explicitly or implicitly elicit advice in the form of question-asking. We also aimed to specifically address topics related to day-to-day social struggles that out-group members could help with. We excluded topics that only in-group members could understand. Thus, the scope of our analysis is the subset of conversations that are "questions" about regular daily experiences, concerns, and challenges. For our analysis, we selected 5 discussion boards: Friendships and Social Skills; Education and Employment; Love, Relationships and Dating; Autism Spectrum Help and Support; PDD-NOS, Social Anxiety and Others. We collected 1,935 threads that were contained in those five discussion boards.

Step 1. Identifying question threads

To build our in-group Q&A dataset, we considered a thread as the unit of analysis. For each thread, we viewed the initial post as the (potential) question and the subsequent posts as the replies, or in-group answers. We wanted to analyze threads that began with a question and determined if a post was a question by using conventions from previous research [25]. Question detection modeling has shown that one must go beyond applying simple heuristics (ending with a question mark and starting with one of the five "*wh*" question words). Indirect requests should be considered questions as well. Therefore, if an initial post had explicit or implicit indicators such as *want, wonder, need, advice, help, suggestion, tip, opinion, feedback, support, problem, issue, trouble, anyone,* or *someone* that garnered any actions by responders, we marked the initial post as a "question post" and included that thread in our subsequent analysis.

As a result of the filtering process of a single coder, we collected 1,277 question threads (1,277 question posts and 20,472 reply posts), and these threads received an average of 17 responses. This represents a significant portion (66%) of the threads in the 5 discussion boards, indicating that Q&A behavior is very common in this online autism community. Furthermore, for 92% (n=1,174), of these 1,277 question threads, at least one person responded with an average first response time of 4.8 days. However, this period would have decreased to 21.6 hours if we had excluded the 10% of the threads did not receive a first response for over a month.

Step 2. Identifying questions for navigating everyday life

From these 1,277 question threads, we wanted to select a random but representative sample of 20 threads that portrayed the variety of everyday life questions the community members were asking. For this fine-grained analysis, we randomly selected threads from Step1. Our goal was to create a subset of 20 question threads to feed into the subsequent out-group analysis (Steps 4-6), but we wanted to make sure that questions were relevant to navigating everyday life and did not require too much expert knowledge in autism. We recruited two additional coders, who were neither part of the research team nor authors. Coders were asked to thoroughly investigate each thread to determine whether the initiating question sought information or advice on how to navigate everyday life (e.g., *how do you find out if you got the job after an interview?*). In addition, we wanted to exclude confidential and/or sensitive inquiries that were too specific to autism itself and that required validation by autism experts. More specifically, we excluded inquiries on the following topics: symptoms associated with autism (e.g., hyper-sensitivity), diagnoses, clinical treatments, and medication.

Step 3. Categorizing questions based on established themes

The Virginia Department of Education has proposed 7 categories of living skills that are necessary for adults with autism to attain independence [27]: 1) grooming/personal hygiene; 2) schedule planning; 3) physical or mental health habits; 4) school, work and professional life; 5) financial planning; 6) household chores management; and 7) leisure and social activity [8]. In order to find example question threads from each of these categories, our three coders (an author and two coders) independently categorized each of the randomly selected question threads accordingly. During this process, two additional categories emerged: 8) communication skills; and 9) initiating and maintaining social relationships. Once we completed the topical categorization, we selected one to three questions from each category so that all topics were covered.

Grooming and personal hygiene (2)
Matching clothes: My mom is continuously telling me that the clothes I wear don't match, even though they always look perfectly fine to me. I don't understand how people decide what matches and what doesn't and how they keep track of it. […] Does anybody else have problems with this?
Daily planning (2)
Difficulty starting the day and doing stuff: It has taken me experiencing countless grumpy, irritable, and depressed weekends to realize I do not do well without a schedule or routine. If I don't start doing something within about 1-3 hours, my day is practically ruined. Does anyone else experience this?
Maintaining good health habits (physical / mental) (2)
Sleep and waking trouble: I often have trouble falling asleep. I could sleep through an explosion. I am told I'm rather violent when someone tries to wake me. Apparently I'm a sleep fighter! Any ideas or suggestions? Sleep aids only make this worse.
School, work and professional life (3)
First day back in school: I went to my first college class this summer, and I started having a panic attack even before I got into the classroom. I started pouring sweat and shaking […]. I felt extremely embarrassed about how I must have looked […] If you have any ideas about what to do to make this better, please let me know.
Financial planning and management (1)
Money management: I seriously suck at not just buying useless stuff. […] The only time I don't buy stuff is when I'm depressed. And even then I'll just go out and buy something to try and make me feel happy (I know how materialistic that sounds). I have a $160 monthly allowance and that's usually spent in two days. Does anyone else have an issue like that?
Managing household chores (3)
How do you cope with power cuts?: Just recently I've been having power cuts at my house and I haven't been able to post when I'm at home and I must say, it really sucked that I actually got to the point where I wanted to actually scream, shout or swear and I managed to survive 3 days of it. Anyways, how do you cope with power cuts?
Leisure and social activity (3)
Friend's wedding: I have a friend who's getting married in a couple months and he just asked me today if I'd be one of his Groomsmen. […] I get really anxious in front of a lot of people, even if the focus isn't on me. Does anyone have any hints on how to keep from having a major incident during the wedding? […]
Initiating and maintaining social relationships (2)
Problem with friendships: Ever since I was a child, I've been overly attached to friends I feel very close to. I get jealous when they hang out with other people. I become crushed when they ignore my friend requests for Facebook. […] I don't want to be overly attached to other people anymore. What should I do to have healthier friendships?
Communication and conversational skills (2)
Problem with phones: Does anyone else there have problems with making/receiving phone calls from people they don't know? I can talk on the phone with friends, but anything involving phone calls to unknown people is a major problem for me. […]

Table 1. Example question posts categorized by areas for navigating everyday life. Note that number next to the category label indicates the total number of questions selected in each category.

Finally, we generated 20 questions for our crowdsourcing experiment presented in subsequent steps of our method. Table 1 shows an example of each of the 9 final question categories that our 20 final question threads fell into. In categorizing the questions into specific areas of daily living skills, we found requests for help in performing day-to-day activities related to home, hygiene, health habits (e.g., food, sleep), financial management, scheduling, or a combination of these areas (e.g., *I'm sharing an apartment with a roommate. How should we divide house chores and the budget for living expenses?*).

However, we found that social activities overlapped with almost every topic. For instance, the study classifies the "Matching clothes" question in Table 1 as primarily a hygiene and grooming question, but it also can be attributed to difficulty in understanding social norms. Rather than create a separate social norms category for this study, and introduce the problem of cross-categorization of questions, we simply point out the overlap between life skills and social skills that are inherent in many questions.

We also identified a distinctive linguistic pattern from our 20 sampled questions. Nine questions included phrases like *"Similar problems?" "Anyone else?"* or *"Is it just me?"* aimed at either gaining empathy or seeking advice. While most question threads were likely to articulate the specific response expected by explicitly asking a question, some of the questions (n=4) appeared to be more in the nature of a self-disclosure. As noted elsewhere, the practice of self-disclosure is an implicit way of eliciting emotional support [24]. In addition, self-disclosing questions often revealed specific details about the individual's personal problems in an effort to solicit coping strategies from others with similar experiences.

Step 4. *Selecting representative answers from in-group responses*

For purposes of a fair comparison with out-group responses, we wanted to determine five in-group community responses directed to the original question poster. However, the reply structure of this community (i.e., who is replying to whom) can become complex as threads get longer. Following Vlahovic et al.'s approach [24], we chose the first response as one of the best answer candidates because it is most likely to be dedicated to the initiating post. We then applied a manual filtering to exclude conversational posts not intending to answer a question as posed. Replies directed to a specific audience by quoting comments or mentioning an audience (@), and follow-up replies generated by the original question asker were also excluded. From the remaining responses, we randomly selected four responses, which we assumed were likely to be answers from community members to the initial question. We used the same procedure for each thread to select five responses (100 responses in total) from the 252 responses generated to the 20 questions.

Step 5. *Generating out-group answers through MTurk*

We created Amazon Mechanical Turk (MTurk) Human Intelligence Tasks (HITs) to generate out-group crowdsourced answers to the 20 questions garnered from Step 3. Each HIT included the following template:

Introduction: Many individuals with autism visit online communities to ask questions about issues they are facing. We would like to know whether people outside of the specific community could provide answers for them. A question from a special autism community will be shown to you. Please read the question carefully, rate your confidence and provide your own answer to the question.
Question Title: Hair Salon **Question Body:** "Do any of you (especially the women) have to mentally prepare yourself to go to the hair salon? I have an appointment on Saturday and I find that I have to mentally prepare myself for not only the touching (I get body shivers from people touching my head) but also because I have to make small talk with the stylist. I just want to get up and out of there as soon as possible but my visits are at the minimum 2 hours."
Tasks: 1. Rate your confidence in being able to answer this question. (1) Not confident at all – (2) Slightly confident – (3) Somewhat confident – (4) Very confident – (5) Extremely confident 2. Explain the reason for your confidence rating: 3. Please answer the question, or explain why you cannot answer:

MTruk workers were provided with brief descriptions of the study objective and the title and body of the question post. They then read the content and provided their own answer to the question or the reason why they could not answer the question. As an optional task, they were asked to rate their confidence in being able to provide an answer and the reason behind the rating. We assigned 20 workers per HIT so that we could collect 400 answers. Each worker was paid $0.20. We refer to the answers generated by these MTurk workers as "out-group crowdsourced answers." In an attempt to determine the demographics of our workers, we sent them a follow-up demographic survey and received responses from 104 workers. As discussed in step 4, we focused on the responses that were intended to answer a question. To build a set of out-group response candidates, we excluded blank responses (n=3), or responses that explicitly stated, "I cannot answer" (n=29). Ultimately, we randomly selected 100 answers (5 per question) from a pool of 368 crowd responses.

Many of the crowdsourced answers arrived very quickly. We paid approximately $90 to collect 400 responses to 20 questions from 149 workers within five hours and nine minutes on MTurk. The first answer arrived within three minutes after we posted the HITs. The demographic information collected on the responding workers demonstrated that the average age was 33.4 and that 51% of the workers were female. The majority of the workers (76%) were from the United States. Most interestingly, 70% of the workers indicated that they either had experience with autism in their personal or professional life. Seven of them had autism, while 40% indicated they regularly interacted with someone on the autism spectrum. With respect to the definition of out-group in this study, responses from the seven autism workers were eliminated from further analysis because they could be considered in-group. When asked to self-rate their own knowledge about autism (none, a little, a lot), 65% of the workers indicated that they knew a little and 29% indicated they knew a lot. Only a few workers (6%) indicated that they knew nothing about autism. Seeing that crowd workers could produce answers more quickly than we saw in the online community, we next evaluated those answers to identify key differences between the groups.

Step 6. Characterizing in-group vs. out-group answers

To evaluate the answers, we characterized the responses from the two sources through several outcome measures to define the quality of the answers. We considered the five following subjective outcome measures in our analysis:

Directness (Yes/No)—*whether a response contains a direct answer*—is a primary measure of determining the quality of an answer [23]. Regardless of the length of the response and how the topic related to the question, this factor considered whether the response did or did not contain an answer to address the main point of the question.

Additional information (Yes/No)—*whether a response contains any other information (positive or negative) beyond the question*—was examined to identify the existence of extra information, or when viewed from the opposite perspective, how concise the response was.

Informational support (Yes/No) was measured to identify the type of social support provided [12]. The existence of informational support was determined by checking *whether the response provides advice, suggestions, or knowledge.*

Emotional support (Yes/No) was another measure of social support provision [12]. Emotional responses *offer empathy, concern, affection, love, trust, acceptance, intimacy, encouragement, or caring.* Both informational and emotional support measures are often used to analyze health-related discourse in online communities [26].

Helpfulness (1-5 scale)—*whether the response helped to address the question*—is used to determine the perceived value of the answer in addressing the issue raised. This was rated was rated on a 5-point scale (1:poor, 2:fair, 3:good, 4:very good, 5:excellent). An excellent answer should convey positive emotions that can relieve a requester's concern as well as provide implementable and useful information.

Three groups of raters participated in the evaluation:

Researchers (n=2)—Two coders (both non-authors) who had already participated in the question classification process described above evaluated all 200 answers using the five measures. These research raters were shown the 20 question sets and the sets of ten related community and crowdsourced answers. Answers were shuffled in random order and the answers' origins were not revealed.

Individuals with autism (n=6)—Raters self-identified as having high-functioning autism participated in the evaluation process to provide a view of how someone with autism perceives the helpfulness of the responses. These raters limited their analysis to the helpfulness measure in order to lessen the cognitive load during the evaluation.

Autism experts (n=11)—We also wanted to include raters who regularly interact with someone with autism (i.e., professionals, parents), and to compare how their ratings differed from the other groups' perspectives. We recruited autism experts at an official

Raters	Intra-class correlation
Researchers (R)	0.79
Individuals with Autism (A)	0.70
Autism experts (E)	0.67
R + A	0.82
R + E	0.72
E + A	0.75
R + A + E	0.79

Table 2. Intra-class correlations for helpfulness between raters.

meeting organized by teachers and staff members who were designing a workplace transition plan for students with autism in the post-school stage. We created an online evaluation form for rating the helpfulness. Due to the time-consuming nature of the rating process, autism expert raters were shown only two randomly sampled answer sets (20 answers for two questions). In total, 11 autism expert raters (vocational and transitional specialists (n=4), special education teachers (n=2), job developers (n=3), a behavior analyst (n=1), and a mother of a son with autism (n=1)) completed the online evaluation. We collected their ratings of about 100 answers corresponding to ten question sets.

RESULTS

Assessing Raters Agreement

For the Yes/No measures (directness, additional information, informational support and emotional support), performed only by the research raters, we converted Yes=1 and No=0 and calculated an average. Krippendorff's α were calculated in order to determine the multi-coder agreement [11]. Measures appear to be internally consistent (directness: α=0.62; additional information: α=0.48; informational support: α=0.71; emotional support: α=0.44), indicating they are in the range of moderate agreement on additional information and emotional support and substantial agreement on directness and informational support.

To assess agreement on the helpfulness scale, we computed intra-class correlations (ICC). ICC allows us to understand what proportion of the total variance within the measure that is explained by the variance between raters [1]. Table 2 shows the ICC values within and between various groups, all indicating strong agreement.

In-group and Out-group Characterization

To evaluate the value of the in-group and out-group answers, Mann-Whitney U tests (two-tailed, reported with a z score and p-value) were conducted to evaluate the statistical significance of the reported non-parametric differences between in-group and out-group answers. Table 3 shows the average score of five measures for the answers from the two sources: in-group community answers and out-group crowdsourced answers. Keeping the high-level findings from the descriptive analysis in mind, we analyzed the qualitatively collected data in order to gain a detailed understanding of the characteristics of the answers in which these patterns occurred.

Answer source	Mean (μ)	Median	SD (σ)	Min	Max
	Directness (z=-4.03, p=0.000053)				
In-group	0.69	0.70	0.26	0	1
Out-group	0.97	1.00	0.06	0.80	1
	Additional Information (z=0.28 p=0.777391)				
In-group	0.25	0.20	0.22	0.00	0.80
Out-group	0.23	0.20	0.20	0.00	0.75
	Informational Support (z=-4.34, p=0.000015)				
In-group	0.41	0.35	0.30	0	1
Out-group	0.91	0.90	0.10	0.70	1
	Emotional Support (z=0.25, p=0.797197)				
In-group	0.38	0.35	0.17	0.10	0.80
Out-group	0.36	0.40	0.22	0.00	0.80
	Helpfulness (z= -4.98, p=0.000001)				
In-group	2.18	2.09	0.48	1.43	3.25
Out-group	3.24	3.22	0.26	2.87	3.87

Table 3. Descriptive statistics for the five outcome measures comparing in-group (N=100) and out-group (N=100) answers for 20 questions. The z statistic is the Mann-Whitney U score.

Directness and Additional Information

The out-group responders were more likely to provide direct answers addressing the question asked, as shown in Table 3 (z=-4.03, p=0.000053). The out-group directness measures were extremely consistent (σ=0.06), as contrasted with the directness of the in-group answers (σ=0.26). Both the in-group and out-group provided some degree of additional information that might positively or negatively affect the ability to comprehend the answers. No statistically significant differences were found between the in-group and out-group on the additional information measure.

We observed, on average, that out-group answers contained fewer words (μ=64.31 words, σ=51.01) than in-group answers (μ=118.49 words, σ=109.39). Regardless of the length of the message, an in-group answer was less likely to contain a direct answer to a question. Our empirical observation determined that in-group community responses were varied and not necessarily related to the original question posted. These community responses included off-topic discussions, and discussions between responders. Even though we excluded the posts between responders and, for every question, included the first response that was likely to provide a direct answer, the results indicate that the chance of receiving a direct answer for the in-group was lower than from the out-group.

The Different Types of Social Support

We were interested in whether out-group differed from the in-group as to the form of social support provided. Table 3 shows that out-group workers provided superior informational value compared to community members (z=-4.34, p=0.000015). The informational value of an in-group answer was dependent on the question at the issue of the question (min=0 to max=1). The groups did not differ statistically in the measure of emotional support. Both groups may equally provide emotional support through their responses, but the results did not present the type of emotional statement (negative or positive) provided. Thus, we revisit this issue by analyzing sampled answers qualitatively.

Is the Answer Helpful?

Helpfulness was rated by investigating whether the response provided a constructive answer that would assist individuals with autism in coping with the challenge identified in the question. All 15 judges rated the out-group answers as more helpful than the in-group answers ($z=-4.98$, $p=0.000001$). Even though the ICC values (Table 2) for each group showed substantial and moderate agreement, we separately examined how individuals with autism and the autism experts perceived the helpfulness. The results showed that the rater with autism rated the helpfulness of the out-group higher than the in-group (in-group μ: 2.20 (σ:0.59), out-group μ: 3.10 (σ: 0.30) $z=-4.79$, $p=0.000002$) as well as autism experts group (in-group μ: 2.16 (σ:0.54), out-group μ: 3.15 (σ: 0.58), $z=-3.20$, $p= 0.001354$).

Qualitative Analysis

Which Out-group Members Provide More Helpful Answers?

While the majority of crowd workers indicated that they were not on the spectrum, many of them (40%) regularly interacted with someone with autism. Over one-half indicated that they knew little or nothing about autism. However, we found no correlations between the helpfulness of the response and 1) the crowd worker's confidence in being able to answer the question, 2) his or her level of knowledge about autism, or 3) the crowd worker's personal connection to someone with autism. The results may be due to most of the questions requiring autism-specific knowledge at the question-sampling stage. Another possible explanation is that the sampled questions likely have common situations occurring in everyone's life, making experience with autism less relevant. One-half of the total crowd responses (n=195) indicated that their past experience was the reason they could answer a question: *"I've overcome spending issues of my own." "I have moved out to a friend's house before for the first time, and I am in almost the same situation."*

Emotional Support

The majority of questions collected through Steps 1-3 elicited subjective opinions. In particular, the in-group community questions often disclosed problems already experienced by the asker and sought feedback from people who have been involved in similar situations, either to receive an opinion or to gain empathy (e.g., *"Last night I went to my school's annual dance. I spent the entire time checking my watch and wanting desperately to leave so that I could go home. There were too many people and too much talking. I felt so overstimulated. Similar problems, advice, anyone?"*). Community responses to this question appeared to have emotional phrases such as *"I felt like drunk, extremely anxious and my head was empty."*, *"Never liked dances either. I always found them boring."*, These comments could help the asker find people in similar situations who might provide fellowship through shared experiences, a big potential advantage for in-group responses.

Surprisingly, out-group answers contained similar emotional statements: *"I feel this way a lot if I am in a situation where there are too many people."* Almost 30% of the crowdsourced responses (n=118) contained similarly sympathetic messages, and some of them affirmed that the problem was not related to autism, but rather was a general issue for everyone: *"You are not alone having this problem. The only difference is that the percentage of this anxiety."*, *"It's natural to worry. Everyone worries about loved ones sometimes."*, *"NO ONE likes going to the dentist! My ex-husband totally freaked out when he had to go and he didn't have autism."*

Socially-appropriate Coping Strategies

Although most in-group answers provided emotional value such as trust and companionship, we found some in-group answers that did not match general social norms and expectations. For instance, in response to a question about dealing with noisy neighbors, one in-group responder suggested: *"Buy a drum kit, wait those neighbors falling asleep, and that's when you practice the living daylights out of that kit. Negotiate with them after, say, three or four sessions."* However, it is unclear if this type of answers can be attributed to informal nature of in-group forums or characteristics of autism. Nevertheless, one of the characteristics for individuals with autism is a difference in social understanding when compared to neurotypicals [19]. Their tendency to take things literally would lead them to misunderstand the nuances of a joke or sarcastic phrases. Thus, the nuanced responses may impact them more than it would for others. While some responses from in-group provided no further advice for coping with the problematic situation, we found that crowd answers commonly contain actionable coping strategies: *"I think that approaching your landlord first, would be a great move. Getting his or her take on the situation will give you another perspective. Also, if you have alerted your landlord with the situation the landlord may be able to do the next steps for you. If this plan is not possible, then I think you should approach the loud people either in passing or in the most non-confrontational way."*

Structured Social and Behavioral Prescriptions

We were also surprised to observe that many crowdsourced responses provided step-by-step coping strategies for various social situations (e.g., feeling isolated on Facebook, extreme anxiety when the partner is away, a panic attack at the first class in the college). One crowd worker offered the following way of relieving stress when away from a partner: *"First, try talking with your partner about how you feel. [...] Talk with him about those worst scenarios you've been imagining. Having a course of action and back-up plan for each scenario will help you both feel more in control. Finally, trust your partner. Try to keep in mind the fact that he's a responsible person who is doing everything possible to keep himself safe."* Many individuals with autism need such assistance in devising explicit rules or strategies for appropriate social behavior [4]. We found that crowdsourced responders prescribed remedies for social and behavioral challenges that are well-suited to the needs of individuals with autism.

DISCUSSION

Our results suggest that crowdsourcing can generate extremely fast, direct, and informational answers from a diverse set of responders with differing perspectives. The crowdsourcing approach shows a potential to provide advice at least as good as that provided by members of a dedicated autism community. In this section, we discuss the implications of these results focusing on the trade-off between the benefits of in-group Q&A behavior and the potential for including an out-group as a supplementary source of support.

Crowds offer quick responses throughout the day

Our investigation reveals that crowd workers are able to provide timely (arguably more timely) answers. For individuals with autism who seek information, the noteworthy speed of crowdsourcing can promise potential support around the clock. This may be particularly helpful since individuals with autism can experience unexpected social situations at any time. In some situations like contextualized health issues, a support-seeker's satisfaction with provided answers depends on what she is seeking in the first place. If she explicitly asks a question to seek informational support and receives only emotional support in return, the requester is likely to be less satisfied [24]. If a requester with autism primarily wants prompt, straight answer to cope with a problem, obtaining responses from crowd workers may be more promising than culling the large volume of conversations often provided by an in-group community. Acknowledging the fact that in-group community has the initiative to seek help, below we propose design directions that enhance the performance of the existing community with the immediate crowdsourced responses.

Crowds *can* answer the autism community's questions

Our findings suggest that crowd workers are able to answer a question asked by individuals with autism, regardless of their knowledge or experience with autism. As we noted, we found that a responder's level of knowledge and experience with autism were not correlated with the helpfulness of the response. While the majority of crowd workers in this study were not on the spectrum, they noted that they have had frustrating situations similar to those that individuals with autism suffer from. About one-half of the crowd workers cited such prior experiences in responding to the questions: *"This definitely happened to me when I've been to a club that I don't want to go to.", "While I'm not autistic, I have issues with being touched sometimes", "As a woman, this is based on my own experience going to the salon every 6-8 weeks."* In addition, some crowd workers showed strong confidence in being able to answer a question because of the relationship between the question topic and their current occupation. For instance, a crowd worker noted in a message that *"I work part time in fashion industry"* as the basis for her ability to answer a question on how to match clothes. For a problem involving workplace conflict, one crowd responder provided advice based on her *"experience as a supervisor, years of coaching experience."* Thus, an extended pool of crowdsourced out-group responders may increase the chance to find potential topical experts in various areas of daily living.

Crowds provide direct and informational support

Our findings suggest that in-group and out-group answers provide different perspectives. In general, the three groups of raters agreed that the out-group answers were more helpful than the in-group answers. One possible reason for this difference may be related to the methodology we used. Given the conversational nature of in-group communities, a collection of answers in a thread may be more valuable than a single post. Unlike the rhetorically-oriented nature of an in-group community, a crowdsourcing platform allows out-group responders to provide isolated and direct answers (i.e., independent judgment [14]). Perhaps by virtue of the isolated nature of crowdsourcing, crowd responders are likely to focus on the concerns of the person asking the question.

Crowds offer helpful advice with emotional support

Online autism communities are intended to engender interaction with a sympathetic group. One might be concerned about the lack of emotional support while engaging in out-group answers. Interestingly, our results suggest our-group answers convey informational value without corresponding loss of the emotional value. We noticed crowd workers sometimes expressed positive emotions such as empathy and encouragement affirming out-group people can also suffer from the same issues. In-group emotional responses were likely to resonate with the poster's suffering, confusion, and frustration (e.g., constantly losing friends, feeling isolated). However, the overexposure to personal, emotionally-laden responses without further helpful insight into their suffering may amplify some negative aspects of life [13]. If an asker were susceptible to absorbing the negative emotions of the responders, the emotional content in the response would no longer be helpful. Further research should address how individuals with autism perceive the value of emotional support provided by in-group members and out-group members differently.

Crowds provide actionable advice with concise language

We found that out-group answers had less words compared to answers provided by community members. While length has been found to be a positive indicator of answer quality in general online Q&A forums [7], overly verbose answers may not convey greater relevant information. More importantly, out-group answers tended to offer social and behavioral prescriptions such as remedies for extreme anxiety when being apart from a partner, coping strategies in a public presentation, and plans of action for first dates in a structured manner (e.g., numbering, bullet points). This strategy resonates with a commonly used autism intervention, SocialStories™, in which scenarios guide the person through the sequence of steps needed to carry out a particular task or learn appropriate behavior for social situations. Prior research has shown that crowd workers are effective in developing social scripts which can be used to assist teachers in generating content for social skills training [4]. Future research should address whether individuals with autism find value in concise and structured, playbook-style answers like those generated by out-group responders.

Crowds broaden the perspective to the autism community

Crowdsourcing provides a wide variety of perspectives obtained via out-group information that can supplement in-group perspective. We found that a majority of the questions we classified were associated with social skills. The fact that members elicited feedback from others with the same core social challenges may indicate that the current in-group structure presents a limited perspective on problem-solving. The notion of broadening the perspective of individuals with autism is a positive endeavor supported by a study of a social networking service used by young adults with autism [8]. The study revealed that members could benefit from obtaining diverse perspectives from a variety of network members, including neurotypical responders such as friends, relatives, parents' friends, and volunteers [8]. Our results demonstrate that such out-group responders could be leveraged with an existing crowdsourcing platform and that out-group answers could be constructive and useful in addressing questions asked by individuals with autism.

While the results of our study are promising, further research may fill existing gaps identified by other studies related to crowdsourcing advice for everyday decisions. The major concerns include the mismatch between crowd workers and question answerers, differing opinions, decoupling context, trust, and cost [10,14]. Our results suggest an opportunity for improving the question-asking experience through a mixture of in-group and out-group support. Crowdsourcing can serve as a supplemental approach to bridge the gaps in existing support provided by in-group communities.

DESIGN OPPORTUNITIES

In this section, we discuss the design opportunities for existing in-group communities that are being repurposed for question-asking and support-seeking. We also propose the design of interfaces or systems that can maximize the benefit of combining in-group members with out-group input.

Motivating to Seek Help from the Crowds

Our study with crowdsourced responders demonstrates that such a crowdsourcing approach can complement in-group communities by providing rapid, socially appropriate answers that offer a broader out-group perspective. Thus, the in-group community could be augmented if it is capable of embedding a crowdsourcing mechanism in some situations, such as when a more immediate or methodical response is needed. A simple visual component such as an "Ask Turk" button could motivate individuals with autism to consider other answer sources when submitting a question. One can imagine that this feature could serve as a "hotline" in which on-demand online volunteers are ready to respond 24/7. We used Amazon Mechanical Turk for this study, but the notion of a hotline serviced by online volunteers suggests that it might be worthwhile to consider the creation of specialized crowd communities. We return to this idea of specialized crowd communities later.

Opportunities for Automation

Individuals with autism may find it difficult to determine if and when they should look to in-group or out-group sources to elicit helpful feedback. We found that out-group sources could provide valuable advice on in-group questions in nine areas of daily activity that were not autism-specific. The manual question filtering and classification performed by coders might be replaced by sophisticated natural language processing techniques. Algorithms could be trained to learn the topics of questions and the level of knowledge about autism required for each topic, and suggest a question-asker to consider seeking advice from the crowd as well.

Our goal with this work was never to replace online communities, but rather to determine ways to improve upon them. As others have found, we saw a preponderance of Q&A behavior and our manual techniques for determining whether an initial post in a thread is a question or not suggests that it might be useful to simply predict whether a post contains a question at all. Automated techniques could attempt to understand different nuances of a question (e.g., is there an immediate informational need or is emotional support being sought). However, directing a question to the out-group should not be automatic. Our suggestion is to augment existing communities by including a user-initiated feature to seek responses from crowds.

Finding a Way to Foster Trust in Strangers

Our autism experts initially expressed skepticism about the credibility and safety of consulting anonymous crowd workers. While our results indicate that strangers may be able to provide direct and helpful answers, it still does not mean that those who care for individuals with autism would be comfortable with all of the out-group answers. To increase trust in responses from crowd workers, potential workers could be given a reminder of the "do's and don'ts" of good answers. The crowd workers in our study represented caregivers (33%) and some autism professionals (4%) without any specific recruiting. These types of crowd workers could also be leveraged to validate answers from other crowd workers. However, this process may inject additional cost and time into the process.

POTENTIAL LIMITATIONS OF OUR STUDY

It is possible that the autism community we sampled is not representative of individuals with autism at large. This issue is mitigated by our empirical observation to characterize several autism communities prior to the study. Our observation reveals that these communities share many similarities which impact the pattern of interaction: discussion board structure and topical discussion board (e.g., social skills : social skills and friendships, work and finding a job : education and employment). Such in-group community discussion boards appear to have the same threading structure composed of initiating posts and reply posts. Thus, we picked a community that already generated a vast amount of threads and that were accessible to our research team.

Our methodology also has shortcomings. First, since out-group membership was critical to our study, we excluded responses generated by crowd workers who stated they had autism. However, we see studying crowd workers that have autism as an exciting future avenue for leveraging their experience to verify the appropriateness of answers. Second, we recognized the imbalanced comparison between selected community threads from a whole conversation and isolated crowd answers. Future research will benefit from the holistic comparison of MTurk answers and community threads. Thirdly, it is also plausible that the helpfulness rating differences between the groups were simply artifacts of worker self-selection or the nature of being paid. The framing of the HIT introduction on MTurk that was visible to potential workers before accepting the HIT may have drawn more individuals with a relationship to autism than what is characteristic of the broader MTurk community. Indeed, we believe that the explicit presentation of the goals and motivations for our published HITs helped us recruit crowd workers that were motivated by the task rather than just the monetary value. In our future work, we hope to explore the possibility of a "philanthropic turk" [4], where online volunteers provide answers not because they are being paid, but because they want to help others in need.

Our work with MTurk responders introduces socio-ethical issues related to the use of a crowdsourcing labor force that is global. One potential drawback is the lack of cultural sensitivity to localized questions about daily living that may often require a nuanced understanding of particular social worlds (e.g., conventions around landlords and apartment rental). To account for cultural contexts and social norms, we envision the creation of specialized crowd communities by leveraging local volunteers who are familiar with the particular contexts of a question asker.

CONCLUSION

The goal of this study was to explore the possibility of crowdsourcing answers to garner a wider perspective of information and advice for individuals with autism. The evaluation of in-group and out-group answers illuminated key differences between the groups. Our results show out-group information obtained through crowdsourcing provides added value with its relatively rapid turnaround time, and a wide variety of responses in a concise and structured manner, without loss of the emotional support when compared with the online community's responses. These differences led to set of design features for augmenting the in-group community support—a nudge to be aware of available answer providers beyond the community, automated question classifier to find better answer source, and a validation mechanism to foster trust. These implications may also encourage researchers to explore issues faced by other specialized communities whose individuals seek advice to navigate their daily lives effectively.

ACKNOWLEDGEMENT

We thank all the individuals that provided the ratings. The final paper was greatly improved by the advice from the anonymous reviewers. This research was supported by the Samsung Fellowship awarded to the first author.

REFERENCES

1. Bartko, J.J. The intraclass correlation coefficient as a measure of reliability. *Psychological reports 19*, 1 (1966), 3–11.
2. Benford, P. The use of Internet-based communication by people with autism. *Ph.D Dissertation. University of Nottingham*, 2008.
3. Bigham, J., Jayant, C., Ji, H., and Little, G. VizWiz: nearly real-time answers to visual questions. *UIST 2010*.
4. Boujarwah, F.A., Abowd, G.D., and Arriaga, R.I. Socially Computed Scripts to Support Social Problem Solving Skills. *CHI 2012*.
5. Burke, M., Kraut, R., and Williams, D. Social use of computer-mediated communication by adults on the autism spectrum. *CSCW 2010*.
6. Burton, M., Brady, E., Brewer, R., and Neylan, C. Crowdsourcing Subjective Fashion Advice Using VizWiz: Challenges and Opportunities. *ASSETS 2012*.
7. Harper, M.F., Raban, D., Rafaeli, S., and Konstan, J.A. Predictors of answer quality in online Q&A sites. *CHI 2008*.
8. Hong, H., Yarosh, S., Kim, J.G., Abowd, G.D., and Arriaga, R.I. Investigating the Use of Circles in Social Networks to Support Independence of Individuals with Autism. *CHI* 2013.
9. Huh, J. and Ackerman, M.S. Collaborative help in chronic disease management: supporting individualized problems. *CSCW 2012*.
10. Jeong, J., Morris, M.R., Teevan, J., and Liebling, D. A Crowd-Powered Socially Embedded Search Engine. *ICWSM 2013*.
11. Krippendorff, K. Reliability in Content Analysis: Some Common Misconceptions and Recommendations. *Human Communication Research 30*, 3 (2004), 411–433.
12. Langford, C.P., Bowsher, J., Maloney, J.P., and Lillis, P.P. Social support: a conceptual analysis. *Journal of advanced nursing 25*, 1 (1997), 95–100.
13. Massimi, M. and Bender, J. Life transitions and online health communities: reflecting on adoption, use, and disengagement. *CSCW 2014*.
14. Morris, M., Inkpen, K., and Venolia, G. Remote Shopping Advice: Enhancing In-Store Shopping with Social Technologies. *CSCW 2014*.
15. Morris, M., Teevan, J., and Panovich, K. What Do People Ask Their Social Networks, and Why? A Survey Study of Status Message Q&A Behavior. *CHI 2010*.
16. Myles, B. and Simpson, R. Understanding the Hidden Curriculum An Essential Social Skill for Children and Youth with Asperger Syndrome. *Intervention in School and Clinic*, (2001).
17. Newton, A.T., Kramer, A.A.D.I., and McIntosh, D. Autism online: a comparison of word usage in bloggers with and without autism spectrum disorders. *CHI 2009*.
18. Ochs, E. and Kremer-Sadlik, T. Autism and the social world: an anthropological perspective. *Discourse Studies 6*, 2 (2004), 147–183.
19. Olney, M. Working with Autism and Other Social Communication Disorders. *Journal of Rehabilitation*, (2000).
20. Palmen, A., Didden, R., and Arts, M. Improving question asking in high-functioning adolescents with autism spectrum disorders Effectiveness of small-group training. *Autism 12*, 1 (2008), 83–98.
21. Schoenebeck, S. The Secret Life of Online Moms: Anonymity and Disinhibition on YouBeMom. com. *ICWSM 2013*.
22. Tajfel, H. Social Psychology of Intergroup Relations. *Annual review of psychology*, (1982), 1–39.
23. Teevan, J., Morris, M., and Panovich, K. Factors Affecting Response Quantity, Quality, and Speed for Questions Asked via Social Network Status Messages. *ICWSM 2011*.
24. Vlahovic, T.A., Wang, Y.-C., Kraut, R.E., and Levine, J.M. Support matching and satisfaction in an online breast cancer support community. *CHI 2014*.
25. Wang, K. and Chua, T. Exploiting salient patterns for question detection and question retrieval in community-based question answering. *Computational Lingui*, (2010), 1155–1163.
26. Wang, Y., Kraut, R., and Levine, J.M. To Stay or Leave? The Relationship of Emotional and Informational Support to Commitment in Online Health Support Groups. *CSCW 2012*.
27. *Autism Spectrum Disorders and the Transition to Adulthood.* Virginia Department of Education, 2010.

Your Location has been Shared 5,398 Times! A Field Study on Mobile App Privacy Nudging

**Hazim Almuhimedi,[1] Florian Schaub,[1] Norman Sadeh,[1]
Idris Adjerid,[2] Alessandro Acquisti,[1] Joshua Gluck,[1]
Lorrie Cranor,[1] Yuvraj Agarwal[1]**

[1]Carnegie Mellon University
{hazim,fschaub,sadeh,acquisti,jgluck,
lorrie,yuvraj.agarwal}@cmu.edu

[2]University of Notre Dame
iadjerid@nd.edu

ABSTRACT

Smartphone users are often unaware of the data collected by apps running on their devices. We report on a study that evaluates the benefits of giving users an app permission manager and sending them nudges intended to raise their awareness of the data collected by their apps. Our study provides both qualitative and quantitative evidence that these approaches are complementary and can each play a significant role in empowering users to more effectively control their privacy. For instance, even after a week with access to the permission manager, participants benefited from nudges showing them how often some of their sensitive data was being accessed by apps, with 95% of participants reassessing their permissions, and 58% of them further restricting some of their permissions. We discuss how participants interacted both with the permission manager and the privacy nudges, analyze the effectiveness of both solutions, and derive some recommendations.

Author Keywords

Mobile; Privacy; Privacy Decision Making; Privacy Nudges.

ACM Classification Keywords

H.5.m. Information Interfaces and Presentation (e.g. HCI): Miscellaneous.

INTRODUCTION

Previous research has shown that smartphone users are often unaware of the data collected by their apps and express surprise and discomfort when they find out (e.g., [14, 26, 30, 11, 13]). Recently, privacy managers such as AppOps (introduced in Android 4.3 but later removed with the introduction of Android 4.4.2), privacy controls in iOS, and ProtectMyPrivacy [5], have offered users more fine-grained control over their privacy. However, to the best of our knowledge, the effectiveness of these fine-grained controls has not yet been evaluated. Privacy decision making is known to be subject to cognitive and behavioral biases, and decision heuristics that often lead to privacy-adverse decisions in favor of short-term benefits [3]. Privacy nudges have been proposed to support users in their privacy decision making [2]. Such nudges aim to make privacy risks more salient and help users move towards privacy settings that better align with their privacy expectations and concerns. One of the goals of our research is to establish to what extent users who have access to fine permission controls might benefit from nudges that raise their awareness of the data collected by their apps, and whether nudges prompt them to review their current permission settings.

In this work, we focus on two research questions: (1) Is access to a fine-grained app permission manager an effective way of helping users review and modify their app permissions? (2) Can privacy nudges, that regularly alert users about sensitive data collected by their apps, enhance the effectiveness of a fine-grained app permission manager? To address these questions, we conducted a 22-day field study in which 23 participants interacted with a permission manager – AppOps on Android – for one week, followed by an 8-day phase in which the permission manager was supplemented with privacy nudges tailored to a participant's installed apps and their data access behavior.

Our mixed methods approach provides rich insights into (1) how and why participants review and restrict app permissions with a permission manager and (2) how they react to privacy nudges alerting them about the data collected by their apps. Our results confirm that users are generally unaware of mobile app data collection practices. Our findings also demonstrate the benefits of fine-grained permission managers and show that the effectiveness of these managers can be significantly enhanced by the delivery of nudges intended to further increase user awareness about mobile app data collection practices.

This work makes the following contributions. First, our study highlights the benefits of a permission manager like AppOps and quantifies the additional benefits that result from supplementing such functionality with privacy nudges. Second, we designed mobile privacy nudges that increase user awareness of data collection practices and effectively motivate users to review and often revise their app permissions. Third, we evaluated the effectiveness of the privacy nudges in a real-world setting. Finally, we derive recommendations for the design of effective privacy nudges on mobile devices based on our results.

CHI 2015, April 18 - 23 2015, Seoul, Republic of Korea.

ACM 978-1-4503-3145-6/15/04...$15.00
http://dx.doi.org/10.1145/2702123.2702210

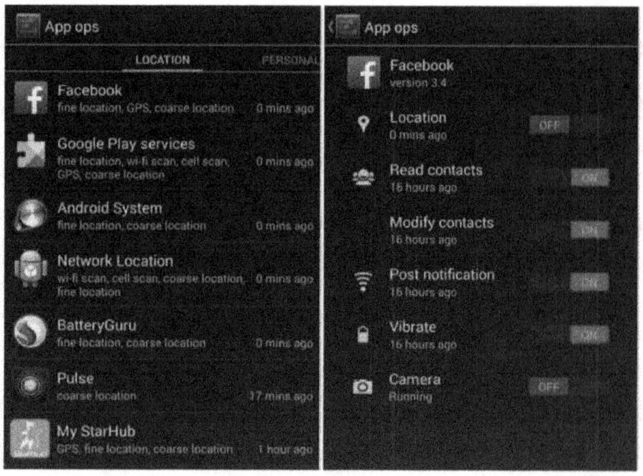

Figure 1. AppOps has four different tabs. Each tab lists all apps that accessed corresponding category of data, e.g., location (*left*). Selecting a specific app opens a screen showing all permissions accessed by the app (*right*).

BACKGROUND AND RELATED WORK

Privacy Controls in Mobile Platforms

Android and iOS provide some privacy safeguards for users. Android displays an app's requested permissions at *install time*, which users have to accept to install it. In Android 4.3, Google included a permission manager, called *AppOps*, that was hidden by default and required an external app to access. AppOps allowed users to selectively grant or restrict permissions for installed apps. AppOps, shown in Figure 1, organizes permissions into four categories: location, personal data (e.g., calendar, phone contacts), messaging (e.g., SMS), and device features (e.g., vibration, notification). In each tab, apps are ordered by most recent access. When selecting a specific app in an AppOps tab, users are shown all permissions for that app. As of Android 4.4.2 AppOps has been made inaccessible [9], unless the device is rooted.

Apple also introduced fine-grained *access time* permissions on a per-feature basis, such as location and contacts, in iOS 5 [33] and expanded it to other features (e.g., camera, calendar, microphone, HealthKit) in iOS 7 and iOS 8. Importantly, app access in iOS is denied by default until the user explicitly grants it. Furthermore, the iOS privacy settings panel groups apps by data type (e.g., location) rather than showing all permissions for a particular app in one place.

Enhancements to Privacy Controls in Mobile Platforms

Several privacy enhancements have been proposed for Android [19, 21, 29] and iOS [5, 10]. Apex [29] retrofits Android to enable selectively granting, denying or constraining access to specific permissions on a per-app basis. AppFence [19] uses taint tracking [12] to provide shadow data to untrusted apps and to block data from leaving the device. ProtectMyPrivacy (PMP) enables iOS jailbroken users to selectively grant or deny apps access to user information, or provide fake information to an app [5]. PMP also provides privacy setting recommendations for new apps to users via crowdsourcing. Even finer grained privacy recommendations can be provided by clustering such privacy decisions into user preference profiles [28, 27].

Asymmetric Information and Privacy Nudges

In privacy contexts, asymmetric or incomplete information refers to a disparity between users' and service providers' knowledge of collection, use, sharing practices, potential consequences, and available protections concerning users' personal information. This phenomenon has been attributed to ineffective communication of privacy risks and protections to users in privacy policies and notices [20]. More recently, researchers have identified a similar information asymmetry in the context of mobile privacy: users are unaware of the data collection performed by mobile apps [14, 30]. This observation has led to alternate proposals for presenting privacy risks to users in a manner that is more usable and salient [24]. However, research focused on privacy contexts finds that information disclosures led to fleeting and even perverse effects on behavior, casting doubts on one time information disclosures' ability to yield better user privacy decision making. For example, Adjerid et al. [4] showed that the impact of simple and readable notices can be thwarted by a mere 15 second delay between showing privacy-relevant information and privacy choices. In light of these limitations, scholars are increasingly turning to alternate methods for communicating relevant privacy information to users, such as privacy nudges [2].

Nudges are "soft-paternalistic" behavioral interventions that do not restrict choice, but attempt to account for bounded rationality in decision making [32]. Within privacy and security contexts, nudges may ameliorate some of the inconsistency in user decision making, such as the dissonance between users stated privacy concerns and actual observed behavior [2, 31]. While privacy nudging has been proposed as a concept, few works have evaluated how privacy nudges can differentially impact user behavior. Wang et al. found that privacy nudges can effectively influence privacy concerns and behavior on Facebook [34].

In the mobile context, the potential for nudges to support privacy decision making is appealing. It may include notifications that, in contrast to traditional notices, highlight the recipients, contexts, or type of personal information being shared via a mobile device [7]. However, most related work has focused on supporting the app installation process by nudging users towards less privacy-invasive apps [8, 17, 25]. Harbach et al. [18] enrich permission dialogs with personalized examples form the user's device to make risks more salient (e.g., showing a personal photo for gallery access). Rather than focusing on app installation, in this work we analyze behavior of installed apps in order to increase awareness of unexpected invasive behavior and surreptitious data access. Balebako et al. [6] propose mobile privacy nudges based on apps' access frequency to specific data and evaluated them in a lab study. Although our work builds on their work, our work differs in two dimensions. First, our work measures the effect of privacy nudges in triggering users to review and adjust their app permissions, whereas theirs measured perception and feeling. Second, our study evaluates privacy nudges in situ, with participants using their own devices 'in the wild,' whereas their study was a lab study and participants did not use their own devices. Fu et al. [16] propose a per app runtime location access notification and contrasted it with the existing location access disclosure method in Android. They showed both that their method is more effective than Android's and showed anecdotal evidence of how their notification affected participants' behavior (e.g., stopped using intrusive apps). Our work extends their work but differs in two dimensions. First, our work measures the effect of privacy nudges in triggering users to review and adjust their app permissions, whereas theirs focused only on transparency.

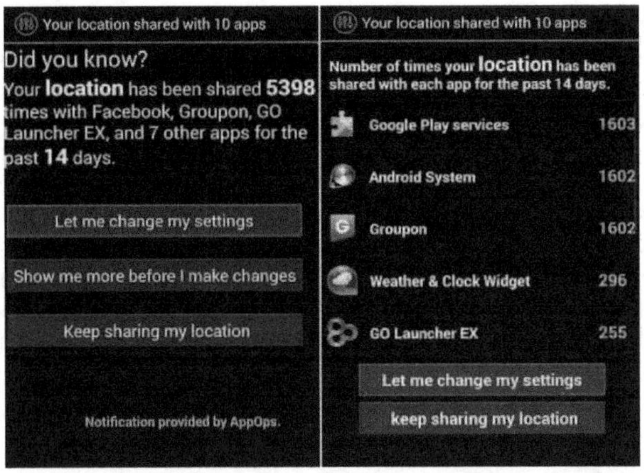

Figure 2. Screenshot of a privacy nudge for location (left) shown to a participant during our study. Nudge content is based on participant's apps and their access to location information. "Let me change my settings" opens AppOps. "Show me more before I make changes" opens the detailed report (right). "Keep Sharing my location" closes the nudge.

Second, their work focused on location access, whereas we also examine phone contacts, calendar, and call logs. Finally, Fisher et al. [15] asked 300 iOS users to take screenshots of their location privacy settings, examined whether users permitted or restricted access to their location, and how to use these decisions to predict future privacy decisions. Our work extends this research, but differs in three dimensions. First, their work focused on location access, whereas we also examine phone contacts, calendar, and call logs. Second, our work combines quantitative and qualitative data to understand why and how users use permission managers, whereas their work only examined users' decisions at one point-of time. Additionally, our work evaluates whether privacy nudges can improve the effectiveness of permission managers, whereas theirs focused on predicting future privacy decisions by users.

MOBILE PRIVACY NUDGE DESIGN

We designed a mobile privacy nudge that provides *concise privacy-relevant information* and *meaningful actions* that reduce the threshold for users to act upon the nudge's content.

Nudge Content

To be effective, a nudge must garner user attention. Prior work has shown that users are unaware of, and surprised by, apps' data access practices and frequency [6, 16, 22], which suggests nudging users to review their app permissions has utility. Therefore, we designed the mobile privacy nudge shown in Figure 2 to display a succinct message describing the number of apps accessing one information type and the total number of accesses in a given period.

The nudge further lists three specific apps that accessed the information in the given period, to concretize the otherwise abstract information. In order to avoid showing only expected apps (e.g., mapping and navigation apps accessing location), the three displayed apps are selected randomly from apps that accessed that information type. The addition of "and 10 other apps" aims to pique the user's interest, and trigger them to review permission settings for the particular information type.

In order to enhance the nudge's credibility, we included cues that establish a relation between the nudge notification and the installed privacy manager (AppOps in our case), such as the AppOps icon and a tag line at the bottom (see Figure 2).

Nudge Response Options

The privacy nudge provides targeted response options to facilitate privacy management (see Figure 2). The "Let me change my settings" option opens AppOps directly. We hypothesized that facilitating access to the permission manager may lead users to review and adjust additional permissions once they switch their focus to privacy management. Since we want nudge users to select this option, it is highlighted.

The second option ("Show me more before I make changes") opens a detailed report, shown in Figure 2, which lists each app's access frequency for the nudge's particular information type, in descending order. The detailed report enables users to investigate which apps accessed the particular information in order to support them in comparing their expectations with apps' data practices. Rather than just naming the option "show me more information," we intentionally indicated that users will also be able to make changes through this option, and imply that this information may help their decision. The detailed report replicates the nudge's other response options to make the provided information actionable. Prior work inspired the detailed report design [6].

The third option ("Keep sharing my [data]") allows users to indicate the status quo is acceptable. Keller et al. [23] recommend employing enhanced active choice to emphasize the desired option (option 1) by "highlighting the losses incumbent in the non-preferred alternative." Therefore, option 3 is adapted to the specific information (i.e. [data] is replaced with "location"). Finally, users can also *ignore* the nudge by pressing the "Home" button or by switching to a another app.

METHODOLOGY

We conducted a field study to gain insights on the effect and perceived utility of mobile privacy managers, as well as the effect and perception of privacy nudges. We implemented our privacy nudges on Android since it supported a permission manager, AppOps, which is accessible on regular non-rooted devices. Thus, our 23 participants were able to use their own phones. Our study received IRB approval.

Implementation of Study Client

We designed a study client app to act as a launcher for AppOps and installed it on participants' phones. Our study client collected information about app permissions accesses for specific information types, which was used to generate personalized privacy nudges for each participant's phone. The required information was obtained by periodically recording logs created by AppOps. The AppOps logs show for each app-permission pair the last time the app tried to access the permission. The logs show when access to a permission was rejected (e.g., after the user restricted an app's access). If the app is currently using a permission, the logs show how long the app has been accessing it. By capturing this information in five minute intervals, we gained detailed insights about apps accessing permissions, as well as the progression of permission changes made by participants via AppOps. Accessing the AppOps logs requires a one-time runtime permission ("GET_APP_OPS_STATS"), which can only be granted if the device is connected via USB after app installation.

In addition to recording access frequency and permission changes, our study client recorded participants opening AppOps, as well as their interaction with displayed privacy nudges. Permission changes had to be recorded periodically, since AppOps does not provide easy access to specific interaction events and modifying AppOps would have required rooting and flashing participants' devices, which we deemed undesirable. Hence, we used the time difference between a participant's recorded response to a privacy nudge and an observed permission adjustment to infer whether it was triggered by the respective nudge.

Study Procedure

Our field study consisted of an entry session, three consecutive field phases lasting 22 days in total, an exit survey, and an optional exit interview. We opted for a within-subjects design as we were interested in observing phone and app usage without interventions in order to establish a baseline, as well as observing interaction with a permission manager with and without supporting privacy nudges.

Entry session: We invited participants to our lab to read and sign our consent form. Because AppOps was only available on Android versions 4.3–4.4.1, participants were required to affirm that they would not update to Android 4.4.2 during the study, and could be disqualified otherwise.

Next, participants completed an online entry survey on a provided computer. The survey asked about general Android usage (e.g., frequently used apps, reasons for installing or uninstalling apps), mobile privacy and security attitudes and behaviors (e.g., screen look use, phone encryption, awareness of apps' permissions), and demographic questions (e.g., gender, age, phone model). While the participant completed the survey, we installed the study client on her phone with the required runtime permission to access AppOps logs, and placed it in a folder named 'Android Apps Behaviors," to make it easily locatable.

Phase 1: Baseline: For the first 7 days of the study, our study client collected data about the participant's installed apps and their data access behavior, without providing access to AppOps or showing privacy nudges. The information collected served as a baseline to better understand participants' phone and app use, and also informed the generation of privacy nudges in phase 3.

Phase 2: AppOps Only: On the first day of the second phase, we made AppOps available through the study client and sent an email and an SMS to participants introducing it. The message subject was "AppOps is now available to you" and it read "AppOps is an app which allows you to selectively grant/deny apps access to your personal information (e.g., location, phone contacts, calendar, SMS messages, etc) on your phone. We just made this app available to you. To use it, go to 'Android Apps Behaviors' folder then click on AppOps." This notification acted as a weak privacy nudge, comparable to seeing a media article or an ad about AppOps. Participants did not receive any further interventions during phase 2, which lasted 7 days.

Phase 3: AppOps Plus Privacy Nudges: In phase 3, which lasted 8 days, participants additionally received one privacy nudge per day, sent at a random time between 11am and 8pm. In our study, we provided nudges for four information types: location, phone contacts, calendar, or call logs. They were selected both because they were shown to be the subject of mobile users' privacy concerns [13], and because initial experiments demonstrated that these four information types constituted the most requested resources by apps, which made it likely that participants' would have apps installed that actually accessed these information types. On the first four days of phase 3, all four nudges were shown in a random order to avoid ordering effect. The same nudges were then repeated in the same order on the last four days of phase 3. The first set of privacy nudges showed access statistics since the beginning of the study (i.e. 14-18 days), the second set showed access statistics for the period since the previous nudge for that data type (i.e. 4 days). If no installed apps had accessed the information type of a scheduled nudge in the respective time period, the next nudge would be shown instead.

Exit Survey and Interviews: After completing phase 3, participants were sent a link to an online exit survey. The survey focused on the participant's experience with AppOps (e.g., prior use of AppOps, AppOps use during study, reasons for using AppOps) and the participant's understanding of, and experience with, the privacy nudges (e.g., meaning of nudge text and options, provided privacy awareness and decision support). Upon completion of the exit survey, participants were compensated with a $30 Amazon gift card.

All participants were further invited to an optional semi-structured one-hour interview and compensated with an additional $10 Amazon gift card. Eight participants responded and were interviewed. The interviews served to gain deeper qualitative insights to participants' experiences with AppOps and the privacy nudges. The interviews were partially tailored to a participant's behavior during the study. For example, we inquired participants' reasons for specific permission changes they made. We further presented them with specific nudges displayed to them when asking about their experiences. All interviews were audio recorded and then coded with categorical codes (i.e. AppOps, the privacy nudges, reasons for app permission changes). We, then, conducted thematic analysis on each of these three categories.

Recruitment

We conducted our study from May to July 2014. Participants were recruited via Craigslist and from a city-wide participant pool maintained by our university. Ads directed prospective participants to a screening survey. Twenty-six respondents, meeting the following criteria, were invited to participate in the study: (1) Adults who have Android phones running Android version 4.3–4.4 (because AppOps is only supported by these Android versions); (2) have a mobile data plan with at least 2 GB/month (as data would have to be transferred during the study); (3) able to visit our lab for the entry session. Three were later disqualified as they upgraded to Android 4.4.2 during the study, which made AppOps inaccessible.

Limitations

Conducting a field study enabled us to evaluate our privacy nudges in-situ on participants' own devices. This increased ecological validity but introduced multiple challenges. First, we were unable to recruit a larger number of participants, because carriers (e.g., AT&T) and OEMs (e.g., Samsung) rolled out updates to Android 4.4.2 (i.e. AppOps removed) around the same time, which significantly shrunk the pool of potential participants. Second, our study client required Internet connectivity. However,

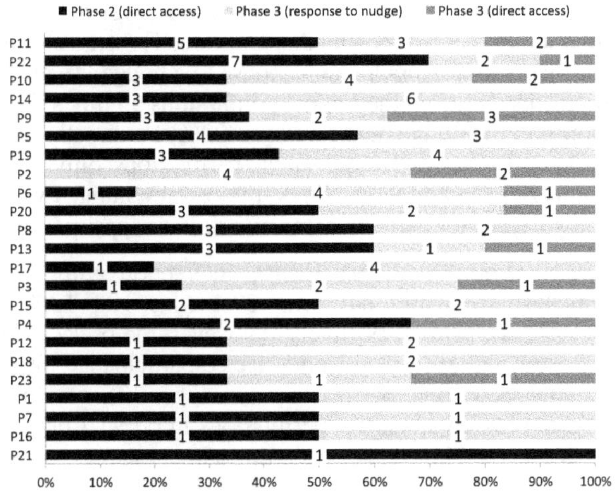

Figure 3. The number of times each participant reviewed their app permissions by opening AppOps in phase 2 & 3. Participants are ordered based on the frequency of reviewing app permissions.

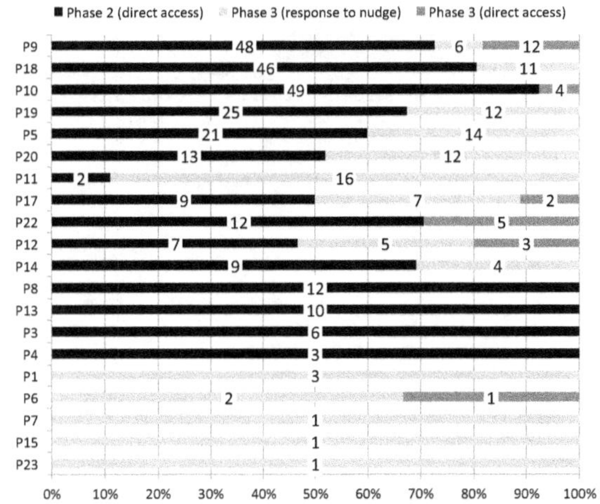

Figure 4. Number of permissions restricted by each participant. Participants are ordered based on (a) the restrictive adjustments they made either in phases 2&3, phase 2, or phase 3, and (b) the frequency of adjustments within each group. P2, P16, & P21 never adjusted their app permissions.

some participants deactivated data connection to conserve data volume or had intermittent connectivity for other reasons. This affected our data collection and caused some nudges to be lost or delivered later than scheduled. We implemented a monitoring tool to identify participants whose devices were not sending back information regularly, and then reminded them via email to remain connected. While this worked, we used this approach sparsely to avoid biasing participants' responses. Due to these technical difficulties, some participants received all eight nudges while others received fewer nudges. In addition, we acknowledge a potential self-selection bias in our participant pool. These limitations may have skewed our results to be more conservative, but we are confident that they did not undermine our findings in general.

RESULTS

We first describe participant demographics and apps usage. Then, we report how participants interacted with the permission manger alone followed by their interaction with the permission manger with accompanying privacy nudges. Finally, we report how participants interacted with nudges and evaluate the effectiveness of the nudge's components.

Demographics

In total, we had 23 participants (65% female; ages 18–44, median=23), of whom 21 owned Samsung devices and 2 owned an HTC One. Based on data collected in phase 1, participants had 89 apps installed on average (SD=22), including services and pre-installed apps. Twenty-one participants (91%) reported never using AppOps before; one had used AppOps, and one was unsure. Moreover, the data collected in phase 1 showed that participants could not access AppOps (e.g. not other launcher app for AppOps installed), until phase 2. Six (26%) of our participants are in information technology related fields and only one of them specializes in computer security. However, our results do not indicate that their background had a significant effect on their behavior. P2 never adjusted his app permissions throughout the study, P13 only adjusted the permissions in phase 2, P6&P7 only adjusted the permissions in phase 3, and P10&P12 adjusted their app permissions in both phases.

In the following, we use two main variables in our analysis:

(1) Reviewing apps' permissions represents how often a participant opened AppOps to review their app permissions regardless of whether they adjusted app permissions.

(2) Adjusting apps' permissions represents how often participants adjusted their app permissions by calculating (a) *restrictive adjustments*, i.e., how often participants restricted any app access to a permission, and (b) *permissive adjustments*, i.e., how often participants permitted an app access to a restricted permission.

Effectiveness of AppOps Without Privacy Nudges

In phase 2, after we made AppOps available, participants reviewed their app permissions 51 times, restricted 76 distinct apps from accessing 272 permissions, and permitted access to one restricted permission.

Reviewing apps' permissions: As Figure 3 shows, 22 participants (95.6%) reviewed their permissions at least once. Of those, 12 participants reviewed their apps' permissions multiple times. Only P2 did not review his permissions in phase 2.

Adjusting apps' permissions: As shown in Figure 4, 15 (65%) participants restricted 272 app-permission pairs for 76 distinct apps, including both participant-installed and pre-installed apps, see Figure 5. Breaking down restrictions by information type, participants restricted apps' access to location 74 times (27%), contacts 57 times (21%), calendar 10 times (4%), and call logs 9 times (3%). Other restricted permissions included: camera 42 (9%), SMS 21 (8%), post notification 19 (7%), and recording audio 15 (6%). Only P10 made a permissive adjustment by permitting the Weather Channel app to send notifications.

In the exist survey, we asked participants if they used AppOps, what they used it for, and why. Most participants reported that they used AppOps to review their app permissions and adjust them if needed. For example, P9 responded: "[I used AppOps] to see what personal information different apps had access to and change that" because "I didn't like that too many apps could access so much information."

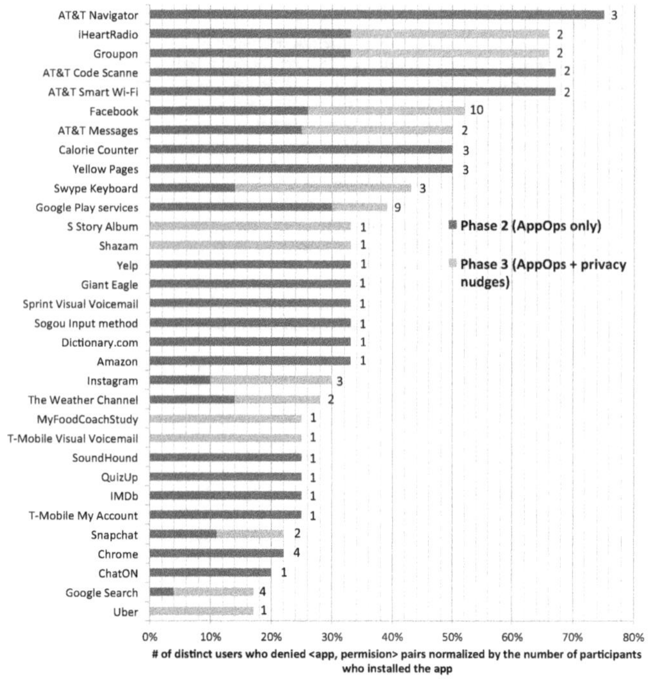

Figure 5. The apps that were revoked permissions in phase 2 & 3. The numbers to the right of the bars are the absolute number of distinct users who revoked at least one permission per app.

In the interviews, participants further explained why they restricted apps' access to permissions. First, participants restricted unused apps, especially pre-installed apps. P10 stated: "I also blocked bunch of AT&T bloatware from accessing any information. I don't use them anyways." Second, participants restricted permissions required for unused functionality. P13 restricted iHeartRadio access to location, explaining: "I know what stations I want listen to no matter where I'm so I turn off the location." Third, participants restricted apps when the purpose to access their personal information is unclear. P4 stated: "[I turned it off] because I can't think of a reason why Inkpad needs my location."

Making the permission manager available to participants led them to actively review their app permissions and adjust them as needed. This indicates clearly that participants wanted to exercise control over apps' access to personal information.

Effectiveness of AppOps with Privacy Nudges

The goal of our nudges was to get users to review their app permissions and adjust them as needed. To that end, we designed the nudges to complement and increase the effectiveness of AppOps. It is important to note that participants' phase 3 behavior is contingent on their phase 2 behavior. For instance, if a participant restricted access to some permissions in phase 2, these restrictions hold in phase 3, and may not require further review or adjustment. Hence, we report and analyze results from phase 3 relative to phase 2.

In phase 3, participants reviewed their apps' permissions 69 times, restricted 47 distinct apps from accessing 122 permissions, and permitted six apps access to six permissions.

Reviewing apps' permissions: As Figure 3 shows, 22 participants (95.6%), with the exception of P21, reviewed their apps' permissions at least once in phase 3. Participants could review their apps' permissions either by opening AppOps directly (same as in phase 2), or by opening AppOps in response to a nudge. Twenty-One participants reviewed their apps' permissions 53 times (78%) in response to the nudge, and 15 times (22%) by directly opening AppOps. P4 reviewed her apps' permissions only once by opening AppOps directly. Thus, the privacy nudges were the primary trigger for participants to review their apps' permissions.

Figure 6 shows that participants' interaction with AppOps declined sharply after day ten: 39% (day 10), 13%, 17%, 22%, 4%, and 9%, respectively. However, the privacy nudges introduced in phase 3 positively affected participants' interest in reviewing their apps' permissions (cf. Figure 3). For instance, P2 did not review his apps' permissions in phase 2 but privacy nudges triggered him to do so six times in phase 3.

Adjusting apps' permissions: Figure 4 shows that 16 (70%) participants restricted 122 app-permission pairs, 14 in direct response to nudges. Ninty-Five (78%) of the restrictive app permission adjustments in phase 3 were made in response to a nudge. Only three participants made permissive adjustments due to loss of app functionality. In the interview, P10 noted that he restricted and later permitted Facebook's access to the clipboard, because he was unable to copy&paste in Facebook. Participants restricted permissions from 47 distinct apps, including both self-installed and pre-installed apps, see Figure 5. Participants restricted 122 permissions such as location 30 (25%), contacts 25 (20%), calendar 8 (7%), and call logs 6 (5%). Other restricted permissions included: post notification 10 (8%), SMS 9 (7%), camera 7 (6%), record audio 7 (6%).

To understand the data further, we analyzed participants' restrictive adjustments in phase 2 & phase 3, and divided them into four groups based on our analysis. We additionally examined the groups' comfort level by analyzing participants' responses to 5-level likert scale question about location, calendar, contacts, and call logs.

Group 1: restrictive adjustments in phases 2 & 3. Although they made restrictive changes already in phase 2, the nudges led 11 participants to make additional adjustments in phase 3. For instance, P11 & P17 restricted 89% and 50% additional permissions. These participants were overall uncomfortable sharing their personal information with apps. This suggests that even active, privacy conscious participants benefited from the additional information provided by privacy nudges, which triggered them to further review and adjust their permissions to better match their privacy preferences.

Group 2: restrictive adjustments in phase 3 only. These five participants made no restrictive adjustments in phase 2. However, the nudges received in phase 3 triggered them to adjust their permissions. These participants were also overall uncomfortable sharing their personal information with apps. This suggests that the nudges provided additional value compared to AppOps alone, triggering them to actively review and adjust their app permissions.

Group 3: restrictive adjustments in phase 2 only. Although the privacy nudges triggered three of these four participants to review their permissions in phase 3, they made no restrictive adjustments. These participants reported mixed levels of comfort sharing

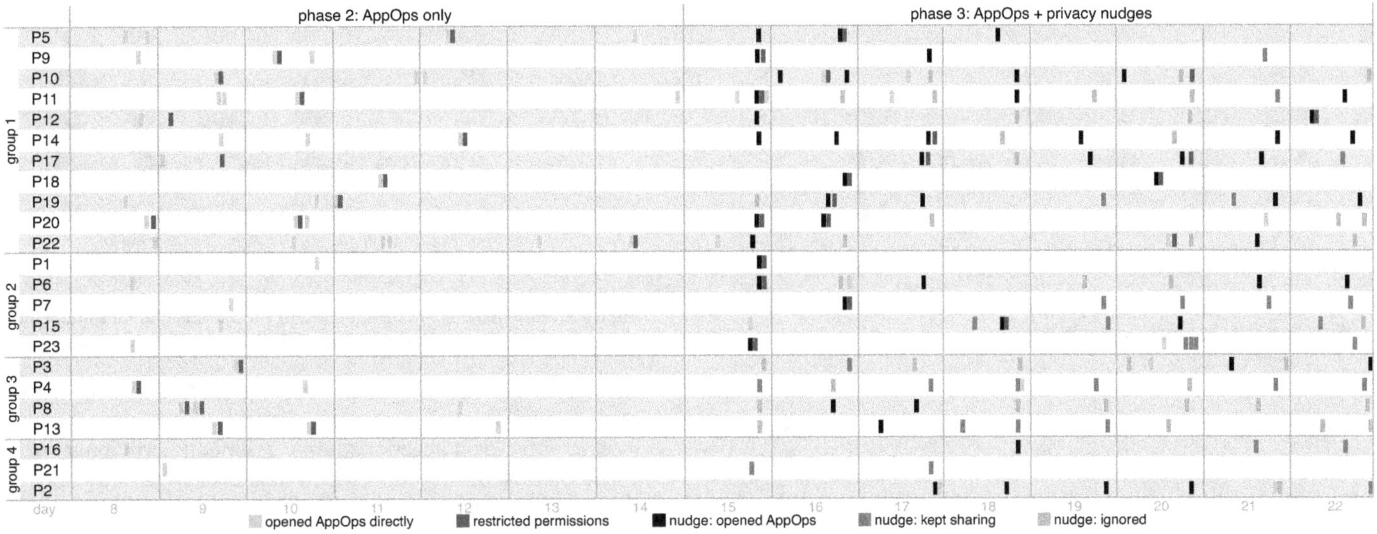

Figure 6. Timeline of participants' interactions with AppOps and the privacy nudges during phase 2 and phase 3. In the X-axis, each column represents a day during phase 2 (7 days) & phase 3 (8 days).

personal information with apps. There are multiple potential explanations for why these participants made no adjustments in phase 3. First, their phase 2 adjustments may have sufficed, particularly for P8 & P13, who adjusted 12 and 10 permissions, respectively. Second, aspects of the nudge affected participants' experience. P4 stated in the interview that she always received the nudges when she was at work and therefore never had time to interact with them. Third, participant-specific issues. In the interview, P13 reported that phase 3 was a very busy week for him, which prevented him from interacting much with the nudges.

Group 4: no restrictive adjustments in either phase. Although the privacy nudges did not trigger these three participants to adjust their permissions, two did review them in response to the nudges. These participants reported being comfortable or neutral sharing their personal information with apps, which may explain the lack of restrictive adjustments.

Interaction with the Nudges

In total, participants received 125 nudges. We report details of how participants interacted with them.

Did participants understand the nudge? In our survey, we presented each participant with a nudge screenshot and asked them about their understanding of the nudge, its options, the trust cues, and the detailed report. All of the participants understood the nudge, the options, and the trust cues ("Notification provided by AppOps"). Nine participants did not understand option two in the nudge ("show me more before I make changes"). Four never chose this option, possibly because they did not understand its meaning or function.

How did participants interact with the nudges? As Figure 7 shows, participants responded to 53 (42%) nudges by choosing "let me change my settings" to open AppOps and 31 (25%) nudges by choosing "keep sharing my [data]." Participants ignored 41 (33%) nudges.

Although some participants may have chosen "keep sharing my [data]" to express satisfaction with how apps were accessing their personal information, our interviews revealed they also used it to close nudges when they came at unsuitable times (e.g., busy at work or about to use another app). P4 stated: "for one [nudge] I said keep sharing because as I said earlier I didn't have time, because if I saw that normally I would have definitely changed it, if I wasn't at work." Similarly, our interviews showed that participants ignored nudges because they received them at unsuitable times. For instance, P19 also explained: "the first time [the nudge] came up I was on a run and it covered my running app. All of a sudden I couldn't hear [my running app] telling me my mileage anymore. So I opened my screen and I swiped [the lock] and that [nudge] was there and I was so confused I hit back so fast it was gone."

Did participants adjust permissions in response to nudges? We counted restrictive apps' permissions adjustments as direct response to the nudge if a participant responded to a nudge by choosing "let me change my settings" and then made these adjustments within 10 minutes. Fourteen (60%) participants made restrictive adjustments in responses to 17 (13.6%) different nudges out of 125 nudges. Of those, three participants made restrictive changes in response to two different nudges. We acknowledge that in some cases the nudge may have led participants to adjust permissions after 10 minutes. P17 made restrictive adjustments within 22 minutes. P1 made three adjustments: one of them within an hour.

The nudges may have had indirect influence on participants' decisions to adjust their app permissions. For instance, a participant might review her app permissions in response to a nudge without adjusting them, and then later open AppOps to adjust app permissions. While these indirect effects are difficult to track, the interviews helped us to identify a noteworthy occurrence. P10 responded to the first nudge by choosing "show me more before I make changes" to open the detailed report and then chose "let me change my setting". However, he never adjusted his app permissions. After a couple of hours, P10 opened AppsOps directly and restricted both the Weather Channel app and HTC Location service access to location. In the interview, P10 described how the nudge helped him realize the Weather Channel app's data access practices mismatched his expectations "this weather app was the most hogging app on my cellphone. I

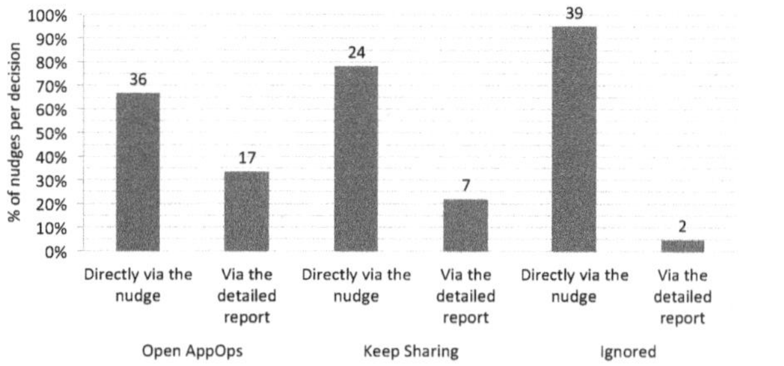

Figure 7. How participants responded to the nudges. The numbers on top of the bars are the absolute numbers.

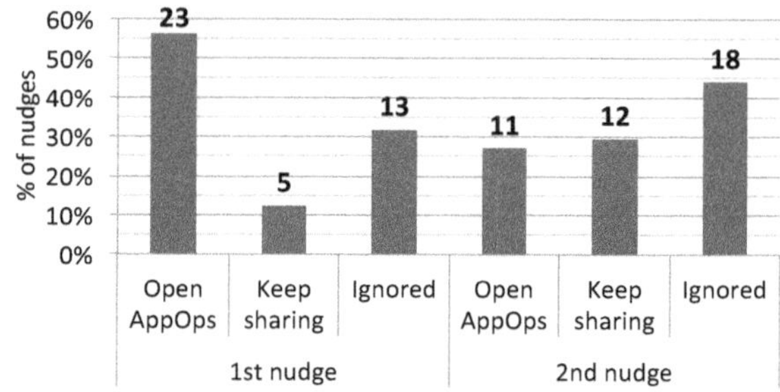

Figure 8. How participants responded to the 1st and the 2nd nudge of the same data type. The numbers on top of the bars are the absolute numbers.

live in a city why do you have to access my location thousands of times in [a] few days? I not only blocked this app, I removed [it]."

To explore whether nudging participants about a particular data type triggered adjusting corresponding permissions, we counted the number of adjustments in which the permission matched the data type in the nudge. As reported earlier, participants restricted their permissions in response to 17 nudges. The response to 15 (88%) nudges included at least one permission that matched the data type in the nudge. Thirty (32%) out of 95 restricted permissions matched the data type featured in the nudge. In other words, 68% of restricted permissions were for data types other than the one in the nudge. A possible explanation for this behavior is how the AppOps UI is structured. If a participant chooses one app, she will be redirected to a new screen listing all the personal information that the selected app has access to, as shown in Figure 1. Thus, it is possible that participants may have initially intended to only adjust the permissions matching the nudge's data type, but adjusted additional permissions as needed. This suggests that the design of the permission manager may sway participants to adjust more permissions than initially intended.

Finally, we explore the effect of the example apps included in the nudge. We checked if participants adjusted permissions for any of the randomly chosen apps in the nudge. As reported earlier, participants restricted their apps' permissions in response to 17 nudges. For nine (53%) nudges, the participants adjusted apps' permissions of at least one of the apps listed in the nudge. For 2 nudges, the participants adjusted the permissions of 2 out of 3 apps listed in the nudge. Out of all 48 apps listed in the 17 nudges, the participants adjusted permissions for 11 (23%) apps, this suggests that example apps listed in the nudge have a moderate effect on participants' decisions to adjust their apps' permissions.

How did participants respond to the 1st and 2nd nudge? In response to their first nudge, 16 (70%) participants chose "let me change my settings", three (13%) choose "Keep sharing my [data]", and four (17%) ignored it. Participants' likelihood to choose "let me change my settings" decreased when they received the second nudge (after 4 days) as Figure 8 shows. This suggests that repeating a nudge about the same data type within a short time may be ineffective, likely because participant preferences do not change within a short time. This leads us to suggest a potential improvement for our nudge. The nudge should provide a mechanism for users to identify apps that they are comfortable sharing their personal information with. Thereafter, the user could receive more pertinent nudges including only unidentified apps.

The detailed report: The main goal of providing a detailed report, as shown in Figure 2, was to give interested participants a closer look at apps' data access patterns. Fourteen participants (61%) chose "show me more before I make changes" to open the detailed report in response to 26 (21%) out of 125 nudges. After opening the detailed report, participants chose "let me change my settings" more often than "keep sharing my [data]" (33% vs. 22%), see Figure 7.

Participants opened the detailed report in eight nudges (47%) before making restrictive adjustments. In each case, the participant made restrictive adjustments for at least one app listed in the detailed report. This suggests that the detailed report is helpful. Though, it is more helpful when the participant intends to make adjustments as the detailed report provided a closer look at the data collection practices of individual apps.

Frequency of access: We explore whether an increase in frequency of personal information accesses by apps correlates with an increase in participants' likelihood to choose "let me change my settings." Using a random effects linear regression, we found a significant correlation ($p<.05$) between the frequency of accessing personal information by apps and participants' likelihood of choosing "let me change my settings," particularly for location ($p<0.01$). This suggests that nudging about apps' frequency of access is effective as it triggered participants to review their apps' permissions, which was the nudge's purpose.

During the interviews, all eight participants indicated that frequencies of access to personal information by apps was the element of the nudge that caught their attention. For instance, P10 explained: "4182 [times] are you kidding me? It felt like I'm being followed by my own phone. It was scary. That number is too high." P17 stated: "the number was huge [356 times], unexpected. Again, big number a bit unexpected."

DISCUSSION

In this section, we discuss the effectiveness of the permission manager and nudges, and how to design more effective nudges based on lessons learned from our study.

Permission Managers Help

Access to a permission manager alone led participants to actively review and change app permissions. All but one of our participants reviewed their app permissions at least once; half of them did so multiple times. Furthermore, the permission manager led more than half of our participants to exercise control over the personal information apps were allowed to access; participants modified permissions of both popular apps and pre-installed apps. In short, our results highlight the value of using permission managers in mobile platforms, because they give users the control they may want and need. However, service providers have taken highly different paths in their handling of such tools. Violations of end users' privacy by app developers have led Apple to provide users with progressively more privacy controls in iOS [33]. On the other hand, Google notoriously removed AppOps from Android phones in 2013 [9]. While no official explanation was provided, this move might be indicative of tensions between Google's advertising-based revenue model and its stated objective of giving users more control over their information.[1] Another possible interpretation might be that this move was motivated by usability concerns, whether concerns over the number of settings made available to users or concerns that users may deny permissions that are necessary for apps to function. Our study however showed that, despite the large number of settings, users generally benefited from having them and we did not see many instances of users complaining about their apps stopping to work.

Nudges Can Increase the Utility of Permission Managers

In addition to making users aware of the permission manager, our goal was to design a nudge that assisted users in better managing their privacy. Our results show that even a simple nudge can help users utilize the permission manager to manage their privacy on mobile devices.

The privacy nudges led participants (both those who had and those who had not used the permission manager before) to review and adjust their permissions. This suggests that nudges help both active users, who may not fully utilize the permission manager alone, and users who otherwise might not have made any adjustments, to act to bring their data sharing into alignment with their privacy preferences.

Privacy nudges are starting to find their way into mobile platforms. Recently, iOS 8 introduced what can be viewed as a form of privacy nudge. Specifically, if a user allows an app to access her location even when not using the app (i.e. in the background), iOS will occasionally ask her whether she wants to continue doing so [1]. This approach is consistent with our findings, which show the benefits of combining permission manager functionality and nudges.

How to Design a More Effective Mobile Privacy Nudge?

We learned valuable lessons from testing mobile privacy nudges with real users on their own devices. Based on those lessons, we offer some suggestions for designing and deploying a more effective mobile privacy nudge.

(1) Personalization: Our results show that users have different privacy preferences for different apps and data types. This suggests that a personalized nudge may be more effective. A personalized nudge could learn which apps the user is or is not comfortable sharing her information with, and nudge accordingly. The nudge could also be customized based on the user's previous decisions. For instance, if the user specified that she is satisfied with an app's data collection practices, this app should not be included in subsequent nudges.

(2) Salient, sticky, but not annoying: We designed our nudge to be full-screen to ensure that it was salient and hard to be ignored. Occasionally, our nudge annoyed some participants, especially when they were using or about to use an app, causing them to quickly dismiss the nudge. To be more effective, a privacy nudge should be salient and sticky, but not annoying. To be salient but not annoying, the nudge may cover part of the screen, like Android's special "Heads-up" notification that covers the top third of the screen. Although this format provides fewer options than a full-screen version, it may be less annoying since it is less disruptive. To be sticky, the nudge could include a "remind me later" option. After a small number of rescheduling (e.g., 2), the nudge could be transformed to a notification and sent to the notification bar.

(3) Configurable: Users have different preferences for receiving privacy nudges. Some participants liked the daily nudges, whereas others indicated they would prefer weekly nudges. Some participants had a time preference to receive the nudge (e.g., at night, on Sunday). Moreover, some participants strongly favored receiving a nudge in form of a notification rather than a full-screen nudge. In light of this, a more effective nudge should accommodate these diverse preferences by allowing users to configure the nudge. Users should be able to easily specify the time(s) when they would like to receive nudges, how often, and the form of delivery (full, heads-up, or regular notification). Whether users will be able or willing to configure these options will need further investigation.

CONCLUSION

In summary, results from our study indicate that Android users benefit from an app permission manager such as App Ops, with a majority of our participants taking advantage of the controls it offers. They also indicate that, even with access to such a manager, user's awareness of the data collected by their apps remains limited. Users would further benefit from receiving nudges that inform them about the sensitive data collected by their apps. The nudges used in this study were fairly simplistic. Moving forward, nudges would benefit from possibly being further personalized, salient, sticky, and configurable but not annoying. In addition, a follow-up study with a larger number of participants and a longer timeframe is required to further validate and refine our findings. In particular, it is still an open question (1) whether privacy nudges would continue to be effective over time due to possible habituation effects, and (2) whether privacy nudges could also be designed to help users as they install new apps.

ACKNOWLEDGMENTS

This research was supported in part by the National Science Foundation under grants CNS 10-1012763 (Nudging Users Towards Privacy) and CNS 13-30596 (Towards Effective Web Privacy Notice & Choice: A Multi-Disciplinary Perspective), in part by IWT SBO Project on Security and Privacy for Online Social Networks (SPION), in part by Google, in part by Samsung, and in part by King Abdulaziz City for Science and Technology.

REFERENCES

1. Apple denies Chinese report that location data are a security risk. `http://on.ft.com/VXpZKR`. Published: 2014-6-12, Accessed: 2014-9-14.

[1] Analysis of Android source code shows that Google has been expanding AppOps code since then (e.g., increasing the number of permissions to control). This suggests that Google may, perhaps, provide mobile users more control in the future.

2. Acquisti, A. Nudging privacy: The behavioral economics of personal information. *IEEE Security & Privacy 7*, 6 (2009), 82–85.

3. Acquisti, A., and Grossklags, J. Privacy and rationality in individual decision making. *IEEE Security & Privacy 3*, 1 (2005), 26–33.

4. Adjerid, I., Acquisti, A., Brandimarte, L., and Loewenstein, G. Sleights of privacy: Framing, disclosures, and the limits of transparency. In *Proc. SOUPS* (2013).

5. Agarwal, Y., and Hall, M. ProtectMyPrivacy: detecting and mitigating privacy leaks on iOS devices using crowdsourcing. In *Proc. MobiSys* (2013).

6. Balebako, R., Jung, J., Lu, W., Cranor, L. F., and Nguyen, C. Little brothers watching you: Raising awareness of data leaks on smartphones. In *Proc. SOUPS* (2013).

7. Balebako, R., Leon, P. G., Almuhimedi, H., Kelley, P. G., Mugan, J., Acquisti, A., Cranor, L. F., and Sadeh, N. Nudging users towards privacy on mobile devices. In *Proc. CHI-PINC* (2011).

8. Choe, E. K., Jung, J., Lee, B., and Fisher, K. Nudging people away from privacy-invasive mobile apps through visual framing. In *Proc. INTERACT* (2013).

9. EFF. Google Removes Vital Privacy Feature From Android, Claiming Its Release Was Accidental. `http://goo.gl/emMQPa`. Published: 2013-12-12, Accessed: 2014-9-14.

10. Egele, M., Kruegely, C., Kirdaz, E., and Vigna, G. PiOS: Detecting privacy leaks in iOS applications. In *Proc. NDSS* (2011).

11. Egelman, S., Felt, A., and Wagner, D. Choice architecture and smartphone privacy: There's a price for that. In *Economics of Info. Sec. & Priv.* Springer, 2013.

12. Enck, W., Gilbert, P., Chun, B.-G., Cox, L. P., Jung, J., McDaniel, P., and Sheth, A. N. Taintdroid: An information flow tracking system for real-time privacy monitoring on smartphones. *Commun. ACM 57*, 3 (2014), 99–106.

13. Felt, A. P., Egelman, S., and Wagner, D. I've got 99 problems, but vibration ain't one: a survey of smartphone users' concerns. In *Proc. SPSM* (2012).

14. Felt, A. P., Ha, E., Egelman, S., Haney, A., Chin, E., and Wagner, D. Android permissions: User attention, comprehension, and behavior. In *Proc. SOUPS* (2012).

15. Fisher, D., Dorner, L., and Wagner, D. Location privacy: user behavior in the field.

16. Fu, H., Yang, Y., Shingte, N., Lindqvist, J., and Gruteser, M. A field study of run-time location access disclosures on android smartphones. *Proc. USEC* (2014).

17. Gates, C., Chen, J., Li, N., and Proctor, R. Effective risk communication for android apps. *IEEE Trans. Depend. Secure Comp. 11*, 3 (May 2014), 252–265.

18. Harbach, M., Hettig, M., Weber, S., and Smith, M. Using personal examples to improve risk communication for security & privacy decisions. In *Proc. CHI* (2014).

19. Hornyack, P., Han, S., Jung, J., Schechter, S., and Wetherall, D. These aren't the droids you're looking for: Retrofitting android to protect data from imperious applications. In *Proc. CCS* (2011).

20. Jensen, C., and Potts, C. Privacy policies as decision-making tools: an evaluation of online privacy notices. In *Proc. CHI* (2004).

21. Jeon, J., Micinski, K., Vaughan, J., Reddy, N., Zhu, Y., Foster, J., and Millstein, T. Dr. Android and Mr. Hide: Fine-grained Security Policies on Unmodified Android. Tech. rep., University of Maryland, 2011.

22. Jung, J., Han, S., and Wetherall, D. Enhancing mobile application permissions with runtime feedback and constraints. In *Proc. SPSM* (2012).

23. Keller, P. A., Harlam, B., Loewenstein, G., and Volpp, K. G. Enhanced active choice: A new method to motivate behavior change. *J. Consum. Psychol. 21*, 4 (2011), 376–383.

24. Kelley, P. G., Bresee, J., Cranor, L. F., and Reeder, R. W. A nutrition label for privacy. In *Proc. SOUPS* (2009).

25. Kelley, P. G., Cranor, L. F., and Sadeh, N. Privacy as part of the app decision-making process. In *Proc. CHI* (2013).

26. Lin, J., Amini, S., Hong, J. I., Sadeh, N., Lindqvist, J., and Zhang, J. Expectation and purpose: understanding users' mental models of mobile app privacy through crowdsourcing. In *Proc. UbiComp* (2012).

27. Lin, J., Liu, B., Sadeh, N., and Hong, J. I. Modeling users' mobile app privacy preferences: Restoring usability in a sea of permission settings. In *Proc. SOUPS* (2014).

28. Liu, B., Lin, J., and Sadeh, N. Reconciling mobile app privacy and usability on smartphones: could user privacy profiles help? In *Proc. WWW* (2014), 201–212.

29. Nauman, M., Khan, S., and Zhang, X. Apex: Extending Android Permission Model and Enforcement with User-defined Runtime Constraints. In *Proc. CCS* (2010).

30. Shklovski, I., Mainwaring, S. D., Skúladóttir, H. H., and Borgthorsson, H. Leakiness and creepiness in app space: Perceptions of privacy and mobile app use. In *Proc. CHI* (2014).

31. Spiekermann, S., Grossklags, J., and Berendt, B. E-privacy in 2nd generation e-commerce: privacy preferences versus actual behavior. In *Proc. EC* (2001).

32. Thaler, R. H., and Sunstein, C. R. *Nudge: Improving decisions about health, wealth, and happiness.* Yale University Press, 2008.

33. Wall Street Journal. Apple Bows to iPhone Privacy Pressures. `http://on.wsj.com/160kjhv`. Published: 2012-2-16, Accessed: 2014-9-14.

34. Wang, Y., Leon, P. G., Acquisti, A., Cranor, L. F., Forget, A., and Sadeh, N. A field trial of privacy nudges for facebook. In *Proc. CHI* (2014).

Can an Algorithm Know the "Real You"? Understanding People's Reactions to Hyper-personal Analytics Systems

Jeffrey Warshaw[1], Tara Matthews[2*], Steve Whittaker[1], Chris Kau[2], Mateo Bengualid[3], Barton A. Smith[2]

[1]University of California at Santa Cruz, CA, USA, {jwarshaw, swhittak}@ucsc.edu

[2]IBM Research - Almaden, CA, USA, taramatthews@gmail.com, {ckau, barton.smith}@us.ibm.com

[3]IBM Argentina, Cordoba, Argentina, benguali@ar.ibm.com

ABSTRACT

Recent research has developed analytics that threaten online self-presentation and privacy by automatically generating profiles of individuals' most personal traits—their personality, values, motivations, and so on. But we know little about people's reactions to personal traits profiles of themselves, or what influences their decisions to share such profiles. We present an early qualitative study of people's reactions to a working *hyper-personal analytics system.* The system lets them see their personality and values profile derived from their own social media text. Our results reveal a paradox. Participants found their personal traits profiles creepily accurate and did not like sharing them in many situations. However, they felt pressured by the social risks of not sharing and showed signs of learned helplessness, leading them to share despite their misgivings. Further, they felt unqualified to significantly modify their profile contents due to a surprising trust in the "expert" algorithm. We explore design implications for hyper-personal analytics systems that consider the needs and preferences of the people being profiled, suggesting ways to enhance the control they feel and the benefits they reap.

Author Keywords

Hyper-personal analytics; privacy; self-presentation; social media; personality; values; user study.

ACM Classification Keywords

H.5.m. Information interfaces and presentation (e.g., HCI): Miscellaneous.

INTRODUCTION

A growing body of research is developing analytics to learn all about individuals' *personal traits* [19]—their personality [15,40], values [4], attitudes [12], and so on—to drive *hyper-personalized* technology user experiences. These new hyper-personal analytics threaten both online self-presentation and privacy, as algorithms sift through people's online behavior to uncover implicit personal traits, which individuals may be unaware they are communicating. With these analytics, anyone with access to text you have posted online could generate a profile of your most intimate personal traits. Market researchers and employers have demonstrated a strong interest in personality profiling, long using small-scale personality profiling as a proxy for consumer behavior [26,39], or to improve hiring decisions [3]. Modern analytics systems have made inferring these traits scalable, and marketing and human resources groups now seek to deploy them widely. As such profiles reach or surpass human judgment of personal traits [41], it is critical to understand how the people being profiled feel about this technology, and how they want the analytics designed and their outputs shared or kept private.

People are already targets of systems that profile them for ads or personalization based on their online behavior [28,29,37]. Recent work has studied how people feel about targeted behavioral profiles of them created by data aggregators, who compile large amounts of information from various sources to identify an individual's demographics, online behaviors, and interests [29,37]. However, the new class of hyper-personal analytics is very different. Rather than just demographics and interests, they aim to be deep-delving portraits of individuals' personal traits and motivations.

We present a qualitative user study of a hyper-personal analytics system. We explore people's reactions to and preferences for interacting with a working system that assesses their *personality* and *values* from text they have posted in social media, similar to [15]. Prior work studying a precursor system highlighted two main user concerns: others' misinterpretation of the user's inferred personal traits, and users wanting control to modify their profile and traits [15]. The system we used to explore people's preferences addressed these two concerns: it provided rich definitions of people's traits in paragraph format, which our pilot participants found easy to interpret. It also added functionality to enable people to modify their profile.

Our method involved participant use of the study profiling system with their own social media posts during an

CHI 2015, April 18–23, 2015, Seoul, Republic of Korea.

ACM 978-1-4503-3145-6/15/04...$15.00.
http://dx.doi.org/10.1145/2702123.2702274

* Current affiliation: Google Inc.

interview. The profiling system was presented to participants as *voluntary, i.e.,* they had the choice to create and share their profile. We presented participants with exercises evaluating and modifying their profile. Participants also evaluated hypothetical scenarios where they had a choice of whether to share their profile, and a real scenario choosing whether to share the profile on their social media account. This enabled us to address the following research questions:

- How do participants *feel* about using a system that auto-generates a profile of their personality and values, from text they posted in social media?
- How *accurate* is the profile? Does it mirror their real and/or online selves?
- How and to what degree do they *modify* the profile and feel *control* over its contents?
- In what situations do they *share* the profile and to what degree do they feel *control* over sharing?

This paper explores the needs and preferences expressed by people viewing, modifying, and sharing their personal traits profile auto-generated by a working hyper-personal analytics system. Our results reveal a paradox: participants found their personal traits profiles creepily accurate and felt uncomfortable sharing them. However, they felt pressured by the social risks of not sharing and showed signs of learned helplessness, leading them to agree to share their profiles in several scenarios despite their discomfort. Further, they felt greater confidence in the algorithm than in their ability to describe their own traits, rarely modifying what they perceived as the algorithm's "expert" assessment. Even though all study scenarios involved purely voluntary profile creation and sharing, multiple participants spontaneously expressed worries that companies could give their profile to a third party without consent or, in many cases, even profile them without their knowledge. We synthesize these results into design implications for hyper-personal analytics systems that provide greater benefits and control for the people being profiled.

RELATED WORK

We review the two main categories of traits derived by the system in the current study, *personality* and *values*; provide context for our study by reviewing other studies of profiling systems; and ground our study in data privacy findings.

Personal Traits Profiled

Two trait taxonomies that have been studied extensively are the Big-5 personality traits (hereafter, Big-5) and Schwartz's basic human values (hereafter, Values). The Big-5 describes five main personality traits for individual differences in affect, behavior, and cognition: *openness-to-experience, conscientiousness, extraversion, agreeableness*, and *neuroticism* [14]. These traits have been studied in multiple domains, showing relations between Big-5 and work performance [3], consumer behavior [11], and relationship success [8].

In contrast to the Big-5, Values describe the beliefs and motivations that guide a person throughout their life. These include four main types of motivations: *self-transcendence, openness-to-change, conservation,* and *self-enhancement* [31]. Schwartz's Values have been validated across 20+ countries [31], and influence a variety of behaviors, including environmental and consumer behavior [26].

Deriving Hyper-personal Traits from Social Media Data

Much prior research has focused on identifying the best predictors for consumer behavior. *Consumer profiling* is an effort to link an individual's buying behaviors to aspects of the individual that might predict their future behavior, such as demographics and interests [39]. With the increase in consumer data available thanks to online shopping and social media, consumer profiling has increasingly incorporated attempts to infer more deeply personal traits based on online behavior through *user modeling*. The last few years have brought several studies that predict an individual's Big-5 or Values from a variety of social media data sources, including Facebook likes [19,41], and linguistic analyses of posted text [4,13,15]. These systems have been shown to have comparable accuracy to a person's friends or family describing their personality [41], a milestone in hyper-personal analytics that could justify their use in supporting or replacing human decision making.

Online Self-presentation Management

The proliferation of social networking sites has given rise to a large amount of HCI research on the ways that people manage their self-presentation online [10,22,34]. Although it is difficult to completely control the implicit cues one communicates in-person (with tone, facial expressions, body language, and so on), prior research argues that the ability to self-curate social media profiles gives people control over the implicit cues others can interpret from their online presence [34], usually by emphasizing positive traits and downplaying negative traits [22]. Hyper-personal analytics systems that automatically infer implicit traits may therefore be seen by people as a threat to attempts to actively manage their self-presentation online.

People's Reactions to Profiling

Many studies have explored people's understanding of and reactions to their data being used to profile them [28,29,37], but these were based on more explicit characteristics: demographics, behaviors, and interests; not personal traits. People show an overall discomfort with being profiled [29], but they also underestimate the depth of inferences that can be drawn from online behavior [28,29]. Only one study we are aware of has explored people's reactions to a hyper-personal analytics system that assesses personal traits, a survey by Gou et al. [15] during which survey respondents interacted with a system that presented a visualization of their automatically-inferred Big-5 and Values. Some respondents expressed a willingness to share their inferred traits in a work setting but were concerned about coworkers misinterpreting the visualization, asking for the ability to correct perceived inaccuracies in the results.

We provide rich, qualitative data about perceived accuracy and acceptability of a hyper-personal analytics system that profiles personality and values derived from social media posts. We also contribute observations of how people modify and share their profile.

Privacy Calculus: Sharing Personal Information

Privacy is the process by which people manage boundaries and disclosure across contexts [25]. Importantly, privacy *attitudes* can differ radically from actual privacy *behavior* [1]. People who claim to have strong general data privacy concerns nonetheless share their data when they see benefits for doing so [6]. This decision-making process is driven by a *privacy calculus*, in which people weigh benefits, risks, and perceived control when considering sharing their data [21]. Because of this, we designed our study so that participants were responding to specific profile sharing scenarios.

People perceive high *benefits* to sharing situations that provide them with new opportunities to enhance their current circumstances. Some benefits to sharing personal information include facilitating socialization [2]; financial benefits, e.g., discounts [9]; and increased convenience, e.g., keeping a credit card on file with an online merchant.

Privacy *risk* factors include concerns about security, third-party sharing, and the potential for social criticism. The possibility of unintentional data leakage is a large security concern, but people are also highly concerned about their data being *purposely* shared with third parties without their consent [30]. Third-party sharing is associated with risks in several domains: in commerce, receiving spam; in work settings, negative ramifications for career or work socialization [38]; in social sharing, humiliation [7]. There are also potential risks attached to *not* sharing: pressure to participate in online networks from peers [16] or work colleagues [38] often leads people to share more than they would like. Perceptions of risk can be affected by system design, for example, calling attention to the specific data at risk when users are making a sharing decision improves risk awareness [17].

Several privacy theories consider perceived *control* over one's data as affecting sharing decisions [21]. People who experience privacy leakages perceive greater risks to sharing and hold their personal information more closely in the future [7]. Such leakages are often accompanied by a sense of "creepiness": an apprehensive, unsettling emotional response to an ambiguous threat to one's sense of control [23,37].

Because of the complexity of privacy decisions, we presented participants with scenarios where they could experience a variety of configurations of benefits, risks, control, and sharing norms, to explore how each of these factors contribute to their willingness to share personal traits profiles.

METHOD

We asked 18 participants to use a hyper-personal analytics system that generated a profile of (a) their Big-5 personality traits [14] and (b) Schwartz's basic human values [31]. Participants logged into their Twitter or Facebook account using this study system and watched their personal traits profile auto-generate from the text they had previously posted. They were first asked to evaluate their profile for accuracy and next given scenarios—both hypothetical and real—in which they were asked to consider modifying and sharing their profile. We conducted semi-structured interviews as participants used the system and analyzed for themes that emerged from their interactions with the system and the scenarios.

Participants

We interviewed 18 participants (9 female, 9 male), ranging in age from 19-59. Participants needed to be either Twitter or Facebook users with enough content for linguistic analysis. Our participants all had >195 tweets or >80 Facebook posts. All participants were recruited from a single global enterprise business at locations in the San Francisco Bay Area. They represent a variety of job roles, including managers, interns, research staff, sales, communications, and administrative assistants.

System

To allow participants to voluntarily create their profile, we modified an existing experimental system, *KnowMe* [15]. It allows a person to login to a Twitter or Facebook account and see their automatically inferred personality traits based on the text they have posted there. The system correlated the relative frequency of categories of words used by the individual with associated Big-5 and Values traits, using a dictionary based on LIWC [35]. The links between these word categories and traits have been previously described in [4,40]. For Twitter accounts, the system pulled up to 200 of the most recent non-retweet tweets; for Facebook, up to 100 of the most recent status updates, wall posts, or comments. Prior work indicates this is enough text for a representative language sample [15].

Our system presented people with a *profile paragraph* of automatically-generated text based on their derived traits (see Figure 1). We arrived at this design following a user-centered design process involving multiple rounds of pilot testing and design iteration to transition from the visualization in [15] to the profile paragraph. In all, 14 pilot participants used *KnowMe* and provided feedback until we arrived at the final design. Initial pilot participants found the visualization difficult to interpret, especially given the complexity of the traits information shown; they felt they needed more explanation on how to interpret the multiple traits together. Pilot participants were most interested in their most extreme Big-5 traits (in relation to the population median), their highest Values, and how their traits combined to create their personality, so we focused the profile paragraph on those. The paragraph therefore contained 3 combined elements: 3 *cross-trait* Big-5

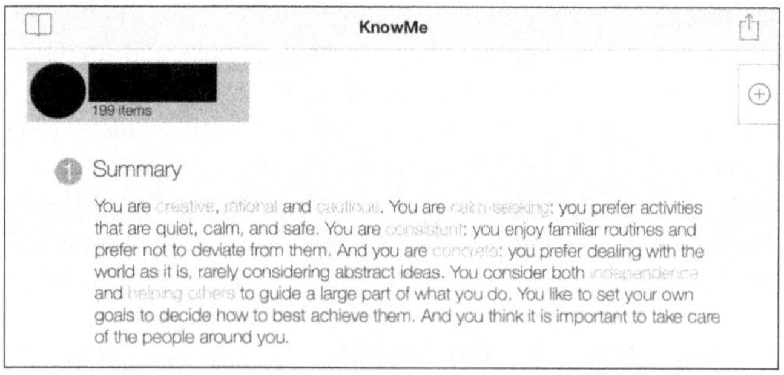

Figure 1. User interface of the study system, showing a derived personality and values profile (P15).

personality terms; 3 Big-5 personality *facet* (subtype) terms and descriptive sentences; and 2 basic *values* terms and descriptive sentences. The cross-trait terms and facets together captured the individual's Big-5 traits. The generated terms are precise; the Big-5 traits are commonly used in psychological and clinical practice [20]. They also include a balance of positive and negative terms (e.g., *cowardly*, *explosive*, *unscrupulous*). We describe how profile terms were generated in the next three sub-sections.

Cross-trait Terms

Pilot participants wanted to better understand how their Big-5 traits affected each other, leading us to add *cross-trait* terms to the final profile paragraph. This is also a more accurate way of describing an individual's personality than focusing on isolated traits, because overall personality involves the combination of multiple traits [14,18].

To create cross-trait terms, we surveyed the Big-5 literature compiling a list of adjectives that have been validated as each describing a specific combination of two Big-5 personality traits (e.g., high *agreeableness* and high *extraversion* may be described as *sociable*, high *agreeableness* and high *neuroticism* as *sentimental*) [14,18]. For combinations of traits that were uncommonly described in prior literature (e.g., high *neuroticism* with low *openness-to-experience*), we created terms and validated them using Mechanical Turk in a procedure similar to [24]. Several of the Turk-validated terms tend to be viewed negatively in Western culture (e.g., *insensitive*, *high-strung*), but we included them to prevent biasing participants by only showing positive terms. The adjective list we generated enabled us to engage with our research questions, so it is useful but not exhaustive or complete.

Following recommendations of our pilot participants, the profile paragraph first provided 3 terms describing a person's most extreme Big-5 traits using a moving window: we showed the term for the first and second most extreme 2 traits of that user, then the second and third most extreme 2 traits, followed by the third and fourth most extreme 2 traits. Although some Big-5 traits can be interpreted as having only one good extreme (e.g., high *agreeableness*), we presented the most extreme traits derived by the system, rather than the most positive traits. Terms that are viewed negatively in Western culture were preceded by a qualifier (e.g., *a bit*, *somewhat*) to provide the user with an honest but slightly hedged description. For example in Figure 1, high *openness* and low *neuroticism* generated the term *creative*; low *neuroticism* and high *conscientiousness* generated the term *rational*; finally, high *conscientiousness* and low *extraversion* generated the term *cautious*.

Facets

Several Big-5 models subdivide traits into facets: subtypes that more specifically describe a predisposition towards an attitude or behavior. We used the IPIP facets [14], which split each Big-5 trait into six facets (e.g., *agreeableness*: *trust*, *cooperation*, *altruism*, *morality*, *modesty*, *sympathy*). We generated terms as well as descriptive sentences for the high and low ends of each facet based on the literature [14].

In the profile paragraph, a user's three most extreme facets were assigned a term and descriptive sentence based on being higher or lower than the population median. For example in Figure 1, the participant's low *excitement-seeking* facet generated the sentence beginning "You are *calm-seeking...*".

Values

Based on [31], we generated terms and descriptive sentences for several values that lay within each values cluster (e.g., the *self-enhancement* cluster contains *gaining social status, ambition, achieving success, high achievement*). For the profile, the system showed the individual's strongest values terms within a descriptive sentence. For example in Figure 1, the participant was strong on *openness-to-change* and *self-transcendence* values, generating the text beginning "You consider both *independence* and *helping others...*".

Interviews

We conducted semi-structured interviews in which 13 out of 18 participants did the following:

1. Used the system to create a *personal traits profile* (on an iPad provided by the interviewer).
2. Examined and discussed the accuracy of, and their reactions to, their profile.
   a. Completed a survey rating the accuracy and valence of each trait in their profile (*survey on profile traits*).
3. For each of 3 to 8 hypothetical and real sharing scenarios:
   a. Modified their profile for that scenario (*profile modification activity*).
   b. Made a decision on whether or not to share (*profile sharing scenarios*).

A control group of 5 participants followed the procedure above minus the ability to modify their profile, to compare participants' perceived control in both conditions. Because few participants changed items in their profile, we included more people in the experimental group to explore profile modification in more detail.

Scenario	Characteristics	Proportion Who Shared
Event Recommender	Non-work, non-reciprocal	.93 (N=14)
Brainstorming Group	Work, non-reciprocal, reported in aggregate	.78 (N=9)
Speed Mentoring	Work, reciprocal	.75 (N=16)
Hobby Group	Non-work, reciprocal	.73 (N=11)
Team Formation	Work, reciprocal	.67 (N=15)
Online Shopping Discount	Non-work, non-reciprocal, shared with third-party	.64 (N=14)
Job Application	Work, non-reciprocal	.59 (N=17)
Actual Account	Shared on user's real social media account	.56 (N=16)

Table 1. Participants were generally willing to share in multiple scenarios.

The first author conducted and coded all interviews. Interviews were face-to-face, lasted 30-80 minutes, were audio recorded, and detailed notes were taken. After the interviews, we reviewed the audio to enhance the notes. We analyzed the notes using open coding (22 codes total), and then iteratively analyzed the concepts and categories from our initial coding for themes, which we report.

Next, we detail the survey on profile accuracy and valence (2a in procedure list above), the profile modification activity (3a), and the profile sharing scenarios (3b).

Survey on Profile Traits

Participants rated each trait shown in their profile in three questions, "*How accurately does '[trait]' describe you?*", "*How positive (good, praising) is the term '[trait]'?*", and "*How negative (bad, critical) is the term '[trait]'?*". Accuracy was rated from (1) "Not at all accurate" to (4) "Completely accurate". Positivity/negativity were rated from (1) "Not at all [positive/negative]" to (4) "Strongly [positive/negative]".

Profile Modification Activity

Prior research shows that people want to modify traits in their profiles [15]. Pilot participants found it difficult to consider the implications of freeform changes, so we built three types of modifications into the study system: *hiding, changing words,* and *adding qualifiers*. So as not to overwhelm participants with choices, we implemented these three modifiers on subsets of the profile where we believed they would be most understandable and useful. *Hiding* removed a trait from view entirely and could be performed on any trait in the profile. *Changing words* was enabled for the cross-trait terms and values elements, so that users could see and choose previously validated alternatives to the terms and descriptions. *Adding qualifiers* was enabled for the Big-5 facet terms. Participants could add understating (e.g., somewhat, sometimes) or exaggerating (e.g., very, quite) qualifiers to any facet term.

Profile Sharing Scenarios

Up to 8 scenarios were presented to participants, each representing a specific situation in which they were asked whether they would voluntarily share their automatically-inferred personal traits profile with the party requesting it. These scenarios systematically explored how different situational contexts affected sharing decisions: audience, reciprocity, third party disclosure, monetary rewards, and recommendations (see Table 1, column 2). We consulted with industry HR professionals to ensure the wording for the *job application* and *team formation* scenarios were true-to-life. Based on prior research, we expected an audience effect, with people showing lower willingness to share with a team leader or hiring manager due to the high risk involved [38]. Prior research on peer pressure and unraveling [16], predicts higher willingness to share when the requesting party shares their profile in return.

We present the *job application* scenario in full, then outline the other scenarios. For each, participants were given the same verbal instruction to talk through their thoughts as they decided whether or not to share their profile:

> *Job application: You are interested in applying to a job posting at an organization that you respect. In order for your application to be considered, you are required to submit a [personality profile]. The job posting mentions that it gives them a better understanding of how you might fit in with the existing organizational culture. It also says that the [personality profile] will be an important part of the evaluation process for your application, but it will not be the sole basis for the hiring decision. If you are hired, your [personality profile] will remain in your employment file with your other application materials.*

The *job application* scenario probed whether the participant would share with a *work* audience to be considered for a job. The organization requesting the profile does not provide personality profiles of current employees so it is classified as *non-reciprocal*.

Three other work scenarios were presented (see Table 1): (1) *Team formation*: sharing with a new work team leader prior to a first group meeting. Participants were shown the leader's profile before deciding (reciprocal). (2) *Brainstorming group*: organizers of a work event to brainstorm ways to improve client service asked for the participant's profile to aggregate with other attendees', in order to understand who takes part in such events (non-reciprocal). (3) *Speed mentoring*: sharing to facilitate meetings with potential career mentors. Participants would receive each mentor's profile after deciding whether to share, but before the meeting (reciprocal).

Three non-work hypothetical scenarios were presented: (1) *Event recommender*: sharing their profile with a company to receive activity recommendations after moving to a new city, based on activities that people similar to them had enjoyed (non-reciprocal). (2) *Hobby group*: the organizer of a hobby group asked participants to submit profiles, promising to share the group's average personality profile for the participant to assess their fit with the group (reciprocal). (3)

Online shopping discount: sharing their profile with their favorite online store for a 50% discount at a favorite online store, with the provision that their profile may be shared with or sold to the store's partners for marketing purposes (non-reciprocal).

Finally, in the *actual account* scenario, participants were invited to post their profile to the social media account from which the profile was derived. This allowed us to compare decisions to share in hypothetical and real scenarios.

RESULTS

Participants found their auto-generated personality profile 'creepily' accurate and expressed discomfort with sharing it in many situations. Nevertheless many said they would share their profile despite strong reservations, and did not modify its contents. Their rationale for these somewhat contradictory reactions revealed several themes. Though participants discussed a series of *risks* and *benefits* to modifying and sharing their profile, the decision was considerably more complex than a simple weighing of the two. Participants felt unqualified to significantly modify their profile contents due to a surprising trust in the "expert" algorithm. They also felt social pressure to share to prove they had nothing bad to hide, coupled with a learned helplessness—a belief that they could not keep their profile private even if they wanted to. Despite the voluntary nature of system use in all presented scenarios, several participants spontaneously expressed worries about potential involuntary deployments of hyper-personal analytics systems. Below, we distinguish feedback based on the presented scenarios from that based on participant speculation about third-party appropriation.

Reactions to System-Inferred Personal Traits Profiles

Accuracy

Participants described the system-generated profiles as surprisingly accurate. 17/18 stated their profile was an accurate representation of their general characteristics as an individual. They discussed the traits in relation to both their online personas and perceptions of their actual selves:

> *"I'd say this is who I am on Twitter for sure. I'm maybe more emotional in my personal life, but things like the [trait 'respecting authority'] would transition over." (P16)*

Even participants who used Twitter primarily for professional reasons, described the profile as characterizing both their online and their offline personality and values:

> *"I'm surprised, actually, that it's really accurate. This is the kind of discussion you usually have with friends or a spouse over a couple of beers... I was thinking, 'my Twitter is a professional account with 1200 followers.' You tend to be a little more professional [and] craft things a little more carefully. It kind of came up with an analysis that's really accurate." (P15)*

In addition to describing the profile's general accuracy, we asked participants to rate each trait in the profile for accuracy, positivity, and negativity. The rating revealed high accuracy overall for cross-traits (M = 3.04, SD = .84), facets (M = 3.44, SD = .73), and values (M = 3.50, SD = .89). Accuracy ratings were moderately correlated with positivity ratings for personality terms (.30 < *r*s < .47) and highly correlated for values terms (.72 < *r*s < .80), echoing psychology research that people view their own traits positively, e.g., [36].

Creepiness

Creepiness was a major theme in participants' reactions to the system's accuracy. Nearly all participants were surprised at the system's accuracy at inferring personal traits. However half (9) explicitly said they felt uncomfortable that it penetrated their carefully crafted online presence to derive fundamental traits like personality and values. Participants described feelings of creepiness over two system aspects: the *personal and implicit inferences* it made, and although the study scenarios gave them the power to not share, the worry that similar systems could be used on their data *without their consent*.

Personal and implicit inferences. Participants expressed a visceral discomfort with their profile revealing personal traits they thought were absent from their online presence. For example, P8 was particularly taken aback by the *values* section of the profile, which was "eerie" in its accuracy given what he felt was a small number of data points (196 tweets):

> *"I don't know how it would derive that from the limited number of tweets that I made... I always thought of that as something that I don't let people on to know very much... I guess I'm a little shocked that it works so well. It's not just like a horoscope or something like that." (P8)*

Participants also described this system as being more invasive than others. These other systems were seen as drawing more *surface level* inferences about them, relating to their consumer behavior rather than personality or values:

> *"It's kind of creepy... I know they do it at the grocery store with your card, Facebook does it, web pages do it... whereas this, I feel like I'm being tracked." (P18)*

Profiling without consent. Even though the current scenarios were framed specifically to allow participants to decline sharing, they were aware and highly uncomfortable that companies could theoretically profile them without their consent or notification. After discussing the scenarios, P10 described unease at the thought of unknown third parties using the system to summarize his character:

> *"Allowing other people to go, 'oh yeah, that's who you are.' That's creepy." (P10)*

Participants felt strongly that their consent to infer these hyper-personal traits should be required, regardless of the privacy settings on their social media posts:

> *"It has to be opt-in. Even if [my Twitter account] is public, I am controlling what I'm putting out. Even if there's an app [letting people look each other up], I wouldn't allow something to be done outside my knowledge. It has to be opt-in, has to be done in that context." (P15)*

(Non-)Modification of Personal Traits Profiles

After logging in and seeing the study system generate their personal traits profile, participants engaged with a series of scenarios (see Table 1), during which they were offered the chance to modify any of the eight items in the profile before deciding whether or not to share it. Participant profiles contained some errors, with 20.7% of all profile terms being rated either 1 ("not at all accurate") or 2 ("slightly accurate"). To our surprise, however, participants made *very few or no changes at all* to resolve these errors in their profile. This was despite all participants understanding how to modify their profile. Of the 13 participants who were given the option to alter aspects of their profile, 6 did not change it for any scenario, 4 changed one item, 2 changed two items, and 1 changed four items. The changes included hiding traits (6 changes), adding understatement qualifiers such as 'somewhat' or 'slightly' (4 changes), and changing words (2 changes). All participants who modified their profile submitted the same changes across scenarios, noting that it was a good representation of their personality and values, and they saw no need for multiple versions.

The surprising accuracy of their profiles seemed to have instilled participants with faith in the system. This faith had an unanticipated effect: participants were reluctant to override the default word choices the system provided. The most common explanation participants gave for not changing their profile was *insecurity that they could craft a better profile than the system.* This feeling of insecurity focused on *changing words;* participants felt more confident when *hiding* or *qualifying* terms.

When participants were ambivalent about how to modify the words in their profile, they consistently trusted the algorithm over their own judgment:

> *"To me, I don't know who's looking at it. I don't know what they're going to be valuing... If it's a government job, maybe I don't want to include 'laid back'. At the end of the day, that's who the system says I am. There's obviously been some type of process where they think this is useful." (P6)*

> *"Each word means something to different people... It's almost impossible to know how others would perceive your profile. I don't think it's ever possible for me to write in a few sentences something that describes me 100%... And so I'm not sure how to change something to make it more accurate." (P2)*

Sharing System-Inferred Personal Traits Profiles

Before and after modifying their profile for each scenario in Table 1, participants were asked to decide whether or not they would share it. Overall, participants did not feel completely comfortable about, or in full control of, their decision to share their profile. Nevertheless they very frequently stated they would share it anyway, whether they modified it or not. Across all hypothetical scenarios, participants shared a mean of 70% of the time. When they were sharing on their *actual* Facebook or Twitter account, 56% of participants shared. These high levels of sharing despite some discomfort and relatively little modification appear contradictory.

While one group of 13 participants could modify their profiles, 5 participants were not offered this ability. There was no noticeable difference in sharing decisions between the two groups, but participants who could change their profile felt more comfortable sharing the modified profile over the original, even though these changes were extremely minor.

Prior work describes people's decisions to share private information as a complex *privacy calculus*, which weighs risks and benefits [21]. An individual's privacy calculus can result in sharing decisions that seem to contradict their stated privacy concerns and preferences [1,7]. To fit this framework, we present our results on participants' sharing decisions in terms of *risks* and *benefits.*

Before presenting risks and benefits, we note that some participants felt the scale was tipped toward the risks but they were helpless to opt-out, even though our scenarios explicitly provided them with this possibility. This is a form of *learned helplessness*, in which people feel they have no power to avert an avoidable negative outcome [32]:

> *"Knowing other companies mine [social media data] is creepy, but it's unstoppable." (P10)*

> *"It's a little eerie, our tweets are public domain unless your [account is] private. I don't see it would be anything that you could stop or prevent. If I could block people from using it, I would." (P8)*

Risks

Three main themes of risks for voluntary sharing emerged: concerns about prejudging based on profile contents, the potential for disclosure to an unknown third-party, and ascribing negative attributes to non-sharers.

Concern about prejudging. The most common concern was being *prejudged*. Participants worried that someone reading their profile would prematurely assess their character before meeting them. A subset of these participants also expressed concerns that profiles might be out of date if they had not posted enough content recently:

> *"I want them to understand my personality when I join and grow rather than them going with something historical." (P15)*

Prejudging was also something participants worried about doing to others in reciprocal scenarios (e.g., team formation, speed mentoring). This participant mentioned a risk of *prejudging others*, explaining others' behavior by invoking their profile:

> *"I would be worried I would look for those traits. When I would talk to you: 'Is that because he's guarded, or because he doesn't like me?'" (P7)*

Third-party disclosure. Participants frequently and spontaneously shared concerns about their profile being shared more widely than the scenario described. They discussed third-party marketers in the non-work scenarios, or managers and peers in the work scenarios. The *online shopping discount* and *job application* scenarios were seen as particularly high risk and had the lowest sharing rates of the hypothetical scenarios (see Table 1). The concern over third-party disclosure confirms results from prior studies of other types of personal information sharing decisions [30].

Ascribing negative attributes to non-sharers. Many participants felt compelled to share their profile to avoid others assuming they were hiding something negative, and being excluded from benefits that sharers would accumulate. In the law literature, this is termed the "unraveling effect" [27]: non-sharing is interpreted as *hiding terrible information*, pressuring non-sharers to share against their wishes. Participants expressed this social pressure both directed at themselves and at others:

> *"[It's] forcing, almost. If they know you decline, that's more of a red flag to them." (P16)*

> *"[If someone hid], I would want to know, what horrible thing was it? You immediately go to the negative." (P18)*

Benefits

Participants ascribed higher benefits to sharing when the scenario involved them getting something in return. This is often described in the literature as exchanging personal data as a *digital currency* [9]. Some participants said they *wanted* to exchange their traits profile for reciprocal sharing, recommendations, and a "trusted source" (the system) to vouch for implicit aspects of their character.

Reciprocal sharing. Although three of our scenarios involved reciprocal sharing, in only one was reciprocity seen as a benefit that would motivate participants to share. The *team formation* scenario enabled participants to make assessments about how well they might fit in a new work group and interact with other members. On the other hand, participants felt that personality profiles were not as useful in other reciprocal sharing scenarios (*speed mentoring* and *hobby group*); instead, other qualities about mentors and fellow hobbyists were more important, like their expertise. In *team formation*, enough value was perceived, so the reciprocity of the sharing became important:

> *"It increased [my willingness to share]. They're asking you to do something that they're already doing." (P6)*

The implication is that reciprocity can motivate people to share, but receiving others' personality information must offer significant value.

Personality-based recommendations. Participants were overwhelmingly positive about sharing their profile to get activity or event recommendations based on people who were like them (e.g., *event recommender* scenario). Participants explained that they believed personality-matched recommendations would be better than seeing just unfiltered recommendations:

> *"I think this is awesome. If you look at Yelp, someone gives [a business] 5 stars, you don't know who that person is or their story." (P6)*

Trusted source vouching for implicit aspects of one's character. Nearly half of participants (8/18, primarily those in service or sales job roles) expressed a strong desire to share their personal traits profile in work settings. For these participants, the study system represented a *trusted source*, since it inferred traits implicitly rather than via self-report, allowing others to verify traits that were hard to demonstrate prior to meeting. This was discussed most frequently in the *job application* scenario:

> *"I wish job applications had this kind of submission. Someone like me who has a lot of between-the-lines interpersonal skills that are hard to build into a resume to show you have that depth. To me, this is what gives people depth and dimension to not only find fit but also give potential employers an idea about what you have as a person... I would much prefer using this data than softer data points about analyzing the way they're talking to me, clothes they're wearing, all the social cues. Nice to go into it, "you've been certified THIS." (P13)*

DISCUSSION

Although there has been much study of user-curated online profiles, we present people's reactions to using a system that automatically generates a hyper-personal profile of their traits and values [15]. We found that people are highly sensitive to the social risks of not sharing and showed signs of learned helplessness, often sharing what they felt were deeply personal, creepily accurate profiles despite strong discomfort. People were more comfortable with sharing their profile when they were able to modify it—even though they did not feel empowered to make many changes. Experiencing the system and scenarios prompted several participants to express discomfort that companies could profile them without their permission or knowledge. This provides additional support for online privacy theories that emphasize that honest disclosure about user data transactions stimulates user comfort with sharing [21].

One of the surprising results from our study was that most participants put more faith in the system than was likely warranted given its still-experimental nature and assessment of very personal traits. They perceived high accuracy even when the system presented participants' negative traits. Again we saw a lack of perceived control. In ambiguous situations, participants trusted the system's word choices *more than their own preferences*. It is fascinating and alarming the degree to which participants trusted the study system to provide a 'character reference'. That an algorithm might be viewed as an *expert on human character*, to officially vouch for a person, puts the computer in a position previously held by people. Although hyper-personal analytics systems may be capable of reaching human-like *accuracy* in assessing traits [41], granting the algorithm this level of "humanity" simultaneously reduces our humanity by supplanting people as the sole judges of character. This result raises the ethical question: even if an algorithm can judge character, should it?

Our participants felt a strong sense of "creepiness" when extrapolating from the study that companies could profile them without their permission using their social media text. In daily life, our personality traits and personal values are implicitly communicated through our behaviors and interactions with others. But such intimate information can be difficult to control in person, with people often feeling better able to curate their self-presentation online [34]. This sense of greater control over online self-presentation may have been undermined when participants saw exactly what the algorithm, and therefore companies that may deploy it, could infer about them. Furthermore, inferring personal traits is generally the purview of other humans. These reasonable concerns could have heightened participant's feelings of creepiness about the study system.

Design Implications

Systems that allow transparency and control over auto-generated profiles are fairly rare [29]. However, people are aware of and uncomfortable with companies deploying profiling systems. This places a requirement on designers to consider users' reactions to their systems whether being profiled is voluntary or involuntary. Our participants offered insights into future designs that include *responsible system defaults* [33]. We also provide user-driven guidance on deployment features that would provide people with a greater comfort with profiling: control over the *content* of inferences made about them, and control over *sharing*. Although these general topics have been studied in prior online privacy work [21,29], our findings indicate that hyper-personal systems are viewed as qualitatively different from traditional consumer profiling systems. Our guidelines address the specific challenges these new systems raise.

Trust in Analytics and the Importance of Defaults

Our results show the importance of default profile wording, and its role in building trust in an analytics system users interact with directly. Participants' initial encounter with a profile they felt accurately described them seemed to instill immediate trust. Including negative traits increased trust further: participants who evaluated a derived trait as both accurate and negative thought it boosted the accuracy of the system beyond a positive item. This finding about people's trust in the system's initial profile extends prior research on the strong effect of system defaults on user behavior [33], showing this effect holds, surprisingly, when people are evaluating descriptions of *their own personality and values*—a topic on which we would expect the person profiled to believe themselves to be expert. Thus, decisions that system builders make regarding the words displayed about traits can significantly impact user experience.

Instilling Control to Modify Derived Profile Contents

Our participants experienced a lack of control over the contents of their personal traits, which reduced their willingness to correct inaccuracies in their profiles. It is therefore critical that designers foster people's ability and confidence to modify their profiles. This is especially important since others might make decisions about a profiled person based on the profile a person shares. First, the fallibility of the algorithm and the potential need for modifications should be communicated. For example, confidence levels for certain terms could be included. This might be suggested by simple visuals such as graying low confidence words or by presenting multiple alternative terms allowing users to choose between them. Second, people's concerns about *hiding terms* and *changing words* were social in nature—they were worried making these modifications could insinuate something negative about their personality—so a social counter-argument might help. For example, the ability to hide traits could be accompanied by statistics about how many others had decided to hide each trait, or by showing how many edits a user typically made to their profile. This type of *social proof* encouragement has been shown to motivate action [5].

Control over Derived Profile Sharing

In line with prior work [21], participant feelings about profile sharing followed a reliable calculus that was *situation-specific*: high benefit scenarios and high perceived control over sharing promoted sharing, but high risk scenarios decreased it. Designers can foster the greatest sense of control over sharing profiles by offering people strong benefits for sharing, and by providing people explicit power to decide whether or not to share their profile.

Our study indicates which use cases designers should target to offer the most benefit to the people profiled: providing *personality-based recommendations*, offering *discounts,* and supporting *reciprocal sharing* of personal traits profiles. Recommendations that, for example, gave insights into the values or personality of an online reviewer, were seen as particularly positive. These represented a new type of filter for products or events that added to other filters participants currently use (e.g., social recommendations). Discounts were seen as providing high economic value for sharing, but were still shared less frequently due to the high risk they represented. Reciprocity was seen as a positive when the user received the other party's profile prior to sharing. However the risk of *unraveling* was very salient, and participants felt pressure to share to avoid assumptions that they had something negative to hide. By providing more information about *contexts of use,* designers could more clearly outline these benefits and potential risks, allowing people to make more informed decisions about profile sharing. Our results indicate that people associated different values to the benefits and risks and should be empowered to choose whether or not their profile is shared. For example, some would exchange it with companies for better recommendations, but others were strongly opposed.

CONCLUSION

New systems that enable companies to generate hyper-personal profiles raise important privacy issues. User reactions to such a system identified significant concerns: the *creepiness* of being accurately profiled by an automatic system, and the desire for *control* over profile contents and privacy. These concerns are complicated by a tendency for people to trust the supposed *impartiality* of an algorithm, which fostered unwillingness to correct profile errors. Future research needs to further investigate user reactions to such systems as they evolve. We also need to develop and evaluate new designs that provide greater user control over hyper-personal profiles, supporting editing and informed sharing, as this type of profiling is deployed more widely.

REFERENCES

1. Acquisti, A., Grossklags, J. Privacy attitudes and privacy behavior. In *Economics of Info. Security*. '04, 165–178.
2. Barkhuus, L., Tashiro, J. Student Socialization in the Age of Facebook. *Proc. CHI*, ('10), 133–142.
3. Barrick, M.R., Mount, M.K. The big five personality dimensions and job performance: A meta-analysis. *Personnel Psychology 44*, ('91), 26.
4. Chen, J., et al. Understanding individuals' personal values from social media word use. *Proc. CSCW*, ('14), 405–414.
5. Cialdini, R.B. *Influence: The Psychology of Persuasion, Revised Edition.* Harper Business, NY, '06.
6. Connelly, K., Khalil, A., Liu, Y. Do I do what I say?: Observed versus stated privacy preferences. In *Human Computer Interaction - INTERACT*. Springer, '07, 620–623.
7. Debatin, B., et al. Facebook and online privacy: Attitudes, behaviors, and unintended consequences. *J. of CMC 15*, ('09), 83–108.
8. Donnellan, M.B., et al. The big five and enduring marriages. *J. of Research in Personality 38*, ('04), 481–504.
9. Egelman, S., Felt, A., Wagner, D. Choice architecture and smartphone privacy: There's a price for that. In *The Economics of Info. Security and Privacy*. '13, 211–236.
10. Ellison, N., Heino, R., Gibbs, J. Managing impressions online: Self-presentation processes in the online dating environment. *J. of CMC 11*, ('06), 415–441.
11. Fraj, E., Martinez, E. Influence of personality on ecological consumer behaviour. *J. of Consumer Beh. 5*, ('06), 167–181.
12. Gao, H., et al. Modeling user attitude toward controversial topics in online social media. *Proc. ICWSM*, ('14).
13. Golbeck, J., et al. Predicting personality from Twitter. *Proc. PASSAT & SOCIALCOM*, ('11), 149–156.
14. Goldberg, L.R. A broad-bandwidth, public-domain, personality inventory measuring the lower-level facets of several Five-Factor models. In *Pers. Psych. in Europe*. '99, 7.
15. Gou, L., Zhou, M.X., Yang, H. KnowMe and ShareMe: Understanding automatically discovered personality traits from social media and user sharing preferences. *Proc. CHI*, ('14), 955–964.
16. Gross, R., Acquisti, A. Information revelation and privacy in online social networks. *Proc. WPSE*, ('05), 71–80.
17. Harbach, M., et al. Using personal examples to improve risk communication for security & privacy decisions. *Proc. CHI*, ('14), 2647.
18. Hofstee, W.K., De Raad, B., Goldberg, L.R. Integration of the big five and circumplex approaches to trait structure. *J. of Personality and Social Psychology 63*, ('92), 146.
19. Kosinski, M., Stillwell, D., Graepel, T. Private traits and attributes are predictable from digital records of human behavior. *PNAS 110*, ('13), 5802–5805.
20. Kotov, R., et al. Linking "big" personality traits to anxiety, depressive, and substance use disorders: A meta-analysis. *Psychological Bulletin 136*, ('10), 768–821.
21. Li, Y. Theories in online information privacy research: A critical review and an integrated framework. *Decision Support Systems 54*, ('12), 471–481.
22. Marwick, A.E., Boyd, D. I tweet honestly, I tweet passionately: Twitter users, context collapse, and the imagined audience. *New Media & Society 13*, ('11), 114–133.
23. McAndrew, F.T., Koehnke, S.S. Creepiness. *Poster presented at SPSP*, ('13).
24. Mohammad, S.M., Turney, P.D. Emotions evoked by common words and phrases: Using mechanical turk to create an emotion lexicon. *Proc. NAACL-HCT*, ('10), 26–34.
25. Palen, L., Dourish, P. Unpacking "Privacy" for a Networked World. *Proc. CHI*, ('03), 129–136.
26. Pepper, M., Jackson, T., Uzzell, D. An examination of the values that motivate socially conscious and frugal consumer behaviours. *Intl. J. of Consumer Studies 33*, ('09), 126–136.
27. Peppet, S.R. Unraveling privacy: The personal prospectus and the threat of a full-disclosure future. *Nw. UL Rev. 105*, ('11), 1153.
28. Rader, E. Awareness of behavioral tracking and information privacy concern in Facebook and Google. *Proc. SOUPS*, '14.
29. Rao, A., Schaub, F., Sadeh, N. *What do they know about me? Contents and concerns of online behavioral profiles.* CMU-CyLab-14-011, '14.
30. Schwaig, K.S., Segars, A.H., Grover, V., Fiedler, K.D. A model of consumers' perceptions of the invasion of information privacy. *Information & Mgmt. 50*, ('13), 1–12.
31. Schwartz, S.H. Universals in the content and structure of values: Theoretical advances and empirical tests in 20 countries. *Advances in Experimental Social Psych. 25*, ('92).
32. Seligman, M.E.P. *Helplessness: On Depression, Development, and Death.* W.H. Freeman & Co., NY, '92.
33. Shah, R.C., Sandvig, C. Software defaults as de facto regulation: The case of the wireless internet. *Information, Communication & Society 11*, ('08), 25–46.
34. Strano, M. User descriptions and interpretations of self-presentation through Facebook profile images. *Cyberpsychol.: J. of Psychosocial Res. on Cyberspace 2*, '02.
35. Tausczik, Y.R., Pennebaker, J.W. The Psychological Meaning of Words: LIWC and Computerized Text Analysis Methods. *J. of Language and Social Psych. 29*, ('10), 24–54.
36. Taylor, S.E., Brown, J.D. Illusion and well-being: A social psychological perspective on mental health. *Psychological Bulletin 103*, ('88), 193–210.
37. Ur, B., et al. Smart, useful, scary, creepy: Perceptions of online behavioral advertising. *Proc. SOUPS*, ('12), 4.
38. Wang, Y., Kobsa, A. Privacy in online social networking at workplace. *Proc. CSE*, ('09), 975–978.
39. Weber, K., Roehl, W.S. Profiling people searching for and purchasing travel products on the world wide web. *J. of Travel Research 37*, ('99), 291–298.
40. Yarkoni, T. Personality in 100,000 Words: A large-scale analysis of personality and word use among bloggers. *Journal of Research in Personality 44*, ('10), 363–373.
41. Youyou, W., Kosinski, M., Stillwell, D. Computer-based personality judgments are more accurate than those made by humans. *PNAS*, ('15), 1-5.

Privacy Tipping Points in Smartphones Privacy Preferences

Fuming Shih[*], **Ilaria Liccardi**[*†], **Daniel J. Weitzner**[*]
{fuming, ilaria, djweitzner}@csail.mit.edu

[*]MIT CSAIL
Cambridge, MA, USA

[†]Oxford e-Research Center
University of Oxford, UK

ABSTRACT

The aim of this research was to understand what affects people's privacy preferences in smartphone apps. We ran a four-week study in the wild with 34 participants. Participants were asked to answer questions, which were used to gather information about their personal context and to measure their privacy preferences, by varying app name and the purpose of data collection.

Our results show that participants shared the most when no information about data access or purpose was given, and shared the least when both of these details were specified. When just one of either purpose or the requesting app was shown, participants shared less when just the purpose was specified than when just the app name was given.

We found that the predominant factor affecting users' choices was the purpose for data access. In our study the purpose varied from being not specified, to vague, to being very specific. Participants were more willing to disclose data when no purpose was specified. When a vague purpose was shown, participants became more privacy-aware and were less willing to disclose their information. When specific purposes were shown, participants were more willing to disclose, provided the purpose for requesting the information appeared to be beneficial to them, while participants shared the least when the purpose for data access was solely beneficial to developers.

Author Keywords

Privacy Preferences; Android; Experience Sampling

ACM Classification Keywords

K.4.1 Computers and Society: Privacy

General Terms

Theory, Human Factors

INTRODUCTION

With the pervasive use of smartphones and advances in sensor technology, context-aware services are an integral part of consumers' daily life. However, while extremely useful in serving and guiding us in our daily activities, smartphones can also be used to silently collect data about us, allowing app companies to create digital dossiers for services like targeted advertisements, extrapolate behavioral patterns valuable for market research. Due to these reasons, smartphones might pose great privacy risks to consumers. Users today have to make decisions regarding disclosure of personal information without being fully aware of the privacy implications behind data collection [11]. This is despite the fact that consumers consider their mobile data as private and are strongly opposed to apps collecting their information from their smartphones and tracking their locations without their consent [33].

Different solutions have been implemented to give users more awareness of what information is collected about them [15]. However, individuals have no way to understand how their data is actually used. A recent report released by the White House addresses these concerns, focusing on the idea of disclosing the range of possible uses for peoples' data [36].

Research [7] has shown that the perceived sensitivity of the collected data affects the willingness of people to disclose the data. This sensitivity is often context-specific and changes dynamically according to the individual's context, such as location and activities [5]. Users should not be expected to consent to the collection of their data for every foreseeable purpose, given the incomplete or missing information [22] they receive when making privacy decisions [2]. Users' privacy concerns rise when they find data collection happening in a context or for a purpose that is unexpected. Such an unpleasant experience leads to a sense of "creepiness" and results in a loss of trust [29]. To ease tensions revolving around data collection, app companies are advised to follow the principle of "respect for context" [35] when harvesting users' data.

In order to properly address users' privacy concerns while simultaneously allowing companies to use mobile data, people should have control of their data in terms of how services can use it, rather than simply granting *carte blanche* access [37]. We are interested in investigating users' choices and which circumstances might lead them to disclosure of their personal information in the form of location and activities. We wanted to investigate effects on privacy preferences by varying the application name and purpose of data collection within real contexts. In particular we are interested in these questions:

1. Do different purposes affect users' willingness to share their data?

CHI 2015, April 18–23, 2015, Seoul, Republic of Korea.

http://dx.doi.org/10.1145/2702123.2702404

2. Are people more likely to share their personal data with apps that they frequently use?
3. Does the type of context (location or activity context) affect people's willingness to share their data? If so, what are the effects and what are the specific contexts?

We applied the Experience Sampling Method (ESM) [8] to elicit responses from users to disclosure of their personal information in the form of their location and activities throughout the day. We developed a framework that creates survey questions customized to an individual's app usage and personal context. We conducted a four week in-the-wild experiment that would prompt users each hour during the day, from 9am to 10pm, asking them to describe their personal context (captured location type, activity context, social surroundings and disclosure preferences), followed by questions asking about their willingness to share contextual data (location or activity type) with familiar apps (gathered from their smartphones) for seven different types of purposes. Purpose types varied from being not specified, to vague, to very specific. Specific purposes varied from being beneficial solely for users, to beneficial solely for developers, to beneficial for both. The main findings were:

1. The more information provided to participants, the more reluctant they were to share personal information. Hence, when presented with *no information* about purpose or data access, participants were willing to share the most.
2. The type of purpose affected a large number (15) of participants' sharing behaviors. Participants were more willing to share for purposes that were beneficial solely to them.
3. The type of app, but not the frequency of use, affected participants' sharing behavior. Participants might share more with less frequently-used apps.
4. Participants were affected in their disclosure behavior according to the type of location they were in.

RELATED RESERCH

Research has shown that many smartphone users lack the knowledge needed to perform changes in privacy control settings and mistakenly trust that the app will protect the privacy of their data [27]. Only few users actually read and understood the implications of permissions requested by Android apps [11], [23]. Many people may still hold unrealistic beliefs about how their data should be treated, and consider information on their smartphones to be private and overwhelmingly reject data collection [33]. Users' privacy expectations often do not reflect current practices. Many apps transmit sensitive data to third parties [10] that users intend to only use on-device.

Given the disparity between users' expectations of privacy [28] and the opaque practices of data collectors [22], researchers have sought to address the privacy issues in the context of consumers' experiences when using apps, by making privacy part of the app selection decision [16], by improving their privacy expectations [24] or by exposing data leakage [6].

Researchers have found that people are willing to disclose their personal information for short-term benefits [2], for perceived beneficial gain (such as monetary rewards) [3], and for high relevance and need for the service provided [13].

Past research has shown that people's privacy preferences for sharing their personal information are *contextual*: sharing current whereabouts [9] [32], [38], updating statuses on social networks [1], [25], configuring context-aware services [17], [19]. In the context of disclosing information to apps, one important factor can be users' trust of data collectors [14]. Knijnenburg and Kobsa found users' willingness to disclose contextual information to recommendation services varied when presented with different justifications for data collection [18]. Tan et. al found developer-specified messages actually affected users' decisions for allowing data access [30]. Their results showed that users were more likely to approve data requests when the purpose for requesting data was displayed.

To model users privacy preferences, Lin [24] used crowdsourced surveys to measure the unexpectedness of certain data accesses by the apps, allowing users to rate apps by comparing their perceived functionality with the actual permissions requested by the app. Toch [31] used a crowdsourcing method to predict each user's privacy preferences for location sharing. While crowdsourcing makes their approach more scalable, crowd opinions only represent users' *a priori* preferences of how an app should work. The results might not reflect users' practical privacy concerns when they actively engage in making "privacy vs. benefit" trade-offs [12].

USER STUDY

We conducted a user study[1] in the wild over a four week period to understand and measure users' privacy preferences toward the sharing of their personal location and activity context with familiar apps for common types of currently-used purposes. We collected their most recent location and enquired about their activities, while also collecting information about apps running on their smartphones. We asked participants to answer a set of *personalized* questions each hour. The questions were personalized based on their location and current activity as well as apps that were familiar to them (already installed). A set of questions contained two segments, and within each segment questions were randomized. The two segments were designed to:

1. **Gather users' personal context** in order to first understand each participant's current state, i.e. where they were (home, work etc.), who they were with (friends, family, colleagues etc.), what were they doing (working, leisure etc.) and who were they willing to share this information with (friends, family, everybody etc.)
2. **Measure users' privacy preferences** in order to understand if the app, the type of purpose and/or the type of location (for example whether they were home or at work) or activity (whether they were working, going somewhere

[1] The study protocol, the rules which participants needed to follow were approved by IRB to ensure subjects' privacy. These details were clearly communicated with participants during information session and documented in the consent form.

etc.) affected participants' willingness to share their personal contexts.

The number of questions varied between sets according to the factors that were present and the way they were shown.

Study Design

Gathering users' personal context

In segment 1, the questions were designed to understand participants' current context in the form of the type of location (Figure 1 (a)), which activity they were currently engaging in (Figure 1 (b)), who was around them (Figure 1 (c)) and who they would have been comfortable sharing the activity they were currently engaging in (Figure 1 (d)). Since we used the answers provided by participants from the activity type question (Figure 1 (c)) within the social sharing attitude questions (Figure 1 (d)), the former would always precede the latter.

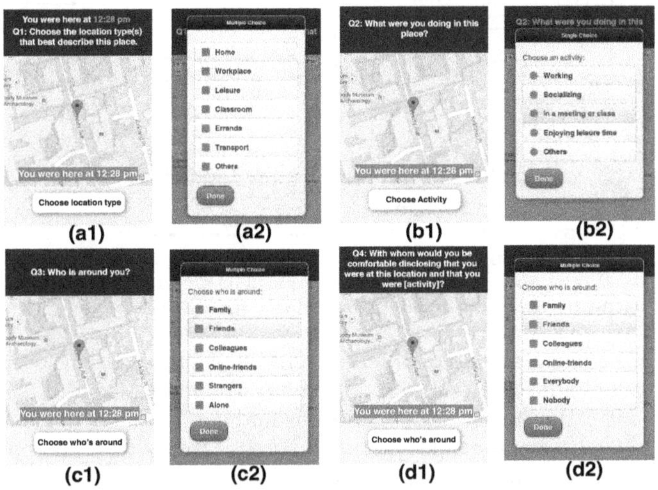

Figure 1. User study questions designed to gather users' personal context in the form of location type (a); activity type (b); social surrounding (c); and social sharing attitudes (d)

Measuring users' privacy preferences

Questions in segment 2 were designed to measure users' privacy preferences. In particular we were interested in testing familiar apps as well as common purposes that have been given as reasons to collect users' data. In order to measure their preferences, we asked questions in which three factors (personal context, app name and purpose) were randomly and evenly selected. Figure 2 shows how the question was presented to participants and where each value condition would appear.

Personal context was set either to the user's current location or the type of activity that the user was currently performing at this location.

App name condition was gathered from the apps used by each user. Usage of each app was measured in the first week of the experiment. According to the amount of usage (low, medium, and high), three apps were randomly selected to be used throughout the study. App usage was calculated individually for each user according to their own level of usage. Questions were also posed with the app name omitted, for a total of four questions.

Purpose condition was randomly selected from six different types of purpose commonly cited for accessing users' personal data. A question was also asked when no purpose was inserted, hence this field was blank (for a total of seven conditions). The types of purposes used were:

- **Vague Purposes**:
  - Without purpose: nothing is displayed;
  - Captures information: "so that the app has your information";
- **User-focused purposes**:
  - Testing needs: "for testing new features";
  - Improving experience: "to improve the app experience for you";
- **User- and developer-focused purposes**:
  - Advertising: "to be used to display personalized ads relevant to you";
- **Developer-focused purposes**:
  - Profiles: "so that the app can learn your daily patterns, to profile you for market research";
  - Revenue needs: "so that it can sell this information and make money".

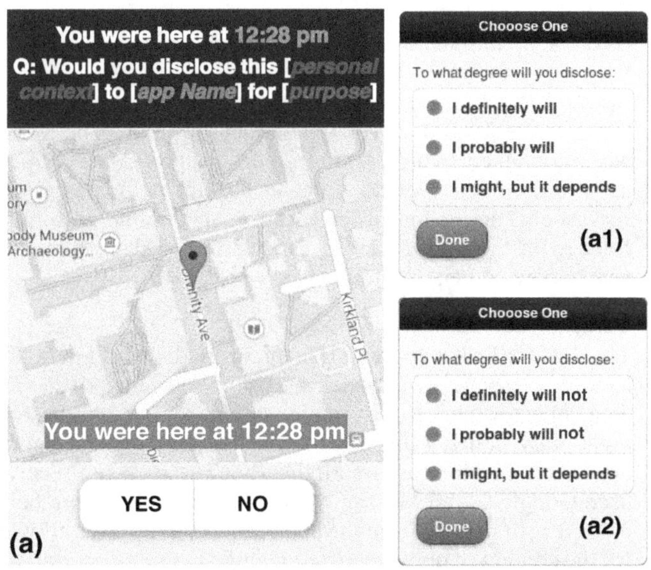

Figure 2. User study questions designed to gather users' willingness (or unwillingness) to share their personal context. Each participant had to choose YES or NO. Afterwards they had to give a rating of positive (a1) or negative (a2) feelings

Randomization of privacy preference questions

To ensure that all factors were collected in an even manner during the *measure users' privacy preferences* part of the study, we introduced a scheme to randomize the appearance of different values for each factor. The privacy preference section of the questions was randomized between two conditions: the *app-specific* and the *purpose-specific* condition.

When the *app-specific* condition was chosen, all seven predefined purposes were shown (including purpose string omitted). First, the study app randomly chose a personal context

- either a location or activity to be used. Then one app name was randomly selected from a predefined list of app names based on each participant's individual frequency of use[2], This app name was shown for each of the seven pre-defined purposes, for a total of seven questions. The purposes appeared in a random order from question to question.

When the *purpose-specific* condition was chosen, the study app randomly selected one purpose from the list of seven purposes, then showed four choices for app names (including the no app option) for both location and activity context (appearance was randomized between questions) for a total of eight questions. The app names appeared in random order from question to question.

The reason for randomly selecting location and activity within the *app-specific* question condition was to avoid overwhelming the participant with an additional seven questions within this set. Similarly, we decided to show both location and activity within the *purpose-specific* condition to present a similar number of questions.

During week 1, information about app usage was collected. Hence, in week 1 when the *purpose-specific* condition was chosen, the study app would show two questions for disclosing activity and location context, with the app name omitted. Table 1 shows that the factors were evenly distributed (please note that *no app* name is larger in to week 1).

Apparatus

We developed a framework to conduct the study. The framework contained two parts: an Android app (*ContextProbe*) used to collect sensor data and to prompt participants with survey questions, and an application server that communicated with the app, received and computed data, then sent new survey content to the app.

ContextProbe app

The *ContextProbe* app has four main modules: 1) data collector, 2) survey, 3) uploader, and 4) message receiver. The data collector module was implemented using a mobile sensing library called *Funf* [4] that allowed the app to schedule data collection tasks periodically. The message receiver used Google Cloud Messaging (GCM) technology to receive pushed notifications from the application server. This allowed for the content of questions to be changed in real-time and tailored according to participants' collected data.

Application server

The application server was developed using Google Apps Script[3], which provides integration across multiple web services on the Google Cloud platform. The application server can run and operate directly on the experimenter's Google Drive space without a complicated setup process. The data handler module on the application stored data uploaded from participants' smartphones in a Google Spreadsheet for easy access and data analysis. The context processor read these data files to compute app usage patterns for each user and used this information as the new content for customizing each participant's survey questions. The cloud messaging module sent GCM contents directly to each participant's phone to update their survey questions.

Framework interactions to create personalized surveys

Figure 3 gives an overview of the architecture of the user study framework and shows step-by-step how different elements interacted with each other to create a customized survey, tailored to each participant's app usage pattern and up-to-date contextual information about their location and activity:

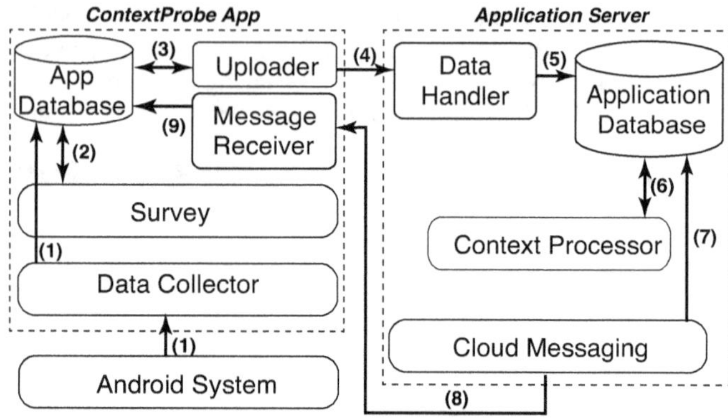

Figure 3. Architecture of the user study framework showing the ContextProbe App and the supporting application server, and how different elements interact in creating a customized survey.

The Data Collector module runs as a background service within the ContextProbe app. Every 15 minutes it collects information about users' locations and continuously listens to system events related to running apps. Every time an app is used, sent to the background or switched between, the event is collected (step 1). Every hour the Survey Module queries the database to gather users' most recent location and captured time. This information is used by the survey module to create survey questions on a map (step 2). The Data Uploader module exports the collected data from the database each hour, including location data, information on running apps, and users' answers, and then uploads data to the remote server (step 3 and 4).

On the application server, the Data Handler module aggregates data collected from different users' smartphones (step 5). The Context Processor module extracts information related to each user's app usage patterns from the collected data on running apps on the users' phones, and identifies candidate apps based on the frequency that each app is used by the user (step 6). The Cloud Messaging module fetches information about the candidate app names for each user and pushes the app names to users' phone (step 7 and 8). The Message Receiver module saves the pushed content, which is used by the Survey Module later to compile new survey questions (step 9).

Procedure

One hour information session

Each participant had to attend a one-hour information session prior to the start of the four week study. This session was used

[2] The app name was chosen from a list of apps divided according their usage frequency; this was based on the captured and collected apps during the first week of the study as aforementioned

[3] https://developers.google.com/apps-script/

to explain how the app worked, to install the app on their smartphone, to allow them to sign the consent form and to familiarize them with the study requirements and respective remuneration.

User Study Requirements
Each participant had to install the *ContextProbe* app. Each user participating in the study had to answer a minimum of 10 sets of questions per day. Each set contained two parts: 1) four initial questions, and 2) 7-8 questions depending on how the questions were randomized. The appearance of the questions was randomized between each part for each set. Users needed 2-5 minutes to read/answer each set of questions i.e. 28-70 minutes a day.

The first set was shown at 9:00 am, the last set at 10:00 pm, for a total of 14 sets a day. A notification was used to alert participants that a new set of question needed to be answered. Participants had up to three hours after the set was first shown to answer all of the questions. We chose to show a set of questions for up to three hours, because we wanted to make sure participants clearly recollected their context. Participants could view the ContextProbe home page to see sets that needed to be answered (marked in green), and sets that had expired, i.e. were not answered within the allotted 3-hours time frame (marked in red). The home page also showed greyed-out buttons indicating the next sets that were not yet available to be answered. If participants did not respond to a minimum of ten sets per day, an automatic warning email was sent to them and the researchers, to inform them that they were not complying with the requirements and that they could be dismissed. If this happened one additional time, the participants and the researcher would both receive an email dismissing the participant from the study. Participants were asked to answer questions as honestly as possible. They were notified in the info session that if random clicking was detected either during or after the study, they would not be paid.

Trustworthiness of the data
Because participants were asked to tag their locations, we stored latitudes and longitudes of these locations and checked whether the tag provided by the participant was the same for the same location, accounting for GPS inaccuracy with a bounding box. We also checked for consistency in context tags (e.g *errands* for the activity label together with *in a class* for the location label. Consistency was checked when the same privacy question was given in the same location. We had a script that automatically checked participants' answers. Participants whose responses appeared to be inconsistent (with a lack of reasonable motivation) were removed.

Semi-Structured Personalized Survey
After analyzing the data for each participant, we enquired about qualitative motivations and reasons for sharing or not sharing context information. We conducted these conversations over email. In the emails we included screenshots of the location, location types, app names and if necessary, type of purpose. Semi-structured surveys were conducted after analyzing the quantitative data. Five different surveys were created to accommodate the five different privacy profile groups. We asked 10-25 tailored questions based on users' answers throughout the four week period.

- Privacy-conscious: Why did you not disclose data at all? From the apps collected from your phone, [app-name] has access to [personal data], did you know?
- Purpose-driven: Why did you not disclose your data to [app-name] for [purpose]? Why did you disclose your data to [app-name] for [purpose]?
- Trust-based: Why did you not disclose [personal data] to [app-name] when you did disclose it to [app-name]?
- Privacy-indifferent: Why did you disclose your data to all apps?
- Location-sensitive: Why do you not disclose your data at [location] rather than [location]? Do apps or purpose not affect you when you are at this [location]?

We looked the answers both between each group and individually. The quotes we present in the paper are examples that reflect common and interesting responses.

RESULTS

Participants
We solicited participation in our study using internal mailing lists and CraigsList announcements. Participation in the study was voluntary and each participant received $120 after completing the whole study. 61 participants attended the one hour information session. Out of these people, three participants did not have an Android device capable of running the app and seven participants never started the study. A total of fifty-one people started the study. Fourteen participants were removed from the study; of these, twelve participants were asked to leave (5 participants in week one; 4 participants in week two and 3 participants in week 3.). Two participants were removed because their responses fell below the allotted threshold of 10 sets per day. Ten participants were removed because their answers were not consistent and they could not provide reasonable explanations and motivation for the inconsistencies. The remaining two participants were asked to stop the study in week one because we could not receive any new GPS location data, even though they reported being in different locations. Thirty-seven participants participated in the entire study. Three participants' responses were removed because due to their type of Android device, information about the apps running on their smartphone could not be collected for the study (they received payment); in addition, one had problems receiving questions due to a poor Internet connection around his neighborhood. Thirty-four people successfully completed the study. Of these, 18 were male (av. age = 25) and 16 female (avg. age = 29). Level of educations varied from having completed high school (4), two-year college degree (7), being an undergraduate student (2), completed four-year college degree (10), completed master degree (4), being a graduate student (3) to advanced graduate work or completed Ph.D (4).

Responses

Over the period of four weeks we gathered 74,713 total responses from the 34 participants (Table 1) for four different conditions (Table 2). We collected 4,212 responses for conditions where *no app name* and *without purpose* were displayed; 25,452 responses for conditions where app names were not displayed, but purposes were displayed (excluding the *without purpose* condition); 6,352 responses where all app condition (excluding *no app name*) were displayed, but *without purposes*; and 38,697 responses where all app names (excluding the *no app name* condition) and all purposes (excluding the *without purpose*) condition were displayed. Questions were evenly distributed for each factor (Table 1).

Table 1. Number of participants' responses grouped by app frequency types (no app name condition is included) for each purpose condition (no purpose condition is included). The total number of responses for each and across conditions is also shown.

TYPES OF PURPOSES	No App	Least Used	Medium Used	Most Used	Total responses
Without Purpose	4,212	2,138	2,069	2,145	**10,564**
Captures Information	4,234	2,196	2,132	2,198	**10,760**
Testing Needs	4,181	2,131	2,059	2,135	**10,506**
Improving Experience	4,278	2,184	2,114	2,186	**10,762**
Ads Needs	4,198	2,110	2,048	2,121	**10,477**
Profiles	4,298	2,224	2,154	2,223	**10,899**
Revenue Needs	4,263	2,182	2,118	2,182	**10,745**
Total responses	**29,664**	**15,165**	**14,694**	**15,190**	**74,713**

Users' privacy profiles

Participants in our study were found to share their personal context according to different factors: usage purpose, trust in the app itself and location type. From Figure 4 (a) & (b) we can see that six participants (P4[4], P15, P23, P27[4], P29[4], P30) shared mostly according to the app that they were using (with the exception of never sharing with any app only when specific purposes were specified). However, the majority of participants (fifteen participants: P3, P5, P6, P10, P11, P13, P14, P16, P17, P18, P19, P24, P25, P26, P33) shared according to the type of purpose (Figure 4 (b)) displayed in each question.

These latter participants did not share their personal information when the purpose specified did not present any conceivable gain to them. Of the remaining participants, eight demonstrated behavior of either always being willing to share their data (P1, P2, P21) or being extremely privacy-sensitive and never sharing (P8, P9, P12, P22, P28). The remaining five participants (P7, P20, P31, P32, P34) showed no effect according to the type of purpose or the app; a closer look at their data showed that they tended not to share their personal information when at particular locations. Among these participants, four participants tended not to share when they were at *home* and one participant tended not to share when at work. Our results highlight five distinct patterns of behavior with respect to privacy preferences:

- **Privacy-conscious users (3)**: These users did not tend to share their personal data. They were very conservative about when to share, and they do not share.
- **Purpose-driven users (15)**: These users shared their personal data according to different purposes. They tended to share data when there was a benefit to them.
- **Trust-based users (6)**: These users trusted certain apps and, no matter the activity or the purpose, would share the data.
- **Privacy-indifferent users (5)**: These users shared their personal data consciously because they saw no problem or harm in doing so.
- **Location-sensitive users (5)**: These users shared their personal data when they were not in a particular location. When they were at a specific location, they tended to never share their location information or the activity they were currently undertaking.

Usage and Collection effects on sharing preferences

Participants in the study tended to share more ($\mu = 3.12$; $\mu_{rank} = 3.04$) when there was no information on the purpose for data collection or which app was collecting it (combination 1) (Table 2). When details were given, such as name of the app requesting the information and the purpose for which it would be used, users tended to share the least ($\mu = 2.71$; $\mu_{rank} = 1.60$; combination 4). When just one of either the purpose or requesting app was shown (data purpose versus data collection), participants tended to share less than when data purpose was specified ($\mu = 2.86$; $\mu_{rank} = 2.50$; combination 3) rather than when the app requesting the data was specified ($\mu = 3.02$; $\mu_{rank} = 2.85$; combination 2) (Table 2).

Table 2. Descriptive statistics and Friedman test for each factor: combination of absence and/or presence of purpose and app name. The mean is calculated using a 5-point Likert-scale (ranging from 5-Will Definitely share to 1-Definitely NOT share). The Friedman test is significant Chi-Square (3, N of Participants = 34) = 25.295, $p < .0001$. Kendall's W is 0.248, indicating fairly strong differences among the four combinations.

	COMBINATIONS APP NAME	PURPOSE	Num. of Responses	Mean (μ)	Std. Dev (σ)	Mean Rank (μ_{rank})
G1	✗	✗	4,212	3.12	0.61	3.04
G2	✓	✗	6,352	3.02	0.65	2.85
G3	✗	✓	25,452	2.86	0.69	2.50
G4	✓	✓	38,697	2.71	0.69	1.60

The Friedman test shows a statistically significant difference in all four groups (Table 2). Post hoc analysis with Wilcoxon conducted with a Bonferroni correction with $p < 0.0083$ ($p = 0.6/6$) shows statistical significance to users' sharing preferences in G1 vs. G3 (Z=-3.198; $p < .001$), G1 vs. G4 (Z= 3.676; $p < .000$), G3 vs. G4 (Z = -3.258; $p < .001$), and G2 vs. G4 (Z = 3.771; $p < .000$).

[4] These participants did not share their personal information when the purposes displayed within the question did not show a conceivable gain to them. Otherwise they based their decision on the app. Even when the purposes displayed within the questions were tailored to have a clear and conceivable gain for them, they still would not share their personal information with certain apps.

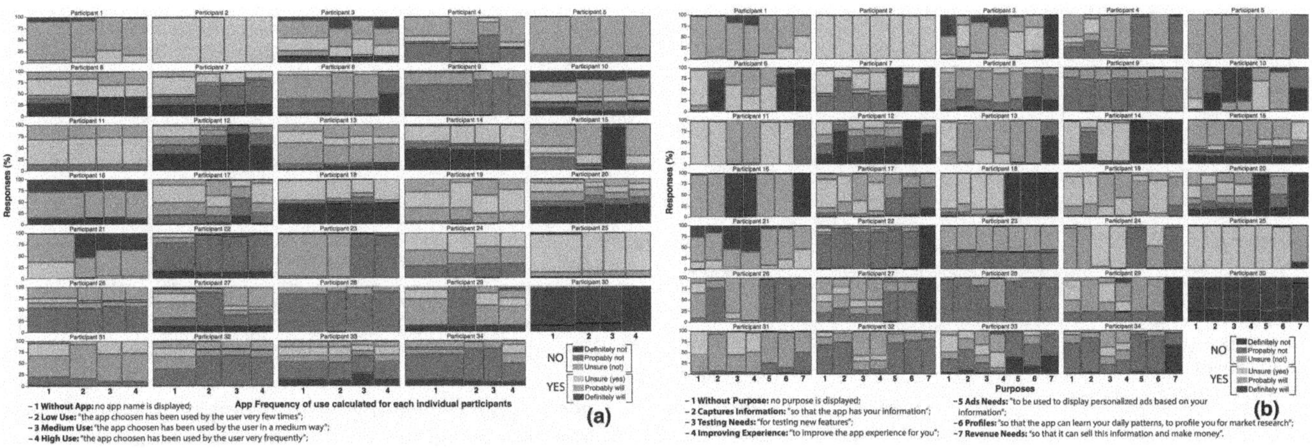

Figure 4. Overview of participants' responses regarding willingness or unwillingness to share their personal information with apps, in the form of either their location or their activities, for six different types of purpose, as well as no purpose.

App effect: Does the frequency or the type of app matter?
Six participants based their decisions to share or not share their personal information on the app they were using.

Frequency of use does not affect willingness to share data, with some participants choosing to share more with less frequently-used apps, rather than the most frequently-used apps. For these participants, the reasons for not wanting to share depended on the type of app. P4 explained that he was afraid that his sensitive information could be used for other purposes by the app (web browser app):

> P4: *"I tend to type in a lot of personal stuff via [browser's name] that I don't want used. That is why I denied its access to my information."*

While P15 was found to be reluctant in sharing personal information with an app (dating app) that had already collected and stored a lot of personal information:

> P15: *"I was just getting a little aggravated with the site [Name], it already had a ton of my data, so no more!"*

P4 in addition tended not to share his personal information (with any type of app, including when the app name was not displayed) when purpose 6 (targeted advertising) and purpose 8 (revenue needs for company) were shown.

P27 and P29 tended not to share their personal information with their least-used apps, however the reasons for these choices are different. For P27, frequency of use and hence familiarity with the app (diet app) was an important factor. P27 explained that once he has established a relationship with an app, he becomes more willing to disclose his personal data, for certain types of purposes that are beneficial to him:

> P(27) *"[...] I didn't use the app, I was not able to establish a relationship with it"*

While P29 explained not wanting to share based on a distrust in the app (banking app) itself:

> P29 *"I feel it's an extreme invasion of privacy letting my bank know where I am during the day. My phone is for leisure, for fun [...]. The less the bank knows about me, the better."*

Similarly to P4, P27 and P29 also tended not to share with any type of app (including when no app name was shown), when purposes did not show any conceivable gain to them (purpose 2,5,6,7).

P23 and P30 instead were unwilling to share their personal data with their mostly frequently used apps. P30's most frequently used app was a social network app and similarly to P15, the reason behind not wanting to share was to avoid giving additional personal data on top of the data already collected and stored by the app. P23 explained concerns that his former employer (bank app developer) would be able to use his personal data:

> P23 *"I used to work for [Company Name] and I would just not want them to have any of my information."*

Participants did not base their decision to share or not share with specific apps on the frequency of (and possible need and desire for) use, but rather on the app itself.

We found that participants denied access to their location to apps which actually requested the location permission on installation. This means that these apps can already collect this data on the user's location. These participants were not aware that this could be happening, underlining the need for clearer and more specific regulation of data purpose rather than data access. Such conflicts are, however, not being addressed enough today by mobile platforms.

Purpose effect: Does the type of purpose matter?
Data usage and collection matters to users when deciding to share their information (Table 2). As we can see from Table 3, Figure 5 and Figure 4(b), the type of purpose affects users' decisions to share or not their personal context.

Participants showed willingness to share their personal context when there was a conceivable gain to them. Participants were prompted to share their personal data for purposes of *testing needs* and *improving app experiences*, their sharing preferences had a $\mu = 3.324$ and $\mu = 3.36$ respectively (Table 3). When the purposes specified were more beneficial for developers (ie. companies), the willingness of participants to

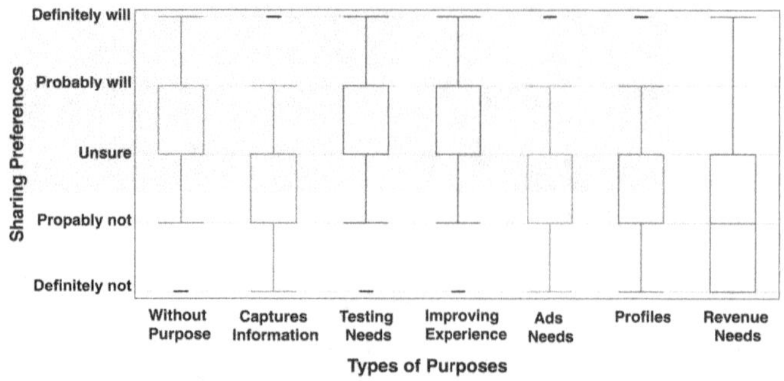

Figure 5. Box plot of participants' responses to sharing of their personal context (location and activity) grouped by different types of purpose (including no purpose).

share dropped, with $\mu = 2.60$ (*ads needs*), $\mu = 2.66$ (*gathering profiles*) and $\mu = 1.96$ (*revenue need*).

Table 3. Descriptive statistics and Friedman test regarding willingness or unwillingness to share, for different types of purposes. Purposes vary according to seven predefined purposes. The Friedman test is significant Chi-Square (6, N = 34) = 126.8, $p < .0001$. Kendall's W is 0.622, indicating fairly strong differences among the seven purposes)

	TYPES OF PURPOSES	N	Mean (μ)	Std. Dev (σ)	Mean Rank (μ_{rank})
1	Without Purpose	34	3.06	0.59	4.94
	Captures Information	34	2.74	0.71	3.28
2	Testing Needs	34	3.34	0.72	5.9
	Improving Experience	34	3.37	0.71	6.06
3	Ads Needs	34	2.61	0.88	3.29
4	Profiles	34	2.66	0.88	3.09
	Revenue Needs	34	1.97	0.91	1.44

When the purpose specified was non-explanatory or non-existent, participants' willingness to share their data differed (Figure 5), even though these two purposes described the same circumstance [20]. When the purpose was non-explanatory and vague, $\mu = 2.74$, while when the purpose was missing, $\mu = 3.05$. This underlines the fact that participants are more willing to share data when they are not aware of what their data is used for.

The appearance of a vague and non-explanatory purpose caused participants to disclose less compared with the results when the purpose was missing. Participants might have been alerted by vague purpose strings, indicating an intention to keep participants' data for other unknown uses (*so that it (the app) can have your information*). P10 and P6 underlined the importance of purpose information:

> P10*"The purpose of the data collection is very important to me. If it is just collecting it to store, I would not be comfortable because I wouldn't know what it is doing with the data".*

> P6*"[...] whether or not to release my location depended on the other factors. [...] it's easy to say "I'm enjoying leisure time" sure, so are 1 billion other people, but having my location is a *lot* more specific, and so I'm less inclined to share that data [...] Purpose of use and nature of app are both extremely important factors in deciding whether or not to disclose the information.*

Similarly, P7 and P29 both had concerns about unknown uses of their personal data.

> P7*"I am not about volunteering information to unknown sources, [...] Just because an app is particularly useful doesn't mean I would grant it a blank check to record and sell my personal data."*

> P29*"I am more sensitive to disclosing data that may have personal information that can be intercepted or used without my permission."*

Effect of context on sharing preferences

While participants were highly affected by the type of purpose and the type of apps shown to them, we found five participants who displayed differences in their sharing behavior based on their location. In Table 4 we reported individual odds ratios representing each participant's willingness to disclose their location in each of the four popular reported places (*home, work, leisure* and *transport*). Three of these participants (P20, P31, P34) showed that when people were in locations other than home, the odds ratio of disclosing at the location is 2 times greater than when at home.

The remaining two participants (P7, P32) showed the opposite, ie. when their current location was among (*work, transport*, or *leisure* the odds of them not disclosing was 1.2 to 3 times larger than when at *home*.

Table 4. Repeated measured logistic regression with *location* context as the predictor variable and participants' disclosure preferences as a binary variable (0 = NOT DISCLOSE; 1 = DISCLOSE). The odds ratios for each context is displayed. The computation is performed per individual participant. The intercept value represents the bias of each participant to respond positively or negatively to disclose their information. The higher the value, the more likely they are to respond (irrespective of context). (***) $p < 0.001$; (**) $p < 0.01$; (*) $p < 0.05$; (+) $p < 0.1$.

PART. ID	INTERCEPT	*Home*	*Work*	*Leisure*	*Transport*
20	0.46***	0.54***	1.40*	1.34	1.05
31	0.51***	0.49***	2.78***	0.66*	1.11
34	0.22***	0.43***	0.94	0.96	0.98
7	0.66***	0.81+	N/A	0.22***	0.53***
32	0.35***	1.04	0.82	0.76	0.62*

However even among these five participants, purpose was a dominant factor affecting their disclosure preferences. When presented with beneficial purposes or no purpose, participants became more willing to disclose, even when the location was labeled as more private to them (e.g. less willing to disclose home for three participants and other locations for the two remaining ones).

Participants' qualitative remarks revealed how they considered these factors together. P20 noted that the sensitivity of disclosed information related to personal context, but also emphasized that purpose was the main factor for disclosing his information:

> P(20)*"I don't like having my home location or home activities available to any app, [...] while I don't mind anyone knowing if I'm running errands or at work. [...] Purpose of use was the most important thing - if it was just for the app developers benefit [...] I didn't want to do it. But if I could get something out of it [...] I was more willing to do it.".*

P7 thought it was fine to disclose his location if it is used appropriately:

> P7 *"[...], I would be fine with an app knowing that I am relaxing in [coffee shop] or at home if it actually put that information to use".*

This observation shows that while users' locations and activities might be helpful in governing the social norms of sharing information with other people [26], these factors are outweighed by purpose when considering disclosing information to apps.

In Android apps, users grant permission prior to installation, allowing apps to use personal information for a variety of unknown purposes. In this study, we have shown that participants based their decisions to share their personal information on the different types of information or a combination of factors: ie. purpose, app and location context. The all-or-nothing decision that the Android OS currently uses could therefore be improved to allow finer-grained control for popular visited locations.

DISCUSSION

Privacy awareness: vague vs. explicit

Our study highlighted the importance of showing *specific information* regarding information about data collection (*app name*) and data usage (*purpose*). As seen in Table 2 participants are more willing to share their personal context when none of this information is displayed. When the appearance of this information is alternated, participants shared less than when information about data usage (*purpose*) was displayed.

Presenting a vague and non-explanatory purpose caused participants to disclose less, compared to when a purpose was missing. Tan et. al [30] reported that users were more willing to disclose their personal information when a purpose was shown in the permission request. This disparity in results might be due to different approaches we took in probing privacy preferences. Tan et. al [30] used an online survey, showing screenshots of permission requests from real apps with hypothetical question about personal data, whereas our study was conducted in the wild with privacy preference questions about participants' real, personal and current contextual information tailored to specific apps that were really used by each participant. Subjects in Tan et. al's study [30] might not have been familiar with the apps shown in the survey, and each subject was given the survey questions once.

In our study, answers from each participant were collected using repeated measures designed to cover all conditions for different purposes. The main goal of conducting the study in the wild with repeated measures was to compare subjects' responses under different conditions, including their physical context (their locations and activities) and different purpose strings presented to them. The aim was to trigger privacy concerns that are more subjective and sample responses from real life situations.

One plausible explanation for the impact of showing a non-explanatory purpose is that privacy awareness was increased. Participants were reminded of the trade-offs [12] between the unpredictable costs (privacy risks) and benefits (functionalities) brought by apps, therefore becoming less willing to disclose personal information. This finding highlights the importance of specificity when describing purpose of data access, since a vague purpose can alert users to possible privacy risks and discourage them from sharing.

Developers are able to collect personal data about users, because to date, mobile platforms lack support for fine-grained control over data collection with specified purposes. Our study suggests that when any explanation, even if vague, is provided for the purpose of data collection, people do get alerted about privacy concerns and make different decisions compared to when no information is displayed.

Purpose matters: give me a reason to share

Differently from previous research [34][17][32] which found that users' preferences for disclosing their locations are contextual, our study demonstrates that users' decisions about whether to disclose context information are affected not only by the sensitivity of the disclosed information itself, but also by the purpose for collecting the data.

In our study, users' contextual information (current location, activity and social surrounding) did not have a significant impact (like purpose) on their privacy preferences for disclosing personal information to apps.

Our results have shown that when control is given to users, they tend to make more specific choices regarding their perceived benefits. For some users, preferences for sharing can be strictly app-specific or location-specific. However, even in these cases participants were unwilling to share their information for some purposes (beneficial to developers).

Our findings confirm that participants used the purpose string to separate data access from data collection and find clues to justify whether such data collection is reasonable or not. As shown in Table 3, the purpose string either increases acceptance of data collection or alerts the user to unfavorable privacy risks that can decrease the willingness of users to disclose personal information to apps.

We analyzed all 34 participants' apps and found that many (85%) of the apps that these users denied access to their location actually request the location permission on installation, meaning that these apps can collect users' locations at any time. This underlines the drawbacks and failings of the current practice of allowing any access to users' personal data without being able to specify and restrict the usage. Such conflicts, however, are not being addressed enough by mobile platforms and they should be addressed by regulations and legislation aimed at helping users to safeguard and protect their right to privacy.

Experiment Limitations

When using experience sampling to probe participants' privacy preferences, we were aware of the natural bias introduced by the time-based triggers as discussed in [21]. For example, *home* and *work* were the predominant places for location context. Therefore we carefully reported the results with appropriate statistical indicators such as odds ratios to show the effects of location context. Our understanding for user location and activity context depends on self-reported data from participants. It is possible that some errors were introduced when annotating the locations.

Our study required the participants to respond to questions fairly frequently (once an hour). It is possible there could be a fatigue effect that caused decays in response rate or lesser quality of data as a result. Due to the monetary incentive and weekly removal of disqualified subjects, we found only a slight decrease in response rate in the final week (5%). They study was conducted with Android smartphone users and might not be completely representative for other smartphone operating systems.

Acknowledgments

Ilaria Liccardi was supported by the European Commission Marie Curie International Outgoing Fellowship grant 2011-301567 *Social Privacy*. Our thanks to Evan W. Patton and our anonymous reviewers for their help, suggestions and insights.

REFERENCES

1. Abdesslem, F. B., Parris, I., and Henderson, T. Mobile experience sampling: Reaching the parts of facebook other methods cannot reach. In *In Privacy and Usability Methods Powwow* (2010).
2. Acquisti, A., and Grossklags, J. Privacy and rationality in individual decision making. *Security Privacy, IEEE* (2005), 26–33.
3. Acquisti, A., and Grossklags, J. When 25 cents is too much: An experiment on willingness-to-sell and willingness-to-protect personal information. In *WEIS* (2007), 12.
4. Aharony, N., Pan, W., Ip, C., Khayal, I., and Pentland, A. Social fmri: Investigating and shaping social mechanisms in the real world. *Pervasive and Mobile Computing 7*, 6 (2011), 643–659.
5. Ahern, S., Eckles, D., Good, N. S., King, S., Naaman, M., and Nair, R. Over-exposed?: privacy patterns and considerations in online and mobile photo sharing. In *Proc. ACM CHI* (2007), 357–366.
6. Balebako, R., Jung, J., Lu, W., Cranor, L. F., and Nguyen, C. "Little Brothers Watching You": Raising Awareness of Data Leaks on Smartphones. In *Proc. of ACM SOUPS* (2013), 12.
7. Bansal, G., Zahedi, F., Gefen, D., et al. The impact of personal dispositions on information sensitivity, privacy concern and trust in disclosing health information online. *Decision Support Systems 49*, 2 (2010), 138–150.
8. Cherubini, M., and Oliver, N. A refined experience sampling method to capture mobile user experience. *Proc. of ACM CHI Workshop of Mobile User Experience Research* (2009), 1–6.
9. Consolvo, S., Smith, I. E., Matthews, T., LaMarca, A., Tabert, J., and Powledge, P. Location disclosure to social relations: why, when, & what people want to share. In *Proc. ACM CHI* (2005), 81–90.
10. Enck, W., Gilbert, P., Chun, B.-G., Cox, L. P., Jung, J., McDaniel, P., and Sheth, A. N. Taintdroid: An information-flow tracking system for realtime privacy monitoring on smartphones. In *Proc. OSDI'10* (2010), 99–106.
11. Felt, A. P., Ha, E., Egelman, S., Haney, A., Chin, E., and Wagner, D. Android permissions: User attention, comprehension, and behavior. In *Proc. ACM SOUP* (2012), 3.
12. Hann, I.-H., Hui, K.-L., Lee, T., and Png, I. Online information privacy: Measuring the cost-benefit trade-off. *Proc. of ICIS* (2002), 1.
13. Hurwitz, J. User choice, privacy sensitivity, and acceptance of personal information collection. In *European Data Protection: Coming of Age*, S. Gutwirth, R. Leenes, P. de Hert, and Y. Poullet, Eds. Springer Netherlands, 2013, 295–312.
14. Joinson, A. N., Reips, U.-D., Buchanan, T., and Schofield, C. B. P. Privacy, trust, and self-disclosure online. *Human–Computer Interaction* (2010), 1–24.
15. Kelley, P. G., Cesca, L., Bresee, J., and Cranor, L. F. Standardizing privacy notices: an online study of the nutrition label approach. In *Proc. of ACM CHI* (2010), 1573–1582.
16. Kelley, P. G., Cranor, L. F., and Sadeh, N. Privacy as part of the app decision-making process. In *Proc. ACM CHI* (2013), 3393–3402.
17. Khalil, A., and Connelly, K. Context-aware telephony: privacy preferences and sharing patterns. In *Proc. ACM CSCW* (2006), 469–478.
18. Knijnenburg, B. P., and Kobsa, A. Helping users with information disclosure decisions: Potential for adaptation. In *Proc. ACM IUI* (2013), 407–416.
19. Knijnenburg, B. P., and Kobsa, A. Making decisions about privacy: information disclosure in context-aware recommender systems. *ACM Transactions on Interactive Intelligent Systems (TiiS) 3*, 3 (2013), 20.
20. Langer, E. Minding matters. *In L. Berkowitz (Ed.), Advances in experimental social psychology (Vol. 22). New York, Academic Press.* (1989).
21. Lathia, N., Rachuri, K. K., Mascolo, C., and Rentfrow, P. J. Contextual dissonance: Design bias in sensor-based experience sampling methods. In *Proc. of ACM UBICOMP* (2013), 183–192.
22. Liccardi, I., Pato, J., and Weitzner, D. J. Improving Mobile App selection through Transparency and Better Permission Analysis. *Journal of Privacy and Confidentiality: Vol. 5: Iss. 2, Article 1.* (2014), 1–55.
23. Liccardi, I., Pato, J., Weitzner, D. J., Abelson, H., and De Roure, D. No technical understanding required: Helping users make informed choices about access to their personal data. In *Proc. ACM Mobiquitous* (2014), 140–150.
24. Lin, J., Amini, S., Hong, J. I., Sadeh, N., Lindqvist, J., and Zhang, J. Expectation and purpose: understanding users' mental models of mobile app privacy through crowdsourcing. In *Proc. of ACM UBICOMP* (2012), 501–510.
25. Mancini, C., Thomas, K., Rogers, Y., Price, B. A., Jedrzejczyk, L., Bandara, A. K., Joinson, A. N., and Nuseibeh, B. From spaces to places: emerging contexts in mobile privacy. In *Proc. ACM UBICOMP* (2009), 1–10.
26. Nissenbaum, H. Privacy as Contextual Integrity. *Washington Law Review 79* (2004), 119.
27. Park, Y. J., and Jang, S. M. Understanding privacy knowledge and skill in mobile communication. *Computers in Human Behavior 38* (2014), 296 – 303.
28. Shilton, K., and Martin, K. E. Mobile privacy expectations in context. In *Proc. of Communication, Information and Internet Policy* (2013).
29. Shklovski, I., Mainwaring, S. D., Skúladóttir, H. H., and Borgthorsson, H. Leakiness and creepiness in app space: Perceptions of privacy and mobile app use. In *Proc. ACM CHI* (2014), 2347–2356.
30. Tan, J., Nguyen, K., Theodorides, M., Negrón-Arroyo, H., Thompson, C., Egelman, S., and Wagner, D. The effect of developer-specified explanations for permission requests on smartphone user behavior. In *Proc. ACM CHI* (2014), 91–100.
31. Toch, E. Crowdsourcing privacy preferences in context-aware applications. *Personal and Ubiquitous Computing* (2014), 129–141.
32. Toch, E., Cranshaw, J., Drielsma, P. H., Tsai, J. Y., Kelley, P. G., Springfield, J., Cranor, L., Hong, J., and Sadeh, N. Empirical models of privacy in location sharing. In *Proc. ACM UBICOMP* (2010), 129–138.
33. Urban, J., Hoofnagle, C., and Li, S. Mobile phones and privacy. In *UC Berkeley Public Law Research Paper* (2012).
34. Venkatanathan, J., Ferreira, D., Benisch, M., Lin, J., Karapanos, E., Kostakos, V., Sadeh, N., and Toch, E. Improving users' consistency when recalling location sharing preferences. In *Proc, of INTERACT (Springer).* 2011, 380–387.
35. White House. Consumer data privacy in a networked world: A framework for protecting privacy and promoting innovation in the global digital economy. 15–19.
36. White House. Big data and privacy: A technological perspective. 40–41.
37. World Economic Forum. Unlocking the value of personal data: From collection to usage.
38. Xie, J., Knijnenburg, B. P., and Jin, H. Location sharing privacy preference: Analysis and personalized recommendation. In *Proc. IUI '14*, IUI '14 (2014), 189–198.

VeilMe: An Interactive Visualization Tool for Privacy Configuration of Using Personality Traits

Yang Wang
University of California Davis
Davis, CA, USA
ywang@ucdavis.edu

Liang Gou
IBM Research - Almaden
San Jose, CA, USA
lgou@us.ibm.com

Anbang Xu
IBM Research - Almaden
San Jose, CA, USA
anbangxu@us.ibm.com

Michelle X. Zhou
Juji Inc.
Saratoga, CA, USA
mzhou@acm.org

Huahai Yang
Juji Inc.
Saratoga, CA, USA
huahai.yang@gmail.com

Hernan Badenes
IBM Argentina
Buenos Aires, Argentina
hdadenes@us.ibm.com

ABSTRACT
With the recent advances in using data analytics to automatically infer one's personality traits from their social media data, users are facing a growing tension between the use of the technology to aid self development in workplace and the privacy concerns of such use. Given the richness of personality data that can be derived today and the varied sensitivity of revealing such data, it is a non-trivial task for users to configure their privacy settings for sharing and protecting their derived personality data. Here we present the design, development, and evaluation of an interactive visualization tool, VeilMe, which helps users configure the privacy settings for the use of their personality portraits derived from social media. Unlike other privacy configuration tools, our tool offers two distinct advantages. First, it presents a novel and intuitive visual interface that aids users in understanding and exploring their own personality traits derived from their social media data, and configuring their privacy preferences. Second, our tool helps users to jump start their privacy settings by suggesting initial sharing strategies based on a set of factors, including the users' personality and target audience. We have evaluated the use of our tool with 124 participants in an enterprise context. Our results show that VeilMe effectively supports various user privacy configuration tasks, and also suggest several design implications, including the approaches to personalized privacy configurations.

Author Keywords
Visual Interface; Personality Traits; Privacy; Sharing Settings; Social Media

ACM Classification Keywords
H.5.2 Information Interfaces and Presentation: User Interfaces - *Interaction Styles*; K.4.1Computers and society: Public Policy Issues - *Privacy*

CHI 2015, April 18 - 23 2015, Seoul, Republic of Korea
Copyright 2015 ACM 978-1-4503-3145-6/15/04 $15.00
http://dx.doi.org/10.1145/2702123.2702293

INTRODUCTION
A person's personality traits — the patterns of individuals' thought, emotion, and behavior, together with the psychological mechanisms behind them — largely impact the person's life outcomes, including their performance in the workplace [9, 2, 30]. Recent advances in psycho-linguistics and machine learning have shown that such traits can now be automatically derived from one's linguistic signals, such as their online social media footprints [11, 37, 40].

Our current work is exploring the use of the derived personality traits to aid employees' self-awareness and self-development in the workplace. In particular, we focus on studying three types of personality traits and their impact on a person's professional life: Big 5 personality [40], human values [3] and fundamental needs [39]. Table 1 summarizes these three types of traits and their use in the workplace.

With the increasing power of gaining deeper insights into themselves, people not only begin to be aware of the potential benefits but have also expressed heightened privacy concerns about revealing these insights about themselves in the workplace. For example, a recent study shows that people perceive a number of benefits and risks of exposing their derived personality traits in the workplace, including self branding and potential misuse of such traits [13]. The users thus have expressed the need of tight controls over the use of such data. While some of their privacy preferences over these data are similar to those on handling their other personal data, such as personal communications (e.g., instant message, email) [24] and work locations [26], the users also want much finer-grained controls over their most intrinsic traits (e.g., exposing Big 5 personality traits but not motivations) due to the power *and* the imperfections of today's data analytics [13].

However, it is a non-trivial task for users to configure their privacy policies for the use of their personality data in the workplace for three main reasons. First, personality data is multi-dimensional and inherently complex for a user to comprehend, let alone setting the privacy policy for each trait. For example, the three types of personality traits that we focus on already include a total of 52 traits (Table 1) at three levels of abstraction. Second, since different personality traits influence a person's professional life differently [30], a user may

Big 5 Personality [40] (Workplace Use: work proficiency, training proficiency, and teamwork [2])	
Openness	Subtraits:*Imagination, Artistic interests, Emotionality, Adventurousness, Intellect, Liberalism*
Conscientiousness	Subtraits:*Self-Efficacy, Orderliness, Dutifulness, Achievement striving, Self-discipline, Cautiousness*
Extraversion	Subtraits: *Friendliness, Gregariousness, Assertiveness, Activity-level, Excitement-seeking, Cheerfulness*
Agreeableness	Subtraits: *Trust, Morality, Altruism, Cooperation, Modesty, Sympathy*
Neuroticism	Subtraits: *Anxiety, Anger, Depression, Self-consciousness, Immoderation, Vulnerability*
Needs [39] (Workplace Use: job incentives, collaboration [39])	
Ideals	a desire for perfection
Harmony	appreciating other people's feeling
Closeness	being connected to family and setting up home
Self-expression	discovering and asserting one's own identity
Excitement	upbeat emotions, and having fun
Curiosity	a desire to discover and grow
Values [3] (Workplace Use: motivations and commitment for jobs [4])	
Self-transcendence	showing concern for the welfare and interests of others
Conservation	emphasizing conformity, tradition, security
Self-enhancement	seeking personal success for oneself
Open-to-change	emphasizing stimulation, self-direction
Hedonism	seeking pleasure and sensuous gratification for oneself

Table 1: The three types of traits used in this work.

not know how to optimize the privacy configurations to balance the benefits and risks of sharing their personality data. Third, there are often many other factors affecting a user's privacy policies over their personality data, including the social groups who can access the data, the purpose of the data use, and the level of trait details to be disclosed.

To help a user effectively configure their privacy policies over the use of their complex personality data without being overwhelmed by the task, we have built an interactive visualization tool, VeilMe. It helps a user to understand, configure, and maintain the sharing preferences of their personality data in the workplace. To help a user jump start the privacy settings, it also suggests an initial set of privacy policies based on a number of factors, including the user's own personality and the privacy policies preferred by other with similar personality.

Compared to existing tools for privacy management and policy authoring and configuration (e.g., [16, 33, 31, 29, 23, 7, 26]), our work offers three unique contributions. First, it introduces a novel but simple visual interface that helps users to effectively explore and understand their personality traits. Second, it supports intuitive visual metaphors and fluid visual interactions that allow users to easily configure their privacy policies involving a number of parameters *simultaneously* based on the "social distance" of target audience. Third, it incorporates several strategies to help users configure their initial privacy policies, which further reduces the users' efforts in their privacy configuration tasks.

To evaluate the effectiveness of VeilMe, we have deployed the tool in a large IT company and conducted a study with 124 participants. Our results are encouraging. It demonstrates the helpfulness of our tool in support of users' privacy configuration tasks over their own personality data. The study has also enriched our understanding on how people use such a tool in the real world and suggested several important design implications, including the effective use of different visual metaphors in configuring privacy policies.

The rest of paper is organized as follows. We first give a brief introduction to the related work, and then present the design rationales and details of VeilMe. Finally, we describe our study design and results, and discuss design implications learned from our study.

RELATED WORK

Personality Modeling on Social Media

There are many research efforts in modeling and analyzing people's traits from various data sources. For example, some work attempts to predict Big 5 personality from essays and conversation scripts [22] and emails [34]. There is also a rich body of work on predicting personal traits from social media, such as extracting an individual's demographics and political orientation from Twitter [28], and inferring one's emotional states from Twitter [6]. Some other efforts use social behavior to predict Big 5 personality [1]. Golbeck et al. show how to predict Big 5 personality from social media [12] by using both linguistic and social behavior signals.

In this work, we used three personality models rooted in psycho-linguistic analysis, including a Big 5 personality model [40] and a model of human values [3] built with LIWC dictionary [37], a model of fundamental needs with a self-constructed dictionary [39]. We implemented the three models in our system with people's twitter data, and the model implementation is beyond the focus of this work.

Privacy about Personal Data

On the other hand, researchers in HCI community show extensive interests in understanding users' privacy preferences of different personal data [15]. Many work has been done to understand personal data including personal communications (e.g., instant message, email, and social media) [24], and location-based activities [18]. Occasionally, there are some work examining the relation among people's privacy and their personality traits. For example, it is showed that people's trust and risk propensity impact their privacy concerns [35], and certain dimensions of Big 5 personality traits influence one's privacy concerns [17, 19]. A recent study shows that people's sharing preferences of such traits are related to several factors in the workplace, including social groups who can access the traits, the control of trait granularity, the trait properties of types and values, and the context of benefits and risks [13].

To sum up, this work of system and visual interface design is grounded in and guided by these studies. Especially, it leverages the results from this work [13] by supporting flexible control over various factors of social groups, trait types and values, trait granularity under in the workplace context.

Interactive User Interface for Privacy Settings

With increasing attention on privacy issues around personal data, some tools have been proposed to assist users to comprehend and configure privacy settings in a networked environment. Some visual interfaces are designed to help people understand their privacy settings. For example, the Facebook audience preview allows users to preview how the individual friends or public to see their profile [16]. Schlegel et. al. used a visual metaphor of eyes to show the amount of personal information accessed by others [33].

Besides supporting the comprehension of privacy settings, other tools are provided for configuring and maintaining such settings. Two notable interactive visualization tools were proposed for security policies configuration. Rode et. al. used a circled pie chart like visualization to show access activity of system files and configure the access policy [31], while Reeder et al. presented an expandable matrix interface to achieve a similar purpose [29] and found this interface is complementary with Facebook audience view [20]. While these tools mainly focus on security and access control on file systems, other tools were proposed for sharing settings of personal data. PViz uses a bubble chart based visual interface to support sharing settings for Facebook and suggests automatically generated social groups to reduce configuration efforts [23]. A similar Venn Diagram interface is used for social network policy configuration for different social groups [7]. MySpace utilizes interactive visualization of physical workplaces to support configuring access policies about availability and location in workplace [26].

To conclude, the visual interface in this work is inspired by above work, but differentiates itself in several ways. This work considers the uniqueness of sharing personality portrait in the workplace setting, such as complicated structure of personality portraits, multiple levels of sharing control on social groups, trait types and values. It is difficult to apply above tools address this problem. Also, this design proposes intuitive visual metaphors to help users understand their personality portraits and configure sharing preferences of portraits.

Privacy Policies Generation

While user interface attempts to help users specify their privacy settings, many other work focuses on generating meaningful privacy preferences for users. These efforts usually take two strategies: rule based and machine learning based approaches. The rule based ones identify important factors impacting sharing, such as information content, social relationship, context, and time, to generate sharing policies for different users or user groups [32, 27]. Meanwhile, some work introduces machine learning techniques to predict a user's sharing preferences with various features, such as social network information [8], sensitivity and visibility of the shared information [21].

In this work, we experimented both rule based and machine learning based strategies which are integrated into our visual interface as the default sharing settings. Personality traits were used as additional features to predict the sharing preferences in our model. The goal here is to find a good default settings strategy to reduce users' efforts to adjust the sharing settings over complicated personality portraits.

VEILME

In this section, we introduce the design goals, implementation details and strategies of generating initial privacy settings in VeilMe.

Design Goals

To help users with the privacy settings for their personality portraits, VeilMe should meet following design goals:

DG1 ***It should provide an intuitive visual representation for personality portrait.*** A user needs to fully understand her personality portrait before she can configure the privacy settings for such traits. In our case, a personality portrait includes multiple dimensions (e.g., "Big 5", "Needs", etc.) and a hierarchical structure (there are sub-traits under Big 5 traits). The goal is to design a scalable visualization of such a personality portrait with a capability of an overview and detail-on-demand.

DG2 ***It should help users to be aware of their privacy settings.*** According to previous literature, it is critical for users to have the awareness of WHAT information (personality traits) can be accessed, by WHOM (social groups), and with HOW MUCH detail (trait sharing granularity). The visual interface should provide users a quick overview of such information.

DG3 ***It should enable users easily control of their sharing preferences.*** It is a non-trivial task to configure the sharing preferences for personality portrait. Users need to control all three factors in a privacy setting: 1) multiple social groups who may access the traits; 2) the personality traits with a multi-dimensional hierarchical structure; 3) sharing granularity of traits. Thus, the system should provide an intuitive user interface for users to easily control these factors.

DG4 ***It should provide a personalized initial privacy setting.*** As mentioned above, it is a tedious process to adjust the sharing preferences of the multi-dimensional hierarchical portraits for various social groups. It would be beneficial to provide a personalized initial default privacy setting to reduce users' efforts on setting adjustment.

User Interface

The user interface of VeilMe is shown in Figure 1. Panel A and B show a user's twitter profile and her latest tweets. Panel C in the middle left shows the visualization, PersonalityGenome, to support interactive exploration of one's personality portrait. On the right is the privacy setting panel (Panel D), where a user can configure her sharing preferences of the personality portrait.

PersonalityGenome Visualization (DG1)

One key component of the VeilMe is to visualize the derived personality portrait for interactive exploration. As mentioned before, the portrait data is both multi-dimensional and hierarchical. It consists of three main trait types: *Big 5 Personality*, *Needs* and *Values* (see Table 1). Within each type, a group of

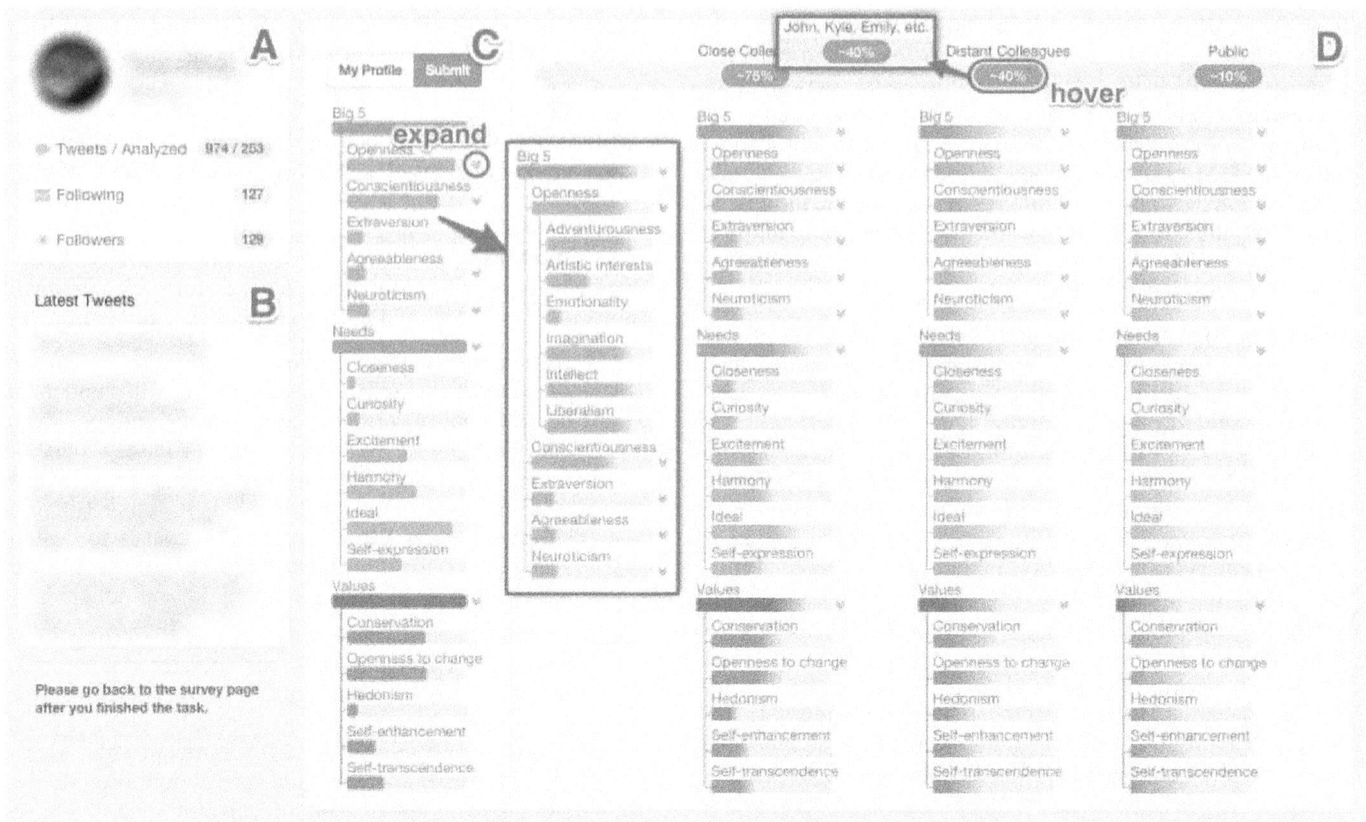

Figure 1: The screenshot of the VeilMe interface. Panel A & B: user's twitter profile and the latest tweets; C: portrait exploration panel; D: privacy setting panel. User can click to expand to reveal traits with sub-traits. When hovering a social distance knob, the input audience names of that group will be shown for user engagement. (Refer to the PDF document for better image quality.)

five to six traits are computed with percentile scores against the population. Furthermore, traits in the *Big 5* type contains sub-traits that constitutes a hierarchical structure.

To visualize this multi-dimensional hierarchical data model, we conducted three design sessions with 10 targeted users and tried three visualization mock-ups including a bar chart, node-link tree and radial space filling tree visualization. With the feedback of balancing functionality and aesthetics, we designed *PersonalityGenome*, a visualization inspired by a genome sequence, as shown in Figure 1 panel C. In this visualization, personality traits are piled together as a genome-like bar sequence. Each bar corresponds a trait. The sub-traits are grouped under a leading bar (indicates the parent trait) with links among them showing the hierarchical structure. Different trait types are colored differently. The length of a filled bar reveals the percentile score of each trait, which is also explicitly shown as text overlay on top. A label of trait name is placed over each bar. A control button on the right of a bar can be used to fold and unfold a trait group. A tooltip popup for a bar displays the definition of the corresponding trait.

Interactive Visualization for Sharing Settings (DG2 & DG3)

The SocialDistance Metaphor

In VeilMe, we incorporated a *SocialDistance* metaphor to achieve effective and efficient privacy control. The design rationale is as follows: people have different self-disclosing tendencies towards different social groups, and the *distance* (denoted as d_{sg}) between a person and a social group impacts her sharing willingness [24, 13]. For example, people tend to share more personal information with family members and close friends, but less to the public. Therefore, in our design, we semantically encode the distance of a social group to control how much information will be disclosed to that group.

As depicted in Figure 1 panel D, we applied the *SocialDistance* metaphor to two levels: 1) the position of social groups on the screen; and 2) the degree of faithfulness for each PersonalityGenome to be shared.

Social groups with different distance d_{sg} are visualized as draggable slider knobs. User can easily drag a knob to adjust the social distance of a specific group; consequently, the faithfulness of her portrait to that group will change accordingly: more faithful is dragged leftward, and more fuzzy is dragged rightward.

Under each social group, an obfuscated copy of the original PersonalityGenome is presented to show how users in that group will perceive of the subject's portrait. We adopted the idea of *k-Anonymity*, a frequently used method in privacy-preserving data mining [36], to develop the *kNN-Anonymity*

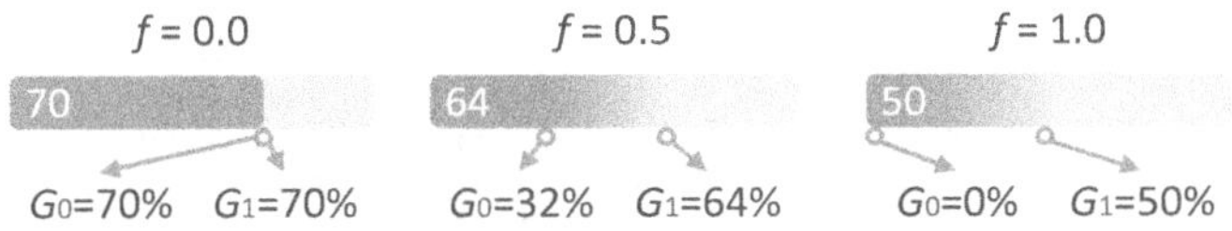

Figure 2: An example of obfuscating a single trait. The fuzziness are, from left to right, 0.0, 0.5 and 1.0, respectively, resulting different $P_{\text{obfuscated}}$ values and gradients.

model for obfuscation of one's PersonalityGenome. The obfuscated portrait can be obtained as:

$$P_{\text{obfuscated}} = kNNA(P_{\text{derived}}, f) \quad (1)$$

where P_{derived} is the derived personality portrait from social footprints and f the injected fuzziness value corresponding to user's interactions. Given a person-specific portrait P_{derived}, The *kNNA* function amalgamates the portraits of the user's k nearest neighbors yielding a obfuscated portrait $P_{\text{obfuscated}}$, from which the user cannot be re-identified.

The number k is mapped from f ($k \in [0, n-1] \leftarrow f \in [0, 1]$) and f is determined by the amount of adjustment on UI. f also controls the level of blurriness,

$$G_0 = P_{\text{obfuscated}} * (1 - f), G_1 = P_{\text{obfuscated}} \quad (2)$$

where G_0 and G_1 are the starting and ending position of the gradient control, respectively. An example of the obfuscation is shown in Figure 2.

One extreme of the *kNN-Anonymity* model is, for example, when $k = 0$, the produced portrait $P_{\text{obfuscated}}$ is the exact portrait P_{derived} of the subject. On the other extreme, when k equals to the number of the population n, $P_{\text{obfuscated}}$ becomes an "averaged" portrait of the whole population.

Multiple Control Levels of Trait Obfuscation

In VeilMe we provide multiple levels of control to adjust the obfuscation of a portrait. Users can either drag the knob to adjust the obfuscation for the whole personality portrait at the social distance level, or click and slide on each trait to adjust the obfuscation individually.

To help users with fast configuration, we also introduced a hierarchical interlocking mechanism. If the obfuscation of a trait is changed explicitly and the resulting obfuscation is different from previous, that specific trait will be locked and its fuzziness will not change until user explicitly unlock it. Otherwise, if not locked, fuzziness of finer grained controls will be overridden by that of its parental traits'. An example of the hierarchical interlocking mechanism is explained in Figure 3. Beside locking, we also allow users to hide traits to prevent from being shared completely.

Strategies for Initial Privacy Settings (DG4)

In our study, we explored different strategies of providing useful initial settings to reduce users' efforts. We examined three strategies: 1) a conservative approach, 2) a rule-based approach and 3) a prediction-based approach.

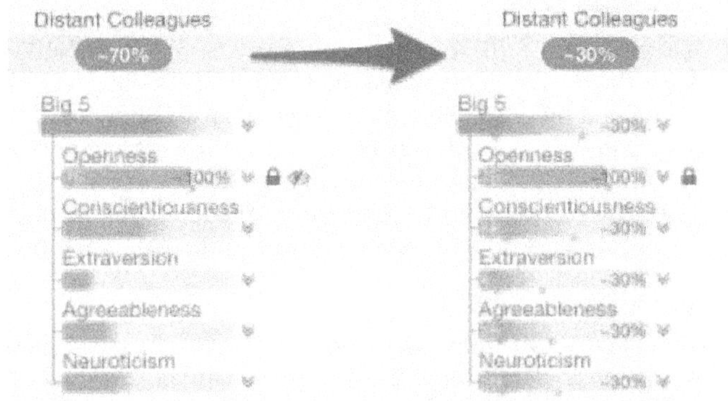

Figure 3: An example of obfuscation and hierarchical interlocking. On the left, the *Distant Colleagues* knob is placed with an overall faithfulness of 70% (30% obfuscation), the child traits inherit the obfuscation level except that obfuscation of trait *Openness* is explicitly changed and locked to 0 (faithfulness 100%). When the knob is dragged rightward to faithfulness 30%, all traits except the locked one are changed.

In the **conservative** approach, we disclosed the least information for all groups with a "privacy pragmatists" assumption [38]. In this approach, all social groups are placed at the far-end on the social distance slider. Traits in PersonalityGenome maintain the lowest level of fidelity. This conservative approach can serve as a baseline when compared with others.

The **rule-based** approach was built upon an observation from previous studies that people tends to share most with close friends and colleagues, but least with the public [24, 13]. From a survey with 224 people of their sharing willingness for different groups [13], we generated an initial settings rule for three default social groups ("close colleagues", "distant colleagues" and "public") with initial faithfulness of 90%, 50% and 10%, respectively.

Lastly in the **prediction-based** approach, we predicted one's sharing willingness for her individual traits towards different social groups based on the derived personality portraits. Again, with sharing willingness ratings from 224 people, we built a kernel (Nadaraya-Watson) regression model for each social group:

$$\mathcal{M}(x) = E[Y|X = x] = \frac{\sum_i^n f(i, x) y_i}{\sum_i^n f(i, x)} \quad (3)$$

where $X_{n \times m}$ is the input portraits ($n = 224$: # of subjects, $m = 16$: # of traits), $Y_{n \times m}$ the output sharing willingness, and $f(i, x)$ a Gaussian kernel with the bandwidth of 0.1.

The model $\mathcal{M}$ can be interpreted as an estimator of weighted average of k nearest neighbors of an incoming portrait. In our study, $k = 7$ gives the highest prediction power (cross-validated) with $R^2 = 0.61$. To prevent potential over-fitting due to limited training samples ($n = 224$) and relative large number of traits ($m = 16$), we applied L1-norm SVM for feature selection, yielding a smaller feature size ($m' = 5$) with marginal drop in prediction accuracy ($R^2 = 0.57$).

EVALUATION

The purpose of the evaluation is to examine how VeilMe meets the design goals mentioned above. This objective can be attained by addressing three questions: Q1) how well the system supports the privacy configuration for sharing personality traits; Q2) what configuration strategies emerge from users' interaction with our system; Q3) how different initial sharing settings affect users' configuration and interaction.

Participants

We invited 1,240 colleagues who have Twitter presence (200+ tweets) as required for extracting personalities. We had 151 completed responses, 124 of which are valid after filtering out unqualified responses based on three criteria (time spent on the tutorials, time spent on the tasks, and one test question for system understanding). Among the valid responses, we had 43 responses for the conservative setting, 40 for the rule-based setting, and 41 for the prediction-based setting. As for demographics, almost half of the participants were from the United States (44.2%), with the rest from Europe (31.4%) and other parts of the world (25.4%), ranging from 25 to 55 in age, most are male (69%), which is representative of a large enterprise or alike. The study took less than 30 minutes to complete and we drew a lottery with $50 Amazon gift card out of 50 people as the compensation for the study.

Procedure

The study consists of two parts: 1) personality portrait exploration, and 2) trait sharing configuration. Each part includes an interactive tutorial, experimental tasks and questions. The whole study was navigated through an online survey.

Personality Portrait Exploration

First, the participants were given the background of the study and the context of personality used in the workplace. Then, they were asked to login with their twitter credentials and the system would lively derive their personality portraits from their tweets. After that, the participants were provided with an interactive tutorial that go through their portraits, and were asked to explore the visualization of their portraits. They were asked to answer three questions about their portrait, including the trait values at both top level (e.g., "Closeness" in Needs) and sub-trait level (e.g. "Cheerfulness" under "Extraversion"), and a trait with maximum score in a trait category. They were also asked to rate how well the results matched their self-assessment. These questions were used to examine how the visualization helped the participants to understand their profile and also to engage them to explore the traits before configuring the sharing preferences. The first question was also used as test questions to filter qualified participants for later analysis.

Trait Sharing Configuration

Before the participants moved to trait sharing tasks, they were solicited for their opinions about the potential benefits and risks of using such personality traits in the workplace. They were first asked to rate the overall benefits and risks identified from previous study [13] (only the top four potential benefits/risks were used) on a 7-likert scale, followed by a task to mark all possible benefits and risks for each trait on top level (not for the sub-traits). With these questions, we want participants to reflect the benefits and risks before they actually used the system to configure their sharing preferences. After answering the benefit and risks questions, the participants were navigated to the sharing preferences setting page. Similarly, an interactive tutorial was popped up to help them go through the interface. At the end of the tutorial, the participants were asked to name three close colleagues and distance colleagues and the input names will be shown on each social group when hovered. The purpose of naming audience they know is to mimic real use scenarios and to engage them to the sharing tasks. The participants were also instructed that the target audience will see the same veiled portrait as they set in the UI, and their preferences will be recorded and used as-is in future deployments.

		Type	Description
Measures	Interaction Log	#Clicks	number of interactions
		ΔChange	amount of value change
		Accuracy	logged vs. reported
	Ctrl. Pref. Rating	PR_{sd}	prefer social dist. level
		PR_{tr}	prefer trait level
	Usability Rating	UR1	easy to explore
		UR2	easy to configure
		UR3	initial setting helpful
		UR4	privacy awareness
		UR5	overall easy to use
Factors	Initial Setting	IS_{con}	conservative setting
		IS_{pred}	prediction-based setting
		IS_{rule}	rule-based setting
	Control Level	CL_g	social distance level
		CL_t	trait level
	Social Group	SG_{cls}	close colleagues
		SG_{dis}	distant colleagues
		SG_{pub}	public

Table 2: Measurements and factors used in the study.

Next, the participants were asked to play with the visual interface and configure their sharing preferences that they feel most conformable. Upon submitting their setting, the participants were asked about their sharing preferences at three levels of social groups, trait categories, and individual traits. The questions include reporting the values of faithfulness for the shared portraits, 7-likert preference rating for adjustment at the two control levels, as well as their comments about their ratings. At last, the participants were asked to answer five usability questions of on a 7-Likert scale (see Figure 4).

Experimental Conditions

To evaluate how different initial setting strategies influence users' sharing preferences, we employed three types of initial settings (*conservative*, *rule-based*, and *prediction-based*) in VeilMe as experimental conditions. The participants were randomly assigned to one of these three conditions to start with and were asked to finish the study described above.

Measures

We used two types of measurements including participants' interaction logs and their subjective ratings (summarized in

Task	Exploration		Configuration		
Questions	Q1	Q2	Q1	Q2	Q3
Accuracy	95.16%	97.99%	93.55%	94.35%	92.74%

Table 3: The accuracy for the trait exploration and the sharing configuration questions.

Table 2). For interaction logs, we counted the number of effective interactions[1] (henceforth referred to as #Clicks) at two control levels (CL) across three default social groups (SG). We also calculated the actual amount of effective change (henceforth referred to as ΔChange). For the subjective ratings, we examined two categories including the adjustment preference ratings (PR) and general usability ratings (UR). The same set of measurements were collected under all three initial settings (IS).

RESULTS AND ANALYSIS

In this section, we report the results of our study and interpret them to answer the evaluation questions proposed earlier. Before diving into these results, we first examined the model performance, and found that the derived traits closely matched the participants' own perception with the means of all self-assessment ratings above 3 (somewhat) out of 5 (perfect). Specifically, we obtained average ratings of 3.45 (sd = 1.21), 3.21 (sd = 1.14), 3.28 (sd = 1.39) for Big 5 personality, values, and needs (more performance discussion in [40, 3, 39, 13]).

Q1: How Helpful VeilMe Is

To answer this question, we assessed the accuracy of the traits exploration and the sharing configuration tasks, and analyzed the usability ratings. Regarding the task accuracies, we compared the values recorded in the system logs and users' answers and found an average accuracy of over 90% was achieved (refer to Table 3), regardless of the initial settings. This indicates the VeilMe interface can effectively support the exploration of the participants' personality portrait and the configuration of their sharing preferences.

As for the usability ratings, VeilMe received around 5 out of 7 for the overall easy-to-use ratings based on the 124 responses (shown in Figure 4). Easy-to-explore obtained the highest ratings of over 5.5 and easy-to-configure also had good ratings of over 5, while privacy-awareness got the lowest ratings around 4.5. Under different initial settings, we did not observe significance for the above ratings. Notably, we found there is a discrepancy in the ratings for the helpfulness-of-the-initial-settings ($F_{1,122} = 7.29, p = 0.008$), and the rule-based strategy received the highest ratings ($\mu = 5.11, sd = 1.8$). We will discuss this in detail later in Q3.

Q2: How Users Interact with VeilMe

We examined the interaction patterns that the participants adopted from two aspects: control levels (CL) and social groups (SG), with different initial settings (IS) strategies.

[1]Effective interactions is defined as the total number of interactions divided by the number of visual elements (i.e. social distance knobs and trait bars) users interacted with.

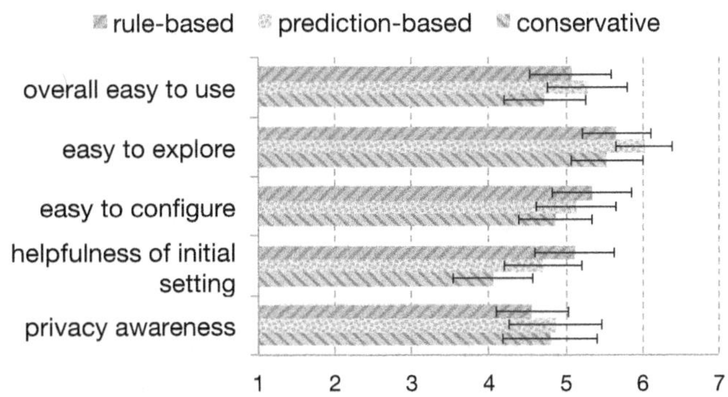

Figure 4: Usability ratings of VeilMe.

	CL×IS			SG×IS		
Measure	Factor	F	p-value	Factor	F	p-value
#Clicks	CL	9.05	0.003***	SG	5.15	0.006***
	IS	0.94	0.391	IS	1.81	0.163
	CL×IS	0.35	0.708	SG×IS	1.02	0.394
ΔChange	CL	1.06	0.347	SG	5.12	0.006***
	IS	1.04	0.308	IS	0.18	0.830
	CL×IS	3.91	0.021*	SG×IS	0.48	0.750
Pref. Rating	CL	8.09	0.005**		N/A	
	IS	4.16	0.017*			
	CL×IS	0.26	0.773			

Table 4: ANOVA analyses of control levels (CL) and social groups (SG) over initial settings (IS).

Interaction Patterns with Control Levels

We first investigated how the participants interacted with both CLs to determine whether it is impacted by the initial settings.

The left part of Table 4 shows two-way ANOVA results for three measurements (#Clicks, ΔChange and preference ratings) over two factors (CL and IS). We can see there is significant difference for #Clicks ($F_{1,244} = 9.12$, $p = 0.003$) at the two control level, but no difference for ΔChange. As shown in Figure 5 (a), we can observed that the participants had more interactions at the social distance level (CL_g). This indicates the participants tend to use the social group knob to configure their sharing preferences rather than adjusting each traits individually.

We also compared the subjective ratings of user's preferences over each CL. We found there is main effect of CL ($F_{1,122} = 8.09$, $p = 0.004$) and participants preferred controlling at the social distance level (PR_{sd}, $\mu = 4.69, sd = 2.0$) than at the trait level (PR_{tr}, $\mu = 3.86, sd = 1.97$), which is consist with the findings from log data and shows that users prefer to use the higher level controls.

Participants' comments also shared the same conclusion that fewer efforts are needed at CL_g. For example, participants commented: "*I found it easiest to do a quick broad brush setting, rather than having to tinker with each trait, which was fiddly and time consuming.*" and "*It's more straightforward to apply settings to the entire group of traits rather than an individual one.*" Interestingly, someone pointed out preferring to control at CL_g is to keep her portrait consistent: "*I think*

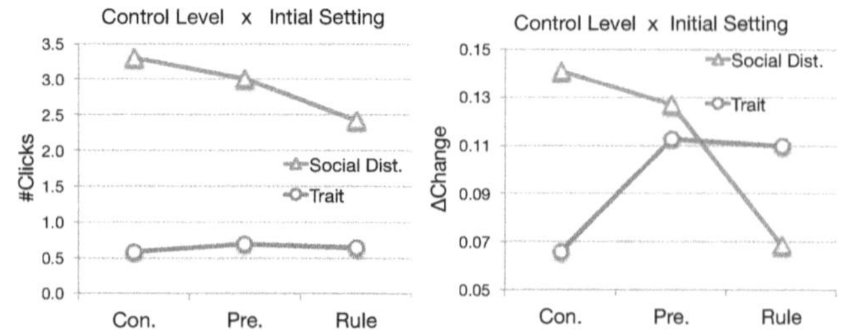

(a) #Clicks (b) ΔChange

Figure 5: Interaction plots over two factors of control level and initial setting for (a)#Clicks and (b)ΔChange.

it's better to share consistently across all the traits so I did not adjust at the finer grained level".

Interaction Patterns with Social Groups

We also studied whether the participants' interactions vary on different social groups. On the right of Table 4 we show two two-way ANOVA results for both #Clicks and ΔChange over factors of SG and IS. We can observe significances for both #Clicks and ΔChange at different SGs ($F_{2,363} = 5.15$, $p = 0.006$ and $F_{2,363} = 5.13$, $p = 0.006$, respectively). Post-hoc Tukey tests show that the #Clicks on SG_{cls} (close colleagues, $\mu = 5.18$) is significantly greater than the #Clicks on SG_{dis} (distant colleagues, $\mu = 3.49$) and SG_{pub} (public, $\mu = 3.18$) with $p = 0.032$ and $p = 0.008$ respectively. Similar results were observed for ΔChange: the ΔChange on SG_{cls} ($\mu = 0.58$) is significantly larger ($p = 0.007$ and $p = 0.04$) than that of SG_{dis} ($\mu = 0.21$) and SG_{pub} ($\mu = 0.282$).

This indicates that participants tend to adjust their preferences for closer social groups. One explanation is that people care more about their personal images presented to people that are close to them (SG_{cls}). Therefore they tend to think carefully and interact more on SG_{cls}. For example, one participant commented, "*Social Groups represent people I would like to interact. It seems easier to set (preferences) by the groups which are familiar for me*".

Q3: How the Initial Settings Work

Lastly we focused on how different ISs help the participants to configure their sharing preferences from two aspects: (1) the overall perceived helpfulness of the participants; and (2) the impact of IS strategies on their interaction patterns.

First, there was a significant impact of IS over participant's perceived helpfulness of the tool ($F_{1,122} = 7.29, p = 0.008$), as mentioned above with Figure 4. The helpfulness ratings of IS_{rule} (the rule-based strategy, $\mu = 5.11, sd = 1.8$) is better than IS_{con} (the conservative strategy, $\mu = 4.1, sd = 1.8$) indicated by a post-hoc test ($p = 0.009$).

Secondly, we did not observe any main effect of IS over the participants' interactions (#Clicks and ΔChange) for both CL and SG. (see Table 4). However, we found there is an interaction effect between CL and IS with $F_{2,242} = 3.91$ and $p = 0.008$ for ΔChange. As depicted in the interaction plot in Figure 5 (b), we can see that participants made more changes at CL_g (social distance level) with IS_{con} (conservative strategy), but made more changes at the CL_t (trait level) with IS_{rule} (rule-based strategy).

The above results from both log data and ratings echo each other and show that our rule-based initial setting worked the best in terms of least efforts for sharing preference configuration, especially at CL_g. However, surprisingly, we did not find that IS_{rule} (prediction-based strategy) performed better than the other two strategies. Also, We did not observe significant patterns between the initial and final settings.

DISCUSSION

In this section, we discuss several important design implications that we have learned from our study, and indicate current limitations in our work and some future research directions.

Effective Use of Visual Metaphors in Aiding Configuration

Traditionally, privacy policy configuration has been supported through the use of basic UI elements, such as buttons and check-boxes. Our study results suggest that it is beneficial to utilize the power of visual metaphors in such a task, especially when the task involves complex parameters. For example, we observed that our participants enjoyed using our "social distance knobs" visual interaction metaphor to rapidly adjust their settings by controlling a number of parameters *simultaneously*. This metaphor is semantically intuitive for our participants to grasp as the "draggable knob" helps them easily control how much to reveal "who I am" to different social groups. Since a metaphor-based design gauges people's cognitive capability for new and complicated tasks with existing knowledge from another and often familiar domain [5], we can extend our work by considering the use of additional visual metaphors. For example, we may design a "social sieve" visual metaphor to reveal the associated benefits and risks when particular pieces of information are filtered by the "sieve". This way a user will have an immediate understanding on what benefits can be gained and what are at risk if s/he chooses to share certain pieces of data. Also we should be careful some caution with visual metaphors, such as interaction constraints imposed by metaphor affordance [5].

Social Groups as a Configuration Proxy

Configuring privacy policies over each personality trait is a tedious task. We observed that our users use "social groups" as a proxy to configure their privacy policies. In particular, they adjust their privacy settings as a whole for each group based on their social distance to the group, instead of specifying policies for each individual traits. This observation echoes the concept of "privacy tension of social boundaries" [25], which states that disclosure boundaries exits among different social groups. While configuring privacy policies at the group level has certainly simplified a user's task, flexibility must be provided to support fine-grained controls and adjustments, e.g. allowing users to split and merge different social groups for more customized settings.

Moreover, special design attention should be paid to the support of different social groups. In our study, we found that our participants made more adjustments about their privacy settings for their "closer" social groups, since they clearly cared more about how their socially "closer" groups perceive their personality traits. This observation implies that we may need to provide different controls to support the privacy policy settings for different groups, e.g., finer-grained controls over groups that have "strong-ties" with the user [10].

Approaches to Personalizing Initial Privacy Settings

To help users jump start their privacy configurations, our current system experimented several approaches to suggest the initial settings to users. While our study shows that providing an initial configuration is helpful, it also reveals that some of the approaches worked better than others. In our case, our simple rule-based approach that suggested initial settings based on a few parameters at a high level worked better than our prediction-based approach that made suggestions based on a prediction model involving a number of fine-grained parameters including the user's personality. These initial settings also directly impacted users' interaction behavior and task performance in our study. This observation seems consistent with the findings in other's work (e.g, [26]), which suggests a template-based approach of sharing settings but does not elaborate whether the granularity of the template would make a difference.

Although a simpler approach demonstrated to be more effective in our study, it does not mean a simpler approach would always work better in the future. A more sophisticated approach can still win if the factors used and their effects can be better modeled. For example, our current prediction-based approach was developed using a small training data set, and the model prediction may be over-fitted and did not predict the preferences accurately enough for new users. While this is a hard problem beyond the scope of this paper, this type of approaches can be greatly improved with more training data and carefully chosen mathematical models. Moreover, we envision a mixed-initiative approach [14], which combines the power of both machines and humans and supports a continuous learning loop involving both sides. The system will first make initial suggestions that users will be willing to adjust, and the users will teach the system to update its prediction model through their behavior and feedback.

Limitations and Future Work

Through our study, we have also observed several limitations in our current work. First, previous studies indicate that privacy control is a long and interactive process within a context [25]. Our current work focused only on understanding participants' interaction behavior during a short time period and have not studied how a temporal context would impact users' behavior in a system like ours. Second, people's privacy concerns are influenced by their trust with the system [13], people might have configured their privacy policies differently if they know more about the quality of a system like ours. However, our current system does not provide users much information to help them assess the quality of our personality analytics, e.g., the evidence showing how the traits are derived and how accurate the derived portraits are. Without such information, our understanding of users' privacy preferences over their personality data is limited. Thus, making our system more transparent by providing users with more information on how the personality traits are derived and the quality of the analytics is one of our future tasks. Our study also revealed several user-desired features that we currently do not support. For example, people want to use the consequences resulted from their privacy policies to guide their behaviors on social media.

CONCLUSION

In this paper, we reported the design, development and evaluation of an interactive visualization tool, VeilMe, to help users configure their privacy preferences of personality portraits derived from social media. VeilMe considers several factors of social groups, personality traits, disclosure level and initial settings in the workplace context. It also employs novel and intuitive visual metaphors to help the exploration of personality portraits, and the comprehension and configuration of sharing preferences. The evaluation results showed that VeilMe can effectively support the sharing configuration, and suggest several design implications including using visual metaphors to aid sharing configuration tasks, using social groups as an efficient configuration proxy, and design tradeoff of approaches for personalized sharing settings.

REFERENCES

1. Adali, S., and Golbeck, J. Predicting personality with social behavior. In *Proc. of ASONAM 2012*, IEEE Computer Society (2012), 302–309.
2. Bellotti, V., and Sellen, A. Design for privacy in ubiquitous computing environments. In *Proc. of ECSCW '93*, Kluwer Academic Publishers (1993), 77–92.
3. Chen, J., Hsieh, G., Mahmud, J. U., and Nichols, J. Understanding individuals' personal values from social media word use. In *Pro. of CSCW'14* (2014), 405–414.
4. Cohen, A. A value based perspective on commitment in the workplace. *International Journal of Intercultural Relations 33*, 4 (2009), 332–345.
5. Cormac, E. R. M. *A Cognitive Theory of Metaphor*. MIT Press, 1990.
6. De Choudhury, M., Counts, S., and Horvitz, E. Predicting postpartum changes in emotion and behavior via social media. In *Proc. of SIGCHI '13* (2013), 3267–3276.
7. Egelman, S., Oates, A., and Krishnamurthi, S. Oops, i did it again: Mitigating repeated access control errors on facebook. In *Proc. of SIGCHI '11*, ACM (2011), 2295–2304.
8. Fang, L., and LeFevre, K. Privacy wizards for social networking sites. In *Proc. of WWW '10*, ACM (2010), 351–360. 00179.
9. Funder, D. C. *The personality puzzle*. WW Norton & Co, 1997.
10. Gilbert, E., and Karahalios, K. Predicting tie strength with social media. In *Proc. of SIGCHI '09*, ACM (2009), 211–220.

11. Golbeck, J., Robles, C., Edmondson, M., and Turner, K. Predicting ersonality from twitter. In *Privacy, security, risk and trust in SocialCom '11* (2011), 149–156.
12. Golbeck, J., Robles, C., and Turner, K. Predicting personality with social media. In *Proc. CHI'11 EA*, ACM (2011), 253–262.
13. Gou, L., Zhou, M. X., and Yang, H. KnowMe and ShareMe: Understanding automatically discovered personality traits from social media and user sharing preferences. In *Proc. of SIGCHI '14*, ACM (2014), 955–964.
14. Horvitz, E. Principles of mixed-initiative user interfaces. In *Proceedings of the SIGCHI Conference on Human Factors in Computing Systems*, CHI '99, ACM (New York, NY, USA, 1999), 159–166. 00675.
15. Iachello, G., and Hong, J. End-user privacy in human-computer interaction. *Foundations and Trends in Human-Computer Interaction 1*, 1 (2007), 1–137.
16. Inc., F. Facebook audience preview, 2014.
17. Junglas, I. A., Johnson, N. A., and Spitzmller, C. Personality traits and concern for privacy: an empirical study in the context of location-based services. *Eur. J. of Info. Sys. 17*, 4 (2008), 387–402.
18. Knijnenburg, B. P., Kobsa, A., and Jin, H. Preference-based location sharing: are more privacy options really better? In *Proc. of SIGCHI '13*, ACM (2013), 2667–2676.
19. Korzaan, M., Brooks, N., and Greer, T. Demystifying personality and privacy: An empirical investigation into antecedents of concerns for information privacy. *Journal of Behavioral Studies in Business 1* (2009), 1–17.
20. Lipford, H. R., Watson, J., Whitney, M., Froiland, K., and Reeder, R. W. Visual vs. compact: A comparison of privacy policy interfaces. In *Proc. of SIGCHI '10*, ACM (2010), 1111–1114.
21. Liu, K., and Terzi, E. A framework for computing the privacy scores of users in online social networks. *ACM Trans. Knowl. Discov. Data 5*, 1 (Dec. 2010).
22. Mairesse, F., Walker, M. A., Mehl, M. R., and Moore, R. K. Using linguistic cues for the automatic recognition of personality in conversation and text. *J. Artif. Intell. Res.(JAIR) 30* (2007), 457–500.
23. Mazzia, A., LeFevre, K., and Adar, E. The PViz comprehension tool for social network privacy settings. In *Proc. of SOUPS '12*, ACM (2012), 13:1–13:12.
24. Olson, J. S., Grudin, J., and Horvitz, E. A study of preferences for sharing and privacy. In *Proc. of CHI '05 EA*, ACM (2005), 1985–1988.
25. Palen, L., and Dourish, P. Unpacking "privacy" for a networked world. In *Proceedings of the SIGCHI Conference on Human Factors in Computing Systems*, CHI '03, ACM (New York, NY, USA, 2003), 129–136.
26. Patil, S., and Lai, J. Who gets to know what when: Configuring privacy permissions in an awareness application. In *Proc. of SIGCHI '05*, ACM (2005), 101–110.
27. Patil, S., Schlegel, R., Kapadia, A., and Lee, A. J. Reflection or action?: How feedback and control affect location sharing decisions. In *Proc. of SIGCHI '14*, ACM (2014), 101–110.
28. Pennacchiotti, M., and Popescu, A.-M. A machine learning approach to twitter user classification. In *ICWSM* (2011).
29. Reeder, R. W., Bauer, L., Cranor, L. F., Reiter, M. K., Bacon, K., How, K., and Strong, H. Expandable grids for visualizing and authoring computer security policies. In *Proc. of SIGCHI '08*, ACM (2008), 1473–1482.
30. Roberts, B. W., Kuncel, N. R., Shiner, R., Caspi, A., and Goldberg, L. R. The power of personality: The comparative validity of personality traits, socioeconomic status, and cognitive ability for predicting important life outcomes. *Persp. on Psy. Sci. 2*, 4 (2007), 313–345.
31. Rode, J., Johansson, C., DiGioia, P., Filho, R. S., Nies, K., Nguyen, D. H., Ren, J., Dourish, P., and Redmiles, D. Seeing further: Extending visualization as a basis for usable security. In *Proc. of SOUPS '06*, ACM (2006), 145–155.
32. Sadeh, N., Hong, J., Cranor, L., Fette, I., Kelley, P., Prabaker, M., and Rao, J. Understanding and capturing people's privacy policies in a mobile social networking application. *Personal Ubiq. Comput. 13*, 6 (2009), 401–412.
33. Schlegel, R., Kapadia, A., and Lee, A. J. Eyeing your exposure: Quantifying and controlling information sharing for improved privacy. In *Proc. of SOUPS '11*, ACM (2011), 14:1–14:14.
34. Shen, J., Brdiczka, O., and Liu, J. Understanding email writers: Personality prediction from email messages. In *User Modeling, Adaptation, and Personalization*. Springer, 2013, 318–330.
35. Smith, H. J., Dinev, T., and Xu, H. Information privacy research: An interdisciplinary review. *MIS quarterly 35*, 4 (2011), 989–1016.
36. Sweeny, L. k-anonymity: A model for protecting privacy. *Int. J. Unc. Fuzz. Knowl. Based Syst. 10*, 05 (2002), 557–570.
37. Tausczik, Y. R., and Pennebaker, J. W. The psychological meaning of words: LIWC and computerized text analysis methods. *J. of Lang.and Soc. Psy. 29*, 1 (2010), 24–54.
38. Westin, A. F., Maurici, D., Business, P. . A., LLP, P. W., and Associates, L. H. a. *E-commerce & Privacy: What Net Users Want*. Privacy & American Business, 1998.
39. Yang, J., and Li, Y. Identifying user needs from social media. Tech. rep., IBM Tech. Report, 2013.
40. Yarkoni, T. Personality in 100,000 words: A large-scale analysis of personality and word use among bloggers. *J. of Res. in Personality 44*, 3 (2010), 363–373.

No News is Good News: Remote Monitoring of Implantable Cardioverter-Defibrillator Patients

Mikael B. Skov[a], Pauline G. Johansen[b], Charlotte S. Skov[b], Astrid Lauberg[b]

[a]Centre for Socio-Interactive Design
Dept. of Computer Science, Aalborg University
Selma Lagerlöfs Vej 300, DK-9220 Aalborg East
dubois@cs.aau.dk

[b]Centre for Cardiovascular Research
Dept. of Cardiology, Aalborg University Hospital
Hobrovej 18-20, DK-9000 Aalborg
{pgb, css, a.lauberg}@rn.dk

ABSTRACT
Implantable cardioverter-defibrillator (ICD) patients have increased safety when connected to remote monitoring as ICD problems and issues are instantly discovered compared to patients without a monitor. While remote monitoring is intrusive in the domestic environment, little HCI research has investigated how people live and interact with such monitoring technologies. We conducted a study with 19 ICD patients and their spouses using diaries and interviews. Our findings illustrate that our participants were satisfied with the monitoring despite the fact that they had almost no knowledge of the data collected and they lacked feedback from the monitor on transmission and operation. Based on our findings, we describe a safety paradox for remote monitoring as participants experienced less safety while being safer, and identify privacy and surveillance concerns in the unequal monitoring of ICD patients.

Author Keywords
Remote monitoring, implantable cardioverter defibrillator, ICD, surveillance, privacy, anxiety

ACM Classification Keywords
H.5.m. Information interfaces and presentation (e.g., HCI): Miscellaneous.

INTRODUCTION
We are witnessing a growing number of technologies that enable remote monitoring (or telecare) where people are being monitored while being at home. Remote monitoring holds enormous potentials in societies where people are currently ageing at an unprecedented rate [28] and where hospital costs are constantly growing. Walker [29] argues that governments around the world are concerned with the impact of the ageing population on aspects of health, social care etc. Thus, previous research on remote monitoring has highly focused on supporting ageing in the home where informal caregivers remotely monitor activities of a relative [2,3,13,28]. Experiences from these studies show that despite good intentions, remote monitoring technology introduces a number of challenges that involves privacy concerns and lack of in-person contact [13].

CHI 2015, April 18 - 23, 2015, Seoul, Republic of Korea
Copyright 2015 ACM 978-1-4503-3145-6/15/04...$15.00
http://dx.doi.org/10.1145/2702123.2702192

This paper deals with remote monitoring of implantable cardioverter-defibrillator (ICD) patients. Such patients are typically those who are at risk of sudden death e.g. due to uncoordinated contraction of the heart muscle [9]. More and more people around the world live with an implanted ICD; in 2009 around 350.000 people worldwide received an ICD, and remote monitoring of these ICD patients holds many potential benefits including reduction in numbers of in-clinic visits [4] and improved patient safety [12,21].

Previous research has found that many ICD patients suffer from anxiety or depression [17] while remote monitoring is found to be intrusive in the private sphere [13]. However, limited HCI research has studied how remote monitoring affects ICD patients and their everyday lives. Furthermore, patients with an ICD are often in a vulnerable situation where they are dependent on external help or support with their disease. Matlock [20] argues for studying the patient perspective when therapies involve trade-offs like reducing number of in-clinic visits and Huber et al. [13] state that little research on preferred types and features of remote monitoring exists.

In this paper, we investigate how ICD patients and spouses live and interact with home monitoring. We studied 19 people (eleven patients and eight spouses) using dairies and interviews. Our findings show that while our participants were satisfied with the monitor and they did not mind being closely monitored, many of them had problems with the *no news is good news* approach, where they are only contacted in case of reported alarms. Most of them had no idea regarding what data the monitor collected and how these data were used. The lack of feedback made them anxious about whether data had been transmitted or if the monitor was working. Based on our findings, we describe a safety paradox for remote monitoring as participants experienced being less safe while actually being safer, and we identify privacy concerns in the monitoring of ICD patients.

RELATED WORK

Previous research has studied opportunities and limitations of remote monitoring for different purposes and in different situations. Often different concepts are used to describe this phenomena, e.g. telemedicine, telecare, telemonitoring, remote monitoring, telehealth, and while they have slightly different meanings, they generally refer to technologies that support people ageing at home through communication with caregivers or support hospital in monitoring patients at home. We will use remote monitoring to denote the activity of monitoring patients over distance and remote monitor to denote the technology that enables such activity.

Remote Monitoring and HCI

While HCI research for several years has investigated how people interact with various technologies at home, we note that previous research has not studied remote monitoring in relation to the everyday lives of ICD patients. Current HCI research on monitoring primarily focuses on supporting people's independence and providing ageing at home [e.g. 2,13,16,25,28]. Two recent papers display opportunities and limitations of remote monitoring systems for informal caregiving e.g. family members [13,28]. Vines et al. [28] studied a pre-release commercial system called SHel for remote activity monitoring and found that the system led to new less-social care work streams. Less person-to-person communication and contact is often raised as a concern for monitoring technologies [16,21]. However, Huber et al. [13] found that their monitoring system did not decrease non-mediated communication during a 6-week study. They speculate that monitoring systems could shape significant relationships while ageing if such systems are designed with sensitivity to primary motivation of the elderly.

In HCI research, privacy concerns are often identified as a key challenge of remote monitoring [3,5,13,20,28]. E.g. participants in the SHel study [28] raised privacy concerns for activities in specific rooms of the house. In particular, they found that activities in and around the bathroom were private and people were anxious about being monitored while in this room. Surprisingly, participants would also sometimes be concerned if none of their caregivers were watching their activities [28]. Birnholtz and Jones-Rounds [3] studied ageing in place for senior people and their need for privacy and awareness and they found a complex relationship between independence and interaction where interaction with other people actually formed the level of perceived independence. Privacy is often discussed in the HCI community, e.g. for hospital systems [30], in the home [23], long-term surveillance and behaviour change [22], and a classification of private moments in the home [7].

Implantable Cardioverter-Defibrillators (ICDs)

Implantable cardioverter-defibrillators (ICDs) are small battery-powered electrical impulse devices that combine a cardioverter and a defibrillator into one implantable unit. Typically, ICD patients are those who are at risk of sudden death for example due to uncoordinated contraction of the cardiac muscle (ventricular fibrillation) or a rapid heart beat (ventricular tachycardia). ICDs are programmed to detect cardiac arrhythmia (an irregular, slower, or faster heartbeat than normal) and correct such arrhythmia by delivering electrical impulse or shock to the heart [17]. Studies have shown that ICD is an effective way of preventing sudden death from cardiac arrest [9]. ICDs are also equipped with wireless capabilities where bidirectional data transmission is possible so professionals like doctors or nurses can retrieve data from the ICD and re-program the ICD through specialized equipment. Research studies have primarily focused on effects of implanting devices, e.g. medical effects related to safety or mortality [9] or psychological effects on anxiety or depression [17,32].

ICD Remote Monitoring

While ICDs can operate without them, remote monitors are technical devices that provide opportunities for retrieving data while patients are at home. This leads to fewer in-clinic patient visits as in-clinic staff can view and monitor data remotely. According to Theuns et al. [27], remote ICD monitors give access to clinical patient information, e.g. heart rate, rhythm electrogram, and they also give access to technical information about the ICD, e.g. battery status. A remote monitor retrieves data from a patient when she is in close proximity to the monitor (less than two meters) and usually at a scheduled time (e.g. when the patient sleeps in her bed during the night) [3]. The remote monitor transmits retrieved data to the remote monitoring system usually located at a clinic. ICDs support bidirectional transmission but remote monitors can only retrieve data and cannot be used for re-programming the device. Numerous studies have investigated benefits and utility evidence of remote monitoring [5,20,21,27] and architectures [14]. Based on previous work and theoretical potentials, Burri and Senouf [5] stress four benefits of remote monitoring namely fewer patient in-clinic visits, reduced costs, improved patient safety, and increased patient satisfaction.

A key benefit of remote monitoring is reduced numbers of in-clinic patient visits [5]. Typically ICD patients without monitoring have follow-up in-clinic visits every 3-6 months and even more frequent as the battery approaches elective replacement. Brugada [4] found that as many as half of the regular in-clinic visits can be skipped without impairing patient safety. Furthermore, potential savings of cost could prove to be quite significant as hospital staff and patients have fewer in-person meetings. However, Burri and Senouf [5] argue that cost savings are quite difficult to measure due to different indirect costs for different countries (e.g. travel expenses or sickness allowance).

Remote monitors improve patient safety as problems and irregularities are reported on a daily basis. Nielsen et al. [21] found that ICD events such as arrhythmia (clinical) or lead impedance issues (technical) often occurred during the first month following a visit to the clinic, hence without remote monitoring such events will be discovered too late. Hindricks et al. [12] found in a recent study that patients with heart failure benefitted significantly on e.g. mortality when connected to a remote monitor service compared to those patients who were not. Finally, remote monitoring can lead to increased patient satisfaction. Studies have shown that patients are generally satisfied with remote monitoring due to fewer in-clinic follow-up visits [19], while Al-Khatib et al. [1] found that some patients actually experience reduced quality of life and lower satisfaction.

While the benefits of remote monitoring are quite evident and significant, a number of negative effects have also been identified. Barriers for acceptance of monitor technologies include reduction of in-person contact with caregivers and hospital staff [13]. Additionally, Denning et al. [8] address security issues on the wireless aspect of ICDs and remote monitors. However, despite the huge proliferation of ICD remote monitoring technologies and at the same time, the invasive nature of such technologies in a private space, we lack understandings and studies on how these technologies are embedded into the lives of ICD patients. In particular, we have yet to understand how implantable ICD patients live and interact with home monitoring systems.

STUDY

The study explores how ICD patients and spouses live and interact with remote monitoring technology and how such technology affects their everyday lives.

Methodological and Ethical Considerations

We had a number of ethical considerations on methodology before we started the study. Cardiac patients live with very severe and chronic diseases and research studies usually show that cardiac patients suffer from e.g. fear of death and anxiety and also, studying them involves intrusiveness in their domestic sphere. When designing our study, we were inspired by the reflections in Maitland and Chalmers [18] who discuss methodological dilemmas in their study on cardiac rehabilitation. Like [18], we chose to use semi-structured interviews as our main data collection technique. We further chose to include a GCP diploma nurse in the interviews trained in cardiac research studies along with an HCI researcher and qualitative research nurse (GCP stands for good clinical practice and is explained here [11]).

We further included diaries as a supplementary unobtrusive technique for capturing information about living with remote monitoring, but also to let the participants reflect upon their medical condition and life situation. While Maitland and Chalmers [18] emphasize that diary writing possibly creates another stressor for cardiac patients during a difficult time, Elliot [10] argues that diaries offer valuable insights into how people construct accounts of illnesses and they provide ways to follow informants as they experience life events or illness episodes. We made diary writing voluntary and five participants chose to write diaries, while one participant (and her spouse) retold her entire cardiac illness history as experienced by them both. We primarily used the diaries for elicitation as illustrated in [6].

Our study was granted ethics approval under the agreement for non-invasive studies at Aalborg University Hospital (AUH) and conducted in compliance with the principles described in the Helsinki Declaration on ethics for medical research involving human subjects [31]. Finally, the study was registered with the Danish Data Protection Agency (no. 2008-58-0028).

The Remote Monitoring Service at AUH

The remote monitoring service at the AUH ICD Clinic currently monitors approximately 700 ICD patients. Over the last decade (2004-2013), AUH has performed a little more than 1000 ICD implantations and currently implants app. 140 ICDs every year.

ICD patients are offered to join this monitoring service without any economical costs for the individual patient (included in the public medicare system in Denmark). A cardiac nurse hands out the remote monitor to the patient after her ICD implantation. The nurse gives instructions on how to install the device and how it operates (e.g. that it retrieves data every night, that ICD clinic staff will contact the patient in case of an alarm), and patients are instructed to contact the clinic if going on vacation for more than three weeks. The monitors transmit data every night to the AUH ICD Clinic over a GSM network. Trained cardiac nurses (and occasionally doctors) examine reported alarms the following day and contact patients over the phone if assessed necessary and call them in for a follow-up. Every twelve to 24 months, patients are called in for scheduled follow-ups at the clinic.

Our participants used one of two remote monitors either the CardioMessenger™ by Biotronik or the Merlin.net™ by St Jude Medical. These monitors retrieve clinical data (heart rate, rhythm electrograms etc.) and technical data (battery status etc.) from the ICDs. For technical descriptions of the included remote monitors, please refer to [5].

Participants

Nineteen people participated in our study including eleven ICD patients (three women) and eight spouses (six women) having in total eight couples, two singles, and one male patient where the spouse did not participate. The patients were between 26 and 77 years old (M=59.5) and they have had an implanted ICD from six months to 14 years (M=5.4). On average, they have had the remote monitor for a little more than a year (M=1.3). Two participants got their remote monitor at the same time they were ICD implanted while nine participants had their ICD for a number of years before receiving the monitor. Based on self-assessment, most of them used the Internet on a daily basis, and all had access to a computer or tablet. Seven patients were retired, three were still active in the labour market, while one was unemployed. Furthermore, they represented different socio-economic backgrounds and holded or had been holding diverse professions e.g. doctor, carpenter, or accountant. All patients (and spouses) lived in their own homes within 40km from Aalborg.

From a clinical perspective, the patients suffered from four different heart diseases. Three of them had ischemic heart disease (where plaque builds up along the inner walls of the heart arteries), two participants had arrythmogenic right ventricular disease (an inherited heart disease), one had cardiomyopathy (weakening of the heart muscle function), and one suffered from ventricular tachycardia (a rapid heart beat). The remaining four participants suffered from several of the above heart diseases. Ten participants had suffered an acute cardiac episode (e.g. cardiac arrest, heart attack) prior to having the ICD implanted while one had the ICD implantation as an elective procedure.

Procedure

We recruited participants using selected inclusion criteria, e.g. both women and men, both living alone and together with a spouse, and at different ages. We contacted potential candidates from the AUH ICD Clinic patient database. Eleven out of 14 contacted patients agreed to participate. Our procedure included two steps namely diary writing and interviews.

(i) *Diary Writing*: We posted an introduction package to the eleven participants including a study information sheet, a consent form, and a diary. The nineteen participants were instructed to keep the diary for a couple of weeks, but some of them kept it for three to four weeks. We contacted the participants once over the phone after two weeks to follow-up on the diary writing and to schedule interview times. Five participants wrote diaries during the period (to different extend), while one patient and her spouse re-told her cardiac illness story in an essay. After four weeks we collected the diaries. The diary study primarily served as an elicitation study, as illustrated in [6], where we analysed the diaries and used findings as interview prompts.

(ii) *Interviews*: We conducted semi-structured interviews with the nineteen participants. All participants chose to be interviewed at home and each interview lasted between 22-55 minutes (M=34.2). Each interview involved two authors and all interviews were audio recorded. Furthermore, we interviewed patients and spouses individually except for two couples who requested to be interviewed together. We developed a questions guideline for the interview including topics on their ICD, the remote monitor etc. Findings from the diaries analysis supplemented the semi-structured interview guide. During the interviews, we saw the location and placement of the remote monitor.

Data Analysis

All interviews were fully transcribed for data analysis. We were inspired by Ricœur [24] in our data analysis where understanding is achieved through a spiral way of thinking. Our data analysis was done in three steps namely naive reading, structured analysis, and critical interpretation and discussion. Researchers from disciplines in nursing and human-computer interaction participated in the analysis. Firstly, our naive reading followed a phenomenological tradition where we read the text several times to identify relevant units of meaning. Secondly, we then conducted a structural analysis alternating between understanding and explanation of the text on what the participants said (units of citation, e.g. a participant saying she doesn't know when the monitoring device last transmitted data), and what they talked about (units of significance, e.g. whether the device is actually working), and finally themes (units of meaning, e.g. safety). Thirdly, we did a critical interpretation where we discussed theme importance including qualifying and motivating them from related research.

FINDINGS

We describe and illustrate our findings under three themes namely satisfaction and safety, surveillance and privacy, and anxiety and feedback. While the themes overlap, they provide structure for illustrating our findings. Table 1 outlines key findings and observations under the themes.

We have anonymized our participants and refer to them as P1-P11 (patients) and S1-S8 (spouses). We sometimes refer to the number of participants behind an observation. E.g. (3/19) would mean three out of all nineteen participants, while (4/11) would refer to four of the eleven ICD patients.

Satisfaction and Safety

Most of our patients had lived with the remote monitor for more than a year (7/11) and at the time of the interview, it had become an integrated part of their lives after some early difficulties when they got the monitor. As instructed by the ICD clinic, all participants had placed their remote monitor next to the bed in their bedrooms and usually on a bedside table (9/11). One participant (P5) had to place the monitor in the windowsill due to poor mobile coverage in his area. But generally they would rarely move or touch the monitor, as they were afraid to make mistakes, or change any functions or setup by mistake. For example, P11 was afraid that her grandchildren would interact with it, so she placed her monitor under the bed out of their reach. Three participants stated that they would bring their monitor when going on vacation, while the remaining eight were either rarely travelling or would not bring it on vacation, but most would call the clinic to inform them if going on vacation.

While our primary focus in this study was how patients and spouses live and interact with the remote monitoring, it was quite clear that the heart diseases and the consequences of these illnesses played very significant roles in the way both patients and spouses would understand their situation and lives also in terms of how they perceived and interacted with the remote monitors. This is not particularly surprising as their heart diseases are extremely severe and can cause heart attacks or cardiac arrest as illustrated in this episode:

I woke up during the night and found P4 making a strange snoring sound, and suddenly she went into spasms, and then became completely inert and lifeless and I panicked and started to shake her ... she woke up but had a very distant look in her eyes ... so I called an ambulance. S4

As this illustrates, anxiety played a prominent role when participants talked about their lives and thus, safety was a major concern and priority to them. All participants (both patients and spouses) expressed average to high satisfaction with their monitor as they felt it primarily provided

Satisfaction and Safety	Surveillance and Privacy	Anxiety and Feedback
Participants were generally satisfied with the monitor as they believed that it provided extra safety for them	Most participants did not mind being monitored closely by the ICD clinic and some were actually pleased with the monitoring	Anxiety played a significant role for all participants as they were concerned about their situation and medical condition
Several were annoyed by the green LED light on the monitoring device and some experienced problems sleeping due to it	Most participants did not know which data the monitor collected, when the data was transmitted, and who examined the data	Several participants did not know whether the monitor was working correctly and had little idea if data had been transmitted
Some lacked the reassurance and safety of small talking with ICD clinic cardiac nurses as they had fewer clinic visits	A few believed that the monitor was able to monitor live and some were concerned with privacy of data interpretation	Lack of feedback through the remote monitor caused participants to be more anxious as they would reflect upon their disease

Figure 1: Key and illustrative findings of our study organized under three themes namely satisfaction and safety, surveillance and privacy, and anxiety and feedback.

additional safety and secondarily reduced the number of required visits to the ICD clinic. As explained by P4: "*...the hospital staff said that the home monitor primarily provides better safety for the patient and secondarily fewer necessary hospital visits ...*" and elaborated by S2: "*... it gives me so much safety when we are at home, because they (i.e. the clinic) can monitor if something is wrong*". Besides, some participants showed high interest in their illnesses and had previously searched for information on the Internet, and some were generally concerned about their illness and situation:

It gives him (P6) a feeling of safety to have a remote monitor, and it probably means more to him than first anticipated because in my opinion he is addicted to safety ... and there is nothing you can do about that. S6

While the participants generally expressed satisfaction with the monitor, several participants described how they were now *living with the green light*. Several participants found that the green LED light on the remote monitor was annoying and disturbing (10/19) and in the beginning, some had found it difficult to actually fall asleep, e.g. P5 said: "*It lights up the entire bedroom*" and this was supported by others who complained that the light was too bright for a dark bedroom (P1,P3). Both included remote monitors have a green LED light for power.

The remote monitor is placed on my bedside table, but it is annoying because I think the light is too bright ... why does it have to be so bright? ... I have tried to put some tape on top of it and I have also tried to place something in front it even though this could affect the data transmission (i.e. between the monitor and the ICD) P1

While some participants ultimately got accustomed to the light, others tried to alleviate the problem themselves by covering or hiding the monitor. Two of them had put tape on top of the LED indicator, one had a towel on top of the entire device, and one covered the device in a pillowcase.

But the green light from the monitor was not only found to be negative, a few participants thought that the green light was either something positive or practical, e.g. P6 said that it was quite convenient for him, as he didn't have to put on the lights when he had to go to bathroom during night.

A few patients were concerned with fewer in-clinic visits as they missed the social interaction with the nurses (4/11):

Well I think it is sad, because you can say, that you are chatting with the clinic nurses while they check my ICD ... they know a lot of things and often it is just something minor that I am worried about P4

During our interviews, we saw that some of the patients lacked the reassurance and safety provided by the cardiac nurses in the ICD clinic, even if it only had to do with small issues or worries. The lack of personal contact seemed to induce anxiety. Also, a few participants did not understand why this was necessary seen from a patient perspective: "*... to visit the hospital twice a year for 30 minutes, I don't think that it is a lot of time to spend on your illness...*" S1

Surveillance and Privacy

Surveillance and privacy are two well-known issues of remote monitoring [3] and previous studies have found that people are often concerned with being monitored and what others can read or infer from surveillance data [20,28].

Almost all participants indicated that they did not mind being closely monitored (18/19). It was quite obvious that their heart illnesses and the severity of their illnesses played a significant role in the way they understood and accepted the monitoring. Previous research has shown similar findings where people with severe health conditions or people feeling vulnerability are more likely to share private data [28]. As illustrated by the following:

The positive thing is that the remote monitor tells someone with knowledge (i.e. hospital staff) that something is wrong ... and the fact that you are being monitored without you noticing it is actually quite nice P2

The green LED light on the remote monitor is cosy and I think that it is just a gentle reminder that someone is looking after me P6

One participant (P11) was concerned with the monitoring and she expressed a number of reservations. In particular, she was concerned about other people being able to view her data, especially if the data could be misinterpreted. We will return to data interpretation later.

Interestingly, some participants were actually surprised to realize that clinic staff would actually monitor and review their data, as illustrated by the spouse of P3:

There was this one time, where the clinic called us, and we actually found out that someone was watching us ... I never expected that anyone would actually sit and monitor us every day and night S3

The latter is in fact incorrect; data is not monitored day and night, only alarms from the monitor are assessed every morning. But still the episode reassured the couple that the monitoring was actually working.

Considering the positive attitudes towards surveillance, we found it interesting and surprising to see that participants in general had limited knowledge on when the monitor was operating, what it retrieves from the ICD, what it transmits to the clinic, and who is looking at the data and when they are looking at the data. Despite these uncertainties, many participants had no severe problems being monitored, but it led to that some of them formed incorrect perceptions on how the monitor would operate and what the clinic staff could interpret from the data.

Some patients knew that the remote monitor would retrieve data from their ICD during the night and then transfer them to the ICD clinic (4/19). P2 said that his monitor retrieved data every night if he was in his bed and retrieval time was set by the ICD clinic. None of the participants knew what kind of data the monitor would collect, and while this is not surprising as such data is extremely complicated and only makes sense to trained professionals, it introduced privacy concerns from a surveillance perspective. In particular, two issues were problematic namely that participants believed that the monitor supported live data feed and issues about how the data could be interpreted.

We were surprised to see that a few participants had got the impression that the remote monitor was providing live feed from their ICD to the clinic (5/19). While this is not only incorrect, it is also a problem as this could prohibit proper action (e.g. call 911) in case of a cardiac episode. P8 was of the impression that the staff at the clinic would monitor him 24/7 in real-time and that they would take immediate and proper action if they observed something wrong in his data. Even after the participating nurse (one of the interviewers) told him that this was not the case (that it would be handled the following day), he found it difficult to believe.

I believe that if something happens to my heart or the pumping function of the heart, people in the ICD clinic will instantly contact me. P8

His spouse (S8) had a slightly different perception on live transmission of data. She thought that the monitor was able to retrieve live data from her husband, but only when he was in close proximity to the remote monitor, that would be in the bedroom. As a result, she would feel more anxious when her husband was in a different room in their house or when he was outside. Most participants knew that the monitor did not transmit live data to the clinic (14/19), e.g. P6 said "*... if I get ill during the night (heart problems), no one from the hospital will contact me immediately or take other kinds of action...*"

During our study, we realized that a few participants (3/19) had formed different understandings of what the data could be used for, and how ICD clinic staff would interpret their data. While the other participants found it unproblematic to be monitored, these three participants were concerned that others (i.e. clinic nurses or doctors) could interpret their data in incorrect ways. This would generate significant privacy concerns as illustrated by the following example where P11 expressed how she thought data could be used:

Anything I do during the day is monitored by the clinic ... at least that is my assumption ... but I have no interest in knowing exactly what they can see ... so I guess that you can see anything ... including if I am physical intimate with someone because my pulse would increase. P11

She continued by stating that she was often almost paranoid about the remote monitor and sometimes refrained from activities e.g. vacuuming, as she had no interest in letting other people know what she was doing.

Anxiety and Feedback

Anxiety played a significant role for our participants, both for patients and their spouses. Some of them were anxious about their general situation as heart patients, e.g. P6 said "*I think it is a deeper anxiety, because you know if your heart stops beating, then you die, and I am afraid that they (hospital staff) will not be able to get the heart to beat again*", while others were anxious about their ICD and in particular they had anxieties about receiving a hurtful shock from the ICD:

I was driving motocross when it gave me a shock, and it feels like being beaten with a shovel ... and then afterwards you just feel weakness in your muscles ... it is definitely not pleasant, one shock is more than enough P9

Previous studies on ICDs and remote monitoring of ICDs have shown similar findings on anxiety [17], but our study also revealed a number of other findings on anxiety and the operation of the monitor. Most participants were aware of the fact that remote monitoring made it safer for them, but different aspects of the monitor made them anxious, for example a few of them would be reminded of their illness when looking at the monitor:

I have put the monitor in a pillowcase (to avoid it) ... it makes me realize and think that I am ill, and of course I know that I am ill, but I don't want to be reminded all the time. P11

P11 further stated that her remote monitor made noises and sounds when it transmitted data during the night and these sounds reminded her of the sounds you would hear at the hospital. On the other hand, she also argued that it provided extra safety and security as she could press a button on the device, which will notify the clinic.

Several expressed that they wanted to live a normal life after they had the ICD implantation and received the monitor. This led to them declining offers or services of the ICD clinic, for example two patients deliberately chose not to join the ICD Café where post implanted ICD patients can meet and share stories in their rehabilitation process.

I have not visited the ICD Café ... actually I don't know it that well ... I want to have as normal a life as possible P10

We discovered another reason for increased anxiety namely due to the way the monitor was designed and functioned. Most participants complained about the lack of feedback from the remote monitor device. This implied that several of them were uncertain whether data had been transmitted and whether the device worked properly.

I miss to receive an OK from the ICD clinic that they have analysed my data today and that everything is ok ... they could send a text message or something so that I could calm down a bit ... the lack of information is really bad for me ... so instead I constantly check my mailbox for letters, because I was told that the clinic would write me in case something was wrong P11

But the clinic staff only uses letters for scheduled follow-ups (every 12-24 months), while they would always call patients on the phone if they received an alarm from the monitor. This lack of feedback constituted a problem for several participants, e.g. P10 once called the clinic to make sure that the communication between his monitor and the clinic was working correctly. While this was confirmed, he was still slightly uncertain, but had over time achieved confidence that it worked correctly. Other participants articulated similar concerns:

Well I assume that the remote monitor regularly transmits data to the clinic P9

Yes, but we never notice when it transmits, it is during the night when we sleep ... actually I don't know whether it has transmitted or not ... we don't hear anything from them, I just assume that it is working S1

But I haven't seen it transmit for a while now ... actually I don't know when the last time was when it transmitted P5

The remote monitor devices in our study provide patients the opportunity to manually initiate transmission of data, e.g. in case the patient feels very anxious and needs some reassurance or if they believe that something has happened with their medical condition. This was done a few times by a few participants:

I just felt that something was wrong, because I could feel my heart and experienced six to eight rapid heart beats and then the heart became normal again ... however they [clinic staff] said there nothing was wrong, it was simply a double heart beat, which was normal according to them P2

The implementation of the ICD remote monitoring system of the AUH ICD Clinic utilizes a procedure where no news is good news. Thus, the clinic would only contact patients if they had bad news (typically an alarm from a monitor). But the lack of feedback from the remote monitor device in combination with this procedure did not work well.

Nothing has happened over the last year where we have had the remote monitor ... so I am in doubt whether it actually works, and it worries me that I cannot find out ... it was my husband (P8) who came home with the monitor and he did the installation, so I don't know whether he did it correctly S8

DISCUSSION

We have studied how patients with ICDs and their spouses live and interact with home monitoring. Our findings show that while our participants were satisfied with their remote monitor, but the lack of system feedback made them more anxious, and further they had very limited knowledge on how the system actually worked and what kind of data the monitor would collect. This led to incorrect understandings of how the system worked. Beside our findings, we identify two other contributions in this paper that advances HCI knowledge on remote monitoring.

Firstly, we observe a paradox of safety where monitoring can prompt or increase anxiety as patients or spouses feel *less safe*, despite the fact that previous research clearly demonstrate that patients are in fact *safer* when connected to a monitoring service.

Secondly, we also see new perspectives of surveillance and privacy, as ICD patients do not hold the same knowledge as clinic staff. Thus, those being monitored have different skills or knowledge that those doing the monitoring. We will elaborate on these contributions in the following, and will also discuss design implications for remote monitoring.

Paradox of Safety

Previous HCI research studies on monitoring technology have largely focused on supporting people's independence and ageing at home [e.g. 2,13,16,28]. Particularly, studies have shown how caregivers like family members can provide safety and comfort through monitoring technology, and Huber et al. argue that monitoring systems could shape significant relationships while ageing at home if they are designed with sensitivity to the primary motivations of the elderly [13].

Our findings extend HCI knowledge on remote monitoring as we found that monitoring technology for ICD patients and spouses can lead to self-reflection of the persons being monitored as they are constantly reminded of their situation (illness). Here we discovered that ICD remote monitoring created a safety paradox of patients *feeling less safe* while actually *being safer* because some of them became more anxious while living with their monitor. Several studies have shown increased patient safety when connected to an ICD monitoring service [5,12,21]. Hindricks et al. [12] found in a recent study with 664 ICD patients that after one year of study, the remote monitoring participants suffering from heart failure had significantly better composite scores (i.e. all-cause deaths, overnight hospital for heart failure, etc.) than participants without monitoring. While previous HCI studies have demonstrated how living with monitoring technology is challenging and complex in itself, i.e. [3,13, 22,28], our findings showed that three issues could affect perceived safety: Lack of feedback, physical appearance of the monitor, and fewer in-clinic visits. Firstly, while remote monitoring offers a powerful tool for cardiac professionals [12,21], the monitor provides little support for ICD patients or spouses while at home. The lack of feedback induced anxiety, and made participants insecure on data retrieval or transmission, e.g. whether the monitor worked correctly.

Furthermore, the physical appearance of the monitor made some participants annoyed or made others reflect upon their situation. For example, the green LED light was found to be highly annoying and some participants tried to cover the monitor. Finally, the lack of contact with hospital staff as a result of fewer in-clinic visits concerned some participants. The latter is in line with findings in previous studies [13,20], and Matlock [20] argues that patients probably decline remote monitoring enrolment, as they prefer the reassurance of coming into a clinic.

For hospitalized patients, Leith [15] saw a similar paradox, where intensive care unit patients sometimes experience increased anxiety when moved from ICU to a general ward, despite the fact that these patients were actually recovering. But the loss of close observation in the ICU made them anxious. Perhaps our safety paradox is best exemplified from the following episode involving a couple from our study. The ICD clinic called them one day as the clinic had received an alarm from P3's monitor, and the nurse called him in for a follow-up. The safety paradox is that for the couple to in fact witness the safety provided by the monitoring system, the patient (P3) had to have a heart incident so the ICD could report an alarm.

Privacy and Surveillance

Privacy and surveillance are two well-known concerns in HCI research on remote monitoring, i.e. [3,5,13,20]. Not surprisingly, HCI research studies have often showed that people find it problematic that other people can see what they are doing [3,22]. While some of our findings support previous HCI research on monitoring and privacy, e.g. people not knowing what is being monitored, our findings also extend current HCI knowledge on how to address such privacy issues.

Most of our participants did not mind being monitored as they could definitely see the benefits. This is in line with the findings in Vines et al. [28] arguing that people with severe health conditions or people feeling vulnerability are more likely to share private data. Vines et al. further argue that home monitoring acceptance is highly dependent upon people's understanding of the data being collected and how this is presented to others. We identified a similar finding, as our participants were generally displeased with their own understanding or had formed misunderstanding of how the device operated. One participant was concerned that others (i.e. clinic staff) could read a lot into her pulse, as the pulse would go up and down. The two included monitors in our study provide no information to the person being monitored on what data it collects and transmits. But ICD data is highly complex with lots of inaccessible information only understandable to professionals. It seems quite clear that such data cannot easily be presented to the patient.

But while previous HCI research on monitoring focuses on people's independence, e.g. technology that provide extra independence by letting people live longer in their own homes [3,13,28], remote monitoring of ICD patients is not about independence but about safety. It also involves very complex data that needs professional interpretation. Vines et al. [28] suggest that to address privacy issues, remote monitors should include mechanisms that present the data that is collected as well as show how data is displayed to others (caregivers).

Our findings illustrate concerns on privacy and surveillance in unequal monitoring, where people being monitored do not have the same knowledge or training as the people doing the monitoring. While we encounter such inequalities in several everyday person-to-person situations (doctor and patient, lawyer and client, etc.), it constitutes a challenge for ICD monitoring technologies. As an example, an ICD alarm (indicating some heart incident) is probably the most important piece of data collected by a ICD monitor, but it needs to be assessed and evaluated by cardiac experts and not simply shown to the patient.

Design Implications: Remote Monitoring Technology

Our findings and contributions point to a number of design implications for ICD remote monitoring technology. More specifically, we identify two implications for the design of monitoring technology namely showing data on the device and physical design of device.

Our first design implication covers data and information shown on the device including recent activities and actions. Clearly, information like time stamp on last data retrieval and data transmission should be integrated in the interfaces of remote monitoring technology. Not only would such data provide reassurance to the users on whether the device is working or not, but it also informs the user on how often and when retrieval and transmission take place. While data about monitoring device operation should definitely be included, designers should also consider how operation data from the ICD could be integrated. A few participants requested positive confirmation from the ICD clinic saying that nothing is wrong (basically the same as no reported alarms). This would reduce anxiety for some patients. But to avoid that the monitor becomes intrusive and prominent in their lives, such information could be integrated using a pull-strategy where users pull information from the monitor (instead of being pushed).

Our second design implication deals with physical design of remote monitoring devices as they are to be placed in private homes. Our study confirmed (like previous studies have shown e.g. [13,26,28]) that people value the lack of physical presence of such devices, where they should work but should not been seen. This was not the case for the included devices in our study, where participants would sometimes hide them or cover them. But on the other hand, other participants valued their presence as it reminded them of being looked after. Therefore, designers should explore physical designs of remote monitoring technology and try to produce physical designs that integrate into a domestic environment - like some of the ideas illustrated in [26].

If we look beyond ICD monitoring, we see avenues where our findings could inspire. We use and rely upon several systems and technologies that only operate and take action if something happens (usually something bad), e.g. fire/smoke alarms, airbags in cars, ABS brakes in cars, but actually also non-critical systems like setting the alarm on a clock. Key issues with such systems include trust, which highly relies on feedback. Now consider that the only way you could test the fire/smoke alarm in your house was by having an actual fire in your house. You could say that this was the experience some of our participants had with their remote monitor.

Methodological and Ethical Considerations: Revisited

We will briefly return to our methodological considerations on involving cardiac patients. As noted, we applied diaries and interviews as data collection techniques. While only five of our participants chose to do the diary part, we found that these diaries provide rich and detailed account of the everyday lives of the patients on e.g. how they treated their heart disease. Also, these accounts provided valuable inputs to our semi-structured interview guide. While five out of nineteen participants is perhaps not overwhelming, we would be reluctant to more strongly encourage participants to write diaries in future studies as some indicated that they did not posses the energy to complete a diary study.

Our interviews highly dealt with their illnesses, medical history, and episodes, and many of them were anxious, also shown in several other studies [17]. As we have illustrated, some participants lacked the informal talks with the clinic nurses as they had fewer scheduled follow-ups, where they gut reassured about minor and fundamental issues related to their disease and ICD. As a result, they would address us with questions and concerns during the interviews. Unlike remote monitoring for ageing at home (e.g. [13,16,21]), we observed that our participants could not easily find replacement for the lack of in-person contact as their issues and questions required cardiac knowledge.

CONCLUSION

While remote monitoring increases patient safety on e.g. mortality, we have limited understanding within HCI on how such technologies are embedded into everyday lives of ICD patients and their families. We studied nineteen people (eleven patients and eight spouses) using dairies and interviews with the aim to uncover how they live and interact with home monitoring. Our findings highlight three themes of remote monitoring on satisfaction and safety, surveillance and privacy, and anxiety and feedback. More specifically, we found that while participants generally were satisfied with being monitored, we also found that the physical design of the monitor gave problems as many of them were annoyed with the green LED light and some lacked the reassurance provided by the follow-up visits at the ICD clinic. Almost all participants did not mind being monitored despite the fact that none of them knew exactly what data the monitor retrieved, when this data was transmitted, and when and how the data was analysed and reviewed at the ICD clinic. A few of them formed strange perceptions on how the system worked and what could be inferred from the data. Finally, participants got anxious due to the lack of feedback, which resulted in that most of them did not know if their monitor worked correctly. Finally, our work shows that remote monitoring can create a safety paradox where patients and spouses feel less safe due to increased anxiety while they are in fact safer. Also, we showed that it is extremely challenging to present the data that is collected to the patient being monitored as well as show how this information is displayed to others.

One avenue for further research on remote monitoring with ICD patients seems apparent namely feedback on collected data from the ICD. Another further research avenue could be to investigate actual safety and perceived safety and how they are inter-related.

ACKNOWLEDGMENTS

We would like to extend our gratitude to the participants for the willingness to take part in our study. We also like to thank Kasper Hornbæk, Jesper Kjeldskov, Jeni Paay, Peter Axel Nielsen, Anders Bruun and the anonymous reviewers for comments on earlier versions of the paper.

REFERENCES

1. Al-Khatib, S. M., Piccini, J. P., Knight, D., Stewart, M., Clapp-Channing, N., and Sanders, G. D. Remote Monitoring of Implantable Cardioverter Defibrillators versus Quarterly Device Interrogations in Clinic: Results from a Randomized Pilot Clinical Trial. *Journal of Cardiovascular Electrophysiology*, Vol. 21, No. 5 (2010), 545–550
2. Ballegaard, S. A., Hansen, T. R., and Kyng, M. Healthcare in Everyday Life – Designing Healthcare Services for Daily Life. *Proc CHI 2008*, Florence, Italy, ACM Press (2008), 1807-1816
3. Birnholtz, J. and Jones-Rounds, M. Independence and Interaction: Understanding Seniors' Privacy and Awareness Needs for Aging in Place. *Proc CHI 2010*, Atlanta, USA, ACM Press (2010), 143-152
4. Brugada, P. What Evidence do we have to Replace In-Hospital Implantable Cardioverter Defibrillator Follow-Up? *Clinical Research in Cardiology*, Vol. 95 (2006), 3-9
5. Burri, H. and Senouf, D. Remote Monitoring and Follow-Up of Pacemakers and Implantable Cardioverter Defibrillators. *Europace*, Vol. 11 (2009), 701-709

6. Carter, S. and Mankoff, J. When Participants do the Capturing: The Role of Media in Diary Studies. *Proc CHI 2005*, Oregon, USA, ACM Press (2005), 899-908
7. Choe, E. K., Consolve, S., Jung, J., Harrison, B., and Kientz, J. A. Living in a Glass House: A Survey of Private Moments in the Home. *Proc UbiComp '11*, Beijing, China, ACM Press (2011), 41-44
8. Denning, T., Borning, A., Friedman, B., Gill, B. T., Kohno, T., and Maisel, W. H. Patients, Pacemakers, and Implantable Defibrillators: Human Values and Security for Wireless Implantable Medical Devices. *Proc CHI 2010*, Atlanta, USA, ACM Press (2010), 917-926
9. DiMarco, J. P. Implantable Cardioverter–Defibrillators. *The New England Journal of Medicine*, Vol. 349, November (2003), 1836-1847
10. Elliott, H. The Use of Diaries in Sociological Research on Health Experience. *Sociological Research Online*, Vol. 2, No. 2 (1997)
11. European Medicines Agency. *Guideline for Good Clinical Practice*. EMEA, (2006)
12. Hindricks, G. et al. Implant-Based Multiparameter Telemonitoring of Patients with Heart Failure (IN-TIME): A Randomised Controlled Trial. *The Lancet*, Vol. 384, No. 9943 (2014), 583-590
13. Huber, L., Shankar, K., Caine, K., Connelly, K., Camp, L. J., Walker, B. A. and Borrero, L. How In-Home Technologies Mediate Caregiving Relationships in Later Life. *International Journal of Human-Computer Interaction*. Vol. 29, No. 7 (2013), 441-455
14. Kumar, S., Kambhatia, K., Hu, F., Lifson, m., and Xiao, Y. Ubiquitous Computing for Remote Cardiac Patient Monitoring: A Survey. *International Journal of Telemedicine and Applications*, Vol. 4 (2008), 1-19
15. Leith, B. A. Patient and Family Members' Perceptions of Transfer from Intensive Care. *Heart and Lung*, Vol. 28, No. 3 (1999), 210-218
16. Lorenzen-Huber, L., Boutain, M., Camp, L. J., Shankar, K., and Connelly, K. H. Privacy, technology, and aging: A Proposed Framework. *Ageing International*, Vol. 36 (2011), 232-252
17. Magyar-Russell, G., Thombs, B. D. et al. The Prevalence of Anxiety and Depression in Adults with Implantable Cardioverter Defibrillators: A Systematic Review. *Journal of Psychosomatic Research*. Elsevier, Vol. 71 (2011), pp. 223-231
18. Maitland, J. and Chalmers, M. Self-Monitoring, Self-Awareness, and Self-Determination in Cardiac Rehabilitation. *Proc CHI 2010*, Atlanta, USA, ACM Press (2010), 1213-1222
19. Masella, C., Zanaboni, P., Di Stasi, F., Gilardi, S., Ponzi, P., and Valsecchi, S. Assessment of a Remote Monitoring System for Implantable Cardioverter Defibrillators. *Journal of Telemedicine and Telecare*, Vol. 14 (2008), 290–294
20. Matlock, D. D. Big Brother is Watching You: What do Patients Think About ICD Home Monitoring? *Ciculation*, American Heart Association, (2010), 319-321
21. Nielsen, J. C. et al. Automatic Home Monitoring of Implantable Cardioverter Defibrillators. *Europace*, Vol. 10 (2008), 729-735
22. Oulasvirta, A., Pihlajamaa, A., Perkiö, J., Ray, R., Vähäkangas, T., Hasu, T., Vainio, N., and Myllymäki, P. Long-Term Effects of Ubiquitous Surveillance in the Home. *Proc UbiComp '13*, Zurich, Switzerland, ACM Press (2013), 41-50
23. Palen, L. and Dourish, P. Unpacking "Privacy" for a Networked World. *Proc CHI 2003*, Fort Lauderdale, USA, ACM Press (2003), 129-136
24. Ricœur, P. *From Text to Action: Essays in Hermeneutics II*, trans. Northwestern University Press, 1991
25. Rogers, W. A. and Fisk A. D. Toward A Psychological Science of Advanced Technology Design for Older Adults. *The Journals of Gerontology Series B: Psychological Sciences and Social Sciences*, Vol. 65 (2010), 645
26. Shanker, K., Camp, L. J., Connely, K., and Huber, L. Aging, Privacy, and Home-Based Computing: Developing a Design Framework. *Pervasive Computing*, October-December (2012), 46-54
27. Theuns, D. A. M. J., Res, J. C. J., and Jordaens, L. J. Home monitoring in ICD therapy: future perspectives. *Europace*, Vol. 5 (2003), 139–142
28. Vines, J., Lindsay, S., Pritchard, G. W., Lie, M., Greathead, D., Olivier, P., and Brittain, K. Making Family Care Work: Dependence, Privacy and Remote Home Monitoring Telecare Systems. *Proc UbiComp '13*, Zurich, Switzerland, ACM Press (2013), 607-616
29. Walker, A. The Economic "Burden" of Ageing and the Prospect of Intergenerational Conflict. *Ageing and Society,* Vol. 10, No. 4 (1990), 377-396
30. Wilcox, L., Morris, D., Tan, D., and Gatewood, J. Designing Patient-Centric Information Displays for Hospitals. *Proc CHI 2010*, Atlanta, USA, ACM Press (2010), 2123-2132
31. World Medical Association. Declaration of Helsinki: Ethical Principles for Medical Research Involving Human Subjects. *64th WMA General Assembly*, Fortaleza, Brazil, October (2013)
32. Zayac, S. and Finch, N. Recipients' of Implanted Cardioverter-Defibrillators Actual and Perceived Adaptation: A Review of the Literature. *Journal of the American Academy of Nurse Practitioners*, Vol. 21 (2009), 549-556

Smart Homes that Monitor Breathing and Heart Rate

Fadel Adib Hongzi Mao Zachary Kabelac Dina Katabi Robert C. Miller
Massachusetts Institute of Technology
32 Vassar Street, Cambridge, MA 02139
{fadel,hongzi,zek,dk,rcm}@mit.edu

ABSTRACT

The evolution of ubiquitous sensing technologies has led to intelligent environments that can monitor and react to our daily activities, such as adapting our heating and cooling systems, responding to our gestures, and monitoring our elderly. In this paper, we ask whether it is possible for smart environments to monitor our vital signs remotely, without instrumenting our bodies. We introduce Vital-Radio, a wireless sensing technology that monitors breathing and heart rate without body contact. Vital-Radio exploits the fact that wireless signals are affected by motion in the environment, including chest movements due to inhaling and exhaling and skin vibrations due to heartbeats. We describe the operation of Vital-Radio and demonstrate through a user study that it can track users' breathing and heart rates with a median accuracy of 99%, even when users are 8 meters away from the device, or in a different room. Furthermore, it can monitor the vital signs of multiple people simultaneously. We envision that Vital-Radio can enable smart homes that monitor people's vital signs without body instrumentation, and actively contribute to their inhabitants' well-being.

Author Keywords Wireless; Vital Signs; Breathing; Smart Homes; Seeing Through Walls; Well-being

Categories and Subject Descriptors H.5.2. Information Interfaces and Presentation: User Interfaces - Input devices and strategies. C.2.2. Network Architecture and Design: Wireless Communication.

INTRODUCTION

The past few years have witnessed a surge of interest in ubiquitous health monitoring [22, 25]. Today, we see smart homes that continuously monitor temperature and air quality and use this information to improve the comfort of their inhabitants [46, 32]. As health-monitoring technologies advance further, we envision that future smart homes would not only monitor our environment, but also monitor our vital signals, like breathing and heartbeats. They may use this information to enhance our health-awareness, answering questions like "Do my breathing and heart rates reflect a healthy lifestyle?" They may also help address some of our concerns by answering questions like "Does my child breathe normally during sleep?" or "Does my elderly parent experience irregular heartbeats?" Furthermore, if non-intrusive in-home continuous monitoring of breathing and heartbeats existed, it would enable healthcare professionals to study how these signals correlate with our stress level and evolve with time and age, which could have a major impact on our healthcare system.

CHI 2015, April 18 - 23 2015, Seoul, Republic of Korea

ACM 978-1-4503-3145-6/15/04...$15.00
http://dx.doi.org/10.1145/2702123.2702200

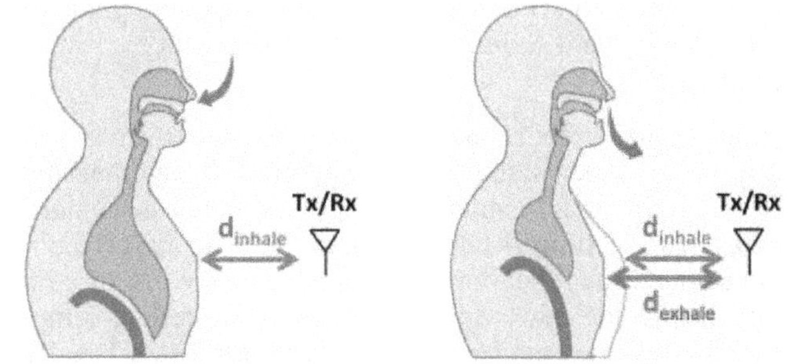

(a) Inhale Motion (b) Exhale Motion

Figure 1—Chest Motion Changes the Signal Reflection Time. (a) shows that when the person inhales, his chest expands and becomes closer to the antenna, hence decreasing the time it takes the signal to reflect back to the device. (b) shows that when the person exhales, his chest contracts and moves away from the antenna, hence the distance between the chest and the antenna increases, causing an increase in the reflection time.

Unfortunately, typical technologies for tracking vital signals require body contact, and most of them are intrusive. Specifically, today's breath monitoring sensors are inconvenient: they require the person to attach a nasal probe [19], wear a chest band [43], or lie on a special mattress [3]. Some heart-rate monitoring technologies are equally cumbersome since they require their users to wear a chest strap [18], or place a pulse oximeter on their finger [21]. The more comfortable technologies such as wristbands do not capture breathing and have lower accuracy for heart rate monitoring [12]. Additionally, there is a section of the population for whom wearable sensors are undesirable. For example, the elderly typically feel encumbered or ashamed by wearable devices [20, 37], and those with dementia may forget to wear them. Children may remove them and lose them, and infants may develop skin irritation from wearable sensors [40].

In this paper, we ask whether it's possible for smart homes to monitor our vital signs remotely – i.e., without requiring any physical contact with our bodies. While past research has investigated the feasibility of sensing breathing and heart rate without direct contact with the body [17, 16, 15, 34, 27, 48, 14], the proposed methods are more appropriate for controlled settings but unsuitable for smart homes: They fail in the presence of multiple users or extraneous motion. They typically require the user to lie still on a bed facing the device. Furthermore, they are accurate only when they are within close proximity to the user's chest.

We introduce Vital-Radio, a new input device for tracking breathing and heartbeats without physical contact with the person's body. Vital-Radio works correctly in the presence of multiple users in the environment and can track the vital signs of the present users simultaneously. Also, Vital-Radio does not require the user to face the device or be aware of its presence. In fact, the user can be sleeping, watching TV, typing on her laptop, or checking her phone. Furthermore, Vital-Radio can accurately track a user's breathing and heart rate even if she is 8 meters away from the device, or in a different room.

Vital-Radio works by using wireless signals to monitor the minute movements due to inhaling, exhaling, and heartbeats. Specifically, it transmits a low-power wireless signal and measures the time it takes for the signal to reflect back to the device. The reflection time depends on the distance of the reflector to the device, and changes as the reflector moves. Fig. 1 illustrates the impact of breathing on the signal's reflection time. When the person inhales, his chest expands and moves forward, reducing the reflection time. In contrast, when the person exhales, his chest contracts moving away from the device, hence increasing the reflection time. Generally, even when the person is not directly facing our device, the wireless signal traverses his body and his vital signs cause periodic changes in the signal's reflection time. Vital-Radio measures these changes and analyzes them to extract breathing and heartbeats.

A key feature of Vital-Radio is its ability to monitor the vital signs of multiple people and operate robustly without requiring the users to lie still. The main challenge in delivering this feature is that any motion in the environment can affect the wireless signal and hence interferes with tracking breathing or heartbeats. Past work addresses this challenge by requiring that only one person be present in front of the device and that the person remains still. In contrast, Vital-Radio recognizes that one can address this problem by building on recent technologies that localize users using wireless signals [6]. Specifically, Vital-Radio first localizes each user in the environment, then zooms in on the signal reflected from each user and analyzes variations in his reflection to extract his breathing and heart rate. By isolating a user's reflection, Vital-Radio also eliminates other sources of interference including noise or extraneous motion in the environment, which may otherwise mask the minute variations due to the user's vital signs. This enables Vital-Radio to monitor multiple users' breathing and heart rates, and to operate at distances up to 8 m from the user or even from behind a wall.

We built a real-time prototype of Vital-Radio and validated its capabilities by conducting experiments with 14 subjects. For baselines, we use FDA-approved breathing and heart rate monitors; these include chest straps for monitoring the inhale-exhale motion and pulse oximeters placed on the subject's finger to monitor their heart rate. In our benchmark evaluation, we ask the users to wear the baseline monitors, while Vital-Radio monitors them remotely without any body contact. We compare the output of Vital-Radio with the ground truth from the FDA-approved baselines, demonstrating that Vital-Radio accurately tracks breathing patterns and heartbeats. Over more than 200 two-minute experiments, our results show that:

- Vital-Radio can accurately track a person's breathing and heart rate without body contact, even when the user is up to 8 meters away from the device, or behind a wall.
- Vital-Radio's median accuracy for breathing is 99.3% (error of 0.09 breath/minute) and for heart rate is 98.5% (0.95 beat/minute) when the person is 1 m away from the device. The accuracy decreases to 98.7% (error of 0.15 breath/minute) and 98.3% (1.1 beat/minute) when the person is 8 m away from the device.
- In an area that spans $8\,m \times 5\,m$, Vital-Radio can monitor the vital signs of up to three individuals with the same accuracy as for one person.

We also perform activity-focused experiments to explore Vital-Radio's monitoring capabilities. Specifically, we demonstrate that Vital-Radio can accurately measure users' breathing and heart rates while they are typing on their computer or using their cell phones. We also demonstrate that Vital-Radio can track sharp changes in vital signs. Specifically, we perform experiments where users are asked to exercise, and show how Vital-Radio accurately tracks the change in breathing and heart rates after exercising.

We believe Vital-Radio takes a significant step toward enabling smart homes that allow people to monitor their vital signals, and that its capabilities can have a significant impact on our health awareness and our health-care system.

RELATED WORK

The desire for non-contact monitoring of vital signs has occupied researchers since the late 70's [29]. Early work presented a proof of concept that the wireless signal is affected by movements of the chest. In these experiments, the person lies still on a bed and the sensor is placed only 3 cm away from the apex of the heart. The results are qualitative with no evaluation of accuracy.

Subsequently, military research explored the potential of building radars that can detect human presence through walls or under rubble by relying on the fact that breathing impacts wireless signals [42, 47, 26, 45]. Specifically, because wireless signals traverse obstacles, they could be used to sense the chest movements of a trapped victim through rubble or enable SWAT teams to sense movement from behind an obstacle and avoid being ambushed. However, since these systems target the military, they typically transmit at excessive power and use military-reserved spectrum bands [47, 45], which is not feasible for consumer devices. More importantly, this line of work generally focused on the detection of users by sensing motion due to their vital signs rather than estimating or monitoring the vital signs themselves.

Recently, the mounting interest in technologies for well-being has led researchers to investigate non-contact methods for analyzing vital signs. Current research on this topic can be divided into two areas: vision-based techniques and wireless systems. Specifically, advances in image processing allowed researchers to amplify visual patterns in video feeds (such as color changes due to blood flow) to detect breathing and heart rate [8, 44]; however, such video-based techniques require the user to face the camera and do not work when he/she turns around or is outside the camera's field of view.

Similarly, advances in wireless transmission systems and signal processing have enabled researchers to detect and analyze human vital signs. Past proposals use one of the following techniques: Doppler radar [17, 16, 15], WiFi [34, 27], or ultra-wideband radar [48, 14, 7]. The key challenge in using wireless signals to extract vital signs is that any motion in the environment affects the signal. Since breathing and heartbeats are minute movements, they can be easily masked by interference from any other source of movement in the environment. Furthermore, the presence of multiple users – even if none of them moves – prevents these systems from operating correctly since the wireless signal will be affected by the combination of their vital signs, making it hard to disentangle the vital signs of each individual. Past proposals deal with this problem by ensuring that there is only one source of motion in the environment: namely, the vital signs of the monitored individual. Hence, their experimental setup has one person, who typically lies still in close proximity to the device [17, 16, 15, 34, 27, 48, 14, 7, 4].

In contrast to these past systems, Vital-Radio has an intrinsic mechanism that enables it to separate different sources of motion in the environment. To do so, Vital-Radio builds on state-of-the-art wireless localization techniques [6], which can identify the distance between the device and different moving objects. Vital-Radio, however, uses these methods to disentangle the incoming signals based on distance, rather than estimate the actual location. This allows it to separate signals reflected off different bodies and body parts. It then analyzes their motion independently to estimate the breathing and heart rate of potentially multiple individuals.

CONTEXT AND SCOPE

We envision that Vital-Radio can be deployed in a smart home to monitor its inhabitants' breathing and heart rates, without body instrumentation. The device can monitor multiple users' vital signs simultaneously, even if some of them are occluded from the device by a wall or a piece of furniture. A single device can monitor users' vital signs at distances up to 8 meters, and hence may be used to cover a studio or a small apartment. One can cover a larger home by deploying multiple Vital-Radio devices in the environment.

Vital-Radio's algorithms run continuously, separating signals from different users, then analyzing the signal from each user independently to measure his/her vital signs. However, when a user walks (or performs a large body motion), the chest motion is mainly impacted by the walk and no longer representative of the breathing and heart rate.[1] At home, there are typically sufficient intervals when a user is quasi-static; these include scenarios where the user is watching TV, typing on a laptop, reading a newspaper, or sleeping. Vital-Radio can use all of these intervals to monitor a user's vital signs, and track how they vary throughout the day.

[1]The vast majority of vital signs monitors, including chest bands that monitor breathing and pulse oximeters that monitor heart rate, cannot provide accurate estimates when the user walks or moves a major limb [35, 28, 11]. To prevent such motion from causing errors in its vital-signs estimates, Vital-Radio automatically detects periods during which the user is quasi-static and computes estimates only during such intervals.

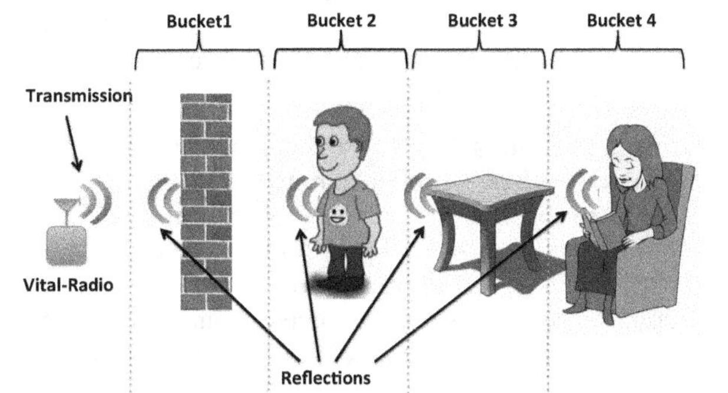

Figure 2—Separating Reflectors into Different Buckets. Vital-Radio uses a radar technique called FMCW to separate the reflections arriving from objects into different buckets depending on the distance between these objects and the device.

THEORY OF OPERATION

Vital-Radio transmits a low power wireless signal and measures the time it takes its signal to travel to the human body and reflect back to its antennas. Knowing that wireless signals travel at the speed of light, we can use the reflection time to compute the distance from the device to the human body. This distance varies slightly and periodically as the user inhales and exhales and his heart beats. Vital-Radio captures these minute changes in distance and uses them to extract the user's vital signs.

However, natural environments have a large number of reflectors, such as walls and furniture as well as multiple users whose bodies all reflect the wireless signal. To address these issues, Vital-Radio's operation consists of three steps:

1. Isolate reflections from different users and eliminate reflections off furniture and static objects.
2. For each user, identify the signal variations that are due to breathing and heartbeats, and separate them from variations due to body or limb motion.
3. Analyze signal variations to extract breathing and heart rates.

In what follows, we describe how these steps enable us to monitor users' vital signs using Vital-Radio.

Step 1: Isolate Reflections from Different Users and Eliminate Reflections off Furniture and Walls

To understand the operation of Vital-Radio, let us consider the scenario in Fig. 2, where the device is placed behind the wall of a room that has two humans and a table. When Vital-Radio transmits a wireless signal, part of that signal reflects off the wall; the other part traverses the wall, reflects off the humans and the table inside the room, and then traverses the wall back to the device.

To isolate signals reflected off different objects, Vital-Radio uses a radar technique called FMCW (Frequency Modulated Carrier Waves). We refer the reader to [6] for a detailed description of how FMCW works. A key property of FMCW that we exploit in this paper is that it enables separating the reflections from different objects into buckets based on their reflection times. Since wireless signals travel at the speed of light, signals reflected off objects at different distances would fall into different buckets.

However, in contrast to past work on localization, which uses FMCW to sense the amount of power arriving from different distances to localize the users, Vital-Radio uses the FMCW technique as a filter –i.e., it uses it to isolate the reflected signals arriving from different distances in the environment into different buckets, before it proceeds to analyze the signals in each of these buckets to extract the vital signs (step 2 below).

Our implementation of FMCW follows the system in [6], where the resolution of FMCW buckets is about 8 cm. This has two implications:

- Reflections from two objects that are separated by at least 8 cm would fall into different buckets. Hence, two users that are few feet apart would naturally fall into different buckets. For example, in Fig. 2, the wall, Bob, the table, and Alice are at different distances from our device, and hence FMCW isolates the signals reflected from each of these entities into different buckets, allowing us to focus on each of them separately.
- Using FMCW as a filter also allows us to isolate some of the limb motion from chest movements due to breathing and heartbeats. For example, the signal reflected off the user's feet will be in a different bucket from that reflected off the user's chest. Thus, having the user move his feet (in place) does not interfere with Vital-Radio's ability to extract the breathing and heart rate.

After bucketing the reflections based on the reflector's distance, Vital-Radio eliminates reflections off static objects like walls and furniture. Specifically, since static objects don't move, their reflections don't change over time, and hence can be eliminated by subtracting consecutive time measurements.

At the end of this step, Vital-Radio would have eliminated all signal reflections from static objects (e.g., walls and furniture), and is left with reflections off moving objects separated into buckets.[2]

Step 2: Identifying Reflections Involving Breathing and Heart Rate

After Vital-Radio isolates reflections from different moving users into separate buckets, it proceeds by analyzing each of these buckets to identify breathing and heart rate. For example, in Fig. 2, we would like to identify whether the user in bucket 2 is quasi-static and his motion is dominated by his vital signs, or whether he is walking around or moving a limb.

To do that, Vital-Radio zooms in on the signal reflection which it isolated in the corresponding bucket. This wireless reflection is a wave; the phase of the wave is related to the distance traveled by the signal as follows [39]:

$$\phi(t) = 2\pi \frac{d(t)}{\lambda}, \quad (1)$$

[2]While unlikely, it is possible that multiple users are at the same distance from the device and hence fall into the same bucket. To deal with such cases, one may deploy multiple devices so that if two users are at the same distance with respect to one device, they are at different distances with respect to another device.

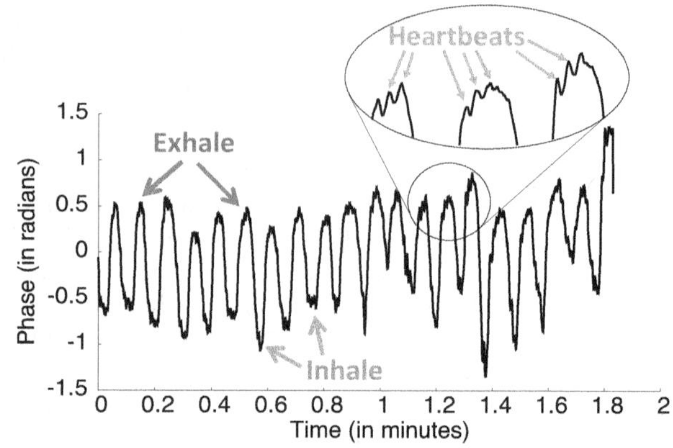

Figure 3—Phase variation due to vital signs. The figure shows the variations in phase due to breathing and heartbeats, where peaks and valleys in the phase correspond to exhale and inhale motions respectively; also, zooming in on the signal allows us to observe the heartbeats modulated on top of the breathing motion.

where λ is the wavelength of the transmitted signal, and $d(t)$ is the traveled distance from the device to the reflector and back to the device. The above equation shows that one can identify variations in $d(t)$ due to inhaling, exhaling, and heartbeats, by measuring the resulting variations in the phase of the reflected signal.

To illustrate how the phase varies with vital signs, let us consider the example in Fig. 1, where a user sits facing the device. When the person inhales, his chest expands and gets closer to the device; and when he exhales, his chest contracts and gets further away from the device. Because the phase and the distance to a reflector are linearly related, Vital-Radio can track a person's breathing. Fig. 3 shows the phase of the captured reflection as a function of time. Specifically, a peak in the phase corresponds to an exhale (highest distance from the device), and a valley in the phase corresponds to an inhale (smallest distance from the device). We note that our implementation uses a wavelength λ around 4.5 cm. According to the above equation, sub-centimeter variations in the chest distance due to breathing cause sub-radian variations in the phase, which is what we observe in the figure.

Similarly, a person's heartbeats cause minute movements of different parts of his body. Specifically, the physiological phenomenon that allows Vital-Radio to extract heart rate from signal reflections is ballistocardiography (BCG). BCG refers to movements of the body synchronous with the heartbeat due to ventricular pump activity [36]. Past work has documented BCG jitters from the head, torso, buttock, etc. [5, 8]. Periodic jitters cause periodic variations in the wireless signal allowing us to capture the heart rate. These movements translate to smaller fluctuations on top of the breathing motion in the wireless reflection as we can see from local peaks in Fig. 3. Note that the periodicity of breathing and heartbeats is independent of the user's orientation. For example, if the user has his back to the device, the valleys become peaks and vice versa, but the same periodicity persists.

Still, an important question to answer is: what happens when a person moves around or moves a limb, and how can Vital-Radio distinguish such motions from breathing and heart-

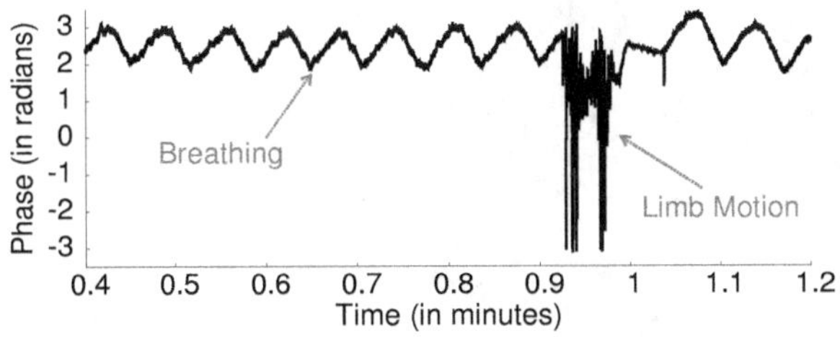

Figure 4—Limb motion affects vital sign monitoring. The figure shows the subject breathing until right before the 1 minute mark where he waves his hand. The device eliminates time intervals when such motion happens.

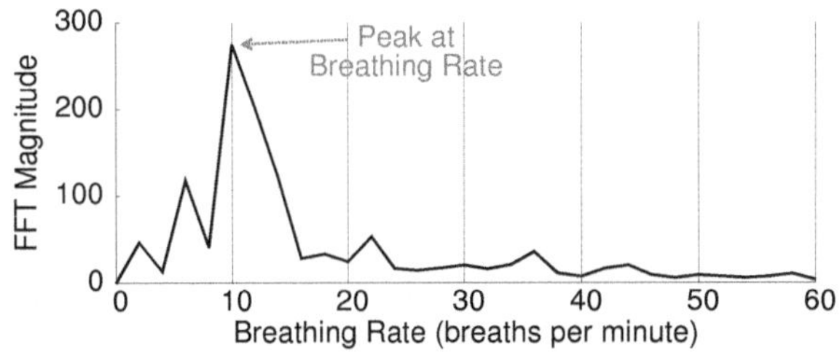

Figure 5—Output of Fourier Transform for Breathing. The figure shows the output of the FFT performed on the phase of the signal of Fig. 3. The FFT exhibits a peak around 10 breaths/minute, providing a coarse estimate of the breathing rate.

beats? To help answer this question, we show in Fig. 4 a scenario where the user waves his hand before the one minute mark resulting in aperiodic phase variations of the signal.

To deal with such scenarios, Vital-Radio exploits that motion due to vital signs is periodic, while body or limb motion is aperiodic. It uses this property to identify intervals of time where a user's whole body moves or where she performs large limb movements and discards them so that they do not create errors in estimating vital signs. To achieve this, Vital-Radio operates on time windows (30 seconds in our implementation). For each window, it measures the periodicity of the signal. If the periodicity is above a threshold, it determines that the dominant motion is breathing and heart rate; otherwise, it discards the window. A typical approach to measure a signal's periodicity is evaluating the sharpness of its *Fourier transform* (or FFT) [10]. Hence, we perform an FFT on each window, choose the FFT's peak frequency, and determine whether the peak's value is sufficiently higher than the average power in the remaining frequencies.[3]

This metric allows us to maintain intervals where a user does not perform large limb movements, including scenarios where the user types on her laptop or checks her phone. This is because, while these movements are indeed aperiodic, they do not mask the breathing or the heart rate since their power does not overwhelm the repetitive movements due to our vital signs.[4] Additionally, in some of these scenarios, the user's hands are stretched out to the laptop and away from his chest as he is typing. As a result, the major part of his typing motion falls into a separate FMCW bucket than the user's chest. Naturally, because the human body is connected, hand movements would still result in muscle stretches and minor shoulder jitters that are close to the user's chest; however, because such movements are weak and aperiodic, they are diluted at the output of the FFT. In contrast, periodic movements due to vital signs are enforced in the FFT operation, which results in maintaining intervals of such quasi-static scenarios.

The above steps allow us to filter out extraneous motion and focus on time windows where the dominant motion for each user is the breathing and heart rate. In the following section, we show how Vital-Radio extracts breathing and heart rate from these intervals.

[3]In our implementation, we choose this peak to be at least $5\times$ above the average power of the remaining frequencies.

[4]Mathematically, these signals would appear as "white noise" in low frequencies, and are filtered out in Step 3 of Vital-Radio's operation.

Step 3: Extracting Breathing and Heart Rate

Breathing Rate Extraction

Because breathing is a periodic motion, we can extract the frequency (rate) of breathing by performing a Fourier transform (an FFT). The peak at the output of the FFT will correspond to the dominant frequency, which in our case is the breathing rate. Specifically, we perform an FFT of the phase signal in Fig. 3 over a 30 second window and plot the output in Fig. 5. The peak of this signal gives us an initial estimate of the person's breathing rate.

However, simply taking the peak of the FFT does not provide an accurate estimate of breathing rate. Specifically, the frequency resolution of an FFT is $1/window\ size$. For a window size of 30 seconds, the resolution of our breath rate estimate is $\approx 0.033Hz$, i.e., 2 breaths/minute. Note that a larger window size provides better resolution, but is less capable of tracking changes in breathing rate. To obtain a more precise measurement, we exploit a well-known property in signal processing which states that: if the signal contains a single dominant frequency, then that frequency can be accurately measured by performing a linear regression on the phase of the complex time-domain signal [33]. Hence, we perform an additional optimization step, whereby we filter the output of the FFT, keeping only the peak and its two adjacent bins; this filtering allows us to eliminate noise caused by extraneous and non-periodic movements. Then, we perform an inverse FFT to obtain a complex time-domain signal $s'(t)$. The phase of $s'(t)$ will be linear and its slope will correspond to the breathing frequency, i.e., the breathing rate. Mathematically, we can compute an accurate estimate of the breathing rate (in terms of breaths per minute) from the following equation:

$$Estimate = 60 \times \frac{slope\{\angle s'(t)\}}{2\pi}, \quad (2)$$

where the factor of 60 transforms this frequency from Hz (i.e., $1/second$) to breaths/minute.

Heart Rate Extraction

Similar to breathing, the heartbeat signal is periodic, and is modulated on top of the breathing signal, as shown in Fig. 3. However, the breathing signal is orders of magnitude stronger than the heartbeat. This leads to a classical problem in FFT's, where a strong signal at a given frequency leaks into other frequencies (i.e., leaks into nearby bins at the output of the FFT) and could mask a weaker signal at a nearby frequency.

To mitigate this leakage, we filter the frequency domain signal around [40-200] beats per minute; this allows us to filter

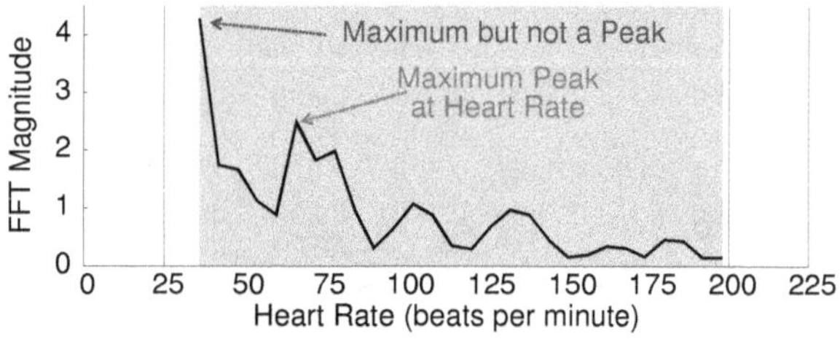

Figure 6—Output of Fourier Transform for Heart Rate. The figure shows the output of the FFT after applying a hanning window and filtering between [40-200] beats/minute. The highest peak (i.e., "local maximum") provides a coarse estimate of the heart rate.

out breathing, which is typically between 8 and 16 breaths per minute [41][5] as well as high frequency noise (which is higher than 200 beats per minute).

We plot the output of this obtained frequency domain signal in Fig. 6, and pick the maximum *peak* of this output as the frequency that corresponds to the heart rate. Note that we do not simply pick the *absolute* maximum of the FFT, because this absolute maximum is typically the first bin after filtering (i.e., around 40 beats/minute), and is due to the leakage from the breathing. In contrast, in this example, the peak occurs at 66 beats/minute.

Similar to breathing, simply taking the peak of the FFT leads to poor resolution. To obtain a more precise estimate of the heart rate, we take an inverse FFT of the signal in the FFT bin corresponding to the heart rate peak and the two adjacent FFT bins. We then regress on the phase of this signal using equation 2. After this regression step, the obtained heart rate is 66.7 beats/minute, whereas the ground truth heart rate obtained from a pulse oximeter is around 66.5 beats/minute.

Finally, we note that for computing heart rate, we use an FFT window of 10 seconds only. This window is long enough to capture the periodicity of heartbeats but it is short enough to quickly react to an increase/decrease in heart rate. Also note that the FFT is computed over overlapping windows that are shifted by 30ms, hence providing a new estimate every 30ms.

IMPLEMENTATION

Our implementation consists of the following components:

Hardware: We reproduced a state-of-the-art FMCW radio designed by past work on wireless localization [6]. The device generates a signal that sweeps from 5.46 GHz to 7.25 GHz every 2.5 milliseconds, transmitting sub-mW power. These parameters are chosen in [6] such that the transmission system is compliant with FCC regulations for consumer electronics.

The FMCW radio connects to a computer over Ethernet. The received signal is sampled (digitized) and transmitted over the Ethernet to the computer for real-time processing.

Software: We implement the signal processing algorithms described in the previous sections in C++. The code runs in realtime, plotting on the screen the breathing and heart rate as function of time and at the same time logs them to a file. The code operates on shifted overlapping FFT windows and generates new estimates every 30ms. The output also shows user motion –i.e., the code tags every 30ms window to show whether the user is quasi-static or performing a major motion.

[5]In fact, this filtering allows us to filter out the breathing signal and its first harmonic.

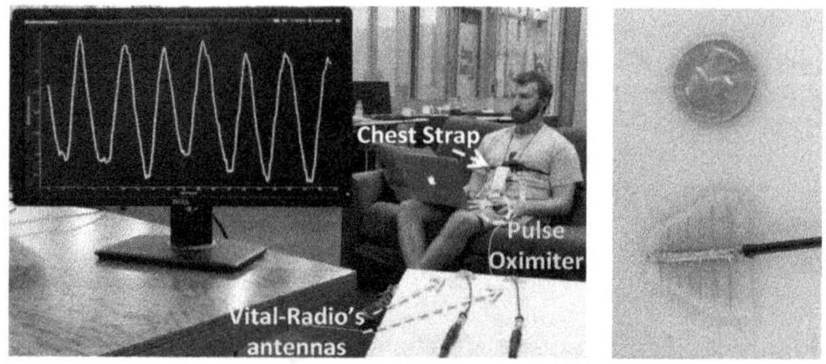

(a) **Setup.** (b) **Antennas.**

Figure 7—Experimental Setup. (a) shows a user sitting about 2.5m away from Vital-Radio's antennas; the user also wears a chest strap and a pulse oximeter, which are connected to the Alice PDx for obtaining ground truth measurements. (b) shows one of Vital-Radio's antennas placed next to a quarter.

EXPERIMENTAL EVALUATION

Participants: To evaluate the performance of Vital-Radio we recruited 14 participants (3 females). These participants were between 21 and 55 years old ($\mu = 31.4$), weighed between 52 and 95 kg ($\mu = 78.3$), and were between 164 and 187 cm tall ($\mu = 175$). During the experiments, the subjects wore their daily attire, including shirts, T-shirts, hoodies, and jackets with different fabric materials.

Ground Truth: To determine Vital-Radio's accuracy, we compare its output against the Alice PDx [1], an FDA approved device for monitoring breathing and heart rate. The Alice PDx is equipped with a chest band and a pulse oximeter. The chest band is strapped around each subject's chest to monitor breathing, and the pulse oximeter is placed on his/her finger to monitor heart rate during the experiment.

Experimental Environment: We perform our experiments in a standard office building; the interior walls are standard double dry walls supported by metal frames with sheet rock on top. The evaluation environment contains office furniture including desks, chairs, couches, and computers.

Throughout the experiments, Vital-Radio's antennas are placed on a table, about 3 feet above the ground as shown in Fig. 7. The user sits at some distance from these antennas and wears the Alice PDx's chest band and pulse oximeter to obtain the ground truth measurements as shown in the figure. In our evaluation, we vary the distance and orientation of the user with respect to Vital-Radio to determine its accuracy in different scenarios as we show in the next section.

Core Experiment: Accuracy Versus Distance

We would like to validate Vital-Radio's ability to monitor a subject's breathing and heart rate at different distances from our device. In this experiment, we place the device in the corner of a large room, whose floor plan is shown in Fig. 8. The device's antennas are pointed toward the center of the room to ensure that they capture motion inside that room. We ask the subject to sit on a chair at marked locations whose distances range from 1 m to 8 m away from the device. In each experi-

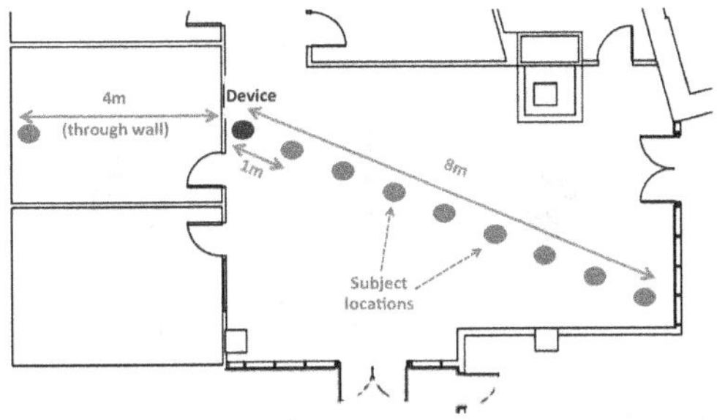

Figure 8—Testbed. The figure shows a layout of our experimental setup, marking the location of Vital-Radio in navy blue, and the different locations where our monitored subjects sat down in red.

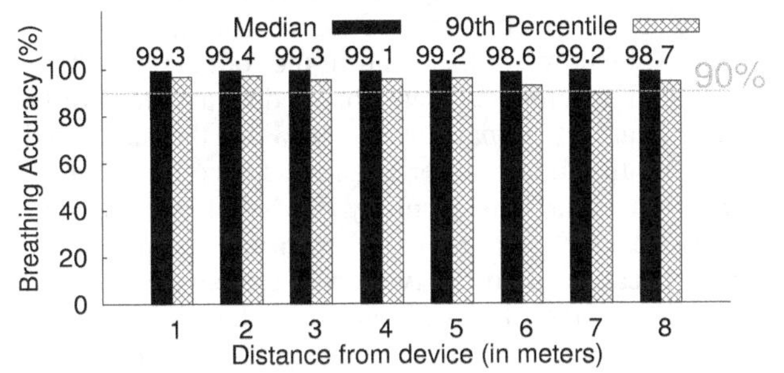

Figure 9—Breathing Accuracy vs Distance. The figure shows Vital-Radio's breathing accuracy versus its distance to the subject.

ment, the subject sits on a chair facing Vital-Radio's antennas and wears the Alice PDx, as shown in Fig. 7.

We run a total of 112 experiments, where we ask each of the 14 subjects to sit at the marked locations from 1m to 8 m.[6] Each experiment lasts for two minutes, during which the user sits facing the device in each of these locations. We extract the breathing and heart rate in real-time using Vital-Radio and log these vital signs using the AlicePDx. During each two minute experiment, Vital-Radio outputs a vital sign estimate every 30 milliseconds, leading to a total of 448,000 measurements across all experiments and all locations.

Based on the ground truth measurements using the Alice PDx, the subjects' breathing rates range from 5 to 23 breaths/minute, while their heart rates vary from 53 to 115 beats/minute. These rates span the range of adult breathing and heart rates [41, 31].[7]

Breathing Rate Accuracy

We compare the output of Vital-Radio with that of the Alice PDx, and plot the median and 90th percentile accuracy of breathing as a function of distance from 1 to 8 meters in Fig. 9. The figure shows that our median accuracy is 99.3% at 1 m and remains as high as 98.7% at 8 m from the device. It also shows that our 90th percentile accuracy is higher than 90% across all these distances.

[6]We limit the experiments to distances of 8 m because the localization accuracy of FMCW-based systems for consumer applications drops beyond this range [6].

[7]We note that one of our subject has a significantly high heart rate of 115 beats/minute. We confirmed with the subject that this value, which was measured with the Alice PDx, is compatible with his medical records. Also one of our subjects has a low breathing rate of 5 breaths/minute, as measured by the Alice PDx. This subject practices yoga on a daily basis.

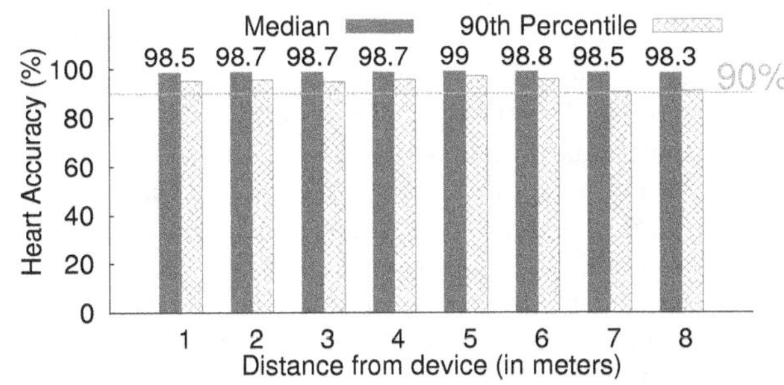

Figure 10—Heart Rate Accuracy vs Distance. The figure shows Vital-Radio's heart rate accuracy versus its distance to the subject.

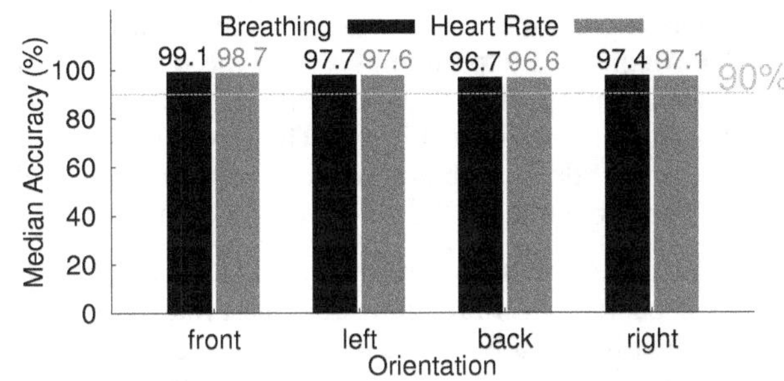

Figure 11—Accuracy versus Orientation. The figure shows Vital-Radio's median accuracy for breathing and heart rate for a user sitting 4 m from the device and facing different directions.

Heart Rate Accuracy

We plot the median and 90th percentile accuracy of heart rate as a function of distance from 1 to 8 meters in Fig. 10. The figure shows that our median accuracy is 98.5% at 1 meter and drops to 98.3% at 8 meters from the device. It also shows that our 90th percentile accuracy remains higher than 90%, even with the subject is 8 m away from the device.

Accuracy in Various Scenarios

Accuracy versus Orientation

To validate that Vital-Radio operates correctly even when subjects do not directly face the device, we run experiments where we ask our subjects to orient themselves in different directions with respect to the device. Specifically, we ask each subject to sit at the 4 m distance from Vital-Radio and we run experiments in four different orientations: subject faces the device, subject has his back to the device, and the subject is facing left or right (perpendicular) to the device.

We plot the median accuracies for breathing and heart rate for these four different orientations in Fig. 11. The figure shows that, indeed, when the user faces the device, the median accuracy of breathing and heart rate is highest (99.1% and 98.7% respectively). However, this accuracy only slightly drops by at most 3% across all the different orientations. Note that the device can detect chest motion even when that motion is perpendicular. This is because when one inhales, his chest expands in all directions, and Vital-Radio can detect a chest side expansion though it is minute.[8]

Next, we validate that Vital-Radio does not require the user to be along a straight line facing the antenna. Specifically, we

[8]Such expansion is no smaller than variations due to heartbeats.

place the antennas at the center of the room, and ask users to sit at a distance of 4 m from the antennas and at angles ranging from $-90°$ to $+90°$ with respect to the pointing direction of the antennas. We perform 20 one-minute experiments with different subjects at different angles. The results show that Vital-Radio can capture the user's vital signs as long as she is at an angle between $-75°$ and $+75°$ with respect to the antenna's pointing direction. Specifically, the median accuracy is above 98% when the user is on a straight line with respect to the antenna, and decreases to 96% at the far edge (i.e., $\pm 75°$).[9]

Through-Wall Accuracy

In order to test the ability of Vital-Radio to measure user's vital signs even when they are in a different room, we run a set of through-wall experiments where the device is placed in a different room than our subjects. Specifically, we use the experimental setup in Fig. 8. The device is kept in the larger room, while the subject sits in an adjacent room behind a wall. The subject faces the device and is about 4 m from it.

Across all experiments, our median accuracies are 99.2% and 90.1% respectively for breathing and heart rate. These results indicate that the breathing rate remains almost the same both in the presence and absence of the wall (at the same distance of 4 m). However, the median heart rate accuracy drops due to the fact that the wall attenuates the heart rate signal significantly (which was already a very minute signal), hence, reducing our signal-to-noise ratio. Still, the heart rate accuracy remains around 90% even in such through-wall scenarios.

Multi-User Accuracy

We are interested in evaluating Vital-Radio's accuracy for multi-user vital sign monitoring. Hence, we perform controlled experiments, where we ask three of our users to sit on a chair at the 2 m, 4 m, and 6 m marks in Fig. 8. In each experiment, Vital-Radio determines that there are 3 users, each at his respective distance from the device, and outputs the vital signs of each; however, the baseline (AlicePDx) can only monitor a single user at any point in time. Hence, to evaluate accuracy, we first connect the baseline to the first user and compare its output to the output of VitalRadio for the user at that distance and for that moment. Then, we move the baseline to the remaining users in succession.

We run 20 experiments with different sets of subjects and plot the accuracies in Fig. 12. The figure shows that Vital-Radio's breathing and heart rate monitoring accuracy is around 98% for all three users. Note also that the median accuracy of the nearest user is higher than that of the further two users because of the increase in distance between these users and the device. These results verify that Vital-Radio can monitor multiple users' vital signs, and that its monitoring accuracy for multiple users is the same as that for a single user.

Next, we would like to confirm that Vital-Radio can accurately capture the vital signs of a quasi-static user while other users are moving in the environment. In principle, Vital-Radio should still operate correctly since FMCW separates reflections from different users based on their distance to the

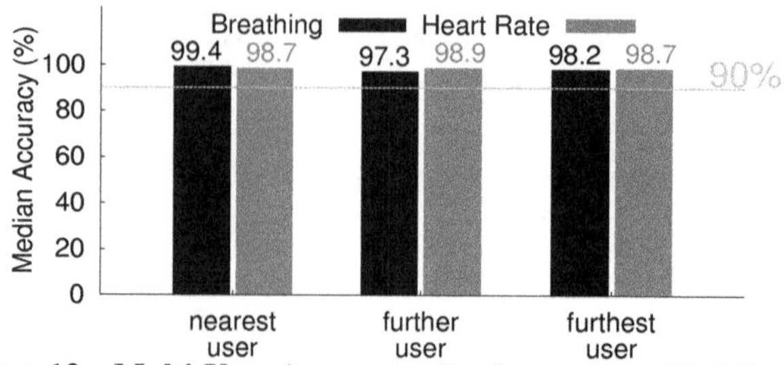

Figure 12—Multi-User Accuracy. The figure shows Vital-Radio's median accuracy in monitoring the vital signs of 3 users simultaneously. The users are sitting at 2 m, 4 m, and 6 m from the device.

device. Hence, we run experiments where we ask one of our subjects to sit on a chair at the 3 m mark in Fig. 8 while asking another subject to walk around in the room. Over 20 experiments with different subjects, the median accuracy of breathing and heart rate remains above 98% for the monitored user as long as the moving user is at a distance of at least 1.5 m away from him. This accuracy drops below 75% when the moving user gets closer than 1 m to the monitored person. This is because when the two users are closer than 1 m, the reflections off their bodies interfere with each other, preventing Vital-Radio from isolating the signal variations due to the monitored user's vital signs.

Activity-Focused Experiments

Daily In-Place Activities

We would like to evaluate Vital-Radio's accuracy in monitoring users as they perform in-place day-to-day activities, such as typing on their laptops, watching TV, or sleeping. Thus, we divided the subjects into two groups: one interacting with their laptops and another interacting with their smartphones. In each experiment, we ask the subject to sit at 4 m from the device and naturally use his/her phone or laptop. Each experiment lasts for 5 minutes; the user reports at the end the activities he/she performed with their laptop or phone. The reports show that the users performed various tasks ranging from checking and responding to their emails to reading news on the web or logging on to Facebook or Instagram. Some users were texting using their phones and one user worked on a problem set on his laptop.

Throughout the experiments where our subjects used their phones, the median accuracies for breathing and heart rate were 99.4% and 98.9% respectively. These accuracies slightly dropped to 99.3% and 98.7% when our subjects were using their laptops. This minor drop in accuracy is expected because using a laptop typically involves slightly larger movements than using a phone, leading to a slight reduction in Vital-Radio's accuracy. Note, however, that these accuracies are almost the same as those when subjects were sitting still at the same distance with respect to our antenna. Hence, Vital-Radio was able to monitor users' breathing and heart rate as they perform day-to-day activities that do not require them to move around their apartments.

Exercising and Health-Awareness

Heart rate recovery – which corresponds to how fast a person's heart rate decreases after exercising – is an important metric for determining how healthy a person's heart is. Specifically, a stronger heart has a fast heart rate recovery, and

[9]This result is expected since Vital-Radio uses log-periodic antennas whose directionality is around 150°.

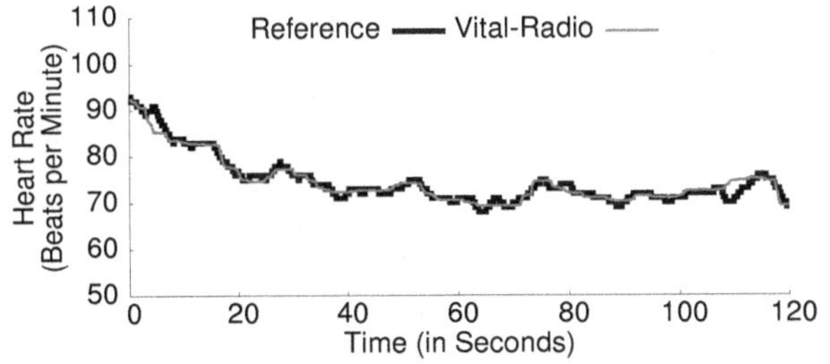

Figure 13—Tracking Heart Rate after Exercising. The figure shows how Vital-Radio' can accurately and in real-time track a user's heart rate as it decreases after exercising.

that recovery rate is a predictor of mortality [13, 24]. Hence, an important way in which Vital-Radio may contribute to a smart home inhabitants' well-being is by accurately measuring the heart rate after users exercise.

To evaluate this capability, we evaluate the accuracy of Vital-Radio's real-time vital sign monitoring after asking our subjects to exercise. Specifically, each of the subjects jumps rope for 2 minutes then sits down on a chair, 4 m away from the device, and breathes normally. During these experiments, we also ask our subjects to wear the Alice PDx chest band and oximeter to obtain ground truth measurements for their vital signs. While both Vital-Radio and Alice PDx cannot accurately measure heart rate during the excessive motion of jumping, they can both measure the vital signs when a user sits down after exercising.

Fig. 13 overlays the heart rate estimated by Vital-Radio (in red) on top of the the ground-truth heart rate of a subject as monitored by the pulse oximeter (in black), throughout a two-minute period after the subject stops exercising. The figure shows that Vital-Radio can effectively track the variations in the heart rate. Note that, throughout this two-minute period, there's a downward trend in the heart rate (from about 93 beats/minute to around 70 beats/minute), which is expected since the subject is in a resting state after exercising. Also, note that throughout this period, the heart rate varies continuously about that trend, and that both the ground truth and Vital-Radio are able to capture these variations.

Across the experiments with multiple subjects, Vital-Radio's median accuracy in measuring breathing and heart rate is 99.4% and 99% respectively, and the 90th percentile is 91.7% and 96.8%. These figures are similar to the accuracy achieved in our previous experiments, where subjects were fully rested, indicating that Vital-Radio can indeed capture our vital signs and track them accurately even as they vary.

LIMITATIONS

In this section, we elaborate on the limitations of Vital-Radio:

1. *Minimum Separation between Users:* Vital-Radio uses FMCW to separate reflections from different users before extracting the per-user vitals. For ideal point reflectors, FMCW can separate reflections from two objects if they are at least C/2B apart [6], where B is the bandwidth and C is the speed of light. For Vital-Radio, this translates to a theoretical minimum separation of 8 cm. However, because a human is not a point reflector, our experiments show that a separation of 1–2 m is needed for high accuracy.
2. *Monitoring Range:* Since Vital-Radio is a wireless system, it requires a minimum signal-to-noise ratio (SNR) to extract the signal from the noise, and this SNR bounds its range and accuracy. Specifically, the maximum distance at which Vital-Radio detects users is 8m. This is because the SNR drops with user distance from the device.
3. *Quasi-static Requirement:* Our implementation measures the vital signs only for quasi-static users (e.g., typing, watching TV). This is because signal variations due to full body motion would otherwise overwhelm the small variations due to vital signs, and prevent Vital-Radio from capturing the minute movements.
4. *Non-human Motion:* Vital-Radio uses FMCW to separate reflections from different objects in space; hence, it can separate the reflection of various moving objects (e.g., humans, fans, pets). It then analyzes the reflections of each moving object to detect breathing. Since the periodicity of breathing is much lower than fans, the device never confuses a fan as a human. Even if the device confuses a fan for a human, it will not affect the vital signs of the real humans since their signals are separated from the fans by FMCW. However, it may still identify the presence of a pet and output its breathing and heart rate assuming it is another user in the environment.

CONCLUSION AND FUTURE OPPORTUNITIES

The HCI community has significant literature on the use of physiological sensing for various applications [38, 30, 9, 23]. In particular, HCI researchers have used physiological sensing to *evaluate user experience* including emotional reactions, stress levels, cognitive performance, and user engagement. But, a key concern with past sensors (e.g., oximeters, EEG, FNIRs, GSR) is that they require direct contact with the user's body, and hence may affect a user's response. In contrast, Vital-Radio doesn't require users to to be aware of its presence, and hence doesn't interfere with user experience.

Additionally, Vital-Radio enables *new interface and interaction capabilities*. For example, it may be incorporated into user interfaces to adapt to a user without requiring him to wear sensors. Also, it can enable environments to adapt the music or lighting by sensing the user's vital signs and inferring his mood. Further, a user walking up to a Vital-Radio-enabled kiosk in an unfamiliar location (such as an airport) might receive customized assistance based on his stress level.

Beyond these applications, we believe that Vital-Radio can impact a wide array of areas in HCI including quantified self, smart homes, elderly care, personal health and well-being, and mobile emotional sensing.[10]

Acknowledgements – The authors thank the members of the NET-MIT group for their feedback, and the reviewers for their insightful comments. This research is supported by NSF. The Microsoft Research PhD Fellowship has supported Fadel Adib. We thank members of the MIT Center for Wireless Networks and Mobile Computing: Amazon.com, Cisco, Google, Intel, MediaTek, Microsoft, and Telefonica for their interest and support.

[10]While we built our radio for flexible development/control, FMCW radios are available on the market [2] and can be used for the above applications once augmented with our algorithm in software.

REFERENCES

1. Alice PDx. `http://www.healthcare.philips.com/main/homehealth/sleep/alicepdx/default.wpd`. Phillips.
2. FMCW Transceivers. `http://www.siversima.com/`. SiversIMA.
3. iBabyGuard. `http://www.ibabyguard.com/`.
4. Kai Medical. `http://www.kaimedical.com/`.
5. Aardal, O., Paichard, Y., Brovoll, S., Berger, T., Lande, T. S., and Hamran, S.-E. Physical working principles of medical radar. *Biomedical Engineering, IEEE Trans. on* (2013).
6. Adib, F., Kabelac, Z., Katabi, D., and Miller, R. C. 3D Tracking via Body Radio Reflections. In *Usenix NSDI* (2014).
7. Anitori, L., de Jong, A., and Nennie, F. Fmcw radar for life-sign detection. In *IEEE Radar Conference* (2009).
8. Balakrishnan, G., Durand, F., and Guttag, J. Detecting pulse from head motions in video. In *IEEE CVPR* (2013).
9. Bargas-Avila, J. A., and Hornbæk, K. Old wine in new bottles or novel challenges: a critical analysis of empirical studies of user experience. In *ACM CHI* (2011).
10. Callahan, J., Cox, D., Hoffman, K., O'shea, D., Pollatsek, H., and Senechal, L. *Calculus in context: the five college calculus project, Chapter 7 (Periodicity)*. WH Freeman, 1995.
11. Chi, Y., Jung, T.-P., and Cauwenberghs, G. Dry-contact and noncontact biopotential electrodes: Methodological review. *Biomedical Engineering, IEEE Reviews in* (2010).
12. CNET. Do wristband heart trackers actually work? A checkup. http://www.cnet.com/news/how-accurate-are-wristband-heart-rate-monitors/.
13. Cole, C. R., Blackstone, E. H., Pashkow, F. J., Snader, C. E., and Lauer, M. S. Heart-rate recovery immediately after exercise as a predictor of mortality. *New England Journal of Medicine* (1999).
14. de Chazal, P., O'Hare, E., Fox, N., and Heneghan, C. Assessment of sleep/wake patterns using a non-contact biomotion sensor. In *IEEE EMBS* (2008).
15. Droitcour, A. D., Boric-Lubecke, O., and Kovacs, G. T. Signal-to-noise ratio in doppler radar system for heart and respiratory rate measurements. *Microwave Theory and Techniques, IEEE Trans.* (2009).
16. Droitcour, Amy D et. al. Range correlation and i/q performance benefits in single-chip silicon doppler radars for noncontact cardiopulmonary monitoring. *Microwave Theory and Techniques, IEEE Trans.* (2004).
17. Fletcher, R., and Han, J. Low-cost differential front-end for doppler radar vital sign monitoring. In *IEEE MTT* (2009).
18. Garmin. Heart Rate Monitor. https://buy.garmin.com/en-US/US/shop-by-accessories/fitness-sensors/heart-rate-monitor/prod10996.html.
19. GigaOm. Could a breath-monitoring headset improve your health? http://gigaom.com/2013/09/20/could-a-breath-monitoring-headset-improve-your-health/.
20. Gokalp, H., and Clarke, M. Monitoring activities of daily living of the elderly and the potential for its use in telecare and telehealth: a review. *TELEMEDICINE and e-HEALTH* (2013).
21. Guard, C. Wireless Wristband Pulse Oximeter CMS-50FW With Software For Sleep Study. `http://www.clinicalguard.com/wireless-wristband-pulse-oximeter-cms50fw-with-software-for-sleep-study-p-455.html`.
22. Healthcare, F. M. Market for embedded health monitoring-gadgets to hit 170M devices by 2017. `http://www.fiercemobilehealthcare.com/story/market-embedded-health-monitoring-gadgets-hit-170m-devices-2017/2012-08-03`.
23. Hirshfield, L. et. Al. Brain measurement for usability testing and adaptive interfaces: an example of uncovering syntactic workload with functional near infrared spectroscopy. In *ACM CHI* (2009).
24. Imai, K. et. Al. Vagally mediated heart rate recovery after exercise is accelerated in athletes but blunted in patients with chronic heart failure. *Journal of the American College of Cardiology* (1994).
25. InformationWeek. Health-Monitoring Devices Market Outpaces Telehealth. `http://www.informationweek.com/mobile/health-monitoring-devices-market-outpaces-telehealth/d/d-id/1104636`.
26. Jia, Y. et. Al. Through-wall-radar localization for stationary human based on life-sign detection. In *IEEE RADAR* (2013).
27. Kaltiokallio, O. et. Al. Non-invasive respiration rate monitoring using a single cots tx-rx pair. In *ACM/IEEE IPSN* (2014).
28. Lanata, A et. Al. Comparative evaluation of susceptibility to motion artifact in different wearable systems for monitoring respiratory rate.
29. Lin, J. et. Al. Microwave apexcardiography. *Microwave Theory and Techniques, IEEE Trans.* (1979).
30. Mahlke, S., and Thüring, M. Studying antecedents of emotional experiences in interactive contexts. In *ACM CHI* (2007).
31. Mayo Clinic. What's a normal resting heart rate? http://www.mayoclinic.org/healthy-living/fitness/expert-answers/heart-rate/faq-20057979.
32. Min, J. et. Al. Toss nturn: Smartphone as sleep and sleep quality detector. In *ACM CHI* (2014).
33. Oppenheim, A., Schafer, R., Buck, J., et al. *Discrete-time signal processing*. Prentice Hall, 1989.
34. Patwari, N. et. Al. Breathfinding: A wireless network that monitors and locates breathing in a home. *Selected Topics in Signal Processing, IEEE Journal of* (2014).
35. Petterson, M. et. Al. The effect of motion on pulse oximetry and its clinical significance. *Anesthesia & Analgesia* (2007).
36. Pinheiro, E., Postolache, O., and Girão, P. Theory and developments in an unobtrusive cardiovascular system representation: ballistocardiography. *The open biomedical engineering journal* (2010).
37. Steele, R., Lo, A., Secombe, C., and Wong, Y. K. Elderly persons perception and acceptance of using wireless sensor networks to assist healthcare. *International journal of medical informatics* (2009).
38. Tan, C. et. Al. Combining think-aloud and physiological data to understand video game experiences. In *ACM CHI* (2014).
39. Tse, D., and Vishwanath, P. *Fundamentals of Wireless Communications*. Cambridge University Press, 2005.
40. U.S. National Library of Medicine MedLine Plus. Heart-respiratory monitor - infantsShare. `http://www.nlm.nih.gov/medlineplus/ency/article/007236.htm`.
41. U.S. National Library of Medicine MedLine Plus. Rapid Shallow Breathing. `http://www.nlm.nih.gov/medlineplus/ency/article/007198.htm`.
42. Venkatesh, S., Anderson, C., Rivera, N., and Buehrer, R. Implementation and analysis of respiration-rate estimation using impulse-based uwb. In *IEEE MILCOMM* (2005).
43. Vivonoetics. Respiration: Single or Dual-Band. `http://vivonoetics.com/products/vivosense/analyzing/respiration-single-or-dual-band/`.
44. Wu, H.-Y., Rubinstein, M., Shih, E., Guttag, J., Durand, F., and Freeman, W. Eulerian video magnification for revealing subtle changes in the world. *ACM SIGGRAPH* (2012).
45. Xu, Y., Wu, S., Chen, C., Chen, J., and Fang, G. A novel method for automatic detection of trapped victims by ultrawideband radar. *Geoscience and Remote Sensing, IEEE Trans. on* (2012).
46. Yang, R. et. Al. Making sustainability sustainable: Challenges in the design of eco-interaction technologies. In *ACM CHI* (2014).
47. Yarovoy, A. et. Al. Uwb radar for human being detection. *Aerospace and Electronic Systems Magazine, IEEE* (2006).
48. Zaffaroni, A., de Chazal, P., Heneghan, C., Boyle, P., Mppm, P. R., and McNicholas, W. T. Sleepminder: an innovative contact-free device for the estimation of the apnoea-hypopnoea index. In *IEEE EMBS* (2009).

Balancing Accuracy and Fun: Designing Camera Based Mobile Games for Implicit Heart Rate Monitoring

Teng Han[2], Xiang Xiao[1], Lanfei Shi[2], John Canny[3], Jingtao Wang[1]

[1]Department of Computer Science,
[2]Intelligent Systems Program,
University of Pittsburgh, Pittsburgh, PA, USA
{teh24@, xiangxiao@cs., las231@, jingtaow@cs.}pitt.edu

[3]Computer Science Division,
University of California at Berkeley,
387 Soda Hall, Berkeley, CA, USA
jfc@cs.berkeley.edu

ABSTRACT

Heart rate monitoring is widely used in clinical care, fitness training, and stress management. However, tracking individuals' heart rates faces two major challenges, namely *equipment availability* and *user motivation*. In this paper, we present a novel technique, LivePulse Games (LPG), to measure users' heart rates in real time by having them play games on unmodified mobile phones. With LPG, the heart rate is calculated by detecting changes in transparency of users' fingertips via the built-in camera of a mobile device. More importantly, LPG integrate users' camera lens covering actions as an essential control mechanism in game play, and detect heart rates implicitly from *intermittent* lens covering actions. We explore the design space and trade-offs of LPG through three rounds of iterative design. In a 12-subject user study, we found that LPG are fun to play and can measure heart rates accurately. We also report the insights for balancing measurement speed, accuracy, and entertainment value in LPG.

Author Keywords

Heart rate, mobile phone, multi-modal interface, game design, serious game, ECG, quantified self.

ACM Classification Keywords

H5.2. Information interfaces and presentation (e.g., HCI): User Interfaces.

General Terms

Design, Experimentation, Human Factors.

INTRODUCTION

Heart rate is one important vital sign in health care [6, 29]. For healthy people, resting heart rate (RHR) is also an essential physiological marker of physical fitness [7, 30, 38], and expected life span [13]. Heart rate has been used in fitness training [19, 20] and competitive sports for managing work-out intensity and balancing physical exertion. Both continual readings of heart rates [5, 15, 37, 33] and heart rate variability, a.k.a. HRV [27, 29, 32, 33], can predict a user's physiological state, including cognitive workload and mental stress levels, in contexts such as computer user interfaces [29, 33], traffic control [29], longitudinal monitoring of emotion and food intake [5], and intelligent tutoring [15]. Therefore, the efficient measurement of heart rate can be of great significance across scenarios involving physical health, mental activities or a combination of both.

CHI 2015, April 18 - 23 2015, Seoul, Republic of Korea
Copyright 2015 ACM 978-1-4503-3145-6/15/04...$15.00
http://dx.doi.org/10.1145/2702123.2702502

Unfortunately, most heart rate measurement methods are either time-consuming [1], or require special measurement equipment [25] that may not be available to a wide audience. For example, manual pulse counting with fingers may be tedious, and inaccurate. More precise methods include the Electrocardiograph (ECG) [22, 25] and pulse oximeters [25, 35]. These dedicated heart rate monitoring devices share at least three disadvantages. First, the costs of these devices could prevent wide adoption in everyday life. Second, it is not convenient to carry and use the devices "on the go". Last but not least, existing methods provide little immediate benefits or *intrinsic motivation* to users and thus may be tedious to track heart rate in a longitudinal setting.

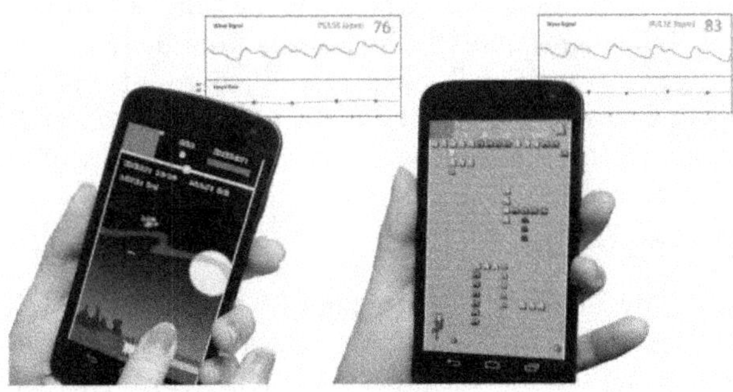

Figure 1. Real-time heart rate measurement via LivePulse Games (left: City Defender, right: Gold Miner).

To overcome the limitations of existing techniques, we have developed LivePulse Games (LPG, figure 1) to measure users' heart rates in real time by having them play serious games on unmodified mobile phones. LPG calculate heart rates by detecting the transparency change of fingertips via the built-in camera (i.e. commodity camera

[1] In both the preparation phase and the actual measurement stage.

based photoplethysmography (PPG) [2, 4, 12, 26]). More importantly, LPG integrate users' camera lens covering actions as essential parts of the game so as to detect heart rate *implicitly* during game play. LPG combine unique designs in both algorithms and game play to achieve accurate and robust heart rate extraction through intermittent finger lens covering actions. With the increasing popularization of smartphones, LPG have the potential to measure heart rate longitudinally in a natural and enjoyable way.

Different from biofeedback games [21, 23, 31] that *use* heart rates to *augment* game play, LPG is a game based approach for heart rate *measurement*. To avoid confounders, we intentionally choose not to use heart rates collected from LPG to change game states at this stage.

This paper offers four important contributions:

- Expanding the design space of camera based heart rate monitoring from continual, explicit signals to *intermittent* and *implicit* signals;
- A robust and accurate algorithm with fast bootstrap time that can detect heart rate from noisy and intermittent signals in real time on mobile devices;
- A set of insights and trade-offs learned from designing engaging LivePulse Games that integrate lens covering actions as an essential control mechanism;
- A 12-subject user study that validates the reported approaches and clarifies the feasibility, usability, and design insights involved.

In the following sections, we first explain in detail the algorithm for detecting human heart rate through intermittent camera lens covering actions; next, we discuss the trade-offs in game design when balancing detection accuracy, detection speed, and game intensity; after that, we share the insights and lessons learned from three rounds of iterative design. Finally, we report the results of a 12-subject user study, including the accuracy of LPG and the impact of game intensity on the speed and accuracy of heart rate measurement.

RELATED WORK

Heart Rate Detection Techniques

The most widely adopted approaches for detecting heart rate are based on Electrocardiography (ECG or EKG, usually in the form factor of chest band, wrist band, or watch) and pulse oximetry (i.e. blood oxygen saturation or blood oxygenation). Researchers have created highly portable, low power, wireless mobile ECG [22] and blood oxygen saturation measurement devices [35] in the past. A state-of-the-art device, the Berkeley Tricorder [22] by Naima and Canny, is capable of measuring a subject's ECG, EMG, respiration, and motion via a 2 by 2 inch Bluetooth device. Despite the steady drop on manufacturing costs [25] for such devices, they are still not readily available for most users in an everyday setting. For example, Depending on the brand, form factor, and communication interface supported, a heart rate monitoring watch (e.g. Omron HR-100CN, MIO Alpha, Basis, or Apple Watch) costs from US$30 to US$350 as of September 2014. Low cost devices like Omron HR-100CN usually do not have digital interfaces for sending data to computers.

LivePulse Games rely on photoplethysmography (PPG) [36] to detect heart rates. Although the fundamental mechanism of PPG through commodity built-in cameras on mobile phones has been explored by both commercial applications (e.g. Instant Heart Rate [12], Cardiograph [4]) and researchers [2, 26] in the past, all existing methods require users to cover and hold the mobile phone camera lens intentionally and steadily for an extended amount of time before receiving heart rate estimates. While these systems eliminated the equipment availability challenge, none of them attempted to address the human *motivation* challenge involved. In comparison, LPG explore the feasibility of extracting heart rates from *implicit, intermittent* lens covering actions during mobile game plays, and design engaging mobile games that balance measurement speed, accuracy and entertainment value.

It's also possible to calculate heart rate by recording and analyzing thermal changes [10], color changes [27, 28], and involuntary motion [1] of human faces in video. However, such approaches are more sensitive to environmental illumination changes and the component analysis (PCA [1] or ICA [27, 28]) techniques used also require users to stay still for an extended amount of time (e.g. 60+ second). Still, facial video analysis from a mobile device's front camera could be an interesting future direction to explore with LivePulse Games.

Heart Rate in Interactions

Heart rate has been used by researchers in fitness training, balancing exertion [19, 20] in social sports, measuring mental workload [29] and stress [32], and developing adaptive intelligent tutoring systems (ITS) [15].

TripleBeat by Oliveira et al. [24] is a mobile fitness training application that uses heart rate measured from an ECG instrumented chestband to encourage runners to better achieve a predefined exercise goal. Nenonen et al. [23] allowed users to control parameters of video games (e.g. speed, slope of the road) by adjusting their heart rate. Mueller et al [19, 20] and Stach et al [31] leveraged the heart rate as an input to balance participants' performance in jogging to motivate people with lower fitness level to "exercise together". Instead of *using* heart rates as a supplemental *input* channel to control the in-game parameters adaptively, LivePulse Games *motivate* users to play games and heart rates are generated as an *implicit output* of game plays.

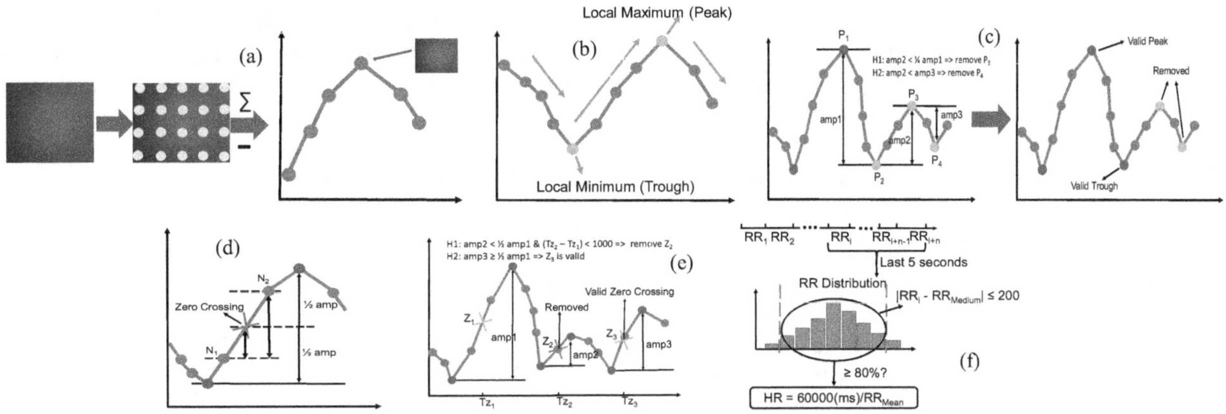

Figure 2. Major steps of the LivePulse algorithm (a. signal preprocessing; b. locating raw local peaks & valleys; c. locating valid peaks & valleys; d. locating raw zero-crossings; e. locating valid zero-crossings; f. calculating heart rate).

A user's changing heart rhythms affect not only the heart itself but also the brain's ability to process information and manage emotion. Researchers have discovered that both the heart rate [37] and heart rate variability (HRV) [32] have strong correlations with stress and persistently elevated heart rate is a sign of chronic stress [37]. It's worth noticing that both heart rate and HRV can and are regularly used for short term stress measurements. In [33], heart rate was a more accurate marker of external stress than HRV. Heart rate will be confounded by physical activity but the user will be aware of whether or not they have been active, and elevated HR otherwise is a sign of stress. Rowe [29] investigated the use of heart rate signals to assess the impact of a monitoring interface on user mental effort. Poh et al [27] demonstrated the feasibility of extracting Heart rate variability (HRV) from 1 minute of continual color facial images[2]. We believe adaptive systems that infer cognitive workload [29], attention [15], or emotion [5] from heart rates could benefit from LivePulse Games' pervasive, non-invasive real-time heart rate monitoring.

Serious Games

Many researchers have explored the use of games as a motivation mechanism for performing desirable but challenging/tedious activities such as education [34], fitness training, behavior change [5], and device calibration [8]. LivePulse Games are serious games designed from the ground up to balance the speed and accuracy of heart rate tracking with fun in game play.

DESIGNING LIVEPULSE GAMES

There are two main challenges in designing LivePulse Games. The first task is to formulate an algorithm that can detect human heart rate *reliably* and *efficiently* on unmodified mobile phones, even during noisy and *sporadic* activities. This task eliminates the need for specialized heart rate monitoring equipment, making it feasible to measure heart rate in different contexts. The second task consists of designing interactions that integrate the slightly "bizarre" requirement in PPG (i.e. covering the camera lens with fingertip and holding it steadily) *naturally* into mobile game play. The second task addresses the motivational challenges in heart rate monitoring, converting heart rate measurement from a dull routine into a fun and engaging activity.

Camera Based Heart Rate Detection

LivePulse Games rely on the back camera of mobile phones to detect heart rates. The underlining theory is: in every cardiac circle, the heart pumps blood to the capillary vessels of a human body, including fingertips. The arrival of fresh blood changes the transparency of fingertips. Such transparency changes correlate directly with heart rates, and can be detected by the built-in camera when the user covers the lens of the camera with her finger tip.

Although camera based heart rate detection algorithms have been reported before [2, 26], the previous algorithms were not optimized for extracting heart rates from *noisy* and *intermittent* covering actions and both algorithms require a long bootstrap time before generating the first estimate (20 seconds in [2], 9 seconds in [26]) in clean and continual measurements. For commercial products such as Instant Heart Rate [12], and Cardiograph [4], their algorithms were never disclosed and neither app could extract heart rates if there are finger movements during the measurement[3]. To achieve better robustness and shorter bootstrap time for noisy, *intermittent* signals from *implicit* user interactions, we designed our own algorithm that meets the speed, accuracy and robustness requirements of LPG.

Instead of using component analysis and then transforming signals to the frequency domain [1, 27, 28], the LivePulse algorithm extracts heart rate information directly from the relatively noisy temporal signal. We made this decision for

[2] In standardized *clinical* diagnosis [18], 24-hour is required for measuring *long-term* HRV. Malik et al [18] also suggested 5 min for reliable *short-term* HRV and 1-2 min as the minimal time HRV in *clinical* use.

[3] According to the authors' experiments in July 2014, the minimal bootstrap time for the 4.0 version of Instant Heart Rate [12] is 7 seconds and 15 seconds of uninterrupted holding is required for a reliable estimate. The app resets its progress when there is significant finger movement during the measurement.

two reasons: 1) Given the intermittent nature of the envisioned usage scenario, we do not assume that consistent, uninterrupted signals will arrive for an extended amount of time, which is usually necessary for transformations such as PCA/ICA; 2) We expect the LivePulse algorithm could run efficiently on mobile devices in real-time and leave enough CPU power to handle the graphics and multimedia effects during game plays.

In the LivePulse algorithm, the camera is set in preview mode, capturing 176x144 pixel color images at a rate of 30 frames per second (a minimal frame rate of 15 fps is required). We disable the automatic focus function and the automatic white balance function to avoid interference with our algorithm. Optionally, we can turn the built-in flashlight on to improve performance in low illumination conditions.

When a lens covering action is detected (LPG uses the *Static LensGesture* detection algorithm in [40]), the LivePulse algorithm extracts heart rates via a 6-step, heuristic based process detailed below.

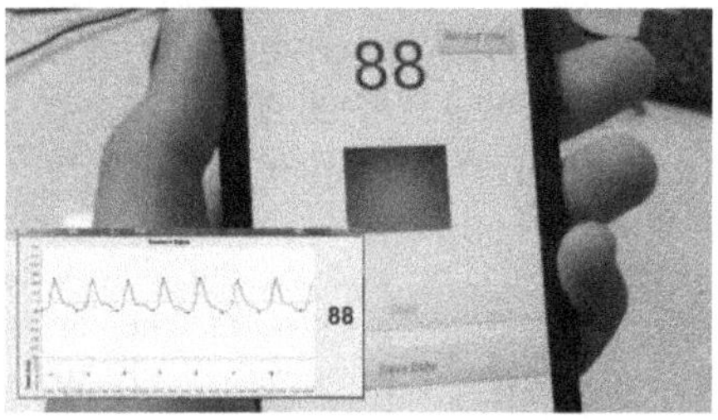

Figure 3. A prototype of LivePulse running on a mobile phone with real-time heart-rate signals shown in a PC application.

Step 1: The LivePulse algorithm first converts each frame into one time-stamped heart beat sample point via equal distance sampling and the summation of 800 points on the Y channel in each frame (Figure 2.a). The signal is flipped in y-axis to match waveform output tradition of existing PPG techniques [36]. *Step 2*: The algorithm then detects all the local peaks and valleys in the converted temporal sequence signal by measuring the local curvature changes (Figure 2.b). *Step 3*: Adjustable threshold based heuristics are applied to eliminate small and noisy local minima/maxima points (Figure 2.c). *Step 4 and 5*: Instead of estimating heart rates from two adjacent peaks/valleys directly, we found that it is more reliable to estimate and interpolate the time stamps of zero-crossing points [4] between peaks and valleys and then derive heart rates from the time differences between two adjacent time stamps of zero-crossing points (Figure 2.d 2.e). *Step 6*: To further improve the robustness of LivePulse, we save and sort the time stamp distances between adjacent zero-crossing points during the past five seconds. Real time heart rate is reported when at least 80% of the time-stamp distances are within a given variation range (25%) (Figure 2.f). Since the heuristic in step 6 doesn't rely on hard coded parameters for noise filtering, it worked robustly in LivePulse Games involving frequent motion gestures.

LivePulse can extract heart rates from people with different skin melanin levels (e.g. white, yellow, black) when the flash is on according to our informal tests.

Figure 3 shows a tool we created for debugging the LivePulse algorithm. Finger transparency information are collected on mobile phones and streamed to a PC for visualization and analysis. After debugging, the actual LivePulse Games run solely on mobile devices in real time.

Intermittent Lens Covering Actions

The above method requires users to cover the camera lens with their fingers for an extended duration. When there are breaks in the heart beat input (caused by releasing the finger from the camera lens), our algorithm suspends updating zero-crossing intervals until a finger covering action is detected. The LivePulse algorithm then applies heuristic steps 1 - 4 on temporal samples after the new covering action, concatenates the first newly detected zero-crossing point, and updates the time stamps for all the follow-up zero-crossing points by subtracting the time gap lapsed between adjacent camera lens covering actions. When compared with existing frequency domain techniques [27, 28], our technique has a short bootstrap latency (mostly 2-3 seconds), and is capable of extracting heart rates from intermittent covering scenarios that existing systems [4, 12] couldn't handle.

From LivePulse to LivePulse Games

In order to make the heart rate monitoring task more engaging, we have designed games that leverage the LivePulse algorithm and integrate heart beat measurement *implicitly* in the game play.

Two major concerns arise when designing LivePulse Games. First, what is the best trade-off in balancing the fun/engaging factor and the measurement accuracy during a game play? Second, what are the effective techniques to integrate lens covering actions required by LivePulse *naturally* into the games?

We clarify the first concern with a thought experiment. According to the working mechanism of LivePulse, the algorithm works best when a user covers the camera lens completely and steadily all the time. Following this trait, in one extreme situation, we could use the camera lens as a "*power switch*", i.e. the game continues when a user covers the camera lens, and pauses when the finger leaves the lens. Although heart rates can be measured with minimal interruptions, such scenario will lead to bad game playing experiences for two reasons: 1) the lens covering action is actually isolated from the actual in-game interactions; and 2) the finger covering action needed becomes an *extra*

[4] The zero crossing line is dynamic, defined as the line with the mean Y values between two adjacent valley and peak (figure 2.d). The time stamps of zero crossing points (i.e. z1, z2, z3 in figure 2.e) are linear interpolated values between two adjacent time stamps.

burden rather than an entertaining factor. As a result, users could feel bored and start to look for equivalent games that do not require lens covering.

In the other extreme situation, if the lens covering action is used as a high frequency input channel, e.g. directly controlling missile firing in a "shoot-em-up" video game, the game play could be engaging and satisfying, but the underlying algorithm may have trouble in getting reliable readings from extremely brief and unstable finger touches.

As illustrated by the two extreme situations, there exists a performance/reliability vs. fun trade-off highlighted in designing LPG. We keep this trade-off in mind and we also run controlled experiments to quantify the trade-offs by manipulating the intensity of games in our user study.

In addition to the brute-force "*power switch*" metaphor, the lens covering gesture can serve as a "*trigger*" to activate an in-game event. In this scenario the camera lens is no different[5] from a push button mounted on the back of the mobile phone. In this mode, the timing and frequency of covering are used in game control. The lens covering gesture can also be used as a "*clutch*" or a gas pedal. In this paradigm, covering the lens steadily will switch certain in-game object into a different mode (e.g. charging, accelerating etc). In the "*clutch*" mode, players use the timing and duration of covering as the primary control mechanism. With these observations in mind, we explore the design space of using lens covering actions by integrating diversified lens control mechanisms in different LivePulse Games.

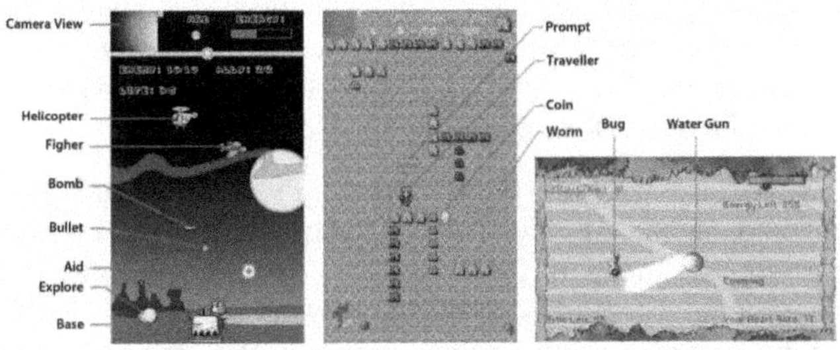

Figure 4. Screenshots of the three games: City Defender (left), Gold Miner (middle), and Bug Defender (right).

There are two supplementary benefits for integrating the unique affordance of users' lens covering gestures in game play. First, this approach could free a user's index finger in the hand holding the phone for game play. This index finger stays idle during most interactions. Second, the edge and bezel of cameras are usually made of different materials and on different surface levels, which could provide natural tactile feedback for direct touch operations on the lens.

When designing LPG, we also explore different combinations of input modalities (touch screen, accelerometer), and interaction types (one-hand, two-hand) in game design. These intentional design space variations allow us to explore the impact of lens covering frequency to heart rate measurement accuracy, as well as the impact of device motion in game play (e.g. wrist rotation, screen tapping) to heart rate measurements.

Through three rounds of iterative design, we created three LivePulse Games: City Defender, Gold Miner, and Bug Defender (figure 4) to test pervasive, non-invasive heart rate monitoring on mobile phones.

City Defender

The City Defender game (figure 4, left) allows users to protect a city by controlling a powerful, but slow anti-aircraft artillery. Users tap on the screen to fire bullets from artillery, move the artillery and collect rescue packages. Each user action costs a certain amount of energy and users lose the ability to fire or move when the energy bar is empty. Users can cover and hold the lens to recharge the energy bar gradually. However, the antiaircraft artillery cannot be moved or fired when the energy bar is charging. Destroying all the enemy fighters clears a stage and being hit by five bombs loses the game.

In order to get high scores in City Defender, users need to make strategic plans on the timing and frequency of four mutually exclusive activities (i.e. firing, charging, collecting rescue packages, and dodging enemy attacks) and execute them properly. For example, collecting a rescue package may not be the right choice if such action moves the artillery to a disadvantaged position.

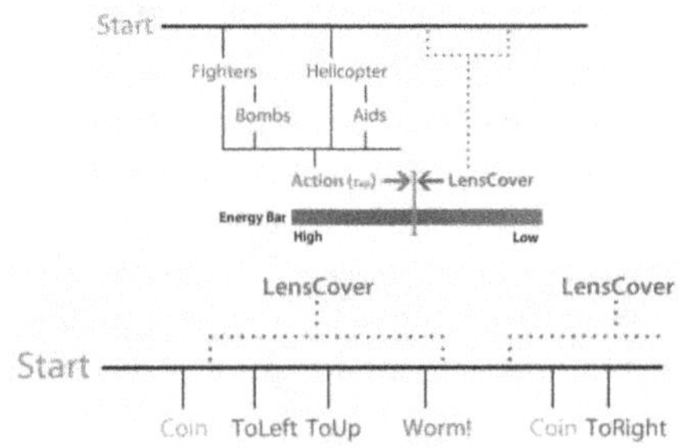

Figure 5. Play workflows for CityDefender (top) and Gold Miner (bottom).

City Defender requires users to perform coordinated actions with both hands. The charging action is completed by the user's index finger on the hand holding the phone, and the firing/moving actions are completed on the touch screen by the other hand. Figure 5 (top) shows the play workflow of City Defender.

Gold Miner

Gold Miner (Figure 4, middle) is similar to the classic snake game on Nokia phones with unique tweaks. In this game, users control an explorer to collect randomly placed coins in the scene. Users tilt the phone in different directions (i.e. left, right, up, and down) to move the explorer. The explorer cannot hit bushes (staying still) or enemy worms (chasing the explorer when the exploring is

---

[5] Despite the 33 ms latency caused by the camera frame rate and the 2.7 ms latency for detecting a lens covering action [40].

moving) during movements. Worms start chasing the explorer only when the explorer is moving. The camera lens is used as a clutch to initiate motion gestures for controlling the explorer in Gold Miner. Releasing the finger from the camera lens will stop both the explorer and the chasing worm.

To become a successful player of Gold Miner, users need to 1) decide wisely on when to move and when to stop (associated with using the lens covering action as a clutch); 2) planning long and feasible moving trajectories and move in-game explorer timely via phone tilting. Figure 5 (bottom) shows the play workflow of Gold Miner.

Bug Defender

Bug Defender (Figure 4, right) is a farming game where users aim to kill worms in their farms. Users cover the camera lens to charge a water gun and tap on the screen fire the water gun and shot at the location tapped. Worms can only be killed when the worm color matches the corresponding screen orientation, i.e. when red worms appear, users need to put the mobile phone in landscape mode and shoot; when blue worms appear, users need to put the mobile phone to portrait mode.

Implementation

LivePulse Games were written in Java running on the Android 4.0 operating system. We used the AndEngine (http://www.andengine.org/) for OpenGL ES encapsulation and game scene management. Excluding third party libraries, the three LivePulse Games have a total of 10,398 lines of code in Java. Our games have been tested on Google Nexus S, Galaxy Nexus, and Nexus 4 smart phones.

Iterative Design Process

LivePulse Games went through three rounds of iterative design. Major design changes were made based on users' comments and feedback in two pilot studies (six subjects and four subjects respectively). LPG were able to extract heart rate information from all the game play sessions, the mean error rate (MER) in the pilot study sessions were satisfactory (< 7%).

In addition to bug fixes, and adding additional in-game feedback (e.g. the low energy alarm, lens covering state), major usability issues identified and addressed through pilot studies include:

Engaging both causal users and "hard-core" players. Pilot study users have highly diversified experiences in mobile game play. While it could take a non-gamer a couple of minutes and a few rounds of trial-and-error to learn to survive in LPG, some "hard-core" players had already felt "not challenging enough" within the same amount of time. To address this issue, we revised LPG to provide multiple levels of intensity under the same play workflow by varying the frequency, number, appearance pattern of enemies (e.g. enemy fighters, coins, and bugs) on screen. We also added the Producer-Consumer pattern [3] to the play flow of each game to increase the diversity of game play and give "hard-core" players opportunities to devise and execute wise strategic plans to unlock higher score and achievements in the game.

Avoiding modality overloading. For example, the initial design of Bug Defender requires input from three different modalities, i.e. screen tapping, lens covering, and screen orientation change. While participants found the idea of multiple input modalities exciting, pilot study results showed that it was also challenging to coordinate three modalities accurately in parallel at the learning stage, even for "hard-core" players. As a result, when adopting multiple input modalities as an engaging factor, we enforce the rule of "no more than two parallel modalities" in initial levels for all the updated LPG.

USER STUDY

Although we have confirmed the feasibility of LivePulse Games in the two pilot studies, a formal user study was necessary to understand the capabilities and limitations of LPG as a new mechanism for implicit heart rate measurement. We had three goals for the study. One was to quantify the accuracy of LPG and observe the impact of LPG play on heart rate (i.e. will playing LPG confound a user's resting heart rate?); The second goal was to quantitatively investigate the trade-offs between game playing intensity, entertainment and the accuracy of heart rate monitoring. Lastly, we were interested in collecting subjective feedback and observing how users play LPG.

Experimental Design

The study consisted of four parts:

Overview. We first gave participants a brief introduction to LivePulse Games and then collected background information of participants. We demonstrated City Defender and Gold Miner to the participants and explained the working mechanisms behind these games.

Measuring Heart Rate Accuracy. We measured participants' heart rates in both resting condition and two gaming settings. In the resting condition, we used a standalone LivePulse application running on a mobile phone (Figure 3) and a pulse oximeter. We let participants sit comfortably in a chair, holding the mobile phone with their left hands, and using the index finger of the left hand to cover the camera lens. We instructed participants to apply comfortable pressure when covering the lens. We attached the pulse oximeter on the index fingers of the participants' right hands. The measurement setting of Gold Miner was the same as the resting condition, because Gold Miner supports one handed game play. Since City Defender requires both hands, we attached the pulse oximeter to the ring finger of the right hand.

Playing Games at Different Intensity Levels. Participants played the City Defender game and the Gold Miner game with three different intensity levels (i.e. 2 games*3 intensity levels = 6 conditions). Different intensities were achieved by manipulating the quantity and appearance frequency of in-game enemies. Participants spent roughly two minutes in

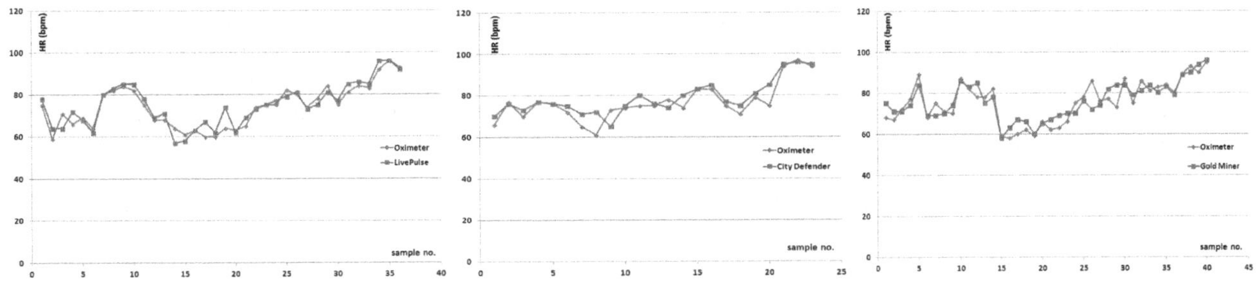

Figure 7. Heart rates (bpm) of 12 subjects (left:resting mode, middle: playing City Defender, right: playing Gold Miner) from LivePulse, LivePulse Games (red) and Oximeter (blue).

each condition. Participants took breaks between different conditions, but they were not allowed to pause or exit from the game in each condition. *The order of conditions was counterbalanced.*

Qualitative Feedback. Closing questionnaires were collected after participants completed all tasks. We also asked participants to comment on each game's difficulty levels, and describe their general feeling towards the LivePulse Games.

Participants and Apparatus

12 participants (3 female) between 19 and 27 years of age participated in our study. All the participants were undergraduate or graduate students in a local university.

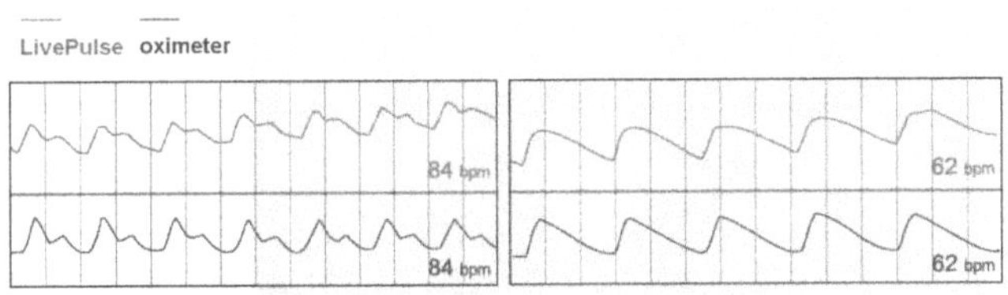

Figure 6. 14 seconds of sample heart beat signals from LivePulse (red) and oximeter (blue).

Our experiments were completed on a Google Galaxy Nexus Smartphone with a 4.65 inch, 720 x 1280 pixels display, 1.2 GHZ dual core ARM Cortex-a9 processor, running Android 4.1. It has a 5 mega-pixel back camera and a LED flash. We also used a CMS 50D pulse oximeter with a USB interface to measure heart rate. This pulse oximeter is an FDA approved, medical grade device. The accuracy of CMS 50D for pulse ratio is +/-2BPM.

EVALUATION RESULTS

LPG were able to extract all the 12 participants' heart rates successfully from all the sessions.

Accuracy

Overall, raw heart beat signals from LivePulse and the oximeter were highly consistent in both beat-to-beat interval and the actual wave shape (Figure 6).

To compare the accuracy of LivePulse quantitatively, we aligned and re-sampled readings from both LivePulse and the oximeter to 20 HZ. When treating the readings from the oximeter as the gold standard, the Mean Error Rate (MER) of LivePulse was 3.9% (-7 ~ +5 bpm, Figure 7, left) in the resting condition, 4.6% (-8 ~ +11 bpm, Figure 7, middle) when playing City Defender, and 5.0% (-14 ~ + 11, Figure 7, right) when playing Gold Miner. Analysis of variance results showed that the differences in heart rate readings from LivePulse and the oximeter were not statistically significant in all the three conditions: LivePulse in resting condition vs. Oximeter($F_{1,\ 11}$ = 1.64, p = 0.13, n.s.), Oximeter vs. City Defender ($F_{1,11}$ = 0.83, p = 0.40, n.s.), Oximeter vs. Gold Miner ($F_{1,11}$ = 0.23, p = 0.82, n.s.). We also computed a Pearson product-moment correlation coefficient and there was a significant positive correlation between readings from LivePulse and oximeter, r = 0.98, t = 15.5, $p < 10^{-7}$.

Considering that the CMS 50D oximeter has an accuracy of +/- 2%, the accuracies of LPG in both resting condition and actual game settings are satisfactory.

Despite the relatively low MER, the maximal absolute difference could be up to 7 bpm in the resting condition, 11 bpm when playing Gold Miner and 14 bpm in Gold Miner. We attribute these outliers to noise caused by finger position/posture changes and background illumination changes. We suspect the higher maximal error rate in Gold Miner was caused by the extensive wrist movements in game plays. These outliers can be further eliminated by applying a low pass filtering algorithm or heuristics [1, 28] in situations where accuracy is more important than responsiveness.

Paradoxically, we didn't observe a major difference in heart rates between the idle mode and two active game play sessions. Among all three conditions tested, subjects' heart rates varied similarly from 56 bpm to 97 bpm. We believe this observation was caused by the "*casual*" style of current LPG and the relatively brief game play sessions. It is possible that the users' heart rates may change significantly when playing more intensive games for an extended amount of time. One piece of interesting future work would be to predict the resting heart rate from heart rate measured in intensive game play sessions via machine learning should these kinds of differences occur.

City Defender

Figure 8 shows a typical 2-minute game playing session when playing City Defender. The top row shows the raw finger transparency readings after scaling (without applying any noise filtering or interpolation algorithms). The second row shows corresponding heart rate estimates. The follow-up rows show the covering states of the lens, major user input, and the major events in the game respectively. As illustrated in Figure 8, finger transparency readings showed up immediately after each lens covering action. The first valid heart rate estimation appeared roughly 20 seconds after the game began. Interestingly, the first one or two raw finger transparency readings (i.e. within 30-60ms) after a lens covering action were usually noisy. The LPG MER can be further reduced by 1% by simply removing the first transparency reading associated with each lens covering action.

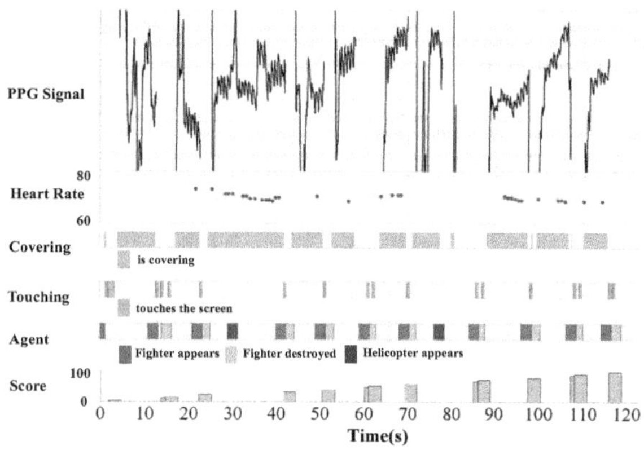

Figure 8. A 2-minute session in City Defender.

In City Defender, with the increase of the in-game intensity, the ratios of valid lens covering sessions[6] and valid lens covering durations[7] decreased consistently (figure 9). The increase of in-game difficulty level led to more frequent switches between lens covering/uncovering actions, as a result, the quality of finger transparency signal drops. In general, around 28% - 37% of lens covering time, or 33% - 43% of the lens covering sessions could generate valid heart rate estimations.

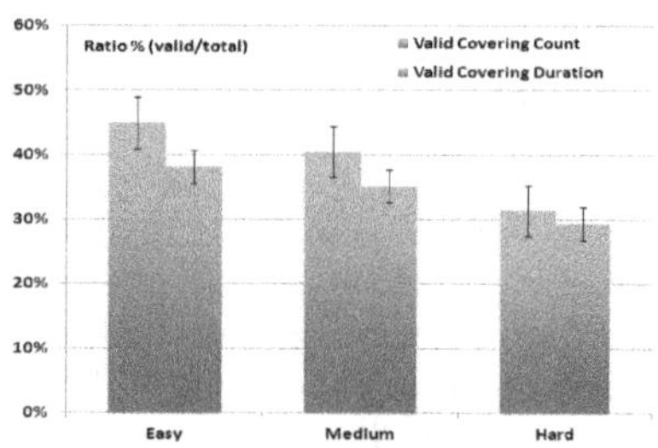

Figure 9. Heart rate estimation quality by difficulty levels in City Defender.

Figure 10 shows the histogram of the covering time needed to generate valid heart rate estimates. In most sessions, LPG generated effective heart rate estimates 2 to 4 seconds after covering the lens. Lens covering actions shorter than 2 seconds were less likely to generate valid heart rate estimates. As a result, when designing a new LivePulse Game, it is imperative to design the game dynamics in a way that a major portion of the in-game lens covering actions are longer than 2 seconds. This empirical parameter also provides an upper bound of game intensity for the current LPG algorithm.

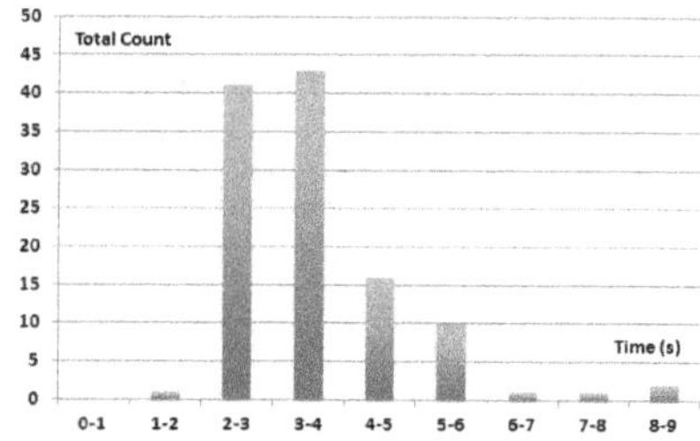

Figure 10. Histogram of time needed to generate the first heart rate estimation in City Defender.

Gold Miner

In Gold Miner, the lens covering action was used as a clutch rather than a trigger. As a result, the lens covering sessions in Gold Miner were fewer but had much longer durations than those in City Defender.

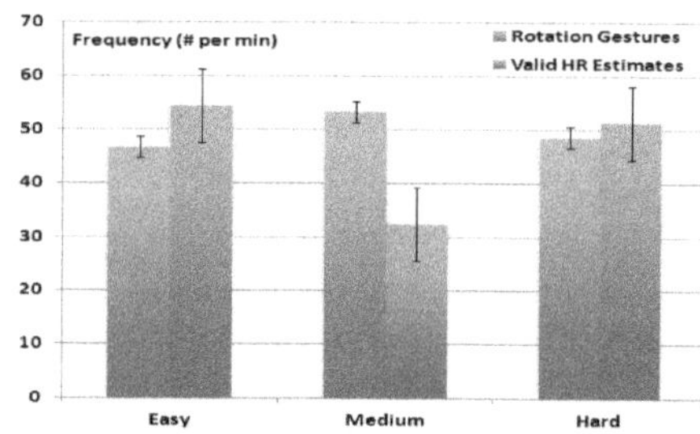

Figure 11: Heart rate estimation quality by difficulty levels in Gold Miner.

Figure 11 shows the impact of game intensity on numbers of rotational gestures detected, and the quality (i.e. number of valid estimates per minute) of heart estimates. Thanks to the strategic planning mechanism in Gold Miner, more intensive levels did not necessarily lead to more frequent rotational gestures and reduced heart rate quality. Although changing intensity level from easy to medium led to more rotational gestures, the number rotational gestures dropped when the intensity level changed from medium to hard. This is because participants started to change game playing strategy when the game intensity reached a certain level. Instead of simply moving the in-game character more frequently, participants started to devise a strategy with less frequent movement but better timing and planning.

DISCUSSIONS

The participants reported highly favorable experiences with LPG. When asked how satisfied with the games overall, the average rating was 4.25 (σ = 0.60) using a five-point Likert scale (5 = strongly favorable, 3 = neutral, 1 = strongly negative). Participants gave an average rating of 4.17 (σ =

[6] Defined as the number of covering sessions that generated heart rate estimates divided by total number of lens covering sessions.

[7] Defined as the total duration of covering sessions that generated heart rate estimates divided by the total duration of lens being covered by finger.

0.80) on the "fun" factor. The average rating was 4.67 (σ = 0.47) on ease of learning.

Sample comments from users include:

'I can get my heart rate after a relaxing game, which is better than barely using the mobile app.'

'I play games frequently and could easily fit a 'healthy' game in. Using an app feels like work'.

'If I do nothing but to wait for a long time, it's boring. But playing game is interesting.'

'I like City Defender. Because 'war game' is more attractive for me. And the difficulty of the game is reasonable, not trivial, but not extremely hard to make me frustrated.'

A few participants commented that the camera lens became a little bit hot after extended game play. This temperature increase was actually caused by heat generated by the LED flash of Google Galaxy Nexus. Interestingly, the flash in Google Nexus S did not have this heating problem. We recommend device manufacturers take the heat emitting ratio into account when choosing LED flash components. Turing on the LED Flash can improve the finger transparency readings in dark environments, but it is not required in indoor conditions with sufficient illumination. One user suggested the idea of changing the bezel of back camera to improve tactile feedback in game play - "*It is better to have a stopper like there are two stoppers on F and J on Query keyboard*".

Although not directly used in the actual game play, participants strongly preferred LPG designs with a small preview window of the back camera. Participants reported that the preview window improved the positioning of fingers on the camera lens when they were concentrating on the game screen. Interestingly, participants believed that the preview window improved their *perceived fluency* and *responsiveness* of game play.

Both non-gamers and frequent mobile game players appreciated the *fun* factors and the *depth* of LPG. In addition to the design of game workflows, fun factors also came from the alternation of input modalities (touch, lens-covering, motion sensing, and orientation matching) as well as the diversity of control paradigms (trigger vs. clutch). The effective mapping of input modalities and control paradigms to in-game challenges is a rich design space for creating engaging games. While increasing the quantity and frequency of enemies was an easy choice for improving the intensity and depth of game play, this approach had limitations on human motor control skills and can also have a negative impact on the quality of heart rate tracking. As demonstrated in the user study, it's important to design LPG such that proficient gamer can discover and leverage winning strategies that rely on *better timing* and better *strategic planning* rather than solely on *higher response frequency*. We hope the depth of LPG perceived by participants could translate to *sustained motivation* in a longitudinal setting.

Based on both quantitative analysis of game playing logs and qualitative feedback collected from the iterative design process and the formal user study, we'd like to recommend the following *preliminary* design suggestions for researchers and practitioners to who are interested in designing similar LPG.

- *Accuracy Guarantee*. It's imperative to design the game playing logic such that there are sufficient lens covering sessions longer than 2 seconds, ideally 4 seconds.
- *Satisfactory Intensity*. Enabling 10 - 15 lens covering actions per minute is a good balance between accuracy and intensity.
- *Alternative Strategy for Hardcore Players*. To achieve a good balance between accuracy and fun in high intensity levels, it's important to design LPG such that proficient gamer can discover and leverage winning strategies that rely on *better timing* and *long-term planning* rather than *higher response frequency*.

CONCLUSION AND FUTURE WORK

We presented LivePulse Games (LPG), a novel technique to measure users' heart rates in real time through serious games on unmodified mobile phones. Major contributions of this paper include: 1) We demonstrated the feasibility of real-time, non-invasive heart rate monitoring during mobile game play; 2) Through a 12-subject user study, we quantified the accuracy of LivePulse in both resting condition and game playing sessions; 3) We studied the impact of game intensity on LPG based heart rate monitoring; 4) We explored the design space and trade-offs of LPG through iterative design.

Our current research has only scratched the surface of LivePulse based heart rate measurement on mobile devices. For example, better algorithms, such as unsupervised Hidden Markov Models [9], can be designed to improve the signal utilization ratio. Output from built-in motion sensors can be leveraged as indicators to signal quality or even compensate noise caused by motions [14].

LPG are not intended for uninterrupted full day heart rate tracking for clinical use. Nevertheless, LPG can still open exciting opportunities on collecting, interpreting and using physiological signals. For example, physical exertion games by Mueller et al [19, 20] can be recreated as a software only solution after certain design changes (e.g. using the "clutch metaphor" for a walkie-talkie style speech interface, touching the camera lens of the phone mounted on the arm or belt to issue voice commands, or talk with other players).

According to a survey by comScore in 2013, 39% of time spent on smartphones was devoted to gaming [17]. Given the preference and popularity of mobile gaming, LPG have the potential to lower the tracking burden of the "quantified self" movement [11], where participants track physiological signals longitudinally, for both wellness improvement and self reflection. The pervasive monitoring of personal physiological signals in non-game settings, e.g. when using LensGesture apps [40], via technologies invented in LPG, can also provide interesting research opportunities for healthcare, personal well-being [5], and adaptive learning [15] in the future.

LivePulseGames are open source software released under BSD license. The current implementation can be downloaded from *http://mips.lrdc.pitt.edu/livepulsegames*. We hope LPG can inspire research prototypes and commercial products that change how people collect, understand, and consume physiological signals.

ACKNOWLEDGEMENTS

We thank Nan Cao, Andrew Head, Jennifer Mankoff, John Wenskovitch and the anonymous reviewers for the help and constructive feedback.

REFERENCES

1. Balakrishnan, G, Durand, F., et al, Detecting Pulse from Head Motions in Video, In *Proc. IEEE CVPR 2013*.
2. Banitsas K., Pelegris P. et al, A Simple Algorithm to Monitor HR for Real Time Treatment Applications, In *Proc. ITAB 2009*.
3. Bjork, S., Patterns in Game Design, *Charles River Media*, 1st ed, 2004.
4. Cardiograph for iOS, https://itunes.apple.com/us/app/cardiograph/id441079429?ls=1&mt=8
5. Carrol, E., Czerwinski, M., Roseway, A., Kapoor, A., d Schraefel, m.c., Food and Mood: An Exploration in Emotional Eating Intervention, In *Proc. ACII 2013*.
6. Cook, S., Togni, M., et al, High heart rate: a cardiovascular risk factor?, European Heart Journal, vol. 27(20), 2006.
7. Cooper, K., Pollock, M., et al, Physical Fitness Levels vs Selected Coronary Risk Factors A Cross-Sectional Study, The Journal of the American Medical Association (JAMA), vol. 236, No. 2, July, 1976.
8. Flatla, D., Gutwin, C., et al, Calibration Games: Making Calibration Tasks Enjoyable by Adding Motivating Game Elements, In *Proc. UIST 2011*.
9. Fridly, J., Snijders, M., et al., Hidden Markov models approach to the analysis of array CGH data, *Journal of Multivariate Analysis*, Vol 90(1), July 2004.
10. Garbey, M., Sun, N., et al, Contact-free Measurement of Cardiac Pulse Based on the Analysis of Thermal Imagery, *IEEE Trans. Biomedical Engineering 54(8),* pp 1418–1426 2007.
11. Hay, T., The Rise of the 'Quantified Self' in Health Care, In *Wall Street Journal*, Aug 13, 2013.
12. Instant Heart Rate for iOS, https://itunes.apple.com/app/instant-heart-rate-measure/id395042892?mt=8
13. Jensen, M., Suadicani, P. et al, Elevated Resting Heart Rate, Physical Fitness and All-Cause Mortality: a 16-year Follow-up in The Copenhagen Male Study, Heart Vol. 99, 2013.
14. Joshi, N., Kang, S.B., et al, Image Deblurring using Inertial Measurement Sensors, In *Proc SIGGRAPH 2010*.
15. Jraidi, I., Chaouachi, M., Frasson, C., A Dynamic Multimodal Approach for Assessing Learners' Interaction Experience, In *Proc. ACM ICMI 2013*.
16. Kristal-Boneh, E., Raifel, M., et al, Heart rate variability in health and disease, *Scand J Work Environ Health*. 1995 Apr;21(2):85-95.
17. Lipsman, A., Aquino, C., 2013 Mobile Future in Focus, comScore whitepaper, released on February 22, 2013.
18. Malik, M., et al, Heart rate variability: standards of measurement, physiological interpretation, and clinical use, Circulation 93:1043–1065,1996
19. Mueller, F., Vetere, F., et al, Jogging Over a Distance Between Europe and Australia, In *Proc. UIST 2010*.
20. Mueller, F., Vetere, F., et al, Balancing Exertion Experiences, In *Proc. CHI 2012*.
21. Nacke, L., Kalyn, M., Biofeedback Game Design: Using Direct and Indirect Physiological Control to Enhance Game Interaction, In *Proc. CHI 2011*.
22. Naima, R., and Canny, J. The Berkeley Tricorder: Ambulatory Health Monitoring, *2009 Sixth International Workshop on Wearable and Implantable Body Sensor Networks*, 53-58.
23. Nenonen, V., Lindblad, A., Using Heart Rate to Control an Interactive Game, In *Proc. CHI 2007*.
24. Oliveira, R., Oliver, N., TripleBeat: Enhancing Exercise Performance with Persuasion, In *Proc. MobileHCI 2009*.
25. Pantelopoulos, A., Bourbakis, N., A Survey on Wearable Biosensor Systems for Health Monitoring, In *Proc. IEEE EMBS 2008*.
26. Pelegris, P., Banitsas, K., et al, A Novel Method to Detect Heart Beat Rate Using a Mobile Phone, In *Proc. IEEE EMBS 2010*.
27. Poh, M., McDuff, D., Picard, R., Advancements in non-contact, multiparameter physiological measurements using a webcam, In *IEEE Trans Biomed Eng*, vol. 58(1), 2011.
28. Poh, M., McDuff, D., Picard, R., Noncontact, Automated Cardiac Pulse Measurements Using Video Imaging and Blind Source Separation, *Optics Express 18 (2010)*: 10762.
29. Rowe, D.R., Sibert, J., and Irwin, D. Heart Rate Variability: Indicator of User State as an Aid to Human-Computer Interaction. In *Proc. CHI 1998*.
30. Scruggs, P., Beveridge, S., Watson, D., Increasing Children's School Time Physical Activity Using Structured Fitness Breaks. Pediatric Exercise Science, 15(2), 2003.
31. Stach, T., Graham, T.C., et al, Heart Rate Control of Exercise Video Games, In Proc. *Graphics Interface 2009*.
32. Singh, D., Saini, B.S. Heart Rate Variability-A Bibliographical Survey, *IETE Journal of research on Biomedical Signal and Image Processing*, vol. 54, no. 3, pp. 209-216, 2008.
33. Sun, D., Canny, J., Paredes, P., MouStress: Detecting Stress from Mouse Motion, In Proc. *CHI 2014*.
34. Tian, F., Lv, F., et al, Let's Play Chinese Characters: Mobile Learning Approaches via Culturally Inspired Group Games, In *Proc. of CHI 2010*.
35. Walker, W., Aroul, P., et al, Mobile Health Monitoring Systems, In Proc. *IEEE EMBS 2009*.
36. Weinman J, Hayat A, Raviv G: Reflection photoplethysmography of arterial-blood volume pulses. In *Med Biol Eng Comput 1977*;
37. Vrijkotte, T., et al, Effects of Work Stress on Ambulatory Blood Pressure, Heart Rate, and Heart Rate Variability, *Hypertension: J. of Ameri. Heart Assoc* Vol. 35, 2000
38. Yar, T., Resting Heart Rate and its Relationship with General and Abdominal Obesity in Young Male Saudi University Students, Pak J Physiol vol. 6(1), 2010.
39. Yun, C., Shastri, D., et al, O' game, Can You Feel My Frustration?: Improving User's Gaming Experience via Stresscam, In *Proc. CHI 2009*.
40. Xiao, X., Han, T., Wang, J., LensGesture: Augmenting Mobile Interactions with Back-of-Device Finger Gestures, In *Proc. ACM ICMI 2013*.

Measuring Photoplethysmogram-Based Stress-Induced Vascular Response Index to Assess Cognitive Load and Stress

Yongqiang Lyu[1], Xiaomin Luo[2], Jun Zhou[1], Chun Yu[1], Congcong Miao[1], Tong Wang[1], Yuanchun Shi[1], Ken-ichi Kameyama[3]

[1]TNLIST, Research Institute of Information Technology, Tsinghua University, Beijing China
[2]BGI (Wuhan) Translational Research Center, Wuhan, China
[3]Interactive Media Lab., Corporate R&D Center, Toshiba Corp., Tokyo, Japan
luyq@tsinghua.edu.cn, luoxm@ luoxm@genomics.org.cn, kenichi.kameyama@toshiba.co.jp

ABSTRACT
Quantitative assessment for cognitive load and mental stress is very important in optimizing human-computer system designs to improve performance and efficiency. Traditional physiological measures, such as heart rate variation (HRV), blood pressure and electrodermal activity (EDA), are widely used but still have limitations in sensitivity, reliability and usability. In this study, we propose a novel photoplethysmogram-based stress induced vascular index (sVRI) to measure cognitive load and stress. We also provide the basic methodology and detailed algorithm framework. We employed a classic experiment with three levels of task difficulty and three stages of testing period to verify the new measure. Compared with the blood pressure, heart rate and HRV components recorded simultaneously, the sVRI reached the same level of significance on the effect of task difficulty/period as the most significant other measure. Our findings showed sVRI's potential as a sensitive, reliable and usable parameter.

Author Keywords
Cognitive Load; Mental Effort; Stress; Stress-Induced Vascular Response Index (sVRI); Photoplethysmogram.

ACM Classification Keywords
H.1.2 [User/Machine Systems Subjects]: Human information processing.

INTRODUCTION
Cognitive load refers to the load that performing a particular task imposes on the human cognitive system [1]. It reflects the demand for both the psychological and physiological resources of cognition, such as working memory, the processing units for visual/spatial and auditory/verbal information, and mental intent. Assessing the cognitive load that a particular system or task imposes on users is very important in human-computer interaction (HCI) design, as the information on cognitive load can be used to improve these systems [2]. Dynamic and real-time assessment of cognitive load is particularly useful for capturing the detailed changes subjects undergo during a task, which supports a precise analysis as well as improvement on design components [2-4] and the collection of continuous psychophysiological data for smart HCI applications [5-7].

In practice, the *mental effort*, which refers to the cognitive resources actually allocated to accommodate a task [1], is often used to reflect the actual cognitive load while participants are working on a task. Mental effort is linked to both cognitive capacity (cognitive resources available) and autonomic intent (arousal). Due to variations in arousal, the same person may perform differently on the same task at different times. Cognitive load or mental effort causes mental *stress*, which occurs when the task's cognitive load exceeds the subject's cognitive capacity, or may also occur when the subjects feel the cognitive load will exceed their cognitive capacity [8]. Mental stress often accompanies the cognitive process when subjects exert mental effort, e.g. executing tasks. This stress may give rise to emotions like anxiety, fatigue, and anger and has an influence on human health [5, 6]. Stress measurement is also very important for affective computing and health-related applications.

Researchers may employ subjective *work/task load* questionnaires [9, 10] to assess cognitive load, or stress state questionnaires [11] to assess the stress. Compared to these subjective measures, objective measures, including behavioral methods, such as behavior measurement and behavioral performance measurement [4, 12, 13], and physiological measures [14-23], such as heart rate variation, blood pressure and skin conductivity, can assess cognitive load and stress more sensitively and accurately. Nevertheless, these measures still suffer from some notable limitations in sensitivity, reliability and usability. Researchers often need to combine multiple measures together to improve the sensitivity and reliability of these measures. However, combining measures in this way is not usable in ubiquitous applications. In the era of ubiquitous

CHI 2015, April 18 - 23 2015, Seoul, Republic of Korea.
Copyright 2015 ACM 978-1-4503-3145-6/15/04...$15.00
http://dx.doi.org/10.1145/2702123.2702399

applications and wearable devices [21-23], reliable and usable measurement of cognitive load and stress is critical.

In this study, we focus on studying a sensitive, reliable and relatively usable (real-time, low-cost, noninvasive and hopefully wearable) physiological measure to assess cognitive load and stress. We propose a PPG-based *stress-induced vascular responses index* (sVRI) to realize the goal by measuring the peripheral vasoconstriction tone (as Figure 1 shows).

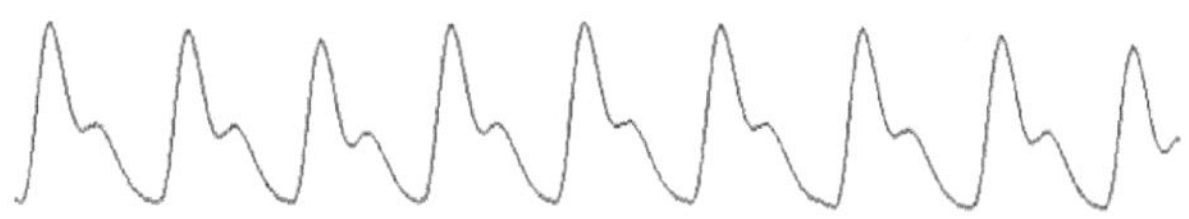

Figure 1. A standard PPG waveform

The main contributions of our work are:

- As an addition to traditional measures, we propose the PPG-based stress-induced vascular response index (sVRI) as a novel physiological measure to assess cognitive load and mental stress, which is verified to be able to differentiate effortful conditions associated with tasks of varying difficulties.
- Differing from previous work, the sVRI employs a relative amplitude ratio between two contours in a PPG waveform, which is sensitive and relatively reliable. The sVRI can output in a nearly real-time fashion at a data rate of one per heartbeat (of the subject). We also found a low standard deviation of sVRI for participants compared to other measures.
- The sVRI shows promising usability in ubiquitous scenarios because of the easy generation of PPG in either a transmission mode or a reflection mode at peripheral parts of body (e.g. fingers, earlobes, forehead) by a low-cost optical-sensing apparatus (e.g. oximeter).

The rest of the paper is organized as follows. First, we analyze the related work on the measures of cognitive load and stress. Second, we provide the basic methodology and the detailed algorithm framework for sVRI. Third, we employ a classic cognitive experiment involving arithmetic calculation of three difficulty levels to examine the performance of sVRI as well as other known physiological measures including blood pressure, heart rate and heart rate variation (HRV). Next, we analyze the experimental results and discuss the limitations of sVRI and the study. Finally, we conclude the study.

RELATED WORK

Subjective measures

We classify the measures available to assess cognitive load and stress into two main categories: subjective and objective. Subjective *work/task load* questionnaires [9, 10] can assess cognitive load by evaluating the characteristics of the tasks that people process, such as task form, complexity, time demand and effort required. Stress state questionnaires [11] can assess mental stress by evaluating three primary categories: task engagement, distress and worry. Although subjective measures may distinguish the cognitive load and stress, they heavily rely on subjective recall and descriptions from participants after the task.

Objective measures: behavioral methods

Although objective methods may not distinguish cognitive load/effort from stress, they are more sensitive, reliable, and usable than subjective methods. The objective methods most commonly used are behavioral methods and physiological methods. Behavioral methods include behavior measurement and behavioral performance measurement. Behavior measurement focuses on user behaviors, such as keyboard and mouse behaviors [5, 6], touch screen behaviors [12], and physical factors of body [13]. Behavior measurement is promising for use in ubiquitous applications in spite of current drawbacks in sensitivity and accuracy. It is also meaningless to assess the cognitive load or stress in a single task only by measuring user performance due to the lack of a control for mental effort investment. However, dual-task-based performance measurement is available. Dual-task analysis is based on the assumption of limited cognitive resources that can be allocated flexibly to the primary task and the secondary task performed simultaneously [4]. The cognitive load induced by one of the tasks is thus assessed by measuring the performance change of that task or the other task. The main disadvantages of dual-task analysis lie in the need for dedicated design of homogeneous dual tasks and the sensitivity and reliability issues due to variable participants' attention [4].

Objective measures: physiological methods

Compared to behavioral measures, physiological measures can directly, sensitively, and reliably reflect subject's internal response to cognitive load and stress. The human body is controlled by nervous systems including the central nervous system (CNS), the autonomic nervous system (ANS), the somatic nervous system, etc. The ANS controls the functions of most organs and thus influences changes in related vital signs [3, 14], such as electrocardiograph (ECG), heart rate (HR), heart rate variation (HRV), pulse rate (PR), pulse rate variation (PRV) respiration, blood pressure (BP), pupil dilation and eye blink. The ANS is composed of the sympathetic nervous system (SNS) and the parasympathetic nervous system (PNS), which inhibit each other. The SNS is responsible for emotional arousal and the physiological adjustments supporting performance, and its activities increase during tasks that require active coping. The PNS inhibits SNS activities and increases its functions during tasks that require passive coping (e.g. response) [16]. Some vital signs are controlled by both the SNS and PNS (dually innervated), while some are controlled only by the sympathetic nervous system (sympathetic-only).

Cognitive load and stress relate to both the SNS and PNS. The dually innervated vital signs actually reflect the production of the both nervous systems. Different modes of the nervous regulations of the two systems may produce the same overt (observed) vital-sign results [15], which may not be informative as to the underlying mechanism [16]. Isolating measures with a specific mapping to the SNS and PNS and then combining them may help assess the cognition and mental process further [16]. SNS activation increases as the central processing complexity of a task increases, and sympathetic-only vital signs are regarded as direct and sensitive indices for autonomic effort, as well as resulting stress in comparison with the PNS-related methods [3, 15-17].

Based on the nervous or biological systems that physiological methods utilize to assess cognitive load or stress, they are split into ANS measures and non-ANS measures. ANS measures are further broken up into dually innervated measures and the sympathetic-only measures.

Non-ANS measures

Some physiological measures available for assessing cognitive load or stress are linked to non-ANS nervous systems. For example, Electroencephalography (EEG) is linked to the central nervous system (CNS) and electromyogram (EMG) is controlled by both the somatic nervous system and the autonomic nervous system [18]. In addition to EEG, neuroimaging techniques, such as positron-emission tomography (PET) and functional magnetic resonance imaging (fMRI) are also very important for measuring brain activation during task execution [4]. Researchers may also employ biomarker-identifying techniques to examine the psychophysiological activities, for example, examining the cortisol or adrenaline in saliva or blood samples [19]. The main drawbacks of non-ANS methods are the complexity of usage, high cost and possible insensitivity to the level of mental effort investment [16].

Dually innervated measures

A range of physiological measures are based on dually innervated vital signs [3, 15], such as the HR/HRV (ECG), respiration, blood pressure, PR/PRV (pulse) and eye activities. Because these measures still suffer from sensitivity and reliability issues, researchers often employ multiple measures to examine the cognitive/mental process of participants in order to improve the assessment sensitivity and reliability. For example, Brouwer et al. [3] used EEG, HRV, respiration, skin conductance, pupil size and eye blink to study the mental effects induced by task difficulties, and found different sensitivities and reliabilities among the measures. Tan et al. proposed a smart video-medicated collaboration system with the user's mental feedback indicated by electrodermal activity (EDA), blood pressure and respiration [7]. Hjortskov et al. [20] also compared the performance of HRV and blood pressure on the effect of mental stress.

These measures have some other drawbacks as well. HRV is inconvenient to measure (multiple ECG leads needed), weak in real time (need at least 2min integral), sensitive to noise (breathing and motion artifacts), and complicated to analyze (manual artifacts corrections are often required and there are multiple components to analyze) [6, 16, 20]. PRV [21, 22] is also dually inverted, which is originated from the heart but may only have comparable sensitivity with HRV for healthy users at rest [24]. Heart rate, respiration, blood pressure (BP) and eye activities are vulnerable to internal and external noise, require obtrusive measurements, and have limitations in their ability to track information in real-time (e.g., BP).

Sympathetic-only measures

Sweat glands are controlled only by SNS, which affect the skin conductivity that is often measured by the electrodermal activity (EDA) method (also known as the galvanic skin response). The effectiveness of EDA has been demonstrated in previous studies [3, 7, 14]. However, EDA may have notable individual differences and is susceptible to the influence from skin conditions as well as ambient temperature and humidity. Over the course of a long testing process, the sweat that leads to EDA changes may be greatly influenced by ambient factors, which can result in sizeable differences between the recorded and actual cognitive and mental response of the user.

Peripheral vasoconstriction is another sympathetic-only vital sign. Iani et al. [16] investigated whether peripheral arterial tone reflects changes in mental effort. Using a modified version of the Sternberg memory task, they found that peripheral arterial tone measured by a pressure-based plethysmograph amplitude was sensitive to task difficulty. Luo et al. [19] reported a strong relationship between participants' PPG amplitudes and cortisol levels. Cortisol is regarded as the biomarker of mental stress. This study verified the physiological linkage between PPG amplitudes and mental stress induced by negative stimuli. Signal-improving techniques for guarding PPG against motion artifacts [25, 26] are also well studied and have been applied in clinical-standard pulse oximeters. Compared with pressure-based plethysmograph measurement, PPG measurement may be more sensitive and stable. PPG amplitudes can also be obtained using only minimal contact, e.g. the surface-sensing method in reflection mode [23], or without contact, e.g. image-based methods via a webcam [21]. PPG amplitudes in the time domain can also be analyzed after converted to the frequency domain [27]. However, PPG amplitudes may have notable temporal changes and individual differences, which can cause severe reliability and usability issues.

STRESS-INDUCED VASCULAR RESPONSE INDEX

In this study, we propose a PPG-based *stress-induced vascular response index* (sVRI) to assess cognitive load (through mental effort) and stress. This index measures a relative ratio of two contours in a PPG waveform, which is sensitive and has limited individual differences. The algorithms for the sVRI also guarantee its reliability and real-time updating.

The featured waveform patterns of sVRI

The effect of mental effort and stress results in peripheral vasoconstriction that is reflected in PPG appearance. Compared with a normal PPG waveform when the participant is in rest (without mental effort), the extracted patterns denoted by the average amplitudes of the two contours as shown in Figure 2, A1 and A2, can show significant differences when a mental task is imposed.

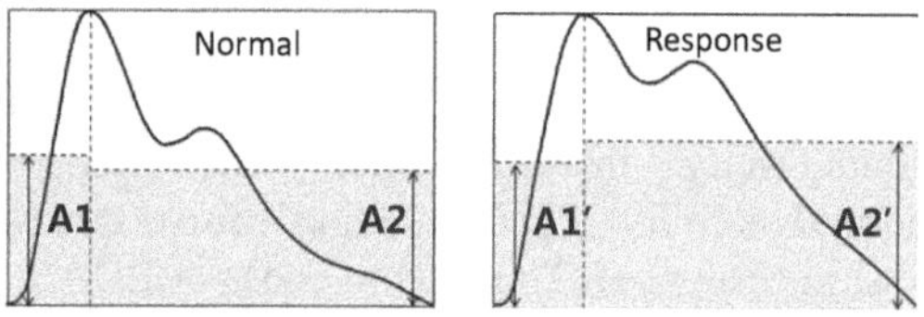

Figure 2. Quantitative response to mental effort, which is reflected in the PPG waveform patterns by the average amplitudes of A1 and A2. A1 and A2 vary (to A1' and A2' respectively) as the vascular response to mental effort.

There is an obvious A2-amplitude elevation in *response* mode in comparison with the *normal* mode. However, A2, A1 and the maximum amplitude of the waveform may have severe temporal changes and individual differences, which causes the notable reliability and usability issues of traditional PPG-based methods. In this study, we define an instant sVRI as:

$$sVRI = \frac{A2}{A1} \quad (1)$$

which can measure dynamic mental effort and stress sensitively and reliably. A1 and A2 are calculated through the area integrals of the two contours of the waveform, and sVRI increases as mental effort or stress increase.

Algorithm framework for reliable and real-time sVRIs

Based on the patterns extracted from the PPG, the sVRI can be implemented as Figure 3 shows. The process starts with the original PPG waveforms, followed by three procedures: the featured pattern extraction (FPE), dynamic sliding windowing (DSW) and statistical index moderating (SIM).

Using the basic signal filtering methods [25, 26], the featured pattern extraction (FPE) can be fed with the high-quality PPG waveforms. In FPE, the average amplitudes of the two contours, A1 and A2, as Figure 2 shows, are calculated by area integral and the instant value of sVRI is calculated using Equation 1.

In order to output reliable and real-time sVRIs, we process the PPG waveforms using the dynamic sliding windowing (DSW) procedure, which frames the PPG waveforms into partially overlapping data windows of varying sizes. One window frames a series of PPG waveforms and outputs one sVRI value.

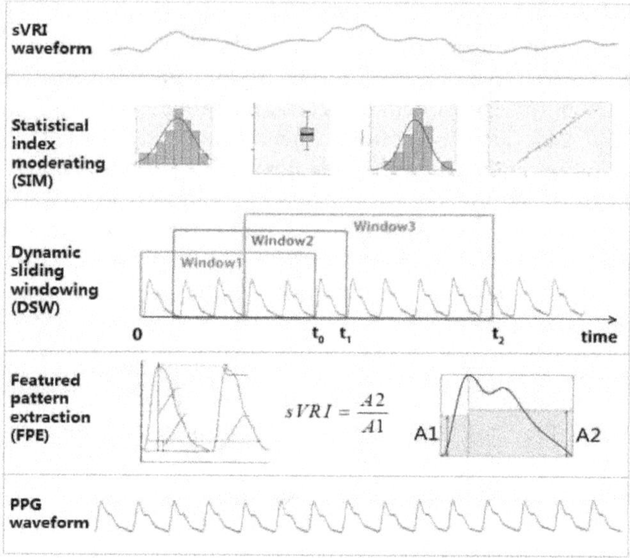

Figure 3. The algorithm framework. Bottom to top: the process begins with the original PPG waveforms; through featured pattern extraction, dynamic windowing and then statistical moderating, the sVRI waveform is achieved.

Although digital filtering in the original PPG (before our algorithms) can mitigate motion artifacts, some distorted waveforms may still exist. Therefore, first, basic digital filtering manipulates the data to select the qualified waveforms to proceed, which is an empirical parameter-based waveform selection scheme. Second, the statistical index moderating (SIM) is invoked to process the window to output a reliable sVRI value corresponding to the window. Third, a new window follows the window before it with certain duration backwards. For instance, as depicted in Figure 3, window 2 (in blue) slides backwards with a pulse beat (similarly with heart rate) after window 1 (in orange). Sometimes, the window might slide with a bigger step to lower the computation required, for example window 3 (in green) move two pulse beats after the window 2, which lowers the data rate for sVRI output. The window sizes may also differ due to the varying proportions of the filtered data. In order to pass enough valid data to the following statistical moderator (SIM), the window sizing process is adopted. For a period with more distorted waveforms, the window size increases and the sVRI data rate decreases.

In order to guarantee the reliability of sVRI, we employ statistical index moderating (SIM) to process and output the sVRI for a window, which assumes a normal distribution holds in the data window. The outliers are filtered by Grubbs' test, which filters out the data too far away from the expectation value (measured by multiples of the standard deviation). The expectation value after filtering is considered as the final output sVRI of the data window. It is noted that this statistical process is actually a pessimistic moderating, which may delay to indicate the sharp mental changes that may be caused by abrupt situations, e.g. a sudden frightening event.

Based on the algorithm flow above, the sVRI is generated in a reliable and real-time fashion with a limited starting delay while the initial data windows are pre-cached.

HYPOTHESES

In this study, we propose the sVRI to assess cognitive load (via mental effort) and stress. We designed an experiment with three task difficulties and three testing periods to evaluate the following specific hypotheses:

Hypotheses A (period effect): The sVRI should show a significant difference between the baseline (before task) and the task-processing period (in task).

Hypotheses B (difficulty effect): The sVRI should show significant differences with the task difficulty varying.

Hypotheses C (monotone effect): The sVRI should increase as mental effort increases, which is induced by greater task difficulty.

METHOD

This study employed a classic mental task of arithmetic calculation using certain digits of number to subtract 6/7/13/77 [28], e.g. using a two-digit number to subtract 7. This task had low requirements for learning [3]. While the participants were performing the tasks, their performance data and physiological data, including sVRIs, were recorded simultaneously. Questionnaires from the participants about their experience were also collected. Finally, the hypotheses were examined based on the analysis of those data.

Participants

There were 40 participants taking part in the experiment. In order to reduce the effects on performance caused by individual capabilities or backgrounds [3], we recruited university students with similar educational backgrounds and arithmetic capabilities. Participants were skilled at arithmetic according to the pretests on their arithmetic capabilities, and none of them had prior experience with the experimental content. Participants were aged between 19 and 25 years old (22 ± 1.7), with 22 males and 18 females. All participants were healthy and did not use any medications. All were right-handed and had normal or corrected-to-normal vision. The experiment was approved by the local ethics committee and performed in according with the ethical standards as laid down in the Declaration of Helsinki. Each participant was paid 40 US dollars.

Apparatus

The sVRI, ECG (for HRV) and blood pressure of the participants were measured throughout the experiment. The PPG for sVRI was measured using a standard clinical finger-clip PPG sensor at a sampling rate of 500HZ [19] and was processed by simultaneous sVRI algorithms. The ECG was measured using a SMOTE PSG device (Compumedics Ltd., Australia) at a sampling rate of 200Hz [24]. Blood pressure was measured by an OMRON HEM-7112 blood pressure monitor. The arithmetic problems were presented on a 19" LCD monitor, and participants used a 101-key standard keyboard to input the answers and then press the Enter key to submit.

Setting

The experiment took place in a sound-attenuated, temperature-controlled and electrically shielded room. Room temperature and humidity during the experiment were held constant. For each participant, the sVRI sensor was placed on the left index finger of the participant; the cuff of the blood pressure monitor was bound to the left upper arm and kept at the same height as the heart of participant. For the ECG, self-adhesive 1 1/2" electrodes with 7% chloride wet gel were attached to the participant's chest in a standard configuration of leads. Once the experiment started, the participant was asked to try to avoid movement.

Stimuli

This study employed a classic mental task format, i.e. the arithmetic calculation that uses certain digits of number to subtract 6/7/13/77 [28]. The task lasted 6 min and the number of completed calculations as well as the number of correct answers were counted and presented to the participants instantly. We set three levels of task difficulties, i.e. *easy*, *medium* and *hard*, and provided a simple and clear GUI for performing the calculations. The main font was black and was presented on a light grey background. In the easy and medium levels, participants had 10 s maximum to complete each calculation, after which it would be counted as wrong and the next question would appear. Real-time results were presented in the interface. In the easy level, participants were asked to subtract 6 or 7 (at random) from random three-digit numbers; while in the medium level, participants were asked to subtract 13 or 77 (at random) from random four-digit numbers. As a special case in this study, the hard level was more challenging; it required participants to calculate the solution to random four-digit numbers subtracted from random five-digit numbers in 15 s. This case was designed to investigate the cognitive load (mental effort) under very high stressors.

Protocol

Each participant was tested individually on three tests (one for each task difficulty) within a two-week period, and was randomly assigned a task difficulty for each test without being told the level of difficulty. Each test lasted about 50 min as shown in Figure 4. At the beginning of the test, the experimenter provided the general information and instructions about the experiment and informed the participants that their physiological responses would be recorded at rest and during mental tasks. The participants were also asked to treat the experiment seriously and to try their best on the task.

The period before the task lasted 30 min, and was composed of a 20min rest period (including preparation time) and a 10min *pre-task* (baseline) period. After attaching the recording devices, the participant was left alone in the room for about 10 min, and was verbally instructed to rest quietly, move as little as possible, and wait for further instructions. In the following 10min pre-task period, an experimenter (only an experimenter in situ) recorded the participant's physiological data as the baseline before starting the arithmetic task. After that, the participant was instructed to complete the arithmetic calculations in 6 min. This was the *in-task* (working) period. When time was up, the participant was instructed to stop and rest for 10 min, which was the *post-task* (recovery) period. The physiological measures were also recorded during the in-task and post-task. In the final 5min period, the participant was asked to fill out questionnaires assessing the feelings about the tasks and the effort on the tasks.

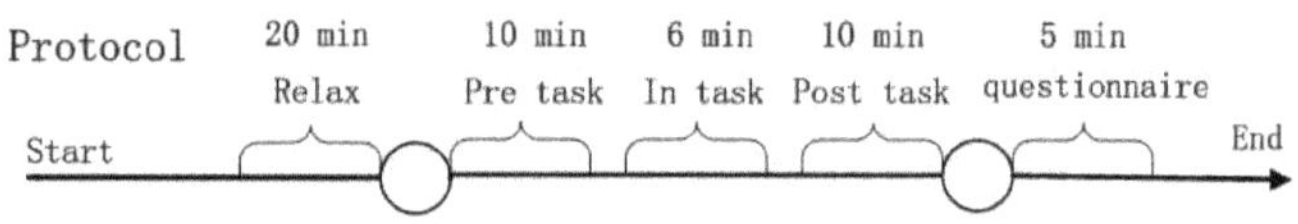

Figure 4. The experiment protocol.

Dependent variables

For each participant, during each of the three task difficulties and during each of the three testing periods, we recorded and determined the values of a range of dependent variables to measure task performance and physiology as described below.

Task performance measures were the amount of total completed calculations (total completions) and the proportion of the correct answers (accuracy). We considered the participants with more correct answers as better performers. In contrast, we considered the participants with many completions but few correct answers, or with few completions but high rate of correctness, as worse performers. In addition, participants also filled out questionnaires subjectively rating task difficulty and their efforts on the task; this data was used to support the performance data.

The raw signals of the PPG for sVRI were recorded via a clinical PPG sensor and processed by the algorithms in this study to form sVRI. We used the average sVRI value in each testing period to examine significance and for comparison with other physiological measures.

The blood pressure (BP) measure includes the systolic and diastolic blood pressures. The blood pressure values are susceptible to human factors, and therefore the measurement process was controlled on human factors in the tests according to the clinical standards. The experimenter read the systolic/diastolic BP values from the BP monitor, who had received prior training in our partner clinics. During the pre/in-task period, BP was recorded three times, and during the post-task period, BP was recorded five times.

As a measure of heart rate (HR), we determined the mean R-R (R-peaks) interval (RRI) from the ECG for each testing period via the Kubios HRV v2.1 (University of Eastern Finland). ECG was recorded throughout the pre, in and post periods.

Based on the R-R intervals, three measures of heart rate variability (HRV) over a 5min period were computed, including the root mean squared successive difference (RMSSD) [3, 14], the high-frequency HRV (HF), and the mid-frequency HRV (MF). HF was the power in the high frequency range of 0.15 – 0.4 Hz of the R-R intervals by Welch's method [3] and MF was the power in the range of 0.04 – 0.15 Hz. The absolute power of the HF and MF within the two bands was submitted to a natural logarithm (ln) transform to approach normal distribution. The RMSSD, HF and MF were all computed via the Kubios HRV software (v2.1, University of Eastern Finland).

Analysis

First, the performance data was examined to confirm task difficulty and participants' effort. A repeated-measures ANOVA was used to analyze the total completions and accuracy as within-subject factors (both corresponded to the three difficulty levels). The Box-plots plots were also used to help justify the outlying performance by assuming the target performance of the participants were compliant with the normal distribution.

Second, each dependent physiological variable was analyzed using a 3*3 repeated-measures ANOVA with the testing period (three levels: pre-task, in-task and post-task) and task difficulty (three levels: easy, medium and hard) as within-subject factors. An effect of a variable varying with the testing period should be reflected by a main effect of the testing period. The effect of a variable varying with the task difficulty was analyzed through the 3 difficulty * 1 in-task period repeated-measures ANOVA because the baselines should not be affected by the task difficulties. The average values of each period were used to analyze the physiological measures.

In the ANOVA tests, a Huynh-Feldt correction of the degrees of freedom was used when the sphericity assumption was violated. Effect sizes for effects as explored by the repeated measures ANOVAs were determined by computing partial eta squared (η^2). Effect sizes for effects as explored by the paired t-tests were determined by computing Cohen's d between pairs of samples. All statistical analysis were performed with the SPSS 13.0 (formerly SPSS Inc. and now IBM, USA) for windows, and were conducted at significance level = 0.05, two-tailed.

RESULTS

Performance Data

Raw Data

First, the performance data was analyzed to confirm 1) if the task difficulties were properly set, and 2) if the participants invested the expected amount of effort.

The performance data is shown in Figure 5. The mean of the total completions was maximal for the easy task (M = 136, SD = 30), intermediate for the medium task (M = 61, SD = 13) and minimal for the hard task (M = 32, SD = 6), F(2, 78) = 511.49, p = 0.000. Similarly, the mean accuracy was maximal for the easy task (M = 99.07%, SD = 2.15%), intermediate for the medium task (M = 84.78%, SD = 12.42%) and minimal for the hard task (M = 58.66%, SD = 21.07%), F(2, 78) = 124.51, p = 0.000.

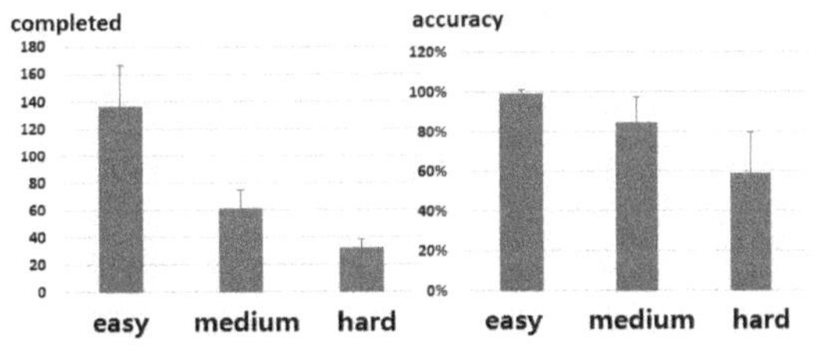

(a) Total completions (b) Accuracy

Figure 5. The performance data (means and SDs) on different task difficulties: (a) the amount of total calculations completed (b) the accuracy.

Filtering Effortless Participants

Recognizing that some participants might have been putting too little effort into the task, we utilized both subjective and objective methods to analyze which participants did not meet our expectation for effort:

1) Using questionnaires. We collected the questionnaires and analyzed participants' feedbacks on how much effort they had invested (a five-point Likert scale) on each task. We found five participants expressed that they might not have invested enough effort during the hard task. Others thought they invested enough effort during all tasks.

2) Using outlying performance analysis. In addition to analyzing the subjective questionnaires, we employed a statistical outlier-filtering method by assuming a normal distribution of the samples. We analyzed the schematic box-plots (Figure 6) with respect to the amount of total completed calculations, the accuracy and the performance degradation respectively. Looking at the number of calculations completed (not shown in Figure 6), we found that there were three outperformers, who we did not exclude from further analysis because our aim was to remove effortless participants. As shown in Figure 6(a), we determined three participants (No. 3, 18 and 39) had significantly worse performance than other participants on one or two tasks. As Figure 6(b) highlights, participant No. 3 was the only negative outlier for the performance degradation between the hard task and the medium task. No outliers found for the performance degradation between the medium task and easy task. We found that participant No.3 was also one of the five participants who, based on self-assessment using the questionnaire, had invested less effort into the tasks, while the other outliers were not. Therefore, we excluded the participant of No.3, and used the data from the remaining *39* participants for further analysis.

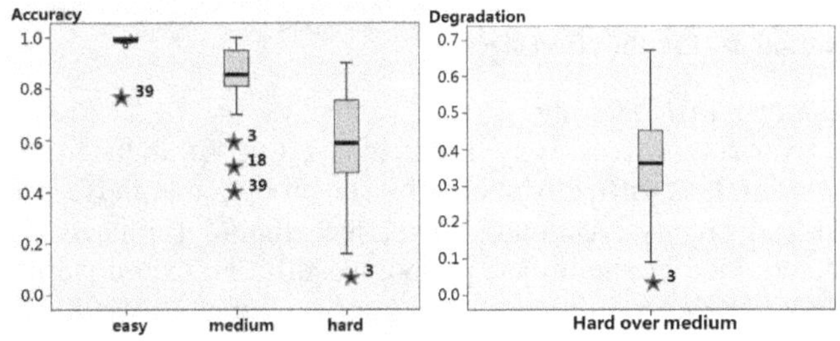

(a) Accuracy. (b) Performance degradation.

Figure 6. Identifying effortless performance. (a) Accuracy vs. task difficulties and (b) Performance degradation calculated as the total completions in hard task over that of medium task.

Physiological data

Effect of testing period

Table 1 shows the mean, and corresponding standard deviations, of all physiological measures during the testing periods and for different task difficulties. The measures are sVRI, systolic blood pressure (sysBP), diastolic blood pressure (diaBP), HR (RRI), RMSSD, MF and HF. A repeated-measures ANOVA of 3 periods (pre, in and post) * 3 difficulties (easy, medium and hard) was performed for each of those measures, which we used to first examine the physiological responses during different testing periods. Table 2 shows the results of the within-subject effects for the in-task period compared to the baseline and post-task

Measure	Easy task			Medium task			Hard task		
	Test period			Test period			Test period		
	Pre (baseline)	In	Post	Pre (baseline)	In	Post	Pre (baseline)	In	Post
sVRI	0.837±0.035	0.878±0.043	0.846±0.035	0.832±0.025	0.892±0.036	0.846±0.023	0.835±0.024	0.900±0.059	0.853±0.027
sysBP	103.4±10.1	116.75±12.4	105.0±10.7	104.0±10.2	118.3±12.56	110.9±30.7	103.3±10.0	118.56±16.1	104.2±10.1
diaBP	64.6±6.5	75.8±8.6	67.1±8.1	65.9±6.6	78.2±8.3	67.5±7.1	64.0±6.3	74.5±8.0	66.4±6.3
HR	830.4±112.2	752.3±111.7	829.0±108.4	839.3±119.1	737.1±107.8	825.1±109.8	849.0±122.8	748.6±164.2	847.9±121.0
RMSSD	36.5±14.2	29.9±14.1	32.8±12.8	39.4±13.8	30.7±10.5	35.4±13.2	38.3±16.1	32.4±14.0	35.3±15.4
MF (ln)	6.23±0.72	6.00±0.70	6.19±0.73	6.59±0.70	6.33±0.78	6.53±0.70	6.40±0.64	6.09±0.80	6.22±0.78
HF(ln)	6.08±0.84	5.56±1.22	5.96±0.89	6.40±0.89	5.82±1.12	6.11±1.04	6.27±1.34	5.83±1.11	6.06±1.07

Table 1. Results of physiological measures. The physiological data were recorded during the pre (baseline), in and post task periods for the easy, medium and hard task difficulty levels respectively.

values. We can see that each physiological measure showed a very significant effect of the testing period: the sVRI, sysBP and diaBP significantly increased, and the HRV measures (HR using RRI, RMSSD, MF and HF) significantly decreased, while participants performed the tasks in comparison with the baselines and post-tasks, ($p < 0.0001$). The results were consistent with previous studies [3, 16, 20].

Measure	Period			
	p	*F*	*df1, df2*	η^2
sVRI	0.000	121.8	1.3, 47.6	0.754
sysBP	0.000	31.02	1.4, 51.6	0.449
diaBP	0.000	180.1	1.4, 52.6	0.826
HR(RRI)	0.000	129.4	1.4, 53.6	0.773
HRV:RMSSD	0.000	23.84	1.72, 65.4	0.385
HRV:MF	0.000	9.85	2, 76	0.206
HRV:HF	0.000	19.56	1.3, 50.8	0.340

Table 2. Within-subject effects of the period by 3*3 repeated-measures ANOVA: p and F values for the main effects of period, η^2 for the effect sizes.

Effect of task difficulty

A variable's sensitivity to mental effort as induced by varying task difficulty should be shown by a main effect of task difficulty. Although this effect should primarily be determined by the in-task period, we still first examined the 3*3 ANOVA results (partially shown in Table 2). We found that the MF ($F(2, 76) = 6.387$, $p = 0.003$), sysBP ($F(1.3, 50.4) = 3.728$, $p = 0.049$) and diaBP ($F(2, 76) = 3.797$, $p = 0.027$) showed significant effects of task difficulty, which suggested that MF and diaBP may vary notably on the baselines according to their full freedom degrees (2 and 76). The sVRI ($F(2.1, 81.3) = 4.601$, $p = 0.011$) and HR ($F(3.3, 124.8) = 2.941$, $p = 0.031$) also showed significant interactive effect of testing period * difficulty with low freedom degrees, which may suggest that the main effects should be primarily reflected by the in-task values.

Next, we analyzed the in-task values of the physiological measures on their own, without the out-of-task values. Table 3 lists the results by using 3 difficulties * 1 period (in-task) repeated measures ANOVA.

Measure	Difficulty			
	p	*F*	*df1, df2*	η^2
sVRI	**0.019** *	4.18	2, 76	0.099
sysBP	**0.002** **	6.66	2, 76	0.149
diaBP	0.054	3.15	1.8, 68.2	0.077
HR (RRI)	**0.025***	4.41	1.5,58.4	0.104
HRV:RMSSD	0.295	1.24	2, 76	0.032
HRV:MF	**0.033***	3.56	2, 76	0.086
HRV:HF	0.139	2.03	2,76	0.051

Table 3. The effect of task difficulty on the in-task physiological values.

We can see that the sVRI, sysBP, HR and MF measures reached significance on the effect of the task difficulty, while the other physiological measures did not. These results were consistent with the findings of previous studies as well [3, 16, 20]. Additionally, in order to eliminate the influence of the baseline on the subsequent measurements, we also examined the change ratio (*cr*) for the in-task *values*, which is defined as:

$$cr = \frac{value - baseline}{baseline} \times 100\% \qquad (2)$$

From the results using change ratios, we found that sVRI (F=5.50, p=0.006), diaBP (F=35.60, p=0.000), HR (F=5.94, p=0.004) and MF (F=5.24, p=0.007) showed greater significance on the effect of task difficulty in comparison with the results obtained without using the change ratios (the results shown in Table 3). However, on the contrary, sysBP (F=3.28, p=0.043) and HF (F=0.91, p=0.409) showed less significance on the results using change ratios. These results may reflect the reliability issues of the blood pressure and HRV measurements, and from these results it can also be concluded that the sVRI was sensitive and reliable.

We also examined the trends of the mean values of the variables reaching significance on task difficulty. Figure 7 shows the trends of the means for the sVRI, sysBP (systolic BP), HR (RR interval) and MF with standard errors. The sVRI and sysBP values were taken from Table 1, and HR and MF used the change ratios to the baselines. The sVRI and sysBP increased and mid frequency decreased with the task difficulty increasing. However, the RR interval did not show the significant decrease (HR's increase) from the medium to hard task, which might suggest the reliability issue of the heart rate.

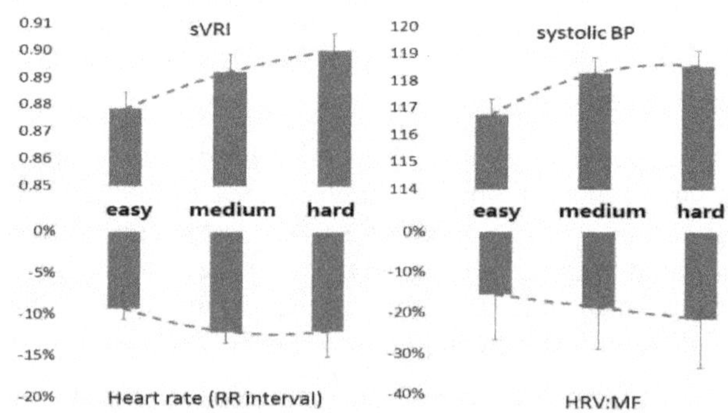

Figure 7. The mean (with standard errors) in-task values of the sVRI, systolic blood pressure, heart rate (RRI) and mid frequency as a function of task difficulty.

Other factors

We also examined the LF/HF (LF is the MF in this study) results for HRV. We found that the LF/HF only showed significance on the testing period (F=5.80, p=0.005), and did not show significance on the difficulty (F=1.34, p=0.269), which was similar with HF. In addition, we checked the 2min HRV using the last 2 minutes in each period for our calculation. We found a slight difference from the 5min HRV: 1) HR, MF and HF still showed significance on the period (p <= 0.001) but the RMSSD was no longer significant (p=0.541). 2) Only MF still maintained significance on the task difficulty (F=6.826, p=0.002), and HR did not (p=0.211).

We also tested for gender effects on the task performance and on the sVRI by t-tests. The gender effects were significant on the total completed calculations but not on the accuracy in the easy and medium tasks (p=0.004 and 0.015 respectively). The sVRI did not show significant gender effects for the three difficulties (p=0.584, 0.050, 0.062 respectively).

Performance and mental effort

We inspected the performance and mental effort using sVRI to understand them better. Figure 8 compares two participants on the performance and sVRI respectively. The performance was the ratio of correct answers (normalized to 1.0 by the best performance), and can be used to evaluate the outcome of the participants objectively. We can see from Figure 8(a) that participant #1 outperformed #2 about 9% in the medium task and about 100% in the hard task. We know the performance is related to individual capability, mental effort, and task complexity. With the task given, it becomes possible to evaluate differences in individual capabilities when mental effort is measurable using sVRI. Figure 8(b) shows the sVRIs in order to display and compare these participants' mental effort. We can see that participant #1 invested less mental effort (smaller sVRI) than #2 during the medium task, but achieved better performance, which implies that participant #1 might have better personal capability. Participant #1 invested increased effort on the hard task, while participant #2 seemed to give up during the hard task according to the large reduction (more than 70%) of the sVRI compared to the medium task. Based on this information, it follows logically that participant #1 still achieved much better performance (about 2x) than participant #2 on the hard task.

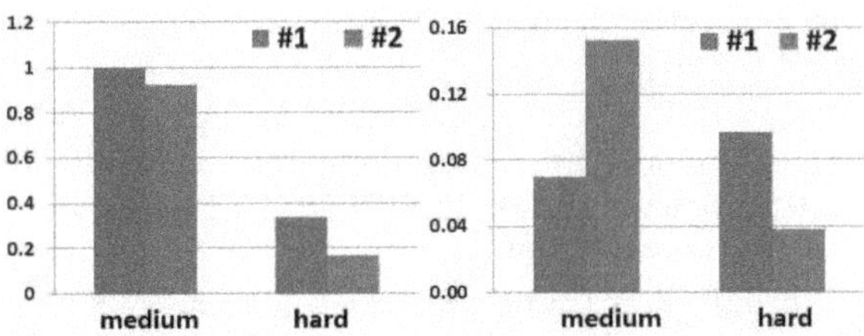

(a) Performance (b) sVRI (mental effort)

Figure 8. Comparing two participants (#1 and #2) on the medium and hard tasks: (a) performance and (b) mental effort displayed using sVRI.

Discussion

Hypotheses

Based on the experimental results, we have confirmed that all the three hypotheses set at the beginning of this study hold.

Comparing the physiological measures

BP and HRV need very careful control to improve their reliability, and their sensitivity may often vary between different trials, which occurred during this study as well as previous studies [3, 16, 20]. The sVRI showed promising sensitivity and reliability in this study. In addition, the sVRI had a small SD in proportion to the mean value, below 5%, while other measures were all above 10%. The sVRI can also output in real-time at the rate of heartbeat (similar with heart rate), while blood pressure needs an air-pumping process (nearly 1 min) and the HRV needs at least a 2min integral. The sVRI is measured nonintrusively via pulse, while other measures may need more body involvement, such as the BP with arm, HRV with ECG (chest), etc.

Ubiquitous usability

We employed a clinical oximeter-based PPG sensor using the transmission mode in this study for our assessment of the sensitivity, reliability and basic usability of the sVRI. PPG waveforms can also be obtained through slight-contact methods by using the reflection mode on the fingers, forehead or earlobes, such as the surface-sensing method [23], or through contactless methods, such as the image-based method using a webcam [21], which may suggest the promising usability of sVRI in ubiquitous applications.

Limitations

The sVRI does not currently differentiate cognitive load from stress despite their differences. The sVRI may be suitable only for measuring autonomic mental effort (cognitive load) and the accompanying stress, and it does not reflect the PNS activities that also correlate to cognitive process and stress since it is sympathetic-only. In addition, high heart rates (e.g. above 120 bpm) may also affect the reliability of sVRI due to more distorted PPG waveforms. Furthermore, the algorithms and experiment still have some limitations in the following two aspects. 1) There were still some odd values appearing in the current output of sVRI, which requires further improvement. 2) The easy task was actually already challenging enough for the university students. The experiment therefore focused too much on the high stressors.

CONCLUSION AND FUTURE WORK

In this paper, we propose the sVRI as a novel physiological measure for assessing cognitive load and stress which can be added to currently known measures. The experiment, based on three levels of task difficulty and three stages of testing periods, showed that the sVRI reached the same level of significance on the effects of task difficulty and period as the highest significance from the blood pressure and HRV components. Our findings also suggested the sVRI's potential as a sensitive, reliable, and usable measure. In future work, we will focus on the current limitations of this method and study its extension for ubiquitous aplications. Futher comparisons with EDA may also be involved.

ACKNOWLEDGMENTS

We thank all the volunteers for their participation in our experiment. We thank all the anonymous reviewers for their insightful comments and helpful suggestions for improving the initial draft of this manuscript. We also gratefully acknowledge the grant from NSFC (#61201357).

REFERENCES

1. Paas, F., Tuovinen, J.E., Tabbers, H., et al. Cognitive Load Measurement as a Means to Advance Cognitive Load Theory. *Educ. Psychol. 38*, 1 (2003), 63-71.
2. Oviatt, S. Human-centered design meets cognitive load theory: designing interfaces that help people think. In *Proc. 14th ACM Multimedia*, ACM (2006), 871-880.
3. Brouwer, A.-M., Hogervorst, M.A., Holewijn, M., et al. Evidence for effects of task difficulty but not learning on neurophysiological variables associated with effort. *Int. J. Psychophysiol. 93*, 2 (2014), 242-252.
4. Brunken, R., Plass, J.L., and Leutner, D. Direct Measurement of Cognitive Load in Multimedia Learning. *Educ. Psychol. 38*, 1 (2003), 53-61.
5. Hernandez, J., Paredes, P., Roseway, A., et al. Under pressure: sensing stress of computer users. In *Proc. CHI 2014*, ACM (2014), 51-60.
6. Sun, D., Paredes, P., and Canny, J. MouStress: detecting stress from mouse motion. In *Proc. CHI 2014*, ACM (2014), 61-70.
7. Tan, C.S.S., Schning, J., Luyten, K., et al. Investigating the effects of using biofeedback as visual stress indicator during video-mediated collaboration. In *Proc. CHI 2014*, ACM (2014), 71-80.
8. Lazarus, R.S. *Psychological stress and the coping process*. McGraw-Hill (1966), New York.
9. Hart, S.G. and Staveland, L.E. Development of NASA-TLX (Task Load Index): Results of Empirical and Theoretical Research. In *Advances in Psychology*, North-Holland (1988), 139-183.
10. Verwey, W.B. and Veltman, H.A. Detecting short periods of elevated workload: A comparison of nine workload assessment techniques. *J. Exp. Psychol. Appl. 2*, 3 (1996), 270-285.
11. Matthews, G., Campbell, S.E., Falconer, S., et al. Fundamental dimensions of subjective state in performance settings: Task engagement, distress, and worry. *Emotion 2*, 4 (2002), 315-340.
12. Gao, Y., Bianchi-Berthouze, N., and Meng, H. What Does Touch Tell Us about Emotions in Touchscreen-Based Gameplay? *ACM Trans. Comput.-Hum. Interact. 19*, 4 (2012), 1-30.
13. Dennerlein, J., Becker, T., Johnson, P., et al. Frustrating computer users increases exposure to physical factors. In *Proceedings of the International Ergonomics Association, Seoul, Korea*(2003).
14. Kreibig, S.D. Autonomic nervous system activity in emotion: A review. *Biol. Psychol. 84*, 3 (2010), 394-421.
15. Berntson, G.G., Cacioppo, J.T., and Quigley, K.S. Autonomic determinism: The modes of autonomic control, the doctrine of autonomic space, and the laws of autonomic constraint. *Psychological. Review 98*, 4 (1991), 459-487.
16. Iani, C., Gopher, D., and Lavie, P. Effects of task difficulty and invested mental effort on peripheral vasoconstriction. *Psychophysiology 41*, 5 (2004), 789-798.
17. Mulder, G. The concept and measurement of mental effort. In *Energetics and human information processing*, Springer (1986), 175-198.
18. Brouwer, A.-M., Hogervorst, M.A., Van Erp, J.B., et al. Estimating workload using EEG spectral power and ERPs in the n-back task. *Journal of neural engineering 9*, 4 (2012), 045008.
19. Luo, L., Xiao, L., Miao, D., et al. The Relationship between Mental Stress Induced Changes in Cortisol Levels and Vascular Responses Quantified by Waveform Analysis: Investigating Stress-Dependent Indices of Vascular Changes. In *ICBEB 2012*, IEEE (2012), 929-933.
20. Hjortskov, N., Rissén, D., Blangsted, A.K., et al. The effect of mental stress on heart rate variability and blood pressure during computer work. *Eur. J. Appl. Physiol. 92*, 1-2 (2004), 84-89.
21. Bousefsaf, F., Maaoui, C., and Pruski, A. Remote detection of mental workload changes using cardiac parameters assessed with a low-cost webcam. *Comput. Biol. Med. 53*(2014), 154-163.
22. Yoo, K.-S. and Lee, W.-H. Mental stress assessment based on pulse photoplethysmography. In *Proc. ISCE 2011*, IEEE (2011), 323-326.
23. Chigira, H., Maeda, A., and Kobayashi, M. Area-based photo-plethysmographic sensing method for the surfaces of handheld devices. In *Proc. UIST 2011*, ACM (2011), 499-508.
24. Schäfer, A. and Vagedes, J. How accurate is pulse rate variability as an estimate of heart rate variability?: A review on studies comparing photoplethysmographic technology with an electrocardiogram. *Int. J. Cardiol. 166*, 1 (2013), 15-29.
25. Wijshoff, R.W.C.G.R., Veen, J., Van Der Lee, A.M., et al. PPG motion artifact handling using a self-mixing interferometric sensor. In *SPIE2011*, SPIE(2011), 78940F-78940F-78913.
26. Wijshoff, R.W.C.G.R., Mischi, M., Veen, J., et al. Reducing motion artifacts in photoplethysmograms by using relative sensor motion: phantom study. *Journal of Biomedical Optics 17*, 11 (2012), 117007-117007.
27. Chen, C.-C., Lin, S.-C., Young, M.-S., et al. Accumulated Mental Stress Study Using the Meridians of Traditional Chinese Medicine with Photoplethysmography. *The Journal of Alternative and Complementary Medicine 20*, 11 (2014), 860-867.
28. Ritter, F.E., Reifers, A.L., Klein, L.C., et al. Lessons from defining theories of stress for cognitive architectures. *Integrated models of cognitive systems*(2007), 254-262.

Fluid Grouping: Quantifying Group Engagement around Interactive Tabletop Exhibits in the Wild

Florian Block[1], James Hammerman[2], Michael Horn[3], Amy Spiegel[4], Jonathan Christiansen[2*], Brenda Phillips[1], Judy Diamond[5], E. Margaret Evans[6], Chia Shen[1]**

[1] School of Engineering and Applied Sciences, Harvard University, [2] STEM Education Evaluation Center, TERC, [3]Northwestern University, [4]University of Nebraska-Lincoln, [5]University of Nebraska State Museum, [6]University of Michigan

[1]{fblock, cshen}@seas.harvard.edu

ABSTRACT
Interactive surfaces are increasingly common in museums and other informal learning environments where they are seen as a medium for promoting social engagement. However, despite their increasing prevalence, we know very little about factors that contribute to collaboration and learning around interactive surfaces. In this paper we present analyses of visitor engagement around several multi-touch tabletop science exhibits. Observations of 629 visitors were collected through two widely used techniques: video study and shadowing. We make four contributions: 1) we present an algorithm for identifying groups within a dynamic flow of visitors through an exhibit hall; 2) we present measures of group-level engagement along with methods for statistically analyzing these measures; 3) we assess the effect of observational techniques on visitors' engagement, demonstrating that consented video studies do not necessarily reflect visitor behavior in more naturalistic circumstances; and 4) we present an analysis showing that groups of two, groups with both children and adults, and groups that take turns spend longer at the exhibits and engage more with scientific concepts.

Author Keywords
Museums; learning; multi-touch tabletops; quantitative methods;

ACM Classification Keywords
H.5.3. Group and Organization Interfaces.

INTRODUCTION
One of the cornerstones of multi-touch technology is its ability to support simultaneous interaction between co-located users. In recent years, multi-touch research has moved out of its infancy and into "the wild" [13, 14, 15, 16, 18, 25, 27, 31]. Large multi-touch displays are now available through several commercial vendors and many real-world applications have emerged. Museums have received particular attention from the research community, as supporting meaningful social interaction is seen as central to learning in informal environments [12, 22]. Several research studies have established that multi-touch technology has the potential to engage visitors in fruitful collaborative learning [14, 15, 16, 25, 31].

Many of these studies are based on qualitative analysis. Surprisingly little quantitative evidence exists that explains clearly the factors contributing to visitor engagement and learning around interactive surfaces. There are numerous challenges and nuances present in assessing group interactions and engagement quantitatively. First, it is not clear what constitutes a visitor group. Museums can be crowded and chaotic environments where acquaintances and strangers form streams of ad hoc visitor groups around exhibits. The composition, size, and interactions within these groups change continuously and spontaneously over time. Studies of group engagement require a systematic definition of groups in these fluid settings as the behavior of individuals around an exhibit will be influenced by other people present. Second, study designs need careful consideration. Museums are free-choice environments. Common recruitment and observation techniques may affect this ecological property, have substantial effects on the very behavior under study and thus inadvertently bias the study outcome. Third, the type of application and its user interface can potentially influence visitor engagement.

In this paper, we present an empirical study of group engagement at the California Academy of Sciences in San Francisco, which receives 2 million annual visitors, and has a very diverse demographic audience. We used two different genres of interactive tabletop exhibits in order to identify factors that are consistent across both types of applications, and two types of study designs. Our concrete contributions are four-fold: after discussing related work and introducing our study designs we present an algorithm for identifying meaningful groups within a continuous flow of visitors.

CHI 2015, April 18 - 23 2015, Seoul, Republic of Korea.
Copyright 2015 ACM 978-1-4503-3145-6/15/04...$15.00.
http://dx.doi.org/10.1145/2702123.2702231

*Jonathan Christiansen is currently at Marywood University.
**Brenda Phillips is currently at Boston University.

Second we present refined measures of group-level engagement along with appropriate statistical analyses. We then make a methodological contribution by examining the effects of different data-collection techniques on group engagement. Finally, we assess the effect of group size, age composition, and overlap with other groups on visitor engagement with the exhibits and their scientific content.

RELATED WORK

Various factors influence group engagement around traditional exhibits. These include the adult and child gender [11, 21, 25], a group's size and age composition [4, 7, 8, 10, 20], and a group's strategy for learning [3]. However, it is unclear if any of the observed effects apply to interactive multi-touch exhibits, which may facilitate different forms of group engagement. Previous HCI research has studied group engagement around interactive tabletops in general [1, 13, 18, 27, 28, 29, 30, 31, 33, 35, 36, 37] and in museums in particular [14, 15, 16, 25, 31]. This includes understanding which gestures are used, how visitors approach surfaces in public spaces, transitions between user groups, and physical and verbal interaction between users [13, 14, 16, 18, 30].

While many "in the wild" studies have assessed engagement with multi-touch technology, the great majority primarily concentrate on *qualitative* analyses of observational data [1, 13, 14, 15, 16, 18, 25, 27, 31]. *Quantitative* analyses of group engagement are less common, particularly for studies that have been conducted outside of laboratory or controlled settings. Peltonen et al. measured distribution of group size and group overlap in front of a public interactive surface located in a shop window [30]; Horn et al. quantified holding times of recruited and non-recruited groups around an interactive game-based exhibit [15]; and Hinrichs et al. quantified occurrences of various multi-touch gestures around an interactive museum exhibit [14]. Other quantitative studies either focus on quantifying engagement around traditional, non-digital exhibits [9, 12, 20, 23] or are conducted in the lab with predetermined group sizes [7, 29, 33, 35, 36, 37].

Our aim, in contrast, is to add to this body of research studies by quantifying group engagement in an ecologically valid environment with natural visitor groups that dynamically form, reconfigure, and disperse. In this context, a significant challenge is to identify groups in a systematic way. Existing work has provided some basic mechanisms of identifying groups based on uninterrupted use [18, 27, 30]. This works for quiet venues, but is problematic when groups overlap [18]. Work on F-formations [19, 34] offers a way of defining and detecting free-standing groups through analyzing orientation and positioning of group members. In museums, however, such spatial characteristic are mostly predetermined by the design of the exhibit space [28]. Here we introduce an algorithm to identify groups based on their temporal formation within continuous periods of usage.

STUDY DESIGN

In this section we will first define measures of engagement for our quantitative study. We then describe our study design, data collection, and research questions.

Measures of Group Engagement

Several methods for quantifying engagement have been proposed. Dwell time (or holding time) is an established measure that is easy to capture and serves as a reasonable proxy for the depth of visitor engagement with exhibits [2, 3, 15, 17]. Following [13, 15, 23, 29], we also measure the frequency of physical and verbal behaviors that we detail in the Study Procedure section. Prior research offers some insight into which group factors may influence engagement and learning in museums. A series of studies have shown that *group size* influences engagement around exhibits [3, 6] and multi-touch tabletops [33]. Another set of studies provides evidence that *age composition* influences learning, highlighting that groups with both children and adults learn best [6, 9, 10, 11]. Third, there is qualitative evidence that the overlap between groups may influence engagement with interactive surfaces in naturalistic, walk-up-and-use scenarios [27, 30].

Applications

The type of application and its user interface can potentially influence visitor engagement around interactive tabletops. In this paper, we consider two different genres of tabletop exhibit to identify factors that are consistent across both applications. In this section we briefly describe both applications to give a sense of the different types of experiences that they provide.

The first application, called DeepTree [5], is an interactive visualization of the Tree of Life in which visitors can browse the evolutionary relationships of over 70,000 species. Visitors can "fly" through the tree to interesting species using a deep zoom interface, view descriptions and rich imagery about species they find, and learn about how any two species in the tree are related. Visitors experience DeepTree as an open ended, exploratory activity, in which they have free control over what they see and do. The second application, *Build-a-Tree* (*BAT*) [15], is a tree-building puzzle game in which visitors reconstruct the evolutionary relationships of different species in increasingly challenging levels. This is done by bumping species together in the correct order.

Both applications are the result of over two years of iterative testing and evaluation involving hundreds of users across several museums [5]. They are now on display in four major museums in the U.S. Both applications have been carefully designed to support collaboration and social engagement [4]. However, even though both applications involve evolutionary trees, the nature of the interaction is very different–one is an open-ended exploratory data visualization, and the other is a puzzle game.

Data Collection

There are several challenges to quantify group interaction in naturalistic settings. First, even though we measure engagement at a group level, we have to collect data at the subject level, as it is almost impossible for a real-time coder to reliably and consistently detect groups as they form. In fact, as we will outline below, even retrospectively identifying groups in a video recording is non-trivial. However, because subjects commonly overlap during the formation of groups, subject-level data is unlikely to be independent. This makes most traditional statistical analyses (such as ANOVAs) that assume independence of observations inapplicable on the subject level.

Secondly, the way in which we conduct observations may influence the way visitors interact with each other and the exhibit. Video recording in public spaces requires visitor consent in most countries. This, in turn, requires consent procedures that may introduce sampling bias and alter visitor behavior, thus undermining the ecological validity of the findings. Alternatively, engagement can be captured by manually coding visitor behavior in real-time. This allows for a more natural flow of visitors and is less intrusive. However, these types of observations present challenges for researchers to accurately measure the range of physical and verbal interactions between group members in real-time.

Our study design seeks to strike a balance between these two methods of observation. To assess the ecological validity of our results, we independently captured engagement twice. In one set of observations, we video recorded visitors using the DeepTree exhibit after obtaining informed consent (Video). For the second set of observations we coded visitor behavior in real-time at both the DeepTree exhibit and the Build-a-Tree exhibit. This was done without video recording or written consent procedures (Naturalistic). This resulted in three independent datasets (Set 1: *Video / DeepTree*; Set 2: *Naturalistic / DeepTree*, and Set 3: *Naturalistic / Build-a-Tree*). Across all three datasets, we used the same engagement variables and real-time coding scheme, as described in the next subsection. All the data were collected at the California Academy of Sciences in San Francisco during the same time of the year. IRB approval was obtained.

Study Procedure and Real-Time Coding

All observations were collected on the floor of the same museum with the general visitor population. In the *Video* condition, the area around the exhibit was cordoned off, and visitors signed a consent form before entering the area. Evaluation staff also actively recruited visitors who were nearby. After giving consent, participants were free to come and go as they pleased. Video and audio of their interaction at the exhibit were recorded. For the naturalistic condition, a sign next to the exhibit informed visitors of an ongoing study, and staff were available to answer questions. Otherwise visitors were entirely free to come and go.

For all of the datasets the same real-time coding scheme was used—the only difference was that coding in the *Video* study utilized the video replay, while in the *Naturalistic* study observers coded engagement on site. To make both study types comparable, the coding scheme was limited to what was accomplishable in real-time, even though the video would have allowed for more sophisticated coding.

The following events were captured. First, arrival and departure times were recorded, from which we could derive dwell times and overlap between visitors. Second, the age range of each visitor was estimated. Third, we developed and refined a coding scheme for social engagement. Our original scheme included 19 codes, but several of these occurred so rarely (<5% of the time) or so frequently (>95% of the time) that they presented insufficient variability and were eliminated in analysis. The following nine social engagement behaviors made up the final set:

- *Prevent Touch* (physical): One visitor prevents another visitor from touching the display.
- *Turn-Taking* (physical): Visitors take turns in taking control of the exhibit.
- *Two Manipulate* (physical): Two visitors manipulate the exhibit at the same time.
- *Pointing* (physical): A visitor points at an element on the screen but does not touch it.
- *Bio Question* (verbal)
- *Bio Statement* (verbal)
- *Negotiation* (verbal): Visitors negotiate what to do.
- *How-To Talk* (verbal): Visitors discuss how to operate the exhibit / user interface.
- *Enjoyment* (affective): A visitor expresses enjoyment.

Following standard museum practice [10, 11], interactions were coded in twenty (20) second intervals – noting that an identified behavior occurred during that interval. This means that even if an engagement behavior occurred multiple times during a twenty second interval, this behavior would be only recorded once during that interval. For each visitor, we can then calculate the percentage of time they experienced engagement behaviors by dividing the number of intervals in which they experienced each behavior by the total number of intervals they spent at the exhibit. For the remainder of this paper, we refer to these percentages as social engagement measures. Note that most social engagement measures can only occur when there are at least two subjects at the table. Consequently, visitors who spent most of their time interacting with the exhibit on their own were excluded from analysis of social engagement (but included in the analysis of dwell time).

Participants

Across all three studies, we collected data from 629 visitors over the course of 10 days, 169 for the *Video* study and 459 across the two *Naturalistic* studies, with 46 young children (~ < 5 years), 149 children (~ 5 – 12y) , 69 teens and 345 adults (20 unknown age group).

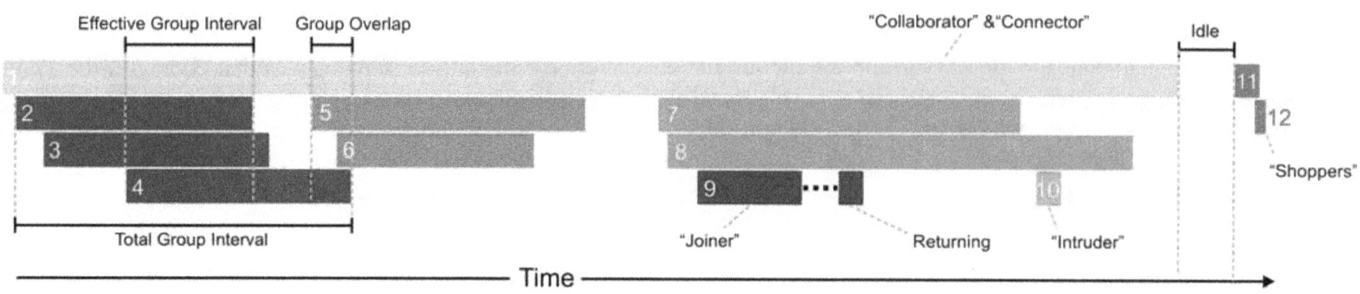

Figure 1. Example of a sequence of visitors spending time at the exhibit and clustering of exclusive groups (color coded).

Research Questions

Based on our measures of engagement, we focus on the following five research questions:

RQ1: How can visitor groups be characterized and quantified in a context in which groups spontaneously form, change over time, and disperse?

RQ2: How does the nature of the observational study affect visitor engagement with interactive exhibits?

RQ3: How does group size and age composition influence engagement?

RQ4: How do overlapping groups influence each other?

RQ5: Are certain types of social engagement associated with longer dwell times?

RQ1 contributes to an algorithmic definition of museum visitor groups. RQ2 addresses issues surrounding study methodologies. RQ3 through RQ5 intend to offer insights into group social engagement around science exhibits on a multi-touch table.

DEFINING GROUPS

While existing observational studies have looked at the formation of groups and their interaction in walk-up-and-use environments, we are not aware of systematic methods for identifying groups within a natural flow of visitors. Some studies have used idle times to cluster sessions and groups of continuous use [18, 27, 30]. However, this is not suitable for busy museums as groups may form and overlap *within* continuous periods of use. An example sequence of arrival and departures of several visitors is shown in Figure 1 (based on real patterns of visitor flow from our data). It illustrates that defining groups by idle time would give us only gross clusters that may contain multiple sub-groups that have come and gone, and thus would fail to detect more fine-grained group formations that overlap with one another. This makes quantitative analysis inaccurate and problematic, whether establishing factors such as group size and age composition, or measuring engagement or dwell time. For instance, it is not clear what we should consider to be the size, composition, and dwell time of this sequence of visitors, since there is only one visitor out of 10 who stays for the entire time, while the others spend vastly varying times at the exhibit in different group constellations.

Methodologically, the need for clearly defining groups arises from two requirements. First, we want to determine the representative group size and age composition in which the group members have *actually* spent most of their time together at the exhibit. Second, we need to analyze engagement on the group level for statistical validity. The experience of many visitors overlaps significantly, which introduces dependencies within our data that makes most statistical analyses inapplicable on the subject level. Through aggregating our engagement per group, we can avoid much of this dependence, which allows us to conduct sound statistical analysis on the group level.

Group Clustering Algorithm

For the purpose of this study, we define shared presence as temporal overlap expressed in percentage of time spent at the exhibit. For instance, if visitors overlap by only 5% of their combined time at the table, they are less likely to influence one another than visitors who spend all of their time together. Note that the percentage of overlap between two visitors is asymmetric when the dwell times of each visitor differ. For instance, visitor 2 in Figure 1 spends 100% of her time with visitor 1, but visitor 1 only spends a small fraction of her time with visitor 2. Our algorithm for identifying groups is based on groups of visitors who all *mutually* overlap for the majority of their time (>50%), so that for any two subjects A and B within a group, A spends most of her time with B, *and* B spends most of her time with A (e.g. visitors 2, 3, and 4). In other words, we select groups of visitors that *share most* of their experience – in this paper referred to as *exclusive groups*.

The core algorithm for this procedure works as follows: 1) calculate pair-wise percentage overlap between all subjects; 2) For each subject, check if there are existing groups in which the subject mutually overlaps with *all* members; 3) if there is exactly one group that meets this criteria, add the subject to the group; if there are multiple groups that meet this criteria, add the subject to the group in which the mutual overlap is highest; if there are no groups, create a new group with the subject as first member. We applied this algorithm to detect groups within our dataset, which clustered our 629 visitors into 354 groups across all three datasets. The visualized results form a sequence chart, such as shown in Figure 1. For illustration, Figure 1 uses color to code exclusive groups determined by the algorithm.

In a second pass, for each exclusive group, the algorithm finds non-members that overlap with *each* member by more than 50%. Note that this time, this overlap is not mutual as otherwise the visitor would have to be a member of the exclusive group. From the perspective of each group, we refer to such visitors who do not spend most of their time with a group, but with whom the group spends most of its time as *collaborators*. For instance, visitor 1, 7 and 8 in Figure 1 are collaborators from the perspective of visitor 9.

The distinction between exclusive group members and collaborators is important in two ways. First, if we want to determine the *actual* predominant configuration in which a group has interacted around the interactive tabletop, we have to consider both the exclusive members, as well as the collaborators of a group. For example, even though the size of the exclusive group of visitor 2, 3 and 4 is three, they have *actually* interacted in a group of size 4 (together with visitor 1). Second, if we aggregate engagement measures on the group level, we need to *exclude* collaborators as by definition, they spend less than 50% of their time with the group and their experiences are not representative of the group. For instance, if we calculate a representative dwell time for the exclusive group formed by visitors 2, 3, and 4, we should only average the dwell times of the exclusive members 2, 3 and 4, but not visitor 1 (who is a collaborator). Similarly, for social engagement measures, only the exclusive group members should be averaged, as their intervals of presence most accurately represent the frequencies of table-wide events of social engagement that happened within the duration of the exclusive group. Note that at the time of data collection, any of the Collaborators' actions would have affected the social engagement coding of other visitors at the table. Consequently, the exclusive groups' aggregated social engagement measures do implicitly reflect the social influence of Collaborators.

In the last step, the algorithm determines the group's effective size and composition (based on the ages of all members and collaborators), as well as its averaged dwell time and social engagement measures (based only on exclusive group membership).

Special Group Types

Based on a review of a visualization of all groups (as shown in Figure 1), we found several noteworthy patterns in the formation of exclusive groups. First, a few visitors (10 out of 629) spend extremely long periods of time (15+ minutes) at the exhibit, overlapping with multiple groups. Such visitors, who we refer to as *Connectors*, are identified as groups of size one by our algorithm (interacting alone) as there is no other visitor with whom they have spent more than 50% of their time. However, Connectors are different from other groups of size one as they do *not* spend the majority of their time alone, but within changing group configurations. As neither a clear group size nor age composition can be assigned for Connectors, we do not consider our 10 connectors as their own group for further

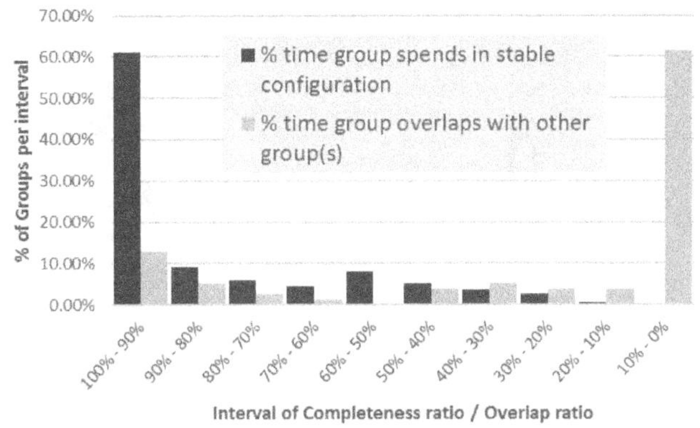

Figure 2. *Completeness Ratio* and *Overlap Ratio* distributions.

analysis in this paper. Note that Connectors *are* counted as collaborators for any group they substantially overlap with, thus, influence the effective size and age composition of groups they collaborate with.

To have a better vocabulary for the qualitative discussion on group engagement, we also identified a few other patterns of visitor flow (who are included in the analysis): *Joiners* and *Intruders* are individuals or groups who approach the table when there is already at least one group present and leave before the initial group departs. However, *Joiners* end up staying with existing groups for more than 2 minutes, while *Intruders* leave before 2 minutes. *Shoppers* are individuals or groups who approach an empty table but leave before 2 minutes. The 2 minute threshold is based on our analysis of dwell time distribution as outlined in the next section.

Stability of Group Configurations and Group Overlap

For each exclusive group, we define the *Completeness Ratio* as the percentage of the total group time spent in the determined configuration of size and age composition. We calculate the Completeness Ratio by dividing the *effective group time* – in which *all* members *and all* collaborators were present – by the *total group time* – in which at least one of the exclusive group members was present (Figure 1 shows the example for exclusive group with members 2, 3 and 4). The higher the *Completeness Ratio*, the more representative the determined group size and age composition is with respect to the aggregated engagement measures. We also define the *Overlap Ratio* as the amount of time any visitor is present who is a member of another exclusive group and *not* a collaborator divided by the *total group time*. The lower the *Overlap Ratio*, the less potential there is for overlapping groups to affect social engagement measures and dwell times. Figure 2 shows a distribution of *Completeness Ratio* and *Overlap Ratio* across all of our groups. More than 60% of our groups spend more than 90% of their time in the determined configuration (purple bar on the left), and have less than 10% overlap with other groups (yellow bar on the right).

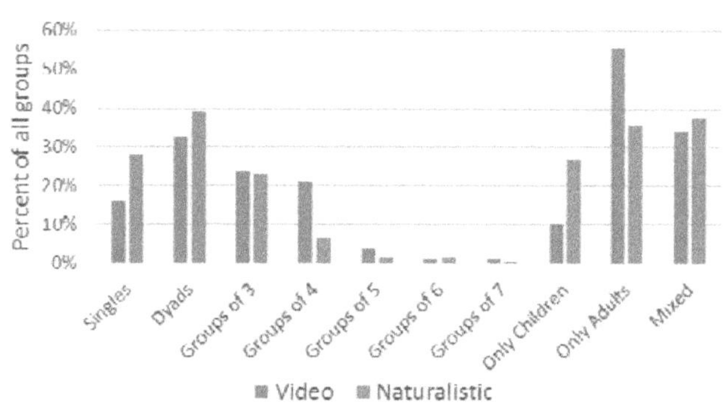

Figure 3. Frequency distribution of group size and age composition, by Study Type.

However, it is important to acknowledge the points between the extremes where around 40% of groups showed various degrees of completeness, as well as overlap with other groups. For instance, 12% of groups overlap with other groups by over 90% — this is the case for all Joiners and Intruders, who spend all their time at the table when an existing group is already present. This means that a minority of dependence of data remains. This can be used to quantify the general "messiness" of group formation in realistic flows of visitors. We could, of course eliminate all groups with overlap, or that are not in a stable configuration for most of their time. This, however, would also exclude cases that are characteristic of the museum context and important to consider when analyzing interaction around multi-touch surfaces. Consequently, we will include all cases in our analysis, and conduct statistical analyses that assume independence of data, even though we acknowledge that some degree of dependence remains.

COMPARING DIFFERENT STUDY TYPES

In this section, we address the question of whether the consent process and video recording in our *Video* setup significantly alter visitor group formation and engagement with the exhibit compared to the *Naturalistic* setups.

Frequencies of Group Size and Age Composition

We analyzed a total of 76 groups for our *Video* dataset and 267 groups for both of our *Naturalistic* datasets. Figure 3 shows the distribution of group size and age composition. The frequencies were significantly different for size and age categories shown in Figure 3 ($N = 343$, *Group Size*: $\chi^2(6) = 19.00, p = .004$; *Age Composition*: $\chi^2(2) = 12.32, p = .002$).

Across all datasets, 35% of groups were dyads (group size = 2), and 22% groups of three. Groups with sizes of 5 and over were rarely observed. In the *Video* data singles are significantly less common than in the *Naturalistic* data (16% vs. 28%), while groups of four are significantly more common in the *Video* data (21% vs. 7%). Overall, this shows that the *Video* study sample is biased towards higher group sizes. Further, *child only* groups were less frequent in the *Video* study (11% vs. 27%), while *adult only* groups were more common (55% vs. 36%). Mixed groups were similarly frequent at around 36% across both study types.

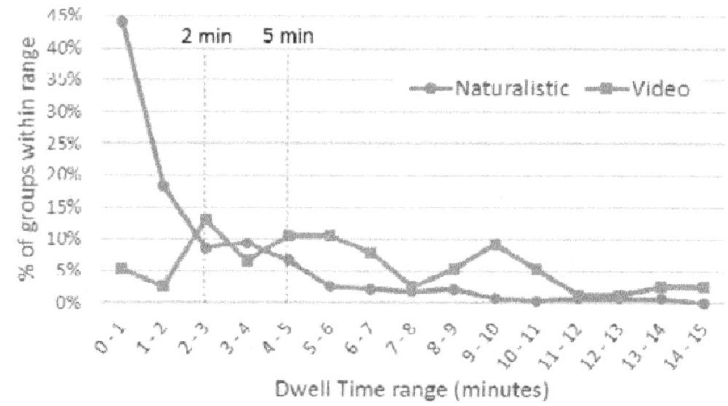

Figure 4. Distribution of dwell times per study type.

Distribution of Dwell Times

The distribution of dwell times is shown in Figure 4. Our two datasets only show comparable distributions of dwell times in the range between 2 and 5 minutes (*Video:* 25% vs. *Naturalistic:* 30%). The ranges below 2 minutes and above 5 minutes are inverse: around 60% of all groups in the *Naturalistic* data engage with the exhibit less than 2 minutes, while only 8% of groups in the *Video* study fall into this range. This shows that in a *Naturalistic* setting, the majority of groups are what we have labelled *Shoppers* and *Intruders*, and suggests that 2 minutes is a suitable threshold for their characterization. Inversely, while almost one half of all groups (49%) in the *Video* study stayed longer than 5 minutes, only 12% of groups stayed over 5 minutes in the *Naturalistic* study. Overall, this shows that dwell time in the *Video* data is strongly skewed towards longer durations compared to the *Naturalistic* data. A One-way ANOVA with factor *Study Type* shows that group dwell time is five times higher in the *Video* study (median 6.0 min) than in the *Naturalistic* study (median 1.2 min) ($F_{1,341} = 106.20, p < .001$). Note that Figure 4 clearly shows that dwell times are not normally distributed. Consequently, for all parametric tests, we use log-transformed dwell time, while reporting the median of the untransformed log times. Kolmogorov-Smirnoff tests showed that all log transformed data were normally distributed ($p > .200$ for all tests).

Differences in Social Engagement Behaviors

We ran Mann-Whitney Tests to compare social engagement measures across our *Video* and *Naturalistic* data (see Table 1 for all significant tests). Alpha was adjusted for multiple comparisons using Bonferroni ($\alpha = 0.005$). Groups in the *Video* study experienced approximately twice the amount of Turn-Taking and Pointing relative to the *Naturalistic* groups, while experiencing significantly less simultaneous interaction and How-To Talk. One interpretation of this result could be that groups who know that they are being recorded resort to more "orderly" forms of interaction, and are more hesitant to show confusion.

Measure	U	P	Video (median)	Naturalistic (median)
Turn-Taking	3325	< .001	20.1%	10.3%
Two Manipulate	4626	.003	31.1%	50.0%
Pointing	4164	< .001	20.5%	8.3%
How-To	4652	.003	23.4%	40.0%

Table 1. Differences in experienced engagement behaviors between *Video* and *Naturalistic* study (Mann-Whitney U).

Discussion
Even though our *Video* methodology encourages a natural flow of visitors and interaction around the table by allowing subjects who had given their consent to come and go as they pleased, there were a series of significant differences compared to the *Naturalistic* data. The consent procedure appears to have deterred / attracted some types of groups more than others, introducing a sampling bias towards larger groups and more adult-only groups and fewer child-only groups. After going through a consent procedure, visitors may also have been less likely to leave after only brief interaction, and more likely to spend time checking out the exhibit they "signed up for". Additionally, awareness of being part of a study may have encouraged a more thorough exploration of the exhibit and more orderly forms of social engagement.

CHARACTERIZING GROUP ENGAGEMENT
In this section, we will assess the effect of group size, age composition, and overlap with other groups on dwell time and social engagement. Given the significant differences between *Video* and *Naturalistic* data, we will analyze each dataset separately, instead of merging all data into a single analysis. Log-transformed dwell times were normally distributed for all analyses. Our social engagement measures are not normally distributed, even after log transformation. Consequently, all analyses of engagement measures use non-parametric Mann-Whitney tests. We adjusted alpha for multiple comparisons using Bonferroni.

Effect of Group Size and Age Composition

Naturalistic Data
We ran an ANOVA with three factors *Group Size* (*1, 2, 3*), *Age Composition* (*children only, adults only, mixed*) and *App Type* (*DeepTree, BAT*) with dependent variable dwell time. We included *App Type* to see if any effects are of a more general nature, or pertain to only one application type. Note that for this analysis we eliminated groups with sizes of four and larger, as we did not have sufficient data (only 7% of all groups consisted of four members, 2% of five, less than 2% of six, and less than 1% of seven members).

There was a significant main effect of *Group Size* ($F_{3,232} = 5.587, p = .004$) on *dwell time*. In the naturalistic studies, groups of two interacted approximately twice as long (median 1.9 minutes) as groups of other sizes ($p < .013$). There was no significant difference between single visitors (median 0.8 minutes), and groups of three (median 1.0 minutes) ($p = 1.000$). There was also a significant main effect of *Age Composition* ($F_{2,232} = 4.466, p = .013$) on *dwell time*. *Child only* groups (median 0.63 minutes) spent significantly less time at the exhibit than *Mixed* groups (median 1.6 minutes) ($p = .003$), and close to significantly less time at the exhibit than *adult only* groups (median 1.6 minutes) ($p = .091$). There was no significant difference between *mixed* groups and *adult only* groups in *dwell time* ($p = .954$). Our results show that groups do not stay longer than individuals, per se. Only dyads were found to engage significantly longer than visitors interacting alone.

There were no significant interactions between *App Type* and *Group Size* ($p = .946$), *App Type* and *Age Composition* ($p = .316$), or *Group Size and Age Composition* ($p = .388$), indicating that the measured main effects on dwell time were consistent across both applications, and independent from one another.

We also analyzed the effect of *Group Size* and *Age Composition* on social engagement. First, we compared differences in social engagement between groups of two and three (single visitors were omitted from the analysis of social engagement). Of our nine measures, only *Two Manipulate* differed significantly, with groups of three experiencing simultaneous interaction of two people 65% of the time (median), while groups of two experienced it only 39% of the time (median) ($U = 2075, p < .001$). While the rate of simultaneous interaction can be expected to go up with increasing group sizes, simultaneous interaction can also indicate increased conflict, which may be one reason for the lower dwell times for groups of three.

Social engagement was also significantly different for different age compositions. Table 2 shows that *mixed* groups experienced significantly more pointing, bio questions, bio statements, how-to talk and enjoyment than *children only* groups. Table 3 shows that compared to *adult only* groups, *mixed* groups experience significantly more preventing touches, two members interacting simultaneously, and negotiation. We believe this nicely captures the facilitating and moderating influence of adults on children in museums [6, 9, 10]. Note that for several social engagement measures, the majority of groups did not experience the relevant behavior at all.

Video Data
We conducted a similar ANOVA for the *Video* data (omitting the factor *App Type*, as we only have data for one application). However, none of the effects of *Group Size* or *Age Composition* from the *Naturalistic* data reoccurred in the *Video* data. There was *no* significant effect of *Group Size* ($F_{6,55} = .472$, $p = .627$) or *Age Composition* ($F_{2,55} = 1.022$, $p = .367$). There were also *no* significant differences of social engagement between groups of two and three, nor between *mixed* groups, *child only* groups, or *adult only* groups.

Measure	U	p	Child only (median)	Mixed (median)
Pointing	1472	< .001	0%	13.2%
Bio Question	1799	.001	0% (mean 6.5%)	0% (mean 15.9%)
Bio Statement	4164	< .001	0%	26.7%
How-To	1771	.003	0%	33.3%
Enjoyment	1833.5	.002	0%	4.3%

Table 2. Differences in social engagement in the *Naturalistic* data between *children only* groups and *mixed* groups (Mann-Whitney U).

Measure	U	p	Mixed (median)	Adults only (median)
Prevent Touch	2063.5	< .001	0% (mean 8.3%)	0% (mean 0.2%)
Two Manipulate	2074.5	< .001	37.5%	0%
Negotiation	1853.5	< .001	25.0%	0%

Table 3. Differences in social engagement in the *Naturalistic* data between *mixed* groups and *adult only* groups (Mann-Whitney U).

Measure	*DeepTree*	*BAT*
Turn-Taking	$r_s = .500, p < .001$	$r_s = .498, p < .001$
Pointing	$r_s = .613, p < .001$	$r_s = .639, p < .001$
Bio Questions	$r_s = .499, p < .001$	$r_s = .585, p < .001$
Bio Statements	$r_s = .599, p < .001$	$r_s = .586, p < .001$
Enjoyment	$r_s = .395, p < .001$	$r_s = .606, p < .001$

Table 4. Engagement measures that significantly correlate with dwell time across both applications in the *Naturalistic* study (Spearman's rho).

Effects of Overlap between Groups

We have determined that a substantial number of groups overlap. Based on our measure of overlap, we examine how the simultaneous presence of multiple groups affects dwell time and social engagement (RQ5).

Naturalistic Data

A Spearman correlation showed no significant correlation between *Overlap Ratio* and dwell time for the *Naturalistic* data (r_s = .056, p = .363). However, the more a group overlapped with another, the more frequently members experienced Two Manipulate, Pointing, Bio Statement, Negotiation, and How-To-Talk ($r_s > .198$, $p < .001$ for all correlations). This means that overlap was generally associated with elevated levels of social engagement around the table, but did not correlate with how long groups stayed at the exhibit. This is interesting, as we expected that social pressure would tend to make existing groups leave prematurely.

Video Data

For the *Video* data, there is a significant negative correlation between *Overlap Ratio* and dwell time (r_s = –.440, $p < .001$), meaning groups stayed longer the less they overlapped with other groups. This indicates that when part of our *Video* study, visitors may have more readily given up space for new groups approaching the table.

Correlation between Social Engagement and Dwell Time

Finally, to address RQ5 we ran non-parametric Spearman correlations between dwell time and each social engagement measure. We conducted this analysis separately for both applications in the *Naturalistic* dataset, focusing on significant correlations that we observed for both. We also ran all correlations for our *Video* data.

Naturalistic Data

Table 4 shows that across both applications, Turn-Taking, Pointing, Bio Questions, Bio Statements, and Enjoyment correlated significantly with dwell time. This means that the longer people interacted with the exhibit, the higher their rate of these engagement behaviors, including, importantly, enjoyment and engagement with scientific concepts.

It is important to note that correlations give us no information about the causal direction of the relationship. In other words, we cannot infer, for instance, that biological talk went up as a consequence of visitors staying longer, or if visitors stayed longer because they engaged in biological talk. Regardless, our findings provide support for the power of dwell time as a proxy for "good" interaction, as it correlates not only with orderly forms of physical activity, but also with enjoyment and engagement with scientific content. From a perspective of interaction design, it is interesting to note that while Turn-taking and Pointing clearly correlated with longer dwell times, Preventing Touch and Two Manipulate did not. This suggests that groups who take turns and do not interfere with one another also tend to spend longer at the exhibit and engage more frequently with the biological content. This is an interesting finding, as much of our interaction design for collaborative learning [4] has involved creating opportunities for simultaneous interaction.

Video Data

We ran the same set of correlations for the *Video* data and found that none of the social engagement measures correlated with dwell time ($p > .05$ for all).

DISCUSSION AND CONCLUSION

As demonstrated in this paper, a systematic and meaningful definition of what constitutes a group in a naturalistic flow of visitors is crucial for the quantitative analysis of engagement and interaction around interactive tabletops in museums. Our algorithm is based on a definition of shared experience as a metric for grouping. We chose this metric based on formal and informal observations of group engagement we conducted throughout the two year development process of both exhibits. We compared the outcome of the algorithm with manual grouping we had done based on the sequence charts. We found that, with a few minor exceptions, the algorithm presented in this paper concurred with our manual grouping, while identifying several mistakes and inconsistencies in the manual grouping. We hope that the proposed grouping algorithm as well as the analysis of overlap and group consistency will benefit future studies of group interactions in public spaces.

In the study setup that most closely reproduced naturalistic conditions, group size, age composition, and the occurrence of certain social behaviors significantly affect how groups engaged with our exhibits. All effects were measured independently across two different types of applications. Our findings have several implications for the design of learning experiences around interactive multi-touch exhibits and visitor research methodology:

Two is better than one and three. Our data suggest that groups do not necessarily engage longer than single visitors per se. We did find evidence that groups of two did engage with the exhibit for significantly longer than visitors who interacted alone, but groups of three did not spend significantly more time at the exhibit than visitors who were alone. This supports existing evidence that social dynamics beyond groups of two are more intricate [28, 33].

Design for small groups, particularly groups of two. Only a small number of people interact with the exhibit in groups of four or larger, so designing for larger groups may not be cost-effective. Instead, focus on designing interactive experiences around groups of two, as dyads spend the most time at the exhibit and show most engagement with the scientific content compared with groups of three.

Provide a meaningful single-user experience. Almost 30% of all visitors interacted with our exhibit on their own. Be sure that a design does not entirely rely on multi-user input and provide means for single visitors to have a meaningful experience.

Entwine playful elements and resources for advanced learners. Groups in which children and adults are mixed spend more time at the exhibit and verbally engage more with scientific content than children alone. Be sure to provide advanced scientific information (e.g. information overlays around the periphery of the display) that can give adults a more meaningful role as facilitators. This reinforces ideas supporting multi-level engagement [6] and synergistic scaffolding [24].

Many visitors will approach the exhibit while it is not in its initial state. Overlap between groups was common, which means that many visitors will enter the experience when others are already interacting. Traditional exhibit designs use reset mechanisms allowing newly joined visitors to start over. There might be opportunities for interactive digital exhibits to provide seamless experiences that are accessible regardless of the state of the exhibit.

Research methodology matters. Throughout the last two sections we have also established significant differences between our two study types. In our *Video* study, the effects on dwell time of group size, age composition, and social engagement were not significant, while more overlap between groups was associated with lower dwell times. These findings are exactly opposite of the *Naturalistic* datasets. Note that our data does not lend itself to identify exactly which factors underlying each study methodology contributed to these behavioral differences. However, we conclude that when quantifying engagement around exhibits, one should *attend carefully to the impact of consent procedures, as they can significantly affect group engagement.* Procedures that require formal consent to enter a small area cordoned off for videotaping significantly alter the flow of visitors to an exhibit and how they engage. If consent for video can be legally and ethically given at a distance in time and space (e.g., upon entering a museum or large exhibit space) then behavior and engagement may more closely resemble naturalistic conditions. If not, be cautious about using videotaped data to draw quantitative conclusions about dwell time or engagement.

LIMITATIONS

While we did take great care to highlight results that we think are ecologically most valid and that are of a more general nature, our results may be specific to the venue in which we have conducted the data collection. Our venue is a busy museum with 2 million annual visitors, and has a very diverse demographic audience. Some of our quantitative findings may or may not apply to other venues.

ACKNOWLEDGEMENTS

We would like to thank Anita Smith, Julie Shattuck, Lauren Hodge and Jim Galdos for their help in collecting the evaluation data, and the California Academy of Sciences for hosting this study. We would also like to thank Heather Lavigne, Joye Thaller and Anna Adams for their help with data processing and analysis. This work is partially supported by the National Science Foundation (DRL-1010889). Any opinions, findings and conclusions or recommendations expressed in this material are those of the authors and do not necessarily reflect the views of the National Science Foundation.

REFERENCES

1. Antle, A.N., Bevans, A., Tanenbaum, J., Seaborn, K. & Wang, S. Futura: design for collaborative learning and game play on a multi-touch digital tabletop. In *Proc. TEI '11*, pp. 93-100, 2010.
2. Benton, D. P. Intergenerational interaction in museums. New York: Columbia University Teachers College. Ed. D. dissertation, 1979.
3. Bitgood, S., Kitazawa, C., Cavender, A. & Nettles, K.A. Study of Social Influence. Poster presented at the 1993 Visitor Studies Conference, Albuquerque, NM, 1977.
4. Block, F. Wigdor, D. Phillips, B. C., Horn, M.S. & Shen, C. FlowBlocks: a multi-touch UI for crowd interaction. In *Proc. UIST '12*, pp. 497-508, 2012.
5. Block, F., Horn, M.S. Phillips, B.C., Diamond, J., Evans, E.M., Chia Shen. The DeepTree Exhibit: Visualizing the Tree of Life to Facilitate Informal Learning. In *TVCG* 18(12), pp. 2789-2798, 2012.
6. Borun, M., Chambers, M. B., Dritsas, J. & Johnson, J. I. Enhancing Family Learning Through Exhibits. In *Curator* 40(4), pp. 279-295, 2010.

7. Buisine, S. Besacier, G., Aoussat, A. & Vernier, F. How do interactive tabletop systems influence collaboration? In *Computers in Human Behavior*, 28(1), 2012.
8. Cone, C., & Kendall, K. Space, time and family interaction: Visitor behavior at the Science Museum of Minnesota. In *Curator*, 21, 345-258, 1978.
9. Crowley, K., Callanan, M. A., Lipson, J. L., Galco, J., Topping, K. & Shrager, J. Shared scientific thinking in everyday parent-child activity. In *Science Education* 85(6), pp. 712-732, 2001.
10. Diamond, J. The behavior of family groups in science museums. In *Curator*, 29(20), pp. 139-154, 1986.
11. Diamond, J., Smith, A. & Bond, A. California Academy of Sciences discovery room. *Curator* 31, 157-166, 1988.
12. Falk, J. H., & Dierking, L. D. *Learning from museums: Visitor experiences and the making of meaning.* Altamira Press, 2000.
13. Fleck, R., Rogers, Y., Yuill, N., Marshall, P., Carr, A., Rick, J. & Bonnett, V. Actions speak loudly with words: unpacking collaboration around the table. In *Proc/ ITS'09*, pp. 189-196, 2009.
14. Hinrichs, U., & Carpendale, S. Gestures in the wild: studying multi-touch gesture sequences on interactive tabletop exhibits. In *Proc. CHI'11*, 3023-3032, 2011.
15. Horn, M., Leong, Z., Block, F., Diamond J., Evans, E.M., Phillips, B. & Shen C. BATs and APEs: Designing an interactive tabletop game for natural history museums. In *Proc. CHI'12*, 2059–2068, 2012.
16. Hornecker, E., ""I don't understand it either, but it is cool" - visitor interactions with a multi-touch table in a museum," In *Proc. ITS'08*, pp.113-120, 1-3 Oct. 2008.
17. Humphrey, T. and Gutwill, J. Fostering active prolonged engagement: The art of creating APE exhibits. Exploratorium (2005).
18. Jacucci, G., Morrison, A., Richard, G.T., Kleimola, J., Peltonen, P., Parisi, L. & Laitinen, T. Worlds of information: designing for engagement at a public multi-touch display. In *Proc. CHI'10*, pp. 2267-2276, 2010.
19. Kendon, A. The F-Formation System: Spatial-Orientational Relations in Face to Face Interaction. In Man Environment Systems(6), pp. 291-296, 1976.
20. Koran, J., Koran, M. & Longino, S. The relationship of age, sex attention, and holding power with two types of science exhibits. In *Curator*, 29(3), pp. 227-224, 1986.
21. Kremer, K. & Mullins, G. Children's gender behavior at science museum exhibits. *Curator*, 35(1), 39-48, 1992.
22. Leinhardt, G., Crowley, K., & Knutson, K. (Eds.). *Learning conversations in museums*. 2002.
23. Leinhardt, G., & Crowley, K. Museum learning as conversational elaboration: a proposal to capture, code, and analyze talk in museums. *Museum Learning Collaborative,* 1998. *http://museumlearning. org/paperresearch. html (accessed March 1, 2007).*
24. Lyons, L. et al. Synergistic Scaffolding of Technologically-enhanced STEM Learning in Informal Institutions. In *Proc. ICLS'14 Vol. 3*, 1456-1465, 2014.
25. Ma, J., Liao, I., Ma, K., Frazier, J. Living Liquid: Design and evaluation of an exploratory visualization tool for museum visitors. In *TVCG* 18(12), pp. 2799-2808, 2012.
26. McManus, P. It's the company you keep… The social determination of learning-related behavior in a science museum. In *International Journal of Museum Management and Curatorhip*, 53, pp. 32-50, 1987.
27. Marshall, P., Morris, R., Rogers, Y., Kreitmayer, S. & Davies, M. 2011. Rethinking 'multi-user': an in-the-wild study of how groups approach a walk-up-and-use tabletop interface. In *CHI'11*, pp. 3033-3042, 2011.
28. Marshall, P., Rogers, Y. & Pantidi, N. Using F-formations to analyse spatial patterns of interaction in physical environments. In *CSCW'11*, 445-454, 2011.
29. Olson, I.C., Leong, Z.A., Wilensky, U. & Horn, M.S. It's just a toolbar!: using tangibles to help children manage conflict around a multi-touch tabletop. In *Proc. TEI'11*, pp. 29-36, 2010.
30. Peltonen, P., Kurvinen, E., Salovaara, A., Jacucci, G., Ilmonen, T., Evans, J, Oulasvirta, A. & Saarikko, P. It's Mine, Don't Touch!: interactions at a large multi-touch display in a city centre. In *CHI'08*, 1285-1294, 2008.
31. Rick, J., Marshall, P., & Yuill, N. Beyond one-size-fits-all: how interactive tabletops support collaborative learning. In *Proc. IDC'11*, pp. 109-117, 2011.
32. Rosenfeld, S. & Turkel, A. A naturalistic study of visitors at an interactive mini-zoo. *Curator*, 25(3), 187-212, 1982.
33. Ryall, K., Forlines, C., Shen, C. & Morris, M.R. Exploring the effects of group size and table size on interactions with tabletop shared-display groupware. In *Proc. CSCW'04*, pp. 284-293, 2004.
34. Setti, F., Russell, C., Bassetti, C. and Cristani, M. F-formation Detection: Individuating Free-standing Conversational Groups in Images. Preprint on arXiv.org, http://arxiv.org/pdf/1409.2702.pdf, 2014.
35. Shaer, O., Strait, M, Valdes, C., Feng, T., Lintz, M. & Wang, H. Enhancing genomic learning through tabletop interaction. In *Proc. CHI'11*, pp. 2817-2826, 2011.
36. Tang, A., Tory, M., Po, B., Neumann, P. & Carpendale, S. Collaborative coupling over tabletop displays. In *Proc. CHI'06*, pp. 1181-1190, 2006.
37. Tse, E., Shen, C., Greenberg, S., Forlines, C. How Pairs Interact Over a Multimodal Digital Table. In *CHI'07*.

Flexible Ecologies and Incongruent Locations

Paul K. Luff[1], Naomi Yamashita[2], Hideaki Kuzuoka[3], Christian Heath[1]

[1] King's College, London
150 Stamford Street, London, UK
<Paul.Luff@kcl.ac.uk,
Christian.Heath@kcl.ac.uk

[2] NTT Communication Science Laboratories,
2-4 Hikaridai Seika-cho
Soraku-gun, Kyoto, Japan
<naomiy@acm.org>

[3] University of Tsukuba, Japan,
1-1-1 Tennoudai
Tsukuba, Ibaraki, Japan
<kuzuoka@iit.tsukuba.ac.jp>

ABSTRACT

In this paper we report on some experiments with a high fidelity media space, t-Room, an immersive system that presents full scale, real-time images of co-participants. The system has been enhanced to provide more flexibility in the ways participants could organise themselves and the materials they are working on. Drawing on some quasi-naturalistic experiments, where the participants were required to undertake a range of complex tasks, we consider the formations they adopt and the issues and problems that arise when they attempt to establish and preserve a common focus and alignment. We conclude by briefly discussing the consequences for developing advanced spaces to support collaborative work and understanding complex video-mediated interaction.

Author Keywords

Media spaces; interaction analysis; CSCW; embodied interaction.

ACM Classification Keywords

H.5.m. Information interfaces and presentation (e.g., HCI): H4.3. Computer-supported cooperative work.

INTRODUCTION

There has been a long-standing interest by researchers and practitioners in human-computer interaction to develop audio-visual and computing infrastructures that support remote collaboration. The focus of most of these systems has been primarily on enabling video mediated communication and collaboration between two participants and increasingly, to provide a common workspace, such as on a tabletop or a shared screen. [13, 16, 20, 25]. The more flexible and contingent forms of cooperation and collaboration we find in many organisational environments, for example in the open-plan office [23], where a number of participants draw on various resources to undertake a particular activity, if only for a few moments, has received less attention. And yet, these complex human and technical arrangements are becoming a pervasive feature of contemporary work. Developing t-Room, an experimental room-sized conferencing system designed to support group-to group collaboration, we examine how multiple participants with access to a variety of electronic and tangible resources, undertake a range of challenging activities that demand highly contingent forms of cooperation and collaboration. In particular, we consider how participants attempt to establish and preserve a common focus and alignment, if only temporarily, and the ways in which they come to recognize and manage incongruities and misunderstandings. The paper therefore is concerned with identifying the problems and practicalities that pervade our attempts to enrich video mediated environments and provide support for complex forms of remote collaboration.

CHI 2015, April 18–23, 2015, Seoul, Republic of Korea.

http://dx.doi.org/10.1145/2702123.2702286

BACKGROUND

Both within the research community and within commercial organisations there is continuing interest in developing audio-visual infrastructures to support collaborative work. In part, this has been motivated by developments in video communication technologies, from early attempts at video-telephony, through prototype media spaces and recently by the great success of computer tools like Skype. Whilst such technologies have shown the potential for supporting informal face-to-face communication, enhancing these systems to support collaborative work has proven more difficult.

Take, for example the great interest in the 1990s in the potential for media spaces to support communication and collaboration in organisations [4]. Although the prototype deployment of this technology revealed how simple video connections facilitated face-to-face communication and various kinds of office sharing, the capabilities available for supporting collaborative tasks were under-utilised. Indeed, such technologies offered little to support activities with and around artefacts like documents, and even undermined participants gaining a common orientation to the critical resources required for collaborative work [8]. In the subsequent years, despite the pervasiveness of different kinds of video technology, the abilities to present moving images in higher and higher fidelity and experiments with various ways of augmented these system, the underlying problems of video supported collaboration remain. Even in a period where the use of Skype is commonplace, video mediated communication remains focused on face-to-face interaction. The tools that are available for collaborative activities tend to be those for sharing electronic documents and these are typically are not very well integrated with the capabilities to support visual communication. For video to support organisational collaboration better ways are needed to support participants to refer to, contribute to and manipulate artefacts and objects.

Perhaps a motivating example would be the kind of support required in intensive multi-party meetings. Often characterised as 'war rooms' [2, 19]. In these, participants plan missions, co-ordinate projects and present proposals for solving problems drawing on a wide range of artefacts including, individual documents, electronic resources, flipcharts and large displays. The spaces in which these participants work therefore involve many different kinds of spaces, on which documents can be added, contributed to or annotated, often simply by the means of attaching PostIt stickers to the displays. The participants can move around this space, and quickly shift between activities; between general discussion of problems, presentation of proposals by individual members to their colleagues and individual detailed work regarding particular concerns. Although such collaboration may be extreme, such flexible and contingent ways of organising activities, requiring the interplay between the individual and the collaborative are common in most forms of everyday work [9].

If we are to support the variety and richness of everyday activities in a dispersed setting then some enhancements to existing technological capabilities seem necessary. One approach that has been of longstanding concern by researchers in human-computer interaction is for participants to meet in some kind of virtual space (through avatars in a collaborative virtual environment CVE, for example). Early studies of such spaces revealed difficulties for participants when they engaged in certain common and apparently simple tasks, like pointing to an object [11] In these spaces, the participants' conduct can become divorced from its environment of action, it being difficult for a colleague to tie a movement of an avatar with an object elsewhere in the space and hence interaction becomes 'fragmented'. As Wong and Gutwin note, recent advances and augmentations to CVEs, such as wider fields of view and enhanced 'pointing devices' such as extensible arms and simulations of laser pointing, go some way in ameliorating these problems, but the fragmented nature of interaction in virtual space persists [26].

The problems of interacting with objects in CVEs resonate with those found when video-mediated interaction is augmented with tools and techniques that go beyond face-to-face communication. Even high fidelity video-mediated systems such as HP's Halo, Cisco's Telepresence. Multiview and BiSI [20, 22] have problems integrating documents within the interaction between participants. In these systems great attention is paid to create a 'blended space' where gaze direction and shifts in body orientation by remote colleagues appear as if those participants were co-present. Partly this is achieved by ensuring the location of participants remain relatively stable, for example, by sitting in a prescribed location constrained by the design of the furniture in the space [22]. However, although this may give a great sense of 'presence', it is hard to integrate other features of the environment within this space and hence document images are placed either above, below or to the side of the images of the participants. Participants' actions, therefore, can be fractured within these environments. It can be difficult to relate the movement of a cursor on one screen with the visible movements of a person on another.

A more recent development in blended spaces seeks to provide for more flexible forms of working. By enclosing a 'room' with video screens and also placing a video tabletop system at the centre of the space, participants are provided with an environment in which they have a variety of ways of collaborating with each other [12]. In t-Room the vertical screens can present both electronic documents and the images of remote participants. It is large enough for several participants to freely move around the space, work in different locations around the desk and also use physical as well as electronic objects in the course of their collaborative activities. In experiments with t-Room, it appeared that despite both transformations in the appearance of conduct and delays between the production and appearance of actions, distributed participants could refer to quite fine details of objects [18]. Unlike other forms of video-mediated interaction, participants seemed able to make sense of their colleagues' actions in the environment. They seemed able to transpose their own conduct into the remote environment, assess their colleague's standpoint and subsequently produce coherent next actions. In short, t-Room seemed to provide resources for participants to assess and draw on the standpoint of a remote colleague. However, in these experiments only one of the screens could be used to display documents and images. Unlike the more flexible and open-ended forms of collaboration found in intensive, multi-party meetings, participants tended to focus around this one screen and participants would usually position themselves around it. In part, the apparent success of t-Room may have been due to stabilities in the orientation and positioning of the participants with respect to features in the environment.

In both CVEs and advanced media spaces, technological advances have seemed to help ameliorate quite fundamental problems that arise when activities are fragmented across geographically dispersed settings. They can help bridge the gaps between the producer of an action, his or her recipients and the local and virtual environments. Nevertheless, even in the most sophisticated collaborative spaces, constraints are placed on the participants, constraints that may impede more flexible forms of collaborative work. We need to better understand the variations and formations of collaborative work, particularly when participants are freer to position and orient themselves within the environment (cf. 6, 15, 24).

A HYBRID COLLABORATION SPACE: T-ROOM

T-Room is an experimental video conferencing system that is intended to support more flexible forms of collaboration. In consists of multiple screens, cameras, and tables. Its design aims to allow several participants to move around the space so they can interact with remote participants, discuss common resources in various locations and shift between individual and collaborative activities. T-Room has different kinds of surfaces available (see Figure 1). A single t-Room consists of eight vertical modules (called Monoliths) arranged in a nonagon (one side left open for participants to enter). It also has at its centre a shared worktable which consists of two 40 inch LCD displays. Each Monolith is made up of a 65 inch LCD panel (resolution of 1920 x 1080) and a high definition video (HDV) camera mounted on the panel. The configuration of video cameras and panels are designed to maintain spatial relationships between distant sites – aiming to support consistent spatial referencing as well as a coherent environment in which to accomplish interaction.

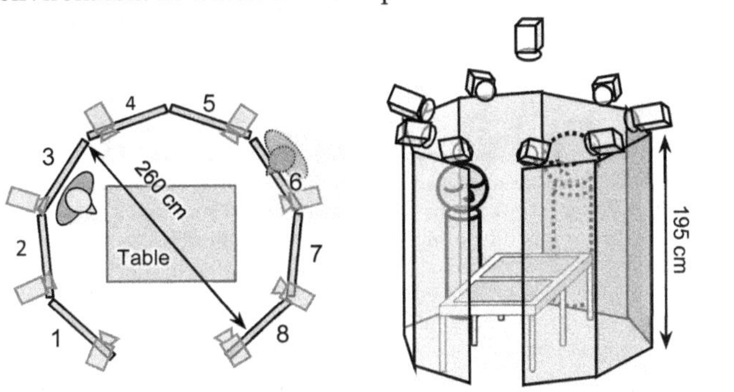

Fig 1: Left: Plan of t-Room showing the position of 8 vertical screens (monoliths). For ease of exposition the monoliths are numbered 1-8: Right: an isometric sketch of the t-Room.

In addition to providing views of the co-participants and the documents on the tabletop, t-Room allows data sharing across sites; distant people can share digital contents such as still images displayed on any monoliths (see [12] for further technical details of the system).

To explore how people collaborated with and through several workspaces, two capabilities were added to t-Room. Firstly, Kinect sensors were mounted above each monolith to provide a multi-touch sensing capability to the monoliths. By the sensors detecting up to two simultaneous touches participants could drag, expand, and shrink the images displayed on the vertical screens. In pilot trials of the new system we found that participants required ways of pointing to the monoliths without activating these sensors. Hence, they had the chance to select a 'virtual button' at the top of each monolith so images displayed would be 'Fixed'. Participants could press this again for a 'Move' setting when they wanted to manipulate the images. Secondly, a simple graphical user interface was developed on an Android tablet to allow participants in each t-Room to look through a collection of images stored on the tablet, select one, and add it to the monolith. They did this by swiping the image upward and then touching the monolith where they wanted the image to appear. This aimed to provide a simple way of moving objects from a private to a public workspace. Participants could also remove an image by dragging it to the bottom of the monolith. Note that the remote participants' body images are overlaid on the still images, allowing participants to collaborate over and around the digital materials.

EXPERIMENTS AND METHODS

Two identical t-Rooms were installed in two distinct rooms in the same building and connected by a gigabit network. One was called the Kyoto Space, the other the Tokyo Space. The network delay for video and audio transmission between the two spaces was up to 0.3-0.4 and 0.2-0.3 seconds, respectively; video and audio were not synchronized.

To explore how people collaborated over large shared workspaces, shifted their attention between locales and collaborated over hybrid combinations of paper and digital documents, we organized a series of quasi-naturalistic experiments that mimic the work practices in intensive design and development meetings. For each experiment two participants were located in the Kyoto Space and two in the Tokyo Space. Four groups of four English–speaking subjects (13 male and 3 female) were recruited for this study and were paid for their participation.

We developed a task for participants to undertake in the experiment that would reflect complex activities required such as searching materials, exchanging information about the materials, sharing the materials with others, annotating them and presenting and discussing plans and solutions with colleagues. In the task, participants were asked to imagine that they were the members of a consultancy pitching to design a major new art exhibition on European art for a museum in Japan. Participants were provided with the following materials: a tablet each, which contained a set of images of paintings; paper materials that described details about the paintings; a floor plan of the museum with 5 rooms; and PostIts of different sizes to draft out pieces of text or diagrams. Note that each tablet had different set of paintings, making participants necessary to exchange information about the paintings that they did not have to hand. In order to induce active discussions, we also emphasized that all the participants should come to an agreement about their proposals.

The task was composed of two parts: In the first part, participants were asked to select paintings for each room (i.e. 15 paintings in total). In doing so, they were asked to discuss and agree on a story line or a theme for the exhibition. For this activity they would need to manage a large number of paper and electronic documents within the space, move these around the space and also be able to refer to them and distinguish which objects their colleagues were referring to. In the second part of the experiment the participants were asked to design an audio guide and the webpage for the art exhibition. This required them to undertake activities like writing and drawing through the space. In both parts of the experiment the participants were free to organise the work as they saw fit and also to work anywhere they liked within the t-Room.

The participants were given a 10 minute introduction to the technology. Each part lasted around 45 minutes followed by a short debriefing to collect the comments of the participants about the use of the system. We collected materials from 6 cameras (3 from each t-Room). Our analysis is concerned with the emergent and sequential character of practical action and the practices in and through which participants collaboratively accomplish activities [7]. In this this case we consider how the participants search for appropriate images, make these visible to colleagues, how they refer to features of the images and recognise these, how they arrange images around the space, and plan, discuss and design related textual materials. The fragments presented here are selected in order to provide a sense of some of the issues and complexities that arise in these brief moments of concerted action. In this paper we focus on the activities of the participants that arose when they are exploring and examining the moving images.

In the data we collected it was apparent that the ability to add documents and images easily to the monoliths using the Kinect, allowed the participants to adopt a wide variety of orientations. To engage in different activities they would frequently adjust their position in the rooms. Nevertheless, there were a few common formations that emerged that were stable for extended periods of collaborative work. We will consider these formations in terms of three simplified categories (cf. [14]): the 'huddle' – a formation where all participants were oriented towards a common artifact; the 'constellation' – a formation where they positioned themselves around the space; and the 'cluster' where they stood in one area of the space, focussed on a collection of objects. Although there was a great variety in how the participants configured themselves and participants would change how they were oriented, for sake of exposition we will focus on these three patterns.

THE 'HUDDLE': CO-PARTICIPATION AROUND A SHARED RESOURCE

Although the participants frequently work on different activities, either as individuals or as a co-present or distributed pair, during the experiments all four participants frequently engaged together in one focused activity. For this they would orient towards an artifact. As in the cases illustrated in Figure 2, where the participants in one of the groups at different times during the task, orient to a monolith on the right, a monolith on the left and documents on the desk, respectively.

Figure 2: Different examples of the Huddle formation using t-Room (all from the Tokyo side). Top: one participant works on a physical document on a monolith to the left, whilst his colleagues monitor him from around the desk. Middle: Two participants, one in Tokyo and one in Kyoto work on a monolith on the right whilst their colleagues monitor what they are doing. Bottom: All four participants collaborate over physical copies of the same document over the desktop.

In the following instance James and Tim in the 'Tokyo Space' and Charles and Runako in the 'Kyoto Space' are oriented in a huddle towards one of the central monoliths (number 3). They have used this monolith to display a lot of images of paintings by Vermeer. Charles has been looking through the paper descriptions on the tabletop and suggests that the "Girl with a Pearl Earring" could also be added. Both James in Tokyo and Runako in Kyoto agree and suggest to 'put' or 'throw that one up' onto the screen. As there already have too many pictures displayed, Charles suggests they remove one first.

All participants are focused on one location and agree to the suggestions to remove an image; three of them pointing to various candidates. However, the participants are all oriented in slightly different ways. Charles is positioned so he can see documents on the tabletop and the screen and also shift attention between them, whilst also monitoring Runako (in the same room) and James and Tim in the remote space. Tim's orientation in Tokyo in some ways parallels Charles's. Although Tim is slightly more oriented to the monolith and to Charles (but away from Runako).

Fragment 1 (Kyoto View)

Fragment 1 (Tokyo View)

J: throw that one up there (er)

R: (so why don't we put up that)

←C: I think I think we should remove one of these

R: yes

T: which one? I think this one is not too hot

Although both Charles and Tim are oriented in similar ways, the technology transforms how they appear to each other with respect to the environment. As the images taken from the video-recordings are complex, we present this and subsequent examples using a series of simplified graphical images reflecting where each participant is positioned, how they are oriented and how they appear to the remote participants. In these, the appearance of the co-participants are shown with dark lines, within the 'wall' of monoliths. The appearance of the remote participants is shown as if they are behind the screen. They are shown lighter (and dashed).

Fragment 1
Kyoto

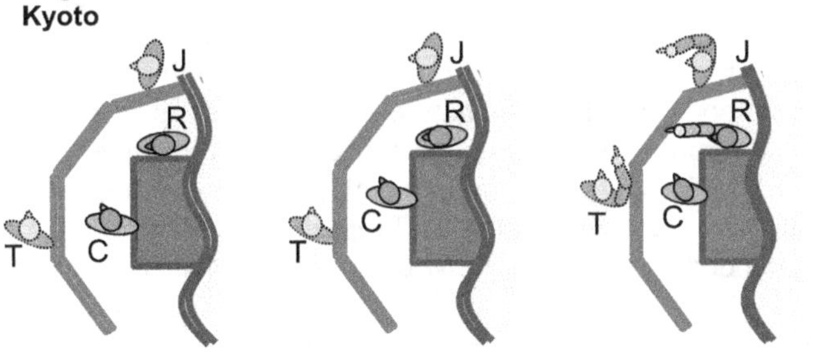

R: so why don't we put up and | C: I think I think we should remove one of these | R: yes T: which one I think this one is not too hot

Tokyo

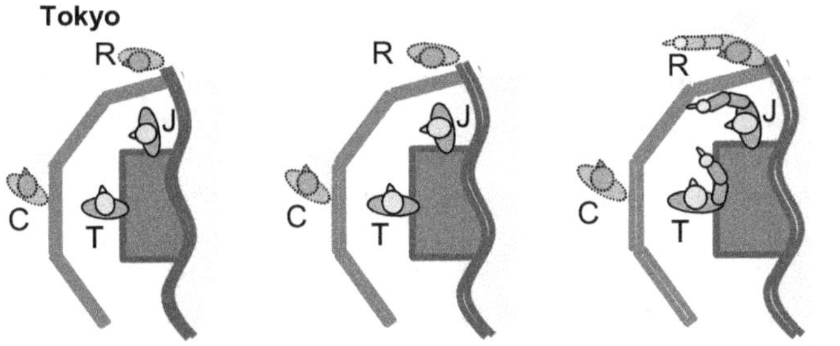

For both Tim and Charles, the other appears closer to the screen. Moreover, when Charles is oriented towards the desk and away from Tim, Charles actually appears to Tim to be oriented towards him. Conversely, when Tim is oriented towards Charles, he appears to Charles as if he is oriented away. The transformation is more marked for Runako and James, who 'share' the same position of the desk. For Runako, she and James are standing back to back. For James, Runako is oriented to his side. Nevertheless, despite these transformations the participants seem to unproblematically contribute to the task. They develop a solution to an emerging problem and agree on which Vermeer painting they should remove.

The way that t-Room has been designed allows the participants to all contribute in their own way towards the task at hand. When engaged in a huddle towards a focal activity, participants point out objects on the screen or the desktop and as they do this, others can see their conduct and respond accordingly. However despite the careful calibration in the design, conduct is transformed through the technology, particularly how the orientations of the participants appears to remote colleagues. And yet, despite these transformations, participants do make sense of the conduct of their colleagues. Objects in the environment are drawn upon to make sense of apparent incongruities in the way activities are presented through the system. A participant will make sense of a colleague's turn towards to away from an object or artefact of concern as one that is related to what they themselves have just done. The participants relying upon colleague's actions in the environment being sequentially relevant in order to accomplish coherent collaborative activities through the mediated environment.

THE 'CONSTELLATION': MANAGING INCONGRUENT LOCATIONS

Another frequently occurring formation the participants adopt is when they are engaged in more disparate activities or more general discussions about the task. In the 'constellation' formation the participants are more spread out around the space. In such a formation they can work on both paper documents and electronic images and also shift orientation back and forth between the monoliths and the desktop. As in the following example where the participants are all engaged in different activities, trying to find paintings for the exhibition. The participants in Tokyo (Pete and Mike) are standing on the left hand side of the desk, whilst the participants in Kyoto (Rich and Guy) are on the right. As we join the fragment, Rich, in Kyoto, has been looking across the space for a while at the monolith opposite. He then asks what one of the paintings is, one of four which are displayed on that monolith. As he asks his question he points across the desk towards the picture in question with his right hand.

Rich's utterance 'whats this one err over (1.0) over (0.6) there?' is accompanied by a number of perturbations including two long pauses. Also before he delivers the gist of his utterance he briefly withdraws his arm before going on to point again, this time reaching out further.

Fragment 2 (Kyoto View)

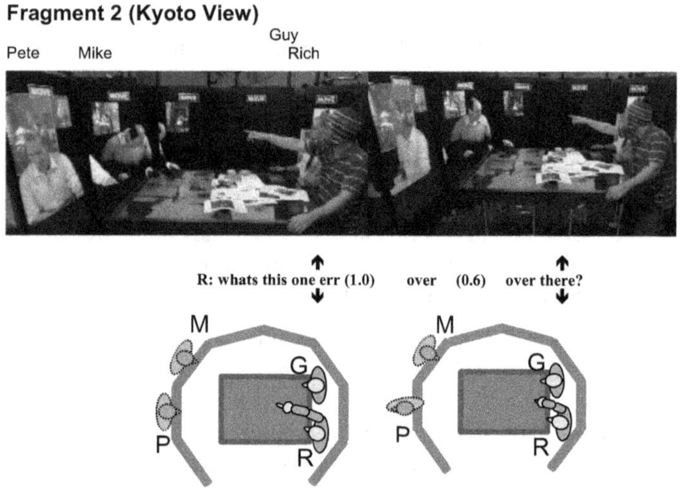

Fragment 2 (Tokyo View)

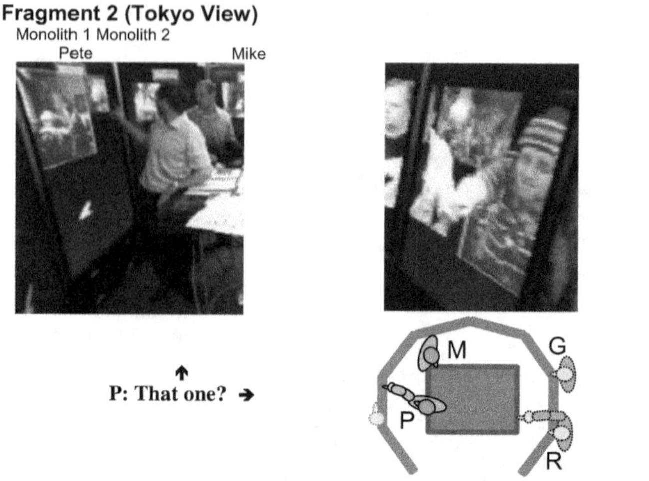

Rich's actions are produced in the light of the conduct of his remote colleagues, who seem to be having some problems identifying where Rich is pointing. As Rich begins his utterance both Pete and Mike in Tokyo look up towards him. Seeing Rich, pointing they turn to the monoliths behind them. But each both look to different screens. Mike looks to his left, at monolith 4 where a painting of a woman sat at harpsichord is displayed. Meanwhile, Pete turns to his right, towards monolith 2, the monolith that is directly behind him. This displays an image that was actually added by Rich. Pete then turns further around and looks across the screens to his right raising his right arm before arriving at an image on that screen (monolith 3). As he points he says 'that one?' which Rich confirms. Pete then answers the original question with the name of the painting ('the Draughtsman'). This seems to successfully identify the picture that Rich is asking about. Despite Pete (and Mike) immediately recognizing the question is for them and Rich's sustained gesture towards the object, there seem to be difficulties identifying which object is being pointed at. In part, this seems to be due to how Ross's conduct appears on the screen.

Although Rich is pointing to the third monolith, the screen to Pete's left, for Pete, Rich appears to be pointing at the second monolith, the screen behind Pete. Hence, Pete turns right around and tries to find an appropriate referent for Rich's point. Rich withdraws his hand as Pete starts to turn. Rich seems sensitive to Pete's difficulties pointing again and moving his finger from left to right, as if to guide Pete towards the correct place.

Although Pete has turned away from Rich and now cannot see these actions on the monolith that is now behind him, an unforeseen feature of t-Room's design seems to assist in Pete orienting to the correct screen. As Rich reaches over to point, the image of Rich's hand is also captured on the first and second monoliths (just noticeable in the bottom left hand corner of the following image of Pete and Mike).

As Pete turns around to the screens these 'hands' become noticeable. So when the hand that previously was behind him and not visible comes into view, and pointing to the right, Pete glances to his right and asks 'that one?'. The 'disembodied hand seems to direct Pete towards the correct image, helping to resolve what seems a problematic referential activity. It might also be noted in this case, that this hand is also visible to Pete's colleague, Matt, seems to engender Matt's reorientation to the correct picture. Having identified the picture, the participants then all go on to other activities.

The problems of identifying the object seem to be due to a variation of what is known as the 'Mona Lisa' effect [1]. However, rather than being an issue with respect to awareness of the direction of gaze through video, in this case, the difficulties seem to be due to the differences between how the production of a gesture is produced and how it appears. The conduct appears different to each of the co-participants. Moreover, when producing the gesture Rich has few resources for assessing how his point is being understood, or indeed the nature of the problem being faced by his remote colleagues. The difficulties are resolved first by Rich drawing on conventional practices for repairing visual conduct (e.g. restarts and repeats [5]) and through an unintended resource of t-Room. Although the visual conduct is presented in a fragmented and curiously disembodied fashion, it seems to help resolve the problem. The appearance of the 'extra' hands' at a sequentially relevant place makes the conduct coherent to the remote participants.

In the following fragment taken from later in the same session the participants are positioned around the table once again. They are discussing the routes visitors might take through the exhibition. Mike in Tokyo notes that they should not begin the route in the museum shop, pointing at a location on the map in front of Pete, his co-present colleague. Pete then suggests a place where visitors could start their route ('the entrance hall'), pointing to a location on the paper plan, just above where Mike has just pointed.

Fragment 3 (Tokyo View)

M :no:: you don't want to start at the museum shop because that's the last (look at everything) when you buy
(.)
R: yeah
G: umm

(.)
P: the entrance hall; (1.3)
P: you can see on my table the way I am pointing right?=
G: =yeah yeah yeah

As Pete does this he looks up to the participants in Kyoto, Guy and Rich, and asks if they can see 'the way' he is pointing. Both Mike and Pete's hands are visible on the projected tabletop and the co-participants in Kyoto confirm that they can see them. The four participants go on to discuss various routes over the plan. Nevertheless, although Pete's actions are visible, it seems unclear to him how they appear in the remote domain. Hence, he has to ask them explicitly whether they can see how he is pointing. It maybe that the transformations in the way images are presented may contribute to this. Although the remote participants are looking down at the table, for them at the right location, for Pete they appear to be looking nearer to them, at their 'own' desk. The technology seems to make such fine work over documents problematic. Although the participants conduct is sequentially appropriate, it is transformed in such a way that the conduct is incongruous within the environment and so hard to tie to a participant's own actions.

In this formation, actions that are directed either towards the large screens or to the tabletop are problematic. The appearance and nature of these actions is transformed and also different for each participant, depending on where they are located and to where they are oriented. These transformations are consequential to the participants, particularly to the person undertaking the action. Hence, they undertake actions to 'repair' what they consider a problem: extending an activity, pausing, restarting an utterance or explicitly requesting clarification of what the other can seen. When participants are divorced from the objects which they are referring to, such problems are more likely to arise and participants have to resolve emerging problems through minor adjustments to their conduct.

THE 'CLUSTER': HYBRID ASYMMETRIES OF ACTION

When engaging in common activities, but not necessarily related to the same focal object, the participants adopted another formation where they positioned themselves in one part of the room, often in a line along one side of the desk. In such a configuration, the remote participants could appear side-by-side, or if they occupied the rough same (virtual) space, behind each other. As in the following instance where the participants are each oriented to different places on the desktops. When we join them they have been looking for one more painting that will go with the Renaissance pictures they have already selected. Tim in Tokyo and Charles in Kyoto are looking over a collection of paper documents on the desktop, whilst Runako in Kyoto looks at a description of one painting on a paper sheet she is holding in front of her. Meanwhile, James in Tokyo rests on the desktop oriented towards Runako and the sheet she is holding. Runako announces she may have a candidate.

Fragment 4 (Kyoto View)

R: I have the one from: (0.7) (it says here) fighting the dragon (.)
(.)
J: ooohh (.) that might be any good (.) do you have that (do you)
R: yea
←T: put it down on the table
R: (Blue one) okay
T: um:: (Naomi) so we can see it
(.)
R: okay
(0.5)
T: where?

Tim, in Kyoto, who is working by Runako's side turns towards her and suggests that she put the sheet down on the tabletop so they can all see the details. As he says this he points to a location in front of him (and to Runako's right) which he has just cleared and where she can put the page down.

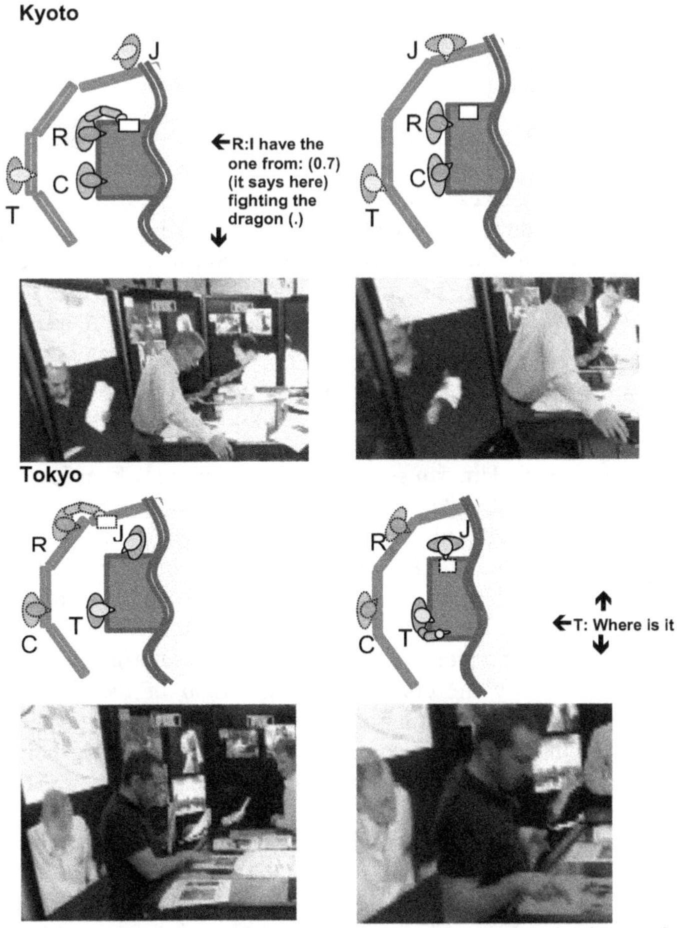

Runako agrees and does put the sheet down, but in front of her and slightly to her left (nearer to James than Tim). Tim sees Runako on the monolith to his left and sees her put the sheet down. Tim then turns to his right and looks down, holding his right hand above a space on the desktop. He then asks 'where is it?' Tim requests Runako to undertake an activity to which she agrees and he sees her take an action to accomplish it and yet he does not seem to be able to determine the location where she undertook that action. Tim's conduct is carefully designed for Runako. He is oriented to Runako, who appears just to his left, and as he asks her to 'put it down on the table so we can see it' he holds his hand over the 'empty space', his finger pointing down. He maintains his hand, still pointing over the space after he sees her put the page down.

Indeed, Tim maintains his point as he inspects a location on the opposite end of the desk to where Runako has placed it. In the design of the gesture Tim assumes that Runako can see his conduct and assess its relevance. It indicates a place on a crowded desk where her document would be visible. In the Kyoto space, Runako appears beside Tim and oriented towards where Tim's hand is being held. And yet, in the Tokyo space, Tim's actions seem very different. Tim appears behind Runako, and so his actions are not visible to Runako. However, in the Kyoto space Tim's colleague, James, is visible to Runako's right. For Runako, when she puts the document down, she can see John's reorientation in its direction, in response to her action. Similarly, her co-present colleague Charles also reorients to the document in front of her.

In spite of standing in a row alongside the desk and having very similar resources available to them in the environment, the participants experience of the space in quite different ways. The range of resources provided by the environment and the detail at which these are presented can support quite subtle actions to be produced and collaborative activities to be performed. However, these very details can also lead to assumptions about how one's own actions are seen and how another's activities can be related to one's own. Although clustered in a close space and oriented towards a common set of objects, the participants have views that are asymmetrical. Tim can see Runako and features of her local environment. Runako can see little of Tim and has few resources for tying his conduct (such as his talk) to the local environment. In other formations when a problem arises the participants can assess that there may be something amiss by monitoring the responses of their remote colleagues. Similarly their actions to repair or resolve the problem can be assessed by the colleagues in the light of their prior conduct. Although having different perspectives within the ecology they do have resources to be able to transpose their actions into the environment of their remote colleagues, and hence can produce concerted collaborative activities. However, in this formation, the asymmetries of video-mediated conduct are more marked. Here, the participants do not have the same resources to make sense of another's action in the environment, and hence their assumptions about how their own actions are visible in the remote environment are undermined. So, despite all participants appearing to have very similar resources available to them, the technology actually produces different ecologies of action for each participant. The technology fractures the environment but in different ways for each participant. This can mean that seemingly subtle differences in where a participant is located or how an action is shaped can have quite marked consequences for how it appears to a remote participant, or whether it is visible at all. Consequently, it can be hard to assess whether or how a colleague orients to one's own conduct. Despite the very rich audio-visual environment in which conduct is presented, the sequential accomplishment of embodied action through the technology can rest on quite fragile foundations.

DISCUSSION

The t-Room system is an advanced video-mediated system that provides a range of resources for participants to collaborate, both within a large space surrounded by numerous (life-sized) images of the remote colleagues, but also multiple locations to place physical and digital documents. With the additional functionality of the Kinect, 't-Room Touch' makes it possible to easily extend the range of places which can be focus of collaborative activities. The size of the system and the range of capabilities it offers allows participants to configure themselves in appropriate locations and orientation to undertake concerted action. When undertaking the tasks the participants made use of this flexibility arranging themselves in many different formations so they could engage in a range of activities and also shift between different forms of collaborative work. They were able to participate in a great variety of activities, including detailed focused work on documents and over images, general multi-party discussions about specific issues and short presentations of their proposals. The participants could also easily shift between these different kinds of activities. Indeed, they seemed to be able to engage in many of the activities found in a range of multiparty workplace activities [9], including those typically found in highly intensive document based collaboration [2].

In order to be able to engage in a diverse range of activities the participants could freely adopt different kinds of configurations. The visual access to the location of their colleagues meant they did not have to engage in any explicit activities to organize themselves. Instead a range of formations emerged so that they could meet the requirements of the task at hand. When adopting these t-Room provided resources by which they could make assumptions about what and how their own actions were visible to their remote colleagues.

Despite the great flexibility it offers, t-Room is not without problems. The technology transforms actions in a variety of ways. These transformations are not unfamiliar in other forms of video-mediated communication. In certain arrangements, the technology fractures the visible presentation of conduct, so a simple gesture, for example, can appear on multiple screens or on different kinds of surfaces. In such cases, an object being referred to, or pointed at, can be divorced from the participant who is undertaking the action (cf [8, 11]), disembodied hands can appear fragmented from other features of participant's conduct. In certain formations, such as when the participants are more spread out (as in the constellation) the 'Mona Lisa' effect can be more apparent. Even when gaze direction is less critical, the nature of video-mediated conduct can make it hard to identify what and where a colleague is referring to. In such cases, it can be hard to tie such features to the ongoing actions of colleagues, and hence the significance of some visible actions is not seen and is consequently ignored. In formations, particularly when participants are side-by-side (or back-to-front), as in the cluster, the technology can fragment the temporal sequence in which actions and their responses are accomplished. Unlike other configurations (cf. [17, 18]) the initial onset of a gesture may not be visible to a co-participant and so when the subsequent action is produced it may not be noticed or its relevance to the ongoing activity not be appropriately assessed.

However, what seems problematic for participants in t-Room is that in endeavouring to support flexible forms of co-participation the resources participants rely upon to produce coherent action are less stable. When adopting a different formation what might have just been assumed to be visible and in what way, may no longer hold. Moreover, the resources for assessing the standpoint of the other also might change. It then seems problematic for participants to design their own actions with regard to another. Although they can draw on a range of everyday interactional practices to attempt to resolve the problems they are facing, such as sustaining a gesture, pausing and restarting an action, they still may not have the means for assessing how such practices are being seen in the remote domain.

It is possible to envisage ways of enhancing t-Room and similar hybrid blended environments that aim to support multiple forms of collaboration. In common with other audio-visual systems, the focus of attention in t-Room's design has been on trying to develop a coherent visual space, so less effort has been paid to the audio environment. It could be possible to provide better ties between talk and visible conduct. So, for example, by more directional presentation of sound, a better sense of where a remote colleague is located could be provided even when they are not visible. As shifts in orientation are critical to collaborative work directional presentation of sound could also help provide a better a sense of shifts in a remote colleague's orientation when they are speaking.

Attention also needs to paid to how in collaborative technologies fragmented images are related to each other [cf. 26]). Digital images could be enhanced (or transformed) in subtle ways, for example, to provide the means to better connect actions that appear on different surfaces and in different spaces (e.g. by transforming the colour and appearance of features of the body). As the problems are different according to the formations that participants adopt, to avoid these enhancements being too intrusive the images could be selectively augmented through the use of sensor systems, like Kinect, detecting the configuration of the participants.

T-Room is a very distinctive kind of system. It is not envisaged, like Halo or Cisco's Telepresence as a commercial system to be deployed for or within organisations. Rather it is more of a workbench to explore how more flexible ways in which participants can engage in tasks and change the ways they participate in activities, for example between multiple participants and collaboration that is not focused around a single location or document. Undertaking experiments with advanced systems like t-Room provide a means for identifying issues regarding video-mediated collaboration. By examining the details of interaction through such spaces it is possible to reveal when there are problems for the participants to undertake concerted action. This is revealed not just by whether a participant explicitly requests some form of clarification or explicitly asks a colleague to undertake an action, but often by the very way a participant designs their conduct through these spaces. In the production of their actions participants often reveal what is problematic and hence what are some of the common assumptions underpinning everyday collaborative actions. Nevertheless, the analysis of these materials is not unproblematic. As may have been noticed from the images presented here, the data are very complex. Analysing video data concerning multiple parties is difficult in its own right, but when each participant not only has a different perspective but that perspective depends on the participants' orientation at a particular moment then analysis becomes particularly difficult. Hence, analysis of mediated collaboration tends to focus on referential actions, rather than the qualities of other types of visible conduct.

Nevertheless, by considering how t-Room and similar technologies fracture and fragment the resources and assumptions on which people rely in everyday interaction, we can get a sense of which practices remain robust and resilient [cf. 3]. It is apparent that supporting coherent action is not just a matter of utilising high fidelity presentations of co-participants and their environment nor of providing greater access to a co-participants' environment, nor of offering advanced ways of tying a participant to features of their environment. Through producing and making visible coherent sequences of actions within an environment, and providing access to colleagues orientations towards objects within that environment throughout those sequences, it is possible for participants to transpose their actions into a remote domain and the actions of others into their own. However, perhaps somewhat ironically, by offering greater flexibility to the ways in which people orient and position themselves within a distributed environment seems to make concerted action more problematic. The nature of these difficulties changes depending on the configuration the participants adopt and their relationship to the artefacts they are oriented to. In this paper we have drawn upon a preliminary set of common formations to consider the nature of these different problems. These formations reflect the stable configurations that the participants adopted (cf. 14) and in each revealed different asymmetries in the interaction between participants. Given the different nature of the asymmetries we need to consider the transitions between them and how participants draw on a sense of a reciprocity of perspectives (cf. 3) in the course of their interaction to make sense of the ongoing conduct.

What studies of complex collaborative technologies bring to light is the need to understand how in everyday work settings participants can produce recognisable actions and make sense of those of others, even when the resources they draw upon and their location do not remain stable. This seems to call for further detailed studies of how participants in settings such as activities that rely on a wide variety of materials produce coherent conduct and make sense of the work of their colleagues. It also suggests that it is worth considering how in organisational environments, even those as seemingly mundane as the open office, participants seamlessly shift from individual to collaborative work, between different orientations and spatial configurations and make sense of the conduct of their colleagues.

ACKNOWLEDGEMENTS
We would like to thank Keiji Hirata and other t-Room members for their support in undertaking the experiments.

REFERENCES

1. Anstis, S.M., Mayhew, J. W & T. Morley, The Perception of Where a Face or Television 'Portrait' Is Looking, *Am Jour of Psychology*, 82, 4 (1969), 474-489
2. Bjorn P. Co-constructing Globally Collaborative Spaces: A Conceptual Study of War Rooms, *Lecture Notes in Business Info Processing* 86, (2011), 16-28.
3. Garfinkel, H. A Conception of and Experiments with Trust as a Condition of Stable Concerted Actions In *Motivation and Social Interaction*. Ronald Press, 1963.
4. Gaver, W.W., et al. Realizing a video environment: EuroPARC's RAVE system. in *Proc CHI 92*. Monterey, CA: (1992), 27-35.
5. Goodwin, C. *Conversational Organisation*. Academic Press: New York and London. 1981.
6. Gergle, D., Clark, A., See What I'm Saying? Using Dyadic Mobile Eye Tracking to Study Collaborative Reference, *CSCW 2011*, pp. 435-444.
7. Heath, C. Hindmarsh, J. & Luff, P. *Video in Qualitative Research*. Sage, London. 2010.
8. Heath, C., & Luff, P. Disembodied Conduct: Communication Through Video in a Multi-Media Environment, in *Proc of CHI '91*, 99-103.
9. Heath, C & Luff, P. *Technology in Action*. Cambridge University Press. 2000.
10. Heath, C., Luff, P., Kuzuoka, H., & Yamazaki, K. Creating Coherent Environments for Collaboration, in Proc of ECSCW 2001, Kluwer, 119-128.
11. Hindmarsh, J., Fraser, M., Heath, C. & Benford, S.. Object-Focused Interaction in Collaborative Virtual Environments. ToCHI, 7, (2000) 477-509.
12. Hirata, K. et al. Video Communication System Supporting Spatial Cues of Mobile Users. In Proceedings of *CollabTech 2008*, IPSJ, 84-97.
13. Ishii, H. & Kobayashi, M. ClearBoard: a seamless medium for shared drawing and conversation with eye contact. *Proc. of CHI'92*, ACM Press, 525-532.
14. Kendon, A. *Conducting Interaction.* Cambridge University Press. Cambridge. 1990.
15. Kunert, A. Kulik, A., Beck, S. & B. Froehlich. Photoportals: shared references in space and time. In *Proc of CSCW 2014.*, 1388-1399.
16. Kuzuoka, H., Yamashita, J., Yamazaki, K. & Yamazaki, A. Agora: A Remote Collaboration System that Enables Mutual Monitoring, *Ext. Abstr. of CHI 1999*, 190-191.
17. Luff, P., Heath, C., Kuzuoka, H., Yamazaki, K. & Yamashita, J.. Handling Documents and Discriminating Objects in Hybrid Spaces In *Proc of the CHI 2006* Montreal, 561-570.
18. Luff, P., Yamashita, N., Kuzuoka, H & Heath, C, Hands on Hitchcock: embodied reference to a moving scene, In *Proc. CHI 2011*, 43-52
19. Mark G. Extreme Collaboration. *Communications of the ACM*, Volume 45 Issue 6, (June 2002), Pages 89-93
20. Minatani, S., Kitahara, I, Kameda, Y. & Ohta, Y. Face-to-Face Tabletop Remote Collaboration in Mixed Reality. *Proc. of ISMAR'07*, (2007), IEEE Comp. Soc., 43-46.
21. Nguyen, D. & Canny, J. MultiView: Spatially Faithful Group Video Conferencing. *Proc of CHI 2005*.
22. O'Hara, K., Kjeldskov, J. & Paay, J., Blended Interaction Spaces for Distributed Team Collaboration. *ToCHI,* 18, 3-3. 2011
23. Salvadori, F. Waiting to talk: Coordinating openings in open plan offices. *4th Intl Conf on Conversation Analysis,* UCLA CA. Jun 25-29, 2014.
24. Tang, A., Pahud, M., Inkpen, K., Benko, H., Tang, J. C., & Buxton, B., Three's Company: Understanding Communication Channels in Three-way Distributed Collaboration. *Proc of CSCW 2010*, 271-280.
25. Tang, J. & Minneman, S. VideoDraw: a video interface for collaborative drawing. *ACM Transactions on Information Systems* 9, 2 (1991), 453-469.
26. Wong, N. & Gutwin, C. Support for deictic pointing in CVEs: still fragmented after all these years'. *Proc of CSCW 2014*, 1377-1387.

Mapping out Work in a Mixed Reality Project Room

Derek Reilly[1], Andy Echenique[2], Andy Wu[3], Anthony Tang[4], W. Keith Edwards[5]

[1]Dalhousie University
Computer Science
Halifax, NS, Canada
reilly@cs.dal.ca

[2] U. C. Irvine
ICS
Irvine, CA, USA
echeniqa@uci.edu

[3]GE Global Research
UX Innovation Lab
San Ramon, CA, USA
andycswu@gmail.com

[4]University of Calgary
Computer Science
Calgary, AB, Canada
tonyt@ucalgary.ca

[4]Georgia Tech
Interactive Computing
Atlanta, GA, USA
keith@cc.gatech.edu

ABSTRACT

We present results from a study examining how the physical layout of a project room and task affect the cognitive maps acquired of a connected virtual environment during mixed-presence collaboration. Results indicate that a combination of physical layout and task impacts cognitive maps of the virtual space. Participants did not form a strong model of how different physical work regions were situated relative to each other in the virtual world when the tasks performed in each region differed. Egocentric perspectives of multiple displays enforced by different furniture arrangements encouraged cognitive maps of the virtual world that reflected these perspectives, when the displays were used for the same task. These influences competed or coincided with document-based, audiovisual and interface cues, influencing collaboration. We consider the implications of our findings on WYSIWIS mappings between real and virtual for mixed-presence collaboration.

Author Keywords

Mixed reality; cross reality; mixed presence; display ecology; cognitive map; spatial cognition

ACM Classification Keywords

H5.3. Information interfaces and presentation (e.g., HCI): Group and Organization Interfaces----Computer Supported Cooperative Work.

INTRODUCTION

Teams in dedicated project rooms actively configure artifacts and space into meaningful regions for work. Over time, space in such rooms takes on special meaning [8,17]. For example, Teasley et al. [24] found that knowledge workers dedicated regions to specific activities, clustered task-relevant artifacts together, and used flipcharts and whiteboards as persistent at-a-glance records of team activity. Architects and designers respond by designing flexible and reconfigurable collaborative workspaces [20,22]. Space provides common ground for collaborators: it comes to take on meaning [8], and bodily action and deictic references become meaningful during collaboration.

CHI 2015, April 18 - 23 2015, Seoul, Republic of Korea

ACM 978-1-4503-3145-6/15/04...$15.00
http://dx.doi.org/10.1145/2702123.2702506

When remote collaborators connect to a project room through audio/video conferencing, the affordances of the space are lost: the remote collaborator cannot easily refer to, nor understand references to, artifacts or regions of the space. Hindmarsh et al. name this problem *fragmented interaction*, referring both to the fragmentation of spaces (between the project room and the remote collaborator's space), as well as the fragmented interaction between collaborators as they encounter referential problems and the repair that needs to take place [9].

One approach to addressing this problem is to use *media spaces*, fusing two or more physical spaces with high-fidelity audio/visual connections, for example, as if collaborators worked on opposite sides of a pane of glass (e.g. Luff et al. [14]). Yet, such setups tend to connect only a single region of a workspace, ignoring other areas that may be relevant, and emphasize face-to-face communication over artifact-centric collaboration.

In contrast to the media space work, our approach has been to consider an artifact-centric fusion that links physical project rooms and virtual spaces, into what we call *mixed reality collaborative spaces*. Remote collaborators access digital documents from within the virtual space, while collocated collaborators work on the same documents through displays embedded in the physical space. In collaboration with industrial design and workspace experts at Steelcase, we have considered ways that physical and virtual environments can be designed together to benefit collaboration, and demonstrated these in a project room called the inSpace lab.

Figure 1. inSpace lab, "strict" WYSIWIS. Visitors to the project room understood the correspondence immediately, but the virtual world was difficult to navigate and use.

In the most literal variation of our approach (Figure 1), the physical project room is reproduced in a virtual world, allowing remote ("in-world") collaborators to join project room collaborators (the "in-room" collaborators) via audio links. Here, collaborators' communicative references to space are meaningful: "front of the room" can be easily understood, and with spatialized audio, "come over here" can be meaningfully understood by all.

This approach begs the question: does a strict What-You-See-Is-What-I-See (WYSIWIS) approach need to be followed, or when and in what ways can a relaxed or non-WYSIWIS approach be used [21]? A relaxed approach might be more effective for getting work done: we can tailor the virtual world to the remote collaborators' user interface (e.g., remove furniture and increase the relative size of documents and workspaces, Figure 2), we no longer need a 1-1 correspondence between displays and in-world content, and we can focus on key connection points for specific collaborative tasks rather than mapping the entire room. We may also want to support opportunistic, *ad hoc* and non-WYSIWIS connections (e.g., opening a virtual world client on a collaborator's laptop in the room).

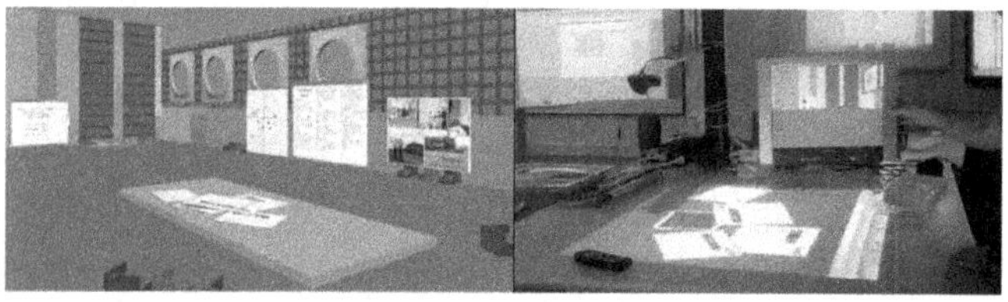

Figure 2. inSpace lab, "relaxed" WYSIWIS. The correspondence needed to be explained to visitors to the project room, but the virtual world was easier to use.

The layout of physical collaborative spaces influences the way people collaborate within that space, with or without digital technology, and sometimes in unanticipated ways [11]. One of the key intuitions guiding our design work was that the physical space may also guide collaboration with remote collaborators [18]. At the same time, our design and prototyping work [18-20] has generated a range of approaches for combining physical and virtual, some requiring strict correspondence, others relaxed correspondence, and others requiring no correspondence.

In this paper we present a study set in the inSpace lab that considers how people build mental models (*cognitive maps*) of a connected virtual space when collaborating. Our results show that the project room's physical layout combined with the collaborative activity impacted the cognitive maps formed by in-room collaborators, and that these effects competed with content and interface cues. Collaborators need ways to reference work materials, maintain awareness of each other's actions, and coordinate next steps. Accurate cognitive maps of the virtual world are only useful if they make it easier to work with remote collaborators. In our study, some of our participant groups worked effectively despite having inaccurate and/or divergent cognitive maps. Some groups were extremely resourceful when figuring out how to coordinate work, testing interface limitations and using both spatial and non-spatial attributes (such as document content) when coordinating. For others, conflicting or inaccurate models led to confusion and breakdowns in collaboration. We consider the implications for WYSIWIS, relaxed WYSIWIS, and non-WYSIWIS approaches to mixed reality collaborative spaces.

BACKGROUND AND MOTIVATION

The mixed reality collaborative spaces concept builds on considerable work addressing the "remote collaborator" problem, in particular work involving *mixed presence* (collocated and remote) collaboration [23], and most directly on three lines of research: media spaces, cooperative buildings, and mixed reality. We briefly touch on this research to illustrate how it has influenced our thinking on collaborative mixed reality workspaces. We then review theories from the psychology literature on how cognitive maps are constructed, and consider how these theories might apply in the mixed reality context.

Connecting Spaces

In the early media space work, which connected physical spaces together using audio-visual links, researchers were interested in preserving the function of the spaces. Bly et al. [3] emphasized connecting functionally similar spaces, for example, placing portals to remote offices in physical hallways, fusing "common areas", and creating shared offices. This early work used the location of a portal as an expression of its function, among other cues (placing coffee pots in view, for example). Buxton describes experiences with a similar system [4], finding that the placement of a media portal relative to the physical work environment impacts expectations and social protocol. These explorations were highly context-specific, however, and general design principles based on room layout are not offered. More recent research has incorporated vision-based tracking with video links to promote collaboration and play (see Hunter et al. [13] for example), yet these emphasize single connection points rather than work environments, and don't permit multiple remote connections.

Architectural & Digital Co-Design

The semantic and functional characteristics of space have been a central part of the cooperative buildings research. For example, Streitz et al. [22] illustrated how technology and architecture could be designed together—the insight being that display surfaces could be designed and configured depending on the function of the spaces they inhabit. These structures provided means for collaborators to engage one another, while also allowing collaborators to reassemble the spaces to support different styles of engagement (just as physical furniture does). Streitz et al. discuss but do not demonstrate an extension to mixed presence collaboration [22]. The swisshouse project [12] applied digital-physical co-design to connect houses in ways that reflect the functional needs of spaces in the home.

Mixed Reality and Cognitive Maps

Dix et al. argue that mixed reality relies on the cognitive process of mapping (drawing connections between) multiple spaces [6]. They identify three types of spaces present in mixed reality systems: the physical environment (*real space*), maps and/or sensed positioning (*measured space*), and the connected digital information (*virtual space*). Interacting with mixed reality systems requires moving from a spatial model of the physical space to a model of the sensed or mapped physical-virtual boundary to interact with the virtual space, which again one must build a model of through its manifestation in the real space. The success of a mixed reality environment will depend on appropriate mappings between these spaces.

Following Dix et al. [6], cognitive maps of the virtual space would impact how shared resources are referenced, how users across the physical-virtual divide maintain awareness of each other, and how they coordinate actions. We now outline research in spatial cognition that considers how such maps are formed.

The Landmark-Route-Survey (LRS) [15] model of spatial knowledge acquisition and its variants emphasize moving through space as the primary way to build cognitive maps. It was unclear to us how moving around our project room could impact a cognitive map of the connected virtual space, since the distances were short and much collaboration occurs while stationary. Colle and Read [5] propose a "gaze viewing mode" of spatial knowledge acquisition, where a spatial model is constructed from visual information, supplementing LRS-mode spatial knowledge. They provide evidence that cognitive maps formed from gaze viewing tend to be structured hierarchically according to distinct physical regions (they dub this the "room effect"), and so it is more difficult to recall the relative location of objects in different subsections of the hierarchy than objects in the same subsection. This effect may also apply to work regions within a project room, and possibly extend to a connected virtual world: one's perception of the relative location in the virtual world of content shown on displays would be influenced by the relative placement of the displays in the physical room if the displays are in the same work region, but not when they are in different work regions.

Physical room layout is not likely the sole determinant of cognitive map formation in a mixed reality collaborative space. As Tversky et al. have noted, cognitive maps are often *collages* of different levels of detail and focus, reflecting the fact that these maps are derived from qualitatively different cues [25]. In particular, non-spatial attributes of shared work documents may have an impact: Hommel and Knuf [10] have shown that grouping in cognitive maps can occur due to non-spatial factors including performing common actions with objects, while Aliakseyeu et al. [1] demonstrate user preference for semantic vs. spatial metaphors on control interfaces for multiple display environments. We anticipated that these factors would also influence cognitive map formation.

EXPERIMENT

We conducted an experiment using a subset of our project room consisting of two regions: a meeting area with a conference table and three large displays, and a brainstorming region comprised of a small table with high seating and a single large landscape display (see Figure 3, left). We expected that our participants would perceive these two regions as distinct. We contrast this with a second, "1-table" room configuration (see Figure 3, right). Display positions were held constant across layouts to avoid perceptual grouping effects based on changes in relative display positions. Each display presented a perspective on a connected virtual world, focused on one shared document plus some of the surrounding virtual world foreground and background (see Figures 4,5).

The experiment was conducted with groups of three participants. A collocated (*in-room*) pair participated in the inSpace project room, while a remote (*in-world*) participant was in an office (Figure 4, top), and used a standard desktop virtual world client to navigate the virtual world connected to the project room. Participants performed two kinds of activities: an itinerary activity and an image search activity. The study employed a counterbalanced 2×2 (Layout × Activity) within-subjects design.

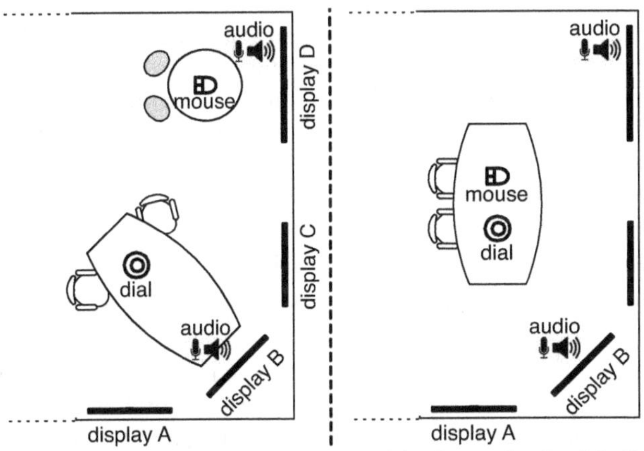

Figure 3. The two room layouts used in the study. 2-table (left) has two work regions, one using displays A-C and one display D. 1-table (right) has a single work area involving all displays.

Inspired by the "room effect" findings of Colle and Read [5], we expected that in the 2-table layout in-room participants would see displays A-C as a single left-to-right virtual world region, and would be less certain about how display D relates to A-C, while in the 1-table layout in-room participants would see displays A-D as a single left-to-right virtual world region.

We anticipated an influence of task on cognitive maps [10], expecting that the itinerary task (which uses display D differently than displays A-C) would amplify the 2-table effect, while the image search task (using displays A-D in the same way) would dampen the 2-table effect.

Following Aliakseyeu et al. [1] and building on our experiences demoing the inSpace lab, we were also interested in seeing what cues collaborators used to work together, and how these cues impacted cognitive maps.

Population and Recruitment

A total of 36 participants (12 groups of 3) were recruited, following two pilot sessions. Participants were drawn from the wider student populations of Georgia Tech and Emory University, through flyers and mailing lists. No specific expertise was required, and familiarity with collaborators was not controlled for. The entire experiment lasted 1½-2 hours, and each participant received $15.

Procedure

Participants first met in the remote participant's room and gave informed consent, after which the collocated pair was escorted to the project room (the remote collaborator did not see the project room). All participants then received training on their respective interfaces, lasting 5-10 minutes.

Participants conducted four group activities: an image search and an itinerary activity (see next section for details) under one layout condition, followed by an image search and an itinerary activity under the other layout condition. Each activity lasted 10-20 minutes. The activities were captured on video using two cameras in the project room, and one in the remote room.

After each activity, the in-room participants were given five minutes to independently sketch, annotate and describe on paper their conception of the virtual environment and the organization of the content within it. They could not see the displays at this time. This was our primary measure of in-room participants' cognitive maps of the virtual world. In order to avoid a learning effect, different virtual world backgrounds were used for each activity.

After the sketching task, in-room participants worked together to place miniature printouts of the documents they used in the activity where they believed they were located on a large top-down printout of the virtual world. This gave an opportunity for each in-room participant to vocalize details of their cognitive map as they relate to the top-down view, and to work out contradictions and disagreements with their partner. The task was captured on video, and a snapshot was taken of the result.

At the end of the experiment, all three participants were brought together for a videotaped 5-10 minute semi-structured interview, to discuss their strategies for collaborating in the activities, and to reflect on their cognitive maps as expressed in the sketching and item placement tasks.

Activities

As discussed, participants engaged in two kinds of group activity: *itinerary* (a simplified holiday itinerary planning exercise), and *image search* (finding a target image among 200 colour-matched photos). Each is detailed here.

Itinerary

In *itinerary*, groups were presented with a set of ~30 attractions, organized into three interest categories (nature, culture, and health and sport). For each category, items were numbered and displayed on a map broken into quadrants, descriptions and hours of operation were provided in a text listing, and labeled photos of points of interest and activities were displayed in a montage (Figure 4). Groups completed one itinerary activity under each layout condition, so materials were prepared for two destinations (Linz and Bologna); the destination-layout pairings were counterbalanced.

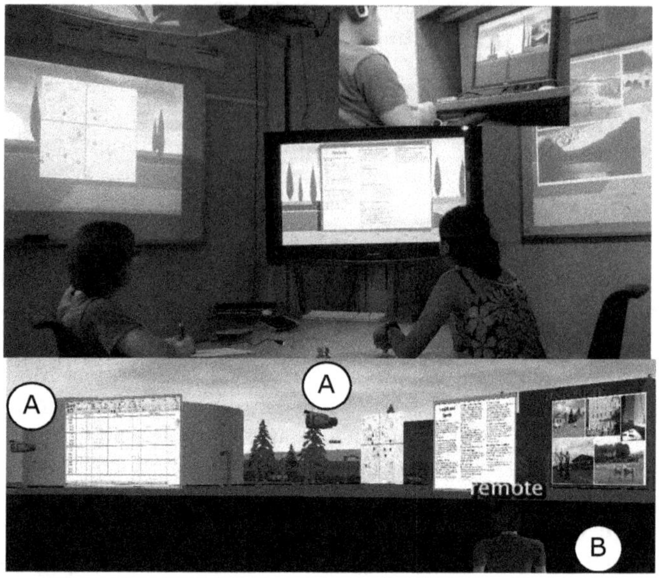

Figure 4 The Itinerary activity. A: cameras show what the in-room participants can see. B: the in-world participant's avatar

Participants selected six items together, choosing at least one from each category, to build a three-day holiday itinerary. Items were scheduled within hours of operation, and a fixed travel time was added if travelling between quadrants in the same day. Participants were asked to set "reasonable durations" for each item on their itinerary. Itinerary planning was split into two subtasks: item selection and scheduling. Participants were told to agree upon six itinerary items during item selection, and then to schedule them on a calendar. Participants were warned if still in the item selection phase after 12 minutes. The calendar displayed the three-day itinerary in an hourly grid (Figure 4, bottom left); items selected to be part of the itinerary could be dragged onto the calendar using a mouse by any collaborator. Participants could return to item selection as needed to review details or make a change to their selected items.

Figure 5 details the collaboration mechanics for the itinerary activity. The calendar was shown on display D, and was the leftmost document in the virtual world. Maps, item text, and photo montages were grouped together by category in-world, and these document groupings were placed in a line. Displays A-C showed map, text and image documents for one category. A dial controller was used to switch between categories: to the right if the dial is rotated clockwise or left if counter-clockwise. If already at the left or right-most category, turning the dial in that direction had no effect. Two audio links (mic and speakers, marked as au1 and au2 in the figure) were set up in the room, one at display D and the other in the center of displays A-C. If the remote collaborator was near the calendar they would be heard at display D, and if they were viewing the same category as the in-room collaborators, they would be heard at displays A-C. Otherwise, audio connection between local and remote collaborators was lost. The remote collaborator could see which category was currently visited by the in-room collaborators via a camera avatar placed in the air above and in front of the category being viewed. Another stationary camera avatar was situated in front of the calendar, indicating that the calendar was always visible to in-room collaborators. The remote collaborator could move their avatar manually using WASD keys, or use 1-4 as hotkeys to jump to the calendar and each of the categories.

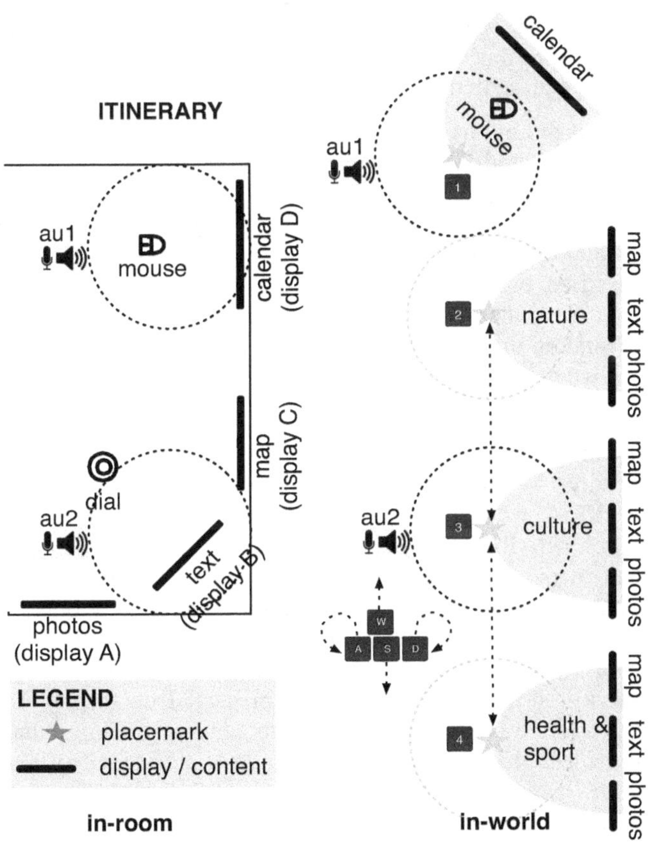

Figure 5 Real-virtual mappings for the Itinerary activity.

Image Search

In *image search* groups located a target image from among 200 colour-matched images presented on four image sets (each set presented images in a 5x10 grid, see Figure 6). Each image set was visible from a separate in-room display. Participants completed 10 rounds, each involving a different set of 200 images. Groups completed an image search activity under each room layout, so two sets of 10x200 images were prepared.

The facilitator described the target image, and then the group worked together to locate the image (no constraints were imposed on strategy). Once a group member located the image, the other group members had to point to it (the remote participant did this using an in-world telepointer). Any round taking more than 2 minutes was aborted by the facilitator.

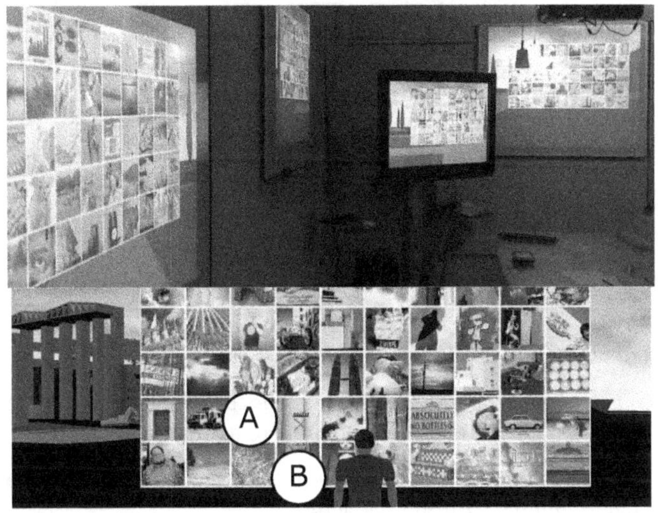

Figure 6 The Image Search activity. A: a telepointer is used to point to images. B: in-world participant's avatar.

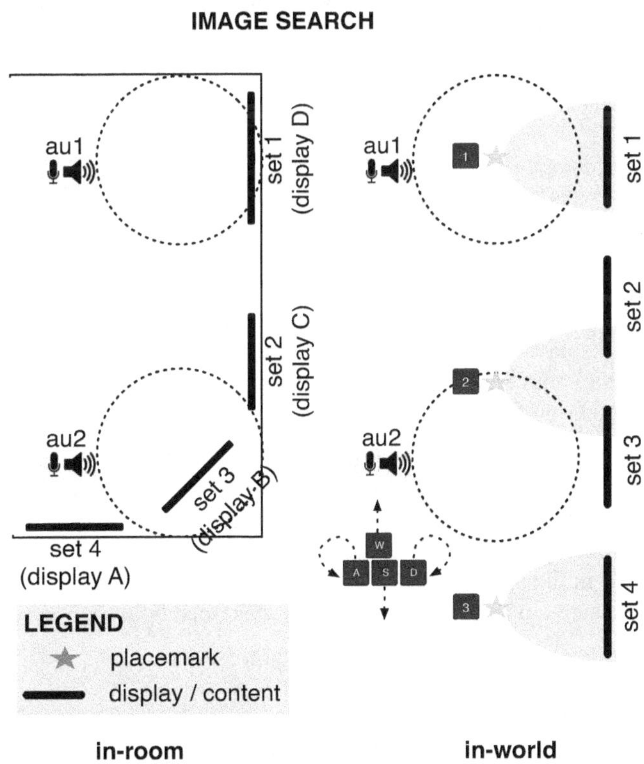

Figure 7 Real-virtual mappings for the Image Search activity.

Figure 7 details the collaboration mechanics for the image search activity. In Image Search, displays A-D each displayed one image set. The sets were presented in the same order in-room as in-world. Audio links (au1, au2) connected displays D and B to the virtual world regions in front of image sets labeled 1 and 3, respectively. Image sets were placed in a straight line in-world, far enough away from each other so that regions surrounding sets 2 and 4 were out of audio range. The remote collaborator could navigate manually using the WASD keys, or jump to a placemark in front of an image set using the 1-4 keys. Video camera avatars in front of image sets 1 and 3 indicated where the audio links were. In this activity, the virtual cameras did not move and there was no indication in-world that sets 2 and 4 were visible in-room.

Measures

Activity Video Coding

We were interested in events that might reflect the impact of cognitive maps, in particular:

Grounding work: local and remote participants talk about how they will collaborate, what each can see, etc.

Synchronization/Coordination: local and remote participants figure out together where to "move to" next.

Spatial reference: local and/or remote participants use spatial language during the activity.

The three video sources were combined, the video was transcribed and interactions were annotated. Following this, an iterative open coding process was followed using the generated text records. Common events were identified during axial coding and these were related back to the higher-level events listed above.

Sketching

Sketches were coded by two individuals who were unaware of their room layout conditions. Sketches were classified according to a set of nominal characteristics reflecting the relative location and organization of all task content, the correspondence of content placement in-world to the layout of displays in the physical project room, the depiction of virtual navigation and/or in-room navigation, and the depiction of the virtual world itself.

Sketching accuracy has previously been shown to correlate strongly with navigation efficacy in virtual environments [1], but using sketching as a means of expressing cognitive maps in general has been both challenged [7] and supported [16] in the spatial cognition literature. We employed several measures in addition to sketching, described below.

Group Content Placement Task and Interview

This data was reviewed for interesting points of disagreement, notable accuracy or inaccuracy in the resulting placements, and the relationship of the placements to the participant sketches.

RESULTS

Sketch Similarity

We considered that similar models of the virtual space would be useful to coordinate work. We assigned a similarity score to *all* pairs of sketches (within groups and across groups) by summing the number of nominal characteristics that were different (i.e., a lower score indicated more similarity). Wilcoxon tests were run on within-group and between-group similarity scores, for both itinerary and image search. Results for itinerary showed no difference in similarity scores within groups (M=4.3) vs. between (M=5.15), Z= -1.49, p = .1353, while results for image search showed a significant increase in similarity within groups (M=1.03) compared to between groups (M=2.71) Z= -4.57, p <.0001.

Cognitive maps appear to converge only when they are used: similar cognitive maps were formed in image search, during which all groups employed a spatial left-to-right or numbering scheme at least once for each activity. By contrast, spatial reference schemes were used (even partially) in only 6 itinerary activities (out of the 24 completed by all groups). All groups used the non-spatial content type (map, text, image, schedule) to reference displays in itinerary—not possible in image search since all displays presented the same type of content.

Impact of Layout and Activity

We considered the placement of the content that appeared on display D (i.e. the schedule in the itinerary activity and leftmost image set in image search) relative to the remaining content in the post-activity sketches. We classified the content on this display as "differentiated" from the other content if it was depicted at a different orientation than *all* other content, and/or separated in space relative to *all* other content.

Z-tests were conducted to compare differentiation in each layout condition across both activities, and then within each activity. An expected main effect was found for activity (Z=2.754, p<.003), with less differentiation in the image search activity (which used all displays in the same way) than in the itinerary activity (which used display D for a separate scheduling subtask), regardless of room layout. No main effect was found for layout (Z=1.252, p=.105), but there was a significant interaction effect of layout and activity, such that the schedule (presented on display D) was differentiated more in the 2-table layout condition than in the 1-table condition for the itinerary activity (Z=1.919, p<.027), but not in the image search activity (Z=0, p=.5). This result suggests that room layout matters when the split in regions corresponds with a split in activity subtask, as was the case in the 2-table itinerary condition.

We also looked in the sketches for a regular placement of content in the virtual world to correspond with the organization of displays in the physical room. Placement didn't need to precisely match the display layout: content might be placed along a straight line, arc, or circle in the sketch, so long as is was positioned in a regular, contiguous pattern. There was a main effect of activity (Z=1.817,p=.035), with the image search activity (using all displays in the same way) encouraging more regular placement of all content (a total of 34/48 image search sketches) than itinerary. There was no main effect of room layout on the presence of such a pattern in the sketches (Z=0,p=.5), and no interaction effect of layout and activity.

After reviewing the sketches for image search, it appeared that the *type* of regular pattern might differ based on layout condition. We found a significant effect of layout (Z=1.873, p<.031) on type of pattern, with more curved and circular patterns in the sketches for the 2-table condition. In the 1-table condition participants had a straight-on view of the displays. In the 2-table condition participants were seated amongst displays A-C, and display D was to the left of and slightly behind their field of view. This suggests that participants mapped their egocentric relationship with the displays into content orientations in the virtual world. We did not capture discussion of curved vs. straight layouts during the image search activity, during top-down placement or in interviews—from this we observe that physical layout can also impact cognitive maps in ways that don't obviously impact collaboration.

Impact of Other Factors

Content Structure

Cognitive maps were influenced by content attributes in the itinerary task. 18/48 itinerary sketches grouped content by type (map, text, image) only, even though the content was organized by category (nature, culture, fitness) then by type in the virtual world (Figure 8). Grouping by content type was also evident in the placement exercise. It is unclear if all such groupings were purely semantic [1], or influenced by the (incorrect) perception that switching between content categories replaced the content on displays A-C instead of jumping to different virtual world regions:

"When turning the dial, I didn't notice that the background was changing"—P7.

Four sketches grouped content by type in a 2-D way with no virtual world, suggesting that a semantic grouping was important. Two in-room participants expressed that a spatial model was not necessary for the itinerary task:

"I... did not need to recall where the [displays] were located, since the four had very specific content that could be... identified as such" –P31.

Interface

Other factors also influenced the cognitive maps of our participants. The dial controller used to move between content categories in the itinerary task rotated clockwise and counter-clockwise; several participants cited this as an indication that the itinerary content was laid out in an arc or circle in the virtual world:

"When we rotated the dial, I assumed we were just rotating around. [The remote participant told] us they were all in a line, but that didn't seem intuitive to me, so I thought he was wrong" –P19.

This is an example of an interface element and layout cue *reinforcing* each other. Many participants also acknowledged the influence of the cove-like orientation of displays A-C:

"I was biased by how the [displays] were laid out in the

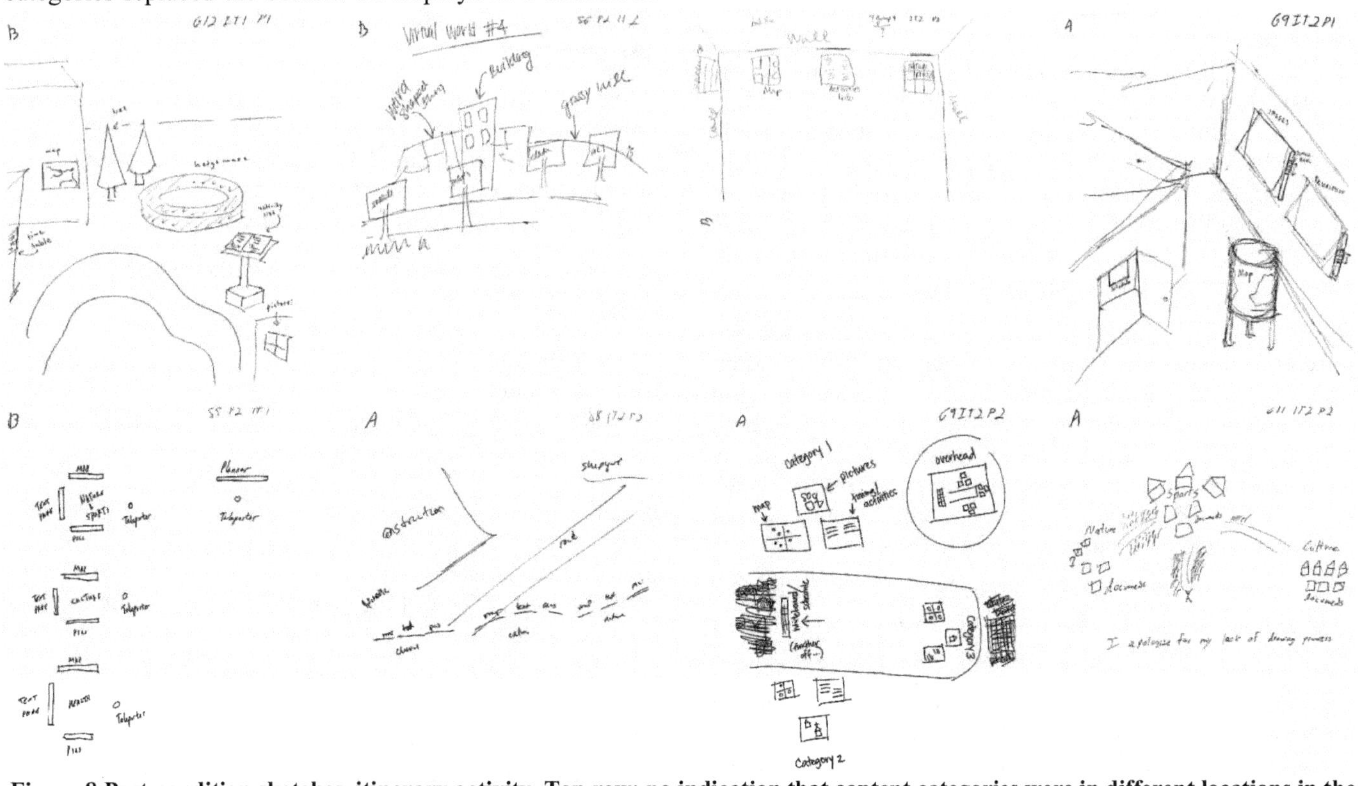

Figure 8 Post-condition sketches, itinerary activity. Top row: no indication that content categories were in different locations in the virtual world. Bottom row: more accurate depictions of how content was laid out.

room in my perception of how things were positioned in the world." – P26

In the image search activity, audio contact played a role in cognitive map formation. Several participants indicated in their sketches or during the interview that the content on displays without audio links was further away in-world, despite the fact that content was presented in l-r order and at the same scale across the in-room displays. This is an example of an interface element and layout cue *conflicting* with each other.

Virtual World

Occasionally, the remote collaborator's avatar would come into view on a display. This gave an indication of the remote participant's location, but only one group used the avatar to coordinate work, and only in image search, while one other group tried to use avatar movement to understand the virtual world layout. If the avatar transited between two displays this didn't necessarily indicate proximity in the virtual world due to the teleport links, and several groups noted this during the activities.

Finally, the virtual world background was sometimes used to infer relationships between the virtual world perspectives on each display. This varied from participant to participant:

"I would look at the background.. the only one [it] didn't work on is the one with the funky houses"—P19.

"It wasn't until the last [condition] that I noticed that there was a background"—P25.

Influence on Collaboration

Image Search

We saw no differences in collaboration style in the 2-table vs. 1-table layout image search conditions, corresponding with our cognitive map results. In-room collaborators could see all four screens while seated in either condition. Groups generally first established a scheme for staying in sync, often testing that locals and remotes could access all image sets, trying to determine whether there was a left-right correspondence, and labelling each image set.

As discussed, all groups used a left-right ordering scheme to refer to image sets. Other approaches were attempted on occasion, including references based on history ("the grid you were just at"), audibility ("the first one you can hear us at"), and image properties ("the image with the apple on the top-right"). Despite the simple document layout in image search and the prevalence of left-right ordering, this did not always structure participants' cognitive maps:

"We would use the first, second, third screen -- we were able to name them. We didn't know what his setup was, but since he never complained, it seemed okay"—P32.

As mentioned, most groups struggled with the "audio holes" at displays B and D, adding reluctance to assume a l-r mapping. Conflicting cues also posed issues for the remote collaborator, particularly when the itinerary task had been done first: since the in-room participants could "jump" from category to category in itinerary and the remote collaborator could see where they were (and where they could be communicated with) based on the camera avatar, remote collaborators sometimes felt the same should be possible in image search ("can you move to set 4?"–P27), becoming confused by the stationary camera avatars in front of sets 1 and 3. The conflicting cues given by audio, camera avatars, and the display layout negatively impacted collaboration as well as cognitive map formation.

Itinerary

Synchronizing transitions between item categories was a source of confusion for some groups, due to the different interfaces used by remote and local collaborators. Remote collaborators usually saw the need to synchronize, since a video camera avatar indicated the item category their collaborators were currently at, while some in-room collaborators did not get the sense that there was movement at all, instead thinking that content was replaced as they turned the dial. Others just didn't seem to realize that coordination was required for transitions. For example, in one instance in-room collaborators in group 3 move from health to nature without saying anything to the remote collaborator, who notices and jumps to nature. When she gets there the in-room collaborators navigate back to health. She jumps again to health and says "hiii... " to re-engage. The local collaborators don't acknowledge, seemingly unaware that contact was lost. The changing virtual world background and the rotation of the dial were not strong enough cues for some in-room collaborators to realize that they were in fact shifting their virtual world location by using the dial.

Most groups used the item category names to manage transitions, although l-r ordering was also used. Again, different interfaces could be a source of confusion when coordinating transitions. In this excerpt, group 2 have finished selecting items in the culture category:

Remote: ok, so you want to go to the other ones?
Local 1: yeah, sure
Remote: ok... number 3 .. number 3
Local 1: number 3?
Remote: nature... nature
((local and remote collaborators transition simultaneously))
Local 2: ((garbled)) nature [((looking at item list))
[where's 3? ...there is no 3
Remote [(looking at item list)
[ok, let's see what we have here, so...
Local 1: [there is no 3
Remote: 3? - no - no - I meant button number 3. Ok... sorry
I have a keyboard... which uh..."
Local 1: ok – which section are you on. Nature?
Remote: nature – nature... I can see you guys

The physical separation imposed by the 2-table condition impacted transitions between item selection and the calendar. Even though all groups selected six items before moving on to the calendar in both layout conditions, seven pairs of in-room collaborators moved back and forth between the calendar and the item content in the 1-table condition vs. one group in the 2-table condition. This clearer split between the two subtasks in the 2-table condition may have influenced (or have been influenced by) the Layout × Activity interaction on cognitive maps discussed earlier. Here, we see how physical layout can either solidify or blur the boundary between subtasks. Other cues can reinforce the boundary and facilitate transition: in the 2-table condition spatialized audio worked alongside layout to establish where the remote participant was during the transition; the only case where in-room collaborators returned to item selection in the 2-table condition was due to hearing the remote collaborator back in that region.

DISCUSSION

Our study explores how layout, activity, and other factors impact cognitive maps – but also sheds some light on how collaboration informs, and is informed by cognitive maps. In-room collaborators' cognitive maps converged when they used them to coordinate. In the 2-table itinerary condition participants were less likely to transition back and forth between calendar and item selection. This simple barrier coincided with a tendency to consider the calendar work area "elsewhere" in the virtual world. If cognitive maps are incomplete, additional time for grounding and coordination is required to ensure that work continues. This is made worse if cues conflict: in image search, collaborators struggled with the relationship between image sets that had a left-right correspondence but different audio connectivity. If cognitive maps are incorrect, coordination can suffer: in the itinerary task, some in-room collaborators would switch categories assuming that their remote collaborators would still be with them.

The results also suggest that when mixed reality is used for collaborative work in spaces like project rooms, the process of building cognitive maps does not strictly follow the physical – sensed – virtual sequence described by Dix et al. [6]. In-room collaborators did form a model of the virtual space based in part on its manifestation in the real world, but this was mediated in part by the room's layout and their egocentric perspective. For *artifact-centric* mixed reality, content semantics can influence cognitive maps, as collaborators use what is most effective to coordinate work [1]. The influence of task on mapping [10] was evident in our artifact-centric activities such that content used in the same task tended to be grouped together; this may also extend to other forms of mixed reality collaboration.

Implications for WYSIWIS In Collaborative Mixed Reality

The utility of real-virtual spatial correspondence can be considered at different scales within a project room. *Between work regions,* if the regions are allotted distinct tasks, and transitions between tasks are infrequent, then spatial correspondence is less important. In such cases it is less important to know "where" a collaborator is than "what" they are doing: permitting relaxed WYSIWIS approaches that concentrate only on connecting individual work regions without considering the room as a whole. Some basic spatial correspondence may still be useful, however: in our itinerary activity the spatialized audio was a useful cue that helped groups manage the transition between subtasks. This relaxed correspondence model is seen in the final inSpace lab setup (shown in Figure 2). If transitions are frequent, spatial correspondence may be more important, to facilitate communication and coordination.

Within a work region (and within a task), the structure and meaning of artifacts are paramount. Where artifacts can be categorized ("health, nature, culture"), spatial correspondence might be less important. If there is a 1-many mapping between an in-room work region and in-world (as with the item selection task in the itinerary activity), anchors for communication and coordination are needed. Document semantics is one possible anchor, as is correspondence in ordering. Clear cues should be available in both physical and virtual workspaces to facilitate coordination.

Within an active set of artifacts (i.e. content that is visible at the same time), if the individual documents can be easily categorized ("map, text, images"), spatial correspondence may be less important, although collaborators may expect that there is one. When there are no distinguishing markers (as in image search), order correspondence is more important. This may be spatial, but needn't be strict – e.g. a line of content in-world can map to a curve in-room.

We employed a form of relaxed WYSIWIS in our study: content placement followed the same left-right order as the displays, but their relative positions and orientations were not equivalent. In both activities, these differences didn't obviously impact collaboration – for example, in image search most groups recognized the left-right correspondence, using spatial language (e.g. "next grid to the right") when coordinating with each other and/or numbering the screens in left to right order. In general, as with other collaborative systems, designers of mixed reality collaborative systems need to prioritize visibility (of action and intent), and facilitate coordination. Spatial correspondence is one tool that must be considered among other aspects (e.g. task workflow, document content, interface cues) in achieving visibility and coordination support.

CONCLUSION

Our study demonstrates that the physical layout of a project room and the activity conducted within it impacts in-room collaborators' cognitive map of the connected virtual world, and that a range of other cues are used to understand real-virtual correspondence during tasks, including audio, input devices, document attributes and virtual world features. It was more important that collaborators could work together with content and coordinate next actions than to share an accurate model of the virtual space. However, conflicting or inadequate cues led to breakdowns in collaboration. Strict and relaxed WYSIWIS approaches are both feasible for mixed reality collaborative spaces, if designs consider the impact of cues influencing perception of the connected virtual space.

ACKNOWLEDGEMENTS

This work was supported by NSF grant IIS-0705569, NSERC grant 418612, and a research collaboration grant from Steelcase Inc.

REFERENCES

1. Aliakseyeu, D., Lucero, A., and Martens, J. Users' quest for an optimized representation of a multi-device space. Personal Ubiquitous Comput. 13, 8 (2009), 599-607.
2. Billinghurst, M., and Weghorst, S. The Use of Sketch Maps to Measure Cognitive Maps of Virtual Environments. In Proceedings of the Virtual Reality Annual International Symposium, (1995), pp 40-47.
3. Bly, S. A., Harrison, S. R., and Irwin, S. Media spaces: bringing people together in a video, audio, and computing environment. Commun. ACM 36, 1 (Jan. 1993), 28-46
4. Buxton, W. Living in Augmented Reality: Ubiquitous Media and Reactive Environments. In Finn, K., Sellen, A. and Wilber, S. (Eds). Video Mediated Communication: 363-384.
5. Colle, H. A., and Reid, G. B. The room effect: Metric spatial knowledge of local and separated regions. Presence:Teleoper.Virtual Environ.7(2)(1998),116–128.
6. Dix, A., Friday, A., Rodden, T., Koleva, B., Muller, H., Ranell, C. and Steed, A. Managing multiple spaces. In: Turner, Phil and Davenport, Elisabeth, (eds.) Spaces, Spatiality and Technology. Springer.
7. Golledge, R.G. Methods and Methodological Issues in Environmental Cognition Research. In *Environmental Knowing,* (Golledge, R.G. and Moore, G.T. Eds.), Dowden, Hutchinson and Ross, Inc., 1976, pp. 300- 313.
8. Harrison, S. and Dourish. P. Re-place-ing space: the roles of place and space in collaborative systems. CSCW 1996: 67-76.
9. Hindmarsh, J., Fraser, M., Heath, C., Benford, S., and Greenhalgh, C.. Fragmented interaction: establishing mutual orientation in virtual environments. CSCW 1998: 217-226.
10. Hommel, B., and Knuf, L. Action related determinants of spatial coding in perception and memory. In Spatial Cognition II, Integrating Abstract Theories, Empirical Studies, Formal Methods, and Practical Applications (2000), Springer-Verlag, pp. 387–398.
11. Huang, E., Mynatt, E., Trimble, J. Displays in the Wild: Understanding the Dynamics and Evolution of a Display Ecology. Pervasive 2006.
12. Huang, J. and Waldvogel, M. The swisshouse: an inhabitable interface for connecting nations. DIS 2004.
13. Hunter, S., Maes, P., Tang, T., Inkpen, K.M. and Hessey, S.M. 2014. WaaZam!: supporting creative play at a distance in customized video environments. CHI 2014: 1197-1206.
14. Luff, P., Heath, C., Kuzuoka, H., Yamazaki, K. and Yamashita, J. Handling documents and discriminating objects in hybrid spaces. CHI 2006: 561-570.
15. Mark, D., Freksa, C., Hirtle, S., Lloyd, R., and Tversky, B. Cognitive models of geographic space. International Journal of Geographical Information Science 13, 8 (1999), 747–774.
16. Newcombe, N. Methods for the Study of Spatial Cognition. In *The Development of Spatial Cognition,* (Cohen, R. Ed.), Hillsdale, New Jersey, Lawrence Erlbaum Associates, 1985, pp. 277-300.
17. Olson, G. M. and Olson, J. S. Distance matters. Hum.Comput. Interact. 15, 2 (Sep. 2000), 139-178.
18. Reilly, D., Mathiasen, N., Salimian, M., Edwards, W.K., Franz, J. and MacKay, B. (2014) SecSpace: Prototyping Usable Privacy and Security for Mixed Reality Collaborative Environments. EICS 2014.
19. Reilly, D., Rouzati, H., Wu, A., Brudvik, J., Hwang, J. Y., and Edwards, W. K. TwinSpace: an Infrastructure for Cross-reality Team Spaces. UIST 2010.
20. Reilly, D., Voida, S., McKeon, M., Le Dantec, C., Edwards, W. K., Mynatt, E. and Mazalek, A. Space Matters: Physical-Digital and Physical-Virtual Codesign in inSpace, IEEE Pervasive Computing 9(3):54-63, 2010
21. Stefik, M., Bobrow, D. G., Foster, G., Lanning, S. and Tatar, D.(1987) WYSIWIS revised: early experiences with multiuser interfaces. *ACM Trans. Inf. Syst.* 5:2, 147-167.
22. Streitz, N. A., Geißler, J., and Holmer, T. 1998. Roomware for Cooperative Buildings: Integrated Design of Architectural Spaces and Information Spaces. 1st intl. Workshop on Cooperative Buildings, London, 4-21.
23. Tang, A., Boyle, M., and Greenberg, S. (2004) Display and presence disparity in Mixed Presence Groupware. OzCHI 2004:73-82.
24. Teasley, S., Covi, L., Krishnan, M., and Olson, J. (2000) How does radical collocation help a team succeed? CSCW 2000: 339-346
25. Tversky, B. (1993) Cognitive maps, cognitive collages, and spatial mental models. In COSIT 1993:4-24.

On Vintage Values: The Experience of Secondhand Fashion Reacquisition

Anne E. Bowser
iSchool
University of Maryland
College Park, MD, USA
abowser1@umd.edu

Oliver L. Haimson
Dept. of Informatics
Univ. of California, Irvine
Irvine, CA, USA
ohaimson@uci.edu

Edward F. Melcer
NYU Polytechnic School of Engineering
Brooklyn, NY, USA
eddie.melcer@nyu.edu

Elizabeth F. Churchill
eBay Research Labs[1]
San Jose, CA, USA
churchill@acm.org

ABSTRACT
Secondhand fashion is a rapidly growing, lucrative market with both off- and online outlets. Studies of secondhand consumption have focused primarily on people's motivations for secondhand shopping, highlighting sustainability and/or thrift. We extend this work by looking at the motivations and practices of secondhand shoppers who are driven instead by style, playfulness and treasure-hunting. We present findings from ethnographic observation and interviews with 13 secondhand shoppers. Three secondhand shopping orientations emerged. *Perfection Seeking* involves seeking items that fit with an individual look or personal brand. These items are seen as unique, and demonstrate an alternative to mainstream fashion and consumption. *Casual curiosity* is less focused, more engaged in browsing, and driven by both secondhand objects and the secondhand experience itself. *Digging* involves the focused pursuit of hidden "gems" or treasures, following the belief that unusual items are waiting to be found. We offer ideas for designing secondhand shopping experiences to support the needs for storytelling, experiential pleasure, and negotiation around durable value.

Author Keywords
Fashion; Recirculation; Value-centered design; Sustainable HCI; eCommerce Consumption; Recycling; Field Study

ACM Classification Keywords
H.5.m. Information interfaces and presentation (e.g., HCI): Miscellaneous.

INTRODUCTION
Secondhand fashion is a growing global phenomenon. As a market sector, the US secondhand retail industry reports annual revenues of $12 billion, with used clothing accounting for 25% of this value [19]. This is not restricted to physical stores; eBay, the world's largest secondhand eCommerce platform, made $11 billion in 2011 [10].

CHI 2015, April 18 – 23, 2015, Seoul, Republic of Korea.

ACM 978-1-4503-3145-6/15/04…$15.00
http://dx.doi.org/10.1145/2702123.2802394

The cultural standing of secondhand fashion is also changing. Once associated almost exclusively with charity donation outlets or "thrift stores" like Goodwill in the US and Oxfam in the UK, secondhand fashion now is found in high end "vintage" stores, in designer-focused consignment stores, and in boutiques that target young and "trendy" shoppers. Diverse online retailers are emerging to challenge established marketplaces like eBay. Examples include The Real Real, Threadflip and Etsy, with premium sales sites like RueLaLa and ideel also featuring more high-end used items. Although commonly associated with thrift, previous studies of secondhand shoppers reveal a broader range of motivations, including nostalgia, eco-consciousness, anti-consumerism, and experiential pleasure [9, 15, 17].

Much HCI research on secondhand shopping has focused on understanding decisions to acquire, preserve, and dispose of objects (or not) for furthering sustainable design [13, 27]. Focusing on the goods themselves, Pierce & Paulos describe secondhand consumption as "acquisition, possession, dispossession and reacquisition." Sustainable HCI research has also focused on fashion, exploring how fashion thinking can support sustainable design [28], or by designing new tools for sustainable consumption [4]. But, despite these early efforts the spaces of fashion and sustainable HCI have yet to fully converge.

Our ethnographic exploration of secondhand fashion, conducted through 13 field interviews with shoppers in the San Francisco Bay Area, is one synergy of fashion and sustainable HCI research. Additionally, we expand previous research on secondhand consumption such as [13, 27, 29] through the use of a method that selects the *experience* and not the *object* as point of entry into understanding key practices. We report a range of experiences related to the values and identities of our shoppers, the objects they select, and the spaces where secondhand interactions unfold. Through distilling these experiences we identify three distinct secondhand fashion consumption orientations, which imply different needs for consumption spaces, both physical and online. Finally, we return to previous research in our discussion, by reflecting on and in some cases expanding the design implications posed by [13, 27, 29].

---

[1] Now at Google

BACKGROUND

Our research contributes to the literature on secondhand consumption, found both within and outside of HCI.

HCI Research on Secondhand Consumption

Our work builds on several secondhand consumption frameworks developed by HCI researchers. Odom et al. examined how the function, symbolism, and material qualities of objects determines how they are valued and preserved [27]. Notably, only one of the qualities these researchers identified—*perceived durability*—is a property of the object itself. *Engagement*, *history*, and *augmentation* are qualities that arise out of the interaction between object and owner, and may occasionally involve third parties as well. These interactions contribute to the "ensoulement" of objects that become precious heirlooms over time [22]. Gegenbauer and Huang extended Odom et al.'s framework through personal inventories with 17 Swedish households [13]. They add one quality inherent in objects—*perceived worth*—and two, *earned functionality,* and *sufficiency,* earned through human use. These researchers also challenged designers to prototype novel technologies based on their extended framework, an exercise that designers found "inspiring." Others studying consumption or preservation of items focused directly on technologies, either generally [12] or by examining classes of devices like PDAs [18].

Our work also builds on Pierce and Paulos' study of secondhand interactions [29]. While [13] and [27] focus primarily on preservation, Pierce and Paulos are interested in the entire re-acquisition cycle, defined as buying, selling, and/or trading of goods (we adopt this definition for our research as well). They advance four reacquisition orientations. *Casual reacquirers* and *necessary reacquirers* are traditional secondhand shoppers, motivated primarily by budget. In contrast, *critical reacquierers* are driven by social, political, or ethical considerations, and *experiential reaquirers* enjoy the experiential or aesthetic qualities associated with reacquisition. Secondhand shoppers that fall within these last two categories, labeled *invested reacquirers*, comprise the population we recruited.

Recognizing that many traditional distinctions between first- and secondhand shopping no longer hold (especially in online spaces), our work is also informed by HCI explorations of fashion thinking and practice. Pan and Blevis explored how fashion concepts can support sustainable design [28]. Their emphasis on the importance of social and community practices, and individual self-expression, is particularly relevant to our work. Juhlin et al's study of mobile technology for supporting clothing selection demonstrates the importance of observing actual dressing practices, and informed our selection of an ethnographic approach [21].

The Secondhand Fashion Experience

Within HCI, work on secondhand consumption often takes an object-centered approach informed by conducting personal inventories [26], an ethnographic methodology used by numerous researchers [12, 13, 18, 27]. In contrast, researchers writing from the perspectives of market research and consumer psychology are more likely to study secondhand shoppers' values, motivations, or experiences.

In these domains, researchers often construct consumer profiles of shoppers with shared values, motivations, and practices. For instance, Guiot and Roux identified four types of secondhand retail shoppers [15], three of which are similar to [29]'s *invested reacquirers*. *Polymorphous enthusiasts* are driven equally by economic motivations and the need to be unique; *thrifty critics* express economic motivations and anti-consumption norms; *nostalgic hedonists* simply enjoy the secondhand experience. A final category, *specialist shoppers*, are only incidentally secondhand consumers (e.g., [29]'s *non-invested reacquirers*). Other research reveals a range of values and motivations. Some secondhand shoppers are driven to craft a unique fashion identity [6]. Others express eco-conscious values. These shoppers may set limits on their consumption, seek out apparel with environmentally preferable attributes (e.g., organic fabrics), buy from local sources, or prefer "classic" styles [17]. Both secondhand shoppers and other recirculaters, such as those who attend swapmeets, may be motivated by anti-consumption, anti-consumerism, or even anti-capitalism [2]. Finally, buyers may be driven by thrift not as a utility but as a moral value linked to sacrifice [3].

The spaces where secondhand fashion consumption unfolds are also of interest. These are recognized as places (as in [16]) formed through the convergence of individuals with distinct values and identities, the objects they buy, sell, gift, or trade, and physical or online spaces [2]. These places are designed to convey a distinct style or taste and to transmit key norms and expectations, including information about price [9]. Within secondhand retail, vintage stores are especially adept at visual merchandising, achieved through a wealth of mechanisms including advertising, display, merchandise selection, merchandise information (such as tags), sales staff, store atmosphere, and store layout [25].

In the case of transient spaces such as vintage markets, which are cyclically built and removed from a space, the opportunity and necessity of mood is particularly salient. Transient spaces establish identity by anchoring to more permanent spaces (such as a restaurant serving food on vintage china), become predictable by giving old vendors preference over newcomers, and maintain a persistent online presence [9]. These practices allow shoppers to form attachments both through their interactional past, described by [23] as former associations with a site, and through their interactional potential. With this background in mind, we present our contribution.

METHODS

We conducted an ethnographic study of 13 re-circulators in the San Francisco Bay Area.

Procedure

Participants were recruited via a snowball sample, soliciting friends of friends and colleagues. We targeted participants who purchased secondhand fashion items "*to craft a unique personal style,*" or those who purchased secondhand "*to enact a set of values*." From our pool of initial respondents we conducted phone screeners with 20 participants. These screeners ranged from 22 to 47 minutes in length, and were designed to confirm two key criteria: (1) consistent engagement with *recirculation of fashion items*, and (2) secondhand consumption for reasons other than budget, i.e. to support a unique personal style or to enact values. Thirteen participants were selected for in-person ethnographic interviews based on fit to the above criteria and availability.

Fieldwork with each participant included a formal sit-down interview followed by exploration of a thrift, consignment, or vintage store. During the interview, participants answered a range of questions regarding personal history, consumption values, shopping preferences, and style. Prior to the interview, we asked each participant to bring or be prepared to talk about *"One piece of clothing and one accessory that you really truly love."* This "homework" [30] was designed to inspire contemplation.

After the sit-down interview, we asked our participants to take us to a favorite stores and *"show us what you do when you go shopping."* In some cases multiple stores were patronized, including a mix of first- and secondhand. We visited thrift stores such as Goodwill and the Salvation Army (N = 5), mid-range consignment stores such as Crossroads and Buffalo Exchange (N = 4), upscale vintage/consignment boutiques (N = 5), and firsthand specialty retailers (such as those specializing in eco fashion; N = 2). Once in the store, we asked participants to *"please 'teach' us how you go [thrifting/ consignment/ vintage shopping], assuming we know nothing about this practice."* This mechanism of "show and tell" is designed to elicit deeper reflections than sit down questions alone, while also providing data regarding participants' actual behavior to balance the biases inherent in self-report [30].

Ethnographic interviews ranged from 1 hour and 45 minutes to 5 hours and 30 minutes, with an average time of 2 hours. Of our 13 participants, 11 shopped alone and 2 requested to participate together. Prior to interviews, all participants signed a consent form to "opt in" to different types of data collection and data sharing. All were compensated for their contribution with Visa gift cards.

Participants

Participants were secondhand shoppers in the San Francisco Bay Area (namely, Albany, Alameda, Berkeley, Campbell, San Francisco, San Jose, and Oakland). Select demographic information is presented in Table 1. The majority of our participants were engaged in multiple types of recirculation, including buying, selling, swapping, gifting, and giving away. Specifically, all 13 purchased both first- and secondhand goods; 9 utilized a mixture of online and offline channels. All 13 reported some experience with selling, although these experiences varied widely. While we did not ask specifically about swapping, 7 participants reported attending swap meets or otherwise sharing clothes. All 13 donated clothing consistently, or had donated clothes in the past. Thus, for our participants, reacquisition was a true landscape, as also observed by [29]. As revealed in Table 1, we interviewed more women then men. This is in line with our snowball sampling procedure, and we do not believe our female skew is a limitation.

	Alias	Age	Gender	Occupation
1	Lucy	20s	F	Retail Employee
2	Rachel	20s	F	Fitness Instructor
3	Alicia	20s	F	eBay Seller
4	Ruth	20s	F	Park Service Ranger
5	Jackson	20s	M	Artist
6	Madeline	20s	F	Radio Host
7	Axel	30s	M	Accountant
8	Maura	30s	F	University Admin.
9	Kiera	30s	F	Special Ed. Teacher
10	Alexandra	30s	F	Student; Law clerk
11	Agnes	40s	F	University Admin.
12	Vivian	40s	F	Jewelry Designer
13	Lidiya	40s	F	Acupuncturist

Table 1. Participant demographics (names have been changed).

Data Collection and Analysis

Two or three researchers were present for each trip. One was primarily responsible for asking contextualized questions, while another documented the experience through audio recordings, photographs, videos, and screen captures. Data analysis was an iterative process that began with debriefing, as researchers shared key insights and contemplated emerging themes immediately following each interview. Following best practices for conducting ethnographic interviews, in addition to debriefing each researcher compiled field notes codifying their reactions in greater depth [30]. Phone and in-person interviews for each participant were recorded and transcribed. These documents were analyzed along with field notes in an iterative process similar to Thematic Analysis. Thematic Analysis is an iterative approach similar to grounded theory considered appropriate when researchers have existing conceptions of key themes [5]. For example, prior to fieldwork we understood secondhand consumption to be a complex reacquisition process driven by values and identity practices, but we did not understand secondhand shoppers' more specific motivations or shopping orientations.

FINDINGS AND DISCUSSION

We report how our participants experienced secondhand retail shopping, and present our typology of three secondhand shopping orientations.

Values and Identities

While participants expressed a number of values, six key themes emerged. These take the form of positive/ negative value pairs: for example, our shoppers valued items that **were** made locally, and **were not** made in the third-world. These value pairs are presented in Table 2. The values expressed by our shoppers are not stable, but rather are negotiated, both across an individual's lifetime, and as practices come into conflict with ideals.

Lifetime Negotiations

The first negotiation is a departure from the values and practices of mainstream consumption. Many participants began shopping with their families. Some participants were drawn to thrift shopping as a practice to support popular "remix style." As Agnes explains: *"I used to subscribe to Seventeen Magazine. And I remember there was an article probably in '79, '80 I think, and it had like you know 'wacky ways to mix your clothes'... So I guess that article, I was like 14 or something, really kind of gave me, confirmed, supported my ideas of what to wear."* Many identify multiple roots. Axel began secondhand shopping to support his own version of remix style (inspired by *GQ Magazine*) while simultaneously acting on anti-consumerist values. Others began secondhand shopping for one reason, and continue for others. Kiera was a recreational thrifter in her teens, but realized the ethical value of her practices after reading the book *No Impact Man*.

Short Term Negotiations

Values also shift in response to different scenarios. For many shoppers, practices often fail to live up to ideals. Maura reported, *"I can't afford to buy everything locally made and I think it's pretty much impossible."* Additional conversations clarify that this is a question of budget and also source: like Kiera, Madeline, and Lucy, Maura reported that it is difficult or undesirable to find items such as bras, underwear, socks, and undershirts secondhand. This example is notable because two negative values come into conflict: the cultural taboo of buying certain (personal) items secondhand, and personal ideals against firsthand consumption (as also noted by [14]).

For Vivian, the information burden of ethical consumption is too severe: "*I'm not informed enough at that level to know, 'Oh if it says from this particular location that means blah blah blah.'*" Kiera sees a solution in secondhand consumption: *"I feel really trapped by the idea of like always trying to look, like where were my clothes made, and so for me the easiest way for me to feel like I'm not contributing to maybe people being paid unfair wages and so forth is to buy things secondhand.*"

The majority of the shoppers we interviewed placed limits on their consumption. For Maura, "*my general rule is, for every piece I bring in, something else has to go out.*" Some, like Ruth, also guard against accumulation: "*I do a big spring cleaning... it's sort of cathartic.*" These restrictions may conflict with other values. Maura tries to limit the amount of clothing she owns, but worries about donation: "*If I get rid of it, it has the potential of going into a landfill, so that sort of bucks up against this waste issue, right?*" While giving items to friends and family directly enhances the likelihood they will be used, this is not always possible.

Value pair	Illustrative Example
Re-constructing consumption/ Embracing consumption myths	On swapping: *"it kind of separates the fun part out of it?...we have bodies and dressing our bodies is like a creative act."* *"You have a bad day and you feel like 'oh I need to buy something' I would fall prey to that more when I was younger."*
Ability to craft an authentic personal style/ Adherence to fashion authority	*"I'm more of a person who sees something in a magazine and then I'm like...how can I make it my own?"* *"I don't like the feeling of being told what I'm supposed to be into right now"*
Fixing or re-purposing/ Unrestrained buying	*"Why I'm so thrifty with clothes and I believe in reusing or repurposing stuff is because of [my Grandmother]. She never wasted anything."* *"With the rise of just really inexpensive fashion... people just buy a lot of stuff and get rid of it really quickly."*
Desire to limit possessions/ Disdain for constant consumption	*"If I'm going to bring in 5 new things, I have to get rid of at least three"* *"We're a consumer nation. We just keep buying stuff."*
Items made locally/ Made globally	*"Somebody got paid to make that here, and they had a job, and it was presumably at least minimum wage."* *"...a chain retailer that probably has their clothing sold in China or you know any sort of sweat shop in a random country."*
Items with meaning/ Generic items	*"I think of clothing a bit like I think of animals? You know they have their own life...they have their stories, they tell stories, they hold stories."* *"I definitely like having things that are more meaningful than just picking them up from say Forever 21"*

Table 2: Common value pairs of the secondhand community

Of course, secondhand shoppers continue to buy despite anti-consumption values. Many construct their consumption to allow intrinsic and social values to outweigh perceived costs. Maura takes pride in her ability to support local artists, *"local women, in particular."* Kiera similarly justifies buying a hat: "*It was pretty and I wanted it, and someone local made it...I rarely buy something that I don't need unless I'm contributing in a way that makes me feel, it's okay to be less frugal.*" Clothing swaps, where guests exchange items in the absence of currency, are more powerful contrasts to mainstream consumption. Lidiya describes taking her step-daughter, who often feels guilty spending money on clothing, to swap meets: *"This thing is*

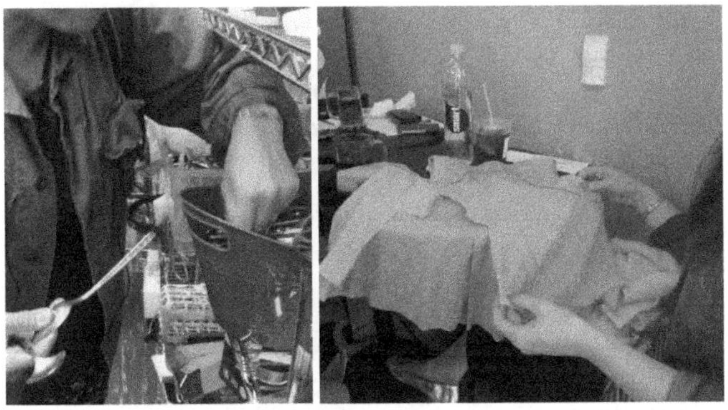

Figure 1. "What gems, within the detritus."

like a total healing balm. This clothes swap. Because we go, and everything is free."

Some researchers suggest that when secondhand markets supplement rather than replace firsthand markets, they contribute to overconsumption [29]. Some experienced re-circulators believe that secondhand consumption may involve even *more* acquisition and dispossession than mainstream retail. Alicia, who makes her living selling secondhand, explains: *"We like have enough money to just keep buying, keep buying. And you'll get rid of stuff. You'll keep changing out your closet. And I'd be hard pressed to find somebody who has something in their closet that they've worn to bits...its kind of unfortunate in a way I feel but it does help my business."*

Negotiated fashion identities

Many participants cultivate signature styles, which often visually distinguish them from mainstream consumers. Madeline, who prefers clothing from the 1960s, is *"affectionately called by good friends the walking couch because of all the patterns that I wear."* Those with strong personal style derive intrinsic pleasure from the act of getting dressed. They also consider style a form of communication [21], both sending and receiving cues: Vivian describes, *"a visual impact of identifying your tribe."* Ruth appreciates *"when people are wearing certain brands that I like, and I know the ethics behind them."*

But style is not always stable. The concept of faceted identities suggests that individuals share different aspects of their selves in different contexts [11]. Many participants expressed faceted style identities. One obvious distinction is between clothing worn during and outside of work. Rachel maintains two separate wardrobes: vintage is *"just for fun."* Kiera will wear the same clothing for work and play, but explains, *"I'll wear an undershirt so that I can have a different top on, and I would take that undershirt off with the same top."* Such manipulations allow her to easily transition from one life context to another.

Maintaining faceted styles frustrates people to varying degrees. Axel, who goes to work *"in the shirt and tie and khaki pants and nice shoes"* would prefer to wear his quirky, vintage-driven style in all life contexts. But others derive pleasure in their ability to, as Lucy explains, *"be a chameleon."* Agnes describes her style as *"this anarchy dressing where anything goes,"* but does not mind dressing differently for work events: *"If everyone else is dressed like that I certainly feel like I fit in, and its comfortable, I wouldn't want to draw attention to myself."* Thus, some who identify primarily with alternative styles still pride in their ability to dress appropriately for mainstream roles.

Objects

The value of secondhand objects is far from static. Objects' values shift in relation to general cultural valuations, or the contextual needs of a buyer. Importantly, individual objects can acquire a nostalgic, transcendent quality, narrated through stories, that drastically enhances their value [22]. Secondhand objects often do not yield to "rational" choices about quality nor to simple price consciousness, but rather are priced through a personal and social evaluation of worth that extends far beyond the properties of the object itself.

Cultural valuation

Most objects must reach a certain age before they are considered "vintage" or "antique" [9]. While Agnes loves a particular style of Japanese spoon, she reported that it lacks market value because *"It's not old enough yet"* (she was quick to qualify that the spoon's young age does not decrease its value for her). Value is also determined by cultural trend. Jackson's success as a seller rests on his ability to find rare pieces, and also to keep on top of a changing market. Alicia searches for pieces cut in *"that retro silhouette that people go crazy over."*

Situational Need

An object's value is elastic in response to situational need. Needs may be practical, as in response to life changes; Ruth had to "*buy a whole new wardrobe*" to fit her new job. Valuation also changes based on emotional or psychological needs. Madeline described her "need" to find a new dress after landing a new DJ gig: *"I'll know I'm going to have a moment where I'm going to look at my closet and go like UH... if I have time and its in my budget I'm going to spend, you know, Thursday night before I go DJ...that will be my time that I'm going to go get that dress. And I'm going to go try my damndest to find that dress."*

The Transcendent Quality of Objects

As noted by [13, 27], objects gain value through the effort exerted in their acquisition. Due to this effort, secondhand consumption is often considered a practice that requires expertise [9]. Agnes's practice involves the act of literally digging (see Figure 1, left) for *"what gems, within the detritus."* Lucy prides on her ability to search and rescue objects from thrift stores and other sources. She showed off a fabric sample salvaged from her company's giveaway bin (see Figure 1, right). She explained, "*We have this sample closet where we keep a lot of the collaborative work...I pull things from those booths quite often, the giveaway bins, they throw away a lot of fabric so I'll bring it in.*" This repurposing is a creative exercise as well as a statement against waste. If Lucy hadn't rescued these fabrics, *"we probably would have just thrown those out."*

But, as secondhand objects acquire value through the effort required to find them, they may also derive value simply from being a part of the secondhand market. For example, if items are purchased from a local consigner, secondhand consumption can also cleanse poor manufacturing practices by essentially re-branding the pieces as local goods. As Axel explains, *"while I'm still buying the same clothing that may have been made in another country at least I know the money isn't going directly to that company, its going to a local business."* Ruth is similarly willing to purchase brands such as Juicy Couture secondhand that she would never consider firsthand—because she is practically and morally opposed to the price, and because she dislikes the conspicuous experience of the Juicy Couture retail space.

Because fashion objects may reflect the values of their designers [28], not all objects can be 'cleansed' through recirculation. The belt Kiera wears (see Figure 2, left) has a detachable buckle, which enables the wearer to utilize both belt and buckle on separate occasions. In contrast, another belt (see Figure 2, right) contains a buckle sewn on to the belt. While Kiera was initially drawn to the belt's aesthetics, she would never purchase this item because of its design. In this way, conspicuous consumption is *"told"* by the way different pieces are constructed; refusing to buy such pieces is a refusal to accept the values they represent. Other participants (including Alicia, Axel, and Lucy) expressed a similar sentiment through their refusal to buy items with obvious logos, even secondhand.

The sacred nature of gifts and inherited items is well understood [7]. Lucy showed off a sweater knitted by her grandmother, remarkable for both its quality and personal association: *"If I wear something of hers, it's just kind of honoring her."* Many participants described items that they would not part with, except possibly to close intimates. The logic underlying these evaluations is that a part of the owner is transferred to an object through use, and strangers would not recognize this value outside of the insider knowledge context that friends and family enjoy.

Yet, secondhand shoppers also find value in possessions touched by unknown others. In some cases, the ability to wonder and re-construct the relationship between an object and its former owner enhances the object's appeal. As Madeline explains, "*it will be a subconscious thought out of nowhere, like, 'I wonder where this piece of clothing was like summer of 1987. Where was this? Was it in a closet? Was it in another crazy girl's box who couldn't give her clothes away?*" Awareness of (and appreciation for) an unknown other is a common value supported through social interaction. Ruth describes how the story of a dress she purchased was shared, first between its previous owner and an employee, and later between that employee and Ruth:

Ruth: "*The other thing that's kind of cool on the back of it, it's got a Moonstone Garnet half-moon pendant? Left there on purpose by the lady who formerly owned it. And she's like, 'I want the next person to have this as well.' Because her husband gave it to her. And she left it with that dress.*"

Researcher: "*How do you know that?*"

Ruth: "*The lady at the store.*"

A final way that objects gain transcendent value is through collective negotiation. Kiera asked one researcher for advice *"as a woman"* (i.e., implicit insider) while trying on a shirt. Ruth will send her mother and sister text messages of items she is considering after trying them on.

Secondhand Sellers and the Construction of "Cool"

Many secondhand shoppers also rely on external experts whose sense of taste helps determine an object's value. Both sellers we interviewed, Jackson and Alicia, are acutely aware of this dependency, and work to convey a sense of taste that enhances the value of the objects they sell. On one hand, these sellers are valued for insider knowledge of their respective retail domains—contemporary fashion for Alicia, and vintage style for Jackson. One fascinating feature of the secondhand market is the degree that brands acquire and lose value over time [11]. Thus, while brand is the traditional authority that determines whether something is "cool," its power diminishes in secondhand retail. Instead, discernment is in the hands of retailers, who act as intermediaries between the totality of secondhand goods and those that reach curated markets. Sellers vet goods in various ways. Jackson does "*market research*" to verify the authenticity of the items he buys, like by learning the "*tells*" of counterfeit pieces. Alicia conducts her research while shopping, evaluating the value of different brands via their performance in secondhand marketplaces such as eBay. Sellers not only value items, but communicate value to potential buyers. This process requires establishing trust, which Jackson claims is crucial in online vintage markets, as buyers must convey and sellers must accept the non-ideal condition of items that still hold value.

An object may be made "cool" by the "cool" person carrying it [31]. Secondhand sellers not only determine

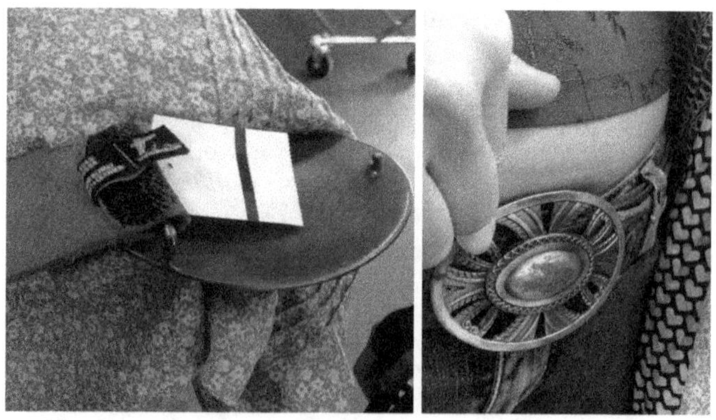

Figure 2. Kiera's belt (left) and a lesser model (right)

whether an object has value, but actively contribute to its value through association with their *personal brand.* Both Jackson and Alicia manage their personal brand to convey a valued sense of taste. For example, both sell on eBay and also maintain a "*professional*" presence on platforms like Pinterst and Instagram. Jackson's Instagram feed shows a rare vintage bike jersey he is extremely proud of finding, but has no intention of selling. Yet, the photo generates market value as testament to Jackson's ability to find and discern what is "cool." Both Jackson and Alicia experimented with the use of digital logos or physical tags to convey their personal brand.

Places

Secondhand shopping is a cultural practice deeply rooted in place. Place is evident in cultural norms regarding secondhand consumption, the influence of geography, and the deliberate design and construction of retail spaces. Many interviewees noted that cultural norms regarding secondhand shopping are changing. This frustrates many who consider theirs a lifelong practice. Agnes, for example, complained that some of her favorite shops are now *"picked over"* by college girls. Cultural norms regarding secondhand consumption are also a function of unique geographies. Vivian speaks to both dependencies:

"I always did consignment shopping, ever since high school. And I would say that, sort of like online dating was just a completely stigmatized thing when it first started and then it would be the cool thing to do, consignment shopping on the East coast was something you maybe did but never would admit to. And here, the friends I got when I came here they loved it as much as I did."

Participants also revealed geographic detriments of "cool." According to Kiera, *"In Colorado I think I probably felt a little more comfortable, you know with the sporty, outdoors-y look? But here kind of that burning man gypsy look... that part of me feels more accepted in California.*" While Kiera appreciates how geography enables her to express multiple facets of her style identity, Lidiya sees the practical benefit of local style, noting that it's easy to find clothes because

Figure 3. Vintage visual merchandising.

"all the women here dress like me." But Agnes describes the Berkeley Baby Boomer aesthetic as *"shapeless, and it looks like you've given up and don't care any more,"* and is irritated by how such clothing clogs the supply line of her favorite store.

Online and offline secondhand spaces are constructed to impart a desired experience, such as through visual merchandising [25]. We observed many such constructions in our ethnographic exploration of retail spaces. For example, color (e.g. vintage paint), material (e.g. racks constructed from old drain pipes), and curation (e.g. by decade) contribute to the "mood" of a space (see Figure 3).

Participants responded to visual cues and noted other sensory experiences. Alicia explained that the feel of a dress is as important as its aesthetic appeal; she is personally drawn to items that feel *"like silk.*" Music in a retail setting conveys a sense of culture. Maura complimented a store's soundtrack, while Kiera hummed as she shopped. Madeline loves the "*familiar*" smell of Mars Vintage; Lucy is drawn to items that smell "*like an antique cedar chest.*" These sensory experiences are not uniformly positive. There are some fabrics Agnes refuses to buy secondhand because of an unpleasant odor that persists "*no matter how many times you wash it.*"

The design of retail environments is also linked to a set of enacted community norms. In "thrift" spaces like Salvation Army and Goodwill, we observed multiple interviewees knock clothing off hangers and then either leave the items on the ground, or throw them carelessly on a nearby rack. In contrast, shoppers who took us to upscale consignment shops or vintage boutiques often explicitly requested that we respect the norms of those places. For example, both Madeline and Lidiya asked us to seek permission from shop employees prior to photographing their space. Finally, the physical design of retail environments affords a set of behaviors. This is most evident in digital spaces; eBay, for example, is currently designed to maximize support for standard keyword search, while platforms such as Etsy and Pinterest make it at least as easy to browse. Physical spaces also support different behaviors, in ways explored below.

Shopping Orientations

As we consider the findings reported above, we identify three primary secondhand fashion orientations: perfection seeking, casual curiosity, and digging.

Perfection seeking shoppers value individuality, and are driven to support a unique personal style. Their orientation is inward, e.g., *it's perfect for **me***; as such, they desire a relatively low level of social interaction during shopping. But, perfection seekers do enjoy sharing their finds with a like-minded community, either by wearing items or through gifting. Offline, these preferences lead perfection seekers to spaces such as vintage stores, boutiques, and, less frequently, medium-sized consignment shops. Online, perfection seeking is facilitated by spaces with extensive search functionality. For example, two perfection seekers used eBay to construct advanced queries and set alerts for new items that fit their exact specifications. For these shoppers, the best items are puzzle pieces that fit perfectly with a unique personal brand. Disappointment takes the form of a promising item that does not quite fit, or a small hole in an otherwise perfect piece.

Casually curious shoppers value social interaction and storytelling. Their orientation is shared, e.g. ***we** are having fun*. They seek interaction with friends (including co-shoppers and via technologies like cell phones), other shoppers, and employees. Casually curious shoppers are passionate about the narratives of pieces, as these carry emotional traces from previous owners. Offline, spaces such as medium-sized consignment shops and large thrift stores (with friends) best support their preferences. Online, they are drawn to visually rich and even interactive websites such as Etsy, Pinterest, and Instagram. These sites are valued for inspiration and user experience above their ability to connect buyers with goods; note that only one of the three examples above is an eCommerce platform. For these shoppers, the most appealing items are those with real or invented stories. Disappointment manifests in a poor experience overall.

The *digging* orientation characterizes the treasure hunters driven to find spectacular things. Their orientation is outward, e.g. *I found **it***. While social interaction during shopping minimizes their engagement with items and efficiency at finding gems, they do enjoy showing off their pieces through social sharing (many of our diggers are passionate users of Instagram). Offline, large thrift stores are the best places for diggers to find gems. Online, diggers are committed explorers of retail spaces. They both search and browse inventories extensively to become familiar with the full range of possibilities prior to making a purchase. Favored items are those salvaged through cleaning or repair. Diggers agonize over missing finds, and wonder about items "*passed over*" during earlier trips.

Unlike researchers such as [1, 6, 29], who believe that consumers fall into one or potentially two orientations or groups, we observe that these orientations are highly fluid. For example, many of our interviewees grappled with the question, *"Do you prefer to shop alone, or with other people?"* Vivian, for example, likes to shop with other people *"because its fun."* She simultaneously noted, *"I don't tend to prefer to go with people because it's slower."* These statements are not contradictions, but demonstrate how different shopping orientations are experienced at different times. When shopping as a compromiser, Vivian delights in social aspects of shopping, in particular the degree that she is respected for her personal taste. When shopping as a digger, Vivian finds joy in "*the treasure hunt aspect, the lottery aspect."* In order to enact this orientation effectively, she must be *"laser focused"* and thus alone. Like our findings on faceted styles, these observations support the faceted or flexible nature of identity (e.g., [11]), and emphasize the need to account for fluidity in design.

The invested orientations advanced by [29] included critical reacquierers, who were motivated by a set of values, and experiential reacquierers, motivated by "positive experiential or aesthetic qualities." To some extent, our orientations can be seen as three subsets of the latter. All of our shoppers are driven by some values, though these were less important overall than *experiences*. Importantly, values are sometimes compromised in a way that orientations are not. When Kiera decided to buy her hat, she prioritized her desire for that hat (and to a lesser extent her desire to support local artists) over her value of anti-consumerism. This decision carries moral weight. When Vivian acts as a digger or a compromiser, she is simply enacting a different aspect of herself, in the absence of critical evaluation.

DISCUSSIONS OF DESIGN

Key work by [27] and later [13] studied how the properties of objects can support sustainable design. Pierce & Paulos similarly focused their study on objects [29], but noted that participants "emphasized ways in which the process of reacquiring was an important, intrinsically valuable experience." We build on this work by taking a perspective that emphasizes experiences first, and objects second. Our investigation was conducted specifically with a future goal to design new interactions that better support people's actual practices. Below, we offer recommendations for designing secondhand experiences to support the practices observed.

Of the attachment categories explored by Odom et al., *histories*, *augmentation*, and *perceived durability* are most relevant here [27]. Regarding *histories,* we note that in secondhand fashion, attachment is formed not only through personal history, but through appreciation of an item's previous existence and owner. Lucy values her grandmother's clothing because it carries traces of her grandmother. Madeline derives similar pleasure from imagining previous owners of her dresses. We also find *augmentation* to support attachment. Recirculators like Axel and Lucy repair or embellish clothing, a process that personalizes and renews these pieces. We observe two distinct types of *durability.* The eBay sellers in our study, Alicia and Jackson, scrutinize items they buy to determine whether their quality and condition offsets their age. By communicating wear and tear through photos and text, they enable potential buyers to replicate this valuation. Buyers and sellers also assess the durability of a piece; as noted in our findings, this value may be individually, jointly, or culturally constructed.

Gegenbauer and Huang identify three additional categories of attachment [13]. Attachment by *earned functionality* occurs when an object is valued "because of the time and effort spent becoming familiar with it" [13]. This category is manifest in our diggers, whose objects acquire value through pursuit. We depart from [13] on a second point: they characterize perceived worth as "of a logical and pragmatic nature, rather than one that is strongly emotional." With the exception of sellers, we find the opposite. Ruth's attachment to her dress with the half moon pendent, for example, is entirely sentimental. Furthermore, Agnes's qualification that flatware that does not hold market value as an antique still holds value *to her* suggests a conscious departure from economic valuation. Thus, the *experienced worth* of objects is subjective and shifting.

Pierce and Paulos offer a number of design "opportunity areas" based on their findings [29]; we re-assert two of these. *Recoding the reacquired and reacquiring* recognizes that many objects are disposed of while some of their value remains. This is a key frustration for Lucy, who repurposes items salvaged from a retailer's giveaway bin, and is expressed in general terms by many of our participants. *Simplifying dispossession* [29] suggests that it should be easier to sell, gift, or donate goods. Participants including Maura described their angst about donating clothing that may be subsequently thrown out. Adding to these reflections, we propose the following suggestions for designing secondhand experiences:

Support the need for pleasure

Observing the same practices performed by our diggers, Pierce and Paulos recognize that pleasure is found in the acquisition experience itself, and caution against over-simplifying reacquisition [29]. We also believe that technology should actively enhance the reacquisition process, like by providing complex sensory experiences around objects and atmospheres. In the near future, tactile feedback could convey the feel of a dress. Further out, olfactory information could be linked to individual objects, either by conveying an actual scent (e.g., to help Agnes avoid certain items) or an ideal scent designed to evoke powerful associations (e.g., Lucy's antique cedar chest). In a similar vein, researchers find that beautiful objects bring pleasure and are more likely to be reused [27, 28]. Designers might provoke users to consider the inherent beauty of objects first, and later to identify a function that fits a particular form.

Observing the practices preferred by our casually curious shoppers, we also understand that pleasure comes from social interaction. Online and offline spaces serving these shoppers should be constructed as social spaces where each user may establish their identity for that particular sociotechnical context, whether through use of a profile page, avatar, or other means.

Support the need for storytelling

Shoppers expressing our casually curious orientation are also inspired by narrative and history. But in secondhand consumption, narrated histories are works in progress. New owners add to existing histories, and determine the salient stories from an object's past. For Leah's pendant narrative, its previous owners' wedding is key historical value; for Tara, discovering the spoons is a narrative that affirms the act of digging itself. This narrative reconstruction is similar to the recoding described by [29], where context helps recode value into 'junk.' To allow narrative reconstruction, design should support rich and varied interpretations (e.g., by augmenting standardized product listing, which are necessary to support search, with human curated tags). To support collective storytelling, design should integrate social and commerce spaces (e.g., by linking spaces for public and private dialogue to a product page). Researchers working in collaboration with Oxfam charity conducted one study where they tagged donated items with RFID and QR codes, allowing shoppers to access "the tales of things" via their Smartphones [8]. These could also be used to let sellers or donators know when their item finds a new owner, thus alleviating concerns expressed by participants like Maura. Though associated privacy implications would need to be carefully considered, those who sell and donate goods may also enjoy seeing how their old items earn new lives. Additionally, HCI design could support storytelling by linking historical data from secondhand items with storytelling applications like Storify and Storehouse to allow users to write items interactive, shareable histories.

Support negotiations around value and durability

In secondhand consumption, two types of gatekeepers construct the value and meaning of items [20]. Human sellers in both online- and offline environments curate 'cool.' Online, algorithms act as gatekeepers through the ordering of search results and curated recommender sites. Alicia and Jackson are far better recommenders than algorithmic systems, and occasionally buy pieces with certain sellers in mind. Effective C2C platforms should offer sellers a place to establish their taste, like through the opportunity to show off goods that both are and are not for sale. Such an infrastructure would also enable recirculates such as Lucy to show off how items that may appear unsalvageable are effectively transformed (e.g., Lucy's planned reconstruction of the shirt in Figure 1). This use case would support Lucy's need for creative individual expression, while also inspiring the larger community to "*recode*" similar goods. Algorithmic solutions might be constructed to match buyers and sellers, or support search and/or browse functionality allowing users to discover items tagged by, for example, decade or mood.

LIMITATIONS AND FUTURE WORK

We conducted 13 ethnographic interviews with secondhand shoppers in the San Francisco Bay Area. Our geographic scope is a limitation of this research, especially in light of our findings about regional culture and style. Comparative studies conducted in other geographies is an area for future research. Recirculation is a cyclical process that involves the acquisition, ownership, and disposal of goods. While we were able to examine acquisition and disposal by watching our participants buying and selling secondhand clothing, these practices were observed over a single day. Future research should examine long-term recirculation behaviors and the practices that unfold over the course of an individual's life, as styles, identities, and values change. Finally, our focus was on shoppers driven by values or identity practices; future HCI research might examine the practices of shoppers driven by economic necessity.

ACKNOWLEDGMENTS

We thank our reviewers for their helpful comments, and our participants for sharing their practices. We thank Daniel Kluver, Oliver Hinder, and Michael Gilbert for their community. Finally, we thank eBay Research Labs: especially Michelle Fulcher, Atish Das Sarma, and Hugo Liu, who helped support this work during summer 2014.

REFERENCES

1. Ailawadi, K., Neslin, S., Luan, J. and Taylor, G. Does retailer CSR enhance behavioral loyalty? A case for benefit segmentation. *International Journal of Research and Marketing, 31,* 2 (2013), 156-167.
2. Albinsson, P. and Perera, Y. Alternative marketplaces in the 21st century: Building community through sharing events. *Jour. of Consumer Behavior, 11* (2012), 303-315.
3. Bardhi, F. and Arnould, E. Thrift shopping: Combining utilitarian thrift and hedonic treat benefits. *Journal of Consumer Behaviour, 4,* 4 (2005), 1572-0817.
4. Bosch, L. and Kanis, M. Encouraging sustainable fashion with a playful recycling system. *Proc. BCS-HCI 2013,* British Computer Society (2013), Article No. 46.
5. Braun, V. and Clarke, V. Using thematic analysis in psychology. *Qualitative Research in Psychology, 3,* 2 (2006), 77-101.
6. Cervellon, M., Carey, L. and Harms, T. Something old, something used: Determinants of women's purchase of vintage fashion vs second-hand fashion. *International Journal of Retail & Distribution Management, 40,* 12 (2012), 956-974.
7. Cheal, D. "Showing them you love them": Gift giving and the dialectic of intimacy. *The Sociological Review, 35,* 1 (1987), 150-169.
8. deJode, M., Barthel, R., Rogers, J., Karpovich, A., Hudson-Smith, A., Quigley, M. and Speed, C. Enhancing the 'second-hand' retail experience with digital object memories. *Proc. Ubicomp* (2012), 451-460.
9. Duffy, K., Hewer, P. and Wilson, J. 'Granny would be proud': On the labours of doing vintage, practices and emergent socialities. *Advances in Consumer Research, 40* (2012), 519-525.
10. eBay beats expectations with $11B in revenue in 2011. http://venturebeat.com/2012/01/19/ebay-q4-earnings/
11. Farnham, S.D. and Churchill, E.F. Faceted identity, faceted lives: Social and technical issues with being yourself online. *Proceedings of CSCW* (2011), 359-368.
12. Gegenbauer, S. and Huang, E. Inspiring the design of longer-loved electronics through an understanding of personal attachment. *Proc. DIS* (2012), 635-644.
13. Gegenbauer, S. and Huang, E. iPods, Ataris, and Polaroids: A personal inventories study of out-of-use electronics in Swiss households. *Proc. Ubicomp* (2012), 531-534.
14. Gregson, N & Crewe, L. Second-hand cultures. *Journal of Design History, 18,* 2 (2005), 214-216.
15. Guiot, D. and Roux, D. A second-hand shoppers' motivation scale: Antecedents, consequences, and implications for retailers. *Journal of Retailing, 86,* 4 (2010), 389-399.
16. Harrison, S. and Dourish, P. Re-placing space: The roles of place and space in collaborative systems. *Proc. CSCW* (1996) 67-76.
17. Hiller-Connell, K. Exploring consumers' perceptions of eco-conscious apparel acquisition behaviors. *Social Responsibility Journal, 7,* 1 (2011), 61-73.
18. Huh, J., Nam, K. and Sharma, N. Finding the lost treasure: Understanding reuse of used computing devices. *Proc. CHI* (2010), 1975-1884.
19. Industry Statistics & Trends. http://www.narts.org/i4a/pages/index.cfm?pageid=3285
20. Juhlin, O. and Zhang, Unpacking social interaction that make us adore: On the aesthetics of mobile phones as shopping items. *Proc. MobileHCI* (2011), 241-250.
21. Juhlin, O., Zhang, Y., Sundbor, C. and Fernaeus, Y. Fashion shape switching: Explorations in outfit-centric design. *Proc. CHI* (2013), 1353-1362.
22. Jung, H., Barzdell, S., Blevis, E., Pierce, J. & Stolterman, E. (2011). How deep is your love: Deep narratives of ensoulment and heirloom status. *Int. J. Design, 5,* 1, 59-71.
23. McCracken, G.D. *Culture and Consumption: New Approaches to the Symbolic Character of Consumer Goods and Activities.* Indiana University Press, 1990.
24. Milligan, M. Interaction past and potential: The social construction of place attachment. *Symbolic Interaction, 21,* 1 (1998), 1-33.
25. Nobbs, K., McColl, J., Shearer, L., Canning, C. & McBride, L. An exploratory study into the strategic significance of visual merchandising: The case of fashion retailing. In Pedroni, M., Ed., *From Production To Consumption.* Oxford: Interdisciplinary Press, 2013.
26. Odom, W. Personal inventories: toward durable human-product relationships. *CHI EA* (2008), 3777-3782.
27. Odom, W., Pierce, J., Stolterman, E. and Blevis, E. Understanding why we preserve some things and discard others in the context of interaction design. *Proc. CHI* (2009), 1053-1062.
28. Pan, Y. and Blevis, E. Fashion thinking: Lessons from fashion and sustainable interaction design, concepts and issues. *Proc. DIS* (2014), 1105-1014.
29. Pierce, J. and Paulos, E. Second-hand interactions: Investigating reacquisition and dispossession practices around domestic objects. *Proc. CHI* (2011), 2385-2394.
30. Portigal, S. *Interviewing Users.* New York: Rosenfeld Media, 2013.
31. Raptis, D., Kjeldskov, J. and Skov, M. Understanding 'cool' in Human-Computer Interaction research and design. *Proc. of CHI* (2013), 53-62.

Your Money's No Good Here: The Elimination of Cash Payment on London Buses

Gary Pritchard
Culture Lab,
School of Computing Science,
Newcastle University, UK
gary.pritchard@ncl.ac.uk

John Vines
Culture Lab,
School of Computing Science,
Newcastle University, UK
john.vines@ncl.ac.uk

Patrick Olivier
Culture Lab,
School of Computing Science,
Newcastle University, UK
p.l.oliver@ncl.ac.uk

ABSTRACT
As digital payments become increasingly important features of economic exchange, traditional forms of payment such as cash are becoming phased out in certain settings. We study one such context—the elimination of cash payment on London buses in July 2014. We conducted ethnographic fieldwork, interviews with drivers and collected online and social media comments before, during and shortly after the introduction of cashless fares. We explore how drivers and passengers were fearful of the change due in part to a lack of information and communication, the anticipation of negative effects on vulnerable passengers and a compromise in freedom, flexibility and surveillance. We highlight the ways cashless payments can alter the social function of money, create new forms of work for drivers and passengers, and if not carefully introduced can cause emotional stress and fears of state surveillance and control.

Author Keywords
Electronic payments; contactless; public transport; cashless.

ACM Classification Keywords
H.5.m. Information interfaces and presentation (e.g., HCI): Miscellaneous.

INTRODUCTION
'Cash takes time to get at, is riskier to carry, and by most estimates, cash costs society as much as 1.5% of GDP. Electronic payments, on the other hand, have been proven to boost economic growth, while advancing financial inclusion.' [22, p.1]

Cashless payments are becoming an important feature of everyday economic exchange. As summarised in this quote by Mastercard, in their report entitled *The Global Journey From Cash to Cashless*, the motivation and enthusiasm surrounding electronic payment is wrapped in a discourse

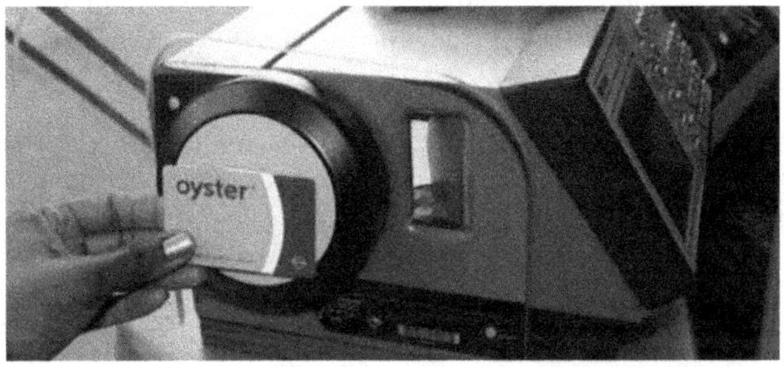

Figure 1. Oyster card being 'tapped in' on a London bus.

of cash being an antiquated burden and an impediment to economic growth and social progress. This perspective is shared by London's transport governing body *Transport for London* (TfL), who on the 6th of July 2014 brought an end to 185-years of allowing passengers to pay cash for bus journeys [35]. This change was heralded as a way of improving the efficiency and reliability of services, to reduce the costs of processing cash, and to give greater convenience and cheaper prices to their customers [35]. As of now, people can only pay for travel on a London bus through a prepaid smartcard (the *Oyster*), a contactless bankcard or pre-paid travel card.

In this paper, we explore the impact that the elimination of cash payments on London's buses has had on bus drivers and passengers. Following a mixed-method approach to data collection, we studied expectations prior to and experience during and shortly after the introduction of the new cashless policy. We conducted interviews with bus drivers and passengers, ethnographic fieldwork at bus depots and on buses, and collected comments from news articles and social media related to the introduction of cashless buses. Our contribution to HCI is three-fold. First, we contribute to the emerging literature on digital payments and money (e.g. [18,30,37]) by studying the impact 'cashless' systems have on the social function of money and the labour involved in their use. Second, we contribute to the study of electronic ticketing and digital technology in public transportation (e.g. [16,25,26]) by highlighting how such systems leave some passengers vulnerable through lack of awareness or lack of infrastructure. Finally, we contribute ways to improve the future introduction of cashless payments in this context.

CHI 2015, April 18 - 23 2015, Seoul, Republic of Korea Copyright is held by the owner/author(s). Publication rights licensed to ACM.
ACM 978-1-4503-3145-6/15/04…$15.00
http://dx.doi.org/10.1145/2702123.2702137

THE OYSTER AND DIGITAL MONEY

An *Oyster* is a near-field communication (NFC) card that is used to pay for public transport in London (Figure 1). They were introduced in 2003, with the intention to replace traditional paper tickets. Instead of paying a driver directly, travellers store credit on their *Oyster* and pay per journey by tapping the card on an electronic reader when entering and exiting the bus. For over a decade the *Oyster* has co-existed with other payment methods—such as cash (coins and banknotes) and travelcards (paper cards that could be purchased at shops and tube stations but not on buses). In 2013, London buses also started to accept contactless payment cards—normal debit and credit cards that use contactless technology to pay for small transactions.

Bus passenger payment habits have been shaped over time by TfL. Over the past decade bus journeys paid by cash have become more expensive, as has the relative cost of travelcards compared to *Oyster*-paid journeys. According to TfL, as of 2013 this has lead to only 1% of all bus journeys made in London being paid for by cash [35]. However, this still equates to approximately 60,000 journeys every day. Furthermore, 86% of those using cash also have an Oyster [35]. As such the 1% figure disguises great complexity and infers that Oyster owners frequently rely on cash as a payment method in certain circumstances.

In early 2014, TfL published a report outlining plans to make all of London's buses 'cashless'. Using the above statistics to highlight the relative lack of cash payments, they noted that: 'Going cashless will remove the delays associated with cash transactions which would also benefit everyone. Cash payers would benefit from cheaper fares, saving around £1 a trip if they switch to *Oyster* pay as you go or contactless payment cards' [35, p.5]. A consultation process involving 37,573 passengers resulted in more negative (67%) than positive (32%) responses to the change, with many people noting the potential problem of being left stranded if an *Oyster* card is out of credit. TfL responded to this by providing concessionary passes to over a third of customers (young people, students, and disabled and older people). They also introduced the 'one more journey scheme' which allows passengers to make one more bus journey with their *Oyster* would allow should they have insufficient credit to travel. With these new procedures in place, the proposal to withdraw cash transaction on buses was put into place on the 6th July 2014.

Money and HCI

The *Oyster* is just one example of the ways digital money, payments and commerce has started to pervade everyday life and this is illustrated through the growth of HCI work studying this area. Areas of particular recent interest include studies of mobile payments (e.g. [19, 20]), peer-to-peer lending and alternative currencies [5] and tools to support decision making around spending [29]. However, somewhat countering these perspectives, studies of financial practices have highlighted the ways people reject technologies that manage the full range of a person's finances [18] or do not provide the necessary level of control [37] or sense of security [36] to be of value. Indeed, these latter works emphasise how the physical and burdensome qualities of cash actually can make managing finances easier than digital payment.

Also related to our work are studies of the implications of introducing cashless payment technologies in public transportation. It has been noted that dwell times can be significantly reduced with prepaid or smartcard payments [34]. A number of studies have examined the *Oyster* specifically as an emblematic example of this technology (e.g. [4, 16, 25]). In their research on public perceptions towards *Oyster*, Poole et al [25] highlighted concerns that using contactless payments may present fewer opportunities to engage in conversation and pleasantries with cashiers and reduce a sense of community. These views were echoed in [26], which highlighted how some (but few) London bus drivers missed the social interaction that disappears when passengers use *Oyster* cards. In a similar vein, Brewer et al observed how a practice of exchanging paper tickets between passengers has been eradicated by the introduction of the 'personal, permanent, and reusable' *Oyster* card [4, p.338]. It has further been illustrated how contactless ticketing systems that are bound to geographical locations can be exclusionary to visitors [25].

One of the greatest concerns surrounding the introduction of contactless payment has been the potential for privacy invasion. Not long after the introduction of the *Oyster* system, the RFID chips on the cards were hacked and instructions on how to do so were made freely available online [13]. Furthermore, there is a tension regarding the collection of data by transport companies and governmental agencies through the use of cards like *Oyster*. It has been highlighted how data from cards can be used to infer travel behaviours, and thus lead to behaviour change interventions [16] or the monitoring of movements of criminals [3]. Along with data hacking and privacy leaking scandals that have surrounded public and private sector organisations in the UK over the last decade, this has promoted underlying tensions between the British public and TfL as to the perceived benefits and costs of this technology (e.g. [40]).

While *Oysters* and similar systems have been studied, this has been done so with the availability of other forms of payment. We were specifically motivated to study what happens when a previously dominant and pervasive mode of payment (cash) was eliminated. Given the availability of cash-based transactions on London's buses for the past 185 years, this brings about a significant change—impacting upon the work of staff and the experiences of those who travel. Furthermore, this provides a rich site for studying the losses and gains presented by electronic ticketing and digital money. As such, our research set out to study the period immediately surrounding the introduction of the no-cash policy, focusing on the ways it impacted drivers' work practices and the experiences of passengers before, during and shortly after its introduction.

METHOD

While the focus of this paper is the elimination of cash payments on London buses in July 2014, our fieldwork and data collection forms part of a larger study on bus driver work practices and use of digital technology. Fieldwork specifically focused on the new cashless policy that began 2 weeks prior to its introduction. However, we began talking informally with bus drivers about the topic when management had consulted them on the policy 15-months prior. We took a mixed-methods approach, based upon interviews with bus drivers and bus passengers, ethnographic fieldwork and online data collection related to the introduction of the new bus policy.

Interviews with drivers

To begin with, around the time of first being informed of the plans for the new cashless policy (April/May 2013) we performed interviews with 10 bus drivers. The lead researcher had pre-existing social relationships with 6 of these participants. These helped the researcher meet other drivers who were comfortable with talking to him and saw him as a 'friend of a friend'. This greatly eased access and acceptance, and participants were very keen to help the research. These initial interviews were undertaken to broadly explore and understand the work practices of London bus drivers and examine the ways in which digital technologies are impacting upon their work (insights from which are published in earlier work [26]). In the following months, the lead author had continual contact with some of these initial participants, through which he was informally kept informed of the upcoming policy change. We followed our initial interviews up with more focused data collection, looking specifically at the new initiative of eliminating cash payments. We interviewed 10 further drivers approximately 1-2 weeks before its introduction. Interviews with drivers were semi-structured, conducted in informal settings and typically lasted for an hour. During these interviews, we discussed how the changes in policy had been communicated to them and the ways in which drivers expected the refusal of cash fares to impact their work. We followed up with these drivers again 2-3 weeks later, to discuss their experiences of the change.

Ethnographic fieldwork

Along with the drivers' interviews, we conducted 3 weeks of focused ethnographic fieldwork where we observed the work practices of bus drivers and informally talked to as many of this occupational group as possible. One of the central tenets of ethnography is the importance of 'being there' [14]. For this reason we spent many hours riding bus routes around London immediately before and after the elimination of cash payment. It's important to note that in the few weeks surrounding the introduction of cashlessness our interviews, observations and fieldwork fed-into each other. As such, we were able to allow interactions with passengers and drivers to inform the focus of our observations and vice-versa. For instance, because both drivers and the public identified tourist zones as likely 'trouble spots' we purposefully rode routes in these areas and asked tourists about their experiences. We also rode in areas on the edge of the city where there are fewer *Oyster* venders, and where TfL run routes alongside other bus operators that still accepted cash. Similarly, we knew from observations that passengers did not always enter the bus in an orderly way. We consequently purposefully engaged with drivers' perspectives about potential changes in boarding before, during and after the new policy.

One of the key considerations in approaching any group for research is the extent to which their setting is open or closed and how this influences what information can be gathered [2]. By definition, public transportation is a very 'open' setting. In contrast, social spaces where drivers can be engaged with more directly and reveal more candid perspectives are 'closed'. The aforementioned pre-established social relationships with a selection of bus drivers endowed automatic trustworthiness and meant that various cultures and conventions of bus-driving work were learnt. Writers have demonstrated how this form of cultural learning aids interaction with informants and smooth immersion into the field [24, 29]. These associations meant that we had access to organized social gatherings with drivers, which typically meant a drink in the pub after their working day. Following on from the traditional 'hanging around' approach first adopted by Whyte [38] in his ethnography of street culture and more recently by Wolf [39] in his work on Canadian outlaw motorcycle-gangs, we spent time around bus garages and depots talking to this occupational group on an informal and serendipitous basis. In all these interactions, the researchers crosschecked information and noted any contradictions. Collins rightly asserts that it is always the case that when someone's experience is incorporated into data, decisions about 'who to trust, what to believe and why something is true are of central importance [6, p. 202].

Gathering passenger perspectives

As well as drivers' perspectives on the changes, we were also interested in the impact that the cashless policy had on bus passengers and the general public. We captured these perspectives in two distinct ways.

First, during ethnographic fieldwork the researcher spoke with members of the public travelling on bus routes about the upcoming changes. These conversations would be spontaneous, serendipitous, and responsive to the context—for example, when an announcement was made on a bus about the upcoming changes, if a passenger had picked up a leaflet related to the changes or if a passenger was seen to be refused boarding due to the new policy.

Second, we compiled public comments responding to news stories on the changes and Twitter data commenting on this issue. On the days surrounding the introduction, we searched for news articles related to the new policy and collected all comments associated with this. Our search identified 12 news reports with comment functionality, which provided us with 745 comments in total. To collect Twitter data, we harvested Tweets between the 1st and 24th of July 2014. We refined our harvesting by restricting the tweets collected to 17 search terms and to the geographical boundary of Greater London. We read through collected Tweets to discard those that were not evidently related to the study. This left us with 532 Tweets in total.

Data integration and analysis

The data presented in this paper is therefore the outcome of a mixed-methods approach. This approach is favoured when studying a complex social phenomenon, like those on display here, because it facilitates an appreciation of 'whole dimensions of social experience' [21, p.13]. Applying more than one method also endows complementarity, allowing the findings from each method to emphasise the other's qualities and incorporate different perspectives and constructions of a phenomenon [9]. This can lead to the creation of new knowledge and reveal different dimensions of a phenomenon and the complex nature of the social world [1, p.128]. This also alerts us to the need to critically evaluate the limitations of our various sources of data. For example, the interview portion of our work gave us depth of understanding but sacrificed berth in terms of number of participants, while the ethnographic fieldwork supported the observation of problematic situations but often we were unable to follow-up with specific passengers and drivers. Twitter and news articles gave us valuable insight into hundreds of passenger views specifically about the policy that would otherwise have been difficult to achieve. These sources also have significant limitations—such as being unable to identify the background and attitudes of those making comments, and comments may not necessarily represent the attitudes of those who make them. However, through combining these multiple sources we are able to mitigate somewhat against each sources limitations.

Once all fieldwork was completed, all of our collected data—anonymised interview transcripts, fieldwork diaries, and anonymised news and Twitter comments—were used as the basis of an inductive qualitative analysis. Following Glaser and Strauss [11] this corpus of data (including field note diaries) was coded at the sentence to paragraph level to develop themes [11]. We then reassembled this data using selective quoting to illustrate these themes. Coding in this manner was a highly effective way to sort all of the research data, especially in light of having gathered such a wide range of material.

FINDINGS

Our analysis highlighted four discreet themes: *communication and anticipation; susceptible passengers and places; negotiating vulnerability and giving leeway;* and *flexibility, choice and surveillance.* All data presented here is anonymised with pseudonyms, and we distinguish different data as belonging to bus drivers (BD), twitter (TW) or news articles (NA).

Communication and anticipation

The early stages of our fieldwork revealed a range of concerns in relation to the upcoming changes. This was particularly so from the drivers. Much of their anxiety stemmed from uncertainty, born from a lack of information from their employers. Initially, most didn't know precisely when cashless fares would be introduced and worried about how they should negotiate this change in practice. Ray for instance explained: *"We have to search the message boards to find these things out. We've got to search things out."* ***(Ray – BD).*** Other drivers explained how they searched on the TfL website out of work hours to look for information related to the changes. It was clear that the lack of communication placed the onus on drivers to seek out information for themselves, which a number of the drivers found relatively stressful.

This information problem was exacerbated by a feeling that the public hadn't been adequately prepared either. One of our bus-driving participants, Gordon, suspected that a lack of publicity was motivated by economic concerns, instead of passenger experience and employee wellbeing. As a result, he and his fellow drivers would inevitably 'get it in the neck': *It seems to me that money is more important than the service for TFL…Yes. It's the drivers that get it in the neck from the passengers.* ***(Gordon – BD).*** A few weeks prior to the introduction, TfL started to produce passenger-oriented information in the form of adverts placed at bus shelters, announcements played over the bus intercom, and leaflets handed out by drivers to cash-paying passengers. These measures however did little to ally the fear from drivers that most of the public were not taking this information onboard. Ray expressed his frustration, explaining how he had diligently given leaflets to all passengers who were paying with cash only to be disappointed when he saw they had all been thrown on the floor.

There was equal fear that the audio announcements played on buses were not heard by passengers. Drivers felt that passengers would *"not take it in"*, *"not speak English"*, *"cant hear it over the bus"* or are just *"wearing headphones"*. Indeed, during fieldwork conducted just prior to the introduction, passengers were not seen to be responsive to the announcements. However, even in those instances where they were responsive, it was not immediately clear what they could do to prepare for the change. In one observed example, an older passenger approached a driver having heard the announcement. Concerned about the consequences the change would have on her niece, the driver responded with: *"you've just heard the announcement did it say ask the driver? No, it said ask TfL."* ***(Nobby - BD).*** While she knew the driver was joking, she still wished to know more information to inform her niece—however, the driver simply repeated the announcement verbatim.

While there were clear concerns about the policy, enthusiasm was also expressed. Drivers spoke fondly of the *Oyster*, as it had sped up boarding times and made their job easier. Bob for instance, felt services now ran more smoothly: *"I relax more, yes. I also think that routes are running smoother actually; we don't waste any time with people"* ***(Bob – BD).*** The new policy was also appreciated because it was perceived as, in the long term, reducing the work and labour of the drivers. Over the last 30 years, the role of London bus driver has been transformed. Some of the more obvious changes include the removal of conductors, meaning drivers acquired the role of receiving payments and issuing tickets. Others that are less obvious relate to being vigilant about suspicious passengers and packages in light of the terrorist attacks on London buses. Trevor explained how he felt: *"There is too much work already, I have to drive, give information to passengers."* ***(Trevor – BD).*** Another driver more forcefully explained how *"we're bus drivers not fucking cashiers"* ***(Gordon – BD).*** There was also a feeling among many of the drivers—but not all—that the new policy would improve their relationship with passengers through, ironically, the need to no longer interact with them.

Problem passengers and places

While drivers had many concerns about how the introduction of cashless fares would impact their work, there were significant ramifications for those passengers who still made cash payments on buses. A primary issue raised in public comments was the potential difficulty it would cause people who only visit London occasionally: "*What happens regarding tourists or people visiting for a day? I mean if you're only going to be in the capital for a day or maybe two at max, are you really going to waste time and money in the form of unused credit getting an Oyster Card?"* ***(JRain – NA).*** The introduction of cashless travel was seen to place an unfair burden on an individual to carefully plan visits to the capital and seek *Oyster* cards in advance of arrival: "*Occasional visitors aren't going to able to access the bus network unless pre-planned. This seems a bit stupid to me."* ***(Geoff – TW).***

Some passengers were seen to be more exposed to the elimination of cash than others. The comments sections of newspapers were full of imagined scenarios of children, older people and lone women left stranded as a result of not having an *Oyster*: "*What happens when a woman or a child from outside London does not have Oyster, or contactless card, only cash, in a dangerous area. At 8 in the evening. In winter-time?"* ***(KarlJ – NA).*** Others highlighted that non-English speakers might find it difficult to become aware of the change. Furthermore, there was an appreciation that the *"one size fits all"* approach to instigating the cashless policy failed to take into account that people may be more or less susceptible to having no credit on their *Oyster* card at different times of the day:

> *"I'm sure most people agree that it's a good idea during the day time because it does save a lot of time and money on many routes, especially tourist areas, which is good of course. But during the night time when there isn't a rush anymore and nobody cares if someone pays with change then I don't see why they don't allow paying by cash. Then there's of course the safety issue of being stranded at midnight. It should be Oyster only during daytime hours, bout 7:30am - 7pm, and then after that we should be able to use cash. The night busses should at least accept cash anyway."* ***(Jonny57 - NA).***

Jonny57 offers a balanced view of the new policy. They suggest a number of benefits to the mass of service users who may be using London's buses at the busiest time of days. However, there was an appreciation that this new policy is perhaps not needed all day, every day, and that at other times there should still be scope for flexibility to account for the heightened vulnerabilities people face travelling in the city at evening time. The fear of being stranded was echoed by others who had experienced an *Oyster* failing to work or vendors closed or out of order:

> *"I think in 4 years I must of paid cash for a bus ticket all of 3 times. But, those times were when I was stranded 10 miles from home at 3 in the morning with an empty Oyster Card. If they want to go cashless 24 hours, fine, but then they'll need to have a way to top up an Oyster 24 hours to go with it. The alternative is people getting into dodgy cabs out of drunken desperation at 4am. That's not a story that ends well."* ***(Barneyfrog66, NA)***

This is not just an issue of time-dependence but also place-dependence, as it was difficult to buy or top up an *Oyster* in some parts of London. Ray, a bus driver in his 50s, noted: "*The problem is that some areas have no places to buy top-up. Clerkenwell for example"* ***(Ray – BD).*** These areas tend to have fewer bus routes operating in their vicinity and are predominantly in more deprived areas of the city. Such gaps in infrastructure are therefore more likely to negatively affect lower-income groups who cannot put large amounts of credit on their card at one time.

Of course, it could be argued that the types of problems Barneyfrog66 and Ray note here might be mitigated against by the 'one more journey' scheme. However, during our fieldwork we observed this scheme being unhelpful for those whose 'one' journey entails changes between buses, tube and rail services. On one occasion, a bus driver was observed denying travel to one passenger during the day. Following up with them later into the journey, it was revealed that this passenger had not realised they had already used their one more journey credit.

Negotiating vulnerability and giving leeway

The reality that some people would be more vulnerable to the new policy than others is not lost on TfL. During our fieldwork—just prior to cashlessness being introduced—bus drivers were issued with a revised operational manual called the *"Big Red Book"*. This included an instruction to refuse passage to those who didn't have an approved method of payment or lacked any 'one more journey' credit: *"Passengers who turn up and attempt to pay with cash should be asked if they have another way to pay for travel. If they have no alternative method of payment, they should be politely refused travel on your bus unless you feel they could be vulnerable."* In an accompanying letter, it was explained how 'vulnerability' should be understood and applied:

"Not everyone is vulnerable all of the time but anyone could be vulnerable at any time. [...] Do not leave anyone stranded if they are vulnerable or clearly in distress. For example:

- *Young or older people*
- *People who could be at risk if left behind, including those in isolated places or at quieter times*
- *People who are disabled, injured, unwell or who have had an accident, assault or similar incident*
- *People who show you a travel support card and may have learning difficulties. Not all impairments are obvious."*

While this new 'vulnerability rule' was a response the types of concerns articulated during public consultation, it prompted further challenges for drivers. In particular, the endowment of more discretionary powers caused unease among some. Jack for instance was anxious that he might wrongly assess someone as 'vulnerable' and be disciplined if a revenue inspector entered the bus and disagreed:

"Yes, well, there's always a risk if Revenue don't agree with you, you can get booked and reported to your manager. Then I'll just see what the manager says and he'll probably see what I say. You can't get everyone right, can you?" ***(Jack – BD)***

Despite these guidelines, drivers' interpretation of 'vulnerability' also differed quite considerably. During an interview, Bobby stated that it was 'common sense' that this provision is for females only: *"It is common sense. If it was a geezer, he is walking, if he hasn't got an Oyster he is walking, I don't care what time of the night it is, he is walking."* ***(Bobby – BD)***. As well as reproducing well meaning but wrongheaded societal-wide prejudice about the fragility of females, this discretion can carry a more aggressive form of prejudice and discrimination. Bobby continued to explain: *"If it is a girl then I won't kick her off, especially if she is pretty. If she's a proper minger and a certain colour, they are fucking getting off. [...] It depends on the people really."* ***(Bobby – BD)***

While the above example is an extreme, a number of drivers explained their difficulty in understanding what vulnerability could or could not mean. As a result of their difficulties in interpreting the guidance, many of the drivers developed a number of pre-emptive coping strategies to be used once the policy was introduced. Despite the explicit guidance from TfL about the enforcement of the 'no cash' policy, drivers explained how they were willing to give passengers some *"leeway"*—in effect some flexibility in allowing people on the bus without payment after the no-cash policy is officially introduced. How long this period of leeway would be differed between drivers—however, it was clear that through conversations with groups of drivers at breaks and outside of work that *"1 or 2 weeks"* was broadly agreed upon. However, there was less agreement about how precisely this leeway would play out in practice. Nobby, for instance, explained the reasons why he gives extra consideration to passengers travelling at a time of day when it when it is difficult to top-up an *Oyster*.

"See, during the day you can tell somebody if it comes up as 'no cash', You can say, "Well, you can go to a shop." But when you do a night bus, at 3AM, the leniency, you can't say that. That's why you've got to be more lenient on the night bus. I'm probably letting on, the last three days or three nights, at least five people on for free. At least. A minimum of five." ***(Nobby – BD)***

A few of our participants also said they would be lenient towards passengers who were displaying obvious signs of distress. This consideration would be independent of perceived vulnerability: *"Well, if they were in distress, sort of panicking. Then you've got to let them on, haven't you? You don't know what problems they've had."* ***(Alan – BD)***. There was also sympathy towards tourists. Alan retells an incident when he let visitors ride for free, feeling that they genuinely didn't know about cashless fares:

"With people who've got on, it's foreigners, European. She put a tenner down and I said, "We don't take cash any more". "Oh", she said. "What can I do?" I said, "Well you need to buy an Oyster or a Travelcard or something." She said, "We're tourists, we've just come over." So I wrote them out the little slips we've got and I said, "When you get to Wimbledon better get yourself an Oyster Card or something." I think she was genuine, you know?" ***(Alan – BD)***

Some of our driver participants coped with refusing people entry by blaming them for being unaware of the change in policy. This tactic of emotionally distancing themselves from passengers isn't effective with tourists. In the above, Alan is not assessing vulnerability; but rather assessing morality, making a normative judgment based on whether the individual deserves passage. We see here that although TfL gave guidelines based on the notional of a 'vulnerable passenger', in practice leeway was usually dependent upon the subjective and personal views of the driver. There are benefits to this type of flexibility but as illustrated, it can lead to the discrimination of certain groups.

Flexibility, choice and surveillance

A major causes of public antagonism towards cashless fares was the perception that it removes an element of flexibility and choice in how people pay for their travel. Some of these criticisms were a matter of personal preference:

"Personally I don't like the idea of not having such simple freedom of use." ***(KennedyClarks - NA)***

"I honestly can't see how people can have a positive reaction to this? In a commerce era where there are more and more ways to pay for things, subtracting rather than adding seems like a step in the wrong direction." ***(Sammonfsih86 - NA)***

The sense of reliance on public transport around London made some of the city's commuters feel it unfair that fundamental changes to payment options had happened on a service that they couldn't 'opt-out' of. Other criticisms of the policy change cited more practical repercussions. Echoing the findings of prior work [36, 37], many online comments stated preferences for using cash because it facilitated a greater awareness of funds and the receipt of paper tickets which acted as records of expenditure: *"I would like to be paid in cash weekly, pay my bills weekly in person whilst receiving a receipt"* ***(MsLelaharvey, - NA)***. In contrast to this, *Oyster* was seen as placing additional barriers to the awareness of credit: *"People don't keep track of how much money they have on their oyster card. I finish work at around 11pm. If I'm short on my card, where can I top it up? I know I have run out a few times"* ***(Gorddtanks - NA)***. Relatedly, some people had clearly experienced failings in the use of *Oyster*, reflecting concerns over its reliability and the perceived seamlessness of the system: *"I had too much taken off my oyster and my bank card doesn't have contactless. I was half an hour late for work"* ***(Billyboob - NA)***.

In the following interview extract, Ray describes how the system's lack of flexibility had played out in practice. Unable to pay for his partner's fare, one passenger had to leave the bus without getting a refund:

"It's very vague. Me personally, I don't think it's going to work. I worked on Monday; the first two hours I had three people on offering me cash. One guy got on with his girlfriend; he had an Oyster Card, she had money in her hand, I said, "Sorry, we don't take cash no more." "Oh, well I've just paid, and I want my girlfriend to come on." "Sorry, but there's nothing I can do about that." "Can I get my money back?" I said, "No.""" ***(Ray - BD)***

Along with removing a flexible payment option, there were some deeper concerns related to the ways in which the *Oyster* might be used for surveillance. As noted in the related work, there are concerns that systems like *Oyster* can be used to gather data for the state. This was not lost on a great many of the public comments on news sites discussing the introduction of the new policy: *"A pathetic decision by the authorities to monitor and control all movement in the capital."; "cashless means every single transaction made will be traceable. Your life will be totally open for review by those who wish to spy on the public."* ***(COYSCOYS - NA)***; and *"Cashless society is not about cost cutting or ease of cash flow it's about control of your money and spying. wake up"* ***(ReginnaJeffrey - NA)***. The somber and cynical opinions about the potential of this technology to track and compile detailed information about passengers was bound up with a fear that this was leading to a dystopian and tyrannical future: *"The first step in getting us to accept a cashless society. Once we are all on plastic money, they can control us."* ***(Flonius77 - TW)***

As well as questions over state surveillance, there were also concerns that personal details would be sold on to third parties. Making electronic payment involuntary allows the mass collection of passenger information that can be stored, matched, retrieved, processed, marketed and circulated:

"I pay for everything in cash because I don't want middle-men monetising my purchasing history." ***(PArisloves - NA)***

"I frickin' hate this; I don't want my financial details known, I don't want the faceless to know where I travelled to, I don't want my life gummed up because my personal habits have been sold on." ***(IAmSmarten - NA)***

None of the online comments we collected articulated any foreseen benefits in collecting and storing this sort of information. This is despite TfL arguing that information will allow them to better plan the transport system and protect commuters from being over-charged.

DISCUSSION

Our findings highlight the myriad of ways that the introduction of compulsory cashless payments on London buses has been negotiated by drivers and passengers. Here we reflect upon four specific issues raised by our study.

Cashless changes the social function of money

The narrative produced by TfL surrounding their elimination of cash payments emphasises the benefits for passengers—reduced boarding times, improved reliability, and efficiency savings to be spent on improving the service. Our fieldwork confirmed some of these claims. There were very few instances of passengers not boarding seamlessly, and many of those spoken to felt that the new system was a *"good idea"*. However at the same time, echoing [4] and [25], we saw occasions where *Oyster* broke social norms around money exchange—reducing engagement between drivers and passengers, and the inability to pay for others.

To gain insight on the implications here, it is useful to first reflect on the social and cultural functions of money, and the ways *Oyster* and the cashless policy undermine these. Sociologist Georg Simmel [32] has argued that the development of money economies came in place of systems of barter and was part of a move from *gemeinshaft* to *gesellschaft*—that is transitioning from a society based on personal relationships to one based on more detached interactions. Simmel viewed money as both the cause and consequence of more impersonal relations. These are ideas alluded to in other classical works in sociology—for example, Karl Marx [23] shared Simmel's understanding of money as impersonal, while emphasising the role it plays in creating and maintaining alienation. We saw the potential for increased separation in the way *Oyster* dramatically reduced the potential for interaction between drivers and passengers—and, indeed, has introduced situations where if these interactions do occur they will likely be adversarial and a result of problems to do with payment.

Perhaps more subtly we also see how the reliance on contactless systems brings with it ramifications for the value of sharing money with others. It is no longer possible to give a fellow passenger small change if they found themselves short of the amount needed for a journey—or for a passenger to pay on the behalf of a partner—or for someone to pay for a friend they owe money to. The implication here is that with the transition to cashless payments comes further qualities of individualisation and removal of spontaneous opportunities of goodness.

Cashless encourages additional emotional labour

For the drivers, there are immediately many more positives than negatives. They no longer need to carry a cash float with them, which also means they no longer have to pay money in at the end of their shift. The majority of drivers considered the reduced need to interact with passengers as a benefit—in some respects a return to the historical role of a bus driver as a driver, and not a *"fucking cashier"*. The sociological literature on work illustrates how prolonged engagement with customers places a significant emotional and psychological strain on employees [15]. Recent studies of London's bus driver's also highlight the various performance-related concerns that heavily impact on drivers work [26, 27]—and issue illustrated in foundational ethnographies of bus driving as well [33]. Therefore, we might infer that the reduced human contact that cashlessness facilitates might actually improve driver wellbeing through reducing one of the performative burdens of this role.

However, the removal of a cash payment option came at some significant cost. First, the run-up to the cashless policy was stressful for many of our bus-driving participants. Their reaction to a lack of information—and an imagined range of negative consequences—inspired coping strategies in advance of the start date. Second, even though these tactics were rarely needed in practice, a range of new problems with passengers did emerge. This included having to gauge the vulnerability of a passenger if they didn't have correct payment, or having to more deeply interrogate *Oyster* users about the validity of their card or their lack of credit. It has been highlighted in workplace studies how the regulation of emotional expression in the duty of work can be considered a form of emotional labour [28], suggesting it is the quality of interaction, and not just its quantity, that places burdens and stresses on workers. Therefore, while the perceived reduction in interactions was seen to be a reduction in labour, those that did occur required greater thought, reflexivity and negotiation of sympathy and meant emotional labour increased.

Cashless brings work

As noted in the previous section, many of the passengers appeared to appreciate the potential efficiency savings of cashless bus payments. For many of the people we spoke to and saw during our ethnographic engagement, it was clear that—in Crabtree et al's [7] words—the *Oyster* was unremarkable. It was something they used, that they saw others using—it was everyday and mundane. This is echoed in the rhetoric surrounding TfL's elimination of cash and the quote from Mastercard that opened this paper—that cash is effortful and burdensome while electronic payments, especially those where there is no need to enter a personal identification number, are effortless, simple and invisible.

However, the narrative surrounding the everyday nature of cashless payments ignores the great amount of work and hidden labour involved in its maintenance and use. While it is not unusual for the hidden labour of employees as a result of new technologies to be highlighted (e.g. [27]), in this case it was the passengers who had to place considerably more effort into the production of this system. There is now a greater need than ever to ensure their *Oyster* is with them at all times and has sufficient credit to complete journeys. This often means that passengers have to seek locations to add credit to their card, keep track of how much remains on it, and—if they are prudent—check on the TfL website to make sure transactions and journeys had been accounted for correctly. While for the most part it appeared that this was not an issue, fear from both drivers and members of the public manifested when journeys were made at times of the day when shops may be closed, when locations around bus stops may be deserted, and when travelling to and from places that are unfamiliar. Indeed, the dangers inherent in running out of credit vividly emerge as the failsafe of cash no longer exists. In many respects, it highlights the 'problem of infrastructure' [10]. It also illustrates how *Oyster* persists into the background until it must 'first be manipulated to bring ordinary activities about' [7, p.555] making the working of *Oyster* the primary activity placing the need to travel into the background. In other words, greater work has to go into seeking places to find credit, or in engaging in dialogue with a bus driver with the hope of being assessed as 'vulnerable' in their eyes—all in order to accomplish the mundane act of using public transport.

Cashless brings fear

Some bus passengers' privacy-related concerns about the introduction of cashless fares—especially in employing the metaphor of 'Big Brother'—reveal a wider cultural fear about computer databases that store and process personal data. Glassner [12] highlights how 'cultures of fear' have become a condition of modern Western societies—a concern that is very apparent here and perhaps more so given the earlier mentioned concerns around state use of *Oyster* data. We must note that those comments discussed are likely to be extreme views—we did not come across any passengers during our journeys that raised these concerns directly to the researchers. Indeed, there are even ways to mitigate against this fear—through using 'pay as you go' *Oyster* cards that do not require registration (albeit come at slightly greater cost). Using this card means transactions are 'counted' but whom they belong to is not. Yet this would possibly not suffice for those whose concerns over surveillance are experienced as a real tension of everyday life. Perhaps in this case there is little that better design can do, but rather —as [8] highlights—to ensure companies, data brokers and governments act responsibly and transparently in the ways which data is used and safeguarded.

Implications for going cashless

While our study was focused on the specific example of *Oyster*, the types of changes being faced in London are likely to occur elsewhere around the world as other municipalities and transport providers introduce cashless payments (or eliminate cash payments). Furthermore, many of the challenges we identified in relation to the elimination of cash payments are illustrative of wider problems with digital payment systems that are increasingly prevalent in our lives. Here we address three specific areas of concern.

First, the issues related to the social function of money are reflective of thinking within the domain of digital payments and banking, which is dominated by bank cards, online services and mobile payments that operate on the basis of a single authenticated account holder. This is, of course, at odds with research that has demonstrated how people desire to share money with those they trust [36], and share passwords with others [18, 31]. Similar sharing practices were important for transport users—couples would pay for each other's travel, parents would pay for their children, friends would pay for travel as a group. Such practices were not just habitual nor whims but often highly pragmatic—it might be easier for large groups to travel together when paying with cash at once, it might be easier for a parent to pay than rely on their child to keep hold of their card, or it's easier to take visitors out on the bus when paying by cash. As such, in line with this work, we call for future cashless systems to take seriously the social value of money and support ways for spontaneously sharing digital money with others. Technically, with some modification there is no reason why cashless payment systems couldn't incorporate flexibility around fares—for example, through the use of buttons either on the card or reader to signify an additional fare. To mitigate against abuse, this could be limited to a single additional fare, which might be changeable through an online account. However, in the specific context of *Oyster*, the primary barrier to paying on the behalf of someone else is policy—which says that all passengers must have a 'valid ticket', and the ticket being the physical *Oyster Card* in itself. As such, we call for changes to policies like this to enable people to spend credit they have purchased in a more flexible manner as they wish.

Second, we saw how the introduction of the policy, and not having a universal payment system to fall back on, placed drivers in the difficult position of assessing another person's vulnerability. Prior work has highlighted how digital technology tends to complicate the occupation of bus driving [26,27], and we see this again in the case of digital payments, although less directly. There might be opportunities here to support drivers in making assessments around passenger vulnerability. Given that drivers are now presented with a plethora of data related to their route already [26], we might imagine that localised information—which might relate the availability of card and credit vendors—would be useful if sensitively presented to drivers in aiding their assessments of the risks of refusing travel to passengers at points along a route. If information overload is a concern, then this could be presented only when stationary at a bus stop, which might communicate with the bus via iBeacons or similar. However, we would argue that a policy of assessing passenger vulnerability is not sustainable in the long term due to its ambiguity, openness to abuse and the stress and scrutiny it places drivers under.

Third, building on the above, there needs to be adequate contingency systems in place for when a person has no credit or card on their person. While the 'one more journey' system for *Oyster* was intended to provide this, we saw it fail when that 'one' journey was actually many small journeys on different buses. It also doesn't account at all for situations where people do not have access to an *Oyster* card in the first place. While one way of resolving this might be to provide better communication channels to citizens about where 'nearby' top-up locations are, it occurs to us that there are more challenging infrastructural issues that should be accounted for prior to introducing cashless public transport. Emergency tickets purchased from basic dispensers at bus shelters that can be shown to drivers for one journey, particularly when boarding from stops known to be in vendor 'black holes', should be a standard contingency. Such tickets could also be purchased from vendors if the traveller is a one-off visitor from out of town—or enables a more regular passenger to keep a small supply of tickets in their wallet for when their credit runs out. This might sound particularly antiquated—and unoriginal, considering similar services are provided in a range of other cities across the world. However, our point is that a universal transport system requires a universal form of payment—and as with universal design this should mean being configurable, accessible and inclusive to all (as alluded by MasterCard in the quote opening this paper), not one-size-fits all.

CONCLUSION

In this paper we have explored the introduction of compulsory cashless payments on London's buses. There is much to gain from cashless technologies like *Oyster*—however, when cash is withdrawn completely there are also substantial losses in the form of the reduced social function of money, heightening the vulnerability of some citizens, and a fear of increased surveillance and control from the state. Our study provided insight into the emerging body of HCI research on the topic of digital money, and highlights the impact the changing nature of money has on a specific occupational group and their service users.

ACKNOWLEDGEMENTS

This work was supported by RCUK Digital Economy Program grant no. EP/G066019/1 SiDE. We would like to thank the anonymous reviewers for their very helpful feedback during the peer-review process.

REFERENCES

1. Alexander, V. D., Thomas, H., Cronin, A.' Fielding, J. and Moran-Ellis, J. 'Mixed methods'. In N. Gilbert (ed.) *Researching Social Life* (3rd edn). London, Sage, 2008.
2. Bell, C. A note on participant observation. *Sociology*, 3, 417-418.
3. BBC News. Oyster data is 'new police tool'. http://news.bbc.co.uk/1/hi/england/london/4800490.stm
4. Brewer, J., Mainwaring, S., and Dourish, P. Aesthetic journeys. In: *Proc. DIS '08*, ACM, 333-341.
5. Collier, B., and Hampshire, R. Sending mixed signals: Multilevel reputation effects in peer-to-peer lending markets. In: *Proc. CSCW '10*, ACM, 197-206.
6. Collins, P. *Black Feminist Thought Knowledge, Consciousness, and the Politics of Empowerment*. New York, Routledge, 1990.

7. Crabtree, A., Mortier, R., Rodden, T., and Tolmie, P. Unremarkable computing: The home network as a part of everyday life. In: *Proc. DIS '12*, ACM, 554-563.
8. De Hert, P., Gutworth, S., Moscibroda, A., Wright, D., and Fuster, G. Legal safeguards for privacy and data protection in ambient intelligence. *Pers Ubi Comp*, 13 (2009), 435-444
9. Deren, S., Oliver-Verez, D., Finlinson, A. et al. Integrating qualitative and quantitative methods: comparing HIV-related risk behaviors among Puerto Rican drug users in Puerto Rico and New York. *Substance Use and Misuse*, 38, 1, 1-24.
10. Edwards, W., Newman, M., and Poole, E. The infrastructure problem in HCI. In: *Proc. CHI '10*, ACM, 423-432.
11. Glaser, B. and Strauss, A. *The discovery of grounded theory: strategies for qualitative research.* Chicago.: Aldine, 1967.
12. Glassner, B. *The culture of feat: Why americans are afraid of the wrong things*. Basic Books, New York, 1999.
13. Garcia, F., de Koning Gans, G., Muijrers, R., et al. Dismantling MIFARE Classic. In: *Proc. ESORICS '08*, Springer, 97-114.
14. Gupta, A. and Ferguson, J. Discipline and practice: "the field" as site, method, and location in anthropology. In: A. Gupta and J. Ferguson (eds.) *Anthropological Locations: Boundaries and Grounds of a Field Science*. Berkley, University of California Press, 1997.
15. Hochschild, A. *The Managed Heart*. Berkley, CA: University of California Press, 1983.
16. Lathia, N., and Capra, L. How smart is your smartcard? Measuring travel behaviours, perceptions, and incentives. In: *Proc. UbiComp 11*, ACM, 291-300.
17. Kaye, J. Understanding Self-reported Password Sharing Strategies. In: *Proc. CHI '11*, ACM, 2619-2622.
18. Kaye, J., McCuiston, M., Gulotta, R., and Shamma, D. Money talks: Tracking personal finances. In: *Proc. CHI '14*, ACM, 521-530.
19. Kumar, D., Martin, D., and O'Neill, J. The times they are a-changin': Mobile payments in India. In: *Proc. CHI '11*, ACM (2011), 1413-1422.
20. Mas, I. and Morawczynski, O. Designing mobile money services: Lessons from M-PESA. *Innovations*, 4 (2), Springer (2009), 77-91.
21. Mason, J. 2006. Mixing methods in a qualitatively driven way. *Qualitative Research*, **6**, 1, 9-25.
22. Mastercard (2013) Cashless Journey: The Global Journey from Cash to Cashless. Cashless Journey Whitepaper. http://tinyurl.com/pfy5g4g
23. Marx, K. Early writings, ed. T.B. Bottomore. New York, McGraw-Hill, 1963.
24. Phillips, S. *The Invisible Culture: Communication in Classroom and Community in Warm Spring Reservation*. Thesis (PhD). University of Pennsylvania, 1975.
25. Poole, E., Le Dantec, C, Eagen, J., and Edwards, W. Reflecting on the invisible: Understanding end-user perceptions of ubiquitous computing. In: *Proc. UbiComp '08*, ACM, 192-201.
26. Pritchard, G., Vines, J., Briggs, P., et al. Digitally driven: how location based services impact the work practices of London bus drivers. In: *Proc. CHI '14*, ACM, 3617-3626.
27. Pritchard, G., Briggs, P., Vines, J., and Olivier, P. How (not) to drive a London bus: Measuring performance in a mobile and remote workplace. In: *Proc. CHI '15*, ACM.
28. Rafaeli, A., and Sutton, R. The expression of emotion in organizational life. In: Cummings L., and Staw, B. (Eds.), *Research in organizational behavior*, 1–42
29. Schensul, S., Schensul, J. and LeCompte, M. *Essential Ethnographic Methods: Observations, Interviews, and Questionnaires*. Walnut Creek, AltaMira Press, 1999.
30. Schwarz, J., Mankoff, J., and Matthews, H. Reflections of everyday activities in spending data. In: *Proc. CHI '09*, ACM, 1737-1740.
31. Singh, S. *Marriage Money: The social shaping of money in marriage & banking*. St. Leonards, Allen & Unwin, 1998.
32. Simmel, G. *The Philosophy of Money*. Trans., ed. T. Bottomore. Boston, Routledge & Kegan Paul, 1978.
33. Slosar, J. Ogre, bandit, and operating employee: The problems and adaptations of the metropolitan bus driver. *Journal of Contemporary Ethnography*, 1, 339-362.
34. Tirachini, A. Bus dwell time: the effect of different fare collection systems, bus floor level and age of passengers. *Transportmetrica A: Transport Science*, 9:1, 28-49.
35. Transport for London. *Going Cashless on TfL Bus Services: Consultation Report*. London, TfL, 2014.
36. Vines, J., Dunphy, P., Blythe, M., et al. The joy of cheques: Trust, paper and eighty sometings. In: *Proc. CSCW '12*, ACM, 147-156.
37. Vines, J., Dunphy, P., and Monk, A. Pay or delay: The role of technology when managing a low income. In: *Proc. CHI '14*, ACM, 501-510.
38. Whyte, W. *Street Corner Society*. Chicago, University of Chicago Press, 1995.
39. Wolf, D. High risk methodology: reflections on leaving an outlaw society. In W. Shaffir and R. Stebbins (eds.) *Experiencing Fieldwork: an Inside View of Qualitative Research*. Newbury Park, Sage, 1991.
40. Xynou, M. Oyster, octopus and metro cards: What happens to our data? http://tinyurl.com/9ror9yc

Informing and Improving Retirement Saving Performance using Behavioral Economics Theory-driven User Interfaces

Junius Gunaratne
New York University
junius@nyu.edu

Oded Nov
New York University
onov@nyu.edu

ABSTRACT

Can human-computer interaction help people make informed and effective decisions about their retirement savings? We applied the behavioral economic theories of endowment effect and loss aversion to the design of novel retirement saving user interfaces. To examine effectiveness, we conducted an experiment in which 487 participants were exposed to one of three experimental user interface designs of a retirement saving simulator, representing endowment effect, loss aversion and control. Users made 34 yearly asset allocation decisions. We found that designs informed by the endowment effect and loss aversion theories and which communicated to savers the long-term implications of their asset allocation choices, led users to adjust their behavior, make larger and more frequent asset allocation changes, and achieve their saving goals more effectively.

Author Keywords

Retirement saving; personal finance; behavioral economics; behavior change; persuasive technology; financial literacy.

INTRODUCTION

Saving for retirement is one of the biggest investments people make in life. Americans are estimated to hold $19.4 trillion in 401(k) retirement accounts [4], however, most Americans have underfunded retirement accounts [9, 17]. Since retirement saving is commonly managed online through user interfaces, HCI can potentially help us understand and inform people who save for retirement. Three aspects of retirement saving make it particularly difficult for non-experts: First, savers have to make repeated decisions about asset allocations that should decrease in risk over time and understand the effects of multiple saving decisions over time. Second, studies show that the majority of people do not assess risk properly [15]. Third, a common mistake retirement savers make is attempting to maximize returns or minimize volatility [15].

To address these issues, in this study we contribute to HCI research by applying the behavioral economic theories of loss aversion and endowment effect to the design of user interface features for retirement saving. The interface highlights saving goals and future investment performance to convey the long-term implications of asset allocation choices. We tested the utility of this approach and measured the effects of different designs on users' behavior.

CHI 2015, April 18–23, 2015, Seoul, Republic of Korea.

http://dx.doi.org/10.1145/2702123.2702408

RELATED WORK

A number of behavioral economic theories explain how information can be reframed to encourage better choices [7, 11]. Prospect Theory, a branch of behavioral economics, shows that people are prone to *loss avers ion*—they have difficulties thinking about the future in present terms, and react more strongly to losses than to gains [10, 11]. Moreover, people tend not to give up what they have even if they get better options, with low costs of switching—a phenomenon known as the *endowment effect*: Kahneman et al showed that after people are given an object they become mentally invested in it [10]. In a financial context, research shows that investors become attached to funds they own and are reluctant to give up what they have [14, 16]. Fryer et al [7] found that employees who were awarded bonuses at the beginning of the year, with the threat of revoking the bonus based on performance, took more action to maintain good performance than employees who were awarded a year-end bonus. Armstrong and Murlis [1] showed that the prospect of getting a bonus can positively influence employee performance if the criteria for determining the rewards are transparent and unbiased.

Prior HCI research explored how to motivate individuals to change their behavior through design interventions in areas such as healthcare informatics and environmental sustainability—sometimes drawing on behavioral economics [6, 13]. Work on persuasive technology [5] has also influenced HCI research studying how technology can change behavior. Lee et al [13] applied the concept of asymmetric comparison in user interfaces to motivate individuals to choose more healthy food choices. Yun et al [19] used intervention techniques for encouraging energy conservation through the use of information dashboards. Similarly, Froehlich et al [6] applied concepts from behavioral economics to promote environmentally sustainable water usage. These studies show that displaying timely feedback and information about deviating from a goal can dramatically affect individual behavior.

Little HCI research, however, focuses on money-saving behavior. In related areas, researchers explore how people manage and think about their money [12, 18], and how real-time information about simulated financial transactions leads to better understanding of economic transactions [3].

STUDY

Setting

To study the effects of feedback on deviation from retirement goals on users' behavior, we created an interactive retirement saving simulator (Figures 1-3). We asked users to save $1.5M over 34 years (2014-2048), a reasonable goal given average annual returns of 7.5%. In each simulation "year" participants allocated fixed yearly savings of $10,000 among the three basic asset classes of stocks, bonds and cash. Stocks are the riskiest asset type, but provide the greatest return. Bonds are less risky, but provide a lower return. Cash has no risk and provides minimal return [2]. Once users clicked "submit" on their chosen asset allocation, they moved to the next simulation year. Users were then presented with market behavior of the previous year as well as their portfolio's performance (see Figures 1-3). To make the market performance realistic, we used (unknown to the users) the Dow Jones Industrial Average for stock data and the Fidelity Investment Grade Bond for bond data, both from 1980 to 2014. Actual market data from 1980 represented the simulated year of 2014, 1981 represented 2015, and so on, ending with the simulated year 2048.

Reward mechanism

We recruited via Amazon Mechanical Turk and limited participation to U.S. users with a record of at least 100 tasks at an approval rate exceeding 99%. To motivate users to achieve a retirement goal rather than maximize returns or evade risks [15], we rewarded goal-driven moderate risk. Consequently, users' compensation was $1.00 default pay and a maximum bonus of $4.00 if they met the $1.5 million retirement goal. Deviation from the goal either positively or negatively led to a proportionally lower bonus. This 4/1 bonus/default compensation ratio represents substantial incentive to achieve the savings goal rather than trying to maximize returns with riskier behavior.

Experimental conditions

The simulator presented asset allocation, and the overall value of the user's investments over time (Figures 1-3). In addition, it included an interactive feature enabling users to check the potential outcomes of asset allocation alternatives before locking in their allocation choice for the year. We randomly assigned users to one of three conditions that applied simplified versions of the behavioral economic concepts of loss aversion and endowment effect. We compared these two conditions to a third control condition. All conditions used an annually compounded future value interest formula to estimate investment performance.

The *endowment effect condition* (Figure 1) displayed the savings goal, the estimated outcome of total retirement funds at retirement based on current asset allocations, and the difference between the goal and estimate. The emphasis on the difference between the goal and the estimated outcome implied that the goal is an endowment. Our application of the endowment effect was based on studies showing how investors become attached to funds and how they react to bonuses [1, 7, 14, 16]. The intervention had elements of loss aversion such that participants saw negative values of lost capital in some cases, viewed negatively by loss-averse users [11]. We expected users to view the $1.5M as an endowment that serves as a reference point [8], and showed them how their choices translate into potentially giving up some of their endowment. We expected users to actively preserve the endowment by adjusting their allocations over time, and allocate more savings toward stocks earlier in their career.

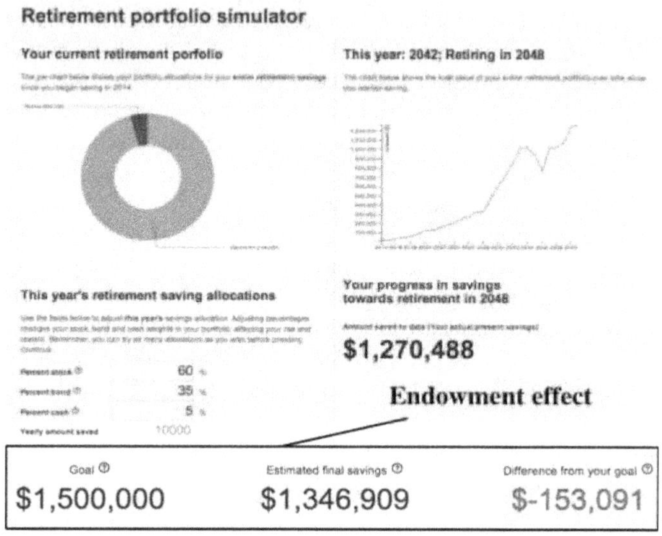

Figure 1. Endowment effect condition.

In the condition emphasizing *loss aversion* (Figure 2), we presented to users three estimates of how the yearly saving ($10,000) would perform in the long run given the time remaining until retirement: worst case value, expected value and best case value. Showing these amounts helps illustrate potential gains or losses. Using an interactive feature of the simulator, participants could adjust the allocation of their savings, to instantly see the long-term performance implications of their choices. The scenarios for low performance are shown and users can also see what happens in an underperforming market, where underperformance in the worst-case scenario can be perceived as a potential loss. The poor performance of cash-dominant allocations can also be perceived as a loss in comparison to high performing stocks. We expected these factors to lead users to save more in stocks and bonds within reason. Our application of loss aversion took into account Odean's [16] study of investors' reluctance to make changes to their portfolios due to hope that depressed values return to their former values over time. To counteract this typical investor behavior we explicitly showed how maintaining underperforming asset allocations could hurt the investor over time.

The *control condition* (Figure 3) presented a UI similar to that of typical commercial online retirement systems, where in addition to the charts, users can modify asset allocations for the current year. We did not present additional information such as estimated savings outcomes.

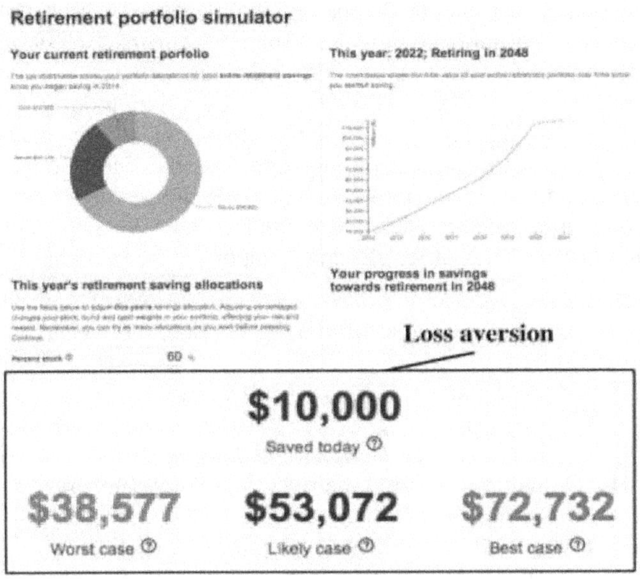

Figure 2. Loss aversion condition.

Both the loss aversion and endowment conditions make users aware of deviating from the goal. What makes these conditions different from a simple goal (and from each other) is how the conditions quantify loss aggregated over time, and show users an amount they could have versus what they will have if they don't change their allocations.

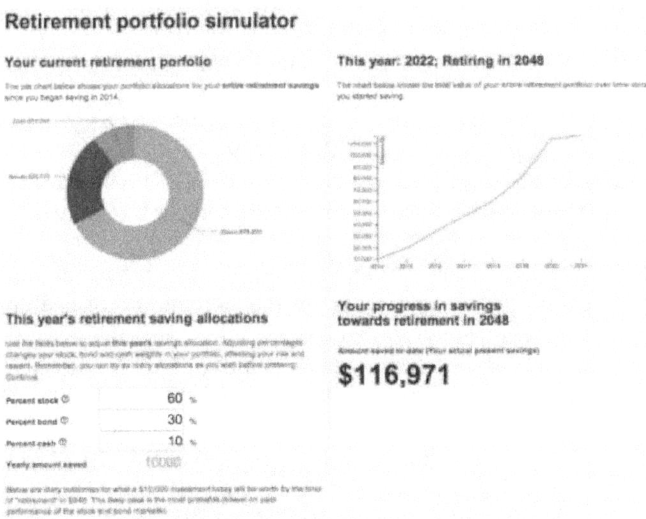

Figure 3. Control condition.

487 users (average age = 34.5, 46.2% women) participated in a between-subjects experiment, divided between the conditions of loss aversion (N=162), endowment effect (N=158) and control (N=167). We recorded gaps between users' savings and their goal, as well as the number and size of asset allocation changes. We compared these using ANOVA and a Bonferroni post-hoc test. In addition, we compared the changes made in yearly allocation: first, we compared the extent to which users changed their allocation during their career. Second, we compared the number of changes made by users throughout the years, across the experimental conditions using ANOVA and a Bonferroni post-hoc test. Finally, we compared the average proportion of stocks across conditions using a chi-square test.

RESULTS

The gap between participants' goal and saving (Table 1) was smallest, on average, in the endowment effect condition ($118k) and bigger (though not significantly) in the loss aversion condition ($124k). Both gaps were significantly smaller ($p<0.05$) than the gap in the control condition ($164k). Users in the loss aversion and the endowment groups made more adjustments to their asset allocations ($p<0.05$), and bigger year-to-year changes in their asset allocations ($p<0.05$) than users in the control group. Users in the endowment group kept more of their savings in stocks, compared to others ($p<0.05$).

In addition, there was a significant difference between the endowment effect and loss aversion conditions, including a difference in the average total saving achieved by users (endowment: 1.501M, loss aversion: 1.443M; $p<0.05$), as well as the likelihood of users to achieve their saving goal (endowment: 0.68, loss aversion: 0.46; $p<0.001$).

Condition	Mean gap from goal ($) / Likelihood of reaching goal	Average number of asset allocation changes	Mean yearly change in asset allocation (%)	Average % of stocks
Endowment effect	118,098* / 0.68*	18.39*	10.24*	70.8*
Loss aversion	124,002* / 0.46	17.68*	9.79*	61.4
Control	*164,640 / 0.45*	*15.00*	*7.46*	*61.5*

Table 1. Comparison between experimental conditions; *significant difference ($p<0.05$) from the control group.

Plotting average stock proportions over time for all conditions shows a decreasing stock portion (Figure 4), such that the endowment effect and loss aversion lines have similar slopes, but the latter is shifted down by 10%.

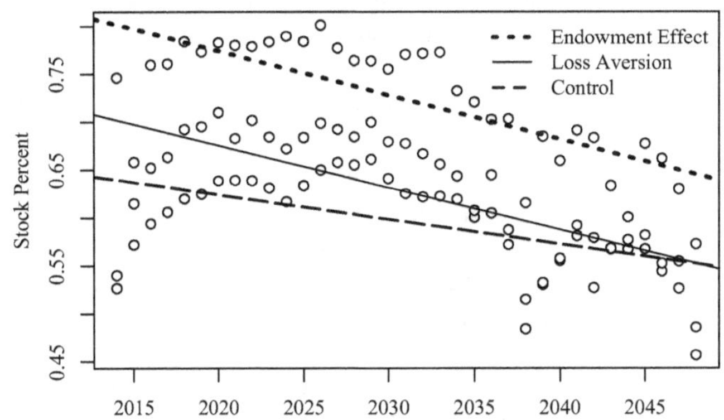

Figure 4. Stock allocation over time: regression lines for endowment effect (top dotted line) loss aversion (middle solid line) and control condition (bottom dashed line).

Participants in the endowment group allocated, on average, the most towards stocks at all points in the study. Loss aversion users allocated 8% more to stocks than the control users at the start of the study, but this difference decreased to zero by the end of the study.

Overall, these comparisons between the conditions and the plotted data illustrate the relationship between experimental conditions, elicited behaviors, and goal attainment.

DISCUSSION AND CONCLUSION

There are many ways to reach a retirement goal through changes in asset allocations over time. Our goal was to inform users as they modified their behavior, enabling them to follow a path to a retirement goal that is most consistent with their risk preferences. On average, users could best reach their savings goal when using the endowment effect interface, followed by the loss aversion interface. The control condition, which is most similar to popular retirement saving interfaces, was least effective. The $1.5M goal required allocation towards stocks, however, increased proportion of stocks is not in itself more risky in the long run, since the alternative—allocating more to "safer" (but lower yield) assets—decreases the likelihood of achieving the goal. Our objective was not to elicit more or less risky behavior, but, given a saving goal, lead participants to take appropriate risks and stay on track toward their goal.

In the endowment condition, we showed a lump sum to the user as the amount she would have saved. The simulator's interactive features showed the endowment being taken away from the user if she made poor choices. Consistent with prior research [8, 10], this framing was likely to make users focus on their goal rather than on maximizing returns, behave as if they were awarded their goal amount, and act to prevent losing it. The results confirmed our hypothesis: users made larger and more frequent allocation changes, and allocated a higher proportion of savings to stocks (see Table 1), suggesting that they were aware of the long-term impacts of their choices. The effects of asset allocation adjustments were transparent to users with changes seen instantly as the user made allocation adjustments. This transparency was likely to influence users in similar ways to unbiased bonuses resulting in behavior analogous to how loss-aversion is applied to bonuses in Fryer's [7] study.

The weaker performance of the loss aversion group can be explained by the fact that users were shown only the likely outcomes of investing the yearly $10,000. In comparison, in the endowment effect condition we showed the likely impact of allocation decisions on the entire portfolio amount. As prior research shows [6], feedback provided at a decision point helps users make better decisions. Providing easy to understand information about long-term outcomes communicated an abstract concept of risk and return, and helped savers make effective asset allocations. Specifically, in the endowment effect and loss aversion conditions the negative outcomes associated with investing too heavily in bonds or cash quickly became evident.

Prior research [17] showed real world applications of behavioral economic theory can help improve retirement saving. Our application of HCI interventions has important design implications: institutions who regulate and manage retirement saving can help the public by utilizing design. In particular, displaying information that emphasizes goals, deviation from goals, and long-term scenarios can be highly effective. Such an approach can help non-expert savers make informed decisions. The findings are also applicable to other contexts of long-term saving or long-term debt.

REFERENCES

[1] Armstrong, M. and Murlis, H., *Reward Management.* 2007.

[2] Sec. and Exch. Comm. *Invest Wisely.* 2014.

[3] Cramer, M. and Hayes, G., The digital economy. *Proc. Interaction Design and Children*, 2013.

[4] Dougherty, C. Retirement Savings Accounts Draw U.S. Consumer Bureau Attention. *Bloomberg*, 2013.

[5] Fogg, B. J., *Persuasive Technology*, 2002.

[6] Froehlich, J., Findlater, L., Ostergren, *et al.*, The design and evaluation of prototype eco-feedback displays for fixture-level water usage data. *Proc. CHI* 2012.

[7] Fryer, R., Levitt, S., *et al.*, Enhancing the efficacy of teacher incentives through loss aversion. NBER, 2012.

[8] Heath, C., Larrick, R., and Wu, G., Goals as reference points.*Cognitive psychology,* 38, 79-109, 1999.

[9] Helman, R., Adams, N., *et al.*, Retirement Confidence Survey. Employee Benefit Research Institute. 2014.

[10] Kahneman, D., Knetsch, J., and Thaler, R., Anomalies. *J. of Econ. Perspectives,* 5, 193-206, 1991.

[11] Kahneman, D. and Tversky, A., Prospect Theory. *Econometrica,* 47, 263-291, 1979.

[12] Kaye, J., McCuistion, M., Gulotta, R., & Shamma, D., Money talks: tracking personal finances. *Proc. CHI* 2014.

[13] Lee, M., Kiesler, S., and Forlizzi, J., Mining behavioral economics to design persuasive technology for healthy choices. *Proc. CHI* 2011.

[14] Matson, B. and Hardy, M. R., *Data Driven Investing: Professional Edition*: Data Driven Publishing , 2004.

[15] Merton, R., The Crisis in Retirement Planning," *Harvard Business Review.* 92, 42-50, 2014.

[16] Odean, T., Are Investors Reluctant to Realize Their Losses? *J. of Finance,* LIII, 1775-1798, 1998.

[17] Thaler, R. and Benartzi, S., Save More Tomorrow. *Journal of Political Economy,* 112, 164-187, 2004.

[18] Vines, J., Dunphy, P. and Monk, A., Pay or delay: the role of technology when managing a low income. *CHI* 2014.

[19] Yun, R., Scupelli, P., *et al.*, Sustainability in the workplace. *Proc. Persuasive Technology* 2013.

Author Index

www.ingramcontent.com/pod-product-compliance
Lightning Source LLC
LaVergne TN
LVHW080101011026
849160LV00013B/1011